ABOUT THE AUTHORS

MIKE DOUCHANT

Douchant was a basketball editor for *The Sporting News* from 1977 to 1991. He also contributed to *The Sporting News Basketball Yearbooks, Official NBA Register,* and *Lindy's College Basketball Yearbook*. During the 1996 NCAA Tournament, Douchant ventured into cyberspace with Prodigy™ to offer his expertise in a basketball Q&A forum.

JIM NANTZ

As the voice of CBS Sports, Nantz has served as the lead play-by-play announcer for college basketball during the regular season and for the NCAA Division I Men's Basketball Championship since 1990. Nantz, a regular golf announcer for CBS Sports since 1986, assumed the anchor position for the network's golf coverage in April 1994. He has hosted the network's coverage of the Masters® Tournament since 1989. Nantz has also covered major sporting events such as the World Swimming and Diving Championships from Madrid, Spain, in 1986, the 1992 and 1994 Olympic Winter Games, the U.S. Open Tennis Championships, and network college and NFL football games. A graduate of the University of Houston with a B.A. in radio/television, Nantz was a member of the golf team and held a variety of broadcasting jobs during his college years.

THESE SPORTS TITLES ARE ALSO AVAILABLE FROM VISIBLE INK PRESS:

Inside Sports Hockey

"Crammed with interesting facts and figures." — *Toronto Star*

By Zander Hollander, 7 1/4" X 9 1/4", paperback, 720 pages, 286 photographs, ISBN 0-7876-0876-9.

Inside Sports World Series Factbook

Inside Sports World Series Factbook presents an in-depth, year-by-year history of the October Classic, from the first Series in 1903 through 1995. Each year's profile includes competing teams, lively narrative, and summary box scores.

Foreword by Mickey Lolich, former Detroit Tiger and 1968 World Series MVP.

By George Cantor, 6" X 9", paperback, 600 pages, 100 photographs, ISBN 0-7876-0821-1.

Hotdogs, Heroes & Hooligans: The Story of Baseball's Major League Teams

"Notable. Monumental." — *Washington Post*

Foreword by Hall of Fame broadcaster Ernie Harwell.

By Michael LaBlanc, 11" X 8 1/2" horizontal, paperback, 593 pages, 300 photos and sports statistics tables, ISBN 0-8103-9748-X.

Bud Collins' Modern Encyclopedia of Tennis

"It's all here... the people, the happenings, the ups and downs from the very beginning to today in the game I love." — Chris Evert

"A must-have for anyone who plays, watches, or just plain enjoys the game." — *Tennis Magazine*

2nd ed., Bud Collins and Zander Hollander, 7 1/4" X 9 1/4", paperback, 700 pages, 250 photos, available Spring 1997.

*These books are available at fine bookstores everywhere
or by calling 1-800-776-6265.*

INSIDE SPORTS MAGAZINE

COLLEGE BASKETBALL

INSIDE
SPORTS
MAGAZINE
COLLEGE
BASKETBALL

Mike Douchant

**With special guest
Jim Nantz**

VISIBLE
INK
PRESS

Detroit ● New York ● Toronto ● London

INSIDE SPORTS COLLEGE BASKETBALL

Copyright © 1995, 1997 by Michael Douchant

Published by **Visible Ink Press™**
A division of Gale Research
835 Penobscot Building
Detroit, MI 48226-4094

Visible Ink Press™ is a trademark of Gale Research

Inside Sports Magazine ©1996 is a registered trademark of Inside Sports Inc.

 otected by all applicable copyright laws, as well as by misappro-
nd other applicable laws.

in any form without permission in writing from the publisher,
brief passages in connection with a review written for inclusion

Most Visible Ink Press™ books are available at special quantity discounts when purchased in bulk by corporations, organizations, or groups. Customized printings, special imprints, messages, and excerpts can be produced to meet your
needs. For more information, contact Special Markets Manager, Gale Research Inc., 835 Penobscot Building, Detroit, MI
48226. Or call 1-800-877-4253.

Art Director: Michelle DiMercurio
Original page design: Mark C. Howell
Front cover photographs of Tony Delk and Derek Anderson: AP/Wide World Photos
Back cover photograph of Tony Delk: AP/Wide World Photos

Library of Congress Cataloging-in-Publication Data
Douchant, Mike, 1951—

    Inside Sports college basketball / Mike Douchant. — 2nd ed.
        p.   cm.
    Includes bibliographical references and index.
    ISBN 0-7876-1033-X
    1. Basketball—United States—History. 2. College sports—-United States—-History. I. Title.
GV885.7.D68 1996
796.323'0973—dc20

96-20071
CIP

Kudos to the numerous relatively obscure small college and high school coaches who are as competent as many of the millionaires club coaches at major universities. Their grateful pupils know the coaches are special and realize they too could have marquee value if the opportunity surfaced at the right place at the right time.

CONTENTS

MY LOVE AFFAIR WITH COLLEGE HOOPS
by Jim Nantz

My affinity for college basketball was pre-destined. It all had to with my upbringing. Born in the great state of North Carolina, I had no choice but to become a rabid follower of the Atlantic Coast Conference and the NCAA Tournament. By age six, I could recite the starting five of every ACC school and often entire rosters. The vital stats of each player; hometown, height and weight, scoring, and rebounding averages were all committed to memory by the end of first grade. I loved to talk the game and relished the chance to dispense with all of this minutiae if anyone would ask. My family thought I was some kind of freak—and to this day I am: I'm crazy about college hoops!

By my teen years the family had been transplanted to New Jersey. Being out of the ACC region was pretty traumatic at first, but thanks to a broadcasting pioneer named C. D. Chesley, the pain soon subsided. Back then, Mr. Chesley had this wild idea to put together a syndicated television package involving the ACC game of the week. Lucky for me, an independent station in Philadelphia carried the games. Each week I would sneak up a rickety ladder and climb into the attic, move the antenna that had been point-ed at New York, and then take dead aim at Philadelphia. The reception was always snowy, but the games were too compelling to turn off. Plus the broadcasters made it even more palatable. Their names were Jim Thacker and Billy Packer. Little did I know back then that I would one day work side-by-side with Billy and call the Final Four.

I often get asked what my credentials are to broadcast the biggest games in college basketball. Usually I explain that it's my job as the play-by-play man to be the point guard on a telecast. I keep the viewer abreast of all the essentials; that includes being in charge of keeping the storylines honest, bringing up any pertinent statistical information, and above all, properly setting up the man I consider the best analyst in the business, Billy Packer. Billy is the expert. As a hot shot guard, he helped Wake Forest make it to the 1962 Final Four. My playing achievements were just a little less impressive. I played two years of varsity basketball at Marlboro High School in New Jersey. I started both years in the backcourt and served as co-captain for my senior season. Now for a confession. My junior year we went 0-22! In one game against Asbury

Park, we trailed 31-0 before we even got the ball across mid-court. My senior season we rebounded to post a 2-20 record. That's right, my high school record was a combined 2-41! Maybe that's why I feel so well-equipped to handle a telecast when the game is a blowout!

Even though my achievements on the floor were anemic, I stayed around the game in college. I attended the University of Houston and was a member of a storied golf program that had won 16 national championships. Regrettably, I was out of my league when it came to Houston golf. By my junior year, I was pursuing a broadcasting career with reckless abandon and had all but traded in my clubs in search of a microphone. My golf coach arranged for me to audition as the public address announcer for the basketball team. Luckily, I won the audition and found myself sitting courtside with a live mike. Somehow, the PA job led to me being named the host of coach Guy Lewis's television show. I've always been so grateful to Guy for allowing me, a young college punk with virtually no experience, to get a start in television. I have to add on a personal note that I want to see Guy Lewis elected to the Basketball Hall of Fame. He took five teams to the Final Four, won 592 games and through integration helped revolutionize college basketball. He also took two players who were barely recruited by anyone and helped develop them into certain future Hall of Famers. I'm talking about Clyde Drexler and Hakeem Olajuwon.

By the time Houston met North Carolina State for the national championship on April 4, 1983, I was two years out of college and working at the CBS affiliate in Salt Lake City. On the day of the title game, the urge to be in Albuquerque was so strong, I asked for the rest of the day off. I got to the Cougars' hotel just in time to hitch a ride on the team bus. Enough time has passed now that I can finally admit to sneaking into The

Pit that night without a pass. I just marched right in past security as I was flanked on both sides by my friends from the team. Once inside, I sat just a few rows up from the baseline over by the Houston bench. Immediately, I looked to my right and realized that I was only ten feet away from the CBS set from which Brent Musburger would host the telecast. Always an admirer of his, I found myself watching the action on the floor and then turning to see Brent's reaction all night long. I studied his every move during the pre-game and halftime shows. I remember thinking he had the greatest job in the world and wistfully longed to sit on that set someday. Oddly enough, three years later Brent shifted from host to play-by-play and guess who was hosting CBS' coverage of the 1986 Final Four from Reunion Arena in Dallas?

I've had the privilege of covering the last eleven Final Fours for CBS. The last six years I've been courtside calling the games with Billy. There is nothing else quite like it. I've never forgotten that my love affair with college basketball started at an early age when my mind loved to absorb every last detail of the game. My dream to be around basketball was fostered sitting next to an antenna in a New Jersey attic, then was developed by knowledgeable people like Guy Lewis.

People have often accused me of having an encyclopedic memory when it comes to sports. It's just not true. I have spent the last 30 years reading and researching a sport I love. There is no better resource that I've come across than *Inside Sports College Basketball*. Mike Douchant has put together the most comprehensive book about the history of the game. Knowing Mike for a long time, I guarantee that he looked at this project as a labor of love. . . . and it shows. Enjoy!

INTRODUCTION
by Mike Douchant

I first decided to write a comprehensive guide to college basketball while browsing through periodicals at book stores. There, I noticed longstanding and respected encyclopedias covering major league baseball, the NFL, and NBA. I found it irksome, given my passion for the game, that a similar comprehensive volume on college basketball wasn't available. If no one else would tackle the project, I'd be willing to take it on. After all, "Final Four" has ascended to a spotlight previously reserved for marquee events such as the Masters, Super Bowl, World Series, Indianapolis 500, Kentucky Derby and major New Year's Day football bowl games. In 1994, the *Encyclopedia of College Basketball* was published. Now an annual publication affiliated with *Inside Sports* magazine, a monthly sports journal showcasing some of the best sportswriters in the world, the *Encyclopedia* has become *Inside Sports College Basketball*. I believe it remains the most authoritative book that anyone can find on college basketball.

I was on the ground floor in helping create publications such as *The Sporting News Basketball Yearbooks, Official NBA Register,* and *Lindy's College Basketball Yearbook.* So I'm well aware that a "repeat" publication needs to be refined in subsequent editions in order to continue to be distinctive and edify diehard fans. I think readers already exposed to the book let alone newcomers will be pleased by much of the fine-tuning.

College basketball in general also needs modification, although the engaging sport remains grand and has become an essential fabric gracing our lives. It has become my goal that whatever level of interest you possess will be piqued and you'll enjoy the vigor of college hoops even more by making yourself familiar with this handy guide.

What's in the Book?

Naturally, the bulk of a much-needed source for today's college hoops fan needs to accentuate major college basketball and the incredibly popular NCAA Division I Tournament. This enterprising edition also includes pertinent material on other significant levels of competition such as the NIT, small colleges (NAIA, NCAA Divisions II and III, and junior colleges), women's basketball, and the Olympics.

I am enamored by the diverse approaches by which the history of college hoops can be portrayed if the information is packaged properly. Thus, in the pages that follow I've tried to deliver a variety of highly readable points to ponder plus relevant statistics and facts that a college basketball fan requires in order to be properly illuminated about the sport.

Acknowledgments

This treasure trove of facts and statistics is unique only because it catalogs the matchless performances of uncommon participants. It couldn't have been achieved without securing input from a variety of basketball aficionados. Therefore, I offer hearty thank-yous and high fives to the following contributors for their mix of clean prose and pertinent stats:

John Duxbury—His painstaking research enlightened year-by-year reviews and made player/coaching records more comprehensive. A glance at the "They Played the Game, Too" section confirms the notion that he is the nation's premier sports historian. Dux was, is, and always will be "The Answer Man." Thanks to Frank Pawloski, the world's No. 1 Army sports expert, for supplying Dux with statistics for Army's undefeated team in 1943–44.

Andy Geerken and Gary Johnson—Their work on the coaches' register was especially efficient. Here is how I think effervescent Dick Vitale would describe Andy, the director of communications for the National Association of Basketball Coaches, and Gary, a statistics coordinator for the NCAA: "They're the 3-R Men, baby! They're Reputable, Reliable and Resourceful."

Michael Johnson—The author of "The Juco Classic" knows more about the history of junior college basketball than anyone who has a pulse. His labor of love in researching J.C. hoops is beyond compare.

Roland Lazenby—As with any project that requires delving into archival material, this book is dependent on precise and relevant analysis on the pioneers of the sport. Roland capitalized on his extensive experience as a sports book author to supply an incisive look at "The Early Years."

Walt Meyer—I value Walt's keen insight and still can't believe some of the salient statistical research he conducted for the "Odds and Ends" chapter.

Wendy Parker—She has honed a witty and well-informed writing style that helps individuals, including me, shed our male basketball chauvinism. In her whirlwind way, she consistently captures how the women have immeasurably improved this decade while the men's game has suffered from inattention to fundamentals such as competent free-throw shooting. The team-oriented women look for passing angles while many self-indulging men look for camera angles to display individualistic "flashdance" routines.

Patrick Premo—A Naismith Memorial Basketball Hall of Fame recommendation proved accurate as Premo supplied invaluable perspective of teams the first half of this century with pre-wire-service national polls.

I'm also appreciative of Harvey Mathews from Philadelphia for lending his expertise on multiple | sport athletes and to Orville Paller from Salt Lake City for reconstructing lost statistics of Utah's 1944 NCAA championship team.

Finally, I'm indebted to college sports information directors from across the country and USA Basketball for providing the vast majority of the photographs and title team statistics.

Of course, Leslie Norback and the folks at Visible Ink Press have my genuine respect for allowing creativity to deviate somewhat from traditional encyclopedia-like volumes while still providing a necessary focus to keep me from going off on too many tangents. I believe the end result is an exceptional, reader-friendly product.

1

THE EARLY YEARS:

1891-1937

As the well-worn legend goes, James Naismith, a young physical education instructor at the YMCA's School for Christian Workers in Springfield, Massachusetts, invented the game of basketball in 1891 to relieve boredom in his winter gym classes.

The school in Springfield trained its students to become managers in the YMCA's network of health clubs around the world. Every winter, the students grew weary of the routine of gymnastics and calisthenics used in their "physical training." They often complained bitterly. In the fall of 1891, the mood seemed nastier than usual, and two instructors had quit rather than deal with the headache. Naismith announced at a faculty meeting that he would take on the problem. He said the students needed an indoors game, one they could learn easily and play in the gym by artificial light.

At first Naismith tried a combination of soccer, lacrosse, and football, but it was too rough. He turned to other options but none worked. "I tried all games that seemed to offer any hope, and studied each one," he later explained in a letter to a friend, "but kept the idea of lacrosse always in mind."

Then, Naismith recalled a childhood game, "Duck on a Rock," where the players attempted to knock a larger, melon-sized rock off a boulder by throwing smaller rocks at it. There seemed to be something to that concept. Plus, he remembered how a rugby team he once played on spent winter days indoors throwing rugby balls into a box.

So he tinkered with a new idea. In late December of 1891 he gave the idea a try, and posted the rules on a bulletin board outside the gym. He first envisioned a game where the players would attempt to throw a soccer ball into a box suspended above the gym floor. But the school janitor, Pops Stebbins, couldn't find any boxes, so he brought Naismith two peach baskets. The railing around the school gym happened to be 10 feet off the floor, so the baskets were set at that height. And because his class held 18 students, Naismith divided them into nine on a side.

"The first words were not very encouraging, when one of the class made the remark,

'Humph, a new game,"' Naismith recalled. "I asked the boys to try it once as a favor to me. They started, and after the ball was first thrown up there was no need of further coaxing."

Naismith's Game Is a Hit

The elements meshed together rather loosely, but all in all the effort was a rousing success. The first hoopsters had been bitten by the bug. One student even suggested that the instructor label the new game "Naismith ball," which Naismith rejected. The student, Frank Mahon, then offered another suggestion—"basket ball."

It wasn't long before lunchtime crowds began gathering to watch the frenetic action of "basket ball" in Naismith's class. It was an awkward game with two teams of nine students attempting to heave a soccer ball into peach baskets suspended 10 feet above the gym floor. But even in its rudimentary stage, it held a peculiar magic. It was fun to play and, almost as important, fun to watch. Basketball rather quickly became a spectator sport. Aided by the YMCA's missionary nature and its network of centers, Naismith's invention soon spread.

On February 12, 1892, the central and Armory Hill branches of the Springfield YMCA staged a boys game that drew a crowd of 100 or so and resulted in a 2-2 tie. "The game is a very pretty one to watch," reported the *Springfield Daily Republican.*

James Naismith: The father of basketball.

By March 12, Naismith's idea was refined enough to weather another public display. The school's faculty took on the students in a game that drew 200 spectators. The students won, 5-1, and Amos Alonzo Stagg, who would go on to fame coaching college football, scored the faculty's only goal. "The most conspicuous figure on the floor was Stagg in the blue Yale uniform, who managed to have a hand in every scrimmage," the *Republican* reported. "His football training hampered him and he was perpetually making fouls by shoving his opponents."

Later that same month, Naismith took a team on a tour of exhibition games in Troy, Albany, and Schenectady, New York, and Newport and Providence, Rhode Island. In April, the Brooklyn YMCA was playing games against other New York branches.

Something of a fad, the game was on its way to rapid distribution. Its popularity among YMCA members and high school athletes grew from there. By the winter of 1893–94, the YMCA in Hartford, Connecticut, had organized a five-team league. The public was invited in to see the games. No admission was charged, except 10 cents for reserved seats. By the end of the winter, more than 10,000 spectators had come to watch the action and the YMCA had collected a $250 profit.

Soon, athletic clubs and high schools took up basketball; then the colleges followed. Women, too, were soon won over by the new game's charm. And before long, "professionals" were attempting to make a few dollars on weekends playing on courts enclosed by wire cages (thus, early basketballers were called "cagers"). By the turn of the century, barnstorming pro teams playing in small Northeastern cities were drawing a few hundred paying fans.

But the real growth in popularity came with the college sport. The early 20th century brought a refinement of rules, and by the 1920s,

THE FIRST RULES On January 15, 1892, James Naismith's "basket ball" rules were printed in the Springfield (Mass.) YMCA School for Christian Workers newspaper, the *Triangle*. They read as follows:

1. The ball may be thrown in any direction with one or both hands.

2. The ball may be batted in any direction with one or both hands (never with the fist).

3. A player cannot run with the ball. The player must throw it from the spot on which he catches it; allowance to be made for a man who catches the ball when running at a good speed.

4. The ball must be held in or between the hands; the arms or body must not be used for holding it.

5. No shouldering, holding, pushing, tripping or striking, in any way the person of an opponent shall be allowed; the first infringement of this rule by any person shall count as a foul, the second shall disqualify him until the next goal is made; or, if there was evident intent to injure the person for the whole of the game, no substitute shall be allowed.

6. A foul is striking at the ball with the fist, violation of Rules 3, 4, and such as described in Rule 5.

7. If either side makes three consecutive fouls, it shall count a goal for the opponents. (Consecutive means without the opponents in the meantime making a foul.)

8. A goal shall be made when the ball is thrown or batted from the ground into the basket and stays there, providing those defending the goal do not touch or disturb the goal. If the ball rests on the edge and the opponent moves the basket, it shall count as a goal.

9. When the ball goes out of bounds, it shall be thrown into the field and played by the person first touching it. In case of a dispute, the umpire shall throw it straight into the field. The thrower-in is allowed five seconds. If he holds it longer, it shall go to the opponent. If any side persists in delaying the game, the umpire shall call a foul on them.

10. The umpire shall be the judge of the men and shall note the fouls and notify the referee when three consecutive fouls have been made. He shall have power to disqualify men according to Rule 5.

11. The referee shall be the judge of the ball and shall decide when the ball is in play, in bounds, to which side it belongs, and shall keep the time. He shall decide when a goal has been made, and keep account of the goals, with any other duties that are usually performed by a referee.

12. The time shall be two fifteen minute halves, with five minutes rest between.

13. The side making the most goals in that time shall be declared the winners. In case of a draw, the game may, by agreement of the captains, be continued until another goal is made.

promoters found they could earn a tidy profit staging college games, the only problem being that the crowds demanded more action and less stalling and fouling and free-throw shooting. The rules makers eventually complied, and the sport bounced along toward a new level of popularity. In 1938 and 1939, with the founding of the National Invitation and the National Collegiate Athletic Association tournaments, basketball found a format that would open the way to mass appeal.

Yet much of the success of the modern game can be traced to the sport's early decades, a fascinating time, complete with strange stories, hot competition, and constantly changing rules.

The New Century

Basketball was born in a time of bicycles and penny arcades and Sunday school picnics. Women wore corsets and full skirts; men sported straw hats, slightly tilted. Community brass bands were a favorite. "There'll Be a Hot Time in the Old Town Tonight" was the hit song. Yet all around there were signs of change in 1891. The newly invented wonders of the world were the trolley car and electric elevator. Ragtime music marked America's quickening, nervous rhythm.

RULES CHANGES DURING THE EARLY YEARS

1895: The free-throw line is moved from 20 feet to 15.

1896: A field goal changes from three to two points, and free throws from three points to one point.

1897: Backboards are first installed.

1901: A dribbler cannot shoot for a field goal and may dribble only once, and then with two hands.

1909: A dribbler is permitted to shoot. The double dribble is made illegal.

1911: Players are disqualified upon committing their fourth personal foul. No coaching is permitted during the progress of a game by anybody connected with their team. A warning is given for the first violation and a free throw is awarded after that.

1914: The bottom of the net is left open.

1915: College, YMCA, and AAU rules are made the same for the first time.

1921: A player is permitted to reenter the game once. Previously, a player could not reenter for the remainder of the game if he exited the contest. Backboards are moved two feet from the wall of the court. Previously, players would "climb" up the padded wall to sink baskets.

1922: Running with the ball changes from a foul to a violation.

1924: A fouled player must shoot his own free throws. Previously, one person usually shot all of his team's foul shots.

1929: The charging foul is introduced.

1931: A "held ball" can be assessed when a closely guarded player is keeping the ball from play for five seconds. The result will be a jump ball.

1933: The 10-second center line is introduced to de-emphasize stalling.

1934: A player is permitted to reenter a game twice.

1936: No offensive player can remain in the free-throw lane, with or without the ball, for longer than three seconds. Following a successful free throw, the team scored upon shall put the ball in play at the end of the court where the goal was scored.

To fill leisure time brought on by industrialization, people hungered for more diversion, and sports provided cheap, quick alternatives. In the spring and summer, they had baseball, and in the fall they had the newfangled game of football. But winters were the dark ages, until quite suddenly in 1891, Naismith introduced some light.

Seemingly overnight, basketball was being played in every YMCA in America.

"It is doubtful if the history of competitive games contains an example of more rapid growth than that shown by basket ball during the first two or three years of its existence," wrote Dr. Joseph E. Raycroft, the coach of the University of Chicago's great early teams. "Even the remarkable spread of baseball in the years immediately following the Civil War was second to this."

Basketball fit just the need for a rigorous indoor game, plus it had the evangelistic fervor of "muscular Christianity" on its side. From Naismith's first class, one student introduced the game in India; another took it to China, and another to Japan. Everywhere the YMCA reached, basketball touched the population. And through students who belonged to YMCAs, the sport eventually worked its way into the colleges. In 1893, W. O. Black left the YMCA's school in Springfield and took the game to Stanford University. A classmate, W. H. Anderson, introduced basketball at Yale. Another Springfield alumnus, Charles Bemus, reportedly started a team at little Geneva College in Pennsylvania as early as 1892. The University of Toronto and Vanderbilt University also reportedly had teams as early as 1893. That same year Amos Alonzo Stagg left Springfield and went to the University of Chicago, where he founded a team in 1894 that played a seven-game schedule against local athletic clubs. Early written accounts indicate that during 1894 students at Yale and Cornell formed teams to play against New England athletic clubs. Temple University, Ohio State University, and Haverford College all started teams shortly thereafter.

The First College Game?

In February of 1895, a team from the Minnesota School of Agriculture and Mining beat Hamline College, 9-3, in what is generally considered the first game between two college teams. Each side, however, played nine players at a time. A month later, a Haverford College team beat Temple, 6-4. In 1896, Stagg's Chicago team defeated a YMCA team composed of University of Iowa students, 15-12, in a game that featured five men on a side. But Penn athletic director Ralph Morgan claimed the first real intercollegiate game occurred when Yale defeated Penn, 32-10, in 1897.

As it had for early football, Yale played a large role in the development of basketball. It was there that the five-man game found its footing, and there that the dribble gained popularity as both a defensive and offensive weapon.

"Yale continued to put a team on the floor in 1898, 1899 and 1900," Morgan wrote, "but no college team was again met until 1899, when Yale played and defeated Cornell in Poughkeepsie, N.Y., by the score of 49-7. In 1900, Yale took a Western trip and played, among other teams, Ohio State and Wisconsin."

Morgan's opinion that Yale and Penn played the first intercollegiate game may reflect

an Eastern bias because historians have found it difficult to determine exactly who played the first game. After a time, it mattered little anyway. Each passing season brought more schools into the fold. After all, basketball was the new game for the new age. Its rapid pace appealed to the young.

"In playing it comes the joy of a quickened pulse and fast-working lungs, the health-giving exercise to all our muscles, the forgetting of all troubles," wrote an elated Southerner in 1902. "There is no game which requires more wind or endurance nor which needs greater agility and deftness."

Despite the game's appeal, a large number of colleges still had no team, leaving basketball to those schools that had gymnasiums. Other colleges, eager to begin the sport, played their games outdoors. Hiram College won an exhibition tournament played outdoors at the 1904 Olympic games in St. Louis. Some colleges continued outdoor competition well into the next decade, and international competition would retain that format even longer.

Some traditionally strong football teams, such as Harvard and Princeton, couldn't seem to get the knack of the new game. Others found almost instant success. The University of Nebraska started a team and created an early dynasty of sorts by closing out the century with 19 wins in a row from 1898–1900. Notre Dame, the most recognized football power in college history, has an unusual historical footnote involving its first basketball captain, John Shillington. Most people know that the sinking of the *Maine* led to the United States' involvement in the Spanish-American War. Few, however, know that Shillington was among those who went down with the ship in the Havana harbor on February 15, 1898. A monument to him—a mounted shell taken from the sunken ship—was erected in front of Brownson Hall, his last home on Notre Dame's campus.

Rules Made to Order

The more colleges became involved in basketball, the more they wanted to have a say in the rules, a situation that grew increasingly awkward early in the new century. The YMCA and the Athletic Amateur Union (AAU) had run the rules committee together, but this arrangement didn't last long. The AAU forbade Yale to play during the 1904–5 season because it was an "unregistered" team, but the school persisted

anyway. The AAU then told Penn that it, too, would lose official sanction if it played a scheduled game against Yale. Penn athletic director Ralph Morgan, then still an undergraduate, was angered by the AAU's position and called a series of meetings in 1905, leading to the formation of the Intercollegiate Athletic Association, the forerunner of the NCAA, and the establishing of a separate set of college rules. Soon afterward, college and AAU officials made peace and began meeting to discuss the rules of their respective games, but they would not merge as a joint rules organization until 1915.

This organizing of the college game helped bring a surge of growth. In 1905, there were an estimated 88 colleges engaged in basketball, with the bulk of them in Pennsylvania, New York, and Ohio. By 1914, these ranks had swelled to 366, with substantial growth in Illinois, Indiana, Iowa, Kansas, Michigan, Minnesota, Missouri, Virginia, and Wisconsin.

This overwhelming acceptance left basketball's earliest promoters both amazed and proud. "More men and boys are playing Basket Ball than are playing any organized sport in America, with the exception of baseball," declared the YMCA's Dr. Luther Gulick in the 1908–9 issue of *Spalding's Guide,* the sport's early yearbook. "It has become the American indoor game."

But, as *Spalding's* editors explained, there simply weren't enough qualified and seasoned officials to keep up with the pace of expansion. Other difficulties stemmed from the evolution of the rules. Drastic changes were made yearly, requiring officials to have the skills of a lawyer to keep pace.

"During 1908, 1909 and 1910, considerable criticism of the game was made, principally from New England, where President (Charles) Eliot of Harvard was a particular foe," wrote Ralph Morgan in 1914. One player acquired 15 fouls in a game against Harvard, which hastened Eliot's complaints. The criticism was answered with a series of revisions, but not to

Eliot's liking. Declaring that "basket ball has become even more brutal than football," Eliot barred the sport at Harvard in 1909. In its official reasoning, the university stated, "The games more closely resembled free fights than friendly athletic contests between amateur teams."

Opponents of Harvard's action suggested the school was merely frustrated by a poor record. But such criticism hastened the sport away from unnecessary roughness. There was little question that Eastern basketball had developed a reputation for forwards who powered and shoved their way near the goal for a score. There was no three-second violation in those days, which left the floor open to sumo-style struggles underneath the hoop.

To counteract the criticism, the rules committee in 1909–10 rescinded its 1908 five-foul rule. Instead, players would be disqualified after four fouls, which reduced the violence somewhat. Some areas of the country even saw the addition of a second referee in 1910.

Playing style was another factor in moving basketball away from brutishness. Observers were already noting the different styles Western teams played. The Mississippi Valley style focused on solid defense, fast-breaking offense and one-handed shots, wrote E. P. O'Neill in the 1906–7 *Spalding's Guide*. "Long, swift passes replace excessive footwork, and the forwards depend on backward one-foot pivots and one-handed throws for shots at goal rather than numerous passes to obtain an unguarded throw. A one-handed shot is more inaccurate than a two-handed shot, but it is not to be guarded without a foul."

Another help in alleviating the inside struggle was the development of the outside shooter. The early game featured forwards and centers as the big scorers, until players such as 5-4 guard Barney Sedran came along. He led City College of New York in scoring from 1909 to 1911. The first of the great set shooters, Sedran would heave 20- and 30-footers into goals with-

out backboards, a skill that carried him on to a celebrated professional career.

Bucknell's John Anderson, the only player to score 50 or more points in a game until George Mikan in 1945, had 80 vs. Philadelphia College of Pharmacy in 1903. No team averaged at least 80 points in a season until 1952.

East Meets West

Perhaps the most important development in the college game was the founding of leagues or conferences. That brought organization and scheduling to the competition. More important, the leagues began setting up training classes for officials.

In May 1901, several schools, including Yale, Harvard, Trinity, Holy Cross, Amherst, and Williams, formed the New England Intercollegiate Basketball League. However, Yale and Harvard dropped out later that year to join the newly formed Eastern Intercollegiate League, the forerunner of the Ivy League. The New England League lasted just one season before folding.

The formation of leagues added a new element of competitiveness to college basketball, setting up the potential for intersectional rivalries. This potential was realized in 1905 when teams from the universities of Wisconsin and Minnesota barnstormed east to take on Columbia, the undefeated champion of the Eastern League.

Emmett Angell coached Wisconsin; his team featured Christian Steinmetz, the first college player to score one thousand points (1903–5), and Bob Zuppke, who would go on to fame as a college football coach. Steinmetz had gained notoriety by scoring what then was the incredible total of 44 points in an 80-10 win over Beloit. In 1905, he would score 50 points in another game. But even his firepower didn't help on the Eastern road trip. The Badgers "played a number of minor games on their trip from the West," reported the 1905–6 edition of *Spalding's*, "and consequently were in excellent condition when they met the Columbia University Five in New York City. As had been predicted by the Eastern critics, the Westerners could not cope with the accurate passing and shooting, or the speedy play of the Blue and White Five, and were handily defeated by the respective scores of 21-15 and 27-15. The victories in these two contests and the winning of the championship of the Eastern colleges gives Columbia the undisputed title of 'Intercollegiate Champions of the United States.'"

If nothing else, the games reflected just how differently the regions approached the game. "Western" teams were used to closely called games, while the Eastern players were glad to mix it up.

"The Minnesota and Wisconsin men played in the style prevalent among most of the girl colleges in the East, that is, the 'no contact' game," sneered Yale's W. C. Hyatt.

Such pettiness aside, Steinmetz was named to the Naismith Memorial Basketball Hall of Fame in 1961. He scored 462 points in a single season, an amazing total in the early years. Harry Fisher, Columbia's leading scorer between 1902 and 1905, was elected to the Hall of Fame in 1973. He scored 13 field goals in a game in 1905, a collegiate record that stood for 45 years. After college, Fisher went on to an esteemed coaching career at Columbia and Army.

Early Conferences

In the 1905–6 season, the big schools of the Midwest met in Chicago to form the "Western Conference," the forerunner of the Big Ten. Members included the universities of Chicago, Minnesota, Wisconsin, Illinois, and Purdue. Similar alliances appeared around the country. The Southern Intercollegiate Athletic Association, featuring Georgia Tech, Auburn, Howard College, Tulane, Vanderbilt, and the University of Georgia, formed for the 1905–6 season and entertained Yale's Southern tour.

The 1908–9 season brought two more major conferences plus the expansion of the Western with Indiana, Iowa, and Northwestern joining the league. The Missouri Valley Conference

formed two divisions, with Kansas, Missouri, and Washington College in the Southern and Nebraska, Ames (Iowa State), and Drake in the Northern.

The Northwest College Conference formed that same season (1908–9) with Oregon Agricultural (Oregon State), Whitman College, Washington State, and the University of Idaho. The next season, the universities of Washington and Oregon also joined the group.

The top program in basketball during the era was the University of Chicago, which compiled a 78-12 record from 1900 to 1909. Chicago's best player was 6-3 center John Schommer, who led the Western League in scoring for three years, averaging just over 10 points per game. A three-time Helms Foundation All-American, he was selected national player of the year in 1909 and would become known in later life for inventing the modern backboard.

"Head and shoulders above all players in the league" is how Wisconsin great Chris Steinmetz described Schommer, who, according to *Spalding's*, had all the assets of a great center—speed, strength, reach, and size. Plus, he could shoot and never loafed on defense, Steinmetz said.

In the backcourt, Chicago had H. O. "Pat" Page, a quick guard and two-time All-American who went on to coaching fame at both Chicago and Butler. Page was named national player of the year in 1910.

Chicago was also one of the first colleges to have a paid coach, Dr. Joseph E. Raycroft. The combination of a paid coach, quick guard, and star center carried Chicago to a 21-2 record and the "national" championship in 1908. But before claiming national honors, Chicago had to battle the University of Wisconsin in Madison before a crowd of 1,500 for the Western title. Chicago won on a last-minute shot by Page, 18-16. The prize was a berth in a two-game playoff with the Eastern champion, Penn. At 8-0, Penn was projected by basketball's Eastern establishment to be the favorite.

But Chicago beat Penn in a two-game series. Although his team lost, Penn's all-conference forward Charles Keinath dazzled a *Spalding's* writer, who reported "his dribbling electrified the crowd, many of whom before had never seen such fancy footwork."

Other conferences, particularly the resuscitated New England League, scoffed that a playoff between two leagues hardly amounted to a national championship. With college leagues springing up in every region of the country, schools were tiring of the Eastern bias. With the help of the New York newspapers, the Eastern League pretentiously announced an "All-America" team each year featuring only Eastern players.

Still, the college game was young and already thirsting to declare a national champion. "The 1908 series had a very good effect on basket ball," declared *Spalding's*, "and the contending teams showed tremendous crowds in Philadelphia and Chicago what a good, wholesome, sportsmanlike game basket ball is."

Chicago finished the 1908–9 season undefeated at 12-0, but despite a clamoring for a championship match against Columbia, the Eastern champion, none could be scheduled. Instead, *Spalding's* listed the various regional league champions, including Georgetown in the Southern, Kansas in the Middle West, Oregon Agriculture in the Northwest, and Williams in New England. The no-championship stalemate would remain for many seasons. Chicago won the Western and Columbia the Eastern again in 1910, but no national championship series between the two leagues could be scheduled.

"The question of intercollegiate supremacy arose, bringing in its wake volumes of idle words, footless arguments and bootless discussions," wrote Oswald Tower, a member of the rules committee, in 1910, "and when all was said and done, no impartial critic could say with any certainty that the best team of this section was better than the best team of any other section."

Great Teams Emerge

The first decade of the new century brought a stunning evolution in basketball. Several teams emerged as powerhouses. Joining the ranks of prominent winners were Dayton, Oregon State, Michigan State, Montana, and Wisconsin. Minnesota won a whopping 107 games during the period.

The next 10 years brought the rise of the Naval Academy with a record of 109-9 from 1910–19, a .924 winning percentage. The University of Texas won 102 games during that period, including a 44-game winning streak beginning in 1913. Other big winners included Virginia, Creighton, California, Virginia Polytechnic, Wisconsin, Illinois, Texas A&M, Kansas State, Syracuse, and numerous other schools.

Despite the flowering of these regional college basketball cultures, the establishment of an annual national champion was further complicated by the difficulties of travel and changes in rules and equipment. Some teams played outdoors. Some used old rules, some new. The official joining of the YMCA, NCAA, and AAU in a rules committee in 1915 helped, but the question of a national champion remained cloudy. Some teams took turns trumpeting their greatness through friendly newspaper editors. Other college teams entered the national AAU competition, hoping that the national title there would stand as evidence that they were the best.

Allen and the Rise of Coaches

The 1908–10 seasons marked a major turning point for the college game. Glass backboards were allowed; out-of-bounds rules were firmed up to eliminate the mad scrambles for the ball out of play; traveling rules were tightened to allow the ball handler only one step; and the double dribble was eliminated.

Despite complaints about roughness, the game was opening up. James Naismith, who had since obtained his degree in medicine and retreated to the faculty at the University of Kansas where he coached that school's team for nine seasons, was particularly pleased with the effect dribbling had on the game.

"The restoration of the dribble has made the game more enjoyable from the standpoint of the spectators as well as the players," he observed. "It has done away with some of the negative features and helped make the game cleaner. This is especially true on large floors, for the chief cause of the roughness was the attempt of the guard to prevent the player with the ball from getting a good, clean throw, and as the player was unable to move, he was unmercifully crowded, and this individual crowding was so evident to the spectators that it made it appear as if the game was exceedingly rough. But with the dribble, if there is no one to whom a player can pass, he can get away from the crowding. The dribble gives the opportunity for the exhibition of skill of the highest order, and spectators show their appreciation of this by bursts of applause that greet the performance of some favorite expert."

With its early success, the college game was beginning to show tinges of commerce. Many programs found they could be self-supporting, even profitable, from ticket sales alone. Dr. Raycroft, Chicago's paid coach, created a stir when he accepted a similar job at Princeton because that school, eager for a winning, big-time program, made him a better offer.

From the game's earliest days, Naismith had believed coaches were unnecessary. "The game isn't meant to be coached; it's meant to be played," he said. But experience proved him wrong. Naismith coached with a philosophy of letting his players play. To this date, he is the only coach in Kansas history with a losing career record.

As schools became more competitive, they wanted men who could make them winners. Yale hired its first professional coach in 1907. About that time Naismith learned what effect a good coach could have. An undergraduate named Forrest "Phog" Allen coached Baker University to an undefeated season, including wins over Kansas and Missouri. Naismith agreed to turn the Kansas coaching job over to Allen for 1907–8. That season Allen coached both Baker and Kansas, and the following season, 1908–9, he added the coaching job at Haskell Institute to his duties. Over two busy seasons, Allen won 116 games. Kansas alone went to a 26-3 record under the young coach in 1908–9 and won the Missouri Valley Conference championship.

Allen earned his medical degree over the next four years at the Kansas City School of Osteopathy, then returned to coaching at Warrensburg Teachers College, where he ran up a 107-7 record and won seven Missouri College Conference championships in seven years. He then returned to Kansas and compiled a career record of 771-233, a .768 winning percentage, good enough for fourth on the all-time list of winningest college coaches.

An autocratic man, Allen pushed college basketball toward the concepts of recruiting and professionalism. Naismith, of course, opposed these things, believing instead in the supremacy of amateurism. He supported the notion of basketball for the fun of it. He and Allen often disagreed over rule changes, but the two men worked together amicably on the Kansas campus for a number of years.

Something of a self-promoter, Allen fancied himself as a "father of basketball coaches." His innovations included a blending of man-to-man and zone defenses, what he called a man defense "with zone principle." His teams ran the standard pattern offense, but Allen believed deeply that the formula for victory in basketball was coaching strategy. His record suggests that he knew what he was talking about.

There were several other excellent coaches in college basketball's formative era. Among them were:

Doc Meanwell: He never played basketball but became one of the early game's most innovative coaches. Meanwell received his medical degree from the University of Maryland in 1909, and became interested in the game while teaching it to children in Baltimore's slums. He became the coach at the University of Wisconsin in 1911 and earned a doctorate in public health there in 1915. In 20 years at Wisconsin and two at the University of Missouri, he won 290 games and six conference titles. He also helped direct the development of the valve-free, hidden-lace ball. As a coach, he believed fiercely that, using the short pass in a pattern offense, a team could work for the right shot. His teams were patient and ran up a 44-1 record in his first three years at Wisconsin. He disdained the dribble and taught tight, tight defense.

Cam Henderson: He coached at two West Virginia colleges, Davis & Elkins first, then at Marshall. From about 1916 to 1930, the standing zone was the defense that ruled college basketball. Henderson's teams played it so well that other coaches copied his innovations. His 611 career victories still rank him among the all-time winningest college coaches.

Doc Carlson: He earned his medical degree at the University of Pittsburgh in 1920, then became basketball coach there in 1922. Carlson invented the "Figure 8" offense and directed two Pitt teams (1928 and 1930) to the mythical national championship. He won 371 games in 31 years at Pitt. Known as one of early basketball's more colorful figures, he was never too consumed with a game to carry on with spectators. A fan in Morgantown, West Virginia, once dumped a bucket of water on Carlson, after the coach continually complained of bad officiating by saying, "This burns me up."

SIZZLING SCORERS

Bucknell's John Anderson exploded for 80 points vs. Philadelphia College of Pharmacy in 1903. To put Anderson's output in perspective, no team averaged at least 80 points in a season until 1952. Anderson's outburst remains a Bucknell single-game scoring record.

The first two decades of the 20th century also saw several other players set what are still school single-game scoring records. Consider:

- Delaware's Liston A. Houston poured in 52 points against Lebanon Valley in the 1909-10 campaign.
- Clemson's J.O. Erwin tallied 58 points against the Butler Guards in the 1911-12 season.
- Toledo's Clark (Pinky) Pittenger pumped in 49 points against Bluffton in the 1918-19 season.

The Fans Arrive

The college game got a glimpse at its future in 1920 when 10,000 fans packed the 168th Street Regimental Armory in New York to see a tournament featuring City College of New York and New York University. The rival New York teams were off to big seasons, and just like that, entrepreneurs saw where the money was. Instead of the usual 1,500 to 2,000 spectators (NYU didn't have a gym and played some games on a Hudson River barge), the game was standing room only. Led by star (and future college coaching legend) Howard Cann, NYU won 39-21 and went on to capture the national AAU title in Atlanta later in the year.

The game helped show college basketball its future—big crowds. The 1920s brought the construction of numerous arenas, many of them in the Midwest. The University of Iowa, for example, built a 16,000-seat facility.

The decade brought more good teams. Montana State led the charge, winning 213 games against 44 defeats between 1920 and 1929. Army, Navy, North Carolina, Cal, Creighton, Oklahoma, Penn State, and CCNY all produced excellent teams.

At Kansas, Phog Allen won six Missouri Valley conference championships in the 1920s, leading Kansas partisans to claim at least two national championships. In 1928, Pittsburgh went 21-0. The Panthers were led by forward Chuck Hyatt and guard Sykes Reed. Hyatt, a three-time college All-American, led the nation in scoring his senior year, 1929–30, and Pitt again earned top rankings with a 23-2 season. During his career, Pitt rang up a 60-7 record. He went on to become an AAU All-American, playing nine seasons for the Phillips 66 Oilers.

Other great players of the 1920s included:

Paul Endacott: Named Helms Foundation Player of the Year in 1923, Endacott was the heart of Phog Allen's undefeated 1923 Kansas team. In 1924, Dr. Naismith declared Endacott the best ever at Kansas. A quarter century later, the appraisals were still high. Allen named him to the national All-Time College Team.

Victor A. Hanson: A three-time All-American for Syracuse, 1925–27, Hanson led the Orangemen to a 48-7 record during his college career and the 1925-26 national championship. He was named national player of the year in 1927, and Grantland Rice named him to the All-Time All-American team in 1952. Hanson played pro basketball with the Cleveland Rosenblums and organized baseball in the New York Yankees' organization. He even coached football at Syracuse from 1930 to 1936 (see Chapter 9).

Branch McCracken: Led Indiana to basketball prominence in the late 1920s. An All-Big Ten selection three years running, he set the conference scoring record his senior year and was named All-American. He later coached the Hoosiers to national championships in 1940 and 1953.

John Roosma: A key player on the great Passaic (N.J.) High School "Wonder Team," Roosma went on to play at the U.S. Military Academy, where he led the Cadets to 33 consecutive wins and an undefeated season. Over three years, he carried Army to a 70-3 record. Later he achieved the rank of colonel in the Army.

Charles Murphy: He led his high school team to the Indiana state title in 1926, then went on to two-time All-America honors at Purdue.

Forrest S. DeBernardi: He scored 50 points in a game for Westminster College in 1920, then went on to become an AAU All-American in 1921, 1922, and 1923. He played three different positions and earned All-American honors at each of them.

John A. "Cat" Thompson: The player largely responsible for Montana State's great success in the 1920s, Thompson was named Helms Foundation player of the year in 1929. During his career, Montana State compiled a 72-4 record. Thompson scored 1,539 points in three years of college play, astronomical numbers for the era.

Harold "Bud" Foster: One of Doc Meanwell's key charges at Wisconsin, Foster led the Badgers to the Western Conference championship in 1929 and was named All-American in 1930.

Early Integration and African-American Teams

African Americans took up basketball shortly after the game's invention, and by the turn of the century were beginning to gain limited prominence. By 1906, black athletic clubs in Brooklyn, New Jersey, and New York had begun sponsoring teams. Soon college programs followed. By 1910, Lincoln University, Howard University, Hampton Institute, and Union University entered the competition.

The 1920s brought limited integration of some college teams. At Columbia, sophomore George Gregory gained notoriety as the All-

Eastern Conference center for 1928–29. Described in *Spalding's* as "the tall colored boy who played center" and as "the graceful Columbia center," Gregory ranked fourth in the conference in scoring and second in free throws made.

Penn athletic director Ralph Morgan wrote, "Gregory had height; he got the tap; he was fast and could shoot. The coaches were clearly right when they selected him (to the all-conference team)."

That same season Western Illinois State Teacher's College had two black players, one of whom, a guard named Page, was selected all-conference. For 1928–29, Southern Cal, the Brooklyn College of Pharmacy, and the Columbia College of Pharmacy teams all had an African-American player.

High school and junior high teams in Pennsylvania showed extensive integration in 1928–29. Elsewhere, from Yankton, South Dakota to Peoria, Illinois, to Warwick, New York, incidents of integration were isolated. But they eventually helped break down the sturdy racial barriers in the college game. In the 1920s, 1930s, and 1940s, noted African-American players began to appear, including Paul Robeson (the future actor and pro football player) at Rutgers, Wilbur Woods at Nebraska, Sadat Singh at Syracuse, and Dolly King at Long Island University.

Star Purdue guard and future UCLA coaching legend John Wooden.

The Last Great Dribble Debate

Basketball seemed to be heading briskly toward its future in the late 1920s, but it paused in 1927 and flirted briefly with the past. Urged on by Wisconsin's Doc Meanwell, who loved the notion of moving the ball only with the short pass, the Joint Rules Committee voted 9-8 to eliminate the dribble. The committee then adjourned to watch the Original Celtics use the passing game to whip the Cleveland Rosenblums for the professional championship. After the game, the committee reconvened, and Meanwell further praised the passing game. But Nat Holman, a member of the Celtics who also coached at CCNY, urged a reconsideration. College players, he argued passionately, were not pros and needed the dribble to maneuver. Upon hearing Holman, the committee voted to keep the dribble in college basketball.

Surviving this threat, the college game was up and running—or off and bouncing—with its big games drawing big crowds. Unknown to many, its greatest legend was already afoot. John Wooden, a quietly determined young guard, had entered Purdue after playing on a high school state championship team in Martinsville, Indiana.

The City Game and the Wonder Five

The moment that college basketball hit the big time isn't exactly clear, but there is little doubt as to the location. The game had kept New York City in its grip since Naismith invented it. Basketball was just the sport to suit Gotham's aggressive nature; it spread quickly across the boroughs, through the YMCAs and athletic clubs. Goals and dirt courts soon appeared on playgrounds around the city, and the neighborhoods came alive with this new competition. Basketball hadn't been born to New Yorkers, but they adopted it as their own.

These feelings only deepened with time. As the game moved into the colleges, the whole city seemed to burn with interest. First came Columbia's big success in 1905. Then dawned the age of "professional" coaches, and New York got its share. Nat Holman, the playmaker for New York's Original Celtics, started at City College of New York in 1919 while still playing pro ball. Ed Kelleher took the coaching job at Fordham in 1922, and Howard Cann went to work at NYU a year later. St. John's hired Buck Freeman, and Lew Andreas took over at upstate Syracuse. Each of these coaches built winning programs, and that in turn built excitement. Within a matter of years, games in small college gyms were packed with 1,500 fans craning their necks for a view of the floor.

The more crowded the games, the more obvious it became that the sport was bursting at the seams. On January 1, 1927, the Palestra opened in Philadelphia, and soon 10,000 spectators crowded inside to see Penn play Princeton. "The Palestra (built for the princely sum of $750,000) was constructed for basketball," wrote Penn's Ralph Morgan.

College basketball, the business, was waiting to be born. All it needed was someone to slap it on the fanny and make it breathe. That someone was a Penn undergraduate, Ned Irish, who witnessed the Palestra phenomenon first hand. A New Yorker, Irish had been working as a part-time sportswriter since high school, making as much as $100 a week from the local papers. When he headed off to college, the New York papers hired him to cover the Philadelphia sports scene. He also worked full time for the *Philadelphia Record*.

Irish returned to New York in 1929 as a sportswriter for the *World-Telegram* and soon made that paper the leader in college basketball coverage (most New York papers virtually ignored the game). For Irish and basketball, the timing couldn't have been better, although the first quake of the Great Depression had already struck. Clair Bee was coaching little Rider College to an 18-3 record, and Freeman had assembled "The Wonder Five" at St. John's. Maturing together for four years, from freshmen to seniors, the "Wonder Five" included 6-5 center Matty Begovich and forward Mack Posnack. The three guards were 5-8 dribble king Mac Kinsbrunner, quick-shooting Allie Schuckman, and defensive specialist Rip Gerson. Freeman packed them into a nifty, Celtics-style post game and let 'em go. In their sophomore season, 1928–29, they ran off an 18-game winning streak on their way to a 23-2 record. They opened the next season, 1929–30, with a 13-game streak, lost a few games, then closed with another run of victories.

Early in the 1930–31 season, the string had grown to 20-something games. The Redmen had grown immensely popular but still played most nights in a packed gym before 1,200 fans. Then, early in 1931, the "Wonder Five" beat CCNY at the 106th Infantry Armory with a record New York crowd of 12,000 watching. Within weeks, Mayor Jimmy Walker was calling on sportswriters to help promote a tripleheader at Madison Square Garden to benefit the Unemployment Relief Fund. Columbia, Fordham, CCNY, Manhattan, St. John's, and NYU were the draw. All had good teams and good records, and 15,000 fans paid to see them play. The Wonder Five beat CCNY again that night to push their win streak to 22. They went on to win 27 in a row and compile a four-year record of 86-8. From there, they toured two years independently, then played five years as the Jewels in the old American League. But the Wonder Five's biggest impact on basketball was the excitement they brought to the city. They had given Irish a hint of things to come.

In 1933, Mayor Walker again set up a basketball benefit, a seven-game extravaganza that attracted 20,000 fans to the Garden, which gave Irish more pause to think. According to some accounts, Irish first hatched the idea of staging big-time games one night as he tore his pants

Stanford star Hank Luisetti was best known for his one-handed shooting style.

while crawling through a window of a little gym in Riverdale to cover a sold-out Manhattan College game. The next season, 1933–34, found the 28-year-old sportswriter plotting to promote a game between NYU and CCNY. He had hoped to play the game at the Garden but a conflict with a boxing match killed the deal. Still, Irish decided to move ahead with his promotional plans. He lined up six dates at the Garden for the following season.

Irish's frantic planning conflicted with his job, and he left the *World-Telegram* a month before the first event. He staked his future on a December 29 doubleheader at the Garden featuring St. John's vs. Westminster and NYU vs. Notre Dame. A sell-out crowd of 16,000 watched, and college basketball, the business, was on its way. Irish's next seven doubleheaders drew 100,000 fans, and he became a rich young man.

From New York, he branched out to Philadelphia, then Buffalo, then other venues. He made vast sums promoting college games. Soon, other promoters picked up his lead with big games from Atlanta to Boston to Chicago.

Bee's Blackbirds vs. Hank's One-Hander

In his writing, author Clair Bee created an ideal athlete, the fictional character Chip Hilton who had it all. Intelligence. Diligence. Honesty. And a nose for victory.

Bee sought to instill those same qualities in the college basketball teams he coached. For the most part, he was overwhelmingly successful. His teams lost just seven games in his seven years of coaching at Rider College. From there, he established a powerhouse at Long Island University from 1931 to 1951. Over those 18 years (Bee missed two seasons while in the service during World War II), his teams won 95 percent of their games, including two NIT titles. LIU's record consisted of winning streaks of 43, 38, 28, and 26 games.

Bee, a small, intense man, was a gentle, scholarly sort, but he could seize on opponents' weaknesses like a mongoose. A thinking man's coach, he held five degrees and authored 44 books, including 23 Chip Hilton volumes. He created the 1-3-1 zone defense and even played a role in bringing the 24-second shot clock to pro basketball (he coached the Baltimore Bullets after leaving LIU in 1951). A native of Grafton, West Virginia, Bee overcame tuberculosis as a child, and his rehabilitation led to an intense involvement with sports.

In his third year at LIU, 1933–34, the Blackbirds finished 27-1, losing only to St. John's and scoring 1,000 points, a benchmark in those days of center jumps after each basket. The next season they ran up a 24-2 record, and suddenly Bee was the toast of New York. In 1935–36, his Blackbirds finished 26-0 with a lineup that fea-

tured Marius Russo (who later pitched for the Yankees), Willie Schwartz, Art Hillhouse, Leo Merson, and Jules Bender. Their one close call on the schedule came against Duquesne in the Garden. Down five points with four minutes to play, the Blackbirds survived on Russo's bucket at the buzzer.

LIU opened the next season on the same note, stretching their winning streak to 43 straight before running into the college game's newest sensation. He was a West Coast player, Stanford's Hank Luisetti, whose polished, running, one-handed shooting style created a stir in those days of set-shooters. Luisetti was 6-3 and handsome, which made him a hero to youngsters on the West Coast. On the East Coast, however, he was virtually unknown until Irish lured Stanford to the Garden.

An invitation from Irish to play at the Garden quickly become a status symbol in 1930s college basketball, and Stanford was definitely among the elite. Luisetti's freshman team went undefeated in 1934–35, and the next year he led Stanford to the Pacific Coast Conference championship. Luisetti's team came East in December of 1936. First, Stanford stopped off in Philadelphia to beat Temple. Then, on December 29, the Indians (called Cardinal now) met Bee's top-ranked LIU team in the Garden. Plump with confidence from their 43-game streak, the Blackbirds were the darlings of the 17,623 spectators. Luisetti didn't open the game with a flashy show of play, but it wasn't long before he wooed the crowd.

Early on, while being guarded by LIU All-American Art Hillhouse, Luisetti fired up his one-hander on the run. "I'll never forget that look on Hillhouse's face," he said years later. "He'd never seen a shot like that. When it hit, I could just see him saying, 'Boy, is this guy lucky.'"

Luisetti went on to score 15, but it was his floor game, passing, and defense that made the difference. Stanford ended LIU's streak that night, 45-31, and the Garden crowd gave Luisetti a standing ovation when he left the floor. "It seemed Luisetti could do nothing wrong," the *New York Times* reported the next morning. "Some of his shots would have been deemed foolhardy if attempted by somebody else, but with Luisetti shooting, these were accepted by the crowd as a matter of course."

The subsequent media attention made Luisetti the darling of college basketball over the remainder of the season and the following year. Stanford traveled about the country, drawing large crowds wherever Luisetti played. And although their coaches frowned on it, schoolboys everywhere began trying to heave up Hank's one-hander.

Stanford returned to New York later that season for a game against CCNY. "I'll quit coaching if I have to teach the one-handed shot to win," declared CCNY coach Nat Holman. "Nobody can convince me that a shot predicated on a prayer is smart basketball."

If Luisetti's shots were prayers, they seemed to get answers. At one point, he popped in 13 consecutive points, and Stanford won, 45-42. The New York newspapers again trumpeted his greatness. Yet Luisetti remained an unselfish player, until finally against Duquesne in Cleveland in 1938, his teammates refused to take shots, feeding his own passes back to him. Luisetti scored 50 that night as Stanford won, 92-27.

Luisetti was twice named national player of the year and led Stanford to three consecutive Pacific titles. He left Stanford in 1938 and was offered a Hollywood deal to make a film, *Campus Confessions,* with Betty Grable. It bombed, and worse, the AAU suspended his amateur status for a season, ruling that he had profited from basketball. Luisetti returned from suspension and went on to star in AAU basketball, but he never followed up his college success with a pro career. He played service ball while in the Navy during World War II and contracted meningitis. Although he won an AAU national

championship in 1951 as a coach, the illness shortened his playing career.

One of the schoolboys affected by Luisetti's example was Jim Pollard, who played at Stanford and later starred with the Minneapolis Lakers. Pollard greatly admired Luisetti: "He was a great guy to watch. He had that charisma about him that everybody liked. Because he was such a graceful ball player and such a great one everybody tried to copy the greatness he had. But Hank was not primarily a scorer. He was a great defensive ball player and an excellent passer. Everybody gives him credit for popularizing the one-hander, which he did. I admit I freely copied it because he was my hero when I was a kid.

"I got to see Hank play a number of times and even played against him frequently in the service for a couple of years. Then when I got out of the service we were going to play together in the Oakland area. I was dying to play with him. He had been hurt during the war when he got spinal meningitis. We scrimmaged about 10 minutes one day. Hank and I took the next three best ball players and just wiped them. Hank was marvelous. But he walked off the floor just like he was drunk. He was weaving; he'd lost his sense of balance. I don't think he ever got on the court again to play."

Tournament Time

Off and on since 1897, the AAU had run a national basketball tournament. The event attracted big interest in Atlanta in 1920, then settled into Kansas City for 1921 and stayed there the next 14 years. But no tournament was held in 1936, and the event moved to Denver.

Angered at the loss of the tournament, Kansas City civic leaders enlisted the help of Dr. Naismith (who was still on the faculty at Kansas) in founding a "national" tournament. The first event in Kansas City in 1937 was actually an eight-team playoff of Midwest conference champions. This tournament organization later flowered into the National Association of

PREMO POWER POLL The first wire-service national poll wasn't conducted until the 1948–49 season by the Associated Press. In an attempt to recognize some of the premier teams in the history of men's college basketball before that time, Patrick M. Premo, a professor of accounting at St. Bonaventure, analyzed every season since 1892–93. Not only did Premo look at each team's opponents and the final scores of each game, but he also reviewed as many of those opponents' games as possible in an attempt to derive a "strength of schedule" for each team.

In the early years, there were often no common opponents, making the evaluations of teams from different regions of the country very difficult. In addition, obtaining information on some schools in the early years was impossible in a number of cases; this accounts for why only a smattering of teams were rankable in the early years. Consequently, some subjectivity was necessary to complete Premo's analysis in reviewing the early years of the sport. Once teams began to oppose clubs outside of their geographic regions, the task of comparing squads became somewhat easier.

In order to avoid confusion, the current name for each school is cited in practically all cases. Premo does not claim that his polls are definitive. They are simply his opinion. But the Premo Power Polls provide a nostalgic trip through the early history of men's college basketball! (See the end of each season's regular-season account in Chapter 2 for the Premo Power Polls in the late 1930s and 1940s. A Premo Power Poll for best teams of each decade is also included at the end of Chapters 1 through 6.)

1892–93

RANKING	TEAM
1	Iowa (2-0-1)7
2	Geneva (1-0)

1893–94

RANKING	TEAM
1	Hiram (Ohio) (1-0)

1894–95

RANKING	TEAM
1	Temple (8-3)

1895–96

RANKING	TEAM
1	Temple (15-7)
2	Yale (8-5)
3	Chicago (5-2)
4	Minnesota (3-2)
5	Bucknell (1-3)

1896–97

RANKING	TEAM
1	Yale (11-5-1)
2	Temple (10-11)
3	Chicago (5-2)
4	Bucknell (4-1)
5	Wabash (1-0)

1897–98

RANKING	TEAM
1	Mount Union (8-1)
2	Yale (12-9)
3	Westminster (Penn.) (4-2)
4	Temple (20-5)
5	Hiram (Ohio) (3-2)

1898–99

RANKING	TEAM
1	Yale (9-1)
2	Allegheny (8-1)
3	Nebraska (4-0)
4	Temple (18-6)
5	Minnesota (7-2)
6	Ohio St. (12-4)
7	Wabash (2-0)
8	Hiram (Ohio) (4-1)
9	Kansas (7-4)
10	Syracuse (1-0-1)

1899–1900

RANKING	TEAM
1	Yale (9-6)
2	Dartmouth (22-4-1)
3	Allegheny (10-4)
4	Nebraska (5-0)
5	Penn St. (7-1)
6	Geneva (8-3)
7	Illinois St. (5-0)
8	Hiram (Ohio) (7-1)
9	Bucknell (6-3)
10	Temple (13-9)

1900–1

RANKING	TEAM
1	Bucknell (12-1)
2	Purdue (12-0)
3	Penn St. (5-1)
4	Yale (10-6)
5	Amherst (4-0)
6	Allegheny (14-2)
7	Minnesota (11-1)
8	Hiram (Ohio) (9-1)
9	Williams (9-2)
10	Dartmouth (11-8)
11	Geneva (10-2)
12	Western Reserve (5-2)
13	Princeton (7-5)
14	Harvard (11-8)
15	Lafayette (4-3)
16	Mount Union (10-6)
17	Syracuse (2-1)
18	Wisc.-Superior (8-2)
19	Michigan St. (3-0)
20	Illinois St. (4-1)

1901–2

RANKING	TEAM
1	Minnesota (15-0)
2	Purdue (11-3)
3	Allegheny (12-1)
4	Amherst (8-0)
5	Iowa (10-2)
6	Williams (12-3)
7	Bucknell (12-2)
8	Wisconsin (7-3)
9	Dartmouth (11-5)
10	Yale (13-8)
11	Penn St. (9-2)
12	Washington (7-0)
13	Colgate (7-2)
14	Harvard (9-5)
15	Pennsylvania (7-2-1)
16	Mount Union (10-2)
17	Lehigh (9-5)
18	Grove City (13-3)
19	Michigan St. (5-0)
20	St. Francis (13-1)

1902–3

RANKING	TEAM
1	Minnesota (13-0)
2	Yale (15-1)
3	Purdue (8-0)
4	Bucknell (10-0)
5	Colgate (7-1)
6	Grove City (13-1)
7	Geneva (10-1)
8	Allegheny (10-2-1)
9	Williams (18-2)
10	Ohio St. (5-2)
11	Columbia (10-6)
12	Princeton (9-6)
13	Wabash (12-3)
14	Hiram (Ohio) (4-1)
15	Wisconsin (5-2)
16	Lehigh (4-2-1)
17	Michigan St. (6-0)
18	Latter Day Sts. (15-1)
19	Wheaton (Ill.) (8-1)
20	Vanderbilt (6-0)

PREMO POWER POLL (CONTD.)

1903–4

RANKING	TEAM
1	Columbia (17-1)
2	Minnesota (11-2)
3	Allegheny (12-2)
4	Purdue (11-2)
5	Holy Cross (10-2)
6	Pennsylvania (10-4)
7	Princeton (10-5)
8	Ohio St. (10-4)
9	Hiram (Ohio) (9-3)
10	Wisconsin (11-4)
11	Williams (15-7)
12	Colgate (12-5)
13	Chicago (7-0)
14	Wheaton (Ill.) (10-3-1)
15	Iowa (6-2)
16	Lehigh (5-2)
17	Washington (5-1)
18	Oregon St. (7-3)
19	Maine (8-2)
20	Illinois St. (7-1)

1904–5

RANKING	TEAM
1	Columbia (19-1)
2	Williams (20-2)
3	Ohio St. (12-2)
4	Allegheny (10-2)
5	Syracuse (16-7)
6	Brown (12-6)
7	Harvard (11-5)
8	Wabash (8-1)
9	Dartmouth (20-10-1)
10	Chicago (9-2)
11	Holy Cross (6-4)
12	Princeton (8-5)
13	Colgate (10-7)
14	Yale (22-13)
15	Butler (6-1)
16	Augustana (Ill.) (9-0)
17	Nebraska (11-5)
18	Penn St. (6-2)
19	Cincinnati (6-3)
20	Dayton (6-1)

1905–6

RANKING	TEAM
1	Wabash (17-1)
2	Dartmouth (16-2)
3	Minnesota (13-2)
4	Wisconsin (12-2)
5	Westminster (Pa.) (12-2)
6	Williams (14-3-1)
7	Pennsylvania (16-4)
8	Bucknell (10-2)
9	Allegheny (13-4)
10	Ohio St. (9-1)
11	Columbia (12-4)
12	Nebraska (12-3)
13	Syracuse (9-3)
14	Harvard (12-4)
15	Holy Cross (12-3)
16	Michigan St. (11-2)
17	Western Reserve (13-3)
18	Wooster (7-3)
19	Oregon St. (10-0)
20	Denison (Ohio) (12-2)

1906–7

RANKING	TEAM
1	Chicago (20-2)
2	Williams (15-1)
3	Wabash (17-2)
4	Columbia (14-4)
5	Allegheny (10-1)
6	Yale (30-6-1)
7	Dartmouth (13-4)
8	Minnesota (10-2)
9	Wisconsin (11-3)
10	Oregon St. (17-1)
11	Westminster (Pa.) (7-1)
12	Bucknell (10-1)
13	Michigan St. (14-2)
14	Dayton (14-0)
15	Grinnell (9-2)
16	Akron (5-2)
17	Lehigh (9-2)
18	CCNY (8-1)
19	Buffalo (6-2)
20	Vanderbilt (6-1)

1907–8

RANKING	TEAM
1	Wabash (24-0)
2	Chicago (21-2)
3	Pennsylvania (23-4)
4	Allegheny (12-0)
5	Wisconsin (10-2)
6	Bucknell (12-0)
7	Grinnell (14-3)
8	Notre Dame (12-4)
9	Syracuse (11-2)
10	Michigan St. (15-5)
11	Dartmouth (11-4)
12	CCNY (9-2)
13	Penn St. (10-4)
14	St. Lawrence (9-2)
15	Lehigh (6-1)
16	Georgetown (5-1)
17	Haskell (24-11)
18	Mount Union (17-3)
19	Washington St. (12-3)
20	Cincinnati (9-0)

1908–9

RANKING	TEAM
1	Chicago (12-0)
2	Swarthmore (12-0)
3	NYU (13-0)
4	Williams (13-1)
5	Columbia (16-1)
6	Ohio St. (11-1)
7	Notre Dame (33-7)
8	Allegheny (11-2)
9	Army (9-2)
10	Grinnell (12-1)
11	Wooster (10-2)
12	Bucknell (9-3)
13	Oregon St. (10-1)
14	Vanderbilt (11-4)
15	Kansas (25-3)
16	Georgia (6-2)
17	Washington (9-1)
18	Dayton (12-2)
19	Illinois St. (9-0)
20	MIT (10-6)

1909–10

RANKING	TEAM
1	Williams (11-0)
2	Columbia (11-1)
3	Army (14-1)
4	Kansas (18-1)
5	VPI (11-0)
6	Cotner (Neb.) (11-0)
7	Centre (Ky.) (20-3)
8	Minnesota (10-3)
9	Kansas St. (11-2-1)
10	Chicago (9-3)
11	Navy (10-1)
12	Ohio St. (11-1)
13	Grinnell (12-1)
14	Iowa (11-3)
15	Allegheny (9-3)
16	NYU (13-4)
17	Swarthmore (9-3)
18	Niagara (13-3)
19	Oberlin (10-3)
20	Oklahoma (8-0)

1910–11

RANKING	TEAM
1	St. John's (14-0)
2	Columbia (13-1)
3	Navy (10-1)
4	Dayton (10-0)
5	Wabash (10-1)
6	Ohio St. (7-2)
7	VPI (11-1)
8	Notre Dame (7-3)
9	Allegheny (9-2)
10	Wesleyan (Conn.) (10-3)
11	Army (9-3)
12	Oberlin (10-2)
13	Washington (11-1)
14	N. Central College (14-2)
15	Grinnell (13-1)
16	Williams (8-2)
17	Wooster (16-4)
18	Oregon (9-3)
19	CCNY (7-2)
20	Union (7-2)

1911–12

RANKING	TEAM
1	Wisconsin (15-0)
2	Purdue (12-0)
3	Grove City (13-0)
4	Allegheny (11-1)
5	Swarthmore (11-1)
6	Wesleyan (Conn.) (13-0)
7	Notre Dame (15-2)
8	Navy (7-1)
9	Beloit (6-2)
10	Columbia (10-2)
11	Dayton (13-0)
12	Oregon St. (16-3)
13	Washington (12-4)
14	Nebraska (14-1)
15	Oregon (9-3)
16	Kentucky (9-0)
17	Syracuse (11-3)
18	St. Lawrence (12-3)
19	Mississippi St. (9-0)
20	Mississippi (10-2)

PREMO POWER POLL (CONTD.)

1912–13

RANKING	TEAM
1	Navy (9-0)
2	Denison (Ohio) (13-1)
3	Dayton (11-0)
4	Wisconsin (14-1)
5	Detroit Mercy (13-0)
6	Georgia (10-1)
7	Akron (7-1)
8	Grinnell (11-0)
9	Army (11-2)
10	Nebraska (17-2)
11	Wesleyan (Conn.) (14-2)
12	Notre Dame (13-2)
13	Catholic (14-3)
14	Penn St. (8-3)
15	Lehigh (12-2)
16	Allegheny (9-2)
17	Virginia (12-3)
18	Utah (21-3)
19	Springfield (6-1)
20	Mississippi St. (11-1)

1913–14

RANKING	TEAM
1	Wisconsin (15-0)
2	Denison (Ohio) (15-1)
3	Navy (10-0)
4	Syracuse (12-0)
5	Cornell (14-2)
6	Lehigh (12-2)
7	St. Mary's (Cal.) (15-0)
8	Nebraska (15-3)
9	Virginia (12-1-1)
10	Grinnell (10-1)
11	Georgia (9-1)
12	Kansas (17-1)
13	Oberlin (7-3)
14	Kentucky (12-2)
15	Duquesne (7-2)
16	Washington (12-2)
17	Catholic (13-4)
18	Tennessee (15-2)
19	Utah (12-2)
20	BYU (10-1)

1914–15

RANKING	TEAM
1	Illinois (16-0)
2	Army (11-2)
3	Navy (9-2)
4	Virginia (17-0)
5	Yale (14-3)
6	Syracuse (10-1)
7	Chicago (9-3)
8	Notre Dame (15-2)
9	Cornell (12-4)
10	Allegheny (10-1)
11	Wabash (7-2)
12	Penn St. (10-3)
13	Seton Hall (15-2)
14	Kansas (16-1)
15	Denison (Ohio) (12-2)
16	Washington (17-2)
17	Whittier (17-3)
18	Texas (14-0)
19	Wisconsin (13-4)
20	Duquesne (12-2)

1915–16

RANKING	TEAM
1	Wisconsin (20-1)
2	Allegheny (10-1)
3	Pittsburgh (16-2)
4	Illinois (13-3)
5	Princeton (16-4)
6	Swarthmore (10-2)
7	Navy (12-2)
8	Nebraska (13-1)
9	Utah (10-0)
10	Missouri (13-3)
11	Kansas St. (13-3)
12	Texas (12-0)
13	Wabash (17-4)
14	Washington St. (18-3)
15	Virginia (11-2)
16	Texas A&M (11-2)
17	Catholic (10-4)
18	Tennessee (12-0)
19	Ripon (15-3)
20	Montana St. (10-1)

1916–17

RANKING	TEAM
1	Washington St. (25-1)
2	California (15-1)
3	Wabash (19-2)
4	Minnesota (15-2)
5	Illinois (13-3)
6	Wisconsin (15-3)
7	Kansas St. (15-2)
8	Navy (11-0)
9	CCNY (15-3)
10	Purdue (11-3)
11	Yale (19-5)
12	Lehigh (15-4)
13	Penn St. (12-2)
14	Syracuse (13-3)
15	Montana St. (19-1)
16	Washington & Lee (13-0)
17	Central Missouri St. (13-2)
18	Georgia (8-1)
19	VPI (17-2)
20	Case Tech (12-1)

1917–18

RANKING	TEAM
1	Syracuse (16-1)
2	Oregon St. (15-0)
3	Penn St. (12-1)
4	Pennsylvania (18-2)
5	Geneva (13-2)
6	Navy (14-2)
7	Princeton (12-3)
8	Stevens (14-0)
9	Wash. & Jefferson (10-2)
10	Union (14-1)
11	Idaho (11-1)
12	Missouri (17-1)
13	Wisconsin (14-3)
14	Springfield (13-3)
15	Virginia (7-1)
16	Centre (10-1)
17	Utah St. (9-0)
18	LSU (12-1)
19	Kentucky (9-2-1)
20	North Carolina St. (12-2)

1918–19

RANKING	TEAM
1	Navy (16-0)
2	Minnesota (13-0)
3	Pennsylvania (15-1)
4	Georgetown (9-1)
5	Penn St. (11-2)
6	Wabash (13-3)
7	Cornell (11-3)
8	Oregon (13-3)
9	Yale (7-2)
10	Idaho (13-2)
11	VPI (18-4)
12	Kansas St. (17-2)
13	Santa Clara (14-1)
14	Missouri (14-3)
15	Bucknell (13-3)
16	Delaware (8-2)
17	Chicago (10-2)
18	Oklahoma (12-0)
19	Washington & Lee (10-3)
20	Texas (17-3)

1918–19 TOP SERVICE TEAMS

RANKING	TEAM
1	Great Lakes NTS (23-7)
2	Camp Dodge (10-1)

1919–20

RANKING	TEAM
1	Pennsylvania (22-1)
2	Missouri (17-1)
3	Penn St. (12-1)
4	NYU (16-1)
5	Georgetown (13-1)
6	Purdue (16-4)
7	Delaware (13-2)
8	Wisconsin (15-1)
9	Navy (14-3)
10	Chicago (11-4)
11	Army (12-2)
12	Westminster (Mo.) (17-0)
13	Texas A&M (19-0)
14	Nebraska (22-2)
15	Syracuse (15-3)
16	Montana St. (13-0)
17	Millikin (22-1)
18	CCNY (13-3)
19	Ripon (11-2)
20	Wyoming (10-1)

1920–21

RANKING	TEAM
1	Missouri (17-1)
2	Pennsylvania (21-2)
3	Navy (18-1)
4	NYU (12-1)
5	Penn St. (14-2)
6	Grove City (15-0)
7	VMI (16-1)
8	Stanford (15-3)
9	Nebraska (12-3)
10	Arizona (7-0)
11	Virginia (11-3)
12	Wisconsin (13-4)
13	Ohio Northern (21-3)
14	Michigan (16-4)
15	Central Mo. St. (22-2)
16	Wabash (21-4)
17	Denison (Ohio) (14-3)
18	Ohio University (16-2)
19	DePauw (12-3)
20	Oberlin (11-1)

PREMO POWER POLL (CONTD.)

1921–22

RANKING	TEAM
1	Missouri (16-1)
2	Kansas (16-2)
3	Army (17-2)
4	Idaho (19-1)
5	Oregon St. (21-2)
6	Wabash (21-3)
7	Holy Cross (14-3)
8	Purdue (15-3)
9	Michigan (15-4)
10	CCNY (10-2)
11	Butler (23-4)
12	Princeton (20-5)
13	Illinois (14-5)
14	Wisconsin (14-5)
15	Pennsylvania (24-3)
16	Texas A&M (18-3)
17	Navy (15-3)
18	Wooster (14-1)
19	Beloit (12-0)
20	Texas (20-4)

1922–23

RANKING	TEAM
1	Army (17-0)
2	Kansas (17-1)
3	Missouri (15-3)
4	Springfield (15-1)
5	Butler (16-4)
6	Iowa (13-2)
7	Penn St. (13-1)
8	N. Texas St. (13-1)
9	Hardin-Simmons (13-1)
10	Marquette (19-2)
11	Grove City (15-2)
12	Idaho (14-3)
13	Wisconsin (12-3)
14	Texas A&M (16-4)
15	West Texas St. (12-4)
16	Navy (14-4)
17	Colgate (14-4)
18	Akron (12-1)
19	Washington (13-3)
20	Denison (Ohio) (12-1)

1923–24

RANKING	TEAM
1	North Carolina (26-0)
2	Kansas (16-3)
3	Navy (15-3)
4	Penn St. (13-2)
5	Texas (23-0)
6	Oklahoma (15-3)
7	Columbia (15-4)
8	Cornell (13-3)
9	Vermont (15-2)
10	USC (15-4)
11	Tulane (22-1)
12	Army (16-2)
13	CCNY (12-1)
14	Beloit (14-0)
15	Creighton (13-2)
16	California (7-3)
17	Alabama (12-4)
18	RPI (11-1)
19	Springfield (13-3)
20	Washington (12-4)

1924–25

RANKING	TEAM
1	Princeton (21-2)
2	Wabash (18-1)
3	Ohio St. (14-2)
4	Kansas (17-1)
5	Syracuse (15-2)
6	Fordham (15-1)
7	Butler (20-4)
8	Oklahoma St. (15-3)
9	Army (12-3)
10	Washburn (15-0)
11	Penn St. (12-2)
12	Creighton (13-2)
13	CCNY (12-2)
14	Dartmouth (12-5)
15	Grove City (15-2)
16	Pennsylvania (17-5)
17	Harvard (11-2)
18	Evansville (11-2)
19	TCU (14-5)
20	Navy (18-5)

1925–26

RANKING	TEAM
1	Syracuse (19-1)
2	Notre Dame (19-1)
3	Kansas (16-2)
4	Columbia (16-2)
5	California (14-0)
6	Oklahoma (11-4)
7	Purdue (13-4)
8	Michigan (12-5)
9	Indiana (12-5)
10	Iowa (12-5)
11	Cincinnati (17-2)
12	Maryland (14-3)
13	Butler (16-5)
14	Oregon (18-4)
15	UCLA (14-2)
16	Lehigh (13-1)
17	North Carolina (20-5)
18	Navy (12-5)
19	Arkansas (15-1)
20	Mississippi (16-2)

1926–27

RANKING	TEAM
1	Notre Dame (19-1)
2	California (13-0)
3	Michigan (14-3)
4	Fordham (18-2)
5	Indiana (13-4)
6	Evansville (16-4)
7	Butler (17-4)
8	Kansas (15-2)
9	Navy (15-2)
10	Oregon (24-4)
11	Vanderbilt (20-4)
12	Syracuse (15-4)
13	West Texas St. (23-3)
14	Western Michigan (16-2)
15	Furman (16-4)
16	Montana St. (30-7)
17	Loyola (Ill.) (15-4)
18	Washington (15-4)
19	Creighton (14-5)
20	Xavier (Ohio) (11-3)

1927–28

RANKING	TEAM
1	Pittsburgh (21-0)
2	Montana St. (36-2)
3	Indiana (15-2)
4	Purdue (15-2)
5	Butler (19-3)
6	Notre Dame (18-4)
7	Arkansas (19-1)
8	Oklahoma (18-0)
9	Fordham (12-1)
10	Springfield (18-2)
11	Georgetown (12-1)
12	Auburn (20-2)
13	Pennsylvania (22-5)
14	USC (22-4)
15	Westminster (Pa.) (17-3)
16	Evansville (14-3)
17	St. John's (18-4)
18	LSU (14-4)
19	Oregon (18-3)
20	Wayne St. (18-1)

1928–29

RANKING	TEAM
1	Montana St. (36-2)
2	San Francisco (21-2)
3	Arkansas (16-1)
4	Michigan (13-3)
5	Butler (17-2)
6	Oklahoma (13-2)
7	Texas (18-2)
8	California (16-4)
9	Wisconsin (15-2)
10	Purdue (13-4)
11	Washington (18-2)
12	Fordham (18-1)
13	West Texas St. (16-2)
14	Loyola (Ill.) (16-0)
15	Notre Dame (15-5)
16	Northwestern (12-5)
17	Pittsburgh (16-5)
18	Westminster (Pa.) (15-2)
19	Washington & Lee (15-1)
20	Creighton (13-4)

1929–30

RANKING	TEAM
1	Alabama (20-0)
2	Syracuse (18-2)
3	Pittsburgh (23-2)
4	Wisconsin (15-2)
5	Duke (18-2)
6	Purdue (13-2)
7	Missouri (15-3)
8	St. John's (23-1)
9	Furman (16-1)
10	USC (15-5)
11	NYU (13-3)
12	Kansas (14-4)
13	Michigan St. (12-4)
14	Western Michigan (17-0)
15	Washington (21-7)
16	Kentucky (16-3)
17	Notre Dame (14-6)
18	Columbia (17-5)
19	CCNY (10-3)
20	Temple (18-3)

PREMO POWER POLL (CONTD.)

1930–31

RANKING	TEAM
1	Northwestern (16-1)
2	St. John's (21-1)
3	Washington (25-3)
4	Columbia (21-2)
5	Georgia (23-2)
6	Pittsburgh (20-4)
7	Syracuse (16-4)
8	Michigan (13-4)
9	Minnesota (13-4)
10	Purdue (12-5)
11	Illinois (12-5)
12	Manhattan (17-2)
13	Furman (15-2)
14	Michigan St. (16-1)
15	Kansas (15-3)
16	Butler (17-2)
17	West Texas St. (17-3)
18	Williams (12-3)
19	Army (12-3)
20	Santa Clara (16-3)

1931–32

RANKING	TEAM
1	Purdue (17-1)
2	Notre Dame (18-2)
3	Minnesota (15-3)
4	Kentucky (15-2)
5	CCNY (16-1)
6	Santa Clara (15-4)
7	St. John's (22-4)
8	Princeton (18-4)
9	Washington St. (22-5)
10	Butler (14-5)
11	Wyoming (18-2)
12	Northwestern (12-5)
13	Creighton (17-4)
14	Arizona (18-2)
15	Providence (19-5)
16	North Carolina (16-5)
17	Michigan St. (12-5)
18	West Texas St. (20-3)
19	Westminster (Pa.) (16-2)
20	Mount Union (16-1)

1932–33

RANKING	TEAM
1	Texas (22-1)
2	South Carolina (21-2)
3	Ohio St. (17-3)
4	Kentucky (20-3)
5	Princeton (19-3)
6	Yale (19-3)
7	Navy (14-2)
8	Syracuse (14-2)
9	Iowa (15-5)
10	St. John's (23-4)
11	Marquette (14-3)
12	TCU (16-4)
13	Northwestern (15-4)
14	Duquesne (15-1)
15	Butler (16-5)
16	Notre Dame (16-6)
17	Creighton (12-5)
18	West Texas St. (20-4)
19	CCNY (13-1)
20	Morgan (28-1)

1933–34

RANKING	TEAM
1	South Carolina (18-1)
2	Kentucky (16-1)
3	Duquesne (19-2)
4	NYU (16-0)
5	Wyoming (26-3)
6	Purdue (17-3)
7	Notre Dame (20-4)
8	Pittsburgh (18-4)
9	Alabama (16-2)
10	Pennsylvania (16-3)
11	DePaul (17-0)
12	Syracuse (15-2)
13	CCNY (14-1)
14	Navy (11-2)
15	LIU-Brooklyn (26-1)
16	Westminster (Pa.) (22-4)
17	North Carolina (18-4)
18	St. John's (16-3)
19	Kansas (16-1)
20	Marquette (15-4)

1934–35

RANKING	TEAM
1	Richmond (20-0)
2	NYU (19-1)
3	Duquesne (18-1)
4	Kentucky (19-2)
5	North Carolina (23-2)
6	Purdue (17-3)
7	LSU (14-1)
8	LIU-Brooklyn (24-2)
9	DePaul (15-1)
10	USC (20-6)
11	Pittsburgh (18-6)
12	Navy (11-3)
13	Pennsylvania (16-4)
14	SMU (14-3)
15	Syracuse (15-2)
16	Illinois (15-5)
17	Wisconsin (15-5)
18	Ohio Wesleyan (17-2)
19	Rutgers (13-3)
20	Westminster (Pa.) (19-3)

1935–36

RANKING	TEAM
1	LIU-Brooklyn (25-0)
2	Notre Dame (22-2-1)
3	Kansas (21-2)
4	Indiana (18-2)
5	Arkansas (24-3)
6	Washington (25-7)
7	DePaul (18-4)
8	Manhattan (17-2)
9	Washington & Lee (18-2)
10	NYU (15-4)
11	Stanford (22-7)
12	St. John's (18-4)
13	Purdue (16-4)
14	Columbia (19-3)
15	George Washington (16-3)
16	Northwestern (13-6-1)
17	Western Kentucky (26-4)
18	Temple (18-6)
19	Duquesne (14-3)
20	Murray St. (23-2)

1936–37

RANKING	TEAM
1	Stanford (25-2)
2	Notre Dame (20-3)
3	LIU-Brooklyn (28-3)
4	Michigan (16-4)
5	Purdue (15-5)
6	Pennsylvania (17-3)
7	Illinois (14-4)
8	George Washington (16-4)
9	USC (19-6)
10	Western Kentucky (21-2)
11	Temple (17-6)
12	Kentucky (17-5)
13	Rhode Island (18-3)
14	Hardin-Simmons (16-1)
15	Oklahoma St. (20-3)
16	Springfield (18-3)
17	Washington St. (24-8)
18	Loyola (Ill.) (16-3)
19	Murray St. (22-3)
20	Ohio Univ. (18-3)

PREMO POWER POLL: BEST TEAMS BY DECADE

1890–99

RANKING	SEASON	TEAM
1	1898–99	Yale (9-1)
2	1898–99	Allegheny (Pa.) (8-1)
3	1898–99	Nebraska (4-0)
4	1897–98	Mt. Union (Ohio) (8-1)
5	1898–99	Temple (18-6)
6	1896–97	Yale (11-5-1)
7	1898–99	Minnesota (7-2)
8	1897–98	Yale (12-9)
9	1897–98	Westminster (Pa.) (4-2)
10	1894–95	Temple (8-3)

1900–9

RANKING	SEASON	TEAM
1	1907–8	Wabash (Ind.) (24-0)
2	1902–3	Minnesota (13-0)
3	1907–8	Chicago (21-2)
4	1901–2	Minnesota (15-0)
5	1906–7	Chicago (20-2)
6	1904–5	Columbia (19-1)
7	1908–9	Chicago (12-0)
8	1902–3	Yale (15-1)
9	1905–6	Wabash (Ind.) (17-1)
10	1903–4	Columbia (17-1)
11	1908–9	Swarthmore (Pa.) (12-0)
12	1906–7	Williams (Mass.) (15-1)
13	1904–5	Williams (Mass.) (20-2)
14	1907–8	Pennsylvania (23-4)
15	1907–8	Allegheny (Pa.) (12-0)
16	1908–9	New York Univ. (13-0)
17	1902–3	Purdue (8-0)
18	1906–7	Wabash (Ind.) (17-2)
19	1904–5	Ohio St. (12-2)
20	1906–7	Columbia (14-4)

PREMO POWER POLL (CONTD.)

1910–19			1920–29			1930–39		
RANKING	SEASON	TEAM	RANKING	SEASON	TEAM	RANKING	SEASON	TEAM
1	1918–19	Navy (16-0)	1	1928–29	Montana St. (36-2)	1	1938–39	LIU-Brooklyn# (23-0)
2	1912–13	Navy (9-0)	2	1927–28	Pittsburgh (21-0)	2	1936–37	Stanford (25-2)
3	1911–12	Wisconsin (15-0)	3	1922–23	Army (17-0)	3	1935–36	LIU-Brooklyn (25-0)
4	1913–14	Wisconsin (15-0)	4	1919–20	Pennsylvania (22-1)	4	1931–32	Purdue (17-1)
5	1918–19	Minnesota (13-0)	5	1925–26	Syracuse (19-1)	5	1937–38	Temple# (23-2)
6	1914–15	Illinois (16-0)	6	1927–28	Montana St. (36-2)	6	1934–35	Richmond (20-0)
7	1910–11	St. John's (14-0)	7	1923–24	North Carolina (26-0)	7	1929–30	Alabama (20-0)
8	1916–17	Washington St. (25-1)	8	1926–27	Notre Dame (19-1)	8	1932–33	Texas (22-1)
9	1911–12	Purdue (12-0)	9	1920–21	Missouri (17-1)	9	1935–36	Notre Dame (22-2-1)
10	1913–14	Denison (Ohio) (15-1)	10	1925–26	Notre Dame (19-1)	10	1936–37	Notre Dame (20-3)
11	1912–13	Denison (Ohio) (13-1)	11	1922–23	Kansas (17-1)	11	1933–34	South Carolina (18-1)
12	1909–10	Williams (Mass.) (11-0)	12	1919–20	Missouri (17-1)	12	1930–31	Northwestern (16-1)
13	1915–16	Wisconsin (20-1)	13	1928–29	San Francisco (21-2)	13	1934–35	NYU (19-1)
14	1916–17	California (15-1)	14	1924–25	Princeton (21-2)	14	1931–32	Notre Dame (18-2)
15	1913–14	Navy (10-0)	15	1921–22	Missouri (16-1)	15	1937–38	Stanford (21-3)
16	1917–18	Syracuse (16-1)	16	1919–20	Penn St. (12-1)	16	1938–39	Bradley (19-3)
17	1910–11	Columbia (13-1)	17	1920–21	Pennsylvania (21-2)	17	1930–31	St. John's (21-1)
18	1911–12	Grove City (Pa.) (13-0)	18	1921–22	Kansas (16-2)	18	1933–34	Kentucky (16-1)
19	1918–19	Pennsylvania (15-1)	19	1928–29	Arkansas (16-1)	19	1932–33	South Carolina (21-2)
20	1916–17	Wabash (Ind.) (19-2)	20	1927–28	Indiana (15-2)	20	1934–35	Duquesne (18-1)
							1935–36	Kansas (21-2)

#–NIT Champion

Intercollegiate Athletics. As such, the NAIA is credited with staging the first national collegiate tournament. Its initial champion in March 1937 was Warrensburg (later to become Central Missouri), a 45-30 winner over Washburn College. The trophy was named for Naismith's wife, Maude.

But, as usual, the "big time" was in New York. Doubleheaders in the larger arenas meant that money was pouring into college basketball. That, in turn, meant that college teams could afford to travel. Figuring there should be a national tournament, the Metropolitan Basketball Writer's Association, a New York sportswriters group, organized the National Invitation Tournament (NIT) to close the 1937–38 season. They hoped to attract the big-name teams and players. Little did they realize they were opening college basketball's billion-dollar future.

MINE EYES HAVE SEEN THE GORY

The quality of the competition might have been suspect, but the first quarter of this century supplied many of the most lopsided results in college basketball history. For instance, an unheard of feat occurred on January 23, 1907, when Dayton blanked Cedarville, 80-0.

In an era where most people believe a ponderous brand of ball was performed, here is a list of some of the obscene margins of more than 70 points:

MARGIN	WINNER	LOSER	SEASON
120	Georgia 122	S.E. Christian 2	1917-18
106	Purdue 112	Indiana State 6	1910-11
101	Texas 10	San Marcos Baptist 1	1915-16
100	California 108	Pomona American Legion 8	1921-22
96	Western Ky. 103	Adairville Independents 7	1922-23
93	Washington 100	Puget Sound 7	1920-21
91	Niagara 100	Rochester YMCA 9	1911-12
90	Niagara 105	Ellicotville YMCA 15	1911-12
88	Georgia 100	Davidson 12	1908-09
83	Texas 89	Southwest Texas 6	1918-19
80	Dayton 80	Cedarville 0	1906-07
80*	Georgia 92	Auburn 12	1912-13
79	Auburn 92	White's Business College 13	1927-28
78	Butler 92	Indiana Law School 14	1921-22
78	Colgate 90	Alfred 12	1921-22
78	Texas 92	Deaf School 14	1909-10
75	Mississippi St. 75	Brownsville Athletic Club 0	1908-09
74	Dayton 75	Lafayette 1	1912-13
74	Delaware 80	Lebanon Valley 6	1909-10
73	Texas 80	St. Edward's 7	1915-16
72	Georgia 90	Auburn 18	1916-17
72	Ottawa 80	Wichita State 8	1912-13
71	Columbus YMCA 74	Auburn 3	1913-14

*Georgia defeated Auburn twice by the same score that season.

EARLY AWARD WINNERS

NCAA CONSENSUS FIRST-TEAM ALL-AMERICANS FROM 1929 TO 1937

1928–29: Thomas Churchill, Oklahoma; Vern Corbin, California; Chuck Hyatt, Pittsburgh; Charles Murphy, Purdue; Joe Schaaf, Pennsylvania; John Thompson, Montana State

1929–30: Chuck Hyatt, Pittsburgh; Charles Murphy, Purdue; Branch McCracken, Indiana; John Thompson, Montana State; Frank Ward, Montana State; John Wooden, Purdue

1930–31: Wes Fesler, Ohio State; George Gregory, Columbia; Joe Reiff, Northwestern; Elwood Romney, Brigham Young; John Wooden, Purdue

1931–32: Louis Berger, Maryland; Ed Krause, Notre Dame; Forest Sale, Kentucky; Les Witte, Wyoming; John Wooden, Purdue

1932–33: Ed Krause, Notre Dame; Elliott Loughlin, Navy; Jerry Nemer, Southern Cal; Joe Reiff, Northwestern; Forest Sale, Kentucky; Don Smith, Pittsburgh

1933–34: Norman Cottom, Purdue; Claire Cribbs, Pittsburgh; Ed Krause, Notre Dame; Hal Lee, Washington; Les Witte, Wyoming

1934–35: Bud Browning, Oklahoma; Claire Cribbs, Pittsburgh; Leroy Edwards, Kentucky; Jack Gray, Texas; Lee Guttero, Southern Cal

1935–36: Vern Huffman, Indiana; Bob Kessler, Purdue; Bill Kinner, Utah; Hank Luisetti, Stanford; John Moir, Notre Dame; Paul Nowak, Notre Dame; Ike Poole, Arkansas

1936–37: Jules Bender, Long Island; Hank Luisetti, Stanford; John Moir, Notre Dame; Paul Nowak, Notre Dame; Jewell Young, Purdue

HELMS FOUNDATION CHAMPIONS FROM 1901 TO 1937   The Helms Foundation of Los Angeles, under the guidance of founder Bill Schroeder, chose national college champions from 1942 to 1982 and researched retroactive No. 1 selections from 1901 to 1941. There are four years when the Helms picks differ from the actual champion since the NIT commenced in 1938–39 (Helms selected LIU), 1940 (Southern Cal), 1944 (Army), and 1954 (Kentucky). Army had a policy against postseason play until accepting a bid to the 1961 NIT. Kentucky rejected a bid to the 1954 NCAA Tournament after the NCAA declared three seniors ineligible.

Multiple Helms national championships from 1901 to 1937 include Chicago (3), Columbia (3), Wisconsin (3), Kansas (2), Minnesota (2), Notre Dame (2), Penn (2), Pittsburgh (2), Syracuse (2), and Yale (2). Only two of these 10 schools won an NCAA Tournament since it started in 1939—Wisconsin (1941) and Kansas (1952 and 1988).

YEAR	CHAMPION (RECORD)	HEAD COACH	TOP PLAYER, POS.
1901	Yale (10-6)	No coach	G. M. Clark, F
1902	Minnesota (15-0)	Louis Cooke	W. C. Deering, F
1903	Yale (15-1)	W. H. Murphy	R. B. Hyatt, F
1904	Columbia (17-1)	No coach	Harry Fisher, F
1905	Columbia (19-1)	No coach	Harry Fisher, F
1906	Dartmouth (16-2)	No coach	George Grebenstein, F
1907	Chicago (22-2)	Joseph Raycroft	John Schammer, C
1908	Chicago (21-2)	Joseph Raycroft	John Schammer, C
1909	Chicago (12-0)	Joseph Raycroft	John Schammer, C
1910	Columbia (11-1)	Harry Fisher	Ted Kiendl, F
1911	St. John's (14-0)	Claude Allen	John Keenan, F-C
1912	Wisconsin (15-0)	Doc Meanwell	Otto Stangel, F
1913	Navy (9-0)	Louis Wenzel	Laurence Wild, F
1914	Wisconsin (15-0)	Doc Meanwell	Gene Van Gent, C
1915	Illinois (16-0)	Ralph Jones	Ray Woods, G
1916	Wisconsin (20-1)	Doc Meanwell	George Lewis, F
1917	Washington State (25-1)	Doc Bohler	Ray Bohler, G
1918	Syracuse (16-1)	Edmund Dollard	Joe Schwarzer, G
1919	Minnesota (13-0)	Louis Cooke	Arnold Oss, F
1920	Penn (22-1)	Lon Jourdet	George Sweeney, F
1921	Penn (21-2)	Edward McNichol	Danny McNichol, G
1922	Kansas (16-2)	Phog Allen	Paul Endacott, G
1923	Kansas (17-1)	Phog Allen	Paul Endacott, G
1924	North Carolina (26-0)	Bo Shepard	Jack Cobb, F
1925	Princeton (21-2)	Al Wittmer	Art Loeb, G
1926	Syracuse (19-1)	Lew Andreas	Vic Hanson, F
1927	Notre Dame (19-1)	George Keagan	John Nykas, C
1928	Pittsburgh (21-0)	Doc Carlson	Chuck Hyatt, F
1929	Montana State (36-2)	Schubert Dyche	John Thompson, F
1930	Pittsburgh (23-2)	Doc Carlson	Chuck Hyatt, F
1931	Northwestern (16-1)	Dutch Lonborg	Joe Reiff, C
1932	Purdue (17-1)	Piggy Lambert	John Wooden, G
1933	Kentucky (20-3)	Adolph Rupp	Forest Sale, F
1934	Wyoming (26-3)	Willard Witte	Les Witte, G
1935	NYU (19-1)	Howard Cann	Sid Gross, F
1936	Notre Dame (22-2-1)	George Keogan	John Moir, F
1937	Stanford (25-2)	John Bunn	Hank Luisetti, F

2

START OF THE
NATIONAL TOURNAMENTS:

1938-49

The NCAA's prize product, the Division I Men's Basketball Tournament, wasn't the NCAA's idea and was literally dumped into the governing body's lap by the National Association of Basketball Coaches (NABC). A group of New York sportswriters staged the first major college tournament, the National Invitation Tournament, in 1938 in New York. But a coalition of NABC members, particularly coaches from the Midwest, felt if there was to be a national tourney, it should be sponsored by a collegiate organization and not scribes, especially those possessing what they perceived to be a "biased" Eastern influence.

Harold Olsen, a former Wisconsin player and Ohio State coach, is accorded much of the credit for unveiling the NCAA Tournament to the American sports scene. The first NCAA Tournament was conducted in 1939, sponsored not by the NCAA but by the NABC. Oddly, Olsen's Ohio State team reached the final of the eight-team event (one from each district) before losing to Oregon, 46-33.

Total attendance for the inaugural NCAA playoff was a meager 15,025, and the venture produced $2,531 worth of red ink. Because the NABC was out of funds, it asked the NCAA to assume responsibility.

"We were darn lucky to get out of debt," said former Wisconsin coach Harold (Bud) Foster, a past president of the NABC. "When the NCAA bailed us out, they provided tickets for all our members.

"It was interesting that Wisconsin played a major role in pulling the basketball tournament out of debt. We had the NCAA boxing tournament in Madison in '39 and drew packed houses. The university turned over $18,000 to the NCAA, and that was the biggest amount the NCAA had received from any source up to that time." Unbelievably, the NCAA sponsored a boxing tournament before it chose to promote basketball in a similar fashion. And wouldn't you know boxing is no longer an NCAA-sanctioned sport?

A more vital fighting led to the following universities among others choosing not to field teams at least one season during World War II: Alabama, Auburn, Ball State, Bradley, Butler, Colorado, Colorado State, Creighton, Dayton,

LUISETTI EXPLODES FOR 50 POINTS Stanford's star player Hank Luisetti ushered in 1938 with a bang. On New Year's Day, Stanford trounced Duquesne, 92-27, in Cleveland, thanks to Luisetti's 50-point outburst. Luisetti was best known for his running one-handed shot.

STANFORD (92)	FG	FT	PTS.
Lafaille	1	0	2
P. Zonne	7	1	15
Huff	1	0	2
Luisetti	23	4	50
Stoefen	5	3	13
Calderwood	1	0	2
Lyon	0	2	2
Lee	0	0	0
Burnett	3	0	6
B. Zonne	0	0	0
Rapp	0	0	0
Heath	0	0	0
TOTALS	**41**	**10**	**92**

DUQUESNE (27)	FG	FT	PTS.
Cristofack	0	1	1
Weitzel	3	1	7
Fortney	3	0	6
Yankitis	2	0	4
Scarry	0	0	0
O'Malley	0	1	1
Neiderberger	0	0	0
Kreilling	1	2	4
Adams	2	0	4
TOTALS	**11**	**5**	**27**
Halftime: Stanford 55-12.			

Duquesne, Eastern Kentucky, Florida, Fordham, Furman, Georgetown, George Washington, Hawaii, Kent, Loyola of Chicago, Loyola Marymount, Manhattan, Massachusetts, Memphis, Miami (Fla.), Mississippi, Mississippi State, New Hampshire, Niagara, Oklahoma City, St. Bonaventure, St. Francis (Pa.), St. Louis, San Francisco, San Jose State, Santa Clara, Seton Hall, Southern Mississippi, Stanford, Syracuse, Tennessee, Utah State, Vermont, Wake Forest, Wichita State, Wyoming and Xavier.

A classic example of the upheaval caused by the war was South Carolina, which had five different coaches in as many seasons from 1941-42 through 1945-46.

Numerous standout players had their college playing careers interrupted by the conflict. For instance, all 11 regulars on Pittsburgh's 1941 Final Four team served in the U.S. military during WWII, and one of them, guard Bob Artman, was killed in action. The following seven two-time first- and second-team NCAA consensus All-Americans had their college careers interrupted while serving in the U.S. armed forces: Charles Black (Kansas) served in the Air Force; Vince Boryla (Notre Dame/Denver); Arnie Ferrin (Utah); Alex Groza (Kentucky), and Gerry Tucker (Oklahoma) served in the Army; Andy Phillip (Illinois) served in the Marine Corps; and Leo Klier (Notre Dame) served in the Navy.

Conflict on the basketball court in the mid-1940s focused on an argument regarding which of the first two imposing big men was best: Oklahoma A&M's Bob Kurland (7-0) or DePaul's George Mikan (6-10). Each of them set school single-game scoring records that still exist. There has been an infatuation with tall players ever since.

It doesn't take a genius to deduce All-American players are all-important to teams, but sheer standouts do not guarantee success in postseason competition. None of the first six two-time NCAA consensus first-team All-Americans in the 1940s reached the NCAA Tournament national semifinals—Dartmouth's Gus Broberg ('40 and '41), North Carolina's George Glamack ('40 and '41), Notre Dame's Leo Klier ('44 and '46), Illinois' Andy Phillip ('42 and '43), NYU's Sid Tanenbaum ('46 and '47) and St. Louis' Ed Macauley ('48 and '49).

The state of Kentucky supplied three of the nation's five winningest programs in the 1940s—Kentucky (1st), Eastern Kentucky (4th) and Western Kentucky (5th). Kansas was the only school west of the Mississippi River to rank among the top 10 programs in winning percentage in the 1930s and Oklahoma A&M was the only institution west of the Mississippi to rank among the top 19 in winning percentage in the 1940s.

The NCAA Tournament struggled with the NIT over which national postseason tourney reigned supreme. The NCAA began to make substantial inroads to stealing some of the NIT's thunder after the first Eastern school (Holy Cross) won the NCAA in 1947.

Holy Cross' coach was Alvin "Doggie" Julian, who previously directed Muhlenberg (Pa.) to the NIT. Muhlenberg had a Navy V-12 program, which resulted in the assignment of many great players to campus. The 1944-45 squad, which fought 15-to-1 favorite St. John's to a one-point game (34-33) in the first round of the NIT, was completely different from the 1943-44 team because of military reassignments. Only one player, Oscar "Red" Baldwin, who played a year for Union (Ky.) College, had any previous college basketball experience.

Several days before Muhlenberg was selected to play in the 1945 NIT, Julian was named head basketball and assistant football coach at Holy Cross. Bud Barker, selected as Julian's replacement, could not coach in 1945-46 because he had to complete some service duty. That made Lee Coker one of the best fill-in coaches in college basketball history. In Coker's first (and only) year as head coach, he led the Mules not only to a 22-3 regular-season record but also to a first-round win in the NIT against Syracuse. What made Coker's achievement all the more amazing was that the team consisted of a senior, two sophomores and the rest freshmen—all the military men had been discharged when the war ended. Muhlenberg, after earning three consecutive NIT appearances with three radically different teams, eventually disappeared from the major-college ranks.

The beginning of separating the haves from the have-nots occurred in 1948, the first year of official classification of schools when 160 universities were designated as major colleges.

1937-38

AT A GLANCE

NIT Champion: Temple (23-2).

New Conference: New England (forerunner of Yankee disbanded in 1976).

New Rule: Center jump after every basket is rescinded.

NCAA Consensus First-Team All-Americans: Meyer "Mike" Bloom, C, Sr., Temple; Hank Luisetti, F, Sr., Stanford; John Moir, F, Sr., Notre Dame; Paul Nowak, C, Sr., Notre Dame; Fred Pralle, G, Sr., Kansas; Jewell Young, F, Sr., Purdue.

Perhaps no player had more of an effect on basketball than Stanford's Hank Luisetti. A couple of decades ahead of his time, he is credited with revolutionizing basketball by introducing his running one-handed shot. Luisetti led Stanford to three consecutive Pacific Coast Conference championships and to a 46-5 record in his final two seasons. Regrettably, it wasn't until the year after his graduation that the NCAA staged its first tourney. The same year of the initial NCAA playoffs, Luisetti starred with legendary Betty Grable in a film called "Campus Confessions." The movie earned him $10,000 from Paramount Pictures. Luisetti (50 points vs. Duquesne; see accompanying box score) and Brown sophomore Harry Platt (48 vs. Northeastern) established what are still single-game school scoring records. Luisetti almost doubled Duquesne's output in a 92-27 victory, contributing to the Dukes' only losing season (6-11) in a 37-year span from 1921 to 1957.

Joe Hagan's 48-foot shot with 12 seconds remaining enabled Kentucky to edge Marquette, 35-33. Showing the state's obsession with hoops success after the game, Gov. Happy Chandler pounded a nail into the floor to mark the spot of the decisive shot. Hagan went to Kentucky to play football, tried out for the basketball team uninvited by coach Adolph Rupp, and was captain of the Wildcats' 1937 football squad.

New York's Madison Square Garden was the mecca of college basketball at the time, however. Long Island University was featured in six of the 12 doubleheaders played in the Garden.

In the Big Ten, Illinois junior forward Lou Boudreau was declared ineligible for further intercollegiate competition in early February because his mother had been given monthly payments by baseball's Cleveland Indians. John Kundla, who later coached the NBA's Minneapolis Lakers to six league titles, was the second-leading scorer for a Minnesota squad that finished second in the Big Ten. Michigan's John Townsend was named to the first five on the Converse All-American team. Fifty-six seasons later (1993–94), his grandson, North Carolina center Eric Montross, would be selected to the first five on the National Association of Basketball Coaches All-American team. All-Americans John Moir and Paul Nowak were joined on Notre Dame's frontcourt by senior captain Ray Meyer, who later became a Hall of Fame coach for DePaul. They helped the Irish compile a 62-8-1 record in their three-year varsity careers. . . . Western Michigan suffered its first losing record (6-12) since its initial competitive season in 1913-14.

Oklahoma A&M lost its Missouri Valley opener to Grinnell before winning 13 consecutive league games en route to a conference crown.

Phog Allen guided Kansas to its seventh title in the 10-year history of the Big Six Conference.

Gail Goodrich of Southern California finished sixth in scoring in the Pacific Coast Conference Southern Division. His son, Gail Goodrich Jr., became an All-American for UCLA in the mid-1960s.

Four starters for New Mexico A&M (now New Mexico State) were named to the first five on the All-Border Conference team after their school went undefeated (18-0) in league competition.

Coach Forrest Twogood guided Idaho to an 11-9 record for the Vandals' only winning season in a 16-year stretch from 1929-30 through 1944-45.

Maryland bowed to Washington & Lee nine consecutive times until defeating the Generals, 36-32. . . . Georgetown was the only team to defeat Temple in Eastern Intercollegiate Conference competition. The Hoyas lost for the fifth consecutive time in their series with Carnegie Tech, 54-31. Carnegie Tech's Melvin Cratsley set a league single-game scoring record with 34 points against West Virginia.

Western Kentucky (30-3/coached by Ed Diddle) lost twice to Bradley but finished with its most victories in school history. Mississippi (22-12/George Bohler) had its winningest season in school history by posting 11 consecutive victories before losing to Georgia Tech in the SEC Tournament final. Ole Miss had just one winning record in its next 12 seasons (14-8 in 1944-45 after not fielding a squad the previous year because of World War II). . . . Alabama's 4-13 record was the school's lone losing mark in a 21-year span from 1927-28 through 1948-49 (did not field a team in 1943-44 because of WWII). . . . South Carolina (3-21) lost more than 20 games for the only time in school history.

1937–38 PREMO POWER POLL

RANKING	SCHOOL
1	Temple# (23-2)
2	Stanford (21-3)
3	Purdue (18-2)
4	Notre Dame (20-3)
5	Oklahoma St. (25-3)
6	Bradley (18-2)
7	Western Kentucky (30-3)
8	Minnesota (16-4)
9	Kansas (18-2)
10	LIU-Brooklyn (23-5)
11	Central Missouri St.+ (24-3)
12	Roanoke (19-2)
13	Rhode Island (19-2)
14	Murray St. (27-4)
15	New Mexico St. (22-3)
16	Oregon (25-8)
17	Arkansas (19-3)
18	Villanova (25-5)
19	Marshall (28-4)
20	Centenary (13-1)

–NIT champion
+ –NAIA champion

1938–39

AT A GLANCE

NCAA Champion: Oregon (29-5; coached by Howard Hobson; won PCC North Division by three games with a 14-2 record).

NIT Champion: Long Island (23-0; coached by Clair Bee).

New Rules: Ball thrown in from out of bounds at mid-court by the team shooting a free throw following a technical foul. Previously, the ball was put into play with a center jump following a technical. The circumference of the ball is established as 30 inches.

NCAA Consensus First-Team All-Americans: Ernie Andres, G, Sr., Indiana; Jimmy Hull, F, Sr., Ohio State; Chet Jaworski, G, Sr., Rhode Island; Irving Torgoff, F, Sr., Long Island; Urgel "Slim" Wintermute, C, Sr., Oregon.

It hasn't always been a pleasant spotlight near or at the top of the national polls for marquee schools Duke, North Carolina and UCLA.

Duke incurred its only losing record (10-12) in a 45-year span from 1927-28 through 1971-72. Meanwhile, rival North Carolina sustained its only losing mark (10-11) in a 30-year stretch from 1920-21 through 1949-50.

UCLA, the most successful school in NCAA Tournament history, was a playoff pretender instead of contender the first year of the national tourney. The Bruins won a non-league game by 57 points (76-19 over LaVerne), but they finished winless in the Pacific Coast Conference's Southern Division for the second straight season. Their senior captain and leading scorer was Bob (Ace) Calkins. During World War II as a navigator on a Flying Fortress, Calkins' plane was shot down and he later died in an Italian prison camp from wounds sustained in the air attack.

Texas toppled Manhattan, 54-32, at Madison Square Garden in front of 18,000 fans, the largest crowd to see a basketball game up to that point. It was the worst defeat dealt to a New York school in the Garden to that time. . . . Intercollegiate doubleheaders, with Loyola and DePaul serving as hosts, made their debut in Chicago with five twinbills at the 132nd Infantry Armory on West Madison Street (capacity 6,000).

Clemson, after recovering from a 2-5 start in regular-season league competition, won the Southern Conference Tournament championship although the Tigers never led at halftime in any of their four tourney games. Tigers athletic director Jess Neely, who also happened to be the school's football coach, rejected an invitation to the NIT because several of the key players were members of the football squad that had to get back for spring practice. The extra workouts on the gridiron might have been the difference in helping Clemson earn an invitation to the Cotton Bowl that year.

The seven-year-old Eastern Intercollegiate Conference agreed to disband at the end of the season. The AP described the league as "one of the best in the nation." Geographical problems had made scheduling difficult for the six members—Carnegie Tech, Georgetown, Penn State, Pittsburgh, Temple and West Virginia. Penn State was the only member never to win outright or share a league regular-season title.

Panzer College of East Orange, N.J., compiled a 20-1 record, losing only to unbeaten LIU (41-35) early in the season. NIT champion LIU played only one game outside New York—vs. La Salle at Philadelphia. . . . Penn State's Max Corbin hit a shot from three quarters length of the floor against West Virginia to send their game into overtime. Penn State won, 46-43, in triple overtime. . . . Defending NIT champion Temple compiled a 10-12 record for coach James Usilton's second losing season in 13 years. Just three days after the end of the campaign, he died of a heart ailment. . . . Rhode Island's school-record 22-game winning streak ended with a 62-50 defeat against Tufts. . . . Brown had a school-record 11-game winning streak in

The 1938–39 champion Oregon Ducks were dubbed "The Tall Firs" due to their size.

George Allen's first season as head coach en route to its highest winning percentage in history (16-4, .800). . . . Lehigh (10-5), coached by Paul Calvert, managed a double-digit victory total for the only time in a 24-year span from 1928-29 through 1951-52.

Stanford's school-record 17-game winning streak was snapped by Dartmouth, 48-47, in the fourth contest of the season. Everett Dean was in his first season as coach of Stanford, which won 55 of its previous 60 games since the end of the 1935-36 campaign.

Emphasis on foreigners isn't a recent phenomenon. Francisco "Kiko" Martinez, a member of the 1936 bronze-medal winning Mexican Olympic team, was the leading scorer for New Mexico A&M (now New Mexico State), which finished with a 20-4 record after losing to NIT champion-to-be LIU in the opening round. . . . Junior college transfer Jesse "Cab" Renick, a full-blooded Choctaw Indian, played guard, center and forward for Missouri Valley co-champion Oklahoma A&M. He was named to the first five on the all-conference team and finished third in the league in scoring. Renick also lettered for the Aggies' football squad. In 1948, while playing for the Phillips 66 Oilers, he was a member of the gold-medal winning U.S. Olympic basketball team.

Alabama, coached by Hank Crisp, finished atop the SEC standings just one year after placing 12th in the 13-team league. . . . Northwestern compiled its first losing record (7-13) in 12 seasons.. . . . Grinnell (Ia.) finished in a tie for third place in the Missouri Valley in its final season as a member of the conference. . . . On the same day (March 11, 1939), Idaho State defeated the University of Mexico City, 32-23, in Pocatello, then lost, 32-30, to the Murtaugh Savages in Rupert, Idaho.

1938–39 PREMO POWER POLL

RANKING	SCHOOL
1	LIU-Brooklyn# (23-0)
2	Bradley (19-3)
3	Loyola (Ill.) (21-1)
4	Oregon* (29-5)
5	St. John's (18-4)
6	Indiana (17-3)
7	USC (20-5)
8	New Mexico St. (20-4)
9	Kentucky (16-4)
10	Ohio St. (16-7)
11	California (24-8)
12	Army (13-2)
13	Duquesne (14-4)
14	Villanova (20-5)
15	Marquette (12-5)
16	Washington (20-5)
17	Colorado (14-4)
18	Notre Dame (15-6)
19	Western Kentucky (22-3)
20	Roanoke (21-3)

#–NIT champion
*–NCAA champion

1939 NCAA Tournament

Summary: Different brands of play and refereeing dominated an era when college basketball was basically a regional game. Intersectional games were rare, although Oregon scheduled games in eight Eastern and Midwest cities (New York, Philadelphia, Buffalo, Cleveland, Detroit, Chicago, Peoria, Ill., and Des Moines). Oregon's slate might have made the Ducks more prepared for the inaugural NCAA Tournament. Another factor was Oregon's height. The Ducks, nicknamed "The Tall Firs" by a sportswriter because they had a 6-8 center and a pair of 6-4 forwards, boasted more size than most teams.

One and Only: John Dick is the only leading scorer in an NCAA Tournament final (15 points as a junior forward for champion Oregon in 1939 against Ohio State) to subsequently

1938–39 NCAA CHAMPION: OREGON

SEASON STATISTICS OF OREGON REGULARS

PLAYER	POS.	CL.	G	PPG
Laddie Gale	F	Sr.	34	12.0
Slim Wintermute	C	Sr.	31	10.0
John Dick	F	Jr.	34	6.7
Wally Johansen	G	Sr.	34	5.7
Bobby Anet	G	Sr.	33	5.4
Bob Hardy	F	Jr.	30	3.8
Ted Sarpola	F	Jr.	27	3.4
Matt Pavalunas	G	Jr.	33	2.7
Ford Mullen	G	Jr.	29	1.2
TEAM TOTALS			**34**	**49.5**

1939 CHAMPIONSHIP GAME

EVANSTON, IL

OREGON (46)	FG	FT-A	PF	PTS.
Gale	2	4-5	1	8
Dick	5	5-5	3	15
Wintermute	2	0-1	1	4
Anet	4	2-3	3	10
Johansen	4	1-2	1	9
Mullen	0	0-0	0	0
Pavalunas	0	0-0	0	0
TOTALS	**17**	**12-16**	**9**	**46**
FT%: .750.				

OHIO STATE (33)	FG	FT-A	PF	PTS.
Hull	5	2-2	2	12
Baker	0	0-1	0	0
Schick	1	0-0	1	2
Dawson	1	0-0	4	2
Lynch	3	1-3	3	7
Maag	0	0-0	0	0
Scott	0	1-1	1	1
Boughner	1	0-0	0	2
Sattler	3	1-2	0	7
Mickelson	0	0-0	2	0
Stafford	0	0-0	0	0
TOTALS	**14**	**5-9**	**13**	**33**
FT%: .556.				
Halftime: Oregon 21-16.				

MOST OUTSTANDING PLAYER
None selected.

1939 CHAMPIONSHIP BRACKET

Regional Semifinals	Regional Finals	National Championship

WESTERN REGIONALS

Oregon
March 20
Texas
— Oregon 56-41

San Francisco, CA
March 21
— Oregon 55-37

Oklahoma
March 20
Utah St.
— Oklahoma 50-39

Evanston, IL
March 27
— Oregon 46-33
NATIONAL CHAMPION

EASTERN REGIONALS

Villanova
March 17
Brown
— Villanova 42-30

Philadelphia, PA
March 18
— Ohio State 53-36

Wake Forest
March 17
Ohio St.
— Ohio St. 64-52

Regional Third Place
March 21
at San Francisco, CA
Utah St. 51, Texas 49

serve as an admiral in the U.S. Navy. Dick commanded the aircraft carrier *Saratoga* for two years and served as chief of staff for all carrier forces in the Western Pacific.

Numbers Game: Only two players scored at least 20 points in the eight tourney games. Ohio State's Jimmy Hull had the high game with 28 points in a 53-36 victory over Villanova in the Eastern Regional final. . . . Oklahoma trailed Oregon by only three points early in the second half of the national semifinals before the Ducks pulled away to win, 55-37.

Putting Things in Perspective: Oregon State, which compiled a 6-10 record in the PCC, defeated Oregon, 50-31.

WINNINGEST PROGRAMS OF THE 1930s

RK.	SCHOOL	W.	L.	PCT.
1	Long Island	198	38	.839
2.	Kentucky	162	34	.827
3.	St. John's	181	40	.819
4.	Kansas	153	37	.805
5.	Syracuse	143	37	.794
6.	Purdue	148	39	.791
7.	Western Kentucky	197	52	.791
8.	Rhode Island	142	39	.785
9.	Notre Dame	170	49	.776
10.	CCNY	120	35	.774

1939–40

AT A GLANCE

NCAA Champion: Indiana (20-3; coached by Branch McCracken; finished in second place in Big Ten with a 9-3 record, which was one game behind Purdue).

NIT Champion: Colorado (17-4; coached by Frosty Cox; won Mountain States Conference by three games with an 11-1 record)

New Rules: Teams have the choice of whether to shoot a free throw or take the ball out-of-bounds at midcourt. If two or more free throws are awarded, the option applies to the final free throw. The backboards move from two to four feet from the end line to permit more movement under the goal.

NCAA Consensus First-Team All-Americans: Gus Broberg, G-F, Jr., Dartmouth; John Dick, F, Sr., Oregon; George Glamack, C, Jr., North Carolina; Bill Hapac, F, Sr., Illinois; Ralph Vaughn, F, Sr., Southern California.

Dr. James Naismith, the inventor of basketball, died at his home in Lawrence, Kansas, at the age of 78. The previous season, Naismith had criticized the use of zone defense in a talk before New York writers, saying: "I have no sympathy with it. The defensive team is stalling which lays back and waits for the offense to come to it. If a soccer team hung back and grouped itself in front of the goal, what could the other team do? The zone is much like that."

Clair Bee, the director of LIU's Department of Physical Education, coached the school's football, basketball, and baseball teams. A *New York Times* article announcing the resumption of football at LIU pointed out that "Bee prefers football to basketball." On Thanksgiving Day, LIU's Dolly King started at center for the basketball team in a 59-41 victory over the alumni after starting at end for the football squad and catching a touchdown pass that afternoon at Ebbets Field in a 35-14 defeat to Catholic University.

North Carolina All-American George Glamack was an inspiration to those fond of individuals overcoming adversity. *The Spalding Guide* noted that "Glamack, who is ambidextrous when on the court, is also so nearsighted that the ball is merely a dim object, but apparently he never looked where he was shooting, depending upon his sense of distance and direction." The secret of "The Blind Bomber" was looking at the black lines on the court. By doing that he knew where he was in reference to the basket and could measure his shot.

Seton Hall's "Wonder Five" finished the season undefeated (19-0), but the Pirates, coached by Honey Russell, didn't participate in either the NCAA tournament or NIT. The first basketball game telecast was on February 28, 1940, when WXBS carried a doubleheader from Madison Square Garden (Pittsburgh vs. Fordham and NYU vs. Georgetown).

Duke became the 12th different school to win the Southern Conference championship in the first 19 years of the league.

Future NBA coaching legend Arnold "Red" Auerbach was George Washington's leading scorer, averaging 8.5 points per game.

Navy's streak of consecutive non-losing seasons ended at 33 when the Midshipmen compiled a 3-11 record.

Ohio Wesleyan defeated Dayton twice in a single season for the third consecutive year. . . . Tennessee sophomore Bernie Mehen, described by Kentucky coach Adolph Rupp as "one of the greatest first-year men of all-time," earned a berth as a forward on the SEC All-Tournament team. . . . Sewanee (Tenn.) dropped out of the SEC after its sixth winless league record in eight years as a member of the conference. . . .Rice (25-4, coached by Buster Brannon) and Toledo (24-6/Harold Anderson) had their winningest season in school history. . . .Washington registered its only losing record (10-15) in a 28-year stretch from 1920-21 through 1947-48.

1939–40 PREMO POWER POLL

RANKING	SCHOOL
1	Indiana* (20-3)
2	USC (20-3)
3	Colorado# (17-4)
4	Duquesne (20-3)
5	Oklahoma St. (26-3)
6	Purdue (16-4)
7	NYU (18-1)
8	Rice (25-4)
9	Kansas (19-6)
10	DePaul (22-6)

1939-40 UNDEFEATED TEAM: SETON HALL (19-0)

COACH: HONEY RUSSELL

SH	OPPONENT	PIRATES HIGH SCORER
45	Alumni 29	Parpan 12
58	Mount St. Mary's 32	Sadowski 13
53	Tulane 25	Davies 9
43	Florida 41	Davies/Sadowski 13
51	William & Mary 35	Sadowski 17
48	at Scranton 32	Sadowski 17
69	Becker 29	Sadowski 14
42	at Kutztown 34	Sadowski 15
50	Loyola (Md.) 40	Sadowski 13
55	at St. Peter's 27	Coyle 13
51	at Brooklyn 34	Fischer 13
44	Rider 32	Davies/Ruthenberg 8
48	St. Francis (Pa.) 36	Davies 17
46	St. Bonaventure 41	Davies 19
53	Kutztown 33	Davies 15
52	Canisius 46	Davies 17
53	Catholic 27	Ryan 13
43	Brooklyn 41	Delany 16
68	Scranton 39	Davies 16

Note: Seton Hall played its home games at five different arenas—East Orange High School, Elizabeth Armory, Orange Armory, Orange High School and Dickinson High School (Jersey City).

INDIVIDUAL STATISTICS FOR SETON HALL REGULARS

PLAYER	POS.	CL.	G.	PPG
Ed Sadowski*	C	Sr.	9	12.2
Bob Davies	F	So.	18	11.8
Bob Fischer	F	So.	18	4.9
John Ruthenberg	G-C	So.	19	4.7
Bob Holm	G	So.	17	4.2
Frank Delany	G-F	Sr.	19	3.8
Bernie Coyle	G-F	Sr.	18	3.7
Nick Parpan	G-F	Jr.	14	3.4
Ken Pine	C	So.	16	3.2
Ray Studwell	F-G	So.	18	1.2

*Sadowski missed half of the season because of a broken kneecap.

1940 NCAA Tournament

Summary: Indiana's "Hurryin' Hoosiers" were noted for their fast break, which emphasized quick ball movement because coach Branch McCracken detested dribbling. The Hoosiers' 60-42 victory over Kansas in the NCAA final marked the highest output for the winner in the championship game until 1950. Kansas newspapers called the blitzing IU team a "tornado" in the wake of the one-sided final. "That tornado was us," boasted Hoosiers guard Marv Huffman, "and we just blew them out of the stadium!"

Outcome for Defending Champion: Oregon (19-12) finished second in the North Division of the Pacific Coast Conference. The Ducks' defeats were by an average margin of just 4.25 points with only two of them by more than six.

Biggest Upset: Heavily favored Southern Cal blew a six-point lead in the closing minutes of a 43-42 setback against Kansas in a national semifinal.

Star Gazing: Huffman, the only senior among Indiana's regulars and the younger brother of former Hoosiers standout Vern Huffman (NCAA consensus All-American in 1936), was named Final Four Most Outstanding Player despite his lowly 4.3-point scoring average for the season. The only game all year when Marv Huffman managed double-digits in scoring was the NCAA final when he tied Jay McCreary with a team-high 12 points. McCreary went on to become LSU's head coach for eight seasons from 1957-58 through 1964-65 before serving as an assistant under Press Maravich when his son,

1939–40 NCAA CHAMPION: INDIANA

SEASON STATISTICS OF INDIANA REGULARS

PLAYER	POS.	CL.	G	PPG
Curly Armstrong	F	Jr.	23	8.9
Herman Schaefer	G-F	Jr.	23	8.0
Bill Menke	C	Jr.	23	7.7
Bob Dro	F-G	Jr.	23	6.3
Jay McCreary	F	Jr.	21	4.5
Marv Huffman	G	Sr.	23	4.3
Andy Zimmer	C	So.	18	1.8
Chet Francis	F	Jr.	14	1.4
Bob Menke	C-F	Jr.	18	1.4
Ralph Dorsey	F	Sr.	20	1.2
James Gridley	G	Jr.	18	1.1
Bill Torphy	G	So.	12	1.0
TEAM TOTALS			**23**	**45.6**

1940 CHAMPIONSHIP GAME

KANSAS CITY, MO

INDIANA (60)	FG	FT-A	PF	PTS.
Schaefer	4	1-1	1	9
McCreary	6	0-0	2	12
W. Menke	2	1-2	3	5
Huffman	5	2-3	4	12
Dro	3	1-1	4	7
Armstrong	4	2-3	3	10
Gridley	0	0-0	0	0
R. Menke	0	0-0	0	0
Zimmer	2	1-1	1	5
Dorsey	0	0-0	0	0
Francis	0	0-0	1	0
TOTALS	**26**	**8-11**	**19**	**60**
FT%: .723.				

KANSAS (42)	FG	FT-A	PF	PTS.
Ebling	1	2-5	0	4
Engleman	5	2-3	3	12
Allen	5	3-4	3	13
Miller	0	2-2	4	2
Harp	2	1-3	1	5
Hunter	0	1-1	0	1
Hogben	2	0-0	0	4
Kline	0	0-0	0	0
Voran	0	1-2	0	1
Sands	0	0-0	0	0
Johnson	0	0-0	0	0
TOTALS	**15**	**12-20**	**11**	**42**
FT%: .600.				

Halftime: Indiana 32-19.

ALL-TOURNAMENT TEAM

Bob Allen, C, Jr., Kansas
Howard Engleman, F, Jr., Kansas
Marvin Huffman, G-F, Sr., Indiana*
Jay McCreary, G-F, Jr., Indiana
Bill Menke, C, Jr., Indiana
* Most Outstanding Tournament Player

Pete, set national scoring records that might never be matched. McCreary's Muncie, Ind., High School team won the 1952 state championship and was runner-up in 1954 to Milan, the later game depicted in the hit movie "Hoosiers."

One and Only: McCracken is the only NCAA consensus first-team All-American (1930) to later coach his alma mater to an NCAA championship. He is one of six NCAA consensus first-team All-Americans to later coach in the NCAA Tournament.

Numbers Game: Bob Allen is the only player to lead an NCAA championship game in scoring while playing for his father. Phog Allen was coach of the Kansas squad that lost the championship game to Indiana despite his son's game-high total of 13 points. . . . . Kansas' Howard Engleman had a tourney-high 21 points in a 50-44 victory over Rice in a Western Regional semifinal. . . . Winning teams usually shot about 30 percent from the floor at this time in the sport's history, but Springfield's 12.7 percent shooting (8 for 63) in an 48-24 opening-round loss to Indiana was particularly paltry. . . . Colorado won the NIT by extending its school-record winning streak to 12 games in a row before the Buffaloes lost both of their outings in the NCAA Tournament.

What If: Indiana would not have appeared in the tourney if Big Ten champion Purdue participated in the event instead of staying home because coach Piggy Lambert wasn't fond of postseason play.

Scoring Leader: Howard Engleman, Kansas (39 points, 13 ppg).

1940–41

AT A GLANCE

NCAA Champion: Wisconsin (20-3; coached by Bud Foster; won Big Ten title by one game with an 11-1 record).

NIT Champion: Long Island (25-2; coached by Clair Bee).

New Rule: Fan-shaped backboards are legalized.

NCAA Consensus First-Team All-Americans: John Adams, F, Sr., Arkansas; Gus Broberg, G-F, Sr., Dartmouth; Howard Engleman, F, Sr., Kansas; Gene Englund, C, Sr., Wisconsin; George Glamack, C, Sr., North Carolina.

Postseason conference tournaments haven't always filled big-time league coffers. According to the *Official Basketball Guide,* "[the SEC Tournament] for the first time in history was a complete financial success, paying the entire expenses of all twelve schools and leaving a substantial amount in the conference treasury. The gross gate was slightly over $15,000."

Dartmouth's Gus Broberg became the first of five players in Ivy League history to win three consecutive scoring championships (the conference was known at the time as the Eastern Intercollegiate League). Broberg played professional basketball briefly before World War II. After enlisting in the Marines as an aviator, he lost his right arm in a plane crash.

1940 CHAMPIONSHIP BRACKET

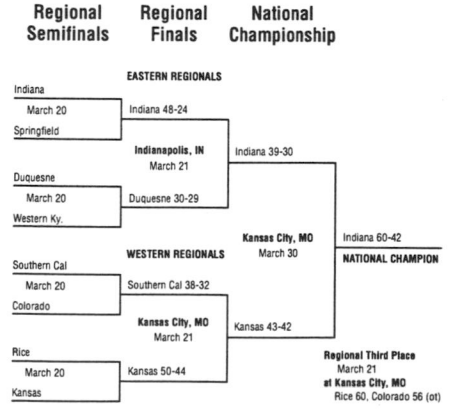

Regional Semifinals	Regional Finals	National Championship
EASTERN REGIONALS		
Indiana		
March 20	Indiana 48-24	
Springfield		
	Indianapolis, IN March 21	Indiana 39-30
Duquesne		
March 20	Duquesne 30-29	
Western Ky.		
		Kansas City, MO March 30 — Indiana 60-42 — **NATIONAL CHAMPION**
WESTERN REGIONALS		
Southern Cal		
March 20	Southern Cal 38-32	
Colorado		
	Kansas City, MO March 21	Kansas 43-42
Rice		
March 20	Kansas 50-44	
Kansas		

Regional Third Place
March 21
at Kansas City, MO
Rice 60, Colorado 56 (ot)

Broberg went on to study law and become a respected judge in Florida.

Iowa State, coached by Louis Menze, earned a share of the Big Six Conference championship after finishing in a tie for last place the previous year. . . . Kansas State's Nichols Gymnasium was packed with legislators when students at the Wildcats' game against archrival Kansas chose to illustrate the danger of cramped seating conditions in the old building by dropping a ketchup-stained dummy from the rafters. . . . Washburn (Kan.) dropped out of the Missouri Valley after its seventh non-winning record in as many seasons in the league. . . . Wittenberg (O.) defeated Dayton for the eighth consecutive year and Mount Union (O.) beat the Flyers for the fourth straight campaign.

Duke opened its season with a 43-39 defeat to Lincoln Memorial and had a 6-9 record after 15 games. The Blue Devils, however, won their last seven games, including two victories over Southern Conference regular-season champion North Carolina, and captured the league tour-nament. Maryland (1-21) won its season finale to avoid going winless.

St. Louis, winless in seven games before meeting Oklahoma A&M, upset the defending Missouri Valley Conference champion, 32-29, in perhaps the biggest upset of the season.

Florida's second-place finish in the SEC was the Gators' highest in the league until 1966–67. Tulane posted it first winning record (8-6) in 11 seasons.

1940–41 PREMO POWER POLL

RANKING	SCHOOL
1	LIU-Brooklyn# (25-2)
2	Wisconsin* (20-3)
3	Washington St. (26-6)
4	Indiana (17-3)
5	Stanford (21-5)
6	Ohio Univ. (18-4)
7	Arkansas (20-3)
8	Duquesne (17-3)
9	Westminster (Pa.) (20-2)
10	Western Kentucky (22-4)
11	Toledo (21-3)
12	Dartmouth (19-5)
13	CCNY (17-5)
14	Washington & Jefferson (15-3)
15	San Diego St. (24-7)
16	Murray St. (25-5)
17	Seton Hall (20-2)
18	Penn St. (15-5)

1940–41 NCAA CHAMPION: WISCONSIN

SEASON STATISTICS OF WISCONSIN REGULARS

PLAYER	POS.	CL.	G	PPG
Gene Englund	C	Sr.	23	13.2
John Kotz	F	So.	23	9.0
Ted Strain	G	Sr.	23	4.8
Charlie Epperson	F	Jr.	22	4.5
Fred Rehm	G	So.	21	3.7
Bob Alwin	G	Jr.	21	2.7
Don Timmerman	C	Sr.	22	1.9
Ed Scheiwe	G	Jr.	17	1.4
TEAM TOTALS			**23**	**43.7**

1941 CHAMPIONSHIP GAME

KANSAS CITY, MO

WISCONSIN (39)	FG	FT-A	PF	PTS.
Epperson	2	0-0	3	4
Schrage	0	0-0	1	0
Kotz	5	2-3	2	12
Englund	5	3-4	2	13
Timmerman	1	0-0	1	2
Rehm	2	0-1	2	4
Strain	0	2-2	1	2
Alwin	1	0-0	0	2
TOTALS	**16**	**7-10**	**12**	**39**

FG%: .254; FT%: .700.

WASHINGTON STATE (34)	FG	FT-A	PF	PTS.
Gentry	0	1-2	1	1
Gilberg	1	0-2	1	2
Butts	1	1-1	1	3
Lindeman	0	3-4	1	3
Zimmerman	0	0-0	0	0
Gebert	10	1-2	1	21
Hunt	0	0-0	0	0
Sundquist	2	0-1	3	4
Hooper	0	0-0	0	0
TOTALS	**14**	**6-12**	**8**	**34**

FG%: .215; FT%: .500.
Halftime: Wisconsin 21-17.

MOST OUTSTANDING PLAYER
John Kotz, F, Soph., Wisconsin

| 19 | Oregon St. (19-9) |
| 20 | Xavier (La.) (29-0) |

#–NIT champion
*–NCAA champion

1941 NCAA Tournament

Summary: Wisconsin, capitalizing on a home court advantage to overcome halftime deficits in the first two rounds of the tourney, captured the crown in a fairy tale script resembling the hit movie *Hoosiers*. In 1940, Wisconsin finished a dismal ninth in the Big Ten and the Badgers' overall record of 5-15 represented their worst mark since joining the Big Ten in 1906. They became the only school to finish more than two games below .500 one season and win the national championship the next year. The 20-3 badgers tied a school single-season record for the most victories.

Outcome for Defending Champion: Indiana (17-3), an eight-point loser to Wisconsin, finished runner-up to the Badgers in the Big Ten. The Hoosiers two other defeats were by a totoal of six points (at Southern Cal and Purdue).

Star Gazing: Washington State center Paul Lindeman (6-7, 230 lbs.) was limited to three points by Wisconsin in the final after he averaged 20 points in the Cougars' first two games. Lindeman scored 26 of the Cougars points in a 48-39 decision over Creighton in the opening round.

One and Only: Howard "Red" Hickey is the only individual to appear in the Final Four before playing and coaching in the NFL at least five seasons apiece. Hickey, a first-team All-Southwest Conference forward for Arkansas, was sufficiently skilled as a tackle in football to make the Razorbacks' all-decade team. Hickey, a lineman for six seasons in the NFL with two different franchises from 1941 through 1948, coached the San Francisco 49ers for five years from 1959 through 1963, compiling a 27-27-1 record.

Numbers Game: The only player to score more than 30 points in a playoff game the first 11 years of the event was North Carolina's George Glamack, who supplied 31 points in a 60-59 loss to Dartmouth in the East Regional third-place game. Glamack had a game-high nine points when the Tar Heels succumbed to Pittsburgh, 26-20, in the opening round in the lowest-scoring contest in NCAA playoff history. . . . Washington State hit an anemic 21.5 percent of its field-goal attempts (14 of 65) in the national final.

Putting Things in Perspective: Amazingly, Wisconsin lost its conference opener by 17 points at Minnesota when the Badgers failed to make a single field goal in the second half before going undefeated through the remainder of their league schedule and the playoffs.

Most Outstanding Player: John Kotz, F, Soph., Wisconsin.

1941 CHAMPIONSHIP BRACKET

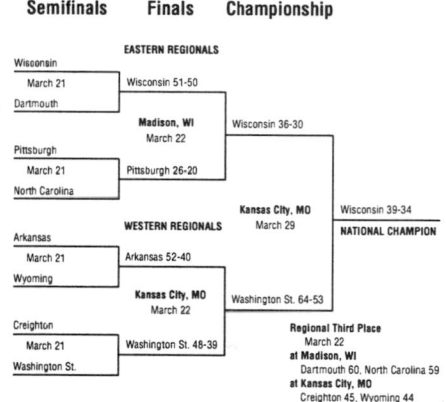

1941–42

AT A GLANCE

NCAA Champion: Stanford (27-4; coached by Everett Dean; won PCC South Division by four games with an 11-1 record).

Everett Dean was Stanford's basketball coach from 1938 to 1951 and baseball coach from 1950 to 1955.

NIT Champion: West Virginia (19-4; coached by Dyke Raese).

NCAA Consensus First-Team All-Americans: Price Brookfield, C, Sr., West Texas State; Bob Davies, G, Sr., Seton Hall; Bob Kinney, C, Sr., Rice; John Kotz, F, Jr., Wisconsin; Andy Phillip, F, Soph., Illinois.

Long Island's Clair Bee was the cream of the crop in the coaching profession, improving his career winning percentage to an astonishing 87.7 (291-41 record) when the Blackbirds compiled a 25-3 mark.

Tennessee held LIU to nine points in the second half in a 36-33 victory in the Sugar Bowl Tournament, snapping LIU's 23-game winning streak.

UCLA continued to struggle, compiling a losing league record for the 15th time in as many seasons as a member of the Pacific Coast Conference. Southern Cal defeated UCLA four times, extending the Trojans' winning streak against the Bruins to 40 games. Arizona's 9-13 record marked the Wildcats' first losing season in 16 years. . . . Brigham Young, coached by Floyd Millet, compiled its best winning percentage in school history (17-3, .850). Two of the Cougars' defeats were to Colorado and the other setback was at Wyoming.

Bob Faught, a 6-5 sophomore center, joined Notre Dame's basketball team in an effort to keep in shape for tennis. He proceeded to lead the Irish in scoring with 9.5 points per game, including 26 in a 55-43 victory over NYU at Madison Square Garden.

Rhode Island defeated New Hampshire, 127-50, in a game where the URI regulars played just the first 16 minutes. . . . Dartmouth (22-4/coached by Ozzie Cowles) had its winningest season in school history. . . . Penn's Lou Jourdet coached the son (Larry Davis) of a player (Lardie Davis) he had on his Penn roster in 1918 and 1919.

Iowa, coached by Rollie Williams, won six consecutive conference games late in the season to end a streak of eight straight non-winning Big Ten records. . . . Wittenberg (O.) defeated Bowling Green for the seventh straight season. . . . Texas Christian notched its first winning record in eight years (13-10).

Kansas' Ralph Miller, who would later be elected to the Naismith Memorial Basketball Hall of Fame after winning 657 games in 38 seasons at three major universities, led the Big Six Conference in scoring. Kansas was eliminated in the NCAA Tournament by Colorado, a school that had four starters who grew up in Kansas.

1941–42 PREMO POWER POLL

RANKING	SCHOOL
1	Stanford* (28-4)
2	LIU-Brooklyn (25-3)
3	Rice (22-5)

4	Colorado (16-2)	
5	West Virginia# (19-4)	
6	Dartmouth (22-4)	
7	Western Kentucky (29-5)	
8	Penn State (18-3)	
9	West Texas St. (28-3)	
10	Duke (22-2)	
11	Tennessee (19-3)	
12	BYU (17-3)	
13	Toledo (23-5)	
14	Kentucky (19-6)	
15	Kansas (17-5)	
16	Arkansas (19-4)	
17	Illinois (18-5)	
18	Creighton (18-5)	
19	CCNY (16-3)	
20	Mount Union (17-1)	

#–NIT champion
*–NCAA champion

1942 NCAA Tournament

Summary: Stanford overcame the title game absence of flu-ridden standout Jim Pollard, who scored 43.4 percent of his team's points in its first two tourney contests. Was it worth it? Stanford (28-4/coached by Everett Dean) took home a meager check for $93.75 to cover its stay in Kansas City to climax the school's all-time winningest season. Pollard popped in a tourney-high 26 points in a 53-47 opening game victory over Rice.

Outcome for Defending Champion: Wisconsin (14-7) finished in a three-way tie for second place in the Big Ten, despite losing its first three conference contests.

Star Gazing: Three Stanford starters—co-captains Don Burness and Bill Cowden and sophomore Howie Dallmar—attended the same high school in San Francisco. Kentucky's final game in an NCAA tournament resulted in a 46-44 verdict over Big Ten titlist Illinois.

One and Only: Dallmar, a 6-5 guard, became the only Final Four Most Outstanding Player to complete his collegiate playing career attending another university (NCAA consensus first-team All-American with Penn in 1945). Sent to Philadelphia by the Navy toward the end of World War II to attend pre-flight training school, Dallmar enrolled at Penn to complete his undergraduate work and to use his final season of sports eligibility (NCAA consensus first-team All-American in 1945). He is also the only Most Outstanding Player to guide a school other than his alma mater to the playoffs. Dallmar posted a 1-1 tourney record with Penn in 1953 before coaching Stanford for 21 years without directing his alma mater to the NCAA playoffs. The principal culprit in denying Dallmar an NCAA appearance with the Cardinal was UCLA's dynasty under John Wooden. Both coaches retired at the end of the 1974–75 season. One of the three defeats for the NCAA champion Bruins that year was at Stanford. Dallmar, an

1942 NCAA CHAMPION: STANFORD

SEASON STATISTICS OF STANFORD REGULARS

PLAYER	POS.	CL.	G	PPG
Jim Pollard	F	Jr.	23	10.5
Ed Voss	C	Jr.	29	8.7
Don Burness	F	Sr.	26	8.5
Howie Dallmar	G	So.	31	7.3
Bill Cowden	G	Sr.	31	5.5
Jack Dana	F	Jr.	27	3.7
Freddie Linari	F	Jr.	25	2.0
Leo McCaffrey	G	Jr.	22	1.0
TEAM TOTALS			**31**	**39.8**

1942 CHAMPIONSHIP GAME

KANSAS CITY, MO

STANFORD (53)	MIN.	FG	FT-A	PF	PTS.
Dana	40	7	0-0	0	14
Burness	9	0	0-0	0	0
Linari	31	3	0-0	0	6
Voss	40	6	1-1	2	13
Cowden	40	2	1-2	3	5
Dallmar	40	6	3-5	0	15
TOTALS	**200**	**24**	**5-8**	**5**	**53**
FT%: .625.					

DARTMOUTH (38)	MIN.	FG	FT-A	PF	PTS.
Myers	29	4	0-1	1	8
Parmer	11	1	0-0	0	2
Munroe	40	5	2-2	1	12
Olsen	40	4	0-1	0	8
Pearson	40	2	2-2	3	6
Skaug	40	1	0-0	2	2
TOTALS	**200**	**17**	**4-6**	**7**	**38**
FT%: .667.					
Halftime: Stanford 24-22.					

MOST OUTSTANDING PLAYER
Howie Dallmar, G, Soph., Stanford

All-NBA first-team selection in 1947–48 when he led the league in assists with the defending champion Philadelphia Warriors, moonlighted in sports the next season in a way practically never done. He played professionally for the Warriors while compiling a 15-8 record in his rookie campaign as coach of Penn.

Numbers Game: Everett Dean, compiling a 3-0 tournament record with champion Stanford, is the only unbeaten coach in NCAA playoff history. He is also the only NCAA basketball championship coach to win a College World Series baseball game for the same school (1953).

Scoring Leaders: Stanford's Jim Pollard and Rice's Chet Palmer (43 points, 21.5 ppg).

1942 CHAMPIONSHIP BRACKET

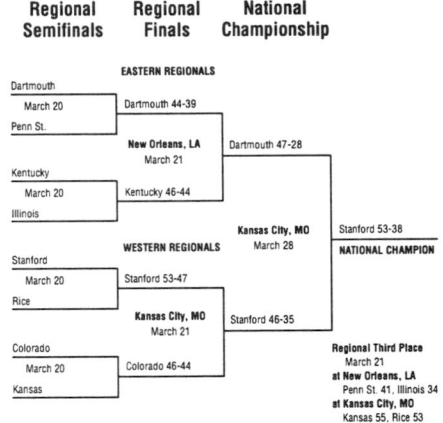

Wyoming head coach Ev Shelton.

New Conference: Metropolitan New York (disbanded after 1962–63 season).

New Rule: Any player eligible to start an overtime period is allowed an extra personal foul, increasing the total for disqualification to five fouls.

NCAA Consensus First-Team All-Americans: Ed Beisser, C, Sr., Creighton; Charles Black, F, Soph., Kansas; Harry Boykoff, C, Soph., St. John's; Bill Closs, C, Sr., Rice; Andy Phillip, F, Jr., Illinois; George Senesky, F, Sr., St. Joseph's.

1942–43

AT A GLANCE

NCAA Champion: Wyoming (31-2; coached by Everett Shelton; won Big Seven Conference by three games with an 11-1 record).

NIT Champion: St. John's (21-3; coached by Joe Lapchick).

Illinois, undefeated in Big Ten competition (12-0) after having four sophomore starters on a league championship squad dubbed "The Whiz Kids" the previous season, placed four players on the first five of the all-conference team—forward Andy Phillip, center Art Mathisen, and guards Gene Vance and Jack

RED CROSS GAMES

For three consecutive years during World War II, the NCAA and NIT champions met in a benefit game at Madison Square Garden in New York to raise money for the Red Cross. The NCAA champions won all three games.

YEAR	OUTCOME
1943	Wyoming (NCAA) 52, St. John's (NIT) 47
1944	Utah (NCAA) 43, St. John's (NIT) 36
1945	Oklahoma A&M (NCAA) 52, DePaul (NIT) 44

Smiley. The fifth Illini starter was named to the second five—forward Ken Menke. Phillip was the first player to average more than 20 points per game for a full season in Big Ten play (21.3). All but Mathisen went on to play professionally.

This is the only year when the Big Ten was not represented in the NCAA Tournament. Illinois, the only Big Ten team to go undefeated in league play in a 30-year span from 1930-31 through 1959-60, didn't participate in a postseason tournament although it ranked first in the final Dunkel Ratings. The school's athletic director declined a bid because he thought it would be unfair to his players to keep them away from their classes for three weeks. The Illini's lone loss was to Camp Grant at Rockford, Ill., where coach Doug Mills played a mostly substitute lineup. Something more pressing dismantled the team at the end of the season when all five starters headed to active duty in the armed forces.

Purdue's streak of winning seasons stopped at 23 when the Boilermakers lost six of seven games in a mid-season stretch to finish with a 9-11 record. . . . St. Louis (11-10), coached by Bob Klenck, ended a string of seven straight losing seasons and began a streak of 19 consecutive winning records. . . . Notre Dame coach George Keogan died of a heart attack on February 17, 1943. In 24 seasons as a college coach (20 with the Irish), he never had a losing record. Keogan passed away before ever appearing in the NIT or NCAA Tournament.

Center Ed Beisser, forward Ralph Langer and guard Dick Nolan finished their three-year varsity careers at Creighton with two Missouri

1942–43 NCAA CHAMPION: WYOMING

SEASON STATISTICS OF WYOMING REGULARS

PLAYER	POS.	CL.	G	PPG
Milo Komenich	C	Jr.	33	16.7
Kenny Sailors	F	Jr.	33	15.0
Jim Weir	F	Jr.	33	10.1
Floyd Volker	F-G	Jr.	33	6.4
Jimmie Reese	F	So.	23	4.3
Lew Roney	G	Jr.	30	2.7
Jim Collins	G	So.	31	2.5
Antone Katana	C	So.	24	1.5
Earl Ray	G	Jr.	19	0.8
TEAM TOTALS			33	59.4

1943 CHAMPIONSHIP GAME

NEW YORK, NY

WYOMING (46)	FG	FT-A	PF	PTS.
Sailors	6	4-5	2	16
Collins	4	0-0	1	8
Weir	2	1-3	2	5
Waite	0	0-0	0	0
Komenich	4	1-4	2	9
Volker	2	1-2	3	5
Roney	0	1-2	1	1
Reese	1	0-0	0	2
TOTALS	19	8-16	11	46
FT%: .500.				

GEORGETOWN (40)	FG	FT-A	PF	PTS.
Reilly	1	0-0	0	2
Potolicchio	1	2-3	1	4
Gabbianelli	1	2-3	3	4
Hyde	0	0-0	0	0
Mahnken	2	2-3	2	6
Hassett	3	0-3	4	6
Finnerty	0	0-0	0	0
Kraus	2	0-1	3	4
Feeney	4	0-0	1	8
Duffey	0	0-0	0	0
TOTALS	14	6-13	14	34
FT%: .462.				
Halftime: Wyoming 18-16.				

MOST OUTSTANDING PLAYER
Kenny Sailors, F, Jr., Wyoming

Valley Conference undisputed championships and one co-championship. The Bluejays were undefeated entering postseason competition but were nipped by Washington & Jefferson, 43-42, in the first round of the NIT. . . . Toledo's undefeated homecourt streak reached 40 games before it was snapped by DePaul, 49-40. . . . Valparaiso, compiling a 17-4 record, claimed to possess the tallest team in the country with a starting lineup averaging 6-6.

Manhattan, boasting eight freshmen among its first 10 players, registered an 18-3 record, including a 42-38 victory over eventual NIT champion St. John's. . . . Syracuse's streak of 18 consecutive winning records ended when the Orangemen compiled an 8-10 mark.

Western Kentucky, coached by Ed Diddle, became the first school to compile 10 consecutive 20-win seasons. . . . Center Don Barksdale's 18-point effort helped UCLA end USC's 42-game winning streak in their series with the Bruins, 42-37. UCLA finished with a 14-7 overall mark for its first winning record in 12 years.

1942–43 PREMO POWER POLL

RANKING	SCHOOL
1	Illinois (17-1)
2	Wyoming* (31-2)
3	Notre Dame (18-2)
4	St. John's# (21-3)
5	Indiana (18-2)
6	Georgetown (22-5)
7	DePaul (19-5)
8	Creighton (19-2)
9	Dartmouth (20-3)
10	Western Kentucky (24-3)
11	Toledo (22-4)
12	Kentucky (17-6)
13	Manhattan (18-3)
14	Penn St. (15-4)
15	Arizona (22-2)
16	Washington & Jefferson (18-5)
17	Kansas (22-6)
18	Detroit (15-5)
19	Fordham (17-6)
20	Tennessee (14-5)

#–NIT champion
*–NCAA champion

1943 NCAA Tournament

Summary: Virtually every university anticipated having players enter the military in the aftermath of the tourney. Wyoming (31-2/ coached by Everett Shelton) had its winningest season in school history despite playing just nine home games during the year. After losing at Duquesne in the fourth contest of the campaign, the Cowboys did not lose a game to another college team the remainder of the year. Their only other setback was to the Denver legion squad. Wyoming would have become the only champion to trail at halftime in every tournament game if the Cowboys didn't score the last three baskets of the first half in the national final to lead Georgetown at intermission (18-16).

Outcome for Defending Champion: Stanford (10-11 overall; 4-4 in conference competition) became one of only two defending champions to compile a losing record. Only two teams in the nine-member PCC posted a worse league mark.

Star Gazing: Wyoming's Kenny Sailors became the fourth consecutive Most Outstanding Player not to be his team's leading scorer for the season. The jump shot that Sailors is credited with inventing is commonplace in today's game, but was unheard of in his day. "If your feet left the floor," Sailors said, "you were a freak."

Biggest Upset: Wyoming went to New York and defeated homestanding St. John's in overtime, 52-47, in a benefit game for the American Red Cross between the NCAA and NIT champions.

One and Only: Wyoming's Shelton later became the only coach to guide teams to the championship game in both the Division I and Division II Tournaments. Shelton directed Sacramento State to a second-place finish in the 1962 Division II Tournament. . . . Sam Mele is the only individual to lead the American League in doubles as a player and manage an A.L. team to a pennant (Minnesota Twins in 1965) after leading a school in scoring in an NCAA Tournament (total of 18 points for NYU in two losses).

Numbers Game: The only team to fail to have at least one player score in double figures in the championship game was Georgetown, a 46-34 loser against Wyoming. . . . DePaul's Ray

Meyer became the first individual to reach the national semifinals in his initial season as a head coach. . . . Texas' John Hargis had a tourney-high 30 points in a 59-55 opening-game victory over Washington.

Scoring Leader: John Hargis, Texas (59 points, 29.5 ppg).

1943 CHAMPIONSHIP BRACKET

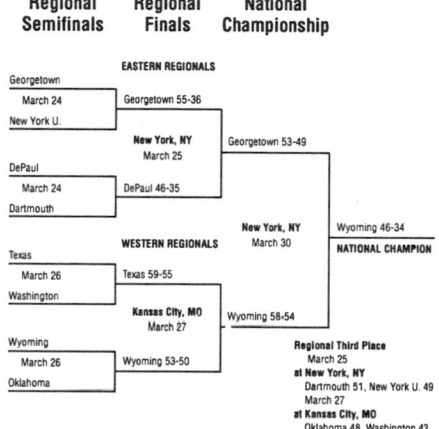

| | Regional Semifinals | Regional Finals | National Championship |

EASTERN REGIONALS

Georgetown
March 24 — Georgetown 55-36
New York U.

New York, NY March 25 — Georgetown 53-49

DePaul
March 24 — DePaul 46-35
Dartmouth

New York, NY March 30 — Wyoming 46-34 NATIONAL CHAMPION

WESTERN REGIONALS

Texas
March 26 — Texas 59-55
Washington

Kansas City, MO March 27 — Wyoming 58-54

Wyoming
March 26 — Wyoming 53-50
Oklahoma

Regional Third Place
March 25
at New York, NY
Dartmouth 51, New York U. 49
March 27
at Kansas City, MO
Oklahoma 48, Washington 43

1943–44

AT A GLANCE

NCAA Champion: Utah (22-4; coached by Vadal Peterson).

NIT Champion: St. John's (18-5; coached by Joe Lapchick).

NCAA Consensus First-Team All-Americans: Bob Brannum, C, Fr., Kentucky; Audley Brindley, C, Jr., Dartmouth; Otto Graham, F, Sr., Northwestern/Colgate; Leo Klier, F, Jr., Notre Dame; Bob Kurland, C, Soph., Oklahoma A&M; George Mikan, C, Soph., DePaul; Allie Paine, G, Jr., Oklahoma.

NCAA champion-to-be Utah was invited to the NCAA playoffs following Arkansas' withdrawal after two of its best players were injured in a horrific automobile accident. The SWC champion declined to participate because of the auto mishap involving the Razorbacks' five starters. Their station wagon, driven by physical education instructor Eugene Norris, had a flat left rear tire about 20 miles outside Fayetteville, Arkansas, while returning from a tune-up game against a military team in Fort Smith. Norris stopped in the right lane on U.S. 71 because the shoulder was too narrow. Norris and two of the starters—Deno Nichols and Ben Jones—were putting the flat in the back of the wagon when a car driven by a local undertaker plowed into the vehicle at full speed. The 28-year-old Norris, escorting the team for the first time, was pronounced dead of internal injuries and extreme shock after arriving at a nearby hospital. Nichols' right leg was broken in two places and both of Jones' legs were broken and his back fractured. Nichols' leg became gangrenous and was amputated just two months after he was married. Jones spent the next two years in various casts and braces.

Another end-of-the-season incident at Arkansas demonstrated how times were different in 1944, and also contributed to the Razorbacks' withdrawal from the tournament. All-SWC guard "Parson" Bill Flynt dropped out of school to become a full-time minister at a Baptist church in Perryville, Arkansas—just before the NCAA Tournament. The Razorbacks tied for the SWC title with Rice, which withdrew from playoff consideration because of military commitments and regulations. Arkansas' only league loss was by 26 points (67-41) at Rice.

St. John's guard Dick McGuire became the first freshman to win the award given by the New York Basketball Writers Association to the outstanding college player in the metropolitan area. McGuire, Cornell center Bob Gale, NYU forward Harry Leggart and Fordham guard Walter Mercer finished the season playing for Dartmouth, where they underwent military training as Navy trainees stationed at the Hanover, N.H., college under the wartime V-12 program. St. John's won the NIT while Dart-

The 1944 NCAA champion Utah Utes, with star freshman and Final Four Most Outstanding Player Arnie Ferrin in back row center (#22).

mouth finished runner-up to Utah in the NCAA tournament.

Rhode Island State (New England) and Dartmouth (Ivy League) each captured its seventh consecutive conference championship. Dartmouth compiled a 19-2 record (.905) under Earl Brown in his only year as coach of the Big Green. The influx of trainees at Dartmouth for the largest V-12 program in the country also included St. John's forward Lionel Baxter, NYU guard Joe Fater and Vermont forward Tom Killick during the regular season before they were shipped out.

Rhode Island State's Ernie Calverley averaged 26.7 points per game, a mark that remained a national record until 1951 and still is a school standard. No individual had had a season scoring average remain in tact longer. He was the first player to score at least 45 points twice in a single season (48 vs. Northwestern and 45 vs. Maine).

The University of Havana became the first foreign team to play at Madison Square Garden, losing to LIU, 40-37. Havana displayed "the most spectacular ball handling seen in New York in many years," according to the *Official Basketball Guide*.

The final Converse-Dunkel Ratings for the season had Army in first, followed by Utah,

Kentucky, DePaul and Western Michigan. Army, under first-year coach Ed Kelleher after going 5-10 the previous season, compiled a 15-0 record in the winter of '44 with three starters (Dale Hall, Doug Kenna and John Hennessey) who had lettered for the school's football squad. The U.S. Military Academy's closest game was its season finale (47-40 over archrival Navy) and its largest margin of victory was its next-to-last game (85-22 over Maryland). Army's basketball arena is named after team captain Edward C. Christl, a first lieutenant the next year when he was killed in Austria. Christl was third in scoring average for the undefeated team.

The University of Chicago's Frank Whittaker became the first African American ever to play for a Big Ten Conference team. . . . Northwestern forward Otto Graham, a quarterback on the school's football squad, became the first athlete ever to earn first-team All-American status in both sports in the same school year. . . . Toledo, after winning more than 20 games each of the previous four seasons, compiled a 5-13 mark for its only losing record in a 20-year span from 1934-35 through 1953-54. . . . Nebraska, 2-13, posted its fewest victories in a season since the 1897-98 campaign.

North Carolina, in Bill Lange's final season as coach of the Tar Heels, posted the best record in the Southern Conference (9-1) just one year after compiling the league's 11th-best mark (8-9).

Washington State sustained its only losing mark (8-19) in a 23-year stretch from 1929-30 through 1951-52 during Jack Friel's 30 seasons as head coach of the Cougars. . . . Southern Cal dropped its last seven games to suffer the Trojans' first losing record in 12 years (8-12).

George Edwards became the first coach to take a Missouri team to the NCAA Tournament and was a classic example showing the assortment of duties coaches had in those days. He was also the school's sports information director at the time and probably encountered difficulty drumming up much publicity because the Tigers had non-winning records seven of the previous nine seasons. Edwards, a former president of the National Association of Basketball Coaches, wrote the NABC creed the organization still embraces.

1943–44 PREMO POWER POLL

RANKING	SCHOOL
1	Army (15-0)
2	Utah* (21-4)
3	Kentucky (19-2)
4	DePaul (22-4)
5	Dartmouth (19-2)
6	St. John's# (18-5)
7	Oklahoma St. (27-6)
8	Bowling Green (22-4)
9	Rice (15-5)
10	Ohio St. (14-7)
11	Western Michigan (15-4)
12	Iowa St. (14-4)

1943-44 UNDEFEATED TEAM: ARMY (15-0)

COACH: ED KELLEHER

ARMY	OPPONENT	ARMY'S HIGH SCORER
80	Swarthmore 29	Faas 20
69	Colgate 44	Hall 18
49	St. John's 36	Hall 21
55	at Columbia 37	Hall 17
49	Penn State 38	Hall 14
55	Coast Guard 37	Kenna 11
58	West Virginia 31	Hall 18
57	at Rochester 43	Hall 23
66	Pittsburgh 32	Christl 16
69	Hobart 36	Hall/Kenna 20
55	Pennsylvania 38	Hall 18
34	Villanova 22	Hall 23
46	New York Univ. 36	Hall 18
85	Maryland 22	Hall 32
47	Navy 40	Kenna 17

INDIVIDUAL STATISTICS FOR ARMY REGULARS

PLAYER	POS.	CL.	G.	PPG
Dale Hall	F	Jr.	15	18.2
Doug Kenna	G	Jr.	15	10.1
Ed Christl	C	Sr.	12	8.3
Bob Faas	F	Sr.	15	7.1
Bill Ekberg	C	Jr.	15	4.7
Jack Hennessey	G	Sr.	15	1.7

1944 NCAA Tournament

Summary: With so many upperclassmen enlisting or been drafted during World War II, Utah had to rely almost entirely on freshmen and sophomores. Utah, entering the NCAA Tournament through the back door after losing to Kentucky in the first round of the NIT, won the NCAA championship game against Dartmouth in overtime (42-40) on freshman Herb Wilkinson's basket from far beyond the top of the key. Utah freshman Arnie Ferrin scored 22 points in the final to help end Dartmouth's school-record 17-game winning streak. Two nights later in a benefit game at Madison Square Garden for the American Red Cross, the Utes defeated yet another favorite, beating NIT titlist St. John's (43-36). St. John's had edged Utah's initial postseason opponent, Kentucky, in the NIT semifinals. Utah's players, all raised within 35 miles of the campus, had an average age of 18 years, six months. Among the four freshman starters was Wat Misaka, a spirited Japanese-American whose country was at war with the homeland of his ancestors. Utah lost its last eight games and 11 of its last 12 the previous season when it compiled a 10-12 record, the Utes' only losing mark in a 16-year span from 1936-37 through 1951-52.

Outcome for Defending Champion: Wyoming, the only school to win the NCAA championship one season and not compete in basketball the next year, did not field a team because of the war. In 1944-45, Wyoming lost its first nine games en route to compiling a 10-18 record.

Star Gazing: Ferrin, Misaka and Fred Sheffield were the only three of this group to earn any more letters with the Utes, which lost both of their NCAA playoff games in 1945. Ferrin was a second-team consensus All-American in 1947, when Utah won the NIT as the 5-8 Misaka restricted unanimous first-team All-American Ralph Beard to two points in a 49-45 triumph over Kentucky in the championship game. Wilkinson played the next three seasons

---

1943–44 NCAA CHAMPION: UTAH

SEASON STATISTICS OF UTAH REGULARS

PLAYER	POS.	CL.	G	PPG
Arnie Ferrin	F	Fr.	21	13.2
Fred Sheffield	C	So.	21	10.4
Herb Wilkinson	G-F	Fr.	21	7.9
Wat Misaka	G	Fr.	20	6.9
Bob Lewis	G	Fr.	20	5.5
Dick Smuin	F-G	Fr.	19	3.7
Bill Kastelic	F	Fr.	14	2.8
TEAM TOTALS			**26**	**52.8**

Note: Statistics are unavailable for Utah's first four games of the season.

1944 CHAMPIONSHIP GAME

NEW YORK, NY

UTAH (42)	MIN.	FG	FT-A	PF	PTS.
Ferrin	45	8	6-7	0	22
Smuin	45	0	0-0	2	0
Sheffield	4	1	0-0	1	2
Misaka	41	2	0-0	1	4
Wilkinson	45	3	1-4	0	7
B. Lewis	45	2	3-3	2	7
TOTALS	**225**	**16**	**10-14**	**6**	**42**

FT%: .714.

DARTMOUTH (40)	MIN.	FG	FT-A	PF	PTS.
Gale	37	5	0-2	1	10
Mercer	19	0	1-1	3	1
Leggat	34	4	0-0	1	8
Nordstrom	8	0	0-0	0	0
Brindley	39	5	1-1	3	11
McGuire	38	3	0-1	3	6
Murphy	17	0	0-0	0	0
Vancisin	19	2	0-0	3	4
Goering	14	0	0-0	0	0
TOTALS	**225**	**19**	**2-5**	**14**	**40**

FT%: .400.
Halftime: Dartmouth 18-17. **Regulation:** Tied 36-36.

MOST OUTSTANDING PLAYER
Arnie Ferrin, F, Fr., Utah

All-American center George Mikan of DePaul.

free block of time in the afternoons to practice during the fall quarter. However, when the winter quarter started his afternoons were no longer free and he had to make a choice between basketball or medical school. He chose medical school and left the team. His place as a starter was taken by Dick Smuin. . . . Iowa State made its only NCAA Tournament appearance until 1985. . . . National runner-up Dartmouth won at least one NCAA playoff game for the fourth consecutive year. The Big Green beat Ohio State, 60-53, in the Eastern Regional final behind Aud Brindley's tourney-high 28 points.

Scoring Leader: Aud Brindley, Dartmouth (52 points, 17.3 ppg).

Highest Scoring Average: Nick Buzolich, Pepperdine (45 points, 22.5 ppg)

for Iowa, where he was an NCAA consensus second-team All-American in 1945. Bob Lewis transferred to Stanford, where he was a three-year letterman from 1947-49.

One and Only: Sheffield, Utah's starting center, is the only Final Four player to finish among the top two high jumpers in four NCAA national track meets. Sheffield, the first athlete to place in the NCAA high jump four consecutive years, was first in 1943 with a best jump of 6-8, second in 1944, tied for first in 1945 and tied for second in 1946.

Numbers Game: Utah is the only championship team to have as many as four freshman starters. Lyman Condie, a second-year medical student, was an original starter for the team. Condie was invited by coach Vadal Peterson to try out for the squad because of a manpower shortage stemming from the war. Condie had a

1944 CHAMPIONSHIP BRACKET

Regional Semifinals	Regional Finals	National Championship
EASTERN REGIONALS		
Dartmouth March 24 Catholic	Dartmouth 63-38	
	New York, NY March 25	Dartmouth 60-53
Ohio St. March 24 Temple	Ohio St. 57-47	
		New York, NY March 28
WESTERN REGIONALS		Utah 42-40 (ot)
Iowa St. March 24 Pepperdine	Iowa St. 44-39	**NATIONAL CHAMPION**
	Kansas City, MO March 25	Utah 40-31
Utah March 24 Missouri	Utah 45-35	

Regional Third Place
March 25
at New York, NY
Temple 55, Catholic 35
at Kansas City, MO
Missouri 61, Pepperdine 46

1944–45

AT A GLANCE

NCAA Champion: Oklahoma A&M (27-4; coached by Hank Iba).

NIT Champion: DePaul (21-3; coached by Ray Meyer).

New Rules: Defensive goaltending is banned, five personal fouls now disqualifies a player (had been four since 1910), an extra foul is not allowed in overtime games, and unlimited substitution is introduced.

NCAA Consensus First-Team All-Americans: Howie Dallmar, G, Sr., Penn; Arnie Ferrin, F, Soph., Utah; Wyndol Gray, F, Soph., Bowling Green; Billy Hassett, G, Jr., Notre Dame; Bill Henry, C, Sr., Rice; Walt Kirk, G, Jr., Illinois; Bob Kurland, C, Jr., Oklahoma A&M; George Mikan, C, Jr., DePaul.

NCAA champion Oklahoma A&M defeated NIT kingpin DePaul, 52-44, at Madison Square Garden in an American Red Cross War Fund benefit game featuring the nation's two premier pivotmen—DePaul's George Mikan and A&M's Bob Kurland. Mikan fouled out of the contest after 14 minutes with the Blue Demons leading, 21-14. Cecil Hankins, the leading pass receiver for A&M's Cotton Bowl winner, scored a game-high 20 points and Kurland contributed 14.

Mikan set a school record with 53 points against Rhode Island State in the NIT semifinals.

Incredibly, three of the NCAA consensus first-team All-Americans previously or later played an entire season for other four-year universities—Penn's Howie Dallmar (previously attended Stanford), Bowling Green's Wyndol Gray (played next season for Harvard) and Notre Dame's Billy Hassett (previously attended Georgetown).

Rice, coached by Joe Davis, managed its most lopsided victory in history (95-22 over Baylor) en route to a school-best 20-1 record. The Owls' lone defeat was against NCAA champion-to-be Oklahoma A&M, 42-28, in the All-College Tournament in Oklahoma City. . . . Winless Baylor (0-17) lost back-to-back games at Arkansas by a total of 126 points (90-30 and 94-28). Nebraska (2-17) ended a school-record streak of 12 consecutive conference defeats by defeating Kansas, 59-45.

In a gigantic mismatch, Kentucky overwhelmed Arkansas State, 75-6, although Alex Groza, the Wildcats' standout freshman center, did not play in the game. Groza led Kentucky to an 11-0 start with an average of 16.5 points per game before he was inducted into the Army.

Iowa's Dick Culberson became the first African American to play for a Big Ten Conference team. The league champion Hawkeyes, coached by Pops Harrison, compiled their best winning percentage in school history with a 17-1 overall record but declined an invitation to the NCAA Tournament. NCAA consensus second-

---

1944–45 NCAA CHAMPION: OKLA. A&M

SEASON STATISTICS OF OKLAHOMA A&M REGULARS

PLAYER	POS.	CL.	G	PPG
Bob Kurland	C	Jr.	31	17.1
Cecil Hankins*	F	Sr.	23	13.3
Weldon Kern	F	Jr.	31	9.8
Doyle Parrack	G	Sr.	19	7.6
J. L. Parks	F	Fr.	31	4.0
Blake Williams	G	Fr.	31	3.8
John Wylie	G	Fr.	28	1.8
Joe Halbert	C	Fr.	20	0.6
TEAM TOTALS			**31**	**54.1**

*First-semester senior.

1945 CHAMPIONSHIP GAME

NEW YORK, NY

OKLAHOMA A&M (49)	FG	FT-A	PF	PTS.
Hankins	6	3-6	3	15
Parks	0	0-0	3	0
Kern	3	0-4	3	6
Wylie	0	0-0	0	0
Kurland	10	2-3	3	22
Parrack	2	0-1	3	4
Williams	1	0-1	1	2
TOTALS	**22**	**5-15**	**16**	**49**

FT%: .333.

NEW YORK UNIV. (45)	FG	FT-A	PF	PTS.
Grenert	5	2-3	3	12
Forman	5	1-2	1	11
Goldstein	0	2-2	2	2
Schayes	2	2-6	2	6
Walsh	0	0-0	2	0
Tanenbaum	2	0-0	2	4
Mangiapane	2	2-4	3	6
Most	1	2-3	2	4
TOTALS	**17**	**11-20**	**17**	**45**

FT%: .550.
Halftime: Oklahoma A&M 26-21.

MOST OUTSTANDING PLAYER
Bob Kurland, C, Jr., Oklahoma A&M

team All-American Max Morris of Northwestern led the Big Ten in scoring in league games (15.8 points per game) after earning MVP honors for the Wildcats' football squad the previous fall as an end.

Temple outlasted Penn State, 63-60, in five overtimes. . . . Dartmouth suffered its first losing record (6-8) in 25 years. . . .St. John's (21-3), coached by Joe Lapchick, finished in third place in the NIT although standouts Harry Boykoff, Dick McGuire and Max Zaslofsky were serving in the U.S. military. Princeton started playing home games in a different arena after University Gymnasium was destroyed by fire.

Oregon (30-13/coached by John Warren) had its winningest season in school history. . . . Davidson compiled a .500 record (9-9), but sustained its most lopsided defeat in history (89-20 at North Carolina). . . . Rensselaer Polytechnic Institute claimed to be the only undefeated college team during the regular season, compiling a 13-0 record before losing to Bowling Green, 60-45, in the opening round of the NIT.

The top five World War II service teams were Norfolk NAS (23-4), Bainbridge NTC (28-5), Great Lakes NTS (32-5), Norfolk NTS (26-8), and Memphis NATTC (31-1).

1945 NCAA Tournament

Summary: The era of the big man arrived. Bob Kurland, continuing his vast improvment in just a couple of years since showing up at Oklahoma A&M as the stereotyped awkward seven-footer, led the Aggies to the NCAA title with 17.1 points per game. They won although Kurland was their only returning letterman. Olkahoma A&M won the national final against New York University, 49-45, although the Aggies hit just five of fifteen free-throw attempts.

Outcome for Defending Champion: Utah (17-4) was eliminated in the opening round, 62-37, when Kurland scored a tourney-high 28 points for A&M. One of the Utes' other setbacks was by 28 points against Ohio State.

Biggest Upset: New York University, featuring just one senior on its roster, erased a 10-point deficit in the final two minutes of regulation on its way to frustrating Ohio State, 70-65, in overtime in the national semifinals.

Numbers Game: Dolph Schayes became the Doogie Howser of Final Four players. He is believed to be the youngest Hall of Famer to appear in an NCAA championship game, joining NYU's varsity lineup in midseason as a 16-year-old freshman and helping the Violets reach

1944–45 PREMO POWER POLL

RANKING	SCHOOL
1	Iowa (17-1)
2	Oklahoma St.* (27-4)
3	DePaul# (21-3)
4	Rice (20-1)
5	Army (14-1)
6	Ohio St. (15-5)
7	Navy (12-2)
8	Kentucky (22-4)
9	Notre Dame (15-5)
10	Bowling Green (24-4)
11	St. John's (21-3)
12	NYU (16-8)
13	Akron (21-2)
14	Muhlenberg (24-4)
15	Rhode Island (20-5)
16	Arkansas (17-9)
17	South Carolina (19-3)
18	Hamline (20-4)
19	Tennessee (18-5)
20	RPI (13-1)

#–NIT champion
*–NCAA champion

1945 CHAMPIONSHIP BRACKET

Regional Semifinals	Regional Finals	National Championship

EASTERN REGIONALS

New York U.
March 22 — New York U. 59-44
Tufts

New York, NY
March 24 — New York U. 70-65 (ot)

Ohio St.
March 22 — Ohio St. 45-37
Kentucky

New York, NY
March 27 — Oklahoma St. 49-45
NATIONAL CHAMPION

WESTERN REGIONALS

Arkansas
March 23 — Arkansas 79-76
Oregon

Kansas City, MO
March 24 — Oklahoma St. 68-41

Oklahoma St.
March 23 — Oklahoma St. 62-37
Utah

Regional Third Place
March 24
at New York, NY
Kentucky 66, Tufts 56
at Kansas City, MO
Oregon 69, Utah 66

the NCAA final against Oklahoma A&M two months before his 17th birthday.

What If: Kentucky (22-4) could have fared better in the playoffs if standout center Alex Groza wasn't inducted into the Army in mid-season.

Putting Things in Perspective: Arkansas' 79-76 victory over Oregon in the opening round shattered the previous two-team tourney scoring record by 36 points.

Scoring Leader: Bob Kurland, Oklahoma A&M (65 points, 21.7 ppg).

Highest Scoring Average: Dick Wilkins, Oregon (44 points, 22 ppg).

1945–46

AT A GLANCE

NCAA Champion: Oklahoma A&M (31-2; coached by Hank Iba; won Missouri Valley title by five games with a 12-0 record).

NIT Champion: Kentucky (28-2; coached by Adolph Rupp; went undefeated in SEC along with LSU).

NCAA Consensus First-Team All-Americans: Leo Klier, F, Sr., Notre Dame; Bob Kurland, C, Sr., Oklahoma A&M; George Mikan, C, Sr., DePaul; Max Morris, F-C, Sr., Northwestern; Sid Tannenbaum, G, Jr., NYU.

Clarence "Nibs" Price completed a unique Rose Bowl-NCAA Tournament double when his California basketball team finished in fourth place in the NCAA playoffs. On January 1, 1929, Price had coached the Cal football squad in its 8-7 defeat to Georgia Tech in the Rose Bowl game that is famous for Roy Riegels' wrong-way run for the Bears.

Purdue's Ward "Piggy" Lambert ended his 29-year coaching career with a 371-152 record. Lambert directed the Boilermakers to six Big Ten titles and five co-championships and holds the conference record for longevity. His final season marked the school's first losing league mark (4-8) since 1919.

George Ratterman, a quarterback for Notre Dame's football team, scored the last 11 points for the Irish in a 56-47 upset of a Kentucky squad that eventually won the NIT.

Oklahoma A&M's Bob Kurland poured in a school-record 58 points in an 86-33 rout of St. Louis.

A then college-record crowd of 22,822 watched Ohio State defeat Northwestern, 53-46, and DePaul upend Notre Dame, 63-47, in a doubleheader at Chicago Stadium. The victory enabled Ohio State to clinch the Big Ten crown in the Buckeyes' regular-season finale. . . . Defending Big Ten champion Iowa won its first two games by a total of 127 points (87-25 over Augustana and 91-26 over South Dakota) and its first five outings by an average margin of 43.6 points. . . . The University of Chicago dropped out of the Big Ten Conference after its fifth consecutive winless league record.

SWC champion Baylor sported its winningest season (25-5) in school history in Bill Henderson's initial full season as the Bears' head coach just one year after they were winless. . . . Guy Lewis became the first Houston player to crack the 3-0point plateau in a game. He later became the Cougars' all-time winningest coach. . . . Kansas State lost a school-record 11 consecutive games en route to a school-worst 4-20 mark. It was the Wildcats' 15th straight non-winning season. They were 3-5 at home for their last losing record there before setting an NCAA record for consecutive home winning seasons that was extended to 50 through 1995-96. . . . Elmore Morgernthaler, a 7-1 center for New Mexico School of Mines, was called the "tallest player in the world" by the Converse Basketball Yearbook. The Boston College transfer scored 12 field goals in an 84-61 victory over Drury (Mo.) in an exhibition game with 12-foot baskets at Kansas City. Field goals counted for three points in the contest.

Boston College fielded its first intercollegiate basketball team since the 1924-25 season and notched a 3-10 record. . . . Connecticut's losing streak against the Coast Guard reached seven consecutive games. . . . Manhattan defeated Villanova 10 consecutive times until losing to the Wildcats, 42-40. . . . The U.S. Merchant Marine Academy (Kings Point) compiled a modest 5-11 record, but two of its victories came against Villanova (43-38) and Maryland (52-25). . . . La Salle lost its last five games to finish with the Explorers' only losing record (9-14) in a 29-year span from 1936-37 through 196-465. . . . George Washington compiled its only losing mark (7-8) in a 25-season stretch from 1929-30 through 1955-56 (did not field squads in 1943-44 and 1944-45 because of World War II).

The Official Basketball Guide reported that "a record-breaking crowd of 8,800 paid admissions" saw Duke's second game with North Carolina "in Duke's big indoor stadium." The Guide went on to note that "this is reputed to be the largest crowd ever to see a game in the South."

Georgia Tech freshman Jim Nolan led the SEC in scoring with 14.6 points per game.

1945–46 PREMO POWER POLL

RANKING	SCHOOL
1	Oklahoma St.* (31-2)
2	Kentucky# (28-2)
3	North Carolina (30-5)
4	Indiana (18-3)
5	DePaul (19-5)
6	Rhode Island (21-3)
7	Ohio St. (16-5)
8	Notre Dame (17-4)
9	West Virginia (24-3)
10	Bowling Green (27-5)
11	NYU (19-3)
12	Kansas (19-2)
13	Illinois (14-7)
14	Wyoming (22-4)
15	Northwestern (15-5)
16	Baylor (25-5)
17	Iowa (14-4)
18	California (30-6)
19	Tennessee St. (26-2)
20	Yale (14-1)

#–NIT champion
*–NCAA champion

1946 NCAA Tournament

Summary: Bob Kurland was the only player for repeat champion Oklahoma A&M to score in double figures in any of the Aggies' three playoff games. Twenty-six different players appeared in A&M's 33 games, but only three scored more than five points in either of the two Final Four frays.

1945–46 NCAA CHAMPION: OKLAHOMA A&M

SEASON STATISTICS OF OKLAHOMA A&M REGULARS

PLAYER	POS.	CL.	G	PPG
Bob Kurland	C	Sr.	33	19.5
Weldon Kern	F	Jr.	25	8.2
J. L. Parks	G	So.	33	5.7
Blake Williams	G	So.	33	4.5
A. L. Bennett	F	So.	22	3.8
Joe Bradley	G	Fr.	30	3.4
Sam Aubrey	F	Sr.	33	3.3
Joe Pitts	F	Fr.	25	1.9
Joe Halbert	C	So.	27	1.3
Paul Geymann	F	Sr.	21	1.0
TEAM TOTALS			**33**	**50.4**

1946 CHAMPIONSHIP GAME

NEW YORK, NY

OKLAHOMA A&M (43)	FG	FT-A	PF	PTS.
Aubrey	0	1-2	1	1
Bennett	3	0-0	4	6
Kern	3	1-3	2	7
Bradley	1	1-2	1	3
Kurland	9	5-9	5	23
Halbert	0	0-0	0	0
Williams	0	2-4	2	2
Bell	0	1-1	1	1
Parks	0	0-0	2	0
TOTALS	**16**	**11-21**	**18**	**43**

FT%: .524.

NORTH CAROLINA (40)	FG	FT-A	PF	PTS.
Dillon	5	6-6	5	16
Anderson	3	2-3	3	8
Paxton	2	0-0	4	4
McKinney	2	1-3	5	5
White	0	1-1	0	1
Thorne	1	0-0	2	2
Jordan	0	4-8	3	4
TOTALS	**13**	**14-21**	**22**	**40**

FT%: .667.
Halftime: Oklahoma A&M 23-17.

MOST OUTSTANDING PLAYER
Bob Kurland, C, Sr., Oklahoma A&M

Star Gazing: Sam Aubrey, who had been seriously wounded in the war, came back to be a regular for A&M although there had been some doubt as to whether he would ever walk again.

One and Only: Kurland became the only player to score more than half of a championship team's points in a single tournament when his 72 points accounted for 51.8 percent of Oklahoma State's output in three games.

Numbers Game: Bones McKinney, who averaged 9.8 points per game as a junior center for NCAA runner-up North Carolina, is the only one of the five individuals to play for and coach a team in the Final Four to average more than 5.5 points per game in the season his alma mater reached the national semifinals. McKinney, who averaged 9.8 points per game for Carolina, coached Wake Forest to the 1962 Final Four.

What If: Ohio State captured the Big Ten Conference crown but was edged by national runnerup-to-be North Carolina (60-57 in overtime) in the East Regional final to finish the season with a 16-5 record. The Buckeyes might have had sufficient firepower to prevent Oklahoma A&M from repeating as NCAA champion had their top two scorers from Final Four teams the previous two years still been around. But Don Grate, a two-time NCAA consensus second-team All-American forward, signed a pro baseball contract as a pitcher with the Philadelphia Phillies prior to his senior year, and center Arnie Risen played just six games in the first semester before becoming academically ineligible and ending the season with a pro franchise in Indianapolis. Risen led the NBA in field-goal percentage three years later when he was the Rochester Royals' top scorer and an All-NBA second-team selection.

Scoring Leader: Bob Kurland, Oklahoma A&M (72 points, 24 ppg).

1946–47

AT A GLANCE

NCAA Champion: Holy Cross (27-3; coached by Doggie Julian).

NIT Champion: Utah (19-5; coached by Vadal Peterson; finished in second place with a 12-2 record behind Wyoming in the Big Seven Conference).

New Conference: Mid-American.

New Rule: Transparent backboards are authorized.

NCAA Consensus First-Team All-Americans: Ralph Beard, G, Soph., Kentucky; Alex Groza, C, Soph., Kentucky; Ralph Hamilton, F, Sr., Indiana; Sid Tannenbaum, G, Sr., NYU; Gerry Tucker, C, Sr., Oklahoma.

Which enterprise was deemed Bob Davies' second job when he pulled off one of the most amazing feats in college basketball history? Davies coached Seton Hall, his alma mater, to a 24-3 record the same season he also earned National Basketball League Most Valuable Player honors (averaged 14.3 points in 43 regular-season and playoff games with the Rochester Royals). The "Blonde Bomber" is credited with inventing the behind-the-back dribble. He was

1946 CHAMPIONSHIP BRACKET

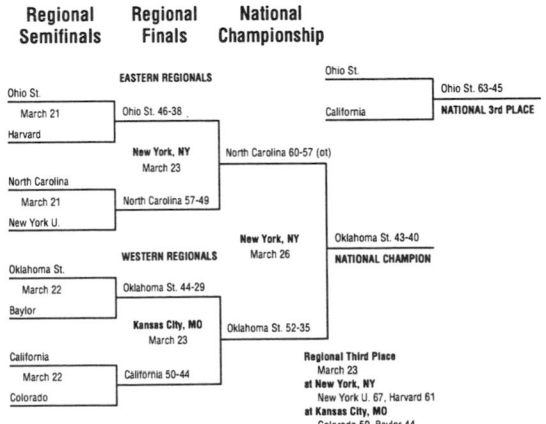

Regional Semifinals	Regional Finals	National Championship

EASTERN REGIONALS

Ohio St.
March 21
Harvard

Ohio St. 46-38

New York, NY
March 23

North Carolina
March 21
New York U.

North Carolina 57-49

North Carolina 60-57 (ot)

Ohio St.

Ohio St. 63-45
NATIONAL 3rd PLACE

California

WESTERN REGIONALS

Oklahoma St.
March 22
Baylor

Oklahoma St. 44-29

Kansas City, MO
March 23

California
March 22
Colorado

California 50-44

Oklahoma St. 52-35

New York, NY
March 26

Oklahoma St. 43-40

NATIONAL CHAMPION

Regional Third Place
March 23
at New York, NY
New York U. 67, Harvard 61
at Kansas City, MO
Colorado 59, Baylor 44

26 years old in his only season as coach of the Pirates.

Kentucky standout center Alex Groza saw limited action in the SEC Tournament because of a back injury, but the Wildcats cruised to victories over Vanderbilt (98-29), Auburn (84-18), Georgia Tech (75-53), and Tulane (55-38). The all-tourney team (considered the all-league team that season) included five Wildcats on the first five—forwards Jack Tingle and Joe Holland, center Wallace "Wah Wah" Jones, and guards Ken Rollins and Ralph Beard. Sophomores Beard and Groza are the only set of underclassmen teammates named NCAA consensus first-team All-Americans in the same year since the start of the NCAA Tournament.

Wisconsin, which finished in ninth place the previous season, won its last Big Ten Conference championship. Defending Big Ten champion Ohio State fell to a tie for sixth place. Wisconsin, involved in a bizarre late-season game to determine the title, was locked in a battle with Purdue atop the standings when the Badgers visited Lafayette, Indiana, on February 24. At halftime, newly-installed wooden bleachers at Lambert Fieldhouse's east grandstand collapsed under the overflow crowd of more than 11,000, crushing three student spectators and injuring hundreds of other patrons. The second half of the ill-fated contest was suspended for more than two weeks until being completed at a neutral site (Evanston, Illinois, High School), where Wisconsin outscored Purdue, 39-26, to claim a belated 72-60 triumph. The Badgers were coached by Bud Foster.

Oklahoma center Gerry Tucker became an NCAA consensus first-team All-American after having his career interrupted for three years while serving in the U.S. Army. He later became coach of the 1956 U.S. Olympic team.

Texas, the "Mighty Mice" team featuring three starters 5-10 or shorter, compiled a 26-2 record with both of its defeats coming by one point (40-39 to defending NCAA champion Oklahoma A&M and 55-54 to Oklahoma in the NCAA Tournament). The Longhorns were coached by Jack Gray, who was hired in the 1936-37 season when he was only 25. In an era of

1946–47 NCAA CHAMPION: HOLY CROSS

SEASON STATISTICS OF HOLY CROSS REGULARS

PLAYER	POS.	CL.	G	PPG
George Kaftan	F-C	So.	28	11.1
Dermie O'Connell	F	So.	29	9.0
Bob Cousy	G-F	Fr.	30	7.6
Ken Haggerty	G	Sr.	29	5.7
Andy Laska	G-F	Fr.	30	5.6
Joe Mullaney	G	So.	30	5.0
Frank Oftring	C-F	Fr.	29	4.6
Bob Curran	F-C	Jr.	30	4.4
Charlie Bollinger	C	So.	26	4.0
Bobbie McMullen	G-F	Fr.	29	3.8
TEAM TOTALS			**30**	**60.9**

1947 CHAMPIONSHIP GAME

NEW YORK, NY

HOLY CROSS (58)	FG	FT-A	PF	PTS.
Kaftan	7	4-9	4	18
O'Connell	7	2-4	3	16
Oftring	6	2-3	5	14
Mullaney	0	0-0	2	0
Haggerty	0	0-0	0	0
Laska	0	0-0	0	0
Curran	0	0-1	2	0
Riley	0	0-0	1	0
McMullen	2	4-4	0	8
Cousy	0	2-2	1	2
Bollinger	0	0-0	0	0
Graver	0	0-0	0	0
TOTALS	**22**	**14-23**	**18**	**58**

FT%: .609.

OKLAHOMA (47)	FG	FT-A	PF	PTS.
Reich	3	2-2	3	8
Courty	3	2-3	4	8
Tucker	6	10-12	3	22
Paine	2	2-2	0	6
Landon	1	0-1	4	2
Waters	0	0-0	0	0
Day	0	0-0	0	0
Pryor	0	1-1	2	1
Merchant	0	0-0	1	0
TOTALS	**15**	**17-21**	**17**	**47**

FT%: .810.
Halftime: Oklahoma 31-28.

MOST OUTSTANDING PLAYER
George Kaftan, F-C, Soph., Holy Cross

slow, deliberate play, Gray's squads were known for their innovative running, pressing style and were one of the first to don white sneakers.

UCLA's Don Barksdale, a second-team selection, became the first African-American player named to an NCAA consensus All-American squad. After a three-year stint in the U.S. Army, he led the Pacific Coast Conference Southern Division in scoring. . . . The top major-college single-game output of the season was a 54-point effort by St. John's Harry Boykoff against St. Francis (N.Y.). . . . Creighton compiled a 17-8 mark in Eddie Hickey's final season as the Bluejays' coach before they suffered nine consecutive non-winning records.

Bowling Green (28-7, coached by Harold Anderson), Holy Cross (27-3, Doggie Julian), Texas (26-2, Jack Gray) and Eastern Kentucky (21-4, Paul McBrayer) had their winningest seasons in school major-college history. It was McBrayer's first year as coach of the Colonels.

Cincinnati, winning more than 10 games for the first time in eight years, compiled a 17-9 record in John Wiethe's first season as coach of the Bearcats. . . . Branch McCracken returned to coach Indiana after taking a three-year leave of absence serving in World War II. . . . Miami of Ohio notched its most lopsided victory in history by overwhelming Wright State, 89-32.

North Carolina State, in Everett Case's first season as coach of the Wolfpack, posted the best record in the 16-team Southern Conference (11-2) just one year after finishing in a tie for ninth place. . . . Washington's Hec Edmundson ended his 29-year coaching career with a 508-204 record. In an 18-year span from 1927-28 through 1944-45, he notched 20-win seasons 11 times.

Kansas posted a 16-11 mark, but Howard Engleman concluded the campaign as coach when Phog Allen was ordered to take a rest after a head injury in mid-season when the Jayhawks were in the midst of a five-game losing

Holy Cross coach Alvin F. (Doggie) Julian.

streak. . . . Kansas State started a streak of 18 consecutive winning seasons by compiling a 14-10 record in the initial campaign of Jack Gardner's second go-around as the Wildcats' coach. Meanwhile, Maryland registered the same 14-10 mark for its only winning season in a 10-year span from 1940-41 through 1949-50.

1946–47 PREMO POWER POLL

RANKING	SCHOOL
1	Kentucky (34-3)
2	Holy Cross* (27-3)
3	Texas (26-2)
4	Duquesne (20-2)
5	Utah# (19-5)
6	Oklahoma (24-7)
7	Western Kentucky (25-4)
8	Notre Dame (20-4)
9	Navy (16-3)
10	Oregon St. (28-5)
11	N. Carolina St. (26-5)
12	Oklahoma St. (24-8)
13	West Virginia (19-3)
14	Arizona (21-3)
15	CCNY (17-6)
16	Wyoming (22-6)
17	LIU-Brooklyn (17-5)
18	Seton Hall (24-3)
19	Wisconsin (16-6)
20	Santa Clara (21-4)

#–NIT champion
*–NCAA champion

1947 NCAA Tournament

Summary: Holy Cross, entering the tourney with 20 consecutive victories, fell behind early in all three tourney contests before rallying to win the title. It was an incredible turnaround for the Crusaders, who compiled a meager 4-9 record two years earlier.

Outcome for Defending Champion: Oklahoma A&M compiled a 24-8 record. The Aggies only double-digit defeat was to St. Louis 38-20.

Star Gazing: The lowest team-leading scoring average for an individual in the season who was named Final Four Most Outstanding Player was compiled by George Kaftan, a forward-center with an 11.1-point average for Holy Cross' NCAA champion, after becoming the first player to score 30 points in a Final Four game (30 in a 60-45 victory over CCNY in East Regional final before tossing in a team-high 18 in a 58-47 triumph over Oklahoma in the national final).

One and Only: Alvin (Doggie) Julian is the only coach of a championship team to subsequently coach another university and compile a winning NCAA playoff record at his last major college job. Julian captured a national title in the middle of his three seasons as coach at Holy Cross before compiling a 4-3 playoff record in three tournament appearances with Dartmouth from 1956 to 1959.

Numbers Game: Seldom-used Ken Pryor's only basket in the tourney, a long jumper in the closing seconds, gave Oklahoma a 55-54 victory over Texas in the national semifinals.

Putting Things in Perspective: Holy Cross suffered its three defeats in successive early-season games. The Crusaders' first two setbacks were by a total of 26 points.

Scoring Leader: George Kaftan, Holy Cross (63 points, 21 ppg).

1947–48

AT A GLANCE

NCAA Champion: Kentucky (36-3; coached by Adolph Rupp; compiled a 9-0 record in the SEC to finish with a better winning percentage that Tulane, which was 13-1).

NIT Champion: St. Louis (24-3; coached by Eddie Hickey; finished in second place in Missouri Valley games behind Oklahoma A&M).

New Rule: Clock stopped on every dead ball the last three minutes of the second half and of every overtime period. This includes every time a basket is scored because the ball is considered dead until put into play again (rule was abolished in 1951).

NCAA Consensus First-Team All-Americans: Ralph Beard, G, Jr., Kentucky; Ed Macauley, C-F, Jr., St. Louis; Jim McIntyre, C, Jr., Minnesota; Kevin O'Shea, G, Soph., Notre Dame; Murray Wier, G, Sr., Iowa.

Long before multi-sport standouts Bo Jackson and Deion Sanders were hailed as jacks of all trades, there was three-sport whiz Dike Eddleman, possibly the most amazing all-around athlete to participate in the Final Four. Eddleman, a 6-3, 180-pound guard-forward for Illinois, was named the Big Ten Most Valuable Player by the *Chicago Tribune* in 1949 when he

1947 CHAMPIONSHIP BRACKET

Regional Semifinals	Regional Finals	National Championship

EASTERN REGIONALS

Holy Cross
March 20
Navy

Holy Cross 55-47

New York, NY
March 22

CCNY
March 20
Wisconsin

CCNY 70-56

Texas

Texas 54-50

NATIONAL 3rd PLACE

CCNY

Holy Cross 60-45

New York, NY
March 25

Holy Cross 58-47

NATIONAL CHAMPION

WESTERN REGIONALS

Texas
March 19
Wyoming

Texas 42-40

Kansas City, MO
March 22

Oklahoma
March 21
Oregon St.

Oklahoma 56-54

Oklahoma 55-54

Holy Cross 58-47

Regional Third Place
March 22
at New York, NY
Wisconsin 50, Navy 49
at Kansas City, MO
Oregon St. 63, Wyoming 46

1947–48 INDIVIDUAL LEADERS

SCORING

PLAYER	PTS.	AVG.
Hankins, Lawrence Tech	630	22.5
Wier, Iowa	399	21.0
Lavelli, Yale	554	20.5
Kudelka, St. Mary's	489	20.4
Vandeweghe, Colgate	385	20.3
Haskins, Hamline	605	19.5
Kok, Arkansas	469	19.5
McIntyre, Minnesota	360	18.9
Hatchett, Rutgers	201	18.3
Berce, Marquette	390	17.7

FIELD GOAL PERCENTAGE

PLAYER	FGM	FGA	PCT.
Petersen, Oregon St.	89	187	.476
Mackin, Muhlenberg	158	338	.467
Coleman, Louisville	136	292	.466
Compton, Louisville	109	241	.452
Karplak, Colorado A&M	77	176	.438
Mann, Bradley	87	199	.437
Brown, Miami (Ohio)	178	417	.427
Walker, Akron	135	316	.427
Dobler, Colorado A&M	106	251	.422
Richter, Cincinnati	122	294	.415
Harman, Kansas St.	76	183	.415

FREE THROW PERCENTAGE

PLAYER	FTM	FTA	PCT.
Urzetta, St. Bonaventure	59	64	.922
Sterling, West Virginia	40	45	.889
Shannon, Kansas St.	55	66	.879
Sharman, USC	38	44	.864
Wylie, Ohio U.	88	102	.863
L. Malamed, CCNY	55	66	.833
Line, Kentucky	48	58	.828
McMullen, Mississippi	70	86	.814
Woodcock, Bucknell	39	48	.813
Nelson, Brigham Young	111	138	.804

1947–48 TEAM LEADERS

SCORING OFFENSE

SCHOOL	PTS.	AVG.
Rhode Island St.	1755	76.3
North Carolina St.	2409	75.3
Bowling Green	2327	70.5
Lawrence Tech	1961	70.0
Bradley	2157	69.6

SCORING DEFENSE

SCHOOL	PTS.	AVG.
Oklahoma A&M	1006	32.5
Alabama	1070	39.6
Creighton	925	40.2
Wyoming	1101	40.8
Siena	1161	41.5

FREE THROW PERCENTAGE

SCHOOL	FTM	FTA	PCT.
Texas	351	481	.730
Michigan	280	411	.681
St. Bonaventure	286	421	.679
DePaul	468	698	.670
New York University	433	646	.670

FIELD GOAL PERCENTAGE

SCHOOL	FGM	FGA	PCT.
Oregon St.	668	1818	.367
Muhlenberg	655	1822	.359
Akron	571	1617	.353
Louisville	709	2028	.350
Bowling Green	918	2639	.348

1947–48 NCAA CHAMPION: KENTUCKY

SEASON STATISTICS OF KENTUCKY REGULARS

PLAYER	POS.	CL.	G	FG%	FT%	PPG
Alex Groza	C	Jr.	39	.377	.629	12.5
Ralph Beard	G	Jr.	38	.362	.591	12.5
Wallace Jones	F-C	Jr.	36	.311	.670	9.3
James Line	F	So.	38	.361	.823	7.0
Ken Rollins	G	Sr.	39	.279	.728	6.6
Cliff Barker	F	Jr.	38	.309	.559	6.5
Dale Barnstable	F	So.	38	.271	.571	4.6
Joe Holland	F	Jr.	38	.280	.511	3.7
Jack Parkinson	G	Sr.	29	.201	.455	3.3
Walt Hirsch	F-G	Fr.	13	.291	.556	2.8
Albert Cummins	G	So.	17	.351	.667	1.9
Jim Jordan	F	So.	30	.148	.720	1.5
Garland Townes	G	Fr.	13	.318	.455	1.5
Roger Day	F	Fr.	11	.278	.778	1.5
Albert Campbell	C	Sr.	15	.222	.571	1.1
Johnny Stough	G	So.	23	.211	.500	0.9
TEAM TOTALS			**39**	**.312**	**.626**	**70.0**

Note: Statistics include three games in Olympic Trials after the NCAA Tournament.

1948 CHAMPIONSHIP GAME

NEW YORK, NY

KENTUCKY (58)	FG	FT-A	PF	PTS.
Jones	4	1-1	3	9
Barker	2	1-3	4	5
Groza	6	2-4	4	14
Beard	4	4-4	1	12
Rollins	3	3-5	3	9
Line	3	1-1	3	7
Holland	1	0-0	1	2
Barnstable	0	0-1	0	0
TOTALS	**23**	**12-19**	**19**	**58**

FT%: .632.

BAYLOR (42)	FG	FT-A	PF	PTS.
Owens	2	1-2	0	5
DeWitt	3	2-4	3	8
Heathington	3	2-4	5	8
Johnson	3	4-7	5	10
Robinson	3	2-4	4	8
Pulley	0	1-1	0	1
Hickman	1	0-0	0	2
Preston	0	0-2	2	0
Srack	0	0-0	0	0
TOTALS	**15**	**12-24**	**19**	**42**

FT%: .500.
Halftime: Kentucky 29-16.

MOST OUTSTANDING PLAYER
Alex Groza, C, Jr., Kentucky

was the leading scorer for the national third-place finisher in basketball. In football, he played both offense and defense, punted and returned kicks, and played in the 1947 Rose Bowl for a team that overwhelmed UCLA, 45-14. He set school season records in 1948 for highest punting average (43 yards per kick) and punt return average (32.8). Eddleman, interrupting his collegiate career by joining the U.S. Army Air Corps during World War II, earned an amazing 11 varsity letters at Illinois. He won three Big Ten high jump titles. But his greatest athletic achievement might have been winning a silver medal in the high jump in the 1948 Olympics in London. The Olympics climaxed an outstanding academic school year for Eddleman. He won the NCAA high jump crown and led Illinois' football and basketball teams in scoring.

Iowa's Murray Wier is acknowledged as the shortest player (5-9) to lead the nation in scoring (21 points per game) although Norm Hankins of Lawrence Tech in Detroit was designated as the major-college scoring leader (22.5 ppg) that season.

North Carolina State, runner-up to Rhode Island State in team offense with 75.3 points per game, became the first school other than the Rhodies ever to average more than 75. The Wolfpack, undefeated in Southern Conference competition (12-0), finished the season with a 29-3 mark when its leading scorer, sophomore Dick Dickey, was sidelined with the mumps in an NIT opening-round defeat to DePaul.

Virginia defeated Duke, 49-39, for the Cavaliers' only victory over the Blue Devils in a 23-game stretch from 1929-30 through 1955-56.

Michigan, coached by Ozzie Cowles, compiled a 10-2 Big Nine mark for its first winning league record in 11 years and first conference title in 19 seasons. . . . Iowa's Murray Wier is acknowledged as the shortest player (5-9) to lead the nation in scoring (21 points per game) although Norm Hankins of Lawrence Tech in Detroit was designated as the major-college

scoring leader (22.5 ppg). Wier was the only senior among the consensus NCAA first-team All-American selections. Ten of the 14 consensus NCAA first- and second-team choices were undergraduates.

Jim Lacy of Loyola (Md.) finished 12th in the nation in scoring with 17.5 points per game but had the nation's single-game high of 44 points against Western Maryland. . . . St. Bonaventure's Sam Urzetta (92.2 percent) became the only player to convert more than 90 percent of his free throws in a single season until 1962. . . . Notre Dame (17-7), coached by Moose Krause, defeated two teams ranked No. 1 in the country in the final month of the regular season—NCAA champion-to-be Kentucky and NIT runner-up NYU. But Notre Dame's school-record homecourt winning streak was snapped at 38 by eventual NIT kingpin St. Louis. . . . Duquesne's Chick Davies ended a 21-year coaching career with a 314-106 record.

Arkansas became the first school to compile 25 consecutive winning seasons. . . . Kansas State, coached by Jack Gardner, ended its streak of 21 consecutive non-winning conference records by capturing the Big Seven title with a 9-3 league mark. It was the Wildcats' first conference crown in 29 seasons.

Kansas' streak of 18 consecutive winning records under coach Phog Allen came to a halt when the Jayhawks lost 10 straight games the second half of the season en route to a 9-15 mark. It was the school's only losing record in a 29-year span through 1957-58.

Washington's Jack Nichols finished his fifth season of varsity competition in the Pacific Coast Conference (three with the Huskies and two as a military trainee during World War II with Southern California). . . . Montana's Bob Cope set a school single-game scoring record by firing in 40 points against Gonzaga (mark later tied). . . . Hamline (Mn.), Lawrence Tech (Mn.), Scranton (Pa.) and Texas Wesleyan competed in their final season at the major-college level.

RANKING	SCHOOL
1	Kentucky* (36-3)
2	St. Louis# (24-3)
3	Holy Cross (26-4)
4	Western Kentucky (28-2)
5	N. Carolina St. (29-3)
6	NYU (22-4)
7	DePaul (22-8)
8	West Virginia (17-3)
9	Michigan (16-6)
10	Oklahoma St. (27-4)
11	Baylor (24-8)
12	Tennessee (20-5)
13	Bowling Green (27-6)
14	Tulane (23-3)
15	Bradley (28-3)
16	Iowa (15-4)
17	Texas (20-5)
18	Illinois (15-5)
19	CCNY (18-3)
20	Columbia (21-3)

#–NIT champion
*–NCAA champion

1948 NCAA Tournament

Summary: Ken Rollins, the lone senior among coach Adolph Rupp's "Fabulous Five," held standout guard Bob Cousy, the leading scorer for defending champion Holy Cross, to just five points in the semifinals. Kentucky's winningest team in school history (36-3 under coach Adolph Rupp) had an excessive amount of maturity since Rollins, Alex Groza, Dale Barnstable, Jim Line, and Cliff Barker were World War II service veterans. Barker, a defensive specialist, was in a German prisoner-of-war camp for 16 months after the crewman's B-17 was shot down in Europe.

Outcome for Defending Champion: Holy Cross finished with a 26-4 record when Kentucky ended the Crusaders' 19-game winning streak. Their most lopsided defeat was to St. Louis, 61-46.

One and Only: Michigan's Pete Elliott became the only player to score a team-high point total in his school's first NCAA Tournament victory the same year he earned All-American honors as a quarterback for a national football champion. Elliott, a second-team pick on the Helms All-American team scored a team-high 15 points in a 66-49 decision over Columbia in the Eastern Regional third-place game. Elliott also earned All-American honors as a quarterback for the Wolverines' 1948 national football champion. He was executive director of the Pro Football Hall of Fame after serving as head football coach at Nebraska (1956), California (1957-59) and Illinois (1960-66), leading Cal and the Illini to Rose Bowl berths.

Numbers Game: Columbia entered the playoffs with just one defeat (in overtime), but Kentucky's Wallace Jones (21), Groza (17), and Beard (15) combined to equal their entire output as the Wildcats prevailed, 76-53, in the first round. Michigan's Ozzie Cowles became the first coach to direct two different schools to the NCAA playoffs for the initial time. He guided Dartmouth to its first tourney appearance in 1941. . . . Wyoming's John Pilch scored a tourney-high 24 points in a 57-47 loss to Washington in the Western Regional third-place game.

Scoring Leader: Alex Groza, Kentucky (54 points, 18 ppg).

Highest Scoring Average: Jack Nichols, Washington (39 points, 19.5 ppg).

1948 CHAMPIONSHIP BRACKET

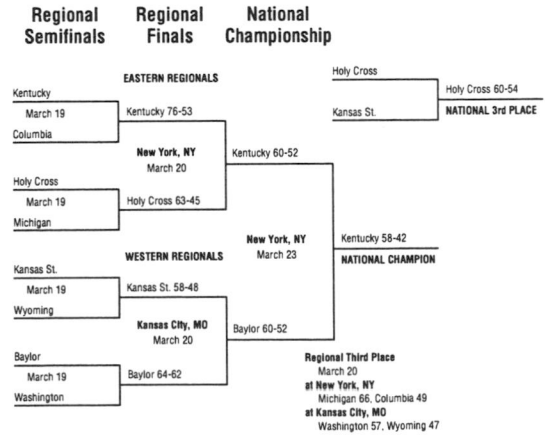

1948–49

NCAA Champion: Kentucky (32-2; coached by Adolph Rupp; compiled a 13-0 SEC record to finish two games ahead of Tulane).

NIT Champion: San Francisco (25-5; coached by Pete Newell).

New Conference: Ohio Valley.

New Rules: Coaches allowed to converse while mingling with players during a timeout. NIT field expands from eight teams to 12.

NCAA Consensus First-Team All-Americans: Ralph Beard, G, Sr., Kentucky; Vince Boryla, F, Sr., Denver; Alex Groza, C, Sr., Kentucky; Tony Lavelli, G, Sr., Yale; Ed Macauley, C-F, Sr., St. Louis.

A weekly ritual began when the Associated Press announced the results of the first weekly basketball poll on January 18, 1949. St. Louis was ranked first in the initial poll, followed by Kentucky, Western Kentucky, Minnesota, Oklahoma A&M, San Francisco, Illinois, Hamline, Villanova, and Utah.

Kentucky, unbeaten in SEC competition for the third consecutive season en route to becoming the only school to win more than 30 games overall in three consecutive campaigns, finished sixth nationally in both team offense and defense. The season's most shocking defeat was the Wildcats' 67-56 setback against Loyola of Chicago in the opening round of the NIT. The defending NCAA champions entered the game ranked No. 1 in the nation in the AP poll. Later, it was disclosed that the Kentucky-Loyola game was one in which UK players allegedly were bribed by gamblers to keep the winning margin under 10 points.

Western Kentucky won 32 consecutive regular-season games until bowing to Eastern Kentucky, 42-40. . . . Oklahoma A&M won the Missouri Valley title, extending the Aggies' streak of finishing first or second in the MVC to 12 consecutive seasons.

Jim Lacy of Loyola (Md.) became the first player to finish his career cracking the 2,000-point plateau. . . . Villanova's Paul Arizin erupted for a school-record 85 points in a 117-25 pounding of Philadelphia NAMC (Naval Air Material Center) after the Wildcats played their previous eight games on the road. The only player to score at least 40 points in two games was Yale's Tony Lavelli. A 52-point uprising by Lavelli against Williams remains a school record.

Muhlenberg registered seven straight victories over Villanova until succumbing to the Wildcats, 62-49. . . . Colgate's Ernie Vandeweghe finished among the nation's top five scorers for the third consecutive season. His son, Kiki, became a standout at UCLA and averaged more than 20 points per game seven consecutive seasons in the NBA from 1981-82 through 1987-88. . . . West Virginia's school-record homecourt winning streak ended at 57 consecutive games with a 34-32 overtime loss to Pittsburgh in the closing contest on the Mountaineers' schedule.

Cliff Wells, Tulane's all-time winningest coach, guided the Green Wave to its only Top 20 appearance in a final wire-service poll by compiling a school-record 24-4 record. Three of Tulane's four defeats were to Kentucky. The only other setback for the Green Wave was by two points at Vanderbilt. It was the third consecutive Tulane team with more than 20 victories. The following excerpt of a letter written by Wells to a high school coach might explain the drive behind Green Wave teams of the Wells era:

"I am a firm believer that condition means stamina. Stamina demands training. Training spells sacrifice. Sacrifice is the highway to desire. If a boy is traveling another road he is lost in every sense of the word. I would not have him on my squad. The athlete at his best learns something different. Not comfortable, ease. Not idleness. Not self-indulgence. Not jaunty contempt for authority. These never win

1948–49 INDIVIDUAL LEADERS

SCORING

PLAYER	PTS.	AVG.
Lavelli, Yale	671	22.4
Arizin, Villanova	594	22.0
Giermak, William & Mary	740	21.8
Senesky, St. Joseph's	483	21.0
Vandeweghe, Colgate	397	20.9
Groza, Kentucky	698	20.5
Goodwin, Rhode Island	433	19.7
Noertker, Virginia	442	19.2
Boryla, Denver	624	18.9
Schaus, West Virginia	442	18.4

FIELD GOAL PERCENTAGE

PLAYER	FGM	FGA	PCT.
Macauley, St. Louis	144	275	.524
Goodwin, Rhode Island	145	291	.498
Brawley, Maryland	78	161	.484
Leverte, Seton Hall	101	210	.481
Boven, Western Michigan	123	257	.479
Share, Bowling Green	193	410	.471
Coleman, Louisville	188	404	.465
Kerris, Loyola (Ill.)	175	382	.458
White, Texas	83	185	.449
Grover, Bradley	98	212	.462

FREE THROW PERCENTAGE

PLAYER	FTM	FTA	PCT.
Schroer, Valparaiso	59	68	.868
Line, Kentucky	43	51	.843
Oftring, Holy Cross	47	56	.839
Dolnics, TCU	99	119	.832
Goodwin, Rhode Island	143	172	.831
Lavelli, Yale	215	261	.824
Palcheff, Washington (Mo.)	65	80	.813
Alston, Xavier	52	64	.813
Cheek, Davidson	75	94	.798
Westerfeld, Cincinnati	50	63	.794

1948–49 TEAM LEADERS

SCORING OFFENSE

SCHOOL	PTS.	AVG.
Rhode Island St.	1575	71.6
Western Kentucky	2028	69.9
Yale	2089	69.6
Bowling Green	2139	69.0
Colgate	1297	68.3

SCORING DEFENSE

SCHOOL	PTS.	AVG.
Oklahoma A&M	985	35.2
Siena	1215	41.9
Wyoming	1509	43.1
Minnesota	912	43.4
St. Bonaventure	1137	43.7

FIELD GOAL PERCENTAGE

SCHOOL	FGM	FGA	PCT.
Muhlenberg	593	1512	.392
Wyoming	674	1777	.379
Loyola (Ill.)	720	1918	.375
Seton Hall	566	1509	.375
Bradley	889	2372	.375

FREE THROW PERCENTAGE

SCHOOL	FTM	FTA	PCT.
Davidson	347	489	.710
Kentucky	514	728	.706
Utah	489	704	.695
Denver	505	730	.692
Valparaiso	340	496	.687

SCORING MARGIN

SCHOOL	OWN	OPP.	MAR.
Kentucky	68.2	43.9	24.3
Tulane	65.6	48.8	16.8
Rhode Island St.	71.6	56.0	15.6
Loyola (Ill.)	61.3	45.7	15.5
Western Kentucky	69.9	54.4	15.5

1948–49 NCAA CHAMPION: KENTUCKY

SEASON STATISTICS OF KENTUCKY REGULARS

PLAYER	POS.	CL.	G	FG%	FT%	PPG
Alex Groza	C	Sr.	34	.423	.726	20.5
Ralph Beard	G	Sr.	34	.299	.713	10.9
Wallace Jones	F-C	Sr.	32	.295	.653	9.7
Cliff Barker	G-F	Sr.	34	.298	.682	7.3
Dale Barnstable	F-G	Jr.	34	.272	.719	6.1
Jim Line	F	Jr.	32	.359	.843	5.7
Walt Hirsch	F-G	So.	34	.321	.688	4.6
Roger Day	F	So.	19	.538	.529	2.7
Garland Townes	G	So.	16	.208	.550	1.9
Johnny Stough	G	Jr.	25	.232	.857	1.5
TEAM TOTALS			**34**	**.328**	**.706**	**68.2**

1949 CHAMPIONSHIP GAME

SEATTLE, WA

KENTUCKY (46)	FG	FT-A	PF	PTS.
Jones	1	1-3	3	3
Line	2	1-2	3	5
Groza	9	7-8	5	25
Beard	1	1-2	4	3
Barker	1	3-3	4	5
Barnstable	1	1-1	1	3
Hirsch	1	0-0	1	2
TOTALS	**16**	**14-19**	**21**	**46**

FT%: .737.

OKLAHOMA A&M (36)	FG	FT-A	PF	PTS.
Yates	1	0-0	1	2
Shelton	3	6-7	4	12
Harris	3	1-1	5	7
Bradley	0	3-6	3	3
Parks	2	3-4	5	7
Jaquet	0	1-2	0	1
McArthur	0	2-2	1	2
Pilgrim	0	2-2	1	2
Smith	0	0-0	1	0
TOTALS	**9**	**18-24**	**21**	**36**

FT%: .750.
Halftime: Kentucky 25-20.

MOST OUTSTANDING PLAYER
Alex Groza, C, Sr., Kentucky

any game. Instead, these: obedience, self-denial, team play and always the inner cry—`I must, I MUST and I will!'"

Another school to register its winningest season in history was William & Mary (24-10/coached by Bernard Wilson).

Ohio University went 6-16 for its first losing season in 15 years. . . . Miami of Ohio suffered its most lopsided defeat in history when the Redskins were clobbered at Cincinnati, 94-36. . . . Bowling Green hasn't won more than 20 games in a season since compiling a 24-7 mark as third-place finisher in the NIT. The Falcons averaged 24.3 victories annually over the last seven seasons in the 1940s despite sustaining losses in that span to Muskingum, Great Lakes, Denison and Baldwin-Wallace. . . . St. Louis' Ed Macauley finished his career as a two-time first-team Al--American after averaging a modest 6.8 points per game in his three-year varsity career at a local high school.

Texas' Slater Martin also set a school record (subsequently tied) with 49 points against TCU. . . . Pacific lost 17 consecutive games in its series with Santa Clara until defeating the Broncos, 60-52. . . . John Wooden began his coaching career at UCLA with a 22-7 record, breaking the Bruins' previous single-season mark of 18 victories, which was set two years earlier under his predecessor, Wilbur Johns. Wooden, who coached two seasons at Indiana State in his home state, had also caught the eye of Minnesota, but UCLA put its offer on the table first and he accepted a first-year salary of $6,000.

1948-49 FINAL NATIONAL POLL

AP	SCHOOL(RECORD)	HEAD COACH
1	Kentucky (32-2)	Adolph Rupp
2	Oklahoma St. (23-5)	Hank Iba
3	St. Louis (22-4)	Eddie Hickey
4	Illinois (21-4)	Harry Combes
5	Western Kentucky (25-4)	Ed Diddle
6	Minnesota (18-3)	Ozzie Cowles
7	Bradley (27-8)	Forddy Anderson
8	San Francisco (25-5)	Pete Newell
9	Tulane (24-4)	Cliff Wells
10	Bowling Green St. (24-7)	Harold Anderson

1949 NCAA Tournament

Summary: Despite returning seven of his top eight scorers from an NCAA titlist, Kentucky coach Adolph Rupp experimented with the Wildcats' lineup until he achieved the chemistry he sought. Cliff Barker was moved from forward to guard and forward Dale Barnstable also played some guard. After an early-season defeat to St. Louis on a last-second tip-in, Kentucky won all of its games until bowing in the NIT to eventual finalist Loyola of Chicago. A couple of years later, Alex Groza, Ralph Beard, and Barnstable admitted in sworn testimony that they accepted $1,500 in bribes to throw the NIT game against Loyola. They also testified they accepted money from gamblers to shave points in other contests. Each received a suspended sentence in return for cooperating with federal officials and were banned by the NBA. Beard and Groza are the only two of the 10 players who started the first NBA All-Star Game in 1951 not to be in the Naismith Memorial Basketball Hall of Fame. Beard admits to taking $700, but not even the gambler, a student who sat on Kentucky's bench, said Beard agreed to shave points. "It's like I told the grand jury," Beard says. "I said, `I would like to know what constitutes guilt. If taking money constitutes guilt, I'm guilty. But if influencing the point spread constitutes guilt, I'm as innocent as anybody ever was.' I was too selfish as a player, too proud of who I was, to ever play less than my best."

Star Gazing: Alex Groza was the brother of football Hall of Famer Lou Groza. Interestingly, a reserve on Kentucky's team early in the season, Joe B. Hall, didn't make the trip to Seattle because he had transferred to the University of the South. Later, he was the Wildcats' coach when they made a trip to the "Emerald City" at the 1984 Final Four.

One and Only: Groza, the Final Four Most Outstanding Player in 1948 and 1949, is the only player to appear at a minimum of two Final Fours and be the game-high scorer in every

Final Four contest in which he played. Despite missing 13 minutes of the second half because of foul trouble, Groza scored 25 points to lead the Wildcats to a 46-36 decision over Oklahoma A&M in the title game. . . . Wyoming fell one victory shy of reaching the Final Four for the third consecutive year. . . . Oklahoma A&M became the only school to reach the NCAA championship game in its first three playoff appearances—won titles in 1945 and 1946.

Numbers Game: Groza and Villanova's Paul Arizin each scored 30 points when Kentucky defeated Villanova, 85-72. It was the only playoff game in which two players scored at least 30 in the same game until 1953.

Scoring Leader: Alex Groza, Kentucky (82 points, 27.3 ppg).

1949 CHAMPIONSHIP BRACKET

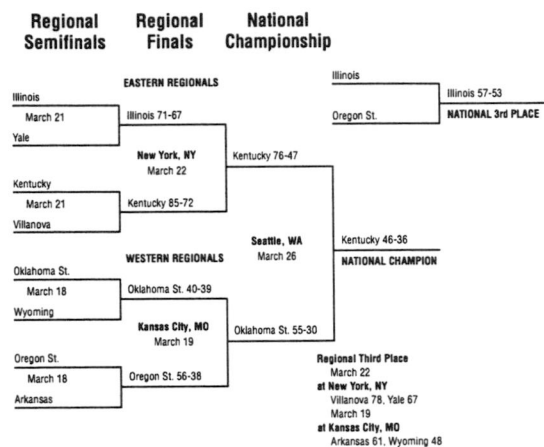

WINNINGEST PROGRAMS OF THE 1940S

RK.	SCHOOL	W.	L.	PCT.
1.	Kentucky	239	42	.851
2.	Oklahoma A&M	237	55	.812
3.	Rhode Island	178	44	.802
4.	Eastern Kentucky	143	37	.794
5.	Western Kentucky	222	66	.771
6.	Tennessee	152	46	.768
7.	Bowling Green	204	66	.756
8.	Notre Dame	162	55	.747
9.	Toledo	176	65	.730
10.	St. John's	162	60	.730

Note: Seton Hall (128-22 record, .853) and Duquesne (118-32, .787) competed in only seven seasons during the decade.

3

THE "GREAT PLAYERS" ERA:
THE 1950s

Kentucky, closing out the 1940s with back-to-back NCAA crowns, continued to excel but represented the best and worst of the 1950s. The Wildcats were virtually invincible on the court, winning at least 20 games every season they competed in the decade. On the other hand, they were party to a widespread gambling-related scandal that barred them from participating one season.

Kentucky coach Adolph Rupp's average record in a 15-year span from 1944-59 was an incredible 27-3. An example of the Wildcats' SEC dominance was their victories over Florida by at least 42 points in a 12-year stretch from 1948-59.

The '50s also marked the emergence of dominating African-American players such as Elgin Baylor, Wilt Chamberlain, Oscar Robertson, and Bill Russell. The athleticism of big men Chamberlain and Russell was stunning. Chamberlain became the only seven-foot center to lead a Final Four in scoring (55 points in two games for 1957 runner-up Kansas) and win a conference high jump title in the same year (Big Eight outdoor meet at a height of 6'5"). Russell, 6-10, did more than lead San Francisco to back-to-back NCAA basketball championships. He was ranked as the world's No. 7 high jumper in the *Track and Field News* rankings for 1956 after winning titles in the West Coast Relays, Pacific AAU meet, and Central California AAU meet. Baylor and Robertson were equally impressive athletes.

Chamberlain, who grew up in Philadelphia, headlined an impressive string of All-Americans from Pennsylvania. He and eight other natives of the Quaker State became NCAA consensus first-team All-Americans a total of 12 times from 1950-58. Joining Chamberlain on this list were Paul Arizin (Villanova), Bill Mlkvy (Temple), Dick Groat (Duke), Ernie Beck (Penn), Tom Gola (La Salle), Dick Ricketts (Duquesne), Don Hennon (Pitt) and Guy Rodgers (Temple). Gola and Ricketts were among freshmen declared eligible for varsity competition in the 1951-52 season by most colleges because of the manpower shortage caused by the Korean War.

The '50s are the long lost glory years for many schools. More than half of the Top 20 teams in the decade in final wire-service polls failed to appear among the Top 20 in comparable rankings the first half of the 1990s. Three schools in the '50s went from the Final Four one year to at least 10 games below .500 the next season.

1949–50

AT A GLANCE

NCAA/NIT Champion: CCNY (24-5; coached by Nat Holman).

NCAA Consensus First-Team All-Americans: Paul Arizin, F, Sr., Villanova; Bob Cousy, G, Sr., Holy Cross; Dick Schnittker, F, Sr., Ohio State; Bill Sharman, G, Sr., Southern California; Paul Unruh, F, Sr., Bradley.

Paul Arizin, who couldn't earn a spot on his high school squad and didn't bother to try out as a Villanova freshman, led the nation in scoring average (25.3 ppg). Arizin's outbursts helped Villanova end Rhode Island State's streak of 14 consecutive seasons leading the nation in offense. The Wildcats averaged 72.8 points per game.

Bob Zawoluk's school-record 65 points for St. John's against St. Peter's was the top one-game barrage during the season.

Butler's Ralph "Buckshot" O'Brien, a 5-9, 150-pound guard, averaged 25.3 points per game in seven games against Big Nine teams.

St. Bonaventure's Sam Urzetta led the nation in free-throw accuracy for the second time in three seasons. Urzetta also went on to win the U.S. Amateur golf title.

Ohio State forward Dick Schnittker earned consensus All-American honors after starting as an end for Ohio State's conference co-championship football squad that defeated California, 17-14, in the Rose Bowl. Cincinnati, coached by John Wiethe, became the only Mid-American team to ever go undefeated in conference competition since the league's

inception in 1947. . . . Bradley (32-5/coached by Forddy Anderson) had its winningest season in school history. Holy Cross (27-4/Buster Sheary) tied its school record for most victories in a single season.

Two future teammates with the Boston Celtics for four seasons led the Pacific Coast Conference in scoring. Washington State's Gene Conley paced the Northern Division with 13.8 points per game while Southern Cal's Bill Sharman led the Southern Division with a 19.8 mark. Both Conley and Sharman also played professional baseball. Speaking of the Celtics, Red Auerbach was an assistant coach and heir apparent to Gerry Gerard at Duke for three months before leaving for a pro job at Tri-Cities. Auerbach was given much credit for grooming Duke All-American Dick Groat.

1949-50 FINAL NATIONAL POLL

AP	SCHOOL (RECORD)	HEAD COACH
1	Bradley (32-5)	Forddy Anderson
2	Ohio State (22-4)	Tippy Dye
3	Kentucky (25-5)	Adolph Rupp
4	Holy Cross (27-4)	Buster Sheary
5	N.C. State (27-6)	Everett Case
6	Duquesne (23-6)	Dudey Moore
7	UCLA (24-7)	John Wooden
8	Western Kentucky (25-6)	Ed Diddle
9	St. John's (24-5)	Frank McGuire
10	La Salle (21-4)	Ken Loeffler
11	Villanova (25-4)	Al Severance
12	San Francisco (19-7)	Pete Newell
13	Long Island (20-5)	Clair Bee
14	Kansas State (17-7)	Jack Gardner
15	Arizona (26-5)	Fred Enke
16	Wisconsin (17-5)	Bud Foster
17	San Jose State (21-7)	Walter McPherson
18	Washington State (19-13)	Jack Friel
19	Kansas (14-11)	Phog Allen
20	Indiana (17-5)	Branch McCracken

TCU finished with a losing record in SWC competition but became the first major-college team to hit 40 percent of its field-goal attempts in a single season. . . . Baylor captured its third straight and final SWC championship. Bears coach Bill Henderson had only two winning records in the next 11 seasons. . . . Tulane's school-record 42-game homecourt winning streak ended when Arkansas edged the Green Wave, 42-41. . . . Kansas (14-11) tied for the Big

1949–50 INDIVIDUAL LEADERS

SCORING

PLAYER	PTS.	AVG.
Arizin, Villanova	735	25.3
Senesky, St. Joseph's	537	22.4
White, Long Island	551	22.0
Lovellette, Kansas	545	21.8
Lavoy, Western Kentucky	671	21.6
Schnittker, Ohio St.	469	21.3
Giermak, William & Mary	646	20.8
Handlan, Washington & Lee	406	20.3
Zawoluk, St. John's	588	20.3
Noertker, Virginia	503	20.1

FIELD GOAL PERCENTAGE

PLAYER	FGM	FGA	PCT.
Moran, Niagara	98	185	.530
Toft, Denver	146	281	.520
McDonald, Toledo	102	200	.510
Arizin, Villanova	260	527	.493
Skendrovich, Duquesne	108	220	.491
Mann, Bradley	135	291	.464
Share, Bowling Green	204	444	.459
Meineke, Dayton	194	424	.458
Beck, Bowling Green	84	186	.452
Pilch, Wyoming	143	317	.451

FREE THROW PERCENTAGE

PLAYER	FTM	FTA	PCT.
Urzetta, St. Bonaventure	54	61	.885
Morrill, Michigan	41	48	.854
Ballots, Temple	73	86	.849
Popp, Baldwin-Wallace	69	83	.831
Sermersheim, Georgia Tech	68	82	.829
Gardiner, St. Louis	53	64	.828
Brawner, Auburn	49	60	.817
Turner, Western Kentucky	84	103	.816
Davis, Pennsylvania	44	54	.815
Norris, Colgate	79	97	.814

1949–50 TEAM LEADERS

SCORING OFFENSE

SCHOOL	PTS.	AVG.
Villanova	2111	72.8
Holy Cross	2251	72.6
St. John's	2093	72.2
Muhlenberg	1651	71.8
Western Kentucky	2216	71.5

SCORING DEFENSE

SCHOOL	PTS.	AVG.
Oklahoma A&M	1059	39.2
Wyoming	1491	41.4
Tulsa	1027	44.7
Washington (Mo.)	1066	46.3
San Francisco	1237	47.6

FIELD GOAL PERCENTAGE

SCHOOL	FGM	FGA	PCT.
Texas Christian	476	1191	.400
Bowling Green	808	2070	.390
Toledo	633	1631	.388
Bradley	999	2588	.386
Akron	676	1752	.386
Wyoming	629	1631	.386

FREE THROW PERCENTAGE

SCHOOL	FTM	FTA	PCT.
Temple	342	483	.708
Colorado	395	576	.686
Auburn	390	574	.679
Duquesne	418	616	.679
Washington St.	456	673	.678

SCORING MARGIN

SCHOOL	OWN	OPP.	MAR.
Holy Cross	72.6	55.4	17.2
Villanova	72.8	55.7	17.1
St. John's	72.2	56.7	15.5
La Salle	69.8	54.8	15.0
North Carolina St.	65.3	51.7	13.7

Seven Conference crown after finishing in last place the previous year. The Jayhawks shared the title after losing an early-season game to Creighton, which was in the midst of nine consecutive non-winning seasons. . . . Nebraska registered the largest ever winning margin in an overtime game with an 85-67 triumph over Iowa State. . . . Clarence Iba became Tulsa's ninth head coach in 12 years.

Coach Lee Patton, who holds the second-best winning percentage in West Virginia history, died in an auto accident late in the season. . . . Kentucky claimed its seventh consecutive SEC Tournament title. The Wildcats sustained just 15 defeats in the last five seasons, with the third setback in that span to Notre Dame, 64-51. . . . Mississippi's Jack Marshall finished his fifth season of varsity competition with an 11.2-point scoring average. . . .Alabama sustained its only losing record (9-12) in a 19-year stretch from

1938-39 through 1957-58 (did not field a squad in 1943-44 because of World War II). . . . Wisconsin, Long Island, San Jose State and Washington State made their lone appearance in the Top 20 of a final wire-service poll. . . . Wayne State (Mich.) competed in its final season at the major-college level.

1950 NCAA Tournament

Summary: CCNY became the only school to win the NCAA playoffs and NIT in the same year. It is also the only former major college to compile a winning playoff record in the NCAA Division I Tournament. The ultimate "Cinderella" squad won the NCAA crown by defeating three teams ranked in the AP top five (second-ranked Ohio State, fifth-ranked North Carolina State, and top-ranked Bradley) although five of CCNY's six leading scorers were sophomores. CCNY, coached by Nat Holman, also defeated

1949–50 NCAA CHAMPION: CCNY

SEASON STATISTICS OF CCNY REGULARS

PLAYER	POS.	CL.	G.	FG%	FT%	PPG
Ed Roman	C	So.	29	.416	.642	16.4
Ed Warner	F	So.	29	.430	.567	14.8
Irwin Dambrot	F	Sr.	29	.371	.580	10.2
Floyd Layne	G	So.	29	.280	.606	6.9
Al Roth	G	So.	29	.288	.515	6.4
Herb Cohen	G	So.	24	.410	.526	5.4
Norm Mager	F	Sr.	29	.353	.629	3.6
Ronald Nadell	G	Jr.	19	.386	.650	2.5
Mike Wittlin	G	Sr.	22	.314	.600	1.7
Joe Galiber	C	Sr.	24	.239	.522	1.4
TEAM TOTALS			29	.363	.577	68.7

1950 CHAMPIONSHIP GAME

NEW YORK, NY

CCNY (71)	FG-A	FT-A	A	PF	PTS.
Dambrot	7-14	1-2	2	0	15
Roman	6-17	0-2	1	5	12
Warner	4-9	6-14	3	2	14
Roth	2-7	1-5	3	2	5
Mager	4-10	6-6	2	3	14
Galiber	0-0	0-0	0	1	0
Layne	3-7	5-6	4	3	11
Nadell	0-0	0-0	1	1	0
TOTALS	**26-64**	**19-35**	**16**	**17**	**71**

FG%: .406. FT%: .543.

BRADLEY (68)	FG-A	FT-A	A	PF	PTS.
Grover	0-10	2-3	3	3	2
Schlictman	0-3	0-0	0	2	0
Unruh	4-9	0-0	2	5	8
Behnke	3-10	3-3	2	4	9
Kelly	0-1	0-2	0	0	0
Mann	2-7	5-5	1	5	9
Preece	6-11	0-0	0	5	12
D. Melchiorre	0-0	0-0	0	0	0
G. Melchiorre	7-16	2-4	5	4	16
Chianakas	5-7	1-3	1	4	11
Stowell	0-0	1-1	0	0	1
TOTALS	**27-74**	**14-21**	**14**	**32**	**68**

FG%: .365. FT%: .667.
Halftime: CCNY 39-32.

MOST OUTSTANDING PLAYER
Irwin Dambrot, F, Sr., CCNY

12th-ranked San Francisco, third-ranked Kentucky, sixth-ranked Duquesne, and Bradley a second time the same year on its way to the NIT title. "Nat was a great coach," said Red Holzman, who played for Holman at CCNY from 1940-42. "He had a lot to do with the development of the game. His philosophy of basketball was great. He preached team basketball, passing the ball to the open man, moving without the ball, unselfishness, defense. He taught me a lot of things that I preached later on (coaching the Knicks to their only two NBA titles)."

Outcome for Defending Champion: Kentucky (25-5) was embarrassed by CCNY, 89-50, in the Wildcats NIT opener. Their other defeats were each by more than 10 points.

Star Gazing: CCNY was the first NCAA champion to have black players in its starting lineup—Floyd Layne, Joe Galiber, and Ed Warner. Alas, midnight struck for the Beavers following their storybook season when four CCNY regulars and other New York-based players were indicted in a point-shaving scandal rocking the sport the following year. After the investigation revealed scholastic records were falsified to allow several recruits admission to CCNY, the school de-emphasized its program in 1953.

One and Only: The worst winning percentage for a Final Four team was compiled by Baylor, which finished with a 14-13 record (.519) after losing both of its Final Four games (to Bradley and North Carolina State).

Numbers Game: UCLA, making its playoff debut under coach John Wooden, led mighty Bradley by seven points with five minutes remaining before the Braves went on a 23-2 spurt to end the game. N.C. State won the national third-place over Baylor, 53-41, although the Wolfpack hit a Final Four low 19.5 percent of its field-goal attempts (15 of 77).

What If: Bob Cousy and Frank Oftring, members of Holy Cross' 1947 NCAA titlist as freshmen, were senior co-captains when the Crusaders won their first 26 games to temporarily earn AP's No. 1 ranking. But they lost four of their last five contests, including both outings in the NCAA playoffs when Cousy went 17 for 61 from the floor (27.9 percent).

1950 CHAMPIONSHIP BRACKET

Regional Semifinals	Regional Finals	National Championship	

EASTERN REGIONALS

North Carolina St.

North Carolina St. 53-41
NATIONAL 3rd PLACE

CCNY
March 23
Ohio St. — CCNY 56-55

New York, NY
March 25 — CCNY 78-73

North Carolina St.
March 24
Holy Cross — North Carolina 87-74

Baylor

WESTERN REGIONALS

New York, NY
March 28 — CCNY 71-68
NATIONAL CHAMPION

Baylor
March 23
Brigham Young — Baylor 56-55

Kansas City, MO
March 25 — Bradley 68-66

Bradley
March 24
UCLA — Bradley 73-59

Regional Third Place
March 25
at New York, NY
Ohio St. 72, Holy Cross 52
at Kansas City, MO
Brigham Young 83, UCLA 62

Putting Things in Perspective: Would CCNY have been able to become the only school to win the NIT and NCAA playoffs in the same season had both of the national postseason tournaments not been staged in New York? Most observers thought CCNY was out of the playoff picture after the Beavers lost three of five games late in the season.

Scoring Leader: Sam Ranzino, North Carolina State (77 points, 25.7 ppg).

1950-51

AT A GLANCE

NCAA Champion: Kentucky (32-2; coached by Adolph Rupp; compiled 14-0 record in SEC to finish four games ahead of Alabama and Vanderbilt).

NIT Champion: Brigham Young (28-9; coached by Stan Watts; finished in first place in Rocky Mountain Conference with a 15-5 record).

New Rule: NCAA Tournament field expands from eight to 16 teams, with 10 conference champions qualifying automatically for the first time (Big Seven, Big Ten, Border, Ivy, Missouri Valley, Pacific Coast, Skyline, Southeastern, Southern, and Southwest).

NCAA Consensus First-Team All-Americans: Clyde Lovellette, C, Jr., Kansas; Gene Melchiorre, G, Sr.,

Long Island University's Clair Bee ended his 21-year college coaching career with a 412-87 record when LIU dropped its program in the wake of a fixing scandal. Star center Sherman White, who had scored 63 points against John Marshall the previous season, and two other Blackbird regulars were implicated and later prosecuted. In all, by the time the investigation was completed, 32 players at seven schools were cited in a plot to fix 86 games. White spent eight months in prison for conspiracy to commit bribery.

"In the first half of the century, Bee was basketball," said Bob Knight, who was befriended by Bee when Knight was at Army and Bee at a local military school. "There wasn't a thing he did that didn't affect the game, and there wasn't a thing that affected the game that he didn't do. He was one of the most singularly brilliant minds ever involved with athletics, and one of the greatest analytical basketball minds we've ever had. He had such a clear, brilliant grasp of what had to be done. He was a coach in the truest sense of the word."

LIU was undefeated at home in its last 13 seasons, compiling an overall 225-3 record at the 800-seat Brooklyn College of Pharmacy. Bee refused to employ a zone defense at home because he thought it would give his team an unfair advantage on a court that was 24 feet shorter than regulation, putting the 10-second line at the rear free-throw line instead of at midcourt. LIU's average record in its last 16 seasons under Bee was 21-4.

The only regular-season defeat for NCAA champion-to-be Kentucky was against St. Louis (43-42) in the opening round of the Sugar Bowl in New Orleans. The Wildcats also bowed to Vanderbilt in the SEC Tournament final (61-57) although the championship trophy already had "Kentucky" engraved on it.

1950–51 INDIVIDUAL LEADERS

SCORING

PLAYER	PTS.	AVG.
Mlkvy, Temple	731	29.2
Handlan, Washington & Lee	656	26.2
Workman, West Virginia	705	26.1
Groat, Duke	831	25.2
Lovellette, Kansas	548	22.8
Slaughter, South Carolina	569	22.8
Hennessey, Villanova	703	22.0
Ove, Valparaiso	469	21.3
Zawoluk, St. John's	654	21.1
Ranzino, N.C. St.	706	20.8

REBOUNDING

PLAYER	REB.	AVG.
Beck, Pennsylvania	556	20.6
Mlkvy, Temple	472	18.9
Christ, Fordham	493	18.4
Payton, Tulane	426	17.8
Darling, Iowa	387	17.6
Nolen, Texas Tech	492	17.6
Deasy, North Carolina	399	17.3

Spivey, Kentucky	567	17.2
Slaughter, South Carolina	413	16.5
Corizzi, Rutgers	339	16.1

ASSISTS

PLAYER	AST.	AVG.
Walker, Toledo	210	7.2
Mlkvy, Temple	176	7.0
Birch, Niagara	193	6.9
Chadwick, Cornell	170	6.8
Regan, Seton Hall	158	5.6
Markham, Wisconsn	99	5.5
Becker, New York	87	5.4
Baird, Holy Cross	114	5.4
Stratton, Colgate	119	5.4
Cox, South Carolina	135	5.4

FIELD GOAL PERCENTAGE

PLAYER	FGM	FGA	PCT.
Meineke, Dayton	240	469	.512
Maguire, Villanova	86	170	.506
Workman, West Virginia	273	558	.489

Rogers, Texas Western	154	317	.486
Slaughter, South Carolina	222	458	.485
Jennerich, Manhattan	76	157	.484
Chambers, William & Mary	199	413	.482
Koffenberger, Maryland	97	202	.480
Sullivan, Alabama	136	284	.479
Jones, Virginia Tech	184	388	.474

FREE THROW PERCENTAGE

PLAYER	FTM	FTA	PCT.
Handlan, Washington & Lee	158	184	.859
McMurray, Wichita	81	95	.853
Preece, Bradley	62	73	.849
Gordon, Temple	53	63	.841
Skoog, Minnesota	52	63	.825
Davis, Pennsylvania	61	74	.824
Matthews, Hardin-Simmons	60	73	.822
Sayre, Virginia Tech	128	156	.821
Travis, Texas Western	84	103	.816
Stange, Iowa St.	66	81	.815

1950–51 TEAM LEADERS

SCORING OFFENSE

SCHOOL	PTS.	AVG.
Cincinnati	1694	77.0
North Carolina St.	2748	76.3
Kentucky	2540	74.7
Virginia Tech	2149	74.1
Gettysburg (Pa.)	1623	73.8

SCORING DEFENSE

SCHOOL	PTS.	AVG.
Texas A&M	1275	44.0
Arkansas	1101	45.9
Oklahoma A&M	1616	46.2
Texas	1256	46.5
Oklahoma City	1423	47.4

FIELD GOAL PERCENTAGE

SCHOOL	FGM	FGA	PCT.
Maryland	481	1210	.398
Virginia Tech	805	2029	.397
Washington & Lee (Va.)	639	1613	.396
Toledo	725	1852	.391
Bradley	941	2427	.388

FREE THROW PERCENTAGE

SCHOOL	FTM	FTA	PCT.
Minnesota	287	401	.716
Virginia Tech	539	756	.713
Oklahoma	383	547	.700
Duke	619	888	.697
Baylor	371	533	.696

SCORING MARGIN

SCHOOL	OWN	OPP.	MAR.
Kentucky	74.7	52.5	22.3
Columbia	72.9	52.7	20.1
Cincinnati	77.0	58.1	18.9
Arizona	69.5	55.4	14.1
Kansas St.	68.8	55.1	13.8

Temple's Bill Mlkvy concluded the season with a school-record 73 points, including 54 consecutive, against Wilkes College to finish with a national-leading 29.2 points per game. He averaged an amazing 39 field-goal attempts per game on his way to setting a school record for highest scoring average in a single season (29.2 points per game). Mlkvy, the Owl without a vowel, was also national runner-up in rebounding (18.9) and assists (7.0). Washington & Lee's Jay Handlan, runner-up to Mlkvy in scoring, set an NCAA record with 71 field-goal attempts (30 made) when he scored 66 points in a game against Furman.

Duke, coached by Harold Bradley, manufactured the greatest comeback in NCAA history by erasing a 32-point deficit in a 74-72 victory over Tulane in the consolation game of the Dixie Classic at Raleigh, N.C. The Blue Devils trailed by 32 points with two minutes remaining in the first half (54-22) and by 29 points at halftime (56-27). Bradley was appointed Duke's coach shortly before the start of the season after Gerry Gerard's cancer no longer was in remission.

North Carolina State won both the Southern Conference regular-season and postseason tourney titles for the fifth consecutive year. . . . North

Carolina lost the first six times the Tar Heels opposed George Washington until clipping the Colonials, 66-60. . . . Clemson, coached by Banks McFadden, compiled its first winning season (11-7) in 12 years. . . . Navy defeated Maryland for the 13th time in 14 games, 51-47.

Columbia, coached by first-year mentor Lou Rossini after Gordon Ridings was sidelined by illness, became the first team in the 50-year history of the Eastern Intercollegiate League to finish its season without a defeat (22-0), but the Lions lost to Illinois, 79-71, in the opening round of the NCAA Tournament. Columbia's leading scorer was 6-4 1/2 sophomore Jack Molinas (14.4 points per game), who later served five years in prison for his role as "master fixer" in point-shaving scandals, was barred from the NBA for betting on his own team and subsequently murdered at his home in California.

Eastern schools supplied 18 consecutive national team scoring leaders until Cincinnati moved atop the list with a 77-point average. . . . Eleven players fouled out of a first-round NIT game in which St. Bonaventure outlasted Cincinnati, 70-67, in double overtime. NIT champion Brigham Young attempted to duplicate CCNY's feat the previous year of winning both the NIT and NCAA, but BYU was eliminated by Kansas State, 64-54, in an NCAA Western Regional final. . . . Connecticut's Bill Corley set a school record when he tallied 51 points against New Hampshire. . . . Rhode Island lost six of its first seven games en route to a 13-15 record for Rams' first losing season in 29 years.

Brigham Young (28-9, coached by Stan Watts), Kansas State (25-4, Jack Gardner) and Cornell (20-5, Roy Greene) had their winningest seasons in school history. Bradley (32-6, Forddy Anderson) tied its school record for most victories in a single season.

Tulane's Mel Payton (31 vs. Mississippi State) and Purdue's Carl McNulty (27 vs. Minnesota) set school single-game rebounding records. . . . Murray State made its lone appearance in the Top 20 of a final wire-service poll. . . . Notre Dame, which finished 13-11, dealt St. Louis (23-4) a shocking 77-70 defeat. The Irish raced to a 46-20 lead at intermission. . . . Northwestern's Ray Ragelis became the last Big Ten individual scoring champ to average fewer than 20 points per game (19.8). . . . Bradley won 32 games for the second straight season.

Texas finished in a tie for first place in the SWC despite compiling its first overall losing record (13-14) in 21 years. One of the two teams to tie Texas was Texas A&M, which posted its only winning mark (17-12) in a 20-year span from 1938-39 through 1957-58. . . . Arizona established an NCAA record for highest rebound margin in a single game by grabbing 84 more rebounds (102-18) than Northern Arizona. The Wildcats, coached by Fred Enke, captured their sixth consecutive Border Conference championship.

1950-51 FINAL NATIONAL POLLS

AP	UPI	SCHOOL (RECORD)	HEAD COACH
1	1	Kentucky (32-2)	Adolph Rupp
2	2	Oklahoma A&M (29-6)	Hank Iba
3	5	Columbia (23-1)	Lou Rossini*
4	3	Kansas State (25-4)	Jack Gardner
5	4	Illinois (22-5)	Harry Combes
6	6	Bradley (32-6)	Forddy Anderson
7	8	Indiana (19-3)	Branch McCracken
8	7	N.C. State (30-7)	Everett Case
9	9	St. John's (26-5)	Frank McGuire
10	11	St. Louis (22-8)	Eddie Hickey
11	10	Brigham Young (28-9)	Stan Watts
12	12	Arizona (24-6)	Fred Enke
13	18	Dayton (27-5)	Tom Blackburn
14	-	Toledo (23-8)	Jerry Bush
15	13	Washington (24-6)	Tippy Dye
16	-	Murray State (21-6)	Harlan Hodges
17	17	Cincinnati (18-4)	John Wiethe
18	-	Siena (19-8)	Dan Cunha
19	-	Southern Cal (21-6)	Forrest Twogood
20	14	Villanova (25-7)	Al Severance
-	14	Beloit, Wis. (18-5)	Dolph Stanley
-	16	UCLA (19-10)	John Wooden
-	18	St. Bonaventure (19-6)	Ed Melvin
-	18	Seton Hall (24-7)	Honey Russell
-	18	Texas A&M (17-12)	John Floyd

*Rossini handled coaching duties at Columbia because of Gordon Ridings' illness.

New Washington coach Tippy Dye became the first coach to guide two different schools to a Top 20 appearance in a final wire-service poll in back-to-back seasons. Washington, the PCC champion, sustained six setbacks by an average

1950–51 NCAA CHAMPION: KENTUCKY

SEASON STATISTICS OF KENTUCKY REGULARS

PLAYER	POS.	CL.	G.	FG%	FT%	PPG	RPG
Bill Spivey	C	Jr.	33	.399	.621	19.2	17.2
Shelby Linville	F	Jr.	34	.389	.757	10.4	9.1
Bobby Watson	G	Jr.	34	.328	.750	10.4	2.5
Frank Ramsey	G	So.	34	.327	.610	10.1	12.8
Cliff Hagan	F-C	So.	20	.367	.738	9.2	8.5
Walt Hirsch*	F	Sr.	30	.285	.706	9.1	8.0
Skip Whitaker	G	Jr.	31	.342	.600	5.2	2.0
Lou Tsioropoulos	F-C	So.	27	.311	.533	3.4	4.8
Dwight Price	F	So.	20	.277	.444	1.7	2.2
C. M. Newton	G	Jr.	18	.229	.454	1.2	0.7
TEAM TOTALS			34	.342	.648	74.7	62.0

*Ineligible for NCAA Tournament as a fourth-year varsity player.

1951 CHAMPIONSHIP GAME

MINNEAPOLIS, MN

KENTUCKY (68)	FG-A	FT-A	REB.	PF	PTS.
Whitaker	4-5	1-1	2	2	9
Linville	2-7	4-8	8	5	8
Spivey	9-29	4-6	21	2	22
Ramsey	4-10	1-3	4	5	9
Watson	3-8	2-4	3	3	8
Hagan	5-6	0-2	4	5	10
Tsioropoulos	1-4	0-0	3	1	2
Newton	0-0	0-0	0	0	0
TOTALS	28-69	12-24	45	23	68

FG%: .406. FT%: .500.

KANSAS STATE (58)	FG-A	FT-A	REB.	PF	PTS.
Head	3-11	2-2	3	2	8
Stone	3-8	6-8	6	2	12
Hitch	6-15	1-1	9	3	13
Barrett	2-12	0-2	3	1	4
Iverson	3-12	1-2	0	3	7
Rousey	2-10	0-0	2	3	4
Gibson	0-2	1-1	1	5	1
Upson	0-1	0-0	2	1	0
Knostman	1-4	1-2	3	1	3
Peck	2-3	0-1	0	0	4
Schuyler	1-2	0-1	1	2	2
TOTALS	23-80	12-20	30	23	58

FG%: .288. FT%: .600.
Halftime: Kansas State 29-27.

MOST OUTSTANDING PLAYER

None selected.

of only 4.5 points. The previous year, Dye directed Ohio State to a 22-4 record and Big Ten title.

So many players fouled out of a game against Tennessee Tech that Morehead State had only three men on the court in the final minutes. Morehead coach Ellis Johnson chose to play the remaining few minutes after referees let him participate only after he had conceded the contest. "What bothered me most," said Johnson after his club lost 90-88, "was that my players wouldn't pass the ball to me."

1951 NCAA Tournament

Summary: The scandal surrounding college basketball had not yet focused intensely on Kentucky when the Wildcats captured their third NCAA title in four years. Kansas State led at halftime (29-27) in the championship game, but guard Ernie Barrett, the Wildcats' leading scorer, was hampered by a sore shoulder and finished with just four points on two of 12 field-goal shooting. Kentucky had edged Illinois, 76-74, in the East Regional final behind center Bill Spivey's tourney-high 28 points. The Wildcats were the only NCAA champion to have six players finish the season with scoring averages higher than nine points per game until UCLA duplicated the feat in 1995.

Outcome for Defending Champion: City College of New York posted a 12-7 record before its last two games (against Manhattan and NYU) were canceled after a fix scandal broke. One of the games CCNY agreed to shave points in was at Madison Square Garden, where the school bowed to visiting Missouri, 54-37.

Star Gazing: Columbia, undefeated entering the tourney (21-0), blew a seven-point, halftime lead and lost in the first round of East Regional against eventual national third-place finisher Illinois (79-71). The Lions' John Azary was outscored by the Illini's Don Sunderlage (25-13) in a battle of All-American candidates. Sunderlage finished the season with 471 points, breaking the Illinois single-season record by 138 points.

Biggest Upset: Oklahoma A&M, entering the tourney with a No. 2 national ranking, fell behind 37-14 at intermission when it was eliminated by Kansas State, 68-44.

Numbers Game: Four teammates outrebounded Kentucky center Bill Spivey in the Wildcats' 79-68 opening-game victory over Louisville before he averaged 16 rebounds per game in their last three tourney contests. . . . Arizona made its only NCAA Tournament appearance until 1976 and San Jose State participated for the only time until 1980.

Putting Things in Perspective: North Carolina State had a 29-4 record after winning the Southern Conference Tournament. But without three standouts (Sam Ranzino, Paul Horvath and Vic Bubas) ineligible for the NCAA playoffs because they were in their fourth year of varsity competition, N.C. State was eliminated in the second round by Illinois (84-70).

1951 CHAMPIONSHIP BRACKET

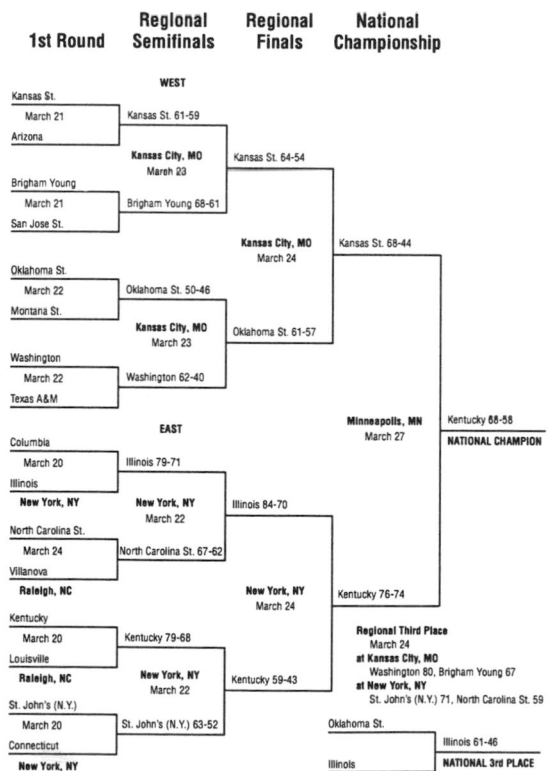

Scoring Leader: Don Sunderlage, Illinois (83 points, 20.75 ppg).

Highest Scoring Average: Bill Kukoy, North Carolina State (69 points, 23 ppg).

Rebounding Leader: Spivey, Kentucky (65 rebounds, 16.3 rpg).

1951–52

AT A GLANCE

NCAA Champion: Kansas (26-2; coached by Phog Allen; won Big Seven title by one game with an 11-1 record).

NIT Champion: La Salle (25-7; coached by Ken Loeffler).

New Rules: Games are played in four 10-minute quarters. Previously, games were played in two 20-minute halves.

NCAA Consensus First-Team All-Americans: Chuck Darling, C, Sr., Iowa; Rod Fletcher, G, Sr., Illinois; Dick Groat, G, Sr., Duke; Cliff Hagan, F, Jr., Kentucky; Clyde Lovellette, C, Sr., Kansas.

Freshmen, thrust to the varsity level because of a manpower shortage stemming from the Korean War, made an impact long before the first half of the 1970s when they permanently gained eligibility. Freshman center Tom Gola led NIT champion La Salle in scoring (17.2 ppg) and rebounding (16.5 rpg). Another standout freshman was Wichita forward Cleo Littleton, who was named to the first five on the All-Missouri Valley Conference team with an 18.5-point scoring average. Other freshmen of influence include: center Jesse Arnelle, lead scorer and rebounder for Penn State; center Dick Hemric, lead scorer and rebounder for Wake Forest; forward-center John Haran averaged 10.1 points and 7.1 rebounds per game for Dayton; guard AL Lifson, North Carolina's lead scorer; and forward Ken Sears, a starter for Santa Clara's Final Four team.

Kansas' Clyde Lovellette became the only Big Eight Conference player ever to lead the nation in scoring (28.4 ppg). Defending scoring champion Bill Mlkvy of Temple plummeted to 42nd (17.4 ppg) by incurring the largest decrease in scoring average (11.8) from one season to the next for any underclassman who ever led the nation in scoring.

Duke's Dick Groat, who would later become a star shortstop in the majors, was national runner-up in scoring and assists. He is the only individual to win an MVP award in major league baseball (1960 with the Pittsburgh Pirates) after being an NCAA consensus first-team basketball All-American. Duke teammate Bernie Janicki set a school single-game record by grabbing 31 rebounds against North Carolina.

Seattle's 5-8 Johnny O'Brien became the first college player to score 1,000 or more points in a season when he amassed 1,051 points in 37 games for a 28.4 average. He had 43 points in a shocking 84-81 victory over the Harlem Globetrotters in a special game played to raise money for the U.S. Olympic Games Fund. The mighty Globetrotters, in an era before they went exclusively to entertainment, usually opened a big lead before going into their crowd-pleasing antics. But they were without ball-handling wizard Marques Haynes against Seattle because he had to appear at his draft board. O'Brien scored most of his points against Globetrotters great Goose Tatum.

Army sophomore Bill Hannon became the shortest player (6-3) ever to lead the nation in rebounding. He averaged 20.9 rebounds per game. . . . Colgate's Al Antinelli fouled out of 15 of 22 games. . . . Dale Hall was in his only season as coach of New Hampshire when the school compiled its only winning record (11-9) in a 26-season span from 1941-42 through 1968-69 (cancelled 1943-44 and 1944-45 campaigns because of World War II).

Field-goal accuracy was only 33.7 percent per game despite an all-time high 140.64 field-goal attempts per outing for both teams.

LSU's Bob Pettit recorded the biggest one-game scoring output of the season with 50 points against Georgia. . . . Kentucky's Cliff Hagan established SEC Tournament records for most points in a single game (42 against Tennessee) and in an entire tourney (110 in four games). . . . Tennessee's Herb Neff set a SEC single-game standard with a school-record 36 rebounds against Georgia Tech.

West Virginia's Mack Isner (31 vs. Virginia Tech) and Iowa's Charles Darling (30 vs. Wisconsin) established school single-game rebounding records.

1951-52 FINAL NATIONAL POLLS

AP	UPI	SCHOOL (RECORD)	HEAD COACH
1	1	Kentucky (29-3)	Adolph Rupp
2	2	Illinois (22-4)	Harry Combes
3	6	Kansas State (19-5)	Jack Gardner
4	4	Duquesne (23-4)	Dudey Moore
5	7	St. Louis (23-8)	Eddie Hickey
6	5	Washington (25-6)	Tippy Dye
7	8	Iowa (19-3)	Bucky O'Connor
8	3	Kansas (28-3)	Phog Allen
9	14	West Virginia (23-4)	Red Brown
10	9	St. John's (25-6)	Frank McGuire
11	18	Dayton (28-5)	Tom Blackburn
12	–	Duke (24-6)	Harold Bradley
13	15	Holy Cross (24-4)	Buster Sheary
14	12	Seton Hall (25-3)	Honey Russell
15	11	St. Bonaventure (21-6)	Ed Melvin
16	10	Wyoming (28-7)	Everett Shelton
17	19	Louisville (20-6)	Peck Hickman
18	–	Seattle (29-8)	Al Brightman
19	20	UCLA (19-12)	John Wooden
20	–	SW Texas State (30-1)	Milton Jowers
–	13	Texas Christian (24-4)	Buster Brannon
–	16	Western Kentucky (26-5)	Ed Diddle
–	17	La Salle (25-7)	Ken Loeffler
–	20	Indiana (16-6)	Branch McCracken

North Carolina lost its last five games to finish with a 12-15 record for the second consecutive season. The Tar Heels then lured coach Frank McGuire away from St. John's after he had guided the Redmen to an average of 25 victories the past three years. . . . Arkansas' streak of non-losing seasons ended at 28 when the Razorbacks dropped five of six SWC games down the stretch to finish with a 10-14 record. . . . Dayton (28-5, coached by Tom Blackburn) and Texas Christian (24-4/Buster Brannon) had their winningest seasons in school history.

Illinois became the only school to lead the Big Ten in scoring five consecutive seasons in league competition. The Illini achieved the feat in Harry Combes' first five years as coach. . . . Arizona's 81-game homecourt winning streak, which started in 1945, was snapped by Kansas State, 76-57. . . . Idaho State (coached by Steve Belko) won its eighth consecutive Rocky Mountain Conference crown and North Carolina State (Everett Case) captured its sixth consecutive Southern Conference Tournament championship.

1952 NCAA Tournament

Summary: Legendary coach Phog Allen, running out of time in his quest to capture an elusive national championship, achieved his goal on the broad shoulders of Clyde Lovellette although his star player got lost in the fog. The night before the semifinals, one of Lovellette's Sigma Chi fraternity brothers, who was in the Coast Guard and stationed on a cutter anchored in Puget Sound, invited Lovellette to dinner on the ship. By the time they were finished, a dense fog moved in and they were unable to make it back to shore. Lovellette spent the night on the ship and didn't get back to his team's hotel until after dawn. Unfazed, he became the only player to crack the 30-point plateau in the national semifinals and final in the same season (33 points against both Santa Clara in the semifinals and St. John's in the final). In a West Regional final, Lovellette poured in a tourney-high 44 points in a 74-55 triumph over St. Louis.

Outcome for Defending Champion: Kentucky (29-3), the first school to lead the nation in

---

1951-52 INDIVIDUAL LEADERS

SCORING

PLAYER	PTS.	AVG.
Lovellette, Kansas	795	28.4
Groat, Duke	780	26.0
Pettit, Louisiana St.	612	25.5
Darling, Iowa	561	25.5
Selvy, Furman	591	24.6
Workman, West Virginia	577	23.1
Retherford, Baldwin-Wallace	457	21.8
Hemric, Wake Forest	629	21.7
Hagan, Kentucky	692	21.6
Clune, Navy	487	21.2

REBOUNDING

PLAYER	REB.	AVG.
Hannon, Army	355	20.9
Dukes, Seton Hall	513	19.7
Beck, Pennsylvania	551	19.0
Tuttle, Creighton	396	18.9
Chamber, William & Mary	509	18.2
Molinas, Columbia	234	18.0
Hemric, Wake Forest	510	17.5

Workman, West Virginia	437	17.5
Gola, La Salle	497	17.1
Peterson, Oregon	465	16.6

ASSISTS

PLAYER	AST.	AVG.
O'Toole, Boston College	213	7.9
Groat, Duke	229	7.6
McLean, Davidson	187	7.5
Friedman, Muhlenberg	168	7.3
Chadwick, Cornell	171	6.9
Simms, Xavier	150	6.3
Holmes, West Virginia	160	6.2
Heim, Xavier	145	6.0
Burch, Pittsburgh	131	6.0
Rhodes, Western Kentucky	182	5.9

FIELD GOAL PERCENTAGE

PLAYER	FGM	FGA	PCT.
Spoelstra, Western Kentucky	178	345	.516
Rogers, Texas Western	136	270	.504
Swanson, Detroit	172	342	.503

Klinar, Virginia Military	98	199	.492
Marshall, Western Kentucky	189	385	.491
Workman, West Virginia	207	430	.481
Lovellette, Kansas	315	660	.477
Patton, Denver	93	198	.470
Daukas, Boston College	136	290	.469
Preston, Hardin-Simmons	117	250	.468

FREE THROW PERCENTAGE

PLAYER	FTM	FTA	PCT.
Chadroff, Miami (Fla.)	99	123	.805
Kenney, Kansas	110	137	.803
Turner, St. Mary's	81	101	.802
Bartlett, Tennessee	93	116	.802
Rerucha, Colorado A&M	76	95	.800
Moore, West Virginia	68	85	.800
Tuttle, New Mexico	87	110	.791
Meineke, Dayton	194	246	.789
Bunt, New York Univ.	85	108	.787
Feiereisel, DePaul	113	144	.785

1951-52 TEAM LEADERS

SCORING OFFENSE

SCHOOL	PTS.	AVG.
Kentucky	2635	82.3
West Virginia	2172	80.4
Louisville	2080	80.0
Duke	2320	77.3
Western Kentucky	2388	77.0

SCORING DEFENSE

SCHOOL	PTS.	AVG.
Oklahoma A&M	1228	45.5
Oklahoma City	1287	47.7

Texas A&M	1159	48.3
New Mexico A&M	1514	48.8
Texas Christian	1395	49.8

FIELD GOAL PERCENTAGE

SCHOOL	FGM	FGA	PCT.
Boston College	787	1893	.416
Western Kentucky	959	2339	.410
Seton Hall	783	1941	.403
Stanford	743	1889	.393
Kansas	748	1906	.392
Furman	691	1761	.392

FREE THROW PERCENTAGE

SCHOOL	FTM	FTA	PCT.
Kansas	491	707	.6944
Pennsylvania	454	654	.6941
Kansas St.	473	684	.692
South Carolina	400	582	.687
Syracuse	430	626	.687

1951–52 NCAA CHAMPION: KANSAS

SEASON STATISTICS OF KANSAS REGULARS

PLAYER	POS.	CL.	G.	FG%	FT%	PPG	RPG
Clyde Lovellette	C	Sr.	31	.474	.728	28.6	13.2
Bob Kenney	F	Sr.	30	.360	.789	13.1	3.8
Bill Hougland	G	Sr.	30	.391	.742	6.8	5.6
Dean Kelley	G	Jr.	31	.397	.605	6.5	3.3
Bill Lienhard	F	Sr.	29	.303	.700	5.8	3.3
Charlie Hoag	F-G	Jr.	21	.303	.564	5.2	3.0
John Keller	F-G	Sr.	27	.388	.767	2.3	2.7
B. H. Born	C	So.	27	.304	.613	1.7	1.2
Bill Heitholt	G-F	Fr.	28	.237	.454	1.5	1.9
Dean Smith	G	Jr.	19	.455	.500	1.5	0.6
Larry Davenport	F	Fr.	22	.324	.700	1.4	1.0
TEAM TOTALS			31	.390	.692	71.3	37.8

Note: Statistics include three games in Olympic Trials after NCAA Tournament.

1952 CHAMPIONSHIP GAME

SEATTLE, WA

Kansas (80)	FG-A	FT-A	REB.	PF	PTS.
Kenney	4-11	4-6	4	2	12
Keller	1-1	0-0	4	2	2
Lovellette	12-25	9-11	17	4	33
Lienhard	5-8	2-2	4	4	12
Kelley	2-5	3-6	3	5	7
Hoag	2-6	5-7	4	5	9
Houghland	2-5	1-3	6	2	5
Davenport	0-0	0-0	0	1	0
Heitholt	0-0	0-0	0	0	0
Born	0-0	0-0	0	0	0
Kelley	0-2	0-0	1	0	0
TOTALS	**28-63**	**24-35**	**43**	**25**	**80**

FG%: .444. **FT%:** .686.

St. John's (63)	FG-A	FT-A	REB.	PF	PTS.
McMahon	6-12	1-4	2	4	13
Davis	1-4	2-3	2	4	4
Zawoluk	7-12	6-11	9	5	20
Duckett	2-5	2-2	2	4	6
MacGilvray	3-8	2-5	10	3	8
Walsh	3-6	0-0	4	3	6
Walker	0-2	0-0	2	4	0
McMorrow	1-3	0-0	0	3	2
Sagona	2-2	0-0	0	5	4
Giancontieri	0-0	0-2	1	0	0
Peterson	0-1	0-0	0	0	0
TOTALS	**25-55**	**13-27**	**32**	**35**	**63**

FG%: .455. **FT%:** .481.
Halftime: Kansas State 41-27.

ALL-TOURNAMENT TEAM

Dean Kelley, G, Jr., Kansas
John Kerr, C, Soph., Illinois
Clyde Lovellette, C, Sr., Kansas*
Ron MacGilvray, G, Sr., St. John's
Bob Zawoluk, C, Sr., St. John's
    * Most Outstanding Tournament Player

scoring with an average of more than 80 points per game (82.3), claimed its ninth consecutive SEC regular-season title. The Wildcats' two regular-season defeats were in non-league play (61-57 at Minnesota and 61-60 vs. St. Louis in the Sugar bowl final in New Orleans).

Biggest Upset: St. John's gained sweet revenge against the nation's top-ranked team. Kentucky humiliated the Redmen by 41 points (81-40) early in the season when the Catholic institution became the first to have a black player on the floor at Lexington, Ky., despite Kentucky coach Adolph Rupp's protests. The African American, Solly Walker, played only a few minutes before he took a hit sidelining him for three weeks. But St. John's, sparked by center Bob Zawoluk's 32 points, avenged the rout by eliminating the Wildcats (64-57) in the East Regional, ending their 23-game winning streak.

One and Only: Lovellette is the only player to lead the nation in scoring average (28.4 ppg) while playing for a team reaching the NCAA Tournament championship game. . . . St. John's is the only school to reach the Final Four after losing a regular-season game by more than 40 points. . . . Princeton forward Dave Sisler is the only son of a member of one of the early classes of baseball Hall of Fame selections (first baseman George Sisler) to start for a school in its first NCAA Tournament appearance.

Numbers Game: St. Louis' Eddie Hickey became the first coach to direct two different schools to NCAA playoff victories in their initial tourney appearances. He guided Creighton to the 1941 NCAA Tournament. . . . Elmer Gross became the first individual to coach his alma mater in the NCAA playoffs after playing in the tourney (Penn State '42). . . . All five Dayton starters fouled out when the Flyers committed an NCAA playoff-record 41 fouls in an 80-61 loss to Illinois in the East Regional semifinals.

What If: Kansas State finished runner-up in the Big Seven Conference to NCAA champion-to-be Kansas, a team the Wildcats defeated at home in Manhattan by 17 points. K-State, ranked 3rd by AP and 6th by UPI after finishing as national runner-up to Kentucky the previous year, lost another matchup against the Jayhawks on a neutral court in overtime.

Scoring Leader: Clyde Lovellette, Kansas (141 points, 35.25 ppg).

1952 CHAMPIONSHIP BRACKET

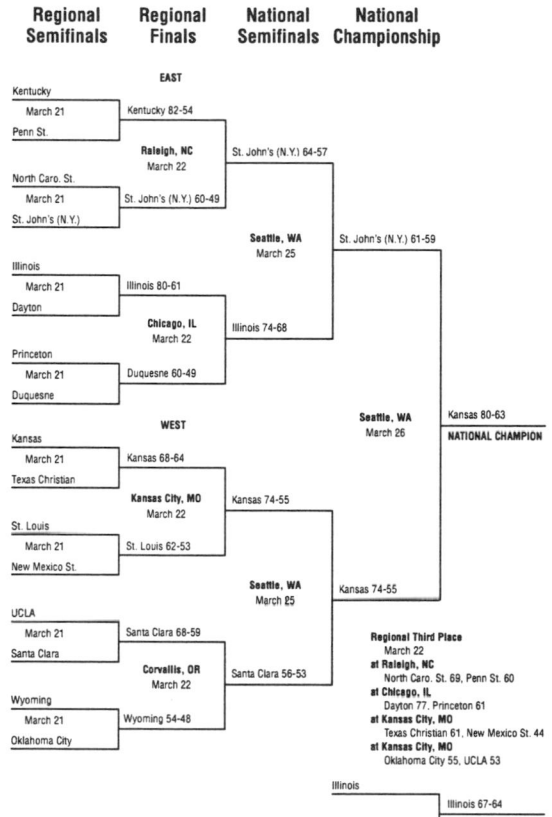

Regional Semifinals	Regional Finals	National Semifinals	National Championship

EAST

Kentucky
March 21
Penn St.

Kentucky 82-54

Raleigh, NC
March 22

North Caro. St.
March 21
St. John's (N.Y.)

St. John's (N.Y.) 60-49

St. John's (N.Y.) 64-57

Illinois
March 21
Dayton

Illinois 80-61

Chicago, IL
March 22

Princeton
March 21
Duquesne

Duquesne 60-49

Illinois 74-68

Seattle, WA
March 25

St. John's (N.Y.) 61-59

WEST

Kansas
March 21
Texas Christian

Kansas 68-64

Kansas City, MO
March 22

St. Louis
March 21
New Mexico St.

St. Louis 62-53

Kansas 74-55

Seattle, WA
March 26

Kansas 80-63

NATIONAL CHAMPION

UCLA
March 21
Santa Clara

Santa Clara 68-59

Corvallis, OR
March 22

Wyoming
March 21
Oklahoma City

Wyoming 54-48

Santa Clara 56-53

Seattle, WA
March 25

Kansas 74-55

Regional Third Place
March 22
at Raleigh, NC
North Caro. St. 69, Penn St. 60
at Chicago, IL
Dayton 77, Princeton 61
at Kansas City, MO
Texas Christian 61, New Mexico St. 44
at Kansas City, MO
Oklahoma City 55, UCLA 53

Illinois
Illinois 67-64
Santa Clara
NATIONAL 3rd PLACE

1952–53

AT A GLANCE

NCAA Champion: Indiana (23-3; coached by Branch McCracken; won Big Ten title by three games with a 17-1 record).

NIT Champion: Seton Hall (31-2; coached by Honey Russell).

New Conference: California Basketball Association (forerunner of West Coast).

New Rules: Teams no longer waive free throws in favor of taking the ball out of bounds. The one-and-one free-throw rule is introduced although the bonus is used only if the first shot misfires. The rule will be in effect the entire game except the last three minutes, when every foul is two shots. The NCAA Tournament bracket expands from 16 teams to 22 and fluctuates between 22 and 25 until 1974.

NCAA Probation: Bradley, Kentucky.

NCAA Consensus First-Team All-Americans: Ernie Beck, F, Sr., Penn; Walter Dukes, C, Jr., Seton Hall; Tom Gola, C-F, Soph., La Salle; Bob Houbregs, C, Sr., Washington; Johnny O'Brien, G, Sr., Seattle.

The season marked the greatest increase in points per game from one year to the next (126.6 to 138.1). College basketball's record book was overhauled when intercollegiate competition was interpreted as being between varsity teams of four-year, degree-granting universities. In effect, the ruling negated games against AAU, service, junior college, alumni and freshman teams. The decision stemmed from 100-point plus outings by Rio Grande's Clarence "Bevo" Francis and Los Angeles State's John Barber. In response to Francis' 113-point performance, Los Angeles State coach Sax Elliott scheduled a game for his team with the Chapman junior varsity and had his players concentrate on scoring and feeding Barber, a 6-6 center. Los Angeles State won, 206-82, as Barber scored 188 points.

Furman (21-6, coached by Lyles Alley) became the first school to average more than 90 points per game (90.2). Furman's Frank Selvy supplied the season's top scoring effort with 63 points against Mercer.

A couple of major rebounding records were established. Seton Hall's Walter Dukes set an NCAA single-season record by retrieving a total of 734 missed shots. William & Mary's Bill Chambers grabbed an NCAA record 51 rebounds in a 105-84 victory against Virginia on Valentine's Day. Chambers later became his alma mater's all-time winningest coach in a nine-year coaching career with the Tribe from 1957-58 through 1965-66.

Niagara outlasted Siena, 88-81, in a six-overtime game. Niagara's Ed Fleming played all

70 minutes and teammate Larry Costello played all but 20 seconds before fouling out. As a result, Fleming had his uniform number changed to 70 and Costello's was changed to 69. Oddly, one of the referees in the game was Max Tabbachi, who had officiated a five-overtime NBA game between Rochester and Indianapolis two seasons ago.

The University of Chicago, a former powerhouse, ended a 45-game losing streak with a 65-52 victory over Illinois-Navy Pier. . . . Cincinnati compiled an 11-13 overall record but finished in a tie for second place in the Mid-American Conference (9-3) in its final year as a member of the league. . . . Seattle's Johnny O'Brien finished among the top six in both field-goal shooting (53.3 percent) and free-throw accuracy (80.8). . . . Western Kentucky's Art Spoelstra, who led the nation in field-goal marksmanship (51.6 per-

cent) the previous season, improved to 52.8 percent yet finished sixth. Three severe heart attacks sidelined Western Kentucky coach Ed Diddle for a time.

The Citadel's Jerry Varn (51 points vs. Piedmont), Washington's Bob Houbregs (49 vs. Idaho) and Penn's Ernie Beck (47 vs. Duke in Dixie Classic at Raleigh, N.C.) set school single-game scoring records. Villanova's Larry Hennessy (29.2 ppg), Beck (25.9) and Houbregs (25.6) set school records for highest scoring average in a single season. Houbregs' outbursts helped Washington finish with a 30-3 mark for its winningest season in history (coached by Tippy Dye).

Northern Arizona set an NCAA record by attempting 79 free throws (46 made) in a game against Arizona. A new free-throw rule

1952–53 INDIVIDUAL LEADERS

SCORING

PLAYER	PTS.	AVG.
Selvy, Furman	738	29.5
Hennessey, Villanova	438	29.2
J. O'Brien, Seattle	884	28.5
Dukes, Seton Hall	861	26.1
Beck, Pennsylvania	673	25.9
Houbregs, Washington	800	25.8
Schlundt, Indiana	661	25.4
Hemric, Wake Forest	623	24.9
Dalton, John Carroll	669	24.8
Pettit, Louisiana St.	519	24.7

REBOUNDING

PLAYER	REB.	AVG.
Conlin, Fordham	612	23.5
Dukes, Seton Hall	734	22.2

Chambers, William & Mary	480	21.8
Quimby, Connecticut	430	20.5
Virostek, Pittsburgh	424	20.2
Estergard, Bradley	540	20.0
Hannon, Army	365	19.2
Holup, George Washington	396	18.0
Lange, Navy	374	17.8
Tuttle, Creighton	438	17.5

FIELD GOAL PERCENTAGE

PLAYER	FGM	FGA	PCT.
Stokes, St. Francis (NY)	147	247	.595
Houbregs, Washington	306	564	.543
E. O'Brien, Seattle	176	325	.542
J. O'Brien, Seattle	276	518	.533
Hoxie, Niagara	125	235	.532
Spoelstra, W. Kentucky	188	356	.528
Gordon, Furman	249	483	.516

Holup, G. Washington	154	301	.512
Nathanic, Seton Hall	111	222	.500
Glowaski, Seattle	199	405	.491

FREE THROW PERCENTAGE

PLAYER	FTM	FTA	PCT.
Weber, Yale	117	141	.830
Dohner, Virginia	96	117	.821
Sharp, Wyoming	163	200	.815
Sheets, Oklahoma A&M	87	107	.813
Matheny, California	101	125	.808
J. O'Brien, Seattle	332	411	.808
Schlundt, Indiana	249	310	.803
Perry, Holy Cross	101	126	.802
Ollrich, Drake	137	171	.801
Beck, Pennsylvania	183	229	.799

1952–53 TEAM LEADERS

SCORING OFFENSE

SCHOOL	PTS.	AVG.
Furman	2435	90.2
Seattle	2818	88.1
George Washington	1890	85.9
Duke	2093	83.7
Miami (Ohio)	1916	83.3

SCORING DEFENSE

SCHOOL	PTS.	AVG.
Oklahoma A&M	1614	53.8
Maryland	1256	54.6

Oklahoma City	1338	55.8
Wyoming	1676	55.9
San Jose St.	1293	56.2

FIELD GOAL PERCENTAGE

SCHOOL	FGM	FGA	PCT.
Furman	936	2106	.444
Niagara	718	1640	.438
Seattle	1019	2350	.434
Seton Hall	914	2129	.429
William & Mary	603	1410	.428

FREE THROW PERCENTAGE

SCHOOL	FTM	FTA	PCT.
George Washington	502	696	.721
Pennsylvania	502	702	.715
Oklahoma City	548	771	.711
Loyola (Ill.)	525	743	.707
Fordham	493	699	.705

1952-53 NCAA CHAMPION: INDIANA

SEASON STATISTICS OF INDIANA REGULARS

PLAYER	POS.	CL.	G.	FG%	FT%	PPG	RPG
Don Schlundt	C	So.	26	.432	.803	25.4	8.5
Bob Leonard	G	Jr.	26	.326	.667	16.3	...
Dick Farley	F	Jr.	26	.443	.694	10.1	...
Burke Scott	G	So.	26	.369	.647	8.0	...
Charles Kraak	F	Jr.	26	.356	.588	7.2	...
Dick White	F	So.	22	.313	.741	5.6	...
Phil Byers	G	So.	23	.347	.542	2.7	...
James DeaKyne	G	Jr.	20	.230	.417	2.3	...
TEAM TOTALS			26	.365	.701	81.2	...

1953 CHAMPIONSHIP GAME

KANSAS CITY, MO

INDIANA (69)	FG-A	FT-A	PF	PTS.
Kraak	5-8	7-10	5	17
DeaKyne	0-0	0-0	1	0
Farley	1-8	0-0	5	2
Schlundt	11-26	8-11	3	30
White	1-5	0-0	2	2
Leonard	5-15	2-4	2	12
Poff	0-1	0-0	0	0
Scott	2-4	2-3	3	6
Byers	0-2	0-0	1	0
TOTALS	**25-69**	**19-28**	**22**	**69**

FG%: .362. FT%: .679.

KANSAS (68)	FG-A	FT-A	PF	PTS.
Patterson	1-3	7-8	3	9
A. Kelley	7-20	6-8	3	20
Davenport	0-1	0-0	0	0
Born	8-27	10-12	5	26
Smith	0-0	1-1	1	1
Alberts	0-1	0-0	1	0
D. Kelley	3-4	2-4	2	8
Reich	2-9	0-0	2	4
TOTALS	**21-65**	**26-33**	**17**	**68**

FG%: .323. FT%: .788.
Halftime: Tied 41-41.

ALL-TOURNAMENT TEAM

B. H. Born, C, Jr., Kansas*
Bob Houbregs, C, Sr., Washington
Dean Kelley, G, Sr., Kansas
Bob Leonard, G, Jr., Indiana
Don Schlundt, C, Soph., Indiana
    * Named Most Outstanding Player

increased attempts from the charity stripe to a staggering 65.8 per game for both teams. . . . LSU established a SEC standard for most lopsided victory by smothering Southwestern (Tenn.), 124-33. . . . Arizona State, coached by Bill Kajikawa, overcame a 1-10 start to finish with its only winning record (13-12) in a 10-year span from 1948-49 through 1957-58. . . . Oklahoma A&M captured its 14th team defense title in 19 seasons although it was the first time a Hank Iba-coached squad allowed as many as 50 points per game (53.8). . . . Colorado's Burdette Haldorson collected 31 points and a school-record 31 rebounds against Oklahoma in the Big Eight Christmas Tournament at Kansas City.

Fordham's Ed Conlin (36 vs, Colgate), Richmond's Walt Lysaght (35 vs. North Carolina in double overtime), Seton Hall's Dukes (34 vs. King's, Pa.), St. Joseph's John Doogan (34 vs. West Chester State), Columbia's Jack Molinas (31 vs. Brown), Wisconsin's Paul Morrow (30 vs. Purdue), Rutgers' Swede Sundstrom (30 vs. Johns Hopkins), Georgia Tech's Eric Crake (27 vs. Georgia) and Pittsburgh's Don Virostek (26 vs. Westminster) also set school single-game

rebounding records. It was one of five times in Conlin's career that he grabbed more than 30 rebounds. Sundstrom tied his record the next season against Army.

Coach Frank McGuire lost six of his first seven games against North Carolina State after leaving St. John's for North Carolina. But McGuire's first contest against the Wolfpack with Carolina was a 70-69 success at Raleigh, ending the Tar Heels' 15-game losing streak against their big rival.

Later, Wake Forest ended N.C. State's streak of six consecutive Southern Conference Tournament championships with a 71-70 victory over the Wolfpack. It was the final Southern Conference tourney before seven of the league's members broke away to form the Atlantic Coast Conference.

Maryland lost to Penn for the twelfth straight time in their series. . . . Tony Packer, the father of former Wake Forest star and current CBS analyst Billy Packer, posted his only winning record (12-8) in 16 years as coach at Lehigh.

It was the Engineers' lone winning season in a 28-year span from 1939-40 through 1966-67.

Dayton, struggling to stay above .500 in its only campaign in an eight-year span through 1957-58 to fail to finish among the nation's Top 20 in a final wire-service poll, pulled off the biggest upset of the season when the Flyers toppled top-ranked Seton Hall, 71-65. The Pirates, who would go on to capture the NIT, entered the road game with a 27-0 record. Seton Hall also lost its next outing (73-67 at Louisville) en route to finishing with a 31-2 mark, a school record for most victories.

B.H. Born was named the Most Outstanding Player during the 1952-53 NCAA Tournament.

1952–53 FINAL NATIONAL POLLS

AP	UPI	SCHOOL	HEAD COACH
1	1	Indiana (23-3)	Branch McCracken
2	2	Seton Hall (31-2)	Honey Russell
3	5	Kansas (19-6)	Phog Allen
4	3	Washington (30-3)	Tippy Dye
5	6	Louisiana State (22-3)	Harry Rabenhorst
6	4	La Salle (25-3)	Ken Loeffler
7	–	St. John's (17-6)	Al DeStefano
8	7	Oklahoma A&M (23-7)	Hank Iba
9	20	Duquesne (21-8)	Dudey Moore
10	13	Notre Dame (19-5)	John Jordan
11	10	Illinois (18-4)	Harry Combes
12	9	Kansas State (17-4)	Jack Gardner
13	17	Holy Cross (20-6)	Buster Sheary
14	–	Seattle (29-4)	Al Brightman
15	–	Wake Forest (22-7)	Murray Greason
16	–	Santa Clara (20-7)	Bob Feerick
17	11	Western Kentucky (25-6)	Ed Diddle
18	8	N.C. State (26-6)	Everett Case
19	14	DePaul (19-9)	Ray Meyer
20	–	SW Missouri State (24-4)	Bob Vanatta
–	12	California (16-10)	Nibs Price
–	14	Wyoming (20-10)	Everett Shelton
–	16	St. Louis (16-11)	Eddie Hickey
–	18	Oklahoma City (18-6)	Doyle Parrack
–	19	Brigham Young (22-8)	Stan Watt

Pete Mullins, the sixth-place finisher in the 1948 Olympic decathlon while competing for Australia, finished as Washington State's leading scorer with 13.3 points per game. He had been the Cougars' second-leading scorer as a sophomore and third-leading scorer as a junior. . . . Big Ten charter member Indiana captured its first undisputed conference championship. Hoosiers coach Branch McCracken had been denied a Big Ten title in his first 11 years at his alma mater despite winning more than 70 percent of his games. . . . Baldwin-Wallace (Oh.) and CCNY competed in their final season at the major-college level.

Utah's Vadal Peterson ended his 26-year coaching career with a 386-223 record. Pitt posted its first winning record (12-11) in eight seasons as Dr. H.C. Carlson ended his 31-year coaching career at the school with a 367-250 record.

Carlson's distaste for recruiting soured him on the game and he retired. One of his last recruiting acts would prove costly to Bob Timmons, his successor, for the next four years. Carlson, looking to break the color line at Pitt, couldn't make up his mind between Ernie Bryant and Maurice Stokes. Carlson chose Bryant, who quit after his freshman year and never played varsity ball. Stokes went on to put St. Francis (Pa.) on the basketball map and became an instant star in the NBA before a disabling disease ended his career.

Stars of the 50's decade: Clyde Lovellette and Oscar Robertson.

1953 NCAA Tournament

Summary: Junior guard Bob Leonard supplied the decisive point by hitting one of two free throws with 27 seconds remaining to give Indiana a 69-68 victory over defending champion Kansas in the final. Don Schlundt, averaging 25.4 points per game for the Hoosiers as a sophomore center, is the only player to never appear in the NBA or ABA after averaging more than 20 for a team reaching the NCAA championship game.

Outcome for Defending Champion: Big Seven champion Kansas finished with a 19-6 record. The Jayhawks' two league losses were by 15 points at Oklahoma and 21 at Oklahoma State.

Star Gazing: B.H. Born, the only Kansas starter taller than 6-1, scored more points in two Final Four games (51) for the national runner-up Jayhawks than he did the entire previous season when he averaged just 1.7 points per game as a sophomore backup to Clyde Lovellette, who was named Most Outstanding Player in powering KU to the 1952 title.

Biggest Upset: George "Rinso" Marquette, the first-year coach at Lebanon Valley (Pa.), guided the Flying Dutchmen to the NCAA Tournament when they received an invitation after La Salle and Seton Hall chosen to go to the NIT. Lebanon Valley's "Seven Dwarfs"—no player was taller than 6-1—won the Middle Atlantic Conference and led the nation in field-goal shooting (47.2 percent). They flogged Fordham, 80-67, in the first round of the East Regional before bowing to Bob Pettit-led LSU, an eventual Final Four team. Lebanon Valley, with a current enrollment of 900 after having 425 students in 1953, remains the smallest school ever to play in the tournament. The leading scorer for Lebanon Valley was Howie Landa, who went on to coach nationally-ranked Mercer County (N.J.) Community College and then serve as an assistant to both the men's and women's teams at UNLV.

One and Only: Kansas' Dean Kelley became the only player to have season scoring averages of fewer than 10 points per game in back-to-back years in which he was named to the All-NCAA Tournament team. He and fellow

1953 CHAMPIONSHIP BRACKET

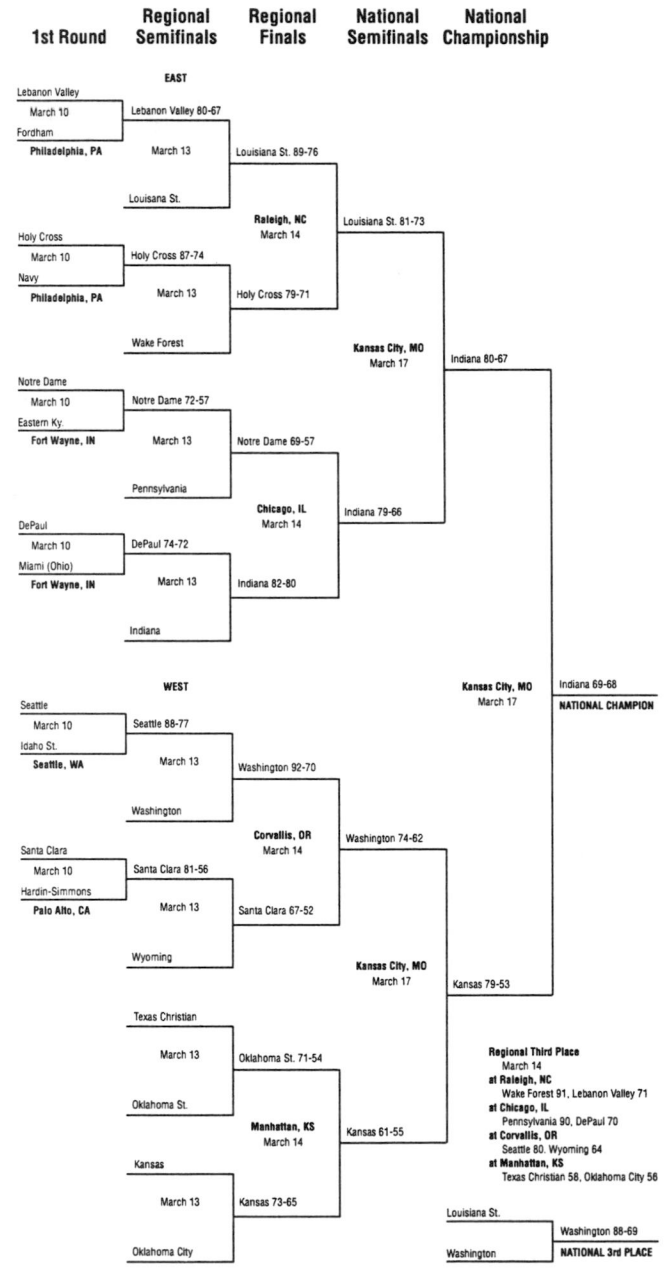

| | Regional Semifinals | Regional Finals | National Semifinals | National Championship |
| 1st Round | | | | |

EAST

Lebanon Valley
March 10
Fordham
Philadelphia, PA

Lebanon Valley 80-67
March 13

Louisana St.

Louisiana St. 89-76

Raleigh, NC
March 14

Holy Cross
March 10
Navy
Philadelphia, PA

Holy Cross 87-74
March 13

Wake Forest

Holy Cross 79-71

Louisiana St. 81-73

Kansas City, MO
March 17

Indiana 80-67

Notre Dame
March 10
Eastern Ky.
Fort Wayne, IN

Notre Dame 72-57
March 13

Pennsylvania

Notre Dame 69-57

Chicago, IL
March 14

Indiana 79-66

DePaul
March 10
Miami (Ohio)
Fort Wayne, IN

DePaul 74-72
March 13

Indiana

Indiana 82-80

Kansas City, MO
March 17

Indiana 69-68
NATIONAL CHAMPION

WEST

Seattle
March 10
Idaho St.
Seattle, WA

Seattle 88-77
March 13

Washington

Washington 92-70

Corvallis, OR
March 14

Santa Clara
March 10
Hardin-Simmons
Palo Alto, CA

Santa Clara 81-56
March 13

Wyoming

Santa Clara 67-52

Washington 74-62

Kansas City, MO
March 17

Kansas 79-53

Texas Christian
March 13

Oklahoma St.

Oklahoma St. 71-54

Manhattan, KS
March 14

Kansas 61-55

Kansas
March 13

Oklahoma City

Kansas 73-65

Regional Third Place
March 14
at Raleigh, NC
Wake Forest 91, Lebanon Valley 71
at Chicago, IL
Pennsylvania 90, DePaul 70
at Corvallis, OR
Seattle 80. Wyoming 64
at Manhattan, KS
Texas Christian 58, Oklahoma City 56

Louisiana St.

Washington

Washington 88-69
NATIONAL 3rd PLACE

guard Allen Kelley are the only set of brothers to play together in two NCAA playoff title games.

Numbers Game: Of the nearly 50 coaches reaching the national semifinals at least twice, Indiana's Branch McCracken is the only one to compile an undefeated Final Four record. He also won the championship in 1940. . . . Seattle's Johnny O'Brien, a 5-8 unanimous first-team All-American, became the only player to score more than 40 points in his first playoff game. He had 42 in an 88-77 victory over Idaho State. . . . Washington's Bob Houbregs had a tourney-high 45 points in a 92-70 scorching of Seattle in the West Regional semifinals. He poured in 42 in an 88-69 trouncing of LSU in the national third-place game.

What If: Mighty Kentucky was barred from playing a competitive schedule.

Putting Things in Perspective: Indiana almost finished undefeated, losing three games during the regular season by a total of five points on field goals scored with fewer than five seconds remaining.

Scoring Leader: Bob Houbregs, Washington (139 points, 34.75 ppg).

1953–54

AT A GLANCE

NCAA Champion: La Salle (26-4; coached by Ken Loeffler).

NIT Champion: Holy Cross (26-2; coached by Buster Sheary).

New Conference: ACC.

New Rule: The Tuesday-Wednesday format for the NCAA Tournament semifinals and final changes to Friday-Saturday.

NCAA Probation: Arizona State.

NCAA Consensus First-Team All-Americans: Tom Gola, C-F, Jr., La Salle; Cliff Hagan, F, Sr., Kentucky; Bob Pettit, C, Sr., Louisiana State; Don Schlundt, C, Jr., Indiana; Frank Selvy, F, Sr., Furman.

Furman forward Frank Selvy scored 100 points vs. Newberry on his way to becoming the

La Salle's Tom Gola.

first three-year player to reach 2,000 points, finishing with 2,538. (See accompanying box for more details.) Selvy (41.7 ppg) and Darrell Floyd (24.3) combined for 66 points per game during the season and are the highest-scoring duo in major-college history. Selvy scored 50 or more in seven games. Despite Selvy's explosions, scoring decreased nationally for the first time in 19 years, from 138.1 the previous season to 137.9.

Teammates Joe Holup (57.2 percent) and Elliott Karver (56.1) finished one-two in the country in field-goal accuracy to help George Washington lead the nation in that category.

Undefeated Kentucky finished among the top 10 in team offense for the eighth consecutive season in which it participated (barred from playing in 1952–53 as the result of an NCAA ruling regarding improper payments to players). LSU tied Kentucky for the SEC championship by going undefeated in league competition for the second straight season opener to obscure visitor Louisiana College, 84-79.

Western Kentucky won 21 consecutive games, an Ohio Valley Conference record, en route to Ed Diddle becoming the first coach to reach the 600-win plateau.

Virginia guard Buzz Wilkinson set ACC Tournament records for most field-goal attempts (13 of 44) and free-throw attempts (16 of 22) when he scored 42 points in a 76-68 first-round defeat against Duke. The ACC's inaugural season marked the only time North Carolina finished fifth or worse in the league standings.

Wade "Swede" Halbrook, a 7-3, 245-pound sophomore, averaged 21.2 points and 11.9 rebounds per game for Oregon State. He was called "the largest man in basketball history" by the *NCAA Basketball Guide*.

Washington compiled an 8-18 mark after finishing among the top 15 the previous three seasons in final wire-service polls. The Huskies, a Final Four team the previous year when they were 30-3, lost their first nine games and 14 of

SELVY SCORES RECORD 100 POINTS   On February 13, 1954, Furman forward Frank Selvy scored 100 points vs. Newberry on his way to becoming the first three-year player to reach 2,000 points. (He wound up with a career total of 2,538.) Making Selvy's 100-point outburst even more amazing was the fact that his mother, watching her son play for the first time, was among several hundred fans from his hometown of Corbin, Kentucky, who made the trip to Furman, located in Greenville, South Carolina, to watch the game. An early indication that something special was in the offing came less than three minutes into the game when the Newberry player (Bobby Bailey) assigned to defend Selvy fouled out.

Selvy's last three field goals came in the game's closing 30 seconds, and the crowning moment was his final basket. "It (the 100-point game) was something that was just meant to be," Selvy said. "My last basket was from past halfcourt just before the final buzzer." Selvy hit 41 of 66 shots from the floor and 18 of 22 from the free-throw line. He played every minute of every game that season.

FURMAN (149)	FG	FT-A	PTS.
Bennett	0	1-1	1
Floyd	12	1-1	25
Fraley	3	0-2	6
Poole	0	0-0	0
Thomas	5	1-1	11
Kyber	0	0-2	0
Roth	0	0-0	0
Gordon	0	0-0	0
Selvy	41	18-22	100
Deardorff	1	1-1	3
Wright	0	0-0	0
Jones	0	1-1	1
Gilreath	1	0-0	2
TOTALS	**63**	**23-31**	**149**

NEWBERRY (95)	FG	FT-A	PTS.
Boland	0	0-0	0
Warner	2	0-4	4
Leitner	6	4-7	16
Bailey	0	1-2	1
Blanko	14	7-10	35
Cone	1	0-0	2
Roth	0	3-4	3
McKlven	1	0-0	2
Davis	13	6-7	32
TOTALS	**37**	**21-34**	**95**

Halftime: Furman 77-44.

their first 15. . . . Guard Ron Livingston, UCLA's leading scorer with 12.5 points per game, won the 1954 NCAA Doubles title in tennis and advanced to the finals in the singles division. He was the first outstanding two-fisted tennis player in college.

Colorado State's 22-7 record marked the first winning season in eight years for the Rams. . . . NIT champion Holy Cross compiled its highest winning percentage in school history (.929). . . . Notre Dame defeated Purdue for the fifteenth time in their last 17 meetings, 78-58.

Furman's Frank Selvy shoots for 2, on his way to 100 points vs. Newberry.

1953-54 FINAL NATIONAL POLLS

AP	UPI	SCHOOL(RECORD)	HEAD COACH
1	2	Kentucky (25-0)	Adolph Rupp
2	11	La Salle (26-4)	Ken Loeffler
3	9	Holy Cross (26-2)	Buster Sheary
4	1	Indiana (20-4)	Branch McCracken
5	3	Duquesne (26-3)	Dudey Moore
6	5	Notre Dame (22-3)	John Jordan
7	–	Bradley (19-13)	Forddy Anderson
8	6	Western Kentucky (29-3)	Ed Diddle
9	–	Penn State (18-6)	Elmer Gross
10	4	Oklahoma A&M (24-5)	Hank Iba
11	14	Southern Cal (19-14)	Forrest Twogood
12	–	George Washington (23-3)	Bill Reinhart
13	10	Iowa (17-5)	Bucky O'Connor
14	8	Louisiana State (20-5)	Harry Rabenhorst
15	20	Duke (22-6)	Harold Bradley
16	–	Niagara (24-6)	Taps Gallagher
17	17	Seattle (26-2)	Al Brightman
18	7	Kansas (16-5)	Phog Allen
19	12	Illinois (17-5)	Harry Combes
20	–	Maryland (23-7)	Bud Millikan
–	13	Colorado State (22-7)	Bill Strannigan
–	14	N.C. State (26-7)	Everett Case
–	16	Oregon State (19-10)	Slats Gill
–	17	Dayton (25-7)	Tom Blackburn
–	19	Rice (23-5)	Don Suman

1954 NCAA Tournament

Summary: After a one-year schedule boycott, Kentucky's undefeated squad declined a bid to the NCAA playoffs because its three fifth-year (postgraduate) stars—Cliff Hagan, Frank Ramsey, and Lou Tsioropoulos—were ineligible. The Wildcats defeated national champion-to-be La Salle by 13 points in the UK Invitation Tournament final on their way to being ranked 1st by AP and 2nd by UPI. UK had just two games tighter than a 12-point decision (77-71 over Xavier and 63-56 over LSU). Sandwiched between those two contests were 16 victories by an average margin of 33.7 points. Without UK, La Salle's achievement lost some of its significance.

Outcome for Defending Champion: Big Ten champion Indiana (20-4) lost its tourney opener to Notre Dame, 65-64. Former Notre Dame athletic director Dick Rosenthal collected 25 points and 15 rebounds for the Irish and helped limit Hoosiers All-American Don Schlundt to one field goal. Indiana's first three defeats were by a total of 44 points.

Star Gazing: Tom Gola is the only individual to be named both NCAA Final Four Most Outstanding Player and NIT Most Valuable Player in his career. Gola led La Salle to the 1954 NCAA crown with a 23-point average. Two years earlier as a freshman when the Explorers won the NIT, he shared the MVP award with teammate Norm Grekin.

Biggest Upset: Penn State, supposedly the final team selected for the NCAA playoffs, reached the Final Four by winning its first three tourney games by at least eight points—knocking off Toledo and a Bob Pettit-led LSU before snapping Notre Dame's 18-game winning streak. The Nittany Lions' 62-50 triumph over Toledo came despite four of 19 field-goal shooting by star Jesse Arnell. Phil Martin scored more than half of Toledo's points (26) in a losing effort.

One and Only: The worst composite winning percentage when four teams arrived at the national semifinals was this year as La Salle (24-4), Bradley (18-12), Penn State (17-5), and Southern California (19-12) combined for a 78-33 record (.703). Southern Cal lost both of its Final Four games (against Bradley and Penn State) to become the only national semifinalist with as many as 14 defeats. Bradley lost the championship game against La Salle to become one of only three Final Four squads to finish a season with more than a dozen defeats.

Junior center Jesse Arnelle led Cinderella-story Penn State to the NCAA Final Four.

1953-54 UNDEFEATED TEAM: UNIVERSITY OF KENTUCKY (25-0)

COACH: ADOLPH RUPP

UK	OPPONENT	UK'S HIGH SCORER
86	Temple 59	Hagan 51
81	at Xavier 66	Ramsey 27
101	Wake Forest 69	Hagan 18
71	at St. Louis 59	Ramsey 21
85	Duke 69	Hagan 27
73	La Salle 60	Hagan 28
74	Minnesota 59	Ramsey 23
77	Xavier 71	Hagan 20
105	Georgia Tech 53	Hagan 34
81	DePaul 63	Hagan/Ramsey 22
94	Tulane 43	Ramsey 26
97	at Tennessee 71	Ramsey 37
85	at Vanderbilt 63	Ramsey 24
99	Georgia Tech* 48	Hagan 23
106	Georgia 55	Ramsay 29
100	Georgia* 68	Unavailable
97	at Florida 55	Hagan 22
88	Mississippi 62	Hagan 38
81	Mississippi State 49	Hagan 26
90	Tennessee 63	Hagan 24
76	at DePaul 61	Unavailable
100	Vanderbilt 64	Hagan 22
109	Auburn* 79	Unavailable
68	at Alabama 43	Hagan 24

SEC PLAYOFF

UK	OPPONENT	UK'S HIGH SCORER
63	Louisiana State* 56	Ramsey 30

*Neutral court games.

INDIVIDUAL STATISTICS FOR KENTUCKY REGULARS

PLAYER	POS.	CL.	G.	PPG
Cliff Hagan	F-C	Sr.	25	24.0
Frank Ramsey	G	Sr.	25	19.6
Lou Tsioropoulos	F	Sr.	25	14.5
Billy Evans	F-G	Jr.	25	8.4
Gayle Rose	G	Jr.	23	6.7
Phil Grawemeyer	F-C	So.	25	5.9
Linville Puckett	G	So.	24	5.1
Bill Bibb	F	So.	16	1.7

1953–54 INDIVIDUAL LEADERS

SCORING

PLAYER	PTS.	AVG.
Selvy, Furman	1209	41.7
Pettit, Louisiana St.	785	31.4
Wilkinson, Virginia	814	30.1
Short, Oklahoma City	696	27.8
Schafer, Villanova	836	27.0
Walowac, Marshall	548	26.1
Marshall, W. Kentucky	829	25.9
Kerr, Illinois	556	25.3
Bianchi, Bowling Green	600	25.0
Palazzi, Holy Cross	670	24.8

REBOUNDING

PLAYER	REB.	AVG.
Quimby, Connecticut	588	22.6
Slack, Marshall	466	22.2

Gola, La Salle	652	21.7
Sundstrom, Rutgers	494	20.6
Koch, St. Louis	502	20.1
Tuttle, Creighton	601	20.0
Russell, San Francisco	403	19.2
Holup, George Washington	484	18.6
Conlin, Fordham	417	17.4
Hannon, Army	381	17.3

FIELD GOAL PERCENTAGE

PLAYER	FGM	FGA	PCT.
Holup, G. Wash.	179	313	.572
Karver, G. Wash.	124	221	.561
Mattick, Okla. A&M	199	358	.556
Hoxie, Niagara	115	211	.545
Spoelstra, W. Kentucky	202	381	.530
Carpenter, Texas Tech	110	214	.514
Shue, Maryland	237	469	.505

Hemric, Wake Forest	225	446	.504
Heim, Xavier	139	277	.502
Schlundt, Indiana	177	354	.500

FREE THROW PERCENTAGE

PLAYER	FTM	FTA	PCT.
Daugherty, Arizona St.	75	86	.872
Kelley, Kansas	75	87	.862
Powell, Florida	166	195	.851
Dalton, John Carroll	189	225	.840
Nystedt, New Mexico	98	118	.831
Short, Oklahoma City	232	282	.823
Costello, Niagara	125	152	.822
Lamkin, DePaul	105	128	.820
Williams, San Jose St.	184	225	.818
Devlin, G. Wash.	115	141	.816

1953–54 TEAM LEADERS

SCORING OFFENSE

SCHOOL	PTS.	AVG.
Furman	2658	91.7
Kentucky	2187	87.5
W. Kentucky	2730	85.3
Duke	2250	83.3
Holy Cross	2329	83.2

SCORING DEFENSE

SCHOOL	PTS.	AVG.
Oklahoma A&M	1539	53.1

Duquesne	1551	53.5
Wyoming	1522	54.4
Oregon State	1585	54.7
Oklahoma City	1370	54.8

FIELD GOAL PERCENTAGE

SCHOOL	FGM	FGA	PCT.
George Washington	744	1632	.456
Holy Cross	871	2018	.432
Niagara	778	1817	.428
Maryland	669	1564	.428
Furman	990	2370	.418

FREE THROW PERCENTAGE

SCHOOL	FTM	FTA	PCT.
Wake Forest	734	1010	.727
Florida	540	746	.724
Tulane	422	583	.724
New Mexico	444	614	.723
Niagara	667	929	.718

1953–54 NCAA CHAMPION: LA SALLE

SEASON STATISTICS OF LA SALLE REGULARS

PLAYER	POS.	CL.	G.	FG%	FT%	PPG	RPG
Tom Gola	C-G	Jr.	30	.407	.732	23.0	21.7
Charlie Singley	F	So.	30	.382	.654	10.7	5.1
Frank Blatcher	F	So.	27	.374	.640	10.4	4.6
Frank O'Hara	G	Sr.	30	.406	.708	9.6	3.7
Fran O'Malley	G-F	So.	30	.345	.697	7.4	4.6
Bob Maples	C-F	So.	30	.404	.554	6.9	4.7
Charles Greenberg	F-G	So.	26	.311	.545	4.7	3.0
John Yodsnukis	C	So.	18	.304	.625	4.6	5.7
Bob Ames	F	So.	14	.300	.769	2.0	0.9
Manuel Gomez	C	So.	16	.167	.462	0.6	0.8
TEAM TOTALS			30	.378	.667	75.4	51.1

1954 CHAMPIONSHIP GAME

KANSAS CITY, MO

LA SALLE (92)	FG	FT-A	PF	PTS.
Singley	8	7-10	4	23
Greenberg	2	1-2	1	5
Maples	2	0-0	4	4
Blatcher	11	1-2	4	23
Gola	7	5-5	5	19
O'Malley	5	1-1	4	11
Yodsnukis	0	0-0	5	0
O'Hara	2	2-3	1	7
TOTALS	37	18-24	28	92

FT%: .750.

BRADLEY (76)	FG	FT-A	PF	PTS.
Petersen	4	2-2	2	10
Babetch	0	0-0	0	0
King	3	6-7	4	12
Gower	0	1-2	1	1
Estergard	3	11-12	1	17
Carney	3	11-17	4	17
Utt	0	0-0	1	0
Kent	8	0-2	2	16
Riley	1	1-2	1	3
TOTALS	22	32-44	16	76

FT%: .727.
Halftime: Bradley 43-42.

ALL-TOURNAMENT TEAM

Jesse Arnelle, C, Jr., Penn State
Bob Carney, G, Sr., Bradley
Tom Gola, C-F, Jr., La Salle*
Roy Irvin, C, Jr., Southern Cal
Chuck Singley, F, Soph., La Salle
   *Named Most Outstanding Player

1954 CHAMPIONSHIP BRACKET

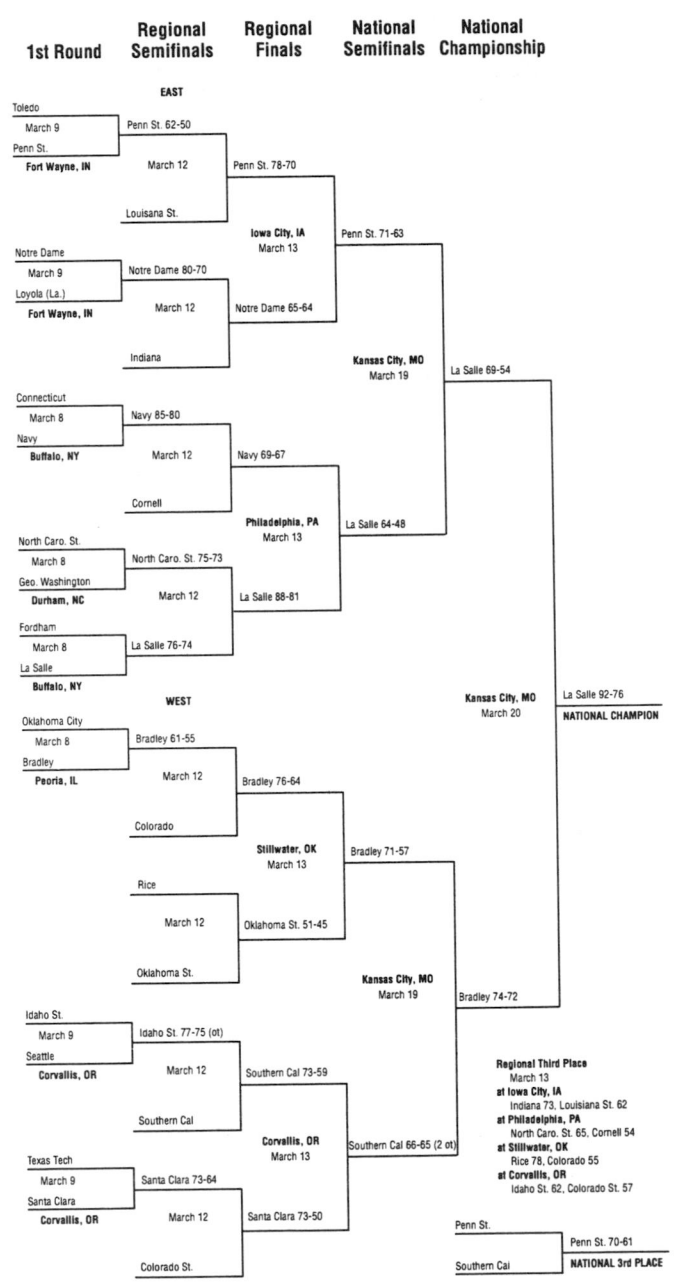

	Regional	Regional	National	National
1st Round	Semifinals	Finals	Semifinals	Championship

EAST

Toledo
March 9
Penn St.
Fort Wayne, IN

Penn St. 62-50
March 12

Louisana St.

Penn St. 78-70

Iowa City, IA
March 13

Penn St. 71-63

Notre Dame
March 9
Loyola (La.)
Fort Wayne, IN

Notre Dame 80-70
March 12

Indiana

Notre Dame 65-64

Kansas City, MO
March 19

La Salle 69-54

Connecticut
March 8
Navy
Buffalo, NY

Navy 85-80
March 12

Cornell

Navy 69-67

Philadelphia, PA
March 13

La Salle 64-48

North Caro. St.
March 8
Geo. Washington
Durham, NC

North Caro. St. 75-73
March 12

La Salle 88-81

Fordham
March 8
La Salle
Buffalo, NY

La Salle 76-74

Kansas City, MO
March 20

La Salle 92-76
NATIONAL CHAMPION

WEST

Oklahoma City
March 8
Bradley
Peoria, IL

Bradley 61-55
March 12

Colorado

Bradley 76-64

Stillwater, OK
March 13

Bradley 71-57

Rice
March 12
Oklahoma St.

Oklahoma St. 51-45

Kansas City, MO
March 19

Bradley 74-72

Idaho St.
March 9
Seattle
Corvallis, OR

Idaho St. 77-75 (ot)
March 12

Southern Cal

Southern Cal 73-59

Corvallis, OR
March 13

Southern Cal 66-65 (2 ot)

Texas Tech
March 9
Santa Clara
Corvallis, OR

Santa Clara 73-64
March 12

Colorado St.

Santa Clara 73-50

Regional Third Place
March 13
at Iowa City, IA
Indiana 73, Louisiana St. 62
at Philadelphia, PA
North Caro. St. 65, Cornell 54
at Stillwater, OK
Rice 78, Colorado 55
at Corvallis, OR
Idaho St. 62, Colorado St. 57

Penn St.

Southern Cal

Penn St. 70-61
NATIONAL 3rd PLACE

Numbers Game: Of the more than 40 different players to score more than 225 points in the playoffs and/or average over 25 points per tournament game (minimum of six games), LSU's Bob Pettit is the only one to score more than 22 points in every postseason contest (six games in 1953 and 1954). He is the only player from that select group to have a single-digit differential between his high game (36 points) and his low game (27). La Salle's output in a 92--6 victory over Bradley in the final represented the most points by a team in a championship game until UCLA's first national crown in 1964. . . . Navy's Jack Clune collected a tourney-high 42 points in an 85-80 opening-game victory over Connecticut. . . . Bradley's Bob Carney became the only player ever to make at least 50 free throws in a single tourney. He was 55 of 70 from the foul line in five games, including a 23 of 26 effort from the charity stripe against Colorado in the Midwest Regional semifinals.

Putting Things in Perspective: Niagara (24-6) defeated La Salle twice by a total of 27 points before finishing in third place in the NIT.

Scoring Leader: Tom Gola, La Salle (114 points, 22.8 ppg).

Highest Scoring Average: Bob Pettit, LSU (61 points, 30.5 ppg).

1954–55

AT A GLANCE

NCAA Champion: San Francisco (28-1; coached by Phil Woolpert; won California Basketball Association by five games with a 12-0 record).

NIT Champion: Duquesne (22-4; coached by Dudey Moore).

New Rules: Games changed back to two 20-minute halves. The one-and-one free-throw is altered so that the bonus shot is given only if the first shot is converted.

NCAA Probation: Miami (Fla.), North Carolina State.

NCAA Consensus First-Team All-Americans: Dick Garmaker, F, Sr., Minnesota; Tom Gola, C-F, Sr., La Salle; Si Green, G, Jr., Duquesne; Dick Ricketts, F-C, Sr., Duquesne; Bill Russell, C, Jr., San Francisco.

National Player of the Year: Gola (24.2 ppg, 19.9 rpg).

National Coach of the Year: Phil Woolpert, San Francisco (28-1/UPI).

David slew Goliath twice in a 23-day period. Kentucky's NCAA-record 129-game home-court winning streak was snapped by Georgia Tech, 59-58, on January 8. Tech guard Joe Helms scored a game-high 23 points, including a one-handed, 12-footer with 11 seconds remaining to end the Wildcats' 54-game regular-season winning streak and 16-year unbeaten streak in the SEC. The Jackets, 2-22 the previous season and 22-73 the previous four years, had lost to Sewanee, 67-66, one game prior to venturing to Lexington, where they had lost 10 times during UK's streak by an average margin of 35 points. Later in January, Tech became the first team to twice defeat Kentucky coach Adolph Rupp in the same season, leading the Wildcats all the way in a 65-59 decision.

Georgia Tech used only five players in both upsets. Despite the pair of setbacks to a team that finished with a losing record (12-13), Rupp improved his career mark to 520-86 (85.8 winning percentage) as the Wildcats went 23-3.

Alabama's George Linn grabbed a rebound in the closing seconds of the first half of a game against North Carolina, turned and made an overhand throw to the basket at the opposite end of the court and made the shot, which was measured at 84 feet, 11 inches.

Alabama was also involved in a bizarre pre-game fight at Kentucky. The Wildcats had a disconcerting tactic of sending their backups to mid-court, where they stood and tried to give their opponents an inferiority complex by staring at them warming up. Bama coach Johnny Dee, however, fought glare with glare. Dee dispatched his reserves to disdainfully assess UK.

1954 ACC Player-of-the-Year Dickie Hemric of Wake Forest.

single-season record for highest rebounding average with 70 per game.

Wake Forest's Dickie Hemric, one of only three starters in the ACC to measure 6-7 or better the previous year in the league's inaugural season, set an ACC single-game record by grabbing a school-record 36 rebounds against Clemson.

Dick Ricketts, Duquesne's all-time leading scorer, grabbed 28 rebounds in a game against Villanova. That's the highest rebounding total for any Dukes player against a major college.

Oregon's Jim Loscutoff established what remains a Pacific-10 Conference record by averaging 17.2 rebounds per game, including a school-record 32 rebounds against Brigham Young. Oregon State's Swede Halbrook set a league mark with 36 rebounds in a game against Idaho. . . . La Salle's Tom Gola finished his career with 2,462 points and 2,201 rebounds. His total of points and rebounds (4,663) is the highest in NCAA history. Gola grabbed a school-record 37 rebounds in a 112-70 victory over Lebanon Valley. . . . Coach Ken Loeffler, after guiding NCAA runner-up La Salle to more than 20 victories each of his six years with the Explorers, left after the season for a similar position at Texas A&M.

Furman's Darrell Floyd, the nation's leading scorer, poured in a national-high 67 points against Morehead State. Floyd's fireworks helped Furman led the nation in scoring for the third consecutive season. . . . Minnesota defeated Purdue, 59-56, in six overtimes in the longest game in Big Ten history. Each team used only six players.

Purdue lost 13 consecutive games to Indiana in their series until the Boilermakers blasted the Hoosiers, 92-67. . . . Bowling Green's school record of 12 consecutive winning seasons ended with a 6-16 worksheet, including the most lopsided defeat in the Falcons' history (109-39 against Dayton).

Virginia guard Buzz Wilkinson set an ACC single-season scoring average record by averaging 32.1 points per game, becoming the first

After exchanging words, players soon were swinging away in a pileup in the middle of the floor and had to be separated by state troopers. The Crimson Tide led midway through the second half before faltering down the stretch and losing, 66-52, providing Kentucky with the one-game cushion the Wildcats needed to stay ahead of Bama in the SEC regular-season race.

Brown's Ed Tooley established an NCAA record for most free-throw attempts in a game with 36 against Amherst (23 made). . . . Marshall's Charlie Slack set an NCAA single-season record for highest rebounding average with 25.6 boards per game. . . . Holy Cross' Tom Heinsohn (42 vs. Boston College) and Connecticut's Art Quimby (40 vs. Boston University) became two of four major-college players in history to grab at least 40 rebounds in a single game. Quimby's boardwork helped Connecticut set an NCAA

major-college player to crack 30 points per game in back-to-back years. Wilkinson still has seven of the eight games in Cavaliers history with more than 42 points.

TCU's Dick O'Neal (49 points vs. Rice) and Kent State's Dan Potopsky (49 vs. Western Michigan) established school single-game scoring records. Virginia's Wilkinson, Clemson's Bill Yarborough (28.3 ppg), William & Mary's Johnny Mahoney (27.3), Penn State's Arnelle (26.1) and Kent State's Potopsky (23.4) set school records for highest scoring average in a single season.

Texas sophomore Raymond Downs averaged 26.1 points per game in Southwest Conference competition, but failed to earn a spot among the first five on the all-league team after the Longhorns lost a school-record 15 consecutive games. . . . Kansas dedicated Allen Fieldhouse on March 1 with a 77-66 victory over Kansas State before a crowd of 17,228. Season tickets the first full season the next year cost $16, which included free parking close to the arena. The Jayhawks had previously played their home games at Hoch Auditorium, which had a seating capacity of 3,800 for basketball. . . . Wichita's Cleo Littleton became the initial player west of the Mississippi to finish his career with more than 2,000 points. . . . Hank Iba absorbed his first losing record (12-13) in 21 seasons as coach at Oklahoma A&M/State.

Seattle didn't finish among the Top 20 in a final wire-service poll for the only time in an eight-year span through 1958-59. . . . New Mexi-

1954–55 INDIVIDUAL LEADERS

SCORING

PLAYER	PTS.	AVG.
Floyd, Furman	897	35.9
Wilkinson, Virginia	898	32.1
Freeman, Ohio St.	409	31.5
Yarbrough, Clemson	651	28.3
O'Neal, Texas Christian	676	28.2
Hemric, Wake Forest	746	27.6
Patterson, Tulsa	773	27.6
Mahoney, William & Mary	656	27.3
Brackeen, Mississippi	599	27.2
Arnelle, Penn St.	731	26.1

REBOUNDING

PLAYER	REB.	PCT.
Slack, Marshall	538	.264
Russell, San Francisco	594	.258

	PTS	PCT
Conlin, Fordham	578	.241
Boldebuck, Houston	453	.221
Sparrow, Detroit	489	.218
Harper, Alabama	456	.205
Holup, G. Wash.	546	.203
Gola, La Salle	618	.203
Quimby, Connecticut	611	.196
McCarvill, Iona	422	.189

FIELD GOAL PERCENTAGE

PLAYER	FGM	FGA	PCT.
O'Connor, Manhattan	147	243	.605
Holup, G. Wash.	223	373	.598
Glowaski, Seattle	144	245	.588
Francis, Dartmouth	117	204	.574
Carpenter, Texas Tech	129	227	.568
Crosthwaite, W. Ky.	156	285	.547
Russell, San Fran.	229	423	.541

Young, Lafayette	143	266	.538
Devlin, G. Wash.	263	490	.537
McCarty, Virginia	236	444	.532

FREE THROW PERCENTAGE

PLAYER	FTM	FTA	PCT.
Scott, W. Texas St.	153	171	.895
Walczak, Marquette	104	118	.881
Barnes, SMU	83	97	.856
Williams, San Jose St.	181	214	.846
Forte, Columbia	187	222	.842
Ryan, Hardin-Simmons	105	125	.840
Blackshear, Texas Tech	83	99	.838
Sears, Santa Clara	197	235	.838
Murdock, Wake Forest	101	121	.835
Stewart, Missouri	88	106	.830

1954–55 TEAM LEADERS

SCORING OFFENSE

SCHOOL	PTS.	AVG.
Furman	2572	95.3
Connecticut	2252	90.1
Virginia	2605	89.8
North Carolina St.	2839	88.7
Marshall	1834	87.3

SCORING DEFENSE

SCHOOL	PTS.	AVG.
San Francisco	1511	52.1
Oklahoma A&M	1333	53.3
Oregon State	1660	55.3
Duquesne	1512	58.2
Santa Clara	1427	59.5

FIELD GOAL PERCENTAGE

SCHOOL	FGM	FGA	PCT.
George Washington	867	1822	.476
Wake Forest	803	1745	.460
Lafayette	760	1700	.447
Manhattan	604	1351	.447
Virginia	935	2115	.442

FREE THROW PERCENTAGE

SCHOOL	FTM	FTA	PCT.
Wake Forest	709	938	.756
Arizona State	832	627	.754
George Washington	615	819	.751
Missouri	550	747	.736
Richmond	641	879	.729

REBOUNDING

SCHOOL	TOTAL REB.	REB.	PCT.
Niagara	2417	1507	.624
St. Louis	2499	1512	.605
Seattle	2219	1336	.602
Kentucky	2800	1680	.600
North Carolina St.	3111	1864	.599

co lost back-to-back games at Southern Cal (103-39) and UCLA (106-41) by a total of 129 points. The defeats are the two most lopsided in Lobos history. . . . George Washington (24-6/coached by Bill Reinhart) and Lafayette (23-3/Butch van Breda Kolff) had their winningest seasons in school history. Lafayette won its last 20 regular-season games, a winning streak that remains a school record.

Manhattan's Ed O'Connor became the first player to lead the nation in field-goal shooting with a mark above 60 percent (60.5). . . . San Jose State's Carroll Williams finished fourth in the country in free-throw shooting with 84.6 percent accuracy. He later became coach at Santa Clara for 22 seasons. . . . Connecticut compiled a 20-5 record, which matched the Huskies' average number of defeats annually in a nine-year span from 1946-47. . . . Western Kentucky's 67-game homecourt winning streak was snapped by Xavier (82-80 in overtime). . . . A pair of Ohio universities, Case Western Reserve and John Carroll, competed in their final season at the major-college level.

1954-55 FINAL NATIONAL POLLS

AP	UPI	SCHOOL(RECORD)	HEAD COACH
1	1	San Francisco (28-1)	Phil Woolpert
2	2	Kentucky (23-3)	Adolph Rupp
3	3	La Salle (26-5)	Ken Loeffler
4	6	N.C. State (28-4)	Everett Case
5	5	Iowa (19-7)	Bucky O'Connor
6	7	Duquesne (22-4)	Dudey Moore
7	4	Utah (24-4)	Jack Gardner
8	9	Marquette (24-3)	Jack Nagle
9	10	Dayton (25-4)	Tom Blackburn
10	8	Oregon State (22-8)	Slats Gill
11	13	Minnesota (15-7)	Ozzie Cowles
12	–	Alabama (19-5)	Johnny Dee
13	12	UCLA (21-5)	John Wooden
14	15	George Washington (24-6)	Bill Reinhart
15	11	Colorado (19-6)	Bebe Lee
16	14	Tulsa (21-7)	Clarence Iba
17	–	Vanderbilt (16-6)	Bob Polk
18	16	Illinois (17-5)	Harry Combes
19	–	West Virginia (19-11)	Fred Schaus
20	18	St. Louis (20-8)	Eddie Hickey
–	17	Niagara (20-7)	Taps Gallagher
–	19	Holy Cross (19-7)	Buster Sheary
–	20	Cincinnati (21-8)	George Smith

1955 NCAA Tournament

Summary: Bill Russell retrieved 25 missed shots in the final while defensive specialist K.C.

Jones, 6-1, held La Salle's three-time consensus first-team All-American Tom Gola, 6-6, without a basket during one 21-minute stretch and outscored him, 24-16, in San Francisco's 77-63 triumph.

Outcome for Defending Champion: La Salle (26-5) won its first three tourney games by an average of 32 points. The Explorers had lost three of their last six outings the first month of the season.

Biggest Upset: Kentucky, ranked second in the country entering the tourney, lost its opener to Marquette, 79-71. Marquette had losing records in 12 of the previous 15 seasons before compiling a 24-3 mark.

One and Only: Bradley is the only school to win at least one playoff game in a year it entered the tournament with a losing record. The Braves were the only team to enter the playoffs with a record of more than 10 games under the .500 mark (7-19). They are the only school to go from the Final Four one year to 20 defeats the next season.

Numbers Game: Utah, which defeated Seattle (108-85) in the West Regional third-place game, was the only school to reach triple figures in scoring in the first 20 tournaments. . . . Terry Rand set a Marquette record for most points in an NCAA playoff game when he poured in a tourney-high 37 in a 90-79 victory over Miami of Ohio. . . . Oklahoma City's Gerald Bullard became the first player to appear in four consecutive NCAA Tournaments. He scored a total of seven points in five playoff games.

What If: ACC regular-season and tournament champion North Carolina State, which defeated eventual national runner-up La Salle, was ineligible to participate in the NCAA Tournament because it was on probation. . . . Kentucky forward Phil Grawemeyer was averaging 13 points per game when he broke his leg against DePaul and missed the Wildcats' last six contests, including a 79-71 defeat to Marquette in their NCAA Tournament opener. UK (23-3) defeated NCAA playoff runner-up La Salle by nine points early in the season.

1955 CHAMPIONSHIP BRACKET

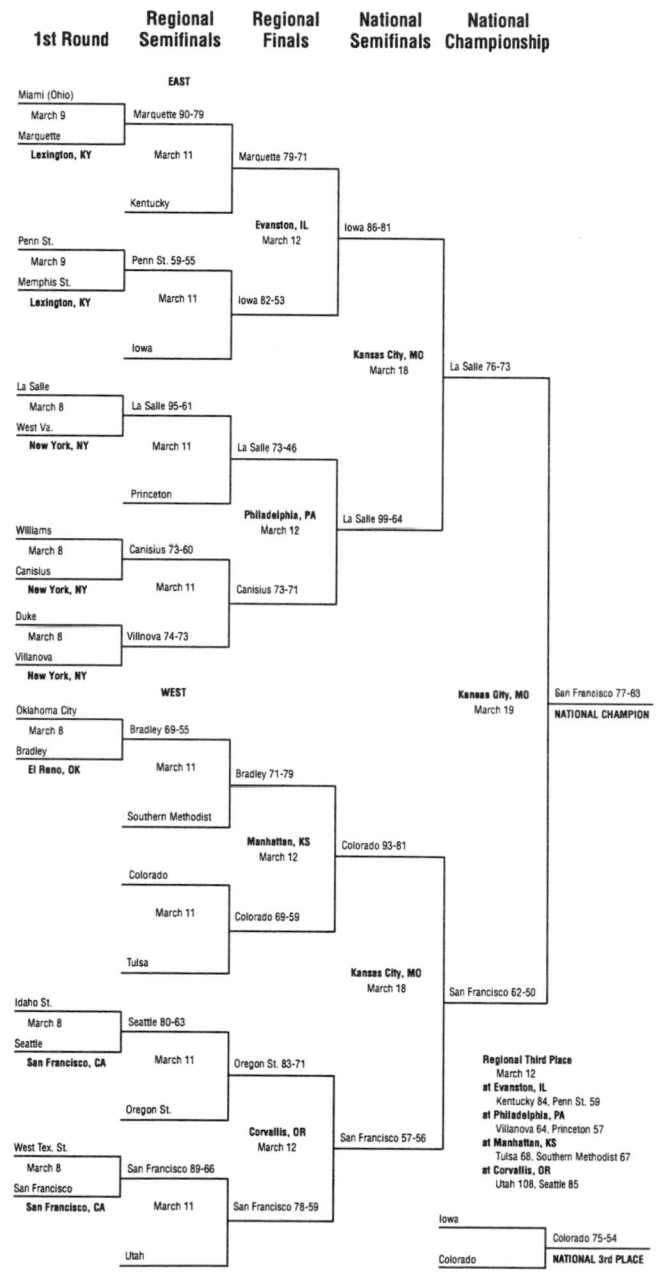

	1st Round	Regional Semifinals	Regional Finals	National Semifinals	National Championship

EAST

Miami (Ohio)
March 9
Marquette
Lexington, KY

Marquette 90-79
March 11

Kentucky

Marquette 79-71

Evanston, IL
March 12

Iowa 86-81

Penn St.
March 9
Memphis St.
Lexington, KY

Penn St. 59-55
March 11

Iowa

Iowa 82-53

Kansas City, MO
March 18

La Salle 76-73

La Salle
March 8
West Va.
New York, NY

La Salle 95-61
March 11

Princeton

La Salle 73-46

Philadelphia, PA
March 12

La Salle 99-64

Williams
March 8
Canisius
New York, NY

Canisius 73-60
March 11

Canisius 73-71

Duke
March 8
Villanova
New York, NY

Villnova 74-73

WEST

Oklahoma City
March 8
Bradley
El Reno, OK

Bradley 69-55
March 11

Southern Methodist

Bradley 71-79

Manhattan, KS
March 12

Colorado 93-81

Colorado
March 11

Colorado 69-59

Tulsa

Kansas City, MO
March 18

San Francisco 62-50

Idaho St.
March 8
Seattle
San Francisco, CA

Seattle 80-63
March 11

Oregon St.

Oregon St. 83-71

Corvallis, OR
March 12

San Francisco 57-56

West Tex. St.
March 8
San Francisco
San Francisco, CA

San Francisco 89-66
March 11

Utah

San Francisco 78-59

Kansas City, MO
March 19

San Francisco 77-63
NATIONAL CHAMPION

Regional Third Place
March 12
at Evanston, IL
Kentucky 84, Penn St. 59
at Philadelphia, PA
Villanova 64, Princeton 57
at Manhattan, KS
Tulsa 68, Southern Methodist 67
at Corvallis, OR
Utah 108, Seattle 85

Iowa

Colorado

Colorado 75-54
NATIONAL 3rd PLACE

1954–55 NCAA CHAMPION: SAN FRANCISCO

SEASON STATISTICS OF SAN FRANCISCO REGULARS

PLAYER	POS.	CL.	G.	FG%	FT%	PPG	RPG
Bill Russell	C	Jr.	29	.541	.590	21.4	20.5
Jerry Mullen	F	Sr.	27	.379	.729	13.6	7.1
K. C. Jones	G	Jr.	29	.358	.674	10.6	5.1
Hal Perry	G	Jr.	29	.372	.750	6.9	1.9
Stan Buchanan	F	Sr.	29	.302	.711	5.2	3.2
Bob Wiebusch	F	Sr.	28	.322	.714	3.6	2.1
Rudy Zannini	G	Sr.	27	.300	.724	1.9	0.4
Dick Lawless	F	Sr.	26	.270	.600	1.8	1.1
Warren Baxter	G	Jr.	19	.524	.706	1.8	0.5
Bill Bush	G	Jr.	25	.333	.556	1.6	1.0
Jack King	F	So.	16	.333	.700	0.9	0.4
Gordon Kirby	C	Sr.	20	.200	.200	0.4	0.7
TEAM TOTALS			29	.396	.657	67.3	45.7

1955 CHAMPIONSHIP GAME

KANSAS CITY, MO

SAN FRANCISCO (77)	FG	FT-A	PF	PTS.
Mullen	4	2-5	5	10
Buchanan	3	2-2	1	8
Russell	9	5-7	1	23
Jones	10	4-4	2	24
Perry	1	2-2	4	4
Wiebusch	2	0-0	0	4
Zannini	1	0-0	0	2
Lawless	1	0-0	0	2
Kirby	0	0-0	1	0
TOTALS	31	15-20	14	77

FG%: .373. FT%: .750.

LA SALLE (63)	FG	FT-A	PF	PTS.
O'Malley	4	2-3	1	10
Singley	8	4-4	1	20
Gola	6	4-5	4	16
Lewis	1	4-9	1	6
Greenberg	1	1-2	4	3
Blatcher	4	0-0	1	8
Maples	0	0-0	0	0
Fredricks	0	0-0	0	0
TOTALS	24	15-23	12	63

FG%: .353. FT%: .652.
Halftime: San Francisco 35-24.

ALL-TOURNAMENT TEAM

Carl Cain, F, Jr., Iowa
Tom Gola, C, Sr., La Salle
K. C. Jones, G, Jr., San Francisco
Jim Ranglos, F, Jr., Colorado
Bill Russell, C, Jr., San Francisco*
*Named Most Outstanding Player

Putting Things in Perspective: The first of San Francisco's back-to-back champions survived a scare in a West Regional and won by one point at Oregon State (57-56). The Beavers would have avenged a 26-point defeat earlier in the season against the Dons if they hadn't missed a last-second shot. A 60-34 verdict over Oregon State was the first of USF's 60 consecutive victories, the longest winning streak in major-college history until UCLA won 88 games in a row from 1971-74.

Scoring Leader: Bill Russell, San Francisco (118 points, 23.6 ppg).

Highest Scoring Average: Bob Patterson, Tulsa (57 points, 28.5 ppg).

1955–56

AT A GLANCE

NCAA Champion: San Francisco (29-0; coached by Phil Woolpert; won WCAC by five games with a 14-0 record).

NIT Champion: Louisville (26-3; coached by Peck Hickman).

New Rules: The two-shot penalty in the last three minutes of a game is eliminated. The one-and-one is now in effect the entire game. The NCAA Tournament goes from two regionals to four.

NCAA Probation: Cincinnati.

NCAA Consensus First-Team All-Americans: Robin Freeman, G, Sr., Ohio State; Si Green, G, Sr., Duquesne; Tom Heinsohn, F, Sr., Holy Cross; Bill Russell, C, Sr., San Francisco; Ron Shavlik, C, Sr., North Carolina State.

National Player of the Year: Russell (20.6 ppg, 21 rpg, 51.3 FG%).

National Coach of the Year: Phil Woolpert, San Francisco (29-0/UPI).

Alabama was ranked fifth by AP and UPI but didn't participate in the NCAA Tournament because of a rules technicality stemming from varsity participation as freshmen by several of the "Rocket 8" star players in 1953. Alabama's squad, dominated by Midwest recruits who didn't survive tryouts to receive scholarships from Notre Dame, became the first opponent to score

1955-56 INDIVIDUAL LEADERS

SCORING LEADERS

PLAYER	PTS.	AVG.
Floyd, Furman	946	33.8
Freeman, Ohio St.	723	32.9
Swartz, Morehead St.	828	28.6
Heinsohn, Holy Cross	740	27.4
McCoy, Michigan St.	600	27.3
Rosenbluth, North Carolina	614	26.7
Hundley, West Virginia	798	26.6
Downs, Texas	580	26.4
Ray, Toledo	563	25.6
Sigler, Louisiana St.	501	25.1

REBOUNDING

PLAYER	REB.	PCT.
Holup, G. Wash.	604	.256
Tyra, Louisville	645	.235

Harper, Alabama	517	.232
Russell, San Francisco	609	.231
Slack, Marshall	520	.215
Inniss, St. Francis (NY)	465	.196
Shavlik, North Carolina St.	545	.193
Heinsohn, Holy Cross	549	.188
Sobieszczyk, DePaul	316	.182
McLaughlin, St. Louis	455	.181

FIELD GOAL PERCENTAGE

PLAYER	FGM	FGA	PCT.
Holup, G. Wash.	200	309	.647
Greer, Marshall	128	213	.601
Johnson, St. Mary's	134	238	.563
Downs, Texas	167	309	.540
Lombardo, Manhattan	172	322	.534
Roberson, Cornell	117	224	.522
Ellis, Niagara	133	255	.522

O'Shea, Alabama	112	218	.514
Russell, San Francisco	246	480	.513
Choice, Indiana	148	290	.510

FREE THROW PERCENTAGE

PLAYER	FTM	FTA	PCT.
Von Weyhe, Rhode Island	180	208	.865
Murdock, Wake Forest	203	237	.857
Molodet, N. Carolina St.	167	196	.852
Miani, Miami (Fla.)	139	166	.837
McCarty, Virginia	163	196	.832
Petcavich, G. Wash.	138	166	.831
Gaudin, Loyola (La.)	130	157	.828
Plump, Butler	94	114	.825
Downs, Texas	246	290	.823
Forte, Columbia	114	139	.820

1955-56 TEAM LEADERS

SCORING OFFENSE

SCHOOL	PTS.	AVG.
Morehead St.	2782	95.9
Marshall	2145	93.3
Illinois	1996	90.7
Furman	2492	89.0
Memphis St.	2385	88.3

SCORING DEFENSE

SCHOOL	PTS.	AVG.
San Francisco	1514	52.2
Oklahoma A&M	1428	52.9
New Mexico A&M	1358	59.0
Tulsa	1537	59.1
San Jose St.	1485	59.4

FIELD GOAL PERCENTAGE

SCHOOL	FGM	FGA	PCT.
George Washington	725	1451	.500
Manhattan	698	1519	.460
DePaul	659	1456	.453
Niagara	739	1653	.447
Wake Forest	777	1754	.443

FREE THROW PERCENTAGE

SCHOOL	FTM	FTA	PCT.
Southern Methodist	701	917	.764
Murray State	590	791	.746
Texas Western	517	698	.741
Illinois	534	725	.737
North Carolina St.	639	869	.735

REBOUNDING

SCHOOL	TOTAL REB.	REB.	PCT.
George Washington	2356	1451	.616
Niagara	2008	1198	.597
San Francisco	2642	1573	.595
St. Louis	2529	1503	.594
Rice	2181	1294	.593

100 points against Kentucky. The 20-6 Wildcats, the SEC's representative to the NCAA Tournament, were whipped by 24 points (101-77 in the Massacre in Montgomery) as 'Bama went on a 27-2 second-half spurt en route to finishing the season with 16 consecutive victories. The Crimson Tide's defeats—at North Carolina and St. John's and against Notre Dame on a neutral court—were in a span of four games.

As incredible as it might seem today, Johnny Dee left Alabama after such a splendid season to coach an amateur team sponsored by the Denver-Chicago Trucking Company. The school wound up failing to participate in the NCAA Tournament for the first time until 1975. Dee later coached at Notre Dame for seven seasons.

Jerry Harper, who set a conference record by averaging 21.5 rebounds per game, garnered 37 points and 26 rebounds for Alabama in its big win over Kentucky. Earlier, he collected 41 points and a school-record 33 rebounds in a 105-71 triumph over Louisiana College.

Alabama's last loss was to Notre Dame (86-80) in the semifinals of the Sugar Bowl Tournament at New Orleans. The Irish defeated Utah, a Top 20 team most of the season, the next evening. The Sugar Bowl was the high point of the campaign for Notre Dame, which absorbed its first losing record (9-15) in 33 years.

Ronnie Shavlik still owns 12 of the top 13 rebounding efforts in North Carolina State history. He cleaned the glass with 25 or more boards six times in his career. His 19.5 rebounds per game average as a senior is still an ACC record. . . . N.C. State captured its sixth Dixie Classic title in the first seven years of the eight-team event.

The original showcase of "Big Four" basketball was considered the No. 1 Christmas holiday tournament in the nation. During the Dixie Classic's heyday, the reams of copy moved nationally prompted Western Union officials to call it "the biggest sporting event in the South." The final year for the Classic was 1960.

North Carolina ended its streak of at least 10 defeats in six consecutive seasons by compiling an 18-5 record. . . . Clemson lost its first 26 games in ACC regular-season play, a league record, before upending Virginia, 75-73. It was the Tigers' only victory in their first 42 meetings against ACC competition.

Ohio State's streak of consecutive non-winning seasons ended at five when the Buckeyes compiled a 16-6 record. . . . Ohio State guard Robin Freeman's only sub-20 point game all season (12 against Illinois) cost him the national scoring title in a battle with Furman's Darrell Floyd (33.8 points per game). Freeman, who finished at 32.9, was 34.3 in all contests except the mediocre contests against the Illini. Floyd poured in a national-high 62 points against The Citadel. However, The Citadel's NCAA-record 37-game losing streak was snapped when the Bulldogs defeated Charleston.

In perhaps the biggest upset of the season, Big Ten runner-up Illinois bowed to Northwest-

ern, 83-82, in the closing game of the season for both teams. Northwestern finished with a 2-20 record. . . . DePaul lost 15 consecutive games to Kentucky before edging the visiting Wildcats, 81-79. . . . The Air Force Academy competed in its inaugural season of basketball, compiling an 11-9 record against freshman teams as Bob Beckel led the way with a 28.1-point scoring average.

Wyoming's Joe Capua (51 points vs. Montana), Texas' Raymond Downs (tied with 49 at Baylor), Eastern Kentucky's Jack Adams (49 vs. Union) and George Washington's Joe Holup (49 vs. Furman) set school single-game scoring records. Holup also established a Southern Conference single-season standard by averaging 23.2 rebounds per game.

Ohio State's Freeman, Morehead State's Dan Swartz (28.6), Alabama's Harper (27.3), Texas' Downs (26.4), Toledo's Jim Ray (25.6), Louisville's Charlie Tyra (23.8) and Cornell's Chuck Rolles (23) set school records for highest scoring average in a single season.

George Washington led the nation's teams in field-goal shooting for the third consecutive season as Holup finished among the top two individuals in that category for the third straight year. He was eighth as a freshman in 1952-53. . . . Marshall's Charlie Slack, 6-5, finished his career as the only major-college player to average more

1955-56 UNDEFEATED TEAM: SAN FRANCISCO (29-0)

COACH: PHIL WOOLPERT

USF	OPPONENT	USF'S HIGH SCORER
70	Chico State 39	Russell 15
58	Southern California 42	Russell 24
72	San Francisco State 47	Russell 20
65	Marquette* 58	Russell 16
82	at DePaul 59	Jones 23
75	at Wichita 65	Russell 17
61	at Loyola of New Orleans 43	Russell 20
79	La Salle* 62	Russell 26
67	Holy Cross* 51	Russell 24
70	UCLA* 53	Russell 17
62	Pepperdine 51	Russell 20
74	Santa Clara 56	Farmer 18
69	at Fresno State 50	Russell 22
33	at California 24	Jones 15
67	San Jose State 40	Russell 21
68	Loyola of Los Angeles 46	Boldt 20
77	at Pacific 60	Russell 24

USF	OPPONENT	USF'S HIGH SCORER
79	Fresno State 46	Russell 23
76	at San Jose State 52	Russell 21
76	at St. Mary's 63	Russell 28
80	at Santa Clara 44	Russell 29
87	Pacific 49	Russell 28
68	at Pepperdine 40	Boldt 14
65	at Loyola of Los Angeles 48	Russell 24
82	St. Mary's 49	Russell 22

NCAA TOURNAMENT

USF	OPPONENT	
72	UCLA* 61	Brown 23
92	Utah* 77	Russell 27
86	Southern Methodist* 68	Farmer 26
83	Iowa* 71	Russell 26

*Neutral court games.

than 22 rebounds per game in three consecutive seasons. Marshall became the first major college to have at least three players average more than 20 points per game—Slack (22.5), Cebe Price (21.2) and Paul Underwood (20.2). . . . Al Inniss of St. Francis (N.Y.) set an NIT and Madison Square Garden college record with 37 rebounds in an NIT first-round game vs. Lafayette.

The Philadelphia Big Five, an unsanctioned alliance including La Salle, Penn, St. Joseph's, Temple and Villanova, began annual round-robin competition at The Palestra. Villanova is the only one of the five schools to fail to rank among the top 10 nationally in winning percentage in a decade since the start of the Big Five—La Salle (4th in '50s), St. Joseph's (7th in '60s), Penn (3rd in '70s) and Temple (5th in '80s). Villanova's highest finish in a decade was 15th in the '60s.

Norm Stewart, finishing 15th in the nation in scoring, averaged 24.1 points per game for Missouri. He would later become his alma mater's all-time winningest coach. . . . St. Bonaventure lost its last five games to finish with its only losing record (11-12) in a 37-year span from 1947-48 through 1983-84.

UCLA had a string of outstanding front-courters during coach John Wooden's career. Surprisingly, the one setting the school record for most rebounds in a single-game was Willie Naulls, who retrieved 28 missed shots against Arizona State. . . . There was a drought of sorts in the Arizona desert. Utah defeated Arizona in back-to-back games by a total of 104 points. A 119-45 setback to the Utes is the most lopsided defeat in Arizona history. Meanwhile, Arizona State also suffered its most lopsided loss (113-63 to Texas Tech). . . . Wyoming, after averaging 22 victories annually the previous 10 years, compiled a 7-19 mark to start a streak of nine consecutive losing records.

Kansas coach Phog Allen retired after 48 seasons with a 746-264 record. His final varsity squad lost a preseason game to the school's freshman team when Philadelphia native Wilt

Chamberlain collected 42 points and 29 rebounds for the frosh. . . . Yale's Howard Hobson, who guided Oregon to a title in the first NCAA Tournament in 1939, retired after a 23-year coaching career with a 400-257 record.

1955–56 FINAL NATIONAL POLLS

AP	UPI	SCHOOL (RECORD)	HEAD COACH
1	1	San Francisco (29-0)	Phil Woolpert
2	2	N.C. State (24-4)	Everett Case
3	3	Dayton (25-4)	Tom Blackburn
4	4	Iowa (20-6)	Bucky O'Connor
5	5	Alabama (21-3)	Johnny Dee
6	7	Louisville (26-3)	Peck Hickman
7	6	SMU (26-4)	Doc Hayes
8	9	UCLA (22-6)	John Wooden
9	12	Kentucky (20-6)	Adolph Rupp
10	8	Illinois (18-4)	Harry Combes
11	–	Oklahoma City (20-7)	Abe Lemons
12	10	Vanderbilt (19-4)	Bob Polk
13	11	North Carolina (18-5)	Frank McGuire
14	15	Holy Cross (22-5)	Roy Leenig
15	14	Temple (27-4)	Harry Litwack
16	–	Wake Forest (19-9)	Murray Greason
17	18	Duke (19-7)	Harold Bradley
18	13	Utah (22-6)	Jack Gardner
19	16	Oklahoma A&M (18-9)	Hank Iba
20	–	West Virginia (21-9)	Fred Schaus
–	16	St. Louis (18-7)	Eddie Hickey
–	18	Canisius (19-7)	Joe Curran
–	18	Seattle (18-11)	Al Brightman

1956 NCAA Tournament

Summary: National champion San Francisco averaged 14-point victories after winning all but two of its regular-season games by double-digit margins. Marquette, 13-11 that season, came closest to USF in a 65-58 decision on a neutral court in the DePaul Invitational. Unanimous first-team All-American Bill Russell averaged 22.8 points in four tournament games as the Dons won each of them by more than 10 points. Their 86-68 victory over SMU in the national semifinals snapped the Mustangs' school-record 20-game winning streak. K. C. Jones was ineligible for the playoffs because he had played one game two years earlier before an appendectomy ended his season, but USF still became the first undefeated champion in NCAA history (29-0, coached by Phil Woolpert). It remains the winningest season in USF history.

Star Gazing: Temple mighty mites Hal Lear (5-11) combined with backcourtmate Guy

Rodgers (6-0) to score 73.5 percent of the Owls' points in two Final Four games. Lear manufactured 61.5 percent of Temple's offense by scoring 40 points in the Owls' 65-59 victory against Connecticut in the East Regional semifinals. He tallied a tourney-high 48 points in a 90-81 triumph over SMU in the national third-place game.

Biggest Upset: North Carolina State, ranked No. 2 in the nation entering the tourney, was stunned in four overtimes in the first round by Canisius, 79-78.

One and Only: San Francisco center Bill Russell became the only player to grab more than 41 rebounds at a Final Four (50) and more than 21 in a championship game (27 against Iowa).

Numbers Game: The record for most rebounds in a playoff game was set by Temple's Fred Cohen with 34 in a 65-59 victory against Connecticut in the East Regional semifinals. Cohen grabbed just five rebounds in the Owls' next contest, a 60-58 win over Canisius.

Putting Things in Perspective: National runner-up Iowa lost four consecutive games and five of six before reeling off 17 straight victories until bowing to San Francisco in the NCAA final, 83-71. Each of the Hawkeyes' starters compiled double-figure scoring averages as they became known as the "Fabulous Five"—Carl Cain (15.8 ppg), Bill Logan (17.7), Sharm Scheuerman (10.1), Bill Schoof (10.8) and Bill Seaberg (13.9). They were the only set of starters to achieve that double-digit distinction and reach the NCAA championship game until 1960 NCAA kingpin Ohio State.

Scoring Leader: Hal Lear, Temple (160 points, 32 ppg; Kentucky's Bob Burrow also averaged 32 ppg).

1955–56 NCAA CHAMPION: SAN FRANCISCO

SEASON STATISTICS OF SAN FRANCISCO REGULARS

PLAYER	POS.	CL.	G.	FG%	FT%	PPG	RPG
Bill Russell	C	Sr.	29	.513	.495	20.6	21.0
K. C. Jones*	G	Sr.	25	.365	.655	9.8	5.2
Hal Perry	G	Sr.	29	.365	.729	9.1	2.0
Carl Boldt	F	Jr.	28	.326	.783	8.6	5.0
Mike Farmer	F	So.	28	.371	.548	8.4	7.8
Gene Brown	G	So.	29	.377	.641	7.1	4.4
Mike Preaseau	F	So.	29	.366	.609	4.1	3.1
Warren Baxter	G	Sr.	26	.301	.667	2.2	0.7
Bill Bush	G	Sr.	22	.208	.625	0.9	0.8
Jack King	F	Jr.	22	.162	.462	0.8	1.0
TEAM TOTALS			29	.388	.604	72.2	54.2

*Ineligible for NCAA Tournament as a fifth-year player.

1956 FINAL FOUR CHAMPIONSHIP GAME

EVANSTON, IL

SAN FRANCISCO (83)	FG	FT-A	PF	PTS.
Boldt	7	2-2	4	16
Farmer	0	0-0	2	0
Preaseau	3	1-2	3	7
Russell	11	4-5	2	26
Nelson	0	0-0	0	0
Perry	6	2-2	2	14
Brown	6	4-4	0	16
Baxter	2	0-0	0	4
TOTALS	35	13-15	13	83

FG%: .402. **FT%:** .867. **Rebounds:** 60 (Russell 27).

IOWA (71)	FG	FT-A	PF	PTS.
Cain	7	3-4	1	17
Schoof	5	4-4	3	14
Logan	5	2-2	3	12
George	0	0-0	0	0
Scheuerman	4	3-4	2	11
Seaberg	5	7-10	1	17
Martel	0	0-0	0	0
McConnell	0	0-0	0	0
TOTALS	26	19-24	10	71

FG%: .325. **FT%:** .792. **Rebounds:** 48 (Logan 15).
Halftime: San Francisco 38-33.

NATIONAL SEMIFINALS
IOWA (83): Cain 8 4 20, Schoof 5 8 18, Logan 13 10 36, Seaberg 1 0 2, Scheuerman 1 2 4, Martel 1 1 3. Team 29 25 83.

TEMPLE (76): Reinfeld 1 0 2, Norman 1 0 2, Fleming 2 0 4, Cohen 3 0 6, Van Patton 1 0 2, Rodgers 12 4 28, Lear 15 2 32. Team 35 6 76.

Halftime: Iowa 39-36.

SAN FRANCISCO (86): Boldt 3 1 7, Farmer 11 4 26, Preaseau 1 0 2, King 0 0 0, Russell 8 1 17, Perry 6 2 14, Brown 5 2 12, Baxter 4 0 8. Team 38 10 86.

SOUTHERN METHODIST (68): Showalter 4 0 8, Krog 3 0 6, McGregor 1 1 3, Krebs 10 4 24, Miller 1 0 2, Miller 1 9 11, Morris 4 2 10, Herrscher 1 2 4. Team 25 18 68.

Halftime: San Francisco 44-32.

ALL-TOURNAMENT TEAM
Carl Cain, F, Sr., Iowa
Hal Lear, G, Sr., Temple*
Bill Logan, C, Sr., Iowa
Hal Perry, G, Sr., San Francisco
Bill Russell, C, Sr., San Francisco
    *Named Most Outstanding Player

1956 CHAMPIONSHIP BRACKET

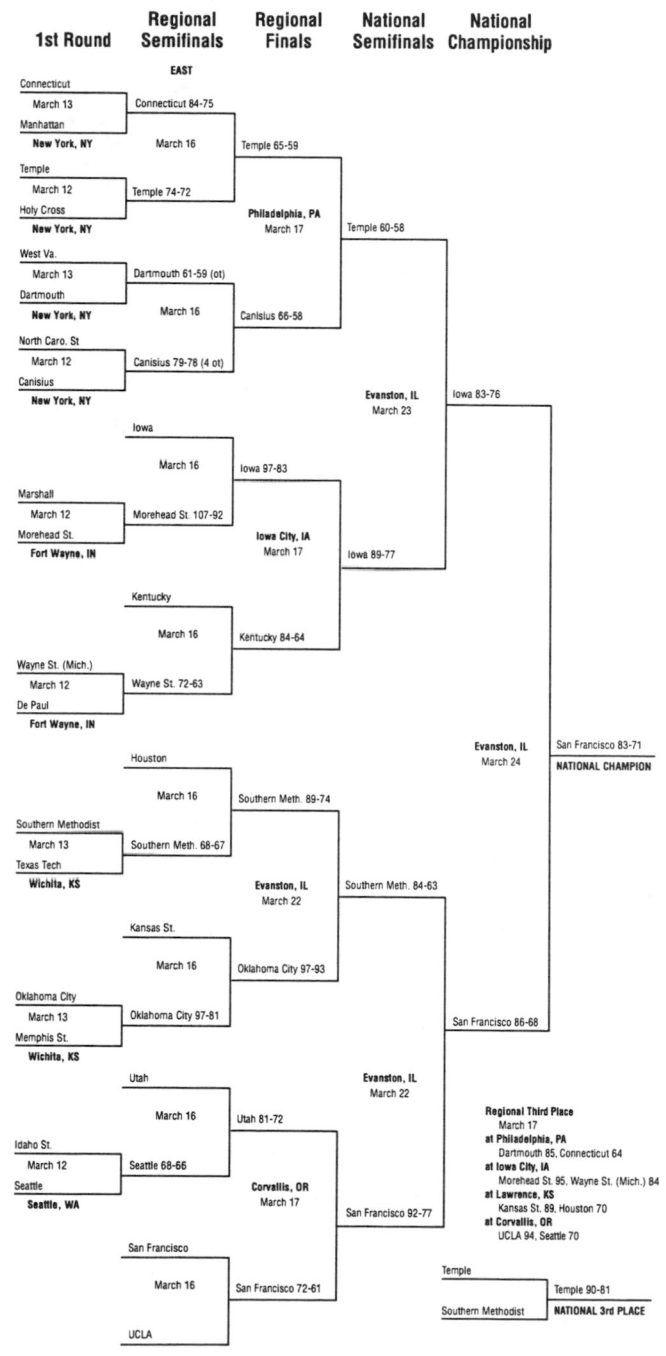

	1st Round	Regional Semifinals	Regional Finals	National Semifinals	National Championship

EAST

Connecticut
March 13
Manhattan
New York, NY
Connecticut 84-75
March 16

Temple
March 12
Holy Cross
New York, NY
Temple 74-72

Temple 65-59

Philadelphia, PA
March 17

West Va.
March 13
Dartmouth
New York, NY
Dartmouth 61-59 (ot)
March 16

North Caro. St
March 12
Canisius
New York, NY
Canisius 79-78 (4 ot)

Canisius 66-58

Temple 60-58

Iowa
March 16
Iowa 97-83

Marshall
March 12
Morehead St.
Fort Wayne, IN
Morehead St. 107-92

Iowa City, IA
March 17

Kentucky
March 16
Kentucky 84-64

Wayne St. (Mich.)
March 12
De Paul
Fort Wayne, IN
Wayne St. 72-63

Iowa 89-77

Evanston, IL
March 23

Iowa 83-76

Houston
March 16
Southern Meth. 89-74

Southern Methodist
March 13
Texas Tech
Wichita, KS
Southern Meth. 68-67

Evanston, IL
March 22

Kansas St.
March 16
Oklahoma City 97-93

Oklahoma City
March 13
Memphis St.
Wichita, KS
Oklahoma City 97-81

Southern Meth. 84-63

Evanston, IL
March 24

San Francisco 83-71

NATIONAL CHAMPION

San Francisco 86-68

Utah
March 16
Utah 81-72

Idaho St.
March 12
Seattle
Seattle, WA
Seattle 68-66

Corvallis, OR
March 17

San Francisco
March 16
San Francisco 72-61

UCLA

San Francisco 92-77

Evanston, IL
March 22

Regional Third Place
March 17
at Philadelphia, PA
Dartmouth 85, Connecticut 64
at Iowa City, IA
Morehead St. 95, Wayne St. (Mich.) 84
at Lawrence, KS
Kansas St. 89, Houston 70
at Corvallis, OR
UCLA 94, Seattle 70

Temple
Southern Methodist
Temple 90-81
NATIONAL 3rd PLACE

1956–57

AT A GLANCE

NCAA Champion: North Carolina (32-0; coached by Frank McGuire; won ACC title by five games with a 14-0 record).

NIT Champion: Bradley (22-7; coached by Chuck Orsborn; finished in second place in the Missouri Valley with a 9-5 record, which was three games behind St. Louis).

New Rules: The free-throw lane is increased from six feet to 12 feet. On the lineup for a free throw, the two spaces adjacent to the end line must be occupied by opponents of the free thrower. Previously, one space was marked "H" for a home team player to occupy, and across the lane the first space was marked "V" for a visiting team player to stand in. Grasping the goal is now classified as a technical foul under unsportsmanlike tactics.

NCAA Probation: Auburn, Florida, Louisville, North Carolina State, Ohio State, Southern Cal, Texas A&M, UCLA, and Washington.

NCAA Consensus First-Team All-Americans: Wilt Chamberlain, C, Soph., Kansas; Chet Forte, G, Sr., Columbia; Rod Hundley, G-F, Sr., West Virginia, Jim Krebs, C, Sr., Southern Methodist; Lennie Rosenbluth, F, Sr., North Carolina; Charlie Tyra, C, Sr., Louisville.

National Player of the Year: Forte (28.9 ppg, 4.5 rpg, 85.2 FT%).

National Coach of the Year: Frank McGuire, North Carolina (27-0/UPI).

West Virginia All-American guard-forward Hot Rod Hundley.

Wilt Chamberlain's varsity debut at Kansas was an immense success as he poured in a school-record 52 points against Northwestern. It is the only existing single-game scoring record achieved in a debut. Chamberlain scored many of the points in his coming-out party against fellow sophomore Joe Ruklick. They would later be NBA teammates after becoming the first two draft choices for the Philadelphia Warriors in 1959. Ruklick averaged only 3.5 points per game in his three-year career as Chamberlain's backup, but supplied one of the most worthy yet long-forgotten assists in hoops history. Ruklick fed Wilt a key pass in the closing seconds of a memorable March 1, 1962, game in Hershey, Pa., that resulted in Chamberlain scoring his 99th and 100th points of the evening.

Chamberlain, who averaged 29.6 points per game in his initial collegiate campaign, would have had a good chance at leading the nation in scoring except for three contests against Iowa State, which limited him to 16 points per game. He set a Big Eight Conference record by averaging 18.7 rebounds per game.

South Carolina's Grady Wallace became the only ACC player to ever lead the nation in scoring (31.2 ppg). It was the fifth consecutive season the scoring title remained in the Palmetto State. Wallace's predecessors were Furman's Frank Selvy and Darell Floyd. Oddly, none of the three were South Carolina natives. Selvy and Wallace were from Kentucky while Floyd was from North Carolina.

The top eight scorers in the country were separated by fewer than 3 1/2 points. The national runner-up in scoring was Mississippi's Joe Gibbon (30), who later pitched in the majors. A couple of other prominent hoopsters who would up in the majors were Ohio State's Frank Howard and Morehead State's Steve Hamilton. Howard was one of the nation's premier rebounders with 15.3 boards per game, including a school-record 32 against Brigham Young. Hamilton led the Eagles in scoring and rebounding. Hamilton became the only athlete to appear in the NCAA Tournament before playing in a World Series (New York Yankees in 1963 and 1964) and an NBA Finals (Minneapolis Lakers rookie in 1959 when they were swept by the Boston Celtics).

Hamilton's boardwork helped Morehead State set an NCAA single-season record for rebounding margin with an average of 25 more caroms per game than its opponents. He set a school single-game standard by retrieving 38 missed shots against Florida State.

Miami of Ohio's Wayne Embry grabbed a school-record 34 rebounds in each of back-to-back games against Eastern Kentucky and Kent State. Niagara's Alex Ellis hauled down a school-record 31 rebounds in two games separated by 10 days (vs. Villanova and Kent State). Cincinnati's Connie Dierking (33 vs. Loyola of New Orleans) and San Jose State's Marv Branstrom (28 at Arizona State) also established school single-game rebounding standards.

Illinois ended San Francisco's 60-game winning streak, 62-33. But the Illini finished out of the final wire-service Top 20 polls for the first time in seven years and posted a non-winning Big Ten record (7-7) for the first time since 1944. . . . Michigan compiled a 13-9 overall record to snap its streak of seven consecutive non-winning seasons. The Wolverines were 8-6 in the Big Ten, finishing ahead of Illinois in the conference race for just the second time in 19 years.

Columbia's 5-9 Chet Forte became the first Ivy League player to score more than 400 points in a conference campaign as he totaled 403 points in 14 games (28.8 per league contest). . . . Harvard (12-9) notched a double-digit victory total for the first time in 10 years. Bucknell compiled a 16-8 record to end its streak of nine consecutive losing seasons. . . . St. Joseph's (17-7) posted its fewest victories in Jack Ramsay's 11 years as coach of the Hawks from 1955-56 through 1965-66. . . . Canisius (22-6, coached by Joseph Curran) had its winningest season in school history.

West Virginia's Hot Rod Hundley (54 points vs. Furman) and Pitt's Don Hennon (45 at Duke) set school single-game scoring records. Hundley's output tied Wallace (vs. Georgia) for the highest single-game outburst during the season. . . . Mississippi State's Jim Ashmore (28.3) and Bailey Howell (25.9) became the first set of teammates in NCAA history to average more than 25 points per game in a single season. Howell (37) and Ashmore (24) combined for 61 points in MSU's first victory over Kentucky in 33 years (89-81) as the Wildcats missed their first 13 field-goal attempts. Howell grabbed a school-record 34 rebounds in a game against LSU.

1956-57 FINAL NATIONAL POLLS

AP	UPI	SCHOOL (RECORD)	HEAD COACH
1	1	North Carolina (32-0)	Frank McGuire
2	2	Kansas (24-3)	Dick Harp
3	3	Kentucky (23-5)	Adolph Rupp
4	4	SMU (22-4)	Doc Hayes
5	5	Seattle (24-3)	John Castellani
6	8	Louisville (21-5)	Peck Hickman
7	11	West Virginia (25-5)	Fred Schaus
8	16	Vanderbilt (17-5)	Bob Polk
9	16	Oklahoma City (19-9)	Abe Lemons
10	10	St. Louis (19-9)	Eddie Hickey
11	7	Michigan State (16-10)	Forddy Anderson
12	–	Memphis State (24-6)	Bob Vanatta
13	6	California (21-5)	Pete Newell
14	9	UCLA (22-4)	John Wooden
15	–	Mississippi State (17-8)	Babe McCarthy
16	–	Idaho State (25-4)	John Grayson
17	19	Notre Dame (20-8)	John Jordan
18	–	Wake Forest (19-9)	Murray Greason
19	–	Canisius (22-6)	Joe Curran
19	–	Oklahoma A&M (17-9)	Hank Iba
–	12	Dayton (19-9)	Tom Blackburn
–	13	Bradley (22-7)	Chuck Orsborn
–	14	Brigham Young (19-9)	Stan Watts
–	15	Indiana (14-8)	Branch McCracken
–	16	Xavier (20-8)	Ned Wulk
–	20	Kansas State (15-8)	Tex Winter

Wake Forest teammates Ernie Wiggins and Jackie Murdock, deadlocked for the national lead in free-throw shooting entering the postseason, finished 1-2 in the country. Wiggins won by hitting all four of his tournament tosses. . . . North Carolina's Lennie Rosenbluth scored an ACC Tournament-record 45 points in a quarterfinal victory over Clemson. He led the NCAA champion-to-be Tar Heels in scoring in 14 of their last 15 outings. . . . South Carolina's Wallace, Columbia's Forte (28.9 ppg), Mississippi State's Ashmore (28.3) and North Carolina's Rosenbluth (28) set school records for highest scoring average in a single season.

Georgia Tech (18-8) won its last five games to end a streak of 11 consecutive seasons with more than 10 defeats. . . . Detroit and Oklahoma State competed in the Missouri Valley Conference for the final season. . . . Creighton (15-6) compiled its first winning record in 10 years. . . . Idaho State made its lone appearance in the Top 20 of a final wire-service poll. . . . Seattle coach John Castellani was hung in effigy on the school's campus after the Elgin Baylor-led Chieftains, seeded No. 1 in the NIT, lost its postseason opener to St. Bonaventure, 85-68.

In one of the strangest games in NIT history, Bradley erased a 21-point deficit to defeat Xavier, 116-81, in the quarterfinals. The Braves outscored Xavier, 72-29, in the second half, setting NIT and Madison Square Garden college records for most points in a half. . . . Bradley wound up winning the NIT with an 84-83 triumph over Memphis State College in the championship game. Memphis State, competing in just its second season as a major college, defeat-

1956–57 INDIVIDUAL LEADERS

SCORING

PLAYER	PTS.	AVG.
Wallace, South Carolina	906	31.2
Gibbon, Mississippi	631	30.0
Baylor, Seattle	743	29.7
Chamberlain, Kansas	800	29.6
Forte, Columbia	694	28.9
Ashmore, Mississippi St.	708	28.3
Rosenbluth, North Carolina	895	28.0
Ebben, Detroit	724	27.8
Howell, Mississippi St.	647	25.9
Dees, Indiana	550	25.0

REBOUNDING

PLAYER	REB.	PCT.
Baylor, Seattle	508	.235
Ellis, Niagara	502	.234

Tyra, Louisville	520	.229
Chamberlain, Kansas	510	.227
Guarilia, G. Wash.	447	.218
Howell, Mississippi St.	492	.212
Ramsey, New York	372	.202
Howard, Ohio State	336	.201
Freeman, Xavier	526	.195
Hamilton, Morehead St.	543	.194

FIELD GOAL PERCENTAGE

PLAYER	FGM	FGA	PCT.
Howell, Mississippi St.	217	382	.568
Inniss, St. Francis (NY)	189	337	.561
Roth, Muhlenberg	162	298	.544
Holtsma, William & Mary	117	216	.542
Ellis, Niagara	209	389	.537
Crosthwaite, Western Ky.	185	349	.530
Francis, Dartmouth	127	243	.523

Downs, Texas	155	298	.520
Richter, N.C. St.	136	262	.519
Nymeyer, Arizona	153	298	.513
Embry, Miami (Ohio)	224	437	.513

FREE THROW PERCENTAGE

PLAYER	FTM	FTA	PCT.
Wiggins, Wake Forest	93	108	.877
Murdock, Wake Forest	161	184	.875
Seitz, N.C. St.	95	109	.872
Ricketts, Duquesne	150	174	.862
Plump, Butler	160	186	.860
Forte, Columbia	224	263	.852
Novalesi, St. Francis (Pa.)	90	106	.849
Simmons, Idaho	101	119	.849
Steinke, Brigham Young	105	124	.847
Dees, Indiana	176	209	.842

1956–57 TEAM LEADERS

SCORING OFFENSE

SCHOOL	PTS.	AVG.
Connecticut	2183	87.3
Ohio	2004	87.1
Marshall	2070	86.3
Memphis St.	2562	85.4
Morehead St.	2301	85.2

SCORING DEFENSE

SCHOOL	PTS.	AVG.
Oklahoma A&M	1420	54.6
San Francisco	1560	55.7
California	1484	57.1
Santa Clara	1260	57.3
Kansas	1583	58.6

FIELD GOAL PERCENTAGE

SCHOOL	FGM	FGA	PCT.
Manhattan	679	1489	.456
Seattle	742	1644	.451
Western Kentucky	802	1788	.449
Lafayette	776	1736	.447
Niagara	756	1693	.447

FREE THROW PERCENTAGE

SCHOOL	FTM	FTA	PCT.
Oklahoma A&M	569	752	.757
Auburn	479	648	.739
Tulane	459	622	.738
Wake Forest	610	827	.738
Memphis St.	714	971	.735
Louisville	513	698	.735

REBOUNDING

SCHOOL	TOT. REB.	REB.	PCT.
Morehead St.	2796	1735	.621
Seattle	2165	1307	.604
Dartmouth	2381	1414	.594
Louisville	2270	1327	.585
Dayton	2871	1676	.584

1956-57 UNDEFEATED TEAM: NORTH CAROLINA (32-0)

COACH: FRANK MCGUIRE

UNC	OPPONENT		UNC'S HIGH SCORER
94	Furman	66	Rosenbluth 47
94	Clemson*	75	Brennan 28
82	George Washington	55	Rosenbluth 27
90	at South Carolina	86	Kearns 29
70	Maryland	61	Rosenbluth 26
64	at New York University	59	Cunningham 16
89	Dartmouth*	61	Rosenbluth 30
83	Holy Cross*	70	Rosenbluth 23
97	Utah*	76	Rosenbluth 36
87	Duke*	71	Rosenbluth 32
63	Wake Forest*	55	Rosenbluth 18
71	at William & Mary	61	Brennan 20
86	Clemson	54	Rosenbluth 34
102	Virginia	90	Rosenbluth 30
83	at North Carolina St.	57	Rosenbluth 29
77	at Western Carolina	59	Rosenbluth 26
65	at Maryland (2OT)	61	Rosenbluth 25
75	Duke	73	Rosenbluth 35
68	at Virginia	59	Rosenbluth 23
72	Wake Forest	69	Rosenbluth 24
86	North Carolina State	57	Rosenbluth 28
75	South Carolina	62	Brennan 26
69	at Wake Forest	64	Rosenbluth 30
86	at Duke	72	Rosenbluth 40

ACC TOURNAMENT

81	Clemson*	61	Rosenbluth 45
61	Wake Forest*	59	Rosenbluth 23
95	South Carolina*	75	Rosenbluth 38

NCAA TOURNAMENT

90	Yale*	74	Rosenbluth 29
87	Canisius*	75	Rosenbluth 39
67	Syracuse*	58	Rosenbluth 23
74	Michigan State* (3OT)	70	Rosenbluth 31
54	Kansas* (3OT)	53	Rosenbluth 20

*Neutral court games.

ed Mississippi State twice, Western Kentucky twice and highly-ranked Louisville.

1957 NCAA Tournament

Summary: A championship game frequently misconstrued as an enormous upset was North Carolina's 54-53 triple-overtime victory against the Wilt Chamberlain-led Kansas. After all, Carolina was undefeated that season (32-0), winning 22 games by at least nine points, and the Tar Heels' top three scorers wound up playing in the NBA, albeit briefly—forwards Lennie Rosenbluth and Pete Brennan and guard Tommy Kearns. Junior center Joe Quigg sank two free throws with six seconds remaining in the third overtime to tie the score and provide the decisive point as North Carolina nipped Kansas, 54-53. Carolina won the national championship by an average of 8.4 points after winning five of its last 11 games against ACC competition by five points or less. The Tar Heels did not outscore their opponents in both halves of any of their five playoff victories, but Rosenbluth bailed them out by scoring at least 20 points in every game. Rosenbluth was Carolina's leading scorer in 27 of their 32 contests, although the Tar Heels won the triple-overtime final after he fouled out with 1:45 remaining in regulation.

Outcome for Defending Champion: San Francisco (22-7) was clobbered by Kansas, 80-56, in the national semifinals. The Dons won their first five games of the season before losing five of their next six.

Star Gazing: Carolina coach Frank McGuire became the first coach to take two different schools to the NCAA championship game. He guided St. John's to a second-place finish in 1952.

Biggest Upset: Kentucky, ranked No. 3 entering the tourney, blew a 12-point halftime lead in an 80-68 setback to Michigan State in the Mideast Regional final. It was only the Wildcats' fifth defeat on their homecourt since 1943.

One and Only: North Carolina became the only school to play in back-to-back triple-overtime games in the playoffs. The Lead in the Tar Heels' 74-70 triumph over Michigan State in the national semifinals changed hands 31 times and the score was tied on 21 occasions. The Spartans' Jack Quiggle made a halfcourt shot that came just after the final buzzer in regulation. Teammate Johnny Green missed a free throw with 11 seconds remaining in the first overtime that would have sealed the verdict for MSU. Brennan grabbed Green's miss. Instead of tossing the ball out to a guard as Brennan normally would do, he dribbled downcourt and hit a game-tying jumper from the foul line at the buzzer.

Numbers Game: Dick Harp became the only individual to play in an NCAA Tournament championship game (with Kansas in 1940 when the Jayhawks lost to Indiana) and later coach his alma mater to a final (KU lost to North Carolina).

Michigan State outrebounded San Francisco (47-6) yet lost the national third-place game to USF, 67-60. The Spartans reached the Final Four despite losing five of six games in a mid-season swoon. . . . Oklahoma City became the first school to participate in six consecutive NCAA playoffs. . . . Rosenbluth fired in a tourney-high 39 points in North Carolina's 87-75 victory over Canisius in the East Regional semifinals. His 42 field-goal attempts (hit 11) in the national semifinals against Michigan State is a Final Four record.

Putting Things in Perspective: Kansas was fortunate SMU shot just 32.1 percent from the floor in their Midwest Regional opener at Dallas. Long before Georgetown tried to minimize distractions, the Jayhawks stayed 30 miles out of

---

1956–57 NCAA CHAMPION: N. CAROLINA

SEASON STATISTICS OF NORTH CAROLINA REGULARS

PLAYER	POS.	CL.	G.	FG%	FT%	PPG	RPG
Lennie Rosenbluth	F	Sr.	32	.483	.758	28.0	8.8
Pete Brennan	F	Jr.	32	.394	.706	14.7	10.4
Tommy Kearns	G	Jr.	32	.434	.711	12.8	3.1
Joe Quigg	C	Jr.	31	.434	.719	10.3	8.6
Bob Cunningham	G	Jr.	32	.393	.598	7.2	6.7
Tony Radovich	G	Sr.	16	.525	.769	3.9	1.8
Bill Hathaway	C	So.	15	.333	.417	2.8	5.0
Stan Groll	G	So.	12	.370	.556	2.1	1.5
Bob Young	C	Sr.	15	.256	.538	1.9	2.1
Ken Rosemond	G	Jr.	15	.400	.556	1.1	0.6
Danny Lotz	F	So.	24	.350	.391	1.0	1.6
TEAM TOTALS			32	.431	.701	79.3	46.7

1957 FINAL FOUR CHAMPIONSHIP GAME

KANSAS CITY, MO

NORTH CAROLINA (54)	FG-A	FT-A	REB.	PF	PTS.
Rosenbluth	8-15	4-4	5	5	20
Cunningham	0-3	0-1	5	4	0
Brennan	4-8	3-7	11	3	11
Kearns	4-8	3-7	1	4	11
Quigg	4-10	2-3	9	4	10
Lotz	0-0	0-0	2	0	0
Young	1-1	0-0	3	1	2
Team			6		
TOTALS	**21-45**	**12-22**	**42**	**21**	**54**

FG%: .467. **FT%:** .545.

KANSAS (53)	FG-A	FT-A	REB.	PF	PTS.
Chamberlain	6-13	11-16	14	3	23
King	3-12	5-6	4	4	11
Elstun	4-12	3-6	4	2	11
Parker	2-4	0-0	0	0	4
Loneski	0-5	2-3	3	2	2
L. Johnson	0-1	2-2	0	1	2
Billings	0-0	0-0	0	2	0
Team			3		
TOTALS	**15-47**	**23-33**	**28**	**14**	**53**

FG%: .319. **FT%:** .697.
Halftime: North Carolina 29-22. **Regulation:** Tied 46-46. **First Overtime:** Tied 48-48. **Second Overtime:** Tied 48-48.

NATIONAL SEMIFINALS

NORTH CAROLINA (74): Rosenbluth 11-42 7-9 29, Cunningham 9-18 3-5 21, Brennan 6-16 2-4 14, Kearns 1-8 4-5 6, Quigg 0-1 2-3 2, Lotz 0-1 0-0 0, Young 1-3 0-1 2, Searcy 0-0 0-0 0. Team 28-89 (.315) 18-27 (.667) 74.

MICHIGAN STATE (70): Quiggle 6-21 8-10 20, Green 4-12 3-6 11, Ferguson 4-8 2-3 10, Hedden 4-20 6-7 14, Wilson 0-3 2-2 2, Andergg 2-7 3-6 7, Bencie 1-6 0-0 2, Scott 2-3 0-2 4. Team 23-80 (.288) 24-36 (.667) 70.

Halftime: Tied 29-29. **Regulation:** Tied 58-58. **First Overtime:** Tied 64-64. **Second Overtime:** Tied 66-66.

KANSAS (80): M. King 6-8 1-1 13, Elstun 8-12 0-0 16, Chamberlain 12-22 8-11 32, Parker 1-1 0-0 2, Loneski 2-6 3-4 7, L. Johnson 1-3 0-2 2, Billings 0-1 0-0 0, Hollinger 1-1 0-1 2, Dater 1-1 0-0 2, Green 1-1 0-0 2, Kindred 0-0 0-2 0, M. Johnson 1-1 0-0 2. Team 34-57 (.597) 12-19 (.632) 80.

SAN FRANCISCO (56): Day 3-14 3-8 9, Dunbar 2-8 0-0 4, Brown 5-14 0-0 10, Farmer 6-15 2-2 14, Preaseau 5-8 2-2 12, Mallen 0-2 0-0 0, L. Johnson 1-3 0-2 2, Koljian 0-1 3-4 3, J. King 0-3 0-0 0, Russell 0-0 0-0 0, Radanovich 0-0 0-1 0, Mancasola 1-2 0-0 2. Team 23-71 (.324) 10-16 (.625) 56.

Halftime: Kansas 38-34.

ALL-TOURNAMENT TEAM

Pete Brennan, F, Jr., North Carolina
Gene Brown, G, Jr., San Francisco
Wilt Chamberlain, C, Soph., Kansas
Johnny Green, C, Soph., Michigan State
Lennie Rosenbluth, F, Sr., North Carolina
*Named Most Outstanding Player

1957 CHAMPIONSHIP BRACKET

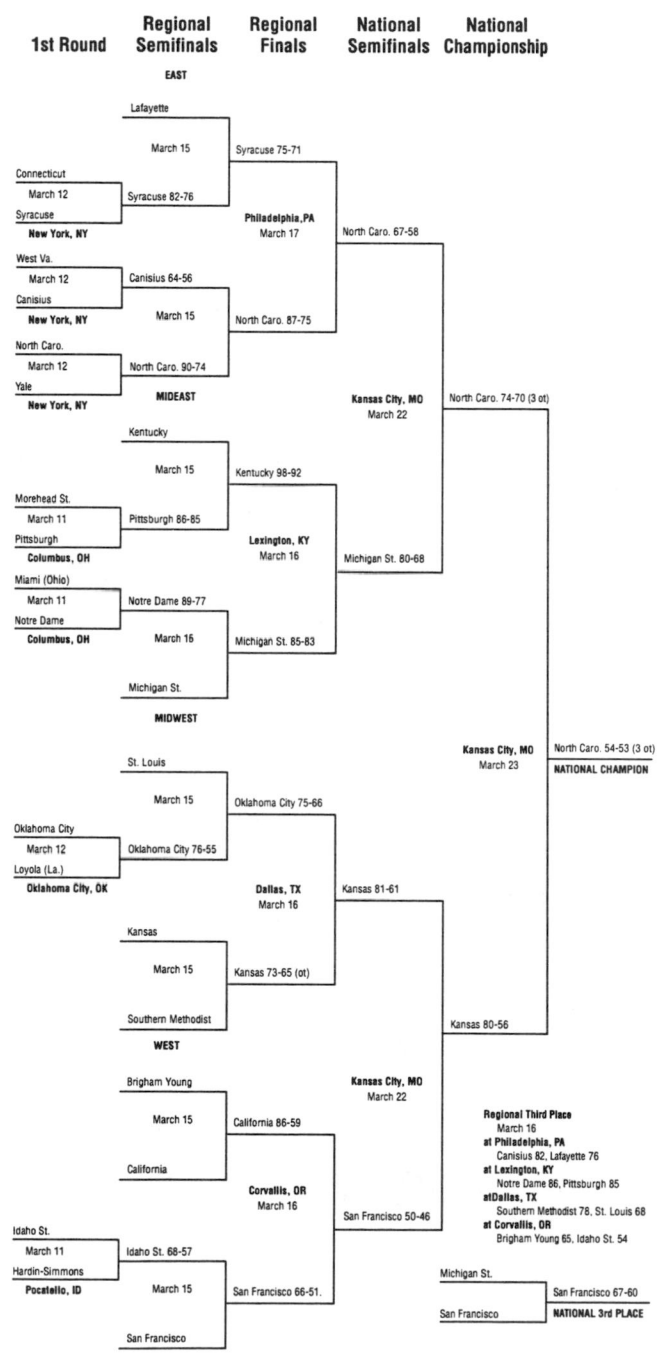

1st Round	Regional Semifinals	Regional Finals	National Semifinals	National Championship

EAST

Lafayette

March 15 — Syracuse 75-71

Connecticut
March 12
Syracuse — Syracuse 82-76
New York, NY

Philadelphia, PA
March 17 — North Caro. 67-58

West Va.
March 12
Canisius — Canisius 64-56
New York, NY

March 15 — North Caro. 87-75

North Caro.
March 12
Yale — North Caro. 90-74
New York, NY

North Caro. 74-70 (3 ot)

MIDEAST

Kentucky

March 15 — Kentucky 98-92

Kansas City, MO
March 22 — North Caro. 74-70 (3 ot)

Morehead St.
March 11
Pittsburgh — Pittsburgh 86-85
Columbus, OH

Lexington, KY
March 16 — Michigan St. 80-68

Miami (Ohio)
March 11
Notre Dame — Notre Dame 89-77
Columbus, OH

March 16 — Michigan St. 85-83

Michigan St.

MIDWEST

Kansas City, MO
March 23 — North Caro. 54-53 (3 ot)
NATIONAL CHAMPION

St. Louis

March 15 — Oklahoma City 75-66

Oklahoma City
March 12
Loyola (La.) — Oklahoma City 76-55
Oklahoma City, OK

Dallas, TX
March 16 — Kansas 81-61

Kansas

March 15 — Kansas 73-65 (ot)

Southern Methodist

Kansas 80-56

WEST

Brigham Young

March 15 — California 86-59

Kansas City, MO
March 22

California

Corvallis, OR
March 16 — San Francisco 50-46

Idaho St.
March 11
Hardin-Simmons — Idaho St. 68-57
Pocatello, ID

March 15 — San Francisco 66-51.

San Francisco

Regional Third Place
March 16
at Philadelphia, PA
Canisius 82, Lafayette 76
at Lexington, KY
Notre Dame 86, Pittsburgh 85
at Dallas, TX
Southern Methodist 78, St. Louis 68
at Corvallis, OR
Brigham Young 65, Idaho St. 54

Michigan St. — San Francisco 67-60

San Francisco — **NATIONAL 3rd PLACE**

town, but some bigots still burned a cross in a yard across from their lodging quarters. And narrow-minded fans at the game punctuated the contest with racial slurs.

Scoring Leader: Lennie Rosenbluth, North Carolina (140 points, 28 ppg).

Highest Scoring Average: Wilt Chamberlain, Kansas (121 points, 30.25 ppg).

Rebounding Leader: Johnny Green, Michigan State (77 rebounds, 19.3 rpg).

1957–58

AT A GLANCE

NCAA Champion: Kentucky (23-6; coached by Adolph Rupp; won SEC title with a 12-2 record, which was one game ahead of Auburn).

NIT Champion: Xavier (19-11; coached by Jim McCafferty).

New Rules: Offensive goaltending is banned. One free throw for each common foul is taken the first six personal fouls by one team in each half, and the one-and-one is employed thereafter. Uniform numbers "1," "2," and any digit greater than "5" are prohibited.

NCAA Probation: Auburn, Florida, Louisville, Memphis State, Montana State, North Carolina State, UCLA, Washington.

NCAA Consensus First-Team All-Americans: Elgin Baylor, F-C, Jr., Seattle; Bob Boozer, F, Jr., Kansas State; Wilt Chamberlain, C, Jr., Kansas; Don Hennon, G, Jr., Pittsburgh; Oscar Robertson, F, Soph., Cincinnati; Guy Rodgers, G, Sr., Temple.

National Player of the Year: Robertson (35.1 ppg, 15.2 rpg, 57.1 FG%).

National Coach of the Year: Tex Winter, Kansas State (22-5/UPI).

Undergraduates stole the spotlight from seniors. Temple guard Guy Rodgers was the only senior among the six NCAA consensus first-team All-Americans.

The three major-college players to average more than 30 points per game this season—Cincinnati's Oscar Robertson (35.1), Seattle's Elgin Baylor (32.5) and Kansas' Wilt Chamberlain (30.1)—each went on to become an All-NBA selection at least 10 times. Baylor finished his college career with an amazing average of more than 50 points and rebounds per game.

Baylor and Robertson each had four games during the year with at least 47 points. Baylor's 60-point uprising against Portland was the highest in the nation. Robertson, Baylor and Chamberlain all averaged more than 15 rebounds per game. Chamberlain set Big Eight Conference records with 36 rebounds against Iowa State (also a school standard) and for scoring average. Robertson is one of only two individuals to be

HUSKERS AVENGE 56-POINT DEFEAT Was it a magic potion? The sad-sack Nebraska Cornhuskers, suffering through another losing season, had been walloped by the Kansas Jayhawks four games earlier, 102-46. But playing in front of their home crowd on February 22, 1958, the Huskers upset the Jayhawks, 43-41. Maybe they had something against the state of Kansas—in their next game, they beat up on No. 1-ranked Kansas State, 55-48.

KANSAS (41)	FG	FT-A	PTS.	NEBRASKA (43)	FG	FT-A	PTS.
Chamberlain	7	4-8	18	Arwood	0	0-1	0
Cleland	0	0-0	0	Fitzpatrick	3	1-1	7
Donaghue	4	1-2	9	Harry	1	0-3	2
Hickman	0	0-0	0	Kubacki	1	0-0	2
J. Johnson	1	1-1	3	Reimers	4	6-8	14
Kindred	1	0-0	2	Smidt	1	4-4	6
Loneski	3	3-6	9	Turner	4	4-7	12
Thompson	0	0-0	0	**TOTALS**	**14**	**15-24**	**43**
TOTALS	**16**	**9-17**	**41**				

Halftime: Nebraska 27-21.

named national player of the year in his first season of varsity competition. The Big O outscored Seton Hall by himself with 56 points in a 118-54 verdict that represents the Pirates' most lopsided defeat in history.

Chamberlain's final college season included one of the most amazing turnarounds in NCAA annals. Nebraska, in the midst of 15 consecutive losing seasons, suffered its most lopsided defeat in school history (margin of 56 points in a 102-46 decision at Kansas) before upsetting the Jayhawks (43-41) four games later in Omaha when backup guard Jim Kubacki hit a 15-foot basket with two seconds remaining. Kubacki, a senior, spent all but the final seven minutes of the game sitting on the bench in street clothes because of a knee injury. When teammate Gary Reimers left the game with leg cramps, Kubacki convinced coach Jerry Bush to let him suit up. Four minutes later, Kubacki entered the game. Nearly three minutes after that, he furnished the fairy-tale ending (see accompanying box). In the Cornhuskers' next outing, they defeated top-ranked Kansas State (55-48), a team that had overwhelmed them by a total of 46 points in two previous matchups.

In Kansas' ensuing contest, the Jayhawks were saddled with their most lopsided defeat in Chamberlain's two-year varsity career when they bowed at Iowa State by six points (48-42). KU's other seven setbacks with Wilt were by two points or in overtime.

Oklahoma lost its last three games but compiled a 13-10 record to end a streak of six consecutive losing seasons. . . . Indiana entered Big Ten competition with a 1-6 record yet won the conference championship. . . . Drake's Red Murrell (51 points vs. Houston in overtime), Lafayette's Bobby Mantz (47 vs. Wilkes) and Marquette's Mike Moran (44 vs. Creighton/later tied) set school single-game scoring records.

Cincinnati's Robertson, Kansas' Chamberlain, Pittsburgh's Don Hennon (26 ppg) and Fordham's Jim Cunningham (25.1) established school records for highest scoring average in a single season.

North Carolina's ACC-record 37-game winning streak ended when the Tar Heels lost to West Virginia, 75-64, in the championship game of the Kentucky Invitational. . . . Maryland, coached by Bud Millikan, became the only school outside the state of North Carolina to win the ACC Tournament in the first 17 years of the event (1954 through 1970). . . . Tennessee Tech, coached by John Oldham, captured the Ohio Valley Conference crown just one season after finishing in last place. . . . Tulane suffered its first losing record (8-15) in 13 seasons.

Dartmouth's Rudy LaRusso grabbed an Ivy League-record 32 rebounds in a game against Columbia. . . . Duquesne defeated Villanova nine consecutive times until bowing to the Wildcats, 69-58. . . . Canisius compiled a 2-19 mark just one year after going 22-6. . . . Seton Hall incurred its only losing record (7-19) in a 14-year span from 1950-51 through 1963-64.

1957-58 FINAL NATIONAL POLLS

AP	UPI	SCHOOL (RECORD)	HEAD COACH
1	1	West Virginia (26-2)	Fred Schaus
2	2	Cincinnati (25-3)	George Smith
3	4	Kansas State (22-5)	Tex Winter
4	3	San Francisco (25-2)	Phil Woolpert
5	5	Temple (27-3)	Harry Litwack
6	6	Maryland (22-7)	Bud Millikan
7	8	Kansas (18-5)	Dick Harp
8	7	Notre Dame (24-5)	John Jordan
9	14	Kentucky (23-6)	Adolph Rupp
10	13	Duke (18-7)	Harold Bradley
11	9	Dayton (25-4)	Tom Blackburn
12	10	Indiana (13-11)	Branch McCracken
13	12	North Carolina (19-7)	Frank McGuire
14	11	Bradley (20-7)	Chuck Orsborn
15	–	Mississippi State (20-5)	Babe McCarthy
16	–	Auburn (16-6)	Joel Eaves
17	19	Michigan State (16-6)	Forddy Anderson
18	19	Seattle (24-7)	John Castellani
19	15	Oklahoma State (21-8)	Hank Iba
20	16	N.C. State (18-6)	Everett Case
–	16	Oregon State (20-6)	Slats Gill
–	18	St. Bonaventure (21-5)	Eddie Donovan
–	19	Wyoming (13-14)	Everett Shelton

Xavier upset the top three seeds on its way to the NIT title—No. 2 Bradley (72-62), No. 3 St. Bonaventure (72-53) and top-seeded Dayton (78-74 in overtime). It was the fifth time in eight seasons that Dayton reached the NIT final and lost.

1957–58 INDIVIDUAL LEADERS

SCORING

PLAYER	PTS.	AVG.
Robertson, Cincinnati	984	35.1
Baylor, Seattle	943	32.5
Chamberlain, Kansas	633	30.1
Howell, Mississippi St.	695	27.8
Murrell, Drake	668	26.7
Coleman, Ky. Wesleyan	639	26.6
Hennon, Pittsburgh	651	26.0
Reed, Oklahoma City	666	25.6
Dees, Indiana	613	25.5
Flora, Washington & Lee	634	25.4

REBOUNDING

PLAYER	REB.	PCT.
Ellis, Niagara	536	.262
Inniss, St. Francis (NY)	477	.248

Baylor, Seattle	559	.235
Chamberlain, Kansas	367	.216
Cincebox, Syracuse	345	.206
McCadney, Fordham	351	.205
Embry, Miami (Ohio)	488	.202
Green, Michigan St.	392	.199
Howell, Mississippi St.	406	.198
Hamilton, Morehead St.	440	.195

FIELD GOAL PERCENTAGE

PLAYER	FGM	FGA	PCT.
Crosthwaite, W. Ky.	202	331	.610
Robertson, Cincinnati	352	617	.571
Brunone, Manhattan	100	178	.562
Goodall, Tulsa	108	194	.557
Greer, Marshall	236	432	.546
Clark, Oklahoma St.	171	317	.539
Mantz, Lafayette	190	354	.537

Aston, St. Francis (Pa.)	120	226	.531
Cunningham, Fordham	176	332	.530
McDonald, G. Wash.	165	314	.525

FREE THROW PERCENTAGE

PLAYER	FTM	FTA	PCT.
Mintz, Davidson	105	119	.882
Myers, Texas Tech	107	123	.870
Clark, Oklahoma St.	160	185	.865
Hobbs, Florida	98	114	.860
Reed, Oklahoma City	206	242	.851
Sidwell, Tennessee Tech	100	118	.847
McCarthy, Notre Dame	132	156	.846
Kennedy, Temple	112	133	.842
Walsh, Detroit	99	118	.839
Adair, Oklahoma St.	97	116	.836
Hennon, Pittsburgh	117	140	.836

1957–58 TEAM LEADERS

SCORING OFFENSE

SCHOOL	PTS.	AVG.
Marshall	2113	88.0
West Virginia	2433	86.9
Cincinnati	2422	86.5
Kentucky Wesleyan	1993	83.0
Notre Dame	2374	81.9

SCORING DEFENSE

SCHOOL	PTS.	AVG.
San Francisco	1363	50.5
Oklahoma St.	1500	51.7
Kansas	1273	55.3
Providence	1332	55.5
Oregon St.	1449	55.7

FIELD GOAL PERCENTAGE

SCHOOL	FGM	FGA	PCT.
Fordham	693	1440	.481
Cincinnati	910	1895	.480
Marshall	817	1740	.470
Seattle	938	2014	.466
Oklahoma St.	620	1346	.461

FREE THROW PERCENTAGE

SCHOOL	FTM	FTA	PCT.
Oklahoma St.	488	617	.791
Marshall	479	608	.788
Oklahoma City	503	667	.754
Stanford	448	603	.743
Kentucky	502	680	.738

REBOUNDING

SCHOOL	TOTAL REB.	REB.	PCT.
Manhattan	2430	1437	.591
Morehead St.	2262	1331	.588
Seattle	2380	1400	.588
Texas Christian	2162	1253	.580
Muhlenberg	2143	1239	.578

The championship game marked one of only two NIT finals matching two schools from the same state (Indiana-Purdue in 1979 was the other). . . . Air Force (17-6, coached by Bob Spear) notched its winningest season in school history. Dartmouth (22-5, Doggie Julian) tied its school record for most victories in a single season. . . . Wyoming (13-14) became the only school with a losing record ever to finish in the Top 20 of a final wire-service poll (19th in UPI). . . . NYU's Howard Cann ended his 35-year coaching career with a 409-232 record.

1958 NCAA Tournament

Summary: Would Kentucky's storied "Fiddlin' Five," a team equaling the most defeats (six) of any Wildcats squad in the previous 15 seasons, snared the title if it didn't enjoy a home-state edge throughout the playoffs (Mideast Regional at Lexington and Final Four at Louisville)? Didn't a highly-partisan crowd give them an emotional lift in the national semi-finals when they trailed Temple by four points and the Owls had the ball with less than a minute and half remaining? UK benefitted from a sub-par performance by Seattle's Elgin Baylor in the national final, where he went 9 for 32 from the floor. Baylor was named Final Four Most Outstanding Player although the award could have gone to Kentucky's Johnny Cox, who collected 22 points and 13 rebounds in a 61-60 victory over Temple and 24 points and 16 rebounds in an 84-72 triumph over Seattle.

Outcome for Defending Champion: North

Carolina (19-7) tied for second place in the ACC after starting center Joe Quigg was sidelined his entire senior season following a leg injury in the team's first big scrimmage. Six of the Tar Heels' defeats were by more than 10 points.

Biggest Upset: West Virginia, ranked No. 1 in the country at the end of the regular season, was upset by Manhattan in the opening round of the East Regional at New York. Jack Powers, the current executive director of the NIT, collected 29 points and 15 rebounds to carry Manhattan (16-10) to an 89-84 victory. Jerry West scored just 10 points in his first NCAA Tournament game for West Virginia, which finished the season with the best winning percentage in school history (26-2, .929).

One and Only: Cox, a 6-4 forward, is the shortest player to lead an NCAA Tournament champion in rebounding (12.6 per game) since the NCAA began keeping rebounding statistics in the early 1950s.

Numbers Game: Arkansas' lone tournament appearance in a 35-year span from 1942 through 1976 was a disaster as the Razorbacks were drilled in two games by Oklahoma State and Cincinnati by an average of 30 points. Cincinnati's Oscar Robertson poured in 56 points in a 97-62 blowout of the Hogs in the Midwest Regional third-place game. . . . Notre Dame grabbed an NCAA playoff-record 86 rebounds in a 94-61 trouncing of Tennessee Tech in the opening round of the Mideast Regional. The Irish had six players with at least eight rebounds, including a game-high 21 by John McCarthy.

What If: West Virginia captain Don Vincent, averaging 12.8 points per game, broke his left leg in the Southern Conference Tournament. The Mountaineers had won by seven points against

1957–58 NCAA CHAMPION: KENTUCKY

SEASON STATISTICS OF KENTUCKY REGULARS

PLAYER	POS.	CL.	G.	FG%	FT%	PPG	RPG
Vern Hatton	G	Sr.	29	.419	.778	17.1	5.0
Johnny Cox	F	Jr.	29	.367	.748	14.9	12.6
John Crigler	F	Sr.	28	.405	.707	13.6	9.9
Adrian Smith	G	Sr.	29	.371	.765	12.4	3.5
Ed Beck	C	Sr.	29	.283	.722	5.6	11.6
Earl Adkins	G	Sr.	19	.453	.742	5.3	1.5
Don Mills	C	So.	20	.253	.625	3.5	5.0
Phil Johnson	F-C	Jr.	22	.306	.517	3.4	5.7
TEAM TOTALS			29	.373	.738	74.7	53.9

1958 FINAL FOUR CHAMPIONSHIP GAME

LOUISVILLE, KY

KENTUCKY (84)	FG-A	FT-A	REB.	PF	PTS.
Cox	10-23	4-4	16	3	24
Crigler	5-12	4-7	14	4	14
Beck	0-1	0-1	3	4	0
Mills	4-9	1-4	5	3	9
Hatton	9-20	12-15	3	3	30
Smith	2-8	3-5	6	4	7
Team			8		
TOTALS	30-73	24-36	55	21	84

FG%: .411. FT%: .667.

SEATTLE (72)	FG-A	FT-A	REB.	PF	PTS.
Frizzell	4-6	8-11	5	3	16
Ogorek	4-7	2-2	11	5	10
Baylor	9-32	7-9	19	4	25
Harney	2-5	0-1	1	1	4
Brown	6-17	5-7	5	5	17
Saunders	0-2	0-0	2	3	0
Piasecki	0-0	0-0	0	0	0
Team			3		
TOTALS	25-69	22-30	46	21	72

FG%: .362. FT%: .733.
Halftime: Seattle 39-36.

NATIONAL SEMIFINALS

KENTUCKY (61): Crigler 3-11 0-2 6, Cox 6-17 10-11 22, Collinsworth 0-0 0-0 0, Beck 3-9 2-2 8, Hatton 5-16 3-4 13, Smith 2-10 8-9 12. Team 19-63 (.302) 23-28 (.821) 61.

TEMPLE (60): Norman 7-17 2-3 16, Brodsky 2-5 0-2 4, Van Patton 1-1 1-2 3, Fleming 3-7 3-6 9, Rodgers 9-24 4-6 22, Kennedy 3-7 0-1 6. Team 25-61 (.410) 10-20 (.500) 60.

Halftime: Tied 31-31.

SEATTLE (73): Ogorek 3-9 1-2 7, Frizzell 2-4 6-7 10, Petrie 0-0 0-0 0, Baylor 9-21 5-7 23, Humphries 0-0 0-0 0, Harney 0-4 0-0 0, Brown 5-6 4-5 14, Saunders 5-11 2-3 12, Piasecki 1-1 3-4 5, Kootnekoff 1-1 0-0 2. Team 26-57 (.456) 21-28 (.750) 73.

KANSAS STATE (51): Boozer 6-15 3-5 15, Frank 6-12 3-4 12, Abbott 0-4 0-0 0, Long 2-6 0-1 4, Fischer 0-1 0-0 0, Parr 2-11 0-1 4, Matuszak 3-8 1-3 7, DeWitz 2-7 2-3 6, Holwerda 0-2 0-0 0. Team 21-66 (.318) 9-17 (.529) 51.

Halftime: Seattle 37-32.

ALL-TOURNAMENT TEAM
Elgin Baylor, C, Jr., Seattle*
Charley Brown, G, Jr., Seattle
Johnny Cox, F, Jr., Kentucky
Vernon Hatton, G, Sr., Kentucky
Guy Rodgers, G, Sr., Temple
*Named Most Outstanding Player

1958 CHAMPIONSHIP BRACKET

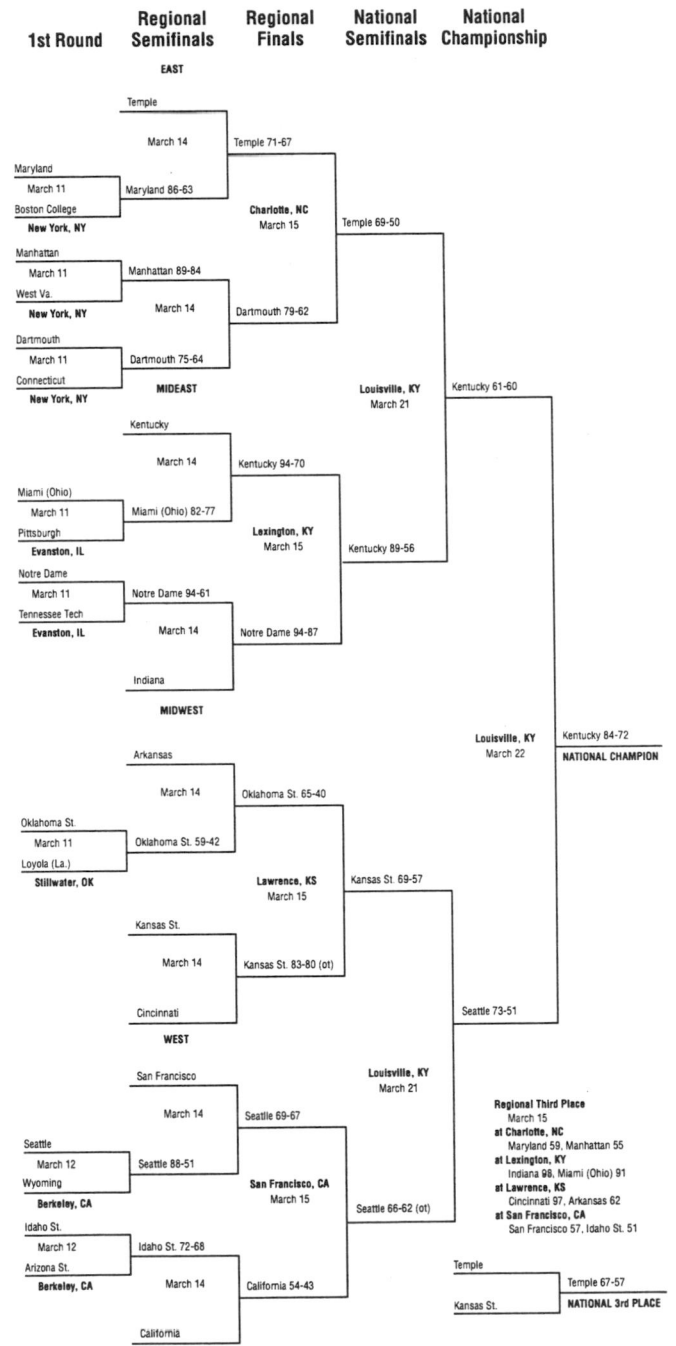

	1st Round	Regional Semifinals	Regional Finals	National Semifinals	National Championship

EAST

Temple

March 14 — Temple 71-67

Maryland
March 11 — Maryland 86-63
Boston College
New York, NY

Charlotte, NC
March 15 — Temple 69-50

Manhattan
March 11 — Manhattan 89-84
West Va.
New York, NY

March 14 — Dartmouth 79-62

Dartmouth
March 11 — Dartmouth 75-64
Connecticut
New York, NY

Louisville, KY
March 21 — Kentucky 61-60

MIDEAST

Kentucky

March 14 — Kentucky 94-70

Miami (Ohio)
March 11 — Miami (Ohio) 82-77
Pittsburgh
Evanston, IL

Lexington, KY
March 15 — Kentucky 89-56

Notre Dame
March 11 — Notre Dame 94-61
Tennessee Tech
Evanston, IL

March 14 — Notre Dame 94-87

Indiana

MIDWEST

Louisville, KY
March 22 — Kentucky 84-72
NATIONAL CHAMPION

Arkansas

March 14 — Oklahoma St. 65-40

Oklahoma St.
March 11 — Oklahoma St. 59-42
Loyola (La.)
Stillwater, OK

Lawrence, KS
March 15 — Kansas St. 69-57

Kansas St.

March 14 — Kansas St. 83-80 (ot)

Cincinnati

WEST

Seattle 73-51

San Francisco

March 14 — Seattle 69-67

Seattle
March 12 — Seattle 88-51
Wyoming
Berkeley, CA

San Francisco, CA
March 15

Louisville, KY
March 21 — Seattle 66-62 (ot)

Idaho St.
March 12 — Idaho St. 72-68
Arizona St.
Berkeley, CA

March 14 — California 54-43

California

Regional Third Place
March 15
at Charlotte, NC
Maryland 59, Manhattan 55
at Lexington, KY
Indiana 98, Miami (Ohio) 91
at Lawrence, KS
Cincinnati 97, Arkansas 62
at San Francisco, CA
San Francisco 57, Idaho St. 51

Temple

Temple 67-57

Kansas St.

NATIONAL 3rd PLACE

NCAA champion-to-be Kentucky, handing the Wildcats just their fifth homecourt defeat in 15 years.

Scoring Leader: Elgin Baylor, Seattle (135 points, 27 ppg).

Highest Scoring Average: Oscar Robertson, Cincinnati (86 points, 43 ppg).

Rebounding Leader: Elgin Baylor, Seattle (91 rebounds, 18.2 rpg).

1958-59

AT A GLANCE

NCAA Champion: California (25-4; coached by Pete Newell; won PCC title with a 14-2 record, which was three games ahead of Washington).

NIT Champion: St. John's (20-6; coached by Joe Lapchick).

New Conference: Middle Atlantic (disbanded in 1974 when ECC is formed).

NCAA Probation: Auburn, Memphis State, North Carolina State, Seattle, Southern Cal, UCLA.

NCAA Consensus First-Team All-Americans: Bob Boozer, F, Sr., Kansas State; Johnny Cox, F, Sr., Kentucky; Bailey Howell, F, Sr., Mississippi State; Oscar Robertson, F, Jr., Cincinnati; Jerry West, F, Jr., West Virginia.

National Player of the Year: Robertson (32.6 ppg, 16.3 rpg, 50.9 FG%).

National Coach of the Year: Eddie Hickey, Marquette (23-6/USBWA).

Mississippi State's Bailey Howell set a school record with 47 points against Union. Mississippi State won its first SEC title with a 13-1 record and finished 24-1 overall, but was forced to bypass the NCAA Tournament because of the opposition of several state officials to interracial games.

Cincinnati's Oscar Robertson became the first player to lead the nation's scorers in both his sophomore and junior seasons. Robertson's brilliance wasn't enough to prevent the Bearcats from losing against California (64-58) in the national semifinals. Guard Mike Mendenhall, the team's co-captain and third-leading scorer (13.5-point average) as one of the nation's top 15 field-goal shooters (51.3 percent), was declared ineligible for the playoffs by the NCAA because he played briefly in the 1955–56 season before missing the remainder of the year nursing a kidney ailment. The season's highest single-game output was 50 points by Air Force's Bob Beckel (school record vs. Arizona) and Rhode Island's Tom Harrington (Brandeis/school record was later tied). Tennessee Tech's Jimmy Hagan established a school mark with 48 points against East Tennessee State (later tied). . . . Marshall's Leo Byrd (29.3 ppg) and Kansas State's Bob Boozer (25.6) set school records for highest scoring average in a single season.

Virginia Tech's Chris Smith (36 vs. Washington & Lee), Ohio University's Dave Scott (34 vs. Marietta), Tennessee Tech's Hagan (30 vs. Morehead State) and Princeton's Carl Belz (29 vs. Rutgers) established school single-game rebounding standards.

Oklahoma State's Arlen Clark set an NCAA record for most successful free throws in a game without a miss when he sank all 24 of his foul shots in a 42-point outburst against Colorado. . . . Kansas, minus All-American center Wilt Chamberlain after he bypassed his senior year of eligibility to join the Harlem Globetrotters, lost seven consecutive games in December. . . . Texas A&M (15-9) compiled a winning record for the first time in eight years.

North Carolina State coach Everett Case, compiling a 320-81 record through 13 seasons, had more victories than any coach in history from his second year through his 13th. . . . West Virginia (29-5, coached by Fred Schaus) went unbeaten in Southern Conference competition for the third consecutive year en route to its winningest season in school history. Kansas State (25-2, Tex Winter) and Dartmouth (22-6, Doggie

Cincinnati's national scoring leader Oscar Robertson comes down with a rebound.

Julian) tied their school records for most victories in a single season. A 22-3 Marquette squad that eventually reached the Mideast Regional final held the ball for the first 11 minutes of a game at Notre Dame. Tom Hawkins scored 18 of his game-high 19 points in the second half to carry the Irish to a 51-35 victory and conclude the season with a 12-13 record. The Warriors concluded the season with a 23-6 record in their year with Eddie Hickey as head coach. After guiding St. Louis to a 24-3 mark in his first season in 1947-48, the Billikens finished in the Top 20 of a final wire-service poll seven times in the next nine years.

Auburn, the only school to rank among the top 35 in both offense and defense, won its first 19 games under coach Joel Eaves before bowing at Kentucky and Tennessee. Auburn's loss at Kentucky snapped the Tigers' school-record 30-game winning streak. . . . Vanderbilt and visiting Baylor play the season finale using experimental rules such as the 24-second shot clock. Vanderbilt trails by as many as 11 points in the second half, but a jumper from the top of the circle by Doug Yates gives the Commodores a 61-60 triumph. "Frankly, I doubt we would have won the game had we been playing under existing rules," said Vandy coach Roy Skinner.

For the first time, Providence fans were able to follow their favorites on radio and the Friars

North Carolina State coach Everett Case and his Wolfpack were on NCAA probation in 1958–59.

made the most of the road opportunity, defeating nationally-ranked Villanova in four overtimes, 90-83, behind Johnny Egan's 39 points. . . . Villanova's George Raveling, who would go on to become one of the nation's most visible coaches, ranked among the top 25 players in the country in field-goal shooting (50.6 percent) and rebounding (15.5 per game). . . . Temple suffered its worst winning percentage in history (6-19, .240) just one year after winning 25 consecutive games en route to the Final Four. . . . Washington & Lee's final season at the Division I level was marred by a 105-24 defeat against Virginia Tech.

Eastern Kentucky won the Ohio Valley Conference crown after finishing in sixth place the previous year. . . . Tennessee Tech and St. Mary's made their lone appearance in the Top 20 of a final wire-service poll. . . . Northwestern,

1958–59 INDIVIDUAL LEADERS

SCORING

PLAYER	PTS.	AVG.
Robertson, Cincinnati	978	32.6
Byrd, Marshall	704	29.3
Hagan, Tennessee Tech	720	28.8
Howell, Mississippi St.	688	27.5
West, West Virginia	903	26.6
Ayersman, Virginia Tech	556	26.5
Hennon, Pittsburgh	617	25.7
Boozer, Kansas St.	691	25.6
Windis, Wyoming	463	24.4
Hawkins, Notre Dame	514	23.4

REBOUNDING

PLAYER	REB.	PCT.
Wright, Pacific	652	.238

Howell, Mississippi St.	379	.220
Smith, Virginia Tech	429	.202
Mealy, Manhattan	240	.201
Cohen, William & Mary	413	.200
Tormohlen, Tennessee	372	.192
Cincebox, Syracuse	365	.188
Danzig, Bucknell	386	.184
Washington, Boston	382	.183

FIELD GOAL PERCENTAGE

PLAYER	FGM	FGA	PCT.
Crosthwaite, W. Ky.	191	296	.645
Carter, Iona	137	225	.609
Kessler, Muhlenberg	153	271	.565
Herdelin, La Salle	144	256	.563
Sanders, New York	131	236	.555
Stith, St. Bonaventure	162	295	.549

Wilson, Furman	157	289	.543
McCraw, Oklahoma City	119	220	.541
Moses, Oklahoma City	158	293	.539
Price, New Mexico St.	209	401	.521

FREE THROW PERCENTAGE

PLAYER	FTM	FTA	PCT.
Clark, Oklahoma St.	201	236	.852
Burgess, Gonzaga	151	178	.848
Neumann, Stanford	127	150	.847
Kaiser, Georgia Tech	106	127	.835
Wendel, Tulsa	185	222	.833
Kennedy, Temple	184	221	.833
Guarilia, G. Wash.	99	119	.832
Siegfried, Ohio St.	136	164	.829
Hagan, Tennessee Tech	212	256	.828
Mills, Kentucky	101	122	.828

1958–59 TEAM LEADERS

SCORING OFFENSE

SCHOOL	PTS.	AVG.
Miami (Fla.)	2190	87.6
West Virginia	2884	84.8
Cincinnati	2519	84.0
Virginia Tech	1758	83.7
Illinois	1815	82.5

SCORING DEFENSE

SCHOOL	PTS.	AVG.
California	1480	51.0
Oklahoma St.	1319	52.8
Idaho St.	1504	53.7
San Jose St.	1352	56.3
Maryland	1296	56.4

FIELD GOAL PERCENTAGE

SCHOOL	FGM	FGA	PCT.
Auburn	593	1216	.488
Cincinnati	970	2062	.470
Oklahoma City	769	1680	.458
St. Bonaventure	724	1584	.457
West Virginia	1075	2355	.456
Mississippi St.	663	1453	.456

FREE THROW PERCENTAGE

SCHOOL	FTM	FTA	PCT.
Tulsa	446	586	.761
Mississippi St.	532	700	.760
George Washington	402	534	.753
Kentucky	570	758	.752
Marshall	472	631	.748

REBOUND PERCENTAGE

SCHOOL	TOT. REB.	REB.	PCT.
Mississippi St.	1719	1012	.589
Iona	1087	1856	.586
Michigan St.	2597	1508	.581
Eastern Kentucky	2346	1361	.580
Gonzaga	2473	1426	.577

coached by William Rohr, wound up in a tie for second place in the Big Ten standings with an 8-6 league record. That is the Wildcats' highest finish since 1934.

Washington won at Iowa, 81-68, to shatter the Hawkeyes' 77-game homecourt winning streak against non-conference opponents. . . . Pacific's Leroy Wright set a West Coast Conference record by averaging 25 rebounds per game. . . . Idaho defeated first-division teams Stanford and UCLA while competing as a member of the Pacific Coast Conference for the final season. . . . Arizona State lost more than 10 games in 13 consecutive seasons until stopping the hemorrhaging by compiling a 17-9 mark in Ned Wulk's second year as head coach. . . . Arizona lost a school-record 16 consecutive games in coach Fred Enke's 34th season with the Wildcats.

1958-59 FINAL NATIONAL POLLS

AP	UPI	SCHOOL (RECORD)	HEAD COACH
1	1	Kansas St. (25-2)	Tex Winter
2	2	Kentucky (24-3)	Adolph Rupp
3	6	Mississippi St. (24-1)	Babe McCarthy
4	8	Bradley (25-4)	Chuck Orsborn
5	4	Cincinnati (26-4)	George Smith
6	5	North Carolina St. (22-4)	Everett Case
7	3	Michigan St. (20-4)	Forddy Anderson
8	10	Auburn (20-2)	Joel Eaves
9	6	North Carolina (20-5)	Frank McGuire
10	11	West Virginia (29-5)	Fred Schaus
11	9	California (25-4)	Pete Newell
12	13	St. Louis (20-6)	John Bennington
13	–	Seattle (23-6)	Vince Cazzetta
14	20	St. Joseph's (22-5)	Jack Ramsay
15	18	St. Mary's (19-6)	Jim Weaver
16	12	Texas Christian (20-6)	Buster Brannon
17	–	Oklahoma City (20-7)	Abe Lemons
18	14	Utah (25-7)	Jack Gardner
19	–	St. Bonaventure (20-3)	Eddie Donovan
20	15	Marquette (23-6)	Eddie Hickey
–	16	Tennessee Tech (16-9)	John Oldham
–	17	St. John's (20-6)	Joe Lapchick
–	18	Navy (18-6)	Ben Carnevale

1959 NCAA Tournament

Summary: Two-time first-team All-American swingman Jerry West was denied an NCAA championship ring when Cal junior center Darrall Imhoff, West's teammate with the Los Angeles Lakers for four seasons in the mid-1960s, tipped in a basket with 17 seconds remaining to give California a 71-70 victory over West Virginia in the NCAA final.

Outcome for Defending Champion: Second-ranked Kentucky (24-3) hit less than one-third of its field-goal attempts in blowing a 15-point lead and absorbing a 76-61 setback against Louisville (19-12). The Wildcats' other two defeats were by a minimum of eight points at Vanderbilt and Mississippi State. Kentucky clobbered Marquette, 98-69, in the Mideast Regional consolation game to become the first school to win at least one game in five consecutive NCAA Tournaments.

Star Gazing: West collected a total of 66 points and 26 rebounds for West Virginia in the national semifinals and final.

Biggest Upset: Kansas State, an 85-75 loser against Cincinnati in the Midwest Regional final, is one of only two teams ranked No. 1 by both AP and UPI entering the tourney to lose by a double-digit margin before the Final Four.

One and Only: Pete Newell became the only U.S. Olympic basketball coach to win the NCAA and NIT titles with different schools. Newell was the 1960 U.S. Olympic basketball coach after capturing national titles with San Francisco (NIT in 1949) and California.

Numbers Game: North Carolina, which won 17 of its first 18 games, lost to Navy, 76-63, in the Tar Heels' only NCAA playoff contest in a nine-year span from 1958 through 1966. The victory improved Navy's record against Carolina to 14-5 since 1919-20, including six triumphs for the Midshipmen in their last seven meetings. . . . Cincinnati's Oscar Robertson scored a tourney-high 39 points in a 98-85 victory over Louisville in the national third-place game. . . . TCU's H.E. Kirchner grabbed a tourney-high 24 rebounds in a 71-65 victory over DePaul in the Midwest Regional third-place game. . . . Michigan State's Johnny Green hauled down 23 rebounds in an 88-81 defeat to Louisville in the Mideast Regional final. Green finished his career with an NCAA Tournament-record rebounding average of 19.7 per game in six playoff contests.

1958–59 NCAA CHAMPION: CALIFORNIA

SEASON STATISTICS OF CALIFORNIA REGULARS

PLAYER	POS.	CL.	G.	FG%	FT%	PPG	RPG
Denny Fitzpatrick	G	Sr.	29	.456	.854	13.3	2.8
Darrall Imhoff	C	Jr.	29	.424	.535	11.3	11.0
Al Buch	G	Sr.	29	.358	.646	9.2	2.8
Bill McClintock	F	So.	28	.416	.561	7.8	7.3
Bob Dalton	F	Sr.	29	.367	.663	7.3	4.6
Jack Grout	F	Sr.	28	.464	.639	5.5	3.7
Dick Doughty	C	Jr.	29	.423	.581	3.4	2.6
Jim Langley	F	Sr.	27	.427	.333	2.6	1.5
Bernie Simpson	G	Sr.	28	.295	.688	2.1	1.3
TEAM TOTALS			**29**	**.406**	**.634**	**63.9**	**45.1**

1959 FINAL FOUR CHAMPIONSHIP GAME

LOUISVILLE, KY

WEST VIRGINIA (70)	FG-A	FT-A	REB.	PF	PTS.
West	10-21	8-12	11	4	28
Akers	5-8	0-1	6	0	10
Clousson	4-7	2-3	4	4	10
Smith	2-5	1-1	2	3	5
Bolyard	1-4	4-4	3	4	6
Retton	0-0	2-2	0	0	2
Ritchie	1-4	2-2	4	0	4
Patrone	2-6	1-2	4	1	5
Team			7		
TOTALS	**25-55**	**20-27**	**41**	**16**	**70**

FG%: .455. FT%: .741.

CALIFORNIA (71)	FG-A	FT-A	REB.	PF	PTS.
McClintock	4-13	0-1	10	1	8
Dalton	6-11	3-4	2	4	15
Imhoff	4-13	2-2	9	3	10
Buch	0-4	2-2	2	3	2
Fitzpatrick	8-13	4-7	2	1	20

Simpson	0-1	0-0	2	2	0
Grout	4-5	2-2	3	1	10
Doughty	3-6	0-0	1	3	6
Team			7		
TOTALS	**29-66**	**13-18**	**38**	**18**	**71**

FG%: .439. FT%: .722.
Halftime: California 39-33.

NATIONAL SEMIFINALS

CALIFORNIA (64): McClintock 2-11 2-4 6, Dalton 2-4 3-4 7, Imhoff 10-25 2-5 22, Fitzpatrick 2-9 0-0 4, Buch 7-15 4-6 18, Grout 2-7 1-2 5, Simpson 1-2 0-0 2. Team 26-73 (.356) 12-21 (.571) 64.

CINCINNATI (58): Robertson 5-16 9-11 19, Wiesenhahn 5-11 0-0 10, Tenwick 2-6 1-1 5, Davis 6-15 1-2 13, Whitaker 4-7 0-2 8, Landfried 0-1 3-5 3, Bouldin 0-0 0-1 0. Team 22-56 (.393) 14-22 (.636) 58.

Halftime: Cincinnati 33-29.

WEST VIRGINIA (94): West 12-21 14-20 38, Akers 2-5 1-2 5, Clousson 5-5 2-2 12, Smith 5-9 2-4 12, Bolyard 4-10 5-7 13, Ritchie 2-6 0-2 4, Patrone 1-4 0-0 2, Retton 3-4 0-0 6, Schertzniger 0-0-0-0 0, Posch 1-2 0-0 2, Goode 0-0 0-0 0, Visnic 0-0 0-0 0. Team 35-66 (.530) 24-37 (.649) 94.

LOUISVILLE (79): Goldstein 6-10 9-9 21, Turner 8-16 2-5 18, Sawyer 2-6 3-4 7, Tieman 1-7 1-1 3, Andrews 9-15 1-1 19, Kitchen 3-7 0-0 6, Leathers 2-8 1-1 5, Geiling 0-0 0-0 0, Stacey 0-0 0-0 0. Team 31-69 (.449) 17-21 (.810) 79.

Halftime: West Virginia 48-32.

ALL-TOURNAMENT TEAM

Denny Fitzpatrick, G, Sr., California
Don Goldstein, F, Sr., Louisville
Darrall Imhoff, C, Jr., California
Oscar Robertson, F, Cincinnati
Jerry West, F, Jr., West Virginia*
*Named Most Outstanding Player

What If: ACC regular-season co-champion and tournament kingpin North Carolina State, which defeated Final Four teams Louisville and Cincinnati, was ineligible for the tourney because of NCAA probation.

Putting Things in Perspective: Oregon, which compiled a 3-13 record in the PCC and 9-16 overall, defeated California, 59-57.

Scoring Leader: Jerry West, West Virginia (160 points, 32 ppg).

Rebounding Leader: Jerry West, Virginia (73 rebounds, 14.6 rpg).

Highest Rebounding Average: H.E. Kirchner, TCU (42 rebounds, 21 rpg

1950–59 PREMO POWER POLL: BEST TEAMS BY DECADE

RANK	SEASON	SCHOOL
1	1955–56	San Francisco* (29-0)
2	1953–54	Kentucky (25-0)
3	1956–57	North Carolina* (32-0)
4	1954–55	San Francisco* (28-1)
5	1950–51	Kentucky* (32-2)
6	1958–59	Kansas St. (25-2)
7	1951–52	Kentucky (29-3)
8	1957–58	Cincinnati (25-3)
9	1952–53	Indiana* (23-3)
10	1956–57	Kansas (24-3)
11	1953–54	Holy Cross# (26-2)
12	1957–58	West Virginia (26-2)
13	1951–52	Kansas* (28-3)
14	1958–59	California* (25-4)
15	1949–50	CCNY#* (24-5)
16	1952–53	Seton Hall# (31-2)
17	1950–51	Illinois (22-5)
18	1957–58	San Francisco (25-2)
19	1953–54	Duquesne (26-3)
20	1950–51	Indiana (19-3)
	1958–59	Cincinnati (26-4)

#–NIT Champion
*–NCAA Tournament Champion

West Virginia's Jerry West whizzes past Louisville's John Turner in the 1959 NCAA Tournament semifinals.

1959 CHAMPIONSHIP BRACKET

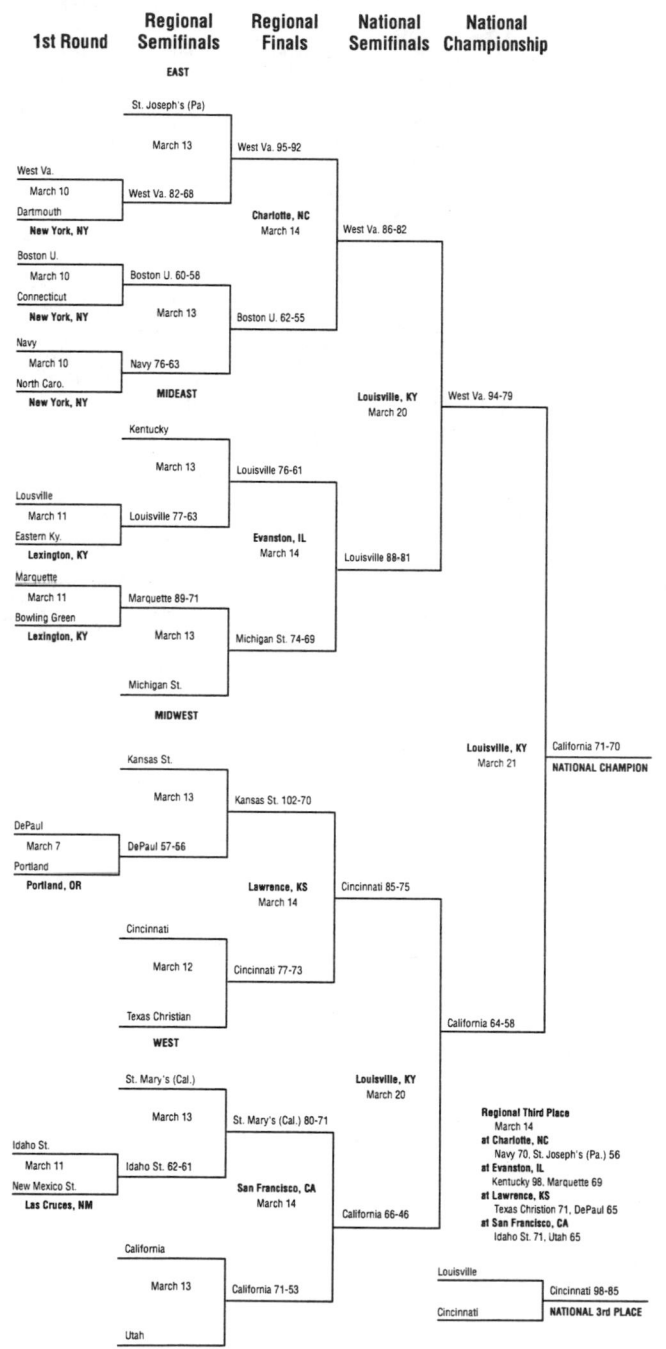

1st Round	Regional Semifinals	Regional Finals	National Semifinals	National Championship

EAST

St. Joseph's (Pa)

March 13 — West Va. 95-92

West Va.
March 10
Dartmouth
New York, NY — West Va. 82-68

Charlotte, NC
March 14 — West Va. 86-82

Boston U.
March 10
Connecticut
New York, NY — Boston U. 60-58

March 13 — Boston U. 62-55

Navy
March 10
North Caro.
New York, NY — Navy 76-63

Louisville, KY
March 20 — West Va. 94-79

MIDEAST

Kentucky

March 13 — Louisville 76-61

Lousville
March 11
Eastern Ky.
Lexington, KY — Louisville 77-63

Evanston, IL
March 14 — Louisville 88-81

Marquette
March 11
Bowling Green
Lexington, KY — Marquette 89-71

March 13 — Michigan St. 74-69

Michigan St.

MIDWEST

Louisville, KY
March 21 — California 71-70

NATIONAL CHAMPION

Kansas St.

March 13 — Kansas St. 102-70

DePaul
March 7
Portland
Portland, OR — DePaul 57-56

Lawrence, KS
March 14 — Cincinnati 85-75

Cincinnati

March 12 — Cincinnati 77-73

Texas Christian

WEST

California 64-58

St. Mary's (Cal.)

March 13 — St. Mary's (Cal.) 80-71

Idaho St.
March 11
New Mexico St.
Las Cruces, NM — Idaho St. 62-61

San Francisco, CA
March 14 — California 66-46

California

March 13 — California 71-53

Utah

Louisville, KY
March 20

Regional Third Place
March 14
at **Charlotte, NC**
Navy 70, St. Joseph's (Pa.) 56
at **Evanston, IL**
Kentucky 96, Marquette 69
at **Lawrence, KS**
Texas Christian 71, DePaul 65
at **San Francisco, CA**
Idaho St. 71, Utah 65

Louisville
Cincinnati — Cincinnati 98-85

NATIONAL 3rd PLACE

Kansas great Wilt Chamberlain.

Kansas coaching greats Dick Harp (left) and Phog Allen.

WINNINGEST PROGRAMS OF THE 1950S

RK.	SCHOOL	W.	L.	PCT.
1.	Kentucky	224	33	.872
2.	N.C. State	240	65	.787
3.	Seattle	233	69	.772
4.	La Salle	209	65	.763
5.	Dayton	228	71	.763
6.	Holy Cross	199	65	.754
7.	Kansas State	179	63	.740
8.	Connecticut	187	67	.736
9.	West Virginia	205	74	.735
10.	Louisville	202	77	.724

4

THE UCLA DYNASTY:

THE 1960s

The 1960s marked the beginning of perhaps the greatest dynasty in the history of sports as UCLA began its march toward 10 NCAA championships in a 12-year span. Center Lew Alcindor staked a claim as the most influential player of all time by propelling the Bruins to 88 victories in 90 games the last three years of the decade. Both of UCLA's defeats with Alcindor manning the middle were by two points.

The South was behind the times but African Americans were finally allowed to play in the ACC, SEC and SWC. The Big Ten had embraced African American players for some time but the only conference member to win more than 70 percent of its games during the decade was Ohio State.

The end of the decade supplied not only Alcindor's dominance but the marvelous showmanship of the M Boys—Pete Maravich (creativity), Rick Mount (long-range shooting) and Calvin Murphy (athleticism of small player). The combination of their influences dictated that college hoops would never be the same again.

Surprisingly, Davidson was the only school other than UCLA to have as many as three dif-

ferent players become an NCAA consensus first- or second-team All-American the last half of the decade (1965 through 1969).

1959–60

AT A GLANCE

NCAA Champion: Ohio State (25-3; coached by Fred Taylor; won Big Ten title with a 13-1 record, which was two games ahead of Indiana).

NIT Champion: Bradley (27-2; coached by Chuck Orsborn; finished in second place in Missouri Valley with a 12-2 record, which was one game behind Cincinnati).

NCAA Probation: Arizona State, Auburn, Montana State, North Carolina State, Seattle.

NCAA Consensus First-Team All-Americans: Darrall Imhoff, C, Sr., California; Jerry Lucas, C, Soph., Ohio State; Oscar Robertson, F, Sr., Cincinnati; Tom Stith, F, Jr., St. Bonaventure; Jerry West, F, Sr., West Virginia.

National Player of the Year: Robertson (33.7 ppg, 14.1 rpg, 52.6 FG%).

National Coach of the Year: Pete Newell, California (28-2/UPI, USBWA).

Tom and Sam Stith combined to average 52 points per game, an NCAA single-season record for brothers on the same team. Tom Stith, runner-up in scoring nationally to Cincinnati's Oscar Robertson, improved from ranking 71st in the country the previous year.

Tom Stith averaged more points per game than Robertson over the last two-thirds of the campaign, but the Big O hung on for the title after averaging over 40 points per game through his senior season's first 10 contests. The season's single-game scoring high was Robertson's school-and Missouri Valley Conference-record 62 points against North Texas State.

Tom Stith poured in 46 points, including a jumper with 15 seconds remaining in triple overtime, in a 90-89 triumph over Providence to extend the Bonnies' homecourt winning streak to 91 consecutive games.

St. Bonaventure's Tom Stith (31.5 ppg), Tennessee Tech's Jimmy Hagan (28.8) and Montana State's Larry Chanay (23.7) set school records for highest scoring average in a single season. . . . Ohio State's Jerry Lucas had the largest-ever margin over the national runner-up in field-goal shooting. Lucas hit 63.7 percent of his shots compared to 57.6 percent for Cincinnati's Paul Hogue. . . William & Mary defeated West Virginia, 94-86, to end the Mountaineers' streak of 56 consecutive victories against Southern Conference competition. . . . West Virginia's Jerry West finished his career as the shortest player (6-3) to score more than 2,300 points and grab more than 1,200 rebounds. West, the Mountaineers' all-time leading rebounder (1,240), tied a school record when he retrieved 31 missed shots in a game against George Washington.

Kentucky's streak of 20-win seasons ended at 14 when the Wildcats compiled an 18-7 record. Excluding the 1952-53 campaign when the Wildcats were banned by the NCAA from competing, it was the first time they didn't finish among the top 10 in a final wire-service poll. . . . Auburn became the first school to lead the

Wake Forest's team captain Dave Budd (left) and Billy Packer.

nation in field-goal shooting by hitting more than half of its shots (52.1 percent). The Tigers also paced the country in free-throw accuracy (77.2 percent) en route to their only SEC regular-season championship. Auburn's team was fondly dubbed "Snow White and the Seven Dwarfs" because white-haired coach Joel Eaves' starting lineup didn't feature a player taller than 6-4.

Bowling Green's James Darrow (52 points vs. Toledo and Marshall), Manhattan's Bob Mealy (51 vs. CCNY), Cornell's George Farley (47 at Princeton) and Arizona's Ernie McCray (46 vs. Los Angeles State) set school single-game scoring records. . . . Houston competed as a member of the Missouri Valley for the final season. . . . Future basketball telecaster Billy Packer was 6 for 35 from the floor for Wake Forest in three ACC Tournament games. It was the last

1959-60 INDIVIDUAL LEADERS

SCORING

PLAYER	PTS.	AVG.
Robertson, Cincinnati	1011	33.7
T. Stith, St. Bonaventure	819	31.5
Darrow, Bowling Green	705	29.4
West, West Virginia	908	29.3
Burgess, Gonzaga	751	28.9
Butler, Niagara	714	28.6
Dischinger, Purdue	605	26.3
Lucas, Ohio St.	710	26.3
DeBusschere, Detroit	691	25.6
Mudd, N. Texas St.	605	25.2

REBOUNDING

PLAYER	REB.	PCT.
Wright, Pacific	380	.234
DeBusschere, Detroit	540	.198

Mortell, Virginia	350	.194
Cohen, William & Mary	471	.194
Smith, Virginia Tech	495	.190
Jones, Niagara	383	.190
Hadnot, Providence	473	.186
Kojis, Marquette	384	.186
Farley, Cornell	466	.185
Jolliff, Ohio	445	.180

FIELD GOAL PERCENTAGE

PLAYER	FGM	FGA	PCT.
Lucas, Ohio St.	283	444	.637
Hogue, Cincinnati	152	264	.576
Gunter, Seton Hall	128	224	.571
Walker, Bradley	244	436	.560
Nordmann, St. Louis	173	310	.558
Dischinger, Purdue	201	368	.546
Hughes, Texas	111	205	.541

Johnson, Minnesota	186	346	.538
Fibbe, Auburn	108	201	.537
Hart, Auburn	108	201	.537

FREE THROW PERCENTAGE

PLAYER	FTM	FTA	PCT.
Waters, Mississippi	103	118	.873
Larese, N. Carolina	131	151	.868
Kaiser, Georgia Tech	164	190	.863
Carl, DePaul	135	158	.854
Smith, Middle Tenn.	144	170	.847
Butler, Niagara	158	187	.845
Pipczynski, Connecticut	102	122	.836
Names, Washington	90	108	.833
Clarke, St. Joseph's	100	121	.826
Adkins, Virginia	109	132	.826

1959-60 TEAM LEADERS

SCORING OFFENSE

SCHOOL	PTS.	AVG.
Ohio St.	2532	90.4
Miami (Fla.)	2427	89.9
West Virginia	2775	89.5
Cincinnati	2602	86.7
Arizona St.	1930	83.9

SCORING DEFENSE

SCHOOL	PTS.	AVG.
California	1486	49.5
Oklahoma St.	1304	52.2
Stanford	1376	55.0
Oregon St.	1458	56.1
Providence	1632	56.3

FIELD GOAL PERCENTAGE

SCHOOL	FGM	FGA	PCT.
Auburn	532	1022	.521
Cincinnati	1035	2025	.511
Ohio St.	1044	2101	.497
Texas	713	1503	.474
Bradley	921	1969	.468

FREE THROW PERCENTAGE

SCHOOL	FTM	FTA	PCT.
Auburn	424	549	.772
Tulane	438	573	.764
North Carolina	542	715	.758
Mississippi	451	600	.752
East Tennessee St.	438	585	.749

REBOUNDING

SCHOOL	TOTAL REB.	REB.	PCT.
Iona	1736	1054	.607
Cornell	2522	1492	.592
Ohio St.	2447	1415	.578
St. Francis (Pa.)	2472	1429	.578
Loyola (Calif.)	2355	1359	.577

year that no ACC school finished among the Top 10 in a final wire-service poll.

Sophomore Dave DeBusschere grabbed a school-record 39 rebounds for Detroit against Central Michigan. It was one of four games in his career that DeBusschere topped the 30-rebound plateau. . . . Dayton's Garry Roggenburk (32 vs. Miami of Ohio), New Mexico's Tom King (26 vs. Wyoming) and Virginia's Bob Mortell (25 vs. Washington & Lee) set school single-game rebounding records. Michigan State's Horace Walker retrieved 28 missed shots in a Big Ten game against Iowa on his way to setting a league record for highest single-season rebound average (18.3 rpg).

Toledo, coached by Eddie Melvin, notched an 18-6 record to end its streak of five consecutive losing marks and start a string of 26 straight winning seasons. . . . Iowa State registered a 15-9 mark in Glen Anderson's first year as head coach. It was the Cyclones' last season with fewer than 10 defeats. . . . Lafayette's streak of consecutive winning seasons ended at 17 when the Leopards compiled a 12-13 record. . . . Hofstra (23-1, coached by Butch van Breda Kolff) posted the best record of any team in the nation, but failed to win the Middle Atlantic Conference College Division-North because its only defeat came against first-place Wagner. . . . Rutgers defeated Penn, 51-44, for the Scarlet Knights' only victory in their first 17 meetings with the Quakers through 1965-66. . . . St. Joseph's achieved its average of 20 victories over the last five years, but one of the Hawks' seven defeats was the most lopsided in school history—by 44 points at Cincinnati (123-79). . . . Connecticut, coached by Hugh Greer, captured its 10th consecutive Yankee Conference championship.

Texas, which finished in the SWC cellar the previous year when its only league triumphs were against Rice, captured the conference crown in Harold Bradley's first season as head coach of the Longhorns. . . . The SWC conducted its final pre-conference tournament, an event that started in the 1951-52 season. . . . John Evans was in his first year as coach for Idaho State when the school won its eighth consecutive Rocky Mountain Conference championship. It was the final season of the league. . . . Utah State (24-5, coached by Cecil Baker) and Miami, Fla. (23-4, Bruce Hale) had their winningest seasons in school history.

1959-60 FINAL NATIONAL POLLS

AP	UPI	SCHOOL (RECORD)	HEAD COACH
1	2	Cincinnati (28-2)	George Smith
2	1	California (28-2)	Pete Newell
3	3	Ohio State (25-3)	Fred Taylor
4	4	Bradley (27-2)	Chuck Orsborn
5	6	West Virginia (26-5)	Fred Schaus
6	5	Utah (26-3)	Jack Gardner
7	10	Indiana (20-4)	Branch McCracken
8	7	Utah State (24-5)	Cecil Baker
9	11	St. Bonaventure (21-5)	Eddie Donovan
10	–	Miami (Fla.) (23-4)	Bruce Hale
11	17	Auburn (19-3)	Joel Eaves
12	12	NYU (22-5)	Lou Rossini
13	8	Georgia Tech (22-6)	John Hyder
14	18	Providence (24-5)	Joe Mullaney
15	19	St. Louis (19-9)	John Bennington
16	–	Holy Cross (20-6)	Roy Leenig
17	9	Villanova (20-6)	Al Severance
18	15	Duke (17-11)	Vic Bubas
19	–	Wake Forest (21-7)	Bones McKinney
20	–	St. John's (17-5)	Joe Lapchick
–	13	Texas (18-8)	Harold Bradley
–	14	North Carolina (18-6)	Frank McGuire
–	16	Kansas State (16-10)	Tex Winter
–	20	Dayton (21-7)	Tom Blackburn

Washington (Mo.) competed in its final season at the major-college level. . . . NYU made its lone appearance in the Top 20 of a final wire-service poll. . . . CCNY's Nat Holman ended his 37-year coaching career early in the season with a 423-190 record. . . . Pete Newell, who coached San Francisco, Michigan State and California, retired after a 14-year coaching career with a 234-123 record. Newell stepped down despite

being named national coach of the year and guiding Cal to a second-place finish in the NCAA Tournament.

1960 NCAA Tournament

Summary: Ohio State became the only titlist to win all of its tournament games by more than 15 points. Center Jerry Lucas, a first-team All-American as a sophomore, averaged 24 points and 16 rebounds in four playoff contests for the Buckeyes. He collected 36 points and 25 rebounds to help them erase a six-point halftime deficit in their Mideast Regional opener against Western Kentucky. Ohio State, playing in the Bay Area (San Francisco) against the nation's top defensive team (California), hit a sizzling 84.2 percent of its first-half field-goal attempts (16-19) en route to a 75-55 victory over the defending champion Bears. Ohio State's five starters—sophomores Lucas, John Havlicek, and Mel Nowell, senior Joe Roberts, and junior Larry Siegfried—were all high school centers. They each scored in double figures in the NCAA final before eventually playing at least two seasons in the NBA, ABA, or both.

Outcome for Defending Champion: The only regular season defeat for California (28-2) was at Southern Cal. (65-57), ending the Bears' 30-game winning streak.

Star Gazing: Oscar Robertson generated glittering averages of 32.6 points per game and 33.7 in leading Cincinnati to the national semifinals in 1959 and 1960, respectively, before the Bearcats were beaten both years by California. The Bears restricted the Big O to a total of 37 points in the two Final Four games as he was just nine of 32 from the floor.

Biggest Upset: Oregon, which lost seven of its last 12 regular-season games, defeated Utah, 65-54, in the West Regional semifinals. Utah, ranked No. 5 by UPI and No. 6 by AP entering the tourney, didn't have a player score more than 10 points against the Ducks.

One and Only: Idaho State became the only school to make as many as eight consecutive

1959-60 NCAA CHAMPION: OHIO STATE

SEASON STATISTICS OF OHIO STATE REGULARS

PLAYER	POS.	CL.	G.	FG%	FT%	PPG	RPG
Jerry Lucas	C	So.	27	.637	.770	26.3	16.4
Larry Siegfried	G	Jr.	28	.466	.750	13.3	3.8
Mel Nowell	G	So.	28	.473	.767	13.1	2.6
John Havlicek	F	So.	28	.462	.716	12.2	7.3
Joe Roberts	F	Sr.	28	.480	.679	11.0	6.9
Richard Furry	F	Sr.	28	.455	.606	5.1	3.3
Bob Knight	F-G	So.	21	.405	.630	3.7	2.0
Howard Nourse	C	Sr.	17	.511	1.000	3.1	2.7
Gary Gearhart	G	So.	19	.404	.438	2.6	1.2
Richie Hoyt	G	Sr.	23	.423	.778	2.5	0.8
David Barker	G	Sr.	16	.407	.167	1.4	0.8
TEAM TOTALS			28	.497	.717	90.4	50.5

1960 FINAL FOUR CHAMPIONSHIP GAME

KANSAS CITY, MO

OHIO STATE (75)	FG-A	FT-A	REB.	PF	PTS.
Havlicek	4-8	4-5	6	2	12
Roberts	5-6	0-0	5	1	10
Lucas	7-9	2-2	10	2	16
Nowell	6-7	3-3	4	2	15
Siegfried	5-6	3-6	1	2	13
Gearhart	0-1	0-0	1	0	0
Cedargren	0-0	1-2	1	1	1
Furry	2-4	0-0	3	1	4
Hoyt	0-1	0-0	0	0	0
Barker	0-0	0-0	0	0	0
Knight	0-1	0-0	0	1	0
Nourse	2-3	0-0	3	1	4
Team			1		
TOTALS	**31-46**	**13-19**	**35**	**13**	**75**

FG%: .674. FT%: .684.

CALIFORNIA (55)	FG-A	FT-A	REB.	PF	PTS.
McClintock	4-15	2-3	3	3	10
Gillis	4-9	0-0	1	1	8
Imhoff	3-9	2-2	5	2	8
Wendell	0-6	4-4	0	2	4
Shultz	2-8	2-2	4	4	6
Mann	3-5	1-1	0	0	7
Doughty	4-5	3-3	6	1	11
Stafford	0-1	1-2	0	1	1
Morrison	0-0	0-0	1	1	0
Averbuck	0-0	0-1	1	0	0
Pearson	0-1	0-0	0	0	0
Alexander	0-0	0-0	0	0	0
Team			7		
TOTALS	**20-59**	**15-18**	**28**	**15**	**55**

FG%: .339. FT%: .833.
Halftime: Ohio State 37-19.

NATIONAL SEMIFINALS

CALIFORNIA (64): McClintock 2-11 2-4 6, Dalton 2-4 3-4 7, Imhoff 10-25 2-5 22, Fitzpatrick 2-9 0-0 4, Buch 7-15 4-6 18, Grout 2-7 1-2 5, Simpson 1-2 0-0 2. Team 26-73 (.356) 12-21 (.571) 64.

CINCINNATI (58): Robertson 5-16 9-11 19, Wiesenhahn 5-11 0-0 10, Tenwick 2-6 1-1 5, Davis 6-15 1-2 13, Whitaker 4-7 0-2 8, Landfried 0-1 3-5 3, Bouldin 0-0 0-1 0. Team 22-56 (.393) 14-22 (.636) 58.

Halftime: Cincinnati 33-29.

WEST VIRGINIA (94): West 12-21 14-20 38, Akers 2-5 1-2 5, Clousson 5-5 2-2 12, Smith 5-9 2-4 12, Bolyard 4-10 5-7 13, Ritchie 2-6 0-2 4, Patrone 1-4 0-0 2, Retton 3-4 0-0 6, Schertzniger 0-0 0-0 0, Posch 1-2 0-0 2, Goode 0-0 0-0 0, Visnic 0-0 0-0 0. Team 35-66 (.530) 24-37 (.649) 94.

LOUISVILLE (79): Goldstein 6-10 9-9 21, Turner 8-16 2-5 18, Sawyer 2-6 3-4 7, Tieman 1-7 1-3 3, Andrews 9-15 1-1 19, Kitchen 3-7 0-0 6, Leathers 2-8 1-1 5, Geiling 0-0 0-0 0, Stacey 0-0 0-0 0. Team 31-69 (.449) 17-21 (.810) 79.

Halftime: West Virginia 48-32.

ALL-TOURNAMENT TEAM

**Darrall Imhoff, C, Sr., California
Jerry Lucas, C, Soph., Ohio State***
**Mel Nowell, G, Soph., Ohio State
Oscar Robertson, F, Sr., Cincinnati
Tom Sanders, C, Sr., New York University
*Named Most Outstanding Player**

NCAA Tournament appearances from the year it participated in the event for the first time (since 1953 under three different coaches). . . . . Ohio State's Fred Taylor became the only coach of an NCAA titlist to previously play major league baseball (first baseman for the Washington Senators in parts of three seasons from 1950 through 1952).

Numbers Game: Ohio State, the only team to lead the nation in scoring offense and win the NCAA championship in the same is also the only champion to win all of its tournament games by more than 15 points. . . . Lucas scored his playoff career-high 36 points in his tournament debut (98-79 victory over Western Kentucky in Mideast Regional semifinal). . . . West

Virginia swingman Jerry West became the only player to score at least 25 points in eight consecutive tournament games (1959 and 1960). West is also the only player to rank among the top five in scoring average in both the NCAA Tournament (30.6 points per game) and NBA playoffs (29.1 ppg).

Scoring Leader: Oscar Robertson, Cincinnati (122 points, 30.5 ppg).

Highest Scoring Average: Jerry West, West Virginia (105 points, 35 ppg).

Rebounding Leader: Tom Sanders, NYU (83 rebounds, 16.6 rpg).

Highest Rebounding Average: Howard Jolliff, Ohio University (65 rebounds, 21.7 rpg).

1960 CHAMPIONSHIP BRACKET

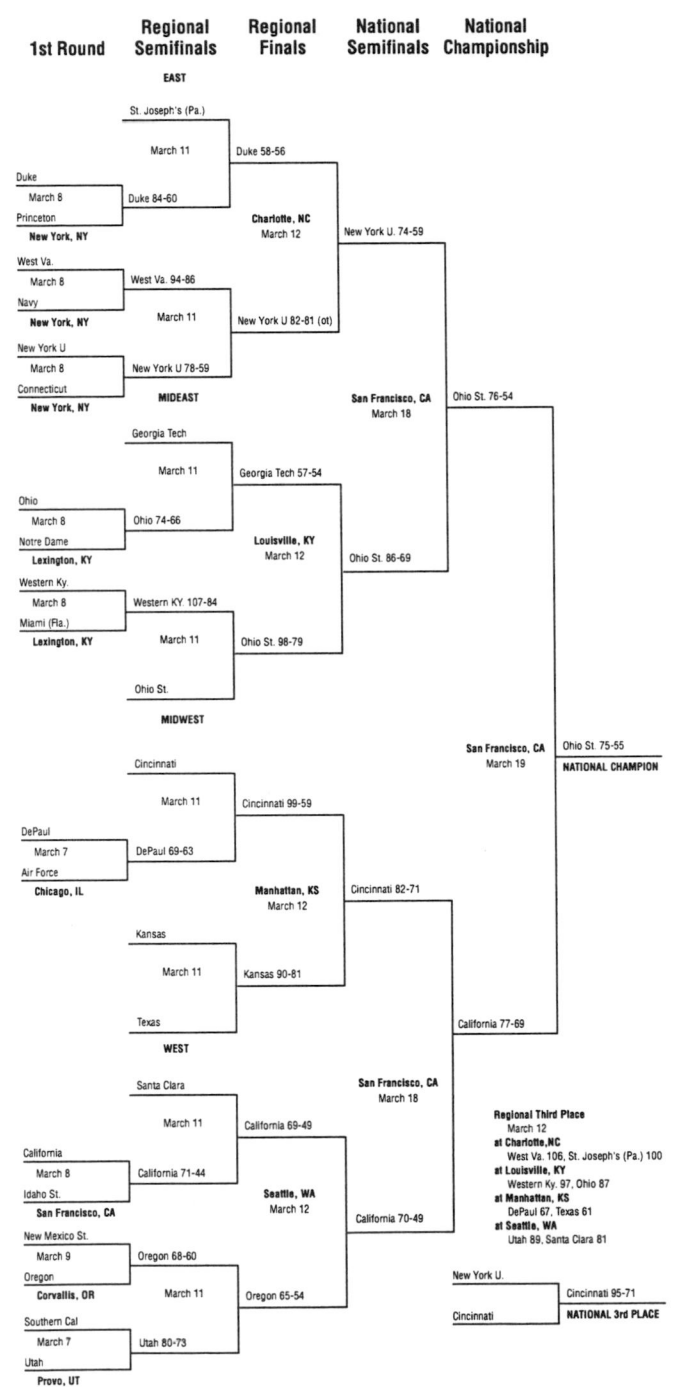

	1st Round	Regional Semifinals	Regional Finals	National Semifinals	National Championship

EAST

St. Joseph's (Pa.)

March 11 — Duke 58-56

Duke
March 8 — Duke 84-60
Princeton
New York, NY

Charlotte, NC
March 12

West Va.
March 8 — West Va. 94-86
Navy
New York, NY
March 11 — New York U 82-81 (ot)

New York U
March 8 — New York U 78-59
Connecticut
New York, NY

New York U. 74-59

MIDEAST

Georgia Tech
March 11 — Georgia Tech 57-54

Ohio
March 8 — Ohio 74-66
Notre Dame
Lexington, KY

Louisville, KY
March 12 — Ohio St. 86-69

Western Ky.
March 8 — Western KY. 107-84
Miami (Fla.)
Lexington, KY
March 11 — Ohio St. 98-79

Ohio St.

MIDWEST

San Francisco, CA
March 18 — Ohio St. 76-54

WEST

Cincinnati
March 11 — Cincinnati 99-59

DePaul
March 7 — DePaul 69-63
Air Force
Chicago, IL

Manhattan, KS
March 12 — Cincinnati 82-71

Kansas
March 11 — Kansas 90-81
Texas
WEST

California 77-69

Santa Clara
March 11 — California 69-49

California
March 8 — California 71-44
Idaho St.
San Francisco, CA

Seattle, WA
March 12 — California 70-49

New Mexico St.
March 9 — Oregon 68-60
Oregon
Corvallis, OR
March 11 — Oregon 65-54

Southern Cal
March 7 — Utah 80-73
Utah
Provo, UT

San Francisco, CA
March 18 — California 77-69

San Francisco, CA
March 19 — Ohio St. 75-55
NATIONAL CHAMPION

Regional Third Place
March 12
at Charlotte,NC
West Va. 106, St. Joseph's (Pa.) 100
at Louisville, KY
Western Ky. 97, Ohio 87
at Manhattan, KS
DePaul 67, Texas 61
at Seattle, WA
Utah 89, Santa Clara 81

New York U.
March — Cincinnati 95-71
Cincinnati
NATIONAL 3rd PLACE

1960–61

AT A GLANCE

NCAA Champion: Cincinnati (27-3; coached by Ed Jucker; won Missouri Valley title with a 10-2 record, which was one game ahead of Bradley).

NIT Champion: Providence (24-5; coached by Joe Mullaney).

NCAA Probation: Auburn, Indiana, Kansas, Loyola (La.), Montana State, North Carolina.

NCAA Consensus First-Team All-Americans: Terry Dischinger, F, Jr., Purdue; Roger Kaiser, G, Sr., Georgia Tech; Jerry Lucas, C, Jr., Ohio State; Tom Stith, F, Sr., St. Bonaventure; Chet Walker, F, Jr., Bradley.

National Player of the Year: Lucas (24.9 ppg, 17.4 rpg, 62.3 FG%).

National Coach of the Year: Fred Taylor, Ohio State (27-1, UPI, USBWA).

Georgia Tech All-American Roger Kaiser.

Scandal reared its ugly head again. The only player to score 40 or more points in a Final Four contest and not eventually play in the NBA was St. Joseph's forward Jack Egan, who scored a tourney-high 42 points in a four-overtime, 127-120 triumph against Utah in the national third-place game. Egan became a third-round draft choice of Philadelphia but forfeited the opportunity to play in the pros when he was implicated in a game-fixing scandal. Egan, who scored a school-record 47 points at Gettysburg earlier in the season (mark subsequently tied), was susceptible to such shenanigans inasmuch as he was the father of two children and his wife had suffered a miscarriage just before the campaign started.

A total of 37 players from 22 schools, including legendary Brooklyn playground hero Connie Hawkins, who spent his freshman year at Iowa, were implicated in point-shaving transgressions.

Indiana's Walt Bellamy set a Big Ten Conference mark with a school-record 33 rebounds in a game against Michigan. Bowling Green's Nate Thurmond established a Mid-American Conference single-season standard by averaging 18.7 rebounds per game.

Gonzaga's Frank Burgess closed his season with a 37-point outburst to win the scoring title with a 32.38 average, edging East Tennessee

1960-61 INDIVIDUAL LEADERS

SCORING

PLAYER	PTS.	AVG.
Burgess, Gonzaga	842	32.4
Chilton, E. Tennessee St.	771	32.1
Stith, St. Bonaventure	830	29.6
Dischinger, Purdue	648	28.2
McGill, Utah	862	27.8
Chappell, Wake Forest	745	26.6
Foley, Holy Cross	688	26.5
Walker, Bradley	656	25.2
Heyman, Duke	629	25.2
Warner, Gettysburg	623	24.9
Lucas, Ohio St.	671	24.9

REBOUNDING

PLAYER	REB.	PCT.
Lucas, Ohio St.	470	.198
Thurmond, Bowling Green	449	.196
Cohen, William & Mary	424	.185
DeBusschere, Detroit	514	.180
Hadnot, Providence	475	.178
Chilton, E. Tennessee St.	403	.175
Bellamy, Indiana	428	.171
Ardon, Tulane	392	.168
Kojis, Marquette	462	.167
Smith, Virginia Tech	362	.164

FIELD GOAL PERCENTAGE

PLAYER	FGM	FGA	PCT.
Lucas, Ohio St.	256	411	.623
Gunter, Seton Hall	200	325	.615
Youngkin, Duke	146	253	.577
Dischinger, Purdue	215	373	.576
Lundy, Lafayette	174	303	.574
Havlicek, Ohio St.	183	321	.570
Ward, Boston College	115	202	.569
Walker, Bradley	238	423	.563
Weiss, Rhode Island	111	199	.558
Hull, Wake Forest	114	206	.553

FREE THROW PERCENTAGE

PLAYER	FTM	FTA	PCT.
Sherard, Army	135	154	.877
Carl, DePaul	161	184	.875
Kaiser, Georgia Tech	176	203	.867
Thompson, Morehead St.	180	208	.865
Carlton, Arkansas	101	117	.863
Siegfried, Ohio St.	123	143	.860
Strickland, Oregon	90	106	.849
Patterson, Clemson	146	173	.844
Zeller, Miami (Ohio)	172	205	.839
Pursiful, Kentucky	99	118	.839

1960-61 TEAM LEADERS

SCORING OFFENSE

SCHOOL	PTS.	AVG.
St. Bonaventure	2479	88.5
Loyola (Ill.)	1989	86.5
West Virginia	2325	86.1
Virginia Tech	1874	85.2
Ohio St.	2383	85.1

SCORING DEFENSE

SCHOOL	PTS.	AVG.
Santa Clara	1314	48.7
San Jose St.	1254	50.2
San Francisco	1440	51.4
California	1192	54.2
Portland	1415	56.6

FIELD GOAL PERCENTAGE

SCHOOL	FGM	FGA	PCT.
Ohio St.	939	1886	.498
St. Bonaventure	1010	2041	.495
Bradley	798	1622	.492
Auburn	500	1018	.491
Utah	1008	2069	.487

FREE THROW PERCENTAGE

SCHOOL	FTM	FTA	PCT.
Tulane	459	604	.760
Ohio St.	505	671	.753
West Texas St.	421	561	.750
W. Kentucky	554	742	.747
Arkansas	428	574	.746

REBOUNDING

SCHOOL	TOTAL REB.	REB.	PCT.
Bradley	2247	1330	.592
Memphis St.	2332	1366	.586
Niagara	1796	1048	.584
Cornell	2406	1384	.575
Cincinnati	2706	1553	.574

State's Tom Chilton, who was second with a 32.13 average. Burgess (against UC Davis), Chilton (Austin Peay) and Purdue's Terry Dischinger (Michigan State) tied for the national high in scoring with 52 points. The outbursts for Burgess and Chilton were school records. . . . Burgess, Chilton, Pacific's Ken Stanley (24 ppg) and Bucknell's Joe Steiner (22) set school records for highest scoring average in a single season. Chilton's average is the highest in Ohio Valley Conference history.

William & Mary's Jeff Cohen (49 points vs. Richmond), Missouri's Joe Scott (46 vs. Nebraska) and Tulane's Jim Kerwin (45 vs. Southeastern Louisiana) set school single-game scoring records. . . . Oklahoma State didn't finish among the top three in national defense rankings for the first time in 26 years. The top four defensive teams were all from the San Francisco Bay Area—Santa Clara (48.7), San Jose State (50.3), San Francisco (51.4) and California (54.2).

Tom Meschery, the West Coast Athletic Conference player of the year, finished his career as St. Mary's all-time leading rebounder. Meschery was born in China in 1938, and placed in a Japanese concentration camp at the beginning of World War II. His father was a white Russian military officer and his mother an employee at the American Consulate in China. The Meschery family was reunited after the war in San Francisco by the Christian Brothers priests. "I went into basketball because it was the fastest way to become accepted," Meschery said. "I was a foreign kid who didn't speak English very well. One of the best ways to be accepted by your playmates is to be good as an athlete."

1960-61 NCAA CHAMPION: CINCINNATI

SEASON STATISTICS OF CINCINNATI REGULARS

PLAYER	POS.	CL.	G.	FG%	FT%	PPG	RPG
Bob Wiesenhahn	F	Sr.	30	.481	.678	17.1	10.0
Paul Hogue	C	Jr.	30	.532	.518	16.8	12.5
Tom Thacker	G-F	So.	30	.396	.684	12.3	9.5
Carl Bouldin	G	Sr.	30	.428	.800	11.7	2.8
Tony Yates	G	So.	30	.486	.602	7.4	3.5
Dale Heidotting	F-C	So.	26	.429	.652	3.6	3.7
Fred Dierking	F-C	Jr.	25	.483	.467	2.6	2.2
Jim Calhoun	G	Jr.	17	.378	.538	2.1	0.5
Tom Sizer	G	Jr.	24	.375	.750	2.0	1.0
Larry Shingleton	G	So.	20	.292	.400	0.9	0.6
Mark Altenau	F	So.	18	.429	.444	0.9	0.6
TEAM TOTALS			30	.457	.633	75.0	51.8

1961 FINAL FOUR CHAMPIONSHIP GAME

KANSAS CITY, MO

CINCINNATI (70)	FG-A	FT-A	REB.	PF	PTS.
Wiesenhahn	8-15	1-1	9	3	17
Thacker	7-21	1-4	7	0	15
Hogue	3-8	3-6	7	3	9
Yates	4-8	5-5	2	3	13
Bouldin	7-12	2-3	4	4	16
Sizer	0-0	0-0	1	0	0
Heidotting	0-0	0-0	0	0	0
Team			6		
TOTALS	**29-64**	**12-19**	**36**	**13**	**70**

FG%: .453. FT%: .632.

OHIO STATE (65)	FG-A	FT-A	REB.	PF	PTS.
Havlicek	1-5	2-2	4	2	4
Hoyt	3-5	1-1	1	3	7
Lucas	10-17	7-7	12	4	27
Nowell	3-9	3-3	3	1	9
Siegfried	6-10	2-3	3	2	14
Knight	1-3	0-0	1	1	2
Gearhart	1-1	0-0	0	1	2
Team			8		
TOTALS	**25-50**	**15-16**	**32**	**14**	**65**

FG%: .500. FT%: .938.
Halftime: Ohio State 39-38. Regulation: Tied 61-61.

NATIONAL SEMIFINALS

CINCINNATI (82): Wiesenhahn 5-7 4-6 14, Thacker 1-7 5-6 7, Hogue 9-16 0-4 18, Bouldin 7-14 7-8 21, Yates 4-6 5-7 13, Heidotting 3-8 1-1 7, Sizer 1-1 0-0 2, Dierking 0-0 0-0 0, Altenau 0-0 0-0 0, Shingleton 0-0 0-0 0, Calhoun 0-0 0-0 0. Team 30-59 (.508) 22-32 (.688) 82.

UTAH (67): Ruffell 6-11 2-2 14, Rhead 2-5 4-6 8, McGill 11-31 3-4 25, Morton 3-9 1-1 7, Rowe 1-3 0-0 2, Crain 2-5 0-1 4, Aufderheide 2-3 2-2 6, Cozby 0-0 0-0 0, Thomas 0-0 1-2 1, Jenson 0-0 0-0 0. Team 27-67 (.403) 13-18 (.722) 67.

Halftime: Cincinnati 35-20.

OHIO STATE (95): Nowell 7-11 1-1 15, Havlicek 5-6 1-2 11, Lucas 10-11 9-10 29, Hoyt 2-6 0-0 4, Siegfried 8-11 5-7 21, Knight 2-5 1-2 5, McDonald 1-4 0-0 2, Gearhart 0-2 2-2 2, Reasbeck 0-1 0-1 0, Lee 1-1 0-0 2, Landes 2-2 0-0 4. Team 38-60 (.633) 19-25 (.760) 95.

ST. JOSEPH'S (69): Lynam 2-5 3-4 7, Hoy 6-17 1-1 13, Majewski 4-12 5-7 13, Egan 3-15 2-3 8, Kempton 5-9 8-8 18, Wynne 1-9 2-2 4, Booth 0-3 2-2 2, Gormley 1-5 2-2 4, Westhead 0-1 0-1 0, Bugey 0-0 0-0 0, Dickey 0-0 0-0 0. Team 22-76 (.289) 25-30 (.833) 69.

Halftime: Ohio State 45-28.

ALL-TOURNAMENT TEAM

Carl Bouldin, G, Sr., Cincinnati
John Egan, F, Sr., St. Joseph's
Jerry Lucas, C, Jr., Ohio State*
Larry Siegfried, G, Sr., Ohio State
Bob Wiesenhahn, F, Sr., Cincinnati
*Named Most Outstanding Player

Sylvester Blye, a 6-5, 220-pound sophomore forward, collected 23 points and 11 rebounds for Seattle in his debut and farewell game, an 86-81 loss to Memphis State. The following day it was discovered that he had played briefly the previous season with the New York Clowns, a touring pro team, and he was declared ineligible for further college competition.

Manhattan compiled its first losing record (8-11) in 25 competitive seasons (did not field teams in 1943-44 and 1944-45 because of World War II).... Connecticut's streak of consecutive winning seasons ended at 15 when the Huskies lost their last five games to finish with an 11-13 mark.... Rutgers (11-10) registered its first winning record in 12 seasons.... St. Bonaventure's 99-game homecourt winning streak, which started in 1948, was snapped by Niagara, 87-77.

Drake stopped Bradley's 46-game homecourt winning streak, 86-76. Mississippi State ended Auburn's 36-game homecourt winning streak, 56-48.... Lehigh lost 34 consecutive games in its series with Lafayette until edging the Leopards, 60-58. VMI lost 32 straight games to Virginia until defeating the Cavaliers, 75-63.

The Citadel's Keith Stowers set a school single-game record by grabbing 23 rebounds against Richmond.... George Washington ended West Virginia's streak of six consecutive Southern Conference Tournament championships. GWU entered the tourney with a 6-16 record. Jon Feldman, 5-10, scored 45 points for the Colonials in the championship game against William & Mary. ... Providence defeated St. Louis in the NIT final, 62-59. It was the third consecutive year for the Friars to beat SLU in the NIT.

Ohio State (27-1, coached by Fred Taylor) had its winningest season in school history. . . . Illinois dropped seven of its last eight games to finish with a losing record (9-15) for the first time in 33 seasons. Jerry Colangelo, who went on to become an executive with several pro sports franchises in Phoenix, led the Illini in field-goal percentage (128 of 279, .459). Among Colangelo's colleagues the previous year at Illinois were guard Mannie Jackson, who became a Honeywell executive and owner of the Harlem Globetrotters, and team manager Dennis Swanson, who became president of ABC Sports. . . . Wichita State's Gene Wiley set a Missouri Valley Conference record by blocking 15 shots against Purdue. . . . Creighton's Dick Hartmann, one of the nation's top rebounders the previous season with 15.1 per game, died in a traffic accident prior to the start of his senior campaign.. . . Colorado State lost to Regis (Co.) for the fifth straight season.

1960-61 FINAL NATIONAL POLLS

AP	UPI	SCHOOL (RECORD)	HEAD COACH
1	1	Ohio St. (27-1)	Fred Taylor
2	2	Cincinnati (27-3)	Ed Jucker
3	3	St. Bonaventure (24-4)	Eddie Donovan
4	4	Kansas St. (23-4)	Tex Winter
5	6	North Carolina (19-4)	Frank McGuire
6	7	Bradley (21-5)	Chuck Orsborn
7	5	Southern Cal (21-8)	Forrest Twogood
8	10	Iowa (18-6)	Sham Scheueman
9	12	West Virginia (23-4)	George King
10	9	Duke (22-6)	Vic Bubas
11	13	Utah (24-7)	Jack Gardner
12	18	Texas Tech (15-10)	Polk Robison
13	–	Niagara (16-5)	Taps Gallagher
14	20	Memphis St. (20-3)	Bob Vanatta
15	10	Wake Forest (19-11)	Bones McKinney
16	8	St. John's (20-5)	Joe Lapchick
17	16	St. Joseph's (25-5)	Jack Ramsay
18	–	Drake (19-7)	Maury John
19	–	Holy Cross (22-5)	Roy Leenig
20	18	Kentucky (19-9)	Adolph Rupp
–	14	St. Louis(21-9)	John Bennington
–	15	Louisville (21-8)	Peck Hickman
–	17	Dayton (20-9)	Tom Blackburn

1961 NCAA Tournament

Summary: Paul Hogue, a 6-9 center who hit just 51.8 percent of his free-throw attempts during the season, sank only two of 10 foul shots in his two previous games before putting Cincin-nati ahead to stay with a pair of pivotal free throws in overtime in a 70-65 championship game victory. Ohio State, undefeated entering the tourney, lost the national final against Cincinnati (70-65 in overtime) after almost getting upset in its opening playoff game at Louisville. Cincinnati's Ed Jucker became the only individual to win an NCAA title in his first full season as head coach at a major university.

Outcome for Defending Champion: Ohio State entered the playoffs undefeated, but needed to overcome a five-point deficit with less than three minutes remaining to escape with a 56-55 triumph at Louisville in the Mideast Regional semifinals. The closest the Buckeyes came to a setback during the regular season were games against St. Bonaventure (84-82 in holiday tournament at Madison Square Garden) and at Iowa (62-61).

Star Gazing: Three-time unanimous first-team All-American Jerry Lucas registered game highs of 27 points and 12 rebounds for the Buckeyes in the championship contest while teammate John Havlicek was limited to four points. Lucas outrebounded Kentucky by himself when he retrieved a tourney-high 30-missed shots in an 87-74 triumph over the Wildcats in the Mideast Regional final.

Biggest Upset: Tom Stith's 29 points weren't enough to keep third-ranked St. Bonaventure from bowing to Wake Forest, 78-73, in the East Regional semifinals.

One and Only: Guard Carl Bouldin became the only athlete to lead his championship team in scoring at the Final Four and play major league baseball in the same year. He helped Cincinnati win the NCAA title with a total of 37 points in two games at Kansas City before pitching in two games later that year for the Washington Senators. . . .Rhode Island's Ernie Calverly became the only individual to coach a team in the playoffs after leading the nation in scoring as a player (26.7 points per game for Rhode Island in 1943-44).

Numbers Game: St. Joseph's Jack Ramsay became the only coach to win an NBA championship (Portland Trail Blazers '77) after directing a college squad to the Final Four. . . . Wake Forest became the only team to ever trail by as many as 10 points at halftime of a tournament game (46-36) and then win the contest by more than 20. The Demon Deacons were behind at intermission (46-36) in the first round of the East Regional before rallying to defeat St. John's (97-74).

What If: ACC regular-season champion North Carolina, which defeated NCAA representative Wake Forest twice by a total of 24 points, was ineligible for postseason competition because of an NCAA probation. . . . Utah, coming off a 26-3 season and with twin towers Billy "The Hill" McGill and Allen Holmes slated to return, were a strong candidate to win it all. The Utes reached the Final Four although Holmes, the 1959 NJCAA Tournament MVP, didn't play after nearly losing his right leg in a summer auto accident. St. Louis finished in a tie for third place in the Missouri Valley after losing All-MVC first-team center Bob"Bevo" Nordmann because of a severe knee injury. The Billikens, who defeated NCAA champion-to-be Cincinnati by 17 points(57-40), lost the NIT final to Providence.

Putting Things in Perspective: Cincinnati lost three times by a total of 44 points in a five-

St. Joseph's (Pa.) coach Jack Ramsay instructs his players.

game stretch early in the season, including the Bearcats' first two Missouri Valley Conference contests.

Scoring Leader: Billy McGill, Utah (119 points, 29.75 ppg).

Rebounding Leader: Jerry Lucas, Ohio State (73 rebounds, 18.3 rpg).

1961 CHAMPIONSHIP BRACKET

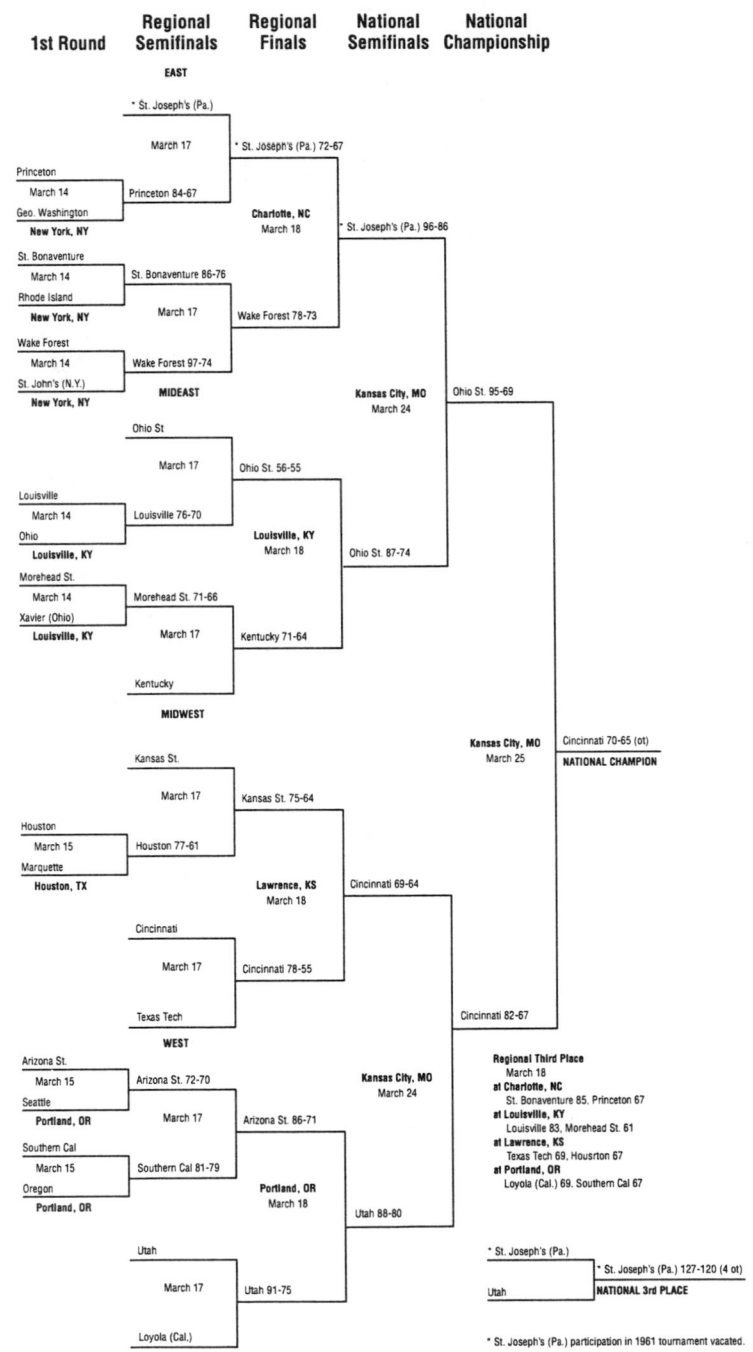

1st Round	Regional Semifinals	Regional Finals	National Semifinals	National Championship

EAST

* St. Joseph's (Pa.)
March 17
* St. Joseph's (Pa.) 72-67

Princeton
March 14
Geo. Washington
New York, NY
Princeton 84-67

Charlotte, NC
March 18
* St. Joseph's (Pa.) 96-86

St. Bonaventure
March 14
Rhode Island
New York, NY
St. Bonaventure 86-76

March 17
Wake Forest 78-73

Wake Forest
March 14
St. John's (N.Y.)
New York, NY
Wake Forest 97-74

MIDEAST

Kansas City, MO
March 24
Ohio St. 95-69

Ohio St
March 17
Ohio St. 56-55

Louisville
March 14
Ohio
Louisville, KY
Louisville 76-70

Louisville, KY
March 18
Ohio St. 87-74

Morehead St.
March 14
Xavier (Ohio)
Louisville, KY
Morehead St. 71-66

March 17
Kentucky 71-64

Kentucky

MIDWEST

Kansas City, MO
March 25
Cincinnati 70-65 (ot)
NATIONAL CHAMPION

Kansas City, MO
March 24
Cincinnati 69-64

Kansas St.
March 17
Kansas St. 75-64

Houston
March 15
Marquette
Houston, TX
Houston 77-61

Lawrence, KS
March 18

Cincinnati
March 17
Cincinnati 78-55

Texas Tech

WEST

Cincinnati 82-67

Arizona St.
March 15
Seattle
Portland, OR
Arizona St. 72-70

March 17
Arizona St. 86-71

Southern Cal
March 15
Oregon
Portland, OR
Southern Cal 81-79

Portland, OR
March 18

Kansas City, MO
March 24

Utah 88-80

Utah
March 17
Utah 91-75

Loyola (Cal.)

Regional Third Place
March 18
at Charlotte, NC
St. Bonaventure 85, Princeton 67
at Louisville, KY
Louisville 83, Morehead St. 61
at Lawrence, KS
Texas Tech 69, Houston 67
at Portland, OR
Loyola (Cal.) 69, Southern Cal 67

* St. Joseph's (Pa.)
* St. Joseph's (Pa.) 127-120 (4 ot)
Utah
NATIONAL 3rd PLACE

* St. Joseph's (Pa.) participation in 1961 tournament vacated.

1961–62

AT A GLANCE

NCAA Champion: Cincinnati (29-2; coached by Ed Jucker; won Missouri Valley playoff title game, 61-46, after tying Bradley with a 10-2 record).

NIT Champion: Dayton (24-6; coached by Tom Blackburn).

NCAA Probation: Indiana, Kansas, Tennessee Tech, Utah.

NCAA Consensus First-Team All-Americans: Len Chappell, C, Sr., Wake Forest; Terry Dischinger, F, Sr., Purdue; Jerry Lucas, C, Sr., Ohio State; Billy McGill, C, Sr., Utah; Chet Walker, F, Sr., Bradley.

National Player of the Year: Lucas (24.9 ppg, 17.4 rpg, 62.3 FG%).

National Coach of the Year: Fred Taylor, Ohio State (27-1/UPI, USBWA).

Ohio State's Jerry Lucas finished his career with the three best single-season rebounding totals in Big Ten Conference history. They were still the top three through the 1993-94 campaign. Lucas became the first player to ever gain five individual national statistical titles in a career (two for rebounding and three for shooting).

National scoring leader Billy McGill (38.8 points per game) accounted for 45.8 percent of Utah's output. That figure was especially impressive because the Utes were sixth in the country in team offense. McGill's season included 12 of the 19 games in school history of more than 40 points and all four contests of at least 50, including a school-record and national-high 60 against Brigham Young.

A deadeye duo–Arkansas' Tommy Boyer (93.3 percent) and Jerry Carlton (88.1)–became the only set to teammates to rank one-two in free-throw accuracy. Boyer's margin of victory in free-throw shooting was the largest in NCAA history. . . . One of the nation's premier field-goal shooters was Iowa's Don Nelson (55.5 percent), who would go on to play and coach in the NBA.. . . Davidson, in its second season under coach Lefty Driesell, posted its first winning record (14-11) since 1948-49.

Wake Forest, coached by Bones McKinney, captured its only undisputed ACC regular-season championship with a 12-2 league record. Wake Forest's Len Chappell scored 30 points or more in an ACC-record eight consecutive games, including an ACC-game mark of 50 against Virginia. A sell-out crowd watching a non-league game between Wake and another top 10 ACC rival, Duke, was enthralled by the Blue Devils' flashy new uniforms as they became the first college team to have player names on the back of the jerseys. Chappell's 37 points weren't enough to prevent a 75-73 loss to Duke, which received 33 points from Art Heyman.

The two highest-scoring teams in the nation were separated by a single basket of compiling duplicate records. Loyola of Chicago and Arizona State both posted 23-4 records, but Loyola scored two more points than the Sun Devils (2,436 to 2,434). . . . Purdue's Terry Dischinger finished his three-year varsity career with a 28.3-point average, but he is the only one of more than 50 two-time consensus first-team All-Americans since 1946 to never participate in the NCAA Tournament or the NIT.

Indiana guard Jimmy Rayl, after averaging a modest four points per game the previous season as a sophomore, exploded for a 29.8-point average to finish sixth in the country. He scored a school-record 56 points against Minnesota. . . . Other players who set school single-game scoring records were Holy Cross' Jack Foley (56 points vs. Connecticut), Brigham Young's Bob Skousen (47 vs. UCLA), Penn State's Gene Harris (46 vs. Holy Cross in Quaker City Classic at Philadelphia) and Minnesota's Eric Magdanz (42 at Michigan/later tied). . . . Utah's McGill, Holy Cross' Foley (33.3), Wake Forest's Chappell (30.1), Indiana's Rayl (29.8) and The Citadel's Gary Daniels (23.9) set school records for highest scoring average in a single season.

Syracuse and Georgetown haven't always been among the Beasts of the East. Syracuse finished with a 2-22 record, the worst mark in university history. The Orangemen lost their first 22 games, including a 63-point setback against NYU (122-59), before ending a school-record 27-

Purdue forward Terry Dischinger.

1961-62 INDIVIDUAL LEADERS

SCORING

PLAYER	PTS.	AVG.
McGill, Utah	1009	38.8
Foley, Holy Cross	866	33.3
Werkman, Seton Hall	793	33.0
Dischinger, Purdue	726	30.3
Chappell, Wake Forest	932	30.1
Rayl, Indiana	714	29.8
Smith, Furman	728	27.0
DeBusschere, Detroit	696	26.8
Duffy, Colgate	611	26.6
Walker, Bradley	687	26.4

REBOUNDING

PLAYER	REB.	PCT.
Lucas, Ohio St.	499	.2112
Silas, Creighton	563	.2108

Glur, Furman	488	.209
Lundy, Lafayette	437	.200
DeBusschere, Detroit	498	.189
Ellis, St. John's	430	.187
Jennings, Murray St.	431	.181
Luyk, Florida	352	.179
Thompson, DePaul	354	.178
Thurmond, Bowling Green	394	.176

FIELD GOAL PERCENTAGE

PLAYER	FGM	FGA	PCT.
Lucas, Ohio St.	237	388	.611
Johns, Auburn	129	221	.584
Green, Colorado St.	203	348	.583
Swain, Florida St.	157	274	.573
Beckman, Memphis St.	206	361	.571
Harger, Houston	145	258	.562
Russell, Nebraska	136	243	.560

McGill, Utah	394	705	.559
Cerkvenik, Arizona St.	101	181	.558
Hadnot, Providence	198	357	.555
Nelson, Iowa	193	348	.555

FREE THROW PERCENTAGE

PLAYER	FTM	FTA	PCT.
Boyer, Arkansas	125	134	.933
Carlton, Arkansas	140	159	.881
Chappelle, Maine	132	151	.874
Foley, Holy Cross	222	256	.867
Williams, Morehead St.	138	160	.863
Sherard, Army	112	130	.862
Komives, Bowling Green	134	156	.859
Loudermilk, SMU	203	239	.849
Reynolds, TCU	100	118	.847
Stroud, Mississippi St.	116	137	.847

1961-62 TEAM LEADERS

SCORING OFFENSE

SCHOOL	PTS.	AVG.
Loyola (Ill.)	2436	90.2
Arizona St.	2434	90.1
Seton Hall	2115	88.1
Indiana	2089	87.0
West Virginia	2562	85.4

SCORING DEFENSE

SCHOOL	PTS.	AVG.
Santa Clara	1302	52.1
Auburn	1254	52.3
San Jose St.	1262	52.6
Cincinnati	1707	55.1
Texas Western	1343	56.0

FIELD GOAL PERCENTAGE

SCHOOL	FGM	FGA	PCT.
Florida St.	709	1386	.512
Utah	883	1812	.487
Ohio St.	952	1961	.485
Memphis St.	736	1530	.481
Bradley	887	1849	.480

FREE THROW PERCENTAGE

SCHOOL	FTM	FTA	PCT.
Arkansas	502	647	.776
Southern Methodist	552	718	.769
Holy Cross	497	650	.765
Memphis St.	367	482	.761
Western Kentucky	538	713	.755

REBOUNDING

SCHOOL	TOTAL REB.	REB.	PCT.
Cornell	2481	1463	.590
Ohio St.	2362	1391	.589
Creighton	2791	1640	.588
DePaul	1989	1161	.584
Delaware	2077	1204	.580

game losing streak with a 73-72 success at Boston College. Meanwhile, Georgetown's streak of seasons with at least 10 defeats ended at eight in a row with a 14-9 mark. The Hoyas, however, lost to Navy for the eighth consecutive time, 64-56, giving them a career 7-31 worksheet against the Midshipmen.

Delaware snapped a streak of eight consecutive losing seasons by compiling an 18-5 record. . . . For the second time in four years, Mississippi State didn't participate in the NCAA Tournament despite compiling the best record in the country (24-1). Mississippi State's only defeat was at Vanderbilt, which finished the season with a .500 mark (12-12). . . . LSU registered its only winning record (13-11) in a 13-year span until legendary Pete Maravich joined the Tigers' varsity in the late 1960s.

The San Francisco Bay Area supplied the leader in team defense for the seventh time in eight years–Santa Clara (52.1). . . . Pepperdine captured the West Coast Conference championship just one year after finishing in sixth place. . . . Creighton's Paul Silas (38 vs. Centenary), St. John's LeRoy Ellis (30 vs. NYU), Washington's Ed Corell (30 vs. Oregon) and Utah's McGill (24 at UCLA) set school single-game rebounding records.

NIT champion Dayton compiled a 24-6 mark but didn't finish the season in the Top 20 of a final wire-service poll. The Tom Blackburn-coached Flyers resided there nine times in the previous 11 years. . . . Butler, making its only NCAA Tournament appearance, enjoyed its last season with fewer than 10 defeats (22-6 record, coached by Paul Hinkle). It is the school's winningest season in history.

1961–62 NCAA CHAMPION: CINCINNATI

SEASON STATISTICS OF CINCINNATI REGULARS

PLAYER	POS.	CL.	G.	FG%	FT%	PPG	RPG
Paul Hogue	C	Sr.	31	.498	.566	16.8	12.4
Ron Bonham	F	So.	31	.455	.760	14.3	5.0
Tom Thacker	G-F	Jr.	31	.405	.612	11.0	8.6
George Wilson	F-C	So.	31	.505	.663	9.2	8.0
Tony Yates	G	Jr.	31	.383	.670	8.2	3.0
Fred Dierking	F	Sr.	28	.433	.588	4.1	2.9
Larry Shingleton	G	Jr.	25	.416	.560	3.9	1.4
Dale Heidotting	F	Jr.	22	.511	.571	3.1	2.3
Tom Sizer	G	Sr.	25	.456	.625	2.7	1.3
Jim Calhoun	G	Sr.	18	.368	.667	1.7	0.4
TEAM TOTALS			31	.447	.632	72.2	49.5

1962 FINAL FOUR CHAMPIONSHIP GAME

LOUISVILLE, KY

OHIO STATE (59)	FG-A	FT-A	REB.	PF	PTS.
Havlicek	5-14	1-2	9	1	11
McDonald	0-1	3-3	1	2	3
Lucas	5-17	1-2	16	3	11
Reasbeck	4-6	0-0	0	4	8
Nowell	4-16	1-1	6	2	9
Doughty	0-1	0-0	2	2	0
Gearhart	1-4	0-0	4	3	0
Bradds	5-7	5-6	4	2	15
TOTALS	24-66	11-14	42	19	59

FG%: .364. FT%: .786. Turnovers: 9.

CINCINNATI (71)	FG-A	FT-A	REB.	PF	PTS.
Bonham	3-12	4-4	6	3	10
Wilson	1-6	4-4	11	2	6
Hogue	11-18	0-2	19	2	22
Thacker	6-14	9-11	6	2	21
Yates	4-8	4-7	1	1	12
Sizer	0-0	0-0	0	0	0
TOTALS	25-58	21-28	43	10	71

FG%: .431. FT%: .750. Turnovers: 8.
Halftime: Cincinnati 37-29.

NATIONAL SEMIFINALS

WAKE FOREST (68): Chappell 10-24 7-11 27, Christie 0-2 1-1 1, Woollard 1-3 1-2 3, Wiedeman 5-16 3-6 13, Packer 8-14 1-2 17, Hull 0-2 0-0 0, McCoy 0-1 2-2 2, Carmichael 0-0 0-0 0, Hassell 1-2 0-0 2, Zawacki 0-0 1-3 1, Koehler 0-1 0-0 0, Brooks 0-1 2-2 2. Team 25-66 (.379) 18-29 (.621) 68.

OHIO STATE (84): Havlicek 9-19 7-9 25, McDonald 5-10 1-2 11, Lucas 8-16 3-4 19, Nowell 2-11 0-0 4, Reasbeck 5-7 0-0 10, Gearhart 2-5 0-0 4, Doughty 2-4 4-4 8, Bradds 0-0 0-1 0, Knight 0-2 0-0 0, Flatt 0-1 2-2 2, Taylor 0-0 0-0 0, Frazier 1-1 0-0 2. Team 34-75 (.453) 16-22 (.727) 84.

Halftime: Ohio State 46-34.

UCLA (70): Blackman 2-3 0-0 4, Cunningham 8-14 3-3 19, Slaughter 1-4 0-0 2, Green 9-16 9-11 27, Hazzard 5-10 2-3 12, Waxman 2-3 2-3 6, Stewart 0-0 0-0 0. Team 27-50 (.540) 16-20 (.800) 70.

CINCINNATI (72): Bonham 8-14 3-6 19, Wilson 1-6 1-2 3, Hogue 12-18 12-17 36, Thacker 1-7 0-0 2, Yates 4-10 2-3 10, Sizer 1-3 0-0 2. Team 27-58 (.466) 18-28 (.643) 72.

Halftime: Tied 37-37.

ALL-TOURNAMENT TEAM

Len Chappell, F-C, Sr., Wake Forest
John Havlicek, F, Sr., Ohio State
Paul Hogue, C, Sr., Cincinnati*
Jerry Lucas, C, Sr., Ohio State
Tom Thacker, F-G, Jr., Cincinnati
     *Named Most Outstanding Player

1961-62 FINAL NATIONAL POLLS

AP	UPI	SCHOOL (RECORD)	HEAD COACH
1	1	Ohio St. (26-2)	Fred Taylor
2	2	Cincinnati (29-2)	Ed Jucker
3	3	Kentucky (23-3)	Adolph Rupp
4	4	Mississippi State (24-1)	Babe McCarthy
5	6	Bradley (21-7)	Chuck Orsborn
6	5	Kansas State (22-3)	Tex Winter
7	10	Utah (23-3)	Jack Gardner
8	9	Bowling Green St. (21-4)	Harold Anderson
9	8	Colorado (19-7)	Sox Walseth
10	13	Duke (20-5)	Vic Bubas
11	13	Loyola of Chicago (23-4)	George Ireland
12	12	St. John's (21-5)	Joe Lapchick
13	7	Wake Forest (22-9)	Bones McKinney
14	11	Oregon State (24-5)	Slats Gill
15	16	West Virginia (24-6)	George King
16	15	Arizona State (23-4)	Ned Wulk
17	18	Duquesne (22-7)	Red Manning
18	19	Utah State (22-7)	Ladell Andersen
19	17	UCLA (18-11)	John Wooden
20	20	Villanova (21-7)	Jack Kraft

Wichita State ended defending champion Cincinnati's 27-game winning streak, 52-51, on Lanny Van Eman's jumper with three seconds remaining. . . . The Border and Skyline conferences disbanded after the season to make way for the Western Athletic Conference. . . . North Carolina's Dean Smith kicked off his illustrious head coaching career with an inauspicious 8-9 record. The Tar Heels lost their first four ACC games in February by an average of 18.5 points in Smith's only losing season.

1962 NCAA Tournament

Summary: Ohio State All-American center Jerry Lucas wrenched his left knee in the national semifinals against Wake Forest, limiting his effectiveness against Cincinnati counterpart Paul Hogue in the Bearcats' 71-59 triumph in the final. In the 1962 national semifinals against UCLA, Hogue scored 14 consecutive points for the Bearcats down the stretch to finish with 36 before Thacker's desperation long-range basket, his only points of the game, gave them a 72-70 triumph. Cincinnati (29-2/coached by Ed Jucker), setting a school single-season record for most victories, is the only school to capture an NCAA championship after earning a berth in the tourney by winning a conference title play-off game (tied atop the Missouri Valley standings with Bradley).

Outcome for Defending Champion: The only Ohio State regular-season defeat in the last two years of the Lucas/John Havlicek era after they won the 1960 NCAA title was at Wisconsin (86-67), ending the Buckeyes' 47-game regular-season winning streak and 27-game Big Ten winning string. Havlicek hit just 3 of 15 field-goal attempts in the contest.

Star Gazing: Tom Thacker, a 6-2 swingman who averaged nine rebounds per game for Cincinnati's back-to-back titlists, is the only individual to play for an NCAA champion, NBA champion (Boston Celtics '68) and ABA champion (Indiana Pacers '70).

One and Only: Dave DeBusschere became the only player to post the highest-scoring game in a single tournament the same year he played major league baseball. DeBusschere scored a tourney-high 38 points for Detroit in a 90-81 defeat against Western Kentucky in the first round of the Mideast Regional. He pitched that summer for the Chicago White Sox. . . . Wake Forest forward Bill Hull became the only individual to play in the Final Four the same year he intercepted a pass in overtime of an AFL championship game (23-yard return by defensive end helped set up game-winning field goal for the Dallas Texans in a 20-17 decision over the Houston Oilers).

Numbers Game: Utah State's Cornell Green became the only athlete to compile one of the top five scoring averages in an NCAA Tournament before playing for an NFL champion. Green, a five-time Pro Bowl defensive back during his 13-year career with the Dallas Cowboys from 1962 through 1973, tied for fourth in scoring average in the '62 playoffs (24.3 points per game in three games). But the Aggies were eliminated by coach John Wooden's first Final Four team at UCLA despite Green's game-high 26 points (73-62 in West Regional semifinals). . . . Wooden's initial Final Four squad (18-11 record) was the only national semifinalist in 20 years from 1960 through 1979 to finish a season with double-digit defeats. The Bruins lost seven of their first 11 games. . . . Ohio State became the only school to reach the Final Four three consecutive years on two separate occasions (1944 through 1946 and 1960 through 1962). . . . Wake Forest became the only school to win back-to-back tourney games by double-digit margins in overtime (10-point victory against Yale and 11-point triumph against St. Joseph's in East Regional). . . . Massachusetts made its only NCAA Tournament appearance until 1992.

What If: Utah (23-3), denied a national post-season tournament appearance for the eighth straight year because it was on NCAA probation, won by nine points at UCLA, an eventual Final Four team. The Utes won 80 percent of their games in that eight-year span. . . . Kansas State, ranked 5th by UPI and 6th by AP the year after being eliminated from the NCAA Tournament by eventual national champion Cincinnati, finished runner-up in the Big Eight Conference to Colorado. The Wildcats' three defeats were in road games against Colorado, Kentucky and Oklahoma State.

Putting Things in Perspective: Cincinnati would have gone undefeated if not for two setbacks by a total of three points in Missouri Valley Conference road games (at Wichita State and Bradley).

Scoring Leader: Len Chappell, Wake Forest (134 points, 26.8 ppg).

Rebounding Leader: Len Chappell, Wake Forest (86 rebounds, 17.2 rpg).

Highest Rebounding Average: Mel Counts, Oregon State (53 rebounds, 17.7 rpg).

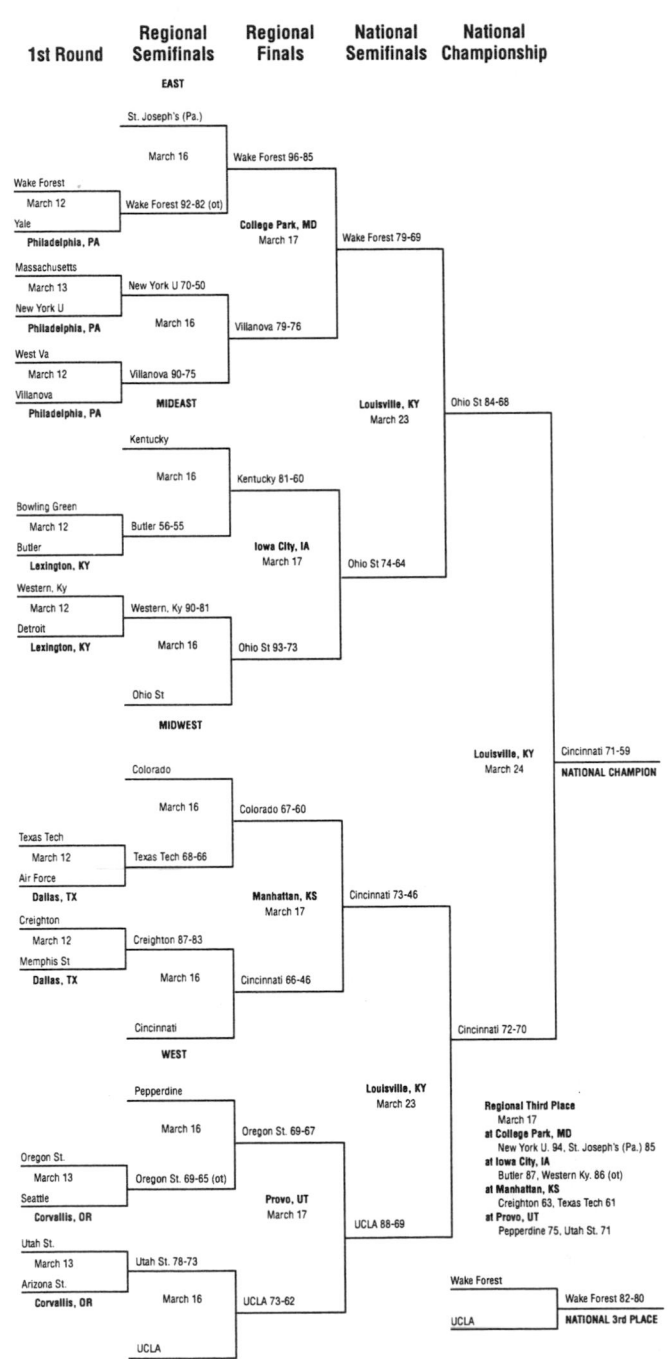

	1st Round	Regional Semifinals	Regional Finals	National Semifinals	National Championship

EAST

St. Joseph's (Pa.)

March 16 — Wake Forest 96-85

Wake Forest
March 12
Yale — Wake Forest 92-82 (ot)

Philadelphia, PA

College Park, MD
March 17 — Wake Forest 79-69

Massachusetts
March 13
New York U — New York U 70-50

Philadelphia, PA

March 16 — Villanova 79-76

West Va
March 12
Villanova — Villanova 90-75

Philadelphia, PA

Louisville, KY
March 23 — Ohio St 84-68

MIDEAST

Kentucky

March 16 — Kentucky 81-60

Bowling Green
March 12
Butler — Butler 56-55

Lexington, KY

Iowa City, IA
March 17 — Ohio St 74-64

Western, Ky
March 12
Detroit — Western, Ky 90-81

Lexington, KY

March 16 — Ohio St 93-73

Ohio St

MIDWEST

Louisville, KY
March 24 — Cincinnati 71-59

NATIONAL CHAMPION

Colorado

March 16 — Colorado 67-60

Texas Tech
March 12
Air Force — Texas Tech 68-66

Dallas, TX

Manhattan, KS
March 17 — Cincinnati 73-46

Creighton
March 12
Memphis St — Creighton 87-83

Dallas, TX

March 16 — Cincinnati 66-46

Cincinnati

WEST

Cincinnati 72-70

Pepperdine

March 16 — Oregon St. 69-67

Oregon St.
March 13
Seattle — Oregon St. 69-65 (ot)

Corvallis, OR

Provo, UT
March 17 — UCLA 88-69

Utah St.
March 13
Arizona St. — Utah St. 78-73

Corvallis, OR

March 16 — UCLA 73-62

UCLA

Louisville, KY
March 23

Regional Third Place
March 17
at College Park, MD
New York U. 94, St. Joseph's (Pa.) 85
at Iowa City, IA
Butler 87, Western Ky. 86 (ot)
at Manhattan, KS
Creighton 63, Texas Tech 61
at Provo, UT
Pepperdine 75, Utah St. 71

Wake Forest

UCLA — Wake Forest 82-80

NATIONAL 3rd PLACE

1962–63

AT A GLANCE

NCAA Champion: Loyola, Ill. (29-2; coached by George Ireland).

NIT Champion: Providence (24-4; coached by Joe Mullaney).

New Conference: Western Athletic.

NCAA Probation: Dayton, Indiana, New Mexico State.

NCAA Consensus First-Team All-Americans: Ron Bonham, F, Jr., Cincinnati; Jerry Harkness, F, Sr., Loyola (Ill.); Art Heyman, F, Sr., Duke; Barry Kramer, F, Jr., NYU; Tom Thacker, F-G, Sr., Cincinnati.

National Player of the Year: Heyman (24.9 ppg, 10.8 rpg).

National Coach of the Year: Ed Jucker, Cincinnati (26-2/UPI, USBWA).

Mississippi State became the first school other than Kentucky to win outright or share three consecutive SEC championships. In order to participate in the NCAA playoffs, Mississippi State coach Babe McCarthy had to sneak out of town in the middle of the night. He left before he was served injunction papers stemming from two segregationist state legislators seeking to prohibit the team from leaving Mississippi and using state funds to travel to the tournament.

Billy Mitts, one of the "Jim Crow" state senators, was a former Mississippi State student body president, but his influence waned when a county sheriff apparently sympathetic to the players' plight graciously left an airport in time for them to board their plane and evade an unpleasant scene.

Mississippi State, an all-white school at the time, had captured SEC championships under McCarthy in 1959, 1961 and 1962. But the Bulldogs—then more popularly known as the Maroons—declined automatic bids to play in the NCAA Tournament those three years because of an unwritten bigoted policy forbidding Mississippi State or Ole Miss athletes to compete in racially integrated contests. Eventu-

al champion Loyola of Chicago, featuring four black starters, fell behind Mississippi State 7-0, but wound up winning the Mideast Regional semifinal game (61-51) in East Lansing, Mich. Incidentally, the next time Mississippi State appeared in the NCAA playoffs was 1991, when the Bulldogs' 13-man roster had 10 blacks.

Loyola of Chicago (29-2, coached by George Ireland) and Arizona State (26-3, Ned Wulk) had their winningest seasons in school history. Miami, Fla. (23-5, Bruce Hale) tied its school record for most victories in a single season. . . . Three of the country's top five point producers were from the East as Seton Hall's Nick Werkman became the first Easterner in 13 years to lead the nation in scoring (29.5 points per game). . . . Duke's Art Heyman finished his three-year career as "Mr. Consistency." He averaged a career-low 24.9 points per game as a senior after averaging 25.2 as a sophomore and 25.3 as a junior.

Dean Smith, in his second year as North Carolina's coach, won at Kentucky, 68-66. The 12th victory of his career came against legendary Kentucky coach Adolph Rupp, who was bypassed by Smith as the all-time winningest major-college coach 34 seasons later. . . . Five of the eight ACC members finished with losing records—Clemson (12-13), N.C. State (10-11), South Carolina (9-15), Maryland (8-13) and Virginia (5-20).

One-eyed Tommy Boyer of Arkansas became the first player to win two consecutive free-throw shooting titles. . . . Bowling Green's Howard Komives set a Mid-American Conference record by hitting 50 consecutive free throws. . . . Two of the nation's top six rebounders—Idaho's Gus Johnson (2nd with 20.3 rpg) and Bowling Green's Nate Thurmond (6th with 16.7 rpg)—had been teammates at Central Hower High School in Akron, Oh. "In my opinion, he (Johnson) was the forerunner to Dr. J (Julius Erving)," Thurmond said. "He was the first guy who was so big (6-6, 235 pounds) and could do so much with the ball." Johnson grabbed a school-record 31 rebounds in a victory over Oregon. He died of brain cancer on April 29, 1987, at the age of 48.

Wichita State ended Cincinnati's 37-game winning streak, 65-64, when Dave Stallworth poured in 46 points for the Shockers. Cincinnati, however, still captured its sixth Missouri Valley Conference championship in as many years as a member of the league. . . . Bradley lost six of eight games in a mid-season tailspin to finish with a 17-9 record, the only season in coach Chuck Orsborn's nine-year stint with the Braves when they didn't win at least two-thirds of their contests. . . . Texas, the epitome of a balanced attack, lost just one SWC game although it didn't have one of the top 10 scorers in the league. Seven Longhorn players averaged seven or more points per game in SWC competition and three other teammates had at least one game of 10 points or more.

Gary Bradds, the successor to Jerry Lucas as Ohio State's principal scoring threat, averaged 28 points per game after posting a 4.7 average the previous season as a sophomore. . . . Indiana guard Jimmy Rayl scored a national-high 56 points against Michigan State, tying a school record he established the previous year.

Illinois' Dave Downey (53 points at Indiana) and Colorado State's Bill Green (48 vs. Denver) set school single-game scoring records. Green (28.2 ppg) and St. Mary's Steve Gray (23.8) established school single-season records for highest scoring average. Green was an award-winning educator in the Bronx, N.Y., at the time of his death in 1994.

Bob Starnes' 50-foot heave at the buzzer enabled Illinois to edge Northwestern, 78-76, helping the Fighting Illini tie Ohio State for the Big Ten title. . . . Kansas finished in the second division of the Big Eight, but managed a four-overtime victory against regular-season co-champion Kansas State in the Big Eight Holiday Tournament.

St. John's (9-15) endured its worst winning percentage since going winless in 1918-19 despite ending an eight-game losing streak to St. Louis, 54-48. . . . Syracuse had lost 50 of 59 games when its mid-season record fell to 3-7. . . . Vermont's Benny Becton (29 vs. Maine) and

Wichita State's Dave Stallworth.

Utah State's Wayne Estes (28 vs. Regis) set school single-game rebounding records.

West Virginia, coached by George King, earned its eighth Southern Conference championship in nine years. . . . Kentucky's streak of

1962-63 INDIVIDUAL LEADERS

SCORING

PLAYER	PTS.	AVG.
Werkman, Seton Hall	650	29.5
Kramer, New York Univ.	675	29.3
Green, Colorado St.	649	28.2
Bradds, Ohio St.	672	28.0
Bradley, Princeton	682	27.3
Robinson, Wyoming	682	26.2
Miles, Seattle	697	25.8
Rayl, Indiana	608	25.3
Heyman, Duke	747	24.9
Crump, Idaho St.	595	24.8

REBOUNDING

PLAYER	REB.	AVG.
Silas, Creighton	557	20.6
Johnson, Idaho	466	20.3

Pokley, Morehead St.	323	17.0
Petersen, Rutgers	389	16.9
Sahm, Notre Dame	438	16.8
Thurmond, Bowling Green	452	16.7
Barnes, Texas Western	428	16.5
Pelkington, Xavier	454	16.2
Jennings, Murray St.	339	16.1
Cunningham, N. Carolina	339	16.1

FIELD GOAL PERCENTAGE

PLAYER	FGM	FGA	PCT.
Harger, Houston	193	294	.656
Raftery, St. Francis (N.Y.)	115	186	.615
Buckley, Duke	130	217	.599
Green, Colorado St.	215	371	.580
Johnson, San Francisco	178	314	.567
Johns, Auburn	119	210	.567
Blackwell, Auburn	123	219	.562
Becker, Arizona St.	225	404	.557
Mullins, Duke	256	466	.549
Cerkvanik, Arizona St.	123	225	.547

FREE THROW PERCENTAGE

PLAYER	FTM	FTA	PCT.
Boyer, Arkansas	147	161	.913
Bradley, Princeton	258	289	.893
Bonham, Cincinnati	173	194	.892
Batchelor, BYU	104	119	.874
Rayl, Indiana	178	204	.873
Stroud, Miss. St.	120	138	.870
Hyland, Princeton	112	129	.868
Ward, South Carolina	118	136	.868
Vadset, Washington St.	119	138	.862
Smith, Furman	204	238	.857

1962-63 TEAM LEADERS

SCORING OFFENSE

SCHOOL	PTS.	AVG.
Loyola (Ill.)	2847	91.8
Miami (Fla.)	2509	89.6
Indiana	2032	84.7
Illinois	2201	84.7
Duke	2496	83.2

SCORING DEFENSE

SCHOOL	PTS.	AVG.
Cincinnati	1480	52.9
Oklahoma St.	1328	53.1
Texas Western	1419	54.6
San Jose St.	1383	57.6
New Mexico	1447	57.9

FIELD GOAL PERCENTAGE

SCHOOL	FGM	FGA	PCT.
Duke	984	1926	.511
Auburn	601	1188	.506
St. Francis (N.Y.)	553	1109	.499
Memphis St.	773	1553	.498
Colorado St.	593	1193	.497

FREE THROW PERCENTAGE

SCHOOL	FTM	FTA	PCT.
Tulane	390	492	.793
Furman	539	708	.761
Princeton	531	699	.760
Cornell	378	498	.759
Florida	533	703	.758

REBOUNDING

SCHOOL	TOTAL REB.	OWN	PCT.
Texas Western	1975	1167	.591
Auburn	1737	1018	.586
Delaware	2116	1239	.586
Davidson	2171	1254	.578
Regis (Colo.)	2089	1205	.577

consecutive season-opener victories ended at 37 when the Wildcats bowed to visiting Virginia Tech, 80-77. Despite the splendid start, the Hokies finished 12-12 for their only non-winning record in a 14-year span from 1955-56 through 1968-69. . . . Tennessee, coming off a dismal 4-19 campaign, posted a respectable 13-11 mark in Ray Mears' initial season as coach of the Volunteers. It was the only season in Mears' 21 years as a coach that he reached double digits in defeats.

Brigham Young incurred its fourth losing record in six seasons. . . . New Mexico compiled a 16-9 record to end a streak of eight consecutive losing seasons with seven or fewer victories. . . . San Francisco captured the West Coast Conference title just one year after finishing in sixth place. . . . Muhlenberg (Pa.) competed in its final season at the major-college level. . . . Connecticut's Hugh Greer ended a 17-year coaching career with a 286-112 record.

1962-63 FINAL NATIONAL POLLS

AP	UPI	SCHOOL (RECORD)	HEAD COACH
1	1	Cincinnati (26-2)	Ed Jucker
2	2	Duke (27-3)	Vic Bubas
3	4	Loyola of Chicago (29-2)	George Ireland
4	3	Arizona State (26-3)	Ned Wulk
5	6	Wichita (19-8)	Ralph Miller
6	7	Mississippi State (22-6)	Babe McCarthy
7	8	Ohio State (20-4)	Fred Taylor
8	5	Illinois (20-6)	Harry Combes
9	11	NYU (18-5)	Lou Rossini
10	9	Colorado (19-7)	Sox Walseth
–	10	Stanford (16-9)	Howie Dallmar
–	12	Texas (20-7)	Harold Bradley
–	13	Providence (24-4)	Joe Mullaney
–	14	Oregon State (22-9)	Slats Gill
–	15	UCLA (20-9)	John Wooden
–	16	St. Joseph's (23-5)	Jack Ramsay
–	16	West Virginia (23-8)	George King
–	18	Bowling Green St. (19-8)	Harold Anderson
–	19	Kansas State (16-9)	Tex Winter
–	19	Seattle (21-8)	Clair Markey*

* Markey coached the Seattle Chieftains in the NCAA Tournament after Vince Cazetta's resignation.

1962–63 NCAA CHAMPION: LOYOLA

SEASON STATISTICS OF LOYOLA OF CHICAGO REGULARS

PLAYER	POS.	CL.	G.	FG%	FT%	PPG	RPG
Jerry Harkness	F	Sr.	31	.504	.725	21.4	7.6
Les Hunter	C	Jr.	31	.530	.731	17.0	11.4
John Egan	G	Jr.	31	.361	.789	13.7	3.6
Vic Rouse	F	Jr.	31	.404	.730	13.5	12.1
Ron Miller	G	Jr.	31	.406	.696	13.3	5.4
Jim Reardon	F	Sr.	14	.321	.813	2.2	2.1
Dan Connaughton	G	So.	17	.424	.625	1.9	1.1
Chuck Wood	F-G	Jr.	17	.393	.714	1.9	1.9
Rich Rochelle	C	Jr.	14	.360	.375	1.5	1.4
TEAM TOTALS			31	.439	.722	91.8	57.7

1963 FINAL FOUR CHAMPIONSHIP GAME

LOUISVILLE, KY

LOYOLA (ILL.) (60)	MIN.	FG-A	FT-A	REB.	A	PF	PTS.
Harkness	45	5-18	4-8	6	0	4	14
Rouse	45	6-22	3-4	12	0	4	15
Hunter	45	6-22	4-4	11	1	3	16
Egan	45	3-8	3-5	3	0	3	9
Miller	45	3-14	0-0	2	0	3	6
Team				11			
TOTALS	225	23-84	14-21	45	1	17	60

FG%: .274. **FT%:** .667. **Turnovers:** 3.

CINCINNATI (58)	MIN.	FG-A	FT-A	REB.	A	PF	PTS.
Bonham	45	8-16	6-6	4	0	3	22
Thacker	45	5-12	3-4	15	3	4	13
Wilson	41	4-8	2-3	13	0	4	10
Yates	45	4-6	1-4	8	1	4	9
Shingleton	45	1-3	2-3	4	0	0	4
Heidotting	4	0-0	0-0	1	0	2	0
Team				7			
TOTALS	225	22-45	14-20	52	4	17	58

FG%: .489. **FT%:** .700. **Turnovers:** 16 (Thacker 7).
Halftime: Cincinnati 29-21. **Regulation:** Tied 54-54.

NATIONAL SEMIFINALS

CINCINNATI (80): Bonham 3-12 8-9 14, Thacker 5-8 4-8 14, Wilson 8-9 8-12 24, Yates 5-9 2-3 12, Shingleton 1-2 0-0 2, Heidotting 0-0 1-2 1, Cunningham 2-3 0-0 4, Meyer 1-1 1-2 3, Smith 1-3 0-2 2, Elasser 1-2 0-1 2, Abernethy 1-2 0-0 2. Team 28-51 (.549) 24-39 (.615) 80.

OREGON STATE (46): Pauly 2-8 0-1 4, Kraus 1-6 1-1 3, Counts 8-14 4-4 20, Peters 1-5 2-2 4, Baker 0-9 0-1 0, Jarvis 1-6 3-4 5, Rossi 1-3 0-0 2, Campbell 0-2 1-1 1, Torgerson 1-2 0-2 2, Hayward 0-2 1-1 1, Benner 2-2 0-0 4. Team 17-59 (.288) 12-15 (.800) 46.

Halftime: Cincinnati 30-27.

LOYOLA OF CHICAGO (94): Harkness 7-18 6-9 20, Rouse 6-12 1-2 13, Hunter 11-20 7-9 29, Egan 4-9 6-7 14, Miller 8-11 2-2 18, Wood 0-1 0-0 0, Rochelle 0-0 0-0 0, Reardon 0-0 0-0 0, Cannaughton 0-0 0-0 0. Team 36-71 (.5-7) 22-29 (.759) 94.

DUKE (75): Heyman 11-30 7-9 29, Mullins 10-20 1-3 21, Buckley 4-10 2-4 10, Schmidt 0-2 0-0 0, Harrison 0-3 2-3 2, Herbster 0-2 0-0 0, Ferguson 1-2 0-0 2, Jamieson 0-0 0-0 0, Cox 0-0 0-0 0, Mann 0-1 0-0 0, Tison 5-12 1-3 11. Team 31-82 (.378) 13-22 (.591) 75.

Halftime: Loyola of Chicago 44-31.

ALL-TOURNAMENT TEAM

Ron Bonham, F, Jr., Cincinnati
Art Heyman, F, Sr., Duke*
Les Hunter, C, Jr., Loyola of Chicago
Tom Thacker, F-G, Sr., Cincinnati
George Wilson, C, Jr., Cincinnati
*Named Most Outstanding Player

1963 NCAA Tournament

Summary: Even some teams outside the South adhered to an accepted standard of "start no more than two blacks at home, or three on the road." When Loyola, featuring four African American starters, upset Cincinnati and the Bearcats' three black starters in the championship game, it was the first time a majority of African-American players participated in the title game. Junior forward Vic Rouse leaped high to redirect center Les Hunter's shot from the free-throw line into the basket to climax the Ramblers' first year in the playoffs. Loyola of Chicago, overcoming 27.4 percent field-goal shooting by committing just three turnovers, won the final against defending NCAA champion Cincinnati (60-58 in overtime). The Ramblers trailed by 15 points in the second half before knotting the score at 54-54 when Jerry Harkness hit a 12-foot jumper with four seconds remaining in regulation. "I never thought we'd lose it," Rouse said. "We came too far to lose it."

One and Only: Oregon State's Terry Baker became the only football Heisman Trophy winner to play in the basketball Final Four. Baker, a quarterback on Oregon State's football squad that defeated Villanova (6-0) in the 1962 Liberty Bowl on his school-record 99-yard run from scrimmage, was the second-leading scorer for the Beavers' basketball team that finished fourth in the national tourney the same academic school year. Teammate Steve Pauly, Oregon State's second-leading rebounder and third-leading scorer, was the only Final Four player to become AAU national champion in the decathlon the same year.

Numbers Game: Loyola of Chicago, using its starting lineup the entire final, is the only school to deploy just five players in a championship game. The starters all averaged more than 13 points per game, making them the lone group to achieve that feat for an NCAA titlist. The Ramblers are the only team to overcome a half-time deficit of as many as eight points (29-21) to win a title game. Loyola of Chicago became the only team to defeat an opponent by at least 50 points in a tournament game (111-42 over Tennessee Tech in the first round of Mideast Regional). . . . Cincinnati coach Ed Jucker won his first 11 NCAA Tournament before bowing in the final to finish his career with an all-time best playoff winning percentage (.917 in minimum of 10 games). . . . Bowling Green's Nate Thurmond grabbed the most rebounds ever in a losing effort in the playoffs when he retrieved a tourney-high 31 missed shots in a 65-60 defeat to Mississippi State in the Southeast Regional third-place game. . . . Rod Thorn tossed in a tourney-high 44 points for West Virginia, but it wasn't enough to prevent a 97-88 setback against St. Joseph's in the East Regional semifinals.

Putting Things in Perspective: Thurmond collected 24 points and 12 rebounds and teammate Howard Komives poured in 32 points in a 92-75 regular-season triumph over NCAA champion-to-be Loyola of Chicago. But Thur-

Idaho's Gus Johnson in action.

mond shot a paltry 29.8 percent from the floor (17 of 57) in three postseason games although the Falcons registered their only NCAA tourney triumph in history (77-72 over Notre Dame).

Scoring Leader: Mel Counts, Oregon State (123 points, 24.6 ppg).

Highest Scoring Average: Barry Kramer, NYU (100 points, 33.3 ppg).

Rebounding Leaders: Bowling Green's Nate Thurmond (70 rebounds, 23.3 rpg) and Loyola's Vic Rouse (70 rebounds, 14 rpg).

1963 CHAMPIONSHIP BRACKET

1st Round	Regional Semifinals	Regional Finals	National Semifinals	National Championship

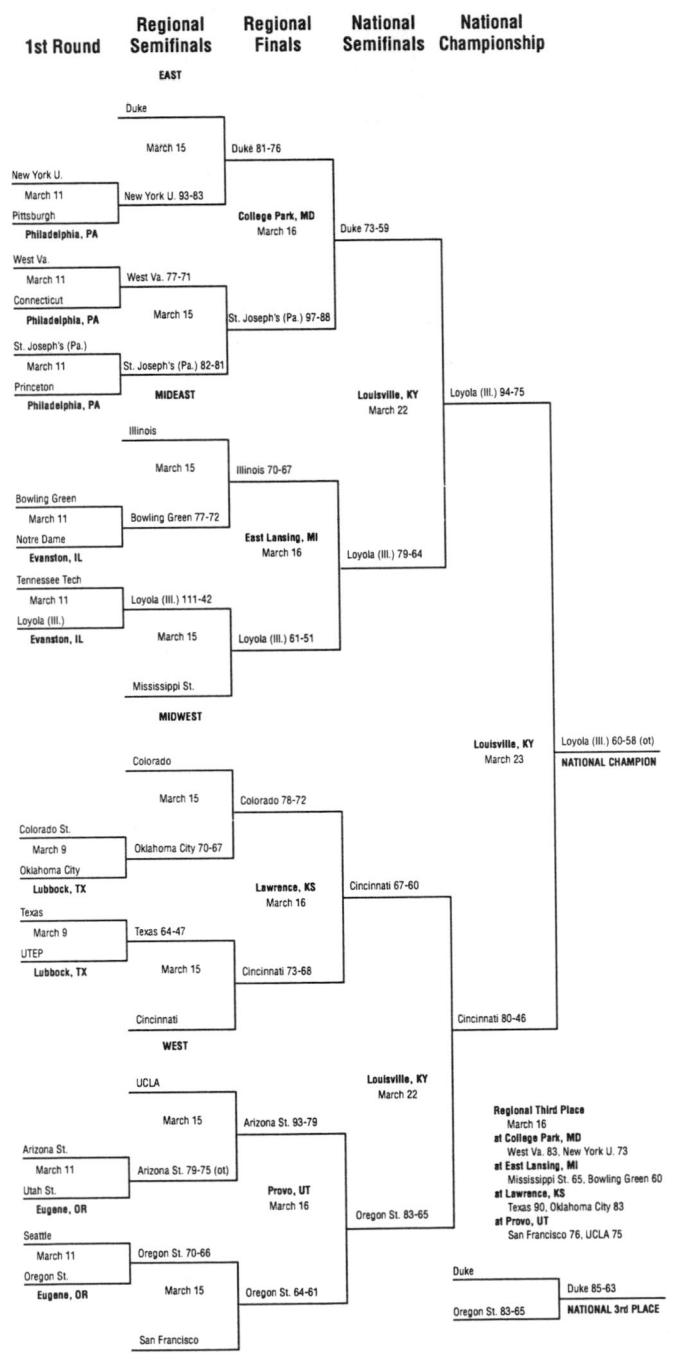

EAST

Duke

March 15 — Duke 81-76

New York U.
March 11
Pittsburgh
Philadelphia, PA

New York U. 93-83

College Park, MD
March 16

West Va.
March 11
Connecticut
Philadelphia, PA

West Va. 77-71

March 15

Duke 73-59

St. Joseph's (Pa.)
March 11
Princeton
Philadelphia, PA

St. Joseph's (Pa.) 82-81

St. Joseph's (Pa.) 97-88

MIDEAST

Louisville, KY
March 22

Loyola (Ill.) 94-75

Illinois

March 15 — Illinois 70-67

Bowling Green
March 11
Notre Dame
Evanston, IL

Bowling Green 77-72

East Lansing, MI
March 16

Tennessee Tech
March 11
Loyola (Ill.)
Evanston, IL

Loyola (Ill.) 111-42

March 15

Loyola (Ill.) 79-64

Loyola (Ill.) 61-51

Mississippi St.

MIDWEST

Louisville, KY
March 23

Loyola (Ill.) 60-58 (ot)

NATIONAL CHAMPION

Colorado

March 15 — Colorado 78-72

Colorado St.
March 9
Oklahoma City
Lubbock, TX

Oklahoma City 70-67

Lawrence, KS
March 16

Cincinnati 67-60

Texas
March 9
UTEP
Lubbock, TX

Texas 64-47

March 15

Cincinnati 73-68

Cincinnati

Cincinnati 80-46

WEST

Louisville, KY
March 22

UCLA

March 15 — Arizona St. 93-79

Arizona St.
March 11
Utah St.
Eugene, OR

Arizona St. 79-75 (ot)

Provo, UT
March 16

Seattle
March 11
Oregon St.
Eugene, OR

Oregon St. 70-66

March 15

Oregon St. 83-65

Oregon St. 64-61

San Francisco

Regional Third Place
March 16
at College Park, MD
West Va. 83, New York U. 73
at East Lansing, MI
Mississippi St. 65, Bowling Green 60
at Lawrence, KS
Texas 90, Oklahoma City 83
at Provo, UT
San Francisco 76, UCLA 75

Duke

Duke 85-63

Oregon St. 83-65

NATIONAL 3rd PLACE

1963-64

Undefeated UCLA won its first of 10 NCAA titles in 12 years, a stretch of dominance that many believe ranks among the greatest achievements in the history of competitive sports. The Bruins had never won a Final Four game despite finishing in a final Top 20 wire-service poll eight times in the previous 14 seasons under coach John Wooden.

UCLA's closest homecourt decision was an 83-79 victory over Illinois despite a school-record 24 rebounds by the Illini's Skip Thoren.

Kentucky set an NCAA single-game record with 108 rebounds against Mississippi. . . . Georgia Tech, coached by Whack Hyder, finished in a tie for second place behind Kentucky in the Southeastern Conference in the Yellow Jackets' final season as a member of the league. . . . Cincinnati's 86-game homecourt winning streak, which started in 1957, was snapped by Kansas, 51-47. Cincinnati finished out of the top 10 of the final AP poll for the first time in seven years.

Defending national scoring champion Nick Werkman of Seton Hall scored almost four points per game more than he did the previous season (from 29.5 to 33.2), but finished runner-up to Bowling Green's Howard Komives, a 6-1 guard who averaged 36.7 points per game after hitting 50 consecutive free throws in his last five games. Komives finished 45th in the country in scoring the previous year with a 20.2 norm. Werkman and Komives were among five players to score more than 32 points per game. Werkman's 52 points against Scranton is still a school record.

Princeton's Bill Bradley set a mark for most points in an Ivy League contest when he poured in 51 against Harvard. . . . Setting school single-game scoring records were Texas Western's Jim Barnes (51 points vs. Western New Mexico), Xavier's Steve Thomas (50 vs. Detroit), Ohio State's Gary Bradds (49 vs. Illinois), Boston College's John Austin (49 vs. Georgetown) and Northwestern's Rich Falk (49 vs. Iowa). . . . Barnes also grabbed a school-record 36 rebounds in the Western New Mexico contest. Bradds' outburst was one of six consecutive 40-point games for him in Big Ten competition.

Komives' average is the highest in Mid-American Conference history. Two of Western Michigan's defeats in its first four games came at Michigan State (101-100) despite Newsome's 45 points and against defending NCAA champion Loyola of Chicago (105-102) despite Newsome's 44 points.

Texas A&M, coached by Shelby Metcalf, captured its first outright Southwest Conference championship since 1923. A&M's Bennie Lenox set a school and Southwest Conference record with a national single-game high of 53 points against Wyoming in the All-College Tournament at Oklahoma City. He was one of 10 different players to score 50 or more in a single game during the season. . . . Creighton's Paul Silas finished his varsity career as the only player in Division I history to average more than 20 rebounds each season of a career that lasted at least three years. He had 13 games with at least 27 rebounds.

Ohio State captured an unprecedented fifth consecutive Big Ten title. The Buckeyes, howev-

1963–64 INDIVIDUAL LEADERS

SCORING

PLAYER	PTS.	AVG.
Komives, Bowling Green	844	36.7
Werkman, Seton Hall	830	33.2
Newsome, W. Michigan	653	32.7
Bradley, Princeton	936	32.3
Barry, Miami (Fla.)	870	32.2
Bradds, Ohio St.	735	30.6
Thomas, Xavier	779	30.0
Austin, Boston College	614	29.2
Barnes, Texas Western	816	29.1
Estes, Utah St.	821	28.3

REBOUNDING

PLAYER	REB.	AVG.
Pelkington, Xavier	567	21.80
Silas, Creighton	631	21.75

Dzik, Detroit	521	20.8
Isaac, Iona	403	20.2
Barnes, Texas Western	537	19.2
Reed, Notre Dame	318	17.7
Sahm, Notre Dame	315	17.5
Kimball, Connecticut	466	17.3
Counts, Oregon St.	489	16.9
Johnson, San Francisco	467	16.7

FIELD GOAL PERCENTAGE

PLAYER	FGM	FGA	PCT.
Holland, Davidson	135	214	.631
DeBerardinis, St. Fr. (Pa.)	112	181	.619
Fisher, Texas	136	222	.613
Nightingale, Rhode I.	139	229	.607
Johnson, San Francisco	206	346	.595
Buckley, Duke	160	271	.590
Thompson, Providence	260	442	.588

Pierce, W. Texas St.	123	210	.586
Bustion, Colorado St.	110	188	.585
Richards, Syracuse	177	305	.580

FREE THROW PERCENTAGE

PLAYER	FTM	FTA	PCT.
Park, Tulsa	121	134	.903
Schultz, Tennessee	101	113	.894
Lee, San Francisco	108	121	.893
Izor, Dayton	95	107	.888
Bailey, N. Texas St.	136	156	.872
Murphy, DePaul	93	107	.869
Geiger, Xavier	119	137	.869
Newsome, W. Michigan	129	149	.866
Vrankovich, Santa Clara	165	191	.864
Perry, Alabama	87	101	.861

1963–64 TEAM LEADERS

SCORING OFFENSE

SCHOOL	PTS.	AVG.
Detroit	2402	96.1
Miami (Fla.)	2575	95.4
Michigan St.	2211	92.1
Weber St.	2288	91.5
Loyola (Ill.)	2556	91.3

SCORING DEFENSE

SCHOOL	PTS.	AVG.
San Jose St.	1307	54.5
Texas Western	1548	55.3
Gettysburg (Pa.)	1363	56.8
New Mexico	1660	57.2
Oklahoma St.	1449	58.0

FIELD GOAL PERCENTAGE

SCHOOL	FGM	FGA	PCT.
Davidson	894	1644	.544
West Texas St.	681	1356	.502
Rhode Island	910	1854	.491
Wichita St.	817	1688	.484
San Francisco	764	1581	.483

FREE THROW PERCENTAGE

SCHOOL	FTM	FTA	PCT.
Miami (Fla.)	593	780	.760
Bowling Green	430	571	.753
Utah	578	769	.752
Kentucky	454	605	.750
Lafayette	454	608	.747

REBOUNDING

SCHOOL	TOTAL REB.	OWN	PCT.
Iona	1673	1071	.640
San Francisco	2343	1410	.602
Cornell	2674	1580	.591
Texas Western	2386	1407	.590
New Mexico	2188	1284	.587

er, saw their 50-game homecourt winning streak snapped when they were dumped by Davidson, 95-73. . . . Senior Terry Holland's nation-leading 63.1 percent field-goal shooting helped Davidson pace the country at 54.4 percent. Holland, who would coach Virginia to the Final Four in 1981 and 1984, is the only Final Four coach to previously lead the nation in a statistical category as a major-college player.

Another player who would become a prominent coach was Providence center John Thompson, who ranked among the nation's top 20 in scoring (26.2 ppg), rebounding (14.5 rpg) and field-goal shooting (58.8 percent). . . . Digger Phelps was graduate assistant coach at Rider when the Broncs stunned NYU, ending the Violets' homecourt winning streak that dated back to 1941.

Forward Joe Caldwell became the only player in Arizona State history to earn first-team all-conference honors on three different occasions–Border (1962) and WAC (1963 and 1964). Jumpin' Joe cleared 6 feet-7 inches in the high jump as a member of the school's track squad. . . . Arizona lost its last three games but registered the Wildcats' first winning record in 10 seasons (15-11).

Duke won a league-record 27 consecutive games against ACC competition (subsequently tied) until bowing at Wake Forest, 72-71. Duke captured the ACC Tournament by an average margin of 23 points. The Blue Devils' trek to the Final Four was unnerving when their 85-seat charter airplane skidded off a rain-slick runway upon landing at Kansas City's Municipal Airport. . . . Clemson won four of its last five games to compile the Tigers' first winning record (13-12) in 12 years. The Tigers notched their first winning record in ACC competition (8-6) since the league's inaugural season in 1953-54. . . . North Carolina junior Billy Cunningham reached double digits in scoring and rebounding in the same game a total of 22 times during the season and on 60 occasions in his three-year varsity career.

Tulane was winless through 22 games until winning its season finale against LSU, 80-68. . . . Kansas State finished first or second in the Big Eight Conference standings for the ninth consecutive season. The Wildcats lost twice to undefeated UCLA by a total of just nine points. . . . Drake, coached by Maury John, earned a share of the Missouri Valley Conference regular-season title after finishing in last place the previous year.

Detroit, coached by Bob Calihan, became the only Michigan Division I team ever to lead the nation in scoring. The 14-11 Titans averaged 96.1 points per game, which was well above the national average of 74.4. . . . Minnesota, coached by John Kundla, compiled a 17-7 record to snap a streak of six consecutive non-winning seasons. . . . DePaul finished in the Top 20 of a final wire-service poll for the only time in a 22-year span from 1953-54 through 1974-75. Texas A&M finished in the Top 20 of a final wire-service poll for the only time in a 28-year span from 1951-52 through 1978-79. . . . Xavier's Bob Pelkington grabbed a school-record 31 rebounds in a game against St. Francis (Pa.).

UCLA's Walt Hazzard dishes one off to a teammate.

Idaho's Tom Moreland set a Big Sky Conference single-game standard by tying a school mark with 31 rebounds against Whitworth. . . . Ben Carnevale was in his 18th season as Navy's coach when the Midshipmen posted their first losing record in 21 years (10-12). . . . Oklahoma State's Hank Iba posted the 700th victory of his college coaching career with an 80-47 triumph over Oklahoma in State's final game of the season.

Pacific ended a streak of seven consecutive losing seasons and started a string of 11 straight

1963-64 NCAA CHAMPION: UCLA

SEASON STATISTICS OF UCLA REGULARS

PLAYER	POS.	CL.	G.	FG%	FT%	PPG	RPG
Gail Goodrich	G	Jr.	30	.458	.711	21.5	5.2
Walt Hazzard	G	Sr.	30	.445	.718	18.6	4.7
Jack Hirsch	F	Sr.	30	.528	.664	14.0	7.6
Kelth Erickson	F	Jr.	30	.403	.623	10.7	9.1
Fred Slaughter	C	Sr.	30	.466	.484	7.9	8.1
Kenny Washington	F-G	So.	30	.458	.627	6.1	4.2
Doug McIntosh	C	So.	30	.519	.500	3.6	4.4
Kim Stewart	F	Sr.	23	.393	.467	2.2	2.0
Rich Levin	F	Jr.	19	.372	.500	2.0	0.6
Mike Huggins	G	Sr.	23	.382	.478	1.6	1.0
Chuck Darrow	G	So.	23	.379	.583	1.6	1.2
Vaughn Hoffman	C	So.	21	.476	.500	1.2	1.3
TEAM TOTALS			30	.455	.644	88.9	55.7

1964 FINAL FOUR CHAMPIONSHIP GAME

KANSAS CITY, MO

UCLA (98)	FG-A	FT-A	REB.	A	PF	PTS.
Goodrich	9-18	9-9	3	1	1	27
Slaughter	0-1	0-0	1	2	0	0
Hazzard	4-10	3-5	3	8	5	11
Hirsch	5-9	3-5	6	6	3	13
Erickson	2-7	4-4	5	1	5	8
McIntosh	4-9	0-0	11	1	2	8
Washington	11-16	4-4	12	1	4	26
Darrow	0-1	3-4	1	0	2	3
Stewart	0-1	0-0	0	0	1	0
Huggins	0-1	0-1	1	2	2	0
Hoffman	1-2	0-0	0	0	0	2
Levin	0-1	0-0	0	0	0	0
TOTALS	**36-76**	**26-32**	**43**	**22**	**25**	**98**

FG%: .474. **FT%:** .813. **Turnovers:** 19.

DUKE (83)	FG-A	FT-A	REB.	A	PF	PTS.
Ferguson	2-6	0-1	1	4	3	4
Buckley	5-8	8-12	9	0	4	18
Tison	3-8	1-1	1	2	2	7
Harrison	1-1	0-0	1	1	2	2
Mullins	9-21	4-4	4	1	5	22
Marin	8-16	0-1	10	1	3	16
Vacendak	2-7	3-3	6	0	4	7
Herbster	1-4	0-2	0	0	0	2
Kitching	1-1	0-0	1	0	0	2
Mann	0-0	3-4	2	0	1	3
Harscher	0-0	0-0	0	0	0	0
Cox	0-0	0-0	0	0	0	0
TOTALS	**32-72**	**19-28**	**35**	**9**	**24**	**83**

FG%: .444. **FT%:** .679. **Turnovers:** 24.
Halftime: UCLA 50-38.

NATIONAL SEMIFINALS

UCLA (90): Goodrich 7-18 0-0 14, Slaughter 2-6 0-0 4, Hazzard 7-10 5-7 19, Hirsch 2-11 0-0 4, Erickson 10-21 8-9 28, McIntosh 3-5 2-3 8, Washington 5-11 3-4 13. Team 36-82 (.439) 18-23 (.783) 90.

KANSAS STATE (84): Moss 3-9 1-1 7, Robinson 2-7 0-1 4, Simons 10-17 4-6 24, Suttner 3-9 0-5 6, Murrell 13-22 3-5 29, Paradis 5-9 0-0 10, Williams 1-1 2-3 4, Nelson 0-1 0-0 0, Gottfrid 0-0 0-0 0, Barnard 0-1 0-0 0. Team 37-76 (.487) 10-21 (.476) 84.

Halftime: UCLA 43-41.

DUKE (91): Ferguson 6-11 0-1 12, Buckley 11-16 3-5 25, Tison 3-10 6-10 12, Harrison 6-15 2-3 14, Mullins 8-19 5-6 21, Marin 1-2 0-0 2, Vacendak 2-5 1-2 5, Herbster 0-0 0-0 0. Team 37-78 (.474) 17-27 (.630) 91.

MICHIGAN (80): Buntin 8-18 3-3 19, Cantrell 6-10 0-0 12, Russell 13-19 5-6 31, Tregoning 3-11 2-2 8, Darden 2-6 1-1 5, Myers 2-5 0-0 4, Pomey 0-1 1-2 1, Herner 0-1 0-0 0. Team 34-71 (.479) 12-14 (.857) 80.

Halftime: Duke 48-39.

ALL-TOURNAMENT TEAM

Bill Buntin, C, Jr., Michigan
Gail Goodrich, G, Jr., UCLA
Walt Hazzard, G, Sr., UCLA*
Jeff Mullins, F, Sr., Duke
Willie Murrell, F, Sr., Kansas State
      *****Named Most Outstanding Player**

1963-64 UNDEFEATED TEAM: UCLA (30-0)

COACH: JOHN WOODEN

UCLA	OPPONENT	UCLA'S HIGH SCORER
113	Brigham Young 71	Hazzard 20
80	Butler 65	Hazzard 21
78	Kansas State* 75	Goodrich 21
74	Kansas* 54	Goodrich 23
112	Baylor* 61	Hazzard 23
95	Creighton* 79	Hazzard 26
95	Yale 65	Goodrich 25
98	Michigan 80	Goodrich 30
83	Illinois 79	Goodrich 21
88	at Washington State 83	Goodrich 28
121	at Washington State 77	Goodrich 21
79	Southern California 59	Hazzard 21
78	Southern California 71	Goodrich 23
84	Stanford 71	Goodrich 23
80	Stanford* 61	Hazzard 31
107	UC Santa Barbara 76	Goodrich/Hazzard 21
87	UC Santa Barbara* 59	Goodrich 31
87	at California 67	Goodrich 26
58	at California 56	Hazzard 17
73	Washington 58	Hazzard 17
88	Washington 60	Goodrich 22
100	at Stanford 88	Hazzard 27
78	at Washington 64	Erickson/Hazzard 21
93	Washington State 56	Hazzard 19
87	California 57	Goodrich 23
91	Southern California 81	Goodrich 23

NCAA TOURNAMENT

95	Seattle* 90	Hazzard 26
76	San Francisco* 72	Hazzard 23
90	Kansas State* 84	Erickson 28
98	Duke* 83	Goodrich 27

*Neutral court games.

winning campaigns by compiling a 15-11 record under first-year coach Dick Edwards. . . . Western Kentucky's Ed Diddle retired after a 42-year coaching career with a 759-302 record. Diddle's teams won an amazing 31 conference championships (13 in the KIAC, 8 in the SIAA and 10 in the OVC). . . . Oregon State's Slats Gill ended his 36-year coaching career with a 599-392 mark. . . . Marquette's Eddie Hickey, who previously coached Creighton and St. Louis, ended his 26-year career with a 435-231 record. Marquette compiled a 5-21 mark, ending Hickey's streak of 21 consecutive winning records.

1963-64 FINAL NATIONAL POLLS

AP	UPI	SCHOOL (RECORD)	HEAD COACH
1	1	UCLA (30-0)	John Wooden
2	2	Michigan (23-5)	Dave Strack
3	4	Duke (26-5)	Vic Bubas
4	3	Kentucky (21-6)	Adolph Rupp
5	6	Wichita (23-6)	Ralph Miller
6	5	Oregon State (25-4)	Slats Gill
7	7	Villanova (24-4)	Jack Kraft
8	8	Loyola of Chicago (22-6)	George Ireland
9	11	DePaul (21-4)	Ray Meyer
10	10	Davidson (22-4)	Lefty Driesell
–	9	Texas Western (25-3)	Don Haskins
–	12	Kansas State (22-7)	Tex Winter
–	13	Drake (21-7)	Maury John
–	13	San Francisco (23-5)	Pete Peletta
–	15	Utah State (21-8)	Ladell Andersen
–	16	New Mexico (23-6)	Bob King
–	16	Ohio State (16-8)	Fred Taylor
–	18	Texas A&M (18-7)	Shelby Metcalf
–	19	Arizona State (16-11)	Ned Wulk
–	19	Providence (20-6)	Joe Mullaney

1964 NCAA Tournament

Summary: UCLA's Kenny Washington was instrumental in helping venerable coach John Wooden capture his first NCAA Tournament championship. Washington, the only player with a single-digit season scoring average (6.1) to tally more than 25 points in a championship game, scored 26 points in a 98-83 triumph over Duke in the final. Washington became the only player to score 25 or more points in a final and not be named to the All-Tournament team. The Bruins won the national championship by a modest average of 7.5 points after gifted guards Gail Goodrich and Walt Hazzard sparked them to 12 double-digit

margin victories in their last 13 regular-season games. Goodrich (21.5 points per game) and Hazzard (18.6 ppg) represent the only backcourt twosome to be the top two scorers on the season for an NCAA championship team. Despite shooting a meager 40.3 percent from the floor and 52.9 percent from the free-throw line, UCLA overcame a 13-point deficit to end San Francisco's 19-game winning streak (76-72) in the West Regional final. Eight of their 30 victories were by seven points or less, including a 58-56 triumph at California. The Bruins became the only school to win an NCAA title one year after appearing in the playoffs and losing their tournament opener by a double-digit margin (93-79 to Arizona State in 1963).

Outcome for Defending Champion: Loyola of Chicago compiled a 22-6 record. The Ramblers' first defeat was in their seventh game (69-58 against Georgetown). Loyola, eliminated in the second round of the national tournament by Michigan, became the only team in the era of three-year eligibility to have four teammates finish their careers at the same time with more than 1,000 points–center Les Hunter (1,472), guards John Egan (1,315) and Ron Miller (1,299), and forward Vic Rouse (1,169).

Star Gazing: Hazzard, the second-leading scorer over the entire season for UCLA's first championship team in 1964 with an average of 18.6 points per game, was named Most Outstanding Player although he was the Bruins' fourth-leading scorer at the Final Four that year. "I never had a better man on the fast break than Walt," UCLA coach John Wooden said. Hazzard had a two-game total of 30 points, finishing behind the scoring aggregates compiled by teammates Goodrich (41), Washington (39) and Keith Erickson (36).

Biggest Upset: Kentucky, ranked No. 3 by UPI and No. 4 by AP entering the tourney, dropped its opener to Ohio, 85-69, when the Wildcats fell behind by 16 points at intermission.

1964 CHAMPIONSHIP BRACKET

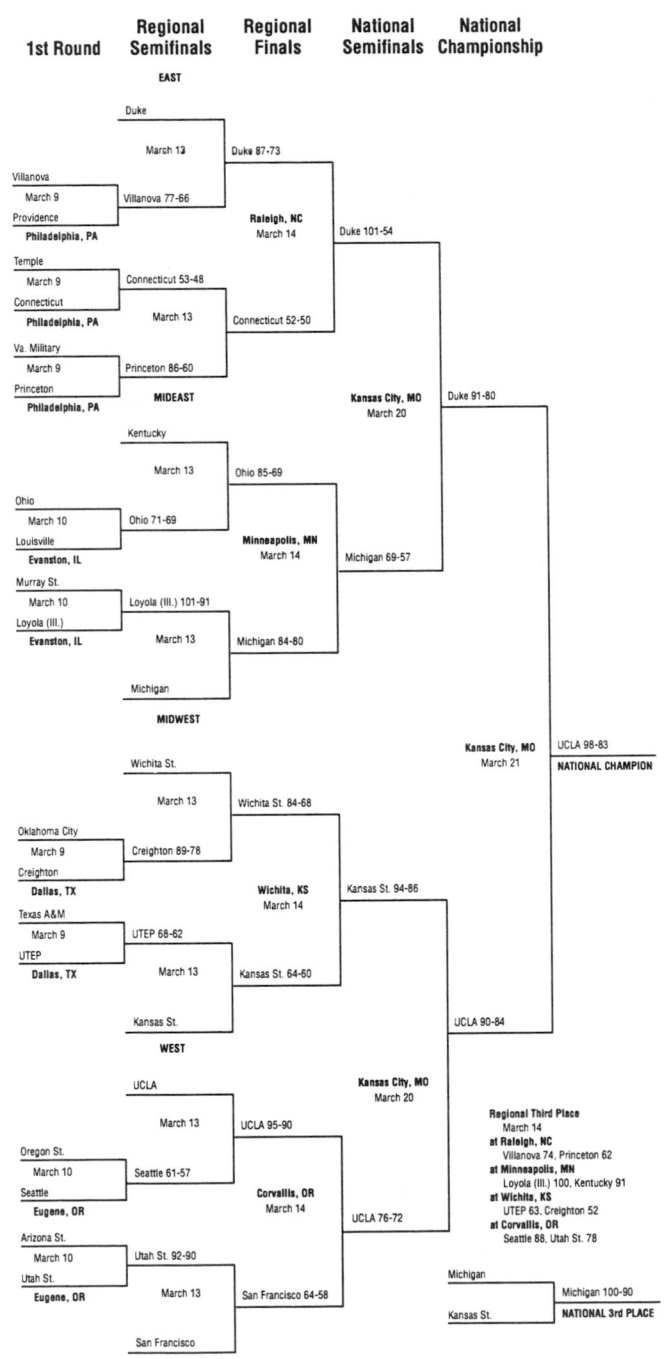

	Regional	Regional	National	National
1st Round	Semifinals	Finals	Semifinals	Championship

EAST

Duke

March 13 — Duke 87-73

Villanova
March 9 — Villanova 77-66
Providence
Philadelphia, PA

Raleigh, NC
March 14 — Duke 101-54

Temple
March 9 — Connecticut 53-48
Connecticut
Philadelphia, PA

March 13 — Connecticut 52-50

Va. Military
March 9 — Princeton 86-60
Princeton
Philadelphia, PA

MIDEAST

Kansas City, MO
March 20 — Duke 91-80

Kentucky
March 13 — Ohio 85-69
Ohio
March 10 — Ohio 71-69
Louisville
Evanston, IL

Minneapolis, MN
March 14 — Michigan 69-57

Murray St.
March 10 — Loyola (Ill.) 101-91
Loyola (Ill.)
Evanston, IL

March 13 — Michigan 84-80

Michigan

MIDWEST

Kansas City, MO
March 21 — UCLA 98-83
NATIONAL CHAMPION

Wichita St.
March 13 — Wichita St. 84-68

Oklahoma City
March 9 — Creighton 89-78
Creighton
Dallas, TX

Wichita, KS
March 14 — Kansas St. 94-86

Texas A&M
March 9 — UTEP 68-62
UTEP
Dallas, TX

March 13 — Kansas St. 64-60

Kansas St.

WEST

UCLA 90-84

Kansas City, MO
March 20 — UCLA 76-72

UCLA
March 13 — UCLA 95-90

Oregon St.
March 10 — Seattle 61-57
Seattle
Eugene, OR

Corvallis, OR
March 14

Arizona St.
March 10 — Utah St. 92-90
Utah St.
Eugene, OR

March 13 — San Francisco 64-58

San Francisco

Regional Third Place
March 14
at Raleigh, NC
Villanova 74, Princeton 62
at Minneapolis, MN
Loyola (Ill.) 100, Kentucky 91
at Wichita, KS
UTEP 63, Creighton 52
at Corvallis, OR
Seattle 88, Utah St. 78

Michigan
Kansas St.

Michigan 100-90
NATIONAL 3rd PLACE

One and Only: Goodrich, a 6-1 junior, became the shortest undergraduate to average more than 20 points per game for an NCAA titlist (21.5 ppg). . . . UCLA's Washington became the only championship team player to have a season scoring average of less than six points per game entering a Final Four but accumulate at least 30 points in the national semifinals and final. Washington had a season scoring average of 5.2 points per game entering the Final Four before erupting for a total of 39 points in victories over Kansas State and Duke. He is the only player with a single-digit season scoring average to score more than 25 points in a championship game (26 against Duke to finish the year with a 6.1-point average). Goodrich scored 27 in the final when he and Washington combined to become the only teammate duo to each score more than 25 in an NCAA final.

Numbers Game: Of the individuals to both play and coach in the NCAA Tournament, Jeff Mullins leads that group in both scoring and rebounding totals. He managed a tourney-high 43 points in an 87-73 victory over Villanova in the East Regional semifinals. Mullins, who later guided UNC Charlotte to the tourney, garnered 200 points and 63 rebounds in eight playoff games to help Duke twice reach the Final Four. . . . Jim "Bad News" Barnes accounted for 61.8 percent of Texas Western's offense by scoring 42 points in the Miners' 68-62 victory against Texas A&M in the first round of the Midwest Regional. In the Miners next game, Barnes was whistled for three quick personal fouls in the opening minutes against Kansas State and spent almost the entire first half on the bench. He was assessed fouls No. 4 and No. 5 early in the second half and fouled out with four points in their 64-60 defeat. . . . Michigan became the only Final Four team ever to have a duo each average more than 23 points per game–guard Cazzie Russell (24.8) and center Bill Buntin (23.2). . . . UCLA had seven players average more than four rebounds per game. . . . Creighton's Paul Silas outrebounded Oklahoma City's Eddie Jackson,

UCLA's Gail Goodrich shoots a jumper in the 1964 NCAA Final against Duke.

27-24, in the Bluejays' 89-78 victory over OCU in the first round of the Midwest Regional.

What If: Wichita (23-6) reached the Midwest Regional final before bowing to Kansas State, 94-86. The Shockers were without standout senior guard Ernie Moore, who was averaging 17.4 points per game when declared ineligible for postseason play.

Scoring Leader: Jeff Mullins, Duke (116 points, 29 ppg).

Highest Scoring Average: Dave Stallworth, Wichita State (59 points, 29.5 ppg).

Rebounding Leader: Paul Silas, Creighton (57 rebounds, 19 rpg).

Highest Rebounding Average: Dave Stallworth, Wichita State (39 rebounds, 19.5 rpg).

1964–65

AT A GLANCE

NCAA Champion: UCLA (28-2; coached by John Wooden; won AAWU title by five games with a 14-0 record).

NIT Champion: St. John's (21-8; coached by Joe Lapchick).

New Rules: Coaches must remain seated on the bench except while the clock is stopped or to direct or encourage players on the court. This rule was to try to help prevent coaches from inciting undesirable crowd behavior toward the referees. NIT field expands from 12 to 14 teams.

NCAA Probation: Miami (Fla.).

NCAA Consensus First-Team All-Americans: Rick Barry, F, Sr., Miami (Fla.); Bill Bradley, F, Sr., Princeton; Gail Goodrich, G, Sr., UCLA; Fred Hetzel, F-C, Sr., Davidson; Cazzie Russell, G, Jr., Michigan.

National Player of the Year: Bradley (30.5 ppg, 11.8 rpg, 53.3 FG%, 88.6 FT%).

National Coaches of the Year: Michigan's Dave Strack (24-4/UPI) and Princeton's Butch van Breda Kolff (23-6/USBWA).

Miami of Florida's Rick Barry led the country in scoring in 1964–65.

Wayne Estes, runner-up to Rick Barry of Miami (Fla.) for the national scoring championship, was electrocuted in a freak accident the evening of February 8. The tragedy occurred less than three hours after Estes scored 48 points against Denver to become Utah State's first player to reach the 2,000-point plateau in his career.

En route back and forth to his off-campus apartment and then a restaurant, Estes was with teammate Delano Lyons and another friend when they passed three times the scene of an auto accident that had killed a Utah State student. The group stopped and inspected the scene briefly. They were returning to their car when Lyons, who is 6-2, noticed a live high-voltage wire dangling in front of him after being dislodged when the victim's car hit a utility pole. Lyons ducked and hollered "Watch it!" to the 6-6 Estes, who was walking behind him. But Estes didn't react quickly enough and the wire carrying 2,700 volts of electricity brushed against his forehead, killing him instantly.

Barry, the only Miami player ever to become an NCAA consensus first- or second-team All-American, was able to stay ahead of Estes in the scoring race by amassing six 50-point games, including a national-high and school record 59 against Rollins. Barry finished the season with an amazing average of 55.7 points and rebounds per contest. He hauled down a school-record 29 rebounds against Oklahoma City.

Western Kentucky's Clem Haskins (55 vs. Middle Tennessee State), Davidson's Fred Hetzel (53 vs. Furman), Utah State's Estes (52 vs. Boston College in overtime at Honolulu), Iona's Warren Isaac (50 vs. Bates), Georgetown's Jim Barry (46 at Fairleigh Dickinson), Middle Tennessee State's Mike Milholland (44 vs. Austin Peay), St. Mary's Jim Moore (43 vs. Sacramento State) and Wisconsin's Ken Barnes (42 vs. Indiana/subsequently tied) established school single-game scoring records.

Haskins' outburst was an Ohio Valley Conference standard. Davidson's Hetzel also grabbed a school-record 27 rebounds in the contest against Furman. MTSU's Miholland grabbed a school-record 32 rebounds in the APSU game. . . . Miami's Barry (37.4 ppg), Utah State's Estes (33.7), Wyoming's Flynn Robinson (27) and Dayton's Henry Finkel (25.3) set school records for highest scoring average in a single season.

Dave Stallworth became the only Wichita State player in history to supply back-to-back 40-point games with 45 and 40 against Loyola of Chicago in overtime and Louisville, respectively, in the last two games of his college career. The midseason graduate was named an NCAA consensus second-team All-American despite play-

ing in just 16 of WSU's 30 games. . . . Wichita State's only No. 1 ranking in school history ended in mid-December when the Shockers were nipped at Michigan, 87-85, on Cazzie Russell's 35-foot basket for the Wolverines at the buzzer.

Princeton's Bill Bradley, who would become a U.S. Senator (D-N.J.), led the country in free-throw shooting. He is the only Princeton player to score 40 or more points in a game, a feat he achieved 11 times. In one of the most memorable college games in Madison Square Garden history, the Tigers lost to Michigan, 80-78, in the semifinals of the Holiday Festival. Bradley fouled out with with 4 1/2 minutes remaining with 41 points and Princeton leading, 76-63. Russell led Michigan's comeback and hit the game-winning basket from 15 feet away with three seconds left

1964–65 INDIVIDUAL LEADERS

SCORING

PLAYER	PTS.	AVG.
Barry, Miami (Fla.)	973	37.4
Estes, Utah St.	641	33.7
Bradley, Princeton	885	30.5
Schellhase, Purdue	704	29.3
Thomas, Xavier	405	28.9
Robinson, Wyoming	701	27.0
Austin, Boston College	673	26.9
Hetzel, Davidson	689	26.5
Beasley, Texas A&M	619	25.8
Russell, Michigan	694	25.7

REBOUNDING

PLAYER	REB.	AVG.
Kimball, Connecticut	483	21.0
Isaac, Iona	480	20.9

Woods, E. Tennessee St.	450	19.6
Barry, Miami (Fla.)	475	18.3
Swagerty, Pacific	473	18.2
Sahm, Notre Dame	393	16.4
Johnson, San Francisco	469	16.2
Branch, Fairfield	208	16.0
Washington, Villanova	442	15.8
Anderson, St. Joseph's	450	15.5

FIELD GOAL PERCENTAGE

PLAYER	FGM	FGA	PCT.
Kehoe, St. Peter's	138	209	.660
Finkel, Dayton	293	450	.651
McKendrick, Rice	152	250	.608
Newton, Auburn	126	208	.606
Johnson, San Francisco	242	405	.598
Hetzel, Davidson	273	471	.580
Kimball, Connecticut	177	311	.569

Chambers, Utah	199	355	.561
Thoren, Illinois	219	391	.560
Stallworth, Wichita St.	153	275	.556
Ritch, Army	140	252	.556

FREE THROW PERCENTAGE

PLAYER	FTM	FTA	PCT.
Bradley, Princeton	272	308	.886
Banko, UC Santa Barbara	156	177	.881
Park, Tulsa	145	165	.879
Estes, Utah St.	137	156	.878
K. McIntyre, St. John's	144	164	.878
Lloyd, Rutgers	127	145	.876
Neuman, Penn	112	129	.868
Barry, Georgetown	110	127	.866
Anderson, W. Michigan	158	183	.863
Barry, Miami (Fla.)	293	341	.859

1964–65 TEAM LEADERS

SCORING OFFENSE

SCHOOL	PTS.	AVG.
Miami (Fla.)	2558	98.4
Brigham Young	2639	94.3
Duke	2310	92.4
Illinois	2213	92.2
Indiana	2200	91.7

SCORING DEFENSE

SCHOOL	PTS.	AVG.
Tennessee	1391	55.64
Oklahoma St.	1503	55.66
New Mexico	1504	55.7
Texas Western	1468	56.5
Oregon St.	1525	58.7

FIELD GOAL PERCENTAGE

SCHOOL	FGM	FGA	PCT.
St. Peter's	579	1089	.532
Davidson	908	1784	.509
San Francisco	931	1893	.492
Duke	942	1921	.490
Manhattan	677	1382	.490

FREE THROW PERCENTAGE

SCHOOL	FTM	FTA	PCT.
Miami (Fla.)	642	807	.796
Morehead St.	487	620	.785
Indiana	464	604	.768
Kentucky	517	675	.766
UC Santa Barbara	482	633	.761

REBOUNDING

SCHOOL	TOTAL REB.	OWN	PCT.
Iona	1896	1191	.628
Tennessee	1997	1207	.604
Florida	1749	1041	.595
Connecticut	2439	1432	.587
New Mexico	2286	1342	.587

1964–65 NCAA CHAMPION: UCLA

SEASON STATISTICS OF UCLA REGULARS

PLAYER	POS.	CL.	G.	FG%	FT%	PPG	RPG
Gail Goodrich	G	Sr.	30	.525	.717	24.8	5.3
Keith Erickson	F	Sr.	29	.443	.725	12.9	8.8
Fred Goss	G	Jr.	30	.442	.729	12.2	3.3
Edgar Lacey	F	So.	30	.469	.579	11.6	10.2
Kenny Washington	F	Jr.	30	.425	.653	9.2	5.0
Mike Lynn	C	So.	30	.503	.581	6.7	5.1
Doug McIntosh	C	Jr.	30	.429	.737	6.5	5.6
TEAM TOTALS			30	.463	.665	86.3	52.0

1965 FINAL FOUR CHAMPIONSHIP GAME

PORTLAND, OR

UCLA (91)	FG-A	FT-A	REB.	PF	PTS.
Erickson	1-1	1-2	1	1	3
Lacey	5-7	1-2	7	3	11
McIntosh	1-2	1-2	0	2	3
Goodrich	12-22	18-20	4	4	42
Goss	4-12	0-0	3	1	8
Washington	7-9	3-4	5	2	17
Lynn	2-3	1-2	6	1	5
Lyons	0-0	0-0	0	1	0
Galbraith	0-0	0-0	0	0	0
Hoffman	1-1	0-0	1	0	2
Levin	0-1	0-0	1	0	0
Chambers	0-0	0-1	0	0	0
Team			6		
TOTALS	33-58	25-33	34	15	91

FG%: .569. FT%: .758. Assists: 4.

MICHIGAN (80)	FG-A	FT-A	REB.	PF	PTS.
Darden	8-10	1-1	4	5	17
Pomey	2-5	0-0	2	2	4
Buntin	6-14	2-4	6	5	14
Russell	10-16	8-10	5	2	28
Tregoning	2-7	1-1	5	5	5
Myers	0-4	0-0	3	2	0
Brown	0-0	0-0	0	0	0
Ludwig	1-2	0-0	0	0	2
Thompson	0-0	0-0	0	0	0
Bankey	0-0	0-0	0	0	0
Clawson	3-4	0-0	0	2	6
Dill	1-2	2-2	1	1	4
Team			7		
TOTALS	33-64	14-18	33	24	80

FG%: .516. FT%: .778. Assists: 2.
Halftime: UCLA 47-34.

NATIONAL SEMIFINALS

MICHIGAN (93): Tregoning 6-9 1-1 13, Darden 6-13 1-3 13, Buntin 7-13 8-10 22, Russell 10-21 8-9 28, Pomey 2-8 2-2 6, Myers 1-4 0-0 2, Thompson 0-1 2-2 2, Dill 0-0 3-4 3, Ludwig 0-0 0-0 0, Clawson 2-2 0-1 4. Team 34-71 (.479) 25-32 (.781) 93.

PRINCETON (76): Bradley 12-25 5-5 29, Haarlow 4-10 1-4 9, Brown 2-6 0-0 4, Walters 5-10 1-2 11, Rodenbach 2-5 2-2 6, Hummer 4-10 4-5 12, Koch 1-4 1-2 3, Kingston 0-1 2-2 2. Team 30-71 (.423) 16-22 (.727) 76.

Halftime: Michigan 40-36.

WICHITA STATE (89): Smith 4-11 0-1 8, Thompson 13-19 10-11 36, Leach 6-14 0-1 12, Pete 6-11 5-5 17, Criss 4-13 0-0 8, Reed 2-3 1-1 5, Davis 1-2 0-0 2, Trope 0-1 0-0 0, Nosich 0-0 1-3 1, Reimond 0-1 0-0 0. Team 36-75 (.480) 17-22 (.773) 89.

UCLA (108): Lacey 9-13 6-10 24, Erickson 1-6 0-0 2, McIntosh 4-5 3-4 11, Goodrich 11-21 6-8 28, Goss 8-13 3-3 19, Washington 4-13 2-4 10, Lynn 5-9 0-0 10, Chambers 0-5 0-0 0, Lyons 2-3 0-0 4, Levin 0-1 0-0 0, Galbraith 0-0-0 0, Hoffman 0-0 0-0 0. Team 44-89 (.494) 20-29 (.690) 108.

Halftime: UCLA 65-38.

ALL-TOURNAMENT TEAM

Bill Bradley, F, Sr., Princeton*
Gail Goodrich, G, Sr., UCLA
Edgar Lacey, F, Soph., UCLA
Cazzie Russell, G, Jr., Michigan
Kenny Washington, F, Jr., UCLA
      *Named Most Outstanding Player

to finish with 27 points. Four of Princeton's five regular-season defeats were by one or two points.

Nebraska suffered its 15th consecutive losing season, but upset top-ranked Michigan, 74-73, on Fred Hare's buzzer-beater. . . . Russell's teammate, Bill Buntin, became the first Michigan player to be chosen in the opening round of an NBA draft. . . . Tennessee (55.64), Oklahoma State (55.66) and New Mexico (55.70) finished one-two-three in team defense in the closest race ever in point prevention. The tight defense helped Oklahoma State captured its only undisputed Big Eight regular-season championship.

North Carolina State's Everett Case retired because of illness early in the 19th season of his coaching career with a 377-134 record. Among

the innovations attributed to him were the time clock, introducing players before a game and cutting down the nets after a big tournament victory. . . . Case's successor was Press Maravich, the father of future All-American Pete Maravich. N.C. State reserve forward Larry Worsley entered the ACC Tournament with a modest 5.2 scoring average. In three tourney games, all of which he entered as a substitute, he scored 12, 15 and 30 points to pace the Wolfpack to the title and earn the Outstanding Player Award. He hit 14 of 19 field-goal attempts in a 91-85 championship game victory over Duke.

Florida defeated Kentucky, 84-68, for the Gators' first victory over the Wildcats since 1934. Florida had lost 18 games to Kentucky in that span. UK also was defeated by St. Louis for the fifth time in the last six seasons, 80-75, although the Billikens' average record in that span was just 16-11. St. Louis also defeated Notre Dame for the 13th time in their last 15 meetings, 75-67.

St. Joseph's (26-3/coached by Jack Ramsay) had its winningest season in school history. Two of St. Joseph's defeats were to Providence. . . . West Virginia (14-15) posted its first losing mark since 1943-44 but still finished in the first division of the Southern Conference. Virginia Tech was runner-up to Davidson in the Southern Conference in the Hokies' final season as a member of the league. . . . Pacific's Keith Swagerty set a West Coast Athletic Conference standard by grabbing a school-record 39 rebounds in a game against UC Santa Barbara.

East Tennessee State's Tommy Woods (38 vs. Middle Tennessee State) and Notre Dame's Walt Sahm (30 vs. Ball State/later tied) set school single-game rebounding records. . . . Illinois' Skip Thoren grabbed more than 20 rebounds three times in a five-game stretch (at Kentucky, at Villanova and vs. Indiana). . . . Wyoming (16-10) chalked up its first winning record in 10 seasons.

1964-65 FINAL NATIONAL POLLS

AP	UPI	SCHOOL (RECORD)	HEAD COACH
1	1	Michigan (24-4)	Dave Strack
2	2	UCLA (28-2)	John Wooden
3	3	St. Joseph's (26-3)	Jack Ramsay
4	4	Providence (24-2)	Joe Mullaney
5	5	Vanderbilt (24-4)	Roy Skinner
6	7	Davidson (24-2)	Lefty Driesell
7	8	Minnesota (19-5)	John Kundla
8	11	Villanova (23-5)	Jack Kraft
9	6	Brigham Young (21-7)	Stan Watts
10	9	Duke (20-5)	Vic Bubas
–	10	San Francisco (24-5)	Pete Peletta
–	12	N.C. State (21-5)	Press Maravich
–	13	Oklahoma State (20-7)	Hank Iba
–	14	Wichita State (21-9)	Gary Thompson
–	15	Connecticut (23-3)	Fred Shabel
–	16	Illinois (18-6)	Harry Combes
–	17	Tennessee (20-5)	Ray Mears
–	18	Indiana (19-5)	Branch McCracken
–	19	Miami, Fla. (22-4)	Bruce Hale
–	20	Dayton (22-7)	Don Donoher

Texas Western bowed to New Mexico, 55-47, for the Miners' only homecourt defeat in a 68-game span at home from 1961 through 1966. . . . Utah coach Jack Gardner had a team finish in last place for the first time in his 29 seasons of coaching. The Utes were in the basement of the six-team WAC with a 3-7 record despite finishing with a 17-9 overall mark. . . . St. John's Joe Lapchick concluded his 20-year coaching career with a 335-129 record after winning the NIT. Indiana's Branch McCracken, who previously coached Ball State, retired after a 32-year coaching career with a 450-231 record.

1965 NCAA Tournament

Summary: Defending champion UCLA, returning only two starters, was overwhelmed in its season opener at Illinois, 110-83. But the Bruins finished the campaign with a 91-80 victory over another Big Ten team, Michigan, in the NCAA final. The Bruins' only other defeat was to another Big Ten squad–87-82 against Iowa in Chicago. Oddly, Michigan didn't lose to either Illinois or Iowa in Big Ten competition. UCLA averaged an even 100 points in its four tourney games to become the only champion to average triple digits in scoring.

Star Gazing: Princeton's Bill Bradley holds the career playoff record for highest free-throw percentage (minimum of 50 attempts). He was 89 of 96 from the foul line (90.6 percent) from 1963 through 1965. In five of his nine playoff games, Bradley made at least 10 free throws while missing no more than one attempt from the charity stripe. He made 16 of 16 free throws against St. Joseph's in the first round of the 1963 East Regional and 13 of 13 foul shots against Providence in the 1965 East Regional final to become the only player to twice convert more than 12 free throws without a miss in a playoff game. Bradley also holds the mark for most points in a single Final Four game (school-record 58 against Wichita State in national third-place game). He scored 39 points in the second half of the consolation contest. The Rhodes Scholar was the only player to have a double-digit season scoring average (30.5 points per game) for Princeton's Final Four team.

One and Only: UCLA's Gail Goodrich became the only guard to score more than 35 points in an NCAA final, erupting for 42 points on 12 of 22 field-goal shooting and 18 of 20 free-throw shooting in a 91-80 triumph over Michigan. His free throws made and attempted remain championship game records. Goodrich averaged 24.6 points per game, a UCLA school record for guards.

Numbers Game: Princeton's Butch van Breda Kolff went on to become the only coach to direct teams to the NCAA Final Four and the NBA Finals (Lakers in 1968 and 1969) and compile a winning NCAA playoff career record (7-5). . . . Wichita State's Gary Thompson became perhaps the first-year coach overcoming the biggest obstacle to reach the national semifinals. The Shockers' roster was depleted in the second half of Thompson's inaugural season after the departures of both of their high NBA draft picks–All-American forward Dave (The Rave) Stallworth and first-round draft choice center Nate Bowman. Stallworth completed his eligibility after the first 16 games and Bowman was declared ineligible for the second semester. Nonetheless, the Missouri Valley Conference champion's roster of primarily local players emerged victorious out of a relatively feeble Midwest Regional field. . . . Michigan's Cazzie Russell became the only player to score more than 25 points in Final Four defeats in back-to-back years. . . . Tony Kimball's 29 rebounds for Connecticut weren't enough to prevent a 67-61 setback against St. Joseph's in their East Regional opener.

What If: Rick Barry-led Miami (Fla.) defeated NCAA playoff first-round winners Houston and Oklahoma City by a total of 35 points, but the Hurricanes were ineligible because of NCAA probation. It was Miami's lone appearance in the Top 20 of a final wire-service poll.

Scoring Leader: Bill Bradley, Princeton (177 points, 35.4 ppg).

Highest Scoring Average: Ollie Johnson, San Francisco (72 points, 36 ppg).

University of Michigan's Cazzie Russell.

Rebounding Leader: Bill Bradley, Princeton (57 rebounds, 11.4 rpg).

Highest Rebounding Average: Ollie Johnson, San Francisco (37 rebounds, 18.5 rpg).

1965 CHAMPIONSHIP BRACKET

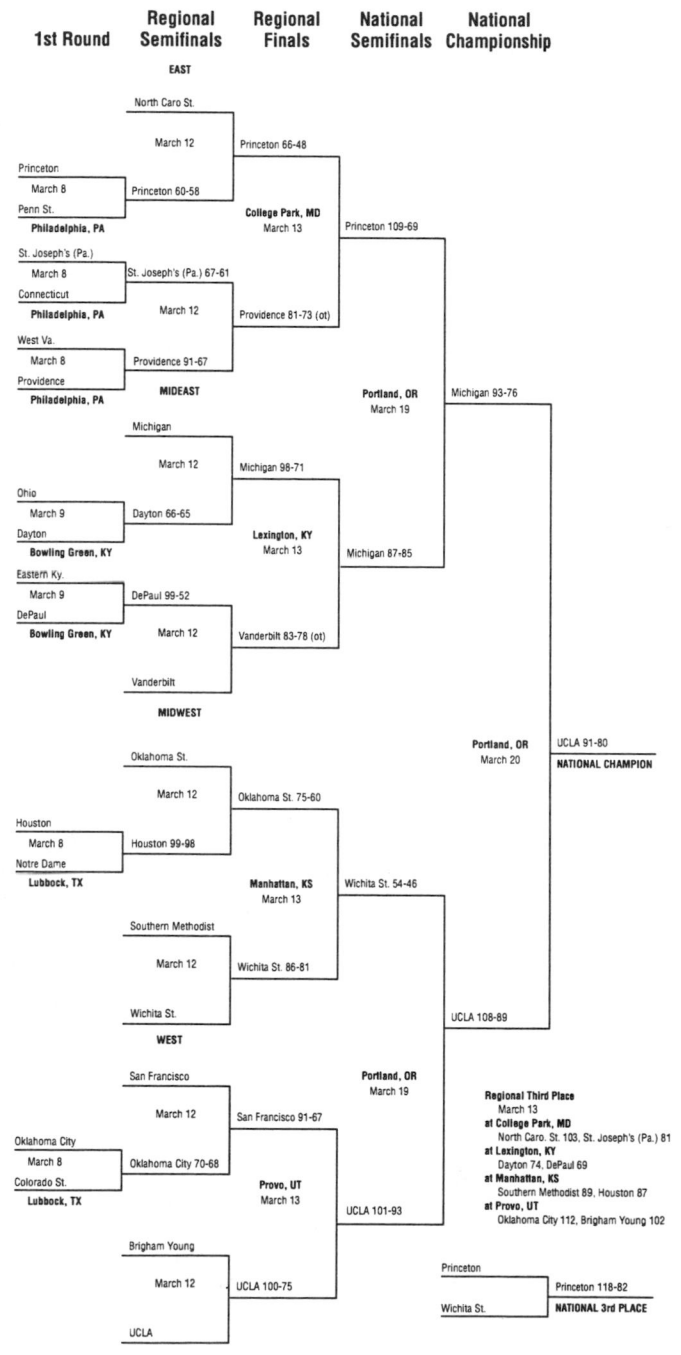

1st Round	Regional Semifinals	Regional Finals	National Semifinals	National Championship

EAST

North Caro St.

March 12 — Princeton 66-48

Princeton
March 8 — Princeton 60-58
Penn St.
Philadelphia, PA

College Park, MD
March 13 — Princeton 109-69

St. Joseph's (Pa.)
March 8 — St. Joseph's (Pa.) 67-61
Connecticut
Philadelphia, PA

March 12 — Providence 81-73 (ot)

West Va.
March 8 — Providence 91-67
Providence
Philadelphia, PA

MIDEAST

Michigan

March 12 — Michigan 98-71

Ohio
March 9 — Dayton 66-65
Dayton
Bowling Green, KY

Portland, OR
March 19 — Michigan 93-76

Lexington, KY
March 13 — Michigan 87-85

Eastern Ky.
March 9 — DePaul 99-52
DePaul
Bowling Green, KY

March 12 — Vanderbilt 83-78 (ot)

Vanderbilt

MIDWEST

Oklahoma St.

March 12 — Oklahoma St. 75-60

Houston
March 8 — Houston 99-98
Notre Dame
Lubbock, TX

Manhattan, KS
March 13 — Wichita St. 54-46

Southern Methodist

March 12 — Wichita St. 86-81

Wichita St.

Portland, OR
March 20 — UCLA 91-80
NATIONAL CHAMPION

UCLA 108-89

WEST

San Francisco

March 12 — San Francisco 91-67

Portland, OR
March 19

Oklahoma City
March 8 — Oklahoma City 70-68
Colorado St.
Lubbock, TX

Provo, UT
March 13 — UCLA 101-93

Brigham Young

March 12 — UCLA 100-75

UCLA

Regional Third Place
March 13
at College Park, MD
North Caro. St. 103, St. Joseph's (Pa.) 81
at Lexington, KY
Dayton 74, DePaul 69
at Manhattan, KS
Southern Methodist 89, Houston 87
at Provo, UT
Oklahoma City 112, Brigham Young 102

Princeton
Wichita St.

Princeton 118-82
NATIONAL 3rd PLACE

THE UCLA DYNASTY: THE 1960s 153

1965-66

AT A GLANCE

NCAA Champion: Texas Western (28-1; coached by Don Haskins).

NIT Champion: Brigham Young (20-5; coached by Stan Watts; finished in second place in WAC with a 6-4 record, which was one game behind Utah).

New Conference: Metropolitan Collegiate (disbanded four years later).

NCAA Consensus First-Team All-Americans: Dave Bing, G, Sr., Syracuse; Clyde Lee, C, Sr., Vanderbilt; Cazzie Russell, G, Sr., Michigan; Dave Schellhase, F, Sr., Purdue; Jimmy Walker, G, Jr., Providence.

National Player of the Year: Russell (30.8 ppg, 8.4 rpg, 51.8 FG%, 82.5 FT%).

National Coach of the Year: Adolph Rupp, Kentucky (27-2/UPI, USBWA).

The best team in the country might have been UCLA's freshman squad. The Bruins' frosh, led by 7-1 Lew Alcindor's 31 points and 21 rebounds, defeated the two-time NCAA champion UCLA varsity, 75-60. The yearlings compiled a 21-0 record, outscoring their opponents 113.2 points per game to 56.6. Starters for what is considered by some as best freshman team in NCAA history included Alcindor (33.1 ppg and 21.5 rpg), forwards Lynn Shackelford (20.9 ppg and 9.3 rpg) and Kent Taylor (7.2 ppg) and guards Lucius Allen (22.4 ppg and 7.8 rpg) and Kenny Heitz (14.3 ppg).

It was a version of Dave's World for the national scoring championship. Purdue forward Dave Schellhase (32.54) edged Idaho State guard Dave Wagnon (32.50) in the closest race in major-college history. Wagnon, who averaged a modest 14.6 points per game the previous season as a junior, averaged 36.4 the second half of his senior campaign before falling one basket short of over-hauling Schellhase. Purdue posted an 8-16 record, leaving Schellhase with the worst mark ever for an NCAA consensus first-team All-

American. He had a national single-game high of 57 points against Michigan.

Cazzie Russell set a Michigan record for most points in a regulation game with 48 against Northwestern. Also establishing school single-game scoring standards were Rutgers' Bob Lloyd (51 points at Delaware/later tied), Texas Tech's Dub Malaise (50 vs. Texas), North Carolina's Bob Lewis (49 vs. Florida State), Tennessee Tech's Ron Filipek (tied with 48 vs. Middle Tennessee State), Rice's Doug McKendrick (47 vs. Georgia Tech), Southern Cal's John Block (45 vs. Washington) and Murray State's Herb McPherson (44 vs. Middle Tennessee State). Lewis' outburst for Carolina capped a six-game stretch during which he averaged 36.1 points per game.

Wagnon, Russell (30.8 ppg), Syracuse's Dave Bing (28.4), Centenary's Tom Kerwin (27.9), Illinois' Don Freeman (27.8) and Texas A&M's John Beasley (27.8) set school records for highest scoring average in a single season. Utah's Jerry Chambers established a Western Athletic Conference single-season record by averaging 28.8 points per game.

Syracuse, after failing to finish among the top 30 in the previous 12 scoring races, won its first national scoring title. Bing grabbed a school-record 25 rebounds in a game against Cornell. . . . One of the most fabled shots in St. Joseph's history came at the Palestra when seldom-used Steve Donches connected on a prayer at the final buzzer to give the Hawks a 71-69 victory over archrival Villanova. . . . Nebraska's string of losing records ended at 15 when the 20-5 Cornhuskers finished in the Top 20 of a final wire-service poll for the only time until 1991. . . . Cincinnati captured the the Missouri Valley Conference crown after finishing in seventh place the previous season. The MVC didn't have a team reach the NCAA Final Four or win the NIT for the first time in eight years. Louisville's Wes Unseld set a MVC single-season record by averaging 19.4 rebounds per game.

Ron Widby punted for Tennessee's football squad in the afternoon in its 27-6 triumph over

1965–66 INDIVIDUAL LEADERS

SCORING

PLAYER	PTS.	AVG.
Schellhase, Purdue	781	32.54
Wagnon, Idaho St.	845	32.50
Russell, Michigan	800	30.8
Chambers, Utah	892	28.8
Bing, Syracuse	794	28.4
Kerwin, Centenary	726	27.9
Freeman, Illinois	668	27.8
Beasley, Texas A&M	668	27.8
Melchionni, Villanova	801	27.6
Lewis, North Carolina	740	27.4

REBOUNDING

PLAYER	REB.	AVG.
Ware, Oklahoma City	607	20.9
Unseld, Louisville	505	19.4

Swagerty, Pacific	514	18.4
Woods, East Tennessee St.	361	17.2
Hayes, Houston	490	16.9
Murrey, Detroit	416	16.6
Wolters, Boston College	431	16.6
Lee, Vanderbilt	412	15.8
Cunningham, Murray St.	390	15.6
Williams, Temple	421	15.0

FIELD GOAL PERCENTAGE

PLAYER	FGM	FGA	PCT.
Hammond, Tulsa	172	261	.659
McKendrick, Rice	168	265	.634
Finkel, Dayton	248	397	.625
Lewis, Duke	161	271	.594
Stephenson, Rhode I.	128	216	.593
Lechman, Gonzaga	145	246	.589
Williams, Temple	195	336	.580
Murrey, Detroit	195	341	.572
Dean, Syracuse	125	219	.571
Hayes, Houston	323	570	.567

FREE THROW PERCENTAGE

PLAYER	FTM	FTA	PCT.
Blair, Providence	101	112	.902
Morawski, Seton Hall	136	153	.889
Lloyd, Rutgers	161	183	.880
Jones, Miami (Fla.)	134	153	.876
Long, Wake Forest	153	176	.869
Beasley, SMU	137	158	.867
Baumann, The Citadel	91	105	.867
Wetzel, Virginia Tech	123	142	.866
Butler, Memphis St.	114	132	.864
Heroman, LSU	132	153	.863

1965–66 TEAM LEADERS

SCORING OFFENSE

SCHOOL	PTS.	AVG.
Syracuse	2773	99.0
Houston	2845	98.1
Oklahoma City	2829	97.6
Loyola (Ill.)	2438	97.5
Brigham Young	2388	95.5

SCORING DEFENSE

SCHOOL	PTS.	AVG.
Oregon St.	1527	54.5
Tennessee	1499	57.7
Oklahoma St.	1523	60.9
Princeton	1425	62.0
Texas Western	1817	62.7

Kansas	1692	62.7
Pennsylvania	1568	62.7

FIELD GOAL PERCENTAGE

SCHOOL	FGM	FGA	PCT.
North Carolina	838	1620	.517
Davidson	877	1713	.512
Syracuse	1132	2271	.498
Brigham Young	946	1898	.498
Seattle	849	1722	.493

FREE THROW PERCENTAGE

SCHOOL	FTM	FTA	PCT.
Auburn	476	601	.792
Austin Peay St.	463	591	.783
Rhode Island	596	770	.774
Murray St.	488	640	.763
Davidson	563	739	.762

REBOUNDING

SCHOOL	TOTAL REB.	OWN	PCT.
Texas Western	2480	1430	.577
Duke	2598	1490	.574
Tennessee	2193	1255	.572
Detroit	2384	1356	.569

Tulsa in the Bluebonnet Bowl and then flew to Shreveport, La., where he scored 18 points that for the Volunteers' basketball team in a 49-43 victory over Centenary in the championship game of the Gulf South Classic. Tennessee handed Kentucky its only regular-season defeat in their SEC finale (69-62). . . . Vanderbilt's Clyde Lee grabbed a school-record 28 rebounds against Mississippi. . . . Tulane competed as a member of the Southeastern Conference for the final season.

Bob Knight embarked on his acclaimed coaching career with an 18-8 record at Army, leading the Cadets to the NIT for the first of four times under him through 1970. Another head coaching newcomer with an 18-8 record was Lou Carnesecca at St. John's. . . . Maryland guard Billy Jones became the first African American to compete in the ACC. . . . Steve Vacendak was named ACC player of the year despite being voted second team all-league. Vacendak finished ninth in the All-ACC balloting after averaging 13.3 points and four rebounds per game for Duke's 26-4 squad.

North Carolina attempted a slowdown game in an effort to upend heavily-favored Duke in the ACC Tournament semifinals but lost, 21-20. The Tar Heels trailed at halftime, 7-5. Entering the tourney, Duke was ranked No. 3 in the AP poll and No. 2 by UPI. No other ACC team was in the Top 20. Duke won its fourth consecutive undisputed regular-season championship although both of its ACC losses were to teams that finished in a three-way tie for last place (South Carolina and Wake Forest).

Rice's only victory of the season (82-70 verdict over Baylor) ended a school-record 28-game

1965–66 NCAA CHAMPION: TEXAS WESTERN

SEASON STATISTICS OF TEXAS WESTERN REGULARS

PLAYER	POS.	CL.	G.	FG%	FT%	PPG	RPG
Bobby Joe Hill	G	Jr.	28	.411	.610	15.0	3.0
David Lattin	C	So.	29	.495	.703	14.0	8.6
Orsten Artis	G	Sr.	28	.470	.867	12.6	3.5
Nevil Shed	F-C	Jr.	29	.494	.755	10.6	7.9
Harry Flournoy	F	Sr.	29	.500	.649	8.3	10.7
Willie Worsley	G	So.	29	.403	.719	8.0	2.3
Willie Cager	F	So.	27	.410	.680	6.6	4.0
Louis Baudoin	F	Jr.	16	.386	.200	2.2	1.3
Jerry Armstrong	F	Sr.	24	.279	.875	1.9	1.4
TEAM TOTALS			29	.445	.700	77.9	49.3

1966 FINAL FOUR CHAMPIONSHIP GAME

COLLEGE PARK, MD

KENTUCKY (65)	FG-A	FT-A	REB.	PF	PTS.
Dampier	7-18	5-5	9	4	19
Kron	3-6	0-0	7	2	6
Conley	4-9	2-2	8	5	10
Riley	8-22	3-4	4	4	19
Jaracz	3-8	1-2	5	5	7
Berger	2-3	0-0	0	0	4
Gamble	0-0	0-0	0	1	0
LeMaster	0-1	0-0	0	1	0
Tallent	0-3	0-0	0	1	0
TOTALS	**27-70**	**11-13**	**33**	**23**	**65**

FG%: .386. FT%: .846.

TEXAS WESTERN (72)	FG-A	FT-A	REB.	PF	PTS.
Hill	7-17	6-9	3	3	20
Artis	5-13	5-5	8	1	15
Shed	1-1	1-1	3	1	3
Lattin	5-10	6-6	9	4	16
Cager	1-3	6-7	6	3	8
Flournoy	1-1	0-0	2	0	2
Worsley	2-4	4-6	4	0	8
TOTALS	**22-49**	**28-34**	**35**	**12**	**72**

FG%: .449. FT%: .824.
Halftime: Texas Western 34-31.

NATIONAL SEMIFINALS

DUKE (79): Marin 11-18 7-10 29, Riedy 2-7 2-2 6, Lewis 9-13 3-3 21, Verga 2-7 0-0 4, Vacendak 7-16 3-3 17, Wendelin 1-4 0-1 2, Liccardo 0-1 0-0 0, Barone 0-0 0-0 0. Team 32-66 (.485) 15-19 (.789) 79.

KENTUCKY (83): Conley 3-5 4-4 10, Riley 8-17 3-4 19, Jaracz 3-5 2-3 8, Dampier 11-20 1-2 23, Kron 5-13 2-2 12, Tallent 1-2 2-2 4, Berger 1-4 5-6 7, Gamble 0-0 0-1 0. Team 32-66 (.485) 19-24 (.792) 83.

Halftime: Duke 42-41.

TEXAS WESTERN (85): Hill 5-20 8-10 18, Artis 10-20 2-3 22, Shed 2-3 5-6 9, Lattin 5-7 1-1 11, Flournoy 3-6 2-2 8, Cager 2-5 1-1 5, Worsley 5-8 2-3 12, Armstrong 0-2 0-1 0. Team 32-71 (.451) 21-27 (.778) 85.

UTAH (78): Tate 0-4 1-3 1, Jackson 3-9 2-2 8, MacKay 4-10 6-9 14, Ockel 1-1 3-5 5, Chambers 14-31 10-12 38, Black 3-8 2-4 8, Lake 1-1 0-0 2, Day 1-2 0-0 2. Team 27-66 (.409) 24-33 (.727) 78.

Halftime: Texas Western 42-39.

ALL-TOURNAMENT TEAM

Jerry Chambers, F, Sr., Utah*
Louie Dampier, G, Jr., Kentucky
Bobby Joe Hill, G, Jr., Texas Western
Jack Marin, F, Sr., Duke
Pat Riley, F, Jr., Kentucky
*****Named Most Outstanding Player**

1965-66 FINAL NATIONAL POLLS

AP	UPI	SCHOOL (RECORD)	HEAD COACH
1	1	Kentucky (27-2)	Adolph Rupp
2	2	Duke (26-4)	Vic Bubas
3	3	Texas Western (28-1)	Don Haskins
4	4	Kansas (23-4)	Ted Owens
5	6	St. Joseph's (24-5)	Jack Ramsay
6	5	Loyola of Chicago (22-3)	George Ireland
7	9	Cincinnati (21-7)	Tay Baker
8	8	Vanderbilt (22-4)	Roy Skinner
9	7	Michigan (18-8)	Dave Strack
10	–	Western Kentucky (25-3)	John Oldham
–	10	Providence (22-5)	Joe Mullaney
–	11	Nebraska (20-5)	Joe Cipriano
–	12	Utah (23-8)	Jack Gardner
–	13	Oklahoma City (24-5)	Abe Lemons
–	14	Houston (23-6)	Guy Lewis
–	15	Oregon State (21-7)	Paul Valenti
–	16	Syracuse (22-6)	Fred Lewis
–	17	Pacific (22-6)	Dick Edwards
–	18	Davidson (21-7)	Lefty Driesell
–	19	Brigham Young (20-5)	Stan Watts
–	19	Dayton (23-6)	Don Donoher

losing streak. . . . Washington State compiled a 15-11 record for its first winning season in 14 years. . . . Montana won 10 of 11 games down the stretch to finish with a 14-10 record and the Grizzlies' only winning season in a 10-year span from 1961-62 through 1970-71. . . . Utah, coached by Jack Gardner, won the WAC title after finishing in last place the previous season. . . . Holy Cross compiled its first losing season in 21 years (10-13) under new coach Jack Donohue, who had guided Power Memorial Academy in New York to a 163-30 record, including 71 consecutive victories with a center named Lew Alcindor.

1966 NCAA Tournament

Summary: Texas Western, now called Texas-El Paso, put the finishing touches on dismantling the prejudiced myth that black athletes couldn't play disciplined basketball by capturing the 1966 title. Texas Western (28-1) had its winningest season in school history. The Miners' Don Haskins was a demanding coach who

UCLA's Lew Alcindor goes high for a rebound.

wouldn't let forward-center Nevil Shed ride back to the hotel with the team after Shed was thrown out in the first half of their 78-76 overtime victory against Cincinnati in the second round. UTEP, featuring an all-black starting lineup with three players 6-1 or shorter in the NCAA final, stunned top-ranked and all-white Kentucky (72-65). Junior college transfer Bobby Joe Hill, one of the Miners' tiny trio, converted steals into layups on consecutive trips down the floor by flustered Kentucky guards to give them a lead they never relinquished. Acclaimed writer Frank Deford, covering the game for Sports Illustrated, said Wildcats coach Adolph Rupp allowed him "into the locker room with the understanding that if Kentucky lost, I wouldn't report on what I saw. Unfortunately, in his anger, Rupp referred to the Texas Western players as 'coons.'" In the wake of UTEP's sterling performance, major Southern schools start-

ed modifying their unwritten directives by recruiting more African-American players.

Outcome for Defending Champion: UCLA (18-8) finished second in the AAWU, failing to win the conference title for the only time in an 18-year span. The Bruins lost back-to-back games to Duke early in the season by a total of 35 points.

Star Gazing: Utah forward Jerry Chambers became the only Final Four Most Outstanding Player to play for a national fourth-place team. He scored a tourney-high 40 points in an 83-74 triumph over Pacific in the West Regional semifinals. . . . Kentucky starting forward Larry Conley didn't later achieve the name recognition of Dick Vitale, but Conley was the other hoops analyst with ESPN from the cable network's inception.

One and Only: Hill, a 5-10, is the shortest player to lead an NCAA champion in scoring average (15 points per game). Hill's 20.2-point average in five tournament games in 1966 doubled the regular-season mark in his career. . . . Utah, the only Western Athletic Conference school ever to reach the Final Four, lost in the national semifinals to future WAC member Texas-El Paso. . . . UTEP is the only current Division I school never to have an NCAA consensus first- or second-team All-American in its history yet capture an NCAA Tournament title.

Numbers Game: Jack Gardner became the only coach to direct two different schools to the Final Four at least twice apiece–Kansas State (4th in 1948 and 2nd in 1951) and Utah (4th in 1961 and 4th in 1966). . . . Elvin Hayes outrebounded Pacific's Keith Swagerty, 28-23, in Houston's 102-91 victory in the West Regional third-place game.

What If: Utah lost two Final Four games by a total of just nine points despite the absence of second-leading scorer and rebounder George Fisher, who sustained a broken leg late in the season. Fisher finished the year with averages of 13.1 points and 9.2 rebounds per game. . . . Texas

1966 CHAMPIONSHIP BRACKET

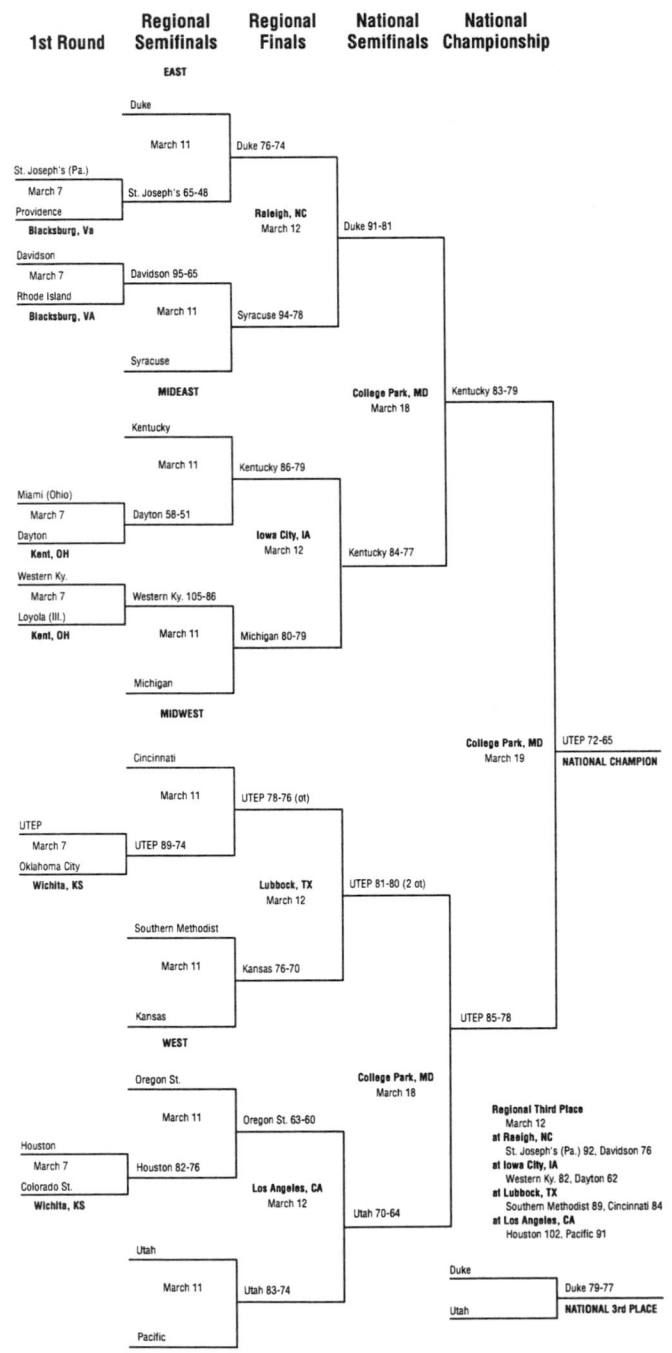

1st Round	Regional Semifinals	Regional Finals	National Semifinals	National Championship

EAST

Duke
March 11   Duke 76-74
St. Joseph's (Pa.)
March 7   St. Joseph's 65-48
Providence
Blacksburg, Va
Davidson
March 7   Davidson 95-65
Rhode Island
Blacksburg, VA   March 11   Syracuse 94-78
Syracuse

Raleigh, NC
March 12   Duke 91-81

MIDEAST

Kentucky
March 11   Kentucky 86-79
Miami (Ohio)
March 7   Dayton 58-51
Dayton
Kent, OH
Western Ky.
March 7   Western Ky. 105-86
Loyola (Ill.)
Kent, OH   March 11   Michigan 80-79
Michigan

Iowa City, IA
March 12   Kentucky 84-77

College Park, MD
March 18   Kentucky 83-79

MIDWEST

Cincinnati
March 11   UTEP 78-76 (ot)
UTEP
March 7   UTEP 89-74
Oklahoma City
Wichita, KS
Southern Methodist
March 11   Kansas 76-70
Kansas

Lubbock, TX
March 12   UTEP 81-80 (2 ot)

WEST

Oregon St.
March 11   Oregon St. 63-60
Houston
March 7   Houston 82-76
Colorado St.
Wichita, KS
Utah
March 11   Utah 83-74
Pacific

Los Angeles, CA
March 12   Utah 70-64

College Park, MD
March 18   UTEP 85-78

College Park, MD
March 19   UTEP 72-65

NATIONAL CHAMPION

Regional Third Place
March 12
at Raleigh, NC
St. Joseph's (Pa.) 92, Davidson 76
at Iowa City, IA
Western Ky. 82, Dayton 62
at Lubbock, TX
Southern Methodist 89, Cincinnati 84
at Los Angeles, CA
Houston 102, Pacific 91

Duke   Duke 79-77
Utah   **NATIONAL 3rd PLACE**

Western had to go into double overtime to nip Kansas, 81-80, in the Midwest Regional final. Jayhawks guard Jo Jo White drilled a 30-footer at the buzzer of the first overtime, but the shot was disallowed when a referee trailing the play saw him step out of bounds moments before releasing the ball.

Scoring and Rebounding Leader: Jerry Chambers, Utah (143 points, 35.75 ppg.; 56 rebounds, 14 rpg).

Highest Rebounding Average: Keith Swagerty, Pacific (42 rebounds, 21 rpg).

1966-67

Providence guard Jimmy Walker after winning the 1966 MVP Award at 1966 Holiday Basketball Festival.

AT A GLANCE

NCAA Champion: UCLA (30-0; coached by John Wooden; won AAWU title by six games with a 14-0 record).

NIT Champion: Southern Illinois (24-2; coached by Jack Hartman).

NCAA Probation: South Carolina.

NCAA Consensus First-Team All-Americans: Lew Alcindor, C, Soph., UCLA; Clem Haskins, G-F, Sr., Western Kentucky; Elvin Hayes, F-C, Jr., Houston; Bob Lloyd, G, Sr., Rutgers; Wes Unseld, C, Jr., Louisville; Bob Verga, G, Sr., Duke; Jimmy Walker, G, Sr., Providence.

National Player of the Year: Alcindor (29 ppg, 15.5 rpg, 66.7 FG%).

National Coach of the Year: John Wooden, UCLA (30-0/AP, UPI, USBWA).

UCLA's Lew Alcindor scored 56 points in his varsity debut against Southern California. Alcindor's opening-game outburst was topped just once all season–by his school record 61 against Washington State. He finished his sophomore season ranked among the top seven in the country in field-goal shooting (first at 66.7 percent), scoring (second at 29 points per game) and rebounding (seventh at 15.5 per game). His scoring average is still the highest in Pacific-10 Conference history.

Alcindor was one of seven players to finish within three points of each other for the national scoring lead. Never have so many major collegians finished so close to the top. Providence's Jimmy Walker won the scoring race with a 30.4 average.

Kent's Doug Grayson set an NCAA record for most consecutive successful field goals in a single game with 16 when he went 18 of 19 from the floor against North Carolina. . . . Rutgers' Bob Lloyd converted 60 consecutive free throws. One of Lloyd's teammates was Jim Valvano, who later made a name for himself as a coach at Iona and North Carolina State. Lloyd went on to serve as coach at his alma mater, where one of his assistants was one low-key Dick Vitale.

Junior forward Don May was instrumental in leading Dayton to the NCAA Final Four.

Houston's mid-sixties teams, coached by Guy Lewis (center), included future NBA stars Elvin Hayes (left) and Don Chaney.

records. . . . Providence's Jimmy Walker (30.4 ppg), Alcindor, Connecticut's Wes Bialosuknia (28), Lloyd (27.9), St. Joseph's Cliff Anderson (26.5) and Duke's Bob Verga (26.1) set school records for highest scoring average in a single season. . . . South Carolina's streak of years with at least 10 defeats ended at 16 when the Gamecocks compiled a 16-7 record to start a string of 15 consecutive winning seasons. Their two regular-season ACC games with Duke were cancelled by the Blue Devils because of USC was on NCAA probation. Duke finished out of the top 10 of the final AP poll for the first time in seven years.

Murray State's Dick Cunningham (36 vs. MacMurray), South Carolina's Gary Gregor (35 vs. Elon at Charlotte), Marquette's Pat Smith (28 vs. Loyola of Chicago), Washington State's Jim

Santa Clara's Bud Ogden (55 points at Pepperdine), Alabama's Mike Nordholz (50 vs. Southern Mississippi in Birmingham Classic) and Montana State's Tom Storm (44 vs. Portland State) established school single-game scoring

1966-67 UNDEFEATED TEAM: UCLA (30-0)

COACH: JOHN WOODEN

UCLA	OPPONENT	BRUINS HIGH SCORER
105	Southern California 90	Alcindor 56
88	Duke 54	Alcindor/Allen 19
107	Duke 87	Alcindor 38
84	Colorado State 74	Alcindor 34
96	Notre Dame 67	Alcindor 25
100	Wisconsin 56	Alcindor 24
91	Georgia Tech 72	Alcindor 18
107	Southern California 83	Alcindor 25
76	at Washington State 67	Alcindor 28
83	at Washington 68	Alcindor 28
96	California 78	Alcindor 26
116	Stanford 78	Alcindor 37
122	Portland 57	Alcindor 27
119	UC Santa Barbara 75	Alcindor 37
82	at Loyola of Chicago 67	Alcindor 35
120	Illinois* 82	Alcindor 45
40	at Southern Cal (OT) 35	Alcindor 13
76	Oregon State 44	Alcindor/Allen 22
100	Oregon 66	Allen 20
34	at Oregon 25	Alcindor 12
72	at Oregon State 50	Alcindor 28
71	Washington 43	Alcindor 37
100	Washington State 78	Alcindor 61
75	at Stanford 47	Alcindor 20
103	at California 66	Alcindor 30
83	Southern California 55	Alcindor 26

NCAA TOURNAMENT

109	Wyoming* 60	Alcindor 29
80	Pacific* 64	Alcindor 38
73	Houston* 58	Shackelford 22
79	Dayton* 64	Alcindor 20

* Neutral court games.

1966-67 INDIVIDUAL LEADERS

SCORING

PLAYER	PTS.	AVG.
Walker, Providence	851	30.4
Alcindor, UCLA	870	29.0
Graham, New York Univ.	688	28.7
Hayes, Houston	881	28.4
Bialosuknia, Connecticut	673	28.0
Lloyd, Rutgers	809	27.9
Gray, Oklahoma City	715	27.5
Anderson, St. Joseph's	690	26.5
Verga, Duke	705	26.1
Tillman, Loyola (Ill.)	553	25.1

REBOUNDING

PLAYER	REB.	AVG.
Cunningham, Murray St.	479	21.8
Beatty, American	458	19.1
Unseld, Louisville	533	19.0
Swagerty, Pacific	518	18.5
May, Dayton	519	16.7
Hayes, Houston	488	15.7
Alcindor, UCLA	466	15.5
Powers, VMI	318	15.1
Lewis, St. Francis (Pa.)	386	14.8
Dove, St. John's	415	14.8

FIELD GOAL PERCENTAGE

PLAYER	FGM	FGA	PCT.
Alcindor, UCLA	346	519	.667
Allen, Bradley	232	373	.622
Lechman, Gonzaga	196	316	.620
Lewis, St. Francis (Pa.)	181	295	.614
Youngblood, Georgia	140	237	.591
Ogden, Santa Clara	186	322	.578
Wagner, Georgia Tech	164	291	.564
Mix, Toledo	227	403	.563
White, Hofstra	161	288	.559
Ware, Virginia Tech	128	230	.557

FREE THROW PERCENTAGE

PLAYER	FTM	FTA	PCT.
Lloyd, Rutgers	255	277	.921
Sandfoss, Morehead St.	106	117	.906
Thompson, Wichita St.	124	137	.905
Sutherland, Clemson	104	116	.897
Cornwall, Syracuse	103	117	.880
Coleman, Missouri	131	150	.873
McPherson, Murray St.	103	118	.873
Chapman, Iowa	114	131	.870
Fritz, Oregon St.	130	150	.867
Heiser, Princeton	93	108	.861

1966-67 TEAM LEADERS

SCORING OFFENSE

SCHOOL	PTS.	AVG.
Oklahoma City	2496	96.0
Northwestern	2009	91.3
UCLA	2687	89.6
Murray St.	2058	89.5
Houston	2765	89.2

SCORING DEFENSE

SCHOOL	PTS.	AVG.
Tennessee	1511	54.0
Memphis St.	1470	56.5
Army	1206	57.4
Princeton	1619	57.8
Kansas	1607	59.5

FIELD GOAL PERCENTAGE

SCHOOL	FGM	FGA	PCT.
UCLA	1082	2081	.520
St. Peter's	773	1498	.516
Bradley	832	1641	.507
Vanderbilt	834	1654	.504
Tulane	843	1679	.502

FREE THROW PERCENTAGE

SCHOOL	FTM	FTA	PCT.
West Texas St.	400	518	.772
Santa Clara	571	742	.770
Kentucky	429	559	.767
Rice	493	648	.761
Georgia	454	598	.759

REBOUNDING

SCHOOL	TOTAL REB.	OWN	PCT.
Florida	2124	1275	.600
Houston	3224	1862	.578
St. Francis (Pa.)	2266	1298	.573
New Mexico	2278	1304	.572
Princeton	2235	1270	.568

1966–67 NCAA CHAMPION: UCLA

SEASON STATISTICS OF UCLA REGULARS

PLAYER	POS.	CL.	G.	FG%	FT%	PPG	RPG
Lew Alcindor	C	So.	30	.667	.650	29.0	15.5
Lucius Allen	G	So.	30	.479	.713	15.5	5.8
Mike Warren	G	Jr.	30	.465	.758	12.7	4.5
Lynn Shackelford	F	So.	30	.480	.821	11.4	5.9
Ken Heitz	F-G	So.	30	.506	.600	6.1	3.2
Bill Sweek	G	So.	30	.479	.565	4.7	2.8
Jim Nielsen	F-C	So.	27	.519	.455	4.6	3.4
Don Saffer	G	Jr.	27	.451	.542	2.9	0.8
Gene Sutherland	G	Jr.	20	.455	.583	1.9	0.8
Neville Saner	F-C	Jr.	24	.308	.667	1.4	1.9
Joe Chrisman	F	Jr.	19	.320	.364	1.1	1.5
TEAM TOTALS			30	.520	.653	89.6	49.8

1967 FINAL FOUR CHAMPIONSHIP GAME

LOUISVILLE, KY

UCLA (79)	MIN.	FG-A	FT-A	REB.	A	PF	PTS.
Heitz	27	2-7	0-0	6	1	2	4
Shackelford	35	5-10	0-2	3	1	1	10
Alcindor	35	8-12	4-11	18	3	0	20
Allen	36	7-15	5-8	9	2	2	19
Warren	35	8-16	1-1	7	0	1	17
Nielsen	4	0-1	0-1	1	0	3	0
Sweek	8	1-1	0-0	0	0	1	2
Saffer	5	2-5	0-0	0	0	1	4
Saner	5	1-1	0-0	2	0	2	2
Chrisman	4	0-0	1-2	1	0	2	1
Sutherland	4	0-0	0-0	0	0	0	0
Lynn	2	0-1	0-0	0	0	0	0
Team				7			
TOTALS	200	34-69	11-25	54	7	15	79

FG%: .493. FT%: .440.

DAYTON (64)	MIN.	FG-A	FT-A	REB.	A	PF	PTS.
May	40	9-23	3-4	17	3	4	21
Sadlier	26	2-5	1-2	7	0	5	5
Obrovac	5	0-2	0-0	2	1	1	0
Klaus	22	4-7	0-0	0	0	1	8
Hooper	34	2-7	2-4	5	2	2	6
Torain	23	3-14	0-0	4	0	3	6
Waterman	23	4-11	2-3	1	2	3	10
Sharpenter	23	2-5	4-5	5	0	1	8
Samanich	1	0-2	0-0	2	0	0	0
Beckman	1	0-0	0-0	0	0	0	0
Inderrieden	1	0-0	0-0	0	0	0	0
Wannemacher	1	0-0	0-0	0	0	0	0
Team				8			
TOTALS	200	26-76	12-18	51	8	20	64

FG%: .342. FT%: .667.
Halftime: UCLA 38-20.

NATIONAL SEMIFINALS

UCLA (73): Heitz 0-0 1-1 1, Shackelford 11-19 0-1 22, Alcindor 6-11 7-13 19, Allen 6-15 5-5 17, Warren 4-10 6-7 14, Nielsen 0-3 0-0 0, Sweek 0-4 0-0 0, Saffer 0-0 0-0 0. Team 27-62 (.435) 19-27 (.704) 73.

HOUSTON (58): Hayes 12-31 1-2 25, Bell 3-11 4-7 10, Kruse 2-5 1-1 5, Grider 2-7 0-0 4, Chaney 3-11 0-2 6, Lentz 1-2 0-3 2, Spain 1-5 0-0 2, Lewis 0-0 0-1 0, Lee 2-3 0-0 4. Team 26-75 (.347) 6-16 (.375) 58.

Halftime: UCLA 39-28.

DAYTON (76): May 16-22 2-6 34, Sadlier 4-7 0-1 8, Obrovac 0-0 0-0 0, Klaus 3-6 9-10 15, Hooper 1-7 3-4 5, Torain 4-14 6-8 14, Wannemacher 0-0 0-2 0, Waterman 0-0 0-0 0. Team 28-56 (.500) 20-31 (.645) 76.

NORTH CAROLINA (62): Miller 6-18 1-1 13, Buntin 1-3 1-1 3, Clark 8-14 3-5 19, Lewis 5-18 1-1 11, Grubar 2-7 3-3 7, Gauntlett 1-4 0-0 2, Brown 0-3 0-0 0, Tuttle 3-5 1-1 7. Team 26-72 (.361) 10-12 (.833) 62.

Halftime: Dayton 29-23.

ALL-TOURNAMENT TEAM

Lew Alcindor, C, Soph., UCLA*
Lucius Allen, G, Soph., UCLA
Elvin Hayes, F, Jr., Houston
Don May, F, Jr., Dayton
Mike Warren, G, Jr., UCLA
*Named Most Outstanding Player

McKean (27 vs. West Virginia) and Portland's Don Lawson (26 vs. Nevada Southern) established school single-game rebounding marks. Cunningham set a single-season Ohio Valley Conference standard by averaging 21.8 rebounds per game.

TCU center James Cash became the first African American to play varsity basketball in the SWC. Cash is now chairman of the Harvard Business School MBA program.. . . Tennessee, coached by Ray Mears, captured its first SEC regular-season championship in 25 years. . . . Kentucky suffered its only non-winning record in coach Adolph Rupp's 41 seasons at the helm when the Wildcats went 13-13. They were 8-10 in league competition for their only losing SEC

mark in history until UK duplicated that record under Eddie Sutton in 1988-89. Kentucky's defeats included a 92-77 setback to visiting Cornell, the only Ivy League team to beat the Wildcats since 1942. The Cornell contest was one of a school-record seven homecourt defeats for the Wildcats. . . . North Carolina finished in the Top 20 of a final wire-service poll for the first time with Dean Smith as head coach. He was in his sixth season as bench boss of the Tar Heels. Carolina defeated Kentucky, 64-55. It was the second of four consecutive victories for Smith against Kentucky coach Adolph Rupp from 1964-65 through 1968-69.

Indiana, coached by Lou Watson, won the Big Ten Conference title after finishing in last place the previous year. . . . The only regular-season defeat for Toledo (23-2) was at Marshall, 96-81. The best season by percentage in the Rockets' history ended with an 82-76 opening-round loss in the NCAA Tournament against Virginia Tech, an opponent they had defeated by 19 points (90-71) in their regular-season finale. . . . Tulsa finished in the Top 20 of a final wire-service poll for the only time in a 26-year span from 1955-56 through 1980-81.

Princeton (25-3, coached by Butch van Breda Kolff) and Pacific (24-4, Dick Edwards) had their winningest seasons in school history. . . . Peck Hickman ended his 23-year coaching career at Louisville with a 443-183 record. He never sustained a losing season. . . . E.C. "Doc" Hayes retired as SMU's coach. The Mustangs did not have a losing record in their last 14 years with him at the helm. In 20 seasons at SMU, Hayes won outright or shared eight SWC titles. No other SWC coach won more than six league championships.

UCLA's Lew Alcindor shoots over a Dayton defender in the NCAA Tournament final.

1966-67 FINAL NATIONAL POLLS

AP	UPI	SCHOOL (RECORD)	HEAD COACH
1	1	UCLA (30-0)	John Wooden
2	2	Louisville (23-5)	Peck Hickman
3	4	Kansas (23-4)	Ted Owens
4	3	North Carolina (26-6)	Dean Smith
5	5	Princeton (25-3)	Butch van Breda Kolff
6	7	Western Kentucky (23-3)	John Oldham
7	6	Houston (27-4)	Guy Lewis
8	9	Tennessee (21-7)	Ray Mears
9	10	Boston College (23-3)	Bob Cousy
10	8	Texas Western (22-7)	Don Haskins
–	11	Toledo (23-2)	Bob Nichols
–	12	St. John's (23-5)	Lou Carnesecca
–	13	Tulsa (19-8)	Joe Swank
–	14	Utah State (22-6)	Ladell Andersen
–	14	Vanderbilt (21-5)	Roy Skinner
–	16	Pacific (24-4)	Dick Edwards
–	17	Providence (21-7)	Joe Mullaney
–	18	New Mexico (19-8)	Bob King
–	19	Duke (18-9)	Vic Bubas
–	20	Florida (21-4)	Tommy Bartlett

1967 NCAA Tournament

Summary: UCLA, starting four sophomores and one junior, won the national championship by a record average of 23.75 points. The Bruins' toughest test was in the West Regional final,

where Pacific trailed by fewer than 10 points in the closing minutes until UCLA pulled away to win by 16 (80-64) behind Lew Alcindor's tourney-high 38 points. The Bruins breezed in the final against Dayton, 79-64, despite hitting just 11 of 25 free-throw attempts. They won 26 of their 30 games by at least 15 points with the only contest in doubt being a 40-35 overtime triumph at Southern Cal in mid-season.

Outcome for Defending Champion: Texas Western compiled a 22-7 record with two of the defeats by double-digit margins against New Mexico State. Bobby Joe Hill, the leading scorer for the Miners' title team, averaged an anemic 4.9 points per game in eight contests.

Biggest Upsets: Dayton wasn't ranked in the UPI top twenty when the Flyers opened the playoffs with a 69-67 overtime triumph against sev-

1967 CHAMPIONSHIP BRACKET

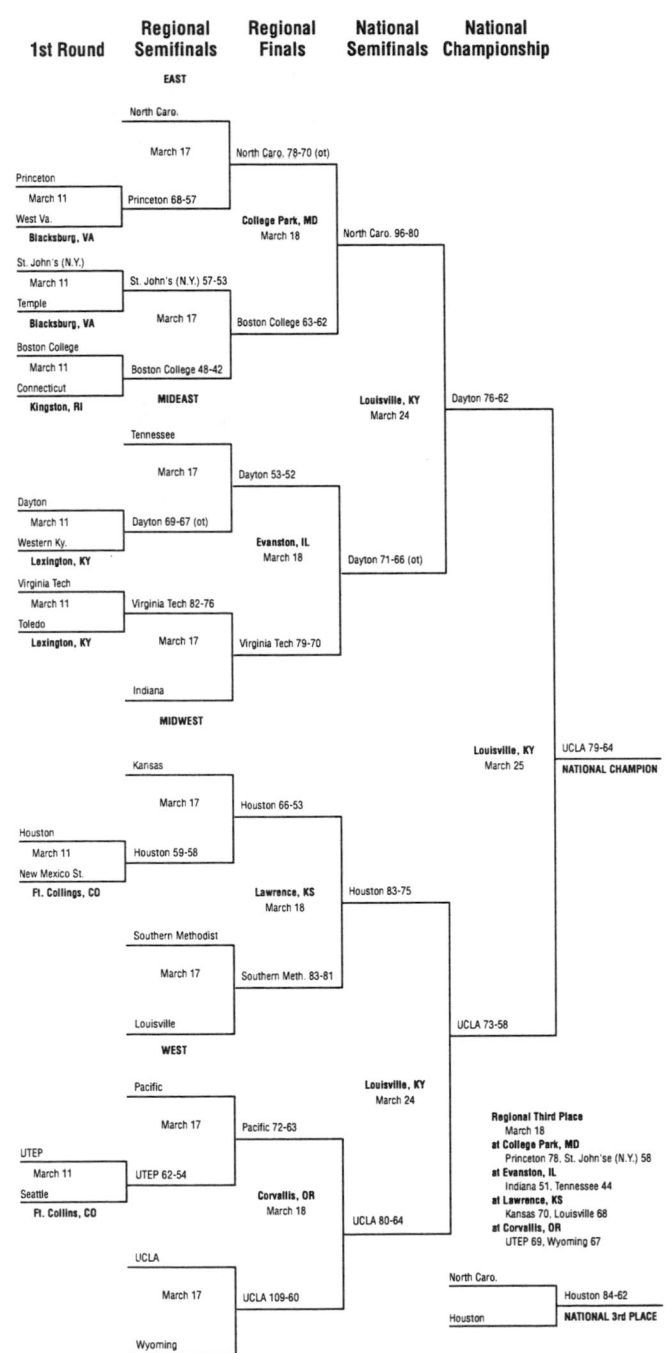

1st Round	Regional Semifinals	Regional Finals	National Semifinals	National Championship

EAST

North Caro.

March 17 — North Caro. 78-70 (ot)

Princeton
March 11
West Va.
Blacksburg, VA

Princeton 68-57

College Park, MD
March 18 — North Caro. 96-80

St. John's (N.Y.)
March 11
Temple
Blacksburg, VA

St. John's (N.Y.) 57-53

March 17 — Boston College 63-62

Boston College
March 11
Connecticut
Kingston, RI

Boston College 48-42

Louisville, KY
March 24 — Dayton 76-62

MIDEAST

Tennessee

March 17 — Dayton 53-52

Dayton
March 11
Western Ky.
Lexington, KY

Dayton 69-67 (ot)

Evanston, IL
March 18 — Dayton 71-66 (ot)

Virginia Tech
March 11
Toledo
Lexington, KY

Virginia Tech 82-76

March 17 — Virginia Tech 79-70

Indiana

MIDWEST

Louisville, KY
March 25 — UCLA 79-54

NATIONAL CHAMPION

Kansas

March 17 — Houston 66-53

Houston
March 11
New Mexico St.
Ft. Collings, CO

Houston 59-58

Lawrence, KS
March 18 — Houston 83-75

Southern Methodist

March 17 — Southern Meth. 83-81

Louisville

WEST

UCLA 73-58

Pacific

March 17 — Pacific 72-63

UTEP
March 11
Seattle
Ft. Collins, CO

UTEP 62-54

Corvallis, OR
March 18 — UCLA 80-64

UCLA
March 17 — UCLA 109-60

Wyoming

Louisville, KY
March 24

Regional Third Place
March 18
at College Park, MD
Princeton 78, St. John'se (N.Y.) 58
at Evanston, IL
Indiana 51, Tennessee 44
at Lawrence, KS
Kansas 70, Louisville 68
at Corvallis, OR
UTEP 69, Wyoming 67

North Caro.

Houston 84-62

Houston

NATIONAL 3rd PLACE

enth-ranked Western Kentucky as Hilltoppers first-team All-American Clem Haskins, playing with his broken wrist in a cast, was limited to eight points. Dayton also defeated two other top ten teams–Tennessee (ranked ninth by UPI) and North Carolina (third)–before getting clobbered by top-ranked UCLA in the national final. . . . Charles Beasley was limited to nine points, but fellow SWC first-team selection Denny Holman picked up the slack with 30 points, including a decisive basket with three seconds remaining, to spark SMU (20-6) to an 83-81 victory over second-ranked Louisville (23-5). Wes Unseld and Butch Beard combined for 32 points and 21 rebounds, but it wasn't enough for the Cardinals, who hit just 5 of their 14 free throws.

One and Only: UCLA is the only NCAA champion since World War II not to have a senior on its roster. . . . Houston is the only school to reach the Final Four (third place) and College World Series championship game (runner-up to Arizona State) in the same year.

Numbers Game: National field-goal accuracy leader UCLA finished among the top 30 teams in that category for the first time in 12 years. . . . Toledo was eliminated in its opener by Virginia Tech when the Rockets' one-two punch of Steve Mix and John Brisker, a pair of forwards who went on to distinguished pro careers, combined to shoot 36.4 percent from the floor (12 of 33). . . . Tennessee, leading the nation in team defense for the second time in three seasons, made its first appearance in the NCAA Tournament. . . . Elvin Hayes' game-high 25 points and tourney-high 24 rebounds weren't enough to prevent Houston's 73-58 setback against UCLA in the national semifinals.

Scoring Leader: Elvin Hayes, Houston (128 points, 25.6 ppg).

Highest Scoring Average: Lew Alcindor, UCLA (106 points, 26.5 ppg).

Rebounding Leader: Don May, Dayton (82 rebounds, 16.4 rpg).

1967-68

AT A GLANCE

NCAA Champion: UCLA (29-1; coached by John Wooden; won AAWU title by three games with a 14-0 record).

NIT Champion: Dayton (21-9; coached by Don Donoher).

New Rules: The dunk shot is deemed illegal during the game and pregame warmup. NIT field expands from 14 teams to 16.

NCAA Probation: Illinois, Mississippi State, South Carolina.

NCAA Consensus First-Team All-Americans: Lew Alcindor, C, Jr., UCLA; Elvin Hayes, F-C, Sr., Houston; Pete Maravich, G, Soph., Louisiana State; Larry Miller, F, Sr., North Carolina; Wes Unseld, C, Sr., Louisville.

National Player of the Year: Hayes (36.8 ppg, 18.9 rpg, 54.9 FG%).

National Coach of the Year: Guy Lewis, Houston (31-2/AP, UPI, NABC, USBWA).

Houston ended UCLA's 47-game winning streak, 71-69, in the Astrodome in what has been called the "Game of the Century." Houston's Elvin Hayes (39 points and 15 rebounds) outdueled injured UCLA center Lew Alcindor (15 points and 12 rebounds while hampered by a scratched left cornea). Hayes, who hit just 59 percent of his free throws in his career, sank two foul shots with 28 seconds remaining to snap a 69-69 deadlock.

Sophomore Pete Maravich scored an amazing 49.3 percent of LSU's points in compiling a 43.8-point average. When Maravich was a prep player, his father, Press, coached at North Carolina State. At the time, the ACC required incoming freshmen to score 800 on their SAT. When Pete apparently had difficulty reaching 800, his father decided that coaching his son was more important than remaining in the ACC. So father and son went to LSU in the SEC. During the 1960s it was widely assumed that the 800 score was the ACC's way of perpetuating segregation. But it

Louisville's Wes Unseld fights off a defender for a rebound.

wound up costing the league one of the most famous white players in history. . . . Maravich's 59-point uprising against Alabama was not the season's single-game high. Houston's Hayes poured in a school-record 62 against Valparaiso. Hayes finished the season with an amazing average of 55.7 points and rebounds per game.

Florida's Neal Walk became the first Southerner in major-college history to pace the nation in rebounding. Walk's school-record tying 31-rebound effort against Alabama was his third game of the season with at least 27 boards. . . . Duke managed just two field goals in a 12-10 defeat against North Carolina State. It was the lowest-scoring game involving at least one major team in 26 years, marking the first time a squad won with fewer than 20 points since 1944. . . . For the only time in ACC history, two members finished the season with at least 20 defeats–Wake Forest (5-21) and Clemson (4-20).

Georgia compiled a 17-8 record to snap a streak of 16 consecutive losing seasons. . . . Tennessee's school-record 33-game homecourt winning streak ended when the Volunteers lost to Auburn, 53-52. . . . Vanderbilt upset three nationally-ranked teams (North Carolina, Davidson, Duke) within a week. But the biggest news at Vanderbilt was Perry Wallace breaking the racial barrier and becoming the first African American to play varsity basketball in the SEC. Wallace is now a Professor of Law at American University. . . . West Virginia finished runner-up to Davidson in the Southern Conference in the Mountaineers' final season as a member of the league.

Establishing school single-game scoring records were Creighton's Bob Portman (51 points vs. Wisconsin-Milwaukee), Connecticut's Bill Corley (51 vs. New Hampshire), Duquesne's Ron Guziak (50 vs. St. Francis, Pa., at Altoona), Southern Illinois' Dick Garrett (46 vs. Centenary), Louisville's Wes Unseld (45 vs. Georgetown, Ky., College) and Massachusetts' Billy Tindall (41 vs. Vermont). . . . Niagara's Calvin Murphy, a 5-9 sophomore, posted the highest single-season scoring average for a major-college player shorter than 6-0 (38.2 points per game). . . . Murphy, Houston's Hayes (36.8 ppg), Creighton's Bob Portman (29.5) and Miami of Ohio's Fred Foster (26.8) set school records for highest scoring average in a single season.

Rudy Tomjanovich, playing his first varsity game for Michigan when the Wolverines christened Crisler Arena, grabbed a still-existing arena record of 27 rebounds in a 96-79 defeat against Kentucky. . . . Houston's Hayes (37 at Centenary), Eastern Kentucky's Garfield Smith (33 vs. Marshall), North Carolina's Rusty Clark (30 vs. Maryland), Notre Dame's Bob Whitmore (tied with 30 vs. St. Norbert), Idaho State's Ed Wilson (30 vs. Pan American), Georgetown's Charlie Adrion (29 vs. George Washington), Bucknell's Craig Greenwood (28 vs. DePauw), Rhode Island's Art Stephenson (28 vs. Brown), St. Bonaventure's Bob Lanier (27 vs. Loyola, Md.), California's Bob Presley (27 vs. St. Mary's) and Western Michigan's Reggie Lacefield (26 at

1967-68 INDIVIDUAL LEADERS

SCORING

PLAYER	PTS.	AVG.
Maravich, LSU	1138	43.8
Murphy, Niagara	916	38.2
Hayes, Houston	1214	36.8
Travis, Oklahoma City	808	29.9
Portman, Creighton	738	29.5
Mount, Purdue	683	28.5
Hill, W. Texas St.	573	27.3
Halimon, Utah St.	671	26.8
Foster, Miami (Ohio)	617	26.8
Walk, Florida	663	26.5

REBOUNDING

PLAYER	REB.	AVG.
Walk, Florida	494	19.8
Smith, E. Kentucky	472	19.7

Hayes, Houston	624	18.9
Unseld, Louisville	513	18.3
Cunningham, Murray St.	410	17.8
Lewis, St. Francis (Pa.)	443	17.7
Wilson, Idaho St.	420	17.5
Cowens, Florida St.	456	16.9
Alcindor, UCLA	461	16.5
Stephenson, Rhode Island	420	16.2

FIELD GOAL PERCENTAGE

PLAYER	FGM	FGA	PCT.
Allen, Bradley	258	304	.655
Hunt, Army	154	248	.621
Alcindor, UCLA	294	480	.613
Unseld, Louisville	294	480	.613
Sorenson, Ohio St.	196	329	.596
Sidle, Oklahoma	189	321	.589
Webster, St. Peter's	279	477	.585

Lanier, St. Bon.	272	466	.584
Bowen, Bradley	185	317	.584
Lienhard, Georgia	213	366	.582

FREE THROW PERCENTAGE

PLAYER	FTM	FTA	PCT.
Heiser, Princeton	117	130	.900
Ward, Centenary	94	106	.887
Carpenter, Pacific	96	109	.881
Luchini, Marquette	107	124	.863
Williams, Rice	113	131	.863
Garrett, S. Ill.	100	116	.862
Montgomery, W. Forest	134	157	.854
Wininger, Butler	97	114	.851
Moeser, Tulane	125	147	.850
Warren, St. John's	102	120	.850
Washington, Miss. St.	96	113	.850

1967-68 TEAM LEADERS

SCORING OFFENSE

SCHOOL	PTS.	AVG.
Houston	3226	97.8
St. Peter's	2630	93.9
UCLA	2802	93.4
Oklahoma City	2492	92.3
Florida St.	2438	90.3

SCORING DEFENSE

SCHOOL	PTS.	AVG.
Army	1448	57.9
Oklahoma St.	1528	58.8
Tennessee	1548	59.5
Villanova	1696	60.6
Princeton	1579	60.7

SCORING MARGIN

SCHOOL	OFF.	DEF.	MAR.
UCLA	93.4	67.2	26.2

Houston	97.8	72.5	25.3
St. Peter's	93.9	76.1	17.8
Columbia	78.8	61.7	17.1
Boston College	88.8	74.9	13.9

WON-LOST PERCENTAGE

SCHOOL	W-L	PCT.
UCLA	29-1	.967
Houston	31-2	.939
St. Bonaventure	23-2	.920
North Carolina	28-4	.875
St. Peter's	24-4	.857

FIELD GOAL PERCENTAGE

SCHOOL	FGM	FGA	PCT.
Bradley	927	1768	.524
St. Peter's	1019	1953	.522
St. Bonaventure	875	1732	.505
UCLA	1161	2321	.500
Louisville	881	1770	.498

FREE THROW PERCENTAGE

SCHOOL	FTM	FTA	PCT.
Vanderbilt	527	684	.770
Mississippi St.	496	645	.769
Nebraska	504	660	.764
Tulane	528	692	.763
Georgia Tech	404	531	.761

REBOUNDS

SCHOOL	REB.	AVG.
Houston	2074	62.8
Northern Illinois	1383	57.6
St. Francis (Pa.)	1434	57.4
Eastern Kentucky	1348	56.2
American	1459	56.1

Illinois State) established school single-game rebounding records. Wilson set a Big Sky Conference standard by averaging 17.5 rebounds per game.

St. Peter's (24-4/coached by Don Kennedy) and Columbia (23-5/Jack Rohan) had their winningest seasons in school history. St. Peter's pounded Duke by 29 points (100-71) to reach the NIT semifinals. . . . Providence's streak of consecutive 20-win seasons under coach Joe Mullaney ended at nine when the Friars lost nine of their last 13 games to finish with an 11-14 record. . . . Long Island, winner of two of the first four NIT titles (1939 and 1941), participated in the NIT for the first time since 1950.

Army (20-5) lost its NIT opener to Notre Dame but the Cadets finished in the top 20 of a final wire-service poll for the only time in school history. . . . Lehigh, coached by Roy Heckman, registered its only winning record (12-11) in a 27-year span from 1953-54 through 1979-80.

Oklahoma City coach Abe Lemons, upset when his team trailed Duke, 49-38, at intermission of its NIT opener, kept his squad on the Madison Square Garden floor for a 10-minute workout. It didn't help as OCU lost, 97-81. . . . Indiana tied for last place in the Big Ten with a 4-10 league record one season after tying for the title with a 10-4 mark.. . . Forward Joe Franklin became Wisconsin's only All-Big Ten first-team

UCLA coaching guru John Wooden.

1967-68 FINAL NATIONAL POLLS

AP	UPI	SCHOOL (RECORD)	HEAD COACH
1	1	Houston (31-2)	Guy Lewis
2	2	UCLA (29-1)	John Wooden
3	3	St. Bonaventure (23-2)	Larry Weise
4	4	North Carolina (28-4)	Dean Smith
5	5	Kentucky (22-5)	Adolph Rupp
6	7	New Mexico (23-5)	Bob King
7	6	Columbia (23-5)	Jack Rohan
8	9	Davidson (24-5)	Lefty Driesell
9	8	Louisville (21-7)	John Dromo
10	11	Duke (22-6)	Vic Bubas
–	10	Marquette (23-6)	Al McGuire
–	12	New Mexico State (23-6)	Lou Henson
–	13	Vanderbilt (20-6)	Roy Skinner
–	14	Kansas State (19-9)	Tex Winter
–	15	Princeton (20-6)	Pete Carril
–	16	Army (20-5)	Bob Knight
–	17	Santa Clara (23-4)	Dick Garibaldi
–	18	Utah (17-9)	Jack Gardner
–	19	Bradley (19-9)	Joe Stowell
–	20	Iowa (16-9)	Ralph Miller

selection in a 38-year span from 1952-53 through 1989-90. He averaged 22.7 points per game and a league-high 13.9 rebounds per contest. . . . Miami of Ohio suffered a season-ending defeat at home against Dayton to finish with the Redskins' only losing record (11-12) in a 16-year stretch from 1962-63 through 1977-78. . . . Texas Christian compiled its first winning mark in nine seasons (15-11) in Johnny Swaim's initial year as coach of the Horned Frogs.

1968 NCAA Tournament

Summary: "I've never come out and said it," UCLA coach John Wooden said, "but it

St. Bonaventure's Bob Lanier stetches to block a shot.

Houston's Elvin Hayes (left) and UCLA's Lew Alcindor go head to head in the 1967–68 NCAA Semifinals.

would be hard to pick a team over the 1968 team. I will say it would be the most difficult team to prepare for and play against offensively and defensively. It created so many problems. It had such great balance.

"We had the big center (Alcindor) who is the most valuable player of all time. Mike Warren was a three-year starter who may have been the most intelligent floor leader ever, going eight complete games once without a turnover. Lucius Allen was a very physical, talented individual who was extremely quick. Lynn Shackleford was a great shooter out of the corner who didn't allow defenses to sag on Jabbar. Mike Lynn didn't have power, but he had as fine a pair of hands around the boards as I have ever seen."

The roster for UCLA's 1968 national champion included six players with double-digit sea-son scoring averages, but senior forward Edgar Lacey dropped off the team with an 11.9-point average following a dispute with Wooden after a highly-publicized mid-season defeat against Houston before 52,693 fans at the Astrodome. Lacey, assigned to defend Cougars star Elvin Hayes early in the game, was annoyed with Wooden for singling him out following Hayes' 29-point first-half outburst. Lacey, the leading rebounder for the Bruins' 1965 NCAA titlist when he was an All-Tournament team selection, missed the 1966-67 campaign because of a fractured left kneecap. Houston, entering the tourney undefeated, lost in the national semifinals against UCLA (101-69) when Hayes, averaging 37.6 points per game entering the Final Four, was restricted to 10 as the Bruins neutralized him by employing a "diamond-and-one" defense with Lynn Shackelford assigned to cover Hayes.

1967–68 NCAA CHAMPION: UCLA

SEASON STATISTICS OF UCLA REGULARS

PLAYER	POS.	CL.	G.	FG%	FT%	PPG	RPG
Lew Alcindor	C	Jr.	28	.613	.616	26.2	16.5
Lucius Allen	G	Jr.	30	.462	.678	15.1	6.0
Mike Warren	G	Sr.	30	.431	.763	12.1	3.7
Lynn Shackelford	F	Jr.	30	.498	.848	10.7	5.0
Mike Lynn	F	Sr.	30	.457	.684	10.3	5.2
Ken Heitz	G	Jr.	27	.500	.743	5.3	2.3
Jim Nielsen	F	Jr.	30	.496	.657	4.6	3.3
Bill Sweek	G	Jr.	27	.471	.654	3.6	1.2
Gene Sutherland	G	Sr.	27	.417	.885	1.6	0.6
Neville Saner	F	Sr.	24	.372	.600	1.5	1.6
TEAM TOTALS			30	.500	.684	93.4	53.4

1968 FINAL FOUR CHAMPIONSHIP GAME

LOS ANGELES, CA

UCLA (78)	MIN.	FG-A	FT-A	REB.	A	PF	PTS.
Shackelford	26	3-5	0-1	2	4	2	6
Lynn	22	1-7	5-7	6	4	2	7
Alcindor	37	15-21	4-4	16	1	4	34
Warren	35	3-7	1-1	3	1	2	7
Allen	35	3-7	5-7	5	5	4	11
Nielsen	10	1-1	0-0	1	0	1	2
Heitz	20	3-6	1-1	2	2	1	7
Sutherland	5	1-2	0-0	2	1	2	2
Sweek	5	0-1	0-0	2	0	0	0
Saner	5	1-3	0-0	2	1	0	2
Team				9			
TOTALS	200	31-60	16-21	48	19	16	78

FG%: .517. FT%: .762. Turnovers: 26.

N. CAROLINA (55)	MIN.	FG-A	FT-A	REB.	A	PF	PTS.
Miller	37	5-13	4-6	6	3	3	14
Bunting	15	1-3	1-2	2	1	5	3
Clark	37	4-12	1-3	8	1	3	9
Scott	35	6-17	0-1	3	2	3	12
Grubar	35	2-5	1-2	0	1	2	5
Fogler	16	1-4	2-2	0	2	0	4
Brown	13	2-5	2-2	5	0	1	6

Tuttle	2	0-0	0-0	0	1	0	0
Frye	3	1-2	0-1	1	0	0	2
Whitehead	1	0-0	0-0	0	0	0	0
Delany	3	0-1	0-0	0	0	0	0
Fletcher	3	0-1	0-0	0	0	0	0
Team				10			
TOTALS	200	22-63	11-19	35	11	17	55

FG%: .349. FT%: .579. Turnovers: 23.
Halftime: UCLA 32-22.

NATIONAL SEMIFINALS

OHIO STATE (66): Howell 6-17 1-2 13, Hosket 4-11 6-9 14, Sorenson 5-17 1-3 11, Schnabel 0-1 0-0 0, Meadors 3-13 2-2 8, Finney 8-13 0-2 16, Smith 2-6 0-0 4, Andreas 0-0 0-0 0, Barclay 0-1 0-0 0, Geddes 0-0 0-0 0. Team 28-79 (.354) 10-18 (.556) 66.

NORTH CAROLINA (80): Miller 10-23 0-1 20, Bunting 4-7 9-10 17, Clark 7-9 1-1 15, Scott 6-16 1-4 13, Grubar 4-9 3-3 11, Fogler 1-2 0-0 2, Brown 0-4 0-0 0, Tuttle 1-1 0-1 2. Team 33-71 (.465) 14-20 (.700) 80.

Halftime: North Carolina 34-27.

HOUSTON (69): Lee 2-15 0-0 4, Hayes 3-10 4-7 10, Spain 4-12 7-10 15, Chaney 5-13 5-7 15, Lewis 2-8 2-2 6, Hamood 3-5 4-6 10, Gribben 0-5 0-1 0, Bell 3-8 3-4 9, Taylor 0-0 0-0 0, Cooper 0-2 0-0 0. Team 22-78 (.282) 25-37 (.676) 69.

UCLA (101): Shackelford 6-10 5-5 17, Lynn 8-10 3-3 19, Alcindor 7-14 5-6 19, Warren 7-18 0-0 14, Allen 9-18 1-2 19, Nielsen 2-3 0-0 4, Heitz 3-6 1-1 7, Sweek 1-1 0-1 2, Sutherland 0-1 0-0 0, Saner 0-2 0-0 0. Team 43-83 (.518) 15-18 (.833) 101.

Halftime: UCLA 53-31.

ALL-TOURNAMENT TEAM

Lew Alcindor, C, Jr., UCLA*
Lucius Allen, G, Jr., UCLA
Larry Miller, F, Sr., North Carolina
Lynn Shackleford, F, Jr., UCLA
Mike Warren, G, Sr., UCLA
*Named Most Outstanding Player

Star Gazing: St. Bonaventure, undefeated entering the tourney (22-0), lost in the East Regional semifinals against North Carolina (91-72) despite 23 points and nine rebounds by consensus second-team All-American Bob Lanier of the Bonnies.

One and Only: Hayes became the only player to lead the playoffs in scoring and rebounding in back-to-back years. Hayes became the only player to lead a tournament in scoring by more than 60 points. Alcindor and his UCLA teammates helped hold Hayes to 10 points in the 1968 national semifinals, but the Big E finished with 167 points in five games. Alcindor was runner-up with 103 points in four games. Hayes became the only player in tournament history to collect more than 40 points and 25 rebounds in the same game when he had tourney highs of 49 points and 27 rebounds in a 94-76 decision over Loyola of Chicago in the opening round of the Midwest Regional. Hayes holds the records for most rebounds in a playoff series (97 in five games as a senior) and career (222 in 13 games). He had five games with at least 24 rebounds, including the first three playoff games in 1968, before being held to five in a 101-69 national semifinal loss against UCLA. Hayes also holds the record for most playoff field goals in a career with 152. He averaged almost 24 field goal attempts per game in helping the Cougars win nine of 13 contests.

1968 CHAMPIONSHIP BRACKET

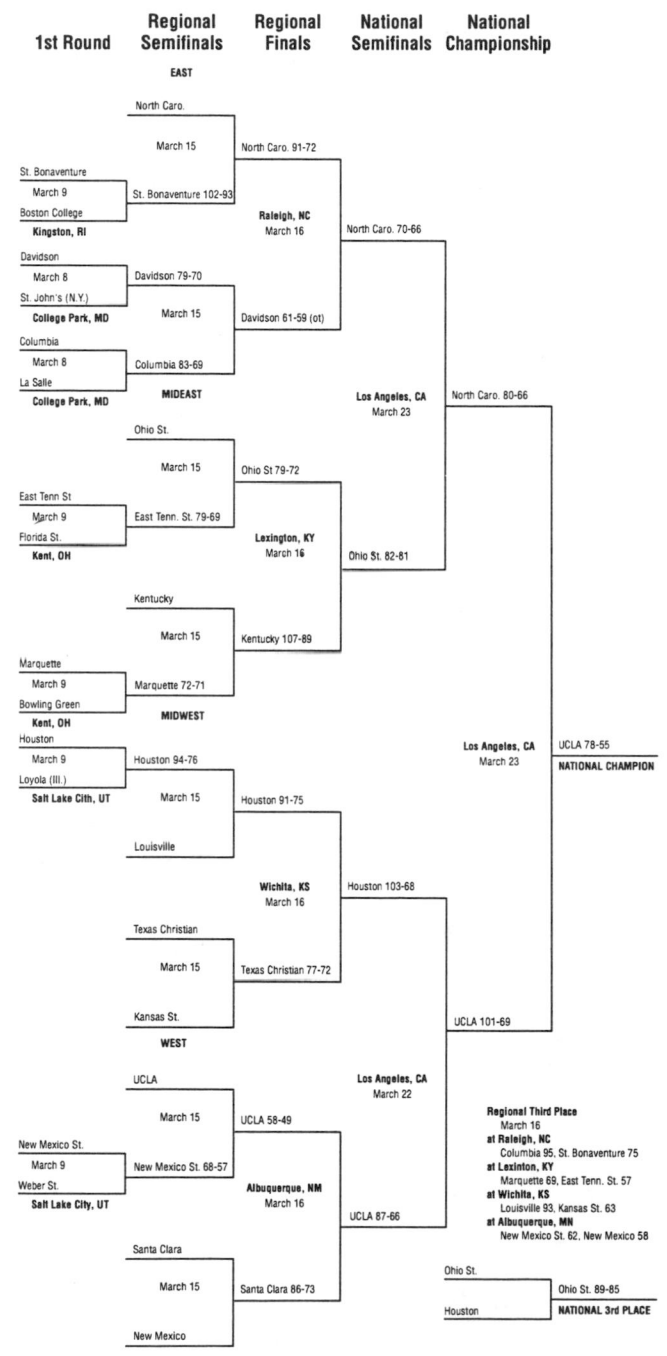

1st Round	Regional Semifinals	Regional Finals	National Semifinals	National Championship

EAST

North Caro.

March 15 — North Caro. 91-72

St. Bonaventure
March 9
Boston College
Kingston, RI — St. Bonaventure 102-93

Raleigh, NC
March 16 — North Caro. 70-66

Davidson
March 8
St. John's (N.Y.)
College Park, MD — Davidson 79-70

March 15 — Davidson 61-59 (ot)

Columbia
March 8
La Salle
College Park, MD — Columbia 83-69

Los Angeles, CA
March 23 — North Caro. 80-66

MIDEAST

Ohio St.

March 15 — Ohio St 79-72

East Tenn St
March 9
Florida St.
Kent, OH — East Tenn. St. 79-69

Lexington, KY
March 16 — Ohio St. 82-81

Kentucky

March 15 — Kentucky 107-89

Marquette
March 9
Bowling Green
Kent, OH — Marquette 72-71

MIDWEST

Houston
March 9
Loyola (Ill.)
Salt Lake Cith, UT — Houston 94-76

March 15 — Houston 91-75

Louisville

Wichita, KS
March 16 — Houston 103-68

Texas Christian

March 15 — Texas Christian 77-72

Kansas St.

Los Angeles, CA
March 23 — UCLA 78-55

NATIONAL CHAMPION

UCLA 101-69

WEST

UCLA

March 15 — UCLA 58-49

New Mexico St.
March 9
Weber St.
Salt Lake City, UT — New Mexico St. 68-57

Los Angeles, CA
March 22

Albuquerque, NM
March 16 — UCLA 87-66

Santa Clara

March 15 — Santa Clara 86-73

New Mexico

Regional Third Place
March 16
at Raleigh, NC
Columbia 95, St. Bonaventure 75
at Lexinton, KY
Marquette 69, East Tenn. St. 57
at Wichita, KS
Louisville 93, Kansas St. 63
at Albuquerque, MN
New Mexico St. 62, New Mexico 58

Ohio St.

Houston — Ohio St. 89-85

NATIONAL 3rd PLACE

Numbers Game: UCLA became the only champion to win its two Final Four games by a total of more than 50 points. The Bruins' 78-55 decision over North Carolina was the most lopsided triumph in championship game history until UNLV demolished Duke in 1990 (103-73). . . . This year marked the only time as many as three Final Four teams returned to the national semifinals for a second consecutive season–UCLA (champion both years under Wooden), Houston (third in '67 and fourth in '68 under Guy Lewis) and North Carolina (fourth in '67 and runner-up in '68 under Dean Smith). . . . Hayes led the tournament in scoring and rebounding by wide margins for fourth-place Houston, but he wasn't named to the all-tournament team.

Putting Things in Perspective: Houston excelled although forward Melvin Bell, the third-leading scorer and second-leading rebounder for the '67 Final Four team, missed the season after undergoing knee surgery.

Scoring and Rebounding Leader: Elvin Hayes, Houston (167 points, 33.4 ppg; 97 rebounds, 19.4 rpg).

Highest Rebounding Average: Wes Unseld, Louisville (20.5 rpg).

1968–69

AT A GLANCE

NCAA Champion: UCLA (29-1; coached by John Wooden; won Pacific-8 title by two games with a 13-1 record, which was two games ahead of Washington State).

NIT Champion: Temple (22-8; coached by Harry Litwack).

NCAA Probation: Florida State, Illinois, La Salle, Mississippi State, St. Bonaventure, Texas-Pan American, Utah State.

NCAA Consensus First-Team All-Americans: Lew Alcindor, C, Sr., UCLA; Spencer Haywood, F-C, Jr., Detroit; Pete Maravich, G, Jr., Louisiana State; Rick Mount, G, Jr., Purdue; Calvin Murphy, G, Jr., Niagara.

National Player of the Year: Alcindor (24 ppg, 14.7 rpg, 63.5 FG%).

National Coaches of the Year: Drake's Maury John (26-5, USBWA) and UCLA's John Wooden (29-1, AP, UPI, NABC).

Pete Maravich, averaging 44.2 points per game, won the national scoring championship by a larger margin than any player in history (10.9 points higher than Purdue guard Rick Mount). Duquesne, one of the nation's top defensive teams, was unbeaten through nine contests by limiting opponents to 57.3 points per game entering the Dukes' outing against LSU in the All-College Tournament final at Oklahoma City. Maravich erupted for 53 points in a 94-91 triumph over Duquesne to give LSU a 7-1 record at that juncture. The Tigers, however, lost their next six SEC assignments despite Maravich's prolific production.

Incredibly, Maravich averaged 46.5 points in 15 road games, compared to 41 at home. Needing 49 in the Tigers' finale at Georgia to set an all-time single-season record, he exploded for 58, including 11 in a second overtime when he climaxed the outburst with a hook shot from midcourt.

A coach who might have wondered about all of the fuss over Maravich was Tennessee's Ray Mears, whose "Chinese" defense restricted Pistol Pete to a 19.8 average in four games over two seasons. No other team held Maravich under 30 points in his first 52 games.

Maravich had three consecutive games with at least 50 points against Division I opponents (66-50-54). His 66-point outburst at Tulane was not the season's single-game high. Niagara's Calvin Murphy claimed that distinction by pouring in a school-record 68 in a 118-110 victory against Syracuse, which finished with its fifth losing record of the decade (9-16).

Mount joined guard Bob Lloyd (Rutgers '67) and forward Larry Miller (North Carolina '68) in an odd category by becoming the third NCAA consensus first-team All-American in as many years to go straight to the ABA and never play in the NBA. . . . Michigan's Rudy Tomjanovich,

1968–69 INDIVIDUAL LEADERS

SCORING

PLAYER	PTS.	AVG.
Maravich, LSU	1148	44.2
Mount, Purdue	932	33.3
Murphy, Niagara	778	32.4
Haywood, Detroit	699	31.8
B. Tallent, G. Washington	723	28.9
Roberts, Utah St.	718	27.6
Curnutt, Miami (Fla.)	661	27.5
Lanier, St. Bonaventure	654	27.3
Travis, Oklahoma City	729	27.0
Morgan, Jacksonville	613	26.7

REBOUNDING

PLAYER	REB.	AVG.
Haywood, Detroit	472	21.5
Lewis, St. Francis (Pa.)	495	20.6

Green, Morehead St.	483	17.9
Walk, Florida	481	17.8
Driscoll, Boston College	498	17.8
Cowens, Florida St.	437	17.5
Brown, Middle Tenn. St.	429	16.5
Ladner, S. Mississippi	411	16.4
Grosso, Louisville	432	16.0
Cross, San Francisco	400	16.0

FIELD GOAL PERCENTAGE

PLAYER	FGM	FGA	PCT.
Alcindor, UCLA	303	477	.635
Bunting, N. Carolina	217	363	.598
Wilkes, Virginia	153	256	.598
Awtrey, Santa Clara	240	406	.591
Lanier, St. Bonaventure	270	460	.587
Lienhard, Georgia	235	404	.582
Smith, Syracuse	177	307	.577

Hayes, Boston Univ.	200	351	.570
Dodds, Wyoming	165	290	.569
Gayeska, Massachusetts	142	250	.568

FREE THROW PERCENTAGE

PLAYER	FTM	FTA	PCT.
Justus, Tennessee	133	147	.905
Finney, Ohio St.	99	110	.900
Thomforde, Princeton	123	137	.898
Ward, Centenary	99	112	.884
Davis, Wake Forest	194	220	.882
Mitchell, W. Texas St.	131	149	.879
Powell, Loyola (La.)	106	121	.876
B. Tallent, G. Washington	155	177	.876
Hagan, Vanderbilt	116	133	.872
Mitchell, VMI	99	114	.868

1968–69 TEAM LEADERS

SCORING OFFENSE

SCHOOL	PTS.	AVG.
Purdue	2605	93.0
Hardin-Simmons	2387	91.9
Kentucky	2542	90.8
Michigan	2153	89.7
Louisiana St.	2316	89.1

SCORING DEFENSE

SCHOOL	PTS.	AVG.
Army	1498	53.5
Tennessee	1651	59.0
Oklahoma St.	1482	59.3
Long Island	1372	59.7
Kansas	1625	60.2

SCORING MARGIN

SCHOOL	OFF.	DEF.	MAR.
UCLA	84.7	63.8	20.9
La Salle	89.0	70.9	18.1

Columbia	77.0	61.3	15.7
Santa Clara	77.0	61.3	15.7
Purdue	93.0	79.1	13.9

WON-LOST PERCENTAGE

SCHOOL	W-L	PCT.
UCLA	29-1	.967
La Salle	23-1	.958
Santa Clara	27-2	.931
Weber St.	27-3	.900
Davidson	27-3	.900

FIELD GOAL PERCENTAGE

SCHOOL	FGM	FGA	PCT.
UCLA	1027	1999	.514
Auburn	734	1461	.502
Southern Mississippi	855	1710	.500
Columbia	689	1380	.499
St. Peter's	913	1847	.494

FREE THROW PERCENTAGE

SCHOOL	FTM	FTA	PCT.
Jacksonville	574	733	.783
Purdue	571	730	.782
Tennessee	438	563	.778
Iowa	573	743	.771
Wake Forest	642	833	.771

REBOUNDING

SCHOOL	REB.	AVG.
Middle Tennessee St.	1685	64.8
St. Francis (Pa.)	1411	58.8
Morehead St.	1583	58.6
Indiana	1354	56.4
Maine	1286	55.9

who coached the Houston Rockets to NBA championships in 1994 and 1995, set a Chicago Stadium college record and school standard with 30 rebounds in a 112-100 overtime defeat to Loyola of Chicago. Earlier in the season in another overtime game, he established a Michigan field-goal record with 21 baskets and tied Cazzie Russell's scoring standard with 48 points in an 89-87 overtime victory against Indiana.

Maine's Jim Stephenson (54 points vs. Colby), Wake Forest's Charlie Davis (51 vs. American University), St. Bonaventure's Bob Lanier (51 vs. Seton Hall), Larry Lewis of St. Francis, Pa. (46 vs. St. Vincent), Western Michi-gan's Gene Ford (46 vs. Loyola of Chicago), Vanderbilt's Tom Hagan (44 at Mississippi State) and Pacific's Bill Stricker (44 vs. Portland) also set school single-game scoring marks. . . . Detroit's Spencer Haywood (32.1 ppg), George Washington's Bob Tallent (28.9), Boston University's Jim Hayes (25.7), Tulane's Johnny Arthurs (25.6), John Conforti (24.3) of St. Francis (N.Y.), Vanderbilt's Hagan (23.4) and Middle Tennessee State's Willie Brown (23.3) set school records for highest scoring average in a single season.

Larry Mikan, the son of Hall of Famer George Mikan, led Minnesota in scoring (18.4 ppg) and rebounding (10.5 rpg). . . . Purdue,

1968–69 NCAA CHAMPION: UCLA

SEASON STATISTICS OF UCLA REGULARS

PLAYER	POS.	CL.	G.	FG%	FT%	PPG	RPG
Lew Alcindor	C	Sr.	30	.635	.612	24.0	14.7
Curtis Rowe	F	So.	30	.502	.678	12.9	7.9
John Vallely	G	Jr.	28	.496	.755	11.0	3.3
Sidney Wicks	F	So.	30	.435	.680	7.5	5.1
Lynn Shackelford	F	Sr.	30	.463	.500	7.0	4.0
Ken Heitz	G	Sr.	30	.467	.684	6.5	2.3
Bill Sweek	G	Sr.	30	.506	.625	6.3	2.2
Steve Patterson	C	So.	29	.527	.750	5.0	3.9
Terry Schofield	G	So.	24	.415	.611	2.7	1.6
John Ecker	F	So.	20	.500	.667	1.6	1.2
Bill Seibert	F	So.	15	.261	.714	1.1	0.8
TEAM TOTALS			30	.513	.648	84.7	50.4

1969 FINAL FOUR CHAMPIONSHIP GAME

LOUISVILLE, KY

UCLA (92)	MIN.	FG-A	FT-A	REB.	A	PF	PTS.
Shackelford	35	3-8	5-8	9	0	3	11
Rowe	37	4-10	4-4	12	3	2	12
Alcindor	36	15-20	7-9	20	0	2	37
Heitz	34	0-3	0-1	3	4	4	0
Vallely	31	4-9	7-10	4	0	3	15
Sweek	10	3-3	0-1	1	0	3	6
Wicks	6	0-1	3-6	4	1	1	3
Schofield	3	1-2	0-0	0	0	0	2
Patterson	5	1-1	2-2	2	0	0	4
Seibert	1	0-0	0-0	1	0	0	0
Farmer	1	0-0	0-0	0	0	1	0
Ecker	1	1-1	0-0	0	0	0	2
Team				5			
TOTALS	200	32-58	28-41	61	8	19	92

FG%: .552. FT%: .683. Turnovers: 19.

PURDUE (72)	MIN.	FG-A	FT-A	REB.	A	PF	PTS.
Gilliam	32	2-14	3-3	11	3	2	7
Faerber	17	1-2	0-0	3	0	5	2
Johnson	27	4-9	3-4	9	0	2	11
Mount	37	12-36	4-5	1	0	3	28
Keller	32	4-17	3-4	4	3	5	11
Kaufman	13	0-0	2-2	5	0	5	2
Bedford	25	3-8	1-3	8	0	3	7
Weatherford	15	1-5	2-2	1	0	3	4
Reasoner	1	0-1	0-1	1	0	2	0
Taylor	1	0-0	0-0	0	0	0	0
Team				5			
TOTALS	200	27-92	18-24	48	6	30	72

FG%: .293. FT%: .750. Turnovers: 4.
Halftime: UCLA 50-41.

NATIONAL SEMIFINALS

NORTH CAROLINA (65): Bunting 7-13 5-7 19, Scott 6-19 4-6 16, Clark 7-9 6-10 20, Fogler 1-4 0-0 2, G. Tuttle 2-4 0-1 4, Delany 0-2 0-0 0, Dedmon 0-1 0-1 0, Brown 1-4 0-0 2, Gipple 0-3 0-0 0, Chadwick 1-2 0-0 2, R. Tuttle 0-1 0-0 0, Eggleston 0-0 0-0 0. Team 25-62 (.403) 15-25 (.600) 65.

PURDUE (92): Gilliam 3-11 0-0 6, Faerber 3-3 2-2 8, Johnson 2-5 1-3 5, Mount 14-28 8-9 36, Keller 9-19 2-3 20, Kaufman 0-1 2-3 2, Weatherford 3-6 1-1 7, Bedford 3-3 0-0 6, Taylor 1-1 0-1 2, Longfellow 0-1 0-0 0, Reasoner 0-0 0-0 0, Young 0-0 0-0 0. Team 38-78 (.487) 16-22 (.727) 92.

Halftime: Purdue 53-30.

DRAKE (82): Pulliam 4-4 4-5 12, Williams 0-1 0-0 0, Wise 5-7 3-4 13, McCarter 10-27 4-4 24, Draper 5-13 2-2 12, Odom 0-2 0-1 0, Wanamaker 4-7 1-1 9, Zeller 4-12 4-6 12, Gwin 0-0 0-1 0. Team 32-83 (.386) 18-24 (.667) 82.

UCLA (85): Shackelford 2-5 2-3 6, Rowe 6-9 2-2 14, Alcindor 8-14 9-16 25, Heitz 3-6 1-3 7, Vallely 9-11 11-14 29, Wicks 0-2 0-0 0, Sweek 0-0 0-0 0, Patterson 0-0 2-2 2, Schofield 0-3 2-4 2. Team 28-50 (.560) 29-44 (.660) 85.

Halftime: UCLA 44-43.

ALL-TOURNAMENT TEAM

Lew Alcindor, C, Sr., UCLA*
Willie McCarter, G, Sr., Drake
Rick Mount, G, Jr., Purdue
Charlie Scott, F-G, Jr., North Carolina
John Vallely, G, Jr., UCLA
    *Named Most Outstanding Player

coached by George King, captured its first Big Ten title in 29 years. . . . Illinois, which didn't have a winning record in any of the previous three seasons, won its first nine contests, including a 97-84 victory at Houston that snapped the Cougars' 59-game homecourt winning streak. . . . Kent State compiled a 14-10 record to end a streak of 16 consecutive losing seasons.

Kentucky became the first school to win 1,000 games. . . . Florida made its only appearance in a national postseason tournament until 1984. The Gators lost to Temple, 82-66, in the first round of the NIT. . . . Notre Dame finished in the Top 20 of a final wire-service poll for the first time since 1958. The Irish dropped its NCAA Tournament opener to Miami of Ohio

when guard Austin Carr broke his foot early in the contest.

Southern Cal ended UCLA's 41-game winning streak, 46-44. It was one of only two defeats for the Bruins during Lew Alcindor's three-year varsity career with both of the setbacks by two points. . . . Santa Clara (27-2/coached by Dick Garibaldi), Davidson (27-3/Lefty Driesell), Weber State (27-3/Phil Johnson), Drake (26-5/Maury John) and Colorado (21-7/Sox Walseth) had their winningest seasons in school history. . . . Santa Clara won its first 21 games before the Broncos absorbed their lone regular-season defeat, a 73-69 decision in double overtime against San Jose State. Weber State became the only Big Sky team ever to go undefeated in

LSU's Pete Maravich (left) was a scoring machine, a three-time All-American—and wore floppy socks!

conference competition since the league's inception in 1964. Colorado captured the Big Eight Conference crown after finishing in a tie for last place the previous year.

Texas Tech did not have a player selected to at least All-SWC second-team honors for the only time from 1957-58 through 1993-94. . . . North Texas (15-10) posted its first winning record in 12 years at the Division I level. . . . Wyoming finished in the Top 20 of a final wire-service poll for the only time in a 22-year span from 1958-59 through 1979-80.

George Washington ended a streak of eight consecutive losing seasons by compiling a 14-11

record. . . . Georgia's Bob Leinhard (32 vs. Sewanee) and Boston College's Terry Driscoll (31 vs. Fordham) set school single-game rebounding records. . . . Duke's Vic Bubas retired after a 10-year coaching career with a 213-67 record. The Blue Devils logged a 15-13 mark in their only season under Bubas without finishing in a final wire-service Top 20 poll. His first-year salary was $9,000. He later became commissioner of the Sun Belt Conference. . . . Virginia lost 22 consecutive games in its series with Duke until defeating the Blue Devils, 81-75.

San Diego's Phil Woolpert, who gained national acclaim as coach of San Francisco's back-to-back NCAA champions in the mid-

1950s, retired after a 16-year coaching career with a 239-164 record. Woolpert spent much of his post-coaching years as a bus driver in the Northwest. . . . Jerry Tarkanian embarked on his major-college coaching career with a 23-3 record (.885) at Long Beach State. Two other first-year head coaches had even higher winning percentages–La Salle's Tom Gola (23-1, .958) and Weber State's Phil Johnson (27-3, .900).

1968-69 FINAL NATIONAL POLLS

AP	UPI	SCHOOL (RECORD)	HEAD COACH
1	1	UCLA (29-1)	John Wooden
2	6	La Salle (23-1)	Tom Gola
3	4	Santa Clara (27-2)	Dick Garibaldi
4	2	North Carolina (27-5)	Dean Smith
5	3	Davidson (27-3)	Lefty Driesell
6	7	Purdue (23-5)	George King
7	5	Kentucky (23-5)	Adolph Rupp
8	8	St. John's (23-6)	Lou Carnesecca
9	10	Duquesne (21-5)	Red Manning
10	15	Villanova (21-5)	Jack Kraft
11	11	Drake (26-5)	Maury John
12	9	New Mexico State (24-5)	Lou Henson
13	20	South Carolina (21-7)	Frank McGuire
14	14	Marquette (24-5)	Al McGuire
15	13	Louisville (21-6)	John Dromo
16	15	Boston College (24-4)	Bob Cousy
17	–	Notre Dame (20-7)	Johnny Dee
18	12	Colorado (21-7)	Sox Walseth
19	20	Kansas (20-7)	Ted Owens
20	–	Illinois (19-5)	Harvey Schmidt
–	17	Weber State (27-3)	Phil Johnson
–	17	Wyoming (19-9)	Bill Strannigan
–	19	Colorado State (17-7)	Jim Williams

1969 NCAA Tournament

Summary: UCLA's Lew Alcindor, climaxing a streak when he became the only player to earn three consecutive Final Four Most Outstanding Player awards, collected 37 points and 20 rebounds in his final college game, a victory against Purdue (92-72). The 37-point outburst was a tourney high and is the fourth-highest point total in championship game history. Teammate Ken Heitz was scoreless in the final but his defense was instrumental in making Boilermakers standout Rick Mount miss 14 consecutive field-goal attempts in one stretch. UCLA coasted despite committing 19 turnovers to four for Purdue. Guard John Vallely, averaging a modest 10.2 points per game entering the Final Four, erupted for 29 points in the national semifinals

and the Bruins needed all of them. They had a nine-point lead with 70 seconds remaining dwindle to one before defeating Drake (85-82) after the Bulldogs missed a go-ahead basket in the waning moments. Alcindor grabbed a tourney-high 21 rebounds in the Drake game. "Drake gave us as much trouble–maybe more–than any team we ever played in the tournament," UCLA coach John Wooden said. "They were a very quick team, and played tough man-to-man (defense)."

One and Only: Alcindor, who later changed his name to Kareem Abdul-Jabbar, is the only individual selected the Final Four's Most Outstanding Player three times (1967 through 1969). Alcindor is the only player to couple three unanimous first-team All-American seasons with three NCAA titles. He is also the only player to hit better than 70 percent of his field-goal attempts in two different NCAA title games ('68 and '69).

Numbers Game: Mount, who scored 122 points in four playoff games, is the only player to lead a single tournament in scoring with more than 120 points and not eventually play in the NBA. He played five seasons in the ABA with four different franchises. Mount (36 points) and Billy Keller (20) accounted for the highest-scoring starting backcourt in a single Final Four game in history when they combined for 56 points in a 92-65 rout of North Carolina in the semifinals. . . . Mount's 36 field-goal attempts against UCLA is an NCAA championship game record. . . . Charlie Scott's second-half heroics enabled Carolina to reach the Final Four for the third consecutive year. Scott connected on 12 of 13 field-goal attempts after intermission in a come-from-behind 85-74 victory over Duke in the ACC Tournament final. The next week in the East Regional final, the 6-5 guard hit 10 of 14 shots from the floor in the second half, including a game-winning 20-foot jumper with three seconds remaining in an 87-85 verdict over Davidson. Scott, the first African American on the Tar Heels' varsity, averaged 7.1 rebounds per game in his three-year career. . . . Santa Clara's

1960–69 PREMO POWER POLL: BEST TEAMS BY DECADE

RANK	SEASON	SCHOOL
1	1967–68	UCLA* (29-1)
2	1966–67	UCLA* (30-0)
3	1968–69	UCLA* (29-1)
4	1959–60	Ohio St.* (25-3)
5	1963–64	UCLA* (30-0)
6	1960–61	Ohio St. (27-1)
7	1959–60	California (28-2)
8	1961–62	Cincinnati* (29-2)
9	1964–65	UCLA* (28-2)
10	1959–60	Cincinnati (28-2)
11	1962–63	Loyola (Ill.)* (29-2)
12	1967–68	Houston (31-2)
13	1961–62	Ohio St. (26-2)
14	1965–66	Texas Western* (28-1)
15	1960–61	Cincinnati* (27-3)
16	1962–63	Cincinnati (26-2)
17	1968–69	La Salle (23-1)
18	1964–65	Michigan (24-4)
19	1960–61	St. Bonaventure (24-4)
20	1965–66	Kentucky (27-2)
	1963–64	Duke (26-5)

*–NCAA Tournament Champion

outstanding frontline of Dennis Awtrey, Bud Ogden and Ralph Ogden combined for 53 points per game before collaborating for just 27 in a 90-52 setback against UCLA in the West Regional final. . . . St. John's lost two of three playoff games despite hitting a tourney series record 87 percent from the free-throw line (47 of 54). The Orangemen were eliminated for the second straight year by Davidson when Wildcats star Mike Maloy hit all 13 of his foul shots in a 79-69 decision. Maloy's accuracy from the charity stripe during his three-year varsity career was less than 70 percent. . . . Backup center Garry Odom averaged a modest 3.8 points and 4.5 rebounds per game on the season, but collected a total of 18 points and 18 rebounds in Drake's two Midwest Regional victories.

What If: La Salle, which defeated NCAA Tournament entrants Villanova, St. Joseph's and Duquesne by a total of 38 points on its way to a No. 2 ranking by AP, was ineligible for the tourney because of NCAA probation.

Putting Things in Perspective: North Carolina starting guard Dick Grubar, averaging 13 points per game, injured a knee in the ACC Tournament and was lost for the NCAA playoffs. A standout defensive player, the senior would have drawn the assignment of facing the explosive Mount, a 36-point scorer in a national semifinal victory over Carolina. . . . Drake nearly pulled off a gigantic upset against UCLA in the national semifinals although the Bulldogs shot just 38.6 percent from the floor.

Scoring Leader: Rick Mount, Purdue (122 points, 30.5 ppg).

Rebounding Leader: Lew Alcindor, UCLA (64 rebounds, 16 rpg).

WINNINGEST PROGRAMS OF THE 1960s

RK.	SCHOOL	W.	L.	PCT.
1.	UCLA	234	52	.818
2.	Cincinnati	214	63	.773
3.	Providence	204	64	.761
4.	Duke	213	67	.761
5.	Kentucky	197	69	.741
6.	Ohio State	188	69	.732
7.	St. Joseph's	201	74	.731
8.	Dayton	207	77	.729
9.	Bradley	197	74	.727
10.	Princeton	188	71	.726

Note: Weber State compiled a 147-36 record (.803) in only seven major-college seasons during the decade.

1969 CHAMPIONSHIP BRACKET

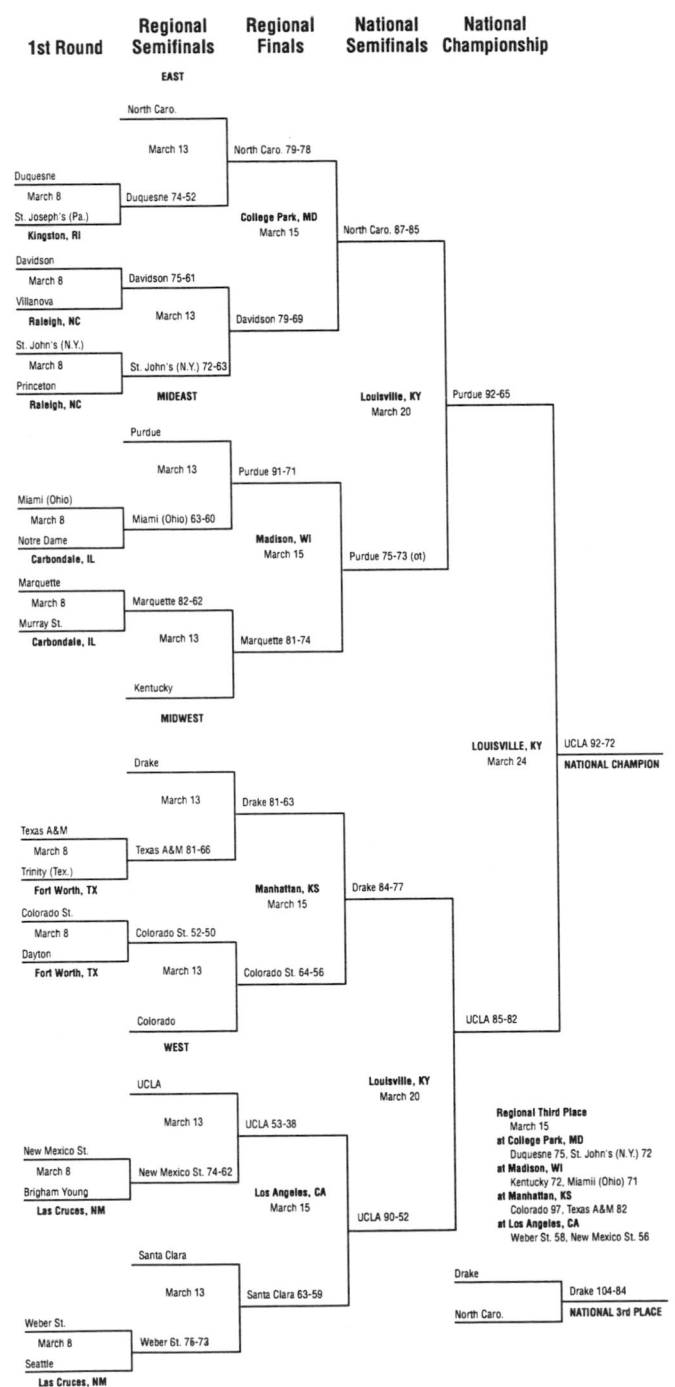

1st Round	Regional Semifinals	Regional Finals	National Semifinals	National Championship

EAST

North Caro.
March 13
North Caro. 79-78
Duquesne
March 8
St. Joseph's (Pa.)
Kingston, RI
Duquesne 74-52
College Park, MD
March 15
North Caro. 87-85

Davidson
March 8
Villanova
Raleigh, NC
Davidson 75-61
March 13
Davidson 79-69
St. John's (N.Y.)
March 8
Princeton
Raleigh, NC
St. John's (N.Y.) 72-63

Louisville, KY
March 20
Purdue 92-65

MIDEAST

Purdue
March 13
Purdue 91-71
Miami (Ohio)
March 8
Notre Dame
Carbondale, IL
Miami (Ohio) 63-60
Madison, WI
March 15
Purdue 75-73 (ot)

Marquette
March 8
Murray St.
Carbondale, IL
Marquette 82-62
March 13
Marquette 81-74
Kentucky

MIDWEST

LOUISVILLE, KY
March 24
UCLA 92-72
NATIONAL CHAMPION

Drake
March 13
Drake 81-63
Texas A&M
March 8
Trinity (Tex.)
Fort Worth, TX
Texas A&M 81-66
Manhattan, KS
March 15
Drake 84-77
Colorado St.
March 8
Dayton
Fort Worth, TX
Colorado St. 52-50
March 13
Colorado St. 64-56
Colorado

WEST

UCLA 85-82

UCLA
March 13
UCLA 53-38
New Mexico St.
March 8
Brigham Young
Las Cruces, NM
New Mexico St. 74-62
Los Angeles, CA
March 15
UCLA 90-52
Santa Clara
March 13
Santa Clara 63-59
Weber St.
March 8
Seattle
Las Cruces, NM
Weber St. 76-73

Louisville, KY
March 20

Regional Third Place
March 15
at College Park, MD
Duquesne 75, St. John's (N.Y.) 72
at Madison, WI
Kentucky 72, Miamii (Ohio) 71
at Manhattan, KS
Colorado 97, Texas A&M 82
at Los Angeles, CA
Weber St. 58, New Mexico St. 56

Drake
North Caro.
Drake 104-84
NATIONAL 3rd PLACE

5

EXPLOSION OF NATIONAL POPULARITY:

THE 1970s

ULA's invincibility began to erode mid-way through the 1970s although the Bruins had an unprecedented six different players become NCAA consensus first-team All-Americans in a five-year stretch from 1974 through 1978 (Bill Walton, Keith Wilkes, Dave Meyers, Richard Washington, Marques Johnson and David Greenwood).

UCLA was the only school to have a better record than Marquette during the decade. Marquette flourished despite having three key front-court players leave school early to turn pro in consecutive seasons in the mid-'70s–Jim Chones (drafted in '72), Larry McNeill ('73) and Maurice Lucas ('74). The Warriors finished in the Top 10 of a final wire-service poll all 10 years.

The NCAA embraced a rule allowing freshman eligibility, accelerating the development of numerous standout players. More and more regal recruits began to bypass illustrious programs to enroll at schools where they could make significant contributions immediately.

The fresh faces became crucial to the game's popularity because of a growing exodus of standouts leaving college with eligibility remaining to join the pros. Following a lawsuit filed by Detroit's Spencer Haywood, the NBA was required by the courts to grant admission to underclassmen. Accordingly, in 1971 the league conducted a separate draft for underclassmen wishing to enter the league because of financial hardship. The next year, such players were included in the regular draft. In 1976, the hardship requirement was eliminated and the current early entry process was implemented whereby any athlete with remaining college eligibility who desires to enter the NBA draft may do so by renouncing his eligibility in a letter to the commissioner postmarked 45 days before the draft.

There wasn't always a pot of gold at the end of the rainbow for standout undergraduates. Among the early defectors who were drafted by NBA teams yet never played in the NBA or ABA included Creighton's Cyril Baptiste (selected by San Francisco in 1971), Jacksonville's David Brent (Los Angeles in 1973), Los Angeles State's Raymond Lewis (Philadelphia in 1973), Ohio University's Walter Luckett (Detroit in 1975) and Illinois State's Cyrus Mann (Boston in 1975).

The flexibility of another year of eligibility fostered player unrest as transferring escalated when athletes didn't receive as much playing time as they thought they should. The Big Ten was hit hard by defections when Kyle Macy left Purdue for Kentucky and Larry Bird enrolled at Indiana State after leaving Indiana. By the end of the decade, there was an explosion of interest in the NCAA Tournament, highlighted by a dream duel between Bird and fellow first-team All-American Magic Johnson of Michigan State.

Illinois is one of the 10 schools with the most Top 20 appearances, but the Illini did not finish in the Top 20 of a final wire-service poll in the 1970s.

North Carolina, starting what eventually became an NCAA Tournament record for consecutive appearances in the playoffs, earned a spot as one of the nation's 10 winningest programs in a decade for the first time.

More colleges moved up to the Division I level than any other decade. The majority of them didn't have longstanding success like they enjoyed as a small school but a select circle went on to eventually reach the national semifinals of the NCAA Tournament or NIT (UAB, Fresno State, Indiana State, Louisiana Tech, UNC Charlotte, Southern Mississippi, Southwestern Louisiana and UNLV).

There was a college arena building boom in the '70s with around 200 arenas constructed in the decade for major colleges, helping college basketball attendance reach 30 million for the first time in the 1978-79 campaign. The Big Ten has led the nation's conferences every season since 1976-77.

The remainder of the Southeastern Conference finally emerged from the dark ages and joined Vanderbilt by having African-American players on their varsity rosters.

The Missouri Valley Conference suffered a series of major defections the first half of the decade. Two-time NCAA champion Cincinnati abandoned ship after the 1969-70 campaign.

Memphis State (1973) and Louisville (1975) left in the aftermath of seasons when they captured MVC titles before reaching the Final Four. St. Louis finished in the first division of the MVC three consecutive years (1971 through 1973) before departing after the 1973-74 season.

The decade closed with Indiana coach Bob Knight in the spotlight for one of a series of occasions in the hot seat. He was charged, and later tried and convicted in absentia, for hitting a Puerto Rican policeman before a practice at the Pan American Games. Knight was sentenced to six months in jail, but the government of Puerto Rico decided in 1987 to drop efforts to extradite him.

1969-70

AT A GLANCE

NCAA Champion: UCLA (28-2; coached by John Wooden; won the Pacific-8 title by three games with a 12-2 record).

NIT Champion: Marquette (26-3; coached by Al McGuire).

New Conference: PCAA (forerunner of Big West).

NCAA Probation: Centenary, Florida State, La Salle, Yale.

NCAA Consensus First-Team All-Americans: Dan Issel, F-C, Sr., Kentucky; Bob Lanier, C, Sr., St. Bonaventure; Pete Maravich, G, Sr., Louisiana State; Rick Mount, G, Sr., Purdue; Calvin Murphy, G, Sr., Niagara.

National Player of the Year: Maravich (44.5 ppg, 5.3 rpg).

National Coach of the Year: John Wooden, UCLA (28-2/AP, UPI, NABC, USBWA).

Duke, North Carolina and North Carolina State haven't always dominated the ACC. South Carolina, ranked No. 1 in preseason polls and considered the favorite to upend UCLA, lost its season opener to visiting Tennessee (55-54) before going unbeaten in ACC regular-season competition and finishing a league-record five games ahead of the Gamecocks' closest rival.

The ACC selected its representative to the NCAA playoffs at the time through its own postseason tourney and seven of the eight previous winners reached the Final Four. But the Gamecocks, featuring a starting lineup with current Georgia Tech coach Bobby Cremins as its only senior, lost against N.C. State in the ACC Tournament final (42-39 in double overtime) when Cremins collected two points, no assists and no rebounds in 49 minutes. Consensus second-team All-American John Roche, entering the ACC Tournament with a 23.8-point average, sustained a severely sprained ankle in the semifinals and wound up averaging just nine points per contest in three ACC tourney outings. . . . South Carolina edged Notre Dame, 84-83, in the championship game of the Sugar Bowl Classic despite an almost perfect game by Irish guard Austin Carr, who hit 14 consecutive field goals in one stretch to go 19 of 24 from the floor, sank all five of his free throws, grabbed six rebounds and did not commit a turnover.

LSU's Pete Maravich set NCAA single-season records for most points (1,381) and highest average (44.5), finishing his career with NCAA career marks for most points (3,667) and highest average (44.2). He also established an NCAA record for most successful free throws in a game when he converted 30 of 31 foul shots against Oregon State. Maravich is the only player in NCAA Division I history to score more than

Purdue All-American guard Rick Mount scores two of his Big Ten record 61 points against Iowa. The Hawkeyes' Fred Brown (left) and John Johnson can only watch.

1,000 points and average over 40 points per game in each of three seasons. He had 56 games with at least 40 points in his three-year career, including a school- and SEC-record 69 at Alabama. No other player has had more than 21 games with a minimum of 40. He averaged

---

MORE THAN 50-50   Two of college basketball's most explosive guns met in a classic high-scoring affair on February 21, 1970. Kentucky, led by Dan Issel, travelled to Louisiana State, led by Pistol Pete Maravich. Although the home team lost, 121-105, fans saw Maravich pump in 64 and Issel "settle" for 51 in a winning effort.

KENTUCKY (121)	FG	FT-A	PTS.	LSU (105)	FG	FT-A	PTS.
Dinwiddie	1	2-2	4	Maravich	23	18-22	64
Parker	9	0-0	18	Sanders	5	1-3	11
Pratt	11	5-8	27	Tribbett	0	2-3	2
Key	1	5-7	7	Hester	8	1-2	17
Issel	19	13-17	51	Newton	4	1-1	9
Mills	6	2-3	14	Hickman	1	0-0	2
Hollenbeck	0	0-0	0	Lang	0	0-0	0
TOTALS	**47**	**27-37**	**121**	**TOTALS**	**41**	**23-31**	**105**

Halftime: Kentucky 56-48. **Fouled Out:** Newton.

1969-70 INDIVIDUAL LEADERS

SCORING

PLAYER	PTS.	AVG.
Maravich, LSU	1381	44.5
Carr, Notre Dame	1106	38.1
Mount, Purdue	708	35.4
Issel, Kentucky	948	33.9
Humes, Idaho St.	733	30.5
Yunkus, Georgia Tech	814	30.1
Tomjanovich, Michigan	722	30.1
Murphy, Niagara	854	29.4
Lanier, St. Bonaventure	757	29.1
Simpson, Michigan St.	667	29.0

REBOUNDING

PLAYER	REB.	AVG.
Gilmore, Jacksonville	621	22.2
Erving, Massachusetts	522	20.9

Cross, San Francisco	467	18.0
Cowens, Florida St.	447	17.2
Stiles, American	378	17.2
Childress, Colorado St.	392	17.0
Haderlein, Loyola Marymount	442	17.0
Brunson, Furman	401	16.0
Lanier, St. Bonaventure	416	16.0

FIELD GOAL PERCENTAGE

PLAYER	FGM	FGA	PCT.
Williams, Florida St.	185	291	.636
Lienhard, Georgia	215	340	.632
Bartolome, Oregon St.	178	286	.622
Chatmon, Baylor	207	345	.600
Cleamons, Ohio St.	211	353	.598
Newton, LSU	143	242	.591
Schoepfer, Boston U.	160	271	.590
Bell, Hofstra	206	353	.584

Cobb, Marquette	158	272	.581
Gilmore, Jacksonville	307	529	.580

FREE THROW PERCENTAGE

PLAYER	FTM	FTA	PCT.
Kaplan, Rutgers	102	110	.927
England, Tennessee	131	146	.897
Finney, Ohio St.	119	134	.888
Murphy, Niagara	222	252	.881
Davis, Wake Forest	196	224	.875
Vidnovic, Iowa	133	152	.875
Newlin, Utah	245	281	.872
Curnutt, Miami (Fla.)	143	166	.861
Foster, Arizona	100	117	.855
Howard, BYU	122	143	.853

1969-70 TEAM LEADERS

SCORING OFFENSE

SCHOOL	PTS.	AVG.
Jacksonville	2809	100.3
Iowa	2467	98.7
Kentucky	2709	96.8
St. Peter's	2247	93.6
Notre Dame	2711	93.5

SCORING DEFENSE

SCHOOL	PTS.	AVG.
Army	1515	54.1
South Carolina	1606	57.4
Fairleigh Dickinson	1409	61.3
Long Island	1532	61.3
Miami (Ohio)	1497	62.4

SCORING MARGIN

SCHOOL	OFF.	DEF.	MAR.
St. Bonaventure	88.4	65.9	22.5

Jacksonville	100.3	78.5	21.8
UCLA	92.0	73.4	18.6
South Carolina	74.0	57.4	16.6
Florida St.	91.7	75.2	16.5

WON-LOST PERCENTAGE

SCHOOL	W-L	PCT.
UCLA	28-2	.933
Jacksonville	27-2	.931
Kentucky	26-2	.929
Pennsylvania	25-2	.926
New Mexico St.	27-3	.900

FIELD GOAL PERCENTAGE

SCHOOL	FGM	FGA	PCT.
Ohio St.	831	1527	.544
Jacksonville	1118	2137	.523
Iowa	959	1834	.523
Georgia Tech	841	1647	.511
Columbia	748	1481	.505

FREE THROW PERCENTAGE

SCHOOL	FTM	FTA	PCT.
Ohio St.	452	559	.809
Iowa	549	704	.780
Rutgers	430	560	.768
Wake Forest	542	706	.768
Boston College	442	581	.761

REBOUNDING

SCHOOL	REB.	AVG.
Florida St.	1451	55.8
Jacksonville	1561	55.8
Western Kentucky	1386	55.4
UNLV	1421	54.7
New Mexico St.	1632	54.4

more than 50 points per game in a 10-game stretch spanning the last three games of 1968-69 and the first seven games of 1969-70. Incredibly, Maravich improved his field-goal accuracy and assists average every year.

Maravich (64) and Kentucky's Dan Issel (51) each scored more than 50 points in the same game on February 21 when the Wildcats won, 121-105 (see accompanying box). It was one of eight times in Issel's senior season that he scored at least 40 to help Kentucky become the most prolific scoring team in SEC history (96.8 points per game). His high was a school-record 53 at Mississippi.

Purdue's Rick Mount set a Big Ten Conference record with 61 points (13 of his 27 field goals would have been behind the current three-point line), but it wasn't enough to prevent a 108-107 setback against visiting Iowa as the Hawkeyes went unbeaten in league play in coach Ralph Miller's final season at their helm before moving to Oregon State. They had gone 5-9 in the Big Ten the previous season.

Iowa had four players average more than 17 points per game on the Hawkeyes' way to a Big Ten-record 102.9-point average. They went undefeated in the league just one year after finishing in a tie for eighth place. Iowa's John Johnson set a school single-game standard with 49 points against Northwestern. . . . Also setting school single-game scoring records were Auburn's John Mengelt (60 points vs. archrival Alabama), Boston University's Jim Hayes (47 vs. Springfield) and John Conforti of St. Francis, N.Y. (45 vs. Wagner). . . . Maravich, Notre Dame's Austin Carr (38.1 ppg), Purdue's Mount (35.4), Kentucky's Issel (33.9), SMU's Gene Phillips (28.5), Iowa's John Johnson (27.9), Butler's Billy Shepherd (27.8), Florida's Andy Owens (27), Northwestern's Dale Kelley (24.3) and Arizona State's Seabern Hill (22.8) set school records for highest scoring average in a single season. . . . Niagara's Calvin Murphy, 5-9, finished his career as the only major-college player in history shorter than 6-0 to score more than 2,500 points. He

has accounted for 19 of the 21 games with more than 40 points in Purple Eagles' history.

Vanderbilt suffered its first losing record (12-14) in 22 seasons. . . . Georgia Tech center Rich Yunkus, a three-time NCAA Academic All-American, twice scored 47 points in a game (vs. Furman and North Carolina). . . . Sophomore Julius Erving set a Massachusetts record with 20.9 rebounds per game in powering the 18-7 Minutemen to their most victories in 60 years of basketball.

Jacksonville (27-2, coached by Joe Williams), New Mexico State (27-3, Lou Henson), St. Bonaventure (25-3, Larry Weise), South Carolina (25-3, Frank McGuire) and Army (22-6, Bob

1969–70 NCAA CHAMPION: UCLA

SEASON STATISTICS OF UCLA REGULARS

PLAYER	POS.	CL.	G.	FG%	FT%	PPG	RPG
Sidney Wicks	F	Jr.	30	.533	.632	18.6	11.9
John Vallely	G	Sr.	30	.486	.721	16.3	3.7
Henry Bibby	G	So.	30	.501	.833	15.6	3.5
Curtis Rowe	F	Jr.	30	.554	.641	15.3	8.7
Steve Patterson	C	Jr.	30	.496	.741	12.5	10.0
John Ecker	F	Jr.	30	.500	.774	3.5	2.5
Kenny Booker	F-G	Jr.	28	.449	.649	3.1	1.5
Terry Schofield	G	Jr.	29	.395	.850	2.7	0.8
Andy Hill	G	So.	24	.289	.714	1.8	0.6
Jon Chapman	C-F	So.	20	.344	.867	1.8	1.7
Rick Betchley	G	So.	23	.462	.625	1.5	0.7
Bill Seibert	F	Jr.	21	.316	.400	1.4	1.6
TEAM TOTALS			30	.496	.696	92.0	50.6

1970 FINAL FOUR CHAMPIONSHIP GAME

COLLEGE PARK, MD

JACKSONVILLE (69)	MIN.	FG-A	FT-A	REB.	A	PF	PTS.
Wedeking	37	6-11	0-0	2	3	2	12
Blevins	19	1-2	1-2	0	1	1	3
Morgan	37	5-11	0-0	4	11	5	10
Burrows	24	6-9	0-0	6	0	1	12
Gilmore	38	9-29	1-1	16	1	5	19
Nelson	16	3-9	2-2	5	0	1	8
Dublin	18	0-5	2-2	1	1	4	2
Baldwin	2	0-0	0-0	0	0	0	0
McIntyre	6	1-3	0-0	3	0	4	2
Hawkins	2	0-1	1-1	1	0	1	1
Selke	1	0-0	0-0	0	0	0	0
Team				2			
TOTALS	200	31-80	7-8	40	17	24	69

FG%: .388. FT%: .875. Turnovers: 18 (Morgan 8).

UCLA (80)	MIN.	FG-A	FT-A	REB.	A	PF	PTS.
Rowe	38	7-15	5-5	8	1	4	19
Patterson	38	8-15	1-4	11	2	1	17
Wicks	38	5-9	7-10	18	3	3	17
Vallely	38	5-10	5-7	7	5	2	15
Bibby	38	2-11	4-4	4	2	1	8

Booker	1	0-0	2-3	0	0	0	2
Seibert	2	0-1	0-0	1	0	1	0
Ecker	2	1-1	0-0	0	0	0	2
Betchley	1	0-0	0-1	0	0	0	0
Chapman	2	0-1	0-0	1	0	0	0
Hill	1	0-0	0-1	0	0	0	0
Schofield	1	0-0	0-0	0	0	0	0
Team				3			
TOTALS	200	28-63	24-35	53	13	12	80

FG%: .444. FT%: .686. Turnovers: 23 (Vallely 7).
Halftime: UCLA 41-36.

NATIONAL SEMIFINALS

JACKSONVILLE (91): Wedeking 7-15 1-1 15, Morgan 6-15 5-6 17, Burrows 2-4 1-1 5, McIntyre 0-3 0-0 0, Gilmore 9-14 11-15 29, Dublin 1-3 9-9 11, Nelson 1-7 10-12 12, Blevins 1-1 0-0 2, R. Baldwin 0-1 0-1 0. Team 27-63 (.429) 37-45 (.822) 91.

ST. BONAVENTURE (83): Kalbaugh 5-8 2-2 12, Hoffman 4-14 2-4 10, Gary 2-7 5-8 9, T. Baldwin 2-10 1-2 5, Gantt 8-17 0-0 16, Kull 4-7 0-0 8, Thomas 7-17 1-2 15, Grys 1-5 2-2 4, Tepas 0-0 2-2 2, Fahey 1-1 0-0 2. Team 34-86 (.395) 15-22 (.682) 83.

Halftime: Jacksonville 42-34.

UCLA (93): Rowe 4-7 7-11 15, Patterson 5-9 2-2 12, Wicks 10-12 2-5 22, Vallely 7-19 9-10 23, Bibby 8-13 3-3 19, Betchley 0-0 0-0 0, Schofield 0-0 0-0 0, Ecker 0-0 0-0 0, Seibert 0-1 0-0 0, Hill 0-0 0-1 0, Chapman 1-1 0-0 2. Team 35-63 (.556) 23-32 (.719) 93.

NEW MEXICO STATE (77): Criss 6-16 7-9 19, Collins 13-23 2-3 28, Burgess 1-6 0-0 2, Smith 4-11 2-3 10, Lacey 3-9 2-3 8, Reyes 1-6 0-0 2, Neal 2-4 0-0 4, Horne 0-4 2-2 2, Moore 1-1 0-0 2, Lefevre 0-0 0-0 0, Franco 0-0 0-0 0, McCarthy 0-0 0-0 0. Team 31-80 (.388) 15-20 (.750) 77.

Halftime: UCLA 48-41.

ALL-TOURNAMENT TEAM

Jimmy Collins, G, Sr., New Mexico State
Artis Gilmore, C, Jr., Jacksonville
Curtis Rowe, F, Jr., UCLA
John Vallely, G, Sr., UCLA
Sidney Wicks, F, Jr., UCLA*
   ***Named Most Outstanding Player**

Knight) had their winningest seasons in school history. . . . Jacksonville became the first school to average more than 100 points per game (100.3). The Dolphins also finished runner-up in four categories–field-goal shooting, rebounding scoring margin and won-lost percentage.

Ohio State, coached by Fred Taylor, led the country in both field-goal shooting (54.4 percent) and free-throw shooting (80.9). The Buckeyes were the first team to hit at least 80 percent of its foul shots in a single season. They were the first team in Big Ten history to have three players average more than 20 points per game–Dave Sorenson (24.2), Jim Cleamons (21.6) and Jody Finney (20.6). . . . Indiana finished in last place in the Big Ten for the fourth time in five seasons. . . . Memphis State finished in the Missouri Valley cellar for the third time in as many seasons, but ended its MVC losing streak at 27 games with an 85-81 victory over Wichita State. Cincinnati was runner-up to Drake in the MVC race in the Bearcats' final season as a member of the league.

Davidson of the Southern Conference became the only school since the start of the NCAA Tournament to go undefeated in back-to-back league seasons with different coaches. Terry Holland succeeded Lefty Driesell after Driesell accepted a similar position at Maryland. . . . Western Kentucky, coached by John Oldham, went unbeaten in Ohio Valley Conference competition for the second time in five seasons. . . . Virginia Tech dropped five of its first six games en route to compiling its only losing record (10-12) in a 31-year span from 1955-56 through 1985-86. . . . Pitt compiled a 12-12 record for its first season in six years with more than seven victories.

Southern Mississippi's Wendell Ladner (32 vs. Pan American), Minnesota's Larry Mikan (28 vs. Michigan), DePaul's Ken Warzynski (28 vs. Harvard), St. Peter's Juan Jiminez (28 vs. Upsala), New Mexico State's Sam Lacey (27 vs. Hardin-Simmons), Brigham Young's Scott Warner (27 at Texas Tech), Tulsa's Dana Lewis (26 vs. McMurry, Tex.), Iowa State's Bill Cain (26 vs. Minnesota) and Weber State's Willie Sojourn-er (25 vs. West Texas State) set school single-game records for most rebounds.

Idaho State won its last four games to compile a 13-11 record for the Bengals' first winning season in eight years. . . . Oklahoma (19-9/coached by John MacLeod), which tied a school record for most defeats the previous season (7-19), lost fewer than 10 games for the first time in 21 years. . . . Oklahoma State's Hank Iba (767-338 record) and Butler's Tony Hinkle (557-393) retired after 41-year coaching careers. Iba served as the United States' head coach for the 1964, 1968 and 1972 Olympic Teams.

Iba, the only coach with six or more NCAA Tournament appearances to reach the regional finals every time, is hailed as the patriarch of basketball's first family of coaches. He had seven of his former Oklahoma State players eventually coach teams into the NCAA playoffs–John Floyd (Texas A&M), Jack Hartman (Kansas State), Don Haskins (Texas-El Paso), Moe Iba (Nebraska), Bud Millikan (Maryland), Doyle Parrack (Oklahoma City) and Eddie Sutton (Creighton, Arkansas, Kentucky, Oklahoma State).

1969-70 FINAL NATIONAL POLLS

AP	UPI	SCHOOL (RECORD)	HEAD COACH
1	1	Kentucky (26-2)	Adolph Rupp
2	2	UCLA (28-2)	John Wooden
3	3	St. Bonaventure (25-3)	Larry Weise
4	5	Jacksonville (27-2)	Joe Williams
5	4	New Mexico State (27-3)	Lou Henson
6	6	South Carolina (25-3)	Frank McGuire
7	7	Iowa (20-5)	Ralph Miller
8	10	Marquette (26-3)	Al McGuire
9	8	Notre Dame (21-8)	Johnny Dee
10	12	N.C. State (23-7)	Norman Sloan
11	14	Florida State (23-3)	Hugh Durham
12	11	Houston (25-5)	Guy Lewis
13	13	Pennsylvania (25-2)	Dick Harter
14	9	Drake (22-7)	Maury John
15	–	Davidson (22-5)	Terry Holland
16	17	Utah State (22-6)	Ladell Andersen
17	17	Niagara (22-7)	Frank Layden
18	17	Western Kentucky (22-3)	John Oldham
19	15	Long Beach State (24-5)	Jerry Tarkanian
20	–	Southern Cal (18-8)	Bob Boyd
–	15	Villanova (22-7)	Jack Kraft
–	20	Cincinnati (21-6)	Tay Baker
–	20	Texas-El Paso (17-8)	Don Haskins

Five generations of major college coaches emanate from Iba, encompassing those coaches who were either players or assistant coaches for

Iba or later generations of coaches with ties to the sage. More than 40 active Division I coaches annually are branches of Iba's coaching tree. "Mr. Iba's system was so sound and he inspired such confidence that there was never any question in my mind that his philosophy offered the best opportunity to be successful," Sutton said. "The things he gave us are as valid today as they were 30 years ago."

1970 NCAA Tournament

Summary: Kentucky, after absorbing just one regular-season defeat (at Vanderbilt), was ranked No. 1 in the nation entering the tourney although starting guard Mike Casey missed the entire campaign in the wake of injuries suffered in an auto accident. UK lost to eventual NCAA Tournament runner-up Jacksonville, 106-100, in the Mideast Regional final. Casey was the Wildcats' leading scorer as a sophomore in 1967-68 with 20 points per game and their second-leading scorer as a junior the next year with a 19.1-point average. JU wound up losing to UCLA in the championship game, 80-69, when the Bruins' Sidney Wicks, 6-8, blocked five shots of 7-2 All-American center Artis Gilmore to help them overcome a nine-point deficit midway through the first half. UCLA enjoyed a 35 to 8 advantage in free-throw attempts, including a 19-2 edge in the opening half. UCLA is the only NCAA titlist to have four players who averaged more than 15 points per game—Wicks (18.6), John Vallely (16.3), Henry Bibby (15.6) and Curtis Rowe (15.3).

Star Gazing: LSU's Pete Maravich became the only three-time first-team All-American to fail to appear in the NCAA playoffs. LSU lost to UCLA by 49 points (133-84) just before Christmas.

One and Only: Notre Dame guard Austin Carr became the only player to score more than 60 points in a single playoff game and the only player to score more than 43 points at least twice. Carr, who tallied a school-record 61 points against Ohio University (Southeast Regional first round), accounted for half of the

Niagara All-American guard Calvin Murphy helped his team reach the Mideast Regional semifinals.

eight games in NCAA Tournament history of more than 46 points. He scored 52 points in the next round, but it wasn't enough to prevent a 109-99 defeat against Kentucky as the Wildcats' Dan Issel scored 44 points in the only tourney game in history to have two players score more than 40. Carr's 52-point playoff outburst is the highest ever in a losing effort.

Numbers Game: The best composite winning percentage when four teams arrived at a Final Four occurred as UCLA (26-2), New Mexico State (26-2), Jacksonville (26-1) and St. Bonaventure (25-1) combined for a 103-6 record (.945). . . . New Mexico State's Sam Lacey grabbed a tourney-high 24 rebounds in an 87-78 triumph over Drake in the Midwest Regional final.

What If: Dave Cowens-led Florida State, which split two games with national runner-up

1970 CHAMPIONSHIP BRACKET

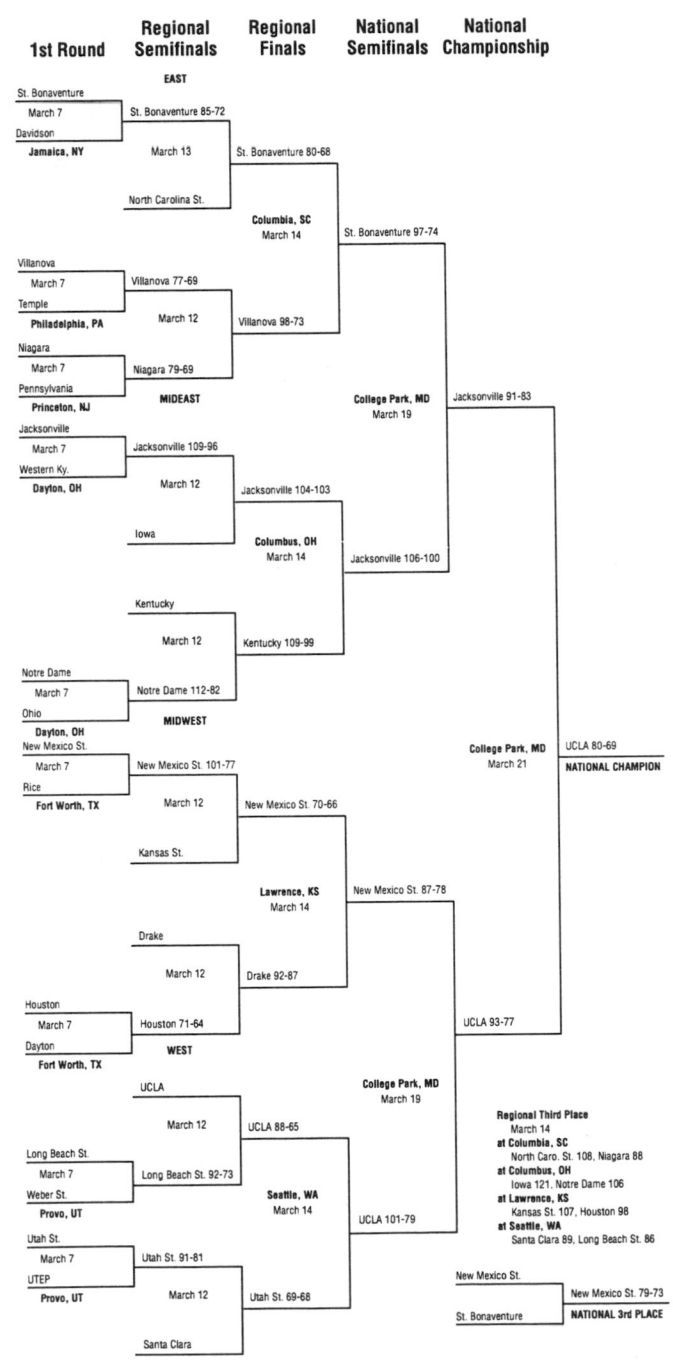

1st Round	Regional Semifinals	Regional Finals	National Semifinals	National Championship

EAST

St. Bonaventure
March 7
Davidson
Jamaica, NY

St. Bonaventure 85-72
March 13

North Carolina St.

St. Bonaventure 80-68

Columbia, SC
March 14

St. Bonaventure 97-74

Villanova
March 7
Temple
Philadelphia, PA

Villanova 77-69
March 12

Niagara
March 7
Pennsylvania
Princeton, NJ

Niagara 79-69

Villanova 98-73

College Park, MD
March 19

Jacksonville 91-83

MIDEAST

Jacksonville
March 7
Western Ky.
Dayton, OH

Jacksonville 109-96
March 12

Iowa

Jacksonville 104-103

Columbus, OH
March 14

Jacksonville 106-100

Kentucky
March 12

Notre Dame
March 7
Ohio
Dayton, OH

Kentucky 109-99

Notre Dame 112-82

MIDWEST

New Mexico St.
March 7
Rice
Fort Worth, TX

New Mexico St. 101-77
March 12

Kansas St.

New Mexico St. 70-66

Lawrence, KS
March 14

New Mexico St. 87-78

Drake
March 12

Houston
March 7
Dayton
Fort Worth, TX

Drake 92-87

Houston 71-64

WEST

UCLA
March 12

UCLA 88-65

Long Beach St.
March 7
Weber St.
Provo, UT

Long Beach St. 92-73

Seattle, WA
March 14

Utah St.
March 7
UTEP
Provo, UT

Utah St. 91-81
March 12

Santa Clara

Utah St. 69-68

UCLA 101-79

UCLA 93-77

College Park, MD
March 19

College Park, MD
March 21

UCLA 80-69
NATIONAL CHAMPION

Regional Third Place
March 14
at Columbia, SC
North Caro. St. 108, Niagara 88
at Columbus, OH
Iowa 121, Notre Dame 106
at Lawrence, KS
Kansas St. 107, Houston 98
at Seattle, WA
Santa Clara 89, Long Beach St. 86

New Mexico St.

St. Bonaventure

New Mexico St. 79-73
NATIONAL 3rd PLACE

Jacksonville (losing at JU by just four points), was ineligible for the tourney because of NCAA probation. . . . St. Bonaventure's only regular-season defeat was by two points at Villanova. But the Bonnies' biggest loss against Villanova was in a 23-point victory over the Wildcats in the East Regional final when All-American center Bob Lanier tore a knee ligament in a freak accident. He was clipped accidentally by future Detroit Pistons teammate Chris Ford, who later became coach of the Boston Celtics.

Scoring Leader: Austin Carr, Notre Dame (158 points, 52.7 ppg).

Rebounding Leader: Artis Gilmore, Jacksonville (93 rebounds, 18.6 rpg).

Highest Rebounding Average: David Hall, Kansas State (40 rebounds, 20 rpg).

1970-71

AT A GLANCE

NCAA Champion: UCLA (29-1; coached by John Wooden; won the Pacific-8 title with a 14-0 record, which was two games ahead of Southern Cal).

NIT Champion: North Carolina (26-6; coached by Dean Smith; won ACC regular-season title with an 11-3 record).

New Rules: A non-jumper may not change his position during a jump ball from the time a referee is ready to make the toss until after the ball is tapped. . . . Any school offered an NCAA Tournament bid must accept it or be prohibited from participating in postseason competition.

NCAA Probation: Centenary, Florida State, Yale.

NCAA Consensus First-Team All-Americans: Austin Carr, G, Sr., Notre Dame; Artis Gilmore, C, Sr., Jacksonville; Jim McDaniels, C, Sr., Western Kentucky; Dean Meminger, G, Sr., Marquette; Sidney Wicks, F, Sr., UCLA.

National Players of the Year: Carr (38 ppg, 7.4 rpg, 51.7 FG%, 81.1 FT%/AP, UPI, Naismith) and Wicks (21.3 ppg, 12.8 rpg, 52.4 FG%/USBWA).

National Coaches of the Year: Villanova's Jack Kraft (23-6, NABC) and Marquette's Al McGuire (28-1, AP, UPI, USBWA).

UCLA's starting frontcourt of Sidney Wicks, Curtis Rowe and Steve Patterson combined to average 51.7 points and 32.6 rebounds per game, making it more productive statistically than any of the Bruins' starting frontcourts with all-time great centers Lew Alcindor and Bill Walton.

UCLA's only defeat was an 89-82 setback at Notre Dame when the Bruins' 48-game nonconference winning streak ended. Notre Dame guard Austin Carr scored 46 points, including 15 of the Irish's last 17.

Over his final two seasons, covering 58 games, Carr scored over 40 points 23 times, broke the 30-point plateau on 46 occasions and

Jacksonville center Artis Gilmore.

1970–71 INDIVIDUAL LEADERS

SCORING

PLAYER	PTS.	AVG.
Neumann, Mississippi	923	40.1
Carr, Notre Dame	1101	38.0
Humes, Idaho St.	777	32.4
McGinnis, Indiana	719	30.0
McDaniels, W. Kentucky	878	29.3
Rinaldi, St. Peter's	687	28.6
Mengelt, Auburn	738	28.4
Phillips, SMU	737	28.3
Meely, Colorado	729	28.0
Brown, Iowa	662	27.6

REBOUNDING

PLAYER	REB.	AVG.
Gilmore, Jacksonville	603	23.2
Washington, American	512	20.5

Erving, Massachusetts	527	19.5
Gianelli, Pacific	509	18.2
Davis, St. John's	479	17.7
Martin, Loyola (Ill.)	387	17.6
Benton, Wichita St.	437	16.8
Kennedy, TCU	416	16.6
Harris, Hardin-Simmons	205	15.8
Frazer, Fairfield	377	15.7

FIELD GOAL PERCENTAGE

PLAYER	FGM	FGA	PCT.
Belcher, Arkansas St.	174	275	.633
Wuycik, North Carolina	182	300	.607
Smith, Syracuse	222	366	.607
Kennedy, TCU	202	340	.594
Szczerbiak, G. Wash.	225	379	.594
Bush, Drake	177	299	.592
Jura, Nebraska	181	306	.592

Sanders, LSU	209	355	.589
Williams, Hardin-Simmons	191	326	.586
Penebacker, Hawaii	165	284	.581

FREE THROW PERCENTAGE

PLAYER	FTM	FTA	PCT.
Starrick, S. Illinois	119	132	.902
Tyler, Brown	128	147	.871
England, Tennessee	143	165	.867
Kaplan, Rutgers	102	118	.864
Davis, Wake Forest	188	218	.862
Wuycik, North Carolina	169	197	.858
Thomason, Pacific	118	138	.855
Bryant, E. Kentucky	122	143	.853
Lowery, Texas Tech	121	143	.846
Phillips, SMU	213	252	.845

1970–71 TEAM LEADERS

SCORING OFFENSE

SCHOOL	PTS.	AVG.
Jacksonville	2598	99.9
Kentucky	2670	95.4
Northern Illinois	2132	92.7
St. Peter's	2221	92.5
Loyola (La.)	2394	92.1

SCORING DEFENSE

SCHOOL	PTS.	AVG.
Fairleigh Dickinson	1236	53.7
Army	1403	58.5
Marquette	1820	62.8
Miami (Ohio)	1591	63.6

SCORING MARGIN

SCHOOL	OFF.	DEF.	MAR.
Jacksonville	99.9	79.0	20.9

Marquette	81.7	62.8	18.9
UCLA	83.5	68.5	15.0
Pennsylvania	81.4	66.8	14.6
Massachusetts	79.7	65.1	14.6

WON-LOST PERCENTAGE

SCHOOL	W-L	PCT.
UCLA	29-1	.967
Marquette	28-1	.966
Pennsylvania	28-1	.966
Southern California	24-2	.923
Kansas	27-3	.900

FIELD GOAL PERCENTAGE

SCHOOL	FGM	FGA	PCT.
Jacksonville	1077	2008	.536
North Carolina	1010	1935	.522
Louisiana St.	897	1725	.520
Loyola (La.)	956	1880	.509
Kentucky	1077	2129	.506

FREE THROW PERCENTAGE

SCHOOL	FTM	FTA	PCT.
Tennessee	538	679	.792
Southern Illinois	460	597	.771
Southern Methodist	552	719	.768
Duke	539	704	.766

REBOUNDING

SCHOOL	REB.	AVG.
Pacific	1643	58.7
West Texas St.	1502	57.8
Hawaii	1596	57.0
Arizona St.	1477	56.8
Los Angeles St.	1458	56.1

was never held under 20. Several of Carr's finest performances came against mighty Kentucky. In four meetings with the Wildcats, he averaged 43 points and shot over 70 percent from the floor. "The fact that he (Carr) could go inside or outside and his ability to shoot with either hand is what made him such a great player," said UK coach Adolph Rupp.

Carr, runner-up to LSU's Pete Maravich in scoring the previous season with a 38-point average, was runner-up again at 38.1 to become the most prolific non-champion ever. Mississippi's Johnny Neumann averaged 40.1 points per game to become the only sophomore in NCAA history other than Maravich (43.8 in 1967-68) to

average more than 40. Neumann, bolstered by a school-record 63-point outburst at LSU, was threatening Maravich's first-year mark until falling off to a 29.4 average his last five contests. Neumann, the only Ole Miss player ever to become an NCAA consensus first- or second-team All-American, had eight games with at least 46 points in his lone varsity campaign.

Neumann, Georgia Tech's Rich Yunkus (30.1 ppg), Western Kentucky's Jim McDaniels (29.3), St. Peter's Rich Rinaldi (28.6), Auburn's John Mengelt (28.4), Colorado's Cliff Meely (28), Massachusetts' Julius Erving (26.9), Boise State's Ron Austin (24.5), Wisconsin's Clarence Sherrod (23.8) and Lamar's Luke Adams (23) set school

Division I records for highest scoring average in a single season.

Bill Smith isn't among the top 15 career scorers in Syracuse history, but the 7-0 center tossed in a school-record 47 points against Lafayette. Also establishing school single-game scoring standards were Idaho State's Willie Humes (53 at Montana State), and SMU's Gene Phillips (51 at Texas). Humes' outburst is a Big Sky Conference record and Phillips' output is the highest ever in a contest between two Southwest Conference teams.

Artis Gilmore, a junior college transfer, finished his two-year career at Jacksonville with an NCAA career rebounding average of 22.7 per game. He is the only player in major-college history to finish his career with averages of more than 22 points and 22 rebounds per game. Gilmore, who grabbed a school-record 34 rebounds against St. Peter's, helped Jacksonville win an unprecedented three national team statistical titles–offense (99.9-point average), scoring margin (20.9) and field-goal shooting (53.6 percent). . . . Also causing something of a sensation at JU was freshman David Brent, a 7-0 center from St. Louis who averaged 36 points and 17 rebounds in head-to-head duels with Gilmore in two frosh-varsity games. Brent, however, never played varsity college basketball.

Big Ten champion Ohio State's only league loss was to visiting Michigan State, 82-70, although the Spartans sustained their fourth of six consecutive losing records in conference competition. . . . Eldon Miller was in his first season as coach at Western Michigan when the Broncos registered a 14-10 mark for their first winning record in nine years.

Defending ACC regular-season champion South Carolina lost its first four league road games, including a 31-30 overtime verdict at Maryland. The Terrapins, finishing in the ACC's second division for the sixth consecutive year, hit 15 of 18 field-goal attempts (83.3 percent) against South Carolina. The Gamecocks finished runner-up to North Carolina in their final season as a member of the ACC. . . . North Carolina forward Dennis Wuycik was second from the floor nationally at 60.7 percent and sixth from the foul line at 85.8 percent. . . . Virginia, coached by Bill Gibson, won 11 of its first 13 games to crack the Top 20 for the first time ever. The Cavaliers faded down the stretch to finish with a 15-11 record, but it was their first winning season in 17 years.

TCU's Eugene "Goo" Kennedy set a SWC standard by grabbing a school-record 28 rebounds against Arkansas. He finished the season with a league-record average of 16 rebounds per game. . . . Arkansas sustained a school-record nine consecutive SWC defeats. The Razorbacks were 1-13 in the SWC despite losing just two league games by a double-digit margin. One of their setbacks was in overtime against Baylor, 111-110. . . . Memphis State compiled an 18-8 record in Gene Bartow's first season as coach of the Tigers. They had sustained at least 17 defeats each of the previous three years.

Fairleigh Dickinson shattered Army's streak of three consecutive scoring defense championships. FDU coach Al LoBalbo previously served as an assistant at Army under Bob Knight. . . . Harvard, which has never captured an Ivy League title, posted its only undisputed second-place finish with an 11-3 conference record.

Arizona State ended a streak of six consecutive losing seasons by compiling a 16-10 record. . . . Colorado State's Mike Childress set a Western Athletic Conference single-season standard by averaging 14.1 rebounds per game.

LaRue Martin's school-record 34 rebounds against Valparaiso weren't enough to keep Loyola of Chicago from losing its 14th consecutive game. Also establishing school single-game rebounding records were Lafayette's Ron Moyer (33 at Gettysburg), UMass' Erving (32 vs. Syracuse), Wichita State's Terry Benton (29 vs. North Texas State), Memphis State's Ronnie Robinson (28 vs. Tulsa), Kansas State's David Hall (27 vs. Oklahoma). Hall later became a professor of law at Northeastern.

Miami (Fla.) dropped its program at the conclusion of the campaign because of dwindling success and finances. The Hurricanes had their first losing record in 15 years the previous season. . . . Alabama suffered its most lopsided defeat in history (122-75 at Southern Cal) but later won at Mississippi, 101-91, for the Crimson Tide's first road victory in four seasons.

Guard Dean Meminger became the first Marquette player to become an NCAA consensus first- or second-team All-American. . . . Marquette (28-1, coached by Al McGuire), Pennsylvania (28-1, Dick Harter), Fordham (26-3, Digger Phelps) and Southern California (24-2, Bob Boyd) had their winningest seasons in school history.

Forward Howard Porter was the first Villanova player since 1950 to become an NCAA consensus first- or second-team All-American. He grabbed a school single-game record of 30 rebounds against St. Peter's. . . . NYU competed in its final season at the major-college level.

1970-71 FINAL NATIONAL POLLS

AP	UPI	SCHOOL (RECORD)	HEAD COACH
1	1	UCLA (29-1)	John Wooden
2	2	Marquette (28-1)	Al McGuire
3	3	Pennsylvania (28-1)	Dick Harter
4	4	Kansas (27-3)	Ted Owens
5	5	Southern Cal (24-2)	Bob Boyd
6	6	South Carolina (23-6)	Frank McGuire
7	7	Western Kentucky (24-6)	John Oldham
8	8	Kentucky (22-6)	Adolph Rupp
9	9	Fordham (26-3)	Digger Phelps
10	10	Ohio State (20-6)	Fred Taylor
11	11	Jacksonville (22-4)	Tom Wasdin
12	14	Notre Dame (20-9)	Johnny Dee
13	13	North Carolina (26-6)	Dean Smith
14	18	Houston (22-7)	Guy Lewis
15	18	Duquesne (21-4)	Red Manning
16	14	Long Beach State (23-5)	Jerry Tarkanian
17	–	Tennessee (21-7)	Ray Mears
18	17	Villanova (23-6)	Jack Kraft
19	16	Drake (21-8)	Maury John
20	11	Brigham Young (18-11)	Stan Watts
–	20	Weber State (21-6)	Phil Johnson

1971 NCAA Tournament

Joe Williams became the only person to be coach of two different universities in back-to-back years when each school made its initial playoff appearance–Jacksonville '70 and Furman '71. Furman compiled a 15-12 record to end a streak of eight consecutive non-winning seasons.

Brigham Young, coached by Stan Watts, captured the WAC title after finishing in seventh place the previous year. . . . Utah's Jack Gardner, who previously coached at Kansas State, ended his 28-year coaching career with a 486-235 record.

Summary: UCLA became the only team to win a national title although its season-leading scorer was held more than 10 points below his average in the championship game, a 68-62 victory over Villanova. Eight of the 10 starters played the entire final. Sidney Wicks, named national player of the year by the U.S. Basketball Writers Association, managed just seven points in a 68-62 victory over Villanova to finish the campaign with a 21.3-point average. The Final Four was tainted when it was disclosed that Villanova star Howard Porter and Western Kentucky standout Jim McDaniels had signed pro contracts before the tourney.

Star Gazing: Julius Erving, leaving Massachusetts with one season of eligibility remaining, didn't participate in the NCAA playoffs despite helping the Minutemen to a composite 41-11 record in 1970 and 1971. He is the only player to score more than 30,000 points in his pro career after never appearing in the NCAA playoffs. UMass was mauled in the first round of the NIT by eventual champion North Carolina, 90-49. . . . Jacksonville blew a 14-point halftime cushion and lost in the first round of the Mideast Regional against eventual Final Four team Western Kentucky (74-72). Western Kentucky's McDaniels outscored Jacksonville's Artis Gilmore, 23-12, in a battle of seven-foot first-team All-Americans.

Biggest Upsets: Marquette, undefeated entering the tourney (26-0), lost in the Mideast Regional semifinals against Ohio State (60-59) after the Warriors' playmaker, unanimous first-team All-American Dean "The Dream"

Meminger, fouled out with five minutes remaining. Teammate Allie McGuire, the coach's son, committed a costly turnover in the closing seconds before Buckeyes guard Allan Hornyak converted a pair of crucial free throws to end Marquette's 39-game winning streak. . . . Penn, undefeated entering the tourney (26-0), lost in the East Regional final against Villanova (90-47) when none of the Quakers players scored more than eight points. Porter, the Final Four Most Outstanding Player, scored 35 points for the Wildcats to more than double the output (16) of three Penn players who wound up in the NBA–Corky Calhoun, Phil Hankinson and Dave Wohl.

One and Only: UCLA center Steve Patterson became the only player to have a single-digit point total in a national semifinal game (six vs. Kansas) and then increase his output by more than 20 points in the championship game (career- and game-high 29 vs. Villanova). "It just shows you what a good team can do," Villanova coach Jack Kraft said. "You hold down Wicks and (Curtis) Rowe as well as we did and that third guy (Patterson) kills you." . . . Western Kentucky became the only Ohio Valley Conference to reach the Final Four. . . . Wicks is the only individual to play for three NCAA titlists after playing in junior college.

Numbers Game: The closest result for UCLA during the Bruins' 38-game tourney winning streak from 1967-73 came in the West Regional final when they had to erase an 11-

UCLA's Sidney Wicks takes careful aim over the outstretched arm of a New Mexico State defender.

point deficit despite 29 percent field-goal shooting to edge Long Beach State (57-55). . . . Drake became the only school to appear in at least three NCAA Tournaments and reach a regional final each time. The Bulldogs, who won the national third-place game in 1969, lost in the Midwest Regional finals in 1970 (against New Mexico State) and 1971 (against Kansas) when their opponents each had just two defeats. . . . Three of Kansas' four playoff games were decid-

1970–71 NCAA CHAMPION: UCLA

SEASON STATISTICS OF UCLA REGULARS

PLAYER	POS.	CL.	G.	FG%	FT%	PPG	RPG
Sidney Wicks	F	Sr.	30	.524	.661	21.3	12.8
Curtis Rowe	F	Sr.	30	.523	.627	17.5	10.0
Steve Patterson	C	Sr.	30	.420	.620	13.0	9.8
Henry Bibby	G	Jr.	30	.376	.835	11.8	3.5
Terry Schofield	G	Sr.	30	.432	.561	6.2	2.4
Kenny Booker	G	Sr.	30	.441	.480	5.5	2.6
Larry Farmer	F	So.	22	.402	.481	3.6	3.7
John Ecker	F	Sr.	26	.438	.882	2.8	2.0
Rick Betchley	G	Jr.	20	.538	.467	1.8	0.7
Larry Hollyfield	F-G	So.	11	.273	.250	1.7	0.7
Andy Hill	G	Jr.	19	.438	.850	1.6	0.2
Jon Chapman	F-C	Jr.	18	.200	.000	0.4	1.3
TEAM TOTALS			30	.453	.651	83.5	52.5

1971 FINAL FOUR CHAMPIONSHIP GAME

HOUSTON, TX

VILLANOVA (62)	MIN.	FG-A	FT-A	REB.	A	PF	PTS.
Smith	40	4-11	1-1	2	0	4	9
Porter	40	10-21	5-6	8	0	1	25
Siemiontkowski	37	9-16	1-2	6	0	3	19
Inglesby	40	3-9	1-1	4	7	2	7
Ford	40	0-4	2-3	5	10	4	2
McDowell	3	0-1	0-0	2	1	0	0
Team				4			
TOTALS	200	26-62	10-13	31	18	14	62

FG%: .419. FT%: .769. Turnovers: 10 (Ford 7).

UCLA (68)	MIN.	FG-A	FT-A	REB.	A	PF	PTS.
Rowe	40	2-3	4-5	8	2	0	8
Wicks	40	3-7	1-1	9	7	2	7
Patterson	40	13-18	3-5	8	4	1	29
Bibby	40	6-12	5-5	2	3	1	17
Booker	5	0-0	0-0	0	0	0	0
Schofield	26	3-9	0-0	1	4	4	6
Betchley	9	0-0	1-2	1	0	1	1
Team				5			
TOTALS	200	27-49	14-18	34	20	9	68

FG%: .551. FT%: .778. Turnovers: 13.
Halftime: UCLA 45-37.

NATIONAL SEMIFINALS

WESTERN KENTUCKY (89): Glover 5-15 2-4 12, Dunn 11-33 3-6 25, McDaniels 10-24 2-4 22, Rose 8-21 2-3 18, Bailey 5-11 2-3 12, Witt 0-1 0-0 0, Sundmacker 0-0 0-0 0. Team 39-105 (.371) 11-20 (.550) 89.

VILLANOVA (92): Smith 5-14 3-6 13, Porter 10-20 2-3 22, Siemiontkowski 11-20 9-10 31, Inglesby 5-10 4-7 14, Ford 3-6 2-2 8, McDowell 2-3 0-3 4. Team 36-73 (.493) 20-31 (.645) 92.

Halftime: Western Kentucky 38-35. **Regulation:** Tied 74-74. **First Overtime:** Tied 85-85.

KANSAS (60): Robisch 7-19 3-6 17, Russell 5-12 2-2 12, Brown 3-8 1-3 7, Stallworth 5-10 2-4 12, Nash 3-9 1-2 7, Kivisto 1-1 1-4 3, Canfield 0-0 0-0 0, Williams 0-1 2-2 2, Mathews 0-0 0-0 0, Douglas 0-0 0-0 0. Team 24-60 (.400) 12-23 (.522) 60.

UCLA (68): Rowe 7-10 2-4 16, Wicks 5-9 11-13 21, Patterson 3-11 0-0 6, Bibby 6-9 6-6 18, Booker 1-2 1-2 3, Schofield 1-3 0-1 2, Farmer 0-2 0-1 0, Betchley 0-0 0-1 0, Ecker 0-1 2-2 2, Hill 0-0 0-0 0, Chapman 0-0 0-0 0. Team 23-47 (.489) 22-30 (.733) 68.

Halftime: UCLA 32-25.

ALL-TOURNAMENT TEAM

Jim McDaniels, C, Sr., Western Kentucky
Steve Patterson, C, Sr., UCLA
Howard Porter, F, Sr., Villanova*
Hank Siemiontkowski, C, Jr., Villanova
Sidney Wicks, F, Sr., UCLA
***Named Most Outstanding Player**

ed by a total of five points. . . . South Carolina appeared in the NCAA Tournament for the first time, becoming the only school to make its inital NCAA playoff appearance in its final year as a league member (ACC) before embracing independent status the next season. The Gamecocks lost the East Regional third-place game to Fordham when the Rams hit all 22 of their free-throw attempts. . . . Notre Dame guard Austin Carr had the two highest-scoring games in the tourney–52 points in a 102-94 triumph over TCU and 47 in a 119-106 setback against Houston. Poo Welch tallied 38 for Houston against the Irish in the Midwest Regional third-place game. . . . BYU's Kresimir Cosic grabbed a playoff-high 23 rebounds in a 91-73 loss to UCLA in the West Regional semifinals.

What If: Southern Cal posted its best record in school history (24-2, .923). USC's defeats were by single-digit margins in Pacific-8 Conference competition against national champion-to-be UCLA. The Trojans ranked 5th in both polls. . . . Houston, minus its third-best scorer and top outside threat Jeff Hickman (declared academically ineligible after the first semester), lost to Final Four-bound Kansas by one point (78-77) in the Midwest Regional semifinals. The Cougars defeated eventual national runner-up Villanova by 15 points on a neutral court early in the season.

Scoring Leader: Jim McDaniels, Western Kentucky (147 points, 29.4 ppg).

Highest Scoring Average: Austin Carr, Notre Dame (125 points, 41.7 ppg).

Rebounding Leader: Clarence Glover, Western Kentucky (89 rebounds, 17.8 rpg).

1971 CHAMPIONSHIP BRACKET

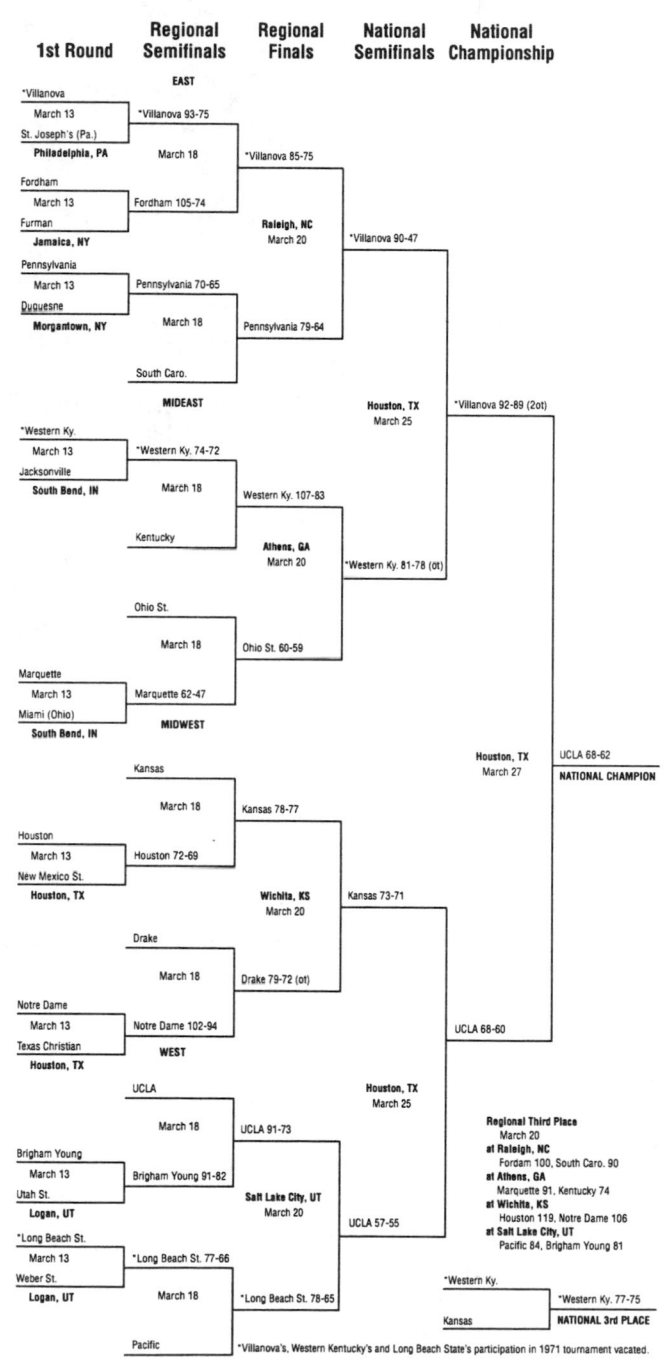

1st Round	Regional Semifinals	Regional Finals	National Semifinals	National Championship

EAST

*Villanova
March 13
St. Joseph's (Pa.)
Philadelphia, PA

*Villanova 93-75
March 18

Fordham
March 13
Furman
Jamaica, NY

Fordham 105-74

*Villanova 85-75

Pennsylvania
March 13
Duquesne
Morgantown, NY

Pennsylvania 70-65
March 18

South Caro.

Pennsylvania 79-64

Raleigh, NC
March 20

*Villanova 90-47

MIDEAST

*Western Ky.
March 13
Jacksonville
South Bend, IN

*Western Ky. 74-72
March 18

Kentucky

Western Ky. 107-83

Athens, GA
March 20

Ohio St.

March 18

Marquette
March 13
Miami (Ohio)
South Bend, IN

Marquette 62-47

Ohio St. 60-59

*Western Ky. 81-78 (ot)

MIDWEST

Kansas

March 18

Houston
March 13
New Mexico St.
Houston, TX

Houston 72-69

Kansas 78-77

Wichita, KS
March 20

Drake

March 18

Notre Dame
March 13
Texas Christian
Houston, TX

Notre Dame 102-94

Drake 79-72 (ot)

Kansas 73-71

WEST

UCLA

March 18

Brigham Young
March 13
Utah St.
Logan, UT

Brigham Young 91-82

UCLA 91-73

Salt Lake City, UT
March 20

*Long Beach St.
March 13
Weber St.
Logan, UT

*Long Beach St. 77-66
March 18

Pacific

*Long Beach St. 78-65

UCLA 57-55

Houston, TX
March 25

*Villanova 92-89 (2ot)

Houston, TX
March 25

UCLA 68-60

Houston, TX
March 27

UCLA 68-62

NATIONAL CHAMPION

Regional Third Place
March 20
at Raleigh, NC
Fordam 100, South Caro. 90
at Athens, GA
Marquette 91, Kentucky 74
at Wichita, KS
Houston 119, Notre Dame 106
at Salt Lake City, UT
Pacific 84, Brigham Young 81

*Western Ky.

Kansas

*Western Ky. 77-75

NATIONAL 3rd PLACE

*Villanova's, Western Kentucky's and Long Beach State's participation in 1971 tournament vacated.

1971-72

AT A GLANCE

NCAA Champion: UCLA (30-0; coached by John Wooden; won Pacific-8 title with a 14-0 record, which was four games ahead of Washington).

NIT Champion: Maryland (27-5; coached by Lefty Driesell; finished in a tie for second place in ACC with an 8-4 record, which was one game behind North Carolina).

NCAA Consensus First-Team All-Americans: Henry Bibby, G, Sr., UCLA; Jim Chones, C, Jr., Marquette; Dwight "Bo" Lamar, G, Jr., Southwestern Louisiana; Bob McAdoo, C, Jr., North Carolina; Ed Ratleff, F-G, Jr., Long Beach State; Tom Riker, C, Sr., South Carolina; Bill Walton, C, Soph., UCLA.

National Player of the Year: Walton (21.1 ppg, 15.5 rpg, 64.0 FG%).

National Coach of the Year: John Wooden, UCLA (30-0/AP, UPI, NABC, USBWA).

Kentucky's Adolph Rupp, called the "Baron of the Bluegrass," retired after a 41-year coaching career with a 875-190 record. Rupp won four NCAA Tournament championships but had a losing NCAA playoff record (10-12) after capturing his last national title in 1958.

UCLA's Bill Walton joined Oscar Robertson (Cincinnati '58) as the only players in history to be named national player of the year in their first season of varsity competition. UCLA set an NCAA single-season record for highest average scoring margin (30.3). Incredibly, the Bruins' average halftime margin (17.4) was greater than any other team over an entire game excluding North Carolina's 17.7.

Long before premier pivotmen such as Georgetown's Patrick Ewing (Jamaica), Dikembe Mutombo (Zaire), Houston's Hakeem Olajuwon (Nigeria), Marist's Rik Smits (Netherlands), New Mexico's Luc Longley (Australia), George Washington's Yinka Dare (Nigeria) and Wake Forest's Tim Duncan (Virgin Islands) arrived from outposts off the mainland U.S., there was an influential international big man by the name of Kresimir Cosic. The Yugoslavian ranked 42nd

Oral Roberts star Richie Fuqua shoots from the outside.

in the country by averaging 22.3 points per game as a junior for Brigham Young.

The nation's top three scorers represented teams playing their initial season at the major-college level–Southwestern Louisiana's Bo Lamar (36.3), Oral Roberts' Richie Fuqua (35.9) and Illinois State's Doug Collins (32.6). Fuqua nearly caught Lamar by averaging 41.4 points to Lamar's 38.7 in their last 10 outings. . . . Lamar and fellow junior Ed Ratleff of Long Beach State became the only set of former high school teammates to be named NCAA consensus first-team All-Americans together. USL's 90-83 early-season victory over visiting Long Beach might have been one of the best intersectional matchups few people have ever heard about. Lamar and Ratleff attended East High in Columbus, Oh., where another one of their teammates was Nick Conner, a starter for Illinois. They were seniors on a 1968-69 high school squad that went undefeated (25-0 record), won the Ohio AA title and extended its winning streak to 49 games. . . . Lamar's explosiveness sparked USL to a 25-4 record for the second consecutive season. He scored 51 points in back-to-back road games at Louisiana Tech and Lamar.

Collins was the star player for Will Robinson, the first black head coach at a predominantly white Division I school. Oddly, Rich Herrin, Collins' high school coach at Benton (Ill.), never had an opportunity to coach an African-American player in his 29 small-town seasons of high-schooling coaching before he was hired by Southern Illinois after the 1984-85 campaign. . . . USL's Lamar, ORU's Fuqua, ISU's Collins, West Virginia's Wil Robinson (29.4 ppg), Central Michigan's Ben Kelso (25.4), Brown's Arnie Berman (25.3), Texas Tech's Greg Lowery (24.5) and Harvard's Jim Fitzsimmons (24.2) set school records for highest scoring average in a single season.

Kansas' Bud Stallworth set a Big Eight Conference game record with 50 points against Missouri. Mizzou, however, made its first Top 20 appearance in a final wire-service poll. . . . Jacksonville's Ernie Fleming (national-high 59 points vs. St. Peter's), Florida's Tony Miller (54 vs. Chicago State), Virginia's Barry Parkhill (51 vs. Baldwin-Wallace), New Mexico State's John Williamson (48 at California), California's John Coughran (47 at Utah State), Fordham's Ken Charles (tied with 46 vs. South Carolina), Georgia's Ronnie Hogue (46 vs. LSU) and Fairfield's George Groom (41 vs. Assumption) set school single-game scoring standards. . . . Parkhill, the first Virginia player to become an NCAA consensus first- or second-team All-American, led the ACC in scoring (21.6 ppg) en route to guiding the Cavaliers to their first-ever Top 20 ranking in a final wire-service poll. Virginia won at Duke for the first time in 32 years and joined the 20-win club for the first time in 44 seasons. The Cavs managed a winning ACC record (8-4) for the only time in the first 25 years of the league's existence.

Southern Illinois' Greg Starrick, who began his college career at Kentucky, finished his career with 90.9 percent free-throw accuracy, an NCAA record. . . . Detroit ended Marquette's 56-game regular-season winning streak, 70-49, and Temple stopped Penn's 48-game regular-season winning streak, 57-52. Marquette's other regular-season defeat was in its regular-season finale at New Mexico State, 73-69. . . . Minnesota center Jim Brewer was annointed as Most Valuable Player in the Big Ten, but he wasn't named to the first- or second-five for either the AP or UPI all-conference teams. The Gophers appeared in the NCAA Tournament for the first time after capturing their first Big Ten title in 35 years. . . . Michigan State's Mike Robinson (27.2 points per game) became the third sophomore in five years to lead the Big Ten in scoring.

North Carolina's three ACC defeats were on the road by a total of five points–at Duke, Maryland (in overtime) and North Carolina State. . . . Providence's Marvin Barnes notched school records of 34 rebounds and 12 blocked shots in a 76-58 victory over Buffalo State. . . . Dartmouth defeated Connecticut for the ninth straight time, 107-89.

Fresno State's streak of 15 consecutive winning seasons ended when the Bulldogs compiled a 9-17 record. . . . Pacific's John Gianelli set a single-season Big West Conference record by averaging 17.9 rebounds per game. Pacific (17-9) posted its last season with fewer than 10 defeats. . . . Hawaii's Bob Nash (30 vs. Arizona State) and Southwestern Louisiana's Roy Ebron (28 at Northwestern State) set school single-game rebounding records.

Notre Dame lost back-to-back road games at Indiana (94-29) and UCLA (114-56) by a total of 123 points in coach Digger Phelps' first season at the Irish helm. Two years later, Notre Dame defeated both teams. . . . Kent State was 7-17 overall, but compiled its only winning Mid-American Conference record (6-4) in the Golden Flashes' first 33 years in the league from 1951-52 through 1983-84.

Maryland (27-5, coached by Lefty Driesell), Florida State (27-6, Hugh Durham) and South-

1971–72 INDIVIDUAL LEADERS

SCORING

PLAYER	PTS.	AVG.
Lamar, Southwestern La.	1054	36.3
Fuqua, Oral Roberts	1006	35.9
Collins, Illinois St.	847	32.6
Robinson, West Virginia	706	29.4
Averitt, Pepperdine	693	28.9
Williamson, New Mexico St.	678	27.1
Kohls, Syracuse	748	26.7
Miller, Florida	507	26.7
Taylor, Murray St.	538	25.6
Martiniuk, St. Peter's	611	25.5
Davidson, West Texas St.	420	17.5
Davis, St. John's	460	17.0
Bradley, Northern Illinois	398	15.9
Jones, Loyola Marymount	395	15.8
Barnes, Providence	424	15.7
Martin, Loyola (Ill.)	329	15.7
Walton, UCLA	466	15.5
Hyland, Iona	350	15.2

REBOUNDING

PLAYER	REB.	AVG.
Washington, American	455	19.8
Gianelli, Pacific	466	17.9

FIELD GOAL PERCENTAGE

PLAYER	FGM	FGA	PCT.
Martens, Abilene Christian	136	204	.667
Fullarton, Xavier	149	229	.651
Stewart, Santa Clara	202	312	.647
Walton, UCLA	238	372	.640
Shaeffer, St. John's	186	294	.633
Jackson, Los Angeles St.	222	362	.613
Ebron, Southwestern La.	283	464	.610
Wuycik, North Carolina	189	310	.610
Robinson, Memphis St.	170	279	.609
Traylor, South Carolina	174	292	.596
Sanders, LSU	171	287	.596

FREE THROW PERCENTAGE

PLAYER	FTM	FTA	PCT.
Starrick, Southern Ill.	148	160	.925
Denny, South Alabama	117	128	.914
Garrett, Southern Ill.	130	146	.890
Bullington, Ball St.	142	161	.882
Sherwin, Army	110	125	.880
Roberts, New Mexico	118	135	.874
Bush, Indiana St.	107	123	.870
Rogers, St. Louis	124	143	.867
Edwards, Tennessee	103	119	.866
Kohls, Syracuse	222	257	.864

1971–72 TEAM LEADERS

SCORING OFFENSE

SCHOOL	PTS.	AVG.
Oral Roberts	2943	105.1
Southwestern Louisiana	2840	97.9
Northern Illinois	2380	95.2
UCLA	2838	94.6
Furman	2592	92.6
Houston	2499	92.6

SCORING DEFENSE

SCHOOL	PTS.	AVG.
Minnesota	1451	58.0
Fairleigh Dickinson	1410	58.8
Texas-El Paso	1636	60.6
Marquette	1836	63.3
Pennsylvania	1780	63.6
Temple	1973	63.6

SCORING MARGIN

SCHOOL	OFF.	DEF.	MAR.
UCLA	94.6	64.3	30.3
North Carolina	89.1	71.4	17.7
Marshall	92.4	76.4	16.0
Florida St.	86.9	71.4	15.5
Long Beach St.	84.9	69.8	15.1

WON-LOST PERCENTAGE

SCHOOL	W-L	PCT.
UCLA	30-0	1.000
Oral Roberts	26-2	.929
Pennsylvania	25-3	.893
Hawaii	24-3	.889
Marquette	25-4	.862
Long Beach St.	25-4	.862
Southwestern Louisiana	25-4	.862

FIELD GOAL PERCENTAGE

SCHOOL	FGM	FGA	PCT.
North Carolina	1031	1954	.528
Abilene Christian	792	1566	.506
South Carolina	894	1773	.504
UCLA	1140	2262	.504
Southwestern Louisiana	1153	2295	.502

FREE THROW PERCENTAGE

SCHOOL	FTM	FTA	PCT.
Lafayette	656	844	.777
Brown	560	725	.772
Southern Illinois	522	687	.760
St. Louis	507	669	.758
Tennessee	450	594	.758

REBOUNDING

SCHOOL	REB.	AVG.
Oral Roberts	1686	60.2
West Texas St.	1444	57.8
Pacific	1495	57.5
Hawaii	1462	56.2
Houston	1515	56.1

western Louisiana (25-4, Beryl Shipley) had their winningest seasons in school Division I history. . . . Marshall finished in the Top 20 of a final wire-service poll for the only time in school history. . . . Loyola (La.) competed in its final season at the major-college level.

Brigham Young's Stan Watts ended his 23-year coaching career with a 371-254 record. His final campaign resulted in his highest winning percentage (21-5 mark). . . . Future Hall of Famer Denny Crum launched his head coaching career at Louisville with a 26-5 record and trip to the Final Four. His predecessor, John Dromo, suffered a heart attack after nine games in 1970-71

and did not complete his fourth season. . . . Coach Bob Knight compiled a 17-8 record in his initial season at Indiana. The Hoosiers ended their longest ever drought out of the Top 20 by cracking the select circle for the first time in eight years.

IU's worst defeat was an 85-71 decision at Northern Illinois when Huskies sophomore Jim Bradley collected 24 points and 20 rebounds shortly before they climbed into the AP Top 20. A last-second 86-85 setback against Illinois State probably cost 21-4 NIU a berth in the NCAA Tournament. Two years later, the 6-9, 230-pound Bradley was ruled ineligible during his senior

UCLA star Bill Walton blocks a shot.

SEASON STATISTICS OF UCLA REGULARS

PLAYER	POS.	CL.	G.	FG%	FT%	PPG	RPG
Bill Walton	C	So.	30	.640	.704	21.1	15.5
Henry Bibby	G	Sr.	30	.450	.806	15.7	3.5
Keith Wilkes	F	So.	30	.531	.696	13.5	8.2
Larry Farmer	F	Jr.	30	.456	.549	10.7	5.5
Greg Lee	G	So.	29	.492	.824	8.7	2.0
Larry Hollyfield	F	Jr.	30	.514	.651	7.3	3.3
Swen Nater	C	Jr.	29	.535	.609	6.7	4.8
Tommy Curtis	G	So.	30	.437	.636	4.1	2.1
Andy Hill	G	Sr.	26	.356	.709	2.7	0.8
Vince Carson	F	So.	28	.400	.667	2.4	2.6
Jon Chapman	F	Sr.	28	.465	.500	1.6	1.6
Gary Franklin	F	So.	26	.412	.438	1.3	1.0
TEAM TOTALS			30	.504	.695	94.6	54.9

1972 FINAL FOUR CHAMPIONSHIP GAME

LOS ANGELES, CA

FLORIDA STATE (76)	MIN.	FG-A	FT-A	REB.	A	PF	PTS.
Garrett	37	1-9	1-1	5	0	1	3
King	31	12-20	3-3	6	1	1	27
Royals	33	5-7	5-6	10	2	5	15
McCray	23	3-6	2-5	6	3	4	8
Samuel	31	3-10	0-0	1	7	1	6
Harris	26	7-13	2-3	6	1	1	16
Petty	9	0-0	1-1	0	2	1	1
Cole	10	0-2	0-0	2	1	1	0
Team				6			
TOTALS	200	31-67	14-19	42	17	15	76

FG%: .463. FT%: .737.

UCLA (81)	MIN.	FG-A	FT-A	REB.	A	PF	PTS.
Wilkes	38	11-16	1-2	10	3	4	23
Farmer	33	2-6	0-0	6	0	2	4
Walton	34	9-17	6-11	20	2	4	24
Lee	16	0-0	0-0	2	4	0	0
Bibby	40	8-17	2-3	3	1	2	18
Curtis	24	4-14	0-1	4	6	1	8
Hollyfield	9	1-6	0-0	2	3	2	2
Nater	6	1-2	0-1	1	0	0	2
Team				2			
TOTALS	200	36-78	9-18	50	19	15	81

FG%: .462. FT%: .500.
Halftime: UCLA 50-39.

NATIONAL SEMIFINALS

NORTH CAROLINA (75): Jones 4-8 1-1 9, Wuycik 7-16 6-6 20, McAdoo 10-19 4-5 24, Previs 1-5 3-6 5, Karl 5-14 1-3 11, Huband 0-1 0-0 0, Chamberlain 2-5 2-3 6, Johnston 0-1 0-0 0, Chambers 0-1 0-1 0-0. Team 29-70 (.414) 17-25 (.680) 75.

FLORIDA STATE (79): Garrett 4-8 3-7 11, King 6-17 10-10 22, Royals 6-8 6-7 18, McCray 3-6 3-6 9, Samuel 2-4 1-4 5, Harris 1-6 2-2 4, Petty 3-5 4-7 10, Gay 0-1 0-0 0. Team 25-55 (.455) 29-43 (.674) 79.

Halftime: Florida State 45-32.

LOUISVILLE (77): Lawhon 0-7 1-2 1, Thomas 2-4 0-0 4, Vilcheck 3-6 0-0 6, Price 11-23 8-9 30, Bacon 5-11 5-7 15, Carter 4-8 0-0 8, Bunton 1-5 1-1 3, Bradley 1-3 0-0 2, Stallings 1-2 0-1 2, Cooper 0-1 2-2 2, Pry 2-3 0-0 4, Meiman 0-1 0-0 0. Team 30-74 (.405) 17-22 (.773) 77.

UCLA (96): Wilkes 5-11 2-2 12, Farmer 6-12 3-5 15, Walton 11-13 11-12 33, Lee 3-6 4-6 10, Bibby 1-5 0-0 2, Curtis 4-5 0-0 8, Hollyfield 3-6 0-0 6, Carson 1-1 0-0 2, Nater 0-0 2-4 2, Hill 1-1 4-4 6, Chapman 0-0 0-1 0, Franklin 0-1 0-0 0. Team 35-61 (.574) 26-34 (.765) 96.

Halftime: UCLA 39-31.

ALL-TOURNAMENT TEAM

Ron King, G, Jr., Florida State
Bob McAdoo, C, Jr., North Carolina
Jim Price, G, Sr., Louisville
Bill Walton, C, Soph., UCLA*
Keith Wilkes, F, Soph., UCLA
*Named Most Outstanding Player

1971-72 UNDEFEATED TEAM: UCLA (30-0)

COACH: JOHN WOODEN

UCLA	OPPONENT	BRUINS HIGH SCORER
105	The Citadel 49	Bibby 26
106	Iowa 72	Bibby 32
110	Iowa State 81	Walton 24
117	Texas A&M 53	Walton 23
114	Notre Dame 56	Bibby 28
119	Texas Christian 81	Walton 31
115	Texas 65	Walton 28
79	Ohio State 53	Walton 14
78	at Oregon State 72	Bibby 17
93	at Oregon 68	Walton 30
118	Stanford 79	Walton 32
82	California 43	Walton 20
92	Santa Clara 57	Wilkes 16
108	Denver 61	Bibby/Farmer 19
92	at Loyola of Chicago 64	Bibby/Walton 18
57	at Notre Dame 32	Bibby 15
81	Southern California 56	Walton 22
89	Washington State 58	Walton 25
109	Washington 70	Walton 27
100	at Washington 83	Walton 31
85	at Washington State 55	Hollyfield/Wilkes 16
92	Oregon 70	Walton 37
91	Oregon State 72	Walton 26
85	at California 71	Walton 24
102	at Stanford 73	Lee 16
79	at Southern California 66	Walton 20

NCAA TOURNAMENT

90	Weber State* 58	Bibby 16
73	Long Beach State* 57	Bibby 23
96	Louisville* 77	Walton 23
81	Florida State* 76	Walton 24

*Neutral court games.

year, finishing his career with averages of 23.1 points and 16.8 rebounds per game. He signed with the ABA's Kentucky Colonels after they purchased his draft rights from San Diego.

Ten years later, Bradley was 29 when he died from a shot in the back in the wee hours of the morning in Portland, Ore., outside a downtown disco two days after his arrest for dealing in a controlled substance. "He was as talented a player as I ever saw," said college and pro standout Dan Issel, who played on two ABA teams with Bradley, "but nobody will ever remember his name because he didn't come close to what he could have been. He could have been as good as anybody who ever played, as far as I'm concerned."

1971-72 FINAL NATIONAL POLLS

AP	UPI	SCHOOL (RECORD)	HEAD COACH
1	1	UCLA (30-0)	John Wooden
2	2	North Carolina (26-5)	Dean Smith
3	3	Pennsylvania (25-3)	Chuck Daly
4	4	Louisville (26-5)	Denny Crum
5	6	Long Beach State (25-4)	Jerry Tarkanian
6	5	South Carolina (24-5)	Frank McGuire
7	7	Marquette (25-4)	Al McGuire
8	8	Southwestern La. (25-4)	Beryl Shipley
9	9	Brigham Young (21-5)	Stan Watts
10	10	Florida State (27-6)	Hugh Durham
11	12	Minnesota (18-7)	Bill Musselman
12	18	Marshall (23-4)	Carl Tacy
13	13	Memphis State (21-7)	Gene Bartow
14	11	Maryland (27-5)	Lefty Driesell
15	15	Villanova (20-8)	Jack Kraft
16	–	Oral Roberts (26-2)	Ken Trickey
17	–	Indiana (17-8)	Bob Knight
18	14	Kentucky (21-7)	Adolph Rupp
19	–	State (18-6)	Fred Taylor
20	–	Virginia (21-7)	Bill Gibson
–	16	State (19-9)	Jack Hartman
–	17	Texas-El Paso (20-7)	Don Haskins
–	19	Missouri (21-6)	Norm Stewart
–	19	Weber State (18-11)	Gene Visscher

1972 NCAA Tournament

Summary: UCLA won the national championship by an average of 18 points. Although the Bill Walton-led Bruins trailed Florida State by a season-high seven points in the first half and the final margin of the championship game was just five (81-76), the outcome never seemed in doubt. Excluding a six-point triumph at Oregon State, they won every other game by at least 13 points.

One and Only: Bo Lamar collected 35 points and a tourney-high 11 assists and Roy Ebron contributed 33 points and 20 rebounds in Division I newcomer Southwestern Louisiana's 112-101 victory over Marshall in the opening round of the Midwest Regional when the Ragin' Cajuns scored the most points in the history of the tourney for a school in its first playoff game.

Numbers Game: Kentucky coach Adolph Rupp's final game was a 73-54 defeat against Florida State in the Mideast Regional final. Rupp is the only coach saddled with more than five regional final losses. Rupp sustained eight such setbacks from 1952 through 1972 by an average margin of 10 points. He also incurred a national quarterfinal reversal in 1945 when the first round of the eight-team event was identified as the regional semifinals. Six of Rupp's first seven "field of eight" defeats were against Big Ten teams, including Ohio State four times. . . . USL's Lamar (36 points vs. Texas) and South Carolina's Tom Riker (36 vs. Villanova) tied for the highest-scoring game in the tourney. . . . Jim Brewer grabbed the most rebounds in a single game (22) to power Minnesota to a 77-72 success against Marquette in the Mideast Regional third-place game.

What If: Marquette probably would have been the team with the best chance to unseat UCLA if Warriors All-American Jim Chones did not terminate his eligibility by signing a professional contract late in the season during the ABA/NBA bidding war. . . . Indiana could have been the Big Ten representative in the NCAA playoffs instead of Minnesota if George McGinnis hadn't left school early for the pros. . . . Kentucky (21-7) might have given runnerup-to-be Florida State more of a challenge in the Mideast Regional if center Tom Payne hadn't left the Wildcats with eligibility remaining to enter the NBA.

Scoring Leader: Jim Price, Louisville (103 points, 25.75 ppg).

Highest Scoring Average: Bo Lamar, Southwestern Louisiana (100 points, 33.3 ppg).

Rebounding Leader: Bill Walton, UCLA (64 rebounds, 16 rpg).

Highest Rebounding Average: Jim Brewer, Minnesota (36 rebounds, 18 rpg).

1972 CHAMPIONSHIP BRACKET

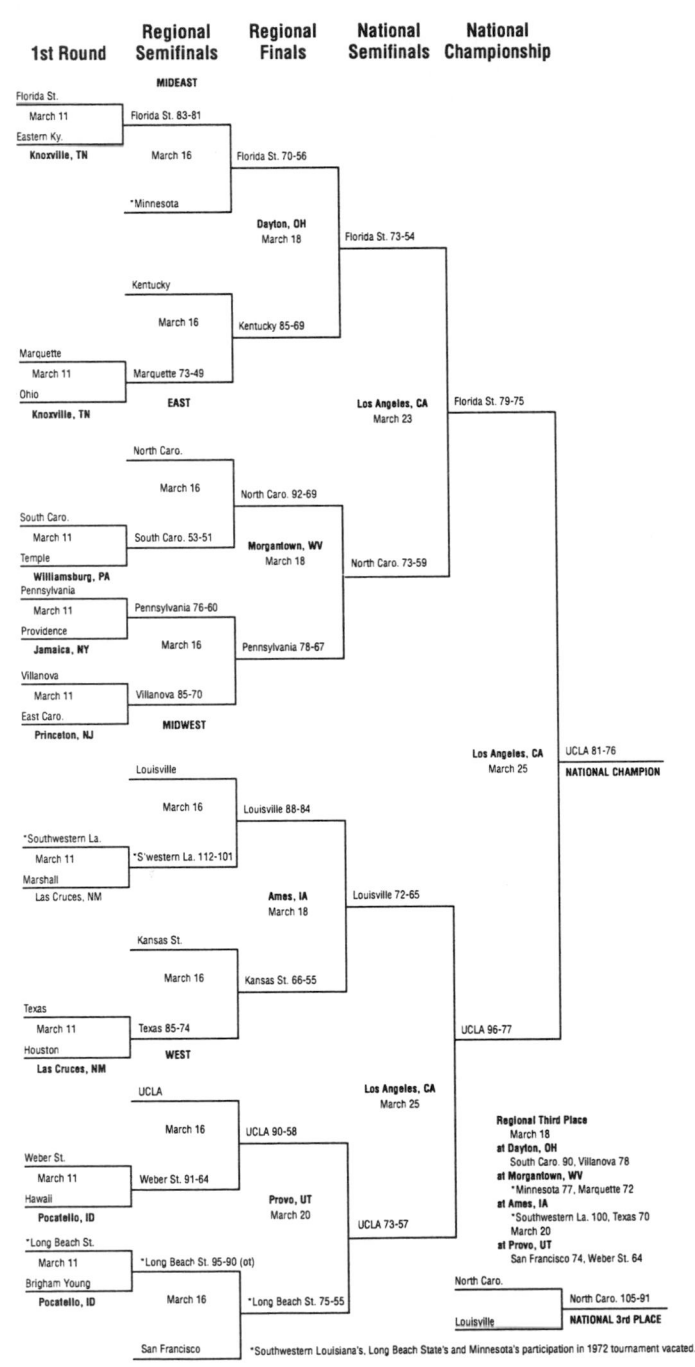

	Regional	Regional	National	National
1st Round	**Semifinals**	**Finals**	**Semifinals**	**Championship**

MIDEAST

Florida St.
March 11 — Florida St. 83-81
Eastern Ky.
Knoxville, TN — March 16 — Florida St. 70-56

*Minnesota

Dayton, OH
March 18 — Florida St. 73-54

Kentucky
March 16 — Kentucky 85-69
Marquette
March 11 — Marquette 73-49
Ohio
Knoxville, TN

EAST

Los Angeles, CA
March 23 — Florida St. 79-75

North Caro.
March 16 — North Caro. 92-69
South Caro.
March 11 — South Caro. 53-51
Temple
Williamsburg, PA

Morgantown, WV
March 18 — North Caro. 73-59

Pennsylvania
March 11 — Pennsylvania 76-60
Providence
Jamaica, NY — March 16 — Pennsylvania 78-67
Villanova
March 11 — Villanova 85-70
East Caro.
Princeton, NJ

MIDWEST

UCLA 81-76
NATIONAL CHAMPION

Louisville
March 16 — Louisville 88-84
*Southwestern La.
March 11 — *S'western La. 112-101
Marshall
Las Cruces, NM

Ames, IA
March 18 — Louisville 72-65

Kansas St.
March 16 — Kansas St. 66-55
Texas
March 11 — Texas 85-74
Houston
Las Cruces, NM

WEST

Los Angeles, CA
March 25 — UCLA 96-77

UCLA
March 16 — UCLA 90-58
Weber St.
March 11 — Weber St. 91-64
Hawaii
Pocatello, ID

Provo, UT
March 20 — UCLA 73-57

*Long Beach St.
March 11 — *Long Beach St. 95-90 (ot)
Brigham Young
Pocatello, ID — March 16 — *Long Beach St. 75-55

San Francisco

Los Angeles, CA
March 25

Regional Third Place
March 18
at Dayton, OH
South Caro. 90, Villanova 78
at Morgantown, WV
*Minnesota 77, Marquette 72
at Ames, IA
*Southwestern La. 100, Texas 70
March 20
at Provo, UT
San Francisco 74, Weber St. 64

North Caro.
March 16 — North Caro. 105-91
Louisville
NATIONAL 3rd PLACE

*Southwestern Louisiana's, Long Beach State's and Minnesota's participation in 1972 tournament vacated.

1972-73

NCAA Champion: UCLA (30-0; coached by John Wooden; won Pacific-8 title by five games with a 14-0 record).

NIT Champion: Virginia Tech (22-5; coached by Don DeVoe).

New Rules: The free throw on the first six common fouls each half by a team is eliminated. . . . Players cannot attempt to create the false impression that they have been fouled in charging-guarding situations or while setting a screen when the contact was only "incidental." A referee can charge the "actor" with a technical foul for unsportsmanlike conduct if, in the referee's opinion, the acting is making a travesty of the game. . . . NCAA bylaws make freshmen eligible to play varsity ball. . . . NCAA Tournament first-round byes determined on the basis of an evaluation of the conference's won-lost record over the previous 10 years in playoff competition.

NCAA Probation: Centenary, Duke, Kansas, New Mexico State, North Carolina State, Western Kentucky.

NCAA Consensus First-Team All-Americans: Doug Collins, G, Sr., Illinois State; Ernie DiGregorio, G, Sr., Providence; Dwight "Bo" Lamar, G, Sr., Southwestern Louisiana; Ed Ratleff, F-G, Sr., Long Beach State; David Thompson, F, Soph., North Carolina State; Bill Walton, C, Jr., UCLA; Keith Wilkes, F, Jr., UCLA.

National Player of the Year: Walton (20.4 ppg, 16.9 rpg, 65.0 FG%).

National Coaches of the Year: Memphis State's Gene Bartow (24-6, NABC) and UCLA's John Wooden (30-0, AP, UPI, USBWA).

UCLA, spearheaded by center Bill Walton, became the first major college in history to compile back-to-back perfect-record seasons. "Walton might have been a better all-around player (than Lew Alcindor)," Bruins coach John Wooden said. "If you were grading a player for every fundamental skill, Walton would rank the highest of any center who ever played."

Illinois State guard Doug Collins became the only white NCAA consensus first-team All-American to play for an African-American head coach (Will Robinson). . . . Oral Roberts, coached by Ken Trickey, established an NCAA record for most field-goal attempts per game with 98.5.

ORU and Southwestern Louisiana finished 1-2 in the team national scoring race for the second consecutive season. . . . Oklahoma City's Ozie Edwards (28.4) and Marvin Rich (25.3) became one of only four sets of teammates in NCAA history to each average more than 25 points per game in a single season.

Marquette's 81-game homecourt winning streak, which started in 1967, was snapped by Notre Dame, 81-79, on guard Dwight Clay's right corner jumper with four seconds remaining. . . . Freshman James "Fly" Williams, the fifth-leading scorer in the country, became a folk hero of sorts by leading Austin Peay State to the Ohio Valley Conference championship after the school finished in last place the previous year. He set an APSU record with 51 points in two different games (against Tennessee Tech and Georgia Southern). Austin Peay finished in the final top 20 of a wire-service poll for the only time in school history.

Los Angeles State's Raymond Lewis (39.9) and Tulsa's Willie Biles (41.6) had staggering scoring averages in their final five games, but they still finished second and third, respectively, in the national scoring race behind Pepperdine's William "Bird" Averitt, who averaged 38.1 points per game in his last 10 contests. Lewis established a Pacific Coast Athletic Association (now Big West Conference) standard by pouring in 53 points in a double overtime game against Long Beach State on his way to a league record 32.9-point scoring average. . . . Averitt supplied the two highest-scoring games in West Coast Conference history when he poured in a school-record 57 points and later 56 in two separate contests against Nevada-Reno. Averitt, a junior college transfer, had 16 games with 37 or more points in his two-year Pepperdine career.

Biles set a Tulsa scoring record with 48 points against Wichita State. Other school single-game scoring standards were set by Virginia Tech's Allan Bristow (52 points vs. George Washington), Dayton's Donald Smith (52 at Loyola of Chicago), Centenary's Robert Parish (50 vs. Lamar), Memphis State's Larry Finch (48 vs.

1972–73 INDIVIDUAL LEADERS

SCORING

PLAYER	PTS.	AVG.
Averitt, Pepperdine	848	33.9
Lewis, Los Angeles St.	789	32.9
Biles, Tulsa	788	30.3
Stewart, Richmond	574	30.2
Williams, Austin Peay	854	29.4
Lamar, Southwestern La.	808	28.9
Edwards, Oklahoma City	767	28.4
Terry, Arkansas	735	28.3
Williamson, New Mexico St.	490	27.2
Collins, Illinois St.	650	26.0

REBOUNDING

PLAYER	REB.	AVG.
Washington, American	511	20.4
Barnes, Providence	571	19.0
Parish, Centenary	505	18.7

Padgett, Nevada-Reno	462	17.8
Bradley, N. Illinois	426	17.8
Walton, UCLA	506	16.9
Kenon, Memphis St.	501	16.7
Campion, Manhattan	402	15.5
Cash, Bowling Green	396	15.2
Baker, UNLV	424	15.1
Perry, Pan American	388	14.9

Note: Parish's rebounding totals were discounted by the NCAA because Centenary was on probation.

FIELD GOAL PERCENTAGE

PLAYER	FGM	FGA	PCT.
Hayes, Lamar	146	222	.658
Walton, UCLA	277	426	.650
Stewart, Santa Clara	186	291	.639
Schaeffer, St. John's	265	420	.631

Losch, Tulane	151	240	.629
Armstead, Rutgers	143	232	.616
Starks, Murray St.	162	264	.614
Taylor, Jacksonville	191	313	.610
Jones, North Carolina	206	343	.601
Minniefield, New Mexico	156	260	.600

FREE THROW PERCENTAGE

PLAYER	FTM	FTA	PCT.
Smith, Dayton	111	122	.910
Jellison, Northeastern	122	136	.897
Palubinskas, LSU	137	153	.895
Johnson, Denver	108	121	.893
J. Lee, Syracuse	93	105	.886
Ritter, Indiana	117	134	.873
Bullington, Ball St.	147	170	.865
Edwards, Oklahoma City	103	120	.858
Floyd, Texas A&M	96	112	.857
Kruger, Kansas St.	90	105	.857

1972–73 TEAM LEADERS

SCORING OFFENSE

SCHOOL	PTS.	AVG.
Oral Roberts	2626	97.3
Southwestern Louisiana	2800	96.6
Austin Peay St.	2700	93.1
North Carolina St.	2509	92.9
Houston	2472	91.6

SCORING DEFENSE

SCHOOL	PTS.	AVG.
Texas-El Paso	1460	56.2
Pennsylvania	1606	57.4
Fairleigh Dickinson	1523	58.6
Air Force	1420	59.2
UCLA	1802	60.1

SCORING MARGIN

SCHOOL	OFF.	DEF.	MAR.
North Carolina St.	92.9	71.1	21.8

UCLA	81.3	60.1	21.2
Long Beach St.	90.1	72.3	17.8
St. Joseph's	77.8	63.0	14.8
Houston	91.6	77.1	14.5

WON-LOST PERCENTAGE

SCHOOL	W-L	PCT.
UCLA	30-0	1.000
North Carolina St.	27-0	1.000
Long Beach St.	26-3	.897
Providence	27-4	.871
Marquette	25-4	.862

FIELD GOAL PERCENTAGE

SCHOOL	FGM	FGA	PCT.
North Carolina	1150	2181	.527
Maryland	1089	2094	.520
North Carolina St.	1054	2028	.520
UCLA	1054	2032	.519
St. John's	932	1804	.517

FREE THROW PERCENTAGE

SCHOOL	FTM	FTA	PCT.
Duke	496	632	.785
Jacksonville	426	547	.779
Rhode Island	313	405	.773
William & Mary	483	636	.759
Tennessee	281	371	.757

REBOUND MARGIN

SCHOOL	OWN	OPP.	MAR.
Manhattan	56.5	38.0	18.5
American	56.7	40.3	16.4
Oral Roberts	66.9	50.3	15.6
UCLA	49.0	33.9	15.1
Houston	54.7	40.8	13.9

St. Joseph's, Ind.) and Arkansas' Martin Terry (47 vs. SMU). Parish did not convert a free throw in his outburst. . . . Averitt (33.9 ppg), Biles (30.3), Austin Peay's Williams (29.5), Arkansas' Martin Terry (28.3), St. John's Billy Schaeffer (24.7), St. Louis' Harry Rogers (24.5) and Finch (24) set school records for highest scoring average in a single season. Averitt's average is a WCC record.. . . Finch, a guard, was the first Memphis State player to become an NCAA consensus first- or second-team All-American.

Villanova compiled a losing record (11-14) for the only time in Jack Kraft's 12 years as the Wildcats' coach. The Wildcats had defeated Boston College 13 straight times until bowing to the Eagles, 82-81. . . . Brown lost 26 consecutive games to Princeton in their series until upending the Tigers, 68-62.. . . Indiana finished in the Top 10 of a final wire-service poll for the first time since 1960.

Davidson (Southern, coached by Terry Holland), Kentucky (SEC, Joe B. Hall) and Weber State (Big Sky, Gene Visscher) each captured its sixth consecutive regular-season league championship. Davidson's crown was its ninth undisputed Southern Conference regular-season title in 10 years. . . . For the first time in ACC Tournament history, the regular-season last-place finisher won a first-round game when Wake Forest (3-9 in the ACC) upset second-place finisher North Carolina State (8-4), 54-52, in overtime.

Houston's only defeat in its last 16 regular-season games was by one point against Eddie Sutton-coached Creighton, 78-77. . . . Arizona's Fred Snowden became the first African-American head coach in the Western Athletic Conference. . . . No league benefited more from year-lings than the WAC in the initial season of freshman eligibility. Arizona freshman Coniel Norman led the WAC in scoring (24 ppg), Utah freshman Mike Sojourner paced the WAC in rebounding (12.3 rpg), Arizona freshman guard Eric Money was an all-league second-team selection and Utah freshman guard Luther (Ticky) Burden led the Utes in scoring although they compiled their first losing record (8-18) in 19 years. . . . Long Beach State (26-3, coached by Jerry Tarkanian) had its winningest season in school history.

1972-73 UNDEFEATED TEAM: UCLA (30-0)

COACH: JOHN WOODEN

UCLA	OPPONENT	BRUINS HIGH SCORER
94	Wisconsin 53	Walton 26
73	Bradley 38	Walton 16
81	Pacific 48	Wilkes 18
98	UC Santa Barbara 67	Walton 30
89	Pittsburgh 73	Wilkes 20
82	Notre Dame 56	Wilkes 18
85	Drake* 72	Walton 29
71	Illinois* 64	Walton 22
64	Oregon 38	Farmer/Wilkes 14
87	Oregon State 61	Wilkes 19
82	at† Stanford 67	Farmer/Hollyfield/Walton 18
69	at California 50	Farmer/Wilkes 18
92	San Francisco 64	Walton 22
101	Providence 77	Farmer 21
87	at Loyola of Chicago 73	Walton 32
82	at Notre Dame 63	Wilkes 20
79	at Southern California 56	Walton 20
88	at Washington State 50	Walton 17
76	at Washington 67	Walton 29
93	Washington 62	Walton 26
96	Washington State 64	Walton 29
72	at Oregon 61	Wilkes 18
73	at Oregon State 67	Walton 21
90	California 65	Walton/Wilkes 15
51	Stanford 45	Walton 23
76	Southern California 56	Walton/Wilkes 17

NCAA TOURNAMENT

98	Arizona State 81	Walton 28
54	San Francisco 39	Farmer 13
70	Indiana* 59	Curtis 22
87	Memphis State* 66	Walton 44

*Neutral court games.

1972-73 UNDEFEATED TEAM: N.C. STATE (27-0)

COACH: NORMAN SLOAN

NCS	1972-73 OPPONENT	WOLFPACK HIGH SCORER
130	Appalachian State 53	Thompson 33
110	Atlantic Christian 40	Thompson 32
44	Georgia Southern 100	Thompson 40
25	South Florida 88	Thompson 30
88	Wake Forest* 83	Thompson 29
68	North Carolina* 61	Thompson 19
103	Davidson* 90	Cafferky 25
97	at Georgia 83	Thompson 26
68	at Virginia 61	Towe 17
94	Duke 87	Towe/Burleson 20
15	Lehigh 53	Burleson 30
87	at Maryland 85	Thompson 37
86	at Clemson 76	Thompson 24
98	at Furman 73	Thompson 27
89	Maryland 78	Thompson 24
64	Virginia 59	Thompson 18
76	North Carolina 73	Thompson 22
68	Clemson* 61	Thompson 30
118	Georgia Tech* 94	Thompson 36
105	East Carolina 70	Thompson 33
81	at Wake Forest 59	Thompson 21
74	at Duke 50	Thompson 31
100	UNC Charlotte 64	Burleson 26
82	at North Carolina 78	Thompson 18
100	Wake Forest 77	Burleson 27

ACC TOURNAMENT

63	Virginia* 51	Burleson/Thompson 14
76	Maryland* 74	Burleson 14

*Neutral court games.

INDIVIDUAL STATISTICS FOR N.C. STATE REGULARS

Player	POS.	CL.	G.	PPG	RPG
David Thompson	F	So.	27	24.7	8.1
Tom Burleson	C	Jr.	27	17.9	12.0
Monte Towe	G	So.	27	10.0	1.7
Rick Holdt	F	Sr.	27	8.3	3.7
Tim Stoddard	F	So.	27	7.9	5.3
Joe Cafferky	G	Sr.	25	7.2	2.1
Greg Hawkins	F	Jr.	25	5.6	3.3
Mark Moeller	G	So.	27	4.7	1.6
Steve Nuce	F	Jr.	26	4.4	2.1
Craig Kuszmaul	G	So.	19	2.4	.9
TEAM TOTALS			27	92.9	46.5

Bucky Waters' fourth and last season as Duke's coach resulted in the Blue Devils' first losing record in 34 years (12-14). . . . Temple's Harry Litwack ended his 21-year coaching career with a 373-193 record. . . . Georgetown's John Thompson started his college coaching career with a 12-14 record, including defeats to St. John's (by 41 points) and Florida State (31), local rivals Maryland (26), American University (22) and George Washington (13) and small school Roanoke (16).

American's Kermit Washington grabbed at least 26 rebounds in each of his last five games to finish the year with a nation-leading 20.4 rebounds per game. He collected 40 points and 26 rebounds in a 90-68 triumph over Georgetown in the Eagles' regular-season finale to preserve his status as the last Division I player to average more than 20 points and 20 rebounds for an entire season. . . . David Vaughn's 34 rebounds for Oral Roberts against Brandeis is the highest single-game total for a major-college player since freshman eligibility was introduced.

Three Texas universities–Abilene Christian, Corpus Christi and Trinity–ended their short stints at the major-college level. Gettsyburg (Pa.) also competed in its final season at the major-college level.

1972-73 FINAL NATIONAL POLLS

AP	UPI	SCHOOL (RECORD)	HEAD COACH
1	1	UCLA (30-0)	John Wooden
2	2	N.C. State (27-0)	Norman Sloan
3	3	Long Beach State (26-3)	Jerry Tarkanian
4	5	Providence (27-4)	Dave Gavitt
5	4	Marquette (25-4)	Al McGuire
6	6	Indiana (22-6)	Bob Knight
7	7	Southwestern La. (24-5)	Beryl Shipley
8	10	Maryland (23-7)	Lefty Driesell
9	7	Kansas State (23-5)	Jack Hartman
10	9	Minnesota (21-5)	Bill Musselman
11	12	North Carolina (25-8)	Dean Smith
12	11	Memphis State (24-6)	Gene Bartow
13	18	Houston (23-4)	Guy Lewis
14	14	Syracuse (24-5)	Roy Danforth
15	17	Missouri (21-6)	Norm Stewart
16	13	Arizona State (19-9)	Ned Wulk
17	15	Kentucky (20-8)	Joe B. Hall
18	20	Pennsylvania (21-7)	Chuck Daly
19	–	Austin Peay State (22-7)	Lake Kelly
20	–	San Francisco (23-5)	Bob Gaillard
–	16	South Carolina (22-7)	Frank McGuire
–	18	Weber State (20-7)	Gene Visscher

1973 NCAA Tournament

Summary: UCLA won the national championship by an average of 16 points. The Bruins' Bill Walton, aided by Greg Lee's tourney-high 14 assists, erupted for a championship game-record 44 points in an 87-66 triumph over Memphis State in the final. Walton had been outscored by fellow center Steve Downing, 26-14, in a 70-59 victory against Indiana in the national semifinals. The Bruins won 26 of their 30 games by a double-digit margin with the closest results being six-point victories against league rivals Oregon State and Stanford.

Star Gazing: This was the last time a champion had just one representative on the All-NCAA Tournament team (Walton).

Biggest Upset: Coach Jerry Tarkanian's fourth consecutive and last tournament team at Long Beach State (26-3) succumbed against San Francisco, 77-67, when two-time consensus first-team All-American Ed Ratleff hit just 4 of 18 field-goal attempts for the 49ers, who were ranked third by UPI.

One and Only: Walton is the only player to have as many as 20 field goals in an NCAA championship game. He was 21 of 22 from the floor against Memphis State.

Numbers Game: Providence's Marvin Barnes hit all 10 of his field-goal attempts in an 87-65 pounding of Pennsylvania in the East Regional semifinals. . . . Memphis State's Larry Kenon had the top two rebounding efforts in the playoffs–22 vs. Providence and 20 vs. South Carolina.

What If: Barnes suffered a dislocated right kneecap in the first half of the national semifinals. The Friars, entering the Final Four with just two defeats, didn't have enough firepower to retain a nine-point halftime lead and wound up losing to Memphis State (98-85). According to legendary CCNY coach Nat Holman, they had gotten off to the best eight-minute start he had ever seen with Barnes dominating inside, Kevin Stacom hitting a couple of long jumpers and Ernie DiGregorio displaying his passing wizardry. . . . Undefeated North Carolina State was

Providence guard Ernie DiGregorio was a key reason the Friars made it to the 1973 NCAA Final Four.

ineligible for the NCAA Tournament because of NCAA probation. The Wolfpack won its first four games by an average margin of 57 points. . . . North Carolina (25-8) might have been the ACC representative in the NCAA playoffs instead of Maryland if Bob McAdoo hadn't left school early for the NBA. . . . Kentucky (20-8) could have possessed the firepower to defeat Indiana in the Mideast Regional final if center Tom Payne hadn't dropped out of college with eligibility remaining. . . . Princeton (16-9) probably would have challenged Penn more to participate in the NCAA playoffs as the Ivy League titlist if guard Brian Taylor hadn't turned pro early. . . . Florida State (18-8) didn't live up to expectations when guard Ron King, the leading scorer for the NCAA Tournament runner-up the previous season, missed the majority of his senior year after dislocating his ankle.

Putting Things in Perspective: Downing and John Ritter, Indiana's top two scorers, were recruited by coach Bob Knight's predecessor, Lou Watson, who compiled a 17-7 mark in his final season (1970-71) when George McGinnis played his only year in college before turning pro.

Scoring Leader: Ernie DiGregorio, Providence (128 points, 25.6 ppg).

Highest Scoring Average: Larry Finch, Memphis State (107 points, 26.75 ppg).

Rebounding Leader: Bill Walton, UCLA (58 rebounds, 14.5 rpg).

1972–73 NCAA CHAMPION: UCLA

SEASON STATISTICS OF UCLA REGULARS

PLAYER	POS.	CL.	G.	FG%	FT%	PPG	RPG
Bill Walton	C	Jr.	30	.650	.569	20.4	16.9
Keith Wilkes	F	Jr.	30	.525	.652	14.8	7.3
Larry Farmer	F	Sr.	30	.511	.701	12.2	5.0
Larry Hollyfield	G	Sr.	30	.466	.492	10.7	2.9
Tommy Curtis	G	Jr.	24	.512	.667	6.4	1.7
Dave Meyers	F	So.	28	.477	.756	4.9	2.9
Greg Lee	G	Jr.	30	.473	.790	4.6	1.3
Swen Nater	C	Sr.	29	.459	.652	3.2	3.3
Pete Trgovich	G-F	So.	25	.382	.400	3.1	1.7
Vince Carson	F	Jr.	26	.514	.471	1.7	2.2
Gary Franklin	F	Jr.	24	.485	.500	1.6	1.3
Bob Webb	G	Jr.	21	.148	.833	0.6	0.2
TEAM TOTALS			30	.519	.632	81.3	49.0

Assists leader: Walton 168.

1973 FINAL FOUR CHAMPIONSHIP GAME

ST. LOUIS, MO

UCLA (87)	MIN.	FG-A	FT-A	REB.	A	PF	PTS.
Wilkes	39	8-14	0-0	7	1	2	16
Farmer	33	1-4	0-0	2	0	2	2
Walton	33	21-22	2-5	13	2	4	44
Lee	34	1-1	3-3	3	14	2	5
Hollyfield	30	4-7	0-0	3	9	4	8
Curtis	11	1-4	2-2	3	0	1	4
Meyers	10	2-7	0-0	3	0	1	4
Nater	7	1-1	0-0	3	0	2	2
Franklin	1	1-2	0-1	1	0	0	2
Carson	1	0-0	0-0	0	0	0	0
Webb	1	0-0	0-0	0	0	0	0
Team				2			
TOTALS	200	40-62	7-11	40	26	18	87

FG%: .645. FT%: .636. **Blocks:** 5. **Turnovers:** 17 (Walton 6). **Steals:** 2.

MEMPHIS ST. (66)	MIN.	FG-A	FT-A	REB.	A	PF	PTS.
Buford	38	3-7	1-2	3	1	1	7
Kenon	34	8-16	4-4	8	3	3	20
Robinson	33	3-6	0-1	7	1	4	6
Laurie	21	0-1	0-0	0	2	0	0
Finch	38	9-21	11-13	1	2	2	29
Westfall	10	0-1	0-0	0	0	5	0
Cook	18	1-4	2-2	0	2	1	4
McKinney	1	0-0	0-0	0	0	0	0
Jones	4	0-0	0-0	0	0	0	0
Tetzlaff	1	0-0	0-2	0	0	1	0
Liss	1	0-1	0-0	0	0	0	0
Andrews	1	0-0	0-0	0	0	0	0
Team				2			
TOTALS	200	24-57	18-24	21	11	17	66

FG%: .421. FT%: .750. **Blocks:** 1. **Turnovers:** 8. **Steals:** 0.
Halftime: Tied 39-39.

NATIONAL SEMIFINALS

MEMPHIS STATE (98): Buford 3-7 0-0 6, Kenon 14-27 0-4 28, Robinson 11-17 2-3 24, Laurie 1-3 2-3 4, Finch 7-16 7-9 21, Cook 3-6 2-3 8, Westfall 2-3 3-4 7, Jones 0-1 0-0 0. Team 41-80 (.513) 16-26 (.615) 98.

PROVIDENCE (85): Crawford 5-12 0-0 10, Costello 5-5 1-1 11, Barnes 5-7 2-3 12, DiGregorio 15-36 2-2 32, Stacom 6-15 3-3 15, King 2-6 0-0 4, Baker 0-0 0-0 0, Dunphy 0-1 1-2 1, Bello 0-0 0-0 0. Team 38-82 (.463) 9-11 (.818) 85.

Halftime: Providence 49-40.

UCLA (70): Wilkes 5-10 3-4 13, Farmer 3-6 1-2 7, Walton 7-12 0-0 14, Lee 0-1 0-0 0, Hollyfield 5-6 0-0 10, Curtis 9-15 4-7 2, Meyers 2-3 0-0 4, Nater 0-0 0-0 0. Team 31-53 (.585) 8-13 (.615) 70.

INDIANA (59): Buckner 3-10 0-1 6, Crews 4-10 0-0 8, Downing 12-20 2-4 26, Green 1-7 0-0 2, Ritter 6-10 1-1 13, Laskowski 1-8 0-0 2, Abernethy 0-1 0-0 0, Smock 0-0 0-0 0, Noort 0-0 0-0 0, Wilson 0-0 0-0 0, Morris 0-0 0-0 0, Ahlfield 0-0 0-0 0, Allen 1-1 0-0 2, Memering 0-0 0-0 0. Team 28-67 (.418) 3-6 (.500) 59.

Halftime: UCLA 40-22.

ALL-TOURNAMENT TEAM

Ernie DiGregorio, G, Sr., Providence
Steve Downing, C, Sr., Indiana
Larry Finch, G, Sr., Memphis State
Larry Kenon, F, Jr., Memphis State
Bill Walton, C, Jr., UCLA*
    *Named Most Outstanding Player

1973 CHAMPIONSHIP BRACKET

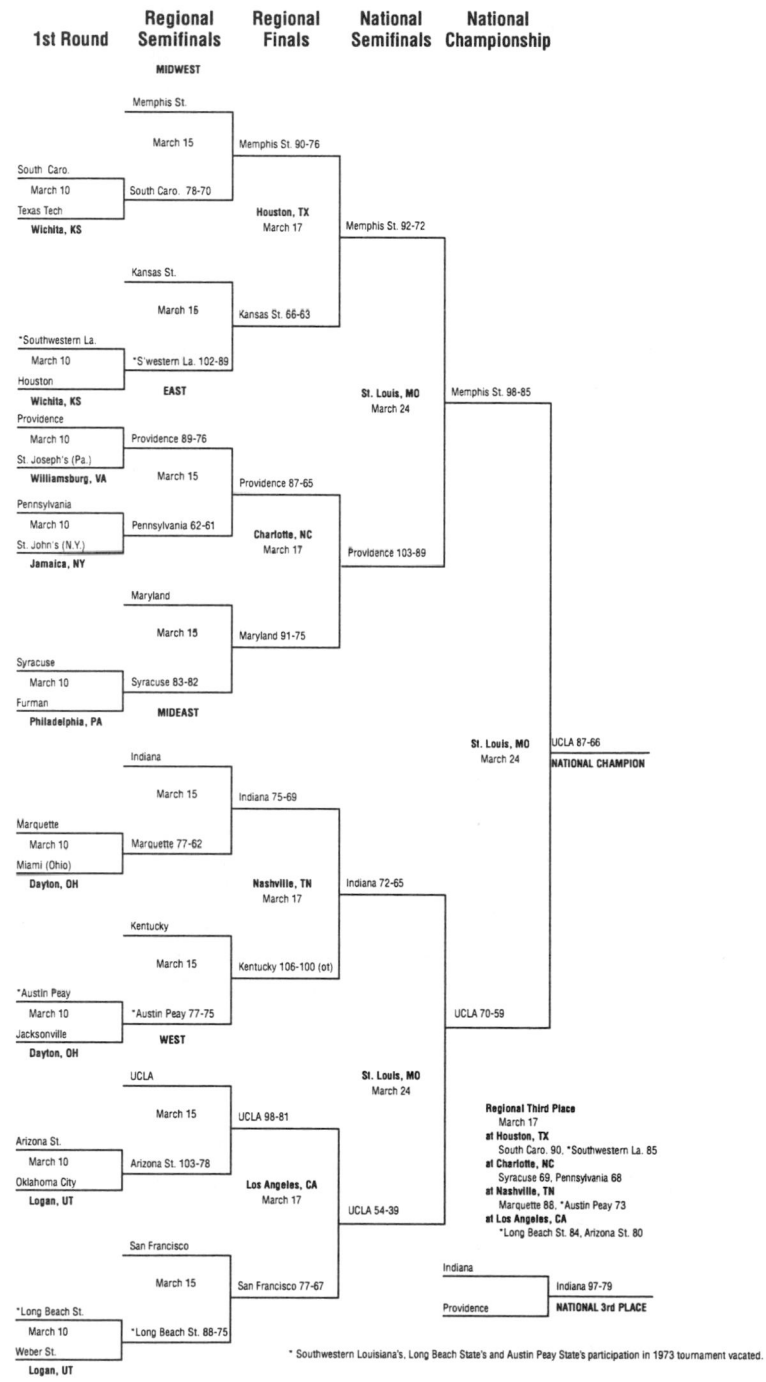

1st Round	Regional Semifinals	Regional Finals	National Semifinals	National Championship

MIDWEST

Memphis St.

March 15 — Memphis St. 90-76

South Caro.
March 10
Texas Tech — South Caro. 78-70
Wichita, KS

Houston, TX
March 17 — Memphis St. 92-72

Kansas St.
March 15 — Kansas St. 66-63

*Southwestern La.
March 10
Houston — *S'western La. 102-89
Wichita, KS

EAST

St. Louis, MO
March 24 — Memphis St. 98-85

Providence
March 10
St. Joseph's (Pa.) — Providence 89-76
Williamsburg, VA

March 15 — Providence 87-65

Pennsylvania
March 10
St. John's (N.Y.) — Pennsylvania 62-61
Jamaica, NY

Charlotte, NC
March 17 — Providence 103-89

Maryland

March 15 — Maryland 91-75

Syracuse
March 10
Furman — Syracuse 83-82
Philadelphia, PA

MIDEAST

St. Louis, MO
March 24 — UCLA 87-66
NATIONAL CHAMPION

Indiana

March 15 — Indiana 75-69

Marquette
March 10
Miami (Ohio) — Marquette 77-62
Dayton, OH

Nashville, TN
March 17 — Indiana 72-65

Kentucky

March 15 — Kentucky 106-100 (ot)

*Austin Peay
March 10
Jacksonville — *Austin Peay 77-75
Dayton, OH

WEST

UCLA 70-59

UCLA

March 15 — UCLA 98-81

Arizona St.
March 10
Oklahoma City — Arizona St. 103-78
Logan, UT

Los Angeles, CA
March 17 — UCLA 54-39

San Francisco

March 15 — San Francisco 77-67

*Long Beach St.
March 10
Weber St. — *Long Beach St. 88-75
Logan, UT

St. Louis, MO
March 24

Regional Third Place
March 17
at Houston, TX
South Caro. 90, *Southwestern La. 85
at Charlotte, NC
Syracuse 69, Pennsylvania 68
at Nashville, TN
Marquette 88, *Austin Peay 73
at Los Angeles, CA
*Long Beach St. 84, Arizona St. 80

Indiana — Indiana 97-79
Providence — **NATIONAL 3rd PLACE**

* Southwestern Louisiana's, Long Beach State's and Austin Peay State's participation in 1973 tournament vacated.

1973-74

AT A GLANCE

NCAA Champion: North Carolina State (30-1; coached by Norman Sloan; won ACC regular-season title by three games with a 12-0 record).

NIT Champion: Purdue (21-9; coached by Fred Schaus; finished in third place in Big Ten with a 10-4 record, which was two games behind co-champions Indiana and Michigan).

CCAT Champion: Indiana (23-5; tied for Big Ten title with a 12-2 record).

New Conferences: ECAC divided to receive multiple automatic qualification berths in the NCAA Tournament.

New Rules: Referees may penalize players for fouls occurring away from the ball (grabbing, illegal screens, etc.). . . . The NCAA Tournament bracket rotation changes for the first time, eliminating East vs. West bracketing in effect since the event's inception. . . . The first public draw to fill oversubscribed orders for Final Four tickets was administered.

NCAA Probation: Centenary, Long Beach State, Louisiana Tech, McNeese State, New Mexico State, Texas-Pan American, Western Kentucky, Wichita State.

NCAA Consensus First-Team All-Americans: Marvin Barnes, C, Sr., Providence; John Shumate, C-F, Soph., Notre Dame; David Thompson, F, Jr., North Carolina State; Bill Walton, C, Sr., UCLA; Keith Wilkes, F, Sr., UCLA.

National Players of the Year: Thompson (26 ppg, 7.9 rpg, 54.7 FG%/AP) and Walton (19.3 ppg, 14.7 rpg, 66.5 FG%/UPI, USBWA, Naismith).

National Coaches of the Year: Marquette's Al McGuire (26-5/NABC); Notre Dame's Digger Phelps (26-3/UPI), and North Carolina State's Norman Sloan (30-1/AP, USBWA).

UCLA's NCAA-record 88-game winning streak ended at Notre Dame, 71-70 (see accompanying box). Notre Dame also ended Indiana's 19-game homecourt winning streak, 73-67, and South Carolina's 34-game homecourt winning streak, 72-68. John Shumate scored at least 24 points in all three streak stoppers.

UCLA's streak of Pacific-8 Conference victories ended at 50 when the Bruins bowed at Oregon State, 61-57. The Bruins were 149-2 at Pauley Pavilion under coach John Wooden.

"When you have the same group for three years, they're a little more difficult to work with. They don't mean to be, but they are," Wooden said. "I can't find fault with my team, but I failed to motivate them. And I'm not talking about won-lost record. In many games we won, I didn't think we displayed intensity and didn't play up to our potential."

Maryland's 65-64 setback at UCLA in the Bruins' second game of the season was the closest and one of only three of their 49 home games during the 88-game winning streak decided by fewer than 11 points.

UCLA's Bill Walton finished his career with an amazing field-goal percentage of 65.1 although he never won a single-season shooting title. Walton is the only player to be a three-time first-team NCAA unanimous All-American and first-team Academic All-American. He shot an NCAA Tournament-record 68.6 percent from the floor in 12 playoff games.

Considered in some quarters as the most incredible comeback in major-college history, North Carolina freshman Walter Davis sent the regular-season finale against Duke into overtime with a 30-foot bank shot, climaxing an eight-point rally in the final 17 seconds of regulation. Carolina won in overtime, 96-92, for its first-ever overtime victory against the Blue Devils. . . . In the lowest-scoring game since 1938, Tennessee and Temple combined for a mere 17 points in the Volunteers' 11-6 victory (see accompanying box). . . . Jerry Tarkanian, the nation's winningest active Division I coach by percentage, lost his home debut at UNLV (82-76 to Texas Tech) after Tarkanian-coached teams never lost a home game in five years at Long Beach State or in six years in junior college.

The nation's top three scorers grew up in New York City—Canisius' Larry Fogle, Pan American's Bruce "Sky" King and Austin Peay State's James "Fly" Williams. Fogle, who set a Canisius record for highest scoring average in a single season (33.4 ppg), enrolled there after Southwestern Louisiana's program was disbanded by the NCAA because of numerous indiscretions. . . . Fogle (55 points vs. St. Peter's) joined the following players who set school single-game scoring records: Appalachian State's Stan Davis (56 vs. Carson-Newman), Providence's Marvin Barnes (52 vs. Austin Peay), Illinois State's Robert "Bubbles" Hawkins (58 vs. Northern Illinois), Tulsa's Willie Biles (tied own mark with 48 vs. St. Cloud, Minn.), Eastern Michigan's Gary Tyson (47 vs. Wheaton), Ball State's Larry Bullington (47 vs. Cleveland State), South Alabama's Eugene Oliver (46 at Southern Mississippi) and Fresno State's Charles Bailey (45 in double overtime at North Texas State). . . . The 6-5 Fogle also grabbed 22 rebounds against St. Peter's, which was one of six games during the season when he retrieved at least 20 missed shots in a game, including a school-record 26 against Catholic.

Providence's Marvin Barnes lets it fly.

UCLA'S 88-GAME WINNING STREAK ENDS

High drama occurred on January 19, 1974 at Notre Dame's Athletic and Convocation Center when the Irish ended UCLA's NCAA-record 88-game winning streak, 71-70. Guard Dwight Clay's fallaway jump shot from the right baseline climaxed a 12-0 spurt in the last three minutes for the Irish. Clay's teammates Gary Brokaw and John Shumate scored 25 and 24 points respectively.

UCLA (70)	FG-A	FT-A	REB.	PTS.
Tommy Curtis	3-11	3-4	1	9
Pete Trgovich	3-5	1-1	0	7
Bill Walton	12-14	0-0	9	24
Dave Meyers	5-10	0-2	7	10
Keith Wilkes	6-16	6-7	5	18
Greg Lee	0-0	2-2	0	2
Marques Johnson	0-0	0-0	0	0
TOTALS	**29-56**	**12-16**	**27**	**70**

FG%: .518. FT%: .750.

NOTRE DAME (71)	FG-A	FT-A	REB.	PTS.
Gary Brokaw	10-16	5-7	3	25
Dwight Clay	2-5	3-4	6	7
John Shumate	11-22	2-4	11	24
Adrian Dantley	4-12	1-1	8	9
Gary Novak	0-2	0-0	0	0
Bill Paterno	2-4	0-0	1	4
Ray Martin	1-1	0-0	2	2
TOTALS	**30-62**	**11-16**	**31**	**71**

FG%: .484. FT%: .687.
Halftime: UCLA 43-34.

LOWEST-SCORING GAME SINCE 1938 Fans attending the December 15, 1973, match at Tennessee between Temple and the Volunteers probably didn't need to worry about missing any action while standing in line for concessions. The two teams combined for 17 points, the lowest total in a game since 1938. Tennessee's Len Kosmalski was "high scorer" with 5 points.

TEMPLE (6)	FG-A	FT-A	REB.	PTS.
Kevin Washington	0-3	0-0	0	0
Joe Anderson	1-3	2-3	4	4
Joe Newman	1-3	0-0	1	2
Rick Trudeau	0-1	0-0	0	0
John Kneib	0-1	0-0	0	0
Tony Moore	0-0	0-0	0	0
TOTALS	**2-11**	**2-3**	**5**	**6**

FG%: .182. FT%: .667.

TENNESSEE (11)	FG-A	FT-A	REB.	PTS.
Ernie Grunfeld	1-3	0-0	2	2
Wayne Tomlinson	0-0	0-0	2	0
Len Kosmalski	2-3	1-2	3	5
Rodney Woods	0-2	0-0	1	0
John Snow	0-1	4-5	1	4
Austin Clark	0-1	0-0	0	0
Team				3
TOTALS	**3-10**	**5-7**	**12**	**11**

FG%: .300. FT%: .714.
Halftime: Tennessee 7-5.

1973–74 INDIVIDUAL LEADERS

PLAYER	PTS.	AVG.
Fogle, Canisius	835	33.4
King, Pan American	681	31.0
Williams, Austin Peay	687	27.5
Stewart, Richmond	663	26.5
Thompson, North Carolina St.	805	26.0
Bullington, Ball St.	664	25.5
Oleynick, Seattle	653	25.1
Outlaw, North Carolina A&T	647	24.9
Biles, Tulsa	641	24.7
Shumate, Notre Dame	703	24.2

REBOUNDING

PLAYER	REB.	AVG.
Barnes, Providence	597	18.7
McCullough, Pan American	358	16.3
Robinson, Kent St.	423	16.3
Campion, Manhattan	419	15.5

Parish, Centenary*	382	15.3
Padgett, Nevada-Reno	395	15.2
McKinney, Baylor	375	15.0
Meriweather, Southern Ill.	387	14.9
Walton, UCLA	398	14.7
Elmore, Maryland	412	14.7
Warner, Maine	350	14.6

Note: Parish's rebounding totals were discounted by the NCAA because Centenary was on probation.

FIELD GOAL PERCENTAGE

PLAYER	FGM	FGA	PCT.
Fleming, Arizona	136	204	.667
Walton, UCLA	232	349	.665
Cox, Mississippi	152	242	.628
Shumate, Notre Dame	281	448	.627
Skinner, Massachusetts	196	316	.620

Carroll, Howard	205	332	.617
Fry, Mississippi St.	141	233	.605
Morgan, Samford	214	354	.605
Garrett, Purdue	276	465	.594
C. Pondexter, Long Beach St.	167	283	.590

FREE THROW PERCENTAGE

PLAYER	FTM	FTA	PCT.
Medlock, Arkansas	87	95	.916
Snow, Tennessee	81	91	.890
Ferrell, Marshall	128	145	.883
Compton, Vanderbilt	89	102	.873
Kruger, Kansas St.	122	140	.871
Cook, Memphis St.	119	138	.862
Johnson, Denver	120	140	.857
Palubinskas, LSU	121	142	.852
Cosey, West Texas St.	80	94	.851
Bullington, Ball St.	154	183	.842

1973–74 TEAM LEADERS

SCORING OFFENSE

SCHOOL	PTS.	AVG.
Maryland-Eastern Shore	2831	97.6
Oral Roberts	2744	94.6
Virginia Commonwealth	2266	94.4
North Carolina St.	2833	91.4
Utah	2726	90.9

SCORING DEFENSE

SCHOOL	PTS.	AVG.
Texas-El Paso	1413	56.5
Temple	1417	56.7
Princeton	1520	58.5
Marquette	1857	59.9
St. Joseph's	1807	60.2

SCORING MARGIN

SCHOOL	OFF.	DEF.	MAR.
UNC Charlotte	90.2	69.4	20.8
UCLA	82.3	62.7	19.6
Long Beach St.	80.2	61.1	19.1
Notre Dame	89.9	73.0	16.9
Maryland	85.7	69.0	16.7

WON-LOST PERCENTAGE

SCHOOL	W-L	PCT.
North Carolina St.	30-1	.968
Maryland-Eastern Shore	27-2	.931
Long Beach St.	24-2	.923
Notre Dame	26-3	.897
Providence	28-4	.875

FIELD GOAL PERCENTAGE

SCHOOL	FGM	FGA	PCT.
Notre Dame	1056	1992	.530
Long Beach St.	887	1680	.528
North Carolina	1015	1952	.520
Massachusetts	878	1709	.514
UNC Charlotte	996	1948	.511
Stetson	781	1529	.511

FREE THROW PERCENTAGE

SCHOOL	FTM	FTA	PCT.
Vanderbilt	477	595	.802
Princeton	332	423	.785
Davidson	488	623	.783
Seattle	366	479	.764
Denver	311	410	.759

REBOUND MARGIN

SCHOOL	OWN	OPP.	MAR.
Massachusetts	43.7	30.7	13.0
Virginia Commonwealth	55.1	42.1	13.0
Arkansas St.	50.3	39.2	11.1
Iona	51.0	40.0	11.0
Maryland	47.0	36.1	10.9

In a remarkable turnaround, Kansas reached the Final Four just one year after compiling an 8-18 record. The Jayhawks (23-7), coached by Ted Owens, were the nation's most-improved team. . . . Mississippi sustained its 14th of 21 consecutive non-winning SEC records but the Rebels handed Arkansas the Hogs' most lopsided defeat in history, 117-66. . . . This season marked won-loss records that were the best (27-2 by Maryland-Eastern Shore) and worst (1-25 by Georgia State) for any first-year Division I schools since classification was first introduced in 1948.

Maryland, ranking fourth in both polls, lost against eventual NCAA champion North Carolina State in the ACC Tournament final (103-100 in overtime) in what some believe might have been the greatest college game ever played (see accompanying box). Three players from each team earned All-American honors during their careers–N.C. State's David Thompson, Tom Burleson and Monte Towe and Maryland's John Lucas, Len Elmore and Tom McMillen. The Terrapins had four players score at least 20 points–Lucas, McMillen, Owen Brown and Mo Howard–in a 20-point victory over 22-6 North Carolina (105-85) in the semifinals. The Terps lost by one point at UCLA in their season opener before dropping both regular-season games against N.C. State by six points and bowing at North Carolina to finish in a tie with the Tar Heels for second place in the ACC standings.

George Washington's Clyde Burwell (33 vs. St. Mary's, Md.), Maine's Bob Warner (28 vs. Trinity), Stanford's Rich Kelley (27 at Kentucky), Southern Illinois' Joe C. Meriweather (27 vs. Indiana State), McNeese State's Henry Ray (27 vs. Texas-Arlington) and Maryland's Elmore (26 at Wake Forest) set school single-game rebounding marks.

South Carolina's school-record 34-game homecourt winning streak ended when the Gamecocks bowed to Notre Dame, 72-68. . . . Rutgers lost 13 consecutive games in its series with Syracuse until defeating the Orangemen,

MOST INCREDIBLE LEAGUE TOURNEY FINAL

MARYLAND VS. NORTH CAROLINA STATE

ACC TOURNAMENT CHAMPIONSHIP GAME (GREENSBORO, NC)

MARCH 9, 1974

Maryland might have been the best team never to appear in the NCAA Tournament. The Terrapins bowed to NCAA champion-to-be North Carolina State, 103-100, in overtime in the ACC Tournament final.

MARYLAND (100)	FG-A	FT-A	REB.	PTS.
Tom McMillen	11-16	0-0	7	22
Owen Brown	7-9	0-0	2	14
Len Elmore	7-12	4-5	13	18
John Lucas	9-20	0-1	3	18
Mo Howard	10-15	2-2	3	22
Tom Roy	3-4	0-0	3	6
Billy Hahn	0-1	0-0	0	0
TOTALS	**47-77**	**6-8**	**31**	**100**

FG%:.610.FT%:.750.

N.C. STATE (103)	FG-A	FT-A	REB.	PTS.
David Thompson	10-24	9-11	5	29
Tim Stoddard	2-3	0-2	6	4
Tom Burleson	18-2	2-4	13	38
Monte Towe	7-11	3-4	2	17
Moe Rivers	4-13	0-1	5	8
Phil Spence	3-4	1-4	6	7
Mark Moeller	0-0	0-0	0	0
TOTALS	**44-80**	**15-26**	**37**	**103**

FG%:.550. FT%:.577.

Halftime: Maryland 55-50. **Regulation:** Tied 97-97.

93-79. . . . Providence (28-4/coached by Dave Gavitt), Pittsburgh (25-4/Buzz Ridl) and Brown (17-9/Gerald Alaimo) had their winningest seasons in school history. Southern California (24-5/Bob Boyd) tied its school single-season record for most victories. . . . Pitt, making its only Top 20 appearance in a final wire-service poll until 1987, won a school-record 22 consecutive games after losing its season opener at West Virginia. The Panthers lost at least 10 contests each of the previous nine years when they posted just one winning record. . . . Seton Hall, coached by current network TV analyst Bill Raftery, compiled a 16-11 record to end a streak of nine consecutive losing seasons.

Furman's Fessor Leonard set a Southern Conference standard with 13 blocked shots against St. Peter's. . . . Alabama made its first Top 20 appearance in a final wire-service poll since 1956. . . . Richmond registered its first winning record (16-12) in 16 years and St. Mary's posted its first winning mark (15-13) in 11 seasons.

Illinois suffered a school-record 11-game losing streak en route to a 5-18 mark in Harv Schmidt's seventh and final season as coach. . . . Lute Olson launched his major college coaching career with a 24-2 record in his lone season at Long Beach State. The only defeats for the probation-shackled 49ers were by two points at Colorado and Marquette.

1973-74 FINAL NATIONAL POLLS

AP	UPI	SCHOOL (RECORD)	HEAD COACH
1	1	N.C. State (30-1)	Norman Sloan
2	2	UCLA (26-4)	John Wooden
3	5	Marquette (26-5)	Al McGuire
4	4	Maryland (23-5)	Lefty Driesell
5	3	Notre Dame (26-3)	Digger Phelps
6	12	Michigan (22-5)	Johnny Orr
7	10	Kansas (23-7)	Ted Owens
8	6	Providence (28-4)	Dave Gavitt
9	9	Indiana (23-5)	Bob Knight
10	11	Long Beach State (24-2)	Jerry Tarkanian
11	–	Purdue (22-8)	Fred Schaus
12	8	North Carolina (22-6)	Dean Smith
13	7	Vanderbilt (23-5)	Roy Skinner
14	19	Alabama (22-4)	C.M. Newton
15	–	Utah (22-8)	Bill Foster
16	14	Pittsburgh (25-4)	Buzz Ridl
17	13	Southern Cal (24-5)	Bob Boyd
18	–	Oral Roberts (23-6)	Ken Trickey
19	16	South Carolina (22-5)	Frank McGuire
20	19	Dayton (20-9)	Don Donoher
–	15	Louisville (21-7)	Denny Crum
–	17	Creighton (23-7)	Eddie Sutton
–	18	New Mexico (22-7)	Norm Ellenberger

Note: This was one of two years that the AP poll was released after the national postseason tournaments.

1974 NCAA Tournament

Summary: North Carolina State, unbeaten in 27 games the previous season when it was ineligible to participate in the national tournament because of an NCAA probation, defeated Marquette in the championship game (76-64) after Warriors coach Al McGuire was assessed two technical fouls late in the first half. The "T" helped the Wolfpack score 10 unanswered points in less than a minute and transform a 28-27 deficit into a comfortable 37-28 lead. The final in N.C. State's home state at Greensboro was anticlimatic after the Wolfpack avenged an 18-point loss to UCLA earlier in the season on a neutral court by ending the Bruins' 38-game playoff winning streak (80-77 in overtime). N.C. State erased an 11-point deficit midway through the second half and a seven-point deficit in the extra session behind David Thompson's 28 points and 10 rebounds to halt UCLA's string of seven consecutive NCAA championships. The Bruins were ripe to be knocked off. The (Bill) Walton Gang also blew a 17-point advantage in its playoff opener before regrouping to outlast Dayton (111-100 in triple overtime). "It was the most disappointing, embarrassing event of my life," Walton said. "I think about it almost daily. If I had one week to bring back and live over, that would be it."

Star Gazing: It's inconceivable to think N.C. State would have won the crown if Thompson didn't recover from a nasty fall to the floor after attempting to block a shot by Pitt in the East Regional final. Thompson, cartwheeling over the shoulders of a teammate, landed with a sickening thud on the back of his head and did not move for four minutes. He regained consciousness, was taken to a hospital and, after getting 15 stitches to mend a head wound, was permitted to return to the arena and watch the end of the game. The mild concussion didn't keep him from being ready for the Final Four, where the junior forward was named Most Outstanding Player. "No matter what you say about Thompson and his ability, you can't exaggerate. He's that good," Wolfpack coach Norman Sloan said.

One and Only: N.C. State starting forward Tim Stoddard is the only individual to play for an NCAA basketball champion and then in a major league baseball World Series (relief pitcher for Baltimore Orioles '79).

Numbers Game: Thompson became the only undergraduate non-center to average more than 23 points per game for a national champion (26 ppg). He tossed in a tourney-high 40 points and teammate Tom Burleson contributed a tourney-high 24 rebounds in a

North Carolina star forward David Thompson.

92-78 victory over Providence in the East Regional semifinals. . . . N.C. State traveled a thorny path during the season to the NCAA title, defeating nine teams that, at the time, were ranked among the nation's Top Five. . . . Texas, winner of just one non-conference game, became the only school with a losing overall record to secure an automatic bid by capturing a regular-season league title.

What If: Two-time consensus first-team All-American forward Keith Wilkes shot better than 50 percent from the floor in his three varsity seasons at UCLA before hitting half of his field-goal attempts in a 12-year NBA career. If only he connected on 41 percent of his field-goal attempts instead of 29.4 percent (5 of 17) in the national semifinals, the Bruins could have defeated N.C. State rather than losing 80-77. . . . Marquette (26-5) might have been more of a match for N.C.

UCLA's Keith (Jamaal) Wilkes moves down the court.

State in the NCAA final if Larry McNeill hadn't left school early for the NBA. . . . Memphis State (19-11) probably would have wound up in the NCAA playoffs instead of the NIT if Larry Kenon hadn't left school with eligibility remaining to turn pro.

1973-74 NCAA CHAMPION: NORTH CAROLINA STATE

SEASON STATISTICS OF N.C. STATE REGULARS

PLAYER	POS.	CL.	G.	FG%	FT%	PPG	RPG
David Thompson	F	Jr.	31	.547	.745	26.0	7.9
Tom Burleson	C	Sr.	31	.516	.654	18.1	12.2
Monte Towe	G	Jr.	31	.517	.811	12.8	2.2
Moe Rivers	G	Jr.	30	.484	.654	12.1	2.9
Phil Spence	F	So.	30	.497	.615	6.0	6.3
Tim Stoddard	F	Jr.	31	.416	.697	5.5	4.5
Steve Nuce	F	Sr.	28	.464	.786	4.4	3.2
Greg Hawkins	F	Sr.	25	.469	.735	2.8	1.4
Mark Moeller	G	Jr.	30	.435	.913	2.7	1.2
TEAM TOTALS			**31**	**.499**	**.708**	**91.4**	**46.8**

1974 FINAL FOUR CHAMPIONSHIP GAME

GREENSBORO, NC

MARQUETTE (64)	MIN.	FG-A	FT-A	REB.	A	PF	PTS.
Ellis	39	6-16	0-0	11	1	5	12
Tatum	20	2-7	0-0	3	1	4	4
Lucas	40	7-13	7-9	13	0	4	21
Walton	25	4-10	0-0	2	2	2	8
Washington	35	3-13	5-8	4	0	3	11
Delsman	5	0-0	0-0	0	0	2	0
Daniels	17	1-3	1-2	0	2	3	3
Campbell	12	2-3	0-0	1	0	3	4
Homan	6	0-4	1-2	6	1	2	1
Brennan	1	0-0	0-0	0	0	1	0
Team				3			
TOTALS	**200**	**25-69**	**14-21**	**43**	**7**	**29**	**64**

FG%: .362. FT%: .667. **Steals:** 9 (Washington 5). **Blocks:** 3.

N.C. STATE (76)	MIN.	FG-A	FT-A	REB.	A	PF	PTS.
Stoddard	26	3-4	2-2	7	2	5	8
Thompson	40	7-12	7-8	7	2	3	21
Burleson	36	6-9	2-6	11	0	4	14
Rivers	40	4-9	6-9	2	5	2	14
Towe	38	5-10	6-7	3	2	1	16
Spence	18	1-2	1-2	3	3	2	3
Moeller	2	0-0	0-0	0	0	0	0
Team				1			
TOTALS	**200**	**26-46**	**24-34**	**34**	**14**	**17**	**76**

FG%: .565. FT%: .706. **Steals:** 12. **Blocks:** 8 (Burleson 7).
Halftime: North Carolina State 39-30.

NATIONAL SEMIFINALS

UCLA (77): Meyers 6-9 0-1 12, Wilkes 5-17 5-5 15, Walton 13-21 3-3 29, Curtis 4-8 3-4 11, Lee 4-11 0-0 8, Johnson 0-3 0-0 0, McCarter 1-2 0-0 2. Team 33-71 (.465) 11-13 (.846) 77.

NORTH CAROLINA STATE (80): Stoddard 4-11 1-2 9, Thompson 12-25 4-6 28, Burleson 9-20 2-6 20, Rivers 3-8 1-2 7, Towe 4-10 4-4 12, Spence 2-3 0-0 4, Hawkins 0-0 0-0 0. Team 34-77 (.442) 12-20 (.600) 80.

Halftime: Tied 35-35. Regulation: Tied 65-65. First Overtime: Tied 67-67.

KANSAS (51): Cook 1-3 2-4 4, Morningstar 5-13 0-0 10, Knight 0-5 0-0 0, Greenlee 3-7 0-0 6, Kivisto 2-7 2-5 6, Suttle 8-13 3-4 19, Smith 3-4 0-0 6. Team 22-52 (.423) 7-13 (.538) 51.

MARQUETTE (64): Ellis 2-9, 1-2 5, Tatum 5-11 4-6 14, Lucas 7-11 4-4 18, Walton 2-7 3-4 7, Washington 5-12 6-11 16, Daniels 0-2 0-0 0, Campbell 0-1 0-0 0, Homan 1-2 0-0 2, Delsman 0-1 2-2 2, Brennan 0-0 0-0 0, Bryant 0-0 0-0 0, Vollmer 0-0 0-0 0, Johnson 0-0 0-0 0. Team 22-56 (.393) 20-29 (.690) 64.

Halftime: Kansas 24-23.

ALL-TOURNAMENT TEAM

Tom Burleson, C, Sr., North Carolina State
Maurice Lucas, C, Jr., Marquette
David Thompson, F, Jr., North Carolina State*
Monte Towe, G, Jr., North Carolina State
Bill Walton, C, Sr., UCLA
*Named Most Outstanding Player

Putting Things in Perspective: Would N.C. State have become kingpin if the Wolfpack did not play at home (East Regional at Raleigh and nearby Greensboro)?

Scoring Leader: David Thompson, North Carolina State (97 points, 24.25 ppg).

Highest Scoring Average: John Shumate, Notre Dame (86 points, 28.7 ppg).

Rebounding Leader: Tom Burleson, North Carolina State (61 rebounds, 15.25 rpg).

Highest Rebounding Average: Marvin Barnes, Providence (51 rebounds, 17 rpg).

1974 CHAMPIONSHIP BRACKET

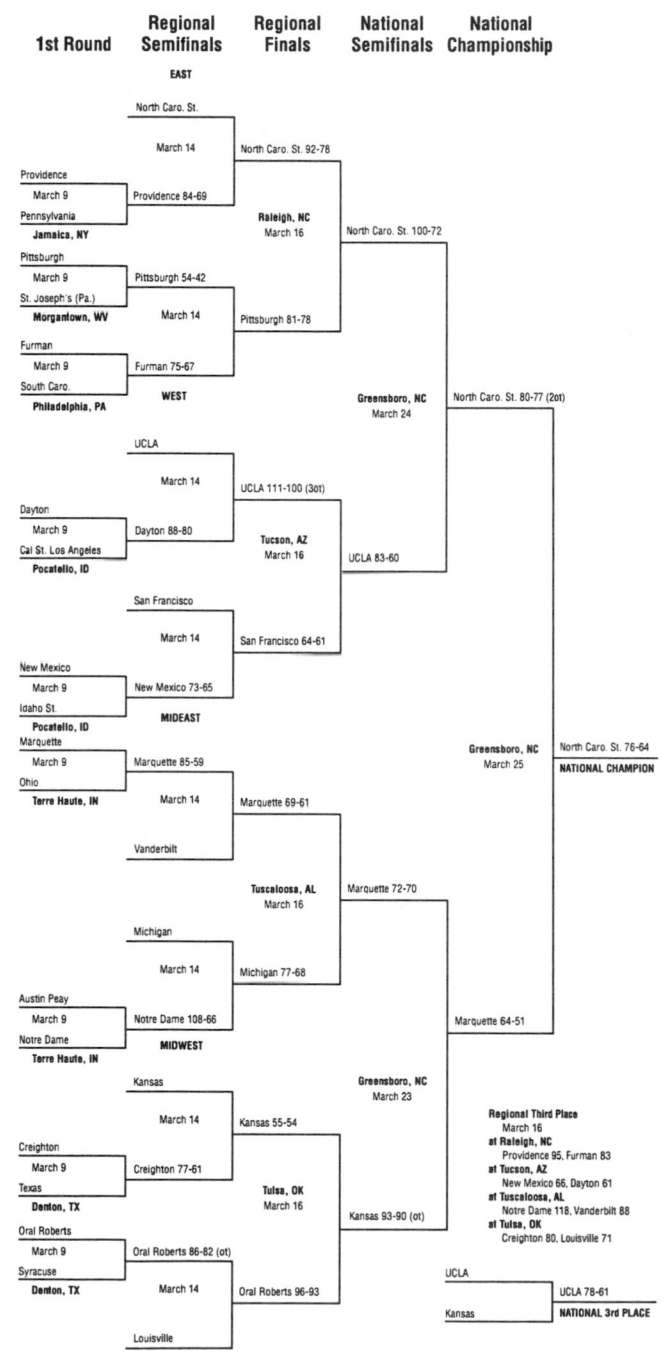

	Regional Semifinals	Regional Finals	National Semifinals	National Championship
1st Round				

EAST

North Caro. St.

North Caro. St. 92-78
March 14

Providence
March 9
Pennsylvania
Jamaica, NY

Providence 84-69

Raleigh, NC
March 16

North Caro. St. 100-72

Pittsburgh
March 9
St. Joseph's (Pa.)
Morgantown, WV

Pittsburgh 54-42
March 14

Pittsburgh 81-78

Furman
March 9
South Caro.
Philadelphia, PA

Furman 75-67

WEST

Greensboro, NC
March 24

North Caro. St. 80-77 (2ot)

UCLA

UCLA 111-100 (3ot)
March 14

Dayton
March 9
Cal St. Los Angeles
Pocatello, ID

Dayton 88-80

Tucson, AZ
March 16

UCLA 83-60

San Francisco

San Francisco 64-61
March 14

New Mexico
March 9
Idaho St.
Pocatello, ID

New Mexico 73-65

MIDEAST

Marquette
March 9
Ohio
Terre Haute, IN

Marquette 85-59
March 14

Marquette 69-61

Vanderbilt

Tuscaloosa, AL
March 16

Marquette 72-70

Greensboro, NC
March 25

North Caro. St. 76-64

NATIONAL CHAMPION

Michigan

Michigan 77-68
March 14

Austin Peay
March 9
Notre Dame
Terre Haute, IN

Notre Dame 108-66

MIDWEST

Marquette 64-51

Kansas

Kansas 55-54
March 14

Greensboro, NC
March 23

Creighton
March 9
Texas
Denton, TX

Creighton 77-61

Tulsa, OK
March 16

Kansas 93-90 (ot)

Oral Roberts
March 9
Syracuse
Denton, TX

Oral Roberts 86-82 (ot)
March 14

Oral Roberts 96-93

Louisville

Regional Third Place
March 16
at Raleigh, NC
Providence 95, Furman 83
at Tucson, AZ
New Mexico 66, Dayton 61
at Tuscaloosa, AL
Notre Dame 118, Vanderbilt 88
at Tulsa, OK
Creighton 80, Louisville 71

UCLA

UCLA 78-61

Kansas

NATIONAL 3rd PLACE

1974-75

AT A GLANCE

NCAA Champion: UCLA (28-3; coached by John Wooden; won Pacific-8 title by two games with a 12-2 record).

NIT Champion: Princeton (22-8; coached by Pete Carril; finished in second place in Ivy League with a 12-2 record, which was one game behind Penn).

NCIT Champion: Drake (19-10; finished in third place in Missouri Valley with a 9-5 record).

New Conference: ECC (spinoff of the Middle Atlantic).

New Rules: A non-jumper on the restraining circle during a jump ball may move around after the ball leaves the referee's hand. . . . A player assessed a foul is no longer required to raise his hand. . . . A 32-team bracket is adopted for the NCAA Tournament and teams other than the conference champion can be chosen on an at-large basis from the same league for the first time.

NCAA Probation: Centenary, Illinois, Long Beach State, Louisiana Tech, Maryland-Eastern Shore, McNeese State, Southern Methodist, Texas-Pan American, Western Kentucky, Wichita State.

NCAA Consensus First-Team All-Americans: Adrian Dantley, F, Soph., Notre Dame; John Lucas, G, Jr., Maryland; Scott May, F, Jr., Indiana; Dave Meyers, F, Sr., UCLA; David Thompson, F, Sr., North Carolina State.

National Player of the Year: Thompson (29.9 ppg, 8.2 rpg, 54.6 FG%).

National Coach of the Year: Bob Knight, Indiana (31-1/AP, UPI, NABC, USBWA).

John Wooden, earning a modest $32,500 base salary in his final season, concluded his 29-year coaching career with a 664-162 record. Wooden, the only coach to compile a double-digit total of Final Four victories, notched a 21-3 Final Four record with UCLA in 12 appearances from 1962-75. He won 94 percent of his games in his last 12 seasons (335-22 record).

"You could probably go back since collegiate basketball first started and never find anyone that has had the impact on the game that he's had," said Hall of Fame Louisville coach Denny Crum, who was an assistant under Wooden. "Not only in style of play, but just in terms of how he approached the game. The way that he dominated college basketball for so many years is mind boggling. You look around and no one can come close to doing what they did at UCLA, and of course Wooden was the architect of all that. He is probably as versatile a teacher as anyone I have ever seen. He was successful with small players, tall players and all different kinds of teams. He was the best. You kind of wish he was still coaching."

Wooden's final defeat was a 103-81 setback at Washington when Huskies reserve Larry Jackson collected 27 points and 14 rebounds. Washington claimed a 52-44 halftime advantage despite being outscored 16-0 at the free-throw line. The victory halted a 12-year losing skid for the Huskies against UCLA dating back to 1963.

Moses Malone, hailed as the country's No. 1 prep player, appeared bound for Maryland to help coach Lefty Driesell fulfill his prophecy of molding the Terrapins into "the UCLA of the East." But to Driesell's chagrin, Malone chose to bypass a collegiate career and went straight from high school to the pros with the Utah Stars of the American Basketball Association.

Richmond's Bob McCurdy won the national scoring title going away with outbursts of 41, 40, 46 and a school-record 53 points (vs. Appalachian State) in a 17-day stretch at the end of the season. As a freshman for Virginia, McCurdy scored 42 points against Maryland's Len Elmore-Tom McMillen freshmen, but subsequently transferred.

North Carolina State tied an ACC standard by extending its league winning streak to 27 consecutive games until Wake Forest, sparked by guard Skip Brown's 25 points, ended the Wolfpack's 37-game winning streak overall, 83-78. N.C. State's David Thompson set a school record with 57 points in 34 minutes against Buffalo State. UNC Charlotte's George Jackson did likewise with 44 points at Samford.

Gene Bartow (left) became coach of the UCLA Bruins after longtime coach John Wooden retired following the 1974–75 season.

McCurdy (32.9 ppg), Thompson (29.9), Iowa State's Hercle Ivy (28.3), Southern Mississippi's Mike Coleman (28.2), New Mexico State's John Williamson (27.2), Arkansas State's Don Scaife (27.1), Tennessee's Bernard King (26.4), Georgia's Jacky Dorsey (25.8) and UNCC's Jackson (24.5) set school records for highest scoring average in a single season.

No Clemson player has scored at least 35 points in a game since freshman Skip Wise poured in 38 in a 76-75 defeat against Pennsylvania in the IPTAY Tournament. . . . North Carolina trailed Wake Forest, 90-82, with only 50 seconds remaining in the first round of the ACC Tournament before the Tar Heels scored the final eight points of regulation and won in overtime, 101-100. Carolina also won the semifinals in overtime against Clemson en route to capturing the ACC Tournament title.

Purdue's Bruce Parkinson set a Big Ten Conference record with 18 assists against Minnesota. . . . Indiana's Bob Knight had one of the all-time greatest coaching staffs. His four assistants all eventually became head coaches for at least two different major colleges–Dave Bliss, Bob Donewald, Mike Krzyzewski and Bob Weltlich.

Texas-El Paso led the nation in team defense

for the third consecutive season under coach Don Haskins, a disciple of former Oklahoma State coach Hank Iba. . . . Penn, coached by Chuck Daly, won its sixth consecutive Ivy League championship. . . . Holy Cross (20-8, coached by George Blaney) was the nation's most-improved team. The Crusaders were 8-18 the previous season. . . . Temple's streak of 15 straight winning seasons ended when the Owls compiled a 7-19 record. Fellow Philadelphia Big 5 member St. Joseph's lost a school record 12 consecutive games en route to its first losing mark in 20 years (8-17).

An NCAA single-season high of 10 schools were on NCAA probation with sanctions prohibiting them from participating in the NCAA Tournament. . . . Long Beach State's 75-game homecourt winning streak, which started in 1968, was snapped in its home opener by San Francisco, 94-84. . . . Pepperdine lost more than 10 games in 12 consecutive seasons until the Waves compiled a 17-8 record. . . . Arizona's Fred Snowden became the first African-American coach to have a team appear in the Top 20 of a final wire-service poll (17th in UPI). The Wildcats were 22-7, with their first five defeats by an average of just three points. The Top 20 appearance was also the first for the school.

Centenary (25-4, coached by Larry Little), Middle Tennessee State (23-5, Jimmy Earle), Stetson (22-4, Glenn Wilkes) and Central Michigan (22-6, Dick Parfitt) had their winningest seasons in school Division I history. . . . Clemson made its lone Top 20 appearance in a final wire-service poll until 1987. The Tigers' Skip Wise became the only freshman to be an All-ACC first-team selection until Kenny Anderson in 1990.

Center Leon Douglas became the only Alabama player ever to become an NCAA consensus first- or second-team All-American. . . . Guard Ron Lee was the first Oregon player since 1940 to become an NCAA consensus first- or second-team All-American. . . . Seattle's Frank Oleynick made game-winning shots at the buzzer in games against Penn State (62-60), St. Mary's (72-70) and Pepperdine (72-71 in overtime) but the Chieftains still finished in the second division of the West Coast Athletic Conference. UNLV captured the WCAC championship in the Rebels' final season as a member of the league.

Northern Arizona's Tom DeBerry set a Big Sky Conference record with 12 steals against Portland State. . . . Stanford, which finished 12-14, upset top-ranked and NCAA champion-to-be UCLA, 64-60, in Howie Dallmar's final season as coach. . . . Pacific (12-14) incurred its first losing record in 12 years. . . . Los Angeles State competed in its final season at the major-college level.

George Ireland, Loyola of Chicago's coach when the Ramblers won the NCAA title in 1963, was forced to resign because of ailing health midway through the campaign. . . . South Florida coach Bill Gibson, 47, died of a heart attack following the season after returning from a recruiting trip. He had suffered a severe heart attack before the start of his only season as coach of the Bulls.

1974-75 FINAL NATIONAL POLLS

AP	UPI	SCHOOL (RECORD)	HEAD COACH
1	2	UCLA (28-3)	John Wooden
2	4	Kentucky (26-5)	Joe B. Hall
3	1	Indiana (31-1)	Bob Knight
4	3	Louisville (28-3)	Denny Crum
5	5	Maryland (24-5)	Lefty Driesell
6	–	Syracuse (23-9)	Roy Danforth
7	9	N.C. State (22-6)	Norman Sloan
8	7	Arizona State (25-4)	Ned Wulk
9	10	North Carolina (23-8)	Dean Smith
10	8	Alabama (22-5)	C.M. Newton
11	6	Marquette (23-4)	Al McGuire
12	–	Princeton (22-8)	Pete Carril
13	–	Cincinnati (23-6)	Gale Catlett
14	14	Notre Dame (19-10)	Digger Phelps
15	–	Kansas State (20-9)	Jack Hartman
16	–	Drake (19-10)	Bob Ortegel
17	14	UNLV (24-5)	Jerry Tarkanian
18	–	Oregon State (19-12)	Ralph Miller
19	–	Michigan (19-8)	Johnny Orr
20	11	Pennsylvania (23-5)	Chuck Daly
–	12	Southern Cal (18-8)	Bob Boyd
–	13	Utah State (21-6)	Dutch Belnap
–	16	Creighton (20-7)	Tom Apke
–	17	Arizona (22-7)	Fred Snowden
–	18	New Mexico State (20-7)	Lou Henson
–	19	Clemson (17-11)	Tates Locke
–	20	Texas-El Paso (20-6)	Don Haskins

Note: This was one of two years that the AP poll was released after the national postseason tournaments. Southern Cal (18th) and Centenary (19th) ranked among the AP's Top 20 before the national tourneys.

1975 NCAA Tournament

Summary: John Wooden's farewell resulted in another NCAA title. Richard Washington scored 54 points in two Final Four outings as a sophomore for UCLA after averaging a modest 4.1 points per game the previous season for the national third-place Bruins. UCLA erased a four-point deficit in the last 50 seconds of regulation to send its national semifinal game against Louisville into overtime. Three Louisville regulars shooting better than 52 percent from the floor for the season (swingman Junior Bridgeman, center Ricky Gallon and guard Phillip Bond) combined to hit 25 percent (6 of 24) in a 75-74 loss against UCLA. Adding insult to injury for the Cardinals was reserve guard Terry Howard missing the front end of a one-and-one free-throw opportunity in the closing seconds of overtime after he converted all 28 of his previous foul shots that season. The Bruins led a charmed life throughout the playoffs. They won their opener in overtime after Michigan's C.J. Kupec missed a shot at the end of regulation and defeated Montana by three points (67-64) in the West Regional semifinals when future pro standout Micheal Ray Richardson scored just two points for the Grizzlies. "I'm sad

1974–75 INDIVIDUAL LEADERS

SCORING

PLAYER	PTS.	AVG.
McCurdy, Richmond	855	32.9
Dantley, Notre Dame	883	30.4
Thompson, N.C. St.	838	29.9
Burden, Utah	747	28.7
Ivy, Iowa St.	737	28.3
Coleman, Southern Miss.	564	28.2
Oleynick, Seattle	709	27.3
Scaife, Arkansas St.	678	27.1
Rogers, Pan American	588	26.7
Adams, Oklahoma	691	26.6

REBOUNDING

PLAYER	REB.	AVG.
Parish, Centenary	447	15.4
Irving, Hofstra	323	15.4
Warner, Maine	352	14.1

Roane, Md.-Eastern Shore	356	13.7
Mayes, Furman	394	13.6
Robinzine, DePaul	338	13.5
Barnett, Samford	350	13.5
Sorrell, Middle Tenn. St.	373	13.3
King, Pan American	293	13.3
Adams, Oklahoma	346	13.3
Hayes, Idaho St.	346	13.3

Note: Parish's rebounding totals were discounted by the NCAA because Centenary was on probation.

FIELD GOAL PERCENTAGE

PLAYER	FGM	FGA	PCT.
King, Tennessee	273	439	.622
Fleischer, Duke	178	287	.620
Meriweather, S. Ill.	229	370	.619
Roundfield, Central Mich.	216	353	.612
Glenn, Southern Ill.	196	321	.611

Allison, Arkansas	172	282	.610
Andreas, Ohio St.	210	347	.605
Kupchak, North Carolina	239	397	.602
Tampa, East Tenn. St.	117	195	.600
Cutter, Western Michigan	134	224	.598

FREE THROW PERCENTAGE

PLAYER	FTM	FTA	PCT.
Oleynick, Seattle	135	152	.888
Caldwell, Florida	102	115	.887
Brookins, Creighton	98	111	.883
Johnson, Auburn	102	116	.879
Kraft, Air Force	83	95	.874
Lee, Syracuse	98	114	.860
Hays, Montana	91	106	.858
Johnson, Morehead St.	91	106	.858
Krueger, Texas	102	119	.857
Rose, NE Louisiana	83	97	.856

1974–75 TEAM LEADERS

SCORING OFFENSE

SCHOOL	PTS.	AVG.
South Alabama	2412	92.8
North Carolina St.	2596	92.7
Houston	2407	92.6
Kentucky	2858	92.2
Illinois St.	2375	91.3

SCORING DEFENSE

SCHOOL	PTS.	AVG.
Texas-El Paso	1491	57.3
New Mexico St.	1601	59.3
Minnesota	1577	60.7
Princeton	1835	61.2
Marquette	1679	62.2

SCORING MARGIN

SCHOOL	OFF.	DEF.	MAR.
UNC Charlotte	88.9	65.2	23.7

Indiana	88.0	65.9	22.1
Maryland	89.9	74.6	15.3
North Carolina St.	92.7	77.9	14.8
Pan American	87.0	73.2	13.8

WON-LOST PERCENTAGE

SCHOOL	W-L	PCT.
Indiana	31-1	.969
Pan American	22-2	.917
Louisville	28-3	.903
UCLA	28-3	.903
UNC Charlotte	23-3	.885

FIELD GOAL PERCENTAGE

SCHOOL	FGM	FGA	PCT.
Maryland	1049	1918	.547
North Carolina	1037	1933	.536
Arkansas	807	1524	.530
Tennessee	927	1756	.528
Duke	864	1672	.517

FREE THROW PERCENTAGE

SCHOOL	FTM	FTA	PCT.
Vanderbilt	530	692	.766
Florida	456	596	.765
Seattle	303	399	.759
Maryland	509	672	.757
Drake	402	533	.754

REBOUND MARGIN

SCHOOL	OWN	OPP.	MAR.
Stetson	47.1	34.7	12.4
South Alabama	52.6	42.2	10.4
Pan American	45.6	35.7	9.9
Maryland	43.5	34.4	9.1
Minnesota	39.6	30.8	8.8

1974–75 NCAA CHAMPION: UCLA

SEASON STATISTICS OF UCLA REGULARS

PLAYER	POS.	CL.	G.	FG%	FT%	PPG	RPG
Dave Meyers	F	Sr.	31	.484	.736	18.3	7.9
Richard Washington	C-F	So.	31	.576	.724	15.9	7.8
Marques Johnson	F	So.	29	.543	.686	11.6	7.1
Pete Trgovich	G	Sr.	31	.431	.640	10.2	3.3
Ralph Drollinger	C	Jr.	31	.532	.659	8.8	7.4
Andre McCarter	G	Jr.	31	.359	.729	7.0	2.3
Jim Spillane	G	So.	29	.396	.762	4.5	1.2
Wilbert Olinde	F	So.	22	.474	.560	3.1	2.0
Casey Corliss	F	So.	21	.522	.850	3.1	1.3
Ray Townsend	G	Fr.	20	.410	.667	1.9	0.7
TEAM TOTALS			31	.479	.703	84.7	45.7

Assists leader: McCarter 156.

1975 FINAL FOUR CHAMPIONSHIP GAME

SAN DIEGO, CA

UCLA (92)	MIN.	FG-A	FT-A	REB.	A	PF	PTS.
Meyers	40	9-18	6-7	11	1	4	24
M. Johnson	24	3-9	0-1	7	1	2	6
Washington	40	12-23	4-5	12	3	4	28
Trgovich	40	7-16	2-4	5	4	4	16
McCarter	40	3-6	2-3	2	14	1	8
Drollinger	16	4-6	2-5	13	0	4	10
Team				5			
TOTALS	200	38-78	16-25	55	23	19	92

FG%: .487. FT%: .640. Blocks: 7. Turnovers: 13 (Washington 5). Steals: 3.

KENTUCKY (85)	MIN.	FG-A	FT-A	REB.	A	PF	PTS.
Grevey	36	13-30	8-10	5	1	4	34
Guyette	24	7-11	2-2	7	3	3	16
Robey	14	1-3	0-0	9	1	5	2
Conner	38	4-12	1-2	5	6	1	9
Flynn	25	3-9	4-5	3	2	4	10
Givens	25	3-10	2-3	6	1	3	8
Johnson	17	0-3	0-0	3	1	3	0

Phillips	16	1-7	2-3	6	0	4	4
Lee	3	1-1	0-0	1	0	0	2
Hall	2	0-0	0-0	0	1	1	0
Team				4			
TOTALS	200	33-86	19-25	49	16	28	85

FG%: .384. FT%: .760. Blocks: 1. Turnovers: 13. Steals: 6.
Halftime: UCLA 43-40.

NATIONAL SEMIFINALS

SYRACUSE (79): Hackett 4-6 6-9 14, Sease 7-11 4-4 18, Seibert 2-3 0-2 4, Lee 10-17 3-3 23, Williams 2-9 0-1 4, King 2-8 1-3 5, Kindel 1-3 1-2 3, Shaw 0-0 0-0 0, Parker 2-3 4-7 8, Byrnes 0-0 0-1 0, Kelley 0-1 0-0 0, Meadors 0-0 0-0 0. Team 30-61 (.492) 19-32 (.594) 79.

KENTUCKY (95): Grevey 5-13 4-5 14, Guyette 2-3 3-4 7, Robey 3-8 3-7 9, Conner 5-9 2-4 12, Flynn 4-9 3-5 11, Givens 10-20 4-8 24, Johnson 2-4 0-0 4, Phillips 5-6 0-2 10, Lee 1-4 0-1 2, Haskins 0-0 2-2 2, Hale 0-1 0-0 0, Hall 0-0 0-0 0, Warford 0-0 0-0 0, Smith 0-1 0-0 0. Team 37-78 (.474) 21-38 (.553) 95.

Halftime: Kentucky 44-32.

LOUISVILLE (74): Murphy 14-28 5-7 33, Cox 5-8 4-11 14, Bunton 3-4 1-2 7, Bridgeman 4-15 4-4 12, Bond 2-6 2-2 6, Whitfield 0-0 0-0 0, Gallon 0-3 0-0 0, Brown 1-1 0-0 2, Wilson 0-0 0-0 0, Howard 0-0 0-1 0. Team 29-65 (.446) 16-27 (.593) 74.

UCLA (75): Meyers 6-16 4-16 16, Johnson 5-10, 0-0 10, Washington 11-19 4-6 26, Trgovich 6-12 0-0 12, McCarter 3-12 0-0 6, Drollinger 1-2 1-2 3, Olinde 0-0 0-0 0, Spillane 1-2 0-0 2. Team 33-73 (.452) 9-14 (.643) 75.

Halftime: Louisville 37-33. **Regulation:** Tied 65-65.

ALL-TOURNAMENT TEAM

Kevin Grevey, F, Sr., Kentucky
Jim Lee, G, Sr., Syracuse
David Meyers, F, Sr., UCLA
Allen Murphy, F, Sr., Louisville
Richard Washington, C-F, Soph., UCLA*
***Named Most Outstanding Player**

I'm getting out, but I'm going out pretty happy, too," Wooden said. "I told them (his team) how proud I was of them. I told them they'd won a national championship but to keep it in perspective. There are other things ahead."

Outcome for Defending Champion: N.C. State (22-6) finished in a three-way tie for second place in the ACC. Despite the presence of national player of the year David Thompson, the ACC Tournament runner-up did not compete in the NCAA playoffs after losing twice against regular-season champion Maryland in league play.

Star Gazing: Indiana, undefeated entering the tourney (29-0), lost the Mideast Regional final against Kentucky (92-90) despite Kent Benson's 33 points and tourney-high 23 rebounds.

Knight said he made a mistake by playing an offensive player (John Laskowski) substantially more minutes (33 to 3) than defensive standout Tom Abernethy. Kentucky prevailed despite 6-of-19 field-goal shooting by leading scorer Kevin Grevey. UK guards Jimmy Dan Conner and Mike Flynn combined to outscore Indiana counterparts Quinn Buckner and Bobby Wilkerson, 39-22.

One and Only: Louisville is the only school to lead UCLA at halftime in the 20 Final Four games for the Bruins' 10 titlists under Wooden. The Cardinals led UCLA at intermission, 37-33, in the national semifinals before bowing to the Bruins in overtime, 75-74.

Numbers Game: North Carolina, starting its streak of being the only school to participate in the NCAA Tournament every year since conferences were first permitted to have more than one representative, became the only school to hit more than 60 percent from the floor in a playoff series. The Tar Heels, who won the East Regional third-place game, sank 113 of 187 shots from the floor (60.4 percent) in three contests. . . . Carolina was eliminated by Syracuse, 78-76, in the East Regional semifinals although Rudy Hackett, the leading scorer and rebounder for the Orangemen, was limited to six points and one rebound. Hackett had three playoff games with at least 28 points and 12 rebounds. . . . Incredibly, Final Four Most Outstanding Players-to-be Jack Givens of Kentucky and Butch Lee of Marquette were blanked in the same game in their freshman season when Kentucky mauled Marquette, 76-54, in the Mideast Regional. . . . Kansas State sustained its third regional final defeat in four years under coach Jack Hartman. Standout Wildcats freshman guard Mike Evans hit only 6 of 21 field-goal attempts in a 95-87 overtime loss to Syracuse in the East Regional final. He was wearing a hockey goalie mask after breaking his nose in the semifinals. . . . Alabama appeared in the NCAA playoffs for the first time. . . . Kansas had a playoff-record six players disqualified because of fouls in a 77-71 defeat to Notre Dame in the opening round of the Midwest Regional. . . . Louisville's Junior Bridgeman (36 points vs. Rutgers) and Mitch Kupchak (36 vs. Boston College) tied for the highest-scoring game in the playoffs.

What If: Kentucky had four regulars shoot better than 50 percent from the floor during the campaign–forward Kevin Grevey, guard Jimmy Dan Conner, and centers Rick Robey and Mike Phillips. If only they combined to hit 44.2 percent of their field-goal attempts instead of 36.5 percent (19 of 52) in the championship game, the Wildcats could have defeated UCLA rather than losing 92-85. . . . Kentucky could have received more of a challenge from Marquette (23-4) in the Mideast Regional if Maurice Lucas had stayed in college and exercised the remainder of his eligibility. . . . In another opener, Michigan (19-8) might have given UCLA more of a contest in the West Regional if Campy Russell didn't left school early. . . . Notre Dame (19-10) probably would have had more of a chance of advancing beyond the regional semifinals if Gary Brokaw didn't leave school early. . . . Arizona (22-7) might have been one of the WAC representatives in the NCAA playoffs instead of Arizona State or Texas-El Paso if Eric Money and Coniel Norman didn't forsake their remaining eligibility.

Putting Things in Perspective: Consensus first-team All-American forward Scott May's broken arm possibly cost Indiana the national crown. May returned to the lineup against Kentucky, but he was rusty and scored just two points.

Scoring Leader: Jim Lee, Syracuse (119 points, 23.8 ppg).

Highest Scoring Average: Adrian Dantley, Notre Dame (92 points, 30.7 ppg).

Rebounding Leader: Richard Washington, UCLA (60 rebounds, 12 rpg).

Highest Rebounding Average: Mike Franklin, Cincinnati (49 rebounds, 16.3 rpg).

1975 CHAMPIONSHIP BRACKET

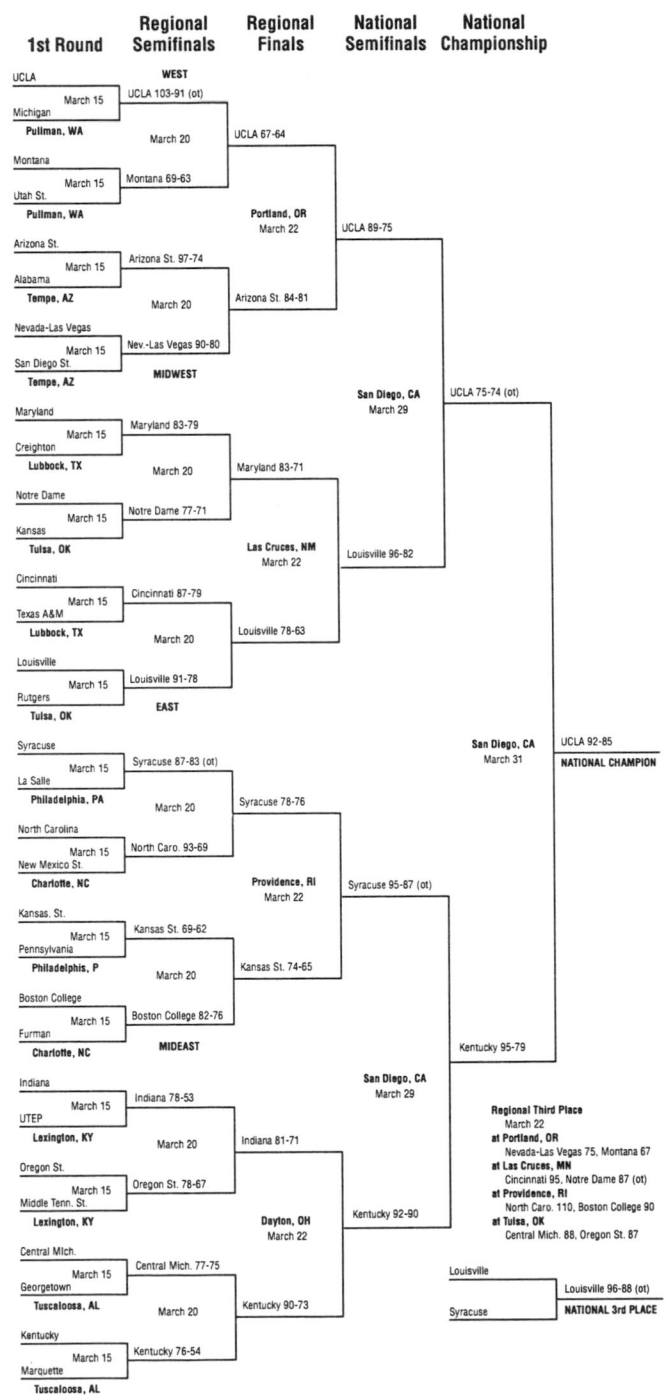

1st Round	Regional Semifinals	Regional Finals	National Semifinals	National Championship

WEST

UCLA
March 15
Michigan
Pullman, WA
UCLA 103-91 (ot)
March 20
UCLA 67-64

Montana
March 15
Utah St.
Pullman, WA
Montana 69-63

Portland, OR
March 22
UCLA 89-75

Arizona St.
March 15
Alabama
Tempe, AZ
Arizona St. 97-74
March 20
Arizona St. 84-81

Nevada-Las Vegas
March 15
San Diego St.
Tempe, AZ
Nev.-Las Vegas 90-80

MIDWEST

San Diego, CA
March 29
UCLA 75-74 (ot)

Maryland
March 15
Creighton
Lubbock, TX
Maryland 83-79
March 20
Maryland 83-71

Notre Dame
March 15
Kansas
Tulsa, OK
Notre Dame 77-71

Las Cruces, NM
March 22
Louisville 96-82

Cincinnati
March 15
Texas A&M
Lubbock, TX
Cincinnati 87-79
March 20
Louisville 78-63

Louisville
March 15
Rutgers
Tulsa, OK
Louisville 91-78

EAST

San Diego, CA
March 31
UCLA 92-85
NATIONAL CHAMPION

Syracuse
March 15
La Salle
Philadelphia, PA
Syracuse 87-83 (ot)
March 20
Syracuse 78-76

North Carolina
March 15
New Mexico St.
Charlotte, NC
North Caro. 93-69

Providence, RI
March 22
Syracuse 95-87 (ot)

Kansas. St.
March 15
Pennsylvania
Philadelphis, P
Kansas St. 69-62
March 20
Kansas St. 74-65

Boston College
March 15
Furman
Charlotte, NC
Boston College 82-76

MIDEAST

Kentucky 95-79

San Diego, CA
March 29

UCLA 92-85

Indiana
March 15
UTEP
Lexington, KY
Indiana 78-53
March 20
Indiana 81-71

Oregon St.
March 15
Middle Tenn. St.
Lexington, KY
Oregon St. 78-67

Dayton, OH
March 22
Kentucky 92-90

Central Mich.
March 15
Georgetown
Tuscaloosa, AL
Central Mich. 77-75
March 20
Kentucky 90-73

Kentucky
March 15
Marquette
Tuscaloosa, AL
Kentucky 76-54

Regional Third Place
March 22
at Portland, OR
Nevada-Las Vegas 75, Montana 67
at Las Cruces, MN
Cincinnati 95, Notre Dame 87 (ot)
at Providence, RI
North Caro. 110, Boston College 90
at Tulsa, OK
Central Mich. 88, Oregon St. 87

Louisville
Louisville 96-88 (ot)
Syracuse
NATIONAL 3rd PLACE

1975–76

AT A GLANCE

NCAA Champion: Indiana (32-0; coached by Bob Knight; won Big Ten title by four games with an 18-0 record).

NIT Champion: Kentucky (20-10; coached by Joe B. Hall; finished in a tie for fourth place in the SEC with an 11-7 record).

New Conferences: Metro (disbanded after 1994-95 season), Southland (moved up from Division II).

New Rules: NCAA Tournament regional third-place games are abolished. . . . NIT field reduced from 16 teams to 12 for one year.

NCAA Probation: Canisius, Centenary, Clemson, Long Beach State, Louisiana Tech, Minnesota, Seton Hall, Southwestern Louisiana.

NCAA Consensus First-Team All-Americans: Kent Benson, C, Jr., Indiana; Adrian Dantley, F, Jr., Notre Dame; John Lucas, G, Sr., Maryland; Scott May, F, Sr., Indiana; Richard Washington, C-F, Jr., UCLA.

National Players of the Year: Dantley (28.6 ppg, 10.1 rpg, 58.8 FG%/USBWA) and May (23.5 ppg, 7.7 rpg, 52.7 FG%/AP, UPI, NABC, Naismith).

National Coaches of the Year: Indiana's Bob Knight (32-0/AP, USBWA); Michigan's Johnny Orr (25-7/NABC), and Rutgers' Tom Young (31-2/UPI).

Tennessee's Ernie Grunfeld.

Indiana tied North Carolina '57 for the all-time record for victories by an undefeated team. The Hoosiers' schedule was one of the most difficult of any NCAA kingpin. In 14 games outside the rigorous Big Ten, their opponents combined to win more than three-fourths of their games excluding the contests with Indiana. "I don't think a team should really give a damn who it's playing against," IU coach Bob Knight said. "It doesn't make any difference who you play, how good they are, how poor you are. It's not a game against an opponent; it's a game against your potential. If it is going to be a good team, every time it goes on the floor it is going to try to play against its potential. When it walks off the floor, it need not look at the scorebord to know if it has played up to its potential or not. It needs only to reflect back on the performance, both individually and collectively, relative to potential, to determine the success of the venture. I think that's the whole essence of athletics."

Indiana (32-0, coached by Bob Knight), Rutgers (31-2, Tom Young), Western Michigan (25-3, Eldon Miller) and North Texas State (22-4, Bill Blakeley) had their winningest seasons in school history. Rutgers made its first Top 20 appearance in a final wire-service poll. North Texas State compiled a 6-20 mark the previous season.

Illinois lost 13 consecutive games against Purdue until the Illini whipped the Boilermakers, 71-63. . . . Purdue (25 of 25) and Wisconsin (22 of 22) combined to sink all 47 of their free-throw attempts in a game on February 7. The Boilermakers won the game, 85-74. It was one of 14 consecutive defeats for the Badgers on the heels of erasing a 22-point deficit in an 82-81

1975–76 INDIVIDUAL LEADERS

SCORING

PLAYER	PTS.	AVG.
Rogers, Pan American	919	36.8
Williams, Portland St.	834	30.9
Furlow, Michigan St.	793	29.4
Dantley, Notre Dame	829	28.6
Carr, North Carolina St.	798	26.6
Dixon, Hardin-Simmons	707	26.2
Tripucka, Lafayette	679	26.1
Birdsong, Houston	730	26.1
Grunfeld, Tennessee	683	25.3
Smith, Missouri	783	25.3

REBOUNDING

PLAYER	REB.	AVG.
Parish, Centenary*	486	18.0
Pellom, Buffalo	420	16.2
Barnett, Samford	354	15.4

Irving, Hofstra	423	14.6
Thomas, Connecticut	402	13.9
Rudd, McNeese St.	328	13.7
Webster, Indiana St.	339	13.6
Terrell, Southern Methodist	374	13.4
Stephens, Drexel	307	13.3
King, Tennessee	325	13.0
Kyle, Cleveland St.	325	13.0

Note: Parish's rebounding totals were discounted by the NCAA because Centenary was on probation.

FIELD GOAL PERCENTAGE

PLAYER	FGM	FGA	PCT.
Moncrief, Arkansas	149	224	.665
Brown, East Tenn. St.	181	274	.661
Thorpe, Virginia Tech	165	251	.657
Shute, Texas-Arlington	136	209	.651
Abrams, S. Illinois	145	224	.647

Cutter, W. Michigan	140	217	.645
Pierson, Georgia St.	187	291	.643
Davis, Florida St.	143	224	.638
Nordhorn, Stetson	146	234	.624
Hillard, Memphis St.	226	366	.617

FREE THROW PERCENTAGE

PLAYER	FTM	FTA	PCT.
Dufelmeier, Loyola (Ill.)	71	80	.888
O'Connell, Stetson	68	77	.883
Drake, Central Mich.	101	115	.878
Furlow, Michigan St.	177	202	.876
Rood, Hofstra	77	88	.875
Brown, Wake Forest	97	111	.874
Carter, Hawaii	117	136	.860
Macy, Purdue	85	99	.859
Rogers, Pan American	197	230	.857
Evans, Kansas St.	70	82	.854

1975–76 TEAM LEADERS

SCORING OFFENSE

SCHOOL	PTS.	AVG.
UNLV	3426	110.5
North Texas St.	2497	96.0
Pan American	2391	95.6
Rutgers	3079	93.3
Notre Dame	2579	88.9

SCORING DEFENSE

SCHOOL	PTS.	AVG.
Princeton	1427	52.9
Texas-El Paso	1480	56.9
Colgate	1390	57.9
Drexel	1364	59.3
Marquette	1742	60.1

SCORING MARGIN

SCHOOL	OFF.	DEF.	MAR.
UNLV	110.5	89.0	21.5
Indiana	82.1	64.8	17.3

Rutgers	93.3	76.9	16.4
UNC Charlotte	84.5	69.0	15.5
Pan American	95.6	80.7	14.9
Florida St.	83.9	69.0	14.9

WON-LOST PERCENTAGE

SCHOOL	W-L	PCT.
Indiana	32-0	1.000
Rutgers	31-2	.939
UNLV	29-2	.935
Marquette	27-2	.931
Western Michigan	25-3	.893

FIELD GOAL PERCENTAGE

SCHOOL	FGM	FGA	PCT.
Maryland	996	1854	.537
Arkansas	910	1715	.531
Oregon St.	839	1594	.526
North Carolina	966	1838	.526
Duke	968	1853	.522

FREE THROW PERCENTAGE

SCHOOL	FGM	FGA	PCT.
Morehead St.	452	577	.783
Bradley	443	572	.774
Central Michigan	328	425	.772
Ohio	412	534	.772
Michigan St.	443	576	.769

REBOUND MARGIN

SCHOOL	OWN	OPP.	MAR.
Notre Dame	46.3	34.1	12.2
Buffalo	51.5	39.7	11.8
Virginia Tech	45.6	35.3	10.3
Connecticut	43.0	32.8	10.2
UNC Charlotte	44.4	34.2	10.2

overtime victory against Ohio State. . . . Minnesota's Mychal Thompson established a Big Ten Conference standard with 12 blocked shots in a game against Ohio State. . . . St. Joseph's had an NCAA-record eight players foul out in a 109-96 defeat in double overtime against Xavier. The victory enabled the Musketeers to compile their first winning record (14-12) in 12 years.

Michigan State's Terry Furlow (50 vs. Iowa) set school Division I single-game scoring records. Furlow became the only Big Ten player to average more than 30 points per game (32.7) in conference competition in a 23-year span from 1970-71 through 1992-93. . . . Furlow (29.4),

Lafayette's Todd Tripucka (26.1), Minnesota's Mychal Thompson (25.9) and Missouri's Willie Smith (25.3) set school records for highest scoring average in a single season.

Missouri, coached by Norm Stewart, captured its first conference crown since 1930. . . . Oregon guard Ron Lee became the only player in Pacific-8 Conference history to be named to the all-league first team four consecutive years. . . . UNLV's only regular-season defeat was at Pepperdine, 93-91.

Tennessee's Ernie Grunfeld (25.3) and Bernard King (25.2) became one of only four sets

COACH: BOB KNIGHT

IU	1975-76 OPPONENT	IU'S HIGH SCORER
84	UCLA* 64	May 33
83	Florida State* 59	May 24
63	Notre Dame 60	May 25
77	Kentucky* (OT) 68	Benson/May 27
93	Georgia 56	May 18
101	Virginia Tech 74	May 27
106	Columbia* 63	Benson 15
97	Manhattan* 61	May 32
76	at St. John's 69	May 29
66	at Ohio State 64	May 24
78	Northwestern 61	Benson 22
80	at Michigan 74	Benson 33
69	at Michigan State 57	Benson 23
83	at Illinois 55	May 27
71	Purdue 67	May 32
85	at Minnesota 76	Abernethy 22
88	at Iowa 73	May 32
114	Wisconsin 61	May 30
72	Michigan (OT) 67	May 27
85	Michigan State 70	Benson 38
58	Illinois 48	Benson 17
74	at Purdue 71	May 26
76	Minnesota 64	Abernethy 22
101	Iowa 81	Buckner 24
96	at Wisconsin 67	May 41
76	at Northwestern 63	May 24
96	Ohio State 67	Benson/May 21

NCAA TOURNAMENT

90	St. John's* 70	May 33
74	Alabama* 69	May 25
65	Marquette* 56	Benson 18
65	UCLA* 51	Benson 16
86	Michigan* 68	May 26

*Neutral court games.

of teammates in NCAA history to each average more than 25 points per game in a single season. King was the first Tennessee to become an NCAA consensus first- or second-team All-American. With King idled by a broken right thumb, half of the Bernie-Ernie show was on the sideline and Grunfeld's 36 points weren't enough to prevent an 81-75 defeat against VMI in the first round of the East Regional. The Volunteers defeated national runner-up Michigan early in the season.

Merlin Wilson became the first Georgetown player to finish his career with at least 1,000 points (1,191) and 1,000 rebounds (1,230). . . . Centenary's Robert Parish finished his career as the only player ever to rank among the national top five in rebounding for four seasons. Parish had a total of 16 games with at least 20 rebounds. . . . North Carolina outlasted Tulane, 113-106, in four overtimes at the Superdome in New Orleans.

Cal State Fullerton's Kerry Davis (27 vs. Central Michigan) and SMU's Ira Terrell (26 vs. New Mexico State) set school single-game rebounding records. . . . Virginia Military (22-10), posting its first winning record in 33 years, earned its only undisputed Southern Conference regular-season championship. VMI was coached by Bill Blair. . . . Washington finished in the Top 20 of a final wire-service poll for the first time since 1953. Centenary, Pepperdine and Western Michigan made the only appearance in a final wire-service in their school history.

1975-76 FINAL NATIONAL POLLS

AP	UPI	SCHOOL (RECORD)	HEAD COACH
1	1	Indiana (32-0)	Bob Knight
2	2	Marquette (27-2)	Al McGuire
3	4	UNLV (29-2)	Jerry Tarkanian
4	3	Rutgers (31-2)	Tom Young
5	5	UCLA (27-5)	Gene Bartow
6	7	Alabama (23-5)	C.M. Newton
7	8	Notre Dame (23-6)	Digger Phelps
8	6	North Carolina (25-4)	Dean Smith
9	9	Michigan (25-7)	Johnny Orr
10	19	Western Michigan (25-3)	Eldon Miller
11	13	Maryland (22-6)	Lefty Driesell
12	16	Cincinnati (25-6)	Gale Catlett
13	14	Tennessee (21-6)	Ray Mears
14	11	Missouri (26-5)	Norm Stewart
15	12	Arizona (24-9)	Fred Snowden
16	–	Texas Tech (25-6)	Gerald Myers
17	–	DePaul (20-9)	Ray Meyer
18	15	Virginia (18-12)	Terry Holland
19	–	Centenary (22-5)	Larry Little
20	–	Pepperdine (22-6)	Gary Colson
–	10	Washington (23-5)	Marv Harshman
–	16	Florida State (21-6)	Hugh Durham
–	18	St. John's (23-6)	Lou Carnesecca
–	19	Princeton (22-5)	Pete Carril

Western Michigan compiled a 25-3 record for its only season without at least 10 defeats in a 35-year span from 1956-57 through 1990-91. Meanwhile, Air Force posted a 16-9 mark for its only season without at least 10 setbacks in a 32-year stretch from 1962-63 through 1993-94.

Ohio State's Fred Taylor ended his 18-year coaching career with a 297-158 record. His final

Indiana guard Quinn Buckner (left) jumps for the rebound as teammate Scott May looks on.

Rutgers' Phil Sellers hauls down a rebound.

season (6-20 mark) represented the most defeats in the Buckeyes' history until 1994-95. . . . Mike Krzyzewski began his distinguished coaching career at Army with a modest 11-14 record, which was eight games better than the previous season for the Cadets when they posted their worst winning percentage in school history (3-22, .120). In 1976-77, Army reached the 20-win plateau.

1976 NCAA Tournament

Summary: Indiana's Scott May and Kent Benson combined for 40.8 points and 16.5 rebounds per game for team winning national championship by an average of 13.2 points. The Hoosiers kept a perfect record intact despite trailing in the second half of three of their five tournament games, including Mideast Regional contests against Alabama and Marquette

accounting for two of the 11 contests they won by single-digit margins. The closest result was a two-point triumph at Ohio State in their Big Ten Conference opener. Knight's alma mater finished in the Big Ten basement that season with a 2-16 league record. Bob Wilkerson collected 19 rebounds and seven assists in a 65-51 victory over UCLA in the national semifinals before captain Quinn Buckner contributed 16 points and eight rebounds in the championship game against Michigan. Trailing by six points at intermission in the final and playing without Wilkerson after the guard sustained a concussion early in the game, the Hoosiers shot 60 percent from the floor in the second half to come from behind and win (86-68). May, Benson and Buckner collaborated for 36 of Indiana's first 38 points in the second half against the Wolverines, an overtime loser at Indiana in Big Ten Conference competition.

1975-76 NCAA CHAMPION: INDIANA

SEASON STATISTICS OF INDIANA REGULARS

PLAYER	POS.	CL.	G.	FG%	FT%	PPG	RPG
Scott May	F	Sr.	32	.527	.782	23.5	7.7
Kent Benson	C	Jr.	32	.578	.684	17.3	8.8
Tom Abernethy	F	Sr.	32	.561	.743	10.0	5.3
Quinn Buckner	G	Sr.	32	.441	.488	8.9	2.8
Bobby Wilkerson	G-F	Sr.	32	.493	.630	7.8	4.9
Wayne Radford	G	So.	30	.563	.712	4.7	2.1
Jim Crews	G	Sr.	31	.468	.857	3.3	0.7
Jim Wisman	G	So.	26	.367	.724	2.5	0.8
Rich Valavicius	F	Fr.	28	.483	.625	2.4	1.8
TEAM TOTALS			32	.517	.698	82.1	41.4

Assists leader: Wilkerson 171. **Steals leader:** Buckner 65.

1976 FINAL FOUR CHAMPIONSHIP GAME

PHILADELPHIA, PA

MICHIGAN (68)	MIN.	FG-A	FT-A	REB.	A	PF	PTS.
Britt	31	5-6	1-1	3	2	5	11
Robinson	38	4-8	0-1	6	5	2	8
Hubbard	31	4-8	2-2	11	0	5	10
Green	39	7-16	4-5	6	2	3	18
Grote	35	4-9	4-6	1	3	4	12
Bergen	5	0-1	0-0	0	0	1	0
Staton	9	2-5	3-4	2	0	3	7
Baxter	6	0-2	0-0	0	0	2	0
Thompson	2	0-0	0-0	0	0	0	0
Hardy	4	1-2	0-0	2	0	0	2
Team				1			
TOTALS	200	27-57	14-19	32	12	25	68

FG%: .474. **FT%:** .737. **Blocks:** 3. **Turnovers:** 19 (Robinson 6). **Steals:** 9.

INDIANA (86)	MIN.	FG-A	FT-A	REB.	A	PF	PTS.
Abernethy	35	4-8	3-3	4	1	2	11
May	39	10-17	6-6	8	2	4	26
Benson	39	11-20	3-5	9	2	3	25
Wilkerson	2	0-1	0-0	0	0	1	0
Buckner	39	5-10	6-9	8	4	4	16
Radford	7	0-1	0-0	1	0	0	0
Crews	12	0-1	2-2	1	4	1	2
Wisman	21	0-1	2-3	1	6	4	2
Valavicius	4	1-1	0-0	0	0	0	2
Haymore	1	1-1	0-0	1	0	0	2
Bender	1	0-0	0-0	0	0	0	0
Team				3			
TOTALS	200	32-61	22-28	36	19	19	86

FG%: .525. **FT%:** .786. **Blocks:** 2. **Turnovers:** 13. **Steals:** 10 (Buckner 5).
Halftime: Michigan 35-29.

NATIONAL SEMIFINALS

MICHIGAN (86): Britt 5-9 1-1 11, Robinson 8-13 4-5 20, Hubbard 8-13 0-3 16, Green 7-16 2-2 16, Grote 4-13 6-6 14, Baxter 2-5 1-2 5, Staton 1-1 2-2 4, Bergen 0-0 0-0 0, Thompson 0-0 0-0 0, Schinnerer 0-0 0-0 0, Hardy 0-1 0-0 0, Jones 0-0 0-0 0, Lillard 0-0 0-0 0. Team 35-70 (.500) 16-21 (.762) 86.

RUTGERS (70): Sellers 5-13 1-3 11, Copeland 7-12 1-1 15, Bailey 1-3 4-6 6, Jordan 6-20 4-4 16, Dabney 5-17 0-1 10, Anderson 3-8 0-1 6, Conlin 2-2 0-0 4, Hefele 1-1 0-0 2. Team 30-76 (.395) 10-16 (.625) 70.

Halftime: Michigan 46-29.

UCLA (51): Washington 6-15 3-4 15, Johnson 6-10 0-1 12, Greenwood 2-5 1-2 5, Townsend 2-10 0-0 4, McCarter 2-9 0-0 4, Drollinger 0-3 2-2 2, Holland 0-2 0-0 0, Spillane 0-2 0-0 0, Smith 3-4 0-0 6, Hamilton 0-1 1-2 1, Vroman 0-0 0-0 0, Lippert 0-0 2-2 2, Olinde 0-0 0-0 0. Team 21-61 (.344) 9-13 (.692) 51.

INDIANA (65): Abernethy 7-8 0-1 14, May 5-16 4-6 14, Benson 6-15 4-6 16, Wilkerson 1-5 3-4 5, Buckner 6-14 0-1 12, Crews 1-1 2-3 4. Team 26-59 (.441) 13-21 (.619) 65.

Halftime: Indiana 34-26.

ALL-TOURNAMENT TEAM

Tom Abernethy, F, Sr., Indiana
Kent Benson, C, Jr., Indiana*
Rickey Green, G, Jr., Michigan
Marques Johnson, F, Jr., UCLA
Scott May, F, Sr., Indiana

*Named Most Outstanding Player

Outcome for Defending Champion: UCLA's 98-game homecourt winning streak, which started in 1970, was snapped by Oregon, 65-45. The Bruins (27-5) won the Pacific-8 title by two games although they were upset at Notre Dame for the third year in a row. Their five defeats were by an average of 16.2 points.

Star Gazing: Rutgers, undefeated entering the tourney (28-0), lost in the national semifinals against Michigan (86-70) when the Scarlet Knights hit a paltry 27.5 percent of their field-goal attempts in the first half. Rutgers' top three scorers for the season–forward Phil Sellers and guards Mike Dabney and Eddie Jordan–combined to shoot 31.4 percent from the floor (16 of 51). John Robinson posted game highs of 20 points and 16 rebounds for the Wolverines.

Biggest Upset: UNLV, ranked third by AP and fourth by UPI entering the tourney, lost to Arizona, 114-109, in overtime in the West Regional semifinals. Arizona, coached by Fred Snowden, participated in the tourney for the first time since its debut in 1951. The Wildcats won their opener, 83-76, against John Thompson-coached Georgetown in the first NCAA playoff game where both coaches were African Americans.

One and Only: Buckner was the only one of the Hoosiers' starting quintet to finish his NBA

1976 CHAMPIONSHIP BRACKET

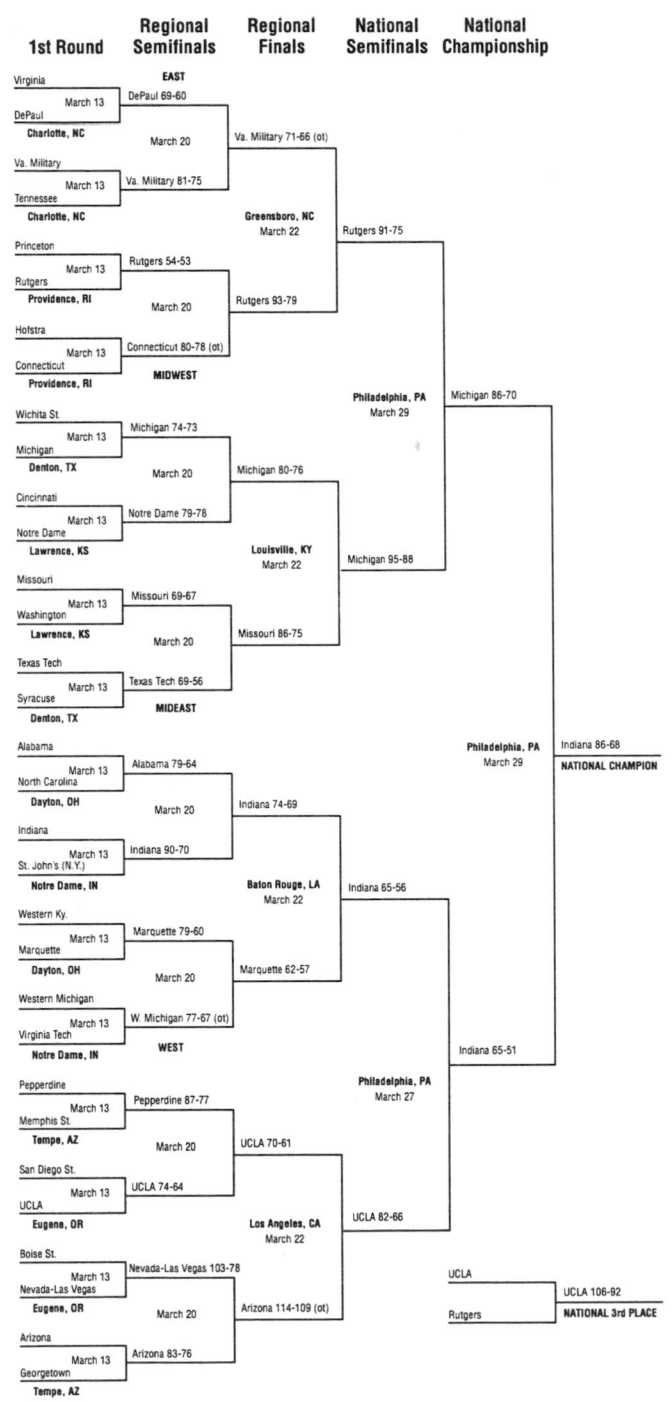

1st Round	Regional Semifinals	Regional Finals	National Semifinals	National Championship

EAST

Virginia
March 13 — DePaul 69-60
DePaul
Charlotte, NC

March 20 — Va. Military 71-66 (ot)

Va. Military
March 13 — Va. Military 81-75
Tennessee
Charlotte, NC

Greensboro, NC
March 22 — Rutgers 91-75

Princeton
March 13 — Rutgers 54-53
Rutgers
Providence, RI

March 20 — Rutgers 93-79

Hofstra
March 13 — Connecticut 80-78 (ot)
Connecticut
Providence, RI

MIDWEST

Wichita St.
March 13 — Michigan 74-73
Michigan
Denton, TX

March 20 — Michigan 80-76

Cincinnati
March 13 — Notre Dame 79-78
Notre Dame
Lawrence, KS

Louisville, KY
March 22 — Michigan 95-88

Missouri
March 13 — Missouri 69-67
Washington
Lawrence, KS

March 20 — Missouri 86-75

Texas Tech
March 13 — Texas Tech 69-56
Syracuse
Denton, TX

Philadelphia, PA
March 29 — Michigan 86-70

MIDEAST

Alabama
March 13 — Alabama 79-64
North Carolina
Dayton, OH

March 20 — Indiana 74-69

Indiana
March 13 — Indiana 90-70
St. John's (N.Y.)
Notre Dame, IN

Baton Rouge, LA
March 22 — Indiana 65-56

Western Ky.
March 13 — Marquette 79-60
Marquette
Dayton, OH

March 20 — Marquette 62-57

Western Michigan
March 13 — W. Michigan 77-67 (ot)
Virginia Tech
Notre Dame, IN

Philadelphia, PA
March 27 — Indiana 65-51

Philadelphia, PA
March 29 — Indiana 86-68
NATIONAL CHAMPION

WEST

Pepperdine
March 13 — Pepperdine 87-77
Memphis St.
Tempe, AZ

March 20 — UCLA 70-61

San Diego St.
March 13 — UCLA 74-64
UCLA
Eugene, OR

Los Angeles, CA
March 22 — UCLA 82-66

Boise St.
March 13 — Nevada-Las Vegas 103-78
Nevada-Las Vegas
Eugene, OR

March 20 — Arizona 114-109 (ot)

Arizona
March 13 — Arizona 83-76
Georgetown
Tempe, AZ

UCLA
Rutgers — UCLA 106-92
NATIONAL 3rd PLACE

career with a winning playoff record and play for a championship team (Boston Celtics in 1984).

Numbers Game: This year marked the last time more than half of a set of NCAA first-team All-Americans participated in the Final Four. The five-man All-American squad included Indiana's Benson and May and UCLA's Richard Washington. . . . Virginia and Western Michigan appeared in the NCAA Tournament for the first time. . . . Missouri guard Willie Smith scored a tourney-high 43 points in a 95-88 loss to Michigan in the Midwest Regional final.

What If: Eventual NBA first-round draft choices Leon Douglas and Reggie King combined to score an average of 31.5 points per game for Alabama in the 1975-76 season. If only this frontcourt duo combined for 22 points instead of 16 in the 1976 Mideast Regional semifinals, the Crimson Tide could have defeated unbeaten Indiana rather than losing 74-69. The Hoosiers were also fortunate when eventual NBA players Butch Lee, Lloyd Walton and Jerome Whitehead struggled from the floor for Marquette in the Mideast Regional final. If only Lee, Walton and Whitehead combined to hit 35.1 percent of their field-goal attempts instead of 21.6 percent (8 of 37), the Warriors could have defeated Indiana rather than losing 65-56. . . . Arizona (24-9) could have given UCLA more of a challenge in the West Regional final if Ticky Burden and Coniel Norman had stayed in college and exercised the remainder of their eligibility. . . . Illinois State (20-7) might have made its first NCAA playoff appearance if Bubbles Hawkins didn't leave school early. . . . Utah (19-8) would have had a good chance of appearing in the playoffs for the first time in 10 years if Mike Sojourner had exercised all of his eligibility.

Putting Things in Perspective: North Carolina sophomore playmaker Phil Ford, a second-team consensus All-American, injured a knee in a pickup game after the ACC Tournament and was ineffective (two points, three assists, five turnovers) in the Tar Heels' 79-64 NCAA Tournament first-round defeat to Alabama.

Scoring Leader: Scott May, Indiana (113 points, 22.6 ppg).

Highest Scoring Average: Willie Smith, Missouri (94 points, 31.3 ppg).

Rebounding Leader: Phil Hubbard, Michigan (61 rebounds, 12.2 rpg).

Highest Rebounding Average: John Thomas, Connecticut (30 rebounds, 15 rpg).

1976–77

AT A GLANCE

NCAA Champion: Marquette (25-7; coached by Al McGuire).

NIT Champion: St. Bonaventure (24-6; coached by Jim Satalin).

New Conference: Eastern Collegiate Basketball League (forerunner of Atlantic 10), New Jersey-New York 7 (disbanded three years later), Sun Belt.

New Rules: The dunk shot is allowed again after an eight-year exile. . . . NIT implements format whereby early-round games are played at locations across the country before the four semifinalists advance to New York.

NCAA Probation: Canisius, Centenary, Clemson, Denver, Minnesota, Montana, Nevada, Southwestern Louisiana, West Texas State.

NCAA Consensus First-Team All-Americans: Kent Benson, C, Sr., Indiana; Otis Birdsong, G, Sr., Houston; Phil Ford, G, Jr., North Carolina; Rickey Green, G, Sr., Michigan; Marques Johnson, F, Sr., UCLA; Bernard King, F, Jr., Tennessee.

National Player of the Year: Johnson (21.4 ppg, 11.1 rpg, 59.1 FG%).

National Coaches of the Year: San Francisco's Bob Gaillard (29-2/AP, UPI); North Carolina's Dean Smith (28-5/NABC), and Arkansas' Eddie Sutton (26-2/USBWA).

The first 38 NCAA national champions, from Oregon (29-5 record in 1938-39) through Indiana (the last unbeaten team with a 32-0 mark in 1975-76), averaged barely over two defeats per season. None of the titlists sustained

Tennessee forward Bernard King.

Roberts' Anthony Roberts finished runner-up in scoring (34 ppg) by averaging 37.3 over the last half of the season, including outbursts of 66 points and 65 (NIT record against Oregon). Portland State's Freeman Williams averaged 40.7 ppg from January 9 through the remainder of the season to lead the country with a 38.8 mark.

Williams poured in 71 points against Southern Oregon–the highest total by a major collegian in 23 years. He averaged 35.3 points on a trip to the South when his team ended New Orleans' 21-game homecourt winning streak, North Texas State's 19-game home streak and Pan American's 20-game home streak in a five-day stretch. . . . Williams (38.8 ppg), Bird (32.8), Hofstra's Rich Laurel (30.3), Louisiana Tech's Mike McConathy (27.5), Nevada-Reno's Edgar Jones (24.7) and Hawaii's Gavin Smith (23.4) set school Division I records for highest scoring average in a single season.

Toledo, en route to its first of five consecutive 20-plus win seasons, ended Indiana's 57-game regular-season winning streak, 59-57, in the inaugural game in the Rockets' Savage Hall. . . . UNC Charlotte (28-5, coached by Lee Rose), Virginia Military (26-4, Charlie Schmaus), Detroit (25-4, Dick Vitale), Old Dominion (25-4, Paul Webb), Idaho State (25-5, Jim Killingsworth), Minnesota (24-3, Jim Dutcher), Austin Peay State (24-4, Lake Kelly), Hofstra (23-7, Roger Gaeckler) and Tennessee (22-6, Ray Mears) had their winningest seasons in school Division I history.

The last 16 VMI coaches have all-time losing records at the school. That's what makes the Keydets' lone appearance in the Top 20 of a final wire-service poll so remarkable (20th in AP). UNCC also finished in the Top 20 of a final wire-service poll for the only time in school annals.

Minnesota, which was on NCAA probation, became the only college ever to have three teammates later average more than 20 points per game in any NBA season–Kevin McHale (12 ppg as a freshman), Mychal Thompson (22 ppg as a junior) and Ray Williams (18 ppg as a senior). . . .

more than six setbacks until Marquette's Al McGuire-coached squad won the title with a 25-7 worksheet. It was the final campaign in McGuire's coaching career, which included 20-win seasons each of his last 11 years. His average record in the last 10 years was 25-4. McGuire's eight previous Marquette teams incurred fewer defeats than his lone NCAA titlist. The Warriors' seven defeats were by an average of four points.

In an amazing turnaround, New Mexico State trailed 28-0 before rallying to defeat Bradley, 117-109 (see accompanying box). It was the largest deficit before scoring for a team to overcome and still win a game. . . . Transfer Larry Bird, who briefly attended Indiana, began to make a name for himself at Indiana State. He averaged 38.3 points per game in his last 15 outings to finish third in the nation in scoring. Oral

SCORING

PLAYER	PTS.	AVG.
Williams, Portland St.	1010	38.8
Roberts, Oral Roberts	951	34.0
Bird, Indiana St.	918	32.8
Birdsong, Houston	1090	30.3
Laurel, Hofstra	908	30.3
Natt, NE Louisiana	782	29.0
McConathy, LSU	716	27.5
Phegley, Bradley	739	27.4
Reynolds, Northwestern (La.)	686	26.4
Hanson, Connecticut	702	26.0

REBOUNDING

PLAYER	REB.	AVG.
Mosley, Seton Hall	473	16.31
Irving, Hofstra	440	16.30
Elmore, Wichita St.	441	15.8

Stephens, Drexel	340	14.8
Landsberger, Arizona St.	359	14.4
King, Tennessee	371	14.3
Bird, Indiana St.	373	13.3
King, Iowa	332	13.3
Jones, Nevada-Reno	355	13.1
Hubbard, Michigan	389	13.0
Hicks, N. Illinois	350	13.0

FIELD GOAL PERCENTAGE

PLAYER	FGM	FGA	PCT.
Senser, W. Chester St.	130	186	.699
Montgomery, VMI	161	247	.652
Moncrief, Arkansas	157	242	.649
Maxwell, UNC Charlotte	244	381	.640
Sowinski, Princeton	163	258	.632
Natt, NE Louisiana	307	493	.623
Cooper, Providence	188	302	.623
Griffin, Wake Forest	198	319	.621

Miller, Cincinnati	180	291	.619
Brewer, Arkansas	199	326	.610
Brown, Iona	150	246	.610

FREE THROW PERCENTAGE

PLAYER	FTM	FTA	PCT.
Smith, UNLV	98	106	.925
Kelly, Vermont	71	77	.922
Thieneman, Va. Tech	98	107	.916
O'Brien, Seattle	89	99	.899
Fagan, Colgate	110	123	.894
DeSantis, Fairfield	116	130	.892
Jonas, Utah	118	133	.887
Mack, Brown	70	79	.886
Hamilton, Iona	68	77	.883
Perry, Holy Cross	156	177	.881
Yoder, Cincinnati	111	126	.881

1976–77 TEAM LEADERS

SCORING OFFENSE

SCHOOL	PTS.	AVG.
UNLV	3426	107.1
Houston	3482	94.1
San Francisco	2904	93.7
North Texas St.	2468	91.4
Detroit	2629	90.7

SCORING DEFENSE

SCHOOL	PTS.	AVG.
Princeton	1343	51.7
Marquette	1900	59.4
Toledo	1604	59.4
Arkansas	1701	60.8
Oregon	1766	60.9

SCORING MARGIN

SCHOOL	OFF.	DEF.	MAR.
UNLV	107.1	87.7	19.4
Clemson	86.6	68.9	17.7
Old Dominion	88.3	70.9	17.4
Detroit	90.7	73.9	16.8
Syracuse	86.9	70.2	16.7

WON-LOST PERCENTAGE

SCHOOL	W-L	PCT.
San Francisco	29-2	.935
Arkansas	26-2	.929
UNLV	29-3	.906
Indiana St.	25-3	.893
Minnesota	24-3	.889

FIELD GOAL PERCENTAGE

SCHOOL	FGM	FGA	PCT.
Arkansas	849	1558	.545
UNC-Wilmington	816	1500	.544
West Texas St.	885	1634	.542
Utah	936	1733	.540
North Carolina	1054	1961	.537

FIELD GOAL PERCENTAGE DEFENSE

SCHOOL	FGM	FGA	PCT.
Minnesota	766	1886	.406
Princeton	548	1336	.410
Oral Roberts	796	1922	.414
Kansas	727	1726	.421
Syracuse	830	1970	.421

FREE THROW PERCENTAGE

SCHOOL	FTM	FTA	PCT.
Utah	499	638	.782
Marquette	446	573	.778
Princeton	391	507	.771
UNLV	610	793	.769
Georgia Tech	434	565	.768

REBOUND MARGIN

SCHOOL	OWN	OPP.	MAR.
Notre Dame	42.4	31.6	10.8
Indiana St.	44.0	33.9	10.1
San Francisco	47.0	37.1	9.9
Arizona	46.7	37.0	9.7
Navy	41.0	32.3	8.7

Minnesota transfer Mark Landsberger set an Arizona State single-game record with 27 rebounds against San Diego State. . . . LSU's Rudy Macklin (32 vs. Tulane), Northeast Louisiana's Calvin Natt (tied with 31 vs. Georgia Southern), Drake's Ken Harris (26 vs. Tulsa) and UNC Charlotte's Cedric Maxwell (tied with 24 at Seton Hall) established school single-game rebounding marks.

Wisconsin's Bill Cofield became the first African-American head coach in the Big Ten. . . . Houston guard Otis Birdsong set a Southwest Conference record by averaging 30.3 points per game. . . . Texas-El Paso's streak of 16 consecutive winning seasons ended when the Miners compiled an 11-15 record. . . .Southwestern Louisiana (21-8) was the nation's most-improved team. The Ragin' Cajuns were 7-19 the previous season. USL's coach was Jim Hatfield.

Arkansas, earning its first appearance in the Top 20 of a final wire-service poll, participated in the NCAA Tournament for the first time in 19 years after becoming the first SWC school in 21 seasons to go undefeated in league play. Guards

Marquette's Bo Ellis was named to the 1977 All-Tournament Team.

Sidney Moncrief (64.9 percent) and Ron Brewer (61 percent) finished among the top 10 nationally in field-goal shooting to help the Razorbacks lead the country in that category. The Hogs clinched the title by shooting 68 percent against Wake Forest in the NCAA Tournament although they lost the game.

UCLA's Marques Johnson, the unanimous national player of the year, didn't mince words when he was asked to express what the return of the dunk meant to him. "It was like I was reborn," Johnson responded.

Notre Dame won at UCLA, 66-63, to snap the Bruins' 115-game nonconference homecourt winning streak.... San Francisco, undefeated until its final regular-season game at Notre Dame (93-82), was a first-round NCAA Tournament loser to UNLV.... Oregon's Greg Ballard set a school

record with 43 points at Oral Roberts in the first round of the NIT. It was his third 40-point outing in a month. Also establishing school single-game scoring standards were Stetson's Mel Daniels (48 points vs. UNC-Wilmington) and Weber State's Stan Mayhew (45 vs. Utah State).

West Virginia forward Bob Huggins, who would later coach Cincinnati to the Final Four, led the fledgling ECBL in free-throw shooting with a mark of 84.4 percent.... Forward Rod Griffin became the first Wake Forest player since 1955 to become an NCAA consensus first- or second-team All-American.... William & Mary finished in the first division of the Southern Conference in its final season as a member of the league. Furman, coached by Joe Williams, tied for first place in the SC after finishing in seventh the previous year.

Long Beach State, coached by Dwight Jones, captured its eighth consecutive Pacific Coast Athletic Association championship.... Nevada-Reno ended a streak of 10 straight losing seasons by compiling a 15-12 record under first-year Wolf Pack coach Jim Carey.... Philadelphia Textile defeated Villanova for the second straight year.... Buffalo competed in its final season at the major-college level.

1976-77 FINAL NATIONAL POLLS

AP	UPI	SCHOOL (RECORD)	HEAD COACH
1	1	Michigan (26-4)	Johnny Orr
2	4	UCLA (24-5)	Gene Bartow
3	5	Kentucky (26-4)	Joe B. Hall
4	6	UNLV (29-3)	Jerry Tarkanian
5	3	North Carolina (28-5)	Dean Smith
6	9	Syracuse (26-4)	Jim Boeheim
7	14	Marquette (25-7)	Al McGuire
8	2	San Francisco (29-2)	Bob Gaillard
9	–	Wake Forest (22-8)	Carl Tacy
10	–	Notre Dame (22-7)	Digger Phelps
11	18	Alabama (25-6)	C.M. Newton
12	19	Detroit (25-4)	Dick Vitale
13	17	Minnesota (24-3)	Jim Dutcher
14	10	Utah (23-7)	Jerry Pimm
15	8	Tennessee (22-6)	Ray Mears
16	11	Kansas State (23-8)	Jack Hartman
17	–	UNC Charlotte (30-5)	Lee Rose
18	7	Arkansas (26-2)	Eddie Sutton
19	13	Louisville (21-7)	Denny Crum
20	–	Virginia Military (26-4)	Charlie Schmaus
–	12	Cincinnati (25-5)	Gale Catlett
–	15	Providence (24-5)	Dave Gavitt
–	16	Indiana State (25-3)	Bob King
–	20	Purdue (20-8)	Fred Schaus

1977 NCAA Tournament

Summary: Tears of joy flowed for coach Al McGuire when Marquette won the championship in his farewell. Marquette overcame halftime deficits to win their first three playoff games against Cincinnati, Kansas State and Wake Forest before trailing most of the second half against UNC Charlotte in the national semifinals. Marquette succeeded in the postseason despite losing five home games, including its last three, to register the Warriors' worst record in 10 years. They lost those home games in Milwaukee Arena, where during one period McGuire's teams were 145-7, including an 81-game winning streak. McGuire, leaving the bench before the game was even over with tears running down his cheeks, pulled away from a hug by long-time assistant Hank Raymonds and made his way to the silence of the locker room. "I want to be alone," McGuire said. "I'm not afraid to cry. All I could think about at the end was–why me? After all the jocks and socks. All the odors in the locker room. All the fights in the gyms. Just the wildness of it all. And to have it end like this ..."

Outcome for Defending Champion: Indiana (14-13) finished fourth in the Big Ten although two defeats to Minnesota were later deemed forfeit victories. The Hoosiers had their league-record 37-game winning streak in regular-season Big Ten competition snapped in their conference opener by Purdue, 80-63. They

---

1976–77 NCAA CHAMPION: MARQUETTE

SEASON STATISTICS OF MARQUETTE REGULARS

PLAYER	POS.	CL.	G.	FG%	FT%	PPG	RPG
Butch Lee	G	Jr.	32	.477	.872	19.6	3.8
Bo Ellis	F	Sr.	32	.507	.752	15.6	8.3
Jerome Whitehead	C	Jr.	32	.517	.581	10.5	8.2
Gary Rosenberger	G	Jr.	32	.471	.760	7.3	1.4
Jim Boylan	G	Jr.	32	.456	.922	7.0	2.8
Ulice Payne	F-G	Jr.	21	.488	.933	4.5	2.6
Bernard Toone	F-C	So.	32	.410	.711	4.4	2.2
Bill Neary	F	Sr.	32	.328	.769	1.7	2.8
Jim Dudley	F	So.	17	.417	.600	1.5	1.7
TEAM TOTALS			32	.472	.778	70.5	36.6

Assists leaders: Boylan 114, Lee 104.

1977 FINAL FOUR CHAMPIONSHIP GAME

ATLANTA, GA

N. CAROLINA (59)	MIN.	FG-A	FT-A	REB.	A	PF	PTS.
Davis	33	6-13	8-10	8	3	4	20
O'Koren	31	6-10	2-4	11	1	5	14
Yonakor	25	3-5	0-0	4	1	0	6
Ford	38	3-10	0-0	2	5	3	6
Kuester	31	2-6	1-2	0	6	5	5
Krafcisin	10	1-1	0-0	0	0	0	2
Zaliagiris	10	2-3	0-0	0	0	3	4
Bradley	5	1-1	0-0	0	0	2	2
Buckley	10	0-1	0-0	0	0	1	0
Wolf	3	0-1	0-0	1	0	0	0
Colescott	1	0-0	0-0	0	0	0	0
Coley	1	0-0	0-0	0	0	0	0
Doughton	1	0-0	0-0	0	0	0	0
Virgil	1	0-0	0-0	0	0	1	0
Team				2			
TOTALS	200	24-51	11-16	28	16	24	59

FG%: .471. FT%: .688. Blocks: 1. Turnovers: 14. Steals: 6.

MARQUETTE (67)	MIN.	FG-A	FT-A	REB.	A	PF	PTS.
Ellis	39	5-9	4-5	9	3	4	14
Neary	12	0-2	0-0	0	0	1	0
Whitehead	39	2-8	4-4	11	2	2	8
Lee	40	6-14	7-7	3	2	1	19
Boylan	33	5-7	4-4	4	0	3	14
Rosenberger	8	1-1	4-4	1	1	1	6
Toone	29	3-6	0-1	0	0	1	6
Team				1			
TOTALS	200	22-47	23-25	29	8	13	67

FG%: .468. FT%: .920. Blocks: 3. Turnovers: 11. Steals: 5.
Halftime: Marquette 39-27.

NATIONAL SEMIFINALS

NORTH CAROLINA (84): Davis 7-7 5-6 19, O'Koren 14-19 3-5 31, Yonakor 5-7 1-4 11, Ford 4-10 4-5 12, Kuester 2-5 5-7 9, Zaliagiris 0-1 0-0 0, Krafcisin 0-0 0-1 0, Buckley 1-5 0-0 2, Bradley 0-1 0-0 0, Wolf 0-1 0-0 0, Colescott 0-0 0-0 0. Team 33-56 (.589) 18-28 (.643) 84.

UNLV (83): Owens 7-15 0-0 14, Gondrezick 4-8 0-0 8, Moffett 6-9 1-2 13, R. Smith 4-11 0-1 8, S. Smith 10-18 0-0 20, T. Smith 6-8 0-2 12, Theus 4-11 0-0 8, Brown 0-0 0-0 0. Team 41-80 (.513) 1-5 (.200) 83.

Halftime: UNLV 49-43.

UNC CHARLOTTE (49): Massey 7-13 0-0 14, King 2-7 0-0 4, Maxwell 5-6 7-9 17, Kinch 1-7 2-2 4, Watkins 2-4 2-3 6, Gruber 2-6 0-0 4, Scott 0-0 0-0 0. Team 19-43 (.442) 11-14 (.788) 49.

MARQUETTE (51): Ellis 2-8 0-0 4, Neary 0-1 0-0 0, Whitehead 10-16 1-2 21, Lee 5-18 1-1 11, Boylan 4-9 0-0 8, Toone 2-6 2-2 6, Rosenberger 0-0 1-2 1. Team 23-58 (.397) 5-7 (.714) 51.

Halftime: Marquette 25-22.

ALL-TOURNAMENT TEAM

Walter Davis, F, Sr., North Carolina
Bo Ellis, F, Sr., Marquette
Butch Lee, G, Jr., Marquette*
Cedric Maxwell, C, Sr., UNC Charlotte
Jerome Whitehead, C, Jr., Marquette
   *Named Most Outstanding Player

Marquette coach Al McGuire went out a winner as the Warriors won the NCAA Championship in his last game.

wound up losing their last four conference road games.

Biggest Upset: Gene Bartow departed after only two seasons as John Wooden's successor following UCLA's 76-75 setback at Idaho State. The Bruins, ranked fourth by UPI entering the tourney, finished with a 24-5 record when guards Roy Hamilton and Brad Holland combined to hit just 8 of 24 field-goal attempts. Idaho State (25-5), prevailing despite shooting just 40.6 percent from the floor, received 27 points and 12 rebounds from Steve Hayes.

One and Only: Cedric "Cornbread" Maxwell is the only player to average more than 20 points and 10 rebounds for an NIT semifinalist one year and an NCAA semifinalist the next season. His UNC Charlotte coach, Lee Rose, became the only individual to coach teams in the NAIA Tournament, NCAA Division III Tournament, NCAA Division II Tournament, NIT and NCAA Division I Tournament. . . . UNLV, which finished in third place, is the only Final Four team to have as many as six players compile a double-digit season scoring average–forwards Eddie Owens (21.8 points per game) and Sam Smith (14.8); guards Glen Gondrezick (14.6), Reggie Theus (14.5) and Robert Smith (12.8), and center Lewis Brown (10.2). The Rebels, averaging 107.1 points as a team on their way to a national third-place finish, also had two other players come close to a double-figure scoring average–guard Tony Smith (9 ppg) and center Larry Moffett (8). Tony Smith was the only one of the eight players in UNLV's regular rotation to never appear in an NBA game.

Numbers Game: Mike O'Koren became the only freshman to score more than 30 points in a national semifinal or championship game. The North Carolina forward scored 31 in an 84-83 victory over UNLV in the national semifinals. . . . Michigan's Phil Hubbard hauled in a tourney-high 26 rebounds in an 86-81 victory over Detroit in the Mideast Regional semifinals. . . . Southern Illinois' Mike Glenn (35 points vs. Arizona), Michigan's Rickey Green (35 vs. Holy Cross) and Hofstra's Rich Laurel (35 vs. Notre Dame) tied for the highest-scoring game in the playoffs.

What If: Guards Phil Ford and John Kuester combined to score 28.4 points per game on 52.7 percent field-goal shooting for North Carolina in the 1976-77 season. If only they combined for 20 points instead of 11 points on 5 of 16 field-goal shooting (31.3 percent) in the championship game, the Tar Heels could have defeated Marquette rather than losing 67-59. . . . Notre Dame (22-7) would have sufficient resources to avoid being edged by Carolina in the East Regional semifinals if Adrian Dantley hadn't defected to the NBA. . . . Big Ten runner-up Minnesota, which defeated national champion Marquette on the Warriors' home court, was ineligible for the NCAA Tournament because of an NCAA probation. . . . Louisville was flying high with a 19-3 record before forward Larry Williams broke his foot against Tulsa in mid-February. The Cardinals went 2-4 to close out the season, erasing memories of an early-season victory at Marquette. . . . Holy Cross, playing without injured standout freshman guard Ronnie Perry (23 points per game), led top-ranked Michigan with less than five minutes remaining before succumbing in the opening round, 92-81. . . . UCLA (24-5) might not have been upset at Idaho State in the West Regional if Richard Washington didn't leave school early for the NBA. . . . Kansas (18-10) probably would have given Kansas State more of a challenge for the Big Eight title if Norm Cook had stayed in college and not turned pro early.

Putting Things in Perspective: North Carolina senior center Tommy LaGarde was averaging 15.1 points and 7.4 rebounds per game when he injured a knee at midseason and was lost for the remainder of the year. Teammate Phil Ford, a first-team consensus All-American and Carolina's leading scorer, hyperextended his shooting elbow (right) in the East Regional semifinals and scored a total of just 20 points in the team's last three playoff games, including six points on 3 of 10 field-goal shooting in a nation-

1977 CHAMPIONSHIP BRACKET

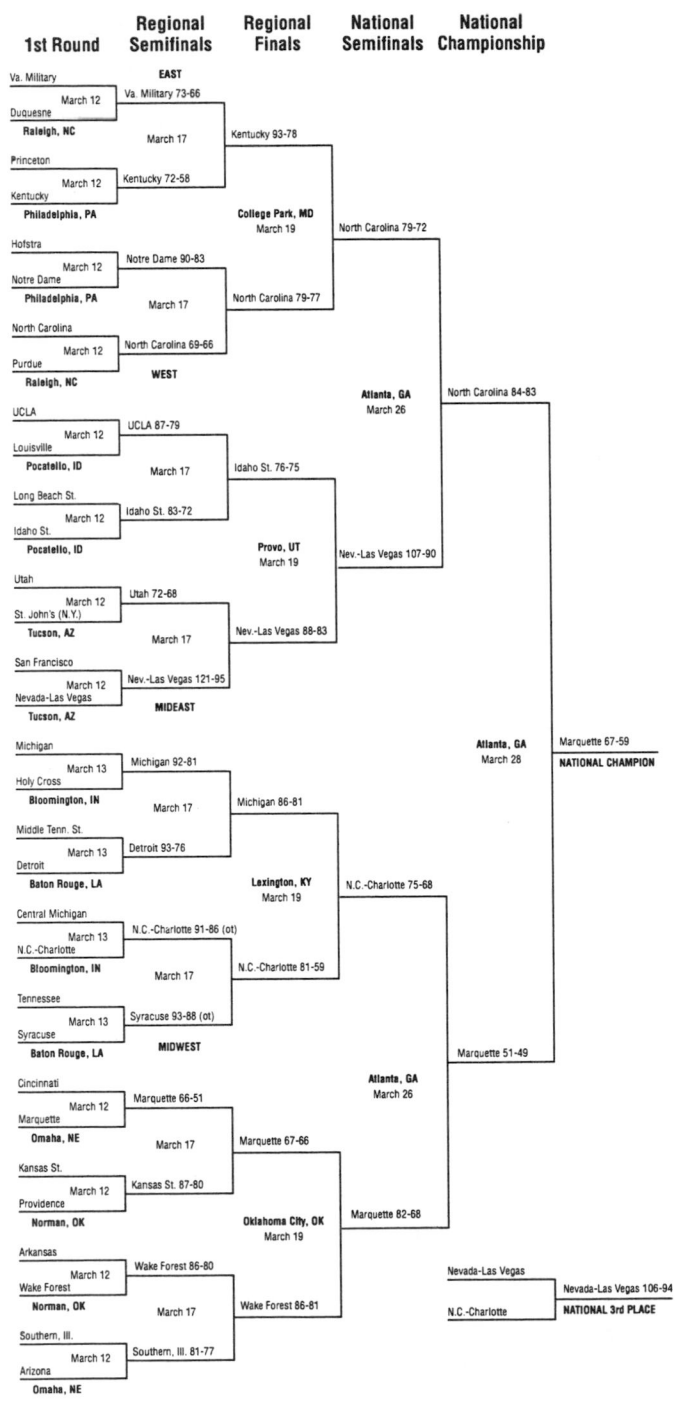

	1st Round	Regional Semifinals	Regional Finals	National Semifinals	National Championship

EAST

Va. Military
March 12 — Va. Military 73-66
Duquesne
Raleigh, NC
March 17 — Kentucky 93-78
Princeton
March 12 — Kentucky 72-58
Kentucky
Philadelphia, PA
College Park, MD March 19 — North Carolina 79-72
Hofstra
March 12 — Notre Dame 90-83
Notre Dame
Philadelphia, PA
March 17 — North Carolina 79-77
North Carolina
March 12 — North Carolina 69-66
Purdue
Raleigh, NC

WEST

North Carolina 84-83

UCLA
March 12 — UCLA 87-79
Louisville
Pocatello, ID
March 17 — Idaho St. 76-75
Long Beach St.
March 12 — Idaho St. 83-72
Idaho St.
Pocatello, ID
Provo, UT March 19 — Nev.-Las Vegas 107-90
Utah
March 12 — Utah 72-68
St. John's (N.Y.)
Tucson, AZ
March 17 — Nev.-Las Vegas 88-83
San Francisco
March 12 — Nev.-Las Vegas 121-95
Nevada-Las Vegas
Tucson, AZ

Atlanta, GA March 26

MIDEAST

Marquette 67-59
NATIONAL CHAMPION

Atlanta, GA March 28

Michigan
March 13 — Michigan 92-81
Holy Cross
Bloomington, IN
March 17 — Michigan 86-81
Middle Tenn. St.
March 13 — Detroit 93-76
Detroit
Baton Rouge, LA
Lexington, KY March 19 — N.C.-Charlotte 75-68
Central Michigan
March 13 — N.C.-Charlotte 91-86 (ot)
N.C.-Charlotte
Bloomington, IN
March 17 — N.C.-Charlotte 81-59
Tennessee
March 13 — Syracuse 93-88 (ot)
Syracuse
Baton Rouge, LA

MIDWEST

Marquette 51-49

Atlanta, GA March 26

Cincinnati
March 12 — Marquette 66-51
Marquette
Omaha, NE
March 17 — Marquette 67-66
Kansas St.
March 12 — Kansas St. 87-80
Providence
Norman, OK
Oklahoma City, OK March 19 — Marquette 82-68
Arkansas
March 12 — Wake Forest 86-80
Wake Forest
Norman, OK
March 17 — Wake Forest 86-81
Southern, Ill.
March 12 — Southern, Ill. 81-77
Arizona
Omaha, NE

Nevada-Las Vegas
Nevada-Las Vegas 106-94
N.C.-Charlotte
NATIONAL 3rd PLACE

al final defeat against Marquette.

Scoring Leader: Cedric Maxwell, UNC Charlotte (123 points, 24.6 ppg).

Highest Scoring Average: Mike Glenn, Southern Illinois (65 points, 32.5 ppg).

Rebounding Leader: Cedric Maxwell, UNC Charlotte (64 rebounds, 12.8 rpg).

Highest Rebounding Average: Phil Hubbard, Michigan (45 rebounds, 15 rpg).

1977-78

AT A GLANCE

NCAA Champion: Kentucky (30-2; coached by Joe B. Hall; won SEC title by three games with a 16-2 record).

NIT Champion: Texas (26-5; coached by Abe Lemons; tied for first place in SWC with a 14-2 record).

New Rule: A seeding process is used in the NCAA Tournament for the first time. A maximum of four automatically-qualifying conference teams are seeded in each of the four regional brackets. These teams are seeded based on their respective conferences' won-lost records in tournament play the previous five years. At-large seeding in each region is based on won-lost records, strength of schedule, and eligibility status of student-athletes for postseason competition.

NCAA Probation: Centenary, Clemson, Hawaii, Idaho, Minnesota, UNLV, Western Carolina.

NCAA Consensus First-Team All-Americans: Larry Bird, F, Jr., Indiana State; Phil Ford, G, Sr., North Carolina; David Greenwood, F, Jr., UCLA; Butch Lee, G, Sr., Marquette; Mychal Thompson, C, Sr., Minnesota.

National Players of the Year: Ford (20.8 ppg, 52.7 FG%, 81.0 FT%/NABC, USBWA, Wooden) and Lee (17.7 ppg, 50.6 FG%, 87.9 FT%).

National Coaches of the Year: Duke's Bill Foster (27-7/shared NABC); Texas' Abe Lemons (26-5/shared NABC); DePaul's Ray Meyer (27-3/USBWA), and Arkansas' Eddie Sutton (32-4/AP, UPI).

Evansville's initial year at the Division I level ended in tragedy when coach Bobby Watson and 13 members of his Purple Aces squad perished in a plane crash just after taking off en route to their fifth game of the season. Their only victory in the first four outings was a 90-83 verdict over Pittsburgh, which finished the season with a winning record (16-11) and tied for third place in the Eastern 8. Mike Duff, hailed as Evansville's most promising player, was among those who died. Duff signed with Missouri but changed his mind and was able to immediately attend Evansville because the Aces weren't affiliated with the national letter of intent. Dick Walters was appointed Watson's successor and guided the Aces to their first NCAA Tournament appearance in 1982.

North Carolina set an NCAA record for highest field-goal percentage in a half by hitting 16 of 17 shots (94.1 percent) after intermission against Virginia. . . . Duke's Mike Gminski became the first player in major-college history to score 1,000 points before his 19th birthday. . . . North Carolina A&T, which compiled a 3-24 record the previous season, improved by 16 1/2 games to 20-8.

UNLV's 72-game homecourt winning streak, which started in 1974, was snapped by New Mexico, 89-76. Before the season started, Rebels coach Jerry Tarkanian filed suit and was granted an injunction to retain his job after the NCAA placed UNLV on probation for 18 rules violations and recommended that Tarkanian be suspended for two years. . . . New Mexico's Marvin Johnson set a Western Athletic Conference record for most points in a league game with a school-record 50 against Colorado State. CSU, however, compiled its only winning WAC record (8-6) in the Rams' first 14 years in the conference. . . . Arizona and Arizona State each compiled a 6-8 mark in WAC competition in their final season as members of the league.

Portland State guard Freeman Williams became the first major collegian to average more than 30 points per game in his career while playing four seasons in Division I. The senior scored 81 points against Rocky Mountain. . . . West Chester State's Joe Senser, the country's No. 3

1977–78 INDIVIDUAL LEADERS

SCORING

PLAYER	PTS.	AVG.
Williams, Portland St.	969	35.9
Bird, Indiana St.	959	30.0
Short, Jackson St.	650	29.5
Mack, East Carolina	699	28.0
Phegley, Bradley	663	27.6
Sanders, Southern (La.)	740	27.4
Carter, VMI	736	26.3
Gerdy, Davidson	670	25.8
Brooks, La Salle	696	24.9
Mitchell, Auburn	671	24.9

REBOUNDING

PLAYER	REB.	AVG.
Williams, N. Texas St.	411	14.7
Taylor, Pan American	368	14.2
Uthoff, Iowa St.	378	14.0
King, Alabama	359	13.3
Natt, NE Louisiana	356	13.2
Searcy, Appalachian St.	359	12.8
Brooks, La Salle	358	12.8
Ruland, Iona	332	12.8
Cooper, New Orleans	343	12.7
Knight, Loyola (Ill.)	343	12.7

FIELD GOAL PERCENTAGE

PLAYER	FGM	FGA	PCT.
Senser, W. Chester St.	135	197	.685
O'Koren, N. Carolina	173	269	.643
Cummings, Cincinnati	212	330	.642
Robey, Kentucky	167	263	.635
Daniels, Stetson	180	284	.634
Young, Fairfield	149	237	.629
Fields, UNC-Wilmington	240	382	.628
Haymore, Mass.	162	259	.625
Macklin, LSU	217	349	.622
Ness, Lafayette	227	368	.617

FREE THROW PERCENTAGE

PLAYER	FTM	FTA	PCT.
Gibson, Marshall	84	89	.944
Tucker, Oklahoma St.	114	125	.912
Williams, J'ville	70	77	.909
Appel, Hofstra	67	74	.905
Perry, Holy Cross	181	201	.900
Macy, Kentucky	115	129	.891
Krivacs, Texas	123	138	.891
Miller, Penn St.	73	82	.890
Stamper, Morehead St.	121	136	.890
Hudson, N. Arizona	92	104	.885

1977–78 TEAM LEADERS

SCORING OFFENSE

SCHOOL	PTS.	AVG.
New Mexico	2731	97.5
Pan American	2487	95.7
Southern (La.)	2653	94.8
Detroit	2730	94.1
Houston	3015	91.4

SCORING DEFENSE

SCHOOL	PTS.	AVG.
Fresno St.	1417	52.5
Princeton	1431	55.0
Marquette	1722	61.5
Arkansas	2218	61.6
Middle Tennessee	1623	62.4

SCORING MARGIN

SCHOOL	OFF.	DEF.	MAR.
UCLA	85.3	67.4	17.9
Detroit	94.1	77.2	16.9
Syracuse	87.8	71.6	16.2
Kansas	81.6	66.4	15.2
Pan American	95.7	80.7	15.0

WON-LOST PERCENTAGE

SCHOOL	W-L	PCT.
Kentucky	30-2	.938
DePaul	27-3	.900
UCLA	25-3	.893
Arkansas	32-4	.889
Detroit	25-4	.862

FIELD GOAL PERCENTAGE

SCHOOL	FGM	FGA	PCT.
Arkansas	1060	1943	.546
Southern (La.)	1107	2031	.545
Kentucky	1040	1922	.541
UNC-Wilmington	809	1499	.540
San Francisco	1020	1907	.535

FIELD GOAL PERCENTAGE DEFENSE

SCHOOL	FGM	FGA	PCT.
Delaware St.	733	1802	.407
Kansas	705	1729	.408
Utah St.	803	1915	.419
Air Force	637	1516	.420
Indiana	723	1720	.420

FREE THROW PERCENTAGE

SCHOOL	FTM	FTA	PCT.
Duke	665	841	.791
Furman	557	721	.773
St. Bonaventure	454	590	.769
Bradley	470	615	.764
Morehead St.	363	475	.764

REBOUND MARGIN

SCHOOL	OWN	OPP.	MAR.
Alcorn St.	52.3	36.0	16.3
Southern (La.)	43.1	31.4	11.7
South Carolina St.	49.1	38.4	10.7
South Alabama	40.0	31.1	8.9
Louisiana St.	46.2	37.5	8.7
Pan American	46.0	37.3	8.7

pass receiver in Division II football in the fall, led the nation in field-goal accuracy for the second consecutive year. . . . Minnesota's Mychal Thompson led the Big Ten Conference in scoring and rebounding, but finished his career as the last NCAA consensus first-team All-American to never participate in the NCAA Tournament.

All five LSU starters fouled out, but the Tigers defeated NCAA champion-to-be Kentucky, 95-94, in overtime. . . . Guard Ron Brewer became the first Arkansas player since 1941 to become an NCAA consensus first- or second-team All-American. . . . South Alabama's stall didn't prevent the Jaguars from losing to New Orleans, 22-20, on Nate Mills' last-second jumper in the final of the Sun Belt Conference Tournament. The next season, the Sun Belt became the first league to experiment with a 45-second shot clock. . . . Fresno State went from last place the previous season in the Pacific Coast Athletic Association to a tie for first under first-year Bulldogs coach Boyd Grant.

Georgetown, coached by John Thompson, earned a spot in the Top 20 of a final wire-service poll for the first time in school history (20th in UPI). Thompson was in his sixth season as

Marquette All-American guard Butch Lee works his way through the defense.

bench boss of the Hoyas. . . . St. Francis (N.Y.) compiled its first winning record in 11 seasons (16-9).

East Carolina's Oliver Mack (47 points vs. USC-Aiken), Old Dominion's Ronnie Valentine (44 at Tulane) and Virginia Military's Ron Carter (42 vs. Long Beach State) set school Division I single-game scoring standards. Mack (27.9 ppg), Ron Carter (26.3), Northeastern's Dave Caligaris (24.6), Montana's Michael Ray Richardson (24.2) and UNC Wilmington's Denny Fields (22.5) set school Division I records for highest scoring average in a single season. VMI's Carter had 19 consecutive games with 20 points or more.

Michigan State finished in the Top 20 of a final wire-service poll for the first time since 1959. . . . Miami of Ohio lost four of five games in a mid-season tailspin but the Redskins (19-9) finished in the final top 20 of a wire-service poll for the only time in school history.

Portland, coached by Jack Avina, compiled its only record with fewer than 10 defeats (19-8) since the 1963-64 campaign. . . . Air Force registered its last winning season with a 15-10 mark. . . . Northern Colorado competed in its final campaign at the major-college level.

Illinois State (24-4/coached by Gene Smithson) and Cal State Fullerton (23-9/Bobby Dye) had their winningest seasons in school Division I history. Texas (26-5, Abe Lemons), Detroit (25-4, David Gaines), Lafayette (23-8, Roy Chipman) and North Texas (22-6, Bill Blakeley) tied their school records for most victories in a single season.

Southern Cal's Cliff Robinson (28 vs. Portland State) and Appalachian State's Tony Searcy (24 vs. High Point) set school Division I single-game rebounding records. . . . Alabama's Reggie King had a string of 13 consecutive games with at least 10 rebounds.. . . Southern Mississippi, coached by second-year mentor M.K. Turk, ended its streak of seven consecutive losing seasons by compiling a 13-12 record.

Purdue's Fred Schaus, who previously coached West Virginia, chose to enter athletic administration, ending his 12-year coaching career with a 251-96 record. The Boilermakers finished in the first division of the Big Ten but they were drubbed in a non-conference game at Indiana State, 91-63, when the Sycamores' Larry Bird collected 26 points, 17 rebounds and eight assists. . . . Chuck Daly left Penn six weeks before the start of the season to become an assistant coach under Billy Cunningham with the Philadelphia 76ers. The Quakers promoted assistant Bob Weinhauer to succeed Daly. . . . Ray Mears, who never had a losing record in his 21-year career at Wittenberg and Tennessee, did not coach the Volunteers because of exhaustion. He then got out of the coaching profession with a 399-135 record.

1977-78 FINAL NATIONAL POLLS

AP	UPI	SCHOOL (RECORD)	HEAD COACH
1	1	Kentucky (30-2)	Joe B. Hall
2	2	UCLA (25-3)	Gary Cunningham
3	7	DePaul (27-3)	Ray Meyer
4	5	Michigan State (25-5)	Jud Heathcote
5	6	Arkansas (32-4)	Eddie Sutton
6	11	Notre Dame (23-8)	Digger Phelps
7	9	Duke (27-7)	Bill Foster
8	3	Marquette (24-4)	Hank Raymonds
9	14	Louisville (23-7)	Denny Crum
10	8	Kansas (24-5)	Ted Owens
11	13	San Francisco (23-6)	Bob Gaillard
12	4	New Mexico (24-4)	Norm Ellenberger
13	15	Indiana (21-8)	Bob Knight
14	18	Utah (23-6)	Jerry Pimm
15	12	Florida State (23-6)	Hugh Durham
16	10	North Carolina (23-8)	Dean Smith
17	19	Texas (26-5)	Abe Lemons
18	–	Detroit (25-4)	Smokey Gaines
19	–	Miami of Ohio (19-9)	Darrell Hedric
20	–	Pennsylvania (20-8)	Bob Weinhauer
–	16	Houston (25-8)	Guy Lewis
–	17	Utah State (21-7)	Dutch Belnap
–	20	Georgetown (23-8)	John Thompson

1978 NCAA Tournament

Summary: Jack Givens sank 18 of 27 field-goal attempts against Duke's zone defense and scored Kentucky's last 16 points of the first half en route to a 41-point performance in a 94-88 triumph in the final. Duke, after finishing in last place in the ACC regular-season standings the previous four years, improved to second one

1977–78 NCAA CHAMPION: KENTUCKY

SEASON STATISTICS OF KENTUCKY REGULARS

PLAYER	POS.	CL.	G.	FG%	FT%	PPG	RPG
Jack Givens	F	Sr.	32	.553	.761	18.1	6.8
Rick Robey	F-C	Sr.	32	.635	.720	14.4	8.2
Kyle Macy	G	So.	32	.536	.891	12.5	2.4
James Lee	F	Sr.	32	.569	.743	10.9	5.2
Mike Phillips	C	Sr.	31	.595	.759	10.2	4.7
Truman Claytor	G	Jr.	32	.466	.774	6.9	0.9
Jay Shidler	G	So.	29	.412	.852	3.7	0.8
Chuck Aleksinas	C	Fr.	27	.569	.694	3.7	2.2
LaVon Williams	F	So.	31	.375	.607	1.9	2.0
Fred Cowan	F	Fr.	19	.500	.667	1.9	0.9
Dwane Casey	G	Jr.	26	.382	.600	1.2	0.7
Tim Stephens	G	So.	19	.333	.857	1.2	0.6
TEAM TOTALS			32	**.541**	**.759**	**84.2**	**36.6**

Assists leader: Macy 178.

1978 FINAL FOUR CHAMPIONSHIP GAME

ST. LOUIS, MO

DUKE (88)	MIN.	FG-A	FT-A	REB.	A	PF	PTS.
Banks	37	6-12	10-12	8	2	2	22
Dennard	31	5-7	0-0	8	2	5	10
Gminski	37	6-16	8-8	12	2	3	20
Harrell	24	2-2	0-0	0	1	3	4
Spanarkel	40	8-16	5-6	2	3	4	21
Suddath	9	1-3	2-3	2	0	1	4
Bender	16	1-2	5-5	1	4	3	7
Goetsch	6	0-1	0-0	1	0	1	0
Team				1			
TOTALS	**200**	**29-59**	**30-34**	**35**	**14**	**22**	**88**

FG%: .492. **FT%:** .882. **Blocks:** 1. **Turnovers:** 17. **Steals:** 6.

KENTUCKY (94)	MIN.	FG-A	FT-A	REB.	A	PF	PTS.
Givens	37	18-27	5-8	8	3	4	41
Robey	32	8-11	4-6	11	0	2	20
Phillips	11	1-4	2-2	2	1	5	4
Macy	38	3-3	3-4	0	8	1	9
Claytor	24	3-5	2-4	0	3	2	8
Lee	20	4-8	0-0	4	2	4	8
Shidler	15	1-5	0-1	1	3	3	2

Aleksinas	1	0-0	0-0	0	0	1	0
Williams	11	1-3	0-0	4	0	2	2
Cowan	8	0-2	0-0	2	0	1	0
Stephens	1	0-0	0-0	0	0	0	0
Courts	1	0-0	0-0	0	0	0	0
Gettelfinger	1	0-0	0-0	0	0	0	0
Casey	0	0-0	0-0	0	0	1	0
TOTALS	**200**	**39-68**	**16-25**	**32**	**20**	**26**	**94**

FG%: .574. **FT%:** .573. **Blocks:** 1. **Turnovers:** 14. **Steals:** 9.
Halftime: Kentucky 45-38.

NATIONAL SEMIFINALS

ARKANSAS (59): Counce 2-2 2-3 6, Delph 5-13 5-6 15, Schall 3-5 0-0 6, Brewer 5-12 6-8 16, Moncrief 5-11 3-7 13, Zahn 1-1 1-2 3, Reed 0-0 0-0 0. Team 21-44 (.477) 17-26 (.654) 59.

KENTUCKY (64): Givens 10-16 3-4 23, Robey 3-6 2-2 8, Phillips 1-6 3-4 5, Macy 2-8 3-4 7, Claytor 1-2 0-1 2, Shidler 3-5 0-0 6, Lee 4-8 5-5 13, Casey 0-0 0-0 0, Stephens 0-0 0-0 0, Cowan 0-0 0-0 0, Williams 0-0 0-0 0. Team 24-51 (.471) 16-20 (.800) 64.

Halftime: Kentucky 32-30.

DUKE (90): Banks 8-15 6-7 22, Dennard 2-3 3-5 7, Gminski 13-17 3-4 29, Harrell 0-2 6-6 6, Spanarkel 4-11 12-12 20, Bender 0-1 2-3 2, Goetsch 1-1 0-0 2, Suddath 1-3 0-0 2. Team 29-53 (.547) 32-37 (.865) 90.

NOTRE DAME (86): Tripucka 5-17 2-2 12, Batton 3-6 4-4 10, Flowers 5-8 0-0 10, Branning 4-10 0-0 8, Williams 8-15 0-1 16, Laimbeer 1-5 5-6 7, Hanzlik 3-8 2-2 8, Jackson 5-6 1-2 11, Wilcox 2-2 0-0 4. Team 36-77 (.468) 14-17 (.824) 86.

Halftime: Duke 43-29.

ALL-TOURNAMENT TEAM

Ron Brewer, G, Sr., Arkansas
Jack Givens, F, Sr., Kentucky*
Mike Gminski, C, Soph., Duke
Rick Robey, F-C, Sr., Kentucky
Jim Spanarkel, G, Jr., Duke
    *Named Most Outstanding Player

game behind North Carolina before winning the ACC Tournament and reaching the Final Four.

Outcome for Defending Champion: Marquette (24-4), making its eighth of 10 consecutive tournament appearances, wasted a five-point, halftime lead and lost in the first round of the Mideast Regional against Miami of Ohio (84-81 in overtime). Current Ohio State coach Randy Ayers collected 20 points and 10 rebounds for the Redskins to help offset national player of the year Butch Lee's 27 points for Marquette.

Star Gazing: DePaul center Dave Corzine scored a tourney-high 46 points in a 90-89 victory over Louisville in the Midwest Regional semifinals. Corzine is the only individual ever to score at least 45 points in the NCAA playoffs and never become an NCAA first- or second-team consensus All-American or Final Four Most Outstanding Player. Corzine broke his finger the day before the regional final and the Blue Demons succumbed to Notre Dame, 84-64.

Biggest Upset: Cal State Fullerton (23-9) had four players score from 18 to 23 points and made 62.1 percent of its field-goal attempts to erase a six-point, halftime deficit and upend fourth-ranked New Mexico, 90-85. Future Laker standout Michael Cooper had an off-game for the Lobos (24-4), sinking just six of 15 field-goal attempts. In the second round, Cal State Fuller-

1978 CHAMPIONSHIP BRACKET

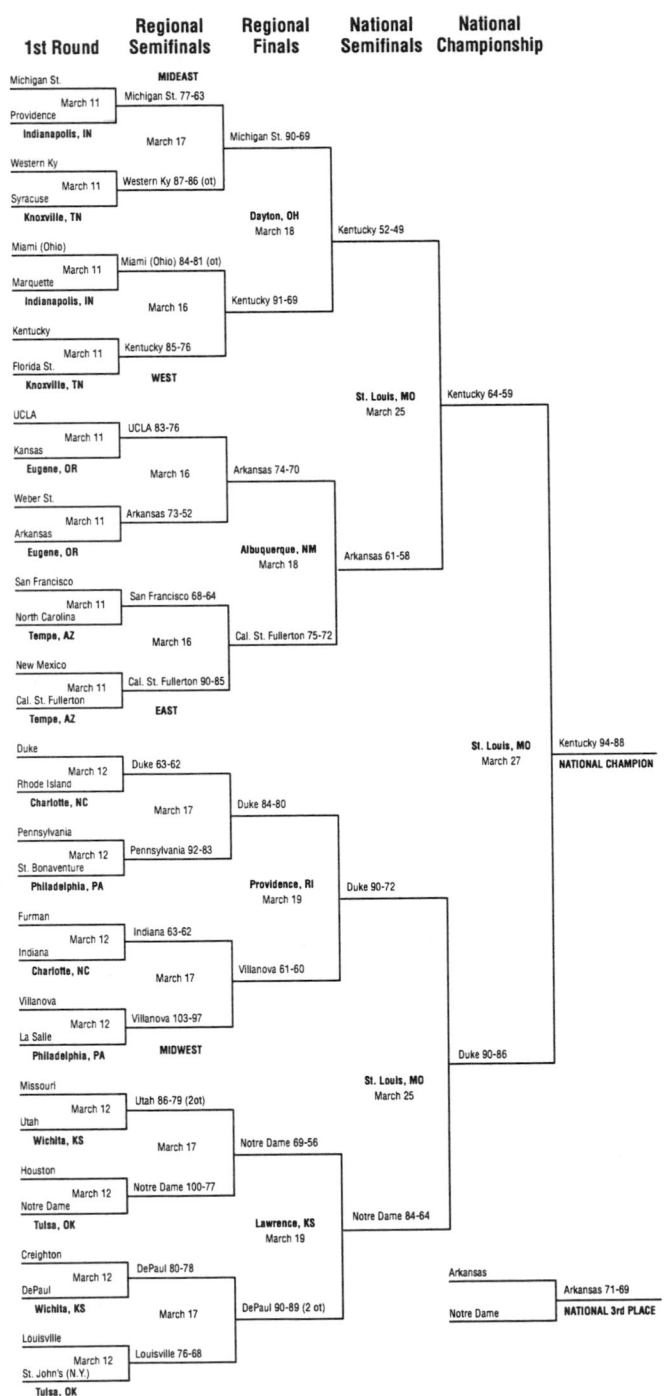

1st Round	Regional Semifinals	Regional Finals	National Semifinals	National Championship

MIDEAST

Michigan St.
March 11
Providence
Indianapolis, IN

Michigan St. 77-63
March 17

Western Ky
March 11
Syracuse
Knoxville, TN

Western Ky 87-86 (ot)

Michigan St. 90-69

Dayton, OH
March 18

Kentucky 52-49

Miami (Ohio)
March 11
Marquette
Indianapolis, IN

Miami (Ohio) 84-81 (ot)
March 16

Kentucky
March 11
Florida St.
Knoxville, TN

Kentucky 85-76

Kentucky 91-69

WEST

St. Louis, MO
March 25

Kentucky 64-59

UCLA
March 11
Kansas
Eugene, OR

UCLA 83-76
March 16

Weber St.
March 11
Arkansas
Eugene, OR

Arkansas 73-52

Arkansas 74-70

Albuquerque, NM
March 18

Arkansas 61-58

San Francisco
March 11
North Carolina
Tempe, AZ

San Francisco 68-64
March 16

New Mexico
March 11
Cal. St. Fullerton
Tempe, AZ

Cal. St. Fullerton 90-85

Cal. St. Fullerton 75-72

EAST

St. Louis, MO
March 27

Kentucky 94-88
NATIONAL CHAMPION

Duke
March 12
Rhode Island
Charlotte, NC

Duke 63-62
March 17

Pennsylvania
March 12
St. Bonaventure
Philadelphia, PA

Pennsylvania 92-83

Duke 84-80

Providence, RI
March 19

Duke 90-72

Furman
March 12
Indiana
Charlotte, NC

Indiana 63-62
March 17

Villanova
March 12
La Salle
Philadelphia, PA

Villanova 103-97

Villanova 61-60

MIDWEST

Duke 90-86

St. Louis, MO
March 25

Missouri
March 12
Utah
Wichita, KS

Utah 86-79 (2ot)
March 17

Houston
March 12
Notre Dame
Tulsa, OK

Notre Dame 100-77

Notre Dame 69-56

Lawrence, KS
March 19

Notre Dame 84-64

Creighton
March 12
DePaul
Wichita, KS

DePaul 80-78
March 17

Louisville
March 12
St. John's (N.Y.)
Tulsa, OK

Louisville 76-68

DePaul 90-89 (2 ot)

Arkansas

Arkansas 71-69
NATIONAL 3rd PLACE

Notre Dame

242 INSIDE SPORTS COLLEGE BASKETBALL

ton overcame a 12-point deficit at intermission to notch a 75-72 triumph over San Francisco (ranked 11th by AP and 13th by UPI). Incredibly, the Titans almost erased a 15-point, halftime deficit in the regional final before losing, 61-58, against Arkansas (ranked 5th by AP and 6th by UPI). Fullerton, participating in its only NCAA playoff, fell short because of 40.3 percent field-goal shooting compared to 61.7 percent for the Razorbacks.

One and Only: Guard Bob Bender, a member of Indiana's 1976 unbeaten NCAA champion before transferring to Duke, became the only player in NCAA Tournament history to play for two different teams in the championship game.

Numbers Game: None of the five NCAA consensus first-team All-Americans advanced to a regional final, let alone the Final Four. . . . Eight of 11 conference regular-season champions failed to win their league postseason tournament. . . . St. John's George Johnson grabbed a tourney-high 20 rebounds in a 76-68 loss to Louisville in the opening round of the Midwest Regional.

What If: Arkansas' acclaimed trio–guards Ron Brewer and Sidney Moncrief and forward Marvin Delph–combined to shoot 55.7 percent from the floor in the 1977-78 season. If only they combined to hit half of their field-goal attempts instead of 41.7 percent (15 of 36) in the national semifinals, the Razorbacks could have defeated eventual champion Kentucky rather than losing 64-59. The Wildcats were fortunate to overcome a five-point halftime deficit in their previous game, a 52-49 victory against Michigan State in the Mideast Regional final. Spartans freshman sensation Magic Johnson hit just two of 10 field-goal attempts and committed six turnovers. Johnson shot a lowly 27.8 percent from the floor (10 of 36) in three tourney games. . . . Phil Hubbard, projected as a first-team All-American for defending Big Ten champion Michigan, missed the season after undergoing knee surgery. . . . North Carolina State (21-10) might have wound up in the NCAA playoffs instead of the NIT if Kenny Carr didn't forgo his final season of eligibility to turn pro.

Scoring Leader: Mike Gminski, Duke (109 points, 21.8 ppg).

Highest Scoring Average: Dave Corzine, DePaul (82 points, 27.3 ppg).

Rebounding Leader: Gene Banks, Duke (50 rebounds, 10 rpg).

Highest Rebounding Average: Greg Kelser, Michigan State (37 rebounds, 12.3 rpg).

1978-79

AT A GLANCE

NCAA Champion: Michigan State (26-6; coached by Jud Heathcote; tied for first place in Big Ten with a 13-5 record).

NIT Champion: Indiana (22-12; coached by Bob Knight; finished in fifth place in Big Ten with a 10-8 record).

New Rules: The NCAA Tournament bracket expands from 32 teams to 40 and each entrant is seeded for the first time. . . . Three-man officiating crews are assigned to all tournament games. . . . NIT field expands from 16 teams to 24.

NCAA Probation: Cincinnati, Grambling, Hawaii, UNLV.

NCAA Consensus First-Team All-Americans: Larry Bird, F-C, Sr., Indiana State; Mike Gminski, C, Jr., Duke; David Greenwood, F, Sr., UCLA; Earvin "Magic" Johnson, G, Soph., Michigan State; Sidney Moncrief, G-F, Sr., Arkansas.

National Player of the Year: Bird (28.6 ppg, 14.9 rpg, 53.2 FG%, 83.1 FT%).

National Coaches of the Year: Indiana State's Bill Hodges (33-1/AP, UPI); DePaul's Ray Meyer (26-6/NABC), and North Carolina's Dean Smith (23-6/USBWA).

A ballyhooed matchup between Indiana State's Larry Bird and Michigan State's Magic Johnson aroused fans and generated the largest basketball game rating (24.1) and share (38) in television history. A share is the percentage of televisions in use at the time.

Michigan State didn't appear anything like a potential NCAA champion in mid-season

Michigan State superstar Earvin "Magic" Johnson.

with a total of 80 points in two contests. Bird, "Hick from French Lick," wasn't able to regain the lead despite pouring in a school-record 49 points against Wichita State in his last regular-season home game.

Denver's Matt Teahan scored the most points in a single game with 61 against Nebraska Wesleyan. Among the other players who set school Division I single-game scoring records were James Madison's Steve Stiepler (51 points vs. Robert Morris), Baylor's Vinnie Johnson (50 vs. TCU), Northern Illinois' Paul Dawkins (47 at Western Michigan), Maryland's Ernest Graham.

Indiana State (33-1, coached by Bill Hodges), Appalachian State (23-6, Bobby Cremins), Nevada-Reno (21-7, Jim Carey), Wagner (21-7, P.J. Carlesimo) and The Citadel (20-7, Les Robinson) had their winningest seasons in school history. Eastern Kentucky (21-8, Ed Byhre) tied its school mark for most victories in a single season. . . . Wagner compiled a 7-19 record the previous season. Indiana State became the first Missouri Valley team in 31 years to go unbeaten in conference competition.

A point-shaving scandal at Boston College led to a 10-year prison sentence for Eagles player Rick Kuhn. Notorious organized crime figure Henry Hill and New York gambler Richard (The Fixer) Perry masterminded a scheme to fix nine Boston College games in concert with Kuhn and teammates Ernie Cobb and Jim Sweeney. Kuhn, the only player convicted, served 2 1/2 years in prison for conspiracy to commit sports bribery and interstate gambling.

American's Ray Voelkel set an NCAA record for most consecutive successful field goals with 25, covering a nine-game span. . . . North Texas State's Jon Manning tossed in 41 points against Baylor to become the only player to score 40 or more in a single game for two different schools against Division I opponents. Manning had scored 43 points in January, 1975 as a freshman for Oklahoma City against Tulsa. . . . UCLA, coached by Gary Cunningham, set an NCAA record with its 13th consecutive regular-season conference championship (Pacific-8/Pacific-10).

when the Spartans were stunned by downtrodden Northwestern (see accompanying box).

Bird was the favorite to lead the nation in scoring until he was limited to four points in a mid-February game against Bradley while Idaho State's Lawrence Butler grabbed the lead

Oklahoma finished in the Top 20 of a final wire-service poll for the first time since the AP started its rankings in 1948-49. LSU placed in a final Top 20 for the first time since 1954. . . . The Big Eight Conference sponsored its 33rd and final holiday tournament. The 1946 and 1947 tourneys were conducted prior to Christmas on the second weekend in December. The remainder of the events were held after Christmas. Pairings were based on the previous year's league standings until 1964, but beginning in 1965 the first-round matchups were based on a set rotation. Missouri and Kansas combined to win the last nine Big Eight Holiday Tournament titles.

The Sun Belt became the first conference to sign a long-term contract with the fledgling ESPN cable network. The Sun Belt is the only league to have its championship televised on ESPN every year since the network's inception. . . . South Alabama, coached by Cliff Ellis, went undefeated in Sun Belt competition after compiling a 3-7 league mark the previous year. USA is the only Sun Belt team ever to go undefeated in conference play since the league's inception in 1977. . . . UNLV led the nation in scoring for the third time in four seasons.

Providence gave coach Dave Gavitt a royal send-off in his final homecourt appearance, defeating Rhode Island, 84-77, after losing to the Rams the previous month by 44 points. The next year, Gavitt became commissioner of the wildly successful Big East Conference. . . . Penn, in one of the most remarkable achievements by a school in any decade, had three different coaches guide the Quakers to a Top 20 finish at least twice apiece in the 1970s–Dick Harter, Chuck Daly and Bob Weinhauer. . . . Massachusetts' streak of 11 consecutive winning seasons ended when the Minutemen compiled a 5-22 record. It was their first of 11 straight losing seasons. UMass' average annual record in that famine was 8-19. . . . Temple made its first Top 20 appearance in a final wire-service poll since 1958. . . . The Ivy League permitted freshman eligibility six years after the rest of the nation embraced the rule.

Michigan State forward Greg Kelser scores on a slam.

Maryland outlasted N.C. State, 124-110, in the highest-scoring game in ACC history. . . . North Carolina blew a 17-point lead midway through the second half at N.C. State, but Dudley Bradley's steal and dunk in the waning seconds gave the Tar Heels a 70-69 victory. . . . Duke's Kenny Dennard set an ACC record with 11 steals in a game against Maryland.

Arizona's Russell Brown established a Pacific-10 Conference record with 19 assists against Grand Canyon. . . . Illinois' Derek Holcomb amassed a school-record 11 blocked shots in a 64-57 victory over South Carolina. Illinois had a 15-0 record after edging Michigan State, 57-55, on Eddie Johnson's shot at the buzzer. But the Illini lost 11 of their last 15 games to finish in seventh place in the Big Ten. It was the sixth of seven consecutive second-division finishes for Illinois.

Alcorn State, entering the NIT with an undefeated record, erased a 16-point deficit in an 80-78 victory at Mississippi State in a key intrastate matchup. . . . Houston didn't have an All-SWC first- or second-team selection for the only time in its first 19 years as a member of the league from 1975-76 through 1993-94. . . . Oklahoma City's Ernie Hill set a Trans America Athletic Conference single-season record by averaging 26.6 points per game.. . . Colorado compiled a 14-13 mark for its first winning record in eight campaigns and Brigham Young posted a 20-8 record to snap a streak of five consecutive losing seasons.

Washington went 11-16 for its only losing mark in 14 seasons under coach Marv Harshman. . . . North Carolina State won the first Great Alaska Shootout, which has blossomed into one of the nation's premier in-season tournaments. . . . Paul Lambert, lured by Auburn from Southern Illinois, died in a tragic motel fire. Auburn filled the coaching vacancy by hiring Sonny Smith from East Tennessee State. Another coach who passed away in the offseason was Stu Aberdeen after his second season at Marshall.

1978-79 FINAL NATIONAL POLLS

AP	UPI	SCHOOL (RECORD)	HEAD COACH
1	1	Indiana State (33-1)	Bill Hodges
2	2	UCLA (25-5)	Gary Cunningham
3	4	Michigan State (26-6)	Jud Heathcote
4	5	Notre Dame (24-6)	Digger Phelps
5	6	Arkansas (25-5)	Eddie Sutton
6	8	DePaul (26-6)	Ray Meyer
7	9	Louisiana State (23-6)	Dale Brown
8	10	Syracuse (26-4)	Jim Boeheim
9	3	North Carolina (23-6)	Dean Smith
10	13	Marquette (22-7)	Hank Raymonds
11	7	Duke (22-8)	Bill Foster
12	17	San Francisco (22-7)	Dan Belluomini
13	19	Louisville (24-8)	Denny Crum
14	–	Pennsylvania (25-7)	Bob Weinhauer
15	14	Purdue (27-8)	Lee Rose
16	–	Oklahoma (21-10)	Dave Bliss
17	–	St. John's (21-11)	Lou Carnesecca
18	–	Rutgers (22-9)	Tom Young
19	–	Toledo (22-7)	Bob Nichols
20	11	Iowa (20-8)	Lute Olson
–	12	Georgetown (24-5)	John Thompson
–	15	Texas (21-8)	Abe Lemons
–	16	Temple (25-4)	Don Casey
–	18	Tennessee (21-12)	Don DeVoe
–	20	Detroit (22-6)	Smokey Gaines

1979 NCAA Tournament

Summary: Indiana State, undefeated entering the tourney (29-0), lost the national final

LOWLY NORTHWESTERN STUNS NCAA CHAMPION-TO-BE

MICHIGAN STATE AT NORTHWESTERN

JANUARY 27, 1979

Northwestern has had more than its share of problems in the Big Ten Conference, but the Wildcats were on top of the world when they shocked Michigan State by 18 points, 83-65, in one of the biggest upsets in NCAA history. Eventual NBA forwards Greg Kelser and Jay Vincent combined to hit just four of 15 field-goal attempts for the Spartans.

MICHIGAN STATE (65)	FG-A	FT-A	REB.	PTS.
Greg Kelser	2-10	0-0	4	4
Ron Charles	2-4	1-2	5	5
Jay Vincent	2-5	2-2	2	6
Magic Johnson	7-22	12-16	10	26
Terry Donnelly	1-2	0-0	0	2
Mike Longaker	1-2	2-2	2	4
Greg Lloyd	1-3	2-2	3	4
Mike Brkovich	4-13	1-1	0	9
Rob Gonzalez	1-1	1-2	0	3
Gerald Busby	1-4	0-0	2	2
Jaimie Huffman	0-0	0-0	0	0
Rick Kaye	0-0	0-1	0	0
Don Brkovich	0-1	0-0	0	0
Team:				10
TOTALS	**22-67**	**21-28**	**38**	**65**

FG%: .328. **FT%:** .750. **Assists:** 15 (Johnson 10). **Steals:** 5. **Blocked Shots:** 2. **Turnovers:** 19 (Johnson 5, M. Brkovich 5). **Fouled Out:** 1 (Vincent).

NORTHWESTERN (83)	FG-A	FT-A	REB.	PTS.
Rod Roberson	6-13	8-9	7	20
Mike Campbell	6-13	4-4	7	16
Brian Jung	1-3	0-2	3	2
Brian Gibson	6-10	4-4	4	16
Jerry Marifke	2-6	8-9	3	12
Bob Klaas	3-7	3-3	7	9
Pete Boeson	1-2	0-0	0	2
Randy Carroll	2-2	0-0	0	4
Bill Fenlon	0-0	0-0	0	0
John Egan	0-0	2-2	1	2
Lyle Dobbins	0-0	0-0	0	0
TOTALS	**27-56**	**29-33**	**42**	**83**

FG%: .482. **FT%:** .879. **Assists:** 19 (Marifke 7). **Steals:** 2. **Blocked Shots:** 2. **Turnovers:** 18 (Roberson 6). **Fouled Out:** 1 (Klaas).

Halftime: Northwestern 39-29.

against Michigan State (75-64) when the Sycamores' Larry Bird, who hit 53.2 percent of his field-goal attempts on the season, made just one-third of his shots from the floor (7 of 21) as a sore thumb limited his shooting effectiveness. Magic Johnson scored a game-high 24 points for the Spartans. Michigan State dominated the 1979 NCAA Tournament, handing every one of its five playoff opponents, a quintet averaging 25.6 victories, their worst defeat of the year–Lamar (31-point margin), LSU (16), Notre Dame (12), Penn (34) and Indiana State (11).

1978–79 INDIVIDUAL LEADERS

SCORING

PLAYER	PTS.	AVG.
Butler, Idaho St.	812	30.1
Bird, Indiana St.	973	28.6
Galis, Seton Hall	743	27.5
Tillman, E. Kentucky	780	26.9
Dawkins, N. Illinois	695	26.7
Gerdy, Davidson	721	26.7
Hill, Oklahoma City	771	26.6
Stroud, Mississippi	709	26.3
Manning, N. Texas St.	699	25.9
Stielper, James Madison	668	25.7

REBOUNDING

PLAYER	REB.	AVG.
Davis, Tennessee St.	421	16.2
Cartwright, San Francisco	455	15.7
Garrett, Southern (La.)	433	15.5
Bird, Indiana St.	505	14.9
Knight, Loyola (Ill.)	386	14.3
Smith, Alcorn St.	398	13.7
Brooks, La Salle	347	13.3
Stephens, Drexel	360	13.3
Lawrence, McNeese St.	343	12.7

FIELD GOAL PERCENTAGE

PLAYER	FGM	FGA	PCT.
Brown, Florida St.	237	343	.691
Ruland, Iona	233	347	.671
Johnson, Oregon St.	197	298	.661
Green, Tenn. St.	120	183	.656
Peck, Miss. St.	154	239	.644
Mercer, Georgia	146	227	.643
Spain, Pan American	145	227	.639
Lawrence, McNeese St.	226	356	.635
Bouie, Syracuse	176	279	.631

FREE THROW PERCENTAGE

PLAYER	FTM	FTA	PCT.
Mauldin, Campbell	70	76	.921
Kanaskie, La Salle	55	60	.917
Krivacs, Texas	101	111	.910
Orner, Butler	70	77	.909
Perry, Holy Cross	178	196	.908
Goetz, San Diego St.	74	82	.902
Sienkiewicz, Villanova	78	87	.897
White, Marshall	85	95	.895
Huggins, S. Illinois	76	85	.894
Marifke, Northwestern	63	71	.887

1978–79 TEAM LEADERS

SCORING OFFENSE

SCHOOL	PTS.	AVG.
UNLV	2700	93.1
Alcorn St.	2678	92.3
Wichita St.	2485	88.8
Syracuse	2660	88.7
New Mexico	2567	88.5

SCORING DEFENSE

SCHOOL	PTS.	AVG.
Princeton	1452	55.8
Dartmouth	1486	57.2
Fresno St.	1632	58.3
Montana	1628	60.3
Indiana	2080	61.2
Marquette	1775	61.2

SCORING MARGIN

SCHOOL	OFF.	DEF.	MAR.
Syracuse	88.7	71.5	17.2
Notre Dame	79.7	64.1	15.6
Indiana St.	86.8	72.8	14.0
Alcorn St.	92.3	78.9	13.4
Michigan St.	75.7	62.6	13.1

WON-LOST PERCENTAGE

SCHOOL	W-L	PCT.
Indiana St.	33-1	.971
Alcorn St.	28-1	.966
Syracuse	26-4	.867
Temple	25-4	.862
Arkansas	25-5	.833
UCLA	25-5	.833

FIELD GOAL PERCENTAGE

SCHOOL	FGM	FGA	PCT.
UCLA	1053	1897	.555
Fairfield	792	1468	.540
Arkansas	849	1587	.535
The Citadel	864	1616	.535
Syracuse	1052	1970	.534

FIELD GOAL PERCENTAGE DEFENSE

SCHOOL	FGM	FGA	PCT.
Illinois	738	1828	.404
Tennessee St.	717	1707	.420
Wyoming	667	1582	.422
Indiana	847	2008	.422
Princeton	548	1287	.426

FREE THROW PERCENTAGE

SCHOOL	FTM	FTA	PCT.
St. Francis (Pa.)	350	446	.785
Kentucky	666	858	.776
Fairfield	513	666	.770
Villanova	394	514	.767
DePaul	517	676	.765

REBOUND MARGIN

SCHOOL	OWN	OPP.	MAR.
Alcorn St.	50.1	36.3	13.8
Tennessee St.	49.7	37.9	11.8
Pittsburgh	41.3	30.6	10.7
Indiana St.	48.2	38.1	10.1
Syracuse	44.1	34.8	9.3

Consequently, most observers don't remember the glaring defect of the Spartans earlier that season when they were defeated by four Big Ten Conference second-division teams. Michigan State required two overtime victories at home to avoid compiling six Big Ten losses in a seven-game span. Four of the Spartans' five Big Ten defeats were to second-division teams, including an 18-point setback against conference cellar dweller Northwestern, which has 25 consecutive losing league records and finished in the Big Ten basement 12 times in one 16-year stretch.

Excluding Northwestern, Michigan State's five other defeats were by a total of just eight points.

Outcome for Defending Champion: Kentucky (19-12) incurred its lowest SEC finish (6th) to that point before losing at home in the first round of the NIT to Clemson before an NIT single-game attendance record of 23,522 spectators. The Wildcats bowed three times to Tennessee by an average of 11.3 points.

Star Gazing: Johnson became the only individual to be named Final Four Most Outstand-

1978–79 NCAA CHAMPION: MICHIGAN STATE

SEASON STATISTICS OF MICHIGAN STATE REGULARS

PLAYER	POS.	CL.	G.	FG%	FT%	PPG	RPG
Greg Kelser	F	Sr.	32	.545	.671	18.8	8.7
Earvin Johnson	G	So.	32	.468	.842	17.1	7.3
Jay Vincent	C	So.	31	.496	.581	12.7	5.2
Ron Charles	F	Jr.	32	.665	.622	8.8	5.1
Mike Brkovich	F	So.	32	.509	.803	7.0	1.8
Terry Donnelly	G	Jr.	32	.535	.754	6.6	1.6
Rob Gonzalez	F	Fr.	28	.581	.800	1.7	1.0
TEAM TOTALS			**32**	**.527**	**.721**	**75.7**	**37.1**

Assists leader: Johnson 269.

1979 FINAL FOUR CHAMPIONSHIP GAME

SALT LAKE CITY, UT

MICH. STATE (75)	MIN.	FG-A	FT-A	REB.	A	PF	PTS.
M. Brkovich	39	1-2	3-7	4	1	1	5
Kelser	32	7-13	5-6	8	9	4	19
Charles	31	3-3	1-2	7	0	5	7
Donnelly	39	5-5	5-6	4	0	2	15
Johnson	35	8-15	8-10	7	5	3	24
Vincent	19	2-5	1-2	2	0	4	5
Gonzalez	3	0-0	0-0	0	0	0	0
Longaker	2	0-0	0-0	0	0	0	0
Team				2			
TOTALS	**200**	**26-43**	**23-33**	**34**	**15**	**19**	**75**

FG%: .605. FT%: .697. Blocks: 2. Turnovers: 16. Steals: 6.

INDIANA STATE (64)	MIN.	FG-A	FT-A	REB.	A	PF	PTS.
Miley	29	0-0	0-1	3	0	1	0
Gilbert	20	2-3	0-4	4	0	4	4
Bird	40	7-21	5-8	13	2	3	19
Nicks	36	7-14	3-6	2	4	5	17
Reed	36	4-9	0-0	0	9	4	8
Heaton	22	4-14	2-2	6	2	2	10
Staley	17	2-2	0-1	3	0	2	4
Nemcek	2	1-1	0-0	0	1	3	2
Team				3			
TOTALS	**200**	**27-64**	**10-22**	**34**	**18**	**24**	**64**

FG%: .422. FT%: .455. Blocks: 2. Turnovers: 10 (Bird 6). Steals: 6 (Bird 5).

Halftime: Michigan State 37-28.

NATIONAL SEMIFINALS

PENNSYLVANIA (67): Price 7-18 4-4 18, Smith 0-6 0-0 0, White 5-12 3-4 13, Salters 1-5 0-0 2, Willis 4-13 1-3 9, Ross 2-6 0-0 4, Hall 3-8 0-1 6, Reynolds 1-3 0-0 2, Leifsen 0-1 1-2 1, Flick 0-6 6-6 6, Jackson 1-2 4-4 6, Kuhl 0-2 0-0 0, Condon 0-0 0-0 0. Team 24-82 (.293) 19-24 (.792) 67.

MICHIGAN STATE (101): M. Brkovich 6-10 0-0 12, Kelser 12-19 4-6 28, Charles 2-2 0-0 4, Donnelly 3-5 0-0 6, Johnson 9-10 11-12 29, Vincent 0-1 3-4 3, Gonzalez 1-5 0-0 2, Longaker 2-2 0-0 4, Lloyd 0-2 6-7 6, Kaye 2-2 1-3 5, Huffman 0-0 0-1 0, Gilkie 0-1 0-0 0, D. Brkovich 1-1 0-1 2. Team 38-60 (.633) 25-34 (.735) 101.

Halftime: Michigan State 50-17.

DEPAUL (74): Watkins 8-11 0-0 16, Aguirre 9-18 1-2 19, Mitchem 6-11 0-0 12, Bradshaw 4-8 0-0 8, Garland 9-18 1-3 19. Team 36-66 (.545) 2-5 (.400) 74.

INDIANA STATE (76): Miley 2-2 0-0 4, Gilbert 6-7 0-1 12, Bird 16-19 3-4 35, Nicks 4-13 2-2 10, Reed 3-5 0-0 6, Heaton 3-6 0-0 6, Staley 1-4 1-2 3. Team 35-56 (.625) 6-9 (.667) 76.

Halftime: Indiana State 45-42.

ALL-TOURNAMENT TEAM

Mark Aguirre, F, Fr., DePaul
Larry Bird, F-C, Sr., Indiana State
Gary Garland, G, Sr., DePaul
Magic Johnson, G, Soph., Michigan State*
Greg Kelser, F, Sr., Michigan State
***Named Most Outstanding Player**

ing Player (Michigan State '79) and NBA Finals Most Valuable Player (Los Angeles Lakers '80) in back-to-back seasons.

Biggest Upset: East Regional No. 1 seed North Carolina lost its opener (72-71 against Penn) in the Tar Heels' home state (Raleigh, N.C.).

One and Only: Indiana State is the only school to reach the Final Four in its one and only NCAA Tournament appearance. The Sycamores won the Midwest Regional final against Arkansas, 73-71, when Bob Heaton shifted the ball from his normal right hand to his left for a short shot that bounced twice on the rim before going down. In the regular season, Heaton kept their unbeaten streak intact by hitting a 55-footer that banked off the glass, knotting the score at New Mexico State and forcing an overtime. . . . Bill Hodges of Indiana State is the only individual to win more than 30 games in earning a trip to the national semifinals in his first season as a head coach. Hodges was named interim coach when Bob King was forced to step down four days before practice started after suffering a stroke in the preseason. The Sycamores, who moved up to Division I status in 1972, haven't compiled a winning season since Hodges guided them to a 16-11 mark the year after Bird departed.

Numbers Game: Penn forward Tony Price is the highest scorer in a tourney for a Final Four team to fail to be named All-Tournament. . . . DePaul forward Mark Aguirre became the first freshman to be named to an NCAA All-Tournament team. . . . Michigan State forward Greg Kelser personally outscored (34 to 18) and outrebounded (13 to 11) Notre Dame's vaunted frontcourt of Kelly Tripucka, Orlando Woolridge and Bill Laimbeer in the Mideast Regional final. . . . MSU guard Terry Donnelly doubled his season scoring average in the second half of the national final with 13 points against Indiana State. . . . David Greenwood's tourney-high 37 points for UCLA weren't enough to prevent a 95-91 setback against DePaul in the West Regional final. . . . St. John's, a No. 10 seed, won three games by an average of three points before losing to Penn by two (64-62) in the East Regional final. . . . Oklahoma made its first NCAA playoff appearance since 1947. . . . Tennessee notched its first NCAA Tournament victory (97-81 over Eastern Kentucky). In 22 years from 1964-85, the Volunteers finished no worse than fourth in the SEC 18 times and won at least 20 games in 13 of those seasons. . . . Lamar's Clarence Kea collected a game-high 33 points and tourney-high 19 rebounds in a 95-87 triumph over Detroit in the opening round of the Mideast Regional.

What If: LSU won the SEC regular-season title despite the absence of standout forward Rudy Macklin, who missed the majority of the year because of an injury. The Tigers were 22-3 entering their regular-season finale but playoff aspirations were defused when leading scorer DeWayne Scales was suspended for repeated conversations with an agent. LSU scored just 19 first-half points in an 87-71 setback against Michigan State in the Mideast Regional semifinals. . . . San Francisco (22-7), not UCLA, might have advanced to the West Regional final against DePaul if Winford Boynes and James Hardy had remained with the Dons instead of turning pro early.

Putting Things in Perspective: Three players who finished their Duke careers with more than 2,000 points (Gene Banks, Mike Gminski and Jim Spanarkel) each compiled lower scoring averages than they manufactured the previous year, when Duke was national runner-up. In 1978, Banks, Gminski and Spanarkel became the only trio to each score at least 20 points in both Final Four games (total of 71 points in 90-86 victory over Notre Dame in the semifinals and 63 in 94-88 setback against Kentucky in the cham-

pionship game). Duke is the only national runner-up to score more than 85 points in an NCAA final. Banks, Gminski and Spanarkel all scored at least 16 points when they combined to shoot 53.5 percent from the floor against St. John's, but none of their teammates managed more than seven points as the Blue Devils blew a five-point halftime lead.

Scoring Leader: Tony Price, Pennsylvania (142 points, 23.7 ppg).

Highest Scoring Average: Bill Cartwright, San Francisco (58 points, 29 ppg).

Rebounding Leader: Larry Bird, Indiana State (67 rebounds, 13.4 rpg).

Highest Rebounding Average: Lionel Green, LSU (31 rebounds, 15.5 rpg).

WINNINGEST PROGRAMS OF THE 1970S

RK.	SCHOOL	W.	L.	PCT.
1.	UCLA	273	27	.910
2.	Marquette	252	40	.863
3.	Pennsylvania	223	56	.799
4.	North Carolina	239	65	.786
5.	Kentucky	223	69	.764
6.	Louisville	224	70	.762
7.	Syracuse	213	69	.755
8.	Long Beach State	203	68	.749
9.	Indiana	208	75	.735
10.	Oral Roberts	161	59	.732

Note: UNC Charlotte compiled a 147-48 record (.754) in seven seasons as a major college during the decade.

1970-79 PREMO POWER POLL: BEST TEAMS BY DECADE

RANK	SEASON	SCHOOL
1	1971–72	UCLA* (30-0)
2	1975–76	Indiana* (32-0)
3	1972–73	UCLA* (30-0)
4	1973–74	North Carolina St.* (30-1)
5	1974–75	Indiana (31-1)
6	1969–70	UCLA* (28-2)
7	1973–74	UCLA (26-4)
8	1970–71	UCLA* (29-1)
9	1977–78	Kentucky* (30-2)
10	1972–73	North Carolina St. (27-0)
11	1969–70	St. Bonaventure (25-3)
12	1970–71	Marquette (28-1)
13	1978–79	Indiana St. (33-1)
14	1976–77	UNLV (29-3)
15	1975–76	Marquette (27-2)
16	1970–71	Pennsylvania (28-1)
17	1969–70	Jacksonville (27-2)
18	1973–74	Maryland (23-5)
19	1974–75	UCLA* (28-3)
20	1977–78	Arkansas (32-4)
	1976–77	North Carolina (28-5)
	1971–72	North Carolina (26-5)
	1978–79	Michigan St.* (26-6)

*–NCAA Tournament Champion

1979 CHAMPIONSHIP BRACKET

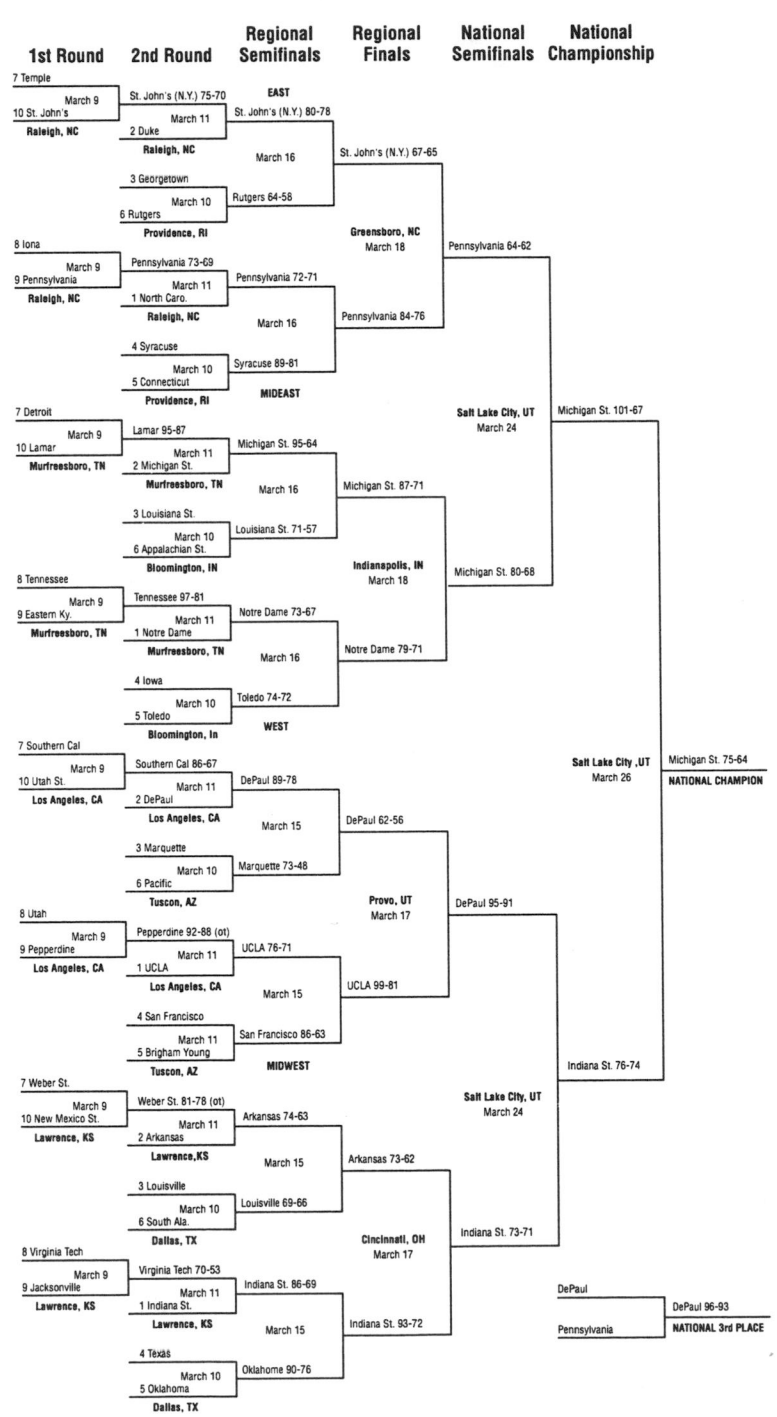

| 1st Round | 2nd Round | Regional Semifinals | Regional Finals | National Semifinals | National Championship |

EAST

7 Temple
March 9
10 St. John's
Raleigh, NC

St. John's (N.Y.) 75-70
March 11
2 Duke
Raleigh, NC

St. John's (N.Y.) 80-78

3 Georgetown
March 10
6 Rutgers
Providence, RI

Rutgers 64-58

March 16

St. John's (N.Y.) 67-65

8 Iona
March 9
9 Pennsylvania
Raleigh, NC

Pennsylvania 73-69
March 11
1 North Caro.
Raleigh, NC

Pennsylvania 72-71

Greensboro, NC
March 18

Pennsylvania 64-62

4 Syracuse
March 10
5 Connecticut
Providence, RI

Syracuse 89-81

March 16

Pennsylvania 84-76

MIDEAST

7 Detroit
March 9
10 Lamar
Murfreesboro, TN

Lamar 95-87
March 11
2 Michigan St.
Murfreesboro, TN

Michigan St. 95-64

3 Louisiana St.
March 10
6 Appalachian St.
Bloomington, IN

Louisiana St. 71-57

March 16

Michigan St. 87-71

8 Tennessee
March 9
9 Eastern Ky.
Murfreesboro, TN

Tennessee 97-81
March 11
1 Notre Dame
Murfreesboro, TN

Notre Dame 73-67

Indianapolis, IN
March 18

Michigan St. 80-68

4 Iowa
March 10
5 Toledo
Bloomington, In

Toledo 74-72

March 16

Notre Dame 79-71

Salt Lake City, UT
March 24

Michigan St. 101-67

WEST

7 Southern Cal
March 9
10 Utah St.
Los Angeles, CA

Southern Cal 86-67
March 11
2 DePaul
Los Angeles, CA

DePaul 89-78

3 Marquette
March 10
6 Pacific
Tuscon, AZ

Marquette 73-48

March 15

DePaul 62-56

8 Utah
March 9
9 Pepperdine
Los Angeles, CA

Pepperdine 92-88 (ot)
March 11
1 UCLA
Los Angeles, CA

UCLA 76-71

Provo, UT
March 17

DePaul 95-91

4 San Francisco
March 11
5 Brigham Young
Tuscon, AZ

San Francisco 86-63

March 15

UCLA 99-81

Salt Lake City, UT
March 24

Indiana St. 76-74

MIDWEST

7 Weber St.
March 9
10 New Mexico St.
Lawrence, KS

Weber St. 81-78 (ot)
March 11
2 Arkansas
Lawrence, KS

Arkansas 74-63

3 Louisville
March 10
6 South Ala.
Dallas, TX

Louisville 69-66

March 15

Arkansas 73-62

8 Virginia Tech
March 9
9 Jacksonville
Lawrence, KS

Virginia Tech 70-53
March 11
1 Indiana St.
Lawrence, KS

Indiana St. 86-69

Cincinnati, OH
March 17

Indiana St. 73-71

4 Texas
March 10
5 Oklahoma
Dallas, TX

Oklahoma 90-76

March 15

Indiana St. 93-72

Salt Lake City, UT
March 26

Michigan St. 75-64
NATIONAL CHAMPION

DePaul

Pennsylvania

DePaul 96-93
NATIONAL 3rd PLACE

6

THE EMERGENCE OF PARITY:
THE 1980s

Parity became a buzzword as 10 different schools won NCAA championships in a 10-year stretch beginning in 1982. Tight title games were the rule rather than the exception. Excluding Georgetown's nine-point victory over Houston in the 1984 final, the other seven NCAA championship games from 1982-89 were decided by an average of two points. Expansion of the NCAA Tournament field to the magic number of 64 helped more and more schools reach the Promised Land for the first time, including long-time major universities such as Auburn, Clemson, Florida, Georgia, Nebraska and Seton Hall.

The 1980s boasted many of the premier centers in college basketball history–from Ralph Sampson to Patrick Ewing to Hakeem Olajuwon to David Robinson to Alonzo Mourning to the start of Shaquille O'Neal's career.

The '80s represented the first decade since the 1920s that Kentucky failed to finish among the top five programs in winning percentage. The Wildcats ranked ninth with a 233-86 record (.730). UCLA, the nation's winningest program each of the two previous decades, didn't finish

among the top 20 in the 1980s when the Bruins had six seasons with at least 10 defeats. North Carolina finished in the top 10 of a final wire-service poll every year in the decade except 1980, when the Tar Heels placed 15th.

The trite "East is Least" cliche came to an abrupt end with the formation of the Big East Conference. The Big East highlighted a conference reshuffling that saw 10 new Division I leagues in a four-year span from 1980-83.

Meanwhile, the Big Ten struggled in the NCAA Tournament midway through the decade, compiling a 20-24 playoff record in a five-year stretch from 1982-86. And the Big Eight began to assert itself more nationally when coaches Johnny Orr (Iowa State) and Billy Tubbs (Oklahoma) entered the league and forced opponents to change their traditional methodical style of play and embrace a more uptempo brand.

The decade also featured the advent of two key playing rules changes (shot clock and three-point basket) and an increased influx of prominent foreign players. The building of large arenas remained a major growth industry when the

'80s closed with 11 conferences having an average seating capacity of at least 10,000.

An obsession in the coaching ranks to have taller players at every position decreased after 5-7 Spud Webb (North Carolina State) and 5-3 Tyrone Bogues (Wake Forest) excelled in the powerful Atlantic Coast Conference. Recruiting took on a new dimension in November 1982 with the start of an "early" signing period.

Ethical questions hovered over coaches because of the escalating influence of sneaker companies and several prominent mentors receiving "kickbacks" for scheduling non-conference games. Evidence that coaching was becoming more and more of a young man's game was exemplified by three universities hiring a 26-year-old head coach–John Griffin (Siena in 1982), Lehigh (Fran McCaffery in 1985) and Niagara (Jack Armstrong in 1989).

1979–80

AT A GLANCE

NCAA Champion: Louisville (33-3; coached by Denny Crum; won Metro title by four games with a 12-0 record).

NIT Champion: Virginia (24-10; coached by Terry Holland; tied for fifth place in ACC with a 7-7 record).

New Conferences: Big East, Midwestern City (forerunner of Midwestern Collegiate), North Atlantic, SWAC (moved up to Division I), Trans America Athletic.

New Rules: The NCAA Tournament bracket expands from 40 teams to 48, including 24 automatic qualifiers and 24 at-large teams. . . . The top 16 seeds receive byes to the second round. . . . The limit of two teams from the same conference allowed in the tournament is lifted. . . . The NIT field expands from 24 teams to 32.

NCAA Probation: Auburn, Cincinnati, East Carolina, Memphis State, Oral Roberts, San Francisco.

NCAA Consensus First-Team All-Americans: Mark Aguirre, F, Soph., DePaul; Michael Brooks, F, Sr., La Salle; Joe Barry Carroll, C, Sr., Purdue; Darrell Griffith, G, Sr., Louisville; Kyle Macy, G, Sr., Kentucky.

National Players of the Year: Aguirre (26.8 ppg, 7.6 rpg, 54.0 FG%/AP, UPI, USBWA, Naismith); Brooks (24.1 ppg, 11.5 rpg, 52.4 FG%/NABC), and Griffith (22.9 ppg, 4.8 rpg, 55.3 FG%/Wooden).

National Coaches of the Year: DePaul's Ray Meyer (26-2/AP, UPI, USBWA) and Iowa's Lute Olson (23-10/NABC).

Perhaps the greatest single crop of freshman recruits took center stage. An alphabetical list of the standout yearlings for the Class of '83 included John Bagley (Boston College), Thurl Bailey (North Carolina State), Sam Bowie (Kentucky), Antoine Carr (Wichita State), Howard Carter (LSU), Terry Cummings (DePaul), Quintin Dailey (San Francisco), Dale Ellis (Tennessee), Sidney Green (UNLV), Clark Kellogg (Ohio State), Cliff Levingston (Wichita State), Jeff Malone (Mississippi State), Rodney McCray (Louisville), John Paxson (Notre Dame), Ralph Sampson (Virginia), Byron Scott (Arizona State), Steve Stipanovich (Missouri), Isiah Thomas (Indiana), LaSalle Thompson (Texas), Dominique Wilkins (Georgia), Rob Williams (Houston) and James Worthy (North Carolina).

Worthy was averaging 12.5 points and 7.4 rebounds per game for North Carolina when he sustained a broken ankle at midseason and was lost for the remainder of the year. The Tar Heels lost their NCAA playoff opener in double overtime against Texas A&M. . . . The NCAA Tournament showed the effect of parity and expansion of the field. This was the only year as many as three Final Four teams finished third or lower in their regular-season league standings–UCLA (fourth in Pacific-10), Purdue (third in Big Ten) and Iowa (fourth in Big Ten). UCLA's streak of 13 consecutive undisputed conference championships was snapped by Oregon State.

Parity also existed among the premier players. La Salle's Michael Brooks scored a national-high 51 points in a 108-106 triple-overtime loss at Brigham Young. Brooks, DePaul's Mark Aguirre and Louisville's Darrell Griffith shared the six nationally-recognized Player of the Year Awards. It is the only time as many as three individuals shared the principal national awards. . . . Aguirre was the first DePaul player since 1946 to become an NCAA consensus first- or second-team All-American. DePaul won its first 25 games of the season until succumbing at Notre Dame, 76-74, in double overtime. Kelly Tripucka scored 28 points for the Irish.

Since the end of World War II, Kansas and Kansas State had never gone two years in a row without either of them gaining at least a portion of the Big Seven/Eight Conference title until Missouri earned its first of four consecutive undisputed regular-season titles. The Tigers, topping 60 percent in shooting from the floor 12 times, established an NCAA single-season record for field-goal percentage (57.2 percent). . . . Murray State, which compiled a 4-22 record the previous season, improved by 16 1/2 games to 23-8. The Racers were coached by Ron Greene. . . . Drake's Lewis "Magic" Lloyd finished national runner-up in scoring (30.2) and rebounding (15).

Maryland guard Greg Manning was sixth nationally in field-goal shooting (64.3 percent)

1979–80 INDIVIDUAL LEADERS

SCORING

PLAYER	PTS.	AVG.
Murphy, Southern (La.)	932	32.1
Lloyd, Drake	815	30.2
Kelly, Texas Southern	753	29.0
Page, New Mexico	784	28.0
Tillman, E. Kentucky	734	27.2
Belcher, St. Bonaventure	646	26.9
Bowers, American	726	26.9
Nicks, Indiana St.	723	26.8
Aguirre, DePaul	749	26.8
Toney, Southwestern La.	627	26.1

REBOUNDING

PLAYER	REB.	AVG.
Smith, Alcorn St.	392	15.1
Lloyd, Drake	406	15.0

Brown, Mississippi St.	389	14.4
Davis, Tennessee St.	347	13.3
Hooker, Murray St.	356	12.3
Grooms, Kent St.	319	12.3
Schoen, St. Francis (Pa.)	303	12.1
Green, Pan American	337	12.0
Ruland, Iona	407	12.0
Martin, Oral Roberts	334	11.9

FIELD GOAL PERCENTAGE

PLAYER	FGM	FGA	PCT.
Johnson, Oregon St.	211	297	.710
Charles, Mich. St.	169	250	.676
Rhone, Centenary	193	290	.666
Bouie, Syracuse	189	289	.654
Brown, Florida St.	230	356	.646
Manning, Maryland	196	305	.643
Ruland, Iona	256	399	.642

Frazier, Missouri	160	252	.635
McCormick, W. Ky.	165	264	.625
Byrd, Marquette	137	220	.623

FREE THROW PERCENTAGE

PLAYER	FTM	FTA	PCT.
Magid, G. Washington	79	85	.929
Nesbit, The Citadel	74	80	.925
Macy, Kentucky	104	114	.912
Manning, Maryland	79	87	.908
White, Gonzaga	116	130	.892
Matthews, Wisc.	127	143	.888
Salters, Penn	86	97	.887
Nehls, Arizona	108	122	.885
Jones, St. Bon.	84	95	.884
Falconiero, Lafayette	98	111	.883

1979–80 TEAM LEADERS

SCORING OFFENSE

SCHOOL	PTS.	AVG.
Alcorn St.	2729	91.0
Drake	2398	88.8
Oral Roberts	2447	87.4
Utah St.	2329	86.3
Syracuse	2575	85.8

SCORING DEFENSE

SCHOOL	PTS.	AVG.
St. Peter's	1563	50.4
Princeton	1654	55.1
Penn St.	1600	57.1
Wyoming	1644	58.7
Fresno St.	1412	58.8

SCORING MARGIN

SCHOOL	OFF.	DEF.	MAR.
Alcorn St.	91.0	73.6	17.4
Syracuse	85.8	70.4	15.4
South Alabama	76.4	64.5	11.9
Weber St.	75.2	63.3	11.9
Georgetown	80.1	68.8	11.3

WON-LOST PERCENTAGE

SCHOOL	W-L	PCT.
Alcorn St.	28-2	.933
DePaul	26-2	.929
Louisville	33-3	.917
Weber St.	26-3	.897
Oregon St.	26-4	.867
Syracuse	26-4	.867

FIELD GOAL PERCENTAGE

SCHOOL	FGM	FGA	PCT.
Missouri	936	1635	.572
Maryland	985	1789	.551
Oregon St.	943	1732	.544
Syracuse	1025	1902	.539
Toledo	923	1724	.535

FIELD GOAL PERCENTAGE DEFENSE

SCHOOL	FGM	FGA	PCT.
Penn St.	543	1309	.415
St. Peter's	590	1396	.423
UNC-Wilmington	719	1685	.427
Wichita St.	776	1818	.427
Old Dominion	775	1814	.427

FREE THROW PERCENTAGE

SCHOOL	FTM	FTA	PCT.
Oral Roberts	481	610	.789
Southern (La.)	417	537	.777
St. Bonaventure	467	610	.766
Utah St.	605	794	.762
Kentucky	609	802	.759

REBOUND MARGIN

SCHOOL	OWN	OPP.	MAR.
Alcorn St.	49.2	33.8	15.4
Tennessee St.	46.5	34.3	12.2
Wyoming	41.0	30.8	10.2
Northeastern	39.2	31.2	8.0
South Alabama	39.3	31.7	7.6

and fourth from the free-throw line (90.8 percent). . . . An 89'3" basket at the buzzer by Virginia Tech's Les Henson after he chased down an errant shot, spun and fired the ball the length of the floor gave the Hokies a 79-77 victory at Florida State. Amazingly, the lefthanded Henson made the shot righthanded!

Lamar's Mike Olliver (50 points at Portland State) and San Jose State's Wally Rank (40 vs. Sacramento State) set school single-game scoring records. . . . Lloyd (30.2 ppg), New Mexico's Kenny Page (28), Eastern Kentucky's James Tillman (27.2), American's Russell Bowers (26.9), Aguirre (26.8), Maine's Rufus Harris (25.6), Cleveland State's Frank Edwards (25.5), Oklahoma State's Ed Odom (24.2) and Washington State's Don Collins (23.1) set school records for highest scoring average in a single season.

Jacksonville's James Ray scored a Sun Belt Conference-record 45 points in a game against South Florida. . . . Syracuse's school-record 57-game homecourt winning streak was snapped in its final game at Manley Field House (52-50 against Georgetown). . . . St. Peter's, coached by ex-Princeton assistant Bob Dukiet, dethroned Princeton as the national leader in scoring defense, yielding only 50.4 points per game–the lowest figure in 19 years. . . . Princeton and Penn tied for the Ivy League title with 11-3 conference records. It was the first time in 17 years that an Ivy champion lost more than two league games. Yale dropped all four of its games against Princeton and Penn, but ended a streak of 11 consecutive losing seasons by compiling a 16-10 mark.

Louisville (33-3, coached by Denny Crum), Iona (29-5, Jim Valvano), Texas A&M (26-8, Shelby Metcalf) and Furman (23-7, Eddie Holbrook) had their winningest seasons in school history. Old Dominion (25-5, Paul Webb) tied its school single-season record for most victories.

Iona made its lone appearance in a final wire-service poll. The Gaels leveled NCAA champion-to-be Louisville, 77-60, late in the regular season at Madison Square Garden. Their leading scorer and rebounder for the third con-

Louisville All-American guard Darrell Griffith sneaks behind the basket for two.

secutive season was center Jeff Ruland. . . . Duquesne, coached by Mike Rice, tied for first place in the Eastern 8 after finishing in seventh the previous year. . . . Massachusetts ended a 29-game losing streak with a 67-44 triumph over Harvard on a neutral court before the Minutemen snapped a 19-game homecourt losing streak with a 69-63 verdict over New Hampshire.

Bradley, coached by Dick Versace, captured the Missouri Valley Conference crown after finishing in a tie for last place the previous year. . . . Alcorn State led the nation in rebounding margin for the third consecutive season. . . . Clemson, boasting three 6-10 starters along its frontline, defeated six teams that were ranked in the AP Top 20 (prior to the game). The Tigers earned an invitation to the NCAA Tournament for the first time. . . . Ohio State finished in the Top 20 of a final wire-service poll for the only time in an 18-year span from 1972-73 through 1989-90.

New Mexico averaged 14,344 fans per home date despite incurring its first losing record (6-22) in 18 years. The Lobos lost most of their roster in the aftermath of investigations by the NCAA and FBI revealing serious indiscretions, specifically altering transcripts of transferring students to make them appear eligible. . . . Idaho, coached by Don Monson, ended a streak of eight consecutive losing seasons by compiling a 17-10 mark.

Weber State (26-3, coached by Neil McCarthy) set a school record with 18 straight victories. . . . Denver and Seattle competed in their final season at the major-college level.. . . South Carolina's Frank McGuire, who previously coached St. John's and North Carolina, retired after a 30-year college coaching career with a 550-235 record. He guided the Gamecocks to six consecutive final Top 20 rankings from 1968-69 through 1973-74.

1979-80 FINAL NATIONAL POLLS

AP	UPI	SCHOOL (RECORD)	HEAD COACH
1	1	DePaul (26-2)	Ray Meyer
2	4	Louisville (33-3)	Denny Crum
3	2	Louisiana State (26-6)	Dale Brown
4	3	Kentucky (29-6)	Joe B. Hall
5	5	Oregon State (26-4)	Ralph Miller
6	6	Syracuse (26-4)	Jim Boeheim
7	7	Indiana (21-8)	Bob Knight
8	8	Maryland (24-7)	Lefty Driesell
9	11	Notre Dame (22-6)	Digger Phelps
10	9	Ohio State (21-8)	Eldon Miller
11	10	Georgetown (26-6)	John Thompson
12	12	Brigham Young (24-5)	Frank Arnold
13	13	St. John's (24-5)	Lou Carnesecca
14	16	Duke (24-9)	Bill Foster
15	15	North Carolina (21-8)	Dean Smith
16	14	Missouri (25-6)	Norm Stewart
17	17	Weber State (26-3)	Neil McCarthy
18	19	Arizona State (22-7)	Ned Wulk
19	–	Iona (29-5)	Jim Valvano
20	–	Purdue (23-10)	Lee Rose
–	18	Texas A&M (26-8)	Shelby Metcalf
–	20	Kansas State (22-9)	Jack Hartman

1980 NCAA Tournament

Summary: All-American Darrell Griffith hit less than 40 percent of his field-goal attempts when Louisville won its first two tourney games in overtime and played only 18 minutes as the Cardinals overcame an eight-point deficit against LSU in the Midwest Regional final. But the high-leaping Griffith, nicknamed "Dr. Dunkenstein," performed at the top of his game at the Final Four. The Cardinals' only returning starter from the previous season hit 23 of 37 shots from the floor against Iowa (80-72) and UCLA (59-54). "I've guarded other guys who could leap high before," Iowa's Bob Hansen said. "But all of them came down." Louisville forward Wiley Brown left his artificial right thumb on the breakfast table before the championship game and managers had to search through hotel garbage to retrieve it. The Cardinals excelled with 6-7 freshman Rodney McCray, who replaced his brother, Scooter, at the center position after Scooter suffered a season-ending knee injury.

Outcome for Defending Champion: Michigan State (12-15 overall; ninth place in Big Ten with 6-12 league mark) became one of only two schools to compile a losing record as defending NCAA champion. The Spartans and Indiana State are the last set of title game participants to fail to qualify for the tournament the next season.

Star Gazing: In a 10-year stretch from 1977 through 1986, Griffith (22.9 points per game) was the only player to average more than 20 the season his school captured a national title. . . . Guard Ronnie Lester, Iowa's leader in scoring average who missed half of the season because of a knee injury, tallied the Hawkeyes' first 10 points in the national semifinals against Louisville before leaving midway through the first half after reinjuring his knee.

Biggest Upset: DePaul was the nation's top-ranked team entering the postseason when the Blue Demons lost their opener (77-71 against UCLA in West Regional).

One and Only: Louisville became the only school to win a Division I championship after capturing a small college national tournament. The Cardinals won the 1948 NAIA Tournament by defeating John Wooden-coached Indiana

1979–80 NCAA CHAMPION: LOUISVILLE

SEASON STATISTICS OF LOUISVILLE REGULARS

PLAYER	POS.	CL.	G.	FG%	FT%	PPG	RPG
Darrell Griffith	G	Sr.	36	.553	.713	22.9	4.8
Derek Smith	F	So.	36	.573	.700	14.8	8.3
Wiley Brown	C-F	So.	36	.519	.610	10.4	5.6
Rodney McCray	F-C	Fr.	36	.543	.647	7.8	7.5
Jerry Eaves	G	So.	34	.514	.667	7.7	1.8
Poncho Wright	G-F	So.	36	.450	.729	6.5	2.5
Roger Burkman	G	Jr.	36	.409	.702	3.9	1.7
Tony Branch	G	Sr.	25	.379	.905	1.6	0.1
Greg Deuser	G	So.	22	.360	.682	1.5	0.5
TEAM TOTALS			36	.521	.686	76.9	38.0

Assists leaders: Griffith 138, Burkman 113, Eaves 82.

1980 FINAL FOUR CHAMPIONSHIP GAME

INDIANAPOLIS, IN

UCLA (54)	MIN.	FG-A	FT-A	REB.	A	PF	PTS.
Wilkes	24	1-4	0-0	6	0	3	2
Vandeweghe	37	4-9	6-6	7	0	3	14
Sanders	34	4-10	2-4	6	0	4	10
Foster	38	6-15	4-4	1	5	3	16
Holton	29	1-3	2-2	2	3	2	4
Pruitt	16	2-8	2-2	6	1	2	6
Daye	13	1-3	0-0	1	2	1	2
Allums	4	0-0	0-0	2	0	0	0
Anderson	5	0-0	0-0	0	0	0	0
Team				3			
TOTALS	200	19-52	16-18	34	11	18	54

FG%: .365. **FT%:** .889. **Blocks:** 3. **Turnovers:** 16. **Steals:** 10 (Foster 6).

LOUISVILLE (59)	MIN.	FG-A	FT-A	REB.	A	PF	PTS.
Brown	34	4-12	0-2	7	3	3	8
Smith	36	3-9	3-4	5	1	2	9
R. McCray	36	2-4	3-4	11	2	4	7
Eaves	30	4-7	0-2	3	3	3	8
Griffith	38	9-16	5-8	2	3	3	23
Burkman	11	0-1	0-0	1	1	4	0
Wright	12	2-4	0-0	4	0	1	4
Branch	3	0-0	0-0	0	0	0	0
Team				3			
TOTALS	200	24-53	11-20	36	13	20	59

FG%: .453. **FT%:** .550. **Blocks:** 5. **Turnovers:** 17. **Steals:** 8.
Halftime: UCLA 28-26.

NATIONAL SEMIFINALS

IOWA (72): Brookins 6-18 2-2 14, Boyle 0-8 0-0 0, Krafcisin 4-5 4-4 12, Lester 4-4 2-2 10, Arnold 9-17 2-2 20, Waite 4-6 1-1 9, Hansen 2-8 3-4 7, Gannon 0-0 0-0 0, Henry 0-0 0-0 0. Team 29-66 (.439) 14-15 (.933) 72.

LOUISVILLE (80): Brown 1-3 0-2 2, Smith 3-7 7-8 13, R. McCray 5-7 4-4 14, Eaves 2-4 4-5 8, Griffith 14-21 6-8 34, Wright 1-2 0-0 2, Burkman 2-3 3-4 7, Branch 0-0 0-0 0, Cleveland 0-0 0-0 0, Pulliam 0-0 0-0 0. Team 28-47 (.596) 24-31 (.774) 80.

Halftime: Louisville 34-29.

PURDUE (62): Morris 5-14 2-2 12, Hallman 1-7 0-0 2, Carroll 8-14 1-4 17, Edmonson 9-16 5-6 23, B. Walker 1-3 4-5 6, Stallings 0-0 0-0 0, Scearce 0-2 0-0 0, Barnes 1-1 0-0 2, S. Walker 0-1 0-0 0. Team 25-58 (.431) 12-17 (.706) 62.

UCLA (67): Wilkes 2-2 0-0 4, Vandeweghe 9-12 6-6 24, Sanders 3-7 6-6 12, Foster 4-7 1-2 9, Holton 1-3 2-2 4, Allums 0-0 0-2 0, Daye 1-5 4-5 6, Sims 0-3 0-0 0, Pruitt 3-7 2-2 8. Team 23-46 (.500) 21-25 (.840) 67.

Halftime: UCLA 33-25.

ALL-TOURNAMENT TEAM

Joe Barry Carroll, C, Sr., Purdue
Rod Foster, G, Fr., UCLA
Darrell Griffith, G, Sr., Louisville*
Rodney McCray, F-C, Fr., Louisville
Kiki Vandeweghe, F, Sr., UCLA
*Named Most Outstanding Player

State in the final. . . . This was the only year no No. 1 seed reached the Final Four.

Numbers Game: Virginia Tech became the only school to erase a halftime deficit of at least 18 points to win a playoff game. The Hokies, Metro Conference runner-up to eventual NCAA champion Louisville, trailed at intermission (48-30) before rallying to edge Western Kentucky (89-85 in overtime) in the first round of the Mideast Regional. . . . Backup swingman Mark Dressler erupted for 32 points on 13 of 16 field-goal shooting to spark Missouri to an 87-84 overtime victory against Notre Dame. The short-handed Tigers, playing without starting forward Curtis Berry (knee surgery), lost their next game in the Midwest Regional semifinals to LSU, 68-63. Suspensions had knocked guard Barry Lau-

rie and center Lex Drum off the Tigers' roster, Kirk Shawver quit and Steve Wallace was declared ineligible in mid-season. . . . LSU's Rudy Macklin (19 rebounds vs. Alcorn State) and Notre Dame's Tracy Jackson (19 vs. Missouri) tied for the best single-game rebounding performances in the playoffs. . . . Lamar needed every one of guard Mike Olliver's tourney-high 37 points to nip Weber State, 87-86, in the opening round of the West Regional. . . . Washington State made its first playoff appearance since 1941. . . . UCLA reached the NCAA title game despite not finishing among the top 10 in the final AP poll for the first time in 14 seasons.

What If: Forwards Kiki Vandeweghe, Mike Sanders and James Wilkes, guards Rod Foster, Michael Holton and Darren Daye, and center

1980 CHAMPIONSHIP BRACKET

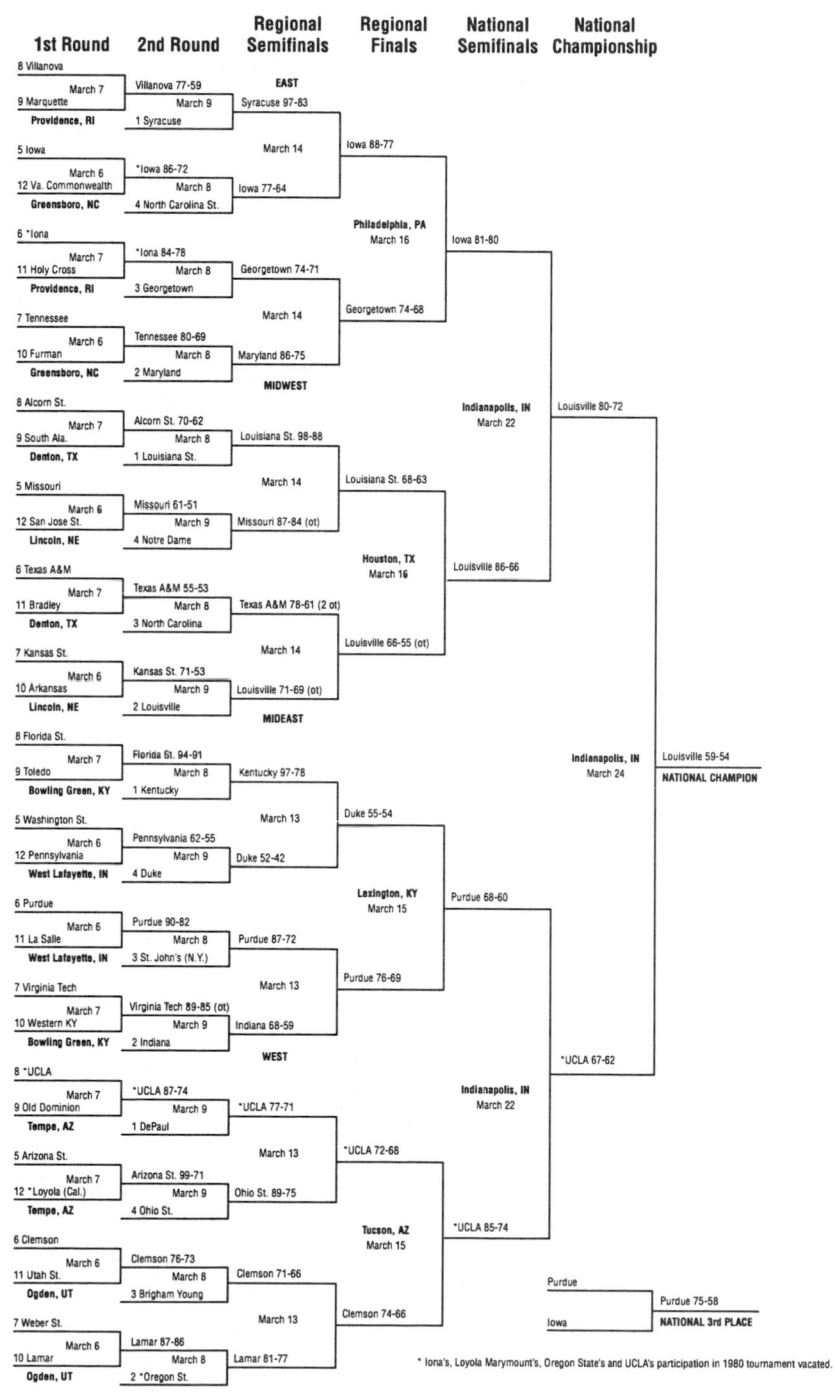

1st Round	2nd Round	Regional Semifinals	Regional Finals	National Semifinals	National Championship

EAST

8 Villanova
March 7
9 Marquette
Providence, RI

Villanova 77-59
March 9
1 Syracuse

Syracuse 97-83

Iowa 88-77

5 Iowa
March 6
12 Va. Commonwealth
Greensboro, NC

*Iowa 86-72
March 8
4 North Carolina St.

Iowa 77-64

March 14

Philadelphia, PA
March 16

Iowa 81-80

6 *Iona
March 7
11 Holy Cross
Providence, RI

*Iona 84-78
March 8
3 Georgetown

Georgetown 74-71

Georgetown 74-68

7 Tennessee
March 6
10 Furman
Greensboro, NC

Tennessee 80-69
March 8
2 Maryland

Maryland 86-75

March 14

MIDWEST

Louisville 80-72

8 Alcorn St.
March 7
9 South Ala.
Denton, TX

Alcorn St. 70-62
March 8
1 Louisiana St.

Louisiana St. 98-88

Louisiana St. 68-63

5 Missouri
March 6
12 San Jose St.
Lincoln, NE

Missouri 61-51
March 9
4 Notre Dame

Missouri 87-84 (ot)

March 14

Houston, TX
March 16

Louisville 86-66

6 Texas A&M
March 7
11 Bradley
Denton, TX

Texas A&M 55-53
March 8
3 North Carolina

Texas A&M 78-61 (2 ot)

Louisville 66-55 (ot)

7 Kansas St.
March 6
10 Arkansas
Lincoln, NE

Kansas St. 71-53
March 9
2 Louisville

Louisville 71-69 (ot)

March 14

MIDEAST

Indianapolis, IN
March 22

8 Florida St.
March 7
9 Toledo
Bowling Green, KY

Florida St. 94-91
March 8
1 Kentucky

Kentucky 97-78

Duke 55-54

Louisville 59-54

NATIONAL CHAMPION

5 Washington St.
March 6
12 Pennsylvania
West Lafayette, IN

Pennsylvania 62-55
March 9
4 Duke

Duke 52-42

March 13

Lexington, KY
March 15

Purdue 68-60

6 Purdue
March 6
11 La Salle
West Lafayette, IN

Purdue 90-82
March 8
3 St. John's (N.Y.)

Purdue 87-72

Purdue 76-69

7 Virginia Tech
March 7
10 Western KY
Bowling Green, KY

Virginia Tech 89-85 (ot)
March 9
2 Indiana

Indiana 68-59

March 13

WEST

*UCLA 67-62

8 *UCLA
March 7
9 Old Dominion
Tempe, AZ

*UCLA 87-74
March 9
1 DePaul

*UCLA 77-71

*UCLA 72-68

Indianapolis, IN
March 22

5 Arizona St.
March 7
12 *Loyola (Cal.)
Tempe, AZ

Arizona St. 99-71
March 9
4 Ohio St.

Ohio St. 89-75

March 13

Tucson, AZ
March 15

*UCLA 85-74

6 Clemson
March 6
11 Utah St.
Ogden, UT

Clemson 76-73
March 8
3 Brigham Young

Clemson 71-66

Clemson 74-66

Purdue

Purdue 75-58

NATIONAL 3rd PLACE

7 Weber St.
March 6
10 Lamar
Ogden, UT

Lamar 87-86
March 8
2 *Oregon St.

Lamar 81-77

March 13

Iowa

* Iona's, Loyola Marymount's, Oregon State's and UCLA's participation in 1980 tournament vacated.

Darrell Allums were proficient enough to eventually play in the NBA after they each shot at least 50 percent from the floor for UCLA in the 1979-80 season. If only they combined to hit 45.5 percent of their field-goal attempts instead of 38.6 percent (17 of 44) in the championship game, the Bruins could have defeated Louisville rather than losing by five points.

Putting Things in Perspective: Louisville lost two of three games in late December, including a 13-point neutral-court defeat to Illinois, which finished with a losing record in Big Ten competition.

Scoring Leader: Joe Barry Carroll, Purdue (158 points, 26.3 ppg).

Highest Scoring Average: Kelvin Ransey, Ohio State (54 points, 27 ppg).

Rebounding Leader: Mike Sanders, UCLA (60 rebounds, 10 rpg).

Highest Rebounding Average: Syracuse's Louis Orr and Maryland's Buck Williams (24 rebounds, 12 rpg).

1980-81

AT A GLANCE

NCAA Champion: Indiana (26- 9; coached by Bob Knight; won Big Ten title by one game over Iowa with a 14- 4 record).

NIT Champion: Tulsa (26- 7; coached by Nolan Richardson; tied for second place in Missouri Valley with an 11- 5 record, which was one game behind Wichita State).

New Conference: MEAC (moved up from Division II).

New Rule: No more than 50 percent of the NCAA Tournament berths shall be filled by automatic qualifiers.

NCAA Probation: UC Santa Barbara, New Mexico, West Texas State.

NCAA Consensus First- Team All- Americans: Mark Aguirre, F, Jr., DePaul; Danny Ainge, G, Sr., Brigham Young; Steve Johnson, C, Sr., Oregon State; Ralph Sampson, C, Soph., Virginia; Isiah Thomas, G, Soph., Indiana.

National Players of the Year: Ainge (24.4 ppg, 4.8 rpg, 51.8 FG%, 82.4 FT%/NABC, Wooden) and Sampson (17.7 ppg, 11.5 rpg, 55.7 FG%/AP, UPI, USBWA, Naismith).

National Coaches of the Year: Kansas State's Jack Hartman (24- 9/shared NABC) and Oregon State's Ralph Miller (26- 2/AP, UPI, shared NABC, USBWA).

Perhaps the national player of the year to struggle the most in a single NCAA Tournament was Virginia sophomore center Ralph Sampson, who had three mediocre playoff games of less than 12 points, including an 11-point outing when the Cavaliers were defeated by North Carolina in the national semifinals. Virginia had captured its only undisputed ACC regular-season title with a 13-1 league record. The Cavaliers sprinted to a 23-0 mark before Notre Dame's Orlando Woolridge ended the streak with a last-second shot, 57-56.

Oregon State's Steve Johnson, who didn't play basketball until his senior year in high school, set an NCAA single-season record by hitting 74.6 percent of his field-goal attempts (235 of 315). He finished his career at 67.8 percent, an NCAA mark with a minimum of 600 baskets. Johnson is the only player to hit more than 70 percent of his field-goal attempts in two different seasons. . . . Oregon State won its first 26 games before the Beavers were blasted in their regular-season finale by visiting Arizona State, 87-67. Guard Byron Scott scored a game-high 25 points for the Sun Devils. Earlier, ASU outlasted UCLA, 78-74, in triple overtime in a game that had nine of its 10 starters go on to NBA careers.

Danny Ainge became the first Brigham Young player since 1953 to earn a spot on an NCAA consensus first- or second-team All-American squad. . . . UC Irvine's Kevin Magee, after an unspectacular high school career in Magnolia, Miss., and brief stints at three colleges, became the first player ever to finish among the top four nationally in scoring, rebounding and field-goal shooting. . . . Colgate's Mike Ferrara (28.6 ppg), UCI's Magee (27.5) and Portland's Jose Slaughter (21.2) set school records for highest scoring average in a single season.

Tulsa became the only school to win more than 25 games the season after a single-digit victory total. The Golden Hurricanes improved to 26-7 from 8-19 after first-year coach Nolan Richardson brought four of his top players from NJCAA champion Western Texas. Tulsa became the first team to capture the NIT after posting a losing record the previous year.. . . Oklahoma

State, coached by Paul Hansen, compiled an 18-9 record to end a streak of 10 consecutive losing seasons. . . . Nebraska coach Joe Cipriano died after a year-long battle with cancer three days before the Cornhuskers' season opener. . . . TCU's Warren Bridges, Darrell Browder and Deckery Johnson each logged an amazing 60 minutes of action during the Horned Frogs' four-overtime, 78-77 victory over Houston.

South Carolina guard Zam Fredrick, entering his senior season with a career scoring average of just 8.1 points per game, ranked in 20th

1980–81 INDIVIDUAL LEADERS

SCORING

PLAYER	PTS.	AVG.
Fredrick, South Carolina	781	28.9
Ferrara, Colgate	772	28.6
Magee, UC Irvine	743	27.5
Lloyd, Drake	762	26.3
Williams, Houston	749	25.0
Jackson, Oklahoma City	719	24.8
Edwards, Cleveland St.	664	24.6
Belcher, St. Bonaventure	637	24.5
Ainge, Brigham Young	782	24.4
McGee, Michigan	732	24.4

REBOUNDING

PLAYER	REB.	AVG.
Watson, Miss. Valley St.	379	14.0
Sappleton, Loyola (Ill.)	374	13.4

Cage, San Diego St.	355	13.1
Magee, UC Irvine	337	12.5
Thompson, Texas	370	12.3
Kellogg, Ohio St.	324	12.0
Atkins, Duquesne	352	11.7
Williams, Maryland	363	11.7
Henry, Oklahoma City	338	11.7
Sampson, Virginia	378	11.5

FIELD GOAL PERCENTAGE

PLAYER	FGM	FGA	PCT.
Johnson, Oregon St.	235	315	.746
Magee, UC Irvine	280	417	.671
Woolridge, Notre Dame	156	240	.650
Williams, Maryland	183	283	.647
Best, Lafayette	164	255	.643
Johnson, UNLV	152	239	.636
Hopson, Idaho	157	247	.636

Payton, Appa. St.	178	281	.633
Palm, Nevada-Reno	204	323	.632
Aleksinas, Conn.	154	244	.631

FREE THROW PERCENTAGE

PLAYER	FTM	FTA	PCT.
Hildahl, Portland St.	76	82	.927
Moore, Nebraska	118	128	.922
Bontrager, O. Roberts	73	81	.901
Stack, N'western	81	90	.900
Leonard, Manhattan	123	138	.891
Simmons, La. Tech	130	146	.890
Greig, Oregon	82	93	.882
Edwards, Cleve. St.	134	152	.882
Wafer, La. Tech	80	91	.879
Ferrara, Colgate	176	201	.876

1980–81 TEAM LEADERS

SCORING OFFENSE

SCHOOL	PTS.	AVG.
UC Irvine	2332	86.4
West Texas St.	2309	85.5
Oklahoma City	2421	83.5
San Francisco	2579	83.2
Long Island	2390	82.4

SCORING DEFENSE

SCHOOL	PTS.	AVG.
Fresno St.	1470	50.7
Princeton	1438	51.4
St. Peter's	1338	51.5
Air Force	1518	56.2
San Jose St.	1699	56.6

SCORING MARGIN

SCHOOL	OFF.	DEF.	MAR.
Wyoming	73.6	57.5	16.1
Oregon St.	76.6	60.9	15.7
Fresno St.	66.1	50.7	15.4
Wichita St.	80.9	66.5	14.4
DePaul	78.9	66.1	12.8
South Alabama	73.8	61.0	12.8

WON-LOST PERCENTAGE

SCHOOL	W-L	PCT.
DePaul	27-2	.931
Oregon St.	26-2	.929
Virginia	29-4	.879
Fresno St.	25-4	.862
Idaho	25-4	.862

FIELD GOAL PERCENTAGE

SCHOOL	FGM	FGA	PCT.
Oregon St.	862	1528	.564
Notre Dame	824	1492	.552
Idaho	816	1484	.550
UC Irvine	934	1703	.548
Pepperdine	918	1709	.537

FIELD GOAL PERCENTAGE DEFENSE

SCHOOL	FGM	FGA	PTS.
Wyoming	637	1589	.401
Penn St.	547	1338	.409
South Florida	701	1682	.417
St. Peter's	521	1248	.417
Air Force	561	1343	.418

FREE THROW PERCENTAGE

SCHOOL	FTM	FTA	PCT.
Connecticut	487	623	.782
Idaho St.	405	522	.776
Davidson	477	626	.762
St. John's	463	612	.757
Tennessee	424	561	.756

REBOUND MARGIN

SCHOOL	OWN	OPP.	MAR.
Northeastern	44.9	32.0	12.9
Wyoming	42.0	30.3	11.7
Wichita St.	44.1	34.0	10.1
Miss. Valley St.	47.1	39.0	8.1
San Francisco	40.1	32.6	7.5

Lute Olson and his Iowa team went to the Final Four in 1980, but they couldn't match that success when the Hawkeyes fell to Wichita State in the opening round of the 1981 tournament.

place at midseason (22.5 ppg) before averaging 36 ppg his last 13 games to finish with a nation-leading mark of 28.9. South Carolina is the only school in NCAA history to have the nation's leading scorer in basketball and leading rusher in football (Heisman Trophy-winner George Rogers with 1,891 yards in 1980) in the same school year. . . . Colgate's Mike Ferrara, runner-up to Fredrick in scoring (28.6), scored a national-high 50 points against Siena.

Michigan's Mike McGee became the only player to score more than 1,500 points in Big Ten Conference competition. . . . Indiana's Ted Kitchel canned all 18 of his free-throw attempts in a 78-61 victory over Illinois, setting a school and Big Ten standard that still stands. . . . Cleveland State's Frank Edwards set a school single-game scoring record with 49 points at Xavier. . . . Loyola of Chicago's Wayne Sappleton established a Midwestern Collegiate Conference single-season standard by averaging 15.2 rebounds per game. The league was called the Midwestern City at the time. Xavier won the title despite compiling a 12-16 record overall.

Louisiana State (31-5, coached by Dale Brown), South Alabama (25-6, Cliff Ellis), American (24-6, Gary Williams), San Jose State (21-9, Bill Berry) and Texas-Arlington (20-8, Bob LeGrand) had their winningest seasons in school Division I history. . . . Texas-Arlington's Albert Culton grabbed a school-record 24 rebounds in a game against Northeastern. . . . West Virginia's 23-10 record snapped a streak of losing more than 10 games in 12 consecutive seasons. . . . The three-point goal was an experimental rule in the Southern Conference. Western Carolina's Ronnie Carr made the first three-pointer in history on November 29, 1980, in Reid Gymnasium against Middle Tennessee State.

Freshman guard John Stockton averaged a modest 3.1 points per game when Gonzaga compiled a 19-8 record for its only season with fewer than 10 defeats in a 25-year span from 1967-68 through 1991-92. . . . National field-goal shooting improved for the eighth consecutive season to 48 percent. . . . Five Mid-American teams tied for first place, the most ever for a Division I conference, with 10-6 league records. . . . Catholic (D.C.) competed in its final season at the major-college level.

1980-81 FINAL NATIONAL POLLS

AP	UPI	SCHOOL (RECORD)	HEAD COACH
1	1	DePaul (27-2)	Ray Meyer
2	2	Oregon State (26-2)	Ralph Miller
3	5	Arizona State (24-4)	Ned Wulk
4	4	Louisiana State (31-5)	Dale Brown
5	3	Virginia (29-4)	Terry Holland
6	6	North Carolina (29-8)	Dean Smith
7	9	Notre Dame (23-6)	Digger Phelps
8	8	Kentucky (22-6)	Joe B. Hall
9	7	Indiana (26-9)	Bob Knight
10	11	UCLA (20-7)	Larry Brown
11	14	Wake Forest (22-7)	Carl Tacy
12	13	Louisville (21-9)	Denny Crum
13	12	Iowa (21-7)	Lute Olson
14	10	Utah (25-5)	Jerry Pimm
15	15	Tennessee (21-8)	Don DeVoe
16	17	Brigham Young (25-7)	Frank Arnold
17	16	Wyoming (24-6)	Jim Brandenburg
18	20	Maryland (21-10)	Lefty Driesell
19	18	Illinois (21-8)	Lou Henson
20	–	Arkansas (24-8)	Eddie Sutton
–	19	Kansas (24-8)	Ted Owens

1981 NCAA Tournament

Summary: North Carolina couldn't cope with two players named Thomas in a 63-50 defeat in the NCAA final. Indiana's Isiah Thomas collected 23 points and five assists and teammate Jim Thomas chipped with eight assists. Jim Thomas, a defensive standout, became the only player who didn't score a total of more than 10 points in two Final Four games (two points in each game) to be named to an All-NCAA Tournament team.

Star Gazing: Isiah Thomas is the only guard among the eight freshmen and sophomores to lead a national titlist in scoring average.

Outcome for Defending Champion: Louisville (21-9) won the Metro Conference regular-season crown by four games after losing six of its first seven non-league contests.

Biggest Upsets: Louisville and 1980 runner-up UCLA succumbed against Arkansas and

1980–81 NCAA CHAMPION: INDIANA

SEASON STATISTICS OF INDIANA REGULARS

PLAYER	POS.	CL.	G.	FG%	FT%	PPG	RPG
Isiah Thomas	G	So.	34	.554	.742	16.0	3.1
Ray Tolbert	F-C	Sr.	35	.588	.740	12.2	6.4
Randy Wittman	G	Jr.	35	.542	.768	10.4	2.3
Landon Turner	F-C	Jr.	33	.561	.717	9.5	3.7
Ted Kitchel	F	Jr.	34	.465	.854	9.2	3.3
Jim Thomas	G	So.	33	.495	.771	3.7	3.2
Tony Brown	G	So.	28	.458	.536	3.3	1.3
Steve Risley	F	Sr.	31	.452	.651	3.0	2.3
Glen Grunwald	F	Sr.	27	.512	.615	1.9	1.2
Phil Isenbarger	F	Sr.	26	.600	.650	1.7	1.2
Steve Bouchie	F	So.	29	.383	.818	1.6	1.6
Chuck Franz	G	So.	21	.583	.875	1.3	0.3
TEAM TOTALS			35	.530	.744	70.0	32.7

Assists leader: I. Thomas 197. **Blocked shots leader:** Tolbert 35. **Steals leader:** I. Thomas 74.

1981 FINAL FOUR CHAMPIONSHIP GAME

PHILADELPHIA, PA

INDIANA (63)	MIN.	FG-A	FT-A	REB.	A	PF	PTS.
Kitchel	4	0-1	0-0	0	0	3	0
Turner	34	5-8	2-2	6	1	5	12
Tolbert	40	1-4	3-6	11	0	0	5
I. Thomas	40	8-17	7-8	2	5	4	23
Wittman	40	7-13	2-2	4	0	2	16
Risley	13	1-1	3-4	4	0	1	5
J. Thomas	29	1-4	0-0	4	8	2	2
Team				2			
TOTALS	200	23-48	17-22	33	14	17	63

FG%: .479. **FT%:** .773. **Blocks:** 1. **Turnovers:** 14. **Steals:** 8.

NORTH CAROLINA (50)	MIN.	FG-A	FT-A	REB.	A	PF	PTS.
Wood	38	6-13	6-9	6	2	4	18
Worthy	31	3-11	1-2	6	2	5	7
Perkins	39	5-8	1-2	8	1	3	11
Pepper	23	2-5	2-2	1	0	1	6
Black	36	3-4	0-0	2	6	5	6
Budko	1	0-1	0-0	1	0	0	0
Doherty	24	1-2	0-1	4	0	4	2
Braddock	4	0-2	0-0	0	1	1	0
Brust	3	0-0	0-0	0	0	0	0
Kenny	1	0-1	0-0	1	0	0	0
TOTALS	200	20-47	10-16	29	12	23	50

FG%: .426. **FT%:** .625. **Blocks:** 2. **Turnovers:** 19 (Doherty 6). **Steals:** 9. **Halftime:** Indiana 27-26.

NATIONAL SEMIFINALS

INDIANA (67): Kitchel 3-8 4-4 10, Turner 7-19 6-7 20, Tolbert 3-7 1-2 7, I. Thomas 6-8 2-3 14, Wittman 3-10 2-2 8, Risley 0-2 1-2 1, J. Thomas 0-4 2-2 2, Bouchie 0-1 0-0 0, Grunwald 1-2 1-2 3, Brown 0-1 0-1 0, Isenbarger 0-1 0-0 0, Franz 0-0 2-2 2, LaFave 0-0 0-0 0. Team 23-63 (.365) 21-27 (.778) 67.

LOUISIANA STATE (49): Mitchell 3-10 3-4 9, Macklin 2-12 0-0 4, Cook 3-5 0-0 6, Martin 2-8 3-7 7, Carter 5-10 0-0 10, Sims 2-8 1-2 5, Jones 0-2 0-1 0, Tudor 1-3 4-4 6, Bergeron 0-0 0-0 0, Costello 0-0 0-0 0, Black 1-1 0-0 2. Team 19-59 (.322) 11-14 (.786) 49.

Halftime: Louisiana State 30-27.

NORTH CAROLINA (78): Wood 14-19 11-13 39, Worthy 2-8 4-7 8, Perkins 4-7 3-5 11, Pepper 0-4 0-0 0, Black 4-6 2-3 10, Doherty 0-1 8-9 8, Braddock 0-1 0-0 0, Kenny 1-1 0-0 2. Team 25-47 (.532) 28-37 (.757) 78.

VIRGINIA (65): Lamp 7-18 4-4 18, Gates 1-1 0-0 2, Sampson 3-10 5-7 11, Wilson 4-7 0-0 8, Jones 5-13 1-1 11, Stokes 0-2 0-0 0, Raker 5-9 3-3 13, Lattimore 1-1 0-0 2. Team 26-61 (.426) 13-15 (.867) 65.

Halftime: Tied 27-27.

ALL-TOURNAMENT TEAM

Jeff Lamp, G, Sr., Virginia
Isiah Thomas, G, Soph., Indiana*
Jim Thomas, G, Soph., Indiana
Landon Turner, F-C, Jr., Indiana
Al Wood, F, Sr., North Carolina
*****Named Most Outstanding Player**

Brigham Young, respectively. It was the last time both championship final teams appeared in the tourney again the following season and lost their opening-round games. . . . DePaul was the nation's top-ranked team entering the tourney for the second consecutive season when the Blue Demons lost their playoff opener again (49-48 against St. Joseph's in Mideast Regional). It was the "Year of the Upset" as second-ranked Oregon State succumbed to Kansas State, 50-48, and third-ranked Arizona State was clobbered by Kansas, 88-71, in their playoff openers. K-State defeated OSU on Rolando Blackman's 17-foot buzzer beater from the right baseline.

One and Only: DePaul became the only school to be top-ranked entering back-to-back tournaments but lose both opening playoff games. St. Joseph's gained its only lead in the second half when an inexcusably unguarded Hawks player named John Smith sank a layup with three seconds left after DePaul's most accurate foul shooter, Skip Dillard, the guy they called "Money" because when he shot 'em, they were as good as in the bank, missed the front end of a one-and-one with 12 seconds remaining.

DePaul did not score a point or take a shot in the final 6 1/2 minutes. A stunned Aguirre, the national player of the year, didn't even throw the ball inbounds and finished the game with one rebound, one assist, no blocked shots, no steals and the only sub-10 scoring output of his college career (eight points). He must have saved his energy for throwing the game ball into Dayton's Great Miami River after the game.

Smith felt no remorse for Aguirre and venerable DePaul coach Ray Meyer. "Aguirre? Why should I? I know one thing, he didn't light us up, did he? And, he did all the (trash) talking. That made me want to dig in and put it to this guy. Who in the hell does he think he is? He sure wasn't doing anything."

Numbers Game: The last player to score the most points in a single game of a tournament and play for a Final Four team was Al Wood. He scored a playoff-high 39 points for North Carolina in the Tar Heels' 78-65 victory against Virginia in the national semifinals before they lost to Indiana in the championship game. In the West Regional final, Wood grabbed a tourney-high 17 rebounds to carry Carolina to an 82-68 triumph over Kansas State. . . . Indiana's Ray Tolbert retrieved 11 missed shots in the NCAA final but finished the season with the lowest rebounding average for a player leading a national titlist in that category (6.4 rpg) since the NCAA began charting rebound statistics. . . . LSU's Rudy Macklin, after averaging 20.5 points per game in his first six NCAA playoff contests, scored a total of four points in two Final Four games. . . . Mississippi made its only NCAA Tournament appearance in school history. . . . Wichita State's Mike Jones hit two long-range baskets in the last 50 seconds to give the Shockers a 66-65 victory over Kansas in the Midwest Regional semifinals in the first game between the schools in 36 years.

What If: Arizona State, ranked third by AP entering the playoffs with a 24-3 record, had the door open to a possible national title when No. 1 seeds DePaul and Oregon State lost their play-off openers at the buzzer. But the Sun Devils, featuring four upperclassmen who combined for a total of more than 35 seasons in the NBA (guards Fat Lever and Byron Scott, center Alton Lister and forward Sam Williams), became one of the biggest busts in tourney history. The door to the Final Four was also slammed shut on them in their opener by Kansas (88-71 in Midwest Regional) when they fell behind by 16 points at intermission. Arizona State had defeated Iowa by eight points early in the season before the Hawkeyes twice upended eventual national champion Indiana in Big Ten Conference competition.

Putting Things in Perspective: Iowa (21-7) defeated Indiana twice by a total of 16 points before the Hawkeyes lost their NCAA playoff opener in the second round against Wichita State on the Shockers' home court. The Hoosiers got off to a modest 7-5 start, including a defeat on a neutral court against Pan American. . . . Wichita State (26-7) was without starting center Ozell Jones (declared ineligible because of a technicality with his high school transcript) when the Shockers bowed to LSU, 96-85, in the Midwest Regional final at the Louisiana Superdome. . . . LSU (31-5) might have fared better at the Final Four if DeWayne Scales didn't defect early to turn pro.

Scoring Leader: Al Wood, North Carolina (109 points, 21.8 ppg).

Highest Scoring Average: Mike Olliver, Lamar (54 points, 27 ppg).

Rebounding Leader: Cliff Levingston, Wichita State (53 rebounds, 13.25 rpg).

1981 CHAMPIONSHIP BRACKET

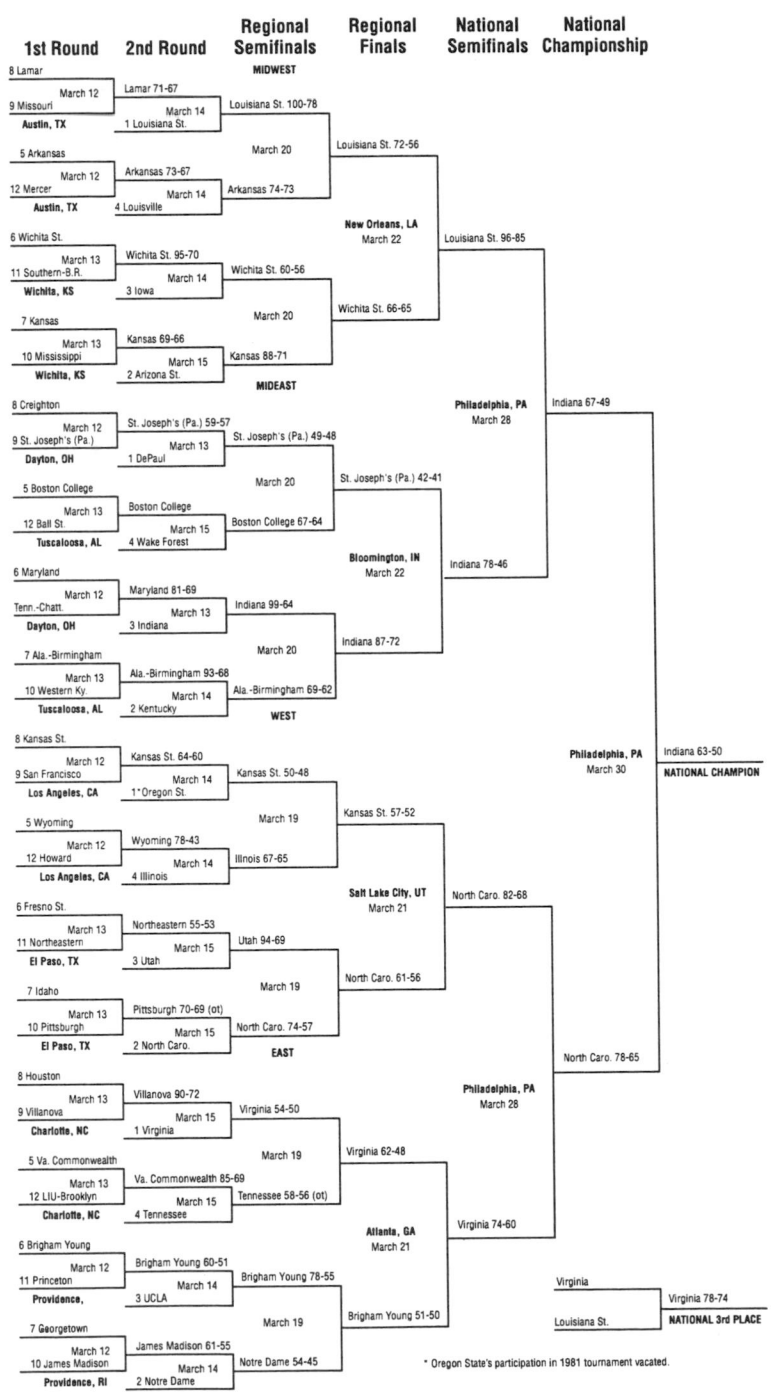

1st Round	2nd Round	Regional Semifinals	Regional Finals	National Semifinals	National Championship

MIDWEST

8 Lamar
March 12
9 Missouri
Austin, TX

Lamar 71-67
March 14
1 Louisiana St.

Louisiana St. 100-78
March 20

5 Arkansas
March 12
12 Mercer
Austin, TX

Arkansas 73-67
March 14
4 Louisville

Arkansas 74-73

Louisiana St. 72-56

6 Wichita St.
March 13
11 Southern-B.R.
Wichita, KS

Wichita St. 95-70
March 14
3 Iowa

Wichita St. 60-56
March 20

New Orleans, LA
March 22

Louisiana St. 96-85

7 Kansas
March 13
10 Mississippi
Wichita, KS

Kansas 69-66
March 15
2 Arizona St.

Kansas 88-71

Wichita St. 66-65

MIDEAST

8 Creighton
March 12
9 St. Joseph's (Pa.)
Dayton, OH

St. Joseph's (Pa.) 59-57
March 13
1 DePaul

St. Joseph's (Pa.) 49-48
March 20

Philadelphia, PA
March 28

Indiana 67-49

5 Boston College
March 13
12 Ball St.
Tuscaloosa, AL

Boston College
March 15
4 Wake Forest

Boston College 67-64

St. Joseph's (Pa.) 42-41

6 Maryland
March 12
Tenn.-Chatt.
Dayton, OH

Maryland 81-69
March 13
3 Indiana

Indiana 99-64
March 20

Bloomington, IN
March 22

Indiana 78-46

7 Ala.-Birmingham
March 13
10 Western Ky.
Tuscaloosa, AL

Ala.-Birmingham 93-68
March 14
2 Kentucky

Ala.-Birmingham 69-62

Indiana 87-72

WEST

8 Kansas St.
March 12
9 San Francisco
Los Angeles, CA

Kansas St. 64-60
March 14
1* Oregon St.

Kansas St. 50-48
March 19

Indiana 63-50
NATIONAL CHAMPION

5 Wyoming
March 12
12 Howard
Los Angeles, CA

Wyoming 78-43
March 14
4 Illinois

Illinois 67-65

Kansas St. 57-52

6 Fresno St.
March 13
11 Northeastern
El Paso, TX

Northeastern 55-53
March 15
3 Utah

Utah 94-69
March 19

Philadelphia, PA
March 30

Salt Lake City, UT
March 21

North Caro. 82-68

7 Idaho
March 13
10 Pittsburgh
El Paso, TX

Pittsburgh 70-69 (ot)
March 15
2 North Caro.

North Caro. 74-57

North Caro. 61-56

EAST

8 Houston
March 13
9 Villanova
Charlotte, NC

Villanova 90-72
March 15
1 Virginia

Virginia 54-50
March 19

North Caro. 78-65

5 Va. Commonwealth
March 13
12 LIU-Brooklyn
Charlotte, NC

Va. Commonwealth 85-69
March 15
4 Tennessee

Tennessee 58-56 (ot)

Virginia 62-48

6 Brigham Young
March 12
11 Princeton
Providence,

Brigham Young 60-51
March 14
3 UCLA

Brigham Young 78-55
March 19

Philadelphia, PA
March 28

Atlanta, GA
March 21

Virginia 74-60

7 Georgetown
March 12
10 James Madison
Providence, RI

James Madison 61-55
March 14
2 Notre Dame

Notre Dame 54-45

Brigham Young 51-50

Virginia

Louisiana St.

Virginia 78-74
NATIONAL 3rd PLACE

* Oregon State's participation in 1981 tournament vacated.

1981-82

AT A GLANCE

NCAA Champion: North Carolina (32-2; coached by Dean Smith; tied for ACC regular-season title with a 12-2 record).

NIT Champion: Bradley (26-10; coached by Dick Versace; won Missouri Valley title by one game with a 13-3 record).

New Conferences: Metro Atlantic Athletic, Northeast.

New Rules: The jump ball is employed only at the beginning of the game and the start of each overtime. An alternating arrow indicates possession in jump-ball situations during the game, with the arrow first pointing in the direction of the team that didn't gain possession of the initial jump ball. . . . All fouls assessed to bench personnel are charged to the head coach. . . . National third-place game in the NCAA Tournament is abolished.

NCAA Probation: Arkansas State, UC Santa Barbara, New Mexico, UCLA, Wichita State.

NCAA Consensus First-Team All-Americans: Terry Cummings, F-C, Jr., DePaul; Quintin Dailey, G, Jr., San Francisco; Eric "Sleepy" Floyd, G, Sr., Georgetown; Ralph Sampson, C, Jr., Virginia; James Worthy, F, Jr., North Carolina.

National Player of the Year: Sampson (15.8 ppg, 11.4 rpg, 56.1 FG%).

National Coaches of the Year: Oregon State's Ralph Miller (25-5/AP); Idaho's Don Monson (27-3/NABC); Missouri's Norm Stewart (27-4/UPI), and Georgetown's John Thompson (30-7/USBWA).

Georgetown's John Thompson took umbrage to depictions of him as the initial African-American coach to direct a team to the Final Four. But the injustices in the past against his race were sufficient reason for placing emphasis on Thompson's achievements with predominantly black rosters. His shooting guard, Sleepy Floyd, became the first Georgetown player to earn a spot on an NCAA consensus first- or second-team All-American squad.

Slowdown tactics that could bore fans to tears embarrassed the prestigious ACC Tournament, helping pave the way for the introduction of a shot clock later in the decade. Despite the presence of standouts such as Michael Jordan, Sam Perkins, James Worthy and Ralph Sampson, only one team scored at least 60 points in the seven ACC Tournament games.

Seton Hall guard Dan Callandrillo averaged 27.4 points per game to set a Big East Conference single-season record. . . . UC Irvine's Kevin Magee became the only player ever to finish two seasons in the top 10 nationally in scoring, rebounding and field-goal shooting. Magee set a school single-game scoring record with 46 points against Loyola Marymount. He also grabbed a school-record 25 rebounds against Long Beach State. . . . Western Illinois'

LONGEST GAME IN HISTORY Cincinnati and Bradley players anticipating their Christmas break in 1981 had a rude awakening on December 21, 1981. The game between the Braves and the Bearcats went into the seventh overtime before hometeam Bradley lost to Cincinnati, 75-73. Bradley's David Thirdkill and Mitchell Anderson led all scorers with 25 and 20 points, respectively.

CINCINNATI (75)	MIN.	FG-A	FT-A	REB.	PTS.
Gaffney	52	6-16	3-4	8	15
Jones	64	8-14	2-5	15	18
Williams	63	3-11	2-3	15	8
Johnson	63	1-4	0-1	1	2
Austin	73	8-19	2-3	7	18
Schloemer	18	3-3	0-0	3	6
McMillan	13	0-2	0-0	2	0
Robinson	24	2-4	2-3	4	6
Campbell	7	1-1	0-0	1	2
Kecman	1	0-1	0-0	0	0
Team				1	
TOTALS	**375**	**32-75**	**11-19**	**57**	**75**

FG%: .427. **FT%:** .579. **Assists:** 18 (Johnson 7). **Steals:** 7. **Blocked Shots:** 0. **Turnovers:** 19. **Fouled Out:** 2 (Gaffney/6th OT, Jones/6th OT).

BRADLEY (73)	MP	FG-A	FT-A	REB.	PTS.
Anderson	65	8-25	4-6	12	20
Thirdkill	68	10-17	5-8	9	25
Reese	73	4-9	6-8	6	14
Scott	68	0-7	2-3	4	2
Mines	6	0-3	0-0	0	0
Winters	69	6-15	0-2	15	12
Cook	10	0-2	0-0	1	0
Mathews	17	0-1	0-0	1	0
Team				2	
TOTALS	**375**	**28-79**	**17-27**	**50**	**73**

FG%: .354. **FT%:** .630. **Assists:** 20 (Scott 8). **Steals:** 12. **Blocked Shots:** 2. **Turnovers:** 15. **Fouled Out:** 2 (Anderson/5th OT, Winter/2nd half).

Halftime: Bradley 40-35. **Regulation:** Tied 61-61. **First Overtime:** Tied 63-63. **Second Overtime:** Tied 65-65. **Third Overtime:** Tied 65-65. **Fourth Overtime:** Tied 67-67. **Fifth Overtime:** Tied 71-71. **Sixth Overtime:** Tied 73-73.

1981–82 INDIVIDUAL LEADERS

SCORING

PLAYER	PTS.	AVG.
Kelly, Texas Southern	862	29.7
Pierce, Rice	805	26.8
Callandrillo, Seton Hall	698	25.9
Magee, UC Irvine	732	25.2
Dailey, San Francisco	755	25.2
Jackson, Centenary	693	23.9
Wiggins, Florida St.	523	23.8
Moss, Northeastern	710	23.7
McLaughlin, C. Michigan	581	23.2
Jakubick, Akron	594	22.8

REBOUNDING

PLAYER	REB.	AVG.
Thompson, Texas	365	13.5
Sappleton, Loyola (Ill.)	376	13.0
Tillis, Cleveland St.	346	12.8
McNamara, California	341	12.6
Clarida, Long Island	369	12.3
Norris, Jackson St.	341	12.2
Magee, UC Irvine	353	12.2
Cobb, Pan American	302	12.1
Cummings, DePaul	334	11.9

FIELD GOAL PERCENTAGE

PLAYER	FGM	FGA	PCT.
McNamara, California	231	329	.702
Ellis, Tennessee	257	393	.654
Phillips, Pepperdine	181	280	.646
Culton, Texas-Arl.	200	311	.643
Magee, UC Irvine	272	424	.642
Pinckney, Villanova	169	264	.640
Hopson, Idaho	158	250	.632
Clarida, Long I.	180	285	.632
Jones, Houston Bap.	178	282	.631
Clark, Miss.	251	403	.623

FREE THROW PERCENTAGE

PLAYER	FTA	FTM	PCT.
Foster, UCLA	95	100	.950
Moore, Nebraska	123	131	.939
Dykstra, W. Ill.	147	161	.913
Williams, Idaho St.	70	78	.897
Master, Kentucky	95	106	.896
McGraw, Siena	112	126	.889
Lee, Boise St.	71	80	.888
Carrabino, Harvard	85	97	.876
Gillam, W. Chester St.	85	97	.876
Engelland, Duke	77	88	.875

1981–82 TEAM LEADERS

SCORING OFFENSE

SCHOOL	PTS.	AVG.
Long Island	2605	86.8
Texas Southern	2429	83.8
North Texas St.	2258	83.6
San Francisco	2527	81.5
Houston	2685	81.4

SCORING DEFENSE

SCHOOL	PTS.	AVG.
Fresno St.	1412	47.1
N.C. St.	1570	49.1
Princeton	1277	49.1
Wyoming	1545	51.5
James Madison	1559	52.0

SCORING MARGIN

SCHOOL	OFF.	DEF.	MAR.
Oregon St.	69.6	55.0	14.6
Georgetown	67.6	53.5	14.2
Idaho	71.3	57.5	13.8
Virginia	70.7	57.2	13.5
Tenn.-Chattanooga	72.6	59.9	12.7

WON-LOST PERCENTAGE

SCHOOL	W-L	PCT.
North Carolina	32-2	.941
DePaul	26-2	.929
Fresno St.	27-3	.900
Idaho	27-3	.900
Virginia	30-4	.882

FIELD GOAL PERCENTAGE

SCHOOL	FGM	FGA	PCT.
UC Irvine	920	1639	.561
Mississippi	696	1281	.543
Pepperdine	929	1714	.542
Tennessee	792	1462	.542
Missouri	815	1511	.539

FIELD GOAL PERCENTAGE DEFENSE

SCHOOL	FGM	FGA	PCT.
Wyoming	584	1470	.397
Georgetown	757	1808	.419
Idaho	696	1662	.419
N.C. St.	621	1481	.419
Missouri	742	1766	.420

FREE THROW PERCENTAGE

SCHOOL	FTM	FTA	PCT.
Western Illinois	447	569	.786
Northwestern St. (La.)	489	624	.784
Western Carolina	481	623	.772
Idaho St.	393	522	.753
Ohio St.	415	552	.752

REBOUND MARGIN

SCHOOL	OWN	OPP.	MAR.
Northeastern	41.2	30.8	10.4
Wyoming	36.4	26.7	9.7
Brigham Young	37.3	29.3	8.0
Alabama	37.3	29.5	7.7
Pepperdine	37.7	30.0	7.6

Joe Dykstra set an NCAA record by converting 64 consecutive free throws (eight-game stretch from December 1 to January 4).

In the longest game in major-college history, Cincinnati outlasted NIT champion-to-be Bradley, 75-73, in seven overtimes (see accompanying box). "That was my biggest thrill as a coach," said Tony Barone, an assistant to Bradley's Dick Versace at the time. "One of their subs made a jump shot that he had no business making–a terrible shot–that went in with two seconds left in the seventh overtime. We threw the ball the length of the court and our center caught it, turned around from the top of the key, shot it and the ball went in and out. Otherwise, it would have been eight overtimes." In another wild overtime affair, Dayton scored the last points in all five extra sessions to outlast Providence, 79-77.

Missouri, coached by Norm Stewart, won its first 19 games and was ranked No. 1 in the country before bowing to visiting Nebraska, 67-51. . . . Fresno State posted the best scoring defense of any team since 1952 (47.1 points per

The Louisiana Superdome hosts the 1982 NCAA Final Four.

game). FSU and Alabama-Birmingham finished in the Top 20 of a final wire-service poll for the only time in school history. . . . Texas, coached by Abe Lemons, got off to a sizzling 14-0 start but finished with a modest 16-11 record after forward Mike Wacker sustained a season-ending knee injury. . . . TCU, coached by Jim Killingsworth, compiled a 16-13 mark to end a streak of nine consecutive losing seasons.

Oregon State's 14.6-point margin of victory was the lowest ever for a school that led the nation in scoring differential. . . . California compiled a 14-13 record for its only winning season in a 10-year span from 1975-76 through 1984-85. . . . Former NCAA champion San Fran-

cisco dropped its program after a 25-6 season because of improprieties frowned upon by the university administration and the NCAA. The Dons averaged 22.5 victories annually in their last 11 years. . . . Rice's Ricky Pierce (26.8 ppg) and San Francisco's Quintin Dailey (25.2) set school records for highest scoring average in a single season.

Cal State Fullerton, which compiled a 4-23 record the previous season, improved by 11 1/2 games to 18-14. The Titans were coached by George McQuarn. . . . Montana State's Doug Hashley grabbed a school-record 24 rebounds in a game against Nevada-Reno. . . . West Virginia finished in the Top 20 of a final wire-service poll for the first time since 1963. The Mountaineers' school-record 23-game winning streak, the longest in the country, was ended at Rutgers, 74-64, in their regular-season finale.

Virginia (30-4, coached by Terry Holland), Fresno State (27-3, Boyd Grant), Idaho (27-3, Don Monson), Tennessee-Chattanooga (27-4, Murray Arnold), James Madison (24-6, Lou Campanelli) and UC Irvine (23-7, Bill Mulligan) had their winningest seasons in school Division I history.

Western Kentucky competed as a member of the Ohio Valley Conference for the final season. . . . West Chester State (Pa.) competed in its final campaign at the major-college level. . . . Notre Dame, incurring its only losing record (10-17) in an 18-year stretch from 1972-73 through 1989-90, finished out of the top 10 of the final AP poll for the first time in seven seasons. . . . The national scoring average decreased for the seventh consecutive season, reaching the lowest point since 1952 with 135.1 points per game (both teams combined). Texas Southern's Harry Kelly led the country in scoring with a 29.7-point average, including a national-high 51 points against Texas College.

1981-82 FINAL NATIONAL POLLS

AP	UPI	SCHOOL (RECORD)	HEAD COACH
1	1	North Carolina (32-2)	Dean Smith
2	2	DePaul (26-2)	Ray Meyer
3	3	Virginia (30-4)	Terry Holland
4	4	Oregon State (25-5)	Ralph Miller
5	5	Missouri (27-4)	Norm Stewart
6	7	Georgetown (30-7)	John Thompson
7	6	Minnesota (23-6)	Jim Dutcher
8	8	Idaho (27-3)	Don Monson
9	9	Memphis State (24-5)	Dana Kirk
10	11	Tulsa (24-6)	Nolan Richardson
11	10	Fresno State (27-3)	Boyd Grant
12	13	Arkansas (23-6)	Eddie Sutton
13	12	Alabama (24-7)	Wimp Sanderson
14	17	West Virginia (27-4)	Gale Catlett
15	14	Kentucky (22-8)	Joe B. Hall
16	16	Iowa (21-8)	Lute Olson
17	–	UAB (25-6)	Gene Bartow
18	19	Wake Forest (21-9)	Carl Tacy
19	–	UCLA (21-6)	Larry Farmer
20	20	Louisville (23-10)	Denny Crum
–	15	Wyoming (23-7)	Jim Brandenburg
–	18	Kansas State (23-8)	Jack Hartman

1982 NCAA Tournament

Summary: Georgetown's early 12-6 lead was the biggest of the game. Freshman guard Michael Jordan swished a 16-foot jumper from the left side with 16 seconds remaining to provide the title game's final points as North Carolina edged Georgetown, 63-62. Georgetown guard Fred Brown's errant pass directly to Tar Heels forward James Worthy prevented the Hoyas from attempting a potential game-winning shot in the closing seconds. Georgetown's Patrick Ewing was called for goaltending five times in the opening minutes of the final. Jordan's heroics came after an inauspicious playoff debut when he collected six points, one rebound, no assists and no steals in 37 minutes of a 52-50 opening-round victory against James Madison in the East Regional.

Outcome for Defending Champion: Indiana (19-10), after losing guard Isiah Thomas early to the NBA, was eliminated in the second round of the Mideast Regional by Alabama-Birmingham, 80-70. The Hoosiers had a four-game losing streak after dropping their first two Big Ten assignments but they rebounded to finish in a tie for second place in the league standings.

Star Gazing: Worthy, the Final Four Most Outstanding Player, hit 20 of 27 field-goal attempts in two Final Four games. He scored a career-high 28 points in the championship game.

Biggest Upsets: DePaul lost its third opener in as many years as a No. 1 seed when the Blue Demons, ranked second nationally, bowed to Boston College, 82-75, in the Midwest Regional. . . . Middle Tennessee State (seeded No. 11) overcame an early 8-0 deficit to defeat Kentucky (No. 6), 50-44, in the first round of the Mideast Regional. No Kentucky player scored more than eight points.

One and Only: Northeastern's Perry Moss was the only player to crack the 30-point plateau in the tourney. He tallied 31 against Villanova.

SEASON STATISTICS OF NORTH CAROLINA REGULARS

PLAYER	POS.	CL.	G.	FG%	FT%	PPG	RPG
James Worthy	F	Jr.	34	.573	.674	15.6	6.3
Sam Perkins	C	So.	32	.578	.768	14.3	7.8
Michael Jordan	G	Fr.	34	.534	.722	13.5	4.4
Matt Doherty	F	So.	34	.519	.772	9.3	3.0
Jimmy Black	G	Sr.	34	.513	.738	7.6	1.7
Jim Braddock	G	Jr.	34	.452	.833	1.9	0.5
Chris Brust	F	Sr.	33	.622	.455	1.7	1.7
Buzz Peterson	G	Fr.	30	.390	.429	1.2	0.5
Jeb Barlow	F	Sr.	28	.387	.444	1.0	0.8
TEAM TOTALS			34	.537	.692	66.7	29.4

Assists leader: Black 213. **Blocked shots leader:** Perkins 53. **Steals leader:** Black 58.

1982 FINAL FOUR CHAMPIONSHIP GAME

NEW ORLEANS, LA

GEORGETOWN (62)	MIN.	FG-A	FT-A	REB.	A	PF	PTS.
E. Smith	35	6-8	2-2	3	5	5	14
Hancock	8	0-2	0-0	0	0	1	0
Ewing	37	10-15	3-3	11	1	4	23
F. Brown	29	1-2	2-2	2	5	4	4
Floyd	39	9-17	0-0	3	5	2	18
Spriggs	30	0-2	1-2	1	0	2	1
Jones	10	1-3	0-0	0	0	0	2
B. Martin	5	0-2	0-0	0	0	1	0
G. Smith	7	0-0	0-0	0	0	1	0
Team				2			
TOTALS	200	27-51	8-9	22	16	20	62

FG%: .529. **FT%:** .889. **Blocks:** 2. **Turnovers:** 12. **Steals:** 11.

N. CAROLINA (63)	MIN.	FG-A	FT-A	REB.	A	PF	PTS.
Doherty	39	1-3	2-3	3	1	0	4
Worthy	38	13-17	2-7	4	0	3	28
Perkins	38	3-7	4-6	7	1	2	10
Black	38	1-4	2-2	3	7	2	4
Jordan	34	7-13	2-2	9	2	2	16
Peterson	7	0-3	0-0	1	1	0	0
Braddock	2	0-0	0-0	0	1	1	0
Brust	4	0-0	1-2	1	1	1	1
Team				2			
TOTALS	200	25-47	13-22	30	14	11	63

FG%: .532. **FT%:** .591. **Blocks:** 1. **Turnovers:** 13. **Steals:** 7.
Halftime: Georgetown 32-31.

NATIONAL SEMIFINALS

HOUSTON (63): Drexler 6-12 5-6 17, Young 1-7 0-1 2, Micheaux 8-14 2-3 18, Rose 10-15 0-2 20, R. Williams 0-8 2-2 2, B. Williams 0-1 0-0 0, Olajuwon 1-3 0-0 2, Davis 1-2 0-0 2, Anders 0-2 0-0 0. Team 27-64 (.422) 9-14 (.643) 63.

NORTH CAROLINA (68): Doherty 2-7 1-2 5, Worthy 7-10 0-0 14, Perkins 9-11 7-7 25, Black 1-2 4-6 6, Jordan 7-14 4-4 18, Peterson 0-0 0-0 0, Brust 0-0 0-0 0, W. Martin 0-0 0-0 0, Braddock 0-0 0-0 0. Team 26-44 (.591) 16-19 (.842) 68.

Halftime: North Carolina 31-29.

LOUISVILLE (46): W. Brown 2-5 0-0 4, D. Smith 4-8 2-4 10, R. McCray 2-5 4-4 8, Gordon 1-6 0-0 2, Eaves 4-9, 0-0 8, Wagner 1-4 0-0 2, Jones 4-7 0-2 8, S. McCray 0-1 0-0 0, Wright 1-3 2-2 4. Team 19-48 (.396) 8-12 (.667) 46.

GEORGETOWN (50): E. Smith 6-10 2-4 14, Hancock 1-3 0-0 2, Ewing 3-8 2-2 8, F. Brown 1-3 2-3 4, Floyd 3-11 7-8 13, Spriggs 2-2 1-3 5, G. Smith 0-0 0-0 0, Jones 2-4 0-0 4, B. Martin 0-0 0-0 0. Team 18-41 (.439) 14-20 (.700) 50.

Halftime: Georgetown 24-22.

ALL-TOURNAMENT TEAM

Patrick Ewing, C, Fr., Georgetown
Sleepy Floyd, G, Sr., Georgetown
Michael Jordan, G, Fr., North Carolina
Sam Perkins, C, Soph., North Carolina
James Worthy, F, Jr., North Carolina*
*Named Most Outstanding Player

Numbers Game: Junior guard Rob Williams, Houston's leader in scoring with a 21.1-point average, missed all eight of his field-goal attempts against the Tar Heels in the national semifinals. Nonetheless, he still finished as the tourney's leading scorer because he scored at least 25 points in three previous outings. Williams left early for the NBA after the season and was joined in the same category by teammates Clyde Drexler in 1983 and Hakeem Olajuwon in 1984 as the Cougars became the only school to have an undergrad selected in the first round of the NBA draft three consecutive years. . . . Virginia's Ralph Sampson grabbed a tourney-high 21 rebounds, but it was in vain when the Cavaliers bowed to Alabama-Birmingham, 68-66, in the Mideast Regional semifinals. . . . Tulsa appeared in the playoffs for the first time since 1955.

What If: Williams, swingman Michael Young and center Hakeem Olajuwon combined to average 40.3 points per game for Houston. If only they collaborated for 12 points instead of two apiece in the national semifinals, the Cougars could have defeated Carolina rather than losing 68-63. . . . It is unlikely that DePaul (26-2) would have been eliminated right away in the tourney if Mark Aguirre didn't forgo his final season of eligibility. . . . Maryland (16-13) might have wound up in the NCAA playoffs instead of the NIT if rebounder deluxe Buck Williams had remained in school instead of turning pro early.

1982 CHAMPIONSHIP BRACKET

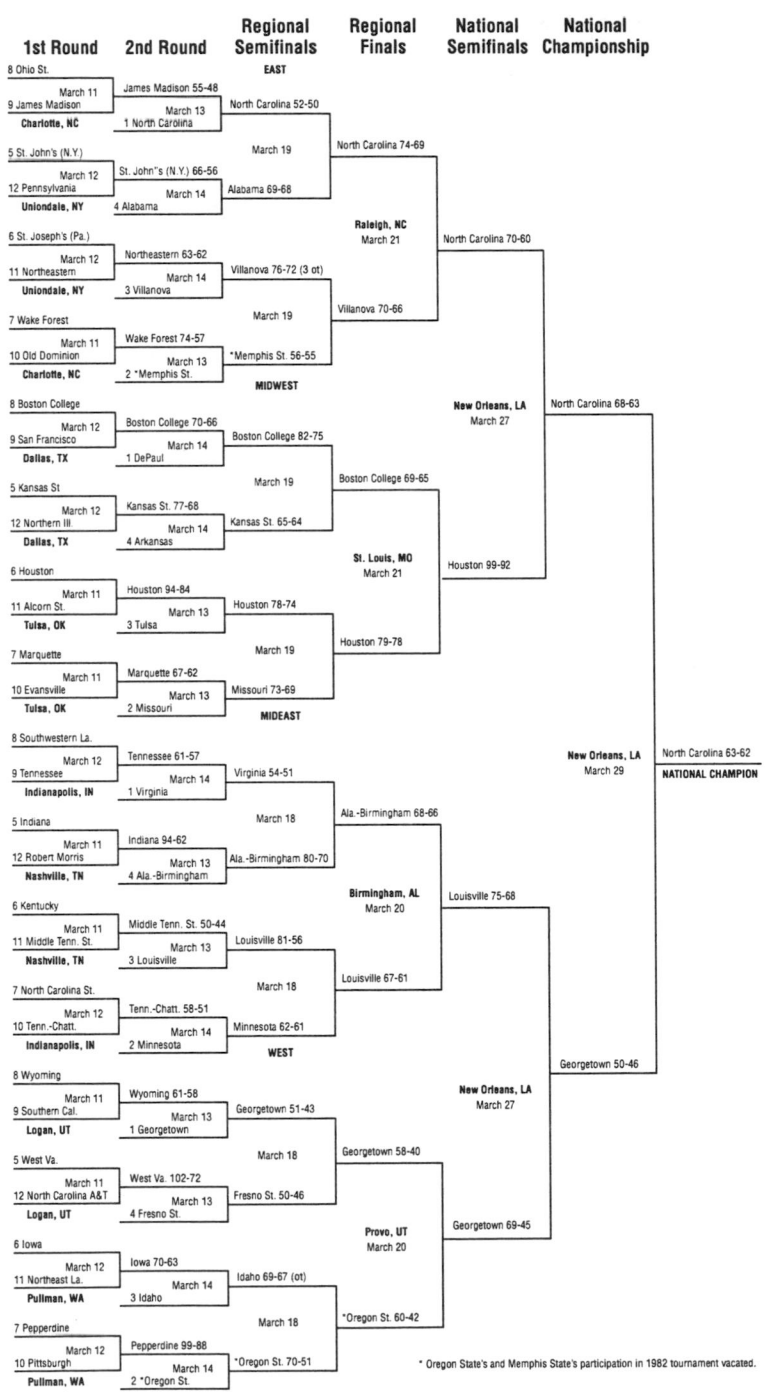

1st Round	2nd Round	Regional Semifinals	Regional Finals	National Semifinals	National Championship

EAST

8 Ohio St.
March 11
9 James Madison
Charlotte, NC
James Madison 55-48
March 13
1 North Carolina
North Carolina 52-50

5 St. John's (N.Y.)
March 12
12 Pennsylvania
Uniondale, NY
St. John"s (N.Y.) 66-56
March 14
4 Alabama
Alabama 69-68

North Carolina 74-69

6 St. Joseph's (Pa.)
March 12
11 Northeastern
Uniondale, NY
Northeastern 63-62
March 14
3 Villanova
Villanova 76-72 (3 ot)

7 Wake Forest
March 11
10 Old Dominion
Charlotte, NC
Wake Forest 74-57
March 13
2 *Memphis St.
*Memphis St. 56-55

Villanova 70-66

Raleigh, NC
March 21
North Carolina 70-60

MIDWEST

8 Boston College
March 12
9 San Francisco
Dallas, TX
Boston College 70-66
March 14
1 DePaul
Boston College 82-75

5 Kansas St
March 12
12 Northern Ill.
Dallas, TX
Kansas St. 77-68
March 14
4 Arkansas
Kansas St. 65-64

Boston College 69-65

6 Houston
March 11
11 Alcorn St.
Tulsa, OK
Houston 94-84
March 13
3 Tulsa
Houston 78-74

7 Marquette
March 11
10 Evansville
Tulsa, OK
Marquette 67-62
March 13
2 Missouri
Missouri 73-69

Houston 79-78

St. Louis, MO
March 21
Houston 99-92

New Orleans, LA
March 27
North Carolina 68-63

MIDEAST

8 Southwestern La.
March 12
9 Tennessee
Indianapolis, IN
Tennessee 61-57
March 14
1 Virginia
Virginia 54-51

5 Indiana
March 11
12 Robert Morris
Nashville, TN
Indiana 94-62
March 13
4 Ala.-Birmingham
Ala.-Birmingham 80-70

Ala.-Birmingham 68-66

6 Kentucky
March 11
11 Middle Tenn. St.
Nashville, TN
Middle Tenn. St. 50-44
March 13
3 Louisville
Louisville 81-56

7 North Carolina St.
March 12
10 Tenn.-Chatt.
Indianapolis, IN
Tenn.-Chatt. 58-51
March 14
2 Minnesota
Minnesota 62-61

Louisville 67-61

Birmingham, AL
March 20
Louisville 75-68

New Orleans, LA
March 27
Georgetown 50-46

North Carolina 63-62
NATIONAL CHAMPION

New Orleans, LA
March 29

WEST

8 Wyoming
March 11
9 Southern Cal.
Logan, UT
Wyoming 61-58
March 13
1 Georgetown
Georgetown 51-43

5 West Va.
March 11
12 North Carolina A&T
Logan, UT
West Va. 102-72
March 13
4 Fresno St.
Fresno St. 50-46

Georgetown 58-40

6 Iowa
March 12
11 Northeast La.
Pullman, WA
Iowa 70-63
March 14
3 Idaho
Idaho 69-67 (ot)

7 Pepperdine
March 12
10 Pittsburgh
Pullman, WA
Pepperdine 99-88
March 14
2 *Oregon St.
*Oregon St. 70-51

*Oregon St. 60-42

Provo, UT
March 20
Georgetown 69-45

* Oregon State's and Memphis State's participation in 1982 tournament vacated.

Putting Things in Perspective: Would North Carolina have captured the crown if the Tar Heels didn't win three games, two of them by a total of just seven points, in familiar surroundings (second round at Charlotte and East Regional at Raleigh)?

Scoring Leader: Rob Williams, Houston (88 points, 17.6 ppg).

Highest Scoring Average: Perry Moss, Northeastern (55 points, 27.5 ppg).

Rebounding Leader: Clyde Drexler, Houston (41 rebounds, 8.2 rpg).

Highest Rebounding Average: Ralph Sampson, Virginia (30 rebounds, 15 rpg).

1982-83

AT A GLANCE

NCAA Champion: North Carolina State (26-10; coached by Jim Valvano; finished in a tie for third place in ACC with an 8-6 record).

NIT Champion: Fresno State (25-10; coached by Boyd Grant; finished in fourth place in PCAA with a 9-7 record).

New Conferences: AMCU (forerunner of Mid-Continent), ECAC South (forerunner of Colonial Athletic).

New Rules: It is no longer a jump-ball situation when the closely guarded five-second count is reached. It is a violation, and the ball is awarded to the defensive team out of bounds. . . . An opening round was added to the NCAA Tournament, requiring the representatives of eight automatic-qualifying conferences to compete for four positions in the 52-team bracket. . . . The current tourney format was established that begins the event the third weekend in March, regional championships on the fourth Saturday and Sunday, and the national semifinals and final the following Saturday and Monday.

NCAA Probation: Oklahoma City, St. Louis, Wichita State.

NCAA Consensus First-Team All-Americans: Dale Ellis, F, Sr., Tennessee; Patrick Ewing, C, Soph., Georgetown; Michael Jordan, G, Soph., North Carolina; Keith Lee, C, Soph., Memphis State; Sam Perkins, C, Jr., North Carolina; Ralph Sampson, C, Sr., Virginia; Wayman Tisdale, C-F, Fr., Oklahoma.

National Player of the Year: Sampson (19 ppg, 11.7 rpg, 60.4 FG%).

National Coaches of the Year: St. John's Lou Carnesecca (28-5/NABC, USBWA); Houston's Guy Lewis (31-3/AP), and UNLV's Jerry Tarkanian (28-3/UPI).

Parity was more than a rhetorical concept this season. In a game hailed as one of the biggest upsets in college basketball history, Ralph Sampson-led Virginia lost at Chaminade, 77-72, in Hawaii.

Virginia also squandered a 10-point lead in the last 4:12 against North Carolina and bowed to the Tar Heels, 64-63, when they scored the game's last 11 points. A tip-in by Michael Jordan cut their deficit to one before his steal and dunk gave Carolina the triumph.

Wayman Tisdale, the first Oklahoma player since 1947 to become an NCAA consensus first- or second-team All-American, was the first

Houston's Clyde Drexler flies past an opponent.

All-American forward Dale Ellis dunks one for the Tennessee Volunteers.

1982–83 INDIVIDUAL LEADERS

SCORING

PLAYER	PTS.	AVG.
Kelly, Texas Southern	835	28.8
Malone, Miss. St.	777	26.8
Yates, George Mason	723	26.8
Bradley, S. Florida	855	26.7
Jakubick, Akron	774	26.7
Goorjian, Loyola (Cal.)	601	26.1
Hughes, Loyola (Ill.)	744	25.7
Tisdale, Oklahoma	810	24.5
Lyons, N. Texas St.	728	24.3
Jackson, Centenary	697	24.0

REBOUNDING

PLAYER	REB.	AVG.
McDaniel, Wichita St.	403	14.4
Giles, S. Caro. St.	360	12.9
Cage, San Diego St.	354	12.6
Halsel, Northeastern	350	12.5
Cross, Maine	310	11.9
Green, UNLV	368	11.9
Kelly, Texas Southern	340	11.7
Sampson, Virginia	386	11.7
Olajuwon, Houston	388	11.4
Mosley, Nevada-Reno	325	11.2

FIELD GOAL PERCENTAGE

PLAYER	FGM	FGA	PCT.
Mikell, East Tenn. St.	197	292	.675
Phillips, Pepperdine	223	338	.660
McDowell, Florida	203	314	.646
Barkley, Auburn	161	250	.644
Best, St. Peter's	138	215	.642
Thorpe, Providence	204	321	.636
Robinson, Nicholls St.	146	231	.632
Johnson, Grambling	205	325	.631
DeBisschop, Fairfield	203	324	.627
Mosley, Nevada-Reno	184	297	.620

FREE THROW PERCENTAGE

PLAYER	FGM	FGA	PCT.
Gonzalez, Colorado	75	82	.915
Fisher, J. Madison	95	104	.913
Waitkus, Brown	97	108	.898
Cox, Vanderbilt	113	126	.897
Hobdy, Grambling	78	87	.897
Dykstra, W. Ill.	156	176	.886
Allen, Nevada-Reno	117	132	.886
Mullin, St. John's	173	197	.878
Price, Ga. Tech	93	106	.877
Gross, UC S. Barbara	140	160	.875

1982–83 TEAM LEADERS

SCORING OFFENSE

SCHOOL	PTS.	AVG.
Boston College	2697	84.3
Syracuse	2612	84.3
South Carolina St.	2353	84.0
Alabama St.	2352	84.0
Houston	2800	82.4

SCORING DEFENSE

SCHOOL	PTS.	AVG.
Princeton	1507	52.0
Fresno St.	1880	53.7
James Madison	1670	53.9
Notre Dame	1619	55.8
Arkansas St.	1651	56.9

SCORING MARGIN

SCHOOL	OFF.	DEF.	MAR.
Houston	82.4	64.9	17.4
Virginia	81.9	65.0	16.9
Oklahoma	82.3	70.7	11.6
North Carolina	77.0	65.7	11.3
St. John's	75.2	63.9	11.3
Wichita St.	82.3	71.0	11.3

WON-LOST PERCENTAGE

SCHOOL	W-L	PCT.
Houston	31-3	.912
UNLV	28-3	.903
Wichita St.	25-3	.893
Louisville	32-4	.889
Arkansas	26-4	.867

FIELD GOAL PERCENTAGE

SCHOOL	FGM	FGA	PCT.
Kentucky	869	1564	.556
Stanford	752	1373	.548
New Orleans	937	1714	.547
Pepperdine	900	1653	.544
Houston Baptist	712	1319	.540

FIELD GOAL PERCENTAGE DEFENSE

SCHOOL	FGM	FGA	PCT.
Wyoming	599	1441	.416
Virginia	863	2071	.417
Idaho	661	1582	.418
Montana	663	1574	.421
Memphis St.	831	1965	.423

FREE THROW PERCENTAGE

SCHOOL	FTM	FGA	PCT.
Western Illinois	526	679	.775
Dayton	453	586	.773
UC Santa Barbara	413	535	.772
William & Mary	470	609	.772
St. John's	649	843	.770

REBOUND MARGIN

SCHOOL	OWN	OPP.	MAR.
Wichita St.	42.4	33.6	8.8
Virginia	40.6	32.3	8.4
Houston	41.6	33.4	8.1
Wyoming	34.7	27.1	7.6
Alcorn St.	39.8	32.9	6.9

freshman to be named an NCAA consensus first-team All-American. None of the NCAA's seven consensus first-team All-Americans reached the national semifinals. . . . Tisdale (24.5 ppg and 10.3 rpg in Big Eight) and Louisiana Tech's Karl Malone (20.9 ppg and 10.3 rpg in Southland) earned league player of the year honors as freshmen. It was the only season in history that two major conferences had a freshman become player of the year.

Houston's Clyde Drexler set a SWC record with 11 steals against Syracuse. . . . Texas Southern's Harry Kelly led the nation in scoring with a 28.8-point average, including a national-high 60 points against Jarvis Christian. . . . Wichita State's Antoine Carr (47 points vs. Southern Illinois), Akron's Joe Jakubick (47 vs. Murray State), North Texas State's Kenneth Lyons (47 vs. Louisiana Tech), Arizona State's Paul Williams (45 at Southern Cal) and South Florida's Charlie Bradley (42 vs. Florida State) established single-game scoring records for their schools. . . . South Florida's Bradley (28.2 ppg) and George Mason's Carlos Yates (26.8) set school records for highest scoring average in a single season.

1982–83 NCAA CHAMPION: N.C. STATE

SEASON STATISTICS OF N.C. STATE REGULARS

PLAYER	POS.	CL.	G.	FG%	FT%	PPG	RPG
Dereck Whittenburg	G	Sr.	22	.467	.800	17.5	2.7
Thurl Bailey	F-C	Sr.	36	.501	.717	16.7	7.7
Sidney Lowe	G	Sr.	36	.461	.776	11.3	3.7
Ernie Myers	G	Fr.	35	.446	.607	11.2	2.5
Lorenzo Charles	F	So.	36	.542	.670	8.1	6.0
Terry Gannon	G	So.	36	.521	.903	7.3	0.8
Cozell McQueen	C	So.	36	.431	.576	3.5	5.6
Alvin Battle	F	Jr.	33	.419	.520	2.7	2.0
George McClain	G	Fr.	25	.375	.500	2.7	0.5
Harold Thompson	F	Jr.	26	.353	.500	0.5	0.5
TEAM TOTALS			36	**.472**	**.689**	74.2	34.4

Assists leader: Lowe 271. **Blocked shots leader:** Bailey 95. **Steals leader:** Lowe 87.

1983 FINAL FOUR CHAMPIONSHIP GAME

ALBUQUERQUE, NM

N.C. STATE (54)	MIN.	FG-A	FT-A	REB.	A	PF	PTS.
Bailey	39	7-16	1-2	5	0	1	15
Charles	25	2-7	0-0	7	0	2	4
McQueen	34	1-5	2-2	12	1	4	4
Whittenburg	39	6-17	2-2	5	1	3	14
Lowe	40	4-9	0-1	0	8	2	8
Battle	4	0-1	2-2	1	1	1	2
Gannon	18	3-4	1-2	1	2	3	7
Myers	1	0-0	0-0	1	0	0	0
Team				2			
TOTALS	200	23-59	8-11	34	13	16	54

FG%: .390. **FT%:** .727. **Blocks:** 2. **Turnovers:** 6. **Steals:** 7 (Lowe 5).

HOUSTON (52)	MIN.	FG-A	FT-A	REB.	A	PF	PTS.
Drexler	25	1-5	2-2	2	0	4	4
Micheaux	18	2-6	0-0	6	0	1	4
Olajuwon	38	7-15	6-7	18	1	1	20
Franklin	35	2-6	0-1	0	3	0	4
Young	30	3-10	0-4	8	1	0	6
Anders	17	4-9	2-5	2	1	2	10
Gettys	20	2-2	0-0	2	2	3	4
Rose	7	0-1	0-0	1	0	2	0
Williams	10	0-1	0-0	4	1	3	0
Team				1			
TOTALS	200	21-55	10-19	44	9	16	52

FG%: .382. **FT%:** .526. **Blocks:** 8 (Olajuwon 7). **Turnovers:** 13. **Steals:** 0. **Halftime:** North Carolina State 33-25.

NATIONAL SEMIFINALS

N.C. STATE (67): Bailey 9-17 2-5 20, Charles 2-2 1-2 5, McQueen 4-5 0-0 8, Whittenburg 8-18, 4-4 20, Lowe 4-6 2-2 10, Battle 0-0 0-0 0, Gannon 1-4 2-2 4. Team 28-52 (.538) 11-15 (.733) 67.

GEORGIA (60): Banks 5-19 3-5 13, Heard 3-5 2-3 8, Fair 2-9 1-2 5, Crosby 5-15 2-2 12, Fleming 7-17 0-0 14, Corhen 3-6 0-1 6, Hartry 1-3 0-0 2, Floyd 0-0 0-0 0. Team 26-74 (.351) 8-13 (.615) 60.

Halftime: North Carolina State 33-32.

LOUISVILLE (81): S. McCray 5-8 0-0 10, R. McCray 3-6 2-8 8, Jones 3-10 6-8 12, Gordon 6-15 5-6 17, Wagner 12-23 0-0 24, Thompson 1-4 4-5 4, Hall 2-4 0-0 4, West 0-0 0-0 0, Valentine 0-0 0-0 0. Team 32-70 (.457) 17-27 (.630) 81.

HOUSTON (94): Drexler 10-15 1-2 21, Micheaux 4-7 0-1 8, Olajuwon 9-14 3-7 21, Franklin 5-8 3-4 13, Young 7-18 2-3 16, Gettys 0-0 0-0 0, Anders 5-9 3-5 13, Rose 0-2 0-0 0, Williams 1-1 0-0 2, Giles 0-0 0-1 0. Team 41-74 (.554) 12-23 (.522) 94.

Halftime: Louisville 41-36.

ALL-TOURNAMENT TEAM

Thurl Bailey, F, Sr., North Carolina State
Sidney Lowe, G, Sr., North Carolina State
Hakeem Olajuwon, C, Soph., Houston*
Milt Wagner, G, Soph., Louisville
Dereck Whittenburg, G, Sr., North Carolina State
*Named Most Outstanding Player

Washington State (since 1950), Wichita State (1965), Oklahoma State (1965) and Boston College (1969) finished in the Top 20 of a final wire-service poll for the first time in a long time. Georgia finished in the Top 20 for the first of just two times in school history. . . . Boston College (25-7/coached by Gary Williams), Georgia (24-10/Hugh Durham), Robert Morris (23-8/Matt Furjanic), South Florida (22-10/Lee Rose) and Northwestern (18-12/Rich Falk) had their winningest seasons in school history. Illinois State (24-7/Bob Donewald) tied its school Division I record for most victories in a single season.

Boston College became the only school since 1952 to lead the nation in scoring with an average under 85 points per game (84.3 ppg).

Falk is the only individual to direct a major college to an existing single-season record for most victories after setting the same school's single-game scoring standard as a player. . . . Illinois State and Tennessee-Chattanooga made their lone appearances in the Top 20 of a final wire-service poll. . . . Missouri, coached by Norm Stewart, became the only Big Eight school to win four consecutive regular-season championships since the league expanded to eight members in 1959. Center Steve Stipanovich and guard Jon Sundvold became the first Mizzou players to earn spots on an NCAA consensus first- or second-team All-American squad.

Tulane's Paul Thompson took a 90-foot inbounds pass from teammate Lamar Baker with one second remaining in double overtime and drilled an off-balance 25-footer to give the Green Wave an 80-79 victory at Florida State. Two nights earlier, a 30-foot buzzer-beater by Tulane's Daryl Moreau was the difference in a 49-47 victory over nationally ranked Memphis State at Tulane Gym (now Fogelman Arena), a snakepit with one of the smallest seating capacities (3,600) among members of elite leagues.

New Orleans lost three consecutive games to LSU the previous four seasons by an average of 26 points before overcoming a school-record 38 turnovers to prevail at LSU, 99-94, in overtime in the first round of the NIT. LSU, which lost to Tulane, 83-72, in the NIT the previous year, is the only school to be eliminated by visiting intrastate rivals in the opening round of back-to-back NITs.

The nation's top shot blocker before the NCAA began charting the statistic nationally was Old Dominion's Mark West, who finished his career with an average of 3.8 rejections per game. . . . Backup guard Marc Campbell of Clemson connected on seven of seven three-point field goals in back-to-back ACC games. . . . Villanova finished in the Top 20 of a final wire-service poll for the only time in a 22-year span from 1972-73 through 1993-94. . . . Defending NCAA champion North Carolina had an 18-game winning streak snapped by visiting Villanova, 56-53. The Tar Heels then lost back-to-back ACC road games at Maryland and North Carolina State to post their longest losing streak during All-American Michael Jordan's three-year career.

Manhattan, coached by Gordon Chiesa, posted its only winning mark (15-13) in a 16-year stretch from 1975-76 through 1990-91. The Jaspers won fewer than 10 games in nine of those seasons. . . . St. Bonaventure broke West Virginia's 39-game homecourt winning streak, 64-63. . . . LIU's Carey Scurry grabbed a school-record 26 rebounds in a game against Marist.

Northwestern compiled its only winning record (18-12) in a 24-year span from 1969-70 through 1992-93. . . . Texas Tech's streak of consecutive winning records ended at 13 when the Red Raiders registered an 11-20 mark.

Wyoming led the nation in field-goal percentage defense for the third consecutive season under coach Jim Brandenburg. . . . Utah State, which compiled a 4-23 record the previous season, improved by 15 games to 20-9. The Aggies were coached by Rod Tueller. . . . Oral Roberts' team voted to boycott when Ken Hayes was fired in mid-season. That put ORU star Mark Acres in the unusual position of having to strike against his father, Dick Acres, who was promoted from assistant to head coach. . . . New Mexico State finished in a tie for third place in the Missouri Valley Conference in the Aggies' final season as a member of the league.

Cal State Fullerton's Leon Wood set a Big West Conference single-season mark by averaging 11 assists per game. UNLV won its first 24 games until bowing at Cal State Fullerton, 86-78. . . . The number of independent schools in Division I decreased from 52 to 19. There had been as many as 79 independents in the mid-1970s. . . . Baltimore competed in its final season at the major-college level.

1982-83 FINAL NATIONAL POLLS

AP	UPI	USA/CNN	SCHOOL (RECORD)	HEAD COACH
1	1	2	Houston (31-3)	Guy Lewis
2	2	3	Louisville (32-4)	Denny Crum
3	3	8	St. John's (28-5)	Lou Carnesecca
4	4	5	Virginia (29-5)	Terry Holland
5	5	9	Indiana (24-6)	Bob Knight
6	6	18	UNLV (28-3)	Jerry Tarkanian
7	7	16	UCLA (23-6)	Larry Farmer
8	8	7	North Carolina (28-8)	Dean Smith
9	9	10	Arkansas (26-4)	Eddie Sutton
10	12	19	Missouri (26-8)	Norm Stewart
11	13	13	Boston College (25-7)	Gary Williams
12	10	6	Kentucky (23-8)	Joe B. Hall
13	11	11	Villanova (24-8)	Rollie Massimino
14	–	15	Wichita State (25-3)	Gene Smithson
15	16	–	UT-Chattanooga (26-4)	Murray Arnold
16	14	1	N.C. State (26-10)	Jim Valvano
17	17	12	Memphis State (23-8)	Dana Kirk
18	15	4	Georgia (24-10)	Hugh Durham
19	19	–	Oklahoma State (24-7)	Paul Hansen
20	20	20	Georgetown (22-10)	John Thompson
–	–	14	Iowa (21-10)	Lute Olson
–	–	17	Ohio State (20-10)	Eldon Miller
–	18	–	Illinois State (24-7)	Bob Donewald
–	–	21	Fresno State (25-10)	Boyd Grant
–	–	22	Utah (18-14)	Jerry Pimm
–	–	23	Syracuse (21-10)	Jim Boeheim
–	–	24	Washington State (23-7)	George Raveling
–	–	25	Tennessee (20-12)	Don DeVoe

An explosive Hakeem Olajuwon steals a Louisville pass in the 1983 NCAA Semifinals.

1983 NCAA Tournament

Summary: Sophomore forward Lorenzo Charles scored only four points in the title game, but two of them came when he converted guard Dereck Whittenburg's off-line desperation shot from well beyond the top of the free-throw circle into a decisive dunk as North Carolina State upset heavily-favored Houston, 54-52. Houston's 17-2 spurt at the start of the second half was in vain. The Cougars, entering the final with a 26-game winning streak, had a seven-point lead midway through the second half before Houston coach Guy Lewis inexplicably went into a spread offense, a ploy for which he was widely criticized. N.C. State, the first titlist with a double-digit loss total, became the only school to have as many as four playoff games decided by one or two points en route to a championship. The Wolfpack defeated Pepperdine in double overtime after trailing by six points with 24 seconds remaining in regulation, erased a 12-point deficit midway through the second half against UNLV and overcame a 10-point deficit against Virginia in the West Regional final. N.C. State capitalized on its six victims combining to shoot an anemic 56.8 percent from the free-throw line.

Outcome for Defending Champion: North Carolina (28-8) was eliminated in the East Regional final by Georgia, 82-77. The Tar Heels won the ACC regular-season title after recovering from a shaky start when they could have lost four of their first six non-league contests if not for a miraculous 70-68 triple-overtime victory against Tulane.

Star Gazing: Hakeem Olajuwon, who collected 41 points and 40 rebounds (tourney-high 22 vs. Louisville and 18 vs. N.C. State) for national runner-up Houston in two Final Four games, is the only Final Four Most Outstanding Player since 1972 not to play for the championship team.

Biggest Upset: The first meeting between in-state rivals Kentucky and Louisville in more

1983 CHAMPIONSHIP BRACKET

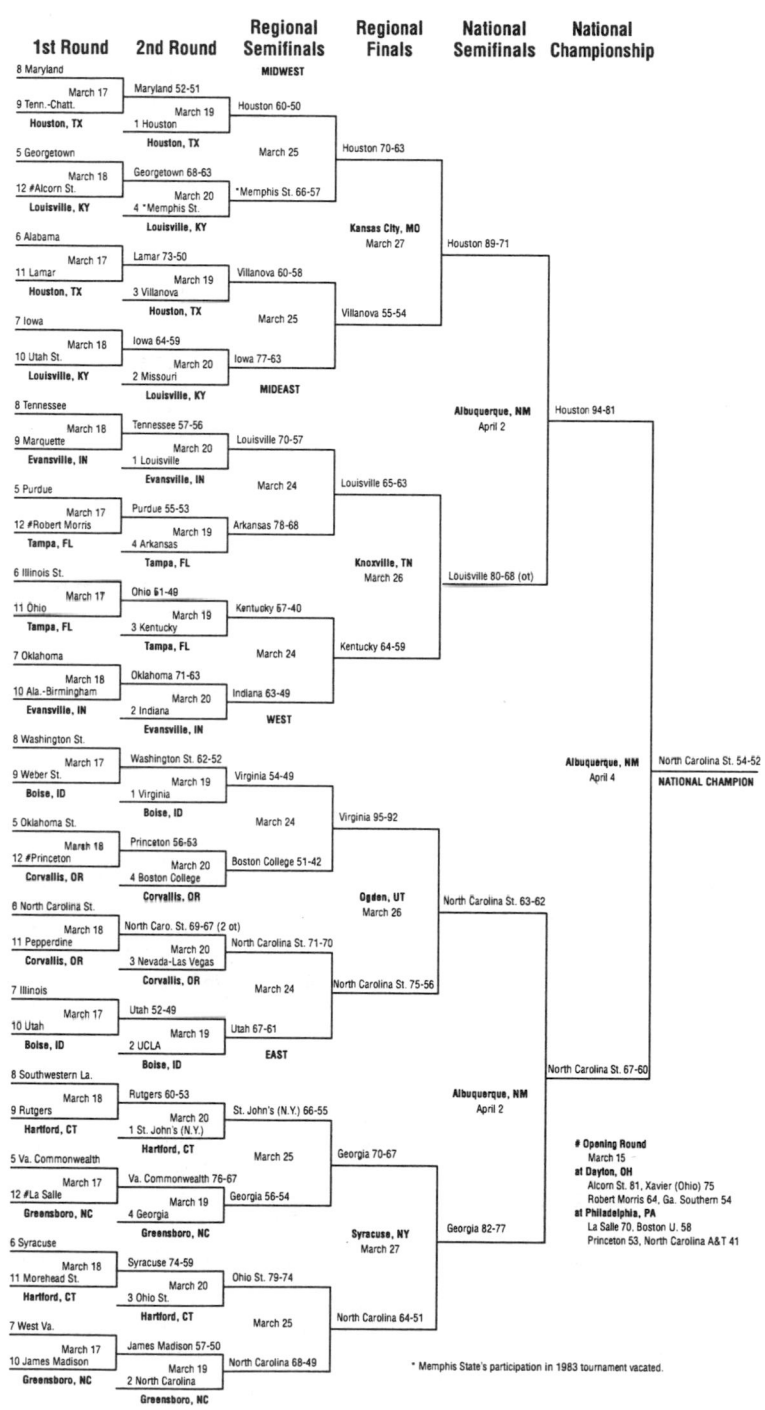

1st Round	2nd Round	Regional Semifinals	Regional Finals	National Semifinals	National Championship

MIDWEST

8 Maryland
March 17
Maryland 52-51
9 Tenn.-Chatt.
Houston, TX
March 19
Houston 60-50
1 Houston
Houston, TX
Houston 70-63

5 Georgetown
March 18
Georgetown 68-63
12 #Alcorn St.
Louisville, KY
March 20
*Memphis St. 66-57
4 *Memphis St.
Louisville, KY

Kansas City, MO
March 27
Houston 89-71

6 Alabama
March 17
Lamar 73-50
11 Lamar
Houston, TX
March 19
Villanova 60-58
3 Villanova
Houston, TX
Villanova 55-54

7 Iowa
March 18
Iowa 64-59
10 Utah St.
Louisville, KY
March 20
Iowa 77-63
2 Missouri
Louisville, KY

Albuquerque, NM
April 2
Houston 94-81

MIDEAST

8 Tennessee
March 18
Tennessee 57-56
9 Marquette
Evansville, IN
March 20
Louisville 70-57
1 Louisville
Evansville, IN
Louisville 65-63

5 Purdue
March 17
Purdue 55-53
12 #Robert Morris
Tampa, FL
March 19
Arkansas 78-68
4 Arkansas
Tampa, FL

Knoxville, TN
March 26
Louisville 80-68 (ot)

6 Illinois St.
March 17
Ohio 51-49
11 Ohio
Tampa, FL
March 19
Kentucky 67-40
3 Kentucky
Tampa, FL
Kentucky 64-59

7 Oklahoma
March 18
Oklahoma 71-63
10 Ala.-Birmingham
Evansville, IN
March 20
Indiana 63-49
2 Indiana
Evansville, IN

Houston 94-81

WEST

8 Washington St.
March 17
Washington St. 62-52
9 Weber St.
Boise, ID
March 19
Virginia 54-49
1 Virginia
Boise, ID
Virginia 95-92

5 Oklahoma St.
March 18
Princeton 56-53
12 #Princeton
Corvallis, OR
March 20
Boston College 51-42
4 Boston College
Corvallis, OR

Ogden, UT
March 26
North Carolina St. 63-62

6 North Carolina St.
March 18
North Caro. St. 69-67 (2 ot)
11 Pepperdine
Corvallis, OR
March 20
North Carolina St. 71-70
3 Nevada-Las Vegas
Corvallis, OR
North Carolina St. 75-56

7 Illinois
March 17
Utah 52-49
10 Utah
Boise, ID
March 19
Utah 67-61
2 UCLA
Boise, ID

Albuquerque, NM
April 4
North Carolina St. 54-52
NATIONAL CHAMPION

Albuquerque, NM
April 2
North Carolina St. 67-60

EAST

8 Southwestern La.
March 18
Rutgers 60-53
9 Rutgers
Hartford, CT
March 20
St. John's (N.Y.) 66-55
1 St. John's (N.Y.)
Hartford, CT
Georgia 70-67

5 Va. Commonwealth
March 17
Va. Commonwealth 76-67
12 #La Salle
Greensboro, NC
March 19
Georgia 56-54
4 Georgia
Greensboro, NC

Syracuse, NY
March 27
Georgia 82-77

6 Syracuse
March 18
Syracuse 74-59
11 Morehead St.
Hartford, CT
March 20
Ohio St. 79-74
3 Ohio St.
Hartford, CT
North Carolina 64-51

7 West Va.
March 17
James Madison 57-50
10 James Madison
Greensboro, NC
March 19
North Carolina 68-49
2 North Carolina
Greensboro, NC

 # Opening Round
March 15
at Dayton, OH
Alcorn St. 81, Xavier (Ohio) 75
Robert Morris 64, Ga. Southern 54
at Philadelphia, PA
La Salle 70, Boston U. 58
Princeton 53, North Carolina A&T 41

* Memphis State's participation in 1983 tournament vacated.

than 24 years was memorable as the Cardinals outscored the Wildcats 18-6 in overtime to reach the Final Four.

One and Only: This was the only year when all of the Final Four teams won their conference tournaments–North Carolina State (ACC), Houston (SWC), Georgia (SEC) and Louisville (Metro). . . . . This was the only year two teams reached the Final Four despite losing an undergraduate player who defected at the end of the previous season to become an NBA first-round draft choice (Georgia forward Dominique Wilkins, the 3rd pick in the 1982 draft and Houston guard Rob Williams, the 19th pick overall). . . . This was also the only year the four No. 2 seeds combined for a losing record (3-4).

Numbers Game: Georgia, seeded No. 4 in the 1983 East Regional in its playoff debut, is the only first-time entrant to be seeded better than fifth since the field expanded to at least 48 teams in 1980. . . . La Salle's Steve Black scored a tourney-high 31 points in a 76-67 setback against Virginia Commonwealth.

What If: Houston swingmen Clyde Drexler and Michael Young and forward Larry Micheaux combined to score 47 points per game. If only they combined for 17 points instead of 14 points in the championship game, the Cougars could have defeated N.C. State rather than losing by two points. Drexler played only 25 minutes after drawing four fouls in the first half. . . . Boston College (25-7 record/without John Bagley), Indiana (24-6/Isiah Thomas), North Carolina (28-8/James Worthy) and Ohio State (20-10/Clark Kellogg) might have advanced farther in the playoffs if standout players had exercised their remaining eligibility instead of turning pro. . . . DePaul (21-12) probably would have participated in the NCAA Tournament instead of the NIT if Terry Cummings didn't defect early to the NBA.

Putting Things in Perspective: Maryland (20-10) defeated N.C. State twice by a total of 14 points before losing in the second round against eventual national runner-up Houston. Virginia (29-5) defeated the Wolfpack twice by a total of 19 points before losing against N.C. State by one point in the West Regional final. N.C. State lost six of eight games in one span. Five of the Wolfpack's six ACC losses were by at least eight points, including back-to-back defeats by 18 points apiece.

Scoring Leader: Dereck Whittenburg, North Carolina State (120 points, 20 ppg).

Highest Scoring Average: Steve Black, La Salle (46 points, 23 ppg).

Rebounding Leader: Hakeem Olajuwon, Houston (65 rebounds, 13 rpg).

1983-84

AT A GLANCE

NCAA Champion: Georgetown (34-3; coached by John Thompson; won Big East title by two games with a 14-2 record).

NIT Champion: Michigan (23-10; coached by Bill Frieder; finished in fourth place in Big Ten with a 10-8 record).

New Rules: Two free throws are taken for each common foul committed within the last two minutes of the second half and the entire overtime periods, if the bonus rule is in effect (rule was rescinded one month into the season). . . . One additional NCAA Tournament opening-round game was established, requiring 10 automatic-qualifying conferences to compete for five positions in the 53-team bracket.

NCAA Probation: San Diego State.

NCAA Consensus First-Team All-Americans: Patrick Ewing, C, Jr., Georgetown; Michael Jordan, G, Jr., North Carolina; Hakeem Olajuwon, C, Jr., Houston; Sam Perkins, C, Sr., North Carolina; Wayman Tisdale, C-F, Soph., Oklahoma.

National Player of the Year: Jordan (19.6 ppg, 5.3 rpg, 55.1 FG%).

National Coaches of the Year: Washington's Marv Harshman (24-7/NABC); Purdue's Gene Keady (22-7/USBWA), and DePaul's Ray Meyer (27-3/AP, UPI).

1983–84 INDIVIDUAL LEADERS

SCORING

PLAYER	PTS.	AVG.
Jakubick, Akron	814	30.1
Jackson, Alabama St.	812	29.0
Durrant, Brigham Young	866	27.9
Hughes, Loyola (Ill.)	800	27.6
Tisdale, Oklahoma	919	27.0
Dumars, McNeese St.	817	26.4
Crawford, U.S. Intl.	614	24.6
Cage, San Diego St.	686	24.5
Burtt, Iona	749	24.2
Wood, Cal St. Full.	719	24.0

REBOUNDING

PLAYER	REB.	AVG.
Olajuwon, Houston	500	13.5
Scurry, Long Island	418	13.5
McDaniel, Wichita St.	393	13.1
Newman, Ark.-Little Rock	348	12.9
Cage, San Diego St.	352	12.6
Cross, Maine	339	12.6
Brown, G. Washington	351	12.1

Sanders, Miss. Valley St.	338	12.1
Binion, N. Carolina A&T	335	11.6
Koncak, SMU	378	11.5

ASSISTS

PLAYER	AST.	AVG.
Lathan, Ill.-Chicago	274	9.4
Tarkanian, UNLV	289	8.5
Gettys, Houston	309	8.4
LaFleur, Northeastern	252	7.9
William, Florida St.	215	7.7
Teague, Boston U.	218	7.5
Weingrad, Hofstra	208	7.4
Smith, Massachusetts	212	7.3
Les, Bradley	158	7.2
Stockton, Gonzaga	201	7.2

FIELD GOAL PERCENTAGE

PLAYER	FGM	FGA	PCT.
Olajuwon, Houston	249	369	.675
Hurt, Alabama	168	253	.664
Ewing, Georgetown	242	368	.658
Green, Oregon St.	134	204	.657
Walker, Utica	125	191	.654
Thornton, UC Irvine	151	236	.640
Barkley, Auburn	162	254	.638
Toomer, Florida A&M	149	234	.637
Boldon, C. Mich.	151	238	.634
Burke, Dartmouth	194	306	.634

FREE THROW PERCENTAGE

PLAYER	FTM	FTA	PCT.
Alford, Indiana	137	150	.913
Carrabino, Harvard	153	169	.905
Mullin, St. John's	169	187	.904
Ferry, Harvard	84	93	.903
Cunningham, UTSA	94	107	.879
Golston, Loyola (Ill.)	128	146	.877
Beasley, Arizona St.	112	128	.875
Potter, O. Roberts	82	94	.872
Arnolie, Penn	82	94	.872
White, UT-Chat.	124	143	.867

1983–84 TEAM LEADERS

SCORING OFFENSE

SCHOOL	PTS.	AVG.
Tulsa	2816	90.8
Alabama St.	2485	88.8
Oklahoma	2953	86.9
Marshall	2589	83.5
Oral Roberts	2569	82.9

SCORING DEFENSE

SCHOOL	PTS.	AVG.
Princeton	1403	50.1
Fresno St.	1802	54.6
Tulane	1535	54.8
Oregon St.	1618	55.8
Illinois	1737	56.0

SCORING MARGIN

SCHOOL	OFF.	DEF.	MAR.
Georgetown	74.3	57.9	16.4
North Carolina	80.1	64.8	15.3
Oklahoma	86.9	72.6	14.3
Lamar	78.5	64.8	13.6
UNLV	82.1	68.7	13.4

WON-LOST PERCENTAGE

SCHOOL	W-L	PCT.
Georgetown	34-3	.919
North Carolina	28-3	.903
DePaul	27-3	.900
Texas-El Paso	27-4	.871
Tulsa	27-4	.871

FIELD GOAL PERCENTAGE

SCHOOL	FGM	FGA	PCT.
Houston Baptist	797	1445	.552
North Carolina	966	1779	.543
Southern Methodist	1023	1892	.541
Navy	873	1616	.540
Maryland	941	1745	.539

FIELD GOAL PERCENTAGE DEFENSE

SCHOOL	FGM	FGA	PCT.
Georgetown	799	2025	.395
DePaul	687	1658	.414
Memphis St.	796	1904	.418
Kentucky	796	1894	.420
Southern (La.)	746	1768	.422

FREE THROW PERCENTAGE

SCHOOL	FTM	FTA	PCT.
Harvard	535	651	.822
North Carolina	551	704	.783
Illinois St.	510	659	.774
Fairfield	508	657	.773
St. Louis	400	521	.768

REBOUND MARGIN

SCHOOL	OWN	OPP.	MAR.
Northeastern	40.1	30.3	9.8
Georgetown	40.0	30.5	9.5
St. Joseph's	39.4	30.3	9.1
Auburn	36.9	28.5	8.5
George Washington	38.3	30.8	7.4

In one of the most ballyhooed regular-season matchups ever, Ralph Sampson-led Virginia defeated fellow center Patrick Ewing and the Georgetown Hoyas, 68-63. Sampson collected 28 points and 16 rebounds compared to Ewing's 16 points and eight rebounds.

In the first regular-season meeting in 61 years between in-state rivals Kentucky and Louisville, the Wildcats whipped the Cardinals, 65-44. Later, Kentucky's Melvin Turpin tied a SEC Tournament record with 42 points against Georgia.

Houston's Hakeem Olajuwon set a SWC record with 16 blocked shots against Arkansas. . . . North Carolina was ranked No. 1 with a 19-0 record when the Tar Heels succumbed at Arkansas, 65-64, in Pine Bluff on a last-second basket by Charles Balentine. . . . Maryland coach Lefty Driesell won his first ACC Tournament in 15 tries.

DePaul coach Ray Meyer (left) retired after the 1983–84 season and was replaced by his son, Joey (right) who was an assistant coach.

Oklahoma's Wayman Tisdale poured in a national-high and school-record 61 points against Texas-San Antonio. St. Joseph's Tony Costner tied a school standard with 47 points against Alaska-Anchorage in the Cable Car Classic at San Francisco. . . . Akron's Joe Jakubick became the nation's only player to average more than 30 points per game in a six-year span from 1980-81 through 1985-86. . . . Jakubick (30.1 ppg), Brigham Young's Devin Durrant (27.9), Loyola of Chicago's Alfredrick Hughes (27.6), San Diego State's Michael Cage (24.5) and Cal State Fullerton's Leon Wood (24) set school Division I records for highest scoring average in a single season.

Harvard, coached by Frank McLaughlin, set an NCAA single-season record for free-throw accuracy (82.2 percent). . . . Lamar's 80-game homecourt winning streak, which started in 1978, was snapped by Louisiana Tech, 68-65, in the Southland Conference Tournament.

Duke appeared in the Top 20 of final wire-service polls for the first time under coach Mike Krzyzewski. The Blue Devils were nine games below .500 after his first three years (38-47), including a school-record 43-point loss against Virginia in the first round of the ACC Tournament to end his third season. "I don't think there ever was a time I was afraid for my job,"

Krzyzewski said in retrospect. "But I was concerned that we'd never achieve what we wanted to achieve at Duke."

Georgia Tech began to assert itself in the Yellow Jackets' fifth year in the ACC. Five ACC home games were decided in the final seconds of play, four of them on the last play of the contest. . . . North Carolina (14-0) and Maryland (9-5) were the only ACC teams to compile winning records in league competition.. . . Temple, coached by John Chaney, went unbeaten in the Atlantic 10 Conference after posting a losing league record the previous year. Northeastern, coached by Jim Calhoun, went unbeaten in North Atlantic Conference competition after finishing in sixth place the previous season with a 4-6 league mark.

Houston (32-5, coached by Guy Lewis), Tulsa (27-4, Nolan Richardson), Northeastern (27-5, Jim Calhoun), Lamar (26-5, Pat Foster), Marshall (25-6, Rick Huckabay), Morehead State (25-6, Wayne Martin), Bucknell (24-5, Charlie Woollum), Miami of Ohio (24-6, Darrell Hedric) and George Mason (21-7, Joe Harrington) had their winningest seasons in school Division I history. Bucknell's record-setting campaign came just two years after the worst season in Bison history (7-20).

Cornell, coached by Tom Miller, compiled a 16-10 record for its first winning season in 17 years. . . . Massachusetts (12-17) lost six of its last seven games but managed to avoid its sixth consecutive season with at least 20 defeats. . . . Richmond, coached by Dick Tarrant, captured the ECAC South title after finishing in last place the previous season.

SMU and Auburn finished in the Top 20 of a final wire-service poll for the first time since 1957 and 1960, respectively. . . . Illinois, coached by Lou Henson, captured its first Big Ten title in 21 years. . . . Arkansas-Little Rock's Donald Newman set a Trans America Athletic Conference single-game record by grabbing 29 rebounds against Centenary.

DePaul's Ray Meyer retired after a 42-year coaching career with a 724-354 record. Meyer, who compiled a 14-16 record in 13 tournament appearances with DePaul, is the only coach to go more than 40 years from his first appearance in the playoffs to his last (1943 to 1984). He averaged 26 victories his last seven seasons after averaging a modest 14 triumphs annually in a 21-year span from 1957-77.

1983-84 FINAL NATIONAL POLLS

AP	UPI	USA/CNN	SCHOOL (RECORD)	HEAD COACH
1	1	4	North Carolina (28-3)	Dean Smith
2	2	1	Georgetown (34-3)	John Thompson
3	3	3	Kentucky (29-5)	Joe B. Hall
4	4	6	DePaul (27-3)	Ray Meyer
5	5	2	Houston (32-5)	Guy Lewis
6	6	5	Illinois (26-5)	Lou Henson
7	8	14	Oklahoma (29-5)	Billy Tubbs
8	7	13	Arkansas (25-7)	Eddie Sutton
9	9	20	Texas-El Paso (27-4)	Don Haskins
10	11	17	Purdue (22-7)	Gene Keady
11	10	12	Maryland (24-8)	Lefty Driesell
12	12	21	Tulsa (27-4)	Nolan Richardson
13	13	10	UNLV (29-6)	Jerry Tarkanian
14	14	22	Duke (24-10)	Mike Krzyzewski
15	15	19	Washington (24-7)	Marv Harshman
16	16	9	Memphis State (26-7)	Dana Kirk
17	20	–	Oregon State (22-7)	Ralph Miller
18	16	18	Syracuse (23-9)	Jim Boeheim
19	–	8	Wake Forest (23-9)	Carl Tacy
20	–	25	Temple (26-5)	John Chaney
–	–	7	Virginia (21-12)	Terry Holland
–	18	11	Indiana (22-9)	Bob Knight
–	–	15	Dayton (21-11)	Don Donoher
–	–	16	Louisville (24-11)	Denny Crum
–	19	–	Auburn (20-11)	Sonny Smith
–	–	23	Michigan (24-9)	Bill Frieder
–	–	24	SMU (25-8)	Dave Bliss

1984 NCAA Tournament

Summary: Georgetown's Patrick Ewing and Houston's Hakeem Olajuwon, the nation's two most celebrated centers who lost their previous title bids on last-second freak plays, clashed in the championship game but the head-to-head duel didn't live up to its lofty billing. It was little consolation to Olajuwon when he played Ewing to a standoff on the backboards (each grabbed nine rebounds) and outscored his rival, 15-10. At the end, Olajuwon was on the national runner-up for the second consecutive season as freshmen Reggie Williams and Michael Graham combined for 33 points to spark the Hoyas to a 84-75 triumph.

1983–84 NCAA CHAMPION: GEORGETOWN

SEASON STATISTICS OF GEORGETOWN REGULARS

PLAYER	POS.	CL.	G.	FG%	FT%	PPG	RPG
Patrick Ewing	C	Jr.	37	.658	.656	16.4	10.0
David Wingate	G-F	So.	37	.435	.721	11.2	3.6
Michael Jackson	G	So.	31	.509	.816	10.1	1.7
Reggie Williams	G-F	Fr.	37	.433	.768	9.1	3.5
Bill Martin	F	Jr.	37	.509	.705	8.9	5.9
Michael Graham	F	Fr.	35	.561	.459	4.9	4.0
Horace Broadnax	G	So.	35	.434	.853	4.8	1.4
Gene Smith	G	Sr.	36	.511	.592	3.7	2.1
Fred Brown	G	Sr.	36	.486	.646	3.2	2.6
Ralph Dalton	C-F	Jr.	36	.569	.574	2.8	2.2
TEAM TOTALS			37	**.509**	**.678**	**74.3**	**40.0**

Assists leader: Jackson 137. Blocked shots leader: Ewing 133. Steals leader: Smith 67.

1984 FINAL FOUR CHAMPIONSHIP GAME

SEATTLE, WA

HOUSTON (75)	MIN.	FG-A	FT-A	REB.	A	PF	PTS.
Winslow	33	0-1	2-2	6	3	4	2
Young	37	8-21	2-3	5	1	3	18
Olajuwon	32	6-9	3-7	9	0	4	15
Franklin	38	8-15	5-6	2	9	3	21
Gettys	29	3-3	0-0	1	7	2	6
Anders	10	2-2	0-2	0	0	0	4
Clark	1	0-0	0-0	0	0	0	0
Anderson	6	1-1	0-0	2	0	0	2
Dickens	6	2-3	1-2	0	0	5	5
Thomas	2	0-0	0-0	0	0	0	0
Giles	2	0-0	0-0	0	0	0	0
Weaver	1	0-0	0-0	0	0	0	0
Orsak	1	1-1	0-0	0	0	0	2
Alexander	1	0-0	0-0	1	0	0	0
Belcher	1	0-0	0-0	0	0	0	0
Team				3			
TOTALS	200	31-56	13-22	29	20	21	75

FG%: .554. FT%: .591. Blocks: 4. Turnovers: 13. Steals: 3.

GEORGETOWN (84)	MIN.	FG-A	FT-A	REB.	A	PF	PTS.
Wingate	32	5-10	6-9	1	3	4	16
Dalton	13	0-0	0-0	2	0	1	0
Ewing	30	4-8	2-2	9	3	4	10
Brown	15	1-2	2-2	4	4	4	4
Jackson	35	3-4	5-5	0	6	4	11
Graham	24	7-9	0-2	5	0	4	14
Williams	26	9-18	1-2	7	3	2	19
Broadnax	8	2-3	0-0	0	0	2	4
Martin	16	3-6	0-0	2	0	0	6
Morris	1	0-0	0-0	0	0	0	0
Team				7			
TOTALS	**200**	**34-60**	**16-22**	**37**	**19**	**25**	**84**

FG%: .567. FT%: .727. Blocks: 6 (Ewing 4). Turnovers: 9. Steals: 0.
Halftime: Georgetown 40-30.

NATIONAL SEMIFINALS

VIRGINIA (47): Miller 6-15 0-0 12, Edelin 1-2 0-0 2, Polynice 4-7 1-1 9, Wilson 5-12 2-2 12, Carlisle 3-14 2-2 8, Stokes 1-1 0-2 2, Sheehey 1-3 0-0 2. Team 21-54 (.389) 5-7 (.714) 47.

HOUSTON (49): Winslow 4-7 0-0 8, Young 8-16 1-4 17, Olajuwon 4-5 4-6 12, Franklin 2-7 2-2 6, Gettys 3-7 0-0 6, Dickens 0-0 0-0 0, Alexander 0-0 0-0 0. Team 21-42 (.500) 7-12 (.583) 49.

Halftime: Houston 25-23. **Regulation:** Tied 43-43.

GEORGETOWN (53): Wingate 5-8 1-2 11, Dalton 0-1 0-0 0, Ewing 4-6 0-0 8, Brown 0-1 0-1 0, Jackson 4-9 4-6 12, Smith 2-4 1-2 5, Martin 1-4 0-0 2, Graham 4-6 0-2 8, Williams 1-7 0-0 2, Broadnax 2-4 1-2 5. Team 23-50 (.460) 7-15 (.467) 53.

KENTUCKY (40): Bowie 3-10 4-4 10, Walker 1-3 2-2 4, Turpin 2-11 1-2 5, Beal 2-8 2-2 6, Master 2-7 2-2 6, Bennett 1-8 0-0 2, Blackmon 2-5 1-2 5, Bearup 0-0 2-2 2, Harden 0-1 0-0 0. Team 13-53 (.245) 14-16 (.875) 40.

Halftime: Kentucky 29-22.

ALL-TOURNAMENT TEAM

Patrick Ewing, C, Jr., Georgetown*
Alvin Franklin, G, Soph., Houston
Michael Graham, F, Fr., Georgetown
Hakeem Olajuwon, C, Jr., Houston
Michael Young, F, Sr., Houston
      *Named Most Outstanding Player

Georgetown became the first Eastern school in 30 years to win an NCAA title. Ewing, the Hoyas' leading scorer on the season, matched the all-time low scoring total for a Final Four Most Outstanding Player with 18 points in two games (fifth on the team), but he was the key component in Georgetown's suffocating defense. The Hoyas led the nation in field-goal percentage defense (39.5 percent) and exhibited their tenacity in the national semifinals when they harassed Kentucky into shooting a dismal 9.1 percent in the second half (3 of 33) en route to a 53-40 victory. Georgetown's Michael Jackson, a 6-1 guard averaging 1.4 rebounds per game entering the Final Four, retrieved 10 missed shots against Kentucky's formidable frontline to help the Hoyas overcome a seven-point halftime deficit in the national semifinals.

Outcome for Defending Champion: North Carolina State (19-14) finished in seventh place in the ACC before losing at home to Florida State in the first round of the NIT. The Wolfpack twice lost five consecutive ACC regular-season games.

Star Gazing: Ewing, the only individual to fail to score more than 10 points in either the national semifinal or championship game in the year he was named Most Outstanding Player, tallied eight points in a 53-40 triumph over Kentucky in the semifinals and 10 in an 84-75 decision over Houston in the final.

Biggest Upset: Many observers predicted Georgetown would meet top-ranked North Carolina in the national final, but the Tar Heels were upset in the East Regional semifinals by Indiana (72-68) when national player of the year Michael Jordan was limited to 13 points, one rebound and one assist.

One and Only: Virginia became the only school to reach the Final Four despite compiling a losing record in conference competition (6-8 in ACC) and succumbing in the first round of its league tournament. The Cavaliers lost nine of 13 games in a mid-season stretch. . . . Georgetown became the only school to win an NCAA championship after enduring a dry spell of more than 30 years without participating in the playoffs. The Hoyas did not appear in the tourney from 1944 through 1974. . . . Georgetown's John Thompson is the only person to play for an NBA championship team (Boston Celtics '65) before coaching an NCAA titlist.

Numbers Game: Dayton forward Roosevelt Chapman became the only non-guard to be the undisputed leading scorer of an NCAA Tournament and not participate in the Final Four (105 points in four games). He poured in a tourney-high 41 points in an 89-85 victory over Oklahoma in the second round of the West Regional. . . . Northeastern hit 75 percent from the floor (33 of 44), including 15 of 17 by freshman Reggie Lewis, in the first round, but bowed to Virginia Commonwealth, 70-69. . . . Arkansas' Alvin Robertson finished his career with an average of six steals in four playoff games. . . . The Big Ten compiled its only winning record (4-3) in a five-year span from 1982-86. . . . Oral Roberts' Mark Acres grabbed a tourney-high 18 rebounds in a 92-83 opening-round

loss to Memphis State. . . . Auburn and Richmond appeared in the NCAA playoffs for the first time.

What If: Eventual top six NBA draft choices Sam Bowie, Melvin Turpin and Kenny Walker combined to shoot 56.4 percent from the floor to help Kentucky register 51.5 percent field-goal accuracy as a team in the 1983-84 season. If only the Wildcats managed to hit 30.3 percent of their second-half field-goal attempts instead of 9.1 percent (3 of 33) in the national semifinals, they could have defeated eventual champion Georgetown rather than blowing a seven-point halftime lead. Kentucky's starters missed all 21 of their field-goal attempts after intermission. The first-round starting frontcourt of Bowie, Turpin and Walker combined to shoot 25 percent from the floor (6 of 24) in the entire game. . . . Houston (32-5) might have possessed the firepower necessary to upend Georgetown in the NCAA final if Clyde Drexler didn't turn pro early. . . . Alabama (18-12, without Ennis Whatley), Illinois (26-5, Derek Harper) and Purdue (22-7, Russell Cross) might have advanced farther in the playoffs if standout players had exercised their remaining eligibility instead of defecting to the NBA. . . . Marquette (17-13) probably would have participated in the NCAA Tournament instead of the NIT if Doc Rivers didn't leave school early for the NBA.

Scoring Leader: Roosevelt Chapman, Dayton (105 points, 26.25 ppg).

Highest Scoring Average: Kevin Mullin, Princeton (56 points, 28 ppg).

Rebounding Leader: Hakeem Olajuwon, Houston (57 rebounds, 11.4 rpg).

Highest Rebounding Average: Keith Lee, Memphis State (37 rebounds, 12.3 rpg).

1984 CHAMPIONSHIP BRACKET

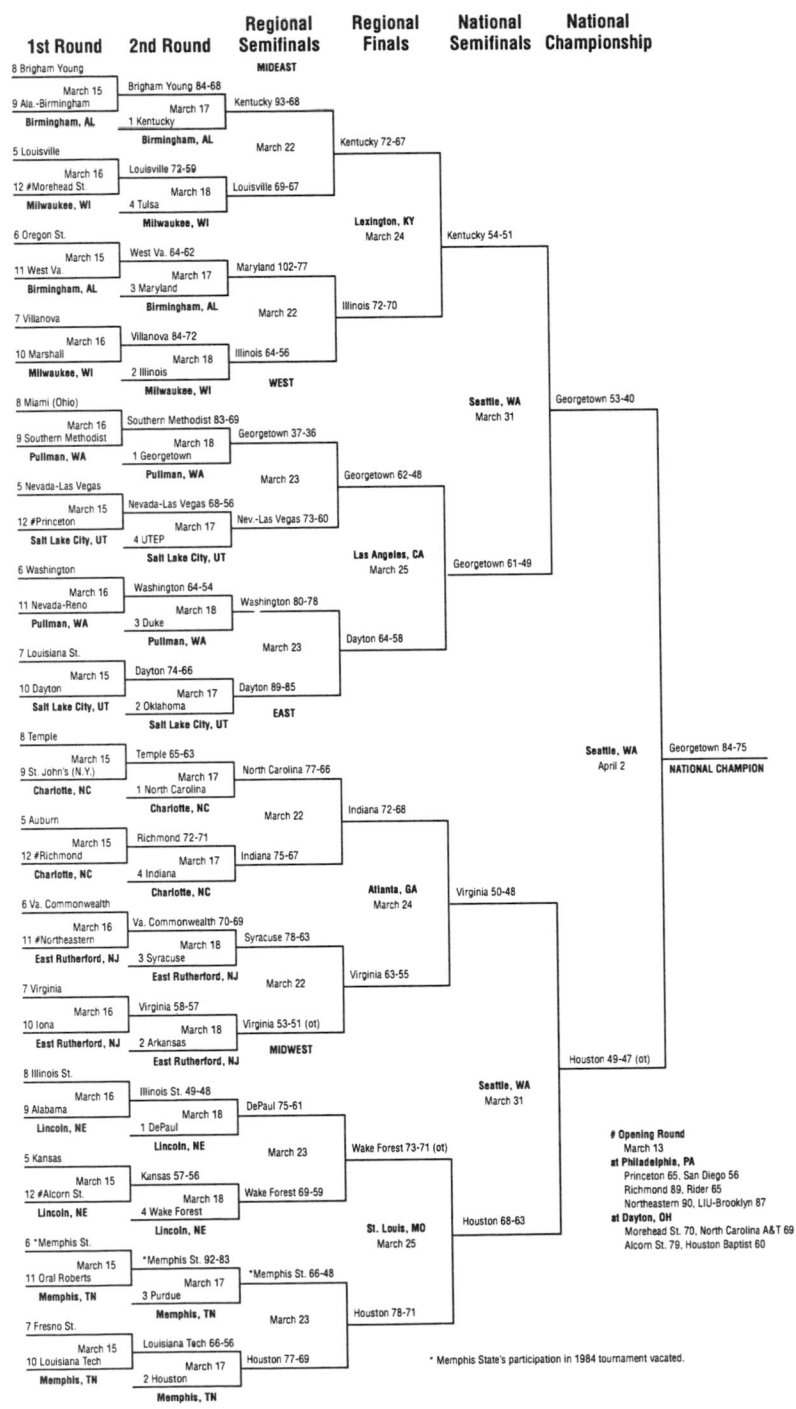

1st Round   **2nd Round**   **Regional Semifinals**   **Regional Finals**   **National Semifinals**   **National Championship**

MIDEAST

8 Brigham Young
March 15
9 Ala.-Birmingham
Birmingham, AL
Brigham Young 84-68
March 17
1 Kentucky
Birmingham, AL
Kentucky 93-68

5 Louisville
March 16
12 #Morehead St.
Milwaukee, WI
Louisville 72-59
March 18
4 Tulsa
Milwaukee, WI
Louisville 69-67

March 22
Kentucky 72-67

6 Oregon St.
March 15
11 West Va.
Birmingham, AL
West Va. 64-62
March 17
3 Maryland
Birmingham, AL
Maryland 102-77

7 Villanova
March 16
10 Marshall
Milwaukee, WI
Villanova 84-72
March 18
2 Illinois
Milwaukee, WI
Illinois 64-56

March 22
Illinois 72-70

Lexington, KY
March 24
Kentucky 54-51

WEST

8 Miami (Ohio)
March 16
9 Southern Methodist
Pullman, WA
Southern Methodist 83-69
March 18
1 Georgetown
Pullman, WA
Georgetown 37-36

5 Nevada-Las Vegas
March 15
12 #Princeton
Salt Lake City, UT
Nevada-Las Vegas 68-56
March 17
4 UTEP
Salt Lake City, UT
Nev.-Las Vegas 73-60

March 23
Georgetown 62-48

6 Washington
March 16
11 Nevada-Reno
Pullman, WA
Washington 64-54
March 18
3 Duke
Pullman, WA
Washington 80-78

7 Louisiana St.
March 15
10 Dayton
Salt Lake City, UT
Dayton 74-66
March 17
2 Oklahoma
Salt Lake City, UT
Dayton 89-85

March 23
Dayton 64-58

Las Angeles, CA
March 25
Georgetown 61-49

Seattle, WA
March 31
Georgetown 53-40

EAST

8 Temple
March 15
9 St. John's (N.Y.)
Charlotte, NC
Temple 65-63
March 17
1 North Carolina
Charlotte, NC
North Carolina 77-66

5 Auburn
March 15
12 #Richmond
Charlotte, NC
Richmond 72-71
March 17
4 Indiana
Charlotte, NC
Indiana 75-67

March 22
Indiana 72-68

6 Va. Commonwealth
March 16
11 #Northeastern
East Rutherford, NJ
Va. Commonwealth 70-69
March 18
3 Syracuse
East Rutherford, NJ
Syracuse 78-63

7 Virginia
March 16
10 Iona
East Rutherford, NJ
Virginia 58-57
March 18
2 Arkansas
East Rutherford, NJ
Virginia 53-51 (ot)

March 22
Virginia 63-55

Atlanta, GA
March 24
Virginia 50-48

Seattle, WA
March 31
Houston 49-47 (ot)

MIDWEST

8 Illinois St.
March 16
9 Alabama
Lincoln, NE
Illinois St. 49-48
March 18
1 DePaul
Lincoln, NE
DePaul 75-61

5 Kansas
March 15
12 #Alcorn St.
Lincoln, NE
Kansas 57-56
March 18
4 Wake Forest
Lincoln, NE
Wake Forest 69-59

March 23
Wake Forest 73-71 (ot)

6 *Memphis St.
March 15
11 Oral Roberts
Memphis, TN
*Memphis St. 92-83
March 17
3 Purdue
Memphis, TN
*Memphis St. 66-48

7 Fresno St.
March 15
10 Louisiana Tech
Memphis, TN
Louisiana Tech 66-56
March 17
2 Houston
Memphis, TN
Houston 77-69

March 23
Houston 78-71

St. Louis, MO
March 25
Houston 68-63

Seattle, WA
April 2
Georgetown 84-75
NATIONAL CHAMPION

Opening Round
March 13
at Philadelphia, PA
Princeton 65, San Diego 56
Richmond 89, Rider 65
Northeastern 90, LIU-Brooklyn 87
at Dayton, OH
Morehead St. 70, North Carolina A&T 69
Alcorn St. 79, Houston Baptist 60

* Memphis State's participation in 1984 tournament vacated.

1984-85

NCAA Champion: Villanova (25-10; coached by Rollie Massimino; tied for third place in Big East with a 9-7 record).

NIT Champion: UCLA (21-12; coached by Walt Hazzard; finished in a three-way tie for third place in Pacific-10 with a 12-6 record).

New Rules: The coaching box is introduced, whereby a coach and all bench personnel must remain in the 28-foot-long coaching box unless seeking information from the scorer's table. . . . The NCAA Tournament bracket was expanded to include 64 teams, eliminating first-round byes.

NCAA Probation: Akron.

NCAA Consensus First-Team All-Americans: Johnny Dawkins, G, Jr., Duke; Patrick Ewing, C, Sr., Georgetown; Keith Lee, C, Sr., Memphis State; Xavier McDaniel, F, Sr., Wichita State; Chris Mullin, G-F, Sr., St. John's; Wayman Tisdale, C-F, Jr., Oklahoma.

National Players of the Year: Ewing (14.6 ppg, 9.2 rpg, 62.5 FG%/AP, NABC, Naismith) and Mullin (19.8 ppg, 4.8 rpg, 52.1 FG%, 82.4 FT%/UPI, USBWA, Wooden).

National Coaches of the Year: St. John's Lou Carnesecca (31-4/UPI, USBWA); Michigan's Bill Frieder (26-4/AP), and Georgetown's John Thompson (35-3/NABC).

Chicago product Ben Wilson, named the top player at the Nike/AFBE Camp in Princeton, N.J., entered his senior season of high school generally regarded as the premier recruit in the nation because of his Magic Johnson-like skills. Just a few days prior to the first game of his senior campaign, Wilson was slain by a gunshot within a block of Simeon High's campus.

There is more to the game than scoring. Georgetown center Patrick Ewing compiled the lowest scoring average ever for a wire-service national player of the year as his forte was intimidation near the basket.

Guard Mark Price became the first Georgia Tech player since 1961 to become an NCAA consensus first- or second-team All-American. . . .

Georgia Tech, after finishing in the ACC's second division in its first five seasons in the league, finished in the Top 20 of a final wire-service poll for the first time since 1960 and earned a three-way share of the league's regular-season title with a 9-5 conference record. No ACC team had previously finished first with more than three defeats. All eight ACC members participated in the two postseason tourneys–five in the NCAA and three in the NIT–but none reached the national semifinals of either event.

North Carolina State, coached by Jim Valvano, finished in a tie for first place in the ACC one year after placing seventh.. . . Wichita State's Xavier McDaniel posted the lowest nation-leading scoring average (27.2) since Villanova's Paul Arizin averaged 25.3 in 1950. . . . McDaniel, Oklahoma's Wayman Tisdale (27), Ball State's Dan Palombizio (26.3), South Alabama's Terry Catledge (25.6) and Texas-San Antonio's Derrick Gervin (25.6), set school Division I records for highest scoring average in a single season.

Memphis State's Keith Lee averaged 19.7 points per game to finish his four-year career with an 18.8 average. His lowest average was 18.3 as a freshman. Lee is the only major-college player to score more than 2,000 points over four seasons and have his highest and lowest average separated by fewer than two points per game.

Georgetown (35-3, coached by John Thompson), Memphis State (31-4, Dana Kirk), St. John's (31-4, Lou Carnesecca), Louisiana Tech (29-3, Andy Russo), Virginia Commonwealth (26-6, J.D. Barnett), San Diego State (23-8, Smokey Gaines), Mercer (22-9, Bill Bibb), Auburn (22-12, Sonny Smith) and Tennessee Tech (19-9, Tom Deaton) had their winningest seasons in school Division I history. Tennessee (22-15, Don DeVoe) and Nevada-Reno (21-10, Sonny Allen) tied their school Division I records for most victories. VCU made its lone appearance in the Top 20 of a final wire-service poll.

Navy center David Robinson began to generate national acclaim by averaging 23.6 points and 11.6 rebounds per game. He averaged a

Oklahoma All-American forward Wayman Tisdale racks up some hang time.

modest 7.6 points and four rebounds per game the previous season as a freshman. . . . Penn State's Craig Collins set an NCAA single-season record for free-throw accuracy by hitting 94 of 98 foul shots (95.9 percent).

Michigan, which was a total of 16 games under .500 in Big Ten competition over the previous six seasons, captured the conference championship with a 16-2 league mark. The Wolverines won a school record 17 consecutive games before being eliminated in the NCAA Tournament by Villanova. . . . Indiana coach Bob Knight tossed a chair across the court during a game against Purdue. He was ejected and suspended for a game by Big Ten commissioner Wayne Duke. . . . Michigan State guard Sam Vincent (23.7 ppg) followed in his brother Jay's footsteps by leading the Big Ten in scoring. Jay, a forward, paced the league in 1979-80 (22.1) and 1980-81 (24.1).

Syracuse snapped Kentucky's streak of eight consecutive seasons leading the nation in attendance. . . . Loyola of Chicago returned to the Top 20 of a final wire-service poll for the first time since 1966. . . . Cleveland State, coached by Kevin Mackey, captured the Mid-Continent Conference championship one year after finishing in seventh place.

Gervin, the younger brother of pro legend George Gervin, established a Texas-San Antonio mark with 51 points against Baylor. Other players setting school single-game scoring records were Loyola of Chicago's Alfredrick Hughes (47 points vs. Detroit), Miami of Ohio's Ron Harper (45 vs. Ball State in Mid-American Conference Tournament semifinals) and George Mason's Carlos Yates (42 vs. Navy). . . . Holy Cross' Jim McCaffrey established a Metro Atlantic Athletic Conference regular-season single-game standard with 46 points against Iona.

LSU was in sixth place in the SEC with a 7-5 record before winning its last six league games to capture the conference crown. The Tigers, coached by Dale Brown, were believed to be the first team ever to win the SEC title with no seniors on its roster. . . . Four Tulane starters, including eventual pro standout John (Hot Rod) Williams, and a reserve were accused of shaving points in two games. Two of the five players, Clyde Eads and Jon Johnson, were granted immunity and testified that the others had also shaved points in exchange for cash and cocaine. Williams was acquitted and nobody served jail time, but university president Eamon Kelly shut down the basketball program for four years.

Cincinnati, which compiled a 3-25 record the previous season, improved by 12 1/2 games to 17-14. The Bearcats were coached by Tony Yates. . . . Princeton lost its first six games against major-college competition to incur its first losing record (11-15) in 32 seasons and St. Bonaventure lost nine of 11 games in a mid-season swoon to sustain its first losing mark (14-15) in 29 years. . . . Army, coached by Les Wothke, posted its only winning record (16-13) since the 1978-79 campaign. . . . Marshall's Bruce Morris hit a basket from 89 feet, 10 inches away as the first-half buzzer sounded against visiting Appalachian State on February 7, 1985. The shot made its way into the Guiness Book of World Records as the longest shot ever recorded in a college game. . . . Oklahoma City competed in its final season at the major-college level.

Southern Cal, coached by Stan Morrison, tied for first place in the Pacific-10 Conference after finishing in eighth the previous year. . . . There were 26 new head coaches at the Division I level, the only year there has been fewer than 34 changes in a season since the number of major universities increased to at least 210 in 1971-72. The changes included Butch van Breda Kolff, who returned to Lafayette 30 years after first coaching at the school from 1951-52 through 1954-55. One of the newcomers was Walt Hazzard, the fifth UCLA coach in 10 years since John Wooden retired. . . . Kentucky's Joe B. Hall retired after a 19-year coaching career with a 373-156 record. Washington's Marv Harshman, who previously coached at Pacific Lutheran and Washington State, retired after a 40-year coaching career with a 642-448 record.

1984-85 FINAL NATIONAL POLLS

AP	UPI	USA/CNN	SCHOOL (RECORD)	HEAD COACH
1	1	2	Georgetown (35-3)	John Thompson
2	2	9	Michigan (26-4)	Bill Frieder
3	3	3	St. John's (31-4)	Lou Carnesecca
4	5	6	Oklahoma (31-6)	Billy Tubbs
5	4	5	Memphis State (31-4)	Dana Kirk
6	6	4	Georgia Tech (27-8)	Bobby Cremins
7	7	7	North Carolina (27-9)	Dean Smith
8	8	8	Louisiana Tech (29-3)	Andy Russo
9	9	20	UNLV (28-4)	Jerry Tarkanian
10	12	13	Duke (23-8)	Mike Krzyzewski
11	11	19	Va. Commonwealth (26-6)	J.D. Barnett
12	10	11	Illinois (26-9)	Lou Henson
13	13	16	Kansas (26-8)	Larry Brown
14	17	12	Loyola of Chicago (27-6)	Gene Sullivan
15	15	17	Syracuse (22-9)	Jim Boeheim
16	18	10	N.C. State (23-10)	Jim Valvano
17	16	–	Texas Tech (23-8)	Gerald Myers
18	14	–	Tulsa (23-8)	Nolan Richardson
19	–	–	Georgia (22-9)	Hugh Durham
20	19	–	Louisiana State (19-10)	Dale Brown
–	–	1	Villanova (25-10)	Rollie Massimino
–	–	14	Auburn (22-12)	Sonny Smith
–	–	15	Boston College (20-11)	Gary Williams
–	–	18	Maryland (25-12)	Lefty Driesell
–	20	–	Michigan State (19-10)	Jud Heathcote
–	–	21	UAB (25-9)	Gene Bartow
–	–	22	Alabama (23-10)	Wimp Sanderson
–	–	23	UCLA (21-12)	Walt Hazzard
–	–	24	Kentucky (18-13)	Joe B. Hall
–	–	25	Arkansas (22-13)	Eddie Sutton

1985 NCAA Tournament

Summary: Villanova became the worst seed (#8 in the Southeast Regional) to win a national championship. The Wildcats shot a championship game-record 78.6 percent from the floor in posting a 66-64 victory against Georgetown, the nation's top-ranked team. The Hoyas' two regular-season defeats were by a total of just three points (against St. John's and Syracuse). Villanova also defeated three other teams with No. 1 or No. 2 seeds (Michigan, North Carolina and Memphis State). The narrow victory over the Hoyas typified Rollie Massimino's NCAA playoff coaching at Villanova as he won 11 of 12 NCAA Tournament games decided by fewer than five points. "It was frustrating," Georgetown guard Horace Broadnax said. "We were right in their faces (on defense) and they kept hitting and hitting." Two years later, it was frustrating and embarrassing for Villanova and Massimino when guard Gary McLain told Sports Illustrated he played the semifinal game against Memphis State while high on cocaine

and was also high when the team met President Reagan at the White House.

Outcome for Defending Champion: Georgetown sustained its two Big East defeats by a total of three points in back-to-back games against St. John's and Syracuse.

Star Gazing: Chris Mullin, after averaging 25.5 points in St. John's first four playoff games, became the only national player of the year (UPI, USBWA and Wooden Award) to score less than 10 points when his school was eliminated in a Final Four contest. The Redmen were routed by Georgetown (77-59) in the national semifinals when Mullin was limited to eight points in 39 minutes.

Biggest Upset: LSU was one of the biggest disappointments in NCAA history. The Tigers, seeded fourth in the Southeast Regional, boasted a roster including eventual NBA first-round draft picks John Williams and Jerry Reynolds and six other players who became NBA draft choices. But they became the only top four seed to lose a opening-round game by more than 20 points when they were trounced by No. 13 seed Navy, 78-55, when David Robinson collected 18 points and a tourney-high 18 rebounds for the Midshipmen.

One and Only: Massimino became the only individual to be more than 10 games below .500 in his initial campaign as a major-college head coach and subsequently guide a team to a national championship. . . . Villanova is the only title team to have a coach with a son on his roster, although guard R.C. Massimino played sparingly.

Numbers Game: St. John's became the only school to defeat a team three times in a season that the opponent captured the NCAA title. The Redmen won their three games against Villanova by a total of 22 points. . . . Nike was crowing when all of the Final Four teams wore its "swoosh" sneakers. . . . Georgetown was the first defending NCAA Tournament champion in 15 years to return to the Final Four the next season. . . . Oklahoma's Wayman Tisdale, who

1984–85 INDIVIDUAL LEADERS

SCORING

PLAYER	PTS.	AVG.
McDaniel, Wichita St.	844	27.2
Hughes, Loyola (Ill.)	868	26.3
Palombizio, Ball St.	762	26.3
Dumars, McNeese St.	697	25.8
Catledge, South Alabama	718	25.6
Gervin, Texas-San Ant.	718	25.6
Tisdale, Oklahoma	932	25.2
Smith, Loyola M'mount	678	25.1
Mitchell, Mercer	774	25.0
Harper, Miami (Ohio)	772	24.9

REBOUNDING

PLAYER	REB.	AVG.
McDaniel, Wichita St.	460	14.8
Benjamin, Creighton	451	14.1
Scurry, Long Island	394	14.1
Towns, Monmouth	319	12.3
Sanders, Miss. Valley St.	344	11.9
Stivrins, Colorado	317	11.7
Robinson, Navy	370	11.6

Catledge, S. Alabama	322	11.5
Neal, Cal St. Full.	326	11.2
Williams, Alabama St.	288	11.1

ASSISTS

PLAYER	AST.	AVG.
Weingard, Hofstra	228	9.5
Golston, Loyola (Ill.)	305	9.2
Les, Bradley	263	8.8
Chisholm, Delaware	224	8.0
Carr, Nebraska	237	7.9
James, Brooklyn	211	7.5
Clarington, Tenn. Tech	210	7.5
Moore, SMU	247	7.5
Teague, Boston	217	7.2
McCarthy, Weber St.	209	7.2

FIELD GOAL PERCENTAGE

PLAYER	FGM	FGA	PCT.
Walker, Utica	154	216	.713
Moore, Creighton	265	393	.674

Hoppen, Nebraska	270	418	.646
Robinson, Navy	302	469	.644
Staves, Southern (La.)	164	257	.638
Salley, Ga. Tech	193	308	.627
Ewing, Georgetown	220	352	.625
Daugherty, N. Carolina	238	381	.625
Bantum, Cornell	163	262	.622
Lavodrama, Houst. Bapt.	186	301	.618

FREE THROW PERCENTAGE

PLAYER	FTM	FTA	PCT.
Collins, Penn St.	94	98	.959
Alford, Indiana	116	126	.921
Eggink, Marist	81	88	.920
Nutt, TCU	77	84	.917
Timko, Youngstown St.	78	86	.907
Hagan, Weber St.	86	95	.905
Burden, St. Louis	93	104	.894
Brooks, Tennessee	146	164	.890
Olson, Wisconsin	73	82	.890
Webster, Harvard	96	108	.889

1984–85 TEAM LEADERS

SCORING OFFENSE

SCHOOL	PTS.	AVG.
Oklahoma	3328	89.9
Alcorn St.	2555	85.2
Southern (La.)	2515	83.8
Loyola (Ill.)	2757	83.5
Utah St.	2292	81.9

SCORING DEFENSE

SCHOOL	PTS.	AVG.
Fresno St.	1696	53.0
Princeton	1429	55.0
Colgate	1451	55.8
Temple	1736	56.0
Illinois	2001	57.2

SCORING MARGIN

SCHOOL	OFF.	DEF.	MAR.
Georgetown	74.3	57.3	17.1
Oklahoma	89.9	75.6	14.4
Navy	78.4	65.3	13.0
Louisiana Tech	77.9	65.1	12.8
Illinois	68.9	57.2	11.7

WON-LOST PERCENTAGE

SCHOOL	W-L	PCT.
Georgetown	35-3	.921
Louisiana Tech	29-3	.906
Memphis St.	31-4	.886
St. John's	31-4	.886
UNLV	28-4	.875

FIELD GOAL PERCENTAGE

SCHOOL	FGM	FGA	PCT.
Navy	946	1726	.548
St. John's	978	1806	.542
North Carolina	1039	1925	.540
Iona	898	1669	.538
Michigan St.	837	1559	.537

FIELD GOAL PERCENTAGE DEFENSE

SCHOOL	FGM	FGA	PCT.
Georgetown	833	2064	.404
Illinois	832	1989	.418
West Virginia	693	1652	.419
Iowa	767	1826	.420
Memphis St.	911	2152	.423

FREE THROW PERCENTAGE

SCHOOL	FTM	FTA	PCT.
Harvard	450	555	.811
Davidson	539	692	.779
Weber St.	495	641	.772
The Citadel	529	688	.769
Texas-San Antonio	454	591	.768

REBOUND MARGIN

SCHOOL	OWN	OPP.	MAR.
Georgetown	39.6	30.5	9.1
Michigan	36.7	28.8	7.9
E. Kentucky	40.8	32.9	7.9
Iowa	41.4	33.8	7.7
Washington	34.3	26.9	7.4

averaged 25.6 points per game in his three-year career, was limited to 11 in a 63-61 setback against Memphis State in the Midwest Regional final. . . . Michigan State's Sam Vincent (32 points vs. Alabama-Birmingham) and Old Dominion's Mark Davis (32 vs. SMU) tied for the highest output in a playoff game.

What If: Center Patrick Ewing, after averaging a modest 13.2 points per game in six Final Four contests with Georgetown, has never averaged fewer than 20 points per game in his eight-year career with the New York Knicks. If only Ewing averaged 14 points per Final Four game by scoring two more points in the 1982 championship game (63-62 defeat against North Carolina) and three more in the 1985 final (66-64 defeat against Villanova), the Hoyas could have captured three national titles in his college career rather than one. . . . ACC champion Georgia

1984–85 NCAA CHAMPION: VILLANOVA

SEASON STATISTICS OF VILLANOVA REGULARS

PLAYER	POS.	CL.	G.	FG%	FT%	PPG	RPG
Ed Pinckney	C	Sr.	35	.600	.730	15.6	8.9
Dwayne McClain	F-G	Sr.	35	.574	.774	14.8	4.1
Harold Pressley	F	Jr.	35	.488	.644	12.0	7.9
Gary McLain	G	Sr.	35	.500	.831	8.0	1.2
Dwight Wilbur	G	Jr.	35	.467	.745	7.5	2.0
Harold Jensen	G	So.	32	.434	.813	4.5	1.2
Mark Plansky	F	Fr.	30	.442	.552	3.3	2.0
Chuck Everson	C	Jr.	32	.514	.565	1.5	1.5
TEAM TOTALS			35	.510	.715	68.7	31.8

Assists leader: McLain 150. **Blocked shots leaders:** Pinckney 64, Pressley 38. **Steals leaders:** Pinckney 54, Pressley 53.

1985 FINAL FOUR CHAMPIONSHIP GAME

LEXINGTON, KY

VILLANOVA (66)	MIN.	FG-A	FT-A	REB.	A	PF	PTS.
Pressley	40	4-6	3-4	4	1	1	11
McClain	40	5-7	7-8	1	3	3	17
Pinckney	37	5-7	6-7	6	5	3	16
Wilbur	5	0-0	0-0	0	1	0	0
McLain	40	3-3	2-2	2	2	2	8
Jensen	34	5-5	4-5	1	2	2	14
Plansky	1	0-0	0-1	0	0	1	0
Everson	3	0-0	0-0	0	0	0	0
Team				3			
TOTALS	200	22-28	22-27	17	14	12	66

FG%: .786. FT%: .815. Blocks: 1. Turnovers: 17. Steals: 8.

GEORGETOWN (64)	MIN.	FG-A	FT-A	REB.	A	PF	PTS.
Martin	37	4-6	2-2	5	1	2	10
Williams	29	5-9	0-2	4	2	3	10
Ewing	39	7-13	0-0	5	2	4	14
Jackson	37	4-7	0-0	0	9	4	8
Wingate	39	8-14	0-0	2	2	4	16
McDonald	2	0-1	0-0	0	0	0	0
Broadnax	13	1-2	2-2	1	2	4	4
Dalton	4	0-1	2-2	0	0	1	2
TOTALS	200	29-53	6-8	17	18	22	64

FG%: .547. FT%: .750. Blocks: 1. Turnovers: 11. Steals: 6.
Halftime: Villanova 29-28.

NATIONAL SEMIFINALS

VILLANOVA (52): Pressley 1-8 1-2 3, McClain 6-9 7-7 19, Pinckney 3-7 6-9 12, Wilbur 0-2 0-0 0, Plansky 1-1 1-3 3, Jensen 3-6 0-0 6, Everson 0-0 0-0 0. Team 16-38 (.421) 20-26 (.769) 52.

MEMPHIS STATE (45): Lee 3-9 4-4 10, Holmes 4-8 0-0 8, Bedford 4-9 0-0 8, Turner 5-13 1-2 11, Askew 1-3 0-1 2, Wilfong 0-1 0-0 0, Boyd 0-2 0-0 0, Bailey 1-1 0-0 2, Becton 1-4 2-2 4. Team 19-50 (.380) 7-9 (.778) 45.

Halftime: Tied 23-23.

ST. JOHN'S (59): Berry 4-8 4-5 12, Glass 4-4 5-7 13, Wennington 4-7 4-5 12, Mullin 4-8 0-0 8, Moses 3-7 0-0 6, Bross 0-0 0-0 0, Jackson 3-4 0-2 6, Jones 1-4 0-0 2, Stewart 0-0 0-0 0, Shurina 0-0 0-0 0, Cornegy 0-0 0-0 0. Team 23-42 (.548) 13-19 (.684) 59.

GEORGETOWN (77): Martin 4-8 4-4 12, Williams 8-15 4-4 20, Ewing 7-12 2-4 16, Jackson 2-5 0-0 4, Wingate 3-8 6-8 12, McDonald 0-1 0-0 0, Floyd 0-0 0-0 0, Broadnax 3-4 3-4 9, Lockhart 0-0 0-0 0, Highsmith 0-1 0-0 0, Mateen 0-1 0-0 0, Dalton 2-2 0-0 4. Team 29-57 (.509) 19-24 (.792) 77.

Halftime: Georgetown 32-28.

ALL-TOURNAMENT TEAM

Patrick Ewing, C, Sr., Georgetown
Harold Jensen, G, Soph., Villanova
Dwayne McClain, F-G, Sr., Villanova
Gary McLain, G, Sr., Villanova
Ed Pinckney, C, Sr., Villanova*
*Named Most Outstanding Player

Tech lost to top-ranked Georgetown, 60-54, in the East Regional final. Sophomore Craig Neal, who later became Georgia Tech's all-time assists leader, missed most of the season because of torn wrist ligaments and could have given the Yellow Jackets some depth. . . . Alabama (23-10, without Ennis Whatley), Auburn (22-12, Charles Barkely), Michigan (26-4, Tim McCormick) and North Carolina (27-9, Michael Jordan) might have advanced farther in the playoffs if standout players had exercised their remaining eligibility instead of defecting to the NBA. . . . UCLA (21-12) probably would have participated in the NCAA Tournament instead of the NIT if Stuart Gray didn't leave school early for the NBA.

Putting Things in Perspective: St. John's (31-4) defeated Villanova three times by a total of 22 points before the Redmen lost against Georgetown in the national semifinals. Georgetown (35-3) defeated the Wildcats twice by a total of nine points before losing to Villanova in the national final. Villanova lost four of five Big East Conference games in one span before dropping its regular-season finale by a whopping 23 points at Pittsburgh. Excluding three setbacks to Georgetown, St. John's only other defeat was by three points to Niagara in Buffalo.

Scoring Leader: Chris Mullin, St. John's (110 points, 22 ppg).

Highest Scoring Average: Rolando Lamb, Virginia Commonwealth (55 points, 27.5 ppg).

Rebounding Leader: Ed Pinckney, Villanova (48 rebounds, 8 rpg).

Highest Rebounding Average: Karl Malone, Louisiana Tech (40 rebounds, 13.3 rpg).

1985 CHAMPIONSHIP BRACKET

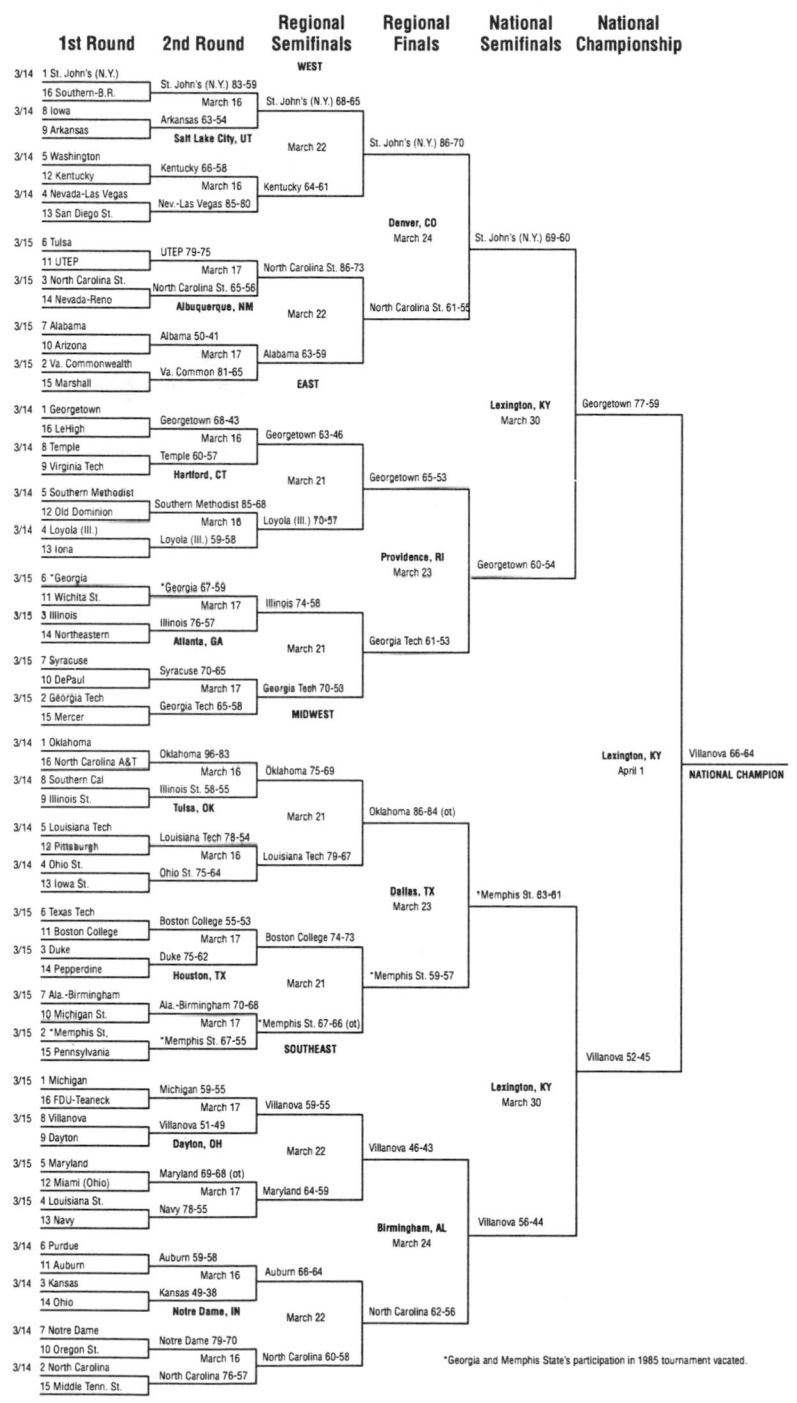

	1st Round	2nd Round	Regional Semifinals	Regional Finals	National Semifinals	National Championship

WEST

3/14 1 St. John's (N.Y.)
16 Southern-B.R.
   St. John's (N.Y.) 83-59
   March 16
   St. John's (N.Y.) 68-65
3/14 8 Iowa
9 Arkansas
   Arkansas 63-54
   Salt Lake City, UT
   March 22
   St. John's (N.Y.) 86-70
3/14 5 Washington
12 Kentucky
   Kentucky 66-58
   March 16
   Kentucky 64-61
3/14 4 Nevada-Las Vegas
13 San Diego St.
   Nev.-Las Vegas 85-80
   Denver, CO
   March 24
   St. John's (N.Y.) 69-60

3/15 6 Tulsa
11 UTEP
   UTEP 79-75
   March 17
   North Carolina St. 86-73
3/15 3 North Carolina St.
14 Nevada-Reno
   North Carolina St. 65-56
   Albuquerque, NM
   March 22
   North Carolina St. 61-55
3/15 7 Alabama
10 Arizona
   Albama 50-41
   March 17
   Alabama 63-59
3/15 2 Va. Commonwealth
15 Marshall
   Va. Common 81-65

EAST

3/14 1 Georgetown
16 LeHigh
   Georgetown 68-43
   March 16
   Georgetown 63-46
3/14 8 Temple
9 Virginia Tech
   Temple 60-57
   Hartford, CT
   March 21
   Georgetown 65-53
3/14 5 Southern Methodist
12 Old Dominion
   Southern Methodist 85-68
   March 16
   Loyola (Ill.) 70-57
3/14 4 Loyola (Ill.)
13 Iona
   Loyola (Ill.) 59-58
   Providence, RI
   March 23
   Georgetown 60-54

3/15 6 *Georgia
11 Wichita St.
   *Georgia 67-59
   March 17
   Illinois 74-58
3/15 3 Illinois
14 Northeastern
   Illinois 76-57
   Atlanta, GA
   March 21
   Georgia Tech 61-53
3/15 7 Syracuse
10 DePaul
   Syracuse 70-65
   March 17
   Georgia Tech 70-53
3/15 2 Georgia Tech
15 Mercer
   Georgia Tech 65-58

MIDWEST

3/14 1 Oklahoma
16 North Carolina A&T
   Oklahoma 96-83
   March 16
   Oklahoma 75-69
3/14 8 Southern Cal
9 Illinois St.
   Illinois St. 58-55
   Tulsa, OK
   March 21
   Oklahoma 86-84 (ot)
3/14 5 Louisiana Tech
12 Pittsburgh
   Louisiana Tech 78-54
   March 16
   Louisiana Tech 79-67
3/14 4 Ohio St.
13 Iowa St.
   Ohio St. 75-64
   Dallas, TX
   March 23
   *Memphis St. 63-61

3/15 6 Texas Tech
11 Boston College
   Boston College 55-53
   March 17
   Boston College 74-73
3/15 3 Duke
14 Pepperdine
   Duke 75-62
   Houston, TX
   March 21
   *Memphis St. 59-57
3/15 7 Ala.-Birmingham
10 Michigan St.
   Ala.-Birmingham 70-68
   March 17
   *Memphis St. 67-66 (ot)
3/15 2 *Memphis St.
15 Pennsylvania
   *Memphis St. 67-55

SOUTHEAST

3/15 1 Michigan
16 FDU-Teaneck
   Michigan 59-55
   March 17
   Villanova 59-55
3/15 8 Villanova
9 Dayton
   Villanova 51-49
   Dayton, OH
   March 22
   Villanova 46-43
3/15 5 Maryland
12 Miami (Ohio)
   Maryland 69-68 (ot)
   March 17
   Maryland 64-59
3/15 4 Louisiana St.
13 Navy
   Navy 78-55
   Birmingham, AL
   March 24
   Villanova 56-44

3/14 6 Purdue
11 Auburn
   Auburn 59-58
   March 16
   Auburn 66-64
3/14 3 Kansas
14 Ohio
   Kansas 49-38
   Notre Dame, IN
   March 22
   North Carolina 62-56
3/14 7 Notre Dame
10 Oregon St.
   Notre Dame 79-70
   March 16
   North Carolina 60-58
3/14 2 North Carolina
15 Middle Tenn. St.
   North Carolina 76-57

National Semifinals / Championship:

Lexington, KY — March 30 — Georgetown 77-59

Lexington, KY — March 30 — Villanova 52-45

Lexington, KY — April 1 — Villanova 66-64 — **NATIONAL CHAMPION**

*Georgia and Memphis State's participation in 1985 tournament vacated.

1985-86

AT A GLANCE

NCAA Champion: Louisville (32-7; coached by Denny Crum; won Metro title by one game over Memphis State with a 10-2 record).

NIT Champion: Ohio State (19-14; coached by Eldon Miller; finished in seventh place in Big Ten with an 8-10 record).

New Conference: Big South.

New Rules: The 45-second clock is introduced with the team in control of the ball having to shoot for a goal within 45 seconds after it attains team control. . . . If a shooter is fouled intentionally and the shot is missed, the penalty will be two shots and possession of the ball out of bounds to the team that was fouled. . . . The head coach may stand throughout the game, while all other bench personnel must remain seated. . . . NCAA Tournament regional competition played at neutral sites. If an institution selected to host this level of competition is a participant in the tourney, it will be bracketed in another regional.

NCAA Probation: Baylor, Idaho State, Southern Illinois.

NCAA Consensus First-Team All-Americans: Steve Alford, G, Jr., Indiana; Walter Berry, F, Jr., St. John's; Len Bias, F, Sr., Maryland; Johnny Dawkins, G, Sr., Duke; Kenny Walker, F, Sr., Kentucky.

National Players of the Year: Berry (23 ppg, 11.1 rpg, 59.8 FG%/AP, UPI, NABC, USBWA, Wooden) and Dawkins (20.2 ppg, 54.9 FG%, 81.2 FT%/Naismith).

National Coaches of the Year: Duke's Mike Krzyzewski (37-3/UPI); Kentucky's Eddie Sutton (32-4/AP, NABC), and Bradley's Dick Versace (32-3/USBWA).

It was one of those moments when time seemed to stand still. The fallout stemming from All-American forward Len Bias' cocaine-induced death just four days after the NBA draft included the ouster of longtime Maryland coach Lefty Driesell.

Another school enduring significant off-the-court transgressions was Minnesota, which was shattered by the arrests of three players on rape charges and the subsequent resignation of coach Jim Dutcher.

Basketball fans in Los Angeles were restless. UCLA's streak of 32 consecutive winning

Houston's Guy Lewis bid adieu to coaching after 30 years.

records in conference competition ended when the Bruins finished fourth in the Pacific-10 with a 9-9 mark. They then became the only defending NIT champion to lose an NIT first-round game at home (80-74 to UC Irvine) since the NIT started playing early-round games away from Madison Square Garden. Meanwhile, Southern Cal showed promise with standout freshmen Tom Lewis, Hank Gathers and Bo Kimble. But all three players wound up transferring and finished their careers with more than 2,000 points–Lewis (Pepperdine), Gathers (Loyola Marymount) and Kimble (Loyola Marymount).

Navy's David Robinson blocked 14 shots in a game against North Carolina-Wilmington en route to finishing the season with an NCAA record 207 rejections. Robinson also grabbed a school-record 25 rebounds in a game against Fairfield. . . . Chicago State's Darron Brittman became the only player ever to average as many as five steals per game in a single season.

New Mexico hit 35 of 43 field-goal attempts (81.4 percent) against Oregon State. It was the second-best team shooting from the floor in a single game in NCAA history. . . . Michigan

1985–86 INDIVIDUAL LEADERS

SCORING

PLAYER	PTS.	AVG.
Bailey, Wagner	854	29.4
Skiles, Michigan St.	850	27.4
Yezbak, U.S. Intl.	755	27.0
Miller, UCLA	750	25.9
Harper, Miami (Ohio)	757	24.4
Curry, Virginia Tech	722	24.1
Lewis, Northeastern	714	23.8
Bias, Maryland	743	23.2
Ross, American	645	23.0
Berry, St. John's	828	23.0

REBOUNDING

PLAYER	REB.	AVG.
Robinson, Navy	455	13.0
Anderson, Houston	360	12.9
Sellers, Ohio St.	416	12.6
Harper, Miami (Ohio)	362	11.7
Krystkowiak, Montana	364	11.4
Berry, St. John's	399	11.1
Hill, Bethune-Cookman	317	10.9
Carter, Loyola (Md.)	304	10.9
Boone, Marquette	319	10.6
Grant, Clemson	357	10.9

ASSISTS

PLAYER	AST.	AVG.
Jackson, St. John's	328	9.1
Chisholm, Delaware	230	8.5

Bogues, Wake Forest	245	8.4
Lee, Xavier	251	8.4
Thomas, Monmouth	205	8.2
Smith, Old Dominion	253	8.2
Harmon, McNeese St.	243	8.1
Davis, Marist	248	8.0
Paguaga, St. Francis (N.Y.)	223	8.0
Moody, N'western St. (La.)	198	7.9

BLOCKED SHOTS

PLAYER	BLK.	AVG.
Robinson, Navy	207	5.9
Perry, Temple	123	4.0
Blake, St. Joseph's	121	3.8
Fonville, Jackson St.	93	3.2
Kitchen, South Florida	89	3.2
Seikaly, Syracuse	97	3.0
Tarpley, Michigan	97	2.9
Sellers, Ohio St.	97	2.9
Martin, North Carolina	81	2.8
Smith, Pittsburgh	81	2.8

STEALS

PLAYER	STL.	AVG.
Brittman, Chicago St.	139	5.0
Paguaga, St. Francis (N.Y.)	120	4.3
Allen, Hofstra	100	3.6
Harper, Miami (Ohio)	101	3.3
Starks, Providence	84	3.2
Robinson, Md.-E. Shore	69	3.1
Anderson, Pan American	97	3.1

Bogues, Wake Forest	89	3.1
Anderson, Drexel	92	3.0
Ware, Florida A&M	76	2.8

FIELD GOAL PERCENTAGE

PLAYER	FGM	FGA	PCT.
Daugherty, N. Carolina	284	438	.648
Norman, Illinois	216	337	.641
Gattison, Old Dom.	218	342	.637
McKey, Alabama	178	280	.636
Thomas, Centenary	182	288	.632
Duckworth, E. Ill.	250	396	.631
Jones, N'western St. (La.)	130	207	.628
Turner, Brown	199	317	.628
Smits, Marist	216	347	.622
Williams, SMU	150	242	.620

FREE THROW PERCENTAGE

PLAYER	FTM	FTA	PCT.
Barton, Dartmouth	65	69	.942
Goodwin, Dayton	95	102	.931
Suder, Duquesne	135	147	.918
Coval, Wm. & Mary	111	121	.917
Androlewicz, Lehigh	84	93	.903
Skiles, Mich. St.	188	209	.900
Bajusz, Cornell	89	99	.899
Waddy, W. Carolina	70	78	.897
Newman, Richmond	153	172	.890
Rucker, Davidson	103	116	.888

1985–86 TEAM LEADERS

SCORING OFFENSE

SCHOOL	PTS.	AVG.
U.S. International	2542	90.8
Cleveland St.	2934	88.9
Oklahoma	3077	87.9
North Carolina	2945	86.6
Syracuse	2674	83.6

SCORING DEFENSE

SCHOOL	PTS.	AVG.
Princeton	1429	55.0
St. Peter's	1539	55.0
Fresno St.	1708	56.9
North Carolina A&T	1732	57.7
Tulsa	1854	57.9

SCORING MARGIN

SCHOOL	OFF.	DEF.	MAR.
Cleveland St.	88.9	69.6	19.3

North Carolina	86.6	69.0	17.6
Syracuse	83.6	68.3	15.3
Memphis St.	82.4	67.4	15.0
Notre Dame	78.9	64.8	14.1

WON-LOST PERCENTAGE

SCHOOL	W-L	PCT.
Duke	37-3	.925
Bradley	32-3	.914
Kansas	35-4	.897
Kentucky	32-4	.889
Cleveland St.	29-4	.879

FIELD GOAL PERCENTAGE

SCHOOL	FGM	FGA	PCT.
Michigan St.	1043	1860	.561
North Carolina	1197	2140	.559
Kansas	1260	2266	.556
Georgia Tech	1008	1846	.546
Illinois	990	1828	.542

FIELD GOAL PERCENTAGE DEFENSE

SCHOOL	FGM	FGA	PCT.
St. Peter's	574	1395	.411
South Florida	621	1499	.414
Texas Christian	711	1713	.415
Georgetown	789	1885	.419
Navy	932	2215	.421

REBOUND MARGIN

SCHOOL	OWN	OPP.	MAR.
Notre Dame	36.4	27.8	8.6
Michigan	37.4	29.2	8.1
Syracuse	41.0	32.9	8.1
Ark.-Little Rock	44.6	36.5	8.1
Cleveland St.	38.4	31.0	7.5

State led the country in both field-goal shooting (56.1 percent) and free-throw shooting (79.9). When Kansas star Danny Manning fouled out with 2:21 remaining in regulation, the Spartans appeared bound to defeat the Jayhawks in the Midwest Regional semifinals in Kansas City. But the game clock stuck at 2:21 for an estimated 15 seconds, allowing KU to overcome a six-point deficit in the last minute before the Jayhawks won in overtime, 96-86.

St. John's Mark Jackson set a Big East Conference single-season record by averaging 9.4 assists per game. The Redmen won 19 consecutive games on their way to 31 victories for the second straight year. . . . Princeton became the only school to lead the nation in scoring defense (55 points per game) despite compiling a non-winning record (13-13). Meanwhile, U.S. International became the only school to lead the country in scoring offense (90.8 ppg) while posting a losing record (8-20).

Penn and Princeton combined to win the previous 17 Ivy League championships before Brown won its only Ivy title after finishing in seventh place the previous year. . . . St. Louis, coached by Rich Grawer, compiled an 18-12 record to end a streak of 12 consecutive losing seasons. . . . Bradley, which posted a 17-13 mark the previous campaign, improved by 12 1/2 games to 32-3. The Braves' made their first Top 20 appearance in a final wire-service poll since 1968. . . . Toledo's streak of 26 consecutive winning seasons ended when the Rockets compiled a 12-17 mark.

Miami (Fla.) and San Francisco resurrected their basketball programs after prolonged absences. . . . Loyola Marymount's streak of non-winning seasons ended at 10 in a row when the Lions compiled a 19-11 record in Paul Westhead's first year as their coach. . . . Wyoming, coached by Jim Brandenburg, tied for the WAC regular-season title just one year after finishing in seventh place.

San Diego State's Anthony Watson (54 points vs. U.S. International), Wagner's Terrance Bailey (49 vs. Brooklyn), Northeastern's

On the rebound: Pervis Ellison of Louisville.

Reggie Lewis (41 vs. Siena) and UC Santa Barbara's Scott Fisher (39 at Montana State) set school single-game scoring standards. Bailey (29.4 ppg) established a school record for highest scoring average in a single season. . . . Youngstown State's Tilman Bevely tied an Ohio Valley Conference single-game mark by pouring in 55 points against Tennessee Tech.

Duke (37-3, coached by Mike Krzyzewski), Kansas (35-4, Larry Brown), Navy (30-5, Paul Evans), Cleveland State (29-4, Kevin Mackey),

Pepperdine (25-5, Jim Harrick), Fairfield (24-7, Mitch Buonaguro) and McNeese State (21-11, Glenn Duhon) had their winningest seasons in school Division I history. Bradley (32-3, Dick Versace), St. John's (31-5, Lou Carnesecca), St. Joseph's (26-6, Jim Boyle), Middle Tennessee State (23-11, Bruce Stewart) and Auburn (22-11, Sonny Smith) tied their school records for most victories in a single season.

Navy finished in the Top 20 of a final wire-service poll for the first time since 1959. Fairfield, under first-year coach Mitch Buonaguro, won the Metro Atlantic Athletic Conference regular-season and postseason conference titles after finishing in last place the previous year.... Texas, coached by Bob Weltlich, tied for first place in the Southwest Conference after compiling losing records in league competition the previous five seasons.... West Texas State competed in its final campaign at the Division I level.... Arkansas' Nolan Richardson became the first African-American head coach in the SWC.... Houston's Guy Lewis ended his 30-year coaching career with a 592-279 record. He didn't have a losing record in any of his last 27 seasons.

1985-86 FINAL NATIONAL POLLS

AP	UPI	USA/CNN	SCHOOL (RECORD)	HEAD COACH
1	1	2	Duke (37-3)	Mike Krzyzewski
2	2	3	Kansas (35-4)	Larry Brown
3	4	4	Kentucky (32-4)	Eddie Sutton
4	3	10	St. John's (31-5)	Lou Carnesecca
5	5	14	Michigan (28-5)	Bill Frieder
6	6	6	Georgia Tech (27-7)	Bobby Cremins
7	7	1	Louisville (32-7)	Denny Crum
8	8	7	North Carolina (28-6)	Dean Smith
9	9	16	Syracuse (26-6)	Jim Boeheim
10	11	21	Notre Dame (23-6)	Digger Phelps
11	10	13	UNLV (33-5)	Jerry Tarkanian
12	12	15	Memphis State (28-6)	Dana Kirk
13	15	19	Georgetown (24-8)	John Thompson
14	13	20	Bradley (32-3)	Dick Versace
15	17	24	Oklahoma (26-9)	Billy Tubbs
16	14	–	Indiana (21-8)	Bob Knight
17	–	8	Navy (30-5)	Paul Evans
18	18	12	Michigan State (23-8)	Jud Heathcote
19	20	25	Illinois (22-10)	Lou Henson
20	16	–	Texas-El Paso (27-6)	Don Haskins
–	–	5	Louisiana State (26-12)	Dale Brown
–	–	9	Auburn (22-11)	Sonny Smith
–	–	11	N.C. State (21-13)	Jim Valvano
–	–	17	Cleveland State (29-4)	Kevin Mackey
–	19	18	Alabama (24-9)	Wimp Sanderson
–	–	22	Iowa State (22-11)	Johnny Orr
–	–	23	DePaul (18-13)	Joey Meyer

1986 NCAA Tournament

Summary: This is the only time a group of teams arrived at the Final Four with a total of at least 125 victories with Louisville (30-7), Duke (36-2), Kansas (35-3) and LSU (26-11) combining for a 127-23 record (.847). LSU had lost 10 of its last 17 regular-season games. The two hottest teams of the group–Louisville (16 consecutive victories and Duke (21)–reached the final, where freshman Pervis Ellison collected 25 points and 11 rebounds to carry the Cardinals to a 72-69 triumph. Louisville's Billy Thompson finished the season with the lowest scoring average to lead an NCAA titlist since 1959 (14.9 points per game). Thompson was the Cardinals' top point producer in the tourney (total of 110 points) after averaging a modest 4.9 ppg in his first seven playoff contests.

Outcome for Defending Champion: Villanova (23-14) finished in fourth place in the Big East before getting eliminated in the second round of the NCAA Tournament by Georgia Tech, 66-61. The Wildcats lost non-league games by double-digit margins to Lamar, UNLV and Missouri.

Star Gazing: Guard Johnny Dawkins scored 13 of Duke's first 25 points in the final and finished the tourney with 153. No other player scored more than 110.

Biggest Upset: Arkansas-Little Rock, a 17 1/2-point underdog, shocked No. 3 seed Notre Dame in the first round of the Midwest Regional (90-83).

One and Only: Cleveland State became the only school seeded in the bottom of a bracket (13 through 16) to reach a Sweet 16. The Vikings, leading the nation in scoring margin, were seeded No. 14 when they won two East Regional games in their only tourney appearance.

Numbers Game: LSU, the No. 11 seed in the Southeast Regional, is the only double-digit seeded team to reach the Final Four. The Tigers reached the national semifinals after finishing in

1985–86 NCAA CHAMPION: LOUISVILLE

SEASON STATISTICS OF LOUISVILLE REGULARS

PLAYER	POS.	CL.	G.	FG%	FT%	PPG	RPG
Billy Thompson	F	Sr.	39	.576	.714	14.9	7.8
Milt Wagner	G	Sr.	39	.495	.862	14.8	3.1
Pervis Ellison	C	Fr.	39	.554	.682	13.1	8.2
Herbert Crook	F	So.	39	.528	.688	11.8	6.5
Jeff Hall	G	Sr.	39	.530	.890	10.3	1.7
Tony Kimbro	F	Fr.	39	.572	.691	5.3	2.5
Mark McSwain	F	Jr.	28	.561	.717	3.6	2.9
Kenny Payne	F	Fr.	34	.437	.773	3.6	1.7
Kevin Walls	G	Fr.	27	.444	.750	2.1	0.4
TEAM TOTALS			39	.531	.733	79.4	37.2

Assists leader: Wagner 165. **Blocked shots leader:** Ellison 92. **Steals leader:** Wagner 52.

1986 FINAL FOUR CHAMPIONSHIP GAME

DALLAS, TX

DUKE (69)	MIN.	FG-A	FT-A	REB.	A	PF	PTS.
Henderson	28	5-15	4-4	4	4	5	14
Alarie	33	4-11	4-4	6	0	5	12
Bilas	26	2-3	0-0	3	0	4	4
Amaker	38	3-10	5-6	2	7	3	11
Dawkins	40	10-19	4-4	4	0	1	24
Ferry	20	1-2	2-2	4	0	2	4
Williams	2	0-1	0-0	0	0	0	0
King	13	0-1	0-1	0	1	2	0
Team				4			
TOTALS	200	25-62	19-21	27	12	22	69

FG%: .403. **FT%:** .905. **Blocks:** 0. **Turnovers:** 14. **Steals:** 13 (Amaker 7).

LOUISVILLE (72)	MIN.	FG-A	FT-A	REB.	A	PF	PTS.
Crook	32	5-9	0-3	12	5	2	10
Thompson	31	6-8	1-3	4	2	4	13
Ellison	35	10-14	5-6	11	1	4	25
Wagner	30	2-6	5-5	3	2	4	9
Hall	33	2-4	0-0	2	2	2	4
McSwain	17	2-4	1-2	3	2	1	5
Walls	8	0-1	0-0	1	0	2	0
Kimbro	14	2-4	2-2	2	2	1	6
Team				1			
TOTALS	200	29-50	14-21	39	16	20	72

FG%: .580. **FT%:** .667. **Blocks:** 7. **Turnovers:** 24 (Crook 9). **Steals:** 5. **Halftime:** Duke 37-34.

NATIONAL SEMIFINALS

KANSAS (67): Manning 2-9 0-0 4, Kellogg 11-15 0-0 22, Dreiling 1-7 4-4 6, Hunter 2-5 1-4 5, Thompson 5-12 3-3 13, Turgeon 1-1 0-0 2, Marshall 6-10 1-1 13, Piper 1-1 0-0 2. Team 29-60 (.483) 9-12 (.750) 67.

DUKE (71): Henderson 3-12 7-8 13, Alarie 4-13 4-6 12, Bilas 1-2 5-7 7, Amaker 2-5 3-4 7, Dawkins 11-17 2-4 24, Strickland 0-1 0-0 0, Ferry 4-5 0-1 8, King 0-0 0-0 0. Team 25-55 (.455) 21-30 (.700) 71.

Halftime: Duke 36-33.

LOUISIANA STATE (77): Williams 7-17 0-1 14, Redden 10-20 2-3 22, Blanton 3-5 3-6 9, Taylor 7-17 2-2 16, N. Wilson 7-15 1-1 15, Brown 0-1 1-2 1. Team 34-75 (.453) 9-15 (.600) 77.

LOUISVILLE (88): Crook 8-13 0-1 16, Thompson 10-11 2-5 22, Ellison 5-11 1-2 11, Wagner 8-16 6-6 22, Hall 6-11 2-2 14, McSwain 1-2 1-3 3, Walls 0-2 0-0 0, Kimbro 0-2 0-0 0. Team 38-68 (.559) 12-17 (.708) 88.

Halftime: Louisiana State 44-36.

ALL-TOURNAMENT TEAM

Mark Alarie, F, Sr., Duke
Tommy Amaker, G, Jr., Duke
Johnny Dawkins, G, Sr., Duke
Pervis Ellison, F-C, Fr., Louisville*
Billy Thompson, F, Sr., Louisville
*Named Most Outstanding Player

a tie for fifth place in the SEC with a .500 record (9-9). . . . Maryland earned the best seed (#5) in tourney history for an at-large squad with a losing conference record (6-8 in the ACC). . . . Nebraska appeared in the NCAA Tournament for the first time. . . . Temple's Tim Perry grabbed a playoff-high 18 rebounds in a 61-50 first-round triumph over Jacksonville in the Midwest Regional. . . . Navy's David Robinson (35 points vs. Syracuse) and Northeastern's Reggie Lewis (35 vs. Oklahoma) tied for the highest-scoring game in the tourney. . . . Kentucky's Kenny Walker hit all 11 of his field-goal attempts in a 71-64 victory over Western Kentucky in the second round of the Southeast Regional. . . . A record four Sun Belt Conference members–UAB, Jacksonville, Old Dominion and Western Kentucky–qualified for the NCAA playoffs.

What If: Forwards Mark Alarie and David Henderson and guard Tommy Amaker combined to make more than 50 percent of their field-goal attempts for Duke in the 1985-86 season. If only they combined to hit 39 percent instead of 33.3 percent (12 of 36) in the championship game, the Blue Devils could have defeated Louisville rather than losing 72-69. . . . Oklahoma (26-9) might have advanced farther in the playoffs if Wayman Tisdale had exercised his remaining eligibility instead of defecting to the NBA. . . . Louisiana Tech (20-14) probably would have participated in the NCAA Tournament instead of the NIT if Karl Malone didn't leave school early for the NBA. . . . LSU (26-12) could have fared better at the Final Four if Jerry Reynolds didn't forsake his final year of eligibility to enter the NBA.

1986 CHAMPIONSHIP BRACKET

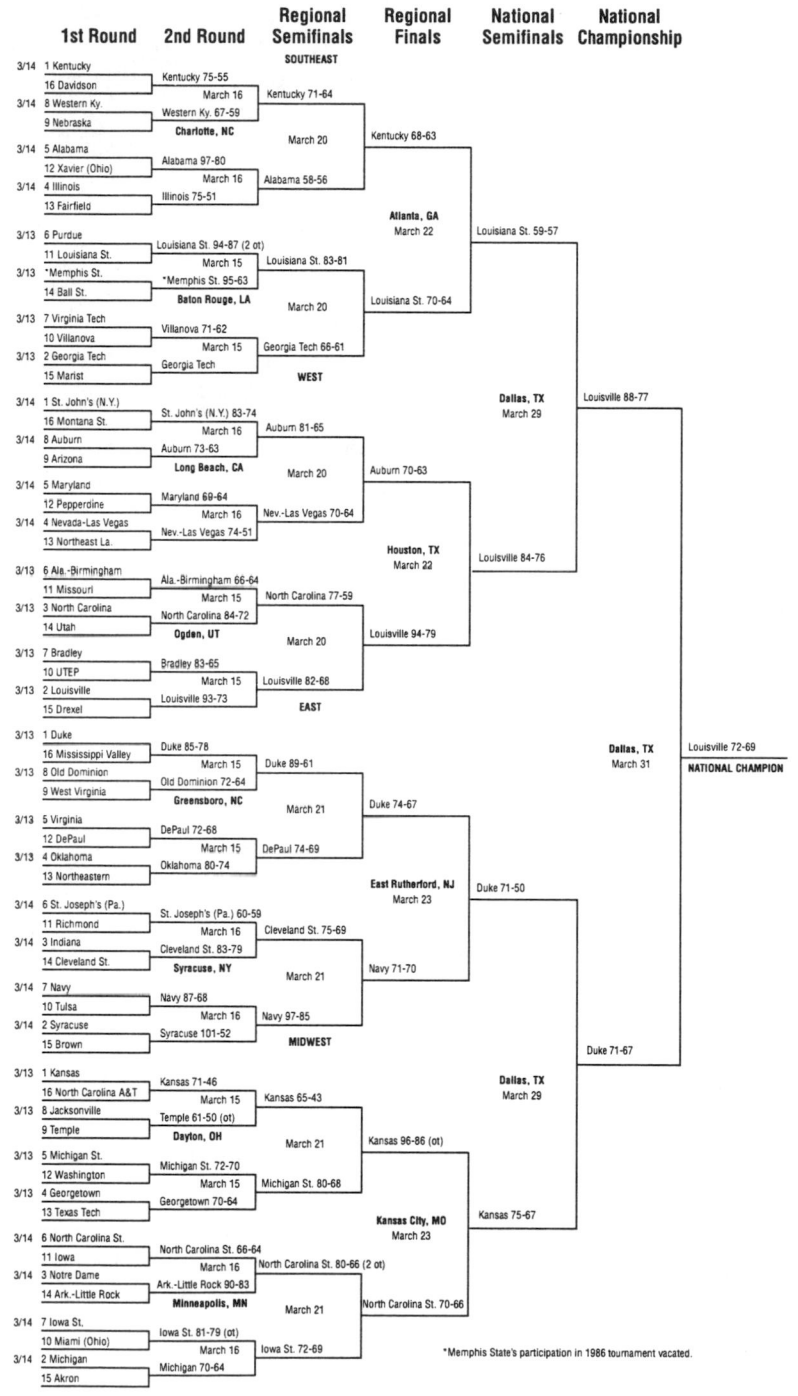

	1st Round	2nd Round	Regional Semifinals	Regional Finals	National Semifinals	National Championship

SOUTHEAST

3/14 1 Kentucky
16 Davidson — Kentucky 75-55
3/14 8 Western Ky.
9 Nebraska — Western Ky. 67-59
March 16 — Kentucky 71-64
Charlotte, NC
3/14 5 Alabama
12 Xavier (Ohio) — Alabama 97-80
3/14 4 Illinois
13 Fairfield — Illinois 75-51
March 16 — Alabama 58-56
March 20 — Kentucky 68-63

3/13 6 Purdue
11 Louisiana St. — Louisiana St. 94-87 (2 ot)
3/13 *Memphis St.
14 Ball St. — *Memphis St. 95-63
March 15 — Louisiana St. 83-81
Baton Rouge, LA
3/13 7 Virginia Tech
10 Villanova — Villanova 71-62
3/13 2 Georgia Tech
15 Marist — Georgia Tech
March 15 — Georgia Tech 66-61
March 20 — Louisiana St. 70-64

Atlanta, GA
March 22 — Louisiana St. 59-57

WEST

3/14 1 St. John's (N.Y.)
16 Montana St. — St. John's (N.Y.) 83-74
3/14 8 Auburn
9 Arizona — Auburn 73-63
March 16 — Auburn 81-65
Long Beach, CA
3/14 5 Maryland
12 Pepperdine — Maryland 69-64
3/14 4 Nevada-Las Vegas
13 Northeast La. — Nev.-Las Vegas 74-51
March 16 — Nev.-Las Vegas 70-64
March 20 — Auburn 70-63

3/13 6 Ala.-Birmingham
11 Missouri — Ala.-Birmingham 66-64
3/13 3 North Carolina
14 Utah — North Carolina 84-72
March 15 — North Carolina 77-59
Ogden, UT
3/13 7 Bradley
10 UTEP — Bradley 83-65
3/13 2 Louisville
15 Drexel — Louisville 93-73
March 15 — Louisville 82-68
March 20 — Louisville 94-79

Houston, TX
March 22 — Louisville 84-76

Dallas, TX
March 29 — Louisville 88-77

EAST

3/13 1 Duke
16 Mississippi Valley — Duke 85-78
3/13 8 Old Dominion
9 West Virginia — Old Dominion 72-64
March 15 — Duke 89-61
Greensboro, NC
3/13 5 Virginia
12 DePaul — DePaul 72-68
3/13 4 Oklahoma
13 Northeastern — Oklahoma 80-74
March 15 — DePaul 74-69
March 21 — Duke 74-67

3/13 6 St. Joseph's (Pa.)
11 Richmond — St. Joseph's (Pa.) 60-59
3/14 3 Indiana
14 Cleveland St. — Cleveland St. 83-79
March 16 — Cleveland St. 75-69
Syracuse, NY
3/14 7 Navy
10 Tulsa — Navy 87-68
3/14 2 Syracuse
15 Brown — Syracuse 101-52
March 16 — Navy 97-85
March 21 — Navy 71-70

East Rutherford, NJ
March 23 — Duke 71-50

Dallas, TX
March 31 — Louisville 72-69

NATIONAL CHAMPION

MIDWEST

3/13 1 Kansas
16 North Carolina A&T — Kansas 71-46
3/13 8 Jacksonville
9 Temple — Temple 61-50 (ot)
March 15 — Kansas 65-43
Dayton, OH
3/13 5 Michigan St.
12 Washington — Michigan St. 72-70
3/13 4 Georgetown
13 Texas Tech — Georgetown 70-64
March 15 — Michigan St. 80-68
March 21 — Kansas 96-86 (ot)

3/14 6 North Carolina St.
11 Iowa — North Carolina St. 66-64
3/14 3 Notre Dame
14 Ark.-Little Rock — Ark.-Little Rock 90-83
March 16 — North Carolina St. 80-66 (2 ot)
Minneapolis, MN
3/14 7 Iowa St.
10 Miami (Ohio) — Iowa St. 81-79 (ot)
3/14 2 Michigan
15 Akron — Michigan 70-64
March 16 — Iowa St. 72-69
March 21 — North Carolina St. 70-66

Kansas City, MO
March 23 — Kansas 75-67

Dallas, TX
March 29 — Kansas 75-67

Duke 71-67

*Memphis State's participation in 1986 tournament vacated.

Putting Things in Perspective: Kansas (35-4) defeated Louisville twice by a total of seven points before losing to Duke in the national semifinals. The Cardinals lost six of 15 games in one stretch the first half of the season.

Scoring Leader: Johnny Dawkins, Duke (153 points, 25.5 ppg).

Highest Scoring Average: Len Bias, Maryland (57 points, 28.5 ppg).

Rebounding Leader: Pervis Ellison, Louisville (57 rebounds, 9.5 rpg).

Highest Rebounding Average: Tim Perry, Temple (26 rebounds, 13 rpg).

1986-87

AT A GLANCE

NCAA Champion: Indiana (30-4; coached by Bob Knight; tied for first place in Big Ten with Purdue with a 15-3 record).

NIT Champion: Southern Mississippi (23-11; coached by M.K. Turk; tied for third place in Metro with a 6-6 record).

New Rules: The three-point field goal is introduced nationwide and set at 19-feet 9 inches from the center of the basket. . . . A coach may leave the confines of the bench at any time without penalty to correct a mistake by a scorer or timer. A technical foul is assessed if there is no mistake (rule changed the next year to a timeout). . . . A television replay may be used to prevent or rectify a scorer's or timer's mistake or a malfunction of the clock. . . . All 64 teams selected for the NCAA Tournament are subjected to drug testing for the first time.

NCAA Probation: Bradley, East Tennessee State, Memphis State.

NCAA Consensus First-Team All-Americans: Steve Alford, G, Sr., Indiana; Danny Manning, F-C, Jr., Kansas; David Robinson, C, Sr., Navy; Kenny Smith, G, Sr., North Carolina; Reggie Williams, F-G, Sr., Georgetown.

National Player of the Year: Robinson (28.2 ppg, 11.8 rpg, 4.5 bpg, 59.1 FG%).

National Coaches of the Year: Temple's John Chaney (32-4/USBWA); Iowa's Tom Davis (30-5/AP); Indiana's Bob Knight (30-4/Naismith); Providence's Rick Pitino (25-9/NABC), and Georgetown's John Thompson (29-5/UPI).

Indiana guard Steve Alford tips one in.

Controversial legislation affecting academic eligibility was implemented. NCAA Bylaw 5-1-(j), introduced as Proposition 48 at the NCAA Convention in 1983, specified that potential qualifers for an athletic scholarship at A Division I school must meet two requirements:

• An accumulative minimum 2.0 GPA in a core curriculum of at least 11 specified academic courses in the areas of English, math, social science and natural or physical science.

• A score of at least 700 on the verbal and math sections of the SAT or a score of 15 on the ACT.

The most prominent recruits who lost their freshman year of eligibility after failing to meet the new scholastic guidelines were Nick Anderson (Illinois), Chris Brooks (West Virginia), Terry Mills (Michigan), Anthony Pendelton (Iowa), Keith Robinson (Notre Dame) and

Rumeal Robinson (Michigan). Pendelton enrolled at Southern Cal after Iowa released him from his letter-of-intent.

Also making an immediate impact was the new three-point field-goal shooting rule. Consider:

• NCAA champion Indiana set an NCAA single-season record by hitting more than half of its three-point field-goal attempts (130 of 256 for 50.8 percent).

• Eastern Kentucky hit 11 consecutive three-point field-goal attempts and was 15 of 18 overall from beyond the arc in a game against North Carolina-Asheville.

• Butler's Darrin Fitzgerald averaged almost 13 three-point field-goal attempts per game on his way to setting an NCAA single-season record for most treys with 158.

• Niagara's Gary Bossert set an NCAA record for most consecutive successful three-pointers in a game with 11 vs. Siena.

UNLV's Mark Wade set an NCAA single-season record with 406 assists. . . . Northeastern's Andre LaFleur finished his career as the tallest player (6-3) with more than 800 assists. He had 894. . . . The turnover in the Division I coaching ranks has never been higher as 66 schools had new mentors. Thirty-five of the new coaches were in their first year at the Division I level. . . . Temple's only Atlantic 10 defeat, a 64-61 setback against West Virginia, snapped the Owls' 33-game McGonigle Hall winning streak.

Horace Grant (21 ppg) became the only Clemson player to average more than 20 points per game since 1969-70. He is the only player in Clemson history to become an NCAA consensus first- or second-team All-American. . . . Virginia Tech incurred its first losing record (10-18) in 32 seasons. . . . Memphis State erased a seven-point deficit in the last 15 seconds to defeat Oral Roberts, 59-58, although the Tigers fell out of the Top 20 for the first time in six years. Memphis State's new head coach was Larry Finch, who was promoted after Dana Kirk encoun-

Syracuse forward Derrick Coleman was named to the 1987 All-Tournament Team.

tered extensive legal problems. . . . James Madison, which compiled a 5-23 record the previous season, improved by 14 games to 20-10.

Forward Ken Norman became the first Illinois player since 1952 to become an NCAA consensus first- or second-team All-American. . . . Colgate ended its 49-game league losing streak and 32-game losing string overall. . . . Among the schools benefitting from the impact of freshmen was Maryland-Baltimore County, which had three yearlings score more than 13 points per game–forwards Gamel Spencer (13.8 ppg) and Duane Faust (13.7 ppg) and guard Larry Simmons (13.5 ppg). . . . Maryland's Bob Wade and Oklahoma State's Leonard Hamilton became the first African-American head coaches in the ACC and Big Eight, respectively. Wade got off on the wrong foot as the Terrapins com-

1986-87 INDIVIDUAL LEADERS

SCORING

PLAYER	PTS.	AVG.
Houston, Army	953	32.9
Hopson, Ohio St.	958	29.0
Robinson, Navy	903	28.2
Bailey, Wagner	788	28.1
Hawkins, Bradley	788	27.2
Fitzgerald, Butler	734	26.2
Elmore, VMI	713	25.5
Ross, American	683	25.3
Queenan, Lehigh	720	24.8
Larkin, Xavier	792	24.7

REBOUNDING

PLAYER	REB.	AVG.
Lane, Pittsburgh	444	13.5
Dudley, Yale	320	13.3
Moore, Loyola (Ill.)	360	12.4
Robinson, Navy	378	11.8
Rowsom, UNC-Wilm.	345	11.5
Agbejemisin, Wagner	333	11.5
McCann, Morehead St.	317	11.3
Stewart, Texas St.	316	10.9
Besselink, Conn.	300	10.7
Anderson, Houston	318	10.6

ASSISTS

PLAYER	AST.	AVG.
Johnson, Southern (La.)	333	10.7
Wade, UNLV	406	10.7
Fairley, Baptist	270	9.6
Bogues, Wake Forest	276	9.6
Van Drost, Wagner	260	9.3
Washington, Mid. Tenn. St.	255	8.8
Manuel, Bradley	237	8.8
Smith, Old Dominion	229	8.2
Davis, Marist	227	8.1
Chisholm, Delaware	220	7.9

BLOCKED SHOTS

PLAYER	BLK.	AVG.
Robinson, Navy	144	4.5
Lewis, Maryland	114	4.4
Fonville, Jackson St.	112	3.9
Blake, St. Joseph's	87	3.6
Comegys, DePaul	108	3.5
Perry, Temple	116	3.2
Baugh, Howard	90	3.2
Smith, Pittsburgh	106	3.2
Smith, Ball St.	86	3.2
Brow, Virginia Tech	86	3.1

STEALS

PLAYER	STL.	AVG.
Fairley, Baptist	114	4.1
Usitalo, Boise St.	105	3.5
Jeter, Delaware St.	96	3.4
Ford, Texas-Arl.	96	3.4
Washington, Mid. Tenn. St.	93	3.2
Davis, Marist	88	3.1
Anderson, Drexel	85	3.0
Williams, Baylor	93	3.0
Chisholm, Delaware	84	3.0
Blye, Md.-E. Shore	68	3.0

FIELD GOAL PERCENTAGE

PLAYER	FGM	FGA	PCT.
Williams, Princeton	163	232	.703
Howard, E. Ky.	156	230	.678
Grant, Clemson	256	390	.656
Godbolt, La. Tech	191	295	.647
Williams, N.C. A&T	174	273	.637
Tate, Arkansas St.	216	339	.637
Leckner, Wyoming	246	390	.631
Manning, Kansas	347	562	.617
Rebholz, Hofstra	139	226	.615
Himes, Davidson	196	319	.614

FREE THROW PERCENTAGE

PLAYER	FTM	FTA	PCT.
Houston, Army	268	294	.912
Johnson, Mich. St.	111	122	.910
Haffner, Evansville	80	88	.909
Blackwell, Temple	123	136	.904
Smith, BYU	103	114	.904
White, Tennessee	165	183	.902
MoPhee, Gonzaga	105	118	.890
Alford, Indiana	160	180	.889
Adams, Hardin-Simm.	87	98	.888
Farmer, Alabama	118	133	.887

THREE-POINT FIELD GOAL PERCENTAGE

PLAYER	FGM	FGA	PCT.
Jones, Pr. View	64	112	.571
Rhodes, S. F. Austin St.	58	106	.547
Davis, G. Mason	45	84	.536
Dimak, S. F. Austin St.	46	86	.535
Alford, Indiana	107	202	.530

THREE-POINT FIELD GOALS PER GAME

PLAYER	FGM	AVG.
Fitzgerald, Butler	158	5.6
Brooks, UC Irvine	111	4.0
Banks, UNLV	152	3.9
Ivory, Miss. Valley St.	109	3.9
Ross, San Diego St.	104	3.7

1986-87 TEAM LEADERS

SCORING OFFENSE

SCHOOL	PTS.	AVG.
UNLV	3612	92.6
North Carolina	3285	91.2
Oklahoma	3028	89.1
Michigan	2821	88.2
Southern (La.)	2706	87.3

SCORING DEFENSE

SCHOOL	PTS.	AVG.
Southwest Missouri St.	1958	57.6
St. Mary's (Calif.)	1766	58.9
Wis.-Green Bay	1714	59.1
Notre Dame	1902	59.4
San Diego	1810	60.3

SCORING MARGIN

SCHOOL	OFF.	DEF.	MAR.
UNLV	92.6	75.5	17.1
North Carolina	91.2	74.9	16.4
Clemson	86.1	71.5	14.6
DePaul	76.2	62.5	13.7
Georgetown	77.8	64.2	13.5

WON-LOST PERCENTAGE

SCHOOL	W-L	PCT.
UNLV	37-2	.949
DePaul	28-3	.903
North Carolina	32-4	.889
Temple	32-4	.889
Indiana	30-4	.882

FIELD GOAL PERCENTAGE

SCHOOL	FGM	FGA	PCT.
Princeton	601	1111	.541
North Carolina	1238	2304	.537
Marshall	946	1777	.532
Clemson	990	1873	.529
Lafayette	813	1544	.527

FIELD GOAL PERCENTAGE DEFENSE

SCHOOL	FGM	FGA	PCT.
San Diego	660	1645	.401
Houston Baptist	740	1835	.403
Jackson St.	703	1721	.408
Navy	814	1961	.415
DePaul	769	1850	.416

FREE THROW PERCENTAGE

SCHOOL	FTM	FTA	PCT.
Alabama	521	662	.787
Army	491	626	.784
Michigan St.	408	529	.771
Northern Iowa	390	507	.769
UC Irvine	532	693	.768

REBOUND MARGIN

SCHOOL	OWN	OPP.	MAR.
Iowa	43.1	31.5	11.5
Pittsburgh	41.5	31.8	9.7
Western Kentucky	39.6	31.5	8.0
Georgetown	40.4	32.4	8.0
Auburn	39.6	32.0	7.6

THREE-POINT FIELD GOAL PERCENTAGE

SCHOOL	FGM	FGA	PCT.
Indiana	130	256	50.8
Miss. Valley St.	161	322	50.0
Stephen F. Austin St.	120	241	49.8
Niagara	128	275	46.5
Eastern Michigan	144	310	46.5

THREE-POINT FIELD GOALS PER GAME

SCHOOL	FGM	AVG.
Providence	280	8.2
UNLV	309	7.9
Eastern Kentucky	216	7.2
Butler	198	7.1
UC Irvine	187	6.7

piled a 9-17 record for their first losing season in 18 years.

Setting school single-game scoring standards were Butler's Darrin Fitzgerald (54 points vs. Detroit), Army's Kevin Houston (53 vs. Fordham in MAAC Tournament opener), Tennessee's Tony White (51 vs. Auburn), Rutgers' Eric Riggins (tied with 51 vs. Penn State in double overtime), Lehigh's Daren Queenan (49 vs. Bucknell in double overtime in ECC Tournament semifinals), Dartmouth's Jim Barton (48 at Brown in OT), Washington State's Brian Quinnett (45 vs. Loyola Marymount) and UNC-Wilmington's Brian Rowsom (39 at East Carolina).

Watson's uprising is the highest in Western Athletic Conference annals and Riggins' outburst is the highest in Atlantic 10 Conference history. Fitzgerald established a Midwestern Collegiate Conference single-season mark by averaging 31.3 points per game. Queenan's record-setting performance came one night after teammate Mike Polaha had moved atop the school single-game scoring chart with 42 points against Drexel in double overtime in the ECC Tournament quarterfinals. . . . Army's Houston (32.9 ppg), Navy's David Robinson (28.2), Georgetown's Reggie Williams (23.6) and Fairfield's Troy Bradford (22.7) set school records for highest scoring average in a single season. . . . Robinson set a record for most points in a Colonial Athletic Association game when he poured in 45 against James Madison. It was one of five contests during the campaign where Robinson scored at least 43 points.

UNLV (37-2, coached by Jerry Tarkanian), Temple (32-4, John Chaney), Syracuse (31-7, Jim Boeheim), Iowa (30-5, Tom Davis), DePaul (28-3, Joey Meyer), Alabama (28-5, Wimp Sanderson), Southwest Missouri State (28-6, Charlie Spoonhour), New Orleans (26-4, Benny Dees), Arkansas-Little Rock (26-11, Mike Newell), Clemson (25-6, Cliff Ellis), San Diego (24-6, Hank Egan) and Southern Mississippi (23-11, M.K. Turk) had their winningest seasons in school Division I history. Northeastern (27-7, Karl Fogel), Marshall

(25-6, Rick Huckabay), Pitt (25-8, Paul Evans), Texas Christian (24-7, Jim Killingsworth) and Central Michigan (22-8, Charles Coles) tied their school Division I records for most victories in a single season. Davis was in his first year as coach of the Hawkeyes.

Central Michigan captured the Mid-American Conference regular-season championship after finishing in a tie for sixth place the previous year. Evansville grabbed a share of the Midwestern Collegiate Conference regular-season crown after finishing in sixth place the previous year. . . . Colorado's 26-game losing streak against Big Eight competition ended when the Buffaloes beat Iowa State, 77-74. . . . Northeast Louisiana lost four of its last five games to suffer its only losing record (13-15) since 1960-61. . . . Texas Christian made its first Top 20 appearance in a final wire-service poll since 1959. . . . Texas-San Antonio's Lennell Moore grabbed a school-record 25 rebounds against Centenary. . . . Utica (N.Y.) competed in its final campaign at the Division I level. . . . Arkansas erased a 21-point deficit midway through the second half and edged Arkansas State, 67-64, in overtime in the first round of the NIT.

1986-87 FINAL NATIONAL POLLS

AP	UPI	USA/CNN	SCHOOL (RECORD)	HEAD COACH
1	1	2	UNLV (37-2)	Jerry Tarkanian
2	3	4	North Carolina (32-4)	Dean Smith
3	2	1	Indiana (30-4)	Bob Knight
4	4	7	Georgetown (29-5)	John Thompson
5	5	9	DePaul (28-3)	Joey Meyer
6	7	5	Iowa (30-5)	Tom Davis
7	6	13	Purdue (25-5)	Gene Keady
8	8	17	Temple (32-4)	John Chaney
9	9	8	Alabama (28-5)	Wimp Sanderson
10	10	3	Syracuse (31-7)	Jim Boeheim
11	11	20	Illinois (23-8)	Lou Henson
12	12	18	Pittsburgh (25-8)	Paul Evans
13	15	22	Clemson (25-6)	Cliff Ellis
14	14	23	Missouri (24-10)	Norm Stewart
15	13	21	UCLA (25-7)	Walt Hazzard
16	19	–	New Orleans (26-4)	Benny Dees
17	–	11	Duke (24-9)	Mike Krzyzewski
18	18	16	Notre Dame (24-8)	Digger Phelps
19	16	25	Texas Christian (24-7)	Jim Killingsworth
20	–	14	Kansas (25-11)	Larry Brown
–	–	6	Providence (25-9)	Rick Pitino
–	–	10	Louisiana State (24-15)	Dale Brown
–	–	15	Florida (23-11)	Norman Sloan
–	17	19	Wyoming (24-10)	Jim Brandenburg
–	19	12	Oklahoma (24-10)	Billy Tubbs
–	19	–	Texas-El Paso (25-7)	Don Haskins
–	–	24	SW Missouri State (28-6)	Charlie Spoonhour

1986–87 NCAA CHAMPION: INDIANA

SEASON STATISTICS OF INDIANA REGULARS

PLAYER	POS.	CL.	G.	FG%	FT%	PPG	RPG
Steve Alford	G	Sr.	34	.474	.889	22.0	2.6
Daryl Thomas	F	Sr.	34	.538	.786	15.7	5.7
Rick Calloway	F	So.	29	.531	.742	12.6	4.3
Dean Garrett	C	Jr.	34	.542	.635	11.4	8.5
Keith Smart	G	Jr.	34	.517	.841	11.2	2.9
Steve Eyl	F	Jr.	34	.648	.674	3.0	3.4
Joe Hillman	G	Jr.	32	.483	.742	2.5	1.2
Kreigh Smith	G-F	Jr.	25	.500	.857	1.5	0.8
Todd Meier	F-C	Sr.	29	.450	.591	1.1	1.5
TEAM TOTALS			34	.513	.767	82.5	35.0

Three-point field goals leader: Alford (107 of 202, .530). Assists leader: Alford 123. Blocked shots leader: Garrett 93. Steals leader: Thomas 45.

1987 FINAL FOUR CHAMPIONSHIP GAME

NEW ORLEANS, LA

SYRACUSE (73)	MIN.	FG-A	FT-A	REB.	A	PF	PTS.
Triche	32	3-9	2-4	1	1	4	8
Coleman	37	3-7	2-4	19	1	2	8
Seikaly	34	7-13	4-6	10	1	3	18
Monroe	32	5-11	0-1	2	3	1	12
Douglas	39	8-15	2-2	2	7	3	20
Brower	9	3-3	1-3	1	0	3	7
Thompson	17	0-2	0-0	3	1	0	0
TOTALS	200	29-60	11-20	38	14	16	73

FG%: .483. FT%: .550. Three-point goals: 4 of 10 (Monroe 2-8, Douglas 2-2). Blocks: 7. Turnovers: 14. Steals: 5.

INDIANA (74)	MIN.	FG-A	FT-A	REB.	A	PF	PTS.
Calloway	14	0-3	0-0	2	1	3	0
Thomas	40	8-18	4-7	7	1	1	20
Garrett	33	5-10	0-0	10	0	4	10
Alford	40	8-15	0-0	3	5	2	23
Smart	35	9-15	3-4	5	6	2	21
Meier	4	0-0	0-1	1	0	0	0
Eyl	13	0-0	0-0	1	1	2	0

1987 NCAA Tournament

Summary: Indiana became the only school to win the NCAA championship in four different decades (previous titles were in 1940, 1953, 1976 and 1987). Junior college recruit Keith Smart, a guard who was Indiana's fifth-leading scorer, tallied 12 of the Hoosiers' last 15 points, including a 15-foot jumper from the left baseline with five seconds remaining to give them a 74-73 victory over Syracuse in the championship game. Indiana's well-balanced attack featured Smart and the four other starters–Steve Alford, Ricky Calloway, Dean Garrett and Daryl Thomas–each having at least one 20-point game and two contests with a minimum of 18 points in the playoffs. IU was fined $10,000 by the NCAA and coach Bob Knight reprimanded

Smith	1	0-0	0-0	1	0	1	0
Hillman	20	0-1	0-0	2	6	2	0
Team				4			
TOTALS	200	30-62	7-12	35	20	17	74

FG%: .484. FT%: .583. Three-point goals: 7 of 11 (Alford 7-10, Smart 0-1). Blocks: 3. Turnovers: 11. Steals: 7.
Halftime: Indiana 34-33.

NATIONAL SEMIFINALS

PROVIDENCE (63): Kipfer 4-10 0-1 8, Lewis 2-12 2-2 7, Duda 2-7 0-1 4, Brooks 4-9 0-0 9, Donovan 3-12 1-1 8, Screen 5-6 7-10 18, Shamsid-Deen 1-2 0-0 2, Conlon 1-1 0-0 2, D. Wright 1-4 0-0 3, S. Wright 1-3 0-0 2, Snedeker 0-0 0-0 0. Team 24-66 (.364) 10-15 (.667) 63.

SYRACUSE (77): Triche 4-10 4-5 12, Coleman 4-6 4-7 12, Seikaly 4-11 8-11 16, Monroe 4-9 6-10 17, Douglas 5-11 2-6 12, Brower 0-1 0-0 0, Thompson 3-5 1-3 7, Harried 0-0 1-2 1. Team 24-53 (.453) 26-44 (.591) 77.

Halftime: Syracuse 36-26. Three-point field goals: Providence (5-19). Syracuse (3-8).

UNLV (93): Paddio 2-13 0-0 6, Gilliam 14-26 4-6 32, Basnight 3-4 0-1 6, Wade 1-6 1-2 4, Banks 12-23 4-6 38, Robinson 0-0 0-0 0, Graham 0-5 1-4 1, Hudson 3-4 0-0 6, Willard 0-1 0-0 0. Team 35-82 (.427) 10-19 (.526) 93.

INDIANA (97): Alford 10-19 11-13 33, Smart 5-7 4-5 14, Garrett 7-10 4-5 18, Calloway 6-10 0-0 12, Thomas 3-5 0-0 6, Meier 0-0 0-0 0, Eyl 3-3 1-2 7, Smith 0-2 0-0 0, Hillman 3-4 1-3 7. Team 37-60 (.617) 21-28 (.750) 97.

Halftime: Indiana 53-47. Three-point field goals: UNLV (13-35). Indiana (2-4).

ALL-TOURNAMENT TEAM

Steve Alford, G, Sr., Indiana
Derrick Coleman, F, Fr., Syracuse
Sherman Douglas, G, Soph., Syracuse
Armon Gilliam, F-C, Sr., UNLV
Keith Smart, G, Jr., Indiana*
*Named Most Outstanding Player

after he banged his fist on the scorer's table during the Midwest regional final against LSU.

Outcome for Defending Champion: Louisville (18-14) won the Metro Conference regular-season championship but didn't participate in a national postseason tournament. The Cardinals started the season by losing all three of their assignments in the Great Alaska Shootout.

Star Gazing: Smart, the Final Four Most Outstanding Player, is the only former junior college player to win the award. Indiana looked to Alford for the final shot, but the All-American guard was covered.

"I wasn't surprised I got the ball," Smart said. "I was surprised it went in." The biggest surprise might have been that he ever enrolled at a major college. As a junior in high school in Baton Rouge, La., he was only 5-3. He grew to 5-7 as a senior, but that season ended early when Smart broke his wrist. Before attending Garden City (Kan.) Community College, he spent a year flipping hamburgers at a fast-food restaurant.

Biggest Upsets: Xavier (13th seed) over Missouri (4), 70-69; Southwest Missouri State (13) over Clemson (4), 65-60, and Austin Peay State (14) over Illinois (3), 68-67.

One and Only: Walt Hazzard is the only Final Four Most Outstanding Player (UCLA '64) to later coach his alma mater in the tournament (1-1 playoff record with the Bruins). . . . UNLV became the only school to win a regional final game in which it trailed by more than 12 points at halftime. The Rebels were behind Iowa at intermission in the West Regional final by 16 points (58-42) before rallying to win (84-81). . . . Iowa became the only school ever to have as many as 14 different players score in a playoff game when the Hawkeyes hammered Santa Clara, 99-76, in the first round of the West Regional.

Numbers Game: Georgetown is the only school to defeat two eventual Final Four teams by double-digit margins in the same conference tournament. The Hoyas whipped Providence by 18 points and Syracuse by 10 to win the Big East Tournament before they were eliminated by Providence in the Southeast Regional final of the NCAA playoffs. . . . Danny Manning is the only player to score more than 62 percent of his team's points in an NCAA Tournament game. He supplied 62.7 percent of Kansas' offense by scoring 42 points in the Jayhawks' 67-63 victory against Southwest Missouri State in the second round of the Southeast Regional. . . . UNLV guard Freddie Banks scored more points than any player in a Final Four game without being selected to the All-Tournament team (38 in a 97-93 defeat in the national semifinals against eventual champion Indiana). . . . The record for most assists in an NCAA playoff game was set by UNLV playmaker Mark Wade with 18 in a 97-93 loss against Indiana (national semifinals). Wade

also established the record for most assists in a single playoff series with 61 in five games. He had at least nine assists in each of the five contests while scoring a total of just 13 points. Wade finished his career with an average of 11.6 assists in eight playoff games. . . . David Robinson furnished 61 percent of Navy's offense by scoring a school-record and tourney-high 50 points in the Middies' 97-82 loss against Michigan in the opening round of the East Regional. . . . Florida appeared in the NCAA Tournament for the first time. . . . Wyoming's Fennis Dembo hit all 16 of his free throws to finish with 41 points in a 78-68 triumph over UCLA in the second round of the West Regional.

What If: Forward Derrick Coleman and guards Stephen Thompson and Howard Triche combined to shoot 51.6 percent from the floor for Syracuse in the 1986-87 season. If only they combined to hit 38.9 percent instead of 33.3 percent (six of 18) in the championship game, the Orangemen could have defeated Indiana rather than losing by one point. Coleman's tourney-high 19 rebounds were in vain in the final. . . . Georgia (18-12, without Cedric Henderson), Louisiana State (24-15, John Williams), North Carolina State (20-15, Chris Washburn), St. John's (21-9, Walter Berry) and Syracuse (31-7, Pearl Washington) might have fared better in the playoffs if standout players had exercised their remaining eligibility instead of defecting to the NBA.

Putting Things in Perspective: Pacific-10 runner-up Arizona, minus standout guard Steve Kerr (knee injury), was eliminated in the first round of the West Regional by Texas-El Paso, 98-91, in overtime.

Scoring Leaders: Indiana's Steve Alford and Syracuse's Rony Seikaly (138 points).

Highest Scoring Averages: Wyoming's Fennis Dembo and UCLA's Reggie Miller (28 ppg).

Rebounding Leader: Derrick Coleman, Syracuse (73 rebounds, 12.2 rpg).

Highest Rebounding Average: Tim Perry, Temple (28 rebounds, 14 rpg).

1987 CHAMPIONSHIP BRACKET

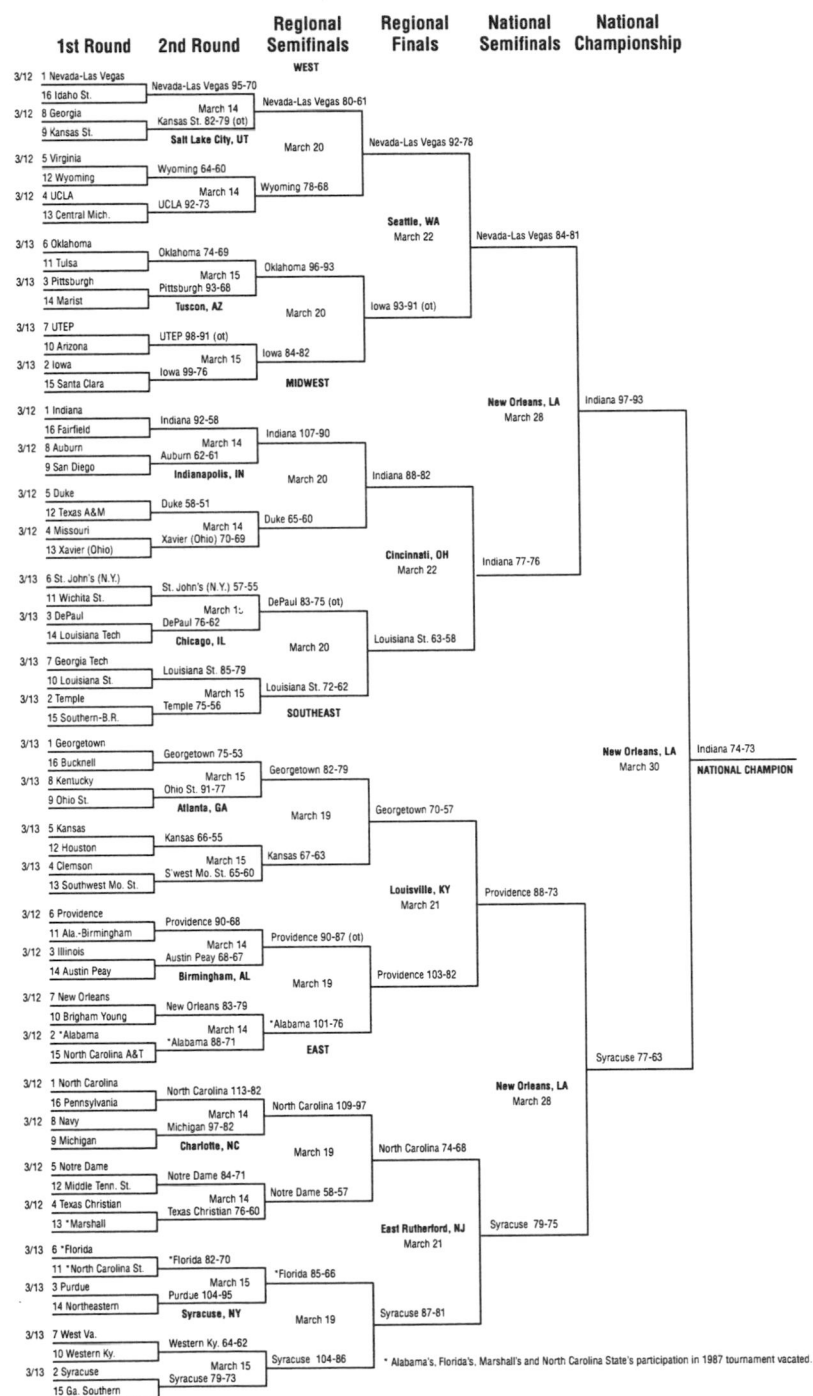

1st Round	2nd Round	Regional Semifinals	Regional Finals	National Semifinals	National Championship

WEST

3/12 1 Nevada-Las Vegas
16 Idaho St.
    Nevada-Las Vegas 95-70
3/12 8 Georgia
9 Kansas St.
    March 14 Kansas St. 82-79 (ot)
    Salt Lake City, UT
    Nevada-Las Vegas 80-61
    March 20

3/12 5 Virginia
12 Wyoming
    Wyoming 64-60
3/12 4 UCLA
13 Central Mich.
    March 14 UCLA 92-73
    Wyoming 78-68

    Nevada-Las Vegas 92-78

    Seattle, WA
    March 22

3/13 6 Oklahoma
11 Tulsa
    Oklahoma 74-69
3/13 3 Pittsburgh
14 Marist
    March 15 Pittsburgh 93-68
    Tuscon, AZ
    Oklahoma 96-93
    March 20

3/13 7 UTEP
10 Arizona
    UTEP 98-91 (ot)
3/13 2 Iowa
15 Santa Clara
    March 15 Iowa 99-76
    Iowa 84-82

    Iowa 93-91 (ot)

    Nevada-Las Vegas 84-81

MIDWEST

3/12 1 Indiana
16 Fairfield
    Indiana 92-58
3/12 8 Auburn
9 San Diego
    March 14 Auburn 62-61
    Indianapolis, IN
    Indiana 107-90
    March 20

3/12 5 Duke
12 Texas A&M
    Duke 58-51
3/12 4 Missouri
13 Xavier (Ohio)
    March 14 Xavier (Ohio) 70-69
    Duke 65-60

    Indiana 88-82

    Cincinnati, OH
    March 22

3/13 6 St. John's (N.Y.)
11 Wichita St.
    St. John's (N.Y.) 57-55
3/13 3 DePaul
14 Louisiana Tech
    March 1? DePaul 76-62
    Chicago, IL
    DePaul 83-75 (ot)
    March 20

3/13 7 Georgia Tech
10 Louisiana St.
    Louisiana St. 85-79
3/13 2 Temple
15 Southern-B.R.
    March 15 Temple 75-56
    Louisiana St. 72-62

    Louisiana St. 63-58

    Indiana 77-76

    New Orleans, LA
    March 28

    Indiana 97-93

SOUTHEAST

3/13 1 Georgetown
16 Bucknell
    Georgetown 75-53
3/13 8 Kentucky
9 Ohio St.
    March 15 Ohio St. 91-77
    Atlanta, GA
    Georgetown 82-79
    March 19

3/13 5 Kansas
12 Houston
    Kansas 66-55
3/13 4 Clemson
13 Southwest Mo. St.
    March 15 S'west Mo. St. 65-60
    Kansas 67-63

    Georgetown 70-57

    Louisville, KY
    March 21

3/12 6 Providence
11 Ala.-Birmingham
    Providence 90-68
3/12 3 Illinois
14 Austin Peay
    March 14 Austin Peay 68-67
    Birmingham, AL
    Providence 90-87 (ot)
    March 19

3/12 7 New Orleans
10 Brigham Young
    New Orleans 83-79
3/12 2 *Alabama
15 North Carolina A&T
    March 14 *Alabama 88-71
    *Alabama 101-76

    Providence 103-82

    Providence 88-73

    New Orleans, LA
    March 30
    NATIONAL CHAMPION

    Indiana 74-73

EAST

3/12 1 North Carolina
16 Pennsylvania
    North Carolina 113-82
3/12 8 Navy
9 Michigan
    March 14 Michigan 97-82
    Charlotte, NC
    North Carolina 109-97
    March 19

3/12 5 Notre Dame
12 Middle Tenn. St.
    Notre Dame 84-71
3/12 4 Texas Christian
13 *Marshall
    March 14 Texas Christian 76-60
    Notre Dame 58-57

    North Carolina 74-68

    East Rutherford, NJ
    March 21

3/13 6 *Florida
11 *North Carolina St.
    *Florida 82-70
3/13 3 Purdue
14 Northeastern
    March 15 Purdue 104-95
    Syracuse, NY
    *Florida 85-66
    March 19

3/13 7 West Va.
10 Western Ky.
    Western Ky. 64-62
3/13 2 Syracuse
15 Ga. Southern
    March 15 Syracuse 79-73
    Syracuse 104-86

    Syracuse 87-81

    Syracuse 79-75

    New Orleans, LA
    March 28

    Syracuse 77-63

* Alabama's, Florida's, Marshall's and North Carolina State's participation in 1987 tournament vacated.

1987-88

AT A GLANCE

NCAA Champion: Kansas (27-11; coached by Larry Brown; finished in third place in Big Eight with a 9-5 record).

NIT Champion: Connecticut (20-14; coached by Jim Calhoun; finished in ninth place in Big East with a 4-12 record).

New Conference: American South (merged with Sun Belt four years later)

New Rule: Each intentional personal foul carries a two-shot penalty plus possession of the ball.

NCAA Probation: Brooklyn, Eastern Washington, Marist, Minnesota, South Carolina, Virginia Tech.

NCAA Consensus First-Team All-Americans: Sean Elliott, F, Jr., Arizona; Gary Grant, G, Sr., Michigan; Hersey Hawkins, G, Sr., Bradley; Danny Manning, F-C, Sr., Kansas; J.R. Reid, C, Soph., North Carolina.

National Players of the Year: Hawkins (36.3 ppg, 7.8 rpg, 52.4 FG%, 84.8 FT%/AP, UPI, USBWA) and Manning (24.8 ppg, 9 rpg, 58.3 FG%/NABC, Naismith, Wooden).

National Coaches of the Year: Kansas' Larry Brown (27-11/Naismith) and Temple's John Chaney (32-2/AP, UPI, NABC, USBWA).

Loyola Marymount, which finished in last place in the West Coast Conference the previous season, went unbeaten in league competition. The Lions became the only team to ever have four players average more than 17 points per game in a season–Hank Gathers (22.5 ppg), Bo Kimble (22.2), Mike Yoest (17.6) and Corey Gaines (17.4). Loyola Marymount, after compiling a 12-16 record the previous year, improved by 14 games to 28-4 to make its lone appearance in the Top 20 of a final wire-service poll.

Sean Elliott became the first Arizona player ever to become an NCAA consensus first- or second-team All-American. Teammate Steve Kerr finished his career with an NCAA-record 38 consecutive games making a three-point field goal. . . . Holy Cross' Glenn Tropf set an NCAA single-season record for three-point field-goal

accuracy by hitting 52 of 82 long-range attempts (63.4 percent). . . . Southern's Avery Johnson set an NCAA single-season record for assists average with 13.3 scoring feeds per game. Johnson, who began his college career at a junior college, averaged 10.7 assists the previous season to become the only player to twice averge double figures in that category. He had 20 or more assists in four games. . . . Oklahoma's Mookie Blaylock, another J.C. transfer, set an NCAA single-season record with 150 steals, including 13 in one game against Centenary.

Lafester Rhodes isn't among Iowa State's top 20 all-time scorers, but he set a school single-game record with 54 points in overtime against Iowa. Other players establishing school single-game marks were Bradley's Hersey Hawkins (63 points at Detroit), Marshall's Skip Henderson (55 vs. The Citadel in Southern Conference Tournament), Central Michigan's Tommie Johnson (53 at Wright State), Rhode Island's Tom Garrick (tied with 50 vs. Rutgers in Atlantic 10 Tournament quarterfinals), Detroit's Archie Tullos (49 vs. Bradley), San Francisco's Keith Jackson (47 at Loyola Marymount) and Drexel's John Rankin (44 vs. Rider) set school single-game records. Ledell Eackles' 45 points against Florida International was a Division I school record for New Orleans. Southern Mississippi's John White tied a Division I school record with 41 points at Virginia Tech.

Hawkins' uprising was also a Missouri Valley Conference mark. Henderson's outburst is a SC Tournament standard. . . . Hawkins (36.3 ppg), Lehigh's Daren Queenan (28.5), Murray State's Jeff Martin (26), Evansville's Marty Simmons (25.9), Southern Illinois' Steve Middleton (25.4), Dartmouth's Jim Barton (24.2), San Jose State's Ricky Berry (24.2), Drexel's Michael Anderson (23.9) and Eastern Michigan's Grant Long (23) set school Division I records for highest scoring average in a single season. Hawkins' average is also a MVC single-season record.

Virginia Tech guard Bimbo Coles scored a Metro Conference-record 51 points in a 141-133

Bradley's Hersey Hawkins (#33) battles an opponent for a rebound.

since 1958 to become an NCAA consensus first- or second-team All-American.

Arizona (35-3, coached by Lute Olson), Oklahoma (35-4, Billy Tubbs), Purdue (29-4, Gene Keady), Loyola Marymount (28-4, Paul Westhead), Rhode Island (28-7, Tom Penders), SMU (28-7, Dave Bliss), Richmond (26-7, Dick Tarrant), Boise State (24-6, Bobby Dye), Fairleigh Dickinson (23-7, Tom Green), UC Santa Barbara (22-8, Jerry Pimm) and Lehigh (21-10, Fran McCaffery) had their winningest seasons in school Division I history. Temple (32-2, John Chaney), Kansas State (25-9, Lon Kruger) and Middle Tennessee State (23-11, Bruce Stewart) tied their school records for most victories in a single season.

St. John's compiled a 17-12 record. It was the closest Lou Carnesecca ever came to a non-winning mark in his 24 years as head coach of the Redmen. . . . Connecticut lost 13 consecutive games to Georgetown in their series until upending the Hoyas, 66-59. . . . Pittsburgh, capturing its lone undisputed Big East Conference regular-season championship, became the only school to feature a roster with as many as eight players who would wind up scoring more than 1,000 points before ending their college careers: seniors Charles Smith and Demetreus Gore, junior Jerome Lane, sophomore Rod Brookin and freshmen Bobby Martin, Jason Matthews, Sean Miller and Darelle Porter.

Marquette incurred its first losing record (10-18) in 24 seasons. . . . Rhode Island and Richmond finished in the Top 20 of a final wire-ser-

double overtime victory over Southern Mississippi. . . . Loyola of Chicago's Kenny Miller became the only freshman ever to lead the nation in rebounding (13.6 per game). . . . Kansas State's Mitch Richmond poured in 35 points in a 72-61 triumph at Kansas, ending the Jayhawks' school and Big Eight-record 55-game homecourt winning streak. Richmond was the first Kansas State player since 1959 to become an NCAA consensus first- or second-team All-American. . . . Guard Mark Macon was the first Temple player

1987–88 INDIVIDUAL LEADERS

SCORING

PLAYER	PTS.	AVG.
Hawkins, Bradley	1125	36.3
Queenan, Lehigh	882	28.5
Mason, Tennessee St.	783	28.0
Hayward, Loyola (Ill.)	756	26.1
Martin, Murray St.	806	26.0
Simmons, Evansville	750	25.9
Middleton, Southern Ill.	711	25.4
Grayer, Iowa St.	811	25.3
Larkin, Xavier	758	25.3
Henderson, Marshall	804	25.1

REBOUNDING

PLAYER	REB.	AVG.
Miller, Loyola (Ill.)	395	13.6
Mack, S. Carolina St.	387	13.3
Lane, Pittsburgh	378	12.2
Sanders, George Mason	339	11.7
White, La. Tech	359	11.6
Canino, Central Conn. St.	321	11.5
Johnson, Baptist	331	11.4
Simmons, La Salle	386	11.4
West, Texas Southern	322	11.1
Coleman, Syracuse	384	11.0

ASSISTS

PLAYER	AST.	AVG.
Johnson, Southern (La.)	399	13.3
Manuel, Bradley	373	12.0
Neal, Georgia Tech	303	9.5
Gaines, L. Marymount	271	8.7
Evans, Temple	294	8.6
Douglas, Syracuse	288	8.2
Smith, Old Dominion	244	8.1
Williams, Holy Cross	234	8.1
Davis, Marist	207	7.7
Brown, Siena	222	7.7

BLOCKED SHOTS

PLAYER	BLK.	AVG.
Blake, St. Joseph's	116	4.0
Smits, Marist	105	3.9
Brown, Canisius	100	3.7
Perry, Temple	118	3.6
Brow, Virginia Tech	100	3.6
Garrett, Indiana	99	3.4
Butts, Bucknell	91	3.4
Campbell, Clemson	88	3.1
Smith, Pittsburgh	96	3.1
Hopkins, Navy	74	3.1

STEALS

PLAYER	STL.	AVG.
Ware, Florida A&M	142	4.9
Johnson, Towson St.	124	4.1
Blaylock, Oklahoma	150	3.8
Workman, Oral Roberts	103	3.6
Johnson, Southern (La.)	106	3.5
Murdock, Providence	90	3.2
Conway, Montana St.	94	3.1
Robertson, Cleveland St.	90	3.0
McDonald, Texas A&M	90	2.9
Strickland, DePaul	75	2.9

FIELD GOAL PERCENTAGE

PLAYER	FGM	FGA	PCT.
Jones, Boise St.	187	283	.661
Brundy, DePaul	194	295	.658
Holifield, Ill. St.	177	273	.648
Basnight, UNLV	184	284	.648
Leckner, Wyoming	181	281	.644
Stuckey, SW Mo. St.	166	259	.641
White, La. Tech	226	354	.638
Perdue, Vanderbilt	234	369	.634
Ambroise, Baptist	171	270	.633
Campbell, Clemson	217	345	.629

FREE THROW PERCENTAGE

PLAYER	FTM	FTA	PCT.
Henson, Kansas St.	111	120	.925
Tullos, Detroit	139	153	.908
Edwards, Indiana	69	76	.908
Barton, Dartmouth	115	127	.906
Smith, Louisville	143	158	.905
Boyd, Memphis St.	111	124	.895
Willingham, S. F. Austin St.	75	84	.893
Harris, Ill. St.	91	102	.892
Nurnberger, S. Ill.	78	88	.886
Lichti, Stanford	174	198	.879

THREE-POINT FIELD GOAL PERCENTAGE

PLAYER	FGM	FGA	PCT.
Tropf, Holy Cross	52	82	.634
Kerr, Arizona	114	199	.573
Joseph, Bucknell	65	116	.560
Jones, Pr. View	85	155	.548
Orlandini, Princeton	60	110	.545

THREE-POINT FIELD GOALS PER GAME

PLAYER	FGM	AVG.
Pollard, Miss. Valley St.	132	4.7
McGill, E. Ky.	104	3.9
Lancaster, Va. Tech	106	3.7
Mooney, Coastal Carolina	102	3.6
Paddio, UNLV	118	3.5

1987–88 TEAM LEADERS

SCORING OFFENSE

SCHOOL	PTS.	AVG.
Loyola Marymount	3528	110.3
Oklahoma	4012	102.9
Southern (La.)	2965	95.6
Xavier	2840	94.7
Iowa	3181	93.6

SCORING DEFENSE

SCHOOL	PTS.	AVG.
Georgia Southern	1725	55.6
Boise St.	1680	56.0
Princeton	1467	56.4
Colorado St.	2007	57.3
St. Mary's (Calif.)	1640	58.6

SCORING MARGIN

SCHOOL	OFF.	DEF.	MAR.
Oklahoma	102.9	81.0	21.9
Arizona	85.1	64.2	20.9
UNLV	84.3	68.2	16.1
Temple	76.8	61.2	15.6
Xavier	94.7	79.5	15.2

WON-LOST PERCENTAGE

SCHOOL	W-L	PCT.
Temple	32-2	.941
Arizona	35-3	.921
Oklahoma	35-4	.897
North Carolina A&T	26-3	.897
Purdue	29-4	.879

FIELD GOAL PERCENTAGE

SCHOOL	FGM	FGA	PCT.
Michigan	1198	2196	.546
Arizona	1147	2106	.545
North Carolina	1013	1892	.535
Purdue	1018	1912	.532
Brigham Young	976	1839	.531

FIELD GOAL PERCENTAGE DEFENSE

SCHOOL	FGM	FGA	PCT.
Temple	777	1981	.392
Marist	617	1537	.401
Kansas	912	2215	.412
UNLV	841	2012	.418
Georgia Southern	640	1529	.419

FREE THROW PERCENTAGE

SCHOOL	FTM	FTA	PCT.
Butler	413	517	.799
Princeton	315	405	.778
Bucknell	477	617	.773
UNC-Asheville	419	543	.772
Auburn	406	527	.770

REBOUND MARGIN

SCHOOL	OFF.	DEF.	MAR.
Notre Dame	36.0	26.2	9.9
South Carolina St.	42.9	33.5	9.4
Ark.-Little Rock	41.3	32.5	8.8
Georgetown	39.2	31.3	7.9
Missouri	41.9	34.3	7.7

THREE-POINT FIELD GOAL PERCENTAGE

SCHOOL	FGM	FGA	PCT.
Princeton	211	429	.492
Prairie View	129	266	.485
Kansas St.	179	370	.484
Arizona	254	526	.483
Bucknell	154	328	.470

THREE-POINT FIELD GOALS PER GAME

SCHOOL	FGM	AVG.
Princeton	211	8.1
Loyola Marymount	251	7.8
Oklahoma	299	7.7
George Mason	219	7.3
Bradley	224	7.2

vice poll for the only time in their history. Xavier finished in the Top 20 of a final wire-service poll for the first time since 1957. . . . Delaware, coached by Steve Steinwedel, snapped a streak of nine straight losing seasons by notching a 19-9 mark. . . . Northeastern's Steve Carney collected a school-record 23 rebounds in a game against Hartford.

North Carolina A&T, coached by Don Corbett, won its seventh consecutive Mid-Eastern Athletic Conference Tournament. . . . Wichita State finished with a 20-10 record despite losing three consecutive early-season games in overtime. . . . SMU, coached by Dave Bliss, captured the SWC regular-season title just one year after finishing in a tie for sixth place. . . . St. Mary's lost more than 10 games in 26 consecutive seasons until the Gaels compiled a 19-9 record. . . . Long Beach State ended a streak of six consecutive losing seasons by registering a 17-12 ledger in Joe Harrington's initial campaign as coach of the 49ers.

1987-88 FINAL NATIONAL POLLS

AP	UPI	USA/CNN	SCHOOL (RECORD)	HEAD COACH
1	1	5	Temple (32-2)	John Chaney
2	2	3	Arizona (35-3)	Lute Olson
3	3	6	Purdue (29-4)	Gene Keady
4	4	2	Oklahoma (35-4)	Billy Tubbs
5	5	4	Duke (28-7)	Mike Krzyzewski
6	6	9	Kentucky (27-6)	Eddie Sutton
7	8	7	North Carolina (27-7)	Dean Smith
8	7	13	Pittsburgh (24-7)	Paul Evans
9	9	16	Syracuse (26-9)	Jim Boeheim
10	10	10	Michigan (26-8)	Bill Frieder
11	12	23	Bradley (26-5)	Stan Albeck
12	11	22	UNLV (26-5)	Jerry Tarkanian
13	14	–	Wyoming (26-6)	Benny Dees
14	13	21	N.C. State (24-8)	Jim Valvano
15	16	19	Loyola Marymount (28-4)	Paul Westhead
16	15	20	Illinois (23-10)	Lou Henson
17	18	14	Iowa (24-10)	Tom Davis
18	–	–	Xavier (26-4)	Pete Gillen
19	17	25	Brigham Young (26-6)	Ladell Andersen
20	20	8	Kansas State (25-9)	Lon Kruger
–	–	1	Kansas (27-11)	Larry Brown
–	–	11	Villanova (24-13)	Rollie Massimino
–	–	12	Rhode Island (28-7)	Tom Penders
–	–	15	Louisville (24-11)	Denny Crum
–	–	17	Vanderbilt (20-11)	C.M. Newton
–	–	18	Richmond (26-7)	Dick Tarrant
–	19	–	Indiana (19-10)	Bob Knight
–	–	24	DePaul (22-8)	Joey Meyer

1988 NCAA Tournament

Summary: The Big Eight went 30 years without winning a Final Four game until Kansas and Oklahoma both won. Kansas won the championship game after losing three previous finals at Kansas City (1940, 1953 and 1957). Danny Manning had a Final Four-record six blocked shots in a 66-59 victory over Duke in the national semifinals. Larry Brown became the only coach to leave an NCAA champion before the next season for another coaching job. After winning the NCAA title, Brown quit the Jayhawks before the start of the next NCAA probation-marred campaign to return to the NBA.

Outcome for Defending Champion: Indiana (19-10) finished fifth in the Big Ten before losing its tourney opener to No. 13 seed Richmond, 72-69. The Hoosiers lost four of their first five league outings.

Star Gazing: Manning became the only one of the more than 60 major-college players to score at least 2,500 career points or average a minimum of 28.5 points per game and play for an NCAA championship team. Manning, the only national player of the year from 1981-91 to play for a national titlist, hit 25 of 45 field-goal attempts and grabbed 28 rebounds at the Final Four.

Biggest Upset: Murray State (14th seed) defeated North Carolina State (3), 78-75.

One and Only: Oklahoma became the only school to compete for the national championship in both football and basketball in the same academic school year (1988). The football Sooners lost to Miami (Fla.) in the Orange Bowl, finishing third in the final wire-service polls.

Numbers Game: Temple, a 63-53 loser against Duke in the East Regional final, is one of only two teams ranked No. 1 by both AP and UPI entering the tourney to lose by a double-digit margin before the Final Four. The Owls finished with 32 victories for the second consecutive season. . . . Oklahoma's Mookie Blaylock set the record for most steals in a playoff series (23 in six games). He had seven steals as a junior guard in an 83-79 championship game loss against Kansas. . . . Bradley's Hersey Hawkins poured in a tourney-high 44 points in

1987–88 NCAA CHAMPION: KANSAS

SEASON STATISTICS OF KANSAS REGULARS

PLAYER	POS.	CL.	G.	FG%	FT%	PPG	RPG
Danny Manning	F-C	Sr.	38	.583	.734	24.8	9.0
Milt Newton	G	Jr.	35	.555	.564	11.6	5.0
Kevin Pritchard	G	So.	37	.486	.739	10.6	2.6
Chris Piper	F	Sr.	34	.537	.705	5.1	3.8
Lincoln Minor	G	Jr.	34	.419	.667	4.8	1.4
Jeff Gueldner	G	So.	34	.422	.681	3.8	2.0
Scooter Barry	G	Jr.	35	.477	.815	3.3	1.3
Keith Harris	F	So.	27	.451	.633	3.1	2.6
Otis Livingston	G	Jr.	27	.650	.613	2.6	1.4
Mike Maddox	F	Fr.	24	.532	.471	2.5	1.5
Mike Masucci	C	Fr.	24	.431	.467	2.1	1.5
TEAM TOTALS			**38**	**.521**	**.690**	**75.3**	**35.6**

Three-point field goals leader: Newton (29 of 64, .453). **Assists leader:** Pritchard 113. **Blocked shots leader:** Manning 73. **Steals leaders:** Manning 70, Pritchard 52.

1988 FINAL FOUR CHAMPIONSHIP GAME

KANSAS CITY, MO

KANSAS (83)	MIN.	FG-A	FT-A	REB.	A	PF	PTS.
Piper	37	4-6	0-0	1	2	3	8
Gueldner	15	1-2	0-0	0	1	0	2
Manning	36	13-24	5-7	7	2	3	31
Pritchard	31	6-7	0-0	0	4	1	13
Newton	32	6-6	1-2	0	1	1	15
Barry	9	0-2	1-2	0	2	1	1
Maddox	1	0-0	0-0	0	0	1	0
Harris	12	1-1	0-0	0	0	2	2
Normore	16	3-3	0-1	0	4	3	7
Minor	11	1-4	2-2	0	1	1	4
Team				1			
TOTALS	**200**	**35-55**	**9-14**	**8**	**17**	**16**	**83**

FG%: .636. **FT%:** .643. **Three-point goals:** 4-6 (Pritchard 1-1, Newton 2-2, Normore 1-1, Gueldner 0-1, Manning 0-1). **Blocks:** 4. **Turnovers:** 23. **Steals:** 11 (Manning 5).

OKLAHOMA (79)	MIN.	FG-A	FT-A	REB.	A	PF	PTS.
Grant	40	6-14	2-3	3	1	4	14
Sieger	40	7-15	1-2	3	7	2	22
King	39	7-14	3-3	2	0	3	17
Blaylock	40	6-13	0-1	3	4	4	14
Grace	34	4-14	3-4	3	7	4	12
Mullins	7	0-0	0-0	0	0	1	0
Team				1			
TOTALS	**200**	**30-70**	**9-13**	**14**	**19**	**18**	**79**

FG%: .429. **FT%:** .692. **Three-point goals:** 10-24 (Sieger 7-13, Blaylock 2-4, Grace 1-7). **Blocks:** 3. **Turnovers:** 15 (Sieger 6). **Steals:** 13 (Blaylock 7). **Halftime:** Tied 50-50.

NATIONAL SEMIFINALS

KANSAS (66): Piper 3-4 4-4 10, Guelder 0-1 0-0 0, Manning 12-21 1-2 25, Pritchard 2-6 2-2 6, Newton 8-14 2-3 20, Barry 1-2 3-4 5, Maddox 0-0 0-0 0, Harris 0-4 0-0 0, Normore 0-0 0-0 0, Minor 0-0 0-0 0, Mattox 0-0 0-0 0. Team 26-52 (.500) 12-15 (.800) 66.

DUKE (59): Ferry 7-22 4-4 19, King 1-4 1-2 3, Brickey 2-9 2-5 6, Snyder 4-10 1-2 9, Strickland 5-13 0-0 10, Koubek 3-5 0-0 8, Abdelnaby 1-2 2-4 4, Smith 0-0 0-0 0, Henderson 0-2 0-0 0, Cook 0-0 0-0 0. Team 23-67 (.343) 10-17 (.588) 59.

Halftime: Kansas 38-27.
Three-point goals: Kansas 2-4 (.500), Duke 3-14 (.214).

ARIZONA (78): Cook 6-13 4-6 16, Elliott 13-23 3-3 31, Tolbert 5-11 1-2 11, McMillan 3-6 0-0 8, Kerr 2-13 0-0 6, Turner 0-0 0-0 0, Mason 0-0 0-0 0, Buechler 2-2 0-0 4, Lofton 1-4 0-0 2. Team 32-72 (.444) 8-11 (.727) 78.

OKLAHOMA (86): Grant 7-14 7-10 21, Sieger 3-8 3-6 10, King 9-16 3-6 21, Blaylock 3-7 1-2 7, Grace 3-10 5-7 13, Mullins 1-1 0-0 3, Wiley 4-8 3-3 11. Team 30-64 (.469) 22-34 (.647) 86.

Halftime: Oklahoma 39-27.
Three-point goals: Arizona 6-23 (.261), Oklahoma 4-14 (.286).

ALL-TOURNAMENT TEAM

Sean Elliott, F, Jr., Arizona
Stacey King, C, Jr., Oklahoma
Danny Manning, F, Sr., Kansas*
Milt Newton, G-F, Jr., Kansas
Dave Sieger, F, Sr., Oklahoma
*Named Most Outstanding Player

a 90-86 setback against Auburn in the opening round of the Southwest Regional. . . . Pitt's Jerome Lane grabbed a tourney-high 20 rebounds in an 80-74 defeat against Vanderbilt in the second round of the Midwest Regional. . . . Kansas State guard William Scott finished his playoff career with 65 percent accuracy from three-point range (26 of 40 in five games). . . . North Carolina lost its fourth regional final in six years. . . . Seton Hall appeared in the NCAA Tournament for the first time. . . . Kentucky became the fourth different SEC school in four years to have its NCAA Tournament participation vacated. The previous SEC offenders were Georgia '85, Alabama '87 and Florida '87.

What If: Forwards Danny Ferry and Robert Brickey and guard Phil Henderson combined to shoot 50 percent from the floor in their Duke careers. If only they combined to hit 39.4 percent of their field-goal attempts instead of 27.3 percent (9 of 33) in the national semifinals, the Blue Devils could have defeated eventual champion Kansas rather than losing 66-59. . . . Kansas State (25-9, without Norris Coleman), Louisiana State (16-14, John Williams), Memphis State (20-12, Vincent Askew) and North Carolina State (24-8, Chris Washburn) might have fared better in the playoffs if standout players had exercised their remaining eligibility instead of defecting to the NBA. . . . Georgia (20-16) probably would

Kansas' Danny Manning (#25) snags a rebound from an opponent.

1988 CHAMPIONSHIP BRACKET

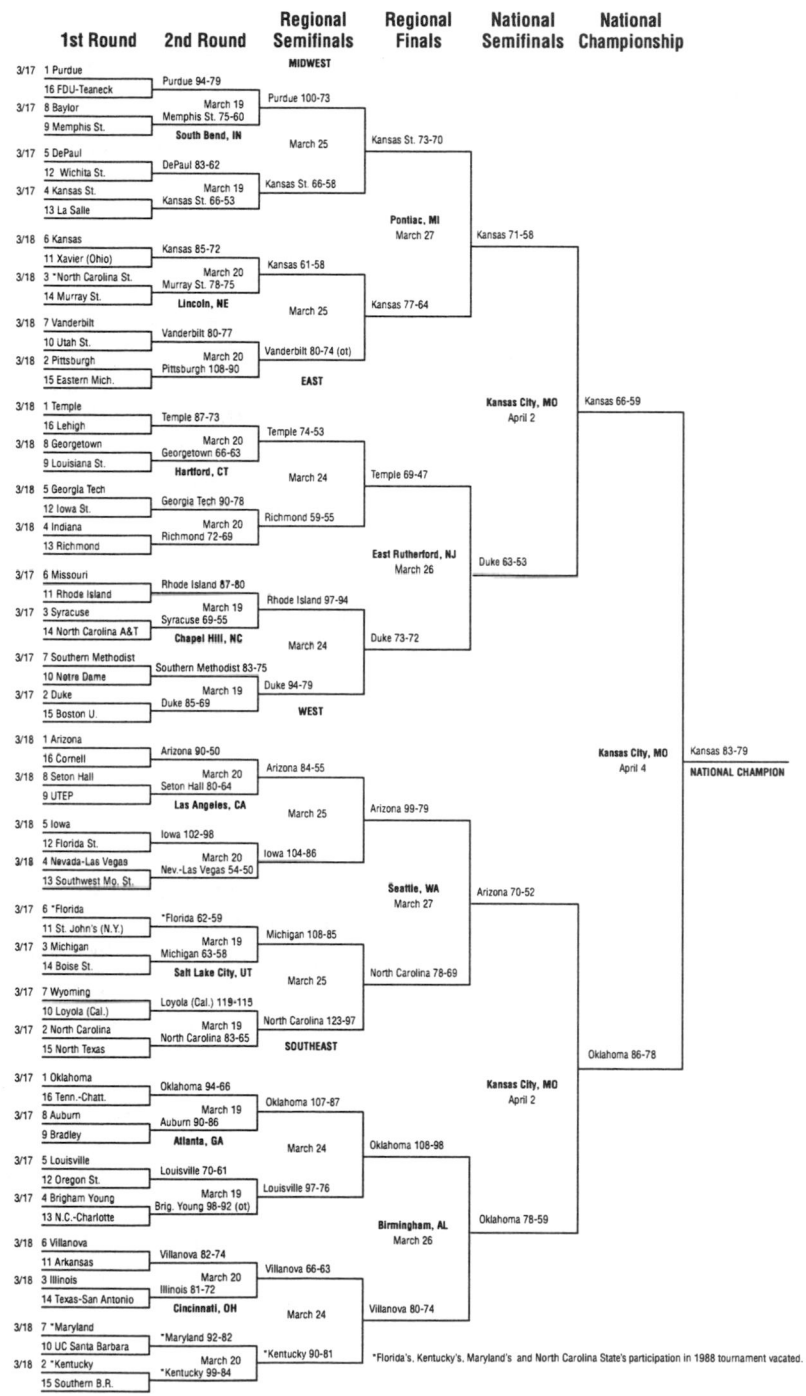

	1st Round	2nd Round	Regional Semifinals	Regional Finals	National Semifinals	National Championship

MIDWEST

3/17 1 Purdue
16 FDU-Teaneck
— Purdue 94-79
3/17 8 Baylor
9 Memphis St.
— Memphis St. 75-60
March 19
Purdue 100-73
South Bend, IN
March 25
Kansas St. 73-70

3/17 5 DePaul
12 Wichita St.
— DePaul 83-62
3/17 4 Kansas St.
13 La Salle
— Kansas St. 66-53
March 19
Kansas St. 66-58

Kansas 71-58

Pontiac, MI
March 27

3/18 6 Kansas
11 Xavier (Ohio)
— Kansas 85-72
3/18 3 *North Carolina St.
14 Murray St.
— Murray St. 78-75
March 20
Kansas 61-58
Lincoln, NE
March 25
Kansas 77-64

3/18 7 Vanderbilt
10 Utah St.
— Vanderbilt 80-77
3/18 2 Pittsburgh
15 Eastern Mich.
— Pittsburgh 108-90
March 20
Vanderbilt 80-74 (ot)

Kansas City, MO
April 2

Kansas 66-59

EAST

3/18 1 Temple
16 Lehigh
— Temple 87-73
3/18 8 Georgetown
9 Louisiana St.
— Georgetown 66-63
March 20
Temple 74-53
Hartford, CT
March 24
Temple 69-47

3/18 5 Georgia Tech
12 Iowa St.
— Georgia Tech 90-78
3/18 4 Indiana
13 Richmond
— Richmond 72-69
March 20
Richmond 59-55

Duke 63-53

East Rutherford, NJ
March 26

3/17 6 Missouri
11 Rhode Island
— Rhode Island 87-80
3/17 3 Syracuse
14 North Carolina A&T
— Syracuse 69-55
March 19
Rhode Island 97-94
Chapel Hill, NC
March 24
Duke 73-72

3/17 7 Southern Methodist
10 Notre Dame
— Southern Methodist 83-75
3/17 2 Duke
15 Boston U.
— Duke 85-69
March 19
Duke 94-79

WEST

Kansas City, MO
April 4

Kansas 83-79
NATIONAL CHAMPION

3/18 1 Arizona
16 Cornell
— Arizona 90-50
3/18 8 Seton Hall
9 UTEP
— Seton Hall 80-64
March 20
Arizona 84-55
Las Angeles, CA
March 25
Arizona 99-79

3/18 5 Iowa
12 Florida St.
— Iowa 102-98
3/18 4 Nevada-Las Vegas
13 Southwest Mo. St.
— Nev.-Las Vegas 54-50
March 20
Iowa 104-86

Arizona 70-52

Seattle, WA
March 27

3/17 6 *Florida
11 St. John's (N.Y.)
— *Florida 62-59
3/17 3 Michigan
14 Boise St.
— Michigan 63-58
March 19
Michigan 108-85
Salt Lake City, UT
March 25
North Carolina 78-69

3/17 7 Wyoming
10 Loyola (Cal.)
— Loyola (Cal.) 119-115
3/17 2 North Carolina
15 North Texas
— North Carolina 83-65
March 19
North Carolina 123-97

Kansas City, MO
April 2

Oklahoma 86-78

SOUTHEAST

3/17 1 Oklahoma
16 Tenn.-Chatt.
— Oklahoma 94-66
3/17 8 Auburn
9 Bradley
— Auburn 90-86
March 19
Oklahoma 107-87
Atlanta, GA
March 24
Oklahoma 108-98

3/17 5 Louisville
12 Oregon St.
— Louisville 70-61
3/17 4 Brigham Young
13 N.C.-Charlotte
— Brig. Young 98-92 (ot)
March 19
Louisville 97-76

Oklahoma 78-59

Birmingham, AL
March 26

3/18 6 Villanova
11 Arkansas
— Villanova 82-74
3/18 3 Illinois
14 Texas-San Antonio
— Illinois 81-72
March 20
Villanova 66-63
Cincinnati, OH
March 24
Villanova 80-74

3/18 7 *Maryland
10 UC Santa Barbara
— *Maryland 92-82
3/18 2 *Kentucky
15 Southern B.R.
— *Kentucky 99-84
March 20
*Kentucky 90-81

*Florida's, Kentucky's, Maryland's and North Carolina State's participation in 1988 tournament vacated.

have participated in the NCAA Tournament instead of the NIT if Cedric Henderson didn't leave school early for the NBA two years ago after his sophomore season.

Putting Things in Perspective: Kansas State (25-9) defeated Kansas twice by a total of 26 points before losing against KU in the Midwest Regional final, 71-58, when Wildcats star Mitch Richmond was restricted to 11 points and four rebounds. Richmond had averaged 25.8 points and 10.2 rebounds in his first five playoff games. Oklahoma (35-4) defeated the Jayhawks twice by eight points in each Big Eight Conference regular-season game before losing against KU in the national final. Kansas lost five games by double-digit margins. The Jayhawks went almost a month without a victory against a Division I opponent as their only win in a mid-season, six-game stretch was against Hampton (Va.). Nebraska, which was 4-10 in the Big Eight when the Cornhuskers' streak of 14 consecutive winning seasons came to an end, defeated Kansas, 70-68.

Scoring Leader: Danny Manning, Kansas (163 points, 27.2 ppg).

Rebounding Leader: Danny Manning, Kansas (56 rebounds, 9.3 rpg).

Highest Rebounding Average: Jerome Lane, Pittsburgh (37 rebounds, 18.5 rpg).

1988-89

AT A GLANCE

NCAA Champion: Michigan (30-7; coached by Bill Frieder and Steve Fisher; finished in third place in Big Ten with a 12-6 record).

NIT Champion: St. John's (20-13; coached by Lou Carnesecca; finished in a tie for seventh place in Big East with a 6-10 record).

New Rules: Neutral courts are used in all rounds of the NCAA Tournament. . . . Bracket rotation for the NCAA tourney was established. . . . Criteria governing automatic qualification for conferences was strengthened.

NCAA Probation: Cincinnati, Cleveland State, Kansas, Marist, Virginia Tech.

NCAA Consensus First-Team All-Americans: Sean Elliott, F, Sr., Arizona; Pervis Ellison, C, Sr., Louisville; Danny Ferry, F-C, Sr., Duke; Chris Jackson, G, Fr., Louisiana State; Stacey King, C, Sr., Oklahoma.

National Players of the Year: Elliott (22.3 ppg, 7.2 rpg, 84.1 FT%/AP, NABC, Wooden) and Ferry (22.6 ppg, 7.4 rpg, 52.2 FG%/UPI, USBWA, Naismith).

National Coaches of the Year: Seton Hall's P.J. Carlesimo (31-7/NABC); Indiana's Bob Knight (27-8/AP, UPI, USBWA), and Duke's Mike Krzyzewski (28-8/Naismith).

The proliferation of parity and the wisdom of expanding the postseason field was never more evident than in the 1989 playoffs. All of the Final Four teams would not have qualified for the NCAA Tournament prior to 1975 when more than one league member could be invited—Michigan (finished in third place in Big Ten Conference), Seton Hall (lost in Big East Tournament semifinals after finishing runner-up to Georgetown in regular-season standings), Duke (lost in ACC Tournament final after finishing in three-way tie for second place behind North Carolina State in regular-season standings) and Illinois (runner-up in Big Ten to Indiana).

LSU edged second-ranked Georgetown, 82-80, on Ricky Blanton's last-second rebound basket before 54,321 fans at the Louisiana Superdome (64,144 paid). . . . LSU guard Chris Jackson became the highest-scoring freshman in major-college history when he averaged 30.2 points per game. His 55 points were in vain in a 113-112 overtime loss at Ole Miss when the Rebels' Gerald Glass offset Jackson's outburst with 53 points. . . . Jackson's 48 points weren't enough to prevent a 104-95 defeat against visiting Florida when the Gators clinched their only SEC regular-season title. Helping Florida along the way was an incredible 81-78 overtime victory at Vanderbilt when the Gators tied the game at the end of regulation after Commodore fans were assessed a two-shot technical for throwing tennis balls at center Dwayne Schintzius, who had previously run afoul of the law while wielding a tennis racket.

Vanderbilt guard Barry Goheen ended his career as one of the premier clutch players in college history. He made six game-winning shots in the closing seconds and sent an NCAA Tournament game into overtime with two three-point baskets in the final five seconds of regulation. . . . Duke's Danny Ferry established an ACC and school single-game record by pouring in 58 points at Miami (Fla.). Also setting a school single-game scoring standard was Eastern Washington's David Peed (44 points against UC Irvine).

La Salle's Lionel Simmons (28.4 ppg), Virginia Tech's Bimbo Coles (26.6), Air Force's Raymond Dudley (26.6), Virginia Commonwealth's Chris Cheeks (23.8), Eastern Illinois' Jay Taylor (23.4) and Peed (20.9) set school Division I records for highest scoring average in a single season.

Memphis State raced to a 24-0 lead at highly-ranked Louisville en route to upending the Cardinals, 72-67. Louisville and Memphis State combined to capture the previous 10 Metro Conference regular-season championships until Florida State moved atop the league standings.

Mr. Clutch: Vanderbilt's Barry Goheen.

Loyola Marymount junior Hank Gathers became the only player to lead the nation in scoring (32.7 points per game) in a season he shot better than 60 percent from the floor (60.8). Gathers collected 41 points and a school-record 29 rebounds in 30 minutes in a 181-150 victory

HIGHEST-SCORING GAME IN HISTORY Loyola Marymount's high scorers met U.S. International on January 31, 1989, in what became the highest-scoring game in history. Marymount defeated U.S. International, 181-150. Marymount's high scorer was Hank Gathers; International's top gun was Steve Smith.

USIU (150)	FG-A	FT-A	REB.	PTS.
Williams	9-12	7-12	5	25
Laffitte	12-18	4-5	7	28
Sterner	5-9	0-0	6	10
Wilson	10-21	1-3	3	21
Smith	11-15	8-8	8	32
Davis	3-4	0-1	3	7
Moore	3-5	0-0	4	6
Judd	3-5	0-0	3	6
Hodges	0-2	0-2	0	0
Howard	6-8	1-4	1	13
Banks	1-2	0-0	0	2
Team			9	
TOTALS	**63-101**	**21-35**	**49**	**150**

FG%: .624. **FT%**: .600. **Three-point shooting:** 3 of 7 (Wilson 0-2, Smith 2-2, Davis 1-2, Hodges 0-1).

LMU (181)	FG-A	FT-A	REB.	PTS.
Stumer	4-11	2-3	5	12
Peabody	2-3	1-2	2	5
Gathers	15-24	11-14	29	41
Fryer	10-24	8-10	2	34
Simmons	10-14	3-4	5	25
Lee	2-2	1-3	1	5
Mister	0-0	1-2	2	1
O'Connell	2-3	1-1	1	5
Lowery	5-9	4-4	4	15
Roscoe	0-0	0-0	0	0
Yoest	3-6	0-0	1	6
Kimble	9-15	0-0	4	20
Knight	1-2	2-2	1	4
Veargason	2-3	0-0	4	4
Morley	0-0	0-0	1	0
Slater	2-3	0-0	0	4
Team			1	
TOTALS	**67-119**	**34-45**	**63**	**181**

FG%: .563. **FT%**: .755. **Three-point shooting:** 13 of 34 (Stumer 2-6, Fryer 6-14, Simmons 2-4, Lowery 1-3, Yoest 0-1, Kimble 2-6). **Halftime:** Loyola Marymount 94-76.

Aside from these famous cardboard fans, all spectators were banned from the 1989 North Atlantic Tournament due to a measles outbreak.

over U.S. International that set an NCAA record for most total points. The scoring orgy left the following numbers of note:

• A field goal was attempted an average of every 11 seconds and a basket was scored an average of every 18.5 seconds.

• The longest span between baskets was 59 seconds.

• A point was scored an average of every 7.25 seconds.

• Seven players amassed more points than minutes played.

Kentucky's NCAA-record streak of consecutive non-losing seasons was stopped at 60 when the Wildcats compiled a 13-19 mark in Eddie Sutton's last year as their coach. The following indiscretions left UK's program in turmoil:

• Chris Mills transferred to Arizona in the wake of a Los Angeles newspaper reporting that Emery Worldwide employees had discovered $1,000 in an accidentally opened package sent to Mills' father by Wildcats assistant Dwane Casey. Teammate Leron Ellis, another product from California, transferred to Syracuse.

• Prize recruit Shawn Kemp, a Proposition 48 casualty, dropped out of school after an alleged theft.

• Starter Eric Manuel's ACT score was

1988–89 INDIVIDUAL LEADERS

SCORING

PLAYER	PTS.	AVG.
Gathers, Loyola Marymount	1015	32.7
Jackson, Louisiana St.	965	30.2
Simmons, La Salle	908	28.4
Glass, Mississippi	841	28.0
Edwards, East Carolina	773	26.7
Dudley, Air Force	746	26.6
Coles, Virginia Tech	717	26.6
Smith, Brigham Young	765	26.4
King, Oklahoma	859	26.0
Taft, Marshall	701	26.0

REBOUNDING

PLAYER	REB.	AVG.
Gathers, Loyola Marymount	426	13.7
Hill, Xavier	403	12.2
Draper, American	336	12.0
Battles, Southern (La.)	360	11.6
Simmons, La Salle	365	11.4
Coleman, Syracuse	422	11.4
Burton, Long Island	309	11.0
Mack, South Carolina St.	361	10.9
Sanders, George Mason	326	10.9
Washington, Weber St.	303	10.8

ASSISTS

PLAYER	AST.	AVG.
Williams, Holy Cross	278	9.9
Corchiani, N.C. St.	266	8.6
Douglas, Syracuse	326	8.6
Payton, Oregon St.	244	8.1
Manuel, Bradley	216	8.0
Timberlake, Boston U.	238	7.9
Overton, La Salle	244	7.6
Richardson, UCLA	236	7.6
Sample, Southern (La.)	234	7.5
McGee, New Mexico	243	7.4

BLOCKED SHOTS

PLAYER	BLK.	AVG.
Mourning, Georgetown	169	5.0
Causwell, Temple	124	4.1
Ogg, UAB	129	3.8
Coleman, Syracuse	127	3.4
Butts, Bucknell	100	3.2
Ellison, Louisville	98	3.2
Henderson, Siena	86	3.1
Green, Rhode Island	85	3.0
West, Texas Southern	90	3.0
Campbell, Clemson	87	3.0
Godfread, Evansville	92	3.0

STEALS

PLAYER	STL.	AVG.
Robertson, Cleveland St.	111	4.0
Blaylock, Oklahoma	131	3.7
Applewhite, Tex. S'thern	105	3.5
Screen, Providence	101	3.5
Lee, Towson St.	98	3.4
Tanner, Rice	94	3.4
Murdock, Providence	97	3.3
Workman, Oral Roberts	93	3.3
Blanks, Texas	111	3.3
Newbern, Minnesota	101	3.3

FIELD GOAL PERCENTAGE

PLAYER	FTM	FTA	PCT.
Davis, Florida	179	248	.722
Burns, Miss. St.	167	249	.671
Davis, Clemson	146	218	.670
Mack, S. Carolina St.	204	306	.667
Parker, Cleve. St.	168	253	.664
Ambroise, Baptist	164	247	.664
Vaught, Michigan	201	304	.661
Stewart, Coppin St.	199	302	.659
Smith, Idaho	185	284	.651
Burke, Wagner	215	331	.650

FREE THROW PERCENTAGE

PLAYER	FTM	FTA	PCT.
Smith, BYU	160	173	.925
Henson, Kansas St.	92	100	.920
Simmons, Md.-Balt. C'nty	83	92	.902
Nurnberger, S. Ill.	129	143	.902
Haffner, Evansville	136	151	.901
Matthews, Pitt	142	158	.899
Blevins, Kent	94	105	.895
Lauritzen, Indiana St.	68	76	.895
Peterson, Yale	111	125	.888
Christian, Appa. St.	76	86	.884

THREE-POINT FIELD GOAL PERCENTAGE

PLAYER	FGM	FGA	PCT.
Calloway, Monmouth	48	82	.585
Tribelhorn, Colo. St.	76	135	.563
Joseph, Bucknell	62	115	.539
Bays, Towson St.	71	132	.538
Anglavar, Marquette	53	99	.535

THREE-POINT FIELD GOALS PER GAME

PLAYER	FGM	AVG.
Pollard, Miss. Vly. St.	124	4.4
Grider, SW La.	122	4.2
Fryer, L. Marymount	126	4.1
Barros, Boston College	112	3.9
McCloud, Florida St.	115	3.8

1988–89 TEAM LEADERS

SCORING OFFENSE

SCHOOL	PTS.	AVG.
Loyola Marymount	3486	112.5
Oklahoma	3680	102.2
Southern (La.)	3015	97.3
Texas	3206	94.3
Louisiana St.	2966	92.7

SCORING DEFENSE

SCHOOL	PTS.	AVG.
Princeton	1430	53.0
St. Mary's (Calif.)	1728	57.6
Boise St.	1767	58.9
Colorado St.	2012	61.0
Idaho	1894	61.1

SCORING MARGIN

SCHOOL	OWN	OPP.	MAR.
St. Mary's (Calif.)	76.1	57.6	18.5
Arizona	84.5	66.9	17.6
Michigan	91.7	74.8	16.9
Duke	86.5	69.8	16.8
Siena	85.0	69.8	15.1

WON-LOST PERCENTAGE

SCHOOL	W-L	PCT.
Ball St.	29-3	.906
Arizona	29-4	.879
Illinois	31-5	.861
Georgetown	29-5	.853
West Virginia	26-5	.839

FIELD GOAL PERCENTAGE

SCHOOL	FGM	FGA	PCT.
Michigan	1325	2341	.566
New Mexico	992	1819	.545
Syracuse	1334	2456	.543
Duke	1163	2166	.537
St. Mary's (Calif.)	859	1606	.535

FIELD GOAL PERCENTAGE DEFENSE

SCHOOL	FGM	FGA	PCT.
Georgetown	795	1993	.399
West Virginia	738	1840	.401
St. Mary's (Calif.)	651	1606	.405
Ball St.	688	1687	.408
Seton Hall	934	2265	.412

FREE THROW PERCENTAGE

SCHOOL	FTM	FTA	PCT.
Brigham Young	527	647	.815
Gonzaga	485	614	.790
Bucknell	590	749	.788
Kent	592	755	.784
Louisiana St.	557	723	.770

REBOUND MARGIN

SCHOOL	OWN	OPP.	MAR.
Iowa	41.4	31.8	9.6
Notre Dame	37.7	28.8	9.0
Missouri	42.1	34.2	7.9
Michigan	37.7	30.3	7.4
Stanford	34.8	27.7	7.1

THREE-POINT FIELD GOAL PERCENTAGE

SCHOOL	FGM	FGA	PCT.
Indiana	121	256	.473
Michigan	196	419	.468
The Citadel	153	328	.466
Colorado St.	141	305	.462
Bucknell	160	347	.461

THREE-POINT FIELD GOALS PER GAME

SCHOOL	FGM	AVG.
Loyola Marymount	287	9.3
Valparaiso	257	8.9
Oral Roberts	216	7.7
Mt. St. Mary's (Md.)	202	7.5
Alabama-Birmingham	247	7.3

1988–89 NCAA CHAMPION: MICHIGAN

SEASON STATISTICS OF MICHIGAN REGULARS

PLAYER	POS.	CL.	G.	FG%	FT%	PPG	RPG
Glen Rice	F	Sr.	37	.577	.832	25.6	6.3
Rumeal Robinson	G	Jr.	37	.557	.656	14.9	3.4
Loy Vaught	F	Jr.	37	.661	.778	12.6	8.0
Terry Mills	C	Jr.	37	.564	.769	11.6	5.9
Sean Higgins	F-G	So.	34	.506	.771	12.4	3.1
Mark Hughes	C-F	Sr.	35	.608	.604	6.8	4.1
Kirk Taylor	G	So.	21	.478	.611	4.5	2.2
Mike Griffin	G-F	Jr.	37	.508	.767	2.7	2.4
J. P. Oosterbaan	C	Jr.	22	.564	.692	2.4	1.2
Demetrius Calip	G	So.	30	.440	.824	2.0	0.6
Rob Pelinka	G	Fr.	26	.360	.700	1.1	0.6
TEAM TOTALS			37	.566	.735	91.7	37.7

Three-point field goals leaders: Rice (99 of 192, .516), Higgins (51 of 110 .464), Robinson (30 of 64, .469). **Assists leaders:** Robinson 233, Mills 104, Griffin 103. **Blocked shots leader:** Mills 49. **Steals leader:** Robinson 70.

1989 FINAL FOUR CHAMPIONSHIP GAME

SEATTLE, WA

MICHIGAN (80)	MIN.	FG-A	FT-A	REB.	A	PF	PTS.
Rice	42	12-25	2-2	1	0	2	31
Hughes	25	1-1	0-0	0	0	2	2
Mills	34	4-8	0-0	3	2	2	8
Griffin	17	0-0	0-0	2	3	4	0
Robinson	43	6-13	9-10	1	11	2	21
Vaught	26	4-8	0-0	2	0	2	8
Calip	11	0-2	0-0	0	1	3	0
Higgins	27	3-10	3-4	2	2	3	10
Team				3			
TOTALS	225	30-67	14-16	14	19	20	80

FG%: .448. **FT%:** .875. **Three-point goals:** 6-16 (Rice 5-12, Higgins 1-4). **Blocks:** 4 (Mills 3). **Turnovers:** 14. **Steals:** 3.

SETON HALL (79)	MIN.	FG-A	FT-A	REB.	A	PF	PTS.
Walker	39	5-9	3-4	3	1	2	13
Gaze	39	1-5	2-2	2	3	3	5
Ramos	33	4-9	1-1	0	1	2	9
Morton	37	11-26	9-10	1	3	3	35
Greene	43	5-13	1-3	0	5	3	13

Avent	11	1-2	0-0	1	1	0	2
Volcy	7	0-0	0-2	0	0	2	0
Cooper	14	0-0	0-0	0	0	1	0
Wigington	2	1-1	0-0	0	0	1	2
Team				2			
TOTALS	225	28-65	16-22	9	14	17	79

FG%: .431. **FT%:** .727. **Three-point goals:** 7-23 (Morton 4-12, Greene 2-5, Gaze 1-5, Walker 0-1). **Blocks:** 2. **Turnovers:** 11. **Steals:** 4. **Halftime:** Michigan 37-32. **Regulation:** Tied 71-71.

NATIONAL SEMIFINALS

ILLINOIS (81): Anderson 6-14 5-6 17, Battle 10-17 8-10 29, Hamilton 5-14 1-2 11, Gill 5-9 1-1 11, Bardo 1-7 4-4 7, Smith 3-5 0-0 6, Small 0-0 0-0 0, Liberty 0-1 0-0 0. Team 30-67 (.448) 19-23 (.826) 81.

MICHIGAN (83): Rice 12-24 2-2 28, Hughes 4-5 1-1 9, Mills 4-8 0-0 8, Griffin 0-1 0-0 0, Robinson 6-13 2-5 14, Calip 0-1 0-0 0, Higgins 5-12 3-3 14, Vaught 5-13 0-0 10. Team 36-77 (.468) 8-11 (.727) 83.

Three-point goals: Illinois 2-8 (.25), Michigan 3-8 (.375). **Halftime:** Michigan 39-38.

DUKE (78): Brickey 0-3 2-2 2, Ferry 13-29 7-11 34, Laettner 4-5 5-7 13, Henderson 4-16 5-6 13, Snyder 3-10 0-0 8, Koubek 0-3 0-0 0, Davis 1-2 0-2 2, Abdelnaby 0-0 0-0 0, Smith 1-4 3-4 6, Palmer 0-0 0-0 0, Burgin 0-0 0-0 0, Buckley 0-0 0-0 0. Team 26-72 (.361) 22-32 (.688) 78.

SETON HALL (95): Walker 6-9 7-7 19, Gaze 7-14 2-2 20, Ramos 3-8 3-3 9, Morton 4-8 5-6 13, Greene 5-9 6-6 17, Avent 3-4 0-0 6, Volcy 1-2 0-1 2, Cooper 3-4 0-0 6, Wigington 0-0 0-1 0, Monteserin 0-0 0-0 0, Katsikis 1-1 0-1 3, Crowley 0-1 0-0 0, Rebimias 0-1 0-0 0, Long 0-1 0-0 0. Team 33-62 (.532) 23-27 (.852) 95.

Three-point goals: Duke 4-16 (.250), Seton Hall 6-12 (.500). **Halftime:** Duke 38-33.

ALL-TOURNAMENT TEAM

Danny Ferry, F, Sr., Duke
Gerald Greene, G, Sr., Seton Hall
John Morton, G, Sr., Seton Hall
Glen Rice, F, Sr., Michigan*
Rumeal Robinson, G, Jr., Michigan
   *Named Most Outstanding Player

questioned when it doubled from the second time he took the test to the third. Manuel eventually transferred.

Syracuse's Sherman Douglas (22 assists against Providence) and Georgetown's Dikembe Mutombo (12 blocked shots against St. John's) set Big East Conference single-game records. . . . Connecticut lost 17 straight games to St. John's in their series until defeating the Redmen, 80-52. Rutgers lost 13 consecutive games to Temple in their series until defeating the Owls, 77-64. . . . Seton Hall and Stanford finished in the Top 20 of a final wire-service poll for the first time since 1953 and 1963, respectively. Todd Lichti was the first Stanford player

since 1942 to become an NCAA first- or second-team All-American. . . . The North Atlantic Tournament was dubbed the MIT (Measles Invitational Tourney) because all spectators were banned because of a measles outbreak.

Illinois (31-5, coached by Lou Henson), Ball State (29-3, Rick Majerus), Missouri (29-8, Norm Stewart), St. Louis (27-10, Rich Grawer), St. Mary's (25-5, Lynn Nance), Siena (25-5, Mike Deane), Evansville (25-6, Jim Crews) and Colorado State (23-10, Boyd Grant) had their winningest seasons in school Division I history. Seton Hall (31-7, P.J. Carlesimo) and Middle Tennessee State (23-8, Bruce Stewart) tied their school single-season records for most victories.

Evansville's Scott Haffner scored a national-high, school-record and Midwestern Collegiate Conference-record 65 points against Dayton. . . . Ball State sustained at least 10 defeats in 24 consecutive seasons until compiling a 29-3 record under coach Rick Majerus. The Cardinals, who compiled a 14-14 record the previous season, improved by 13 games en route to their lone appearance in the Top 20 of a final wire-service poll. . . . Illinois State posted winning records in its first 18 seasons in Division I until the Redbirds compiled a 13-17 mark in Bob Donewald's last year as their coach.

A bench-clearing brawl forced referees to eject most of Indiana State's team when the Sycamores lost, 84-69, to visiting Wichita State. ISU was forced to play the second half with only four players, ending the contest with just two on the floor after a couple of them fouled out. . . . Arkansas-Little Rock's Carl Brown had the most points ever in a Trans America Athletic Conference game with 46 against Centenary. . . . Houston Baptist competed in its final season at the Division I level.

The NIT semifinalists all won their third-round games on the road for the only time in the event's history–Alabama-Birmingham (at Connecticut), Michigan State (at Villanova), St. Louis (at New Mexico) and St. John's (at Ohio State). New Mexico sustained its fourth home-court defeat in the last four years in the NIT, fifth in six seasons and sixth since 1979.

Oregon State's Ralph Miller, who previously coached at Wichita State and Iowa, retired after a 38-year coaching career with a 657-382 record. C.M. Newton, who coached Transylvania, Alabama and Vanderbilt, ended his coaching career with a 509-375 record when he became athletic director at his alma mater (Kentucky). Norman Sloan, who previously coached Presbyterian, The Citadel and North Carolina State, was forced out at Florida, ending his 37-year coaching career with a 624-393 record. Texas A&M's Shelby Metcalf finished his career as the SWC's all-time winningest coach.

1988-89 FINAL NATIONAL POLLS

AP	UPI	USA/CNN	SCHOOL (RECORD)	HEAD COACH
1	1	7	Arizona (29-4)	Lute Olson
2	2	5	Georgetown (29-5)	John Thompson
3	3	3	Illinois (31-5)	Lou Henson
4	5	12	Oklahoma (30-6)	Billy Tubbs
5	4	8	North Carolina (29-8)	Dean Smith
6	8	11	Missouri (29-8)	Norm Stewart*
7	9	6	Syracuse (30-8)	Jim Boeheim
8	6	10	Indiana (27-8)	Bob Knight
9	7	4	Duke (28-8)	Mike Krzyzewski
10	10	1	Michigan (30-7)	Bill Frieder**
11	11	2	Seton Hall (31-7)	P.J. Carlesimo
12	13	13	Louisville (24-9)	Denny Crum
13	12	21	Stanford (26-7)	Mike Montgomery
14	15	16	Iowa (23-10)	Tom Davis
15	14	9	UNLV (29-8)	Jerry Tarkanian
16	16	22	Florida State (22-8)	Pat Kennedy
17	19	18	West Virginia (26-5)	Gale Catlett
18	–	19	Ball State (29-3)	Rick Majerus
19	18	14	N.C. State (22-9)	Jim Valvano
20	20	–	Alabama (23-8)	Wimp Sanderson
–	–	15	Virginia (22-11)	Terry Holland
–	17	20	Arkansas (25-7)	Nolan Richardson
–	–	17	Minnesota (19-12)	Clem Haskins
–	–	23	Texas-El Paso (26-7)	Don Haskins
–	–	24	South Alabama (23-9)	Ronnie Arrow
–	–	25	UCLA (21-10)	Jim Harrick

* Rich Daly coached Missouri the last 10 games of the season after Stewart became ill.

** Steve Fisher coached Michigan the last six games of the season after replacing Frieder.

1989 NCAA Tournament

Summary: Michigan, guided by interim coach Steve Fisher, became the NCAA titlist to win its two Final Four games by the fewest total of points (three). Sean Higgins' last-second rebound basket gave the Wolverines an 83-81 victory against Illinois in the national semifinals before Rumeal Robinson sank two free throws with three seconds remaining in overtime in an 80-79 triumph against Seton Hall in the final. In the first overtime final since 1963, Seton Hall guard John Morton had the highest scoring output (35 points with 17 in the last eight minutes of regulation to help the Pirates erase a 12-point deficit) of any player for the losing team in a championship game. Since the introduction of seeding in 1979, this was the only year the championship game did not include at least one No. 1 or No. 2 seed (Michigan and Seton Hall were both No. 3 seeds). The roster Fisher inherited at the start of the playoffs included four future NBA first-round draft choices–Terry Mills, Glen Rice, Robinson and Loy Vaught.

What was the pressure of a one-and-one opportunity for a 65.6 percent free-throw shooter after he had gone one-on-one with the street? Previously, the Jamaican-born Robinson had no place to live at all. He was a 12-year-old street urchin deserted by his mother after they moved to Cambridge, Mass., a Boston suburb.

"Somewhere along the line," Robinson said. "I think I was blessed. I feel no bitterness. I have not been cheated. I do not know why my mother did not want me. I do not know why my biological father died the day before I was to meet him. But I also do not know why I was so lucky to find my adoptive parents. It is not so much bad luck or good luck. It is ... only how it is ... how God wants it."

Outcome for Defending Champion: Kansas (19-12) finished in sixth place in the Big Eight. The Jayhawks suffered their most lopsided defeat ever at home in Allen Fieldhouse (91-66 to Missouri).

Star Gazing: Rice, the Final Four Most Outstanding Player, became the only player to score more than 25 points in two games at a single Final Four from 1975-94. Rice holds the records for most three-point baskets and points in a playoff series (27 treys and 184 points in six games). The senior forward hit 12 of 17 from three-point range on his way to a total of 66 points in Southeast Regional semifinal and final victories over North Carolina (92-87) and Virginia (102-65). Rice's liberal use of the three-pointer enabled him to become the only player from a national champion to average more than 25 points per game in a title season (25.6) since David Thompson finished with a 26-point average for North Carolina State in 1974.

Biggest Upsets: Middle Tennessee State (13th seed) over Florida State (4), 97-83, and Siena (14) over Stanford (3), 80-78. MTSU, sparked by freshman guard Mike Buck's six-for-six shooting from three-point range, overcame a 17-point deficit with 16 minutes remaining. Siena guard Marc Brown poured in 32 points, including a pair of decisive free throws with

three seconds remaining, to spoil Stanford's first playoff appearance since 1942.

One and Only: Illinois became the only school to defeat the NCAA champion-to-be twice in one season by at least 12 points when the Illini swept Michigan in Big Ten competition.

Numbers Game: Of the more than 60 different players to score at least 2,500 points and/or rank among the top 25 in career scoring average, Arizona's Sean Elliott finished his career as the only one to have a winning NCAA playoff record in his career plus post higher scoring, rebounding and field-goal shooting career playoff averages than he compiled in the regular season. . . . Xavier became the only school to have the misfortune of opposing eventual national champions in the first round in back-to-back years (Kansas '88 and Michigan '89). . . . The worst composite conference record in one year of the NCAA playoffs was posted by the SEC, which had all five of its entrants lose their first-round games, with four of them bowing by more than 10 points. Independent South Carolina, a recent addition to SEC, was also drubbed in its opening-round game, giving the six current SEC members a 13.7-point average margin of defeat. . . . North Carolina State's Rodney Monroe scored a tourney-high 40 points in a 102-96 victory over Iowa in the second round of the East Regional. . . . Notre Dame's LaPhonso Ellis grabbed a tourney-high 18 rebounds in an 81-65 triumph over Vanderbilt in the opening round of the East Regional.

What If: Forward Nick Anderson (55.3 percent) and center Lowell Hamilton (53.4 percent) rank among the top five Illinois players in career field-goal shooting. If only they combined for 46.4 percent field-goal shooting instead of 39.3 percent (11 of 28) in the national semifinals, the Illini could have defeated eventual champion Michigan rather than losing 83-81. The Wolverines also dodged a bullet against Seton Hall in their narrow title game victory as Pirates forward Andrew Gaze was restricted to one field goal after contributing at least six baskets in each of the previous four playoff games. . . . DePaul (21-12/without Rod Strickland), Kansas State (19-11/Norris Coleman), Memphis State (21-11/Sylvester Gray), North Carolina State (22-9/Charles Shackleford) and Pittsburgh (17-13/Jerome Lane) might have fared better in the playoffs if standout players had exercised their remaining eligibility instead of defecting to the NBA. . . . Miami, Fla. (19-12) could have appeared in the tourney for the first time since 1960 if Tito Horford didn't leave school early for the pros.

Putting Things in Perspective: Illinois (31-5) defeated Michigan twice by a total of 28 points before losing to the Wolverines by two points in the national semifinals. Indiana (27-8) defeated the Wolverines twice by a total of two points before losing against eventual national runner-up Seton Hall in the West Regional semifinals. Michigan suffered defeats in five of 10 Big Ten games in one span after losing on a neutral court to obscure Alaska-Anchorage, 70-66.

Scoring Leader: Glen Rice, Michigan (184 points, 30.7 ppg).

Rebounding Leader: Daryll Walker, Seton Hall (58 rebounds, 9.7 rpg).

Highest Rebounding Average: Stanley Brundy, DePaul (30 rebounds, 15 rpg).

WINNINGEST PROGRAMS OF THE 1980S

RK.	SCHOOL	W.	L.	PCT.
1.	North Carolina	281	63	.817
2.	UNLV	271	65	.807
3.	Georgetown	269	69	.796
4.	DePaul	235	67	.778
5.	Temple	225	78	.743
6.	Syracuse	243	87	.736
7.	Texas-El Paso	227	82	.735
8.	Oklahoma	245	90	.731
9.	Kentucky	233	86	.730
10.	St. John's	228	85	.728

1980–89 PREMO POWER POLL: BEST TEAMS BY DECADE

RANK	SEASON	SCHOOL
1	1983–84	Georgetown* (34-3)
2	1981–82	North Carolina* (32-2)
3	1984–85	Georgetown (35-3)
4	1982–83	Houston (31-3)
5	1985–86	Duke (37-3)
6	1979–80	Louisville* (33-3)
7	1983–84	North Carolina (28-3)
8	1986–87	Indiana* (30-4)
9	1984–85	St. John's (31-4)
10	1980–81	Oregon St. (26-2)
11	1987–88	Oklahoma (35-4)
12	1988–89	Arizona (29-4)
13	1986–87	UNLV (37-2)
14	1979–80	DePaul (26-2)
15	1981–82	Virginia (30-4)
16	1983–84	DePaul (27-3)
17	1987–88	Arizona (35-3)
18	1980–81	DePaul (27-2)
19	1985–86	Kansas (35-4)
20	1982–83	Louisville (32-4)
	1988–89	Georgetown (29-5)

*–NCAA Tournament Champion

1989 CHAMPIONSHIP BRACKET

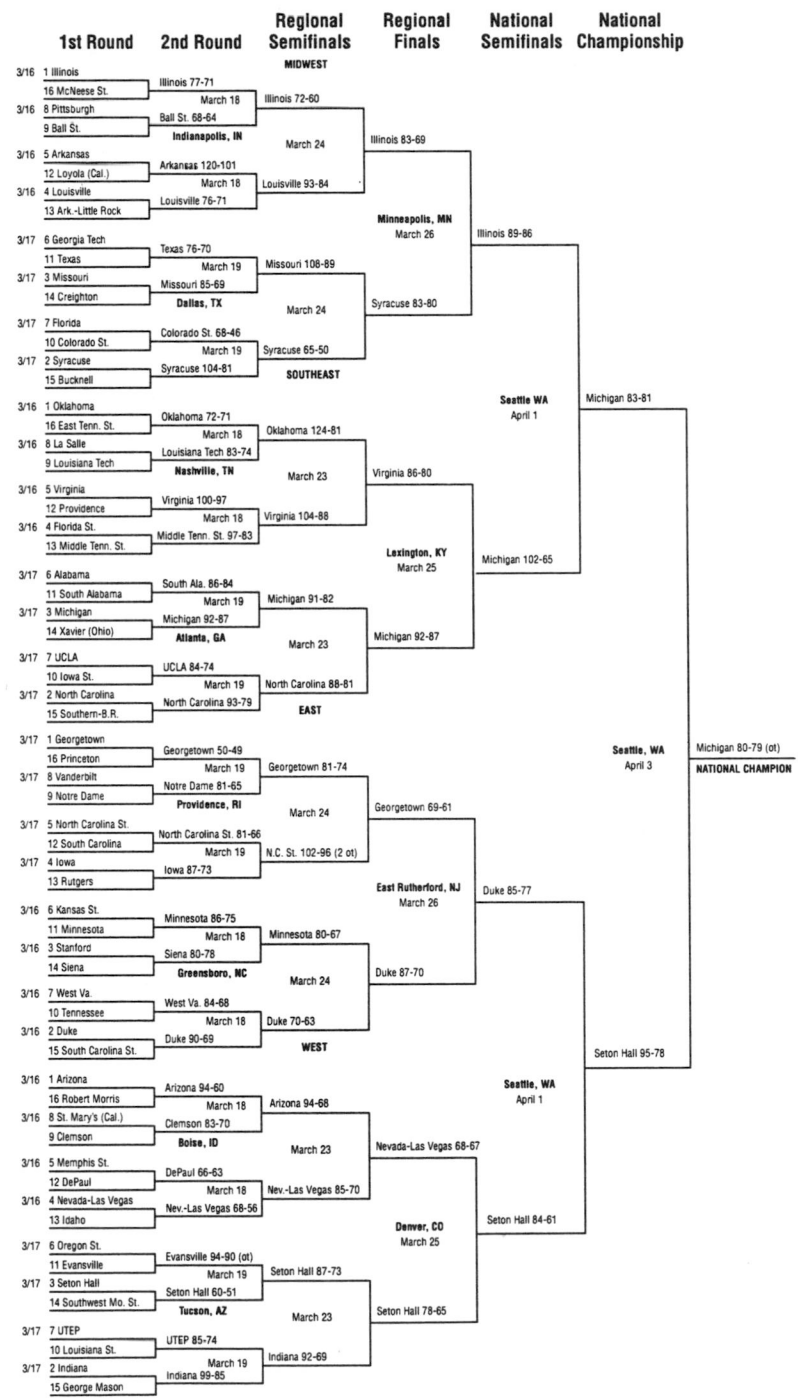

	1st Round	2nd Round	Regional Semifinals	Regional Finals	National Semifinals	National Championship

MIDWEST

- 3/16 1 Illinois
- 3/16 16 McNeese St. — Illinois 77-71 — March 18 — Illinois 72-60
- 3/16 8 Pittsburgh
- 3/16 9 Ball St. — Ball St. 68-64
- **Indianapolis, IN** — March 24 — Illinois 83-69
- 3/16 5 Arkansas
- 3/16 12 Loyola (Cal.) — Arkansas 120-101 — March 18
- 3/16 4 Louisville
- 3/16 13 Ark.-Little Rock — Louisville 76-71 — Louisville 93-84
- **Minneapolis, MN** — March 26 — Illinois 89-86
- 3/17 6 Georgia Tech
- 3/17 11 Texas — Texas 76-70 — March 19 — Missouri 108-89
- 3/17 3 Missouri
- 3/17 14 Creighton — Missouri 85-69
- **Dallas, TX** — March 24 — Syracuse 83-80
- 3/17 7 Florida
- 3/17 10 Colorado St. — Colorado St. 68-46 — March 19
- 3/17 2 Syracuse
- 3/17 15 Bucknell — Syracuse 104-81 — Syracuse 65-50

Seattle WA — April 1 — Michigan 83-81

SOUTHEAST

- 3/16 1 Oklahoma
- 3/16 16 East Tenn. St. — Oklahoma 72-71 — March 18 — Oklahoma 124-81
- 3/16 8 La Salle
- 3/16 9 Louisiana Tech — Louisiana Tech 83-74
- **Nashville, TN** — March 23 — Virginia 86-80
- 3/16 5 Virginia
- 3/16 12 Providence — Virginia 100-97 — March 18
- 3/16 4 Florida St.
- 3/16 13 Middle Tenn. St. — Middle Tenn. St. 97-83 — Virginia 104-88
- **Lexington, KY** — March 25 — Michigan 102-65
- 3/17 6 Alabama
- 3/17 11 South Alabama — South Ala. 86-84 — March 19 — Michigan 91-82
- 3/17 3 Michigan
- 3/17 14 Xavier (Ohio) — Michigan 92-87
- **Atlanta, GA** — March 23 — Michigan 92-87
- 3/17 7 UCLA
- 3/17 10 Iowa St. — UCLA 84-74 — March 19
- 3/17 2 North Carolina
- 3/17 15 Southern-B.R. — North Carolina 93-79 — North Carolina 88-81

Seattle, WA — April 3 — Michigan 80-79 (ot) **NATIONAL CHAMPION**

EAST

- 3/17 1 Georgetown
- 3/17 16 Princeton — Georgetown 50-49 — March 19 — Georgetown 81-74
- 3/17 8 Vanderbilt
- 3/17 9 Notre Dame — Notre Dame 81-65
- **Providence, RI** — March 24 — Georgetown 69-61
- 3/17 5 North Carolina St.
- 3/17 12 South Carolina — North Carolina St. 81-66 — March 19
- 3/17 4 Iowa
- 3/17 13 Rutgers — Iowa 87-73 — N.C. St. 102-96 (2 ot)
- **East Rutherford, NJ** — March 26 — Duke 85-77
- 3/16 6 Kansas St.
- 3/16 11 Minnesota — Minnesota 86-75 — March 18 — Minnesota 80-67
- 3/16 3 Stanford
- 3/16 14 Siena — Siena 80-78
- **Greensboro, NC** — March 24 — Duke 87-70
- 3/16 7 West Va.
- 3/16 10 Tennessee — West Va. 84-68 — March 18
- 3/16 2 Duke
- 3/16 15 South Carolina St. — Duke 90-69 — Duke 70-63

Seattle, WA — April 1 — Seton Hall 95-78

WEST

- 3/16 1 Arizona
- 3/16 16 Robert Morris — Arizona 94-60 — March 18 — Arizona 94-68
- 3/16 8 St. Mary's (Cal.)
- 3/16 9 Clemson — Clemson 83-70
- **Boise, ID** — March 23 — Nevada-Las Vegas 68-67
- 3/16 5 Memphis St.
- 3/16 12 DePaul — DePaul 66-63 — March 18
- 3/16 4 Nevada-Las Vegas
- 3/16 13 Idaho — Nev.-Las Vegas 68-56 — Nev.-Las Vegas 85-70
- **Denver, CO** — March 25 — Seton Hall 84-61
- 3/17 6 Oregon St.
- 3/17 11 Evansville — Evansville 94-90 (ot) — March 19 — Seton Hall 87-73
- 3/17 3 Seton Hall
- 3/17 14 Southwest Mo. St. — Seton Hall 60-51
- **Tucson, AZ** — March 23 — Seton Hall 78-65
- 3/17 7 UTEP
- 3/17 10 Louisiana St. — UTEP 85-74 — March 19
- 3/17 2 Indiana
- 3/17 15 George Mason — Indiana 99-85 — Indiana 92-69

7

THE SOUTH RISES AGAIN:
THE 1990s

T here won't be a special convention to change the name of the sport to "Y'all Ball," but the South has risen again! At least in college basketball. Five of the six NCAA Tournament champions from 1991 through 1996 came from two "Southern" conferences–the ACC and SEC.

The first half of the 1990s featured the national dominance of two ACC schools–Duke and North Carolina. Developing what many believe is the nation's foremost rivalry, Duke and Carolina or both were represented on the NCAA consensus All-American first- and second-team all but one year (1990) from 1976 through 1995. They combined for more NCAA Tournament victories than the total of over 20 Division I conferences since the playoff field expanded to 64 teams in 1985. Their playoff prowess enabled the ACC to win more than 70 percent of its tourney games.

The Southeastern Conference, however, compiled the best NCAA playoff record from 1994 through 1996. Many of the nation's premier leagues were gone by the middle of the decade–Big Eight (merged with four SWC mem-

bers to form Big 12), Great Midwest (majority of alliance wound up in newly formed Conference USA), Metro (members joined Atlantic 10, Colonial and C-USA) and Southwest (members joined Big 12, C-USA and WAC).

The impact of Proposition 48's academic requirements for freshman eligibility escalated, leading to more emphasis on junior college recruits. Debate over Proposition 48 among other legislative matters fostered an atmosphere whereby the Black Coaches Association (BCA) threatened boycotts for what it thought was discrimination.

1989-90

AT A GLANCE

NCAA Champion: UNLV (35-5; coached by Jerry Tarkanian; tied for first place with New Mexico State in Big West with a 16-2 record).

NIT Champion: Vanderbilt (21-14; coached by Eddie Fogler; tied for seventh place in SEC with a 7-11 record).

Hank Gathers, Loyola Marymount's rising star, collapsed during 1990 NCC Tournament play and tragically died soon after.

The most tragic moment in the history of any league tourney occurred in the semifinals of the West Coast Conference Tournament at Loyola Marymount when Hank Gathers, the league's all-time scoring leader and a two-time tourney MVP, collapsed on his home court during the Lions' game with Portland. He died later that evening of a heart ailment and the tournament was suspended. The Lions still earned an NCAA Tournament bid because of their regular-season crown and advanced to the West Regional final behind the heroics of Bo Kimble, who was Gathers' longtime friend from Philadelphia.

Loyola Marymount, leading the nation in point production for the third consecutive season under coach Paul Westhead, set an NCAA record for highest scoring average per game (122.4). The Lions scored at least 99 points in all but two of their 32 games. They also established a mark for largest-ever margin over the national runner-up (21.1 over Oklahoma). Gathers and Kimble became the only set of teammates to surpass the 2,250-point plateau. Kimble (35.3 ppg), Gathers (29) and Jeff Fryer (22.7) combined for 87 points per game to become the highest-scoring trio in a single season in Division I history. Kimble had four games with at least 50 points.

La Salle's only regular-season defeat was against Loyola Marymount, 121-116. The Explorers made their first Top 20 appearance in a final wire-service poll since 1969. La Salle's Lionel Simmons ended his career with an NCAA-record 115 consecutive games scoring in double figures.

Oregon State's Gary Payton (58 points vs. Southern Cal in OT), LMU's Kimble (54 at St. Joseph's), Nevada-Reno's Kevin Franklin (48 at Loyola Marymount), St. Louis' Anthony Bonner (45 in overtime at Loyola of Chicago) and Harvard's Ralph James (41 at Penn) set school single-game scoring records. Marquette guard Tony Smith tied a school mark with 44 points in an 82-65 loss at Wisconsin. . . . Kimble (35.3 ppg), Ohio's Dave Jamerson (31.2), Duquesne's Mark Stevenson (27.2), Towson State's Kurk Lee (26), Marquette's Smith (23.8) and San Diego's John Jerome (19.3) established school Division I records for highest scoring average in a single season.

Northwestern's Todd Leslie set an NCAA record for most consecutive successful three-point baskets with 15 in a span covering four games.

OU's Jamerson set an NCAA standard (later tied) for most three-point field goals in a game with 14 vs. Charleston (S.C.) en route to a 60-point outing that is a school and Mid-American Conference record.

Georgia Tech's perimeter marksmen Dennis Scott (27.7), Brian Oliver (21.3) and Kenny Anderson (20.6) were known in Hoopdom as Lethal Weapon 3 when they became the first ACC trio to all average more than 20 points per game in the same season. They were also the only threesome ever to achieve the feat for a Final Four team. Anderson, the sixth Tech player in eight years to be named ACC Rookie of the Year, had his best all-around game when he collected 32 points, 12 rebounds and 18 assists in a 93-92 triumph over Pittsburgh. The Yellow Jackets' six ACC defeats were by a total of 14 points. . . . Georgia, coached by Hugh Durham, captured its lone SEC regular-season title one year after finishing ninth in the 10-team league.

La Salle (30-2, coached by Speedy Morris), Xavier (28-5, Pete Gillen), Michigan State (28-6,

Guard Kenny Anderson—one-third of Georgia Tech's "Lethal Weapon 3"—launches a shot.

Jud Heathcote), Georgia Tech (28-7, Bobby Cremins), Southern Illinois (26-8, Rich Herrin), Penn State (25-9, Bruce Parkhill), Hawaii (25-10, Riley Wallace), Northern Iowa (23-9, Eldon Miller) and Kent (21-8, Jim McDonald) had their

North Carolina State coach Jim Valvano was one of college basketball's most colorful characters.

a tie for first place, made its first appearance in the top 20 of a final wire-service poll for the first time since 1965. . . . Michigan State, coached by Jud Heathcote, won the Big Ten title just one year after finishing in a tie for eighth place. . . . Oklahoma gave Northeastern Illinois a rude welcome to Division I basketball with a 95-point victory (146-51).

Kentucky had eight different players hit a three-point basket in a 104-73 victory over Furman on December 19, 1989. Four days later, Kentucky (53) and Southwestern Louisiana combined for an NCAA-record 84 three-point field-goal attempts. The Wildcats averaged an NCAA-record 28.9 three-point attempts per game during the season. . . . SEC cellar dweller Florida snapped a 14-game losing streak by leveling LSU, 76-63. Among O'Neal's teammates were Chris Jackson and Stanley Roberts.

Purdue's Steve Scheffler overcame dyslexia to finish with a Big Ten career record for field-goal shooting (minimum of 400 baskets). He hit 68.5 percent of his field-goal attempts (408 of 596). . . . Clemson, en route to capturing its only ACC regular-season title, closed out its first perfect month of February in 70 years (8-0) with a 97-93 victory over fifth-ranked Duke. The Tigers were coached by Cliff Ellis. . . . North Carolina didn't finish among the top 10 in a final AP poll for the first time in 10 years.

Seton Hall guard Marko Lokar, a native of Italy making his first college start, scored a Big East Conference-freshman record 41 points against Pittsburgh. In his total of 33 other games with the Pirates this season and a portion of next year, Lokar scored 99 points with only two double-digit outings (15 and 12). Lokar, a pacifist, was opposed to war of any kind and left school because of the reaction he received following his refusal to wear an American flag on his uniform along with the remainder of his teammates during the Gulf War.

Texas-El Paso's school-record 31-game homecourt winning streak ended when the Miners lost to Indiana, 69-66. UTEP coach Don

winningest seasons in school Division I history. Tennessee Tech (19-9, Frank Harrell) tied a school single-season mark for most victories.

Connecticut, improving from a tie for seventh place in the Big East the previous season to

1989-90 INDIVIDUAL LEADERS

SCORING

PLAYER	PTS.	AVG.
Kimble, L. Marymount	1131	35.3
Bradshaw, U.S. Intl.	875	31.3
Jamerson, Ohio U.	874	31.2
Ford, Miss. Valley St.	808	29.9
Rogers, Alabama St.	831	29.7
Gathers, L. Marymount	754	29.0
Brooks, Tenn. St.	690	28.8
Jackson, LSU	889	27.8
Scott, Ga. Tech	970	27.7
Stevenson, Duquesne	788	27.2

REBOUNDING

PLAYER	REB.	AVG.
Bonner, St. Louis	456	13.8
McArthur, UC Santa Barb.	377	13.0
Hill, Xavier	402	12.6
Campbell, SW Mo. St.	363	12.5
Ceballos, Cal St. Full.	362	12.5
Shahid, S. Florida	383	12.4
Draper, American	354	12.2
Coleman, Syracuse	398	12.1
O'Neal, LSU	385	12.0
Weatherspoon, S. Miss.	371	11.6

ASSISTS

PLAYER	AST.	AVG.
Lehmann, Drexel	260	9.3
Mitchell, SW La.	264	9.1
Jennings, East Tenn. St.	297	8.7
Livingston, Idaho	262	8.5
Anderson, Ga. Tech	285	8.1
Payton, Oregon St.	235	8.1
Edmond, TCU	234	8.1
Corchiani, N.C. St.	238	7.9
Porter, Pittsburgh	229	7.9
Holt, Prairie View	213	7.9

BLOCKED SHOTS

PLAYER	BLK.	AVG.
Green, Rhode I.	124	4.8
Mutombo, Georgetown	128	4.1
Roberson, Vermont	114	3.8
Williams, Stetson	121	3.8
Roland, Marshall	101	3.6
O'Neal, LSU	115	3.6
Stevenson, Prairie View	97	3.6
Harris, Texas A&M	108	3.5
Longley, New Mexico	117	3.4
Palmer, Dartmouth	85	3.4

STEALS

PLAYER	STL.	AVG.
McMahon, E. Wash.	130	4.5
Dowdell, Coastal Caro.	109	3.8
Henefeld, Conn.	138	3.7
Robinson, Centenary	104	3.5
Payton, Oregon St.	100	3.4
Tanner, Rice	95	3.4
Corchiani, N.C. St.	95	3.2
Rogers, Alabama St.	86	3.1
Giles, Florida A&M	89	3.1
Brown, J'ville	88	3.0

FIELD GOAL PERCENTAGE

PLAYER	FGM	FGA	PCT.
Campbell, SW Mo. St.	192	275	.698
Scheffler, Purdue	173	248	.698
Spencer, Louisville	188	276	.681
Parker, Cleve. St.	155	236	.657
Hill, Evansville	180	278	.647
Stewart, Coppin St.	233	361	.645
Shahid, S. Florida	201	314	.640
French, Hardin-Simm.	212	338	.627
Keefe, Stanford	210	335	.627
Davis, Clemson	205	328	.625

FREE THROW PERCENTAGE

PLAYER	FTM	FTA	PCT.
Robbins, New Mexico	101	108	.935
Joseph, Bucknell	144	155	.929
Jackson, LSU	191	210	.910
Kennedy, UAB	111	123	.902
Henson, Kansas St.	101	112	.902
Matthews, Pittsburgh	141	158	.892
Shreffler, Evansville	84	95	.884
Recasner, Washington	99	112	.884
Venable, Bowling Green	114	129	.884
Franklin, Nevada-Reno	68	77	.883

THREE-POINT FIELD GOAL PERCENTAGE

PLAYER	FGM	FGA	PCT.
Lapin, Princeton	71	133	.534
Iuzzolino, St. Francis (Pa.)	79	153	.516
Oberbrunner, Wisc.-GB	47	93	.505
Mayberry, Arkansas	65	129	.504
Pernell, Holy Cross	81	161	.503

THREE-POINT FIELD GOALS MADE PER GAME

PLAYER	FGM	AVG.
Jamerson, Ohio U.	131	4.7
Grider, SW La.	131	4.5
Alberts, Akron	122	4.4
Fryer, L. Marymount	121	4.3
Brooks, Tenn. St.	95	4.0

1989-90 TEAM LEADERS

SCORING OFFENSE

SCHOOL	PTS.	AVG.
Loyola Marymount	3918	122.4
Oklahoma	3243	101.3
Southern (La.)	3078	99.3
U.S. International	2738	97.8
Centenary	2877	95.9

SCORING DEFENSE

SCHOOL	PTS.	AVG.
Princeton	1378	51.0
Ball St.	1935	58.6
Colorado St.	1778	59.3
Wisc.-Green Bay	1913	59.8
Northern Illinois	1710	61.1

SCORING MARGIN

SCHOOL	OFF.	DEF.	MAR.
Oklahoma	101.3	80.4	21.0
Kansas	92.1	72.3	19.7
Georgetown	81.5	64.8	16.7
Arkansas	95.6	79.8	15.8
Southern (La.)	99.3	84.1	15.2

WON-LOST PERCENTAGE

SCHOOL	W-L	PCT.
La Salle	30-2	.938
UNLV	35-5	.875
Arkansas	30-5	.857
Kansas	30-5	.857
Xavier	28-5	.848

FIELD GOAL PERCENTAGE

SCHOOL	FGM	FGA	PCT.
Kansas	1204	2258	.533
Louisville	1097	2078	.528
Princeton	592	1133	.523
Purdue	778	1491	.522
Loyola Marymount	1456	2808	.519

DEFENSIVE FIELD GOAL PERCENTAGE

SCHOOL	FGM	FGA	PCT.
Georgetown	713	1929	.370
Arizona	780	1990	.392
Ball St.	715	1789	.400
Alabama	784	1952	.402
South Carolina	660	1630	.405

FREE THROW PERCENTAGE

SCHOOL	FTM	FTA	PCT.
Lafayette	461	588	.784
Vanderbilt	742	956	.776
Wisc.-Green Bay	411	532	.773
Murray St.	540	703	.768
Bucknell	502	657	.764

REBOUND MARGIN

SCHOOL	OWN	OPP.	MAR.
Georgetown	44.8	34.0	10.8
Xavier	40.4	30.0	10.4
Ball St.	39.5	30.9	8.6
Michigan St.	38.1	29.8	8.4
Notre Dame	37.9	29.6	8.2

THREE-POINT FIELD GOAL PERCENTAGE

SCHOOL	FGM	FGA	PCT.
Princeton	208	460	45.2
Brigham Young	140	311	45.0
Western Michigan	177	394	44.9
Holy Cross	181	404	44.8
Northwestern	116	260	44.6

THREE-POINT FIELD GOALS MADE

SCHOOL	FGM	AVG.
Kentucky	281	10.0
Loyola Marymount	298	9.3
Southwestern La.	251	8.7
East Tenn. St.	285	8.4
Dayton	261	8.2

UNLV's Anderson Hunt.

Georgia Tech's Brian Oliver reaches for the hoop.

Haskins missed much of the season when doctors order him to abandon his coaching duties because of an acute case of laryngitis. . . . New Mexico's Rob Robbins set a Western Athletic Conference record by converting 52 consecutive free-throw attempts. . . . Pacific lost 19 consecutive games to UC Irvine in their series before upending the Anteaters, 70-58. . . . UC Santa Barbara's Eric McArthur set a school single-game record with 28 rebounds against New Mexico State.

Massachusetts (17-14, coached by John Calipari) posted its first winning record in 12 years. . . . Hardin-Simmons (Tex.) competed in its final season at the Division I level. . . . Tennessee's Wade Houston became the first African-American head coach in the SEC. . . . National personality Jim Valvano was forced out as coach at N.C. State. The Wolfpack had entered the season on a sour note after the publication of "Personal Fouls," a book alleging a wide range of wrongdoing at the school. Valvano became an ESPN/ABC commentator who died three years later after a courageous fight against cancer.

1989-90 FINAL NATIONAL POLLS

AP	UPI	USA/CNN	SCHOOL (RECORD)	HEAD COACH
1	1	11	Oklahoma (27-5)	Billy Tubbs
2	2	1	UNLV (35-5)	Jerry Tarkanian
3	3	5	Connecticut (31-6)	Jim Calhoun
4	4	7	Michigan State (28-6)	Jud Heathcote
5	5	14	Kansas (30-5)	Roy Williams
6	6	10	Syracuse (26-7)	Jim Boeheim
7	8	4	Arkansas (30-5)	Nolan Richardson
8	9	15	Georgetown (24-7)	John Thompson
9	7	3	Georgia Tech (28-7)	Bobby Cremins
10	10	6	Purdue (22-8)	Gene Keady
11	11	20	Missouri (26-6)	Norm Stewart
12	13	19	La Salle (30-2)	Speedy Morris
13	15	18	Michigan (23-8)	Steve Fisher
14	12	21	Arizona (25-7)	Lute Olson
15	14	2	Duke (29-9)	Mike Krzyzewski
16	16	24	Louisville (27-8)	Denny Crum
17	17	13	Clemson (26-9)	Cliff Ellis
18	18	–	Illinois (21-8)	Lou Henson
19	–	–	Louisiana State (23-9)	Dale Brown
20	–	8	Minnesota (23-9)	Clem Haskins
21	–	9	Loyola Marymount (26-6)	Paul Westhead
22	–	–	Oregon State (22-7)	Jim Anderson
23	19	16	Alabama (26-9)	Wimp Sanderson
24	20	–	New Mexico State (26-5)	Neil McCarthy
25	–	17	Xavier (28-5)	Pete Gillen
–	–	12	Texas (24-9)	Tom Penders
–	–	22	Ball State (26-7)	Dick Hunsaker
–	–	23	UCLA (22-11)	Jim Harrick
–	–	25	North Carolina (21-13)	Dean Smith

20 WINNINGEST PROGRAMS OF 1990-96

RK.	SCHOOL	W.	L.	PCT.
1.	Kansas	194	44	.815
2.	Kentucky	184	45	.803
3.	Arkansas	195	49	.799
4.	Arizona	179	46	.796
5.	Massachusetts	183	53	.775
6.	Connecticut	175	53	.768
7.	UCLA	170	53	.762
8.	North Carolina	184	58	.760
9.	Wis.-Green Bay	160	53	.751
10.	Syracuse	166	58	.741
11.	Duke	178	63	.739
12.	Indiana	164	60	.732
13.	New Mexico State	159	60	.726
14.	Cincinnati	164	62	.726
15.	Princeton	137	52	.725
16.	Utah	162	63	.720
17.	UNLV	153	61	.715
18.	Purdue	155	63	.711
19.	Montana	145	60	.707
20.	New Mexico	169	72	.701

1990 NCAA Tournament

Summary: UNLV's 103-73 rout of Duke when the Rebels became the only team to score more than 100 points in a championship game established a record for widest margin of victory in a final. UNLV forced Duke's starting backcourt, Bobby Hurley and Phil Henderson, into a total of 11 turnovers. Larry Johnson, 6-7, finished with the highest rebounding average for a player on an NCAA titlist (11.4 rpg) since North Carolina State's Tom Burleson (12.2 in 1973-74).

Outcome for Defending Champion: Michigan (23-8) finished third in the Big Ten after dropping three of four conference contests late in the season.

Star Gazing: UNLV guard Anderson Hunt is the only Final Four Most Outstanding Players since 1954 to never play in the NBA.

Biggest Upset: Northern Iowa (14th seed) defeated Missouri (3), 74-71.

One and Only: Georgia Tech guard Kenny Anderson became the only freshman on a Final Four team to score more than 20 points in as many as four tournament games.

Numbers Game: Georgia Tech is the only Final Four team to have three players each average more than 20 points per game in the same season. The trio, known as Lethal Weapon 3, included Dennis Scott (27.7), Brian Oliver (21.3) and Anderson (20.6). . . . Each Final Four participant received more than $1.47 million, a whopping increase of about 2,870 percent in just 20 years. Trying to minimize emphasis on the intrinsic dollar value of "six-figure shots" taken by players, the NCAA implemented a new revenue-sharing formula beginning with the next season. . . . The record for most three-point field goals in a playoff game was set by Loyola Marymount senior guard Jeff Fryer with 11 (149-115 victory over defending NCAA champion Michigan in the second round of the West Regional). Fryer (41) and Bo Kimble (37) became the only set of teammates to score more than 35 points in the same tourney game when they combined for 78 vs. Michigan in the highest-scoring game in NCAA playoff history. Kimble had poured in a tourney-high 45 points in a 111-92 triumph over New Mexico State in the opening round. The Lions set an NCAA record for highest scoring average in a playoff series (105.8 in four games). . . . Michigan's Loy Vaught grabbed a

1989–90 NCAA CHAMPION: UNLV

SEASON STATISTICS OF UNLV REGULARS

PLAYER	POS.	CL.	G.	FG%	FT%	PPG	RPG
Larry Johnson	F	Jr.	40	.624	.767	20.6	11.4
Anderson Hunt	G	So.	39	.481	.663	15.9	2.2
David Butler	C	Sr.	33	.487	.728	15.8	7.4
Stacey Augmon	F	Jr.	39	.553	.671	14.2	6.9
Greg Anthony	G	Jr.	39	.457	.682	11.2	3.0
Moses Scurry	F-C	Sr.	30	.520	.560	7.7	4.1
Travis Bice	G	So.	33	.480	.818	4.3	0.6
Barry Young	F	Jr.	39	.380	.680	4.2	2.0
James Jones	F	Sr.	31	.527	.550	3.9	2.8
Stacey Cvjanovich	G	Sr.	33	.362	.900	2.6	1.1
TEAM TOTALS			40	.508	.699	93.5	41.7

Three-point field goals leaders: Hunt (99 of 258, .384), Anthony (45 of 120 .375), Bice (36 of 75, .480), Young (31 of 96, .323). **Assists leaders:** Anthony 289, Hunt 158, Augmon 143. **Blocked shots leaders:** Johnson 56, Augmon 49. **Steals leaders:** Anthony 106, Augmon 69, Johnson 65.

1990 FINAL FOUR CHAMPIONSHIP GAME

DENVER, CO

UNLV (103)	MIN.	FG-A	FT-A	REB.	A	PF	PTS.
Johnson	30	8-12	4-4	2	2	3	22
Augmon	26	6-7	0-1	2	7	5	12
Butler	27	1-4	2-2	0	3	3	4
Hunt	31	12-16	1-2	0	2	0	29
Anthony	30	5-11	3-4	1	6	3	13
Cvjanovich	10	1-2	2-2	1	2	2	5
Bice	9	0-1	0-C	0	0	0	2
Rice	2	0-2	0-0	0	0	0	0
Young	12	2-2	0-0	0	0	1	5
Jones	8	4-5	0-0	0	0	2	8
Scurry	12	2-5	1-2	3	0	2	5
Jeter	3	0-0	0-0	0	0	0	0
Team				2			
TOTALS	200	41-67	13-17	11	24	23	103

FG%: .612. **FT%:** .765. **Three-point goals:** 8-14 (Hunt 4-7, Johnson 2-2, Cvjanovich 1-1, Young 1-1, Rice 0-1, Bice 0-1, Anthony 0-1). **Blocks:** 3. **Turnovers:** 17. **Steals:** 16 (Anthony 5).

DUKE (73)	MIN.	FG-A	FT-A	REB.	A	PF	PTS.
Brickey	24	2-4	0-2	1	2	2	4
Laettner	29	5-12	5-6	5	5	4	15
Abdelnaby	24	5-7	4-6	4	0	3	14
Henderson	32	9-20	2-2	1	0	2	21

Hurley	32	0-3	2-2	0	3	3	2
Hill	8	0-2	0-0	1	1	0	0
Davis	21	2-5	2-3	1	0	1	6
McCaffrey	9	1-3	2-2	0	0	1	4
Koubek	14	1-4	0-0	2	0	0	2
Palmer	2	0-0	3-4	0	0	0	3
Buckley	3	0-0	0-0	0	0	0	0
Cook	2	1-1	0-0	0	0	0	2
Team				6			
TOTALS	200	26-61	20-27	21	11	16	73

FG%: .426. **FT%:** .741. **Three-point goals:** 1-11 (Henderson 1-8, Hurley 0-2, Koubek 0-1). **Blocks:** 3. **Turnovers:** 23 (Henderson 6, Hurley 5). **Steals:** 5. **Halftime:** UNLV 47-35.

NATIONAL SEMIFINALS

GEORGIA TECH (81): Scott 8-17 6-9 29, Mackey 2-3 0-0 4, McNeil 2-4 0-1 4, Anderson 7-14 1-2 16, Oliver 9-18 6-9 24, Brown 2-3 0-0 4, Barnes 0-0 0-0 0. Team 30-59 (.508) 13-21 (.619) 81.

UNLV (90): Johnson 5-11 4-4 15, Augmon 9-16 3-3 22, Butler 6-10 1-3 13, Hunt 7-15 1-2 20, Anthony 4-9 3-7 14, Cvjanovich 0-0 0-0 0, Young 0-0 0-0 0, Jones 0-0 0-0 0, Scurry 3-4 0-0 6. Team 34-65 (.523) 12-19 (.632) 90.

Three-point goals: Georgia Tech 8-21 (.381), UNLV 10-15 (.667). **Halftime:** Georgia Tech 53-46.

DUKE (97): Brickey 8-10 1-3 17, Laettner 5-7 9-12 19, Abdelnaby 8-12 4-5 20, Henderson 10-21 5-5 28, Hurley 0-2 3-6 3, Hill 0-0 0-0 0, Davis 1-4 3-4 5, McCaffrey 0-1 3-4 3, Koubek 1-4 0-0 2, Buckley 0-0 0-0 0, Cook 0-0 0-0 0. Team 33-61 (.541) 28-39 (.718) 97.

ARKANSAS (83): Whitby 0-2 0-0 0, Linn 0-1 0-0 0, Marks 0-0 0-0 0, Day 8-17 7-7 27, Howell 5-9 7-8 18, Credit 2-3 1-4 5, Mayberry 6-18 0-0 12, Bowers 1-6 0-0 2, Murry 2-5 0-0 5, Hawkins 2-4 2-2 6, Miller 1-3 1-2 3, Huery 2-5 1-3 5. Team 29-73 (.397) 19-26 (.731) 83.

Three-point goals: Duke 3-9 (.333), Arkansas 6-21 (.286). **Halftime:** Duke 46-43.

ALL-TOURNAMENT TEAM

Stacey Augmon, F, Jr., UNLV
Phil Henderson, G, Sr., Duke
Anderson Hunt, G, Soph., UNLV*
Larry Johnson, F, Jr., UNLV
Dennis Scott, F, Jr., Georgia Tech
    *Named Most Outstanding Player

tourney-high 21 rebounds in a 76-70 victory over Illinois State in the first round of the West Regional. . . . Louisville's LaBradford Smith finished his playoff career with 95.7 percent accuracy from the free-throw line (45 of 47 in eight games).

What If: Anderson averaged 27 points per game in his first four tournament contests as a freshman for Georgia Tech. If only he reached that figure in his fifth game instead of scoring 16 points in the national semifinals, the Yellow Jackets could have defeated eventual champion UNLV rather than blowing a seven-point half-time lead and losing 90-81. . . . Illinois (21-8, without Nick Anderson), Indiana (18-11, Jay Edwards) and North Carolina (21-13, J.R. Reid) might have fared better in the playoffs if standout players had exercised their remaining eligibility instead of defecting to the NBA. . . . Memphis State (18-12) probably would have participated in the NCAA Tournament instead of the NIT if Sylvester Gray didn't leave school early for the NBA two years earlier after his sophomore season.

Scoring Leader: Dennis Scott, Georgia Tech (153 points, 30.6 ppg).

1990 CHAMPIONSHIP BRACKET

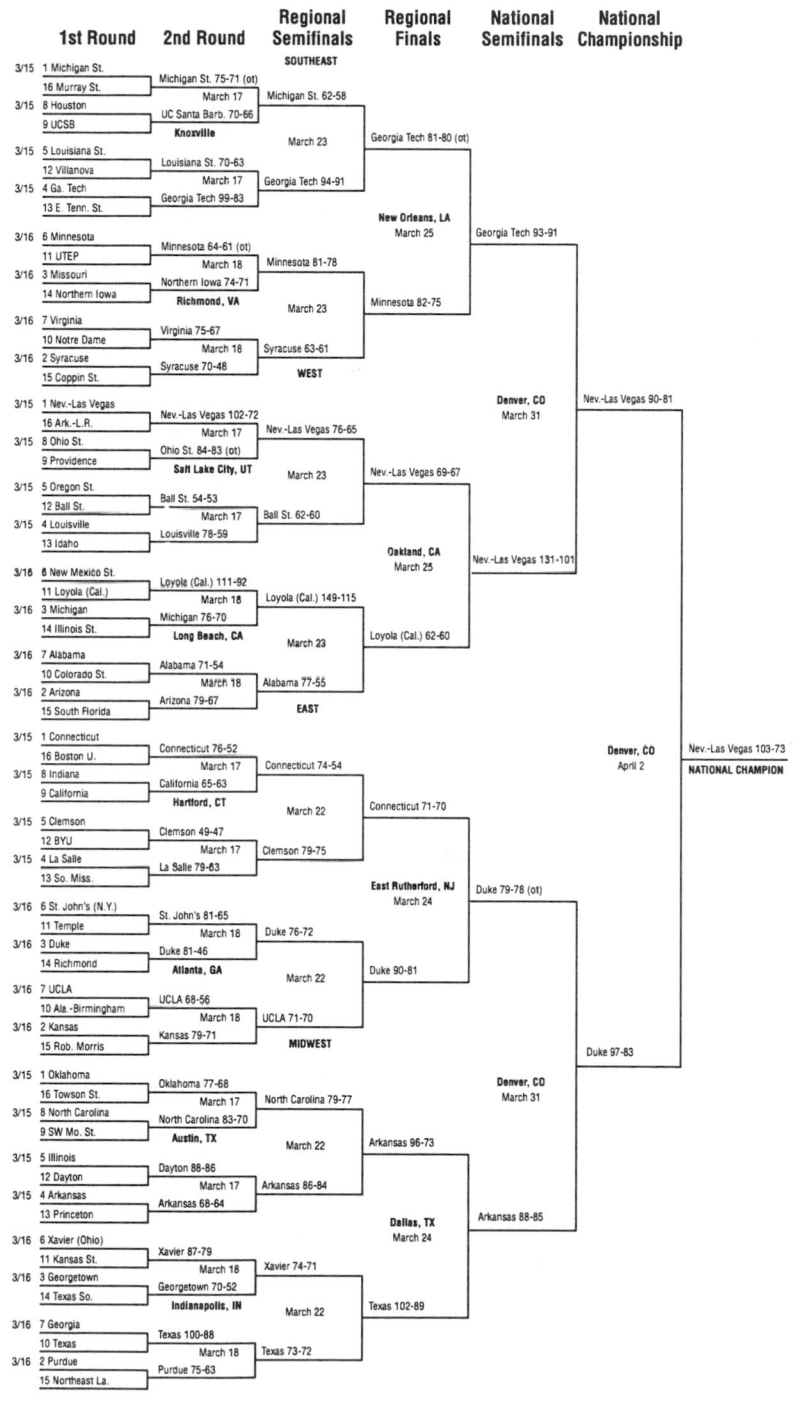

1st Round	2nd Round	Regional Semifinals	Regional Finals	National Semifinals	National Championship

SOUTHEAST

3/15 1 Michigan St.
16 Murray St.
Michigan St. 75-71 (ot)
March 17 — Michigan St. 62-58
3/15 8 Houston
9 UCSB
UC Santa Barb. 70-66
Knoxville
March 23 — Georgia Tech 81-80 (ot)
3/15 5 Louisiana St.
12 Villanova
Louisiana St. 70-63
March 17 — Georgia Tech 94-91
3/15 4 Ga. Tech
13 E. Tenn. St.
Georgia Tech 99-83

New Orleans, LA
March 25 — Georgia Tech 93-91

3/16 6 Minnesota
11 UTEP
Minnesota 64-61 (ot)
March 18 — Minnesota 81-78
3/16 3 Missouri
14 Northern Iowa
Northern Iowa 74-71
Richmond, VA
March 23 — Minnesota 82-75
3/16 7 Virginia
10 Notre Dame
Virginia 75-67
March 18 — Syracuse 63-61
3/16 2 Syracuse
15 Coppin St.
Syracuse 70-48

WEST

3/15 1 Nev.-Las Vegas
16 Ark.-L.R.
Nev.-Las Vegas 102-72
March 17 — Nev.-Las Vegas 76-65
3/15 8 Ohio St.
9 Providence
Ohio St. 84-83 (ot)
Salt Lake City, UT
March 23 — Nev.-Las Vegas 69-67
3/15 5 Oregon St.
12 Ball St.
Ball St. 54-53
March 17 — Ball St. 62-60
3/15 4 Louisville
13 Idaho
Louisville 78-59

Oakland, CA
March 25 — Nev.-Las Vegas 131-101

3/16 6 New Mexico St.
11 Loyola (Cal.)
Loyola (Cal.) 111-92
March 18 — Loyola (Cal.) 149-115
3/16 3 Michigan
14 Illinois St.
Michigan 76-70
Long Beach, CA
March 23 — Loyola (Cal.) 62-60
3/16 7 Alabama
10 Colorado St.
Alabama 71-54
March 18 — Alabama 77-55
3/16 2 Arizona
15 South Florida
Arizona 79-67

Georgia Tech 93-91

Nev.-Las Vegas 90-81

Denver, CO
March 31

EAST

3/15 1 Connecticut
16 Boston U.
Connecticut 76-52
March 17 — Connecticut 74-54
3/15 8 Indiana
9 California
California 65-63
Hartford, CT
March 22 — Connecticut 71-70
3/15 5 Clemson
12 BYU
Clemson 49-47
March 17 — Clemson 79-75
3/15 4 La Salle
13 So. Miss.
La Salle 79-63

East Rutherford, NJ
March 24 — Duke 79-78 (ot)

3/16 6 St. John's (N.Y.)
11 Temple
St. John's 81-65
March 18 — Duke 76-72
3/16 3 Duke
14 Richmond
Duke 81-46
Atlanta, GA
March 22 — Duke 90-81
3/16 7 UCLA
10 Ala.-Birmingham
UCLA 68-56
March 18 — UCLA 71-70
3/16 2 Kansas
15 Rob. Morris
Kansas 79-71

MIDWEST

3/15 1 Oklahoma
16 Towson St.
Oklahoma 77-68
March 17 — North Carolina 79-77
3/15 8 North Carolina
9 SW Mo. St.
North Carolina 83-70
Austin, TX
March 22 — Arkansas 96-73
3/15 5 Illinois
12 Dayton
Dayton 88-86
March 17 — Arkansas 86-84
3/15 4 Arkansas
13 Princeton
Arkansas 68-64

Dallas, TX
March 24 — Arkansas 88-85

3/16 6 Xavier (Ohio)
11 Kansas St.
Xavier 87-79
March 18 — Xavier 74-71
3/16 3 Georgetown
14 Texas So.
Georgetown 70-52
Indianapolis, IN
March 22 — Texas 102-89
3/16 7 Georgia
10 Texas
Texas 100-88
March 18 — Texas 73-72
3/16 2 Purdue
15 Northeast La.
Purdue 75-63

Nev.-Las Vegas 131-101

Duke 97-83

Denver, CO
March 31

Nev.-Las Vegas 90-81

Duke 97-83

Denver, CO
April 2

Nev.-Las Vegas 103-73
NATIONAL CHAMPION

Highest Scoring Average: Bo Kimble, Loyola Marymount (143 points, 35.75 ppg).

Rebounding Leader: Larry Johnson, UNLV (75 rebounds, 12.5 rpg).

Highest Rebounding Average: Loy Vaught, Michigan (38 rebounds, 19 rpg).

1990-91

AT A GLANCE

NCAA Champion: Duke (32-7; coached by Mike Krzyzewski; won ACC regular-season title by one game over North Carolina with an 11-3 record).

NIT Champion: Stanford (20-13; coached by Mike Montgomery; finished in a five-way tie for fifth place in Pacific-10 with an 8-10 record).

New Conference: Patriot League.

New Rules: Beginning with a team's 10th personal foul in a half, two free throws are awarded for each common foul, except player-control fouls. . . . Three free throws are awarded when a shooter is fouled during an unsuccessful three-point attempt. . . . The definition of "home court" in the NCAA Tournament is amended to include playing no more than three games of a regular-season schedule, excluding league tournaments, in one arena. . . . A preliminary round is used for six of 33 eligible conferences to identify the 30 automatic-qualifying leagues. The conferences with the lowest rankings in the Ratings Percentage Index (RPI) must compete for the available automatic-qualifying positions.

NCAA Probation: Illinois, Kentucky, Marshall, Maryland, Missouri, Northwestern (La.) State, Robert Morris, Southeastern Louisiana.

NCAA Consensus First-Team All-Americans: Kenny Anderson, G, Soph., Georgia Tech; Jim Jackson, G-F, Soph., Ohio State; Larry Johnson, F, Sr., UNLV; Shaquille O'Neal, C, Soph., Louisiana State; Billy Owens, F, Jr., Syracuse.

National Players of the Year: Johnson (22.7 ppg, 10.9 rpg, 66.2 FG%, 81.8 FT%/NABC, USBWA, Naismith, Wooden) and O'Neal (27.6 ppg, 14.7 rpg, 5 bpg, 62.8 FG%/AP, UPI).

National Coaches of the Year: Ohio State's Randy Ayers (27-4/AP, Naismith, USBWA); Duke's Mike Krzyzewski (32-7/NABC), and Utah's Rick Majerus (30-4/UPI).

UNLV's Larry Johnson in motion.

Defending champion UNLV, the first team to enter the NCAA Tournament undefeated since Indiana State in 1979, was upset by Duke in the national semifinals. Still, the Rebels will go down as one of the greatest teams in history if only because they're the only squad to have at least four teammates score a minimum of 1,500 points: Stacey Augmon (2,011), Greg Anthony (1,738), Anderson Hunt (1,632) and Larry Johnson (1,617).

U.S. International's Kevin Bradshaw, a Navy veteran who started his college career at Bethune-Cookman, set a single-game record for most points against a major college opponent with 72 vs. Loyola Marymount. Loyola Marymount, a 186-140 winner in the game, established an NCAA record for most points by a team. Bradshaw, who had three other games with at least 53 points, finished his career as the

1990–91 INDIVIDUAL LEADERS

SCORING

PLAYER	PTS.	AVG.
Bradshaw, U.S. International	1054	37.6
Ford, Miss. Valley St.	915	32.7
McDade, Wisc.-Milw.	830	29.6
Rogers, Alabama St.	852	29.4
Lowery, L. Marymount	884	28.5
Phills, Southern (La.)	795	28.4
O'Neal, LSU	774	27.6
Taft, Marshall	764	27.3
Monroe, N.C. St.	836	27.0
Brandon, Oregon	745	26.6

REBOUNDING

PLAYER	REB.	AVG.
O'Neal, LSU	411	14.7
Jones, Murray St.	469	14.2
Stewart, Coppin St.	403	13.4
Burroughs, J'ville	350	13.0
Kidd, Middle Tenn. St.	370	12.3
Weatherspoon, S'ern Miss.	355	12.2
Johnson, New Orleans	367	12.2
Davis, Delaware St.	366	12.2
Mutombo, Georgetown	389	12.2
Davis, Clemson	340	12.1

ASSISTS

PLAYER	AST.	AVG.
Corchiani, N.C. St.	299	9.6
Tirado, J'ville	259	9.3
Lowery, L. Marymount	283	9.1
Jennings, East Tenn. St.	301	9.1
Anthony, UNLV	310	8.9
Usher, Tenn. Tech	233	8.3
Smart, San Francisco	237	8.2
Johnson, Sam Houston St.	193	8.0

Cody, Texas-Arl.	229	7.9
Bernard, SW Mo. St.	257	7.6

BLOCKED SHOTS

PLAYER	BLK.	AVG.
Bradley, BYU	177	5.2
Lewis, Maryland	143	5.1
O'Neal, LSU	140	5.0
Mutombo, Georgetown	151	4.7
Roberson, Vermont	104	3.7
Williams, Stetson	113	3.6
Earl, Iowa	106	3.3
McIlvaine, Marquette	92	3.3
Longley, New Mexico	95	3.2
Lopez, Fordham	100	3.0

STEALS

PLAYER	STL.	AVG.
Usher, Tenn. Tech	104	3.7
Burrell, Connecticut	112	3.6
Murdock, Providence	111	3.5
McDade, Wisc.-Milw.	97	3.5
Smith, St. Francis (N.Y.)	100	3.4
Davis, Delaware St.	84	3.4
Ellison, Texas-San Ant.	97	3.3
Jennings, East Tenn. St.	109	3.3
Phills, Southern (La.)	90	3.2
Baldwin, N'western	90	3.2

FIELD GOAL PERCENTAGE

PLAYER	FGM	FGA	PCT.
Miller, Arkansas	254	361	.704
Kidd, Middle Tenn. St.	173	247	.700
Freeman, Akron	175	250	.700
James, St. Francis (N.Y.)	149	215	.693
Kennedy, E. Mich.	240	352	.682

Lightfoot, Montana St.	130	196	.663
Brooks, West Va.	222	335	.663
Johnson, UNLV	308	465	.662
Alexander, Iowa St.	294	446	.659
Longley, New Mex.	229	349	.656

FREE THROW PERCENTAGE

PLAYER	FTM	FTA	PCT.
Archbold, Butler	187	205	.912
Lewis, Monmouth	91	101	.901
Alexander, Okla. St.	96	107	.897
Jennings, East Tenn. St.	136	152	.895
Monroe, N.C. St.	162	183	.885
Iuzzolino, St. Francis (Pa.)	215	243	.885
Bird, Indiana St.	82	94	.872
Marcelic, S. Utah	81	93	.871
Geter, Ohio	137	158	.867
Kennedy, UAB	167	193	.865

THREE-POINT FIELD GOAL PERCENTAGE

PLAYER	FGM	FGA	PCT.
Jennings, East Tenn. St.	84	142	.592
Bennett, Wisc.-GB	80	150	.533
Iuzzolino, St. Francis (Pa.)	103	195	.528
Richardson, L. Marymount	61	116	.526
Mitchell, Samford	41	78	.526

THREE-POINT FIELD GOALS PER GAME

PLAYER	FGM	AVG.
Phills, Southern (La.)	123	4.4
Schmitz, Mo.-KC	116	4.0
Herdman, UC Irvine	112	3.7
Day, Radford	106	3.7
Jackson, Princeton	95	3.5

1990–91 TEAM LEADERS

SCORING OFFENSE

SCHOOL	PTS.	AVG.
Southern (La.)	2924	104.4
Loyola Marymount	3211	103.6
Arkansas	3783	99.6
UNLV	3420	97.7
Oklahoma	3363	96.1

SCORING DEFENSE

SCHOOL	PTS.	AVG.
Princeton	1320	48.9
Northern Illinois	1781	57.5
Yale	1508	58.0
Wisconsin-Green Bay	1893	61.1
Georgetown	1964	61.4

SCORING MARGIN

SCHOOL	OFF.	DEF.	MAR.
UNLV	97.7	71.0	26.7
Arkansas	99.6	80.4	19.2
East Tennessee St.	94.0	76.8	17.3
Ohio St.	84.6	68.5	16.2
North Carolina	87.6	71.6	16.0

WON-LOST PERCENTAGE

SCHOOL	W-L	PCT.
UNLV	34-1	.971
Arkansas	34-4	.895

Princeton	24-3	.889
Utah	30-4	.882
Ohio St.	27-4	.871

FIELD GOAL PERCENTAGE

SCHOOL	FGM	FGA	PCT.
UNLV	1305	2441	.535
Indiana	1043	1955	.534
New Mexico	868	1644	.528
Brooklyn	656	1262	.520
Kansas	1086	2097	.518

DEFENSIVE FIELD GOAL PERCENTAGE

SCHOOL	FGM	FGA	PCT.
Georgetown	680	1847	.368
Northern Illinois	616	1587	.388
Connecticut	682	1753	.389
New Orleans	725	1837	.395
Middle Tennessee St.	793	2007	.395

FREE THROW PERCENTAGE

SCHOOL	FTM	FTA	PCT.
Butler	725	922	.786
Monmouth	422	547	.771
Air Force	483	627	.770
Northwestern	470	612	.768
Wyoming	654	853	.767

REBOUND MARGIN

SCHOOL	OWN	OPP.	MAR.
New Orleans	41.7	32.4	9.3
Murray St.	43.4	34.6	8.7
Stanford	37.9	29.4	8.5
UNLV	42.5	34.8	7.7
Northern Illinois	35.5	28.0	7.5

THREE-POINT FIELD GOAL PERCENTAGE

SCHOOL	FGM	FGA	PCT.
Wisconsin-Green Bay	189	407	.464
Southern Utah St.	158	353	.448
St. Francis (Pa.)	238	534	.446
Eastern Illinois	200	457	.438
Northern Illinois	133	305	.436

THREE-POINT FIELD GOALS PER GAME

SCHOOL	G.	FGM	AVG.
Texas-Arlington	29	265	9.1
East Tennessee St.	33	301	9.1
Dayton	29	256	8.8
UC Irvine	30	263	8.8
Kentucky	28	242	8.6

only player to transfer from one major college to another and score more than 2,750 points. He had 2,804.

Missouri-Kansas City's Ronnie Schmitz (51 points vs. U.S. International), Georgia Tech's Kenny Anderson (50 vs. Loyola Marymount), Wisconsin-Milwaukee's Von McDade (50 at Illinois), Georgia State's Chris Collier (49 vs. Butler), Columbia's Buck Jenkins (47 vs. Harvard), Radford's Doug Day (43 vs. Central Connecticut State) and UAB's Andy Kennedy (41 vs. St. Louis) set single-game scoring records for their schools. . . . Collier's barrage is a Trans America Athletic Conference standard. Georgia State shuffled games because his religious convictions as a Worldwide Church of God member prohibited him from normal earthly activities such as playing on the Sabbath (Friday nights or before sundown on Saturdays). . . . McDade (29.6 ppg), Oregon's Terrell Brandon (26.6), Fairleigh Dickinson's Desi Wilson (23.8), Kevin Green of Loyola, Md. (22.1) and UAB's Kennedy (21.8) set school records for highest scoring average in a single season. Wilson went on to play professional baseball as an outfielder.

Providence guard Eric Murdock established a Big East Conference record with 48 points against Pittsburgh. . . . La Salle guards Randy Woods (46) and Doug Overton (45) became the only set of teammates in history to score more than 40 points in a single game when they combined for 91 in a 133-118 victory at Loyola Marymount. . . . A national high of 15 different teams averaged more than 90 points per game. Meanwhile, Princeton, limiting its opponents to 48.9 points per game under coach Pete Carril, set a record for highest-ever margin over the runner-up in team defense (8.6 fewer than Northern Illinois). . . . Connecticut set an NCAA mark for largest lead at the start of a game before an opponent scored, racing to a 32-0 advantage in a victory over New Hampshire. Later, New Hampshire's NCAA-record 32 consecutive homecourt defeats was snapped when the Wildcats defeated Holy Cross, 72-56.

UNLV's Stacey Augmon prepares to dish it off to a teammate.

Indiana State set an NCAA record for most consecutive successful free throws by converting 49 in a row in two games in mid-February. . . . LSU's Shaquille O'Neal became the only player in SEC history to lead the league in scoring, rebounding, field-goal percentage and blocked shots in the same season. . . . Florida freshman guard Craig Brown scored an NCAA-record 13 points in the second overtime period of the Gators' 91-81 victory at Mississippi. . . . East Tennessee State's Keith "Mister" Jennings (5-7) became the first player under 5-10 to finish his career with more than 900 assists. He had 938.

Arkansas (34-4, coached by Nolan Richardson), Utah (30-4, Rick Majerus), East Tennessee State (28-5, Alan LeForce), Eastern Michigan (26-7, Ben Braun), Nebraska (26-8, Danny Nee), Northern Illinois (25-6, Jim Molinari), Creighton (24-8, Tony Barone), St. Francis, Pa. (24-8, Jim

1990–91 NCAA CHAMPION: DUKE

SEASON STATISTICS OF DUKE REGULARS

PLAYER	POS.	CL.	G.	FG%	FT%	PPG	RPG
Christian Laettner	C-F	Jr.	39	.575	.802	19.8	8.7
Billy McCaffrey	G	So.	38	.481	.832	11.6	1.8
Thomas Hill	G-F	So.	39	.552	.743	11.5	3.6
Bobby Hurley	G	So.	39	.423	.728	11.3	2.4
Grant Hill	F-G	Fr.	36	.516	.609	11.2	5.1
Brian Davis	G-F	Jr.	39	.456	.730	7.6	4.1
Greg Koubek	F	Sr.	38	.435	.813	5.9	2.9
Antonio Lang	F-C	Fr.	36	.606	.526	4.3	2.6
Crawford Palmer	C	Jr.	38	.646	.825	3.6	2.0
Marty Clark	G	Fr.	23	.448	.625	2.1	0.7
TEAM TOTALS			**39**	**.511**	**.726**	**87.7**	**36.3**

Three-point field goals leaders: Hurley (76 of 188, .404), Koubek (32 of 76, .421). **Assists leader:** Hurley 289. **Blocked shots leader:** Laettner 44. **Steals leaders:** Laettner 75, T. Hill 59.

1991 FINAL FOUR CHAMPIONSHIP GAME

INDIANAPOLIS, IN

KANSAS (65)	MIN.	FG-A	FT-A	REB.	A.	PF.	PTS.
Jamison	29	1-10	0-0	4	5	4	2
Maddox	19	2-4	0-0	3	4	3	4
Randall	33	7-9	3-6	10	2	4	18
Brown	31	6-15	0-0	4	1	1	16
Jordan	34	4-6	1-2	0	3	0	11
Richey	4	0-1	0-0	1	0	0	0
Woodberry	18	1-4	0-0	4	0	4	2
Tunstall	11	1-5	0-0	1	0	3	2
Wagner	3	1-1	0-0	1	0	0	2
Scott	15	3-9	0-0	2	0	1	6
Johanning	3	1-1	0-0	2	1	1	2
TOTALS	**200**	**27-65**	**4-8**	**32**	**16**	**21**	**65**

FG%: .415. **FT%:** .500. **Three-point goals:** 7 of 18 (Jamison 0-2, Randall 1-1, Brown 4-11, Jordan 2-2, Richey 0-1, Tunstall 0-1). **Blocks:** 2. **Turnovers:** 14. **Steals:** 10 (Jamison 4).

DUKE (72)	MIN.	FG-A	FT-A	REB.	A.	PF.	PTS.
Koubek	17	2-4	0-0	4	0	1	5
G. Hill	28	4-6	2-8	8	3	1	10
Laettner	32	3-8	12-12	10	0	3	18
Hurley	40	3-5	4-4	1	9	1	12
T. Hill	23	1-5	0-0	4	1	2	3
McCaffrey	26	6-8	2-2	1	0	1	16
Lang	1	0-0	0-0	0	0	0	0
Davis	24	4-5	0-2	2	1	4	8
Palmer	9	0-0	0-0	0	0	0	0
Team				1			
TOTALS	**200**	**23-41**	**20-28**	**31**	**14**	**13**	**72**

FG%: .561. **FT%:** .714. **Three-point goals:** 6 of 10 (Koubek 1-2, Hurley 2-4, T. Hill 1-1, McCaffrey 2-3). **Blocks:** 2. **Turnovers:** 18. **Steals:** 6.
Halftime: Duke 42-34.

NATIONAL SEMIFINALS

DUKE (79): Koubek 1-6 0-0 2, G. Hill 5-8 1-1 11, Laettner 9-14 9-11 28, Hurley 4-7 1-1 12, T. Hill 2-6 2-2 6, McCaffrey 2-3 1-2 5, Lang 0-0 0-0 0, Davis 6-12 3-4 15, Palmer 0-0 0-0 0. Team 29-56 (.518) 17-21 (.810) 79.

UNLV (77): Johnson 5-10 3-4 13, Augmon 3-10 0-1 6, Ackles 3-6 1-2 7, Hunt 11-20 3-5 29, Anthony 8-18 1-1 19, Gray 1-2 0-0 2, Spencer 0-2 1-2 1. Team 31-68 (.456) 9-15 (.600) 77.

Three-point goals: Duke 4-8 (.500), UNLV 6-15 (.400).
Halftime: UNLV 43-41.

KANSAS (79): Jamison 4-8 1-3 9, Maddox 4-10 2-2 10, Randall 6-11 4-6 16, Brown 1-10 0-3 3, Jordan 4-11 6-13 16, Richey 1-1 2-4 4, Woodberry 0-0 2-2 2, Tunstall 1-5 2-5 5, Wagner 0-1 0-0 0, Scott 6-9 2-3 14, Johanning 0-0 0-0 0. Team 27-66 (.409) 21-36 (.583) 79.

NORTH CAROLINA (73): Lynch 5-8 3-6 13, Fox 5-22 3-3 13, Chilcutt 2-8 0-0 4, Rice 1-6 3-4 5, Davis 9-16 5-5 25, Montross 3-4 0-1 6, Sullivan 0-0 0-0 0, Harris 0-2 0-0 0, Rodl 0-1 0-0 0, Phelps 1-1 0-1 2, Reese 2-5 0-3 5, Rozier 0-0 0-0 0, Cherry 0-0 0-0 0, Salvadori 0-0 0-0 0, Wenstrom 0-0 0-0 0. Team 28-73 (.384) 14-23 (.609) 73.

Three-point goals: Kansas 4-14 (.286), North Carolina 3-18 (.167).
Halftime: Kansas 43-34.

ALL-TOURNAMENT TEAM

Anderson Hunt, G, Jr., UNLV
Bobby Hurley, G, Soph., Duke
Christian Laettner, C, Jr., Duke*
Bill McCaffrey, G, Soph., Duke
Mark Randall, F, Sr., Kansas
    *Named Most Outstanding Player

Baron), Murray State (24-9, Steve Newton) and Arkansas State (23-9, Nelson Catalina) had their winningest seasons in Division I school history. Ohio State (27-4, Randy Ayers), Siena (25-10, Mike Deane), St. Peter's (24-7, Ted Fiore) and Texas-Arlington (20-9, Mark Nixon) tied their single-season school Division I records for most victories.. . . Arkansas authored an Southwest Conference championship in the Razorbacks' final season as a member of the league.

Utah captured the WAC championship just one year after finishing in a tie for sixth place. ETSU made its lone appearance in the Top 20 of a final wire-service poll. Nebraska set its school standard on the heels of three consecutive seventh-place Big Eight finishes. . . . Mississippi State and Nebraska finished in the Top 20 of a final wire-service poll for the first time since 1963 and 1966, respectively. Eastern Michigan and Southern Mississippi made their lone appearance in the Top 25 of a final wire-service poll. . . . Georgetown (19-13) sustained its most defeats since coach John Thompson's first season in 1972-73, but the Hoyas led the nation in field-goal percentage defense for the third consecutive year.

Louisville's NCAA record of consecutive winning seasons was snapped at 46 when the

Cardinals went 14-16. . . . Michigan's streak of seven straight 20-win seasons ended when the Wolverines compiled a 14-15 mark. . . . Ohio State, coached by Randy Ayers, captured its first Big Ten title in 20 years. . . . Wisconsin lost 26 consecutive games to Purdue in their series until the Badgers blasted the Boilermakers, 66-44. . . . Northwestern (0-18), finishing in the Big Ten cellar for the seventh straight year, became the first team to go winless in conference competition since the University of Chicago went 0-12 in 1945-46 in its last season as a member of the league.

Rice, coached by Scott Thompson, compiled a 16-14 record for its first winning season in 20 years. . . . St. Francis (N.Y.) ended a streak of 11 consecutive losing records by compiling a 15-14 mark. . . . Vermont's string of consecutive losing seasons was snapped at nine when the Catamounts compiled a 15-13 record. . . . Radford, which registered a 7-22 record the previous season, improved by 15 games to 22-7 under coach Oliver Purnell.

Drake, with nine freshmen on its roster, pulled off perhaps the biggest upset of the season with a 94-93 victory at Arizona State in Rudy Washington's head coaching debut with the Bulldogs. . . . Brigham Young's Shawn Bradley established a Western Athletic Conference mark by blocking 14 shots in a game against Eastern Kentucky. . . . North Carolina's Dean Smith set a national coaching record with his 24th 20-win season.

Furman, coached by Butch Estes, tied for first place in the Southern Conference after finishing in a tie for sixth the previous season. . . . South Alabama, coached by Ronnie Arrow, captured the Sun Belt Conference crown after finishing in last place the previous year. . . . Tom Young, who previously coached Catholic, American and Rutgers, was forced out at Old Dominion, ending a 31-year coaching career with a 524-328 record.

Long-time Michigan assistant Mike Boyd was appointed head coach at Cleveland State

less than a month before the start of official workouts after the Vikings' Kevin Mackey was fired following his confession to substance-abuse and alcohol problems. Mackey had been confronted about rumors concerning his off-the-court activities on numerous occasions, but he denied it all. School officials appeared to wonder how many times Mackey had lied about other topics, particularly his actions in the recruitment of 7-7 Manute Bol, which resulted in three years of NCAA Probation.

1990-91 FINAL NATIONAL POLLS

AP	UPI	USA/CNN	SCHOOL (RECORD)	HEAD COACH
1	1	2	UNLV (34-1)	Jerry Tarkanian
2	2	5	Arkansas (34-4)	Nolan Richardson
3	3	9	Indiana (29-5)	Bob Knight
4	4	4	North Carolina (29-6)	Dean Smith
5	5	8	Ohio State (27-4)	Randy Ayers
6	6	1	Duke (32-7)	Mike Krzyzewski
7	8	16	Syracuse (26-6)	Jim Boeheim
8	7	10	Arizona (28-7)	Lute Olson
9	–	17	Kentucky (22-6)	Rick Pitino
10	10	12	Utah (30-4)	Rick Majerus
11	9	19	Nebraska (26-8)	Danny Nee
12	12	3	Kansas (27-8)	Roy Williams
13	11	6	Seton Hall (25-9)	P.J. Carlesimo
14	13	13	Oklahoma State (24-8)	Eddie Sutton
15	17	22	New Mexico State (23-6)	Neil McCarthy
16	14	25	UCLA (23-9)	Jim Harrick
17	15	24	East Tenn. State (28-5)	Alan LeForce
18	20	–	Princeton (24-3)	Pete Carril
19	16	–	Alabama (23-10)	Wimp Sanderson
20	19	7	St. John's (23-9)	Lou Carnesecca
21	18	–	Mississippi State (20-9)	Richard Williams
22	21	–	Louisiana State (20-10)	Dale Brown
23	25	–	Texas (23-9)	Tom Penders
24	–	–	DePaul (20-9)	Joey Meyer
25	–	–	Southern Miss. (21-8)	M.K. Turk
–	–	15	Connecticut (20-11)	Jim Calhoun
–	–	18	Eastern Michigan (26-7)	Ben Braun
–	23	20	Georgetown (19-13)	John Thompson
–	–	21	Pittsburgh (21-12)	Paul Evans
–	22	–	Michigan State (19-11)	Jud Heathcote
–	24	23	N.C. State (20-11)	Les Robinson

1991 NCAA Tournament

Summary: Duke required nine appearances at the Final Four until the resolute Blue Devils finally won a national title. The Blue Devils' Mike Krzyzewski joined UCLA's John Wooden as the only other coach to lead a school to four consecutive Final Fours. Their shocking 79-77 win over defending champion UNLV was the Rebels' lone defeat.

1991 CHAMPIONSHIP BRACKET

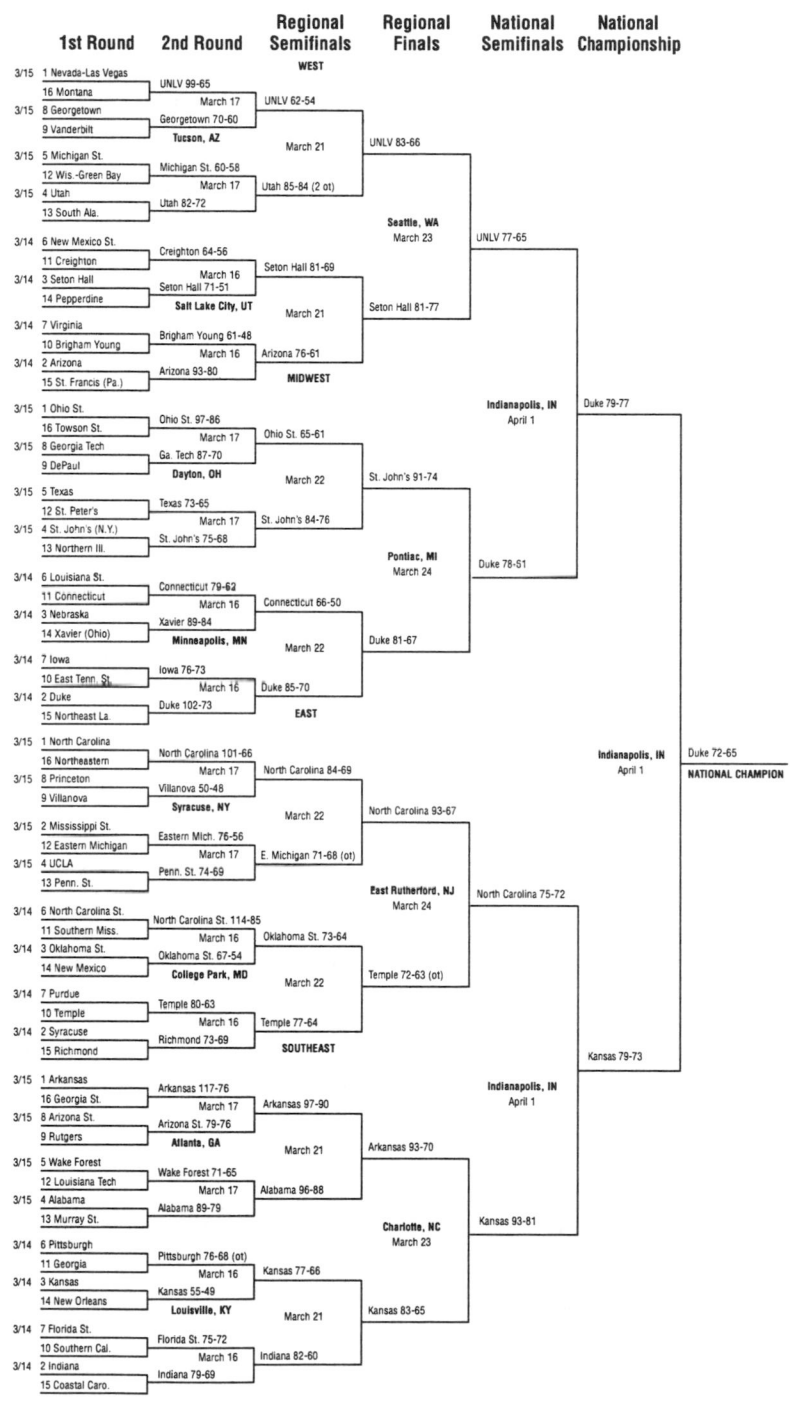

		Regional	Regional	National	National
1st Round	**2nd Round**	**Semifinals**	**Finals**	**Semifinals**	**Championship**

WEST

3/15 1 Nevada-Las Vegas
16 Montana — UNLV 99-65
March 17 — UNLV 62-54
3/15 8 Georgetown
9 Vanderbilt — Georgetown 70-60
Tucson, AZ — UNLV 83-66
3/15 5 Michigan St.
12 Wis.-Green Bay — Michigan St. 60-58
March 17 — Utah 85-84 (2 ot)
3/15 4 Utah
13 South Ala. — Utah 82-72
Seattle, WA
March 23 — UNLV 77-65
3/14 6 New Mexico St.
11 Creighton — Creighton 64-56
March 16 — Seton Hall 81-69
3/14 3 Seton Hall
14 Pepperdine — Seton Hall 71-51
Salt Lake City, UT — Seton Hall 81-77
March 21
3/15 7 Virginia
10 Brigham Young — Brigham Young 61-48
March 16 — Arizona 76-61
3/14 2 Arizona
15 St. Francis (Pa.) — Arizona 93-80

MIDWEST

Indianapolis, IN
April 1 — Duke 79-77

3/15 1 Ohio St.
16 Towson St. — Ohio St. 97-86
March 17 — Ohio St. 65-61
3/15 8 Georgia Tech
9 DePaul — Ga. Tech 87-70
Dayton, OH — St. John's 91-74
March 22
3/15 5 Texas
12 St. Peter's — Texas 73-65
March 17 — St. John's 84-76
3/15 4 St. John's (N.Y.)
13 Northern Ill. — St. John's 75-68
Pontiac, MI
March 24 — Duke 78-S1
3/14 6 Louisiana St.
11 Connecticut — Connecticut 79-62
March 16 — Connecticut 66-50
3/14 3 Nebraska
14 Xavier (Ohio) — Xavier 89-84
Minneapolis, MN — Duke 81-67
March 22
3/14 7 Iowa
10 East Tenn. St. — Iowa 76-73
March 16 — Duke 85-70
3/14 2 Duke
15 Northeast La. — Duke 102-73

EAST

3/15 1 North Carolina
16 Northeastern — North Carolina 101-66
March 17 — North Carolina 84-69
3/15 8 Princeton
9 Villanova — Villanova 50-48
Syracuse, NY — North Carolina 93-67
March 22
3/15 2 Mississippi St.
12 Eastern Michigan — Eastern Mich. 76-56
March 17 — E. Michigan 71-68 (ot)
3/15 4 UCLA
13 Penn. St. — Penn. St. 74-69
East Rutherford, NJ
March 24 — North Carolina 75-72
3/14 6 North Carolina St.
11 Southern Miss. — North Carolina St. 114-85
March 16 — Oklahoma St. 73-64
3/14 3 Oklahoma St.
14 New Mexico — Oklahoma St. 67-54
College Park, MD — Temple 72-63 (ot)
March 22
3/14 7 Purdue
10 Temple — Temple 80-63
March 16 — Temple 77-64
3/14 2 Syracuse
15 Richmond — Richmond 73-69

Indianapolis, IN
April 1 — Duke 72-65
NATIONAL CHAMPION

SOUTHEAST

3/15 1 Arkansas
16 Georgia St. — Arkansas 117-76
March 17 — Arkansas 97-90
3/15 8 Arizona St.
9 Rutgers — Arizona St. 79-76
Atlanta, GA — Arkansas 93-70
March 21
3/15 5 Wake Forest
12 Louisiana Tech — Wake Forest 71-65
March 17 — Alabama 96-88
3/15 4 Alabama
13 Murray St. — Alabama 89-79
Charlotte, NC
March 23 — Kansas 93-81
3/14 6 Pittsburgh
11 Georgia — Pittsburgh 76-68 (ot)
March 16 — Kansas 77-66
3/14 3 Kansas
14 New Orleans — Kansas 55-49
Louisville, KY — Kansas 83-65
March 21
3/14 7 Florida St.
10 Southern Cal. — Florida St. 75-72
March 16 — Indiana 82-60
3/14 2 Indiana
15 Coastal Caro. — Indiana 79-69

Indianapolis, IN
April 1 — Kansas 79-73

North Carolina 75-72

Star Gazing: Christian Laettner became the only player with at least 10 championship game free-throw attempts to convert all of them (12 of 12 against Kansas).

Biggest Upsets: Richmond (15th seed) over Syracuse (2), 73-69; Xavier (14) over Nebraska (3), 89-84, and Penn State (13) over UCLA (4), 74-69. UCLA was without standout freshman forward Ed O'Bannon, who missed the season because of a severe knee injury.

One and Only: North Carolina's Dean Smith became the only coach to direct teams to Final Fours in four different decades, but the Tar Heels lost against Kansas in the national semifinals to give him nine Final Four defeats. No other coach has more than seven Final Four setbacks. . . . Eddie Sutton became the only coach to guide four different schools to the NCAA Tournament when his alma mater, Oklahoma State, earned a bid.

Numbers Game: Duke became the only school to reach the NCAA Tournament final in back-to-back seasons after losing by double-digit margins in its conference tournament (defeated by 11 points against Georgia Tech in the 1990 ACC Tournament semifinals before getting trounced in the 1991 ACC Tournament final by 22 points against North Carolina).

What If: Forward Larry Johnson and guard Stacey Augmon combined for 37 points per game on 61 percent field-goal shooting in their two years together as teammates at UNLV. If only they had combined for 22 points instead of 19 points on 40 percent field-goal shooting (8 of 20) in the national semifinals, the seemingly invincible Rebels could have defeated eventual champion Duke rather than losing 79-77. . . . Georgia Tech (17-13, without Dennis Scott), Indiana (29-5, Jay Edwards), Louisiana State (20-10, Chris Jackson) and Michigan (23-8, Sean Higgins) might have fared better in the playoffs if standout players had exercised their remaining eligibility instead of defecting to the NBA. . . . Houston (18-11) probably would have participated in the NCAA Tournament instead of the NIT if Carl Herrera didn't leave school early for the NBA.

Scoring Leader: Christian Laettner, Duke (125 points, 20.8 ppg).

Highest Scoring Average: Terry Dehere, Seton Hall (97 points, 24.3 ppg).

Rebounding Leader: Larry Johnson, UNLV (51 rebounds, 10.2 rpg).

Highest Rebounding Averages: Ohio State's Perry Carter and Oklahoma State's Byron Houston (36 rebounds, 12 rpg).

1991-92

AT A GLANCE

NCAA Champion: Duke (35-2; coached by Mike Krzyzewski; won ACC regular-season title by three games over Florida State with a 14-2 record).

NIT Champion: Virginia (20-13; coached by Jeff Jones; tied for fourth place in ACC with an 8-8 record).

New Conference: Great Midwest (merged with teams from the Metro to form Conference USA four years later).

New Rules: Contact technical fouls count toward the five fouls for player disqualification and toward team fouls in reaching bonus free-throw situations. . . . The shot clock is reset when the ball strikes the basket ring, not when a shot leaves the shooter's hands as it had been since the rule was introduced in 1986.

NCAA Probation: Auburn, Maryland, UNLV, Northwestern (La.) State, Texas A&M.

NCAA Consensus First-Team All-Americans: Jim Jackson, G-F, Jr., Ohio State; Christian Laettner, F-C, Sr., Duke; Harold Miner, G, Jr., Southern California; Alonzo Mourning, C, Sr., Georgetown; Shaquille O'Neal, C, Jr., Louisiana State.

National Players of the Year: Jackson (22.4 ppg, 6.8 rpg, 81.1 FT%/UPI) and Laettner (21.5 ppg, 7.9 rpg, 57.5 FG%, 81.5 FT%/AP, NABC, USBWA, Naismith, Wooden).

National Coaches of the Year: Tulane's Perry Clark (21-8/UPI, USBWA); Duke's Mike Krzyzewski (34-2/Naismith); Southern Cal's George Raveling (24-6/NABC), and Kansas' Roy Williams (27-5/AP).

Cincinnati coach Bob Huggins argues a call.

Duke's Christian Laettner hit a dramatic decisive last-second shot against Kentucky in overtime after receiving a long inbounds pass in the East Regional final. The game is acknowledged as one of the most suspenseful in NCAA history (see accompanying box).

Virginia's NIT title enabled Jeff Jones to become the only person to win NIT crowns as a player (Virginia guard in 1980) and as a coach. His father, Bob Jones, had been coach of Kentucky Wesleyan when it won the 1973 NCAA Division II crown. . . . Embattled coach Jerry Tarkanian was forced out at UNLV, but not before the Rebels captured their 10th consecutive Big West Conference championship.

Tarkanian's 307 victories in his last 10 seasons is by far the most successful 10-year stretch in major-college history.

Jackson State guard Lindsey Hunter, who would become a first-round draft choice of the Detroit Pistons the next year, set an NCAA record with 26 three-point field-goal attempts (11 made) in a game at Kansas. . . . San Francisco's Tomas Thompson set an NCAA standard for most three-pointers in a game without a miss (subsequently tied) when he hit all eight of his attempts from beyond the arc against Loyola Marymount.

Georgetown's Alonzo Mourning finished his career with an NCAA record 453 blocked

MOST EXCITING PLAYOFF GAME FINISH

DUKE VS. KENTUCKY IN EAST REGIONAL FINAL

AT THE SPECTRUM, PHILADELPHIA, PA

MARCH 28, 1992

Guard Sean Woods' successful go-ahead bank shot in the waning moments of overtime appeared to have him destined to go down in Kentucky lore. But that was before a miracle pass by Grant Hill and pressure-packed outside jumper by Christian Laettner lifted NCAA champion-to-be Duke to a 104-103 victory over the Wildcats in the NCAA Tournament.

KENTUCKY (103)	MP	FG-A	FT-A	REB.	PTS.
Jamal Mashburn	43	11-16	3-3	10	28
John Pelphrey	25	5-7	3-3	1	16
Gimel Martinez	23	2-4	0-0	0	5
Sean Woods	38	9-15	2-2	2	21
Richie Farmer	15	2-3	4-6	1	9
Deron Feldhaus	37	2-6	1-2	1	5
Dale Brown	30	6-11	3-5	3	18
Travis Ford	7	0-2	0-0	1	0
Aminu Timberlake	5	0-0	1-2	0	1
Andre Riddick	1	0-0	0-0	0	0
Junior Braddy	1	0-1	0-0	0	0
Totals	**225**	**37-65**	**12-22**	**21**	**103**

FG%: .569. **FT%:** .739. 3-PT. **FG:** 12-22 (Mashburn 3-4, Pelphrey 3-4, Brown 3-5, Martinez 1-2, Farmer 1-2, Woods, 1-1, Feldhaus 0-2, Ford 0-1, Braddy 0-1). **Assists:** 24 (Woods 9). **Steals:** 12. **Blocked Shots:** 0. **Turnovers:** 12. **Fouled Out:** 2 (Mashburn, Martinez).

DUKE (104)	MP	FG-A	FT-A	REB.	PTS.
Antonio Lang	21	2-2	0-1	3	4
Brian Davis	38	3-6	7-10	5	13
Christian Laettner	43	10-10	10-10	7	31
Bobby Hurley	45	6-12	5-6	3	22
Thomas Hill	34	6-10	5-5	3	19
Grant Hill	37	5-10	1-2	10	11
Cherokee Parks	6	2-2	0-0	0	4
Marty Clark	1	0-0	0-0	0	0
Totals	**225**	**34-52**	**28-34**	**31**	**104**

FG%: .654. **FT%:** .824. 3-PT. **FG:** 8-16 (Hurley 5-10, T. Hill 2-3, Laettner 1-1, Davis 0-2). **Assists:** 23 (Hurley 10). **Steals:** 8. **Blocked Shots:** 3. **Turnovers:** 20. **Fouled Out:** 1 (Davis).

Halftime: Duke 50-45. **Regulation:** Tied 93-93.

shots. Joining Ralph Sampson (Virginia), David Robinson (Navy) and J.R. Reid (North Carolina), Mourning became the fourth center in 10 years to earn NCAA consensus first-team All-American recognition after playing high school basketball in Virginia.

LSU's Shaquille O'Neal concluded his three-year career with a total of six games with at least 10 blocked shots. He is the only player to twice average at least five rejections per game in a season. O'Neal was one of six SEC players to be selected in the first round of the NBA draft, including three from conference newcomer Arkansas.

Height doesn't always determine who excels at blocked shots and field-goal shooting. Vermont's Kevin Roberson finished his career as the shortest player (6-7) to block more than three shots per game (3.65) and Massachusetts' William Herndon finished his career as the shortest player (6-3) to hit more than 63 percent of his field-goal attempts.

Morehead State's Brett Roberts (53 points vs. Middle Tennessee State), Colgate's Jonathan Stone (52 vs. Brooklyn) and Hartford's Vin Baker (44 vs. Lamar) established school Division I single-game scoring records. . . . Maryland's Walt Williams (26.8 ppg), Southern Cal's Harold Miner (26.3), Stanford's Adam Keefe (25.3) and UC Santa Barbara's Lucius Davis (22.2) set school records for highest scoring average in a single season.

Missouri's Jeff Warren established a Big Eight Conference record by hitting 24 consecutive field-goal attempts. . . . Forward Byron Houston was the first Oklahoma State player since 1954 to become an NCAA consensus first- or second-team All-American. . . . Delaware (27-4/coached by Steve Steinwedel) had its winningest season in school history. Southern Cal (24-6/George Raveling) tied its school single-season mark for most victories. . . . Massachusetts made its initial Top 20 appearance in a final wire-service poll.

Cincinnati (29-5, coached by Bob Huggins), tying its record for most victories in a single season, did not appear in a final wire-service national poll or the NCAA Tournament for 14 consecutive years until highlighting the Great Midwest Conference's inaugural season by reaching the Final Four. It was the first time for

1991–92 INDIVIDUAL LEADERS

SCORING

PLAYER	PTS.	AVG.
Roberts, Morehead St.	815	28.1
Baker, Hartford	745	27.6
Ford, Miss. Valley St.	714	27.5
Woods, La Salle	847	27.3
Rogers, Alabama St.	764	27.3
Williams, Maryland	776	26.8
Miner, Southern Cal	789	26.3
Lowery, Loyola Marymount	675	26.0
Cunningham, Bethune-Cookman	744	25.7
Casebier, Evansville	634	25.4

REBOUNDING

PLAYER	REB.	AVG.
Jones, Murray St.	431	14.4
O'Neal, Louisiana St.	421	14.0
Burroughs, Jacksonville	370	13.2
Keefe, Stanford	355	12.2
White, Southern (La.)	367	12.2
Sims, Youngstown St.	327	11.7
Ellis, Notre Dame	385	11.7
Stokes, SW La.	370	11.6
Johnson, San Francisco	309	11.4
Henderson, Fairfield	318	11.4
Smith, TCU	386	11.4

ASSISTS

PLAYER	AST.	AVG.
Usher, Tenn. Tech	254	8.8
Crawford, New Mexico St.	282	8.5
Smart, San Francisco	241	8.3
Soares, Nevada	227	7.8
Evans, Miss. St.	219	7.8
Walker, L. Marymount	218	7.8
Dale, S. Miss.	222	7.7
Hurley, Duke	237	7.6

Miller, Marquette	221	7.6
Yelding, S. Alabama	184	7.1

BLOCKED SHOTS

PLAYER	BLK	AVG.
O'Neal, LSU	157	5.2
Mourning, Georgetown	160	5.0
Roberson, Vermont	139	5.0
Earl, Iowa	121	4.0
Baker, Hartford	100	3.7
Van Dyke, UTEP	116	3.5
Horry, Alabama	121	3.5
Jaxon, New Mexico	109	3.3
Chandler, Nebraska	91	3.1
Outlaw, Houston	97	3.1

STEALS

PLAYER	STL.	AVG.
Snipes, NE Illinois	86	3.4
Burcy, Chicago St.	85	3.3
Corbitt, Cent. Conn. St.	88	3.1
Mitchell, Wisc.-Milw.	78	3.1
Soares, Nevada	90	3.1
White, Southern (La.)	93	3.1
Higgins, Maine	95	3.0
Usher, Tenn. Tech	86	3.0
Evans, Miss. St.	83	3.0
Mee, W. Ky.	94	2.9

FIELD GOAL PERCENTAGE

PLAYER	FGM	FGA	PCT.
Outlaw, Houston	156	228	.684
Kidd, Middle Tenn. St.	156	235	.664
Fish, UNC-Wilm.	206	319	.646
McDowell, Texas-Arl.	184	287	.641
Spencer, UNLV	174	273	.637
Robinson, Mo.-KC	199	314	.634

Peplowski, Mich. St.	168	266	.632
Hupmann, Evansville	159	252	.631
Ellis, Notre Dame	227	360	.631
Solis, Brooklyn	150	238	.630

FREE THROW PERCENTAGE

PLAYER	FTM	FTA	PCT.
MacLean, UCLA	197	214	.921
Adkins, UNC-Wilm.	78	85	.918
Shreffler, Evansville	78	85	.918
Hildebrand, Liberty	114	125	.912
Lauritzen, Indiana St.	82	91	.901
Goodman, Utah St.	82	92	.891
Anderson, Old Dom.	96	108	.889
Schmitz, Mo.-KC	76	86	.884
Breslin, Holy Cross	91	103	.883
Marcelic, S. Utah St.	135	153	.882

THREE-POINT FIELD GOAL PERCENTAGE

PLAYER	FGM	FGA	PCT.
Wightman, W. Mich.	48	76	.632
Laettner, Duke	54	97	.557
Barker, Valparaiso	61	117	.521
Batle, Auburn	71	139	.511
Bennett, Wisc.-GB	95	186	.511

THREE-POINT FIELD GOALS PER GAME

PLAYER	FGM	AVG.
Day, Radford	117	4.0
Alberts, Akron	110	3.9
Woods, La Salle	121	3.9
McKelvey, Portland	106	3.8
Hurd, La Salle	113	3.6

1991–92 TEAM LEADERS

SCORING OFFENSE

SCHOOL	PTS.	AVG.
Northwestern St. (La.)	2660	95.0
Oklahoma	2838	94.6
Southern (La.)	2809	93.6
Georgia Southern	2836	91.5
Loyola Marymount	2552	91.1

SCORING DEFENSE

SCHOOL	PTS.	AVG.
Princeton	1349	48.2
Wisc.-Green Bay	1659	55.3
Southwest Missouri St.	1761	56.8
Monmouth	1701	58.7
Ball St.	1959	59.4

SCORING MARGIN

SCHOOL	OFF.	DEF.	MAR.
Indiana	83.4	65.8	17.6
Kansas	84.5	68.1	16.4
Arizona	84.8	68.8	16.0
Cincinnati	79.0	63.1	15.9
Duke	88.0	72.6	15.3

WON-LOST PERCENTAGE

SCHOOL	W-L	PCT.
Duke	34-2	.944

UNLV	26-2	.929
Delaware	27-4	.871
Montana	27-4	.871
Massachusetts	30-5	.857

FIELD GOAL PERCENTAGE

SCHOOL	FGM	FGA	PCT.
Duke	1108	2069	.536
Liberty	790	1519	.520
UNLV	817	1583	.516
Kansas	975	1892	.515
Wisc.-Green Bay	759	1481	.512

FIELD GOAL PERCENTAGE DEFENSE

SCHOOL	FGM	FGA	PCT.
UNLV	628	1723	.364
Princeton	445	1169	.381
Montana	685	1736	.395
Connecticut	734	1843	.398
Charleston Southern	592	1486	.398
Utah	730	1832	.398

FREE THROW PERCENTAGE

SCHOOL	FTM	FTA	PCT.
Northwestern	497	651	.763
Bucknell	550	722	.762
Monmouth	414	544	.761
Washington St.	554	729	.760
Drexel	524	692	.757

REBOUND MARGIN

SCHOOL	OWN	OPP.	MAR.
Delaware	42.1	33.8	8.3
Montana	40.6	32.4	8.2
Wake Forest	36.8	29.1	7.7
Providence	42.8	35.3	7.5
Michigan	40.4	33.0	7.5

THREE-POINT FIELD GOAL PERCENTAGE

SCHOOL	FGM	FGA	PCT.
Wisc.-Green Bay	204	437	.467
Auburn	182	403	.452
Western Michigan	120	267	.449
Louisiana Tech	161	359	.448
Duke	171	394	.434

THREE-POINT FIELD GOALS PER GAME

SCHOOL	FGM	AVG.
La Salle	294	9.5
Northwestern	259	9.3
N.C. St.	265	8.8
Kentucky	317	8.8
Texas-Arlington	255	8.8

a first-year league member to advance to the national semifinals since UNC Charlotte represented the Sun Belt Conference in 1977, which coincidentally was the last year Cincinnati had participated in the event.

Western Michigan, coached by Bob Donewald, compiled a 21-9 record to end a streak of nine consecutive losing seasons. . . . Prairie View (0-28) became the first team to go winless in an entire season since The Citadel went 0-17 in 1955. . . . Miami (Fla.) compiled a 1-17 league record in its inaugural season in the Big East, but the Hurricanes won their Big East Tournament debut with an 83-71 decision over Pittsburgh. . . . Syracuse finished out of the top 10 of a final AP poll for the first time in seven years.

North Carolina, trailing by 20 points with less than 15 minutes remaining, rallied to edge Wake Forest, 80-78, on a last-second shot by Brian Reese. That rates as the largest deficit the Tar Heels have ever had to overcome for a victory. . . . Tulane appeared in a final wire-service poll for the first time since the AP's initial rankings in 1949. . . . Liberty, after compiling a 5-23 record the previous season, improved by 16 1/2 games to 22-7. . . . Tennessee Tech's Van Usher led the nation in assists one year after pacing the country in steals.

Wyoming's Reginald Slater (27 against Troy State) and UNC-Wilmington's Matt Fish (20 in triple overtime at American) set school single-game rebounding records. . . . Arizona's 71-

Grant Hill jumps head and shoulders above Michigan's Jalen Rose in the 1992 NCAA final.

game homecourt winning streak, which started in 1987, was snapped by UCLA, 89-87. . . . Lucius Davis Jr. finished his career at UC Santa Barbara with 1,420 points. He and his father are believed to be the only father-son combination to score more than 1,400 points apiece for schools that are currently at the Division I level. Lucius Davis Sr. scored 1,511 points in three seasons for Fresno State (1968-70) shortly before the Bulldogs moved up to Division I. . . . St. John's Lou Carnesecca ended his 24-year college coaching career with a 526-200 record. He is the only major-college coach to survive more than 20 seasons with nothing but winning records at least five games above .500.

1991-92 FINAL NATIONAL POLLS

AP	UPI	USA/CNN	SCHOOL (RECORD)	HEAD COACH
1	1	1	Duke (34-2)	Mike Krzyzewski
2	2	7	Kansas (27-5)	Roy Williams
3	4	4	Ohio State (26-6)	Randy Ayers
4	3	8	UCLA (28-5)	Jim Harrick
5	6	2	Indiana (27-7)	Bob Knight
6	9	6	Kentucky (29-7)	Rick Pitino
7	–	–	UNLV (26-2)	Jerry Tarkanian
8	7	11	Southern Cal (24-6)	George Raveling
9	8	10	Arkansas (26-8)	Nolan Richardson
10	5	16	Arizona (24-7)	Lute Olson
11	10	9	Oklahoma State (28-8)	Eddie Sutton
12	14	5	Cincinnati (29-5)	Bob Huggins
13	13	19	Alabama (26-9)	Wimp Sanderson
14	11	20	Michigan State (22-8)	Jud Heathcote
15	17	3	Michigan (25-9)	Steve Fisher
16	12	18	Missouri (21-9)	Norm Stewart
17	21	15	Massachusetts (30-5)	John Calipari
18	15	12	North Carolina (23-10)	Dean Smith
19	18	13	Seton Hall (23-9)	P.J. Carlesimo
20	16	14	Florida State (22-10)	Pat Kennedy
21	20	24	Syracuse (22-10)	Jim Boeheim
22	19	23	Georgetown (22-10)	John Thompson
23	22	–	Oklahoma (21-9)	Billy Tubbs
24	23	–	DePaul (20-9)	Joey Meyer
25	–	25	Louisiana State (21-10)	Dale Brown
–	–	17	Memphis State (23-11)	Larry Finch
–	–	21	Georgia Tech (23-12)	Bobby Cremins
–	–	22	Texas-El Paso (27-7)	Don Haskins
–	24	–	St. John's (19-11)	Lou Carnesecca
–	25	–	Tulane (21-8)	Perry Clark

Indiana's Calbert Cheaney drives through Michigan's Rob Pelinka (left) and Jimmy King.

1992 NCAA Tournament

Summary: Christian Laettner became the NCAA Tournament's all-time leading scorer and teammate Bobby Hurley became the tourney's all-time leader in assists as the Blue Devils became the first school since UCLA (1967-73) to repeat as national champion. Hurley took up the slack with 26 points when Laettner was limited to eight points in an 81-78 decision over Indiana in the national semifinals. Laettner closed out his college career with a game-high 19 points in the championship game against Michigan, which became the only school to ever lead an NCAA final at halftime and end up losing the game by at least 20 points. Duke coach Mike Krzyzewski did the unthinkable and temporarily passed UCLA legend John Wooden (47-10, .8246) for the top spot in all-time NCAA playoff winning percentage (minimum of 20 games). Hurley was selected Final Four Most Outstanding Player although dissenters believed that Duke teammate Grant Hill deserved the honor instead. In the two Final Four games, Hill had more field goals than Hurley (14 to 10), outshot him from the floor (61 percent to 41.7), blocked more shots (5 to 0), outrebounded him (16 to 3) and accumulated just as many assists (11 each). Moreover, Hurley's 3 of 12 field-goal shooting in the final against Michigan was the worst marksmanship from the floor for a Final Four Most Outstanding Player in a championship game since Elgin Baylor of runner-up Seattle went 9 of 32 against Kentucky in 1958. It was the second consecutive year for the Final Four Most Outstanding Player to come from Duke and manage just three baskets and shoot less than 50 percent from the

1991–92 NCAA CHAMPION: DUKE

SEASON STATISTICS OF DUKE REGULARS

PLAYER	POS.	CL.	G.	FG%	FT%	PPG	RPG
Christian Laettner	C	Sr.	35	.575	.815	21.5	7.9
Thomas Hill	G	Jr.	36	.534	.768	14.6	3.4
Grant Hill	F-G	So.	33	.611	.733	14.0	5.7
Bobby Hurley	G	Jr.	31	.433	.789	13.2	2.0
Brian Davis	F	Sr.	36	.481	.740	11.2	4.5
Antonio Lang	F	So.	34	.562	.657	6.4	4.1
Cherokee Parks	C	Fr.	34	.571	.725	5.0	2.4
Marty Clark	G	So.	34	.541	.778	2.9	0.8
Erik Meek	C	Fr.	25	.579	.500	2.5	1.2
Kenny Blakeney	G	So.	29	.565	.650	1.4	0.9
TEAM TOTALS			36	.536	.748	88.0	34.1

Three-point field goals leaders: Hurley (59 of 140, .421), Laettner (54 of 97, .557), T. Hill (37 of 91, .407). **Assists leaders:** Hurley 237, G. Hill 134. **Blocked shots leaders:** Parks 35, Laettner 32. **Steals leaders:** Laettner 74, T. Hill 60.

1992 FINAL FOUR CHAMPIONSHIP GAME

MINNEAPOLIS, MN

MICHIGAN (51)	MIN.	FG-A	FT-A	REB.	A.	PF.	PTS.
Webber	30	6-12	2-5	11	1	4	14
Jackson	16	0-1	0-0	1	2	1	0
Howard	29	4-9	1-3	3	0	3	9
Rose	37	5-12	1-2	5	4	4	11
King	40	3-10	0-0	2	1	1	7
Riley	19	2-6	0-0	4	1	2	4
Voskuil	15	1-2	2-2	3	3	2	4
Pelinka	10	1-2	0-0	2	1	0	2
Hunter	2	0-0	0-0	0	0	0	0
Talley	1	0-2	0-0	1	0	0	0
Bossard	1	0-1	0-0	0	0	0	0
Seter	1	0-1	0-0	1	0	0	0
Armer	1	0-0	0-0	0	0	0	0
TOTALS	200	22-58	6-12	35	13	17	51

FG%: .379. **FT%:** .500. **Three-point goals:** 1 of 11 (King 1-2, Rose 0-3, Webber 9-2, Howard 0-1, Voskuil 0-1, Talley 0-1, Bossard 0-1). **Blocks:** 3 (Jackson 2). **Turnovers:** 20 (Howard 4, Rose 4). **Steals:** 8 (Webber 2, Rose 2, King 2).

DUKE (71)	MIN.	FG-A	FT-A	REB.	A.	PF.	PTS.
Lang	31	2-3	1-2	4	0	1	5
G. Hill	36	8-14	2-2	10	5	2	18
Laettner	35	6-13	5-6	7	0	1	19
Hurley	36	3-12	2-2	3	7	4	9
T. Hill	34	5-10	5-8	7	0	2	16
Parks	13	1-3	2-2	3	0	3	4
Davis	10	0-2	0-0	0	0	0	0
Ast	1	0-0	0-0	1	0	0	0
Clark	1	0-0	0-0	0	0	0	0
Blakeney	1	0-0	0-0	0	0	0	0
Burt	1	0-0	0-0	0	0	0	0
Meek	1	0-0	0-0	0	0	0	0
TOTALS	200	25-57	17-22	37	12	13	71

FG%: .439. **FT%:** .773. **Three-point goals:** 4 of 9 (Laettner 2-4, Hurley 1-3, T. Hill 1-2). **Blocks:** 4 (G. Hill 2). **Turnovers:** 14 (Laettner 7). **Steals:** 9 (G. Hill 3).

Halftime: Michigan 31-30.

NATIONAL SEMIFINALS

DUKE (81): Lang 1-5 2-2 4, Davis 1-3 3-7 5, Laettner 2-8 4-7 8, T. Hill 3-10 4-5 11, Hurley 7-12 6-8 26, G. Hill 6-9 2-4 14, Parks 3-5 2-3 8, Clark 0-0 5-6 5. Team 23-52 (.442) 28-42 (.667) 81.

INDIANA (76): Cheaney 4-13 2-4 11, Henderson 6-9 2-2 15, Nover 3-4 2-2 9, Bailey 4-8 0-0 9, Reynolds 1-4 0-0 2, Meeks 1-2 1-2 3, Anderson 1-6 0-1 2, G. Graham 6-9 5-5 18, Leary 3-3 0-0 9. Team 29-58 (.500) 12-16 (.750) 78.

Halftime: Indiana 42-37.

MICHIGAN (76): Webber 8-12 0-2 16, Jackson 1-2 1-2 3, Howard 3-9 6-7 12, Rose 4-13 5-6 13, King 5-9 4-4 17, Talley 1-3 2-3 4, Riley 1-1 0-0 2, Voskuil 2-4 4-5 9. Team 25-53 (.471) 22-29 (.758) 76.

CINCINNATI (72): Nelson 2-2 0-0 4, Jones 5-13 2-2 14, Blount 0-3 1-2 1, Buford 6-17 4-4 18, Van Exel 7-15 5-10 21, Martin 4-10 2-3 10, Scott 0-0 0-0 0, Jackson 0-1 0-0, Gibson 2-3 0-0 4. Team 26-64 (.406) 14-21 (.667) 72.

Halftime: Cincinnati 41-38.

ALL-TOURNAMENT TEAM

Grant Hill, F, Soph., Duke
Bobby Hurley, G, Jr., Duke*
Christian Laettner, C, Sr., Duke
Jalen Rose, G, Fr., Michigan
Chris Webber, F, Fr., Michigan
   *Named Most Outstanding Player

floor in the title game. In 1991, Laettner hit 3 of 8 field-goal attempts against Kansas. Duke became the 18th NCAA Tournament champion to win at least two playoff games by fewer than six points when the Blue Devils edged Kentucky (104-103 in overtime in East Regional final) and Indiana (81-78 in national semifinals). Massachusetts might have been facing Duke instead of Kentucky if not for a critical, and controversial, technical foul assessed to Minutemen coach John Calipari by referee Lenny Wirtz.

Star Gazing: Hurley, 6-0, was the shortest player to be selected Final Four Most Outstanding Player since 5-11 Hal Lear led Temple to a national third-place finish in 1956. The only Final Four Most Outstanding Player shorter than Hurley from a championship team was 5-11 Kenny Sailors of Wyoming '43. Hurley shot a mediocre 41 percent from the floor in his career with the Blue Devils, but his playmaking and intangibles helped them win 18 of 20 NCAA playoff games. He holds the career record for most playoff assists (145) although his bid to become the first player to start four consecutive NCAA finals was thwarted when California upset Duke in the second round of the 1993 Midwest Regional despite Hurley's career-high 32 points.

Biggest Upsets: East Tennessee State (14th seed) over Arizona (3), 87-80, and Southwestern Louisiana (13) over Oklahoma (4), 87-83.

One and Only: Guard Jalen Rose is the only freshman to finish with the highest season scoring average for a team reaching the NCAA Tournament championship game. He averaged 17.6 points per game for national runner-up Michigan. Rose and Chris Webber became the only set of freshman teammates to be named to an NCAA All-Tournament team.

Numbers Game: All three Final Four game winners trailed at halftime. . . . Duke defied a recent trend by becoming the first top-ranked team in 10 years entering the NCAA Tournament to win the national title. The previous five top-ranked teams failed to reach the championship game. . . . The final between Duke and Michigan was the most-watched basketball game in television history. An estimated 53 million viewers took in all or part of the title game in the United States' TV homes covered by the Nielsen ratings. CBS estimated that an additional 10 percent of the total audience watched the 1992 final away from home: in taverns, dormitories and other venues that Nielsen doesn't survey. That's more than 100 times the initial viewing audience estimated at 500,000 in 1946, when the championship game (Oklahoma State defeated North Carolina, 43-40) was televised locally for the first time in New York by WCBS-TV. . . . Four of Michigan's Fab Five Freshmen—Rose (107 points), Webber (98), Jimmy King (83) and Juwan Howard (82)—ranked among the top six freshman scorers in a single tournament in the last 13 years. . . . UNLV's streak of tournament appearances ended at nine when the Rebels were on NCAA Probation. . . . Iowa State compiled the worst league record (5-9 in the Big Eight) of any team ever to receive an at-large invitation. . . . Tulane appeared in the NCAA playoffs for the first time in school history. . . . Duke won all nine of its NCAA playoff games against Big East and Big Ten teams in a three-year span from 1990-92.

What If: Forwards Calbert Cheaney and Eric Anderson shot better than 50 percent from the floor in their careers for Indiana. If only they had combined to hit 36.8 percent of their field-goal attempts instead of 26.3 percent (5 of 19) in the national semifinals, the Hoosiers could have defeated eventual champion Duke rather than having a five-point halftime lead evaporate and losing 81-78. . . . Kentucky coach Rick Pitino was criticized in some quarters for leaving Grant Hill unguarded for his approximate 80-foot pass to Laettner with 2.1 seconds remaining in overtime in the East Regional. . . . Arizona (24-7, without Brian Williams), Georgia Tech (23-12, Kenny Anderson), Louisiana State (21-10, Chris Jackson), Temple (17-13, Donald Hodge) and Syracuse (22-10, Billy Owens) might have fared better in the playoffs if standout players had exercised their remaining eligibility instead of defecting to the NBA.

Putting Things in Perspective: Duke came close to becoming the eighth NCAA champion to go undefeated. The Blue Devils' two losses were by a total of just six points (ACC road games against North Carolina and Wake Forest to start and end a stretch of five of six contests away from home from February 5-23).

Scoring Leader: Christian Laettner, Duke (115 points, 19.2 ppg).

Highest Scoring Average: Jamal Mashburn, Kentucky (96 points, 24 ppg).

Rebounding Leader: Chris Webber, Michigan (58 rebounds, 9.7 rpg).

Highest Rebounding Average: Doug Edwards, Florida State (32 rebounds, 10.7 rpg).

1992 CHAMPIONSHIP BRACKET

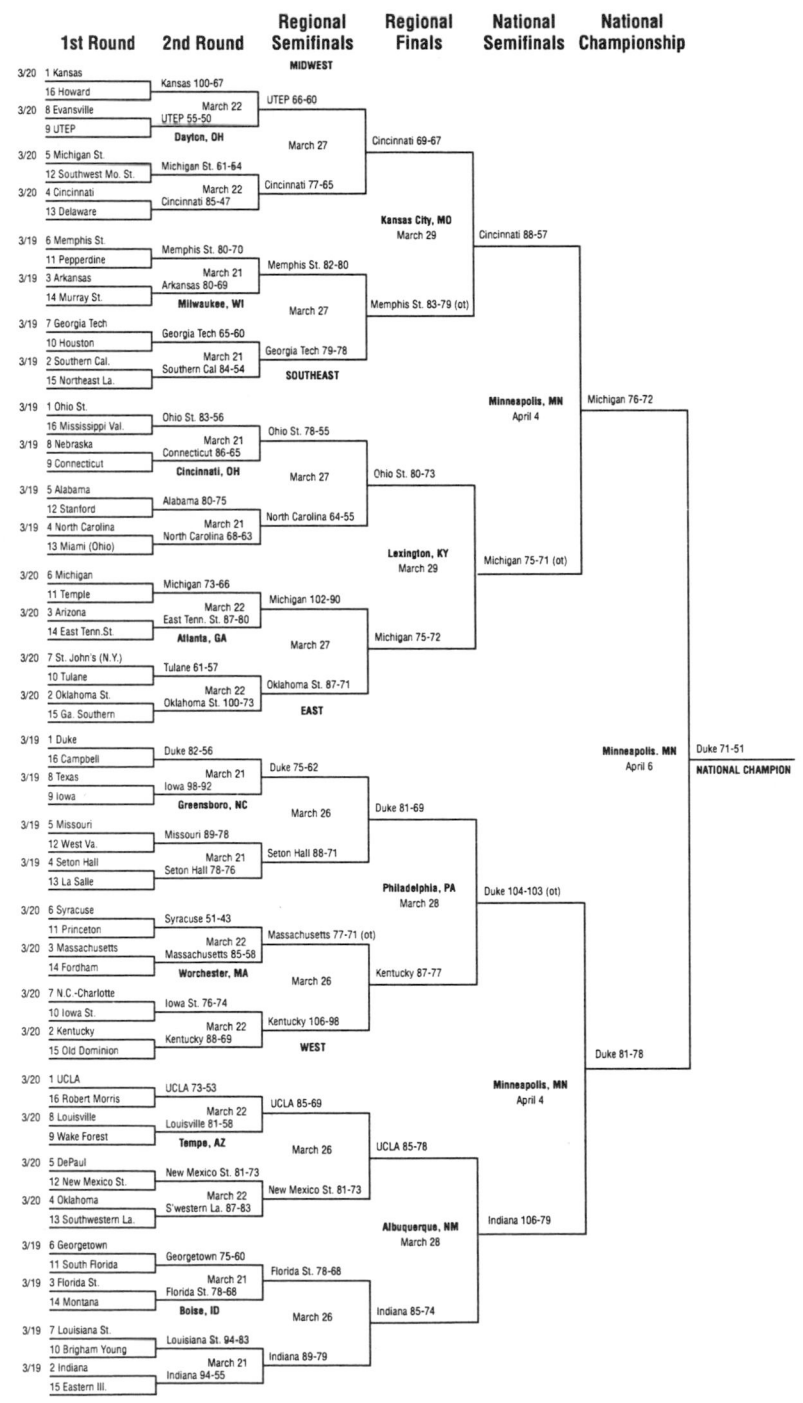

		Regional Semifinals	Regional Finals	National Semifinals	National Championship

1st Round   **2nd Round**

MIDWEST

3/20 1 Kansas
16 Howard — Kansas 100-67
3/20 8 Evansville — March 22 UTEP 55-50 — UTEP 66-60
9 UTEP — **Dayton, OH**
— March 27 — Cincinnati 69-67
3/20 5 Michigan St.
12 Southwest Mo. St. — Michigan St. 61-64
3/20 4 Cincinnati — March 22 Cincinnati 85-47 — Cincinnati 77-65
13 Delaware
— **Kansas City, MO** March 29 — Cincinnati 88-57
3/19 6 Memphis St.
11 Pepperdine — Memphis St. 80-70
3/19 3 Arkansas — March 21 Arkansas 80-69 — Memphis St. 82-80
14 Murray St. — **Milwaukee, WI**
— March 27 — Memphis St. 83-79 (ot)
3/19 7 Georgia Tech
10 Houston — Georgia Tech 65-60
3/19 2 Southern Cal. — March 21 Southern Cal 84-54 — Georgia Tech 79-78
15 Northeast La. — **SOUTHEAST**

— **Minneapolis, MN** April 4 — Michigan 76-72

3/19 1 Ohio St.
16 Mississippi Val. — Ohio St. 83-56
3/19 8 Nebraska — March 21 Connecticut 86-65 — Ohio St. 78-55
9 Connecticut — **Cincinnati, OH**
— March 27 — Ohio St. 80-73
3/19 5 Alabama
12 Stanford — Alabama 80-75
3/19 4 North Carolina — March 21 North Carolina 68-63 — North Carolina 64-55
13 Miami (Ohio)
— **Lexington, KY** March 29 — Michigan 75-71 (ot)
3/20 6 Michigan
11 Temple — Michigan 73-66
3/20 3 Arizona — March 22 East Tenn. St. 87-80 — Michigan 102-90
14 East Tenn.St. — **Atlanta, GA**
— March 27 — Michigan 75-72
3/20 7 St. John's (N.Y.)
10 Tulane — Tulane 61-57
3/20 2 Oklahoma St. — March 22 Oklahoma St. 100-73 — Oklahoma St. 87-71
15 Ga. Southern — **EAST**

— **Minneapolis, MN** April 6 — Duke 71-51 **NATIONAL CHAMPION**

3/19 1 Duke
16 Campbell — Duke 82-56
3/19 8 Texas — March 21 Iowa 98-92 — Duke 75-62
9 Iowa — **Greensboro, NC**
— March 26 — Duke 81-69
3/19 5 Missouri
12 West Va. — Missouri 89-78
3/19 4 Seton Hall — March 21 Seton Hall 78-76 — Seton Hall 88-71
13 La Salle
— **Philadelphia, PA** March 28 — Duke 104-103 (ot)
3/20 6 Syracuse
11 Princeton — Syracuse 51-43
3/20 3 Massachusetts — March 22 Massachusetts 85-58 — Massachusetts 77-71 (ot)
14 Fordham — **Worchester, MA**
— March 26 — Kentucky 87-77
3/20 7 N.C.-Charlotte
10 Iowa St. — Iowa St. 76-74
3/20 2 Kentucky — March 22 Kentucky 88-69 — Kentucky 106-98
15 Old Dominion — **WEST**

— **Minneapolis, MN** April 4 — Duke 81-78

3/20 1 UCLA
16 Robert Morris — UCLA 73-53
3/20 8 Louisville — March 22 Louisville 81-58 — UCLA 85-69
9 Wake Forest — **Tempe, AZ**
— March 26 — UCLA 85-78
3/20 5 DePaul
12 New Mexico St. — New Mexico St. 81-73
3/20 4 Oklahoma — March 22 S'western La. 87-83 — New Mexico St. 81-73
13 Southwestern La.
— **Albuquerque, NM** March 28 — Indiana 106-79
3/19 6 Georgetown
11 South Florida — Georgetown 75-60
3/19 3 Florida St. — March 21 Florida St. 78-68 — Florida St. 78-68
14 Montana — **Boise, ID**
— March 26 — Indiana 85-74
3/19 7 Louisiana St.
10 Brigham Young — Louisiana St. 94-83
3/19 2 Indiana — March 21 Indiana 94-55 — Indiana 89-79
15 Eastern Ill.

1992-93

AT A GLANCE

NCAA Champion: North Carolina (34-4; coached by Dean Smith; won ACC regular-season title by two games over Florida State with a 14-2 record).

NIT Champion: Minnesota (22-10; coached by Clem Haskins; finished in a tie for fifth place in Big Ten with a 9-9 record).

New Rule: Unsportsmanlike technical fouls, in addition to contact technical fouls, count toward the five fouls for player disqualification and the team fouls in reaching bonus free-throw situations.

NCAA Probation: Middle Tennessee State, Syracuse, Texas-Pan American, Tulsa.

NCAA Consensus First-Team All-Americans: Calbert Cheaney, F, Sr., Indiana; Anfernee Hardaway, G, Jr., Memphis State; Bobby Hurley, G, Sr., Duke; Jamal Mashburn, F, Jr., Kentucky; Chris Webber, F, Soph., Michigan.

National Player of the Year: Cheaney (22.4 ppg, 6.4 rpg, 54.9 FG%).

National Coaches of the Year: Vanderbilt's Eddie Fogler (28-6/AP, UPI, NABC, USBWA) and North Carolina's Dean Smith (34-4/Naismith).

North Carolina coach Dean Smith goes out of his way to emphasize senior leadership and always has his seniors featured on the cover of the Tar Heels' media guide even if they play sparingly. Carolina had several heroes on its way to capturing the national championship, but none loomed larger than senior forward George Lynch, who turned in double doubles (double figures in scoring and rebounding) in his last four games as the Tar Heels won the East Regional at East Rutherford, N.J., and the Final Four at New Orleans.

One of Carolina's four defeats was at Wake Forest when Demon Deacons guard Randy Childress erupted for 18 second-half points in less than four minutes. Carolina almost had another setback, but the Tar Heels erased a 19-point deficit with less than nine minutes remaining against Florida State to upend the Seminoles, 82-77. The biggest comeback of the season, however, came when Virginia Commonwealth overcame a 26-point deficit midway through the second half to post a 95-91 overtime triumph at South Florida. Guard Kenny Harris, a transfer from North Carolina, tallied 30 points in the final 15 minutes for VCU.

Florida State became the only school in history to have five active 1,000-point career scorers on their roster at the same time (no transfers from other four-year schools)—Douglas Edwards, Rodney Dobard, Sam Cassell, Chuck Graham and Bob Sura. Cassell was a junior college transfer. . . . Georgia Tech (19-11) averaged 11 defeats annually over the last five seasons despite having an NBA first-round draft choice each year. The Yellow Jackets ended defending NCAA champion Duke's 23-game winning streak, 80-79. . . . Duke's Bobby Hurley finished his career with an NCAA-record 1,076 assists. He had 33 games with at least 10 scoring feeds.

Iowa had a legitimate shot at the Big Ten title until forward Chris Street, the Hawkeyes' leading rebounder, died in an auto accident. . . . Wisconsin's Michael Finley set a Big Ten record with 10 steals against Purdue. . . . Purdue compiled a 9-5 homecourt record for the Boilermakers' worst winning percentage (.643) in Mackey Arena since the 14,123-seat facility opened in 1967-68. One of their homecourt defeats was to Northwestern, 62-59, when the Wildcats snapped a 41-game road losing streak. . . . Indiana coach Bob Knight was suspended for one game after a sideline outburst in a victory against Notre Dame. During the tirade, Knight screamed at his son, Pat, and kicked him in the leg.

Mississippi Valley State guard Alphonso Ford finished his Division I career as the only player to score more than 700 points and average more than 25 points per game in each of four seasons. . . . Connecticut's Scott Burrell finished his career as the tallest player (6-7) to amass more than 300 steals. He had 310. Burrell is the only individual to be a first-round selec-

1992–93 INDIVIDUAL LEADERS

SCORING

PLAYER	PTS.	AVG.
Guy, Texas-Pan Am.	556	29.3
Rider, UNLV	814	29.1
Best, Tenn. Tech	799	28.5
Baker, Hartford	792	28.3
Hunter Jackson St.	907	26.7
Ford, Miss. Valley St.	728	26.0
Edwards, Wright St.	757	25.2
Ross, Appa. St.	683	24.4
Robinson, Purdue	676	24.1
Sykes, Grambling St.	644	23.9

REBOUNDING

PLAYER	REB.	AVG.
Kidd, Middle Tenn. St.	386	14.8
Scales, Southern (La.)	393	12.7
Jackson, Nicholls St.	325	12.5
Dunkley, Delaware	367	12.2
Callahan, Northeastern	340	12.1
Johnson, New Orleans	346	11.9
Rogers, Tenn. St.	339	11.7
Rose, Drexel	330	11.4
Smith, Providence	375	11.4
Brown, Colgate	317	11.3

ASSISTS

PLAYER	AST.	AVG.
Crawford, New Mex. St.	310	9.1
Thomas, UNLV	248	8.6
Woods, Wright St.	253	8.4
Hurley, Duke	262	8.2
Evans, Miss. St.	235	8.1
Kidd, California	222	7.7
Miller, Marquette	213	7.6
Haggerty, Baylor	189	7.3
Browne, Lamar	195	7.2
Capers, Arizona St.	200	7.1

BLOCKED SHOTS

PLAYER	BLK.	AVG.
Ratliff, Wyoming	124	4.4
Wright, Clemson	124	4.1
Outlaw, Houston	114	3.8
Rogers, Tenn. St.	93	3.2
Wilson, E. Mich.	96	3.2
Dunkley, Delaware	96	3.2
Dobard, Florida St.	111	3.2
Popa, Miami (Fla.)	85	3.1
Hart, Iona	80	3.1
Thurman, W. Ill.	83	3.1

STEALS

PLAYER	STL.	AVG.
CALIFORNIA	110	3.8
Goodman, Utah St.	102	3.8
Woods, Wright St.	109	3.6
Bright, Bucknell	94	3.2
Mee, W. Ky.	100	3.1
Myers, St. Francis (N.Y.)	81	3.1
Woods, Charleston	84	3.1
Johnson, Canisius	79	3.0
Peyton, Bucknell	88	3.0
Evans, Oklahoma	97	3.0

FIELD GOAL PERCENTAGE

PLAYER	FGM	FGA	PCT.
Outlaw, Houston	196	298	.658
Grant, Xavier	223	341	.654
Hart, Iona	151	231	.654
Parks, Duke	161	247	.652
Trent, Ohio	194	298	.651
Nahar, Wright St.	190	296	.642
Peplowski, Mich. St.	161	252	.639
Lunsford, Ala. St.	142	223	.637
Kidd, Middle Tenn. St.	167	265	.630
Gay, Winthrop	194	309	.628

FREE THROW PERCENTAGE

PLAYER	FTM	FTA	PCT.
Grant, Utah	104	113	.920
Breslin, Holy Cross	100	111	.901
Lake, Montana	71	79	.899
Schmidt, Valparaiso	70	78	.897
Hartzell, UNC-G'boro	72	81	.889
Holman, Kent	69	78	.885
Ford, Kentucky	104	118	.881
Baldwin, N'western	66	75	.880
Burgess, Radford	109	124	.879
Houston, Tenn.	165	188	.878

THREE-POINT FIELD GOAL PERCENTAGE

PLAYER	FGM	FGA	PCT.
Anderson, Kent	44	82	.537
Moore, S. Houston St.	73	137	.533
Morton, Louisville	51	96	.531
Ford, Kentucky	101	191	.529
Graham, Indiana	57	111	.514

THREE-POINT FIELD GOALS PER GAME

PLAYER	FGM	AVG.
Haslett, S. Miss.	109	4.2
Smith, Arizona St.	113	4.2
Alberts, Akron	107	4.1
Veney, Lamar	106	3.9
Day, Radford	116	3.7

1992–93 TEAM LEADERS

SCORING OFFENSE

SCHOOL	PTS.	AVG.
Southern (La.)	3011	97.1
Northwestern St. (La.)	2357	90.7
UNLV	2592	89.4
Wright St.	2674	89.1
Oklahoma	2850	89.1

SCORING DEFENSE

SCHOOL	PTS.	AVG.
Princeton	1421	54.7
Yale	1444	55.5
Miami (Ohio)	1775	57.3
Cincinnati	1871	58.5
Southwest Missouri St.	1813	58.5

SCORING MARGIN

SCHOOL	OFF.	DEF.	MAR.
North Carolina	86.1	68.3	17.8
Kentucky	87.5	69.8	17.7
Cincinnati	74.5	58.5	16.0
Duke	86.4	71.2	15.2
Indiana	86.5	71.6	14.9

WON-LOST PERCENTAGE

SCHOOL	W-L	PCT.
North Carolina	34-4	.895
Indiana	31-4	.886
Kentucky	30-4	.882
New Orleans	26-4	.867
Michigan	31-5	.861

FIELD GOAL PERCENTAGE

SCHOOL	FGM	FGA	PCT.
Indiana	1076	2062	.522
Northeast Louisiana	1015	1946	.522
James Madison	848	1634	.519
Wright St.	987	1912	.516
Kansas	1109	2154	.515

FIELD GOAL PERCENTAGE DEFENSE

SCHOOL	FGM	FGA	PCT.
Marquette	634	1613	.393
George Washington	708	1794	.395
Arizona	710	1776	.400
Utah	737	1831	.403

FREE THROW PERCENTAGE

SCHOOL	FTM	FTA	PCT.
Utah	476	602	.791
Charleston Southern	408	526	.776
Valparaiso	412	532	.774
Indiana St.	445	580	.767
Brigham Young	697	909	.767

REBOUND MARGIN

SCHOOL	OWN	OPP.	MAR.
Massachusetts	43.9	32.8	11.2
Iowa	42.8	31.7	11.1
Idaho	39.6	29.3	10.3
Arizona	43.1	34.2	9.0
North Carolina	41.1	32.2	8.9

THREE-POINT FIELD GOAL PERCENTAGE

SCHOOL	FGM	FGA	PCT.
Valparaiso	214	500	.428
Princeton	204	479	.426
Indiana	197	464	.425
Kent	162	384	.422
Miami (Ohio)	218	522	.418

THREE-POINT FIELD GOALS PER GAME

SCHOOL	FGM	AVG.
Lamar	271	10.0
Kentucky	340	10.0
Arizona St.	263	9.4
UNC-Asheville	235	8.7
Southern Cal	259	8.6

tion by both the NBA (20th pick overall by the Charlotte Hornets) and major league baseball (righthanded pitcher was 26th pick overall by the Seattle Mariners as a high school senior in 1989). . . . Guard Terry Dehere became the first Seton Hall player since 1953 to earn a spot on an NCAA consensus first- or second-team All-American squad. . . . Georgetown incurred its worst ever finish in the Big East (eighth place) one year after finishing in a tie for first.

Oklahoma State center Bryant Reeves became the first player to lead the Big Eight in scoring, rebounding and field-goal shooting since Kansas' Wilt Chamberlain achieved the feat in 1956-57. . . . Marquette's Jim McIlvaine blocked 13 shots in a game against Northeastern Illinois. . . . J.R. Rider set a UNLV Division I school record with 44 points against Nevada-Reno. UNLV's 59-game homecourt winning streak was ended by Louisville, 90-86.

Towson State's Devin Boyd (46 points at Maryland-Baltimore County), Wright State's Bill Edwards (45 vs. Morehead State) and Portland's Matt Houle (43 vs. San Francisco) established school Division I single-game scoring standards. Boyd's barrage is a Big South Conference standard.. . . Rider (29.1 ppg), Hartford's Vin Baker (28.3), Edwards (25.2), Appalachian State's Billy Ross (24.4), Weber State's Stan Rose (23.2) and Long Beach State's Lucious Harris (23.1) set school Division I records for highest scoring average in a single season.

Tennessee became the first school ever to have nine successive seasons with one or more players scoring at least 600 points. The Volunteers' principal point producers in that stretch were Michael Brooks, Tony White, Dyron Nix and Allan Houston. Despite the presence of so many prolific scorers, the Vols didn't win an NCAA Tournament game in that span and posted just two winning SEC records. . . . Tennessee State, which compiled a 4-24 record the previous season, improved by 14 1/2 games to 19-10. Tennessee State, coached by Frankie Allen, captured the Ohio Valley Conference regular-sea-

son crown after finishing in last place the previous year. . . . George Washington and Western Kentucky finished in the Top 20 of a final wire-service poll for the first time since 1955 and 1971, respectively. GWU participated in the NCAA Tournament for the first time since 1961. . . . Forward Tony Dunkin of Coastal Carolina in the Big South Conference became the only player to be named MVP four times in a Division I league. He originally signed with Jacksonville, but left the Dolphins' program before ever playing for them.

North Carolina (34-4, coached by Dean Smith), Michigan (31-5, Steve Fisher), Vanderbilt (28-6, Eddie Fogler), Northeast Louisiana (26-5, Mike Vining) and Colgate (18-10, Jack Bruen) had their winningest seasons in school history. New Orleans (26-4, Tim Floyd) tied its school single-season record for most victories. . . . Vandy made its first Top 20 appearance in a final wire-service poll since 1974. Guard Billy McCaffrey became the first Vanderbilt player since 1966 to earn a spot on an NCAA consensus first- or second-team All-American squad.

Arkansas closed out playing in historic Barnhill Arena on a sour note when the Razorbacks' 36-game conference winning streak at home was snapped by Auburn, 100-89, as the Tigers shot 74 percent from the floor in the second half. . . . Lamar had an NCAA-record 23 three-pointers in a 103-76 victory over Louisiana Tech. Lamar's Keith Veney had two games with 11 three-pointers in a nine-day span in early February against Prairie View A&M and Arkansas-Little Rock. Veney transferred after the season to Marshall. . . . Texas-Pan American's Greg Guy, who averaged a mere 3.3 points per game the previous season in three games for Fresno State before transferring, became the only national scoring champion to average fewer than 14 the season before capturing the scoring title (29.3 ppg).

Drake's Curt Smith became the first player in Missouri Valley Conference history to lead the league in scoring, assists and steals in the

A distressed Jason Kidd disputes a call.

years. . . . New Hampshire lost more than 20 games for the seventh straight season. . . . Maryland-Eastern Shore's Rob Chavez became a novelty of sorts as the first white coach at a predominantly black Division I school.

A big story was 29-year-old Todd Bozeman, who was promoted at California following a controversial midseason firing of Lou Campanelli. For the first time in its 66-year history, the National Association of Basketball Coaches publicly condemned the dismissal of one of its member coaches. The NABC's principal concern was the absence of due process after Campanelli was accused of verbally abusing the Cal players. Campanelli, who I think did an outstanding job rejuvenating Cal basketball, subsequently filed a $5 million lawsuit against the school, charging the administration violated due process by not properly warning him that it disapproved of his treatment of players.

same season. . . . SMU, coached by John Shumate, captured the SWC regular-season title just one year after finishing in seventh place. . . . Western Kentucky lost 12 consecutive times to Louisville in their series until clipping the Cardinals, 78-77. WKU made its first Top 20 appearance in a final wire-service poll since 1971. . . . Louisiana Tech's string of nine consecutive 20-win seasons ended abruptly when the Bulldogs posted a 7-21 record. . . . New Orleans' Ervin Johnson grabbed a school-record 27 rebounds in a game against Lamar.

Fordham defeated St. John's, 60-55, breaking a 23-game losing streak in the Rams' series with the Redmen. . . . Princeton, coached by Pete Carril, led the nation in team defense for the fifth consecutive season and 11th time in 18 years. . . . Columbia (16-10), coached by Jack Rohan, compiled its first winning record in 11

1992-93 FINAL NATIONAL POLLS

AP	UPI	USA/CNN	SCHOOL (RECORD)	HEAD COACH
1	1	5	Indiana (31-4)	Bob Knight
2	4	3	Kentucky (30-4)	Rick Pitino
3	3	2	Michigan (31-5)	Steve Fisher
4	2	1	North Carolina (34-4)	Dean Smith
5	5	12	Arizona (24-4)	Lute Olson
6	6	11	Seton Hall (28-7)	P.J. Carlesimo
7	7	6	Cincinnati (27-5)	Bob Huggins
8	8	8	Vanderbilt (28-6)	Eddie Fogler
9	9	4	Kansas (29-7)	Roy Williams
10	10	9	Duke (24-8)	Mike Krzyzewski
11	11	7	Florida State (25-10)	Pat Kennedy
12	12	10	Arkansas (22-9)	Nolan Richardson
13	13	19	Iowa (23-9)	Tom Davis
14	16	22	Massachusetts (24-7)	John Calipari
15	14	15	Louisville (22-9)	Denny Crum
16	15	14	Wake Forest (21-9)	Dave Odom
17	18	–	New Orleans (20-10)	Tim Floyd
18	19	–	Georgia Tech (19-11)	Bobby Cremins
19	17	20	Utah (24-7)	Rick Majerus
20	24	16	Western Kentucky (20-11)	Ralph Willard
21	–	–	New Mexico (24-7)	Dave Bliss
22	20	–	Purdue (18-10)	Gene Keady
23	22	–	Oklahoma State (20-9)	Eddie Sutton
24	25	–	New Mexico State (26-8)	Neil McCarthy
25	21	–	UNLV (21-8)	Rollie Massimino
–	–	13	Temple (20-13)	John Chaney
–	–	17	California (21-9)	Todd Bozeman*
–	23	18	Virginia (21-10)	Jeff Jones
–	–	21	George Washington (21-9)	Mike Jarvis
–	–	23	Xavier (24-6)	Pete Gillen
–	–	24	UCLA (22-11)	Jim Harrick
–	–	25	Minnesota (22-10)	Clem Haskins

*Bozeman coached the Bears' last 13 games (11-2 record) after replacing Lou Campanelli.

1993 NCAA Tournament

Summary: George Lynch, North Carolina's top rebounder and second-leading scorer, made four big plays in the closing moments of the title game. With Michigan leading, 67-66, he and Eric Montross blocked away a driving layup by Jimmy King. That led to a fastbreak basket by Derrick Phelps and put the Tar Heels ahead to stay with just over three minutes remaining. After a missed Michigan shot, Lynch hit a turnaround jumper from the middle of the lane with 2:28 remaining to increase Carolina's lead to 70-67. On an inbounds play after UNC regained possession, Lynch lofted a perfect pass to Montross for a dunk. The Wolverines rallied to trim the deficit to 73-71 before Lynch and Phelps trapped Chris Webber on the sideline with just 11 seconds remaining and Michigan's consensus first-team All-American called a fateful timeout his team did not have. Donald Williams wrapped the game up with four consecutive free throws.

Outcome for Defending Champion: Duke's streak of five consecutive trips to the Final Four ended when the Blue Devils lost against California in the second round of the Midwest Regional (82-77) despite Grant Hill's eight steals. Duke guard Bobby Hurley was thwarted in his bid to become the first player to start four consecutive NCAA finals, but he is the only player to be credited with more than 125 assists in the tournament. He had 145 scoring feeds in 20 playoff games. Hurley also has more career three-pointers in the NCAA playoffs than anyone (42).

Star Gazing: Final Four Most Outstanding Player Donald Williams scored 25 points in each Final Four game for North Carolina to become the first guard to score at least 25 in both the national semifinals and final since Rick Mount for runner-up Purdue in 1969. The previous guard for a championship team to score at least 25 points in both the national semifinals and final was UCLA's Gail Goodrich in 1965.

Biggest Upsets: In terms of point spreads, Arizona's 64-61 first-round defeat in the West Regional against 20-point underdog Santa Clara was the biggest upset in NCAA playoff history. The Wildcats, ranked fifth by AP entering the tournament, lost against Santa Clara although they scored 25 consecutive points in a 10-minute span bridging the first and second halves. The setback gave Lute Olson five opening-round defeats as coach at Arizona and lowered his record to 2-8 in down-to-the-wire tourney games decided in overtime or in regulation by fewer than six points. . . . Another first-round shocker was Georgia Tech getting smothered by Southern (93-78), leaving Bobby Cremins of the Yellow Jackets as the only coach to ever lose as many as five playoff games against opponents with double-digit seeds.

One and Only: Williams is the only player to average fewer than four points per game as a freshman and then be named Final Four Most Outstanding Player the next season as a sophomore. After averaging an unsightly 2.2 points per game for North Carolina in 1991-92, he finished with a 14.3-point average in 1992-93. . . . Dean Smith became the first coach in NCAA Tournament history to reach the 50-win plateau in playoff competition when he raised his record of playoff appearances to 23 and North Carolina won its opening game for the 13th consecutive year.

Quote of Note: Webber's family took his mental lapse in stride and showed time heals all wounds when his father, Mayce, acquired a vanity license plate that said "Timeout," a reference to his son's excruciating blunder. "It's no big deal," the younger Webber said. "I'm not happy it happened. But I know it's going to help me in some way. It made me a man. It made me grow up a lot faster than if it hadn't happened."

Numbers Game: Purdue forward Glenn Robinson had the highest-scoring game of the tourney when he tossed in 36 points in a first-round loss against Rhode Island. . . . Carolina's Smith and the other three coaches at the Final Four—Michigan's Steve Fisher, Kentucky's Rick

1992-93 NCAA CHAMPION: N. CAROLINA

SEASON STATISTICS OF NORTH CAROLINA REGULARS

PLAYER	POS.	CL.	G.	FG%	FT%	PPG	RPG
Eric Montross	C	Jr.	38	.615	.684	15.8	7.6
George Lynch	F	Sr.	38	.501	.667	14.7	9.6
Donald Williams	G	So.	37	.458	.829	14.3	1.9
Brian Reese	F	Jr.	35	.507	.692	11.4	3.6
Derrick Phelps	G	Jr.	36	.457	.675	8.1	4.4
Pat Sullivan	F	Jr.	38	.518	.789	6.4	2.4
Kevin Salvadori	C-F	Jr.	38	.458	.704	4.5	3.6
Henrik Rodl	G	Sr.	38	.496	.658	4.3	1.5
Matt Wenstrom	C	Sr.	33	.557	.593	2.5	1.4
Scott Cherry	G	Sr.	33	.606	.714	2.1	0.7
Dante Calabria	G	Fr.	35	.462	.778	1.8	0.8
TEAM TOTALS			38	.506	.706	86.1	41.1

Three-point field goals leader: Williams (83 of 199, .417). **Assists leaders:** Phelps 196, Rodl 136, Reese 83. **Blocked shots leaders:** Montross 47, Salvadori 45. **Steals leaders:** Lynch 89, Phelps 82.

1993 FINAL FOUR CHAMPIONSHIP GAME

NEW ORLEANS, LA

N. CAROLINA (77)	MIN.	FG-A	FT-A	REB.	A.	PF.	PTS.
Reese	27	2-7	4-4	5	3	1	8
Lynch	28	6-12	0-0	10	1	3	12
Montross	31	5-11	6-9	5	0	2	16
Phelps	36	4-6	1-2	3	6	0	9
Williams	31	8-12	4-4	1	1	1	25
Sullivan	14	1-2	1-2	1	1	2	3
Salvadori	18	0-0	2-2	4	1	1	2
Rodl	11	1-4	0-0	0	0	0	2
Calabria	1	0-0	0-0	0	0	0	0
Wenstrom	2	0-1	0-0	0	0	0	0
Cherry	1	0-0	0-0	0	0	0	0
TOTALS	200	27-55	18-23	29	13	10	77

FG%: .491. **FT%:** .789. **Three-point goals:** 5 of 11 (Reese 0-1, Phelps 0-1, Williams 5-7, Rodl 0-2). **Blocks:** 4. **Turnovers:** 10 (Phelps 5). **Steals:** 7.

MICHIGAN (71)	MIN.	FG-A	FT-A	REB.	A.	PF.	PTS.
Webber	33	11-18	1-2	11	1	2	23
Jackson	20	2-3	2-2	1	1	5	6
Howard	34	3-8	1-1	7	3	3	7
Rose	40	5-12	0-0	1	4	3	12
King	34	6-13	2-2	6	4	2	15
Riley	14	1-3	0-0	3	1	1	2
Pelinka	17	2-4	0-0	2	1	1	6
Talley	14	0-0	0-0	0	1	1	0
Voskuil	4	0-1	0-0	0	1	0	0
Team				2			
TOTALS	200	30-62	6-7	33	17	18	71

FG%: .484. **FT%:** .857. **Three-point goals:** 5 of 15 (Webber 0-1, Rose 2-6, King 1-5, Pelinka 2-3). **Blocks:** 4. **Turnovers:** 14 (Rose 6). **Steals:** 4. **Halftime:** North Carolina 42-36.

NATIONAL SEMIFINALS

MICHIGAN (81): Webber 10-17 7-9 27, Jackson 4-7 3-5 11, Howard 6-12 5-7 17, Rose 6-16 6-7 18, King 1-3 0-0 2, Riley 2-4 0-0 4, Pelinka 0-1 2-2 2, Voskuil 0-0 0-0 0. Team 29-61 (.475) 23-30 (.767) 81.

KENTUCKY (78): Mashburn 10-18 5-9 26, Prickett 1-6 7-7 9, Dent 2-6 2-2 6, Ford 3-10 4-4 12, Brown 6-10 0-0 16, Rhodes 0-1 1-2 1, Riddick 2-4 0-1 4, Martinez 0-3 0-0 0, Brassow 0-0 0-0 0, Delk 1-3 2-2 4, Braddy 0-0 0-0 0. Team 25-61 (.410) 21-26 (.808) 78.

Three-point goals: Michigan 0-4, Kentucky 7-21 (.333).

Halftime: Michigan 40-35. **Regulation:** Tied 71-71.

KANSAS (68): Hancock 2-5 2-2 6, Scott 3-5 2-2 8, Pauley 2-5 1-1 5, Walters 7-15 0-0 19, Jordan 7-13 0-0 19, Rayford 0-0 0-0 0, Woodberry 2-5 0-0 4, Richey 1-4 0-0 2, Ostertag 0-2 2-2 2, Gurley 1-2 0-0 3, Pearson 0-1 0-0 0. Team 25-57 (.439) 7-7 (1.000) 68.

NORTH CAROLINA (78): Lynch 5-12 4-6 14, Reese 3-5 1-2 7, Montross 9-14 5-8 23, Phelps 1-3 1-2 3, Williams 7-11 6-6 25, Sullivan 0-2 0-0 0, Rodl 0-0 0-0 0, Cherry 0-0 0-0 0, Salvadori 3-5 0-0 6, Wenstrom 0-0 0-0 0, Calabria 0-0 0-0 0, Davis 0-0 0-0 0, Stephenson 0-0 0-0 0, Geth 0-0 0-0 0. Team 28-52 (.538) 17-24 (.708) 78.

Three-point goals: Kansas 11-20 (.550), North Carolina 5-7 (.714). **Halftime:** North Carolina 40-36.

ALL-TOURNAMENT TEAM

George Lynch, F, Sr., North Carolina
Jamal Mashburn, F, Jr., Kentucky
Eric Montross, C, Jr., North Carolina
Chris Webber, F, Soph., Michigan
Donald Williams, G, Soph., North Carolina*
*Named Most Outstanding Player

Pitino and Kansas' Roy Williams–had all won more than 70 percent of their NCAA playoff games at that stage in their careers. Fisher, improving his tourney record to 17-3 (.850) by reaching the national final for the third time in five years, moved ahead of Hall of Famer John Wooden (47-10, .825) for the highest winning percentage in tournament history (minimum of 20 games). . . . Three No. 1 seeds reached the Final Four for the only time since seeding was introduced in 1979. . . . The Big East suffered a down year when consecutive tourney appearances for Georgetown (14) and Syracuse (10) came to an end. Syracuse was on NCAA proba-

tion . . . . California freshman guard Jason Kidd's inside baskets on deft moves in the closing seconds helped boost the Bears to victories over two schools making their 10th consecutive NCAA playoff appearance–Duke and LSU. . . . Florida State's Sam Cassell converted all seven of his three-point field-goal attempts in a 94-63 trouncing of Tulane in the second round of the Southeast Regional. . . . East Carolina became the eighth school to participate in the NCAA Tournament despite entering the playoffs with a losing record (13-16 after winning Colonial Athletic Association Tournament). The Pirates' first-round opponent was North Carolina, which handed them their 39th defeat in as many games against the four schools from their state that were charter members of the ACC. . . . The ACC and Big Eight tied for the most playoff representatives with six apiece. The ACC notched at least 12 tourney triumphs for the fifth consecutive year. . . . Manhattan and George Washington made their first NCAA playoff appearance since 1958 and 1961, respectively. . . . Temple became the first at-large team in seven years to win fewer than 60 percent of its games but still reach a regional semifinal. The Owls advanced all the way to the West Regional final, where they blew an eight-point, second-half lead and lost against Michigan. . . . Tennessee's Allan Houston (2,801 points) joined LSU's Pete Maravich (3,667 from 1968-70), Portland State's Freeman Williams (3,249 from 1975-78), Texas Southern's Harry Kelly (3,066 from 1980-83) and Houston's Otis Birdsong (2,832 from 1974-77) as players to score more than 2,800 points in their major-college careers but never participate in the NCAA Tournament. . . . Arkansas' Darrell Hawkins had eight steals in a opening-round victory over Holy Cross.

What If: Webber absorbed a good deal of grief after his baffling call for a timeout prevented Michigan from having an opportunity to tie the score or take the lead against North Carolina. But why wasn't a Wolverine guard back to bring the ball up after Webber grabbed a rebound off a missed free throw? Webber became the fourth player to secure NCAA All-Tournament team status in back-to-back sea-

sons without winning a national championship either year as Michigan became the third school to lose two consecutive tourney finals. . . . Indiana was a No. 1 seed entering the tournament, but many experts didn't pick the Hoosiers to reach the Final Four, let alone win the national crown, after star forward Alan Henderson was hampered by a knee injury. . . . Georgia Tech (19-11, without Kenny Anderson), Louisiana State (22-11, Shaquille O'Neal) and UCLA (22-11, Tracy Murray) might have fared better in the playoffs if standout players had exercised their remaining eligibility instead of defecting to the NBA. . . . Ohio State (15-13, without Jim Jackson) and Southern Cal (18-12, Harold Miner) probably would have participated in the NCAA Tournament instead of the NIT if All-Americans didn't leave school early for the NBA.

Overcoming Adversity: North Carolina, which finished with a 34-4 record, lost back-to-back ACC road games at Wake Forest (88-62) and Duke (81-67) by a total of 40 points. The Tar Heels' other two defeats were against Michigan (79-78 at Rainbow Classic in Honolulu) and Georgia Tech (77-75 in ACC Tournament final when Phelps missed the game because of an injury).

Scoring Leader: Donald Williams, North Carolina (118 points, 19.7 ppg).

Highest Scoring Average: Calbert Cheaney, Indiana (106 points, 26.5 ppg).

Rebounding Leader: Chris Webber, Michigan (68 rebounds, 11.3 rpg).

1993 CHAMPIONSHIP BRACKET

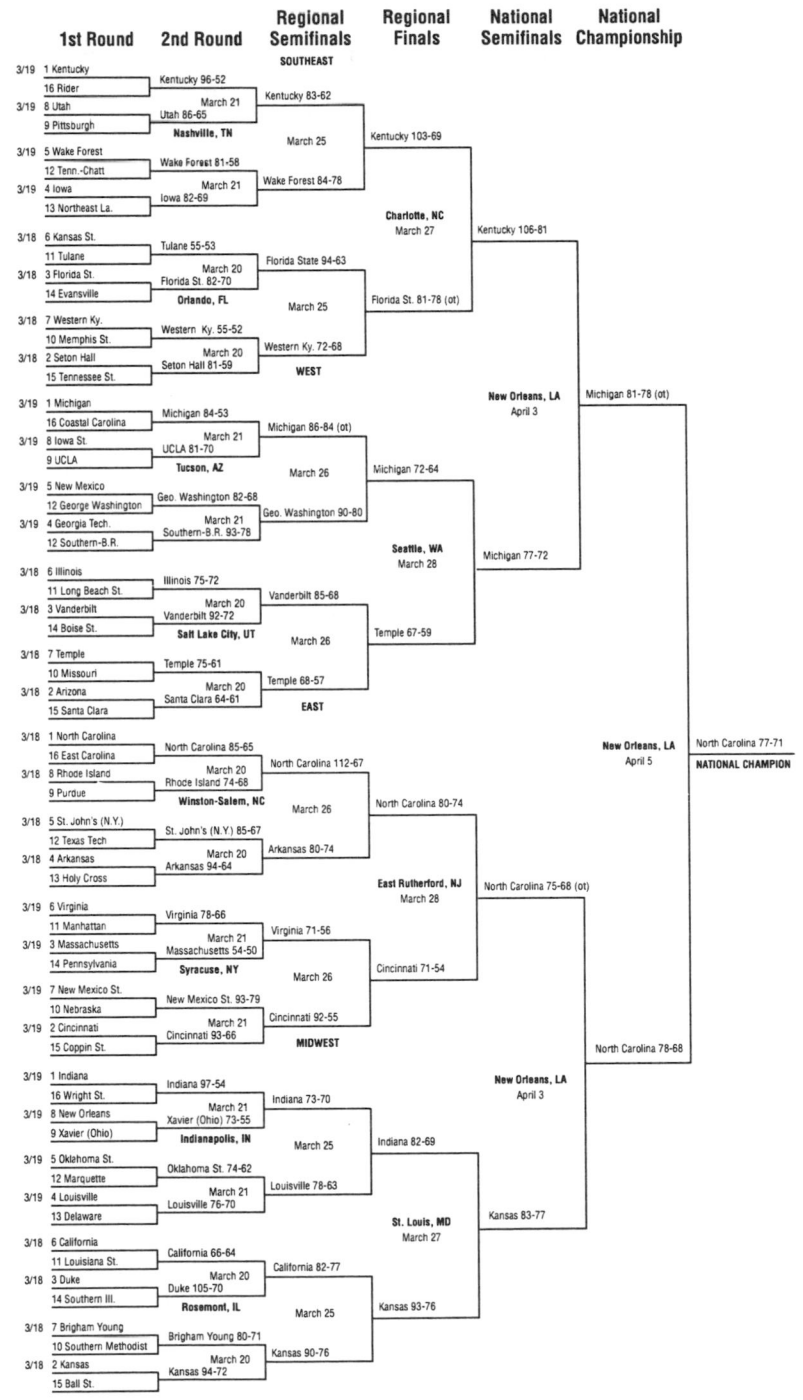

1st Round	2nd Round	Regional Semifinals	Regional Finals	National Semifinals	National Championship

SOUTHEAST

3/19 1 Kentucky
16 Rider
Kentucky 96-52
3/19 8 Utah
9 Pittsburgh
March 21
Utah 86-65
Nashville, TN
Kentucky 83-62
March 25
Kentucky 103-69

3/19 5 Wake Forest
12 Tenn.-Chatt.
Wake Forest 81-58
3/19 4 Iowa
13 Northeast La.
March 21
Iowa 82-69
Wake Forest 84-78

Charlotte, NC
March 27
Kentucky 106-81

3/19 6 Kansas St.
11 Tulane
Tulane 55-53
3/18 3 Florida St.
14 Evansville
March 20
Florida St. 82-70
Orlando, FL
Florida State 94-63
March 25
Florida St. 81-78 (ot)

3/18 7 Western Ky.
10 Memphis St.
Western Ky. 55-52
3/18 2 Seton Hall
15 Tennessee St.
March 20
Seton Hall 81-59
Western Ky. 72-68

WEST

New Orleans, LA
April 3
Michigan 81-78 (ot)

3/19 1 Michigan
16 Coastal Carolina
Michigan 84-53
3/19 8 Iowa St.
9 UCLA
March 21
UCLA 81-70
Tucson, AZ
Michigan 86-84 (ot)
March 26
Michigan 72-64

3/19 5 New Mexico
12 George Washington
Geo. Washington 82-68
3/19 4 Georgia Tech.
12 Southern-B.R.
March 21
Southern-B.R. 93-78
Geo. Washington 90-80

Seattle, WA
March 28
Michigan 77-72

3/18 6 Illinois
11 Long Beach St.
Illinois 75-72
3/18 3 Vanderbilt
14 Boise St.
March 20
Vanderbilt 92-72
Salt Lake City, UT
Vanderbilt 85-68
March 26
Temple 67-59

3/18 7 Temple
10 Missouri
Temple 75-61
3/18 2 Arizona
15 Santa Clara
March 20
Santa Clara 64-61
Temple 68-57

EAST

New Orleans, LA
April 5
North Carolina 77-71

NATIONAL CHAMPION

3/18 1 North Carolina
16 East Carolina
North Carolina 85-65
3/18 8 Rhode Island
9 Purdue
March 20
Rhode Island 74-68
Winston-Salem, NC
North Carolina 112-67
March 26
North Carolina 80-74

3/18 5 St. John's (N.Y.)
12 Texas Tech
St. John's (N.Y.) 85-67
3/18 4 Arkansas
13 Holy Cross
March 20
Arkansas 94-64
Arkansas 80-74

East Rutherford, NJ
March 28
North Carolina 75-68 (ot)

3/19 6 Virginia
11 Manhattan
Virginia 78-66
3/19 3 Massachusetts
14 Pennsylvania
March 21
Massachusetts 54-50
Syracuse, NY
Virginia 71-56
March 26
Cincinnati 71-54

3/19 7 New Mexico St.
10 Nebraska
New Mexico St. 93-79
3/19 2 Cincinnati
15 Coppin St.
March 21
Cincinnati 93-66
Cincinnati 92-55

MIDWEST

North Carolina 78-68

New Orleans, LA
April 3
Kansas 83-77

3/19 1 Indiana
16 Wright St.
Indiana 97-54
3/19 8 New Orleans
9 Xavier (Ohio)
March 21
Xavier (Ohio) 73-55
Indianapolis, IN
Indiana 73-70
March 25
Indiana 82-69

3/19 5 Oklahoma St.
12 Marquette
Oklahoma St. 74-62
3/19 4 Louisville
13 Delaware
March 21
Louisville 76-70
Louisville 78-63

St. Louis, MO
March 27
Kansas 83-77

3/18 6 California
11 Louisiana St.
California 66-64
3/18 3 Duke
14 Southern Ill.
March 20
Duke 105-70
Rosemont, IL
California 82-77
March 25
Kansas 93-76

3/18 7 Brigham Young
10 Southern Methodist
Brigham Young 80-71
3/18 2 Kansas
15 Ball St.
March 20
Kansas 94-72
Kansas 90-76

1993-94

AT A GLANCE

NCAA Champion: Arkansas (31-3; coached by Nolan Richardson; won SEC Western Division title by two games over Alabama with a 14-2 record).

NIT Champion: Villanova (20-12; coached by Steve Lappas; finished in a three-way tie for fourth place in Big East with a 10-8 record).

New Rules: Shot clock reduced to 35 seconds from 45, five-second defensive pressure call is eliminated, game clock stopped in the last minute after every basket and trash-talking prohibited.

NCAA Consensus First-Team All-Americans: Grant Hill, F-G, Sr., Duke; Jason Kidd, G, Soph., California; Donyell Marshall, F, Jr., Connecticut; Glenn Robinson, F, Jr., Purdue; Clifford Rozier, C-F, Jr., Louisville.

National Player of the Year: Robinson (30.3 ppg, 10.1 rpg).

National Coaches of the Year: Purdue's Gene Keady (29-5/shared NABC); Arkansas' Nolan Richardson (31-3/Naismith, shared NABC); Saint Louis' Charlie Spoonhour (23-6/USBWA), and Missouri's Norm Stewart (28-4/AP, UPI).

A glaring lack of fundamentals was apparent as shooting percentages continued to decrease. Free-throw shooting across the country dipped to 67.1 percent, the lowest mark since 1959. Teams shot an all-time low 34.5 percent from three-point range.

Purdue junior Glenn Robinson became the first Big Ten player to lead the country in scoring (30.3 points per game) since Purdue's Dave Schellhase in 1966. Robinson was at his best against the Big Ten's elite, scoring 73 in two games against Michigan and 72 in two outings against Indiana. Robinson's early departure to the NBA left the Patriot League as the only Division I conference in history ever to return two of the top three leading scorers in the country–Holy Cross' Rob Feaster (28 ppg) and Colgate's Tucker Neale (26.6 ppg).

Donyell Marshall, the first Connecticut player ever to become an NCAA consensus

Purdue's Glenn Robinson became the first Big Ten player since 1966 to lead the country in scoring.

first- or second-team All-American, hit 39 of 40 free throws in averaging 37.7 points per game in three contests against St. John's as the Redmen absorbed their first losing record since 1962-63. . . . Houston's streak of 34 consecutive non-losing

Connecticut forward Donyell Marshall concentrates at the free throw line.

seasons came to an halt when the Cougars compiled a 8-19 record. . . . Kentucky tied an NCAA record by overcoming a 31-point, second-half deficit in a 99-95 victory at LSU (see accompanying box). The deflating defeat contributed to ending LSU's streak of 17 consecutive non-losing records. . . . Louisville's Clifford Rozier set an NCAA record by hitting all 15 of his field-goal attempts in a game against Eastern Kentucky. . . . Auburn's Wesley Person finished his career with 2,066 points to join his brother, Chuck (2,311), as the only sibling combination to score more than 2,000 for the same school.

Cleveland State (39) and Kent (36) established an NCAA standard for most points in overtime periods, both teams, when they combined for 75 in the Vikings' 104-101, four-overtime triumph. . . . Southern (La.) posted the widest margin of victory in major-college history (97 points) with a 154-57 victory over Patton College. . . . Dartmouth had nine different players hit a three-pointer, an NCAA record, in a game against Boston College. . . . Providence's Michael Smith set a Big East Conference record by grabbing 26 rebounds against Syracuse. . . . Vermont sophomore guard Eddie Benton set a school and North Atlantic Conference record with 54 points against Drexel.

Marist's Danny Basile converted all 60 of his free-throw attempts in Northeast Conference regular-season play. Teammate Izett Buchanan set a school record and Northeast Conference standard with 51 points at Long Island University. . . . Also establishing school single-game scoring records were Siena's Doremus Bennerman (51 points vs. Kansas State in NIT third-place game), Idaho's Orlando Lightfoot (50 at Gonzaga), Winthrop's Melvin Branham (45 at Charleston Southern) and Nebraska's Eric Piatkowski (42 vs. Oklahoma in Big Eight Tournament quarterfinals). Excluding Lightfoot, the remainder of Idaho's team scored just 19 points in a 76-69 setback at Gonzaga. . . . Western Carolina's Frankie King (26.9 ppg), Vermont's Benton (26.4), Siena's Bennerman (26), Marist's Buchanan (25.4), Idaho's Lightfoot (25.4), California's Lamond Murray (24.3), Arizona's Khalid Reeves (24.2) and Northern Iowa's Randy Blocker (23) set school Division I records for highest scoring average in a single season.

Cal's Murray and teammate Jason Kidd became the first Bears players since 1960 to earn spots on an NCAA consensus first- or second-team All-American squad. It was also the first Top 20 appearance in a final wire-service poll for Cal since 1960. . . . Missouri went unbeaten in the Big Eight after finishing in seventh place the previous year. . . . Guard Donnie Boyce scored 20 consecutive second-half points for Colorado and finished with 46 but it wasn't enough to prevent an 83-68 defeat at Oklahoma State.

Askia Jones exploded for a national-high and Big Eight Conference-record 62 points in just 28 minutes and tied an NCAA single-game

1993-94 INDIVIDUAL LEADERS

SCORING

PLAYER	PTS.	AVG.
Robinson, Purdue	1030	30.3
Feaster, Holy Cross	785	28.0
Scales, Southern	733	27.1
King, W. Carolina	752	26.9
Neale, Colgate	771	26.6
Benton, Vermont	687	26.4
Bennerman, Siena	858	26.0
Dumas, Mo.-Kansas City	753	26.0
Jones, Air Force	663	25.5
Buchanan, Marist	685	25.4
Trent, Ohio U.	837	25.4
Lightfoot, Idaho	710	25.4

REBOUNDING

PLAYER	REB.	AVG.
Lambert, Baylor	355	14.8
Scales, Southern	384	14.2
Kubel, N'western (La.)	341	13.1
Warren, Va. C'wealth	336	12.4
Rose, Drexel	371	12.4
Vaughn, Memphis	335	12.0
Jackson, Nicholls St.	311	12.0
Simon, New Orleans	355	11.8
Stewart, UNLV	256	11.6
Rogers, Tennessee St.	358	11.5
Smith, Providence	344	11.5

ASSISTS

PLAYER	AST.	AVG.
Kidd, California	272	9.1
Edwards, Texas A&M	265	8.8
Miller, Marquette	274	8.3
O'Bryant, Nevada	232	8.3
Abdullah, Providence	241	8.0
Nathan, Northeast La.	179	7.8
Smart, San Francisco	204	7.6
Pogue, Campbell	207	7.4

Thomas, UNLV	205	7.3
Haggerty, Baylor	161	7.3

BLOCKED SHOTS

PLAYER	BLK.	AVG.
Livingston, Howard	115	4.4
McIlvaine, Marquette	142	4.3
Ratliff, Wyoming	114	4.1
Vaughn, Memphis	107	3.8
Duncan, Wake Forest	124	3.8
Camby, Massachusetts	105	3.6
Cato, South Alabama	85	3.5
Marshall, Connecticut	111	3.3
McDonald, New Orleans	96	3.2
Fleury, UMBC	80	3.2

STEALS

PLAYER	STL.	AVG.
Griggs, S'western La.	120	4.0
Walker, San Francisco	109	3.9
Cradle, Long Island	79	3.8
Kidd, California	94	3.1
Tyler, Texas	87	3.1
Ceasar, LSU	80	3.0
Black, Texas-Pan Am	80	3.0
Thompson, Oklahoma St.	99	2.9
Robertson, Dayton	78	2.9
Golden, Tennessee	78	2.9
Walton, Alcorn St.	63	2.9

FIELD GOAL PERCENTAGE

PLAYER	FGM	FGA	PCT.
Atkinson, Long Beach St.	141	203	.695
Wade, SW Texas St.	232	356	.652
Miller, Mich. St.	162	249	.651
Thomas, Illinois	207	327	.633
Swinson, Auburn	234	371	.631
Ritter, James Madison	230	366	.628

Williamson, Arkansas	237	436	.626
Ardayfio, Army	180	289	.623
Lunsford, Alabama St.	163	263	.620
Rozier, Louisville	247	400	.618

FREE THROW PERCENTAGE

PLAYER	FGM	FGA	PCT.
Basile, Marist	84	89	.944
Evans, Troy St.	72	77	.935
Schmidt, Valparaiso	75	81	.926
Hildebrand, Liberty	149	161	.925
Culuko, James Madison	117	127	.921
Yoder, Colorado St.	107	117	.915
Ford, Kentucky	103	113	.912
Hoover, Notre Dame	76	84	.905
Cline, Morehead St.	73	81	.901
Tucker, N. Illinois	71	79	.899

THREE-POINT FIELD GOAL PERCENTAGE

PLAYER	FGM	FGA	PCT.
Kell, Evansville	62	123	.504
Santiago, Fresno St.	64	128	.500
Born, Tenn.-Chat.	67	135	.496
Young, Canisius	53	109	.486
Eisley, Boston College	91	188	.484

THREE-POINT FIELD GOALS PER GAME

PLAYER	FGM	AVG.
Brown, UC Irvine	122	4.7
Hicks, Coastal Carolina	115	4.4
Durden, Cincinnati	102	4.1
Haslett, Southern Miss.	112	3.7
Townes, La Salle	100	3.7
Ross, George Mason	99	3.7

standard with 14 three-pointers, boosting Kansas State to a 115-77 rout of visiting Fresno State in the NIT quarterfinals. Jones poured in 28 of his Big Eight-record 45 second-half points in the first 7:12 after intermission. His final total, spurred by nine consecutive successful three-point shots bridging the first and second halves, was the second-highest in major-college post-season history. . . . Texas, coached by Tom Penders, captured the SWC regular-season championship just one year after finishing in seventh place. . . . Texas-Pan American's Greg Guy (29.3 ppg in '93 to 19.2) became the only defending national scoring champion other than Temple's Bill Mlkvy (29.2 in '51 to 17.4 in '52) to have a scoring average decrease of more than 10 points per game.

Florida (29-8, coached by Lon Kruger), Wisconsin-Green Bay (27-7, Dick Bennett), Ohio University (25-8, Larry Hunter), Gonzaga (22-8, Dan Fitzgerald), Rider (21-9, Kevin Bannon) and Maine (20-9, Rudy Keeling) had their winningest seasons in school Division I history. Purdue (29-5, Gene Keady), Texas (26-8, Tom Penders), Siena (25-8, Mike Deane) and Canisius (22-7, John Beilein) tied their school single-season Division I marks for most victories.

Saint Louis compiled a 23-6 record to finish in a final wire-service poll for the first time since 1961. Fellow Great Midwest member Marquette compiled a 24-9 mark to finish in a final national poll for the first time since 1979. . . . Dayton's lone Great Midwest victory came against Saint

SCORING OFFENSE

SCHOOL	PTS.	AVG.
Southern (La.)	2727	101.0
Troy St.	2634	97.6
Arkansas	3176	93.4
Texas	3119	91.7
Murray St.	2611	90.0

SCORING DEFENSE

SCHOOL	PTS.	AVG.
Princeton	1361	52.3
Temple	1697	54.7
Wisconsin-Green Bay	1872	55.1
Alabama-Birmingham	1806	60.2
Marquette	2040	61.8

SCORING MARGIN

SCHOOL	OFF.	DEF.	MAR.
Arkansas	93.4	75.6	17.9
Connecticut	84.9	68.6	16.3
Arizona	89.3	74.4	14.9
Southern (La.)	101.0	87.7	13.3
North Carolina	85.6	72.4	13.2

WON-LOST PERCENTAGE

TEAM	W-L	PCT.
Arkansas	31-3	.912
Pennsylvania	25-3	.893
Missouri	28-4	.875
Charleston (S.C.)	24-4	.857
Connecticut	29-5	.853
Purdue	29-5	.853

FIELD GOAL PERCENTAGE

SCHOOL	FGM	FGA	PCT.
Auburn	854	1689	.506
Michigan St.	944	1875	.503
Radford	793	1580	.502
James Madison	890	1783	.499
North Carolina	1091	2188	.499

DEFENSIVE FIELD GOAL PERCENTAGE

SCHOOL	FGM	FGA	PCT.
Marquette	750	2097	.358
Temple	621	1686	.368
Wisconsin-Green Bay	664	1777	.374
Kansas	823	2147	.383
Alabama-Birmingham	661	1718	.385

FREE THROW PERCENTAGE

SCHOOL	FTM	FTA	PCT.
Colgate	511	665	.768
Wisconsin-Green Bay	462	607	.761
Iowa St.	521	687	.758
Davidson	529	704	.751
Vanderbilt	557	742	.751

REBOUND MARGIN

SCHOOL	OWN	OPP.	MAR.
Utah St.	38.4	29.8	8.6
North Carolina	43.7	35.3	8.5
Idaho	41.5	33.1	8.4
UCLA	43.9	36.2	7.7
Baylor	50.3	42.7	7.6

THREE-POINT FIELD GOAL PERCENTAGE

SCHOOL	FGM	FGA	PCT.
Indiana	182	401	.454
Robert Morris	139	323	.430
Evansville	244	570	.428
Oklahoma St.	258	619	.417
Montana	150	369	.407

THREE-POINT FIELD GOALS PER GAME

SCHOOL	FGM	AVG.
Troy St.	262	9.7
New Mexico	300	9.7
Vermont	240	8.9
Arkansas	301	8.9
Kentucky	301	8.9

SCORING DEFENSE

SCHOOL	PTS.	AVG.
Oklahoma A&M	1539	53.1
Duquesne	1551	53.5
Wyoming	1522	54.4
Oregon State	1585	54.7
Oklahoma City	1370	54.8

FIELD GOAL PERCENTAGE

SCHOOL	FGM	FGA	PCT.
George Washington	744	1632	.456
Holy Cross	871	2018	.432
Niagara	778	1817	.428
Maryland	669	1564	.428
Furman	990	2370	.418

Louis (82-77 in overtime) when guard Shawn Haughn hit all eight of his shots from beyond the three-point arc. . . . Valparaiso, ending its streak of 16 consecutive losing seasons, compiled a 20-8 record.

La Salle went 11-16 for its first losing record in 18 years. . . . Canisius captured the Metro Atlantic Athletic Conference regular-season crown after finishing in sixth place the previous year. . . . Pepperdine's WCC record of 38 consecutive victories against conference opponents (six in postseason tourney play) ended when the Waves were edged by San Francisco, 75-72.

Appalachian State's Ricky Need finished his four-year career with an NCAA record for field-goal shooting (69 percent, 412 of 597). . . . Clemson overcame a halftime deficit against North Carolina to defeat the Tar Heels after trailing at intermission against them for the first time since

1993-94 FINAL NATIONAL POLLS

AP	UPI	USA/CNN	SCHOOL (RECORD)	HEAD COACH
1	2	9	North Carolina (28-7)	Dean Smith
2	1	1	Arkansas (31-3)	Nolan Richardson
3	3	5	Purdue (29-5)	Gene Keady
4	4	7	Connecticut (29-5)	Jim Calhoun
5	5	6	Missouri (28-4)	Norm Stewart
6	6	2	Duke (28-6)	Mike Krzyzewski
7	8	13	Kentucky (27-7)	Rick Pitino
8	7	15	Massachusetts (28-7)	John Calipari
9	9	3	Arizona (29-6)	Lute Olson
10	10	10	Louisville (28-6)	Denny Crum
11	11	8	Michigan (24-8)	Steve Fisher
12	12	18	Temple (23-8)	John Chaney
13	13	12	Kansas (27-8)	Roy Williams
14	15	4	Florida (29-8)	Lon Kruger
15	14	14	Syracuse (23-7)	Jim Boeheim
16	16	–	California (22-8)	Todd Bozeman
17	17	22	UCLA (21-7)	Jim Harrick
18	18	16	Indiana (21-9)	Bob Knight
19	19	21	Oklahoma State (24-10)	Eddie Sutton
20	21	24	Texas (26-8)	Tom Penders
21	29	17	Marquette (24-9)	Kevin O'Neill
22	24	–	Nebraska (20-10)	Danny Nee
23	23	23	Minnesota (21-12)	Clem Haskins
24	22	–	Saint Louis (23-6)	Charlie Spoonhour
25	–	–	Cincinnati (22-10)	Bob Huggins
–	–	11	Boston College (23-11)	Jim O'Brien
–	–	19	Tulsa (23-8)	Tubby Smith
–	–	20	Maryland (18-12)	Gary Williams
–	25	–	UAB (22-8)	Gene Bartow
–	–	25	Pennsylvania (25-3)	Fran Dunphy

1954. . . . Former national coaches of the year Butch van Breda Kolff and Johnny Orr retired from Hofstra and Iowa State, respectively.

1994 NCAA Tournament

Summary: Arkansas, boasting a roster with 11 different players who had a season high in scoring of more than 10 points, ended a SEC dry spell in the NCAA playoffs. Despite having an average of three first-round NBA draft choices annually in 15 years since 1979, no current member of the 12-team SEC reached the NCAA Tournament championship game in that span although every school participated in the playoffs at least once. Arkansas' title vindicated coach Nolan Richardson, who probably would have been dismissed in 1987 after his second season with the Hogs if they didn't rally from a 21-point second-half deficit in the NIT to edge Arkansas State, 67-64, in overtime. But that wasn't the most strain he faced that year because his 16-year-old daughter, Yvonne, died of leukemia. Richardson was also a leading figure in a national controversy concerning alleged racial injustices. Pressure was also intense on Scotty Thur-

man with the shot clock winding down and the score tied with 40 seconds remaining when he lofted a three-point attempt over Duke's Antonio Lang that hit nothing but net. Thurman attributed his ability to get off such a high arc shot to an age-old drill shooting over a defender with a broomstick his coach at Ruston (La.) High School employed during practices. "He made a great play," Duke guard Chris Collins said of Thurman after the Razorbacks' 76-72 victory. "The national championship, less than a minute left, tie game–he made a great shot."

Outcome for Defending Champion: North Carolina's streak of 13 consecutive trips to a regional semifinal ended when the Tar Heels lost to Boston College in the second round. The Tar Heels (28-7) finished in second place in the ACC after incurring at least five league losses for the fourth time in six years. Their only non-conference setback was to Massachusetts in the Preseason NIT.

Star Gazing: Final Four Most Outstanding Player Corliss Williamson of Arkansas briefly surpassed Bill Walton's playoff field-goal shoot-

---

UK ERASES HUGE SECOND-HALF DEFICIT ON THE ROAD

KENTUCKY AT LOUISIANA STATE
FEBRUARY 14, 1994

In one of the most amazing comebacks of all time, Kentucky trailed by 31 points (68-37) with 15 1/2 minutes remaining in the second half at LSU before rallying to frustrate the Tigers, 99-95.

KENTUCKY (99)	FG-A	FT-A	REB.	PTS.
Tony Delk	3-8	1-2	7	9
Chris Harrison	3-4	0-1	2	8
Travis Ford	3-8	2-2	2	10
Andre Riddick	4-6	1-2	5	9
Rodrick Rhodes	3-9	4-6	3	11
Jeff Brassow	5-7	0-2	1	14
Jeff Sheppard	0-1	0-0	1	0
Anthony Epps	0-0	0-0	0	0
Jared Prickett	1-4	0-2	0	2
Walter McCarty	9-14	1-2	8	23
Gimel Martinez	6-10	1-2	3	13
Totals	**37-71**	**10-21**	**33**	**99**

FG%: .521. **FT%:** .476. **Three-point shooting:** 15 of 37 (Delk 2-7, Harrison 2-3, Ford 2-5, Rhodes 1-6, Brassow 4-6, McCarty 4-7, Martinez 0-3). **Assists:** 25 (Ford 12). **Steals:** 7. **Blocked Shots:** 4. **Turnovers:** 18 (Delk 5).

LSU (95)	FG-A	FT-A	REB.	PTS.
Jamie Brandon	3-10	6-8	8	13
Andre Owens	1-2	2-2	1	4
Sean Gipson	0-2	0-0	4	0
Ronnie Henderson	12-19	4-4	2	36
Lenear Burns	1-4	0-1	7	2
Clarence Ceasar	10-18	8-11	10	32
Brandon Titus	1-1	3-9	2	5
Glover Jackson	0-0	0-0	0	0
Roman Rubchenko	1-4	1-2	4	3
Totals	**29-60**	**24-37**	**40**	**95**

FG%: .483. **FT%:** .649. **Three-point shooting:** 13 of 24 (Brandon 1-3, Owens 0-1, Henderson 8-13, Ceasar 4-7). **Assists:** 19 (Owens 7). **Steals:** 8. **Blocked Shots:** 3. **Turnovers:** 20.

Halftime: LSU 48-32.

1993 NCAA CHAMPION: ARKANSAS

SEASON STATISTICS OF ARKANSAS REGULARS

PLAYER	POS.	CL.	G.	FG%	FT%	PPG	RPG
Corliss Williamson	F	So.	34	.626	.700	20.4	7.7
Scotty Thurman	G-F	So.	34	.469	.732	15.9	4.5
Al Dillard	G	Jr.	34	.404	.786	8.9	1.1
Corey Beck	G	Jr.	34	.506	.667	8.8	3.9
Clint McDaniel	G	Jr.	31	.407	.754	8.1	2.8
Dwight Stewart	C	Jr.	34	.463	.647	8.0	5.0
Darnell Robinson	C	Fr.	27	.457	.577	7.6	4.7
Roger Crawford	G	Sr.	30	.556	.679	7.4	1.9
Davor Rimac	G	Jr.	34	.455	.786	4.8	1.9
Lee Wilson	C	Fr.	30	.493	.580	3.4	3.1
Ken Biley	F	Sr.	18	.655	.667	2.8	2.1
Elmer Martin	F	Jr.	27	.308	.692	1.3	1.2
Ray Biggers	F	Jr.	18	.172	.438	1.1	2.2
TEAM TOTALS			34	.488	.680	93.4	41.6

Three-point field goals leaders: Thurman (85 of 198, .429), Dillard (75 of 183, .410), McDaniel (38 of 108, .352), Steward (37 of 95, .389), Rimac (32 of 79, .405). **Assists leaders:** Beck 169, Thurman 103. **Blocked shots leader:** Williamson 39. **Steals leaders:** Beck 68, McDaniel 53, Thurman 47.

1994 FINAL FOUR CHAMPIONSHIP GAME

CHARLOTTE, NC

DUKE (72)	MIN.	FG-A	FT-A	REB.	A.	PF.	PTS.
Lang	34	6-9	3-3	5	3	5	15
Hill	38	4-11	3-5	14	6	3	12
Parks	30	7-10	0-1	7	0	3	14
Capel	35	6-16	0-0	5	4	3	14
Collins	34	4-11	0-0	0	1	1	12
Clark	15	1-6	1-2	1	3	2	3
Meek	14	1-2	0-0	7	0	1	2
Team				5			
TOTALS	200	29-65	7-11	44	17	18	72

FG%: .446. **FT%:** .636. **Three-point goals:** 7 of 20 (Hill 1-4, Capel 2-6, Collins 4-8, Clark 0-2). **Blocks:** 7 (Hill 3). **Turnovers:** 23 (Hill 9, Capel 6, Lang 5). **Steals:** 5 (Hill 3).

ARKANSAS (76)	MIN.	FG-A	FT-A	REB.	A.	PF.	PTS.
Biley	3	0-0	0-0	0	0	1	0
Williamson	35	10-24	3-5	8	3	3	23
Stewart	29	3-11	0-0	9	4	3	6
Beck	35	5-11	5-8	10	4	3	15

Thurman	36	6-13	0-0	5	1	2	15
McDaniel	32	2-5	2-4	2	3	2	7
Robinson	12	1-5	0-0	2	0	1	2
Dillard	8	1-5	1-2	1	0	1	4
Rimac	5	0-1	0-0	0	0	0	0
Wilson	5	2-2	0-0	4	0	1	4
Team				3			
TOTALS	200	30-77	11-19	44	15	17	76

FG%: .390. **FT%:** .579. **Three-point goals:** 5 of 18 (Stewart 0-5, Beck 0-1, Thurman 3-5, McDaniel 1-3, Dillard 1-4). **Blocks:** 3. **Turnovers:** 12 (Williamson 5). **Steals:** 11 (Stewart 4).
Halftime: Arkansas 34-33.

NATIONAL SEMIFINALS

ARIZONA (82): Owes 7-15 2-2 16, Geary 2-6 0-0 4, Blair 4-7 0-1 8, Reeves 6-19 8-9 20, Stoudamire 5-24 4-4 16, Flanagan 1-1 0-0 2, McLean 1-1 0-0 2, Williams 5-7 0-0 14, Rigdon 0-0 0-0 0, Richey 0-0 0-0 0, Brown 0-0 0-0 0, Kelley 0-0 0-0 0. Team 31-80 (.388) 14-16 (.875) 82.

ARKANSAS (91): Stewart 2-5 1-2 7, Williamson 11-18 7-9 29, Robinson 5-9 2-3 12, Beck 2-5 4-8 9, Thurman 5-13 4-6 14, McDaniel 4-10 2-2 12, Dillard 2-7 0-0 6, Wilson 1-2 0-2 2, Rimac 0-1 0-0 0. Team 32-70 (.457) 20-32 (.625) 91.

Three-point goals: Arizona 6-32, Arkansas 7-24 (.292).
Halftime: Tied 41-41.

FLORIDA (65): Thompson 1-3 2-4 4, DeClercq 7-11 0-2 14, Hill 6-17 4-6 16, Brown 3-9 0-0 8, Cross 3-14 2-4 10, Kuisma 0-2 2-2 2, Anderson 4-6 1-2 9, Dyrkolbotn 0-0 0-0 0, Williams 1-1 0-0 2. Team 25-63 (.397) 11-20 (.550) 65.

DUKE (70): Lang 3-6 6-6 12, Hill 8-13 6-8 25, Parks 4-11 3-4 11, Capel 3-10 1-1 9, Collins 1-4 0-0 2, Clark 3-6 0-0 8, Meek 0-1 3-4 3, Newton 0-0 0-0 0. Team 22-51 (.431) 19-23 (.826) 70.

Three-point goals: Florida 4-9 (.444), Duke 7-14 (.500).
Halftime: Florida 39-32.

ALL-TOURNAMENT TEAM

Corey Beck, G, Jr., Arkansas
Grant Hill, G, Sr., Duke
Antonio Lang, F, Sr., Duke
Scotty Thurman, G-F, Soph., Arkansas
Corliss Williamson, F, Soph., Arkansas*
Named Most Outstanding Player

ing record (68.6 percent) before missing his first five shots in the final against Duke's Cherokee Parks and finishing the game 10 of 24 from the floor. Williamson's Final Four heroics overshadowed a brilliant performance against him by Michigan's Juwan Howard in a regional final. Howard outscored Williamson (30-12) and outrebounded him (13-6), but the Wolverines concentrated so much on "Big Nasty" that Arkansas hit 10 three-pointers.

One and Only: Richardson became the only coach to win national championships in junior college (1980 with Western Texas), the NIT (1981 with Tulsa) and the NCAA. . . . Duke guard Chris Collins became the first championship game player to be the son of a former NCAA consensus All-American. His father, NBA analyst Doug Collins, was an All-American for Illinois State the year after playing for the 1972 U.S. Olympic team.

Numbers Game: Skip Prosser of Loyola (Md.) became the only active coach to engineer a turnaround that included an NCAA playoff appearance in his first full year at a new job although the school registered a record of more than 20 games below .500 the previous season. The Greyhounds, 2-25 in 1993-94, improved by 13 1/2 games when Prosser assumed control and compiled a 17-13 mark. . . . Gary Williams, leading Maryland to the Midwest Regional semifinals, became the only individual to win games while coaching schools from the three conferences with the best winning percentages in NCAA Tournament history reflecting actual membership–ACC, Big East and Big Ten. He is also the only coach to win games with as many as three different schools (Boston College, Maryland and Ohio State) although they were seeded ninth or worse. . . . Duke's Mike Krzyzewski became the only coach to win his first seven NCAA regional finals. . . . Boston College's Jim O'Brien defeated two of the three coaches with at least 40 tourney victories (North Carolina's Dean Smith and Indiana's Bob Knight in back-to-back East Regional games). . . . Arizona guard Khalid Reeves (20th in scoring with 24.2 points per game) was the only player ranking among the nation's top 60 scorers, top 30 in assists and top 30 rebounders to participate in the Final Four. . . . Fourteen of 17 worst-seeded winners in the tournament shot better behind the three-point arc, by an average of 43.8 percent to 27.5 percent. . . . Wisconsin tied Brown for the longest drought in NCAA Tournament history for schools previously participating in the playoffs. The Badgers' last appearance was in 1947. Brown didn't earn a bid from 1940 through 1985. . . . Saint Louis appeared in the playoffs for the first time since 1957.

What Might Have Been: Alabama (20-10, without James Robinson), Kentucky (27-7, Jamal Mashburn), Michigan (24-8, Chris Webber), Seton Hall (17-13, Luther Wright) and Wake Forest (21-12, Rodney Rogers) might have fared better in the playoffs if standout players had exercised their remaining eligibility instead of defecting to the NBA. . . . Brigham Young (22-10) probably would have participated in the NCAA Tournament instead of the NIT if Shawn Bradley didn't leave school early for the NBA.

Overcoming Adversity: Arkansas lost two of three SEC road games from January 8-19 and nearly lost three of four but capitalized on Thurman's three-pointer with nine seconds remaining to escape with a 65-64 victory at Tennessee, which finished with the league's worst record (2-14). Thurman scored a season-low seven points against the Volunteers. The Hogs also almost lost at home to a second-division team, but LSU missed two shots in the final 10 seconds to fall short, 84-83, in the only game at Arkansas' brand new Walton Arena that would be less than a double-digit victory. Later, Arkansas erased a four-point deficit in the last 12 seconds of regulation and two-point deficit with less than 20 seconds remaining in overtime to win at LSU, 108-105.

Scoring Leader: Khalid Reeves, Arizona (137 points, 27.4 ppg).

Highest Scoring Average: Gary Collier, Tulsa (94 points, 31.3 ppg).

Rebounding Leader: Cherokee Parks, Duke (55 rebounds, 9.2 rpg).

Highest Rebounding Average: Juwan Howard, Michigan (51 rebounds, 12.8 rpg).

1994 CHAMPIONSHIP BRACKET

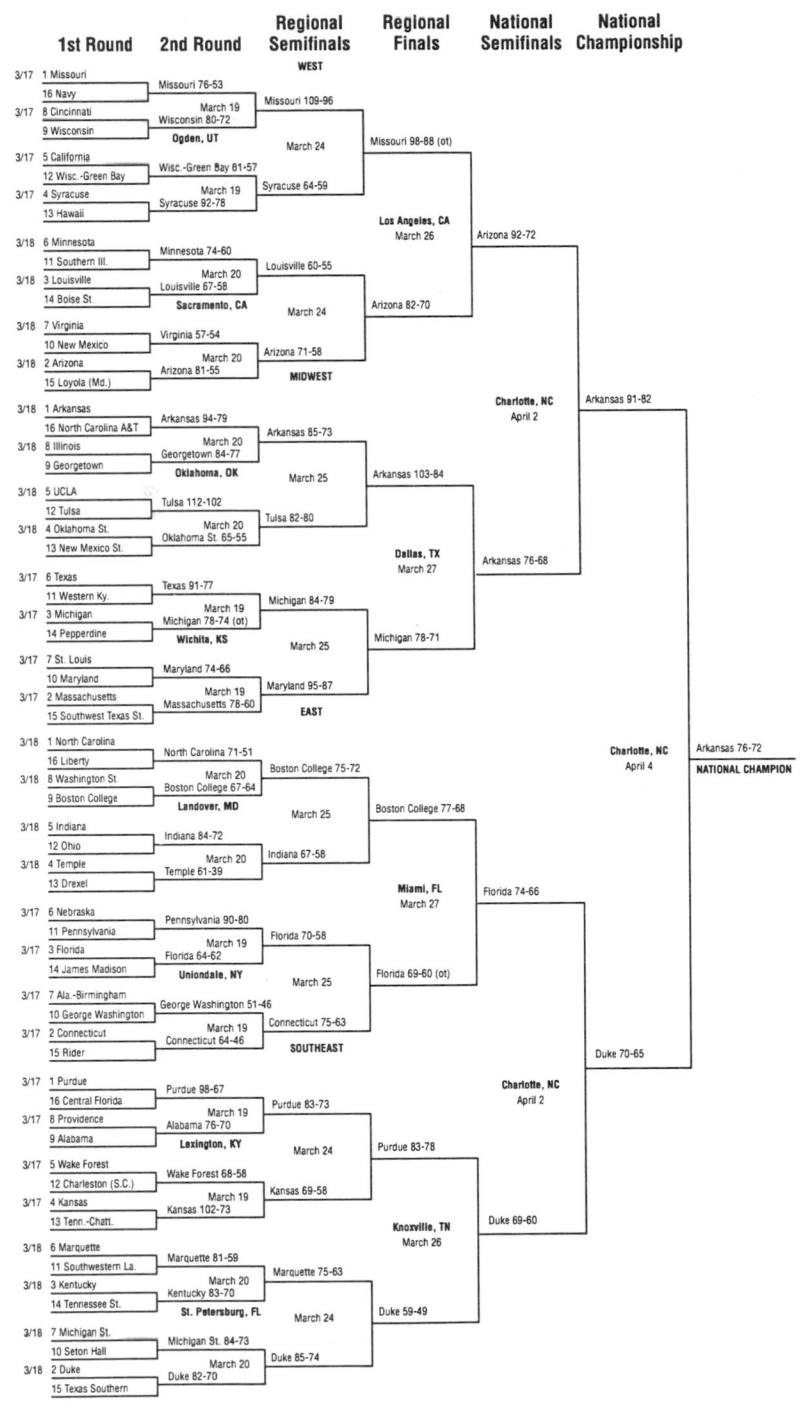

	1st Round	2nd Round	Regional Semifinals	Regional Finals	National Semifinals	National Championship

WEST

3/17 1 Missouri
16 Navy — Missouri 76-53
3/17 8 Cincinnati
9 Wisconsin — Wisconsin 80-72 — March 19 — Missouri 109-96
Ogden, UT
3/17 5 California
12 Wisc.-Green Bay — Wisc.-Green Bay 81-57 — March 24
3/17 4 Syracuse
13 Hawaii — Syracuse 92-78 — March 19 — Syracuse 64-59 — Missouri 98-88 (ot)

3/18 6 Minnesota
11 Southern Ill. — Minnesota 74-60
3/18 3 Louisville
14 Boise St. — Louisville 67-58 — March 20 — Louisville 60-55 — **Los Angeles, CA** March 26
Sacramento, CA
3/18 7 Virginia
10 New Mexico — Virginia 57-54 — March 24 — Arizona 82-70 — Arizona 92-72
3/18 2 Arizona
15 Loyola (Md.) — Arizona 81-55 — March 20 — Arizona 71-58

MIDWEST

3/18 1 Arkansas
16 North Carolina A&T — Arkansas 94-79
3/18 8 Illinois
9 Georgetown — Georgetown 84-77 — March 20 — Arkansas 85-73
Oklahoma, OK
3/18 5 UCLA
12 Tulsa — Tulsa 112-102 — March 25 — Arkansas 103-84
3/18 4 Oklahoma St.
13 New Mexico St. — Oklahoma St. 65-55 — March 20 — Tulsa 82-80 — **Dallas, TX** March 27

3/17 6 Texas
11 Western Ky. — Texas 91-77
3/17 3 Michigan
14 Pepperdine — Michigan 78-74 (ot) — March 19 — Michigan 84-79
Wichita, KS
3/17 7 St. Louis
10 Maryland — Maryland 74-66 — March 25 — Michigan 78-71 — Arkansas 76-68
3/17 2 Massachusetts
15 Southwest Texas St. — Massachusetts 78-60 — March 19 — Maryland 95-87

EAST

3/18 1 North Carolina
16 Liberty — North Carolina 71-51
3/18 8 Washington St.
9 Boston College — Boston College 67-64 — March 20 — Boston College 75-72
Landover, MD
3/18 5 Indiana
12 Ohio — Indiana 84-72 — March 25 — Boston College 77-68
3/18 4 Temple
13 Drexel — Temple 61-39 — March 20 — Indiana 67-58 — **Miami, FL** March 27

3/17 6 Nebraska
11 Pennsylvania — Pennsylvania 90-80
3/17 3 Florida
14 James Madison — Florida 64-62 — March 19 — Florida 70-58
Uniondale, NY
3/17 7 Ala.-Birmingham
10 George Washington — George Washington 51-46 — March 25 — Florida 69-60 (ot) — Florida 74-66
3/17 2 Connecticut
15 Rider — Connecticut 64-46 — March 19 — Connecticut 75-63

SOUTHEAST

3/17 1 Purdue
16 Central Florida — Purdue 98-67
3/17 8 Providence
9 Alabama — Alabama 76-70 — March 19 — Purdue 83-73
Lexington, KY
3/17 5 Wake Forest
12 Charleston (S.C.) — Wake Forest 68-58 — March 24 — Purdue 83-78
3/17 4 Kansas
13 Tenn.-Chatt. — Kansas 102-73 — March 19 — Kansas 69-58 — **Knoxville, TN** March 26

3/18 6 Marquette
11 Southwestern La. — Marquette 81-59
3/18 3 Kentucky
14 Tennessee St. — Kentucky 83-70 — March 20 — Marquette 75-63
St. Petersburg, FL
3/18 7 Michigan St.
10 Seton Hall — Michigan St. 84-73 — March 24 — Duke 59-49 — Duke 69-60
3/18 2 Duke
15 Texas Southern — Duke 82-70 — March 20 — Duke 85-74

National Semifinals / Championship

Charlotte, NC April 2 — Arkansas 91-82

Charlotte, NC April 2 — Duke 70-65

Charlotte, NC April 4 — Arkansas 76-72 — **NATIONAL CHAMPION**

1994-95

AT A GLANCE

NCAA Champion: UCLA (31-2; coached by Jim Harrick; won Pacific-10 title by three games with a 16-2 record).

NIT Champion: Virginia Tech (25-10; coached by Bill Foster; finished in a tie for fourth place in the Metro with a 6-6 record).

New Rules: Voted to restrict scoring to a tap-in when play is resumed by a throw-in and three-tenths (.3) of a second or less remain on the game clock or shot clock. . . . A player whose uniform has blood on it does not have to leave the game if medical personnel judges the uniform to be nonsaturated. . . . Expanded backcourt violation exceptions to a defensive player who receives the ball while in the air. . . . Expanded the fighting rule to include coaches and team personnel. . . . The inner circle at midcourt is eliminated.

NCAA Probation: Alabama State, Coastal Carolina, Northeastern Illinois.

NCAA Consensus First-Team All-Americans: Ed O'Bannon, F, Sr., UCLA; Shawn Respert, G, Sr., Michigan State; Joe Smith, C, Soph., Maryland; Jerry Stackhouse, F, Soph., North Carolina; Damon Stoudamire, G, Sr., Arizona.

National Players of the Year: O'Bannon (20.4 ppg, 8.3 rpg, 1.9 spg, 53.3 FG%/USBWA, Wooden); Respert (25.6 ppg, 4 rpg, 86.9 FT%, 47.4 3FG%/NABC), and Smith (20.8 ppg, 10.6 rpg, 2.9 bpg, 57.8 FG%/AP, UPI, Naismith).

National Coaches of the Year: Miami's Leonard Hamilton (15-13/UPI); UCLA's Jim Harrick (31-2/NABC, Naismith), and Oklahoma's Kelvin Sampson (23-9/AP, USBWA).

A couple of high profile coaches for the Western conference departed before the season started under unusual circumstances. Southern Cal's George Raveling stepped down in the aftermath of a serious auto accident and UNLV's Rollie Massimino was pressured to resign after a series of questionable activities.

Tim Grgurich, Massimino's successor, left the Rebels after seven games due to health reasons. Howie Landa and Cleveland Edwards served as interim coaches the remainder of UNLV's sorriest season in history (11-15).

Baylor coach Darrel Johnson was dismissed before the season started because of academic irregularities. Three Baylor assistant coaches–Gary Thomas, Troy Drummond and Kevin Gray–were sentenced to three years probation, assigned 50 hours of community service and fined from $1,000 to $1,500 apiece for helping three recruits cheat. The coaches had been convicted by a federal jury of conspiracy and mail and wire fraud charges. They were found guilty of giving junior college players term papers and of changing their test scores. The mail fraud and wire fraud charges were filed because the Postal Service and fax equipment were used in the process. Johnson was acquitted, but Gray and Thomas said Johnson condoned the wrongdoing. They gave depositions to the NCAA that said the cheating "was always discussed in meetings" with Johnson.

Duke coach Mike Krzyzewski compiled a 9-3 record before missing the remainder of the season recovering from back surgery and exhaustion. Pete Gaudet, a designated restricted-earnings assistant earning an anemic $16,000 annually under NCAA rules, filled in for Krzyzewski. The Blue Devils promptly lost their first nine ACC games for the first time and finished with the most defeats in school history (13-18 mark). Their demise included blowing a 23-point lead with less than 15 minutes remaining against Virginia and bowing to the Cavaliers in double overtime, 91-88.

Tommy Joe Eagles, hired by New Orleans after he was forced out by Auburn at the end of the previous season, died of a heart attack during the summer. . . . James Madison's Lefty Driesell became the first coach to register at least 125 victories for three different schools. He previously achieved the feat for Davidson and Maryland. . . . Michigan State's Jud Heathcote, who previously coached Montana, retired with a 420-273 record.

Wisconsin's Michael Finley tied a school single-game record with 42 points in a 92-76 loss at Eastern Michigan. The Badgers trailed

1994–95 INDIVIDUAL LEADERS

SCORING

PLAYER	PTS.	AVG.
Thomas, Texas Christian	781	28.9
King, Western Carolina	743	26.5
Sykes, Grambling	684	26.3
Ford, Ill.-Chicago	707	26.2
Roberts, Southern (La.)	680	26.2
Townes, La Salle	699	25.9
Griffin, Long Island	723	25.8
Respert, Michigan St.	716	25.6
Feaster, Holy Cross	672	24.9
Smith, Wis.-Milwaukee	661	24.5

REBOUNDING

PLAYER	REB.	AVG.
Thomas, Texas Christian	393	14.6
Rose, Drexel	404	13.5
Trent, Ohio Univ.	423	12.8
Callahan, Northeastern	364	12.6
Duncan, Wake Forest	401	12.5
Foyle, Colgate	371	12.4
Carpenter, Eastern Mich.	343	11.8
Awojobi, Boston Univ.	365	11.8
Mann, Miss. Valley	317	11.7
Ensminger, Valparaiso	315	11.3

ASSISTS

PLAYER	AST.	AVG.
Haggerty, Baylor	284	10.1
McCants, George Mason	251	9.3
Miglinieks, UC Irvine	245	8.4
Snow, Michigan State	217	7.8
Vaughn, Kansas	238	7.7
Foster, South Alabama	203	7.5
Miller, Marquette	248	7.5
Hassan Sanders, Southern (La.)	179	7.5
Washington, Nicholls State	213	7.3
Stoudamire, Arizona	220	7.3
O'Bryant, Nevada	211	7.3

BLOCKED SHOTS

PLAYER	BLK.	AVG.
Closs, Central Conn.	139	5.3
Ratliff, Wyoming	144	5.1
Foyle, Colgate	147	4.9
Fleury, UMBC	124	4.6
Coleman, Tenn. Tech	122	4.5
Duncan, Wake Forest	135	4.2
Gilpin, Dartmouth	92	3.5
Bennett, Arizona State	115	3.5
Aluma, Liberty	97	3.5
Camby, Massachusetts	103	3.4

STEALS

PLAYER	STL.	AVG.
Anderson, Texas	101	3.4
Black, Tex.-Pan American	94	3.4
Langley, George Mason	87	3.3
Washington, Nicholls St.	88	3.0
Ceasar, LSU	66	3.0
Iverson, Georgetown	89	3.0
McNeil, St. Bonaventure	90	2.9
Young, Fresno State	81	2.9
Strickland, Nebraska	89	2.9
Walker, San Francisco	80	2.9

FIELD-GOAL PERCENTAGE

PLAYER	FGM	FGA	PCT.
Kline-Ruminski, BGSU	181	265	.683
Spain, Davidson	141	210	.671
Wallace, N. Carolina	238	364	.654
Dampier, Mississippi St.	153	239	.640
Koul, George Wash.	160	253	.632
McNaull, Long Beach St.	156	248	.629
Hendrickson, Wash. St.	183	292	.627
McCulloch, Fresno St.	152	244	.623
Coleman, Tenn. Tech	168	270	.622
Robinson, E. Carolina	181	293	.618

FREE-THROW PERCENTAGE

PLAYER	FTM	FTA	PCT.
Bibb, Tennessee Tech	106	117	.906
Hartzell, N.C.-Greensboro	97	108	.898
Brown, Murray State	189	211	.896
Cornett, Texas-Arlington	70	79	.886
Johnson, Eastern Ky.	123	139	.885
Basile, Marist	74	84	.881
Nash, Santa Clara	153	174	.879
Rillie, Gonzaga	87	99	.879
Barker, Valparaiso	72	82	.878
Heary, Navy	105	120	.875

THREE-POINT FG PERCENTAGE

PLAYER	FGM	FGA	PCT.
Jackson, Evansville	53	95	.558
Kegler, Penn	58	114	.509
Westlake, Wis.-Green Bay	87	174	.500
Calabria, N. Carolina	66	133	.496
Hightower, Marshall	46	95	.484
Lake, Montana	76	157	.484

THREE-POINT FIELD GOALS PER GAME

PLAYER	FGM	AVG.
Taylor, Southern (La.)	109	4.4
Respert, Michigan St.	119	4.3
Roberts, Southern (La.)	108	4.2
Rutherford, Okla. St.	146	3.9
Townes, La Salle	103	3.8

EMU by 33 points at halftime (50-17). Finley was among three players on Proviso East's Illinois state Class AA championship in 1991 who were all drafted by NBA teams–Sherell Ford (Illinois-Chicago) and Finley in the first round and Donnie Boyce (Colorado) in the second round. Ford was the nation's fourth-leading scorer as a senior and Boyce finished his career as Colorado's all-time leading scorer.

Corey Beck distributed 30 assists in three games to spark Arkansas to the Rainbow Classic championship in Hawaii. It was the Razorbacks' first in-season tournament title in 26 years. Rainbow Classic runner-up Iowa defeated Duke in the opening round, ending the Blue Devils' 14-game winning streak against Big Ten teams. . . . Maryland's pair of two-point victories over Duke enabled the Terrapins to gain a share of the ACC regular-season crown and end their streak of nine consecutive defeats in College Park and 15 overall to the Blue Devils. The ACC's four-way tie for the regular-season title was the first in league history. . . . Randolph Childress poured in an ACC Tournament-record 107 points to catapult Wake Forest to its first championship since 1962. . . . Indiana's 50-game homecourt winning streak, which began in 1991, was ended by Michigan, 65-52. . . . A school-record 11 blocked shots by freshman center Samaki Walker helped Louisville nip Kentucky, 88-86, for the Cardinals' first victory over the Wildcats since 1989. . . . Central Connecticut State's Keith Closs had a national-high 13 rejections in a game against St. Francis (Pa.).

Kentucky clobbered Notre Dame, 97-58, handing the Fighting Irish its most lopsided

1994–95 TEAM LEADERS

SCORING OFFENSE

SCHOOL	PTS.	AVG.
Texas Christian	2529	93.7
Southern (La.)	2425	93.3
Texas	2787	92.9
George Mason	2499	92.6
Troy State	2468	91.4

SCORING DEFENSE

SCHOOL	PTS.	AVG.
Princeton	1501	57.7
Wis.-Green Bay	1767	58.9
Temple	1792	59.7
Miami of Ohio	1827	60.9
Manhattan	1929	62.2

SCORING MARGIN

SCHOOL	OFF.	DEF.	MAR.
Kentucky	87.4	69.0	18.4
Massachusetts	80.9	65.7	15.1
Pennsylvania	82.2	67.5	14.7
UCLA	87.5	73.9	13.7
Montana State	84.2	70.8	13.4

WON-LOST PERCENTAGE

SCHOOL	W-L	PCT.
UCLA	31-2	.939
Western Kentucky	27-4	.871
Massachusetts	29-5	.853
Connecticut	28-5	.848
Kentucky	28-5	.848

FIELD-GOAL PERCENTAGE

SCHOOL	FGM	FGA	PCT.
Washington St.	902	1743	.517
UCLA	1079	2102	.513
North Carolina	1044	2055	.508
Montana State	930	1832	.508
Bowling Green	721	1427	.505

FIELD-GOAL PERCENTAGE DEFENSE

SCHOOL	FGM	FGA	PCT.
Alabama	771	2048	.376
Kansas	768	2032	.378
Marquette	747	1957	.382
Mississippi St.	698	1821	.383
Manhattan	670	1747	.384

FREE-THROW PERCENTAGE

SCHOOL	FTM	FTA	PCT.
Brigham Young	617	798	.773
Murray State	553	719	.769
Wake Forest	475	622	.764
Samford	472	622	.759
Iowa State	610	806	.757

REBOUND MARGIN

SCHOOL	OWN	OPP.	MAR.
Navy	40.6	29.6	11.0
Utah State	40.9	30.4	10.5
Texas Tech	43.3	33.5	9.8
Utah	39.7	30.0	9.8
Miss. Valley	47.0	38.3	8.8

THREE-POINT FIELD GOAL PERCENTAGE

SCHOOL	FGM	FGA	PCT.
Southern Utah	244	571	.427
Evansville	181	424	.427
Wis.-Green Bay	188	451	.417
Arizona	245	593	.413
North Carolina	266	648	.410

THREE-POINT FIELD GOALS PER GAME

SCHOOL	FGM	AVG.
Troy State	287	10.6
Samford	279	10.3
Vermont	268	9.9
Baylor	265	9.5
Marshall	253	9.4

homecourt defeat this century. In their next outing, the Wildcats lost at home to Mississippi State, 76-71, for the first time since 1967. . . . In Mississippi State's previous game, the Bulldogs hit five three-pointers in the last 1 1/2 minutes to nearly erase a 12-point deficit against Auburn but they fell short, 70-69. Mississippi State finished with a Top 20 appearance in a final wire-service poll for the first time since 1963. . . . LSU redshirt freshman Randy Livingston was leading the nation with 10 assists per game in mid-season before he was sidelined for the year because of his third knee injury since signing with the Tigers.

Connecticut remained the nation's only undefeated team through mid-January by overcoming a 25-point deficit in an 85-76 victory at Pittsburgh. The Huskies went on to become the only team ever to defeat Georgetown three times in a Big East Conference campaign. . . . Miami (Fla.) lost its first 29 Big East road games until upsetting St. John's, 82-79. The Hurricanes, winless in league play the previous year, finished with the greatest one-season turnaround in conference history by compiling a 9-9 Big East record. . . . Kerry Kittles became the first Villanova player since 1971 to earn a spot on an NCAA consensus first- or second-team All-American squad.

Canisius lost 27 consecutive games on St. Bonaventure's home court in Olean, N.Y., until edging the Bonnies, 76-74. Later, St. Bonaventure defeated Temple for the first time in 25 games with a 78-64 triumph in overtime. . . . Eddie Benton became Vermont's all-time leading scorer midway through his junior season.

The Metro, in its final season of existence, was the only conference in the country to have each member post a winning overall record. . . . Tennessee-Chattanooga's John Oliver averaged a modest 10.9 points per game, but he exploded for a school-record 42 in a game against Georgia Southern. . . . Southern's Tim Roberts scored a national-high 56 points against Faith Baptist.

UCLA (31-2, coached by Jim Harrick), Manhattan (26-5, Fran Fraschilla), Wake Forest (26-6, Dave Odom), Virginia Tech (25-10, Bill Foster), Portland (21-8, Rob Chavez) and New Hampshire (19-9, Gib Chapman) had their winningest seasons in school Division I history. Manhattan was the first school to reach the 20-win plateau. . . . Massachusetts' game at Rutgers was suspended at halftime because of a student protest stemming from racial remarks by the Rutgers president.

Randy Rutherford poured in 45 points in Oklahoma State's regular-season finale at Kansas but the Jayhawks won, 78-62, when Cowboys All-Big Eight center Bryant Reeves went scoreless. Reeves and Rutherford were the nation's only set of teammates to each score more than 700 points during the season. . . . Oregon swept its Pacific-10 series with intrastate rival Oregon State for the first time since 1961. Oregon won more than 16 games for the first time since the 1976-77 campaign. . . . California finished in a tie for eighth place in the Pacific-10 despite becoming the first school in league history to win at UCLA's Pauley Pavilion three consecutive times (100-93). Cal is the only team registering a league record at least eight games under .500 (5-13) to win a road game against a conference rival that later became NCAA champion.

Point guard Steve Nash converted all 21 of his free throws in a 75-71 victory over St. Mary's on his way to becoming the first Santa Clara player to top the WCC in scoring (20.9 points per game) since Mike Gervasoni averaged 20.1 in 1966-67. Nash, a native of British Columbia, scored 40 points, nailing eight three-pointers, to help the Broncos end Gonzaga's 34-game home-court winning streak, 73-68. They went on to clinch their first WCC regular-season title since 1970.

TCU's Kurt Thomas became the third player to lead the nation in scoring and rebounding.

Thomas averaged only 1.9 points per game as a freshman in 1990-91. . . . TCU's Thomas (28.9 ppg) and Long Island's Joe Griffin (25.8) set school records for highest scoring average in a single season. . . . Kareem Townes set a La Salle single-game scoring record with 52 points against Loyola of Chicago. . . . Pitt forward Orlando Antigua signed with the Harlem Globetrotters after the season. He became the first non-African-American player with the Globetrotters since Bob Karstens in 1942-43.

Marquette's Tony Miller dished out a school single-game record of 17 assists against Memphis en route to finishing his career as the only player at any level of the NCAA to collect 1,000 points, 500 rebounds and 900 assists. . . . Eastern Michigan's Kareem Carpenter set a school single-game rebounding mark with a national-high 27 against Western Michigan. Carpenter also hauled down 26 rebounds in a contest against Central Michigan. . . . Western Illinois (20-8) posted the nation's most-improved record, improving from a 7-20 mark the previous year. WIU was coached by Jim Kerwin.

1994-95 FINAL NATIONAL POLLS

AP	UPI	USA/NABC	SCHOOL (RECORD)	HEAD COACH
1	1	1	UCLA (31-2)	Jim Harrick
2	2	5	Kentucky (28-5)	Rick Pitino
3	3	9	Wake Forest (26-6)	Dave Odom
4	5	3	North Carolina (28-6)	Dean Smith
5	4	10	Kansas (25-6)	Roy Williams
6	6	2	Arkansas (32-7)	Nolan Richardson
7	7	7	Massachusetts (29-5)	John Calipari
8	8	6	Connecticut (28-5)	Jim Calhoun
9	9	23	Villanova (25-8)	Steve Lappas
10	11	11	Maryland (26-8)	Gary Williams
11	10	20	Michigan State (22-6)	Jud Heathcote
12	12	19	Purdue (25-7)	Gene Keady
13	14	8	Virginia (25-9)	Jeff Jones
14	16	4	Oklahoma State (27-10)	Eddie Sutton
15	13	25	Arizona (23-8)	Lute Olson
16	15	13	Arizona State (24-9)	Bill Frieder
17	19	-	Oklahoma (23-9)	Kelvin Sampson
18	17	12	Mississippi St. (22-8)	Richard Williams
19	18	22	Utah (28-6)	Rick Majerus
20	20	21	Alabama (23-10)	Dave Hobbs
21	-	-	Western Kentucky (27-4)	Matt Kilcullen
22	-	16	Georgetown (21-10)	John Thompson
23	22	18	Missouri (20-9)	Norm Stewart
24	22	-	Iowa State (23-11)	Tim Floyd
25	21	17	Syracuse (20-10)	Jim Boeheim
	24	-	Oregon (19-9)	Jerry Green
	25	-	Stanford (20-9)	Mike Montgomery
-	-	14	Memphis (24-10)	Larry Finch
-	-	15	Tulsa (24-8)	Tubby Smith
-	-	24	Texas (23-7)	Tom Penders

Sacramento State's NCAA-record 55-game losing streak on the road ended with a 68-56 success at Loyola of Chicago. . . . Wyoming's Theo Ratliff blocked 11 shots in each of back-to-back games against Mississippi State and San Diego State. . . . Brad Snyder, Northern Arizona's leading scorer, was killed in a one-vehicle accident late in the season.

1995 NCAA Tournament

Summary: It was a return to glory for UCLA. Playmaker deluxe Tyus Edney played only three minutes in the final because of a sprained right wrist, but his replacement, Cameron Dollar, played like a million dollars. "I was definitely tight and tense at the beginning," said Dollar, who committed just one turnover. "Then I got going and it turned out to be just another game, like any other day in the playground." Edney played the role of Wizard of Westwood II with a series of breathtaking drives and baskets in the first five playoff games, including a length-of-the-court game-winner against Missouri in the second round. Teammate Ed O'Bannon collected 30 points and 17 rebounds in an 89-78 victory over Arkansas for one of the best title game performances in history. O'Bannon became only the third different player to amass at least 30 points and 15 rebounds in a championship game, joining Clyde Lovellette (Kansas '52) and Lew Alcindor (UCLA '68 & '69). During a crucial five-game stretch in February, O'Bannon averaged 27.8 points and nine rebounds per game. Toby Bailey became the only freshman to score more than 25 points in a national championship game when he tallied 26 after managing just two in the semifinals against Oklahoma State. UCLA became the only champion other than Kentucky '51 to have six players finish the season with scoring averages higher than nine points per game.

Outcome for Defending Champion: Arkansas reached the NCAA championship game after winning its first two tourney assignments by a total of three points after blowing double-digit second-half leads. The Razorbacks'

victory margin entering the Final Four, 3.8, was the slimmest of any team reaching the national semifinals since the tournament expanded to 64 teams in 1985). The Hogs had 13 wins by five or fewer points entering the NCAA final after kicking off the season with a 24-point defeat to Massachusetts in the Tip-Off Classic at Springfield, Mass.

Star Gazing: Alabama center Antonio McDyess had the highest-scoring game in the tourney with 39 points against Penn in overtime in the first round. . . . North Carolina center Rasheed Wallace, the third-leading field-goal shooter in the country (65.4 percent), had just one field-goal attempt in the last 27 minutes as the Tar Heels went more than 12 1/2 minutes without a basket.

Biggest Upset: Old Dominion outlasted Villanova, 89-81, in triple overtime although Monarchs star Odell Hodge missed most of the season because of a severe injury to his left knee.

One and Only: Bob Weltlich became the only coach to earn automatic qualification for two different schools by winning conference tournaments after compiling losing records in regular-season league competition. He was coach of No. 6 seed Mississippi in the 1981 SEC Tournament (8-10) and No. 8 seed Florida International (4-12) in the '95 TAAC Tournament.

Numbers Game: There were six overtime games in the first two rounds of the tourney. Alabama (24) and Penn (18) set a record for most points by both teams in one overtime period when they combined for 42 in Alabama's 91-85 triumph. . . . Michigan coach Steve Fisher won his first 12 NCAA playoff games decided by fewer than six points or in overtime before bowing to Western Kentucky, 82-76, in overtime in the opening round. . . . The Big Ten didn't have a representative among the final 16 entrants for the first time since the NCAA field expanded to at least 16 teams in 1951. All six Big Ten squads would have been eliminated in the opening round if Wisconsin-Green Bay hadn't missed a last-second shot against Purdue. . . .

1994-95 NCAA CHAMPION: UCLA

SEASON STATISTICS FOR UCLA REGULARS

PLAYER	POS.	CL.	G.	FG%	FT%	PPG	RPG
Ed O'Bannon	F	Sr.	33	.533	.785	20.4	8.3
Tyus Edney	G	Sr.	32	.497	.764	14.3	3.1
Charles O'Bannon	F	So.	33	.554	.739	13.6	6.1
George Zidek	C	Sr.	33	.553	.731	10.6	5.4
Toby Bailey	G	Fr.	33	.484	.564	10.5	4.8
J.R. Henderson	F-C	Fr.	33	.547	.675	9.2	4.2
Cameron Dollar	G	So.	33	.354	.659	3.4	1.9
Ike Nwankwo	C	So.	23	.571	.538	2.7	1.6
Kris Johnson	F	Fr.	21	.420	.706	2.6	1.7
omm'A Givens	F-C	Fr.	25	.381	.563	1.6	1.3
TEAM TOTALS			33	.513	.709	87.5	40.4

Three-point field goals leaders: E. O'Bannon (55 of 127, .433), Edney (25 of 66, .379), Bailey (20 of 73, .274). Assists leaders: Edney 216, C. O'Bannon 110, Dollar 103, E. O'Bannon 81. Blocked shots leader: C. O'Bannon 38. Steals leaders: Edney 74, E. O'Bannon 64, Dollar 54.

1995 FINAL FOUR CHAMPIONSHIP GAME

SEATTLE, WA

UCLA (89)	Min.	FG-A	FT-A	Reb.	A	PF	Pts.
O'Bannon	36	4-10	3-4	9	6	1	11
O'Bannon	40	10-21	9-11	17	3	2	30
Zidek	29	5-8	4-7	6	0	4	14
Edney	3	0-0	0-0	0	0	0	0
Bailey	39	12-20	1-2	9	3	3	26
Dollar	36	1-4	4-5	3	8	4	6
Henderson	17	1-5	0-0	2	1	1	2
Team				4			
TOTALS	200	33-68	21-29	50	21	15	89

FG%: .485. FT%: .724. Three-point goals: 2 of 7 (E. O'Bannon 1 of 4, Bailey 1 of 2, Dollar 0 of 1). Blocks: 4. Turnovers: 20 (E. O'Bannon 5). Steals: 11 (Dollar 4).

ARKANSAS (78)	MIN.	FG-A	FT-A	REB.	A	PF	PTS.
Thurman	32	2-9	0-0	3	1	2	5
Williamson	33	3-16	6-10	4	6	1	12
Martin	6	1-2	0-0	3	1	2	3
McDaniel	35	5-10	3-4	3	1	5	16
Beck	25	4-6	1-2	3	2	3	11
Stewart	22	5-10	1-2	5	0	4	12
Dillard	15	2-4	0-0	2	1	1	6
Robinson	10	2-3	0-0	2	0	3	4

Rimac	12	1-1	0-0	2	3	0	2
Wilson	7	3-4	1-2	0	0	1	7
Williams	1	0-0	0-0	0	0	0	0
Garrett	2	0-0	0-0	0	0	0	0
Team				4			
TOTALS	200	28-65	12-20	31	15	22	78

FG%: .431. FT%: .600. Three-point goals: 10 of 28 (Thurman 1 of 7, Martin 1 of 2, McDaniel 3 of 7, Beck 2 of 3, Stewart 1 of 5, Dillard 2 of 3, Robinson 0 of 1). Blocks: 4. Turnovers: 18. Steals: 15 (McDaniel 4, Williamson 4). Halftime: UCLA 40-39.

NATIONAL SEMIFINALS

UCLA (74): C. O'Bannon 7-9 5-5 19, E. O'Bannon 6-14 1-2 15, Zidek 2-4 2-2 6, Edney 6-12 9-11 21, Bailey 1-2 0-0 2, Dollar 1-1 7-8 9, Henderson 1-6 0-0 2, Dempsey 0-0 0-0 0, Nwankwo 0-0 0-0 0, Givens 0-0 0-0 0, Johnson 0-1 0-0 0, Myers 0-0 0-0 0. Team 24-49 (.490) 24-28 (.857) 74.

OKLAHOMA STATE (61): Pierce 1-4 0-1 2, Collins 2-6 0-0 6, Reeves 8-16 9-9 25, Rutherford 4-13 3-4 15, Owens 1-4 0-0 3, Roberts 5-7 0-2 10, Skaer 0-0 0-0 0, Alexander 0-0 0-0 0, Baum 0-0 0-0 0, Nelson 0-0 0-0 0, Miles 0-0 0-0 0. Team 21-50 (.420) 12-16 (.750) 61.

Three-point goals: UCLA 2-7 (.286). Oklahoma State 7-19 (.368). Halftime: Tied 37-37.

NORTH CAROLINA (68): Stackhouse 4-7 7-10 18, Calabria 1-10 0-0 2, Wallace 4-6 2-4 10, D. Williams 7-19 0-0 19, McInnis 3-9 5-6 13, Sullivan 1-2 2-4 4, Zwikker 0-1 0-0 0, Landry 1-2 0-0 2, S. Williams 0-0 0-0 0. Team 21-56 (.375) 16-24 (.667) 68.

ARKANSAS (75): Thurman 2-10 0-0 6, Williamson 10-17 1-1 21, Martin 1-1 0-0 3, McDaniel 3-7 4-4 13, Beck 2-9 0-0 5, Dillard 0-5 0-0 0, Rimac 2-8 0-0 6, Stewart 6-10 0-2 15, Wilson 1-3 2-2 4, Robinson 1-4 0-0 2. Team 28-74 (.378) 7-9 (.778) 75.

Three-point goals: North Carolina 10-28 (.357). Arkansas 12-34 (.353). Halftime: North Carolina 38-34.

ALL-TOURNAMENT TEAM

Toby Bailey, G, Fr., UCLA
Clint McDaniel, G, Sr., Arkansas
Ed O'Bannon, F, Sr., UCLA*
Bryant Reeves, C, Sr., Oklahoma State
Corliss Williamson, F, Jr., Arkansas

*Named Most Outstanding Player.

Oregon made its first playoff appearance since 1961.

What Might Have Been: Brigham Young (22-10, without Shawn Bradley), Cincinnati (22-12, Dontonio Wingfield), Connecticut (28-5, Donyell Marshall), Louisville (19-14, Cliff Rozier), Michigan (17-14, Juwan Howard, Jalen Rose and Chris Webber) and Purdue (25-7, Glenn Robinson) might have fared better in the playoffs if standout players had exercised their remaining eligibility instead of defecting to the NBA. . . . Clemson (15-13, without Sharone Wright) and George Washington (18-14, Yinka Dare) probably would have participated in the NCAA Tournament instead of the NIT if prominent big men didn't leave school early for the NBA. . . . California (13-14) likely would have been bound for the NCAA playoffs if Jason Kidd and Lamond Murray didn't forsake their remaining eligibility to turn pro early.

Putting Things in Perspective: Massachusetts and Virginia were eliminated in regional finals after each of them lost standouts guards. Michael Williams was dismissed from UMass' team for disciplinary reasons. Virginia's Cory

1995 CHAMPIONSHIP BRACKET

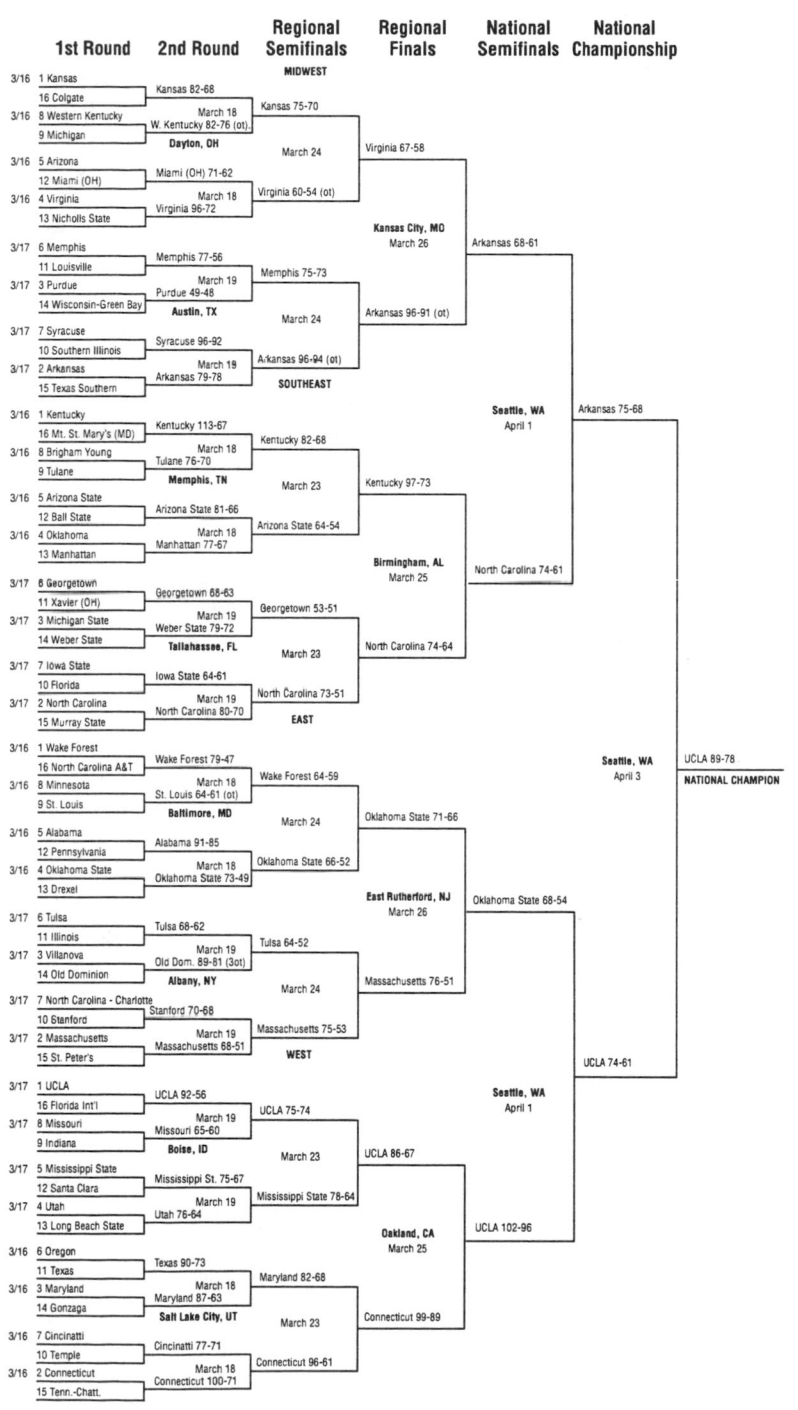

1st Round	2nd Round	Regional Semifinals	Regional Finals	National Semifinals	National Championship

MIDWEST

3/16 1 Kansas
16 Colgate — Kansas 82-68
3/16 8 Western Kentucky — March 18 W. Kentucky 82-76 (ot)
9 Michigan — **Dayton, OH** — Kansas 75-70
3/16 5 Arizona
12 Miami (OH) — Miami (OH) 71-62 — March 24
3/16 4 Virginia — March 18 Virginia 96-72 — Virginia 60-54 (ot) — Virginia 67-58
13 Nicholls State

Kansas City, MO March 26 — Arkansas 68-61

3/17 6 Memphis
11 Louisville — Memphis 77-56
3/17 3 Purdue — March 19 Purdue 49-48 — Memphis 75-73
14 Wisconsin-Green Bay — **Austin, TX** — March 24
3/17 7 Syracuse — Syracuse 96-92 — Arkansas 96-91 (ot)
10 Southern Illinois — March 19 Arkansas 79-78 — Arkansas 96-94 (ot)
3/17 2 Arkansas
15 Texas Southern

SOUTHEAST

Seattle, WA April 1 — Arkansas 75-68

3/16 1 Kentucky
16 Mt. St. Mary's (MD) — Kentucky 113-67
3/16 8 Brigham Young — March 18 Tulane 76-70 — Kentucky 82-68
9 Tulane — **Memphis, TN** — March 23
3/16 5 Arizona State — Arizona State 81-66 — Kentucky 97-73
12 Ball State — March 18 Manhattan 77-67 — Arizona State 64-54
3/16 4 Oklahoma
13 Manhattan

Birmingham, AL March 25 — North Carolina 74-61

3/17 6 Georgetown
11 Xavier (OH) — Georgetown 68-63
3/17 3 Michigan State — March 19 Weber State 79-72 — Georgetown 53-51
14 Weber State — **Tallahassee, FL** — March 23
3/17 7 Iowa State — Iowa State 64-61 — North Carolina 74-64
10 Florida — March 19 North Carolina 80-70 — North Carolina 73-51
3/17 2 North Carolina
15 Murray State

EAST

Seattle, WA April 3 — UCLA 89-78 **NATIONAL CHAMPION**

3/16 1 Wake Forest
16 North Carolina A&T — Wake Forest 79-47
3/16 8 Minnesota — March 18 St. Louis 64-61 (ot) — Wake Forest 64-59
9 St. Louis — **Baltimore, MD** — March 24
3/16 5 Alabama — Alabama 91-85 — Oklahoma State 71-66
12 Pennsylvania — March 18 Oklahoma State 73-49 — Oklahoma State 66-52
3/16 4 Oklahoma State
13 Drexel

East Rutherford, NJ March 26 — Oklahoma State 68-54

3/17 6 Tulsa
11 Illinois — Tulsa 68-62
3/17 3 Villanova — March 19 Old Dom. 89-81 (3ot) — Tulsa 64-52
14 Old Dominion — **Albany, NY** — March 24
3/17 7 North Carolina - Charlotte — Stanford 70-68 — Massachusetts 76-51
10 Stanford — March 19 Massachusetts 68-51 — Massachusetts 75-53
3/17 2 Massachusetts
15 St. Peter's

WEST

Seattle, WA April 1 — UCLA 74-61

3/17 1 UCLA
16 Florida Int'l — UCLA 92-56
3/17 8 Missouri — March 19 Missouri 65-60 — UCLA 75-74
9 Indiana — **Boise, ID** — March 23
3/17 5 Mississippi State — Mississippi St. 75-67 — UCLA 86-67
12 Santa Clara — March 19 Utah 76-64 — Mississippi State 78-64
3/17 4 Utah
13 Long Beach State

Oakland, CA March 25 — UCLA 102-96

3/16 6 Oregon
11 Texas — Texas 90-73
3/16 3 Maryland — March 18 Maryland 87-63 — Maryland 82-68
14 Gonzaga — **Salt Lake City, UT** — March 23
3/16 7 Cincinnati — Cincinnati 77-71 — Connecticut 99-89
10 Temple — March 18 Connecticut 100-71 — Connecticut 96-61
3/16 2 Connecticut
15 Tenn.-Chatt.

Alexander, who became an NBA first-round draft choice as an undergraduate, was injured.

Scoring Leader: Corliss Williamson, Arkansas (125 points, 20.8 ppg).

Highest Scoring Average: Darryl Wilson, Mississippi State (73 points, 24.3 ppg).

Rebounding Leader: Ed O'Bannon, UCLA (54 rebounds, 9 rpg).

Highest Rebounding Average: Tim Duncan, Wake Forest (43 rebounds, 14.3 rpg).

1995-96

AT A GLANCE

NCAA Champion: Kentucky (34-2; coached by Rick Pitino; won SEC Eastern Division by seven games with a 16-0 record).

NIT Champion: Nebraska (21-14; coached by Danny Nee; finished in seventh place in the Big Eight with a 4-10 record).

New Conference: Conference USA.

New Rules: All unsportsmanlike technical fouls charged to anyone on the bench count toward the team foul total. . . . Teams are allowed one 20-second timeout per half.

NCAA Probation: Alcorn State, Baylor, Georgia Southern, Morgan State, New Mexico State.

NCAA Consensus First-Team All-Americans: Ray Allen, G-F, Jr., Connecticut; Marcus Camby, C, Jr., Massachusetts; Tony Delk, G, Sr., Kentucky; Tim Duncan, C, Jr., Wake Forest; Allen Iverson, G, Soph., Georgetown; Kerry Kittles, G-F, Sr., Villanova.

National Players of the Year: Camby (20.5 ppg, 8.1 rpg, 3.9 bpg/AP, NABC, Naismith, USBWA, Wooden) and Allen (23.4 ppg, 6.5 rpg, 81.0 FT%).

National Coaches of the Year: Purdue's Gene Keady (26-6; 15-3 in Big Ten/AP, UPI, USBWA) and Massachusetts' John Calipari (35-2; 15-1 in Eastern Division of Atlantic 10/NABC, Naismith).

The Big East became the only conference ever to have three different members represented among the NCAA consensus first-team All-American selections. But second-team All-American John Wallace was the only All-Big East standout to appear with his team at the Final Four, however.

Connecticut became the first Big East team to post the league's undisputed best record in back-to-back seasons. . . . St. John's (11-16) compiled its worst mark in 33 years, giving the Red Storm three consecutive non-winning records for the first time since 1918-20. . . . West Virginia's 84-63 defeat against Boston College was the Mountaineers' worst homecourt loss since bowing to Westminster, 102-80, in the 1954-55 season. . . . Coach Lefty Driesell sustained his first losing record in 33 seasons when James Madison went 10-20. Davidson, Driesell's first head coaching outpost, became the first Southern Conference school in 21 years to go undefeated in league competition.

Massachusetts captured both the regular-season and postseason conference tournament titles for the fifth consecutive year. UMass won its first 26 games before bowing to visiting George Washington, 86-76, when Minutemen coach John Calipari was banished midway through the first half after receiving two technical fouls. Earlier, GWU finally was able to capitalize on its homecourt advantage against Temple by overwhelming the visiting Owls, 64-47. Temple had won its first 13 games at GWU's Smith Center. . . . George Washington (21-8, .724) posted its best winning percentage in 41 years while North Carolina lost three homecourt games for the first time in the same time frame.

Duke still had difficulty in the ACC despite the return of coach Mike Krzyzewski. The Blue Devils' blew double-digit leads in their first six ACC defeats and visiting Illinois hit less than half of its free throws but still ended Duke's 95-game homecourt winning streak against non-conference competition, 75-65. Later, however, the Illini lost its first five Big Ten games for the first time since the 1930-31 season. . . . Georgia Tech, despite entering conference play with six defeats in its previous seven non-league games, captured the ACC regular-season championship after winning a school-record seven consecutive league games. The Yellow Jackets almost overcame an 18-point, second-half deficit in the ACC Tournament final but bowed to Wake Forest, 75-74. . . . Wake Forest's Tim Duncan set an ACC Tournament record with with a total of 56 rebounds.

Alabama's Roy Rogers set a SEC record with a national-high 14 blocked shots in a game at Georgia but it wasn't enough to prevent a 68-55 setback against the Bulldogs. . . . Kentucky became the first SEC team in 40 years to go undefeated in league regular-season competition. The Wildcats won all but one of their regular-season SEC games by double digits but (insert SEC Tournament final vs. Mississippi State). It was MSU's first-ever SEC Tournament title. . . . Arkansas' season unraveled when junior college signees Sunday Adebayo and Jesse Pate were forced off the team late in the year because of questions about their academic eligibility. . . . Mississippi State's program came under scrunity when a suspect student and standout forward Dontae' Jones "earned" 36 junior college credits the previous summer (regular classes and correspondence courses) in order to gain his eligibility. . . . Mississippi Valley State's Marcus Mann grabbed a national-high 28 rebounds in a game against Jackson State.

Dayton's Chris Daniels ranked second in the nation in field-goal percentage when he died because of a heart ailment. His brother, Antonio, hit a layup in the closing seconds to give Bowling Green a 72-70 victory over Eastern Michigan in Antonio's first game after his sibling's death. . . . Marcus Brown set a Murray State single-game scoring record with 45 points against Washington (Mo.). His barrage tied Vermont guard Eddie Benton (45 vs. Hartford) for highest single-game output in the nation.

Texas Tech, coached by James Dickey, became only the fourth team in the 82-year history of the Southwest Conference to go undefeated in league competition. . . . New Mexico

State recruited a freshman for a scholarship for the first time in the '90s. . . . Arizona refused to play at St. Joseph's because of a snow storm although Philadelphia's airport did not close. St. Joe's coach Phil Martelli said he was so upset by the Wildcats' decision he would to play them again, even if the teams were paired in the NCAA Tournament. The decision cost the Hawks national exposure on a cable network.

Central Connecticut's Keith Closs set a national record for highest average of blocked shots per game when he rejected 6.4 field-goal attempts per outing. . . . Penn's winning streak against Ivy League competition ended at 48 when the Quakers were edged at Dartmouth, 54-53. . . . Penn State closed out 67 years at Rec Hall in style, getting off to its best start in school history (won first 11 games under first-year coach Jerry Dunn) before opening Bryce Jordan Center.

1995-96 FINAL NATIONAL POLLS

AP	UPI	USA/NABC	SCHOOL (RECORD)	HEAD COACH
1	1	2	Massachusetts (35-2)	John Calipari
2	2	1	Kentucky (34-2)	Rick Pitino
3	3	8	Connecticut (32-3)	Jim Calhoun
T4	6	7	Georgetown (29-8)	John Thompson
T4	5	5	Kansas (29-5)	Roy Williams
T4	4	15	Purdue (26-6)	Gene Keady
7	7	6	Cincinnati (28-5)	Bob Huggins
8	8	10	Texas Tech (30-2)	James Dickey
9	9	9	Wake Forest (26-6)	Dave Odom
10	12	17	Villanova (26-7)	Steve Lappas
11	11	11	Arizona (26-7)	Lute Olson
12	10	12	Utah (27-7)	Rick Majerus
13	14	13	Georgia Tech (24-12)	Bobby Cremins
14	13	19	UCLA (23-8)	Jim Harrick
15	15	3	Syracuse (29-9)	Jim Boeheim
16	16	–	Memphis (22-8)	Larry Finch
17	18	20	Iowa State (24-9)	Tim Floyd
18	17	–	Penn State (21-7)	Jerry Dunn
19	22	4	Mississippi St. (26-8)	Richard Williams
20	21	23	Marquette (23-8)	Mike Deane
21	19	22	Iowa (23-9)	Tom Davis
22	20	21	Virginia Tech (23-6)	Bill Foster
23	–	25	New Mexico (28-5)	Dave Bliss
24	23	14	Louisville (22-12)	Denny Crum
25	24	24	North Carolina (21-11)	Dean Smith
–	25	–	Stanford (20-9)	Mike Montgomery
–	–	16	Georgia (21-10)	Tubby Smith
–	–	18	Arkansas (20-13)	Nolan Richardson

Wisconsin-Green Bay went undefeated in league play, making the Midwestern Collegiate Conference the first non-divisional alliance in 25 years (Princeton and Penn in the Ivy League in 1969 and 1970, respectively) to have two dif-

THE SOUTH RISES AGAIN: THE 1990s

1995–96 INDIVIDUAL LEADERS

SCORING

PLAYER	PTS.	AVG.
Granger, Texas Southern	648	27.0
Brown, Murray St.	767	26.4
B. Wells, Austin Peay	789	26.3
Williams, Hampton	669	25.7
B. Wells, Ball St.	712	25.4
McCollum, W. Caro.	751	25.0
Iverson, Georgetown	926	25.0
Benton, Vermont	636	24.5
Alosa, New Hampshire	624	24.0
Allen, Conn.	818	23.4

REBOUNDING

PLAYER	REB.	AVG.
Mann, Miss. Valley St.	394	13.6
Rose, Drexel	409	13.2
Foyle, Colgate	364	12.6
Duncan, Wake Forest	395	12.3
Farley, Mercer	349	12.0
Ensminger, Valparaiso	368	11.5
DeLaney, Charleston	330	11.4
Tomidy, Marist	329	11.3
Lollis, Montana St.	340	11.3
Snowden, Harvard	289	11.1

ASSISTS

PLAYER	AST.	AVG.
Miglinieks, UC Irvine	230	8.5
McCants, George Mason	223	8.3
Pogue, Campbell	183	8.0
Williams, McNeese St.	200	7.4
Sims, Syracuse	281	7.4
Knight, Stanford	212	7.3
Turner, UC Santa Barbara	190	7.3
Geary, Arizona	231	7.0
Fizdale, San Diego	195	7.0
Hutchins, Marquette	215	6.9

BLOCKED SHOTS

PLAYER	BLK.	AVG.
Closs, Central Conn.	178	6.4
Foyle, Colgate	165	5.7
Rogers, Alabama	156	4.9
James, Florida A&M	119	4.4
Tomidy, Marist	113	3.9
Aluma, Liberty	113	3.9
Camby, Mass.	128	3.9
Duncan, Wake Forest	120	3.8

STEALS

PLAYER	STL.	AVG.
Williams, McNeese St.	118	4.4
Rhodes, Maryland	110	3.7
Taylor, Jackson St.	106	3.7
Salahuddin, Long Beach St.	101	3.6
Hoard, NE Ill.	97	3.6

FIELD-GOAL PERCENTAGE

PLAYER	FGM	FGA	PCT.
Lollis, Montana St.	212	314	.675
Watts, Nevada	145	221	.656
Abrams, Centenary	187	286	.654
Koul, George Wash.	163	254	.642
Mott, Coppin St.	208	326	.638
Jamison, North Caro.	201	322	.624
Caldwell, Tennessee St.	110	178	.618
Smith, Delaware	173	282	.613
Mann, Miss. Valley St.	251	415	.605
Fincher, Eastern Ky.	148	245	.604
Potapenko, Wright St.	198	328	.604

FREE-THROW PERCENTAGE

PLAYER	FTM	FTA	PCT.
Dillard, Sam Houston St.	63	68	.926
Cross, Stanford	81	88	.920
Howard, UNCC	93	103	.903
Billet, Rutgers	72	80	.900
Nash, Santa Clara	101	113	.894
Grimm, Missouri	100	113	.885
Wilson, Evansville	75	85	.882
Carter, Middle Tenn. St.	104	118	.881
Simms, UMBC	74	84	.881
Alexander, Stetson	123	140	.879

THREE-POINT FIELD GOAL PERCENTAGE

PLAYER	FGM	FGA	PCT.
Stafford,. W. Caro.	58	110	.527
Peral, Wake Forest	51	100	.510
Tebbs, Weber St.	50	100	.500
Brown, Central Mich.	51	104	.490
Fontaine, Wash. St.	66	136	.485

THREE-POINT FIELD GOALS PER GAME

PLAYER	FGM	AVG.
Young, Fresno St.	120	4.1
McLinton, James Madison	122	4.1
Veney, Marshall	111	4.0
Marshall, Northeast La.	115	3.8
Hudson, Southern Illinois	93	3.7
Lueking, Army	99	3.7

ferent schools go undefeated in conference competition in back-to-back seasons. Xavier achieved the feat the previous year. . . . Iowa State finished in the Top 20 of a final wire-service poll for the only time in school history. Penn State and Marquette reached that plateau for the first time since 1954 and 1979, respectively. . . . Former Indiana All-American Steve Alford became coach at Southwest Missouri State, where his father, Sam, joined him as an assistant in an unusual twist. . . . Minnesota became the first Big Ten team with a winning league record not to receive an at-large bid to the NCAA Tournament.

Massachusetts (35-2, coached by John Calipari), Connecticut (32-3, Jim Calhoun), Texas Tech (30-2, James Dickey), New Mexico (28-5, Dave Bliss), Drexel (27-4, Bill Herrion), Villanova (26-7, Steve Lappas), Mississippi State (26-8, Richard Williams), Iowa State (24-9, Tim Floyd), Marist (22-7, Dave Magarity) and Valparaiso (21-11, Homer Drew) had their winningest seasons in school Division I history. Wake Forest (26-6, Dave Odom) tied its school record for most victories in a single season.

Calipari accepted a five-year, $15 million deal after the season to coach the NBA's New Jersey Nets. His departure came just a couple days after a scandal erupted involving national player of the year Marcus Camby and a Hartford, Conn.-based agent. Camby, who exited Umass to make himself available for the NBA draft, admitted receiving improper gifts in college and filed a criminal complaint stemming from allega-

1995–96 TEAM LEADERS

SCORING OFFENSE

SCHOOL	PTS.	AVG.
Troy State	2551	94.5
Kentucky	3292	91.4
Marshall	2560	91.4
George Mason	2443	90.5
Southern (La.)	2521	90.0

SCORING DEFENSE

SCHOOL	PTS.	AVG.
Princeton	1498	51.7
Wis.-Green Bay	1620	55.9
South Alabama	1571	58.2
Temple	1922	58.2
N.C.-Wilmington	1694	58.4

SCORING MARGIN

SCHOOL	OFF.	DEF.	MAR.
Kentucky	91.4	69.4	22.1
Connecticut	82.6	64.7	17.9
Drexel	82.6	66.3	16.3
Davidson	84.3	68.2	16.0
Kansas	80.6	65.3	15.4

WON-LOST PERCENTAGE

SCHOOL	W-L	PCT.
Massachusetts	35-2	.946
Kentucky	34-2	.944
Texas Tech	30-2	.938
Connecticut	32-3	.914
Drexel	27-4	.871

FIELD-GOAL PERCENTAGE

SCHOOL	FGM	FGA	PCT.
UCLA	897	1698	.528
Colorado St.	851	1683	.506
Coppin St.	828	1650	.502
Montana St.	898	1800	.499
Weber St.	880	1766	.498

FIELD-GOAL PERCENTAGE DEFENSE

SCHOOL	FGM	FGA	PCT.
Temple	670	1741	.385
Marquette	682	1772	.385
Mississippi St.	803	2084	.385
Connecticut	840	2175	.386
Kansas	777	2008	.387
Massachusetts	812	2098	.387

FREE-THROW PERCENTAGE

SCHOOL	FTM	FTA	PCT.
Utah	649	828	.784
Weber St.	519	675	.769
Brigham Young	587	767	.765
Stanford	558	736	.758
Va. Military	469	623	.753

REBOUND MARGIN

SCHOOL	OWN	OPP.	MAR.
Miss. Valley	48.3	36.8	11.6
Utah St.	39.5	29.5	10.0
Utah	39.6	30.0	9.6
Iowa	40.5	31.4	9.1
Connecticut	43.4	34.4	9.0

THREE-POINT FIELD GOAL PERCENTAGE

SCHOOL	FGM	FGA	PCT.
Weber St.	245	577	.425
Wake Forest	260	618	.421
Penn St.	197	482	.409
Connecticut	258	633	.408
N.C.-Greensboro	205	503	.406

THREE-POINT FIELD GOALS PER GAME

SCHOOL	FGM	AVG.
Troy St.	300	11.1
Marshall	284	10.1
N.C. St.	292	9.4
Southern Ill.	268	9.2
Stanford	243	9.0
Southern (La.)	252	9.0
Auburn	287	9.0

tions that he was blackmailed by a would-be agent attempting to woo him as a client.

Venerable coaches Pete Carril (Princeton), Lou Henson (Illinois) and Jim Phelan (Mount St. Mary's) retired with postseason teams. Another high profile coach, UAB's Gene Bartow, also retired.

1996 NCAA Tournament

Summary: Kentucky's air of invincibility dissipated when the Wildcats' 27-game winning streak was shattered by Mississippi State in the SEC Tournament final. UK quickly regrouped, however, and the Big Blue showed clearly in the NCAA playoffs that it was the nation's premier team. Kentucky's dominance in the Midwest Regional led some observers to again believe the Wildcats were untouchable, but two rugged games at the Final Four revealed that the principal difference between the Wildcats and the

remainder of the field was roster depth. UK, entering the Final Four with an opportunity to become the first NCAA kingpin to win all of its playoff games by at least 20 points, won both Final Four games by a single-digit margin. Massachusetts and Syracuse cut double-digit second-half deficits to two at the Final Four against the 'Cats before faltering as they captured their first NCAA title since 1978. National player of the year Marcus Camby finished with 25 points and eight rebounds in the semifinals for UMass, but at one point he went almost 16 minutes without a field goal. Freshman Ron Mercer gave Kentucky a big boost with 20 points in the final after scoring just four points in the regional. The Wildcats won the final despite shooting 38 percent from the floor, the lowest for a winner in 33 years. Kentucky's Tony Delk tied a championship game record with seven three-pointers. In historical terms, there is probably only one other titlist that had

1996 FINAL FOUR CHAMPIONSHIP GAME

SEASON STATISTICS FOR KENTUCKY REGULARS

PLAYER	POS.	CL.	G.	FG%	FT%	PPG	RPG
Tony Delk	G	Sr.	36	.494	.800	17.8	4.2
Antoine Walker	F	So.	36	.463	.631	15.2	8.4
Walter McCarty	F-C	Sr.	36	.543	.721	11.3	5.7
Derek Anderson	G-F	Jr.	36	.509	.784	9.4	3.4
Ron Mercer	G-F	Fr.	36	.457	.785	8.0	2.9
Mark Pope	C	Sr.	36	.482	.683	7.6	5.2
Anthony Epps	G	Jr.	36	.438	.817	6.7	3.1
Jeff Sheppard	G	Jr.	34	.520	.621	5.5	2.1
Wayne Turner	G	Fr.	35	.533	.625	4.5	1.5
Allen Edwards	G	So.	35	.463	.739	3.3	1.1
Nazr Mohammed	C	Fr.	16	.448	.458	2.3	1.5
Oliver Simmons	F	Fr.	21	.481	.556	1.8	1.1
TEAM TOTALS			33	**.513**	**.709**	**87.5**	**40.4**

Three-point field goals leaders: Delk (93 of 210, .443), Epps (43 of 105, .410). Assists leaders: Epps 175, Walker 104, McCarty 92, Anderson 88. Blocked shots leader: McCarty 51, Pope 44. Steals leaders: Delk 67, Anderson 61, Walker 61, Epps 55.

EAST RUTHERFORD, NJ

SYRACUSE (67)	MIN.	FG-A	FT-A	REB.	A.	PF.	PTS.
Burgan	39	7-10	2-5	8	1	5	19
Wallace	38	11-19	5-5	10	1	5	29
Hill	28	3-9	1-1	10	1	2	7
Sims	38	2-5	1-2	2	7	2	6
Cipolla	35	3-8	0-0	1	2	1	6
Reafsnyder	13	0-1	0-0	4	0	0	0
Janulis	8	0-0	0-0	2	0	2	0
Nelson	1	0-0	0-0	0	0	0	0
Team	1						
TOTALS	**200**	**26-52**	**9-13**	**37**	**12**	**17**	**67**

FG%: .500. FT%: .692. Three-point goals: 6-15 (Burgan 3-5, Wallace 2-3, Sims 1-4, Cipolla 0-3). Blocks: 2. Turnovers: 24 (Sims 7, Wallace 6, Burgan 5). Steals: 6 (Cipolla 4).

KENTUCKY (76)	MIN.	FG-A	FT-A	REB.	A.	PF.	PTS.
Anderson	16	4-8	1-1	4	1	2	11
Walker	32	4-12	3-6	9	4	2	11
McCarty	19	2-6	0-0	7	3	3	4
Delk	37	8-20	1-2	7	2	2	24
Epps	35	0-6	0-0	4	7	1	0
Pope	27	1-6	2-2	3	2	3	4
Mercer	24	8-12	1-1	2	2	3	20
Sheppard	7	1-2	0-1	2	0	3	2
Edwards	3	0-1	0-0	0	1	0	0
Team	2						
TOTALS	**200**	**28-73**	**8-13**	**38**	**22**	**19**	**76**

FG%: .384. FT%: .615. Three-point goals: 12-27 (Delk 7-12, Mercer 3-4, Anderson 2-3, Walker 0-1, Sheppard 0-1, Edwards 0-1, Pope 0-2, Epps 0-3). Blocks: 1. Turnovers: 15 (Pope 4). Steals: 11 (Walker 4). Halftime: Kentucky 42-33.

NATIONAL SEMIFINALS

MISSISSIPPI STATE (69): Walters 5-9 0-0 10, Jones 6-16 2-2 16, Dampier 4-6 4-4 12, Bullard 4-9 0-0 11, Wilson 7-16 0-0 20, Hughes 0-0 0-0 0, Washington 0-0 0-0 0, Hyche 0-0 0-0 0. Team 26-56 (.464) 6-6 (1.000) 69.

SYRACUSE (77): Burgan 6-11 5-6 19, Wallace 6-14 8-10 21, Hill 7-11 1-2 15, Sims 3-5 4-4 11, Cipolla 3-9 2-2 9, Reafsnyder 1-3 0-0 2, Janulis 0-2 0-0 0. Team 26-55 (.473) 20-24 (.833) 77.

Three-point goals: Mississippi State 11-28 (.393). Syracuse 5-12 (.417). Halftime: Tied 36-36.

KENTUCKY (81): Walker 5-10 4-5 14, McCarty 4-8 0-0 8, Delk 7-16 5-9 20, Epps 3-6 0-0 7, Pope 1-2 6-6 8, Sheppard 2-2 3-4 7, Turner 1-2 0-0 2, Mercer 4-6 0-1 9, Edwards 0-0 0-0 0. Team 28-55 (.509) 22-30 (.733) 81.

MASSACHUSETTS (74): Dingle 4-6 0-0 8, Bright 7-14 1-2 15, Camby 9-18 7-9 25, E. Padilla 2-10 1-2 6, Travieso 3-7 2-2 10, Weeks 0-2 1-2 s1, Clarke 1-2 1-2 3, Norville 1-1 0-0 2, Nunez 0-0 0-0 0, G. Padilla 2-4 0-0 4. Team 29-64 (.453) 13-19 (.684) 74.

Three-point goals: Kentucky 3-9 (.333). Massachusetts 3-9 (.333). Halftime: Kentucky 36-28.

ALL-TOURNAMENT TEAM

Todd Burgan, G-F, Soph., Syracuse
Marcus Camby, C, Jr., Massachusetts
Tony Delk, G, Sr., Kentucky*
Ron Mercer, F-G, Fr., Kentucky
John Wallace, F, Sr., Syracuse
    *Named Most Outstanding Player.

as much depth as UK. Seven players for UCLA's first championship team in 1964 averaged more than four rebounds per game.

Outcome for Defending Champion: UCLA won the Pacific-10 championship but the Bruins were eliminated in the first round of the NCAA Tournament when Princeton coach Pete Carril bowed out in style with a 43-41 victory reminiscent of how many games were played several decades ago.

Star Gazing: Coach Jim Boeheim of runner-up Syracuse gave counterpart Rick Pitino of champion Kentucky Pitino's first full-time coaching job in 1976, when Boeheim was promoted to bench boss by the Orangemen. Boe-

heim came to New York and called Pitino on Pitino's wedding day, offering him an assistant's job, and was so persistent Pitino eventually met with him for 2 1/2 hours at a hotel right after the wedding. "I kept calling my wife every half-hour, telling her I'd be up (to the room)," Pitino recalled.

Biggest Upsets: The biggest upset in the tourney might not have been Princeton over UCLA. It could have been Drexel over Memphis, 75-63. Drexel has had an outstanding run the last three seasons, but Memphis had as much talent as any team in the country. . . . Western Carolina missed a three-point shot at the buzzer that would have beaten Purdue and

1996 CHAMPIONSHIP BRACKET

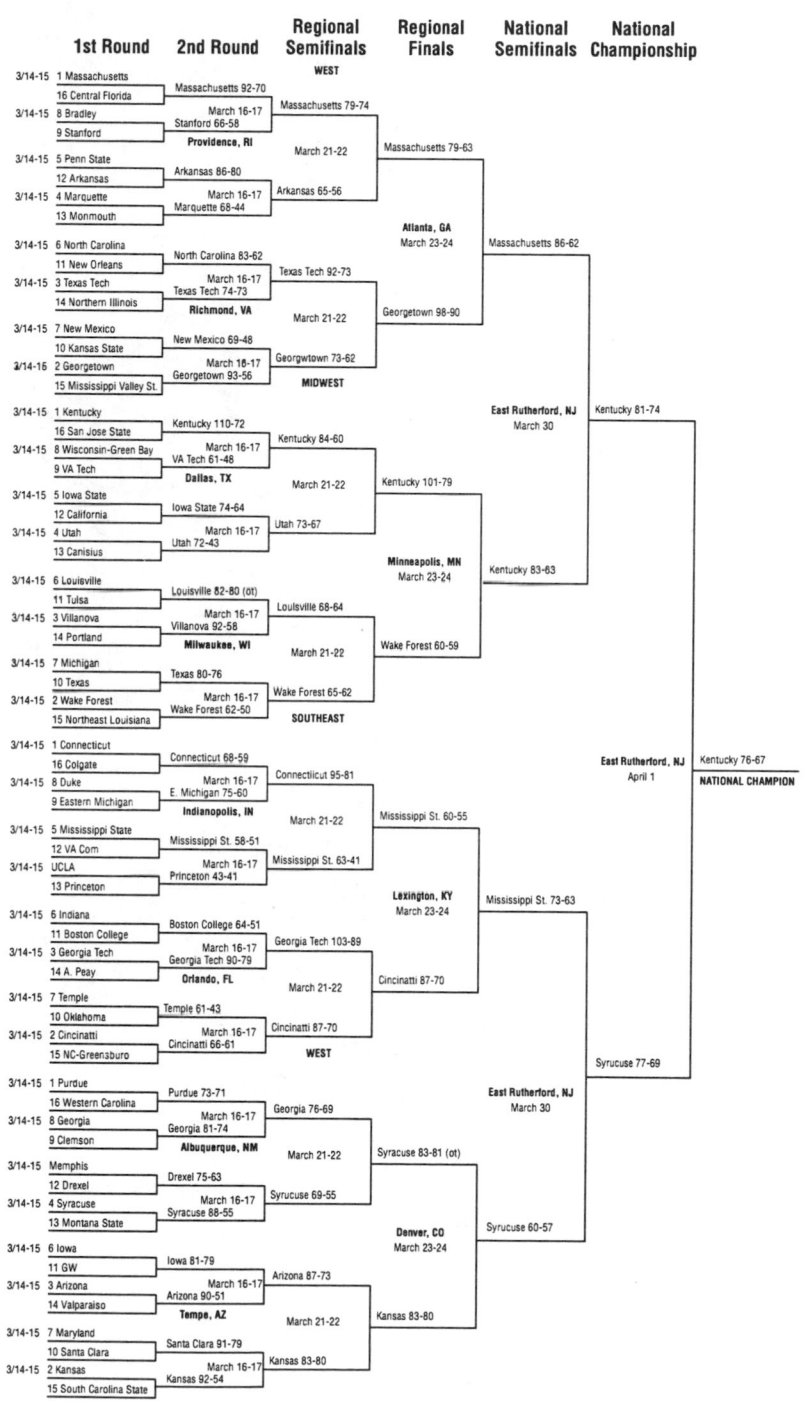

	1st Round	2nd Round	Regional Semifinals	Regional Finals	National Semifinals	National Championship

WEST

3/14-15 1 Massachusetts — Massachusetts 92-70
16 Central Florida
3/14-15 8 Bradley — March 16-17 Stanford 66-58 — Massachusetts 79-74
9 Stanford
Providence, RI
3/14-15 5 Penn State — Arkansas 86-80
12 Arkansas
3/14-15 4 Marquette — March 16-17 Marquette 68-44 — Arkansas 65-56
13 Monmouth
Massachusetts 79-63

Atlanta, GA March 23-24

3/14-15 6 North Carolina — North Carolina 83-62
11 New Orleans
3/14-15 3 Texas Tech — March 16-17 Texas Tech 74-73 — Texas Tech 92-73
14 Northern Illinois
Richmond, VA
3/14-15 7 New Mexico — New Mexico 69-48
10 Kansas State
3/14-16 2 Georgetown — March 16-17 Georgetown 93-56 — Georgwtown 73-62
15 Mississippi Valley St.
Georgetown 98-90

Massachusetts 86-62

East Rutherford, NJ March 30

MIDWEST

3/14-15 1 Kentucky — Kentucky 110-72
16 San Jose State
3/14-15 8 Wisconsin-Green Bay — March 16-17 VA Tech 61-48 — Kentucky 84-60
9 VA Tech
Dallas, TX
3/14-15 5 Iowa State — Iowa State 74-64
12 California
3/14-15 4 Utah — March 16-17 Utah 72-43 — Utah 73-67
13 Canisius
Kentucky 101-79

Kentucky 81-74

Minneapolis, MN March 23-24

3/14-15 6 Louisville — Louisville 82-80 (ot)
11 Tulsa
3/14-15 3 Villanova — March 16-17 Villanova 92-58 — Louisville 68-64
14 Portland
Milwaukee, WI
3/14-15 7 Michigan — Texas 80-76
10 Texas
3/14-15 2 Wake Forest — March 16-17 Wake Forest 62-50 — Wake Forest 65-62
15 Northeast Louisiana
Wake Forest 60-59

Kentucky 83-63

SOUTHEAST

East Rutherford, NJ April 1

Kentucky 76-67

NATIONAL CHAMPION

3/14-15 1 Connecticut — Connecticut 68-59
16 Colgate
3/14-15 8 Duke — March 16-17 E. Michigan 75-60 — Connectiicut 95-81
9 Eastern Michigan
Indianopolis, IN
3/14-15 5 Mississippi State — Mississippi St. 58-51
12 VA Com
3/14-15 UCLA — March 16-17 Princeton 43-41 — Mississippi St. 63-41
13 Princeton
Mississippi St. 60-55

Lexington, KY March 23-24

3/14-15 6 Indiana — Boston College 64-51
11 Boston College
3/14-15 3 Georgia Tech — March 16-17 Georgia Tech 90-79 — Georgia Tech 103-89
14 A. Peay
Orlando, FL
3/14-15 7 Temple — Temple 61-43
10 Oklahoma
3/14-15 2 Cincinnati — March 16-17 Cincinnati 66-61 — Cincinnati 87-70
15 NC-Greensburo
Cincinnati 87-70

Mississippi St. 73-63

East Rutherford, NJ March 30

Mississippi St. 73-63

Syrucuse 77-69

WEST

3/14-15 1 Purdue — Purdue 73-71
16 Western Carolina
3/14-15 8 Georgia — March 16-17 Georgia 81-74 — Georgia 76-69
9 Clemson
Albuquerque, NM
3/14-15 Memphis — Drexel 75-63
12 Drexel
3/14-15 4 Syracuse — March 16-17 Syracuse 88-55 — Syrucuse 69-55
13 Montana State
Syracuse 83-81 (ot)

Denver, CO March 23-24

3/14-15 6 Iowa — Iowa 81-79
11 GW
3/14-15 3 Arizona — March 16-17 Arizona 90-51 — Arizona 87-73
14 Valparaiso
Tempe, AZ
3/14-15 7 Maryland — Santa Clara 91-79
10 Santa Clara
3/14-15 2 Kansas — March 16-17 Kansas 92-54 — Kansas 83-80
15 South Carolina State
Kansas 83-80

Syracuse 60-57

made the Catamounts the first No. 16 seed winner in tourney history.

One and Only: First-year Georgia mentor Tubby Smith became the only coach to guide three consecutive teams to regional semifinals despite not being accorded a top four seed during the span. His two previous clubs were at Tulsa.

Numbers Game: Kentucky was a 13 1/2-point favorite in the NCAA final against Syracuse. That is the largest championship game spread since UCLA was a 16-point choice vs. Florida State in 1972 (Bruins won 81-76). . . . The NCAA succumbed to network pressure and moved the title game to 9:22 p.m. ET, but CBS' 18.3 rating for the championship contest was the lowest since 1972. . . . Central Florida became the second consecutive Trans America Athletic Conference team to enter the NCAA playoffs with an 11-18 record after earning a berth by winning the TAAC Tournament. . . . Canisius made its first appearance in the tourney since 1957. . . . When will the Southeastern Conference receive the respect it deserves? The SEC, boasting two teams at the Final Four for the second time in three years, compiled more NCAA Tournament victories than any league over the last three seasons. . . . The Big Ten came within eight points of going 0-11 in the NCAA playoffs the last two seasons. . . . The last four defeats for Indiana coach Bob Knight were to worse-seeded opponents. . . . Michigan's lack of maturity was exemplified when the Wolverines were assessed a technical for calling yet another timeout in the closing seconds of a playoff game while being out of timeouts. They apparently weren't making a vow to avoid Chris Webber's blunder when several of their standouts had their infamous auto accident at 5 a.m. earlier in the season. . . . Texas Tech had as many players foul out in its 98-90 loss to Georgetown in the East Regional semifinals (three) as the Red Raiders totaled in their first 34 games. . . . None of the first six NCAA champions in the '90s reached a regional final. . . . Eastern Michigan's Brian Tolbert tallied a tourney-high 36 points in a second-

After the end of the 1996 season, Calipari accepted a $15 million deal to coach the NBA's New Jersey Nets.

round setback against Connecticut in the Southeast Regional. . . . Montana State's Quadre Lollis hit 12 of 13 field-goal attempts in an opening-round loss to Syracuse in the West Regional.

What Might Have Been: Arkansas (20-13, without Corliss Williamson and Scotty Thurman), Maryland (17-13, Joe Smith), Memphis (22-8, David Vaughn) and North Carolina (21-11, Jerry Stackhouse and Rasheed Wallace) might have fared better in the playoffs if standout players had exercised their remaining eligibility instead of declaring early for the NBA draft. . . . Alabama probably would have participated in the NCAA Tournament instead of the NIT if Antonio McDyess didn't defect early for the NBA. . . . Wake Forest struggled in the tourney when guard Tony Rutland missed his first 15 shots in NCAA playoff play. Rutland eventually underwent reconstructive surgery on his right knee after tearing a ligament in the ACC Tournament title game. . . . UConn's chances to earning its first berth at the Final Four diminished when standout freshman guard Ricky Moore was idled by a shoulder injury. . . . Center Tim Young was out with a bulging disk in his lower back for Stanford, which trailed by just one point in the closing seconds vs. top-ranked UMass. . . . Virginia might have avoided becoming one of the nation's most underachieving teams if guard Cory Alexander hadn't left early for the NBA.

NCAA DIVISION I TOURNAMENT DATES AND SITES

1997 FIRST AND SECOND ROUNDS

East: Lawrence Joel Veterans Memorial Coliseum, Winston-Salem, NC (March 13 and 15, 1997). Civic Arena, Pittsburgh (March 14 and 16, 1997).

Southeast: The Pyramid, Memphis (March 13 and 15, 1997). Charlotte Coliseum, Charlotte, NC (March 14 and 16, 1997).

Midwest: The Palace of Auburn Hills, Auburn Hills, MI (March 13 and 15, 1997). Kemper Arena, Kansas City (March 14 and 16, 1997).

West: Jon M. Huntsman Center, Salt Lake City (March 13 and 15, 1997). McKale Center, Tucson, AZ (March 14 and 16, 1997).

1997 REGIONALS

East: Carrier Dome, Syracuse, NY (March 21 and 23, 1997).

Southeast: Birmingham-Jefferson Civic Center, Birmingham, AL (March 21 and 23, 1997).

Midwest: Alamodome, San Antonio, TX (March 20 and 22, 1997).

West: San Jose Arena, San Jose, CA (March 20 and 22, 1997).

1997 FINAL FOUR

RCA Dome, Indianapolis (March 29 and 31, 1997).

The East Regional winner will oppose the Southeast Regional champion and the Midwest Regional winner will oppose the West Regional champion in the national semifinals.

1998 FIRST AND SECOND ROUNDS

East: Hartford Civic Center, Hartford, CT (March 12 and 14, 1998). USAir Arena, Landover, MD (March 13 and 15, 1998).

Southeast: The Omni, Atlanta (March 12 and 14, 1998). Rupp Arena, Lexington, KY (March 13 and 15, 1998).

Midwest: Myriad Convention Center, Oklahoma City, OK (March 12 and 14, 1998). United Center, Chicago (March 13 and 15, 1998).

West: Arco Arena, Sacramento, CA (March 12 and 14, 1998). Boise State University Pavilion, Boise, ID (March 13 and 15, 1998).

1998 REGIONALS

East: Greensboro Coliseum, Greensboro, NC (March 19 and 21, 1998).

Southeast: ThunderDome, St. Petersburg, FL (March 20 and 22, 1998).

Midwest: Kiel Center, St. Louis (March 20 and 22, 1998).

West: Arrowhead Pond, Anaheim, CA (March 19 and 21, 1998).

1998 FINAL FOUR

Alamodome, San Antonio, TX (March 28 and 30, 1998).

The East Regional winner will oppose the West Regional champion and the Midwest Regional winner will oppose the Southeast Regional champion in the national semifinals.

1999 FIRST AND SECOND ROUNDS

East: FleetCenter, Boston (March 11 and 13, 1999). Charlotte Coliseum, Charlotte, NC (March 12 and 14, 1999).

Southeast: Orlando Arena, Orlando, FL (March 11 and 13, 1999). Louisiana Superdome, New Orleans (March 12 and 14, 1999).

Midwest: Bradley Center, Milwaukee (March 11 and 13, 1999). RCA Dome, Indianapolis (March 12 and 14, 1999).

West: Key Arena, Seattle (March 11 and 13, 1999). McNichols Sports Arena, Denver (March 12 and 14, 1999).

1999 REGIONALS

East: Carrier Dome, Syracuse, NY (March 18 and 20, 1999).

Southeast: Thompson-Boling Arena, Knoxville, TN (March 19 and 21, 1999).

Midwest: Trans World Dome, St. Louis (March 18 and 20, 1999).

West: America West Arena, Phoenix (March 19 and 21, 1999).

1999 FINAL FOUR

ThunderDome, St. Petersburg, FL (March 27 and 29, 1999).

The East Regional winner will oppose the Midwest Regional champion and the West Regional winner will oppose the Southeast Regional champion in the national semifinals.

2000 FINAL FOUR

RCA Dome, Indianapolis (April 1 and 3, 2000).

The East Regional winner will oppose the Southeast Regional champion and the West Regional winner will oppose the Midwest Regional champion in the national semifinals.

2001 FINAL FOUR

Metrodome, Minneapolis (March 31 and April 2, 2001).

The East Regional winner will oppose the West Regional champion and the Southeast Regional winner will oppose the Midwest Regional champion in the national semifinals.

2002 FINAL FOUR

Georgia Dome, Atlanta (March 30 and April 1, 2002).

The East Regional winner will oppose the Midwest Regional champion and the Southeast Regional winner will oppose the West Regional champion in the national semifinals.

8

NATIONAL INVITATION
TOURNAMENT (NIT)

The Final Four hasn't eternally been the final word in national postseason competition, although it appears that's the case. The NCAA Tournament, which previously played second fiddle to the National Invitation Tournament (NIT), seems to haughtily look down upon the NIT as little more than an acronymn contest for derisive entries such as National Insignificant Tournament, Not Influential Tournament, Nominally Important Tournament, No Interest Tournament, Nearly Ignominious Tournament, Naturally Impaired Tournament, Never Impressionable Tournament, and so on.

But the NIT was once superior to the NCAA Tournament during an era when airplanes did not dominate the transportation industry, television was in its infancy, and New York's Madison Square Garden was the place to be if a team wanted extensive national exposure. If ever there was a concept whose time had arrived, it was the NIT in 1938. If ever there was a location to conduct a national tourney at a time when the sports page was the principal place to get sports news, it was in New York because of Gotham's close to 20 daily newspapers.

Too many were saying for too long such provincial comments as the West was best, the East was least, the North couldn't forth, and the South was all mouth. Finally, basketball could designate a national champion. Originated by the Metropolitan Basketball Writers Association, responsibility for administering the NIT was transferred two years later to local colleges, and a group first known as the Metropolitan Intercollegiate Basketball Committee, and in 1948, as the Metropolitan Intercollegiate Basketball Association (MIBA).

And the NIT lived up to its billing. In 1939, the NIT final featured two unbeaten teams when Long Island University defeated Loyola of Chicago, 44-32 (see accompanying box score).

In the early years, the NIT was an extravaganza so hot the NCAA playoffs were actually scheduled after the NIT to prevent the lukewarm reception given the NCAA from turning completely frigid by going head-to-head against what was clearly basketball's showcase event. Such schedule modifications allowed City College of New York to become the only school to win both titles in the same year (1950) and permitted Utah to win the 1944 NCAA crown after the Utes were eliminated in the opening round of the NIT by eventual third-place finisher Kentucky (46-38). The final year teams participated in both national tournaments was 1952, when Dayton, Duquesne, St. John's, and St. Louis doubled up on postseason participation. St. John's was runner-up to Kansas in the NCAA Tournament that year after the Redmen lost their opener in the NIT against La Salle (51-45). Western Kentucky (28-2, .933), the 1948 NIT third-place finisher, and Seton Hall (31-2, .939), the 1953 NIT champion, led the nation in winning percentages those seasons.

Some observers believe the 1948 NIT, starting the tourney's second decade, was the best from a strength standpoint. If there had been a national poll at the time, it is believed that five of the nation's top seven teams were in the NIT, which was won that year by Ed Macauley-led St. Louis University.

In each of the first two years the Associated Press conducted national rankings (1949 and 1950), five of the top 10 teams participated in the NIT. The four seeded teams in the 1949 NIT all were upset in the quarterfinals after receiving first-round byes—Kentucky, St. Louis, Western Kentucky, and Utah. Four of the 12 teams in the 1953 and 1960 NIT fields were schools ranked in the top 10 of the final AP and/or UPI polls. In

HOW NIT FIELD HAS INCREASED

A committee of New York writers decided that the inaugural NIT would have two local teams, two from elsewhere in the East, and two from the Midwest or Far West. Three years later, the 1941 NIT included three New York area schools in the first eight-team format.

The final year of the 1940s posed a dilemma when local teams failed to compile sterling records, however. Faced with forgoing any local draws, the NIT made a drastic change and expanded the field to 12 teams, adding an opening round to eliminate four entrants. The 1949 opening-round pair of doubleheaders was a dark day and evening for Big Apple hoops as CCNY, Manhattan, NYU, and St. John's dropped their openers by an average of 18.75 points.

Here is how the NIT field has increased over the years:

1938 (6 entrants), 1941 (8), 1949 (12), 1965 (14), 1968 (16), 1979 (24), and 1980 (32).

Note: The NIT went back to a twelve-team field for one year (1976).

1954, the last four NIT survivors (Holy Cross, Duquesne, Niagara, and Western Kentucky) combined to win 91 percent of their games entering the semifinals, while their NCAA counterparts (La Salle, Bradley, Penn State, and Southern Cal) combined to win barely over 70 percent

POSTSEASON BATTLE OF UNBEATENS   On March 22, 1939, the NIT final game, held at New York's Madison Square Garden, featured two unbeaten teams—Loyola of Chicago and Long Island University. That game marked the only time in major-college history that two undefeated major colleges met in a national postseason tournament. LIU defeated Loyola, 44-32. LIU finished with a 24-0 record and Loyola 21-1.

LIU (44)	FG	FT	PTS.
Torgoff	5	2	12
King	0	0	0
Kaplowitz	4	1	9
Schwartz	0	2	2
Scharf	0	0	0
Sewitch	0	1	1
Lobelin	0	0	0
Newman	1	1	3
Shelly	1	0	2
Bromberg	2	1	5
Schechtman	4	1	9
Zeitlin	0	1	1
TOTALS	**17**	**10**	**44**

LOYOLA (32)	FG	FT	PTS.
Hogan	2	0	4
Schell	1	0	2
O'Brien	4	1	9
Graham	1	0	2
Novak	0	1	1
Kautz	3	0	6
Driscoll	0	0	0
Wenskus	4	0	8
TOTALS	**15**	**2**	**32**

of their games. Niagara, the third-place finisher in the NIT, defeated 1954 NCAA champion La Salle twice during the regular season by a total of 27 points.

The NCAA final was also conducted at Madison Square Garden seven times in eight years from 1943 to 1950. NIT crowds averaged more than 18,000 fans per game from 1945 through 1948. But after a point-shaving scandal in 1951 turned New York into a basketball cesspool, the Final Four didn't come anywhere close to the Big Apple, until the semifinals and final were held at the Meadowlands in East Rutherford, New Jersey, in 1996.

NCAA Puts on the Pressure

The NCAA, making it mandatory in the mid-1950s for any team winning its conference to participate in the NCAA playoffs, methodically set in motion the forces pressuring the majority of major schools into selecting its national tournament over the NIT. Xavier, right smack in the middle of some bizarre circumstances, is a vivid example of that turbulence. NIT champion-to-be Louisville was ranked 4th in the nation by AP in mid-February when it lost by 40 points at Xavier (99-59). Two years later, Xavier lost 10 of its final 15 regular-season games after a 10-1 start and the NIT asked the Musketeers to give back its NIT bid. But Xavier said no and went on to win the 1958 NIT title.

The issue of "choice" came to a head in 1970 when Marquette, an independent school at the time coached by feisty Al McGuire, won the NIT

St. Louis' Ed Macauley (white uniform, jumping) fights off a defender in a 1949 NIT game.

after rejecting an NCAA at-large invitation because the Warriors were going to be placed in the NCAA Midwest Regional (Fort Worth, Texas) instead of closer to home in the Mideast Regional (Dayton, Ohio). McGuire's snub led the NCAA to decree that any school offered an NCAA bid must accept it or be prohibited from participating in postseason competition.

The NIT, although imperiled by the NCAA's self-serving maneuvers, more than held its own with the NCAA Tournament

Western Kentucky has made 11 NIT appearances, including a second-place finish in 1942. Shown here are members of the 1947–48 team, which took third place in the NIT (from left): Don Ray, John Oldham, Odie Spears, coach E. A. Diddle, Oran McKinney, Dee Gibson, and assistant coach Ted Hornback.

because of some scintillating storylines. The final NIT at the old Garden in 1967 belonged to a so-called "small" school, Southern Illinois, sparked by a smooth swingman named Walt Frazier. He wasn't Clyde yet, but the future Knick was well on his way.

The competitive NIT, boasting three double overtime games in 1971, was a stark contrast to the "UCLA Invitational." Seemingly invincible UCLA captured seven consecutive NCAA titles from 1967 to 1973 by winning 28 tournament games by an average of almost 18 points per contest. In 1973, the Bruins' four tournament vic-

tories were by an average of 16 points, including a 21-point triumph over Memphis State in the championship game. Meanwhile, NIT champion Virginia Tech won four exciting postseason games that year by a total of five points, including a game-winning basket at the buzzer in overtime in the final against Notre Dame. The next year, seven of the 12 NIT games in the first round and quarterfinals were decided by four points or less.

Exacerbating the tug of war between the two events was a short-lived, eight-team tournament ostensibly to showcase league runners-up but principally introduced to hamper the NIT field. The new tourney was called the Collegiate Commissioners Association Tournament in 1974, when Indiana won the title at St. Louis, and then changed to the National Commissioners Invitational Tournament in 1975, when Drake won the title at Louisville.

The bottom line: Once network television made its move, it left virtually no choice for schools to choose between the national postseason events. The NCAA inflicted another blow to the NIT in 1978 when NCAA Productions started televising all of the NCAA Tournament games. The occasionally acrimonious battle was over as TV made the NCAA playoffs larger, more affluent, and more visible than it ever fantasized it could become.

While the NCAA pulled strings like a master puppeteer, the NIT's influence eroded. Prominent active coaches such as Lute Olson and Eddie Sutton have never appeared in the NIT. The last consensus first-team All-American to participate in the NIT was forward Larry Bird of Indiana State, a loser at Rutgers in the 1978 quarterfinals. The last wire-service top 10 team to appear in the NIT was North Carolina, a first-round loser against Purdue in 1974.

NIT in Recent Years

The NIT championship games the first half of the 1980s were precursors to bigger things to come. In a five-year span from 1980 through 1984 when the NCAA field ranged from 48 to 52 teams, Virginia (1980 NIT champion), DePaul (1983 runner-up), and Michigan (1984 champion) became NCAA regional No. 1 seeds the year after reaching an NIT final. Tulsa was a no. 3 seed under coach Nolan Richardson in the 1982 NCAA Tournament after capturing the '81 NIT by winning its last three games by a total of five points. But when the NCAA bracket was increased to 64 in 1985, the move effectively denied the NIT access even to the vast majority of up-and-coming teams. In effect, the NIT champion was reduced to proclaiming "We're

FALSE START

Does an NIT crown serve as a springboard to future success for budding powers? The 11 NIT titlists from 1985 through 1995 combined for a losing national postseason tournament record (9-10) the year after capturing an NIT championship–NCAA (6-8) and NIT (3-2). Here is a breakdown of how the NIT champions fared the next season since the NCAA Tournament expanded to 64 teams in 1985:

YEAR	NIT CHAMPION	PERFORMANCE THE FOLLOWING SEASON
1985	UCLA	15-14 record; 9-9 in Pac-10 (4th place); no postseason.
1986	Ohio State	20-13; 9-9 in Big Ten (6th); lost in NCAA 2nd round.
1987	Southern Miss.	19-11; 5-7 in Metro (7th); lost in NIT 2nd round.
1988	Connecticut	18-13; 6-10 in Big East (T7th); lost in NIT 3rd round.
1989	St. John's	24-10; 10-6 in Big East (4th); lost in NCAA 2nd round.
1990	Vanderbilt	17-13; 11-7 in SEC (4th); lost in NCAA 1st round.
1991	Stanford	18-11; 10-8 in Pac-10 (4th); lost in NCAA 1st round.
1992	Virginia	21-10; 9-7 in ACC (5th); lost in NCAA regional semifinal.
1993	Minnesota	21-12; 10-8 in Big Ten (T4th); lost in NCAA 2nd round.
1994	Villanova	25-8; 14-4 in Big East (2nd); lost in NCAA 1st round.
1995	Virginia Tech	23-6; 13-3 in Atlantic 10 (T1st/W); lost in 2nd round.

No. 65!" although anywhere from nine to 13 teams out of the NIT draw made the NCAA field the following year since the NCAA expanded to 64 entrants.

The NIT has made several strategic alterations over the years, but they've had little impact on how the event is perceived from a national scope. Attendance slipped to an all-time low in 1976 although national power Kentucky won the title. In 1977, former executive director Pete Carlesimo saved the NIT by implementing a plan whereby early-round games were played at campus sites and locations across the country before the four semifinalists advanced to New York. In 1985, the NIT started a preseason tournament, which evolved into the nation's premier in-season tourney and now probably carries as much clout, if not more, than the postseason NIT. Coaches are fond of the preseason NIT because those games are exempt

ACTIVE COACHES WITH NIT TITLES
(THROUGH 1996)

COACH	SCHOOL(YEAR)
Dean Smith	North Carolina ('71)
Lefty Driesell	Maryland ('72)
Don DeVoe	Virginia Tech ('73)
Bob Knight	Indiana ('79)
Nolan Richardson	Tulsa ('81)
Bill Frieder	Michigan ('84)
Eldon Miller	Ohio State ('86)
Jim Calhoun	Connecticut ('88)
Eddie Fogler	Vanderbilt ('90)
Mike Montgomery	Stanford ('91)
Jeff Jones	Virginia ('92)
Clem Haskins	Minnesota ('93)
Steve Lappas	Villanova ('94)
Bill Foster	Virginia Tech ('95)
Danny Nee	Nebraska ('96)

Lenny Wilkens (#14) was a star for the Providence Friars when they were a dominant team in the early 1960s NIT tournaments.

from counting against their regular-season limit of contests.

The memories and tradition of the NIT are marvelous, yet one occasionally wonders how much longer the postseason event can survive when it became so contrived that second- and third-round matchups aren't announced until after the previous games are played. Although the NIT has tinkered with a rule making certain every semifinalist played at least one road game before getting to New York, it is perceived as a tournament awarding home games on the basis of gate-receipt potential or to favor teams bringing the most fans or publicity or both to Madison Square Garden for the tourney's semifinals and final.

Texas-El Paso coach Don Haskins was irked in 1993 when the Miners were consigned to Georgetown's on-campus, 2,200-seat McDonough Gym for a second-round game after UTEP had a near-capacity crowd of 11,800 for a first-round contest against Houston. Haskins, according to AP, called the decision political. "They (NIT officials) want to have Georgetown in New York (for the semifinals and final)," he said. "It's all politics." In 1994, Coppin State, undefeated in the Mid-Eastern Athletic Conference and 22-8 overall with a difficult non-league schedule, rightfully thought the selection process was unjust when it was left out of the NIT.

The NIT's first nine champions lost a total of 25 games, but its eleven titlists from 1986 through 1996 combined to go 24 gamesbelow .500 just in conference competition, including a 4-12 league mark compiled by 1988 Big East cellar dweller Connecticut and a 4-10 league record registered by 1996 Big Eight seventh place team Nebraska. The NIT's "final four" participants combined to average more than 13 defeats per team in the first 12 years after the NCAA field expanded to 64 entrants, including a grim 19-18 mark by 1985 NIT fourth-place finisher Louisville. Louisville was the only school to win two NCAA titles from 1977 to 1986. The 1985 NIT finalists (UCLA and Indiana) have combined for 15 NCAA championships.

"NIT! NIT! NIT!" is chanted at some games by taunting crowds seeking to ridicule opponents who have the potential to participate in

Oregon's Ron Lee was Most Valuable Player of the 1975 NIT.

NIT FINAL GAME SUMMARY

YEAR	CHAMPION	RUNNER-UP	MOST VALUABLE PLAYER
1938	Temple	Colorado	Don Shields, Temple
1939	Long Island Univ.	Loyola of Chicago	Bill Lloyd, St. John's
1940	Colorado	Duquesne	Bob Doll, Colorado
1941	Long Island Univ.	Ohio University	Frank Baumholtz, Ohio
1942	West Virginia	Western Kentucky	Rudy Baric, West Virginia
1943	St. John's	Toledo	Harry Boykoff, St. John's
1944	St. John's	DePaul	Bill Kotsores, St. John's
1945	DePaul	Bowling Green St.	George Mikan, DePaul
1946	Kentucky	Rhode Island	Ernie Calverley, Rhode Island
1947	Utah	Kentucky	Vern Gardner, Utah
1948	St. Louis	New York Univ.	Ed Macauley, St. Louis
1949	San Francisco	Loyola of Chicago	Don Lofgan, San Francisco
1950	CCNY	Bradley	Ed Warner, CCNY
1951	Brigham Young	Dayton	Roland Minson, Brigham Young
1952	La Salle	Dayton	Tom Gola and Norm Grekin, La Salle
1953	Seton Hall	St. John's	Walter Dukes, Seton Hall
1954	Holy Cross	Duquesne	Togo Palazzi, Holy Cross
1955	Duquesne	Dayton	Maurice Stokes, St. Francis (Pa.)
1956	Louisville	Dayton	Charlie Tyra, Louisville
1957	Bradley	Memphis St.	Win Wilfong, Memphis St.
1958	Xavier	Dayton	Hank Stein, Xavier
1959	St. John's	Bradley	Tony Jackson, St. John's
1960	Bradley	Providence	Lenny Wilkens, Providence
1961	Providence	St. Louis	Vin Ernst, Providence
1962	Dayton	St. John's	Bill Chmielewski, Dayton
1963	Providence	Canisius	Ray Flynn, Providence
1964	Bradley	New Mexico	Lavern Tart, Bradley
1965	St. John's	Villanova	Ken McIntyre, St. John's
1966	Brigham Young	New York Univ.	Bill Melchionni, Villanova
1967	Southern Illinois	Marquette	Walt Frazier, Southern Illinois
1968	Dayton	Kansas	Don May, Dayton
1969	Temple	Boston College	Terry Driscoll, Boston College
1970	Marquette	St. John's	Dean Meminger, Marquette
1971	North Carolina	Georgia Tech	Bill Chamberlain, N. Carolina
1972	Maryland	Niagara	Tom McMillen, Maryland
1973	Virginia Tech	Notre Dame	John Shumate, Notre Dame
1974	Purdue	Utah	Mike Sojourner, Utah
1975	Princeton	Providence	Ron Lee, Oregon
1976	Kentucky	UNC Charlotte	Cedric Maxwell, UNC Charlotte
1977	St. Bonaventure	Houston	Greg Sanders, St. Bonaventure
1978	Texas	N.C. State	Jim Krivacs and Ron Baxter, Texas
1979	Indiana	Purdue	Butch Carter and Ray Tolbert, Indiana
1980	Virginia	Minnesota	Ralph Sampson, Virginia
1981	Tulsa	Syracuse	Greg Stewart, Tulsa
1982	Bradley	Purdue	Mitchell Anderson, Bradley
1983	Fresno St.	DePaul	Ron Anderson, Fresno St.
1984	Michigan	Notre Dame	Tim McCormick, Michigan
1985	UCLA	Indiana	Reggie Miller, UCLA
1986	Ohio State	Wyoming	Brad Sellers, Ohio State
1987	Southern Miss.	La Salle	Randolph Keys, Southern Miss.
1988	Connecticut	Ohio State	Phil Gamble, Connecticut
1989	St. John's	St. Louis	Jayson Williams, St. John's
1990	Vanderbilt	St. Louis	Scott Draud, Vanderbilt
1991	Stanford	Oklahoma	Adam Keefe, Stanford
1992	Virginia	Notre Dame	Bryant Stith, Virginia
1993	Minnesota	Georgetown	Voshon Lenard, Minnesota
1994	Villanova	Vanderbilt	Doremus Bennerman, Siena
1995	Virginia Teach	Marquette	Shawn Smith, Virgina Tech
1996	Nebraska	St. Joseph's	Erick Strickland, Nebraska

the NCAA Tournament but who are on the fence to make it and apparently may have to settle for the NIT. CBS analyst Billy Packer once called the NIT "a gerrymandering tournament with no accountability."

Although NIT-picking observers think the postseason NIT should be taken off life support, the mood in New York is to retain a stiff upper lip. "We think the NIT is still a service to college basketball," said Jack Powers, the NIT's executive director. "Our early-round games frequently play to packed arenas and we still draw reasonably well in the Garden. Because of parity all across the country, there is a place for the teams in our tournament."

MOST NIT APPEARANCES
(THROUGH 1996)

SCHOOL	APPEARANCES
St. John's*	26
Bradley*	17
Dayton	17
Duquesne	16
Fordham	16
Manhattan	16
St. Louis	16
Providence	14
New Mexico	13
DePaul	12
Louisville	12
St. Bonaventure	12
St. Peter's	12
Temple	12
Villanova	12
Holy Cross	11
La Salle	11
Marquette	11
Memphis State	11
St. Joseph's	11
Seton Hall	11
Utah	11
Western Kentucky	11
West Virginia	11
Bowling Green State	10
Clemson	10
Nebraska	10
Niagara	10

*St. John's (5) and Bradley (4) have the most NIT championships.

9

PLAYER REGISTER

W ho were the premier players in major-college history? There's excellence everywhere one turns ... so many greats to choose from ... so many divergent opinions on a seemingly endless list of standout individuals ... so many dilemmas separating pertinent facts from school-submitted fax.

Citing qualifications for determining the cream of the crop is a no-win situation. But in order to whittle the illustrious field of candidates to a manageable number, there must be criteria. Following are the standards used in *Inside Sports College Basketball* to determine the greatest college players of all time. There is an emphasis on NBA achievements so as not to forget numerous star players who left college with eligibility remaining.

- NCAA consensus first-team All-American selection or two-time NCAA consensus second-team All-American selection since the NCAA started compiling national statistics in 1948.

- Two-time NCAA consensus first- or second-team All-American selection from the start of the national tournament in 1939 until the NCAA began keeping national statistics.

- Two-time NCAA consensus first-team All-American selection from 1929 until the start of the NCAA Tournament.

- Averaged more than 30 points per game or scored more than 2,750 points in major-college career.

- Collected more than 2,000 points and 1,500 rebounds.

- Led the nation in scoring and rebounding in the same season.

- Two-time national scoring leader.

- Averaged more than 20 points and 20 rebounds per game in college career.

- Two-time All-NCAA Tournament team selection.

- NBA or ABA Most Valuable Player.

- NBA Finals Most Valuable Player.

- Scored more than 15,000 points in NBA and/or ABA career.

- All-NBA first-, second- or third-team selection a minimum of four times.

- Territorial pick or one of the top two choices in an NBA draft since 1955.

The following are abbreviations used throughout this chapter, first in the text, then in the statistical tables.

ABA	American Basketball Association
AP	Associated Press
BAA	Basketball Association of America
NABC	National Association of Basketball Coaches
NBA	National Basketball Association
NBL	National Basketball League
NCAA	National Collegiate Athletic Association
NIT	National Invitation Tournament
ppg	Points per game
UPI	United Press International
USBWA	United States Basketball Writers Association
G	Games played
FGM	Field goals made
FGA	Field goal attempts
FG%	Field goal percentage
FTM	Free throws made
FTA	Free throw attempts
FT%	Free throw percentage
Reb.	Rebounds
Avg.	Average number of rebounds or points per game
Pts.	Points

KAREEM ABDUL-JABBAR
see Lew Alcindor

MAHDI ABDUL-RAHMAD
see Walt Hazzard

MAHMOUD ABDUL-RAUF
see Chris Jackson

MARK AGUIRRE
DePaul
6-6 – F
Chicago, Ill.

Named national player of the year by AP, UPI, and USBWA in 1980.... Naismith Award winner in 1980.... NCAA unanimous first-team All-American in 1980 and 1981.... Leading scorer and second-leading rebounder for 1979 national third-place team (26-6 record).... Member of All-NCAA Tournament team in 1979.... Averaged 20.6 points and 6.1 rebounds in seven NCAA Tournament games from 1979 to 1981 (4-3 record).... Member of 1980 U.S. Olympic team.... Selected as an undergraduate by the Dallas Mavericks in first round of 1981 NBA draft (1st pick overall).

Season	G	FGM	FGA	FG%	FTM	FTA	FT%	Reb.	Avg.	Pts.	Avg.
1978–79	32	302	581	.520	163	213	.765	244	7.6	767	24.0
1979–80	28	281	520	.540	187	244	.766	213	7.6	749	26.8
1980–81	29	280	481	.582	106	137	.774	249	8.6	666	23.0
Totals	89	863	1582	.546	456	594	.768	706	7.9	2182	24.5

DANNY AINGE
Brigham Young
6-5 – G
Eugene, Ore.

Named national player of the year by NABC in 1981.... Wooden Award winner in 1981.... NCAA unanimous first-team All-American in 1981.... Averaged 17.8 points in six NCAA Tournament games from 1979 to 1981 (3-3 record).... Selected by the Boston Celtics in second round of 1981 NBA draft (31st pick overall) after he played three years in the American League as an infielder with the Toronto Blue Jays.

Season	G	FGM	FGA	FG%	FTM	FTA	FT%	Reb.	Avg.	Pts.	Avg.
1977–78	30	243	473	.514	146	169	.864	173	5.8	632	21.1
1978–79	27	206	376	.548	86	112	.768	102	3.8	498	18.4
1979–80	29	229	430	.533	97	124	.782	114	3.9	555	19.1
1980–81	32	309	596	.518	164	199	.824	152	4.8	782	24.4
Totals	118	987	1875	.526	493	604	.816	541	4.6	2467	20.9

LEW ALCINDOR
UCLA
7-2 – C
New York, N.Y.

Named national player of the year by AP, UPI, and the USBWA in 1967 and 1969.... Naismith Award winner in 1969.... NCAA unanimous first-team All-American in 1967, 1968, and 1969.... Led the nation in field-goal shooting in 1967 and 1969.... Named Final Four Most Outstanding Player in 1967, 1968, and 1969.... Leading scorer and rebounder for NCAA champions in 1967 (30-0 record), 1968 (29-1) and 1969 (29-1).... Averaged 25.3 points and 16.8 rebounds in 12 NCAA Tournament games from 1967 to 1969 (12-0 record).... Selected by the Milwaukee Bucks in first round of 1969 NBA draft (1st pick overall).... Changed his name to Kareem Abdul-Jabbar.

Season	G	FGM	FGA	FG%	FTM	FTA	FT%	Reb.	Avg.	Pts.	Avg.
1966–67	30	346	519	.667	178	274	.650	466	15.5	870	29.0
1967–68	28	294	480	.613	146	237	.616	461	16.5	734	26.2
1968–69	30	303	477	.635	115	188	.612	440	14.7	721	24.0
Totals	88	943	1476	.639	439	699	.628	1367	15.5	2325	26.4

STEVE ALFORD
Indiana
6-2 – G
New Castle, Ind.

NCAA unanimous first-team All-American in 1987 and consensus first-team All-American in 1986.... Led the nation in free-throw percentage in 1984.... Leading scorer for 1987 NCAA champion (30-4 record).... Named to All-NCAA Tournament team in 1987.... Averaged 21.3 points in 10 NCAA Tournament games in 1984, 1986 and 1987 (8-2 record).... Averaged 21.6 points in five NIT games for 1985 runner-up.... Member of 1984 U.S. Olympic team.... Selected by the Dallas Mavericks in second round of 1987 NBA draft (26th pick overall).

Season	G	FGM	FGA	FG%	FTM	FTA	FT%	Reb.	Avg.	Pts.	Avg.
1983–84	31	171	289	.592	137	150	.913	82	2.6	479	15.5
1984–85	32	232	431	.538	116	126	.921	101	3.2	580	18.1
1985–86	28	254	457	.556	122	140	.871	75	2.7	630	22.5
1986–87	34	241	508	.474	160	180	.889	87	2.6	749	22.0
Totals	125	898	1685	.533	535	596	.898	345	2.8	2438	19.5

Three-point field goals: 107 of 202 (.530) in 1986–87.

LUCIUS ALLEN
UCLA
6-2 – G
Kansas City, Mo.

NCAA consensus second-team All-American in 1968.... Named to All-NCAA Tournament team in 1967 and 1968.... Second-leading scorer for NCAA champions in 1967 (30-0 record) and 1968 (29-1).... Averaged 15.1 points and 6.8 rebounds in eight NCAA Tournament games in 1967 and 1968 (8-0 record).... Selected by the Seattle SuperSonics in first round of 1969 NBA draft (3rd pick overall).

Season	G	FGM	FGA	FG%	FTM	FTA	FT%	Reb.	Avg.	Pts.	Avg.
1966–67	30	187	390	.479	92	129	.713	175	5.8	466	15.5
1967–68	30	186	403	.462	80	118	.678	181	6.0	452	15.1
1968–69				Did not play because of academic problems.							
Totals	60	373	793	.470	172	247	.696	356	5.9	918	15.3

RAY ALLEN
Connecticut
6-5 – G/F
Dalzell, S.C.

Named national player of the year by UPI in 1996. . . . NCAA unanimous first-team All-American in 1996. . . . Ranked among the nation's leading scorers in 1995 (34th) and 1996 (10th). . . . Averaged 19.5 points and seven rebounds in 10 NCAA Tournament games from 1994-96 (7-3 record).

Season	G.	FGM	FGA	FG%	FTM	FTA	FT%	Reb.	Avg.	Pts.	Avg.
1993-94	34	158	310	.510	80	101	.792	155	4.6	429	12.6
1994-95	32	255	521	.489	80	110	.727	218	6.8	675	21.1
1995-96	35	292	618	.472	119	147	.810	228	6.5	818	23.4
Totals	101	705	1449	.487	279	358	.779	601	6.0	1922	19.0

Three-point field goals: 33 of 82 (.402) in 1993-94, 85 of 191 (.445) in 1994-95 and 115 of 247 (.466) in 1995-96. **Totals:** 233 of 520 (.448).

KENNY ANDERSON
Georgia Tech
6-1 – G
Queens, N.Y.

NCAA unanimous first-team All-American in 1991.... Second-leading scorer and leader in assists for 1990 Final Four team (28-7 record).... Averaged 25.7 points and five assists in seven NCAA Tournament games in 1990 and 1991 (5-2 record).... Selected as an undergraduate by the New Jersey Nets in first round of 1991 NBA draft (2nd pick overall).

Season	G	FGM	FGA	FG%	FTM	FTA	FT%	Reb.	Avg.	Pts.	Avg.
1989–90	35	283	549	.515	107	146	.733	193	5.5	721	20.6
1990–91	30	278	636	.437	155	187	.829	171	5.7	776	25.9
Totals	65	561	1185	.473	262	333	.787	364	5.6	1497	23.0

Three-point field goals: 48 for 117 (.410) in 1989–90 and 65 for 185 (.351) in 1990–91. **Totals:** 113 for 302 (.374).

NATE ARCHIBALD
Texas-El Paso
6-1 – G
Bronx, N.Y.

Scored 36 points in his only NCAA Tournament game in 1970.... Averaged 29.5 Points in one junior college season at Arizona Western.... Selected by the Cincinnati Royals in second round of 1970 NBA draft (19th pick overall).... Elected to Naismith Memorial Basketball Hall of Fame in 1990.

Season	G	FGM	FGA	FG%	FTM	FTA	FT%	Reb.	Avg.	Pts.	Avg.
1967–68	23	131	281	.466	102	140	.729	81	3.5	364	15.8
1968–69	25	199	374	.532	161	194	.830	69	2.8	559	22.4
1969–70	25	180	351	.513	176	225	.782	66	2.6	536	21.4
Totals	73	510	1006	.507	439	559	.785	216	2.9	1459	20.0

PAUL ARIZIN
Villanova
6-4 – F
Philadelphia, Pa.

Consensus first-team All-American in 1950.... Led the nation in scoring in 1950.... Averaged 26 points in two NCAA Tournament games in 1949 (1-1 record).... Selected by the Philadelphia Warriors in first round of 1950 NBA draft.... Elected to Naismith Memorial Basketball Hall of Fame in 1977.

Season	G	FGM	FGA	FG%	FTM	FTA	FT%	Reb.	Avg.	Pts.	Avg.
1947–48	24	101			65	98	.663			267	11.1
1948–49	27	210			174	233	.747			594	22.0
1949–50	29	260	527	.493	215	278	.773			735	25.3
Totals	80	571			454	609	.745			1596	20.0

JOHN AUSTIN
Boston College
6-0 – G
Hyattsville, Md.

Ranked among the nation's leading scorers in 1964 (8th), 1965 (7th) and 1966 (22nd). . . . Ranked 18th in the nation in free-throw percentage in 1966. . . . Did not play in NCAA Tournament. . . . Scored 40 points in one NIT game in 1965. Did not play in 1966 NIT because of a foot injury. . . . Selected by the Celtics in fourth round of 1966 NBA draft (38th pick overall).

Season	G.	FGM	FGA	FG%	FTM	FTA	FT%	Reb.	Avg.	Pts.	Avg.
1963-64	21	235	489	.481	144	191	.754	125	6.0	614	29.2
1964-65	25	231	514	.449	211	267	.790	100	4.0	673	26.9
1965-66	22	189	470	.402	170	202	.842	75	3.4	548	24.9
Totals	68	655	1473	.445	525	660	.795	300	4.4	1835	27.0

WILLIAM (BIRD) AVERITT
Pepperdine
6-1 – G
Hopkinsville, Ky.

Led the nation in scoring in 1973.... Did not play in NCAA Tournament or NIT.... Selected as an undergraduate by the San Diego Conquistadors in second round of 1973 ABA special circumstance draft.

Season	G	FGM	FGA	FG%	FTM	FTA	FT%	Reb.	Avg.	Pts.	Avg.
1971–72	24	263	638	.412	167	225	.742	147	6.1	693	28.9
1972–73	25	352	753	.467	144	211	.682	92	3.7	848	33.9
Totals	49	615	1391	.442	311	436	.713	239	4.9	1541	31.4

CHARLES BARKLEY
Auburn
6-6 – F
Leeds, Ala.

Collected 23 points and 17 rebounds in one NCAA Tournament game in 1984.... Leading scorer (18 points per game) for 1992 U.S. Olympic team.... Selected as an undergraduate by the Philadelphia 76ers in first round of 1984 NBA draft (5th pick overall).

Season	G	FGM	FGA	FG%	FTM	FTA	FT%	Reb.	Avg.	Pts.	Avg.
1981–82	28	144	242	.595	68	107	.636	275	9.8	356	12.7
1982–83	28	161	250	.644	82	130	.631	266	9.5	404	14.4
1983–84	28	162	254	.638	99	145	.683	265	9.5	423	15.1
Totals	84	467	746	.626	249	382	.652	806	9.6	1183	14.1

JIM BARNES
Texas-El Paso
6-8 – F/C
Tuckerman, Ark.

Averaged 17.8 points and 11 rebounds in four NCAA Tournament games in 1963 and 1964 (2-2 record).... Averaged 29.8 points in two junior college seasons at Cameron (Okla.).... Member of 1964 U.S. Olympic team.... Selected by the New York Knicks in first round of 1964 NBA draft (1st pick overall).

Season	G	FGM	FGA	FG%	FTM	FTA	FT%	Reb.	Avg.	Pts.	Avg.
1962–63	26	166	330	.503	160	210	.762	428	16.5	492	18.9
1963–64	28	299	532	.562	218	295	.738	537	19.2	816	29.1
Totals	54	464	862	.540	378	505	.748	965	17.8	1308	24.2

MARVIN BARNES
Providence
6-9 – F/C
Providence, R.I.

NCAA unanimous first-team All-American in 1974.... Led the nation in rebounding in 1974.... Second-leading scorer and leading rebounder for 1973 national fourth-place team (27-4 record).... Averaged 17.1 points and 13.1 rebounds in eight NCAA Tournament games from 1972 to 1974 (5-3 record).... Selected by the Philadelphia 76ers in first round of 1974 NBA draft (2nd pick overall), but he chose to sign a contract with the ABA's Spirits of St. Louis.

Season	G	FGM	FGA	FG%	FTM	FTA	FT%	Reb.	Avg.	Pts.	Avg.
1971–72	27	236	462	.511	112	173	.647	424	15.7	584	21.6
1972–73	30	237	436	.544	237	436	.544	571	19.0	549	18.3
1973–74	32	297	596	.498	112	164	.683	597	18.7	706	22.1
Totals	89	770	1494	.515	461	773	.596	1592	17.9	1839	20.7

RICK BARRY
Miami (Fla.)
6-7 – F
Roselle Park, N.J.

NCAA unanimous first-team All-American in 1965.... Did not play in NCAA Tournament.... Averaged 19.3 points in three NIT games in 1963 and 1964 (1-2 record).... Selected by the San Francisco Warriors in second round of 1965 NBA draft.... Elected to Naismith Memorial Basketball Hall of Fame in 1986.

Season	G	FGM	FGA	FG%	FTM	FTA	FT%	Reb.	Avg.	Pts.	Avg.
1962–63	24	162	341	.475	131	158	.829	351	14.6	455	19.0
1963–64	27	314	572	.549	242	287	.843	448	16.6	870	32.2
1964–65	26	340	651	.522	293	341	.859	475	18.3	973	37.4
Totals	77	816	1564	.522	666	786	.847	1274	16.5	2298	29.8

ELGIN BAYLOR
Seattle
6-6 – F
Washington, D.C.

NCAA unanimous first-team All-American in 1958 and consensus second-team All-American in 1957.... Led the nation in rebounding in 1957.... Named Final Four Most Outstanding Player in 1958.... Leading scorer and rebounder for 1958 national runner-up (24-7 record).... Averaged 27 points in five NCAA Tournament games in 1958 (4-1 record).... Selected as a junior eligible by the Minneapolis Lakers in first round of 1958 NBA draft.... Elected to Naismith Memorial Basketball Hall of Fame in 1976.

Season	G	FGM	FGA	FG%	FTM	FTA	FT%	Reb.	Avg.	Pts.	Avg.
1954–55*	26	332	651	.510	150	232	.647	492	20.5	814	31.3
1955–56			Sat out season after transferring from College of Idaho								
1956–57	25	271	555	.488	201	251	.801	508	20.3	743	29.7
1957–58	29	353	697	.506	237	308	.769	559	19.3	943	32.5
Totals	80	956	1903	.502	588	791	.743	1559	20.0	2500	31.3

* Rebounds available for 24 of 26 games he played for the College of Idaho his freshman season.

RALPH BEARD
Kentucky
5-11 – G
Louisville, Ky.

NCAA unanimous first-team All-American in 1947 and 1948, and consensus first-team All-American in 1949.... Second-leading scorer for NCAA champions in 1948 (36-3) and 1949 (32-2).... Averaged 9.2 points in six NCAA Tournament games in 1948 and 1949 (6-0 record).... Averaged 12 points in seven NIT games in 1946 (champion), 1947 (runner-up), and 1949 (opening-game loser).... Member of 1948 U.S. Olympic team.... Selected by the Chicago Stags in first round of 1949 BAA draft but a corporation including him and several Kentucky teammates was granted an NBL franchise (the Indianapolis Olympians). When the BAA and NBL merged that summer to form the NBA, the Olympians represented one of the franchises involved in the merger.

Season	G	FGM	FGA	FG%	FTM	FTA	FT%	Reb.	Avg.	Pts.	Avg.
1945–46	30	111			57	110	.518			279	9.3
1946–47	37	157	469	.335	78	115	.678			392	10.6
1947–48	38	194	536	.362	88	149	.591			476	12.5
1948–49	34	144	481	.299	82	115	.713			370	10.9
Totals	139	606			305	489	.624			1517	10.9

ERNIE BECK
Penn
6-4 – F
Philadelphia, Pa.

NCAA consensus first-team All-American in 1953.... Led the nation in rebounding in 1951.... Averaged 23.5 points in two NCAA Tournament games in 1953 (1-1 record).... Selected by the Philadelphia Warriors in 1953 NBA draft.

Season	G	FGM	FGA	FG%	FTM	FTA	FT%	Reb.	Avg.	Pts.	Avg.
1950–51	27	230	532	.432	98	181	.541	556	20.6	558	20.7
1951–52	29	229	561	.408	138	197	.701	551	19.0	596	20.6
1952–53	26	245	625	.392	183	229	.799	450	17.3	673	25.9
Totals	82	704	1718	.410	419	607	.690	1557	19.0	1827	22.3

WALT BELLAMY
Indiana
6-11 – C
New Bern, N.C.

NCAA consensus second-team All-American in 1961.... Did not play in NCAA Tournament.... Member of 1960 U.S. Olympic team.... Selected by the Chicago Packers in first round of 1961 NBA draft (1st pick overall).... Elected to Naismith Memorial Basketball Hall of Fame in 1993.

Season	G	FGM	FGA	FG%	FTM	FTA	FT%	Reb.	Avg.	Pts.	Avg.
1958–59	22	148	289	.512	86	141	.610	335	15.2	382	17.4
1959–60	24	212	396	.535	113	161	.702	324	13.5	537	22.4
1960–61	24	195	389	.501	132	204	.647	428	17.8	522	21.8
Totals	70	555	1074	.517	331	506	.654	1087	15.5	1441	20.6

KENT BENSON
Indiana
6-11 – C
New Castle, Ind.

NCAA unanimous first-team All-American in 1976 and consensus first-team All-American in 1977.... Final Four Most Outstanding Player in 1976.... Leading rebounder and second-leading scorer for undefeated 1976 NCAA champion (32-0 record).... Averaged 19.6 points and 10.9 rebounds in eight NCAA Tournament games in 1975 and 1976 (7-1 record).... Named MVP of 1974 Collegiate Commissioners Association Tournament in powering Indiana to title.... Selected by the Milwaukee Bucks in first round of 1977 NBA draft (1st pick overall).

Season	G	FGM	FGA	FG%	FTM	FTA	FT%	Reb.	Avg.	Pts.	Avg.
1973–74	27	113	224	.504	24	40	.600	222	8.2	250	9.3
1974–75	32	198	366	.541	84	113	.743	286	8.9	480	15.0
1975–76	32	237	410	.578	80	117	.684	282	8.8	554	17.3
1976–77	23	174	346	.503	108	144	.750	241	10.5	456	19.8
Totals	114	722	1346	.536	296	414	.715	1031	9.0	1740	15.3

WALTER BERRY
St. John's
6-8 – F/C
Bronx, N.Y.

Named national player of the year by AP, UPI, USBWA, and NABC in 1986.... Wooden Award winner in 1986.... NCAA unanimous first-team All-American in 1986.... Second-leading scorer for 1985 Final Four team (31-4 record).... Averaged 20.6 points and 8.6 rebounds in seven NCAA Tournament games in 1985 and 1986 (5-2 record).... Averaged 28.9 points and 14 rebounds in one junior college season at San Jacinto (Tex.).... Selected as an undergraduate by the Portland Trail Blazers in first round of 1986 NBA draft (14th pick overall).

Season	G	FGM	FGA	FG%	FTM	FTA	FT%	Reb.	Avg.	Pts.	Avg.
1982–83			Did not play first year at St. John's due to academic problems.								
1984–85	35	231	414	.558	134	187	.717	304	8.7	596	17.0
1985–86	36	327	547	.598	174	248	.702	399	11.1	828	23.0
Totals	71	558	961	.581	308	435	.708	703	9.9	1424	20.1

LEN BIAS
Maryland
6-8 – F
Landover, Md.

NCAA unanimous first-team All-American in 1986 and consensus second-team All-American in 1985.... Averaged 18.7 points and 7.4 rebounds in nine NCAA Tournament games from 1983 to 1986 (5-4 record).... Selected by the Boston Celtics in first round of 1986 NBA draft (2nd pick overall) but died of a cocaine overdose two days later.

Season	G	FGM	FGA	FG%	FTM	FTA	FT%	Reb.	Avg.	Pts.	Avg.
1982–83	30	86	180	.478	42	66	.636	125	4.2	217	7.2
1983–84	32	211	372	.567	66	86	.767	145	4.5	488	15.3
1984–85	37	274	519	.528	153	197	.777	251	6.8	701	18.9
1985–86	32	267	491	.544	209	242	.864	224	7.0	743	23.2
Totals	131	838	1562	.536	470	591	.795	745	5.7	2149	16.4

Three-point field goals: 3 of 11 (.273) in 1982–83.

HENRY BIBBY
UCLA
6-1 – G
Franklinton, N.C.

NCAA consensus first-team All-American in 1972.... Second-leading scorer for undefeated 1972 NCAA champion (30-0 record), third-leading scorer for 1970 champion (28-2), and fourth-leading scorer for 1971 champion (29-1).... Averaged 15.2 points and 4.4 rebounds in 12 NCAA Tournament games from 1970 to 1972 (12-0 record).... Selected by the New York Knicks in fourth round of 1972 NBA draft (58th pick overall).

Season	G	FGM	FGA	FG%	FTM	FTA	FT%	Reb.	Avg.	Pts.	Avg.
1969–70	30	189	377	.501	90	108	.833	105	3.5	468	15.6
1970–71	30	137	364	.376	81	97	.835	105	3.5	355	11.8
1971–72	30	183	407	.450	104	129	.806	106	3.5	470	15.7
Totals	90	509	1148	.443	275	334	.823	316	3.5	1293	14.4

DAVE BING
Syracuse
6-3 – G
Washington, D.C.

NCAA unanimous first-team All-American in 1966.... Averaged 15 points and 10 rebounds in two NCAA Tournament games in 1966 (1-1 record).... Collected 31 points and nine rebounds in one NIT game in 1964.... Selected by the Detroit Pistons in first round of 1966 NBA draft (2nd pick overall).... Elected to Naismith Memorial Basketball Hall of Fame in 1989.

Season	G	FGM	FGA	FG%	FTM	FTA	FT%	Reb.	Avg.	Pts.	Avg.
1963–64	25	215	460	.467	126	172	.733	206	8.2	556	22.2
1964–65	23	206	444	.464	121	162	.747	277	12.0	533	23.2
1965–66	28	308	569	.541	178	222	.802	303	10.8	794	28.4
Totals	**76**	**729**	**1473**	**.495**	**425**	**556**	**.764**	**786**	**10.3**	**1883**	**24.8**

LARRY BIRD
Indiana State
6-9 – F
French Lick, Ind.

Named national player of the year by AP, UPI, USBWA, and NABC in 1979.... Naismith Award and Wooden Award winner in 1979.... NCAA unanimous first-team All-American in 1978 and 1979.... Member of All-NCAA Tournament team in 1979.... Leading scorer and rebounder for 1979 national runner-up (33-1 record).... Averaged 27.2 points and 13.4 rebounds in five NCAA Tournament games in 1979 (4-1 record).... Averaged 31.3 points and 11.7 rebounds in three NIT games in 1977 and 1978 (1-2 record).... Member of 1992 U.S. Olympic team.... Selected as a junior eligible by the Boston Celtics in first round of 1978 NBA draft (6th pick overall).

Season	G	FGM	FGA	FG%	FTM	FTA	FT%	Reb.	Avg.	Pts.	Avg.
1974–75	Left Indiana University before the start of the season.										
1975–76	Sat out the season after transferring to Indiana State.										
1976–77	28	375	689	.544	168	200	.840	373	13.3	918	32.8
1977–78	32	403	769	.524	153	193	.793	369	11.5	959	30.0
1978–79	34	376	707	.532	221	266	.831	505	14.9	973	28.6
Totals	**94**	**1154**	**2165**	**.533**	**542**	**659**	**.822**	**1247**	**13.3**	**2850**	**30.3**

OTIS BIRDSONG
Houston
6-4 – G
Winter Haven, Fla.

NCAA consensus first-team All-American in 1977.... Did not play in NCAA Tournament.... Averaged 29 points in four NIT games for 1977 runner-up.... Selected by the Kansas City Kings in first round of 1977 NBA draft (2nd pick overall).

Season	G	FGM	FGA	FG%	FTM	FTA	FT%	Reb.	Avg.	Pts.	Avg.
1973–74	26	154	312	.494	64	92	.696	110	4.2	372	14.3
1974–75	26	268	460	.583	104	143	.727	122	4.7	640	24.6
1975–76	28	302	582	.519	126	191	.660	176	6.3	730	26.1
1976–77	36	452	794	.569	186	249	.747	159	4.4	1090	30.3
Totals	**116**	**1176**	**2148**	**.547**	**480**	**675**	**.711**	**567**	**4.9**	**2832**	**24.4**

CHARLES BLACK
Kansas
6-4 – F
Topeka, Kans.

NCAA consensus first-team All-American in 1943 and second-team All-American in 1946.... Averaged 17 points in two NCAA Tournament games in 1942 (1-1 record).

Season	G	FGM	FGA	FG%	FTM	FTA	FT%	Reb.	Avg.	Pts.	Avg.
1941–42	22	101			43	76	.566			245	11.1
1942–43	18	82			42					206	11.4
1943–44	Military Service (Air Force)										
1944–45	Military Service (Air Force)										
1945–46	20	122			82					326	16.3
1946–47	27	107			91	144	.632			305	11.3
Totals	**87**	**412**			**278**					**1082**	**12.4**

ROLANDO BLACKMAN
Kansas State
6-6 – G
Brooklyn, N.Y.

Averaged 14.8 points and 4.5 rebounds in six NCAA Tournament games in 1980 and 1981 (4-2 record).... Member of 1980 U.S. Olympic team.... Selected by the Dallas Mavericks in first round of 1981 NBA draft (9th pick overall).

Season	G	FGM	FGA	FG%	FTM	FTA	FT%	Reb.	Avg.	Pts.	Avg.
1977–78	29	127	269	.472	61	93	.656	187	6.4	315	10.9
1978–79	28	200	392	.510	83	113	.735	110	3.9	483	17.3
1979–80	31	226	419	.539	100	145	.690	145	4.7	552	17.8
1980–81	33	202	380	.532	90	115	.783	165	5.0	494	15.0
Totals	**121**	**755**	**1460**	**.517**	**334**	**466**	**.717**	**607**	**5.0**	**1844**	**15.2**

RON BONHAM
Cincinnati
6-5 – F
Muncie, Ind.

NCAA consensus first-team All-American in 1963 and consensus second-team All-American in 1964.... Second-leading scorer for 1962 NCAA champion (29-2 record) and leading scorer for 1963 national runner-up (26-2).... Member of All-NCAA Tournament team in 1963.... Averaged 17.8 points in eight NCAA Tournament games in 1962 and 1963 (7-1 record).... Selected by the Boston Celtics in second round of 1964 NBA draft.

Season	G	FGM	FGA	FG%	FTM	FTA	FT%	Reb.	Avg.	Pts.	Avg.
1961–62	31	174	382	.455	95	125	.760	156	5.0	443	14.3
1962–63	28	208	449	.463	173	194	.892	178	6.4	589	21.0
1963–64	26	222	430	.516	190	232	.819	155	6.0	634	24.4
Totals	**85**	**604**	**1261**	**.479**	**458**	**551**	**.831**	**489**	**5.8**	**1666**	**19.6**

RON BOONE
Idaho State
6-2 – G
Omaha, Nebr.

Averaged 25.2 points in one junior college season at Iowa Western.... Did not play in NCAA Tournament or NIT.... Selected by the Dallas Chaparrals in eighth round of 1968 ABA draft.

Season	G	FGM	FGA	FG%	FTM	FTA	FT%	Reb.	Avg.	Pts.	Avg.
1965–66	10	46	119	.387	17	26	.654	95	9.5	109	10.9
1966–67	25	199	416	.478	160	215	.744	128	5.1	558	22.3
1967–68	26	223	519	.430	108	159	.679	110	4.2	554	21.3
Totals	**61**	**468**	**1054**	**.444**	**285**	**400**	**.713**	**333**	**5.5**	**1221**	**20.0**

BOB BOOZER
Kansas State
6-8 – F
Omaha, Nebr.

NCAA unanimous first-team All-American in 1959 and consensus first-team All-American in 1958.... Leading scorer and rebounder for 1958 national fourth-place team (22-5 record).... Averaged 22 points and 10.7 rebounds in six NCAA Tournament games in 1958 and 1959 (4-2 record).... Member of 1960 U.S. Olympic team.... Selected by the Cincinnati Royals in first round of 1959 NBA draft.

Season	G	FGM	FGA	FG%	FTM	FTA	FT%	Reb.	Avg.	Pts.	Avg.
1956–57	23	136	307	.443	178	231	.771	237	10.3	450	19.6
1957–58	27	195	441	.442	154	215	.716	281	10.4	544	20.1
1958–59	27	247	578	.427	197	258	.764	306	11.3	691	25.6
Totals	**77**	**578**	**1326**	**.436**	**529**	**704**	**.751**	**824**	**10.7**	**1685**	**21.9**

VINCE BORYLA
Notre Dame/Denver
6-5 – F
East Chicago, Ind.

NCAA consensus first-team All-American in 1949.... Did not play in NCAA Tournament or NIT.... Member of 1948 U.S. Olympic team.

Season	G	FGM	FGA	FG%	FTM	FTA	FT%	Reb.	Avg.	Pts.	Avg.
1944–45	20	130			62	94	.660			322	16.1
1945–46	21	128	369	.347	65	93	.699			321	15.3
1946–47		Military Service (Army)									
1947–48		Military Service (Army)									
1948–49	33	212			200	253	.791			624	18.9
Totals	74	470			327	440	.743			1267	17.1

Note: Attended Notre Dame his first two seasons before enrolling at Denver for final year in college.

SAM BOWIE
Kentucky
7-1 – C
Lebanon, Pa.

NCAA consensus second-team All-American in 1981.... Leading rebounder and third-leading scorer for 1984 Final Four team (29-5 record).... Averaged 9.7 points and 8.7 rebounds in seven NCAA Tournament games in 1980, 1981 and 1984 (4-3 record).... Member of 1980 U.S. Olympic team.... Selected by the Portland Trail Blazers in first round of 1984 NBA draft (2nd pick overall).

Season	G	FGM	FGA	FG%	FTM	FTA	FT%	Reb.	Avg.	Pts.	Avg.
1979–80	34	165	311	.531	110	144	.764	276	8.1	440	12.9
1980–81	28	185	356	.520	118	164	.720	254	9.1	488	17.4
1981–82		Did not play because of a leg injury.									
1982–83		Did not play because of a leg injury.									
1983–84	34	133	258	.516	91	126	.722	313	9.2	357	10.5
Totals	96	483	925	.522	319	434	.735	843	8.8	1285	13.4

GARY BRADDS
Ohio State
6-8 – C
Jamestown, Ohio

Named national player of the year by AP and UPI in 1964.... NCAA unanimous first-team All-American in 1964 and consensus second-team All-American in 1963.... Sixth-leading scorer for 1962 national runner-up (26-2 record).... Averaged 6.3 points and 3.8 rebounds in four NCAA Tournament games in 1962 (3-1 record).... Selected by the Baltimore Bullets in first round of 1964 NBA draft.

Season	G	FGM	FGA	FG%	FTM	FTA	FT%	Reb.	Avg.	Pts.	Avg.
1961–62	26	50	72	.694	23	40	.575	72	2.8	123	4.7
1962–63	24	237	453	.523	198	248	.798	312	13.0	672	28.0
1963–64	24	276	527	.524	183	231	.792	322	13.4	735	30.6
Totals	74	563	1052	.535	404	519	.778	706	9.5	1530	20.7

BILL BRADLEY
Princeton
6-5 – F
Crystal City, Mo.

Named national player of the year by AP, UPI, and USBWA in 1965.... NCAA unanimous first-team All-American in 1964 and 1965.... Led the nation in free-throw percentage in 1965.... Final Four Most Outstanding Player in 1965.... Leading scorer and rebounder for 1965 national third-place team (23-6 record).... Averaged 33.7 points and 12 rebounds in nine NCAA Tournament games from 1963 to 1965 (5-4 record).... Member of 1964 U.S. Olympic team.... Selected as a territorial pick by the New York Knicks in 1965 NBA draft.... Elected to Naismith Memorial Basketball Hall of Fame in 1982.

Season	G	FGM	FGA	FG%	FTM	FTA	FT%	Reb.	Avg.	Pts.	Avg.
1962–63	25	212	445	.476	258	289	.893	306	12.2	682	27.3
1963–64	29	338	648	.522	260	306	.850	360	12.4	936	32.3
1964–65	29	306	574	.533	273	308	.886	342	11.8	885	30.5
Totals	83	856	1667	.513	791	903	.876	1008	12.1	2503	30.2

SHAWN BRADLEY
Brigham Young
7-6 – C
Castle Dale, Utah

Led NCAA with 5.2 blocked shots per game in 1991.... Averaged nine points, seven rebounds, and six blocked shots in two NCAA Tournament games in 1991 (1-1 record).... Selected as an undergraduate by the Philadelphia 76ers in first round of 1993 NBA draft (2nd pick overall) after spending two years in Australia on a Mormon mission.

Season	G	FGM	FGA	FG%	FTM	FTA	FT%	Reb.	Avg.	Pts.	Avg.
1990–91	34	187	361	.518	128	185	.692	262	7.7	503	14.8

Three-point field goals: 1 of 1 in 1990–91.

JIM BREWER
Minnesota
6-9 – F
Maywood, Ill.

NCAA consensus second-team All-American in 1973.... Averaged 12 points and 18 rebounds in two NCAA Tournament games in 1972 (1-1 record).... Averaged 13.5 points in two NIT games in 1973 (1-1 record).... Member of 1972 U.S. Olympic team.... Selected by the Cleveland Cavaliers in first round of 1973 NBA draft (2nd pick overall).

Season	G	FGM	FGA	FG%	FTM	FTA	FT%	Reb.	Avg.	Pts.	Avg.
1970–71	24	166	413	.402	67	104	.644	331	13.8	399	16.6
1971–72	25	95	260	.365	54	113	.482	275	11.0	244	9.8
1972–73	26	147	317	.464	72	102	.706	301	11.6	366	14.1
Totals	75	408	990	.412	193	319	.605	907	12.1	1009	13.5

GUS BROBERG
Dartmouth
6-1 – G/F
Torrington, Conn.

NCAA consensus first-team All-American in 1940 and 1941.... Averaged 19 points in two NCAA Tournament games in 1941 (1-1 record).

Season	G	FGM	FGA	FG%	FTM	FTA	FT%	Reb.	Avg.	Pts.	Avg.
1938–39	23	127			64	76	.842			318	13.8
1939–40	21	124			57	60	.950			305	14.5
1940–41	23	141			61	76	.803			343	14.9
Totals	67	392			182	212	.858			966	14.4

MICHAEL BROOKS
La Salle
6-7 – F
Philadelphia, Pa.

Named national player of the year by NABC in 1980.... NCAA consensus first-team All-American in 1980.... Averaged 32 points and 13 rebounds in two NCAA Tournament games in 1978 and 1980 (0-2 record).... Leading scorer (13.2 ppg) for 1980 U.S. Olympic team.... Selected by the San Diego Clippers in first round of 1980 NBA draft (9th pick overall).

Season	G	FGM	FGA	FG%	FTM	FTA	FT%	Reb.	Avg.	Pts.	Avg.
1976–77	29	241	490	.492	97	152	.638	311	10.7	579	20.0
1977–78	28	288	490	.588	120	164	.732	358	12.8	696	24.9
1978–79	26	245	443	.553	116	161	.720	347	13.3	606	23.3
1979–80	31	290	553	.524	167	237	.705	356	11.5	747	24.1
Totals	114	1064	1976	.538	500	714	.700	1372	12.0	2628	23.1

JOE (JELLY BEAN) BRYANT
La Salle
6-9 – F
Philadelphia, Pa.

Collected 25 points and 14 rebounds in one NCAA Tournament game in 1975. . . . Selected as a hardship case by the Golden State Warriors in first round of 1975 NBA draft (14th pick overall). Draft rights sold to Philadelphia 76ers.

Season	G.	FGM	FGA	FG%	FTM	FTA	FT%	Reb.	Avg.	Pts.	Avg.
1973-74	26	200	440	.455	86	123	.699	282	10.8	486	18.7
1974-75	29	256	495	.517	120	165	.727	330	11.4	632	21.8
Totals	55	456	935	.488	206	288	.715	612	11.1	1118	20.3

BILL BUNTIN
Michigan
6-7 – F/C
Detroit, Mich.

NCAA consensus second-team All-American in 1965.... Leading rebounder and second-leading scorer for 1964 national third-place team (23-5 record) and 1965 national runner-up (24-4).... Named to All-NCAA Tournament team in 1964.... Averaged 22.6 points and 11.4 rebounds in eight NCAA Tournament games in 1964 and 1965 (6-2 record).... Selected as a territorial pick by the Detroit Pistons in 1965 NBA draft.

Season	G	FGM	FGA	FG%	FTM	FTA	FT%	Reb.	Avg.	Pts.	Avg.
1962–63	24	211	491	.430	112	161	.696	376	15.7	534	22.3
1963–64	27	238	481	.495	151	192	.786	338	12.5	627	23.2
1964–65	28	221	454	.487	122	159	.767	323	11.5	564	20.1
Totals	79	670	1426	.470	385	512	.752	1037	13.1	1725	21.8

CARL CAIN
Iowa
6-3 – G
Freeport, Ill.

Member of All-NCAA Tournament team in 1955 and 1956.... Second-leading scorer and rebounder for 1955 national fourth-place team (19-7 record) and 1956 national runner-up (20-6).... Averaged 20.1 points in eight NCAA Tournament games in 1955 and 1956 (5-3 record).... Member of 1956 U.S. Olympic team.... Selected by the Rochester Royals in 1956 NBA draft (did not play in league).

Season	G	FGM	FGA	FG%	FTM	FTA	FT%	Reb.	Avg.	Pts.	Avg.
1953–54	22	106	248	.427	71	119	.597			283	12.9
1954–55	26	133	333	.399	94	140	.671	244	9.4	360	13.8
1955–56	26	165	403	.409	81	112	.723	257	9.9	411	15.8
Totals	74	404	984	.411	246	371	.663			1054	14.2

JOE CALDWELL
Arizona State
6-5 – F
Los Angeles, Calif.

Averaged 22.2 points in five NCAA Tournament games from 1962-64 (2-3 record).... Selected by the Detroit Pistons in first round of 1964 NBA draft (2nd pick overall).

Season	G	FGM	FGA	FG%	FTM	FTA	FT%	Reb.	Avg.	Pts.	Avg.
1961–62	27	141	291	.485	73	115	.635	285	10.6	355	13.1
1962–63	29	239	523	.457	93	152	.612	314	10.8	571	19.7
1963–64	27	231	521	.443	127	193	.658	330	12.2	589	21.8
Totals	83	611	1335	.458	293	460	.637	929	11.2	1515	18.3

MARCUS CAMBY
Massachusetts
6-11 – C
Hartford, Conn.

Named national player of the year by AP, NABC, USBWA in 1996. . . . Earned Naismith and Wooden Awards in 1996. . . . NCAA unanimous first-team All-American in 1996. . . . Ranked among the nation's leaders in blocked shots in 1994 (6th with 3.6 bpg), 1995 (10th with 3.4 bpg) and 1996 (7th with 3.9 bpg). . . . Ranked 43rd in the nation in scoring in 1996. . . . Leading scorer and rebounder for 1996 Final Four team in NCAA Tournament (35-2 record). . . . Averaged 17.9 points, 7.7 rebounds and 3.9 blocked shots in 11 NCAA Tournament games from 1994-96 (8-3 record).

Season	G.	FGM	FGA	FG%	FTM	FTA	FT%	Reb.	Avg.	Pts.	Avg.
1993-94	29	117	237	.494	62	104	.596	185	6.4	296	10.2
1994-95	30	166	302	.550	83	129	.643	186	6.2	416	13.9
1995-96	33	256	537	.477	163	233	.700	268	8.1	675	20.5
Totals	92	539	1076	.501	308	466	.661	639	6.9	1387	15.1

Three-point field goals: 0 of 4 in 1993-94, 1 of 1 in 1994-95 and 0 of 8 in 1995-96. **Totals:** 1 of 13 (.077).

AUSTIN CARR
Notre Dame
6-3 – G
Washington, D.C.

Named national player of the year by AP and UPI in 1971.... Naismith Award winner in 1971.... NCAA unanimous first-team All-American in 1971 and consensus second-team All-American in 1970.... Averaged 41.3 points and 7.6 rebounds in seven NCAA Tournament games from 1969 to 1971 (2-5 record).... Selected by the Cleveland Cavaliers in first round of 1971 NBA draft (1st pick overall).

Season	G	FGM	FGA	FG%	FTM	FTA	FT%	Reb.	Avg.	Pts.	Avg.
1968–69	16	143	294	.486	67	85	.788	84	5.3	353	22.1
1969–70	29	444	799	.556	218	264	.826	240	8.3	1106	38.1
1970–71	29	430	832	.517	241	297	.811	214	7.4	1101	38.0
Totals	74	1017	1925	.528	526	646	.814	538	7.3	2560	34.6

KENNY CARR
North Carolina State
6-7 – F
Hyattsville, Md.

Ranked among the nation's leading scorers in 1976 (5th) and 1977 (42nd). . . . Did not play in NCAA Tournament. . . . Averaged 18.7 points in three games for third-place team in 1976 NIT (2-1 record). . . . Member of 1976 U.S. Olympic team (6.8 ppg, 3.2 rpg, 55.6 FG%). . . . Selected as an undergraduate (after junior season) by the Lakers in first round of 1977 NBA draft (6th pick overall).

Season	G	FGM	FGA	FG%	FTM	FTA	FT%	Reb.	Avg.	Pts.	Avg.
1974-75	28	158	301	.525	70	101	.693	201	7.2	386	13.8
1975-76	30	322	607	.530	154	218	.706	310	10.3	798	26.6
1976-77	28	230	467	.493	128	198	.646	278	9.9	588	21.0
Totals	86	710	1375	.516	352	517	.681	789	9.2	1772	20.6

JOE BARRY CARROLL
Purdue
7-1 – C
Denver, Colo.

NCAA unanimous first-team All-American in 1980.... Leading scorer and rebounder for 1980 national third-place team (23-10 record).... Member of All-NCAA Tournament team in 1980.... Averaged 23 points and 9.6 rebounds in seven NCAA Tournament games in 1977 and 1980 (5-2 record).... Averaged 25.2 points and 8 rebounds in five NIT games for 1979 runner-up.... Selected by the Golden State Warriors in first round of 1980 NBA draft (1st pick overall).

Season	G	FGM	FGA	FG%	FTM	FTA	FT%	Reb.	Avg.	Pts.	Avg.
1976-77	28	93	187	.497	34	54	.630	206	7.4	220	7.9
1977-78	27	163	312	.522	95	143	.664	288	10.7	421	15.6
1978-79	35	318	545	.583	162	253	.640	352	10.1	798	22.8
1979-80	33	301	558	.539	134	203	.660	302	9.2	736	22.3
Totals	123	875	1602	.546	425	653	.651	1148	9.3	2175	17.7

BILL CARTWRIGHT
San Francisco
6-11 – C
Elk Grove, Calif.

NCAA consensus second-team All-American in 1977 and 1979.... Averaged 24.6 points and nine rebounds in five NCAA Tournament games from 1977 to 1979 (2-3 record).... Scored 5 points in one NIT game in 1976.... Selected by the New York Knicks in first round of 1979 NBA draft (3rd pick overall).

Season	G	FGM	FGA	FG%	FTM	FTA	FT%	Reb.	Avg.	Pts.	Avg.
1975-76	30	151	285	.530	72	98	.735	207	6.9	374	12.5
1976-77	31	241	426	.566	118	161	.733	262	8.5	600	19.4
1977-78	21	168	252	.667	96	131	.733	213	10.1	432	20.6
1978-79	29	268	443	.605	174	237	.734	455	15.7	710	24.5
Totals	111	828	1406	.589	460	627	.734	1137	10.2	2116	19.1

WILT CHAMBERLAIN
Kansas
7-1 – C
Philadelphia, Pa.

NCAA unanimous first-team All-American in 1957 and 1958.... Final Four Most Outstanding Player in 1957.... Leading scorer and rebounder for 1957 national runner-up (24-3 record).... Averaged 30.3 points and 15.5 rebounds in four NCAA Tournament games in 1957 (3-1 record).... Selected as a territorial choice by the Philadelphia Warriors in first round of 1959 NBA draft after he played one season with the Harlem Globetrotters.... Elected to Naismith Memorial Basketball Hall of Fame in 1978.

Season	G	FGM	FGA	FG%	FTM	FTA	FT%	Reb.	Avg.	Pts.	Avg.
1956-57	27	275	588	.468	250	399	.627	510	18.9	800	29.6
1957-58	21	228	482	.473	177	291	.608	367	17.5	633	30.1
Totals	48	503	1070	.470	427	690	.619	877	18.3	1433	29.9

TOM CHAMBERS
Utah
6-10 – F/C
Boulder, Colo.

Averaged 12.8 points and seven rebounds in five NCAA Tournament games from 1978 to 1981 (2-3 record).... Selected by the San Diego Clippers in first round of 1981 NBA draft (8th pick overall).

Season	G	FGM	FGA	FG%	FTM	FTA	FT%	Reb.	Avg.	Pts.	Avg.
1977-78	28	69	139	.496	40	64	.625	104	3.7	178	6.4
1978-79	30	206	379	.544	69	127	.543	266	8.9	481	16.0
1979-80	28	195	359	.543	92	129	.713	244	8.7	482	17.2
1980-81	30	221	372	.594	115	155	.742	262	8.7	557	18.6
Totals	116	691	1249	.553	316	475	.665	876	7.6	1698	14.6

LEN CHAPPELL
Wake Forest
6-8 – F/C
Portage Area, Pa.

NCAA consensus first-team All-American in 1962.... Leading scorer and rebounder for 1962 national third-place team (22-9 record).... Member of All-NCAA Tournament team in 1962.... Averaged 27.6 points and 17.1 rebounds in eight NCAA Tournament games in 1961 and 1962 (6-2 record).... Selected by the Syracuse Nationals in first round of 1962 NBA draft.

Season	G	FGM	FGA	FG%	FTM	FTA	FT%	Reb.	Avg.	Pts.	Avg.
1959-60	28	166	372	.446	156	228	.684	350	12.5	488	17.4
1960-61	28	271	538	.504	203	286	.710	393	14.0	745	26.6
1961-62	31	327	597	.548	278	383	.726	470	15.2	932	30.1
Totals	87	764	1507	.507	637	897	.710	1213	13.9	2165	24.9

CALBERT CHEANEY
Indiana
6-7 – F/G
Evansville, Ind.

Named national player of the year by AP, UPI, NABC, and USBWA in 1993.... Won Naismith Award and Wooden Award in 1993.... NCAA unanimous first-team All-American in 1993.... Leading scorer and third-leading rebounder for 1992 Final Four team (27-7 record).... Averaged 21.5 points and 7.7 rebounds in 13 NCAA Tournament games from 1990-93 (9-4 record).... Selected by the Washington Bullets in first round of 1993 NBA draft (6th pick overall).

Season	G	FGM	FGA	FG%	FTM	FTA	FT%	Reb.	Avg.	Pts.	Avg.
1989-90	29	199	348	.572	72	96	.750	133	4.6	495	17.1
1990-91	34	289	485	.596	113	141	.801	188	5.5	734	21.6
1991-92	34	227	435	.522	112	140	.800	166	4.9	599	17.6
1992-93	35	303	552	.549	132	166	.795	223	6.4	785	22.4
Totals	132	1018	1820	.559	429	543	.790	710	5.4	2613	19.8

Three-point field goals: 25 of 51 (.490) in 1989-90, 43 of 91 (.473) in 1990-91, 33 of 86 (.384) in 1991-92, and 47 of 110 (.427) in 1992-93. **Totals:** 148 of 338 (.438).

JIM CHONES
Marquette
6-11 – C
Racine, Wisc.

NCAA consensus first-team All-American in 1972.... Averaged 22 points and 12 rebounds in three NCAA Tournament games in 1971 (2-1 record).... Signed as an undergraduate by the ABA's New York Nets in 1972.... Drafted by the Los Angeles Lakers in second round of 1973 NBA draft (30th pick overall); rights traded to the Cleveland Cavaliers for a first-round draft choice, May 17, 1974.

Season	G	FGM	FGA	FG%	FTM	FTA	FT%	Reb.	Avg.	Pts.	Avg.
1970–71	29	230	401	.574	60	113	.531	333	11.5	520	17.9
1971–72	21	180	349	.516	72	105	.686	250	11.9	432	20.6
Totals	50	410	750	.547	132	218	.606	583	11.7	952	19.0

JEFF COHEN
William & Mary
6-7 – F/C
Kenosha, Wisc.

Did not play in NCAA Tournament or NIT.... Selected by the Chicago Packers in second round of 1961 NBA draft (did not play in league).

Season	G	FGM	FGA	FG%	FTM	FTA	FT%	Reb.	Avg.	Pts.	Avg.
1957–58	29	146	341	.428	113	164	.689	371	12.8	405	14.0
1958–59	24	150	342	.439	95	142	.669	413	17.2	395	16.5
1959–60	26	230	458	.502	168	232	.724	471	18.1	628	24.2
1960–61	24	193	404	.478	189	246	.768	424	17.7	575	24.0
Totals	103	719	1545	.465	565	784	.721	1679	16.3	2003	19.4

DERRICK COLEMAN
Syracuse
6-9 – F
Detroit, Mich.

NCAA unanimous first-team All-American in 1990.... Leading rebounder and fourth-leading scorer for 1987 national runner-up (31-7 record).... Averaged 12.4 points and 11.1 rebounds in 14 NCAA Tournament games from 1987 to 1990 (10-4 record).... Selected by the New Jersey Nets in first round of 1990 NBA draft (1st pick overall).

Season	G	FGM	FGA	FG%	FTM	FTA	FT%	Reb.	Avg.	Pts.	Avg.
1986–87	38	173	309	.560	107	156	.686	333	8.8	453	11.9
1987–88	35	176	300	.587	121	192	.630	384	11.0	474	13.5
1988–89	37	227	395	.575	171	247	.692	422	11.4	625	16.9
1989–90	33	194	352	.551	188	263	.715	398	12.1	591	17.9
Totals	143	770	1356	.568	587	858	.684	1537	10.7	2143	15.0

Three-point field goals: 1 of 6 (.167) in 1987–88, 0 of 8 in 1988–89, and 15 of 41 (.366) in 1989–90. **Totals:** 16 of 55 (.291).

DOUG COLLINS
Illinois State
6-6 – G
Benton, Ill.

NCAA consensus first-team All-American in 1973.... Did not play in NCAA Tournament or NIT.... Member of 1972 U.S. Olympic team.... Selected by the Philadelphia 76ers in first round of 1973 NBA draft (1st pick overall).

Season	G	FGM	FGA	FG%	FTM	FTA	FT%	Reb.	Avg.	Pts.	Avg.
1970–71	26	273	609	.448	197	235	.838	166	6.4	743	28.6
1971–72	26	352	704	.500	143	177	.808	133	5.1	847	32.6
1972–73	25	269	565	.476	112	137	.818	126	5.0	650	26.0
Totals	77	894	1878	.476	452	549	.823	425	5.5	2240	29.1

BOB COUSY
Holy Cross
6-1 – G
Queens, N.Y.

NCAA unanimous first-team All-American in 1950.... Third-leading scorer for 1947 NCAA champion (27-3 record).... Averaged 10.6 points in eight NCAA Tournament games from 1947 to 1950 (5-3 record).... NBA rights to 1950 first-round draft choice were drawn out of a hat by the Boston Celtics for $8,500 in dispersal of Chicago Stags franchise.... Elected to Naismith Memorial Basketball Hall of Fame in 1970.

Season	G	FGM	FGA	FG%	FTM	FTA	FT%	Reb.	Avg.	Pts.	Avg.
1946–47	30	91			45					227	7.6
1947–48	30	207			72	108	.667			486	16.2
1948–49	27	195			90	134	.672			480	17.8
1949–50	30	216	659	.328	150	199	.754			582	19.4
Totals	117	709			357					1775	15.2

DAVE COWENS
Florida State
6-9 – C
Newport, Ky.

Collected 11 points and four rebounds in one NCAA Tournament game in 1968.... Selected by the Boston Celtics in first round of 1970 NBA draft (4th pick overall).... Elected to Naismith Memorial Basketball Hall of Fame in 1990.

Season	G	FGM	FGA	FG%	FTM	FTA	FT%	Reb.	Avg.	Pts.	Avg.
1967–68	27	206	383	.538	96	131	.733	456	16.9	508	18.8
1968–69	25	202	384	.526	104	164	.634	437	17.5	588	20.3
1969–70	26	174	355	.490	115	169	.680	447	17.2	463	17.8
Totals	78	582	1122	.519	315	464	.679	1340	17.2	1479	19.0

JOHNNY COX
Kentucky
6-4 – F
Hazard, Ky.

NCAA consensus first-team All-American in 1959.... Leading rebounder and second-leading scorer for 1958 NCAA champion (23-6 record).... Member of All-NCAA Tournament team in 1958.... Averaged 18.9 points in eight NCAA Tournament games from 1957 to 1959 (6-2 record).... Selected by the New York Knicks in fourth round of 1959 NBA draft.

Season	G	FGM	FGA	FG%	FTM	FTA	FT%	Reb.	Avg.	Pts.	Avg.
1956–57	28	203	490	.414	138	180	.767	310	11.1	544	19.4
1957–58	29	173	471	.367	86	115	.748	365	12.6	432	14.9
1958–59	27	188	464	.405	109	146	.747	329	12.2	485	18.0
Totals	84	564	1425	.396	333	441	.755	1004	12.0	1461	17.4

CLAIRE CRIBBS
Pittsburgh
6-2 – G
Jeannette, Pa.

NCAA consensus first-team All-American in 1934 and 1935.

STATISTICS NOT AVAILABLE.

TERRY CUMMINGS
DePaul
6-9 – F
Chicago, Ill.

NCAA unanimous first-team All-American in 1982.... Averaged 16.3 points and 9.7 rebounds in three NCAA Tournament games from 1980 to 1982 (0-3 record).... Selected as an undergraduate by the San Diego Clippers in first round of 1982 NBA draft (2nd pick overall).

Season	G	FGM	FGA	FG%	FTM	FTA	FT%	Reb.	Avg.	Pts.	Avg.
1979–80	28	154	303	.508	89	107	.832	263	9.4	397	14.2
1980–81	29	151	303	.498	75	100	.750	260	9.0	377	13.0
1981–82	28	244	430	.567	136	180	.756	334	11.9	624	22.3
Totals	85	549	1036	.530	300	387	.775	857	10.1	1398	16.4

BILLY CUNNINGHAM
North Carolina
6-6 – F
Brooklyn, N.Y.

Did not play in NCAA Tournament or NIT.... Selected by the Philadelphia 76ers in first round of 1965 NBA draft.... Elected to Naismith Memorial Basketball Hall of Fame in 1985.

Season	G	FGM	FGA	FG%	FTM	FTA	FT%	Reb.	Avg.	Pts.	Avg.
1962–63	21	186	380	.489	105	170	.618	339	16.1	477	22.7
1963–64	24	233	526	.443	157	249	.631	379	15.8	623	26.0
1964–65	24	237	481	.493	135	213	.634	344	14.3	609	25.4
Totals	69	656	1387	.473	397	632	.628	1062	15.4	1709	24.8

QUINTIN DAILEY
San Francisco
6-3 – G
Baltimore, Md.

NCAA consensus first-team All-American in 1982.... Averaged 24 points in two NCAA Tournament games in 1981 and 1982 (0-2 record).... Selected as an undergraduate by the Chicago Bulls in first round of 1982 NBA draft (7th pick overall).

Season	G	FGM	FGA	FG%	FTM	FTA	FT%	Reb.	Avg.	Pts.	Avg.
1979–80	29	154	292	.527	85	134	.634	107	3.7	393	13.6
1980–81	31	267	467	.572	159	208	.764	170	5.5	693	22.4
1981–82	30	286	524	.546	183	232	.789	156	5.2	755	25.2
Totals	90	707	1283	.551	427	574	.744	433	4.8	1841	20.5

LOUIE DAMPIER
Kentucky
6-0 – G
Indianapolis, Ind.

NCAA consensus second-team All-American in 1966 and 1967.... Second-leading scorer for 1966 national runner-up (27-2 record).... Averaged 22.8 points and 6.3 rebounds in four NCAA Tournament games in 1966 (3-1 record).... Selected by the Kentucky Colonels in first round of 1967 ABA draft.

Season	G	FGM	FGA	FG%	FTM	FTA	FT%	Reb.	Avg.	Pts.	Avg.
1964–65	25	171	334	.512	84	100	.840	123	4.9	426	17.0
1965–66	29	249	482	.517	114	137	.832	144	5.0	612	21.1
1966–67	26	219	443	.494	99	119	.832	142	5.5	537	20.7
Totals	80	639	1259	.508	297	356	.834	409	5.1	1575	19.7

MEL DANIELS
New Mexico
6-9 – C
Detroit, Mich.

NCAA consensus second-team All-American in 1967.... Averaged 18.3 points in three NIT games in 1965 and 1967 (1-2 record).... Averaged 22.6 points in one junior college season at Burlington (Iowa).... Selected by the Minnesota Muskies in first five rounds of 1967 ABA draft.

Season	G	FGM	FGA	FG%	FTM	FTA	FT%	Reb.	Avg.	Pts.	Avg.
1964–65	27	178	366	.486	111	182	.609	302	11.2	467	17.3
1965–66	23	191	394	.485	107	145	.738	238	10.3	489	21.2
1966–67	27	225	468	.481	131	191	.686	313	11.6	581	21.5
Totals	77	594	1228	.484	349	518	.674	853	11.1	1537	20.0

ADRIAN DANTLEY
Notre Dame
6-5 – F
Washington, D.C.

Named national player of the year by USBWA in 1976.... NCAA unanimous first-team All-American in 1975 and 1976.... Averaged 25.4 points and 8.3 rebounds in eight NCAA Tournament games from 1974 to 1976 (4-4 record).... Member of 1976 U.S. Olympic team who holds U.S. record for highest scoring average in a single Olympiad (19.3 points per game).... Selected as an undergraduate by the Buffalo Braves in first round of 1976 NBA draft (6th pick overall).

Season	G	FGM	FGA	FG%	FTM	FTA	FT%	Reb.	Avg.	Pts.	Avg.
1973–74	28	189	339	.558	133	161	.826	255	9.7	511	18.3
1974–75	29	315	581	.542	253	314	.806	296	10.2	883	30.4
1975–76	29	300	510	.588	229	294	.779	292	10.1	829	28.6
Totals	86	804	1430	.562	615	769	.800	843	9.8	2223	25.8

CHUCK DARLING
Iowa
6-8 – C
Denver, Colo.

NCAA unanimous first-team All-American in 1952.... Did not play in NCAA Tournament or NIT.... Member of 1956 U.S. Olympic team.... Selected by the Rochester Royals in 1952 NBA draft (did not play in league).

Season	G	FGM	FGA	FG%	FTM	FTA	FT%	Reb.	Avg.	Pts.	Avg.
1949–50	19	67	212	.316	41	65	.631			175	9.2
1950–51	22	139	376	.370	80	120	.667	387	17.6	358	16.3
1951–52	22	204	489	.417	153	218	.702			561	25.5
Totals	63	410	1077	.381	274	403	.680			1094	17.4

BRAD DAUGHERTY
North Carolina
7-0 – C
Swannanoa, N.C.

NCAA consensus second-team All-American in 1986.... Led the nation in field-goal shooting in 1986.... Averaged 14.2 points and 8.8 rebounds in 12 NCAA Tournament games from 1983 to 1986 (8-4 record).... Selected by the Cleveland Cavaliers in first round of 1986 NBA draft (1st pick overall).

Season	G	FGM	FGA	FG%	FTM	FTA	FT%	Reb.	Avg.	Pts.	Avg.
1982–83	35	110	197	.558	67	101	.663	181	5.2	287	8.2
1983–84	30	128	210	.610	59	87	.678	167	5.6	315	10.5
1984–85	36	238	381	.625	147	198	.742	349	9.7	623	17.3
1985–86	34	284	438	.648	119	174	.684	306	9.0	687	20.2
Totals	133	760	1226	.620	392	560	.700	1003	7.5	1912	14.2

Three-point field goals: 0 of 1 in 1982–83.

BOB DAVIES
Seton Hall
6-1 – G
Harrisburg, Pa.

NCAA first-team All-American in 1942.... Did not play in NCAA Tournament.... Averaged 11.3 points in three NIT games for 1941 third-place finisher (1-2 record).... Signed as a free agent in 1945 by the NBL's Rochester Royals, which transferred to the BAA for 1948–49 campaign before the NBL and BBA merged to form the NBA for the 1949–50 season.... Coached his alma mater to a 24-3 record in 1946–47, which was the same season he also earned NBL Most Valuable Player honors (averaged 14.3 points in 43 regular-season and playoff games with Rochester).... Elected to Naismith Memorial Basketball Hall of Fame in 1969.

Season	G	FGM	FGA	FG%	FTM	FTA	FT%	Reb.	Avg.	Pts.	Avg.
1939–40	18	78			56					212	11.8
1940–41	22	91			42					224	10.2
1941–42	19	81			63					225	11.8
Totals	59	250			161					661	11.2

WALTER DAVIS
North Carolina
6-6 – G/F
Charlotte, N.C.

Second-leading scorer and rebounder for 1977 national runner-up (28-5 record).... Named to All-NCAA Tournament team in 1977.... Averaged 14.1 points and 5.4 rebounds in eight NCAA Tournament games from 1975 to 1977 (5-3 record; did not play in 1977 opener).... Scored 18 points in one NIT game in 1974.... Member of 1976 U.S. Olympic team.... Selected by the Phoenix Suns in first round of 1977 NBA draft (5th pick overall).

Season	G	FGM	FGA	FG%	FTM	FTA	FT%	Reb.	Avg.	Pts.	Avg.
1973–74	27	161	322	.500	65	82	.793	126	4.7	387	14.3
1974–75	31	200	396	.505	98	130	.754	195	6.3	498	16.1
1975–76	29	190	351	.541	101	130	.777	166	5.7	481	16.6
1976–77	32	203	351	.578	91	117	.778	183	5.7	497	15.5
Totals	119	754	1420	.531	355	459	.773	670	5.6	1863	15.7

JOHNNY DAWKINS
Duke
6-2 – G
Washington, D.C.

Naismith Award winner in 1986.... NCAA unanimous first-team All-American in 1986 and consensus first-team All-American in 1985.... Leading scorer, runner-up in assists and third-leading rebounder for 1986 national runner-up (37-3 record).... Named to All-NCAA Tournament team in 1986.... Averaged 23.8 points and 5.3 rebounds in nine NCAA Tournament games from 1984 to 1986 (6-3 record).... Selected by the San Antonio Spurs in first round of 1986 NBA draft (10th pick overall).

Season	G	FGM	FGA	FG%	FTM	FTA	FT%	Reb.	Avg.	Pts.	Avg.
1982–83	28	207	414	.500	73	107	.682	115	4.1	506	18.1
1983–84	34	263	547	.481	133	160	.831	138	4.1	659	19.4
1984–85	31	225	455	.495	132	166	.795	141	4.5	582	18.8
1985–86	40	331	603	.549	147	181	.812	142	3.6	809	20.2
Totals	133	1026	2019	.508	485	614	.790	536	4.0	2556	19.2

Three-point field goals: 19 of 54 (.352) in 1982–83.

DAVE DEBUSSCHERE
Detroit
6-5 – F
Detroit, Mich.

Scored 38 points and grabbed 19 rebounds in one NCAA Tournament game in 1962.... Averaged 19 points in two NIT games in 1960 and 1961....

Selected as a territorial pick by the Detroit Pistons in first round of 1962 NBA draft.... Elected to Naismith Memorial Basketball Hall of Fame in 1982.

Season	G	FGM	FGA	FG%	FTM	FTA	FT%	Reb.	Avg.	Pts.	Avg.
1959–60	27	288	656	.433	115	196	.587	540	20.0	691	25.6
1960–61	27	256	636	.403	86	155	.555	514	19.0	598	22.1
1961–62	26	267	616	.433	162	242	.669	498	19.2	696	26.8
Totals	80	811	1917	.423	363	593	.612	1552	19.4	1985	24.8

ARCHIE DEES
Indiana
6-8 – C
Mt. Carmel, Ill.

NCAA consensus second-team All-American in 1958.... Averaged 26.5 points and 14.5 rebounds in two NCAA Tournament games in 1958 (1-1 record).... Selected by the Cincinnati Royals in first round of 1958 NBA draft (2nd pick overall).

Season	G	FGM	FGA	FG%	FTM	FTA	FT%	Reb.	Avg.	Pts.	Avg.
1955–56	22	140	332	.422	103	127	.811			383	17.4
1956–57	22	187	440	.425	176	209	.842			550	25.0
1957–58	24	230	480	.479	153	186	.823	345	14.4	613	25.5
Totals	68	557	1252	.445	432	522	.828			1546	22.7

TONY DELK
Kentucky
6-1 – G
Brownsville, Tenn.

NCAA consensus first-team All-American in 1996. . . . Leading scorer for 1996 NCAA Tournament champion (34-2 record). . . . Member of 1996 All-NCAA Tournament team when he was named Final Four Most Outstanding Player (44 points, 9 rebounds). . . . Averaged 14.5 points in 17 NCAA Tournament games from 1993-96 (14-3 record).

Season	G.	FGM	FGA	FG%	FTM	FTA	FT%	Reb.	Avg.	Pts.	Avg.
1992-93	30	47	104	.452	24	33	.727	57	1.9	136	4.6
1993-94	34	200	440	.455	69	108	.639	153	4.5	564	16.6
1994-95	33	207	433	.478	60	89	.674	110	3.3	551	16.7
1995-96	36	229	464	.494	88	110	.800	150	4.2	639	17.8
Totals	133	683	1441	.474	241	340	.709	470	3.5	1890	14.2

Three-point field goals: 18 of 51 (.353) in 1992-93, 95 of 254 (.374) in 1993-94, 77 of 197 (.391) in 1994-95 and 93 of 210 (.443) in 1995-96. **Totals:** 283 of 712 (.397).

ERNIE DIGREGORIO
Providence
6-0 – G
North Providence, R.I.

NCAA consensus first-team All-American in 1973.... Leading scorer for national fourth-place team in 1973 (27-4 record).... Member of All-NCAA Tournament team in 1973.... Averaged 24.2 points and 6.5 assists in six NCAA Tournament games in 1972 and 1973 (3-3 record).... Averaged 21.5 points in two NIT games in 1971.... Selected by the Buffalo Braves in first round of 1973 NBA draft (3rd pick overall).

Season	G	FGM	FGA	FG%	FTM	FTA	FT%	Reb.	Avg.	Pts.	Avg.
1970–71	28	217	451	.481	88	106	.830	112	4.0	522	18.6
1971–72	27	192	440	.436	93	116	.802	81	3.0	477	17.7
1972–73	31	348	728	.478	65	81	.802	99	3.2	761	24.5
Totals	86	757	1619	.468	246	303	.812	292	3.4	1760	20.5

TERRY DISCHINGER
Purdue
6-7 – F
Terre Haute, Ind.

NCAA unanimous first-team All-American in 1961 and 1962, and consensus second-team All-American in 1960.... Did not play in NCAA Tournament or NIT.... Member of 1960 U.S. Olympic team.... Selected by the Chicago Zephyrs in second round of 1962 NBA draft.

Season	G	FGM	FGA	FG%	FTM	FTA	FT%	Reb.	Avg.	Pts.	Avg.
1959–60	23	201	368	.546	203	260	.781	328	14.3	605	26.3
1960–61	23	215	373	.576	218	261	.835	308	13.4	648	28.2
1961–62	24	217	404	.537	292	350	.834	322	13.4	726	30.3
Totals	70	633	1145	.553	713	871	.819	958	13.7	1979	28.3

CLYDE DREXLER
Houston
6-6 – F/G
Houston, Tex.

NCAA second-team All-American in 1983.... Second-leading scorer and leading rebounder for 1982 Final Four team (25-8 record) and second-leading scorer and second-leading rebounder for 1983 national runner-up (31-3).... Averaged 13.4 points and 6.9 rebounds in 11 NCAA Tournament games from 1981 to 1983 (8-3 record).... Member of 1992 U.S. Olympic team.... Selected as an undergraduate by the Portland Trail Blazers in first round of 1983 NBA draft (14th pick overall).

Season	G	FGM	FGA	FG%	FTM	FTA	FT%	Reb.	Avg.	Pts.	Avg.
1980–81	30	153	303	.505	50	85	.588	314	10.5	356	11.9
1981–82	32	206	362	.569	73	120	.608	336	10.5	485	15.2
1982–83	34	236	440	.536	70	95	.737	298	8.8	542	15.9
Totals	96	595	1105	.538	193	300	.643	948	9.9	1383	14.4

WALTER DUKES
Seton Hall
6-10 – C
Rochester, N.Y

NCAA unanimous first-team All-American in 1953.... One of six players to average more than 20 points and 20 rebounds per game in his career.... Did not play in NCAA Tournament.... NIT Most Valuable Player in 1953.... Averaged 22.5 points in four NIT games in 1952 (first-round loser) and 1953 (champion).... Played two full seasons with the Harlem Globetrotters before signing with the New York Knicks, who picked him in the 1953 NBA draft.

Season	G	FGM	FGA	FG%	FTM	FTA	FT%	Reb.	Avg.	Pts.	Avg.
1951–52	26	169	402	.420	186	280	.664	513	19.7	524	20.2
1952–53	33	272	574	.474	317	426	.744	734	22.2	861	26.1
Totals	59	441	976	.452	503	706	.712	1247	21.1	1385	23.5

JOE DUMARS
McNeese State
6-3 – G
Natchitoches, La.

Did not play in NCAA Tournament or NIT.... Selected by the Detroit Pistons in first round of 1985 NBA draft (18th pick overall).

Season	G	FGM	FGA	FG%	FTM	FTA	FT%	Reb.	Avg.	Pts.	Avg.
1981–82	29	206	464	.444	115	160	.719	64	2.1	527	18.2
1982–83	29	212	487	.435	140	197	.711	128	4.4	569	19.6
1983–84	31	275	586	.469	267	324	.824	164	5.3	817	26.4
1984–85	27	248	501	.495	201	236	.852	132	4.9	697	25.8
Totals	116	941	2038	.462	723	917	.788	488	4.2	2610	22.5

Three-point field goals: 5 of 8 (.625) in 1982–83.

TIM DUNCAN
Wake Forest
6-10 – C
St. Croix, Virgin Islands

NCAA unanimous first-team All-American in 1996.... Ranked among the nation's leading rebounders in 1995 (5th) and 1996 (4th).... Ranked among the nation's leaders in blocked shots in 1994 (5th with 3.8 bpg), 1995 (6th with 4.2 bpg) and 1996 (8th with 3.8 bpg).... Averaged 17.1 points, 13.7 rebounds and 4.7 blocked shots in nine NCAA Tournament games from 1994-96 (6-3 record).

Season	G.	FGM	FGA	FG%	FTM	FTA	FT%	Reb.	Avg.	Pts.	Avg.
1993–94	33	120	220	.545	82	110	.745	317	9.6	323	9.8
1994–95	32	208	352	.591	118	159	.742	401	12.5	537	16.8
1995–96	32	228	411	.555	149	217	.687	395	12.3	612	19.1
Totals	97	556	983	.566	349	486	.718	1113	11.5	1472	15.2

Three-point field goals: 1 of 1 (1.000) in 1993-94, 3 of 7 (.429) in 1994-95 and 7 of 23 (.304) in 1995-96. **Totals:** 11 of 31 (.355).

OZIE EDWARDS
Oklahoma City
6-4 – F/G
Chicago, Ill.

Ranked among the nation's leading scorers in 1972 (33rd) and 1973 (7th).... Ranked 8th in the nation in free-throw percentage in 1973.... Collected 31 points and nine rebounds in one NCAA Tournament game in 1973.... Played two junior college seasons for Eastern Oklahoma A&M.... Selected by the Cavaliers in third round of 1973 NBA draft (39th pick overall; did not play in league).

Season	G.	FGM	FGA	FG%	FTM	FTA	FT%	Reb.	Avg.	Pts.	Avg.
1971-72	26	248	566	.438	99	123	.805	214	8.2	595	22.9
1972-73	27	332	736	.451	103	120	.858	210	7.8	767	28.4
Totals	53	580	1302	.445	202	243	.831	424	8.0	1362	25.7

SEAN ELLIOTT
Arizona
6-8 – F
Tucson, Ariz.

Named national player of the year by AP and NABC in 1989.... Wooden Award winner in 1989.... NCAA unanimous first-team All-American in 1988 and 1989.... Member of All-NCAA Tournament team in 1988.... Leading scorer and rebounder for 1988 Final Four team (35-3 record).... Averaged 23.6 points and 6.8 rebounds in 10 NCAA Tournament games from 1986 to 1989 (6-4 record).... Selected by the San Antonio Spurs in first round of 1989 NBA draft (3rd pick overall).

Season	G	FGM	FGA	FG%	FTM	FTA	FT%	Reb.	Avg.	Pts.	Avg.
1985–86	32	187	385	.486	125	167	.749	171	5.3	499	15.6
1986–87	30	209	410	.510	127	165	.770	181	6.0	578	19.3
1987–88	38	263	461	.570	176	222	.793	219	5.8	743	19.6
1988–89	33	237	494	.480	195	232	.841	237	7.2	735	22.3
Totals	133	896	1750	.512	623	786	.793	808	6.1	2555	19.2

Three-point field goals: 33 of 89 (.371) in 1986–87, 41 of 87 (.471) in 1987–88 and 66 of 151 (.437) in 1988–89. **Totals:** 140 of 327 (.428).

DALE ELLIS
Tennessee
6-7 – F
Marietta, Ga.

NCAA consensus first-team All-American in 1983 and consensus second-team All-American in 1982.... Averaged 14.5 points and 5.5 rebounds in eight NCAA Tournament games from 1980 to 1983 (4-4 record).... Selected by the Dallas Mavericks in first round of 1983 NBA draft (9th pick overall).

Season	G	FGM	FGA	FG%	FTM	FTA	FT%	Reb.	Avg.	Pts.	Avg.
1979–80	27	81	182	.445	31	40	.775	96	3.6	193	7.1
1980–81	29	215	360	.597	83	111	.748	185	6.4	513	17.7
1981–82	30	257	393	.654	121	152	.796	189	6.3	635	21.2
1982–83	32	279	464	.601	166	221	.751	209	6.5	724	22.6
Totals	118	832	1399	.595	401	524	.765	679	5.8	2065	17.5

PERVIS ELLISON
Louisville
6-9 – F/C
Savannah, Ga.

NCAA consensus first-team All-American in 1989.... Final Four Most Outstanding Player in 1986.... Member of All-NCAA Tournament team in 1986.... Third-leading scorer and leading rebounder for 1986 NCAA champion (32-7 record).... Averaged 17 points and 10.1 rebounds in 12 NCAA Tournament games in 1986, 1988, and 1989 (10-2 record).... Selected by the Sacramento Kings in first round of 1989 NBA draft (1st pick overall).

Season	G	FGM	FGA	FG%	FTM	FTA	FT%	Reb.	Avg.	Pts.	Avg.
1985–86	39	210	379	.554	90	132	.682	318	8.2	510	13.1
1986–87	31	185	347	.533	100	139	.719	270	8.7	470	15.2
1987–88	35	235	391	.601	146	211	.692	291	8.3	617	17.6
1988–89	31	227	369	.615	92	141	.652	270	8.7	546	17.6
Totals	136	857	1486	.577	428	623	.687	1149	8.4	2143	15.8

Three-point field goals: 1 of 2 (.500) in 1987–88 and 0 of 1 in 1988–89. **Totals:** 1 of 3 (.333).

LEN ELMORE
Maryland
6-9 – C
New York, N.Y.

NCAA consensus second-team All-American in 1974. . . . Ranked 10th in the nation in rebounding in 1974. . . . Averaged 12 points and 12 rebounds in two NCAA Tournament games in 1973 (1-1 record). . . . Averaged 16.5 points and 13.8 rebounds in four NIT games for 1972 champion. . . . Selected by the Bullets in first round of 1974 NBA draft (13th pick overall). Selected by the Pacers in first round of 1973 ABA undergraduate draft.

Season	G	FGM	FGA	FG%	FTM	FTA	FT%	Reb.	Avg.	Pts.	Avg.
1971-72	32	126	273	.462	95	126	.754	351	11.0	347	10.8
1972-73	26	112	239	.469	37	61	.607	290	11.2	261	10.0
1973-74	28	170	324	.525	69	91	.758	412	14.7	409	14.6
Totals	86	408	836	.488	201	278	.723	1053	12.2	1017	11.8

ALEX ENGLISH
South Carolina
6-7 – F
Columbia, S.C.

Averaged 16.8 points and 11 rebounds in four NCAA Tournament games in 1973 and 1974 (2-2 record).... Averaged 15.5 points in two NIT games in 1975.... Selected by the Milwaukee Bucks in second round of 1976 NBA draft (23rd pick overall).

Season	G	FGM	FGA	FG%	FTM	FTA	FT%	Reb.	Avg.	Pts.	Avg.
1972–73	29	189	368	.514	44	70	.629	306	10.6	422	14.6
1973–74	27	209	395	.529	75	112	.670	237	8.8	493	18.3
1974–75	28	199	359	.554	49	77	.636	244	8.7	447	16.0
1975–76	27	258	468	.551	94	134	.701	277	10.3	610	22.6
Totals	111	855	1590	.538	262	393	.667	1064	9.6	1972	17.8

KEITH ERICKSON
UCLA
6-5 – F
El Segundo, Calif.

Leading rebounder and fourth-leading scorer for 1964 NCAA Tournament champion (30-0 record). . . . Second-leading scorer and rebounder for 1965 NCAA champion (28-2). . . . Averaged 11.6 points and 6.8 rebounds in 10 NCAA Tournament games from 1963-65 (8-2 record). . . . Played one junior college season at El Camino (Calif.). . . . Selected by the San Francisco Warriors in fourth round of 1965 NBA draft (25th pick overall).

Season	G.	FGM	FGA	FG%	FTM	FTA	FT%	Reb.	Avg.	Pts.	Avg.
1962-63	28	58	163	.356	25	39	.641	170	6.1	141	5.0
1963-64	30	127	315	.403	66	106	.623	272	9.1	320	10.7
1964-65	29	147	332	.443	79	109	.725	255	8.8	373	12.9
Totals	87	332	810	.410	170	254	.669	697	8.0	834	9.6

JULIUS ERVING
Massachusetts
6-6 – F
Roosevelt, N.Y.

One of six players to average more than 20 points and 20 rebounds per game in his career.... Did not play in NCAA Tournament.... Averaged 15.5 points in two NIT games in 1970 and 1971 (0-2 record).... Selected by the Milwaukee Bucks in first round of 1972 NBA draft (12th pick overall) although he was already playing in the ABA after signing as an undergraduate free agent with the Virginia Squires.... Elected to Naismith Memorial Basketball Hall of Fame in 1993.

Season	G	FGM	FGA	FG%	FTM	FTA	FT%	Reb.	Avg.	Pts.	Avg.
1969–70	25	238	468	.509	167	230	.726	522	20.9	643	25.7
1970–71	27	286	609	.470	155	206	.752	527	19.5	727	26.9
Totals	52	524	1077	.487	322	436	.739	1049	20.2	1370	26.3

PATRICK EWING
Georgetown
7-0 – C
Cambridge, Mass.

Named national player of the year by AP and NABC in 1985.... Naismith Award winner in 1985.... NCAA unanimous first-team All-American in 1984 and 1985, and consensus first-team All-American in 1983.... Final Four Most Outstanding Player in 1984.... Member of All-NCAA Tournament team in 1982, 1984, and 1985.... Leading scorer and rebounder for 1984 NCAA champion (34-3 record) and 1985 national runner-up (35-3).... Second-leading scorer and leading rebounder for 1982 national runner-up (30-7).... Averaged 14.2 points and eight rebounds in 18 NCAA Tournament games from 1982 to 1985 (15-3 record).... Member of 1984 and 1992 U.S. Olympic teams .... Selected by the New York Knicks in first round of 1985 NBA draft (1st pick overall).

Season	G	FGM	FGA	FG%	FTM	FTA	FT%	Reb.	Avg.	Pts.	Avg.
1981–82	37	183	290	.631	103	167	.617	279	7.5	469	12.7
1982–83	32	212	372	.570	141	224	.629	325	10.2	565	17.7
1983–84	37	242	368	.658	124	189	.656	371	10.0	608	16.4
1984–85	37	220	352	.625	102	160	.638	341	9.2	542	14.6
Totals	143	857	1382	.620	470	740	.635	1316	9.2	2184	15.3

ARNIE FERRIN
Utah
6-4 – F
Ogden, Utah

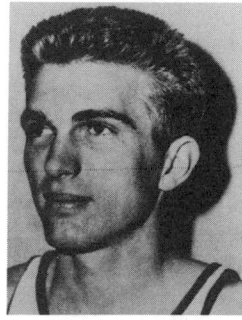

NCAA consensus first-team All-American in 1945 and second-team All-American in 1947 and 1948.... Final Four Most Outstanding Player in 1944.... Leading scorer with 13.3 points per game during 1944 tournament for NCAA champion (22-4 record).... Did not play in the 1945 playoffs after entering the service the day after the regular season ended.... Averaged 13.5 points in four NIT games in 1944 (first-round loser) and 1947 (champion).

Season	G	FGM	FGA	FG%	FTM	FTA	FT%	Reb.	Avg.	Pts.	Avg.
1943–44	24	127			47					301	12.5
1944–45	18									315	17.4
1945–46	Military Service (Army)										
1946–47	20	82			63					227	11.4
1947-48	20	96			90					282	14.1
Totals	82									1125	13.7

DANNY FERRY
Duke
6-10 – F/C
Bowie, Md.

Named national player of the year by UPI and NABC in 1989.... Naismith Award winner in 1989.... NCAA unanimous first-team All-American in 1989 and consensus second-team All-American in 1988.... Member of All-NCAA Tournament team in 1989.... Leading scorer and rebounder for Final Four teams in 1988 (28-7 record) and 1989 (28-8).... Sixth-leading scorer and second-leading rebounder for 1986 national runner-up (37-3).... Averaged 14.2 points and 6.9 rebounds in 19 NCAA Tournament games from 1986-89 (15-4 record).... Selected by the Los Angeles Clippers in first round of 1989 NBA draft (2nd pick overall); the Clippers subsequently traded his draft rights to the Cleveland Cavaliers.

Season	G	FGM	FGA	FG%	FTM	FTA	FT%	Reb.	Avg.	Pts.	Avg.
1985–86	40	91	198	.460	54	86	.628	221	5.5	236	5.9
1986–87	33	172	383	.449	92	109	.844	256	7.8	461	14.0
1987–88	35	247	519	.476	135	163	.828	266	7.6	667	19.1
1988–89	35	300	575	.522	146	193	.756	260	7.4	791	22.6
Totals	143	810	1675	.484	427	551	.775	1003	7.0	2155	15.1

Three-point field goals: 25 of 63 (.397) in 1986–87, 38 of 109 (.349) in 1987–88, and 45 of 106 (.425) in 1988–89. **Totals:** 108 of 278 (.388).

VERN FLEMING
Georgia
6-5 – G
Long Island, N.Y.

Leading scorer for 1983 Final Four team (24-10 record).... Averaged 14.3 points, seven rebounds and four assists in four NCAA Tournament games in 1983 (3-1 record).... Averaged 12.6 points and 4.3 rebounds in seven NIT games in 1981 (eliminated in second round), 1982 (lost in semifinals)

and 1984 (eliminated in first round).... Member of 1984 U.S. Olympic team (7.7 ppg, 2.7 rpg).... Selected by the Pacers in first round of 1984 NBA draft (18th pick overall).

Season	G.	FGM	FGA	FG%	FTM	FTA	FT%	Reb.	Avg.	Pts.	Avg.
1980-81	30	108	225	.480	85	122	.697	80	2.7	301	10.0
1981-82	31	117	236	.496	73	114	.640	120	3.9	307	9.9
1982-83	34	227	424	.535	121	169	.716	158	4.6	575	16.9
1983-84	30	248	493	.503	98	130	.754	120	4.0	594	19.8
Totals	125	700	1378	.508	377	535	.705	478	3.8	1777	14.2

ROD FLETCHER
Illinois
6-4 – G
Champaign, Ill.

NCAA consensus first-team All-American in 1952.... Second-leading scorer for 1952 national third-place finisher (22-4 record) and third-leading scorer for 1951 national third-place finisher (22-5).... Averaged 14 points in eight NCAA Tournament games in 1951 and 1952 (6-2 record).... Selected by the Minneapolis Lakers in 1952 NBA draft (did not play in league).

Season	G	FGM	FGA	FG%	FTM	FTA	FT%	Reb.	Avg.	Pts.	Avg.
1949–50	22	39	176	.222	24	48	.500			102	4.6
1950–51	27	115	338	.340	60	111	.541			290	10.7
1951–52	22	90	311	.289	65	116	.560			245	11.1
Totals	71	244	825	.296	149	275	.542			637	9.0

DARRELL FLOYD
Furman
6-1 – G/F
Morehead, Ky.

NCAA consensus second-team All-American in 1955 and 1956.... Led the nation in scoring in 1955 and 1956.... Did not play in NCAA Tournament or NIT.... Selected by the St. Louis Hawks in third round of 1956 NBA draft (did not play in league).

Season	G	FGM	FGA	FG%	FTM	FTA	FT%	Reb.	Avg.	Pts.	Avg.
1953–54	18	185	417	.444	68	81	.840	141	7.8	438	24.3
1954–55	25	344	796	.432	209	267	.783	208	8.3	897	35.9
1955–56	28	339	850	.399	268	350	.766	262	9.4	946	33.8
Totals	71	868	2063	.421	545	698	.781	611	8.6	2281	32.1

ERIC (SLEEPY) FLOYD
Georgetown
6-3 – G
Gastonia, N.C.

NCAA unanimous first-team All-American in 1982.... Member of All-NCAA Tournament team in 1982.... Leading scorer and third-leading rebounder for 1982 national runner-up (30-7 record).... Averaged 18 points in 10 NCAA Tournament games from 1979 to 1982 (6-4 record).... Selected by the New Jersey Nets in first round of 1982 NBA draft (13th pick overall).

Season	G	FGM	FGA	FG%	FTM	FTA	FT%	Reb.	Avg.	Pts.	Avg.
1978–79	29	177	388	.456	126	155	.813	119	4.1	480	16.6
1979–80	32	246	444	.554	106	140	.757	98	3.1	598	18.7
1980–81	32	237	508	.467	133	165	.806	133	4.2	607	19.0
1981–82	37	249	494	.504	121	168	.720	127	3.4	619	16.7
Totals	130	909	1834	.496	486	628	.774	477	3.7	2304	17.7

ALPHONSO FORD
Mississippi Valley State
6-1 – G
Greenwood, Miss.

Scored 16 points in one NCAA Tournament game in 1992.... Selected by the Philadelphia 76ers in second round of 1993 NBA draft (did not play in league).

Season	G	FGM	FGA	FG%	FTM	FTA	FT%	Reb.	Avg.	Pts.	Avg.
1989–90	27	289	656	.441	126	171	.737	133	4.9	808	29.9
1990–91	28	325	668	.487	179	234	.765	167	6.0	915	32.7
1991–92	26	255	567	.450	137	181	.757	145	5.6	714	27.5
1992–93	28	252	578	.436	148	187	.791	147	5.3	728	26.0
Totals	109	1121	2469	.454	590	773	.763	592	5.4	3165	29.0

Three-point field goals: 104 of 288 (.361) in 1989–90, 86 of 260 (.331) in 1990–91, 67 of 221 (.303) in 1991–92, and 76 of 216 (.352) in 1992–93.

Totals: 333 of 985 (.338).

PHIL FORD
North Carolina
6-2 – G
Rocky Mount, N.C.

Named national player of the year by NABC and USBWA in 1978.... Wooden Award winner in 1978.... NCAA unanimous first-team All-American in 1978, consensus first-team All-American in 1977 and consensus second-team All-American in 1977.... Leading scorer for 1977 national runner-up (28-5 record).... Averaged 14.7 points and 4.9 assists in 10 NCAA Tournament games from 1975 to 1978 (6-4 record).... Member of 1976 U.S. Olympic team.... Selected by the Kansas City Kings in first round of 1978 NBA draft (2nd pick overall).

Season	G	FGM	FGA	FG%	FTM	FTA	FT%	Reb.	Avg.	Pts.	Avg.
1974–75	31	191	370	.516	126	161	.783	85	2.7	508	16.4
1975–76	29	206	387	.532	128	164	.780	51	1.8	540	18.6
1976–77	33	230	431	.534	157	184	.853	63	1.9	617	18.7
1977–78	30	238	452	.527	149	184	.810	62	2.1	625	20.8
Totals	123	865	1640	.527	560	693	.808	261	2.1	2290	18.6

CHET FORTE
Columbia
5-9 – G
Hackensack, N.J.

Named national player of the year by UPI in 1957.... NCAA consensus first-team All-American in 1957.... Did not play in NCAA Tournament or NIT.... Selected by the Cincinnati Royals in seventh round of 1957 NBA draft (did not play in league).

Season	G	FGM	FGA	FG%	FTM	FTA	FT%	Reb.	Avg.	Pts.	Avg.
1954–55	25	186	465	.400	187	222	.842	100	4.0	559	22.4
1955–56	16	122	288	.424	114	139	.820	82	5.1	358	22.4
1956–57	24	235	583	.403	224	263	.852	108	4.5	694	28.9
Totals	65	543	1336	.406	525	624	.841	290	4.5	1611	24.8

ROBIN FREEMAN
Ohio State
5-11 – G
Cincinnati, Ohio

NCAA unanimous first-team All-American in 1956 and consensus second-team All-American in 1955.... Did not play in NCAA Tournament or NIT.... Selected by the St. Louis Hawks in fourth round of 1956 NBA draft (did not play in league).

Season	G	FGM	FGA	FG%	FTM	FTA	FT%	Reb.	Avg.	Pts.	Avg.
1953–54	22	185	461	.401	95	122	.779			465	21.1
1954–55	13	149	341	.437	111	137	.810			409	31.5
1955–56	22	259	562	.461	205	253	.810			723	32.9
Totals	57	593	1364	.435	411	512	.803			1597	28.0

RICHIE FUQUA
Oral Roberts
6-4 – G
Chattanooga, Tenn.

NCAA consensus second-team All-American in 1972.... Did not play in NCAA Tournament.... Averaged 30.7 points in three NIT games in 1972 and 1973 (1-2 record).... Selected by the Boston Celtics in fourth round of 1973 NBA draft (did not play in league).

Season	G	FGM	FGA	FG%	FTM	FTA	FT%	Reb.	Avg.	Pts.	Avg.
1969–70	31	228	483	.472	105	147	.714	154	5.0	561	18.1
1970–71	26	353	701	.504	120	171	.702	116	4.5	826	31.8
1971–72	28	423	941	.450	160	210	.762	140	5.0	1006	35.9
1972–73	26	269	713	.377	73	130	.562	113	4.3	611	23.5
Totals	111	1273	2838	.449	458	658	.696	523	4.7	3004	27.1

Note: Oral Roberts was a Division II school in his first two seasons.

DICK GARMAKER
Minnesota
6-3 – F
Hibbing, Mich.

NCAA consensus first-team All-American in 1955.... Did not play in NCAA Tournament or NIT.... Played 1950–51 and 1951–52 seasons at Hibbing (Minn.) Junior College.... Selected by the Minneapolis Lakers in both the 1954 and 1955 NBA drafts (territorial pick in 1955).

Season	G	FGM	FGA	FG%	FTM	FTA	FT%	Reb.	Avg.	Pts.	Avg.
1952–53				Sat out season under Big Ten rules for junior college transfers.							
1953–54	22	147	327	.450	181	251	.721	155	7.0	475	21.6
1954–55	22	186	507	.367	161	209	.770	185	8.4	533	24.2
Totals	44	333	834	.399	342	460	.743	340	7.7	1008	22.9

ERIC (HANK) GATHERS
Loyola Marymount
6-7 – F/C
Philadelphia, Pa.

NCAA consensus second-team All-American in 1990.... Led the nation in scoring and rebounding in 1989.... Averaged 21.3 points and 13.7 rebounds in three NCAA Tournament games in 1988 and 1989 (1-2 record; died of heart ailment before the 1990 tournament in which the Lions were 3-1).

Season	G	FGM	FGA	FG%	FTM	FTA	FT%	Reb.	Avg.	Pts.	Avg.
1985–86	28	90	170	.529	53	92	.576	143	5.1	233	8.3
1986–87				Sat out entire year after transferring from Southern Cal.							
1987–88	32	304	541	.562	113	208	.543	278	8.7	721	22.5
1988–89	31	419	689	.608	177	315	.562	426	13.7	1015	32.7
1989–90	26	314	528	.595	126	222	.568	281	10.8	754	29.0
Totals	117	1127	1928	.585	469	837	.560	1128	9.6	2723	23.3

Three-point field goals: 0 of 1 in 1987–88 and 0 of 1 in 1989–90. **Totals:** 0 of 2.

ARMON GILLIAM
UNLV
6-9 – F
Bethel Park, Pa.

NCAA consensus second-team All-American in 1987.... Leading scorer and rebounder for 1987 Final Four team (37-2 record).... Averaged 21.5 points and 9.3 rebounds in 10 NCAA Tournament games from 1985 to 1987 (7-3 record).... Averaged 16.9 points and 8.3 rebounds in one junior college season at Independence (Kans.).... Selected by the Phoenix Suns in first round of 1987 NBA draft (2nd pick overall).

Season	G	FGM	FGA	FG%	FTM	FTA	FT%	Reb.	Avg.	Pts.	Avg.
1983–84	Sat out the entire season as a redshirt.										
1984–85	31	136	219	.621	98	150	.653	212	6.8	370	11.9
1985–86	37	221	418	.529	140	190	.737	315	8.5	582	15.7
1986–87	39	359	598	.600	185	254	.728	363	9.3	903	23.2
Totals	107	716	1235	.580	423	594	.712	890	8.3	1855	17.3

ARTIS GILMORE
Jacksonville
7-2 – C
Chipley, Fla.

NCAA unanimous first-team All-American in 1971.... Led the nation in rebounding in 1970 and 1971.... Only player to average more than 22 points and 22 rebounds per game in his career.... Leading scorer and rebounder for 1970 national runner-up (27-2 record).... Named to All-NCAA Tournament team in 1970.... Averaged 24 points and 19.2 rebounds in six NCAA Tournament games in 1970 and 1971 (4-2 record).... Averaged 22.5 points in two junior college seasons at Gardner-Webb (N.C.).... Selected by the Chicago Bulls in seventh round of 1971 NBA draft (117th pick overall) and by the Kentucky Colonels in first round of 1971 ABA draft.

Season	G	FGM	FGA	FG%	FTM	FTA	FT%	Reb.	Avg.	Pts.	Avg.
1969–70	28	307	529	.580	128	202	.634	621	22.2	742	26.5
1970–71	26	229	405	.565	112	188	.596	603	23.2	570	21.9
Totals	54	536	934	.574	240	390	.615	1224	22.7	1312	24.3

GEORGE GLAMACK
North Carolina
6-6 – C
Allentown, Pa.

NCAA consensus first-team All-American in 1940 and 1941.... Averaged 20 points in two NCAA Tournament games in 1941 (0-2 record).

Season	G	FGM	FGA	FG%	FTM	FTA	FT%	Reb.	Avg.	Pts.	Avg.
1938–39		Statistics not available.									
1939–40		Statistics not available.									
1940–41	28									578	20.6
Totals		Totals not available.									

GERALD GLASS
Mississippi
6-6 – G/F
Greenwood, Miss.

Ranked among the nation's leading scorers in 1989 (4th) and 1990 (19th).... Did not play in NCAA Tournament.... Scored 29 points in one NIT game in 1989.... Selected by the Timberwolves in first round of 1990 NBA draft (20th pick overall).

Season	G.	FGM	FGA	FG%	FTM	FTA	FT%	Reb.	Avg.	Pts.	Avg.
1985-86	31	168	303	.554	52	72	.722	203	6.5	388	12.5
1986-87	33	360	595	.605	134	191	.702	414	12.5	861	26.1
1987-88	Sat out the entire season after transferring from Delta State.										

1988-89	30	326	613	.532	148	201	.736	255	8.5	841	28.0
1989-90	30	284	580	.490	109	148	.736	229	7.6	723	24.1
Totals	124	1138	2091	.544	443	612	.724	1101	8.9	2813	22.7

Three-point field goals: 7 of 27 (.259) in 1986-87, 41 of 109 (.376) in 1988-89 and 46 of 122 (.377) in 1989-90. **Totals:** 94 of 258 (.364).

MIKE GMINSKI
Duke
6-11 – C
Monroe, Conn.

NCAA consensus first-team All-American in 1979 and consensus second-team All-American in 1980.... Named to All-NCAA Tournament team in 1978.... Leading rebounder and second-leading scorer for 1978 national runner-up (27-7 record).... Averaged 19.8 points and 8.3 rebounds in nine NCAA Tournament games from 1978 to 1980 (6-3 record).... Selected by the New Jersey Nets in first round of 1980 NBA draft (7th pick overall).

Season	G	FGM	FGA	FG%	FTM	FTA	FT%	Reb.	Avg.	Pts.	Avg.
1976–77	27	175	340	.515	64	91	.703	289	10.7	414	15.3
1977–78	32	246	450	.547	148	176	.841	319	10.0	640	20.0
1978–79	30	218	420	.519	129	177	.729	275	9.2	565	18.8
1979–80	33	262	487	.538	180	214	.841	359	10.9	704	21.3
Totals	122	901	1697	.531	521	658	.792	1242	10.2	2323	19.0

TOM GOLA
La Salle
6-6 – F
Philadelphia, Pa.

Named national player of the year by UPI in 1955.... NCAA unanimous first-team All-American in 1954 and 1955, and consensus first-team All-American in 1953.... Final Four Most Outstanding Player in 1954.... Named to All-NCAA Tournament teams in 1954 and 1955.... Leading scorer and rebounder for 1954 NCAA champion (26-4 record) and 1955 national runner-up (26-5).... Averaged 22.9 points in 10 NCAA Tournament games in 1954 and 1955 (9-1 record).... Co-Most Valuable Player of 1952 NIT with teammate Norm Grekin.... Averaged 14 points in five NIT games in 1952 (champion) and 1953 (opening-game loser).... Selected as a territorial choice by the Philadelphia Warriors in 1955 NBA draft.... Elected to Naismith Memorial Basketball Hall of Fame in 1975.

Season	G	FGM	FGA	FG%	FTM	FTA	FT%	Reb.	Avg.	Pts.	Avg.
1951–52	29	192	528	.364	121	170	.712	497	17.1	505	17.4
1952–53	28	186	451	.412	145	186	.780	434	15.5	517	18.5
1953–54	30	252	619	.407	186	254	.732	652	21.7	690	23.0
1954–55	31	274	624	.439	202	267	.757	618	19.9	750	24.2
Totals	118	904	2222	.407	654	877	.746	2201	18.7	2462	20.9

GAIL GOODRICH
UCLA
6-1 – G
Pasadena, Calif.

NCAA unanimous first-team All-American in 1965.... Named to All-NCAA Tournament team in 1964 and 1965.... Leading scorer and fourth-leading rebounder for NCAA champions in 1964 (30-0 record) and 1965 (28-2).... Averaged 23.5 points and four rebounds in 10 NCAA Tournament games from 1963 to 1965 (8-2 record).... Selected as a territorial pick by the Los Angeles Lakers in 1965 NBA draft.

Season	G	FGM	FGA	FG%	FTM	FTA	FT%	Reb.	Avg.	Pts.	Avg.
1962–63	29	117	280	.418	66	103	.641	101	3.5	300	10.3
1963–64	30	243	530	.458	160	225	.711	156	5.2	646	21.5
1964–65	30	277	528	.525	190	265	.717	158	5.3	744	24.8
Totals	89	637	1338	.476	416	593	.702	415	4.7	1690	19.0

OTTO GRAHAM
Northwestern/Colgate
6-0 – F
Waukegan, Ill.

NCAA consensus first-team All-American in 1944 and second-team All-American in 1943.... Did not play in NCAA Tournament or NIT.

Season	G	FGM	FGA	FG%	FTM	FTA	FT%	Reb.	Avg.	Pts.	Avg.
1941–42	21	103			86					292	13.9
1942–43	16	86			51					223	13.9
1943–44	17	75			37					187	11.0
Totals	54	264			174					702	13.0

Note: 1943–44 statistics include four games with Colgate in which he had a total of 28 field goals and eight free throws.

GARY GRANT
Michigan
6-3 – G
Canton, Ohio

NCAA unanimous first-team All-American in 1988.... Averaged 11.2 points and 6.1 assists in nine NCAA Tournament games from 1985-88 (5-4 record).... Selected by the Seattle SuperSonics in first round of 1988 NBA draft (15th pick overall); they promptly traded his draft rights to the Los Angeles Clippers.

Season	G	FGM	FGA	FG%	FTM	FTA	FT%	Reb.	Avg.	Pts.	Avg.
1984–85	30	169	307	.550	49	60	.817	76	2.5	387	12.9
1985–86	33	172	348	.494	58	78	.744	104	3.2	402	12.2
1986–87	32	286	533	.537	111	142	.782	159	5.0	716	22.4
1987–88	34	269	508	.530	135	167	.808	116	3.4	717	21.1
Totals	129	896	1696	.528	353	447	.790	455	3.5	2222	17.2

Three-point field goals: 33 of 68 (.485) in 1986–87 and 44 of 99 (.444) in 1987–88. **Totals:** 77 of 167 (.461).

DON GRATE
Ohio State
6-2 – F
Greenfield, Ohio

NCAA consensus second-team All-American in 1944 and 1945.... Leading scorer for 1944 national semifinalist (14-7 record) and second-leading scorer for 1945 national semifinalist (15-5).... Averaged 11.3 points in four NCAA Tournament games in 1944 and 1945 (2-2 record).... Signed pro baseball contract with the Philadelphia Phillies as a pitcher prior to his senior season.

Season	G	FGM	FGA	FG%	FTM	FTA	FT%	Reb.	Avg.	Pts.	Avg.
1943–44	21									272	13.0
1944–45	20	95			46					236	11.8
Totals	41									508	12.4

RICKEY GREEN
Michigan
6-0 – G
Chicago, Ill.

NCAA unanimous first-team All-American in 1977.... Named to All-NCAA Tournament team in 1976.... Leading scorer for 1976 national runner-up (25-7 record).... Averaged 18.6 points, 4.5 rebounds and 5 assists in eight NCAA Tournament games in 1976 and 1977 (6-2 record).... Averaged 19 points in two junior college seasons at Vincennes (Ind.).... Selected by the Golden State Warriors in first round of 1977 NBA draft (16th pick overall).

Season	G	FGM	FGA	FG%	FTM	FTA	FT%	Reb.	Avg.	Pts.	Avg.
1975–76	32	266	542	.491	106	135	.785	117	3.7	638	19.9
1976–77	28	224	464	.483	98	128	.766	81	2.9	546	19.5
Totals	60	490	1006	.487	204	263	.776	198	3.3	1184	19.7

SI GREEN
Duquesne
6-3 – G
Brooklyn, N.Y.

NCAA unanimous first-team All-American in 1956 and consensus first-team All-American in 1955.... Did not play in NCAA Tournament.... Averaged 21.3 points in eight NIT games in 1954 (runner-up), 1955 (champion), and 1956 (lost in quarterfinals).... Selected by the Rochester Royals in 1956 NBA draft.

Season	G	FGM	FGA	FG%	FTM	FTA	FT%	Reb.	Avg.	Pts.	Avg.
1953–54	29	151	377	.401	88	146	.603	239	8.2	390	13.4
1954–55	25	206	470	.438	139	235	.591	341	13.6	551	22.0
1955–56	27	241	570	.423	180	258	.698	356	13.2	662	24.5
Totals	81	598	1417	.422	407	639	.637	936	11.6	1603	19.8

DAVID GREENWOOD
UCLA
6-9 – F
Los Angeles, Calif.

NCAA unanimous first-team All-American in 1978 and consensus first-team All-American in 1979.... Seventh-leading scorer and fourth-leading rebounder for 1976 national third-place team (27-5 record).... Averaged 13.9 points and 7.7 rebounds in 12 NCAA Tournament games from 1976 to 1979 (8-4 record).... Selected by the Chicago Bulls in first round of 1979 NBA draft (2nd pick overall).

Season	G	FGM	FGA	FG%	FTM	FTA	FT%	Reb.	Avg.	Pts.	Avg.
1975–76	31	62	122	.508	28	35	.800	114	3.7	152	4.9
1976–77	29	202	395	.511	80	112	.714	280	9.7	484	16.7
1977–78	28	196	364	.538	97	133	.729	319	11.4	489	17.5
1978–79	30	247	421	.587	102	126	.810	309	10.3	596	19.9
Totals	118	707	1302	.543	307	406	.756	1022	8.7	1721	14.6

HAL GREER
Marshall
6-2 – G
Huntington, W.V.

Scored 12 points in his only NCAA Tournament game in 1956.... Selected by the Syracuse Nationals in second round of 1958 NBA draft (14th pick overall).... Elected to Naismith Memorial Basketball Hall of Fame in 1981.

Season	G	FGM	FGA	FG%	FTM	FTA	FT%	Reb.	Avg.	Pts.	Avg.
1955–56	23	128	213	.601	101	145	.697	153	6.6	357	15.5
1956–57	24	167	329	.508	119	156	.763	332	13.8	453	18.9
1957–58	24	236	432	.546	95	114	.833	280	11.7	567	23.6
Totals	71	531	974	.545	315	415	.759	765	10.8	1377	19.4

KEVIN GREVEY
Kentucky
6-5 – F
Hamilton, O. (Taft H.S.)

NCAA consensus second-team All-American in 1975. . . . Ranked 20th in the nation in scoring in 1975. . . . Leading scorer and third-leading rebounder for 1975 NCAA Tournament runner-up (26-5 record). . . . Averaged 19.4 points, 5.6 rebounds and 3.9 assists in seven NCAA Tournament games in 1973 and 1975 (5-2 record). . . . Named to 1975 All-NCAA Tournament team. . . . Selected by the Bullets in first round of 1975 NBA draft (18th pick overall).

Season	G.	FGM	FGA	FG%	FTM	FTA	FT%	Reb.	Avg.	Pts.	Avg.
1972-73	28	236	441	.535	52	76	.684	168	6.0	524	18.7
1973-74	25	232	457	.508	83	100	.830	180	7.2	547	21.9
1974-75	31	303	592	.512	124	157	.790	199	6.4	730	23.5
Totals	84	771	1490	.517	259	333	.778	547	6.5	1801	21.4

ROD GRIFFIN
Wake Forest
6-6 – F
Fairmont, N.C.

NCAA consensus second-team All-American in 1977 and 1978. . . . Averaged 21.3 points and 6.3 rebounds in three NCAA Tournament games in 1977 (2-1 record). . . . Selected by the Denver Nuggets in first round of 1978 NBA draft (17th pick overall).

Season	G	FGM	FGA	FG%	FTM	FTA	FT%	Reb.	Avg.	Pts.	Avg.
1974–75	25	142	290	.490	64	97	.660	190	7.6	348	13.9
1975–76	27	190	367	.518	102	135	.756	242	9.0	482	17.9
1976–77	26	198	319	.621	136	174	.782	224	8.6	532	20.5
1977–78	29	243	424	.573	137	191	.717	291	10.0	623	21.5
Totals	107	773	1400	.552	439	597	.735	947	8.9	1985	18.6

DARRELL GRIFFITH
Louisville
6-4 – G
Louisville, Ky.

Wooden Award winner in 1980. . . . NCAA unanimous first-team All-American in 1980. . . . Final Four Most Outstanding Player in 1980. . . . Leading scorer and fourth-leading rebounder for 1980 NCAA champion (33-3 record). . . . Averaged 20.3 points and 4.7 rebounds in 10 NCAA Tournament games from 1977-80 (7-3 record). . . . Selected by the Utah Jazz in first round of 1980 NBA draft (2nd pick overall).

Season	G	FGM	FGA	FG%	FTM	FTA	FT%	Reb.	Avg.	Pts.	Avg.
1976–77	28	150	299	.502	59	93	.634	109	3.8	359	12.8
1977–78	30	240	460	.522	78	110	.709	162	5.4	558	18.6
1978–79	32	242	487	.497	107	151	.709	140	4.4	591	18.5
1979–80	36	349	631	.553	127	178	.713	174	4.8	825	22.9
Totals	126	981	1877	.523	371	532	.697	585	4.6	2333	18.5

DICK GROAT
Duke
6-0 – G
Swissvale, Pa.

NCAA unanimous first-team All-American in 1952 and consensus second-team All-American in 1951. . . . Finished second in the nation in assists with 7.6 per game in 1952. . . . Did not play in NCAA Tournament or NIT. . . . Appeared in College World Series in 1952. . . . Selected by the Fort Wayne Pistons in 1952 NBA draft.

Season	G	FGM	FGA	FG%	FTM	FTA	FT%	Reb.	Avg.	Pts.	Avg.
1949–50	19	109	256	.426	57	98	.582			275	14.5
1950–51	33	285	713	.400	261	331	.789			831	25.2
1951–52	30	288	700	.411	204	281	.726			780	26.0
Totals	82	682	1669	.409	522	710	.735			1886	23.0

ALEX GROZA
Kentucky
6-7 – C
Martins Ferry, Ohio

NCAA consensus first-team All-American in 1947 and 1949, and consensus second-team All-American in 1948. . . . Final Four Most Outstanding Player in 1948 and 1949. . . . Leading scorer for NCAA champions in 1948 (36-3 record) and 1949 (32-2). . . . Averaged 22.7 points in six NCAA Tournament games in 1948 and 1949 (6-0 record). . . . Averaged 13.3 points in four NIT games in 1947 (runner-up) and 1949 (opening-game loser). . . . Leading scorer (11.1 points per game) for 1948 U.S. Olympic team. . . . Selected by the Indianapolis Olympians in 1949 NBA draft.

Season	G	FGM	FGA	FG%	FTM	FTA	FT%	Reb.	Avg.	Pts.	Avg.
1944–45	10	62			41					165	16.5
1945–46		Military Service (Army)									
1946–47	37	146	372	.392	101	160	.631			393	10.6
1947–48	39	200	530	.377	88	140	.629			488	12.5
1948-49	34	259	612	.423	180	248	.726			698	20.5
Totals	120	667			410					1744	14.5

CLIFF HAGAN
Kentucky
6-4 – F/C
Owensboro, Ky.

NCAA consensus first-team All-American in 1952 and 1954. . . . Leading scorer for 1954 undefeated team that chose not to participate in national postseason competition (25-0 record). . . . Fifth-leading scorer for 1951 NCAA champion (32-2). . . . Averaged 12 points in six NCAA Tournament games in 1951 and 1952 (5-1 record). . . . Selected by the Boston Celtics in third round of 1953 NBA draft; draft rights traded to St. Louis Hawks after he served two years in the military. . . . Elected to Naismith Memorial Basketball Hall of Fame in 1977.

Season	G	FGM	FGA	FG%	FTM	FTA	FT%	Reb.	Avg.	Pts.	Avg.
1950–51	20	69	188	.367	45	61	.738	169	8.5	183	9.2
1951–52	32	264	633	.417	164	235	.698	528	16.5	692	21.6
1952–53		Kentucky prohibited from playing because of NCAA probation.									
1953–54	25	234	514	.455	132	191	.691	338	13.5	600	24.0
Totals	77	567	1335	.425	341	487	.700	1035	13.4	1475	19.2

DALE HALL
Army
5-10 – F
Parsons, Kans.

NCAA consensus second-team All-American in 1944 and 1945.... Did not play in NCAA Tournament or NIT.

Season	G	FGM	FGA	FG%	FTM	FTA	FT%	Reb.	Avg.	Pts.	Avg.
1942–43	12	41			11					93	7.8
1943–44	15	122			29					273	18.2
1944–45	15	91			31					213	14.2
Totals	42	254			71					579	13.8

ANFERNEE HARDAWAY
Memphis State
6-7 – G
Memphis, Tenn.

NCAA unanimous first-team All-American in 1993.... Averaged 17.6 points, 5.4 rebounds, and five assists in five NCAA Tournament games in 1992 and 1993 (3-2 record).... Selected as an undergraduate by the Golden State Warriors in first round of 1993 NBA draft (3rd pick overall); draft rights promptly traded to the Orlando Magic.

Season	G	FGM	FGA	FG%	FTM	FTA	FT%	Reb.	Avg.	Pts.	Avg.
1990–91			Did not play—failed to meet requirements of Proposition 48.								
1991–92	34	209	483	.433	103	158	.652	237	7.0	590	17.4
1992–93	32	249	522	.477	158	206	.767	273	8.5	729	22.8
Totals	66	458	1005	.456	261	364	.717	510	7.7	1319	20.0

Three-point field goals: 69 of 190 (.363) in 1991–92 and 73 of 220 (.332) in 1992–93. **Totals:** 142 of 410 (.346).

JERRY HARKNESS
Loyola of Chicago
6-2 – F
New York, N.Y.

NCAA consensus first-team All-American in 1963.... Leading scorer and third-leading rebounder for 1963 NCAA champion (29-2 record).... Averaged 21.2 points and nine rebounds in five NCAA Tournament games in 1963 (5-0 record).... Averaged 15.7 points in three games for 1962 NIT third-place team.... Selected by the New York Knicks in second round of 1963 NBA draft (10th pick overall).

Season	G	FGM	FGA	FG%	FTM	FTA	FT%	Reb.	Avg.	Pts.	Avg.
1960–61	23	185	372	.497	150	198	.758	198	8.6	520	22.6
1961–62	27	202	438	.461	163	229	.712	234	8.7	567	21.0
1962–63	31	244	484	.504	174	240	.725	236	7.6	662	21.4
Totals	81	631	1294	.488	487	667	.730	668	8.2	1749	21.6

CLEM HASKINS
Western Kentucky
6-3 – G/F
Campbellsville, Ky.

NCAA consensus first-team All-American in 1967.... Averaged 17 points and 11.3 rebounds in four NCAA Tournament games in 1966 and 1967 (2-2 record).... Averaged 17 points in two NIT games in 1965.... Selected by the Chicago Bulls in first round of 1967 NBA draft (3rd pick overall).

Season	G	FGM	FGA	FG%	FTM	FTA	FT%	Reb.	Avg.	Pts.	Avg.
1964–65	27	252	561	.449	129	190	.679	293	10.9	633	23.4
1965–66	28	213	461	.462	146	189	.772	280	10.0	572	20.4
1966–67	21	170	377	.451	135	167	.808	236	11.2	475	22.6
Totals	76	635	1399	.454	410	546	.751	809	10.6	1680	22.1

JOHN HAVLICEK
Ohio State
6-5 – G/F
Bridgeport, Ohio

NCAA consensus second-team All-American in 1962.... Fourth-leading scorer and second-leading rebounder on 1960 NCAA champion (25-3 record), third-leading scorer and second-leading rebounder on 1961 national runner-up (27-1), and second-leading scorer and rebounder on 1962 national runner-up (26-2).... Named to All-NCAA Tournament team in 1962.... Averaged 13 points and 8.8 rebounds in 12 NCAA Tournament games from 1960 to 1962 (10-2 record).... Selected by the Boston Celtics in first round of 1962 NBA draft.... Elected to Naismith Memorial Basketball Hall of Fame in 1983.

Season	G	FGM	FGA	FG%	FTM	FTA	FT%	Reb.	Avg.	Pts.	Avg.
1959–60	28	144	312	.462	53	74	.716	205	7.3	341	12.2
1960–61	28	173	321	.539	61	87	.701	244	8.7	407	14.5
1961–62	28	196	377	.520	83	109	.761	271	9.7	475	17.0
Totals	84	513	1010	.508	197	270	.730	720	8.6	1223	14.6

HERSEY HAWKINS
Bradley
6-3 – G
Chicago, Ill.

Named national player of the year by AP, UPI and NABC in 1988.... NCAA unanimous first-team All-American in 1988.... Led the nation in scoring in 1988.... Averaged 29 points and 7.3 rebounds in three NCAA Tournament games in 1986 and 1988 (1-2 record).... Collected 13 points and 10 rebounds in one NIT game in 1985.... Member of 1988 U.S. Olympic team.... Selected by the Los Angeles Clippers in first round of 1988 NBA draft (6th pick overall); draft rights promptly traded to the Philadelphia 76ers.

Season	G	FGM	FGA	FG%	FTM	FTA	FT%	Reb.	Avg.	Pts.	Avg.
1984–85	30	179	308	.581	81	105	.771	182	6.1	439	14.6
1985–86	35	250	461	.542	156	203	.768	200	5.7	656	18.7
1986–87	29	294	552	.533	169	213	.793	195	6.7	788	27.2
1987–88	31	377	720	.524	284	335	.848	241	7.8	1125	36.3
Totals	125	1100	2041	.539	690	856	.806	818	6.5	3008	24.1

Three-point field goals: 31 of 108 (.287) in 1986–87 and 87 of 221 (.394) in 1987–88. **Totals:** 118 of 329 (.359).

ELVIN HAYES
Houston
6-9 – F
Rayville, La.

Named national player of the year by AP, UPI, and USBWA in 1968.... NCAA unanimous first-team All-American in 1967 and 1968.... Member of All-NCAA Tournament team in 1967.... Leading scorer and rebounder for 1967 national third-place team (27-4 record) and 1968 fourth-place team (31-2).... Averaged 27.5 points and 17.4 rebounds in 13 NCAA Tournament games from 1966 to 1968 (9-4 record).... Selected by the San Diego Rockets in first round of 1968 NBA draft (1st pick overall).... Elected to Naismith Memorial Basketball Hall of Fame in 1989.

Season	G	FGM	FGA	FG%	FTM	FTA	FT%	Reb.	Avg.	Pts.	Avg.
1965–66	29	323	570	.567	143	257	.556	490	16.9	789	27.2
1966–67	31	373	750	.497	135	227	.595	488	15.7	881	28.4
1967–68	33	519	945	.549	176	285	.618	624	18.9	1214	36.8
Totals	93	1215	2265	.536	454	769	.590	1602	17.2	2884	31.0

SPENCER HAYWOOD
Detroit
6-8 – F/C
Detroit, Mich.

NCAA unanimous first-team All-American in 1969.... Led the nation in rebounding in 1969.... Did not play in NCAA Tournament or NIT.... Averaged 28.2 points and 22.1 rebounds in one junior college season at Trinidad State (Colo.).... Leading scorer (16.1 points per game) for 1968 U.S. Olympic team.... Signed as an undergraduate free agent by the ABA's Denver Rockets in 1969.

Season	G	FGM	FGA	FG%	FTM	FTA	FT%	Reb.	Avg.	Pts.	Avg.
1968–69	24	288	508	.567	195	254	.768	530	22.1	771	32.1

WALT HAZZARD
UCLA
6-2 – G
Philadelphia, Pa.

Named national player of the year by USBWA in 1964.... NCAA unanimous first-team All-American in 1964.... Second-leading scorer for undefeated 1964 NCAA champion (30-0 record) and third-leading scorer for 1962 fourth-place finisher (18-11).... Final Four Most Outstanding Player and member of All-NCAA Tournament team in 1964.... Averaged 16.2 points and 5.7 rebounds in 10 NCAA Tournament games from 1962 to 1964 (6-4 record).... Member of 1964 U.S. Olympic team.... Selected as a territorial pick by the Los Angeles Lakers in first round of 1964 NBA draft.... Changed his name to Mahdi Abdul-Rahmad.

Season	G	FGM	FGA	FG%	FTM	FTA	FT%	Reb.	Avg.	Pts.	Avg.
1961–62	28	134	338	.396	102	143	.713	163	5.8	370	13.2
1962–63	29	170	380	.447	133	193	.689	170	5.9	473	16.3
1963–64	30	204	458	.445	150	209	.718	142	4.7	558	18.6
Totals	87	508	1176	.432	385	545	.706	475	5.5	1401	16.1

TOM HEINSOHN
Holy Cross
6-7 – F
Union City, N.J.

NCAA consensus first-team All-American in 1956.... Collected 26 points and 20 rebounds in one NCAA Tournament game in 1956.... Averaged 18.3 points in four NIT games in 1954 (champion) and 1955 (first-round loser).... Selected as a territorial pick by the Boston Celtics in 1956 NBA draft.... Elected to Naismith Memorial Basketball Hall of Fame in 1985.

Season	G	FGM	FGA	FG%	FTM	FTA	FT%	Reb.	Avg.	Pts.	Avg.
1953–54	28	175	364	.481	94	142	.662	300	10.7	444	15.9
1954–55	26	232	499	.465	141	215	.656	385	14.8	605	23.3
1955–56	27	254	630	.403	232	304	.763	569	21.1	740	27.4
Totals	81	661	1493	.443	467	661	.707	1254	15.4	1789	22.1

NED (DICKIE) HEMRIC
Wake Forest
6-6 – F/C
Jonesville, N.C.

NCAA consensus second-team All-American in 1955.... Averaged 29 points and 17.5 rebounds in two NCAA Tournament games in 1953 (1-1 record).... Selected by the Boston Celtics in 1955 NBA draft.

Season	G	FGM	FGA	FG%	FTM	FTA	FT%	Reb.	Avg.	Pts.	Avg.
1951–52	24	182	413	.441	174	310	.561	447	18.6	538	22.4
1952–53	25	212	452	.469	199	336	.592	416	16.6	623	24.9
1953–54	28	225	446	.504	230	310	.742	424	15.1	680	24.3
1954–55	27	222	429	.517	302	403	.749	515	19.1	746	27.6
Totals	104	841	1740	.483	905	1359	.666	1802	17.3	2587	24.9

DON HENNON
Pittsburgh
5-9 – G
Wampum, Pa.

NCAA consensus first-team All-American in 1958 and consensus second-team All-American in 1959.... Averaged 25.8 points in four NCAA Tournament games in 1957 and 1958 (1-3 record).... Selected by the Cincinnati Royals in sixth round of 1959 NBA draft.

Season	G	FGM	FGA	FG%	FTM	FTA	FT%	Reb.	Avg.	Pts.	Avg.
1956–57	27	225	541	.416	123	149	.826	95	3.5	573	21.2
1957–58	25	267	654	.408	117	140	.836	118	4.7	651	26.0
1958–59	24	231	632	.366	155	191	.812	105	4.4	617	25.7
Totals	76	723	1827	.396	395	480	.823	318	4.2	1841	24.2

FRED HETZEL
Davidson
6-8 – F/C
Washington, D.C.

NCAA unanimous first-team All-American in 1965 and consensus second-team All-American in 1964.... Did not play in NCAA Tournament.... Selected by the San Francisco Warriors in first round of 1965 NBA draft.

Season	G	FGM	FGA	FG%	FTM	FTA	FT%	Reb.	Avg.	Pts.	Avg.
1962–63	27	245	460	.533	144	181	.796	359	13.3	634	23.5
1963–64	26	273	498	.548	163	211	.773	351	13.5	709	27.3
1964–65	26	273	471	.580	143	178	.803	384	14.8	689	26.5
Totals	79	791	1429	.554	450	570	.789	1094	13.8	2032	25.7

ART HEYMAN
Duke
6-5 – F
Rockville Center, N.Y.

Named national player of the year by AP, UPI, and USBWA in 1963.... NCAA unanimous first-team All-American in 1963 and consensus second-team All-American in 1962.... Leading scorer and rebounder for 1963 national third-place team (27-3 record).... Averaged 22.3 points and 10.5 rebounds in four NCAA Tournament games in 1963 (3-1 record).... Selected by the New York Knicks in first round of 1963 NBA draft.

Season	G	FGM	FGA	FG%	FTM	FTA	FT%	Reb.	Avg.	Pts.	Avg.
1960–61	25	229	488	.469	171	263	.650	272	10.9	629	25.2
1961–62	24	219	506	.433	170	276	.616	269	11.2	608	25.3
1962–63	30	265	586	.452	217	314	.691	324	10.8	747	24.9
Totals	79	713	1580	.451	558	853	.654	865	10.9	1984	25.1

GRANT HILL
Duke
6-8 – G/F
Reston, Va.

NCAA unanimous first-team All-American in 1994 and consensus second-team All-American in 1993.... Fifth-leading scorer and second-leading rebounder for 1991 NCAA championship team (32-7 record), second-leading rebounder and third-leading scorer for 1992 NCAA championship team (34-2), and leading scorer and second-leading rebounder for 1994 NCAA runner-up (28-6).... Named to All-NCAA Tournament team in 1992 and

1994.... Averaged 13.5 points, 6.7 rebounds, and 4.3 assists in 20 NCAA Tournament games from 1991 to 1994 (18-2 record).... Selected by the Detroit Pistons in first round of 1994 NBA draft (3rd pick overall).

Season	G	FGM	FGA	FG%	FTM	FTA	FT%	Reb.	Avg.	Pts.	Avg.
1990–91	36	160	310	.516	81	133	.609	183	5.1	402	11.2
1991–92	33	182	298	.611	99	135	.733	187	5.7	463	14.0
1992–93	26	185	320	.578	94	126	.746	166	6.4	468	18.0
1993–94	34	218	472	.462	116	165	.703	233	6.9	591	17.4
Totals	129	745	1400	.532	390	559	.698	769	6.0	1924	14.9

Three-point field goals: 1 of 2 (.500) in 1990–91, 0 of 1 in 1991–92, 4 of 14 (.286) in 1992–93, and 39 of 100 in 1993–94. **Totals:** 44 of 117 (.376).

PAUL HOGUE
Cincinnati
6-9 – C
Knoxville, Tenn.

Leading scorer and rebounder for 1962 NCAA champion (29-2 record), leading rebounder and second-leading scorer for 1961 NCAA champion (27-3), and third-leading scorer and second-leading rebounder for 1960 national third-place team (28-2).... Averaged 18.4 points and 13.3 rebounds in 12 NCAA Tournament games from 1960 to 1962 (11-1 record).... Named to All-NCAA Tournament team in 1962.... Selected by the New York Knicks in first round of 1962 NBA draft (2nd pick overall).

Season	G	FGM	FGA	FG%	FTM	FTA	FT%	Reb.	Avg.	Pts.	Avg.
1959–60	30	152	264	.576	63	130	.485	331	11.0	367	12.2
1960–61	30	208	391	.532	87	168	.518	374	12.5	503	16.8
1961–62	31	211	424	.498	99	175	.566	383	12.4	521	16.8
Totals	91	571	1079	.529	249	473	.526	1088	12.0	1391	15.3

JOE HOLUP
George Washington
6-6 – C
Swoyersville, Pa.

Led the nation in field-goal shooting in 1954 and 1956.... Led the nation in rebounding in 1956.... Scored 13 points in one NCAA Tournament game in 1954.... Selected by the Syracuse Nationals in first round of 1956 NBA draft.

Season	G	FGM	FGA	FG%	FTM	FTA	FT%	Reb.	Avg.	Pts.	Avg.
1952–53	22	154	301	.512	119	167	.713	396	18.0	427	19.4
1953–54	26	179	313	.572	189	255	.741	484	18.6	547	21.0
1954–55	30	223	373	.598	155	208	.745	546	18.2	601	20.0
1955–56	26	200	309	.647	251	331	.758	604	23.2	651	25.0
Totals	104	756	1296	.583	714	961	.743	2030	19.5	2226	21.4

BOB HOUBREGS
Washington
6-7 – F/C
Seattle, Wash.

NCAA unanimous first-team All-American in 1953 and consensus second-team All-American in 1952.... Leading scorer and rebounder for 1953 national third-place team (30-3 record).... Member of All-NCAA Tournament team in 1953.... Averaged 27.4 points in seven NCAA Tournament games in 1951 and 1953 (5-2 record).... Selected by the Milwaukee Hawks in 1953 NBA draft.... Elected to Naismith Memorial Basketball Hall of Fame in 1986.

Season	G	FGM	FGA	FG%	FTM	FTA	FT%	Reb.	Avg.	Pts.	Avg.
1950–51	30							292	9.7	408	13.6
1951–52	28	189	440	.430	142	195	.728	298	10.6	520	18.6
1952–53	33	325	604	.538	196	264	.742	381	11.5	846	25.6
Totals	91							971	10.7	1774	19.5

ALLAN HOUSTON
Tennessee
6-6 – G
Louisville, Ky.

Did not play in NCAA Tournament.... Averaged 25.8 points and 6.5 rebounds in four NIT games in 1990 and 1992 (2-2 record).... Selected by the Detroit Pistons in first round of 1993 NBA draft (11th pick overall).

Season	G	FGM	FGA	FG%	FTM	FTA	FT%	Reb.	Avg.	Pts.	Avg.
1989–90	30	203	465	.437	120	149	.805	88	2.9	609	20.3
1990–91	34	265	550	.482	177	205	.863	104	3.1	806	23.7
1991–92	34	223	492	.453	189	225	.840	180	5.3	717	21.1
1992–93	30	211	454	.465	165	188	.878	145	4.8	669	22.3
Totals	128	902	1961	.460	651	767	.849	517	4.0	2801	21.9

Three-point field goals: 83 of 192 (.432) in 1989–90, 99 of 231 (.429) in 1990–91, 82 of 196 (.418) in 1991–92, and 82 of 198 (.414) in 1992–93. **Totals:** 346 of 817 (.424).

BAILEY HOWELL
Mississippi State
6-7 – F
Middleton, Tenn.

NCAA unanimous first-team All-American in 1959 and consensus second-team All-American in 1958.... Led the nation in field-goal percentage in 1957.... Did not play in NCAA Tournament or NIT.... Selected by the Detroit Pistons in first round of 1959 NBA draft.

Season	G	FGM	FGA	FG%	FTM	FTA	FT%	Reb.	Avg.	Pts.	Avg.
1956–57	25	217	382	.568	213	285	.747	492	19.7	647	25.9
1957–58	25	226	439	.515	243	315	.771	406	16.2	695	27.8
1958–59	25	231	464	.498	226	292	.774	379	15.2	688	27.5
Totals	75	674	1285	.525	682	892	.765	1277	17.0	2030	27.1

LOU HUDSON
Minnesota
6-5 – G/F
Greensboro, N.C.

Did not play in NCAA Tournament or NIT.... Selected by the St. Louis Hawks in first round of 1966 NBA draft (4th pick overall).

Season	G	FGM	FGA	FG%	FTM	FTA	FT%	Reb.	Avg.	Pts.	Avg.
1963–64	24	191	435	.439	53	85	.624	191	8.0	435	18.1
1964–65	24	231	463	.499	96	123	.780	247	10.3	558	23.3
1965–66	17	143	303	.472	50	77	.649	138	8.1	336	19.8
Totals	65	565	1201	.470	199	285	.698	576	8.1	1329	20.4

ALFREDRICK HUGHES
Loyola of Chicago
6-5 – F
Chicago, Ill.

Averaged 15.3 points and 7.3 rebounds in three NCAA Tournament games in 1985 (2-1 record).... Selected by the San Antonio Spurs in first round of 1985 NBA draft (14th pick overall).

Season	G	FGM	FGA	FG%	FTM	FTA	FT%	Reb.	Avg.	Pts.	Avg.
1981–82	29	216	538	.401	70	109	.642	177	6.1	502	17.3
1982–83	29	318	711	.447	108	188	.574	254	8.8	744	25.7
1983–84	29	326	655	.498	148	209	.708	237	8.2	800	27.6
1984–85	33	366	756	.484	136	195	.697	314	9.5	868	26.3
Totals	120	1226	2660	.461	462	701	.659	982	8.2	2914	24.3

WILLIE HUMES
Idaho State
6-1 – F
Madison, Ind.

Did not play in NCAA Tournament or NIT.... Averaged 22.6 points and 6.5 rebounds in two junior college seasons at Vincennes (Ind.).... Selected by the Atlanta Hawks in sixth round of 1971 NBA draft (did not play in league).

Season	G	FGM	FGA	FG%	FTM	FTA	FT%	Reb.	Avg.	Pts.	Avg.
1969–70	24	278	620	.448	177	237	.747	151	6.3	733	30.5
1970–71	24	287	723	.397	203	272	.746	187	7.8	777	32.4
Totals	48	565	1343	.421	380	509	.747	338	7.0	1510	31.5

ROD HUNDLEY
West Virginia
6-4 – G/F
Charleston, W.V.

NCAA consensus first-team All-American in 1957 and consensus second-team All-American in 1956.... Averaged 17.3 points in three NCAA Tournament games from 1955 to 1957 (0-3 record).... Selected by the Cincinnati Royals in 1957 NBA draft (1st pick overall).

Season	G	FGM	FGA	FG%	FTM	FTA	FT%	Reb.	Avg.	Pts.	Avg.
1954–55	30	260	756	.344	191	255	.749	244	8.1	711	23.7
1955–56	30	290	814	.356	218	326	.669	392	13.1	798	26.6
1956–57	29	235	648	.363	201	254	.791	305	10.5	671	23.1
Totals	89	785	2218	.354	610	835	.731	941	10.6	2180	24.5

ANDERSON HUNT
UNLV
6-2 – G
Detroit, Mich.

Second-leading scorer and leader in assists for 1990 NCAA champion (35-5 record) and second-leading scorer for 1991 national runner-up (34-1).... Member of All-NCAA Tournament team in 1990 and 1991.... Averaged 14.4 points and 3.2 assists in 15 NCAA Tournament games from 1989 to 1991 (13-2 record).... Left school with one season of eligibility remaining, but he wasn't drafted by an NBA team.

Season	G	FGM	FGA	FG%	FTM	FTA	FT%	Reb.	Avg.	Pts.	Avg.
1987–88			Sat out the season as a Proposition 48 casualty.								
1988–89	37	158	396	.399	48	70	.686	64	1.7	443	12.0
1989–90	39	230	478	.481	61	92	.663	87	2.2	620	15.9
1990–91	33	218	455	.479	28	42	.667	53	1.6	569	17.2
Totals	109	606	1329	.456	137	204	.672	204	1.9	1632	15.0

Three-point field goals: 79 of 218 (.362) in 1988–89, 99 of 258 (.384) in 1989–90, and 105 of 263 (.399) in 1990–91. Totals: 283 of 739 (.383).

BOBBY HURLEY
Duke
6-0 – G
Jersey City, N.J.

NCAA unanimous first-team All-American in 1993.... Holds NCAA career record for most assists.... Final Four Most Outstanding Player in 1992.... Third-leading scorer and leader in assists for 1992 NCAA champion (34-2 record), fourth-leading scorer and leader in assists for 1991 NCAA champion (32-7), and fifth-leading scorer and leader in assists for 1990 Final Four team (29-9).... Averaged 12 points and 8.1 assists in 20 NCAA Tournament games from 1990 to 1993 (18-2 record).... Selected by the Sacramento Kings in first round of 1993 NBA draft (7th pick overall).

Season	G	FGM	FGA	FG%	FTM	FTA	FT%	Reb.	Avg.	Pts.	Avg.
1989–90	38	92	262	.351	110	143	.769	68	1.8	335	8.8
1990–91	39	141	333	.423	83	114	.728	93	2.4	441	11.3
1991–92	31	123	284	.433	105	133	.789	61	2.0	410	13.2
1992–93	32	157	373	.421	143	178	.803	84	2.6	545	17.0
Totals	140	513	1252	.410	441	568	.776	306	2.2	1731	12.4

Three-point field goals: 41 of 115 (.357) in 1989–90, 76 of 188 (.404) in 1990–91, 59 of 140 (.421) in 1991–92, and 88 of 209 (.421) in 1992–93. Totals: 264 of 652 (.405).

CHUCK HYATT
Pittsburgh
6-0 – F
Uniontown, Pa.

NCAA consensus first-team All-American in 1929 and 1930.... Elected to Naismith Memorial Basketball Hall of Fame in 1959.

Season	G	FGM	FGA	FG%	FTM	FTA	FT%	Reb.	Avg.	Pts.	Avg.
1927–28		110			46					266	
1928–29		118			64					300	
1929–30		138			38					314	
Totals		366			148					880	

DARRALL IMHOFF
California
6-10 – C
Alhambra, Calif.

NCAA unanimous first-team All-American in 1960.... Second-leading scorer and leading rebounder for 1959 NCAA champion (25-4 record).... Leading scorer and rebounder for 1960 national runner-up (28-2).... Member of All-NCAA Tournament team in 1959 and 1960.... Averaged 14 points in 10 NCAA Tournament games from 1958 to 1960 (9-1 record; did not play in 1958 West Regional final defeat).... Member of 1960 U.S. Olympic team.... Selected by the New York Knicks in first round of 1960 NBA draft (3rd pick overall).

Season	G	FGM	FGA	FG%	FTM	FTA	FT%	Reb.	Avg.	Pts.	Avg.
1957–58	16	6	17	.353	2	5	.400	23	1.4	14	0.9
1958–59	29	134	316	.424	61	114	.535	318	11.0	329	11.3
1959–60	30	154	346	.445	102	162	.630	371	12.4	410	13.7
Totals	75	294	679	.433	165	281	.587	712	9.5	753	10.0

DAN ISSEL
Kentucky
6-9 – F/C
Batavia, Ill.

NCAA unanimous first-team All-American in 1970 and consensus second-team All-American in 1969.... Averaged 29.3 points and 11.3 rebounds in six NCAA Tournament games from 1968 to 1970 (3-3 record).... Selected by the Kentucky Colonels in first round of 1970 ABA draft.... Elected to Naismith Memorial Basketball Hall of Fame in 1993.

Season	G	FGM	FGA	FG%	FTM	FTA	FT%	Reb.	Avg.	Pts.	Avg.
1967–68	27	171	390	.438	102	154	.662	328	12.1	444	16.4
1968–69	28	285	534	.534	176	232	.759	381	13.6	746	26.6
1969–70	28	369	667	.553	210	275	.764	369	13.2	948	33.9
Totals	83	825	1591	.519	488	661	.738	1078	13.0	2138	25.8

ALLEN IVERSON
Georgetown
6-1 – G
Hampton, Va. (Bethel H.S.) ·

NCAA consensus first-team All-American in 1996. . . . Ranked among the nation's leading scorers in 1995 (46th) and 1996 (7th). . . . Ranked among the nation's leaders in steals in 1995 (6th with 3 spg) and 1996 (7th with 3.4 spg). . . . Averaged 23.9 points and four rebounds in seven NCAA Tournament games in 1995 and 1996 (5-2 record).

Season	G.	FGM	FGA	FG%	FTM	FTA	FT%	Reb.	Avg.	Pts.	Avg.
1994-95	30	203	520	.390	172	250	.688	99	3.3	613	20.4
1995-96	37	312	650	.480	215	317	.678	141	3.8	926	25.0
Totals	67	515	1170	.440	387	567	.683	240	3.6	1539	23.0

Three-point field goals: 35 of 151 (.232) and 87 of 238 (.366) in 1995-96. **Totals:** 122 of 389 (.314).

CHRIS JACKSON
Louisiana State
6-1 – G
Gulfport, Miss.

NCAA consensus first-team All-American in 1989 and 1990.... Compiled highest scoring average for a freshman in NCAA history.... Averaged 20.7 points in three NCAA Tournament games in 1989 and 1990 (1-2 record).... Selected as an undergraduate by the Denver Nuggets in first round of 1990 NBA draft (3rd pick overall).... Changed his name to Mahmoud Abdul-Rauf.

Season	G	FGM	FGA	FG%	FTM	FTA	FT%	Reb.	Avg.	Pts.	Avg.
1988–89	32	359	739	.486	163	200	.815	108	3.4	965	30.2
1989–90	32	305	662	.461	191	210	.910	81	2.5	889	27.8
Totals	64	664	1401	.474	354	410	.863	189	3.0	1854	29.0

Three-point field goals: 84 of 216 (.389) in 1988–89 and 88 of 246 (.358) in 1989–90. **Totals:** 172 of 462 (.372).

JIM JACKSON
Ohio State
6-6 – G
Toledo, Ohio

NCAA unanimous first-team All-American in 1992 and consensus first-team All-American in 1991.... Averaged 17.7 points, 6.4 rebounds, and 4.4 assists in nine NCAA Tournament games from 1990 to 1992 (6-3 record).... Selected as an undergraduate by the Dallas Mavericks in first round of 1992 NBA draft (4th pick overall).

Season	G	FGM	FGA	FG%	FTM	FTA	FT%	Reb.	Avg.	Pts.	Avg.
1989–90	30	194	389	.499	73	93	.785	166	5.5	482	16.1
1990–91	31	228	441	.517	112	149	.752	169	5.5	585	18.9
1991–92	32	264	535	.493	146	180	.811	217	6.8	718	22.4
Totals	93	686	1365	.503	331	422	.784	552	5.9	1785	19.2

Three-point field goals: 21 of 59 (.356) in 1989–90, 17 of 51 (.333) in 1990–91, and 44 of 108 (.407) in 1991–92. **Totals:** 82 of 218 (.376).

TONY JACKSON
St. John's
6-4 – F
Brooklyn, N.Y.

NCAA consensus second-team All-American in 1960 and 1961.... Collected 26 points and six rebounds in one NCAA Tournament game in 1961.... NIT Most Valuable Player in 1959.... Averaged 19.8 points in five NIT games in 1959 (champion) and 1960 (opening-game loser).... Selected by the New York Knicks in third round of 1961 NBA draft (24th pick overall).

Season	G	FGM	FGA	FG%	FTM	FTA	FT%	Reb.	Avg.	Pts.	Avg.
1958–59	26	215	470	.457	91	130	.700	401	15.4	521	20.0
1959–60	25	187	456	.410	157	196	.801	286	11.4	531	21.2
1960–61	25	203	400	.508	145	180	.806	310	12.4	551	22.0
Totals	76	605	1326	.456	393	506	.777	997	13.1	1603	21.1

CHESTER (CHET) JAWORSKI
Rhode Island
5-11 – G
Worcester, Mass.

NCAA consensus first-team All-American in 1939.... Led the nation in scoring in 1938 and 1939.... Did not play in NCAA Tournament or NIT.

Season	G	FGM	FGA	FG%	FTM	FTA	FT%	Reb.	Avg.	Pts.	Avg.
1936–37										301	
1937–38	21	177			87					441	21.0
1938–39	21	201			73					475	22.6
Totals										1217	

DENNIS JOHNSON
Pepperdine
6-4 – G
Compton, Calif.

Averaged 13 points and six rebounds in two NCAA Tournament games in 1976 (1-1 record).... Played two junior college seasons at Los Angeles Harbor (Calif.).... Selected as an undergraduate by the Seattle SuperSonics in second round of 1976 NBA draft (29th pick overall).

Season	G	FGM	FGA	FG%	FTM	FTA	FT%	Reb.	Avg.	Pts.	Avg.
1975–76	27	181	378	.479	63	112	.563	156	5.8	425	15.7

EARVIN (MAGIC) JOHNSON
Michigan State
6-9 – G
Lansing, Mich.

NCAA unanimous first-team All-American in 1979.... Final Four Most Outstanding Player and member of All-NCAA Tournament team in 1979.... Second-leading scorer and rebounder for 1979 national champion (26-6 record).... Averaged 17.8 points, eight rebounds, and 9.5 assists in eight NCAA Tournament games in 1978 and 1979 (7-1 record).... Member of 1992 U.S. Olympic team.... Selected as an undergraduate by the Los Angeles Lakers in first round of 1979 NBA draft (1st pick overall).

Season	G	FGM	FGA	FG%	FTM	FTA	FT%	Reb.	Avg.	Pts.	Avg.
1977–78	30	175	382	.458	161	205	.785	237	7.9	511	17.0
1978–79	32	173	370	.468	202	240	.842	234	7.3	548	17.1
Totals	62	348	752	.463	363	445	.816	471	7.6	1059	17.1

EDDIE JOHNSON
Illinois
6-7 – F
Chicago, Ill.

Averaged 17 points and eight rebounds in two NCAA Tournament games in 1981 (1-1 record).... Averaged 18.6 points and 8.4 rebounds in five NIT games for 1980 third-place team.... Selected by the Kansas City Kings in second round of 1981 NBA draft (29th pick overall).

Season	G	FGM	FGA	FG%	FTM	FTA	FT%	Reb.	Avg.	Pts.	Avg.
1977–78	27	100	234	.427	20	27	.741	84	3.1	220	8.1
1978–79	30	168	405	.415	26	49	.531	170	5.7	362	12.1
1979–80	35	266	576	.462	78	119	.655	310	8.9	610	17.4
1980–81	29	219	443	.494	62	82	.756	267	9.2	500	17.2
Totals	121	753	1658	.454	186	277	.671	831	6.9	1692	14.0

GUS JOHNSON
Idaho
6-6 – F
Akron, Ohio

Did not play in NCAA Tournament or NIT.... Played two junior college seasons at Boise (Idaho) JC.... Selected by the Baltimore Bullets in second round of 1963 NBA draft (11th pick overall).

Season	G	FGM	FGA	FG%	FTM	FTA	FT%	Reb.	Avg.	Pts.	Avg.
1959–60			Left the University of Akron before the start of the season.								
1962–63	23	188	438	.429	62	105	.590	466	20.3	438	19.0

KEVIN JOHNSON
California
6-1 – G
Sacramento, Cal.

Did not play in NCAA Tournament.... Averaged 25.8 points and 4.8 assists in four NIT games in 1986 and 1987 (2-2 record).... Selected by the Cleveland Cavaliers in first round of 1987 NBA draft (7th pick overall).

Season	G	FGM	FGA	FG%	FTM	FTA	FT%	Reb.	Avg.	Pts.	Avg.
1983–84	28	98	192	.510	75	104	.721	83	3.0	271	9.7
1984–85	27	127	282	.450	94	142	.662	104	3.9	348	12.9
1985–86	29	164	335	.490	123	151	.815	104	3.6	451	15.6
1986–87	34	212	450	.471	113	138	.819	132	3.9	585	17.2
Totals	115	601	1259	.477	405	535	.757	423	3.7	1655	14.0

Three-point field goals: 48 of 124 (.387) in 1986–87.

LARRY JOHNSON
UNLV
6-7 – F
Dallas, Tex.

Named national player of the year by NABC and USBWA in 1991.... Naismith Award and Wooden Award winner in 1991.... NCAA unanimous first-team All-American in 1991 and consensus first-team All-American in 1990.... Named to All-NCAA Tournament team in 1990.... Leading scorer and rebounder for 1990 NCAA champion (35-5 record) and 1991 Final Four team (34-1).... Averaged 20.2 points and 11.5 rebounds in 11 NCAA Tournament games in 1990 and 1991 (10-1 record).... Averaged 26 points and 11.6 rebounds in two junior college seasons at Odessa (Tex.).... Selected by the Charlotte Hornets in first round of 1991 NBA draft (1st pick overall).

Season	G	FGM	FGA	FG%	FTM	FTA	FT%	Reb.	Avg.	Pts.	Avg.
1989–90	40	304	487	.624	201	262	.767	457	11.4	822	20.6
1990–91	35	308	465	.662	162	198	.818	380	10.9	795	22.7
Totals	75	612	952	.643	363	460	.789	837	11.2	1617	21.6

Three-point field goals: 13 of 38 (.342) in 1989–90 and 17 of 48 (.354) in 1990–91. **Totals:** 30 of 86 (.349).

MARQUES JOHNSON
UCLA
6-7 – F
Los Angeles, Calif.

Named national player of the year by AP, UPI, USBWA, and NABC in 1977.... Naismith Award and Wooden Award winner in 1977.... NCAA unanimous first-team All-American in 1977.... Member of All-NCAA Tournament team in 1976.... Third-leading scorer and rebounder for 1975 national champion (28-3 record).... Second-leading scorer and rebounder for 1976 national third-place team (27-5).... Averaged 14.6 points and 8.6 rebounds in 16 NCAA Tournament games from 1974 to 1977 (13-3 record).... Selected by the Milwaukee Bucks in first round of 1977 NBA draft (3rd pick overall).

Season	G	FGM	FGA	FG%	FTM	FTA	FT%	Reb.	Avg.	Pts.	Avg.
1973–74	27	83	131	.634	28	38	.737	90	3.3	194	7.2
1974–75	29	138	254	.543	59	86	.686	205	7.1	335	11.6
1975–76	32	223	413	.540	106	140	.757	301	9.4	552	17.3
1976–77	27	244	413	.591	90	145	.621	301	11.1	578	21.4
Totals	115	688	1211	.568	283	409	.692	897	7.8	1659	14.4

STEVE JOHNSON
Oregon State
6-10 – C
San Bernardino, Calif.

NCAA consensus first-team All-American in 1981.... Led the nation in field-goal percentage in 1980 and 1981.... Averaged 20 points and 12 rebounds in two NCAA Tournament games in 1980 and 1981 (0-2 record).... Collected 22 points and eight rebounds in one NIT game in 1979.... Selected by the Kansas City Kings in first round of 1981 NBA draft (7th pick overall).

Season	G	FGM	FGA	FG%	FTM	FTA	FT%	Reb.	Avg.	Pts.	Avg.
1976–77	28	159	267	.596	61	91	.670	156	5.6	379	13.5
1977–78	3	26	45	.578	8	13	.615	29	9.7	60	20.0
1978–79	27	197	298	.661	104	169	.615	178	6.6	498	18.4
1979–80	30	211	297	.710	87	145	.600	207	6.9	509	17.0
1980–81	28	235	315	.746	119	174	.684	215	7.7	589	21.0
Totals	116	828	1222	.678	379	592	.640	785	6.8	2035	17.5

Note: Missed most of 1977–78 season after suffering a broken left foot.

K. C. JONES
San Francisco
6-1 – G
San Francisco, Calif.

NCAA consensus second-team All-American in 1956.... Third-leading scorer for 1955 champion (28-1 record) and second-leading scorer for undefeated 1956 champion (29-0).... Member of All-NCAA Tournament team in 1955.... Averaged 13.6 points in five NCAA Tournament games in 1955.... Ineligible to play in 1956 NCAA Tournament because he was playing his fifth season of college basketball.... Member of 1956 U.S. Olympic team.... Selected by the Boston Celtics in second round of 1956 NBA draft.... Elected to Naismith Memorial Basketball Hall of Fame in 1988.

Season	G	FGM	FGA	FG%	FTM	FTA	FT%	Reb.	Avg.	Pts.	Avg.
1951–52	24	44	128	.344	46	64	.719	94	3.9	134	5.6
1952–53	23	63	159	.396	79	149	.544			205	8.9
1953–54	1	3	12	.250	2	2	1.000	3	3.0	8	8.0
1954–55	29	105	293	.358	97	144	.674	148	5.1	307	10.6
1955–56	25	76	208	.365	93	142	.655	130	5.2	245	9.8
Totals	102	291	800	.364	319	501	.637			901	8.8

Note: Missed majority of 1953–54 season after undergoing an appendectomy.

WALLACE (WAH WAH) JONES

Kentucky
6-4 – F/C
Harlan, Ky.

NCAA consensus second-team All-American in 1949. . . . Third-leading scorer for back-to-back NCAA Tournament champions in 1948 (36-3 record) and 1949 (32-2). . . . Averaged 9.7 points in six NCAA Tournament games in 1948 and 1949 (6-0 record). . . . Averaged 9.9 points in seven NIT games in 1946, j1947 and 1949 (5-2 record). . . . Member of 1948 U.S. Olympic team (7.2 ppg). . . . Selected by the Washington Capitols in 1949 BAA draft. One of five former Kentucky players who obtained a franchise in the National Basketball League in 1949 before the BAA and NBL merged to form the NBA.

MICHAEL JORDAN

North Carolina
6-6 – G/F
Wilmington, N.C.

NCAA unanimous first-team All-American in 1983 and 1984.... Named national player of the year by AP, UPI, USBWA, and NABC in 1984.... Naismith Award and Wooden Award winner in 1984.... Member of All-NCAA Tournament team in 1982.... Third-leading scorer and rebounder for 1982 national champion (32-2 record).... Member of 1984 and 1992 U.S. Olympic teams.... Averaged 16.5 points and 4.2 rebounds in 10 NCAA Tournament games from 1982 to 1984 (8-2 record).... Selected as an undergraduate by the Chicago Bulls in first round of 1984 NBA draft (3rd pick overall).

Season	G	FGM	FGA	FG%	FTM	FTA	FT%	Reb.	Avg.	Pts.	Avg.
1981–82	34	191	358	.534	78	108	.722	149	4.4	460	13.5
1982–83	36	282	527	.535	123	167	.737	197	5.5	721	20.0
1983–84	31	247	448	.551	113	145	.779	163	5.3	607	19.6
Totals	101	720	1333	.540	314	420	.748	509	5.0	1788	17.7

Three-point field goals: 34 of 76 (.447) in 1982–83.

GEORGE KAFTAN

Holy Cross
6-3 – F
New York, N.Y.

NCAA consensus second-team All-American in 1947 and 1948.... Final Four Most Outstanding Player in 1947.... Leading scorer for 1947 NCAA champion (27-3 record) and second-leading scorer for 1948 national third-place team (26-4).... Averaged 17.3 points in six NCAA Tournament games in 1947 and 1948 (5-1 record).

Season	G	FGM	FGA	FG%	FTM	FTA	FT%	Reb.	Avg.	Pts.	Avg.
1945–46	15	90			57					237	15.8
1946–47	28	119			72					310	11.1
1947–48	30	187			94					468	15.6
1948–49	14	68			26					162	11.6
Totals	87	464			249					1177	13.5

ROGER KAISER

Georgia Tech
6-1 – G
Dale, Ind.

NCAA consensus first-team All-American in 1961 and consensus second-team All-American in 1960.... Averaged 26 points and 5.5 rebounds in two NCAA Tournament games in 1960 (1-1 record).... Selected by the Chicago Packers in fourth round of 1961 NBA draft (did not play in league).

Season	G	FGM	FGA	FG%	FTM	FTA	FT%	Reb.	Avg.	Pts.	Avg.
1958–59	26	138	342	.404	106	127	.835	182	7.0	382	14.7
1959–60	28	237	503	.471	164	190	.863	154	5.5	638	22.8
1960–61	26	216	517	.418	176	203	.867	106	4.1	608	23.4
Totals	80	591	1362	.434	446	520	.858	442	5.5	1628	20.4

DEAN KELLEY

Kansas
6-0 – G
McCune, Kans.

Named to All-NCAA Tournament team in 1952 and 1953.... Fourth-leading scorer for 1952 NCAA champion (28-3 record) and third-leading scorer for 1953 national runner-up (19-6).... Averaged 9.8 points in eight NCAA Tournament games in 1952 and 1953 (7-1 record).... Member of 1952 U.S. Olympic team.... Selected by the Fort Wayne Pistons in 1953 NBA draft (did not play in the league).

Season	G	FGM	FGA	FG%	FTM	FTA	FT%	Reb.	Avg.	Pts.	Avg.
1950–51	18	7			0	4	.000			14	0.8
1951–52	31	77	194	.397	49	81	.605	101	3.3	203	6.5
1952–53	25	81	236	.343	80	115	.696	76	3.0	242	9.7
Totals	74	165			129	200	.645			459	6.2

HARRY KELLY

Texas Southern
6-7 – F
Jackson, Miss.

Led the nation in scoring in 1982 and 1983.... Did not play in NCAA Tournament or NIT.... Selected by the Atlanta Hawks in fourth round of 1983 NBA draft (did not play in league).

Season	G	FGM	FGA	FG%	FTM	FTA	FT%	Reb.	Avg.	Pts.	Avg.
1979–80	26	313	612	.511	127	163	.779	205	7.8	753	29.0
1980–81	26	252	538	.468	112	149	.751	205	7.9	616	23.7
1981–82	29	336	658	.511	190	260	.730	337	11.6	862	29.7
1982–83	29	333	736	.452	169	222	.761	340	11.7	835	28.8
Totals	110	1234	2544	.485	598	794	.753	1085	9.9	3066	27.9

JASON KIDD

California
6-4 – G
Oakland, Calif.

NCAA unanimous first-team All-American in 1994.... Led the nation in steals with 3.8 per game in 1993.... Averaged 13 points, 7.8 rebounds, 9.5 assists, and four steals in four NCAA Tournament games in 1993 and 1994 (2-2 record).... Selected as an undergraduate by the Dallas Mavericks in first round of 1994 NBA draft (2nd pick overall).

Season	G	FGM	FGA	FG%	FTM	FTA	FT%	Reb.	Avg.	Pts.	Avg.
1992–93	29	133	287	.463	88	134	.657	142	4.9	378	13.0
1993–94	30	166	352	.472	117	169	.692	207	6.9	500	16.7
Totals	59	299	639	.468	205	303	.677	349	5.9	878	14.9

Three-point field goals: 24 of 84 (.286) in 1992–93 and 51 of 141 (.362) in 1993–94. **Totals:** 75 of 225 (.333).

BERNARD KING
Tennessee
6-7 – F
Brooklyn, N.Y.

NCAA consensus first-team All-American in 1977 and consensus second-team All-American in 1976.... Led the nation in field-goal percentage in 1975.... Collected 23 points and 12 rebounds in one NCAA Tournament game in 1977.... Selected as an undergraduate by the New Jersey Nets in first round of 1977 NBA draft (7th pick overall).

Season	G	FGM	FGA	FG%	FTM	FTA	FT%	Reb.	Avg.	Pts.	Avg.
1974–75	25	273	439	.622	115	147	.782	308	12.3	661	26.4
1975–76	25	260	454	.573	109	163	.669	325	13.0	629	25.2
1976–77	26	278	481	.578	116	163	.712	371	14.3	672	25.8
Totals	76	811	1374	.590	340	473	.719	1004	13.2	1962	25.8

STACEY KING
Oklahoma
6-10 – C
Lawton, Okla.

NCAA unanimous first-team All-American in 1989.... Member of All-NCAA Tournament team in 1988.... Leading scorer and rebounder for 1988 national runner-up (35-4 record).... Averaged 20.5 points and 7.8 rebounds in 12 NCAA Tournament games from 1987 to 1989 (9-3 record).... Selected by the Chicago Bulls in first round of 1989 NBA draft (6th pick overall).

Season	G	FGM	FGA	FG%	FTM	FTA	FT%	Reb.	Avg.	Pts.	Avg.
1985–86	14	26	67	.388	32	43	.744	53	3.8	84	6.0
1986–87	28	71	162	.438	54	87	.621	108	3.8	196	7.0
1987–88	39	337	621	.543	195	289	.675	332	8.5	869	22.3
1988–89	33	324	618	.524	211	294	.718	332	10.1	859	26.0
Totals	114	758	1468	.516	492	713	.690	825	7.2	2008	17.6

Three-point field goals: 0 of 1 in 1986–87 and 0 of 1 in 1987–88. **Totals:** 0 of 2.

   Note: Missed 1986 NCAA Tournament because of academic problems.

BOB KINNEY
Rice
6-6 – C
San Antonio, Tex.

NCAA consensus first-team All-American in 1942 and consensus second-team All-American in 1941.... Averaged 10 points in four NCAA Tournament games in 1940 and 1942 (1-3 record).

Season	G	FGM	FGA	FG%	FTM	FTA	FT%	Reb.	Avg.	Pts.	Avg.
1939–40	27	145			48					338	12.5
1940–41	24	128			96	144	.667			352	14.7
1941–42	27	147			75	136	.551			369	13.7
Totals	78	420			219					1059	13.6

KERRY KITTLES
Villanova
6-5 – G/F
New Orleans, La. (St. Augustine H.S.)

NCAA consensus first-team All-American in 1996 and second-team All-American in 1995.... Ranked among the nation's leading scorers in 1995 (31st) and 1996 (44th).... Averaged 20.3 points and 6.3 rebounds in three NCAA Tournament games in 1995 and 1996 (1-2 record).... Averaged 21.2 points, 6.8 rebounds and 4.2 assists in five NIT games for 1994

Season	G	FGM	FGA	FG%	FTM	FTA	FT%	Reb.	Avg.	Pts.	Avg.
1992-93	27	108	224	.482	37	55	.673	94	3.5	294	10.9
1993-94	32	233	516	.452	91	129	.705	207	6.5	630	19.7
1994-95	33	264	504	.524	92	120	.767	201	6.1	706	21.4
1995-96	30	216	475	.455	103	145	.710	213	7.1	613	20.4
Totals	122	821	1719	.478	323	449	.719	715	5.9	2243	18.4

Three-point field goals: 41 of 95 (.432) in 1992-93, 73 of 209 (.349) in 1993-94, 86 of 209 (.411) in 1994-95 and 78 of 193 (.404) in 1995-96. **Totals:** 278 of 706 (.394).

LEO KLIER
Notre Dame
6-1 – F
Washington, Ind.

NCAA consensus first-team All-American in 1944 and 1946.

Season	G	FGM	FGA	FG%	FTM	FTA	FT%	Reb.	Avg.	Pts.	Avg.
1942–43	3	4			0	0				8	2.7
1943–44	19	117			59	98	.602			293	15.4
1944–45		Military Service (Navy)									
1945–46	21	147	513	.287	61	115	.530			355	16.9
Totals	43	268			120	213	.563			656	15.3

JOHN KOTZ
Wisconsin
6-3 – F
Rhinelander, Wisc.

NCAA consensus first-team All-American in 1942 and second-team All-American in 1943.... Second-leading scorer for 1941 NCAA champion (20-3 record).... Final Four Most Outstanding Player in 1941.... Averaged 12.3 points in three NCAA Tournament games in 1941.

Season	G	FGM	FGA	FG%	FTM	FTA	FT%	Reb.	Avg.	Pts.	Avg.
1940–41	23	79			47					205	8.9
1941–42	21	125			75					325	15.5
1942–43	21	114			79					307	14.6
Totals	65	318			201					837	12.9

BARRY KRAMER
New York University
6-4 – F
Schenectady, N.Y.

NCAA consensus first-team All-American in 1963.... Averaged 25.2 points and 9.3 rebounds in six NCAA Tournament games in 1962 and 1963 (3-3 record).... Averaged 21.3 points in four NIT games for 1964 fourth-place team.... Selected by the San Francisco Warriors in first round of 1964 NBA draft.

Season	G	FGM	FGA	FG%	FTM	FTA	FT%	Reb.	Avg.	Pts.	Avg.
1961–62	24	152	349	.436	120	161	.745	219	9.1	424	17.7
1962–63	23	220	463	.475	235	283	.830	276	12.0	675	29.3
1963–64	27	209	488	.428	150	198	.758	195	7.2	568	21.0
Totals	74	581	1300	.447	505	642	.787	690	9.3	1667	22.5

ED (MOOSE) KRAUSE
Notre Dame
6-3 – C
Chicago, Ill.

NCAA consensus first-team All-American in 1932, 1933, and 1934.

Season	G	FGM	FGA	FG%	FTM	FTA	FT%	Reb.	Avg.	Pts.	Avg.
1931–32	18	48		42						138	7.7
1932–33	21	77		59						213	10.1
1933–34	23	76		44						196	8.5
Totals	62	201		145						547	8.8

JIM KREBS
SMU
6-8 – C
Webster Groves, Mo.

NCAA consensus first-team All-American in 1957.... Leading scorer and rebounder for 1965 national fourth-place team (26-4 record).... Averaged 21.6 points in nine NCAA Tournament games from 1955-57 (4-5 record).... Selected by the Minneapolis Lakers in first round of 1957 NBA draft (3rd pick overall).

Season	G	FGM	FGA	FG%	FTM	FTA	FT%	Reb.	Avg.	Pts.	Avg.
1954–55	26	209	478	.437	137	189	.725	228	8.8	555	21.3
1955–56	30	228	532	.429	118	156	.756	299	10.0	574	19.1
1956–57	26	233	486	.479	158	200	.790	313	12.0	624	24.0
Totals	82	670	1496	.448	413	545	.758	840	10.2	1753	21.4

BOB KURLAND
Oklahoma A&M
7-0 – C
St. Louis, Mo.

NCAA consensus first-team All-American in 1944, 1945, and 1946.... Final Four Most Outstanding Player in 1945 and 1946.... Leading scorer for NCAA champions in 1945 (27-4 record) and 1946 (31-2).... Averaged 22.8 points in six NCAA Tournament games in 1945 and 1946 (6-0 record).... Averaged 13.7 points in three NIT games for 1944 fourth-place finisher (1-2 record).... Member of 1948 and 1952 U.S. Olympic teams.... Elected to Naismith Memorial Basketball Hall of Fame in 1961.

Season	G	FGM	FGA	FG%	FTM	FTA	FT%	Reb.	Avg.	Pts.	Avg.
1942–43	21	22		9						53	2.5
1943–44	33	182		80						444	13.5
1944–45	31	214		101						529	17.1
1945–46	33	257		129						643	19.5
Totals	118	675		319						1669	14.1

CHRISTIAN LAETTNER
Duke
6-11 – C/F
Angola, N.Y.

Named national player of the year by AP, UPI, USBWA, and NABC in 1992.... Naismith Award and Wooden Award winner in 1992.... NCAA unanimous first-team All-American in 1992 and consensus second-team All-American in 1991.... Final Four Most Outstanding Player in 1991.... Member of All-NCAA Tournament team in 1991 and 1992.... Leading scorer and rebounder for 1992 national champion (34-2 record), what about 1991 (32-7) and 1990 (29-9).... Averaged 17.7 points and 7.3 rebounds in 23 NCAA Tournament games from 1989 to 1992 (21-2 record).... Member of 1992 U.S. Olympic team.... Selected by the Minnesota Timberwolves in first round of 1992 NBA draft (3rd pick overall).

Season	G	FGM	FGA	FG%	FTM	FTA	FT%	Reb.	Avg.	Pts.	Avg.
1988–89	36	115	159	.723	88	121	.727	170	4.7	319	8.9
1989–90	38	194	380	.511	225	269	.836	364	9.6	619	16.3
1990–91	39	271	471	.575	211	263	.802	340	8.7	771	19.8
1991–92	35	254	442	.575	189	232	.815	275	7.9	751	21.5
Totals	148	834	1452	.574	713	885	.806	1149	7.8	2460	16.6

Three-point field goals: 1 of 1 in 1988–89, 6 of 12 (.500) in 1989–90, 18 of 53 (.340) in 1990–91, and 54 of 97 (.557) in 1991–92. **Totals:** 79 of 163 (.485).

DWIGHT (BO) LAMAR
Southwestern Louisiana
6-1 – G
Columbus, Ohio

NCAA unanimous first-team All-American in 1972 and consensus first-team All-American in 1973.... Led the nation in scoring in 1972.... Averaged 29.2 points in six NCAA Division I Tournament games in 1972 and 1973 (3-3 record).... Averaged 33.2 points in five NCAA Division II Tournament games for 1971 national third-place team.... Selected by the San Diego Conquistadors in first round of 1973 ABA draft (1st pick overall).

Season	G	FGM	FGA	FG%	FTM	FTA	FT%	Reb.	Avg.	Pts.	Avg.
1969–70	26	253	608	.416	81	107	.757	132	5.1	587	22.6
1970–71	29	424	910	.466	196	261	.751	102	3.5	1044	36.0
1971–72	29	429	949	.452	196	268	.731	78	2.7	1054	36.3
1972–73	28	339	741	.457	130	166	.783	94	3.4	808	28.9
Totals	112	1445	3208	.450	603	802	.752	406	3.6	3493	31.2

BOB LANIER
St. Bonaventure
6-11 – C
Buffalo, N.Y.

NCAA unanimous first-team All-American in 1970 and consensus second-team All-American in 1968.... Leading scorer and rebounder for 1970 national fourth-place team (25-3 record).... Averaged 25.2 points and 14.2 rebounds in six NCAA Tournament games in 1968 and 1970 (4-2 record).... Selected by the Detroit Pistons in first round of 1970 NBA draft (1st pick overall).

Season	G	FGM	FGA	FG%	FTM	FTA	FT%	Reb.	Avg.	Pts.	Avg.
1967–68	25	272	466	.584	112	175	.640	390	15.6	656	26.2
1968–69	24	270	460	.587	114	181	.630	374	15.5	654	27.3
1969–70	26	308	549	.561	141	194	.727	416	16.0	757	29.1
Totals	75	850	1475	.576	367	550	.667	1180	15.7	2067	27.6

TONY LAVELLI
Yale
6-3 – G
Somerville, Mass.

NCAA consensus first-team All-American in 1949 and consensus second-team All-American in 1946 and 1948.... Led the nation in scoring in 1949.... Averaged 17.5 points in two NCAA Tournament games in 1949 (0-2 record).... Selected by the Boston Celtics in 1949 NBA draft.

Season	G	FGM	FGA	FG%	FTM	FTA	FT%	Reb.	Avg.	Pts.	Avg.
1945–46	15	124			72	90	.800			320	21.3
1946–47	25	152			115	159	.723			419	16.8
1947–48	27	196			162	212	.764			554	20.5
1948–49	30	228	652	.350	215	261	.824			671	22.4
Totals	97	700			564	722	.781			1964	20.2

ALFRED (BUTCH) LEE
Marquette
6-2 – G
Bronx, N.Y.

Named national player of the year by AP and UPI in 1978.... Naismith Award winner in 1978.... NCAA unanimous first-team All-American in 1978 and consensus second-team All-American in 1977.... Final Four Most Outstanding Player and member of All-NCAA Tournament team in 1977.... Leading scorer and third-leading rebounder for 1977 NCAA champion (25-7 record).... Averaged 16 points in 10 NCAA Tournament games from 1975 to 1978 (7-3 record).... Selected by the Atlanta Hawks in first round of 1978 NBA draft (10th pick overall).

Season	G	FGM	FGA	FG%	FTM	FTA	FT%	Reb.	Avg.	Pts.	Avg.
1974–75	26	85	188	.452	45	56	.804	63	2.4	215	8.3
1975–76	29	160	354	.452	77	98	.786	104	3.6	397	13.7
1976–77	32	239	501	.477	150	172	.872	121	3.8	628	19.6
1977–78	28	182	360	.506	131	149	.879	87	3.1	495	17.7
Totals	115	666	1403	.475	403	475	.848	375	3.3	1735	15.1

CLYDE LEE
Vanderbilt
6-9 – C
Nashville, Tenn.

NCAA unanimous first-team All-American in 1966 and consensus second-team All-American in 1965.... Averaged 26 points and 17.5 rebounds in two NCAA Tournament games in 1965 (1-1 record).... Selected by the San Francisco Warriors in first round of 1966 NBA draft (3rd pick overall).

Season	G	FGM	FGA	FG%	FTM	FTA	FT%	Reb.	Avg.	Pts.	Avg.
1963–64	25	176	410	.429	119	176	.676	391	15.6	471	18.8
1964–65	28	239	516	.463	153	228	.671	420	15.0	631	22.5
1965–66	26	218	457	.477	153	206	.743	412	15.8	589	22.7
Totals	79	633	1383	.458	425	610	.697	1223	15.5	1691	21.4

KEITH LEE
Memphis State
6-10 – C/F
West Memphis, Ark.

NCAA unanimous first-team All-American in 1985 and consensus first-team All-American in 1983.... Consensus second-team All-American in 1984.... Leading scorer and rebounder for 1985 Final Four team (31-4 record).... Averaged 18.3 points and 8.9 rebounds in 12 NCAA Tournament games from 1982 to 1985 (8-4 record).... Selected by the Chicago Bulls in first round of 1985 NBA draft (11th pick overall); draft rights promptly traded to the Cleveland Cavaliers.

Season	G	FGM	FGA	FG%	FTM	FTA	FT%	Reb.	Avg.	Pts.	Avg.
1981–82	29	199	370	.538	134	178	.753	320	11.0	532	18.3
1982–83	31	220	438	.502	141	172	.820	336	10.8	581	18.7
1983–84	33	245	453	.541	117	151	.775	357	10.8	607	18.4
1984–85	35	266	536	.496	156	200	.780	323	9.2	688	19.7
Totals	128	930	1797	.518	548	701	.782	1336	10.4	2408	18.8

BOB LLOYD
Rutgers
6-1 – G
Upper Darby, Pa.

NCAA consensus first-team All-American in 1967.... Led the nation in free-throw percentage in 1967.... Did not play in NCAA Tournament.... Averaged 32.3 points in four NIT games for 1967 third-place team.... Selected by the Minnesota Muskies in first five rounds of 1967 ABA draft.

Season	G	FGM	FGA	FG%	FTM	FTA	FT%	Reb.	Avg.	Pts.	Avg.
1964–65	24	237	543	.436	127	145	.876	72	3.0	601	25.0
1965–66	24	237	517	.458	161	183	.880	70	2.9	635	26.5
1966–67	29	277	579	.478	255	277	.921	96	3.3	809	27.9
Totals	77	751	1639	.458	543	605	.898	238	3.1	2045	26.6

CLYDE LOVELLETTE
Kansas
6-9 – C
Terre Haute, Ind.

NCAA consensus first-team All-American in 1951 and 1952.... Led the nation in scoring in 1952.... Leading scorer and rebounder for 1952 NCAA champion (28-3 record).... Final Four Most Outstanding Player in 1952.... Averaged 35.3 points in four NCAA Tournament games in 1952.... Leading scorer (14.1 points per game) for 1952 U.S. Olympic team.... Selected by the Minneapolis Lakers in 1952 NBA draft.... Elected to Naismith Memorial Basketball Hall of Fame in 1987.

Season	G	FGM	FGA	FG%	FTM	FTA	FT%	Reb.	Avg.	Pts.	Avg.
1949–50	25	214	499	.429	117	181	.646	192	7.7	545	21.8
1950–51	24	245	554	.442	58	89	.652	237	9.9	548	22.8
1951–52	28	315	660	.477	165	224	.737	357	12.8	795	28.4
Totals	77	774	1713	.452	340	494	.688	786	10.2	1888	24.5

JERRY LUCAS
Ohio State
6-8 – C
Middletown, Ohio

Named national player of the year by AP, UPI, and USBWA in 1961 and 1962.... NCAA unanimous first-team All-American in 1960, 1961, and 1962.... Led the nation in field-goal percentage in 1960, 1961, and 1962.... Led nation in rebounding in 1961 and 1962.... Final Four Most Outstanding Player in 1960 and 1961.... Member of All-NCAA Tournament team in 1960, 1961, and 1962.... Leading scorer and rebounder for 1960 NCAA champion (25-3 record) and national runners-up in 1961 (27-1) and 1962 (26-2).... Averaged 22.2 points and 16.4 rebounds in 12 NCAA Tournament games from 1960 to 1962 (10-2 record).... Tied with Oscar Robertson for scoring leadership (17 points per game) on 1960 U.S. Olympic team.... Selected as a territorial pick by the Cincinnati Royals in first round of 1962 NBA draft (did not play professionally in 1962–63 after signing with the Cleveland Pipers before they dropped out of the American Basketball League prior to the start of the season).... Elected to Naismith Memorial Basketball Hall of Fame in 1979.

Season	G	FGM	FGA	FG%	FTM	FTA	FT%	Reb.	Avg.	Pts.	Avg.
1959–60	27	283	444	.637	144	187	.770	442	16.4	710	26.3
1960–61	27	256	411	.623	159	208	.764	470	17.4	671	24.9
1961–62	28	237	388	.611	135	169	.799	499	17.8	609	21.8
Totals	82	776	1243	.624	438	564	.777	1411	17.2	1990	24.3

JOHN LUCAS
Maryland
6-3 – G
Durham, N.C.

NCAA consensus first-team All-American in 1975 and 1976.... Averaged 22.2 points in five NCAA Tournament games in 1973 and 1975 (3-2 record).... Selected by the Houston Rockets in first round of 1976 NBA draft (1st pick overall).

Season	G	FGM	FGA	FG%	FTM	FTA	FT%	Reb.	Avg.	Pts.	Avg.
1972–73	30	190	353	.538	45	64	.703	83	2.8	425	14.2
1973–74	28	253	495	.511	58	77	.753	82	2.9	564	20.1
1974–75	24	186	339	.549	97	116	.836	100	4.2	469	19.5
1975–76	28	233	456	.511	91	117	.778	109	3.9	557	19.9
Totals	110	862	1643	.525	291	374	.778	374	3.4	2015	18.3

ANGELO (HANK) LUISETTI
Stanford
6-2 – F
San Francisco, Calif.

NCAA consensus All-American in 1936, 1937, and 1938.... Led the nation in scoring in 1936 and 1937.... Did not play in NCAA Tournament or NIT.... Elected to Naismith Memorial Basketball Hall of Fame in 1959.

Season	G	FGM	FGA	FG%	FTM	FTA	FT%	Reb.	Avg.	Pts.	Avg.
1935–36	29									416	14.3
1936–37	24									410	17.1
1937–38	27									465	17.2
Totals	80									1291	16.1

BOB MCADOO
North Carolina
6-9 – F/C
Greensboro, N.C.

NCAA consensus first-team All-American in 1972.... Named to All-NCAA Tournament team in 1972.... Leading scorer and rebounder for 1972 national third-place team (29-5 record).... Averaged 20.5 points and 14 rebounds in four NCAA Tournament games in 1972 (3-1 record).... Averaged 21.9 points and 10.5 rebounds in two junior college seasons at Vincennes (Ind.).... Selected as an undergraduate by the Buffalo Braves in first round of 1972 NBA draft (2nd pick overall).

Season	G	FGM	FGA	FG%	FTM	FTA	FT%	Reb.	Avg.	Pts.	Avg.
1971–72	31	243	471	.516	118	167	.707	312	10.1	604	19.5

ED MACAULEY
St. Louis
6-8 – C/F
St. Louis, Mo.

NCAA unanimous first-team All-American in 1949 and consensus first-team All-American in 1948.... Led the nation in field-goal percentage in 1949.... Did not play in NCAA Tournament.... NIT Most Valuable Player in 1948.... Averaged 16.5 points in four NIT games in 1948 (champion) and 1949 (first-round loser).... Selected as a territorial pick by the St. Louis Bombers of the Basketball Association of America in 1949.... Elected to Naismith Memorial Basketball Hall of Fame in 1960.

Season	G	FGM	FGA	FG%	FTM	FTA	FT%	Reb.	Avg.	Pts.	Avg.
1945–46	23	94			71					259	11.3
1946–47	28	141			104					386	13.8
1947–48	27	132	324	.407	104	159	.654			368	13.6
1948–49	26	144	275	.524	116	153	.758			404	15.5
Totals	104	511			395					1417	13.6

XAVIER MCDANIEL
Wichita State
6-7 – F
Columbia, S.C.

NCAA consensus first-team All-American in 1985.... One of only two players in NCAA history to lead the nation in scoring and rebounding in the same season (1985); also led the nation in rebounding in 1983.... Collected 22 points and 11 rebounds in one NCAA Tournament game in 1985.... Collected 16 points and 10 rebounds in one NIT game in 1984.... Selected by the Seattle SuperSonics in first round of 1985 NBA draft (4th pick overall).

Season	G	FGM	FGA	FG%	FTM	FTA	FT%	Reb.	Avg.	Pts.	Avg.
1981–82	28	68	135	.504	27	43	.628	103	3.7	163	5.8
1982–83	28	223	376	.593	80	148	.541	403	14.4	526	18.8
1983–84	30	251	445	.564	117	172	.680	393	13.1	619	20.6
1984–85	31	351	628	.559	142	224	.634	460	14.8	844	27.2
Totals	117	893	1584	.564	366	587	.624	1359	11.6	2152	18.4

JIM MCDANIELS
Western Kentucky
7-0 – C
Scottsdale, Ky.

NCAA consensus first-team All-American in 1971.... Leading scorer and rebounder for 1971 national third-place team (24-6 record).... Member of All-NCAA Tournament team in 1971.... Averaged 29.3 points and 12.2 rebounds in six NCAA Tournament games in 1970 and 1971 (4-2 record).... Selected by the Utah Stars in first round of a "secret" ABA draft in January 1971 before signing a contract with the ABA (no specific team) sometime before the end of the season.

Season	G	FGM	FGA	FG%	FTM	FTA	FT%	Reb.	Avg.	Pts.	Avg.
1968–69	26	273	544	.502	98	152	.645	324	12.5	644	24.8
1969–70	25	305	535	.570	106	141	.752	340	13.6	716	28.6
1970–71	30	357	684	.522	164	221	.742	454	15.1	878	29.3
Totals	81	935	1763	.530	368	514	.716	1118	13.8	2238	27.6

ANTONIO MCDYESS
Alabama
6-9 – F/C
Quitman, Miss.

Ranked 27th in the nation in rebounding in 1995. . . . Averaged 21.3 points and 15 rebounds in four NCAA Tournament games in 1994 and 1995 (2-2 record). . . . Selected by the Los Angeles Clippers in first round of 1995 NBA draft (2nd pick overall). Draft rights promptly traded to the Denver Nuggets.

Season	G.	FGM	FGA	FG%	FTM	FTA	FT%	Reb.	Avg.	Pts.	Avg.
1993-94	26	132	234	.564	32	60	.533	210	8.1	296	1.4
1994-95	33	185	361	.512	88	132	.667	337	10.2	458	13.9
Totals	59	317	595	.533	120	192	.625	547	9.3	754	12.8

Three-point field goals: 0 of 1 in 1994-95.

BILLY MCGILL
Utah
6-9 – C
Los Angeles, Calif.

NCAA unanimous first-team All-American in 1962 and consensus first-team All-American in 1961.... Led the nation in scoring in 1962.... Leading scorer and rebounder for 1961 national fourth-place team (23-8 record).... Averaged 23.7 points and 10.7 rebounds in seven NCAA Tournament games in 1960 and 1961 (4-3 record).... Selected by the Chicago Zephyrs in first round of 1962 NBA draft.

Season	G	FGM	FGA	FG%	FTM	FTA	FT%	Reb.	Avg.	Pts.	Avg.
1959–60	29	179	374	.479	92	138	.667	285	9.8	450	15.5
1960–61	31	343	650	.528	176	249	.707	430	13.9	862	27.8
1961–62	26	394	705	.559	221	302	.732	391	15.0	1009	38.8
Totals	86	916	1729	.530	489	689	.710	1106	12.9	2321	27.0

GEORGE MCGINNIS
Indiana
6-8 – F
Indianapolis, Ind.

Did not play in NCAA Tournament or NIT.... Signed as an undergraduate free agent by the ABA's Indiana Pacers in 1971 in lieu of 1972 first-round draft choice.

Season	G	FGM	FGA	FG%	FTM	FTA	FT%	Reb.	Avg.	Pts.	Avg.
1970–71	24	283	615	.460	153	249	.614	352	14.7	719	30.0

KEVIN MCHALE
Minnesota
6-10 – F/C
Hibbing, Minn.

Did not play in NCAA Tournament.... Averaged 12 points in five NIT games for 1980 runner-up.... Selected by the Boston Celtics in first round of 1980 NBA draft (3rd pick overall).

Season	G	FGM	FGA	FG%	FTM	FTA	FT%	Reb.	Avg.	Pts.	Avg.
1976–77	27	133	241	.552	58	77	.753	218	8.1	324	12.0
1977–78	26	143	242	.591	54	77	.701	192	7.4	340	13.1
1978–79	27	202	391	.517	79	96	.823	259	9.6	483	17.9
1979–80	32	236	416	.567	85	107	.794	281	8.8	557	17.4
Totals	112	714	1290	.553	276	357	.773	950	8.5	1704	15.2

JIM MCINTYRE
Minnesota
6-10 – C
Minneapolis, Minn.

NCAA consensus first-team All-American in 1948.,.. Did not play in NCAA Tournament or NIT.... Did not play in NBA although several teams held his rights (Rochester Royals, Tri-Cities Blackhawks, and Milwaukee Hawks). He chose instead to get involved in the Youth for Christ Movement although he did play two seasons (1952–53 and 1953–54) with the Akron Goodyears in the National Industrial Basketball League.

Season	G	FGM	FGA	FG%	FTM	FTA	FT%	Reb.	Avg.	Pts.	Avg.
1945–46	20	74			47					195	9.8
1946–47	21	107			100					314	15.0
1947–48	19	125			110					360	18.9
1948–49	21	126			102	146	.699			354	16.9
Totals	81	432			359					1223	15.1

KYLE MACY
Kentucky
6-3 – G
Peru, Ind.

NCAA unanimous first-team All-American in 1980.... Third-leading scorer for 1978 NCAA champion (30-2 record).... Averaged 10.3 points in seven NCAA Tournament games in 1978 and 1980 (6-1 record).... Scored 20 points in one NIT game in 1979.... Selected as a junior eligible by the Phoenix Suns in first round of 1979 NBA draft (22nd pick overall).

Season	G	FGM	FGA	FG%	FTM	FTA	FT%	Reb.	Avg.	Pts.	Avg.
1975–76	27	144	293	.491	85	99	.859	75	2.8	373	13.8
1976–77		Sat out the season after transferring from Purdue.									
1977–78	32	143	267	.536	115	129	.891	76	2.4	401	12.5
1978–79	31	179	355	.504	112	129	.868	82	2.6	470	15.2
1979–80	35	218	415	.525	104	114	.912	85	2.4	540	15.4
Totals	125	684	1330	.514	416	471	.883	318	2.5	1784	14.3

JEFF MALONE
Mississippi State
6-4 – G
Macon, Ga.

Did not play in NCAA Tournament or NIT.... Selected by the Washington Bullets in first round of 1983 NBA draft (10th pick overall).

Season	G	FGM	FGA	FG%	FTM	FTA	FT%	Reb.	Avg.	Pts.	Avg.
1979–80	27	139	303	.459	42	51	.824	90	3.3	320	11.9
1980–81	27	219	447	.490	105	128	.820	113	4.2	543	20.1
1981–82	27	225	410	.549	52	70	.743	111	4.1	502	18.6
1982–83	29	323	608	.531	131	159	.824	106	3.7	777	26.8
Totals	110	906	1768	.512	330	408	.809	420	3.8	2142	19.5

KARL MALONE
Louisiana Tech
6-9 – F
Summerfield, La.

Averaged 19.6 points and 12 rebounds in five NCAA Tournament games in 1984 and 1985 (3-2 record).... Member of 1992 U.S. Olympic team.... Selected as an undergraduate by the Utah Jazz in 1985 NBA draft (13th pick overall).

Season	G	FGM	FGA	FG%	FTM	FTA	FT%	Reb.	Avg.	Pts.	Avg.
1981–82		Did not play because he was academically ineligible.									
1982–83	28	217	373	.582	152	244	.623	289	10.3	586	20.9
1983–84	32	220	382	.576	161	236	.682	282	8.8	601	18.8
1984–85	32	216	399	.541	97	170	.571	288	9.0	529	16.5
Totals	92	653	1154	.566	410	650	.631	859	9.3	1716	18.7

DANNY MANNING
Kansas
6-10 – F/C
Greensboro, N.C.

NCAA unanimous first-team All-American in 1987 and 1988, and consensus second-team All-American in 1986.... Named national player of the year by NABC in 1988.... Naismith Award and Wooden Award winner in 1988.... Member of All-NCAA Tournament team in 1988 when he was Final Four Most Outstanding Player.... Leading scorer and rebounder for 1988 NCAA champion (27-11 record), and leading scorer and second-leading rebounder for 1986 Final Four team (35-4).... Member of 1988 U.S. Olympic team.... Averaged 20.5 points and 7.3 rebounds in 16 NCAA Tournament games from 1985-88 (13-3 record).... Selected by the Los Angeles Clippers in first round of 1988 NBA draft (1st pick overall).

Season	G	FGM	FGA	FG%	FTM	FTA	FT%	Reb.	Avg.	Pts.	Avg.
1984–85	34	209	369	.566	78	102	.765	258	7.6	496	14.6
1985–86	39	279	465	.600	95	127	.748	245	6.3	653	16.7
1986–87	36	347	562	.617	165	226	.730	342	9.5	860	23.9
1987–88	38	381	653	.583	171	233	.734	342	9.0	942	24.8
Totals	147	1216	2049	.593	509	688	.740	1187	8.1	2951	20.1

Three-point field goals: 1 of 3 (.333) in 1986–87 and 9 of 26 (.346) in 1987–88. **Totals:** 10 of 29 (.345).

PETE MARAVICH
Louisiana State
6-5 – G
Raleigh, N.C.

NCAA unanimous first-team All-American in 1968, 1969, and 1970.... Named national player of the year by AP, UPI, and USBWA in 1970.... Naismith Award winner in 1970.... Led the nation in scoring in 1968, 1969, and 1970.... Did not play in NCAA Tournament.... Averaged 25.7 points, five rebounds, and 7.7 assists in three NIT games for 1970 fourth-place team (did not play in one game).... Selected by the Atlanta Hawks in first round of 1970 NBA draft (3rd pick overall).... Elected to Naismith Memorial Basketball Hall of Fame in 1986.

Season	G	FGM	FGA	FG%	FTM	FTA	FT%	Reb.	Avg.	Pts.	Avg.
1967–68	26	432	1022	.423	274	338	.811	195	7.5	1138	43.8
1968–69	26	433	976	.444	282	378	.746	169	6.5	1148	44.2
1969–70	31	522	1168	.447	337	436	.773	164	5.3	1381	44.5
Totals	83	1387	3166	.438	893	1152	.775	528	6.4	3667	44.2

STEPHON MARBURY
Georgia Tech
6-1 – G
Brooklyn, N.Y.

NCAA consensus second-team All-American in 1996.... Averaged 20.3 points, 6.8 rebounds and 4.2 assists in three NCAA Tournament games in 1996 (2-1 record).

Season	G	FGM	FGA	FG%	FTM	FTA	FT%	Reb.	Avg.	Pts.	Avg.
1995–96	36	235	514	.457	121	164	.738	161	4.5	679	18.9

Three-point field goals: 88 of 238 (.370) in 1995-96.

DONYELL MARSHALL
Connecticut
6-9 – F
Reading, Pa.

NCAA unanimous first-team All-American in 1994.... Averaged 17.2 points and 10.4 rebounds in five NCAA Tournament games in 1992 and 1994 (3-2 record).... Collected 22 points and 12 rebounds in one NIT game in 1993.... Selected as an undergraduate by the Minnesota Timberwolves in first round of 1994 NBA draft (4th pick overall).

Season	G	FGM	FGA	FG%	FTM	FTA	FT%	Reb.	Avg.	Pts.	Avg.
1991–92	30	125	295	.424	69	93	.742	183	6.1	334	11.1
1992–93	27	166	332	.500	107	129	.829	210	7.8	459	17.0
1993–94	34	306	599	.511	200	266	.752	302	8.9	853	25.1
Totals	91	597	1226	.487	376	488	.770	695	7.6	1646	18.1

Three-point field goals: 15 of 62 (.242) in 1991–92, 20 of 54 (.370) in 1992–93, and 41 of 132 in 1993–94. **Totals:** 76 of 248 (.306).

LARUE MARTIN
Loyola of Chicago
6-11 – C
Chicago, Ill.

Did not play in NCAA Tournament or NIT.... Selected by the Portland Trail Blazers in first round of 1972 NBA draft (1st pick overall).

Season	G	FGM	FGA	FG%	FTM	FTA	FT%	Reb.	Avg.	Pts.	Avg.
1969–70	24	168	332	.506	63	100	.630	346	14.4	399	16.6
1970–71	22	166	406	.409	80	127	.630	387	17.6	412	18.7
1971–72	21	159	359	.443	93	114	.816	329	15.7	411	19.6
Totals	67	493	1097	.449	236	341	.692	1062	15.9	1222	18.2

SLATER (DUGIE) MARTiN
Texas
5-10 – G
Houston, Tex.

Ranked 22nd in the nation in free-throw percentage in 1948 and 32nd in scoring in 1949.... Averaged 13.7 points in three NCAA Tournament games in 1947 (2-1 record).... Scored seven points in one game in 1948 NIT.... Second-leading scorer for third-place team in 1947 NCAA Tournament (26-2 record).... Selected by the Minneapolis Lakers in Basketball Association of American draft in 1949.... Elected to Naismith Memorial Basketball Hall of Fame in 1981.

Season	G.	FGM	FTM	FTA	FT%	Pts.	Avg.
1943-44	14	75	34		....	184	13.1
1944-45 and 1945-46			Military Service (Navy)				
1946-47	27	109	37	...	...	255	9.4
1947-48	25	126	65	85	.765	317	12.7
1948-49	24	165	54	...	...	384	16.0
Totals	90	475	190	...	...	1140	12.7

JAMAL MASHBURN
Kentucky
6-8 – F
Bronx, N.Y.

NCAA unanimous first-team All-American in 1993.... Leading scorer and rebounder for 1993 Final Four team (30-4 record).... Averaged 21.4 points and eight rebounds in nine NCAA Tournament games in 1992 and 1993 (7-2 record).... Selected as an undergraduate by the Dallas Mavericks in first round of 1993 NBA draft (4th pick overall).

Season	G	FGM	FGA	FG%	FTM	FTA	FT%	Reb.	Avg.	Pts.	Avg.
1990–91	28	137	289	.474	64	88	.727	195	7.0	362	12.9
1991–92	36	279	492	.567	151	213	.709	281	7.8	767	21.3
1992–93	34	259	526	.492	130	194	.670	284	8.4	714	21.0
Totals	98	675	1307	.516	345	495	.697	760	7.8	1843	18.8

Three-point field goals: 23 of 82 (.280) in 1990–91, 58 of 132 (.439) in 1991–92, and 66 of 180 (.367) in 1992–93. **Totals:** 147 of 394 (.373).

DON MAY
Dayton
6-4 – F
Dayton, Ohio

NCAA consensus second-team All-American in 1967 and 1968.... Leading scorer and rebounder for 1967 national runner-up (25-6 record).... Named to All-NCAA Tournament team in 1967.... Averaged 20.1 points and 12.9 rebounds in eight NCAA Tournament games in 1966 and 1967 (5-3 record).... Most Valuable Player of 1968 NIT.... Averaged 26.5 points in four NIT games for 1968 champion.... Selected by the New York Knicks in third round of 1968 NBA draft (30th pick overall).

Season	G	FGM	FGA	FG%	FTM	FTA	FT%	Reb.	Avg.	Pts.	Avg.
1966–66	29	238	505	.471	114	166	.687	331	11.4	590	20.3
1966–67	31	258	543	.475	173	213	.812	519	16.7	689	22.2
1967–68	30	239	509	.470	223	284	.785	451	15.0	701	23.4
Totals	90	735	1557	.472	510	663	.769	1301	14.5	1980	22.0

SCOTT MAY
Indiana
6-7 – F
Sandusky, Ohio

Named national player of the year by AP, UPI, and NABC in 1976.... Naismith Award winner in 1976.... NCAA unanimous first-team All-American in 1976 and consensus first-team All-American in 1975.... Leading scorer and second-leading rebounder for undefeated 1976 NCAA champion (32-0 record).... Named to All-NCAA Tournament team in 1976.... Averaged 14.4 points and 4.9 rebounds in eight NCAA Tournament games in 1975 and 1976 (7-1 record).... Leading rebounder (6.2 rpg) and second-leading scorer (16.7 ppg) for 1976 U.S. Olympic team.... Selected by the Chicago Bulls in first round of 1976 NBA draft (2nd pick overall).

Season	G	FGM	FGA	FG%	FTM	FTA	FT%	Reb.	Avg.	Pts.	Avg.
1972–73	Did not play because he was academically ineligible.										
1973–74	28	154	313	.492	43	56	.768	150	5.4	351	12.5
1974–75	30	204	400	.510	82	107	.766	199	6.6	490	16.3
1975–76	32	308	584	.527	136	174	.782	245	7.7	752	23.5
Totals	90	666	1297	.513	261	337	.774	594	6.6	1593	17.7

CEDRIC (CORNBREAD) MAXWELL
UNC Charlotte
6-8 – F/C
Kinston, N.C.

Leading scorer and rebounder for 1977 NCAA fourth-place finisher (30-5 record).... Named to All-NCAA Tournament team in 1977.... Averaged 24.6 points and 12.8 rebounds in five NCAA Tournament games in 1977 (3-2 record).... NIT Most Valuable Player in 1976 when he averaged 27.3 points and 11.5 rebounds in four games for second-place finisher.... Selected by the Boston Celtics in first round of 1977 NBA draft (12th pick overall).

Season	G	FGM	FGA	FG%	FTM	FTA	FT%	Reb.	Avg.	Pts.	Avg.
1973–74	26	98	154	.636	41	77	.532	161	6.2	237	9.1
1974–75	26	127	237	.535	64	88	.727	230	8.8	318	12.2
1975–76	29	201	371	.541	177	215	.823	350	12.1	579	20.0
1976–77	31	244	381	.640	202	263	.768	376	12.1	690	22.3
Totals	112	670	1143	.586	484	643	.753	1117	10.0	1824	16.3

GENE MELCHIORRE
Bradley
5-8 – G
Highland Park, Ill.

NCAA consensus first-team All-American in 1951.... Second-leading scorer for 1950 NCAA runner-up (32-5 record).... Averaged 15.3 points in three NCAA Tournament games for 1950 national runner-up.... Averaged 16.7 points in six NIT games for 1949 fourth-place team and 1950 runner-up.... Selected by the Baltimore Bullets in 1951 NBA draft (did not play in league).

Season	G	FGM	FGA	FG%	FTM	FTA	FT%	Reb.	Avg.	Pts.	Avg.
1947–48	31	111	279	.398	82	137	.599			304	9.8
1948–49	34	142	328	.433	116	177	.655			400	11.8
1949–50	37	153	384	.398	134	202	.663			440	11.9
1950–51	35	138			161					437	12.5
Totals	137	544			493					1581	11.5

DEAN MEMINGER
Marquette
6-1 – G
New York, N.Y.

NCAA unanimous first-team All-American in 1971.... Averaged 18.2 points and 5.7 rebounds in six NCAA Tournament games in 1969 and 1971 (4-2 record).... Averaged 17.8 points in four NIT games for 1970 champion.... NIT Most Valuable Player in 1970.... Selected by the New York Knicks in first round of 1971 NBA draft (16th pick overall).

Season	G	FGM	FGA	FG%	FTM	FTA	FT%	Reb.	Avg.	Pts.	Avg.
1968–69	29	172	409	.421	131	233	.562	187	6.4	475	16.4
1969–70	29	184	400	.460	178	279	.638	142	4.9	546	18.8
1970–71	29	216	425	.508	184	250	.736	117	4.0	616	21.2
Totals	87	572	1234	.464	493	762	.647	446	5.1	1637	18.8

DAVE MEYERS
UCLA
6-8 – F
La Habra, Calif.

NCAA unanimous first-team All-American in 1975.... Leading scorer and rebounder for 1975 NCAA champion (28-3 record), third-leading scorer and rebounder for 1974 national third-place team (26-4), and sixth-leading scorer for undefeated 1973 NCAA champion (30-0).... Member of All-NCAA Tournament team in 1975.... Averaged 12.7 points and 6.8 rebounds in 13 NCAA Tournament games from 1973 to 1975 (12-1 record).... Selected by the Los Angeles Lakers in first round of 1975 NBA draft (2nd pick overall). Rights promptly traded to the Milwaukee Bucks.

Season	G	FGM	FGA	FG%	FTM	FTA	FT%	Reb.	Avg.	Pts.	Avg.
1972–73	28	52	109	.477	34	45	.756	82	2.9	138	4.9
1973–74	30	144	295	.488	54	77	.701	171	5.7	342	11.4
1974–75	31	230	475	.484	106	144	.736	244	7.9	566	18.3
Totals	89	426	879	.485	194	266	.729	497	5.6	1046	11.8

GEORGE MIKAN
DePaul
6-10 – C
Joliet, Ill.

NCAA consensus first-team All-American in 1944, 1945 and 1946.... Led the nation in scoring in 1945 and 1946.... Final Four Most Outstanding Player in 1955.... Leading scorer for 1943 Final Four team (19-5 record).... Averaged 15.5 points in two NCAA Tournament games in 1943 (1-1 record).... NIT Most Valuable Player in 1945.... Leading scorer in NIT in 1944 and 1945 when he averaged 28.2 points in six games.... Signed by the NBA's Chicago Stags in 1946.... Elected to Naismith Memorial Basketball Hall of Fame in 1959.

Season	G	FGM	FGA	FG%	FTM	FTA	FT%	Reb.	Avg.	Pts.	Avg.
1942–43	24	97			77	111	.694			271	11.3
1943–44	26	188			110	169	.651			486	18.7
1944–45	24	218			122	199	.613			558	23.3
1945–46	24	206			143	186	.769			555	23.1
Totals	98	709			452	665	.680			1870	19.1

LARRY MILLER
North Carolina
6-4 – F
Catasauqua, Pa.

NCAA consensus first-team All-American in 1968 and consensus second-team All-American in 1967.... Leading scorer and second-leading rebounder for 1968 national runner-up (28-4 record) and 1967 national fourth-place team (26-6).... Member of All-NCAA Tournament team in 1968.... Averaged 17.5 points and 9.1 rebounds in eight NCAA Tournament games in 1967 and 1968 (5-3 record).... Selected by the Los Angeles Stars in first five rounds of 1968 ABA draft.

Season	G	FGM	FGA	FG%	FTM	FTA	FT%	Reb.	Avg.	Pts.	Avg.
1965–66	27	219	400	.548	127	187	.679	277	10.3	565	20.9
1966–67	32	278	553	.503	144	218	.661	299	9.3	700	21.9
1967–68	32	268	545	.492	181	256	.707	258	8.1	717	22.4
Totals	91	765	1498	.511	452	661	.684	834	9.2	1982	21.8

HAROLD MINER
Southern California
6-5 – G
Inglewood, Calif.

NCAA unanimous first-team All-American in 1992.... Averaged 19 points and five rebounds in three NCAA Tournament games in 1991 and 1992 (1-2 record).... Selected as an undergraduate by the Miami Heat in first round of 1992 NBA draft (12th pick overall).

Season	G	FGM	FGA	FG%	FTM	FTA	FT%	Reb.	Avg.	Pts.	Avg.
1989–90	28	206	436	.472	106	126	.841	101	3.6	578	20.6
1990–91	29	235	519	.453	152	190	.800	159	5.5	681	23.5
1991–92	30	250	571	.438	232	286	.811	211	7.0	789	26.3
Totals	87	691	1526	.453	490	602	.814	471	5.4	2048	23.5

Three-point field goals: 60 of 142 (.423) in 1989–90, 59 of 175 (.337) in 1990–91, and 57 of 162 (.352) in 1991–92. **Totals:** 176 of 479 (.367).

MIKE MITCHELL
Auburn
6-7 – F
Atlanta, Ga.

Did not play in NCAA Tournament or NIT.... Selected by the Cleveland Cavaliers in first round of 1978 NBA draft (15th pick overall).

Season	G	FGM	FGA	FG%	FTM	FTA	FT%	Reb.	Avg.	Pts.	Avg.
1974–75	25	204	426	.479	53	98	.541	286	11.4	461	18.4
1975–76	26	210	431	.487	66	96	.688	249	9.6	486	18.7
1976–77	26	229	429	.534	47	69	.681	220	8.5	505	19.4
1977–78	27	283	544	.520	105	135	.778	241	8.9	671	24.9
Totals	104	926	1830	.506	271	398	.681	996	9.6	2123	20.4

BILL MLKVY
Temple
6-4 – F
Palmerton, Pa.

NCAA unanimous first-team All-American in 1951.... Led the nation in scoring in 1951.... Second in the nation in rebounding and assists in 1951.... Did not play in NCAA Tournament or NIT.... Selected by the Philadelphia Warriors in 1952 NBA draft.

Season	G	FGM	FGA	FG%	FTM	FTA	FT%	Reb.	Avg.	Pts.	Avg.
1949–50	24	152			86	110	.782			390	16.3
1950–51	25	303	964	.314	125	181	.691	472	18.9	731	29.2
1951–52	24	169			80	103	.777	379	15.8	418	17.4
Totals	73	624			291	394	.739			1539	21.1

STAN MODZELEWSKI
Rhode Island
5-11 – G
Worcester, Mass.

NCAA consensus second-team All-American in 1941 and 1942.... Led the nation in scoring in 1940, 1941, and 1942.... Did not play in NCAA Tournament.... Averaged 14 points in two NIT first-round defeats in 1941 and 1942.... . Changed his name to Stan Stutz.

Season	G	FGM	FGA	FG%	FTM	FTA	FT%	Reb.	Avg.	Pts.	Avg.
1939–40	22	210			89					509	23.1
1940–41	25	178			107					463	18.5
1941–42	22	182			106	131	.809			470	21.4
Totals	69	570			302					1442	20.9

JOHN MOIR
Notre Dame
6-2 – F
Niagara Falls, N.Y.

NCAA consensus first-team All-American in 1937 and 1938.

Season	G	FGM	FGA	FG%	FTM	FTA	FT%	Reb.	Avg.	Pts.	Avg.
1935–36	23	112			36					260	11.3
1936–37	22	113			64					290	13.2
1937–38	22	92			46					230	10.5
Totals	67	317			146					780	11.6

SIDNEY MONCRIEF
Arkansas
6-3 – G
Little Rock, Ark.

NCAA consensus first-team All-American in 1979.... Led the nation in field-goal percentage in 1976.... Leading rebounder and second-leading scorer for 1978 national third-place team (32-4 record).... Averaged 17 points and 7.1 rebounds in nine NCAA Tournament games from 1977 to 1979 (6-3 record).... Selected by the Milwaukee Bucks in first round of 1979 NBA draft (5th pick overall).

Season	G	FGM	FGA	FG%	FTM	FTA	FT%	Reb.	Avg.	Pts.	Avg.
1975–76	28	149	224	.665	56	77	.727	213	7.6	354	12.6
1976–77	28	157	242	.649	117	171	.684	235	8.4	431	15.4
1977–78	36	209	354	.590	203	256	.793	278	7.7	621	17.3
1978–79	30	224	400	.560	212	248	.855	289	9.6	660	22.0
Totals	122	739	1220	.606	588	752	.782	1015	8.3	2066	16.9

ERIC MONTROSS
North Carolina
7-0 – C
Indianapolis, Ind.

NCAA consensus second-team All-American in 1993 and 1994.... Leading scorer and second-leading rebounder for 1993 NCAA champion (34-4 record).... Fourth-leading rebounder and sixth-leading scorer for 1991 Final Four team (29-6).... Named to All-NCAA Tournament team in 1993.... Averaged 13.9 points and 6.9 rebounds in 16 NCAA Tournament games from 1991 to 1994 (13-3 record).... Selected by the Boston Celtics in first round of 1994 NBA draft (9th pick overall).

Season	G	FGM	FGA	FG%	FTM	FTA	FT%	Reb.	Avg.	Pts.	Avg.
1990–91	35	81	138	.587	41	67	.612	148	4.2	203	5.8
1991–92	31	140	244	.574	68	109	.624	218	7.0	348	11.2
1992–93	38	222	361	.615	156	228	.684	290	7.6	600	15.8
1993–94	35	183	327	.560	110	197	.558	285	8.1	476	13.6
Totals	139	626	1070	.585	375	601	.624	941	6.8	1629	11.7

MAX MORRIS
Northwestern
6-1 – C-F
West Frankfort, Ill.

NCAA consensus first-team All-American in 1946 and second-team All-American in 1945.... Did not play in NCAA Tournament or NIT.

Season	G	FGM	FGA	FG%	FTM	FTA	FT%	Reb.	Avg.	Pts.	Avg.
1943–44			Earned letter in football at the University of Illinois.								
1944–45	19									292	15.4
1945–46	20	133			78					344	17.2
Totals	39									636	16.3

RICK MOUNT
Purdue
6-4 – G
Lebanon, Ind.

NCAA unanimous first-team All-American in 1969 and 1970.... Leading scorer with 30.5-point average in four NCAA Tournament games for 1969 national runner-up (23-5 record).... Member of All-NCAA Tournament team in 1969.... Selected by the Indiana Pacers in 1970 ABA draft.

Season	G	FGM	FGA	FG%	FTM	FTA	FT%	Reb.	Avg.	Pts.	Avg.
1967–68	24	259	593	.437	165	195	.846	67	2.8	683	28.5
1968–69	28	366	710	.515	200	236	.847	90	3.2	932	33.3
1969–70	20	285	582	.490	138	166	.831	54	2.7	708	35.4
Totals	72	910	1885	.483	503	597	.843	211	2.9	2323	32.3

ALONZO MOURNING
Georgetown
6-10 – C
Chesapeake, Va.

NCAA consensus first-team All-American in 1992 and consensus second-team All-American in 1990.... Led the nation in blocked shots (five per game) in 1989.... Averaged 15.3 points, 8.5 rebounds, and 3.7 blocked shots in 10 NCAA Tournament games from 1989 to 1992 (6-4 record).... Selected by the Charlotte Hornets in first round of 1992 NBA draft (2nd pick overall).

Season	G	FGM	FGA	FG%	FTM	FTA	FT%	Reb.	Avg.	Pts.	Avg.
1988–89	34	158	262	.603	130	195	.667	248	7.3	447	13.1
1989–90	31	145	276	.525	220	281	.783	265	8.5	510	16.5
1990–91	23	105	201	.522	149	188	.793	176	7.7	363	15.8
1991–92	32	204	343	.595	272	359	.758	343	10.7	681	21.3
Totals	120	612	1082	.566	771	1023	.754	1032	8.6	2001	16.7

Three-point field goals: 1 of 4 (.250) in 1988–89, 0 of 2 in 1989–90, 4 of 13 (.308) in 1990–91, and 6 of 23 (.261) in 1991–92. **Totals:** 11 of 42 (.262).

CHRIS MULLIN
St. John's
6-6 – G/F
Brooklyn, N.Y.

Named national player of the year by UPI and USBWA in 1985.... Wooden Award winner in 1985.... NCAA unanimous first-team All-American in 1985 and consensus second-team All-American in 1984.... Leading scorer and third-leading rebounder for 1985 Final Four team (31-4 record).... Averaged 20.7 points, 4.3 rebounds, and 3.9 assists in 10 NCAA Tournament games from 1982 to 1985 (6-4 record).... Member of 1984 and 1992 U.S. Olympic teams.... Selected by the Golden State Warriors in first round of 1985 NBA draft (7th pick overall).

Season	G	FGM	FGA	FG%	FTM	FTA	FT%	Reb.	Avg.	Pts.	Avg.
1981–82	30	175	328	.534	148	187	.791	97	3.2	498	16.6
1982–83	33	228	395	.577	173	197	.878	123	3.7	629	19.1
1983–84	27	225	394	.571	169	187	.904	120	4.4	619	22.9
1984–85	35	251	482	.521	192	233	.824	169	4.8	694	19.8
Totals	125	879	1599	.550	682	804	.848	509	4.1	2440	19.5

CALVIN MURPHY
Niagara
5-9 – G
Norwalk, Conn.

NCAA consensus first-team All-American in 1969 and 1970, and consensus second-team All-American in 1968.... Averaged 29.3 points and 6.3 rebounds in three NCAA Tournament games in 1970 (1-2 record).... Selected by the San Diego Rockets in second round of 1970 NBA draft (18th pick overall).

Season	G	FGM	FGA	FG%	FTM	FTA	FT%	Reb.	Avg.	Pts.	Avg.
1967–68	24	337	772	.437	242	288	.840	118	4.9	916	38.2
1968–69	24	294	700	.420	190	230	.826	87	3.6	778	32.4
1969–70	29	316	692	.457	222	252	.881	103	3.6	854	29.4
Totals	77	947	2164	.438	654	770	.849	308	4.0	2548	33.1

CHARLES (STRETCH) MURPHY
Purdue
6-6 – C
Marion, Ind.

NCAA consensus first-team All-American in 1929 and 1930.... Elected to Naismith Memorial Basketball Hall of Fame in 1960.

Season	G	FGM	FGA	FG%	FTM	FTA	FT%	Reb.	Avg.	Pts.	Avg.
1927–28	17	70			37					177	10.4
1928–29	17	76			54					206	12.1
1929–30	15	73			44					190	12.7
Totals	49	219			135					573	11.7

LARRY NANCE
Clemson
6-10 – F/C
Anderson, S.C.

Averaged 14.5 points and 9.3 rebounds in four NCAA Tournament games in 1980 (3-1 record).... Averaged 15.3 points and 6 rebounds in three NIT games in 1979 and 1981 (1-2 record).... Selected by the Phoenix Suns in first round of 1981 NBA draft (20th pick overall).

Season	G	FGM	FGA	FG%	FTM	FTA	FT%	Reb.	Avg.	Pts.	Avg.
1977–78	25	35	75	.467	8	17	.471	78	3.1	78	3.1
1978–79	29	137	264	.519	49	77	.636	210	7.2	323	11.1
1979–80	32	174	338	.515	98	164	.598	259	8.1	446	13.9
1980–81	31	207	360	.575	80	116	.690	237	7.6	494	15.9
Totals	117	553	1037	.533	235	374	.628	784	6.7	1341	11.5

CHARLES (COTTON) NASH
Kentucky
6-5 – F
Lake Charles, La.

NCAA unanimous first-team All-American in 1964 and consensus second-team All-American in 1962 and 1963.... Averaged 17.5 points and 9.8 rebounds in four NCAA Tournament games in 1962 (1-3 record).... Selected by the Los Angeles Lakers in second round of 1964 NBA draft (14th pick overall).

Season	G	FGM	FGA	FG%	FTM	FTA	FT%	Reb.	Avg.	Pts.	Avg.
1961–62	26	221	489	.452	166	218	.761	345	13.3	608	23.4
1962–63	25	176	471	.374	162	236	.686	300	12.0	514	20.6
1963–64	27	248	588	.422	152	198	.768	317	11.7	648	24.0
Totals	78	645	1548	.417	480	652	.736	962	12.3	1770	22.7

CALVIN NATT
Northeast Louisiana
6-6 – F
Bastrop, La.

NCAA consensus second-team All-American in 1979.... Did not play in NCAA Tournament.... Collected 38 points and 8 rebounds in one NIT game in 1979.... Selected by the New Jersey Nets in first round of 1979 NBA draft (8th pick overall).

Season	G	FGM	FGA	FG%	FTM	FTA	FT%	Reb.	Avg.	Pts.	Avg.
1975–76	25	207	371	.558	102	129	.791	274	11.0	516	20.6
1976–77	27	307	493	.623	168	226	.743	340	12.6	782	29.0
1977–78	27	220	401	.549	136	186	.731	356	13.2	576	21.3
1978–79	29	283	506	.559	141	178	.792	315	10.9	707	24.4
Totals	108	1017	1771	.574	547	719	.761	1285	11.9	2581	23.9

JOHNNY NEUMANN
Mississippi
6-6 – F/G
Memphis, Tenn.

NCAA consensus second-team All-American in 1971.... Led the nation in scoring in 1971.... Did not play in NCAA Tournament or NIT.... Signed as an undergraduate free agent by the Memphis Pros of the ABA in 1971.

Season	G	FGM	FGA	FG%	FTM	FTA	FT%	Reb.	Avg.	Pts.	Avg.
1970–71	23	366	792	.462	191	250	.764	152	6.6	923	40.1

PAUL NOWAK
Notre Dame
6-6 – C
South Bend, Ind.

NCAA consensus first-team All-American in 1936, 1937, and 1938.

Season	G	FGM	FGA	FG%	FTM	FTA	FT%	Reb.	Avg.	Pts.	Avg.
1935–36	23	65			31					161	7.0
1936–37	21	56			40					152	7.2
1937–38	23	68			37					173	7.5
Totals	67	189			108					486	7.3

ED O'BANNON
UCLA
6-8 – F
Lakewood, Calif.

Named national player of the year by USBWA in 1995.... Wooden Award winner in 1995.... NCAA unanimous first-team All-American in 1995.... Ranked 47th in the nation in scoring in 1995.... Leading scorer and rebounder for 1995 NCAA Tournament champion (31-2 record).... Final Four Most Outstanding Player in 1995 (45 points, 25 rebounds).... Named to 1995 All-NCAA Tournament team.... Averaged 15.5 points and 7.8 rebounds in 13 NCAA Tournament games from 1992-95 (10-3 record).... Selected by the New Jersey Nets in first round of 1995 NBA draft (9th pick overall).

Season	G.	FGM	FGA	FG%	FTM	FTA	FT%	Reb.	Avg.	Pts.	Avg.
1990-91	Sat out the entire season because of an injury to his left knee.										
1991-92	23	32	77	.416	17	27	.630	70	3.0	83	3.6
1992-93	33	208	386	.539	116	164	.707	230	7.0	550	16.7
1993-94	28	191	395	.484	111	149	.745	245	8.8	509	18.2
1994-95	33	247	463	.533	124	158	.785	275	8.3	673	20.4
Totals	117	678	1321	.513	368	498	.739	820	7.0	1815	15.5

Three-point field goals: 2 of 8 (.250) in 1991-92, 18 of 40 (.450) in 1992-93, 16 of 56 (.286) in 1993-94 and 55 of 127 (.433) in 1994-95. **Totals:** 91 of 231 (.394).

JOHNNY O'BRIEN
Seattle
5-8 – G
South Amboy, N.J.

NCAA unanimous first-team All-American in 1953 and consensus second-team All-American in 1952.... Averaged 32 points in three NCAA Tournament games in 1953 (2-1 record).... Selected by the Milwaukee Hawks in 1953 NBA draft.

Season	G	FGM	FGA	FG%	FTM	FTA	FT%	Reb.	Avg.	Pts.	Avg.
1950–51	37	275	484	.568	216	290	.745			766	20.7
1951–52	37	345	646	.534	361	475	.760			1051	28.4
1952–53	32	284	535	.531	348	430	.809	173	5.4	916	28.6
Totals	106	904	1665	.543	925	1195	.774			2733	25.8

Note: Seattle was classified a Division II school in 1951 and 1952.

MIKE O'KOREN
North Carolina
6-8 – F
Jersey City, N.J.

NCAA consensus second-team All-American in 1979 and 1980.... Leading rebounder and third-leading scorer for 1977 national runner-up (28-5 record).... Member of All-NCAA Tournament team in 1977.... Averaged 15.8 points and 8.6 rebounds in eight NCAA Tournament games from 1977 to 1980 (4-4 record).... Selected by the New Jersey Nets in first round of 1980 NBA draft (6th pick overall).

Season	G	FGM	FGA	FG%	FTM	FTA	FT%	Reb.	Avg.	Pts.	Avg.
1976–77	33	172	298	.577	114	157	.726	217	6.6	458	13.9
1977–78	27	173	269	.643	122	163	.748	180	6.7	468	17.3
1978–79	28	135	259	.521	144	188	.766	202	7.2	414	14.8
1979–80	29	163	298	.547	99	152	.651	216	7.4	425	14.7
Totals	117	643	1124	.572	479	660	.726	815	7.0	1765	15.1

HAKEEM OLAJUWON
Houston
7-0 – C
Lagos, Nigeria

NCAA consensus first-team All-American in 1984.... Led the nation in rebounding, field-goal percentage, and blocked shots (5.6 per game) in 1984.... Final Four Most Outstanding Player in 1983.... Second-leading scorer and leading rebounder for 1984 national runner-up (32-5 record), third-leading scorer and leading rebounder for 1983 national runner-up (31-3), and sixth-leading scorer and third-leading rebounder for 1982 Final Four team (25-8).... Member of All-NCAA Tournament team in 1983 and 1984.... Averaged 15.1 points and 10.2 rebounds in 15 NCAA Tournament games from 1982-84 (12-3 record).... Selected as an undergraduate by the Houston Rockets in first round of 1984 NBA draft (1st pick overall).

Season	G	FGM	FGA	FG%	FTM	FTA	FT%	Reb.	Avg.	Pts.	Avg.
1980–81	Did not play first year after coming to the U.S. from Nigeria.										
1981–82	29	91	150	.607	58	103	.563	179	6.2	240	8.3
1982–83	34	192	314	.611	88	148	.595	388	11.4	472	13.9
1983–84	37	249	369	.675	122	232	.526	500	13.5	620	16.8
Totals	100	532	833	.639	268	483	.555	1067	10.7	1332	13.3

SHAQUILLE O'NEAL
Louisiana State
7-1 – C
San Antonio, Tex.

Named national player of the year by AP and UPI in 1991.... NCAA unanimous first-team All-American in 1991 and 1992.... Led the nation in rebounding in 1991 and in blocked shots (5.2 per game) in 1992.... Averaged 24 points, 13.2 rebounds, and 5.8 blocked shots in five NCAA Tournament games from 1990-92 (2-3 record).... Selected as an undergraduate by the Orlando Magic in first round of 1992 NBA draft (1st pick overall).

Season	G	FGM	FGA	FG%	FTM	FTA	FT%	Reb.	Avg.	Pts.	Avg.
1989–90	32	180	314	.573	85	153	.556	385	12.0	445	13.9
1990–91	28	312	497	.628	150	235	.638	411	14.7	774	27.6
1991–92	30	294	478	.615	134	254	.528	421	14.0	722	24.1
Totals	90	786	1289	.610	369	642	.575	1217	13.5	1941	21.6

KEVIN O'SHEA
Notre Dame
6-1 – G
San Francisco, Calif.

NCAA unanimous first-team All-American in 1948 and consensus second-team All-American in 1950.... Did not play in NCAA Tournament or NIT.... Selected by the Minneapolis Lakers in 1950 NBA draft.

Season	G	FGM	FGA	FG%	FTM	FTA	FT%	Reb.	Avg.	Pts.	Avg.
1946–47	22	91	261	.349	28	57	.491			210	9.5
1947–48	23	100	316	.316	65	106	.613			265	11.5
1948–49	22	85	268	.317	62	92	.674			232	10.5
1949–50	24	133	390	.341	92	141	.652			358	14.9
Totals	91	409	1235	.331	247	396	.624			1065	11.7

BILLY OWENS
Syracuse
6-9 – F
Carlisle, Pa.

NCAA unanimous first-team All-American in 1991.... Averaged 18.9 points and 8.6 rebounds in eight NCAA Tournament games from 1989 to 1991 (5-3 record).... Selected as an undergraduate by the Sacramento Kings in first round of 1991 NBA draft (3rd pick overall); traded to the Golden State Warriors before the start of his rookie season.

Season	G	FGM	FGA	FG%	FTM	FTA	FT%	Reb.	Avg.	Pts.	Avg.
1988–89	38	196	376	.521	94	145	.648	263	6.9	494	13.0
1989–90	33	228	469	.486	127	176	.722	276	8.4	602	18.2
1990–91	32	282	554	.509	157	233	.674	371	11.6	744	23.3
Totals	103	706	1399	.505	378	554	.682	910	8.8	1840	17.9

Three-point field goals: 8 of 36 (.222) in 1988–89, 19 of 60 (.317) in 1989–90, and 23 of 58 (.397) in 1990–91. **Totals:** 50 of 154 (.325).

ROBERT PARISH
Centenary
7-0 – C
Shreveport, La.

Led the nation in rebounding in 1975 and 1976.... Did not play in NCAA Tournament or NIT.... Selected by the Golden State Warriors in first round of 1976 NBA draft (8th pick overall).

Season	G	FGM	FGA	FG%	FTM	FTA	FT%	Reb.	Avg.	Pts.	Avg.
1972–73	27	285	492	.579	50	82	.610	505	18.7	620	23.0
1973–74	25	224	428	.523	49	78	.628	382	15.3	497	19.9
1974–75	29	237	423	.560	74	112	.661	447	15.4	548	18.9
1975–76	27	288	489	.589	93	134	.694	486	18.0	669	24.8
Totals	108	1034	1832	.564	266	406	.655	1820	16.9	2334	21.6

JOHN PAXSON
Notre Dame
6-2 – G
Kettering, Ohio

NCAA consensus second-team All-American in 1982 and 1983.... Averaged five points in three NCAA Tournament games in 1980 and 1981 (1-2 record).... Scored 17 points in one NIT game in 1983.... Selected by the San Antonio Spurs in first round of 1983 NBA draft (19th pick overall).

Season	G	FGM	FGA	FG%	FTM	FTA	FT%	Reb.	Avg.	Pts.	Avg.
1979–80	27	42	87	.483	41	55	.745	34	1.3	125	4.6
1980–81	29	113	218	.518	61	89	.685	53	1.8	287	9.9
1981–82	27	185	346	.535	72	93	.774	55	2.0	442	16.4
1982–83	29	219	411	.533	74	100	.740	63	2.2	512	17.7
Totals	112	559	1062	.526	248	337	.736	205	1.8	1366	12.2

GARY PAYTON
Oregon State
6-3 – G
Oakland, Calif.

NCAA unanimous first-team All-American in 1990.... Averaged 18 points, four rebounds, and seven assists in three NCAA Tournament games from 1988 to 1990 (0-3 record).... Averaged 15.5 points and six assists in two NIT games in 1987 (1-1 record).... Selected by the Seattle SuperSonics in first round of 1990 NBA draft (2nd pick overall).

Season	G	FGM	FGA	FG%	FTM	FTA	FT%	Reb.	Avg.	Pts.	Avg.
1986–87	30	153	333	.459	55	82	.671	120	4.0	374	12.5
1987–88	31	180	368	.489	58	83	.699	103	3.3	449	14.5
1988–89	30	208	438	.475	105	155	.677	122	4.1	603	20.1
1989–90	29	288	571	.504	118	171	.690	135	4.7	746	25.7
Totals	120	829	1710	.485	336	491	.684	480	4.0	2172	18.1

Three-point field goals: 13 of 35 (.371) in 1986–87, 31 of 78 (.397) in 1987–88, 82 of 213 (.385) in 1988–89, and 52 of 156 (.333) in 1989–90. **Totals:** 178 of 482 (.369).

SAM PERKINS
North Carolina
6-10 – F/C
Latham, N.Y.

NCAA consensus first-team All-American in 1983 and 1984, and consensus second-team All-American in 1982.... Second-leading scorer and leading rebounder for 1982 NCAA champion (32-2 record).... Second-leading scorer and rebounder for 1981 national runner-up (29-8).... Named to All-NCAA Tournament team in 1982.... Averaged 15.8 points and 8.6 rebounds in 15 NCAA Tournament games from 1981 to 1984 (12-3 record).... Member of U.S. Olympic team in 1984.... Selected by the Dallas Mavericks in first round of 1984 NBA draft (4th pick overall).

Season	G	FGM	FGA	FG%	FTM	FTA	FT%	Reb.	Avg.	Pts.	Avg.
1980–81	37	199	318	.626	152	205	.741	289	7.8	550	14.9
1981–82	32	174	301	.578	109	142	.768	250	7.8	457	14.3
1982–83	35	218	414	.527	145	177	.819	330	9.4	593	16.9
1983–84	31	195	331	.589	155	181	.856	298	9.6	545	17.6
Totals	135	786	1364	.576	561	705	.796	1167	8.6	2145	15.9

Three-point field goals: 12 of 28 (.429) in 1982–83.

BOB PETTIT
Louisiana State
6-9 – F/C
Baton Rouge, La.

NCAA consensus first-team All-American in 1954 and consensus second-team All-American in 1953.... Leading scorer and rebounder for 1953 national fourth-place team (22-3 record).... Averaged 30.5 points in six NCAA Tournament games in 1953 and 1954 (3-3 record).... Selected by the Milwaukee Hawks in first round of 1954 NBA draft.... Elected to Naismith Memorial Basketball Hall of Fame in 1970.

Season	G	FGM	FGA	FG%	FTM	FTA	FT%	Reb.	Avg.	Pts.	Avg.
1951–52	23	237	549	.432	115	192	.599	315	13.1	589	25.6
1952–53	21	193	394	.490	133	215	.619	263	16.3	519	24.7
1953–54	25	281	573	.490	223	308	.724	432	17.3	785	31.4
Totals	69	711	1516	.469	471	715	.659	1010	14.6	1893	27.4

ANDY PHILLIP
Illinois
6-2 – F
Granite City, Ill.

NCAA consensus first-team All-American in 1942 and 1943, and consensus second-team All-American in 1947.... Averaged 5.5 points in two NCAA Tournament games in 1942 (0-2 record).... Elected to Naismith Memorial Basketball Hall of Fame in 1961.

Season	G	FGM	FGA	FG%	FTM	FTA	FT%	Reb.	Avg.	Pts.	Avg.
1941–42	23	87			58					232	10.1
1942–43	18	131			43	57	.754			305	16.9
1943–44		Military Service (Marine Corps)									
1944–45		Military Service (Marine Corps)									
1945–46		Military Service (Marine Corps)									
1946–47	20	81			30	61	.492			192	9.6
Totals	61	299			131					729	12.0

MARK PRICE
Georgia Tech
6-0 – G
Enid, Okla.

NCAA consensus second-team All-American in 1985.... Averaged 17.9 points in seven NCAA Tournament games in 1985 and 1986 (5-2 record).... Collected 13 points and five assists in one NIT game in 1984.... Selected by the Dallas Mavericks in second round of 1986 NBA draft (25th pick overall); rights promptly traded to the Cleveland Cavaliers for a 1989 second-round draft choice and cash.

Season	G	FGM	FGA	FG%	FTM	FTA	FT%	Reb.	Avg.	Pts.	Avg.
1982–83	28	201	462	.435	93	106	.877	105	3.8	568	20.3
1983–84	29	191	375	.509	70	85	.824	61	2.1	452	15.6
1984–85	35	223	462	.483	137	163	.840	71	2.0	583	16.7
1985–86	34	233	441	.528	124	145	.855	94	2.8	590	17.4
Totals	126	848	1740	.487	424	499	.850	331	2.6	2193	17.4

Three-point field goals: 73 of 166 (.440) in 1982–83.

FRANK RAMSEY
Kentucky
6-3 – F
Madisonville, Ky.

NCAA consensus second-team All-American in 1954.... Second-leading scorer for undefeated 1954 team that chose not to participate in national postseason competition (25-0 record).... Second-leading rebounder and fourth-leading scorer for 1951 NCAA champion (32-2).... Averaged 11.2 points in six NCAA Tournament games in 1951 and 1952 (5-1 record).... Selected by the Boston Celtics in first round of 1953 NBA draft.... Elected to Naismith Memorial Basketball Hall of Fame in 1981.

Season	G	FGM	FGA	FG%	FTM	FTA	FT%	Reb.	Avg.	Pts.	Avg.
1950–51	34	135	413	.327	75	123	.610	434	12.8	345	10.1
1951–52	32	185	470	.394	139	214	.650	383	12.0	509	15.9
1952–53		Kentucky prohibited from playing because of NCAA probation.									
1953–54	25	179	430	.416	132	181	.729	221	8.8	490	19.6
Totals	91	499	1313	.380	346	518	.668	1038	11.4	1344	14.8

SAM RANZINO
North Carolina State
6-1 – G/F
Gary, Ind.

NCAA consensus first-team All-American in 1951.... Leading scorer for 1950 national third-place team (27-6 record).... Averaged 25.7 points in three NCAA Tournament games in 1950 (2-1 record; he and star teammates Paul Horvath and Vic Bubas were ineligible for the 1951 NCAA Tournament because they were in their fourth season of varsity competition).... Averaged 13 points in two NIT opening-game defeats (1948 and 1951).... Selected by the Rochester Royals in 1951 NBA draft.

Season	G	FGM	FGA	FG%	FTM	FTA	FT%	Reb.	Avg.	Pts.	Avg.
1947–48	32	105			46	71	.648			256	8.0
1948–49	33	157			67	97	.691			381	11.5
1949–50	33	241	721	.334	142	197	.721			624	18.9
1950–51	34	241	760	.317	224	305	.734	220	6.5	706	20.8
Totals	132	744			479	670	.715			1967	14.9

ED RATLEFF
Long Beach State
6-6 – F/G
Columbus, Ohio

NCAA unanimous first-team All-American in 1972 and 1973.... Averaged 18.8 points and 7.3 rebounds in nine NCAA Tournament games from 1971 to 1973 (6-3 record).... Member of 1972 U.S. Olympic team.... Selected by the Houston Rockets in first round of 1973 NBA draft (6th pick overall).

Season	G	FGM	FGA	FG%	FTM	FTA	FT%	Reb.	Avg.	Pts.	Avg.
1970–71	27	218	485	.449	103	132	.780	239	8.9	539	20.0
1971–72	29	250	517	.484	121	157	.771	220	7.6	621	21.4
1972–73	29	275	549	.501	110	138	.797	251	8.7	660	22.8
Totals	85	743	1551	.479	334	427	.782	710	8.4	1820	21.4

J. R. REID
North Carolina
6-9 – F/C
Virginia Beach, Va.

NCAA unanimous first-team All-American in 1988.... Averaged 20.4 points and 8.5 rebounds in 10 NCAA Tournament games from 1987 to 1989 (7-3 record).... Member of 1988 U.S. Olympic team.... Selected as an undergraduate by the Charlotte Hornets in 1989 NBA draft (5th pick overall).

Season	G	FGM	FGA	FG%	FTM	FTA	FT%	Reb.	Avg.	Pts.	Avg.
1986–87	36	198	339	.584	132	202	.653	268	7.4	528	14.7
1987–88	33	222	366	.607	151	222	.680	293	8.9	595	18.0
1988–89	27	164	267	.614	101	151	.669	170	6.3	429	15.9
Totals	96	584	972	.601	384	575	.668	731	7.6	1552	16.2

JOE REIFF
Northwestern
6-2 – F
Chicago, Ill.

NCAA consensus first-team All-American in 1931 and 1933.

Season	G	FGM	FGA	FG%	FTM	FTA	FT%	Reb.	Avg.	Pts.	Avg.
1930–31	12	43			37					123	10.3
1931–32	12	36			32					104	8.7
1932–33	12	53			61					167	13.9
Totals	36	132			130					394	10.9

Note: Statistics are for Big Ten Conference games only.

JESSE (CAB) RENICK
Oklahoma A&M
6-2 – G

NCAA consensus second-team All-American in 1940. . . . Averaged 8.5 points in two NIT games for 1940 third-place team. . . . Played two seasons in junior college. . . . Member of 1948 U.S. Olympic team (5.6 ppg).

Season	G.	FGM	FTM	Pts.	Avg.
1938-39	14	52	24	128	9.1
1939-40	12	37	20	94	7.8

Note: (Statistics are for conference games only.)

SHAWN RESPERT
Michigan State
6-3 – G
Detroit, Mich.

Named national player of the year by the NABC in 1995. . . . NCAA unanimous first-team All-American in 1995. . . . Ranked among the nation's leading scorers in 1993 (63rd), 1994 (16th) and 1995 (8th). . . . Ranked among the nation's leaders in free-throw percentage in 1993 (27th) and 1995 (13th). . . . Ranked 8th in the nation in three-point field-goal percentage and 2nd in three-pointers per game with 4.3 in 1995. . . . Averaged 21 points in five NCAA Tournament games in 1992, 1994 and 1995 (2-3 record). . . . Collected 20 points and four assists in one NIT game in 1993. . . . Selected by the Portland Trail Blazers in first round of 1995 NBA draft (8th pick overall). Draft rights promptly traded to the Milwaukee Bucks.

Season	G.	FGM	FGA	FG%	FTM	FTA	FT%	Reb.	Avg.	Pts.	Avg.
1990-91	1	0	2	.000	0	0	.000	0	0.0	0	0.0
1991-92	30	173	344	.503	68	78	.872	64	2.1	474	15.8
1992-93	28	192	399	.481	119	139	.856	111	4.0	563	20.1
1993-94	32	272	562	.484	142	169	.840	127	4.0	778	24.3
1994-95	28	229	484	.473	139	160	.869	111	4.0	716	25.6
Totals	119	866	1791	.484	468	546	.857	413	3.5	2531	21.3

Three-point field goals: 60 of 132 (.455) in 1991-92, 60 of 140 (.429) in 1992-93, 92 of 205 (.449) in 1993-94 and 119 of 251 (.474) in 1994-95. **Totals:** 331 of 728 (.455).

(Missed majority of 1990-91 season recovering from knee injury he suffered in high school playoffs.)

GLEN RICE
Michigan
6-7 – F/G
Flint, Mich.

NCAA consensus second-team All-American in 1989. . . . Leading scorer and second-leading rebounder for 1989 NCAA champion (30-7 record). . . . Final Four Most Outstanding Player in 1989. . . . Named to All-NCAA Tournament team in 1989. . . . Averaged 23.7 points and 6.3 rebounds in 13 NCAA Tournament games from 1986 to 1989 (10-3 record). . . . Selected by the Miami Heat in first round of 1989 NBA draft (4th pick overall).

Season	G	FGM	FGA	FG%	FTM	FTA	FT%	Reb.	Avg.	Pts.	Avg.
1985–86	32	105	191	.550	15	25	.600	97	3.0	225	7.0
1986–87	32	226	402	.562	85	108	.787	294	9.2	540	16.9
1987–88	33	308	539	.571	79	98	.806	236	7.2	728	22.1
1988–89	37	363	629	.577	124	149	.832	232	6.3	949	25.6
Totals	134	1002	1761	.569	303	380	.797	859	6.4	2442	18.2

Three-point field goals: 3 of 12 (.250) in 1986–87, 33 of 77 (.429) in 1987–88, and 99 of 192 (.516) in 1988–89. **Totals:** 135 of 281 (.480).

DICK RICKETTS
Duquesne
6-8 – F/C
Pottstown, Pa.

NCAA consensus first-team All-American in 1955 and consensus second-team All-American in 1954. . . . Averaged 18 points in two NCAA Tournament games in 1952 (1-1 record). . . . Averaged 17.8 points in 13 NIT games in 1952 (fourth place), 1953 (third place), 1954 (runner-up), and 1955 (champion). . . . Selected by the St. Louis Hawks in 1955 NBA draft.

Season	G	FGM	FGA	FG%	FTM	FTA	FT%	Reb.	Avg.	Pts.	Avg.
1951–52	27	130	331	.393	76	105	.724	290	10.7	336	12.4
1952–53	29	229	637	.359	148	226	.655	318	11.0	606	20.9
1953–54	29	205	488	.420	88	121	.727	301	10.4	498	17.2
1954–55	26	174	435	.400	175	225	.778	450	17.3	523	20.1
Totals	111	738	1891	.390	487	677	.719	1359	12.2	1963	17.7

TOM RIKER
South Carolina
6-10 – C
Oyster Bay, N.Y.

NCAA consensus first-team All-American in 1972. . . . Averaged 23.6 points and 10.2 rebounds in five NCAA Tournament games in 1971 and 1972 (2-3 record). . . . Selected by the New York Knicks in first round of 1972 NBA draft (8th pick overall).

Season	G	FGM	FGA	FG%	FTM	FTA	FT%	Reb.	Avg.	Pts.	Avg.
1969–70	28	143	277	.516	101	151	.669	251	9.0	387	13.8
1970–71	29	148	313	.473	110	173	.636	231	8.0	406	14.0
1971–72	28	208	375	.555	134	187	.717	292	10.4	550	19.6
Totals	85	499	965	.517	345	511	.675	774	9.1	1343	15.8

OSCAR ROBERTSON
Cincinnati
6-5 – G/F
Indianapolis, Ind.

Named national player of the year by UPI and USBWA in 1958, 1959, and 1960. . . . NCAA unanimous first-team All-American in 1958, 1959, and 1960. . . . Led the nation in scoring in 1958, 1959, and 1960. . . . Leading scorer and rebounder for national third-place teams in 1959 (26-4 record) and 1960 (28-2). . . . Member of All-NCAA Tournament team in 1959 and 1960. . . . Averaged 32.4 points and 13.1 rebounds in 10 NCAA Tournament games from 1958 to 1960 (7-3 record).... Tied with Jerry Lucas for scoring leadership (17 points per game) on 1960 U.S. Olympic team.... Selected as a territorial pick by the Cincinnati Royals in 1960 NBA draft.... Elected to Naismith Memorial Basketball Hall of Fame in 1979.

Season	G	FGM	FGA	FG%	FTM	FTA	FT%	Reb.	Avg.	Pts.	Avg.
1957–58	28	352	617	.571	280	355	.789	425	15.2	984	35.1
1958–59	30	331	650	.509	316	398	.794	489	16.3	978	32.6
1959–60	30	369	701	.526	273	361	.756	424	14.1	1011	33.7
Totals	88	1052	1968	.535	869	1114	.780	1338	15.2	2973	33.8

RICK ROBEY
Kentucky
6-10 – F/C
New Orleans, La.

NCAA consensus second-team All-American in 1978.... Ranked 4th in the nation in field-goal percentage in 1978.... Leading rebounder and second-leading scorer for 1978 NCAA Tournament champion (30-2 record).... Leading rebounder and third-leading scorer for 1975 NCAA Tournament runner-up (26-5).... Named to 1978 All-NCAA Tournament team.... Averaged 10.7 points and 6.7 rebounds in 13 NCAA Tournament games in 1975, 1977 and 1978 (11-2 record).... Did not play in postseason for 1976 NIT champion because of a knee injury.... Selected by the Pacers in first round of 1978 NBA draft (3rd pick overall).

Season	G.	FGM	FGA	FG%	FTM	FTA	FT%	Reb.	Avg.	Pts.	Avg.
1974-75	31	135	248	.544	51	63	.810	214	6.9	321	10.4
1975-76	12	73	130	.562	41	56	.732	90	7.5	187	15.6
1976-77	30	158	276	.572	111	161	.689	273	9.1	427	14.2
1977-78	32	167	263	.635	126	175	.720	261	8.2	460	14.4
Totals	105	533	917	.581	329	455	.723	838	8.0	1395	13.3

DAVID ROBINSON
Navy
7-0 – C
Woodbridge, Va.

Named national player of the year by AP, UPI, USBWA, and NABC in 1987.... Wooden Award and Naismith Award winner in 1987.... NCAA unanimous first-team All-American in 1987 and consensus second-team All-American in 1986.... Led the nation in rebounding in 1986.... Led the nation in blocked shots in 1986 (5.9 per game) and 1987 (4.5 per game).... Averaged 28.6 points and 12.3 rebounds in seven NCAA Tournament games from 1985 to 1987 (4-3 record).... Member of 1988 and 1992 U.S. Olympic teams.... Selected by the San Antonio Spurs in first round of 1987 NBA draft (1st pick overall).

Season	G	FGM	FGA	FG%	FTM	FTA	FT%	Reb.	Avg.	Pts.	Avg.
1983–84	28	86	138	.623	42	73	.575	111	4.0	214	7.6
1984–85	32	302	469	.644	152	243	.626	370	11.6	756	23.6
1985–86	35	294	484	.607	208	331	.628	455	13.0	796	22.7
1986–87	32	350	592	.591	202	317	.637	378	11.8	903	28.2
Totals	127	1032	1683	.613	604	964	.627	1314	10.3	2669	21.0

Three-point field goals: 1 for 1 in 1986–87.

GLENN ROBINSON
Purdue
6-8 – F
Gary, Ind.

Named national player of the year by AP, UPI, USBWA, and NABC in 1994.... Wooden Award and Naismith Award winner in 1994.... NCAA unanimous first-team All-American in 1994.... Led the nation in scoring in 1994.... Averaged 31.4 points and 9.8 rebounds in five NCAA Tournament games in 1993 and 1994 (3-2 record).... Selected by the Milwaukee Bucks in first round of 1994 NBA draft (1st pick overall).

Season	G	FGM	FGA	FG%	FTM	FTA	FT%	Reb.	Avg.	Pts.	Avg.
1991–92			Sat out the entire season as a Proposition 48 casualty.								
1992–93	28	246	519	.474	152	205	.741	258	9.2	676	24.1
1993–94	34	368	762	.483	215	270	.796	344	10.1	1030	30.3
Totals	62	614	1281	.479	367	475	.773	602	9.7	1706	27.5

Three-point field goals: 32 of 80 (.400) in 1992–93 and 79 of 208 (.380) in 1993–94. Totals: 111 of 288 (.385).

JOHN ROCHE
South Carolina
6-3 – G
New York, N.Y.

NCAA consensus second-team All-American in 1970 and 1971.... Averaged 11 points in two NCAA Tournament defeats in 1971.... Averaged 21 points in two NIT games in 1969 (1-1 record).... Selected by the Phoenix Suns in first round of 1971 NBA draft (14th pick overall).

Season	G	FGM	FGA	FG%	FTM	FTA	FT%	Reb.	Avg.	Pts.	Avg.
1968–69	28	239	507	.471	184	226	.814	73	2.6	662	23.6
1969–70	28	222	469	.473	179	216	.829	70	2.5	623	22.3
1970–71	29	205	493	.416	215	262	.821	67	2.3	625	21.6
Totals	85	666	1469	.453	578	704	.821	210	2.5	1910	22.5

GUY RODGERS
Temple
6-0 – G
Philadelphia, Pa.

NCAA unanimous first-team All-American in 1958 and consensus second-team All-American in 1957.... Leading scorer for 1958 national third-place team (27-3 record).... Member of All-NCAA Tournament team in 1958.... Averaged 17.9 points in nine NCAA Tournament games in 1956 and 1958 (7-2 record).... Averaged 23.3 points in three NIT games for 1957 third-place team.... Selected as a territorial pick by the Philadelphia Warriors in 1958 NBA draft.

Season	G	FGM	FGA	FG%	FTM	FTA	FT%	Reb.	Avg.	Pts.	Avg.
1955–56	31	243	552	.440	87	155	.561	186	6.0	573	18.5
1956–57	29	216	565	.382	159	224	.710	202	7.0	591	20.4
1957–58	30	249	564	.441	105	171	.614	199	6.6	603	20.1
Totals	90	708	1681	.421	351	550	.638	587	6.5	1767	19.6

MARSHALL ROGERS
Pan American
6-2 – G
St. Louis, Mo.

Led the nation in scoring in 1976 after finishing 9th in 1975.... Ranked 9th in the nation in free-throw percentage in 1976.... Did not play in NCAA Tournament or NIT.... Selected by the Golden State Warriors in second round of 1976 NBA draft (34th pick overall).

Season	G.	FGM	FGA	FG%	FTM	FTA	FT%	Reb.	Avg.	Pts.	Avg.
1972-73	18	52	152	.342	34	51	.667	46	2.6	138	7.7
1973-74			Sat out the entire season after transferring from Kansas.								
1974-75	22	248	546	.454	92	123	.748	134	6.1	588	26.7
1975-76	25	361	683	.529	197	230	.857	122	4.9	919	36.8
Totals	65	661	1381	.479	323	404	.800	302	4.6	1645	25.3

LENNIE ROSENBLUTH
North Carolina
6-5 – F
New York, N.Y.

NCAA consensus first-team All-American in 1957.... Leading scorer and second-leading rebounder for undefeated 1957 NCAA champion (32-0 record).... Member of All-NCAA Tournament team in 1957.... Averaged 28 points and 9.2 rebounds in five NCAA Tournament games in 1957 (5-0 record).... Selected by the Philadelphia Warriors in first round of 1957 NBA draft (6th pick overall).

Season	G	FGM	FGA	FG%	FTM	FTA	FT%	Reb.	Avg.	Pts.	Avg.
1954–55	21	189	444	.426	158	222	.712	246	11.7	536	25.5
1955–56	23	227	496	.458	160	217	.737	264	11.5	614	26.7
1956–57	32	305	631	.483	285	376	.758	280	8.8	895	28.0
Totals	76	721	1571	.459	603	815	.740	790	10.4	2045	26.9

CURTIS ROWE
UCLA
6-7 – F
Los Angeles, Calif.

NCAA consensus second-team All-American in 1971. . . . Second-leading scorer and rebounder for NCAA Tournament champions in 1971 (29-1 record) and 1969 (29-1). . . . Fourth-leading scorer and third-leading rebounder for 1970 NCAA Tournament champion (28-2). . . . Named to 1970 All-NCAA Tournament team. . . . Averaged 13.8 points and 11.6 rebounds in 12 NCAA Tournament games from 1969-71 (12-0 record). . . . Selected by the Detroit Pistons in first round of 1971 NBA draft (11th pick overall).

Season	G.	FGM	FGA	FG%	FTM	FTA	FT%	Reb.	Avg.	Pts.	Avg.
1968-69	30	144	287	.502	99	146	.678	237	7.9	387	12.9
1969-70	30	168	303	.554	123	192	.641	260	8.7	459	15.3
1970-71	30	207	396	.523	111	177	.627	299	10.0	525	17.5
Totals	90	519	986	.526	333	515	.647	796	8.8	1371	15.2

CLIFFORD ROZIER
Louisville
6-9 – F/C
Bradenton, Fla.

NCAA consensus first-team All-American in 1994.... Averaged 8.3 points and 5.5 rebounds in 11 NCAA Tournament games in 1991 (five games with North Carolina), 1993, and 1994 (8-3 record).... Fifth-leading rebounder and seventh-leading scorer for North Carolina's 1991 Final Four team (29-6 record).... Selected as an undergraduate by the Golden State Warriors in first round of 1994 NBA draft (16th pick overall).

Season	G	FGM	FGA	FG%	FTM	FTA	FT%	Reb.	Avg.	Pts.	Avg.
1990–91	34	64	136	.471	39	69	.565	101	3.0	167	4.9
1991–92					Sat out the season after transferring from North Carolina.						
1992–93	31	192	342	.561	104	183	.568	338	10.9	488	15.7
1993–94	34	247	400	.618	122	224	.545	377	11.1	616	18.1
Totals	99	503	898	.560	265	476	.557	816	8.2	1271	12.8

Three-point field goals: 0 of 2 in 1992–93 and 0 of 1 in 1993–94. **Totals:** 0 of 3.

BILL RUSSELL
San Francisco
6-9 – C
Oakland, Calif.

Named national player of the year by UPI in 1956.... NCAA unanimous first-team All-American in 1956 and consensus first-team All-American in 1955.... One of six players to average more than 20 points and 20 rebounds per game in his career.... Final Four Most Outstanding Player in 1955.... Leading scorer and rebounder for NCAA championship teams in 1955 (28-1 record) and 1956 (29-0).... Member of All-NCAA Tournament team in 1955 and 1956.... Averaged 23.2 points in nine NCAA Tournament games in 1955 and 1956 (9-0 record).... Leading scorer (14.1 points per game) for 1956 U.S. Olympic team.... Selected by the Boston Celtics in first round of 1956 NBA draft (3rd pick overall).... Elected to Naismith Memorial Basketball Hall of Fame in 1974.

Season	G	FGM	FGA	FG%	FTM	FTA	FT%	Reb.	Avg.	Pts.	Avg.
1953–54	21	150	309	.485	117	212	.552	403	19.2	417	19.9
1954–55	29	229	423	.541	164	278	.590	594	20.5	622	21.4
1955–56	29	246	480	.513	105	212	.495	609	21.0	597	20.6
Totals	79	625	1212	.516	386	702	.550	1606	20.3	1636	20.7

CAZZIE RUSSELL
Michigan
6-5 – G
Chicago, Ill.

Named national player of the year by AP, UPI, and USBWA in 1966.... NCAA unanimous first-team All-American in 1965 and 1966, and consensus second-team All-American in 1964.... Leading scorer and third-leading rebounder for 1964 national third-place team (23-5 record) and 1965 runner-up (24-4).... Member of All-NCAA Tournament team in 1965.... Averaged 24.6 points and 7.4 rebounds in eight NCAA Tournament games from 1964 to 1966 (5-3 record; didn't play in 1964 national third-place game because of a swollen ankle).... Selected by the New York Knicks in first round of 1966 NBA draft (1st pick overall).

Season	G	FGM	FGA	FG%	FTM	FTA	FT%	Reb.	Avg.	Pts.	Avg.
1963–64	27	260	507	.513	150	178	.843	244	9.0	670	24.8
1964–65	27	271	558	.486	152	186	.817	213	7.9	694	25.7
1965–66	26	308	595	.518	184	223	.825	219	8.4	800	30.8
Totals	80	839	1660	.505	486	587	.828	676	8.5	2164	27.1

FOREST (AGGIE) SALE
Kentucky
6-4 – F/C
Lawrenceburg, Ky.

NCAA consensus first-team All-American in 1932 and 1933.

Season	G	FGM	FGA	FG%	FTM	FTA	FT%	Reb.	Avg.	Pts.	Avg.
1930–31										62	
1931–32	17									235	13.8
1932–33	23									324	14.0
Totals										621	

RALPH SAMPSON
Virginia
7-4 – C
Harrisonburg, Va.

Named national player of the year by AP, UPI, and USBWA in 1981, 1982, and 1983, and by NABC in 1982 and 1983.... Wooden Award winner in 1982 and 1983.... Naismith Award winner in 1981, 1982, and 1983.... NCAA unanimous first-team All-American in 1981, 1982, and 1983.... Leading rebounder and second-leading scorer for 1981 national third-place team (29-4 record).... Averaged 16.4 points and 11.3 rebounds in 10 NCAA Tournament games from 1981 to 1983 (7-3 record).... NIT Most Valuable Player in 1980.... Averaged 19.2

points and 13.8 rebounds in five NIT games for 1980 champion.... Selected by the Houston Rockets in first round of 1983 NBA draft (1st pick overall).

Season	G	FGM	FGA	FG%	FTM	FTA	FT%	Reb.	Avg.	Pts.	Avg.
1979–80	34	221	404	.547	66	94	.702	381	11.2	508	14.9
1980–81	33	230	413	.557	125	198	.631	378	11.5	585	17.7
1981–82	32	198	353	.561	110	179	.615	366	11.4	506	15.8
1982–83	33	250	414	.604	126	179	.704	386	11.7	629	19.1
Totals	132	899	1584	.568	427	650	.657	1511	11.4	2228	16.9

Three-point field goals: 3 of 5 (.600) in 1982–83.

DOLPH SCHAYES
New York University
6-8 – F/C
Bronx, N.Y.

Third-leading scorer for 1945 national runner-up (16-8 record).... Averaged 8.8 points in five NCAA Tournament games in 1945 and 1946 (3-2 record).... Averaged 10 points in three NIT games for 1948 runner-up.... Selected by the Tri-Cities Hawks in 1948 National Basketball League draft before his rights were acquired by the Syracuse Nationals of the NBA.... Elected to Naismith Memorial Basketball Hall of Fame in 1972.

Season	G	FGM	FGA	FG%	FTM	FTA	FT%	Reb.	Avg.	Pts.	Avg.
1944–45	11	46			23					115	10.5
1945–46	22	54			41					149	6.8
1946–47	21	66			63					195	9.3
1947–48	26	124			108					356	13.7
Totals	80	290			235					815	10.2

DAVE SCHELLHASE
Purdue
6-4 – F
Evansville, Ind.

NCAA unanimous first-team All-American in 1966 and consensus second-team All-American in 1965.... Led the nation in scoring in 1966.... Did not play in NCAA Tournament or NIT.... Selected by the Chicago Bulls in first round of 1966 NBA draft (10th pick overall).

Season	G	FGM	FGA	FG%	FTM	FTA	FT%	Reb.	Avg.	Pts.	Avg.
1963–64	24	213	441	.483	163	211	.773	271	11.3	589	24.5
1964–65	24	249	559	.445	206	262	.786	195	8.1	704	29.3
1965–66	24	284	611	.465	213	276	.772	255	10.6	781	32.5
Totals	72	746	1611	.463	582	749	.777	721	10.0	2074	28.8

DON SCHLUNDT
Indiana
6-10 – C
South Bend, Ind.

NCAA consensus first-team All-American in 1954 and consensus second-team All-American in 1953.... Leading scorer and rebounder for 1953 NCAA champion (23-3 record).... Member of All-NCAA Tournament team in 1953.... Averaged 27 points in six NCAA Tournament games in 1953 and 1954 (5-1 record).... Selected by the Syracuse Nationals in 1955 NBA draft (never played in league).

Season	G	FGM	FGA	FG%	FTM	FTA	FT%	Reb.	Avg.	Pts.	Avg.
1951–52	22	131	289	.453	114	171	.667	158	7.2	376	17.1
1952–53	26	206	477	.432	249	310	.803	220	8.5	661	25.4
1953–54	24	177	354	.500	229	296	.774	267	11.1	583	24.3
1954–55	22	169	377	.448	234	299	.783	215	9.8	572	26.0
Totals	94	683	1497	.456	826	1076	.768	860	9.1	2192	23.3

DICK SCHNITTKER
Ohio State
6-5 – F
Sandusky, Ohio

NCAA unanimous first-team All-American in 1950.... Averaged 21.5 points in two NCAA Tournament games in 1950 (1-1 record).... Selected by the Washington Capitols in 1950 NBA draft.

Season	G	FGM	FGA	FG%	FTM	FTA	FT%	Reb.	Avg.	Pts.	Avg.
1946–47	2	1	1	1.000	0	0				2	1.0
1947–48	20	116	281	.413	90	120	.750			322	16.1
1948–49	19	125	275	.455	86	125	.688			336	17.7
1949–50	22	158	390	.405	153	204	.750			469	21.3
Totals	63	400	947	.422	329	449	.733			1129	17.9

CHARLIE SCOTT
North Carolina
6-5 – G/F
New York, N.Y.

NCAA consensus second-team All-American in 1969 and 1970.... Leading scorer and third-leading rebounder for 1969 national fourth-place team (27-5 record).... Second-leading scorer and fourth-leading rebounder for 1968 national runner-up (28-4).... Member of All-NCAA Tournament team in 1969.... Averaged 21.2 points and 5.3 rebounds in eight NCAA Tournament games in 1968 and 1969.... Scored 26 points in one NIT game in 1970.... Selected by the Washington Capitols in first round of "secret" ABA draft in January 1970; NBA rights traded by the Boston Celtics to the Phoenix Suns for future considerations, March 14, 1972.

Season	G	FGM	FGA	FG%	FTM	FTA	FT%	Reb.	Avg.	Pts.	Avg.
1967–68	32	234	490	.478	94	141	.667	191	6.0	562	17.6
1968–69	32	290	577	.503	134	191	.702	226	7.1	714	22.3
1969–70	27	281	611	.460	169	215	.786	232	8.6	731	27.1
Totals	91	805	1678	.480	397	547	.726	649	7.1	2007	22.1

FRANK SELVY
Furman
6-3 – F
Corbin, Ky.

NCAA consensus first-team All-American in 1954 and consensus second-team All-American in 1953.... Holds NCAA record for most points in a single game with 100 against Newberry on February 13, 1954.... Led the nation in scoring in 1953 and 1954.... Did not play in NCAA Tournament or NIT.... Selected by the Baltimore Bullets in 1954 NBA draft.

Season	G	FGM	FGA	FG%	FTM	FTA	FT%	Reb.	Avg.	Pts.	Avg.
1951–52	24	223	556	.401	145	199	.729			591	24.6
1952–53	25	272	646	.421	194	263	.738			738	29.5
1953–54	29	427	941	.454	355	444	.800	400	13.8	1209	41.7
Totals	78	922	2143	.430	694	906	.766			2538	32.5

BILL SHARMAN
Southern California
6-1 – G
Porterville, Calif.

NCAA consensus first-team All-American in 1950.... Did not play in NCAA Tournament or NIT.... Selected by the Washington Capitols in second round of 1950 NBA draft.... Elected to Naismith Memorial Basketball Hall of Fame in 1975.

Season	G	FGM	FGA	FG%	FTM	FTA	FT%	Reb.	Avg.	Pts.	Avg.
1946–47	10	16			9	12	.750			41	4.1
1947–48	24	100			38	44	.864			238	9.9
1948–49	24	142			98	125	.784			382	15.9
1949–50	24	171	421	.406	104	129	.806			446	18.6
Totals	82	429			249	310	.803			1107	13.5

RON SHAVLIK
North Carolina State
6-9 – C
Denver, Colo.

NCAA consensus first-team All-American in 1956 and consensus second-team All-American in 1955.... Averaged 19.3 points in four NCAA Tournament games in 1954 and 1956 (2-2 record).... Selected by the New York Knicks in 1956 NBA draft.

Season	G	FGM	FGA	FG%	FTM	FTA	FT%	Reb.	Avg.	Pts.	Avg.
1953–54	33	204	536	.381	115	203	.567	441	13.4	523	15.8
1954–55	32	260	646	.402	187	267	.700	581	18.2	707	22.1
1955–56	28	177	429	.413	156	227	.687	545	19.5	510	18.2
Totals	93	641	1611	.398	458	697	.657	1567	16.8	1740	18.7

JOHN SHUMATE
Notre Dame
6-9 – F/C
Elizabeth, N.J.

NCAA unanimous first-team All-American in 1974.... Averaged 28.7 points and eight rebounds in three NCAA Tournament games in 1974 (2-1 record).... Averaged 23.8 points and 8.8 rebounds in four NIT games for 1973 runner-up.... Selected with eligibility remaining by the Phoenix Suns in first round of 1974 NBA draft (4th pick overall).

Season	G	FGM	FGA	FG%	FTM	FTA	FT%	Reb.	Avg.	Pts.	Avg.
1971–72					Sat out the entire season because of a blood clot in a lung.						
1972–73	30	257	434	.592	117	179	.654	365	12.2	631	21.0
1973–74	29	281	448	.627	141	196	.719	319	11.0	703	24.2
Totals	59	538	882	.610	258	375	.688	684	11.6	1334	22.6

PAUL SILAS
Creighton
6-7 – F/C
Oakland, Calif.

Holds NCAA record for most rebounds in a three-year career.... Led the nation in rebounding in 1963.... One of six players to average more than 20 points and 20 rebounds in his career.... Averaged 17.5 points in six NCAA Tournament games in 1962 and 1964 (3-3 record).... Selected by the St. Louis Hawks in second round of 1964 NBA draft (12th pick overall).

Season	G	FGM	FGA	FG%	FTM	FTA	FT%	Reb.	Avg.	Pts.	Avg.
1961–62	25	213	524	.406	125	215	.581	563	22.5	551	22.0
1962–63	27	220	531	.414	133	228	.583	557	20.6	573	21.2
1963–64	29	210	529	.397	117	194	.603	631	21.8	537	18.5
Totals	81	643	1584	.406	375	637	.589	1751	21.6	1661	20.5

LIONEL SIMMONS
La Salle
6-7 – F
Philadelphia, Pa.

Named national player of the year by AP, UPI, NABC, and USBWA in 1990.... Naismith Award and Wooden Award winner in 1990.... NCAA unanimous first-team All-American in 1990 and consensus second-team All-American in 1989.... Averaged 26.5 points and 12 rebounds in four NCAA Tournament games from 1988 to 1990 (1-3 record).... Averaged 23.4 points and 10.4 rebounds in five NIT games for 1987 runner-up.... Selected by the Sacramento Kings in first round of 1990 NBA draft (7th pick overall).

Season	G	FGM	FGA	FG%	FTM	FTA	FT%	Reb.	Avg.	Pts.	Avg.
1986–87	33	263	500	.526	142	186	.763	322	9.8	670	20.3
1987–88	34	297	613	.485	196	259	.757	386	11.4	792	23.3
1988–89	32	349	716	.487	189	266	.711	365	11.4	908	28.4
1989–90	32	335	653	.513	146	221	.661	356	11.1	847	26.5
Totals	131	1244	2482	.501	673	932	.722	1429	10.9	3217	24.6

Three-point field goals: 2 of 6 (.333) in 1986–87, 2 of 8 (.250) in 1987–88, 21 of 56 (.375) in 1988–89, and 31 of 65 (.477) in 1989–90. **Totals:** 56 of 135 (.415).

JOE SMITH
Maryland
6-10 – C
Norfolk, Va.

Named national player of the year by AP and UPI in 1995.... Naismith award winner in 1995.... NCAA unanimous first-team All-American in 1995.... Ranked 38th in the nation in scoring, 18th in rebounding, 30th in field-goal percentage and 17th in blocked shots per game with 2.9 in 1995.... Averaged 20.8 points and 12.2 rebounds in six NCAA Tournament games in 1994 and 1995 (4-2 record).... Selected as an undergraduate (after sophomore season) by the Golden State Warriors in first round of 1995 NBA draft (1st pick overall).

Season	G.	FGM	FGA	FG%	FTM	FTA	FT%	Reb.	Avg.	Pts.	Avg.
1993-94	30	206	395	.522	168	229	.734	321	10.7	582	19.4
1994-95	34	245	424	.578	209	282	.741	362	10.6	708	20.8
Totals	64	451	819	.551	377	511	.738	683	10.7	1290	20.2

Three-point field goals: 2 of 5 (.400) in 1993-94 and 9 of 21 (.429) in 1994-95. **Totals:** 11 of 26 (.423).

KENNY SMITH
North Carolina
6-3 – G
Queens, N.Y.

NCAA unanimous first-team All-American in 1987.... Averaged 13.4 points and 6.6 assists in 13 NCAA Tournament games from 1984 to 1987 (9-4 record).... Selected by the Sacramento Kings in first round of 1987 NBA draft (6th pick overall).

Season	G	FGM	FGA	FG%	FTM	FTA	FT%	Reb.	Avg.	Pts.	Avg.
1983–84	23	83	160	.519	44	55	.800	40	1.7	210	9.1
1984–85	36	173	334	.518	98	114	.860	92	2.6	444	12.3
1985–86	34	164	318	.516	80	99	.808	75	2.2	408	12.0
1986–87	34	208	414	.502	71	88	.807	76	2.2	574	16.9
Totals	127	628	1226	.512	293	356	.823	283	2.2	1636	12.9

Three-point field goals: 87 of 213 (.408) in 1986–87.

RIK SMITS
Marist
7-4 – C
Eindhoven, Holland

Averaged 19 points and three rebounds in two NCAA Tournament games in 1986 and 1987 (0-2 record).... Selected by the Indiana Pacers in first round of 1988 NBA draft (2nd pick overall).

Season	G	FGM	FGA	FG%	FTM	FTA	FT%	Reb.	Avg.	Pts.	Avg.
1984–85	29	132	233	.567	60	104	.577	162	5.6	324	11.2
1985–86	30	216	347	.622	98	144	.681	242	8.1	530	17.7
1986–87	21	157	258	.609	109	151	.722	171	8.1	423	20.1
1987–88	27	251	403	.623	166	226	.735	236	8.7	668	24.7
Totals	107	756	1241	.609	433	625	.693	811	7.6	1945	18.2

BILL SPIVEY
Kentucky
7-0 – C
Warner Robins, Ga.

NCAA unanimous first-team All-American in 1951.... Leading scorer and rebounder for 1951 NCAA champion (32-2 record).... Averaged 18 points and 13.8 rebounds in four NCAA Tournament games in 1951 (4-0 record).... Scored 15 points in one NIT game in 1950.... Allegedly wasn't drafted by any NBA team because of possible repercussions stemming from a game-fixing scandal involving Kentucky.

Season	G	FGM	FGA	FG%	FTM	FTA	FT%	Reb.	Avg.	Pts.	Avg.
1949–50	30	225	619	.363	128	176	.727			578	19.3
1950–51	33	252	632	.399	131	211	.621	567	17.2	635	19.2
Totals	63	477	1251	.381	259	387	.669			1213	19.3

Note: Didn't play in 1951–52 because of a knee injury at the start of the season and then later was dropped from Kentucky's team because of possible involvement in the game-fixing scandals.

JERRY STACKHOUSE
North Carolina
6-6 – F
Kinston, N.C., and Mouth of Wilson, Va.

NCAA unanimous first-team All-American in 1995. . . . Averaged 15.6 points and 7.1 rebounds in seven NCAA Tournament games in 1994 and 1995 (5-2 record). . . . Selected as an undergraduate (after sophomore season) by the Philadelphia 76ers in first round of 1995 NBA draft (3rd pick overall).

Season	G.	FGM	FGA	FG%	FTM	FTA	FT%	Reb.	Avg.	Pts.	Avg.
1993-94	35	138	296	.466	150	205	.732	176	5.0	428	12.2
1994-95	34	215	416	.517	185	260	.712	280	8.2	652	19.2
Totals	69	353	712	.496	335	465	.720	456	6.6	1080	15.7

Three-point field goals: 2 of 20 (.100) in 1993-94 and 37 of 90 (.411) in 1994-95. **Totals:** 39 of 110 (.355).

DAVE STALLWORTH
Wichita State
6-7 – F
Dallas, Tex.

NCAA unanimous first-team All-American in 1964 and consensus second-team All-American in 1965.... Averaged 29.5 points and 19.5 rebounds in two NCAA Tournament games in 1964 (1-1 record).... Averaged 17 points in two NIT games in 1962 and 1963 (0-2 record).... Selected by the New York Knicks in second round of 1965 NBA draft.

Season	G	FGM	FGA	FG%	FTM	FTA	FT%	Reb.	Avg.	Pts.	Avg.
1961–62	7	56	127	.441	28	35	.800	64	9.1	140	20.0
1962–63	27	222	421	.527	165	199	.829	275	10.2	609	22.6
1963–64	29	283	518	.546	203	279	.728	294	10.1	769	26.5
1964–65	16	153	275	.556	94	139	.676	194	12.1	400	25.0
Totals	79	714	1341	.532	490	652	.752	827	10.5	1918	24.3

Note: Did not play for national fourth-place team in 1965 NCAA play-offs because his eligibility expired after the first semester.

STEVE STIPANOVICH
Missouri
6-10 – C
St. Louis, Mo.

NCAA consensus second-team All-American in 1983.... Averaged 11.9 points and 6.6 rebounds in seven NCAA Tournament games from 1980-83 (3-4 record).... Selected by the Indiana Pacers in first round of 1983 NBA draft (2nd pick overall).

Season	G	FGM	FGA	FG%	FTM	FTA	FT%	Reb.	Avg.	Pts.	Avg.
1979–80	31	180	331	.598	85	127	.669	199	6.4	445	14.4
1980–81	32	143	286	.500	120	162	.741	237	7.4	406	12.7
1981–82	31	140	278	.504	79	104	.760	248	8.0	359	11.6
1982–83	34	246	454	.542	134	187	.717	300	8.8	626	18.4
Totals	128	709	1319	.538	418	580	.721	984	7.7	1836	14.3

TOM STITH
St. Bonaventure
6-5 – F
Brooklyn, N.Y.

NCAA unanimous first-team All-American in 1961 and consensus first-team All-American in 1960.... Averaged 29 points in three NCAA Tournament games in 1961 (2-1 record).... Averaged 24.8 points in five NIT games in 1959 (opening-game loser) and 1960 (fourth place).... Selected by the New York Knicks in first round of 1961 NBA draft (2nd pick overall).

Season	G	FGM	FGA	FG%	FTM	FTA	FT%	Reb.	Avg.	Pts.	Avg.
1958–59	22	162	295	.549	79	129	.612	224	10.2	403	18.3
1959–60	26	318	614	.518	183	261	.701	296	11.4	819	31.5
1960–61	28	327	622	.526	176	265	.664	191	6.8	830	29.6
Totals	76	807	1531	.527	438	655	.669	711	9.4	2052	27.0

JOHN STOCKTON
Gonzaga
6-1 – G
Spokane, Wash.

Did not play in NCAA Tournament or NIT.... Member of 1992 U.S. Olympic team.... Selected by the Utah Jazz in first round of 1984 NBA draft (16th pick overall).

Season	G	FGM	FGA	FG%	FTM	FTA	FT%	Reb.	Avg.	Pts.	Avg.
1980–81	25	26	45	.578	26	35	.743	11	0.4	78	3.1
1981–82	27	117	203	.576	69	102	.676	67	2.5	303	11.2
1982–83	27	142	274	.518	91	115	.791	87	3.2	375	13.9
1983–84	28	229	397	.577	126	182	.692	66	2.4	584	20.9
Totals	107	514	919	.559	312	434	.719	231	2.2	1340	12.5

MAURICE STOKES
St. Francis (Pa.)
6-6 – C
Pittsburgh, Pa.

Did not play in NCAA Tournament.... NIT Most Valuable Player in 1955.... Averaged 31 points in six NIT games in 1954 (quarterfinals loser) and 1956 (fourth-place team).... Selected by the Rochester Royals in first round of 1955 NBA draft (2nd pick overall).

Season	G	FGM	FGA	FG%	FTM	FTA	FT%	Reb.	Avg.	Pts.	Avg.
1951–52	30	206	450	.458	93	166	.560			505	16.8
1952–53	18	170	331	.514	77	125	.616	397	22.1	417	23.2
1953–54	26	234	549	.426	132	190	.695	689	26.5	600	23.1
1954–55	28	302	707	.427	156	218	.716	733	26.2	760	27.1
Totals	102	912	2037	.448	458	699	.655	1617		2282	22.4

DAMON STOUDAMIRE
Arizona
5-10 – G
Portland, Ore.

NCAA unanimous first-team All-American in 1995. . . . Ranked 20th in the nation in scoring, 13th in three-point field-goal percentage, 7th in three-point field goals per game with 3.7 and 10th in assists in 1995. . . . Averaged 16.1 points and 5.1 assists in eight NCAA Tournament games from 1992-95 (4-4 record). . . . Selected by the Toronto Raptors in first round of 1995 NBA draft (7th pick overall).

Season	G.	FGM	FGA	FG%	FTM	FTA	FT%	Ast.	Avg.	Pts.	Avg.
1991-92	30	76	167	.455	37	48	.771	76	2.5	217	7.2
1992-93	28	99	226	.438	72	91	.791	159	5.7	309	11.0
1993-94	35	217	484	.448	112	140	.800	208	5.9	639	18.3
1994-95	30	222	466	.476	128	155	.825	220	7.3	684	22.8
Totals	123	614	1343	.457	349	434	.804	663	5.4	1849	15.0

Three-point field goals: 28 of 69 (.406) in 1991-92, 39 of 102 (.382) in 1992-93, 93 of 265 (.351) in 1993-94 and 112 of 241 (.465) in 1994-95. **Totals:** 272 of 677 (.402).

STAN STUTZ
see **Stan Modzelewski**

SID TANNENBAUM
New York University
6-0 – G
Brooklyn, N.Y.

NCAA consensus first-team All-American in 1946 and 1947.... Second-leading scorer for 1945 national runner-up (16-8 record).... Averaged 9.8 points in five NCAA Tournament games in 1945 and 1946 (3-2 record).

Season	G	FGM	FGA	FG%	FTM	FTA	FT%	Reb.	Avg.	Pts.	Avg.
1943–44	16	88			34					210	13.1
1944–45	24	121			60					302	12.6
1945–46	22	113			58					284	12.9
1946–47	21	117			44					278	13.2
Totals	83	439			196					1074	12.9

TOM THACKER
Cincinnati
6-2 – F/G
Covington, Ky.

NCAA consensus first-team All-American in 1963.... Third-leading scorer and rebounder for 1961 NCAA champion (27-3 record), third-leading scorer and second-leading rebounder for 1962 NCAA champion (29-2), and second-leading scorer and rebounder for 1963 national runner-up (26-2).... Member of All-NCAA Tournament team in 1962 and 1963.... Averaged 12 points and 9.3 rebounds in 12 NCAA Tournament games from 1961 to 1963 (11-1 record).... Selected as a territorial pick by the Cincinnati Royals in 1963 NBA draft.

Season	G	FGM	FGA	FG%	FTM	FTA	FT%	Reb.	Avg.	Pts.	Avg.
1960–61	30	139	531	.396	91	133	.684	284	9.5	369	12.3
1961–62	31	134	331	.405	74	121	.612	266	8.6	342	11.0
1962–63	28	169	357	.473	103	155	.665	281	10.0	441	15.8
Totals	89	442	1219	.363	268	409	.655	831	9.3	1152	12.9

REGGIE THEUS
UNLV
6-7 – G
Inglewood, Calif.

Fourth-leading scorer and fifth-leading rebounder for 1977 national third-place team (29-3 record).... Averaged 13.9 points and 4.1 rebounds in seven NCAA Tournament games in 1976 and 1977 (5-2 record).... Selected as an undergraduate by the Chicago Bulls in first round of 1978 NBA draft (9th pick overall).

Season	G	FGM	FGA	FG%	FTM	FTA	FT%	Reb.	Avg.	Pts.	Avg.
1975–76	31	68	163	.417	48	60	.800	53	1.7	184	5.9
1976–77	32	178	358	.497	108	132	.818	145	4.5	464	14.5
1977–78	28	181	389	.465	167	207	.807	191	6.8	529	18.9
Totals	91	427	910	.469	323	399	.810	389	4.3	1177	12.9

ISIAH THOMAS
Indiana
6-1 – G
Chicago, Ill.

NCAA unanimous first-team All-American in 1981.... Final Four Most Outstanding Player in 1981.... Led 1981 NCAA champion in scoring and assists (26-9 record).... Averaged 19.7 points and 7.9 assists in seven NCAA Tournament games in 1980 and 1981 (6-1 record).... Member of 1980 U.S. Olympic team.... Selected as an undergraduate by the Detroit Pistons in first round of 1981 NBA draft (2nd pick overall).

Season	G	FGM	FGA	FG%	FTM	FTA	FT%	Reb.	Avg.	Pts.	Avg.
1979–80	29	154	302	.510	115	149	.772	116	4.0	423	14.6
1980–81	34	212	383	.554	121	163	.742	105	3.1	545	16.0
Totals	63	366	685	.534	236	312	.756	221	3.5	968	15.4

KURT THOMAS
Texas Christian
6-9 – F
Dallas, Tex.

Led the nation in scoring and rebounding in 1995. Ranked 58th in the nation in scoring in 1994. Ranked 30th in the nation in blocked shots with 2.4 per game in 1995. . . . Did not play in NCAA Tournament. . . . Did not play in 1992 NIT after sustaining a fractured left tibia. . . . Selected by the Miami Heat in first round of 1995 NBA draft (10th pick overall).

Season	G.	FGM	FGA	FG%	FTM	FTA	FT%	Reb.	Avg.	Pts.	Avg
1990-91	28	8	18	.444	7	14	.500	13	0.5	23	0.8
1991-92	21	58	119	.487	34	51	.667	114	5.4	150	7.1
1992-93	Missed the entire season after suffering a severe leg injury.										
1993-94	27	224	440	.509	98	152	.645	262	9.7	558	20.7
1994-95	27	288	526	.548	202	283	.714	393	14.6	781	28.9
Totals	103	578	1103	.524	341	500	.682	782	7.6	1512	14.7

Three-point field goals: 0 of 2 in 1990-91, 12 of 46 (.261) in 1993-94 and 3 of 12 (.250) in 1994-95. **Totals:** 15 of 60 (.250).

DAVID THOMPSON
North Carolina State
6-4 – F
Shelby, N.C.

Named national player of the year by UPI, USBWA, and NABC in 1975, and by AP in 1974 and 1975.... Naismith Award winner in 1975.... NCAA unanimous first-team All-American in 1973, 1974, and 1975.... Final Four Most Outstanding Player and member of All-NCAA Tournament team in 1974.... Leading scorer and second-leading rebounder for 1974 NCAA champion (30-1 record).... Averaged 24.3 points and 7.3 rebounds in four NCAA Tournament games in 1974 (4-0 record).... Selected as an undergraduate by the Virginia Squires in first round of 1975 ABA draft; rights traded to the Denver Nuggets, July 14, 1975.

Season	G	FGM	FGA	FG%	FTM	FTA	FT%	Reb.	Avg.	Pts.	Avg.
1972–73	27	267	469	.569	132	160	.825	220	8.1	666	24.7
1973–74	31	325	594	.547	155	208	.745	245	7.9	805	26.0
1974–75	28	347	635	.546	144	197	.731	229	8.2	838	29.9
Totals	86	939	1698	.553	431	565	.763	694	8.1	2309	26.8

JOHN (CAT) THOMPSON
Montana State
5-10 – F
St. George, Utah

NCAA consensus first-team All-American in 1929 and 1930.... Elected to Naismith Memorial Basketball Hall of Fame in 1962.

Season	G	FGM	FGA	FG%	FTM	FTA	FT%	Reb.	Avg.	Pts.	Avg.
1926–27	12	69			29					167	13.9
1927–28	38	274			81					629	16.6
1928–29	36	262			73					597	16.6
1929–30	12	45			18					108	9.0

Note: Statistics in 1926–27 and 1929–30 are for conference games only.

MYCHAL THOMPSON
Minnesota
6-10 – F/C
Nassau, Bahamas

NCAA unanimous first-team All-American in 1978 and consensus second-team All-American in 1977.... Did not play in NCAA Tournament or NIT.... Selected by the Portland Trail Blazers in first round of 1978 NBA draft (1st pick overall).

Season	G	FGM	FGA	FG%	FTM	FTA	FT%	Reb.	Avg.	Pts.	Avg.
1974–75	23	114	215	.530	59	78	.756	176	7.7	287	12.5
1975–76	25	264	461	.573	119	171	.696	312	12.5	647	25.9
1976–77	27	251	414	.606	93	132	.705	240	8.9	595	22.0
1977–78	21	194	362	.536	75	119	.630	228	10.9	463	22.0
Totals	96	823	1452	.567	346	500	.692	956	10.0	1992	20.8

ROD THORN
West Virginia
6-4 – F/G
Princeton, W.V.

NCAA consensus second-team All-American in 1962 and 1963.... Averaged 29.3 points and 8.8 rebounds in four NCAA Tournament games in 1962 and 1963 (2-2 record).... Selected by the Baltimore Bullets in first round of 1963 NBA draft.

Season	G	FGM	FGA	FG%	FTM	FTA	FT%	Reb.	Avg.	Pts.	Avg.
1960–61	24	192	416	.462	61	106	.575	299	12.5	445	18.5
1961–62	29	259	586	.442	170	241	.705	351	12.1	688	23.7
1962–63	29	241	557	.433	170	221	.769	262	9.0	652	22.5
Totals	82	692	1559	.444	401	568	.706	912	11.1	1785	21.8

NATE THURMOND
Bowling Green State
6-11 – C
Akron, Ohio

NCAA consensus second-team All-American in 1963.... Averaged 17.5 points and 21 rebounds in four NCAA Tournament games in 1962 and 1963 (1-3 record).... Selected by the San Francisco Warriors in first round of 1963 NBA draft.... Elected to Naismith Memorial Basketball Hall of Fame in 1984.

Season	G	FGM	FGA	FG%	FTM	FTA	FT%	Reb.	Avg.	Pts.	Avg.
1960–61	24	170	427	.398	87	129	.674	449	18.7	427	17.8
1961–62	25	163	358	.455	67	113	.593	394	15.8	393	15.7
1962–63	27	206	466	.442	124	197	.629	452	16.7	536	19.9
Totals	76	539	1251	.431	278	439	.633	1295	17.0	1356	17.8

WAYMAN TISDALE
Oklahoma
6-8 – F
Tulsa, Okla.

NCAA unanimous first-team All-American in 1984 and 1985, and consensus first-team All-American in 1983.... Averaged 22.6 points and 9.6 rebounds in seven NCAA Tournament games from 1983 to 1985 (4-3 record).... Leading rebounder (6.4 rpg) for 1984 U.S. Olympic team.... Selected as an undergraduate by the Indiana Pacers in first round of 1985 NBA draft (2nd pick overall).

Season	G	FGM	FGA	FG%	FTM	FTA	FT%	Reb.	Avg.	Pts.	Avg.
1982–83	33	338	583	.580	134	211	.635	341	10.3	810	24.5
1983–84	34	369	639	.577	181	283	.640	329	9.7	919	27.0
1984–85	37	370	640	.578	192	273	.703	378	10.2	932	25.2
Totals	104	1077	1862	.578	507	767	.661	1048	10.1	2661	25.6

RUDY TOMJANOVICH
Michigan
6-8 – F
Hamtramck, Mich.

Did not play in NCAA Tournament or NIT.... Selected by the San Diego Rockets in first round of 1970 NBA draft (2nd pick overall).

Season	G	FGM	FGA	FG%	FTM	FTA	FT%	Reb.	Avg.	Pts.	Avg.
1967–68	24	210	446	.471	49	78	.628	323	13.5	469	19.5
1968–69	24	269	541	.497	79	131	.603	340	14.2	617	25.7
1969–70	24	286	604	.474	150	200	.750	376	15.7	722	30.1
Totals	72	765	1591	.481	278	409	.680	1039	14.4	1808	25.1

KELLY TRIPUCKA
Notre Dame
6-6 – F/G
Bloomfield, N.J.

NCAA consensus second-team All-American in 1979 and 1981.... Third-leading scorer and rebounder for 1978 national fourth-place team (23-8 record).... Averaged 16 points and 4.8 rebounds in 11 NCAA Tournament games from 1978 to 1981 (6-5 record).... Selected by the Detroit Pistons in first round of 1981 NBA draft (12th pick overall).

Season	G	FGM	FGA	FG%	FTM	FTA	FT%	Reb.	Avg.	Pts.	Avg.
1977–78	31	141	247	.571	80	108	.741	161	5.2	362	11.7
1978–79	29	143	277	.516	129	151	.854	125	4.3	415	14.3
1979–80	23	150	270	.556	115	151	.762	151	6.6	415	18.0
1980–81	29	195	354	.551	137	168	.815	169	5.8	527	18.2
Totals	112	629	1148	.548	461	578	.798	606	5.4	1719	15.3

GERRY TUCKER
Oklahoma
6-4 – C
Winfield, Kans.

NCAA consensus first-team All-American in 1947 and consensus second-team All-American in 1943.... Leading scorer for 1947 national runner-up (24-7 record).... Averaged 16.6 points in five NCAA Tournament games in 1943 and 1947 (3-2 record).

Season	G	FGM	FGA	FG%	FTM	FTA	FT%	Reb.	Avg.	Pts.	Avg.
1941–42	12	71			44					186	15.5
1942–43	26	144			85					373	14.3
1943–44		Military Service (Army)									
1944–45		Military Service (Army)									
1945–46		Military Service (Army)									
1946–47	31	111			103	136	.757			325	10.5
Totals	69	326			232					884	12.8

JACK TWYMAN
Cincinnati
6-6 – F
Pittsburgh, Pa.

Did not play in NCAA Tournament.... Averaged 19.7 points in three NIT games for 1955 third-place finisher (2-1 record).... Selected by the Rochester Royals in second round of 1955 NBA draft (10th pick overall).... Elected to Naismith Memorial Basketball Hall of Fame in 1982.

Season	G	FGM	FGA	FG%	FTM	FTA	FT%	Reb.	Avg.	Pts.	Avg.
1951–52	16	27	83	.325	13	27	.481	55	3.4	67	4.2
1952–53	24	136	323	.421	89	143	.622	362	15.1	361	15.0
1953–54	21	174	443	.393	110	145	.759	347	16.5	458	21.8
1954–55	29	285	628	.454	142	192	.740	478	16.5	712	24.6
Totals	90	622	1477	.421	354	507	.698	1242	13.8	1598	17.8

CHARLIE TYRA
Louisville
6-8 – C
Louisville, Ky.

NCAA consensus first-team All-American in 1957.... Did not play in NCAA Tournament.... NIT Most Valuable Player in 1956.... Averaged 20.2 points in six NIT games in 1954 (first-round loser), 1955 (second-round loser), and 1956 (champion).... Selected by the Detroit Pistons in first round of 1957 NBA draft (2nd pick overall).

Season	G	FGM	FGA	FG%	FTM	FTA	FT%	Reb.	Avg.	Pts.	Avg.
1953–54	13	36	82	.439	13	38	.342	84	6.5	85	6.5
1954–55	27	149	379	.393	100	158	.633	368	13.6	398	14.7
1955–56	29	262	592	.443	166	256	.648	645	22.2	690	23.8
1956–57	26	193	452	.427	169	234	.722	520	20.0	555	21.3
Totals	95	640	1505	.425	448	686	.653	1617	17.0	1728	18.2

PAUL UNRUH
Bradley
6-4 – F
Toulon, Ill.

NCAA unanimous first-team All-American in 1950.... Leading scorer for 1950 national runner-up (32-5 record).... Averaged 9.3 points in three NCAA Tournament games in 1950.... Averaged 16.1 points in eight NIT games in 1947 (first-round loser), 1949 (fourth place), and 1950 (runner-up).... Selected by the Indianapolis Olympians in second round of 1950 NBA draft (did not play in league).

Season	G	FGM	FGA	FG%	FTM	FTA	FT%	Reb.	Avg.	Pts.	Avg.
1946–47	32	156	465	.335	71	115	.617			383	12.0
1947–48	29	176	461	.382	103	157	.656			455	15.7
1948–49	35	202	522	.387	105	156	.673			509	14.5
1949–50	37	189	480	.394	97	149	.651			475	12.8
Totals	133	723	1928	.375	376	577	.652			1822	13.7

WES UNSELD
Louisville
6-7 – C
Louisville, Ky.

NCAA unanimous first-team All-American in 1967 and 1968.... Averaged 20.5 points and 17.5 rebounds in four NCAA Tournament games in 1967 and 1968 (1-3 record).... Collected 35 points and 26 rebounds in one NIT game in 1966.... Selected by the Baltimore Bullets in first round of 1968 NBA draft (2nd pick overall).... Elected to the Naismith Memorial Basketball Hall of Fame in 1987.

Season	G	FGM	FGA	FG%	FTM	FTA	FT%	Reb.	Avg.	Pts.	Avg.
1965–66	26	195	374	.521	128	202	.634	505	19.4	518	19.9
1966–67	28	201	374	.537	121	177	.684	533	19.0	523	18.7
1967–68	28	234	382	.613	177	275	.644	513	18.3	645	23.0
Totals	82	630	1130	.558	426	654	.651	1551	18.9	1686	20.6

JOHN VALLELY
UCLA
6-2 – G
Corona Del Mar, Calif.

Named to All-NCAA Tournament team in 1969 and 1970.... Second-leading scorer for NCAA champion in 1970 (28-2 record) and third-leading scorer for NCAA champion in 1969 (29-1).... Averaged 16.4 points in eight NCAA Tournament games in 1969 and 1970 (8-0 record).... Averaged 23.3 points and 9.7 rebounds in two junior college seasons at Orange Coast (Calif.).... Selected by the Atlanta Hawks in first round of 1970 NBA draft (14th pick overall).

Season	G	FGM	FGA	FG%	FTM	FTA	FT%	Reb.	Avg.	Pts.	Avg.
1968–69	28	116	234	.496	77	102	.755	91	3.3	309	11.0
1969–70	30	192	395	.486	106	147	.721	111	3.7	490	16.3
Totals	58	308	629	.490	183	249	.735	202	3.5	799	13.8

DICK VAN ARSDALE
Indiana
6-5 – F
Indianapolis, Ind.

Did not play in NCAA Tournament or NIT.... Selected by the New York Knicks in third round of 1965 NBA draft (18th pick overall).

Season	G	FGM	FGA	FG%	FTM	FTA	FT%	Reb.	Avg.	Pts.	Avg.
1962–63	24	95	225	.422	102	142	.718	213	8.9	292	12.2
1963–64	24	178	396	.449	179	223	.803	298	12.4	535	22.3
1964–65	24	146	327	.446	121	142	.852	208	8.7	413	17.2
Totals	72	419	948	.442	402	507	.793	719	10.0	1240	17.2

BOB VERGA
Duke
6-0 – G
Sea Girt, N.J.

NCAA consensus first-team All-American in 1967 and consensus second-team All-American in 1966.... Second-leading scorer for national third-place team in 1966.... Averaged 15.5 points in four NCAA Tournament games in 1966 (3-1 record).... Scored 24 points in one NIT game in 1967.... Selected by the Kentucky Colonels in first five rounds of 1967 ABA draft.

Season	G	FGM	FGA	FG%	FTM	FTA	FT%	Reb.	Avg.	Pts.	Avg.
1964–65	25	229	431	.531	76	116	.655	84	3.4	534	21.4
1965–66	28	216	441	.490	87	119	.731	113	4.0	519	18.5
1966–67	27	283	614	.461	139	179	.777	102	3.8	705	26.1
Totals	80	728	1486	.490	302	414	.729	299	3.7	1758	22.0

NEAL WALK
Florida
6-9 – C
Miami Beach, Fla.

Led the nation in rebounding in 1968.... Did not play in NCAA Tournament.... Scored 26 points in one NIT game in 1969.... Selected by the Phoenix Suns in first round of 1969 NBA draft (2nd pick overall).

Season	G	FGM	FGA	FG%	FTM	FTA	FT%	Reb.	Avg.	Pts.	Avg.
1966–67	25	109	210	.519	70	97	.722	206	8.2	288	11.5
1967–68	25	239	507	.471	185	244	.758	494	19.8	663	26.5
1968–69	27	224	449	.499	201	278	.723	464	17.2	649	24.0
Totals	77	572	1166	.491	456	619	.737	1164	15.1	1600	20.8

CHET WALKER
Bradley
6-6 – F
Benton Harbor, Mich.

NCAA unanimous first-team All-American in 1962 and consensus first-team All-American in 1961.... Did not play in NCAA Tournament.... Averaged 23.5 points in four NIT games in 1960 (champion) and 1962 (first-round loser).... Selected by the Syracuse Nationals in second round of 1962 NBA draft (14th pick overall).

Season	G	FGM	FGA	FG%	FTM	FTA	FT%	Reb.	Avg.	Pts.	Avg.
1959–60	29	244	436	.560	144	234	.615	388	13.4	632	21.8
1960–61	26	238	423	.563	180	250	.720	327	12.6	656	25.2
1961–62	26	268	500	.536	151	236	.640	321	12.3	687	26.4
Totals	81	750	1359	.552	475	720	.660	1036	12.8	1975	24.4

JIMMY WALKER
Providence
6-3 – G
Boston, Mass.

NCAA unanimous first-team All-American in 1967 and consensus first-team All-American in 1966.... Led the nation in scoring in 1967.... Averaged 20 points in four NCAA Tournament games in 1965 and 1966 (2-2 record).... Averaged 36.5 points in two NIT games in 1967 (1-1 record).... Selected by the Detroit Pistons in first round of 1967 NBA draft (1st pick overall).

Season	G	FGM	FGA	FG%	FTM	FTA	FT%	Reb.	Avg.	Pts.	Avg.
1964–65	26	211	444	.475	110	143	.769	158	6.1	532	20.5
1965–66	27	248	488	.508	166	215	.772	182	6.7	662	24.5
1966–67	28	323	659	.490	205	256	.801	169	6.0	851	30.4
Totals	81	782	1591	.492	481	614	.783	509	6.3	2045	25.2

KENNY WALKER
Kentucky
6-8 – F
Roberta, Ga.

NCAA unanimous first-team All-American in 1986 and consensus second-team All-American in 1985.... Second-leading scorer and third-leading rebounder for 1984 Final Four team (29-5 record).... Averaged 16.1 points and 5.8 rebounds in 14 NCAA Tournament games from 1983 to 1986 (10-4 record).... Selected by the New York Knicks in first round of 1986 NBA draft (5th pick overall).

Season	G	FGM	FGA	FG%	FTM	FTA	FT%	Reb.	Avg.	Pts.	Avg.
1982–83	31	88	144	.611	51	77	.662	151	4.9	227	7.3
1983–84	34	171	308	.555	80	109	.734	200	5.9	422	12.4
1984–85	31	246	440	.559	218	284	.768	315	10.2	710	22.9
1985–86	36	260	447	.582	201	263	.764	276	7.7	721	20.0
Totals	132	765	1339	.571	550	733	.750	942	7.1	2080	15.8

BILL WALTON
UCLA
6-11 – C
La Mesa, Calif.

NCAA unanimous first-team All-American in 1972, 1973, and 1974.... Named national player of the year by UPI and USBWA in 1972, 1973, and 1974, and by AP in 1972 and 1973.... Naismith Award winner in 1972, 1973, and 1974.... Final Four Most Outstanding Player in 1972 and 1973.... Leading scorer and rebounder for undefeated NCAA champions in 1972 (30-0 record) and

1973 (30-0) and national third-place team in 1974 (26-4).... Member of All-NCAA Tournament team in 1972, 1973, and 1974.... Averaged 21.2 points and 14.7 rebounds in 12 NCAA Tournament games from 1972 to 1974 (11-1 record).... Selected by the Portland Trail Blazers in first round of 1974 NBA draft (1st pick overall).... Elected to Naismith Memorial Basketball Hall of Fame in 1993.

Season	G	FGM	FGA	FG%	FTM	FTA	FT%	Reb.	Avg.	Pts.	Avg.
1971–72	30	238	372	.640	157	223	.704	466	15.5	633	21.1
1972–73	30	277	426	.650	58	102	.569	506	16.9	612	20.4
1973–74	27	232	349	.665	58	100	.580	398	14.7	522	19.3
Totals	87	747	1147	.651	273	425	.642	1370	15.7	1767	20.3

MIKE WARREN
UCLA
5-11 – G
South Bend, Ind.

Named to All-NCAA Tournament team in 1967 and 1968.... Third-leading scorer for NCAA champions in 1967 (30-0 record) and 1968 (29-1).... Averaged 13.6 points and 4.9 rebounds in eight NCAA Tournament games in 1967 and 1968 (8-0 record).... Selected by the Seattle SuperSonics in 14th round of 1968 NBA draft (did not play in league).

Season	G	FGM	FGA	FG%	FTM	FTA	FT%	Reb.	Avg.	Pts.	Avg.
1965–66	26	162	368	.440	108	146	.740	96	3.7	432	16.6
1966–67	30	144	310	.465	94	124	.758	134	4.5	382	12.7
1967–68	30	152	353	.431	58	76	.763	111	3.7	362	12.1
Totals	86	458	1031	.444	260	346	.751	341	4.0	1176	13.7

KERMIT WASHINGTON
American
6-8 – C/F
Washington, D.C.

NCAA consensus second-team All-American in 1973.... Led the nation in rebounding in 1972 and 1973.... One of six players to average more than 20 points and 20 rebounds per game in his career.... Did not play in NCAA Tournament.... Collected 29 points and 15 rebounds in one NIT game in 1973.... Selected by the Los Angeles Lakers in first round of 1973 NBA draft (5th pick overall).

Season	G	FGM	FGA	FG%	FTM	FTA	FT%	Reb.	Avg.	Pts.	Avg.
1970–71	25	173	370	.468	119	183	.650	512	20.5	465	18.6
1971–72	23	193	355	.544	96	144	.667	455	19.8	482	21.0
1972–73	25	211	426	.495	98	132	.742	511	20.4	520	20.8
Totals	73	577	1151	.501	313	459	.682	1478	20.2	1467	20.1

RICHARD WASHINGTON
UCLA
6-10 – F/C
Portland, Ore.

NCAA consensus first-team All-American in 1976.... Leading scorer and second-leading rebounder for national third-place team in 1976 (27-5 record), second-leading scorer and rebounder for 1975 NCAA champion (28-3), and eighth-leading scorer and fifth-leading rebounder for 1974 national third-place team (26-4).... Final Four Most Outstanding Player in 1975.... Member of All-NCAA Tournament team in 1975.... Averaged 16.1 points and 7.6 rebounds in 13 NCAA Tournament games from 1974 to 1976 (12-1 record; did not play in 1974 national semifinal defeat).... Selected as an undergraduate by the Kansas City Kings in first round of 1976 NBA draft (3rd pick overall).

Season	G	FGM	FGA	FG%	FTM	FTA	FT%	Reb.	Avg.	Pts.	Avg.
1973–74	24	41	80	.513	17	34	.500	66	2.8	99	4.1
1974–75	31	204	354	.576	84	116	.724	242	7.8	492	15.9
1975–76	32	276	538	.513	92	125	.736	274	8.6	644	20.1
Totals	87	521	972	.536	193	275	.702	582	6.7	1235	14.2

MAYCE (CHRIS) WEBBER
Michigan
6-9 – F
Detroit, Mich.

NCAA unanimous first-team All-American in 1993.... Leading scorer and rebounder for 1993 NCAA runner-up (31-5 record), and leading rebounder and second-leading scorer for 1992 NCAA runner-up (25-9).... Named to All-NCAA Tournament team in 1992 and 1993.... Averaged 17.9 points, 10.5 rebounds, and 2.7 blocked shots in 12 NCAA Tournament games in 1992 and 1993 (10-2 record).... Selected as an undergraduate by the Orlando Magic in first round of 1993 NBA draft (1st pick overall); draft rights promptly traded to the Golden State Warriors.

Season	G	FGM	FGA	FG%	FTM	FTA	FT%	Reb.	Avg.	Pts.	Avg.
1991–92	34	229	412	.556	56	113	.496	340	10.0	528	15.5
1992–93	36	281	454	.619	101	183	.552	362	10.1	690	19.2
Totals	70	510	866	.589	157	296	.530	702	10.0	1218	17.4

Three-point field goals: 14 of 54 (.259) in 1991–92 and 27 of 80 (.338) in 1992–93. **Totals:** 41 of 134 (.306).

NICK WERKMAN
Seton Hall
6-3 – F
Trenton, N.J.

Led the nation in scoring in 1963.... Did not play in NCAA Tournament or NIT.... Selected by the Boston Celtics in fifth round of 1964 NBA draft (did not play in league).

Season	G	FGM	FGA	FG%	FTM	FTA	FT%	Reb.	Avg.	Pts.	Avg.
1961–62	24	271	563	.481	251	347	.723	413	17.2	793	33.0
1962–63	22	221	502	.440	208	325	.640	278	12.6	650	29.5
1963–64	25	320	734	.436	190	308	.617	345	13.8	830	33.2
Totals	71	812	1799	.451	649	980	.662	1036	14.6	2273	32.0

JERRY WEST
West Virginia
6-3 – G/F
Cabin Creek, W.V.

NCAA unanimous first-team All-American in 1959 and 1960.... Final Four Most Outstanding Player in 1959.... Leading scorer and rebounder for 1959 national runner-up (29-5 record).... Member of All-NCAA Tournament team in 1959.... Averaged 30.6 points and 13.8 rebounds in nine NCAA Tournament games from 1958 to 1960 (6-3 record).... Member of 1960 U.S. Olympic team.... Selected by the Los Angeles Lakers in first round of 1960 NBA draft (2nd pick overall).... Elected to Naismith Memorial Basketball Hall of Fame in 1979.

Season	G	FGM	FGA	FG%	FTM	FTA	FT%	Reb.	Avg.	Pts.	Avg.
1957–58	28	178	359	.496	142	194	.732	311	11.1	498	17.8
1958–59	34	340	656	.518	223	320	.697	419	12.3	903	26.6
1959–60	31	325	645	.504	258	337	.766	510	16.5	908	29.3
Totals	93	843	1660	.508	623	851	.732	1240	13.3	2309	24.8

PAUL WESTPHAL
Southern California
6-4 – G
Redondo Beach, Calif.

Did not play in NCAA Tournament or NIT.... Selected by the Boston Celtics in first round of 1972 NBA draft (10th pick overall).

Season	G	FGM	FGA	FG%	FTM	FTA	FT%	Reb.	Avg.	Pts.	Avg.
1969–70	26	147	277	.531	84	110	.764	68	2.6	378	14.5
1970–71	26	157	328	.479	109	150	.727	84	3.2	423	16.3
1971–72	14	106	219	.484	72	95	.758	74	5.3	284	20.3
Totals	66	410	824	.498	265	355	.746	226	3.4	1085	16.4

JO JO WHITE
Kansas
6-3 – G
St. Louis, Mo.

NCAA consensus second-team All-American in 1968 and 1969.... Averaged 17.3 points and 6.5 rebounds in four NCAA Tournament games in 1966 and 1967 (2-2 record).... Averaged 13.8 points and 3.5 rebounds in four NIT games for 1968 runner-up.... Member of 1968 U.S. Olympic team.... Selected by the Boston Celtics in first round of 1969 NBA draft (9th pick overall).

Season	G	FGM	FGA	FG%	FTM	FTA	FT%	Reb.	Avg.	Pts.	Avg.
1965–66	9	44	112	.393	14	26	.538	68	7.6	102	11.3
1966–67	27	170	416	.409	59	72	.819	150	5.6	399	14.8
1967–68	30	188	462	.407	83	115	.722	107	3.6	459	15.3
1968–69	18	134	286	.469	58	79	.734	84	4.7	326	18.1
Totals	84	536	1276	.420	214	292	.733	409	4.9	1286	15.3

SIDNEY WICKS
UCLA
6-8 – F/C
Los Angeles, Calif.

Named national player of the year by USBWA in 1971.... NCAA unanimous first-team All-American in 1971 and consensus second-team All-American in 1970.... Leading scorer and rebounder for NCAA champions in 1970 (28-2 record) and 1971 (29-1).... Fourth-leading scorer and third-leading rebounder for 1969 NCAA champion (29-1).... Final Four Most Outstanding Player in 1970.... Member of All-NCAA Tournament team in 1970 and 1971.... Averaged 13.3 points and 9.3 rebounds in 12 NCAA Tournament games from 1969 to 1971 (12-0 record).... Averaged 26 points and 19.5 rebounds in one season of junior college basketball at Santa Monica Community College.... Selected by the Portland Trail Blazers in first round of 1971 NBA draft (2nd pick overall).

Season	G	FGM	FGA	FG%	FTM	FTA	FT%	Reb.	Avg.	Pts.	Avg.
1968–69	30	84	193	.435	58	100	.580	153	5.1	226	7.5
1969–70	30	221	415	.533	117	185	.632	357	11.9	559	18.6
1970–71	30	244	466	.524	150	227	.661	384	12.8	638	21.3
Totals	90	549	1074	.511	325	512	.635	894	9.9	1423	15.8

MURRAY WIER
Iowa
5-9 – G
Muscatine, Iowa

NCAA consensus first-team All-American in 1948.... Led the nation in scoring in 1948.... Did not play in NCAA Tournament.... Selected by the Tri-Cities Blackhawks in 1948 NBL draft.

Season	G	FGM	FGA	FG%	FTM	FTA	FT%	Reb.	Avg.	Pts.	Avg.
1944–45	17	58			18	33	.545			134	7.9
1945–46	18	57			39	62	.629			153	8.5
1946–47	18	105	348	.302	62	93	.667			272	15.1
1947–48	19	152	429	.354	95	136	.699			399	21.0
Totals	72	372			214	324	.660			958	13.3

LENNY WILKENS
Providence
6-1 – G
Brooklyn, N.Y.

NCAA consensus second-team All-American in 1960.... Did not play in NCAA Tournament.... NIT Most Valuable Player in 1960.... Averaged 20.3 points in eight NIT games in 1959 (fourth place) and 1960 (runner-up).... Selected by the St. Louis Hawks in first round of 1960 NBA draft.... Elected to Naismith Memorial Basketball Hall of Fame in 1988.

Season	G	FGM	FGA	FG%	FTM	FTA	FT%	Reb.	Avg.	Pts.	Avg.
1957–58	24	137	316	.434	84	130	.646	190	7.9	358	14.9
1958–59	27	167	390	.428	89	144	.618	188	7.0	423	15.7
1959–60	29	157	362	.434	98	140	.700	205	7.1	412	14.2
Totals	80	461	1068	.432	271	414	.655	583	7.3	1193	14.9

JAMAAL WILKES
see Keith Wilkes

KEITH WILKES
UCLA
6-7 – F
Santa Barbara, Calif.

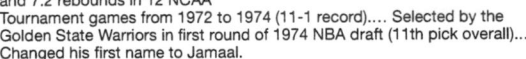
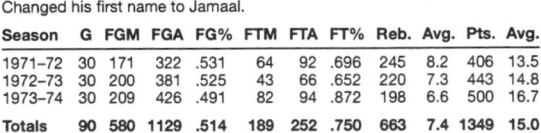

NCAA unanimous first-team All-American in 1974 and consensus first-team All-American in 1973.... Second-leading scorer and rebounder for undefeated 1973 NCAA champion (30-0 record) and 1974 third-place team (26-4).... Third-leading scorer and second-leading rebounder for undefeated 1972 NCAA champion (30-0).... Member of All-NCAA Tournament team in 1972.... Averaged 15 points and 7.2 rebounds in 12 NCAA Tournament games from 1972 to 1974 (11-1 record).... Selected by the Golden State Warriors in first round of 1974 NBA draft (11th pick overall).... Changed his first name to Jamaal.

Season	G	FGM	FGA	FG%	FTM	FTA	FT%	Reb.	Avg.	Pts.	Avg.
1971–72	30	171	322	.531	64	92	.696	245	8.2	406	13.5
1972–73	30	200	381	.525	43	66	.652	220	7.3	443	14.8
1973–74	30	209	426	.491	82	94	.872	198	6.6	500	16.7
Totals	90	580	1129	.514	189	252	.750	663	7.4	1349	15.0

DOMINIQUE WILKINS
Georgia
6-8 – F
Washington, N.C.

Did not play in NCAA Tournament.... Averaged 21.5 points and 9 rebounds in six NIT games in 1981 (second-round loser) and 1982 (semifinals loser).... Selected as an undergraduate by the Utah Jazz in first round of 1982 NBA draft (3rd pick overall).

Season	G	FGM	FGA	FG%	FTM	FTA	FT%	Reb.	Avg.	Pts.	Avg.
1979–80	16	135	257	.525	27	37	.730	104	6.5	297	18.6
1980–81	31	310	582	.533	112	149	.752	234	7.5	732	23.6
1981–82	31	278	526	.529	103	160	.644	250	8.1	659	21.3
Totals	78	723	1365	.530	242	346	.699	588	7.5	1688	21.6

RICHARD (BUZZ) WILKINSON
Virginia
6-2 – G
Pineville, W. Va.

Ranked among the nation's leading scorers in 1953 (16th), 1954 (3rd) and 1955 (2nd). . . . Did not play in NCAA Tournament or NIT. . . . Selected by the Celtics in 1955 NBA draft, but his career was shortened by an automobile accident.

Season	G.	FGM	FGA	FG%	FTM	FTA	FT%	Reb.	Avg.	Pts.	Avg.
1952-53	23	188	145		197		.736			521	22.7
1953-54	27	288	767	.375	238	306	.778	174	6.4	814	30.1
1954-55	28	308	740	.416	282	366	.770	178	6.4	898	32.1
Totals	78	784			665					2233	28.6

CHARLES (BUCK) WILLIAMS
Maryland
6-8 – F
Rocky Mount, N.C.

Averaged 16.5 points and 12.5 rebounds in four NCAA Tournament games in 1980 and 1981 (2-2 record).... Averaged 10.5 points and 14 rebounds in two NIT games in 1979.... Selected as an undergraduate by the New Jersey Nets in first round of 1981 NBA draft (3rd pick overall).

Season	G	FGM	FGA	FG%	FTM	FTA	FT%	Reb.	Avg.	Pts.	Avg.
1978–79	30	120	206	.583	60	109	.550	323	10.8	300	10.0
1979–80	24	143	236	.606	85	128	.664	242	10.1	371	15.5
1980–81	31	183	283	.647	116	182	.637	363	11.7	482	15.5
Totals	85	446	725	.615	261	419	.623	928	10.9	1153	13.6

FREEMAN WILLIAMS
Portland State
6-4 – G
Los Angeles, Calif.

NCAA consensus second-team All-American in 1978.... Led the nation in scoring in 1977 and 1978.... Did not play in NCAA Tournament or NIT.... Selected by the Boston Celtics in first round of 1978 NBA draft (8th pick overall).

Season	G	FGM	FGA	FG%	FTM	FTA	FT%	Reb.	Avg.	Pts.	Avg.
1974–75	26	186	435	.428	64	81	.790	89	3.4	436	16.8
1975–76	27	356	781	.456	122	155	.787	111	4.1	834	30.9
1976–77	26	417	838	.498	176	221	.796	126	4.8	1010	38.8
1977–78	27	410	872	.470	149	191	.780	132	4.9	969	35.9
Totals	106	1369	2926	.468	511	648	.789	458	4.3	3249	30.7

REGGIE WILLIAMS
Georgetown
6-7 – F/G
Baltimore, Md.

NCAA unanimous first-team All-American in 1987.... Fourth-leading scorer for 1984 NCAA champion (34-3 record) and 1985 national runner-up (35-3).... Averaged 15.3 points and 5.5 rebounds in 17 NCAA Tournament games from 1984 to 1987 (14-3 record).... Selected by the Los Angeles Clippers in first round of 1987 NBA draft (4th pick overall).

Season	G	FGM	FGA	FG%	FTM	FTA	FT%	Reb.	Avg.	Pts.	Avg.
1983–84	37	130	300	.433	76	99	.768	131	3.5	336	9.1
1984–85	35	168	332	.506	80	106	.755	200	5.7	416	11.9
1985–86	32	227	430	.528	109	149	.732	261	8.2	563	17.6
1986–87	34	284	589	.482	156	194	.804	294	8.6	802	23.6
Totals	138	809	1651	.490	421	548	.768	886	6.4	2117	15.3

Three-point field goals: 78 of 202 (.386) in 1986–87.

GEORGE WILSON
Cincinnati
6-8 – C/F
Chicago, Ill.

Named to All-NCAA Tournament team in 1963.... Fourth-leading scorer and third-leading rebounder for 1962 NCAA champion (29-2 record) and third-leading scorer and leading rebounder for 1963 national runner-up (26-2).... Averaged 13.1 points and 8.9 rebounds in eight NCAA Tournament games in 1962 and 1963 (7-1 record).... Member of 1964 U.S. Olympic team.... Selected as a territorial choice by the Cincinnati Royals in 1964 NBA draft.

Season	G	FGM	FGA	FG%	FTM	FTA	FT%	Reb.	Avg.	Pts.	Avg.
1961–62	31	109	216	.505	67	101	.663	248	8.0	285	9.2
1962–63	28	160	299	.535	101	170	.594	314	11.2	421	15.0
1963–64	26	164	343	.478	90	173	.520	326	12.5	418	16.1
Totals	85	433	858	.505	258	444	.581	888	10.4	1124	13.2

LES WITTE
Wyoming
6-0 – F
Lincoln, Nebr.

NCAA consensus first-team All-American in 1932 and 1934.

Season	G	FGM	FGA	FG%	FTM	FTA	FT%	Reb.	Avg.	Pts.	Avg.
1930–31	23									274	11.9
1931–32	20									238	11.9
1932–33	23									234	10.2
1933–34	27									323	12.0
Totals	93									1069	11.5

JOHN WOODEN
Purdue
5-10 – G
Martinsville, Ind.

NCAA consensus first-team All-American in 1930, 1931, and 1932.... Elected to Naismith Memorial Basketball Hall of Fame as a player in 1960.

Season	G	FGM	FGA	FG%	FTM	FTA	FT%	Reb.	Avg.	Pts.	Avg.
1929–30	13	45			26					116	8.9
1930–31	17	53			34	49	.694			140	8.2
1931–32	18	79			61	86	.709			219	12.2
Totals	48	177			121					475	9.9

Reggie Lewis (center) holds up his new jersey after the Boston Celtics selected him as their first pick in the 1987 NBA draft; Celtics president Red Auerbach (left) looks on. Lewis was a college star in the Celtics' backyard, scoring over 2700 points for Northeastern University. Tragedy struck in July 1993 when Lewis died of a heart attack after tests revealed he had a heart condition.

JAMES WORTHY
North Carolina
6-9 – F
Gastonia, N.C.

NCAA consensus first-team All-American in 1982.... Final Four Most Outstanding Player in 1982.... Leading scorer and second-leading rebounder for 1982 NCAA champion (32-2 record).... Third-leading scorer and leading rebounder for 1981 national runner-up (29-8).... Averaged 15.3 points and 5.5 rebounds in 10 NCAA Tournament games in 1981 and 1982 (9-1 record).... Selected as an undergraduate by the Los Angeles Lakers in first round of 1982 NBA draft (1st pick overall).

Season	G	FGM	FGA	FG%	FTM	FTA	FT%	Reb.	Avg.	Pts.	Avg.
1979–80	14	74	126	.587	27	45	.600	104	7.4	175	12.5
1980–81	36	208	416	.500	96	150	.640	301	8.4	512	14.2
1981–82	34	203	354	.573	126	187	.674	215	6.3	532	15.6
Totals	**84**	**485**	**896**	**.541**	**249**	**382**	**.652**	**620**	**7.4**	**1219**	**14.5**

JEWELL YOUNG
Purdue
6-0 – F
Lafayette, Ind.

NCAA consensus first-team All-American in 1937 and 1938.

Season	G	FGM	FGA	FG%	FTM	FTA	FT%	Reb.	Avg.	Pts.	Avg.
1935–36	20	74			29	43	.674			177	8.9
1936–37	20	97			49	65	.754			243	12.2
1937–38	20	117			55	73	.753			289	14.5
Totals	**60**	**288**			**133**	**181**	**.735**			**709**	**11.8**

10

COACH DIRECTORY

Determining the greatest coaches in college basketball history is an inexact science. Actually, many of the most efficient coaches toiled in anonymity at obscure schools with inferior talent. Nonetheless, here is a look at the achievements of major-college coaches who met any of the following criteria:

- At least one NCAA championship team.

- Directed two or more teams to the Final Four.

- Total of 600 victories (minimum of 20 seasons in Division I).

- Won more than two-thirds of games in career with at least 20 years in Division I.

- At least 10 NCAA Tournament appearances or 20 NCAA playoff decisions.

- Named to Naismith Memorial Basketball Hall of Fame with more than 200 major-college victories.

- Directed at least six teams to the Top 20 of a final wire-service poll or at least three teams to the Top 10 of a final wire-service poll.

JIM BOEHEIM
Syracuse '66
Lyons, N.Y.

Coach of 1987 and 1996 NCAA Tournament runner-up. . . . Coach of 1981 NIT runner-up. . . . Coach of three Big East Tournament champions–1981, 1988 and 1992. . . . Assistant coach at Syracuse under Roy Danforth for seven seasons from 1970-76.

Year	School	Overall	League	Finish	Postseason
76–77	Syracuse	26-4			NCAA (1-1)
77–78	Syracuse	22-6			NCAA (0-1)
78–79	Syracuse	26-4			NCAA (1-1)
79–80	Syracuse	26-4	5-1	T1st (Big East)	NCAA (1-1)
80–81	Syracuse	22-12	6-8	6th (Big East)	NIT (4-1)
81–82	Syracuse	16-13	7-7	T5th (Big East)	NIT (1-1)
82–83	Syracuse	21-10	9-7	5th (Big East)	NCAA (1-1)
83–84	Syracuse	23-9	12-4	T2d (Big East)	NCAA (1-1)
84–85	Syracuse	22-9	9-7	T3d (Big East)	NCAA (1-1)
85–86	Syracuse	26-6	14-2	T1st (Big East)	NCAA (1-1)
86–87	Syracuse	31-7	12-4	T1st (Big East)	NCAA (5-1)
87–88	Syracuse	26-9	11-5	2d (Big East)	NCAA (1-1)
88–89	Syracuse	30-8	10-6	3d (Big East)	NCAA (3-1)
89–90	Syracuse	26-7	12-4	T1st (Big East)	NCAA (2-1)
90–91	Syracuse	26-6	12-4	1st (Big East)	NCAA (0-1)
91–92	Syracuse	22-10	10-8	T5th (Big East)	NCAA (1-1)
92–93	Syracuse	20-9	10-8	3d (Big East)	Probation
93–94	Syracuse	23-7	13-5	2d (Big East)	NCAA (2-1)
94–95	Syracuse	20-10	12-6	3rd (Big East)	NCAA (1-1)
95–96	Syracuse	29-9	12-6	2nd (Big East 7)	NCAA (5-1)

20-Year Coaching Record: 483-159 (.752) at Syracuse; 176-92 (.657) in Big East; 26-14 (.650) in Big East Tournament; 27-17 (.614) in NCAA Tournament; 5-2 (.714) in NIT.

DALE BROWN
Minot St. '57
Minot, N.D.

Guided LSU to Final Four appearances in 1981 (4th) and 1986 (T-3rd). . . . Second-winningest coach in SEC history (behind Adolph Rupp) in both overall and SEC games. . . . Led Tigers to 15 consecutive postseason tournaments (1979-93). . . . Coach of 1980 SEC Tournament champion. . . . Assistant coach on Ladell Andersen's staff at Utah State (1966-71) before a one-year stint under Marv Harshman at Washington State (1971-72).

Year	School	Overall	League	Finish	Postseason
72–73	LSU	14-10	9-9	5th (SEC)	DNP
73–74	LSU	12-14	6-12	8th (SEC)	DNP
74–75	LSU	10-16	6-12	7th (SEC)	DNP
75–76	LSU	12-14	5-13	9th (SEC)	DNP
76–77	LSU	15-12	8-10	5th (SEC)	DNP
77–78	LSU	18-9	12-6	2d (SEC)	DNP
78–79	LSU	23-6	14-4	1st (SEC)	NCAA (1-1)
79–80	LSU	26-6	14-4	2d (SEC)	NCAA (2-1)
80–81	LSU	31-5	17-1	1st (SEC)	NCAA (3-2)
81–82	LSU	14-14	11-7	T4th (SEC)	NIT (0-1)
82–83	LSU	19-13	10-8	T2d (SEC)	NIT (0-1)
83–84	LSU	18-11	11-7	T3d (SEC)	NCAA (0-1)
84–85	LSU	19-10	13-5	1st (SEC)	NCAA (0-1)
85–86	LSU	26-12	9-9	5th (SEC)	NCAA (4-1)
86–87	LSU	24-15	8-10	T6th (SEC)	NCAA (3-1)
87–88	LSU	16-14	10-8	T4th (SEC)	NCAA (0-1)
88–89	LSU	20-12	11-7	T4th (SEC)	NCAA (0-1)
89–90	LSU	23-9	12-6	T2d (SEC)	NCAA (1-1)
90–91	LSU	20-10	13-5	T1st (SEC)	NCAA (0-1)
91–92	LSU	21-10	12-4	2d-W (SEC)	NCAA (1-1)
92–93	LSU	22-10	9-7	2d-W (SEC)	NCAA (0-1)
93–94	LSU	11-16	5-11	5th-W (SEC)	DNP
94–95	LSU	12-15	6-10	5th (SEC West)	DNP
95–96	LSU	12-17	4-12	6th (SEC West)	DNP

24-Year Coaching Record: 438-281 (.609) at LSU; 235-187 (.557) in Southeastern Conference; 12-17 (.414) in SEC Tournament; 15-14 (.517) in NCAA Tournament; 0-2 in NIT.

JIM CALHOUN
American International '67
Braintree, Mass.

Coach of 1988 NIT champion. . . . Coach of five North Atlantic Conference Tournament champions–1981, 1982, 1984, 1985 and 1986. . . . Coach of two Big East Tournament champions–1990 and 1996. . . . Assistant coach at his alma mater for two seasons (1966-67 and 1967-68).

Year	School	Overall	League	Finish	Postseason
72–73	Northeastern	19-7	–	–	DNP
73–74	Northeastern	14-11	–	–	DNP
74–75	Northeastern	12-12	–	–	DNP
75–76	Northeastern	12-13	–	–	DNP
76–77	Northeastern	12-14	–	–	DNP
77–78	Northeastern	14-12	–	–	DNP
78–79	Northeastern	13-13	–	–	DNP
79–80	Northeastern	19-8	–	–	DNP
80–81	Northeastern	24-6		NCAA	(1-1)
81–82	Northeastern	23-7	8-1	1st (NAC)	NCAA (1-1)
82–83	Northeastern	13-15	4-6	6th (NAC)	DNP
83–84	Northeastern	27-5	14-0	1st (NAC)	NCAA (1-1)
84–85	Northeastern	22-9	13-3	T1st (NAC)	NCAA (0-1)
85–86	Northeastern	26-5	16-2	1st (NAC)	NCAA (0-1)
86–87	Connecticut	9-19	3-13	T8th (Big East)	DNP
87–88	Connecticut	20-14	4-12	9th (Big East)	NIT (5-0)
88–89	Connecticut	18-13	6-10	T7th (Big East)	NIT (2-1)
89–90	Connecticut	31-6	12-4	T1st (Big East)	NCAA (3-1)
90–91	Connecticut	20-11	9-7	T3rd (Big East)	NCAA (2-1)
91–92	Connecticut	20-10	10-8	T5th (Big East)	NCAA (1-1)
92–93	Connecticut	15-13	9-9	T4th (Big East)	NIT (0-1)
93–94	Connecticut	29-5	16-2	1st (Big East) NCAA (2-1)
94–95	Connecticut	28-5	16-2	1st (Big East)	NCAA (3-1)
95–96	Connecticut	32-3	17-1	1st (Big East 6)	NCAA (2-1)

24-Year Coaching Record: 472-236 (.667) overall; 250-137 (.646) in 14 years at Northeastern; 222-99 (.692) in first 10 years at Connecticut; 55-12 (.821) in five years in North Atlantic Conference; 102-68 (.600) in Big East Conference; 13-2 (.867) in NAC Tournament; 10-8 (.556) in Big East Tournament; 16-11 (.593) in NCAA Tournament; 7-2 in NIT (.778).

GALE CATLETT
West Virginia '63
Hedgesville, W.V.

Winningest coach in West Virginia and Atlantic 10 Conference history. . . . Directed West Virginia to NIT semifinals (4th) in 1981. . . . Coached Cincinnati to two Metro Tournament titles (1976 and 1977). . . . Directed West Virginia to back-to-back Atlantic 10 Tournament championships in 1983 and 1984. . . . Assistant coach under Richmond's Lew Mills, Davidson's Lefty Driesell, Kansas' Ted Owens and Kentucky's Adolph Rupp.

Year	School	Overall	League	Finish	Postseason
72–73	Cincinnati	17-9			DNP
73–74	Cincinnati	19-8			NIT (0-1)
74–75	Cincinnati	23-6			NCAA (2-1)
75–76	Cincinnati	25-6	2-1	(Metro 6)	NCAA (0-1)
76–77	Cincinnati	25-5	4-2	2d (Metro 7)	NCAA (0-1)
77–78	Cincinnati	17-10	6-6	T4th (Metro 7)	DNP
78–79	West Va.	16-12	7-3	T2d (East. 8)	DNP
79–80	West Va.	15-14	4-6	7th (East. 8)	DNP
80–81	West Va.	23-10	9-4	3d (East. 8)	NIT (3-2)
81–82	West Va.	27-4	13-1	1st (East. 8)	NCAA (1-1)
82–83	West Va.	23-8	10-4	T1st-W (Atl. 10)	NCAA (0-1)
83–84	West Va.	20-12	9-9	T4th (Atl. 10)	NCAA (1-1)
84–85	West Va.	20-9	9-7	1st (Atl. 10)	NIT (0-1)
85–86	West Va.	22-11	15-3	T2d (Atl. 10)	NCAA (0-1)
86–87	West Va.	23-8	15-3	2d (Atl. 10)	NCAA (0-1)
87–88	West Va.	18-14	12-6	3d (Atl. 10)	NIT (0-1)
88–89	West Va.	26-5	17-1	1st (Atl. 10)	NCAA (1-1)
89–90	West Va.	16-12	11-7	T3d (Atl. 10)	DNP
90–91	West Va.	17-14	10-8	T3d (Atl. 10)	NIT (1-1)
91–92	West Va.	20-12	10-6	3d (Atl. 10)	NCAA (0-1)
92–93	West Va.	17-12	7-7	6th (Atl. 10)	NIT (1-1)
93–94	West Va.	17-12	8-8	T3d (Atl. 10)	NIT (1-1)
94–95	West Va.	13-13	7-9	T6th (Atl. 10)	DNP
95–96	West Va.	12-15	7-11	4th (Big East 6)	DNP

24-Year Coaching Record: 471-241 (.662) overall; 126-44 (.741) in six years at Cincinnati; 345-197 (.637) in first 18 years at West Virginia; 12-9 (.571) in Metro Conference; 180-87 (.674) in Atlantic 10 Conference; 7-11 (.389) in Big East Conference; 5-1 (.833) in Metro Tournament; 21-15 (.583) in Atlantic 10 Tournament; 0-1 in Big East Tournament; 5-10 (.333) in NCAA Tournament; 6-8 (.429) in NIT.

JOHN CHANEY
Bethune-Cookman '55
Philadelphia, Pa.

Earned national coach of the year awards from the USBWA in 1987 and from AP, UPI, NABC and USBWA in 1988. . . . Coach of NCAA Division II champion in 1978 and third-place finisher in 1979. . . . Won four Atlantic 10 Conference Tournament titles (1985, 1987, 1988, 1990).

Year	School	Overall	League	Finish	Postseason
72–73	Cheyney St.	23-5	12-2	1st-E (Pa. Conf.)	NCAA-II (1-1)
73–74	Cheyney St.	19-7	11-1	T1st-E (Pa. Conf.)	DNP
74–75	Cheyney St.	16-9	9-5	2d-E (Pa. Conf.)	DNP
75–76	Cheyney St.	24-5	11-1	1st-E (Pa. Conf.)	NCAA-II (2-1)
76–77	Cheyney St.	20-8	10-2	1st-E (Pa. Conf.)	NCAA-II (1-1)
77–78	Cheyney St.	27-2	12-0	1st-E (Pa. Conf.)	NCAA-II (5-0)
78–79	Cheyney St.	24-7	12-0	1st-E (Pa. Conf.)	NCAA-II (4-1)
79–80	Cheyney St.	23-5	12-0	1st-E (Pa. Conf.)	NCAA-II (1-1)
80–81	Cheyney St.	21-8	9-3	T1st-E (Pa. Conf.)	NCAA-II (1-1)
81–82	Cheyney St.	28-3	11-1	1st-E (Pa. Conf.)	NCAA-II (2-1)
82–83	Temple	14-15	5-9	3d-E (Atl. 10)	DNP
83–84	Temple	26-5	18-0	1st (Atl. 10)	NCAA (1-1)
84–85	Temple	25-6	15-3	2d (Atl. 10)	NCAA (1-1)
85–86	Temple	25-6	15-3	T2d (Atl. 10)	NCAA (1-1)
86–87	Temple	32-4	17-1	1st (Atl. 10)	NCAA (1-1)
87–88	Temple	32-2	18-0	1st (Atl. 10)	NCAA (3-1)
88–89	Temple	18-12	15-3	2d (Atl. 10)	NIT (0-1)
89–90	Temple	20-11	15-3	1st (Atl. 10)	NCAA (0-1)
90–91	Temple	24-10	13-5	2d (Atl. 10)	NCAA (3-1)
91–92	Temple	17-13	11-5	2d (Atl. 10)	NCAA (0-1)
92–93	Temple	20-13	8-6	T2d (Atl. 10)	NCAA (3-1)
93–94	Temple	23-8	12-4	2d (Atl. 10)	NCAA (1-1)
94–95	Temple	19-11	10-6	T2nd (Atl. 10)	NCAA (0-1)
95–96	Temple	20-13	12-4	2nd (A10 East)	NCAA (1-1)

24-Year Coaching Record: 540-188 (.742) overall; 225-59 (.792) in 10 years at Cheyney State; 315-129 (.709) in first 14 years at Temple; 107-17 (.863) in Pennsylvania Conference; 184-52 (.780) in Atlantic 10 Conference; 27-10 (.730) in Atlantic 10 Tournament; 15-12 (.556) in NCAA Division I Tournament; 0-1 in NIT; 18-7 (.720) in NCAA Division II Tournament.

BOBBY CREMINS
South Carolina '70
Bronx, N.Y.

Led Georgia Tech to Final Four appearance in 1990. . . . Naismith national coach of the year in 1990. . . . His three ACC Tournament championships (1985, 1990 and 1993) are second only to Dean Smith's among active ACC coaches. . . . Led Appalachian State to 1979 Southern Conference Tournament title. . . . Served as an assistant coach at Point Park (Pa.) and under Frank McGuire at South Carolina.

Year	School	Overall	League	Finish	Postseason
75–76	Appala. St.	13-14	6-6	5th (Southern)	DNP
76–77	Appala. St.	17-12	8-4	3d (Southern)	DNP
77–78	Appala. St.	15-13	9-3	1st (Southern)	DNP
78–79	Appala. St.	23-6	11-3	1st (Southern)	NCAA (0-1)
79–80	Appala. St.	12-16	6-10	T6th (Southern)	DNP
80–81	Appala. St.	20-9	11-5	T1st (Southern)	DNP
81–82	Ga. Tech	10-16	3-11	8th (ACC)	DNP
82–83	Ga. Tech	13-15	4-10	6th (ACC)	DNP
83–84	Ga. Tech	18-11	6-8	T5th (ACC)	NIT (0-1)
84–85	Ga. Tech	27-8	9-5	T1st (ACC)	NCAA (3-1)
85–86	Ga. Tech	27-7	11-3	2d (ACC)	NCAA (2-1)
86–87	Ga. Tech	16-13	7-7	5th (ACC)	NCAA (0-1)
87–88	Ga. Tech	22-10	8-6	4th (ACC)	NCAA (1-1)
88–89	Ga. Tech	20-12	8-6	5th (ACC)	NCAA (0-1)
89–90	Ga. Tech	28-7	8-6	T3d (ACC)	NCAA (4-1)
90–91	Ga. Tech	17-13	6-8	T5th (ACC)	NCAA (1-1)
91–92	Ga. Tech	23-12	8-8	T4th (ACC)	NCAA (2-1)
92–93	Ga. Tech	19-11	8-8	6th (ACC)	NCAA (0-1)
93–94	Ga. Tech	16-13	7-9	6th (ACC)	NIT (0-1)
94–95	Ga. Tech	18-12	8-8	5th (ACC)	DNP
95–96	Ga. Tech	24-12	13-3	1st (ACC)	NCAA (2-1)

21-Year Coaching Record: 398-242 (.622) overall; 100-70 (.588) in six years at Appalachian State; 298-172 (.634) in first 15 years at Georgia Tech; 51-31 (.622) in Southern Conference; 114-106 (.518) in Atlantic Coast Conference; 10-5 (.667) in Southern Conference Tournament; 15-12 (.556) in ACC Tournament; 15-11 (.577) in NCAA Tournament; 0-2 in NIT.

DENNY CRUM
UCLA '58
San Fernando, Calif.

Reached NCAA Final Four six times–1972 (fourth), 1975 (third), 1980 (champion), 1982 (tied for third), 1983 (tied for third) and 1986 (champion). . . . Coach of 1985 NIT fourth-place team. . . . Coach of 11 Metro Conference Tournament champions–1978, 1980, 1981, 1983, 1986, 1988, 1989, 1990, 1993, 1994 and 1995. . . . Assistant coach at UCLA for six seasons under John Wooden from 1959-'71 sandwiched around six-year stint at Pierce (Calif.) Community College. . . . Elected to Naismith Memorial Basketball Hall of Fame in 1994.

Year	School	Overall	League	Finish	Postseason
71–72	Louisville*	26-5	12-2	T1st (Mo. Valley)	NCAA (2-2)
72–73	Louisville	23-7	11-3	2d (Mo. Valley)	NIT (1-1)
73–74	Louisville	21-7	11-1	1st (Mo. Valley)	NCAA (0-2)
74–75	Louisville	28-3	12-2	1st (Mo. Valley)	NCAA (4-1)
75–76	Louisville	20-8	2-1	(Metro)	NIT (0-1)
76–77	Louisville	21-7	6-1	1st (Metro)	NCAA (0-1)
77–78	Louisville	23-7	9-3	2d (Metro)	NCAA (1-1)
78–79	Louisville	24-8	9-1	1st (Metro)	NCAA (1-1)
79–80	Louisville	33-3	12-0	1st (Metro)	NCAA (5-0)

80–81	Louisville	21-9	11-1	1st (Metro)	NCAA (0-1)
81–82	Louisville	23-10	8-4	T2d (Metro)	NCAA (3-1)
82–83	Louisville	32-4	12-0	1st (Metro)	NCAA (3-1)
83–84	Louisville	24-11	11-3	T1st (Metro)	NCAA (2-1)
84–85	Louisville	19-18	6-8	T4th (Metro)	NIT (3-2)
85–86	Louisville	32-7	10-2	1st (Metro)	NCAA (6-0)
86–87	Louisville	18-14	9-3	1st (Metro)	DNP
87–88	Louisville	24-11	9-3	1st (Metro)	NCAA (2-1)
88–89	Louisville	24-9	8-4	T2d (Metro)	NCAA (2-1)
89–90	Louisville	27-8	12-2	1st (Metro)	NCAA (1-1)
90–91	Louisville	14-16	4-10	8th (Metro)	DNP
91–92	Louisville	19-11	7-5	T2d (Metro)	NCAA (1-1)
92–93	Louisville	22-9	11-1	1st (Metro)	NCAA (2-1)
93–94	Louisville	26-6	10-2	1st (Metro)	NCAA (2-1)
94–95	Louisville	19-14	7-5	T2nd (Metro)	NCAA (0-1)
95–96	Louisville	22-12	10-4	2nd (C-USA White)	NCAA (2-1)

*Won Missouri Valley Conference playoff game against regular-season co-champion Memphis State (83-72) to earn invitation to NCAA Tournament.

25-Year Coaching Record: 585-224 (.723) at Louisville; 46-8 (.852) in four years in Missouri Valley Conference; 173-59 (.746) in 20 years in Metro Conference; 10-4 (.714) in first year in Conference USA; 33-9 (.786) in Metro Conference Tournament; 1-1 (.500) in C-USA Tournament; 39-20 (.661) in NCAA Tournament; 4-4 (.500) in NIT.

TOM DAVIS
Wisconsin-Platteville '60
Ridgeway, Wis.

Named AP national coach of the year in 1987. . . . Assistant coach at Maryland under Lefty Driesell and at American University under Tom Young.

Year	School	Overall	League	Finish	Postseason
71-72	Lafayette	21-6	7-3	T2nd (Mid. Atl./W)	NIT (1-1)
72-73	Lafayette	16-10	7-3	1st (Mid. Atl./W)	DNP
73-74	Lafayette	17-9	7-3	T2nd (Mid. Atl./W)	DNP
74-75	Lafayette	22-6	7-1	1st (ECC/W)	NIT (0-1)
75-76	Lafayette	19-7	9-1	1st (ECC/W)	DNP
76-77	Lafayette	21-6	9-1	1st (ECC/W)	DNP
77-78	Boston Col.	15-11	....	....	DNP
78-79	Boston Col.	21-9	....	....	DNP
79-80	Boston Col.	19-10	2-4	5th (Big East)	NIT (0-1)
80-81	Boston Col.	23-7	10-4	1st (Big East)	NCAA (2-1)
81-82	Boston Col.	22-10	8-6	4th (Big East)	NCAA (3-1)
82-83	Stanford	14-14	6-12	8th (Pac-10)	DNP
83-84	Stanford	19-12	8-10	T5th (Pac-10)	DNP
84-85	Stanford	11-17	3-15	10th (Pac-10)	DNP
85-86	Stanford	14-16	8-10	T5th (Pac-10)	DNP
86-87	Iowa	30-5	14-4	3rd (Big Ten)	NCAA (3-1)
87-88	Iowa	24-10	12-6	T3rd (Big Ten)	NCAA (2-1)
88-89	Iowa	23-10	10-8	4th (Big Ten)	NCAA (1-1)
89-90	Iowa	12-16	4-14	T8th (Big Ten)	DNP
90-91	Iowa	21-11	9-9	T5th (Big Ten)	NCAA (1-1)
91-92	Iowa	19-11	10-8	5th (Big Ten)	NCAA (1-1)
92-93	Iowa	23-9	11-7	T3rd (Big Ten)	NCAA (1-1)
93-94	Iowa	11-16	5-13	T10th (Big Ten)	DNP
94-95	Iowa	21-12	9-9	T7th (Big Ten)	NIT (2-1)
95-96	Iowa	23-9	11-7	4th (Big Ten)	NCAA (1-1)

25-Year Coaching Record: 481-259 (.650) overall; 116-44 (.725) in six years at Lafayette; 100-47 (.680) in five years at Boston College; 58-59 (.496) in four years at Stanford; 207-109 (.655) in first 10 years at Iowa; 46-12 (.793) in Middle Atlantic/East Coast Conference; 20-14 (.588) in Big East Conference; 25-47 (.347) in Pacific-10 Conference; 95-85 (.528) in first 10 years in Big Ten Conference; 1-3 (.250) in Big East Conference Tournament; 15-9 (.625) in NCAA Tournament; 3-4 (.429) in NIT.

CHARLES (LEFTY) DRIESELL
Duke '54
Norfolk, Va.

Coach of 1972 NIT champion. . . . Coach of five conference tournament champions–three in Southern Conference (1966, 1968 and 1969), one in ACC (1984) and one in Colonial Athletic Association (1994).

Year	School	Overall	League	Finish	Postseason
60–61	Davidson	9-14	2-10	9th (Southern)	DNP
61–62	Davidson	14-11	5-6	5th (Southern)	DNP
62–63	Davidson	20-7	8-3	2d (Southern)	DNP
63–64	Davidson	22-4	9-2	1st (Southern)	DNP
64–65	Davidson	24-2	12-0	1st (Southern)	DNP
65–66	Davidson	21-7	11-1	1st (Southern)	NCAA (1-2)
66–67	Davidson	15-12	8-4	2d (Southern)	DNP
67–68	Davidson	24-5	9-1	1st (Southern)	NCAA (2-1)
68–69	Davidson	27-3	9-0	1st (Southern)	NCAA (2-1)
69–70	Maryland	13-13	5-9	6th (ACC)	DNP
70–71	Maryland	14-12	5-9	T6th (ACC)	DNP
71–72	Maryland	27-5	8-4	T2d (ACC)	NIT (4-0)
72–73	Maryland	23-7	7-5	3d (ACC)	NCAA (1-1)
73–74	Maryland	23-5	9-3	T2d (ACC)	DNP
74–75	Maryland	24-5	10-2	1st (ACC)	NCAA (2-1)
75–76	Maryland	22-6	7-5	T2d (ACC)	DNP
76–77	Maryland	19-8	7-5	4th (ACC)	DNP
77–78	Maryland	15-13	3-9	T6th (ACC)	DNP
78–79	Maryland	19-11	6-6	4th (ACC)	NIT (1-1)
79–80	Maryland	24-7	11-3	1st (ACC)	NCAA (1-1)
80–81	Maryland	21-10	8-6	4th (ACC)	NCAA (1-1)
81–82	Maryland	16-13	5-9	5th (ACC)	NIT (1-1)
82–83	Maryland	20-10	8-6	T3d (ACC)	DNP
83–84	Maryland	24-8	9-5	2nd (ACC)	NCAA (1-1)
84–85	Maryland	25-12	8-6	T4th (ACC)	NCAA (2-1)
85–86	Maryland	19-14	6-8	6th (ACC)	NCAA (1-1)
88–89	J. Madison	16-14	6-8	T5th (CAA)	DNP
89–90	J. Madison	20-11	11-3	1st (CAA)	NIT (0-1)
90–91	J. Madison	19-10	12-2	1st (CAA)	NIT (0-1)
91–92	J. Madison	21-11	12-2	T1st (CAA)	NIT (0-1)
92–93	J. Madison	21-9	11-3	T1st (CAA)	NIT (0-1)
93–94	J. Madison	20-10	10-4	T1st (CAA)	NCAA (0-1)
94–95	J. Madison	16-13	9-5	3rd (CAA)	DNP
95–96	J. Madison	10-20	6-10	T6th (CAA)	DNP

34-Year Coaching Record: 667-322 (.674) overall; 176-65 (.730) in nine years at Davidson; 348-159 (.686) in 17 years at Maryland; 143-98 (.593) in first eight years at James Madison; 73-27 (.730) in Southern Conference; 122-100 (.550) in ACC; 77-37 (.675) in Colonial Athletic Association; 15-5 (.750) in Southern Conference Tournament; 17-16 (.515) in ACC Tournament; 11-7 (.611) in CAA Tournament; 15-13 (.536) in NCAA Tournament; 6-6 (.500) in NIT.

STEVE FISHER
Illinois St. '67
Herrin, Ill.

Reached NCAA Final Four three times–1989 (champion), 1992 (runner-up) and 1993 (runner-up). . . . Assistant coach at Western Michigan under Les Wothke for three seasons from 1980-82 and at Michigan under Bill Frieder for seven seasons from 1983-89.

Year	School	Overall	League	Finish	Postseason
88–89	Michigan	6-0*			NCAA (6-0)
89–90	Michigan	23-8	12-6	3d (Big Ten)	NCAA (1-1)
90–91	Michigan	14-15	7-11	8th (Big Ten)	NIT (0-1)
91–92	Michigan	25-9	11-7	3d (Big Ten)	NCAA (5-1)
92–93	Michigan	31-5	15-3	2d (Big Ten)	NCAA (5-1)
93–94	Michigan	24-8	13-5	2d (Big Ten)	NCAA (3-1)
94–95	Michigan	17-14	11-7	3rd (Big Ten)	NCAA (0-1)
95–96	Michigan	20-12	10-8	T5th (Big Ten)	NCAA (0-1)

*Promoted from assistant to head coach just before the start of the 1989 playoffs after Frieder announced he had accepted the head coaching position at Arizona State.

Eight-Year Coaching Record: 160-71 (.693) at Michigan; 79-47 (.627) in Big Ten; 20-6 (.769) in NCAA Tournament; 0-1 in NIT.

BILL FRIEDER
Michigan '64
Saginaw, Mich.

Coach of 1984 NIT champion. . . . Assistant under Johnny Orr for seven years at Michigan.

Year	School	Overall	League	Finish	Postseason
80–81	Michigan	19-11	8-10	7th (Big Ten)	IT (2-1)
81–82	Michigan	8-19	7-11	T7th (Big Ten)	DNP
82–83	Michigan	16-12	7-11	9th (Big Ten)	DNP
83–84	Michigan	24-9	11-7	4th (Big Ten)	NIT (5-0)
84–85	Michigan	26-4	16-2	1st (Big Ten)	NCAA (1-1)
85–86	Michigan	28-5	14-4	1st (Big Ten)	NCAA (1-1)
86–87	Michigan	20-12	10-8	5th (Big Ten)	NCAA (1-1)
87–88	Michigan	26-8	13-5	2nd (Big Ten)	NCAA (2-1)
88–89	Michigan	24-7	12-6	3rd (Big Ten)	NCAA*
89–90	Arizona St.	15-16	6-12	T7th (Pac-10)	NIT (0-1)
90–91	Arizona St.	20-10	10-8	3rd (Pac-10)	NCAA (1-1)
91–92	Arizona St.	19-14	9-9	6th (Pac-10)	NIT (1-1)
92–93	Arizona St.	18-10	11-7	T3rd (Pac-10)	NIT (0-1)
93–94	Arizona St.	15-13	10-8	T4th (Pac-10)	NIT (0-1)
94–95	Arizona St.	24-9	12-6	3rd (Pac-10)	NCAA (2-1)
95–96	Arizona St.	11-16	6-12	8th (Pac-10)	DNP

*Replaced by Michigan assistant Steve Fisher just before the start of the 1989 playoffs after announcing he had accepted the head coaching position at Arizona State.

16-Year Coaching Record: 313-175 (.641) overall; 191-87 (.687) in nine years at Michigan; 122-88 (.581) in first seven years at Arizona State; 98-64 (.605) in Big Ten Conference; 64-62 (.508) in Pacific-10 Conference; 2-1 (.667) in Pacific-10 Tournament; 8-6 (.571) in NCAA Tournament; 8-5 (.615) in NIT.

JIM HARRICK
Charleston '60
Charleston, W.V.

Earned national coach of the year awards from NABC and Naismith in 1995. . . . Coach of NCAA Tournament champion in 1995. . . . Assistant under Dutch Belnap for four years at Utah State and under Gary Cunningham for two years at UCLA.

Year	School	Overall	League	Finish	Postseason
79–80	Pepperdine	17-11	9-7	T5th (WCAC)	NIT (0-1)
80–81	Pepperdine	16-12	11-3	T1st (WCAC)	DNP
81–82	Pepperdine	22-7	14-0	1st (WCAC)	NCAA (1-1)
82–83	Pepperdine	20-9	10-2	1st (WCAC)	NCAA (0-1)
83–84	Pepperdine	15-13	6-6	T4th (WCAC)	DNP
84–85	Pepperdine	23-9	11-1	1st (WCAC)	NCAA (0-1)
85–86	Pepperdine	25-5	13-1	1st (WCAC)	NCAA (0-1)
86–87	Pepperdine	12-18	5-9	7th (WCAC)	DNP
87–88	Pepperdine	17-13	8-6	4th (WCAC)	NIT (0-1)
88–89	UCLA	21-10	13-5	T3d (Pac-10)	NCAA (1-1)
89–90	UCLA	22-11	11-7	4th (Pac-10)	NCAA (2-1)
90–91	UCLA	23-9	11-7	2d (Pac-10)	NCAA (0-1)
91–92	UCLA	28-5	16-2	1st (Pac-10)	NCAA (3-1)
92–93	UCLA	22-11	11-7	T3d (Pac-10)	NCAA (1-1)
93–94	UCLA	21-7	13-5	T2nd (Pac-10)	NCAA (0-1)
94–95	UCLA	31-2	16-2	1st (Pac-10)	NCAA (6-0)
95–96	UCLA	23-8	16-2	1st (Pac-10)	NCAA (0-1)

17-Year Coaching Record: 358-160 (.691) overall; 167-97 (.633) in nine years at Pepperdine; 191-63 (.752) in first eight years at UCLA; 87-35 (.713) in West Coast Athletic Conference; 107-37 (.743) in Pacific-10 Conference; 3-2 (.600) in WCAC Tournament; 3-2 (.600) in Pac-10 Tournament; 14-11 (.560) in NCAA Tournament; 0-2 in NIT.

DON HASKINS
Oklahoma State '53
Enid, Okla.

Coach of 1966 NCAA Tournament champion. . . . Coach of four Western Athletic Conference Tournament champions–1984, 1986, 1989 and 1990. . . . U.S. Olympic team assistant coach in 1972.

Year	School	Overall	League	Finish	Postseason
61–62	Texas West.*	18-6			DNP
62–63	Texas West.*	19-7			NCAA (0-1)
63–64	Texas West.*	25-3			NCAA (2-1)
64–65	Texas West.*	16-9			NIT (0-1)
65–66	Texas West.*	28-1			NCAA (5-0)
66–67	Texas West.*	22-6			NCAA (2-1)
67–68	Texas-El Paso	14-9			DNP
68–69	Texas-El Paso	16-9			DNP
69–70	Texas-El Paso	17-8	10-4	1st (WAC)	NCAA (0-1)
70–71	Texas-El Paso	15-10	9-5	T2d (WAC)	NIT (4-0)
71–72	Texas-El Paso	20-7	9-5	T2d (WAC)	NIT (0-1)
72–73	Texas-El Paso	16-10	6-8	5th (WAC)	DNP
73–74	Texas-El Paso	18-7	8-6	5th (WAC)	DNP
74–75	Texas-El Paso	20-6	10-4	2d (WAC)	NCAA (0-1)
75–76	Texas-El Paso	19-7	9-5	T2d (WAC)	DNP
76–77	Texas-El Paso	11-15	3-11	8th (WAC)	DNP
77–78	Texas-El Paso	10-16	2-12	8th (WAC)	DNP
78–79	Texas-El Paso	11-15	3-9	T6th (WAC)	DNP
79–80	Texas-El Paso	20-8	10-4	T2d (WAC)	NIT (1-1)
80–81	Texas-El Paso	18-12	9-7	4th (WAC)	NIT (1-1)
81–82	Texas-El Paso	20-8	11-5	T2d (WAC)	DNP
82–83	Texas-El Paso	19-10	11-5	T1st (WAC)	NIT (0-1)
83–84	Texas-El Paso	27-4	13-3	1st (WAC)	NCAA (0-1)
84–85	Texas-El Paso	22-10	12-4	1st (WAC)	NCAA (1-1)
85–86	Texas-El Paso	27-6	12-4	1st (WAC)	NCAA (0-1)
86–87	Texas-El Paso	25-7	13-3	1st (WAC)	NCAA (1-1)
87–88	Texas-El Paso	23-10	10-6	4th (WAC)	NCAA (0-1)
88–89	Texas-El Paso	26-7	11-5	T2d (WAC)	NCAA (1-1)
89–90	Texas-El Paso	21-11	10-6	T3d (WAC)	NCAA (0-1)
90–91	Texas-El Paso	16-13	7-9	T5th (WAC)	DNP
91–92	Texas-El Paso	27-7	12-4	T1st (WAC)	NCAA (2-1)
92–93	Texas-El Paso	21-13	10-8	4th (WAC)	NIT (1-1)
93–94	Texas-El Paso	18-12	8-10	T6th (WAC)	DNP
94–95	Texas-El Paso	20-10	13-5	T2nd (WAC)	NIT (1-1)
95–96	Texas-El Paso	13-16	4-14	9th (WAC)	DNP

*School's official name was Texas Western until 1967.

Note: UTEP had a 10-3 record in 1995-96 when he was sidelined for the remainder of the season by a heart ailment.

35-Year Coaching Record: 678-314 (.683) at Texas-El Paso; 5-3 (.625) in Border Conference; 245-173 (.586) in Western Athletic Conference; 21-8 (.724) in WAC Tournament; 14-13 (.519) in NCAA Tournament; 4-7 (.364) in NIT.

BOB HUGGINS
West Virginia '77
Gnadenhutten, O.

Guided Cincinnati to Final Four in 1992. . . . Captured a total of six conference tournaments–one with Akron (OVC in 1986) and five with Cincinnati (all four Great Midwest from 1992 through 1995 and first of Conference USA in 1996). . . . Served as an assistant coach under Joedy Gardner for one season at West Virginia and under Eldon Miller for two seasons at Ohio State.

Year	School	Overall	League	Finish	Postseason
80-81	Walsh (O.)	14-16	9-5	T3rd (Mid-Ohio)	DNP
81-82	Walsh (O.)	23-9	11-3	1st (Mid-Ohio)	DNP
82-83	Walsh (O.)	34-1	14-0	1st (Mid-Ohio)	NAIA (0-1)
84-85	Akron	12-14	6-8	6th (OVC)	DNP
85-86	Akron	22-8	10-4	T1st (OVC)	NCAA (0-1)
86-87	Akron	21-9	9-5	T2nd (OVC)	NIT (0-1)
87-88	Akron	21-7	–	–	DNP
88-89	Akron	21-8	–	–	NIT (0-1)
89-90	Cincinnati	20-14	9-5	T2nd (Metro)	NIT (1-1)
90-91	Cincinnati	18-12	8-6	3rd (Metro)	NIT (1-1)
91-92	Cincinnati	29-5	8-2	T1st (GMC)	NCAA (4-1)
92-93	Cincinnati	27-5	8-2	1st (GMC)	NCAA (3-1)
93-94	Cincinnati	22-10	7-5	4th (GMC)	NCAA (0-1)
94-95	Cincinnati	22-12	7-5	T3rd (GMC)	NCAA (1-0)
95-96	Cincinnati	28-5	11-3	1st (C-USA Blue)	NCAA (3-1)

15-Year Coaching Record: 334-135 (.712) overall; 71-26 (.732) in three years at Walsh (O.); 97-46 (.693) in five years at Akron; 166-63 (.725) in first seven years at Cincinnati; 25-17 (.595) in Ohio Valley Conference; 17-11 (.607) in Metro Conference; 30-14 (.682) in Great Midwest Conference; 11-3 (.786) in Conference USA; 3-1 (.750) in Ohio Valley Tournament; 1-2 (.333) in Metro Tournament; 10-0 (1.000) in Great Midwest Tournament; 3-0 in C-USA Tournament; 11-6 (.647) in NCAA Tournament; 2-4 (.333) in NIT; 0-1 in NAIA Tournament.

GENE KEADY
Kansas State '58
Larned, Kans.

Named national coach of the year by all of the major awards in 1996, by USBWA in 1984 and co-coach of the year (with Nolan Richardson) by the NABC in 1994. . . . Member of National Junior College Basketball Hall of Fame (as player and coach). Compiled 187-48 record (.796) in eight seasons at Hutchinson (Kan.) Community College. . . . Guided three Purdue teams to NIT semifinal round–1981 (3rd), 1982 (2nd) and 1993 (4th). . . . Assistant coach at Arkansas under Eddie Sutton for four seasons from 1975-78.

Year	School	Overall	League	Finish	Postseason
78–79	Western Ky.	17-11	7-5	T2d (OVC)	DNP
79–80	Western Ky.	21-8	10-2	T1st (OVC)	NCAA (0-1)
80–81	Purdue	21-11	10-8	4th (Big Ten)	NIT (4-1)
81–82	Purdue	18-14	11-7	5th (Big Ten)	NIT (4-1)
82–83	Purdue	21-9	11-7	T2d (Big Ten)	NCAA (1-1)
83–84	Purdue	22-7	15-3	T1st (Big Ten)	NCAA (0-1)
84–85	Purdue	20-9	11-7	T3d (Big Ten)	NCAA (0-1)
85–86	Purdue	25-10	11-7	T4th (Big Ten)	NCAA (1-1)
86–87	Purdue	25-5	15-3	T1st (Big Ten)	NCAA (2-1)
87–88	Purdue	29-4	16-2	1st (Big Ten)	NCAA (2-1)
88–89	Purdue	15-16	8-10	T6th (Big Ten)	DNP
89–90	Purdue	22-8	13-5	2d (Big Ten)	NCAA (1-1)
90–91	Purdue	17-12	9-9	T5th (Big Ten)	NCAA (0-1)
91–92	Purdue	18-15	8-10	T6th (Big Ten)	NIT (2-1)
92–93	Purdue	18-10	9-9	T5th (Big Ten)	NCAA (0-1)
93–94	Purdue	29-5	14-4	1st (Big Ten)	NCAA (3-1)
94–95	Purdue	25-7	15-3	1st (Big Ten)	NCAA (1-1)
95–96	Purdue	26-6	15-3	1st (Big Ten)	NCAA (1-1)

18-Year Coaching Record: 386-167 (.698) overall; 38-19 (.667) in two years at Western Kentucky; 348-148 (.702) in first 16 years at Purdue; 17-7 (.708) in Ohio Valley Conference; 191-97 (.663) in Big Ten Conference; 10-13 (.435) In NCAA Tournament; 10-3 (.769) in NIT.

BOB KNIGHT
Ohio St. '62
Orrville, Ohio

Named national coach of the year by NABC in 1975; by AP and USBWA in 1976, 1976 and 1989; by UPI in 1976 and 1989, and by Naismith in 1987. . . . Reached NCAA Final Four five times–1973 (third), 1976 (champion), 1981 (champion), 1987 (champion) and 1992 (tied for third). . . . Coach of five NIT semifinalists–1966 (fourth), 1969 (fourth), 1970 (third), 1979 (champion) and 1985 (runner-up). . . . Coach of 1974 Collegiate Commissioners Association Tournament champion. . . . Winningest coach in Big Ten Conference history. . . . U.S. Olympic team coach in 1984. . . . Assistant coach at Army under Tates Locke for two seasons (1963-64 and 1964-65). . . . Elected to Naismith Memorial Basketball Hall of Fame in 1990.

Year	School	Overall	League	Finish	Postseason
65–66	Army	18-8			NIT (2-2)
66–67	Army	13-8			DNP
67–68	Army	20-5			NIT (0-1)
68–69	Army	18-10			NIT (2-2)
69–70	Army	22-6			NIT (3-1)
70–71	Army	11-13			DNP
71–72	Indiana	17-8	9-5	T3d (Big Ten)	NIT (0-1)
72–73	Indiana	22-6	11-3	1st (Big Ten)	NCAA (3-1)
73–74	Indiana	23-5	12-2	T1st (Big Ten)	CCA (3-0)
74–75	Indiana	31-1	18-0	1st (Big Ten)	NCAA (2-1)
75–76	Indiana	32-0	18-0	1st (Big Ten)	NCAA (5-0)
76–77	Indiana*	14-13	9-9	5th (Big Ten)	DNP
77–78	Indiana	21-8	12-6	T2d (Big Ten)	NCAA (1-1)
78–79	Indiana	22-12	10-8	5th (Big Ten)	NIT (4-0)
79–80	Indiana	21-8	13-5	1st (Big Ten)	NCAA (1-1)
80–81	Indiana	26-9	14-4	1st (Big Ten)	NCAA (5-0)
81–82	Indiana	19-10	12-6	T2d (Big Ten)	NCAA (1-1)
82–83	Indiana	24-6	13-5	1st (Big Ten)	NCAA (1-1)
83–84	Indiana	22-9	13-5	3d (Big Ten)	NCAA (2-1)
84–85	Indiana	19-14	7-11	7th (Big Ten)	NIT (4-1)
85–86	Indiana	21-8	13-5	2d (Big Ten)	NCAA (0-1)
86–87	Indiana	30-4	15-3	T1st (Big Ten)	NCAA (6-0)
87–88	Indiana	19-10	11-7	5th (Big Ten)	NCAA (0-1)
88–89	Indiana	27-8	15-3	1st (Big Ten)	NCAA (2-1)
89–90	Indiana	18-11	8-10	7th (Big Ten)	NCAA (0-1)
90–91	Indiana	29-5	15-3	T1st (Big Ten)	NCAA (2-1)

Future coaching success stories: Mike Krzyzewski

Year	School	Overall	League	Finish	Postseason
91–92	Indiana	27-7	14-4	2d (Big Ten)	NCAA (4-1)
92–93	Indiana	31-4	17-1	1st (Big Ten)	NCAA (3-1)
93–94	Indiana	21-9	12-6	3d (Big Ten)	NCAA (2-1)
94–95	Indiana	19-12	11-7	T3rd (Big Ten)	NCAA (0-1)
95–96	Indiana	19-12	12-6	T2nd (Big Ten)	NCAA (0-1)

*Overall record is 16-11 and Big Ten mark is 11-7 in fourth place if include two forfeit victories awarded from Minnesota after the season.

31-Year Coaching Record: 676-249 (.731) overall; 102-50 (.671) in six years at Army; 574-199 (.743) in first 25 years at Indiana; 314-124 (.717) in Big Ten; 40-17 (.702) in NCAA Tournament; 15-8 (.652) in NIT; 3-0 in Collegiate Commissioners Association Tournament.

MIKE KRZYZEWSKI
Army '69
Chicago, Ill.

UPI national coach of the year in 1986. . . . Naismith national coach of the year in 1989 and NABC national coach of the year in 1991. . . . Coach of 1991 and 1992 NCAA champions. . . . Reached NCAA Final Four seven times in nine years from 1986-94. . . . Coach of three ACC Tournament champions–1986, 1988 and 1992. . . . U.S. Olympic team assistant coach in 1992. . . . Assistant coach at Indiana under Bob Knight for one season in 1974-75.

Year	School	Overall	League	Finish	Postseason
75–76	Army	11-14			DNP
76–77	Army	20-8			DNP
77–78	Army	19-9			NIT (0-1)
78–79	Army	14-11			DNP
79–80	Army	9-17			DNP
80–81	Duke	17-13	6-8	6th (ACC)	NIT (2-1)
81–82	Duke	10-17	4-10	T6th (ACC)	DNP
82–83	Duke	11-17	3-11	7th (ACC)	DNP
83–84	Duke	24-10	7-7	3d (ACC)	NCAA (0-1)
84–85	Duke	23-8	8-6	4th (ACC)	NCAA (1-1)
85–86	Duke	37-3	12-2	1st (ACC)	NCAA (5-1)
86–87	Duke	24-9	9-5	3d (ACC)	NCAA (2-1)
87–88	Duke	28-7	9-5	3d (ACC)	NCAA (4-1)
88–89	Duke	28-8	9-5	T2d (ACC)	NCAA (4-1)
89–90	Duke	29-9	9-5	2d (ACC)	NCAA (5-1)
90–91	Duke	32-7	11-3	1st (ACC)	NCAA (6-0)
91–92	Duke	34-2	14-2	1st (ACC)	NCAA (6-0)
92–93	Duke	24-8	10-6	T3d (ACC)	NCAA (1-1)
93–94	Duke	28-5	12-4	1st (ACC)	NCAA (5-1)
94–95	Duke*	9-3	0-1	9th (ACC)	DNP
95–96	Duke	18-13	8-8	T4th (ACC)	NCAA (0-1)

*Missed the last 19 games of 1994-95 season because of a back ailment.

21-Year Coaching Record: 449-198 (.694) overall; 73-59 (.553) in five years at Army; 376-139 (.730) in first 16 years at Duke; 131-88 (.598) in ACC; 17-12 (.586) in ACC Tournament; 39-10 (.796) in NCAA Tournament; 2-2 (.500) in NIT.

ROLLIE MASSIMINO
Vermont '56
Hillside, N.J.

Coach of NCAA national champion in 1985. . . . Coach of 1977 NIT third-place team. . . . Coach of two Eastern Athletic Association Tournament champions–1978 and 1980. . . . Assistant coach at Penn under Chuck Daly for three seasons from 1972-'74. . . . New coach at Cleveland State.

Year	School	Overall	League	Finish	Postseason
69–70	Stony Brook	19-6	9-0	1st (K'bocker)	NCAA-III (0-1)
70–71	Stony Brook	15-10	7-2	T2d (K'bocker)	DNP
73–74	Villanova	7-19			DNP
74–75	Villanova	9-18			DNP
75–76	Villanova	16-11			DNP
76–77	Villanova	23-10	6-1	2d (ECBL East)	NIT (3-1)
77–78	Villanova	23-9	7-3	T1st (East. 8)	NCAA (2-1)
78–79	Villanova	15-13	9-1	1st (East. 8)	DNP
79–80	Villanova	23-8	7-3	T1st (East. 8)	NCAA (1-1)
80–81	Villanova	20-11	8-6	T3d (Big East)	NCAA (1-1)
81–82	Villanova	24-8	11-3	1st (Big East)	NCAA (2-1)
82–83	Villanova	24-8	12-4	T1st (Big East)	NCAA (2-1)
83–84	Villanova	19-12	12-4	T2d (Big East)	NCAA (1-1)
84–85	Villanova	25-10	9-7	T3d (Big East)	NCAA (6-0)
85–86	Villanova	23-14	10-6	4th (Big East)	NCAA (1-1)
86–87	Villanova	15-16	6-10	6th (Big East)	NIT (0-1)
87–88	Villanova	24-13	9-7	T3d (Big East)	NCAA (3-1)
88–89	Villanova	18-16	7-9	5th (Big East)	NIT (2-1)
89–90	Villanova	18-15	8-8	T5th (Big East)	NCAA (0-1)
90–91	Villanova	17-15	7-9	T7th (Big East)	NCAA (1-1)
91–92	Villanova	14-15	11-7	4th (Big East)	NIT (0-1)
92–93	UNLV	21-8	13-5	2d (Big West)	NIT (0-1)
93–94	UNLV	15-12	10-8	T5th (Big West)	DNP

23-Year Coaching Record: 425-276 (.606) overall; 34-16 (.680) in two years at SUNY-Stony Brook; 357-241 (.597) in 19 years at Villanova; 36-20 (.643) in first two years at UNLV; 16-2 (.889) in two years in Knickerbocker Conference; 29-8 (.784) in four years in Eastern 8 Conference; 110-80 (.579) in 12 years in Big East Conference; 23-13 (.639) in Big West Conference; 9-2 (.818) in Eastern 8 Tournament; 13-12 (.520) in Big East Tournament; 2-2 (.500) in Big West Tournament; 0-1 in NCAA Division III Tournament; 20-10 (.667) in NCAA Division I Tournament; 5-5 (.500) in NIT.

ROBERT (LUTE) OLSON
Augsburg (Minn.) '57
Mayville, N.D.

Named national coach of the year by NABC in 1980. . . . Reached NCAA Final Four three times–1980 (fourth with Iowa), 1988 (tied for third with Arizona) and 1994 (tied for third with Arizona). . . . Coach of three Pacific-10 Conference Tournament champions–1988, 1989 and 1990. . . . Coached at Long Beach City College, including the 1971 California community college champion.

Year	School	Overall	League	Finish	Postseason
73–74	L. Beach St.	24-2	12-0	1st (PCAA)	Probation
74–75	Iowa	10-16	7-11	7th (Big Ten)	DNP
75–76	Iowa	19-10	9-9	5th (Big Ten)	DNP
76–77	Iowa	20-7	12-6	4th (Big Ten)	DNP
77–78	Iowa	12-15	5-13	8th (Big Ten)	DNP
78–79	Iowa	20-8	13-5	T1st (Big Ten)	NCAA (0-1)
79–80	Iowa	23-10	10-8	4th (Big Ten)	NCAA (4-2)

80–81	Iowa	21–7	13–5	2d (Big Ten)	NCAA (0-1)
81–82	Iowa	21–8	12–6	T2d (Big Ten)	NCAA (1-1)
82–83	Iowa	21–10	10–8	5th (Big Ten)	NCAA (2-1)
83–84	Arizona	11–17	8–10	T5th (Pac-10)	DNP
84–85	Arizona	21–10	12–6	T3d (Pac-10)	NCAA (0-1)
85–86	Arizona	23–9	14–4	1st (Pac-10)	NCAA (0-1)
86–87	Arizona	18–12	13–5	2d (Pac-10)	NCAA (0-1)
87–88	Arizona	35–3	17–1	1st (Pac-10)	NCAA (4-1)
88–89	Arizona	29–4	17–1	1st (Pac-10)	NCAA (2-1)
89–90	Arizona	25–7	15–3	T1st (Pac-10)	NCAA (1-1)
90–91	Arizona	28–7	14–4	1st (Pac-10)	NCAA (2-1)
91–92	Arizona	24–7	13–5	3d (Pac-10)	NCAA (0-1)
92–93	Arizona	24–4	17–1	1st (Pac-10)	NCAA (0-1)
93–94	Arizona	29–6	14–4	1st (Pac-10)	NCAA (4-1)
94–95	Arizona	23–8	13–5	2nd (Pac-10)	NCAA (0-1)
95–96	Arizona	26–7	13–5	2nd (Pac-10)	NCAA (2-1)

23-Year Coaching Record: 507-194 (.723) overall; 24-2 (.943) in one year at Long Beach State; 167-91 (.647) in nine years at Iowa; 316-101 (.758) in first 13 years at Arizona; 12-0 in Pacific Coast Athletic Association; 91-71 (.562) in Big Ten; 180-52 (.776) in Pacific-10; 9-1 (.900) in Pacific-10 Tournament; 22-18 (.550) in NCAA Tournament.

RICK PITINO
Massachusetts '74
New York, N.Y.

Reached NCAA Final Four on three occasions–once with Providence (1987) and twice with Kentucky (1993 and 1996). The '96 team won the national title. . . . Coach of North Atlantic Conference Tournament champion in 1983 and SEC Tournament champions from 1992 through 1995. . . . Compiled a 90-74 regular-season record and 6-7 playoff mark in two seasons as coach of the NBA's New York Knicks (1987-88 and 1988-89). . . . Assistant coach at Hawaii under Bruce O'Neil for two seasons (1974-75 and 1975-76), Syracuse under Jim Boeheim for two seasons (1976-77 and 1977-78) and with the Knicks under Hubie Brown for two seasons (1983-84 and 1984-85).

Year	School	Overall	League	Finish	Postseason
78–79	Boston U.	17–9			DNP
79–80	Boston U.	21–9			NIT (0-1)
80–81	Boston U.	13–14			DNP
81–82	Boston U.	19–9	6–2	4th (N. Atl.)	DNP
82–83	Boston U.	21–10	8–2	T1st (N. Atl.)	NCAA (0-1)
85–86	Prov.	17–14	7–9	5th (Big East)	NIT (2-1)
86–87	Prov.	25–9	10–6	T4th (Big East)	NCAA (4-1)
89–90	Kentucky	14–14	10–8	T4th (SEC)	Probation
90–91	Kentucky	22–6	14–4	1st (SEC)	Probation
91–92	Kentucky	29–7	12–4	1st (SEC East)	NCAA (3-1)
92–93	Kentucky	30–4	13–3	2d (SEC East)	NCAA (4-1)
93–94	Kentucky	27–7	12–4	T1st (SEC East)	NCAA (1-1)
94–95	Kentucky	28–5	14–2	1st (SEC East)	NCAA (3-1)
95-96	Kentucky	34–2	16–0	1st (SEC East)	NCAA (6-0)

14-Year College Coaching Record: 315-119 (.726) overall; 91-51 (.641) in five years at Boston University; 42-23 (.646) in two years at Providence; 182-45 (.802) in first seven years at Kentucky; 14-4 (.778) in North Atlantic Conference; 17-15 (.531) in Big East Conference; 91-25 (.784) in SEC; 21-6 (.778) in postseason conference tournaments; 17-5 (.773) in NCAA Tournament; 2-2 (.500) in NIT.

NOLAN RICHARDSON
Texas-El Paso '65
El Paso, Tex.

Received Naismith Award as national coach of the year and shared similar NABC award in 1994. . . . Coach of three Final Four teams–1990 (tied for third place), 1994 (champion) and 1995 (runner-up). . . . Coach of 1981 NIT champion. . . . Coach of five conference tournament champions–Missouri Valley (1982 and 1984) and Southwest Conference (1989, 1990 and 1991). . . . Coach at Western Texas Junior College for three seasons, including the 1980 NJCAA championship team that compiled a 37-0 record.

Year	School	Overall	League	Finish	Postseason
80–81	Tulsa	26–7	11–5	T2d (Mo. Valley)	NIT (5-0)
81–82	Tulsa	24–6	12–4	T2d (Mo. Valley)	NCAA (0-1)
82–83	Tulsa	19–12	11–7	T3d (Mo. Valley)	NIT (0-1)
83–84	Tulsa	27–4	13–3	T1st (Mo. Valley)	NCAA (0-1)
84–85	Tulsa	23–8	12–4	1st (Mo. Valley)	NCAA (0-1)

85–86	Arkansas	12–16	4–12	7th (SWC)	DNP
86–87	Arkansas	19–14	8–8	5th (SWC)	NIT (1-1)
87–88	Arkansas	21–9	11–5	T2d (SWC)	NCAA (0-1)
88–89	Arkansas	25–7	13–3	1st (SWC)	NCAA (1-1)
89–90	Arkansas	30–5	14–2	1st (SWC)	NCAA (4-1)
90–91	Arkansas	34–4	15–1	1st (SWC)	NCAA (3-1)
91–92	Arkansas	26–8	13–3	1st (SEC West)	NCAA (1-1)
92–93	Arkansas	22–9	10–6	1st (SEC West)	NCAA (2-1)
93–94	Arkansas	31–3	14–2	1st (SEC West)	NCAA (6-0)
94–95	Arkansas	32–7	12–4	T1st (SEC West)	NCAA (5-1)
95–96	Arkansas	20–13	9–7	T2nd (SEC West)	NCAA (2-1)

16-Year Coaching Record: 391-132 (.748) overall; 119-37 (.763) in five years at Tulsa; 272-95 (.741) in first 11 years at Arkansas; 59-23 (.720) in Missouri Valley Conference; 65-31 (.677) in SWC; 58-22 (.725) in SEC; 11-3 (.786) in MVC Tournament; 10-3 (.769) in SWC Tournament; 6-5 (.545) in SEC Tournament; 24-11 (.686) in NCAA Tournament; 6-2 (.750) in NIT.

WINFREY (WIMP) SANDERSON
North Alabama '59
Florence, Ala.

Only second coach in SEC history (Kentucky's Adolph Rupp) to win three consecutive SEC Tournament titles (1989-91). Also, led 'Bama to SEC postseason tournament titles in 1982 and 1987 for a total of five. . . . Served as an assistant for 20 years at Alabama under Hayden Riley and C.M. Newton.

Year	School	Overall	League	Finish	Postseason
80–81	Alabama	18–11	10–8	4th (SEC)	NIT (1-1)
81–82	Alabama	24–7	12–6	3d (SEC)	NCAA (1-1)
82–83	Alabama	20–12	8–10	T8th (SEC)	NCAA (0-1)
83–84	Alabama	18–12	10–8	5th (SEC)	NCAA (1-1)
84–85	Alabama	23–10	11–7	T3d (SEC)	NCAA (2-1)
85–86	Alabama	24–9	13–5	T2d (SEC)	NCAA (2-1)
86–87*	Alabama	28–5	16–2	1st (SEC)	NCAA (2-1)
87–88	Alabama	14–17	6–12	T8th (SEC)	DNP
88–89	Alabama	23–8	12–6	T2d (SEC)	NCAA (0-1)
89–90	Alabama	26–9	12–6	T2d (SEC)	NCAA (2-1)
90–91	Alabama	23–10	12–6	3d (SEC)	NCAA (2-1)
91–92	Alabama	26–9	10–6	3d (SEC)	NCAA (1-1)
94–95	UALR	17–12	9–9	T5th (Sun Belt)	DNP
95–96	UALR	23–7	14–4	T1st (Sun Belt)	NIT (0-1)

*NCAA Tournament games later vacated by action of the NCAA.

14-Year Coaching Record: 307-138 (.690) overall; 267-119 (.692) in 12 years at Alabama; 40-19 (.678) in first two years at Arkansas-Little Rock; 17-12 (.586); 132-82 (.617) in Southeastern Conference; 23-13 (.639) in Sun Belt Conference; 25-7 (.781) in SEC Tournament; 4-2 (.667) in Sun Belt Conference Tournament; 12-10 (.545) in NCAA Tournament; 1-2 (.333) in NIT.

DEAN SMITH
Kansas '53
Topeka, Kans.

NABC national coach of the year in 1977 and USBWA national coach of the year in 1979. . . . All-time winningest coach in NCAA Tournament competition. . . . Reached NCAA Final Four 10 times–1967 (fourth), 1968 (runner-up), 1969 (fourth), 1972 (third), 1977 (runner-up), 1981 (runner-up), 1982 (champion), 1991 (tied for third), 1993 (champion) and 1995 (tied for third). . . . Coach of 1971 NIT champion and 1973 third-place team. . . . Coach of 12 ACC Tournament champions–1967, 1968, 1969, 1972, 1975, 1977, 1979, 1981, 1982, 1989, 1991 and 1994. . . . U.S. Olympic team coach in 1976. . . . Assistant coach under Kansas' Dick Harp, Air Force's Bob Spear and North Carolina's Frank McGuire. . . . Elected to Naismith Memorial Basketball Hall of Fame in 1982.

Year	School	Overall	League	Finish	Postseason
61–62	N. Caro.	8–9	7–7	T4th (ACC)	DNP
62–63	N. Caro.	15–6	10–4	3d (ACC)	DNP
63–64	N. Caro.	12–12	6–8	5th (ACC)	DNP
64–65	N. Caro.	15–9	10–4	T2d (ACC)	DNP
65–66	N. Caro.	16–11	8–6	T3d (ACC)	DNP
66–67	N. Caro.	26–6	12–2	1st (ACC)	NCAA (2-2)
67–68	N. Caro.	28–4	12–2	1st (ACC)	NCAA (3-1)
68–69	N. Caro.	27–5	12–2	1st (ACC)	NCAA (2-2)

69–70	N. Caro.	18-9	9-5	T2d (ACC)	NIT (0-1)
70–71	N. Caro.	26-6	11-3	1st (ACC)	NIT (4-0)
71–72	N. Caro.	26-5	9-3	1st (ACC)	NCAA (3-1)
72–73	N. Caro.	25-8	8-4	2d (ACC)	NIT (3-1)
73–74	N. Caro.	22-6	9-3	T2d (ACC)	NIT (0-1)
74–75	N. Caro.	23-8	8-4	T2d (ACC)	NCAA (2-1)
75–76	N. Caro.	25-4	11-1	1st (ACC)	NCAA (0-1)
76–77	N. Caro.	28-5	9-3	1st (ACC)	NCAA (4-1)
77–78	N. Caro.	23-8	9-3	1st (ACC)	NCAA (0-1)
78–79	N. Caro.	23-6	9-3	T1st (ACC)	NCAA (0-1)
79–80	N. Caro.	21-8	9-5	T2d (ACC)	NCAA (0-1)
80–81	N. Caro.	29-8	10-4	2d (ACC)	NCAA (4-1)
81–82	N. Caro.	32-2	12-2	T1st (ACC)	NCAA (5-0)
82–83	N. Caro.	28-8	12-2	T1st (ACC)	NCAA (2-1)
83–84	N. Caro.	28-3	14-0	1st (ACC)	NCAA (1-1)
84–85	N. Caro.	27-9	9-5	T1st (ACC)	NCAA (3-1)
85–86	N. Caro.	28-6	10-4	3d (ACC)	NCAA (1-1)
86–87	N. Caro.	32-4	14-0	1st (ACC)	NCAA (3-1)
87–88	N. Caro.	27-7	11-3	1st (ACC)	NCAA (3-1)
88–89	N. Caro.	29-8	9-5	T2d (ACC)	NCAA (2-1)
89–90	N. Caro.	21-13	8-6	T3d (ACC)	NCAA (2-1)
90–91	N. Caro.	29-6	10-4	2nd (ACC)	NCAA (4-1)
91–92	N. Caro.	23-10	9-7	3d (ACC)	NCAA (2-1)
92–93	N. Caro.	34-4	14-2	1st (ACC)	NCAA (6-0)
93–94	N. Caro.	26-7	11-5	2d (ACC)	NCAA (1-1)
94–95	N. Carolina	28-6	12-4	T1st (ACC)	NCAA (4-1)
95–96	N. Carolina	21-11	10-6	3rd (ACC)	NCAA (1-1)

35-Year Coaching Record: 851-247 (.775) at North Carolina; 353-131 (.729) in ACC; 55-23 (.705) in ACC Tournament; 61-26 (.701) in NCAA Tournament; 7-3 (.700) in NIT.

DEAN'S ALMOST ATOP LIST

Dean Smith, entering his 36th year as North Carolina's head coach with 851 victories, is on a pace to bypass Kentucky legend Adolph Rupp and become the all-time winningest major-college coach late in the 1996-97 season or early in the 1997-98 campaign. Smith entered this season needing 26 triumphs to move atop the list. The Tar Heels averaged 26 wins annually the previous 30 seasons. Here is a list of the coaches with more than 600 victories through 1995-96:

RANK	COACH	WINS
1.	Adolph Rupp	876
2.	Dean Smith*	851
3.	Henry Iba	767
4.	Ed Diddle	759
5.	Phog Allen	746
6.	Ray Meyer	724
T7.	Don Haskins*	678
T7.	Norm Stewart*	678
9.	Bob Knight*	676
10.	Ralph Miller	674
11.	Lefty Driesell*	667
12.	John Wooden	664
13.	Lou Henson	661
T14.	Marv Harshman	653
T14.	Jerry Tarkanian*	653
16.	Gene Bartow	646
17.	Cam Henderson	630
18.	Norman Sloan	627

*Active coaches.

Notes: Miller was forced to forfeit 17 of his victories with Oregon State. . . . Six NCAA Tournament victories for Tarkanian at Long Beach State were voided by the NCAA. . . . Forfeit victories are not included for Knight (two), Henson (two), Bartow (one) and Harshman (one). . . . Louisville's Denny Crum is expected to crack the 600-win plateau sometime during the 1996-97 season.

NORM STEWART
Missouri '56
Shelbyville, Mo.

UPI national coach of the year in 1982 and 1994. Also named by AP in 1994. . . . Coach of six Big Eight Conference champions–1978, 1982, 1987, 1989, 1991 and 1993. . . . Winningest coach in Big Eight Conference history. . . . Coach of NCAA Division II fourth-place team in 1964. . . . Assistant coach at Missouri under Sparky Stalcup for four seasons from 1958-'61.

Year	School	Overall	League	Finish	Postseason
61–62	N. Iowa	19-5	8-4	T1st (N. Cent.)	DNP
62–63	N. Iowa	15-8	8-4	2d (N. Cent.)	DNP
63–64	N. Iowa	23-4	11-1	1st (N. Cent.)	NCAA-II (3-2)
64–65	N. Iowa	16-7	8-4	2d (N. Cent.)	DNP
65–66	N. Iowa	13-7	9-3	2d (N. Cent.)	DNP
66–67	N. Iowa	11-11	6-6	T2d (N. Cent.)	DNP
67–68	Missouri	10-16	5-9	6th (Big Eight)	DNP
68–69	Missouri	14-11	7-7	5th (Big Eight)	DNP
69–70	Missouri	15-11	7-7	T3d (Big Eight)	DNP
70–71	Missouri	17-9	9-5	T2d (Big Eight)	DNP
71–72	Missouri	21-6	10-4	2d (Big Eight)	NIT (0-1)
72–73	Missouri	21-6	9-5	T2d (Big Eight)	NIT (0-1)
73–74	Missouri	12-14	3-11	T7th (Big Eight)	DNP
74–75	Missouri	18-9	9-5	3d (Big Eight)	DNP
75–76	Missouri	26-5	12-2	1st (Big Eight)	NCAA (2-1)
76–77	Missouri	21-8	9-5	T2d (Big Eight)	DNP
77–78	Missouri	14-16	4-10	T6th (Big Eight)	NCAA (0-1)
78–79	Missouri	13-15	8-6	T2d (Big Eight)	DNP
79–80	Missouri	25-6	11-3	1st (Big Eight)	NCAA (2-1)
80–81	Missouri	22-10	10-4	1st (Big Eight)	NCAA (0-1)
81–82	Missouri	27-4	12-2	1st (Big Eight)	NCAA (1-1)
82–83	Missouri	26-8	12-2	1st (Big Eight)	NCAA (0-1)
83–84	Missouri	16-14	5-9	T6th (Big Eight)	DNP
84–85	Missouri	18-14	7-7	T3d (Big Eight)	NIT (0-1)
85–86	Missouri	21-14	8-6	T3d (Big Eight)	NCAA (0-1)
86–87	Missouri	24-10	11-3	1st (Big Eight)	NCAA (0-1)
87–88	Missouri	19-11	7-7	4th (Big Eight)	NCAA (0-1)
88–89	Missouri	29-8	10-4	2d (Big Eight)	NCAA (2-1)
89–90	Missouri	26-6	12-2	1st (Big Eight)	NCAA (0-1)
90–91	Missouri	20-10	8-6	4th (Big Eight)	Probation
91–92	Missouri	21-9	8-6	T2d (Big Eight)	NCAA (1-1)
92–93	Missouri	19-14	5-9	7th (Big Eight)	NCAA (0-1)
93–94	Missouri	28-4	14-0	1st (Big Eight)	NCAA (3-1)
94–95	Missouri	20-9	8-6	4th (Big Eight)	NCAA (1-1)
95–96	Missouri	18-15	6-8	6th (Big Eight)	NIT (1-1)

35-Year Coaching Record: 678-334 (.670) overall; 97-42 (.698) in six years at Northern Iowa; 581-292 (.666) in first 29 years at Missouri; 50-22 (.694) in North Central Conference; 246-160 (.606) in Big Eight Conference; 29-14 (.674) in Big Eight Tournament; 12-15 (.444) in NCAA Division I Tournament; 1-4 (.200) in NIT; 0-1 in National Commissioners Invitational Tournament; 3-2 (.600) in NCAA Division II Tournament.

EDDIE SUTTON
Oklahoma St. '58
Bucklin, Kans.

Named national coach of the year by USBWA in 1977, by AP and UPI in 1978, and by AP and NABC in 1986. . . . Coach of two NCAA Tournament Final Four teams–1978 with Arkansas (3rd) and 1995 with Oklahoma State (tied for third). . . . Only coach to guide four different colleges to the NCAA playoffs. . . . Coach of six conference tournament champions–SWC (1977, 1979 and 1982 with Arkansas), SEC (1986 and 1988 with Kentucky) and Big Eight (1995 with Oklahoma State). . . . Assistant coach at Oklahoma State under Henry Iba for one season (1958-59). . . . Coach at Southern Idaho Junior College for three seasons from 1967-'69.

Year	School	Overall	League	Finish	Postseason
69–70	Creighton	15-10			DNP
70–71	Creighton	14-11			DNP
71–72	Creighton	15-11			DNP
72–73	Creighton	15-12			DNP
73–74	Creighton	23-6			NCAA (2-1)
74–75	Arkansas	17-9	11-3	T2d (SWC)	DNP
75–76	Arkansas	19-9	9-7	4th (SWC)	DNP
76–77	Arkansas	26-2	16-0	1st (SWC)	NCAA (0-1)
77–78	Arkansas	32-4	14-2	T1st (SWC)	NCAA (4-1)
78–79	Arkansas	25-5	13-3	T1st (SWC)	NCAA (2-1)

79–80	Arkansas	21-8	13-3	2d (SWC)	NCAA (0-1)
80–81	Arkansas	24-8	13-3	1st (SWC)	NCAA (2-1)
81–82	Arkansas	23-6	12-4	1st (SWC)	NCAA (0-1)
82–83	Arkansas	26-4	14-2	2d (SWC)	NCAA (1-1)
83–84	Arkansas	25-7	14-2	2d (SWC)	NCAA (0-1)
84–85	Arkansas	22-13	10-6	T2d (SWC)	NCAA (1-1)
85–86	Kentucky	32-4	17-1	1st (SEC)	NCAA (3-1)
86–87	Kentucky	18-11	10-8	T3d (SEC)	NCAA (0-1)
87–88	Kentucky	27-6	13-5	1st (SEC)	NCAA (2-1)
88–89	Kentucky	13-19	8-10	T6th (SEC)	DNP
90–91	Okla. St.	24-8	10-4	T1st (Big Eight)	NCAA (2-1)
91–92	Okla. St.	28-8	8-6	T2d (Big Eight)	NCAA (2-1)
92–93	Okla. St.	20-9	8-6	T2d (Big Eight)	NCAA (1-1)
93–94	Okla. St.	24-10	10-4	2d (Big Eight)	NCAA (1-1)
94–95	Okla. State	27-10	10-4	2nd (Big Eight)	NCAA (4-1)
95–96	Okla. State	17-10	7-7	T4th (Big Eight)	DNP

26-Year Coaching Record: 572-220 (.722) overall; 82-50 (.621) in five years at Creighton; 260-75 (.776) in 11 years at Arkansas; 90-40 (.692) in four years at Kentucky; 140-55 (.718) in first six years at Oklahoma State; 139-35 (.799) in Southwest Conference; 48-24 (.667) in Southeastern Conference; 53-31 (.631) in Big Eight Conference; 13-7 (.650) in SWC Tournament; 6-2 (.750) in SEC Tournament; 8-5 (.615) in Big Eight Tournament; 27-18 (.600) in NCAA Tournament.

JERRY TARKANIAN
Fresno State '55
Pasadena, Calif.

UPI national coach of the year in 1983. . . . Coach of 1990 NCAA champion. . . , Reached NCAA Final Four four times in 15 years from 1977-91. . . . Compiled highest career winning percentage in Division I history. . . . Coach of seven Big West Tournament champions–1983, 1985, 1986, 1987, 1989, 1990 and 1991. . . . Compiled a 9-11 record in brief stint with NBA's San Antonio Spurs at the start of 1992-93 season. . . . Compiled a 212-26 (.891) record in seven seasons as coach at two community colleges in California.

Year	School	Overall	League	Finish	Postseason
68-69	Long Beach St.	23-3	11-1	1st (CCAA)	DNP
69-70	Long Beach St.	24-5	10-0	1st (PCAA)	NCAA (1-2)
70-71	Long Beach St.	24-5	10-0	1st (PCAA)	NCAA (2-1)
71-72	Long Beach St.	25-4	10-2	1st (PCAA)	NCAA (2-1)
72-73	Long Beach St.	26-3	10-2	1st (PCAA)	NCAA (2-1)
73-74	UNLV	20-6	10-4	3rd (WCAC)	DNP
74-75	UNLV	24-5	13-1	1st (WCAC)	NCAA (2-1)
75-76	UNLV	29-2	–	–	NCAA (1-1)
76-77	UNLV	29-3	–	–	NCAA (4-1)
77-78	UNLV	20-8	–	–	Probation
78-79	UNLV	21-8	–	–	Probation
79-80	UNLV	23-9	–	–	NIT (3-2)
80-81	UNLV	16-12	.–	–	DNP
81-82	UNLV	20-10	.–	–	NIT (1-1)
82-83	UNLV	28-3	15-1	1st (PCAA)	NCAA (0-1)
83-84	UNLV	29-6	16-2	1st (PCAA)	NCAA (2-1)
84-85	UNLV	28-4	17-1	1st (PCAA)	NCAA (1-1)
85-86	UNLV	33-5	16-2	1st (PCAA)	NCAA (2-1)
86-87	UNLV	37-2	18-0	1st (PCAA)	NCAA (4-1)
87-88	UNLV	28-6	15-3	1st (PCAA)	NCAA (1-1)
88-89	UNLV	29-8	16-2	1st (Big West)	NCAA (3-1)
89-90	UNLV	35-5	16-2	T1st (Big West)	NCAA (6-0)
90-91	UNLV	34-1	18-0	1st (Big West)	NCAA (4-1)
91-92	UNLV	26-2	18-0	1st (Big West)	Probation
95-96	Fresno State	22-11	13-5	3rd (WAC)	NIT (2-1)

25-Year College Coaching Record: 653-136 (.828) overall; 122-20 (.859) in five years at Long Beach State; 509-105 (.829) in 19 years at UNLV; 22-11 (.667) in first year at Fresno State; 23-5 (.821) in West Coast Athletic Conference; 205-17 (.923) in Pacific Coast Athletic Association/Big West Conference; 13-5 (.722) in Western Athletic Conference; 24-2 (.923) in Big West Tournament; 1-1 (.500) in WAC Tournament; 37-16 (.698) in NCAA Tournament; 6-4 (.600) in NIT.

TARK ALERT

If Fresno State competes in 30 games in the 1996-97 season, the Bulldogs need to win at least 24 contests to keep Jerry Tarkanian atop the list of winningest coaches by percentage in NCAA history. Here are the coaches with the five highest winning percentages:

COACH,	SCHOOLS	RECORD	PCT.
1. **Jerry Tarkanian,**	Long Beach St./UNLV/Fresno St.	653-136	.828

The only year he failed to win at least 20 games was 1980-81 (16-12 mark).

2. **Clair Bee,**	Rider/Long Island University	412-87	.826

Lost more than five games in a season just once in his first 14 years.

3. **Adolph Rupp,**	Kentucky	876-190	.822

Never compiled a losing won-loss record in his 41 seasons as a head coach.

4. **John Wooden,**	Indiana State/UCLA	664-162	.804

Worst mark was 14-12 in 1959-60 before winning 10 NCAA titles in 12 years.

5. **Dean Smith,**	North Carolina	851-247	.775

Won at least 25 games an amazing 21 seasons with a high of 34 in 1992-93.

JOHN THOMPSON
Providence '64
Washington, D.C.

Named national coach of year by USBWA in 1982, by the NABC in 1985 and by UPI in 1987. . . . Reached NCAA Final Four three times–1982 (runner-up), 1984 (champion) and 1985 (runner-up). . . . Coach of two NIT semifinalists–1978 (fourth) and 1993 (runner-up). . . . Coach of six Big East Conference Tournament champions–1980, 1982, 1984, 1985, 1987 and 1989. . . . U.S. Olympic head coach in 1988 and assistant coach in 1976.

Year	School	Overall	League	Finish	Postseason
72–73	Georgetown	12-15			DNP
73–74	Georgetown	13-13			DNP
74–75	Georgetown	18-10			NCAA (0-1)
75–76	Georgetown	21-7			NCAA (0-1)
76–77	Georgetown	19-9			NIT (0-1)
77–78	Georgetown	23-8			NIT (2-2)
78–79	Georgetown	24-5			NCAA (0-1)
79–80	Georgetown	26-6	5-1	T1st (Big East)	NCAA (0-1)
80–81	Georgetown	20-12	9-5	2d (Big East)	NCAA (0-1)
81–82	Georgetown	30-7	10-4	2d (Big East)	NCAA (4-1)
82–83	Georgetown	22-10	11-5	4th (Big East)	NCAA (1-1)
83–84	Georgetown	34-3	14-2	1st (Big East)	NCAA (5-0)
84–85	Georgetown	35-3	14-2	2d (Big East)	NCAA (5-1)
85–86	Georgetown	24-8	11-5	3d (Big East)	NCAA (1-1)
86–87	Georgetown	29-5	12-4	T1st (Big East)	NCAA (3-1)
87–88	Georgetown	20-10	9-7	T3d (Big East)	NCAA (1-1)
88–89	Georgetown	29-5	13-3	1st (Big East)	NCAA (3-1)
89–90	Georgetown	24-7	11-5	3d (Big East)	NCAA (1-1)
90–91	Georgetown	19-13	8-8	6th (Big East)	NCAA (1-1)
91–92	Georgetown	22-10	12-6	T1st (Big East)	NCAA (1-1)
92–93	Georgetown	20-13	8-10	8th (Big East)	NIT (4-1)
93–94	Georgetown	19-12	10-8	T4th (Big East)	NCAA (1-1)
94–95	Georgetown	21-10	11-7	4th (Big East)	NCAA (2-1)
95–96	Georgetown	29-8	13-5	1st (Big East 7)	NCAA (3-1)

24-Year Coaching Record: 553-208 (.727) at Georgetown; 181-87 (.675) in Big East Conference; 31-11 (.738) in Big East Tournament; 34-18 (.654) in NCAA Tournament; 6-4 (.600) in NIT.

BILLY TUBBS
Lamar '58
Tulsa, Okla.

Directed Oklahoma to 12 consecutive 20-win seasons (1982-93), a Big Eight best. . . . Took the Sooners to postseason play his last 13 years with them (9 NCAA/4 NIT) before moving to TCU. . . . His '88 OU squad advanced to the national championship game against Kansas. . . . OU teams advanced to NIT semifinals in 1982 (T3rd) and 1991 (2nd). . . . Led Oklahoma to three Big Eight Tournament championships–1985, 1988 and 1990.

Year	School	Overall	League	Finish	Postseason
71–72	S'western	12-14	7-5	T2d (Big St.)	DNP
72–73	S'western	19-8	9-3	2d (Big St.)	DNP
76–77	Lamar	12-17	6-4	3d (Southland)	DNP
77–78	Lamar	18-9	8-2	T1st (Southland)	DNP
78–79	Lamar	23-9	8-1	1st (Southland)	NCAA (1-1)
79–80	Lamar	22-11	8-2	1st (Southland)	NCAA (2-1)
80–81	Oklahoma	9-18	4-10	7th (Big Eight)	DNP
81–82	Oklahoma	22-11	8-6	3d (Big Eight)	NIT (3-1)
82–83	Oklahoma	24-9	10-4	2d (Big Eight)	NCAA (1-1)
83–84	Oklahoma	29-5	13-1	1st (Big Eight)	NCAA (0-1)
84–85	Oklahoma	31-6	13-1	1st (Big Eight)	NCAA (3-1)
85–86	Oklahoma	26-9	8-6	T3d (Big Eight)	NCAA (1-1)
86–87	Oklahoma	24-10	9-5	T2d (Big Eight)	NCAA (2-1)
87–88	Oklahoma	35-4	12-2	1st (Big Eight)	NCAA (5-1)
88–89	Oklahoma	30-6	12-2	1st (Big Eight)	NCAA (2-1)
89–90	Oklahoma	27-5	11-3	2d (Big Eight)	NCAA (1-1)
90–91	Oklahoma	20-15	5-9	T6th (Big Eight)	NIT (4-1)
91–92	Oklahoma	21-9	8-6	T2d (Big Eight)	NCAA (0-1)
92–93	Oklahoma	20-12	7-7	T5th (Big Eight)	NIT (1-1)
93–94	Oklahoma	15-13	6-8	5th (Big Eight)	NIT (0-1)
94-95	TCU	16-11	8-6	T3rd (SWC)	DNP
95-96	TCU	15-15	6-8	4th (SWC)	DNP

22-Year Coaching Record: 470-226 (.675) overall; 31-22 (.585) in two years at Southwestern (Tex.); 75-46 (.620) in four years at Lamar; 333-132 (.716) in 14 years at Oklahoma; 31-26 (.544) in first two years at Texas Christian; 30-9 (.769) in Southland Conference; 126-70 (.643) in Big Eight Conference; 14-14 (.500) in Southwest Conference; 18-11 (.621) in Big Eight Tournament; 0-2 (.000) in SWC Tournament; 18-11 (.621) in NCAA Tournament; 8-4 (.667) in NIT.

ROY WILLIAMS
North Carolina '72
Skyland, N.C.

USBWA national coach of the year in 1990. . . . Reached NCAA Final Four two times–1991 (runner-up) and 1993 (tied for third). . . . Coach of 1992 Big Eight Tournament champion. . . . Assistant coach at North Carolina under Dean Smith for 10 seasons from 1979-88.

Year	School	Overall	League	Finish	Postseason
88–89	Kansas	19-12	6-8	6th (Big Eight)	Probation
89–90	Kansas	30-5	11-3	T2d (Big Eight)	NCAA (1-1)
90–91	Kansas	27-8	10-4	T1st (Big Eight)	NCAA (5-1)
91–92	Kansas	27-5	11-3	1st (Big Eight)	NCAA (1-1)
92–93	Kansas	29-7	11-3	1st (Big Eight)	NCAA (4-1)
93–94	Kansas	27-8	9-5	3d (Big Eight)	NCAA (2-1)
94–95	Kansas	25-6	11-3	1st (Big Eight)	NCAA (2-1)
95–96	Kansas	29-5	12-2	1st (Big Eight)	NCAA (3-1)

Eight-Year Coaching Record: 213-56 (.792) at Kansas; 81-31 (.723) in Big Eight Conference; 10-7 (.588) in Big Eight Tournament; 18-7 (.720) in NCAA Tournament.

STERLING START

Kansas' Roy Williams (213-56, .792) tied former North Carolina State coach Everett Case (1947-54) for most victories in a head coach's first eight seasons. Williams needs to guide the Jayhawks to 28 triumphs in the 1996-97 campaign to keep pace with Case. Here is a list of Case and the three other coaches before Williams to register more than 200 wins through their first nine seasons:

COACH, TEAM	SEASONS	W.	L.	PCT.
Everett Case, N.C. State	1947-55	241	56	.811
Jerry Tarkanian, Long Beach St./UNLV	1969-77	224	36	.862
Denny Crum, Louisville	1972-80	219	55	.799
Jim Boeheim, Syracuse	1977-85	204	71	.742

Former College Coaching Greats

FORREST (PHOG) ALLEN
Kansas '06
Independence, Mo.

Elected to Naismith Memorial Basketball Hall of Fame in 1959.... U.S. Olympic team assistant coach in 1952.... Reached NCAA Final Four three times—1940 (2nd), 1952 (1st), and 1953 (2nd).... His 1922 and 1923 Kansas teams were selected as national champions by the Helms Foundation.... Holds the NCAA career record for most years coached.

Year	School	Overall	League	Finish	Postseason
05–6	Baker	18-3			
06–7	Baker	14-0			
07–8	Baker	13-6			
07–8	Kansas	18-6	6-0	1st (MVC)	
08–9	Kansas	25-3	8-2	1st (MVC)	
08–9	Haskell	27-5			
12–13	Central Mo. St.	11-7			
13–14	Central Mo. St.	15-4			
14–15	Central Mo. St.	13-4			
15–16	Central Mo. St	9-4			
16–17	Central Mo. St.	13-2			
17–18	Central Mo. St.	9-4			
18–19	Central Mo. St.	14-6			
19–20	Kansas	10-7	9-7	3d (MVC)	
20–21	Kansas	10-8	10-8	4th (MVC)	
21–22	Kansas	16-2	15-1	T1st (MVC)	
22–23	Kansas	17-1	16-0	1st (MVC)	
23–24	Kansas	16-3	15-1	1st (MVC)	
24–25	Kansas	17-1	15-1	1st (MVC)	
25–26	Kansas	16-2	16-2	1st (MVC)	
26–27	Kansas	15-2	10-2	1st (MVC)	
27–28	Kansas	9-9	9-9	4th (MVC)	
28–29	Kansas	3-15	2-8	T5th (Big Six)	
29–30	Kansas	14-4	7-3	2d (Big Six)	
30–31	Kansas	15-3	7-3	1st (Big Six)	
31–32	Kansas	13-5	7-3	1st (Big Six)	
32–33	Kansas	13-4	8-2	1st (Big Six)	
33–34	Kansas	16-1	9-1	1st (Big Six)	
34–35	Kansas	15-5	12-4	2d (Big Six)	
35–36	Kansas	21-2	10-0	1st (Big Six)	Olympic Playoffs (3-2)
36–37	Kansas	15-4	8-2	T1st (Big Six)	
37–38	Kansas	18-2	9-1	1st (Big Six)	DNP
38–39	Kansas	13-7	6-4	3d (Big Six)	DNP
39–40	Kansas	19-6	8-2	T1st (Big Six)	NCAA (2-1)
40–41	Kansas	12-6	7-3	T1st (Big Six)	DNP
41–42	Kansas	17-5	8-2	T1st (Big Six)	NCAA (1-1)
42–43	Kansas	22-6	10-0	1st (Big Six)	DNP
43–44	Kansas	17-9	5-5	3d (Big Six)	DNP
44–45	Kansas	12-5	7-3	2d (Big Six)	DNP
45–46	Kansas	19-2	10-0	1st (Big Six)	DNP
46–47	Kansas	8-5	5-5	T3d (Big Six)	DNP

Year	School	Overall	League	Finish	Postseason
47–48	Kansas	9-15	4-8	T6th (Big Seven)	DNP
48–49	Kansas	12-12	3-9	T6th (Big Seven)	DNP
49–50	Kansas	14-11	8-4	T1st (Big Seven)	DNP
50–51	Kansas	16-8	8-4	T2d (Big Seven)	DNP
51–52	Kansas	26-2	11-1	1st (Big Seven)	NCAA (4-0)
52–53	Kansas	19-6	10-2	1st (Big Seven)	NCAA (3-1)
53–54	Kansas	16-5	10-2	T1st (Big Seven)	DNP
54–55	Kansas	11-10	5-7	5th (Big Seven)	DNP
55–56	Kansas	14-9	6-6	5th (Big Seven)	DNP

Note: Coached two teams during the 1907-8 and 1908-9 seasons.

48-Year Coaching Record: 746-264 (.739) overall; 45-9 (.833) in three years at Baker; 27-5 (.844) in one year at Haskell; 84-31 (.730) in seven years at Central Missouri State; 588-218 (.730) in 39 years at Kansas; 115-31 (.788) in Missouri Valley Conference; 210-94 (.691) in Big Eight Conference; 10-3 (.769) in NCAA Tournament.

FORDDY ANDERSON
Stanford '42
Gary, Ind.

One of only 10 coaches to take two different teams to the Final Four.... Reached NCAA Final Four three times—1950 (2nd with Bradley), 1954 (2nd with Bradley), and 1957 (4th with Michigan State).... Led Bradley to fourth-place finish in 1949 NIT and second-place finish in 1950 NIT.... Assistant coach under Everett Dean at Stanford while completing work for college degree following World War II.

Year	School	Overall	League	Finish	Postseason
46–47	Drake	18-11	8-4	T2d (MVC)	DNP
47–48	Drake	14-12	5-5	3d (MVC)	DNP
48–49	Bradley	27-8	6-4	3d (MVC)	NIT (2-2)
49–50	Bradley	32-5	11-1	1st (MVC)	NCAA (2-1); NIT (2-1)
50–51	Bradley	32-6	11-3	T2d (MVC)	DNP
51–52	Bradley	17-12			DNP
52–53	Bradley	15-12			Probation
53–54	Bradley	19-13			NCAA (4-1)
54–55	Mich. St.	13-9	8-6	4th (Big Ten)	DNP
55–56	Mich. St.	13-9	7-7	5th (Big Ten)	DNP
56–57	Mich. St.	16-10	10-4	T1st (Big Ten)	NCAA (2-2)
57–58	Mich. St.	16-6	9-5	3d (Big Ten)	DNP
58–59	Mich. St.	19-4	12-2	1st (Big Ten)	NCAA (1-1)
59–60	Mich. St.	10-11	5-9	8th (Big Ten)	DNP
60–61	Mich. St.	7-17	3-11	9th (Big Ten)	DNP
61–62	Mich. St.	8-14	3-11	T9th (Big Ten)	DNP
62–63	Mich. St.	4-16	3-11	9th (Big Ten)	DNP
63–64	Mich. St.	14-10	8-6	T4th (Big Ten)	DNP
64–65	Mich. St.	5-18	1-13	10th (Big Ten)	DNP
65–66	Hiram Scott	12-3			
66–67	Hiram Scott	19-4			
67–68	Hiram Scott	15-5			
68–69	Hiram Scott	13-8			
69–70	Hiram Scott	10-11			

24-Year Coaching Record: 368-234 (.611) overall; 32-23 (.582) in two years at Drake; 142-56 (.717) in six years at Bradley; 125-124 (.502) in 11 years at Michigan State; 69-31 (.690) in five years at Hiram Scott; 41-17 (.707) in Missouri Valley Conference; 69-85 (.448) in Big Ten Conference; 9-5 (.643) in NCAA Tournament; 4-3 (.571) in NIT.

HAROLD ANDERSON
Otterbein '24
Akron, O.

Elected to Naismith Memorial Basketball Hall of Fame in 1984.... Directed teams to NIT semifinals in 1942 (4th), 1945 (2nd) and 1949 (3rd).... Instrumental in starting NABC East-West All-Star Game.

Year	School	Overall	League	Finish	Postseason
34–35	Toledo	13-3			
35–36	Toledo	12-4			
36–37	Toledo	18-4			
37–38	Toledo	14-6			DNP
38–39	Toledo	17-10			DNP
39–40	Toledo	24-6			DNP
40–41	Toledo	21-3			DNP

Year	School	Overall	League	Finish	Postseason
41–42	Toledo	23-5			NIT (1-2)
42–43	Bowling Green	18-5			DNP
43–44	Bowling Green	22-4			NIT (0-1)
44–45	Bowling Green	24-4			NIT (2-1)
45–46	Bowling Green	27-5			NIT (0-1)
46–47	Bowling Green	28-7			DNP
47–48	Bowling Green	27-6			NIT (0-1)
48–49	Bowling Green	24-7			NIT (3-1)
49–50	Bowling Green	19-11			DNP
50–51	Bowling Green*	10-4			DNP
51–52	Bowling Green	17-10			DNP
52–53	Bowling Green	12-15			DNP
53–54	Bowling Green	17-7	10-3	2nd (MAC)	NIT (1-1)
54–55	Bowling Green	6-16	5-9	T5th (MAC)	DNP
55–56	Bowling Green	4-19	1-11	7th (MAC)	DNP
56–57	Bowling Green	14-9	7-5	T3rd (MAC)	DNP
57–58	Bowling Green	15-8	6-6	4th (MAC)	DNP
58–59	Bowling Green	18-8	9-3	T1st (MAC)	NCAA (0-1)
59–60	Bowling Green	10-14	6-6	T3rd (MAC)	DNP
60–61	Bowling Green	10-14	4-8	T5th (MAC)	DNP
61–62	Bowling Green	21-4	11-1	1st (MAC)	NCAA (0-1)
62–63	Bowling Green	19-8	9-3	1st (MAC)	NCAA (1-2)

* Took leave of absence for health reasons. Bowling Green was 15-12 overall.

29-Year Coaching Record: 504-226 (.690) overall; 142-41 (.776) in eight years at Toledo; 362-185 (.662) in 21 years at Bowling Green; 134-107 (.556) in Mid-American Conference; 1-4 (.200) in NCAA Tournament; 7-8 (.467) in NIT.

LEW ANDREAS
Syracuse '21
Sterling, Ill.

His 1926 team was selected as national champion by the Helms Foundation.

Year	School	Overall	League	Finish	Postseason
24–25	Syracuse	14-2			
25–26	Syracuse	19-1			
26–27	Syracuse	15-4			
27–28	Syracuse	10-6			
28–29	Syracuse	11-4			
29–30	Syracuse	18-2			
30–31	Syracuse	16-4			
31–32	Syracuse	13-7			
32–33	Syracuse	14-2			
33–34	Syracuse	15-2			
34–35	Syracuse	15-2			
35–36	Syracuse	12-5			
36–37	Syracuse	13-4			
37–38	Syracuse	13-5			DNP
38–39	Syracuse	14-4			DNP
39–40	Syracuse	10-8			DNP
40–41	Syracuse	14-5			DNP
41–42	Syracuse	15-6			DNP
42–43	Syracuse	8-10			DNP
44–45	Syracuse	7-12			DNP
45–46	Syracuse	23-4			NIT (0-1)
46–47	Syracuse	19-6			DNP
47–48	Syracuse	11-13			DNP
48–49	Syracuse	18-7			DNP
49–50	Syracuse	18-9			NIT (1-1)

25-Year Coaching Record: 355-134 (.726) overall; 1-2 (.333) in NIT.

JUSTIN (SAM) BARRY
Wisconsin '16 (after playing three sports at Lawrence College)
Madison, Wis.

Elected to Naismith Memorial Basketball Hall of Fame in 1978.... Reached Final Four with USC in 1940 (3rd).... Coached USC's baseball team to College World Series championship in 1948.

Year	School	Overall	League	Finish	Postseason
18–19	Knox	9-2			
19–20	Knox	8-6			

Year	School	Overall	League	Finish	Postseason
20-21	Knox	10-2			
21-22	Knox	11-5			
22-23	Iowa	13-2	11-1	T1st (Big Ten)	
23-24	Iowa	7-10	4-8	9th (Big Ten)	
24-25	Iowa	6-10	5-7	7th (Big Ten)	
25-26	Iowa	12-5	8-4	T1st (Big Ten)	
26-27	Iowa	9-8	7-5	T4th (Big Ten)	
27-28	Iowa	6-11	3-9	T7th (Big Ten)	
28-29	Iowa	9-8	5-7	7th (Big Ten)	
29-30	Southern Cal	15-5	7-2	1st (PCC-S)	
30-31	Southern Cal	8-8	5-4	2nd (PCC-S)	
31-32	Southern Cal	10-12	8-3	T1st (PCC-S)	
32-33	Southern Cal	18-5	10-1	1st (PCC-S)	
33-34	Southern Cal	16-8	9-3	1st (PCC-S)	
34-35	Southern Cal	20-6	11-1	1st (PCC-S)	
35-36	Southern Cal	14-12	8-4	T1st (PCC-S)	
36-37	Southern Cal	19-6	8-4	2nd (PCC-S)	
37-38	Southern Cal	17-9	6-6	3rd (PCC-S)	DNP
38-39	Southern Cal	20-5	9-3	T1st (PCC-S)	DNP
39-40	Southern Cal	20-3	10-2	1st (PCC-S)	NCAA (1-1)
40-41	Southern Cal	15-10	6-6	T2nd (PCC-S)	DNP
44-45	Southern Cal	15-9	2-2	2nd (PCC-S)	DNP
45-46	Southern Cal	14-7	8-4	2nd (PCC-S)	DNP
46-47	Southern Cal	10-14	2-10	4th (PCC-S)	DNP
47-48	Southern Cal	14-10	7-5	2nd (PCC-S)	DNP
48-49	Southern Cal	14-10	8-4	2nd (PCC-S)	DNP
49-50	Southern Cal	16-8	7-5	2nd (PCC-S)	DNP

29-Year Coaching Record: 375-216 (.635) overall; 38-15 (.717) in four years at Knox; 53-54 (.495) in seven years at Iowa; 260-138 (.653) in 18 years at Southern California; 43-41 (.512) in Big Ten Conference; 137-76 (.643) in Pacific Coast Conference; 1-1 (.500) in NCAA Tournament.

GENE BARTOW
Northeast Missouri State '53
Browning, Mo.

NABC national coach of the year in 1973.... Reached NCAA Final Four two times–1973 (runner-up with Memphis State) and 1976 (third with UCLA).... Coach of NIT third-place teams in 1989 and 1993.... Coach of four Sun Belt Conference Tournament champions–1982, 1983, 1984 and 1987.... Assistant coach at UC Santa Barbara under Art Gallon in 1960-61.

Year	School	Overall	League	Finish	Postseason
61-62	Central Mo. St.	16-6	7-3	3rd (MIAA)	DNP
62-63	Central Mo. St.	17-6	7-3	T2nd (MIAA)	DNP
63-64	Central Mo. St.	14-9	6-4	T2nd (MIAA)	DNP
64-65	Valparaiso	13-12	5-7	T3rd (ICC)	DNP
65-66	Valparaiso	19-9	7-5	4th (ICC)	NCAA DII (1-1)
66-67	Valparaiso	21-8	7-5	2nd (ICC)	NCAA DII (2-1)
67-68	Valparaiso	11-15	3-9	6th (ICC)	DNP
68-69	Valparaiso	16-12	4-4	T2nd (ICC)	NCAA DII (1-1)
69-70	Valparaiso	13-13	2-6	5th (ICC)	DNP
70-71	Memphis State	18-8	8-6	T4th (Mo. Valley)	DNP
71-72	Memphis State*	21-7	12-2	T1st (Mo. Valley)	NIT (0-1)
72-73	Memphis State	24-6	12-2	1st (Mo. Valley)	NCAA (3-1)
73-74	Memphis State	19-11	–	–	NIT (1-1)
74-75	Illinois	8-18	4-14	T9th (Big Ten)	Probation
75-76	UCLA	27-5	12-2	1st (Pacific-10)	NCAA (4-1)
76-77	UCLA	24-5	11-3	1st (Pacific-10)	NCAA (1-1)
78-79	UAB	15-11	–	–	DNP
79-80	UAB	18-12	10-4	T2nd (Sun Belt)	NIT (0-1)
80-81	UAB	23-9	9-3	T1st (Sun Belt)	NCAA (2-1)
81-82	UAB	25-6	9-1	1st (Sun Belt)	NCAA (2-1)
82-83	UAB	19-14	9-5	3rd (Sun Belt)	NCAA (0-1)
83-84	UAB	23-11	8-6	5th (Sun Belt)	NCAA (0-1)
84-85	UAB	25-9	11-3	2nd (Sun Belt)	NCAA (1-1)
85-86	UAB	25-11	9-5	T3rd (Sun Belt)	NCAA (1-1)
86-87	UAB	21-11	10-4	3rd (Sun Belt)	NCAA (0-1)
87-88	UAB	16-15	7-7	5th (Sun Belt)	DNP
88-89	UAB	22-12	8-6	4th (Sun Belt)	NIT (4-1)
89-90	UAB	22-9	12-2	1st (Sun Belt)	NCAA (0-1)
90-91	UAB	18-13	9-5	2nd (Sun Belt)	NIT (0-1)
91-92	UAB	20-9	4-6	5th (Great Midwest)	NIT (0-1)
92-93	UAB	21-14	5-5	4th (Great Midwest)	NIT (4-1)
93-94	UAB	22-8	8-4	T2nd (Great Midwest)	NCAA (0-1)
94-95	UAB	14-16	5-7	6th (Great Midwest)	DNP
95-96	UAB	16-14	6-8	T2nd (C-USA Red)	DNP

*Lost Missouri Valley Conference playoff game against regular-season co-champion Louisville (83-72) for automatic berth in NCAA Tournament.

34-Year Coaching Record: 646-354 (.646) overall if don't include forfeit victory over Oregon State in 1975-76; 47-21 (.691) in three years at Central Missouri State; 93-69 (.574) in six years at Valparaiso; 82-32 (.719) in four years at Memphis State; 8-18 (.308) in one year at Illinois; 51-10 (.836) in two years at UCLA; 365-204 (.641) in 18 years at UAB; 20-10 (.667) in Missouri Intercollegiate Athletic Association; 28-36 (.438) in Indiana Collegiate Conference; 32-10 (.762) in Missouri Valley; 4-14 (.222) in Big Ten; 23-5 (.821) in Pacific-10; 111-51 (.685) in Sun Belt; 22-22 (.500) in Great Midwest; 6-8 (.429) in Conference USA; 19-8 (.704) in Sun Belt Tournament; 0-4 in Great Midwest Tournament; 0-1 in C-USA Tournament; 4-3 (.571) in NCAA Division II Tournament with Valparaiso; 14-12 (.538) in NCAA Division I Tournament; 9-7 (.563) in NIT.

CLAIR BEE
Waynesburg '25
Grafton, W.V.

Elected to Naismith Memorial Basketball Hall of Fame in 1967.... Coached LIU-Brooklyn to NIT titles in 1939 and 1941.... Second on the all-time coaches list for career winning percentage.... Compiled a 34-116 record with the NBA's Baltimore Bullets from 1952–53 through 1954–55.

Year	School	Overall	League	Finish	Postseason
28–29	Rider	19-3			
29–30	Rider	17-2			
30–31	Rider	17-2			
31–32	LIU-Bk'lyn	16-4			
32–33	LIU-Bk'lyn	6-11			
33–34	LIU-Bk'lyn	26-1			
34–35	LIU-Bk'lyn	24-2			
35–36	LIU-Bk'lyn	25-0			
36–37	LIU-Bk'lyn	28-3			
37–38	LIU-Bk'lyn	23-5			NIT (0-1)
38–39	LIU-Bk'lyn	23-0			NIT (3-0)
39–40	LIU-Bk'lyn	19-4			NIT (0-1)
40–41	LIU-Bk'lyn	25-2			NIT (3-0)
41–42	LIU-Bk'lyn	25-3			NIT (0-1)
42–43	LIU-Bk'lyn	13-6			DNP
45–46	LIU-Bk'lyn	14-9			DNP
46–47	LIU-Bk'lyn	17-5			NIT (0-1)
47–48	LIU-Bk'lyn	17-4			DNP
48–49	LIU-Bk'lyn	18-12			DNP
49–50	LIU-Bk'lyn	20-5			NIT (0-1)
50–51	LIU-Bk'lyn	20-4			DNP

21-Year Coaching Record: 412-87 (.826) overall; 53-7 (.883) in three years at Rider; 359-80 (.818) in 18 years at LIU-Brooklyn; 6-5 (.545) in NIT.

TOM BLACKBURN
Wilmington '31
Peebles, O.

Coached Dayton to NIT title in 1962. Reached NIT semifinals in 1951 (2nd), 1952 (2nd) 1955 (2nd), 1956 (2nd), 1958 (2nd) and 1961 (4th)..

Year	School	Overall	League	Finish	Postseason
47-48	Dayton	12-14			DNP
48-49	Dayton	16-14			NCIT (1-1)
49-50	Dayton	24-8			DNP
50-51	Dayton	27-5			NIT (3-1)
51-52	Dayton	28-5			NCAA (1-1): NIT (3-1)
52-53	Dayton	16-13			DNP
53-54	Dayton	25-7			NIT (1-1)
54-55	Dayton	25-4			NIT (2-1)
55-56	Dayton	25-4			NIT (2-1)
56-57	Dayton	19-9			NIT (1-1)
57-58	Dayton	25-4			NIT (2-1)
58-59	Dayton	14-12			DNP
59-60	Dayton	21-7			NIT (1-1)
60-61	Dayton	20-9			NIT (1-2)
61-62	Dayton	24-6			NIT (4-0)
62-63	Dayton	16-10			DNP
63-64	Dayton	15-10			DNP

Note: Blackburn died March 6, 1964, a little over one day before Dayton's final game. Assistant Don Donoher handled the team in the Flyers' last three outings although the contest are part of Blackburn's record.

17-Year Coaching Record: 352-141 (.714) at Dayton; 1-1 (.500) in NCAA Tournament; 20-10 (.667) in NIT; 1-1 (.500) in National Catholic Invitational Tournament.

HAROLD BRADLEY
Hartwick '34
Oneonta, N.Y.

Coached two different schools to NCAA Tournament.

Year	School	Overall	League	Finish	Postseason
47-48	Hartwick	14-8			
48-49	Hartwick	18-5			
49-50	Hartwick	18-5			
50-51	Duke	20-13	13-6	T4th (Southern)	DNP
51-52	Duke	24-6	13-3	3rd (Southern)	DNP
52-53	Duke	18-8	12-4	6th (Southern)	DNP
53-54	Duke	22-6	9-1	1st (ACC)	DNP
54-55	Duke	20-8	11-3	2nd (ACC)	NCAA (0-1)
55-56	Duke	19-7	10-4	T3rd (ACC)	DNP
56-57	Duke	13-11	8-6	3rd (ACC)	DNP
57-58	Duke	18-7	11-3	1st (ACC)	DNP
58-59	Duke	13-12	7-7	T3rd (ACC)	DNP
59-60	Texas	18-8	11-3	1st (SWC)	NCAA (0-2)
60-61	Texas	14-10	8-6	4th (SWC)	DNP
61-62	Texas	16-8	8-6	4th (SWC)	DNP
62-63	Texas	20-7	13-1	1st (SWC)	NCAA (2-1)
63-64	Texas	15-9	8-6	T3rd (SWC)	DNP
64-65	Texas	16-9	10-4	T1st (SWC)	DNP
65-66	Texas	12-12	7-7	T4th (SWC)	DNP
66-67	Texas	14-10	8-6	T2nd (SWC)	DNP

20-Year Coaching Record: 337-169 (.666) overall; 50-18 (.735) in three years at Hartwick; 167-78 (.682) in nine years at Duke; 125-73 (.631) in eight years at Texas; 38-13 (.745) in Southern Conference; 56-24 (.700) in Atlantic Coast Conference; 73-39 (.652) in Southwest Conference; 4-3 (.571) in Southern Conference Tournament; 6-6 (.500) in ACC Tournament; 2-4 (.333) in NCAA Tournament.

LARRY BROWN
North Carolina '63
Long Beach, N.Y.

Naismith coach of the year in 1988.... Coach of 1988 NCAA champion, 1980 runner-up, and 1986 Final Four team.... Coach of two Big Eight Conference Tournament champions—1984 and 1986.... U.S. Olympic team assistant coach in 1980.... Compiled a 229-107 (.682) regular-season record and 20-22 (.476) playoff mark in four seasons as coach in the ABA from 1972-73 through 1975-76 before compiling a 481-377 (.561) regular-season record and 29-32 (.475) playoff mark in his first 11 years as coach of five different NBA franchises from 1976-77 through 1993-94.... Assistant coach at North Carolina under Dean Smith for two seasons (1965-66 and 1966-67).

Year	School	Overall	League	Finish	Postseason
79-80	UCLA	22-10	12-6	4th (Pac-10)	NCAA (5-1)
80-81	UCLA	20-7	13-5	3d (Pac-10)	NCAA (0-1)
83-84	Kansas	22-10	9-5	2d (Big Eight)	NCAA (1-1)
84-85	Kansas	26-8	11-3	2d (Big Eight)	NCAA (1-1)
85-86	Kansas	35-4	13-1	1st (Big Eight)	NCAA (4-1)
86-87	Kansas	25-11	9-5	T2d (Big Eight)	NCAA (2-1)
87-88	Kansas	27-11	9-5	3d (Big Eight)	NCAA (6-0)

Seven-Year College Coaching Record: 177-61 (.744) overall; 42-17 (.712) in two years at UCLA; 135-44 (.754) in five years at Kansas; 25-11 (.694) in Pacific-10 Conference; 51-19 (.729) in Big Eight; 10-3 (.769) in Big Eight Tournament; 19-6 (.760) in NCAA Tournament.

VIC BUBAS
N.C. St. '51
Gary, Ind.

Reached NCAA Final Four three times—1963 (3rd), 1964 (2nd), and 1966 (3rd).... Coach of four Atlantic Coast Conference Tournament champions—1960, 1963, 1964, and 1966.... Assistant coach under Everett Case at his alma mater from 1951-52 through 1958-59.

Year	School	Overall	League	Finish	Postseason
59-60	Duke	17-11	7-7	4th (ACC)	NCAA (2-1)
60-61	Duke	22-6	10-4	3d (ACC)	DNP
61-62	Duke	20-5	11-3	2d (ACC)	DNP
62-63	Duke	27-3	14-0	1st (ACC)	NCAA (3-1)
63-64	Duke	26-5	13-1	1st (ACC)	NCAA (3-1)
64-65	Duke	20-5	11-3	1st (ACC)	DNP
65-66	Duke	26-4	12-2	1st (ACC)	NCAA (3-1)
66-67	Duke	18-9	9-3	2d (ACC)	NIT (0-1)
67-68	Duke	22-6	11-3	2d (ACC)	NIT (1-1)
68-69	Duke	15-13	8-6	T3d (ACC)	DNP

10-Year Coaching Record: 213-67 (.761) overall; 106-32 (.768) in Atlantic Coast Conference; 22-6 (.786) in ACC Tournament; 11-4 (.733) in NCAA Tournament; 1-2 (.333) in NIT.

JOHN CALIPARI
Clarion (Pa.) State '82
Pittsburgh, Pa.

Coach of Final Four team in 1996.... Coach of last five Atlantic 10 Conference Tournament champions—1992, 1993, 1994, 1995 and 1996.... Directed Massachusetts to fourth-place finish in 1991 NIT.... Assistant coach at Kansas under Larry Brown.

Year	School	Overall	League	Finish	Postseason
88-89	Massachusetts	10-18	5-13	8th (Atl. 10)	DNP
89-90	Massachusetts	17-14	10-8	6th (Atl. 10)	NIT (0-1)
90-91	Massachusetts	20-13	10-8	T3rd (Atl. 10)	NIT (3-2)
91-92	Massachusetts	30-5	13-3	1st (Atl. 10)	NCAA (2-1)
92-93	Massachusetts	24-7	11-3	1st (Atl. 10	NCAA (1-1)
93-94	Massachusetts	28-7	14-2	1st (Atl. 10)	NCAA (1-1)
94-95	Massachusetts	29-5	13-3	1st (Atl. 10)	NCAA (3-1)
95-96	Massachusetts	35-2	15-1	1st (Atl. 10/E)	NCAA (4-1)

Eight-Year Coaching Record: 193-71 (.731) at Massachusetts; 79-37 (.681) in Atlantic 10; 14-3 (.824) in Atlantic 10 Tournament; 11-5 (.688) in NCAA Tournament; 3-3 (.500) in NIT.

HOWARD CANN
N.Y.U. '20
New York, N.Y.

Elected to Naismith Memorial Basketball Hall of Fame in 1967.... Coach of Helms Foundation national champion in 1935.... Reached Final Four in 1945 (2nd).... NIT runner-up in 1948.... Reached NIT semifinals in 1938 (4th).... Competed in the 1920 Olympics as a shot putter.... Coached NYU's football squad in 1932 and 1933.

Year	School	Overall	League	Finish	Postseason
23-24	New York U.	8-8			
24-25	New York U.	7-7			
25-26	New York U.	10-4			
26-27	New York U.	4-7			
27-28	New York U.	8-6			
28-29	New York U.	13-5			
29-30	New York U.	13-3			
30-31	New York U.	9-6			
31-32	New York U.	6-6			
32-33	New York U.	11-4			
33-34	New York U.	16-0			
34-35	New York U.	18-1			
35-36	New York U.	14-4			
36-37	New York U.	10-6			
37-38	New York U.	16-8			NIT (1-2)
38-39	New York U.	11-11			DNP

39-40	New York U.	18-1				DNP
40-41	New York U.	13-6				DNP
41-42	New York U.	12-7				DNP
42-43	New York U.	16-6				NCAA (0-2)
43-44	New York U.	7-7				DNP
44-45	New York U.	14-7				NCAA (2-1)
45-46	New York U.	19-3				NCAA (1-1)
46-47	New York U.	12-9				DNP
47-48	New York U.	22-4				NIT (2-1)
48-49	New York U.	12-8				NIT (0-1)
49-50	New York U.	8-11				DNP
50-51	New York U.	12-4				DNP
51-52	New York U.	17-8				NIT (0-1)
52-53	New York U.	9-11				DNP
53-54	New York U.	9-9				DNP
54-55	New York U.	7-13				DNP
55-56	New York U.	10-8				DNP
56-57	New York U.	8-13				DNP
57-58	New York U.	10-11				DNP

35-Year Coaching Record: 409-232 (.638) at New York University; 3-4 (.429) in NCAA Tournament; 3-5 (.375) in NIT.

LOU CARNESECCA
St. John's '46
Manhattan, N.Y.

Named national coach of the year by NABC and USBWA in 1983, and by UPI and USBWA in 1985.... Coach of 1985 NCAA Final Four team.... Coach of three NIT semifinalists—1970 (runner-up), 1975 (fourth place), and 1989 (champion).... Compiled 114-138 record in three seasons with ABA's New York Nets from 1970–71 through 1972–73.... Assistant coach at St. John's for nine seasons under Joe Lapchick from 1957 to 1965.... Elected to Naismith Memorial Basketball Hall of Fame in 1991.

Year	School	Overall	League	Finish	Postseason
65–66	St. John's	18-8			NIT (0-1)
66–67	St. John's	23-5			NCAA (1-1)
67–68	St. John's	19-8			NCAA (0-1)
68–69	St. John's	23-6			NCAA (1-1)
69–70	St. John's	21-8			NIT (3-1)
73–74	St. John's	20-7			NIT (0-1)
74–75	St. John's	21-10			NIT (2-2)
75–76	St. John's	23-6			NCAA (0-1)
76–77	St. John's	22-9			NCAA (0-1)
77–78	St. John's	21-7			NCAA (0-1)
78–79	St. John's	21-11			NCAA (3-1)
79–80	St. John's	24-5	5-1	T1st (Big East)	NCAA (0-1)
80–81	St. John's	17-11	8-6	T3d (Big East)	NIT (0-1)
81–82	St. John's	21-9	9-5	3d (Big East)	NCAA (1-1)
82–83	St. John's	28-5	12-4	T1st (Big East)	NCAA (1-1)
83–84	St. John's	18-12	8-8	T4th (Big East)	NCAA (0-1)
84–85	St. John's	31-4	15-1	1st (Big East)	NCAA (4-1)
85–86	St. John's	31-5	14-2	T1st (Big East)	NCAA (1-1)
86–87	St. John's	21-9	10-6	T4th (Big East)	NCAA (1-1)
87–88	St. John's	17-12	8-8	T5th (Big East)	NCAA (0-1)
88–89	St. John's	20-13	6-10	T7th (Big East)	NIT (5-0)
89–90	St. John's	24-10	10-6	4th (Big East)	NCAA (1-1)
90–91	St. John's	23-9	10-6	2d (Big East)	NCAA (3-1)
91–92	St. John's	19-11	12-6	T1st (Big East)	NCAA (0-1)

24-Year College Coaching Record: 526-200 (.725) overall; 127-69 (.648) in Big East; 12-11 (.522) in Big East Tournament; 17-20 (.459) in NCAA Tournament; 10-6 (.625) in NIT.

BEN CARNEVALE
N.Y.U. '38
Somerville, N.J.

Elected to Naismith Memorial Basketball Hall of Fame in 1969.... U.S. Olympic team manager in 1968.... Reached Final Four in 1946 (2nd).... Coached two different schools to NCAA Tournament.... Guided North Carolina to 1945 Southern Conference Tournament championship.... Played for Howard Cann at NYU before serving in the U.S. Navy (1942-44).

Year	School	Overall	League	Finish	Postseason
44-45	N. Carolina	22-6	11-3	4th (Southern)	DNP
45-46	N. Carolina	30-5	13-1	1st (Southern)	NCAA (2-1)
46-47	Navy	16-3			NCAA (0-2)
47-48	Navy	10-7			DNP
48-49	Navy	12-9			DNP
49-50	Navy	14-7			DNP
50-51	Navy	16-6			DNP
51-52	Navy	16-7			DNP
52-53	Navy	16-5			NCAA (0-1)
53-54	Navy	18-8			NCAA (2-1)
54-55	Navy	11-9			DNP
55-56	Navy	10-9			DNP
56-57	Navy	15-8			DNP
57-58	Navy	10-10			DNP
58-59	Navy	18-6			NCAA (2-1)
59-60	Navy	16-6			NCAA (0-1)
60-61	Navy	10-9			DNP
61-62	Navy	13-8			NIT (0-1)
62-63	Navy	9-9			DNP
63-64	Navy	10-12			DNP
64-65	Navy	10-10			DNP
65-66	Navy	7-12			DNP

22-Year Coaching Record: 309-171 (.644) overall; 52-11 (.825) in two years at North Carolina; 257-160 (.616) in 20 years at the United States Naval Academy; 24-4 (.857) in Southern Conference; 4-1 (.800) in Southern Conference Tournament; 6-7 (.462) in NCAA Tournament; 0-1 in NIT.

PETE CARRIL
Lafayette '52
Bethlehem, Pa.

Captured the Ivy League's only NIT championship in 1975.... Won two Ivy League playoff games (1981 and 1996).... Incurred only one losing record in 30 seasons at Princeton.

Year	School	Overall	League	Finish	Postseason
66-67	Lehigh	11-12	–	Middle Atlantic	DNP
67-68	Princeton	20-6	12-2	T1st (Ivy)	DNP
68-69	Princeton	19-7	14-0	1st (Ivy)	NCAA (0-1)
69-70	Princeton	16-9	9-5	3rd (Ivy)	DNP
70-71	Princeton	14-11	9-5	T3rd (Ivy)	DNP
71-72	Princeton	20-7	12-2	2nd (Ivy)	NIT (1-1)
72-73	Princeton	16-9	11-3	2nd (Ivy)	DNP
73-74	Princeton	16-10	11-3	T2nd (Ivy)	DNP
74-75	Princeton	22-8	12-2	2nd (Ivy)	NIT (4-0)
75-76	Princeton	22-5	13-1	1st (Ivy)	NCAA (0-1)
76-77	Princeton	21-5	13-1	1st (Ivy)	NCAA (0-1)
77-78	Princeton	17-9	11-3	T2nd (Ivy)	DNP
78-79	Princeton	14-12	7-7	3rd (Ivy)	DNP
79-80	Princeton	15-15	11-3	T1st (Ivy)	DNP
80-81	Princeton	18-10	13-1	T1st (Ivy)	NCAA (0-1)
81-82	Princeton	13-13	9-5	T2nd (Ivy)	DNP
82-83	Princeton	20-9	12-2	1st (Ivy)	NCAA (2-1)
83-84	Princeton	18-10	10-4	1st (Ivy)	NCAA (1-1)
84-85	Princeton	11-15	7-7	T4th (Ivy)	DNP
85-86	Princeton	13-13	7-7	T4th (Ivy)	DNP
86-87	Princeton	16-9	9-5	T2nd (Ivy)	DNP
87-88	Princeton	17-9	9-5	3rd (Ivy)	DNP
88-89	Princeton	19-8	11-3	1st (Ivy)	NCAA (0-1)
89-90	Princeton	20-7	11-3	1st (Ivy)	NCAA (0-1)
90-91	Princeton	24-3	14-0	1st (Ivy)	NCAA (0-1)
91-92	Princeton	22-6	12-2	1st (Ivy)	NCAA (0-1)
92-93	Princeton	15-11	7-7	4th (Ivy)	DNP
93-94	Princeton	18-8	11-3	2nd (Ivy)	DNP
94-95	Princeton	16-10	10-4	T2nd (Ivy)	DNP
95-96	Princeton	22-7	12-2	T1st (Ivy)	NCAA (1-1)

30-Year College Coaching Record: 525-273 (.658) overall; 11-12 (.478) in one year at Lehigh; 514-261 (.663) in 29 years at Princeton; 314-96 (.766) in Ivy League; 4-11 (.267) in NCAA Tournament; 5-1 (.833) in NIT.

EVERETT CASE
Wisconsin '23
Anderson, Ind.

Elected to Naismith Memorial Basketball Hall of Fame in 1981.... Reached Final Four in 1950 (3rd).... Coach of six Southern Conference Tournament champions—1947, 1948, 1949, 1950, 1951, and 1953.... Coach of four Atlantic Coast Conference Tournament champions—1954, 1955, 1956, and 1959.

Year	School	Overall	League	Finish	Postseason
46–47	N.C. St.	26-5	11-2	1st (Southern)	NIT (2-1)
47–48	N.C. St.	29-3	12-0	1st (Southern)	NIT (0-1)
48–49	N.C. St.	25-8	14-1	1st (Southern)	DNP
49–50	N.C. St.	27-6	12-2	1st (Southern)	NCAA (2-1)
50–51	N.C. St.	30-7	13-1	1st (Southern)	NCAA (1-2): NIT (0-1)
51–52	N.C. St.	24-10	12-2	2d (Southern)	NCAA (1-1)
52–53	N.C. St.	26-6	13-3	1st (Southern)	DNP
53–54	N.C. St.	26-7	5-3	4th (ACC)	NCAA (2-1)
54–55	N.C. St.	28-4	12-2	1st (ACC)	DNP
55–56	N.C. St.	24-4	11-3	T1st (ACC)	NCAA (0-1)
56–57	N.C. St.	15-11	7-7	T4th (ACC)	DNP
57–58	N.C. St.	18-6	10-4	T2d (ACC)	DNP
58–59	N.C. St.	22-4	12-2	T1st (ACC)	DNP
59–60	N.C. St.	11-15	5-9	6th (ACC)	DNP
60–61	N.C. St.	16-9	8-6	4th (ACC)	DNP
61–62	N.C. St.	11-6	10-4	3d (ACC)	DNP
62–63	N.C. St.	10-11	5-9	T4th (ACC)	DNP
63–64	N.C. St.	8-11	4-10	T7th (ACC)	DNP
64–65	N.C. St.	1-1	0-1		DNP

19-Year Coaching Record: 377-134 (.738) overall; 87-11 (.888) in Southern Conference; 89-60 (.597) in Atlantic Coast Conference; 20-1 (.952) in Southern Conference Tournament; 15-7 (.682) in ACC Tournament; 6-6 (.500) in NCAA Tournament; 2-3 (.400) in NIT.

HARRY COMBES
Illinois '37
Monticello, Ill.

Reached NCAA Final Four three times—1949 (3rd), 1951 (3rd), and 1952 (3rd).

Year	School	Overall	League	Finish	Postseason
47–48	Illinois	15-5	7-5	T3d (Big Ten)	DNP
48–49	Illinois	21-4	10-2	1st (Big Ten)	NCAA (2-1)
49–50	Illinois	14-8	7-5	T3d (Big Ten)	DNP
50–51	Illinois	22-5	13-1	1st (Big Ten)	NCAA (3-1)
51–52	Illinois	22-4	12-2	1st (Big Ten)	NCAA (3-1)
52–53	Illinois	18-4	14-4	2d (Big Ten)	DNP
53–54	Illinois	17-5	10-4	T3d (Big Ten)	DNP
54–55	Illinois	17-5	10-4	T2d (Big Ten)	DNP
55–56	Illinois	18-4	11-3	2d (Big Ten)	DNP
56–57	Illinois	14-8	7-7	7th (Big Ten)	DNP
57–58	Illinois	11-11	5-9	T8th (Big Ten)	DNP
58–59	Illinois	12-10	7-7	T5th (Big Ten)	DNP
59–60	Illinois	16-7	8-6	T3d (Big Ten)	DNP
60–61	Illinois	9-15	5-9	7th (Big Ten)	DNP
61–62	Illinois	15-8	7-7	T4th (Big Ten)	DNP
62–63	Illinois	20-6	11-3	T1st (Big Ten)	NCAA (1-1)
63–64	Illinois	13-11	6-8	T6th (Big Ten)	DNP
64–65	Illinois	18-6	10-4	3d (Big Ten)	DNP
65–66	Illinois	12-12	8-6	T3d (Big Ten)	DNP
66–67	Illinois	12-12	6-8	7th (Big Ten)	DNP

20-Year Coaching Record: 316-150 (.678) overall; 174-104 (.626) in Big Ten Conference; 9-4 (.692) in NCAA Tournament.

CHARLES (CHICK) DAVIES
Duquesne '34
New Castle, Pa.

Reached NCAA Final Four in 1940 (tied for third place).... Coach of second-place finisher in 1940 NIT.

Year	School	Overall	League	Finish	Postseason
24–25	Duquesne	12-6			
25–26	Duquesne	15-4			
26–27	Duquesne	16-4			
27–28	Duquesne	15-7			
28–29	Duquesne	12-8			
29–30	Duquesne	18-10			
30–31	Duquesne	12-6			
31–32	Duquesne	14-6			
32–33	Duquesne	15-1			
33–34	Duquesne	19-2			
34–35	Duquesne	18-1			
35–36	Duquesne	14-3			
36–37	Duquesne	13-6			
37–38	Duquesne	6-11			DNP
38–39	Duquesne	14-4			DNP
39–40	Duquesne	20-3			NCAA (1-1); NIT (2-1)
40–41	Duquesne	17-3			NIT (0-1)
41–42	Duquesne	15-6			DNP
42–43	Duquesne	12-7			DNP
46–47	Duquesne	20-2			NIT (0-1)
47–48	Duquesne	17-6			DNP

21-Year Coaching Record: 314-106 (.748) overall; 1-1 (.500) in NCAA Tournament; 2-3 (.400) in NIT.

EVERETT DEAN
Indiana '21
Salem, Ind.

Elected to Naismith Memorial Basketball Hall of Fame in 1966.... Coached Stanford to the 1942 NCAA championship.

Year	School	Overall	League	Finish	Postseason
21–22	Carleton	14-2		1st (Midwest)	
22–23	Carleton	17-2		1st (Midwest)	
23–24	Carleton	14-0		1st (Midwest)	
24–25	Indiana	12-5	8-4	T2d (Western)	
25–26	Indiana	12-5	8-4	T1st (Western)	
26–27	Indiana	13-4	9-3	2d (Western)	
27–28	Indiana	15-2	10-2	T1st (Western)	
28–29	Indiana	7-10	4-8	8th (Western)	
29–30	Indiana	8-9	7-5	T4th (Western)	
30–31	Indiana	9-8	5-7	6th (Western)	
31–32	Indiana	8-10	4-8	7th (Western)	
32–33	Indiana	10-8	6-6	T6th (Western)	
33–34	Indiana	13-7	6-6	T5th (Western)	
34–35	Indiana	14-6	8-4	T1st (Western)	
35–36	Indiana	18-2	11-1	T1st (Western)	
36–37	Indiana	13-7	6-6	T6th (Western)	
37–38	Indiana	10-10	4-8	8th (Western)	DNP
38–39	Stanford	16-9	6-6	3d (PCC-S)	DNP
39–40	Stanford	14-9	6-6	2d (PCC-S)	DNP
40–41	Stanford	21-5	10-2	1st (PCC-S)	DNP
41–42	Stanford	27-4	11-1	1st (PCC-S)	NCAA (3-0)
42–43	Stanford	10-10	4-4	T2d (PCC-S)	DNP
45–46	Stanford	6-18	0-12	4th (PCC-S)	DNP
46–47	Stanford	15-16	5-7	3d (PCC-S)	DNP
47–48	Stanford	15-11	3-9	T3d (PCC-S)	DNP
48–49	Stanford	19-9	5-7	3d (PCC-S)	DNP
49–50	Stanford	11-14	3-9	4th (PCC-S)	DNP
50–51	Stanford	12-14	5-7	3d (PCC-S)	DNP

28-Year Coaching Record: 374-217 (.633) overall; 45-4 (.918) in three years at Carleton; 162-93 (.635) in 14 years at Indiana; 167-120 (.582) in 11 years at Stanford; 96-72 (.571) in Western Conference (forerunner of Big Ten); 53-70 (.431) in Pacific Coast Conference-South Division; 3-0 in NCAA Tournament.

ED DIDDLE
Centre '21
Columbia, Ky.

Elected to Naismith Memorial Basketball Hall of Fame in 1971.... Coach of four Ohio Valley Conference Tournament champions—1949, 1952, 1953, and 1954.... Coach of second-place finisher in 1942 NIT, third-place finisher in 1948, and fourth-place finisher in 1954.... Tied with DePaul's Ray Meyer for the NCAA career record for most years coached at one school with 42 seasons.

Year	School	Overall	League	Finish	Postseason
22–23	Western Ky.	12-2			
23–24	Western Ky.	9-9			
24–25	Western Ky.	8-6			
25–26	Western Ky.	10-4	KIAC		
26–27	Western Ky.	12-7	KIAC		
27–28	Western Ky.	10-7	KIAC		
28–29	Western Ky.	8-10	KIAC		
29–30	Western Ky.	4-12	KIAC		
30–31	Western Ky.	11-3	KIAC		
31–32	Western Ky.	15-8	KIAC		
32–33	Western Ky.	16-6	KIAC		
33–34	Western Ky.	28-8	KIAC		
34–35	Western Ky.	24-3	KIAC		
35–36	Western Ky.	26-4	KIAC		
36–37	Western Ky.	21-2	KIAC		
37–38	Western Ky.	30-3	KIAC		DNP
38–39	Western Ky.	22-3	KIAC		DNP
39–40	Western Ky.	24-6	KIAC		NCAA (0-1)
40–41	Western Ky.	22-4	KIAC		DNP
41–42	Western Ky.	29-5	KIAC		NIT (2-1)
42–43	Western Ky.	24-3	3-1	T2d (KIAC)	NIT (0-1)
43–44	Western Ky.	13-9		KIAC	DNP
44–45	Western Ky.	17-10		KIAC	DNP
45–46	Western Ky.	15-19	2-6	8th (KIAC)	DNP
46–47	Western Ky.	25-4	6-2	2d (KIAC)	DNP
47–48	Western Ky.	28-2	10-0	1st (KIAC)	NIT (2-1)
48–49	Western Ky.	25-4	8-2	1st (OVC)	NIT (0-1)
49–50	Western Ky.	25-6	8-0	1st (OVC)	NIT (1-1)
50–51	Western Ky.	19-10	4-4	4th (OVC)	DNP
51–52	Western Ky.	26-5	9-1	1st (OVC)	NIT (1-1)
52–53	Western Ky.	25-6	8-2	2d (OVC)	NIT (0-1)
53–54	Western Ky.	29-3	9-1	1st (OVC)	NIT (1-2)
54–55	Western Ky.	18-10	8-2	1st (OVC)	DNP
55–56	Western Ky.	16-12	7-3	T1st (OVC)	DNP
56–57	Western Ky.	17-9	9-1	T1st (OVC)	DNP
57–58	Western Ky.	14-11	5-5	3d (OVC)	DNP
58–59	Western Ky.	16-10	8-4	2d (OVC)	DNP
59–60	Western Ky.	21-7	10-2	1st (OVC)	NCAA (2-1)
60–61	Western Ky.	18-8	9-3	T1st (OVC)	DNP
61–62	Western Ky.	17-10	11-1	1st (OVC)	NCAA (1-2)
62–63	Western Ky.	5-16	3-9	7th (OVC)	DNP
63–64	Western Ky.	5-16	3-11	8th (OVC)	DNP

Note: No regular-season standings, only postseason conference tournaments, for the Kentucky Intercollegiate Athletic Conference except for one season through 1944–45. The SIAA Tournament included champions and at-large teams from various southern conferences.

42-Year Coaching Record: 759-302 (.715) overall; 21-9 (.700) in Kentucky Intercollegiate Athletic Conference; 119-51 (.700) in Ohio Valley Conference; 54-7 (.885) in KIAC Tournament; 35-7 (.833) in Southern Intercollegiate Athletic Association Tournament; 3-4 (.429) in NCAA Tournament; 7-9 (.438) in NIT.

DON DONOHER
Dayton '54
Toledo, O.

Coached Dayton to NIT title in 1968. . . . Reached Final Four of NCAA Tournament in 1967 (2nd). . . . One of 10 coaches to take his first three teams to the NCAA Tournament. . . . Assistant coach for 1984 gold medal-winning U.S. Olympic team.

Year	School	Overall	League	Finish	Postseason
64-65	Dayton	22-7			NCAA (2-1)
65-66	Dayton	23-6			NCAA (1-2)
66-67	Dayton	25-6			NCAA (4-1)
67-68	Dayton	21-9			NIT (4-0)
68-69	Dayton	20-7			NCAA (0-1)
69-70	Dayton	19-8			NCAA (0-1)
70-71	Dayton	18-9			NIT (0-1)
71-72	Dayton	13-13			DNP
72-73	Dayton	13-13			DNP
73-74	Dayton	20-9			NCAA (1-2)
74-75	Dayton	10-16			DNP
75-76	Dayton	14-13			DNP
76-77	Dayton	16-11			DNP
77-78	Dayton	19-10			NIT (1-1)
78-79	Dayton	19-10			NIT (1-1)
79-80	Dayton	13-14			DNP
80-81	Dayton	18-11			NIT (1-1)
81-82	Dayton	21-9			NIT (2-1)
82-83	Dayton	18-10			DNP
83-84	Dayton	21-11			NCAA (3-1)
84-85	Dayton	19-10			NCAA (0-1)
85-86	Dayton	17-13			NIT (0-1)
86-87	Dayton	13-15			DNP
87-88	Dayton	13-18			DNP
88-89	Dayton	12-17	6-6	4th (MCC)	DNP

Note: Became an assistant coach at Dayton in January, 1963 (had previously been in private business and a part-time scout and assistant high school coach). He was in charge of the Flyers for their last three outings in 1963-64 although the contests are considered part of the record for coach Tom Blackburn, who passed away a little over one day before the final game.

25-Year Coaching Record: 437-275 (.614) at Dayton; 6-6 (.500) in Midwestern Collegiate Conference; 1-1 (.500) in MCC Tournament; 11-10 (.524) in NCAA Tournament; 9-6 (.600) in NIT.

BRUCE DRAKE
Oklahoma '29
Oklahoma City, Okla.

Elected to Naismith Memorial Basketball Hall of Fame in 1972.... U.S. Olympic Team coach in 1956.... Reached NCAA Final Four two times—1939 (tied for third) and 1947 (2nd).... Assistant coach under Hugh McDermott at Oklahoma.

Year	School	Overall	League	Finish	Postseason
38–39	Oklahoma	12-9	7-3	T1st (Big Six)	NCAA (1-1)
39–40	Oklahoma	12-7	8-2	T1st (Big Six)	DNP
40–41	Oklahoma	6-12	5-5	4th (Big Six)	DNP
41–42	Oklahoma	11-7	8-2	T1st (Big Six)	DNP
42–43	Oklahoma	18-9	7-3	2d (Big Six)	NCAA (1-1)
43–44	Oklahoma	15-8	9-1	T1st (Big Six)	DNP
44–45	Oklahoma	12-13	5-5	T3d (Big Six)	DNP
45–46	Oklahoma	11-10	7-3	2d (Big Six)	DNP
46–47	Oklahoma	24-7	8-2	1st (Big Six)	NCAA (2-1)
47–48	Oklahoma	13-9	7-5	T2d (Big Seven)	DNP
48–49	Oklahoma	14-9	9-3	T1st (Big Seven)	DNP
49–50	Oklahoma	12-10	6-6	T3d (Big Seven)	DNP
50–51	Oklahoma	14-10	6-6	4th (Big Seven)	DNP
51–52	Oklahoma	7-17	4-8	T4th (Big Seven)	DNP
52–53	Oklahoma	8-13	5-7	T4th (Big Seven)	DNP
53–54	Oklahoma	8-13	4-8	6th (Big Seven)	DNP
54–55	Oklahoma	3-18	1-11	7th (Big Seven)	DNP

17-Year Coaching Record: 200-181 (.525) overall; 106-80 (.570) in Big Eight Conference (previously known as Big Six and Big Seven); 4-3 (.571) in NCAA Tournament.

HUGH DURHAM
Florida St. '59
Louisville, Ky.

One of only three coaches in NCAA history to win at least 200 games at two Division I schools.... His Florida State squad was runner-up to UCLA in the 1972 NCAA Tournament finals, and his 1983 Georgia team reached the national semifinals.... Guided Georgia to 1982 NIT semifinals (T3rd).... Led Georgia to 1983 SEC Tournament title.... Assistant coach at his alma mater under Bud Kennedy.

Year	School	Overall	League	Finish	Postseason
66–67	Florida St.	11-15			DNP
67–68	Florida St.	19-8			NCAA (0-1)
68–69	Florida St.	18-8			Probation
69–70	Florida St.	23-3			Probation
70–71	Florida St.	17-9			Probation
71–72	Florida St.	27-6			NCAA (4-1)
72–73	Florida St.	18-8			DNP
73–74	Florida St.	18-8			DNP
74–75	Florida St.	18-8			DNP
75–76	Florida St.	22-5			DNP
76–77	Florida St.	16-11	2-4	5th (Metro)	DNP
77–78	Florida St.	23-6	11-1	1st (Metro)	NCAA (0-1)
78–79	Georgia	14-14	7-11	7th (SEC)	DNP
79–80	Georgia	14-13	7-11	T6th (SEC)	DNP
80–81	Georgia	19-12	9-9	5th (SEC)	NIT (1-1)
81–82	Georgia	19-12	10-8	6th (SEC)	NIT (3-1)
82–83	Georgia	24-10	9-9	T4th (SEC)	NCAA (3-1)
83–84	Georgia	17-13	8-10	T7th (SEC)	NIT (0-1)
84–85*	Georgia	22-9	12-6	2d (SEC)	NCAA (1-1)
85–86	Georgia	17-13	9-9	T5th (SEC)	NIT (1-1)
86–87	Georgia	18-12	10-8	T3d (SEC)	NCAA (0-1)
87–88	Georgia	20-16	8-10	7th (SEC)	NIT (1-1)
88–89	Georgia	15-16	6-12	9th (SEC)	DNP
89–90	Georgia	20-9	13-5	1st (SEC)	NCAA (0-1)
90–91	Georgia	17-13	9-9	5th (SEC)	NCAA (0-1)
91–92	Georgia	15-14	7-9	4th-E (SEC)	DNP
92–93	Georgia	15-14	8-8	4th-E (SEC)	NIT (0-1)
93–94	Georgia	14-16	7-9	4th-E (SEC)	DNP

* NCAA Tournament games later vacated by action of the NCAA

28-Year Coaching Record: 510-301 (.629); 230-95 (.708) in 12 years at Florida State; 280-206 (.576) in first 16 years at Georgia; 13-5 (.722) in Metro Conference; 139-143 (.493) in Southeastern Conference; 1-2 (.333) in Metro Tournament; 17-15 (.531) in SEC Tournament; 8-8 (.500) in NCAA Tournament; 6-6 (.500) in NIT.

CLARENCE (HEC) EDMUNDSON
Idaho '10
Moscow, Idaho

Year	School	Overall	League	Finish	Postseason
16–17	Idaho	8-8			
17–18	Idaho	12-1			
20–21	Washington	18-4	10-4	3d (PCC)	
21–22	Washington	13-5	11-5	4th (PCC)	
22–23	Washington	12-4	5-3	T1st (PCC-N)	
23–24	Washington	12-4	7-2	1st (PCC-N)	
24–25	Washington	14-7	5-5	T3d (PCC-N)	
25–26	Washington	10-6	5-5	4th (PCC-N)	
26–27	Washington	15-4	7-3	T2d (PCC-N)	
27–28	Washington	22-6	9-1	1st (PCC-N)	
28–29	Washington	18-2	10-0	1st (PCC-N)	
29–30	Washington	21-7	12-4	1st (PCC-N)	
30–31	Washington	25-3	14-2	1st (PCC-N)	
31–32	Washington	19-6	12-4	1st (PCC-N)	
32–33	Washington	22-6	10-6	2d (PCC-N)	
33–34	Washington	20-5	14-2	1st (PCC-N)	
34–35	Washington	16-8	11-5	2d (PCC-N)	
35–36	Washington	25-7	13-3	1st (PCC-N)	
36–37	Washington	15-11	11-5	T1st (PCC-N)	
37–38	Washington	29-7	13-7	2d (PCC-N)	DNP
38–39	Washington	20-5	11-5	2d (PCC-N)	DNP
39–40	Washington	10-15	6-10	4th (PCC-N)	DNP
40–41	Washington	12-13	7-9	T3d (PCC-N)	DNP
41–42	Washington	18-7	10-6	2d (PCC-N)	DNP
42–43	Washington	24-7	12-4	1st (PCC-N)	NCAA (0-2)
43–44	Washington	26-6	15-1	1st (PCC-N)	DNP
44–45	Washington	22-18	5-11	4th (PCC-N)	DNP
45–46	Washington	14-14	6-10	4th (PCC-N)	DNP
46–47	Washington	16-8	8-8	3d (PCC-N)	DNP

29-Year Coaching Record: 508-204 (.713) overall; 20-9 (.690) in two years at Idaho; 488-195 (.714) in 27 years at Washington; 259-130 (.666) in Pacific-10 (Pacific Coast Conference); 0-2 in NCAA Tournament.

HAROLD BUD FOSTER
Wisconsin '30
Mason City, Iowa

Elected to Naismith Memorial Basketball Hall of Fame in 1964.... Coach of 1941 NCAA championship team.

Year	School	Overall	League	Finish	Postseason
34–35	Wisconsin	15-5	9-3	T1st (Big Ten)	DNP
35–36	Wisconsin	11-9	4-8	8th (Big Ten)	DNP
36–37	Wisconsin	8-12	3-9	T8th (Big Ten)	DNP
37–38	Wisconsin	10-10	5-7	7th (Big Ten)	DNP
38–39	Wisconsin	10-10	4-8	7th (Big Ten)	DNP
39–40	Wisconsin	5-15	3-9	9th (Big Ten)	DNP
40–41	Wisconsin	20-3	11-1	1st (Big Ten)	NCAA (3-0)
41–42	Wisconsin	14-7	10-5	T2d (Big Ten)	DNP
42–43	Wisconsin	12-9	6-6	T4th (Big Ten)	DNP
43–44	Wisconsin	12-9	9-3	T2d (Big Ten)	DNP
44–45	Wisconsin	10-11	4-8	T6th (Big Ten)	DNP
45–46	Wisconsin	4-17	1-11	9th (Big Ten)	DNP
46–47	Wisconsin	16-6	9-3	1st (Big Ten)	NCAA (1-1)
47–48	Wisconsin	12-8	7-5	T3d (Big Ten)	DNP
48–49	Wisconsin	12-10	5-7	7th (Big Ten)	DNP
49–50	Wisconsin	17-5	9-3	2d (Big Ten)	DNP
50–51	Wisconsin	10-12	7-7	T4th (Big Ten)	DNP
51–52	Wisconsin	10-12	5-9	7th (Big Ten)	DNP
52–53	Wisconsin	13-9	10-8	5th (Big Ten)	DNP
53–54	Wisconsin	12-10	6-8	T5th (Big Ten)	DNP
54–55	Wisconsin	10-12	5-9	T6th (Big Ten)	DNP
55–56	Wisconsin	6-16	4-10	T8th (Big Ten)	DNP
56–57	Wisconsin	5-17	3-11	9th (Big Ten)	DNP
57–58	Wisconsin	8-14	3-11	10th (Big Ten)	DNP
58–59	Wisconsin	3-19	1-13	10th (Big Ten)	DNP

25-Year Coaching Record: 265-267 (.498) overall; 143-182 (.440) in Big Ten Conference; 4-1 (.800) in NCAA Tournament.

JACK GARDNER
Southern Cal '32
Redlands, Calif.

Elected to Naismith Memorial Basketball Hall of Fame in 1983.... Reached NCAA Final Four four times—1948 (4th with Kansas St.), 1951 (2nd with Kansas St.), 1961 (4th with Utah), and 1966 (4th with Utah).

Year	School	Overall	League	Finish	Postseason
39–40	Kansas St.	6-12	2-8	T4th (Big Six)	DNP
40–41	Kansas St.	6-12	3-7	5th (Big Six)	DNP
41–42	Kansas St.	8-10	3-7	5th (Big Six)	DNP
46–47	Kansas St.	14-10	3-7	T5th (Big Six)	DNP
47–48	Kansas St.	22-6	9-3	1st (Big Seven)	NCAA (1-2)
48–49	Kansas St.	13-11	8-4	3d (Big Seven)	DNP
49–50	Kansas St.	17-7	8-4	T1st (Big Seven)	DNP
50–51	Kansas St.	25-4	11-1	1st (Big Seven)	NCAA (3-1)
51–52	Kansas St.	19-5	10-2	2d (Big Seven)	DNP
52–53	Kansas St.	17-4	9-3	2d (Big Seven)	DNP
53–54	Utah	12-14	7-7	T4th (Sky. Eight)	DNP
54–55	Utah	24-4	13-1	1st (Sky. Eight)	NCAA (1-1)
55–56	Utah	22-6	12-2	1st (Sky. Eight)	NCAA (1-1)
56–57	Utah	19-8	10-4	2d (Sky. Eight)	NIT (0-1)
57–58	Utah	20-7	9-5	T2d (Sky. Eight)	NIT (0-1)
58–59	Utah	21-7	13-1	1st (Sky. Eight)	NCAA (0-2)
59–60	Utah	26-3	13-1	1st (Sky. Eight)	NCAA (1-1)
60–61	Utah	23-8	12-2	T1st (Sky. Eight)	NCAA (2-2)
61–62	Utah	23-3	13-1	1st (Sky. Eight)	Probation
62–63	Utah	12-14	5-5	3d (WAC)	DNP
63–64	Utah	19-9	4-6	T4th (WAC)	DNP
64–65	Utah	17-9	3-7	6th (WAC)	DNP
65–66	Utah	23-8	7-3	1st (WAC)	NCAA (2-2)
66–67	Utah	15-11	5-5	T3d (WAC)	DNP
67–68	Utah	17-9	5-5	T2d (WAC)	DNP
68–69	Utah	13-13	5-5	T3d (WAC)	DNP
69–70	Utah	18-11	9-5	T2d (WAC)	NIT (1-1)
70–71	Utah	15-11	9-5	T2d (WAC)	DNP

28-Year Coaching Record: 486-235 (.674) overall; 147-81 (.645) in 10 years at Kansas State; 339-154 (.688) in 18 years at Utah; 66-46 (.589) in Big Eight Conference (Big Six, Big Seven); 102-24 (.810) in Skyline Eight Conference; 52-46 (.531) in Western Athletic Conference; 12-12 (.500) in NCAA Tournament; 1-3 (.250) in NIT.

AMORY SLATS GILL
Oregon St. '24
Salem, Oreg.

Elected to Naismith Memorial Basketball Hall of Fame in 1967.... Reached NCAA Final Four two times—1949 (4th) and 1963 (4th).

Year	School	Overall	League	Finish	Postseason
28–29	Oregon St.	12-8	4-6	4th (PCC-N)	
29–30	Oregon St.	14-13	7-9	4th (PCC-N)	
30–31	Oregon St.	19-9	9-7	3d (PCC-N)	
31–32	Oregon St.	12-12	8-8	3d (PCC-N)	
32–33	Oregon St.	21-6	12-4	1st (PCC-N)	
33–34	Oregon St.	14-10	7-9	3d (PCC-N)	
34–35	Oregon St.	19-9	12-4	1st (PCC-N)	
35–36	Oregon St.	16-9	10-6	2d (PCC-N)	
36–37	Oregon St.	11-14	5-11	4th (PCC-N)	
37–38	Oregon St.	17-16	6-14	5th (PCC-N)	DNP
38–39	Oregon St.	13-11	6-10	4th (PCC-N)	DNP
39–40	Oregon St.	27-11	12-4	1st (PCC-N)	DNP
40–41	Oregon St.	19-9	9-7	2d (PCC-N)	DNP
41–42	Oregon St.	18-9	11-5	1st (PCC-N)	DNP
42–43	Oregon St.	19-9	8-8	4th (PCC-N)	DNP
43–44	Oregon St.	8-16	5-11	T3d (PCC-N)	DNP
44–45	Oregon St.	20-8	10-6	3d (PCC-N)	DNP
45–46	Oregon St.	13-11	10-6	2d (PCC-N)	DNP
46–47	Oregon St.	28-5	13-3	1st (PCC-N)	NCAA (1-1)
47–48	Oregon St.	21-13	10-6	T1st (PCC-N)	DNP
48–49	Oregon St.	24-12	12-4	1st (PCC-N)	NCAA (1-2)
49–50	Oregon St.	13-14	8-8	T2d (PCC-N)	DNP
50–51	Oregon St.	14-18	6-10	T4th (PCC-N)	DNP
51–52	Oregon St.	9-19	3-13	5th (PCC-N)	DNP
52–53	Oregon St.	11-18	6-10	4th (PCC-N)	DNP
53–54	Oregon St.	19-10	11-5	1st (PCC-N)	DNP
54–55	Oregon St.	22-8	15-1	1st (PCC-N)	NCAA (1-1)
55–56	Oregon St.	8-18	5-11	T7th (PCC)	DNP
56–57	Oregon St.	11-15	6-10	6th (PCC)	DNP
57–58	Oregon St.	20-6	12-4	T1st (PCC)	DNP
58–59	Oregon St.	13-13	7-9	6th (PCC)	DNP
59–60	Oregon St.*	9-3			DNP
60–61	Oregon St.	14-12			DNP
61–62	Oregon St.	24-5			NCAA (2-1)
62–63	Oregon St.	22-9			NCAA (3-2)
63–64	Oregon St.	25-4			NCAA (0-1)

* Missed 14 games (6-8 record) in 1959–60 because of illness. Replaced by Paul Valenti, who later succeeded him.

36-Year Coaching Record: 599-392 (.604) overall; 265-229 (.536) in Pacific-10 Conference (Pacific Coast); 8-8 (.500) in NCAA Tournament.

HUGH GREER
Connecticut '26
Suffield, Conn.

Finished lower than second place in Yankee Conference just once in 17 seasons.

Year	School	Overall	League	Finish	Postseason
46–47*	Conn.	12-0	5-0	2d (Yankee)	DNP
47–48	Conn.	17-6	6-1	1st (Yankee)	DNP
48–49	Conn.	19-6	7-1	1st (Yankee)	DNP
49–50	Conn.	17-8	5-2	2d (Yankee)	DNP
50–51	Conn.	22-4	6-1	1st (Yankee)	NCAA (0-1)
51–52	Conn.	20-7	6-1	1st (Yankee)	DNP
52–53	Conn.	17-4	5-1	1st (Yankee)	DNP
53–54	Conn.	23-3	7-0	1st (Yankee)	NCAA (0-1)
54–55	Conn.	20-5	7-0	1st (Yankee)	NIT (0-1)
55–56	Conn.	17-11	6-1	1st (Yankee)	NCAA (1-2)
56–57	Conn.	17-8	8-0	1st (Yankee)	NCAA (0-1)
57–58	Conn.	17-10	10-2	1st (Yankee)	NCAA (0-1)
58–59	Conn.	17-7	8-2	1st (Yankee)	NCAA (0-1)
59–60	Conn.	17-9	8-2	1st (Yankee)	NCAA (0-1)
60–61	Conn.	11-13	6-4	3d (Yankee)	DNP
61–62	Conn.	16-8	7-3	T2d (Yankee)	DNP
62–63	Conn.	7-3	9-1	1st (Yankee)	DNP

* Greer coached only last 12 games of 16-2 season and 6-1 conference record.

17-Year Coaching Record: 286-112 (.719) overall; 116-22 (.841) in Yankee Conference; 1-8 (.111) in NCAA Tournament; 0-1 in NIT.

JOE B. HALL
Sewanee '51
Cynthiana, Ky.

Reached NCAA Final Four three times—1975 (2nd), 1978 (1st), and 1984 (tied for third).... Led Kentucky to 1976 NIT title.... Coach of 1984 Southeastern Conference Tournament champion.

Year	School	Overall	League	Finish	Postseason
59–60	Regis (Colo.)	10-11			DNP
60–61	Regis (Colo.)	10-10			DNP
61–62	Regis (Colo.)	10-11			DNP
62–63	Regis (Colo.)	15-9			DNP
63–64	Regis (Colo.)	12-9			DNP
64–65	Central Mo. St.	19-6	9-1	1st (MIAA)	NCAA-II (1-1)
72–73	Kentucky	20-8	14-4	1st (SEC)	NCAA (1-1)
73–74	Kentucky	13-13	9-9	T4th (SEC)	DNP
74–75	Kentucky	26-5	15-3	T1st (SEC)	NCAA (4-1)
75–76	Kentucky	20-10	11-7	T4th (SEC)	NIT (4-0)
76–77	Kentucky	26-4	16-2	T1st (SEC)	NCAA (2-1)
77–78	Kentucky	30-2	16-2	1st (SEC)	NCAA (5-0)
78–79	Kentucky	19-12	10-8	6th (SEC)	NIT (0-1)
79–80	Kentucky	29-6	15-3	1st (SEC)	NCAA (1-1)
80–81	Kentucky	22-6	15-3	2d (SEC)	NCAA (0-1)
81–82	Kentucky	22-8	13-5	T1st (SEC)	NCAA (0-1)
82–83	Kentucky	23-8	13-5	1st (SEC)	NCAA (2-1)
83–84	Kentucky	29-5	14-4	1st (SEC)	NCAA (3-1)
84–85	Kentucky	18-13	11-7	T3d (SEC)	NCAA (2-1)

19-Year Coaching Record: 373-156 (.705) overall; 57-50 (.533) in five years at Regis (Colorado); 19-6 (.760) in one year at Central Missouri State; 297-100 (.748) in 13 years at Kentucky; 9-1 (.900) in Missouri Intercollegiate Athletic Association; 172-62 (.735) in Southeastern Conference; 10-6 (.625) in SEC Tournament; 20-9 (.690) in NCAA Tournament; 4-1 (.800) in NIT; 1-1 (.500) in NCAA Division II Tournament.

MARV HARSHMAN
Pacific Lutheran '42
Lake Stevens, Wash.

Named national coach of the year by the NABC in 1984.... Elected to Naismith Memorial Basketball Hall of Fame in 1984.

Year	School	Overall	League	Finish	Postseason
45–46	Pac. Luth.	10-18	3-13	4th (WIAC)	DNP
46–47	Pac. Luth.	15-14	6-6	3d (WIAC)	DNP
47–48	Pac. Luth.	17-15	12-3	1st (WIAC)	DNP
48–49	Pac. Luth.	25-7	11-3	T2d (Evergreen)	DNP
49–50	Pac. Luth.	19-8	8-6	4th (Evergreen)	DNP
50–51	Pac. Luth.	20-11	10-4	T2d (Evergreen)	DNP
51–52	Pac. Luth.	22-10	7-5	3d (Evergreen)	DNP
52–53	Pac. Luth.	16-10	8-4	T2d (Evergreen)	DNP
53–54	Pac. Luth.	18-10	8-4	2d (Evergreen)	DNP
54–55	Pac. Luth.	17-6	10-2	T1st (Evergreen)	DNP
55–56	Pac. Luth.	25-6	15-3	1st (Evergreen)	DNP
56–57	Pac. Luth.	28-1	12-0	1st (Evergreen)	DNP
57–58	Pac. Luth.	21-6	12-0	1st (Evergreen)	DNP
58–59	Wash. St.	10-16	3-13	8th (PCC-N)	DNP
59–60	Wash. St.	13-13			DNP
60–61	Wash. St.	10-16			DNP
61–62	Wash. St.	8-18			DNP
62–63	Wash. St.	5-20			DNP
63–64	Wash. St.	5-21	2-13	6th (Pac-8)	DNP
64–65	Wash. St.	9-17	6-8	5th (Pac-8)	DNP
65–66	Wash. St.	15-11	6-8	4th (Pac-8)	DNP

		Overall	League	Finish	Postseason
66–67	Wash. St.	15–11	8–6	2d (Pac-8)	DNP
67–68	Wash. St.	16–9	8–6	3d (Pac-8)	DNP
68–69	Wash. St.	18–8	11–3	2d (Pac-8)	DNP
69–70	Wash. St.	19–7	9–5	2d (Pac-8)	DNP
70–71	Wash. St.	12–14	2–12	7th (Pac-8)	DNP
71–72	Washington	20–6	10–4	2d (Pac-8)	DNP
72–73	Washington	16–11	6–8	T5th (Pac-8)	DNP
73–74	Washington	16–10	7–7	4th (Pac-8)	DNP
74–75	Washington	16–10	6–8	T5th (Pac-8)	DNP
75–76	Washington	23–5	10–4	3d (Pac-8)	NCAA (0-1)
76–77	Washington	17–10	8–6	T3d (Pac-8)	DNP
77–78	Washington	14–13	6–8	T5th (Pac-8)	DNP
78–79	Washington	11–16	6–12	T8th (Pac-10)	DNP
79–80	Washington	18–10	9–9	5th (Pac-10)	NIT (0-1)
80–81	Washington	14–13	8–10	T5th (Pac-10)	DNP
81–82	Washington	19–10	11–7	4th (Pac-10)	NIT (1-1)
82–83	Washington	16–15	7–11	T6th (Pac-10)	DNP
83–84	Washington	24–7	15–3	T1st (Pac-10)	NCAA (2-1)
84–85	Washington	22–10	13–5	T1st (Pac-10)	NCAA (0-1)

40-Year Coaching Record: 654-449 (.589) overall; 253-122 (.675) in 13 years at Pacific Lutheran; 155-181 (.461) in 13 years at Washington State; 246-146 (.628) in 14 years at Washington; 21-22 (.488) in Washington Intercollegiate Athletic Conference; 101-31 (.765) in Evergreen Intercollegiate Conference; 176-177 (.499) in Pacific-10 Conference (Pacific Coast-Northern, Pacific-8); 2-3 (.400) in NCAA Tournament; 1-2 (.333) in NIT.

JACK HARTMAN
Oklahoma State '49
Shidler, Okla.

Named NABC national co-coach of the year in 1981. . . . Coached Southern Illinois to NIT title in 1967. . . . Led Kansas State to two Big Eight Tournament titles (1977 and 1980). . . . Coached 1983 U.S. Pan American team to gold medal. . . . Compiled a 147-39 record in seven years (1955-56 through 1961-62) at junior college level for Coffeyville (Kan.), where he went undefeated (32-0) in his final season. . . . Graduate assistant between his high school coaching and stint at Coffeyville under legendary Hank Iba at Oklahoma State. . . . Played as a pro quarterback for Saskatchewan in the Canadian Football League.

Year	School	Overall	League	Finish	Postseason
62–63	Southern Ill.	20–10			DNP
63–64	Southern Ill.	15–10			DNP
64–65	Southern Ill.	20–6			DNP
65–66	Southern Ill.	21–7			DNP
66–67	Southern Ill.	24–2			NIT (4-0)
67–68	Southern Ill.	13–11			DNP
68–69	Southern Ill.	16–8			NIT (0-1)
69–70	Southern Ill.	13–10			DNP
70–71	Kansas State	11–15	6–8	T5th (Big Eight)	DNP
71–72	Kansas State	19–9	12–2	1st (Big Eight)	NCAA (1-1)
72–73	Kansas State	23–5	12–2	1st (Big Eight)	NCAA (1-1)
73–74	Kansas State	19–8	11–3	2nd (Big Eight)	DNP
74–75	Kansas State	20–9	10–4	2nd (Big Eight)	NCAA (2-1)
75–76	Kansas State	20–8	11–3	2nd (Big Eight)	NIT (0-1)
76–77	Kansas State	24–7	11–3	1st (Big Eight)	NCAA (1-1)
77–78	Kansas State	18–11	7–7	T4th (Big Eight)	DNP
78–79	Kansas State	16–12	8–6	T2nd (Big Eight)	DNP
79–80	Kansas State	22–9	8–6	T2nd (Big Eight)	NCAA (1-1)
80–81	Kansas State	24–9	9–5	T2nd (Big Eight)	NCAA (3-1)
81–82	Kansas State	23–8	10–4	2nd (Big Eight)	NCAA (2-1)
82–83	Kansas State	12–16	4–10	T6th (Big Eight)	DNP
83–84	Kansas State	14–15	5–9	T6th (Big Eight)	DNP
84–85	Kansas State	14–14	5–9	T5th (Big Eight)	DNP
85–86	Kansas State	16–14	4–10	7th (Big Eight)	DNP

24-Year Coaching Record: 439-233 (.653) overall; 142-64 (.689) in eight years at Southern Illinois; 295-169 (.643) in 16 years at Kansas State; 133-91 (.594) in Big Eight Conference; 13-8 (.619) in Big Eight Tournament; 11-7 (.611) in NCAA Tournament; 4-2 (.667) in NIT.

GEORGE (JUD) HEATHCOTE
Washington State '50
Port Orchard, Wash.

Named national coach of the year by NABC in 1990.... Coach of 1979 NCAA champion.... Coach of 1989 NIT fourth-place team.... Served as an assistant coach at Washington State under Marv Harshman from 1965 to 1971.

Year	School	Overall	League	Finish	Postseason
71–72	Montana	14–12	7–7	T5th (Big Sky)	DNP
72–73	Montana	13–13	7–7	4th (Big Sky)	DNP
73–74	Montana*	19–8	11–3	T1st (Big Sky)	DNP
74–75	Montana	21–8	13–1	1st (Big Sky)	NCAA (1-2)
75–76	Montana	13–12	7–7	5th (Big Sky)	DNP
76–77	Mich. St.	12–15	9–9	5th (Big Ten)	DNP
77–78	Mich. St.	25–5	15–3	1st (Big Ten)	NCAA (2-1)
78–79	Mich. St.	26–6	13–5	T1st (Big Ten)	NCAA (5-0)
79–80	Mich. St.	12–15	6–12	9th (Big Ten)	DNP
80–81	Mich. St.	13–14	7–11	8th (Big Ten)	DNP
81–82	Mich. St.	12–16	7–11	T7th (Big Ten)	DNP
82–83	Mich. St.	17–13	9–9	T6th (Big Ten)	NIT (1-1)
83–84	Mich. St.	16–12	9–9	5th (Big Ten)	DNP
84–85	Mich. St.	19–10	10–8	T5th (Big Ten)	NCAA (0-1)
85–86	Mich. St.	23–8	12–6	3d (Big Ten)	NCAA (2-1)
86–87	Mich. St.	11–17	6–12	7th (Big Ten)	DNP
87–88	Mich. St.	10–18	5–13	8th (Big Ten)	DNP
88–89	Mich. St.	18–15	6–12	T8th (Big Ten)	NIT (3-2)
89–90	Mich. St.	28–6	15–3	1st (Big Ten)	NCAA (2-1)
90–91	Mich. St.	19–11	11–7	T3d (Big Ten)	NCAA (1-1)
91–92	Mich. St.	22–8	11–7	T3d (Big Ten)	NCAA (1-1)
92–93	Mich. St.	15–13	7–11	T8th (Big Ten)	NIT (0-1)
93–94	Mich. St.	20–12	10–8	T4th (Big Ten)	NCAA (1-1)

* Lost Big Sky Conference playoff game against regular-season co-champion Idaho St. (60-57) for automatic berth in NCAA Tournament.

23-Year Coaching Record: 398-267 (.598) overall; 80-53 (.602) in five years at Montana; 318-214 (.598) in first 18 years at Michigan State; 45-25 (.643) in Big Sky Conference; 168-156 (.519) in Big Ten Conference; 15-9 (.625) in NCAA Tournament; 4-4 (.500) in NIT.

BILL HENDERSON
Howard Payne
Ballinger, Tex. '25

Reached Final Four two times—1948 (2d) and 1950 (4th).... Assistant coach under Ralph Wolf at Baylor.

Year	School	Overall	League	Finish	Postseason
41–42	Baylor	11–9	6–6	T3d (SWC)	DNP
42–43	Baylor	6–14	3–9	7th (SWC)	DNP
45–46	Baylor	25–5	11–1	1st (SWC)	NCAA (0-2)
46–47	Baylor	11–11	6–6	4th (SWC)	DNP
47–48	Baylor	24–8	11–1	1st (SWC)	NCAA (2-1)
48–49	Baylor	14–10	9–3	T1st (SWC)	DNP
49–50	Baylor	14–13	8–4	1st (SWC)	NCAA (1-2)
50–51	Baylor	8–16	3–9	6th (SWC)	DNP
51–52	Baylor	6–18	5–7	T3d (SWC)	DNP
52–53	Baylor	10–11	6–6	4th (SWC)	DNP
53–54	Baylor	12–11	6–6	3d (SWC)	DNP
54–55	Baylor	13–11	7–5	4th (SWC)	DNP
55–56	Baylor	6–17	3–9	5th (SWC)	DNP
56–57	Baylor	9–15	6–6	3d (SWC)	DNP
57–58	Baylor	5–19	3–11	8th (SWC)	DNP
58–59	Baylor	11–13	7–7	4th (SWC)	DNP
59–60	Baylor	12–12	6–8	6th (SWC)	DNP
60–61	Baylor	4–20	2–12	8th (SWC)	DNP

19-Year Coaching Record: 201-233 (.463) overall; 108-116 (.482) in Southwest Conference; 3-5 (.375) in NCAA Tournament.

CAM HENDERSON
Salem '17
Joe Town, W.V.

Coach of 1947 NAIA Tournament champion.

Year	School	Overall	League	Finish	Postseason
19–20	Muskingum	10–8			
20–21	Muskingum	20–4			
21–22	Muskingum	8–10			
22–23	Muskingum	6–11			
23–24	Davis & Elkins	10–7			
24–25	Davis & Elkins	22–0			
25–26	Davis & Elkins	15–4			
26–27	Davis & Elkins	23–3			

Year	School	Overall	League	Finish	Postseason
27–28	Davis & Elkins	24-4			
28–29	Davis & Elkins	20-5			
29–30	Davis & Elkins	22-3			
30–31	Davis & Elkins	17-4			
31–32	Davis & Elkins	19-2			
32–33	Davis & Elkins	15-8			
33–34	Davis & Elkins	11-6			
34–35	Davis & Elkins	27-4			
35–36	Marshall	6-10	1-9	T5th (Buckeye)	
36–37	Marshall	23-8	9-1	T1st (Buckeye)	
37–38	Marshall	28-4			NAIA (1-1)
38–39	Marshall	22-5			DNP
39–40	Marshall	25-4			DNP
40–41	Marshall	14-9			DNP
41–42	Marshall	15-9			DNP
42–43	Marshall	10-7			DNP
43–44	Marshall	15-7			DNP
44–45	Marshall	17-9			DNP
45–46	Marshall	24-10			DNP
46–47	Marshall	32-5			NAIA (5-0)
47–48	Marshall	22-11			NAIA (1-1)
48–49	Marshall	16-12	2-2	4th (OVC)	DNP
49–50	Marshall	15-9	5-4	3d (OVC)	DNP
50–51	Marshall	13-13	2-6	6th (OVC)	DNP
51–52	Marshall	15-11	5-7	4th (OVC)	DNP
52–53	Marshall	20-4			DNP
53–54	Marshall	12-9	6-7	4th (MAC)	DNP
54–55	Marshall	17-4	10-4	2d (MAC)	DNP

35-Year Coaching Record: 630-243 (.722) overall; 44-33 (.571) in four years at Muskingum; 225-50 (.818) in 12 years at Davis & Elkins; 361-160 (.693) in 20 years at Marshall; 10-10 (.500) in Buckeye Conference; 14-19 (.424) in Ohio Valley Conference; 16-11 (.593) in Mid-American Conference; 7-2 (.778) in NAIA Tournament.

LOU HENSON
New Mexico State '55
Okay, Okla.

Coach of two NCAA Final Four teams—1970 (third with New Mexico St.) and 1989 (tied for third with Illinois).... Coach of 1980 NIT third-place team.

Year	School	Overall	League	Finish	Postseason
62–63	Hardin-Simm.	10-16			DNP
63–64	Hardin-Simm.	20-6			DNP
64–65	Hardin-Simm.	17-8			DNP
65–66	Hardin-Simm.	20-6			DNP
66–67	New Mex. St.	15-11			NCAA (0-1)
67–68	New Mex. St.	23-6			NCAA (2-1)
68–69	New Mex. St.	24-5			NCAA (1-2)
69–70	New Mex. St.	27-3			NCAA (4-1)
70–71	New Mex. St.	19-8			NCAA (0-1)
71–72	New Mex. St.	19-6			DNP
72–73	New Mex. St.	12-14	6-8	T5th (Mo. Valley)	Probation
73–74	New Mex. St.	14-11	7-6	T3d (Mo. Valley)	Probation
74–75	New Mex. St.	20-7	11-3	2d (Mo. Valley)	NCAA (0-1)
75–76	Illinois	14-13	7-11	T7th (Big Ten)	DNP
76–77	Illinois*	14-16	6-12	7th (Big Ten)	DNP
77–78	Illinois	13-14	7-11	7th (Big Ten)	DNP
78–79	Illinois	19-11	7-11	7th (Big Ten)	DNP
79–80	Illinois	22-13	8-10	T6th (Big Ten)	NIT (4-1)
80–81	Illinois	21-8	12-6	3d (Big Ten)	NCAA (1-1)
81–82	Illinois	18-11	10-8	6th (Big Ten)	NIT (1-1)
82–83	Illinois	21-11	11-7	T2d (Big Ten)	NCAA (0-1)
83–84	Illinois	26-5	15-3	T1st (Big Ten)	NCAA (2-1)
84–85	Illinois	26-9	12-6	2d (Big Ten)	NCAA (2-1)
85–86	Illinois	22-10	11-7	T4th (Big Ten)	NCAA (1-1)
86–87	Illinois	23-8	13-5	4th (Big Ten)	NCAA (0-1)
87–88	Illinois	23-10	12-6	T3d (Big Ten)	NCAA (1-1)
88–89	Illinois	31-5	14-4	2d (Big Ten)	NCAA (4-1)
89–90	Illinois	21-8	11-7	T4th (Big Ten)	NCAA (0-1)
90–91	Illinois	21-10	11-7	T3d (Big Ten)	Probation
91–92	Illinois	13-15	7-11	8th (Big Ten)	DNP
92–93	Illinois	19-13	11-7	T3d (Big Ten)	NCAA (1-1)
93–94	Illinois	17-11	10-8	T4th (Big Ten)	NCAA (1-1)
94–95	Illinois	19-12	10-8	T5th (Big Ten)	NCAA (0-1)
95–96	Illinois	18-13	7-11	9th (Big Ten)	NIT (0-1)

* Overall record is 16-14 and Big Ten mark is 8-10, including two forfeit victories awarded from Minnesota after the season.

34-Year Coaching Record: 661-333 (.665) overall; 67-36 (.650) in four years at Hardin-Simmons; 173-71 (.709) in nine years at New Mexico State; 421-226 (.651) in 21 years at Illinois; 24-17 (.585) in Missouri Valley Conference; 214-164 (.566) in Big Ten Conference; 19-19 (.500) in NCAA Tournament; 5-3 (.625) in NIT.

EDGAR (EDDIE) HICKEY
Creighton '27
Sioux City, Iowa, and Spalding, Neb.

Elected to Naismith Memorial Basketball Hall of Fame in 1978. . . . Named USBWA national coach of the year in 1959. . . . Coached St. Louis to NIT title in 1948. Reached NIT semifinals with Creighton in 1942 (3rd) and Marquette in 1963 (3rd). . . . Served in U.S. Navy during World War II.

Year	School	Overall	League	Finish	Postseason
35-36	Creighton	13-6	8-4	T1st (MVC)	
36-37	Creighton	11-9	8-4	2nd (MVC)	
37-38	Creighton	11-14	7-7	4th (MVC)	DNP
38-39	Creighton	11-12	7-7	5th (MVC)	DNP
39-40	Creighton	11-9	8-4	2nd (MVC)	DNP
40-41	Creighton	18-7	9-3	1st (MVC)	NCAA (1-1)
41-42	Creighton	19-5	9-1	T1st (MVC)	NIT (2-1)
42-43	Creighton	19-2	10-0	1st (MVC)	NIT (0-1)
46-47	Creighton	19-8	7-5	4th (MVC)	DNP
47-48	St. Louis	24-3	8-2	2nd (MVC)	NIT (3-0)
48-49	St. Louis	22-4	8-2	2nd (MVC)	NIT (0-1)
49-50	St. Louis	17-9	8-4	2nd (MVC)	DNP
50-51	St. Louis	22-8	11-3	T2nd (MVC)	NIT (1-1)
51-52	St. Louis	23-8	9-1	1st (MVC)	NCAA (1-1)
52-53	St. Louis	16-11	5-5	T2nd (MVC)	NIT (0-1)
53-54	St. Louis	14-12	4-6	4th (MVC)	DNP
54-55	St. Louis	20-8	8-2	T1st	(MVC)
55-56	St. Louis	18-7	8-4	T2nd	(MVC)
56-57	St. Louis	19-9	12-2	1st (MVC)	NCAA (0-2)
57-58	St. Louis	16-10	9-5	3rd (MVC)	DNP
58-59	Marquette	23-6			NCAA (1-2)
59-60	Marquette	13-12			DNP
60-61	Marquette	16-11			NCAA (0-1)
61-62	Marquette	15-11			DNP
62-63	Marquette	20-9			NIT (2-1)
63-64	Marquette	5-21			DNP

26-Year Coaching Record: 435-231 (.653) overall; 132-72 (.647) in nine years at Creighton; 211-89 (.703) in 11 years at St. Louis; 92-70 (.568) in six years at Marquette; 163-71 (.697) in Missouri Valley Conference; 3-7 (.300) in NCAA Tournament; 9-9 (.500) in NIT.

BERNARD (PECK) HICKMAN
Western Kentucky '35
Central City, Ky.

Coached team to the NIT title in 1956.... Led Louisville to five NCAA Tournament appearances, including a fourth-place finish in 1959.... Coach of 1948 NAIA Tournament champion.

Year	School	Overall	League	Finish	Postseason
44-45	Louisville	16-3		KIAC	DNP
45-46	Louisville	22-6	10-2	2d (KIAC)	DNP
46-47	Louisville	17-6	5-3	5th (KIAC)	DNP
47-48	Louisville	29-6	7-3	2d (KIAC)	NAIB (5-0)
48-49	Louisville	23-10	6-3	3d (OVC)	DNP
49-50	Louisville	21-11			DNP
50-51	Louisville	19-7			NCAA (0-1)
51-52	Louisville	20-6			NIT (0-1)
52-53	Louisville	22-6			NIT (1-1)
53-54	Louisville	22-7			NIT (0-1)
54-55	Louisville	19-8			NIT (1-1)
55-56	Louisville	26-3			NIT (3-0)
56-57	Louisville	21-5			Probation
57-58	Louisville	13-12			DNP
58-59	Louisville	19-12			NCAA (3-2)
59-60	Louisville	15-11			DNP
60-61	Louisville	21-8			NCAA (2-1)
61-62	Louisville	15-10			DNP

62–63	Louisville	14-11			DNP
63–64	Louisville	15-10			NCAA (0-1)
64–65	Louisville	15-10			DNP
65–66	Louisville	16-10			NIT (0-1)
66–67	Louisville	23-5			NCAA (0-2)

Note: No regular-season standings, only postseason conference tournament, for the Kentucky Intercollegiate Athletic Conference in 1944–45.

23-Year Coaching Record: 443-183 (.708) overall; 22-8 (.733) in Kentucky Intercollegiate Athletic Conference; 6-3 (.667) in Ohio Valley Conference; 5-3 (.625) in Kentucky Intercollegiate Athletic Conference Tournament; 2-1 (.667) in Ohio Valley Conference Tournament; 5-7 (.417) in NCAA Tournament; 5-5 (.500) in NIT; 5-0 in NAIB.

PAUL (TONY) HINKLE
University of Chicago '21
Chicago, Ill.

Elected to Naismith Memorial Basketball Hall of Fame in 1965. . . . A three-sport coach at Butler where his teams won over 1,000 games in football, basketball and baseball. . . . One of seven NCAA coaches to serve 40 or more years. . . . Only two individuals have coached more seasons (42) with one school. . . . Coached Great Lakes Naval Training Center basketball team to a 33-3 record in 1942-43 and a 31-3 mark in 1943-44.

Year	School	Overall	League	Finish	Postseason
26-27	Butler	17-4			
27-28	Butler	17-3			
28-29	Butler	17-2			
29-30	Butler	13-7			
30-31	Butler	17-2			
31-32	Butler	14-5			
32-33	Butler	16-5	9-1	1st (MVC)	
33-34	Butler	14-7	9-1	1st (MVC)	
34-35	Butler	13-7			
35-36	Butler	6-15			
36-37	Butler	6-14			
37-38	Butler	11-12			DNP
38-39	Butler	14-6			DNP
39-40	Butler	17-6			DNP
40-41	Butler	13-9			DNP
41-42	Butler	13-9			DNP
45-46	Butler	12-8			DNP
46-47	Butler	16-7	6-2	T1st (MAC)	DNP
47-48	Butler	14-7	4-2	2nd (MAC)	DNP
48-49	Butler	18-5	8-2	2nd (MAC)	DNP
49-50	Butler	12-12	6-4	T2nd (MAC)	DNP
50-51	Butler	5-19	3-7	5th (ICC)	DNP
51-52	Butler	12-12	8-2	1st (ICC)	DNP
52-53	Butler	14-9	7-3	T1st (ICC)	DNP
53-54	Butler	13-12	7-3	T1st (ICC)	DNP
54-55	Butler	10-14	8-4	T2nd (ICC)	DNP
55-56	Butler	14-9	8-4	T2nd (ICC)	DNP
56-57	Butler	11-14	6-6	5th (ICC)	DNP
57-58	Butler	15-10	10-2	2nd (ICC)	NIT (0-1)
58-59	Butler	19-9	10-2	1st (ICC)	NIT (1-1)
59-60	Butler	15-11	10-2	2nd (ICC)	DNP
60-61	Butler	15-11	10-2	1st (ICC)	DNP
61-62	Butler	22-6	10-2	1st (ICC)	NCAA (2-1)
62-63	Butler	16-10	10-2	2nd (ICC)	DNP
63-64	Butler	13-13	9-3	2nd (ICC)	DNP
64-65	Butler	11-15	5-7	T3rd (ICC)	DNP
65-66	Butler	16-10	8-4	3rd (ICC)	DNP
66-67	Butler	9-17	5-7	5th (ICC)	DNP
67-68	Butler	11-14	6-6	4th (ICC)	DNP
68-69	Butler	11-15	4-4	T2nd (ICC)	DNP
69-70	Butler	15-11	6-2	T1st (ICC)	DNP

41-Year Coaching Record: 557-393 (.586) at Butler; 18-2 (.900) in Missouri Valley Conference; 24-10 (.706) in Mid-American Conference; 150-74 (.670) in Indiana Collegiate Conference; 2-1 (.667) in NCAA Tournament; 1-2 (.333) in NIT.

HOWARD HOBSON
Oregon '26
Portland, Oreg.

Elected to Naismith Memorial Basketball Hall of Fame in 1965. . . . U.S. Olympic team manager in 1952. . . . Coach of 1939 NCAA champion.

Year	School	Overall	League	Finish	Postseason
32–33	S. Oreg.	19-5			
33–34	S. Oreg.	23-5			
34–35	S. Oreg	26-5			
35–36	Oregon	20-11	7-9	4th (PCC-N)	DNP
36–37	Oregon	20-9	11-5	T1st(PCC-N)	DNP
37–38	Oregon	25-8	14-6	1st (PCC-N)	DNP
38–39	Oregon	29-5	14-2	1st (PCC-N)	NCAA (3-0)
39–40	Oregon	19-12	10-6	2d (PCC-N)	DNP
40–41	Oregon	18-18	7-9	T3d (PCC-N)	DNP
41–42	Oregon	12-15	7-9	4th (PCC-N)	DNP
42–43	Oregon	19-10	10-6	2d (PCC-N)	DNP
43–44	Oregon	16-10	11-5	2d (PCC-N)	DNP
45–46	Oregon	16-17	8-8	3d (PCC-N)	DNP
46–47	Oregon	18-9	7-9	4th (PCC-N)	DNP
47–48	Yale	14-13	4-8	6th (EIBL)	DNP
48–49	Yale	22-8	9-3	1st (EIBL)	NCAA (0-2)
49–50	Yale	17-9	7-5	T3d (EIBL)	DNP
50–51	Yale	14-13	4-8	5th (EIBL)	DNP
51–52	Yale	14-14	4-8	T5th (EIBL)	DNP
52–53	Yale	10-15	6-6	T3d (EIBL)	DNP
53–54	Yale	12-14	7-7	4th (EIBL)	DNP
54–55	Yale	3-21	3-11	T6th (Ivy)	DNP
55–56	Yale	15-11	7-7	T5th (Ivy)	DNP

23-Year Coaching Record: 401-257 (.609) overall; 68-15 (.819) in three years at Southern Oregon; 212-124 (.631) in 11 years at Oregon; 121-118 (.506) in nine years at Yale; 106-74 (.589) in Pacific Coast Conference; 51-63 (.447) in Ivy League (Eastern Intercollegiate Basketball League); 3-2 (.600) in NCAA Tournament.

TERRY HOLLAND
Davidson '64
Clinton, N.C.

Reached NCAA Final Four with Virginia in 1981 (3d) and 1984 (tied for 3d). . . . Coach of 1980 NIT champion. . . . Coach of 1970 Southern Conference Tournament champion with Davidson and 1976 Atlantic Coast Conference Tournament champion with Virginia. . . . Assistant coach under Lefty Driesell at Davidson from 1969–70 through 1973–74.

Year	School	Overall	League	Finish	Postseason
69–70	Davidson	22-5	10-0	1st (Southern)	NCAA (0-1)
70–71	Davidson	15-11	9-1	1st (Southern)	DNP
71–72	Davidson	19-9	8-2	1st (Southern)	NIT (0-1)
72–73	Davidson	18-9	9-1	1st (Southern)	DNP
73–74	Davidson	18-9	7-3	3d (Southern)	DNP
74–75	Virginia	12-13	4-8	5th (ACC)	DNP
75–76	Virginia	18-12	4-8	6th (ACC)	NCAA (0-1)
76–77	Virginia	12-17	2-10	6th (ACC)	DNP
77–78	Virginia	20-8	6-6	4th (ACC)	NIT (0-1)
78–79	Virginia	19-10	7-5	3d (ACC)	NIT (1-1)
79–80	Virginia	24-10	7-7	5th (ACC)	NIT (5-0)
80–81	Virginia	29-4	13-1	1st (ACC)	NCAA (4-1)
81–82	Virginia	30-4	12-2	1st (ACC)	NCAA (1-1)
82–83	Virginia	29-5	12-2	1st (ACC)	NCAA (2-1)
83–84	Virginia	21-12	6-8	5th (ACC)	NCAA (4-1)
84–85	Virginia	17-16	3-11	8th (ACC)	NIT (2-1)
85–86	Virginia	19-11	7-7	4th (ACC)	NCAA (0-1)
86–87	Virginia	21-10	8-6	4th (ACC)	NCAA (0-1)
87–88	Virginia	13-18	5-9	6th (ACC)	DNP
88–89	Virginia	22-11	9-5	T2d (ACC)	NCAA (3-1)
89–90	Virginia	20-12	6-8	T4th (ACC)	NCAA (1-1)

21-Year Coaching Record: 418-216 (.659) overall; 92-43 (.681) in five years at Davidson; 326-173 (.653) in 16 years at Virginia; 43-7 (.860) in Southern Conference; 111-103 (.519) in Atlantic Coast Conference; 15-15 (.500) in ACC Tournament; 7-4 (.636) in Southern Conference Tournament; 15-10 (.600) in NCAA Tournament; 8-4 (.667) in NIT.

NAT HOLMAN
Savage School of Phys.
Ed. '17
New York, N.Y.

Elected to Naismith Memorial Basketball Hall of Fame in 1964.... Coach of NCAA and NIT titlists in 1950, the only time a team won both crowns in the same year. Also finished fourth in 1947 NCAA Tournament.... Coach of 1941 NIT third-place finisher.

Year	School	Overall	League	Finish	Postseason
19–20	CCNY	13-3			
20–21	CCNY	11-4			
21–22	CCNY	10-2			
22–23	CCNY	12-1			
23–24	CCNY	12-1			
24–25	CCNY	12-2			
25–26	CCNY	9-5			
26–27	CCNY	9-3			
27–28	CCNY	11-4			
28–29	CCNY	9-5			
29–30	CCNY	11-3			
30–31	CCNY	12-4			
31–32	CCNY	16-1			
32–33	CCNY	13-1			
33–34	CCNY	14-1			
34–35	CCNY	10-6			
35–36	CCNY	10-4			
36–37	CCNY	10-6			
37–38	CCNY	13-3			DNP
38–39	CCNY	11-6			DNP
39–40	CCNY	8-8			DNP
40–41	CCNY	17-5			NIT (2-1)
41–42	CCNY	16-3			NIT (0-1)
42–43	CCNY	8-10			DNP
43–44	CCNY	6-11			DNP
44–45	CCNY	12-4			DNP
45–46	CCNY	14-4			DNP
46–47	CCNY	17-6			NCAA (1-2)
47–48	CCNY	18-3			DNP
48–49	CCNY	17-8			NIT (0-1)
49–50	CCNY	24-5			NCAA (3-0); NIT (4-0)
50–51	CCNY	12-7			DNP
51–52	CCNY	8-11			DNP
54–55	CCNY	8-10			DNP
55–56	CCNY	4-14			DNP
58–59	CCNY	6-12			DNP
59–60	CCNY	0-4			DNP

37-Year Coaching Record: 423-190 (.690) overall; 4-2 (.667) in NCAA Tournament; 6-3 (.667) in NIT.

HENRY (HANK) IBA
Westminster, Mo. '28
Easton, Mo.

Elected to Naismith Memorial Basketball Hall of Fame in 1968.... U.S. Olympic Team coach in 1964, 1968, and 1972.... Reached Final Four on four occasions—1945 (1st), 1946 (1st), 1949 (2d), and 1951 (4th).... Coach of three teams that reached NIT semifinals—1938 (3d), 1940 (3d), and 1944 (4th).... Holds the NCAA career record for most games coached at 1,105.

Year	School	Overall	League	Finish	Postseason
29–30	NW Mo. St.	31-0	16-0	1st (MIAA)	
30–31	NW Mo. St.	32-6	3-5	T3d (MIAA)	
31–32	NW Mo. St.	26-2	7-1	1st (MIAA)	
32–33	NW Mo. St.	12-6	6-2	1st (MIAA)	
33–34	Colorado	11-8	7-5	2d (RMC)	
34–35	Okla. St.	9-9	5-7	T5th (MVC)	
35–36	Okla. St.	16-8	8-4	T1st (MVC)	

Year	School	Overall	League	Finish	Postseason
36–37	Okla. St.	20-3	11-1	1st (MVC)	
37–38	Okla. St.	25-3	13-1	1st (MVC)	NIT (1-1)
38–39	Okla. St.	19-8	11-3	T1st (MVC)	DNP
39–40	Okla. St.	26-3	12-0	1st (MVC)	NIT (1-1)
40–41	Okla. St.	18-7	8-4	2d (MVC)	DNP
41–42	Okla. St.	20-6	9-1	T1st (MVC)	DNP
42–43	Okla. St.	14-10	7-3	T2d (MVC)	DNP
43–44	Okla. St.	27-6		Mo. Valley	NIT (1-2)
44–45	Okla. St.	27-4		Mo. Valley	NCAA (3-0)
45–46	Okla. St.	31-2	12-0	1st (MVC)	NCAA (3-0)
46–47	Okla. St.	24-8	8-4	T2d (MVC)	DNP
47–48	Okla. St.	27-4	10-0	1st (MVC)	DNP
48–49	Okla. St.	23-5	9-1	1st (MVC)	NCAA (2-1)
49–50	Okla. St.	18-9	7-5	T3d (MVC)	DNP
50–51	Okla. St.	29-6	12-2	1st (MVC)	NCAA (2-2)
51–52	Okla. St.	19-8	7-3	2d (MVC)	DNP
52–53	Okla. St.	23-7	8-2	1st (MVC)	NCAA (1-1)
53–54	Okla. St.	24-5	9-1	1st (MVC)	NCAA (1-1)
54–55	Okla. St.	12-13	5-5	3d (MVC)	DNP
55–56	Okla. St.	18-9	8-4	T2d (MVC)	NIT (0-1)
56–57	Okla. St.	17-9	8-6	T3d (MVC)	DNP
57–58	Okla. St.	21-8			NCAA (2-1)
58–59	Okla. St.	11-14	5-9	T5th (Big Eight)	DNP
59–60	Okla. St.	10-15	4-10	T7th (Big Eight)	DNP
60–61	Okla. St.	15-10	9-5	3d (Big Eight)	DNP
61–62	Okla. St.	14-11	7-7	4th (Big Eight)	DNP
62–63	Okla. St.	16-9	7-7	5th (Big Eight)	DNP
63–64	Okla. St.	15-10	7-7	T4th (Big Eight)	DNP
64–65	Okla. St.	20-7	12-2	1st (Big Eight)	NCAA (1-1)
65–66	Okla. St.	4-21	2-12	7th (Big Eight)	DNP
66–67	Okla. St.	7-18	2-12	7th (Big Eight)	DNP
67–68	Okla. St.	10-16	3-11	T7th (Big Eight)	DNP
68–69	Okla. St.	12-13	5-9	T6th (Big Eight)	DNP
69–70	Okla. St.	14-12	5-9	T7th (Big Eight)	DNP

41-Year Coaching Record: 767-338 (.694) overall; 101-14 (.878) in four years at Northwest Missouri St.; 11-8 (.579) in one year at Colorado; 655-316 (.675) in 36 years at Oklahoma St.; 32-8 (.800) in Missouri Intercollegiate Athletic Association; 7-5 (.583) in Rocky Mountain Conference; 187-57 (.766) in Missouri Valley Conference; 68-100 (.405) in Big Eight Conference; 15-7 (.682) in NCAA Tournament; 3-5 (.375) in NIT.

GEORGE IRELAND
Notre Dame '36
Prairie du Chien, Wisc.

Coach of 1963 NCAA champion and 1962 NIT third-place finisher.

Year	School	Overall	League	Finish	Postseason
51–52	Loyola (Ill.)	17-8			DNP
52–53	Loyola (Ill.)	8-15			DNP
53–54	Loyola (Ill.)	7-15			DNP
54–55	Loyola (Ill.)	13-11			DNP
55–56	Loyola (Ill.)	10-14			DNP
56–57	Loyola (Ill.)	14-10			DNP
57–58	Loyola (Ill.)	16-8			DNP
58–59	Loyola (Ill.)	11-13			DNP
59–60	Loyola (Ill.)	10-12			DNP
60–61	Loyola (Ill.)	15-8			DNP
61–62	Loyola (Ill.)	23-4			NIT (2-1)
62–63	Loyola (Ill.)	29-2			NCAA (5-0)
63–64	Loyola (Ill.)	22-6			NCAA (2-1)
64–65	Loyola (Ill.)	11-14			DNP
65–66	Loyola (Ill.)	22-3			NCAA (0-1)
66–67	Loyola (Ill.)	13-9			DNP
67–68	Loyola (Ill.)	15-9			NCAA (0-1)
68–69	Loyola (Ill.)	9-14			DNP
69–70	Loyola (Ill.)	13-11			DNP
70–71	Loyola (Ill.)	4-20			DNP
71–72	Loyola (Ill.)	8-14			DNP
72–73	Loyola (Ill.)	8-15			DNP
73–74	Loyola (Ill.)	12-14			DNP
74–75	Loyola (Ill.)	8-6			DNP

24-Year Coaching Record: 318-255 (.555) overall; 7-3 (.700) in NCAA Tournament; 2-1 (.667) in NIT.

ED JUCKER
Cincinnati '40
Cincinnati, Ohio

Named national coach of the year by UPI and the USBWA in 1963.... Led Cincinnati to three consecutive Final Four appearances—1961 (1st), 1962 (1st), and 1963 (2d).... Holds the NCAA Tournament all-time record (minimum of 10 games) for highest winning percentage at 91.7% (11-1).

Year	School	Overall	League	Finish	Postseason
45–46	King's Pt.	14-0			DNP
46–47	King's Pt.	12-4			DNP
48–49	Rensselaer	13-3			DNP
49–50	Rensselaer	12-3			DNP
50–51	Rensselaer	9-9			DNP
51–52	Rensselaer	4-11			DNP
52–53	Rensselaer	8-9			DNP
60–61	Cincinnati	27-3	10-2	1st (MVC)	NCAA (4-0)
61–62	Cincinnati	29-2	10-2	T1st (MVC)	NCAA (4-0)
62–63	Cincinnati	26-2	11-1	1st (MVC)	NCAA (3-1)
63–64	Cincinnati	17-9	6-6	T4th (MVC)	DNP
64–65	Cincinnati	14-12	5-9	7th (MVC)	DNP
72–73	Rollins	13-11			DNP
73–74	Rollins	18-9			NCAA II (1-2)
74–75	Rollins	15-7			DNP
75–76	Rollins	19-6	8-2	2d (Sunshine)	NCAA II(1-1)
76–77	Rollins	16-9	6-4	T2d (Sunshine)	DNP

17-Year Coaching Record: 266-109 (.709) overall; 26-4 (.867) in two years at King's Point; 46-35 (.568) in five years at Rensselaer; 113-28 (.801) in five years at Cincinnati; 81-42 (.659) in five years at Rollins; 42-20 (.667) in Missouri Valley Conference; 14-6 (.700) in Sunshine St. Conference; 11-1 (.917) in NCAA Tournament; 2-3 (.400) in NCAA Division II Tournament.

ALVIN (DOGGIE) JULIAN
Bucknell '23
Reading, Pa.

Elected to Naismith Memorial Basketball Hall of Fame in 1967.... Led Holy Cross to two NCAA Final Four appearances—1947 (1st) and 1948 (3d).... Compiled a 47-81 record as coach of the NBA's Boston Celtics in 1948–49 and 1949–50.

Year	School	Overall	League	Finish	Postseason
27–28	Albright	6-13			
28–29	Albright	3-13			
36–37	Muhlenberg	9-9			
37–38	Muhlenberg	9-11			
38–39	Muhlenberg	13-8			
39–40	Muhlenberg	11-9			
40–41	Muhlenberg	13-10			
41–42	Muhlenberg	17-7	9-3	2d (Eastern Pa.)	
42–43	Muhlenberg	13-8	7-3	2d (Eastern Pa.)	
43–44	Muhlenberg	20-5			NIT (0-1)
44–45	Muhlenberg	24-4			DNP
45–46	Holy Cross	12-3			DNP
46–47	Holy Cross	27-3			NCAA (3-0)
47–48	Holy Cross	26-4			NCAA (2-1)
50–51	Dartmouth	3-23	1-11	7th (EIBL)	DNP
51–52	Dartmouth	11-19	4-8	T5th (EIBL)	DNP
52–53	Dartmouth	12-14	5-7	T5th (EIBL)	DNP
53–54	Dartmouth	13-13	5-9	6th (EIBL)	DNP
54–55	Dartmouth	18-7	9-5	4th (Ivy)	DNP
55–56	Dartmouth	18-11	10-4	1st (Ivy)	NCAA (2-1)
56–57	Dartmouth	18-7	10-4	2d (Ivy)	DNP
57–58	Dartmouth	22-5	11-3	1st (Ivy)	NCAA (2-1)
58–59	Dartmouth	22-6	14-1	1st (Ivy)	NCAA (0-1)
59–60	Dartmouth	14-9	10-4	2d (Ivy)	DNP
60–61	Dartmouth	5-19	4-10	T6th (Ivy)	DNP
61–62	Dartmouth	6-18	3-11	T6th (Ivy)	DNP
62–63	Dartmouth	7-18	2-12	8th (Ivy)	DNP
63–64	Dartmouth	2-23	0-14	8th (Ivy)	DNP
64–65	Dartmouth	4-21	1-13	8th (Ivy)	DNP
65–66	Dartmouth	3-21	0-14	8th (Ivy)	DNP
66–67	Dartmouth	7-17	1-13	8th (Ivy)	DNP

32-Year College Coaching Record: 388-358 (.520) overall; 9-26 (.257) in two years at Albright; 129-71 (.645) in nine years at Muhlenberg; 65-10 (.867) in three years at Holy Cross; 185-251 (.424) in 17 years at Dartmouth; 16-6 (.727) in Eastern Pennsylvania Collegiate League; 90-143 (.386) in Ivy League (Eastern Intercollegiate Basketball League); 9-4 (.692) in NCAA Tournament; 0-1 in NIT Tournament.

FRANK KEANEY
Bates '11
Boston, Mass.

Led Rhode Island to a fourth-place finish in 1945 NIT and a second-place finish in 1946 NIT.... Elected to Naismith Memorial Basketball Hall of Fame in 1960.

Year	School	Overall	League	Finish	Postseason
21–22	Rhode I.	3-7			
22–23	Rhode I.	9-4			
23–24	Rhode I.	9-6			
24–25	Rhode I.	11-5			
25–26	Rhode I.	8-8			
26–27	Rhode I.	13-4			
27–28	Rhode I.	15-5			
28–29	Rhode I.	15-1			
29–30	Rhode I.	10-5			
30–31	Rhode I.	13-4			
31–32	Rhode I.	13-3			
32–33	Rhode I.	14-4			
33–34	Rhode I.	13-3			
34–35	Rhode I.	12-6			
35–36	Rhode I.	13-5			
36–37	Rhode I.	18-3	8-0	1st (New England)	
37–38	Rhode I.	19-2	8-0	1st (New England)	DNP
38–39	Rhode I.	17-4	7-1	1st (New England)	DNP
39–40	Rhode I.	19-3	8-0	1st (New England)	DNP
40–41	Rhode I.	21-4	7-1	T1st (New England)	NIT (0-1)
41–42	Rhode I.	18-4	8-0	1st (New England)	NIT (0-1)
42–43	Rhode I.	16-3	7-1	1st (New England)	DNP
43–44	Rhode I.	14-6		New England	DNP
44–45	Rhode I.	20-5		New England	NIT (1-2)
45–46	Rhode I.	21-3	4-0	1st (New England)	NIT (2-1)
46–47	Rhode I.	17-3	4-1	3d (Yankee)	DNP
47–48	Rhode I.	16-7	5-1	2d (Yankee)	DNP

27-Year Coaching Record: 387-117 (.768) overall; 57-3 (.950) in New England Conference; 9-2 (.818) in Yankee Conference; 3-5 (.375) in NIT.

GEORGE KEOGAN
Minnesota
Detroit Lakes, Minn.

Coach of Notre Dame teams in 1927 and 1936 that were selected as national champions by the Helms Foundation.... Elected to Naismith Memorial Basketball Hall of Fame in 1961.

Year	School	Overall	League	Finish	Postseason
15–16	St. Louis	13-6			
18–19	Allegheny	14-1			
19–20	Valparaiso	12-8			
20–21	Valparaiso	19-5			
23–24	Notre Dame	15-8			
24–25	Notre Dame	11-11			
25–26	Notre Dame	19-1			
26–27	Notre Dame	19-1			
27–28	Notre Dame	18-4			
28–29	Notre Dame	15-5			
29–30	Notre Dame	14-6			
30–31	Notre Dame	12-8			
31–32	Notre Dame	18-2			
32–33	Notre Dame	16-6			
33–34	Notre Dame	20-4			
34–35	Notre Dame	13-9			
35–36	Notre Dame	22-2-1			
36–37	Notre Dame	20-3			
37–38	Notre Dame	20-3			DNP
38–39	Notre Dame	15-6			DNP
39–40	Notre Dame	15-6			DNP

Year	School	Overall	League	Finish	Postseason
40–41	Notre Dame	17-5			DNP
41–42	Notre Dame	16-6			DNP
42–43	Notre Dame	12-1			DNP

24-Year Coaching Record: 385-117 (.767) overall; 13-6 (.684) in one year at St. Louis; 14-1 (.933) in one year at Allegheny; 31-13 (.705) in two years at Valparaiso; 327-97 (.771) In 20 years at Notre Dame.

JACK KRAFT
St. Joseph's '42
Philadelphia, Pa.

Named NABC national coach of the year in 1971. . . . Reached Final Four with Villanova in 1971 (2nd). . . . Reached NIT semifinals with Villanova in 1963 (4th), 1965 (2nd) and 1966 (3rd). . . . Coached two different schools to NCAA Tournament.

Year	School	Overall	League	Finish	Postseason
61-62	Villanova	21-7			NCAA (2-1)
62-63	Villanova	19-10			NIT (2-2)
63-64	Villanova	24-4			NCAA (2-1)
64-65	Villanova	23-5			NIT (2-1)
65-66	Villanova	18-11			NIT (3-1)
66-67	Villanova	17-9			NIT (0-1)
67-68	Villanova	19-9			NIT (1-1)
68-69	Villanova	21-9			NCAA (0-1)
69-70	Villanova	22-7			NCAA (2-1)
70-71	Villanova	23-6			NCAA (4-1)
71-72	Villanova	20-8			NCAA (1-2)
72-73	Villanova	11-14			DNP
73-74	Rhode Island	11-14	5-5	4th (Yankee)	DNP
74-75	Rhode Island	5-20	3-6	5th (Yankee)	DNP
75-76	Rhode Island	14-12			DNP
76-77	Rhode Island	13-13			DNP
77-78	Rhode Island	24-7			NCAA (0-1)
78-79	Rhode Island	20-9			NIT (0-1)
79-80	Rhode Island	15-13			DNP
80-81	Rhode Island	21-8	10-3	1st (Eastern 8)	NIT (0-1)

20-Year Coaching Record: 361-191 (.654) overall; 238-95 (.725) in 12 years at Villanova; 123-96 (.562) in eight years at Rhode Island; 8-11 (.421) in Yankee Conference; 10-3 (.769) in Eastern Eight Conference; 1-1 (.500) in Eastern Eight Tournament; 11-8 (.579) in NCAA Tournament; 8-8 (.500) in NIT.

WARD (PIGGY) LAMBERT
Wabash '11
Crawfordsville, Ind.

Coach of 1932 team that was selected as national champion by the Helms Foundation.... Elected to Naismith Memorial Basketball Hall of Fame in 1960.

Year	School	Overall	League	Finish	Postseason
16–17	Purdue	11-3	7-2	3d (Big Ten)	
18–19	Purdue	6-8	4-7	7th (Big Ten)	
19–20	Purdue	16-4	8-2	2d (Big Ten)	
20–21	Purdue	13-7	8-4	T1st (Big Ten)	
21–22	Purdue	15-3	8-1	1st (Big Ten)	
22–23	Purdue	9-6	7-5	T4th (Big Ten)	
23–24	Purdue	12-5	7-5	T4th (Big Ten)	
24–25	Purdue	9-5	7-4	4th (Big Ten)	
25–26	Purdue	13-4	8-4	T1st (Big Ten)	
26–27	Purdue	12-5	9-3	T2d (Big Ten)	
27–28	Purdue	15-2	10-2	T1st (Big Ten)	
28–29	Purdue	13-4	9-3	3d (Big Ten)	
29–30	Purdue	13-2	10-0	1st (Big Ten)	
30–31	Purdue	12-5	8-4	2d (Big Ten)	
31–32	Purdue	17-1	11-1	1st (Big Ten)	
32–33	Purdue	11-7	6-6	T5th (Big Ten)	
33–34	Purdue	17-3	10-2	1st (Big Ten)	
34–35	Purdue	17-3	9-3	T1st (Big Ten)	
35–36	Purdue	16-4	11-1	T1st (Big Ten)	
36–37	Purdue	15-5	8-4	4th (Big Ten)	
37–38	Purdue	18-2	10-2	1st (Big Ten)	DNP
38–39	Purdue	12-7	6-6	5th (Big Ten)	DNP
39–40	Purdue	16-4	10-2	1st (Big Ten)	DNP
40–41	Purdue	13-7	6-6	6th (Big Ten)	DNP
41–42	Purdue	14-7	9-6	T5th (Big Ten)	DNP
42–43	Purdue	9-11	6-6	T4th (Big Ten)	DNP
43–44	Purdue	11-10	8-4	T4th (Big Ten)	DNP
44–45	Purdue	9-11	6-6	4th (Big Ten)	DNP
45–46	Purdue	7-7	2-4	8th (Big Ten)	DNP

29-Year Coaching Record: 371-152 (.709) overall; 228-105 (.685) in Big Ten Conference.

JOE LAPCHICK
St. John's '27
New York, N.Y.

Led St. John's to NIT titles in 1943, 1944, 1959, and 1965.... Elected to Naismith Memorial Basketball Hall of Fame in 1966.... Compiled a 326-247 record (.569) as coach of the New York Knicks for nine seasons (1947–48 through 1955–56), reaching the NBA Finals in 1951 and 1952.

Year	School	Overall	League	Finish	Postseason
36–37	St. John's	13-7			
37–38	St. John's	15-4			DNP
38–39	St. John's	18-4			NIT (1-2)
39–40	St. John's	15-4			NIT (0-1)
40–41	St. John's	11-6			DNP
41–42	St. John's	16-5			DNP
42–43	St. John's	21-3			NIT (3-0)
43–44	St. John's	18-5			NIT (3-0)
44–45	St. John's	21-3			NIT (2-1)
45–46	St. John's	17-6			NIT (0-1)
46–47	St. John's	16-7			NIT (0-1)
56–57	St. John's	14-9			DNP
57–58	St. John's	18-8			NIT (2-2)
58–59	St. John's	20-6			NIT (4-0)
59–60	St. John's	17-8			NIT (0-1)
60–61	St. John's	20-5			NCAA (0-1)
61–62	St. John's	21-5			NIT (2-1)
62–63	St. John's	9-15			DNP
63–64	St. John's	14-11			DNP
64–65	St. John's	21-8			NIT (4-0)

20-Year Coaching Record: 335-129 (.722) overall; 0-1 in NCAA Tournament; 21-10 (.677) in NIT.

GUY LEWIS
Houston '47
Arp, Tex.

Named national coach of the year by AP, UPI, and the USBWA in 1968, and again by AP in 1983.... Reached NCAA Final Four five times—1967 (3d), 1968 (4th), 1982 (tied for 3d), 1983 (2d), and 1984 (2d).... Coach of four Southwest Conference Tournament champions—1978, 1981, 1983, and 1984.... Assistant under Alden Pasche at Houston for three seasons from 1953–54 through 1955–56.

Year	School	Overall	League	Finish	Postseason
56–57	Houston	10-16	5-9	5th (MVC)	DNP
57–58	Houston	9-16	4-10	6th (MVC)	DNP
58–59	Houston	12-14	6-8	5th (MVC)	DNP
59–60	Houston	13-12	6-8	4th (MVC)	DNP
60–61	Houston	17-11			NCAA (1-2)
61–62	Houston	21-6			NIT (0-1)
62–63	Houston	15-11			DNP
63–64	Houston	16-10			DNP
64–65	Houston	19-10			NCAA (1-2)
65–66	Houston	23-6			NCAA (2-1)
66–67	Houston	27-4			NCAA (4-1)
67–68	Houston	31-2			NCAA (3-2)
68–69	Houston	16-10			DNP

Year	School	Overall	League	Finish	Postseason
69–70	Houston	25-5			NCAA (1-2)
70–71	Houston	22-7			NCAA (2-1)
71–72	Houston	20-7			NCAA (0-1)
72–73	Houston	23-4			NCAA (0-1)
73–74	Houston	17-9			DNP
74–75	Houston	16-10			DNP
75–76	Houston	17-11	7-9	6th (SWC)	DNP
76–77	Houston	29-8	13-3	2d (SWC)	NIT (3-1)
77–78	Houston	25-8	11-5	3d (SWC)	NCAA (0-1)
78–79	Houston	16-15	6-10	T6th (SWC)	DNP
79–80	Houston	14-14	8-8	T4th (SWC)	DNP
80–81	Houston	21-9	10-6	T2d (SWC)	NCAA (0-1)
81–82	Houston	25-8	11-5	2d (SWC)	NCAA (4-1)
82–83	Houston	31-3	16-0	1st (SWC)	NCAA (4-1)
83–84	Houston	32-5	15-1	1st (SWC)	NCAA (4-1)
84–85	Houston	16-14	8-8	T5th (SWC)	NIT (0-1)
85–86	Houston	14-14	8-8	6th (SWC)	DNP

30-Year Coaching Record: 592-279 (.680) overall; 21-35 (.375) in Missouri Valley Conference; 113-63 (.642) in Southwest Conference; 18-7 (.720) in SWC Tournament; 26-18 (.591) in NCAA Tournament; 3-3 (.500) in NIT.

HARRY LITWACK
Temple '30
Philadelphia, Pa.

Elected to Naismith Memorial Basketball Hall of Fame in 1975.... Led team to 1969 NIT title and third-place finish in 1957 NIT.... Reached NCAA Final Four two times—1956 (3d) and 1958 (3d).... Assistant coach at Temple under Jimmy Usilton, Ernie Messikomer, and Josh Cody.... Assistant under Ed Gottlieb of the NBA's Philadelphia Warriors in 1950–51.

Year	School	Overall	League	Finish	Postseason
52–53	Temple	16-10			DNP
53–54	Temple	15-12			DNP
54–55	Temple	11-10			DNP
55–56	Temple	27-4			NCAA (4-1)
56–57	Temple	20-9			NIT (2-1)
57–58	Temple	27-3			NCAA (3-1)
58–59	Temple	6-19	4-7	9th (Mid. Atl.)	DNP
59–60	Temple	17-9	9-2	3d (Mid. Atl.)	NIT (0-1)
60–61	Temple	20-8	9-1	2d (Mid. Atl.)	NIT (1-1)
61–62	Temple	18-9	8-2	2d (Mid. Atl.)	NIT (1-1)
62–63	Temple	15-7	6-3	4th (Mid. Atl.)	DNP
63–64	Temple	17-8	6-1	1st (Mid. Atl.)	NCAA (0-1)
64–65	Temple	14-10		4th (Mid. Atl.)	DNP
65–66	Temple	21-7		2d (Mid. Atl.)	NIT (1-1)
66–67	Temple	20-8		1st (Mid. Atl.)	NCAA (0-1)
67–68	Temple	19-9		3d (Mid. Atl.)	NIT (0-1)
68–69	Temple	22-8		1st (Mid. Atl.)	NIT (4-0)
69–70	Temple	15-13	2-3	T2d (Mid. Atl.-E)	NCAA (0-1)
70–71	Temple	13-12	3-3	4th (Mid. Atl.-E)	DNP
71–72	Temple	23-8	6-0	1st (Mid. Atl.-E)	NCAA (0-1)
72–73	Temple	17-10	5-1	2d (Mid. Atl.-E)	DNP

21-Year Coaching Record: 373-193 (.659) overall; 58-23 (.716) in Middle Atlantic Conference; 7-6 (.538) in NCAA Tournament; 9-6 (.600) in NIT.

KEN LOEFFLER
Penn St. '24
Beaver Falls, Pa.

Led La Salle to 1952 NIT championship and 1954 NCAA title. Also directed team to second-place finish in 1955 NCAA Tournament.... Elected to the Naismith Memorial Basketball Hall of Fame in 1964.... Coach of the NBA's St. Louis Bombers in 1946–47 and 1947–48 and Providence Steamrollers in 1948–49, guiding Bombers to the league's best regular-season record in 1947–48.

Year	School	Overall	League	Finish	Postseason
28–29	Geneva	14-5			
29–30	Geneva	10-9			
30–31	Geneva	13-10			
31–32	Geneva	13-7		(Eastern Pa.)	
32–33	Geneva	13-6	10-2	1st (Eastern Pa.)	
33–34	Geneva	13-9	11-1	1st (Eastern Pa.)	
34–35	Geneva	16-7			
35–36	Yale	8-16	6-6	3d (Ivy)	
36–37	Yale	12-8	7-5	3d (Ivy)	
37–38	Yale	7-12	3-9	7th (Ivy)	DNP
38–39	Yale	4-16	3-9	6th (Ivy)	DNP
39–40	Yale	13-6	7-5	3d (Ivy)	DNP
40–41	Yale	10-12	4-8	4th (Ivy)	DNP
41–42	Yale	7-12	3-9	6th (Ivy)	DNP
49–50	La Salle	21-4			NIT (1-1)
50–51	La Salle	22-7			NIT (0-1)
51–52	La Salle	24-5			NIT (4-0)
52–53	La Salle	25-3			NIT (0-1)
53–54	La Salle	26-4			NCAA (5-0)
54–55	La Salle	26-5			NCAA (4-1)
55–56	Texas A&M	6-18	3-9	T5th (SWC)	DNP
56–57	Texas A&M	7-17	3-9	T6th (SWC)	Probation

22-Year College Coaching Record: 310-198 (.610) overall; 92-53 (.634) in seven years at Geneva; 61-82 (.427) in seven years at Yale; 144-28 (.837) in six years at La Salle; 13-35 (.271) in two years at Texas A&M; 33-51 (.393) in Eastern Intercollegiate Basketball League (forerunner of Ivy League); 6-18 (.250) in Southwest Conference; 9-1 (.900) in NCAA Tournament; 5-3 (.625) in NIT.

JAMES (BABE) MCCARTHY
Mississippi State '49
Baldwyn, Miss.

Three-time SEC coach of the year.... World War II transport pilot was also called to active duty during the Korean War. He coached an Air Force team in Memphis while in the service.... Coached four ABA teams–New Orleans (1967-68 through 1969-70), Memphis (1970-71 and 1971-72), Dallas (1972-73) and Kentucky (1973-74).

Year	School	Overall	League	Finish	Postseason
55-56	Miss. State	12-12	6-8	T6th (SEC)	DNP
56-57	Miss. State	17-8	9-5	T3rd (SEC)	DNP
57-58	Miss. State	20-5	9-5	T3rd (SEC)	DNP
58-59	Miss. State	24-1	13-1	1st (SEC)	DNP
59-60	Miss. State	12-13	5-9	9th (SEC)	DNP
60-61	Miss. State	19-6	11-3	1st (SEC)	DNP
61-62	Miss. State	24-1	13-1	T1st (SEC)	DNP
62-63	Miss. State	22-6	12-2	1st (SEC)	NCAA (1-1)
63-64	Miss. State	9-17	4-10	11th (SEC)	DNP
64-65	Miss. State	10-16	6-10	8th (SEC)	DNP
66-67	George Wash.	6-18	5-7	6th (Southern)	DNP

11-Year College Coaching Record: 175-103 (.629) overall; 169-85 (.665) in 10 years at Mississippi State; 6-18 (.250) in one year at George Washington; 88-54 (.620) in Southeastern Conference; 5-7 (.417) in Southern Conference; 0-1 in Southern Conference Tournament; 1-1 (.500) in NCAA Tournament.

BRANCH MCCRACKEN
Indiana '30
Monrovia, Ind.

Led Indiana to two NCAA Tournament championships—1940 and 1953.... Only coach to participate in at least two Final Fours and win all of his games there.... Elected to Naismith Memorial Basketball Hall of Fame as a player in 1960.

Year	School	Overall	League	Finish	Postseason
30–31	Ball St.	9-5	8-5	6th (Ind. Col.)	
31–32	Ball St.	9-7		(Indiana Col.)	
32–33	Ball St.	7-9		(Indiana Col.)	
33–34	Ball St.	9-10		(Indiana Col.)	
34–35	Ball St.	9-9		(Indiana Col.)	
35–36	Ball St.	13-7		3d (Indiana Col.)	

Year	School	Overall	League	Finish	Postseason
36–37	Ball St.	13-6		(Indiana Col.)	
37–38	Ball St.	17-4		(Indiana Col.)	DNP
38–39	Indiana	17-3	9-3	2d (Western)	DNP
39–40	Indiana	20-3	9-3	2d (Western)	NCAA (3-0)
40–41	Indiana	17-3	10-2	2d (Western)	DNP
41–42	Indiana	15-6	10-5	T2d (Western)	DNP
42–43	Indiana	18-2	11-2	2d (Western)	DNP
46–47	Indiana	12-8	8-4	T2d (Western)	DNP
47–48	Indiana	8-12	3-9	T8th (Western)	DNP
48–49	Indiana	14-8	6-6	T4th (Big Ten)	DNP
49–50	Indiana	17-5	7-5	T3d (Big Ten)	DNP
50–51	Indiana	19-3	12-2	2d (Big Ten)	DNP
51–52	Indiana	16-6	9-5	4th (Big Ten)	DNP
52–53	Indiana	23-3	17-1	1st (Big Ten)	NCAA (4-0)
53–54	Indiana	20-4	12-2	1st (Big Ten)	NCAA (1-1)
54–55	Indiana	8-14	5-9	T6th (Big Ten)	DNP
55–56	Indiana	13-9	6-8	T6th (Big Ten)	DNP
56–57	Indiana	14-8	10-4	T1st (Big Ten)	NCAA (1-1)
57–58	Indiana	13-11	10-4	1st (Big Ten)	NCAA (1-1)
58–59	Indiana	11-11	7-7	T5th (Big Ten)	DNP
59–60	Indiana	20-4	11-3	2d (Big Ten)	DNP
60–61	Indiana	15-9	8-6	T4th (Big Ten)	Probation
61–62	Indiana	13-11	7-7	T4th (Big Ten)	Probation
62–63	Indiana	13-11	9-5	3d (Big Ten)	Probation
63–64	Indiana	9-15	5-9	8th (Big Ten)	Probation
64–65	Indiana	19-5	9-5	4th (Big Ten)	DNP

32-Year Coaching Record: 450-231 (.661) overall; 86-57 (.601) in eight years at Ball State; 364-174 (.677) in 24 years at Indiana; 210-116 (.644) in Big Ten Conference; 9-2 (.818) in NCAA Tournament.

AL McGUIRE
St. John's '51
Brooklyn, N.Y.

Named national coach of the year by AP, UPI, and the USBWA in 1971, and by the NABC in 1974.... Coached Marquette to the NIT title in 1970 and the NCAA championship in 1977. His 1974 Marquette squad finished runner-up to North Carolina State in the NCAA Tournament and his 1967 team lost to Southern Illinois in the NIT final.... Elected to Naismith Memorial Basketball Hall of Fame in 1991.... Assistant coach at Dartmouth under Doggie Julian.

Year	School	Overall	League	Finish	Postseason
57–58	Belmont Abbey	24-3			
58–59	Belmont Abbey	21-2			
59–60	Belmont Abbey	19-6			
60–61	Belmont Abbey	17-7			
61–62	Belmont Abbey	16-9			NAIA (0-1)
62–63	Belmont Abbey	6-19			
63–64	Belmont Abbey	6-18			
64–65	Marquette	8-18			DNP
65–66	Marquette	14-12			DNP
66–67	Marquette	21-9			NIT (3-1)
67–68	Marquette	23-6			NCAA (2-1)
68–69	Marquette	24-5			NCAA (2-1)
69–70	Marquette	26-3			NIT (4-0)
70–71	Marquette	28-1			NCAA (2-1)
71–72	Marquette	25-4			NCAA (1-2)
72–73	Marquette	25-4			NCAA (2-1)
73–74	Marquette	26-5			NCAA (4-1)
74–75	Marquette	23-4			NCAA (0-1)
75–76	Marquette	27-2			NCAA (2-1)
76–77	Marquette	26-6			NCAA (5-0)

20-Year Coaching Record: 405-143 (.739) overall; 110-63 (.636) in seven years at Belmont Abbey; 295-80 (.787) in 13 years at Marquette; 20-9 (.690) in NCAA Tournament; 7-1 (.875) in NIT; 0-1 in NAIA Tournament.

FRANK McGUIRE
St. John's '36
New York, N.Y.

Coached 11 years at St. Xavier H.S. (126-39).... Only coach to win more than 100 games for three colleges—St. John's (103), North Carolina (164), and South Carolina (283).... Directed North Carolina to an undefeated record (32-0) en route to the 1957 NCAA Tournament title.... Led St. John's to back-to-back NIT third-place finishes in 1950 and 1951.... Named national coach of the year by UPI in 1957.... Also served as head baseball coach at St. John's, where he took the Redmen to the 1949 College World Series.... Elected to Naismith Memorial Basketball Hall of Fame in 1976.... Guided North Carolina to 1957 ACC Tournament title and South Carolina to the 1971 ACC Tournament championship.... Compiled 49-31 regular-season record for the NBA's Philadelphia Warriors in 1961–62.

Year	School	Overall	League	Finish	Postseason
47–48	St. John's	12-11			DNP
48–49	St. John's	16-9			NIT (0-1)
49–50	St. John's	24-5			NIT (2-1)
50–51	St. John's	26-5			NCAA (2-1); NIT (2-1)
51–52	St. John's	25-5			NCAA (3-1); NIT (0-1)
52–53	N. Carolina	17-10	15-6	8th (Southern)	DNP
53–54	N. Carolina	11-10	5-6	5th (ACC)	DNP
54–55	N. Carolina	10-11	8-6	T4th (ACC)	DNP
55–56	N. Carolina	18-5	11-3	T1st (ACC)	DNP
56–57	N. Carolina	32-0	14-0	1st (ACC)	NCAA (5-0)
57–58	N. Carolina	19-7	10-4	T2d (ACC)	DNP
58–59	N. Carolina	20-5	12-2	T1st (ACC)	NCAA (0-1)
59–60	N. Carolina	18-6	12-2	T1st (ACC)	DNP
60–61	N. Carolina	19-4	12-2	1st (ACC)	Probation
64–65	S. Carolina	6-17	2-12	8th (ACC)	DNP
65–66	S. Carolina	11-13	4-10	T6th (ACC)	DNP
66–67	S. Carolina	16-7	8-4	3d (ACC)	Probation
67–68	S. Carolina	15-7	9-5	4th (ACC)	Probation
68–69	S. Carolina	21-7	11-3	2d (ACC)	NIT (1-1)
69–70	S. Carolina	25-3	14-0	1st (ACC)	DNP
70–71	S. Carolina	23-6	10-4	2d (ACC)	NCAA (0-2)
71–72	S. Carolina	24-5			NCAA (2-1)
72–73	S. Carolina	22-7			NCAA (2-1)
73–74	S. Carolina	22-5			NCAA (0-1)
74–75	S. Carolina	19-9			NIT (1-1)
75–76	S. Carolina	18-9			DNP
76–77	S. Carolina	14-12			DNP
77–78	S. Carolina	16-12			DNP
78–79	S. Carolina	15-12			DNP
79–80	S. Carolina	16-11			DNP

30-Year College Coaching Record: 550-235 (.701) overall; 102-36 (.739) in five years at St. John's; 164-58 (.739) in nine years at North Carolina; 283-142 (.666) in 16 years at South Carolina; 15-6 (.714) in Southern Conference; 142-63 (.693) in Atlantic Coast Conference (84-25, .771, at UNC; 58-38, .604, at USC); 0-1 (.000) in Southern Conference Tournament; 17-12 (.586) in ACC Tournament (8-6, .571, at UNC; 9-6, .600, at USC); 14-8 (.636) in NCAA Tournament; 6-6 (.500) in NIT.

DR. WALTER MEANWELL
Maryland '09
Leeds, England

Led teams to nine conference titles in the first 12 seasons of his 22-year career.... Coach of Wisconsin teams in 1912, 1914, and 1916 that were selected as national champions by the Helms Foundation.... Elected to Naismith Memorial Basketball Hall of Fame in 1959.... Charter member of the National Association of Basketball Coaches.

Year	School	Overall	League	Finish	Postseason
11–12	Wisconsin	15-0	12-0	1st (Big Ten)	
12–13	Wisconsin	14-1	11-1	1st (Big Ten)	
13–14	Wisconsin	15-0	12-0	1st (Big Ten)	
14–15	Wisconsin	13-4	8-4	3d (Big Ten)	
15–16	Wisconsin	20-1	11-1	1st (Big Ten)	
16–17	Wisconsin	15-3	9-3	4th (Big Ten)	
17–18	Missouri	17-1	15-1	1st (MVC)	
19–20	Missouri	17-1	17-1	1st (MVC)	
20–21	Wisconsin	13-4	8-4	T1st (Big Ten)	
21–22	Wisconsin	14-5	8-4	T2d (Big Ten)	
22–23	Wisconsin	12-3	11-1	T1st (Big Ten)	

23–24	Wisconsin	11-5	8-4	T1st (Big Ten)	
24–25	Wisconsin	6-11	3-9	9th (Big Ten)	
25–26	Wisconsin	8-9	4-8	T8th (Big Ten)	
26–27	Wisconsin	10-7	7-5	T4th (Big Ten)	
27–28	Wisconsin	13-4	9-3	T3d (Big Ten)	
28–29	Wisconsin	15-2	10-2	T1st (Big Ten)	
29–30	Wisconsin	15-2	8-2	2d (Big Ten)	
30–31	Wisconsin	8-9	4-8	T7th (Big Ten)	
31–32	Wisconsin	8-10	3-9	T8th (Big Ten)	
32–33	Wisconsin	7-13	4-8	8th (Big Ten)	
33–34	Wisconsin	14-6	8-4	T2d (Big Ten)	

22-Year Coaching Record: 280-101 (.735) overall; 246-99 (.713) in 20 years at Wisconsin; 34-2 (.944) in two years at Missouri; 158-80 (.660) in Big Ten Conference; 32-2 (.941) in Missouri Valley Conference.

RAY MEARS
Miami (Ohio) '49
Dover, Ohio

Coached Wittenberg to 1961 NCAA College Division championship.... His 1969 Tennessee squad finished third in the NIT.

Year	School	Overall	League	Finish	Postseason
56–57	Wittenberg	15-6	11-3	3d (Ohio)	DNP
57–58	Wittenberg	19-3	14-1	2d (Ohio)	DNP
58–59	Wittenberg	19-3	13-1	1st (Ohio)	NCAA DII (1-1)
59–60	Wittenberg	22-2	12-0	1st (Ohio)	DNP
60–61	Wittenberg	25-4	10-0	1st (Ohio)	NCAA DII (5-0)
61–62	Wittenberg	21-5	10-2	2d (Ohio)	NCAA DII (2-1)
62–63	Tennessee	13-11	6-8	7th (SEC)	DNP
63–64	Tennessee	16-8	9-5	T2d (SEC)	DNP
64–65	Tennessee	20-5	12-4	2d (SEC)	DNP
65–66	Tennessee	18-8	10-6	T3d (SEC)	DNP
66–67	Tennessee	21-7	15-3	1st (SEC)	NCAA (0-2)
67–68	Tennessee	20-6	13-5	2d (SEC)	DNP
68–69	Tennessee	21-7	13-5	2d (SEC)	NIT (3-1)
69–70	Tennessee	16-9	10-8	5th (SEC)	DNP
70–71	Tennessee	21-7	13-5	2d (SEC)	NIT (1-1)
71–72	Tennessee	19-6	14-4	T1st (SEC)	DNP
72–73	Tennessee	15-9	13-5	T2d (SEC)	DNP
73–74	Tennessee	17-9	12-6	3d (SEC)	DNP
74–75	Tennessee	18-8	12-6	T3d (SEC)	DNP
75–76	Tennessee	21-6	14-4	2d (SEC)	NCAA (0-1)
76–77	Tennessee	22-6	16-2	T1st (SEC)	NCAA (0-1)

21-Year Coaching Record: 399-135 (.747) overall; 121-23 (.840) in six years at Wittenberg; 278-112 (.713) in 15 years at Tennessee; 70-7 (.909) in Ohio Conference; 182-76 (.705) in Southeastern Conference; 0-4 in NCAA Tournament; 4-2 (.667) in NIT; 8-2 (.800) in NCAA College Division Tournament.

RAY MEYER
Notre Dame '38
Chicago, Ill.

Elected to Naismith Memorial Basketball Hall of Fame in 1978.... Coached three teams to the NIT championship game (1944, 1945, and 1983), winning the title in 1945. His 1948 squad finished fourth at the NIT.... Twice took teams to NCAA Final Four—1943 (T3d) and 1979 (3d).... Shares the longest coaching tenure (42 years) at one school with Western Kentucky's Ed Diddle.... Named coach of the year by UPI and AP in 1980 and 1984, by the USBWA in 1978 and 1980, and by the NABC in 1979.... Assistant coach at Notre Dame under George Keogan for two years in 1940–41 and 1941–42.

Year	School	Overall	League	Finish	Postseason
42–43	DePaul	19-5			NCAA (1-1)
43–44	DePaul	22-4			NIT (2-1)
44–45	DePaul	21-3			NIT (3-0)
45–46	DePaul	19-5			DNP
46–47	DePaul	16-9			DNP
47–48	DePaul	22-8			NIT (1-2)
48–49	DePaul	16-9			DNP
49–50	DePaul	12-13			DNP
50–51	DePaul	13-12			DNP
51–52	DePaul	19-8			DNP
52–53	DePaul	19-9			NCAA (1-2)
53–54	DePaul	11-10			DNP
54–55	DePaul	16-6			DNP
55–56	DePaul	16-8			NCAA (0-1)
56–57	DePaul	8-14			DNP
57–58	DePaul	8-12			DNP
58–59	DePaul	13-11			NCAA (1-2)
59–60	DePaul	17-7			NCAA (2-1)
60–61	DePaul	17-8			NIT (0-1)
61–62	DePaul	13-10			DNP
62–63	DePaul	15-8			NIT (0-1)
63–64	DePaul	21-4			NIT (0-1)
64–65	DePaul	17-10			NCAA (1-2)
65–66	DePaul	18-8			NIT (0-1)
66–67	DePaul	17-8			DNP
67–68	DePaul	13-12			DNP
68–69	DePaul	14-11			DNP
69–70	DePaul	12-13			DNP
70–71	DePaul	8-17			DNP
71–72	DePaul	12-11			DNP
72–73	DePaul	14-11			DNP
73–74	DePaul	16-9			DNP
74–75	DePaul	15-10			DNP
75–76	DePaul	20-9			NCAA (1-1)
76–77	DePaul	15-12			DNP
77–78	DePaul	27-3			NCAA (2-1)
78–79	DePaul	26-6			NCAA (4-1)
79–80	DePaul	26-2			NCAA (0-1)
80–81	DePaul	27-2			NCAA (0-1)
81–82	DePaul	26-2			NCAA (0-1)
82–83	DePaul	21-12			NIT (4-1)
83–84	DePaul	27-3			NCAA (1-1)

42-Year Coaching Record: 724-354 (.672); 14-16 (.467) in NCAA Tournament; 10-8 (.556) in NIT.

RALPH MILLER
Kansas '42
Chanute, Kans.

Elected to Naismith Memorial Basketball Hall of Fame in 1987.... Recorded 33 winning records in 38 seasons at three schools.... Compiled eight 20-win seasons during the 1980s.... Named national coach of the year by UPI, USBWA, and NABC in 1981. Voted coach of the year by AP in 1981 and 1982.... Played college basketball for Phog Allen at Kansas.

Year	School	Overall	League	Finish	Postseason
51–52	Wichita	11-19	2-8	6th (MVC)	DNP
52–53	Wichita	16-11	3-7	6th (MVC)	DNP
53–54	Wichita	27-4	8-2	2d (MVC)	NIT (0-1)
54–55	Wichita	17-9	4-6	4th (MVC)	DNP
55–56	Wichita	14-12	7-5	4th (MVC)	DNP
56–57	Wichita	15-11	8-6	T4th (MVC)	DNP
57–58	Wichita	14-12	6-8	4th (MVC)	DNP
58–59	Wichita	14-12	7-7	4th (MVC)	DNP
59–60	Wichita	14-12	6-8	T4th (MVC)	DNP
60–61	Wichita	18-8	6-6	4th (MVC)	DNP
61–62	Wichita	18-9	7-5	3d (MVC)	NIT (0-1)
62–63	Wichita	19-8	7-5	2d (MVC)	NIT (0-1)
63–64	Wichita	23-6	10-2	T1st (MVC)	NCAA (1-1)
64–65	Iowa	14-10	8-6	5th (Big Ten)	DNP
65–66	Iowa	17-7	8-6	3d (Big Ten)	DNP
66–67	Iowa	16-8	9-5	3d (Big Ten)	DNP
67–68	Iowa	16-9	9-5	T1st (Big Ten)	DNP
68–69	Iowa	12-12	5-9	T8th (Big Ten)	DNP
69–70	Iowa	20-5	14-0	1st (Big Ten)	NCAA (1-1)
70–71	Oregon St.	12-14	4-10	6th (Pac-8)	DNP
71–72	Oregon St.	18-10	9-5	T3d (Pac-8)	DNP
72–73	Oregon St.	15-11	6-8	T5th (Pac-8)	DNP
73–74	Oregon St.	13-13	6-8	5th (Pac-8)	DNP
74–75	Oregon St.	19-12	10-4	2d (Pac-8)	NCAA (1-2)
75–76#	Oregon St.	18-9	10-4	T2d (Pac-8)	DNP
76–77	Oregon St.	16-13	8-6	T3d (Pac-8)	DNP
77–78	Oregon St.	16-11	9-5	2d (Pac-8)	DNP
78–79	Oregon St.	18-10	11-7	3d (Pac-10)	NIT (0-1)
79–80*	Oregon St.	26-4	16-2	1st (Pac-10)	NCAA (0-1)
80–81*	Oregon St.	26-2	17-1	1st (Pac-10)	NCAA (0-1)
81–82*	Oregon St.	25-5	16-2	1st (Pac-10)	NCAA (2-1)
82–83	Oregon St.	20-11	12-6	T3d (Pac-10)	NIT (2-1)
83–84	Oregon St.	22-7	15-3	T1st (Pac-10)	NCAA (0-1)

84–85	Oregon St.	22-9	12-6	T3d (Pac-10)	NCAA (0-1)
85–86	Oregon St.	12-15	8-10	T5th (Pac-10)	DNP
86–87	Oregon St.	19-11	10-8	T3d (Pac-10)	NIT (1-1)
87–88	Oregon St.	20-11	12-6	T2d (Pac-10)	NCAA (0-1)
88–89	Oregon St.	22-8	13-5	T3d (Pac-10)	NCAA (0-1)

#–15 wins later forfeited by action of the NCAA Council.

*–NCAA Tournament games later vacated by action of the NCAA.

38-Year Coaching Record: 674-370 (.646) overall; 220-133 (.623) in 13 years at Wichita State (Wichita); 95-51 (.651) in six years at Iowa; 359-186 (.659) in 19 years at Oregon State; 81-75 (.519) in Missouri Valley Conference; 54-30 (.643) in Big Ten Conference; 204-114 (.642) in Pacific-10 Conference; 3-3 (.500) in Pac-10 Tournament; 5-11 (.313) in NCAA Tournament; 3-6 (.333) in NIT.

DONALD (DUDEY) MOORE
Duquesne '34
Pittsburgh, Pa.

Led Duquesne to the semifinal round of the NIT on five occasions—1950 (4th), 1952 (4th), 1953 (3d), 1954 (2d), and 1955 (1st).

Year	School	Overall	League	Finish	Postseason
48–49	Duquesne	17-5			DNP
49–50	Duquesne	23-6			NIT (1-2)
50–51	Duquesne	16-11			DNP
51–52	Duquesne	23-4			NIT (1-2); NCAA (1-1)
52–53	Duquesne	21-8			NIT (3-1)
53–54	Duquesne	26-3			NIT (2-1)
54–55	Duquesne	22-4			NIT (3-0)
55–56	Duquesne	17-10			NIT (1-1)
56–57	Duquesne	16-7			DNP
57–58	Duquesne	10-12			DNP
58–59	La Salle	16-7			DNP
59–60	La Salle	16-6			DNP
60–61	La Salle	15-7			DNP
61–62	La Salle	16-9			DNP
62–63	La Salle	16-8			NIT (0-1)

15-Year Coaching Record: 270-107 (.716) overall; 191-70 (.732) in 10 years at Duquesne; 79-37 (.681) in five years at La Salle; 1-1 (.500) in NCAA Tournament; 11-8 (.579) in NIT.

JOE MULLANEY
Holy Cross '49
Mineola, N.Y.

Coached Providence to NIT titles in 1961 and 1963. Reached NIT semifinals in 1959 (4th) and 1960 (2nd). . . . Served as an FBI agent after brief playing career with the Celtics. . . . Coached in the NBA (Los Angeles Lakers), ABA (Kentucky Colonels, Utah Stars and Memphis Sounds), Italy and CBA (Pensacola).

Year	School	Overall	League	Finish	Postseason
54-55	Norwich	16-5	5-1		1st (GMC) DNP
55-56	Providence	14-8			DNP
56-57	Providence	15-9			DNP
57-58	Providence	18-6			DNP
58-59	Providence	20-7			NIT (2-2)
59-60	Providence	24-5			NIT (3-1)
60-61	Providence	24-5			NIT (4-0)
61-62	Providence	20-6			NIT (0-1)
62-63	Providence	24-4			NIT (3-1)
63-64	Providence	20-6			NCAA (0-1)
64-65	Providence	24-2			NCAA (2-1)
65-66	Providence	22-5			NCAA (0-1)
66-67	Providence	21-7			NIT (1-1)
67-68	Providence	11-14			DNP
68-69	Providence	14-10			DNP
78-79	Brown	8-18	6-8	T4th (Ivy)	DNP
79-80	Brown	12-14	9-5	3rd (Ivy)	DNP
80-81	Brown	9-17	5-9	T4th (Ivy)	DNP
81-82	Providence	10-17	2-12	T7th (Big East)	DNP
82-83	Providence	12-19	4-12	8th (Big East)	DNP

83-84	Providence	15-14	5-11	T7th (Big East)	DNP
84-85	Providence	11-20	3-13	8th (Big East)	DNP

22-Year College Coaching Record: 364-218 (.625) overall; 16-5 (.762) in one year at Norwich; 319-164 (.660) in 18 years at Providence; 29-49 (.372) in three years at Brown; 5-1 (.833) in Green Mountain Conference; 20-22 (.476) in Ivy League; 14-48 (.226) in Big East Conference; 2-4 (.333) in Big East Tournament; 2-3 (.400) in NCAA Tournament; 13-5 (.722) in NIT.

PETE NEWELL
Loyola (Calif.) '40
Vancouver, B.C.

Guided California to back-to-back NCAA Final Four appearances in 1959 (1st) and 1960 (2d). . . . Named national coach of the year by UPI and the USBWA in 1960. . . . Elected to Naismith Memorial Basketball Hall of Fame in 1978. . . . Coach of gold medal-winning 1960 U.S. Olympic Team. . . . Led San Francisco to 1949 NIT title.

Year	School	Overall	League	Finish	Postseason
46–47	San Fran.	13-14			DNP
47–48	San Fran.	13-11			DNP
48–49	San Fran.	25-5			NIT (4-0)
49–50	San Fran.	19-7			DNP
50–51	Mich. St.	10-11	5-9	7th (Big Ten)	DNP
51–52	Mich. St.	13-9	6-8	T5th (Big Ten)	DNP
52–53	Mich. St.	13-9	11-7	T3d (Big Ten)	DNP
53–54	Mich. St.	9-13	4-10	8th (Big Ten)	DNP
54–55	California	9-16	1-11	4th (PCC-S)	DNP
55–56	California	17-8	10-6	T3d (PCC)	DNP
56–57	California	21-5	14-2	1st (PCC)	NCAA (1-1)
57–58	California	19-9	12-4	T1st (PCC)	NCAA (1-1)
58–59	California	25-4	14-2	1st (PCC)	NCAA (4-0)
59–60	California	28-2	11-1	1st (AAWU)	NCAA (4-1)

14-Year Coaching Record: 234-123 (.655) overall; 70-37 (.654) in four years at San Francisco; 45-42 (.517) in four years at Michigan State; 119-44 (.730) in six years at California; 26-34 (.433) in Big Ten Conference; 62-26 (.705) in Pacific-10 Conference (Pacific Coast Conference/AAWU); 10-3 (.769) in NCAA Tournament; 4-0 in NIT.

FRANK (BUCKY) O'CONNER
Drake '38
Newton, Iowa

Took Iowa to back-to-back NCAA Final Four appearances in 1955 (4th) and 1956 (2d). . . . Assistant coach at Iowa under Pops Harrison and Rollie Williams.

Year	School	Overall	League	Finish	Postseason
49–50	Iowa	6-5	5-5	5th (Big Ten)	DNP
51–52	Iowa	19-3	11-3	2d (Big Ten)	DNP
52–53	Iowa	12-10	9-9	6th (Big Ten)	DNP
53–54	Iowa	17-5	11-3	2d (Big Ten)	DNP
54–55	Iowa	19-7	11-3	1st (Big Ten)	NCAA (2-2)
55–56	Iowa	20-6	13-1	1st (Big Ten)	NCAA (3-1)
56–57	Iowa	8-14	4-10	8th (Big Ten)	DNP
57–58	Iowa	13-9	7-7	6th (Big Ten)	DNP

Eight-Year Coaching Record: 114-59 (.659) in eight years at Iowa; 71-41 (.634) in Big Ten Conference; 5-3 (.625) in NCAA Tournament.

JOHN OLDHAM
Western Kentucky '48
Hartford, Ky.

Guided Western Kentucky to Final Four of 1971 NCAA Tournament (3rd). . . . Directed Western Kentucky to Ohio Valley Conference Tournament titles in 1965 and 1966. . . . Played two seasons in the NBA with Fort Wayne.

Year	School	Overall	League	Finish	Postseason
55-56	Tenn. Tech	14-7	7-3	T1st (OVC)	DNP
56-57	Tenn. Tech	9-11	1-9	6th (OVC)	DNP
57-58	Tenn. Tech	17-9	8-2	1st (OVC)	NCAA (0-1)
58-59	Tenn. Tech	16-9	7-5	3rd (OVC)	DNP
59-60	Tenn. Tech	13-9	7-5	T3rd (OVC)	DNP
60-61	Tenn. Tech	6-13	3-9	6th (OVC)	DNP
61-62	Tenn. Tech	16-6	7-5	T2nd (OVC)	DNP
62-63	Tenn. Tech	16-8	8-4	T1st (OVC)	NCAA (0-1)
63-64	Tenn. Tech	11-11	7-7	T4th (OVC)	DNP
64-65	Western Ky.	18-9	10-4	2nd (OVC)	NIT (1-1)
65-66	Western Ky.	25-3	14-0	1st (OVC)	NCAA (2-1)
66-67	Western Ky.	23-3	13-1	1st (OVC)	NCAA (0-1)
67-68	Western Ky.	18-7	9-5	3rd (OVC)	DNP
68-69	Western Ky.	16-10	9-5	3rd (OVC)	DNP
69-70	Western Ky.	22-3	14-0	1st (OVC)	NCAA (0-1)
70-71	Western Ky.	24-6	12-2	1st (OVC)	NCAA (4-1)

16-Year College Coaching Record: 264-124 (.680) overall; 118-83 (.587) in nine years at Tennessee Tech; 146-41 (.781) in seven years at Western Kentucky; 136-66 (.673) in Ohio Valley Conference; 8-2 (.800) in OVC Tournament; 6-6 (.500) in NCAA Tournament; 1-1 (.500) in NIT.

HAROLD OLSEN
Wisconsin '17
Rice Lake, Wisc.

Directed Ohio State to title game (runner-up to Oregon) in first NCAA Tournament in 1939. . . . Finished in third place in 1946 NCAA Tournament. . . . Elected to Naismith Memorial Basketball Hall of Fame in 1959. . . . Compiled a 95-63 record (.601) as coach of the NBA's Chicago Stags for three seasons (1946–47 through 1948–49).

Year	School	Overall	League	Finish	Postseason
18–19	Bradley	5-7			
19–20	Ripon	10-2			
20–21	Ripon	9-3			
21–22	Ripon	7-5			
22–23	Ohio St.	4-11	1-11	T9th (Western)	
23–24	Ohio St.	12-5	7-5	T4th (Western)	
24–25	Ohio St.	14-2	11-1	1st (Western)	
25–26	Ohio St.	10-7	6-6	5th (Western)	
26–27	Ohio St.	11-6	6-6	7th (Western)	
27–28	Ohio St.	5-12	3-9	T7th (Western)	
28–29	Ohio St.	9-8	6-6	T5th (Western)	
29–30	Ohio St.	4-11	1-9	9th (Western)	
30–31	Ohio St.	4-13	3-9	9th (Western)	
31–32	Ohio St.	9-9	5-7	6th (Western)	
32–33	Ohio St.	17-3	10-2	T1st (Western)	
33–34	Ohio St.	8-12	4-8	T8th (Western)	
34–35	Ohio St.	13-6	8-4	T4th (Western)	
35–36	Ohio St.	12-8	5-7	T6th (Western)	
36–37	Ohio St.	13-7	7-5	5th (Western)	
37–38	Ohio St.	12-8	7-5	T3d (Western)	DNP
38–39	Ohio St.	16-7	10-2	1st (Western)	NCAA (2-1)
39–40	Ohio St.	13-7	8-4	3d (Western)	DNP
40–41	Ohio St.	10-10	7-5	T3d (Western)	DNP
41–42	Ohio St.	6-14	4-11	9th (Western)	DNP
42–43	Ohio St.	8-9	5-7	T6th (Western)	DNP
43–44	Ohio St.	14-7	10-2	1st (Western)	NCAA (1-1)
44–45	Ohio St.	15-5	10-2	2d (Western)	NCAA (1-1)
45–46	Ohio St.	16-5	10-2	1st (Western)	NCAA (2-1)
50–51	N'western	12-10	7-7	T4th (Big Ten)	DNP
51–52	N'western	7-15	4-10	T8th (Big Ten)	DNP

30-Year College Coaching Record: 305-234 (.566); 5-7 (.416) in one year at Bradley; 26-11 (.703) in three years at Ripon; 255-192 (.570) in 24 years at Ohio State; 19-25 (.432) in two years at Northwestern; 165-152 (.521) in Big Ten Conference (154-135, .533, at OSU; 11-17, .393, at NU); 6-4 (.600) in NCAA Tournament.

JOHNNY ORR
Beloit, Wis. '49
Taylorville, Ill.

All-time winningest coach at Michigan (209) and Iowa State (218), joining Ralph Miller (Wichita State and Oregon State) as the only individuals to be the winningest coaches at two different schools. . . . First Big Ten coach to lead his team to four consecutive NCAA berths. . . . Named national coach of the year by the NABC in 1976. . . . Led Michigan to the 1976 NCAA Tournament title game versus Indiana. . . . His 1977 Michigan team was ranked No. 1 in the final wire service polls. . . . Assistant at Wisconsin under John Erickson and under Dave Strack at Michigan.

Year	School	Overall	League	Finish	Postseason
63–64	Mass.	15-9	5-5	3d (Yankee)	DNP
64–65	Mass.	13-11	8-2	2d (Yankee)	DNP
65–66	Mass.	11-13	5-5	3d (Yankee)	DNP
68–69	Michigan	13-11	7-7	4th (Big Ten)	DNP
69–70	Michigan	10-14	5-9	6th (Big Ten)	DNP
70–71	Michigan	19-7	12-2	2d (Big Ten)	NIT (1-1)
71–72	Michigan	14-10	9-5	T3d (Big Ten)	DNP
72–73	Michigan	13-11	6-8	T5th (Big Ten)	DNP
73–74	Michigan	22-5	12-2	T1st (Big Ten)	NCAA (1-1)
74–75	Michigan	19-8	12-6	2d (Big Ten)	NCAA (0-1)
75–76	Michigan	25-7	14-4	2d (Big Ten)	NCAA (4-1)
76–77	Michigan	26-4	16-2	1st (Big Ten)	NCAA (2-1)
77–78	Michigan	16-11	11-7	T4th (Big Ten)	DNP
78–79	Michigan	15-12	8-10	6th (Big Ten)	DNP
79–80	Michigan	17-13	8-10	T6th (Big Ten)	NIT (2-1)
80–81	Iowa St.	9-18	2-12	8th (Big Eight)	DNP
81–82	Iowa St.	10-17	5-9	6th (Big Eight)	DNP
82–83	Iowa St.	13-15	5-9	5th (Big Eight)	DNP
83–84	Iowa St.	16-13	6-8	T4th (Big Eight)	NIT (0-1)
84–85	Iowa St.	21-13	7-7	3d (Big Eight)	NCAA (0-1)
85–86	Iowa St.	22-11	9-5	2d (Big Eight)	NCAA (2-1)
86–87	Iowa St.	13-15	5-9	6th (Big Eight)	DNP
87–88	Iowa St.	20-12	6-8	T5th (Big Eight)	NCAA (0-1)
88–89	Iowa St.	17-12	7-7	T4th (Big Eight)	NCAA (0-1)
89–90	Iowa St.	10-18	4-10	6th (Big Eight)	DNP
90–91	Iowa St.	12-19	6-8	5th (Big Eight)	DNP
91–92	Iowa St.	21-13	5-9	T6th (Big Eight)	NCAA (1-1)
92–93	Iowa St.	20-11	8-6	T2d (Big Eight)	NCAA (0-1)
93–94	Iowa St.	14-13	4-10	T6th (Big Eight)	DNP

29-Year Coaching Record: 466-346 (.574) overall; 39-33 (.542) in three years at Massachusetts; 209-113 (.649) in 12 years at Michigan; 218-200 (.522) in 14 years at Iowa State; 18-12 (.600) in Yankee Conference; 120-72 (.625) in Big Ten Conference; 81-117 (.409) in Big Eight Conference; 7-14 (.333) in Big Eight Tournament; 10-10 (.500) in NCAA Tournament; 3-3 (.500) in NIT.

CHUCK (OZZIE) ORSBORN
Bradley '39
Deerfield, Ill.

Coached Bradley to NIT titles in 1957, 1960 and 1964. Reached NIT semifinals in 1959 (2nd). . . . Played one year of minor league baseball following graduation. . . . Joined Bradley's coaching staff as an assistant in 1947.

Year	School	Overall	League	Finish	Postseason
56-57	Bradley	22-7	9-5	2nd (MVC)	NIT (3-0)
57-58	Bradley	20-7	12-2	2nd (MVC)	NIT (0-1)
58-59	Bradley	25-4	12-2	2nd (MVC)	NIT (2-1)
59-60	Bradley	27-2	12-2	2nd (MVC)	NIT (3-0)
60-61	Bradley	21-5	9-3	2nd (MVC)	DNP
61-62	Bradley	21-7	10-2	T1st (MVC)	NIT (0-1)
62-63	Bradley	17-9	6-6	T3rd (MVC)	DNP
63-64	Bradley	23-6	7-5	3rd (MVC)	NIT (3-0)
64-65	Bradley	18-9	9-5	T2nd (MVC)	NIT (0-1)

Nine-Year Coaching Record: 194-56 (.776) at Bradley; 86-32 (.729) in Missouri Valley Conference; 11-4 (.733) in NIT.

TED OWENS
Oklahoma '51
Hollis, Okla.

Reached NCAA Final Four two times—1971 (4th) and 1974 (4th)....
Finished runner-up in the 1968 NIT.... Led Kansas to 1981 Big Eight
Tournament title.... Assistant at Oklahoma under Bruce Drake in 1951–52
and at Kansas under Dick Harp from 1960–61 through 1963–64.

Year	School	Overall	League	Finish	Postseason
64–65	Kansas	17-8	9-5	2d (Big Eight)	DNP
65–66	Kansas	23-4	13-1	1st (Big Eight)	NCAA (1-1)
66–67	Kansas	23-4	13-1	1st (Big Eight)	NCAA (1-1)
67–68	Kansas	22-8	10-4	2d (Big Eight)	NIT (3-1)
68–69	Kansas	20-7	9-5	T2d (Big Eight)	NIT (0-1)
69–70	Kansas	17-9	8-6	2d (Big Eight)	DNP
70–71	Kansas	27-3	14-0	1st (Big Eight)	NCAA (2-2)
71–72	Kansas	11-15	7-7	T4th (Big Eight)	DNP
72–73	Kansas	8-18	4-10	T6th (Big Eight)	Probation
73–74	Kansas	23-7	13-1	1st (Big Eight)	NCAA (2-2)
74–75	Kansas	19-8	11-3	1st (Big Eight)	NCAA (2-2)
75–76	Kansas	13-13	6-8	T4th (Big Eight)	DNP
76–77	Kansas	18-10	8-6	4th (Big Eight)	DNP
77–78	Kansas	24-5	13-1	1st (Big Eight)	NCAA (0-1)
78–79	Kansas	18-11	8-6	T2d (Big Eight)	DNP
79–80	Kansas	15-14	7-7	T3d (Big Eight)	DNP
80–81	Kansas	24-8	9-5	T2d (Big Eight)	NCAA (2-1)
81–82	Kansas	13-14	4-10	7th (Big Eight)	DNP
82–83	Kansas	13-16	4-10	T7th (Big Eight)	DNP
85–86	Oral Roberts	10-18	5-7	5th (MW Coll.)	DNP
86–87	Oral Roberts	11-17	5-7	T5th (MW Coll.)	DNP

21-Year College Coaching Record: 369-217 (.594) overall; 348-182 (.657)
in 19 years at Kansas; 21-35 (.375) in two years at Oral Roberts; 170-96
(.639) in Big Eight Conference; 10-14 (.417) in Midwestern Collegiate Conference; 10-6 (.625) in Big Eight Tournament; 0-2 in MCC Tournament; 10-
10 (.500) in NCAA Tournament; 3-2 (.600) in NIT.

VADAL PETERSON
Utah '20
Huntsville, Utah

After losing to Kentucky in NIT, led the Utes to NCAA title in 1944....
Coached Utah to NIT title in 1947.

Year	School	Overall	League	Finish	Postseason
27–28	Utah	6-11	5-7	T2d-W (RMC)	
28–29	Utah	8-9	3-9	4th-W (RMC)	
29–30	Utah	13-11	4-8	4th-W (RMC)	
30–31	Utah	20-5	8-4	1st-W (RMC)	
31–32	Utah	12-8	8-4	T1st-W (RMC)	
32–33	Utah	13-9	9-3	T1st-W (RMC)	
33–34	Utah	14-9	7-5	T2d-W (RMC)	
34–35	Utah	8-8	5-7	3d-W (RMC)	
35–36	Utah	9-13	4-8	4th-W (RMC)	
36–37	Utah	17-7	7-5	T1st-W (RMC)	
37–38	Utah	17-4	10-2	T1st (RMC)	DNP
38–39	Utah	12-7	7-5	T3d (MSC)	DNP
39–40	Utah	18-4	8-4	2d (MSC)	DNP
40–41	Utah	14-7	9-3	2d (MSC)	DNP
41–42	Utah	13-7	7-5	4th (MSC)	DNP
42–43	Utah	10-12	1-7	3d-W (MSC)	DNP
43–44	Utah	21-4			NIT (0-1); NCAA (3-0)
44–45	Utah	17-4			NCAA (0-2)
45–46	Utah	12-8	8-4	3d (MSC)	DNP
46–47	Utah	19-5	10-2	2d (MSC)	NIT (3-0)
47–48	Utah	11-9	6-4	T2d (MSC)	DNP
48–49	Utah	24-8	14-6	2d (MSC)	NIT (0-1)
49–50	Utah	26-18	8-12	5th (MSC)	DNP
50–51	Utah	23-13	12-8	3d (MSC)	DNP
51–52	Utah	19-9	8-6	4th (MSC)	DNP
52–53	Utah	10-14	5-9	T5th (MSC)	DNP

26-Year Coaching Record: 386-223 (.634) in 26 years at Utah; 70-62
(.530) in Rocky Mountain Conference; 103-75 (.579) in Mountain States
Conference; 3-2 (.600) in NCAA Tournament; 3-2 (.600) in NIT.

RICHARD (DIGGER) PHELPS
Rider '63
Beacon, N.Y.

Named UPI national coach of the year in 1974.... Reached Final Four in
1978 NCAA Tournament (4th).... NIT runner-up in 1973 and 1984....
Coached two different schools to NCAA Tournament.... Compiled 65-20
record in four seasons as freshman coach for Penn from 1966-67 through
1969-70.

Year	School	Overall	League	Finish	Postseason
70-71	Fordham	26-3			NCAA (2-1)
71-72	Notre Dame	6-20			DNP
72-73	Notre Dame	18-12			NIT (3-1)
73-74	Notre Dame	26-3			NCAA (2-1)
74-75	Notre Dame	19-10			NCAA (1-2)
75-76	Notre Dame	23-6			NCAA (1-1)
76-77	Notre Dame	22-7			NCAA (1-1)
77-78	Notre Dame	23-8			NCAA (3-2)
78-79	Notre Dame	24-6			NCAA (2-1)
79-80	Notre Dame	22-6			NCAA (0-1)
80-81	Notre Dame	23-6			NCAA (1-1)
81-82	Notre Dame	10-17			DNP
82-83	Notre Dame	19-10			NIT (0-1)
83-84	Notre Dame	21-12			NIT (4-1)
84-85	Notre Dame	21-9			NCAA (1-1)
85-86	Notre Dame	23-6			NCAA (0-1)
86-87	Notre Dame	24-8			NCAA (2-1)
87-88	Notre Dame	20-9			NCAA (0-1)
88-89	Notre Dame	21-9			NCAA (1-1)
89-90	Notre Dame	16-13			NCAA (0-1)
90-91	Notre Dame	12-20			DNP

21-Year Coaching Record: 419-200 (.677) overall; 26-3 (.897) in one year
at Fordham; 393-197 (.666) in 20 years at Notre Dame; 17-17 (.500) in
NCAA Tournament; 7-3 (.700) in NIT.

JACK RAMSAY
St. Joseph's '49
Philadelphia, Pa.

Elected to Naismith Memorial Basketball Hall of Fame in 1992....
Reached Final Four in 1961 NCAA Tournament (3rd).... Reached NIT
semifinals in 1956 (3rd).... Compiled 864-783 record in 21 seasons as an
NBA coach, including an NBA title with Portland in 1977.... General
Manager of Philadelphia for three years (1967-69).

Year	School	Overall	League	Finish	Postseason
55-56	St. Joseph's	23-6			NIT (2-1)
56-57	St. Joseph's	17-7			DNP
57-58	St. Joseph's	18-9			NIT (1-1)
58-59	St. Joseph's	22-5			NCAA (0-2)
59-60	St. Joseph's	20-7			NCAA (0-2)
60-61	St. Joseph's	25-5			NCAA (3-1)
61-62	St. Joseph's	18-10			NCAA (0-2)
62-63	St. Joseph's	23-5			NCAA (2-1)
63-64	St. Joseph's	18-10			NIT (1-1)
64-65	St. Joseph's	26-3			NCAA (1-2)
65-66	St. Joseph's	24-5			NCAA (2-1)

11-Year College Coaching Record: 234-72 (.765) at St. Joseph's; 8-11
(.421) in NCAA Tournament; 4-3 (.571) in NIT.

LEE ROSE
Transylvania '58
Lexington, Ky.

In second year at UNC Charlotte, guided the 49ers to the Final Four....
Coached Purdue to third-place finish in 1980 NCAA Tournament.... His
1976 UNC Charlotte squad advanced to the NIT championship game, as
did his 1979 Purdue team.... Guided UNCC to the Sun Belt Tournament
championship in 1977.... Assistant coach at Transylvania from 1961–62
through 1963–64 and at Cincinnati under Tay Baker from 1965–66 through
1967–68.... Assistant coach in the NBA with the San Antonio Spurs
(1986–87 and 1987–88), New Jersey Nets (1988–89), and Milwaukee Bucks
(1991–92).

Year	School	Overall	League	Finish	Postseason
64–65*	Transylvania	21-10			NAIA (0-1)
68–69	Transylvania	20-7			NCAA DII (1-1)
69–70	Transylvania	21-7			NCAA DII (0-2)
70–71	Transylvania	21-3			DNP
71–72	Transylvania	21-6			NCAA DII (0-2)
72–73	Transylvania	20-7			NCAA DII (1-2)
73–74	Transylvania	16-10			DNP
74–75	Transylvania	20-7			NCAA DIII (1-1)
75–76	UNC Charl.	24-6			NIT (3-1)
76–77	UNC Charl.	28-5	5-1	1st (Sun Belt)	NCAA (3-2)
77–78	UNC Charl.	20-7	9-1	1st (Sun Belt)	DNP
78–79	Purdue	27-8	13-5	T1st (Big Ten)	NIT (4-1)
79–80	Purdue	23-10	11-7	3d (Big Ten)	NCAA (5-1)
80–81	S. Fla.	18-11	7-5	4th (Sun Belt)	NIT (0-1)
81–82	S. Fla.	17-11	4-6	4th (Sun Belt)	DNP
82–83	S. Fla.	22-10	8-6	4th (Sun Belt)	NIT (1-1)
83–84	S. Fla.	17-11	9-5	T2d (Sun Belt)	DNP
84–85	S. Fla.	18-12	6-8	T4th (Sun Belt)	NIT (1-1)
85–86	S. Fla.	14-14	5-9	T6th (Sun Belt)	DNP

* Interim head coach.

19-Year Coaching Record: 388-162 (.705) overall; 160-57 (.737) in eight years at Transylvania; 72-18 (.800) in three years at UNC Charlotte; 50-18 in two years at Purdue; 106-69 (.606) in six years at South Florida; 24-12 (.667) in Big Ten Conference; 53-41 (.564) in Sun Belt Conference (14-2, .875, at UNCC; 39-39, .500, at USF); 6-7 (.462) in Sun Belt Tournament (2-1, .667, at UNCC; 4-6, .400, at USF); 8-3 (.727) in NCAA Division I Tournament; 9-5 (.643) in NIT; 0-1 in NAIA Tournament; 2-7 (.222) in NCAA Division II Tournament; 1-1 (.500) in NCAA Division III Tournament.

ADOLPH RUPP
Kansas '23
Halstead, Kans.

Coached teams to four NCAA titles (1948, 1949, 1951, and 1958).... His 1942 squad finished tied for third in the 1942 NCAA Tournament and his 1966 team was runner-up to Texas Western.... Elected to Naismith Memorial Basketball Hall of Fame in 1968.... Named national coach of the year by UPI in 1959 and 1966, and by the USBWA in 1966.... Directed Kentucky to 1946 NIT title. Coached UK to NIT championship game again in 1947. His 1944 UK team finished fourth at NIT.... Coach of 1933 Kentucky team that was selected as national champion by the Helms Foundation.... Holds NCAA career record for most victories.... Coached Kentucky to an SEC-record 24 conference and 13 tournament titles.... Played college ball for Phog Allen at Kansas.

Year	School	Overall	League	Finish	Postseason
30–31	Kentucky	15-3			
31–32	Kentucky	15-2			
32–33	Kentucky	20-3	8-0	1st (SEC)	
33–34	Kentucky	16-1	11-0		
34–35	Kentucky	19-2	11-0	T1st (SEC)	
35–36	Kentucky	15-6	6-2		
36–37	Kentucky	17-5	5-3	1st (SEC)	
37–38	Kentucky	13-5	6-0		DNP
38–39	Kentucky	16-4	5-2	1st (SEC)	DNP
39–40	Kentucky	15-6	4-4	1st (SEC)	DNP
40–41	Kentucky	17-8	8-1		DNP
41–42	Kentucky	19-6	6-2	1st (SEC)	NCAA (1-1)
42–43	Kentucky	17-6	8-1		DNP
43–44	Kentucky	19-2	0-0		NIT (2-1)
44–45	Kentucky	22-4	4-1	1st (SEC)	NCAA (1-1)
45–46	Kentucky	28-2	6-0	1st (SEC)	NIT (3-0)
46–47	Kentucky	34-3	11-0	1st (SEC)	NIT (2-1)
47–48	Kentucky	36-3	9-0	1st (SEC)	NCAA (3-0)
48–49	Kentucky	32-2	13-0	1st (SEC)	NIT (0-1), NCAA (3-0)
49–50	Kentucky	25-5	11-2	1st (SEC)	NIT (0-1)
50–51	Kentucky	32-2	14-0	1st (SEC)	NCAA (4-0)
51–52	Kentucky	29-3	14-0	1st (SEC)	NCAA (1-1)
53–54	Kentucky	25-0	14-0	T1st (SEC)	DNP
54–55	Kentucky	23-3	12-2	1st (SEC)	NCAA (1-1)
55–56	Kentucky	20-6	12-2	2d (SEC)	NCAA (1-1)
56–57	Kentucky	23-5	12-2	1st (SEC)	NCAA (1-1)
57–58	Kentucky	23-6	12-2	1st (SEC)	NCAA (4-0)
58–59	Kentucky	24-3	12-2	T2d (SEC)	NCAA (1-1)
59–60	Kentucky	18-7	10-4	3d (SEC)	DNP
60–61	Kentucky	19-9	10-4	T2d (SEC)	NCAA (1-1)
61–62	Kentucky	23-3	13-1	T1st (SEC)	NCAA (1-1)
62–63	Kentucky	16-9	8-6	5th (SEC)	DNP
63–64	Kentucky	21-6	11-3	1st (SEC)	NCAA (0-2)
64–65	Kentucky	15-10	10-6	5th (SEC)	DNP
65–66	Kentucky	27-2	15-1	1st (SEC)	NCAA (3-1)
66–67	Kentucky	13-13	8-10	T5th (SEC)	DNP
67–68	Kentucky	22-5	15-3	1st (SEC)	NCAA (1-1)
68–69	Kentucky	23-5	16-2	1st (SEC)	NCAA (1-1)
69–70	Kentucky	26-2	17-1	1st (SEC)	NCAA (1-1)
70–71	Kentucky	22-6	16-2	1st (SEC)	NCAA (0-2)
71–72	Kentucky	21-7	14-4	T1st (SEC)	NCAA (1-1)

Note: Kentucky did not field a team in 1952–53. From 1933 to 1950 the SEC champion was determined by a tournament, except for 1935.

41-Year Coaching Record: 875-190 (.822) at Kentucky; 397-75 (.845) in Southeastern Conference; 57-6 (.905) in SEC Tournament; 30-18 (.625) in NCAA Tournament; 7-4 (.636) in NIT.

EVERETT SHELTON
Phillips '23
Cunningham, Kans.

Elected to Naismith Memorial Basketball Hall of Fame in 1979.... Directed Wyoming to 1943 NCAA title.... Won 850 games in a 46-year coaching career that included eight years at the high school level and eight years at AAU.

Year	School	Overall	League	Finish	Postseason
23–24	Phillips	11-16			
24–25	Phillips	15-5			
25–26	Phillips	22-8			
39–40	Wyoming	7-10	3-9	T5th (MSC)	DNP
40–41	Wyoming	13-6	10-2	1st (MSC)	NCAA (0-2)
41–42	Wyoming	15-5	9-3	T2d (MSC)	DNP
42–43	Wyoming	31-2	4-0	1st-E (MSC)	NCAA (3-0)
44–45	Wyoming	10-17			DNP
45–46	Wyoming	22-4	10-2	1st (MSC)	DNP
46–47	Wyoming	22-6	11-1	1st (MSC)	NCAA (0-2)
47–48	Wyoming	18-9	6-4	T2d (MSC)	NCAA (0-2)
48–49	Wyoming	25-10	15-5	1st (MSC)	NCAA (0-2)
49–50	Wyoming	25-11	13-7	T2d (MSC)	DNP
50–51	Wyoming	26-11	13-7	2d (MSC)	DNP
51–52	Wyoming	28-7	13-1	1st (MSC)	NCAA (1-1)
52–53	Wyoming	20-10	12-2	1st (MSC)	NCAA (0-2)
53–54	Wyoming	19-9	10-4	2d (MSC)	DNP
54–55	Wyoming	17-9	9-5	T3d (MSC)	DNP
55–56	Wyoming	7-19	5-9	T6th (MSC)	DNP
56–57	Wyoming	6-19	4-10	7th (MSC)	DNP
57–58	Wyoming	13-14	10-4	1st (MSC)	NCAA (0-1)
58–59	Wyoming	4-22	1-13	T7th (MSC)	DNP
59–60	Sacra. St.	10-13	6-4	3d (Far West.)	DNP
60–61	Sacra. St.	18-8	8-2	2d (Far West.)	DNP
61–62	Sacra. St.	21-10	10-2	1st (Far West.)	NCAA Div. II (4-1)
62–63	Sacra. St.	10-16	4-8	6th (Far West.)	DNP
63–64	Sacra. St.	8-18	6-6	T4th (Far West.)	DNP
64–65	Sacra. St.	10-16	4-8	6th (Far West.)	DNP
65–66	Sacra. St.	10-16	6-6	T4th (Far West.)	DNP
66–67	Sacra. St.	15-11	10-4	T2d (Far West.)	DNP
67–68	Sacra. St.	16-10	9-5	3d (Far West.)	DNP

31-Year Coaching Record: 494-347 (.587) overall; 328-201 (.620) in 19 seasons at Wyoming; 221-133 (.624) in Mountain States Conference; 63-45 (.583) in Far Western Conference; 4-12 (.250) in NCAA Tournament; 4-1 (.800) in NCAA College Division Tournament.

ROY SKINNER
Presbyterian '52
Paducah, Ky.

Four-time SEC coach of the year coached first African-American player in the SEC (Perry Wallace). . . . Coach of Paducah (Ky.) Junior College before becoming an assistant at Vanderbilt under Bob Polk in 1957.

Year	School	Overall	League	Finish	Postseason
58-59	Vanderbilt	14-10	8-6	T5th (SEC)	DNP
61-62	Vanderbilt	12-12	6-8	T6th (SEC)	DNP
62-63	Vanderbilt	16-7	9-5	4th (SEC)	DNP

63–64	Vanderbilt	19-6	8-6	T4th (SEC)	DNP
64–65	Vanderbilt	24-4	15-1	1st (SEC)	NCAA (1-1)
65–66	Vanderbilt	22-4	13-3	2nd (SEC)	DNP
66–67	Vanderbilt	21-5	14-4	T2nd (SEC)	DNP
67–68	Vanderbilt	20-6	12-6	3rd (SEC)	DNP
68–69	Vanderbilt	15-11	9-9	T5th (SEC)	DNP
69–70	Vanderbilt	12-14	8-10	6th (SEC)	DNP
70–71	Vanderbilt	13-13	9-9	T4th (SEC)	DNP
71–72	Vanderbilt	16-10	10-8	4th (SEC)	DNP
72–73	Vanderbilt	20-6	13-5	T2nd (SEC)	DNP
73–74	Vanderbilt	23-5	15-3	T1st (SEC)	NCAA (0-2)
74–75	Vanderbilt	15-11	10-8	5th (SEC)	DNP
75–76	Vanderbilt	16-11	12-6	3rd (SEC)	DNP

16-Year Coaching Record: 278-135 (.673) at Vanderbilt; 171-97 (.638) in Southeastern Conference; 1-3 (.250) in NCAA Tournament.

NORMAN SLOAN
North Carolina St. '51
Anderson, Ind.

Led alma mater North Carolina State to the national championship in 1974.... Named national coach of the year in 1974 by AP and the USBWA.... Selected as head coach of 1980 British Olympic team.... Guided N.C. State to third place (1976) and second place (1978) showings at the NIT. His 1986 Florida team advanced to NIT semifinals (4th).... Coached N.C. State to 1970, 1973, and 1974 ACC Tournament titles.... Assistant coach at Memphis State under Eugene Lambert for one year in 1955–56.

Year	School	Overall	League	Finish	Postseason
51–52	P'byterian	21-7			
52–53	P'byterian	11-15	4-2	2d (S.C. Little 4)	
53–54	P'byterian	17-8	4-2	2d (S.C. Little 4)	
54–55	P'byterian	20-6	6-0	1st (S.C. Little 4)	
56–57	The Citadel	11-14	5-9	7th (Southern)	DNP
57–58	The Citadel	16-11	9-6	4th (Southern)	DNP
58–59	The Citadel	15-5	7-4	3d (Southern)	DNP
59–60	The Citadel	15-8	8-4	4th (Southern)	DNP
60–61	Florida	15-11	9-5	4th (SEC)	DNP
61–62	Florida	12-11	8-6	4th (SEC)	DNP
62–63	Florida	12-14	5-9	T8th (SEC)	DNP
63–64	Florida	12-10	6-8	T9th (SEC)	DNP
64–65	Florida	18-7	11-5	T3d (SEC)	DNP
65–66	Florida	16-10	9-7	T5th (SEC)	DNP
66–67	N.C. St.	7-19	2-12	8th (ACC)	DNP
67–68	N.C. St.	16-10	9-5	T3d (ACC)	DNP
68–69	N.C. St.	15-10	8-6	T3d (ACC)	DNP
69–70	N.C. St.	23-7	9-5	T2d (ACC)	NCAA (1-1)
70–71	N.C. St.	13-14	5-9	T6th (ACC)	DNP
71–72	N.C. St.	16-10	6-6	T4th (ACC)	DNP
72–73	N.C. St.	27-0	12-0	1st (ACC)	Probation
73–74	N.C. St.	30-1	12-0	1st (ACC)	NCAA (4-0)
74–75	N.C. St.	22-6	8-4	T2d (ACC)	DNP
75–76	N.C. St.	21-9	7-5	T2d (ACC)	NIT (3-1)
76–77	N.C. St.	17-11	6-6	5th (ACC)	DNP
77–78	N.C. St.	21-10	7-5	3d (ACC)	NIT (3-1)
78–79	N.C. St.	18-12	3-9	6th (ACC)	DNP
79–80	N.C. St.	20-8	9-5	T2d (ACC)	NCAA (0-1)
80–81	Florida	12-16	5-13	8th (SEC)	DNP
81–82	Florida	5-22	2-16	10th (SEC)	DNP
82–83	Florida	13-18	5-13	10th (SEC)	DNP
83–84	Florida	16-13	11-7	T3d (SEC)	NIT (0-1)
84–85	Florida	18-12	9-9	T5th (SEC)	NIT (0-1)
85–86	Florida	19-14	10-8	4th (SEC)	NIT (3-2)
86–87*	Florida	23-11	12-6	2d (SEC)	NCAA (2-1)
87–88*	Florida	23-12	11-7	T2d (SEC)	NCAA (1-1)
88–89	Florida	21-13	13-5	1st (SEC)	NCAA (0-1)

* NCAA Tournament games later vacated by action of the NCAA.

37-Year Coaching Record: 627-395 (.614) overall; 69-36 (.657) in four years at Presbyterian; 57-38 (.600) in four years at The Citadel; 266-127 (.677) in 14 years at North Carolina State; 235-194 (.548) in 15 years at Florida; 29-23 (.558) in Southern Conference; 103-77 (.573) in Atlantic Coast Conference; 126-124 (.504) in Southeastern Conference; 2-4 (.333) in Southern Conference Tournament; 14-11 (.560) in ACC Tournament; 5-9 (.357) in SEC Tournament; 8-5 (.615) in NCAA Tournament; 9-6 (.600) in NIT.

GEORGE SMITH
Cincinnati '35
Mount Vernon, Ohio

Reached NCAA Final Four two times—1959 (3d) and 1960 (3d).... His 1955 Cincinnati squad finished third in the NIT.... Voted national coach of the year by the Rockne Club in 1960.... Assistant at Cincinnati under John Wiethe for four seasons from 1948–49 through 1951–52.

Year	School	Overall	League	Finish	Postseason
52–53	Cincinnati	11-13	9-3	2d (MAC)	DNP
53–54	Cincinnati	11-10			DNP
54–55	Cincinnati	21-8			NIT (2-1)
55–56	Cincinnati	17-7			Probation
56–57	Cincinnati	15-9			DNP
57–58	Cincinnati	25-3	13-1	1st (MVC)	NCAA (1-1)
58–59	Cincinnati	26-4	13-1	1st (MVC)	NCAA (3-1)
59–60	Cincinnati	28-2	13-1	1st (MVC)	NCAA (3-1)

Eight-Year Coaching Record: 154-56 (.733) in eight years; 9-3 (.750) in Mid-American Conference; 39-3 (.929) in Missouri Valley Conference; 7-3 (.700) in NCAA Tournament; 2-1 (.667) in NIT.

DAVE STRACK
Michigan '45
Indianapolis, Ind.

Guided Michigan to back-to-back Final Four appearances in 1964 (3d) and 1965 (2d).... Voted UPI national coach of the year in 1965.... Assistant at Michigan under Bill Perigo for 10 years from 1949–50 through 1958–59.

Year	School	Overall	League	Finish	Postseason
59–60	Idaho	11-15			DNP
60–61	Michigan	6-18	2-12	10th (Big Ten)	DNP
61–62	Michigan	7-17	5-9	8th (Big Ten)	DNP
62–63	Michigan	16-8	8-6	4th (Big Ten)	DNP
63–64	Michigan	23-5	11-3	T1st (Big Ten)	NCAA (3-1)
64–65	Michigan	24-4	13-1	1st (Big Ten)	NCAA (3-1)
65–66	Michigan	18-8	11-3	1st (Big Ten)	NCAA (1-1)
66–67	Michigan	8-16	2-12	10th (Big Ten)	DNP
67–68	Michigan	11-13	6-8	6th (Big Ten)	DNP

Nine-Year Coaching Record: 124-104 (.544) overall; 11-15 (.423) in one year at Idaho; 113-89 (.559) in eight years at Michigan; 58-54 (.518) in Big Ten Conference; 7-3 (.700) in NCAA Tournament.

FRED TAYLOR
Ohio St. '50
Zanesville, Ohio

Coached Ohio State to NCAA title in 1960. Finished runner-up to Cincinnati in 1961 and 1962. Finished third in fourth Final Four appearance in 1968.... Elected to Naismith Memorial Basketball Hall of Fame in 1985.... Named coach of the year by UPI and USBWA in 1961 and 1962.... Assistant coach under Floyd Stahl until succeeding him.

Year	School	Overall	League	Finish	Postseason
58–59	Ohio St.	11-11	7-7	T5th (Big Ten)	DNP
59–60	Ohio St.	25-3	13-1	1st (Big Ten)	NCAA (4-0)
60–61	Ohio St.	27-1	14-0	1st (Big Ten)	NCAA (3-1)
61–62	Ohio St.	26-2	13-1	1st (Big Ten)	NCAA (3-1)
62–63	Ohio St.	20-4	11-3	T1st (Big Ten)	DNP
63–64	Ohio St.	16-8	11-3	T1st (Big Ten)	DNP
64–65	Ohio St.	12-12	6-8	6th (Big Ten)	DNP

65–66	Ohio St.	11-13	5-9	8th (Big Ten)	DNP
66–67	Ohio St.	13-11	6-8	T7th (Big Ten)	DNP
67–68	Ohio St.	21-8	10-4	T1st (Big Ten)	NCAA (3-1)
68–69	Ohio St.	17-7	9-5	T2d (Big Ten)	DNP
69–70	Ohio St.	17-7	8-6	T3d (Big Ten)	DNP
70–71	Ohio St.	20-6	13-1	1st (Big Ten)	NCAA (1-1)
71–72	Ohio St.	18-6	10-4	2d (Big Ten)	DNP
72–73	Ohio St.	14-10	8-6	T3d (Big Ten)	DNP
73–74	Ohio St.	9-15	4-10	8th (Big Ten)	DNP
74–75	Ohio St.	14-14	8-10	6th (Big Ten)	DNP
75–76	Ohio St.	6-20	2-16	10th (Big Ten)	DNP

18-Year Coaching Record: 297-158 (.653) at Ohio State; 158-102 (.608) in Big Ten Conference; 14-4 (.778) in NCAA Tournament.

JIM VALVANO
Rutgers '67
Seaford, N.Y.

Directed North Carolina State to a stunning 54-52 win over top-ranked Houston to capture the 1983 NCAA championship.... Coached N.C. State to 1983 and 1987 ACC Tournament titles.... Assistant under Bill Foster at Rutgers for two seasons (1967–68 and 1968–69) and under Dee Rowe at Connecticut for two seasons (1970–71 and 1971–72).

Year	School	Overall	League	Finish	Postseason
68–69	Johns Hopkins	3-14	3-9	10th-S (Mid. Atl.)	DNP
72–73	Bucknell	11-14	6-4	T2d-W (Mid. Atl.)	DNP
73–74	Bucknell	8-16	2-8	T5th-W (Mid. Atl.)	DNP
74–75	Bucknell	14-12	4-4	T3d-W (ECC)	DNP
75–76	Iona	11-15			DNP
76–77	Iona	15-10			DNP
77–78	Iona	17-10			DNP
78–79	Iona	23-6			NCAA (0-1)
79–80*	Iona	29-5			NCAA (1-1)
80–81	N.C. St.	14-13	4-10	7th (ACC)	DNP
81–82	N.C. St.	22-10	7-7	4th (ACC)	NCAA (0-1)
82–83	N.C. St.	26-10	8-6	T3d (ACC)	NCAA (6-0)
83–84	N.C. St.	19-14	4-10	7th (ACC)	NIT (0-1)
84–85	N.C. St.	23-10	9-5	T1st (ACC)	NCAA (3-1)
85–86	N.C. St.	21-13	7-7	4th (ACC)	NCAA (3-1)
86–87*	N.C. St.	20-15	6-8	6th (ACC)	NCAA (0-1)
87–88*	N.C. St.	24-8	10-4	2d (ACC)	NCAA (0-1)
88–89	N.C. St.	22-9	10-4	1st (ACC)	NCAA (2-1)
89–90	N.C. St.	18-12	6-8	T4th (ACC)	Probation

* NCAA Tournament games later vacated by action of the NCAA

19-Year Coaching Record: 338-214 (.612) overall; 3-14 (.176) in one year at Johns Hopkins; 33-42 (.440) in three years at Bucknell; 95-46 (.674) in five years at Iona; 209-114 (.647) in 10 years at North Carolina State; 11-21 (344) in Middle Atlantic Conference; 4-4 (.500) in East Coast Conference; 71-69 (.507) in Atlantic Coast Conference; 9-8 (.529) in ACC Tournament; 15-8 (.652) in NCAA Tournament; 0-1 in NIT.

STAN WATTS
Brigham Young '38
Murray, Utah

Coached BYU to NIT titles in 1951 and 1966. . . . Served as chairman of the NCAA Tournament Committee in 1976 and 1977. . . . Coached multiple sports at Dixie Junior College in St. George, Utah, before being named head baseball coach and freshman basketball and football coach at BYU in 1947.

Year	School	Overall	League	Finish	Postseason
49-50	BYU	22-12	14-6	1st (RMC)	NCAA (1-1)
50-51	BYU	28-9	15-5	1st (RMC)	NCAA (1-2), NIT (3-0)

A young Jim Valvano (far right) got his start in coaching as an assistant under Rutgers' Bill Foster (far left) in the late 1960s.

51-52	BYU	14-10	9-5	2nd (MSC)	DNP
52-53	BYU	22-8	11-3	2nd (MSC)	NIT (0-1)
53-54	BYU	18-11	9-5	2nd (MSC)	NIT (0-1)
54-55	BYU	13-13	10-4	2nd (MSC)	DNP
55-56	BYU	18-8	10-4	2nd (MSC)	DNP
56-57	BYU	19-9	11-3	1st (MSC)	NCAA (1-1)
57-58	BYU	13-13	9-5	2nd (MSC)	DNP
58-59	BYU	15-11	8-6	4th (MSC)	DNP
59-60	BYU	8-17	5-9	5th (MSC)	DNP
60-61	BYU	15-11	9-5	3rd (MSC)	DNP
61-62	BYU	10-16	5-9	4th (MSC)	DNP
62-63	BYU	12-14	6-4	2nd (WAC)	DNP
63-64	BYU	13-12	5-5	3rd (WAC)	DNP
64-65	BYU	21-7	8-2	1st (WAC)	NCAA (0-2)
65-66	BYU	20-5	6-4	2nd (WAC)	NIT (3-0)
66-67	BYU	14-10	8-2	T1st (WAC)	DNP
67-68	BYU	13-12	4-6	T4th (WAC)	DNP
68-69	BYU	16-12	6-4	T1st (WAC)	NCAA (0-1)
69-70	BYU	8-18	4-10	7th (WAC)	DNP
70-71	BYU	18-11	10-4	1st (WAC)	NCAA (1-2)
71-72	BYU	21-5	12-2	1st (WAC)	NCAA (0-1)

23-Year Coaching Record: 371-254 (.594) at Brigham Young; 29-11 (.725) in Rocky Mountain Conference; 96-58 (.623) in Mountain States Conference; 69-43 (.616) in Western Athletic Conference; 4-10 (.286) in NCAA Tournament; 6-2 (.750) in NIT.

FRED (TEX) WINTER
Southern California '47
Wellington, Tex.

Owns best winning percentage in Kansas State history (.691).... Guided K-State to two Final Fours—1958 (4th) and 1964 (4th).... Named national coach of the year by UPI in 1958.... His 1959 K-State squad finished No. 1 in both the final AP and UPI polls.... Assistant under Jack Gardner at Kansas St. for four seasons (1947–48 through 1950–51).... Longtime Chicago Bulls assistant compiled a 51-78 record as head coach of the Houston Rockets in 1971–72 and 1972–73.

Year	School	Overall	League	Finish	Postseason
51–52	Marquette	12-14			DNP
52–53	Marquette	13-11			DNP
53–54	Kansas St.	11-10	5-7	T4th (Big Seven)	DNP
54–55	Kansas St.	11-10	6-6	T3d (Big Seven)	DNP
55–56	Kansas St.	17-8	9-3	1st (Big Seven)	NCAA (1-1)
56–57	Kansas St.	15-8	8-4	2d (Big Seven)	DNP
57–58	Kansas St.	22-5	10-2	1st (Big Seven)	NCAA (3-2)
58–59	Kansas St.	25-2	14-0	1st (Big Eight)	NCAA (1-1)
59–60	Kansas St.	16-10	10-4	T1st (Big Eight)	DNP
60–61	Kansas St.	23-4	13-1	1st (Big Eight)	NCAA (1-1)
61–62	Kansas St.	22-3	12-2	2d (Big Eight)	DNP
62–63	Kansas St.	16-9	11-3	T1st (Big Eight)	DNP
63–64	Kansas St.	22-7	12-2	1st (Big Eight)	NCAA (2-2)
64–65	Kansas St.	12-13	5-9	T6th (Big Eight)	DNP
65–66	Kansas St.	14-11	9-5	3d (Big Eight)	DNP
66–67	Kansas St.	17-8	9-5	4th (Big Eight)	DNP
67–68	Kansas St.	19-9	11-3	1st (Big Eight)	NCAA (0-2)
68–69	Washington	13-13	6-8	4th (Pac-8)	DNP
69–70	Washington	17-9	7-7	5th (Pac-8)	DNP
70–71	Washington	15-13	6-8	5th (Pac-8)	DNP
73–74	N'western	9-15	3-11	9th (Big Ten)	DNP
74–75	N'western	6-20	4-14	T9th (Big Ten)	DNP
75–76	N'western	12-14	7-11	T7th (Big Ten)	DNP
76–77	N'western	9-18	7-11	T7th (Big Ten)	DNP
77–78	N'western	8-19	4-14	T9th (Big Ten)	DNP
78–79	Long Beach St.	16-12	7-7	T4th (PCAA)	DNP
79–80	Long Beach St.	21-9	11-3	2d (PCAA)	NIT (1-1)
80–81	Long Beach St.	15-13	9-5	T3d (PCAA)	DNP
81–82	Long Beach St.	12-16	7-7	T4th (PCAA)	DNP
82–83	Long Beach St.	13-16	6-10	7th (PCAA)	DNP

30-Year College Coaching Record: 454-333 (.577) overall; 25-25 (.500) in two years at Marquette; 262-117 (.691) in 15 years at Kansas State; 45-35 (.563) in three years at Washington; 44-87 (.336) in five years at Northwestern; 78-69 (.531) in five years at Long Beach State; 106-36 (.746) in Big Eight Conference; 19-23 (.452) in Pacific-10 Conference (Pacific-8); 24-61 (.282) in Big Ten Conference; 40-32 (.556) in Big West Conference (PCAA); 6-5 (.545) in Big West Tournament (PCAA); 8-9 (.471) in NCAA Tournament; 1-1 (.500) in NIT.

JOHN WOODEN
Purdue '32
Martinsville, Ind.

From 1964 to 1975, UCLA won an NCAA-record 10 national titles, including seven straight from 1967 though 1973.... Elected to Naismith Memorial Basketball Hall of Fame as a coach in 1972.... Named national coach of the year by AP in 1967, 1969, 1970, 1972, and 1973; by UPI in 1964, 1967, 1969, 1970, 1972, and 1973; by the USBWA in 1964, 1967, 1970, 1972, and 1973; and by the NABC in 1969, 1970, and 1972.... His 1962 team finished fourth in the NCAA Tournament and his 1974 squad finished third.... Won 13 conference titles in his last 14 years.

Year	School	Overall	League	Finish	Postseason
46–47	Indiana St.	17-8			DNP
47–48	Indiana St.	27-7			NAIA (4-1)
48–49	UCLA	22-7	10-2	1st-S (PCC)	DNP
49–50	UCLA	24-7	10-2	1st-S (PCC)	NCAA (0-2)
50–51	UCLA	19-10	9-4	T1st-S (PCC)	DNP

Phil Woolpert was elected to the National Basketball Hall of Fame in 1992.

51–52	UCLA	19-12	8-4	1st-S (PCC)	NCAA (0-2)
52–53	UCLA	16-8	6-6	3d-S (PCC)	DNP
53–54	UCLA	18-7	7-5	2d-S (PCC)	DNP
54–55	UCLA	21-5	11-1	1st-S (PCC)	DNP
55–56	UCLA	22-6	16-0	1st (PCC)	NCAA (1-1)
56–57	UCLA	22-4	13-3	T2d (PCC)	Probation
57–58	UCLA	16-10	10-6	3d (PCC)	DNP
58–59	UCLA	16-9	10-6	T3d (PCC)	DNP
59–60	UCLA	14-12	7-5	2d (AAWU)	DNP
60–61	UCLA	18-8	7-5	2d (AAWU)	DNP
61–62	UCLA	18-11	10-2	1st (AAWU)	NCAA (2-2)
62–63	UCLA	20-9	8-5	T1st (AAWU)	NCAA (0-2)
63–64	UCLA	30-0	15-0	1st (AAWU)	NCAA (4-0)
64–65	UCLA	28-2	14-0	1st (AAWU)	NCAA (4-0)
65–66	UCLA	18-8	10-4	2d (AAWU)	DNP
66–67	UCLA	30-0	14-0	1st (AAWU)	NCAA (4-0)
67–68	UCLA	29-1	14-0	1st (AAWU)	NCAA (4-0)
68–69	UCLA	29-1	13-1	1st (Pac-8)	NCAA (4-0)
69–70	UCLA	28-2	12-2	1st (Pac-8)	NCAA (4-0)
70–71	UCLA	29-1	14-0	1st (Pac-8)	NCAA (4-0)
71–72	UCLA	30-0	14-0	1st (Pac-8)	NCAA (4-0)
72–73	UCLA	30-0	14-0	1st (Pac-8)	NCAA (4-0)
73–74	UCLA	26-4	12-2	1st (Pac-8)	NCAA (3-1)
74–75	UCLA	28-3	12-2	1st (Pac-8)	NCAA (5-0)

29-Year Coaching Record: 664-162 (.804) overall; 44-15 (.746) in two years at Indiana State; 620-147 (.808) in 27 years at UCLA; 304-74 (.810) In Pacific-10 Conference; 47-10 (.825) in NCAA Tournament; 4-1 (.800) in NAIA Tournament.

PHIL WOOLPERT
Loyola (La.) '40
Los Angeles, Calif.

Coached San Francisco to back-to-back NCAA titles in 1955 and 1956 before finishing third in 1957.... Named national coach of the year by UPI in 1955 and 1956.... Elected to Naismith Memorial Basketball Hall of Fame in 1991.... Freshman coach at San Francisco under Pete Newell in 1948–49 and 1949–50 while coaching St. Ignatius High School.... Coached the San Francisco Saints for one season in the old American Basketball League.

Year	School	Overall	League	Finish	Postseason
50–51	San Fran.	9-17			DNP
51–52	San Fran.	11-13			DNP
52–53	San Fran.	10-11	6-2	T1st (CBA)	DNP
53–54	San Fran.	14-7	8-4	2d (CBA)	DNP
54–55	San Fran.	28-1	12-0	1st (CBA)	NCAA (5-0)
55–56	San Fran.	29-0	14-0	1st (WCAC)	NCAA (4-0)
56–57	San Fran.	21-7	12-2	1st (WCAC)	NCAA (3-1)
57–58	San Fran.	25-2	12-0	1st (WCAC)	NCAA (1-1)
58–59	San Fran.	6-20	3-9	6th (WCAC)	DNP
62–63	San Diego	4-15			DNP
63–64	San Diego	13-13			DNP
64–65	San Diego	14-11			DNP
65–66	San Diego	17-11			DNP
66–67	San Diego	13-11			DNP
67–68	San Diego	15-10			DNP
68–69	San Diego	10-15			DNP

16-Year College Coaching Record: 239-164 (.593) overall; 153-78 (.662) in nine years at San Francisco; 86-86 (.500) in seven years at San Diego; 67-17 (.798) in West Coast Conference (CBA/WCAC); 13-2 (.867) in NCAA Tournament.

11

THEY PLAYED THE GAME, TOO

There is a theory in some quarters that basketball players are the most versatile team sport athletes in the world. What other sport demands such an abundance of speed, strength, stamina, coordination, quickness, jumping ability, teamwork, timing, guile, and creativity?

Long before Michael Jordan abandoned hoops for baseball, or before Charlie Ward mulled over a choice between basketball and football, or before the widespread jacks-of-all-trades fascination with football/baseball standouts Bo Jackson and Deion Sanders, there was a host of college basketball players who also excelled in other fields of endeavor. Some of the names will surprise you. Here is a summary of former college hoopsters who made a bigger name for themselves off the hardwood—in other sports, as prominent businessmen, and as entertainers.

MAJOR LEAGUE BASEBALL PLAYERS

MARK ACRE, New Mexico State

Appeared in 77 games as a reliever for the Oakland A's in 1994 and 1995 seasons. Compiled a 5-1 record in the strike-shortened '94 campaign. He made it to the majors despite posting a 2-10 record and 8.14 ERA at NMSU. . . . The 6-8, 225-pound forward-center averaged 1.9 points and 1.2 rebounds per game while playing sparingly for the Aggies in 1988–89 and 1989–90 after averaging 25.1 points and 9.6 rebounds per game in his final junior college season at the College of the Siskiyous in Weed, Calif.

JERRY ADAIR, Oklahoma State

Hit .254 in 1,165 games in 13 seasons (1958–70) with the Baltimore Orioles, Chicago White Sox, Boston Red Sox, and Kansas City Athletics. Set a major league record for highest fielding average (.994) and fewest errors (five) by a second baseman in a season in 1964 and set a major league record for consecutive errorless games by a second baseman (89) in 1964 and 1965.... Before signing a pro baseball contract, he played two varsity seasons of basketball at Oklahoma State (third-leading scorer with a 9.7-points-per-game average in 1956–57 and second-leading scorer with an 11.9 average in 1957–58). Ranked among the nation's top 11 free-throw shooters both seasons.

JOE ADCOCK, Louisiana State

First baseman hit .277 with 336 home runs and 1,122 RBIs in 17 seasons (1950–66) with the Cincinnati Reds, Milwaukee Braves, Cleveland Indians, and the Los Angeles/California Angels. Hit four homers and a double for the Braves against the Brooklyn Dodgers on July 31, 1954, setting a major league record for most total bases in a game (18). Braves' regular first baseman for 1957 and 1958 National League champions.... He played three seasons (1944–45 through 1946–47) at LSU as a 6-4, 190-pound center. Leading scorer with an 18.6-points-per-game average on the 1945–46 Tigers team that compiled an 18-3 record and lost against Kentucky in the Southeastern Conference Tournament final. Set SEC Tournament record with 15 field goals in a game against Tulane in 1946.

BILL ALMON, Brown

Signed $90,000 bonus contract with the San Diego Padres after becoming the first player selected in the 1974 baseball draft. Shortstop hit .254 in 15 seasons (1974–88) with the Padres, Montreal Expos, New York Mets, Chicago White Sox, Oakland A's, Pittsburgh Pirates, and Philadelphia Phillies.... The 6-3, 175-pound guard averaged 6.4 points per game for the 1971–72 Brown freshman team and 2.5 ppg for the 1972–73 varsity.

WALTER ALSTON, Miami of Ohio

Baseball Hall of Famer managed the Brooklyn and Los Angeles Dodgers for 23 seasons (1954–76), winning seven National League pennants and three World Series.... The 6-2, 195-pound Alston lettered in basketball at Miami in 1932–33, 1933–34, and 1934–35. Scored 10 of Miami's 15 points in a 32-15 defeat against Indiana in his senior season. Charter member of alma mater's Athletic Hall of Fame.

GEORGE ALTMAN, Tennessee State

First baseman hit .269 with 102 home runs in nine seasons (1959–67) with the Chicago Cubs, St. Louis Cardinals, and New York Mets.... The 6-4 forward earned four letters on Tennessee A&I teams that compiled an 88-17 from 1951–52 through 1954–55. The school appeared in the NAIA Tournament in 1953 and 1954.

ELDON AUKER, Kansas State

Pitcher who compiled a 130-101 record in 10 seasons (1933–42) with the Detroit Tigers, Boston Red Sox, and St. Louis Browns. Led American League in winning percentage in 1935 with .720 mark (18-7 record). Appeared in 1934 and 1935 World Series with the Tigers, hurling a complete game, 10-4 victory over the St. Louis Cardinals in Game Four of the '34 Series.... Three-year basketball letterman was named to the first five on the All-Big Six team in his final college season (1931–32).... The *Spalding Official Basketball Guide* called the 6-2 guard an "outstanding performer, with height, endurance and skill beyond the ordinary."

STEVE BARBER, Riverside City College

Pitcher compiled a 1-0 record in 22 games with the Minnesota Twins in 1970 and 1971.... Starting guard for Jerry Tarkanian-coached community college powers that combined for a 64-6 record in 1964–65 and 1965–66.

FRANKIE BAUMHOLTZ, Ohio University

Outfielder hit .290 in 1,019 games in 10 seasons (1947–49, 1951–57) with the Chicago Cubs, Cincinnati Reds, and Philadelphia Phillies. Led National League in pinch hits in 1955 and 1956.... First player in Ohio U. history to score 1,000 points in a career. Led the school to three-year record of 49-18. Capped college career by earning MVP honors in 1941 NIT as he led the tourney in scoring with 53 points in three games for the second-place Bobcats. Named to first five on Converse 1940–41 All-America team.... Earned second-team all-league honors with the Youngstown Bears in the National Basketball League in 1945–46 and the Cleveland Rebels in the Basketball Association of America in 1946–47.

LOUIS (BOZEY) BERGER, Maryland

Infielder hit .236 in six seasons (1932, 1935 through 1939) with the Cleveland Indians, Chicago White Sox, and Boston Braves.... The 6-2 forward led Maryland to the 1931 Southern Conference championship with a league-high 19.1-point scoring average in conference competition. Maryland's first basketball All-American was an NCAA consensus first-team selection the next year as a senior.

LOU BOUDREAU, Illinois

Baseball Hall of Famer was an infielder for 15 seasons (1938–52) with the Cleveland Indians and Boston Red Sox. Managed Indians, Red Sox, Kansas City Athletics, and Chicago Cubs, starting his managerial career at the age of 24 in 1942. As player-manager in 1948, the shortstop led Cleveland to the American League title and earned MVP honors by hitting .355 with 116 RBIs.... Played two varsity basketball seasons at Illinois (1936–37 and 1937–38). As a sophomore, he led the Illini in scoring with an 8.7-point average as the team shared the Big Ten Conference title. Compiled 8.8 average the next year. After helping the Illini upset St. John's in a game at Madison Square Garden, the *New York Daily News* described him as "positively brilliant" and said he "set up countless plays in breathtaking fashion." ... Averaged 8.2 points per game for the Hammond (Ind.) Ciesar All-Americans in the National Basketball League in 1938–39.

CARL BOULDIN, Cincinnati

Compiled 3-8 pitching record in four seasons (1961–64) with the Washington Senators....

Starting guard and co-captain as a senior on 1961 NCAA champion. Averaged 2.8 points per game as a sophomore, 5.8 as a junior, and 11.7 as a senior. The Bearcats reached the Final Four all three of his varsity seasons (third-place finishes in 1959 and 1960), compiling an 81-9 record in that span.... Sketch in school guide: "Poised, unruffled backcourt leader. Exceptionally fine ball handler and playmaker possesses clever offensive moves. Especially dependable in clutch situations."

RALPH BRANCA, New York University

Compiled an 88-68 pitching record in 12 seasons (1944–54, 1956) with the Brooklyn Dodgers, Detroit Tigers, and New York Yankees. Appeared in 1947 and 1949 World Series with the Dodgers. Best remembered for throwing the pitch that Bobby Thomson of the New York Giants hit for a homer in the decisive game of the 1951 playoff for the National League title.... A 6-2, 190-pound center, he was the sixth-leading scorer for NYU in 1943–44 with an average of 3.8 points per game.

BOB CERV, Nebraska

Outfielder played 12 seasons (1951–62) with the New York Yankees, Kansas City Athletics, Los Angeles Angels, and Houston Colt .45s. Played in the 1955, 1956, and 1960 World Series with the Yankees. In 1958, he batted .305 with 38 home runs and 104 RBIs for Kansas City.... He averaged 6.2 points per game for the Cornhuskers in four varsity seasons (1946–47 through 1949–50), ranking fourth on the school's career scoring list when he finished his career.... Excerpt from school guide: "One of the finest defensive guards to perform on the Nebraska maples. Combines unusual speed with a sixth sense of timing to steal the ball or tie up the ball handler."

MARTY CLARY, Northwestern

Pitcher compiled a 5-14 record in 58 games with the Atlanta Braves in 1987, 1989, and 1990.... The 6-4 guard was a letterman with the

Wildcats in 1982 and 1983. He hit 82.8 percent of his free throws (24 of 29).

GENE CONLEY, Washington State

Compiled a 91-96 pitching record in 11 seasons (1952, 1954–63) with the Boston/Milwaukee Braves, Philadelphia Phillies, and Boston Red Sox. Three-time All-Star Game performer finished second in the National League rookie of the year voting in 1954 when he had a 14-9 record and 2.97 ERA for the Braves.... Led the Cougars and Pacific Coast Conference Northern Division in scoring in 1949–50 as a sophomore (13.3 points per game) in his only season of varsity basketball before signing a pro contract. Played six seasons in the NBA with the Boston Celtics and New York Knicks, averaging 5.9 points and 6.3 rebounds per game. Member of Celtic championship teams in 1959, 1960, and 1961.... Excerpt in school guide: "Unusually fast and active for a boy his size (6-7, 215 pounds)."

ROGER CRAIG, North Carolina State

Former National League pitcher and manager. Compiled a 74-98 record and 3.83 ERA in 12 seasons (1955–66) with the Brooklyn/Los Angeles Dodgers, New York Mets, St. Louis Cardinals, Cincinnati Reds, and Philadelphia Phillies. Led N.L. in losses with the Mets in 1962 (10-24) and 1963 (5-22). Pitched in seven World Series games with the Dodgers and Cardinals. Managed 10 seasons with the San Diego Padres and San Francisco Giants, winning the 1989 N.L. title with the Giants.... The 6-4, 180-pound forward scored 33 points as a member of the 1949–50 N.C. State freshman basketball team before signing a pro baseball contract.

GUY CURTRIGHT, Northeast Missouri State

Outfielder hit .276 with Chicago White Sox from 1943 to 1946. Set major league rookie record (subsequently broken) with a 26-game hitting streak.... Two-time all-conference selection as a 5-11, 200-pound forward in the Missouri Intercollegiate Athletic Association. Led Bulldog basketball team in scoring each of his four seasons.

ALVIN DARK, Louisiana State

Infielder hit .289 in 14 years (1946, 1948-60) with the Boston Braves, New York Giants, St. Louis Cardinals, Chicago Cubs and Philadelphia Phillies. He hit a career-high .322 with the Braves in 1948 when he won the Rookie of the Year award. Dark led the N.L. in doubles with the Giants with 41 in 1951 and paced the league's shortstops three times each in putouts and double plays. He hit .323 in three World Series ('48 with Braves, '51 and '54 with Giants). Dark compiled a 994-954 record in 13 years (1961-64, 1966-71, 1974, 1975, 1977) as manager of the Giants, Kansas City-Oakland A's, Cleveland Indians and San Diego Padres. He won the '62 N.L. pennant with the Giants and '74 World Series with Oakland. As a sophomore in 1942, Dark was a 5-11, 160-pound tailback who led LSU in rushing (433 yards in 60 carries) and passing (completed 40 of 106 passes for 556 yards and five touchdowns). . . . Member of LSU's 1942-43 basketball squad before entering military service during World War II.

WALT DROPO, Connecticut

First baseman hit .270 with 152 home runs and 704 RBIs in 13 seasons from 1949 to 1961 with the Boston Red Sox, Detroit Tigers, Chicago White Sox, Cincinnati Reds, and Baltimore Orioles. Named American League Rookie of the Year in 1950 after hitting .322 with 34 homers and a league-leading 144 RBIs for the Red Sox. Tied major league record with 12 consecutive hits in 1952.... The 6-5 Dropo averaged 21.7 points per game in 1942–43, 21 in 1945–46, and 19.7 in 1946–47 in a Huskies career interrupted by World War II. The first player in UConn history to average 20 points for a season, he has the second-highest scoring average in school annals (20.7).

SAMMY ESPOSITO, Indiana

Utility infielder hit .207 in 560 games during 10-year career (1952, 1955–63) with the Chicago White Sox and Kansas City Athletics. Saw action in two World Series games in 1959 with the White Sox. Baseball coach at North Carolina State from 1967 through 1987, leading the Wolfpack to third-place finish in 1968 College World Series.... Played one season (1951–52) of varsity basketball at Indiana before signing pro baseball contract, averaging seven points per game as a starting guard for the Hoosiers. Assistant basketball coach at N.C. State for 14 years, including the 1974 NCAA champion.... Sketch in school guide: "Only 5-9, he is fast, a peerless playmaker and one of the best defensive men on the squad."

DARRELL EVANS, Pasadena City College

Infielder-outfielder hit .248 with 414 homers and 1,254 RBIs in 21 seasons (1969–89) with the Atlanta Braves, San Francisco Giants, and Detroit Tigers. Led the American League with 40 homers for the Tigers in 1985, becoming the oldest player to win a home run title in the majors (38).... As a sophomore for Pasadena (Calif.) City College in 1966–67, he was a member of a Jerry Tarkanian-coached club that won the state junior college crown.

DAN FIFE, Michigan

Pitcher compiled a 3-2 record in 14 games with the Minnesota Twins in 1973 and 1974.... The father of Michigan guard Dugan Fife averaged 12.6 points per game as the Wolverines' third-leading scorer each year in three varsity seasons (1968–69 through 1970–71).... Excerpt from school guide: "One of the most intense players in country. Greatest hustler in the whole Big Ten."

JOHNNY GEE, Michigan

One of the tallest players ever to play major league baseball. Compiled 7-12 record in 44 games during six seasons (1939, 1941, 1943–46) with the Pittsburgh Pirates and New York Giants.... Senior captain of Wolverines team in 1936–37 that compiled a 16-4 record and third-place finish in the Big Ten. The 6-9, 225-pounder was sixth in the Big Ten in scoring that season with an average of 8.8 points per game.... In his history of Michigan basketball, Jeff Mortimer

wrote: "Gee looked upon a rebound as something that was his property unless it could be taken away by force."

JOE GIBBON, Mississippi

Compiled a 61-65 record and 3.52 ERA in 419 games during 13 seasons (1960–72) with the Pittsburgh Pirates, San Francisco Giants, Cincinnati Reds, and Houston Astros. Pitched in two games in 1960 World Series for the Pirates.... Finished four-year career as the Rebels' leader in career scoring (1,601 points for 18.9 average) and rebounds (827 for 9.6 average). Nation's second-leading scorer as a senior in 1956–57 with an average of 30 points per game, finishing ahead of Seattle's Elgin Baylor (29.7) and Kansas' Wilt Chamberlain (29.7). Named to first team on Helms Foundation All-America squad and second team on United Press All-America team.... School guide described him as "Ole Miss' big weapon, a portsided, long-range bomber who is accurate from the corner, from the front and through crowded defenses for drive-in baskets."

BOB GIBSON, Creighton

Baseball Hall of Famer compiled a 251-174 pitching record with 3,117 strikeouts and 2.91 ERA in 17 seasons (1959–75) with the St. Louis Cardinals. Notched a 7-3 mark and 1.89 ERA in nine games in the 1964, 1967, and 1968 World Series. Set a World Series record with 17 strikeouts against the Detroit Tigers on October 2, 1968.... First Creighton player to average 20 points per game for his career (20.2). Led school in scoring in 1955-56 (40th in the country with 22 ppg) and 1956–57 and was second-leading scorer in 1954–55 before playing one season (1957–58) with the Harlem Globetrotters.... Sketch from school brochure: "Possesses outstanding jump shot and for height (6-1) is a terrific rebounder."

DALLAS GREEN, Delaware

New York Mets manager compiled 20-22 pitching record in eight seasons (1960–67) with the Philadelphia Phillies, Washington Senators, and Mets. Managed the Phillies to victory over the Kansas City Royals in 1980 World Series.... The 6-5 Green played two seasons of varsity basketball for the Blue Hens, averaging 6.5 points per game in 22 games as a sophomore in 1953–54 and 12.1 points in 21 games as a junior in 1954–55, when he was the school's second-leading scorer and rebounder (10.6 per game).

DICK GROAT, Duke

Shortstop hit .286 in 1,929 games in 14 seasons (1952, 1955–67) with the Pittsburgh Pirates, St. Louis Cardinals, Philadelphia Phillies, and San Francisco Giants. Eight-time All-Star Game performer started on World Championship teams with the Pirates in 1960 and Cardinals in 1964.... Named College Basketball Player of the Year by the Helms Foundation in 1950–51. Nation's fourth-leading scorer as a junior (25.2 points per game) and runner-up as a senior (26 ppg). Averaged 14.5 as a sophomore in 1949–50. Scored 48 points against North Carolina on February 29, 1952. Played 26 games in the NBA, averaging 11.9 points per game for the Fort Wayne Pistons in 1952–53.... In 1951, Virginia coach Gus Tebell said Groat is "the finest player I've seen in the South in my 27 years of coaching. An All-American on anybody's team. I recall the brilliance of Hank Luisetti and I must put Groat in the same category with him. Excellent shot and remarkable ballhandler."

TONY GWYNN, San Diego State

San Diego Padres outfielder hit .336 in first 14 seasons (1982–95), winning National League batting titles—1984, 1987, 1988, 1989, 1994 and 1995. Played in 11 All-Star games. Holds National League record for most years leading league in singles (six). Won a Gold Glove five times (1986-87-89-90-91). . . . Averaged 8.6 points and 5.5 assists per game in 107 games with the Aztecs in four seasons (1977–78 through 1980–81). The 5-11, 170-pound guard was named second-team All-Western Athletic Conference as both a junior and senior. Led WAC in assists as both a sophomore and junior and was third as a senior. Led San Diego State in steals each of his last three seasons. Selected in the 10th round of 1981 NBA draft by the San Diego Clippers.

ED HALICKI, Monmouth (N.J.)

Pitcher compiled a 55-66 record in seven seasons (1974–80) with the San Francisco Giants and California Angels. His best season was 1977 when he posted a 16-12 record for the Giants. Hurled a no-hitter for them vs. the New York Mets on August 24, 1975.... The 6-7, 220-pound forward-center collected 1,777 points and 1,266 rebounds in four seasons (1968–69 through 1971–72). Holds Monmouth single-game rebounding record with 40 in his junior year. Named to NAIA All-American third team as a senior when he led the Hawks in scoring with 21 points per game.

STEVE HAMILTON, Morehead State

Lefthanded pitcher compiled a 40-31 record, 3.05 ERA, and 42 saves in 421 games during 12 seasons (1961–72) with the Cleveland Indians, Washington Senators, New York Yankees, Chicago White Sox, San Francisco Giants, and Chicago Cubs. Appeared in 1963 and 1964 World Series with the Yankees.... Averaged 17.9 points and 16.4 rebounds per game in four-year college basketball career (1954–55 through 1957–58), leading the Eagles in scoring and rebounding as a junior and senior. He ranked 15th in the country in scoring as a junior (24.2 ppg) and among the nation's top 10 rebounders as a senior (19.1 rpg). The 6-7, 195-pound forward-center averaged 18.5 points in four NCAA Tournament games in 1956 and 1957. He had a 51-point game against Ohio University as a junior. He also lettered as a pole vaulter in track. Currently the athletic director at his alma mater, he averaged 4.5 points and 3.4 rebounds per game in two seasons with the NBA's Minneapolis Lakers. He is the only athlete to play in the World Series and the NBA Finals (rookie in 1959 when the Lakers were swept by the Boston Celtics).

ATLEE HAMMAKER, East Tennessee State

Pitcher for more than ten seasons with four different teams—Kansas City Royals, San Francisco Giants, San Diego Padres, and Chicago White Sox. His best year was 1983 when he posted a 10-9 record and National League-best 2.25 ERA for the Giants. . . . The 6-2, 185-pound guard averaged 5.3 points per game as a freshman in 1976–77 and 4.9 as a sophomore in 1977–78. . . . Excerpt from school guide: "Probably most exciting player on club. Has ability to come off the bench and provide much needed spark at times."

CHUCK HARMON, Toledo

Utilityman for four seasons (1954–57) with the Cincinnati Reds, St. Louis Cardinals, and Philadelphia Phillies. . . . Second-leading scorer for the Rockets as a sophomore in 1946–47 (13.6 points per game) and as a junior in 1947–48 (8.8). As a freshman starter in 1942–43, the swingman was Toledo's second-leading scorer in the NIT on a 22-4 team that finished runner-up to St. John's. . . . Sketch in school guide: "Master of tricky play and a whirlwind on the backboards."

BILLY HARRELL, Siena

Infielder hit .231 in 173 games with the Cleveland Indians (1955, 1957, 1958) and Boston Red Sox (1961). . . . The 6-1, 180-pounder averaged 10.3 points per game in three seasons of varsity basketball for Siena. When he finished his college career, he held school records for most points in a season (396 in 1951–52), career and game (28 against Arizona State in 1951) and most rebounds in a season (387 in 1949–50). . . . Excerpt from school guide: "Seems to have steel springs for legs and extension hooks for hands. Can reach the top of the backboard if necessary. Shifty and speedy. Has variety of shots. He'll often pass up scoring chance to give ball to teammate."

RICK HERRSCHER, Southern Methodist

Played 35 games as an infielder-outfielder for the 1962 New York Mets team that finished with a 40-120 record. . . . Averaged 11.5 points per game in three seasons (1955–56 through 1957–58) of varsity basketball as a 6-3, 185-pound swingman. Led team with 17.5 average as a senior. Helped Mustangs win two Southwest Conference titles. Member of SMU squad that reached the 1956 Final Four. . . . Excerpt from school guide: "Captain is most versatile cager ever to play for the Mustangs. He possesses great finesse and can fake and evade the man who is guarding him. He knows all the tricks of a postman. His outside shot demands the respect of all opponents. He is an excellent feeder."

ORAL HILDEBRAND, Butler

Compiled 83-78 record in 10 seasons (1931–40) with the Cleveland Indians, St. Louis Browns, and New York Yankees. Named to 1933 American League All-Star Game team. Pitched four shutout innings as fourth-game starter for Yankees in 1939 World Series after posting 10-4 record during the season. . . . Three-year letterman (1927–28 through 1929–30) on Butler teams that combined for a 48-11 record. Senior captain scored 32 points in 24 minutes in a game against Evansville. Named to second five on 1928–29 *College Humor Magazine* All-American team and third five on 1929–30 *College Humor* All-American squad.

JAY HOOK, Northwestern

Compiled a 39-62 pitching record in eight seasons (1957 through 1964) with the Cincinnati Reds and New York Mets. . . . The 6-2, 185-pound swingman was the Wildcats' third-leading scorer as a sophomore with 10.7 points per game. He had a 5.3-point average the next season (1956–57).

FRANK HOWARD, Ohio State

New York Mets coach was outfielder/first baseman for 16 seasons from 1958 to 1973 with the Los Angeles Dodgers, Washington Senators, Texas Rangers, and Detroit Tigers. In 1,902 major league games, he hit .273 with 382 home runs and 1,119 RBIs. Howard led the American League in homers with 44 in 1968 and 1970.... Played three seasons (1955–56 through 1957–58) of varsity basketball with the Buckeyes, leading them in both scoring and rebounding as a junior (20.1 points and 15.3 rebounds) and senior (16.9 and 13.6). He was 54th in the country in scoring as a junior. Finished college career as OSU's third-leading career scorer and leading rebounder. The 6-6, 220-pound Howard was a first-team All-American selection by the U.S. Basketball Writers/*Look Magazine,* Converse, and NEA as a junior when he ranked eighth in the nation in rebounding.... Excerpt from school guide: "One of the strongest players in college basketball and one of the top rebounders. Shoots very well from the outside."

RON JACKSON, Western Michigan

First baseman for seven seasons with the Chicago White Sox and Boston Red Sox (1954–60).... Second-team All-Mid-American Conference choice in 1952, 1953, and 1954. The 6-6, 225-pound center led WMU in scoring in 1952–53 (15.7 points per game) and 1953–54 (19.7).... Excerpt from sketch in *Dell Basketball Magazine:* "Scores with one-hand flip inside, has a good one-hand push near the foul circle, a two-hand set from the side well out. Good pass, good speed, good rebound, and his team's strongest defensive player to boot."

DAVE JOHNSON, Texas A&M

Baltimore Orioles manager guided New York Mets to victory over Boston Red Sox in 1986 World Series. Hit .261 as an infielder in 13-year career (1965–75, 1977–78) with the Baltimore Orioles, Atlanta Braves, Philadelphia Phillies, and Chicago Cubs. Hit 43 homers for the Braves in 1973.... Averaged 1.7 points per game as a sophomore in his only varsity season (1961–62) with the Aggies before signing a pro baseball contract in 1962.

DUANE JOSEPHSON, Northern Iowa

Catcher hit .258 in eight seasons with the Chicago White Sox (1965–70) and Boston Red

Sox (1971–72) ... Averaged 13.4 points per game as a 6–0, 190-pound guard in three varsity seasons (1961-62 through 1963–64) at what was then call the State College of Iowa. Led the team in scoring as a junior and senior and was named to the All-North Central Conference team both of those seasons. Averaged 17.4 points in five NCAA College Division Tournament games in 1964 when SCI finished fourth.

HOWIE JUDSON, Illinois

Compiled 17-37 pitching record in seven seasons with the Chicago White Sox (1948–52) and Cincinnati Reds (1953 and 1954).... Lettered in basketball with the Illini as a freshman in 1943–44 and as a sophomore in 1944–45 (third-leading scorer with average of 8.5 points per game).

CHARLIE KELLER, Maryland

Outfielder hit .286 with 189 home runs and 760 RBIs in 13 seasons (1939–43 and 1945–52) with the New York Yankees and Detroit Tigers. Hit .306 for the Yanks in 19 World Series games (1939, 1941–43).... Three-year basketball letterman with the Terrapins from 1934–35 through 1936–37.

DON KESSINGER, Mississippi

Infielder played 16 seasons (1964–79) with the Chicago Cubs, St. Louis Cardinals, and Chicago White Sox. Managed White Sox in 1979. Led National League shortstops in putouts three times, assists four times, and double plays four times. Played in six All-Star Games.... Selected to the 10-man All-Southeastern Conference team all three of his varsity seasons (1961–62 through 1963–64) as he ranked among the nation's top 45 scorers each year. In scoring for all games, he ranked third in the SEC as a sophomore (21.4 points per game), second as a junior (21.8), and second as a senior (23.5). He scored 49 points against Tulane on February 2,

Mississippi basketball star Don Kessinger became a six-time All-Star shortstop in the major leagues.

Speedy Arizona guard Kenny Lofton turned into a speedy Cleveland Indian rookie of the year.

1963, and 48 against Tennessee 10 nights later.... Excerpt from school guide: "One of the nation's most gifted athletes, he features every shot in the book but the specifics are one-handed push shots, usually a jumper, and driving layups."

JERRY KINDALL, Minnesota

Infielder hit .213 in nine seasons (1956–58, 1960–65) with the Chicago Cubs, Cleveland Indians, and Minnesota Twins. Baseball coach at Arizona for more than 20 years, leading the Wildcats to three College World Series titles (1976, 1980, and 1986).... Played two seasons of varsity basketball for Minnesota, averaging 1.4 points per game as a sophomore in 1954–55 and 6.9 as a junior in 1955–56.... Excerpt from school guide: "Exceptionally quick reflexes and a good eye are his main attributes although he also has tremendous spring making him a good rebounder."

JIM KONSTANTY, Syracuse

National League MVP and All-Star in 1950 when he pitched in a major league record 74 games, all in relief, and compiled a 16-7 record and 2.66 ERA for the N.L. champion Philadelphia Phillies. Lost 1950 World Series opener to the New York Yankees as a starter, 1-0, before relieving in two other Series games. Compiled career record of 66-48 in 11 seasons (1944, 1946, 1948–56) with the Cincinnati Reds, Boston Braves, Phillies, Yankees, and St. Louis Cardinals.... Member of 1937–38 and 1938–39 Syracuse basketball teams.

CAL KOONCE, Campbell

Compiled a 47-49 record in 10 seasons with the Chicago Cubs, New York Mets, and Boston Red Sox (1962–71). He was a reliever for the 1969 Amazin' Mets World Series champions.... Standout basketball player for Campbell in 1960 and 1961 when the North Carolina-based school was a junior college.

SANDY KOUFAX, Cincinnati

Baseball Hall of Famer compiled a 165-87

record and 2.76 ERA in 12 seasons as a lefthanded pitcher with the Brooklyn (1955–57) and Los Angeles (1958–66) Dodgers. Led the National League in ERA in each of his last five seasons. Was 25-5 in 1963, 26-8 in 1965, and 27-9 in 1966 when he won the Cy Young Award. Named N.L. MVP in 1963. Pitched four no-hit games. Compiled a 4-3 record and 0.95 ERA in eight World Series games in 1959, 1963, 1965, and 1966.... Attended Cincinnati one year on a combination basketball/baseball scholarship before signing a pro baseball contract. Third-leading scorer with 9.7-point average as a 6-1, 190-pound forward for the Bearcats' freshman team in 1953–54.... Ed Jucker, coach of Cincinnati's NCAA titlists in 1961 and 1962, coached the Bearcats' 1953–54 freshman team. Jucker said of Koufax's basketball ability: "He could jump extremely well, was a strong kid and a good driver. He would have made a fine varsity player. We certainly could have used him."

KENNY LOFTON, Arizona

Three-time Gold Glove outfielder led the Cleveland Indians with a .325 batting mark (fourth in the A.L.) and paced majors with 70 stolen bases in 1993. Started major league career with the Houston Astros in 1991. After being traded to Cleveland, he hit .285 for the Indians in 1992 and led the A.L. in stolen bases with 66, a record for an A.L. rookie. Played in All-Star Game in 1994 and 1995, when he led the A.L. in stolen bases with 60 and 54, respectively. . . . Averaged 4.8 points and 2.6 assists per game in four seasons (1985–86 through 1988–89) with the Wildcats. Set school records for steals in a season (67 in 1988–89) and career (200). Member of team that compiled a 35-3 record and reached the 1988 Final Four.

JERRY LUMPE, Southwest Missouri State

Infielder hit .268 in 12-year career (1956–67) with the New York Yankees, Kansas City Athletics, and Detroit Tigers. Played in 1957 and 1958 World Series with the Yankees.... Member of Southwest Missouri squads that won 1952 and 1953 NAIA Tournament titles.

DON LUND, Michigan

Outfielder hit .240 in seven-year career (1945, 1947–49, 1952–54) with the Brooklyn Dodgers, St. Louis Browns, and Detroit Tigers.... First-round selection as a fullback/linebacker by the Chicago Bears in the 1945 NFL draft. Rejected $100 a game offer from the Bears and never played pro football.... He was a starting guard as a junior for the Wolverines' basketball team and starting center as a senior.... In his history of Michigan basketball, Jeff Mortimer wrote of the school's World War II squads: "Lund, rejected for military service because of a trick knee, was the mainstay of these teams." ... Following his playing career, he served as baseball coach at Michigan (won 1962 College World Series), farm system director for the Tigers, and associate athletic director at his alma mater.

TONY LUPIEN, Harvard

First baseman hit .268 in six seasons (1940, 1942–45, and 1948) with the Boston Red Sox, Philadelphia Phillies, and Chicago White Sox. The former baseball coach at Dartmouth was co-author of the book *The Imperfect Diamond: The Story of Baseball's Reserve Clause and the Men Who Fought to Change It*.... The 5-10, 185-pound guard was captain of the 1938–39 Harvard basketball squad. The previous season, he was the school's second-leading scorer in conference competition with 5.4 points per game.

TED LYONS, Baylor

Baseball Hall of Famer spent entire career with the Chicago White Sox (1923–42, 1946) after never playing in the minors. Managed White Sox from 1946 through 1948. Three-time 20-game winner compiled a 260-230 record and 3.67 ERA in 594 games. Pitched no-hitter against Boston Red Sox in 1926.... Earned four basketball letters at Baylor from 1919–20 through 1922–23. Consensus first-team selection on All-

Southwest Conference squad as a sophomore and senior.

BILL McCAHAN, Duke

Pitcher for four seasons (1946–49) with the Philadelphia Athletics. Hurled seven-inning shutout in his first major league game and no-hitter vs. Washington on September 3, 1947.... Three-year letterman for Duke basketball teams that finished second in the Southern Conference Tournament in 1940 and won title in 1941 and 1942. Named to United Press all-tourney team in 1942 when the 5-11, 200-pound guard finished second on the Blue Devils in scoring. Played briefly for the Syracuse Nationals in the National Basketball League in the 1946-47 season.

BEN McDONALD, Louisiana State

Pitcher signed free-agent contract with the Milwaukee Brewers after the 1995 season. Compiled a 58-53 mark with the Baltimore Orioles from 1989 through 1995, including a team-record seven victories to start the 1994 campaign... Played in 32 games, starting six, as a 6-6 freshman forward for LSU in 1986–87. Averaged 2.8 points per game with a high of 13 against Auburn. Played in six basketball games the next season before concentrating on his baseball career.

MEL McGAHA, Arkansas

Former manager of the Cleveland Indians (1962) and Kansas City Athletics (June 11, 1964–May 14, 1965).... The first player in Arkansas history to earn four letters in basketball (1943–44 through 1946–47). Played for the New York Knickerbockers of the Basketball Association of America in 1948–49.

SAM MELE, New York University

Major league outfielder (1947–56) and manager of Minnesota Twins (1961–67). Hit .267 in 1,046 games with the Boston Red Sox, Washington Senators, Chicago White Sox, Baltimore Orioles, Cincinnati Reds, and Cleveland Indians. Led American League with 36 doubles for the Senators in 1951 and drove in six runs in one

inning in a 1952 game for the White Sox. Managed Twins in 1965 when they won A.L. title.... The 6-0, 180-pound guard played two seasons of varsity basketball before entering the military. Named to the first five on the All-Metropolitan New York team as a sophomore in 1942–43 when he was the Violets' leading scorer in the NCAA Tournament (losses against Georgetown and Dartmouth).

EDDIE O'BRIEN, Seattle

Infielder-outfielder played five seasons (1953, 1955–58) with the Pittsburgh Pirates, hitting .236 in 231 games. Twin brother of former major leaguer Johnny O'Brien, a teammate at Seattle.... Averaged 12.1 points per game in 1950–51, 10.6 in 1951–52, and 16.5 in 1952–53. Third-team All-American selection on Converse and United Press All-American squads as a senior. Averaged 15.3 points per game in three NCAA Tournament games in 1953. Finished college career as Seattle's second-leading career scorer (behind Johnny) with 1,237 points.

JOHNNY O'BRIEN, Seattle

Infielder/pitcher played six seasons (1953, 1955–59) with the Pittsburgh Pirates, St. Louis Cardinals, and Milwaukee Braves. Hit .250 and compiled 1-3 pitching record in 339 games. Twin brother of former major leaguer Eddie O'Brien, a teammate at Seattle.... The 5-9, 160-pound guard scored 2,733 points in three varsity seasons (1950–51 through 1952–53), averaging 20.7 points per game as a sophomore, 28.4 as a junior, and 28.6 as a senior. Scored 51 points against Gonzaga on February 15, 1953. NCAA consensus All-American second-team choice as a junior and consensus first-team selection as a senior. Averaged 32 points per game in three games in the 1953 NCAA Tournament. Became first college player to score 1,000 points in a season when he scored 1,051 in 37 games in 1951–52.

LOU PINIELLA, Tampa

Seattle Mariners manager hit .291 as an outfielder during 18 seasons (1964, 1968–84) with the Baltimore Orioles, Cleveland Indians,

Kansas City Royals, and New York Yankees. Named American League Rookie of the Year in 1969 after hitting .282 for the Royals. Hit .319 in 22 World Series games with the Yankees in 1976, 1977, 1978, and 1981. Also managed the Yankees (1986–88) and Cincinnati Reds (1990–92). Led the Reds to a four-game sweep of the Oakland A's in the 1990 World Series.... Accepted a college basketball scholarship in 1961 after establishing a Tampa city single-season high school scoring record that stood until 1984. Less than a year after enrolling at UT, he signed a baseball contract with the Cleveland Indians.

PAUL POPOVICH, West Virginia

Infielder hit .233 in 11 seasons (1964, 1966–75) with the Chicago Cubs, Los Angeles Dodgers, and Pittsburgh Pirates. Went three-for-three in pinch-hitting appearances for the Pirates in 1974 National League Championship series.... Averaged 3.3 points per game in a reserve role in his one season (1959–60) of varsity basketball with the Mountaineers before signing pro baseball contract. Led freshman team in scoring with 18.8 average. Teammate of Jerry West on squad that compiled a 26-5 record and played in the 1960 NCAA Tournament.... Excerpt from school guide: "Brings poise and confidence, born of extensive baseball training."

CURTIS PRIDE, William & Mary

Outfielder made major league debut with Montreal Expos in 1993 and hit .444 in 10 games. Born with 95 percent hearing disability, he is one of few deaf athletes to ever play major league baseball.... Averaged 5.6 points and 3.1 assists in four seasons (1986–87 through 1989–90) with the Tribe. The 6-0, 185-pound guard led team in steals three times and in assists twice. Named to the Colonial Athletic Association All-Rookie team as a freshman and to the CAA All-Defensive team as a sophomore and junior.... Excerpt from school guide: "Strong player for his size. Exceptionally quick player has moves to penetrate. Frustrates other ball handlers with his ability to make the big steal."

DENNIS RASMUSSEN, Creighton

Compiled 91-76 record in his first 10 seasons (1984–93) with the San Diego Padres, New York Yankees, Cincinnati Reds, Chicago Cubs, and Kansas City Royals.... The 6-7, 215-pound forward averaged 5.1 points per game in three seasons (1977–78 through 1979–80) for Creighton before signing a pro baseball contract.... Excerpt from school guide: "Super sub proved a valuable contributor. Anchoring an important sixth-man role, Rasmussen sparks the Bluejay offense with deadeye shooting."

RON REED, Notre Dame

Compiled 146-140 pitching record and 3.46 ERA in 19 seasons (1966–84) with the Atlanta Braves, St. Louis Cardinals, Philadelphia Phillies, and Chicago White Sox. Pitched for Phillies in 1980 and 1983 World Series.... The 6-5, 205-pound forward averaged 18.9 points and 14.3 rebounds in three varsity seasons (1962–63 through 1964–65). Averaged 20 points and 17.7 rebounds as a junior and 21 points and 13.2 rebounds as a senior. Named to Helms Foundation 36-man All-American team as a senior.... Third-round selection of the Detroit Pistons in the 1965 NBA draft, he played two seasons with the franchise, averaging eight points and 6.4 rebounds per game.

STEVE RENKO, Kansas

Compiled 134-146 pitching record in 15 seasons (1969–83) with the Montreal Expos, Chicago Cubs, Chicago White Sox, Oakland Athletics, Boston Red Sox, California Angels, and Kansas City Royals.... Averaged 9.9 points and 5.8 rebounds per game as a sophomore before concentrating on his career as a football quarterback and baseball pitcher.... Excerpt from school guide: "Versatile shooter, tough rebounder and promising playmaker."

DAVE RICKETTS, Duquesne

Catcher hit .249 in six seasons (1962, 1965, 1967–70) with the St. Louis Cardinals and Pittsburgh Pirates. Played with Cardinals in 1967, and 1968 World Series. Coach, instructor and minor league manager in the Cardinals' organization since 1976.... The 6-2, 190-pound guard was a three-year starter who led the Dukes in scoring in his senior season with a 17.9 average in 1956–57, finishing fourth in the nation in free-throw percentage with an 86.2 mark. Sophomore member of team that compiled a 22-4 record and finished sixth in the final AP poll after winning the NIT.

DICK RICKETTS, Duquesne

Compiled a 1-6 pitching record in his only season with the St. Louis Cardinals in 1959.... The 6-8, 215-pound forward/center was a second-team consensus All-American choice as a junior in 1953-54 and first five consensus All-American selection as a senior in 1954-55. Averaged 17.7 points and 12.2 rebounds per game in starting all 111 games in his four-year Duquense career. First-round pick of the Milwaukee Hawks in the 1955 NBA draft. Played three seasons in the NBA with the St. Louis Hawks and Rochester/Cincinnati Royals, averaging 9.6 points and 6.3 rebounds per game.... Following pro sports career, he was an executive with Eastman Kodak. Died of leukemia on March 6, 1988.

MEL ROACH, Virginia

Utilityman hit .238 in eight years (1953, 1954 and 1957-62) with the Milwaukee Braves, Chicago Cubs and Philadelphia Phillies. The longtime backup to Red Schoendienst hit .309 in 44 games in 1958 and .300 in 48 games in 1960 for the Braves. . . . The 6-1, 190-pounder earned a letter by averaging 9.3 points per game in the 1952-53 season before receiving a substantial bonus from the Braves.

ROBIN ROBERTS, Michigan State

Baseball Hall of Famer compiled a 286-245 record in 19 seasons (1948–66) with the Philadelphia Phillies, Baltimore Orioles, Houston Astros, and Chicago Cubs. Twenty-game winner for six consecutive seasons with the Phillies (1950–55)....

Played three seasons of basketball with the Spartans. Averaged 10.6 points per game as a freshman (team's third-leading scorer as he was eligible because of WWII), 9.8 as a sophomore (second-leading scorer), and 9.0 as a junior (second-leading scorer). Forward led team in field-goal percentage as a junior.... Sketch from school basketball guide: "Regarded by newsmen as one of the greatest players today in college basketball. A poll by the *Detroit Free Press* named him the 'most valuable' collegiate player in Michigan. He is not especially fast, but he's extremely well-coordinated, passes exceptionally well, and is a beautiful one-hand shot artist."

JACKIE ROBINSON, UCLA

Member of Baseball Hall of Fame was an infielder who hit .311 and was a regular on six National League pennant winners with the Brooklyn Dodgers in 10 seasons (1947–56).... Football, basketball and track standout at Pasadena City College in 1937–38 and 1938–39. Named to All-Southern California Junior College Conference Western Division all-star basketball team both years, a span in which UCLA was winless in league competition. First athlete in UCLA history to letter in football, basketball, baseball, and track. Forward compiled highest scoring average in the Pacific Coast Conference both seasons at UCLA (12.3 points per league game in 1939–40 and 11.1 in 1940–41). In his last UCLA athletic contest, he accounted for more than half of the Bruins' output with 20 points in a 52-37 loss to Southern Cal.

GARRY ROGGENBURK, Dayton

Lefthanded pitcher compiled a 6-9 record during five seasons (1963, 1965, 1966, 1968, 1969) with the Minnesota Twins, Boston Red Sox, and Seattle Pilots.... The 6-6, 190-pound forward led the Flyers in scoring all three of his varsity seasons (16.1 points per game as a sophomore and junior and 16 ppg as a senior) and led the team in rebounding as a sophomore (13.8 per game) and junior (12.5). Named to third team on Helms All-American squad as a senior in 1962 when Dayton won the NIT.

ROBERT (RED) ROLFE, Dartmouth

Third baseman hit .289 in 10 years with the New York Yankees. The four-time All-Star led the A.L. in triples with 15 in 1936 and paced the A.L. in hits (213), doubles (46) and runs (139) in 1939. Rolfe appeared in six of the seven World Series from 1936 through his final season in 1942. He compiled a 278-256 record in four years as a manger of the Detroit Tigers from 1949-52. . . . The 5-11 1-2, 170-pounder appeared in two basketball games for Dartmouth as a freshman in 1927-28 and four contests as a junior in 1929-30. . . . He coached the Toronto Huskies of the Basketball Association of America for the last 44 games of the 1946-47 season.

MARIUS RUSSO, Long Island University

Compiled a 45-34 record and 3.13 ERA in six seasons (1939–43, 1946) with the New York Yankees. Registered a pair of 2-1 World Series victories (over the Brooklyn Dodgers in 1941 and St. Louis Cardinals in 1943).... Played on two of the premier teams in college basketball history when LIU went 24-2 in 1934–35 and 26-0 in 1935–36. Named to the first five on the 1935–36 Metropolitan New York Basketball Writers Association All-Star Team.

TED SAVAGE, Lincoln (Mo.)

Director of target marketing for the St. Louis Cardinals. Outfielder hit .233 in nine seasons (1962–63, 1965–75) with the Philadelphia Phillies, Pittsburgh Pirates, St. Louis Cardinals, Chicago Cubs, Los Angeles Dodgers, Cincinnati Reds, Milwaukee Brewers, and Kansas City Royals.... The 6-0, 175-pounder led Jefferson City, Missouri-based Lincoln in scoring with an average of 13.5 points per game in 1955–56.

DON SCHWALL, Oklahoma

Compiled a 49-48 pitching record in seven seasons (1961–67) with the Boston Red Sox, Pittsburgh Pirates, and Atlanta Braves. Named American League Rookie of the Year in 1961 when he posted a 15-7 mark and 3.22 ERA for the Red Sox.... As a 6-5, 190-pound sophomore forward in 1956–57, he led the Sooners in rebounding with 8.7 per game and finished as the team's second-leading scorer with a 15.9-point average. Scored 23, 20, and 30 points in three defeats against Wilt Chamberlain-led Kansas. Dropped off OU squad in December of junior year after signing a bonus contract with the Red Sox for a reported $50,000.... Excerpt from school guide: "Became highest scoring sophomore in Sooner history. Tremendous rebounder and has exceptional speed for a man his size. Can work inside or outside."

JEFF SHAW, Rio Grande

Pitcher for the Montreal Expos after previously playing for the Cleveland Indians.... He averaged 1.3 points per game as a 6-2, 170-pound freshman guard on the 1984–85 Rio Grande squad that compiled a 31-5 record and reached the second round of the NAIA Tournament.

ROLLIE SHELDON, Connecticut

Compiled a 38-36 pitching record in five seasons (1961, 1962, and 1964–1966) with the New York Yankees, Kansas City Athletics, and Boston Red Sox. He was 11-5 as a rookie with the American League champion Yankees.... The 6-4 sophomore forward was the third-leading scorer with 13.5 points per game for the Huskies' NCAA Tournament basketball team in 1959–60. He also averaged 7.1 rebounds per game.

NORM SIEBERN, Southwest Missouri State

First baseman-outfielder hit .272 with 132 home runs in 12 seasons (1956, 1958–68) with the New York Yankees, Kansas City Athletics, Baltimore Orioles, California Angels, San Francisco Giants, and Boston Red Sox. Played in 1956 and 1958 World Series with the Yankees and 1967 World Series with the Red Sox.... Member of Southwest Missouri squads that won back-to-back NAIA Tournament titles in 1952 and 1953.

SONNY SIEBERT, Missouri

Compiled a 140-114 pitching record in 12 seasons (1964–75) with the Cleveland Indians, Boston Red Sox, Texas Rangers, St. Louis Cardinals, San Diego Padres, and Oakland A's. Pitched a no-hitter for the Indians against the Washington Senators on June 10, 1966. Selected for All-Star Game in 1966 and 1971.... A 6-3 guard, he played two seasons of varsity basketball for the Tigers (1956–57 and 1957–58) before signing a pro baseball contract. Averaged 13.4 points per game as a sophomore (school record at the time for scoring by a first-year player) and 16.7 as a junior. Led Mizzou in scoring in his junior season, including a 31-point outburst against Oklahoma on February 15, 1958.... Sketch in school guide: "Feathery jump shooter who owns a wide repertoire of shots. Handles the ball well to clear many of his shot tries. Good driver can play either outside or in."

JOHN SIMMONS, New York University

Outfielder with the Washington Senators in 1949.... Starting guard averaged 8.7 points per game for NYU's 17-6 NCAA Tournament team in 1943.

LEE SMITH, Northwestern (La.) State

All-time major league career saves leader, notching 471 in 16 seasons with the Chicago Cubs, Boston Red Sox, St. Louis Cardinals, New York Yankees, Baltimore Orioles, and California Angels. Set a record in 1991 (subsequently broken) for most saves in a season by a National League pitcher with 47 for the Cardinals. Six-time All-Star finished 1995 season with a 2.95 ERA in 943 games.... The 6-5, 215-pound forward averaged 3.4 points and 1.9 rebounds per game with the Demons in his only season of college basketball.

TIM STODDARD, North Carolina State

Pitched in 485 games, all as a reliever, in 13 seasons (1975, 1978–89) with the Chicago White Sox, Baltimore Orioles, Chicago Cubs, San Diego Padres, New York Yankees, and Cleveland Indians. Compiled a 41-35 record with 3.95 ERA and 76 saves. Recorded 26 saves for the Orioles in 1980 the year after being the winning pitcher for them in Game Four of the 1979 World Series against the Pittsburgh Pirates.... Played three seasons (1972–73 through 1974–75) of varsity basketball at N.C. State as a 6-7, 230-pound forward. Averaged 7.9 points and 5.3 rebounds as a sophomore, 5.5 and 4.5 as a junior, and 5.6 and 4.8 as a senior as the Wolfpack won 69 of 76 games in that span. Starting forward opposite David Thompson on 1974 NCAA champion.... Sketch in school guide: "Filled a vital role as a starter with his rebounding and defensive play. Has proven himself a clutch performer on numerous occasions."

TED TAPPE, Washington State

Outfielder with Cincinnati Reds (1950 and 1951) and Chicago Cubs (1955).... The 6-3, 185-pound guard was the leading scorer in the 1949 NJCAA national tournament with 81 points in four games in helping Olympic Junior College (Bremerton, Wash.) to a fourth-place finish. He was the third-leading scorer (6.8 points per game) in his only season with the Cougars before signing a pro baseball contract.

JIM UMBRICHT, Georgia

Compiled a 9-5 record and 3.00 ERA in 88 games in five seasons (1959–63) with the Pittsburgh Pirates and Houston Colt .45s before dying of cancer on April 9, 1964.... Three-year basketball letterman captained the Georgia team as a senior in 1951–52.

CECIL UPSHAW, Centenary

Reliever compiled a 34-36 record with 3.13 ERA and 86 saves in nine seasons (1966–69, 1971–75) with the Atlanta Braves, Houston Astros, Cleveland Indians, New York Yankees, and Chicago White Sox. Posted 2.84 ERA in three relief appearances for the Braves in 1969 National League Championship Series. Led Braves in saves five times, including career-high 27 for 1969 N.L. Western Division champions.... The 6-6, 185-pound forward averaged 13.7 points and six rebounds per game from 1961–62 through 1963–64. Led team in scoring as a junior (15.4) and finished as Centenary's third-leading career scorer.... Excerpt from school guide: "Deadly shooter from the corner but lacks strength to battle the boards with the bigger boys."

INMAN (COOT) VEAL, Auburn

Infielder for six seasons (1958–63) with the Detroit Tigers, Washington Senators, and Pittsburgh Pirates. Named to *The Sporting News* Rookie All-Star Team in 1958 after hitting .256 for the Tigers.... Led Auburn in scoring as a sophomore in his only season of varsity basketball (10.9 points per game in 1951–52) before signing a pro baseball contract.

BOB VEALE, Benedictine College (Kan.)

Compiled a 120-95 pitching record and 3.08 ERA in 13 seasons (1962–74) with the Pittsburgh Pirates and Boston Red Sox. Lefthander led National League in strikeouts with 250 in 1964, the first of four consecutive years he won at least 16 games. Two-time N.L. All-Star twice struck out 16 batters in a game.... Scored 1,160 points in three seasons (1955–56 through 1957–58) as a 6-5, 205-pound center for the Atchison (Kan.)-based school that was then called St. Benedict's.

PRESTON WARD, Southwest Missouri State

First baseman-outfielder hit .253 in nine seasons (1948, 1950, 1953–59) with the Brooklyn Dodgers, Chicago Cubs, Pittsburgh Pirates, Cleveland Indians, and Kansas City Athletics.... The 6-4, 190-pound Ward was the second-leading scorer on Southwest Missouri's Teams in 1946–47 (8.1 points per game) and 1948–49 (12.2). Named to the first five on the All-Missouri Intercollegiate Athletic Association team both of those seasons.

BILLY WERBER, Duke

Infielder hit .271 in 11 seasons (1930, 1933–42) with the New York Yankees, Boston Red Sox, Philadelphia Athletics, Cincinnati Reds, and New York Giants. Led American League in stolen bases in 1934, 1935, and 1937. Regular third baseman on the Reds' National League pennant winners in 1939 and 1940. First player to bat in a televised major league game (Reds vs. Brooklyn on August 26, 1939).... First Duke player to earn All-American honors in basketball. He was named to the 10-man Christy Walsh Syndicate All-American team following his senior season in 1929–30 when the Blue Devils were 18-2. Second-leading scorer on Southern Conference Tournament runner-up as both a junior and senior.

SAMMY WHITE, Washington

Catcher hit .262 in 11 seasons with the Boston Red Sox (1951–59), Milwaukee Braves (1961), and Philadelphia Phillies (1962).... Averaged 10.1 points per game as a 6-3, 195-pound forward with the Huskies in three varsity seasons (1946–47 through 1948–49). Named to first five on All-Pacific Coast Conference Northern Division team as a junior and senior.... Sketch in school guide: "White's variations on traditional tosses not only make him a treacherous offensive weapon, but one of the greatest crowd pleasers to perform under the Husky banner in many a moon. Perhaps the fastest man on club, and although his forte is offensive punch, he is far from impotent on defense."

DAVE WINFIELD, Minnesota

Outfielder hit .283 with 465 home runs, 1,833 RBIs and 3,110 hits in 22 seasons (1973-88, 1990-95) with the San Diego Padres, New York Yankees, California Angels, Toronto Blue Jays, Minnesota Twins and Cleveland Indians. Played in 12 All-Star Games after never playing in the minors. . . . Reached 3,000-hit mark during 1993 season.... Played two seasons of varsity basketball as a 6-6, 220-pound forward with the Gophers, averaging 6.9 points and 5.4 rebounds per game as a junior in 1971–72 and 10.5 points and 6.1 rebounds as a senior in 1972–73.... Selected by the Atlanta Hawks in the fifth round of the 1973 NBA draft and the Utah Stars in the sixth round of the 1973 ABA draft. Didn't play college football, but chosen in 17th round of the 1973 NFL draft by the Minnesota Vikings.... Excerpt from school guide: "Recruited out of intramural ranks to lend depth, became a starter and was a giant in the stretch drive. Amazing athlete leaps like a man catapulted. Soft touch from medium range."

BOBBY WINKLES, Illinois Wesleyan

Coached Arizona State to College World Series titles in 1965, 1967, and 1969 before managing the California Angels in 1973 and through the first 74 games of 1974. Reggie Jackson, Rick Monday, and Sal Bando were among the more than 20 future major leaguers he coached at ASU.... Led Illinois Wesleyan in scoring as a senior in 1950–51 (12 points per game). The 5-9, 170-pound guard was a first-team selection in the College Conference of Illinois.

CHUCK WORKMAN, Central Missouri State

Outfielder-third baseman hit .242 in six seasons (1938, 1941, 1943–46) with the Cleveland Indians, Boston Braves, and Pittsburgh Pirates. Finished second in the National League in home runs in 1945 with 25 for the Braves.... Led team in scoring as sophomore (8.9 points per game in 1934–35) and junior (10.5) and was second-leading scorer as a senior (9.5). Leading scorer in tourney with 38 points in three games when Central Missouri won the first National Intercollegiate Tournament (now NAIA Tournament) at Kansas City in 1937.... First five selection on the Missouri Intercollegiate Athletic Association all-star team as a sophomore and junior.

FOOTBALL STANDOUTS

WARREN AMLING, Ohio State

College Football Hall of Famer is one of few athletes to earn consensus All-American honors at two positions (guard in 1945 and tackle in 1946). Member of 1944 Ohio State football team that finished with a 9-0 record, won the Big Ten title, and finished second behind Army in the final Associated Press poll.... Three-year letterman for the Buckeyes' basketball team from 1944–45 through 1946–47. Starting guard on Final Four squads in 1945 and 1946. Second-team All-Big Ten selection in basketball in 1945–46.

KEN ANDERSON, Augustana (Ill.)

Quarterback passed for 32,838 yards and 197 touchdowns in 16 seasons (1975–85) with the Cincinnati Bengals. Played in three NFL Pro Bowl games and one Super Bowl.... Swingman finished Augustana career as the fifth-leading scorer in school history with 1,044 points. Led team in field goal and free throw shooting as a freshman and sophomore. High school teammate of college and pro star Dan Issel.... Quote from Augustana coach Jim Borcherding in school guide: "His outstanding ability and leadership qualities make him an inspiration both to his teammates and to the fans."

DOUG ATKINS, Tennessee

Member of College Football Hall of Fame and Pro Football Hall of Fame. Eight-time Pro Bowl game participant played 17 seasons (1953–69) as a defensive end in the NFL with the Cleveland Browns, Chicago Bears, and New Orleans Saints.... Originally enrolled on a basketball scholarship at Tennessee, where he played one season of varsity basketball before concentrating on football. The 6-5, 210-pound center averaged 9.9 points per game for the 1950–51 Volunteers, ranking third on the team in scoring.

MORRIS (RED) BADGRO, Southern Cal

Pro Football Hall of Famer was an offensive and defensive end with the New York Yankees

(1927), New York Giants (1930–35), and Brooklyn Dodgers (1936) in an NFL career that was interrupted by a stint in major league baseball. Hit .257 in two seasons (1929 and 1930) as an outfielder with the St. Louis Browns.... Earned varsity basketball letters for the Trojans in 1924–25 and 1926–27. Named to the first five on the All-Pacific Coast Conference team as a forward in 1926–27 when he was USC's MVP.

AL (BUBBA) BAKER, Colorado State

Played in three Pro Bowl games during 13-year NFL career from 1978–90 as a defensive end with the Detroit Lions, St. Louis Cardinals, Cleveland Browns, and Minnesota Vikings. Named NFC rookie of the year by *The Sporting News* in 1978.... Averaged 4.1 points and 3.5 points per game as a 6-6, 255-pound forward-center for the CSU Rams from 1974–75 through 1977–78.

TERRY BAKER, Oregon State

College Football Hall of Famer won the 1962 Heisman Trophy as a senior quarterback after rushing 115 times for 538 yards (4.7 per carry), completing 112 of 203 passes for a nation-leading 1,738 yards and 15 touchdowns. He also led the country in total offense (2,276 yards) and touchdowns responsible (24). His 99-yard run from scrimmage for a TD accounted for the only points in a 6-0 victory against Villanova in the Liberty Bowl. Played in the NFL with the Los Angeles Rams (1963–65) and in the Canadian Football League with Edmonton (1967).... The 6-3 guard averaged 7.4 points per game in 1960–61, 10.7 in 1961–62, and 13.4 in 1962–63. Second-leading scorer for Beavers squad that reached the 1963 Final Four.... Excerpt from school guide: "Referred to by *Sports Illustrated* as 'Best Athlete in College.' Leader of fastbreak offense."

ERICH BARNES, Purdue

Defensive back intercepted 45 passes in 14 seasons with the Chicago Bears, New York Giants, and Cleveland Browns. Played in six Pro Bowls and six NFL championship games.... He

was a 6-3, 190-pound forward-center who played briefly for the Boilermakers' varsity basketball team as a sophomore in 1955–56.

ROOSEVELT BARNES, Purdue

Linebacker with the Detroit Lions in the NFL (1982–85).... Member of 1980 Final Four team. Played briefly for Fort Wayne in the CBA.... Excerpt from school's NIT guide: "Known around the Big Ten as a defensive specialist. Probably Purdue's most emotional cager. Quickness, strength and jumping ability are his strongest assets."

CLIFF BATTLES, West Va. Wesleyan College

Halfback became member of College Football and Pro Football Halls of Fame. Led the NFL in rushing as a rookie in 1932 and in his final season in 1937. First NFL player to rush for 200 yards in a game (215 yards in 16 carries for the Boston Redskins against the New York Giants in 1933).... Played four seasons of varsity basketball in college.

SAMMY BAUGH, Texas Christian

College Football and Pro Football Hall of Famer is considered by many as the finest quarterback in history. Consensus All-American in 1936. Passed for 21,886 yards and 186 touchdowns in 16 years (1937–52) with the Washington Redskins. Led the NFL in passing five times, in punting five times, and in pass interceptions once. Held almost all NFL passing records when he retired.... Three-year letterman in basketball at TCU was an honorable mention selection on the All-Southwest Conference team as a senior in 1936–37.

DICK BEETSCH, Northern Iowa

Set NCAA Small College Division (now Division II) record for most pass receptions in a season in 1953 when he caught 54 passes for 837 yards and nine touchdowns as a sophomore.... He averaged 12 points per game in four seasons of basketball, leading the team in scoring as a sophomore (13.3 ppg) and senior (13.8).

JIM BENTON, Arkansas

Standout end with the Cleveland Rams, Chicago Bears, and Los Angeles Rams (1938–40, 1942–47) after leading the nation's major-college players in pass receptions in 1937. Starter on two NFL champions (Bears '43 and Rams '45). Caught 288 passes for 4,801 yards and 45 touchdowns, finishing NFL career ranked second behind all-time great Don Hutson in pass receptions, receiving yardage, and receiving touchdowns. Led league in pass receptions in 1946 and in pass reception yardage in 1945 and 1946. Caught 10 passes for 303 yards in a 1945 game.... The 6-3, 185-pound forward was the Razorbacks' third-leading scorer in SWC play (7.2 points per game) as a senior in 1937–38 when they won the league title with an 11-1 mark and compiled a 19-3 overall record.

MATT BLAIR, Northeastern Oklahoma A&M

Linebacker played 12 years with the Minnesota Vikings (1974-85) after being their second-round draft choice out of Iowa State. He intercepted 16 passes and recovered 16 fumbles, appeared in six Pro Bowl games and two Super Bowls during his pro career. . . . Played in 1970 NJCAA Tournament with team that finished in seventh place.

MATT BLUNDIN, Virginia

Quarterback was a second-round pick by the Kansas City Chiefs in the NFL draft after passing for 2,696 yards and 25 touchdowns in his college career. Named ACC offensive football player of the year as a senior.... Started most of his sophomore basketball season, when he averaged six points and 5.8 rebounds per game. The 6-7, 230-pound forward finished his four-year basketball career with averages of 3.6 points and 4.5 rebounds. He averaged 4.7 points and 5.6

rebounds in seven NCAA Tournament games from 1989–91.

ALBIE BOOTH, Yale

College Football Hall of Famer was an All-American single wing tailback in 1929, 1930, and 1931. Gained nationwide attention when he scored all of Yale's points in a 21-13 victory over Army.... The 5-6, 145-pound forward was named to the All-Eastern Intercollegiate League second five as a senior in 1930–31.

GEORGE BORK, Northern Illinois

First college football player to pass for more than 3,000 yards in a season (completed 244 of 374 passes for 3,077 yards and 32 touchdowns in nine games in 1963). Led NCAA college division in passing and total offense in 1962 and 1963.... Led the Interstate Intercollegiate Athletic Conference in scoring and was named to the first team on the IIAC all-star squad as a junior in 1961–62 (21.7 points per game) and as a senior in 1962–63 (23.2). Had a 44-point game against Winona State on February 20, 1962.

ORDELL BRAASE, South Dakota

Defensive end with the Baltimore Colts in 12 NFL seasons (1957–68). Played in two Pro Bowl games and four NFL championship games. Member of 1958, 1959, and 1968 NFL championship teams.... The 6-4, 215-pound center in basketball was a first-team selection in the All-North Central Conference when he averaged 7.8 points per game in 1952–53 and 11 points in 1953–54.

DARRELL (PETE) BREWSTER, Purdue

Receiver caught 210 passes for 3,758 yards and 21 touchdowns in nine seasons (1952–60) with the Cleveland Browns and Pittsburgh Steelers. Played in two Pro Bowl games and started for Cleveland in five NFL championship games. Member of the Browns' 1954 an 1955 NFL champions.... The 6-3, 200-pound forward-center was the Boilermakers' fourth-leading scorer as a junior (6.8 points per game) and senior (5.9 ppg).

JOHNNY BRIGHT, Drake

Canadian Football League Hall of Famer ranked second on the CFL all-time rushing list at the end of his 13-year career. He led the nation's major college players in total offense yardage in 1949 (1,950) and 1950 (2,400) and finished fifth in the 1951 Heisman Trophy voting. Concluded career as major college leader in all-time total offense yardage (5,903).... Scored 35 points in 17 games for the 1949–50 Bulldogs basketball team.

JIM BROWN, Syracuse

Movie actor is member of College Football Hall of Fame and Pro Football Hall of Fame. Earned All-American honors in football and lacrosse. Averaged 6.2 yards per carry as a senior in 1956 and scored 43 points in a game against Colgate. Established NFL career records for yards rushing (12,312), rushing attempts (2,359), rushing average (5.2 per carry), touchdowns (126), and years leading league in rushing (eight) in his nine seasons (1957–65) with the Cleveland Browns.... Averaged 14.9 points per game for the Orangemen basketball team as a sophomore and 11.3 as a junior. He is reluctant to specifically say why he quit the team before his senior season when Syracuse participated in the NCAA Tournament for the first time, but indicated it was because of a racial quota. "They basically didn't want to start more than two blacks although nobody could outrun, outjump, or outshoot me," Brown said.... Excerpt from school guide: "Brownie is a powerfully built youth, who helps under the boards, and is an excellent shot as well."

FRANK BROYLES, Georgia Tech

Arkansas athletic director compiled 149-62-6 record in 20 seasons as head football coach at Missouri (1957) and Arkansas (1958–76). Guided 10 teams to bowl games, winning the AP and UPI national title in 1964.... Four-year starting

guard in basketball for Tech. Named to second five on the SEC All-Tournament team in 1944, 1945, and 1947. Second-leading scorer for Tech with a 10.4-point average as a senior in 1946–47.

BOB CAREY, Michigan State

Consensus All-American was captain and leading pass receiver on undefeated and untied 1951 MSU football team. First-round choice of the Los Angeles Rams in 1952 finished his NFL career with the Chicago Bears in 1958.... A forward-center in basketball, he averaged 8.8 points per game in three varsity seasons.... Excerpt from school guide: "Extremely fast for his size (6-5, 220). Ranks as finest all-around athlete in school history."

HAROLD CARMICHAEL, Southern (La.)

Wide receiver caught 590 passes for 8,985 yards and 79 touchdowns in 14-year career with the Philadelphia Eagles (1971–83) and Dallas Cowboys (1984). Four-time Pro Bowl Game participant established an NFL record for most consecutive games with a pass reception (127).... Former Southern basketball coach Dick Mack said Carmichael was a starter his last two seasons with the Jaguars and their top rebounder.

CHUCK CARNEY, Illinois

College Football Hall of Famer was a consensus All-American choice as an end in 1920. Only Illini athlete to earn All-American honors in both football and basketball.... The Helms Foundation named him to its 10-man All-American basketball teams for the 1919–20 and 1921–22 seasons and named him player of the year for the 1921–22 season. Led the Big Ten in scoring with 15.7 points per game in 1919-20 and 14.3 in 1921-22.... Sketch in *Spalding Official Basketball Guide*: "Possessed of reach, height, speed and a good eye for the basket, he had all the requisites of a star. No guard was able to hold him in check."

REG CAROLAN, Idaho

Played seven seasons (1962-68) in the NFL with the San Diego Chargers and Kansas City Chiefs as an offensive and defensive end. He was an eighth-round draft choice of the Los Angeles Rams in 1961. Caught 23 passes for 364 yards and five touchdowns. . . . The 6-6, 235-pounder played three varsity years (1960-62) with Idaho's basketball team, averaging four points and 4.7 rebounds per game.

RICK CASARES, Florida

Fullback for 12 NFL seasons (1955–66) with the Chicago Bears, Washington Redskins, and Miami Dolphins. Led league in rushing (1,136 yards) and touchdowns (14) in 1957. Ranks second on Bears career rushing list behind Walter Payton with 5,675 yards.... The 6-2, 205-pound forward led the Gators in scoring and rebounding in both of his varsity seasons—14.9 points and 11.3 rebounds as a sophomore in 1951–52 and 15.5 points and 11.5 rebounds as a junior in 1952–53.

LYNN CHANDNOIS, Michigan State

Halfback amassed 2,093 yards, 6.5-yard rushing average, 31 touchdowns and 20 interceptions. He was a unanimous All-American as a senior with the Spartans in 1949 when he averaged 6.9 yards per carry in 129 rushing attempts and returned seven pass interceptions for a nation-leading 183 yards. The three-time All-Pro played seven seasons with the Pittsburgh Steelers after entering the NFL as a first-round draft choice in 1950. The halfback accounted for over 1,500 yards in total offense in 1953. He returned three kickoffs for touchdowns en route to setting team records for kickoff return average in a career (29.6) and a single season (league-high 35.2 in 1952). Gale Sayers (30.6) is the only NFL player to finish his career with a higher kickoff return average than Chandnois, who also led the NFL in that category in 1951 (32.5). . . . The 6-

2 sophomore forward scored 15 points in 11 games for the school's basketball squad in 1946-47 and 1947-48.

SAM CLANCY, Pittsburgh

Defensive end had 49 sacks in his first 11 seasons in pro football with the Seattle Seahawks, Cleveland Browns, and Indianapolis Colts in the NFL and Pittsburgh and Memphis in the USFL. Played in two AFC championship games with the Browns.... The 6-7, 235-pound basketball center was a member of the gold-medal winning U.S. team in the 1979 Pan American Games. Averaged 14.4 points and 11.6 rebounds per game for Pitt from 1977–78 through 1980–81. Chosen in the third round of 1981 NBA draft by the Phoenix Suns after finishing his college career as the Panthers' all-time leading rebounder. Played 1981–82 season with Billings in the CBA, averaging 11.5 points and 8.3 rebounds per game.... Quote in school guide from West Virginia coach Gale Catlett: "Clancy is Superman in shorts. He's one of the best players I've seen and that includes some great ones."

EARL (DUTCH) CLARK, Colorado College

Member of College Football and Pro Football Halls of Fame. Halfback and quarterback was named to All-NFL team in six of his seven seasons with Portsmouth (1931–32) and Detroit (1934–38). Led NFL in scoring in 1932, 1935, and 1936. Player-coach of Detroit (1937–38) and head coach of Cleveland Rams (1939–42). First-team QB on the 1928 AP All-America team. Scored at least one touchdown in 21 consecutive college football games.... The 6-0, 180-pounder was an All-Rocky Mountain Conference choice in basketball all four seasons (first team as a freshman and senior, second team as a junior, and third team as a sophomore).... Sketch in *Spalding Official Guide*: "There isn't a man who could match Clark as a floor guard. The best dribbler ever to bounce a ball in the conference."

GEORGE CONNOR, Notre Dame

College Football and Pro Football Hall of Famer was Outland Trophy winner (outstanding interior lineman) as a tackle on Notre Dame's 1946 national championship team. Consensus All-American football choice in 1946 and 1947. Earned All-American honors as a tackle at Holy Cross in 1943 before transferring to Notre Dame. Played offensive and defensive tackle and linebacker with the Chicago Bears from 1948 through 1955, earning All-NFL first-team honors from 1949 through 1953.... Averaged 2.5 points per game as a 6-3, 225-pound center on the Irish's 1946–47 basketball team.

CHARLIE COWAN, New Mexico Highlands

Three-time Pro Bowl game participant was an offensive tackle for 15 seasons with the Los Angeles Rams (1961–75).... The 6-4, 260-pound basketball center averaging 15 points and 15.6 rebounds per game in his college career (20.7 points and 18.3 rebounds as a junior and 19.5 points and 18.3 rebounds as a senior).... Excerpt from school guide: "Rugged under the basket but moves with the grace of a cat playing at the post. He will drive the basket from either side and also has a good hook shot."

HERBERT (FRITZ) CRISLER, Chicago

College Football Hall of Famer compiled 116-32-9 record in 18 seasons as football coach at Minnesota (1930-31), Princeton (1932-37), and Michigan (1938-47). The only team he coached with a losing record was in his first year. His last seven Michigan teams finished in the top 10 in the final Associated Press Poll. The 1947 Wolverines had a 10-0 record, defeated Southern Cal in the Rose Bowl (49-0), and finished second in the final AP poll behind Notre Dame.... Named to third five on All-Big Ten basketball team in 1919–20 when the University of Chicago was a member of the league.

ED DANOWSKI, Fordham

All-American halfback in 1933. He completed 311 of 645 passes for 3,867 yards and 39 touchdowns, rushed 455 times for 1,232 yards and punted 31 times for 37.9-yard average in pro career with the New York Giants from 1934-

39 and 1941. Member of NFL champions in 1934 and 1938. Received NFL first-team all-league honors in 1935 and 1938.... Earned a letter with Fordham's basketball team in 1932-33.

ERNIE DAVIS, Syracuse

Heisman Trophy winner in 1961. Halfback was consensus All-American choice in 1960 and 1961 after Syracuse won the 1959 national championship. College Football Hall of Famer averaged 6.6 yards per carry and scored 35 touchdowns. Selected by the Washington Redskins as the first player picked in the 1962 NFL draft. His rights were acquired for the great Bobby Mitchell by the Cleveland Browns, who signed Davis that summer before he was diagnosed with leukemia. He never played in the NFL and died on May 18, 1963.... A 6-2, 205-pound forward on the 1960–61 Syracuse varsity basketball team, his rebound average (9.6) was highest on the team and his scoring average (10.2) ranked second.

GLENN DAVIS, Army

College Football Hall of Famer was a consensus All-American in 1944, 1945, and 1946. The 5-9, 170-pound halfback averaged 8.3 yards per carry and scored 59 touchdowns for Army teams that compiled a 34-2-2 record in his four seasons. Won Heisman Trophy in 1946 and was runner-up in 1944 and 1945. Played with the Los Angeles Rams in the NFL in 1950 and 1951.... Member of Army basketball teams as a junior in 1944–45 and as a senior in 1945–46.

LEN DAWSON, Purdue

Pro Football Hall of Famer completed 2,136 for 28,731 yards and 239 touchdowns in 19 seasons (1957–75) with the Cleveland Browns, Dallas Texans, and Kansas City Chiefs. Quarterbacked the Chiefs to victory over the Minnesota Vikings in Super Bowl following 1969 season.... Played in two games as a 6-0, 180-pound guard for Purdue's basketball team in the 1956–57 season.

VERN DEN HERDER, Central College

Defensive lineman played in four Super Bowls with the Miami Dolphins during his 12-year NFL career (1971–82). Starting defensive left end on undefeated 1972 Miami team (17-0).... The 6-6, 220-pound basketball center finished his four-season career at Central College as the Pella, Iowa-based school's all-time leading scorer (15.5 ppg) and rebounder (12.4 rpg). He grabbed a school-record 29 rebounds in a game his senior season (1970–71).

MIKE DITKA, Pittsburgh

College Football and Pro Football Hall of Famer is a network analyst and former coach of the Chicago Bears. The tight end caught 427 passes for 5,812 yards and 43 touchdowns in 12 NFL seasons (1961–72) with the Chicago Bears, Philadelphia Eagles, and Dallas Cowboys. Coached Super Bowl winner in 1985 season when Bears compiled an 18-1 overall record. Registered 112-68 mark in 11 years (1982–92) as coach of the Bears.... Played two seasons as a 6-2, 205-pound forward for the Panthers, averaging 2.8 points and 2.6 rebounds per game.... Sketch in school basketball guide: "A natural athlete who never quits. If Pitt wins a few games, there is a good chance he will be in the thick of things."

VINCE DOOLEY, Auburn

Won national championship in 1980 and six SEC titles as coach at Georgia. Compiled a 201-66-10 record as 20 teams played in bowl games in his 25 seasons (1964–88).... Averaged 6.3 points per game as a starting guard in 1951–52 in his only season of varsity basketball at Auburn before he concentrated on football.

JACK DUGGER, Ohio State

Consensus All-American end on the 1944 OSU football team that finished second behind Army in the final AP poll. Played pro football with three different franchises from 1946 to 1949.... Three-year letterman in basketball was a 6-4, 205-pound starting forward for the Buck-eyes' Final Four teams in 1944 and 1945. Played briefly for the Syracuse Nationals in the National Basketball League in 1946–47.

PETE ELLIOTT, Michigan

Pro Football Hall of Fame executive director earned All-American honors as a quarterback on the Wolverines' 1948 national champion. Former head coach at Nebraska (1956), California (1957–59) and Illinois (1960–66) led Cal, and the Illini to Rose Bowl berths.... A four-year starter as a 6-0, 190-pound guard on Michigan teams from 1945–46 through 1948–49. Captain of squad as a sophomore and member of Big Ten championship team in 1947–48. First-team all-conference choice as a junior and second-team selection as a senior. Second-team pick on Helms All-American team in 1947–48.... Excerpt from school guide: "At times his defensive work was almost uncanny as he held high-scoring opposition practically scoreless in several games. Outstanding at recovering rebounds."

RAY EVANS, Kansas

College Football Hall of Famer earned All-American honors as a back in 1942 and 1947 in a career interrupted by World War II. Led nation's major-college players in passes attempted (200) and completed (101) and interceptions (10) in 1942 for a rare triple crown. Played in NFL with the Pittsburgh Steelers in 1948 before becoming a prominent Kansas City bank official.... Four-year basketball letterman was the second-leading scorer in 1942 NCAA Tournament for the Jayhawks. Earned Helms Foundation All-American honors in 1941–42 and 1942–43.

WILBUR (WEEB) EWBANK, Miami of Ohio

Pro Football Hall of Famer is only head coach to win championships in both the NFL (Baltimore Colts in 1958 and 1959) and AFL (New York Jets in 1968).... Two-year basketball letterman at Miami (1926–27 and 1927–28) was head basketball coach at Brown University in 1946–47.

BEATTIE FEATHERS, Tennessee

Became first NFL player to rush for 1,000 yards or more in season when he had 1,004 yards (9.9 per carry) as a rookie with the Chicago Bears in 1934. College Football Hall of Famer was a consensus All-American halfback in 1933. Played seven seasons in the NFL with the Bears (1934–37), Brooklyn Dodgers (1938–39) and Green Bay Packers (1940).... Regular on the 1931–32 Volunteers' basketball squad.

WES FESLER, Ohio State

College Football Hall of Famer was consensus All-American end in 1928, 1929, and 1930. Named to Grantland Rice's all-time All-American team in 1939. Coach at Pittsburgh (1946), Ohio State (1947–50), and Minnesota (1951–53).... The 6-0, 185-pounder was a second-team All-Big Ten basketball selection as a sophomore and a first-team choice as a senior.

JIM FINKS, Tulsa

Recently deceased NFL executive was a defensive back and quarterback with the Pittsburgh Steelers (1949–55). Selected to the Pro Bowl following 1952 season after leading NFL in touchdown passes with 20. Led NFL in passes attempted (344), passes completed (165), and passing yardage (2,270) in 1955. Played with Calgary in the Canadian Football League in 1957.... The 6-0, 170-pound Finks was a four-year varsity basketball player at Tulsa, leading the team in scoring average as a sophomore with 8.9 points per game in 1946–47. Held school single-game scoring record at the time with 28 points against Drake.

ARNOLD GALIFFA, Army

College Football Hall of Famer was a consensus All-American selection in 1949 and fin-

ished fourth in voting for Heisman Trophy. Quarterback of Cadet teams that compiled a 31-2-3 record from 1946 through 1949. Played in the NFL and CFL.... Army's third-leading scorer in basketball as a freshman (6.2 points per game) and as a junior (9.1) before becoming second-leading scorer as a senior (9.2).... Served as an aide to Gen. Matthew Ridgeway and Gen. Mark Clark during the Korean War before becoming an executive with U.S. Steel.

PETE GENT, Michigan State

Flanker and tight end caught 68 passes for 989 yards and four touchdowns with the Dallas Cowboys from 1964–68.... Author of several novels, including *North Dallas Forty* and *The Franchise*. His most recent title is *The Conquering Heroes,* a cynical look at a fictional renegade college basketball program.... Averaged 17.4 points and 8.3 rebounds per game in leading the Spartans in scoring each of his three varsity seasons (1961–62 through 1963–64). The 6-4, 200-pound forward scored 34 points against Bowling Green State in his senior year when he ranked 62nd in the country in scoring with 21.1 ppg.... Excerpt from school guide: "Fine playmaker with excellent ability in shooting, driving, dribbling and passing. Hardnosed competitor."

GEORGE GIPP, Notre Dame

College Football Hall of Famer earned All-American football honors in 1919 and 1920. Legendary halfback scored 12 points in four games for the 1918–19 Irish basketball team.

OTTO GRAHAM, Northwestern

Member of College Football and Pro Football Halls of Fame. Quarterback earned All-American honors and finished third in Heisman Trophy voting as a senior in 1943. Played 10 seasons (1946–55) with the Cleveland Browns and led team to championship game each year (All-American Football Conference from 1946 to 1949 and NFL from 1950 to 1955). Compiled a 105-17-4 record in regular-season pro competition, completing 1,464 of 2,626 passes for 23,584 yards and 174 touchdowns.... Played three seasons of varsity basketball, finishing second in the Big Ten in scoring as a sophomore (13.1 points per game) and as a junior (15.8). The 6-0 forward earned second-team All-Big Ten honors in 1941–42 and first five honors in 1942–43. Also played for Colgate as a senior. NCAA consensus first-team All-American in 1944 and second-team All-American in 1943. Left Northwestern with the highest scoring total in school history with more than 600 points. Played one season with the Rochester Royals in the National Basketball League, averaging 5.2 points per game for the 1945–46 squad that won the NBL title.

HARRY (BUD) GRANT, Minnesota

Former NFL and CFL end and coach. Played with Philadelphia in the NFL from 1951 to 1952 and Winnipeg of the CFL from 1953 to 1956. Caught 88 passes for 4,197 yards and 20 touchdowns in six pro seasons, leading the CFL in pass receptions in 1953, 1954, and 1956. Coached Winnipeg in the CFL (1957–66) and Minnesota in the NFL (1967–85). Coach of four CFL champions and four NFL Super Bowl teams.... Third-leading scorer for the Gophers' basketball squad in 1948–49 (8.5 points per game) after being named team MVP the previous season over first-team All-American Jim McIntyre. Finished 13th in the Big Ten in scoring in 1946–47 with a 9.3 average. Played two seasons in the NBA, including a rookie year when he was a member of the Minneapolis Lakers' 1950 championship team.

CORNELL GREEN, Utah State

Intercepted 34 passes in 13 years as a defensive back with the Dallas Cowboys (1962–74). Played in five Pro Bowl games and two Super Bowls.... Finished his three-year varsity career as Utah State's all-time leading scorer with 1,890 points. The 6-4 forward led the Aggies in scoring

with 21.2 points per game in 1959–60 (34th in the nation), 20.3 in 1960–61 (57th) and 25.6 in 1961–62 (13th). Held under 10 points only once in college career and scored 46 against New Mexico on March 3, 1962. The school's all-time leading rebounder set a single-season record with 403 boards in 1959–60. Helms Foundation second-team All-American as a senior, when he averaged 24.3 points per game in three NCAA Tournament contests.... Review of his career in school guide: "He had an array of moves and shots that ranged from quick reverse pivots under the hoop to overpowering physical strength as a rebounder and tap shot artist."

BOB GRIESE, Purdue

TV analyst and member of College Football and Pro Football Halls of Fame. Quarterback played 14 seasons (1967–80) with the Miami Dolphins, completing 1,926 of 3,429 passes for 25,093 yards and 192 touchdowns. Played in six Pro Bowl games and three Super Bowls.... As a 6-1, 185-pound sophomore guard in 1964–65, he scored 22 points in 16 games in his only varsity basketball season with the Boilermakers.

GEORGE HALAS, Illinois

Pro Football Hall of Famer compiled a 324-151-31 record as an NFL coach, guiding the Chicago Bears to seven NFL titles. His 40-year NFL coaching career also included stints with the Decatur/ Chicago Staleys.... The 6-0, 175-pound Halas was a starting guard for the Illini team that won the Big Ten basketball title in 1916–17 with a 10-2 record.

He was captain of the squad the next season before entering the armed forces.

DALE HALL, Army

Successor to legendary Red Blaik as football coach at Army. Compiled w4-4-1, 6-3-1 and 6-4 records from 1959 to 1961.… Named college basketball player of the year by *The Sporting News* in 1943–44 when he was the leading scorer (18.2 points per game) for a Cadet team that compiled a 15-0 record and was ranked No. 1 in the nation by the Dick Dunkel rankings. The next season as a senior, he was the team scoring leader (14.2 ppg) for a 14-1 squad. NCAA consensus second-team All-American in 1944 and 1945. Recipient of the Army Athletic Association trophy presented annually to the man who renders "the most valuable service to athletics during his cadet career."

VIC HANSON, Syracuse

Consensus All-American end in 1926 served as head football coach at his alma mater from 1930 through 1936, compiling a 33-21-5 record, including a 7-1-1 mark in 1931.… Forward was named to Helms Athletic Foundation 10-man All-American basketball teams selected in 1943 for the 1924–25, 1925–26, and 1926–27 seasons. Naismith Memorial Hall of Famer was designated college basketball player of the year by Helms in his senior season.

WAYNE HARDIN, Pacific

Head football coach at U.S. Naval Academy (1959–64) and Temple (1970–82). Coached Heisman Trophy winner Roger Staubach in 1963 when Navy finished second in the nation in the final AP poll with a 9-2 record.… Letterman on four Pacific basketball teams in the late 1940s.

KEVIN HARDY, Notre Dame

Defensive end and tackle for four seasons in the NFL with three different teams. Two-time All-American with the Irish, including 1966 as a junior on the school's national championship football team.… The 6-5, 260-pound forward-center averaged 2.1 points and 2.3 rebounds per game in his one season of basketball (1964–65).

TOM HARMON, Michigan

Two-time consensus All-American halfback won Heisman Trophy in 1940. Played two seasons (1946 and 1947) with the Los Angeles Rams following World War II military service.… Averaged 7.6 points per game as a sophomore in 1938–39 and led the Wolverines in scoring in five contests. Posted 2.5-point average the next year as a junior.… Michigan coach Bennie Oosterbaan said Harmon "had a great fake and cut, a great shot, and aggressiveness."

HOWARD (RED) HICKEY, Arkansas

Coach of San Francisco 49ers (1959–63) after playing end for the Cleveland and Los Angeles Rams (1941–42, 1945–48). Finished sixth in the NFL in pass receptions in 1941. Member of the Rams' 1945 NFL title team.… The 6-2, 195-pound guard was a second-team All-Southwest Conference choice as a sophomore and junior and a first-team selection as a senior. He was a member of the 1941 team that won the SWC title with a 12-0 record, finished 20-3 overall, and reached the Final Four in its NCAA Tournament debut.

ELROY (CRAZY LEGS) HIRSCH, Wisconsin/Michigan

Member of College Football and Pro Football Halls of Fame. Played halfback, defensive back, and offensive end as a pro with the Chicago Rockets of the All-American Football Conference and Los Angeles Rams of the NFL. Caught 387 passes and scored 66 touchdowns as a pro. Played in four NFL championship games.… Starting center for the Wolverines' basketball team while undergoing military training there.… Sketch in Michigan guide: "Naval transfer from Wisconsin was a big aid, chiefly through his flaming competitive spirit."

PAUL HORNUNG, Notre Dame

College Football and Pro Football Hall of Famer earned All-American honors as a quarterback in 1955 and 1956. Won Heisman Trophy as a senior after finishing fifth as a junior. Played nine seasons as a halfback with the Green Bay Packers, leading the NFL in scoring in 1959, 1960, and 1961. Played in five NFL championship games.... Played varsity basketball for the Irish as a sophomore, averaging 6.1 points per game in 10 contests.

PERCY HOWARD, Austin Peay State

Wide receiver failed to catch a pass in eight regular-season games for the Dallas Cowboys in 1975, but caught a 34-yard touchdown pass from Roger Staubach for their final TD in a 21-17 loss to the Pittsburgh Steelers in Super Bowl X.... Averaged 12.4 points and 7.3 rebounds per game in three varsity seasons (1972–73 through 1974–75) for the Governors as a 6-4, 215-pound forward. He averaged seven points and seven rebounds per game in four NCAA Tournament contests in 1973 and 1974 as a teammate of the celebrated James "Fly" Williams.

JIM LEE HOWELL, Arkansas

New York Giants end (1937–42, 1946–48) and head coach (1954–60). Started for them in four NFL championship games, including 1938 titlist. Coach of Giants team that routed the Chicago Bears, 47-7, in 1956 NFL title game. Also guided New York to 1958 and 1959 NFL championship games.... A 6-5, 200-pounder, he was named to the first five on the All-Southwest Conference team in his senior season (1935–36) as a member of an Arkansas squad that won the league title, compiled a 24-3 record and participated in the U.S. Olympic basketball trials.

JOHNNY JOHNSON, San Jose State

Rushed for 3,147 yards in his first four seasons in the NFL. Played first three pro years with the Phoenix Cardinals before he was traded to the New York Jets and led the Jets in rush-

ing in 1993. Appeared in Pro Bowl following rookie season. As a junior at San Jose State in 1988, he was the first player in NCAA history to rush for more than 1,200 yards (1,219) and catch at least 60 passes (61) in a single season.... Averaged 11.2 points and 6.5 rebounds per game as a 6-3, 210-pound junior forward in 1988–89. Led the Spartans in scoring (23 points) and rebounding (12) in a 95-66 loss to UNLV.

ED (TOO TALL) JONES, Tennessee State

Defensive lineman with the Dallas Cowboys for 15 seasons (1974–78, 1980–89). Appeared in three Super Bowls and three Pro Bowl games.... He was a 6-8, 230-pound backup post player when he averaged 1.7 points and 2.6 rebounds for the Tigers in his freshman and sophomore seasons (1969–70 and 1970–71).

RALPH (SHUG) JORDAN, Auburn

Compiled a 176-83-6 record as head football coach at his alma mater from 1951 to 1975. Led Auburn to berths in 12 bowl games and an AP national title in 1957 with a 10-0 record.... Three-year basketball letterman was captain of the team in his junior season (1930–31).

JOE KAPP, California

Quarterback with Calgary (1959–60) and Vancouver (1961–66) in the Canadian Football League and Minnesota (1967–69) and Boston (1970) in the NFL. Member of CFL Hall of Fame. Passed for 28,836 yards and 194 touchdowns in his pro career. Finished fifth in Heisman Trophy voting in 1958 when he led Cal to a Rose Bowl berth.... The Bears won Pacific Coast Conference titles both years (1956–57 and 1957–58) when he was a 6-3, 195-pound backup forward.... Sketch in school guide: "Powerfully built player has an excellent long jump shot."

LARRY KELLEY, Yale

Heisman Trophy winner in 1936. End earned All-American football honors in 1934, 1935, and 1936.... The 6-1, 190-pound swingman finished 12th in the Eastern Intercollegiate League in scoring in 1935–36 and was seventh in the league in scoring the next season. Honorable mention on all-league team as a junior.

GLENN KILLINGER, Penn State

College Football Hall of Famer was a 1921 consensus All-American as a quarterback-halfback. He played in the NFL with the Canton Bulldogs (1921) and New York Giants (1926).... Three-year basketball letterman on teams that compiled an overall record of 37-5. Captain of team as a senior in 1920–21.

BILLY KILMER, UCLA

Quarterback with the San Francisco 49ers, New Orleans Saints, and Washington Redskins (1961–62, 1964, 1966, 1967–78).... Scored eight points in six games for coach John Wooden's 1959–60 UCLA basketball team.... Excerpt from school guide: "Tried basketball, but his football ankle failed to allow him to perform at his best."

NILE KINNICK, Iowa

Heisman Trophy winner as a quarterback-halfback in 1939 when he rushed and passed for 1,012 yards, intercepted eight passes, punted for a 39.9-yard average, and averaged 11.9 yards on punt returns and 25.1 yards on kickoff returns. Phi Beta Kappa graduate was selected by the Philadelphia Eagles in the first round of 1940 NFL draft.... Bypassed pro football to attend law school. He was killed in a plane crash in 1943 while serving in the Navy during World War II.... The 5-8, 165-pounder played basketball for Iowa during his sophomore year, averaging 6.1 points per game as the team's second-leading scorer.

TERRY KIRBY, Virginia

Miami Dolphins running back started as a rookie and was their leading pass receiver and second-leading rusher after being a third-round pick in the 1993 NFL draft. Set Virginia career rushing record with 3,348 yards on 567 carries.... Averaged 3.4 points per game as a freshman in 1989–90 and 2.1 as a sophomore in 1990–91. Scored 18 points in seven minutes of playing time (hitting 8 of 10 field-goal attempts) against North Carolina State on January 31, 1990.

RON KRAMER, Michigan

Offensive end for 10 seasons (1957 and 1959–67) with Green Bay Packers and Detroit Lions. Caught 229 passes for 3,272 yards and 16 touchdowns in the NFL.... The 6-3, 220-pound forward-center led the Wolverines in scoring as a sophomore (16 points per game) and as a junior (20.4) before finishing second on the team as a senior (14.5). Second-team All-American selection by Converse and third-team pick by National Association of Basketball Coaches as a senior.... Excerpt from school guide: "Can leap and battle as well as shoot, and he's an inspirational type of player who picks up his teammates when he's in there."

JOHN LATTNER, Notre Dame

Consensus All-American halfback won Heisman Trophy in 1953 after finishing fifth in the Heisman voting the previous year. College Football Hall of Famer helped the Irish compile a 23-4-2 record in his three varsity football seasons (1951–53). Played with the Pittsburgh Steelers in the NFL in 1954 before suffering a career-ending knee injury while in military service.... Scored 12 points in four games for the 1951–52 Notre Dame basketball team as a 6-2 forward.

ELMER LAYDEN, Notre Dame

College Football Hall of Famer was a fullback in the famed Four Horseman backfield of the 1920s. Consensus All-American selection in 1924. Head football coach of the Irish from 1934 through 1940, compiling a 47-12-2 record. His 1938 Notre Dame team was named national champion by the Dickinson System.... NFL commissioner from 1941–46.... Scored seven points in 10 games for the 1922–23 Notre Dame basketball squad.

DAVE LOGAN, Colorado

Wide receiver caught 263 passes for 4,250 yards and 24 touchdowns in nine seasons (1976–84) with the Cleveland Browns and Denver Broncos.... Averaged 14.1 points and 6.3 rebounds per game in 58 varsity basketball games for the Buffaloes from 1972–73 through 1975–76 (missed 1974–75 because of a knee injury). Team's second-leading scorer as both a sophomore and senior.

JOHN LUJACK, Notre Dame

Heisman Trophy winner in 1947 after finishing third in voting the previous year. In his three years as quarterback, the College Football Hall of Famer helped the Irish win a national championship each season and a 26-1-1 record overall. Was quarterback, defensive back, and kicker for the Chicago Bears from 1948 through 1951, leading them in scoring all four years. He intercepted a team-high eight passes as a rookie and holds the franchise record for most passing yards in a game with 468 in a 1949 contest.... Averaged 3.4 points per game as a starting guard for Notre Dame's basketball team in 1943–44.

LAMAR LUNDY, Purdue

Member of the "Fearsome Foursome" for the Los Angeles Rams in his 13–year NFL career (1957-69).... He averaged 10.5 points and 8.5 rebounds per game in three varsity seasons, leading the Boilermakers in rebounding as a junior and senior. He finished 30th in the country in field-goal shooting (48.1 percent) in 1957.... Sketch in school guide: "The most improved player in the Big Ten. The 6-6, 225-pound Lundy was more often than not the equal of or better than opposing centers reaching 6-8 or 6-9. His unusual speed and defensive ability make him a valuable asset."

BOB MacLEOD, Dartmouth

College Football Hall of Famer was consensus All-American halfback in 1938 when he finished fourth in Heisman Trophy voting. Three-year letterman on Dartmouth football teams that compiled a 21-3-3 record under the legendary Red Blaik. Selected by Brooklyn in the first round of the 1939 NFL draft.... Ranked among the Eastern Intercollegiate League's top 20 scorers all three years in college for Dartmouth teams that won the league his last two seasons. Named to first five on all-league team as a senior and second team as a junior.

JACK (CY) McCLAIREN, Bethune-Cookman

Split end with the Pittsburgh Steelers from 1955 through 1960. Finished third in the NFL in pass receptions with 46 in 1957.... A 6-4, 210-pound forward-center in basketball, he was a two-time All-Southern Intercollegiate Athletic Conference selection. In the championship game of the 1953 SIAC tourney, he scored 36 points to lead his team to victory over Xavier of New Orleans. Served as head basketball coach at his alma mater for 31 seasons before retiring following the 1992–93 campaign.

BANKS McFADDEN, Clemson

College Football Hall of Famer became Clemson's first football All-American in 1939. The halfback finished eighth in the Heisman Trophy voting that year. Selected by the Brooklyn Dodgers in the first round (third player overall) of the 1940 NFL draft. Finished fourth in rushing in the NFL in 1940, averaging 6.3 yards per carry, before entering military service.... Led Clemson in scoring in each of his three seasons on his way to becoming the school's first All-American basketball player. The 6-3, 175-pound center was named to the first five on the Southern Conference all-tournament team three times.

KEITH McKELLER, Jacksonville (Ala.) State

Buffalo Bills tight end has played in four Super Bowl games.... Starting center on Jacksonville State's 1985 NCAA Division II championship team. Led Gulf South Conference in rebounding each of his first three seasons and finished second as a senior. Four-time all-league pick averaged 12.5 points and 10.1 rebounds per game in his career (1982–83 through 1985–86).

GEORGE MARTIN, Oregon

Defensive end who played 14 seasons (1975–88) with the New York Giants. Started for the 1986 Giants team that defeated the Denver Broncos, 39-20, in the Super Bowl. Scored six touchdowns in his NFL career (84-yard run with blocked field goal, three pass interception returns, and two runs with fumble recoveries).... The 6-5, 225-pound forward-center averaged just over 10 points and 10 rebounds per game for the Ducks' freshman squad in 1971–72. He played briefly for the varsity the next season.

PETE METZELAARS, Wabash (Ind.)

Tight end played in five AFC championship games and four Super Bowls in his 13-year career (1982–94) with the Seattle Seahawks and Buffalo Bills. He led the Bills with 68 receptions in 1993.... As a 6-8, 235-pound center at Wabash, he averaged 19.2 points and 11.4 rebounds per game in four varsity seasons. Set NCAA Division III field-goal shooting records for a single season (75.3 percent in 1981–82 as a senior) and career (72.4). Led Wabash to the 1982 Division III Tournament title, scoring a tourney record 129 points in five games and earning tourney outstanding player honors. Collected 45 points and 13 rebounds in the championship game.

DON MILLER, Notre Dame

Halfback in Irish's famous "Four Horsemen" backfield. College Football Hall of Famer earned All-American honors in 1923 and 1924. Former president of the U.S. Attorney's Association was a longtime judge and attorney in Ohio.... Played for Notre Dame's basketball team in 1922–23 and 1923–24.

GEORGE MUSSO, Millikin (Ill.)

Pro Football Hall of Famer played for seven divisional winners and four NFL title teams. The 6-2, 270-pound guard and tackle played for 12 seasons (1933–44) with the Chicago Bears. As a collegian, he played against future president Ronald Reagan, who attended Eureka. As a member of the Bears in 1935, Musso played against future president Gerald Ford in the Bears-College All-Star Game in Chicago.... Three-year basketball letterman in college.

ERNIE NEVERS, Stanford

Member of College Football and Pro Football Halls of Fame. He was a consensus All-American selection as a senior fullback in 1925 before playing in the NFL with the Duluth Eskimos (1926–27) and Chicago Cardinals (1929–31). Set NFL record with a 40-point game against the Chicago Bears in 1929.... Compiled a 6-12 pitching record in three seasons (1926–28) with the St. Louis Browns.... Lettered in basketball at Stanford as a sophomore and junior. Named to the All-Pacific Coast Conference second five as a junior.... Historians say he was a fine shooter, an excellent dribbler, tough on defense, and generally a terrifying figure for the opposition. The *Spalding Basketball Guide* said: "He is almost as good a basketball player as he is a football star. With his speed, weight and general all-around ability, he was a stellar performer."

GIFFORD NIELSEN, Brigham Young

Quarterback finished sixth in Heisman Trophy voting in 1976. In three seasons at BYU (1975–77), he completed 415 of 708 passes for 5,833 yards and 55 touchdowns. Played six seasons in the NFL with the Houston Oilers (1978–83).... The 6-5, 190-pound forward-guard averaged 6.5 points and 2.7 rebounds per game in 44 varsity contests during the 1973–74 and 1974–75 seasons. Fourth-leading scorer on 1974–75 squad with an 8.7 average.

ELMER OLIPHANT, Purdue/Army

One of the legendary athletes in the history of college sports. Earned nine letters (three in football and two each in basketball, baseball, and track) at Purdue before graduating in 1914. Won 12 letters at Army (U.S. Military Academy) in football, basketball, baseball, track, boxing, and hockey before graduating in 1918. Consensus All-American halfback in 1916 and 1917.... The 5-7, 175-pound Oliphant was named to the 10-man All-American basketball teams selected in 1957 by the Helms Foundation for the 1913–14 and 1914–15 seasons.... *Spalding's Official Basketball Guide* called him "the fastest and most aggressive floor worker in the conference."

BENNIE OOSTERBAAN, Michigan

College Football Hall of Famer coached Michigan's football team to a 63-33-4 record in 11 seasons (1948-58). His first team finished with a 9-0 record and was voted national champion in the AP poll. Won Big Ten titles in 1948, 1949, and 1950.... In 1943, the Helms Athletic Foundation named him to its 10-man All-American basketball teams it selected for the 1926–27 and 1927–28 seasons. Finished third in Big Ten scoring in 1926–27 (9.3 points per game) and led conference as a senior the next year (10.8 ppg).

R. C. OWENS, College of Idaho

Split end caught 206 passes for 3,285 yards and 22 touchdowns in his eight seasons (1957–64) with the San Francisco 49ers, Baltimore Colts, and New York Giants. Gained fame as the receiver on "Alley-Oop" pass play in which he made receptions by leaping high above pass defenders. Became the first 49er to gain 1,000 yards on pass receptions in a season when he caught 55 passes for 1,032 yards in 1961.... The 6-3, 195-pound center had three standout basketball seasons. He averaged 23.5 points and 27.1 rebounds per game in 1952–53 and finished third in the nation among NCAA small college rebounders. Led in rebounding the next season with 27.1 per game while also averaging 23.5 points. In 1954–55, on a team that also included all-time great Elgin Baylor (31.3 ppg and 20.5 rpg), Owens averaged 18.1 ppg and 21.3 rpg. Owens was named to AAU All–American team in 1956-57 as a member of the Seattle Buchan Bakers.

ARA PARSEGHIAN, Miami of Ohio

College Football Hall of Famer compiled a 170-58-6 record as coach at Miami of Ohio (1951–55), Northwestern (1956–63), and Notre Dame (1964–74). Guided Notre Dame to three national football titles (1964, 1966, and 1973). Halfback on Cleveland Browns team that won All-American Football Conference title in 1948.... Played for Miami basketball squads in 1946–47 and 1947–48.

JOE PATERNO, Brown

Penn State's head coach since 1966 guided the Nittany Lions to national championships in 1983 and 1986. Entering 1994, he had compiled a 257-69-3 record, including a 15-8-1 record in bowl games.... He earned varsity basketball letters at Brown in 1947–48 and 1948–49. His 7.3-points-per-game scoring average in 1947–48 was second highest on the team.

HAL PATTERSON, Kansas

Canadian Football League Hall of Famer averaged 20.6 yards per pass reception in his 14-year career with 460 catches for 9,473 yards and 64 touchdowns. He also played defensive back for Montreal and Hamilton.... Named to NJCAA All-Tournament team in 1952 when he averaged 20 points per game for Garden City (Kan.) before enrolling at Kansas. The 6-1, 185-pound forward averaged 9.5 ppg in 1952–53 for the Jayhawks' NCAA runner-up and averaged 11.2 ppg the next season. Excerpt from school guide: "Fierce battler. Exceptionally high jumper under the backboards. Good close range shooter."

PRESTON PEARSON, Illinois

Did not play college football, but rushed for 3,609 yards in 941 carries, caught 254 passes for 3,095 yards, and returned 114 kickoffs for 2,801 yards in 14 NFL seasons (1967–80) with the Baltimore Colts, Pittsburgh Steelers, and Dallas Cowboys. Played in five Super Bowl games.... Guard-forward averaged 8.7 points and six rebounds per game as a senior in 1966–67 to finish his three-year varsity career with 5.2 ppg and

3.6 rpg.... Excerpt from school guide: "Aggressive, scrappy play made him a crowd favorite. Although he's not big (6-1, 190) by present basketball standards, Preston is one of the strongest men in any game."

DICK PLASMAN, Vanderbilt

Member of two NFL championship teams with the Chicago Bears (1940 and 1941) and one with the Chicago Cardinals (1947). Led Bears in pass receptions in 1939 and 1941.... Starter as 6-5 center on basketball team in 1934–35 and 1935–36. Named to the second five on the 1936 SEC All-Tournament team.

ART POWELL, San Jose State

Offensive end caught 512 passes for 8,699 yards and 85 touchdowns in 11 seasons (1957, 1959–68) in the Canadian Football League, AFL, and NFL. Led AFL in pass reception yards in 1962 and 1963 and in touchdowns on pass receptions in 1960 (14) and 1963 (16). Played in four AFL All-Star Games. Led the nation's major-college players in pass receptions as a sophomore in 1956 with 40 before signing CFL contract the next year.... The 6-2, 190-pound forward averaged 10.5 points and 8.2 rebounds per game in nine contests for the Spartans varsity basketball team in 1956–57.

GREG PRUITT, Oklahoma

Consensus All-American running back was third in the Heisman Trophy voting in 1971 and second in 1972. Rushed for 5,672 yards in 12 seasons (1973–84) with the Cleveland Browns and Los Angeles Raiders.... A 5-10, 180-pound guard in basketball, he averaged 13.3 points per game in three contests for the 1969–70 Sooners freshman team before concentrating on football.

RAY RAMSEY, Bradley

Offensive and defensive halfback in the All-America Football Conference from 1947 through 1949 with three different franchises (Chicago Rockets, Brooklyn Dodgers, and Chicago Hornets) before playing in the NFL for four seasons from 1950 through 1953 with the Chicago Cardinals. Led the Rockets in pass receptions, punt returns, kickoff returns, and scoring and finished second in rushing as a rookie in 1947. Tied for second in the NFL in pass interceptions with 10 in his final season.... Led Bradley's basketball team in scoring in 1941–42 (12.3 ppg) and 1942–43 (13.3 ppg) before having his career interrupted by World War II. He was captain of the Braves' 1946–47 squad that compiled a 25-7 record.

WAYNE RASMUSSEN, South Dakota State

Defensive back intercepted 16 passes for 189 yards in nine seasons (1964–72) with the Detroit Lions.... A guard in basketball, he averaged 11.6 points per game in three varsity seasons. He was named MVP in the eight-team 1963 NCAA College Division Tournament after scoring a tourney high 56 points in three games to lead the Jackrabbits to the national title.... Excerpt from school guide: "An intense competitor, he's at his best when the chips are down and the going is toughest. Ability to start quickly and shift immediately into full speed are assets that make him a strong driver. He plays tall for his height (6-1)."

GEORGE RATTERMAN, Notre Dame

Quarterback with Buffalo in the All-American Football Conference, New York Yankees and Cleveland Browns in the NFL, and Montreal Alouettes in the CFL. Played in AAFC championship game in 1948 and NFL championship games in 1953, 1954, and 1955. Second-team QB on Notre Dame's 1946 national championship football team.... Third-leading scorer with 11.7 points per game as 6-0 forward on 1944–45 Irish basketball team that compiled a 15-5 record and 8.6 ppg on 1945–46 squad that went 17-4. Scored 4.9 ppg as a senior reserve. In 1945–46, he scored Notre Dame's last 11 points in a 56-47 upset of Kentucky club that finished with a 28-2 mark.... Sketch in school guide: "Considered one of the 'slickest' players in college ball."

PAT RICHTER, Wisconsin

Tight end with Washington Redskins for nine seasons after being their first-round pick in

the 1962 NFL draft. Caught 99 passes for 1,315 yards and 14 touchdowns and averaged 41.9 yards per punt on 338 punts for the Redskins. Consensus football All-American in 1962 at Wisconsin, where he is now the athletic director. Led school's baseball team in hits, home runs, and RBIs for three consecutive seasons.... Three-year letterman in basketball collected 103 points and 145 rebounds in 38 games as a 6-5, 230-pound center.

ANDRE RISON, Michigan State

Wide receiver averaged almost 80 receptions per year in his first five seasons in the NFL with the Indianapolis Colts (1989) and Atlanta Falcons (1990–93). Played in four Pro Bowl games in that span, leading the Falcons in pass receptions (fourth in NFL with 86) and touchdowns (15) in 1993.... The 6-1, 185-pound guard in basketball, was a backup for the Spartans in two seasons (1985–86 and 1987–88).

GENE RONZANI, Marquette

Halfback-quarterback with the Chicago Bears for eight seasons and coach of the Green Bay Packers from 1950–53. Played in three NFL championship games (1933, 1934, and 1937). Led Bears in passing in 1934 and in rushing in 1935.... A 5-10 guard in basketball, he was the Warriors' fourth-leading scorer in 1931–32 (3.8 points per game) and third-leading scorer in 1932–33 (3.5 ppg).

BOBBY ROSS, Virginia Military Institute

Compiled a 39-25 record in his first four seasons as coach of the San Diego Chargers (1992-95), leading them to AFC Western Division titles in 1992 and 1994 with 11-5 marks and a spot in the Super Bowl following the 1994 campaign (49-26 loss to the San Francisco 49ers). Regis-

Football was—and continues to be—Andre Rison's forte, but he did spend some time as a backup guard for the Michigan State Spartans in the mid-1980s.

tered a 90-74 record in 15 seasons as a college head coach for The Citadel, Maryland and Georgia Tech. His 1990 Georgia Tech squad won UPI national title by finishing with a 11-0-1 mark.... The 5-10, 160-pound Ross averaged three points per game as a freshman for the 1955-56 VMI varsity basketball team.

OTTO SCHNELLBACHER, Kansas

Defensive back intercepted 34 passes in four pro seasons. Led AAFC with 11 interceptions for the New York Yankees in 1948 and led NFL with 11 in 1951 for the New York Giants. Named to All-NFL team in 1951 by AP and UPI.... Averaged 11 points per game in four-year basketball career at Kansas, earning All-Big Six/Seven Conference honors each season. The 6-3, 180-pound forward ranked second on the school's career scoring list when his career ended at the conclusion of the 1947–48 campaign. Averaged 6.4 ppg in 43 games for the Providence Steamrollers and St. Louis Bombers as a rookie in the Basketball Association of America the next season.

WEAR SCHOONOVER, Arkansas

End was Arkansas' initial football first-team All-American (Grantland Rice in 1929).... All-SWC basketball selection in 1928, 1929, and 1930 when the Razorbacks extended their streak of league titles to five in a row. Selected as a senior to the second five on *College Humor Magazine*'s All-American team.

JOE SENSER, West Chester (Pa.) State

Tight end caught 165 passes for 1,822 yards and touchdowns in four-year career (1980–82, 1984) with the Minnesota Vikings. Selected for the Pro Bowl following the 1981 season in which he caught 79 passes for 1,004 yards and eight touchdowns.... Averaged 11.4 points and 7.4 rebounds per game and shot 66.2 percent from the floor in his four-year college basketball career as a 6-5, 230-pound center. Led NCAA Division I in field-goal shooting in 1976–77 (69.9 percent) and 1977–78 (68.5).

ART SHELL, Maryland-Eastern Shore

Pro Football Hall of Famer has been head coach of the Los Angeles Raiders since 1989. Offensive tackle for the Raiders from 1968 to 1982 played in eight Pro Bowl games.... Two-year basketball letterman as a 6-5, 265-pound center at school that was then known as Maryland State College.... Sketch from school guide: "Pure muscle. Amazing agility. Uncompromising under the boards, nobody pushes big Art without a battle."

VERNON (CATFISH) SMITH, Georgia

College Football Hall of Famer was a consensus All-American end as a senior in 1931. Scored all of Georgia's points and was a standout on defense in a shocking 15-0 upset of Yale in his sophomore season.... Three-year basket-

ball letterman was senior captain and starting center on Bulldogs team that defeated Duke in the semifinals and North Carolina in the final to win the 1932 Southern Conference Tournament. Named to second five on the all-tourney team.

NORMAN SNEAD, Wake Forest

The first-round draft choice played for five NFL teams (Washington Redskins, Philadelphia Eagles, Minnesota Vikings, New York Giants and San Francisco 49ers) during a 16-year career (1961-76) that saw him play in three Pro Bowl games. He completed 2,276 of 4,353 passes for 30,797 yards and 196 touchdowns. Snead led the NFL in pass completion percentage in 1972 (60.3%). The only Wake Forest quarterback to earn All-American honors was first team All-ACC in 1959 and 1960 as a junior and senior when he led the league in passing and total offense. Snead passed for a career-high 424 yards for Washington against Pittsburgh in 1963. He led the NFL in passing for the Giants in 1972 with 2,307 yards. . . . Played in four basketball games as a senior, averaging 7.8 points and three rebounds per game. He shot 61.8 percent from the floor (13 of 21). Two of his teammates were All-American Len Chappell and CBS announcer-to-be Billy Packer.

J. NEIL (SKIP) STAHLEY, Penn State

Head football coach for Delaware (1934), Brown (1941–43), George Washington (1946–47), Toledo (1948–49) and Idaho (1954–60). Backfield coach of the NFL's Chicago Cardinals in 1953.... Leading scorer for Penn State's basketball team in 1928–29 and captain of the squad the next season.

ROGER STAUBACH, Navy

College Football and Pro Football Hall of Famer won Heisman Trophy in 1963. Passed for 3,571 yards and rushed for 682 in his career at Navy (1961–64). Quarterback in four Super Bowls during his 11 seasons with the Dallas Cowboys. Five-time Pro Bowl player passed for 22,700 yards and 153 touchdowns.... Averaged 9.3 points per game for the 1961–62 Navy plebe (freshman) basketball team. The 6-2, 190-pound forward scored five points in four games for Midshipmen varsity squad the next season.

JOE STYDAHAR, West Virginia

Member of College Football and Pro Football Halls of Fame. Earned All-American honors as a 6-4, 230-pound tackle in 1935. Played nine seasons (1936–42, 1945–46) with the Chicago Bears after being their first-round pick in the first NFL draft in 1936. Named to All-NFL team four times from 1937 through 1940. Coached Los Angeles Rams (1950–51) and Chicago Cardinals (1953–54), leading Rams to 1951 NFL title.... Four-year basketball letterman was captain of the Mountaineers' 1934–35 team that compiled a 16-6 record. Selected to the first five on West Virginia's Pre-World War II team that was named as part of the university's all-time basketball squad.

HUGH (BONES) TAYLOR, Tulane/Okla. City

Offensive end caught 272 passes for 5,233 yards and 58 touchdowns in eight seasons (1947–54) with the Washington Redskins. Led NFL in average per reception in 1950 (21.4 yards) and 1952 (23.4) and in touchdown receptions (nine) in 1949. Led Redskins in pass receptions from 1949 through 1954. Coach of Houston Oilers in the AFL in 1965.... Lettered in basketball for Tulane and Oklahoma City, leading OCU in scoring as a senior with 11.4 points per game.

LIONEL TAYLOR, New Mexico Highlands

First player in pro football history to catch 100 passes in a season holds the all-time AFL record for most pass receptions in a career with 587 as a wide receiver for the Denver Broncos (1960–66) and Houston Oilers (1967–68). Led AFL in pass receptions in 1960 (92), 1961 (100), 1962 (77), 1963 (78), and 1965 (85). Caught 13 passes in a single game in 1964.... The 6-2, 205-pounder averaged 16 points per game during his basketball career, leading the team in scoring average with 13.6 ppg in 1955–56 and 20.3 in 1956–57.

OTIS TAYLOR, Prairie View

Wide receiver caught 410 passes for 7,306 yards and 57 touchdowns in 11 seasons (1965–75) with the Kansas City Chiefs. He also rushed 30 times for a 5.4-yard average and three touchdowns. Taylor led the AFL in average per reception in 1966 (22.4 yards) and led the NFL in pass reception yardage in 1971 (1,110). Played in two Super Bowl games and caught 10 passes for 128 yards and a touchdown.... He was a backup small forward in the Prairie View era after the school's glory years with Zelmo Beaty. Former Prairie View coach Leroy Moore remembers Taylor for his "all-around great athletic ability."

ARNOLD TUCKER, Army

Quarterback on the great Army football teams that compiled a 27-0-1 record from 1944 through 1946, winning national titles the first two years. Earned All-American honors as a junior and senior. Won the Sullivan Award in 1946 as the nation's outstanding amateur athlete. Tied for the national lead in pass interceptions with eight in 1946 and finished fifth in the Heisman Trophy voting.... Played basketball as a Navy V-12 trainee at Miami (Fla.) and Florida prior to entering West Point. Played three seasons of basketball for Army and was captain of the team as a senior.

EMLEN TUNNELL, Toledo

Pro Football Hall of Famer played in nine Pro Bowl games. Defensive back established career records for interceptions (79), yards gained on interceptions (1,282) and yards gained on punt returns (2,209) in 14 seasons (1948–61) with the New York Giants and Green Bay Packers.... The 6-1, 180-pound forward was a top reserve for the 1942–43 Toledo basketball team that compiled a 22-4 record and finished second in the NIT.

BOB VOIGTS, Northwestern

All-American football tackle in 1938 and head football coach for his alma mater from 1946 to 1954. Starter on 1936 Northwestern team that won the only Big Ten football title in the school's history (6-0 in league play and 7-1 overall). Coach of the only Northwestern team ever to play in the Rose Bowl. The Wildcats, ranked seventh in the final AP poll in 1946, finished second in the Big Ten behind national champion Michigan, compiled an 8-2 overall record, and defeated California, 20-14, in the Rose Bowl.... The 5-11, 205-pound Voigts was a three-year letterman in basketball and captain of the team his senior season.

VIRGIL WAGNER, Millikin (Ill.)

Canadian Football League Hall of Famer played halfback for the Montreal Alouettes from 1946 through 1954. Led CFL in scoring in 1947, 1948, and 1949 and tied for scoring title in 1946. Scored two touchdowns for the Alouettes in their 28-15 victory over Calgary in the 1949 Grey Cup game (CFL championship).... Second-leading scorer for Millikin's basketball team in 1941–42 and 1942–43.

CHARLIE WARD, Florida State

Heisman Trophy winner and consensus All-American quarterback captured the 1993 Sullivan Award winner as the nation's top amateur athlete. Led the Seminoles to 1993 national title by passing for 3,032 yards and 27 touchdowns and rushing for 339 yards and four touchdowns. Passed and rushed for 6,636 yards in his college football career.... Averaged 8.1 points and 4.4 assists per game in his four-year basketball career (1990–91 through 1993–94). The 6-2 guard set a school career record with 238 steals.... Excerpt from school guide: "Lightning quick defender excels in every facet of the game. Great decision maker and poised leader."

JAMES WHATLEY, Alabama

Tackle and end for the NFL's Brooklyn Dodgers from 1936 to 1938. Starting tackle for 1934 Alabama football team that compiled a 10-0 record and defeated Stanford, 29-13, in the Rose Bowl. All-SEC first-team selection and All-American second-team pick in football in 1935.... The 6-4 1/2 center in basketball was a sophomore starter and fourth-leading scorer in the league

for the 1933–34 squad that won the school's first SEC title and compiled a 16-2 record. He was a first-team selection on the All-SEC Tournament team in 1934 and 1936. Whatley served as head basketball coach at Western Carolina, Mississippi (1946–47 through 1948–49), and Georgia (1949–50 and 1950–51).

RON WIDBY, Tennessee

Averaged 42 yards per punt in six seasons (1968–73) with the Dallas Cowboys and Green Bay Packers. Played in the Pro Bowl following the 1971 season and appeared in 1970 and 1971 NFL title games with the Cowboys.... He averaged 14.5 points and 8.3 rebounds as a sophomore, 17.3 points and eight rebounds as a junior, and 22.1 points and 8.7 rebounds as a senior. The 6-4, 210-pound forward scored 50 points vs. LSU as a senior on his way to becoming SEC player of the year in 1967. Named to second five on AP All-American team and third five on UPI All-American team in 1966–67. He played briefly with the New Orleans Buccaneers in the ABA in 1967–68.

DICK WILKINS, Oregon

Standout end caught 68 passes for 1,050 yards and seven touchdowns in his pro career with the Los Angeles Dons of the All-American Football Conference (1949) and Dallas Texans (1952) and New York Giants (1954) of the NFL. Wilkins led the Texans with 32 catches in 1952. He was the leading pass receiver (27 catches for 520 yards and five touchdowns) on 1948 Oregon team that featured quarterback Norm Van Brocklin, compiled a 9-2 mark and won the Pacific Coast Conference championship. The Ducks lost to SMU, 21-13, in the Cotton Bowl that season despite his four receptions for 57 yards, including a 24-yard touchdown pass from Van Brocklin.... The 6-2, 185-pound forward was the leading scorer (12.6-point average) for the Ducks in

1944-45 when they compiled a 30-13 record and participated in the NCAA Tournament. He was their leading scorer in the 1945 playoffs on his way to becoming the first Oregon player to crack the 1,000-point plateau.

BILLY WILSON, San Jose State

Split end caught 407 passes for 5,902 yards in 10 seasons (1951-60) with the San Francisco 49ers. He was a Pro Bowl selection six consecutive years (1955-60) and was named to wire-service All-Pro teams in 1955 and 1957. Wilson led the NFL in receptions three consecutive years–1954 (60 catches), 1956 (60) and 1957 (52). Caught 10 touchdown passes his last three years at San Jose State after spending 19 months in the Pacific with the Navy. . . . The 6-3, 175-pound center averaged 3.3 points per game and grabbed a total of 80 rebounds as a senior letterman for the basketball Spartans in 1950-51 after playing sparingly the previous two years. He scored 107 points in 44 games during three varsity seasons. Wilson collected two points and seven rebounds in a 68-61 opening-round loss to Brigham Young in the NCAA Tournament.

LAWRENCE (LONNIE) WRIGHT, Colorado State

Cornerback had a total of five interceptions in two seasons (1966 and 1967) with the AFL's Denver Broncos although he never played a down of college football. He became the first player in professional sports history to compete in football and basketball (Denver Rockets) simultaneously. Wright posted a pro best scoring average of 16.4 points per game in 1968-69 during his five-year ABA career. . . . The 6-2, 205-pound swingman averaged 17.9 points per game in three varsity seasons (1963-64 through 1965-66), pacing CSU in scoring all three seasons (14.1 ppg as a sophomore, 19.7 as a junior and 20.9 as a senior). He collected 25 points and 10 rebounds in two NCAA Tournament games in 1965 and 1966.

BOB ZUPPKE, Wisconsin

College Football Hall of Famer compiled a 131-81-13 record as head football coach at Illinois from 1913 through 1941. Directed the Illini to four national titles (1914, 1919, 1923, and 1927) and seven Big Ten championships.... Two-year letterman on Wisconsin's basketball team. The seven-man 1904–5 squad was called the "Western intercollegiate champions" by *Spalding's Official Basketball Guide*.

BOXING, GOLF, TENNIS, AND TRACK STARS

JIM BAUSCH, Kansas

Olympic decathlon champion in 1932 won the Sullivan Award that year as the nation's outstanding amateur athlete. Member of College Football Hall of Fame and Track and Field Hall of Fame played in the NFL in 1933.... Starter for 1929–30 Jayhawks basketball team that compiled a 13-game winning streak on its way to a 14-4 record and second-place finish in the Big Six Conference.... The *Spalding Official Basketball Guide* said that he "solved the center problem which had bothered Kansas for several seasons."

JOE CAMPBELL, Purdue

Professional Golfers Association Rookie of the Year in 1959. Won Texas Open (1961), Baton Rouge Open (1962), and Tucson Open (1966) before a back injury ended his PGA Tour career. NCAA golf champion in 1955 has been coach of eight Purdue golf teams that won Big Ten titles.... Averaged 7.7 points per game in three seasons of varsity basketball. The 5-7, 165-pound guard was the team's third-leading scorer (11.9 ppg) and leading free-throw shooter (73.6 percent) as a senior in 1956–57.

OTIS DAVIS, Oregon

Double gold medal winner in track and field in the 1960 Olympic Games. Won the 400 meters with a world record time of 44.9 seconds and anchored the 1600-meter relay team as it set a world record of 3.02.2.... Played briefly for the Ducks' basketball team in 1957–58 after transferring from Los Angeles City College.

WALTER (BUDDY) DAVIS, Texas A&M

Winner of gold medal in 1952 Olympic Games high jump with a leap of 6 feet, 8 inches. Won AAU high jump titles in 1952 and 1953. Set then-world high jump record of 6 feet, 11 inches in 1953.... Played three seasons of varsity basketball with the Aggies, averaging 9.9 points per game as a sophomore, 12.1 as a junior (NCAA Tournament team), and 15.1 as a senior. First five selection on All-Southwest Conference team as both a junior and senior. Held school season (362 points) and career (952 points) scoring records when he graduated in 1952. Named to Helms Foundation All-American third team as a junior. The 6-8, 210-pound center-forward averaged 4.8 points and 4.3 rebounds in five seasons (1953–54 through 1957–58) in the NBA with the Philadelphia Warriors and St. Louis Hawks. Member of two NBA championship teams— Warriors in 1956 and Hawks in 1958.

JAMES (BUSTER) DOUGLAS, Coffeyville (Kan.) Community College

Won world heavyweight boxing title with a 10th-round knockout of Mike Tyson in Tokyo on February 10, 1990. Lost title to Evander Holyfield on a third-round KO in Las Vegas on October 23, 1990.... A 6-4, 210-pound forward, he averaged nine points and eight rebounds per game for the 1978–79 Coffeyville team that compiled a 25-8 record. He scored 20 points and grabbed 18 rebounds in an 89-65 rout of Tunxis County CC (Conn.) in the NJCAA national tournament.

DWIGHT (DIKE) EDDLEMAN, Illinois

Member of 1948 U.S. Olympic track and field team finished fourth in the high jump with a mark of 6 feet, 4³⁄₄ inches. Won 1948 NCAA high jump title (6 feet, 7 inches), placed fourth in 1946, and tied for second in 1947. Holds Illini football records for highest punting average in a season (43 yards per kick in 1948), longest punt (88 yards vs. Iowa in 1948), punt return average in a season (32.8 in 1948), and longest punt return (92 yards vs. Western Michigan in 1947).... Led Illinois basketball squad in scoring

in 1947–48 (13.9 points per game) and 1948–49 (13.1). The 6-3, 180-pound guard-forward was named to the second five on Associated Press All-American team in 1947–48 and 1948–49 and first team on Converse All-American team in 1948–49. Played four seasons in the NBA (1949–50 through 19522-53) with the Tri-Cities Black-hawks, Milwaukee Hawks, and Fort Wayne Pistons.

RAFER JOHNSON, UCLA

Former world record holder in the decathlon. Won gold medal in the decathlon in the 1955 Pan American Games and the 1960 Olympic Games and was runner-up in the 1956 Olympics. Won Sullivan Award in 1960 as the nation's No. 1 amateur athlete.... Lettered in basketball with the Bruins two seasons as a 6-3 forward-guard. Averaged 2.5 points per game in 1957–58 and 8.2 points in 1958–59. Third-leading scorer and rebounder on 1958–59 team that he led in field-goal percentage (50.7).... Sketch in school guide: "Had to miss practice sessions because of his duties as the Associated Students (student body) president, and, as a result, hasn't come along as fast as hoped for. But this great athlete figures to be mighty valuable."

RANDY MATSON, Texas A&M

Former world record holder in the shot put became first shot putter to exceed 70 feet with a toss of 70 feet, 7¹⁄₄ inches in 1965. Won gold medal in shot put in 1968 Olympic Games and silver medal in 1964. Won both shot put and discus in the 1966 and 1967 NCAA and AAU meets. Sullivan Award winner in 1967 as the nation's outstanding amateur athlete.... In his only season of varsity basketball (1965–66), the 6-6¹⁄₂, 250-pound forward-center averaged 8.2 points and 10.1 rebounds per game. In Southwest Conference competition, he finished third in field-goal shooting (54.9 percent) and fifth in rebounding (10 rpg).

JESSE MORTENSEN, Southern Cal

Track and Field Hall of Famer coached his alma mater to seven NCAA titles (1951, 1952, 1953, 1954, 1955, 1958, and 1961) and a 79-0 mark in dual meets. He won the AAU and NCAA javelin title in 1929 and was AAU decathlon champion in 1931.... Three-year basketball letterman was named to the first five on the Pacific Coast Conference all-league team in 1927–28 and 1929–30. The forward-center was the third-leading scorer in the PCC Southern Division as a sophomore (10.8 points per game) and fourth-leading scorer as a junior (6.4). Third-team All-American selection on 1928–29 *College Humor Magazine* team and first-team choice on 1929–30 Christy Walsh Syndicate squad.

PETER MULLINS, Washington State

Sixth-place finisher in the 1948 Olympic Games decathlon as a member of the Australian team.... Captain as a senior in 1952–53 when he led the Cougars' basketball squad with 13.3 points per game. He was the school's second-leading scorer as a sophomore (8 ppg) and third-leading scorer as a junior (8.7 ppg).

STEVE PAULY, Oregon State

AAU decathlon champion in 1963 after finishing third in 1962.... Played three seasons (1960–61 through 1962–63) of varsity basketball with the Beavers as a 6-4, 200-pound guard-forward. Third-leading scorer on team as both a junior (11.5 points per game) and senior (9.2). Scoring average was 6.2 as a sophomore. Helped Oregon State reach 1963 Final Four by scoring 21 points against Arizona State in West Regional final.... Sketch in school guide: "Big, fairly quick and can shoot. Can also play defense with the best of 'em."

JOHN RAMBO, Long Beach State

Bronze medal winner in the high jump in the 1964 Olympic Games with a jump of 7 feet, 1 inch, which was two inches under his career best mark. NCAA high jump champion in 1964 before winning the AAU indoor high jump championships in 1967 and 1969.... The 6-7, 195-pound forward averaged 19.8 points and 11 rebounds per game in two years (California Collegiate Athletic Association first-team all-star choice in 1963–64 and 1964–65). He led the 49ers in scoring (20.3 points per game) and rebounding (12.7) in his second season. Had a 42-point, 31-rebound outing against San Diego.

MARTY RIESSEN, Northwestern

Nine times ranked among the top 10 men's singles tennis players in the United States. Member of five U.S. Davis Cup teams (1963, 1965, 1967, 1973, 1981).... A 6-1, 170-pound guard, he averaged 6.5 points per game for Northwestern from 1961–62 through 1963–64.... Sketch in school guide: "Reputation as a rugged, poised performer. Cool head makes him a logical floor leader."

HARLOW ROTHERT, Stanford

Member of two U.S. Olympic track and field teams placed seventh in the shot put in 1928 and won silver medal in the event in 1932. NCAA shot put champion in 1928, 1929, and 1930. Second in discus in 1930 AAU meet and fourth in 1930 AAU decathlon.... A 6-2, 225-pounder, he was named to the 10-man Helms Foundation 1928–29 All-American team selected in 1943.... Excerpt from *Spalding Basketball Guide*: "The opinion seemed to be nearly unanimous that Rothert is the best guard in the (Pacific Coast) conference. Rangy and aggressive, he is clever at getting the ball off the backboard and putting it back in play, and is a dangerous scorer when in shooting distance."

VIC SEIXAS, North Carolina

Tennis Hall of Famer was Wimbledon champion in 1953. Ranked No. 1 in the U.S. in 1951, 1954, and 1957. Member of U.S. Davis Cup

team from 1951 through 1957, he shared French and Australian doubles titles with Tony Trabert in 1953.... Scored six points in one basketball game for the Tar Heels in 1946–47.

FRED SHEFFIELD, Utah

First athlete to place in NCAA high jump for four consecutive years. Finished first with a best jump of 6-8 in 1943, second in 1944, tied for first in 1945, and tied for second in 1946.... The 6-2, 165-pounder was the starting center as a junior for the 1943–44 Utah team that won the NCAA Tournament and compiled a 22-4 record. Played for the Philadelphia Warriors in the Basketball Association of America in 1946–47 and Sunbury in the Eastern Basketball League in 1948–49.

JACK TORRANCE, Louisiana State

Broke world shot put record five times in the 1930s. Mark of 57 feet, 1 inch set in 1934 stood as the world record until 1948. Helped LSU win NCAA track title in 1933 with a first-place finish in the shot put and third-place finish in the discus throw. All-SEC lineman in 1933 when he captained the Tigers' undefeated football team (7-0-3). Played tackle with the Chicago Bears in 1939 and 1940.... A 6-3, 240-pound center in basketball, he finished third in the SEC in scoring in 1931–32 and 10th in 1933–34.

TONY TRABERT, Cincinnati

International Tennis Hall of Famer won NCAA singles title in 1951 before winning singles titles in French (1954 and 1955), United States (1955), and Wimbledon (1955) tournaments. Ranked the No. 1 men's player in the world by the *London Daily Telegraph* in 1953 and 1955.... Played two seasons of varsity basketball for the Bearcats in a college career interrupted by military service. Averaged 6.9 points in 22

games in 1950–51 and scored 11 points in four games in 1953–54. Starting guard as a 6-0 sophomore for the '51 team that played in the NIT and had an 18-4 record.... Sketch in school guide: "Great surprise in early basketball drills. His improvement has been rapid and he should be a great help to the club."

SAMMY URZETTA, St. Bonaventure

United States Amateur golf champion in 1950 when he defeated all-time great Frank Stranahan on the 39th hole in the title match in one of the biggest surprises in the tourney's history. *Sport* magazine called him a "pre-tourney 100-1 shot." ... Averaged 6.2 points per game in four-year varsity career with the Bonnies from 1946–47 through 1949–50. Led nation in free-throw percentage as a sophomore (92.2 percent) and senior (88.5).... Sketch in school guide: "One of the finest floor men in college. Equally adept at scoring from underneath or out front. One of the best defensive men in the business."

RICK WANAMAKER, Drake

Winner of the decathlon title in 1971 Pan American Games, 1971 National AAU meet, and 1970 NCAA meet.... Averaged 4.8 points per game in three-year varsity career with the Bulldogs (1967–68 through 1969–70). Drake won the national third-place game in 1969 after his nine points and seven rebounds weren't enough to prevent an 85-82 loss against UCLA in the NCAA Tournament semifinals.... Sketch in school guide: "Without batting an eye, he batted away a Lew Alcindor shot. When Alcindor hesitated to come out to the top of the key to cover him, the lanky lad popped in a couple of quick jumpers. Wanamaker forced Dick Fosbury to make his first seven-foot jump of the season in the Drake Relays. Rick cleared 6-11."

CELEBRATED ACTORS, BUSINESSMEN, AND POLITICIANS

ROBERT B. ADAMS, Canisius

Served in the U.S. Army for 31 years, retir-

Known as David Adkins when he played for the University of Denver, comedian Sinbad now has his own TV show.

ing with the rank of major general, before he was appointed commissioner of the New York State Office of General Services by Governor Mario Cuomo. Listed in *Who's Who in America* and *Who's Who of American Business Leaders*.... Third-leading scorer (9.2 points per game) as a senior for Canisius' first NCAA Tournament team in 1955.

DAVID ADKINS, Denver

Comedian known as "Sinbad" has a show by that name on the Fox Network. He vaulted to TV prominence as a co-star on the hit series *A Different World*.... Adkins averaged 4.2 points and 4.4 rebounds for the Pioneers in his varsity career (1974–75 through 1977–78) when they were classified as a major college independent. He never shot less than 50 percent from the floor in any of his four seasons.

BOB AMES, La Salle

Director of the Central Intelligence Agency's Office of Analysis of the Near East and South Asia in 1983 when he was killed in Beirut. A truck loaded with TNT on a suicide mission rammed into the facility where Ames was staying while serving as a liaison trying to allay contacts among the Lebanese, Syrians, and Israelis in hopes of calming the escalating discord.... Backup forward for La Salle's 1954 NCAA titlist and 1955 national runner-up in his sophomore and junior seasons.

NOLAN ARCHIBALD, Weber State

President and chief executive officer of Black & Decker. He is on the Board of Directors for ITT. Named to National Junior College Athletic Association All-America second team in 1966 when he averaged 25.3 points per game for Dixie College (Utah). The 6-5, 195-pound forward averaged 15.2 points and 9 rebounds per game as a junior at Weber State and 11.9 points and 7.1 rebounds as a senior. Named to second five on All-Big Sky Conference all-star team in 1967–68.

JESSE ARNELLE, Penn State

Founding partner of San Francisco-based Arnelle & Hastie, one of the first minority-owned national corporate law firms in America. The four-year football letterman and one of the finest ends ever to play for the Nittany Lions is vice president of his alma mater's board of trustees.... The 6-5, 220-pound Arnelle averaged 20.2 points per game in 10 NCAA Tournament games in 1952, 1954, and 1955. He remains the school's all-time leader in scoring (2,138 points) and rebounding (1,238) after pacing the Nittany Lions in those two categories all four varsity seasons. He had 15 games of 30 or more points. Arnelle averaged 4.7 points per game in one season in the NBA (1955–56) with the Fort Wayne Pistons.

SCOTTY BAESLER, Kentucky

Mayor of Lexington, Ky., for 10 years before representing Kentucky's Sixth District in the U.S.

House of Representatives. The Democrat ran for governor in 1994. . . . The 5-11, 180-pound guard averaged 8.4 points per game in three varsity seasons (1960–61 through 1962–63). Scored 26 points as a junior against Southern California. Senior captain hit 16 of 17 free throws in a game against Vanderbilt.... Sketch in school guide: "Typifies the 'we ain't scared of nothing' attitude of 'Fearless Five.' The self-made man type that sportswriters like to laud in success stories."

RICHARD T. (DICK) BAKER, Ohio State

Managing partner and CEO of major accounting firm Ernst and Ernst for 13 years, starting in 1964. Accounting Hall of Famer served on the boards of directors of such firms as General Electric, Anheuser-Busch, and Hershey Foods.... Three-year letterman was Ohio State's second-leading scorer as a starting senior forward for a team that finished runner-up to Oregon in the first NCAA Tournament in 1939. He scored a game-high 25 points for the Buckeyes in their tourney opener, a 64-52 victory over Wake Forest.

BILL BRADLEY, Princeton

United States senator (D-N.J.).... Elected to Naismith Memorial Basketball Hall of Fame in 1982. Averaged 30.2 points and 12.1 rebounds per game in three varsity seasons as a 6-5 forward. Scored 58 points against Wichita State in the national third-place game in 1965 when he was named Most Outstanding Player in the NCAA Tournament. Averaged 33.7 points in nine playoff games from 1963 through 1965. Named college player of the year as a senior in 1964–65 season by Associated Press, United Press International, and the United States Basketball Writers Association.... Member of gold-medal winning U.S. basketball team in the 1964 Olympic Games. Played 10 seasons in the NBA with the New York Knicks, averaging 12.4 points, 3.4 assists, and 3.2 rebounds per game. Member of 1970 and 1973 NBA championship teams.

LLOYD VERNET (BEAU) BRIDGES, UCLA

Actor with the hit movie *The Fabulous Baker Boys* among his credits.... Averaged 0.6 points and 1.4 rebounds per game for the Bruins' 1960–61 freshman team that compiled a 20-2 record. He was a frosh teammate of Fred Slaughter, the starting center for UCLA's first NCAA championship team in 1964.

AVERY BRUNDAGE, Illinois

AAU president in the 1930s before becoming president of the International Olympic Committee from 1952 to 1972. Competed in the decathlon and pentathlon in the 1912 Olympic Games.... Basketball letterman with the Illini in 1907–8.

DR. CALVIN W. BURNETT, St. Louis

President of Coppin State in Baltimore since 1970. Listed in *Who's Who in America*.... Three-year letterman averaged 5.2 points and 8.2 rebounds per game with the Billikens (1956–57 through 1958–59). The 6-5, 190-pound forward led team in rebounding with 14.9 per game as a sophomore.... Excerpt from sketch in school guide: "Strong, fast and a fine competitor, Cal favors a leaping one-hander from medium range. He is 'sure death' on follows."

JAMES B. BURNS, Northwestern

U.S. attorney for the Northern Illinois District.... Career average of 19.5 points per game in leading the Wildcats in scoring each of his three varsity seasons (1964–65 through 1966–67). The 6-4 guard was Northwestern's all-time leading scorer when he finished his career. Named to third five on AP and NABC All-American teams as a senior.... Sketch in school guide: "Converted forward is especially effective driving the baseline for acrobatic layups." ... Played briefly for the Chicago Bulls in the NBA and Dallas Chaparrals in the ABA in the 1967–68 season.

WAYNE CALLOWAY, Wake Forest

Former Chairman of the Board and CEO of PepsiCo. earned $1 million in salary and a $2 million bonus before retiring in 1994. The business administration major scored 29 points in 15 games for the Demon Deacons in 1957–58 as a 6-1, 180-pound guard. "One of the unique aspects of being on a team is that you clearly learn to share responsibility and share the credit," Calloway says. "You find out that there is definitely a reason for working together. In today's business world, you discover this in a hurry. You only get so far by yourself."

JAMES CASH, Texas Christian

Became the first black tenured professor at Harvard in 1976. He was named chairman of the Harvard Business School MBA program in 1992.... The first African-American to play in the Southwest Conference averaged 13.9 points and 11.6 rebounds per game in three seasons from 1966–67 through 1968–69. The 6-6, 220-pound center had a 37-point game and 26-, 25-, and 23-rebound games for TCU. He was the SWC's leading rebounder as a senior with 12.9 per game.

TED CASSIDY, Stetson

Actor played the role of Lurch in the TV comedy *The Addams Family* in the 1960s.... He died prematurely during a heart bypass operation in 1975.... The 6-9, 245-pounder played four seasons for Stetson in the first half of the 1950s after a mysterious brief stint at West Liberty State College. When his college career was interrupted one year because of academic problems, he served as a disc jockey for two different radio stations. Cassidy, a sophomore member of the Stetson squad that participated in the 1953 NAIA Tournament, was the team's leading scorer (17.7 ppg) and rebounder (10.7 rpg) as a senior in 1954–55.

DALE COMEY, Connecticut

Former Executive Vice President of ITT, a global enterprise with sales in excess of $23 bil-

lion specializing in diversified products and services in three areas—financial and business, manufactured products, and Sheraton Hotels. He earned more than $1 million per year before retiring. Comey averaged nine points per game in three varsity seasons after leading the school's freshman team in scoring (16 ppg). The 5-9, 150-pound guard was an All-Yankee Conference second-team selection as a senior when he scored 17 points in a 77-71 defeat to West Virginia in the first round of the 1963 NCAA Tournament.

KEVIN (CHUCK) CONNORS, Seton Hall

Longtime star of the television series *The Rifleman*.... Played major league baseball with the Brooklyn Dodgers (1949) and Chicago Cubs (1951).... Scored 32 points in 15 varsity games for Seton Hall in 1941–42 before leaving school for military service. The 6-5, 190-pound forward-center played for the Rochester Royals in the National Basketball League in 1945–46 and Boston of the Basketball Association of America in 1946-47 and 1947–48.

MIKE CONNORS, UCLA

Real name of actor, who had a hit TV series (*Mannix*), is Jay Kerkon O'Hanian.... The 6-1, 180-pounder averaged 4.6 points per game for the Bruins' 1946–47 freshman team that compiled a 15-3 record.

DR. DENTON COOLEY, Texas

World famous heart surgeon has performed about 20,000 open-heart operations.... Three-year letterman (1938–39 through 1940–41) on Texas teams that combined for a 51-21 record. He saw action in both of the Longhorns' games in the inaugural NCAA Tournament in 1939 after they captured the Southwest Conference championship.

KRESIMIR COSIC, Brigham Young

Deputy ambassador to the United States for Croatia. He died of cancer in May, 1995, at the age of 46. A 6-11, 195-pound center, he averaged 19.1 points and 11.6 rebounds per game in three-year varsity career (1970–71 through 1972–73). Led the Cougars in rebounding all three seasons and led in scoring as a junior and senior. Earned All-American honors in 1971–72 (Coaches fourth team and UPI third team) and 1972–73 (Coaches fourth team and Helms Foundation 36-man team). Member of Yugoslavian Olympic teams.

MICHAEL CRICHTON, Harvard

Nationally-acclaimed fiction writer has authored numerous best-selling novels, including *Andromeda Strain* (1969), *The Terminal Man* (1972), *The Great Train Robbery* (1975), *Jurassic Park* (1991) and *Disclosure* (1994) and *The Lost World* (1995). *Jurassic Park* was made into one of the biggest blockbuster movies of all-time, grossing more than $900 million worldwide in its first release alone. He also serves as co-executive producer for the NBC hit series *ER*. . . . The tallest player (6-8) on Harvard's squad as a sophomore in 1961–62 scored three points (all free throws) in nine games. He averaged 6.3 points per game in 12 outings for Harvard's freshman team the previous year when his best performance was a 16-point, 14-rebound effort against Andover.

R. HAL DEAN, Grinnell (Ia.)

Former chairman of Ralston Purina Company.... Played basketball for Grinnell when it was a member of the Missouri Valley Conference. In 1936–37, he was named to the second five on the All-MVC team and finished fifth in league scoring with an average of 7.5 points per game. The next season, he was again named to the All-MVC second five and finished 16th in conference scoring with an average of 6.5 per game.... The *Spalding Official Guide* described him as a "sparkplug" and "one of the Midland's best guards."

JOHN DICK, Oregon

Retired with the rank of admiral after 32 years of service in the U.S. Navy. Commanded the aircraft carrier *Saratoga* for two years and served as chief of staff for all carrier forces in the Western Pacific.... Starting junior forward for first NCAA Tournament champion in 1939 when he led the Ducks in scoring in three play-off games, including a game-high 15 points in the final against Ohio State. NCAA consensus first-team All-American the next season when he paced the Pacific Coast Conference Northern Division in scoring with 183 points in 16 games.

JAY DICKEY, Arkansas

Republican member of the U.S. House of Representatives from the Fourth District of Arkansas that includes President Clinton's birthplace (Hope, Ark.).... Dickey scored eight points in six games for the Razorbacks' basketball team in 1959–60 before he was stricken with polio.

ROBERT J. DOLE, Kansas

In 1996, Dole stepped down from his Senator's seat after 27 years to devote time to his presidential campaign. Senate majority leader from 1985 to 1987 and in 1995. Republican nominee for vice president of the U.S. in 1976.... Member of Kansas freshman basketball team in 1942–43 before enlisting in the Army during World War II.

DR. EDDIE DURNO, Oregon

U.S. congressman in 1961 and 1962 lost primary for U.S. Senate before serving as Oregon chairman for Barry Goldwater's presidential campaign in 1964. Durno was a physician in Medford, Oregon, for more than 30 years after graduating cum laude from Harvard Medical School.... Scored half of Oregon's entire point total as a sophomore forward in 1918–19 when he led the league in scoring for the Pacific Coast Conference titlist. Named to Helms Foundation 10-man All-American team for the 1920–21 season (selected in 1943).... Excerpt from *Spalding Basketball Guide*: "He is small, but makes up for

In his college days, Ray Flynn (left) was a star Providence guard; he "grew up" to become mayor of Boston and U.S. ambassador to the Vatican.

and dribbling. He makes long shots as well as short ones from any angle on the floor."

DR. PAUL ALLEN EBERT, Ohio State

Director of the American College of Surgeons since 1986. Nationally-recognized authority on children's thoracic and cardiovascular surgery is listed in *Who's Who in America*.... Earned All-American recognition by averaging more than 20 points per game each of his three varsity seasons (1951–52 through 1953–54). All-Big Ten choice each year finished his career as the school's career scoring leader. Had a 40-point game against Michigan as a sophomore. He was second in the Big Ten in scoring as a sophomore (20.1 ppg) and junior (21.7) and third as a senior (23.5).

DR. HARRY F. EDWARDS, San Jose State

Nationally-known liberal sociologist and special consultant for the San Francisco 49ers.... The 6-8, 240-pound center averaged 10 points and 5.9 rebounds per game in three seasons of varsity basketball (1961–62 through 1963–64). He was the Spartans' second-leading scorer (10.2) and rebounder (5.8) as a senior.

CLIFF EHRLICH, Brown

Senior vice-president of the Marriott Corporation is listed in *Who's Who in America*.... The 6-

4, 200-pound forward was a three-year letterman (1957–58 through 1959–60). He led Brown in scoring as a junior with 13.9 points per game and was named to the second five on the All-Ivy League team.

RAY FLYNN, Providence

U.S. Ambassador to the Vatican for President Clinton was former mayor of Boston. . . . Averaged 12.5 points per game as a 6-0 guard in his three varsity seasons with the Friars (1960-61 through 1962-63). As a senior captain, he tied with John Thompson for team scoring honors with an average of 18.9 points per game. Member of NIT championship teams in 1961 and 1963, winning NIT Most Valuable Player award in 1963 after leading tourney in scoring with 83 points in three games. . . . Sketch in school guide: "One of the fiercest competitors and greatest outside shooters in Providence history. Admired by his teammates for his intense devotion to basketball, manifested by his constant effort to improve."

GILBERT (GIB) FORD, Texas

President of Converse. . . . The 6-4, 190-pound guard-forward averaged 7.6 points and 5.9 rebounds per game in three varsity seasons (1951–52 through 1953–54). Leading rebounder (7.8 per game) and third-leading scorer (9.8 ppg) as a junior. Earned a spot on the 1956 U.S. Olympic team as a member of the Armed Forces All-Stars while serving in the Air Force.

CHET FORTE, Columbia

Former director of *Monday Night Football* on ABC Television. Nine-time Emmy Award winner also produced or directed Olympic Games, World Series, and Indianapolis 500 before a gambling addiction cost him almost $4 million and led to a guilty plea to fraud and tax evasion charges. Forte, who last bet in April 1988, has been host of a San Diego radio show and was slated to return to the NFL in 1994 to direct several games on NBC. . . . The 5-9, 145-pound guard averaged 24.8 points per game in three varsity seasons (1954–55 through 1956–57). Named college player of the year by UPI as a senior when he was the nation's fifth-leading scorer (28.9 ppg) and ranked sixth in free-throw shooting (85.2 percent).

GARY FRANKS, Yale

Republican member of 102nd and 103rd Congresses from 5th Connecticut District. He was one of two black GOP House members after the 1994 election. . . . The 6-1, 175-pound guard led the Yale freshman squad with a 25-point scoring average in 1971-72. He averaged 7.8 points per game in 59 varsity games in three seasons (1972-73 through 1974-75).

AL GORE, Harvard

Vice President in Bill Clinton's administration was a Democratic senator from Tennessee. . . . Gore averaged 2.8 points per game for Harvard's 12-4 freshman team in 1965–66.

STEDMAN GRAHAM, Hardin-Simmons

Longtime beau of TV personality Oprah Winfrey is president of a sports marketing and consulting firm with offices in Chicago and Washington, D.C. He founded Athletes Against Drugs in 1985 and is a regular columnist for *Inside Sports* magazine. . . . The 6-6, 200-pound forward averaged 10.7 points and 7.4 rebounds per game in his three-year varsity career, averaging 12.3 ppg and 10 rpg as a junior in 1972-73, and 15.2 ppg and 8.5 rpg as a senior in 1973-74. He played his freshman season in junior college at Weatherford (Tex.).

LEE H. HAMILTON, DePauw (Ind.)

Chairman of the House Foreign Affairs Committee represents Indiana's Ninth District in the U.S. House of Representatives. . . . Ranked fourth on DePauw's career scoring list when he graduated in 1952. Led team in scoring as a junior (11.4 points per game) and was the second-leading scorer as a sophomore (9.8 ppg) and senior (10.9 ppg).

HARRY HOPKINS, Grinnell (Ia.)

Advisor to President Franklin D. Roosevelt

(1933–45), including stint as secretary of commerce (1938–40). Headed the Federal Emergency Relief Administration and the Works Progress Administration during the Depression.... Played varsity basketball for Grinnell in 1910–11 and 1911–12. *Scarlet and Black,* the school newspaper, said Hopkins was the game's "bright and shining light" when Grinnell upset Missouri Valley Conference champion Kansas, 17-16, on February 22, 1911.

DR. FREDERICK L. HOVDE, Minnesota

President of Purdue University (1946–70)....
Fourth-leading scorer for Gophers in Big Ten basketball competition in 1928–29.... Described by *Spalding's Official Basketball Guide* as "a small, hard driving floor man."

MANNIE JACKSON, Illinois

Senior vice president, Honeywell, Inc., head of International and Home Building Control unit. The owner of the Harlem Globetrotters, a team he played for after graduating from Illinois, is the ultimate rags to riches story. Jackson was born in a boxcar in East St. Louis.... Three-year starter averaged 11.1 points per game in 1957–58, 13.6 in 1958–59, and 16.4 in 1959–60. Named to second five on UPI All-Big Ten team as a senior after finishing 10th in the league in scoring. Had 32-point game against Iowa as a senior captain. Finished Illini career as fourth-leading scorer in school history with 922 points.... Excerpt from school guide: "A spring-legged jump shooter played forward his first year before being shifted to guard. Quick hands and an excellent eye for the basket."

E. HENRY (HANK) KNOCHE,
Colorado/Washington & Jefferson

Deputy director of the Central Intelligence Agency in 1976 under President-to-be George Bush.... Led the Mountain States (Big Seven) Conference in scoring in 1945–46 with a 16.4-points-per-game average before transferring from Colorado to Washington & Jefferson to play on a 16-4 team with two of his brothers. The father of American University coach Chris Knoche, he was reputedly the first player selected in the NBA's first college draft in 1947 by the Pittsburgh Ironmen although the league doesn't have any official draft records prior to 1949.

BILL LAURIE, Memphis State

Former high school basketball coach breeds and trains horses at Crown Center Farms, south of Columbia, Mo. In May 1996, he presented Missouri with the largest single, private gift in the school's history–$10 million, which was earmarked as seed money for a new 17,000-seat, $50 million arena. His wife, Nancy, is the daughter of the late Bud Walton and niece of the late Sam Walton, the brothers who founded Wal-Mart. . . . Laurie, reared in Versailles, Mo., was a 5-10 guard who averaged 3.9 points per game for the Memphis State team that lost to UCLA in the 1973 NCAA Tournament final.

ART LINKLETTER, San Diego State

Longtime radio and television personality was master of ceremonies of such popular shows as *People Are Funny* and *Art Linkletter's House Party.*... Three-year letterman led the Aztecs in scoring in 1932–33 (7 points per game) and 1933–34 (8.8 ppg). Named to Southern California Intercollegiate Athletic Conference all-star team as a sophomore and senior. Captain of team as a senior when he finished second in conference competition in scoring.

JIM LUISI, St. Francis (N.Y.)

Actor played part of Lt. Chapman on television series *The Rockford Files*... Led the Terriers in scoring in 1949–50 (14.7 points per game) and 1950–51 (14.6). Finished his career in third place on the school's career scoring list. Played briefly for the Baltimore Bullets in the NBA in 1953–54.... Excerpt from school guide: "Shooting ability and deceptive dribbling, together with his

Maryland center Tom McMillen became a politician after his successful 11-year career in the NBA.

Physical Fitness under Bill Clinton. Former member of the U.S. House of Representatives from Maryland.... The 6-11 center averaged 20.5 points and 9.8 rebounds per game in three seasons for Maryland from 1971–72 through 1973–74. Member of 1972 U.S. Olympic team.... Averaged 8.1 points and four rebounds in 11 NBA seasons (1975–76 through 1985–86) with the Buffalo Braves, New York Knicks, Atlanta Hawks, and Washington Bullets.

REV. EDWARD A. MALLOY, C.S.C., Notre Dame

President of the University of Notre Dame.... The 6-4, 190-pound guard-forward scored two points in three games as a sophomore in 1960–61, 19 in 11 games as a junior in 1961–62, and six in seven games as a senior in 1962–63. He was a high school teammate of John Thompson, a star center for Providence who played briefly in the NBA before becoming coach at Georgetown.

JAMES E. MARTIN, Auburn

The 14th president of Auburn (1984–1992) was a scholarship basketball player at the same school. A three-year letterman, he started as a 6-6 sophomore center in 1951–52, when he was runner-up in scoring (9.1 points per game) and led in rebounding (eight per game). Averaged 7.1 points and 6.8 rebounds in his three-year varsity career.

TONY MASIELLO, Canisius

Mayor of Buffalo.... Averaged 15.1 points and 8.9 rebounds per game in three varsity seasons (1966–67 through 1968–69). The 6-4, 190-pound forward led Canisius in scoring and rebounding as a junior (18.2 ppg, 10.5 rpg) and senior (19.9 ppg, 9.3 rpg). He culminated his college career with 35 points in an 83-79 victory over Calvin Murphy-led Niagara.... Excerpt from school guide: "Became captain of the Golden Griffins through concentrated team play and aggressive individual performance. Backbone of the team."

indomitable courage in the face of the toughest opposition, make him an invaluable asset."

TOM McMILLEN, Maryland

Co-chairman of President's Council on

HENRY (HANK) NOWAK, Canisius

Never received less than 75 percent of the general electorate vote while representing Buffalo area for nine terms (1975–93) in the U.S. House of Representatives.... Leading rebounder for the only three Canisius teams to participate in the NCAA Tournament. He averaged 19.4 points per game in nine NCAA playoff contests. Led the Golden Griffins in scoring as a senior (51st in the country with 20.1 ppg). The school's all-time leading rebounder (880) is third in career scoring (1,449 points).... Excerpt from school guide: "Quiet and unassuming lad when off the court, but when going up for a tap or rebound, he becomes transformed into a whirling mass of arms and legs."

JAY KERKON O'HANION

see MIKE CONNORS

DR. HUNTER RAWLINGS III, Haverford (Pa.)

President of the University of Iowa.... The 6-7 center was a four-year starter in college. As a senior in 1965–66, he averaged 16.2 points and 16.4 rebounds per game and was named MVP in the Southern College Division of the Middle Atlantic Conference after leading his team to a 13-3 league record.

PAUL ROBESON, Rutgers

World renowned singer and actor.... He was a 6-3, 215-pound center for the Scarlet Knights' basketball team.... Earned Phi Beta Kappa honors from Rutgers when he graduated in 1919. Earned law degree from Columbia, financing way through school by playing pro football with the Akron Pros and Milwaukee Badgers.

TOM SELLECK, Southern Cal

Television and movie star who won an Emmy in 1984 for his work on *Magnum, P.I.* Was a 6-4, 200-pound forward with the Trojans. After serving as captain of the basketball team at Los Angeles Valley Community College, he scored four points in seven games for USC in 1965–66 and was scoreless in three games in 1966–67....

Excerpt from school guide: "Agile and quick performer who adds depth on front line. Business administration major is good jumper with fine mobility. Rapidly improving shooter has impressed coaches with his hustle in practice. Needs to work on defense."

DR. KENNETH A. SHAW, Illinois State

Chancellor of Syracuse University represented the Big East Conference on the NCAA Presidents Commission.... Known as "Buzz" in college, he was a 6-2, 185-pound guard who averaged 12.9 points per game in his varsity career. He led the Redbirds in scoring as a junior with a 15-point average. Set school records (subsequently broken) for most games played (108) and highest career free-throw percentage (.831).

C. J. (PETE) SILAS, Georgia Tech

Chairman and chief executive officer of Phillips Petroleum Company.... The 6-6, 180-pound forward led the Yellow Jackets in scoring in each of his three varsity seasons (11.6 points per game in 1950–51, 17.8 ppg in 1951–52, and 17 ppg in 1952–53). He set school records at the time for points in a game (39) and in a season (393 as a junior). Member of gold-medal winning U.S. Pan American Games team in 1955 while serving in the Armed Forces.

SINBAD

see DAVID ADKINS

GEORGE SMATHERS, Florida

Prominent Washington lobbyist after representing Florida as a congressman from 1947-51 and Senator from 1951-69. The Democrat was a chairman of the Select Committee on Small Business in the late 1960s. Lettered on Gator teams from 1933–34 through 1935–36. Captain of squad his senior season.

PAUL TAGLIABUE, Georgetown

NFL commissioner since October 26, 1989.... Averaged 11.4 points and nine rebounds per game in three varsity seasons as a 6-5 forward.

Led the Hoyas in rebounding as a sophomore and junior and was second-leading rebounder as a senior captain.... Sketch in school guide: "One of the toughest competitors ever to wear the Blue and Gray. At his best when the going gets toughest. Fierce rebounder, an excellent shooter and a tireless performer. President of his class."

JOSEPH P. (JOE) TEASDALE, Benedictine College

Former governor of Missouri (1977–81) gained national attention by walking across the state while campaigning.... Member of 1953–54 team from Kansas (then called St. Benedict's) that compiled a 24-5 record en route to winning the NAIA Tournament. Converted 19 of 20 free throws the next season in a game against William Jewell College on his way to finishing as the team's second-leading scorer with an 11.9-point average.

MONROE TROUT, Harvard

Considered among the trading elite on Chicago's volatile commodity markets. According to the New York Times, his Trout Trading Company earned profits in 69 of 79 consecutive months, an outstanding ratio.... He set a school record for season field-goal shooting (65.9 percent) as a sophomore in 1981–82. The 6-9 center averaged 10 and 10.6 points per game in his sophomore and junior seasons before slipping to 3.4 ppg as a senior.

MORRIS (MO) UDALL, Arizona

Former member of the U.S. House of Representatives and former candidate for the Democratic Party's presidential nomination.... He was the Wildcats' second-leading scorer with an average of 10 points per game on the 1946–47 team that won the Border Conference title and finished with a 21-3 record. The next year, he was the leading scorer (13.3 average) on a squad that successfully defending its league crown. The 6-5, 200-pound forward-center was named to the first five on the 1947–48 Border Conference all-star team and finished second in the

league in scoring. He played with the Denver Nuggets in the National Basketball League in 1948–49.

HAL UPLINGER, Long Island

Gained notoriety as the television producer for Bob Geldolf's "Live Aids Concert." The California television and marketing executive also served as the executive director of the World Games, a sort of Olympics for non-Olympic sports. . . . Averaged 8.3 points per game in 20 games as a starter for the 1950-51 LIU squad. Scored a game-high 25 points for Los Angeles City College in the 1950 NJCAA Tournament final when that school captured the title. Played one season (1953-54) in the NBA with Baltimore under his LIU coach (Clair Bee).... Excerpt from LIU guide: "Works like a beaver under the backboards, utilizing his 6-4 frame in a way that belies his placid appearance."

REV. MAURICE E. VAN ACKEREN, S.J., Creighton

Former chancellor of Rockhurst College in Kansas City.... First-team All-Missouri Valley Conference selection as a sophomore (second-leading scorer in league) and junior (leading scorer) and second-team choice as a senior (third-leading scorer). Creighton tied for the MVC title his first two years and won the conference crown with an 8-0 record and finished with 17-4 overall mark his senior year in 1932 when he captained the team.

RICHARD VINROOT, North Carolina

Mayor of Charlotte.... The 6-7, 210-pound center played briefly for the Tar Heels in coach Dean Smith's first two seasons (1961–62 and 1962–63).... Excerpt from school guide: "Diligent worker. President of junior and senior classes."

ROBERT JAMES WALLER, Northern Iowa

Best-selling author of *The Bridges of Madison County* and *Slow Waltz in Cedar Bend. Puerto Vallarata Squeeze* is his most recent best-seller. Averaged 11.8 points per game as a 6-0 guard in three

UCLA star guard Mike Warren went on to become the likable Officer Bobby Hill on TV's Hill Street Blues.

earn their first NCAA Tournament appearance in the college division.

LLOYD WARD, Michigan State

He was President/Central Division Frito-Lay, Inc. before becoming President of Maytag Appliance. . . . The 5-10, 165-pound guard averaged 4.8 points per game in three varsity seasons (1967-68 through 1969-70) with the Spartans. He was their sixth-leading scorer as a senior with an average of 7.3 ppg.

MIKE WARREN, UCLA

Television star who portrayed Officer Bobby Hill on *Hill Street Blues*.... The 5-11, 160-pound guard averaged 16.6 points per game in 1965–66 as a sophomore, 12.7 in 1966–67 as a junior, and 12.1 in 1967–68 as a senior. He was an All-NCAA Tournament selection in 1967 and 1968 when the Bruins won national titles by combining for a 59-1 record. Warren was named to Converse and Helms All-American squads as a junior. In his senior season, he was named to the 10-man United States Basketball Writers Association All-American team and was a third five selection on the Associated Press and United Press International All-American squads.... Excerpt from school guide: "Named on the Academic All-American first team. One of UCLA's all-time great ball handlers as well as being an outstanding driver and jump shooter."

BYRON (WHIZZER) WHITE, Colorado

Former U.S. Supreme Court Justice.... Finished second in 1937 Heisman Trophy voting after rushing for national-leading 1,121 yards, passing for 475, returning punts and kickoffs for 746, punting for a 42.5-yard average, intercepting four passes, and scoring a nation-leading 122 points. Played three seasons in the NFL with the Pittsburgh Steelers (1938) and Detroit Lions (1940–41). Led the NFL in rushing in 1938 and 1940 and in punt returns in 1941.... In a low-scoring era of basketball, he averaged 6.8 points per game for the Buffaloes in conference play in three varsity seasons (1935–36 through 1937–38). Third-team all-league as a sophomore (Rocky

varsity seasons (1959–60 through 1961–62). Earned All-North Central Conference honors as a senior when he finished 10th in the league in scoring (14.2 ppg) and fourth in free-throw shooting (78.4 percent). Helped the Panthers

Mountain) and first team as a junior (RMC) and senior (Mountain States).... After Colorado's 48-47 victory over NYU in the 1938 NIT, the *New York Times* wrote that "White was the guiding genius of the team and its steadying influence. The Rhodes Scholar, with a build as solid as an oak tree, was all-powerful on defense and an excellent shot when he chose."

DR. JOHN EDGAR WIDEMAN, Penn

Award-winning writer/novelist is an English literature professor at the University of Massachusetts. Books authored include *Hurry Home* (1969), *The Lynchers* (1973), *Sent for You Yesterday* (1983), *Brothers and Keepers* (1984), and *Philadelphia Fire* (1990). Rhodes Scholar has been listed in Who's Who in America.... The 6-1, 180-pound forward led Penn in scoring as a junior (13.2 points per game in 1961–62) and as a senior (13.8 ppg in 1962–63). Also led the Quakers in rebounding as a junior (7.6 per game).

KENNY WOLFE, Harvard

Producer for ABC's Monday Night Football.... The 6-2, 165-pound guard was an honorable mention All-Ivy League pick as a senior in 1973–74 when he was the team's third-leading scorer with 9.8 points per game. Wolfe averaged seven points per game in his three-year varsity career.

RON WYDEN, UC Santa Barbara

Won USA's first vote-by-mail congressional election in January 1996 for Senate seat vacated by Republican Bob Packwood after Packwood resigned following a long ethics investigation into sexual harassment and misconduct charges. Democratic member of the House of Representatives from Oregon for 16 years was Vice Chairman of the Subcommittee on Health and the Environment that dealt with the tobacco industry. Wyden and California Representative Howard Berman were the two most vocal advocates to force the tobacco companies to reveal their research findings on nicotine addictions. Wyden then served on the House Committee on Oversight and Investigations. . . . The 6-3 1/2, 175-pound forward averaged 17.4 points per game for the Gaucho freshman team in 1967-68 before averaging 2.6 ppg as a sophomore. Excerpt from school guide: "Great ability to get offensive rebounds and get the shot back up despite his height limitations. Plays very hard and is a fierce competitor."

SMEDES YORK, North Carolina State

Former mayor of Raleigh, N.C., was one of the city's most successful businessmen and civic leaders. . . . The 6-4, 200-pounder played briefly for the Wolfpack as a sophomore and junior (1961-62 and 1962-63).

12

WOMEN'S HOOPS

As the 1980s drew to a close, an influential sportswriter took a gander at the state of women's athletics and wondered why, with more females than ever taking up sports and fitness activities, there wasn't more interest in women's team sports. Figure skating, gymnastics, tennis, swimming and golf were more identifiable with women participants and spectators, who easily related to the personality factor in individual sports. Where were the matinee idols in women's basketball? After the bodacious Cheryl Miller completed her career at Southern Cal in 1986, the sport lacked a personality to drive it. All sports do. Before the Magic Johnson-Larry Bird rivalry that emerged in the 1980s, for example, the NBA didn't have any particular sizzle. Women's basketball without Miller continued to grow both on the court and in the stands, but something was missing. The game's biggest supporters and those in the media sensed that it could reach a point of breaking out, of emerging more into the mainstream of sports. But when? And how? And who would do it? The questions got a decisive answer during the 1994-95 season, when a band of unlikely heroines from the University of Con-

necticut stormed to a perfect 35-0 championship season, giving women's college basketball a higher profile. As a result, the game has exploded onto the scene with Final Four sellouts, broader corporate sponsorship and professional marketing and generous television that promises to yield more going into the 21st century.

"We've put women's basketball into the minds of a lot of people," said UConn coach Geno Auriemma, a relentless chatterbox and amateur stand-up comic, in the moments after winning the title over favored Tennessee. "We went 35-0 and won the national championship. I can't be eloquent at this time. I'm sure it was a great show today. It was great basketball." Actually, the keys to the Huskies' success, and the reasons why they became a national sports story, are loaded into his comments. For only the third time, a women's team won a national title undefeated, with UConn joining Louisiana Tech in 1981 and the 1986 Texas team. No other team has won as many games en route to a spotless record and an NCAA championship. That in itself gets attention, no matter where you play. That UConn is in the backyard of the New York media market is no coincidence. Once the newspapers began picking up the story as the season went along, the television stations followed. That bred spoof treatment on "Saturday Night Live," and post-title appearances on David Letterman, Regis & Kathie Lee, and other yak-yak shows. Why such a fuss? Auriemma originally drew the attention of the media several years ago, and still has a difficult time pulling himself away from postgame press conferences. Sarcastic one-liners and articulate, lucid remarks on the game keep scribes happy and writing.

WOMEN'S FINAL NATIONAL RANKINGS

1994-95

AP	USA/CNN	SCHOOL (RECORD)	HEAD COACH
1	1	Connecticut (35-0)	Geno Auriemma
2	5	Colorado (30-3)	Ceal Barry
3	2	Tennessee (34-3)	Pat Summitt
4	3	Stanford (30-3)	Tara VanDerveer
5	7	Texas Tech (33-4)	Marsha Sharp
6	8	Vanderbilt (28-7)	Jim Foster
7	16	Penn State (26-5)	Rene Portland
8	10	Louisiana Tech (28-5)	Leon Barmore
9	12	Western Kentucky (28-4)	Paul Sanderford
10	6	Virginia (27-5)	Debbie Ryan
11	11	North Carolina (30-5)	Sylvia Rhyne Hatchell
12	4	Georgia (28-5)	Andy Landers
13	14	Alabama (22-9)	Rick Moody
14	13	Washington (25-9)	Chris Gabrecht
15	20	Arkansas (23-7)	Gary Blair
16	9	Purdue (24-8)	Lin Dunn
17	18	Florida (24-9)	Carol Ross
18	15	George Washington (26-6)	Joe McKeown
19	22	Mississippi (21-8)	Van Chancellor
20	17	Duke (22-9)	Gail Goestenkors
21	21	Oregon State (21-8)	Judy Spoelstra
22	–	San Diego State (24-6)	Beth Burns
23	23	Kansas (20-11)	Marian Washington
24	19	N.C. State (21-10)	Kay Yow
25	–	Old Dominion (27-6)	Wendy Larry
–	24	Drake (25-6)	Lisa Bluder
–	25	Montana (26-7)	Robin Selvig

In Connecticut, the state the size of a bread box, UConn basketball is big-time. Fans who couldn't get tickets to men's games ended up selling out Gampel Pavilion for the women. But lots of teams have good players, top-notch coaches and loyal fans. Why this team? As UConn began drawing national notice, the players became more than athletes. Like Cheryl Miller a decade before, they became personalities, sweethearts to some, who identified with their visible enjoyment of the game on the court and their example away from it. The 1995

national player of the year, Rebecca Lobo, is a classic example. A finesse forward with great outside shooting range and terrific passing ability, Lobo exemplified everything UConn was all about: unselfishness, teamwork, hustle and enthusiasm. Point guard Jennifer Rizzotti and strong forward Jamelle Elliott manifested those qualities in a blue-collar fashion. Kara Wolters, a 6-7 enforcer, is probably the most dominating post player in the game since Anne Donovan played for Old Dominion in the early 1980s. With the Gotham and New England press chronicling every game and the team having to hide from reporters and fans on occasion to get some privacy, UConn tapped into something few other women's teams ever have done. "I don't think you can top this," Auriemma said. "Thirty-five-and-oh and national champions is about as well as you can do."

The signs of an explosion were apparent in the years leading up to Lobo & Co. In UConn's first Final Four trip in 1991, the exciting, and excitable Virginia guard tandem of Dawn Staley and Tammi Reiss generated vast media attention, although the Cavaliers fell short of getting the brass ring. Upsets were abounding in the NCAA tournament, which for many years was a predictable exercise in which the top women's teams advanced with little suspense. New programs were getting through to the Sweet 16 and making their entries into the national rankings. The supply of gifted athletes with exciting games kept increasing. In the two years before UConn made its historic, dazzling run, the Final Four was loaded with players who helped elevate public perception about women players. Not since Miller has a single player attracted the raves as Sheryl Swoopes did during the two seasons she played for Texas Tech. From 1991 to 1993, the junior college transfer scored 1,645 points, grabbed 597 rebounds and turned heads with her smooth, complete offensive game and full-court talents. The Lady Raiders won the 1993 national championship as she broke Bill Walton's NCAA title game record by scoring 47 points against Ohio State. At halftime of that

The 1996 U.S. Women's Olympic Basketball Team.

game, women's media guru Mel Greenberg, who has seen every championship since the early 1970s, made a bold declaration: "This is better than Miller." A year later, an unheralded North Carolina team faced the unenviable task in the title contest of trying to topple Louisiana Tech, which shocked No. 1 Tennessee in the regionals. Charlotte Smith had been enjoying a sterling year after an inauspicious start to her college career, but not even she could have imagined how the basketball gods would annoint her. With less than a second remaining and Tech leading by 57-56 in a rather lackluster contest, Smith set up for a three-point shot, found herself wide open on a fake off the inbounds pass, and nailed the trey at the buzzer.

Never had there been such an ending for a women's title game.

Building on the excitement from the close of the 1995-96 season and the best women's TV ratings, as ESPN took over exclusive coverage of the NCAA Tournament, another major development took place. Following the end of an undefeated tour by the U.S. National team against college squads, the National Basketball Association announced that by the summer of 1997, it would launch a summer professional league for women. The announcement came on the heels of the organization of the American Basketball League (ABL) by several Silicon Valley investors, who were tentatively scheduling to begin play in the fall of 1996. The ABL had signed 10 of the national team (later Olympic) players to contracts, promising an average salary of $70,000. But the NBA league, endorsed heartily by Commissioner David Stern, might be the one that sticks. After many failed efforts at a women's pro league in the late 1970s and early 1980s, very little has happened in that direction. The TV sports marketplace has become even more crowded, and comparisons between men's and women's basketball haven't gone away. However, the national team has been able to show how much better women (like men) become as they grow into their late 20s and beyond. To see a beefy Lisa Leslie, an even quicker and more well-rounded Sheryl Swoopes and the 30ish veterans Teresa Edwards and Katrina McClain is to see what a women's pro league would look like. As these players become more well-known to average sports fans, and as they are on television and written about in the papers more frequently, the fan base is expected to grow. The NBA has a built-in system for its league to make it and even make a profit. Starting up, there will be eight teams, all in NBA cities and playing in NBA arenas with the staff of that NBA franchise managing daily operations. Throw in a national TV contract, the league's phenomenal marketing and promotional divisions as well as its licensed merchandise line, and this is perhaps the best, and maybe the best last chance, for a women's league to last in the United States.

WOMEN'S FINAL NATIONAL RANKINGS

1995-96

AP	USA/CNN	SCHOOL (RECORD)	HEAD COACH
1	5	Louisiana Tech (31-2)	Leon Barmore
2	3	Connecticut (34-4)	Geno Auriemma
3	4	Stanford (29-3)	Any Tucker/Marianne Stanley
4	1	Tennessee (32-4)	Pat Summitt
5	2	Georgia (28-5)	Andy Landers
6	10	Old Dominion (29-3)	Wendy Larry
7	9	Iowa (27-4)	Angie Lee
8	13	Penn State (27-7)	Rene Portland
9	12	Texas Tech (27-5)	Marsha Sharp
10	11	Alabama (24-8)	Rick Moody
11	6	Virginia (26-7)	Debbie Ryan
12	7	Vanderbilt (23-8)	Jim Foster
13	19	Duke (26-7)	Gail Goestenkors
14	17	Clemson (23-8)	Jim Davis
15	–	Purdue (20-11)	Lin Dunn
16	22	Florida (21-9)	Carol Ross
17	18	Colorado (26-9)	Ceal Barry
18	20	Wisconsin (21-8)	Jane Albright-Dieterle
19	8	Auburn (23-9)	Joe Ciampi
20	–	Kansas (22-10)	Marian Washington
21	–	Oregon State (19-9)	Aki Hill
22	–	Notre Dame (23-8)	Muffet McGraw
23	–	N.C. State (20-10)	Kay Yow
T24	–	Mississippi (18-11)	Van Chancellor
T24	25	Texas (21-9)	Jody Conradt
–	14	Stephen F. Austin (27-4)	Royce Chadwick
–	16	San Francisco (24-8)	Mary Hile and Bill Nepfel
–	23	DePaul (21-10)	Doug Bruno
–	24	Colorado State (26-5)	Greg Williams

The Early Years

To understand how women have gotten to this point in their basketball development, it's necessary to look back at the beginnings. Those origins coincided with the invention of basketball itself, but progress lagged for many decades until the 1970s.

Just months after Dr. James Naismith put up his first peach basket in Springfield, Mass., a physical education teacher at a nearby women's college asked him to explain the new game of "basket ball" in hopes of introducing it to her students. In early 1892, Lithuanian-born Senda Berenson adopted the same general concept of the game as Naismith, but rewrote a substantial portion of his original rule book to suit prevailing Victorian assumptions of femininity and the kind of physical stress that females could endure. Not surprisingly, the first contests that Berenson organized at Smith College limited players to one of three sections of the court and prohibited them from snatching the ball from an opponent.

Other women teachers flocked to write their own rules. Games sprung up at Mount Holyoke College and at Sophie Newcomb College (now part of Tulane University), where women played 11 to a side, and all were restricted to a small portion of the floor. Players could guard opponents only vertically, and the no-snatch rule, which would dominate most women's rules for years, continued to apply. In some places dribbling was not allowed and defenders could not try to steal or bat away an opponent's pass. Bounce passes also were taboo for many years. All these rules were part of an effort to eliminate the roughness that Berenson and her peers found appalling in the basketball games they saw men play.

The controls on women's rules, which fit like the typical corset of the day, began a pattern of events that steered women's basketball for more than 70 years, until women began playing the five-player version that exists today. Women physical educators steadfastly believed that the purpose of basketball and any other sport was for the fitness and well-being of the athlete, and not for competition's sake. Basketball simply was too rough for societal acceptance and their own ideals of physical activity, so future rules revisions that opened up the game came slowly and in some instances, with great reluctance.

As a result, the experience of women in basketball has been drastically different from that of men, although they've been playing just as long. It also explains women's delayed entry into more competitive brands of basketball, and why the women's college game today, despite dramatic progress in the last 20 years, lacks the overt commercialization of men's basketball. The perspective and approach of women leaders, both in the physical education realm through the 1960s and by feminist-minded coaches and athletic administrators since then, in some ways resonate with the values and aspirations of the founders of the women's game.

In addition to the restrictive rules, Berenson and colleagues emphasized the importance of only women teaching and coaching female athletes. This issue has become a highly volatile aspect of the contentious gender equity debate currently roaring through college athletic departments, in which male coaching candidates occasionally are bypassed in favor of women.

One other turn-of-the-century issue still has delicate ramifications and is a hot-button topic that surfaces in larger question of women's rights in sports. Arguments raged for years about whether females would be made more masculine if they undertook athletic pursuits. Then and now, women coaches and teachers

pleaded that such activity ideally fosters the well-being, health, vitality, self-image, and confidence of young women. Discussions of women, sports, and sexuality often are laced with connotations of what constitutes feminine nature. Ardent women's sports leaders now contend that health benefits from sports are necessary for all girls and women, and charge their critics routinely engage in homophobic scare tactics to stunt women's advances in athletics.

In April 1896, four years after Berenson published the first Spalding rules for women, the first known women's intercollegiate varsity basketball game was played. Stanford defeated California 2-1 after playing two 20-minute halves, precisely the same time rules that govern the current women's college game. Each team played with nine players and although 700 people cheered with interest, they all were women. At California's request, men were strictly forbidden from watching women compete. Women teachers across the country feared a co-ed audience would prevent them from fulfilling their educational ideals, which did not include spectators who may be interested in something besides their athletic abilities. This philosophy, rooted in the creed of universal participation, rather than elite competition by a talented few, did not pass easily from the scene.

But there was more than a sporadic staging of women's basketball in colleges and high schools between 1900 and 1920. This reflected a new-found sense of independence by some women and a desire by others to strive for more competition than what was offered in intramural programs. While they are the forerunners of the pro-competition feminists in the 1970s and 1980s, and descended from the earliest American women's rights leaders, neither were they terribly interested in upsetting the societal equilibrium of the time. Ironically, as many American women were expressing some limited social freedoms by adopting a Jazz Age flapper lifestyle, women physical education teachers took steps to force female athletic participation into a very narrow domain. They worried that women would not be allowed to take part in sports activities at all if they veered too far away from traditional cultural prescriptions that still dominated educational institutions. Throughout the first half of the 20th century, women's athletic experiences in the educational realm consisted mostly of "play days," large intramural events that emphasized the values their teachers held dear.

Women's collegiate competition whittled away quickly in the 1920s and did not return on a significant national scale until the late 1960s. High school teams were more commonplace and were most popular in the South and some parts of the Midwest. But the Amateur Athletic Union, which was virtually all male, eyed women's basketball and other women's sports to increase its membership and offerings for athletes. Naturally, the women teachers resisted, and in the early 1920s, tenaciously fought the AAU's efforts. They feared a pro-competition avenue opening for women that they regarded as exploitive and exclusive. Some leaders quickly met to form organizations that worked to oppose women's participation in the Olympic games and denied attempts by the AAU to be affiliated with them.

The AAU fanned the flames by proposing to nationalize women's basketball rules and speed up the game to augment high-level competition. It wasn't until the 1930s that the AAU was allowed membership in women's sports groups. By then, pockets of basketball hotbeds were creating unprecedented opportunities for girls and women. The earliest national-caliber players hailed not from college campuses but from factory and mill towns and thousands of high school communities that placed their female basketball teams on a rare pedestal of respect and admiration.

Women's Basketball Tournaments Increase

That tradition was especially passionate in Iowa, where the famous girls high school bas-ketball tournament got its start in the mid-1920s. The Iowa Girls High School Athletic Union (IGHSAU) was set up expressly to offer interscholastic basketball competition at the same time other states were moving in the opposite direction. Eventually, the girls tournament would come to outdraw the boys and offer a fervent rallying point for fans in Des Moines all the way down to the smallest farming villages. It was as if all the controversies about how females should play basketball missed Iowa completely; the men who set up the IGHSAU firmly believed that girls would benefit from the experience regardless of their life's ambitions. In 1985, however, the six-player tournament got some competition when a five-player option was offered for the first time. By 1993, six-player basketball had been phased out altogether. All across the South, industrial leagues sprang up between the world wars, providing substantial competition for working women and others who wanted to continue playing after high school. Between 1927 and 1932, a Dallas insurance firm, Employers Casualty Company, built a powerful team called the Golden Cyclones that won an AAU national tournament and featured future Olympic champion and golfing legend Babe Didrikson. Two other Dallas teams, the Sunoco Oil Company Oilers and the Schepps Aces, also won national titles, fueling rivalries that were widely reported in the local papers. The Depression forced numerous companies to disband their teams, and the Golden Cyclones were an early victim.

Southern industrial teams continued to dominate the AAUs in the post-war period, producing most of the players on the first American women's national teams. However, a number of college teams cropped up into the fray, signalling the very earliest calls for a pro-varsity existence that was still at least a generation away.

Another Texas school, Wayland Baptist in the Panhandle region, was one of the first institutions to offer basketball scholarships to women. Claude Hutcherson, who sponsored the team, known as the Flying Queens, also arranged for first class travel. They flew to major competition in such places as Mexico and Madison Square Garden in a fleet of Beechcraft Bonanzas he owned. During the 1950s, the Flying Queens locked horns for national supremacy with Nashville Business College (NBC), which boasted Nera White, who later would be inducted into the Naismith Memorial Basketball Hall of Fame. The United States won the first two women's World Championship tournaments in 1953 and 1957, primarily with players from NBC and Hutcherson's Flying Queens.

Away from the playing courts, women's sports leaders actively debated the possibility of strengthening interscholastic competition. Some more traditionally-minded women balked, arguing that women would adopt male patterns of athletic behavior they believed were corrupting and contrary to the best interests of student-athletes. A host of rules changes opened the doors even further. By 1961, the six-player game allowed two players on each side to rove full-court, and an unlimited dribble was permitted five years later. And in 1969, as the first organization devoted to women's varsity collegiate competition was formed, another dramatic new set of rules, ironically introduced on an experimental basis, permanently changed the look of women's basketball. The five-player, full-court game also was played with a 30-second shot clock to speed up the tempo. Not only was this a reward for elite players, but it symbolized the advent of modern college basketball for women.

AIAW and Title IX

As the women's liberation movement gathered steam in the late 1960s, the first major intercollegiate women's basketball tournament set off a wave of activity that permanently changed the game. Although disputes continued for the rest of the decade over how scholarships, recruiting, professional coaches, and competition would be implemented, women had decided firmly that intercollegiate play was a positive and necessary development in increasing women's opportunities in sports.

The National Collegiate Athletic Association had refused repeatedly to sponsor championships for women. In 1966, however, a group of women's sports leaders created the Commission on Intercollegiate Athletics for Women (CIAW) to look into that possibility, piquing the interest of the NCAA. The two groups would clash for 15 years until the NCAA usurped women's separate administration of varsity sports in 1981.

In 1969, a physical education teacher at West Chester (Pa.) State College quietly planted the seeds for championship-oriented competition. Carol Eckman organized the first women's invitational tournament, attracting top college teams from around the nation and showcasing the college game for the first time. Her West Chester team won the title and the event continued for two more years. The CIAW evolved into the Association of Intercollegiate Athletics for Women (AIAW), which first offered a national basketball championship tournament for the 1971–72 season.

But the biggest instrument toward full competition for women came in 1972 when Congress passed a package of laws to order sex equity in education. Title IX of those Education Amendments strictly prohibited federal funds to schools, colleges, and universities that practiced sex discrimination, whether it was in the biology lab or on the basketball court. The most celebrated Title IX cases, however, involved women's athletics, and many of those controversies rage today. It was not until the late 1970s, as the NCAA's interest in sponsoring women's sports soared, that nominal enforcement of Title IX began.

Reflecting the education-oriented philosophies of the AIAW, small colleges coached by prominent women physical education teachers dominated the early years. Immaculata College, a tiny, all-women's institution outside Philadelphia, won the first three titles behind the play of center Theresa Shank; now Theresa Grentz, she is the respected coach at Rutgers and of the 1992 U.S. Olympic team. Two of her teammates also would become leading coaches: Rene Portland of Penn State, and Marianne Stanley, who led Old Dominion to three national titles. Immaculata's coach was Cathy Rush, who like her peers received little or no stipend for coaching. However, after leaving coaching in the late 1970s, she opened up a girls sports camp business and has been a color analyst on women's television games.

Delta State University in Cleveland, Miss., won the next three titles, from 1975 to 1977. Alumna Margaret Wade was brought in to start the program from scratch in 1973, and she relied on a supremely talented local player, 6-3 Lusia Harris, the first true athletic center in the women's college game, to help lead the way. Both are in the Naismith Memorial Basketball Hall of Fame.

The early AIAW years weren't lost on a sports media intrigued by chronicling what was then a novelty. When Queens College played host to the 1973 AIAW national tournament, reporters from all the New York papers, including the *New York Times*, profiled players and coaches and ran box scores. Players congregated in a hospitality room to enjoy juice, cookies, and fellowship after games.

Two years later, New York again was the center of attention as Madison Square Garden officials invited Queens and Immaculata to face off in what became at the time the largest crowd in the United States to watch a women's game. Nearly 12,000 spectators saw Immaculata win in a preliminary to a men's game, a normal practice in women's basketball until the 1980s. Players warmed up to Helen Reddy's popular song that began: "I Am Woman, Hear Me Roar." The Garden was the site for in-season tournaments sponsored by Manufacturers Hanover that featured top college teams throughout the 1970s. The first Kodak All-American team, started by Rush, was unveiled in 1975, and is considered the most prestigious women's All-American honor today.

Although women played with a shot clock to speed up the game, it generally remained mechanical and lacked widespread athleticism for a number of years. The AIAW's first guidelines prohibited females who received athletic scholarships from competing in its sanctioned events. This ban eventually was struck down after a female college tennis player went to court. Scholarships were awarded in limited quantities beginning in 1974, a practice that eventually would benefit large, public universities. The smaller schools, with limited resources, would be pushed out of the national scope by the end of the decade.

Other AIAW policies reflected the leaders' beliefs that the interests of athletes should come first. Student-athletes had to maintain academic averages required of all students at their schools. Women players also could transfer and play immediately at their new college, since other students who transferred could participate in other extracurricular activities once they became academically eligible. No women's basketball team took greater advantage of this rule than Tennessee, which emerged nationally in large part because of transfers. Coach Pat Head persuaded 1976 Olympic teammates Pat Roberts and Cindy Brogdon to transfer to her program. They closed out their careers with the Lady Volunteers and helped Tennessee reach the upper echelon of the AIAW tournament for the first time.

The Olympic team, which won a silver medal, was perhaps the most telling indicator of how women's basketball in the United States had progressed. After being throttled by the Soviets, who boasted a starting lineup with a 7-2 center and a 6-8 forward, American coaches began searching for taller, more athletically-inclined players. They found one in Anne Donovan, a thin 6-8 player from a strong high school program in New Jersey. She joined Old Dominion in time to help win a national championship and later became a national player of the year and a three-time Olympian.

By 1978, big schools were becoming fixtures on the national scene and at the first AIAW Final Four played at UCLA. The home team, led by

UCLA All-American Ann Meyers celebrates her team's 1978 AIAW national championship.

All-American Ann Meyers, won the title by defeating Maryland in the finals. This ushered in a new period of women's basketball as the recruiting of female players and the professionalization of coaches began in earnest. Many of the women physical education teachers who pioneered the college game were going back to the classroom. Their protégés, in many cases former players barely out of college, filled full-time positions and took the initial steps toward emulating their men's counterparts. They attended camps and tournaments that showcased top high school players, went on publicity tours, and informally organized for their professional common good.

Media attention stepped up that same season, when *Philadelphia Inquirer* reporter Mel Greenberg began the first Associated Press women's basketball poll. Those rankings framed the sport for reporters and gave schools fodder for press releases and brochures. *Parade Magazine* also began choosing girls' high school All-American basketball teams that served as a useful recruiting resource.

The 1978 Final Four also marked the end of the remarkable career of Carol Blazejowski, who set a women's record by averaging 38.6 points per game that season for Montclair (N.J.) State College. She is widely considered the finest jump shooter ever to play women's basketball and once scored 52 points in a game at Madison Square Garden. As she bowed out, the most decorated women's player ever jumped into prominence. Lynette Woodard of Kansas was the first true all-around athlete to play women's college basketball, starting at all five positions during her career. She scored 3,649 points, only 18 behind Pete Maravich's all-time college mark and became an All-American, Olympian, and the first woman to suit up for the Harlem Globetrotters.

Old Dominion's 1979 and 1980 national title teams exemplified more than basketball supremacy; they were an entertaining band of players who captured the attention of basketball fans in general. Flashy guard Nancy Lieberman was a street-tough New Yorker who learned the game playing against men in the playgrounds of Harlem. Center Inge Nissen, a native of Denmark, was a worldly traveler who occasionally smoked cigarettes and drank coffee during halftime. Their coach, Marianne Stanley, came on the scene after her predecessor, the fiery Pam Parsons, was the subject of complaints from players.

By the time Old Dominion rose to the top, televised women's games were not unprecedented. The first TV game was carried by NBC in 1975 between Immaculata and Maryland. NBC also carried the national title game beginning in 1978 through the early 1980s, although regular season games virtually were non-existent on the tube.

And it was over television that the final rifts between the AIAW and the NCAA erupted, resulting in an ugly, visible dispute marked by the lawsuits, intense rhetoric, and power struggles that highlight recent battles over gender equity. Title IX had forced initial compliance with its provisions in regard to use of facilities, travel and recruiting budgets, and more playing opportunities for athletes, but they hardly amounted to a drop in the basket of what women's sports leaders expected and later would demand.

AIAW leaders were optimistic as the 1970s drew to a close that a lucrative TV contract and other corporate sponsorships could lead to greater self-sufficiency. In 1980, the AIAW signed a four-year contract with NBC that amounted to $200,000 per year in television rights alone and worked other deals to help pay for partial travel expenses for national tournament teams, something it declined to do previously. But the very progress of the AIAW, and of Title IX, led to the ultimate demise of the women-dominated group. Greater demand for scholarship aid, calls from outspoken feminists for equity to match the exact level of support for men's programs, and takeover caveats from the NCAA forced their hand.

The NCAA offered a women's basketball tournament for the 1981–82 season that included promises for more television exposure and program expansion and full reimbursement for travel and expenses to the championships. That last pledge prompted most athletic directors to go with the NCAA, since their costs would be minimized and they were under Title IX threats to broaden women's offerings. Even many women basketball coaches, especially from bigger schools, thought the change would enhance the sport.

The AIAW staged its final basketball tournament the same year, but lost nearly $10,000 in the process. Rutgers defeated Texas in the Palestra in Philadelphia, but only a handful of the nation's top teams remained with the AIAW. Louisiana Tech won the first NCAA women's title on live TV and before a sold-out crowd of more than 10,000 in Norfolk, Va.

Trying to stay alive, the AIAW filed an antitrust lawsuit soon after, but later its members voted to disband. The novel experiment of a student-centered model of college sports was in place for only 11 seasons, but it opened the doors to high-level competition and produced many of the elite coaches who have controlled women's basketball since the 1980s. How they handled their new association with the NCAA proved to be an exciting experience although somewhat contentious.

The NCAA Digs In: Coming of Age in a Time of Transition

With the bitter breakup of the AIAW still fresh in their minds, women's sports leaders looked ahead to a future under the NCAA umbrella with some trepidation. Title IX was nowhere closer to being enforced, and large numbers of women coaches were leaving their positions. Men began filling many of those jobs, especially in basketball, and women feared they were losing their grip on the control of women's athletics.

But on the court, women's basketball experienced a virtual explosion of growth and interest in the 1980s. Players with superb athletic as well as basketball skills were starring in all parts of the country. Many would become Olympic stars later in the decade, as the United States replaced the Soviet Union as the dominant force in international women's basketball.

Just months after Louisiana Tech won the first NCAA title in 1982, elite coaches awaited the recruiting decision of a California teenager who came to personify the sport in an unprecedented fashion. Cheryl Miller finally cast her lot with USC, noting its major media market and academic program in public relations. Not only was Miller one of the most gifted women ever to play basketball, but her personal flair and theatrics attracted national attention and gave the sport an unmistakable identity.

She would become the first four-time Kodak All-American, and in her first two seasons guided USC to national championships. USC fans loved her emotional fury, as she pumped her fists in the air after a spectacular play. Opposing coaches and fans were infuriated when she blew kisses to the crowd or slammed down a ball after a call didn't go her way. However she was perceived by individual supporters or foes, Miller meant one thing to women's basketball. She injected personality, pizazz, and a sense of the dramatic. For once, the game was the viable entertainment option its leaders hoped it would be.

USC reached the title game in Miller's senior season, but lost to Texas in 1986. She was the leading scorer for the 1984 Olympic team that won the gold medal in Los Angeles, and continued a sports career in broadcasting after graduation. In late 1993, she took over the coaching reins at her alma mater.

There was no lack of exciting players and teams to challenge USC. In the Deep South, the Southeastern Conference asserted itself as the best league in the nation. Tennessee had been strong since the 1970s, but with the NCAA era came an increase in funding and commitment at schools like Auburn and Georgia. LSU, Vanderbilt, and Mississippi also were regular contenders for postseason play.

Georgia turned heads by recruiting some of the top high school players in the country. In 1981, Janet Harris, a 6-3 center from Chicago, headed to Georgia to begin a migration that continues today. In the next two years, homegrown talent in guard Teresa Edwards and center Katrina McClain would join forces on one of the most talented teams ever to play. Georgia reached the Final Four in 1983 and in 1985 was favored to win the national title, but was tripped up by Old Dominion in the championship game.

TRACK STAR JOYNER-KERSEE WAS CAGER, TOO

There's an argument in some sexist quarters that women's basketball is inferior because of an absence of female players with all-around athletic skills. It's easy to refute that stance, however, when one recalls Jackie Joyner-Kersee, acknowledged as the greatest female athlete in history.

Joyner, a four-year starter, averaged 9.6 points and 6.2 rebounds per game in her UCLA basketball career from 1980–81 through 1982–83 and 1984–85.

Later, she earned national acclaim with an extraordinary track and field career. Her achievements include:

- Won five medals in Olympic track and field competition, including the gold medal in the heptathlon in 1988 and 1992 and the long jump in 1988.

- Established women's world heptathlon record (7,290 points) and women's American long jump record (24 feet, 5 1/2 inches).

- Earned Sullivan Award as the nation's premier amateur athlete in 1986.

- Named Female Athlete of the Year by the Associated Press in 1987.

What Georgia and other SEC schools embodied was the full acceptance of recruiting as a tool to advance the game. As gifted athletes who played nearly year-round on national teams and in summer leagues, these players represented the kind of student-athlete that AIAW leaders abhorred. These young women were tied down to their athletic obligations like male athletes had been for years, and there were no signs of turning back. Even more women coaches with physical education backgrounds left the profession, leaving the door open to men and women who fit the new prototype.

A win-at-all-costs recruiting mentality began to materialize at the highest levels of women's basketball, since there aren't nearly the numbers of blue chip players as come out of boys high school ranks. Toward the end of the AIAW era, a scandal rocked women's basketball badly enough to illustrate that women could fall victim to the corrupting influences the game's pioneers dreaded would happen.

When coach Pam Parsons left Old Dominion in 1977 because of protests from her players, she latched on at South Carolina, turning that school into an instant power. She embarked on a national recruiting effort—landing Evelyn Johnson, the talented younger sister of Magic Johnson, among others—to build her program. South Carolina reached the AIAW Final Four in 1980 and was a favorite to get back. But allegations of illegal recruiting, financial and academic activities, and sexual improprieties jolted the school and the sport and led to Parsons' resignation early in the 1980–81 season. A *Sports Illustrated* article detailing the situation included accusations that she was personally involved with one of her players, a charge she vehemently denied. Parsons sued the magazine for libel, but later was convicted of perjury.

The AIAW believed in self-policing of rules violations, but the South Carolina imbroglio clearly demonstrated that approach could not control flagrant abuses. The only major recruiting scandal during the NCAA era was widely reported around the country. Northeast Louisiana made the national rankings in the mid-1980s because of aggressive, nationwide recruiting. When a Mississippi high school star, 6-4 Chana Perry, caught college coaches' attention in 1983, Northeast Louisiana boosters allegedly offered her use of automobiles and other gifts and promised her jobs after graduation. An assistant provided illegal transportation and lodging during a recruiting trip and Perry was given an illegal tryout while still in high school.

Perry signed with Northeast Louisiana and in 1985 helped her team to the Final Four. But soon after, the NCAA placed the school on probation, giving it the maximum penalty for a women's program: it was not eligible for postseason play. Perry also was not allowed to play there any longer and finished her career at San Diego State.

A host of new schools reached prominent levels during the 1980s, especially from the major conferences. In the Atlantic Coast Conference, Maryland and North Carolina State received a new rival in Virginia, which dominated into the early 1990s behind the guard play of Dawn Staley. The Big Ten featured annual clashes between Ohio State and Iowa, and Purdue entered the fray toward the end of the decade. Colorado and Kansas were the most solid programs in the Big Eight. USC owned the Pacific-10 during the Miller years, but budding programs at Washington and Stanford would shift the balance northward in years to come.

Texas had the Southwest Conference all to itself, winning 188 consecutive league games and leading the nation in attendance for most of the 1980s. In 1986, the Lady Longhorns became the only NCAA champion to go undefeated, posting a 34-0 record and featuring the play of freshman forward Clarissa Davis, who earned Final Four MVP honors. She was one of four players on that team later to become an All-American, and one of three from Texas to make an Olympic team. Injuries cut short Davis' career, but not before she scored 45 points at Tennessee before a world record crowd of nearly 25,000 fans in early 1987.

And Tennessee, after several tries without success, finally won a national title in 1987, the first of three in five seasons for coach Pat Head Summitt, who had learned the recruiting game very well. She developed a pipeline to Michigan to sign the best of that state's deep talent base, and went to Florida to get Bridgette Gordon, a smooth forward who keyed her first title and a repeat performance in 1989. The Lady Volunteers won the crown again in 1991, making Summitt the only women's coach to earn three NCAA championships.

The advent of tougher academic requirements, such as Proposition 48, also changed the national picture. Tara VanDerveer left Ohio State to revive the Stanford program in 1985. She also recruited nationwide for top prep athletes, but many of them were class valedictorians and honor students. Five years later, Stanford won the national title and duplicated the feat in 1992. The 1990 Final Four, played in the spacious 25,000-seat arena on the Tennessee campus, marked another women's watershed. Although Tennessee had been ousted in the regionals, Summitt and other school officials persuaded partisan fans to come. More than 20,000 spectators watched Stanford, led by Knoxville-area native Jennifer Azzi, take the crown.

The Final Four's first advance sellout in 1993 was a fitting finale for Texas Tech senior Sheryl Swoopes, who electrified the crowd of more than 15,000 in Atlanta with a 47-point performance against Ohio State in the title game. That broke Bill Walton's Final Four record of 44 points in 1973 and made her a household name in basketball circles.

Off-the-court issues dominated news stories and NCAA policies in the early 1990s. Women sports activists stepped up efforts to push women coaches for plum jobs, and men coaches complained of reverse discrimination. And the concept of gender equity became a major source of controversy. The NCAA Task Force on Gender Equity mapped out a plan to make athletic programs comply with Title IX toward the end of the decade. But feminist demands for resources proportionate to female student enrollment placed women at severe odds with some athletic directors and football coaches, who saw their revenue-producing programs threatened.

Several basketball programs faced extinction as the 1990s opened. Oklahoma suddenly dropped its women's team during the 1990 Final Four, but threats of a lawsuit forced a change in plans. Similar pressure was put on athletic administrators at William & Mary, which proposed cutting women's basketball for financial reasons. That decision also was reversed after extensive reports appeared in major newspapers and magazines.

In 1984, Title IX was imperiled when the U.S. Supreme Court ruled that the law did not apply if specific departments of an educational institution received no federal funds. The ruling threatened to remove athletics from the realm of Title IX, but Congress overrode the court's action in 1988 by passing the Civil Rights Restoration Act, which mandated universal Title IX compliance.

Southeastern Louisiana's Robin Roberts (right) is now a successful ESPN reporter.

Women's basketball coaches began to enter the high rent district in terms of salary and benefits in the early 1990s. No less than a half dozen coaches received six-figure contracts following the 1992–93 season, with the equal pay component of gender equity a major factor. Summitt, VanDerveer, Virginia's Debbie Ryan, and several others received the same base pay as the men's coaches at their schools. Others came close to the male standard. After coaching Texas Tech to the 1993 title, Marsha Sharp received a Lexus automobile from the school as a bonus. It was featured on the cover of the school's media guide the next season.

But an equal pay dispute at USC erupted into a full-scale controversy in late 1993. Marianne Stanley, who had retooled the program into a winner, demanded the same salary as

WOMEN'S CHAMPIONSHIPS, ATTENDANCE, AND TV

With judicious placement of host schools in the bracket, the NCAA women's championship almost doubled in attendance in a 10-year span from 2,455 per session in 1983 to 4,800 in 1992. There has also been an increase in the size of the field. In an era of gender equality, the bracket expanded from 32 to 40 teams in 1988, from 40 to 48 the next year, and from 48 to the same size as the men's tournament (64) in 1994. Another possible change is moving the dates of the women's tourney so it isn't overshadowed as much by the men's event.

Prior to the NCAA's first women's tournament in 1982, several alterations occurred under the auspices of the former governing body, the Association of Intercollegiate Athletics for Women (AIAW). In 1978, the 16-team, one-site event (games were played morning, noon, and night) was transformed into sectional play (four at each regional). A year later, the AIAW field was increased to 24. It decreased to 16 in its 11th and final competition in 1982, when the majority of noteworthy Division I schools chose to compete in the first NCAA championship.

Women's basketball, with few national personalities, is a difficult sell for the television networks. But NCAA executives, terrified of strident cries from Title IX muckrakers, mandated that a women's package be part of CBS' billion dollar deal to carry the men's Final Four. One of the trade-offs, however, was forcing the women's semifinals and final to be played on back-to-back days. The format is rigorous for any athlete to endure and can be a deterrent to the women putting their best foot forward on national TV in the championship game. The lack of time to physically recuperate didn't stop Texas Tech's Sheryl Swoopes from scoring more points, 47, than any player, male or female, ever managed in an NCAA final in 1993 when she helped the Red Raiders outlast Ohio State (84-82). Swoopes was acknowledged as the best women's player since Southern Cal's Cheryl Miller in the mid-1980s.

The women's championship game has been telecast on CBS since 1987 although it hasn't generated the audience a network needs to keep it going and growing. The ratings for the first six finals were abysmal, starting with a somewhat promising 6.1 (18 share) in 1987 but falling to as low as a 3.7 (11 share) in 1990. But Swoopes' performance in a close game in 1993 helped the women notch a 5.5 rating, a 34 percent increase from the previous year and the highest since 1987. The highest-rated women's basketball game came in 1982, when Louisiana Tech defeated Cheyney on CBS in the NCAA's first female championship game. It drew a 7.3 rating.

In addition to Swoopes' pristine performance, here are other factors demonstrating why women's basketball might be on the horizon of becoming a legitimate form of sports entertainment:

- The four teams at Atlanta in 1993 were Final Four first-timers, showing perhaps the women's game could be on the verge of extensive parity similar to the men.

- In 1993, there was the first advance sellout since the women embraced a Final Four format in 1978.

- The ladies generated enough attention to make the Las Vegas bookmakers' lines.

men's coach George Raveling during contract negotiations. The school offered her slightly less, near the $100,000 mark, a figure she rejected. Her contract expired and Cheryl Miller was hired, but Stanley filed an $8 million sex discrimination lawsuit. She sought reinstatement for the 1993–94 season, but her petition was rejected by the U.S. Supreme Court.

Women's coaches rushed to Stanley's side, publicly blasting USC and suggesting boycotts against the Miller-coached team. But the school contended that since Raveling's team produces revenue and the women lose money, the pressures on them to produce are different and therefore their job descriptions were not the same.

Despite the internal squabbles, women's college basketball continued to attract more fans and media interest. Attendance records have been set every season during the NCAA period, to more than four million for the 1992–93 season. The NCAA tournament was expanded three times and now matches the men's 64-team field. Television exposure also increased, as various schools and conferences signed their own deals and the NCAA demanded several women's games as part of its men's tournament package awarded to CBS.

Marketing, promotions, and business deals will dictate the viability of women's basketball in the sports market-

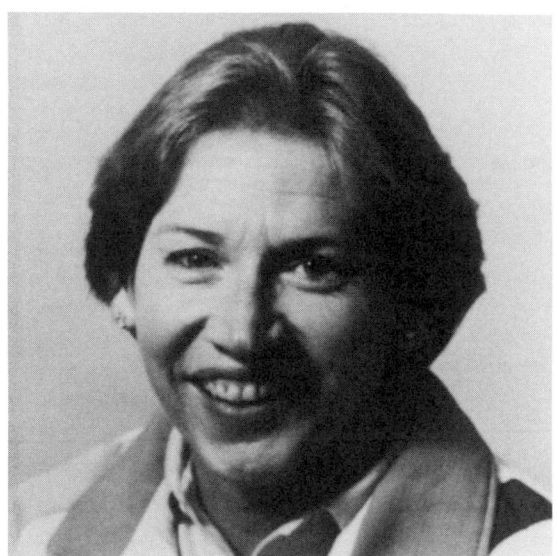

Coach Sylvia Hatchell and her North Carolina team won the 1994 NCAA Championship.

history, became one of ESPN's top announcers. In their struggles to achieve full equality, however, women in basketball still cling to some of the educational precepts that have formed the game's heritage. Finding a balance between those ideals will continue to be their biggest challenge as women's basketball moves into its second century.

AIAW CHAMPIONS

YEAR	CHAMPION	COACH	RUNNER-UP	SITE
1972	Immaculata	Cathy Rush	West Chester	West Chester, Pa.
1973	Immaculata	Cathy Rush	Queens (N.Y.)	Flushing, N.Y.
1974	Immaculata	Cathy Rush	Miss. College	Manhattan, Kans.
1975	Delta St.	Margaret Wade	Immaculata	Harrisonburg, Va.
1976	Delta St.	Margaret Wade	Immaculata	University Park, Pa.
1977	Delta St.	Margaret Wade	LSU	Minneapolis
1978	UCLA	Billie Moore	Maryland	Los Angeles
1979	Old Dominion	Marianne Stanley	La. Tech	Greensboro, N.C.
1980	Old Dominion	Marianne Stanley	Tenn.	Mt. Pleasant, Mich.
1981	Louisiana Tech	Sonja Hogg	Tenn.	Eugene, Ore.
1982	Rutgers	Theresa Grentz	Texas	Philadelphia

NCAA WOMEN'S CHAMPIONS

YEAR	CHAMPION	COACH	RUNNER-UP	SITE
1982	La. Tech	Sonja Hogg	Cheyney (Pa.)	Norfolk, Va.
1983	Southern Cal	Linda Sharp	La. Tech	Norfolk, Va.
1984	Southern Cal	Linda Sharp	Tennessee	Los Angeles
1985	Old Dominion	Marianne Stanley	Georgia	Austin, Tex.
1986	Texas	Jody Conradt	Southern Cal	Lexington, Ky.
1987	Tennessee	Pat Summitt	La. Tech	Austin, Tex.
1988	La. Tech	Leon Barmore	Auburn	Tacoma, Wash.
1989	Tennessee	Pat Summitt	Auburn	Tacoma, Wash.
1990	Stanford	Tara VanDerveer	Auburn	Knoxville, Tenn.
1991	Tennessee	Pat Summitt	Virginia	New Orleans
1992	Stanford	Tara VanDerveer	W. Kentucky	Los Angeles
1993	Texas Tech	Marsha Sharp	Ohio State	Atlanta
1994	N. Carolina	Sylvia Hatchell	La. Tech	Richmond, Va.
1995	Connecticut	Geno Auriemma	Tennessee	Minneapolis, MN
1996	Tennessee	Pat Summitt	Georgia	Charlotte, NC

NCAA OUTSTANDING PLAYER AWARD WINNERS

1982: Janice Lawrence, Louisiana Tech
1983: Cheryl Miller, Southern Cal
1984: Cheryl Miller, Southern Cal
1985: Tracy Claxton, Old Dominion
1986: Clarissa Davis, Texas
1987: Tonya Edwards, Tennessee
1988: Erica Westbrooks, Louisiana Tech
1989: Bridgette Gordon, Tennessee
1990: Jennifer Azzi, Stanford
1991: Dawn Staley, Virginia
1992: Molly Goodenbour, Stanford
1993: Sheryl Swoopes, Texas Tech
1994: Charlotte Smith, North Carolina
1995: Rebecca Lobo, Connecticut

place. Coaches sign endorsement contracts, speak before civic and business groups, and are positioning themselves to administer the sport when their coaching days are concluded. Recruiting and evaluation camps and tournaments have helped prepare high school players for the rigors of the college game. Developmental programs have been started by USA Basketball to foster intense competition at a younger age and instill a wider range of basketball skills. International events such as the Olympics and professional leagues for women in Europe have continued the playing careers of elite players, some of whom are competing into their 30s.

The chaste beginnings of women's basketball 100 years ago have given way completely to a modern sport that reflects the emancipation of women in society. For instance, Robin Roberts, who still ranks among the top five scorers and rebounders in Southeastern Louisiana women's

WOMEN'S AWARDS

BRODERICK AWARD

Voted on by a national panel of women's collegiate athletic directors. First presented by the late Thomas Broderick, an athletic outfitter.

1977: Lucy Harris, Delta State
1978: Ann Meyers, UCLA
1979: Nancy Lieberman, Old Dominion
1980: Nancy Lieberman, Old Dominion
1981: Lynette Woodward, Kansas
1982: Pam Kelly, Louisiana Tech
1983: Anne Donovan, Old Dominion
1984: Cheryl Miller, Southern Cal
1985: Cheryl Miller, Southern Cal
1986: Kamie Ethridge, Texas
1987: Katrina McClain, Georgia
1988: Teresa Weatherspoon, La. Tech
1989: Bridgette Gordon, Tennessee
1990: Jennifer Azzi, Stanford
1991: Dawn Staley, Virginia
1992: Dawn Staley, Virginia
1993: Sheryl Swoopes, Texas Tech

WADE TROPHY

Voted on by the National Association for Girls and Women in Sports (NAGWS) and awarded for academics and community service as well as player performance. Presented in the name of former Delta State coach Margaret Wade.

1978: Carol Blazejowski, Montclair State
1979: Nancy Lieberman, Old Dominion
1980: Nancy Lieberman, Old Dominion
1981: Lynette Woodward, Kansas
1982: Pam Kelly, Louisiana Tech
1983: LaTaunya Pollard, Long Beach State
1984: Janice Lawrence, Louisiana Tech
1985: Cheryl Miller, Southern Cal
1986: Kamie Ethridge, Texas
1987: Shelly Pennefather, Villanova
1988: Teresa Weatherspoon, Louisiana Tech
1989: Clarissa Davis, Texas
1990: Jennifer Azzi, Stanford
1991: Daedra Charles, Tennessee
1992: Susan Robinson, Penn State
1993: Karen Jennings, Nebraska
1994: Carol Ann Shudlick, Minnesota
1995: Rebecca Lobo, Connecticut

NAISMITH TROPHY

Voted on by a panel of coaches, sportswriters and broadcasters. Presented by the Atlanta Tip-Off Club in the name of Dr. James Naismith, the inventor of basketball.

1983: Anne Donovan, Old Dominion
1984: Cheryl Miller, Southern Cal
1985: Cheryl Miller, Southern Cal
1986: Cheryl Miller, Southern Cal
1987: Clarissa Davis, Texas
1988: Sue Wicks, Rutgers
1989: Clarissa Davis, Texas
1990: Jennifer Azzi, Stanford
1991: Dawn Staley, Virginia

1992: Dawn Staley, Virginia
1993: Sheryl Swoopes, Texas Tech
1994: Lisa Leslie, Southern Cal
1995: Rebecca Lobo, Connecticut
1996: Saudia Roundtree, Georgia

WOMEN'S BASKETBALL COACHES ASSOCIATION

Voted on by WBCA members and presented by Rawlings.

1983: Anne Donovan, Old Dominion
1984: Janice Lawrence, Louisiana Tech
1985: Cheryl Miller, Southern Cal
1986: Cheryl Miller, Southern Cal
1987: Katrina McClain, Georgia
1988: Michelle Edwards, Iowa
1989: Clarissa Davis, Texas
1990: Venus Lacey, Louisiana Tech
1991: Dawn Staley, Virginia
1992: Dawn Staley, Virginia
1993: Sheryl Swoopes, Texas Tech
1994: Lisa Leslie, Southern Cal
1995: Rebecca Lobo, Connecticut

CONVERSE COACH OF THE YEAR

Award voted on by the Women's Basketball Coaches Association and presented by Converse athletic outfitters.

1983: Pat Summitt, Tennessee
1984: Jody Conradt, Texas
1985: Jim Foster, St. Joseph's
1986: Jody Conradt, Texas
1987: Theresa Grentz, Rutgers
1988: Vivian Stringer, Iowa
1989: Tara VanDerveer, Stanford
1990: Kay Yow, North Carolina State
1991: Rene Portland, Penn State
1992: Ferne Labati, Miami (Fla.)
1993: Vivian Stringer, Iowa
1994: Marsha Sharp, Texas Tech
1995: Pat Summitt, Tennessee

NAISMITH COACH OF THE YEAR

1987: Pat Summitt, Tennessee
1988: Leon Barmore, Louisiana Tech
1989: Pat Summitt, Tennessee
1990: Tara VanDerveer, Stanford
1991: Debbie Ryan, Virginia
1992: Chris Weller, Maryland
1993: Vivian Stringer, Iowa
1994: Pat Summitt, Tennessee
1995: Geno Auriemma, Connecticut
1996: Andy Landers, Georgia

KODAK ALL-AMERICAN SELECTIONS

Voted on by the Women's Basketball Coaches Association. Selections broken down by major and small schools started in 1983.

1974-75

Carolyn Bush, Wayland Baptist (Tex.); Marianne Crawford, Immaculata (Pa.); Nancy Dunkle, Cal State Fullerton; Lusia Harris, Delta State (Miss.); Jan Irby, William Penn (Iowa); Ann Meyers, UCLA; Brenda Moeller, Wayland Baptist (Tex.); Debbie Oing, Indiana; Sue Rojcewicz, Southern Connecticut State; Susan Yow, Elon (N.C.).

1975-76

Carol Blazejowski, Montclair State (N.J.); Cindy Brogdon, Mercer (Ga.); Nancy Dunkle, Cal State Fullerton; Doris Felderhoff, Stephen F. Austin (Tex.); Lusia Harris, Delta State (Miss.); Susie Kudma, William Penn (Iowa); Ann Meyers, UCLA; Marianne Crawford Stanley, Immaculata (Pa.); Pearl Worrell, Wayland Baptist (Tex.); Susan Yow, North Carolina State.

1976-77

Carol Blazejowski, Montclair State (N.J.); Nancy Dunkle, Cal State Fullerton; Rita Easterling, Mississippi College; Susie Snider Eppers, Baylor; Doris Felderhoff, Stephen F. Austin (Tex.); Lusia Harris, Delta State (Miss.); Charlotte Lewis, Illinois State; Ann Meyers, UCLA; Patricia Roberts, Tennessee; Mary Scharff, Immaculata (Pa.).

1977-78

Genia Beasley, North Carolina State; Carol Blazejowski, Montclair State (N.J.); Debbie Brock, Delta State (Miss.); Cindy Brogdon, Tennessee; Julie Gross, Louisiana State; Althea Gwyn, Queens (N.Y.); Kathy Harston, Wayland Baptist (Tex.); Nancy Lieberman, Old Dominion; Ann Meyers, UCLA; Lynette Woodard, Kansas.

1978-79

Cindy Brogdon, Tennessee; Carol Chason, Valdosta State (Ga.); Pat Colasardo, Montclair State (N.J.); Denise Curry, UCLA; Nancy Lieberman, Old Dominion; Jill Rankin, Wayland Baptist (Tex.); Susan Taylor, Valdosta State (Ga.); Rosie Walker, Stephen F. Austin (Tex.); Franci Washington, Ohio State; Lynette Woodard, Kansas.

1979-80

Denise Curry, UCLA; Tina Gunn, Brigham Young; Pam Kelly, Louisiana Tech; Nancy Lieberman, Old Dominion; Inge Nissen, Old Dominion; Jill Rankin, Wayland Baptist (Tex.); Susan Taylor, Valdosta State (Ga.); Rosie Walker, Stephen F. Austin (Tex.); Holly Warlick, Tennessee; Lynette Woodard, Kansas.

1980-81

Denise Curry, UCLA; Anne Donovan, Old Dominion; Pam Kelly, Louisiana; Kris Kirchner, Rutgers; Carol Menken, Oregon State; Cindy Noble, Tennessee; LaTaunya Pollard, Long Beach State; Bev Smith, Oregon; Valerie Walker, Cheyney (Pa.); Lynette Woodard, Kansas.

1981-82

Jerilynn Harper, Tennessee Tech; Janet Harris, Georgia; Pam Kelly, Louisiana Tech; Barbara Kennedy, Clemson; June Olkowski, Rutgers; Mary Ostrowski, Tennessee; Bev Smith, Oregon; Valerie Still, Kentucky; Angela Turner, Louisiana Tech; Valerie Walker, Cheyney (Pa.).

1982-83

Priscilla Gary, Kansas State; Tanya Haave, Tennessee; Anne Donovan, Old Dominion; Janice Lawrence, Louisiana Tech; Paula McGee, Southern California; Cheryl Miller, Southern California; Jasmina Perazic, Maryland; LaTaunya Pollard, Long Beach State; Valerie Still, Kentucky; Joyce Walker, Louisiana State.

1983-84

Tresa Brown, North Carolina; Janet Harris, Georgia; Becky Jackson, Auburn; Yolanda Laney, Cheyney (Pa.); Janice Lawrence, Louisiana Tech; Pam McGee, Southern California; Cheryl Miller, Southern California; Arnette Smith, Texas; Marilyn Stephens, Temple; Joyce Walker, Louisiana State.

1984-85

Anucha Browne, Northwestern; Sheila Collins, Tennessee; Kirsten Cummings, Long Beach State; Medina Dixon, Old Dominion; Teresa Edwards, Georgia; Kamie Ethridge, Texas; Pam Gant, Louisiana Tech; Janet Harris, Georgia; Eun Jung Lee, Northeast Louisiana; Cheryl Miller, Southern California.

1985-86

Cindy Brown, Long Beach State; Teresa Edwards, Georgia; Kamie Ethridge, Texas; Wanda Ford, Drake; Jennifer Gillom, Mississippi; Pam Leake, North Carolina; Lillie Mason, Western Kentucky; Katrina McClain, Georgia; Cheryl Miller, Southern California; Sue Wicks, Rutgers.

1986-87

Cindy Brown, Long Beach State; Clarissa Davis, Texas; Tracey Hall, Ohio State; Donna Holt, Virginia; Andrea Lloyd, Texas; Katrina McClain, Georgia; Vickie Orr, Auburn; Shelly Pennefather, Villanova; Teresa Weatherspoon, Louisiana Tech; Sue Wicks, Rutgers.

1987-88

Michelle Edwards, Iowa; Bridgette Gordon, Tennessee; Tracey Hall, Ohio State; Donna Holt, Virginia; Suzie McConnell, Penn State; Vickie Orr, Auburn; Penny Toler, Long Beach State; Teresa Weatherspoon, Louisiana Tech; Sue Wicks, Rutgers; Beverly Williams, Texas.

1988-89

Jennifer Azzi, Stanford; Vicky Bullett, Maryland; Clarissa Davis, Texas; Bridgette Gordon, Tennessee; Nora Lewis, Louisiana Tech; Nikita Lowry, Ohio State; Vickie Orr, Auburn; Chana Perry, San Diego State; Deanna Tate, Maryland; Penny Toler, Long Beach State.

1989-90

Jennifer Azzi, Stanford; Daedra Charles, Tennessee; Portia Hill, Stephen F. Austin (Tex.); Dale Hodges, St. Joseph's; Carolyn Jones, Auburn; Venus Lacy, Louisiana Tech; Franthea Price, Iowa; Wendy Scholtens, Vanderbilt; Dawn Staley, Virginia; Andrea Stinson, North Carolina State.

1990-91

Kerry Bascom, Connecticut; Daedra Charles, Tennessee; Dana Chatman, Louisiana State; Delmonica DeHorney, Arkansas; Sonja Henning, Stanford; Joy Holmes, Purdue; Carolyn Jones, Auburn; Genia Miller, Cal State Fullerton; Dawn Staley, Virginia; Andrea Stinson, North Carolina State.

1991-92

Shannon Cate, Montana; Dena Head, Tennessee; MaChelle Joseph, Purdue; Rosemary Kasiorek, West Virginia; Tammi Reiss, Virginia; Susan Robinson, Penn State; Frances Savage, Miami (Fla.); Dawn Staley, Virginia; Sheryl Swoopes, Texas Tech; Val Whiting, Stanford.

1992-93

Andrea Congreaves, Mercer (Ga.); Toni Foster, Iowa; Lauretta Freeman, Auburn; Heidi Gillingham, Vanderbilt; Lisa Harrison, Tennessee; Katie Smith, Ohio State; Karen Jennings, Nebraska; Sheryl Swoopes, Texas Tech; Milica Vukadinovic, California; Val Whiting, Stanford.

1993-94

Jessica Barr, Clemson; Janice Felder, Southern Mississippi; Niesa Johnson, Alabama; Lisa Leslie, Southern California; Rebecca Lobo, Connecticut; Nikki McCray, Tennessee; Andrea Nagy, Florida International; Tonya Sampson, North Carolina; Carol Ann Shudlick, Minnesota; Natalie Williams, UCLA.

1994-95

Angela Acock, Kansas; Niesa Johnson, Alabama; Vickie Johnson, Louisiana Tech; Rebecca Lobo, Connecticut; Stacey Lovelace, Purdue; Nikki McCray, Tennessee; Wendy Palmer, Virginia; Jennifer Risotti, Connecticut; Shelly Sheetz, Colorado; Charlotte Smith, North Carolina.

All-Time Great Women's Players

JENNIFER AZZI
Stanford
5-8 – G
Oak Ridge, Tenn.

1990 recipient of Wade Trophy and Naismith National Player of the Year Award. . . . Two-time Pacific-10 Player of the Year when she was also a Kodak All-American first team selection (1989 and 1990). . . . Named MVP of the 1990 NCAA Final Four when she led Stanford to a 32-1 record and the NCAA Tournament title. . . . The Cardinal compiled a 101-23 mark during her four seasons.

Year	G	FGM	FGA	FG%	FTM	FTA	FT%	Reb.	Avg.	Pts.	Avg.
86-87	27	91	201	.453	65	95	.684	100	3.7	247	9.2
87-88	32	139	321	.433	57	72	.792	126	3.9	405	12.7
88-89	31	180	331	.544	100	127	.787	129	4.2	513	16.6
89-90	32	159	320	.497	83	104	.798	121	3.8	469	14.7
Totals	122	569	1173	.485	305	398	.766	476	3.9	1634	13.4

Three-point shooting: 70 of 172 (.407) in 1987-88, 53 of 107 (.495) in 1988-89 and 68 of 154 (.442) in 1989-90. Totals: 191 of 433 (.441).

LORRI BAUMAN
Drake
6-3 – C
Des Moines, Iowa

The first woman to score 3,000 points while playing a majority of her games under NCAA auspices. . . . Still holds seven NCAA tournament marks, including 50 points in a game in the 1982 West Regional final in a loss to Maryland. . . . Only one of nine women to score more than 3,000 points and collect more than 1,000 rebounds. . . . Drake qualified for three NCAA Tournament trips during her career. . . . In 120 games, she missed double figures in scoring only four times. . . . Played six-on-six basketball in high school in Iowa, averaging 48 points per game as a senior.

Year	G	FGM	FGA	FG%	FTM	FTA	FT%	Reb.	Avg.	Pts.	Avg.
80–81	28	263	465	.566	212	264	.803	248	8.9	738	26.4
81–82	35	273	513	.532	275	325	.846	372	9.2	821	23.5
82–83	28	264	445	.593	209	251	.833	264	9.4	737	26.3
83–84	29	304	508	.598	211	250	.844	216	7.4	819	28.2
Totals	120	1104	1931	.572	907	1090	.832	1050	8.8	3115	26.0

CAROL BLAZEJOWSKI
Montclair State
5-11 – F
Cranford, N.J.

Still holds women's career scoring average (31.7 points) and season average (38.6) and is third on the all-time women's scoring charts (3,199 points). . . . Was inducted in the Naismith Hall of Fame in 1993. . . . Owns the women's single-season scoring mark with 1,235 points as a senior. . . . A three-time Kodak All-American and the first Wade Trophy winner. . . . Helped Montclair State reach the first AIAW Final Four in 1978. . . . Montclair also played in two other AIAW national tournaments. . . . Continues to play on barnstorming teams in the Northeast. . . . Currently is director of licensing for the National Basketball Association.

Year	G	FGM	FGA	FG%	FTM	FTA	FT%	Reb.	Avg.	Pts.	Avg.
74–75	17	138	320	.430	57	80	.711	171	10.0	333	19.6
75–76	25	298	540	.551	116	150	.773	255	10.2	712	28.5
76–77	27	393	695	.565	133	167	.796	272	10.1	919	34.0
77–78	32	515	905	.569	205	245	.837	317	9.9	1235	38.6
Totals	101	1344	2460	.550	511	642	.795	1015	10.4	3199	31.7

CATHY BOSWELL
Illinois State
5-11 – F
Joliet, Ill.

Illinois State's all-time leading women's scorer (2,005 points) holds six school records and is the only woman athlete at the school to have her number retired. . . . Twice a finalist for the Wade Trophy.

Year	G	FGM	FGA	FG%	FTM	FTA	FT%	Reb.	Avg.	Pts.	Avg.
79–80	33	242	490	.494	51	84	.607	301	9.1	535	16.2
80–81	36	274	537	.510	101	119	.849	343	9.5	649	18.0
81–82	22	165	347	.476	28	44	.636	159	7.2	358	16.3
82–83	30	208	444	.468	47	62	.758	257	8.6	463	15.4
Totals	121	889	1818	.489	227	309	.735	1060	8.8	2005	16.6

DEBBIE BROCK
Delta State
4-11 – G
Forest City, Miss.

The tiny guard played for three AIAW national championship teams from 1975 to 1977. . . . Averaged only 7 points a game during her career, but was known for her excellent passing to future Hall of Fame teammate Lusia Harris. . . . An All-American her final two seasons. . . . Scored 22 points in the 1977 national title game against LSU from what now is the 3-point range.

Year	G	FGM	FGA	FG%	FTM	FTA	FT%	Reb.	Avg.	Pts.	Avg.
74–75	25	63	119	.529	65	77	.844	60	2.4	191	7.6
75–76	34	65	128	.507	62	78	.794	111	3.2	192	5.6
76–77	35	100	221	.452	65	77	.844	78	2.2	95	7.6
77–78	32	85	200	.425	85	103	.825	94	2.9	255	7.9
Totals	126	313	668	.469	277	335	.827	343	2.7	903	7.1

CINDY BROGDON
Mercer/Tennessee
5-10 – F
Buford, Ga.

The second all-time leading women's scorer with 3,240 points. . . . Tennessee made its first trip to the Final Four in her senior year in 1979. . . . Played her first two seasons for Mercer before transferring. . . . Was a two-time Kodak All-American, once at each school.

Year	G	FGM	FGA	FG%	FTM	FTA	FT%	Reb.	Avg.	Pts.	Avg.
75–76	30	348	706	.490	206	247	.830	319	10.6	902	30.1
76–77	28	335	690	.490	174	216	.810	286	10.2	844	30.1
77–78	31	286	593	.482	102	118	.864	238	7.6	674	21.7
78–79	39	344	639	.538	96	118	.813	185	4.7	784	20.1
Totals	128	1313	2628	.500	578	699	.827	1028	8.3	3240	25.0

ANUCHA BROWNE
Northwestern
6-1 – F
Brooklyn, N.Y.

Holds 24 school records and is Northwestern's first Kodak All-American (1985). . . . As a senior, she led the country in scoring with 30.5 points a game. . . . Set an NCAA record by scoring 30 points or more in six consecutive games. . . . The second all-time leading scorer in Big Ten history with 2,307 points, she was a three-time all-league pick and twice was its Player of the Year. . . . A finalist for the Wade Trophy and the Naismith Award.

Year	G	FGM	FGA	FG%	FTM	FTA	FT%	Reb.	Avg.	Pts.	Avg.
81–82	29	136	266	.511	74	116	.638	174	6.0	346	11.9
82–83	27	221	396	.558	110	170	.647	249	9.2	552	20.4
83–84	26	221	481	.459	112	179	.651	271	10.4	554	21.3
84–85	28	341	666	.512	173	254	.681	257	9.2	855	30.5
Totals	110	919	1809	.508	469	719	.652	951	8.6	2307	21.0

VICKY BULLETT
Maryland
6-2 – F/C
Martinsburg, W.V.

A two-time Kodak All-American.... The leading scorer and rebounder in school history.... Leading scorer and rebounder on Maryland's 1989 Final Four team.... Helped team to two Atlantic Coast Conference titles.... A three-time All-ACC pick.

Year	G	FGM	FGA	FG%	FTM	FTA	FT%	Reb.	Avg.	Pts.	Avg.
85–86	21	87	175	.470	44	61	.721	135	6.4	218	10.4
86–87	29	197	357	.552	49	77	.636	243	8.4	443	15.3
87–88	32	243	404	.602	95	134	.709	303	9.6	581	18.2
88–89	32	289	503	.675	108	136	.794	287	9.0	688	21.4
Totals	114	816	1439	.567	296	408	.725	888	7.8	1928	16.9

DENISE CURRY
UCLA
6-1 – F
Davis, Calif.

UCLA's all-time leading scorer (3,198 points) and rebounder (1,310 boards) who played on 1978 AIAW national championship team as a freshman.... Set a collegiate record by scoring in double figures in all 130 games of her career.... A three-time Kodak All-American who helped the Bruins to two West Coast Athletic Association titles and two AIAW national appearances.... Holds 14 UCLA career records.... Currently an assistant coach at the University of California.

Year	G	FGM	FGA	FG%	FTM	FTA	FT%	Reb.	Avg.	Pts.	Avg.
77–78	30	280	451	.621	50	65	.769	273	9.1	610	20.3
78–79	34	355	586	.606	93	115	.809	340	10.0	803	23.6
79–80	30	361	599	.604	133	149	.893	337	11.2	855	28.5
80–81	36	390	647	.603	150	192	.781	360	10.0	930	25.8
Totals	130	1386	2283	.607	426	521	.818	1310	10.1	3198	24.6

CLARISSA DAVIS-WRIGHTSIL
Texas
6-1 – F
San Antonio, Tex.

The all-time Southwest Conference career scoring and third-best scorer in school history despite being cut down by injuries during her career (knee injury as junior).... Was MVP of the 1986 Final Four as a freshman as Texas won the NCAA title.... A two-time Kodak All-American and Wade Trophy winner.... Also named National Player of the Year as a senior by Naismith, Champion Products, and the USBWA/Mercedes.... Scored 45 points in 97-78 Texas win at Tennessee in which a world attendance record (24,563) was set.... Established a Texas record by scoring 843 points during senior year.... Currently playing professional basketball in Turkey, where her husband also is a pro player.

Year	G	FGM	FGA	FG%	FTM	FTA	FT%	Reb.	Avg.	Pts.	Avg.
85–86	34	180	309	.583	99	150	.660	262	7.7	459.	13.5
86–87	26	196	340	.576	91	146	.632	217	8.3	483	18.6
87–88	9	93	145	.641	37	50	.740	87	9.7	223	24.8
88–89	32	324	585	.559	188	262	.718	316	9.9	843	26.3
Totals	101	793	1379	.580	415	608	.680	882	8.7	2008	19.8

ANNE DONOVAN
Old Dominion
6-8 – C
Ridgewood, N.J.

Old Dominion's all-time leading scorer and rebounder played for two national championship squads and two gold medal Olympic squads.... The first exceptionally tall impact player in women's college basketball.... A four-year starter, she was leading scorer and rebounder as a freshman, playing alongside All-Americans Nancy Lieberman and Inge Nissen on national title team.... A three-time Kodak All-American and the 1983 National Player of the Year.

Year	G	FGM	FGA	FG%	FTM	FTA	FT%	Reb.	Avg.	Pts.	Avg.
79–80	38	290	460	.630	68	126	.539	491	12.9	648	17.0
80–81	35	377	591	.638	125	175	.714	569	16.2	879	25.1
81–82	28	240	375	.640	99	142	.697	412	14.7	579	14.7
82–83	35	263	428	.614	87	130	.669	504	14.4	613	17.5
Totals	136	1170	1854	.631	379	573	.661	1976	14.5	2719	19.9

TERESA EDWARDS
Georgia
5-11 – G
Cairo, Ga.

A two-time Kodak All-American and three-time Olympian. . . . Played on Georgia's Final Four teams in 1983 and 1985. . . . Jersey number was the first to be retired for a Georgia basketball player, male or female. . . . Named all-SEC three times. . . . Has played professionally in Italy, Japan, Spain and France. . . . Her international play has spanned from 1981 to the 1996 Olympics and she has participated in 13 major competitions.

Year	G	FGM	FGA	FG%	FTM	FTA	FT%	Reb.	Avg.	Pts.	Avg.
82–83	33	189	412	.459	52	82	.634	73	2.2	430	13.0
83–84	33	207	397	.521	51	65	.785	81	2.5	465	14.1
84–85	30	203	385	.527	58	79	.734	84	2.8	464	15.5
85–86	32	274	491	.558	82	104	.788	146	4.6	630	19.7
Totals	128	873	1685	.518	243	330	.736	384	3.0	1989	15.5

PEGGIE GILLOM
Mississippi
6-0 – F
Abbeville, Miss.

The leading scorer and rebounder in school history.... Led Ole Miss to two AIAW regional tournament trips.... Was a finalist for the Wade Trophy in 1980... Drafted by the Dallas Diamonds of the Women's Professional Basketball League in 1980 and played one season before returning to Ole Miss, where she has been an assistant coach since 1981.... Her younger sister, Jennifer, also scored more than 2,000 points for the Lady Rebels, earned a gold medal with the 1988 U.S. Olympic team, and is the school's only Kodak All-American.

Year	G	FGM	FGA	FG%	FTM	FTA	FT%	Reb.	Avg.	Pts.	Avg.
76–77	28	159	314	.506	41	67	.612	240	8.6	359	12.8
77–78	40	312	583	.535	97	132	.735	329	8.2	721	8.0
78–79	39	288	571	.504	116	152	.763	341	8.7	692	17.7
79–80	37	293	652	.449	128	181	.707	361	9.8	714	19.3
Totals	144	1052	2120	.496	382	532	.718	1271	8.8	2486	17.3

BRIDGETTE GORDON
Tennessee
6-0 – F
DeLand, Fla.

The all-time leading scorer and most decorated player in school history.... Led Tennessee to its first two national championships in 1987 and 1989, and is one of three Lady Volunteers to reach the Final Four in all four of her college seasons. No other women's program holds that distinction.... A two-time Kodak All-American and MVP of the 1989 Final Four.... The all-time leading scorer in NCAA women's tournament history with 388 points and a 21.6 average.... Tennessee was 115-21 during her career, winning two SEC titles, and she was the league's Player of the Year twice.... Led her professional team to the Italian League championship in 1991.

Year	G	FGM	FGA	FG%	FTM	FTA	FT%	Reb.	Avg.	Pts.	Avg.
85–86	34	206	429	.480	69	109	.633	209	6.2	418	14.2
86–87	34	222	459	.484	115	160	.719	232	6.8	559	16.4
87–88	33	286	529	.541	106	151	.702	225	6.8	687	20.8
88–89	36	298	557	.535	131	188	.697	251	7.0	733	20.4
Totals	137	1012	1974	.513	421	608	.692	917	6.1	2460	18.0

JERILYNN HARPER
Tennessee/Tennessee Tech
6-1 – F
Jefferson City, Tenn.

The second all-time career scorer for one of the early powers from the Southeast.... Helped Tech to appearances in the National Women's Invitational Tournament and the first NCAA tournament in 1982.... Owns 10 of the top 11 individual single-game scoring records at Tech.... Scored 40 or more points six different times in her career and in 32 games scored 30 points or more.... Played her freshman year at Tennessee, where she was a reserve on the 1979 Final Four team, before transferring to Tennessee Tech.

Year	G	FGM	FGA	FG%	FTM	FTA	FT%	Reb.	Avg.	Pts.	Avg.
78–79	37	152	271	.561	61	84	.726	170	4.6	365	9.9
79–80	27	159	293	.543	78	100	.780			396	14.7
80–81	34	410	653	.628	191	242	.789			1011	29.7
81–82	31	343	601	.571	191	242	.784			831	26.8
Totals	129	1064	1818	.585	521	668	.780	961	7.4	2603	20.2

JANET HARRIS
Georgia
6-3 – F/C
Chicago, Ill.

Georgia's all-time leading scorer and rebounder, a three-time Kodak All-American, and a member of two U.S. National Sports teams.... Took Georgia to the NCAA Final Four in 1983 and 1985.... Is one of three Georgia women's players to have a jersey number retired.... While at Georgia, the team earned four straight NCAA Tournament trips.... A three-time All-SEC selection, she led Georgia to consecutive league crowns in 1983 and 1984.

Year	G	FGM	FGA	FG%	FTM	FTA	FT%	Reb.	Avg.	Pts.	Avg.
81–82	30	281	517	.533	101	160	.631	371	12.4	663	22.4
82–83	34	299	537	.557	94	155	.606	397	11.7	692	20.4
83–84	33	249	472	.528	88	126	.698	279	8.5	584	17.8
84–85	34	298	503	.592	104	147	.707	351	10.3	700	20.6
Totals	131	1127	2029	.555	387	588	.658	1398	10.7	2641	20.2

LUSIA HARRIS STEWART
Delta State
6-3 – C
Minter City, Miss.

The first female college player to be inducted into the Naismith Basketball Hall of Fame in 1992.... The first prototypical modern center in the women's college game.... Led the Lady Statesmen to three consecutive AIAW national titles from 1975 to 1977. She was MVP of all three national tournaments.... A member of the 1976 silver medal U.S. Olympic team, she scored the first points ever by a female player in the Olympics.... The Olympians' top scorer (15.0) and rebounder (7.0).... A three-time All-American and two-time national Player of the Year.... The nation's top scorer as a junior, averaging 31.2 points.... Delta State's first women's basketball recruit after a 40-year layoff.... Currently a high school teacher and coach in Ruleville, Miss.

Year	G	FGM	FGA	FG%	FTM	FTA	FT%	Reb.	Avg.	Pts.	Avg.
73–74	18	147	226	.650	58	103	.563	252	14.0	352	19.6
74–75	28	300	458	.655	107	145	.738	400	14.3	707	25.3
75–76	34	457	738	.619	146	217	.672	514	15.1	1060	31.2
76–77	35	363	579	.627	136	200	.680	496	14.2	862	24.6
Totals	115	1266	2001	.633	447	665	.672	1662	14.5	2979	25.9

PAM KELLY
Louisiana Tech
6-0 – F
Columbia, La.

Captained Louisiana Tech to national titles in 1981 and 1982 as the Lady Techsters rolled up a dominating record of 69-1 over those seasons, prompting one coach to proclaim they had the two best teams in America.... The school's career leader in points (2,979) and rebounds (1,511) as well as in 19 other categories.... A three-time Kodak All-American and the 1982 Wade Trophy winner.... A member of the Louisiana Tech Hall of Fame and the Louisiana College Athlete of the Year in 1981.... Scored in double figures in 140 of her 153 college games, and notched rebounding double-figure games 80 times.... Had a career-high of 41 points against UCLA as a senior.... The Lady Techsters were 143-10 during her career.

Year	G	FGM	FGA	FG%	FTM	FTA	FT%	Reb.	Avg.	Pts.	Avg.
78–79	38	273	564	.484	62	92	.674	372	9.8	721	19.0
79–80	45	369	710	.520	79	114	.693	491	10.9	932	20.7
80–81	34	204	449	.454	53	70	.757	322	9.5	595	17.5
81–82	36	280	435	.644	171	247	.692	326	9.1	732	20.3
Totals	153	1126	2158	.522	365	531	.687	1511	9.8	2979	19.4

BARBARA KENNEDY
Clemson
6-1 – F/C
Rome, Ga.

A Kodak All-American selection in 1981–82, when she averaged 29 points a game, currently the 10th best seasonal average in NCAA history.... Still holds the Atlantic Coast Conference record for career scoring average and is the league's career rebounding leader... Clemson was 84-42 during her career, qualifying for three AIAW tournaments and the first NCAA women's tournament.... She scored the first points in NCAA women's tournament history against Penn State on March 12, 1982.... A member of the Clemson Athletic Hall of Fame, she also was a Clemson assistant coach and is now an athletic academic counselor at the school.

Year	G	FGM	FGA	FG%	FTM	FTA	FT%	Reb.	Avg.	Pts.	Avg.
78–79	29	227	477	.476	87	130	.669	248	8.6	541	18.7
79–80	36	382	729	.524	89	137	.650	298	8.3	853	23.7
80–81	31	348	722	.482	115	175	.657	306	9.9	811	26.2
81–82	31	392	760	.516	124	172	.721	400	12.9	908	29.3
Totals	127	1349	2688	.502	415	614	.676	1252	9.9	3113	24.5

JANICE LAWRENCE
Louisiana Tech
6-3 – C
Lucedale, Miss.

A three-time Kodak All-American and a national Player of the Year who guided the Lady Techsters to two national titles in 1980–81 and 1981–82. Those title teams were among the most dominating in women's college annals, going a collective 69-1.... The MVP of the first NCAA Women's Final Four in 1982.... The national player of the year in 1984 as well as the Wade Trophy winner.

Year	G	FGM	FGA	FG%	FTM	FTA	FT%	Reb.	Avg.	Pts.	Avg.
80–81	34	192	326	.589	123	189	.651	283	8.3	507	14.9
81–82	36	202	363	.556	124	174	.713	253	7.0	528	14.7
82–83	33	272	455	.598	141	222	.635	301	9.1	685	20.7
83–84	32	268	433	.619	147	207	.710	301	8.1	683	21.3
Totals	135	934	1577	.592	535	792	.676	1097	8.1	2403	17.8

LISA LESLIE
Southern Cal
6-5 – F/C
Inglewood, Calif.

The first four-time All-Pac-10 selection since Cheryl Miller and the 1994 national player of the year.... A three-time All-American.... Third in USC scoring charts (2,414 points), scoring average (20.1 per game) and fourth in rebounds (1,214).... Developed from a thin, gangly high school star into a muscular, strong, dominating post player for the 1996 U.S. Olympic team.... Scored 101 points in the first half of a high school game before the opposing team left the court at halftime.

Year	G	FGM	FGA	FG%	FTM	FTA	FT%	Reb.	Avg.	Pts.	Avg.
90–91	30	241	504	.478	98	145	.676	299	10.0	582	19.4
91–92	31	262	476	.550	106	152	.697	261	8.4	632	20.4
92–93	29	211	378	.558	119	162	.735	285	9.8	543	18.7
94–94	30	259	464	.558	138	201	.687	369	12.3	657	21.9
Totals	120	973	1822	.534	461	660	.698	1214	10.1	2414	20.1

NANCY LIEBERMAN CLINE
Old Dominion
5-10 – G
Far Rockaway, N.Y.

One of the first flash-and-dash players of the modern women's era.... She was captain of two national championship teams and a three-time Kodak All-American.... The 1980 national Player of the year.... Named to the 1976 U.S. Olympic team as an 18-year-old high school graduate.... A first-round draft choice of the Dallas Diamonds in 1980, leading them to a league title.... Was a physical trainer and confidante of tennis champion Martina Navratilova.... Has played in the U.S. Basketball League and currently has several basketball and sports marketing businesses in operation.... Wrote an autobiography entitled *Lady Magic* for the nickname she earned because of her fancy passing abilities.

Year	G	FGM	FGA	FG%	FTM	FTA	FT%	Reb.	Avg.	Pts.	Avg.
76–77	27	240	507	.473	88	117	.709	272	10.1	563	20.9
77–78	34	281	651	.432	119	163	.730	325	9.6	681	20.2
78–79	36	243	500	.478	139	176	.790	276	7.7	625	17.4
79–80	37	203	390	.533	145	186	.779	294	7.9	561	15.2
Totals	134	973	2056	.472	486	642	.757	1167	8.7	2430	18.1

REBECCA LOBO
Connecticut
6-4 – F
Southwick, Mass.

The most-decorated player in Big East history helped Connecticut to a historic 35-0 record and NCAA championship in 1995.... A member of the 1996 U.S. Olympic team.... Made appearances on David Letterman and other shows and was a magazine cover girl during the Huskies' stretch drive for the title.... Was national player of the year as a senior and was an academic Phi Beta Kappa.... Has written a book with her mother, whose fight with cancer earned national headlines during Lobo's final two seasons.... Big East's career rebounding leader (1,268) and second in UConn scoring (2,133).... A two-time All-American and four-time All-Big East pick.

Year	G	FGM	FGA	FG%	FTM	FTA	FT%	Reb.	Avg.	Pts.	Avg.
91-92	29	167	338	.494	82	117	.701	228	7.9	416	14.3
92-93	29	189	421	.449	77	119	.647	326	11.2	484	16.7
93-94	33	243	445	.546	138	187	.738	371	11.2	635	19.2
94-95	35	238	476	.500	104	154	.675	343	9.8	598	17.1
Totals	126	837	1680	.498	401	577	.695	1268	10.1	2133	16.9

Three-point shooting: 0 of 1 in 1991-92, 29 of 85 (.341) in 1992-93, 11 of 34 (.324) in 1993-94 and 18 of 51 (.353) in 1994-95. Totals: 58 of 171 (.339).

KATRINA MCCLAIN
Georgia
6-2 – C
Charleston, S.C.

The 1987 Player of the Year by Champion Products, the Women's Basketball News Service, the American Women's Sports Foundation, and the *Shreveport Journal*.... A two-time All-American and two-time Olympian.... Was named to two All-SEC teams.... Starting center on Georgia team that reached the 1985 national title game.

Year	G	FGM	FGA	FG%	FTM	FTA	FT%	Reb.	Avg.	Pts.	Avg.
83–84	33	137	197	.695	66	95	.695	254	7.7	340	10.3
84–85	29	164	262	.626	70	105	.667	234	8.1	398	13.7
85–86	31	262	396	.662	137	176	.778	314	10.1	661	21.3
86–87	32	310	552	.562	176	240	.733	391	12.2	796	24.9
Totals	125	873	1407	.620	449	616	.729	1193	9.5	2195	17.6

SUZIE MCCONNELL SERIO
Penn State
5-5 – G
Pittsburgh, Pa.

A 1988 Kodak All-American and a two-time Olympian.... The NCAA's all-time women's assists leader, totaling 1,307 for an average of 10.2 a game.... Guided the Nittany Lions to four NCAA Tournament berths.... Named the Frances Pomeroy Naismith winner in 1988 as the top small player in the country.... Had 71 double-figure assist games.... Currently a high school and AAU coach in Pittsburgh.

Year	G	FGM	FGA	FG%	FTM	FTA	FT%	Reb.	Avg.	Pts.	Avg.
84–85	33	157	343	.458	101	136	.743	93	2.8	415	12.6
85–86	32	148	335	.442	86	109	.789	94	2.9	382	11.9
86–87	30	169	337	.502	68	94	.723	141	4.7	418	13.9
87–88	33	255	511	.499	116	143	.811	165	5.0	682	20.6
Totals	128	729	1526	.478	371	482	.770	493	3.9	1897	14.8

NIKKI MCCRAY
Tennessee
5-11 – G/F
Collierville, Tenn.

The leader and defensive ace of a Lady Vol program that during her career had a record of 122-11, the best four-year stretch in school history, and reached the NCAA title game in 1995.... A two-time SEC player of the year and All-American.... A two-time Naismith player of the year finalist. . . Ranks among the Top 20 in Tennessee records in steals (second with 292) and points (seventh with 1,572).... Tennessee went undefeated in the SEC during her last three seasons, going 33-0 during the regular season and won two SEC tournament titles.... Originally signed as a Proposition 48 non-qualifier, but gained an extra season of eligibility following NCAA academic revisions.... A member of the 1996 U.S. Olympic team.

Year	G	FGM	FGA	FG%	FTM	FTA	FT%	Reb.	Avg.	Pts.	Avg.
91-92	31	87	174	.500	39	53	.736	114	3.7	215	6.9
92-93	32	133	286	.465	83	115	.722	145	4.5	349	10.9
93-94	33	213	421	.506	111	158	.703	231	7.0	537	16.3
94-95	31	193	392	.492	83	122	.680	182	5.9	471	15.2
Totals	127	626	1273	.492	316	448	.705	672	5.3	1572	12.4

Three-point shooting: 2 of 10 (.200) in 1991-92 and 2 of 15 (.133) in 1994-95. Totals: 4 of 25 (.160).

PAM MCGEE
Southern Cal
6-3 – F/C
Flint, Mich.

A Kodak All-American in 1984 as a senior.... Member of national title teams in 1983 and 1984.... The identical twin of USC forward Paula McGee.... Was a finalist for the Wade Trophy in 1983 and the Naismith Award in 1984.... USC's all-time leader in career field-goal shooting.

Year	G	FGM	FGA	FG%	FTM	FTA	FT%	Reb.	Avg.	Pts.	Avg.
80–81	34	217	398	.545	75	148	.506	294	8.6	509	14.8
81–82	27	219	381	.575	91	143	.636	312	11.6	529	19.6
82–83	33	249	408	.610	110	174	.632	329	10.0	608	18.4
83–84	33	250	420	.595	68	131	.519	320	8.7	568	17.2
Totals	127	935	1607	.582	365	596	.613	1255	9.9	2214	17.4

PAULA MCGEE
Southern Cal
6-3 – F/C
Flint, Mich.

Was a Kodak All-American in 1981 and 1983.... Helped the Trojans to national titles in 1983 and 1984.... The identical twin of USC forward Pam McGee.... No other USC freshman, including Cheryl Miller, scored as many points (683).

Year	G	FGM	FGA	FG%	FTM	FTA	FT%	Reb.	Avg.	Pts.	Avg.
80–81	34	289	567	.510	105	165	.636	318	9.4	683	20.1
81–82	27	226	461	.490	94	130	.723	278	10.3	546	20.2
82–83	33	282	493	.572	68	91	.747	305	9.2	632	19.2
83–84	33	207	393	.527	71	110	.645	259	7.8	485	14.7
Totals	127	993	1941	.524	338	496	.681	1160	9.1	2346	17.5

CAROL MENKEN SCHAUDT
Oregon State
6-5 – C
Jefferson, Ore.

A 1981 Kodak All-American and 1984 U.S. Olympian.... Owns a majority of Oregon State's individual women's records, despite playing only three seasons for the Beavers after one year of junior college ball.... As a senior, led the nation in field-goal percentage, hitting 75 percent of her shots and helping OSU to a 22-6 record, one of its best ever.... Once scored 51 points in a game.... A three-time all-conference selection of the Northwest College Women's Sports Association.

Year	G	FGM	FGA	FG%	FTM	FTA	FT%	Reb.	Avg.	Pts.	Avg.
78–79	22	239	379	.630	106	173	.612	274	12.5	584	26.5
79–80	31	353	518	.681	125	217	.576	325	10.5	831	26.8
80–81	28	363	484	.750	102	161	.634	302	10.9	828	29.6
Totals	81	955	1381	.692	333	551	.604	901	11.1	2243	27.7

ANN MEYERS
UCLA
5-8 – G
LaHabra, Calif.

Inducted into the Naismith Basketball Hall of Fame in 1993.... With late husband, baseball great Don Drysdale, made history by becoming part of first married couple to both be elected into the halls of fame of their respective sports.... Team captain of 1978 AIAW national championship as a senior.... First woman awarded an athletic scholarship at UCLA.... Older brother Dave Meyers played on national title teams at UCLA in early 1970s.... Drafted by the Indiana Pacers in 1978, the first woman ever selected by an NBA team... Played two seasons for the New Jersey Gems of the Women's Professional Basketball League.

Year	G	FGM	FGA	FG%	FTM	FTA	FT%	Reb.	Avg.	Pts.	Avg.
74–75	23	183	346	.529	56	73	.767	191	8.3	422	18.3
75–76	23	129	303	.426	65	89	.730	189	8.2	323	14.0
76–77	22	160	317	.505	82	99	.828	161	7.3	402	18.3
77–78	29	221	420	.526	96	120	.800	278	9.6	538	18.6
Totals	97	693	1386	.500	299	381	.785	819	8.4	1685	17.4

CHERYL MILLER
Southern Cal
6-3 – F
Riverside, Calif.

A four-time All-American and three-time Naismith Award winner.... Led USC to national titles in 1983 and 1984 and the championship game in 1986.... Named 1980s Player of the Decade by the WBCA and the U.S. Basketball Writers Association.... USC career leader in points, rebounds, field goals, free throws, and steals.... Scored a state-record 105 points in a high school game.... The first four-time *Parade* high school All-American, male or female.... The only USC basketball player, male or female, to have her number retired.... Was a sports commentator for ABC-TV and ESPN before being named USC's head coach in September 1993.... Grew up in an athletic family, with an older brother formerly a major league baseball prospect and younger brother, Reggie, currently starring for the NBA's Indiana Pacers.

Year	G	FGM	FGA	FG%	FTM	FTA	FT%	Reb.	Avg.	Pts.	Avg.
82–83	33	268	486	.551	137	186	.737	320	9.7	673	20.4
83–84	33	281	493	.570	164	218	.752	350	10.6	726	22.0
84–85	30	302	572	.528	201	289	.753	474	15.8	805	26.8
85–86	32	308	506	.609	198	263	.753	390	12.2	814	25.4
Totals	128	1159	2057	.563	702	956	.734	1534	12.0	3018	23.6

KIM MULKEY ROBERTSON
Louisiana Tech
5-4 – G
Hammond, La.

Piloted Lady Techsters to national titles in 1981 and 1982.... A two-time Kodak All-American, she won 1984 Francis Pomeroy Naismith Award as the best women's player under 5-6.... Also selected as an Academic All-American twice.... Currently an assistant coach at Louisiana Tech.

Year	G	FGM	FGA	FG%	FTM	FTA	FT%	Reb.	Avg.	Pts.	Avg.
80–81	34	88	172	.512	76	118	.644	46	1.4	252	7.4
81–82	36	77	158	.487	46	76	.605	56	1.6	200	5.6
82–83	31	78	159	.491	53	85	.624	55	1.8	209	6.7
83–84	32	101	205	.493	81	120	.675	72	2.3	283	8.8
Totals	133	344	694	.496	256	399	.642	229	1.7	944	7.1

INGE NISSEN
Old Dominion
6-5 – C
Randers, Denmark

Member of dominating Old Dominion national title teams in 1979 and 1980.... Second-leading scorer and rebounder in school history.... A two-time Kodak All-American.... Currently an assistant coach at Florida International.... Lady Monarch MVP three times.... Established a school single-game record with 28 rebounds.... One of the first foreign female players to excel in the college game, she recruits many European players as a coach.... Played on professional title teams in Denmark, Norway, and France .... Holds the National Women's Invitational Tournament mark with 20 field goals in a game.... Played briefly in the now-defunct U.S. women's pro leagues.

Year	G	FGM	FGA	FG%	FTM	FTA	FT%	Reb.	Avg.	Pts.	Avg.
76–77	32	255	408	.523	82	152	.539	410	12.8	592	18.5
77–78	32	257	544	.472	148	209	.708	378	11.8	662	20.7
78–79	34	300	576	.521	148	198	.747	339	9.9	749	22.0
79–80	37	252	576	.437	140	199	.703	382	10.3	644	17.4
Totals	135	1064	2184	.487	518	758	.683	1509	11.2	2647	19.6

JUNE OLKOWSKI
Rutgers
6-0 – F
Philadelphia, Pa.

The only Rutgers player to have her jersey number retired.... Was captain and second-leading scorer of 1982 team that won the final AIAW national championship... A two-time Kodak All-American.... Has been an assistant coach at Auburn and Maryland and a head coach at Arizona and Butler, where she has been since the 1993–94 season.

Year	G	FGM	FGA	FG%	FTM	FTA	FT%	Reb.	Avg.	Pts.	Avg.
78–79	32	197	426	.462	102	152	.671	304	9.5	496	15.5
79–80	30	186	379	.491	91	138	.659	225	7.5	463	15.4
80–81	17	101	190	.532	54	78	.692	95	5.6	256	15.1
81–82	24	116	261	.444	53	73	.726	156	6.5	285	11.9
Totals	103	600	1256	.480	300	441	.680	780	7.7	1500	14.8

VICKIE ORR
Auburn
6-3 – C
Decatur, Ala.

A three-time Kodak All-American.... Was a finalist for the Champion/WBCA and Naismith Player of the Year Awards.... Led Auburn to national championship games in 1988 and 1989 ... Was SEC Player of the Year in 1988 ... Was named an assistant coach at Auburn in 1992.

Year	G	FGM	FGA	FG%	FTM	FTA	FT%	Reb.	Avg.	Pts.	Avg.
85–86	30	165	297	.555	65	98	.663	233	7.8	395	13.2
86–87	33	239	396	.604	72	110	.656	252	7.6	550	16.7
87–88	35	248	461	.538	69	90	.767	237	6.8	565	16.1
88–89	33	212	374	.567	101	135	.748	284	8.6	525	15.9
Totals	131	864	1528	.565	307	433	.709	1006	7.7	2035	15.5

SHELLY PENNEFATHER
Villanova
6-1 – F
Utica, N.Y.

The all-time leading career scorer (2,408 points) in school history and for the Philadelphia Big Five .... A two-time All-American and the 1987 Wade Trophy winner.... Named to the All-Big East team three times, and was the league's MVP three times as well.... Is the Big East's women's career scoring and rebounding leader.... Villanova won two Big East regular-season crowns and averaged 23 wins a season during her career.... The first Big East player, male or female, to earn the conference's player of the week award three consecutive times.... Was inducted into the Big Five Hall of Fame in 1993.... She played professionally in Japan for four seasons.... Currently is a member of the Order of St. Claire, a cloistered nunnery in Virginia.

Year	G	FGM	FGA	FG%	FTM	FTA	FT%	Reb.	Avg.	Pts.	Avg.
83–84	29	220	411	.535	64	82	.780	253	9.7	504	19.4
84–85	29	245	459	.534	54	73	.740	317	10.9	544	18.8
85–86	31	302	527	.573	81	99	.818	293	9.5	685	22.1
86–87	31	306	523	.585	68	82	.768	308	9.9	675	21.8
Totals	120	1073	1920	.558	262	336	.779	1171	9.7	2408	20.0

LATAUNYA POLLARD
Long Beach State
5-10 – G/F
East Chicago, Ind.

One of just 13 women players with 3,000 career points or more.... Instrumental in turning Long Beach State into a national power in the early 1980s.... The 1983 Wade Trophy winner and a three-time All-American....

Villanova's Shelly Pennefather maneuvers around the opposition's defense.

Twice named the player of the year by the West Coast Athletic Association.... Holds four major career and three single season school records, including scoring, scoring average, and field goals made.... Guided the 49ers to four postseason bids (three AIAW and one NCAA).... A prototype full-court athlete who helped speed up the transition game in women's basketball.... Was such a popular figure during her college days that she once rode on the City of Long Beach float at the Tournament of Roses parade.

Year	G	FGM	FGA	FG%	FTM	FTA	FT%	Reb.	Avg.	Pts.	Avg.
79–80	34	295	570	.518	70	94	.745	176	5.1	660	19.4
80–81	34	325	602	.540	83	121	.686	193	5.8	733	21.6
81–82	29	292	540	.541	117	154	.760	177	6.1	701	24.2
82–83	31	376	721	.521	155	201	.771	275	8.9	907	29.2
Totals	128	1288	2433	.530	425	570	.745	821	6.4	3001	23.5

JILL RANKIN
Wayland Baptist/Tennessee
6-3 – C
Phillips, Tex.

A Kodak All-American in her only season at Tennessee, which went 35-5 and finished second in the AIAW national tournament.... The last national caliber player at Wayland Baptist, a tiny Texas Panhandle school that was one of the first institutions to give women basketball scholarships as early as the 1950s.... Helped Wayland reach three AIAW national tournaments during its college-era heyday in the late 1970s and was a Kodak choice as a junior.... Scored 81 points in a high school game.

Year	G	FGM	FGA	FG%	FTM	FTA	FT%	Reb.	Avg.	Pts.	Avg.
76–77	36	218	368	.592	91	131	.695	257	7.0	527	14.6
77–78	38	259	426	.607	76	121	.628	262	6.9	594	15.6
78–79	34	410	698	.587	180	234	.769	305	9.0	1000	29.4
79–80	38	296	536	.552	138	172	.802	277	7.3	730	19.2
Totals	146	1183	2028	.583	485	658	.737	1101	7.6	2851	19.2

THERESA SHANK GRENTZ
Immaculata
5-10 – C
Springfield, Pa.

The first dominating center in women's college basketball.... A two-time All-American who paced Immaculata to the first three AIAW national championships from 1972 to 1974.... Bypassed an opportunity to try out for the 1976 Olympic team to get married and begin a family.... One of the first women's coaches to earn a professional salary that did not include teaching duties.... Taught elementary school after graduation before being named head coach at St. Joseph's.... Went to Rutgers in 1977 and coached the last AIAW national championship team in 1982.

Year	G	FGM	FGA	FG%	FTM	FTA	FT%	Reb.	Avg.	Pts.	Avg.
70–71	3	58	101	.574	8	11	.727	44	14.6	66	22.0
71–72	20	188	321	.585	120	170	.705	389	19.4	496	24.8
72–73	16	124	247	.500	59	90	.655	269	16.8	307	19.1
73–74	20	123	257	.478	76	114	.660	263	13.1	322	16.1
Totals	59	493	926	.532	263	385	.683	965	16.3	1191	20.2

BEV SMITH
Oregon
5-11 – F
Salmon Arm, B.C.

The only Oregon player to be named a Kodak All-American (1981 and 1982).... Is the school's career rebounding leader and second leading all-time scorer.... Owns or shares 12 school records... A four-year starter, she led the Ducks to a 103-20 record, two AIAW national tournament appearances, and one trip to the NCAA tourney.... Was nominated for the Wade Trophy twice.... MVP of the National Women's Invitational Tournament as a freshman.... Played for the 1984 Canadian Olympic team and in the 1979 World Championships.

Year	G	FGM	FGA	FG%	FTM	FTA	FT%	Reb.	Avg.	Pts.	Avg.
78–79	25	166	356	.466	47	86	.547	323	12.9	379	15.2
79–80	27	240	441	.544	99	129	.767	367	13.6	579	21.4
80–81	32	259	485	.534	114	157	.726	376	11.8	632	19.8
81–82	26	192	400	.480	89	119	.748	296	11.4	473	18.2
Totals	110	857	1682	.510	349	491	.711	1362	12.4	2063	18.8

DAWN STALEY
Virginia
5-6 – G
Philadelphia, Pa.

Named national player of the year as a junior and senior by a variety of organizations.... Was a three-time Kodak All-American.... Led Virginia to three Final Four appearances.... Named the 1991 Honda-Broderick Cup Award winner, signifying the top collegiate woman athlete.... Was MVP of the 1991 Final Four, sharing a single-game record of 28 points in a losing effort against Tennessee in the national title game.... The NCAA career steals leader with 454.... The only player in ACC history, male or female, to register at least 2,000 points, 700 rebounds, 700 assists and 400 steals.... The first woman in school history to score 2,000 points.... Led Virginia to an ACC tournament title and

was a two-time league Player of the Year.... Learned the game on the same playgrounds as former Loyola Marymount All-Americans Hank Gathers and Bo Kimble.

Year	G	FGM	FGA	FG%	FTM	FTA	FT%	Reb.	Avg.	Pts.	Avg.
88–89	31	197	431	.457	147	177	.831	158	5.1	574	18.5
89–90	32	203	449	.452	132	169	.781	214	6.7	574	17.9
90–91	34	176	391	.450	108	131	.824	209	6.1	495	14.6
91–92	34	177	366	.484	118	146	.808	191	5.6	492	14.5
Totals	131	753	1637	.460	505	623	.811	772	5.9	2135	16.3

Three-point shooting: 33 of 93 (.355) in 1988-89, 36 of 104 (.346) in 1989-90, 35 of 108 (.324) in 1990-91 and 20 of 66 (.303) in 1991-92, Totals: 124 of 371 (.334).

MARIANNE CRAWFORD STANLEY
Immaculata
5-6 – G
Upper Darby, Pa.

A two-time All-American who played on two AIAW national championship teams.... Considered one of the first guards to speed up the game with a full-court transition game and heady point guard play.... Played on the same Immaculata teams with Theresa Grentz, head coach at Rutgers, and Rene Portland of Penn State.... Averaged nearly six assists a game during her career.... Was an assistant coach at Immaculata for one season before beginning her head coaching career at Old Dominion, where she coached three national championship teams.... Moved to USC in 1989 before suing the school on equal pay grounds.

Year	G	FGM	FGA	FG%	FTM	FTA	FT%	Reb.	Avg.	Pts.	Avg.
72–73	16	74	158	.468	56	81	.691	83	5.1	204	12.7
73–74	20	65	168	.386	41	65	.630	62	3.1	171	8.5
74–75	26	86	219	.392	45	70	.642	80	3.0	217	8.3
75–76	27	60	147	.408	34	51	.666	63	2.3	154	5.7
Totals	89	692	285	.418	176	267	.659	288	3.2	746	8.3

VALERIE STILL
Kentucky
6-1 – F/C
Cherry Hill, N.J.

The all-time leading scorer, male or female, in Kentucky basketball history with 2,763 points.... A two-time All-American and finalist for the Wade Trophy.... Led the Lady Kats to their best season ever as a senior, reaching the NCAA Tournament and achieving a No. 4 national ranking.... Guided Kentucky to its only SEC tournament championship in 1982 by averaging 30 points and 11 rebounds in three games and earning MVP honors.... She holds nearly a dozen school career records.... The only woman at Kentucky to have her jersey retired.... Began her playing career in Europe shortly after graduation and is currently playing there, perhaps the most longevity of any American female.... The younger sister of former Kansas City Chiefs All-Pro lineman Art Still.

Year	G	FGM	FGA	FG%	FTM	FTA	FT%	Reb.	Avg.	Pts.	Avg.
79–80	29	256	463	.553	129	183	.700	403	13.9	641	22.1
80–81	30	260	447	.581	108	154	.701	329	10.9	628	20.9
81–82	32	329	565	.582	136	199	.683	457	14.3	794	24.8
82–83	28	273	456	.599	154	212	.726	336	12.0	700	25.0
Totals	119	1118	1931	.580	527	748	.700	1525	12.8	2763	23.2

SHERYL SWOOPES
Texas Tech
6-0 – F
Brownfield, Tex.

Played just two years of major college basketball, but as a senior guided Texas Tech to the NCAA championship in 1993.... She shattered Bill

Walton's Final Four single-game scoring record of 44 points by tallying 47 against Ohio State in the title contest.... Was a unanimous national Player of the Year and twice earned Kodak All-American honors.... Scored in double figures in all but two of her 66 games at Texas Tech and finished as the school's second all-time scoring leader with 1,645 points.... Was the national Junior College Player of the Year at South Plains Junior College in Texas, where she holds 28 school records.

Year	G	FGM	FGA	FG%	FTM	FTA	FT%	Reb.	Avg.	Pts.	Avg.
91–92	32	275	527	.503	135	167	.808	285	8.9	690	21.6
92–93	34	356	652	.546	211	243	.868	312	9.2	955	28.0
Totals	66	631	1179	.535	346	410	.843	597	9.0	1645	24.9

Three-point shooting: 25 of 61 (.410) in 1991-92 and 32 of 78 (.410) in 1992-93. Totals: 57 of 139 (.410).

JOYCE WALKER
LSU
5-8 – G
Seattle, Wash.

A two-time Kodak All-American and the school's career scoring leader with 2,906 points.... The only player in LSU history to rank in the Top 10 in scoring, rebounding, assists, steals, and blocked shots.... Second-leading SEC career scoring leader at 24.9 points, she also leads the league in career field goals made and attempted.... Helped LSU to an AIAW national tournament appearance as a freshman and to the NCAA regionals in her senior season.

Year	G	FGM	FGA	FG%	FTM	FTA	FT%	Reb.	Avg.	Pts.	Avg.
80–81	30	277	489	.566	67	107	.626	157	5.2	621	20.7
81–82	30	340	500	.676	67	99	.677	136	4.5	747	24.9
82–83	27	312	540	.578	120	161	.745	186	6.9	744	27.6
83–84	30	330	619	.533	134	165	.812	119	4.0	794	26.5
Totals	117	1259	2238	.562	388	532	.729	598	5.1	2906	24.8

ROSIE WALKER
Stephen F. Austin
6-1 – F
Dallas, Tex.

Despite playing only two years, is one of the most decorated players in school history.... A two-time All-American at Stephen F. Austin after being named a junior college All-American.... Holds seven school records in all.... The Ladyjacks recorded a 57-11 during her two seasons and one national AIAW tournament trip.... Scored 30 or more points in 18 different games.

Year	G	FGM	FGA	FG%	FTM	FTA	FT%	Reb.	Avg.	Pts.	Avg.
78–79	35	395	607	.650	122	174	.701	448	12.8	912	26.0
79–80	31	263	390	.674	123	170	.724	354	11.4	649	20.9
Totals	66	658	997	.660	245	344	.712	802	12.2	1561	23.7

TERESA WEATHERSPOON
Louisiana Tech
5-8 – G
Pineland, Tex.

The all-time assists leader in Louisiana Tech history who guided the Lady Techsters to their third national title in 1988.... A two-time Kodak All-

American and the 1988 Wade Trophy Winner.... Also the 1988 recipient of the Honda/Broderick Cup, awarded to the top collegiate female athlete in all sports.... Named to the all-Women's Final Four team twice.... In 1993 became one of the first two Americans to play professional basketball in Russia as a member of the Moscow Red Army team.

Year	G	FGM	FGA	FG%	FTM	FTA	FT%	Reb.	Avg.	Pts.	Avg.
84–85	33	72	140	.514	51	100	.510	127	3.8	195	5.9
85–86	32	110	226	.487	61	112	.545	125	3.9	281	8.7
86–87	33	122	234	.521	67	95	.705	137	4.2	311	9.4
87–88	33	119	249	.478	57	86	.663	144	4.4	300	9.1
Totals	131	423	849	.498	236	393	.601	533	4.1	1087	8.3

LYNETTE WOODARD
Kansas
6-0 – F
Wichita, Kans.

The all-time women's scoring leader, with 3,649 points, only 18 points shy of Pete Maravich's career college record... A four-time All-American and two-time Olympian, captaining the 1984 U.S. gold medal squad.... The 1981 Wade Trophy Winner, awarded to the top female collegian.... Selected the Big Eight's Player of the Decade for the 1980s.... A member of the Kansas and National High School Athletic Halls of Fame.... Paced Kansas to a 108-32 record and three AIAW national tournament appearances.... Holds eight career, eight single-season, and five single-game school records.... Was the first woman to play for the Harlem Globetrotters.... Played professionally in Italy and Japan and briefly was a Kansas assistant coach.... Currently is athletic director for Kansas City public schools.... The first female inducted into the GTE Academic All-American Hall of Fame in 1992.

Year	G	FGM	FGA	FG%	FTM	FTA	FT%	Reb.	Avg.	Pts.	Avg.
77–78	33	366	736	.497	101	152	.664	490	14.8	833	25.2
78–79	38	519	924	.562	139	212	.656	545	14.3	1177	31.0
79–80	37	372	738	.504	137	192	.714	389	10.5	881	23.8
80–81	31	315	594	.533	128	186	.688	310	10.0	758	24.5
Totals	139	1572	2992	.525	505	742	.681	1734	12.4	3649	26.3

All-Time Great Women's Coaches

LEON BARMORE
Louisiana Tech '67

The winningest coach by percentage in women's college basketball history.... Served as an assistant and associate head coach and was co-head coach with Sonja Hogg for three seasons before getting the job to himself in 1985.... Tech won two national titles while he was an assistant and again in 1988.... Named co-Coach of the Decade for the 1980s by the U.S. Basketball Writers Association.... Named Naismith National Coach of the Year in 1988.... Until 1990–91, Tech had never finished lower than fifth in the final regular-season AP poll.... Lady Techsters upset No. 1 Tennessee and Southern Cal to reach the 1994 Final Four, losing only on a last-second shot by North Carolina in the finals.

Year	School	Overall	League	Postseason
82–83	La. Tech	26-6		NCAA Runnerup
83–84	La. Tech	30-3		NCAA Final Four
84–85	La. Tech	29-4		NCAA Regional
85–86	La. Tech	27-5		NCAA Regional
86–87	La. Tech	30-3		NCAA Runnerup
87–88	La. Tech	32-2	8-0 (ASC)	NCAA Champion
88–89	La. Tech	32-4	12-0 (ASC)	NCAA Final Four
89–90	La. Tech	32-1	14-0 (ASC)	NCAA Final Four
90–91	La. Tech	18-12	10-4 (ASC)	NCAA 1st Round
91–92	La. Tech	20-10	11-3 (SBC)	NCAA 1st Round
92–93	La. Tech	26-6	13-1 (SBC)	NCAA Regional
93–94	La. Tech	32-3	14-0 (SBC)	NCAA Runnerup
93–94	La. Tech	31-4	14-0 (SBC)	NCAA Runnerup
94–95	La. Tech	28-5	14-0 (SBC)	NCAA Sweet 16
95–96	La. Tech	32-2	14-0 (SBC)	NCAA Elite

14-Year Coaching Record: 398-63 (.863) at Louisiana Tech; 35-13 (.729) in NCAA Tournament.

JOE CIAMPI
Mansfield '68

The 12th winningest active Division I coach who led the Lady Tigers to the NCAA title game in 1988, 1989 and 1990. . . . National coach of the year in 1987, 1989 and 1993. . . . He has coached four All-Americans and three Olympians: Vickie Orr in 1988, Carolyn Jones in 1992 and Ruthie Bolton-Holifield in 1996. . . . Coached Auburn to SEC regular-season titles in 1987, 1988 and 1989 and the SEC Tournment championship in 1981, 1987 and 1990. . . . The fourth-winningest coach in NCAA tournament history had had 12 teams qualify for the NCAA Tournament. . . . Coached at Army when Mike Krzyzewski was the men's coach there. . . . Auburn held an NCAA homecourt winning streak at 68 games from 1986-91 that was broken by Tennessee.

Year	School	Overall	League	Postseason
77-78	Army	19-6		
78-79	Army	20-4		
79-80	Auburn	17-13		
80-81	Auburn	26-7		SEC Tr. Champs
81-82	Auburn	24-5		NCAA Tournament
82-83	Auburn	24-8	6-2 (SEC)	NCAA 2nd Round
83-84	Auburn	19-10	5-3 (SEC)	
84-85	Auburn	25-6	5-3 (SEC)	NCAA 2nd Round
85-86	Auburn	24-6	6-3 (SEC)	NCAA Sweet 16
86-87	Auburn	31-2	8-1 (SEC)	NCAA Elite 8
87-88	Auburn	32-3	9-0 (SEC)	NCAA Runner-up
88-89	Auburn	32-2	9-0 (SEC)	NCAA Runner-up
89-90	Auburn	28-7	7-2 (SEC)	NCAA Runner-up
90-91	Auburn	26-6	7-2 (SEC)	NCAA Elite 8
91-92	Auburn	17-12	4-7 (SEC)	
92-93	Auburn	25-4	9-2 (SEC)	NCAA Sweet 16
93-94	Auburn	20-10	6-5 (SEC)	NCAA 2nd Round
94-95	Auburn	17-10	5-6 (SEC)	
95-96	Auburn	23-9	6-5 (SEC)	NCAA Elite 8

19-Year Coaching Record: 421-72 (.853) overall; 39-10 (.795) in two years at Army; 410-120 (.773) in first 17 years at Auburn; 92-41 (.691) in SEC.

JODY CONRADT
Baylor '63

The all-time winningest coach in women's college basketball history and the only coach with more than 600 career victories. . . . Her 1986 Texas team went 34-0 and finished as the only undefeated women's NCAA title team ever. . . . Earned Southwest Conference Coach of the Year honors four times and was the National Coach of the Year in 1980 and 1986. . . . Texas won a record 188 consecutive SWC victories until Arkansas snapped the string during the 1989-90 season. . . . Texas also was the national attendance leader during the 1980s. . . . Coached the U.S. to a gold medal in the 1987 Pan American Games. . . . Women's athletic director at Texas since 1992. . . . A young 1993-94 Lady Longhorn team upset defending NCAA champion Texas Tech with a last-second shot to win the Southwest Conference Tournament.

Year	School	Overall	League	Postseason
69-70	Sam Houston St.	15-4		
70-71	Sam Houston St.	20-6		
71-72	Sam Houston St.	19-6		
72-73	Sam Houston St.	20-7		
73-74	UT-Arlington	9-14		
74-75	UT-Arlington	11-14		
75-76	UT-Arlington	23-11		
76-77	Texas	36-10		AIAW Regional
77-78	Texas	29-10		AIAW Regional
78-79	Texas	37-4		AIAW Regional
79-80	Texas	33-4		5th AIAW
80-81	Texas	28-8		AIAW Nationals
81-82	Texas	35-4		2nd AIAW
82-83	Texas	30-3	8-0 (SWC)	NCAA Regional
83-84	Texas	32-3	16-0 (SWC)	NCAA Regional
84-85	Texas	28-3	16-0 (SWC)	NCAA Regional
85-86	Texas	34-0	16-0 (SWC)	NCAA Champion
86-87	Texas	31-2	16-0 (SWC)	NCAA Final Four
87-88	Texas	32-3	16-0 (SWC)	NCAA Regional
88-89	Texas	27-5	16-0 (SWC)	NCAA Regional
89-90	Texas	27-5	15-1 (SWC)	NCAA Regional
90-91	Texas	21-9	14-2 (SWC)	NCAA 1st Round
91-92	Texas	21-10	13-4 (SWC)	NCAA 2nd Round
92-93	Texas	22-8	13-1 (SWC)	NCAA 2nd Round
93-94	Texas	22-9	10-4 (SWC)	NCAA 2nd Round
94-95	Texas	12-16	7-7 (SWC)	
95-96	Texas	21-9	13-1 (SWC)	NCAA 1st Round

27-Year Coaching Record: 675-187 (.783) overall; 64-23 (.736) in four years at Sam Houston State; 43-39 (.524) in three years at Texas-Arlington; 558-125 (.816) in first 20 years at Texas; 189-19 (.908) in Southwest Conference; 69-25 (.739) in the postseason.

SUE GUNTER
Peabody '62

She is the only women's coach with as many as 30 years of heading coaching experience. . . . Was an All-American AAU player in 1960 for Nashville Business College. . . . The first women's coach to earn 200 career victories at two different schools. . . . Coached LSU to the SEC Tournament championship in 1991. . . . Her LSU team won the National Women's Invitational Tournament in 1985.

Year	School	Overall	League	Postseason
62-63	Middle Tenn. St.	N/A		
63-64	Middle Tenn. St.	N/A		
64-65	Stephen F. Austin	N/A		
65-66	Stephen F. Austin	N/A		
66-67	Stephen F. Austin	N/A		
67-68	Stephen F. Austin	N/A		
69-70	Stephen F. Austin	6-4		
70-71	Stephen F. Austin	12-2		
71-72	Stephen F. Austin	19-9		
72-73	Stephen F. Austin	21-6		
73-74	Stephen F. Austin	27-7		AIAW Tr.
74-75	Stephen F. Austin	32-8		AIAW Tr.
75-76	Stephen F. Austin	30-4		
76-77	Stephen F. Austin	28-6		AIAW Regional
77-78	Stephen F. Austin	25-13		AIAW Tr.
78-79	Stephen F. Austin	30-5		AIAW Regional
79-80	Stephen F. Austin	27-6		AIAW Regional
82-83	LSU	20-7	6-2 (SEC)	
83-84	LSU	23-7	5-3 (SEC)	NCAA Regional
84-85	LSU	20-9	4-4 (SEC)	NWIT Champion
85-86	LSU	27-6	6-3 (SEC)	NCAA Regionals
86-87	LSU	20-8	6-3 (SEC)	NCAA 2nd Round
87-88	LSU	18-11	6-3 (SEC)	NCAA 1st Round
88-89	LSU	19-11	5-4 (SEC)	NCAA Regional
89-90	LSU	21-9	4-5 (SEC)	NCAA 1st Round
90-91	LSU	24-7	5-4 (SEC)	NCAA 2nd Round
91-92	LSU	16-13	4-7 (SEC)	
92-93	LSU	9-18	0-11 (SEC)	
93-94	LSU	11-16	2-9 (SEC)	
94-95	LSU	7-20	1-10 (SEC)	
95-96	LSU	21-11	4-7 (SEC)	

32-Year Coaching Record: 522-240 (.685) overall; 266-87 (.704) at Stephen F. Austin State; 256-153 (.625) in first 14 years at LSU; 58-75 (.436) in Southeastern Conference; 33-31 (.516) in postseason.

SONJA HOGG
Louisiana Tech '70

Began the famed Louisiana Tech program and coached it to national titles in 1981 and 1982. . . . Set a women's single-season record of 40 victories in 1979-90. . . . The 1980-81 team that went 34-0 is only one of two women's teams to go undefeated in a season. . . . In her later years at Tech, became a marketing and public relations ambassador for the team, leaving Leon Barmore to handle on-court responsibilities. . . . Left Tech in 1985 and became a high school coach in Texas briefly in the late 1980s. . . . Was director of marketing for the women's athletic department at Texas and also was the chief fundraiser for a women's basketball hall of fame to be built near Jackson, Tenn. . . . Named head coach at Baylor in April 1994.

Year	School	Overall	League	Postseason
74-75	La. Tech	13-9		
75-76	La. Tech	19-10		
76-77	La. Tech	22-9		AIAW Regional
77-78	La. Tech	20-8		AIAW Regional
78-79	La. Tech	34-4		AIAW Tr.
79-80	La. Tech	40-5		AIAW Final Four
80-81	La. Tech	34-0		AIAW Champions
81-82	La. Tech	35-1		NCAA Champions

82–83	La. Tech	31-2		NCAA Final Four
83–84	La. Tech	30-3		NCAA Final Four
84–85	La. Tech	29-4		NCAA Regional
94–95	Baylor	13-14	4-10 (SWC)	
95–96	Baylor	11-19	3-11 (SWC)	

13-Year Coaching Record: 331-88 (.689) overall; 307-55 (.848) in 11 years at Louisiana Tech; 24-33 (.421) in first two years at Baylor; 37-11 (.771) in postseason.

LUCILLE KYVALLOS
Springfield College

One of the pioneering college coaches of the early 1970s.... Queens participated in the earliest National Invitation Tournament and later became an AIAW runnerup under her tutelage.... The college coach of former Immaculata mentor Cathy Rush.... Helped organize the first women's college game at Madison Square Garden in 1975 in which her team was defeated by Immaculata before a crowd of more than 12,000 spectators.... Was named the first recipient of the U.S. Basketball Writers Association's Pioneer Award in 1990 .... Still a member of the physical education faculty at Queens.

Year	School	Overall	League	Postseason
62–66	W. Chester St.	54-2		
68–69	Queens	N/A		
69–70	Queens	N/A		W. Carolina Inv.
70–71	Queens	N/A		
71–72	Queens	27-2		AIAW Tournament
72–73	Queens	22-5		2nd AIAW Tr.
73–74	Queens	22-4		
74–75	Queens	19-8		
75–76	Queens	20-5		
76–77	Queens	18-13		
77–78	Queens	24-3		
78–79	Queens	N/A		
79–80	Queens	23-6		

Incomplete 16-Year Coaching Record: 229-48 (.826) overall; 54-2 (.964) at West Chester State; 175-46 (.791) at Queens.

ANDY LANDERS
Tennessee Tech '74

Only one of four coaches to take team to Final Four four times. Georgia reached it the last two seasons, but lost to SEC rival Tennessee both times. . . . Built Lady Bulldogs from scratch into a contending program largely on recruiting. . . . One of the first women's coaches to actively recruit from around the country. . . . Georgia got to NCAA title game in 1985 with future Olympians Teresa Edwards and Teresa McClain. . . . Seventh among active Division I coaches in winning percentage. . . . Registered 82 wins at Roane State (Tenn.) Junior College. . . . Has earned Naismith national coach of the year honors in 1986, 1987 and 1996. . . . Georgia is seventh in NCAA Tournament wins and 10th in winning percentage in the postseason. . . . SEC coach of the year in 1984 and 1991. . . . The Lady Dogs have gone to 13 NCAA Tournaments and have won five SEC titles under Landers. . . . He has coached eight Kodak All-Americans.

Year	School	Overall	League	Postseason
79-80	Georgia	16-12		
80-81	Georgia	27-10		NWIT Champions
81-82	Georgia	21-9	4-3 (SEC)	NCAA Tournament
82-83	Georgia	27-7	4-5 (SEC)	NCAA Final Four
83-84	Georgia	30-3	8-1 (SEC)	NCAA Sweet 16
84-85	Georgia	29-5	7-1 (SEC)	NCAA Runner-up
85-86	Georgia	30-2	9-0 (SEC)	NCAA Sweet 16
86-87	Georgia	27-5	7-2 (SEC)	NCAA Sweet 16
87-88	Georgia	21-10	5-4 (SEC)	NCAA Sweet 16
88-89	Georgia	23-7	6-3 (SEC)	NCAA Sweet 16
89-90	Georgia	25-5	6-3 (SEC)	NCAA 2nd Round
90-91	Georgia	28-4	9-0 (SEC)	NCAA Elite 8
91-92	Georgia	19-11	6-5 (SEC)	
92-93	Georgia	21-13	5-6 (SEC)	NCAA 2nd Round
93-94	Georgia	17-11	5-6 (SEC)	
94-95	Georgia	28-5	9-2 (SEC)	NCAA Final Four
95-96	Georgia	28-5	10-1 (SEC)	NCAA Runner-up

17-Year Coaching Career: 417-124 (.770) at Georgia; 100-41 (.709) in SEC.

DARLENE MAY
Cal State Fullerton '67

The winningest coach in Division II history, topping the 500-victory mark early in the 1993–94 season and is third among all active women's coaches.... Coached three national championship teams and eight AIAW and NCAA Final Four teams.... Cal Poly-Pomona has never finished below first place in conference play.... Has won the Converse national Division II Coach of the Year award two times.... Also has had a distinguished officiating career, becoming the first woman to referee a women's Olympic contest during the 1984 games in Los Angeles, including the bronze medal game.... Retired after 1993–94 season.

Year	School	Overall	League	Postseason
74–75	Cal Poly-Pomona	16-6		5th AIAW
75–76	Cal Poly-Pomona	20-6		8th AIAW
76–77	Cal Poly-Pomona	28-6	10-0 (SCAA)	5th AIAW
77–78	Cal Poly-Pomona	31-4	10-0 (SCAA)	
78–79	Cal Poly-Pomona	24-7	10-0 (SCAA)	
79–80	Cal Poly-Pomona	27-13	9-1 (SCAA)	6th AIAW
80–81	Cal Poly-Pomona	30-9	12-0 (CCAA)	AIAW Final Four
81–82	Cal Poly-Pomona	29-7	12-0 (CCAA)	NCAA Champion
82–83	Cal Poly-Pomona	29-3	11-0 (CCAA)	NCAA Final Four
83–84	Cal Poly-Pomona	22-7	11-1 (CCAA)	
84–85	Cal Poly-Pomona	26-7	11-1 (CCAA)	NCAA Champion
85–86	Cal Poly-Pomona	30-3	12-0 (CCAA)	NCAA Champion
86–87	Cal Poly-Pomona	29-3	11-1 (CCAA)	NCAA Final Four
87–88	Cal Poly-Pomona	28-4	12-0 (CCAA)	NCAA Regional
88–89	Cal Poly-Pomona	28-6	11-1 (CCAA)	NCAA Final Four
89–90	Cal Poly-Pomona	29-4	12-0 (CCAA)	NCAA Final Four
90–91	Cal Poly-Pomona	22-9	11-1 (CCAA)	NCAA Regional
91–92	Cal Poly-Pomona	23-6	12-0 (CCAA)	
92–93	Cal Poly-Pomona	27-3	11-1 (CCAA)	NCAA Regional
93–94	Cal Poly-Pomona	21-6	9-1 (CCAA)	NCAA 1st Round

19-Year Coaching Record: 519-119 (.813) overall; 195-8 (.961) in the Southern California Athletic Association and California Collegiate Athletic Association.

BILLIE JEAN MOORE
Washburn '66

Coached Cal State Fullerton and UCLA to national championships during a 24-year career that culminated with her retirement in April 1993.... Won the first AIAW Final Four in 1978 in her first year at UCLA.... Her Fullerton team won a national crown in her first year on the job there, predating the official beginning of the AIAW tournament.... Also coached the first U.S. women's Olympic team to a silver medal in 1976.... Teams went to postseason play 16 out of 24 seasons, winning nine conference titles and eight national Top 10 finishes.

Year	School	Overall	League	Postseason
69–70	CS Fullerton	17-1		NIT Champion
70–71	CS Fullerton	20-1		
71–72	CS Fullerton	19-1		3rd AIAW
72–73	CS Fullerton	13-1		
73–74	CS Fullerton	19-2		
74–75	CS Fullerton	19-2		3rd AIAW
75–76	CS Fullerton	14-5		
76–77	CS Fullerton	19-2		
77–78	UCLA	27-3	8-0 (WCAA)	AIAW Champion
78–79	UCLA	24-10	7-1 (WCAA)	4th AIAW
79–80	UCLA	18-12	9-3 (WCAA)	AIAW Regional
80–81	UCLA	29-7	9-3 (WCAA)	5th AIAW
81–82	UCLA	16-14	7-5 (WCAA)	
82–83	UCLA	18-11	9-5 (WCAA)	NCAA Regional
83–84	UCLA	17-12	6-8 (WCAA)	
84–85	UCLA	20-10	10-4 (WCAA)	NCAA Regional
85–86	UCLA	12-16	3-5 (Pac West)	
86–87	UCLA	18-10	11-7 (Pac-10)	
87–88	UCLA	19-11	12-6 (Pac-10)	
88–89	UCLA	12-16	8-10 (Pac-10)	
89–90	UCLA	17-12	12-6 (Pac-10)	NCAA 1st Round
90–91	UCLA	15-13	10-8 (Pac-10)	
91–92	UCLA	21-10	12-6 (Pac-10)	NCAA Regional
92–93	UCLA	13-14	8-10 (Pac-10)	

24-Year Coaching Record: 436-196 (.689) overall; 140-15 (.903) at Cal State Fullerton; 296-181 (.620) at UCLA; 73-35 (.579) in Pacific-10 games; 59-18 (.766) in postseason games.

UCLA coach Billie Moore hoists the 1978 AIAW trophy, cheered on by her team.

CATHY RUSH
West Chester State

A women's coaching pioneer who led Immaculata to the first three AIAW national titles... Three of her former players are distinguished college coaches—Theresa Grentz (Rutgers), Rene Portland (Penn State), and Marianne Stanley (formerly of Old Dominion, Pennsylvania, and USC).... Made history in 1975 when Immaculata played Queens in Madison Square Garden, drawing nearly 12,000 spectators.... After retiring in 1977, got into sports camp business for girls, her current occupation.... She runs the camps with her husband, NBA referee Ed Rush.... Is a commentator on women's TV games.... Named the 1994 recipient of the U.S. Basketball Writers Association's Pioneer Award.

Year	School	Overall	League	Postseason
70–71	Immaculata	12-2		
71–72	Immaculata	20-1		AIAW champion
72–73	Immaculata	20-0		AIAW champion
73–74	Immaculata	20-1		AIAW champion
74–75	Immaculata	23-3		AIAW runnerup
75–76	Immaculata	25-3		AIAW nationals
76–77	Immaculata	29-6		AIAW nationals

7-Year Coaching Record: 149-16 (.903) overall.

MARSHA SHARP
Wayland Baptist '75

Bumped Texas out of the top spot in the Southwest Conference for most of the 1990s, culminating with the NCAA championship in 1993. In fact, she used a former Lady Longhorn signee Sheryl Swoopes to guide Tech to the top. . . . Received a $1 million, five-year contract following the 1995-96 season. . . . Lady Raiders usually outdraw the men's team and filled the Tech football stadium with 40,000 fans for a post-title pep rally. . . . National coach of the year in 1993. . . . Tech has gone to five straight Sweet 16 trips in the NCAA Tournament. . . . SWC coach of the year six times, including five of the last seven years. . . . Tech has gone to 11 postseason tournaments and has had 11 20-win-plus seasons. . . . Has recruited most of her players from Texas, especially the Panhandle region, but is starting to attract national prep stars. . . . Was a graduate assistant at Wayland for renowned coach Dean Weese. Weese's brother, Linden, has been on Tech's staff for all of her 14 seasons.

Year	School	Overall	League	Postseason
82-83	Texas Tech	22-9	6-2 (SWC)	Women's NIT
83-84	Texas Tech	23-7	13-3 (SWC)	NCAA Tournament
84-85	Texas Tech	24-8	12-4 (SWC)	Women's NIT
85-86	Texas Tech	21-9	13-3 (SWC)	NCAA 2nd Round
86-87	Texas Tech	18-11	10-6 (SWC)	
87-88	Texas Tech	17-13	9-7 (SWC)	
88-89	Texas Tech	17-13	9-7 (SWC)	
89-90	Texas Tech	20-11	11-5 (SWC)	NCAA 2nd Round
90-91	Texas Tech	23-8	12-4 (SWC)	NCAA 2nd Round
91-92	Texas Tech	27-5	13-1 (SWC)	NCAA Sweet 16
92-93	Texas Tech	31-3	13-1 (SWC)	NCAA Champion
93-94	Texas Tech	28-5	12-2 (SWC)	NCAA Sweet 16
94-95	Texas Tech	33-4	13-1 (SWC)	NCAA Sweet 16
95-96	Texas Tech	27-4	13-1 (SWC)	NCAA Sweet 16

14-Year Coaching Record: 331-110 (.751) at Texas Tech; 159-47 (.771) in SWC.

BOB SPENCER
Parsons College '57

Retired following 1992–93 season with 578 wins, the second most of any women's coach ever, trailing only Jody Conradt of Texas.... A native of Iowa, a girls high school hotbed where he coached some of the first women's intercollegiate teams in the mid-1960s.... Started programs at John F. Kennedy College and William Penn College, two of the earliest Midwestern college powers.... William Penn won seven Iowa AIAW titles, six regional crowns, and a national ranking in each of his eight seasons.... The 1973 team finished fourth in the AIAW national tournament.

Year	School	Overall	League	Postseason
66–70	JFK	73-42		
71–73	Parsons	67-39		

73–81	William Penn	40-43		
81–82	Fresno St.	8-17		
82–83	Fresno St.	15-12		
83–84	Fresno St.	18-11		
84–85	Fresno St.	20-9		
85–86	Fresno St.	21-9		
86–87	Fresno St.	22-8	12-6	(Big W.)
87–88	Fresno St.	16-12	11-7	(Big W.)
88–89	Fresno St.	18-12	9-9	(Big W.)
89–90	Fresno St.	21-12	11-7	(Big W.)
90–91	Fresno St.	16-13	9-9	(Big W.)
91–92	Fresno St.	13-15	7-11	(Big W.)
92–93	Fresno St.	10-17	4-10	(WAC)

27-Year Coaching Record: 578-274 (.678) overall; 198-137 (.591) at Fresno State.

MARIANNE STANLEY
Immaculata '76

A three-time national championship coach who left USC in an equal pay dispute in September 1993 and sued the institution.... Won two AIAW and one NCAA title at Old Dominion, becoming the only women's coach to win crowns in both associations.... Revived the USC program in her final two seasons, as the Trojans reached the regional finals and regionals.... Two-time national Coach of the Year (1979, 1985).... Old Dominion won titles in 1979 and 1980 and the NCAA crown in 1985.... In her first season of college coaching, Old Dominion won the National Women's Invitational Tournament.... An All-American player at Immaculata (Pa.) College, which won two national titles while she was there.... Hired to market women's basketball at Stanford while her lawsuit is pending.

Year	School	Overall	League	Postseason
77–78	Old Dominion	30-4		NWIT Champion
78–79	Old Dominion	35-1		AIAW Champion
79–80	Old Dominion	37-1		AIAW Champion
80–81	Old Dominion	28-7		AIAW Final Four
81–82	Old Dominion	22-6		AIAW Regional
82–83	Old Dominion	29-6		NCAA Final Four
83–84	Old Dominion	24-5		NCAA Regional
84–85	Old Dominion	31-3		NCAA Champion
85–86	Old Dominion	15-13		
86–87	Old Dominion	18-13		NCAA Regional
87–88	Pennsylvania	6-20		
88–89	Pennsylvania	5-21		
89–90	USC	8-19	6-12 (Pac-10)	
90–91	USC	18-12	11-7 (Pac-10)	NCAA 2nd Round
91–92	USC	23-8	14-4 (Pac-10)	NCAA Regional
92–93	USC	22-7	14-4 (Pac 10)	NCAA Regional

16-Year Coaching Record: 351-146 (.706) overall; 269-59 (.820) at Old Dominion; 11-41 (.212) at Pennsylvania; 71-46 (.606) at USC; 56-27 (.674) in the Pacific-10 Conference; 17-7 (.708) in the NCAA Tournament. . . . Served as interim co-coach at Stanford during 1995-96 season, helping Cardinal to Final Four, then named head coach at California in April 1996.

C. VIVIAN STRINGER
Slippery Rock '70

The 1993 Converse National Coach of the Year after guiding Iowa to its first Final Four appearance and overcoming the death of her husband early in the season.... Coached Cheyney State (Pa.) College to the first women's NCAA title game in 1982.... Also Converse Coach of the Year in 1988.... Iowa has won outright or shared six Big Ten championships since she arrived in 1983.

Year	School	Overall	League	Postseason
71–83	Cheyney St.	251-51		
83–84	Iowa	17-10	11-7 (Big 10)	
84–85	Iowa	20-8	14-4 (Big 10)	
85–86	Iowa	22-7	15-3 (Big 10)	NCAA 2nd Round
86–87	Iowa	26-5	17-1 (Big 10)	NCAA Regional
87–88	Iowa	29-2	17-1 (Big 10)	NCAA Regional
88–89	Iowa	27-5	16-2 (Big 10)	NCAA Regional
89–90	Iowa	23-6	15-3 (Big 10)	NCAA 2nd Round
90–91	Iowa	21-9	13-5 (Big 10)	NCAA 2nd Round
91–92	Iowa	25-4	16-2 (Big 10)	NCAA 2nd Round

Year	School	Overall	League	Postseason
92–93	Iowa	27-4	16-2 (Big 10)	NCAA Final Four
93–94	Iowa	21-7	13-5 (Big 10)	NCAA 2nd Round
94–95	Iowa	11-17	6-10 (Big 10)	
95–96	Rutgers	13-15	8-10 (Big East)	

25-Year Coaching Record: 533-150 (.780) overall; 269-84 (.762) in 12 years at Iowa; 13-15 (.464) in first year at Rutgers; 141-45 (.758) in Big Ten; 8-10 (.400) in Big East; 11-9 (.550) in NCAA tournament.

PAT HEAD SUMMITT
Tennessee-Martin '74

Only women's coach to win four national titles (1987, 1989, 1991, 1996).... Earned her 500th career win in the first game of the 1993–94 season, becoming the second winningest active Division I coach behind Jody Conradt of Texas.... Coached the U.S. women to the 1984 Olympic gold medal, and played on the first Olympic team in 1976 that won a silver medal.... Her teams have qualified for 11 Final Fours and have won 20 or more games 17 consecutive seasons.... The Naismith National Coach of the Year in 1987, 1989, and 1994.... Named co-coach of the decade for the 1980s by the U.S. Basketball Writers Association.... The first woman to receive the John Bunn Award given by the Naismith Basketball Hall of Fame in 1990.... An inductee of the Women's Sports Foundation Hall of Fame in 1990.

Year	School	Overall	League	Postseason
74–75	Tennessee	16-8		
75–76	Tennessee	16-11		
76–77	Tennessee	28-5		3rd AIAW
77–78	Tennessee	27-4		1st AIAW Poll
78–79	Tennessee	30-9		AIAW Final Four
79–80	Tennessee	33-5		2nd AIAW
80–81	Tennessee	25-6		2nd AIAW
81–82	Tennessee	22-10		NCAA Final Four
82–83	Tennessee	25-8	7-1 (SEC)	NCAA Regional
83–84	Tennessee	23-10	7-1 (SEC)	2nd Final Four
84–85	Tennessee	22-10	4-4 (SEC)	NCAA Regional
85–86	Tennessee	24-10	5-4 (SEC)	NCAA Final Four
86–87	Tennessee	28-6	6-3 (SEC)	NCAA Champion
87–88	Tennessee	31-3	8-1 (SEC)	NCAA Final Four
88–89	Tennessee	35-2	8-1 (SEC)	NCAA Champion
89–90	Tennessee	27-6	8-1 (SEC)	NCAA Regional
90–91	Tennessee	30-5	6-3 (SEC)	NCAA Champion
91–92	Tennessee	28-3	10-1 (SEC)	NCAA Regional
92–93	Tennessee	29-3	11-0 (SEC)	NCAA Regional
93–94	Tennessee	31-2	11-0 (SEC)	NCAA Regionals
94–95	Tennessee	31-3	11-0 (SEC)	NCAA Runner-up
95–96	Tennessee	31-4	9-2 (SEC)	NCAA Champion

22-Year Coaching Record: 492-133 (.787) at Tennesseee; 111-22 (.834) in Southeastern Conference; 118-31 (.791) in postseason play; 63-4 (.940) in international play.

TARA VANDERVEER
Indiana '76

The 1996 U.S. Olympic coach who turned Stanford from a downtrodden Pac-10 program to a two-time national champion. . . . Cardinal have reached five Final Fours during her tenure, even in the 1995-96 season, when she was away preparing for the Olympics. Amy Tucker, her long-time assistant, and Marianne Stanley were co-coaches in 1995-96. . . . The national coach of the year in 1990, when Stanford won its first national title, and previously in 1988. . . . Considered one of the best strategists in the women's game, has been talked about as a professional men's coach. . . . Stanford has excelled with top-notch players who also are academic standouts inthe classroom. . . . Cardinal have won seven Pac-10 titles and been to the NCAA Sweet 16 or better the last nine seasons. . . . At Ohio State, the Buckeyes won the Big Ten four times. . . . Played for Indiana and watched Bobby Knight's practices intently. . . . During high school, became the team mascot so she could watch the boys' teams and follow its strategy.

Year	School	Overall	League	Postseason
78–79	Idaho	17-8		
79–80	Idaho	25-6		AIAW Tournament
80–81	Ohio State	17-15		
81–82	Ohio State	20-7		
82–83	Ohio State	23-5		
83–84	Ohio State	22-7		NCAA Tournament
84–85	Ohio State	28-3		NCAA Elite 8
85–86	Stanford	13-15	1-7 (Pac-10)	
86–87	Stanford	14-14	8-10 (Pac-10)	
87–88	Stanford	17-5	14-4 (Pac-10)	NCAA Sweet 16
88–89	Stanford	28-3	18-0 (Pac-10)	NCAA Elite 8
89–90	Stanford	32-1	17-1 (Pac-10)	NCAA Champion
90–91	Stanford	26-6	16-2 (Pac-10)	NCAA Final Four
91–92	Stanford	30-3	15-3 (Pac-10)	NCAA Champion
92–93	Stanford	26-6	15-3 (Pac-10)	NCAA Sweet 16
93–94	Stanford	25-6	15-3 (Pac-10)	NCAA Elite 8
94–95	Stanford	30-3	17-1 (Pac-10)	NCAA Final Four

17-Year Coaching Record: 403-113 (.781) overall; 42-14 (.750) in two years at Idaho; 110-37 (.748) in five years at Ohio State; 251-62 (.802) in 10 years at Stanford.

MARGARET WADE
Delta State

Became the first woman college coach inducted into the Naismith Basketball Hall of Fame in 1984.... Coached Delta State to three AIAW national titles from 1975 to 1977, and collected a career record of 157-23 in six seasons.... Revived a dormant Delta State program and retired from coaching in 1979. Her star player, Lusia Harris Stewart, also is a member of the Hall of Fame.... Came to Delta State to teach physical education in 1959 and began a women's varsity program there 14 years later.... Her Delta State team, nicknamed the "Cadillac Kids," once posed for a *Sports Illustrated* photograph along with Wade seated on the hood of a Cadillac.... The Wade Trophy, given to the top woman player each season, is named after her.

Year	School	Overall	League	Postseason
73–74	Delta State	16-2		
74–75	Delta State	28-0		AIAW Champion
75–76	Delta State	33-1		AIAW Champion
76–77	Delta State	32-3		AIAW Champion
77–78	Delta State	27-5		AIAW Tournament
78–79	Delta State	21-12		AIAW Tournament

6-Year Coaching Record: 157-23 (.872) overall.

DEAN WEESE
Wayland Baptist College

Ushered tiny Wayland Baptist College from an AAU powerhouse into a national contender on the women's college scene during the mid-1980s. Wayland won two AAU championships and finished fifth or higher in the AIAW nationals five times in his six seasons.... Wayland was one of the first colleges to offer basketball scholarships to women and his teams were instantly dominant in Texas when the AIAW era began.... Was honored with the 1991 Pioneer Award by the U.S. Basketball Writers Association.... Since leaving Wayland, has been a successful high school coach in west Texas, currently coaching at Levelland High School.

Year	School	Overall	League	Postseason
73–74	Wayland Baptist	37-5		AAU Champion; 5th AIAW
74–75	Wayland Baptist	34-1		AAU Champion; 5th AIAW
75–76	Wayland Baptist	34-5		2nd AAU; 3rd AIAW
76–77	Wayland Baptist	31-5		
77–78	Wayland Baptist	33-5		4th AIAW
78–79	Wayland Baptist	24-10		AIAW Quarterfinals

6-Year College Coaching Record: 193-91 (.862) overall.

CHRIS WELLER
Maryland '66

Has spent most of her adult life at Maryland as a student, coach, and administrator.... The Naismith and U.S. Basketball Writers Association national Coach of the Year in 1992.... A two-time ACC Coach of the Year whose teams have won a record eight ACC titles.... Has missed coaching in a national tournament only twice.... Played basketball and lacrosse and swam during college career.... Coach of the U.S. Jones Cup team in 1992 and the 1994 U.S. Select Team.

Year	School	Overall	League	Postseason
75–76	Maryland	20-4		
76–77	Maryland	17-6		
77–78	Maryland	27-4	5-1 (ACC)	2nd AIAW
78–79	Maryland	22-7	6-1 (ACC)	AIAW Regional
79–80	Maryland	21-9	5-2 (ACC)	AIAW Regional
80–81	Maryland	19-9	5-2 (ACC)	AIAW Regional
81–82	Maryland	25-7	6-1 (ACC)	NCAA Final Four
82–83	Maryland	26-5	10-3 (ACC)	NCAA Regional
83–84	Maryland	19-10	10-4 (ACC)	NCAA Regional
84–85	Maryland	9-18	4-10 (ACC)	
85–86	Maryland	17-13	6-8 (ACC)	NCAA Regional
86–87	Maryland	15-14	6-8 (ACC)	
87–88	Maryland	26-6	12-2 (ACC)	NCAA Regional
88–89	Maryland	29-3	13-1 (ACC)	NCAA Final Four
89–90	Maryland	19-11	7-7 (ACC)	NCAA Regional
90–91	Maryland	17-13	9-5 (ACC)	NCAA Regional
91–92	Maryland	25-6	13-3 (ACC)	NCAA Regional
92–93	Maryland	22-8	11-5 (ACC)	NCAA 2nd Round
93–94	Maryland	15-13	8-8 (ACC)	
94–95	Maryland	11-18	2-14 (ACC)	
95–96	Maryland	13-14	7-9 (ACC)	

21-Year Coaching Record: 414-198 (.676) at Maryland; 145-94 (.606) in Atlantic Coast Conference.

KAY YOW
East Carolina '64

The second-winningest coach in ACC history trails only Maryland's Chris Weller. . . . Coached the 1988 U.S. Olympic team to the gold medal in Seoul. . . . The Wolfpack have won four ACC crowns and have gone to postseason play 17 times. . . . Only five other women's coaches have won 400 games or more at one school. . . . N.C. State has gotten to 11 ACC Tournament title games. . . . Has coached eight All-Americans and 21 All-ACC players. . . . From a coaching family. Her sister, Debbie, coached at Kentucky and
Florida and is now the athletic director at Maryland. Another sister, Susan, coached at Drake and Kansas State and played for Kay one season at N.C. State. . . . Had a mastectomy after being diagnosed with breast cancer but then went on to her Olympic duties. . . . Only Jody Conradt, Pat Summitt, Vivian Stringer, and Sue Gunter have won more games in their careers. . . . The WBCA coach of the year in 1990. . . . Pack has gone to Sweet 16 seven times.

Year	School	Overall	League	Postseason
71-72	Elon (N.C.)	5-11		
72-73	Elon (N.C.)	13-3		
73-74	Elon (N.C.)	20-1		
74-75	Elon (N.C.)	19-4		
75-76	N.C. State	19-7		Women's NIT
76-77	N.C. State	21-3		AIAW Tournament
77-78	N.C. State	29-5		AIAW Tournament
78-79	N.C. State	27-7		AIAW Regionals
79-80	N.C. State	28-8		AIAW 2nd Round
80-81	N.C. State	21-10		AIAW Tournament
81-82	N.C. State	24-7		NCAA Sweet 16
82-83	N.C. State	22-8		NCAA 1st Round
83-84	N.C. State	23-9		NCAA Sweet 16
84-85	N.C. State	25-6		NCAA 2nd Round
85-86	N.C. State	18-11		NCAA 1st Round
86-87	N.C. State	24-7		NCAA Sweet 16
87-88	N.C. State	10-17		
88-89	N.C. State	24-7		NCAA Sweet 16
89-90	N.C. State	25-6		NCAA Sweet 16
90-91	N.C. State	27-6		NCAA Sweet 16
91-92	N.C. State	16-12		
92-93	N.C. State	14-13		
93-94	N.C. State	13-14		
94-95	N.C. State	21-10		NCAA Sweet 16
95-96	N.C. State	20-10		NCAA 2nd Round

25-Year Coaching Record: 508-202 (.715) overall; 57-19 (.750) in four years at Elon; 451-183 (.679) in 21 years at N.C. State.

WOMEN'S FINAL NATIONAL RANKINGS

1993-94

AP	USA/CNN	SCHOOL (RECORD)	HEAD COACH
1	5	Tennessee (31-2)	Pat Summitt
2	6	Penn State (28-3)	Rene Portland
3	7	Connecticut (30-3)	Geno Auriemma
4	1	North Carolina (33-2)	Sylvia Hatchell
5	10	Colorado (27-5)	Ceal Barry
6	2	Louisiana Tech (31-4)	Leon Barmore
7	9	Southern Cal (26-4)	Cheryl Miller
8	3	Purdue (29-5)	Lin Dunn
9	11	Texas Tech (28-5)	Marsha Sharp
10	12	Virginia (27-5)	Debbie Ryan
11	8	Stanford (25-6)	Tara VanDerveer
12	13	Vanderbilt (25-8)	Jim Foster
13	15	Iowa (21-7)	Vivian Stringer
14	14	Seton Hall (27-5)	Phyllis Mangina
15	17	Kansas (22-6)	Marian Washington
16	4	Alabama (26-7)	Rick Moody
17	18	Montana (25-5)	Robin Selvig
18	21	Washington (21-8)	Chris Gabrecht
19	24	Fla. International (25-4)	Cindy Russo
20	25	Florida (22-7)	Carol Ross
21	–	Boise State (23-6)	June Daugherty
22	16	Southern Miss. (26-5)	Kay James
23	20	Mississippi (24-9)	Van Chancellor
24	–	Bowling Green (26-4)	Jaci Clark
25	23	Texas (22-9)	Jody Conradt
–	19	Texas A&M (23-8)	Candi Harvey
–	22	Clemson (20-10)	Jim Davis

WOMEN'S FINAL NATIONAL RANKINGS

1992-93

AP	USA/CNN	SCHOOL (RECORD)	HEAD COACH
1	4	Vanderbilt (30-3)	Jim Foster
2	5	Tennessee (29-3)	Pat Summitt
3	2	Ohio State (28-4)	Nancy Darsch
4	3	Iowa (27-4)	Vivian Stringer
5	1	Texas Tech (31-3)	Marsha Sharp
6	7	Stanford (26-6)	Tara VanDerveer
7	10	Auburn (25-4)	Joe Ciampi
8	13	Penn State (22-6)	Rene Portland
9	6	Virginia (26-6)	Debbie Ryan
10	9	Colorado (27-4)	Ceal Barry
11	18	Maryland (22-8)	Chris Weller
12	11	Stephen F. Austin (28-5)	Gary Blair
13	12	Western Kentucky (24-7)	Paul Sanderford
14	8	Louisiana Tech (26-6)	Leon Barmore
15	14	Southern Cal (22-7)	Marianne Stanley
16	19	Texas (22-8)	Jody Conradt
17	15	North Carolina (23-7)	Sylvia Hatchell
18	23	Vermont (28-1)	Cathy Inglese
19	–	Bowling Green (25-5)	Jaci Clark
20	20	Miami, Fla. (24-7)	Ferne Labati
21	21	Georgia (21-13)	Andy Landers
22	22	Nebraska (23-8)	Angela Beck
23	24	Hawaii (??-?)	Vince Goo
24	–	Kansas (21-9)	Marian Washington
25	–	Northern Illinois (24-6)	Jane Albright-Dieterle
25	–	Oklahoma State (23-9)	Dick Haterman
–	16	Georgetown (23-7)	Patrick Knapp
–	17	SW Missouri State (23-9)	Cheryl Burnett
–	25	Alabama (22-9)	Rick Moody

WOMEN'S FINAL NATIONAL RANKINGS

1991-92

AP	USA/CNN	SCHOOL (RECORD)	HEAD COACH
1	2	Virginia (32-2)	Debbie Ryan
2	5	Tennessee (28-3)	Pat Summitt
3	1	Stanford (30-3)	Tara VanDerveer
4	13	Stephen F. Austin (28-3)	Gary Blair
5	6	Mississippi (29-3)	Van Chancellor
6	9	Miami, Fla. (30-2)	Ferne Labati
7	10	Iowa (25-4)	Vivian Stringer
8	8	Maryland (25-6)	Chris Weller
9	14	Penn State (24-7)	Rene Portland
10	4	SW Missouri State (31-3)	Cheryl Burnett
11	16	Purdue (23-7)	Lin Dunn
12	15	Texas Tech (27-5)	Marsha Sharp
13	7	Vanderbilt (22-9)	Jim Foster
14	11	West Virginia (26-4)	Scott Harrelson
15	3	Western Kentucky (27-8)	Paul Sanderford
16	20	George Washington (25-7)	Joe McKeown
17	25	Kansas (25-6)	Marian Washington
18	17	Alabama (23-7)	Rick Moody
19	23	Texas (21-10)	Jody Conradt
20	19	Clemson (21-10)	Jim Davis
21	24	Creighton (28-4)	Bruce Rasmussen
22	–	Houston (22-8)	Jessie Kenlaw
23	12	Southern Cal (23-8)	Marianne Stanley
24	21	UC Santa Barbara (27-5)	Mark French
25	22	Vermont (29-1)	Cathy Inglese
–	18	UCLA (21-10)	Billie Jean Moore

WOMEN'S FINAL NATIONAL RANKINGS

1989-90

AP	USA/CNN	SCHOOL (RECORD)	HEAD COACH
1	4	Louisiana Tech (32-1)	Leon Barmore
2	1	Stanford (32-1)	Tara VanDerveer
3	7	Washington (28-3)	Chris Gobrecht
4	5	Tennessee (27-6)	Pat Summitt
5	15	UNLV (27-3)	Jim Bolla
6	9	Stephen F. Austin (28-3)	Gary Blair
7	13	Georgia (25-5)	Andy Landers
8	6	Texas (27-5)	Jody Conradt
9	2	Auburn (28-7)	Joe Ciampi
10	18	Iowa (23-6)	Vivian Stringer
11	10	N.C. State (25-6)	Kay Yow
12	3	Virginia (29-6)	Debbie Ryan
13	22	Northwestern (24-5)	Don Perrelli
14	20	Long Beach State (25-8)	Joan Bonvicini
15	14	Purdue (23-7)	Lin Dunn
16	24	Hawaii (26-4)	Vince Goo
17	21	Northern Illinois (26-5)	Jane Albright-Dieterle
18	11	Providence (27-5)	Bob Foley
19	16	South Carolina (24-9)	Nancy Wilson
20	23	Southern Miss. (27-5)	Kay James
21	25	Tennessee Tech (26-5)	Bill Worrell
22	8	Arkansas (25-5)	John Sutherland
23	–	Louisiana State (21-9)	Sue Gunter
24	12	Mississippi (22-10)	Van Chancellor
25	–	St. Joseph's (24-7)	Jim Foster
–	17	Vanderbilt (23-11)	Phil Lee
–	19	Clemson (22-10)	Jim Davis

WOMEN'S FINAL NATIONAL RANKINGS

1990-91

AP	USA/CNN	SCHOOL (RECORD)	HEAD COACH
1	9	Penn State (29-2)	Rene Portland
2	2	Virginia (31-3)	Debbie Ryan
3	6	Georgia (28-4)	Andy Landers
4	1	Tennessee (30-5)	Pat Summitt
5	14	Purdue (26-3)	Lin Dunn
6	5	Auburn (26-6)	Joe Ciampi
7	10	N.C. State (27-6)	Kay Yow
8	18	Louisiana State (24-7)	Sue Gunter
9	12	Arkansas (28-4)	John Sutherland
10	11	Western Kentucky (29-3)	Paul Sanderford
11	3	Stanford (26-6)	Tara VanDerveer
12	13	Washington (24-5)	Chris Gobrecht
13	4	Connecticut (29-5)	Geno Auriemma
14	19	Stephen F. Austin (26-5)	Gary Blair
15	24	Providence (26-6)	Bob Foley
16	25	Texas (21-9)	Jody Conradt
17	22	UNLV (25-7)	Jim Bolla
18	17	Long Beach State (24-8)	Joan Bonvicini
19	–	Mississippi (20-9)	Van Chancellor
20	–	Rutgers (23-7)	Theresa Grentz
21	8	Clemson (22-11)	Jim Davis
22	23	Northwestern (21-9)	Don Perrelli
23	21	Iowa (21-9)	Vivian Stringer
24	7	Lamar (29-4)	Al Barbre
25	16	Oklahoma State (27-6)	Dick Haterman
–	15	James Madison (26-5)	Sheila Moorman
–	20	Vanderbilt (19-12)	Phil Lee

WOMEN'S FINAL NATIONAL RANKINGS

1988-89

AP	USA/CNN	SCHOOL (RECORD)	HEAD COACH
1	1	Tennessee (35-2)	Pat Summitt
2	2	Auburn (32-2)	Joe Ciampi
3	4	Louisiana Tech (32-4)	Leon Barmore
4	5	Stanford (28-3)	Tara VanDerveer
5	3	Maryland (29-3)	Chris Weller
6	6	Texas (27-5)	Jody Conradt
7	7	Long Beach State (30-5)	Joan Bonvicini
8	11	Iowa (23-6)	Vivian Stringer
9	19	Colorado (27-4)	Ceal Barry
10	18	Georgia (23-7)	Andy Landers
11	16	Stephen F. Austin (30-4)	Gary Blair
12	8	Mississippi (23-8)	Van Chancellor
13	10	N.C. State (24-7)	Kay Yow
14	9	Ohio State (24-6)	Nancy Darsch
15	17	Purdue (24-6)	Lin Dunn
16	12	UNLV (27-7)	Jim Bolla
17	22	South Carolina (23-7)	Nancy Wilson
18	–	La Salle (28-3)	John Miller
19	–	Western Kentucky (22-9)	Paul Sanderford
20	21	Old Dominion (23-9)	Wendy Larry
–	13	Clemson (20-11)	Jim Davis
–	14	Louisiana State (19-11)	Sue Gunter
–	15	Virginia (21-10)	Debbie Ryan
–	20	Rutgers (24-7)	Theresa Grentz
–	23	St. Joseph's (23-8)	Jim Foster
–	24	Tennessee Tech (22-8)	Bill Worrell
–	25	James Madison (26-4)	Sheila Moorman

WOMEN'S FINAL NATIONAL RANKINGS

1987-88

AP	USA/CNN	SCHOOL (RECORD)	HEAD COACH
1	3	Tennessee (31-3)	Pat Summitt
2	6	Iowa (29-2)	Vivian Stringer
3	2	Auburn (32-3)	Joe Ciampi
4	5	Texas (32-3)	Jody Conradt
5	1	Louisiana Tech (32-2)	Leon Barmore
6	9	Ohio State (25-5)	Nancy Darsch
7	4	Long Beach State (28-6)	Joan Bonvicini
8	11	Rutgers (27-5)	Theresa Grentz
9	8	Maryland (26-6)	Chris Weller
10	7	Virginia (27-5)	Debbie Ryan
11	16	Washington (25-5)	Chris Gobrecht
12	12	Mississippi (24-7)	Van Chancellor
13	14	Stanford (27-5)	Tara VanDerveer
14	15	James Madison (27-4)	Sheila Moorman
15	13	Southern Cal (22-8)	Linda Sharp
16	17	Montana (28-2)	Robin Selvig
17	10	Georgia (21-10)	Andy Landers
18	23	New Mexico State (26-3)	Joe McKeown
19	18	Stephen F. Austin (29-5)	Gary Blair
20	–	La Salle (25-5)	John Miller
–	19	Western Kentucky (26-8)	Paul Sanderford
–	20	Clemson (21-9)	Jim Davis
–	21	St. Joseph's (24-8)	Jim Foster
–	22	DePaul (27-4)	Doug Bruno
–	24	South Carolina (23-11)	Nancy Wilson
–	25	Houston (22-7)	Greg Williams

WOMEN'S FINAL NATIONAL RANKINGS

1985-86

AP	USA/CNN	SCHOOL (RECORD)	HEAD COACH
1	1	Texas (34-0)	Jody Conradt
2	4	Georgia (30-2)	Andy Landers
3	2	Southern Cal (31-5)	Linda Sharp
4	7	Louisiana Tech (27-5)	Leon Barmore
5	3	Western Kentucky (32-4)	Paul Sanderford
6	14	Virginia (26-3)	Debbie Ryan
7	9	Auburn (24-6)	Joe Ciampi
8	12	Long Beach State (29-5)	Joan Bonvicini
9	8	Louisiana State (27-6)	Sue Gunter
10	10	Rutgers (29-4)	Theresa Grentz
11	6	Mississippi (24-8)	Van Chancellor
12	17	Ohio State (23-7)	Nancy Darsch
13	13	Penn State (24-8)	Rene Portland
14	19	Iowa (22-7)	Vivian Stringer
15	5	Tennessee (24-10)	Pat Summitt
16	15	North Carolina (23-9)	Jennifer Alley
17	16	James Madison (28-4)	Sheila Moorman
18	22	Southern Illinois (25-4)	Cindy Scott
19	18	Oklahoma (24-7)	Maura McHugh
20	25	Vanderbilt (22-9)	Phil Lee
–	11	NE Louisiana (26-3)	Linda Harper
–	20	Montana (27-4)	Robin Selvig
–	21	Texas Tech (21-9)	Marsha Sharp
–	23	Drake (22-8)	Carole Baumgarten
–	24	St. Joseph's (22-7)	Jim Foster

WOMEN'S FINAL NATIONAL RANKINGS

1986–87

AP	USA/CNN	SCHOOL (RECORD)	HEAD COACH
1	3	Texas (31-2)	Jody Conradt
2	6	Auburn (31-2)	Joe Ciampi
3	2	Louisiana Tech (30-3)	Leon Barmore
4	4	Long Beach State (33-3)	Joan Bonvicini
5	5	Rutgers (30-3)	Theresa Grentz
6	9	Georgia (27-5)	Andy Landers
7	1	Tennessee (28-6)	Pat Summitt
8	11	Mississippi (25-5)	Van Chancellor
9	7	Iowa (26-5)	Vivian Stringer
10	8	Ohio State (26-5)	Nancy Darsch
11	10	Virginia (26-5)	Debbie Ryan
12	15	James Madison (27-4)	Sheila Moorman
13	12	N.C. State (24-7)	Kay Yow
14	19	Louisiana State (20-8)	Sue Gunter
15	16	Penn State (23-7)	Rene Portland
16	13	Southern Illinois (28-3)	Cindy Scott
17	22	Villanova (27-4)	Harry Perretta
18	21	Vanderbilt (23-10)	Phil Lee
19	14	Southern Cal (22-8)	Linda Sharp
20	18	Washington (23-7)	Chris Gobrecht
–	17	Old Dominion (18-13)	Marianne Stanley
–	20	Oregon (23-7)	Elwin Heiny
–	23	Western Kentucky (24-9)	Paul Sanderford
–	24	St. Joseph's (23-9)	Jim Foster
–	25	Drake	Susan Yow

WOMEN'S FINAL NATIONAL RANKINGS

1984-85

AP	SCHOOL (RECORD)	HEAD COACH
1	Texas (28-3)	Jody Conradt
2	NE Louisiana (30-2)	Linda Harper
3	Long Beach State (28-3)	Joan Bonvioini
4	Louisiana Tech (29-4)	Leon Barmore
5	Old Dominion (31-3)	Marianne Stanley
6	Mississippi (29-3)	Van Chancellor
7	Ohio State (28-3)	Tara VanDerveer
8	Georgia (29-5)	Andy Landers
9	Penn State (28-5)	Rene Portland
10	Auburn (25-7)	Joe Ciampi
11	Washington (26-2)	Joyce Sake
12	N.C. State (25-6)	Kay Yow
13	Tennessee (22-10)	Pat Summitt
14	Western Kentucky (29-6)	Paul Sanderford
15	Southern Cal (20-9)	Linda Sharp
16	UNLV (25-6)	Jim Bolla
17	St. Joseph's (25-5)	Jim Foster
18	UCLA (20-10)	Billie Jean Moore
19	Texas Tech (24-8)	Marsha Sharp
20	San Diego State (21-9)	Earnest Riggins

WOMEN'S FINAL NATIONAL RANKINGS

1983-84

AP	SCHOOL (RECORD)	HEAD COACH
1	Texas (32-3)	Jody Conradt
2	Louisiana Tech (30-3)	Leon Barmore
3	Georgia (30-3)	Andy Landers
4	Old Dominion (24-5)	Marianne Stanley
5	Southern Cal (29-4)	Linda Sharp
6	Long Beach State (25-6)	Joan Bonvicini
7	Kansas State (25-6)	Lynn Hickey
8	Louisiana State (23-7)	Sue Gunter
9	Cheyney, Pa. (25-5)	Winthrop McGriff
10	Mississippi (24-6)	Van Chancellor
11	Missouri (25-6)	Joann Rutherford
12	Alabama (23-9)	Ken Weeks
13	NE Louisiana (23-4)	Linda Harper
14	North Carolina (24-8)	Jennifer Alley
15	Tennessee (23-10)	Pat Summitt
16	N.C. State (23-9)	Kay Yow
17	Maryland (19-10)	Chris Weller
18	Virginia (22-7)	Debbie Ryan
19	Ohio State (22-7)	Tara VanDerveer
20	UT-Chattanooga (26-5)	Sharon Fanning

WOMEN'S FINAL NATIONAL RANKINGS

1982-83

AP	SCHOOL (RECORD)	HEAD COACH
1	Southern Cal (30-2)	Linda Sharp
2	Louisiana Tech (26-6)	Leon Barmore
3	Texas (30-3)	Jody Conradt
4	Old Dominion (29-6)	Marianne Stanley
5	Cheyney, Pa. (27-3)	Vivian Stringer
6	Long Beach State (24-7)	Joan Bonvicini
7	Maryland (26-5)	Chris Weller
8	Penn State (26-7)	Rene Portland
9	Georgia (27-7)	Andy Landers
10	Tennessee (25-8)	Pat Summitt
11	Arizona State (23-7)	Juliene Simpson
12	Kentucky (23-5)	Terry Hall
13	Mississippi (26-6)	Van Chancellor
14	Auburn (24-8)	Joe Ciampi
15	Missouri (23-6)	Joann Rutherford
16	N.C. State (22-8)	Kay Yow
17	Kansas State (25-6)	Lynn Hickey
18	North Carolina (22-8)	Jennifer Alley
19	Oregon State (24-6)	Aki Hill
20	Louisiana State (20-7)	Sue Gunter

WOMEN'S FINAL NATIONAL RANKINGS

1981-82

AP	SCHOOL (RECORD)	HEAD COACH
1	Louisiana Tech (35-1)	Sonja Hogg
2	Cheyney, Pa. (26-3)	Vivian Stringer
3	Maryland (25-7)	Chris Weller
4	Tennessee (22-10)	Pat Summitt
5	Texas (35-4)	Jody Conradt
6	Southern Cal (22-4)	Linda Sharp
7	Old Dominion (22-6)	Marianne Stanley
8	Rutgers	Theresa Grentz
9	Long Beach State (23-6)	Joan Bonvicini
10	Penn State (24-6)	Rene Portland
11	Villanova	Harry Perretta
12	N.C. State (24-6)	Kay Yow
13	Kentucky (24-8)	Terry Hall
14	Kansas State (26-6)	Lynn Hickey
15	South Carolina (22-8)	Terry Kelly
16	Drake (28-7)	Carole Baumgarten
17	Memphis State (26-5)	Mary Lou Johns
18	Arizona State (24-7)	Juliene Simpson
19	Oregon (20-5)	Elwin Heiny
20	Missouri (24-9)	Joann Rutherford

WOMEN'S FINAL NATIONAL RANKINGS

1980-81

AP	SCHOOL
1	Louisiana Tech
2	Tennessee
3	Old Dominion
4	Southern Cal
5	Cheyney, Pa.
6	Long Beach State
7	UCLA
8	Maryland
9	Rutgers
10	Kansas
11	Kentucky
12	Oregon
13	N.C. State
14	Stephen F. Austin
15	Illinois State
16	Texas
17	Jackson State
18	Minnesota
19	Oregon
20	Clemson

WOMEN'S FINAL NATIONAL RANKINGS

1979-80

AP	SCHOOL
1	Old Dominion
2	Tennessee
3	Louisiana Tech
4	South Carolina
5	Stephen F. Austin
6	Maryland
7	Texas
8	Rutgers
9	Long Beach State
10	N.C. State
11	Kansas
12	Cheyney, Pa.
13	Kansas State
14	Kentucky
15	Northwestern
16	Mercer
17	Oregon
18	Central Mo. State
19	San Francisco
20	Brigham Young

WOMEN'S FINAL NATIONAL RANKINGS

1977-78

AP	SCHOOL
1	Tennessee
2	Wayland Baptist
3	N.C. State
4	Montclair State
5	UCLA
6	Maryland
7	Queens, N.Y.
8	Valdosta State
9	Delta State
10	Louisiana State
11	St. Joseph's
12	Old Dominion
13	Missouri
14	Stephen F. Austin
15	Texas
16	Ohio State
17	Penn State
18	Southern Conn. St.
19	Memphis State
20	Mississippi

WOMEN'S FINAL NATIONAL RANKINGS

1978-79

AP	SCHOOL
1	Old Dominion
2	Louisiana Tech
3	Tennessee
4	Texas
5	Stephen F. Austin
6	UCLA
7	Rutgers
8	Maryland
9	Cheyney, Pa.
10	Wayland Baptist
11	N.C. State
12	Valdosta State
13	Penn State
14	Kansas
15	South Carolina
16	Northwestern
17	UNLV
18	Long Beach State
19	Fordham
20	Montclair State

WOMEN'S FINAL NATIONAL RANKINGS

1976-77

AP	SCHOOL
1	Delta State
2	Immaculata
3	St. Joseph's
4	Cal St. Fullerton
5	Tennessee
6	Tennessee Tech
7	Wayland Baptist
8	Montclair State
9	Stephen F. Austin
10	N.C. State
11	Louisiana State
12	Baylor
13	UCLA
14	Old Dominion
15	Southeastern La.
16	Maryland
17	Michigan State
18	Miss. College
19	Southern Conn. St.
20	Kansas State

13

SMALL COLLEGES:

J.C., DIVISIONS II & III, AND NAIA

Junior College Action

Junior college players were perceived by many observers for an extended period as the rogues of recruiting. But now they are in vogue throughout the vast majority of major four-year universities because of an improved image amid the advent of stiffer academic requirements for Division I freshman eligibility.

Although many tunnel-vision Division I coaches were once standoffish, it seems as if virtually everyone except Ivy League schools are flocking toward J.C. recruits these days, especially after "juco" signees frequented the rosters of recent Final Four teams—Arkansas (1990, 1994 and 1995), Cincinnati (1992), Indiana (1987), Kansas (1988, 1991 and 1993), Kentucky (1993), Mississippi State (1996), Oklahoma (1988), Oklahoma State (1995), Syracuse (1996) and UNLV (1987, 1990 and 1991). For instance, five of Cincinnati's nine regulars in 1992 were former junior college players.

It wasn't too long ago when only a splinter group of maverick coaches were bold enough to liberally dot their rosters with J.C. players stereotyped as discipline problems, academic risks or simply unsuitable to go directly from high school

to major college programs. "Jucoland" was labeled by misguided observers as little more than basketball rehabilitation where free-lance players enjoyed free rein to make Great Plains arenas their own personal H-O-R-S-E stables.

But now major colleges aren't nearly so reluctant to bring "quick fix" junior college players aboard for two seasons. It is no longer demeaning to recruit at the juco level because the entire recruiting process is based on the law of supply and demand and harsher academic requirements at the NCAA level increase the amount of talent at the J.C. level.

The talent pool in the NJCAA Tournament might have never been greater than in 1968, when eight of the 10 members of the All-Tournament Team either eventually played or were at least drafted by the NBA and/or ABA, and a ninth All-Tournament Team member played several years with the Harlem Globetrotters.

The misconceptions regarding junior college basketball aren't helped when network TV pulls a snafu such as when it was mistakenly inferred that recent Kentucky guard Dale Brown was the first instance of the Wildcats recruiting a junior college player. Actually, Hall of Fame coach Adolph Rupp, a Kansas native, regularly attended the NJCAA Tournament at Hutchinson, Kan., in the 1950s and recruited four tournament MVPs or leading scorers. Two of the four didn't play much for Kentucky or transferred, but the other two–Bob Burrow (Lon Morris) and Sid Cohen (Kilgore)–proved to be pivotal players for the Wildcats and were selected in the NBA draft. Burrow was an NCAA consensus second-team All-American in 1956. Guard Adrian Smith, a key member of Kentucky's 1958 NCAA champion, was also a junior college recruit.

Two decades earlier, Alabama, after finishing 12th in the 13-team SEC in 1937-38 with a 4-12 record, topped the league's regular-season standings the next year with a 13-4 mark. Bama's squad included three junior college graduates, led by center George Prather, who was named to the SEC All-Tournament first five.

The Big Ten Conference has never had an abundance of junior college players. But J.C. transfer Dick Garmaker scored 37 points for Minnesota in his first league game in 1954 before becoming an NCAA consensus All-American the next year.

Success has not been limited to just basketball ability. The most notable student-athlete to come out of junior college might be Nolan Archibald, an Academic All-American selection as a senior and player for Weber State's first NCAA Tournament team in 1968. An All-American selection at Dixie Junior College in his native state of Utah, Archibald graduated cum laude from Weber State before earning an M.S. degree in business administration from the Harvard Business School in 1970. As Black & Decker's chairman of the board, president and chief executive officer since 1986, he heads a $5 billion corporation. Archibald is one of the youngest CEOs of a publicly held Fortune 100 company and has been recognized by Fortune and Business Week as one of the nation's outstanding managers.

A glance at NBA rosters and the backgrounds of many of the nation's prominent Divi-

Southeastern Oklahoma's Dennis Rodman slams one home, though he went on to become an NBA rebounding machine.

sion I coaches suggests there probably never should have been a stigma attached to the J.C. ranks. One seldom hears NBA commentators credit a J.C. beginning, but approximately 40

NBA players annually played for a two-year school at some point in their college careers, including recent regulars Mookie Blaylock, Anthony Bowie, Sam Cassell, Cedric Ceballos, Blue Edwards, Kevin Edwards, Craig Ehlo, Kevin Gamble, Winston Garland, Armon Gilliam, Harvey Grant, Avery Johnson, Larry Johnson, Nate McMillan, Ken Norman, Robert Pack, Ricky Pierce, Mitch Richmond, J.R. Rider, Alvin Robertson, Dennis Rodman, Latrell Sprewell, John Starks, Nick Van Exel, Spud Webb, Gerald Wilkins, Kenny Williams and Kevin Willis. Embellishing junior college credentials even more are all-time pro greats with a J.C. connection such as Tiny Archibald, Ron Boone, Fred Brown, Mack Calvin, Michael Cooper, Artis Gilmore, Spencer Haywood, Lionel Hollins, Dennis Johnson, Gus Johnson, Vinnie Johnson, Jim Loscutoff, Bob McAdoo and Paul Pressey.

Former Riverside (Calif.) City and Pasadena (Calif.) City coach Jerry Tarkanian, who wound up at his alma mater (Fresno State) after leaving UNLV, is among about 40 active Division I head coaches who previously served in a similar capacity at a junior college. The list includes the following high profile coaches: Louisville's Denny Crum (Pierce, CA), Purdue's Gene Keady (Hutchinson, KS), Arizona's Lute Olson (Long Beach City, CA), Arkansas' Nolan Richardson (Western Texas), St. Louis' Charlie Spoonhour (Moberly, MO, and Southeastern, IA), and Oklahoma State's Eddie Sutton (Southern Idaho). Among the former major-college mentors who guided teams to the NCAA Tournament after coaching at the J.C. level are Dick Motta (Weber, UT), Maury John (Moberly, MO) and Jack Hartman (Coffeyville, KS). Hartman took two of his

NJCAA CHAMPIONS

YEAR	CHAMPION (RECORD)		
1949	Tyler, TX (36-1)	1973	Mercer County, NJ (34-3)
1951	Tyler, TX (36-3)	1974	Mercer County, NJ (32-2)
1952	Wharton, TX (34-4)	1975	Western Texas (36-1)
1953	El Dorado, KS (24-7)	1976	Southern Idaho (34-1)
1954	Moberly, MO (22-8)	1977	Independence, KS (34-2)
1955	Moberly, MO (29-4/)	1978	Independence, KS (28-7)
1956	Kilgore, TX (27-5)	1979	Three Rivers, MO (37-3)
1957	San Angelo, TX (31-2)	1980	Western Texas (37-0)
1958	Kilgore, TX (27-2)	1981	Westark, AR (32-5)
1959	Weber, UT (34-3)	1982	Midland, TX (34-4)
1960	Parsons, KS (25-6)	1983	San Jacinto, TX (35-2)
1961	Pueblo, CO (31-2)	1984	San Jacinto, TX (35-2)
1962	Coffeyville, KS (32-0)	1985	Dixie, UT (35-1)
1963	Independence, KS (26-3)	1986	San Jacinto, TX (37-0)
1964	Dodge City, KS (29-2	1987	Southern Idaho (37-1)
1965	Vincennes, IN (28-6)	1988	Hutchinson, KS (36-2)
1966	Moberly, MO (29-5)	1989	NE Oklahoma A&M (36-4)
1967	Moberly, MO (31-2)	1990	Connors State, OK (35-2)
1968	San Jacinto, TX (44-2)	1991	Aquinas, TN (32-3)
1969	Paducah, KY (23-5)	1992	Three Rivers, MO (35-3)
1970	Vincennes, IN (29-4/)	1993	Pensacola, FL (31-5)
1971	Ellsworth, IA (26-7)	1994	Hutchinson, KS (35-4)
1972	Vincennes, IN (33-0)	1995	Okaloosa-Walton, FL (31-6)
		1996	Sullivan, KY (27-10)

Multiple NJCAA titles by school: Moberly (4), San Jacinto (4), Independence (3), Vincennes (3), Hutchinson (2), Kilgore (2), Mercer County (2), Southern Idaho (2), Three Rivers (2), Tyler (2), Western Texas (2).

Most NJCAA titles by state: Texas (13/seven different schools), Kansas (9/six different schools), Missouri (6/two different schools).

J.C. stars (Paul Henry and Lou Williams) with him to Southern Illinois, where he coached eight years before moving to Kansas State.

Southern Idaho has produced more NCAA Division I head coaches than any other junior college. Joining Sutton at that level were Boyd Grant (Fresno State and Colorado State), Jerry Hale (Oral Roberts) and Fred Trenkle (San Diego State).

Tarkanian, Crum and Olson never coached in the NJCAA Tournament. California community college administrators conduct an in-state tournament because they don't want athletes from their more than 90 men's programs to participate in national competition.

The NJCAA Tournament is a five-day, 16-team, 26-game double-elimination affair. It has been played in Hutchinson, Kansas, since 1949.

1940s and 1950s Odds and Trends: Former NFL commissioner Pete Rozelle was athletic publicity director at Compton (Calif.) College in 1946–47 when the school played 26 consecutive games without calling a timeout en route to their 36-4 record. . . . Longtime NBA coach Lowell (Cotton) Fitzsimmons is believed to hold the record for the longest shot made in NJCAA Tournament history. Fitzsimmons, playing for Hannibal-LaGrange (Mo.), hit a basket estimated at 70 feet just before the end of the first half of the 1952 national third-place game. The next year, Fitzsimmons averaged 25.4 points per game. Incidentally, Fitzsimmons was coach of Moberly (Mo.) when the school won back-to-back national titles in 1966 and 1967. . . . John Keller, a swingman on 1950 national third-place finisher Garden City (Kan.), became a member of the Clyde Lovellette-led Kansas team that won the 1952 NCAA Tournament. Keller was among the Jayhawks' seven players on the 1952 U.S. Olympic team as he became the first former NJCAA Tournament player to earn a gold medal in the Olympics. . . . Another Garden City product, forward Hal Patterson, was an All-Tournament team selection in 1952 before playing for Kansas' NCAA runner-up in 1953. He also was an end who was named to the Canadian Football League Hall of Fame after a 14-year career (1954–67) during which he averaged 20.6 yards per pass reception with 460 catches for 9,473 yards and 64 touchdowns. . . . Network television announcer Gary Bender is the son of Herb Bender, who coached Dodge City (Kan.) to five consecutive national junior college tournament appearances from 1948 to 1952. . . . Jim Carey, a member of the back-to-back champions for Moberly (Mo.) in 1954 and 1955, is the only tourney participant to have played and coached on an NJCAA champion. He guided Ellsworth (Iowa) to the 1971 title. . . . "Jungle Jim" Loscutoff of Grant Tech (Calif.) was the first NJCAA Tournament alumnus to reach the NBA. After graduating from Oregon, he enjoyed a successful career with the Boston Celtics from 1956 through 1964, a period in which they won seven NBA championships.

1960s and 1970s Odds and Trends: The 1962 Jack Hartman-coached Coffeyville (Kan.) became the first undefeated team (32-0) to win the NJCAA Tournament. . . . The leading rebounder for 1963 runner-up Moberly (Mo.) was 6-3 Larry "Butch" Mantle, a younger brother of New York Yankees Hall of Famer Mickey Mantle. . . . Allegany Community College of Cumberland, Md., defeated Baltimore Institute, 210-23, on February 8, 1964. Allegany led 90-8 at halftime and hit 92 of 127 field-goal attempts in the debacle. . . . Longtime pro standout Artis Gilmore, the NJCAA Tournament's first seven-footer, had a disappointing juco tourney experience. His Gardner-Webb (N.C.) teams lost their openers in 1968 and 1969. . . . Essex County of Newark, N.J., set a NJCAA scoring record in a 210-67 rout of Englewood Cliffs during the 1973–74 season. Essex led at halftime, 110-29. Essex's Lou Grimsley scored 44 points on 22 of 26 field-goal shooting.

1980s and 1990s Odds and Trends: An NJCAA Tournament standard is listed in *The Guinness Book of World Records.* In a 1982 first-round game against Mercer County, Dixie College's Chris McMullin (later a player for Utah State) hit 29 free throws without a miss. . . . The NJCAA employs a ticket purchasing plan similar to those used by pro teams and high profile colleges. Season-ticket holders have the right to repurchase their seats for the next year in the 6,800-seat Hutchinson (Kan.) Sports Arena as long as they renew before a May 31 deadline. Consequently, except for standing-room-only tickets, the tournament has sold out nine months in advance every year since 1979. . . . No individual has played on both an NJCAA and an NCAA Division I championship team. The two players to come closest were guards Jerry Tetzlaff of Ellsworth (1971) and Terry Brown of Northeastern Oklahoma A&M (1989). Tetzlaff played sparingly for 1973 NCAA runner-up Memphis State, and Brown was a starter and three-point specialist for 1991 NCAA runner-up Kansas. Elmore Spencer of Connors (1990) was a center on UNLV's team that was undefeated until getting upset by eventual champion Duke in the 1991 NCAA semifinals. . . . No college team ever blew a game more incredibly than Shasta (Calif.) in its 1990 contest against Butte

(Calif.). Shasta squandered an 18-point lead in the final 77 seconds of regulation. Then, the Knights assembled an 11-point advantage only to see that margin evaporate, too. They finally lost in double overtime, 116-115. . . . Alex Dillard of Southern Union State (Ala.) tied a NJCAA Tournament single-game record in 1993 by hitting nine three-pointers. He later set a single-game SEC record for Arkansas by canning 12 treys against Delaware State. . . . In 1996, Gene (Central Florida) and Randy (Butler County, KS) Smithson became the first father-son coaching combination to direct teams to the NJCAA Tournament. One day prior to the tourney, Randy accepted the head coaching position at Wichita State, where Gene had coached from 1978-79 through 1985-86.

Divisions II and III: Bevo and Friends

The spotlight on Division I leaves the vast majority of Division II and III players toiling in virtual obscurity. But perhaps the greatest folk hero in college basketball history was a small-college player named Clarence "Bevo" Francis, who set an all-time collegiate scoring record with 113 points for Rio Grande (Ohio) College in a 134-95 victory over Hillsdale on February 2, 1954 (see accompanying box for box score). Francis' revolutionary jump shot helped him average 46.5 points per game that season.

Francis proved he could score against major-college teams by pouring in 39 points vs. Villanova, 41 vs. Providence, 48 vs. Miami (Fla.), 34 vs. North Carolina State, 32 vs. Wake Forest, 48 vs. Butler, and 49 and 41 vs. Creighton. Rio Grande won the Providence, Miami, Wake Forest, and Butler games and the first Creighton contest.

"I really don't remember much about the 113-point game," said Francis, a factory worker who was selected by the Philadelphia Warriors in the 1956 draft but couldn't reach a contract agreement with them and never played in the NBA. "It was just another time when I was double- and triple-teamed. Their coach told me after the game that if he could have dressed out, he would have guarded me, too."

No stat sheet exists to detail how many shots the 6-9 Francis attempted en route to his 37 field goals against Hillsdale. "Most of them were outside," he said. "With the three-pointer, I know I would have come close to 150 points."

The scoring outburst might not have had much of an impact on him because he scored even more points—116—as a freshman the previous season against Ashland (Ky.) Junior College. Francis averaged 50.1 points that year for a 39-0 team that reportedly generated sufficient gate receipts to save the school from bankruptcy. However, his single-game total against Ash-

---

BEVO BREAKS LOOSE! On February 2, 1954, Hillsdale visited Rio Grande in a game that featured the amazing scoring of Clarence "Bevo" Francis. In an era where there was no three-point zone, Francis wowed the crowd with an all-time scoring total of 113 points (see accompanying text for more details).

HILLSDALE (91)	FG	FT	PTS.
Lowry	4	1	9
Helsted	6	7	19
Kincannon	0	3	3
Wagner	1	0	2
Davis	7	11	25
Sewell	0	3	3
Fake	0	2	2
Neff	4	4	12
Check	1	1	3
Allinder	1	2	4
Thiendeck	1	0	2
Vushan	2	0	4
Tallmen	1	1	3
TOTALS	**28**	**35**	**91**

RIO GRANDE (134)	FG	FT	PTS.
Wiseman	1	2	4
Barr	1	0	2
Ripperger	2	5	9
Francis	38	37	113
McKenzie	0	0	0
Vyhnalek	0	0	0
Moses	1	0	2
Gossett	0	1	1
Weiher	1	0	2
Myers	0	1	1
TOTALS	**44**	**46**	**134**

Pan American's Luke Jackson (far right) comes down hard with a rebound, accidentally kicking Rockhurst College's Dick Hennier in an NAIA tournament game in the mid-1960s.

land and his season average were later expunged from the NCAA record book because 27 of the opponents for Rio Grande (pronounced RYE-o Grand) were junior colleges, military teams, and vocational schools.

Bevo got his nickname because his father was fond of Beve Beer, a root beer-type soft drink. Francis rejected offers from larger universities to follow his Wellsville, Ohio, high school coach, Newt Oliver, to a college with an enrollment of 92 full-time students. Francis, who had a wife and an infant when he arrived at Rio Grande, left school after his sophomore season and signed a three-year contract worth $13,000 annually to play on a national barnstorming tour for a team that opposed the Harlem Globetrotters.

Francis' scoring exploits completely overshadowed the rebounding records established by Tom Hart, a 6-4 center for Middlebury. Hart finished his career in 1955–56 with an average of 27.6 rebounds per game, including an average of 29.5 in each of the previous two years. His career average and his season standards are still NCAA marks.

The most recognizable small-college coach in history probably is Clarence "Bighouse" Gaines, who compiled 828 victories in 47 seasons at Winston-Salem State. Gaines' prize pupil was future Hall of Famer Earl "The Pearl" Monroe, a 6-3 guard who averaged 41.5 points per game for the Rams' 1967 College Division titlist. Winston-Salem was the first historically black college to win an NCAA basketball championship. Monroe's presence at Winston-Salem overshadowed one of the most remarkable

NCAA DIVISION II CHAMPIONS

YEAR	CHAMPION	(RECORD)
1957	Wheaton (Ill.)	(28-1)
1958	South Dakota	(22-5)
1959	Evansville (Ind.)	(21-6)
1960	Evansville (Ind.)	(25-4)
1961	Wittenberg (Ohio)	(25-4)
1962	Mt. St. Mary's (Md.)	(24-6)
1963	South Dakota State	(22-5)
1964	Evansville (Ind.)	(26-3)
1965	Evansville (Ind.)	(29-0)
1966	Kentucky Wesleyan	(24-6)
1967	Winston-Salem State (N.C.)	(30-2)
1968	Kentucky Wesleyan	(28-3)
1969	Kentucky Wesleyan	(25-5)
1970	Philadelphia Textile (Pa.)	(29-2)
1971	Evansville (Ind.)	(22-8)
1972	Roanoke (Va.)	(28-4)
1973	Kentucky Wesleyan	(24-6)
1974	Morgan State (Md.)	(28-5)
1975	Old Dominion (Va.)	(25-6)
1976	Puget Sound (Wash.)	(27-7)
1977	Tennessee-Chattanooga	(27-5)
1978	Cheyney State (Pa.)	(27-2)
1979	North Alabama	(22-9)
1980	Virginia Union	(26-4)
1981	Florida Southern	(24-8)
1982	District of Columbia	(25-5)
1983	Wright State (Ohio)	(28-4)
1984	Central Missouri State	(29-3)
1985	Jacksonville State (Ala.)	(30-1)
1986	Sacred Heart (Conn.)	(30-4)
1987	Kentucky Wesleyan	(28-5)
1988	Lowell (Mass.)	(27-7)
1989	North Carolina Central	(28-4)
1990	Kentucky Wesleyan	(31-2)
1991	North Alabama	(29-4)
1992	Virginia Union	(30-3)
1993	Cal State-Bakersfield	(33-0)
1994	Cal State-Bakersfield	(27-6)
1995	Southern Indiana	(29-4)
1996	Fort Hays State (K.S.)	(34-0)

Most Division II titles by school: Kentucky Wesleyan (6), Evansville (5).

Note: Known as the college division from 1957 through 1973.

NCAA DIVISION III CHAMPIONS

YEAR	CHAMPION	(RECORD)
1975	Lemoyne-Owen (Tenn.)	(27-5)
1976	Scranton (Pa.)	(27-5)
1977	Wittenberg (Ohio)	(23-5)
1978	North Park (Ill.)	(29-2)
1979	North Park (Ill.)	(26-5)
1980	North Park (Ill.)	(28-3)
1981	Potsdam State (N.Y.)	(30-2)
1982	Wabash (Ohio)	(24-4)
1983	Scranton (Pa.)	(19-7)
1984	Wisconsin-Whitewater	(27-4)
1985	North Park (Ill.)	(26-4)
1986	Potsdam State (N.Y.)	(32-0)
1987	North Park (Ill.)	(28-3)
1988	Ohio Wesleyan	(27-5)
1989	Wisconsin-Whitewater	(29-2)
1990	Rochester (N.Y.)	(27-5)
1991	Wisconsin-Platteville	(28-3)
1992	Calvin (Mich.)	(31-1)
1993	Ohio Northern	(28-2)
1994	Lebanon Valley (Pa.)	(28-4)
1995	Wisconsin-Platteville	(31-0)
1996	Rowan (N.J.)	(28-4)

Most Division III titles by school: North Park (5), Potsdam State (2), Scranton (2), Wisconsin-Platteville (2), Wisconsin-Whitewater (2).

achievements in hoop history. The next season, 6-6 William English outscored the opposition by himself with 77 points for the Rams in a 146–74 victory over Fayetteville.

Joining Monroe among the most memorable players in the small-college ranks were George Gervin (Eastern Michigan), Walt Frazier (Southern Illinois), Jerry Buse (Evansville), and Jerry Sloan (Evansville), but many were lost in the shuffle as schools shed small-college status to be classifed as major colleges or had a dual affiliation with the NAIA. After several unsuccessful attempts to restructure its membership in the early 1970s, the NCAA conducted its first-ever special convention at Chicago in August 1973, to realign schools for legislative and competitive purposes. The outcome was to divide the membership by creating Divisions I, II, and III. Division III schools were grouped together because they don't award athletic scholarships. Division II has in the neighborhood of 220 members while Division III usually has between 310 and 325.

The 32-team Division II Tournament introduced an "Elite Eight" finals format in 1989, with quarterfinal pairings at one site featuring teams from eight regions (East, Great Lakes, New England, North Central, South, South Atlantic, South Central, and West). Springfield, Massachusetts, was the site of the finals for 14 consecutive seasons before the event was moved to Louisville in 1995.

Division III has a 40-team bracket. Wittenberg, the only school to win national titles at both Division II (1961) and Division III (1977), was host of four Division III Tournament semifinals and finals from 1989 through 1992. Buffalo State was designated as host of the event from 1993 through 1995.

Working Their Way Up the Ladder

Cash cow or not, no one should be able to accuse the NCAA's hierarchy of unabashed favoritism for the Division I ranks. After all, a couple of the NCAA's key administrators—Executive Director Cedric Dempsey and Assistant Executive Director for Enforcement and Eligibility Appeals David Berst—have prominent small-college backgrounds.

Dempsey was a former basketball coach at Albion (Michigan), his alma mater. He was named Michigan Intercollegiate Athletic Association Most Valuable Player in basketball in 1953-54. The 6-3 forward finished second in the nation in the 1951-52 NCAA small college rebounding statistics with 21.6 per game. The next season, he finished eighth with 19.5 per game.

Berst was a starting center in basketball and pitcher in baseball for MacMurray (Ill.) from 1965-68. The 6-5 Berst averaged 6.3 points and four rebounds per game in basketball and still holds the school's baseball record for best earned-run average in a career (2.15). He subsequently became a coach in both sports at his alma mater.

NAIA Tournament

Perhaps no postseason competition factors in endurance in such a brief span as much as the National Association of Intercollegiate Athletics Tournament (NAIA). When 32 of the finest small colleges in the country collide, a champion emerges after winning five games in one week. The NAIA Tournament is also a grueling test for spectators. Fans sit through more than 12 hours of basketball each of three consecutive days covering the first two rounds of the 32-team event.

There have been numerous NAIA players to warrant such attention, however. These former NAIA Tournament standouts went on to play at least three seasons in the NBA and/or ABA: Dick Barnett (Tennessee State), John Barnhill (Tennessee State), Billy Ray Bates (Kentucky State), Zelmo Beaty (Prairie View A&M), M. L. Carr (Guilford), World B. Free (Guilford), Joe Fulks (Murray State), Travis Grant (Kentucky State), Luke Jackson (Pan American), Kevin Loder (Alabama State), Vern Mikkelsen (Hamline), Earl Monroe (Winston-Salem State), Terry Porter (Wisconsin-Stevens Point), Willis Reed (Grambling), Dennis Rodman (Southeastern Oklahoma), Jack Sikma (Illinois Wesleyan), Elmore Smith (Kentucky State), Al Tucker (Oklahoma Baptist), and Foots Walker (West Georgia).

"We're Goin' to Kansas City" served as the theme song for countless small schools across the country for the final time in 1993. After being a fixture for more than 40 years as the Kansas City masterpiece, the week-long marathon shifted along with the NAIA headquarters to Tulsa, beginning in 1994. Attendance had waned in Kansas City for more than a decade, but the principal reason for the move was to escape what had overshadowed the NAIA for years:

the nearby headquarters of the NCAA, the Big Eight Conference Tournament, the NFL (Chiefs), and major league baseball (Royals).

The NAIA split into two divisions in 1992. NAIA Division II schools, which conduct a 24-team national tournament, are those that distribute no more than five scholarships.

Divisions II & III and NAIA Roundup

1940s Odds and Trends: York (Neb.) College, with an enrollment of 50, upset Akron, 52-49, in the first round of the NAIA Tournament before losing to North Texas, 51-49, in the second round. Brothers Jim and Wayne Kaeding scored 78 of York's 101 points. . . . North Carolina College's Rocky Roberson scored 58 points in a game against Shaw in the 1942–43 season for what was believed to be a college record at the time. . . . Howie Schultz, a star for Hamline (Minn.) in the early 1940s, replaced Jackie Robinson at first base in Robinson's first regular-season game for the Brooklyn Dodgers in 1947. . . . More than 100 current NCAA Division I schools previously competed in the NAIA Tournament. Thirteen of the 17 different colleges to win NAIA titles from 1941 through 1963 are currently classified as NCAA Division I institutions. One of the 13 universities is Southeast Missouri State, which captured the 1943 crown after losing its first four games of the season. . . . CIAA champion West Virginia State was the nation's only undefeated college team in 1947–48, finishing with a 23-0 record. The squad, coached by Mark Cardwell, included future NBA players Bob Wilson and Earl Lloyd. . . . UCLA legend John Wooden was in his final season as coach of Indiana State when the

NAIA/NAIB CHAMPIONS

YEAR	CHAMPION	RECORD
1937	Central Missouri St.	(17-3)
1938	Central Missouri St.	(24-3)
1939	Southwestern (Kans.)	(21-2)
1940	Tarkio (Mo.)	(20-4)
1941	San Diego St. (Calif.)	(24-7)
1942	Hamline (Minn.)	(20-2)
1943	Southeast Missouri St.	(19-6)
1944	No tournament due to World War II	
1945	Loyola (La.)	(19-5)
1946	Southern Illinois	(20-6)
1947	Marshall (W.V.)	(32-5)
1948	Louisville (Ky.)	(29-6)
1949	Hamline (Minn.)	(29-1)
1950	Indiana St.	(27-8)
1951	Hamline (Minn.)	(27-2)
1952	Southwest Missouri St.	(27-5)
1953	Southwest Missouri St.	(24-4)
1954	St. Benedict's (Kans.)	(24-5)
1955	East Texas St.	(29-5)
1956	McNeese St. (La.)	(33-3)
1957	Tennessee St.	(31-4)
1958	Tennessee St.	(31-3)
1959	Tennessee St.	(32-1)
1960	Southwest Texas St.	(28-3)
1961	Grambling (La.)	(30-4)
1962	Prairie View A&M (Tex.)	(27-3)
1963	Pan American (Tex.)	(26-6)
1964	Rockhurst (Mo.)	(27-6)
1965	Central St. (Ohio)	(30-0)
1966	Oklahoma Baptist	(26-7)
1967	St. Benedict's (Kans.)	(27-2)
1968	Central St. (Ohio)	(29-4)
1969	Eastern New Mexico	(24-7)
1970	Kentucky St.	(29-3)
1971	Kentucky St.	(31-2)
1972	Kentucky St.	(28-5)
1973	Guilford (N.C.)	(29-5)
1974	West Georgia	(29-4)

YEAR	CHAMPION	RECORD
1975	Grand Canyon (Ariz.)	(30-3)
1976	Coppin State (Md.)	(39-2)
1977	Texas Southern	(31-5)
1978	Grand Canyon (Ariz.)	(30-3)
1979	Drury (Mo.)	(33-2)
1980	Cameron (Okla.)	(36-3)
1981	Bethany Nazarene (Okla.)	(36-6)
1982	Spartanburg (S.C.)	(27-5)
1983	Charleston (S.C.)	(33-5)
1984	Fort Hays St. (Kans.)	(35-2)
1985	Fort Hays St. (Kans.)	(35-3)
1986	David Lipscomb (Tenn.)	(35-4)
1987	Washburn (Kans.)	(35-4)
1988	Grand Canyon (Ariz.)	(37-6)
1989	St. Mary's (Tex.)	(28-5)
1990	Birmingham Southern (Ala.)	(31-3)
1991	Oklahoma City	(34-3)
1992	Oklahoma City	(38-0)
1993	Hawaii Pacific	(30-4)
1994	Oklahoma City	(28-7)
1995	Birmingham Southern (Ala.)	(35-2)
1996	Oklahoma City	(32-6)

YEAR	DIVISION II CHAMPION	RECORD
1992	Grace, Indiana	(35-2)
1993	Willamette, Ore.	(29-4)
1994	Eureka, Ill.	(27-4)
1995	Bethel, Ind.	(38-2)
1996	Albertson, Idaho	(31-3)

* St. Benedict's is now known as Benedictine College.

Most NAIA titles by school: Grand Canyon (3), Hamline (3), Kentucky State (3), Oklahoma City (3), Tennessee State (3).

Most NAIA Tournament appearances: Central Washington (24), Wisconsin-Eau Claire (20).

Sycamores lost to Louisville in the 1948 final. The all-tourney first five included Beloit's Johnny Orr, who went on to become a longtime major-college coach. Two years later, Indiana State won the NAIA title. . . . Tennessee State, coached by Henry A. Kean, was the nation's only undefeated team in 1948–49 with a 24-0 record. The Tigers' leading scorers, Clarence Wilson and Joshua Grider, were both eventually longtime standouts with the Harlem Globetrotters. . . . Hamline (Minn.), the 1949 NAIA champion, had two players—center Vern Mikkelsen and forward Hal Haskins—on Converse's first three five-man All-American teams.

1950s Odds and Trends: Morris Harvey's George King became the first college player to average 30 or more points per game in a seson when he led the nation's small-college players with a 31.2-point average in 1949–50. . . . The

John Barnhill (left) and Dick Barnett—each of whom went on to NBA careers—were members of Tennessee State, the first historically black institution to participate in post-season competition.

man/outfielder Norm Siebern. . . . West Virginia Tech averaged more than 100 points per game four consecutive seasons from 1954–55 through 1957–58. . . . McNeese State's Bill Reigel, playing for his third college in six seasons, led the nation's small-college players with a 33.9-point average when he paced McNeese to the 1956 NAIA Tournament title. Reigel had averaged 18 points per game for the Duquesne freshman team in 1950–51 and 16.3 points per game for the Duke varsity in 1952–53 before entering military service. He later coached McNeese for three seasons from 1971–72 through 1973–74. . . . Western Illinois missed an opportunity to become the nation's only undefeated college team in 1957–58 when it lost to Tennessee State, 85-73, in the NAIA Tournament championship game. Western had defeated Tennessee State, 79-76, earlier in the season. It was one of three consecutive NAIA titles won by Tennessee State, which boasted future pros Dick Barnett, John Barnhill, and Ben Warley. . . . Davis & Elkins' Paul Wilcox, 6-6, became the only player to lead the NAIA in scoring (22.6 ppg) and rebounding (22.3 rpg) in the same season (1958–59).

1960s Odds and Trends: The NAIA All-Stars upset NCAA champion Ohio State, 76-69, in a first-round games in the 1960 Olympic Trials. The NAIA zone defense limited Buckeye All-American Jerry Lucas to 14 points. . . . Midwestern (Tex.) defeated Austin College, 14-11, in overtime in 1964. Midwestern held a 4-1 halftime lead and the teams were tied at 8-8 at the end of regulation. Midwestern had won an earlier game that season with Austin by 40 points, 92-52. . . . Sam Alford, father of former Indiana All-American guard Steve Alford, led the NAIA in free-throw shooting in 1963–64. The elder Alford hit 91.2 percent of his foul shots for Franklin (Ind.) that season. . . . Youngstown State's John McElroy became the shortest player (6-0) ever to score 70 or more points in a game involving NCAA colleges when he scored 72 against Wayne State (Mich.) on February 26, 1969.

1970s and 1980s Odds and Trends: Doug Williams, a 32-year-old Air Force veteran,

first black college to take the floor in an integrated national collegiate tournament was Tennessee State (then Tennessee A&I) in 1953. Hall of Famer John McLendon coached Tennessee State to three consecutive national titles (1957–59). Oddly, the '53 Tennessee State team defeated McLendon-coached North Carolina College for the opportunity to go to Kansas City. . . . Southwest Missouri, winning the 1953 crown to become the first school to capture back-to-back titles with a 32-team format, played the last 3_ minutes of its semifinal game with only four players on the court after encountering foul problems. The principal reason Southwest Missouri was shorthanded stemmed from two squad members being in spring training on their way to playing 12 seasons of major league baseball—infielder Jerry Lumpe and first base-

earned NAIA first-team All-American honors for St. Mary's (Tex.) in 1969–70 when he averaged 18.9 points per game. He scored 24 in a 76-66 upset of Houston. . . . Elmore Smith, a 7-0 center for 1970 NAIA champion Kentucky State, was called for goaltending 12 times in a 116-98 defeat to Eastern Michigan. . . . Tennessee State edged Oglethorpe, 7-4, on February 16, 1971, in what is believed to be the lowest-scoring college game since the center jump was eliminated prior to the 1937–38 season. Tennessee State had overwhelmed Oglethorpe, 82-43, earlier in the season. . . . Birmingham-Southern's Russell Thompson scored 25 points without making a field-goal attempt in a 55-46 victory over Florence State in the 1970–71 season. He converted 25 of 28 free throws. . . . Kentucky State's Travis "Machine Gun" Grant set the single-game NAIA Tournament scoring record with 60 points against Minot State in 1972. Grant finished his four-year college career with 4,045 points and a 33.4-point average. . . . Guilford (N.C.) and Tennessee State are the only

Despite being called for goaltending 12 times in a late 1960s game, Kentucky State's Elmore Smith (right) holds the collegiate record for most rebounds in a season.

two small colleges to have two players score more than 20 points per game in an NBA season—World B. Free and Bob Kaufmann attended Guilford, and Dick Barnett and Truck Robinson attended Tennessee State. . . . Guilford won the 1973 NAIA Tournament with a lineup that included included three future NBA players—Free, M. L. Carr, and Greg Jackson. Guilford's top reserve was Steve Hankins, a 6-6, 220-pound, 28-year-old Marine Corps veteran who had served 44 months in Vietnam and was one

of the military pallbearers at President John F. Kennedy's funeral. . . . Leon Gobczynski, a 6-10 center, averaged 36.1 points per game for Millikin (Ill.) in the 1973–74 season despite being blanked by Augustana (Ill.) in an 88-61 defeat. Gobczynski, who had scored 43 points in an earlier game that year between the two teams, missed all nine of his field-goal attempts in 36 minutes of playing time. . . . Albany (Ga.) State's Major Jones led NCAA Division II rebounders with an average of 22.5 per game. Jones, 6-9, is

HUMBLE PIE

Many of the biggest names in coaching have had to rebound from embarrassing defeats that won't be cited on their resumes. Here is an alphabetical list of high-profile active coaches who lost games to non-Division I colleges at some point in their careers.

COACH, SCHOOL	GAMES LOST	COACH, SCHOOL	GAMES LOST
Rick Barnes, Clemson	Lost at Chaminade (Hawaii) in 1991-92 while coaching Providence.	Leonard Hamilton, Miami (Fla.)	Lost at BYU-Hawaii in 1987-88 while coaching Oklahoma State.
Dave Bliss, New Mexico	Lost to Eastern New Mexico in 1991-92.	Jim Harrick, UCLA	Lost at Abilene (Tex.) Christian in 1984-85 while coaching Pepperdine.
Jim Calhoun, Connecticut	Lost to American International (Mass.), Bridgeport (Mass.) and Assumption (Mass.) in 1972-73 and Brandeis (Mass.) in 1974-75 while coaching Northeastern.	Don Haskins, Texas-El Paso	Lost to Louisiana College in 1977-78.
		Mike Krzyzewski, Duke	Lost to SUNY-Buffalo, Scranton (Pa.) and King's College (Pa.) in 1975-76 while coaching Army.
Bobby Cremins, Georgia Tech	Lost to Lenoir-Rhyne (N.C.) in 1975-76 and 1977-78 while coaching Appalachian State.	John MacLeod, Notre Dame	Lost to Samford (Ala.) in 1971-72 while coaching Oklahoma.
Denny Crum, Louisville	Lost at Chaminade (Hawaii) in 1983-84 and 1984-85.	Jim O'Brien, Boston College	Lost at Florida Tech in 1988-89.
		Dave Odom, Wake Forest	Lost at Alaska-Anchorage in 1993-94.
Tom Davis, Iowa	Lost to Chico State in 1982-83 while coaching Stanford and to UC Riverside in 1988-89.	Rick Pitino, Kentucky	Lost to Adelphi (N.Y.) in 1978-79 while coaching Boston University.
		Norm Stewart, Missouri	Lost at Alaska-Anchorage in 1985-86.
Lefty Driesell, James Madison	Lost to Catawba (N.C.) twice in 1960-61 and to Carson-Newman (Tenn.) and Erskine (S.C.) in 1961-62 while coaching Davidson.	John Thompson, Georgetown	Lost to Assumption (Mass.) in 1971-72 and 1973-74, Randolph-Macon (Va.) in 1971-72 and 1974-75, and Roanoke (Va.) in 1972-73.
Bill Frieder, Arizona State	Lost to Alaska-Anchorage on a neutral court in 1988-89 while coaching Michigan.	Billy Tubbs, TCU	Lost to Ohio Northern in 1980-81 while coaching Oklahoma.

the last Division I or Division II player to average at least 20 per game. . . . Amherst's Jim Rehnquist, son of Supreme Court Justice William Rehnquist, finished fifth in NCAA Division III scoring with an average of 27.8 points per game. . . . Salem College's (W. Va.) Archie Talley set an NAIA record for most points in a season (1,347) in 1975–76 when he averaged 40.8 per game. . . . Dave Robbins, who is white, became coach at Virginia Union in 1978-79 in the predominately black CIAA. Robbins went on to win more CIAA tournaments than any coach in league history. . . . Former Phoenix Suns coach Paul Westphal guided Grand Canyon to the 1988 NAIA title.

1990s Odds and Trends: Central Arkansas ranks among the top three schools for most NAIA Tournament appearances with 14 through 1994 but none of those were when 1992 U.S. basketball Olympian Scottie Pippen of the Chicago Bulls played for the Bears. . . . Missouri and Texas are the states with the most different colleges to win the tournament with six apiece. . . . The 1992 NAIA championship game going into overtime wasn't a rarity. Four of the eight finals from 1981 through 1988 required extra sessions. Nine of the last 11 championship games were decided in

overtime or by fewer than six points in regulation. . . . Bob Hoffman was deprived of becoming the first coach in NAIA history to guide men's and women's champions when No. 1 seed Oklahoma Baptist bowed to Hawaii Pacific, 88-83, in the 1993 championship game. Hoffman had directed Southern Nazarene (Okla.) to the 1989 NAIA women's title. . . . John Pierce of Lipscomb (Tenn.) became college basketball's all-time leading scorer after totaling 33 points in his 1993–94 regular-season finale, a 119-102 triumph over Cumberland Pierce; his 4,110 total career points broke former roommate Phil Hutcheson's mark of 4,106 set in the 1990 NAIA Tournament.

Modest Backgrounds

Small colleges have supplied many of the biggest names in coaching. Recently-retired Gene Bartow began his coaching career at Central Missouri State, a Division II power that lists Division I championship coaches Phog Allen of Kansas and Joe B. Hall of Kentucky among its former head coaches. Allen posted an 84-31 record in seven seasons at Central Missouri from 1913 to 1919, Bartow was 47-21 in three seasons from 1962 to 1964, and Hall was 19-6 in one season (1964–65).

Central Missouri, winner of the first two NAIA Tournaments in 1937 and 1938, captured the NCAA Division II crown in 1984 under Lynn Nance, the coach at St. Mary's (Calif.) in 1989 when the Gaels made their first NCAA Tournament appearance in 30 years. Another former CMSU coach, Louisiana Tech's Jim Wooldridge, directed Southwest Texas State to its first-ever NCAA playoff appearance in 1994.

Here is an alphabetical list including a striking number of prominent active major-college coaches who worked their way up the ladder after graduating from a small school:

Current Iowa coach Tom Davis graduated from small college Wisconsin-Platteville in 1960.

DIVISION I COACH	ALMA MATER
Dana Altman	Eastern New Mexico '80
Rick Barnes	Lenoir-Rhyne (N.C.) '76
J. D. Barnett	Winona (Minn.) State '66
Dick Bennett	Ripon (Wisc.) '65
Dale Brown	Minot (N.D.) State '57
Jim Calhoun	American International (Mass.) '67
John Chaney	Bethune-Cookman (Fla.) '55
Perry Clark	Gettysburg (Pa.) '74
Gary Colson	David Lipscomb (Tenn.) '56
Tom Davis	Wisconsin-Platteville '60
Mike Deane	Potsdam (N.Y.) State '74
James Dickey	Central Arkansas '76
Bob Donewald	Hanover (Ind.) '64
Steve Fisher	Illinois State '67
Bill Foster	Carson-Newman (Tenn.) '58
Leonard Hamilton	Tennessee-Martin '71
Jim Harrick	Morris Harvey (W. Va.) '60
Rich Herrin	McKendree (Ill.) '56
Ben Jobe	Fisk (Tenn.) '56
Pat Kennedy	King's (Pa.) '75
Steve Lappas	City College of New York '77
Nick Macarchuk	Fairfield (Conn.) '63
John MacLeod	Bellarmine (Ky.) '59
Neil McCarthy	Sacramento (Calif.) State '65
Eldon Miller	Wittenberg (Ohio) '61
Jim Molinari	Illinois Wesleyan '77
Danny Nee	St. Mary of the Plains (Kan.) '71
Dave Odom	Guilford (N.C.) '65
Lute Olson	Augsburg (Minn.) '56
Kevin O'Neill	McGill (Montreal, Canada) '79
Bruce Parkhill	Lock Haven (Pa.) '71
Oliver Purnell	Old Dominion (Va.) '75
Kelvin Sampson	Pembroke (N.C.) State '78
Wimp Sanderson	Florence (Ala.) State '59
Herb Sendek	Carnegie Mellon '85
Sonny Smith	Milligan (Tenn.) '58
Tubby Smith	High Point (N.C.) '73
Charlie Spoonhour	Ozarks (Ark.) '61
Jerry Tarkanian	Fresno (Calif.) State '55
Billy Tubbs	Lamar (Tex.) '58

Notes: Bethune-Cookman, Fairfield, Fresno State, Illinois State, Lamar, and Old Dominion, are now classified as NCAA Division I colleges. . . . Several of these coaches who graduated from small colleges started their careers at major universities before transferring—Barnett (Missouri), Calipari (North Carolina-Wilmington), Harrick (Marshall), Molinari (Kansas State), and Nee (Marquette). . . . Morris Harvey College is now the University of Charleston and Florence State is now the University of North Alabama.

FROM PEON TO PEDESTAL

Here is an alphabetical list of some of the most prominent major-college players who started their careers and played for small colleges before transferring.

PLAYER	(SMALL COLLEGE/MAJOR COLLEGE)
Henry Akin	(William Carey, Miss./Morehead State)
Elgin Baylor	(College of Idaho/Seattle)
Larry Bergh	(Tuskegee, Ala./Weber State)
Anthony Bethune	(Lock Haven, Pa./Hartford)
Don Boldebuck	(Nebraska Wesleyan/Houston)
Jimmy Bolden	(St. Mary's, Mich./Wichita State)
Tom Boswell	(South Carolina State/South Carolina)
Jim Boylan	(Assumption, Mass./Marquette)
Bob Davies	(Franklin & Marshall, Pa./Seton Hall)
Dick Dickey	(DePauw, Ind./North Carolina State)
Gerald Glass	(Delta State, Miss./Ole Miss)
John Harrell	(North Carolina Central/Duke)
Avery Johnson	(Cameron, Okla./Southern, La.)
Maynard Johnson	(Macalester, Minn./Minnesota)
Willie Jones	(Buffalo State/Vanderbilt)
Marcus Kennedy	(Ferris State, Mich./Eastern Michigan)
LeRoy King	(Monmouth, Ill./Northwestern)
Tony Massop	(Sacramento State/Kansas State)
Bob McCann	(Upsala, N.J./Morehead State)
Tucker Neale	(Ashland, O./Colgate)
Arnie Risen	(Eastern Kentucky/Ohio State)
Frank Schade	(Wisconsin-Eau Claire/Texas-El Paso)
Bill Simonovich	(Hamline, Minn./Minnesota)
Ron Simpson	(Adelphi, N.Y./Rider)
Tom Wahl	(Mankato State, Minn./Nebraska)
Haywoode Workman	(Winston-Salem State/Oral Roberts)

Purvis Short was a standout for Jackson State University.

SMALL-SCHOOL STANDOUTS

Here is an alphabetical list of the career statistics for a smattering of recognizable small-college stars.

PLAYER	SCHOOL	LAST YEAR	G.	FG%	FT%	RPG	PPG
Brooms Abramovic, Salem (W.V.)		1943	97				22.2
Jerry Anderson, SW Missouri		1955	106		.657		9.4
Al Attles, North Carolina A&T		1960	53	.561	.636		13.1
Dick Barnett, Tennessee St.		1959	136				23.6
John Barnhill, Tennessee St.		1959	103				13.8
Zelmo Beaty, Prairie View (Tex.)		1962	108	.655	.775	19.0	24.7
Manute Bol, Bridgeport (C.T.)		1985	31	.611	.595	13.5	22.5
Ron Bontemps, Beloit (Wis.)		1951	83				21.3
Don Buse, Evansville		1972	84	.497	.784	6.3	17.0
M. L. Carr, Guilford (N.C.)		1973	111	.573	.618	11.4	18.0
Fred Carter, Mount St. Mary's		1969	84	.429	.581	10.8	21.9
Barry Clemens, Ohio Wesleyan		1965	94	.466	.719	13.1	20.3
Sweetwater Clifton, Xavier (La.)		1943	18				18.7
E.C. Coleman, Houston Baptist		1973	94	.585	.640	13.6	19.0
Bob Dandridge, Norfolk (Va.) St.		1969	77	.578	.745	13.0	22.6
Mike Davis, Virginia Union		1969	77	.578	.745	13.0	22.6
John Drew, Gardner-Webb (N.C.)		1974	51	.518	.692	11.0	25.2
Mario Elie, Amer. Intl.		1985	120	.555	.767	8.3	17.7
Clarence "Bevo" Francis, Rio Grande		1954	66				48.6
Walt Frazier, Southern Illinois		1967	50	.471	.751	10.6	17.7
Lloyd Free, Guilford (N.C.)		1975	85	.485	.731	6.5	23.6
Joe Fulks, Murray St.		1943	47		.665		13.2
Mike Gale, Elizabeth City State		1971	62	.522	.678	15.6	19.6
Harry Gallatin, Northeast Missouri		1948	62				13.2
George Gervin, Eastern Michigan		1972	39	.582	.776	14.4	26.8
Travis "Machine Gun" Grant, Kentucky St.		1972	121	.638	.774	9.4	33.4
Mike Green, Louisiana Tech		1973	102	.580	.723	15.4	22.9
Hal Haskins, Hamline (Minn.)		1950	120				17.1
Cleo Hill, Winston-Salem State		1961	108	.444	.743	6.8	23.2
Wilbur Holland, New Orleans		1975	109	.471	.787	4.6	22.8
Bob Hopkins, Grambling (La.)		1956	126	.423	.738	17.4	29.8
Phil Hutcheson, Lipscomb (Tenn.)		1990	155				26.5
Luke Jackson, Pan American (Tex.)		1964	77	.544	.730	18.5	24.1
Phil Jackson, North Dakota		1967	86	.510	.738	12.9	19.9
Clemon Johnson, Florida A&M		1978	109	.528	.589	13.7	12.7
George Johnson, Dillard (Ga.)		1970	90	.472	.590	15.0	12.3
Mickey Johnson, Aurora (Ill.)		1974	94	.561	.660	20.9	26.1
Caldwell Jones, Albany (Ga.) St.		1973	109	.606	.674	20.3	20.5
Earl Jones, District of Columbia		1984	109	.541	.776	10.7	23.4
James Jones, Grambling (La.)		1967	104				20.3
Sam Jones, North Carolina Central		1957	100	.463	.697	9.0	17.7
Wilbert Jones, Albany (Ga.) St.		1969	117	.481	.687	14.2	17.2
Bob Kauffman, Guilford (N.C.)		1968	113			15.9	22.8
Jerome Kersey, Longwood (Va.)		1984	103	.507	.607	11.3	17.0
George King, Morris Harvey (W.V.)		1950	105				24.1
Bob Love, Southern (La.)		1965	104	.561	.749	11.2	23.1
Bob Mabry, Rio Grande (Ohio)		1970	104			21.8	22.7
Rick Mahorn, Hampton (Va.) Institute		1980	119	.534	.682	12.3	20.3
Peter Martin, Midamerica Nazarene		1992	56	.696	.756	10.1	34.0
Vern Mikkelsen, Hamline (Minn.)		1949	104				13.6
Earl Monroe, Winston-Salem (N.C.) St.		1967	110				26.7
Otto Moore, Pan American (Tex.)		1968	105	.486	.616	16.0	17.9
Jackie Moreland, Louisiana Tech		1960	70	.421	.773	16.5	21.3
Charles Oakley, Virginia Union		1985	117	.609	.627	14.0	20.3
Joe Pace, UMES/Coppin State		1976	116	.545	.657	18.1	18.3
Curtis Perry, Southwest Missouri		1970	105	.460	.623	13.6	17.5
John Pierce, Lipscomb (Tenn.)		1994	148	.658	.771	10.1	28.5
Scottie Pippen, Central Arkansas		1987	93	.563	.695	8.1	17.2
Terry Porter, Wisconsin-Stevens Point		1985	117	.589	.796	3.8	13.5
Willis Reed, Grambling (La.)		1964	122	.597	.740	15.2	18.7
Len "Truck" Robinson, Tennessee St.		1974	111	.521	.645	13.5	20.3
Dennis Rodman, Southeastern Oklahoma		1986	96	.637	.625	15.7	25.7
Dan Roundfield, Central Michigan		1975	79	.542	.631	13.1	16.7
Woody Sauldsberry, Texas Southern		1955	29				18.5
Bruce Seals, Xavier (La.)		1973	53	.520	.617	13.0	22.2
Purvis Short, Jackson (Miss.) St.		1978	104	.534	.733	9.3	23.4
Jack Sikma, Illinois Wesleyan		1977	107	.592	.765	13.1	21.2
James Silas, Stephen F. Austin (Tex.)		1972	99	.572	.803	4.7	18.7
Jerry Sloan, Evansville		1965	85	.403	.721	12.4	15.5
Elmore Smith, Kentucky St.		1971	85	.584	.566	22.6	21.3
Randy Smith, Buffalo St.		1971	74	.497	.657	13.2	23.1
Scott Steagall, Millikin (Ill.)		1951	98				21.7
Maurice Stokes, St. Francis (Pa.)		1955	102	.448	.655		22.4
Sedale Threatt, West Virginia Tech		1983	120	.498	.724	3.7	20.7
Dave Twardzik, Old Dominion		1972	82	.506	.799	5.5	20.2
Charles "Chico" Vaughn, Southern Ill.		1962	85	.439	.737	7.8	24.5
Clarence "Foots" Walker, West Georgia		1974	61	.492	.760	7.4	20.9
Ben Warley, Tennessee St.		1960	74	.424	.843	10.3	13.8
Don "Slick" Watts, Xavier (La.)		1973	80	.490	.620	4.2	17.6
Marvin Webster, Morgan St. (Md.)		1975	114	.524	.658	19.9	17.5
Larry Wright, Grambling (La.)		1976	86		.771		23.7

Notes: Statistics for Attles and Gale are available for only their last two of four seasons. . . . The freshman statistics for Barnhill and Sauldsberry are unavailable. . . . L. Jackson (Texas Southern) and E. Smith (Wiley, Tex., College) played for other schools, but those statistics are unavailable. . . . Warley's complete statistics are unavailable and the figures listed are based on available stats. . . . Central Michigan, Coppin State, Eastern Michigan, Evansville, Florida A&M, Grambling, Jackson State, Louisiana Tech, Maryland-Eastern Shore, Morgan State, Mount St. Mary's, Murray State, New Orleans, North Carolina A&T, Old Dominion, Pan American, Prairie View, St. Francis (Pa.), Southern (La.), Southern Illinois, Southwest Missouri State, Stephen F. Austin State, Tennessee State, and Texas Southern subsequently moved up to NCAA Division I status.

14

THE OLYMPIC GAMES

Dr. James Naismith is credited for inventing the game of basketball in 1891, but it was not until June, 1932, in Geneva, Switzerland that an international federation was formed to focus solely on basketball. Three years later, the International Basketball Federation (FIBB) was officially recognized by the International Olympic Committee (IOC), helping pave the path for men's basketball to be implemented at the 1936 Berlin Summer Olympic Games. The FIBB is the forerunner of the International Basketball Federation (FIBA).

Naismith's protege, Dr. F.C. "Phog" Allen, was the driving force behind the addition of basketball to the Olympic Games. During the late 1920s and early 1930s, he conducted a personal crusade trying to coax Olympic officials to include the sport before it finally paid off.

The Amateur Athletic Union (AAU) was recognized as the organization that would be responsible for United States teams in international competitions when the U.S joined FIBA as a member in 1934. Various committees controlled the selection of the U.S. Olympic teams and coaching staffs. For instance, the Games

Committee selected from eight teams at the 1960 Olympics Trials–three AAU squads, the NCAA Tournament champion, an NCAA university all-star team, an NCAA college all-star team, an Armed Forces all-star team, and a National Association of Intercollegiate Athletics (NAIA) all-star team.

Just prior to the 1972 Olympics, FIBA revoked its recognition of the AAU and instructed the U.S. to form a new organization containing representation from the numerous basketball outlets in the country. In 1974, the Amateur Basketball Federation of the United States of America (ABAUSA) was formed. ABAUSA changed its name to USA Basketball in October, 1989. Shortly thereafter FIBA modified its rules to allow professional basketball players to participate in international competitions, allowing the National Basketball Association to assemble a series of "Dream Teams".

Olympics basketball has gone full circle, returning to a global mockery although if Croatia and Yugoslavia could send a united squad, the U.S. "Dream Team" would certainly face an opponent capable of giving it a close contest. But boundaries limit U.S. challengers because Croatia is a separate country now. Croatia, led by forwards Toni Kukoc (Chicago Bulls) and Dino Radja (Boston Celtics) and center Zan Tabak (Toronto Raptors), and Yugoslavia, powered by center Vlade Divac (Los Angeles Lakers) and guard Sasha Danilovic (Miami Heat), were expected to compete with Lithuania in a "Battle for the Silver Medal" at Atlanta in 1996.

Meanwhile, the U.S. Women's National Team created what it hoped was a blueprint for success by fielding its squad more than a year in advance of the 1996 Olympics, paying players an annual salary of $50,000. The ladies also became a "dream team" of sorts, winning their first 39 exhibition games against U.S. colleges and foreign opponents by an average margin of almost 35 points. The $3 million long-range project enabled the U.S. to assemble a more mature female roster (average age of 27 compared to 21 in the '76 and '80 Olympics).

Teresa Edwards (Georgia '86) became the first four-time U.S. basketball Olympian. But Edwards represented the favored U.S. women's team lone shortcoming, an average height of just 5-11. By contrast, imposing foreign opponents such as Ukraine (10 players taller than 6-0), China (six) and Russia (six) possessed much more size.

Men's Basketball

1936   BERLIN, GERMANY

MEDAL WINNERS: 1. U.S. (5-0); 2. Canada (5-1); 3. Mexico (5-2).

U.S. COACH: James Needles, Universal Pictures (Calif.).

FAST FACT: The Phillips Oilers, winners of the national AAU title, defeated Kentucky, the 1948 NCAA champion, in the final game of the U.S. Olympic Trials (53-49). Each of the finalists wound up with five representatives on the U.S. squad. NIT champion St. Louis rejected an invitation to the eight-team Olympic Trials because the school's administration believed the players would miss too much class time. Jesse "Cab" Renick, one of the U.S. team members from the Oilers, was a full-blooded Choctaw Indian and NCAA consensus second-team All-American with Oklahoma A&M in 1940.

U.S. MEN'S RESULTS

U.S. 2, Spain 0*
U.S. 52, Estonia 28
U.S. 56, Philippines 23
U.S. 25, Mexico 10
U.S. 19, Canada 8

* The U.S. was awarded a forfeit victory when its first opponent (Spain) failed to appear because of the Spanish civil war.

U.S. MEN'S ROSTER AND STATISTICS

PLAYER	POS.	AFFILIATION/SCHOOL	PPG.
Sam Balter	G	Universal Pictures (UCLA)	8.5
Ralph Bishop	F	Washington	2.0
Joe Fortenberry	C	Globe Oilers (Wichita State)	14.5
John Gibbons	G	Globe Oilers (Southwestern)	6.0
Francis Johnson	G	Globe Oilers (Wichita State)	10.0
Carl Knowles	F	Universal Pictures (UCLA)	3.0
Frank Lubin	F	Universal Pictures (UCLA)	11.0
Art Mollner	G	Universal Pictures (L.A.J.C.)	2.0
Don Piper	G	Universal Pictures (UCLA)	2.0
Jack Ragland	G	Globe Oilers (Wichita State)	3.5
Willard Schmidt	C	Globe Oilers (Creighton)	8.0
Carl Shy	G	Universal Pictures (UCLA)	5.0
Dwayne Swanson	F	Universal Pictures (USC)	2.0
William Wheatley	F	Globe Oilers (Kansas Wesleyan)	4.5

Note: The team was divided into two seven-man units, each of whom played one game and then sat out the next contest.

1948   LONDON, ENGLAND

MEDAL WINNERS: 1. U.S. (8-0); 2. France (5-2); 3. Brazil (7-1).

U.S. COACH: Omar Browning, Phillips Oilers (Okla.).

FAST FACT: The Phillips Oilers, winners of the national AAU title, defeated Kentucky, the 1948 NCAA champion, in the final game of the U.S. Olympic Trials (53-49). Each of the finalists wound up with five representatives on the U.S. squad. NIT champion St. Louis rejected an invitation to the eight-team Olympic Trials because the school's administration believed the players would miss too much class time.

U.S. MEN'S RESULTS

U.S. 86, Switzerland 21
U.S. 53, Czechoslovakia 28
U.S. 59, Argentina 57
U.S. 66, Egypt 28
U.S. 61, Peru 33
U.S. 63, Uruguay 28
U.S. 71, Mexico 40
U.S. 65, France 21

U.S. MEN'S ROSTER AND STATISTICS

PLAYER	POS.	AFFILIATION/SCHOOL	PPG.
Cliff Barker	F	Kentucky	3.8
Don Barksdale	C	Oakland Bittners (UCLA)	9.0
Ralph Beard	G	Kentucky	3.7
Lewis Beck	G	Phillips Oilers (Oregon State)	4.7
Vince Boryla*	G	Denver Nuggets (Notre Dame)	5.6
Gordon Carpenter	C-F	Phillips Oilers (Kansas)	7.0
Alex Groza	C	Kentucky	11.1
Wallace Jones	C-F	Kentucky	7.2
Bob Kurland	C	Phillips Oilers (Oklahoma State)	9.3
Ray Lumpp	G	NYU	7.2
R. C. Pitts	F	Phillips Oilers (Arkansas)	7.8
Jesse Renick	G	Phillips Oilers (Oklahoma State)	5.6
Jack Robinson	G	Baylor	2.6
Ken Rollins	G	Kentucky	4.0

* Boryla played two seasons at Notre Dame (1944–45 and 1945–46) and then served in the military for two years before finishing his college career at the University of Denver (1948–49).

1952   HELSINKI, FINLAND

MEDAL WINNERS: 1. U.S. (8-0); 2. Soviet Union (6-2); 3. Uruguay (5-3).

U.S. COACH: Warren Womble, Peoria Caterpillars (Ill.).

FAST FACT: U.S. Olympic team captain Ron Bontemps was a high school (Taylorville, Ill.) and college (Illinois and Beloit, Wisc.) teammate of former Massachusetts, Michigan, and Iowa State coach Johnny Orr. Their 1944 state high school championship team compiled a 45-0 record. Bontemps averaged a team-high 22 points per game for a Beloit squad that earned a bid to the 1951 NIT after defeating larger schools such as Washington State, Marshall, San Jose State, and Loyola (III.). Beloit had an enrollment of 1,060 students.

U.S. MEN'S RESULTS

U.S. 66, Hungary 48
U.S. 72, Czechoslovakia 47
U.S. 57, Uruguay 44
U.S. 86, USSR 58
U.S. 103, Chile 55
U.S. 57, Brazil 53
U.S. 85, Argentina 76
U.S. 36, USSR 25

U.S. MEN'S ROSTER AND STATISTICS

PLAYER	POS.	AFFILIATION/SCHOOL	PPG.
Ron Bontemps	G	Peoria Caterpillars (III./Beloit)	7.1
Marcus Freiberger	C	Peoria Caterpillars (Oklahoma)	6.3
Wayne Glasgow	G-F	Phillips 66ers	4.5
Charlie Hoag	G-F	Kansas	2.9
Bill Hougland	G	Kansas	6.0
John Keller	G-F	Kansas	1.5
Dean Kelley	G	Kansas	0.7
Bob Kenney	F	Kansas	10.9
Bob Kurland	C	Phillips 66ers (Oklahoma State)	9.6
Bill Lienhard	F	Kansas	4.0
Clyde Lovellette	C-F	Kansas	14.1
Frank McCabe	F	Peoria Caterpillars (Marquette)	3.0
Dan Pippin	G	Peoria Caterpillars (Missouri)	7.0
Howie Williams	G	Peoria Caterpillars (Purdue)	3.4

1956   MELBOURNE, AUSTRALIA

MEDAL WINNERS: 1. U.S. (8-0); 2. Soviet Union (5-3); 3. Uruguay (6-2).

U.S. COACH: Gerald Tucker, Phillips 66ers (OK).

FAST FACT: The XVIth Olympiad was held during the United States' winter season (Nov. 22–Dec. 1) because the seasons are reversed in Australia; this delayed Bill Russell's NBA debut. Swingman Gib Ford became president of Converse after serving in the Air Force.

U.S. MEN'S RESULTS

U.S. 98, Japan 40
U.S. 101, Thailand 29
U.S. 121, Philippines 53
U.S. 85, Bulgaria 44
U.S. 113, Brazil 51
U.S. 85, USSR 55
U.S. 101, Uruguay 38
U.S. 89, USSR 55

U.S. MEN'S ROSTER AND STATISTICS

PLAYER	POS.	AFFILIATION/SCHOOL	PPG.
Dick Boushka	F	Wichita Vickers (St. Louis Univ.)	8.0
Carl Cain	F	Iowa	1.5
Chuck Darling	C	Phillips 66ers (Iowa)	9.3
Bill Evans	G	U.S. Armed Forces (Kentucky)	6.8
Gib Ford	G-F	U.S. Armed Forces (Texas)	4.9
Burdette Haldorson	F	Phillips 66ers (Colorado)	8.6
Bill Hougland	F	Phillips 66ers (Kansas)	5.8
Bob Jeangerard	F	Phillips 66ers (Colorado)	12.5
K. C. Jones	G	San Francisco	10.9
Bill Russell	C	San Francisco	14.1
Ron Tomsic	G	U.S. Armed Forces (Stanford)	11.1
Jim Walsh	G	Phillips 66ers (Stanford)	9.1

1960   ROME, ITALY

MEDAL WINNERS: 1. U.S. (8-0); 2. Soviet Union (6-2); 3. Brazil (6-2).

U.S. COACH: Pete Newell, California.

FAST FACT: Eight members of the 12-man U.S. roster in 1960 went on to play at least nine seasons in the NBA. Jay Arnette, one of the four who didn't have a prolonged NBA career (three years with the Cincinnati Royals), was a Texas teammate and Olympic opponent of Albert Almanza, the third-leading scorer for the Mexican team that finished in eleventh place.

U.S. MEN'S RESULTS

U.S. 88, Italy 54
U.S. 125, Japan 66
U.S. 107, Hungary 63
U.S. 104, Yugoslavia 42
U.S. 108, Uruguay 50
U.S. 81, USSR 57
U.S. 112, Italy 81
U.S. 90, Brazil 63

U.S. MEN'S ROSTER AND STATISTICS

PLAYER	POS.	AFFILIATION/SCHOOL	PPG.
Jay Arnette	F	Texas	2.9
Walter Bellamy	C	Indiana	7.9
Bob Boozer	F	Peoria Caterpillars (Kansas State)	6.8
Terry Dischinger	F	Purdue	11.8
Burdette Haldorson	F	Phillips 66ers (Colorado)	2.9
Darrall Imhoff	C	California	4.8
Allen Kelley	G	Peoria Caterpillars (Kansas)	0.8
Lester Lane	G	Wichita Vickers (Oklahoma)	5.9
Jerry Lucas	F-C	Ohio State	17.0
Oscar Robertson	F	Cincinnati	17.0
Adrian Smith	G	U.S. Armed Forces (Kentucky)	10.9
Jerry West	G	West Virginia	13.8

1964   TOKYO, JAPAN

MEDAL WINNERS: 1. U.S. (9-0); 2. Soviet Union (8-1); 3. Brazil (6-3).

U.S. COACH: Hank Iba, Oklahoma State.

FAST FACT: Current UNC Charlotte coach Jeff Mullins compiled the lowest scoring average on the 12-man U.S. roster despite averaging 24.2 points per game for NCAA runner-up Duke. Mullins scored 14 of his 18 points against Puerto Rico in the semifinals.

U.S. MEN'S RESULTS

U.S. 78, Australia 45
U.S. 77, Finland 51
U.S. 60, Peru 45
U.S. 83, Uruguay 28
U.S. 69, Yugoslavia 61
U.S. 86, Brazil 53
U.S. 116, South Korea 50
U.S. 62, Puerto Rico 42
U.S. 73, USSR 59

U.S. MEN'S ROSTER AND STATISTICS

PLAYER	POS.	AFFILIATION/SCHOOL	PPG.
Jim Barnes	C	Texas Western	8.5
Bill Bradley	G-F	Princeton	10.1
Larry Brown	G	Goodyear Wingfoots (N. Carolina)	4.1
Joe Caldwell	G-F	Arizona State	9.0
Mel Counts	C	Oregon State	6.6
Dick Davies	G	Goodyear Wingfoots (LSU)	3.4
Walt Hazzard	G-F	UCLA	3.8
Luke Jackson	F	Pan American	10.0
Pete McCaffrey	F	Goodyear Wingfoots (St. Louis Univ.)	5.1
Jeff Mullins	G-F	Duke	2.3
Jerry Shipp	G	Phillips 66ers (SE Oklahoma State)	12.4
George Wilson	F-C	Chicago Jamaco Saints (Cincinnati)	5.4

1968   MEXICO CITY, MEXICO

MEDAL WINNERS: 1. U.S. (9-0); 2. Yugoslavia (7-2); 3. Soviet Union (8-1).

U.S. COACH: Hank Iba, Oklahoma State.

Houston's Ken Spain was part of the 1968 Olympic basketball team.

FAST FACT: Spencer Haywood, the leading scorer for the U.S. squad, was at that time the youngest player (19) to ever earn a spot on the U.S. Olympic basketball team. The U.S. team probably would have featured a different leading scorer and most assuredly would have averaged more than 67 points in its last three games if LSU's Pete Maravich, the nation's leading scorer as a sophomore (43.8 ppg), had been named to the squad.

U.S. MEN'S RESULTS

U.S. 81, Spain 46
U.S. 93, Senegal 36
U.S. 96, Philippines 75
U.S. 73, Yugoslavia 58
U.S. 95, Panama 60
U.S. 100, Italy 61
U.S. 61, Puerto Rico 56
U.S. 75, Brazil 63
U.S. 65, Yugoslavia 50

U.S. MEN'S ROSTER AND STATISTICS

PLAYER	POS.	AFFILIATION/SCHOOL	PPG.
Mike Barrett	G	U.S. Armed Forces (West Va. Tech)	6.2
John Clawson	G	U.S. Armed Forces (Michigan)	3.6
Don Dee	F	St. Mary of the Plains (Kans.)	4.7
Calvin Fowler	G	Goodyear Wingfoots (St. Francis, Pa.)	6.4
Spencer Haywood	C	Trinidad State J.C. (Colo.)	16.1
Bill Hosket	F	Ohio State	8.6
Jim King	F	Goodyear Wingfoots (Oklahoma State)	1.8
Glynn Saulters	G	Northeast Louisiana	5.3
Charlie Scott	F-G	North Carolina	8.0
Mike Silliman	F	U.S. Armed Forces (Army)	9.0
Ken Spain	C	Houston	4.4
Jo Jo White	G	Kansas	11.7

MEDAL WINNERS: 1. Soviet Union (9-0); 2. U.S. (8-1); 3. Cuba (7-2).

U.S. COACH: Hank Iba, Oklahoma State.

FAST FACT: The United States' 62-game Olympic winning streak ended in the most controversial game in international basketball history. In the final game, three seconds were put back on the clock on two separate occasions before the USSR's Aleksander Belov received a length-of-the-court pass between two American players and converted a game-winning layup. UCLA's Bill Walton became a postdefeat whipping boy in some quarters for not playing on the team. Iba is the only individual ever to coach three different U.S. Olympic squads.

U.S. MEN'S RESULTS

U.S. 66, Czechoslovakia 35
U.S. 81, Australia 55
U.S. 67, Cuba 48
U.S. 61, Brazil 54
U.S. 96, Egypt 31
U.S. 72, Spain 56
U.S. 99, Japan 33
U.S. 68, Italy 38
USSR 51, U.S. 50

U.S. MEN'S ROSTER AND STATISTICS

PLAYER	POS.	AFFILIATION/SCHOOL	PPG.
Mike Bantom	F	St. Joseph's	7.7
Jim Brewer	F-C	Minnesota	7.6
Tom Burleson	C	North Carolina State	3.4
Doug Collins	G	Illinois State	7.3
Kenny Davis	G	Marathon Oil (Georgetown College)	1.8
Jim Forbes	F	Texas-El Paso	5.1
Tom Henderson	G	St. Jacinto J.C. (Tex.)	9.2
Bobby Jones	F	North Carolina	4.1
Dwight Jones	C	Houston	9.2
Kevin Joyce	G	South Carolina	5.3
Tom McMillen	F	Maryland	6.8
Ed Ratleff	F-G	Long Beach State	6.4

MEDAL WINNERS: 1. U.S. (7-0); 2. Yugoslavia (5-2); 3. Soviet Union (5-2).

U.S. MEN'S COACH: Dean Smith, North Carolina.

FAST FACT: Seven members of the 12-man U.S. roster were from coach Dean Smith's conference although the ACC didn't notch a victory in the 1976 NCAA Tournament. One of the non-ACC players was Notre Dame forward Adrian Dantley, who managed the highest-ever scoring average for a U.S. player in a single Olympiad (19.3 points per game).

U.S. MEN'S RESULTS

U.S. 106, Italy 86
U.S. 95, Puerto Rico 94
U.S. 112, Yugoslavia 93
U.S. 2, Egypt 0*
U.S. 81, Czechoslovakia 76
U.S. 95, Canada 77
U.S. 95, Yugoslavia 74

* The U.S. was awarded a forfeit victory when Egypt withdrew for political reasons.

U.S. MEN'S ROSTER AND STATISTICS

PLAYER	POS.	AFFILIATION/SCHOOL	PPG.	RPG.
Tate Armstrong	G	Duke	2.7	0.4
Quinn Buckner	G	Indiana	7.3	3.0
Kenny Carr	F	North Carolina State	6.8	3.2
Adrian Dantley	F	Notre Dame	19.3	5.7
Walter Davis	F-G	North Carolina	4.3	1.7
Phil Ford	G	North Carolina	11.3	2.2
Ernie Grunfeld	F	Tennessee	3.5	0.7
Phil Hubbard	F	Michigan	4.7	3.8
Mitch Kupchak	C	North Carolina	12.5	5.7
Tom LaGarde	C	North Carolina	6.7	1.8

Scott May	F	Indiana		16.7	6.2
Steve Sheppard	F-G	Maryland		1.5	1.0

1980   MOSCOW, SOVIET UNION

MEDAL WINNERS: 1. Yugoslavia (8-0); 2. Italy (5-3); 3. Soviet Union (6-2).

U.S. MEN'S COACH: Dave Gavitt, Providence.

FAST FACT: Argentina, Canada, China, Mexico, Puerto Rico, and the U.S. all qualified for the Olympics, but they boycotted the Moscow Games in protest of the Soviet Union's invasion of Afghanistan. A key member of the gold-medal winning Yugoslavian team was Kresimir Cosic, who had led Brigham Young in scoring in 1971-72 (22.3 ppg) and 1972-73 (20.2 ppg).

U.S. MEN'S ROSTER AND STATISTICS

PLAYER	POS.	SCHOOL	PPG.	RPG.
Mark Aguirre	F	DePaul	11.3	5.0
Rolando Blackman	G-F	Kansas State	8.0	4.7
Sam Bowie	C	Kentucky	11.8	6.9
Michael Brooks	F	La Salle	13.2	6.0
Bill Hanzlik	G	Notre Dame	1.8	1.0
Alton Lister	C	Arizona State	1.7	1.0
Rodney McCray	F	Louisville	0.6	0.8
Isiah Thomas	G	Indiana	9.5	2.0
Darnell Valentine	G	Kansas	5.7	2.0
Danny Vranes	F	Utah	6.8	2.8
Buck Williams	F	Maryland	4.9	4.0
Al Wood	F-G	North Carolina	10.0	2.9

Note: Statistics are for six games (5-1 record) in the "Gold Medal Series" in various U.S. cities against NBA All-Star teams.

1984   LOS ANGELES, CALIFORNIA, USA

MEDAL WINNERS: 1. U.S. (8-0); 2. Spain (6-2); 3. Yugoslavia (7-1).

U.S. MEN'S COACH: Bob Knight, Indiana.

FAST FACT: Political repercussions persisted as the Soviet bloc countries boycotted the Olympic Games in Los Angeles. Holy Cross coach Jack Donohue, who guided the Canadian National Team to a fourth place finish, previously coached Power Memorial Academy in New York to a 160-30 record, including 71 consecutive victories with center Lew Alcindor in his lineup.

U.S. MEN'S RESULTS

U.S. 97, China 49
U.S. 89, Canada 68
U.S. 104, Uruguay 68
U.S. 120, France 62
U.S. 101, Spain 68
U.S. 78, West Germany 67
U.S. 78, Canada 59
U.S. 96, Spain 65

U.S. MEN'S ROSTER AND STATISTICS

PLAYER	POS.	SCHOOL	PPG.	RPG.
Steve Alford	G	Indiana	10.3	3.3
Patrick Ewing	C	Georgetown	11.0	5.6
Vern Fleming	G	Georgia	7.7	2.7
Michael Jordan	G-F	North Carolina	17.1	3.0
Joe Kleine	C	Arkansas	3.4	2.0
Jon Koncak	C	SMU	3.3	2.4
Chris Mullin	G-F	St. John's	11.6	2.5
Sam Perkins	F-C	North Carolina	8.1	5.4
Alvin Robertson	G	Arkansas	7.8	2.8
Wayman Tisdale	F	Oklahoma	8.6	6.4
Jeff Turner	F	Vanderbilt	1.6	2.1
Leon Wood	G	Cal State Fullerton	5.9	2.0

St. Joseph's Mike Bantom, shown here in a regular season game, averaged nearly 8 points per game for the 1972 Olympic basketball team.

1988   SEOUL, SOUTH KOREA

MEDAL WINNERS: 1. Soviet Union (7-1); 2. Yugoslavia (6-2); 3. U.S. (7-1).

U.S. MEN'S COACH: John Thompson, Georgetown.

FAST FACT: Hersey Hawkins, the team's top outside threat, was sidelined because of an injury when the U.S. sustained a semifinal loss to the USSR in the first Olympic matchup between the superpowers since the controversial 1972 final in Munich.

U.S. MEN'S RESULTS

U.S. 97, Spain 53
U.S. 76, Canada 70
U.S. 102, Brazil 87
U.S. 108, China 57
U.S. 102, Egypt 35
U.S. 94, Puerto Rico 57
USSR 82, U.S. 76
U.S. 78, Australia 49

U.S. MEN'S ROSTER AND STATISTICS

PLAYER	POS.	SCHOOL	PPG.	RPG.
Willie Anderson	G	Georgia	5.0	1.9
Stacey Augmon	F	UNLV	1.2	1.8
Bimbo Coles	G	Virginia Tech	7.1	1.8
Jeff Grayer	F-G	Iowa State	6.9	3.4
Hersey Hawkins	G	Bradley	8.8	1.0
Dan Majerle	F-G	Central Michigan	14.1	4.8

North Carolina State's Kay Yow coached the 1988 women's Olympic basketball team to a gold medal.

Danny Manning	F	Kansas	11.4	6.0
J. R. Reid	F-C	North Carolina	6.0	3.3
Mitch Richmond	G-F	Kansas State	8.9	3.4
David Robinson	C	Navy	12.8	6.8
Charles D. Smith	F	Pittsburgh	7.8	4.1
Charles E. Smith	G	Georgetown	8.6	1.3

1992 BARCELONA, SPAIN

MEDAL WINNERS: 1. U.S. (8-0); 2. Croatia (6-2); 3. Lithuania (6-2).

U.S. MEN'S COACH: Chuck Daly, New Jersey Nets.

FAST FACT: "Dream Team I," which won its eight games by an average of 43.8 points, was assembled after international rules, which previously prevented only NBA players from being eligible for Olympic basketball, were changed by the FIBA membership on April 7, 1989, by virtue of a 56-13 vote in favor of "open competition." Three University of Houston products participated in the 1992 Games–David Diaz (Venezuela), Clyde Drexler (U.S.), and Carl Herrera (Venezuela), and a fourth, Rolando Ferreira, was cut by the Brazilian squad just prior to the competition.

U.S. MEN'S RESULTS

U.S. 116, Angola 48
U.S. 103, Croatia 70
U.S. 111, Germany 68
U.S. 127, Brazil 83
U.S. 122, Spain 81
U.S. 115, Puerto Rico 77
U.S. 127, Lithuania 76
U.S. 117, Croatia 85

U.S. MEN'S ROSTER AND STATISTICS

PLAYER	POS.	NBA TEAM/SCHOOL	PPG.	RPG.
Charles Barkley	F	Phoenix Suns (Auburn)	18.0	4.1
Larry Bird	F	Boston Celtics (Indiana State)	8.4	3.8
Clyde Drexler	G	Portland Trail Blazers (Houston)	10.5	3.0
Patrick Ewing	C	New York Knicks (Georgetown)	9.5	5.3
Earvin "Magic" Johnson	G	Los Angeles Lakers (Michigan St.)	8.0	2.3
Michael Jordan	G	Chicago Bulls (North Carolina)	14.9	2.4
Christian Laettner*	F	Duke	4.8	2.5
Karl Malone	F	Utah Jazz (Louisiana Tech)	13.0	5.3

Chris Mullin	F-G	Golden State Warriors (St. John's)	12.9	1.6
Scottie Pippen	F	Chicago Bulls (Central Arkansas)	9.0	2.1
David Robinson	C	San Antonio Spurs (Navy)	9.0	4.1
John Stockton	G	Utah Jazz (Gonzaga)	2.8	0.3

* Drafted by the Minnesota Timberwolves.

1996 ATLANTA, GEORGIA, USA

U.S. MEN'S COACH: Lenny Wilkens, Atlanta Hawks.

U.S. MEN'S ROSTER

PLAYER	POS.	NBA TEAM (SCHOOL)
Charles Barkley	F	Phoenix Suns (Auburn)
Anfernee Hardaway	G	Orlando Magic (Memphis State)
Grant Hill	F-G	Detroit Pistons (Duke)
Karl Malone	F	Utah Jazz (Louisiana Tech)
Reggie Miller	G	Indiana Pacers (UCLA)
Hakeem Olajuwon	C	Houston Rockets (Univ. of Houston)
Shaquille O'Neal	C	Orlando Magic (Louisiana State)
Gary Payton	F	Seattle Sonics (Oregon State)
Scottie Pippen	F	Chicago Bulls (Central Arkansas)
Mitch Richmond	G	Sacramento Kings (Kansas State)
David Robinson	C	San Antonio Spurs (Navy)
John Stockton	G	Utah Jazz (Gonzaga)

Women's Basketball

1976 MONTREAL, QUEBEC, CANADA

MEDAL WINNERS: 1. Soviet Union (5-0); 2. U.S. (3-2); 3. Bulgaria (3-2).

U.S. WOMEN'S COACH: Billie Jean Moore, Cal State Fullerton.

U.S. WOMEN'S RESULTS

Japan 84, U.S. 71
U.S. 95, Bulgaria 79
U.S. 89, Canada 75
USSR 112, U.S. 77
U.S. 83, Czechoslovakia 67

U.S. WOMEN'S LEADING SCORERS

PLAYER	POS.	SCHOOL	PPG.
Lusia Harris	F	Delta State (Miss.)	15.2
Nancy Dunkle	C	Cal State Fullerton	13.0
Patricia Roberts	F	Tennessee	12.0
Ann Meyers	G	UCLA	9.6

1980 MOSCOW, SOVIET UNION

MEDAL WINNERS: 1. Soviet Union (6-0); 2. Bulgaria (4-2); 3. Yugoslavia (4-2).

U.S. WOMEN'S COACH: Sue Gunter, Stephen F. Austin State (Tex.).

U.S. WOMEN'S LEADING SCORERS

PLAYER	POS.	SCHOOL	PPG.
Denise Curry	F	UCLA	17.8
Cindy Noble	C	Tennessee	13.8
Rosie Walker	F	Stephen F. Austin State	12.7
LaTaunya Pollard	F	Long Beach State	12.0
Carol Blazejowski	G	Montclair State (N.J.)	10.7
Tara Heiss	G	Maryland	5.7
Anne Donovan	C	Old Dominion	5.2

Note: Statistics are for six of seven games (6-1 record) in the FIBA Pre-Olympic Qualifying Tournament in Bulgaria.

1984

LOS ANGELES, CALIFORNIA, USA

MEDAL WINNERS: 1. U.S. (6-0); 2. South Korea (4-2); 3. Canada (3-3).

U.S. WOMEN'S COACH: Pat Head Summitt, Tennessee.

U.S. WOMEN'S RESULTS

U.S. 83, Yugoslavia 55
U.S. 81, Australia 47
U.S. 84, South Korea 47
U.S. 91, China 55
U.S. 92, Canada 61
U.S. 85, South Korea 55

U.S. WOMEN'S LEADING SCORERS

PLAYER	POS.	SCHOOL	PPG.
Cheryl Miller	F	Southern Cal	16.5
Lynette Woodard	G	Kansas	10.5
Janice Lawrence	C	Louisiana Tech	9.5
Cindy Noble	C	Tennessee	8.7
Anne Donovan	C	Old Dominion	7.5
Denise Curry	F	UCLA	7.0
Pam McGee	C	Southern Cal	6.2

1988

SEOUL, SOUTH KOREA

MEDAL WINNERS: 1. U.S. (5-0); 2. Yugoslavia (3-2); 3. Soviet Union (3-2).

U.S. WOMEN'S COACH: Kay Yow, North Carolina State.

U.S. WOMEN'S RESULTS

U.S. 87, Czechoslovakia 81
U.S. 101, Yugoslavia 74
U.S. 94, China 79
U.S. 102, USSR 88
U.S. 77, Yugoslavia 70

U.S. WOMEN'S LEADING SCORERS

PLAYER	POS.	SCHOOL	PPG.
Katrina McClain	F	Georgia	17.6
Teresa Edwards	G	Georgia	16.6
Cynthia Cooper	G	Southern Cal	14.2
Bridgette Gordon	F	Tennessee	8.8
Suzie McConnell	G	Penn State	8.4
Cindy Brown	F	Long Beach State	8.0
Andrea Lloyd	F	Texas	6.6

1992

BARCELONA, SPAIN

MEDAL WINNERS: 1. Unified Team (5-0); 2. China (4-1); 3. U.S. (4-1).

U.S. WOMEN'S COACH: Theresa Grentz, Rutgers.

U.S. WOMEN'S RESULTS

U.S. 111, Czechoslovakia 55
U.S. 114, Spain 59
U.S. 93, China 67
Unified 79, U.S. 73
U.S. 88, Cuba 74

U.S. WOMEN'S LEADING SCORERS

PLAYER	POS.	SCHOOL	PPG.
Medina Dixon	F	Old Dominion	15.8
Clarissa Davis	F	Texas	13.0
Teresa Edwards	F	Georgia	12.6
Katrina McClain	F	Georgia	11.4

Louisiana Tech's Karl Malone went on to stardom in the NBA as the Utah Jazz's "Mailman" and as a member of the 1992 Olympic "Dream Team."

Cynthia Cooper	G	Southern Cal	7.6
Vickie Orr	F	Auburn	7.6
Tammy Jackson	C	Florida	7.2
Suzie McConnell	G	Penn State	6.8
Daedra Charles	C	Tennessee	6.2

1996

ATLANTA, GEORGIA, USA

U.S. WOMEN'S COACH: Tara VanDenveer, Stanford.

FAST FACT: Teresa Edwards has played professionally in Italy, Japan, Spain, and France.

U.S. WOMEN'S ROSTER

PLAYER	POS.	SCHOOL
Jennifer Azzi	G	Stanford '90
Ruthie Bolton	G	Auburn '89
Teresa Edwards	G	Georgia '86
Venus Lacy	C	Louisiana Tech '90
Lisa Leslie	C-F	Southern Cal '94
Rebecca Lobo	C-F	Connecticut '95
Katrina McClain	C-F	Georgia '87
Nikki McCray	G	Tennessee '95
Carla McGhee	C-F	Tennessee '90
Dawn Staley	G	Virginia '92
Katy Steding	F	Stanford '90
Sheryl Swoopes	G-F	Texas Tech '93

U.S. MEN'S ALL-TIME OLYMPIC GAMES ROSTER

PLAYER	COLLEGE	YEAR(S)
Mark Aguirre	DePaul	1980
Steve Alford	Indiana	1984
Willie Anderson	Georgia	1988
Tate Armstrong	Duke	1976
Jay Arnette	Texas	1960
Stacey Augmon	UNLV	1988
Sam Balter*	UCLA	1936
Mike Bantom	St. Joseph's	1972
Cliff Barker	Kentucky	1948
Charles Barkley**	Auburn	1992, 1996
Don Barksdale*	UCLA	1948
Jim Barnes	Texas Western	1964
Mike Barrett*	West Virginia Tech	1968
Ralph Beard	Kentucky	1948
Lewis Beck*	Oregon State	1948
Walt Bellamy	Indiana	1960
Larry Bird**	Indiana State	1992
Ralph Bishop	Washington	1936
Rolando Blackman	Kansas State	1980
Ron Bontemps	Illinois/Beloit (Wis.)	1962
Bob Boozer	Kansas State	1960
Vince Boryla*	Notre Dame/Denver	1948
Dick Boushka*	St. Louis	1956
Sam Bowie	Kentucky	1980
Bill Bradley	Princeton	1964
Jim Brewer	Minnesota	1972
Michael Brooks	La Salle	1980
Larry Brown*	North Carolina	1964
Quinn Buckner	Indiana	1976
Tom Burleson	North Carolina State	1972
Carl Cain	Iowa	1956
Joe Caldwell	Arizona State	1964
Gordon Carpenter*	Kansas	1948
Kenny Carr	North Carolina State	1976
John Clawson*	Michigan	1968
Bimbo Coles	Virginia Tech	1988
Doug Collins	Illinois State	1972
Mel Counts	Oregon State	1964
Adrian Dantley	Notre Dame	1976
Chuck Darling*	Iowa	1956
Dick Davies*	Louisiana State	1964
Kenny Davis*	Georgetown College (Ky.)	1972
Walter Davis	North Carolina	1976
Don Dee	St. Mary of the Plains (Kan.)	1968
Terry Dischinger	Purdue	1960
Clyde Drexler**	Houston	1992
Bill Evans*	Kentucky	1956
Patrick Ewing	Georgetown	1984, 1992
Vern Fleming	Georgia	1984
Jim Forbes	Texas-El Paso	1972
Gib Ford*	Texas	1956
Phil Ford	North Carolina	1976
Joe Fortenberry*	Wichita State	1936
Calvin Fowler*	St. Francis (Pa.)	1968
Marcus Freiberger*	Oklahoma	1952
John Gibbons*	Southwestern College (Kan.)	1936
Wayne Glasgow*	Oklahoma	1952
Jeff Grayer	Iowa State	1988
Alex Groza	Kentucky	1948
Ernie Grunfeld	Tennessee	1976
Burdette Haldorson*	Colorado	1956, 1960
Bill Hanzlik	Notre Dame	1980
Anfernee Hardaway	Memphis State	1996
Hersey Hawkins	Bradley	1988
Spencer Haywood	Trinidad State J.C. (Co.)	1968
Walt Hazzard	UCLA	1964
Tom Henderson	San Jacinto J.C. (Tex.)	1972
Grant Hill	Duke	1996
Charles Hoag	Kansas	1952
Bill Hosket	Ohio State	1968
Bill Hougland*	Kansas	1952, 1956
Phil Hubbard	Michigan	1976
Darrall Imhoff	California	1960
Luke Jackson	Pan American (Tex.)	1964
Bob Jeangerard*	Colorado	1956
Francis Johnson*	Wichita State	1936
Magic Johnson**	Michigan State	1992
Bobby Jones	North Carolina	1972
Dwight Jones	Houston	1972
K.C. Jones	San Francisco	1956
Wallace Jones	Kentucky	1948
Michael Jordan	North Carolina	1984, 1992
Kevin Joyce	South Carolina	1972
John Keller	Kansas	1952
Allen Kelley*	Kansas	1960
Dean Kelley	Kansas	1952
Bob Kenney	Kansas	1952
Jimmy King*	Oklahoma State	1968
Joe Kleine	Arkansas	1984
Carl Knowles*	UCLA	1936
Jon Koncak	Southern Methodist	1984
Mitch Kupchak	North Carolina	1976
Bob Kurland*	Oklahoma State	1948, 1952
Christian Laettner	Duke	1992
Tom LaGarde	North Carolina	1976
Lester Lane*	Oklahoma	1960
Bill Lienhard	Kansas	1952
Alton Lister	Arizona State	1980
Clyde Lovellette	Kansas	1952
Frank Lubin*	UCLA	1936
Jerry Lucas	Ohio State	1960
Ray Lumpp	New York University	1948
Dan Majerle	Central Michigan	1988
Karl Malone**	Louisiana Tech	1992, 1996
Danny Manning	Kansas	1988
Scott May	Indiana	1976
Frank McCabe*	Marquette	1952
Pete McCaffrey*	St. Louis	1964
Rodney McCray	Louisville	1980
Tom McMillen	Maryland	1972
Reggie Miller	UCLA	1996
Art Moliner*	Los Angeles J.C.	1936
Chris Mullin	St. John's	1984, 1992
Jeff Mullins	Duke	1964
Hakeem Olajuwon	Houston	1996
Shaquille O'Neal	Louisiana State	1996
Gary Payton	Seattle Sonics	1996
Sam Perkins	North Carolina	1984
Don Piper*	UCLA	1936
Scottie Pippen**	Central Arkansas	1992, 1996
Dan Pippin*	Missouri	1952
R.C. Pitts*	Arkansas	1948
Jack Ragland*	Wichita State	1936
Ed Ratleff	Long Beach State	1972
J.R. Reid	North Carolina	1988
Jesse Renick*	Oklahoma State	1948
Mitch Richmond	Kansas State	1988, 1996
Alvin Robertson	Arkansas	1984
Oscar Robertson	Cincinnati	1960
David Robinson	Navy	1988-92-96
Jack Robinson	Baylor	1948
Ken Rollins	Kentucky	1948
Bill Russell	San Francisco	1956
Glynn Saulters	Northeast Louisiana	1968
Willard Schmidt*	Creighton	1936
Charlie Scott	North Carolina	1968
Steve Sheppard	Maryland	1976
Jerry Shipp*	Southeastern Oklahoma State	1964
Carl Shy*	UCLA	1936
Mike Silliman	Army	1968
Adrian Smith*	Kentucky	1960
Charles D. Smith	Pittsburgh	1988
Charles E. Smith	Georgetown	1988
Ken Spain	Houston	1968
John Stockton**	Gonzaga	1992, 1996
Dwayne Swanson*	Southern California	1936
Isiah Thomas	Indiana	1980
Wayman Tisdale	Oklahoma	1984
Ron Tomsic*	Stanford	1956
Jeff Turner	Vanderbilt	1984
Darnell Valentine	Kansas	1980
Danny Vranes	Utah	1980
Jim Walsh*	Stanford	1956
Jerry West	West Virginia	1960
William Wheatley*	Kansas Wesleyan	1936
Jo Jo White	Kansas	1968
Buck Williams	Maryland	1980
Howie Williams*	Purdue	1952
George Wilson*	Cincinnati	1964
Al Wood	North Carolina	1980
Leon Wood	Cal State Fullerton	1984

*Played for an armed services or independent team when named an Olympian.

**NBA player when named an Olympian.

U.S. WOMEN'S ALL-TIME OLYMPIC GAMES ROSTER

PLAYER	COLLEGE	YEAR(S)
Jennifer Azzi	Stanford	1996
Carol Blazejowski	Montclair (N.J.) State	1980
Ruthie Bolton	Auburn	1996
Cathy Boswell	Illinois State	1984
Cindy Brogdon	Tennessee	1976
Cindy Brown	Long Beach State	1988
Vicky Bullett	Maryland	1988, 1992
Daedra Charles	Tennessee	1992
Cynthia Cooper	Southern California	1988, 1992
Denise Curry	UCLA	1980, 1984
Clarissa Davis	Texas	1992
Medina Dixon	Old Dominion	1992
Anne Donovan	Old Dominion	1980, 1984, 1988
Nancy Dunkle	Cal State Fullerton	1976
Teresa Edwards	Georgia	1984, 1988, 1992, 1996
Kamie Ethridge	Texas	1988
Jennifer Gillom	Mississippi	1988
Bridgette Gordon	Tennessee	1988
Lusia Harris	Delta State (Miss.)	1976
Pat Head	Tennessee-Martin	1976
Tara Heiss	Maryland	1980
Lea Henry	Tennessee	1984
Tammy Jackson	Florida	1992
Carolyn Jones	Auburn	1992
Kris Kirchner	Maryland	1980
Venus Lacy	Louisiana Tech	1996
Janice Lawrence	Louisiana Tech	1984
Lisa Leslie	Southern California	1996

PLAYER	COLLEGE	YEAR(S)
Charlotte Lewis	Illinois State	1976
Nancy Lieberman	Far Rockaway High (N.Y.)	1976
Andrea Lloyd	Texas	1988
Rebecca Lobo	Connecticut	1996
Gail Marquis	Queens College	1976
Katrina McClain	Georgia	1988, 1992, 1996
Suzie McConnell	Penn State	1988, 1992
Nikki McCray	Tennessee	1996
Pam McGee	Southern California	1984
Carla McGhee	Tennessee	1996
Carol Menken-Schaudt	Oregon State	1984
Ann Meyers	UCLA	1976
Cheryl Miller	Southern California	1984
Debra Miller	Boston University	1980
Kim Mulkey	Louisiana Tech	1984
Cindy Noble	Tennessee	1980, 1984
Mary Anne O'Connor	Southern Connecticut State	1976
Vickie Orr	Auburn	1992
LaTaunya Pollard	Long Beach State	1980
Jill Rankin	Tennessee	1980
Patricia Roberts	Tennessee	1976
Sue Rojcewicz	Southern Connecticut State	1976
Juliene Simpson	John F. Kennedy College	1976
Dawn Staley	Virginia	1996
Katy Steding	Stanford	1996
Sheryl Swoopes	Texas Tech	1996
Rosie Walker	Stephen F. Austin State	1980
Holly Warlick	Tennessee	1980
Teresa Weatherspoon	Louisiana Tech	1988, 1992
Lynette Woodard	Kansas	1980, 1984

15

CONFERENCE DIRECTORY

T he nation's NCAA Division I schools have been in a frenetic restructuring of conferences although the quest for megaleagues might be a delusion because they're vying for television revenue that simply doesn't exist anymore as network sports divisions operate at ample deficits.

Only three Division I conferences remained intact since the late 1980s–the Ivy League, Pacific-10 and West Coast. Although the TV well is dry and no amount of realigning will alter the marketplace, more than one-fourth of the nearly 300 Division I schools changed conferences or shed independent status so far in the 1990s.

A time-honored argument rages each season on the court: Which conference plays the best basketball? The debate attained new heights since the Big East's initial campaign, 1980, the year the NCAA Tournament expanded its field to 48 teams. Naturally, the NCAA playoffs are an accurate barometer to determine the longstanding or recent strength of a league. Consider the following achievements:

• The ACC is the only league to have each of its members play at least 10 games in the NCAA playoffs. Incredibly, all nine ACC members have winning NCAA Tournament records and advanced to the Sweet 16 since the field expanded to 64 teams. Perhaps the greatest testimony to the ACC's consistent brilliance was the league's average of 11 NCAA Tournament victories annually from 1983 through 1995.

• The Big East is the only league to have three representatives at a single Final Four– Georgetown, St. John's and Villanova in 1985 after they all defeated ACC members in 1985 regional finals. The Big East has had eight different schools win undisputed league titles since its formation in 1980. Last season, the Big East became the only conference ever to have three different members represented on the NCAA consensus first-team All-American squad.

• Entering the 1997 NCAA Tournament, the Big Ten had the most Final Four teams (33) and most different members win the NCAA title (five).

• The Big Eight portion of the new Big 12 sent more teams (six) to the 1992 NCAA Tournament than any league and tied the ACC for the most playoff delegates in 1993 with six. In 1988,

Kansas and Oklahoma enabled the Big Eight to become the only league to have two members meet in the NCAA final from 1986-94.

• The Atlantic 10 and Conference USA were the only leagues to have five 20-win teams in 1995-96. Current A10 members combined to win more NIT titles than any league (11). C-USA is the only league with all of its members having reached the national semifinals of the NCAA Tournament or NIT at some point in their history.

• The Pacific-10, with nine of its 10 schools advancing to the national semifinals at least once, boasts the highest percentage of present league members to reach the Final Four.

• In 1994, the SEC compiled the best winning percentage in a single tourney for a league with at least three entrants (12-3 record, .800). The SEC has won more NCAA Tournament games than any conference over the last three seasons.

Putting provincialism aside, here are vital facts on Division I conferences. Each season is denoted by a single year. For example, the ACC's first season in 1953-54 is listed as 1954. The numbers in parentheses after schools with regular-season champions denote undisputed titles first and then ties. Totals for NCAA Tournament records reflect current conference membership.

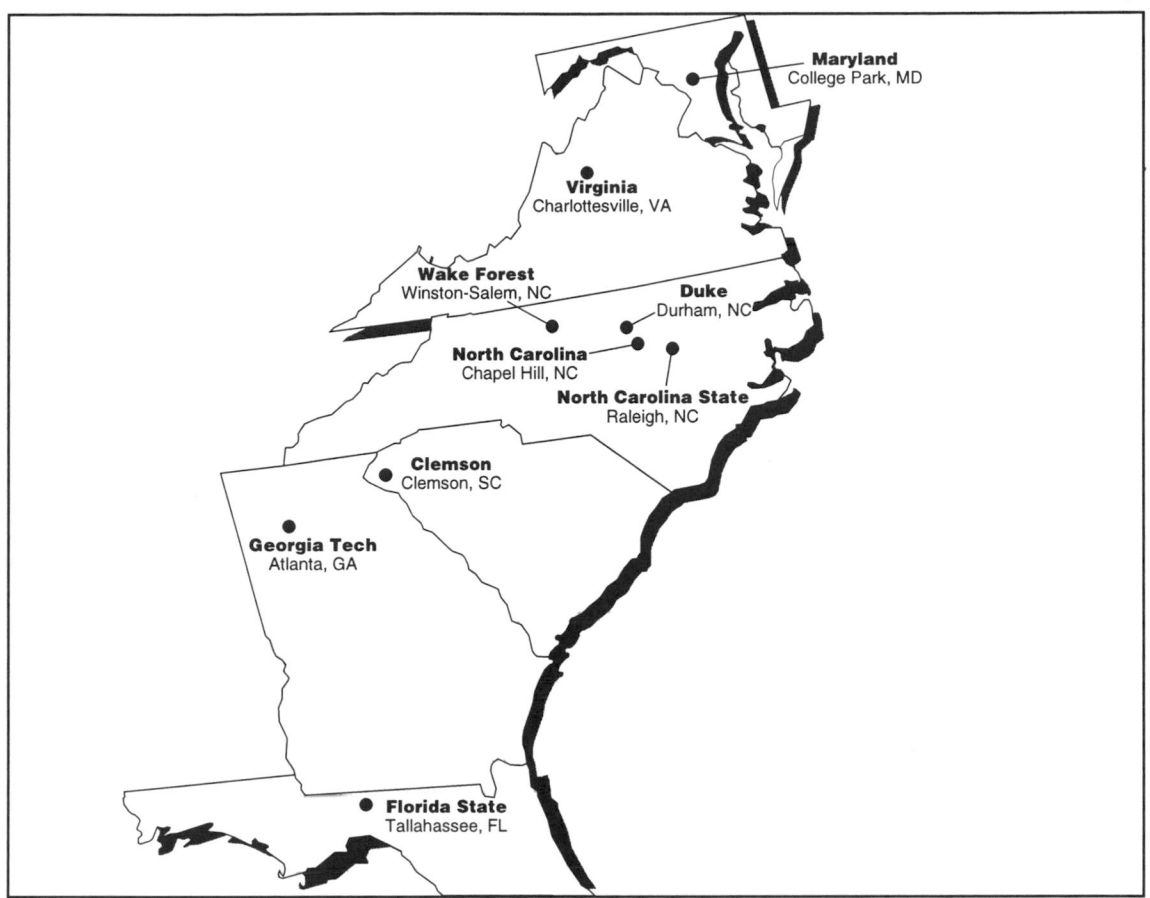

ATLANTIC COAST

ADDRESS: 6011 Landmark Center Boulevard, P.O. Drawer ACC, Greensboro, NC 27419-6999.

PHONE/FAX: (910) 854-8787/8797.

CURRENT MEMBERS: Clemson (1954-97), Duke (1954-97), Florida State (1992-97), Georgia Tech (1980-97), Maryland (1954-97), North Carolina (1954-97), North Carolina State (1954-97), Virginia (1954-97), Wake Forest (1954-97).

FORMER MEMBER: South Carolina (1954-71).

NCAA TOURNAMENT RECORD: 229-114 (.668).

NCAA TITLES (7) : Duke (1991 and 1992), North Carolina (1957-82-93), North Carolina State (1974 and 1983).

NIT TITLES (4) : Maryland (1972), North Carolina (1971), Virginia (1980 and 1992).

ALL-TIME SCORING LEADER: Johnny Dawkins, Duke (2,556 points from 1983-86). Dickie Hemric of Wake Forest (1952-55) scored 2,587 points, but the first two seasons of his career preceded the formation of the ACC.

SINGLE-SEASON SCORING LEADERS: Buzz Wilkinson, Virginia (32.1 points per game in 1954-55) and Dennis Scott, Georgia Tech (960 points in 1989-90).

REGULAR-SEASON CHAMPIONS: Clemson (1 outright-0 ties), Duke (11-0), Georgia Tech (1-1), Maryland (2-1), North Carolina (14-8), North Carolina State (4-3), South Carolina (1-0), Virginia (1-3), Wake Forest (1-2).

ACC TOURNAMENT TITLES: North Carolina (13; 1957-67-68-69-72-75-77-79-81-82-89-91-94), N.C. State (10; 1954-55-56-59-65-70-73-74-83-87), Duke (9; 1960-63-64-66-78-80-86-88-92), Wake Forest (4; 1961-62-95-96), Georgia Tech (3; 1985-90-93), Maryland (2; 1958 and 1984), South Carolina (1; 1971), Virginia (1; 1976).

YEAR-BY-YEAR CHAMPIONS (incl. conference records): 1954—Duke (9-1); **1955**—N.C. State (12-2); **1956**—North Carolina (11-3), N.C. State (11-3); **1957**—North Carolina (14-0); **1958**—Duke (11-3); **1959**—North Carolina (12-2), N.C. State (12-2); **1960**—North Carolina (12-2), Wake Forest (12-2); **1961**—North Carolina (12-2); **1962**—Wake Forest (12-2); **1963**—Duke (14-0); **1964**—Duke (13-1); **1965**—Duke (11-3); **1966**—Duke (12-2); **1967**—North Carolina (12-2); **1968**—North Carolina (12-2); **1969**—North Carolina (12-2); **1970**—South Carolina (14-0); **1971**—North Carolina (11-3); **1972**—North Carolina (9-3); **1973**—N.C. State (12-0); **1974**—N.C. State (12-0); **1975**—Maryland (10-2); **1976**—North Carolina (11-1); **1977**—North Carolina (9-3); **1978**—North Carolina (9-3); **1979**—Duke (9-3), North Carolina (9-3); **1980**—Maryland (11-3); **1981**—Virginia (13-1); **1982**—North Carolina (12-2), Virginia (12-2); **1983**—North Carolina (12-2), Virginia (12-2); **1984**—North Carolina (14-0); **1985**—Georgia Tech (9-5), North Carolina (9-5), N.C. State (9-5); **1986**—Duke (12-2); **1987**—North Carolina (14-0); **1988**—North Carolina (11-3); **1989**—N.C. State (10-4); **1990**—Clemson (10-4); **1991**—Duke (11-3); **1992**—Duke (14-2); **1993**—North Carolina (14-2); **1994**—Duke (12-4); **1995**—Maryland (12-4), North Carolina (12-4), Virginia (12-4), Wake Forest (12-4); **1996**—Georgia Tech (13-3).

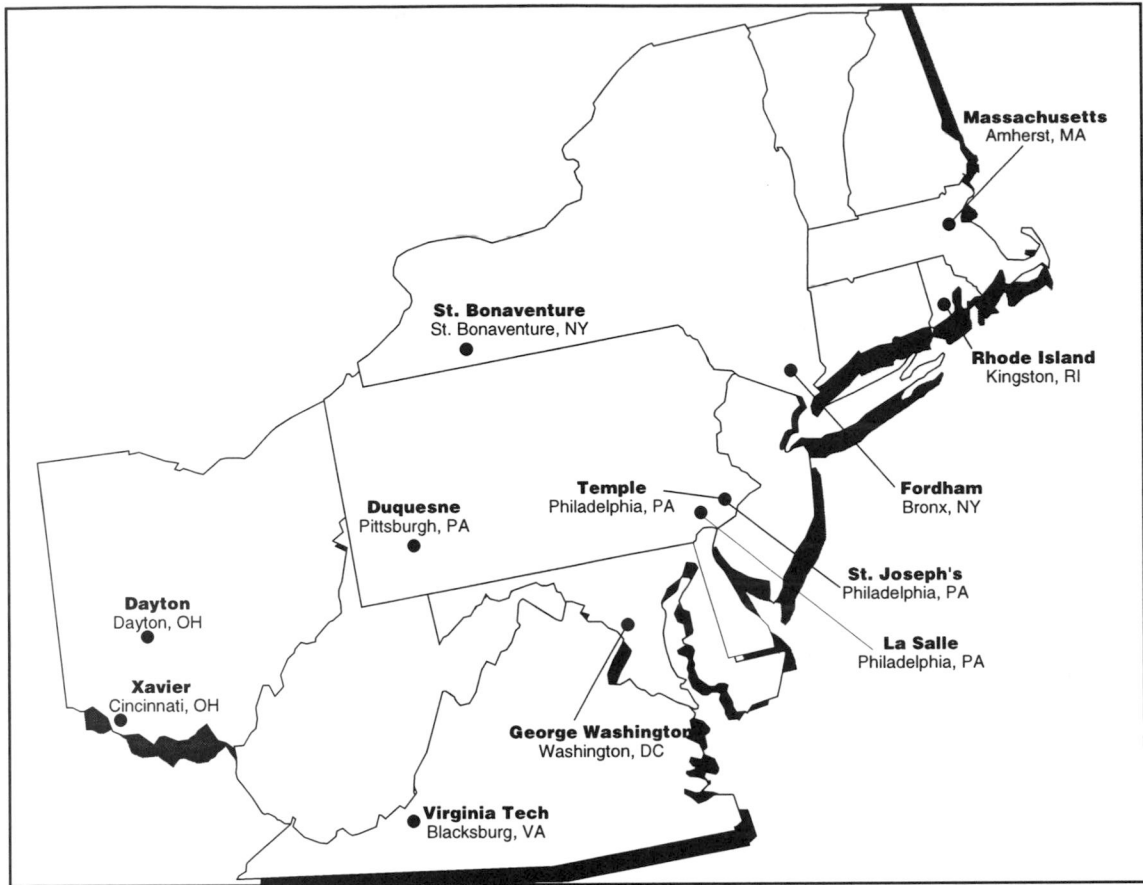

ATLANTIC 10

ADDRESS: 2 Penn Center Plaza, Suite 1410, Philadelphia, PA 19102.

PHONE/FAX: (215) 751-0500/0770.

PREVIOUS NAMES: Eastern Collegiate Basketball League (1977), Eastern Athletic Association or Eastern 8 (1978 through 1982).

CURRENT MEMBERS: Dayton (1996 and 1997), Duquesne (1977-97 except for 1993), Fordham (1996 and 1997), George Washington (1977-97), La Salle (1996 and 1997), Massachusetts (1977-97), Rhode Island (1981-97), St. Bonaventure (1980-97), St. Joseph's (1983-97), Temple (1983-97), Virginia Tech (1996-), Xavier (1996 and 1997).

FORMER MEMBERS: Penn State (1977-79 and 1983-91), Pittsburgh (1977-82), Rutgers (1977-95), West Virginia (1977-95), Villanova (1977-80).

NCAA TOURNAMENT RECORD: 44-41 (.518).

NCAA TITLES (1) : La Salle (1954) won its NCAA title before the conference was formed.

NIT TITLES (11) : Dayton (1962 and 1968), Duquesne (1955), La Salle (1952), St. Bonaventure (1977), Temple (1938 and 1969), Virginia Tech (1973 and 1995), West Virginia (1942) and Xavier (1958) won before joining Atlantic 10.

ALL-TIME SCORING LEADER: Mark Macon, Temple (2,609 points from 1988-91).

SINGLE-SEASON SCORING LEADER: Mark Stevenson, Duquesne (788 points and 27.2 ppg in 1989-90).

REGULAR-SEASON CHAMPIONS: Duquesne (0 outright-2 ties), George Washington (0-1), Massachusetts (5-0), Penn State (0-1), Rhode Island (0-1), Rutgers (3-2), St. Bonaventure (0-1), St. Joseph's (1-0), Temple (4-0), Villanova (1-2), Virginia Tech (0-1), West Virginia (3-2).

ATLANTIC 10 TOURNAMENT TITLES: Massachusetts (5; 1992-93-94-95-96), Temple (4; 1985-87-88-90), Pittsburgh (2; 1981 and 1982), Rutgers (2; 1979 and 1989), Villanova (2; 1978 and 1980), West Virginia (2; 1983 and 1984), Duquesne (1; 1977), Penn State (1; 1991), St. Joseph's (1; 1986).

YEAR-BY-YEAR CHAMPIONS (incl. conference records): 1977—Rutgers (7-1/E), Penn State (5-5/W), West Virginia (5-5/W); **1978**—Rutgers (7-3), Villanova (7-3); 1979—Villanova (9-1); **1980**—Duquesne (7-3), Rutgers (7-3), Villanova (7-3); **1981**—Duquesne (10-3), Rhode Island (10-3); **1982**—West Virginia (13-1); **1983**—Rutgers (11-3/E), St. Bonaventure (10-4/W), West Virginia (10-4/W); **1984**—Temple (18-0); **1985**—West Virginia (16-2); **1986**—St. Joseph's (16-2); **1987**—Temple (17-1); **1988**—Temple (18-0); **1989**—West Virginia (17-1); **1990**—Temple (15-3); **1991**—Rutgers (14-4); **1992**—Massachusetts (13-3); **1993**—Massachusetts (11-3); **1994**—Massachusetts (14-2); **1995**—Massachusetts (13-3); **1996**—Massachusetts (15-1/E), George Washington (13-3/W), Virginia Tech (13-3/W).

Note: The Atlantic 10 had Eastern and Western Divisions for one season in 1982–83. The league resumed divisional play in 1996.

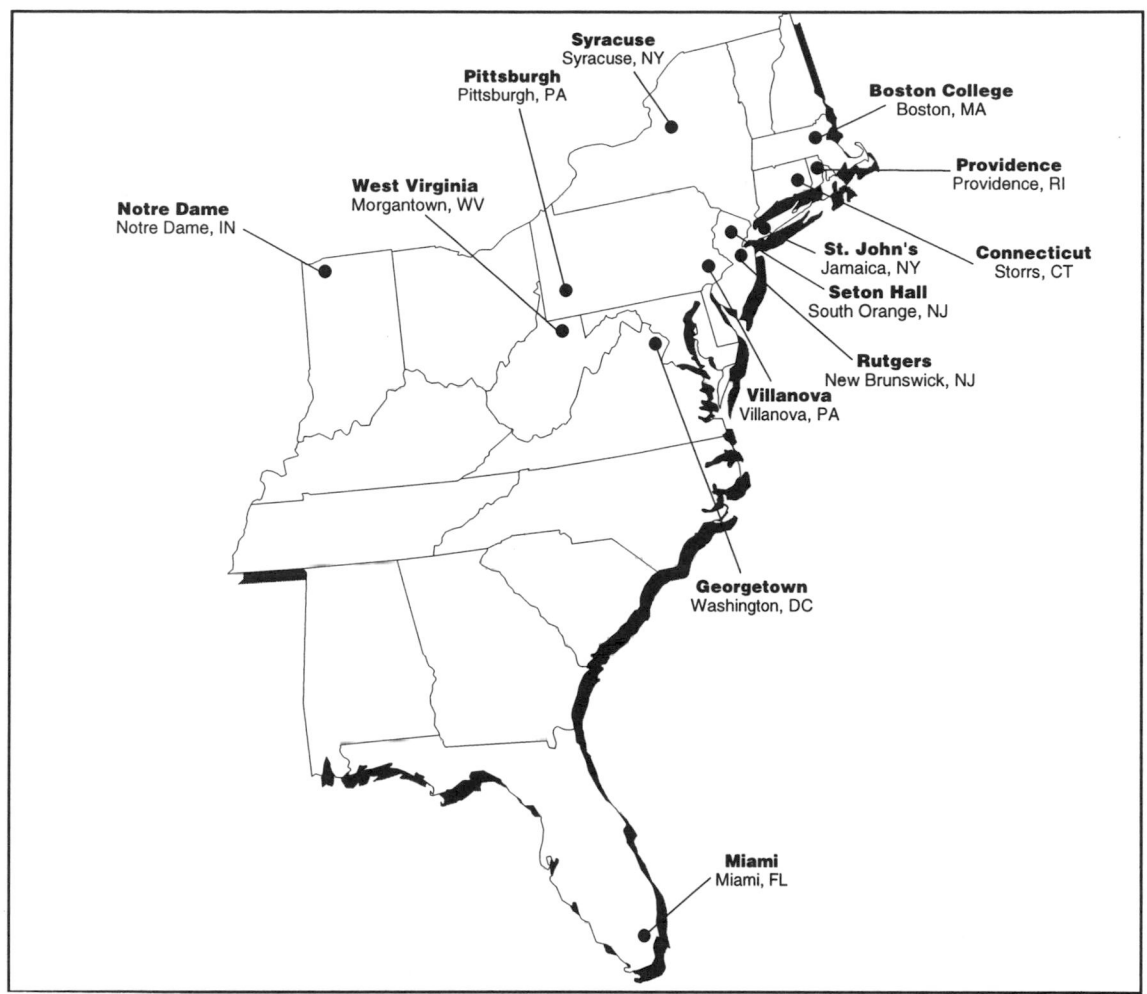

BIG EAST

ADDRESS: 56 Exchange Terrace, Providence, RI 02903.

PHONE/FAX: (401) 453-0660, 272-9108/751-8540.

CURRENT MEMBERS: Boston College (1980-97), Connecticut (1980-97), Georgetown (1980-97), Miami, Fla. (1992-97), Notre Dame (1996 and 1997), Pittsburgh (1983-97), Providence (1980-97), Rutgers (1996 and 1997), St. John's (1980-97), Seton Hall (1980-97), Syracuse (1980-97), Villanova (1981-97), West Virginia (1996 and 1997).

NCAA TOURNAMENT RECORD: 134-79 (.629).

NCAA TITLES (2) : Georgetown (1984) and Villanova (1985).

NIT TITLES (10) : Connecticut (1988), Providence (1961 and 1963), St. John's (1943-44-59-65-89), Seton Hall (1953), Villanova (1994). Three of the titles were earned since the formation of the league.

ALL-TIME SCORING LEADER: Terry Dehere, Seton Hall (2,494 points from 1990-93).

REGULAR-SEASON CHAMPIONS: Boston College (1 outright-1 tie), Connecticut (3-1), Georgetown (3-3), Pittsburgh (1-1), St. John's (1-4), Seton Hall (1-1), Syracuse (1-4), Villanova (1-1).

Big East Tournament Titles: Georgetown (6; 1980-82-84-85-87-89), Syracuse (3; 1981-88-92), Connecticut (2; 1990 and 1996), St. John's (2; 1983 and 1986), Seton Hall (2; 1991 and 1993), Providence (1; 1994), Villanova (1; 1995).

YEAR-BY-YEAR CHAMPIONS (incl. conference records): 1980— Georgetown (5-1), St. John's (5-1), Syracuse (5-1); **1981**—Boston College (10-4); **1982**—Villanova (11-3); **1983**—Boston College (12-4), St. John's (12-4), Villanova (12-4); **1984**—Georgetown (14-2); **1985**—St. John's (15-1); **1986**—St. John's (14-2), Syracuse (14-2); **1987**—Georgetown (12-4), Pittsburgh (12- 4), Syracuse (12-4); **1988**—Pittsburgh (12-4); **1989**—Georgetown (13-3); **1990**—Connecticut (12-4), Syracuse (12-4); **1991**—Syracuse (12-4); **1992**—Georgetown (12-6), St. John's (12-6), Seton Hall (12-6); **1993**—Seton Hall (14-4); **1994**—Connecticut (16-2); **1995**—Connecticut (16-2); **1996**—Connecticut (17-1/BE 6), Georgetown (13-5/BE 7).

Note: League split into two divisions in 1996–Big East 7 (Georgetown, Miami, Pittsburgh, Providence, Rutgers, Seton Hall and Syracuse) and Big East 6 (Boston College, Connecticut, Notre Dame, St. John's, Villanova and West Virginia).

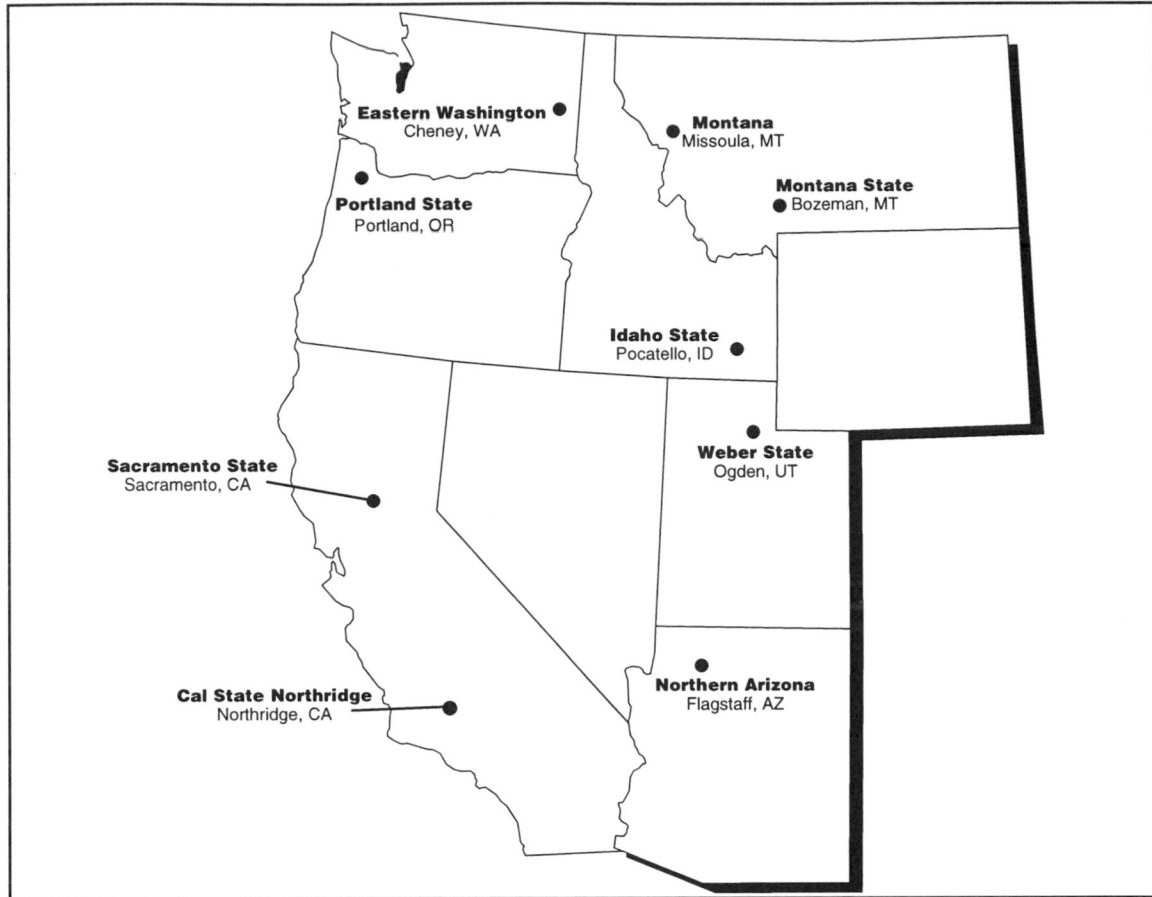

BIG SKY

ADDRESS: Post Office Box 1459, Ogden, UT 84402.

PHONE/FAX: (801) 392-1978/5568.

CURRENT MEMBERS: Cal State Northridge (since 1997), Eastern Washington (1988-97), Idaho State (1964-97), Montana (1964-97), Montana State (1964-97), Northern Arizona (1971-97), Portland State (since 1997), Sacramento State (since 1997), Weber State (1964-97).

FORMER MEMBERS: Boise State (1971-96), Gonzaga (1964-79), Idaho (1964-96), Nevada-Reno (1980-92).

NCAA TOURNAMENT RECORD: 9-31 (.225).

ALL-TIME SCORING LEADER: Orlando Lightfoot, Idaho (2,102 points from 1992-94).

SINGLE-SEASON SCORING LEADER: Dave Wagnon, Idaho State (32.5 points per game in 1965-66).

REGULAR-SEASON CHAMPIONS: Boise State (1 outright-2 ties), Gonzaga (0-2), Idaho (4-1), Idaho State (1-3), Montana (4-3), Montana State (3-1), Nevada-Reno (1-1), Northern Arizona (0-1), Weber State (10-5).

BIG SKY TOURNAMENT TITLES: Boise State (4; 1976-88-93-94), Idaho (4; 1981-82-89-90), Weber State (5; 1978-79-80-83-95), Idaho State (2; 1977 and 1987), Montana (2; 1991 and 1992), Montana State (2; 1986 and 1996), Nevada (2; 1984 and 1985).

YEAR-BY-YEAR CHAMPIONS (incl. conference records): 1964—Montana State (8-2); **1965**—Weber State (8-2); **1966**—Gonzaga (8-2), Weber State (8-2); **1967**—Gonzaga (7-3), Montana State (7-3); **1968**—Weber State (12-3); **1969**—Weber State (15-0); **1970**—Weber State (12-3); **1971**—Weber State (12-2); **1972**—Weber State (10-4); **1973**—Weber State (13-1); **1974**—Idaho State (11-3)*, Montana, (11-3); **1975**—Montana (13-1); **1976**—Boise State (9-5), Idaho State (9-5), Weber State (9-5); **1977**—Idaho State (13-1); **1978**—Montana (12-2); **1979**—Weber State (10-4); **1980**—Weber State (13-1); **1981**—Idaho (12-2); **1982**—Idaho (13-1); **1983**—Nevada (10-4), Weber State (10-4); **1984**—Weber State (12-2); **1985**—Nevada (11-3); **1986**—Montana (9-5), Northern Arizona (9-5); **1987**—Montana State (12-2); **1988**—Boise State (13-3); **1989**—Boise State (13-3), Idaho (13-3); **1990**—Idaho (13-3); **1991**—Montana (13-3); **1992**—Montana (14-2); **1993**—Idaho (11-3); **1994**—Idaho State (10-4), Weber State (10-4); **1995**—Montana (11-3), Weber State (11-3); 1996—**Montana State (11-3).**

*Won playoff.

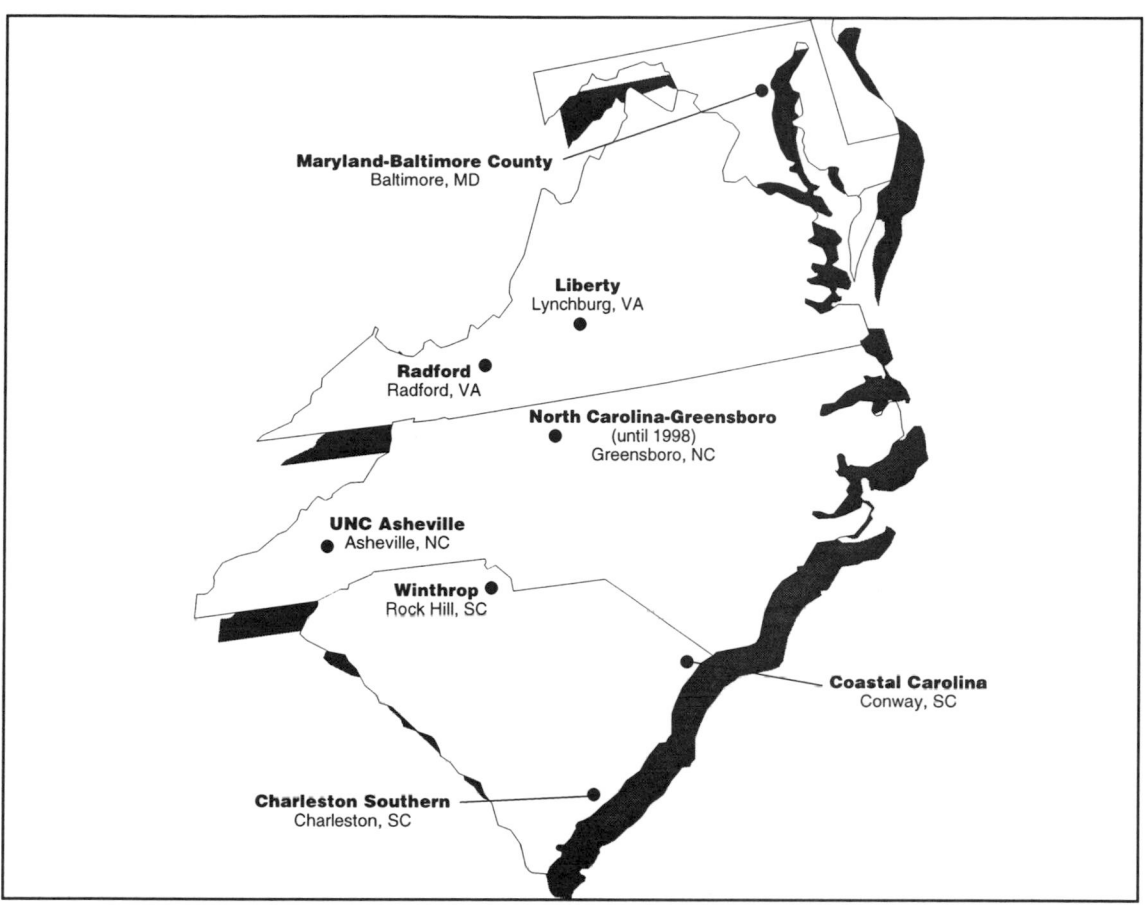

BIG SOUTH

ADDRESS: 1551 21st Avenue North, Suite 11, Myrtle Beach, SC 29577.

PHONE/FAX: (803) 448-9998/626-7167.

CURRENT MEMBERS: Charleston Southern (1986-97), Coastal Carolina (1986-97), Liberty (1992-97), Maryland-Baltimore County (1993-97), UNC Asheville (1986-97), North Carolina-Greensboro (1993-97; slated to join the Southern Conference in 1998), Radford (1986-97), Winthrop (1986-97),

FORMER MEMBERS: Armstrong State (1986 and 1987), Augusta (1986-91), Campbell (1986-94), Davidson (1991 and 1992), Towson State (1993-95).

NCAA TOURNAMENT RECORD: 0-5 (.000).

ALL-TIME SCORING LEADER: Tony Dunkin, Coastal Carolina (2,151 points from 1990-93).

REGULAR-SEASON CHAMPIONS: Charleston Southern (2 outright-0 ties), Coastal Carolina (4-0), UNC Greensboro (2-0), Radford (1-0), Towson State (2-0).

BIG SOUTH TOURNAMENT TITLES: Charleston Southern (3; 1986-87-95), Coastal Carolina (3; 1990-91-93), Liberty (1; 1994), Campbell (1; 1992), UNC Asheville (1; 1989), UNC Greensboro (1; 1996), Winthrop (1; 1988).

YEAR-BY-YEAR CHAMPIONS (incl. conference records): 1986— Charleston Southern (5-1); **1987**—Charleston Southern (12-2); **1988**—Coastal Carolina (9-3); **1989**—Coastal Carolina (9-3); **1990**—Coastal Carolina (11-1); **1991**—Coastal Carolina (13-1); **1992**—Radford (12-2); **1993**—Towson State (14-2); **1994**—Towson State (16-2); **1995**—UNC Greensboro (14-2); **1996**—UNC Greensboro (11-3).

Note: In August 1996, the headquarters will be moving to Charlotte, North Carolina.

BIG TEN

ADDRESS: 1500 West Higgins Road, Park Ridge, IL 60068-6300.

PHONE/FAX: (847) 696-1010/1110.

PREVIOUS NAMES: Intercollegiate Conference of Faculty Representatives or Western Conference, Big Nine (1947 and 1948).

CURRENT MEMBERS: Illinois (1896-97), Indiana (1899-97), Iowa (1899-97), Michigan (1896-97), Michigan State (1949-97), Minnesota (1896-97), Northwestern (1896-97), Ohio State (1912-97), Penn State (1993-97), Purdue (1896-97), Wisconsin (1896-97).

FORMER MEMBER: University of Chicago (1906-46).

NCAA TOURNAMENT RECORD: 213-127 (.626).

NCAA TITLES (9) : Indiana (1940-53-76-81-87), Michigan (1989), Michigan State (1979), Ohio State (1960), Wisconsin (1941).

NIT TITLES (5) : Indiana (1979), Michigan (1984), Minnesota (1993), Ohio State (1986), Purdue (1974).

ALL-TIME SCORING LEADER: Calbert Cheaney, Indiana (2,613 points from 1990-93).

SINGLE-SEASON SCORING LEADER: Rick Mount, Purdue (35.4 points per game in 1969-70).

REGULAR-SEASON CHAMPIONS: Chicago (3 outright-3 ties), Illinois (6-6), Indiana (11-8), Iowa (4-4), Michigan (7-5), Michigan State (3-3), Minnesota (4-4), Northwestern (1-1), Ohio State (10-5), Purdue (12-9), Wisconsin (7-7).

YEAR-BY-YEAR CHAMPIONS (incl. conference records): 1906—Minnesota (6-1); 1907—Chicago (6-2), Minnesota (6-2), Wisconsin (6-2); 1908—Chicago (7-1), Wisconsin (7-1) 1909—Chicago (12-0); 1910—Chicago (9-3); 1911—Minnesota (8-4), Purdue (8-4); 1912—Wisconsin (12-0); 1913—Wisconsin (11-1); 1914—Wisconsin (12-0); 1915—Illinois (12-0); 1916—Wisconsin (11-1); 1917—Illinois (10-2), Minnesota (10-2); 1918—Wisconsin (9-3); 1919—Minnesota (10-0); 1920—Chicago (10-2); 1921—Michigan (8-4), Purdue (8-4), Wisconsin (8-4); 1922—Purdue (8-1); 1923—Iowa (11-1), Wisconsin (11-1); 1924—Chicago (8-4), Illinois (8-4), Wisconsin (8-4); 1925—Ohio State (11-1); 1926—Indiana (8-4), Iowa (8-4), Michigan (8-4), Purdue (8-4); 1927—Michigan (10-2); 1928—Indiana (10-2), Purdue (10-2); 1929—Michigan (10-2), Wisconsin (10-2); 1930—Purdue (10-0); 1931—Northwestern (11-1); 1932—Purdue (11-1); 1933—Northwestern (10-2), Ohio State (10-2); 1934—Purdue (10-2); 1935—Illinois (9-3), Purdue (9-3), Wisconsin (9-3); 1936—Indiana (11-1), Purdue (11-1); 1937—Illinois (10-2), Minnesota (10-2); 1938—Purdue (10-2); 1939—Ohio State (10-2); 1940—Purdue (10-2); 1941—Wisconsin (11-1); 1942—Illinois (13-2); 1943—Illinois (12-0); 1944—Ohio State (10-2); 1945—Iowa (11-1); 1946—Ohio State (10-2); 1947—Wisconsin (9-3); 1948—Michigan (10-2); 1949—Illinois (10-2); 1950—Ohio State (11-1); 1951—Illinois (13-1); 1952—Illinois (12-2); 1953—Indiana (17-1); 1954—Indiana (12-2); 1955—Iowa (11-3); 1956—Iowa (13-1); 1957—Indiana (10-4), Michigan State (10-4); 1958—Indiana (10-4); 1959—Michigan State (12-2); 1960—Ohio State (13-1); 1961—Ohio State (14-0); 1962—Ohio State (13-1); 1963—Illinois (11-3), Ohio State (11-3); 1964—Michigan (11-3), Ohio State (11-3); 1965—Michigan (13-1); 1966—Michigan (11-3); 1967—Indiana (10-4), Michigan State (10-4); 1968—Iowa (10-4), Ohio State (10-4); 1969—Purdue (13-1); 1970—Iowa (14-0); 1971—Ohio State (13-1); 1972—Minnesota (11-3); 1973—Indiana (11-3); 1974—Indiana (12-2), Michigan (12-2); 1975—Indiana (18-0); 1976—Indiana (18-0); 1977—Michigan (16-2); 1978—Michigan State (15-3); 1979—Iowa (13-5), Michigan State (13-5), Purdue (13-5); 1980—Indiana (13-5); 1981—Indiana (14-4); 1982—Minnesota (14-4); 1983—Indiana (13-5); 1984—Illinois (15-3), Purdue (15-3); 1985—Michigan (16-2); 1986—Michigan (14-4); 1987—Indiana (15-3), Purdue (15-3); 1988—Purdue (16-2); 1989—Indiana (15-3); 1990—Michigan State (15-3); 1991—Indiana (15-3), Ohio State (15-3); 1992—Ohio State (15-3); 1993—Indiana (17-1); 1994—Purdue (14-4); 1995—Purdue (15-3); 1996—Purdue (15-3).

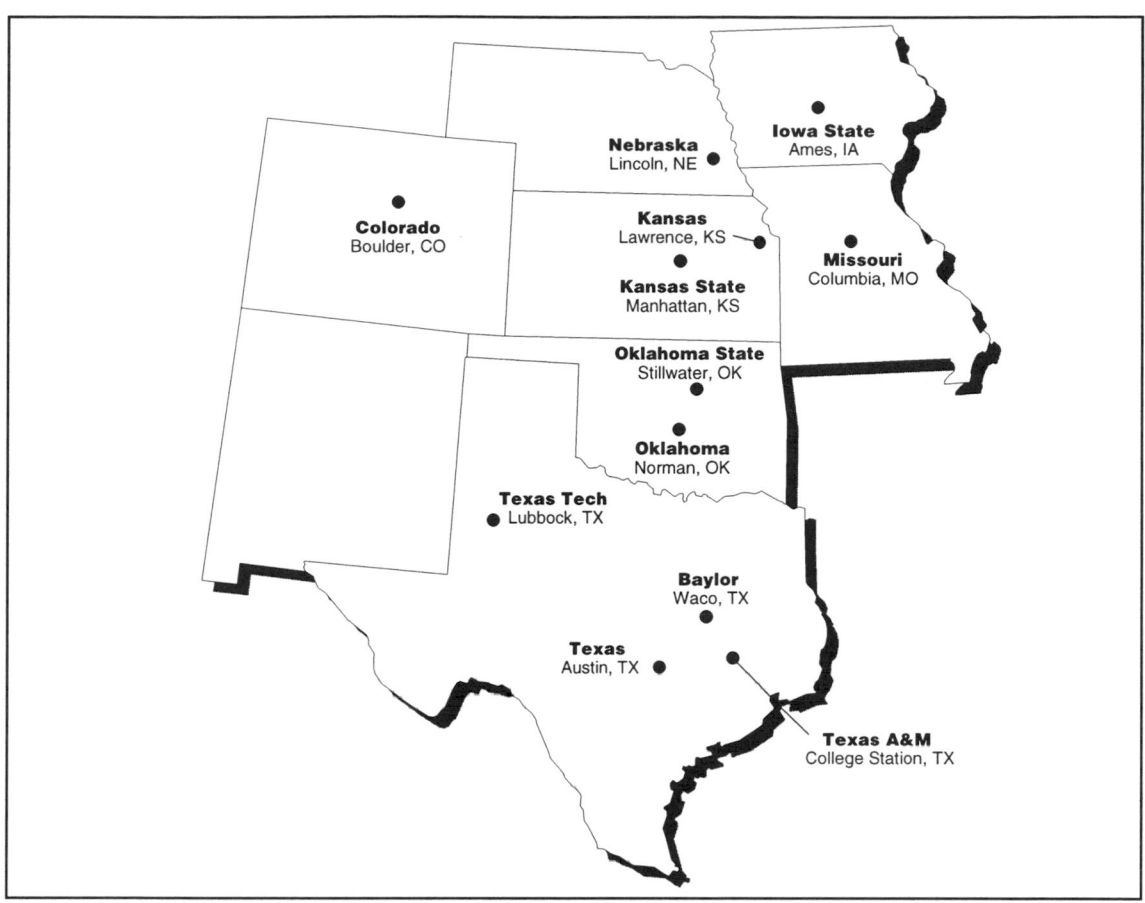

BIG TWELVE

TEMPORARY ADDRESS: 2201 Stemmons Freeway, 28th Fl., Dallas, TX 75207.

TELEPHONE/FAX: (312) 742-1212/2046

MEMBERS Baylor (1997-), Colorado (1997-), Iowa State (1997-), Kansas (1997-), Kansas State (1997-), Missouri (1997-), Nebraska (1997-), Oklahoma (1997-), Oklahoma State (1997-), Texas (1997-), Texas A&M (1997-), Texas Tech (1997-).

NCAA TITLES (2): Kansas (1952 and 1988) won championships as a member of the Big Eight before the Big Twelve was formed.

NIT TITLES (2): Texas (1978) and Nebraska (1996) won championships while members of the SWC and Big Eight, respectively, before the Big Twelve was formed.

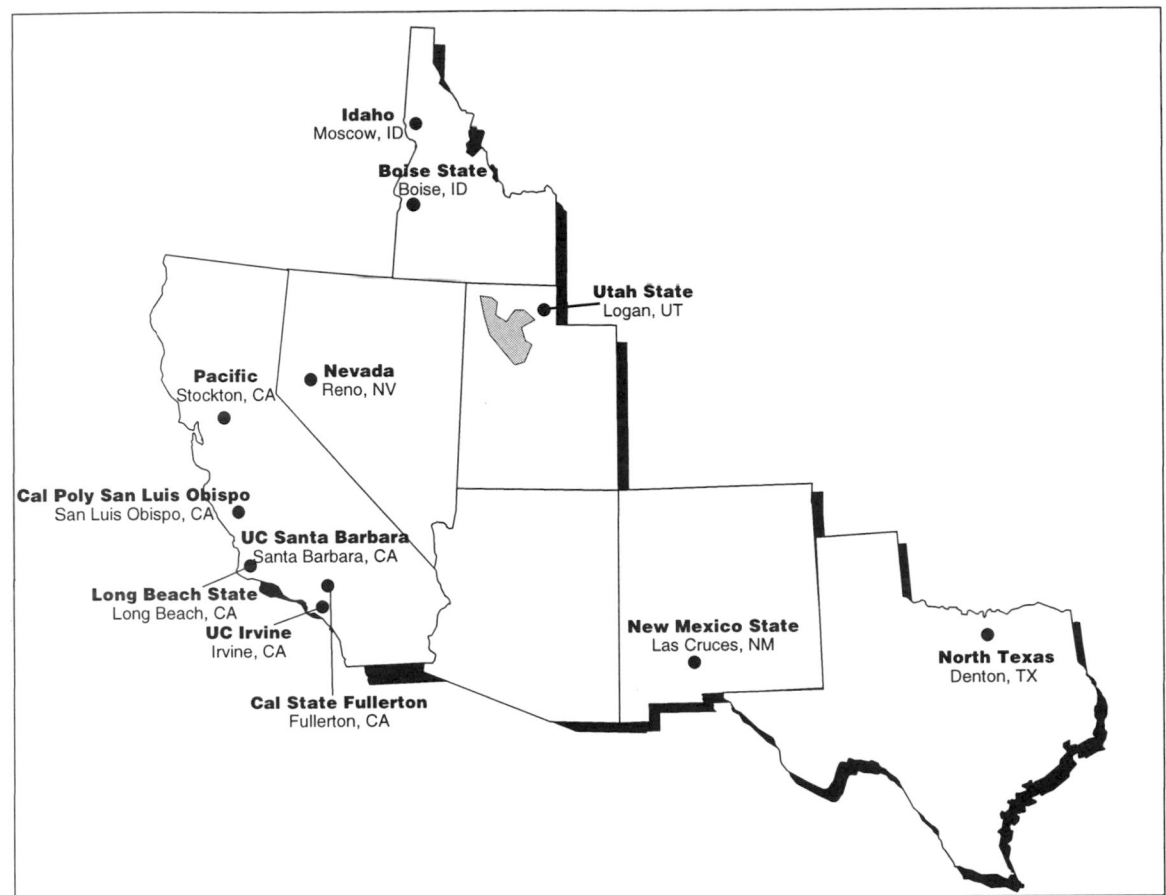

BIG WEST

ADDRESS: 2 Corporate Park, Suite 206, Irvine, CA 92714.

PHONE/FAX: (714) 261-2525/2528.

PREVIOUS NAME:: Pacific Coast Athletic Association (1970-88).

CURRENT MEMBERS: Boise State (1997-), UC Irvine (1978-97), Cal Poly San Luis Obispo (1997-), UC Santa Barbara (1970-74 and 1977-97), Cal State Fullerton (1975-97), Idaho (1997-), Long Beach State (1970-97), Nevada (1993-97), New Mexico State (1984-97), North Texas (1997-), Pacific (1972-97), Utah State (1979-97).

FORMER MEMBERS: Cal State Los Angeles (1970-74), Fresno State (1970-92), San Diego State (1970-78), San Jose State (1970-96), UNLV (1983-96).

NCAA TOURNAMENT RECORD: 37-37 (.500).

NCAA TITLES (1) : UNLV (1990).

ALL-TIME SCORING LEADER: Lucious Harris, Long Beach State (2,312 points from 1990-93).

SINGLE SEASON SCORING LEADERS: Armon Gilliam, UNLV (903 points in 1986-87) and Raymond Lewis, Cal State Los Angeles (32.9 points per game in 1972-73).

REGULAR-SEASON CHAMPIONS: Cal State Fullerton (0 outright-1 tie), Fresno State (2-1), Long Beach State (7-2), New Mexico State (2-1), Pacific (1-0), San Diego State (0-2), UNLV (9-1), Utah State (2-0).

BIG WEST TOURNAMENT TITLES: UNLV (7; 1983-85-86-87-89-90-91), Fresno State (3; 1981-82-84), Long Beach State (3; 1977, 1993 and 1995), New Mexico State (2; 1992 and 1994), San Jose State (2; 1980 and 1996), Cal State Fullerton (1; 1978), Pacific (1; 1979), San Diego State (1; 1976), Utah State (1; 1988).

YEAR-BY-YEAR CHAMPIONS (incl. conference records): 1970—Long Beach State (10-0); **1971**—Long Beach State (10-0); **1972**—Long Beach State (10-2); **1973**—Long Beach State (10-2); **1974**—Long Beach State (12-0); **1975**—Long Beach State (8-2); **1976**—Cal State Fullerton (6-4), Long Beach State (6-4); **1977**—Long Beach State (9-3), San Diego State (9-3); **1978**—Fresno State (11-3), San Diego State (11-3); **1979**—Pacific (11-3); **1980**—Utah State (11-2); **1981**—Fresno State (12-2); **1982**—Fresno State (13-1); **1983**—UNLV (15-1); **1984**—UNLV (16-2); **1985**—UNLV (17-1); **1986**—UNLV (16-2); **1987**—UNLV (18-0); **1988**—UNLV (15-3); **1989**—UNLV (16-2); **1990**—New Mexico State (16-2), UNLV (16-2); **1991**—UNLV (18-0); **1992**—UNLV (18-0); **1993**—New Mexico State (15-3); **1994**—New Mexico State (12-6); **1995**—Utah State (14-4); **1996**—Long Beach State (12-6).

Note: League split into two divisions (Eastern and Western) for the 1996-97 season.

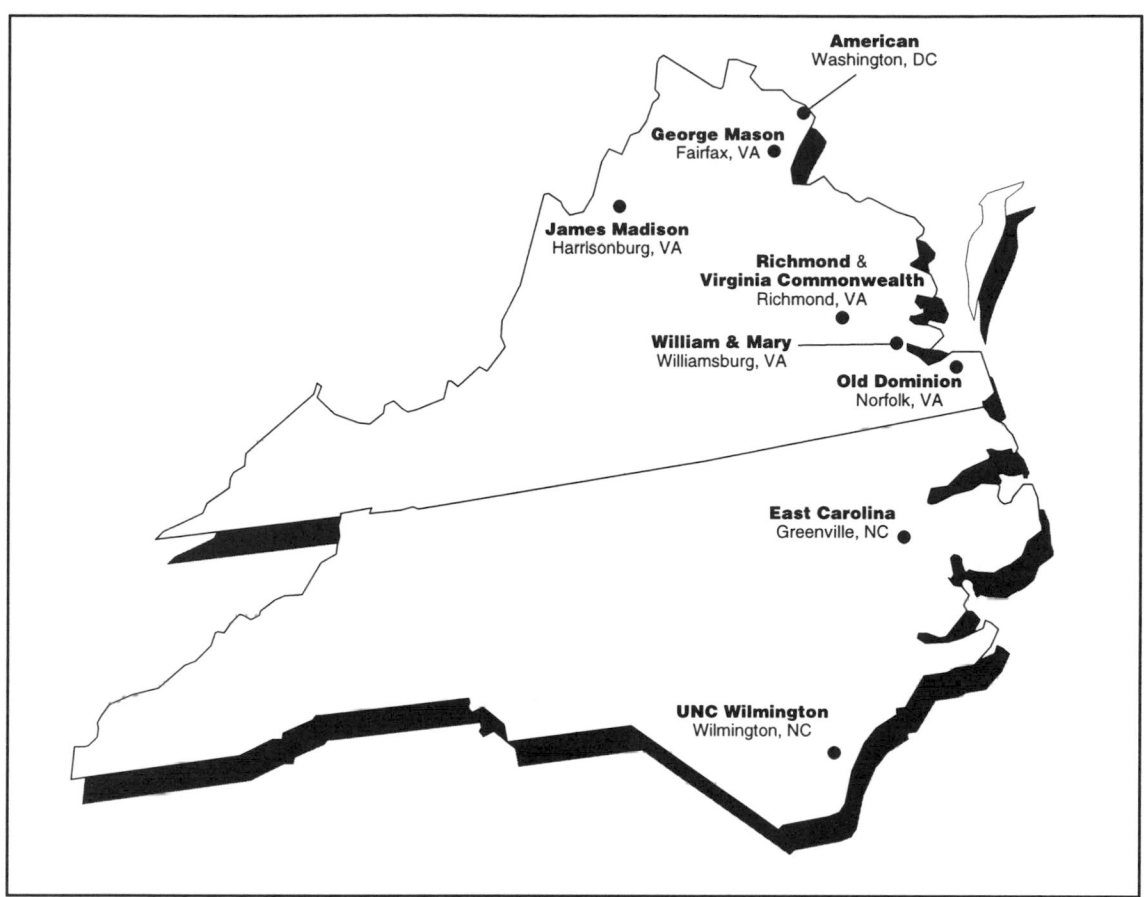

Map showing member locations:
- **American** — Washington, DC
- **George Mason** — Fairfax, VA
- **James Madison** — Harrisonburg, VA
- **Richmond & Virginia Commonwealth** — Richmond, VA
- **William & Mary** — Williamsburg, VA
- **Old Dominion** — Norfolk, VA
- **East Carolina** — Greenville, NC
- **UNC Wilmington** — Wilmington, NC

COLONIAL ATHLETIC ASSOCIATION

ADDRESS: 8625 Patterson Avenue, Richmond, VA 23229-6349.

PHONE/FAX: (804) 754-1616/1830.

PREVIOUS NAME: ECAC South (1983-86).

CURRENT MEMBERS: American (1985-97), East Carolina (1983-97), George Mason (1983-97), James Madison (1983-97), UNC Wilmington (1985-97), Old Dominion (1992-97), Richmond (1983-97), Virginia Commonwealth (1996 and 1997), William & Mary (1983-97).

FORMER MEMBER: Navy (1983-91).

NCAA TOURNAMENT RECORD: 11-15 (.423).

ALL-TIME SCORING LEADER: David Robinson, Navy (2,669 points from 1984-87).

REGULAR-SEASON CHAMPIONS: James Madison (2 outright-3 ties), Navy (2-1), Old Dominion (1-2), Richmond (3-2), Virginia Commonwealth (1-0), William & Mary (1-0).

CAA TOURNAMENT TITLES: Richmond (4; 1984-88-90-91), Navy (3; 1985-86-87), James Madison (2; 1983 and 1994), Old Dominion (2; 1992 and 1995), East Carolina (1; 1993), George Mason (1; 1989), Virginia Commonwealth (1; 1996).

YEAR-BY-YEAR CHAMPIONS (incl. conference records): 1983—William & Mary (9-0); **1984**—Richmond (7-3); **1985**—Navy (11-3), Richmond (11-3); **1986**—Navy (13-1); **1987**—Navy (13-1); **1988**—Richmond (11-3); **1989**—Richmond (13-1); **1990**—James Madison (11-3); **1991**—James Madison (12-2); **1992**—James Madison (12-2), Richmond (12-2); **1993**—James Madison (11-3), Old Dominion (11-3); **1994**—James Madison (10-4), Old Dominion (10-4); **1995**—Old Dominion (12-2); **1996**—Virginia Commonwealth (14-2).

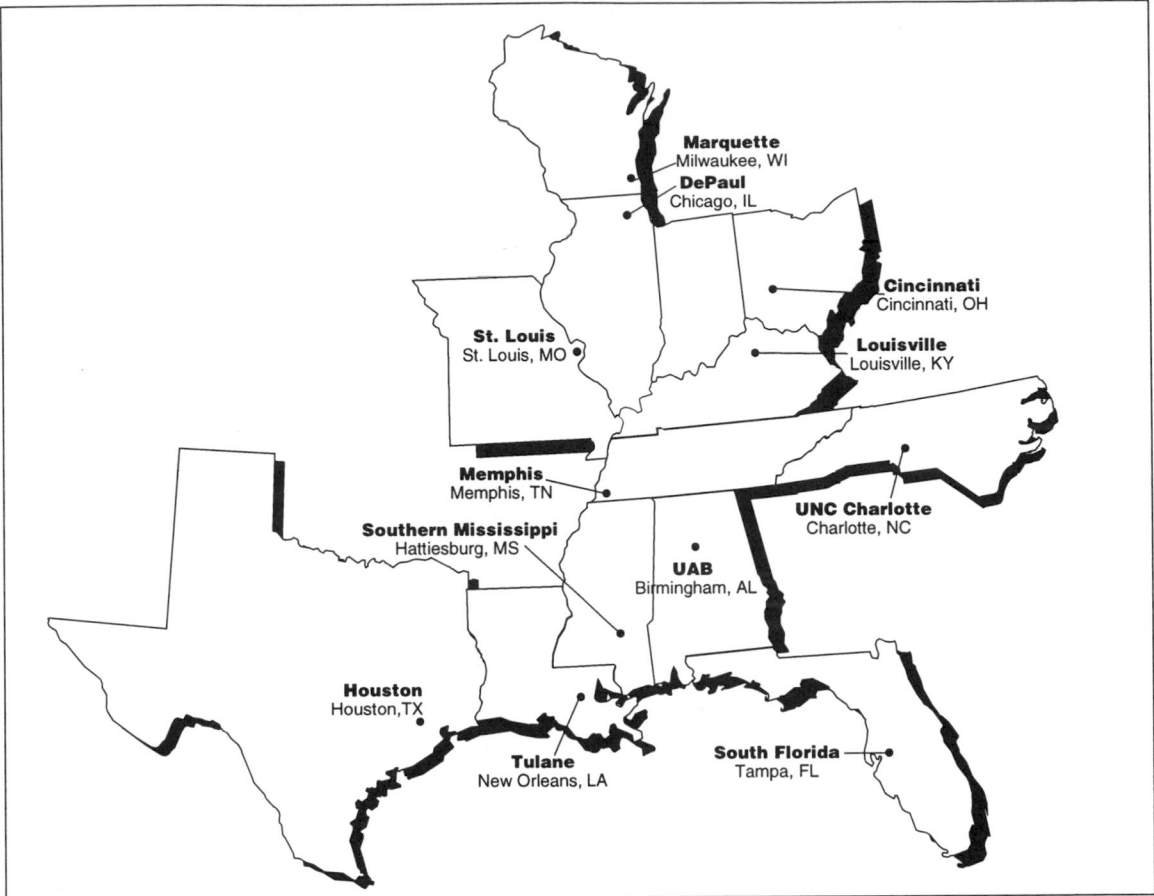

CONFERENCE USA

ADDRESS: 35 East Wacker Drive, Suite 650, Chicago, IL 60601.

PHONE/FAX: (312) 553-0483/0495.

CURRENT MEMBERS: UAB (1996-), Cincinnati (1996-), DePaul (1996-), Houston (1997-), Louisville (1996-), Marquette (1996-), Memphis (1996-), UNC Charlotte (1996-), Saint Louis (1996-), South Florida (1996-), Southern Mississippi (1996-), Tulane (1996-).

NCAA TOURNAMENT RECORD: 6-4 (.600).

NCAA Titles (5): Cincinatti (1961 and 1962), Louisville (1980 and 1986) and Marquette (1977) won championships before the C-USA was formed.

NIT Titles (5): DePaul (1945), Louisville (1956), Marquette (1970), Saint Louis (1948) and Southern Mississippi (1987) won championships before the C-USA was formed.

REGULAR-SEASON CHAMPIONS: Cincinnati (0 outright-1 tie), Memphis (0-1).

C-USA TOURNAMENT TITLES: Cincinnati (1; 1996).

YEAR-BY-YEAR CHAMPIONS (incl. conference records): 1996—Cincinnati (11-3/Blue), Memphis (11-3/White).

Note: League started with three divisions—Red, White, and Blue. Team with the best overall league record is considered its regular-season champion.

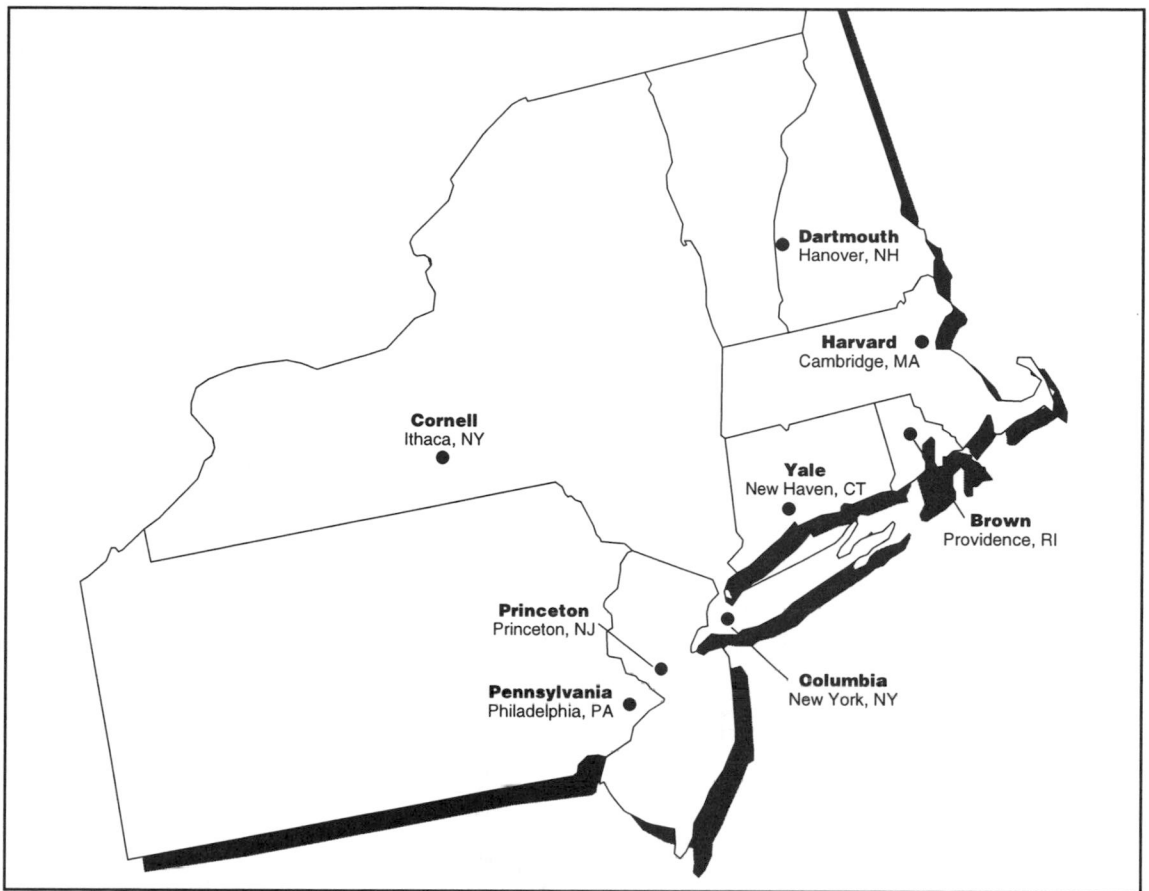

IVY LEAGUE

ADDRESS: 120 Alexander Street, Princeton, NJ 08544.

PHONE/FAX: (609) 258-6426/1690.

PREVIOUS NAME: Eastern Intercollegiate Basketball League (1902-54).

CURRENT MEMBERS: Brown (1954-97), Columbia (1902-97), Cornell (1902-97), Dartmouth (1912-97), Harvard (1902-09 and 1934-97), Pennsylvania (1904-97), Princeton (1902-97), Yale (1902-97).

NCAA TOURNAMENT RECORD: 37-60 (.381).

NIT TITLES (1) : Princeton (1975).

ALL-TIME SCORING LEADER: Bill Bradley, Princeton (2,503 points from 1963-65).

SINGLE-SEASON SCORING LEADER: Bill Bradley, Princeton (32.3 points per game in 1963-64).

REGULAR-SEASON CHAMPIONS: Brown (1 outright-0 ties), Columbia (12-5), Cornell (3-2), Dartmouth (9-3), Penn (25-7), Princeton (18-13), Yale (9-1).

YEAR-BY-YEAR CHAMPIONS (incl. conference records): 1902—Yale (6-2); **1903**—Yale (7-1); **1904**—Columbia (10-0); **1905**—Columbia (8-0); **1906**—Pennsylvania (9-1); **1907**—Yale (9-1); **1908**—Pennsylvania (8-0); **1909**—Columbia (7-1)*; **1910**—Columbia (6-0)*; **1911**—Columbia (7-1); **1912**—Columbia (8-2); **1913**—Cornell (7-1); **1914**—Columbia (8-2), Cornell (8-2); **1915**—Yale (8-2); **1916**—Pennsylvania (8-2), Princeton (8-2); **1917**—Yale (9-1); **1918**—Pennsylvania (9-1); **1919**—Pennsylvania (7-1); **1920**—Pennsylvania (10-0); **1921**—Pennsylvania (9-1); **1922**—Princeton (9-2); **1923**—Yale (7-3); **1924**—Cornell (8-2); **1925**—Princeton (9-1); **1926**—Columbia (9-1); **1927**—Dartmouth (7-3), Princeton (7-3); **1928**—Pennsylvania (7-3), Princeton (7-3); **1929**—Pennsylvania (8-2); **1930**—Columbia (9-1); **1931**—Columbia (10-0); **1932**—Columbia (8-2), Princeton (8-2); **1933**—Yale (8-2); **1934**—Pennsylvania (10-2); **1935**—Columbia (10-2), Pennsylvania (10-2); **1936**—Columbia (12-0); **1937**—Pennsylvania (12-0); **1938**—Dartmouth (8-4); **1939**—Dartmouth (10-2); **1940**—Dartmouth (11-1); **1941**—Dartmouth (10-2); **1942**—Dartmouth (10-2), Princeton (10-2); **1943**—Dartmouth (11-1); **1944**—Dartmouth (8-0); **1945**—Pennsylvania (5-1); **1946**—Dartmouth (7-1); **1947**—Columbia (11-1); **1948**—Columbia (11-1); **1949**—Yale (9-3); **1950**—Princeton (11-1); **1951**—Columbia (12-0); **1952**—Princeton (10-2); **1953**—Pennsylvania (10-2); **1954**—Cornell (12-3); **1955**—Princeton (11-4); **1956**—Dartmouth (10-4); **1957**—Yale (12-2); **1958**—Dartmouth (11-3); **1959**—Dartmouth (14-1); **1960**—Princeton (11-3); **1961**—Princeton (11-3); **1962**—Yale (13-1); **1963**—Princeton (12-3); **1964**—Princeton (12-2); **1965**—Princeton (13-1); **1966**—Pennsylvania (12-2); **1967**—Princeton (13-1); **1968**—Columbia (13-2); **1969**—Princeton (14-0); **1970**—Pennsylvania (14-0); **1971**—Pennsylvania (14-0); **1972**—Pennsylvania (13-1); **1973**—Pennsylvania (12-2); **1974**—Pennsylvania (13-1); **1975**—Pennsylvania (13-1); **1976**—Princeton (14-0); **1977**—Princeton (13-1); **1978**—Pennsylvania (12-2); **1979**—Pennsylvania (13-1); **1980**—Pennsylvania (11-3), Princeton (11-3); **1981**—Pennsylvania (13-1), Princeton (13-1); **1982**—Pennsylvania (12-2); **1983**—Princeton (12-2); **1984**—Princeton (10-4); **1985**—Pennsylvania (10-4); **1986**—Brown (10-4); **1987**—Pennsylvania (10-4); **1988**—Cornell (11-3); **1989**—Princeton (11-3); **1990**—Princeton (11-3); **1991**—Princeton (14-0); **1992**—Princeton (12-2); **1993**—Pennsylvania (14-0); **1994**—Pennsylvania (14-0); **1995**—Pennsylvania (14-0); **1996**—Pennsylvania (12-2), Princeton* (12-2).

*Won playoff.

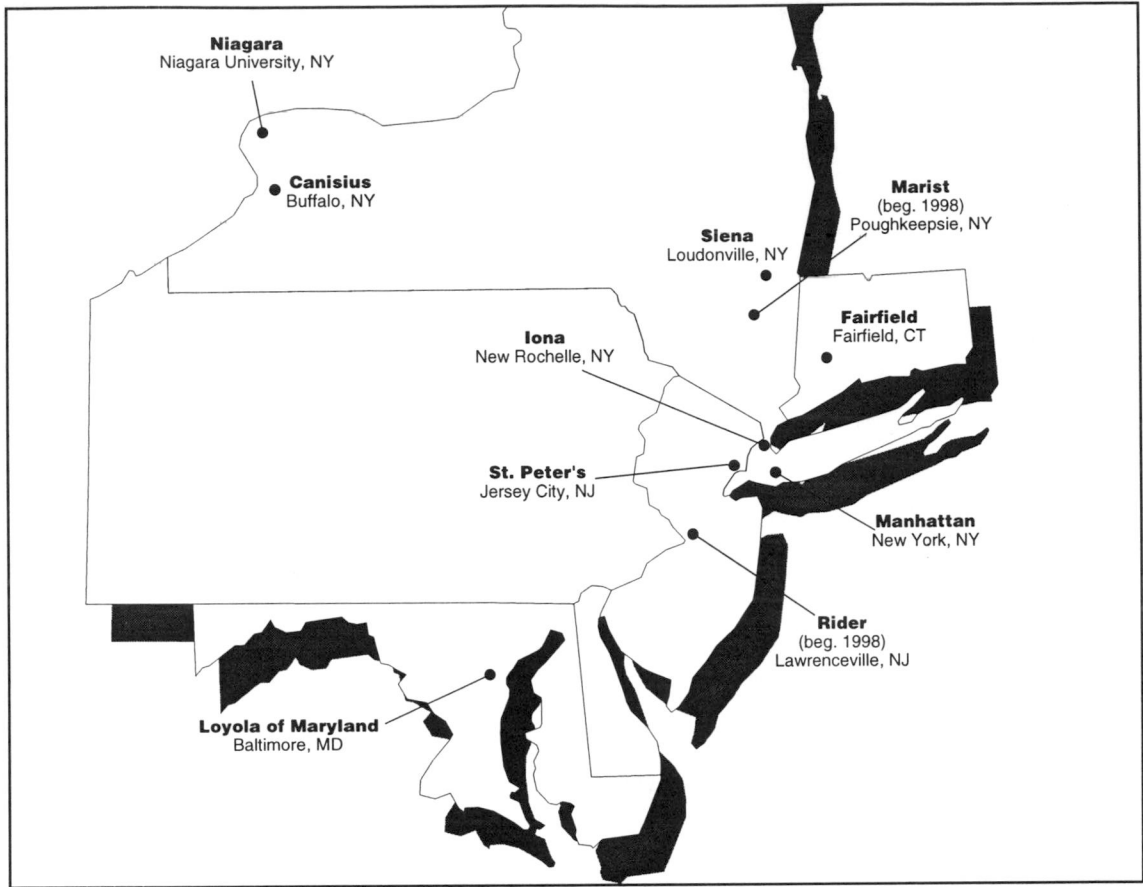

METRO ATLANTIC ATHLETIC

ADDRESS: 1090 Amboy Avenue, Edison, NJ 08837-2847.

PHONE/FAX: (908) 225-0202/5440.

CURRENT MEMBERS: Canisius (1990-97), Fairfield (1982-97), Iona (1982-97), Loyola, Md. (1990-97), Manhattan (1982-97), Niagara (1990-97), St. Peter's (1982-97), Siena (1990-97). Marist and Rider are slated to join the MAAC in 1998.

FORMER MEMBERS: Army (1982-90), Fordham (1982-90), Holy Cross (1984-90), La Salle (1984-92).

NCAA TOURNAMENT RECORD: 2-14 (.125).

ALL-TIME SCORING LEADER: Lionel Simmons, La Salle (3,217 points from 1987-90).

REGULAR-SEASON CHAMPIONS: Canisius (1 outright-0 ties), Fairfield (1-1), Holy Cross (1-0), Iona (2-2), La Salle (3-1), Manhattan (3-0), St. Peter's (2-1), Siena (1-0).

MAAC TOURNAMENT TITLES: La Salle (4), Iona (3), Fairfield (2), Fordham (1), Loyola, Md. (1), Manhattan (1), St. Peter's (1).

YEAR-BY-YEAR CHAMPIONS (incl. conference records): 1982—St. Peter's (9-1); **1983**—Iona (8-2); **1984**—Iona (11-3), La Salle (11-3), St. Peter's (11-3); **1985**—Iona (11-3); **1986**—Fairfield (13-1); **1987**—St. Peter's (11-3); **1988**—La Salle (14-0); **1989**—La Salle (13-1); **1990**—Holy Cross (14-2/N), La Salle (16-0/S); **1991**—Siena (12-4); **1992**—Manhattan (13-3); **1993**—Manhattan (12-2); **1994**—Canisius (12-2); **1995**—Manhattan (12-2); **1996**—Fairfield (10-4), Iona (10-4).

Note: The MAAC had North and South Divisions for one season in 1989–90.

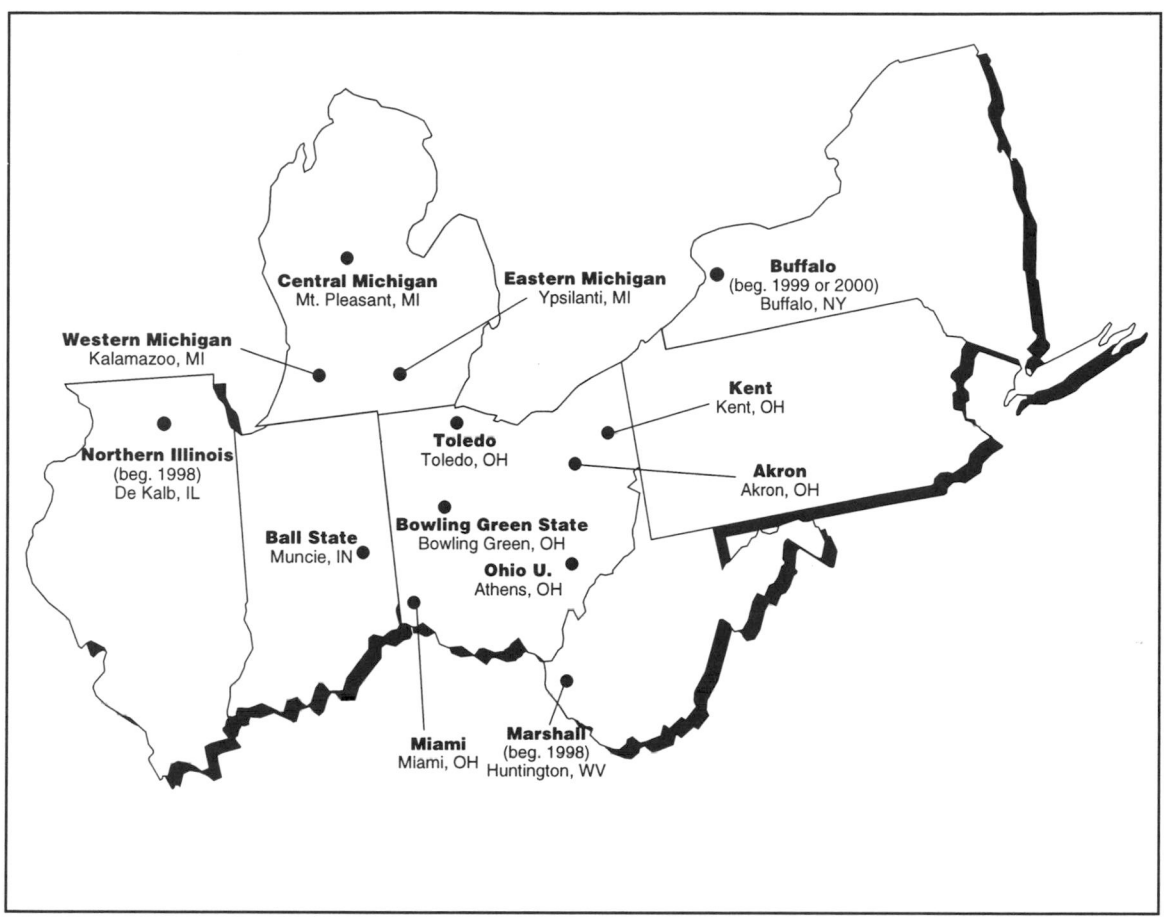

MID-AMERICAN

ADDRESS: Four SeaGate, Suite 102, Toledo, OH 43604.

PHONE/FAX: (419) 249-7177/7199.

CURRENT MEMBERS: Akron (1993-97), Ball State (1976-97), Bowling Green State (1954-97), Central Michigan (1973-97), Eastern Michigan (1975-97), Kent (1952-97), Miami of Ohio (1948-97), Ohio (1947-97), Toledo (1952-97), Western Michigan (1948-97). Marshall and Northern Illinois are slated to join the league in 1998 and Buffalo a year or two later.

FORMER MEMBERS: Butler (1947-50), Cincinnati (1947-53), Marshall (1954-69), Northern Illinois (1976-86), Wayne State (1947), Western Reserve (1947-55).

NCAA TOURNAMENT RECORD: 19-51 (.271).

ALL-TIME SCORING LEADER: Ron Harper, Miami of Ohio (2,377 points from 1983-86).

SINGLE-SEASON SCORING LEADERS: Dave Jamerson, Ohio (874 points in 1989-90) and Howard Komives, Bowling Green State (36.7 points per game in 1963-64).

REGULAR-SEASON CHAMPIONS: Ball State (3 outright-2 ties), Bowling Green State (4-2), Butler (0-1), Central Michigan (2-2), Cincinnati (4-1), Eastern Michigan (3-0), Marshall (1-0), Miami of Ohio (13-5), Northern Illinois (0-1), Ohio (7-2), Toledo (3-3), Western Michigan (1-2).

MAC TOURNAMENT TITLES: Ball State (6; 1981-86-89-90-93-95), Eastern Michigan (3; 1988-91-96), Ohio (3; 1983-85-94), Miami of Ohio (2; 1984 and 1992), Central Michigan (1; 1987), Northern Illinois (1; 1982), Toledo (1; 1980).

YEAR-BY-YEAR CHAMPIONS (incl. conference records): **1947**—Butler (6-2), Cincinnati (6-2); **1948**—Cincinnati (7-2); **1949**—Cincinnati (9-1); **1950**—Cincinnati (10-0); **1951**—Cincinnati (7-1); **1952**—Miami of Ohio (9-3), Western Michigan (9-3); **1953**—Miami of Ohio (10-2); **1954**—Toledo (10-2); **1955**—Miami of Ohio (11-3); **1956**—Marshall (10-2); **1957**—Miami of Ohio (11-1); **1958**—Miami of Ohio (12-0); **1959**—Bowling Green (9-3), Miami of Ohio (9-3); **1960**—Ohio U. (10-2); **1961**—Ohio U. (10-2); **1962**—Bowling Green (11-1); **1963**—Bowling Green (9-3); **1964**—Ohio U. (10-2); **1965**—Miami of Ohio (11-1), Ohio U. (11-1); **1966**—Miami of Ohio (11-1); **1967**—Toledo (11-1); **1968**—Bowling Green (10-2); **1969**—Miami of Ohio (10-2); **1970**—Ohio U. (9-1); **1971**—Miami of Ohio (9-1); **1972**—Ohio U. (7-3), Toledo (7-3); **1973**—Miami of Ohio (9-2); **1974**—Ohio U. (9-3); **1975**—Central Michigan (10-4); **1976**—Western Michigan (15-1); **1977**—Central Michigan (13-3), Miami of Ohio (13-3); **1978**—Miami of Ohio (12-4); **1979**—Central Michigan (13-3), Toledo (13-3)*; **1980**—Toledo (14-2); **1981**—Ball State (10-6), Bowling Green (10-6), Northern Illinois (10-6), Toledo (10-6), Western Michigan (10-6); **1982**—Ball State (12-4); **1983**—Bowling Green (15-3); **1984**—Miami of Ohio (16-2); **1985**—Ohio U. (14-4); **1986**—Miami of Ohio (16-2); **1987**—Central Michigan (14-2); **1988**—Eastern Michigan (14-2); **1989**—Ball State (14-2); **1990**—Ball State (13-3); **1991**—Eastern Michigan (13-3); **1992**—Miami of Ohio (13-3); **1993**—Ball State (14-4), Miami of Ohio (14-4); **1994**—Ohio U. (14-4); **1995**—Miami of Ohio (16-2); **1996**—Eastern Michigan (14-4)

*Won playoff.

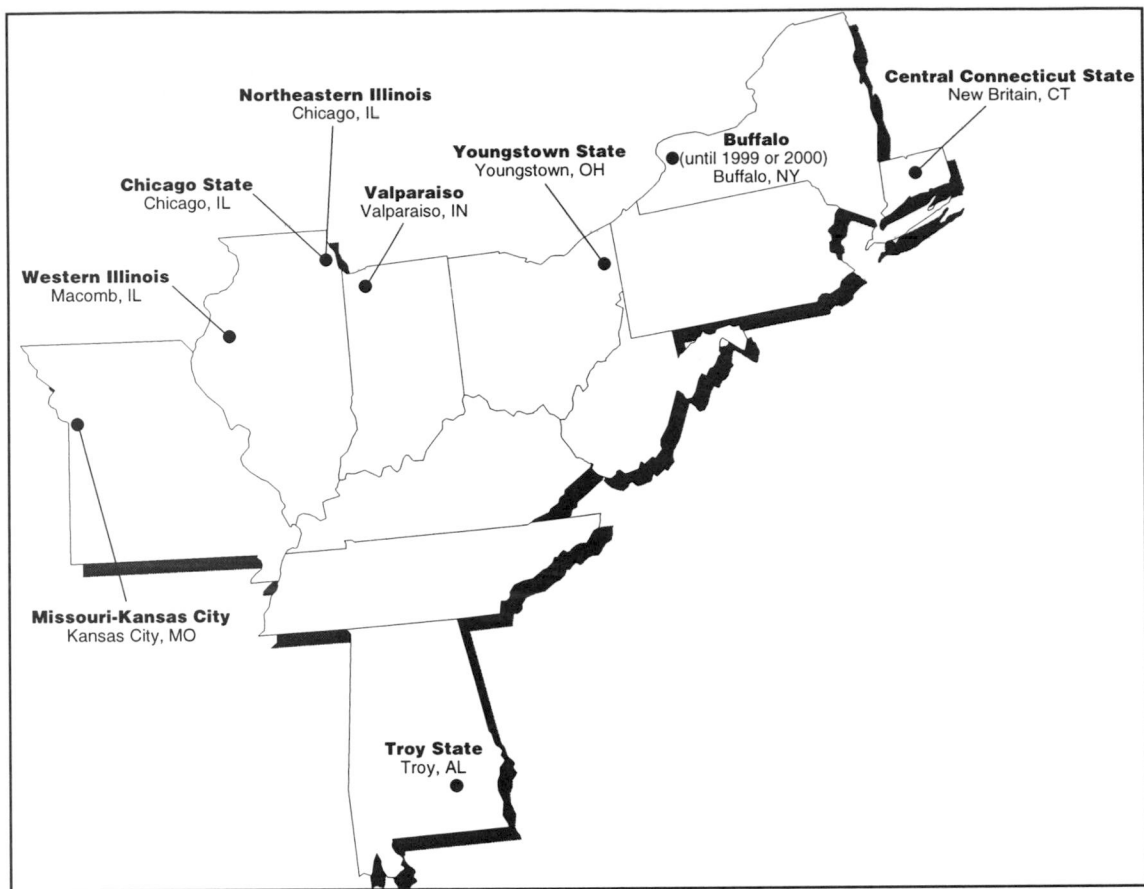

MID-CONTINENT

ADDRESS: 40 Shuman Boulevard, Suite 118, Naperville, IL 60563.

PHONE/FAX: (708) 416-7560/7564.

PREVIOUS NAME: Association of Mid-Continent Universities (1983-89).

CURRENT MEMBERS: Buffalo(1995-97; plans to join Mid-American in 1999 or 2000), Central Connecticut State (1995-97), Chicago State (1995-97), Missouri-Kansas City (1995-97), Northeastern Illinois (1995-97), Troy State (1995-97), Valparaiso (1983-97), Western Illinois (1983-97), Youngstown State (1992-97).

FORMER MEMBERS: Akron (1991 and 1992), Cleveland State (1983-94), Eastern Illinois (1983-96), Illinois-Chicago (1983-94), Northern Illinois (1991-94), Northern Iowa (1983-91), Southwest Missouri State (1983-90), Wisconsin-Green Bay (1983-94), Wisconsin-Milwaukee (1993 and 1994), Wright State (1992-94).

NCAA TOURNAMENT RECORD: 5-12 (.294).

ALL-TIME SCORING LEADER: Tony Bennett, Wisconsin-Green Bay (2,285 points from 1989-92).

REGULAR-SEASON CHAMPIONS: Cleveland State (3 outright-0 ties), Illinois-Chicago (1-0), Northern Illinois (1-0), Southwest Missouri State (4-0), Valparaiso (2-0), Western Illinois (1-0), Wisconsin-Green Bay (2-0).

MID-CONTINENT TOURNAMENT TITLES: Eastern Illinois (2; 1985 and 1992), Southwest Missouri State (2; 1987 and 1991), Valparaiso (2; 1995 and 1996), Wisconsin-Green Bay (2; 1990 and 1994), Cleveland State (1; 1986), Northern Iowa (1; 1989), Western Illinois (1; 1984), Wright State (1; 1993).

YEAR-BY-YEAR CHAMPIONS (incl. conference records): 1983—Western Illinois (9-3); **1984**—Illinois-Chicago (12-2); **1985**—Cleveland State (11-3); **1986**—Cleveland State (13-1); **1987**—Southwest Missouri State (13-1); **1988**—Southwest Missouri State (12-2); **1989**—Southwest Missouri State (10-2); **1990**—Southwest Missouri State (11-1); **1991**—Northern Illinois (14-2); **1992**—Wisconsin-Green Bay (14-2); **1993**—Cleveland State (15-1); **1994**—Wisconsin-Green Bay (15-3); **1995**—Valparaiso (14-4); **1996**—Valparaiso (13-5).

Note: Cleveland State would have won the 1989 regular-season championship instead of Southwest Missouri State had the Vikings' league games counted. But Cleveland State was on NCAA probation and was declared ineligible by the league so that the Mid-Continent Conference wouldn't risk losing its automatic bid to the NCAA Tournament.

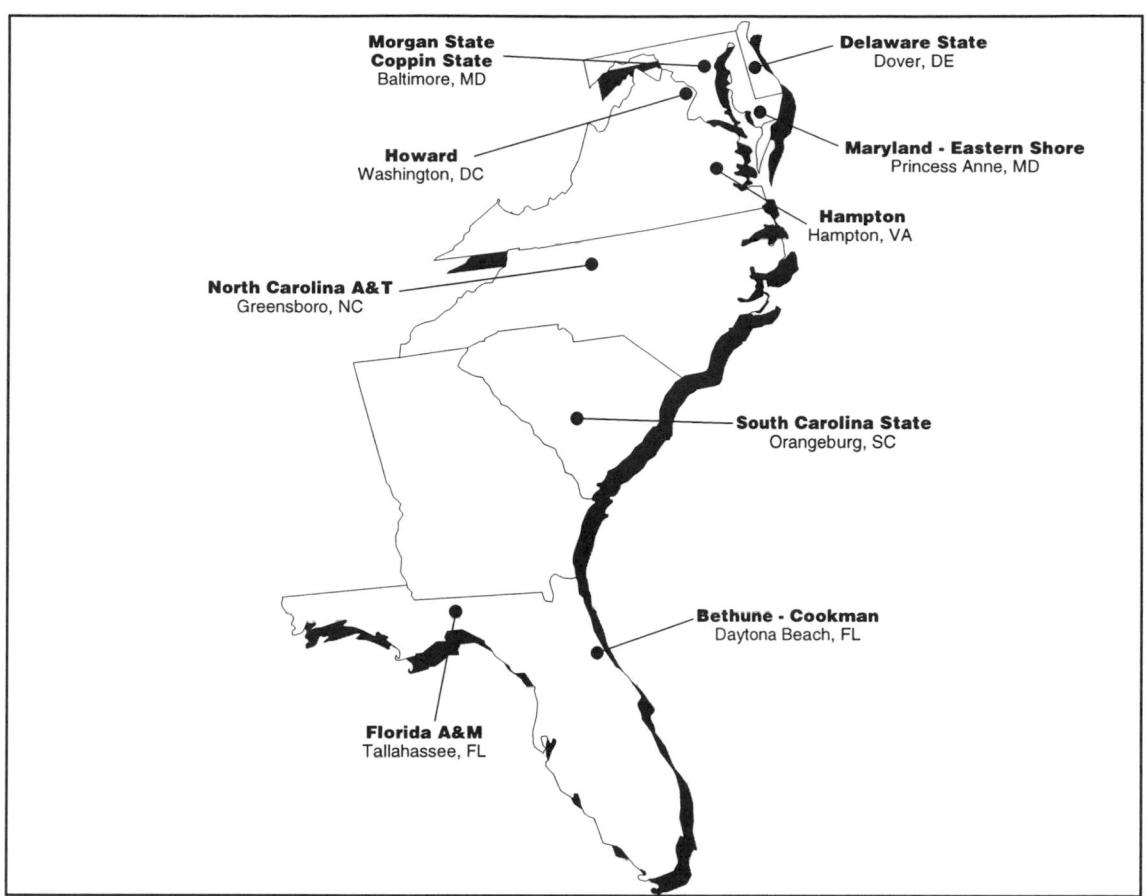

Morgan State
Coppin State
Baltimore, MD

Delaware State
Dover, DE

Howard
Washington, DC

Maryland - Eastern Shore
Princess Anne, MD

Hampton
Hampton, VA

North Carolina A&T
Greensboro, NC

South Carolina State
Orangeburg, SC

Bethune - Cookman
Daytona Beach, FL

Florida A&M
Tallahassee, FL

MID-EASTERN ATHLETIC

ADDRESS: 102 North Elm Street, Suite 401, P.O. Box 21205, Greensboro, NC 27401.

PHONE/FAX: (910) 275-9961/9964.

CURRENT MEMBERS: Bethune-Cookman (1981-97), Coppin State (1986-97), Delaware State (1972-97), Florida A&M (1980-97), Hampton (1996 and 1997), Howard (1972-97), Maryland-Eastern Shore (1972-79 and 1983-97), Morgan State (1972-80 and 1985-97), North Carolina A&T (1972-97), South Carolina State (1972-97).

FORMER MEMBER: North Carolina Central (1972-80).

NCAA TOURNAMENT RECORD: 0-15 (.000).

ALL-TIME SCORING LEADER: Tom Davis, Delaware State (2,274 points from 1988-91).

DIVISION I REGULAR-SEASON CHAMPIONS (SINCE 1972): Coppin State (6 outright-0 ties), Howard (3-1), Maryland-Eastern Shore (1-1), Morgan State (0-2), North Carolina A&T (10-2), South Carolina State (2-0).

MEAC TOURNAMENT TITLES (SINCE 1981): North Carolina A&T (9; 1982-83-84-85-86-87-88-94-95), Coppin State (2; 1990 and 1993), Howard (2; 1981 and 1992), South Carolina State (2; 1989 and 1996), Florida A&M (1; 1991).

YEAR-BY-YEAR CHAMPIONS (incl. conference records): 1972—North Carolina A&T (9-3); **1973**—Maryland-Eastern Shore (10-2); **1974**—Maryland-Eastern Shore (11-1), Morgan State (11-1); **1975**—North Carolina A&T (10-2); **1976**—Morgan State (11-1), North Carolina A&T (11-1); **1977**—South Carolina State (10-2); **1978**—North Carolina A&T (11-1); **1979**—North Carolina A&T (11-1); **1980**—No standings; **1981**—North Carolina A&T (7-3); **1982**—North Carolina A&T (10-2); **1983**—Howard (11-1); **1984**—North Carolina A&T (9-1); **1985**—North Carolina A&T (10-2); **1986**—North Carolina A&T (12-2); **1987**—Howard (13-1); **1988**—North Carolina A&T (16-0); **1989**—South Carolina State (14-2); **1990**—Coppin State (15-1); **1991**—Coppin State (14-2); **1992**—Howard (12-4), North Carolina A&T (12-4); **1993**—Coppin State (16-0); **1994**—Coppin State (16-0); **1995**—Coppin State (15-1); **1996**—Coppin State (14-2).

Note: The MEAC moved up to Division I status in 1981.

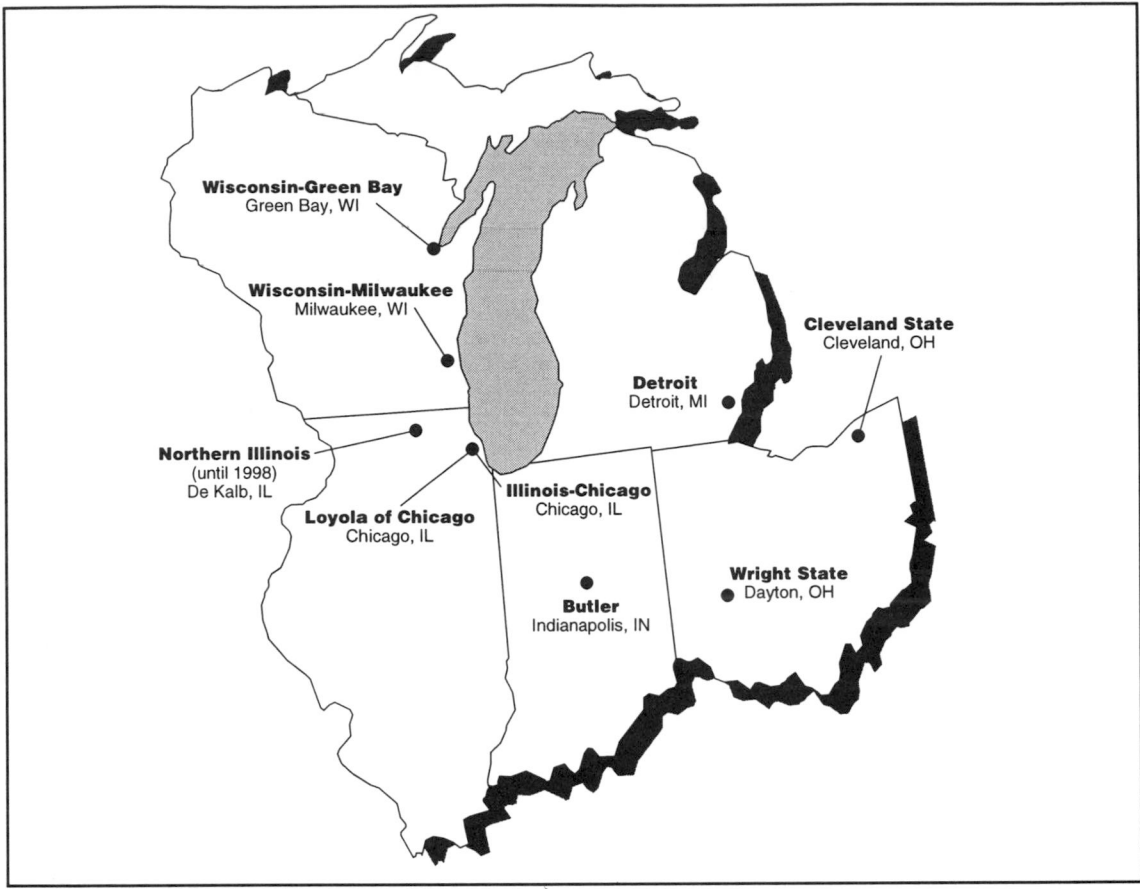

MIDWESTERN COLLEGIATE

ADDRESS: Pan American Plaza, 201 South Capitol Avenue, Suite 500, Indianapolis, IN 46225.

PHONE/FAX: (317) 237-5622/5620.

PREVIOUS NAME: Midwestern City (1980-85).

CURRENT MEMBERS: Butler (1980-97), Cleveland State (1995-97), Detroit (1981-97), Illinois-Chicago (1995-97), Loyola of Chicago (1980-97), Northern Illinois (1995-97; plans to join Mid-American in 1998), Wisconsin-Green Bay (1995-97), Wisconsin-Milwaukee (1995-97), Wright State (1995-97).

FORMER MEMBERS: Dayton (1989-93), Duquesne (1993), Evansville (1980-94), La Salle (1993-95), Marquette (1990 and 1991), Oklahoma City (1980-85), Oral Roberts (1980-87), St. Louis (1983-91), Xavier (1980-95).

NCAA TOURNAMENT RECORD: 9-19 (.321).

NCAA TITLES (1): Loyola of Chicago (1963) won its NCAA title before the conference was formed.

ALL-TIME SCORING LEADER: Alfredrick Hughes, Loyola of Chicago (2,906 points from 1982-85).

SINGLE-SEASON SCORING LEADER: Alfredrick Hughes, Loyola of Chicago (868 points in 1984-85 and 27.6 points per game in 1983-84).

REGULAR-SEASON CHAMPIONS: Evansville (3 outright-2 ties), Loyola of Chicago (3-1), Oral Roberts (1-0), Wisconsin-Green Bay (1-0), Xavier (7-1).

MCC TOURNAMENT TITLES: Xavier (6; 1983-86-87-88-89-91), Evansville (3; 1982-92-93), Oral Roberts (2; 1980 and 1984), Dayton (1; 1990), Detroit Mercy (1; 1994), Loyola of Chicago (1; 1985), Northern Illinois (1; 1996), Oklahoma City (1; 1981), Wisconsin-Green Bay (1; 1995).

YEAR-BY-YEAR CHAMPIONS (incl. conference records): 1980—Loyola of Chicago (5-0); **1981**—Xavier (8-3); **1982**—Evansville (10-2); **1983**—Loyola of Chicago (12-2); **1984**—Oral Roberts (11-3); **1985**—Loyola of Chicago (13-1); **1986**—Xavier (10-2); **1987**—Evansville (8-4), Loyola of Chicago (8-4); **1988**—Xavier (9-1); **1989**—Evansville (10-2); **1990**—Xavier (12-2); **1991**—Xavier (11-3); **1992**—Evansville (8-2); **1993**—Evansville (12-2), Xavier (12-2); **1994**—Xavier (8-2); **1995**—Xavier (14-0); **1996**—Wisconsin-Green Bay (16-0).

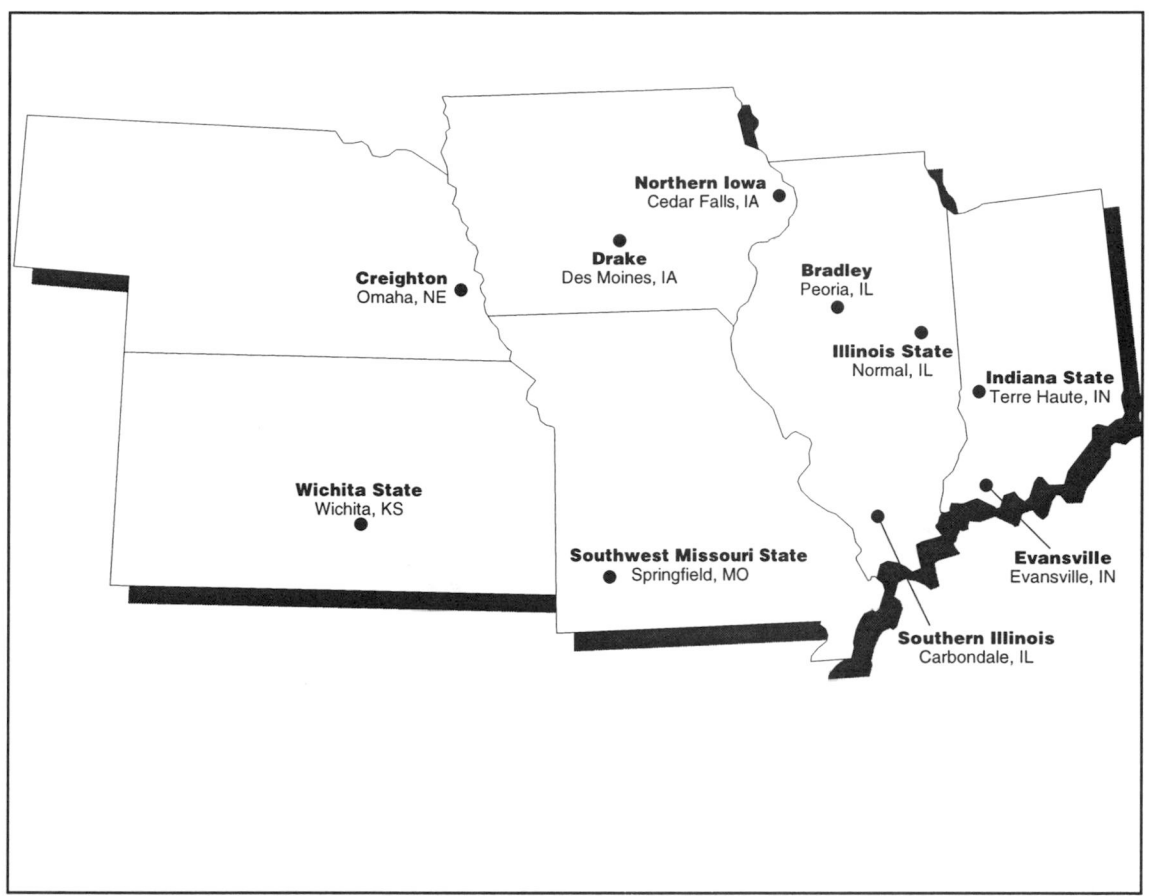

MISSOURI VALLEY

ADDRESS: 1000 St. Louis Union Station, Suite 333, St. Louis, MO 63103.

PHONE/FAX: (314) 421-0339/3505.

PREVIOUS NAME: Missouri Valley Intercollegiate Athletic Association.

CURRENT MEMBERS: Bradley (1949-51 and 1956-97), Creighton (1929-48 and 1977-97), Drake (1908-51 and 1957-97), Evansville (1995-97), Ill. St. (1981-97), Ind. St. (1977-97), Northern Iowa (1992-97), SIU (1975-97), SW Mo. St. (1991-97), Wichita St. (1946-97).

FORMER MEMBERS: Butler (1933 and 1934), Cincinnati (1958-70), Detroit (1950-57), Grinnell, Ia. (1919-39), Houston (1951-60), Iowa State (1908-28), Kansas (1908-28), Kansas State (1914-28), Louisville (1965-75), Memphis State (1968-73), Missouri (1908-28), Nebraska (1908-28), NM. St. (1971-83), North Texas State (1958-75), Oklahoma (1920-28), Okla. A&M (1926-57), St. Louis (1938-74), Tulsa (1935-96), Washburn, Kan. (1935-41), Washington, Mo. (1908-47), West Texas State (1971-86).

NCAA TOURNAMENT RECORD: 69-67 (.507).

NIT TITLES (5) : Bradley (1957-60-64-82), SIU (1967).

ALL-TIME SCORING LEADER: Hersey Hawkins, Bradley (3,008 points from 1985-88).

SINGLE-SEASON SCORING LEADER: Hersey Hawkins, Bradley (36.3 points per game in 1987-88).

REGULAR-SEASON CHAMPIONS (SINCE 1929): Bradley (6 outright-1 tie), Butler (2-0), Cincinnati (6-1), Creighton (6-5), Drake (1-6), Houston (1-0), Ill. St. (1-2), Ind. St. (1-0), Louisville (4-3), Memphis State (1-1), NM. St. (0-1), Okla. A&M (9-4), St. Louis (3-2), SIU (1-2), Tulsa (4-2), Washington, Mo. (1-2), Wichita St. (4-1).

MVC TOURNAMENT TITLES: Creighton (4; 1978-81-89-91), SIU (4; 1977-93-94-95), Tulsa (4; 1982-84-86-96), Bradley (2; 1980 and 1988), Ill. St. (2; 1983 and 1990), Wichita St. (2; 1985 and 1987), Ind. St. (1; 1979), SW Mo. St. (1; 1992).

YEAR-BY-YEAR CHAMPIONS (incl. conference records): 1929—Washington, Mo. (7-0); **1930**—Creighton (6-2), Washington, Mo. (6-2); **1931**—Creighton (5-3), Okla. A&M (5-3), Washington, Mo. (5-3); **1932**—Creighton (8-0); **1933**—Butler (9-1); **1934**—Butler (9-1); **1935**—Creighton (8-4), Drake (8-4); **1936**—Creighton (8-4), Drake (8-4), Okla. A&M (8-4); **1937**—Okla. A&M (11-1); **1938**—Okla. A&M (13-1); **1939**—Drake (11-3), Okla. A&M (11-3); **1940**—Okla. A&M (12-0); **1941**—Creighton (9-3); **1942**—Creighton (9-1), Okla. A&M (9-1); **1943**—Creighton (10-0); **1944**—No competition due to WWII; **1945**—No competition due to WWII; **1946**—Okla. A&M (12-0); **1947**—St. Louis (11-1); **1948**—Okla. A&M (10-0); **1949**—Okla. A&M (9-1); **1950**—Bradley (11-1); **1951**—Okla. A&M (12-2); **1952**—St. Louis (9-1); **1953**—Okla. A&M (8-2); **1954**—Okla. A&M (9-1); **1955**—St. Louis (8-2), Tulsa (8-2); **1956**—Houston (9-3); **1957**—St. Louis (12-2); **1958**—Cincinnati (13-1); **1959**—Cincinnati (13-1); **1960**—Cincinnati (13-1); **1961**—Cincinnati (10-2); **1962**—Bradley (10-2), Cincinnati (10-2)*; **1963**—Cincinnati (11-1); **1964**—Drake (10-2), Wichita St. (10-2)*; **1965**—Wichita St. (11-3); **1966**—Cincinnati (10-4); **1967**—Louisville (12-2); **1968**—Louisville (14-2); **1969**—Drake (13-3), Louisville (13-3)*; **1970**—Drake (14-2); **1971**—Drake (9-5)*, Louisville (9-5), St. Louis (9-5); **1972**—Louisville (12-2)*, Memphis (12-2); **1973**—Memphis (12-2); **1974**—Louisville (11-1); **1975**—Louisville (12-2); **1976**—Wichita St. (10-2); **1977**—NM. St. (8-4), SIU (8-4); **1978**—Creighton (12-4); **1979**—Ind. St. (16-0); **1980**—Bradley (13-3); **1981**—Wichita St. (12-4); **1982**—Bradley (13-3); **1983**—Wichita St. (17-1); **1984**—Ill. St. (13-3), Tulsa (13-3); **1985**—Tulsa (12-4); **1986**—Bradley (13-3); **1987**—Tulsa (11-3); **1988**—Bradley (12-2); **1989**—Creighton (11-3); **1990**—SIU (10-4); **1991**—Creighton (12-4); **1992**—Ill. St. (14-4), SIU (14-4); **1993**—Ill. St. (13-5); **1994**—Tulsa (15-3); **1995**—Tulsa (15-3); **1996**—Bradley (15-3).

*Won playoff.

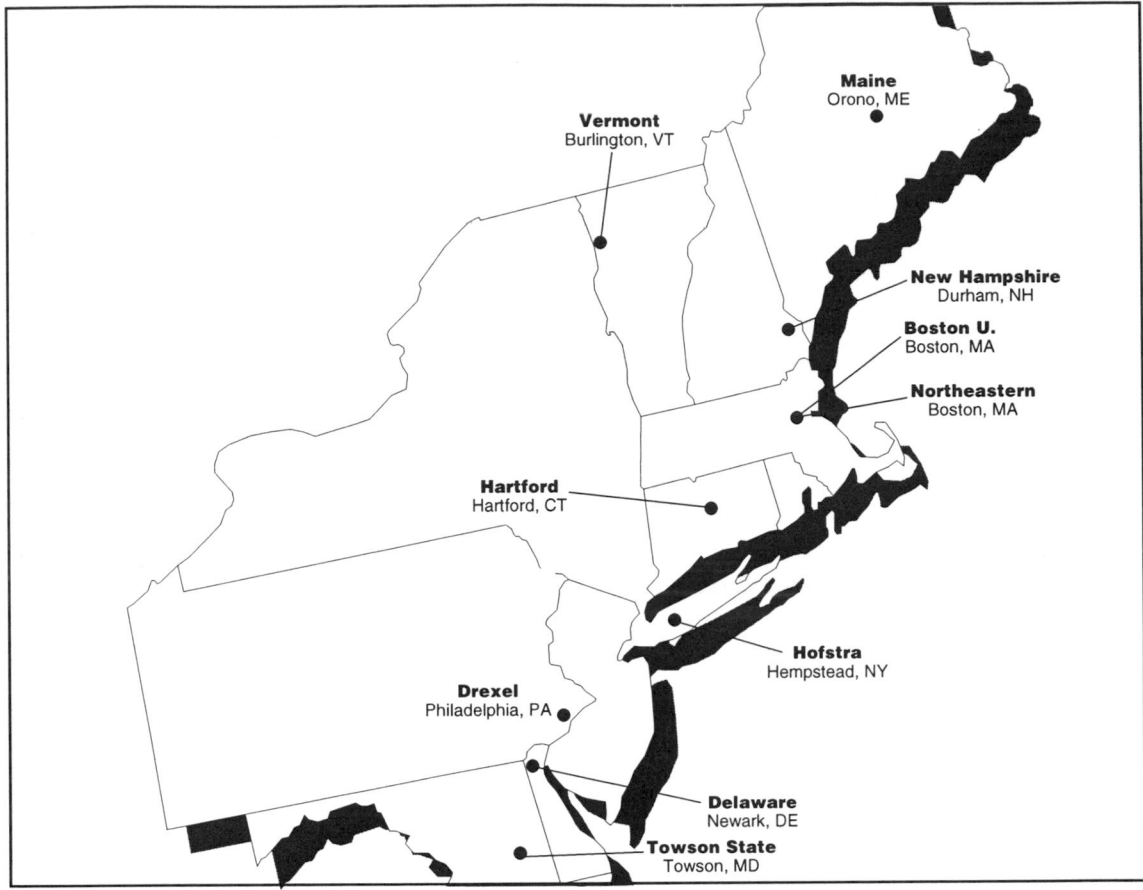

The map shows: Maine (Orono, ME), Vermont (Burlington, VT), New Hampshire (Durham, NH), Boston U. (Boston, MA), Northeastern (Boston, MA), Hartford (Hartford, CT), Hofstra (Hempstead, NY), Drexel (Philadelphia, PA), Delaware (Newark, DE), Towson State (Towson, MD).

NORTH ATLANTIC

ADDRESS: 32 Main Street, P.O. Box 69, Orono, ME 04473.

PHONE/FAX: (207) 866-2383/7524.

PREVIOUS NAMES: ECAC North (1980-82), ECAC North Atlantic (1983-89).

CURRENT MEMBERS: Boston University (1980-97), Delaware (1992-97), Drexel (1992-97), Hartford (1986-97), Hofstra (1995-97), Maine (1980-97), New Hampshire (1980-97), Northeastern (1980-97), Towson State (1996 and 1997), Vermont (1980-97).

FORMER MEMBERS: Canisius (1980-89), Colgate (1980-90), Holy Cross (1980-83), Niagara (1980-89), Rhode Island (1980), Siena (1985-89).

NCAA TOURNAMENT RECORD: 5-17 (.227).

ALL-TIME SCORING LEADER: Reggie Lewis, Northeastern (2,709 points from 1984-87).

SINGLE-SEASON SCORING LEADERS: Vin Baker, Hartford (792 points in 1992-93) and Mike Ferrara, Colgate (28.6 points per game in 1980-81).

REGULAR-SEASON CHAMPIONS: Boston University (0 outright-2 ties), Canisius (0-1), Delaware (1-0), Drexel (3-1), New Hampshire (0-1), Northeastern (6-4), Siena (2-0).

NAC TOURNAMENT TITLES: Northeastern (7; 1981-82-84-85-86-87-91), Boston University (3; 1983-88-90), Drexel (3; 1994-95-96), Delaware (2; 1992 and 1993), Holy Cross (1; 1980), Siena (1; 1989).

YEAR-BY-YEAR CHAMPIONS (incl. conference records): **1982**—Northeastern (8-1); **1983**—Boston U. (8-2), New Hampshire (8-2); **1984**—Northeastern (14-0); **1985**—Canisius (13-3), Northeastern (13-3); **1986**—Northeastern (16-2); **1987**—Northeastern (17-1); **1988**—Siena (16-2); **1989**—Siena (16-1); **1990**—Boston U. (9-3), Northeastern (9-3); **1991**—Northeastern (8-2); **1992**—Delaware (14-0); **1993**—Drexel (12-2), Northeastern (12-2); **1994**—Drexel (12-2); **1995**—Drexel (12-4); **1996**—Drexel (17-1).

Note: As of July 1, 1996, the conference name was changed to AMERICA EAST.

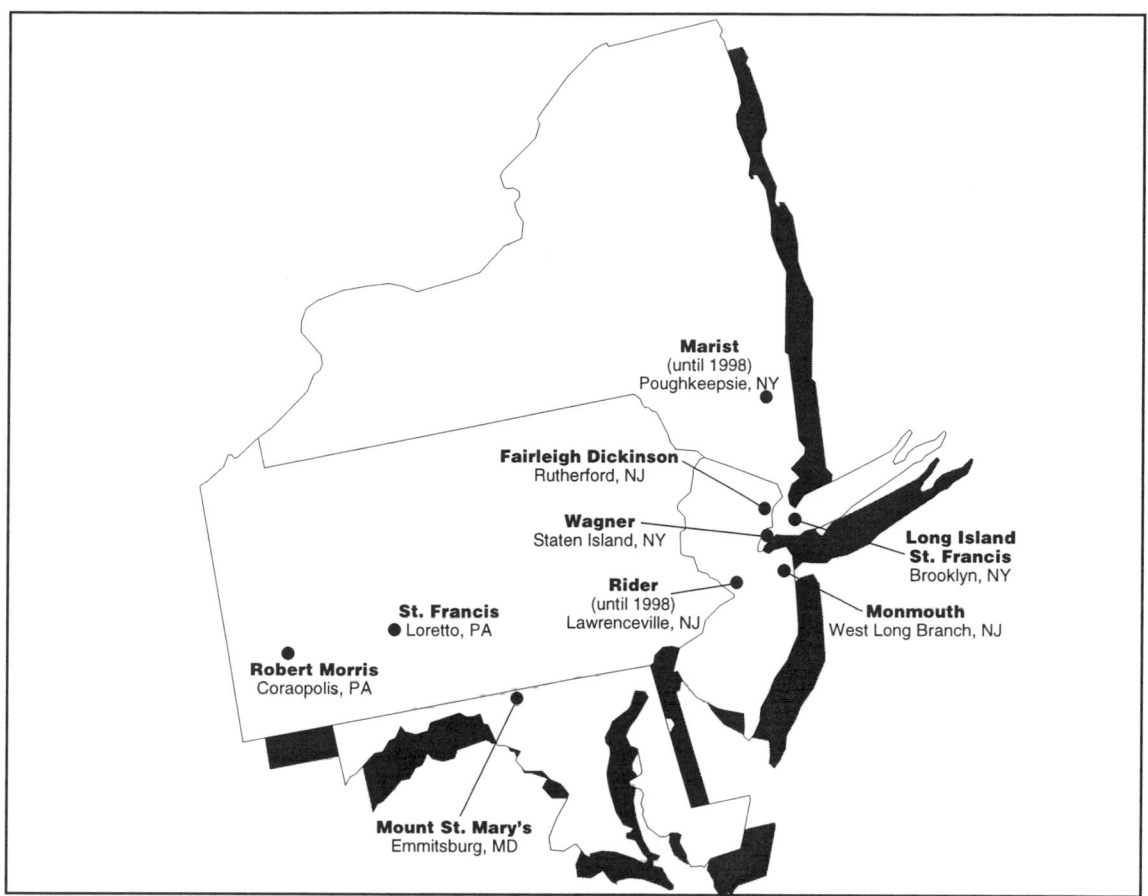

NORTHEAST

ADDRESS: 900 Route 9, Suite 120, Woodbridge, NJ 07095.

PHONE/FAX: (908) 636-9119/6496.

PREVIOUS NAME: ECAC Metro (1982-88).

CURRENT MEMBERS: Fairleigh Dickinson (1982-97), Long Island (1982-97), Marist (1982-97), Monmouth (1986-97), Mount St. Mary's (1990-97), Rider (1993-97), Robert Morris (1982-97), St. Francis, N.Y. (1982-97), St. Francis, Pa. (1982-97), Wagner (1982-97). Marist and Rider are slated to join the MAAC in 1998.

FORMER MEMBERS: Baltimore (1982 and 1983), Loyola, Md. (1982-89), Siena (1982-84), Towson State (1982).

NCAA TOURNAMENT RECORD: 1-15 (.063).

NIT TITLES (2): Long Island (1939 and 1941). Both titles occurred before the league was formed.

ALL-TIME SCORING LEADER: Terrance Bailey, Wagner (2,591 points from 1984-87).

SINGLE-SEASON SCORING LEADER: Terrance Bailey, Wagner (29.4 points per game in 1985-86).

REGULAR-SEASON CHAMPIONS: Fairleigh Dickinson (2 outright-2 ties), Long Island (1-1), Marist (2-1), Mount St. Mary's (1-0), Rider (3-0), Robert Morris (5-1), St. Francis, Pa. (0-1).

NORTHEAST TOURNAMENT TITLES: Robert Morris (5; 1982-83-89-90-92), Fairleigh Dickinson (2; 1985 and 1988), Marist (2; 1986 and 1987), Rider (2; 1993 and 1994), Long Island (1; 1984), Mount St. Mary's (1; 1995), Monmouth (1; 1996), St. Francis, Pa. (1; 1991).

YEAR-BY-YEAR CHAMPIONS (incl. conference records): 1982—Fairleigh Dickinson (12-3/North), Robert Morris (9-5/South); **1983**—Long Island (11-3/N), Robert Morris (12-2/S); **1984**—Long Island (11-5), Robert Morris (11-5); **1985**—Marist (11-3); **1986**—Fairleigh Dickinson (13-3); **1987**—Marist (15-1); **1988**—Fairleigh Dickinson (13-3), Marist (13-3); **1989**—Robert Morris (12-4); **1990**—Robert Morris (12-4); **1991**—Fairleigh Dickinson (13-3), St. Francis, Pa. (13-3); **1992**—Robert Morris (12-4); **1993**—Rider (14-4); **1994**—Rider (14-4); **1995**—Rider (13-5); **1996**—Mount St. Mary's (16-2).

Note: The NEC had North and South Divisions in its first two seasons in 1982 and 1983.

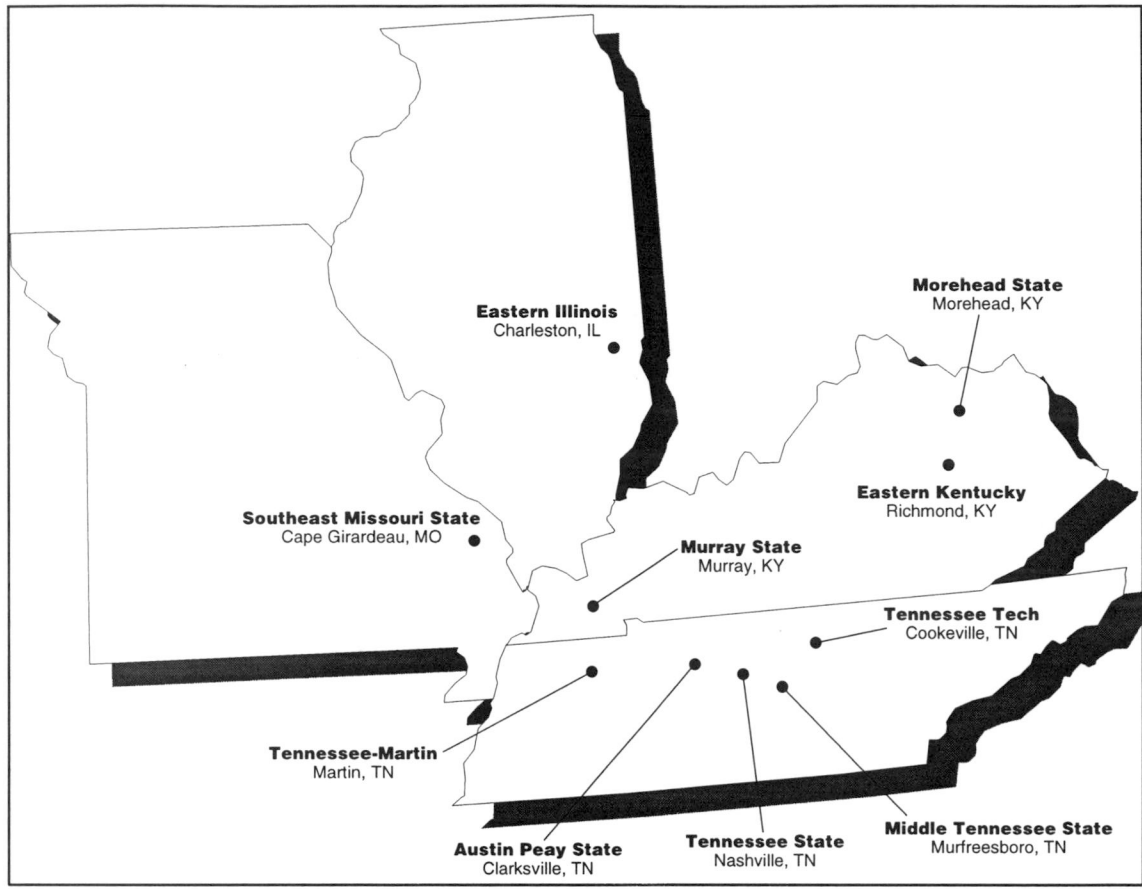

Eastern Illinois
Charleston, IL

Morehead State
Morehead, KY

Eastern Kentucky
Richmond, KY

Southeast Missouri State
Cape Girardeau, MO

Murray State
Murray, KY

Tennessee Tech
Cookeville, TN

Tennessee-Martin
Martin, TN

Austin Peay State
Clarksville, TN

Tennessee State
Nashville, TN

Middle Tennessee State
Murfreesboro, TN

OHIO VALLEY

ADDRESS: 278 Franklin Road, Suite 103, Brentwood, TN 37027.

PHONE/FAX: (615) 371-1698/1788.

CURRENT MEMBERS: Austin Peay State (1964-97), Eastern Illinois (1997-), Eastern Kentucky (1949-97), Middle Tennessee State (1953-97), Morehead State (1949-97), Murray State (1949-61 and 1963-97), Southeast Missouri State (1992-97), Tennessee-Martin (1993-97), Tennessee State (1988-97), Tennessee Tech (1949-97).

FORMER MEMBERS: Akron (1981-87), East Tennessee State (1959-78), Evansville (1949-52), Marshall (1949-52), Western Kentucky (1949-82), Youngstown State (1982-88).

NCAA TOURNAMENT RECORD: 20-47 (.299).

ALL-TIME SCORING LEADER: Joe Jakubick, Akron (2,583 points from 1981-84).

SINGLE-SEASON SCORING LEADERS: Jim McDaniels, Western Kentucky (878 points in 1970-71) and Tom Chilton, east Tennessee State (32.1 points per game in 1960-61).

REGULAR-SEASON CHAMPIONS: Akron (0 outright-1 tie), Austin Peay State (2-1), Eastern Kentucky (4-2), East Tennessee State (0-2), Middle Tennessee State (2-3), Morehead State (1-7), Murray State (9-6), Tennessee State (1-1), Tennessee Tech (2-2), Western Kentucky (13-6).

OVC TOURNAMENT TITLES: Western Kentucky (10; 1949-52-53-54-65-66-76-78-80-81), Murray State (7; 1951-64-88-90-91-92-95), Middle Tennessee State (5; 1975-77-82-85-89), Eastern Kentucky (3; 1950-55-79), Austin Peay (2; 1987 and 1996), Morehead State (2; 1983 and

1984), Tennessee State (2; 1993 and 1994), Akron (1; 1986), Tennessee Tech (1; 1967).

YEAR-BY-YEAR CHAMPIONS (incl. conference records): 1949—Western Kentucky (8-2); **1950**—Western Kentucky (8-0); **1951**—Murray State (9-3); **1952**—Western Kentucky (9-1); **1953**—Eastern Kentucky (9-1); **1954**—Western Kentucky (9-1); **1955**—Western Kentucky (8-2); **1956**—Morehead State (7-3), Tennessee Tech (7-3), Western Kentucky (7-3); **1957**—Morehead State (9-1), Western Kentucky (9-1); **1958**—Tennessee Tech (8-2); **1959**—Eastern Kentucky (10-2); **1960**—Western Kentucky (10-2); **1961**—Eastern Kentucky (9-3), Morehead State (9-3), Western Kentucky (9-3); **1962**—Western Kentucky (11-1); **1963**—Morehead State (8-4), Tennessee Tech (8-4); **1964**—Murray State (11-3); **1965**—Eastern Kentucky (13-1); **1966**—Western Kentucky (14-0); **1967**—Western Kentucky (13-1); **1968**—East Tennessee State (10-4), Murray State (10-4); **1969**—Morehead State (11-3), Murray State (11-3); **1970**—Western Kentucky (14-0); **1971**—Western Kentucky (12-2); **1972**—Eastern Kentucky (9-5), Morehead State (9-5), —Western Kentucky (9-5); **1973**—Austin Peay (11-3); **1974**—Austin Peay (10-4), Morehead State (10-4); **1975**—Middle Tennessee State (12-2); **1976**—Western Kentucky (11-3); **1977**—Austin Peay (13-1); **1978**—East Tennessee State (10-4), Middle Tennessee State (10-4); **1979**—Eastern Kentucky (9-3); **1980**—Murray State (10-2), Western Kentucky (10-2); **1981**—Western Kentucky (12-2); **1982**—Murray State (13-3); **1983**—Murray State (11-3); **1984**—Morehead State (12-2); **1985**—Tennessee Tech (11-3); **1986**—Akron (10-4), Middle Tennessee State (10-4); **1987**—Middle Tennessee State (11-3); **1988**—Murray State (13-1); **1989**—Middle Tennessee State (10-2), Murray State (10-2); **1990**—Murray State (10-2); **1991**—Murray State (10-2); **1992**—Murray State (11-3); **1993**—Tennessee State (13-3); **1994**—Murray State (15-1); **1995**—Murray State (11-5), Tennessee State (11-5); **1996**—Murray State (12-4).

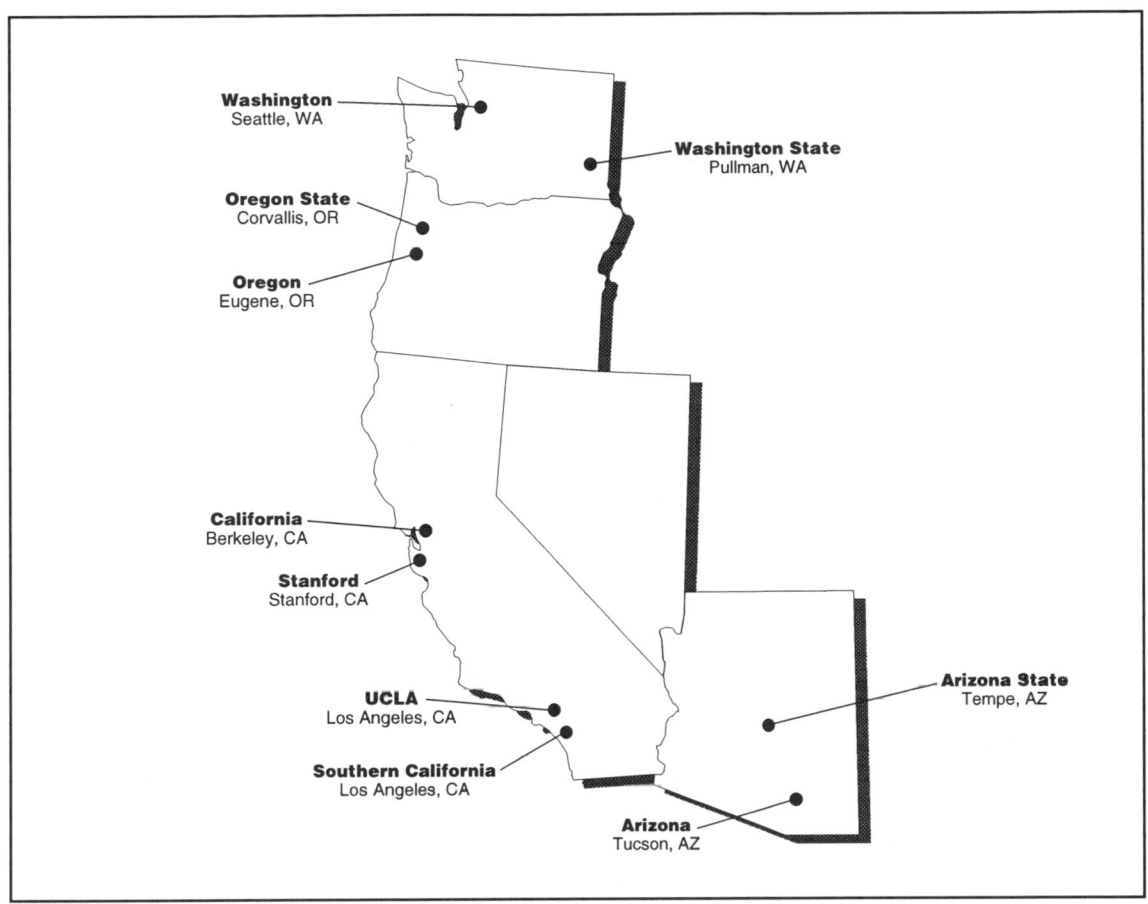

PACIFIC-10

ADDRESS: 800 South Broadway, Suite 400, Walnut Creek, CA 94596.

PHONE/FAX: (510) 932-4411/4601.

PREVIOUS NAMES: Pacific Coast Conference (1916-59), Athletic Association of Western Universities (1960-68), Pacific-8 (1969-78).

CURRENT MEMBERS: Arizona (1979-97), Arizona St. (1979-97), California (1916-97), Oregon (1916-59 and 1965-97), Oregon St. (1916-59 and 1965-97), USC (1922-97), Stanford (1917-97), UCLA (1928-97), Washington (1916-97), Washington St. (1917-59 and 1964-97).

FORMER MEMBERS: Idaho (1922-59), Montana (1924-29).

NCAA TOURNAMENT RECORD: 141-95 (.597).

NCAA TITLES (14) : California (1959), Oregon (1939), UCLA (1964-65-67-68-69-70-71-72-73-75-95), Stanford (1942).

NIT TITLES (2): Stanford (1991), UCLA (1985).

ALL-TIME SCORING LEADER: Don MacLean, UCLA (2,608 points from 1989-92).

SINGLE-SEASON SCORING LEADER: Lew Alcindor, UCLA (29 points per game in 1966-67).

REGULAR-SEASON CHAMPIONS (SINCE 1916): Arizona (6 outright-1 tie), California (10-4), Idaho (2-0), Oregon (2-1), Oregon St. (8-4), USC (6-1), Stanford (5-2), UCLA (24-2), Washington (6-3), Washington St. (2-0).

PACIFIC-10 TOURNAMENT TITLES: Arizona (3; 1988-89-90), UCLA (1; 1987).

YEAR-BY-YEAR CHAMPIONS (incl. conference records): 1916—California (5-3), Oregon St. (5-3); **1917**—Washington St. (8-1); **1918**—No league competition; **1919**—Oregon (11-3); **1920**—Stanford (9-1); **1921**—California (8-3), Stanford (8-3); **1922**—Idaho (7-0); **1923**—Idaho (5-3/North)*;

1924—California (5-3/South)*; **1925**—California (3-1/S)*; **1926**—California (5-0/S)*; **1927**—California (5-0/S)*; **1928**—Southern Cal (6-3/S)*; **1929**—California (9-0/S)*; **1930**—Southern Cal (7-2/S)*; **1931**—Washington (14-2/N)*; **1932**—California (8-3/S)*; **1933**—Oregon St. (12-4/N)*; **1934**—Washington (14-2/N)*; **1935**—Southern Cal (11-1/S)*; **1936**—Stanford (8-4/S)*; **1937**—Stanford (10-2/S)*; **1938**—Stanford (10-2/S)*; **1939**—Oregon (14-2/N)*; **1940**—Southern Cal (10-2/S)*; **1941**—Washington St. (13-3/N)*; **1942**—Stanford (11-1/S)*; **1943**—Washington (12-4/N)*; **1944**—Washington (15-1/N), California (4-0/S); **1945**—Oregon (11-5/N), UCLA (3-1/S); **1946**—California (11-1/S)*; **1947**—Oregon St. (13-3/N)*; **1948**—Washington (10-6/N)*; **1949**—Oregon St. (12-4/N)*; **1950**—UCLA (10-2/S)*; **1951**—Washington (11-5/N)*; **1952**—UCLA (8-4/S)*; **1953**—Washington (15-1/N)*; **1954**—Southern Cal (8-4/S)*; **1955**—Oregon St. (15-1/N)*; **1956**—UCLA (16-0); **1957**—California (14-2); **1958**—California (12-4), Oregon St. (12-4); **1959**—California (14-2); **1960**—California (11-1); **1961**—Southern Cal (9-3); **1962**—UCLA (10-2); **1963**—Stanford (7-5), UCLA (7-5); **1964**—UCLA (15-0); **1965**—UCLA (14-0); **1966**—Oregon St. (12-2); **1967**—UCLA (14-0); **1968**—UCLA (14-0); **1969**—UCLA (13-1); **1970**—UCLA (12-2); **1971**—UCLA (14-0); **1972**—UCLA (14-0); **1973**—UCLA (14-0); **1974**—UCLA (12-2); **1975**—UCLA (12-2); **1976**—UCLA (12-2); **1977**—UCLA (11-3); **1978**—UCLA (14-0); **1979**—UCLA (15-3); **1980**—Oregon St. (16-2); **1981**—Oregon St. (17-1); **1982**—Oregon St. (16-2); **1983**—UCLA (15-3); **1984**—Oregon St. (15-3), Washington (15-3); **1985**—Southern Cal (13-5), Washington (13-5); **1986**—Arizona (14-4); **1987**—UCLA (14-4); **1988**—Arizona (17-1); **1989**—Arizona (17-1); **1990**—Arizona (15-3), Oregon St. (15-3); **1991**—Arizona (14-4); **1992**—UCLA (16-2); **1993**—Arizona (17-1); **1994**—Arizona (14-4); **1995**—UCLA (16-2); **1996**—UCLA (16-2).

*Won divisional playoff.

Note: The PCC had North and South Divisions from 1923 to 1955. No official league competition in 1917-18.

PATRIOT LEAGUE

ADDRESS: 3897 Adler Place, Building C, Suite 310, Bethlehem, PA 18017.

PHONE/FAX: (610) 691-2414/8414.

CURRENT MEMBERS: Army (1991-97), Bucknell (1991-97), Colgate (1991-97), Holy Cross (1991-97), Lafayette (1991-97), Lehigh (1991-97), Navy (1992-97).

FORMER MEMBER: Fordham (1991-95).

NCAA TOURNAMENT RECORD: 0-5 (.000).

REGULAR-SEASON CHAMPIONS: Bucknell (1 outright-2 ties), Colgate (0-3), Fordham (1-2), Holy Cross (0-1), Navy (0-2).

PATRIOT TOURNAMENT TITLES: Colgate (2; 1995 and 1996), Fordham (2; 1991 and 1992), Holy Cross (1; 1993), Navy (1; 1994).

YEAR-BY-YEAR CHAMPIONS (incl. conference records): 1991—Fordham (11-1); **1992**—Bucknell (11-3), Fordham (11-3); **1993**—Bucknell (13-1); **1994**—Colgate (9-5), Fordham (9-5), Holy Cross (9-5), Navy (9-5); **1995**—(11-3); Colgate (11-3); **1996**—Colgate (9-3), Navy (9-3).

SOUTHEASTERN

ADDRESS: 2201 Civic Center Boulevard, Birmingham, AL 35203-1103.

PHONE/FAX: (205) 458-3010/3031.

CURRENT MEMBERS: Alabama (1933-97), Arkansas (1992-97), Auburn (1933-97), Florida (1933-97), Georgia (1933-97), Kentucky (1933-97), Louisiana State (1933-97), Mississippi (1933-97), Mississippi State (1933-97), South Carolina (1992-97), Tennessee (1933-97), Vanderbilt (1933-97).

FORMER MEMBERS: Georgia Tech (1933-64), Sewanee (1933-40), Tulane (1933-66).

NCAA TOURNAMENT RECORD: 158-109 (.592).

NCAA TITLES (7) : Arkansas (1994), Kentucky (1948-49-51-58-78-96).

NIT TITLES (3) : Kentucky (1946 and 1976), Vanderbilt (1990).

ALL-TIME SCORING LEADER: Pete Maravich, LSU (3,667 points from 1968-70).

SINGLE-SEASON SCORING LEADER: Pete Maravich, LSU (44.5 points per game in 1969-70).

REGULAR-SEASON CHAMPIONS: Alabama (5 outright-2 ties), Arkansas (3-1), Auburn (1-0), Florida (1-1), Georgia (1-0), Georgia Tech (1-0), Kentucky (31-10), Louisiana State (4-4), Mississippi State (4-3), Tennessee (2-4), Tulane (1-0), Vanderbilt (2-1).

SEC TOURNAMENT TITLES: Kentucky (20; 1933-37-39-40-42-44-45-46-47-48-49-50-52-84-86-88-92-93-94-95), Alabama (6; 1934-1982-87-89-90-91), Tennessee (4; 1936-41-43-79), Auburn (1; 1985), Georgia (1; 1983), Georgia Tech (1; 1938), Louisiana State (1; 1980), Mississippi (1; 1981), Mississippi State (1; 1996), Vanderbilt (1; 1951).

YEAR-BY-YEAR CHAMPIONS (incl. conference records): **1933**—Kentucky (8-0); **1934**—Kentucky (11-0); **1935**—Kentucky (11-0), Louisiana State (12-0); **1936**—Kentucky (6-2); **1937**—Georgia Tech (10-0); **1938**—Kentucky (6-0); **1939**—Alabama (13-4); **1940**—Alabama (14-4); **1941**—Kentucky (8-1); **1942**—Tennessee (7-1); **1943**—Kentucky (8-1); **1944**—Tulane (4-0); **1945**—Kentucky (4-1), Tennessee (8-2); **1946**—Kentucky (6-0), Louisiana State (8-0); **1947**—Kentucky (11-0); **1948**—Kentucky (9-0); **1949**—Kentucky (13-0); **1950**—Kentucky (11-2); **1951**—Kentucky (14-0); **1952**—Kentucky (14-0); **1953**—Louisiana State (13-0); **1954**—Kentucky (14-0), Louisiana State (14-0); **1955**—Kentucky (12-2); **1956**—Alabama (14-0); **1957**—Kentucky (12-2); **1958**—Kentucky (12-2); **1959**—Mississippi State (13-1); **1960**—Auburn (12-2); **1961**—Mississippi State (11-3); **1962**—Kentucky (13-1), Mississippi State (13-1); **1963**—Mississippi State (12-2); **1964**—Kentucky (11-3); **1965**—Vanderbilt (15-1); **1966**—Kentucky (15-1); **1967**—Tennessee (15-3); **1968**—Kentucky (15-3); **1969**—Kentucky (16-2); **1970**—Kentucky (17-1); **1971**—Kentucky (16-2); **1972**—Kentucky (14-4), Tennessee (14-4); **1973**—Kentucky (14-4); **1974**—Alabama (15-3), Vanderbilt (15-3); **1975**—Alabama (15-3), Kentucky (15-3); **1976**—Alabama (15-3); **1977**—Kentucky (16-2), Tennessee (16-2); **1978**—Kentucky (16-2); **1979**—Louisiana State (14-4); **1980**—Kentucky (15-3); **1981**—Louisiana State (17-1); **1982**—Kentucky (13-5), Tennessee (13-5); **1983**—Kentucky (13-5); **1984**—Kentucky (14-4); **1985**—Louisiana State (13-5); **1986**—Kentucky (17-1); **1987**—Alabama (16-2); **1988**—Kentucky (13-5); **1989**—Florida (13-5); **1990**—Georgia (13-5); **1991**—Louisiana State (13-5), Mississippi State (13-5); **1992**—Kentucky (12-4/E), Arkansas (13-3/W); **1993**—Vanderbilt (14-2/E), Arkansas (10-6/W); **1994**—Florida (12-4/E), Kentucky (12-4/E), Arkansas (14-2/W); **1995**—Kentucky (14-2/E), Arkansas (12-4/W), Mississippi State (12-4/W); **1996**—Kentucky (16-0/E), Mississippi State (10-6/W).

*Won playoff game.

Note: The SEC introduced Eastern and Western Divisions for the first time in the 1991–92 season.

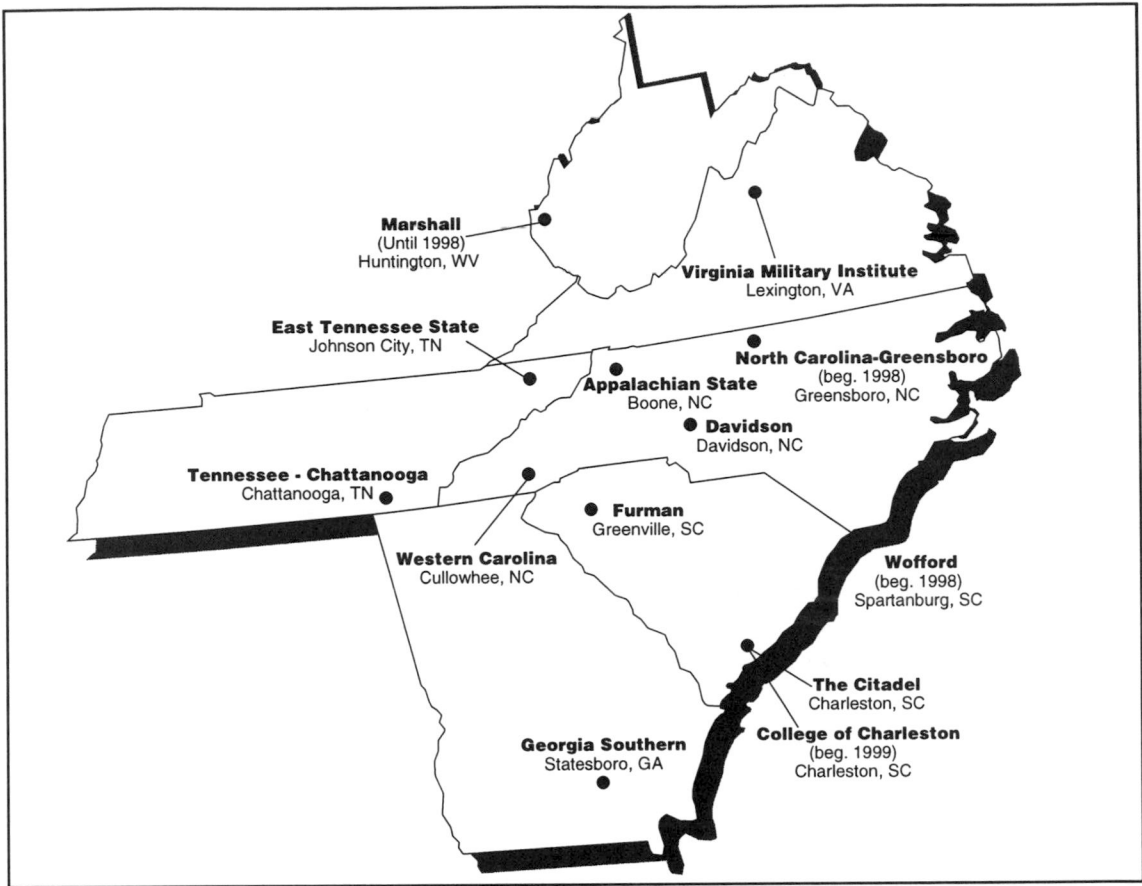

Marshall
(Until 1998)
Huntington, WV

Virginia Military Institute
Lexington, VA

East Tennessee State
Johnson City, TN

North Carolina-Greensboro
(beg. 1998)
Greensboro, NC

Appalachian State
Boone, NC

Davidson
Davidson, NC

Tennessee - Chattanooga
Chattanooga, TN

Furman
Greenville, SC

Western Carolina
Cullowhee, NC

Wofford
(beg. 1998)
Spartanburg, SC

The Citadel
Charleston, SC

College of Charleston
(beg. 1999)
Charleston, SC

Georgia Southern
Statesboro, GA

SOUTHERN

ADDRESS: One West Pack Square, Suite 1508, Asheville, NC 28801.

PHONE/FAX: (704) 255-7872/251-5006.

PREVIOUS NAME: Southern Intercollegiate Athletic.

CURRENT MEMBERS: Appalachian St. (1973-97), The Citadel (1937-97), Davidson (1937-88 and 1993-97), ETSU (1980-97), Furman (1937-97), Ga Southern (1993-97), Marshall (1978-97; plans to join Mid-American in 1998), UTC (1978-97), VMI (1926-97), W. Caro. (1978-97). NC-Greensboro and Wofford (S.C.) are slated to join the league in 1998. The College of Charleston is slated to join the league in 1999.

FORMER MEMBERS: Al (1922-32), Auburn (1922-32), Clemson (1922-53), Duke (1929-53), E. Caro. (1966-1977), GWU (1942 and 1943 and 1946-70), Ga (1922-32), Ga Tech (1922-32), Uk (1922-32), LSU (1923-32), Maryland (1924-53), Ms (1923-32), MSU. (1922-32), NC (1922-53), NC St. (1922-53), Richmond (1937-76), University of the South (1924-32), SC (1923-53), Tennessee (1922-32), Tulane (1923-32), Vanderbilt (1923-32), Virginia (1922-37), Virginia Tech (1922-65), Wake Forest (1937-53), Wash.& Lee (1922-58), W. Va. (1951-68), William & Mary (1937-77).

NCAA TOURNAMENT RECORD: 26-54 (.325).

ALL-TIME SCORING LEADER: Skip Henderson, Marshall (2,574 points from 1985-88).

SINGLE-SEASON SCORING LEADER: Frank Selvy, Furman (41.7 points per game in 1953-54).

REGULAR-SEASON CHAMPIONS: Al (1 outright-0 ties), Appalachian St. (2-1), Auburn (1-0), Davidson (10-1), ETSU (1-2), Furman (3-2), GWU (1-1), Ga (1-0), Marshall (4-0), Maryland (0-1), NC (7-0), NC St. (6-0), SC (4-0), UTC (8-3), Tulane (1-0), Virginia (1-0), VMI (1-1), Virginia Tech (1-0), Wake Forest (1-0), Wash.& Lee (3-0), W. Caro. (1-0), W. Va. (9-1).

SC TOURNAMENT TITLES: W. Va. (10), NC (8), NC St. (7), UT-Chattanooga (7), Furman (6), Davidson (5), Duke (5), ETSU (4), GWU (3), Marshall (3), VMI (3), Wash.& Lee (3), Al (1), Appalachian St. (1), Clemson (1), E. Caro. (1), Ga (1), Maryland (1), Ms (1), MSU. (1), SC (1), Vanderbilt (1), Wake Forest (1), W. Caro. (1).

YEAR-BY-YEAR CHAMPIONS (incl. conference records): 1922—Virginia (5-0); **1923**—NC (5-0); **1924**—Tulane (10-0); **1925**—NC (8-0); **1926**—Uk (8-0); **1927**—SC (9-1); **1928**—Auburn (12-1); **1929**—Wash.& Lee (7-1); **1930**—Al (10-0); **1931**—Ga (15-1); **1932**—Uk (9-1), Maryland (9-1); **1933**—SC (3-0); **1934**—SC (6-0); **1935**—NC (12-1); **1936**—Wash.& Lee (10-1); **1937**—Wash.& Lee (11-1); **1938**—NC (13-3); **1939**—Wake Forest (15-3); **1940**—Duke (13-2); **1941**—NC (14-1); **1942**—Duke (15-1); **1943**—Duke (12-1); **1944**—NC (9-1); **1945**—SC (9-0); **1946**—NC (13-1); **1947**—NC St. (11-2); **1948**—NC St. (12-0); **1949**—NC St. (14-1); **1950**—NC St. (12-2); **1951**—NC St. (13-1); **1952**—W. Virginia (15-1); **1953**—NC St. (13-3); **1954**—GWU (10-0); **1955**—W. Virginia (9-1); **1956**—GWU (10-2), W. Virginia (10-2); **1957**—W. Virginia (12-0); **1958**—W. Virginia (12-0); **1959**—W. Virginia (11-0); **1960**—Va. Tech (12-1); **1961**—W. Virginia (11-1); **1962**—W. Virginia (12-1); **1963**—W. Virginia (11-2); **1964**—Davidson (9-2); **1965**—Davidson (12-0); **1966**—Davidson (11-1); **1967**—W. Virginia (9-1); **1968**—Davidson (9-1); **1969**—Davidson (9-0); **1970**—Davidson (10-0); **1971**—Davidson (9-1); **1972**—Davidson (8-2); **1973**—Davidson (9-1); **1974**—Furman (11-1); **1975**—Furman (12-0); **1976**—Va. Military (9-3); **1977**—Furman (8-2), Va. Military (8-2); **1978**—Appalachian St. (9-3); **1979**—Appalachian St. (11-4); **1980**—Furman (14-1); **1981**—Appalachian St. (11-5), Davidson (11-5), Tenn.-Chat. (11-5); **1982**—Tenn.-Chat. (15-1); **1983**—Tenn.-Chat. (15-1); **1984**—Marshall (13-3); **1985**—Tenn.-Chat. (14-2); **1986**—Tenn.-Chat. (12-4); **1987**—Marshall (15-1); **1988**—Marshall (14-2); **1989**—Tenn.-Chat. (10-4); **1990**—E. Tenn. St. (12-2); **1991**—E. Tenn. St. (11-3), Furman (11-3), Tenn.-Chat. (11-3); **1992**—E. Tenn. St. (12-2), Tenn.-Chat. (12-2); **1993**—Tenn.-Chat. (16-2); **1994**—Tenn.-Chat. (14-4); **1995**—Marshall (10-4/N), UTC (11-3/S), **1996**—Davidson (14-0/N), W. Caro. (10-4/S).

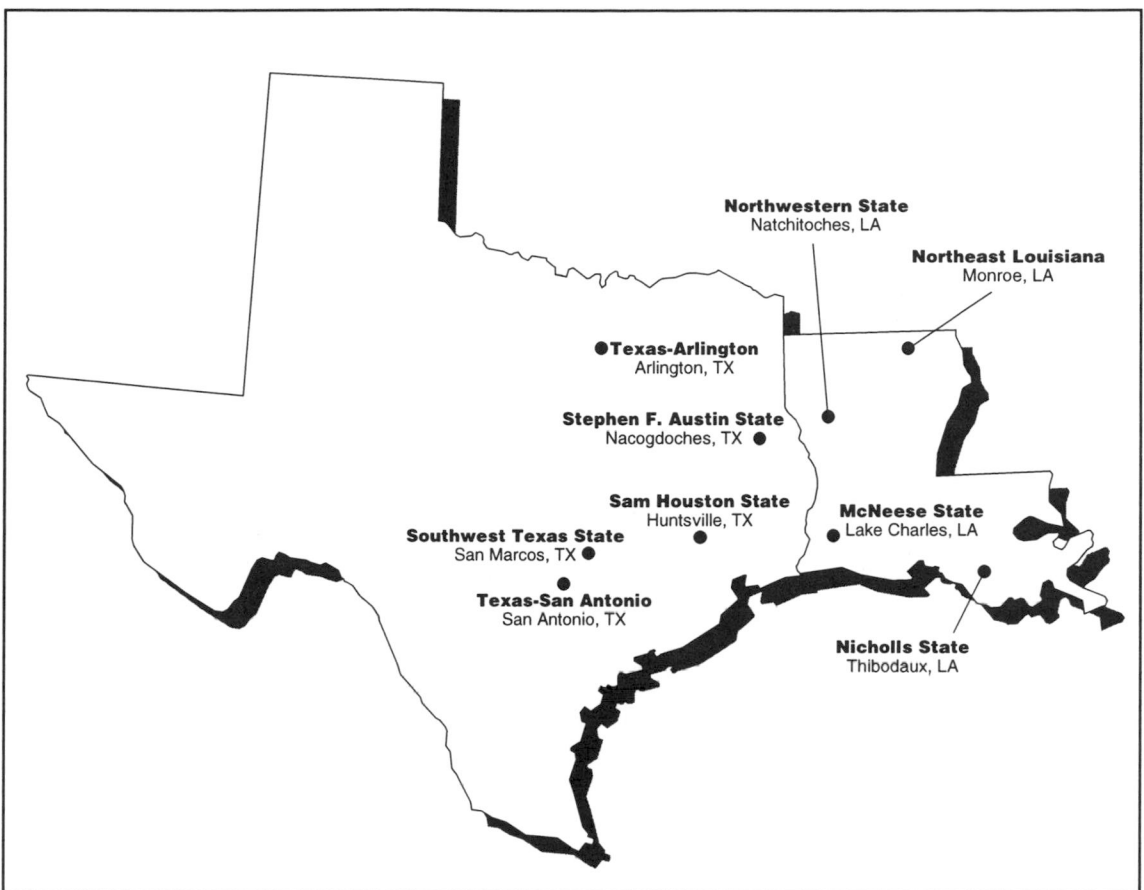

Northwestern State
Natchitoches, LA

Northeast Louisiana
Monroe, LA

●**Texas-Arlington**
Arlington, TX

Stephen F. Austin State
Nacogdoches, TX ●

Sam Houston State
Huntsville, TX

McNeese State
Lake Charles, LA

Southwest Texas State
San Marcos, TX ●

Texas-San Antonio
San Antonio, TX

Nicholls State
Thibodaux, LA

SOUTHLAND

ADDRESS: 8150 North Central Expressway, Suite 930, Dallas, TX 75206.

PHONE/FAX: (214) 750-7522/8077.

CURRENT MEMBERS: McNeese State (1973-97), Nicholls State (1992-97), Northeast Louisiana (1983-97), Northwestern State, La. (1988-97), Sam Houston State (1988-97), Stephen F. Austin State (1988-97), Southwest Texas State (1988-97), Texas-Arlington (1969-86 and 1988-97), Texas-San Antonio (1992-97).

FORMER MEMBERS: Abilene Christian (1969-73), Arkansas State (1969-87), Lamar (1969-87), Louisiana Tech (1972-87), North Texas (1983-96), Southwestern Louisiana (1972-82), Trinity, Tex. (1969-72).

NCAA TOURNAMENT RECORD: 11-22 (.333).

ALL-TIME SCORING LEADER: Dwight "Bo" Lamar, Southwestern Louisiana (3,493 points from 1970-73).

SINGLE-SEASON SCORING LEADER: Dwight "Bo" Lamar, Southwestern Louisiana (36.3 points per game in 1971-72).

REGULAR-SEASON CHAMPIONS (SINCE 1964): Abilene Christian (2 outright-1 tie), Arkansas State (3-1), Lamar (7-1), Louisiana Tech (5-0), McNeese State (1-1), Nicholls State (1-0), Northeast Louisiana (6-0), North Texas (2-0), Southwestern Louisiana (2-0), Texas-San Antonio (1-0), Trinity (1-0).

SLC TOURNAMENT TITLES: Northeast Louisiana (6; 1986-90-91-92-93-96), Louisiana Tech (3; 1984-85-87), Lamar (2; 1981 and 1983), McNeese State (1; 1989), Nicholls State (1; 1995), North Texas (1; 1988), Southwestern Louisiana (1; 1982), Southwest Texas State (1; 1994).

YEAR-BY-YEAR CHAMPIONS (incl. conference records): 1964—Lamar (7-1); **1965**—Abilene Christian (6-2), Arkansas State (6-2); **1966**—Abilene Christian (8-0); **1967**—Arkansas State (8-0); **1968**—Abilene Christian (6-2); **1969**—Trinity, Tex. (7-1); **1970**—Lamar (7-1); **1971**—Arkansas State (6-2); **1972**—Southwestern Louisiana (8-0); **1973**—Southwestern Louisiana (12-0); **1974**—Arkansas State (4-0); **1975**—McNeese State (6-2); **1976**—Louisiana Tech (9-1); **1977**—Southwestern Louisiana (8-2); **1978**—Lamar (8-2), McNeese State (8-2); **1979**—Lamar (9-1); **1980**—Lamar (8-2); **1981**—Lamar (8-2); **1982**—Southwestern Louisiana (8-2); **1983**—Lamar (9-3); **1984**—Lamar (11-1); **1985**—Louisiana Tech (11-1); **1986**—Northeast Louisiana (9-3); **1987**—Louisiana Tech (9-1); **1988**—North Texas (12-2); **1989**—North Texas (10-4); **1990**—Northeast Louisiana (13-1); **1991**—Northeast Louisiana (13-1); **1992**—Texas-San Antonio (15-3); **1993**—Northeast Louisiana (17-1); **1994**—Northeast Louisiana (15-3); **1995**—Nicholls State (17-1); **1996**—Northeast Louisiana (13-5).

Note: The SLC moved up to Division I status in 1976.

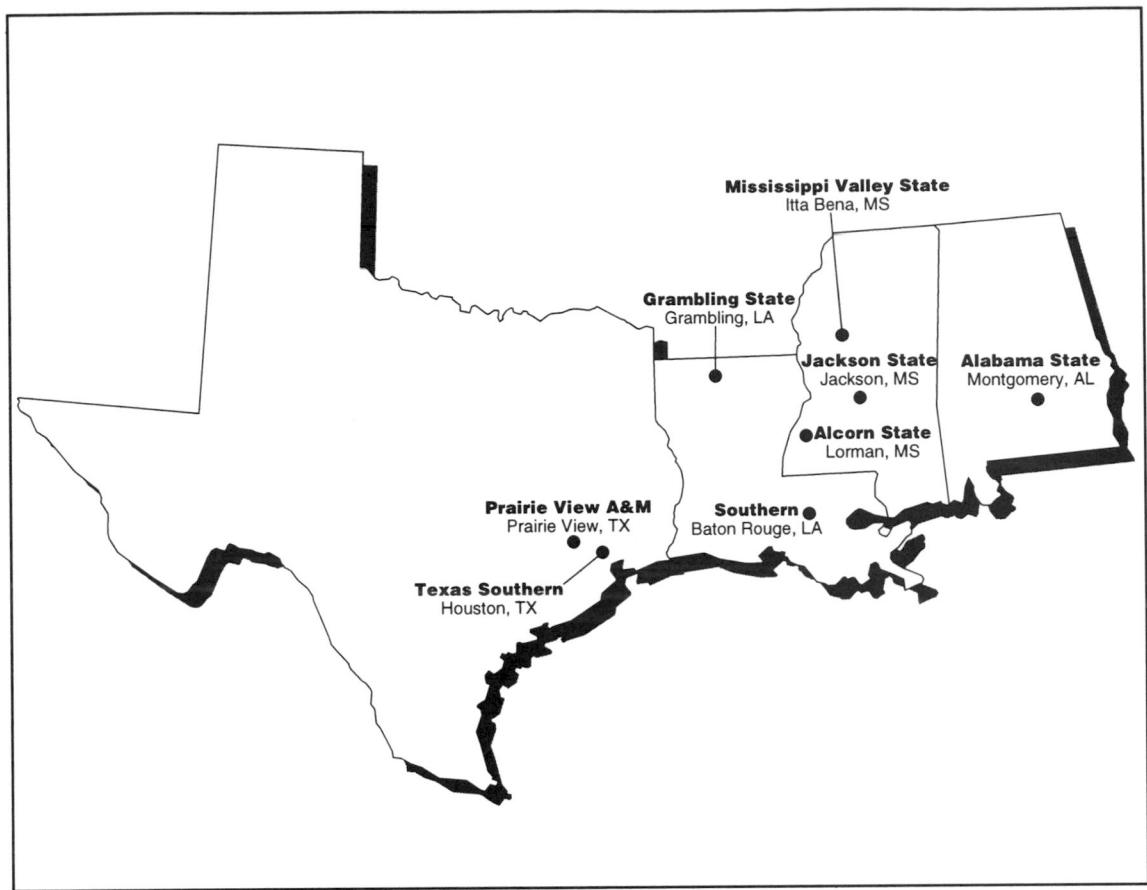

Mississippi Valley State
Itta Bena, MS

Grambling State
Grambling, LA

Jackson State
Jackson, MS

Alabama State
Montgomery, AL

Alcorn State
Lorman, MS

Prairie View A&M
Prairie View, TX

Southern
Baton Rouge, LA

Texas Southern
Houston, TX

SOUTHWESTERN ATHLETIC

ADDRESS: 1500 Sugar Bowl Drive, Louisiana Superdome, New Orleans, LA 70112.

PHONE/FAX: (504) 523-7573/7513.

CURRENT MEMBERS: Alabama State (1983-97), Alcorn State (1963-97), Grambling State (1959-97), Jackson State (1959-97), Mississippi Valley State (1969-97), Prairie View A&M (1921-97 except for 1990-91), Southern (1935-97), Texas Southern (1955-97).

FORMER MEMBERS: Arkansas AM&N (1937-70), Bishop (1921-56), Langston (1932-57), Paul Quinn (1921-29), Sam Houston (1921-59), Texas College (1921-61), Wiley (1921-68).

NCAA TOURNAMENT RECORD: 4-16 (.200).

ALL-TIME SCORING LEADER: Harry Kelly, Texas Southern (3,066 points from 1980-83).

REGULAR-SEASON CHAMPIONS (SINCE JOINING NCAA IN 1957): Alcorn State (7 outright-5 ties), Arkansas AM&N (0-1), Grambling (6-3), Jackson State (5-5), Mississippi Valley State (0-2), Prairie View (2-0), Southern (3-4), Texas Southern (6-2).

SWAC TOURNAMENT TITLES (SINCE 1980): Southern (6; 1981-85-87-88-89-93), Alcorn State (4; 1980-82-83-84), Mississippi Valley State (3; 1986-92-96), Texas Southern (3; 1990-94-95).

YEAR-BY-YEAR CHAMPIONS: 1957—Texas Southern; **1958**—Texas Southern; **1959**—Grambling; **1960**—Grambling; **1961**—Prairie View; **1962**—Prairie View; **1963**—Grambling; **1964**—Grambling, Jackson State; **1965**—Southern; **1966**—Alcorn State, Grambling; **1967**—Alcorn State, Arkansas AM&N, Grambling; **1968**—Alcorn State, Jackson State; **1969**—Alcorn State; **1970**—Jackson State; **1971**—Grambling; **1972**—Grambling; **1973**—Alcorn State; **1974**—Jackson State; **1975**—Jackson State; **1976**—Alcorn State; **1977**—Texas Southern; **1978**—Jackson State, Southern; **1979**—Alcorn State; **1980**—Alcorn State; **1981**—Alcorn State, Southern; **1982**—Alcorn State, Jackson State; **1983**—Texas Southern; **1984**—Alcorn State; **1985**—Alcorn State; **1986**—Alcorn State, Southern; **1987**—Grambling; **1988**—Southern; **1989**—Grambling, Southern, Texas Southern; **1990**—Southern; **1991**—Jackson State; **1992**—Mississippi Valley State, Texas Southern; **1993**—Jackson State; **1994**—Texas Southern; **1995**—Texas Southern; **1996**—Jackson State, Mississippi Valley State.

Note: The SWAC, which started in 1921, moved up to Division I status in 1980. . . . There was no postseason tourney in 1991.

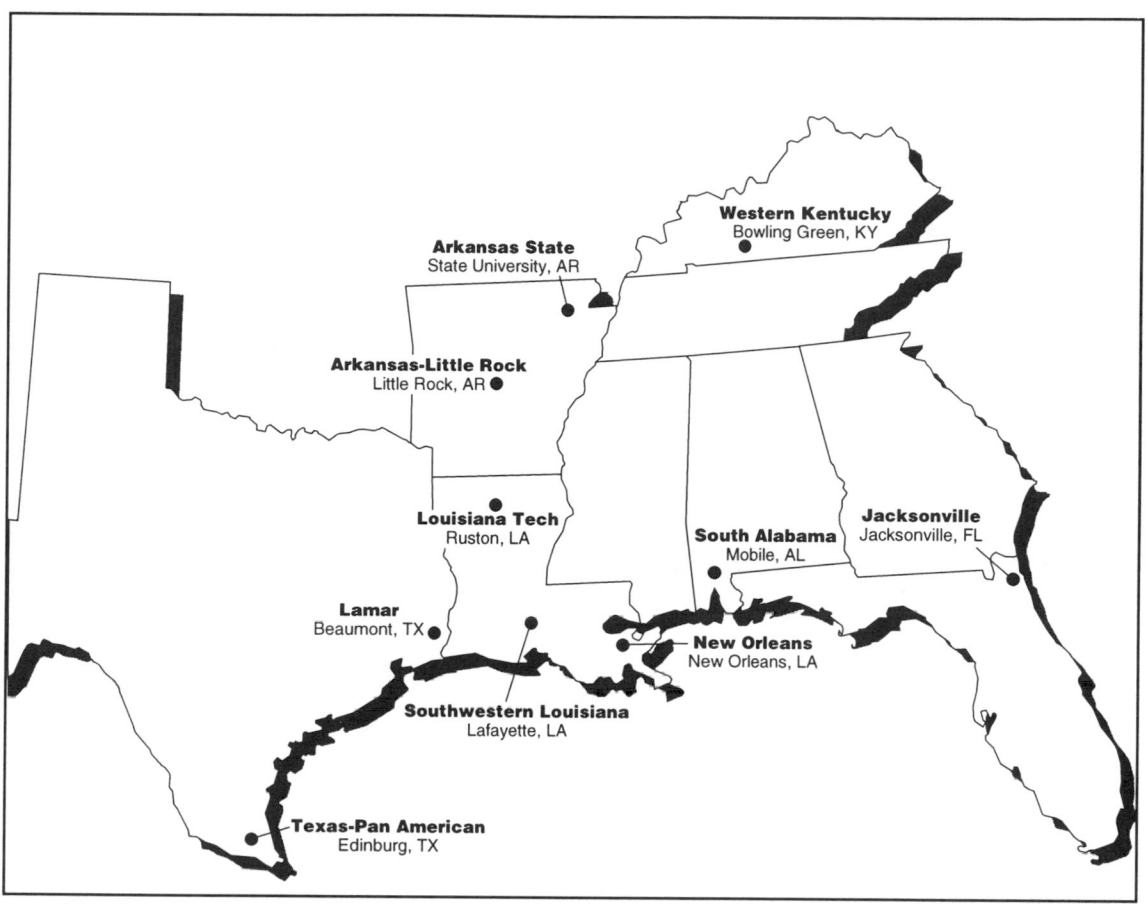

SUN BELT

ADDRESS: One Galleria Boulevard, Suite 2115, Metairie, LA 70001.

PHONE/FAX: (504) 834-6600/6806.

CURRENT MEMBERS: Arkansas-Little Rock (1992-97), Arkansas State (1992-97), Jacksonville (1977-97), Lamar (1992-97), Louisiana Tech (1992-97), New Orleans (1977-80 and 1992-97), South Alabama (1977-97), Southwestern Louisiana (1992-97), Texas-Pan American (1992-97), Western Kentucky (1983-97).

FORMER MEMBERS: Central Florida (1992), Georgia State (1977-81), UNC Charlotte (1977-91), Old Dominion (1983-91), South Florida (1977-91), UAB (1980-91), Virginia Commonwealth (1980-91).

NCAA TOURNAMENT RECORD: 21-34 (.382).

ALL-TIME SCORING LEADER: Charlie Bradley, South Florida (2,273 points from 1982-85).

SINGLE-SEASON SCORING LEADERS: Charlie Bradley, South Florida (901 points in 1982-83) and Greg Guy, Texas-Pan American (29.3 points per game in 1992-93).

REGULAR-SEASON CHAMPIONS: Arkansas-Little Rock (0 outright-1 tie), Louisiana Tech (0-1), New Orleans (1-1), UNC Charlotte (3-0), Old Dominion (1-1), South Alabama (4-1), Southwestern Louisiana (0-1), UAB (2-1), Virginia Commonwealth (2-2), Western Kentucky (3-0).

SUN BELT TOURNAMENT TITLES: UAB (4; 1982-83-84-87), Virginia Commonwealth (3; 1980-81-85), Jacksonville (2; 1979 and 1986), New Orleans (2; 1978 and 1996), UNC Charlotte (2; 1977 and 1988), South Alabama (2; 1989 and 1991), Southwestern Louisiana (2; 1992 and 1994), Western Kentucky (2; 1993 and 1995), South Florida (1; 1990).

YEAR-BY-YEAR CHAMPIONS (incl. conference records): 1977—UNC Charlotte (5-1); **1978**—UNC Charlotte (9-1); **1979**—South Alabama (10-0); **1980**—South Alabama (12-2); **1981**—Alabama-Birmingham (9-3), South Alabama (9-3), Virginia Commonwealth (9-3); **1982**—Alabama-Birmingham (9-1); **1983**—Old Dominion (12-2), Virginia Commonwealth (12-2); **1984**—Virginia Commonwealth (11-3); **1985**—Virginia Commonwealth (12-2); **1986**—Old Dominion (11-3); **1987**—Western Kentucky (12-2); **1988**—UNC Charlotte (11-3); **1989**—South Alabama (11-3); **1990**—Alabama-Birmingham (12-2); **1991**—South Alabama (11-3); **1992**—Louisiana Tech (13-3); **1993**—New Orleans (18-0); **1994**—Western Kentucky (14-4); **1995**—Western Kentucky (17-1); **1996**—Arkansas-Little Rock (14-4), New Orleans (14-4).

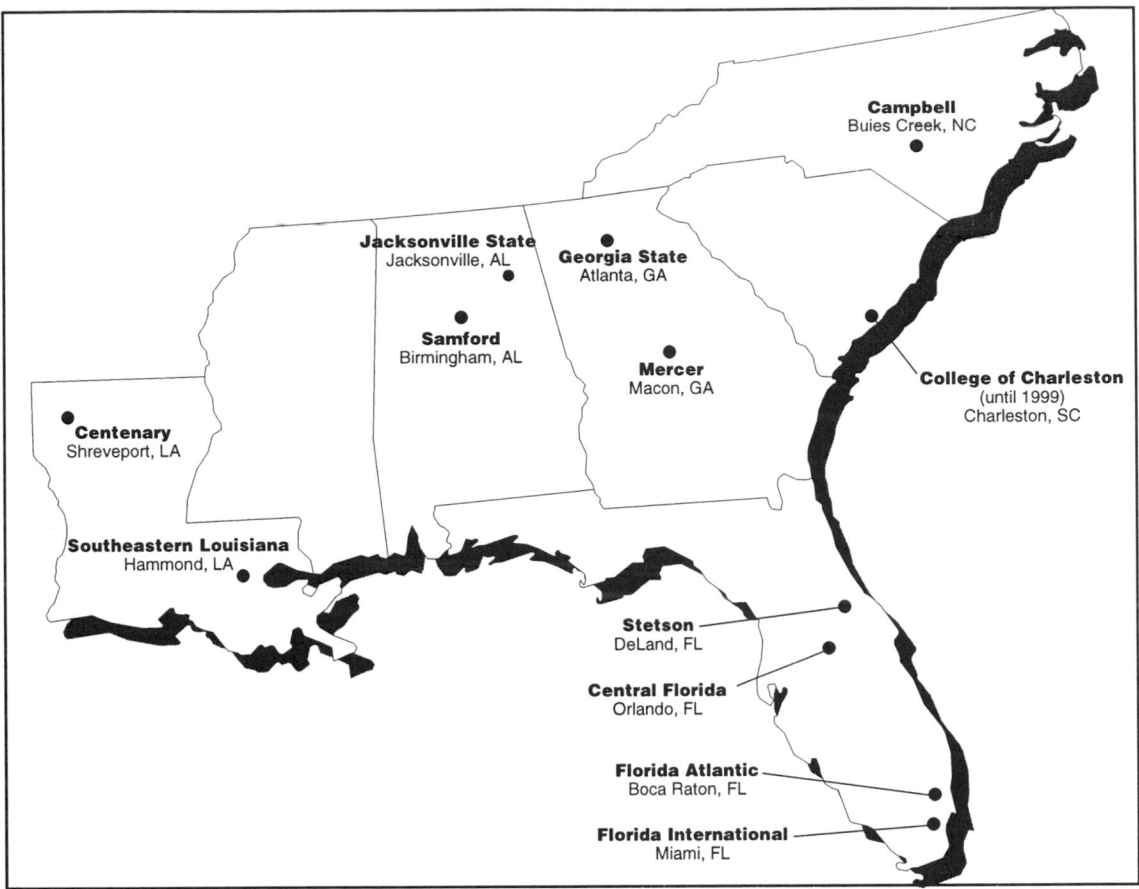

TRANS AMERICA ATHLETIC

ADDRESS: The Commons, Suite 108-B, 3370 Vineville Avenue, Macon, GA 31204.

PHONE/FAX: (912) 474-3394/4272.

CURRENT MEMBERS: Campbell (1995-97), Centenary (1980-97), Central Florida (1994-97), College of Charleston, S.C. (1994-97; will join the Southern Conference in 1999), Florida Atlantic (1996 and 1997), Florida International (1992-97), Georgia State (1985-97), Jacksonville, Ala., State (1996 and 1997), Mercer (1980-97), Samford (1980-97), Southeastern Louisiana (1992-97), Stetson (1987-97).

FORMER MEMBERS: Arkansas-Little Rock (1981-91), Georgia Southern (1981-92), Hardin-Simmons (1980-90), Houston Baptist (1980-89), Northeast Louisiana (1980-82), Northwestern State, La. (1981-84), Texas-Pan American (1980), Texas-San Antonio (1987-91).

NCAA TOURNAMENT RECORD: 1-16 (.059).

ALL-TIME SCORING LEADER: Willie Jackson, Centenary (2,535 points from 1981-84).

SINGLE-SEASON SCORING LEADERS: Sam Mitchell, Mercer (774 points in 1984-85) and Ernie Hill, Oklahoma City (26.6 points per game in 1978-79).

REGULAR-SEASON CHAMPIONS: Arkansas-Little Rock (4 outright-1 tie), Centenary (1-0), College of Charleston (3-0), Florida International (1-0), Georgia Southern (3-1), Houston Baptist (2-0), Northeast Louisiana (2-0), Texas-San Antonio (1-0).

TAAC TOURNAMENT TITLES: Arkansas-Little Rock (3; 1986-89-90), Georgia Southern (3; 1983-87-92), Central Florida (2; 1994 and 1996), Mercer (2; 1981 and 1985), Northeast Louisiana (2; 1979 and 1982), Centenary (1; 1980), Florida International (1; 1995), Georgia State (1; 1991), Houston Baptist (1; 1984), Texas-San Antonio (1; 1988).

YEAR-BY-YEAR CHAMPIONS (incl. conference records): 1980—Northeast Louisiana (6-0); **1981**—Houston Baptist (9-3); **1982**—Arkansas-Little Rock (12-4); **1983**—Arkansas-Little Rock (12-2); **1984**—Houston Baptist (11-3); **1985**—Georgia Southern (11-3); **1986**—Arkansas-Little Rock (12-2); **1987**—Arkansas-Little Rock (16-2); **1988**—Arkansas-Little Rock (15-3), Georgia Southern (15-3); **1989**—Georgia Southern (16-2); **1990**—Centenary (14-2); **1991**—Texas-San Antonio (12-2); **1992**—Georgia Southern (13-1); **1993**—Florida International (9-3); **1994**—College of Charleston (14-2); **1995**—College of Charleston (15-1); **1996**—College of Charleston (15-1).

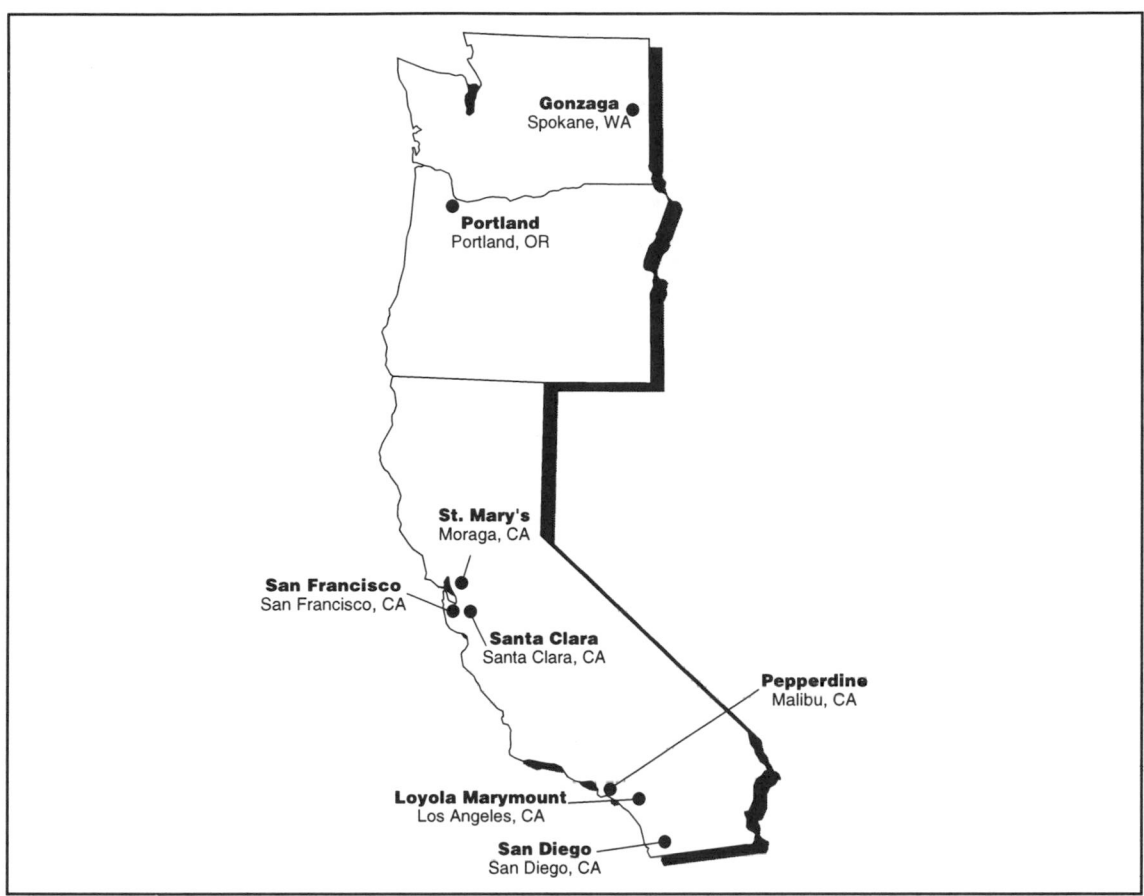

WEST COAST

ADDRESS: 400 Oyster Point Boulevard, Suite 221, South San Francisco, CA 94080.

PHONE/FAX: (415) 873-8622/7846.

PREVIOUS NAMES: California Basketball Association (1953-55) and West Coast Athletic (1956-88).

CURRENT MEMBERS: Gonzaga (1980-97), Loyola Marymount (1956-97), Pepperdine (1956-97), Portland (1977-97), St. Mary's (1953-97), San Diego (1980-97), San Francisco (1953-97), Santa Clara (1953-97).

FORMER MEMBERS: UC Santa Barbara (1965-69), Fresno State (1956 and 1957), Nevada-Reno (1970-79), Pacific (1953-71), San Jose State (1953-69), Seattle (1972-80), UNLV (1970-75).

NCAA TOURNAMENT RECORD: 44-50 (.468).

NCAA TITLES (2) : San Francisco (1955 and 1956).

ALL-TIME SCORING LEADER: Eric "Hank" Gathers, Loyola Marymount (2,490 points from 1988-90).

SINGLE-SEASON SCORING LEADERS: Greg "Bo" Kimble, Loyola Marymount (1,131 points in 1989-90) and William "Bird" Averitt, Pepperdine (33.9 points per game in 1972-73).

REGULAR-SEASON CHAMPIONS: Gonzaga (1 outright-1 tie), Loyola Marymount (3-0), Pacific (3-0), Pepperdine (9-1), St. Mary's (2-1), San Diego (2-0), San Francisco (13-2), Santa Clara (7-1), UNLV (1-0).

WCC TOURNAMENT TITLES: Pepperdine (3; 1991-92-94), Loyola Marymount (2; 1988 and 1989), Santa Clara (2; 1987 and 1993), Gonzaga (1; 1995), Portland (1; 1996).

YEAR-BY-YEAR CHAMPIONS (incl. conference records): 1953—San Francisco (6-2), Santa Clara (6-2)*; **1954**—Santa Clara (9-3); **1955**—San Francisco (12-0); **1956**—San Francisco (14-0); **1957**—San Francisco (12-2); **1958**—San Francisco (12-0); **1959**—St. Mary's (11-1); **1960**—Loyola Marymount (9-3), Santa Clara (9-3)*; **1961**—Loyola Marymount (10-2); **1962**—Pepperdine (11-1); **1963**—San Francisco (10-2); **1964**—San Francisco (12-0); **1965**—San Francisco (13-1); **1966**—Pacific (13-1); **1967**—Pacific (14-0); **1968**—Santa Clara (13-1); **1969**—Santa Clara (13-1); **1970**—Pacific (11-3), Santa Clara (11-3)*; **1971**—Pacific (12-2); **1972**—San Francisco (13-1); **1973**—San Francisco (12-2); **1974**—San Francisco (12-2); **1975**—UNLV (13-1); **1976**—Pepperdine (10-2); **1977**—San Francisco (14-0); **1978**—San Francisco (12-2); **1979**—San Francisco (12-2); **1980**—San Francisco (11-5), St. Mary's (11-5); **1981**—Pepperdine (11-3), San Francisco (11-3); **1982**—Pepperdine (14-0); **1983**—Pepperdine (10-2); **1984**—San Diego (9-3); **1985**—Pepperdine (11-1); **1986**—Pepperdine (13-1); **1987**—San Diego (13-1); **1988**—Loyola Marymount (14-0); **1989**—St. Mary's (12-2); **1990**—Loyola Marymount (13-1); **1991**—Pepperdine (13-1); **1992**—Pepperdine (14-0); **1993**—Pepperdine (11-3); **1994**—Gonzaga (12-2); **1995**—Santa Clara (12-2); **1996**—Gonzaga (10-4), Santa Clara (10-4).

*Won playoff.

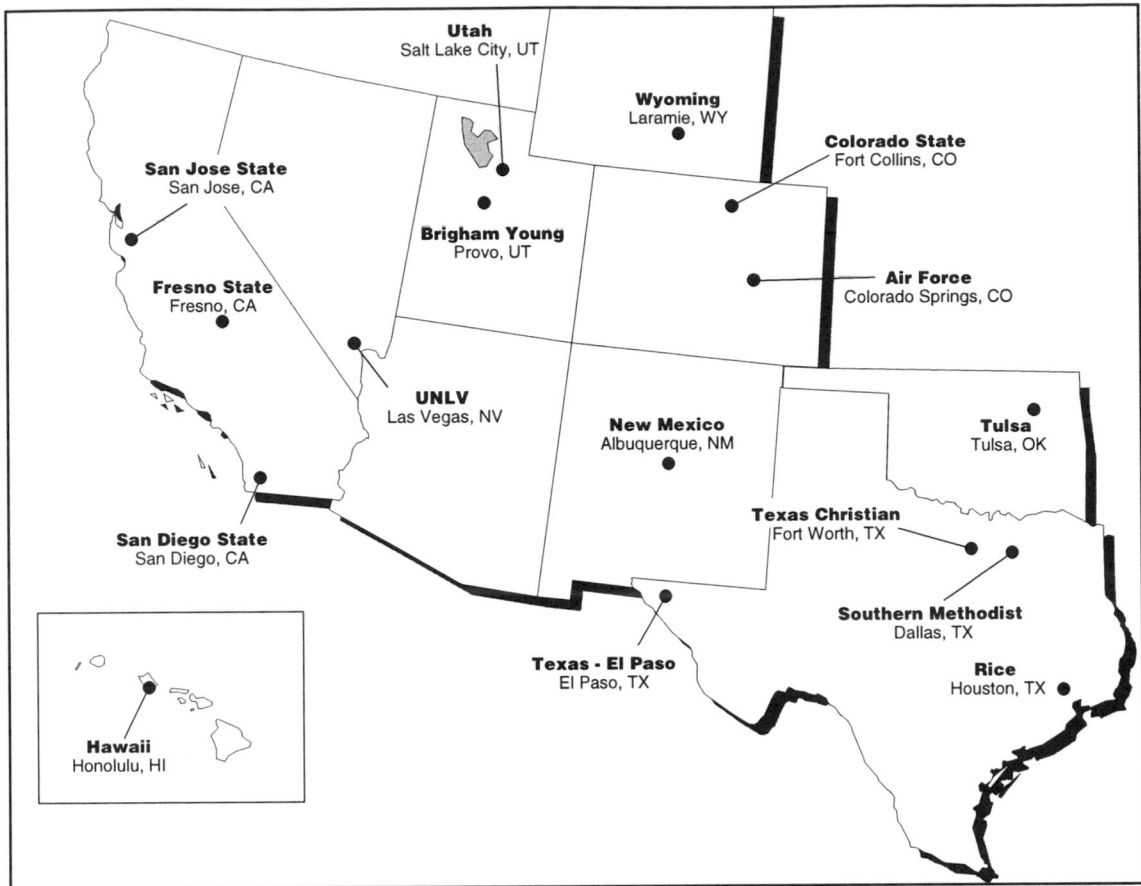

WESTERN ATHLETIC

ADDRESS: 9250 East Costilla Avenue, Suite 300, Englewood, CO 80112-3643.

TELEPHONE/FAX: (303) 799-9221/3888.

CURRENT MEMBERS: Air Force (1981-97), Brigham Young (1963-97), Colorado State (1970-97), Fresno State (1993-97), Hawaii (1980-97), New Mexico (1963-97), Rice (1997-), San Diego State (1979-97), San Jose State (1997-), Southern Methodist (1997-), Texas Christian (1997-), Texas-El Paso (1970-97), Tulsa (1997-), UNLV (1996 and 1997), Utah (1963-97), Wyoming (1963-97).

FORMER MEMBERS: Arizona (1963-78), Arizona State (1963-78).

NCAA TOURNAMENT RECORD: 41-64 (.390).

NCAA TITLES (1) : Texas-El Paso (1966). UTEP won the championship before joining the WAC.

NIT TITLES (4) : Brigham Young (1951 and 1966), Fresno State (1983), Utah (1947). The only one of the four NIT titles won as a member of the WAC was BYU in 1966.

ALL-TIME SCORING LEADER: Danny Ainge, Brigham Young (2,467 points from 1978-81).

SINGLE-SEASON SCORING LEADER: Jerry Chambers, Utah (28.8 points per game in 1965-66).

REGULAR-SEASON CHAMPIONS: Arizona (1 outright-0 ties), Arizona State (3-1), Brigham Young (6-5), Colorado State (1-1), New Mexico (4-1), Texas-El Paso (4-3), Utah (5-4), Wyoming (1-4).

WAC TOURNAMENT TITLES: Texas-El Paso (4; 1984-86-89-90), Brigham Young (2; 1991 and 1992), New Mexico (2; 1993 and 1996), Wyoming (2; 1987 and 1988), Hawaii (1; 1994), San Diego State (1; 1985), Utah (1; 1995).

YEAR-BY-YEAR CHAMPIONS (incl. conference records): 1963—Arizona State (9-1); **1964**—Arizona State (7-3), New Mexico (7-3); **1965**—Brigham Young (8-2); **1966**—Utah (7-3); **1967**—Brigham Young (8-2), Wyoming (8-2); **1968**—New Mexico (8-2); **1969**—Brigham Young (6-4), Wyoming (6-4); **1970**—Texas-El Paso (10-4); **1971**—Brigham Young (10-4); **1972**—Brigham Young (12-2); **1973**—Arizona State (10-4); **1974**—New Mexico (10-4); **1975**—Arizona State (12-2); **1976**—Arizona (11-3); **1977**—Utah (11-3); **1978**—New Mexico (13-1); **1979**—Brigham Young (10-2); **1980**—Brigham Young (13-1); **1981**—Utah (13-3), Wyoming (13-3); **1982**—Wyoming (14-2); **1983**—Brigham Young (11-5), Texas-El Paso (11-5), Utah (11-5); **1984**—Texas-El Paso (13-3); **1985**—Texas-El Paso (12-4); **1986**—Texas-El Paso (12-4), Utah (12-4), Wyoming (12-4); **1987**—Texas-El Paso (13-3); **1988**—Brigham Young (13-3); **1989**—Colorado State (12-4); **1990**—Brigham Young (11-5), Colorado State (11-5); **1991**—Utah (15-1); **1992**—Brigham Young (12-4), Texas-El Paso (12-4); **1993**—Brigham Young (15-3), Utah (15-3); **1994**—New Mexico (14-4); **1995**—Utah (15-3); **1996**—Utah (15-3).

Note: League split into two divisions in 1997–Mountain and Pacific.

FORMER MAJOR COLLEGE CONFERENCES

AMERICAN WEST (1995 AND 1996):

Cal Poly joined the Big West and Cal State Northridge and Sacramento State joined Big Sky.

MEMBERS: Cal Poly San Luis Obispo, Cal State Northridge, Sacramento State and Southern Utah.

REGULAR-SEASON CHAMPIONS: Cal Poly SLO (1 outright-0 ties), Southern Utah (1-0).

AWC TOURNAMENT TITLES: Southern Utah (2; 1995 and 1996).

YEAR-BY-YEAR CHAMPIONS (incl. conference records): 1995—Southern Utah (6-0); **1996**—Cal Poly SLO (5-1).

AMERICAN SOUTH (1988-91)

Merged with the Sun Belt.

MEMBERS: Arkansas State (1988-91), Lamar (1988-91), Louisiana Tech (1988-91), New Orleans (1988-91), Southwestern Louisiana (1988-91), Texas-Pan American (1988-91).

NCAA TOURNAMENT RECORD: 1-3 (.250).

REGULAR-SEASON CHAMPIONS: Arkansas State (0 outright-1 tie), Louisiana Tech (0-2), New Orleans (1-3).

AMERICAN SOUTH TOURNAMENT TITLES: Louisiana Tech (3; 1988-89-91), New Orleans (1; 1990).

YEAR-BY-YEAR CHAMPIONS (incl. conference records): 1988—Louisiana Tech (7-3), New Orleans (7-3); **1989**—New Orleans (7-3); **1990**—Louisiana Tech (8-2), New Orleans (8-2); **1991**—Arkansas State (9-3), New Orleans (9-3).

BIG EIGHT (1919-96):

Combined with half of Southwest Conference to form Big 12.

PREVIOUS NAMES: Big Six (1929 through 1947), Big Seven (1948 through 1958).

MEMBERS: Colorado (1948-96), Iowa State (1929-96), Kansas (1929-96), Kansas State (1929-96), Missouri (1929-96), Nebraska (1929-96), Oklahoma (1929-96), Oklahoma State (1959-96).

NCAA TOURNAMENT RECORD: 137-109 (.557).

NCAA TITLES (2) : Kansas (1952 and 1988).

NIT TITLES (1) : Nebraska (1996).

ALL-TIME SCORING LEADER: Danny Manning, Kansas (2,951 points from 1985-88).

SINGLE-SEASON SCORING LEADERS: Danny Manning, Kansas (942 points in 1987-88) and Wilt Chamberlain, Kansas (30.1 points per game in 1957-58).

REGULAR-SEASON CHAMPIONS: Colorado (3 outright-2 ties), Iowa State (2-2), Kansas (22-8), Kansas State (12-3), Missouri (9-2), Nebraska (0-3), Oklahoma (7-5), Oklahoma State (1-1).

BIG EIGHT TOURNAMENT TITLES: Missouri (6; 1978-82-87-89-91-93), Kansas (4; 1981-84-86-92), Oklahoma (4; 1979-85-88-90), Kansas State (2; 1977 and 1980), Iowa State (1; 1996), Nebraska (1; 1994), Oklahoma State (2; 1983 and 1995).

YEAR-BY-YEAR CHAMPIONS (incl. conference records): 1929—Oklahoma (10-0); **1930**—Missouri (8-2); **1931**—Kansas (7-3); **1932**—Kansas (7-3); **1933**—Kansas (8-2); **1934**—Kansas (9-1); **1935**—Iowa State (8-2); **1936**—Kansas (10-0); **1937**—Nebraska (8-2); **1938**—Kansas (9-1); **1939**—Missouri (7-3), Oklahoma (7-3); **1940**—Kansas (8-2)*, Missouri (8-2), Oklahoma (8-2); **1941**—Iowa State (7-3), Kansas (7-3); **1942**—Kansas (8-2), Oklahoma (8-2); **1943**—Kansas (10-0); **1944**—Iowa State (9-1), Oklahoma (9-1); **1945**—Iowa State (8-2); **1946**—Kansas (10-0); **1947**—Oklahoma (8-2); **1948**—Kansas State (9-3); **1949**—Nebraska (9-3), Oklahoma (9-3); **1950**—Kansas (8-4), Kansas State (8-4), Nebraska (8-4); **1951**—Kansas State (11-1); **1952**—Kansas (11-1); **1953**—Kansas (10-2); **1954**—Colorado (10-2), Kansas (10-2); **1955**—Colorado (11-1); **1956**—Kansas State (9-3); **1957**—Kansas (11-1); **1958**—Kansas State (10-2); **1959**—Kansas State (14-0); **1960**—Kansas (10-4)*, Kansas State (10-4); **1961**—Kansas State (13-1); **1962**—Colorado (13-1); **1963**—Colorado (11-3), Kansas State (11-3);

1964—Kansas State (12-2); **1965**—Oklahoma State (12-2); **1966**—Kansas (13-1); **1967**—Kansas (13-1); **1968**—Kansas State (11-3); **1969**—Colorado (10-4); **1970**—Kansas State (10-4); **1971**—Kansas (14-0); **1972**—Kansas State (12-2); **1973**—Kansas State (12-2); **1974**—Kansas (13-1); **1975**—Kansas (11-3); **1976**—Missouri (12-2); **1977**—Kansas State (11-3); **1978**—Kansas (13-1); **1979**—Oklahoma (10-4); **1980**—Missouri (11-3); **1981**—Missouri (10-4); **1982**—Missouri (12-2); **1983**—Missouri (12-2); **1984**—Oklahoma (13-1); **1985**—Oklahoma (13-1); **1986**—Kansas (13-1); **1987**—Missouri (11-3); **1988**—Oklahoma (12-2); **1989**—Oklahoma (12-2); **1990**—Missouri (12-2); **1991**—Kansas (10-4), Oklahoma State (10-4); **1992**—Kansas (11-3); **1993**—Kansas (11-3); **1994**—Missouri (14-0); **1995**—Kansas (11-3); **1996**—Kansas (12-2).

*Won playoff.

Note: Kansas won 13 of the 21 Missouri Valley Intercollegiate Athletic Association titles from 1908-28.

BORDER (1932-62):

Disbanded when the WAC was formed.

MEMBERS: Arizona (1932-61), Arizona State (1932-62), Hardin-Simmons (1942-62), New Mexico (1932-42 and 1945-51), New Mexico State (1932-62), Northern Arizona (1932-53), Texas-El Paso (1936-62), Texas Tech (1933-56), West Texas State (1942-62).

NCAA TOURNAMENT RECORD: 2-13 (.133).

REGULAR-SEASON CHAMPIONS: Arizona (7 outright-2 ties), Arizona State (2-2), Hardin-Simmons (0-1), New Mexico (1-0), New Mexico State (4-4), Texas Tech (5-1), Texas Western (2-1), West Texas A&M (2-2).

YEAR-BY-YEAR CHAMPIONS (incl. conference records): 1933—Texas Tech; **1934**—Texas Tech; **1935**—Texas Tech; **1936**—Arizona; **1937**—New Mexico State; **1938**—New Mexico State; **1939**—New Mexico State; **1940**—New Mexico State; **1941**—DNP; **1942**—West Texas A&M; **1943**—West Texas A&M; **1944**—Northern Arizona; **1945**—New Mexico; **1946**—Arizona*; **1947**—Arizona; **1948**—Arizona; **1949**—Arizona; **1950**—Arizona; **1951**—Arizona; **1952**—New Mexico State, West Texas A&M; **1953**—Arizona, Hardin-Simmons; **1954**—Texas Tech; **1955**—Texas Tech, West Texas A&M; **1956**—Texas Tech; **1957**—Texas Western; **1958**—Arizona State; **1959**—Arizona State, New Mexico State, Texas Western; **1960**—New Mexico State; **1961**—Arizona State, New Mexico State; **1962**—Arizona State.

*Won tournament for official title.

EASTERN INTERCOLLEGIATE (1933-39)

REGULAR-SEASON CHAMPIONS: Carnegie Tech (0 outright-2 ties), Georgetown (0-1), Pittsburgh (2-3), Temple (1-1), West Virginia (0-1).

YEAR-BY-YEAR CHAMPIONS (incl. conference records): 1933—Pittsburgh (7-1); **1934**—Pittsburgh (8-0); **1935**—Pittsburgh (6-2)*, West Virginia (6-2); **1936**—Carnegie Tech (7-3)*, Pittsburgh (7-3); **1937**—Pittsburgh (7-3)*, Temple (7-3); **1938**—Temple (9-1); **1939**—Carnegie Tech (6-4), Georgetown (6-4).

*Won playoff game.

GREAT MIDWEST (1992-95):

Most of league merged with Metro to form Conference USA.

MEMBERS: Cincinnati (1992-95), Dayton (1994 and 1995), DePaul (1992-95), Marquette (1992-95), Memphis (1992-95), Saint Louis (1992-95), UAB (1992-95).

NCAA TOURNAMENT RECORD: 16-13 (.552).

REGULAR-SEASON CHAMPIONS: Cincinnati (1 outright-1 tie), DePaul (0-1), Marquette (1-0), Memphis (1-0).

GMC TOURNAMENT TITLES: Cincinnati (all 4).

YEAR-BY-YEAR CHAMPIONS (incl. conference records): 1992—Cincinnati (8-2), DePaul (8-2), **1993** —Cincinnati (8-2); **1994**—Marquette (10-2); **1995**—Memphis (9-3).

GULF STAR (1985-87):

Members joined Southland or became independents before joining Trans America Athletic.

MEMBERS: Nicholls State (1985-87), Northwestern State (1985-87), Sam Houston State (1985-87), Southeastern Louisiana (1985-87), Southwest Texas State (1985-87), Stephen F. Austin State (1985-87).

REGULAR-SEASON CHAMPIONS: Sam Houston State (1986), Southeastern Louisiana (1985), Stephen F. Austin State (1987).

YEAR-BY-YEAR CHAMPIONS (incl. conference records): 1985—Southeastern Louisiana (9-1); **1986**—Sam Houston State (9-1); **1987**—Stephen F. Austin (10-0).

METRO (1976-95):

Much of league merged with Great Midwest to form Conference USA.

MEMBERS: Cincinnati (1976-91), Florida State (1977-91), Georgia Tech (1976-78), Louisville (1976-95), Memphis State (1976-91), UNC Charlotte (1992-95), St. Louis (1976-82), South Carolina (1984-91), Southern Mississippi (1983-95), South Florida (1992-95), Tulane (1976-85 and 1990-95), Virginia Commonwealth (1992-95), Virginia Tech (1979-95).

NCAA TITLES (2) : Louisville (1980 and 1986).

NIT TITLES (1) : Southern Mississippi (1987).

ALL-TIME SCORING LEADER: Bimbo Coles, Virginia Tech (2,484 points from 1987-90).

NCAA TOURNAMENT RECORD: 48-42 (.533).

REGULAR-SEASON CHAMPIONS: Florida State (2 outright-0 ties), Louisville (11-1), Memphis State (2-1), UNC Charlotte (1-0), Southern Mississippi (1-0), Tulane (1-0).

METRO TOURNAMENT TITLES: Louisville (11; 1978-80-81-83-86-88-89-90-93-94-95), Memphis State (4; 1982-84-85-87), Cincinnati (2; 1976 and 1977), Florida State (1; 1991), UNC Charlotte (1; 1992), Virginia Tech (1; 1979).

YEAR-BY-YEAR CHAMPIONS (incl. conference records): 1976—Tulane (1-0); **1977**—Louisville (6-1); **1978**—Florida State (11-1); **1979**—Louisville (9-1); **1980**—Louisville (12-0); **1981**—Louisville (11-1); **1982**—Memphis (10-2); **1983**—Louisville (12-0); **1984**—Louisville (11-3), Memphis (11-3); **1985**—Memphis (13-1); **1986**—Louisville (10-2); **1987**—Louisville (9-3); **1988**—Louisville (9-3); **1989**—Florida State (9-3); **1990**—Louisville (12-2); **1991**—Southern Miss. (10-4); **1992**—Tulane (8-4); **1993**—Louisville (11-1); **1994**—Louisville (10-2); **1994**—Louisville (10-2); **1995**—UNC Charlotte (8-4)

Note: Tulane's 1976 "title" is not recognized because the most league games any member played in that inaugural season was three.

METROPOLITAN COLLEGIATE (1966-69):

Disbanded with eight members, including Fairleigh Dickinson, Hofstra, Iona, Long Island, Manhattan, St. Peter's, Seton Hall and Wagner.

MEMBERS: Fairleigh Dickinson (1966-69), Hofstra (1966-69), Iona (1966-69), Long Island (1966-69), Manhattan (1966-69), New York University (1966 and 1967), St. Peter's (1966-69), St. Francis, N.Y. (1966-68), Seton Hall (1966-69), Wagner (1966-69).

REGULAR-SEASON CHAMPIONS: Manhattan (1 outright-2 ties), St. Francis, N.Y. (0-1), St. Peter's (1-2).

YEAR-BY-YEAR CHAMPIONS (incl. conference records): 1966—Manhattan (8-1); **1967**—Manhattan (7-2), St. Francis, N.Y. (7-2), St. Peter's (7-2); **1968**—St. Peter's (8-0); **1969**—Manhattan (7-1), St. Peter's (7-1).

MIDDLE ATLANTIC/EAST COAST (1959-94):

Middle Atlantic (1959-74) split into Eastern and Western sections the last five years of its existence before the majority of members wound up forming the ECC (1975-92 and '94). The ECC, which featured a divisional format its first nine years, merged with the Mid-Continent prior to start of 1994-95 season.

MEMBERS: American (1967-84), Brooklyn (1992), Bucknell (1959-90), Buffalo (1992 and 1994), Central Connecticut State (1991-94), Chicago State (1994), Delaware (1959-91), Drexel (1959-91), Gettysburg (1959-74), Hofstra (1966-94), Lafayette (1959-83), Lehigh (1959-90), Maryland-Baltimore County (1991 and 1992), Muhlenberg (1959-64), Northeastern Illinois (1994), Rider (1967-92), Rutgers (1959-62), St. Joseph's (1959-82), Temple (1959-82), Towson State (1983-92), Troy State (1994), West Chester State (1966-74).

NCAA TOURNAMENT RECORD: 12-37 (.245).

ECC REGULAR-SEASON CHAMPIONS: American (1 outright-2 ties), Bucknell (5-1), Drexel (1-0), Hofstra (1-3), Lafayette (5-2), La Salle (1-2), Lehigh (0-1), Rider (1-1), St. Joseph's (2-0), Temple (2-1), Towson State (1-1), West Chester State (1-0).

ECC TOURNAMENT TITLES: La Salle (4; 1975-78-80-83), Hofstra (3; 1976-77-94), Towson State (3; 1990-91-92), Bucknell (2; 1987 and

1989), Lehigh (2; 1985 and 1988), St. Joseph's (2; 1981 and 1982), Drexel (1; 1986), Rider (1; 1984), Temple (1; 1979).

YEAR-BY-YEAR CHAMPIONS (incl. conference records): 1959—St. Joseph's (7-0); **1960**—St. Joseph's (7-1); **1961**—St. Joseph's (8-0); **1962**—St. Joseph's (9-1); **1963**—St. Joseph's (8-0); **1964**—Temple (6-1); **1965**—St. Joseph's*; **1966**—St. Joseph's*; **1967**—Temple*; **1968**—La Salle*; **1969**—Temple*, St. Joseph's**; **1970**—St. Joseph's (5-0/E), Temple** (E), Lafayette (7-3/W), Lehigh (7-3/W), Rider (7-3/W); **1971**—St. Joseph's** (6-0/E), Lafayette (9-1/W); **972**—Temple** (6-0/E), Rider (8-2/W); **1973**—St. Joseph's** (6-0/E), Lafayette (7-3/W); **1974**—La Salle (5-1/E), St. Joseph's** (5-1/E), Rider (8-2/W); **1975**—American (5-1/E), La Salle (5-1/E), Lafayette (7-1/W); **1976**—St. Joseph's (4-1/E), Lafayette (9-1/W); **1977**—Temple (4-1/E), Hofstra (4-1/E), Lafayette (9-1/W); **1978**—La Salle (5-0/E), lafayette (10-0/W); **1979**—Temple (10-0/E), Bucknell (11-5/W); **1980**—St. Joseph's (10-1/E), Bucknell (13-3/W), Lafayette (13-3/W); **1981**—American (11-0/E), Lafayette (8-8/W), Rider (8-8/W); **1982**—Temple (11-0/E), West Chester State (8-8/W); **1983**—American (7-2/E), La Salle (7-2/E), Hofstra (7-2/E), Rider (10-3/W); **1984**—Bucknell (14-2); **1985**—Bucknell (10-4); **1986**—Drexel (11-3); **1987**—Bucknell (11-3); **1988**—Lafayette (11-3); **1989**—Bucknell (11-3); **1990**—Towson State (8-6); Hofstra (8-6), Lehigh (8-6), **1991**—Towson State (10-2); **1992**—Hofstra (10-2).

*No formal conference competition. Champion based on best regular-season record.

**Won playoff.

Note: ECC had a four-team playoff from 1970-74 with openers matching No. 1 in East vs. No. 2 in West and No. 1 in West vs. No. 2 in East.

MOUNTAIN STATES (1938-62 EXCEPT FOR 1944 AND 1945):

Seven members dropped out of the Rocky Mountain and formed the Mountain States Intercollegiate Athletic Conference after the 193c-37 season. The Mountain States was also informally known as the Big Seven before being dubbed the Skyline Six and then Eight (after Montana and New Mexico joined in 1952. Four teams from the Skyline and two from the Border Conference formed the Western Athletic Conference in 1962.

MEMBERS: Brigham Young (1938-62), Colorado State (1938-47), Colorado A&M/State (1938-62), Montana (1952-62), Montana State (1952-62), New Mexico (1952-62), Utah (1938-62), Utah State (1938-62), Wyoming (1938-62).

NCAA TOURNAMENT RECORD: 20-34 (.370).

REGULAR-SEASON CHAMPIONS: Brigham Young (4 outright-1 tie), Colorado (3-1), Colorado State (1-1), Utah (6-2), Wyoming (7-1).

YEAR-BY-YEAR CHAMPIONS: 1938—Colorado (10-2); Utah (10-2); **1939**—Colorado (10-2); **1940**—Colorado (11-1); **1941**—Wyoming (10-2); **1942**—Colorado 911-1); **1943**—Wyoming (4-0/E), Brigham Young (7-1/W); **1944**—No conference competition; **1945**—Utah (8-0); **1946**—Wyoming (10-2); **1947**—Wyoming (11-1); **1948**—Brigham Young (8-2); **1949**—Wyoming (15-5); **1950**—Brigham Young (14-6); **1951**—Brigham Young (15-5); **1952**—Wyoming (13-1); **1953**—Wyoming (12-2); **1954**—Colorado A&M (12-2); **1955**—Utah (13-1); **1956**—Utah (12-2); **1957**—Brigham Young (11-3); **1958**—Wyoming (10-4); **1959**—Utah (13-1); **1960**—Utah (13-1); **1961**—Colorado State (12-2), Utah (12-2)* ; **1962**—Utah (13-1).

*Won playoff.

NEW ENGLAND/YANKEE (1937-75):

Rhode Island won first eight championships, Connecticut won 17 titles in 20 years from 1948-67 and Massachusetts won outright or shared seven of last eight titles.

MEMBERS: Boston University (1973-76), Connecticut (1938-43 and 1946-76), Maine (1938-43 and 1946-76), Massachusetts (1947-76), New Hampshire (1938-43 and 1946-76), Northeastern (1938-43 and 1946), Rhode Island (1938-43 and 1946-76), Vermont (1947-76).

NCAA TOURNAMENT RECORD: 3-15 for Yankee (.167).

REGULAR-SEASON CHAMPIONS: Connecticut (15 outright-4 ties), Massachusetts (6-2), Rhode Island (10-4).

YEAR-BY-YEAR CHAMPIONS (incl. conference records): 1937—Rhode Island (8-0); **1938**—Rhode Island (8-0); **1939**—Rhode Island (7-1); **1940**—Rhode Island (8-0); **1941**—Connecticut (7-1), Rhode Island (7-1); **1942**—Rhode Island (8-0); **1943**—Rhode Island (7-1); **1944**—DNP; **1945**—DNP; **1946**—Rhode Island (4-0); **1947**—Vermont (1-0)*; **1948**—Connecticut (6-1); **1949**—Connecticut (7-1); **1950**—Rhode Island (6-1); **1951**—Connecticut (6-1); **1952**—Connecticut (6-1); **1953**—Connecticut (5-1); **1954**—Connecticut; **1955**—Connecticut; **1956**—Connecticut (6-1); **1957**—Connecticut (8-0); **1958**—Connecticut (10-0); **1959**—Connecticut (8-2); **1960**—Connecticut (8-2); **1961**—Rhode Island (9-1); **1962**—Massachusetts (8-2); **1963**—Connecticut (9-1); **1964**—Connecticut (8-2), Rhode Island (8-2); **1965**—Connecticut (10-0); **1966**—Connecticut (9-1), Rhode Island (9-1); **1967**—Connecticut (9-1); **1968**—Massachusetts (8-2), Rhode Island (8-2); **1969**—Massachusetts (9-1); **1970**—Connecticut (8-2), Massachusetts (8-2); **1971**—Massachusetts (10-0); **1972**—Rhode Island (8-2); **1973**—Massachusetts (10-2); **1974**—Massachusetts (11-1); **1975**—Massachusetts (10-2).

*Connecticut had the most league victories in the 1946-47 campaign with a 6-1 mark when the conference changed its name to Yankee.

ROCKY MOUNTAIN (1922-60):

Divisional format from 1925-37.

MEMBERS: Adams State (1958-63), Brigham Young (1925-37), Colorado (1923-37), Colorado A&M/State (1924-37), Colorado College (1923-63), Colorado School of Mines (1923-63), Colorado Teachers (1925-34) Denver (1923-37), Greeley State/Colorado State College/Northern Colorado (1935-63), Idaho State (1950-60), Montana State (1925-57 except for 1948), Utah (1925-37), Utah Agricultural/State (1925-37), Western State/Colorado Western (1925-63), Wyoming (1923-37).

REGULAR-SEASON CHAMPIONS: Brigham Young (2 outright-2 ties), Colorado (2-1), Colorado College (7-0), Colorado State (5-2), Denver (0-1), Idaho State (9-0), Montana State (8-3), Northern Colorado (5-0), Utah (2-3), Utah State (2-1), Wyoming (5-1).

YEAR-BY-YEAR CHAMPIONS: 1922—Colorado Col.; **1923**—Colorado Col. (7-1); **1924**—Colorado Col. (9-1); **1925**—Colorado Col. (10-3/E), Brigham Young (5-3/W); **1926**—Colorado State Col.(13-1/E), Utah (8-4/W); **1927**—Colorado Col. (12-2/E), Montana State (10-2/W); **1928**—Wyoming (9-3/E), Montana State (11-1/W); **1929**—Colorado (10-2/E), Montana State (11-1); **1930**—Colorado (11-3/E)Montana State (7-5/W), Utah State (7-5/W); **1931**—Wyoming (11-1/E), Utah (8-4/W); **1932**—Wyoming (12-0/E), Brigham Young (8-4/W), Utah (8-4/W); **1933**—Wyoming (12-2/E), Colorado State (12-2/E), Brigham Young (9-3/W), Utah (9-3/W); **1934**—Wyoming (14-0/E), Brigham Young (9-3/W); **1935**—Northern Colorado (9-3/E), Utah State (9-3/W); **1936**—Wyoming (11-3/E), Utah (9-3/W); **1937**—Denver (10-2/E), Colorado (10-2/E), Montana State (7-5/W), Utah (7-5/W); **1938**—Montana State (10-0); **1939**—Northern Colorado (7-3); **1940**—Northern Colorado (3-1); **1941**—Northern Colorado (9-5); **1942**—Northern Colorado (6-2); **1943**—Northern Colorado (5-3); **1944**—Colorado College (6-0); **1945**—Colorado College (2-0); **1946**—Colorado State (7-1); **1947**—Montana State (7-1); **1948**—Colorado State (5-1); **1949**—Colorado State (7-1); **1950**—Montana State (9-1); **1951**—Montana State (9-1); **1952**—Colorado State (8-2), Montana State (8-2); **1953**—Idaho State (10-0); **1954**—Idaho State (9-1); **1955**—Idaho State (9-1); **1956**—Idaho State (9-1); **1957**—Idaho State (12-0); **1958**—Idaho State (10-0); **1959**—Idaho State (9-1); **1960**—Idaho State (8-0).

SOUTHWEST (1915-96):

League disbanded with schools joining three different conferences (Big 12, Conference USA and WAC).

MEMBERS: Arkansas (1924-91), Baylor (1915-96), Houston (1976-96), Oklahoma A&M (1918 and 1922-25), Phillips, Okla. (1920), Rice (1915-96), Southern Methodist (1919-96), Southwestern, Tex. (1915 and 1916), Texas (1915-96), Texas A&M (1915-96), Texas Christian (1924-96), Texas Tech (1958-96).

NCAA TOURNAMENT RECORD: 75-89 (.457).

NIT TITLES (1) : Texas (1978).

ALL-TIME SCORING LEADER: Terrence Rencher, Texas (2,306 points from 1992-95).

SINGLE-SEASON SCORING LEADER: Otis Birdsong, Houston (30.3 points per game in 1976-77).

REGULAR-SEASON CHAMPIONS: Arkansas (14 outright-8 ties), Baylor (3-2), Houston (2-1), Oklahoma A&M (1-0), Rice (4-6), Southern Methodist (8-5), Texas (12-10), Texas A&M (9-2), Texas Christian (8-2), Texas Tech (4-2).

SWC TOURNAMENT TITLES: Arkansas (6; 1977-79-82-89-90-91), Houston (5; 1978-81-83-84-92), Texas Tech (5; 1976-85-86-93-96), Texas (2; 1994 and 1995), Texas A&M (2; 1980 and 1987), SMU (1; 1988).

YEAR-BY-YEAR CHAMPIONS (incl. conference records): 1915—Texas (5-0); **1916**—Texas (6-0); **1917**—Texas (7-1); **1918**—Rice (7-3); **1919**—Texas (11-2); **1920**—Texas A&M (16-0); **1921**—Texas A&M (10-2); **1922**—Texas A&M (13-3); **1923**—Texas A&M (15-3); **1924**—Texas (20-0); **1925**—Oklahoma A&M (12-2); **1926**—Arkansas (11-1); **1927**—Arkansas (8-2); **1928**—Arkansas (12-0); **1929**—Arkansas (11-1); **1930**—Arkansas (10-2); **1931**—Texas Christian (9-3); **1932**—Baylor (10-2); **1933**—Texas (11-1); **1934**—Texas Christian (10-2); **1935**—Arkansas (9-3), Rice (9-3), Southern Methodist (9-3); **1936**—Arkansas (11-1); **1937**—Southern Methodist (10-2); **1938**—Arkansas (11-1); **1939**—Texas (10-2); **1940**—Rice (10-2); **1941**—Arkansas (12-0); **1942**—Arkansas (10-2), Rice (10-2); **1943**—Rice (9-3), Texas (9-3); **1944**—Arkansas (11-1), Rice (11-1); **1945**—Rice (12-0); **1946**—Baylor (11-1); **1947**—Texas (12-0); **1948**—Baylor (11-1); **1949**—Arkansas (9-3)*, Baylor (9-3); Rice (9-3); **1950**—Arkansas (8-4), Baylor (8-4); **1951**—Texas (8-4), Texas A&M (8-4); **1952**—Texas Christian (11-1); **1953**—Texas Christian (9-3); **1954**—Rice (9-3)*, Texas (9-3); **1955**—Southern Methodist (9-3); **1956**—Southern Methodist (12-0); **1957**—Southern Methodist (11-1); **1958**—Arkansas (9-5)*, Southern Methodist (9-5); **1959**—Texas Christian (12-2); **1960**—Texas (11-3); **1961**—Texas Tech (11-3); **1962**—Southern Methodist (11-3), Texas Tech (11-3)*; **1963**—Texas (13-1); **1964**—Texas A&M (13-1); **1965**—Southern Methodist (10-4)*, Texas (10-4); **1966**—Southern Methodist (11-3); **1967**—Southern Methodist (12-2); **1968**—Texas Christian (9-5); **1969**—Texas A&M (12-2); **1970**—Rice (10-4); **1971**—Texas Christian (11-3); **1972**—Southern Methodist (10-4), Texas (10-4)*; **1973**—Texas Tech (12-2); **1974**—Texas (11-3); **1975**—Texas A&M (12-2); **1976**—Texas A&M (14-2); **1977**—Arkansas (16-0); **1978**—Arkansas (14-2), Texas (14-2); **1979**—Arkansas (13-3), Texas (13-3); **1980**—Texas A&M (14-2); **1981**—Arkansas (13-3); **1982**—Arkansas (12-4); **1983**—Houston (16-0); **1984**—Houston (15-1); **1985**—Texas Tech (12-4); **1986**—Texas (12-4), Texas A&M (12-4), Texas Christian (12-4); **1987**—Texas Christian (14-2); **1988**—Southern Methodist (12-4); **1989**—Arkansas (13-3); **1990**—Arkansas (14-2); **1991**—Arkansas (15-1); **1992**—Houston (11-3), Texas (11-3); **1993**—Southern Methodist (12-2); **1994**—Texas (12-2); **1995**—**Texas (11-3), Texas Tech (11-3)**; 1996—**Texas Tech (14-0)**.

*Won playoff.

BASKETBALL ORGANIZATIONS

AMATEUR ATHLETIC UNION (AAU)

6571 Forum Drive, Suite 200
Orlando, FL 32821
Phone/Fax: (407) 363-6170/6171

BLACK COACHES ASSOCIATION (BCA)

Rudy Washington, Executive Director
1900 13th Street, Suite 200
Boulder, CO 80302
Phone/Fax: (515) 327-1248/(303) 449-3813

COLLEGE SPORTS INFORMATION DIRECTORS OF AMERICA

c/o Fred Nuesch
Texas A&M-Kingsville
Campus Box 114A
Kingsville, TX 78363
Phone/Fax: (512) 595-3908/0389

COMMUNITY COLLEGE LEAGUE OF CALIFORNIA

2017 "O" Street
Sacramento, CA 95814
Phone/Fax: (916) 444-8641/2954

INTERNATIONAL BASKETBALL FEDERATION (FIBA)

Post Office Box 700607
D-81306 Munchen Germany
Phone/Fax: 011 4989 7481 580/5888

NAISMITH MEMORIAL HALL OF FAME

1150 West Columbus Avenue
Springfield, MA 01101-0179
Phone/Fax: (413) 781-6500/1939

NATIONAL ASSOCIATION OF BASKETBALL COACHES (NABC)

9300 West 110th Street, Suite 640
Overland Park, KS 66210-1486
Phone/Fax: (913) 469-1001/1390

NATIONAL ASSOCIATION OF INTERCOLLEGIATE ATHLETICS (NAIA)

6120 South Yale Avenue, Suite 1450
Tulsa, OK 74136-4223
Phone/Fax: (918) 494-8828/8841

NATIONAL COLLEGIATE ATHLETIC ASSOCIATION (NCAA)

6201 College Boulevard
Overland Park, KS 66211-2422
Phone/Fax: (913) 339-1906/1950

NATIONAL INVITATION TOURNAMENT (NIT)

Downtown Athletic Club
19 West Street, Suite 2010
New York, NY 10004
Phone/Fax: (212) 425-6510/785/0594

NATIONAL JUNIOR COLLEGE ATHLETIC ASSOCIATION (NJCAA)

P.O. Box 7305
Colorado Springs, CO 80933-7305
Phone/Fax: (719) 590-9788/7324

UNITED STATES BASKETBALL WRITERS ASSOCIATION (USBWA)

c/o Joe Mitch, Executive Director
1000 St. Louis Union Station, Suite 333
St. Louis, MO 63103
Phone/Fax: (314) 421-0339/3505

USA BASKETBALL

5465 Mark Dabling Boulevard
Colorado Springs, CO 80918-3842
Phone/Fax: (719) 590-4800/4811

WOMEN'S BASKETBALL COACHES ASSOCIATION (WBCA)

4646 B Lawrenceville Highway
Lilburn, GA 30247-3620
Phone/Fax: (770) 279-8027/8473

16

SCHOOL DIRECTORY

In 1950, 145 schools were classified as major colleges. Forty years later, the number of NCAA Division I institutions had more than doubled to in excess of 300. Here are vital facts for those schools that meet any of the following criteria:

- Classified as major colleges for more than 40 years.

- Had at least one player earn a spot as an NCAA consensus first- or second-team All-American.

- Won at least one NCAA Tournament game.

- Reached the NIT semifinals.

- Member of a conference that supplied an NCAA champion.

- Participated in one of the two national runner-up tournaments in 1974 or 1975.

AIR FORCE

OFFICIAL NAME: United States Air Force Academy.
NICKNAME: Falcons.
ADDRESS: Building 2169, Room 1050, Colorado Springs, CO 80840-5461.

PHONE/FAX: (719) 472-2313/3798.
ENROLLMENT: 4,400.
ARENA: Clune Arena (Capacity-6,007; Year Opened-1968).
SCHOOL COLORS: Blue and Silver.
CONFERENCE: Western Athletic.
NCAA TOURNAMENT APPEARANCES (2): 1960 and 1962; 0-2 record.
NIT APPEARANCES: None.
ALL-TIME SCORING LEADER: Raymond Dudley (2,178 points from 1987-90).
ALL-TIME REBOUNDING LEADER: Reggie Jones (776 from 1978-81).

ALABAMA

OFFICIAL NAME: University of Alabama.
NICKNAME: Crimson Tide.
ADDRESS: Post Office Box 870391, Tuscaloosa, AL 35487-0391.
PHONE/FAX: (205) 348-6084/8841.
ENROLLMENT: 20,000.
ARENA: Coleman Coliseum (Capacity-15,043; Year Opened-1968).
SCHOOL COLORS: Crimson and White.
CONFERENCE: Southeastern.
FINAL AP TOP 10 RANKINGS (4): 1956-75-76-87.
NCAA TOURNAMENT APPEARANCES: (14) 1975-76-82-83-84-85-86-87-89-90-91-92-94-95; 15-14 record (.517); never reached regional final.
NIT APPEARANCES (7): 1973-77-79-80-81-93-96; 13-10 record (.565); finished 4th in 1973, 4th in 1977, 3rd in 1979 and 4th in 1996.
ALL-TIME SCORING LEADER: Reggie King (2,168 points from 1976-79).
ALL-TIME REBOUNDING LEADER: Jerry Harper (1,688 from 1953-56).
NCAA CONSENSUS SECOND-TEAM ALL-AMERICANS (1): Leon Douglas (1975).

ALCORN STATE

OFFICIAL NAME: Alcorn State University.

NICKNAME: Braves.

ADDRESS: Post Office Box 510, Lorman, MS 39096.

PHONE/FAX: (601) 877-6466/3821.

ENROLLMENT: 3,300.

ARENA: Davey L. Whitney Complex (Capacity-7,000; Year Opened-1974).

SCHOOL COLORS: Purple and Old Gold.

CONFERENCE: Southwestern Athletic.

NCAA DIVISION I TOURNAMENT APPEARANCES (4): 1980-82-83-84; 3-4 record (.429).

NCAA DIVISION II TOURNAMENT APPEARANCES (1): 1969; 1-1 record (.500).

NAIA TOURNAMENT APPEARANCES (7): 1967-68-73-74-75-76-77; 11-7 record (.611); finished 2nd in 1974 and 3rd in 1975.

NIT APPEARANCES (2): 1979 and 1985; 1-2 record (.333).

ALL-TIME SCORING LEADER: Richard Smith (2,527 points from 1953-56 when school was classified at the NAIA level).

ALL-TIME REBOUNDING LEADER: Alfred Milton (1,432 from 1972-75 when school was classified as a small college).

AMERICAN

OFFICIAL NAME: American University.

NICKNAME: Eagles.

ADDRESS: 224 Bender Arena, 4400 Massachusetts Avenue, NW, Washington, DC 20016-8005.

PHONE/FAX: (202) 885-3032/3033.

ENROLLMENT: 11,500.

ARENA: Bender Arena (Capacity-5,000; Year Opened-1988).

SCHOOL COLORS: Red, White and Blue.

CONFERENCE: Colonial Athletic Association.

NCAA DIVISION I TOURNAMENT APPEARANCES: None.

NCAA DIVISION II TOURNAMENT APPEARANCES (3): 1958-59-60; 6-3 record (.667).

NAIA TOURNAMENT APPEARANCES (2): 1950 and 1951; 0-2 record.

NIT APPEARANCES (3): 1973-81-82; 0-3 record.

ALL-TIME SCORING LEADER: Russell "Boo" Bowers (2,065 points from 1978-81).

ALL-TIME REBOUNDING LEADER: Kermit Washington (1,478 from 1971-73).

NCAA CONSENSUS SECOND-TEAM ALL-AMERICANS (1): Kermit Washington (1973).

ARIZONA

OFFICIAL NAME: University of Arizona.

NICKNAME: Wildcats.

ADDRESS: McKale Center, Tucson, AZ 85721.

PHONE/FAX: (602) 621-4163/2681.

ENROLLMENT: 35,305.

ARENA: McKale Center (Capacity-14,257; Year Opened-1973).

SCHOOL COLORS: Cardinal and Navy.

CONFERENCE: Pacific-10.

FINAL AP TOP 10 RANKINGS (6): 1988-89-91-92-93-94.

NCAA TOURNAMENT APPEARANCES (15): 1951-76-77-85-86-87-88-89-90-91-92-93-94-95-96; 17-15 record (.531); reached Final Four in 1988 (T3rd) and 1994 (T3rd).

NIT APPEARANCES (3): 1946-50-51; 0-3 record.

CCAT RECORD: 2-1 to finish 2nd in 1975.

ALL-TIME SCORING LEADER: Sean Elliott (2,535 points from 1986-89).

ALL-TIME REBOUNDING LEADER: Al Fleming (1,190 from 1973-76).

NCAA CONSENSUS FIRST-TEAM ALL-AMERICANS (3): Sean Elliott (1988 and 1989), Damon Stoudamire (1995).

NCAA CONSENSUS SECOND-TEAM ALL-AMERICANS (1): Khalid Reeves (1994).

ARIZONA STATE

OFFICIAL NAME: Arizona State University.

NICKNAME: Sun Devils.

ADDRESS: IAC Building, Room 105, Tempe, AZ 85287-2505.

PHONE/FAX: (602) 965-6592/5408.

ENROLLMENT: 42,625.

ARENA: University Activity Center (Capacity-14,198; Year Opened-1974).

SCHOOL COLORS: Maroon and Gold.

CONFERENCE: Pacific-10.

FINAL AP TOP 10 RANKINGS (3): 1963-75-81.

NCAA TOURNAMENT APPEARANCES (11): 1958-61-62-63-64-73-75-80-81-91-95; 11-12 record (.478); regional runner-up in 1961, 1963 and 1975.

NAIA TOURNAMENT APPEARANCES (2): 1948 and 1953; 2-2 record (.500).

NIT APPEARANCES (5): 1983-90-92-93-94; 2-5 record (.286).

CCAT RECORD: 0-1 in 1974.

ALL-TIME SCORING LEADER: Ron Riley (1,834 points from 1993-96).

ALL-TIME REBOUNDING LEADER: Tony Cerkvenik (1,022 from 1960-63).

ARKANSAS

OFFICIAL NAME: University of Arkansas.

NICKNAME: Razorbacks.

ADDRESS: Post Office Box 7777, Fayetteville, AR 72702.

PHONE/FAX: (501) 575-2751/7481.

ENROLLMENT: 14,600.

ARENA: Bud Walton Arena (Capacity-19,200; Year Opened-1993).

SCHOOL COLORS: Cardinal and White.

CONFERENCE: Southeastern.

FINAL AP TOP 10 RANKINGS (9): 1978-79-83-84-90-91-92-94-95.

NCAA TOURNAMENT APPEARANCES (22): 1941-45-49-58-77-78-79-80-81-82-83-84-85-88-89-90-91-92-93-94-95-96; 37-22 record (.627); reached Final Four in 1941 (T3rd), 1945 (T3rd), 1978 (3rd), 1990 (T3rd), 1994 (1st) and 1995 (2nd).

NIT APPEARANCES (1): 1987; 1-1 record (.500).

ALL-TIME SCORING LEADER: Todd Day (2,395 points from 1989-92).

ALL-TIME REBOUNDING LEADER: Sidney Moncrief (1,015 from 1976-79).

NCAA CONSENSUS FIRST-TEAM ALL-AMERICANS (3): Ike Poole (1936), John Adams (1941), Sidney Moncrief (1979).

NCAA CONSENSUS SECOND-TEAM ALL-AMERICANS (4): Ron Brewer (1978), Darrell Walker (1983), Corliss Williamson (1994 and 1995).

ARKANSAS-LITTLE ROCK

OFFICIAL NAME: University of Arkansas at Little Rock (UALR).

NICKNAME: Trojans.

ADDRESS: 2801 South University Avenue, Little Rock, AR 72204.

PHONE/FAX: (501) 569-3449/3030.

ENROLLMENT: 12,420.

ARENA: Barton Coliseum (Capacity-8,303; Year Opened-1952).

SCHOOL COLORS: Maroon and Gold.

CONFERENCE: Sun Belt.

NCAA TOURNAMENT APPEARANCES (3): 1986-89-90; 1-3 record (.250).

NIT APPEARANCES (3): 1987-88-96; 3-4 record (.429); finished 4th in 1987.

ALL-TIME SCORING LEADER: James Scott (1,731 points from 1988-91).

ALL-TIME REBOUNDING LEADER: Larry Johnson (1,315 from 1975-78 when school was classified as a small college).

ARKANSAS STATE

OFFICIAL NAME: Arkansas State University.

NICKNAME: Indians.

ADDRESS: Post Office Box 1000, State University, AR 72467.

PHONE/FAX: (501) 972-2541/3367.

ENROLLMENT: 9,820.

ARENA: Convocation Center (Capacity-10,563; Year Opened-1987).

SCHOOL COLORS: Scarlet and Black.

CONFERENCE: Sun Belt.

NCAA DIVISION I TOURNAMENT APPEARANCES: None.

NCAA DIVISION II TOURNAMENT APPEARANCES (6): 1958-60-62-63-66-67; 5-7 record (.417).

NIT APPEARANCES (4): 1987-88-89-91; 4-4 record (.500).

NAIA TOURNAMENT APPEARANCES (2): 1947 and 1949; 0-2 record.

ALL-TIME SCORING LEADER: Jerry Rook (2,153 points from 1962-65 when school was classified as a small college).

ALL-TIME REBOUNDING LEADER: John Belcher (1,166 from 1969-72; school was classified as a small college his first two years).

ARMY

OFFICIAL NAME: United States Military Academy.

NICKNAMES: Black Knights, Cadets.

ADDRESS: 639 Howard Road, West Point, NY 10996-9906.

PHONE/FAX: (914) 938-3512/446-2556.

ENROLLMENT: 4,200.

ARENA: Christl Arena (Capacity-5,043; Year Opened-1985).

SCHOOL COLORS: Black, Gold and Gray.

CONFERENCE: Patriot League.

NCAA TOURNAMENT APPEARANCES: None.

NIT APPEARANCES (8): 1961-64-65-66-68-69-70-78; 13-10 record (.565); finished 3rd in 1964, 3rd in 1965, 4th in 1966, 4th in 1969 and 3rd in 1970.

ALL-TIME SCORING LEADER: Kevin Houston (2,325 points from 1984-87).

ALL-TIME REBOUNDING LEADER: Gary Winton (1,168 from 1975-78).

NCAA CONSENSUS SECOND-TEAM ALL-AMERICANS (2): Dale Hall (1944 and 1945).

AUBURN

OFFICIAL NAME: Auburn University.

NICKNAME: Tigers.

ADDRESS: Post Office Box 351, Auburn, AL 36831-0351.

PHONE/FAX: (334) 844-9701/9708.

ENROLLMENT: 22,120.

ARENA: Beard-Eaves Memorial Coliseum (Capacity-10,108; Year Opened-1969).

SCHOOL COLORS: Burnt Orange and Navy Blue.

CONFERENCE: Southeastern.

FINAL AP TOP 10 RANKINGS (1): 1959.

NCAA TOURNAMENT APPEARANCES (5): 1984-85-86-87-88; 7-5 record (.583); regional runner-up in 1986.

NIT APPEARANCES (3): 1993-95-96; 0-3 record.

ALL-TIME SCORING LEADER: Chuck Person (2,311 points from 1983-86).

ALL-TIME REBOUNDING LEADER: Mike Mitchell (996 from 1975-78).

AUSTIN PEAY STATE

OFFICIAL NAME: Austin Peay State University.

NICKNAME: Governors.

ADDRESS: Box 4515, Clarksville, TN 37044.

PHONE/FAX: (615) 648-7561/7562.

ENROLLMENT: 8,200.

ARENA: Dunn Center (Capacity-9,092; Year Opened-1975).

SCHOOL COLORS: Red and White.

CONFERENCE: Ohio Valley.

NCAA DIVISION I TOURNAMENT APPEARANCES (4): 1973-74-87-96; 2-5 record (.286).

NCAA DIVISION II TOURNAMENT APPEARANCES (4): 1958-60-61-63; 3-6 record (.333).

NAIA TOURNAMENT APPEARANCES (1): 1957; 0-1 record.

NIT APPEARANCES: None.

ALL-TIME SCORING LEADER: Tom Morgan (1,850 points in 1953 and from 1956-58 when school was classified as a small college).

ALL-TIME REBOUNDING LEADER: Tom Morgan (1,431 in 1953 and from 1956-58 when school was classified as a small college).

BALL STATE

OFFICIAL NAME: Ball State University.

NICKNAME: Cardinals.

ADDRESS: HP 120, Muncie, IN 47306-0929.

PHONE/FAX: (317) 285-8242/8929.

ENROLLMENT: 20,717.

ARENA: University Arena (Capacity-11,500; Year Opened-1992).

SCHOOL COLORS: Cardinal and White.

CONFERENCE: Mid-American.

NCAA DIVISION I TOURNAMENT APPEARANCES (6): 1981-86-89-90-93-95; 3-6 record (.333).

NCAA DIVISION II TOURNAMENT APPEARANCES (1): 1964; 0-2 record.

NAIA TOURNAMENT APPEARANCES (1): 1957; 1-1 record (.500).

NIT APPEARANCES (2): 992; 0-2 record.

ALL-TIME SCORING LEADER: Ray McCallum (2,109 points from 1980-83).

ALL-TIME REBOUNDING LEADER: Ed Butler (1,231 from 1962-64 when school was classified as a small college).

BAYLOR

OFFICIAL NAME: Baylor University.

NICKNAME: Bears.

ADDRESS: 3031 Dutton, Waco, TX 76711.

PHONE/FAX: (817) 755-3066/1369.

ENROLLMENT: 12,500.

ARENA: Ferrell Center (Capacity-10,084; Year Opened-1988).

SCHOOL COLORS: Green and Gold.

CONFERENCE: Big 12.

NCAA TOURNAMENT APPEARANCES (4): 1946-48-50-88; 3-6 record (.333); reached Final Four in 1948 (2nd) and 1950 (4th).

NIT APPEARANCES (2): 1987 and 1990; 0-2 record.

ALL-TIME SCORING LEADER: Terry Teagle (2,189 points from 1979-82).

ALL-TIME REBOUNDING LEADER: Jerry Mallett (877 from 1955-57).

BOISE STATE

OFFICIAL NAME: Boise State University.

NICKNAME: Broncos.

ADDRESS: 1910 University Drive, Boise, ID 83725.

PHONE/FAX: (208) 385-3868/3361.

ENROLLMENT: 15,060.

ARENA: BSU Pavilion (Capacity-12,380; Year Opened-1982).

SCHOOL COLORS: Blue and Orange.

CONFERENCE: Big West.

NCAA DIVISION I TOURNAMENT APPEARANCES (4): 1976-88-93-94; 0-4 record.

NCAA DIVISION II TOURNAMENT APPEARANCES (1): 1970; 1-1 record (.500).

NIT APPEARANCES (3): 1987-89-91; 1-3 record (.250).

ALL-TIME SCORING LEADER: Tanoka Beard (1,944 points from 1990-93).

ALL-TIME REBOUNDING LEADER: Bill Otey (805 from 1969 and 1970 when school was classified as a small college).

BOSTON COLLEGE

NICKNAME: Eagles.

ADDRESS: Conte Forum 321, Chestnut Hill, MA 02167.

PHONE/FAX: (617) 552-3004/4903.

ENROLLMENT: 9,165.

ARENA: Silvio O. Conte Forum (Capacity-8,606; Year Opened-1988).

SCHOOL COLORS: Maroon and Gold.

CONFERENCE: Big East.

FINAL AP TOP 10 RANKINGS (1): 1967.

NCAA TOURNAMENT APPEARANCES (10): 1958-67-68-75-81-82-83-85-94-96; 15-11 record (.577); regional runner-up in 1967, 1982 and 1994.

NIT APPEARANCES (9): 1965-66-69-74-80-84-88-92-93; 15-10 record (.600); finished 2nd in 1969, 3rd in 1974 and 4th in 1988.

ALL-TIME SCORING LEADER: Dana Barros (2,342 points from 1986-89).

ALL-TIME REBOUNDING LEADER: Terry Driscoll (1,071 from 1967-69).

BOSTON UNIVERSITY

NICKNAME: Terriers.

ADDRESS: 285 Babcock Street, Boston, MA 02215.

PHONE/FAX: (617) 353-2872/4286.

ENROLLMENT: 13,665.

ARENA: Case Gym (Capacity-2,500; Year Opened-1971).

SCHOOL COLORS: Scarlet and White.

CONFERENCE: North Atlantic.

NCAA TOURNAMENT APPEARANCES (4): 1959-83-88-90; 2-4 record (.333); regional runner-up in 1959.

NIT APPEARANCES (2): 1980 and 1986; 0-2 record.

ALL-TIME SCORING LEADER: Drederick Irving (1,931 points from 1985-88).

ALL-TIME REBOUNDING LEADER: James Garvin (935 from 1971-73).

BOWLING GREEN STATE

OFFICIAL NAME: Bowling Green State University.

NICKNAME: Falcons.

ADDRESS: BGSU Athletic Department, Bowling Green, OH 43403-0030.

PHONE/FAX: (419) 372-7076/6015.

ENROLLMENT: 17,000.

ARENA: Anderson Arena (Capacity-5,000; Year Opened-1960).

SCHOOL COLORS: Brown and Orange.

CONFERENCE: Mid-American.

FINAL AP TOP 10 RANKINGS (2): 1949 and 1962.

NCAA TOURNAMENT APPEARANCES (4): 1959-62-63-68; 1-5 record (.167).

NIT APPEARANCES (10): 1944-45-46-48-49-54-80-83-90-91; 6-10 record (.375); finished 2nd in 1945 and 3rd in 1949.

NCIT Record: 1-1 in 1975.

ALL-TIME SCORING LEADER: Howard Komives (1,834 points from 1962-64).

ALL-TIME REBOUNDING LEADER: Nate Thurmond (1,295 from 1961-63).

NCAA CONSENSUS FIRST-TEAM ALL-AMERICANS (1): Wyndol Gray (1945 before playing for Harvard the next season).

NCAA CONSENSUS SECOND-TEAM ALL-AMERICANS (1): Nate Thurmond (1963).

BRADLEY

OFFICIAL NAME: Bradley University.

NICKNAME: Braves.

ADDRESS: 1501 West Bradley Avenue, Peoria, IL 61625.

PHONE/FAX: (309) 677-2624/2626.

ENROLLMENT: 6,000.

ARENA: Carver Arena (Capacity-10,825; Year Opened-1982).

SCHOOL COLORS: Red and White.

CONFERENCE: Missouri Valley.

FINAL AP TOP 10 RANKINGS (8): 1949-50-51-54-59-60-61-62.

NCAA TOURNAMENT APPEARANCES (7): 1950-54-55-80-86-88-96; 9-7 record (.563); reached Final Four in 1950 (2nd) and 1954 (2nd).

NIT APPEARANCES (17): 1938-39-47-49-50-57-58-59-60-62-64-65-68-82-85-94-95; 24-14 record (.632); finished 3rd in 1939, 4th in 1949, 2nd in 1950, 1st in 1957, 2nd in 1959, 1st in 1960, 1st in 1964 and 1st in 1982.

CCAT RECORD: 1-1 in 1974.

ALL-TIME SCORING LEADER: Hersey Hawkins (3,008 points from 1985-88).

ALL-TIME REBOUNDING LEADER: Dick Estergard (1,414 from 1952-54).

NCAA CONSENSUS FIRST-TEAM ALL-AMERICANS (5): Paul Unruh (1950), Gene Melchiorre (1951), Chet Walker (1961 and 1962), Hersey Hawkins (1988).

BRIGHAM YOUNG

OFFICIAL NAME: Brigham Young University.

NICKNAME: Cougars.

ADDRESS: 30 Smith Fieldhouse, Provo, UT 84602.

PHONE/FAX: (801) 378-4911/3520.

ENROLLMENT: 27,000.

ARENA: Marriott Center (Capacity-22,700; Year Opened-1971).

SCHOOL COLORS: Royal Blue and White.

CONFERENCE: Western Athletic.

FINAL AP TOP 10 RANKINGS (2): 1965 and 1972.

NCAA TOURNAMENT APPEARANCES (18): 1950-51-57-65-69-71-72-79-80-81-84-87-88-90-91-92-93-95; 11-21 record (.344); regional runner-up in 1950, 1951 and 1981.

NAIA TOURNAMENT APPEARANCES (2): 1948 and 1949; 2-2 record (.500).

NIT APPEARANCES (7): 1951-53-54-66-82-86-94; 9-5 record (.643); finished 1st in 1951 and 1966.

ALL-TIME SCORING LEADER: Danny Ainge (2,467 points from 1978-81).

ALL-TIME REBOUNDING LEADER: Michael Smith (922 from 1984-89; missed 1984-85 and 1985-86 seasons while on a LDS mission).

NCAA CONSENSUS FIRST-TEAM ALL-AMERICANS (2): Elwood Romney (1931), Danny Ainge (1981).

NCAA CONSENSUS SECOND-TEAM ALL-AMERICANS (4): Mel Hutchins (1951), Joe Richey (1953), Devin Durrant (1984), Michael Smith (1988).

BROWN

OFFICIAL NAME: Brown University.

NICKNAME: Bears.

ADDRESS: Box 1932, Providence, RI 02912.

PHONE/FAX: (401) 863-2219, 2259/1436.

ENROLLMENT: 5,500.

ARENA: Pizzitola Sports Center (Capacity-2,800; Year Opened-1989).

SCHOOL COLORS: Seal Brown, Cardinal Red and White.

CONFERENCE: Ivy League.

NCAA TOURNAMENT APPEARANCES (2): 1939 and 1986; 0-2 record.

NIT APPEARANCES: None.

ALL-TIME SCORING LEADER: Arnie Berman (1,668 points from 1970-72).

ALL-TIME REBOUNDING LEADER: Phil Brown (931 from 1973-75).

BUCKNELL

OFFICIAL NAME: Bucknell University.

NICKNAME: Bison.

ADDRESS: Lewisburg, PA 17837-2005.

PHONE/FAX: (717) 524-1227/1660.

ENROLLMENT: 3,400.

ARENA: Davis Gymnasium (Capacity-2,300; Year Opened-1938).

SCHOOL COLORS: Orange and Blue.

CONFERENCE: Patriot League.

NCAA TOURNAMENT APPEARANCES (2): 1987 and 1989; 0-2 record.

NIT APPEARANCES: None.

ALL-TIME SCORING LEADER: Al Leslie (1,973 points from 1978-81).

ALL-TIME REBOUNDING LEADER: Hal Danzig (1,134 from 1957-59).

BUTLER

OFFICIAL NAME: Butler University.

NICKNAME: Bulldogs.

ADDRESS: 4600 Sunset Avenue, Indianapolis, IN 46208.

PHONE/FAX: (317) 283-9375/9808.

ENROLLMENT: 4,200.

ARENA: Hinkle Fieldhouse (11,043).

SCHOOL COLORS: Blue and White.

CONFERENCE: Midwestern Collegiate.

NCAA TOURNAMENT APPEARANCES (1): 1962; 2-1 record (.333).

NIT APPEARANCES (5): 1958-59-85-91-92; 1-5 record (.167).

ALL-TIME SCORING LEADER: Chad Tucker (2,321 points from 1984-88; sat out most of 1986-87 season because of shoulder injury).

ALL-TIME REBOUNDING LEADER: Daryl Mason (961 from 1972-74).

CALIFORNIA

OFFICIAL NAME: University of California (At Berkeley).

NICKNAME: Golden Bears.

ADDRESS: Memorial Stadium, Berkeley, CA 94720.

PHONE/FAX: (510) 642-5363/643-7778.

ENROLLMENT: 31,000.

ARENAS: Harmon Arena (Capacity-6,578; Year Opened-1933) and Oakland/Alameda County Coliseum (Capacity-15,025; Year Opened-1966).

SCHOOL COLORS: Blue and Gold.

CONFERENCE: Pacific-10.

FINAL AP TOP 10 RANKINGS (1): 1960.

NCAA TOURNAMENT APPEARANCES (9): 1946-57-58-59-60-90-93-94-96; 14-9 record (.609); reached Final Four in 1946 (4th), 1959 (1st) and 1960 (2nd).

NIT APPEARANCES (3): 1986-87-89; 3-3 record (.500).

ALL-TIME SCORING LEADER: Lamond Murray (1,688 points from 1992-94).

ALL-TIME REBOUNDING LEADER: Bob McKeen (1,019 from 1952-55).

NCAA CONSENSUS FIRST-TEAM ALL-AMERICANS (3): Vern Corbin (1929), Darrall Imhoff (1960), Jason Kidd (1994).

NCAA CONSENSUS SECOND-TEAM ALL-AMERICANS (2): Andy Wolfe (1948), Lamond Murray (1994).

UC IRVINE

OFFICIAL NAME: University of California (At Irvine).

NICKNAME: Anteaters.

ADDRESS: Campus and University Drive, Irvine, CA 92717.

PHONE/FAX: (714) 856-5814/5260.

ENROLLMENT: 16,700.

ARENA: Bren Events Center (Capacity-5,000; Year Opened-1987).

SCHOOL COLORS: Blue and Gold.

CONFERENCE: Big West.

NCAA DIVISION I TOURNAMENT APPEARANCES: None.

NCAA DIVISION II TOURNAMENT APPEARANCES (4): 1968-69-72-75; 2-6 record (.250).

NIT APPEARANCES (2): 1982 and 1986; 2-2 record (.500).

ALL-TIME SCORING LEADER: Tod Murphy (1,778 points from 1983-86).

ALL-TIME REBOUNDING LEADER: Dave Baker (926 from 1972-75 when school was classified as a small college).

NCAA CONSENSUS SECOND-TEAM ALL-AMERICANS (1): Kevin Magee (1982).

UC SANTA BARBARA

OFFICIAL NAME: University of California (At Santa Barbara).

NICKNAME: Gauchos.

ADDRESS: Ward Memorial Freeway, Santa Barbara, CA 93106.

PHONE/FAX: (805) 893-3428/4537.

ENROLLMENT: 18,200.

ARENA: The Thunderdome (Capacity-6,000; Year Opened-1979).

SCHOOL COLORS: Blue and Gold.

CONFERENCE: Big West.

NCAA DIVISION I TOURNAMENT APPEARANCES (2): 1988 and 1990; 1-2 record (.333).

NCAA DIVISION II TOURNAMENT APPEARANCES (2): 1961 and 1963; 3-2 record (.600).

NAIA TOURNAMENT APPEARANCES (1): 1941; finished 4th with 3-2 record (.600).

NIT APPEARANCES (3): 1989-92-93; 0-3 record.

ALL-TIME SCORING LEADER: Carrick DeHart (1,687 points from 1987-90).

ALL-TIME REBOUNDING LEADER: Eric McArthur (904 from 1987-90).

CAL STATE FULLERTON

OFFICIAL NAME: California State University (At Fullerton).

NICKNAME: Titans.

ADDRESS: 800 North State College Boulevard, Fullerton, CA 92634-9480.

PHONE/FAX: (714) 773-3970/3141.

ENROLLMENT: 22,000.

ARENA: Titan Gym (Capacity-4,000; Year Opened-1964).

SCHOOL COLORS: Navy, Orange and White.

CONFERENCE: Big West.

NCAA TOURNAMENT APPEARANCES (1): 1978; reached regional final with a 2-1 record.

NIT APPEARANCES (2): 1983 and 1987; 0-2 record.

ALL-TIME SCORING LEADER: Leon Wood (1,876 points from 1982-84 after transferring from Arizona).

ALL-TIME REBOUNDING LEADER: Tony Neal (1,115 from 1982-85).

NCAA CONSENSUS SECOND-TEAM ALL-AMERICANS (1): Leon Wood (1984).

CANISIUS

OFFICIAL NAME: Canisius College.

NICKNAME: Golden Griffins.

ADDRESS: 2001 Main Street, Buffalo, NY 14208.

PHONE/FAX: (716) 888-2970/2980.

ENROLLMENT: 4,865.

ARENAS: Koessler Athletic Center (Capacity-1,800; Year Opened-1968) and Marine Midland Arena (Capacity-20,000; Year Opened-1996).

SCHOOL COLORS: Blue and Gold.

CONFERENCE: Metro Atlantic Athletic.

NCAA TOURNAMENT APPEARANCES (4): 1955-56-57-96; 6-4 record (.600); regional runner-up in 1955 and 1956.

NIT APPEARANCES (5): 1944-63-85-94-95; 5-5 record (.500); finished 2nd in 1963 and 4th in 1995.

ALL-TIME SCORING LEADER: Ray Hall (2,226 points from 1982-85).

ALL-TIME REBOUNDING LEADER: Henry Nowak (880 from 1955-57).

NCAA CONSENSUS SECOND-TEAM ALL-AMERICANS (1): Larry Fogle (1974).

CENTRAL MICHIGAN

OFFICIAL NAME: Central Michigan University.

NICKNAME: Chippewas.

ADDRESS: 100 Rose Arena, Mount Pleasant, MI 48859.

PHONE/FAX: (517) 774-3277/7324.

ENROLLMENT: 16,450.

ARENA: Dan Rose Arena (Capacity-5,200; Year Opened-1973).

SCHOOL COLORS: Maroon and Gold.

CONFERENCE: Mid-American.

NCAA DIVISION I TOURNAMENT APPEARANCES (3): 1975-77-87; 2-3 record (.400).

NCAA DIVISION II TOURNAMENT APPEARANCES (3): 1965-70-71; 3-3 record (.500).

NAIA TOURNAMENT APPEARANCES (2): 1966 and 1967; 2-2 record (.500).

NIT APPEARANCES (1): 9; 0-1 record.

ALL-TIME SCORING LEADER: Melvin McLaughlin (2,071 points from 1980-83).

ALL-TIME REBOUNDING LEADER: Dan Roundfield (1,031 from 1973-75).

CINCINNATI

OFFICIAL NAME: University of Cincinnati.

NICKNAME: Bearcats.

ADDRESS: 340 Shoemaker Center, Cincinnati, OH 45221-0021.

PHONE/FAX: (513) 556-5191/0619.

ENROLLMENT: 36,000.

ARENA: Myrl Shoemaker Center (Capacity-13,176; Year Opened-1989).

SCHOOL COLORS: Red and Black.

CONFERENCE: Conference USA.

FINAL AP TOP 10 RANKINGS (9): 1958-59-60-61-62-63-66-93-96.

NCAA TOURNAMENT APPEARANCES (15): 1958-59-60-61-62-63-66-75-76-77-92-93-94-95-96; 31-14 record (.689); reached Final Four in 1959 (3rd), 1960 (3rd), 1961 (1st), 1962 (1st), 1963 (2nd) and 1992 (3rd).

NIT APPEARANCES (8): 1951-55-57-70-74-85-90-91; 5-8 record (.385); finished 3rd in 1955.

ALL-TIME SCORING LEADER: Oscar Robertson (2,973 points from 1958-60).

ALL-TIME REBOUNDING LEADER: Oscar Robertson (1,338 from 1958-60).

NCAA CONSENSUS FIRST-TEAM ALL-AMERICANS (5): Oscar Robertson (1958, 1959 and 1960), Ron Bonham (1963), Tom Thacker (1963).

NCAA CONSENSUS SECOND-TEAM ALL-AMERICANS (2): Ron Bonham (1964), Danny Fortson (1996).

THE CITADEL

NICKNAME: Bulldogs.

ADDRESS: Charleston, SC 29409.

PHONE/FAX: (803) 953-5120/4058.

ENROLLMENT: 2,000.

ARENA: McAlister Field House (Capacity-6,200; Year Opened-1939).

SCHOOL COLORS: Citadel Blue and White.

CONFERENCE: Southern.

NCAA TOURNAMENT APPEARANCES:: None.

NIT APPEARANCES: None.

ALL-TIME SCORING LEADER: Regan Truesdale (1,661 points from 1982-85).

ALL-TIME REBOUNDING LEADER: Ray Graves (924 from 1958-60).

CLEMSON

OFFICIAL NAME: Clemson University.

NICKNAME: Tigers.

ADDRESS: 100 Perimeter Road, Post Office Box 31, Clemson, SC 29633.

PHONE/FAX: (803) 365-2114/656-0299.

ENROLLMENT: 17,665.

ARENA: Littlejohn Coliseum (Capacity-11,020; Year Opened-1968).

SCHOOL COLORS: Purple and Orange.

CONFERENCE: Atlantic Coast.

NCAA TOURNAMENT APPEARANCES (5): 1980-87-89-90-96; 6-5 record (.545); regional runner-up in 1980.

NIT APPEARANCES (10): 1975-79-81-82-85-86-88-93-94-95; 6-10 record (.375).

ALL-TIME SCORING LEADER: Elden Campbell (1,880 points from 1987-90).

ALL-TIME REBOUNDING LEADER: Tree Rollins (1,311 from 1974-77).

NCAA CONSENSUS SECOND-TEAM ALL-AMERICANS (1): Horace Grant (1987).

CLEVELAND STATE

OFFICIAL NAME: Cleveland State University.

NICKNAME: Vikings.

ADDRESS: Convocation Center, 2000 Prospect Avenue, Cleveland, OH 44115.

PHONE/FAX: (216) 687-4818/523-7257.

ENROLLMENT: 17,135.

ARENA: Henry J. Goodman Arena (Capacity-13,610; Year Opened-1991).

SCHOOL COLORS: Forest Green and White.

CONFERENCE: Midwestern Collegiate.

NCAA TOURNAMENT APPEARANCES (1): 1986; 2-1 record (.667).

NIT APPEARANCES (2): 1987 and 1988; 2-2 record (.500).

ALL-TIME SCORING LEADER: Ken "Mouse" McFadden (2,256 points from 1986-89).

ALL-TIME REBOUNDING LEADER: Weldon Kytle (1,241 from 1962-65 when school was classified as a small college).

COLGATE

OFFICIAL NAME: Colgate University.

NICKNAME: Red Raiders.

ADDRESS: 13 Oak Drive, Hamilton, NY 13346-1398.

PHONE/FAX: (315) 824-7602/7977.

ENROLLMENT: 2,700.

ARENA: Cotterell Court (Capacity-3,091; Year Opened-1966).

SCHOOL COLORS: Maroon, Gray and White.

CONFERENCE: Patriot League.

NCAA TOURNAMENT APPEARANCES (2): 1995 and 1996; 0-2 record.

NIT APPEARANCES: None.

ALL-TIME SCORING LEADER: Tucker Neale (2,075 points from 1993-95; played freshman season for Ashland University, a Division II school in Ohio, before sitting out one year as a medical redshirt).

ALL-TIME REBOUNDING LEADER: Jack Nichols (1,082 from 1955-57).

NCAA CONSENSUS SECOND-TEAM ALL-AMERICANS (1): Ernie Vandeweghe (1949).

COLORADO

OFFICIAL NAME: University of Colorado.

NICKNAME: Buffaloes.

ADDRESS: CU Fieldhouse Annex, Box 357, Boulder, CO 80309.

PHONE/FAX: (303) 492-5626/3811.

ENROLLMENT: 25,090.

ARENA: Coors Events/Conference Center (Capacity-11,198; Year Opened-1979).

SCHOOL COLORS: Silver, Gold and Black.

CONFERENCE: Big 12.

FINAL AP TOP 10 RANKINGS (2): 1962 and 1963.

NCAA TOURNAMENT APPEARANCES (8): 1940-42-46-54-55-62-63-69; 8-10 record (.444); reached Final Four in 1942 (T3rd) and 1955 (3rd).

NIT APPEARANCES (4): 1938-40-91-95; 7-3 record (.700); finished 2nd in 1938, 1st in 1940 and 3rd in 1991.

ALL-TIME SCORING LEADER: Donnie Boyce (1,995 points from 1992-95).

ALL-TIME REBOUNDING LEADER: Cliff Meely (971 from 1969-71).

NCAA CONSENSUS SECOND-TEAM ALL-AMERICANS (2): Jack Harvey (1940), Bob Doll (1942).

COLORADO STATE

OFFICIAL NAME: Colorado State University.

NICKNAME: Rams.

ADDRESS: 202 B Moby Arena, Fort Collins, CO 80523.

PHONE/FAX: (303) 491-5067/1348.

ENROLLMENT: 20,600.

ARENA: Moby Arena (Capacity-10,000; Year Opened-1966).

SCHOOL COLORS: Green and Gold.

CONFERENCE: Western Athletic.

NCAA TOURNAMENT APPEARANCES (7): 1954-63-65-66-69-89-90; 3-8 record (.273); regional runner-up in 1969.

NIT APPEARANCES (4): 1961-62-88-96; 4-4 record (.500); finished 3rd in 1988.

ALL-TIME SCORING LEADER: Pat Durham (1,980 points from 1986-89).

ALL-TIME REBOUNDING LEADER: Pat Durham (851 from 1986-89).

NCAA CONSENSUS SECOND-TEAM ALL-AMERICANS (1): Bill Green (1963).

COLUMBIA

OFFICIAL NAME: Columbia University.

NICKNAME: Lions.

ADDRESS: 406 Dodge Physical Fitness Center, New York, NY 10027.

PHONE/FAX: (212) 854-2534/8168.

ENROLLMENT: 4,000.

ARENA: Levien Gymnasium (Capacity-3,408; Year Opened-1974).

SCHOOL COLORS: Columbia Blue and White.

CONFERENCE: Ivy League.

FINAL AP TOP 10 RANKINGS (2): 1951 and 1968.

NCAA TOURNAMENT APPEARANCES (3): 1948-51-68; 2-4 record (.333).

NIT APPEARANCES: None.

ALL-TIME SCORING LEADER: Buck Jenkins (1,766 points from 1990-93).

ALL-TIME REBOUNDING LEADER: Frank Thomas (1,022 from 1954-56).

NCAA CONSENSUS FIRST-TEAM ALL-AMERICANS (2): George Gregory (1931), Chet Forte (1957).

CONNECTICUT

OFFICIAL NAME: University of Connecticut.

NICKNAMES: Huskies, UConn.

ADDRESS: 2095 Hillside Road, U-78, Storrs, CT 06269-3078.

PHONE/FAX: (80)486-3531/5085

ENROLLMENT: 25,885.

ARENAS: Harry A. Gampel Pavilion (Capacity-8,241; Year Opened-1990) and Hartford Civic Center (Capacity-16,294; Year Opened-1981).

SCHOOL COLORS: National Flag Blue and White.

CONFERENCE: Big East.

FINAL AP TOP 10 RANKINGS (4): 1990-94-95-96.

NCAA TOURNAMENT APPEARANCES (19): 1951-54-56-57-58-59-60-63-64-65-67-76-79-90-91-92-94-95-96; 17-20 record (.459); regional runner-up in 1964, 1990 and 1995.

NIT APPEARANCES (9): 1955-74-75-80-81-82-88-89-93; 9-8 record (.529); finished 1st in 1988.

ALL-TIME SCORING LEADER: Chris Smith (2,145 points from 1989-92).

ALL-TIME REBOUNDING LEADER: Art Quimby (1,716 from 1952-55).

NCAA CONSENSUS FIRST-TEAM ALL-AMERICANS (2): Donyell Marshall (1994), Ray Allen (1996).

CORNELL

OFFICIAL NAME: Cornell University.

NICKNAME: Big Red.

ADDRESS: Box 729, Ithaca, NY 14851.

PHONE/FAX: (607) 255-3752/9791.

ENROLLMENT: 12,900.

ARENA: Newman Arena (Capacity-4,750; Year Opened-1989).

SCHOOL COLORS: Carnellian Red and White.

CONFERENCE: Ivy League.

NCAA TOURNAMENT APPEARANCES (2): 1954 and 1988; 0-3 record.

NIT APPEARANCES: None.

ALL-TIME SCORING LEADER: John Bajusz (1,663 points from 1984-87).

ALL-TIME REBOUNDING LEADER: George Farley (1,089 from 1958-60).

CREIGHTON

OFFICIAL NAME: Creighton University.

NICKNAME: Bluejays.

ADDRESS: Vinardi Athletic Center, 2500 California Plaza, Omaha, NE 68178-0810.

PHONE/FAX: (402) 280-2488/2495.

ENROLLMENT: 6,340.

ARENA: Omaha Civic Auditorium (Capacity-9,481; Year Opened-1954).

SCHOOL COLORS: Blue and White.

CONFERENCE: Missouri Valley.

NCAA TOURNAMENT APPEARANCES (9): 1941-62-64-74-75-78-81-89-91; 7-10 record (.412); regional runner-up in 1941.

NIT APPEARANCES (5): 1942-43-77-84-90; 2-5 record (.286); finished 3rd in 1942.

ALL-TIME SCORING LEADER: Bob Harstad (2,110 points from 1988-91).

ALL-TIME REBOUNDING LEADER: Paul Silas (1,751 from 1962-64).

NCAA CONSENSUS FIRST-TEAM ALL-AMERICANS (1): Ed Beisser (1943).

DARTMOUTH

OFFICIAL NAME: Dartmouth College.

NICKNAME: Big Green.

ADDRESS: 6083 Alumni Gym, Hanover, NH 03755-3512.

PHONE/FAX: (603) 646-2468/1286.

ENROLLMENT: 4,200.

ARENA: Leede Arena (Capacity-2,100; Year Opened-1986).

SCHOOL COLORS: Dartmouth Green and White.

CONFERENCE: Ivy League.

NCAA TOURNAMENT APPEARANCES (7): 1941-42-43-44-56-58-59; 10-7 record (.588); reached Final Four in 1942 (2nd) and 1944 (2nd).

NIT APPEARANCES: None.

ALL-TIME SCORING LEADER: Jim Barton (2,158 points from 1986-89).

ALL-TIME REBOUNDING LEADER: Rudy LaRusso (1,239 from 1957-59).

NCAA CONSENSUS FIRST-TEAM ALL-AMERICANS (3): Gus Broberg (1940 and 1941), Audley Brindley (1944).

NCAA CONSENSUS SECOND-TEAM ALL-AMERICANS (1): George Munroe (1942).

DAVIDSON

OFFICIAL NAME: Davidson College.

NICKNAME: Wildcats.

ADDRESS: Davidson, NC 28036.

PHONE/FAX: (704) 892-2374/2636.

ENROLLMENT: 1,550.

ARENA: John M. Belk Arena (Capacity-5,700; Year Opened-1989).

SCHOOL COLORS: Red and Black.

CONFERENCE: Southern.

FINAL AP TOP 10 RANKINGS (4): 1964-65-68-69.

NCAA TOURNAMENT APPEARANCES (5): 1966-68-69-70-86; 5-6 record (.455); regional runner-up in 1968 and 1969.

NIT APPEARANCES (3): 1972-94-96; 0-3 record.

ALL-TIME SCORING LEADER: John Gerdy (2,487 points from 1976-79).

ALL-TIME REBOUNDING LEADER: Mike Maloy (1,111 from 1968-70).

NCAA CONSENSUS FIRST-TEAM ALL-AMERICANS (1): Fred Hetzel (1965).

NCAA CONSENSUS SECOND-TEAM ALL-AMERICANS (3): Fred Hetzel (1964), Dick Snyder (1966), Mike Maloy (1969).

DAYTON

OFFICIAL NAME: University of Dayton.

NICKNAME: Flyers.

ADDRESS: 300 College Park, Dayton, OH 45469-1238.

PHONE/FAX: (513) 229-4460/4461.

ENROLLMENT: 6,300.

ARENA: University of Dayton Arena (Capacity-13,455; Year Opened-1969).

SCHOOL COLORS: Red and Blue.

CONFERENCE: Atlantic 10.

FINAL AP TOP 10 RANKINGS (2): 1955 and 1956.

NCAA TOURNAMENT APPEARANCES (10): 1952-65-66-67-69-70-74-84-85-90; 13-12 record (.520); reached Final Four in 1967 (2nd).

NIT APPEARANCES (17): 951-52-54-55-56-57-58-60-61-62-68-71-78-79-81-82-86; 29-16 record (.644); finished 2nd in 1951, 2nd in 1952, 2nd in 1955, 2nd in 1956, 2nd in 1958, 4th in 1961, 1st in 1962 and 1st in 1968.

ALL-TIME SCORING LEADER: Roosevelt Chapman (2,233 points from 1981-84).

ALL-TIME REBOUNDING LEADER: John Horan (1,341 from 1952-55).

NCAA CONSENSUS SECOND-TEAM ALL-AMERICANS (5): Don Meineke (1952), Bill Uhl (1956), Don May (1967 and 1968), Jim Paxson (1979).

DEPAUL

OFFICIAL NAME: DePaul University.

NICKNAME: Blue Demons.

ADDRESS: 1011 West Belden Avenue, Chicago, IL 60614.

PHONE/FAX: (312) 325-7525/7531.

ENROLLMENT: 16,745.

ARENA: Rosemont Horizon (Capacity-17,500; Year Opened-1980).

SCHOOL COLORS: Royal Blue and Scarlet.

CONFERENCE: Conference USA.

FINAL AP TOP 10 RANKINGS (8): 1964-78-79-80-81-82-84-87.

NCAA TOURNAMENT APPEARANCES (20): 1943-53-56-59-60-65-76-78-79-80-81-82-84-85-86-87-88-89-91-92; 20-23 record (.465); reached Final Four in 1943 (T3rd) and 1979 (3rd).

NIT APPEARANCES (12): 1940-44-45-48-61-63-64-66-83-90-94-95; 13-13 record (.500); finished 4th in 1940, 2nd in 1944, 1st in 1945, 4th in 1948 and 2nd in 1983.

ALL-TIME SCORING LEADER: Mark Aguirre (2,182 points from 1979-81).

ALL-TIME REBOUNDING LEADER: Dave Corzine (1,151 from 1975-78).

NCAA CONSENSUS FIRST-TEAM ALL-AMERICANS (6): George Mikan (1944, 1945 and 1946), Mark Aguirre (1980 and 1981), Terry Cummings (1982).

NCAA CONSENSUS SECOND-TEAM ALL-AMERICANS (1): Dick Triptow (1944).

DETROIT

OFFICIAL NAME: University of Detroit.

NICKNAME: Titans.

ADDRESS: 4001 West McNichols Road, Post Office Box 19900, Detroit, MI 48219-0900.

PHONE/FAX: (313) 993-1745/1765.

ENROLLMENT: 7,800.

ARENAS: Calihan Hall (Capacity-8,837; Year Opened-1952) and Cobo Arena (Capacity-11,143; Year Opened-1960).

SCHOOL COLORS: Red, White and Blue.

CONFERENCE: Midwestern Collegiate.

NCAA TOURNAMENT APPEARANCES (3): 1962-77-79; 1-3 record (.250).

NIT APPEARANCES (4): 1960-61-65-78; 2-4 record (.333).

ALL-TIME SCORING LEADER: John Long (2,167 points from 1975-78).

ALL-TIME REBOUNDING LEADER: Dave DeBusschere (1,552 from 1960-62).

NCAA CONSENSUS FIRST-TEAM ALL-AMERICANS (1): Spencer Haywood (1969).

NCAA CONSENSUS SECOND-TEAM ALL-AMERICANS (1): Bob Calihan (1939).

DRAKE

OFFICIAL NAME: Drake University.

NICKNAME: Bulldogs.

ADDRESS: Drake Fieldhouse, Des Moines, IA 50311.

PHONE/FAX: (515) 271-3012/3015.

ENROLLMENT: 4,000.

ARENA: Knapp Center (Capacity-7,002; Year Opened-1992).

SCHOOL COLORS: Blue and White.

NCAA TOURNAMENT APPEARANCES (3): 1969-70-71; 5-3 record (.625); reached Final Four in 1969 (3rd).

NAIA TOURNAMENT APPEARANCES (1): 1938; 0-1 record.

NIT APPEARANCES (3): 1964-81-86; 1-3 record (.250).

NCIT RECORD: 3-0 to finish 1st in 1975.

ALL-TIME SCORING LEADER: Phillip "Red" Murrell (1,657 points from 1956-58).

NCAA CONSENSUS FIRST-TEAM ALL-AMERICANS: Melvin Mathis (854 from 1983-86).

DREXEL

OFFICIAL NAME: Drexel University.

NICKNAME: Dragons.

ADDRESS: 32nd and Chestnut Streets, Philadelphia, PA 19104.

PHONE/FAX: (215) 590-8945/8668.

ENROLLMENT: 4,703.

ARENA: Physical Education Athletic Center (Capacity-2,300; Year Opened-1975).

SCHOOL COLORS: Navy Blue and Gold.

CONFERENCE: North Atlantic.

NCAA DIVISION I TOURNAMENT APPEARANCES (4): 1986-94-95-96; 1-4 record (.200).

NCAA DIVISION II TOURNAMENT APPEARANCES (4): 1957-60-66-67; 0-7 record.

NIT APPEARANCES: None.

ALL-TIME SCORING LEADER: Michael Anderson (2,208 points from 1985-88).

ALL-TIME REBOUNDING LEADER: Malik Rose (1,514 from 1993-96).

DUKE

OFFICIAL NAME: Duke University.

NICKNAME: Blue Devils.

ADDRESS: Post Office Box 90555, 118 Cameron Indoor Stadium, Durham, NC 27708-0555.

PHONE/FAX: (919) 684-2633/2489.

ENROLLMENT: 6,130.

ARENA: Cameron Indoor (Capacity-9,314; Year Opened-1939).

SCHOOL COLORS: Royal Blue and White.

CONFERENCE: Atlantic Coast.

FINAL AP TOP 10 RANKINGS (17): 1958-61-62-63-64-65-66-68-78-85-86-88-89-91-92-93-94.

NCAA TOURNAMENT APPEARANCES (20): 1955-60-63-64-66-78-79-80-84-85-86-87-88-89-90-91-92-93-94-96; 56-18 record (.757); reached Final Four in 1963 (3rd), 1964 (2nd), 1966 (3rd), 1978 (2nd), 1986 (2nd), 1988 (T3rd), 1989 (T3rd), 1990 (2nd), 1991 (1st), 1992 (1st) and 1994 (2nd).

NIT APPEARANCES (5): 1967-68-70-71-81; 5-6 record (.455); finished 4th in 1971.

ALL-TIME SCORING LEADER: Johnny Dawkins (2,556 points from 1983-86).

ALL-TIME REBOUNDING LEADER: Mike Gminski (1,242 from 1977-80).

NCAA CONSENSUS FIRST-TEAM ALL-AMERICANS (10): Dick Groat (1952), Art Heyman (1963), Bob Verga (1967), Mike Gminski (1979), Johnny Dawkins (1985 and 1986), Danny Ferry (1989), Christian Laettner (1992), Bobby Hurley (1993), Grant Hill (1994).

NCAA CONSENSUS SECOND-TEAM ALL-AMERICANS (11): Ed Koffenberger (1947), Dick Groat (1951), Art Heyman (1962), Jeff Mullins (1964), Jack Marin (1966), Bob Verga (1966), Jim Spanarkel (1979), Mike Gminski (1980), Danny Ferry (1988), Christian Laettner (1991), Grant Hill (1993).

DUQUESNE

OFFICIAL NAME: Duquesne University.

NICKNAME: Dukes.

ADDRESS: A.J. Palumbo Center, 600 Forbes Avenue, Pittsburgh, PA 15282.

PHONE/FAX: (412) 396-6560/6210.

ENROLLMENT: 8,600.

ARENA: A.J. Palumbo Center (Capacity-6,200; Year Opened-1988).

SCHOOL COLORS: Red and Blue.

CONFERENCE: Atlantic 10.

FINAL AP TOP 10 RANKINGS (6): 1950-52-53-54-55-69.

NCAA TOURNAMENT APPEARANCES (5): 1940-52-69-71-77; 4-5 record (.444); reached Final Four in 1940 (T3rd).

NIT APPEARANCES (16): 1940-41-47-50-52-53-54-55-56-62-64-68-70-80-81-94; 17-18 record (.486); finished 2nd in 1940, 4th in 1950, 4th in 1952, 3rd in 1953, 2nd in 1954, 1st in 1955 and 4th in 1962.

ALL-TIME SCORING LEADER: Dick Ricketts (1,963 points from 1952-55).

ALL-TIME REBOUNDING LEADER: Dick Ricketts (1,496 from 1952-55).

NCAA CONSENSUS FIRST-TEAM ALL-AMERICANS (3): Dick Ricketts (1955), Si Green (1955 and 1956).

NCAA CONSENSUS SECOND-TEAM ALL-AMERICANS (2): Chuck Cooper (1950), Dick Ricketts (1954).

EAST CAROLINA

OFFICIAL NAME: East Carolina University.

NICKNAME: Pirates.

ADDRESS: Ward Sports Medicine Building, Greenville, NC 27858-4353.

PHONE/FAX: (919) 328-4522/4528.

ENROLLMENT: 17,570.

ARENA: Williams Arena at Minges Coliseum (Capacity-7,500; Year Opened-1995).

SCHOOL COLORS: Purple and Gold.

CONFERENCE: Colonial Athletic Association.

NCAA TOURNAMENT APPEARANCES (2): 1972 and 1993; 0-2 record.

NAIA TOURNATMENT APPEARANCES (2): 1953 and 1954; 0-2 record.

NIT APPEARANCES: None.

NCIT RECORD: 0-1 in 1975.

ALL-TIME SCORING LEADER: Bobby Hodges (2,018 points from 1951-54 when school was classified as a small college).

ALL-TIME REBOUNDING LEADER: Bill Otte (969 from 1961-64 when school was classified as a small college).

EASTERN KENTUCKY

OFFICIAL NAME: Eastern Kentucky University.

NICKNAMES: Colonels, Maroons.

ADDRESS: 205 Begley Building, Richmond, KY 40475-3105.

PHONE/FAX: (606) 622-1253/1230.

ENROLLMENT: 15,725.

ARENA: McBrayer Arena (Capacity-6,500; Year Opened-1962).

SCHOOL COLORS: Maroon and White.

CONFERENCE: Ohio Valley.

NCAA TOURNAMENT APPEARANCES (5): 1953-59-65-72-79; 0-5 record.

NAIA TOURNAMENT APPEARANCES (2): 1945 and 1946; 3-2 record (.600); finished 3rd in 1945.

NIT APPEARANCES: None.

ALL-TIME SCORING LEADER: Antonio Parris (1,723 points from 1984-87).

ALL-TIME REBOUNDING LEADER: Mike Smith (977 from 1989-92).

EASTERN MICHIGAN

OFFICIAL NAME: Eastern Michigan University.

NICKNAME: Eagles.

ADDRESS: 200 Bowen Field House, Ypsilanti, MI 48197.

PHONE/FAX: (313) 487-0317/485-3840.

ENROLLMENT: 25,835.

ARENA: Bowen Field House (Capacity-5,600; Year Opened-1955).

SCHOOL COLORS: Dark Green and White.

CONFERENCE: Mid-American.

NCAA DIVISION I TOURNAMENT APPEARANCES (3): 1988-91-96; 3-3 record (.500).

NCAA DIVISION II TOURNAMENT APPEARANCES (1): 1972; 3-2 record (.600); finished 4th in 1972.

NAIA TOURNAMENT APPEARANCES (4): 1968-69-70-71; 8-4 record (.667); finished 2nd in 1971.

NIT APPEARANCES (1): 1995; 0-1 record.

ALL-TIME SCORING LEADER: Kennedy McIntosh (2,219 points from 1968-71 when school was classified Division II).

ALL-TIME REBOUNDING LEADER: Kennedy McIntosh (1,426 from 1968-71 when school was classified Division II).

EAST TENNESSEE STATE

OFFICIAL NAME: East Tennessee State University.

NICKNAME: Buccaneers.

ADDRESS: Johnson City, TN 37614.

PHONE/FAX: (615) 929-4220/6138.

ENROLLMENT: 12,105.

ARENA: Memorial Center (Capacity-12,000; Year Opened-1977).

SCHOOL COLORS: Blue and Gold.

CONFERENCE: Southern.

NCAA DIVISION I TOURNAMENT APPEARANCES (5): 1968-89-90-91-92; 2-6 record (.250).

NCAA DIVISION II TOURNAMENT APPEARANCES (1): 1957; 1-1 record (.500).

NAIA TOURNAMENT APPEARANCES (3): 1953-54-56; 0-3 record.

NIT APPEARANCES (1): 1983; 0-1 record.

ALL-TIME SCORING LEADER: Greg Dennis (2,204 points from 1989-92).

NCAA CONSENSUS SECOND-TEAM ALL-AMERICANS (1): Keith "Mister" Jennings (1991).

EVANSVILLE

OFFICIAL NAME: University of Evansville.

NICKNAME: Aces.

ADDRESS: 1800 Lincoln Avenue, Evansville, IN 47722.

PHONE/FAX: (812) 479-2350/2199.

ENROLLMENT: 2,600.

ARENA: Roberts Stadium (Capacity-12,300; Year Opened-1956).

SCHOOL COLORS: Purple and White.

CONFERENCE: Missouri Valley.

NCAA DIVISION I TOURNAMENT APPEARANCES (4): 1982-89-92-93; 1-4 record (.200).

NCAA DIVISION II TOURNAMENT APPEARANCES (15): 1957-58-59-60-61-62-63-64-65-66-68-71-72-74-76; 40-10 record (.800); finished first five times (1959-60-64-65-71) and third once (1958).

NAIA TOURNAMENT APPEARANCES (4): 1941-42-51-55; 3-4 record (.429).

NIT APPEARANCES (2): 1988 and 1994; 1-2 record (.333).

ALL-TIME SCORING LEADER: Larry Humes (2,236 points from 1964-66 when school was classified as a small college).

ALL-TIME REBOUNDING LEADER: Dale Wise (1,197 from 1959-61 when school was classified as a small college).

NCAA CONSENSUS SECOND-TEAM ALL-AMERICANS (1): Wilfred Doerner (1942).

FAIRFIELD

OFFICIAL NAME: Fairfield University.

NICKNAME: Stags.

ADDRESS: Fairfield, CT 06430-7524.

PHONE/FAX: (203) 254-4000/4117.

ENROLLMENT: 2,900.

ARENA: Alumni Hall (Capacity-2,479; Year Opened-1959).

School Color: Cardinal Red.

CONFERENCE: Metro Atlantic Athletic.

NCAA DIVISION I TOURNAMENT APPEARANCES (2): 1986 and 1987; 0-2 record.

NCAA DIVISION II TOURNAMENT APPEARANCES (3): 1960-61-62; 2-4 record (.333).

NIT APPEARANCES (4): 1973-74-78-96; 1-4 record (.200).

ALL-TIME SCORING LEADER: Tony George (2,006 points from 1983-86).

ALL-TIME REBOUNDING LEADER: Drew Henderson (1,080 from 1990-93).

FLORIDA

OFFICIAL NAME: University of Florida.

NICKNAME: Gators.

ADDRESS: Post Office Box 14485, Gainesville, FL 32604.

PHONE/FAX: (352) 375-4683/4809.

ENROLLMENT: 40,000.

ARENA: Stephen C. O'Connell Center (Capacity-12,000; Year Opened-1980).

SCHOOL COLORS: Orange and Blue.

CONFERENCE: Southeastern.

NCAA TOURNAMENT APPEARANCES (5): 1987-88-89-94-95; 7-5 record (.583); reached Final Four in 1994 (T3rd).

NIT APPEARANCES (6): 1969-84-85-86-92-93; 6-8 record (.429); finished 4th in 1986 and 1992.

ALL-TIME SCORING LEADER: Ronnie Williams (2,090 points from 1981-84).

ALL-TIME REBOUNDING LEADER: Neal Walk (1,181 from 1967-69).

FLORIDA STATE

OFFICIAL NAME: Florida State University.

NICKNAME: Seminoles.

ADDRESS: Moore Athletic Center, Post Office Drawer 2195, Tallahassee, FL 32316, or West Pensacola & Stadium Drive, 32306-4043.

PHONE/FAX: (904) 644-1403/3820.

ENROLLMENT: 29,000.

ARENA: Tallahassee-Leon County Civic Center (Capacity-12,500; Year Opened-1981).

SCHOOL COLORS: Garnet and Gold.

CONFERENCE: Atlantic Coast.

FINAL AP TOP 10 RANKINGS (1): 1972.

NCAA TOURNAMENT APPEARANCES (9): 1968-72-78-80-88-89-91-92-93; 11-9 record (.550); reached Final Four in 1972 (2nd).

NAIA TOURNAMENT APPEARANCES (2): 1951 and 1955; 3-2 record (.600).

NIT APPEARANCES (2): 1984 and 1987; 2-2 record (.500).

ALL-TIME SCORING LEADER: Bob Sura (2,130 points from 1992-95).

ALL-TIME REBOUNDING LEADER: Dave Cowens (1,340 from 1968-70).

FORDHAM

OFFICIAL NAME: Fordham University.

NICKNAME: Rams.

ADDRESS: Rose Hill Gym, Bronx, NY 10458-9993.

PHONE/FAX: (718) 817-4240/4244.

ENROLLMENT: 14,500.

ARENA: Rose Hill Gym (Capacity-3,470; Year Opened-1926).

SCHOOL COLORS: Maroon and White.

CONFERENCE: Atlantic 10.

FINAL AP TOP 10 RANKINGS (1): 1971.

NCAA TOURNAMENT APPEARANCES (4): 1953-54-71-92; 2-4 record (.333).

NIT APPEARANCES (16): 1943-58-59-63-65-68-69-72-81-82-83-84-85-88-90-91; 5-17 record (.227); finished 4th in 1943.

ALL-TIME SCORING LEADER: Ed Conlin (1,886 points from 1952-55).

ALL-TIME REBOUNDING LEADER: Ed Conlin (1,930 from 1952-55).

NCAA CONSENSUS SECOND-TEAM ALL-AMERICANS (1): Bob Hassmiller (1939).

FRESNO STATE

OFFICIAL NAME: Fresno State University.

NICKNAME: Bulldogs.

ADDRESS: 5305 North Campus Drive, Fresno, CA 93740-0027.

PHONE/FAX: (209) 278-2509/4689.

ENROLLMENT: 19,600.

ARENA: Selland Arena (Capacity-10,159; Year Opened-1966).

SCHOOL COLORS: Cardinal and Blue.

CONFERENCE: Western Athletic.

NCAA DIVISION I TOURNAMENT APPEARANCES (3): 1981-82-84; 1-3 record (.250).

NCAA DIVISION II TOURNAMENT APPEARANCES (7): 1958-60-62-63-64-65-66; 8-8 record (.500).

NIT APPEARANCES (4): 1983-85-94-96; 11-3 record (.786); finished 1st in 1983.

ALL-TIME SCORING LEADER: Wil Hooker (1,739 points from 1989-92).

ALL-TIME REBOUNDING LEADER: Gary Alcorn (1,080 from 1957-59).

FURMAN

OFFICIAL NAME: Furman University.

NICKNAME: Paladins.

ADDRESS: 3300 Poinsett Highway, Greenville, SC 29613.

PHONE/FAX: (803) 294-2061/3061.

ENROLLMENT: 2,500.

ARENA: Greenville Memorial Auditorium (Capacity-5,344; Year Opened-1958).

SCHOOL COLORS: Purple and White.

CONFERENCE: Southern.

NCAA TOURNAMENT APPEARANCES (6): 1971-73-74-75-78-80; 1-7 record (.125).

NIT APPEARANCES (1): 1991; 0-1 record.

ALL-TIME SCORING LEADER: Frank Selvy (2,538 points from 1952-54).

ALL-TIME REBOUNDING LEADER: Jonathan Moore (1,242 from 1977-80).

NCAA CONSENSUS FIRST-TEAM ALL-AMERICANS (1): Frank Selvy (1954).

NCAA CONSENSUS SECOND-TEAM ALL-AMERICANS (3): Frank Selvy (1953), Darrell Floyd (1955 and 1956).

GEORGE WASHINGTON

OFFICIAL NAME: George Washington University.

NICKNAME: Colonials.

ADDRESS: Smith Center, Room 107, 600 22nd Street NW, Washington, DC 20052.

PHONE/FAX: (202) 994-8604/2713.

ENROLLMENT: 17,000.

ARENA: Charles E. Smith Center (Capacity-5,000; Year Opened-1975).

SCHOOL COLORS: Buff and Blue.

CONFERENCE: Atlantic 10.

NCAA TOURNAMENT APPEARANCES (5): 1954-61-93-94-96; 3-5 record (.375).

NIT APPEARANCES (2): 1991 and 1995; 0-2 record.

ALL-TIME SCORING LEADER: Joe Holup (2,226 points from 1953-56).

ALL-TIME REBOUNDING LEADER: Joe Holup (2,030 from 1953-56).

GEORGETOWN

OFFICIAL NAME: Georgetown University.

NICKNAME: Hoyas.

ADDRESS: 37th & O Streets, Washington, DC 20057.

PHONE/FAX: (202) 687-2492/2491.

ENROLLMENT: 6,180.

ARENA: USAir Arena (Capacity-19,500; Year Opened-1973).

SCHOOL COLORS: Blue and Gray.

CONFERENCE: Big East.

FINAL AP TOP 10 RANKINGS (7): 1982-84-85-87-89-90-96.

NCAA TOURNAMENT APPEARANCES (20): 1943-75-76-79-80-81-82-83-84-85-86-87-88-89-90-91-92-94-95-96; 36-19 record (.655); reached Final Four in 1943 (2nd), 1982 (2nd), 1984 (1st) and 1985 (2nd).

NIT APPEARANCES (5): 1953-70-77-78-93; 6-6 record (.500); finished 4th in 1978 and 2nd in 1993.

ALL-TIME SCORING LEADER: Eric Floyd (2,304 points from 1979-82).

ALL-TIME REBOUNDING LEADER: Patrick Ewing (1,316 from 1982-85).

NCAA CONSENSUS FIRST-TEAM ALL-AMERICANS (7): Sleepy Floyd (1982), Patrick Ewing (1983, 1984 and 1985), Reggie Williams (1987), Alonzo Mourning (1992), Allen Iverson (1996).

NCAA CONSENSUS SECOND-TEAM ALL-AMERICANS (1): Alonzo Mourning (1990).

GEORGIA

OFFICIAL NAME: University of Georgia.

NICKNAME: Bulldogs.

ADDRESS: Post Office Box 1472, Athens, GA 30613.

PHONE/FAX: (706) 542-1621/1140.

ENROLLMENT: 28,690.

ARENA: Georgia Coliseum (Capacity-10,512; Year Opened-1963).

SCHOOL COLORS: Red and Black.

CONFERENCE: Southeastern.

NCAA TOURNAMENT APPEARANCES (6): 1983-85-87-90-91-96; 6-6 record (.500); reached Final Four in 1983 (T3rd).

NIT APPEARANCES (7): 1981-82-84-86-88-93-95; 6-7 record (.462); reached semifinals in 1982.

ALL-TIME SCORING LEADER: Litterial Green (2,111 points from 1989-92).

ALL-TIME REBOUNDING LEADER: Bob Lienhard (1,116 from 1968-70).

GEORGIA TECH

OFFICIAL NAME: Georgia Institute of Technology.

NICKNAMES: Yellow Jackets, Rambling Wreck.

ADDRESS: 150 Bobby Dodd Way, N.W., Atlanta, GA 30332-0455.

PHONE/FAX: (404) 894-5445/853-2674.

ENROLLMENT: 13,000.

ARENA: Alexander Memorial Coliseum (Capacity-10,026; Year Opened-1957).

SCHOOL COLORS: Old Gold and White.

CONFERENCE: Atlantic Coast.

FINAL AP TOP 10 RANKINGS (3): 1985-86-90.

NCAA TOURNAMENT APPEARANCES (11): 1960-85-86-87-88-89-90-91-92-93-96; 16-11 record (.593); reached Final Four in 1990 (T3rd).

NIT APPEARANCES (4): 1970-71-84-94; 4-4 record (.500); finished 2nd in 1971.

ALL-TIME SCORING LEADER: Rich Yunkus (2,232 points from 1969-71).

ALL-TIME REBOUNDING LEADER: Malcolm Mackey (1,205 from 1990-93).

NCAA CONSENSUS FIRST-TEAM ALL-AMERICANS (2): Roger Kaiser (1961), Kenny Anderson (1991).

NCAA CONSENSUS SECOND-TEAM ALL-AMERICANS (3): Roger Kaiser (1960), Mark Price (1985), Dennis Scott (1990).

GONZAGA

OFFICIAL NAME: Gonzaga University.

NICKNAME: Zags.

ADDRESS: East 502 Boone Avenue, Spokane, WA 99258.

PHONE/FAX: (509) 328-4220/484-2830.

ENROLLMENT: 5,000.

ARENA: Charlotte Y. Martin Centre (Capacity-4,000; Year Opened-1965).

SCHOOL COLORS: Blue, Red and White.

CONFERENCE: West Coast.

NCAA TOURNAMENT APPEARANCES (1): 1995; 0-1 record.

NAIA TOURNAMENT APPEARANCES (2): 1948 and 1953; 1-2 record (.333).

NIT APPEARANCES (2): 1994 and 1996; 1-2 record (.333).

ALL-TIME SCORING LEADER: Frank Burgess (2,196 points from 1959-61).

ALL-TIME REBOUNDING LEADER: Jerry Vermillion (1,670 from 1952-55).

NCAA CONSENSUS SECOND-TEAM ALL-AMERICANS (1): Frank Burgess (1961).

HARVARD

OFFICIAL NAME: Harvard University.

NICKNAME: Crimson.

ADDRESS: 60 John F. Kennedy Street, Cambridge, MA 02138.

PHONE/FAX: (617) 495-2206/2130.

ENROLLMENT: 6,675.

ARENA: Lavicks Pavilion at the Briggs Athletic Center (Capacity-2,083; Year Opened-1995).

SCHOOL COLORS: Crimson, Black and White.

CONFERENCE: Ivy League.

NCAA TOURNAMENT APPEARANCES (1): 1946; 0-2 record.

NIT APPEARANCES: None.

ALL-TIME SCORING LEADER: Joe Carrabino (1,880 points from 1982-85).

ALL-TIME REBOUNDING LEADER: Ron Mitchell (803 from 1989-92).

HAWAII

OFFICIAL NAME: University of Hawaii.

NICKNAME: Rainbows.

ADDRESS: 1337 Lower Campus Road, Honolulu, HI 96822.

PHONE/FAX: (808) 956-7523/4470.

ENROLLMENT: 19,810.

ARENA: Special Events Arena (Capacity-10,225; Year Opened-1994).

SCHOOL COLORS: Green and White.

CONFERENCE: Western Athletic.

NCAA TOURNAMENT APPEARANCES (2): 1972 and 1994; 0-2 record.

NAIA TOURNAMENT APPEARANCES (1): 1949; 0-1 record.

NIT APPEARANCES (4): 1971-74-89-90; 4-4 record (.500).

ALL-TIME SCORING LEADER: Chris Gaines (1,734 points from 1987-90).

ALL-TIME REBOUNDING LEADER: Melton Werts (1,098 from 1973-76).

HOLY CROSS

OFFICIAL NAME: Holy Cross College.

NICKNAME: Crusaders.

ADDRESS: 1 College Street, Worcester, MA 01610-2395.

PHONE/FAX: (508) 793-2583/2309.

ENROLLMENT: 2,600.

ARENA: Hart Recreation Center (Capacity-3,600; Year Opened-1975).

SCHOOL COLORS: Royal Purple and White.

CONFERENCE: Patriot League.

FINAL AP TOP 10 RANKINGS (2): 1950 and 1954.

NCAA TOURNAMENT APPEARANCES (8): 1947-48-50-53-56-77-80-93; 7-8 record (.467); reached Final Four in 1947 (1st) and 1948 (3rd).

NIT APPEARANCES (11): 1952-54-55-60-61-62-75-76-79-81-90; 10-10 record (.500); finished 1st in 1954 and 3rd in 1961.

ALL-TIME SCORING LEADER: Ronnie Perry (2,524 points from 1977-80).

ALL-TIME REBOUNDING LEADER: Tom Heinsohn (1,254 from 1954-56).

NCAA CONSENSUS FIRST-TEAM ALL-AMERICANS (2): Bob Cousy (1950), Tom Heinsohn (1956).

NCAA CONSENSUS SECOND-TEAM ALL-AMERICANS (3): George Kaftan (1947 and 1948), Jack Foley (1962).

HOUSTON

OFFICIAL NAME: University of Houston.

NICKNAME: Cougars.

ADDRESS: Department of Athletics, Houston, TX 77204-6742.

PHONE/FAX: (713) 743-9404/9411.

ENROLLMENT: 33,000.

ARENA: Hofheinz Pavilion (Capacity-10,060; Year Opened-1969).

SCHOOL COLORS: Scarlet and White.

CONFERENCE: Conference USA.

FINAL AP TOP 10 RANKINGS (4): 1967-68-83-84.

NCAA TOURNAMENT APPEARANCES (18): 1956-61-65-66-67-68-70-71-72-73-78-81-82-83-84-87-90-92; 26-23 record (.531); reached Final Four in 1967 (3rd), 1968 (4th), 1982 (T3rd), 1983 (2nd) and 1984 (2nd).

NAIA TOURNAMENT APPEARANCES (2): 1946 and 1947; 2-2 record (.500).

NIT APPEARANCES (6): 1962-77-85-88-91-93; 4-6 record (.400); finished 2nd in 1977.

ALL-TIME SCORING LEADER: Elvin Hayes (2,884 points from 1966-68).

ALL-TIME REBOUNDING LEADER: Elvin Hayes (1,602 from 1966-68).

NCAA CONSENSUS FIRST-TEAM ALL-AMERICANS (4): Elvin Hayes (1967 and 1968), Otis Birdsong (1977), Hakeem Olajuwon (1984).

NCAA CONSENSUS SECOND-TEAM ALL-AMERICANS (1): Clyde Drexler (1983).

IDAHO

OFFICIAL NAME: University of Idaho.

NICKNAME: Vandals.

ADDRESS: East End Kibbie Dome, Moscow, ID 83843.

PHONE/FAX: (208) 885-0211/0255.

ENROLLMENT: 14,395.

ARENA: Kibbie ASUI Dome (Capacity-10,000; Year Opened-1975).

SCHOOL COLORS: Silver and Gold.

CONFERENCE: Big West.

FINAL AP TOP 10 RANKINGS (1): 1982.

NCAA TOURNAMENT APPEARANCES (4): 1981-82-89-90; 1-4 record (.200).

NIT APPEARANCES (1): 1983; 0-1 record.

ALL-TIME SCORING LEADER: Orlando Lightfoot (2,102 points from 1992-94).

ALL-TIME REBOUNDING LEADER: Deon Watson (877 from 1991-94).

IDAHO STATE

OFFICIAL NAME: Idaho State University.

NICKNAME: Bengals.

ADDRESS: Post Office Box 8124, Pocatello, ID 83209.

PHONE/FAX: (208) 236-3651/3659.

ENROLLMENT: 12,450.

ARENA: Holt Arena (Capacity-8,721; Year Opened-1970).

SCHOOL COLORS: Orange and Black.

CONFERENCE: Big Sky.

NCAA TOURNAMENT APPEARANCES (11): 1953-54-55-56-57-58-59-60-74-77-87; 8-13 record (.381); regional runner-up in 1977.

NAIA TOURNAMENT APPEARANCES (1): 1938; 1-1 record (.500).

NIT APPEARANCES: None.

ALL-TIME SCORING LEADER: Les Roh (1,964 points from 1953-56 when school was classified as a small college).

ALL-TIME REBOUNDING LEADER: Steve Hayes (1,147 from 1974-77).

ILLINOIS

OFFICIAL NAME: University of Illinois.

NICKNAME: Fighting Illini.

ADDRESS: 1817 South Neil, Suite 201, Champaign, IL 61820.

PHONE/FAX: (217) 333-1390/5540.

ENROLLMENT: 35,000.

ARENA: Assembly Hall (Capacity-16,450; Year Opened-1963).

SCHOOL COLORS: Orange and Blue.

CONFERENCE: Big Ten.

FINAL AP TOP 10 RANKINGS (7): 1949-51-52-56-63-84-89.

NCAA TOURNAMENT APPEARANCES (17): 1942-49-51-52-63-81-83-84-85-86-87-88-89-90-93-94-95; 21-18 record (.538); reached Final Four in 1949 (3rd), 1951 (3rd), 1952 (3rd) and 1989 (T3rd).

NIT APPEARANCES (3): 1980-82-96; 5-3 record (.625); finished 3rd in 1980.

ALL-TIME SCORING LEADER: Deon Thomas (2,129 points from 1991-94).

ALL-TIME REBOUNDING LEADER: Efrem Winters (853 from 1983-86).

NCAA CONSENSUS FIRST-TEAM ALL-AMERICANS (5): Bill Hapac (1940), Andy Phillip (1942 and 1943), Walt Kirk (1945), Rod Fletcher (1952).

NCAA CONSENSUS SECOND-TEAM ALL-AMERICANS (4): Andy Phillip (1947), Bill Erickson (1949), Ken Norman (1987), Kendall Gill (1990).

ILLINOIS STATE

OFFICIAL NAME: Illinois State University.

NICKNAME: Redbirds.

ADDRESS: Horton Field House 133, College at Delaine, Normal, IL 61790-7130.

PHONE/FAX: (309) 438-3825/5634.

ENROLLMENT: 21,000.

ARENA: Redbird Arena (Capacity-10,600; Year Opened-1989).

SCHOOL COLORS: Red and White.

CONFERENCE: Missouri Valley.

NCAA DIVISION I TOURNAMENT APPEARANCES (4): 1983-84-85-90; 2-4 record (.333).

NCAA DIVISION II TOURNAMENT APPEARANCES (5): 1957-62-67-68-69; 6-7 record (.462); finished 4th in 1967.

NAIA TOURNAMENT APPEARANCES (1): 1959; 2-1 record (.667).

NIT APPEARANCES (7): 1977-78-80-87-88-95-96; 7-7 record (.500).

ALL-TIME SCORING LEADER: Doug Collins (2,240 points from 1971-73).

ALL-TIME REBOUNDING LEADER: Ron deVries (1,033 from 1972-74).

NCAA CONSENSUS FIRST-TEAM ALL-AMERICANS (1): Doug Collins (1973).

INDIANA

OFFICIAL NAME: Indiana University.

NICKNAME: Hoosiers.

ADDRESS: Assembly Hall, Bloomington, IN 47405.

PHONE/FAX: (812) 855-2421/9401.

ENROLLMENT: 35,000.

ARENA: Assembly Hall (Capacity-17,357; Year Opened-1971).

SCHOOL COLORS: Cream and Crimson.

CONFERENCE: Big Ten.

FINAL AP TOP 10 RANKINGS (16): 1951-53-54-60-73-74-75-76-80-81-83-87-89-91-92-93.

NCAA TOURNAMENT APPEARANCES (25): 1940-53-54-58-67-73-75-76-78-80-81-82-83-84-86-87-88-89-90-91-92-93-94-95 -96; 50-20 record (.714); reached Final Four in 1940 (1st), 1953 (1st), 1973 (3rd), 1976 (1st), 1981 (1st) and 1992 (T3rd).

NIT APPEARANCES (3): 1972-79-85; 8-2 record (.800); finished 1st in 1979 and 2nd in 1985.

CCAT RECORD: 3-0 to finish 1st in 1974.

ALL-TIME SCORING LEADER: Calbert Cheaney (2,613 points from 1990-93).

ALL-TIME REBOUNDING LEADER: Alan Henderson (1,091 from 1992-95).

NCAA CONSENSUS FIRST-TEAM ALL-AMERICANS (13): Branch McCracken (1930), Vern Huffman (1936), Ernie Andres (1939), Ralph Hamilton (1947), Don Schlundt (1954), Scott May (1975 and 1976), Kent Benson (1976 and 1977), Isiah Thomas (1981), Steve Alford (1986 and 1987), Calbert Cheaney (1993).

NCAA CONSENSUS SECOND-TEAM ALL-AMERICANS (9): Marv Huffman (1940), Bill Garrett (1951), Don Schlundt (1953 and 1955), Bob Leonard (1954), Archie Dees (1958), Walt Bellamy (1961), Randy Wittman (1983), Jay Edwards (1989).

INDIANA STATE

OFFICIAL NAME: Indiana State University.

NICKNAME: Sycamores.

ADDRESS: ISU Arena, 4th & Chestnut, Terre Haute, IN 47809.

PHONE/FAX: (812) 237-4160/4157.

ENROLLMENT: 11,570.

ARENA: Hulman Center (Capacity-10,200; Year Opened-1972).

SCHOOL COLORS: Blue and White.

CONFERENCE: Missouri Valley.

FINAL AP TOP 10 RANKINGS (1): 1979.

NCAA DIVISION I TOURNAMENT APPEARANCES (1): 1979; finished 2nd with a 4-1 record.

NCAA DIVISION II TOURNAMENT APPEARANCES (3): 1966-67-68; 5-4 record (.556); finished 2nd in 1968.

NAIA TOURNAMENT APPEARANCES (12): 1942-43-46-48-49-50-52-53-54-59-62-63; 25-12 record (.676); finished 1st in 1950, 2nd in 1946 and 1948, 3rd in 1953, and 4th in 1949.

NIT APPEARANCES (2): 1977 and 1978; 1-2 record (.333).

ALL-TIME SCORING LEADER: Larry Bird (2,850 points from 1977-79).

ALL-TIME REBOUNDING LEADER: Larry Bird (1,247 from 1977-79).

NCAA CONSENSUS FIRST-TEAM ALL-AMERICANS (2): Larry Bird (1978 and 1979).

NCAA CONSENSUS SECOND-TEAM ALL-AMERICANS (2): Duane Klueh (1948).

IONA

OFFICIAL NAME: Iona College.

NICKNAME: Gaels.

ADDRESS: 715 North Avenue, New Rochelle, NY 10801-1890.

PHONE/FAX: (914) 633-2334/2072.

ENROLLMENT: 7,500.

ARENA: Mulcahy Center (Capacity-3,200; Year Opened-1975).

SCHOOL COLORS: Maroon and Gold.

CONFERENCE: Metro Atlantic Athletic.

NCAA TOURNAMENT APPEARANCES (4): 1979-80-84-85; 1-4 record (.200).

NIT APPEARANCES (3): 1982-83-96; 1-3 record (.250).

ALL-TIME SCORING LEADER: Steve Burtt (2,534 points from 1981-84).

ALL-TIME REBOUNDING LEADER: Warren Isaac (1,124 from 1963-65).

IOWA

OFFICIAL NAME: University of Iowa.

NICKNAME: Hawkeyes.

ADDRESS: 205 Carver-Hawkeye Arena, Iowa City, IA 52242.

PHONE/FAX: (319) 335-9411/9417.

ENROLLMENT: 28,000.

ARENA: Carver-Hawkeye Arena (Capacity-15,500; Year Opened-1983).

SCHOOL COLORS: Old Gold and Black.

CONFERENCE: Big Ten.

FINAL AP TOP 10 RANKINGS (6): 1952-55-56-61-70-87.

NCAA TOURNAMENT APPEARANCES (17): 1955-56-70-79-80-81-82-83-85-86-87-88-89-91-92-93-96; 23-19 record (.548); reached Final Four in 1955 (4th), 1956 (2nd) and 1980 (4th).

NIT APPEARANCES (1): 1995; 2-1 record (.667).

ALL-TIME SCORING LEADER: Roy Marble (2,116 points from 1986-89).

ALL-TIME REBOUNDING LEADER: Kevin Kunnert (914 from 1971-73).

NCAA CONSENSUS FIRST-TEAM ALL-AMERICANS (2): Murray Wier (1948), Chuck Darling (1952).

NCAA CONSENSUS SECOND-TEAM ALL-AMERICANS (2): Richard Ives (1945), Herb Wilkinson (1945).

IOWA STATE

OFFICIAL NAME: Iowa State University.
NICKNAME: Cyclones.
ADDRESS: Olsen Building Annex, Ames, IA 50011.
PHONE/FAX: (515) 294-3372/0558.
ENROLLMENT: 22,755.

ARENA: James H. Hilton Coliseum (Capacity-14,020; Year Opened-1971).

SCHOOL COLORS: Cardinal and Gold.

CONFERENCE: Big 12.

NCAA TOURNAMENT APPEARANCES (9): 1944-85-86-88-89-92-93-95-96; 6-9 record (.400); reached Final Four in 1944 (T3rd).

NIT APPEARANCES (1): 1984; 0-1 record.

ALL-TIME SCORING LEADER: Jeff Grayer (2,502 points from 1985-88).

ALL-TIME REBOUNDING LEADER: Dean Uthoff (1,233 from 1977-80).

NCAA CONSENSUS SECOND-TEAM ALL-AMERICANS (1): Gary Thompson (1957).

JACKSONVILLE

OFFICIAL NAME: Jacksonville University.
NICKNAME: Dolphins.
ADDRESS: 2800 University Boulevard North, Jacksonville, FL 32211.
PHONE/FAX: (904) 744-7402/743-0067.
ENROLLMENT: 2,400.
ARENA: Jacksonville Coliseum (Capacity-9,150; Year Opened-1960).
SCHOOL COLORS: Green and White.
CONFERENCE: Sun Belt.
FINAL AP TOP 10 RANKINGS (1): 1970.
NCAA TOURNAMENT APPEARANCES (5): 1970-71-73-79-86; 4-5 record (.444); reached Final Four in 1970 (2nd).
NAIA TOURNAMENT APPEARANCES (1): 1965; 0-1 record.
NIT APPEARANCES (4): 1972-74-80-87; 5-5 record (.500); finished 3rd in 1972 and 4th in 1974.
ALL-TIME SCORING LEADER: Ralph Tiner (2,184 points from 1962-65 when school was classified as a small college).
ALL-TIME REBOUNDING LEADER: Artis Gilmore (1,224 in 1970 and 1971).
NCAA CONSENSUS FIRST-TEAM ALL-AMERICANS (1): Artis Gilmore (1971).

JAMES MADISON

OFFICIAL NAME: James Madison University.
NICKNAME: Dukes.
ADDRESS: Harrisonburg, VA 22807.
PHONE/FAX: (703) 568-6154/3703.
ENROLLMENT: 11,500.

ARENA: JMU Convocation Center (Capacity-7,612; Year Opened-1982).

SCHOOL COLORS: Purple and Gold.

CONFERENCE: Colonial Athletic Association.

NCAA DIVISION I TOURNAMENT APPEARANCES (4): 1981-82-83-94; 3-4 record (.429).

NCAA DIVISION II TOURNAMENT APPEARANCES (2): 1974 and 1976; 0-3 record.

NIT APPEARANCES (5): 1987-90-91-92-93; 0-5 record.

ALL-TIME SCORING LEADER: Steve Stiepler (2,126 points from 1977-80).

ALL-TIME REBOUNDING LEADER: Steve Stiepler (917 from 1977-80).

KANSAS

OFFICIAL NAME: University of Kansas.
NICKNAME: Jayhawks.
ADDRESS: 104 Allen Fieldhouse, Lawrence, KS 66045.
PHONE/FAX: (913) 864-3417/7944.
ENROLLMENT: 25,240.

ARENA: Allen Fieldhouse (Capacity-16,300; Year Opened-1955).

SCHOOL COLORS: Crimson and Blue.

CONFERENCE: Big 12.

FINAL AP TOP 10 RANKINGS (15): 1952-53-57-58-66-67-71-74-78-86-90-92-93-95-96.

NCAA TOURNAMENT APPEARANCES (25): 1940-42-52-53-57-60-66-67-71-74-75-78-81-84-85-86-87-88-90-91-92-93-94-95-96; 54-25 record (.684); reached Final Four in 1940 (2nd), 1952 (1st), 1953 (2nd), 1957 (2nd), 1971 (4th), 1974 (4th), 1986 (T3rd), 1988 (1st), 1991 (2nd) and 1993 (T3rd).

NIT APPEARANCES (2): 1968 and 1969; 3-2 record (.600); finished 2nd in 1968.

ALL-TIME SCORING LEADER: Danny Manning (2,951 points from 1985-88).

ALL-TIME REBOUNDING LEADER: Danny Manning (1,187 from 1985-88).

NCAA CONSENSUS FIRST-TEAM ALL-AMERICANS (9): Fred Pralle (1938), Howard Engleman (1941), Charles Black (1943), Clyde Lovellette (1951 and 1952), Wilt Chamberlain (1957 and 1958), Danny Manning (1987 and 1988).

NCAA CONSENSUS SECOND-TEAM ALL-AMERICANS (7): Charles Black (1946), Walt Wesley (1966), Joseph "Jo Jo" White (1968 and 1969), Isaac "Bud" Stallworth (1972), Danny Manning (1986), Jacque Vaughn (1996).

KANSAS STATE

OFFICIAL NAME: Kansas State University.
NICKNAME: Wildcats.
ADDRESS: 144 Bramlage Coliseum, 1800 College Avenue, Manhattan, KS 66502.
PHONE/FAX: (913) 532-6735/6093.
ENROLLMENT: 20,775.

ARENA: Fred Bramlage Coliseum (Capacity-13,500; Year Opened-1988).

SCHOOL COLORS: Purple and White.

CONFERENCE: Big 12.

FINAL AP TOP 10 RANKINGS (7): 1951-52-58-59-61-62-73.

NCAA TOURNAMENT APPEARANCES (22): 1948-51-56-58-59-61-64-68-70-72-73-75-77-80-81-82-87-88-89-90-93-96; 27-26 record (.509); reached Final Four in 1948 (4th), 1951 (2nd), 1958 (4th) and 1964 (4th).

NIT APPEARANCES (3): 1976-92-94; 4-4 record (.500); finished 4th in 1994.

CCAT RECORD: 0-1 in 1974.

ALL-TIME SCORING LEADER: Mike Evans (2,115 points from 1975-78).

ALL-TIME REBOUNDING LEADER: Ed Nealy (1,071 from 1979-82).

NCAA CONSENSUS FIRST-TEAM ALL-AMERICANS (2): Bob Boozer (1958 and 1959).

NCAA CONSENSUS SECOND-TEAM ALL-AMERICANS (3): Ernie Barrett (1951), Dick Knostman (1953), Mitch Richmond (1988).

KENT

OFFICIAL NAME: Kent University.
NICKNAME: Golden Flashes.
ADDRESS: MAC Center, Kent, OH 44242-0001.
PHONE/FAX: (216) 672-2110/2112.
ENROLLMENT: 29,785.
ARENA: Memorial Athletic and Convocation Center (Capacity-6,327; Year Opened-1950).
SCHOOL COLORS: Blue and Gold.
CONFERENCE: Mid-American.
NCAA TOURNAMENT APPEARANCES: None.
NIT APPEARANCES (3): 1985-89-90; 0-3 record.
ALL-TIME SCORING LEADER: Burrell McGhee (1,710 points from 1977-79).
ALL-TIME REBOUNDING LEADER: Trent Grooms (1,012 from 1977-80).

KENTUCKY

OFFICIAL NAME: University of Kentucky.
NICKNAME: Wildcats.
ADDRESS: Memorial Coliseum, Avenue of Champions, Lexington, KY 40506-0019.
PHONE/FAX: (606) 257-8000/323-4310.
ENROLLMENT: 24,200.
ARENA: Rupp Arena (Capacity-24,000; Year Opened-1976).
SCHOOL COLORS: Blue and White.
CONFERENCE: Southeastern.
FINAL AP TOP 10 RANKINGS (31): 1949-50-51-52-54-55-56-57-58-59-62-64-66-68-69-70-71-75-77-78-80-81-84-86 -88-91-92-93-94-95-96.
NCAA TOURNAMENT APPEARANCES (38): 1942-45-48-49-51-52-55-56-57-58-59-61-62-64-66-68-69-70-71-72-73-75-77-78 -80-81-82-83-84-85-86-87-88-92-93-94-95-96; 72-34 record (.679); reached Final Four in 1942 (T3rd), 1948 (1st), 1949 (1st), 1951 (1st), 1958 (1st), 1966 (2nd), 1975 (2nd), 1978 (1st), 1984 (T3rd), 1993 (T3rd) and 1996 (1st).
NIT APPEARANCES (7): 1944-46-47-49-50-76-79; 11-5 record (.688); finished 3rd in 1944, 1st in 1946, 2nd in 1947 and 1st in 1976.
ALL-TIME SCORING LEADER: Dan Issel (2,138 points from 1968-70).
ALL-TIME REBOUNDING LEADER: Dan Issel (1,078 from 1968-70).
NCAA CONSENSUS FIRST-TEAM ALL-AMERICANS (18): Forest Sale (1932 and 1933), Leroy Edwards (1935), Bob Brannum (1944), Ralph Beard (1947, 1948 and 1949), Alex Groza (1947 and 1949), Bill Spivey (1951), Cliff Hagan (1952 and 1954), Johnny Cox (1959), Charles "Cotton" Nash (1964), Dan Issel (1970), Kyle Macy (1980), Kenny Walker (1986), Jamal Mashburn (1993).
NCAA CONSENSUS SECOND-TEAM ALL-AMERICANS (18): Bernie Opper (1939), Jack Parkinson (1946), Alex Groza (1948), Wallace Jones (1949), Frank Ramsey (1954), Bob Burrow (1956), Charles "Cotton" Nash (1962 and 1963), Louie Dampier (1966 and 1967), Dan Issel (1969), Kevin Grevey (1975), Jack Givens (1978), Rick Robey (1978), Sam Bowie (1981), Mel Turpin (1984), Kenny Walker (1985), Tony Delk (1996).

LAFAYETTE

OFFICIAL NAME: Lafayette College.
NICKNAME: Leopards.
ADDRESS: 17 Watson Hall, Easton, PA 18042-1768.

PHONE/FAX: (610) 250-5122/5127.
ENROLLMENT: 2,000.
ARENA: Allan P. Kirby Field House (Capacity-3,500; Year Opened-1973).
SCHOOL COLORS: Maroon and White.
CONFERENCE: Patriot League.
NCAA TOURNAMENT APPEARANCES (1): 1957; 0-2 record.
NIT APPEARANCES (5): 1955-56-72-75-80; 1-5 record (.167).
ALL-TIME SCORING LEADER: Tracy Tripucka (1,973 points from 1970-72).
ALL-TIME REBOUNDING LEADER: Jim Radcliff (1,148 from 1955-57).

LAMAR

OFFICIAL NAME: Lamar University.
NICKNAME: Cardinals.
ADDRESS: Post Office Box 10066, Beaumont, TX 77710.
PHONE/FAX: (409) 880-2323/2338.
ENROLLMENT: 9,110.
ARENA: Montagne Center (Capacity-10,080; Year Opened-1984).
SCHOOL COLORS: Red and White.
CONFERENCE: Sun Belt.
NCAA DIVISION I TOURNAMENT APPEARANCES (4): 1979-80-81-83; 5-4 record (.556).
NCAA DIVISION II TOURNAMENT APPEARANCES (5): 1960-62-63-64-66; 5-5 record (.500).
NIT APPEARANCES (4): 1982-84-85-86; 2-4 record (.333).
ALL-TIME SCORING LEADER: Mike Olliver (2,518 points from 1978-81).
ALL-TIME REBOUNDING LEADER: Clarence Kea (1,143 from 1977-80).

LA SALLE

OFFICIAL NAME: La Salle University.
NICKNAME: Explorers.
ADDRESS: 1900 West Olney Avenue, Box 805, Philadelphia, PA 19141-1199.
PHONE/FAX: (215) 951-1513/1694.
ENROLLMENT: 5,800.
ARENA: CoreStates Spectrum (Capacity-8,952; Year Opened-1967).
SCHOOL COLORS: Blue and Gold.
CONFERENCE: Atlantic 10.
FINAL AP TOP 10 RANKINGS (5): 1950-53-54-55-69.
NCAA TOURNAMENT APPEARANCES (11): 1954-55-68-75-78-80-83-88-89-90-92; 11-10 record (.524); reached Final Four in 1954 (1st) and 1955 (2nd).
NIT APPEARANCES (11): 1948-50-51-52-53-63-65-71-84-87-91; 9-10 record (.474); finished 1st in 1952 and 2nd in 1987.
ALL-TIME SCORING LEADER: Lionel Simmons (3,217 points from 1987-90).
ALL-TIME REBOUNDING LEADER: Tom Gola (2,201 from 1952-55).
NCAA CONSENSUS FIRST-TEAM ALL-AMERICANS (5): Tom Gola (1953, 1954 and 1955), Michael Brooks (1980), Lionel Simmons (1990).
NCAA CONSENSUS SECOND-TEAM ALL-AMERICANS (2): Ken Durrett (1971), Lionel Simmons (1989).

LEHIGH

OFFICIAL NAME: Lehigh University.
NICKNAME: Engineers.
ADDRESS: 641 Taylor Street, Bethlehem, PA 18015-3187.
PHONE/FAX: (610) 758-3174/4407.

ENROLLMENT: 4,400.

ARENA: Stabler Arena (Capacity-5,600; Year Opened-1979).

SCHOOL COLORS: Brown and White.

CONFERENCE: Patriot League.

NCAA TOURNAMENT APPEARANCES (2): 1985 and 1988; 0-2 record.

NIT APPEARANCES: None.

ALL-TIME SCORING LEADER: Daren Queenan (2,703 points from 1985-88).

ALL-TIME REBOUNDING LEADER: Daren Queenan (1,013 from 1985-88).

LONG BEACH STATE

OFFICIAL NAME: California State University (At Long Beach).

NICKNAME: 49ers.

ADDRESS: 1250 Bellflower Boulevard, Long Beach, CA 90840.

PHONE/FAX: (310) 985-7978/8197.

ENROLLMENT: 27,445.

ARENA: The Pyramid (Capacity-5,000; Year Opened-1994).

SCHOOL COLORS: Black and Gold.

CONFERENCE: Big West.

FINAL AP TOP 10 RANKINGS (3): 1972-73-74.

NCAA DIVISION I TOURNAMENT APPEARANCES (7): 1970-71-72-1973-77-93-95; 7-8 record (.467); regional runner-up in 1971 and 1972.

NCAA DIVISION II TOURNAMENT APPEARANCES (1): 1961; 1-1 record (.500).

NIT APPEARANCES (3): 1980-88-90; 2-3 record (.400).

ALL-TIME SCORING LEADER: Lucious Harris (2,312 points from 1990-93).

ALL-TIME REBOUNDING LEADER: Francois Wise (896 from 1977-80).

NCAA CONSENSUS FIRST-TEAM ALL-AMERICANS (2): Ed Ratleff (1972 and 1973).

LONG ISLAND

OFFICIAL NAME: Long Island University.

NICKNAME: Blackbirds.

ADDRESS: University Plaza, Brooklyn, NY 11201.

PHONE/FAX: (718) 488-1420/780-4046.

ENROLLMENT: 9,500.

ARENA: Schwartz Athletic Center (Capacity-1,700; Year Opened-1963).

SCHOOL COLORS: Blue and White.

CONFERENCE: Northeast.

NCAA DIVISION I TOURNAMENT APPEARANCES (2): 1981 and 1984; 0-2 record.

NCAA DIVISION II TOURNAMENT APPEARANCES (3): 1965-66-67; 6-3 record (.667).

NIT APPEARANCES (9): 1938-39-40-41-42-47-50-68-82; 7-7 record (.500); finished 1st in 1939 and 1941.

ALL-TIME SCORING LEADER: Joe Griffin (1,830 points from 1992-95).

ALL-TIME REBOUNDING LEADER: Carey Scurry (1,013 from 1983-85; played freshman season in junior college).

NCAA CONSENSUS FIRST-TEAM ALL-AMERICANS (2): Jules Bender (1937), Irving Torgoff (1939).

NCAA CONSENSUS SECOND-TEAM ALL-AMERICANS (2): Oscar Schechtman (1941), Sherman White (1950).

LOUISIANA STATE

OFFICIAL NAME: Louisiana State University.

NICKNAME: Tigers.

ADDRESS: Post Office Box 25095, Baton Rouge, LA 70894-5095.

PHONE/FAX: (504) 388-8226/1861.

ENROLLMENT: 24,750.

ARENA: Pete Maravich Assembly Center (Capacity-14,164; Year Opened-1972).

SCHOOL COLORS: Purple and Gold.

CONFERENCE: Southeastern.

FINAL AP TOP 10 RANKINGS (4): 1953-79-80-81.

NCAA TOURNAMENT APPEARANCES (15): 1953-54-79-80-81-84-85-86-87-88-89-90-91-92-93; 17-18 record (.486); reached Final Four in 1953 (4th), 1981 (4th) and 1986 (T3rd).

NIT APPEARANCES (3): 1970-82-83; 2-4 record (.333); finished 4th in 1970.

ALL-TIME SCORING LEADER: Pete Maravich (3,667 points from 1968-70).

ALL-TIME REBOUNDING LEADER: Durand "Rudy" Macklin (1,276 from 1977-81; missed 1978-79 season because of a broken leg).

NCAA CONSENSUS FIRST-TEAM ALL-AMERICANS (8): Bob Pettit (1954), Pete Maravich (1968, 1969 and 1970), Chris Jackson (1989 and 1990), Shaquille O'Neal (1991 and 1992).

NCAA CONSENSUS SECOND-TEAM ALL-AMERICANS (2): Bob Pettit (1953), Durand "Rudy" Macklin (1981).

LOUISIANA TECH

OFFICIAL NAME: Louisiana Tech University.

NICKNAME: Bulldogs.

ADDRESS: Post Office Box 3166TS, Ruston, LA 71272.

PHONE/FAX: (318) 257-3144/3757.

ENROLLMENT: 10,380.

ARENA: Thomas Assembly Center (Capacity-8,000; Year Opened-1982).

SCHOOL COLORS: Columbia Blue and Red.

CONFERENCE: Sun Belt.

FINAL AP TOP 10 RANKINGS (1): 1985.

NCAA DIVISION I TOURNAMENT APPEARANCES (5): 1984-85-87-89-91; 4-5 record (.444).

NCAA DIVISION II TOURNAMENT APPEARANCES (2): 1967 and 1971; 2-2 record (.500).

NAIA TOURNAMENT APPEARANCES (4): 1942-46-53-55; 1-4 record (.200).

NIT APPEARANCES (4): 1986-88-90-92; 5-4 record (.556); finished 3rd in 1986.

ALL-TIME SCORING LEADER: Mike Green (2,340 points from 1970-73 when school was classified as a small college).

ALL-TIME REBOUNDING LEADER: Mike Green (1,575 from 1970-73 when school was classified as a small college).

LOUISVILLE

OFFICIAL NAME: University of Louisville.

NICKNAME: Cardinals.

ADDRESS: Belknap Campus, Louisville, KY 40292.

PHONE/FAX: (502) 852-6581/7401.

ENROLLMENT: 23,000.

ARENA: Freedom Hall (Capacity-18,865; Year Opened-1956).

SCHOOL COLORS: Red, Black and White.

CONFERENCE: Conference USA.

FINAL AP TOP 10 RANKINGS (11): 1956-57-67-68-72-75-78-80-83-86-94.

NCAA TOURNAMENT APPEARANCES (26): 1951-59-61-64-67-68-72-74-75-77-78-79-80-81-82-83-84-86-88-89-90-92-93-94 -95-96; 45-28 record (.616); reached Final Four in 1959 (4th), 1972 (4th), 1975 (3rd), 1980 (1st), 1982 (T3rd), 1983 (T3rd) and 1986 (1st).

NAIA TOURNAMENT APPEARANCES (1): 1948; won title with a 5-0 record.

NIT APPEARANCES (12): 1952-53-54-55-56-66-69-70-71-73-76-85; 10-12 record (.455); finished 1st in 1956 and 4th in 1985.

ALL-TIME SCORING LEADER: Darrell Griffith (2,333 points from 1977-80).

ALL-TIME REBOUNDING LEADER: Charlie Tyra (1,617 from 1954-57).

NCAA CONSENSUS FIRST-TEAM ALL-AMERICANS (6): Charlie Tyra (1957), Wes Unseld (1967 and 1968), Darrell Griffith (1980), Pervis Ellison (1989), Clifford Rozier (1994).

NCAA CONSENSUS SECOND-TEAM ALL-AMERICANS (1): Jim Price (1972).

LOYOLA (ILL.)

OFFICIAL NAME: Loyola University.

NICKNAME: Ramblers.

ADDRESS: 6525 North Sheridan Road, Chicago, IL 60626.

PHONE/FAX: (312) 508-2575/3884.

ENROLLMENT: 15,885.

ARENAS: Alumni Gym (Capacity-2,975; Year Opened-1926) and Rosemont Horizon (Capacity-17,500; Year Opened-1980).

SCHOOL COLORS: Maroon and Gold.

CONFERENCE: Midwestern Collegiate.

FINAL AP TOP 10 RANKINGS (3): 1963-64-66.

NCAA TOURNAMENT APPEARANCES (5): 1963-64-66-68-85; 9-4 record (.692); reached Final Four in 1963 (1st).

NAIA TOURNAMENT APPEARANCES (1): 1943; 0-1 record.

NIT APPEARANCES (4): 1939-49-62-80; 6-4 record (.600); finished 2nd in 1939, 2nd in 1949 and 3rd in 1962.

ALL-TIME SCORING LEADER: Alfredrick Hughes (2,914 points from 1982-85).

ALL-TIME REBOUNDING LEADER: LaRue Martin (1,062 from 1970-72).

NCAA CONSENSUS FIRST-TEAM ALL-AMERICANS (1): Jerry Harkness (1963).

NCAA CONSENSUS SECOND-TEAM ALL-AMERICANS (1): Michael Novak (1939).

LOYOLA MARYMOUNT

OFFICIAL NAME: Loyola Marymount University.

NICKNAME: Lions.

ADDRESS: 7900 Loyola Boulevard, Los Angeles, CA 90045-2699.

PHONE/FAX: (310) 338-7643/2703.

ENROLLMENT: 3,900.

ARENA: Albert Gersten Pavilion (Capacity-4,156; Year Opened-1982).

SCHOOL COLORS: Crimson and Blue.

CONFERENCE: West Coast.

NCAA TOURNAMENT APPEARANCES (5): 1961-80-88-89-90; 5-5 record (.500); regional runner-up in 1990.

NAIA TOURNAMENT APPEARANCES (1): 1955; 0-1 record.

NIT APPEARANCES (1): 1986; 1-1 record (.500).

ALL-TIME SCORING LEADER: Eric "Hank" Gathers (2,490 points from 1988-90; played his freshman season at Southern Cal in 1985-86).

ALL-TIME REBOUNDING LEADER: Jim Haderlein (1,161 from 1969-71).

NCAA CONSENSUS SECOND-TEAM ALL-AMERICANS (2): Eric "Hank" Gathers (1990), Greg "Bo" Kimble (1990).

MANHATTAN

OFFICIAL NAME: Manhattan College.

NICKNAME: Jaspers.

ADDRESS: Manhattan College Parkway, Riverdale, NY 10471-4098.

PHONE/FAX: (718) 920-0228/543-8802.

ENROLLMENT: 3,400.

ARENA: Draddy Gymnasium (Capacity-3,000; Year Opened-1979).

SCHOOL COLORS: Kelly Green and White.

CONFERENCE: Metro Atlantic Athletic.

NCAA TOURNAMENT APPEARANCES (4): 1956-58-93-95; 2-5 record (.286).

NAIA TOURNAMENT APPEARANCES (1): 1948; 2-1 record (.667).

NIT APPEARANCES (16): 1943-49-53-54-55-57-59-65-66-70-73-74-75-92-94-96; 6-17 record (.261); finished 4th in 1953.

ALL-TIME SCORING LEADER: Keith Bullock (1,992 points from 1990-93).

ALL-TIME REBOUNDING LEADER: Bill Campion (1,070 from 1973-75).

MARQUETTE

OFFICIAL NAME: Marquette University.

NICKNAME: Golden Eagles.

ADDRESS: 1212 West Wisconsin Avenue, Milwaukee, WI 53233.

PHONE/FAX: (414) 288-7447/6519.

ENROLLMENT: 10,750.

ARENA: Bradley Center (Capacity-18,592; Year Opened-1988).

SCHOOL COLORS: Blue and Gold.

CONFERENCE: Conference USA.

FINAL AP TOP 10 RANKINGS (10): 1955-70-71-72-73-74-76-77-78-79.

NCAA TOURNAMENT APPEARANCES (20): 1955-59-61-68-69-71-72-73-74-75-76-77-78-79-80-82-83-93-94-96; 28-21 record (.571); reached Final Four in 1974 (2nd) and 1977 (1st).

NIT APPEARANCES (11): 1956-63-67-70-81-84-85-86-87-90-95; 18-9 record (.667); finished 3rd in 1963, 2nd in 1967 and 1995, and 1st in 1970.

ALL-TIME SCORING LEADER: George Thompson (1,773 points from 1967-69).

ALL-TIME REBOUNDING LEADER: Don Kojis (1,222 from 1959-61).

NCAA CONSENSUS FIRST-TEAM ALL-AMERICANS (3): Dean Meminger (1971), Jim Chones (1972), Alfred "Butch" Lee (1978).

NCAA CONSENSUS SECOND-TEAM ALL-AMERICANS (3): Earl Tatum (1976), Alfred "Butch" Lee (1977), Sam Worthen (1980).

MARSHALL

OFFICIAL NAME: Marshall University.

NICKNAME: Thundering Herd.

ADDRESS: 400 Hal Greer Boulevard, Huntington, WV 25755.

PHONE/FAX: (304) 696-5275/2325.

ENROLLMENT: 12,530.

ARENA: Henderson Center (Capacity-10,250; Year Opened-1981).

SCHOOL COLORS: Green and White.

CONFERENCE: Southern.

NCAA TOURNAMENT APPEARANCES (5): 1956-72-84-85-87; 0-5 record.

NAIA TOURNAMENT APPEARANCES (3): 1938-47-48; 7-2 record (.778); finished 1st in 1947.

NIT APPEARANCES (4): 1967-68-73-88; 2-5 record (.286); finished 4th in 1967.

ALL-TIME SCORING LEADER: Skip Henderson (2,574 points from 1985-88).

ALL-TIME REBOUNDING LEADER: Charlie Slack (1,916 from 1953-56).

NCAA CONSENSUS SECOND-TEAM ALL-AMERICANS (1): Leo Byrd (1959).

MARYLAND

OFFICIAL NAME: University of Maryland.

NICKNAMES: Terrapins, Terps.

ADDRESS: Post Office Box 295, College Park, MD 20741-0295, or 1102 Cole Field House, Campus Drive, 20742.

PHONE/FAX: (301) 314-7064/9094.

ENROLLMENT: 30,370.

ARENA: Cole Field House (Capacity-14,500; Year Opened-1955).

SCHOOL COLORS: Red, White, Black and Gold.

CONFERENCE: Atlantic Coast.

FINAL AP TOP 10 RANKINGS (6): 1958-73-74-75-80-95.

NCAA TOURNAMENT APPEARANCES (13): 1958-73-75-80-81-83-84-85-86-88-94-95-96; 17-13 record (.567); regional runner-up in 1973 and 1975.

NIT APPEARANCES (4): 1972-79-82-90; 7-3 record (.700); finished 1st in 1972.

ALL-TIME SCORING LEADER: Len Bias (2,149 points from 1983-86).

ALL-TIME REBOUNDING LEADER: Len Elmore (1,053 from 1972-74).

NCAA CONSENSUS FIRST-TEAM ALL-AMERICANS (5): Louis Berger (1932), John Lucas (1975 and 1976), Len Bias (1986), Joe Smith (1995).

NCAA CONSENSUS SECOND-TEAM ALL-AMERICANS (5): Tom McMillen (1973), Len Elmore (1974), Albert King (1980), Len Bias (1985), Walt Williams (1992).

MASSACHUSETTS

OFFICIAL NAME: University of Massachusetts-Amherst.

NICKNAMES: Minutemen, UMass.

ADDRESS: Boyden Building, Mullins Center, Amherst, MA 01003.

PHONE/FAX: (413) 545-2439/1556.

ENROLLMENT: 16, 825.

ARENA: William D. Mullins Memorial Center (Capacity-9,493; Year Opened-1992).

SCHOOL COLORS: Maroon and White.

CONFERENCE: Atlantic 10.

FINAL AP TOP 10 RANKINGS (3): 1994-95-96.

NCAA TOURNAMENT APPEARANCES (6): 1962-92-93-94-95-96; 11-6 record (.647); reached Final Four in 1996 (T3rd).

NIT APPEARANCES (8): 1970-71-73-74-75-77-90-91; 5-9 record (.357); finished 4th in 1991.

ALL-TIME SCORING LEADER: Jim McCoy (2,374 points from 1989-92).

ALL-TIME REBOUNDING LEADER: Lou Roe (1,070 from 1992-95).

NCAA CONSENSUS FIRST-TEAM ALL-AMERICANS (1): Marcus Camby (1996).

NCAA CONSENSUS SECOND-TEAM ALL-AMERICANS (1): Lou Roe (1995).

MEMPHIS

OFFICIAL NAME: University of Memphis.

NICKNAME: Tigers.

ADDRESS: Athletic Office Building, Memphis, TN 38152.

PHONE/FAX: (901) 678-2337/4134.

ENROLLMENT: 21,500.

ARENA: The Pyramid (Capacity-20,142; Year Opened-1991).

SCHOOL COLORS: Blue and Gray.

CONFERENCE: Conference USA.

FINAL AP TOP 10 RANKINGS (2): 1982 and 1985.

NCAA TOURNAMENT APPEARANCES (16): 1955-56-62-73-76-82-83-84-85-86-88-89-92-93-95-96; 18-16 record (.529); reached Final Four in 1973 (2nd) and 1985 (T3rd).

NAIA TOURNAMENT APPEARANCES (2): 1951 and 1952; 3-2 record (.600).

NIT APPEARANCES (11): 1957-60-61-63-67-72-74-75-77-90-91; 6-11 record (.353); finished 2nd in 1957.

ALL-TIME SCORING LEADER: Keith Lee (2,408 points from 1982-85).

ALL-TIME REBOUNDING LEADER: Keith Lee (1,336 from 1982-85).

NCAA CONSENSUS FIRST-TEAM ALL-AMERICANS (3): Keith Lee (1983 and 1985), Anfernee Hardaway (1993).

NCAA CONSENSUS SECOND-TEAM ALL-AMERICANS (2): Larry Finch (1973), Keith Lee (1984).

MIAMI (FLA.)

OFFICIAL NAME: University of Miami.

NICKNAME: Hurricanes.

ADDRESS: Post Office Box 248167, Coral Gables, FL 33124-0814.

PHONE/FAX: (305) 284-3244/2807.

ENROLLMENT: 13,155.

ARENA: Miami Arena (Capacity-15,388; Year Opened-1988).

SCHOOL COLORS: Orange, Green and White.

CONFERENCE: Big East.

FINAL AP TOP 10 RANKINGS (1): 1960.

NCAA TOURNAMENT APPEARANCES (1): 1960; 0-1 record.

NAIA TOURNAMENT APPEARANCES (1): 1949; 0-1 record.

NIT APPEARANCES (4): 1961-63-64-95; 1-4 record (.200).

ALL-TIME SCORING LEADER: Rick Barry (2,298 points from 1963-65).

ALL-TIME REBOUNDING LEADER: Rick Barry (1,274 from 1963-65).

NCAA CONSENSUS FIRST-TEAM ALL-AMERICANS (1): Rick Barry (1965).

MIAMI (OHIO)

OFFICIAL NAME: Miami University.

NICKNAME: Redskins.

ADDRESS: 230 Millett Hall, Oxford, OH 45056.

PHONE/FAX: (513) 529-4327/6729.

ENROLLMENT: 16,000.

ARENA: Millett Hall (Capacity-9,200; Year Opened-1968).

SCHOOL COLORS: Red and White.

CONFERENCE: Mid-American.

NCAA TOURNAMENT APPEARANCES (14): 1953-55-57-58-66-69-71-73-78-84-85-86-92-95; 4-16 record (.200).

NIT APPEARANCES (4): 1970-93-94-96; 2-4 record (.333).

ALL-TIME SCORING LEADER: Ron Harper (2,377 points from 1983-86).

ALL-TIME REBOUNDING LEADER: Ron Harper (1,119 from 1983-86).

NCAA CONSENSUS SECOND-TEAM ALL-AMERICANS (1): Ron Harper (1986).

MICHIGAN

OFFICIAL NAME: University of Michigan.

NICKNAME: Wolverines.

ADDRESS: 1000 South State Street, Ann Arbor, MI 48109-2201.

PHONE/FAX: (313) 763-1381/747-1188.

ENROLLMENT: 36,845.

ARENA: Crisler Arena (Capacity-13,562; Year Opened-1967).

SCHOOL COLORS: Maize and Blue.

CONFERENCE: Big Ten.

FINAL AP TOP 10 RANKINGS (11): 1964-65-66-74-76-77-85-86-88-89-93.

NCAA TOURNAMENT APPEARANCES (19): 1948-64-65-66-74-75-76-77-85-86-87-88-89-90-92-93-94-95-96; 40-18 record (.690); reached Final Four in 1964 (3rd), 1965 (2nd), 1976 (2nd), 1989 (1st), 1992 (2nd) and 1993 (2nd).

NIT APPEARANCES (5): 1971-80-81-84-91; 10-4 record (.714); finished 1st in 1984.

ALL-TIME SCORING LEADER: Glen Rice (2,442 points from 1986-89).

ALL-TIME REBOUNDING LEADER: Rudy Tomjanovich (1,039 from 1968-70).

NCAA CONSENSUS FIRST-TEAM ALL-AMERICANS (5): Cazzie Russell (1965 and 1966), Rickey Green (1977), Gary Grant (1988), Chris Webber (1993).

NCAA CONSENSUS SECOND-TEAM ALL-AMERICANS (8): Cazzie Russell (1964), Bill Buntin (1965), Henry Wilmore (1972), Michael "Campy" Russell (1974), Phil Hubbard (1977), Glen Rice (1989), Rumeal Robinson (1990), Jalen Rose (1994).

MICHIGAN STATE

OFFICIAL NAME: Michigan State University.

NICKNAME: Spartans.

ADDRESS: Fourth Floor, Olds Hall, East Lansing, MI 48824-1044.

PHONE/FAX: (517) 355-2271/353-9636.

ENROLLMENT: 40,645.

ARENA: Jack Breslin Student Events Center (Capacity-15,138; Year Opened-1989).

SCHOOL COLORS: Green and White.

CONFERENCE: Big Ten.

FINAL AP TOP 10 RANKINGS (4): 1959-78-79-90.

NCAA TOURNAMENT APPEARANCES (11): 1957-59-78-79-85-86-90-91-92-94-95; 17-11 record (.607); reached Final Four in 1957 (4th) and 1979 (1st).

NIT APPEARANCES (4): 1983-89-93-96; 5-5 record (.500); finished 4th in 1989.

ALL-TIME SCORING LEADER: Shawn Respert (2,531 points from 1991-95; missed majority of 1990-91 season recovering from knee injury sustained in high school playoffs).

ALL-TIME REBOUNDING LEADER: Greg Kelser (1,092 from 1976-79).

NCAA CONSENSUS FIRST-TEAM ALL-AMERICANS (2): Earvin "Magic" Johnson (1979), Shawn Respert (1995).

NCAA CONSENSUS SECOND-TEAM ALL-AMERICANS (3): Johnny Green (1959), Scott Skiles (1986), Steve Smith (1991).

MIDDLE TENNESSEE STATE

OFFICIAL NAME: Middle Tennessee State University.

NICKNAME: Blue Raiders.

ADDRESS: Box 20, Murfreesboro, TN 37132.

PHONE/FAX: (615) 898-2450/5626.

ENROLLMENT: 17,385.

ARENA: Hale Arena (Capacity-11,520; Year Opened-1972).

SCHOOL COLORS: Navy Blue and White.

CONFERENCE: Ohio Valley.

NCAA TOURNAMENT APPEARANCES (6): 1975-77-82-85-87-89; 2-6 record (.250).

NAIA TOURNAMENT APPEARANCES (1): 1955; 0-1 record.

NIT APPEARANCES (2): 1986 and 1988; 2-2 record (.500).

ALL-TIME SCORING LEADER: Robert Taylor (1,622 points from 1990-93).

ALL-TIME REBOUNDING LEADER: Warren Kidd (1,048 from 1990-93).

MINNESOTA

OFFICIAL NAME: University of Minnesota.

NICKNAME: Golden Gophers.

ADDRESS: 208 Bierman Athletic Building, 516 15th Avenue SE, Minneapolis, MN 55455-0101.

PHONE/FAX: (612) 625-4090/0359.

ENROLLMENT: 39,000.

ARENA: Williams Arena (Capacity-14,300; Year Opened-1928).

SCHOOL COLORS: Maroon and Gold.

CONFERENCE: Big Ten.

FINAL AP TOP 10 RANKINGS (4): 1949-65-73-82.

NCAA TOURNAMENT APPEARANCES (6): 1972-82-89-90-94-95; 8-6 record (.571); regional runner-up in 1990.

NIT APPEARANCES (7): 1973-80-81-83-92-93-96; 13-6 record (.684); finished 2nd in 1980 and 1st in 1993.

ALL-TIME SCORING LEADER: Voshon Lenard (2,103 points from 1992-95).

ALL-TIME REBOUNDING LEADER: Mychal Thompson (956 from 1975-78).

NCAA CONSENSUS FIRST-TEAM ALL-AMERICANS (3): Jim McIntyre (1948), Dick Garmaker (1955), Mychal Thompson (1978).

NCAA CONSENSUS SECOND-TEAM ALL-AMERICANS (3): Jim McIntyre (1949), Jim Brewer (1973), Mychal Thompson (1977).

MISSISSIPPI

OFFICIAL NAME: University of Mississippi.

NICKNAME: Rebels.

ADDRESS: Fraternity Row, Post Office Box 217, University, MS 38677.

PHONE/FAX: (601) 232-7522/7006.

ENROLLMENT: 12,540.

ARENA: C.M. "Tad" Smith Coliseum (Capacity-8,135; Year Opened-1966).

SCHOOL COLORS: Cardinal Red and Navy Blue.

CONFERENCE: Southeastern.

NCAA TOURNAMENT APPEARANCES (1): 1981; 0-1 record.

NIT APPEARANCES (5): 1980-82-83-87-89; 4-5 record (.444).

ALL-TIME SCORING LEADER: John Stroud (2,328 points from 1977-80).

ALL-TIME REBOUNDING LEADER: Walter Actwood (945 from 1974-77).

NCAA CONSENSUS SECOND-TEAM ALL-AMERICANS (1): Johnny Neumann (1971).

MISSISSIPPI STATE

OFFICIAL NAME: Mississippi State University.

NICKNAME: Bulldogs.

ADDRESS: Post Office Drawer 5308, Mississippi State, MS 39762.

PHONE/FAX: (601) 325-2703/2563.

ENROLLMENT: 13,575.

ARENA: Humphrey Coliseum (Capacity-9,419; Year Opened-1975).

SCHOOL COLORS: Maroon and White.

CONFERENCE: Southeastern.

FINAL AP TOP 10 RANKINGS (3): 1959-62-63.

NCAA TOURNAMENT APPEARANCES (4): 1963-91-95-96; 7-4 record (.636); reached Final Four in 1996 (T3rd).

NIT APPEARANCES (3): 1979-90-94; 1-3 record (.250).

ALL-TIME SCORING LEADER: Jeff Malone (2,142 points from 1980-83).

ALL-TIME REBOUNDING LEADER: Bailey Howell (1,277 from 1957-59).

NCAA CONSENSUS FIRST-TEAM ALL-AMERICANS (1): Bailey Howell (1959).

NCAA CONSENSUS SECOND-TEAM ALL-AMERICANS (1): Bailey Howell (1958).

MISSOURI

OFFICIAL NAME: University of Missouri.

NICKNAMES: Tigers, Mizzou.

ADDRESS: Box 677, Hearnes Center, Columbia, MO 65205.

PHONE/FAX: (573) 882-3241/4720.

ENROLLMENT: 23,440.

ARENA: Hearnes Center (Capacity-13,349; Year Opened-1972).

SCHOOL COLORS: Old Gold and Black.

CONFERENCE: Big 12.

FINAL AP TOP 10 RANKINGS (4): 1982-83-89-94.

NCAA TOURNAMENT APPEARANCES (16): 1944-76-78-80-81-82-83-86-87-88-89-90-92-93-94-95; 13-16 record (.448); regional runner-up in 1944, 1976 and 1994.

NIT APPEARANCES (4): 1972-73-85-96; 1-4 record (.200).

NCIT Record: 0-1 in 1975.

ALL-TIME SCORING LEADER: Derrick Chievous (2,580 points from 1985-88).

ALL-TIME REBOUNDING LEADER: Doug Smith (1,053 from 1988-91).

NCAA CONSENSUS SECOND-TEAM ALL-AMERICANS (5): Steve Stipanovich (1983), Jon Sundvold (1983), Doug Smith (1990), Anthony Peeler (1992), Melvin Booker (1994).

MONTANA

OFFICIAL NAME: University of Montana.

NICKNAME: Grizzlies.

ADDRESS: Adams Fieldhouse, Missoula, MT 59812.

PHONE/FAX: (406) 243-6899/6859.

ENROLLMENT: 11,755.

ARENA: Dahlberg Arena (Capacity-8,950; Year Opened-1953).

SCHOOL COLORS: Copper, Silver and Gold.

CONFERENCE: Big Sky.

NCAA TOURNAMENT APPEARANCES (3): 1975-91-92; 1-4 record (.200).

NAIA TOURNAMENT APPEARANCES (2): 1948 and 1950; 0-2 record.

NIT APPEARANCES (3): 1985-86-95; 0-3 record.

ALL-TIME SCORING LEADER: Larry Krystkowiak (2,017 points from 1983-86).

ALL-TIME REBOUNDING LEADER: Larry Krystkowiak (1,105 from 1983-86).

MONTANA STATE

OFFICIAL NAME: Montana State University.

NICKNAME: Bobcats.

ADDRESS: 426 Culbertson Hall, Bozeman, MT 59717.

PHONE/FAX: (406) 994-5133/4102.

ENROLLMENT: 10,400.

ARENA: Worthington Arena (Capacity-7,828; Year Opened-1956).

SCHOOL COLORS: Blue and Gold.

CONFERENCE: Big Sky.

NCAA TOURNAMENT APPEARANCES (3): 1951-86-96; 0-3 record.

NAIA TOURNAMENT APPEARANCES (6): 1946-47-52-54-55-56; 1-6 record (.143).

NIT APPEARANCES (1): 1987; 0-1 record.

ALL-TIME SCORING LEADER: Larry Chanay (2,034 points from 1957-60).

ALL-TIME REBOUNDING LEADER: Jack Gillespie (1,011 from 1967-69).

NCAA CONSENSUS FIRST-TEAM ALL-AMERICANS (3): John Thompson (1929 and 1930), Frank Ward (1930).

MOREHEAD STATE

OFFICIAL NAME: Morehead State University.

NICKNAME: Eagles.

ADDRESS: Morehead, KY 40351.

PHONE/FAX: (606) 783-2500/2550.

ENROLLMENT: 8,340.

ARENA: Ellis T. Johnson Arena (Capacity-6,500; Year Opened-1981).

SCHOOL COLORS: Blue and Gold.

CONFERENCE: Ohio Valley.

NCAA TOURNAMENT APPEARANCES (5): 1956-57-61-83-84; 4-6 record (.400).

NAIA TOURNAMENT APPEARANCES (2): 1942 and 1951; 0-2 record.

NIT APPEARANCES: None.

ALL-TIME SCORING LEADER: Herbie Stamper (2,072 points from 1976-79).

ALL-TIME REBOUNDING LEADER: Steve Hamilton (1,675 from 1955-58).

MURRAY STATE

OFFICIAL NAME: Murray State University.

NICKNAME: Racers.

ADDRESS: Stewart Stadium, Murray, KY 42071.

PHONE/FAX: (502) 762-4270/6814.

ENROLLMENT: 8,190.

ARENA: Cutchin Fieldhouse/Racer Arena (Capacity-5,550; Year Opened-1954), construction is underway for a new MSU Regional Special Events Center.

SCHOOL COLORS: Blue and Gold.

CONFERENCE: Ohio Valley.

NCAA TOURNAMENT APPEARANCES (7): 1964-69-88-90-91-92-95; 1-7 record (.125).

NAIA TOURNAMENT APPEARANCES (7): 1938-39-41-42-43-50-52; 16-8 record (.667); finished 2nd in 1941 and 1952, 3rd in 1938 and 4th in 1943.

NIT APPEARANCES (6): 1980-82-83-89-94-96; 2-5 record (.286).

ALL-TIME SCORING LEADER: Jeff Martin (2,484 points from 1986-89).

ALL-TIME REBOUNDING LEADER: Ronald "Popeye" Jones (1,374 from 1989-92).

NAVY

OFFICIAL NAME: United States Naval Academy.

NICKNAME: Midshipmen.

ADDRESS: 566 Brownson Road, Ricketts Hall, Annapolis, MD 21402-5000.

PHONE/FAX: (410) 268-6226/269-6779.

ENROLLMENT: 4,200.

ARENA: Alumni Hall (Capacity-5,710; Year Opened-1991).

SCHOOL COLORS: Navy Blue and Gold.

CONFERENCE: Patriot League.

NCAA TOURNAMENT APPEARANCES (9): 1947-53-54-59-60-85-86-87-94; 8-10 record (.444); regional runner-up in 1947, 1954 and 1986.

NIT APPEARANCES (1): 1962; 0-1 record.

ALL-TIME SCORING LEADER: David Robinson (2,669 points from 1984-87).

ALL-TIME REBOUNDING LEADER: David Robinson (1,314 from 1984-87).

NCAA CONSENSUS FIRST-TEAM ALL-AMERICANS (2): Elliott Loughlin (1933), David Robinson (1987).

NCAA CONSENSUS SECOND-TEAM ALL-AMERICANS (1): David Robinson (1986).

NEBRASKA

OFFICIAL NAME: University of Nebraska.

NICKNAMES: Cornhuskers, Huskers.

ADDRESS: 116 South Stadium, Post Office Box 880123, Lincoln, NE 68588-0123.

PHONE/FAX: (402) 472-2263/2005.

ENROLLMENT: 25,000.

ARENA: Devaney Sports Center (Capacity-14,200; Year Opened-1976).

SCHOOL COLORS: Scarlet and Cream.

CONFERENCE: Big 12.

NCAA TOURNAMENT APPEARANCES (5): 1986-91-92-93-94; 0-5 record.

NIT APPEARANCES (10): 1967-78-80-83-84-85-87-89-95-96; 17-9 record (.654); finished tied for 3rd in 1983, 3rd in 1987 and 1st in 1996.

ALL-TIME SCORING LEADER: Dave Hoppen (2,167 points from 1983-86).

ALL-TIME REBOUNDING LEADER: Leroy Chalk (782 from 1969-71).

NEVADA

OFFICIAL NAME: University of Nevada.

NICKNAME: Wolf Pack.

ADDRESS: 1664 North Virginia Street, Lawlor Annex/232, Reno, NV 89557-0041.

PHONE: (702) 784-4600.

ENROLLMENT: 12,500.

ARENA: Lawlor Events Center (Capacity-11,200; Year Opened-1983).

SCHOOL COLORS: Silver and Blue.

CONFERENCE: Big West.

NCAA DIVISION I TOURNAMENT APPEARANCES (2): 1984 and 1985; 0-2 record.

NCAA DIVISION II TOURNAMENT APPEARANCES (4): 1957-61-64-66; 1-6 record (.143).

NIT APPEARANCES (1): 1979; 1-1 record (.500).

NAIA TOURNAMENT APPEARANCES (1): 1946; 2-1 record (.667).

ALL-TIME SCORING LEADER: Edgar Jones (1,877 points from 1976-79).

ALL-TIME REBOUNDING LEADER: Pete Padgett (1,464 from 1973-76).

NEW MEXICO

OFFICIAL NAME: University of New Mexico.

NICKNAME: Lobos.

ADDRESS: South Campus, Albuquerque, NM 87131.

PHONE/FAX: (505) 277-2026/0142.

ENROLLMENT: 23,755.

ARENA: University Arena/The Pit (Capacity-18,018; Year Opened-1966).

SCHOOL COLORS: Cherry and Silver.

CONFERENCE: Western Athletic.

FINAL AP TOP 10 RANKINGS (1): 1968.

NCAA TOURNAMENT APPEARANCES (7): 1968-74-78-91-93-94-96; 3-8 record (.273).

NAIA TOURNAMENT APPEARANCES (1): 1947; 0-1 record.

NIT APPEARANCES (13): 1964-65-67-73-79-84-85-86-87-88-89-90-92; 13-14 record (.481); finished 2nd in 1964 and 4th in 1990.

ALL-TIME SCORING LEADER: Luc Longley (1,769 points from 1988-91).

ALL-TIME REBOUNDING LEADER: Luc Longley (922 from 1988-91).

NCAA CONSENSUS SECOND-TEAM ALL-AMERICANS (1): Mel Daniels (1967).

NEW MEXICO STATE

OFFICIAL NAME: New Mexico State University.

NICKNAME: Aggies.

ADDRESS: Box 30001, Department 3145, Las Cruces, NM 88003-8001.

PHONE/FAX: (505) 646-3929/2425.

ENROLLMENT: 15,165.

ARENA: Pan American Center (Capacity-13,071; Year Opened-1968).

SCHOOL COLORS: Crimson and White.

CONFERENCE: Big West.

FINAL AP TOP 10 RANKINGS (1): 1970.

NCAA TOURNAMENT APPEARANCES (15): 1952-59-60-67-68-69-70-71-75-79-90-91-92-93-94; 10-17 record (.370); reached Final Four in 1970 (3rd).

NAIA TOURNAMENT APPEARANCES (4): 1938-50-51-52; 5-4 record (.556).

NIT APPEARANCES (3): 1939-89-95; 3-3 record (.500).

ALL-TIME SCORING LEADER: Albert "Slab" Jones (1,758 points from 1977-80).

ALL-TIME REBOUNDING LEADER: Sam Lacey (1,265 from 1968-70).

NCAA CONSENSUS SECOND-TEAM ALL-AMERICANS (1): Jimmy Collins (1970).

NEW ORLEANS

OFFICIAL NAME: University of New Orleans.

NICKNAME: Privateers.

ADDRESS: Lakefront Arena, New Orleans, LA 70148.

PHONE/FAX: (504) 286-6284, 7027/7240.

ENROLLMENT: 15,570.

ARENA: Kiefer UNO Lakefront Arena (Capacity-10,000; Year Opened-1983).

SCHOOL COLORS: Royal Blue and Silver.

CONFERENCE: Sun Belt.

NCAA DIVISION I TOURNAMENT APPEARANCES (4): 1987-91-93-96; 1-4 record (.200).

NCAA DIVISION II TOURNAMENT APPEARANCES (4): 1971-72-74-75; 9-6 record (.600); finished 2nd in 1975 and 4th in 1974.

NIT APPEARANCES (5): 1983-88-89-90-94; 4-5 record (.444).

ALL-TIME SCORING LEADER: Mel Henderson (1,854 points from 1970-73 when school was classified as a small college).

ALL-TIME REBOUNDING LEADER: Ervin Johnson (1,287 from 1990-93).

NIAGARA

OFFICIAL NAME: Niagara University.

NICKNAME: Purple Eagles.

ADDRESS: LL O'Shea Hall, Niagara University, NY 14109-2009.

PHONE/FAX: (716) 286-8588/8581.

ENROLLMENT: 3,000.

ARENAS: Niagara Falls Convention Center (Capacity-6,000; Year Opened-1974) and Gallagher Center (Capacity-3,200; Year Opened-1949).

SCHOOL COLORS: Purple, White and Gold.

CONFERENCE: Metro Atlantic Athletic.

NCAA TOURNAMENT APPEARANCES (1): 1970; 1-2 record (.333).

NIT APPEARANCES (10): 1950-53-54-55-56-58-61-72-76-87; 8-10 record (.444); finished 3rd in 1954 and 2nd in 1972.

ALL-TIME SCORING LEADER: Calvin Murphy (2,548 points from 1968-70).

ALL-TIME REBOUNDING LEADER: Alex Ellis (1,533 from 1956-58).

NCAA CONSENSUS FIRST-TEAM ALL-AMERICANS (2): Calvin Murphy (1969 and 1970).

NCAA CONSENSUS SECOND-TEAM ALL-AMERICANS (1): Calvin Murphy (1968).

NORTH CAROLINA

OFFICIAL NAME: University of North Carolina (At Chapel Hill).

NICKNAME: Tar Heels.

ADDRESS: Post Office Box 2126, Chapel Hill, NC 27515-2126, or Smith Center, Skipper Bowles Drive, 27514.

PHONE/FAX: (919) 962-2123/0612.

ENROLLMENT: 24,063.

ARENA: Smith Center (Capacity-21,572; Year Opened-1986).

SCHOOL COLORS: Carolina Blue and White.

CONFERENCE: Atlantic Coast.

FINAL AP TOP 10 RANKINGS (24): 1957-59-61-67-68-69-72-75-76-77-79-81-82-83-84-85-86-87-88-89-91-93-94-95 .

NCAA TOURNAMENT APPEARANCES (30): 1941-46-57-59-67-68-69-72-75-76-77-78-79-80-81-82-83-84-85-86-87-88-89-90 -91-92-93-94-95-96; 68-30 record (.694); reached Final Four in 1946 (2nd), 1957 (1st), 1967 (4th), 1968 (2nd), 1969 (4th), 1972 (3rd), 1977 (2nd), 1981 (2nd), 1982 (1st), 1991 (T3rd), 1993 (1st) and 1995 (T3rd).

NIT APPEARANCES (4): 1970-71-73-74; 7-3 record (.700); finished 1st in 1971 and 3rd in 1973.

ALL-TIME SCORING LEADER: Phil Ford (2,290 points from 1975-78).

ALL-TIME REBOUNDING LEADER: Sam Perkins (1,167 from 1981-84).

NCAA CONSENSUS FIRST-TEAM ALL-AMERICANS (15): George Glamack (1940 and 1941), Lennie Rosenbluth (1957), Larry Miller (1968), Bob McAdoo (1972), Phil Ford (1977 and 1978), James Worthy (1982), Michael Jordan (1983 and 1984), Sam Perkins (1983 and 1984), Kenny Smith (1987), J.R. Reid (1988), Jerry Stackhouse (1995).

NCAA CONSENSUS SECOND-TEAM ALL-AMERICANS (17): John Dillon (1946), Pete Brennan (1958), Lee Shaffer (1960), Larry Miller (1967), Charlie Scott (1969 and 1970), Bobby Jones (1974), Phil Ford (1976), Mitch Kupchak (1976), Mike O'Koren (1979 and 1980), Al Wood (1981), Sam Perkins (1982), Brad Daugherty (1986), Eric Montross (1993 and 1994), Rasheed Wallace (1995).

NORTH CAROLINA STATE

OFFICIAL NAME: North Carolina State University.

NICKNAME: Wolfpack.

ADDRESS: Post Office Box 8501, Case Athletic Center, Cates Avenue, Raleigh, NC 27695-8501.

PHONE/FAX: (919) 515-2102/2898.

ENROLLMENT: 26,685.

ARENA: Reynolds Coliseum (Capacity-12,400; Year Opened-1949); Entertainment and Sports Arena (21,660) is slated to be ready in 1998.

SCHOOL COLORS: Red and White.

CONFERENCE: Atlantic Coast.

FINAL AP TOP 10 RANKINGS (9): 1950-51-55-56-59-70-73-74-75.

NCAA TOURNAMENT APPEARANCES (17): 1950-51-52-54-56-65-70-74-80-82-83-85-86-87-88-89-91; 27-16 record (.628); reached Final Four in 1950 (3rd), 1974 (1st) and 1983 (1st).

NIT APPEARANCES (6): 1947-48-51-76-78-84; 7-6 record (.538); finished 3rd in 1947, 3rd in 1976 and 2nd in 1978.

ALL-TIME SCORING LEADER: Rodney Monroe (2,551 points from 1988-91).

ALL-TIME REBOUNDING LEADER: Ronnie Shavlik (1,598 from 1954-56).

NCAA CONSENSUS FIRST-TEAM ALL-AMERICANS (5): Sam Ranzino (1951), Ronnie Shavlik (1956), David Thompson (1973, 1974 and 1975).

NCAA CONSENSUS SECOND-TEAM ALL-AMERICANS (3): Dick Dickey (1948), Ronnie Shavlik (1955), Tom Burleson (1973).

NORTHEASTERN

OFFICIAL NAME: Northeastern University.

NICKNAME: Huskies.

ADDRESS: 380 Huntington Avenue, Boston, MA 02215.

PHONE/FAX: (617) 373-2691/3152.

ENROLLMENT: 12,000.

ARENA: Matthews Arena (Capacity-6,000; Year Opened-1909).

SCHOOL COLORS: Red and Black.

CONFERENCE: North Atlantic.

NCAA DIVISION I TOURNAMENT APPEARANCES (7): 1981-82-84-85-86-87-91; 3-7 record (.300).

NCAA DIVISION II TOURNAMENT APPEARANCES (6): 1962-63-64-66-67-68; 8-6 record (.571).

NIT APPEARANCES: None.

ALL-TIME SCORING LEADER: Reggie Lewis (2,708 points from 1984-87).

ALL-TIME REBOUNDING LEADER: Mark Halsel (1,115 from 1981-84).

NORTHEAST LOUISIANA

OFFICIAL NAME: Northeast Louisiana University.

NICKNAME: Indians.

ADDRESS: Malone Stadium, Monroe, LA 71209-2500.

PHONE/FAX: (318) 342-5460/5464.

ENROLLMENT: 11,555.

ARENA: Ewing Coliseum (Capacity-8,000; Year Opened-1971).

SCHOOL COLORS: Maroon and Gold.

CONFERENCE: Southland.

NCAA DIVISION I TOURNAMENT APPEARANCES (7): 1982-86-90-91-92-93-96; 0-7 record.

NAIA TOURNAMENT APPEARANCES (1): 1970; 1-1 record (.500).

NIT APPEARANCES: 1979 and 1988; 0-2 record.

ALL-TIME SCORING LEADER: Calvin Natt (2,581 points from 1976-79).

ALL-TIME REBOUNDING LEADER: Calvin Natt (1,285 from 1976-79).

NCAA CONSENSUS SECOND-TEAM ALL-AMERICANS (1): Calvin Natt (1979).

NORTHERN IOWA

OFFICIAL NAME: University of Northern Iowa.

NICKNAME: Panthers.

ADDRESS: UNI-Dome, Cedar Falls, IA 50614.

PHONE/FAX: (319) 273-6354/3602.

ENROLLMENT: 12,800.

ARENA: UNI-Dome (Capacity-10,000; Year Opened-1976).

SCHOOL COLORS: Purple and Old Gold.

CONFERENCE: Missouri Valley.

NCAA DIVISION I TOURNAMENT APPEARANCES (1): 1990; 1-1 record (.500).

NCAA DIVISION II TOURNAMENT APPEARANCES (3): 1962-64-79; 5-4 record (.556); finished 4th in 1964.

NAIA TOURNAMENT APPEARANCES (4): 1946-48-49-53; 2-4 record (.333).

NIT APPEARANCES: None.

ALL-TIME SCORING LEADER: Jason Reese (2,033 points from 1987-90).

ALL-TIME REBOUNDING LEADER: Pete Spoden (1,104 from 1961-64 when school was classified as a small college).

NORTHWESTERN

OFFICIAL NAME: Northwestern University.

NICKNAME: Wildcats.

ADDRESS: 1501 Central Street, Evanston, IL 60201-1699.

PHONE/FAX: (708) 491-7503/8818.

ENROLLMENT: 7,400.

ARENA: Welsh-Ryan Arena (Capacity-8,117; Year Opened-1952).

SCHOOL COLORS: Purple and White.

CONFERENCE: Big Ten.

NCAA TOURNAMENT APPEARANCES: None.

NIT APPEARANCES (2): 1983 and 1994; 2-2 record (.500).

ALL-TIME SCORING LEADER: Billy McKinney (1,900 points from 1974-77).

ALL-TIME REBOUNDING LEADER: Joe Ruklick (868 from 1957-59).

NCAA CONSENSUS FIRST-TEAM ALL-AMERICANS (4): Joe Reiff (1931 and 1933), Otto Graham (1944/also played with Colgate), Max Morris (1946).

NCAA CONSENSUS SECOND-TEAM ALL-AMERICANS (2): Otto Graham (1943), Max Morris (1945).

NOTRE DAME

OFFICIAL NAME: University of Notre Dame.

NICKNAME: Fighting Irish.

ADDRESS: Joyce Athletic and Convocation Center, Notre Dame, IN 46556.

PHONE/FAX: (219) 631-7516/7941.

ENROLLMENT: 9,850.

ARENA: Joyce Athletic and Convocation Center (Capacity-11,418; Year Opened-1968).

SCHOOL COLORS: Gold and Blue.

CONFERENCE: Big East.

FINAL AP TOP 10 RANKINGS (12): 1953-54-58-70-74-76-77-78-79-80-81-86.

NCAA TOURNAMENT APPEARANCES (24): 1953-54-57-58-60-63-65-69-70-71-74-75-76-77-78-79-80-81-85-86-87-88-89-90 ; 25-28 record (.472); reached Final Four in 1978 (4th).

NIT APPEARANCES (5): 1968-73-83-84-92; 14-5 record (.737); finished 3rd in 1968, 2nd in 1973, 2nd in 1984 and 2nd in 1992.

ALL-TIME SCORING LEADER: Austin Carr (2,560 points from 1969-71).

ALL-TIME REBOUNDING LEADER: Tom Hawkins (1,318 from 1957-59).

NCAA CONSENSUS FIRST-TEAM ALL-AMERICANS (17): Ed "Moose" Krause (1932, 1933 and 1934), John Moir (1936, 1937 and 1938), Paul Nowak (1936, 1937 and 1938), Leo Klier (1944 and 1946), Billy Hassett (1945), Kevin O'Shea (1948), Austin Carr (1971), John Shumate (1974), Adrian Dantley (1975 and 1976).

NCAA CONSENSUS SECOND-TEAM ALL-AMERICANS (9): Bob Rensberger (1943), Billy Hassett (1946), Kevin O'Shea (1950), Tom Hawkins (1959), Austin Carr (1970), Kelly Tripucka (1979 and 1981), John Paxson (1982 and 1983).

OHIO UNIVERSITY

NICKNAME: Bobcats.

ADDRESS: Convocation Center, Athens, OH 45701-2979.

PHONE/FAX: (614) 593-1298/2420.

ENROLLMENT: 18,500.

ARENA: Convocation Center (Capacity-13,000; Year Opened-1968).

SCHOOL COLORS: Hunter Green and White.

CONFERENCE: Mid-American.

NCAA TOURNAMENT APPEARANCES (10): 1960-61-64-65-70-72-74-83-85-94; 4-11 record (.267); regional runner-up in 1964.

NIT APPEARANCES (3): 1941-69-95; 4-3 record (.571); finished 2nd in 1941.

ALL-TIME SCORING LEADER: Dave Jamerson (2,336 points from 1986-90; missed 1986-87 season because of a knee injury).

ALL-TIME REBOUNDING LEADER: John Deveraux (957 from 1981-84).

NCAA CONSENSUS SECOND-TEAM ALL-AMERICANS (1): Frank Baumholtz (1941).

OHIO STATE

OFFICIAL NAME: Ohio State University.

NICKNAME: Buckeyes.

ADDRESS: 410 Woody Hayes Drive, 124 St. John Arena, Columbus, OH 43210-1166.

PHONE/FAX: (614) 292-6861/8547.

ENROLLMENT: 52,180.

ARENA: St. John Arena (Capacity-13,276; Year Opened-1956); new 19,560-seat facility is scheduled to open in 1998-99.

SCHOOL COLORS: Scarlet and Gray.

CONFERENCE: Big Ten.

FINAL AP TOP 10 RANKINGS (9): 1950-60-61-62-63-71-80-91-92.

NCAA TOURNAMENT APPEARANCES (18): 1939-44-45-46-50-60-61-62-68-71-80-82-83-85-87-90-91-92; 31-17 record (.646); reached Final Four in 1939 (2nd), 1944 (T3rd), 1945 (T3rd), 1946 (3rd), 1960 (1st), 1961 (2nd), 1962 (2nd) and 1968 (3rd).

NIT APPEARANCES (6): 1979-84-86-88-89-93; 13-6 record (.684); finished 4th in 1979, 1st in 1986 and 2nd in 1988.

ALL-TIME SCORING LEADER: Dennis Hopson (2,096 points from 1984-87).

ALL-TIME REBOUNDING LEADER: Jerry Lucas (1,411 from 1960-62).

NCAA CONSENSUS FIRST-TEAM ALL-AMERICANS (10): Wes Fesler (1931), Jimmy Hull (1939), Dick Schnittker (1950), Robin Freeman (1956), Jerry Lucas (1960, 1961 and 1962), Gary Bradds (1964), Jim Jackson (1991 and 1992).

NCAA CONSENSUS SECOND-TEAM ALL-AMERICANS (9): Don Grate (1944 and 1945), Robin Freeman (1955), Frank Howard (1957), Larry Siegfried (1961), John Havlicek (1962), Gary Bradds (1963), Kelvin Ransey (1980), Dennis Hopson (1987).

OKLAHOMA

OFFICIAL NAME: University of Oklahoma.

NICKNAME: Sooners.

ADDRESS: 180 West Brooks, Room 235, Norman, OK 73019.

PHONE/FAX: (405) 325-8231/7623.

ENROLLMENT: 24,500.

ARENA: Lloyd Noble Center (Capacity-11,100; Year Opened-1975).

SCHOOL COLORS: Crimson and Cream.

CONFERENCE: Big 12.

FINAL AP TOP 10 RANKINGS (5): 1984-85-88-89-90.

NCAA TOURNAMENT APPEARANCES (15): 1939-43-47-79-83-84-85-86-87-88-89-90-92-95-96; 20-15 record (.571); reached Final Four in 1939 (3rd), 1947 (2nd) and 1988 (2nd).

NIT APPEARANCES (6): 1970-71-82-91-93-94; 9-6 record (.600); finished in tie for 3rd in 1982 and 2nd in 1991.

ALL-TIME SCORING LEADER: Wayman Tisdale (2,661 points from 1983-85).

ALL-TIME REBOUNDING LEADER: Wayman Tisdale (1,048 from 1983-85).

NCAA CONSENSUS FIRST-TEAM ALL-AMERICANS (8): Thomas Churchill (1929), Omar "Bud" Browning (1935), Allie Paine (1944), Gerry Tucker (1947), Wayman Tisdale (1983, 1984 and 1985), Stacey King (1989).

NCAA CONSENSUS SECOND-TEAM ALL-AMERICANS (3): James McNatt (1940), Gerry Tucker (1943), Daron "Mookie" Blaylock (1989).

OKLAHOMA STATE

OFFICIAL NAME: Oklahoma State University.
NICKNAME: Cowboys.
ADDRESS: Gallagher-Iba Arena, Stillwater, OK 74078.
PHONE/FAX: (405) 744-5749/7754.
ENROLLMENT: 18,500.

ARENA: Gallagher-Iba Arena (Capacity-6,381; Year Opened-1938).

SCHOOL COLORS: Orange and Black.

CONFERENCE: Big 12.

FINAL AP TOP 10 RANKINGS (4): 1949-51-53-54.

NCAA TOURNAMENT APPEARANCES (14): 1945-46-49-51-53-54-58-65-83-91-92-93-94-95; 25-13 record (.658); reached Final Four in 1945 (1st), 1946 (1st), 1949 (2nd), 1951 (4th) and 1995 (T3rd).

NIT APPEARANCES (6): 1938-40-44-56-89-90; 5-7 record (.417); finished 3rd in 1938, 3rd in 1940 and 4th in 1944.

ALL-TIME SCORING LEADER: Byron Houston (2,374 points from 1989-92).

ALL-TIME REBOUNDING LEADER: Byron Houston (1,190 from 1989-92).

NCAA CONSENSUS FIRST-TEAM ALL-AMERICANS (3): Bob Kurland (1944, 1945 and 1946).

NCAA CONSENSUS SECOND-TEAM ALL-AMERICANS (4): Jesse "Cab" Renick (1940), Gale McArthur (1951), Bob Mattick (1954), Byron Houston (1992).

OLD DOMINION UNIVERSITY

OLD DOMINION

OFFICIAL NAME: Old Dominion University.
NICKNAME: Monarchs.
ADDRESS: Athletic Administration Building, Norfolk, VA 23529-0201.
PHONE/FAX: (804) 683-3372/3119.
ENROLLMENT: 17,000.

ARENA: Norfolk Scope (Capacity-10,253; Year Opened-1971).

SCHOOL COLORS: Slate Blue and Silver.

CONFERENCE: Colonial Athletic Association.

NCAA DIVISION I TOURNAMENT APPEARANCES (6): 1980-82-85-86-92-95; 2-6 record (.250).

NCAA DIVISION II TOURNAMENT APPEARANCES (7): 1969-70-71-73-74-75-76; 15-8 record (.652); finished 1st in 1975, 2nd in 1971 and 4th in 1976.

NIT APPEARANCES (8): 1977-79-81-83-84-88-93-94; 4-8 record (.333).

ALL-TIME SCORING LEADER: Ronnie Valentine (2,204 points from 1977-80).

ALL-TIME REBOUNDING LEADER: Randy Leddy (1,153 from 1963-66 when school was classified as a small college).

ORAL ROBERTS

OFFICIAL NAME: Oral Roberts University.
NICKNAME: Golden Eagles.
ADDRESS: 7777 South Lewis Avenue, Tulsa, OK 74171.
PHONE/FAX: (918) 495-7102/7123.
ENROLLMENT: 4,515.
ARENA: Mabee Center (Capacity-10,575; Year Opened-1972).
SCHOOL COLORS: Navy Blue, Vegas Gold and White.
CONFERENCE: Independent.

NCAA TOURNAMENT APPEARANCES (2): 1974 and 1984; 2-2 record (.500); regional runner-up in 1974.

NAIA TOURNAMENT APPEARANCES (1): 1990; 2-1 record (.667).

NIT APPEARANCES (5): 1972-73-75-77-82; 2-5 record (.286).

ALL-TIME SCORING LEADER: Greg Sutton (3,070 points from 1989-91; played freshman season at Langston in 1986-87).

ALL-TIME REBOUNDING LEADER: Eddie Woods (1,365 from 1971-74).

NCAA CONSENSUS SECOND-TEAM ALL-AMERICANS (1): Richie Fuqua (1972).

OREGON

OFFICIAL NAME: University of Oregon.
NICKNAME: Ducks.
ADDRESS: Len Casanova Athletic Center, 2727 Leo Harris Parkway, Eugene, OR 97401-8835.
PHONE/FAX: (541) 346-5488/5449.

ENROLLMENT: 17,100.
ARENA: McArthur Court (Capacity-9,738; Year Opened-1927).
SCHOOL COLORS: Emerald Green and Lemon Yellow.
CONFERENCE: Pacific-10.

NCAA TOURNAMENT APPEARANCES (5): 1939-45-60-61-95; 6-4 record (.600); reached Final Four in 1939 (1st).

NIT APPEARANCES (6): 1975-76-77-84-88-90; 5-6 record (.455); finished 3rd in 1975.

ALL-TIME SCORING LEADER: Ron Lee (2,085 points from 1973-76).

ALL-TIME REBOUNDING LEADER: Greg Ballard (1,114 from 1974-77).

NCAA CONSENSUS FIRST-TEAM ALL-AMERICANS (2): Urgel "Slim" Wintermute (1939), John Dick (1940).

NCAA CONSENSUS SECOND-TEAM ALL-AMERICANS (3): Bob Anet (1939), Ron Lee (1975), Greg Ballard (1977).

OREGON STATE

OFFICIAL NAME: Oregon State University.
NICKNAME: Beavers.
ADDRESS: 209 Gill Coliseum, Corvallis, OR 97331.
PHONE/FAX: (503) 737-3720/3072.
ENROLLMENT: 15,550.

ARENA: Gill Coliseum (Capacity-10,400; Year Opened-1949).

SCHOOL COLORS: Orange and Black.

CONFERENCE: Pacific-10.

FINAL AP TOP 10 RANKINGS (5): 1955-64-80-81-82.

NCAA TOURNAMENT APPEARANCES (16): 1947-49-55-62-63-64-66-75-80-81-82-84-85-88-89-90; 12-19 record (.387); reached Final Four in 1949 (4th) and 1963 (4th).

NIT APPEARANCES (3): 1979-83-87; 3-3 record (.500).

ALL-TIME SCORING LEADER: Gary Payton (2,172 points from 1987-90).

ALL-TIME REBOUNDING LEADER: Mel Counts (1,375 from 1962-64).

NCAA CONSENSUS FIRST-TEAM ALL-AMERICANS (2): Steve Johnson (1981), Gary Payton (1990).

NCAA CONSENSUS SECOND-TEAM ALL-AMERICANS (3): John Mandic (1942), Dave Gambee (1958), Mel Counts (1964).

PACIFIC

OFFICIAL NAME: University of the Pacific.

NICKNAME: Tigers.

ADDRESS: 3601 Pacific Avenue, Stockton, CA 95211.

PHONE/FAX: (209) 946-2479/2757.

ENROLLMENT: 4,000.

ARENA: Alex G. Spanos Center (Capacity-6,150; Year Opened-1981).

SCHOOL COLORS: Orange and Black.

CONFERENCE: Big West.

NCAA TOURNAMENT APPEARANCES (4): 1966-67-71-79; 2-5 record (.286); regional runner-up in 1967.

NAIA TOURNAMENT APPEARANCES (1): 1951; 0-1 record.

NIT APPEARANCES: None.

ALL-TIME SCORING LEADER: Ron Cornelius (2,065 points from 1978-81).

ALL-TIME REBOUNDING LEADER: Keith Swagerty (1,505 from 1965-67).

PENN

OFFICIAL NAME: University of Pennsylvania.

NICKNAME: Quakers.

ADDRESS: 235 South 33rd Street, Weightman Hall South, Philadelphia, PA 19104-6322.

PHONE/FAX: (215) 898-6128/1747.

ENROLLMENT: 9,300.

ARENA: Palestra (Capacity-8,700; Year Opened-1927).

SCHOOL COLORS: Red and Blue.

CONFERENCE: Ivy League.

FINAL AP TOP 10 RANKINGS (2): 1971 and 1972.

NCAA TOURNAMENT APPEARANCES (16): 1953-70-71-72-73-74-75-78-79-80-82-85-87-93-94-95; 13-18 record (.419); reached Final Four in 1979 (4th).

NIT APPEARANCES (1): 1981; 0-1 record.

ALL-TIME SCORING LEADER: Ernie Beck (1,827 points from 1951-53).

ALL-TIME REBOUNDING LEADER: Ernie Beck (1,557 from 1951-53).

NCAA CONSENSUS FIRST-TEAM ALL-AMERICANS (3): Joe Schaaf (1929), Howie Dallmar (1945), Ernie Beck (1953).

PENN STATE

OFFICIAL NAME: Penn State University.

NICKNAME: Nittany Lions.

ADDRESS: 101D Bryce Jordan Center, University Park, PA 16802.

PHONE/FAX: (814) 865-1757/863-3165.

ENROLLMENT: 31,400.

ARENA: Bryce Jordan Center (Capacity-15,300; Year Opened-1996).

SCHOOL COLORS: Blue and White.

CONFERENCE: Big Ten.

FINAL AP TOP 10 RANKINGS (1): 1954.

NCAA TOURNAMENT APPEARANCES (7): 1942-52-54-55-65-91-96; 7-9 record (.438); reached Final Four in 1954 (3rd).

NIT APPEARANCES (6): 1966-80-89-90-92-95; 9-6 record (.600); finished 3rd in 1990 and 1995.

ALL-TIME SCORING LEADER: Jesse Arnelle (2,138 points from 1952-55).

ALL-TIME REBOUNDING LEADER: Jesse Arnelle (1,238 from 1952-55).

PEPPERDINE

OFFICIAL NAME: Pepperdine University.

NICKNAME: Waves.

ADDRESS: 24255 Pacific Coast Highway, Malibu, CA 90263.

PHONE/FAX: (310) 456-4333/4322.

ENROLLMENT: 7,450.

ARENA: Firestone Fieldhouse (Capacity-3,104; Year Opened-1973).

SCHOOL COLORS: Blue, Orange and White.

CONFERENCE: West Coast.

NCAA TOURNAMENT APPEARANCES (11): 1944-62-76-79-82-83-85-86-91-92-94; 4-12 record (.250).

NAIA TOURNAMENT APPEARANCES (7): 1942-43-45-46-50-51-52; 11-7 record (.611); finished 2nd in 1945 and 3rd in 1946.

NIT APPEARANCES (4): 1980-88-89-93; 2-4 record (.333).

ALL-TIME SCORING LEADER: Dane Suttle (1,702 points from 1980-83).

ALL-TIME REBOUNDING LEADER: Dana Jones (1,031 from 1991-94).

PITT

OFFICIAL NAME: University of Pittsburgh.

NICKNAME: Panthers.

ADDRESS: Post Office Box 7436, Pittsburgh, PA 15213.

PHONE/FAX: (412) 648-8240/8248.

ENROLLMENT: 13,500.

ARENAS: Fitzgerald Field House (Capacity-6,798; Year Opened-1951) and Civic Arena (Capacity-17,500; Year Opened-1961).

SCHOOL COLORS: Blue and Gold.

CONFERENCE: Big East.

FINAL AP TOP 10 RANKINGS (1): 1988.

NCAA TOURNAMENT APPEARANCES (13): 1941-57-58-63-74-81-82-85-87-88-89-91-93; 8-14 record (.364); reached Final Four in 1941 (T3rd).

NIT APPEARANCES (6): 1964-75-80-84-86-92; 4-6 record (.400).

ALL-TIME SCORING LEADER: Charles Smith (2,045 points from 1985-88).

ALL-TIME REBOUNDING LEADER: Sam Clancy (1,342 from 1978-81).

NCAA CONSENSUS FIRST-TEAM ALL-AMERICANS (6): Chuck Hyatt (1929 and 1930), Don Smith (1933), Claire Cribbs (1934 and 1935), Don Hennon (1958).

NCAA CONSENSUS SECOND-TEAM ALL-AMERICANS (3): Don Hennon (1959), Billy Knight (1974), Jerome Lane (1988).

PORTLAND

OFFICIAL NAME: University of Portland.

NICKNAME: Pilots.

ADDRESS: 5000 N. Willamette Boulevard, Portland, OR 97203-5798.

PHONE/FAX: (503) 283-7117/7242.

ENROLLMENT: 2,700.

ARENA: Earle A. Chiles Center (Capacity-5,000; Year Opened-1984).

SCHOOL COLORS: Purple and White.

CONFERENCE: West Coast.

NCAA TOURNAMENT APPEARANCES (2): 1959 and 1996; 0-2 record.

NAIA TOURNAMENT APPEARANCES (9): 1942-49-50-51-52-53-54-57-58; 5-10 record (.333); finished 4th in 1952.

NIT APPEARANCES: None.

ALL-TIME SCORING LEADER: Jose Slaughter (1,940 points, 1979-82).

ALL-TIME REBOUNDING LEADER: Rick Raivio (910, 1977-80).

PRINCETON

OFFICIAL NAME: Princeton University.

NICKNAME: Tigers.

ADDRESS: Post Office Box 71, Jadwin Gymnasium, Princeton, NJ 08544.

PHONE/FAX: (609) 258-3568/4477.

ENROLLMENT: 4,500.

ARENA: Jadwin Gymnasium (Capacity-7,500; Year Opened-1969).

SCHOOL COLORS: Orange and Black.

CONFERENCE: Ivy League.

FINAL AP TOP 10 RANKINGS (1): 1967.

NCAA TOURNAMENT APPEARANCES (19): 1952-55-60-61-63-64-65-67-69-76-77-81-83-84-89-90-91-92-96; 12-23 record (.343); reached Final Four in 1965 (3rd).

NIT APPEARANCES (2): 1972 and 1975; 5-1 record (.833); finished 1st in 1975.

ALL-TIME SCORING LEADER: Bill Bradley (2,503 points from 1963-65).

ALL-TIME REBOUNDING LEADER: Bill Bradley (1,008 from 1963-65).

NCAA CONSENSUS FIRST-TEAM ALL-AMERICANS (2): Bill Bradley (1964 and 1965).

PROVIDENCE

OFFICIAL NAME: Providence College.

NICKNAME: Friars.

ADDRESS: River Avenue & Eaton Street, Providence, RI 02918.

PHONE/FAX: (401) 865-2272/2583.

ENROLLMENT: 3,545.

ARENA: Civic Center (Capacity-13,106; Year Opened-1972).

SCHOOL COLORS: Black and White.

CONFERENCE: Big East.

FINAL AP TOP 10 RANKINGS (3): 1965-73-74.

NCAA TOURNAMENT APPEARANCES (12): 1964-65-66-72-73-74-77-78-87-89-90-94; 11-13 record (.458); reached Final Four in 1973 (4th) and 1987 (T3rd).

NAIA TOURNAMENT APPEARANCES (1): 1951; 0-1 record.

NIT APPEARANCES (14): 1959-60-61-62-63-67-71-75-76-86-91-93-95-96; 28-15 record (.651); finished 4th in 1959, 2nd in 1960, 1st in 1961, 1st in 1963 and 4th in 1993.

ALL-TIME SCORING LEADER: Jimmy Walker (2,045 points from 1964-67).

ALL-TIME REBOUNDING LEADER: Marvin Barnes (1,592 from 1971-74).

NCAA CONSENSUS FIRST-TEAM ALL-AMERICANS (4): Jimmy Walker (1966 and 1967), Ernie DiGregorio (1973), Marvin Barnes (1974).

NCAA CONSENSUS SECOND-TEAM ALL-AMERICANS (2): Lenny Wilkens (1960), Eric Murdock (1991).

PURDUE

OFFICIAL NAME: Purdue University.

NICKNAME: Boilermakers.

ADDRESS: Room 15 - Mackey Arena, West Lafayette, IN 47907-1790.

PHONE/FAX: (317) 494-3200/5447.

ENROLLMENT: 34,685.

ARENA: Mackey Arena (Capacity-14,123; Year Opened-1967).

SCHOOL COLORS: Old Gold and Black.

CONFERENCE: Big Ten.

FINAL AP TOP 10 RANKINGS (7): 1969-84-87-88-90-94-96.

NCAA TOURNAMENT APPEARANCES (15): 1969-77-80-83-84-85-86-87-88-90-91-93-94-95-96; 18-15 record (.545); reached Final Four in 1969 (2nd) and 1980 (3rd).

NIT APPEARANCES (6): 1971-74-79-81-82-92; 18-5 record (.783); finished 1st in 1974, 2nd in 1979, 3rd in 1981 and 2nd in 1982.

NCIT RECORD: 1-1 in 1975.

ALL-TIME SCORING LEADER: Rick Mount (2,323 points from 1968-70).

ALL-TIME REBOUNDING LEADER: Joe Barry Carroll (1,148 from 1977-80).

NCAA CONSENSUS FIRST-TEAM ALL-AMERICANS (16): Charles "Stretch" Murphy (1929 and 1930), John Wooden (1930, 1931 and 1932), Norman Cottom (1934), Bob Kessler (1936), Jewell Young (1937 and 1938), Terry Dischinger (1961 and 1962), Dave Schellhase (1966), Rick Mount (1969 and 1970), Joe Barry Carroll (1980), Glenn Robinson (1994).

NCAA CONSENSUS SECOND-TEAM ALL-AMERICANS (3): Terry Dischinger (1960), Dave Schellhase (1965), Glenn Robinson (1993).

RHODE ISLAND

OFFICIAL NAME: University of Rhode Island.

NICKNAME: Rams.

ADDRESS: Mackal Fieldhouse, Kingston, RI 02881.

PHONE/FAX: (401) 874-2409/5354.

ENROLLMENT: 11,500.

ARENAS: Keaney Gymnasium (Capacity-4,000; Year Opened-1953) and Providence Civic Center (Capacity-13,106; Year Opened-1972).

SCHOOL COLORS: Light Blue, Dark Blue and White.

CONFERENCE: Atlantic 10.

NCAA TOURNAMENT APPEARANCES (5): 1961-66-78-88-93; 3-5 record (.375).

NIT APPEARANCES (9): 1941-42-45-46-79-81-87-92-96; 7-10 record (.412); finished 4th in 1945 and 2nd in 1946.

ALL-TIME SCORING LEADER: Steve Chubin (2,154 points from 1963-66; missed 1964-65 season because he was academically ineligible).

ALL-TIME REBOUNDING LEADER: Art Stephenson (1,048 from 1966-68).

NCAA CONSENSUS FIRST-TEAM ALL-AMERICANS (1): Chet Jaworski (1939).

NCAA CONSENSUS SECOND-TEAM ALL-AMERICANS (2): Stan Modzelewski (1941 and 1942).

RICE

OFFICIAL NAME: Rice University.

NICKNAME: Owls.

ADDRESS: Post Office Box 1892, 6100 South Main, Houston, TX 77251-1892.

PHONE/FAX: (713) 527-4034/6019.

ENROLLMENT: 2,600.

ARENA: Autry Court (Capacity-5,000; Year Opened-1950).

SCHOOL COLORS: Blue and Gray.

CONFERENCE: Western Athletic.

NCAA TOURNAMENT APPEARANCES (4): 1940-42-54-70; 2-5 record (.286); regional runner-up in 1940 and 1942.

NIT APPEARANCES (3): 1943-91-93; 1-3 record (.250).

ALL-TIME SCORING LEADER: Brent Scott (1,906 points from 1990-93).

ALL-TIME REBOUNDING LEADER: Brent Scott (1,049 from 1990-93).

NCAA CONSENSUS FIRST-TEAM ALL-AMERICANS (3): Bob Kinney (1942), Bill Closs (1943), Bill Henry (1945).

NCAA CONSENSUS SECOND-TEAM ALL-AMERICANS (2): Bob Kinney (1941), Bill Henry (1944).

RICHMOND

OFFICIAL NAME: University of Richmond.

NICKNAME: Spiders.

ADDRESS: Robins Center, Richmond, VA 23173.

PHONE/FAX: (804) 289-8365/8820.

ENROLLMENT: 2,800.

ARENA: Robins Center (Capacity-9,171; Year Opened-1972).

SCHOOL COLORS: Blue and Red.

CONFERENCE: Colonial Athletic Association.

NCAA TOURNAMENT APPEARANCES (5): 1984-86-88-90-91; 5-5 record (.500).

NIT APPEARANCES (4): 1982-85-89-92; 2-4 record (.333).

ALL-TIME SCORING LEADER: John Newman (2,383 points from 1983-86).

ALL-TIME REBOUNDING LEADER: Ken Daniel (1,255 from 1953-56).

ROBERT MORRIS

OFFICIAL NAME: Robert Morris College.

NICKNAME: Colonials.

ADDRESS: Narrows Run Road, Coraopolis, PA 15108-1189.

PHONE/FAX: (412) 262-8314/8557.

ENROLLMENT: 5,300.

ARENA: Charles L. Sewall Center (Capacity-3,056; Year Opened-1985).

SCHOOL COLORS: Blue and White.

CONFERENCE: Northeast.

NCAA TOURNAMENT APPEARANCES (5): 1982-83-89-90-92; 1-5 record (.167).

NIT APPEARANCES: None.

ALL-TIME SCORING LEADER: Myron Walker (1,965 points from 1991-94).

ALL-TIME REBOUNDING LEADER: Anthony Dickens (751 from 1986-90; missed 1986-87 season because of a hip injury).

RUTGERS

OFFICIAL NAME: Rutgers, The State University of New Jersey.

NICKNAME: Scarlet Knights.

ADDRESS: Post Office Box 1149, Piscataway, NJ 08855-1149.

PHONE/FAX: (908) 445-4200/3063.

ENROLLMENT: 33,585.

ARENA: Louis Brown Athletic Center (Capacity-9,000; Year Opened-1978).

SCHOOL COLORS: Scarlet and White.

CONFERENCE: Big East.

FINAL AP TOP 10 RANKINGS (1): 1976.

NCAA TOURNAMENT APPEARANCES (6): 1975-76-79-83-89-91; 5-7 record (.417); reached Final Four in 1976 (4th).

NIT APPEARANCES (9): 1967-69-73-74-77-78-82-90-92; 10-9 record (.526); finished 3rd in 1967 and 1978.

ALL-TIME SCORING LEADER: Phil Sellers (2,399 points from 1973-76).

ALL-TIME REBOUNDING LEADER: Phil Sellers (1,115 from 1973-76).

NCAA CONSENSUS FIRST-TEAM ALL-AMERICANS (1): Bob Lloyd (1967).

NCAA CONSENSUS SECOND-TEAM ALL-AMERICANS (1): Phil Sellers (1976).

ST. BONAVENTURE

OFFICIAL NAME: St. Bonaventure University.

NICKNAME: Bonnies.

ADDRESS: Reilly Center, St. Bonaventure, NY 14778.

PHONE/FAX: (716) 375-2319/2383.

ENROLLMENT: 2,300.

ARENA: Reilly Center (Capacity-6,000; Year Opened-1966).

SCHOOL COLORS: Brown and White.

CONFERENCE: Atlantic 10.

FINAL AP TOP 10 RANKINGS (4): 1960-61-68-70.

NCAA TOURNAMENT APPEARANCES (4): 1961-68-70-78; 6-6 record (.500); reached Final Four in 1970 (4th).

NIT APPEARANCES (12): 1951-52-57-58-59-60-64-71-77-79-83-95; 17-13 record (.567); finished 3rd in 1952, 4th in 1957, 3rd in 1958, 4th in 1960, 3rd in 1971 and 1st in 1977.

ALL-TIME SCORING LEADER: Greg Sanders (2,238 points from 1975-78).

ALL-TIME REBOUNDING LEADER: Bob Lanier (1,180 from 1968-70).

NCAA CONSENSUS FIRST-TEAM ALL-AMERICANS (3): Tom Stith (1960 and 1961), Bob Lanier (1970).

NCAA CONSENSUS SECOND-TEAM ALL-AMERICANS (1): Bob Lanier (1968).

ST. FRANCIS (N.Y.)

OFFICIAL NAME: St. Francis College.

NICKNAME: Terriers.

ADDRESS: 180 Remsen Street, Brooklyn Heights, NY 11201.

PHONE/FAX: (718) 522-2300/1274.

ENROLLMENT: 1,910.

ARENA: Physical Education Center (Capacity-1,400; Year Opened-1971).

SCHOOL COLORS: Royal Blue, Red and White.

CONFERENCE: Northeast.

NCAA TOURNAMENT APPEARANCES: None.

NAIA TOURNAMENT APPEARANCES (1): 1955; 0-1 record.

NIT APPEARANCES (3): 1954-56-63; 3-4 record (.429); finished 4th in 1956.

ALL-TIME SCORING LEADER: Darrwin Purdie (1,613 points from 1986-89).

ALL-TIME REBOUNDING LEADER: Jerome Williams (1,018 from 1972-74).

ST. FRANCIS (PA.)

OFFICIAL NAME: St. Francis College of Pennsylvania.

NICKNAME: Red Flash.

ADDRESS: Maurice Stokes Athletics Center, Loretto, PA 15940.

PHONE/FAX: (814) 472-3128/3044.

ENROLLMENT: 1,200.

ARENA: DeGol Arena, Stokes Center (Capacity-3,500; Year Opened-1972).

SCHOOL COLORS: Red and White.

CONFERENCE: Northeast.

NCAA TOURNAMENT APPEARANCES (1): 1991; 0-1 record.

NAIA TOURNAMENT APPEARANCES (1): 1948; 0-1 record.

NIT APPEARANCES (3): 1954-55-58; 3-4 record (.429); finished 4th in 1955.

ALL-TIME SCORING LEADER: Joe Anderson (2,301 points from 1988-91).

ALL-TIME REBOUNDING LEADER: Maurice Stokes (1,819 from 1953-55 when school was classified as a small college; rebounding statistics weren't kept in 1951-52).

ST. JOHN'S

OFFICIAL NAME: St. John's University.

NICKNAME: Red Storm.

ADDRESS: 8000 Utopia Parkway, Jamaica, NY 11439.

PHONE/FAX: (718) 990-6367/969-8468.

ENROLLMENT: 19,500.

ARENAS: Alumni Hall (Capacity-6,008; Year Opened-1961) and Madison Square Garden (Capacity-19,876).

SCHOOL COLORS: Red and White.

CONFERENCE: Big East.

FINAL AP TOP 10 RANKINGS (8): 1950-51-52-53-69-83-85-86.

NCAA TOURNAMENT APPEARANCES (23): 1951-52-61-67-68-69-73-76-77-78-79-80-82-83-84-85-86-87-88-90-91-92-93; 23-25 record (.479); reached Final Four in 1952 (2nd) and 1985 (T3rd).

NIT APPEARANCES (26): 1939-40-43-44-45-46-47-49-50-51-52-53-58-59-60-62-65-66-70-71-72-74-75-81 -89-95; 41-29 record (.586); finished 4th in 1939, 1st in 1943, 1st in 1944, 3rd in 1945, 3rd in 1950, 3rd in 1951, 2nd in 1953, 4th in 1958, 1st in 1959, 2nd in 1962, 1st in 1965, 2nd in 1970, 4th in 1972, 4th in 1975 and 1st in 1989.

ALL-TIME SCORING LEADER: Chris Mullin (2,440 points from 1982-85).

ALL-TIME REBOUNDING LEADER: George Johnson (1,240 from 1975-78).

NCAA CONSENSUS FIRST-TEAM ALL-AMERICANS (3): Harry Boykoff (1943), Chris Mullin (1985), Walter Berry (1986).

NCAA CONSENSUS SECOND-TEAM ALL-AMERICANS (8): Bob Zawoluk (1952), Alan Seiden (1959), Tony Jackson (1960 and 1961), Lloyd "Sonny" Dove (1967), Chris Mullin (1984), Mark Jackson (1987), Malik Sealy (1992).

ST. JOSEPH'S

OFFICIAL NAME: St. Joseph's University.

NICKNAME: Hawks.

ADDRESS: 5600 City Avenue, Philadelphia, PA 19131.

PHONE/FAX: (610) 660-1707/1727.

ENROLLMENT: 2,700.

ARENA: Alumni Memorial Fieldhouse (Capacity-3,200; Year Opened-1949).

SCHOOL COLORS: Crimson and Gray.

CONFERENCE: Atlantic 10.

FINAL AP TOP 10 RANKINGS (2): 1965 and 1966.

NCAA TOURNAMENT APPEARANCES (14): 1959-60-61-62-63-65-66-69-71-73-74-81-82-86; 12-18 record (.400); reached Final Four in 1961 (3rd).

NIT APPEARANCES (11): 1956-58-64-72-79-80-84-85-93-95-96; 9-11 record (.450); finished 3rd in 1956 and 2nd in 1996.

ALL-TIME SCORING LEADER: Bernard Blunt (1,985 points from 1991-95; missed majority of 1993-94 season because of kneecap injury).

ALL-TIME REBOUNDING LEADER: Cliff Anderson (1,288 from 1965-67).

NCAA CONSENSUS FIRST-TEAM ALL-AMERICANS (1): George Senesky (1943).

NCAA CONSENSUS SECOND-TEAM ALL-AMERICANS (1): Matt Guokas (1966).

SAINT LOUIS

OFFICIAL NAME: Saint Louis University.

NICKNAME: Billikens.

ADDRESS: 3672 West Pine Boulevard, St. Louis, MO 63108.

PHONE/FAX: (314) 977-2524/7193.

ENROLLMENT: 11,300.

ARENA: Kiel Center (Capacity-20,000; Year Opened-1994).

SCHOOL COLORS: Blue and White.

CONFERENCE: Conference USA.

FINAL AP TOP 10 RANKINGS (4): 1949-51-52-57.

NCAA TOURNAMENT APPEARANCES (4): 1952-57-94-95; 2-5 record (.286); regional runner-up in 1952.

NIT APPEARANCES (16): 1948-49-51-52-53-55-56-59-60-61-63-65-87-89-90-96; 18-15 record (.545); finished 1st in 1948, 2nd in 1961, 2nd in 1989 and 2nd in 1990.

ALL-TIME SCORING LEADER: Anthony Bonner (1,972 points from 1987-90).

ALL-TIME REBOUNDING LEADER: Anthony Bonner (1,424 from 1987-90).

NCAA CONSENSUS FIRST-TEAM ALL-AMERICANS (2): Ed Macauley (1948 and 1949).

ST. MARY'S

OFFICIAL NAME: St. Mary's College.

NICKNAME: Gaels.

ADDRESS: Post Office Box 5100, Moraga, CA 94575.

PHONE/FAX: (510) 631-4402/4405.

ENROLLMENT: 4,000.

ARENA: McKeon Pavilion (Capacity-3,500; Year Opened-1978).

SCHOOL COLORS: Blue and Red.

CONFERENCE: West Coast.

NCAA TOURNAMENT APPEARANCES (2): 1959 and 1989; 1-2 record (.333); regional runner-up in 1959.

NIT APPEARANCES: None.

ALL-TIME SCORING LEADER: David Vann (1,738 points from 1979-82).

ALL-TIME REBOUNDING LEADER: Tom Meschery (916 from 1959-61).

ST. PETER'S

OFFICIAL NAME: St. Peter's College.

NICKNAME: Peacocks.

ADDRESS: 2641 Kennedy Boulevard, Jersey City, NJ 07306-5997.

PHONE/FAX: (201) 915-9101/9102.

ENROLLMENT: 3,355.

ARENA: Yanitelli Center (Capacity-3,200; Year Opened-1975).

SCHOOL COLORS: Blue and White.

CONFERENCE: Metro Atlantic Athletic.

NCAA TOURNAMENT APPEARANCES (2): 1991 and 1995; 0-2 record.

NAIA TOURNAMENT APPEARANCES (2): 1953 and 1954; 3-2 record (.600).

NIT APPEARANCES (12): 1957-58-67-68-69-75-76-80-82-84-87-89; 5-13 record (.278); finished 4th in 1968.

ALL-TIME SCORING LEADER: Willie Haynes (1,730 points from 1986-89).

ALL-TIME REBOUNDING LEADER: Pete O'Dea (1,033 from 1966-68).

SAN DIEGO

OFFICIAL NAME: University of San Diego.

NICKNAME: Toreros.

ADDRESS: 5998 Alcala Park, San Diego, CA 92110-2492.

PHONE/FAX: (619) 260-4745/292-0388.

ENROLLMENT: 6,200.

ARENA: USD Sports Center (Capacity-2,500; Year Opened-1963).

SCHOOL COLORS: Columbia Blue, Navy and White.

CONFERENCE: West Coast.

NCAA DIVISION I TOURNAMENT APPEARANCES (2): 1984 and 1987; 0-2 record.

NCAA DIVISION II TOURNAMENT APPEARANCES (5): 1966-73-74-78-79; 4-6 record (.400).

NIT APPEARANCES: None.

ALL-TIME SCORING LEADER: Stan Washington (1,472 points from 1972-74 when school was classified as a small college).

ALL-TIME REBOUNDING LEADER: Gus Magee (948 from 1967-70 when school was classified as a small college).

SAN DIEGO STATE

OFFICIAL NAME: San Diego State University.

NICKNAME: Aztecs.

ADDRESS: Athletics Building, Room 109, San Diego, CA 92182.

PHONE/FAX: (619) 594-5547/6541.

ENROLLMENT: 27,000.

ARENA: San Diego Sports Arena (Capacity-13,741); a new 12,000-seat on-campus facility called the Student Activities Center is slated to open in 1997.

SCHOOL COLORS: Scarlet and Black.

CONFERENCE: Western Athletic.

NCAA DIVISION I TOURNAMENT APPEARANCES (3): 1975-76-85; 0-3 record.

NCAA DIVISION II TOURNAMENT APPEARANCES (3): 1957-67-68; 5-3 record (.625).

NAIA TOURNAMENT APPEARANCES (5): 1939-40-41-42-56; 15-4 record (.789); finished 1st in 1941 and 2nd in 1939 and 1940.

NIT APPEARANCES (1): 1982; 0-1 record.

ALL-TIME SCORING LEADER: Michael Cage (1,846 points from 1981-84).

ALL-TIME REBOUNDING LEADER: Michael Cage (1,317 from 1981-84).

NCAA CONSENSUS SECOND-TEAM ALL-AMERICANS (1): Michael Cage (1984).

SAN FRANCISCO

OFFICIAL NAME: University of San Francisco.

NICKNAME: Dons.

ADDRESS: 2130 Fulton, San Francisco, CA 94117-1080.

PHONE/FAX: (415) 666-6161/2929.

ENROLLMENT: 7,000.

ARENA: Memorial Gymnasium (Capacity-5,300; Year Opened-1958).

SCHOOL COLORS: Green and Gold.

CONFERENCE: West Coast.

FINAL AP TOP 10 RANKINGS (5): 1949-55-56-58-77.

NCAA TOURNAMENT APPEARANCES (15): 1955-56-57-58-63-64-65-72-73-74-77-78-79-81-82; 21-13 record (.618); reached Final Four in 1955 (1st), 1956 (1st) and 1957 (3rd).

NIT APPEARANCES (4): 1949-50-66-76; 5-3 record (.625); finished 1st in 1949.

ALL-TIME SCORING LEADER: Bill Cartwright (2,116 points from 1976-79).

ALL-TIME REBOUNDING LEADER: Bill Russell (1,606 from 1954-56).

NCAA CONSENSUS FIRST-TEAM ALL-AMERICANS (3): Bill Russell (1955 and 1956), Quintin Dailey (1982).

NCAA CONSENSUS SECOND-TEAM ALL-AMERICANS (5): Don Lofgran (1950), K.C. Jones (1956), Mike Farmer (1958), Bill Cartwright (1977 and 1979).

SAN JOSE STATE

OFFICIAL NAME: San Jose State University.

NICKNAME: Spartans.

ADDRESS: 1 Washington Square, San Jose, CA 95192.

PHONE/FAX: (408) 924-1217/1291.

ENROLLMENT: 30,000.

ARENA: The Event Center (Capacity-5,000; Year Opened-1989).

SCHOOL COLORS: Gold, White and Blue.

CONFERENCE: Western Athletic.

NCAA TOURNAMENT APPEARANCES (3): 1951-80-96; 0-3 record.

NAIA TOURNAMENT APPEARANCES (2): 1948 and 1949; 3-2 record (.600).

NIT APPEARANCES (1): 1981; 0-1 record.

ALL-TIME SCORING LEADER: Ricky Berry (1,767 points from 1986-88 after transferring from Oregon State).

ALL-TIME REBOUNDING LEADER: Marv Branstrom (864 from 1956-58).

SANTA CLARA

OFFICIAL NAME: Santa Clara University.

NICKNAME: Broncos.

ADDRESS: Toso Pavilion, Santa Clara, CA 95053.

PHONE/FAX: (408) 554-4661/6942.

ENROLLMENT: 7,800.

ARENA: Toso Pavilion (Capacity-5,000; Year Opened-1975).

SCHOOL COLORS: Bronco Red and White.

CONFERENCE: West Coast.

FINAL AP TOP 10 RANKINGS (1): 1969.

NCAA TOURNAMENT APPEARANCES (10): 1952-53-54-60-68-69-70-87-95-96; 10-12 record (.455); reached Final Four in 1952 (4th).

NIT APPEARANCES (4): 1984-85-88-89; 2-4 record (.333).

ALL-TIME SCORING LEADER: Kurt Rambis (1,735 points from 1977-80).

ALL-TIME REBOUNDING LEADER: Dennis Awtrey (1,135 from 1968-70).

NCAA CONSENSUS SECOND-TEAM ALL-AMERICANS (1): Bud Ogden (1969).

SETON HALL

OFFICIAL NAME: Seton Hall University.

NICKNAME: Pirates.

ADDRESS: 400 South Orange Avenue, South Orange, NJ 07079.

PHONE/FAX: (201) 761-9497/9493.

ENROLLMENT: 10,200.

ARENA: Meadowlands Arena (Capacity-20,029; Year Opened-1981).

SCHOOL COLORS: Blue and White.

CONFERENCE: Big East.

FINAL AP TOP 10 RANKINGS (2): 1953 and 1993.

NCAA TOURNAMENT APPEARANCES (6): 1988-89-91-92-93-94; 12-6 record (.667); reached Final Four in 1989 (2nd).

NIT APPEARANCES (11): 1941-51-52-53-55-56-57-74-77-87-95; 6-13 record (.316); finished 4th in 1941, 4th in 1951 and 1st in 1953.

ALL-TIME SCORING LEADER: Terry Dehere (2,494 points from 1990-93).

ALL-TIME REBOUNDING LEADER: Walter Dukes (1,697 from 1951-53).

NCAA CONSENSUS FIRST-TEAM ALL-AMERICANS (2): Bob Davies (1942), Walter Dukes (1953).

NCAA CONSENSUS SECOND-TEAM ALL-AMERICANS (1): Terry Dehere (1993).

SIENA

OFFICIAL NAME: Siena College.

NICKNAME: Saints.

ADDRESS: 515 Loudon Road, Loudonville, NY 12211-1462.

PHONE/FAX: (518) 783-2411/2992.

ENROLLMENT: 2,700.

ARENAS: Alumni Recreation Center (Capacity-4,000; Year Opened-1974) and Knickerbocker Arena (Capacity-15,500).

SCHOOL COLORS: Green and Gold.

CONFERENCE: Metro Atlantic Athletic.

NCAA DIVISION I TOURNAMENT APPEARANCES (1): 1989; 1-1 record (.500).

NCAA DIVISION II TOURNAMENT APPEARANCES (1): 1974; 2-1 record (.667).

NIT APPEARANCES (3): 1988-91-94; 6-3 record (.667); finished 3rd in 1994.

ALL-TIME SCORING LEADER: Marc Brown (2,284 points from 1988-91).

ALL-TIME REBOUNDING LEADER: Lee Matthews (1,037 from 1990-93).

SOUTH ALABAMA

OFFICIAL NAME: University of South Alabama.

NICKNAME: Jaguars.

ADDRESS: 1107 HPELS Building, Mobile, AL 36688-0002.

PHONE/FAX: (334) 460-7121/7297.

ENROLLMENT: 12,465.

ARENA: Mobile Civic Center (Capacity-10,000; Year Opened-1964).

SCHOOL COLORS: Red, Blue and White.

CONFERENCE: Sun Belt.

NCAA TOURNAMENT APPEARANCES (4): 1979-80-89-91; 1-4 record (.200).

NIT APPEARANCES (2): 1981 and 1984; 3-2 record (.600).

ALL-TIME SCORING LEADER: Jeff Hodge (2,221 points from 1986-89).

ALL-TIME REBOUNDING LEADER: Terry Catledge (932 from 1983-85).

SOUTH CAROLINA

OFFICIAL NAME: University of South Carolina.

NICKNAME: Gamecocks.

ADDRESS: Rex Enright Athletic Center, 1300 Rosewood Drive, Columbia, SC 29208.

PHONE/FAX: (803) 777-5204/2967.

ENROLLMENT: 26,130.

ARENA: Carolina Coliseum/Frank McGuire Arena (Capacity-12,401; Year Opened-1968).

SCHOOL COLORS: Garnet and Black.

CONFERENCE: Southeastern.

FINAL AP TOP 10 RANKINGS (3): 1970-71-72.

NCAA TOURNAMENT APPEARANCES (5): 1971-72-73-74-89; 4-6 record (.400); never reached regional final.

NIT APPEARANCES (6): 1969-75-78-83-91-96; 7-6 record (.538).

ALL-TIME SCORING LEADER: Alex English (1,972 points from 1973-76).

ALL-TIME REBOUNDING LEADER: Lee Collins (1,159 from 1953-56).

NCAA CONSENSUS FIRST-TEAM ALL-AMERICANS (1): Tom Riker (1972).

NCAA CONSENSUS SECOND-TEAM ALL-AMERICANS (4): Grady Wallace (1957), John Roche (1970 and 1971), Kevin Joyce (1973).

SOUTH FLORIDA

OFFICIAL NAME: University of South Florida.

NICKNAME: Bulls.

ADDRESS: 4202 East Fowler Avenue, PED 214, Tampa, FL 33620.

PHONE/FAX: (813) 974-4086/5328.

ENROLLMENT: 37,000.

ARENA: Sun Dome (Capacity-10,411; Year Opened-1980).

SCHOOL COLORS: Green and Gold.

CONFERENCE: Conference USA.

NCAA TOURNAMENT APPEARANCES (2): 1990 and 1992; 0-2 record.

NIT APPEARANCES (5): 1981-83-85-91-95; 4-5 record (.444).

ALL-TIME SCORING LEADER: Charlie Bradley (2,319 points from 1982-85).

ALL-TIME REBOUNDING LEADER: Hakim Shahid (893 from 1987-90).

SOUTHERN

OFFICIAL NAME: Southern University & A&M.

NICKNAME: Jaguars.

ADDRESS: Post Office Box 9942, Baton Rouge, LA 70813.

PHONE/FAX: (504) 771-2601/4400.

ENROLLMENT: 9,500.

ARENA: F.G. Clark Activity Center (Capacity-7,500; Year Opened-1976).

SCHOOL COLORS: Columbia Blue and Gold.

CONFERENCE: Southwestern Athletic.

NCAA DIVISION I TOURNAMENT APPEARANCES (6): 1981-85-87-88-89-93; 1-6 record (.143).

NCAA DIVISION II TOURNAMENT APPEARANCES (3): 1974-75-77; 1-5 record (.167).

NAIA TOURNAMENT APPEARANCES (1): 1965; 2-1 record (.667).

NIT APPEARANCES (1): 1990; 0-1 record.

ALL-TIME SCORING LEADER: Frankie Sanders (2,141 points from 1976-78).

ALL-TIME REBOUNDING LEADER: Jervaughn Scales (1,099 from 1992-94).

SOUTHERN CAL

OFFICIAL NAME: University of Southern California.

NICKNAME: Trojans.

ADDRESS: Heritage Hall, Los Angeles, CA 90089-0602.

PHONE/FAX: (213) 740-8480/7584.

ENROLLMENT: 28,375.

ARENA: Los Angeles Sports Arena (Capacity-15,509; Year Opened-1959).

SCHOOL COLORS: Cardinal and Gold.

CONFERENCE: Pacific-10.

FINAL AP TOP 10 RANKINGS (3): 1961-71-92.

NCAA TOURNAMENT APPEARANCES (9): 1940-54-60-61-79-82-85-91-92; 6-11 record (.353); reached Final Four in 1940 (T3rd) and 1954 (4th).

NIT APPEARANCES (3): 1973-93-94; 2-3 record (.400).

CCAT/NCIT RECORD: 2-2 in 1974 (runner-up) and 1975 (eliminated in first round).

ALL-TIME SCORING LEADER: Harold Miner (2,048 points from 1990-92).

ALL-TIME REBOUNDING LEADER: Ron Riley (1,067 from 1970-72).

NCAA CONSENSUS FIRST-TEAM ALL-AMERICANS (5): Jerry Nemer (1933), Lee Guttero (1935), Ralph Vaughn (1940), Bill Sharman (1950), Harold Miner (1992).

NCAA CONSENSUS SECOND-TEAM ALL-AMERICANS (3): Gene Rock (1943), John Rudometkin (1962), Gus Williams (1975).

SOUTHERN ILLINOIS

OFFICIAL NAME: Southern Illinois University (At Carbondale).

NICKNAME: Salukis.

ADDRESS: SIU Arena, Carbondale, IL 62901.

PHONE/FAX: (618) 453-7235/2648.

ENROLLMENT: 24,870.

ARENA: SIU Arena (Capacity-10,014; Year Opened-1964).

SCHOOL COLORS: Maroon and White.

CONFERENCE: Missouri Valley.

NCAA DIVISION I TOURNAMENT APPEARANCES (4): 1977-93-94-95; 1-4 record (.200).

NCAA DIVISION II TOURNAMENT APPEARANCES (7): 1959-61-62-63-64-65-66; 17-9 record (.654); finished 2nd in 1965 and 1966, 3rd in 1962 and 4th in 1963.

NAIA TOURNAMENT APPEARANCES (5): 1945-46-47-48-60; 8-5 record (.615); finished 1st in 1946 and 4th in 1945.

NIT APPEARANCES (7): 1967-69-75-89-90-91-92; 6-6 record (.500); finished 1st in 1967.

ALL-TIME SCORING LEADER: Charlie Vaughn (2,088 points from 1959-62 when school was classified as a small college).

ALL-TIME REBOUNDING LEADER: Seymour Bryson (1,244 from 1956-59 when school was classified as a small college).

SOUTHERN METHODIST

OFFICIAL NAME: Southern Methodist University.

NICKNAME: Mustangs.

ADDRESS: SMU Box 216, 6024 Airline, Dallas, TX 75275-0216.

PHONE/FAX: (214) 768-2883/2044.

ENROLLMENT: 5,435.

ARENA: Moody Coliseum (Capacity-8,998; Year Opened-1956).

SCHOOL COLORS: Red and Blue.

CONFERENCE: Western Athletic.

FINAL AP TOP 10 RANKINGS (2): 1956 and 1957.

NCAA TOURNAMENT APPEARANCES (10): 1955-56-57-65-66-67-84-85-88-93; 10-12 record (.455); reached Final Four in 1956 (4th).

NIT APPEARANCES (1): 1986; 0-1 record.

CCAT RECORD: 0-1 in 1974.

ALL-TIME SCORING LEADER: Gene Phillips (1,931 points from 1969-71).

ALL-TIME REBOUNDING LEADER: Jon Koncak (1,169 from 1982-85).

NCAA CONSENSUS FIRST-TEAM ALL-AMERICANS (1): Jim Krebs (1957).

NCAA CONSENSUS SECOND-TEAM ALL-AMERICANS (1): Jon Koncak (1985).

SOUTHERN MISSISSIPPI

OFFICIAL NAME: University of Southern Mississippi.

NICKNAME: Golden Eagles.

ADDRESS: Southern Station, Box 5161, Hattiesburg, MS 39406-5161.

PHONE/FAX: (601) 266-4503/4507.

ENROLLMENT: 13,000.

ARENA: Reed Green Coliseum (Capacity-8,095; Year Opened-1965).

SCHOOL COLORS: Black and Gold.

CONFERENCE: Conference USA.

NCAA TOURNAMENT APPEARANCES (2): 1990 and 1991; 0-2 record.

NAIA TOURNAMENT APPEARANCES (4): 1952-53-54-55; 2-4 record (.333).

NIT APPEARANCES (6): 1981-86-87-88-94-95; 6-5 record (.545); finished 1st in 1987.

ALL-TIME SCORING LEADER: Nick Revon (2,135 points from 1951-54 when school was classified as a small college).

ALL-TIME REBOUNDING LEADER: Clarence Weatherspoon (1,320 from 1989-92).

SOUTHWESTERN LOUISIANA

OFFICIAL NAME: University of Southwestern Louisiana.

NICKNAME: Ragin' Cajuns.

ADDRESS: 201 Reinhardt Drive, Lafayette, LA 70506-4297.

PHONE/FAX: (318) 482-6331/6649.

ENROLLMENT: 16,500.

ARENA: Cajundome (Capacity-12,000; Year Opened-1985).

SCHOOL COLORS: Vermilion and White.

CONFERENCE: Sun Belt.

FINAL AP TOP 10 RANKINGS (2): 1972 and 1973.

NCAA TOURNAMENT APPEARANCES (6): 1972-73-82-83-92-94; 4-7 record (.364).

NIT APPEARANCES (3): 1980-84-85; 6-4 record (.600); finished 4th in 1984.

ALL-TIME SCORING LEADER: Dwight "Bo" Lamar (3,493 points from 1970-73).

ALL-TIME REBOUNDING LEADER: Roy Ebron (1,064 from 1971-73).

NCAA CONSENSUS FIRST-TEAM ALL-AMERICANS (2): Dwight "Bo" Lamar (1972 and 1973).

SOUTHWEST MISSOURI STATE

OFFICIAL NAME: Southwest Missouri State University.

NICKNAME: Bears.

ADDRESS: 901 South National, Springfield, MO 65804.

PHONE/FAX: (417) 836-5402/4868.

ENROLLMENT: 17,440.

ARENA: Hammons Student Center (Capacity-8,858; Year Opened-1976).

SCHOOL COLORS: Maroon and White.

CONFERENCE: Missouri Valley.

NCAA DIVISION I TOURNAMENT APPEARANCES (5): 1987-88-89-90-92; 1-5 record (.167).

NCAA DIVISION II TOURNAMENT APPEARANCES (10): 1958-59-66-67-68-69-70-73-74-78; 23-10 record (.697); finished 2nd in 1959, 1967, 1969 and 1974.

NAIA TOURNAMENT APPEARANCES (6): 1939-43-49-52-53-54; 15-4 record (.789); finished 1st in 1952 and 1953, and 3rd in 1954.

NIT APPEARANCES (3): 1986-91-93; 5-3 record (.625).

ALL-TIME SCORING LEADER: Daryel Garrison (1,975 points from 1972-75 when school was classified as a small college).

ALL-TIME REBOUNDING LEADER: Curtis Perry (1,424 from 1967-70 when school was classified as a small college).

STANFORD

OFFICIAL NAME: Stanford University.

NICKNAME: Cardinal.

ADDRESS: Encina Gym, Stanford, CA 94305.

PHONE/FAX: (415) 723-4418/725-2957.

ENROLLMENT: 13,075.

ARENA: Maples Pavilion (Capacity-7,391; Year Opened-1968).

SCHOOL COLORS: Cardinal and White.

CONFERENCE: Pacific-10.

NCAA TOURNAMENT APPEARANCES (5): 1942-89-92-95-96; 5-4 record (.556); reached Final Four in 1942 (1st).

NIT APPEARANCES (4): 1988-90-91-94; 6-3 record (.667); finished 1st in 1991.

ALL-TIME SCORING LEADER: Todd Lichti (2,336 points from 1986-89).

ALL-TIME REBOUNDING LEADER: Adam Keefe (1,119 from 1989-92).

NCAA CONSENSUS FIRST-TEAM ALL-AMERICANS (3): Hank Luisetti (1936, 1937 and 1938).

NCAA CONSENSUS SECOND-TEAM ALL-AMERICANS (2): Don Burness (1942), Todd Lichti (1989).

SYRACUSE

OFFICIAL NAME: Syracuse University.

NICKNAME: Orangemen.

ADDRESS: Manley Field House, Syracuse, NY 13244-5020.

PHONE/FAX: (315) 443-2608/2076.

ENROLLMENT: 10,200.

ARENA: Carrier Dome (Capacity-33,000; Year Opened-1980).

SCHOOL COLOR: Orange.

CONFERENCE: Big East.

FINAL AP TOP 10 RANKINGS (10): 1975-77-79-80-86-87-88-89-90-91.

NCAA TOURNAMENT APPEARANCES (23): 1957-66-73-74-75-76-77-78-79-80-83-84-85-86-87-88-89-90-91-92-94-95-96; 35-24 record (.593); reached Final Four in 1975 (4th), 1987 (2nd) and 1996 (2nd).

NIT APPEARANCES (8): 1946-50-64-67-71-72-81-82; 7-8 record (.467); finished 2nd in 1981.

ALL-TIME SCORING LEADER: Lawrence Moten (2,334 points from 1992-95).

ALL-TIME REBOUNDING LEADER: Derrick Coleman (1,537 from 1987-90).

NCAA CONSENSUS FIRST-TEAM ALL-AMERICANS (3): Dave Bing (1966), Derrick Coleman (1990), Billy Owens (1991).

NCAA CONSENSUS SECOND-TEAM ALL-AMERICANS (4): Dwayne "Pearl" Washington (1985), Rony Seikaly (1988), Sherman Douglas (1989), John Wallace (1996).

TEMPLE

OFFICIAL NAME: Temple University.

NICKNAME: Owls.

ADDRESS: 1900 North Broad Street-109-00, McGonigle Hall-047-00, Philadelphia, PA 19122.

PHONE/FAX: (215) 204-7445/7499.

ENROLLMENT: 33,000.

ARENA: McGonigle Hall (Capacity-3,900; Year Opened-1969).

SCHOOL COLORS: Cherry and White.

CONFERENCE: Atlantic 10.

FINAL AP TOP 10 RANKINGS (3): 1958-87-88.

NCAA TOURNAMENT APPEARANCES (20): 1944-56-58-64-67-70-72-79-84-85-86-87-88-90-91-92-93-94-95-96; 23-20 record (.535); reached Final Four in 1956 (3rd) and 1958 (3rd).

NIT APPEARANCES (12): 1938-57-60-61-62-66-68-69-78-81-82-89; 13-10 record (.565); finished 1st in 1938, 3rd in 1957 and 1st in 1969.

ALL-TIME SCORING LEADER: Mark Macon (2,609 points from 1988-91).

ALL-TIME REBOUNDING LEADER: John Baum (1,042 from 1967-69).

NCAA CONSENSUS FIRST-TEAM ALL-AMERICANS (3): Meyer "Mike" Bloom (1938), Bill Mlkvy (1951), Guy Rodgers (1958).

NCAA CONSENSUS SECOND-TEAM ALL-AMERICANS (2): Guy Rodgers (1957), Mark Macon (1988).

TENNESSEE

OFFICIAL NAME: University of Tennessee.

NICKNAME: Volunteers.

ADDRESS: Post Office Box 15016, 1720 Volunteer Boulevard, Knoxville, TN 37901.

PHONE/FAX: (423) 974-1212/1269.

ENROLLMENT: 26,580.

ARENA: Thompson-Boling Arena (Capacity-24,535; Year Opened-1987).

SCHOOL COLORS: Orange and White.

CONFERENCE: Southeastern.

FINAL AP TOP 10 RANKINGS (1): 1967.

NCAA TOURNAMENT APPEARANCES (9): 1967-76-77-79-80-81-82-83-89; 5-10 record (.333); never reached regional final.

NIT APPEARANCES (9): 1945-69-71-84-85-88-90-92-96; 12-9 record (.571); finished 3rd in 1969 and 1985.

CCAT/NCIT RECORD: 0-2 in 1974 and 1975.

ALL-TIME SCORING LEADER: Allan Houston (2,801 points from 1990-93).

ALL-TIME REBOUNDING LEADER: Gene Tormohlen (1,113 from 1957-59).

NCAA CONSENSUS FIRST-TEAM ALL-AMERICANS (2): Bernard King (1977), Dale Ellis (1983).

NCAA CONSENSUS SECOND-TEAM ALL-AMERICANS (3): Bernard King (1976), Ernie Grunfeld (1977), Dale Ellis (1982).

TENNESSEE-CHATTANOOGA

OFFICIAL NAME: University of Tennessee-Chattanooga.

NICKNAME: Moccasins.

ADDRESS: 615 McCallie Avenue, Chattanooga, TN 37403.

PHONE/FAX: (615) 755-4618/4610.

ENROLLMENT: 8,325.

ARENA: UTC Arena (Capacity-11,218; Year Opened-1982).

SCHOOL COLORS: Navy Blue and Old Gold.

CONFERENCE: Southern.

NCAA DIVISION I TOURNAMENT APPEARANCES (7): 1981-82-83-88-93-94-95; 1-7 record (.125).

NCAA DIVISION II TOURNAMENT APPEARANCES (5): 1961-73-75-76-77; 11-5 record (.688); finished 1st in 1977 and 2nd in 1976.

NIT APPEARANCES (4): 1984-85-86-87; 3-4 record (.429).

ALL-TIME SCORING LEADER: Wayne Goldon (2,384 points from 1974-77 when school was classified as a small college).

ALL-TIME REBOUNDING LEADER: David Bryan (1,059 from 1966-69 when school was classified as a small college).

TENNESSEE TECH

OFFICIAL NAME: Tennessee Tech University.

NICKNAME: Golden Eagles.

ADDRESS: Box 5057, Cookeville, TN 38505.

PHONE/FAX: (615) 372-3088/6139.

ENROLLMENT: 8,240.

ARENA: Eblen Center (Capacity-10,152; Year Opened-1977).

SCHOOL COLORS: Purple and Gold.

CONFERENCE: Ohio Valley.

NCAA TOURNAMENT APPEARANCES (2): 1958 and 1963; 0-2 record.

NIT APPEARANCES (1): 1985; 0-1 record.

ALL-TIME SCORING LEADER: Earl Wise (2,196 points from 1987-90).

ALL-TIME REBOUNDING LEADER: Jimmy Hagan (1,108 from 1958-60).

TEXAS

OFFICIAL NAME: University of Texas-Austin.

NICKNAME: Longhorns.

ADDRESS: Post Office Box 7399, Austin, TX 78713.

PHONE/FAX: (512) 471-7437/6040.

ENROLLMENT: 47,905.

ARENA: Frank Erwin Center (Capacity-16,042; Year Opened-1977).

SCHOOL COLORS: Burnt Orange and White.

CONFERENCE: Big 12.

NCAA TOURNAMENT APPEARANCES (15): 1939-43-47-60-63-72-74-79-89-90-91-92-94-95-96; 14-18 record (.438); reached Final Four in 1943 (3rd) and 1947 (3rd).

NIT APPEARANCES (4): 1948-78-80-86; 6-3 record (.667); finished 1st in 1978.

ALL-TIME SCORING LEADER: Terrence Rencher (2,306 points from 1992-95).

ALL-TIME REBOUNDING LEADER: LaSalle Thompson (1,027 from 1980-82).

NCAA CONSENSUS FIRST-TEAM ALL-AMERICANS (1): Jack Gray (1935).

NCAA CONSENSUS SECOND-TEAM ALL-AMERICANS (1): John Hargis (1947).

TEXAS A&M

OFFICIAL NAME: Texas A&M University.

NICKNAME: Aggies.

ADDRESS: Koldus Building, Room 222, College Station, TX 77843-1228.

PHONE/FAX: (409) 845-5725/0564.

ENROLLMENT: 43,255.

ARENA: G. Rollie White Coliseum (Capacity-7,500; Year Opened-1954); Reed Arena is slated to open in the 1997-98 season (12,500).

SCHOOL COLORS: Maroon and White.

CONFERENCE: Big 12.

NCAA TOURNAMENT APPEARANCES (6): 1951-64-69-75-80-87; 3-7 record (.300); never reached regional final.

NIT APPEARANCES (5): 1979-82-85-86-94; 4-5 record (.444).

ALL-TIME SCORING LEADER: Vernon Smith (1,778 points from 1978-81).

ALL-TIME REBOUNDING LEADER: Vernon Smith (978 from 1978-81).

TEXAS CHRISTIAN

OFFICIAL NAME: Texas Christian University.

NICKNAME: Horned Frogs.

ADDRESS: TCU Box 32924, Ft. Worth, TX 76129.

PHONE/FAX: (817) 921-7969/7964.

ENROLLMENT: 6,990.

ARENA: Daniel-Meyer Coliseum (Capacity-7,166; Year Opened-1961).

SCHOOL COLORS: Purple and White.

CONFERENCE: Western Athletic.

NCAA TOURNAMENT APPEARANCES (6): 1952-53-59-68-71-87; 5-6 record (.455); regional runner-up in 1968.

NIT APPEARANCES (3): 1983-86-92; 4-3 record (.571).

ALL-TIME SCORING LEADER: Darrell Browder (1,886 points from 1980-83).

ALL-TIME REBOUNDING LEADER: Reggie Smith (966 from 1989-92).

TEXAS-EL PASO

OFFICIAL NAME: University of Texas-El Paso.

NICKNAME: Miners.

ADDRESS: 201 Baltimore, El Paso, TX 79968.

PHONE/FAX: (915) 747-5330/5444.

ENROLLMENT: 17,500.

ARENA: Special Events Center (Capacity-12,222; Year Opened-1977).

SCHOOL COLORS: Orange, Blue and White.

CONFERENCE: Western Athletic.

FINAL AP TOP 10 RANKINGS (3): 1966-67-84.

NCAA TOURNAMENT APPEARANCES (14): 1963-64-66-67-70-75-84-85-86-87-88-89-90-92; 14-13 record (.519); reached Final Four in 1966 (1st).

NAIA TOURNAMENT APPEARANCES (1): 1941; 0-1 record.

NIT APPEARANCES (7): 1965-72-80-81-83-93-95; 4-7 record (.364).

ALL-TIME SCORING LEADER: Antoine Gillespie (1,706 points from 1993-95; missed 1991-92 season after failing to meet the academic requirements of Proposition 48).

ALL-TIME REBOUNDING LEADER: Jim Barnes (965 in 1963 and 1964).

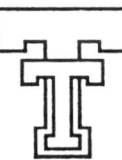

TEXAS TECH

OFFICIAL NAME: Texas Tech University.

NICKNAME: Red Raiders.

ADDRESS: Post Office Box 43021, Lubbock, TX 79409-3021.

PHONE/FAX: (806) 742-2770/1970.

ENROLLMENT: 25,000.

ARENA: Lubbock Municipal Coliseum (Capacity-8,174; Year Opened-1956).

SCHOOL COLORS: Red and Black.

CONFERENCE: Big 12.

FINAL AP TOP 10 RANKINGS (1): 1996.

NCAA TOURNAMENT APPEARANCES (9): 1954-56-61-62-73-76-85-86-96; 5-10 record (.333); never reached regional final.

NAIA TOURNAMENT APPEARANCES (2): 1942 and 1949; 3-2 record (.600).

NIT APPEARANCES (2): 1979 and 1995; 0-2 record.

ALL-TIME SCORING LEADER: Rick Bullock (2,118 points from 1973-76).

ALL-TIME REBOUNDING LEADER: Jim Reed (1,330 from 1954-56).

TOLEDO

OFFICIAL NAME: University of Toledo.

NICKNAME: Rockets.

ADDRESS: Glass Bowl Stadium, Toledo, OH 43606.

PHONE/FAX: (419) 537-3790/3795.

ENROLLMENT: 24,540.

ARENA: John F. Savage Hall (Capacity-9,000; Year Opened-1976).

SCHOOL COLORS: Midnight Blue and Gold.

CONFERENCE: Mid-American.

NCAA TOURNAMENT APPEARANCES (4): 1954-67-79-80; 1-4 record (.200).

NIT APPEARANCES (3): 1942-43-81; 4-4 record (.500); finished 4th in 1942 and 2nd in 1943.

CCAT RECORD: 1-1 in 1974.

ALL-TIME SCORING LEADER: Ken Epperson (2,016 points from 1982-85).

ALL-TIME REBOUNDING LEADER: Ken Epperson (960 from 1982-85).

TULANE

OFFICIAL NAME: Tulane University.

NICKNAME: Green Wave.

ADDRESS: James W. Wilson Jr. Center for Athletics, New Orleans, LA 70118.

PHONE/FAX: (504) 865-5506/5512.

ENROLLMENT: 11,485.

ARENA: Avron B. Fogelman Arena (Capacity-3,600; Year Opened-1933).

SCHOOL COLORS: Olive Green and Sky Blue.

CONFERENCE: Conference USA.

FINAL AP TOP 10 RANKINGS (1): 1949.

NCAA TOURNAMENT APPEARANCES (3): 1992-93-95; 3-3 record (.500).

NIT APPEARANCES (4): 1982-83-94-96; 7-4 record (.636); finished 3rd in 1996.

ALL-TIME SCORING LEADER: Anthony Reed (1,896 points from 1990-93).

ALL-TIME REBOUNDING LEADER: Jack Ardon (1,062 from 1960-62).

TULSA

OFFICIAL NAME: The University of Tulsa.

NICKNAME: Golden Hurricane.

ADDRESS: 600 South College, Tulsa, OK 74104-3189.

PHONE/FAX: (918) 631-2395/3913.

ENROLLMENT: 4,600.

ARENA: Maxwell Convention Center (Capacity-8,659; Year Opened-1964); a Student Life and Convocation Complex is in the planning stages.

SCHOOL COLORS: Old Gold, Royal Blue and Crimson.

CONFERENCE: Western Athletic.

FINAL AP TOP 10 RANKINGS (1): 1982.

NCAA TOURNAMENT APPEARANCES (9): 1955-82-84-85-86-87-94-95-96; 5-9 record (.357).

NIT APPEARANCES (7): 1953-67-69-81-83-90-91; 5-6 record (.455); finished 1st in 1981.

ALL-TIME SCORING LEADER: Steve Harris (2,272 points from 1982-85).

ALL-TIME REBOUNDING LEADER: Bob Goodall (776 from 1958-60).

NCAA CONSENSUS SECOND-TEAM ALL-AMERICANS (1): Paul Pressey (1982).

UAB

OFFICIAL NAME: University of Alabama at Birmingham.

NICKNAME: Blazers.

ADDRESS: 115 UAB Arena, Birmingham, AL 35294-1160.

PHONE/FAX: (205) 934-0722/7505.

ENROLLMENT: 16,660.

ARENA: UAB Arena (Capacity-8,500; Year Opened-1988).

SCHOOL COLORS: Green, Gold and White.

CONFERENCE: Conference USA.

NCAA TOURNAMENT APPEARANCES (9): 1981-82-83-84-85-86-87-90-94; 6-9 record (.400); reached regional final in 1982.

NIT APPEARANCES (5): 1980-89-91-92-93; 8-5 record (.615); finished 3rd in 1989 and 1993.

ALL-TIME SCORING LEADER: Steve Mitchell (1,867 points from 1983-86).

ALL-TIME REBOUNDING LEADER: Jerome Mincy (933 from 1983-86).

UCLA

NICKNAME: Bruins.

ADDRESS: J.D. Morgan Center, 405 Hilgard Avenue, Los Angeles, CA 90024.

PHONE/FAX: (310) 206-6831/825-8664.

ENROLLMENT: 35,500.

ARENA: Pauley Pavilion (Capacity-12,819; Year Opened-1965).

SCHOOL COLORS: Navy Blue and Gold.

CONFERENCE: Pacific-10.

FINAL AP TOP 10 RANKINGS (21): 1950-56-64-65-67-68-69-70-71-72-73-74-75-76-77-78-79-81-83-92-95.

NCAA TOURNAMENT APPEARANCES (32): 1950-52-56-62-63-64-65-67-68-69-70-71-72-73-74-75-76-77-78-79-80-81-83-87 -89-90-91-92-93-94-95-96; 74-25 record (.747); reached Final Four in 1962 (4th), 1964 (1st), 1965 (1st), 1967 (1st), 1968 (1st), 1969 (1st), 1970 (1st), 1971 (1st), 1972 (1st), 1973 (1st), 1974 (3rd), 1975 (1st), 1976 (3rd), 1980 (2nd) and 1995 (1st).

NIT APPEARANCES (2): 1985 and 1986; finished 1st in 1985.

ALL-TIME SCORING LEADER: Don MacLean (2,608 points from 1989-92).

ALL-TIME REBOUNDING LEADER: Bill Walton (1,370 from 1972-74).

NCAA CONSENSUS FIRST-TEAM ALL-AMERICANS (18): Walt Hazzard (1964), Gail Goodrich (1965), Lew Alcindor (1967, 1968 and 1969), Sidney Wicks (1971), Henry Bibby (1972), Bill Walton (1972, 1973 and 1974), Keith Wilkes (1973 and 1974), Dave Meyers (1975), Richard Washington (1976), Marques Johnson (1977), David Greenwood (1978 and 1979), Ed O'Bannon (1995).

NCAA CONSENSUS SECOND-TEAM ALL-AMERICANS (4): Don Barksdale (1947), Lucius Allen (1968), Sidney Wicks (1970), Don MacLean (1992).

UNC CHARLOTTE

NICKNAME: 49ers.

ADDRESS: 9201 University City Boulevard, Charlotte, NC 28223-0001.

PHONE/FAX: (704) 547-4937/4918.

ENROLLMENT: 15,650.

ARENA: Dale F. Halton Arena (Capacity-9,600; Year Opened-1996).

SCHOOL COLORS: Green and White.

CONFERENCE: Conference USA.

NCAA TOURNAMENT APPEARANCES (4): 1977-88-92-95; 3-5 record (.375); reached Final Four in 1977 (4th).

NIT APPEARANCES (3): 1976-89-94; 3-3 record (.500); finished 2nd in 1976.

ALL-TIME SCORING LEADER: Henry Williams (2,383 points from 1989-92).

ALL-TIME REBOUNDING LEADER: Cedric "Cornbread" Maxwell (1,117 from 1974-77).

UNLV

NICKNAME: Runnin' Rebels.

ADDRESS: 4505 Maryland Parkway, Las Vegas, NV 89154.

PHONE/FAX: (702) 895-3207/0989.

ENROLLMENT: 20,240.

ARENA: Thomas & Mack Center (Capacity-18,500; Year Opened-1983).

SCHOOL COLORS: Scarlet and Gray.

CONFERENCE: Western Athletic.

FINAL AP TOP 10 RANKINGS (8): 1976-77-83-85-87-90-91-92.

NCAA DIVISION I TOURNAMENT APPEARANCES (12): 1975-76-77-83-84-85-86-87-88-89-90-91; 30-11 record (.732); reached Final Four in 1977 (3rd), 1987 (T3rd), 1990 (1st) and 1991 (T3rd).

NCAA DIVISION II TOURNAMENT APPEARANCES (4): 1965-67-68-69; 4-5 record (.444).

NIT APPEARANCES (3): 1980-82-93; 4-4 record (.500); finished 4th in 1980.

ALL-TIME SCORING LEADER: Eddie Owens (2,221 points from 1974-77).

ALL-TIME REBOUNDING LEADER: Sidney Green (1,276 from 1980-83).

NCAA CONSENSUS FIRST-TEAM ALL-AMERICANS (2): Larry Johnson (1990 and 1991).

NCAA CONSENSUS SECOND-TEAM ALL-AMERICANS (4): Sidney Green (1983), Armon Gilliam (1987), Stacey Augmon (1991), Isaiah "J.R." Rider (1993).

UTAH

OFFICIAL NAME: University of Utah.

NICKNAME: Utes.

ADDRESS: Jon Huntsman Center, Salt Lake City, UT 84112.

PHONE/FAX: (801) 581-3510/4358.

ENROLLMENT: 26,600.

ARENA: Jon Huntsman Center (Capacity-15,000; Year Opened-1969).

SCHOOL COLORS: Crimson and White.

CONFERENCE: Western Athletic.

FINAL AP TOP 10 RANKINGS (4): 1955-60-62-91.

NCAA TOURNAMENT APPEARANCES (18): 1944-45-55-56-59-60-61-66-77-78-79-81-83-86-91-93-95-96; 22-21 record (.512); reached Final Four in 1944 (1st), 1961 (4th) and 1966 (4th).

NIT APPEARANCES (11): 1944-47-49-57-58-70-74-87-88-92-95; 11-9 record (.550); finished 1st in 1947, 2nd in 1974 and 3rd in 1992.

ALL-TIME SCORING LEADER: Josh Grant (2,000 points from 1989-93; missed most of 1991-92 season because of a knee injury).

ALL-TIME REBOUNDING LEADER: Billy McGill (1,106 from 1960-62).

NCAA CONSENSUS FIRST-TEAM ALL-AMERICANS (3): Bill Kinner (1936), Arnie Ferrin (1945), Billy McGill (1962).

NCAA CONSENSUS SECOND-TEAM ALL-AMERICANS (9): Arnie Ferrin (1944, 1947 and 1948), Vern Gardner (1947 and 1949), Billy McGill (1961), Luther "Ticky" Burden (1975), Danny Vranes (1981), Keith Van Horn (1996).

UTAH STATE

OFFICIAL NAME: Utah State University.

NICKNAME: Aggies.

ADDRESS: 700 North & 800 East, Logan, UT 84322.

PHONE/FAX: (801) 797-1361/2615.

ENROLLMENT: 17,435.

ARENA: Smith Spectrum (Capacity-10,270; Year Opened-1970).

SCHOOL COLORS: Navy Blue and White.

CONFERENCE: Big West.

FINAL AP TOP 10 RANKINGS (1): 1960.

NCAA TOURNAMENT APPEARANCES (11): 1939-62-63-64-70-71-75-79-80-83-88; 5-13 record (.278); regional runner-up in 1939 and 1970.

NAIA TOURNAMENT APPEARANCES (1): 1952; 1-1 record (.500).

NIT APPEARANCES (5): 1960-67-78-84-95; 2-5 record (.286); finished 3rd in 1960.

ALL-TIME SCORING LEADER: Greg Grant (2,127 points from 1983-86).

ALL-TIME REBOUNDING LEADER: Cornell Green (1,067 from 1960-62).

NCAA CONSENSUS SECOND-TEAM ALL-AMERICANS (1): Wayne Estes (1965).

VALPARAISO

OFFICIAL NAME: Valparaiso University.

NICKNAME: Crusaders.

ADDRESS: Athletics-Recreation Center (ARC), Valparaiso, IN 46383.

PHONE/FAX: (219) 464-5232/5762.

ENROLLMENT: 3,760.

ARENA: Athletics-Recreation Center (Capacity-4,500; Year Opened-1984).

SCHOOL COLORS: Brown and Gold.

CONFERENCE: Mid-Continent.

NCAA DIVISION I TOURNAMENT APPEARANCES (1): 1996; 0-1 record.

NCAA DIVISION II TOURNAMENT APPEARANCES (5): 1962-66-67-69-73; 7-5 record (.583).

NAIA TOURNAMENT APPEARANCES (2): 1938 and 1943; 1-2 record (.333).

ALL-TIME SCORING LEADER: Tracy Gipson (1,785 points from 1990-93).

ALL-TIME REBOUNDING LEADER: Chris Ensminger (910 from 1993-96).

NCAA CONSENSUS SECOND-TEAM ALL-AMERICANS (1): Bob Dille (1944).

VANDERBILT

OFFICIAL NAME: Vanderbilt University.

NICKNAME: Commodores.

ADDRESS: Post Office Box 120158, Nashville, TN 37212.

PHONE/FAX: (615) 322-4121/343-7064.

ENROLLMENT: 9,300.

ARENA: Memorial Gymnasium (Capacity-15,311; Year Opened-1952).

SCHOOL COLORS: Black and Gold.

CONFERENCE: Southeastern.

FINAL AP TOP 10 RANKINGS (4): 1957-65-66-93.

NCAA TOURNAMENT APPEARANCES (6): 1965-74-88-89-91-93; 5-7 record (.417); regional runner-up in 1965.

NIT APPEARANCES (6): 1983-87-90-92-94-96; 13-5 record (.722); finished 1st in 1990 and 2nd in 1994.

ALL-TIME SCORING LEADER: Phil Cox (1,725 points from 1982-85).

ALL-TIME REBOUNDING LEADER: Clyde Lee (1,223 from 1964-66).

NCAA CONSENSUS FIRST-TEAM ALL-AMERICANS (1): Clyde Lee (1966).

NCAA CONSENSUS SECOND-TEAM ALL-AMERICANS (2): Clyde Lee (1965), Billy McCaffrey (1993).

VILLANOVA

OFFICIAL NAME: Villanova University.

NICKNAME: Wildcats.

ADDRESS: Jake Nevin Field House, 800 Lancaster Avenue, Villanova, PA 19085-1674.

PHONE/FAX: (610) 519-4120/7323.

ENROLLMENT: 5,995.

ARENAS: John E. duPont Pavilion (Capacity-6,500; Year Opened-1986) and CoreStates Spectrum (Capacity-18,060).

SCHOOL COLORS: Blue and White.

CONFERENCE: Big East.

FINAL AP TOP 10 RANKINGS (5): 1964-65-69-95-96.

NCAA TOURNAMENT APPEARANCES (23): 1939-49-51-55-62-64-69-70-71-72-78-80-81-82-83-84-85-86-88-90-91-95-96; 36-23 record (.610); reached Final Four in 1939 (T3rd), 1971 (2nd) and 1985 (1st).

NIT APPEARANCES (12): 1959-60-63-65-66-67-68-77-87-89-92-94; 19-12 record (.613); finished 4th in 1963, 2nd in 1965, 3rd in 1966, 3rd in 1977 and 1st in 1994.

ALL-TIME SCORING LEADER: Kerry Kittles (2,243 points from 1993-96).

ALL-TIME REBOUNDING LEADER: Howard Porter (1,317 from 1969-71).

NCAA CONSENSUS FIRST-TEAM ALL-AMERICANS (2): Paul Arizin (1950), Kerry Kittles (1996).

NCAA CONSENSUS SECOND-TEAM ALL-AMERICANS (2): Howard Porter (1971), Kerry Kittles (1995).

VIRGINIA

OFFICIAL NAME: University of Virginia.

NICKNAME: Cavaliers.

ADDRESS: Post Office Box 3785, University Hall, Alderman & Massie Roads, Charlottesville, VA 22903.

PHONE/FAX: (804) 982-5500/5525.

ENROLLMENT: 18,010.

ARENA: University Hall (Capacity-8,457; Year Opened-1965).

SCHOOL COLORS: Orange and Blue.

CONFERENCE: Atlantic Coast.

FINAL AP TOP 10 RANKINGS (3): 1981-82-83.

NCAA TOURNAMENT APPEARANCES (13): 1976-81-82-83-84-86-87-89-90-91-93-94-95; 21-13 record (.618); reached Final Four in 1981 (3rd) and 1984 (T3rd).

NIT APPEARANCES (7): 1941-72-78-79-80-85-92; 13-5 record (.722); finished 1st in 1980 and 1992.

ALL-TIME SCORING LEADER: Bryant Stith (2,516 points from 1989-92).

ALL-TIME REBOUNDING LEADER: Ralph Sampson (1,511 from 1980-83).

NCAA CONSENSUS FIRST-TEAM ALL-AMERICANS (3): Ralph Sampson (1981, 1982 and 1983).

NCAA CONSENSUS SECOND-TEAM ALL-AMERICANS (2): Barry Parkhill (1972), Jeff Lamp (1981).

VIRGINIA COMMONWEALTH

OFFICIAL NAME: Virginia Commonwealth University.

NICKNAME: Rams.

ADDRESS: VCU Box 2003, Richmond, VA 23284-2003.

PHONE/FAX: (804) 828-7000/9723.

ENROLLMENT: 22,000.

ARENA: Richmond Coliseum (Capacity-12,500; Year Opened-1971); Stuart C. Sigel Convocation and Recreation Center is slated to open in the 1998-99 season (Capacity-7,500).

SCHOOL COLORS: Black and Gold.

CONFERENCE: Colonial Athletic Association.

NCAA TOURNAMENT APPEARANCES (6): 1980-81-83-84-85-96; 4-6 record (.400).

NIT APPEARANCES (3): 1978-88-93; 2-3 record (.400).

ALL-TIME SCORING LEADER: Len Creech (2,019 points from 1965-69 when school was classified as a small college; missed 1967-68 season).

ALL-TIME REBOUNDING LEADER: Lorenza Watson (1,143 from 1976-79).

VIRGINIA MILITARY

OFFICIAL NAME: Virginia Military Institute.

NICKNAME: Keydets.

ADDRESS: Lexington, VA 24450.

PHONE/FAX: (703) 464-7253/7583.

ENROLLMENT: 1,300.

ARENA: Cameron Hall (Capacity-5,800; Year Opened-1981).

SCHOOL COLORS: Red, White and Yellow.

CONFERENCE: Southern.

NCAA TOURNAMENT APPEARANCES (3): 1964-76-77; 3-3 record (.500); regional runner-up in 1976.

NIT APPEARANCES: None.

ALL-TIME SCORING LEADER: Gay Elmore (2,423 points from 1983-87; missed majority of 1982-83 season because of leg and wrist injuries).

ALL-TIME REBOUNDING LEADER: Dave Montgomery (1,068 from 1975-78).

VIRGINIA TECH

OFFICIAL NAME: Virginia Polytechnic Institute & State University.

NICKNAME: Hokies.

ADDRESS: Jamerson Athletic Center, Blacksburg, VA 24061-0502.

PHONE/FAX: (703) 231-6725/6984.

ENROLLMENT: 22,235.

ARENA: Cassell Coliseum (Capacity-9,971; Year Opened-1962).

SCHOOL COLORS: Chicago Maroon and Burnt Orange.

CONFERENCE: Atlantic 10.

NCAA TOURNAMENT APPEARANCES (7): 1967-76-79-80-85-86-96; 5-7 record (.417); regional runner-up in 1967.

NIT APPEARANCES (7): 1966-73-77-82-83-84-95; 17-5 record (.773); finished 1st in 1973 and 1995, and 3rd in 1984.

ALL-TIME SCORING LEADER: Vernell "Bimbo" Coles (2,484 points from 1987-90).

ALL-TIME REBOUNDING LEADER: Chris Smith (1,508 from 1958-61).

NCAA CONSENSUS SECOND-TEAM ALL-AMERICANS (1): Dell Curry (1986).

WAKE FOREST

OFFICIAL NAME: Wake Forest University.

NICKNAME: Demon Deacons.

ADDRESS: Post Office Box 7265, Athletic Center, Wingate Drive, Winston-Salem, NC 27109.

PHONE/FAX: (910) 759-5640/5140.

ENROLLMENT: 3,600.

ARENA: Lawrence Joel Memorial Coliseum (Capacity-14,407; Year Opened-1989).

SCHOOL COLORS: Old Gold and Black.

CONFERENCE: Atlantic Coast.

FINAL AP TOP 10 RANKINGS (3): 1977-95-96.

NCAA TOURNAMENT APPEARANCES (14): 1939-53-61-62-77-81-82-84-91-92-93-94-95-96; 21-14 record (.600); reached Final Four in 1962 (3rd).

NIT APPEARANCES (2): 1983 and 1985; 3-2 record (.600); finished in tie for 3rd in 1983.

ALL-TIME SCORING LEADER: Dickie Hemric (2,587 points from 1952-55).

ALL-TIME REBOUNDING LEADER: Dickie Hemric (1,802 from 1952-55).

NCAA CONSENSUS FIRST-TEAM ALL-AMERICANS (2): Len Chappell (1962), Tim Duncan (1996).

NCAA CONSENSUS SECOND-TEAM ALL-AMERICANS (5): Dickie Hemric (1955), Rod Griffin (1977 and 1978), Rodney Rogers (1993), Randolph Childress (1995).

WASHINGTON

OFFICIAL NAME: University of Washington.

NICKNAME: Huskies.

ADDRESS: Graves Building, Seattle, WA 98195.

PHONE/FAX: (206) 543-2230/5000.

ENROLLMENT: 34,000.

ARENA: Hec Edmundson Pavilion (Capacity-7,900; Year Opened-1927).

SCHOOL COLORS: Purple and Gold.

CONFERENCE: Pacific-10.

FINAL AP TOP 10 RANKINGS (2): 1952 and 1953.

NCAA TOURNAMENT APPEARANCES (8): 1943-48-51-53-76-84-85-86; 8-9 record (.471); reached Final Four in 1953 (3rd).

NIT APPEARANCES (4): 1980-82-87-96; 3-4 record (.429).

ALL-TIME SCORING LEADER: Christian Welp (2,073 points from 1984-87).

ALL-TIME REBOUNDING LEADER: Doug Smart (1,051 from 1957-59).

NCAA CONSENSUS FIRST-TEAM ALL-AMERICANS (2): Hal Lee (1934), Bob Houbregs (1953).

NCAA CONSENSUS SECOND-TEAM ALL-AMERICANS (2): Jack Nichols (1948), Bob Houbregs (1952).

WASHINGTON STATE

OFFICIAL NAME: Washington State University.

NICKNAME: Cougars.

ADDRESS: Bohler Gym, Room M-8, Pullman, WA 99164-1602.

PHONE/FAX: (509) 335-2684/0267.

ENROLLMENT: 17,500.

ARENA: Friel Court (Capacity-12,058; Year Opened-1973).

SCHOOL COLORS: Crimson and Gray.

CONFERENCE: Pacific-10.

NCAA TOURNAMENT APPEARANCES (4): 1941-80-83-94; 3-4 record (.429); reached Final Four in 1941 (2nd).

NIT APPEARANCES (3): 1992-95-96; 4-3 record (.571).

ALL-TIME SCORING LEADER: Steve Puidokas (1,894 points from 1974-77).

ALL-TIME REBOUNDING LEADER: Steve Puidokas (992 from 1974-77).

NCAA CONSENSUS SECOND-TEAM ALL-AMERICANS (3): Paul Lindemann (1941), Gale Bishop (1943), Vince Hanson (1945).

WEBER STATE

OFFICIAL NAME: Weber State University.

NICKNAME: Wildcats.

ADDRESS: Wildcat Stadium, Ogden, UT 84408-2702.

PHONE/FAX: (801) 626-6010/6490.

ENROLLMENT: 14,500.

ARENA: Dee Events Center (Capacity-12,000; Year Opened-1977).

SCHOOL COLORS: Royal Purple and White.

CONFERENCE: Big Sky.

NCAA TOURNAMENT APPEARANCES (11): 1968-69-70-71-72-73-78-79-80-83-95; 5-12 record (.294).

NIT APPEARANCES (1): 1984; 1-1 record (.500).

ALL-TIME SCORING LEADER: Bruce Collins (2,019 points from 1977-80).

ALL-TIME REBOUNDING LEADER: Willie Sojourner (1,143 from 1969-71).

WEST VIRGINIA

OFFICIAL NAME: West Virginia University.

NICKNAME: Mountaineers.

ADDRESS: Post Office Box 0877, Morgantown, WV 26507-0877.

PHONE/FAX: (304) 293-2821/4105.

ENROLLMENT: 22,710.

ARENA: WVU Coliseum (Capacity-14,000; Year Opened-1970).

SCHOOL COLORS: Old Gold and Blue.

CONFERENCE: Big East.

FINAL AP TOP 10 RANKINGS (6): 1952-57-58-59-60-61.

NCAA TOURNAMENT APPEARANCES (17): 1955-56-57-58-59-60-62-63-65-67-82-83-84-86-87-89-92; 11-17 record (.393); reached Final Four in 1959 (2nd).

NIT APPEARANCES (11): 1942-45-46-47-68-81-85-88-91-93-94; 12-12 record (.500); finished 1st in 1942, 3rd in 1946, 4th in 1947 and 4th in 1981.

ALL-TIME SCORING LEADER: Jerry West (2,309 points from 1958-60).

ALL-TIME REBOUNDING LEADER: Jerry West (1,240 from 1958-60).

NCAA CONSENSUS FIRST-TEAM ALL-AMERICANS (3): Rod Hundley (1957), Jerry West (1959 and 1960).

NCAA CONSENSUS SECOND-TEAM ALL-AMERICANS (4): Mark Workman (1952), Rod Hundley (1956), Rod Thorn (1962 and 1963).

WESTERN KENTUCKY

OFFICIAL NAME: Western Kentucky University.

NICKNAME: Hilltoppers.

ADDRESS: College Heights, Bowling Green, KY 42101.

PHONE/FAX: (502) 745-4298/3444.

ENROLLMENT: 15,400.

ARENA: E.A. Diddle Arena (Capacity-11,300; Year Opened-1963).

SCHOOL COLORS: Red and White.

CONFERENCE: Sun Belt.

FINAL AP TOP 10 RANKINGS (6): 1949-50-54-66-67-71.

NCAA TOURNAMENT APPEARANCES (16): 1940-60-62-66-67-70-71-76-78-80-81-86-87-93-94-95; 15-17 record (.469); reached Final Four in 1971 (3rd).

NAIA TOURNAMENT APPEARANCES (1): 1938; 0-1 record.

NIT APPEARANCES (11): 1942-43-48-49-50-52-53-54-65-82-92; 8-12 record (.400); finished 2nd in 1942, 3rd in 1948 and 4th in 1954.

ALL-TIME SCORING LEADER: Jim McDaniels (2,238 points from 1969-71).

ALL-TIME REBOUNDING LEADER: Ralph Crosthwaite (1,309 from 1955-59; missed 1955-56 season for disciplinary reasons).

NCAA CONSENSUS FIRST-TEAM ALL-AMERICANS (2): Clem Haskins (1967), Jim McDaniels (1971).

NCAA CONSENSUS SECOND-TEAM ALL-AMERICANS (1): Tom Marshall (1954).

WESTERN MICHIGAN

OFFICIAL NAME: Western Michigan University.

NICKNAME: Broncos.

ADDRESS: University Arena, Kalamazoo, MI 49008-5166.

PHONE/FAX: (616) 387-4138/4139.

ENROLLMENT: 26,675.

ARENA: University Arena (Capacity-5,800; Year Opened-1957 as Read Fieldhouse; renovated as University Arena for 1995).

SCHOOL COLORS: Brown and Gold.

CONFERENCE: Mid-American.

FINAL AP TOP 10 RANKINGS (1): 1976.

NCAA TOURNAMENT APPEARANCES (1): 1976; 1-1 record (.500).

NIT APPEARANCES (1): 1992; 0-1 record.

ALL-TIME SCORING LEADER: Manny Newsome (1,786 points from 1962-64).

ALL-TIME REBOUNDING LEADER: Paul Griffin (1,008 from 1973-76).

WICHITA STATE

OFFICIAL NAME: Wichita State University.

NICKNAME: Shockers.

ADDRESS: Campus Box 18, Wichita, KS 67260-0018.

PHONE/FAX: (316) 689-3265/3336.

ENROLLMENT: 15,000.

ARENA: Levitt Arena (Capacity-10,656; Year Opened-1955).

SCHOOL COLORS: Yellow and Black.

CONFERENCE: Missouri Valley.

FINAL AP TOP 10 RANKINGS (2): 1963 and 1964.

NCAA TOURNAMENT APPEARANCES (7): 1964-65-76-81-85-87-88; 6-8 record (.429); reached Final Four in 1965 (4th).

NAIA TOURNAMENT APPEARANCES (2): 1945 and 1946; 0-2 record.

NIT APPEARANCES (7): 1954-62-63-66-80-84-89; 1-7 record (.125).

ALL-TIME SCORING LEADER: Cleo Littleton (2,164 points from 1952-55).

ALL-TIME REBOUNDING LEADER: Xavier McDaniel (1,359 from 1982-85).

NCAA CONSENSUS FIRST-TEAM ALL-AMERICANS (2): Dave Stallworth (1964), Xavier McDaniel (1985).

NCAA CONSENSUS SECOND-TEAM ALL-AMERICANS (1): Dave Stallworth (1965).

WILLIAM & MARY

OFFICIAL NAME: College of William & Mary.

NICKNAME: Tribe.

ADDRESS: Post Office Box 399, Williamsburg, VA 23187.

PHONE/FAX: (757) 221-3368/3412.

ENROLLMENT: 5,300.

ARENA: William & Mary Hall (Capacity-10,000; Year Opened-1969).

SCHOOL COLORS: Green, Gold and Silver.

CONFERENCE: Colonial Athletic Association.

NCAA TOURNAMENT APPEARANCES:: None.

NIT APPEARANCES (1): 1983; 0-1 record.

ALL-TIME SCORING LEADER: Chet Giermak (2,052 points from 1947-50).

ALL-TIME REBOUNDING LEADER: Jeff Cohen (1,679 from 1958-61).

WISCONSIN

OFFICIAL NAME: University of Wisconsin (At Madison).

NICKNAME: Badgers.

ADDRESS: 1440 Monroe Street, Madison, WI 53711.

PHONE/FAX: (608) 262-1811/8184.

ENROLLMENT: 40,305.

ARENA: UW Field House (Capacity-11,500; Year Opened-1930); Kohl Center (Capacity-16,500) is slated to open in 1998.

SCHOOL COLORS: Cardinal and White.

CONFERENCE: Big Ten.

NCAA TOURNAMENT APPEARANCES (3): 1941-47-94; 5-2 record (.714); reached Final Four in 1941 (1st).

NIT APPEARANCES (4): 1989-91-93-96; 3-4 record (.429).

ALL-TIME SCORING LEADER: Michael Finley (2,147 points from 1992-95).

ALL-TIME REBOUNDING LEADER: Claude Gregory (904 from 1978-81).

NCAA CONSENSUS FIRST-TEAM ALL-AMERICANS (2): Gene Englund (1941), John Kotz (1942).

NCAA CONSENSUS SECOND-TEAM ALL-AMERICANS:: (2): John Kotz (1943), Don Rehfeldt (1950).

WISCONSIN-GREEN BAY

OFFICIAL NAME: University of Wisconsin (At Green Bay).

NICKNAME: Phoenix.

ADDRESS: Phoenix Sports Center, 2420 Nicolet Drive, Green Bay, WI 54311-7001.

PHONE/FAX: (414) 465-2145/2357.

ENROLLMENT: 5,000.

ARENA: Brown County Veterans Memorial Arena (Capacity-5,600; Year Opened-1958).

SCHOOL COLORS: Red, Green and White.

CONFERENCE: Midwestern Collegiate.

NCAA DIVISION I TOURNAMENT APPEARANCES (4): 1991-94-95-96; 1-4 record (.200).

NCAA DIVISION II TOURNAMENT APPEARANCES (6): 1974-76-77-78-79-81; 13-8 record (.619); finished 2nd in 1978 and 1979, and 4th in 1981.

NAIA TOURNAMENT APPEARANCES (1): 1973; 2-1 record (.667).

NIT APPEARANCES (2): 1990 and 1992; 1-2 record (.333).

ALL-TIME SCORING LEADER: Tony Bennett (2,285 points from 1989-92).

ALL-TIME REBOUNDING LEADER: Dennis Woelffer (947 from 1970-73 when school was classified as a small college).

WYOMING

OFFICIAL NAME: University of Wyoming.

NICKNAME: Cowboys.

ADDRESS: Post Office Box 3414, Fieldhouse-North Addition, Laramie, WY 82071-3414.

PHONE/FAX: (307) 766-2256/2346.

ENROLLMENT: 11,000.

ARENA: Arena-Auditorium (Capacity-15,028; Year Opened-1982).

SCHOOL COLORS: Brown and Yellow.

CONFERENCE: Western Athletic.

NCAA TOURNAMENT APPEARANCES (13): 1941-43-47-48-49-52-53-58-67-81-82-87-88; 8-18 record (.308); reached Final Four in 1943 (1st).

NIT APPEARANCES (4): 1968-69-86-91; 5-4 record (.556); finished 2nd in 1986.

ALL-TIME SCORING LEADER: Fennis Dembo (2,311 points from 1985-88).

ALL-TIME REBOUNDING LEADER: Reginald Slater (1,197 from 1989-92).

NCAA CONSENSUS FIRST-TEAM ALL-AMERICANS (3): Les Witte (1932 and 1934), Ken Sailors (1943).

NCAA CONSENSUS SECOND-TEAM ALL-AMERICANS (1): Ken Sailors (1946).

XAVIER

OFFICIAL NAME: Xavier University.

NICKNAME: Musketeers.

ADDRESS: 3800 Victory Parkway, Cincinnati, OH 45207-6114.

PHONE/FAX: (513) 745-3416/2825.

ENROLLMENT: 6,125.

ARENA: Cincinnati Gardens (Capacity-10,400; Year Opened-1949).

SCHOOL COLORS: Blue and White.

CONFERENCE: Atlantic 10.

NCAA TOURNAMENT APPEARANCES:: (10): 1961-83-86-87-88-89-90-91-93-95; 5-10 record (.333).

NAIA TOURNAMENT APPEARANCES (1): 1948; finished 4th with 3-2 record (.600).

NIT APPEARANCES (5): 1956-57-58-84-94; 10-4 record (.714); finished 1st in 1958.

ALL-TIME SCORING LEADER: Byron Larkin (2,696 points from 1985-88).

ALL-TIME REBOUNDING LEADER: Tyrone Hill (1,380 from 1987-90).

YALE

OFFICIAL NAME: Yale University.

NICKNAMES: Elis, Bulldogs.

ADDRESS: Box 208216, New Haven, CT 06520-8216.

PHONE/FAX: (203) 432-1455/1454.

ENROLLMENT: 5,200.

ARENA: Payne Whitney Gymnasium (Capacity-3,100; Year Opened-1932).

School Colors: Yale Blue and White.

CONFERENCE: Ivy League.

NCAA TOURNAMENT APPEARANCES (3): 1949-57-62; 0-4 record.

NIT APPEARANCES: None.

ALL-TIME SCORING LEADER: Butch Graves (2,090 points from 1981-84).

ALL-TIME REBOUNDING LEADER: Ed Robinson (1,182 from 1955-57).

NCAA CONSENSUS FIRST-TEAM ALL-AMERICANS (1): Tony Lavelli (1949).

NCAA CONSENSUS SECOND-TEAM ALL-AMERICANS (2): Tony Lavelli (1946 and 1948).

FORMER MAJOR COLLEGES WITH AN NCAA CONSENSUS FIRST TEAM ALL-AMERICAN

Denver: Vince Boryla (1949 after playing two previous seasons for Notre Dame)

New York University: Sid Tannenbaum (1946 and 1947), Barry Kramer (1963)

Seattle: Johnny O'Brien (1953), Elgin Baylor (1957)

West Texas State: Price Brookfield (1942)

Note: Denver, which de-emphasized its program in 1980, is slated to ready to NCAA Division I status in the 1998-1999 season.

FORMER MAJOR COLLEGES WITH AT LEAST ONE NATIONAL POSTSEASON VICTORY

SCHOOL/LAST YEAR IN DIVISION I NCAA	NIT	CURRENT STATUS
City College of New York/1953 4-2	6-3	Division III
Muhlenberg (Pa.)/1963 0-0	1-4	Division III
New York University/1971 9-9	13-10	Division III
Oklahoma City/1985 8-13	0-2	NAIA
Seattle/1980 10-13	0-2	NAIA
Washington and Jefferson (Pa.) 0-0	2-1	Division III
Wayne State (Mich.)/1950 1-2	0-0	Division II

Note: Three of these schools finished at least two seasons ranked among the Top 20 in a final AP or UPI poll–NYU (1960 and 1963), Oklahoma City (1953-57-59) and Seattle (1952-53-54-56-57-58-59-63).

THE NAME GAME

Here is a look at some of the name changes since 1920 of current Division I schools:

- Arizona State (Tempe Teachers until 1945)
- Auburn (formerly Alabama Poly)
- Boise State (Boise College until 1974)
- Cal State Fullerton (formerly Orange County State College, Orange State College and California State College at Fullerton)
- Charleston Southern (formerly Baptist)
- Cleveland State (Fenn College until 1965)
- Colorado State (Colorado Agriculture until 1935, Colorado State College until 1941, and Colorado A&M until 1957)
- Detroit (Detroit Mercy for several years after the University of Detroit and Mercy College of Detroit merged in 1990)
- Duke (Trinity until 1925)
- Grambling State (formerly Grambling College)
- Idaho State (Idaho State College until 1963)
- Kent (formerly Kent State)
- Loyola Marymount (Loyola University until 1930, merged with Marymount College in 1968, and name changed in 1973)
- Memphis (West Tennessee Normal until 1925, West Tennessee Teachers until 1941, Memphis State College until 1958 and Memphis State University until 1994)
- Nevada (formerly Nevada-Reno)
- New Mexico State (New Mexico Agriculture until 1933, New Mexico State College until 1942, and New Mexico A&M until 1960)
- New Orleans (LSU in New Orleans–LSUNO–until 1974)
- Northern Colorado (formerly Colorado State College)
- Northern Iowa (formerly State College of Iowa)
- North Texas (formerly North Texas State)
- Oklahoma State (Oklahoma A&M until 1957)
- Oregon State (Oregon Agriculture until 1927)
- Portland (Columbia University until 1935)
- Rhode Island (formerly Rhode Island State College)
- San Francisco (St. Ignatius until 1930)
- Southern Mississippi (Hattiesburg Teachers until 1940 and Mississippi Southern until 1962)
- Southern Utah State (formerly Branch Agricultural College)
- Tennessee State (Tennessee A&I until merger with University of Tennessee at Nashville in 1979)
- Texas-El Paso (Texas Mines until 1949 and Texas Western until 1967; tried to implement acronymn UTEP, but it wasn't accepted)
- Texas-Pan American (formerly Pan American)
- Tulsa (Henry Kendall until 1921)
- UAB (formerly Alabama-Birmingham)
- UCLA (Los Angeles Normal until 1919 and UC Southern Branch until 1930)
- UNLV (Nevada Southern until 1969)
- Utah State (Utah Agriculture until 1932)
- Wichita State (Fairmount until 1927 and Wichita until 1964)
- Wisconsin-Milwaukee (Wisconsin State Normal School until 1927, Milwaukee State Teachers College until 1951 and Wisconsin State College-Milwaukee until 1956)

17

NCAA HONORS

Excluding specialty publications, there are six nationally-recognized Player of the Year awards. None of them, however, comes anywhere close to being the equivalent to college football's undisputed most prestigious honor, the Heisman Trophy. The reason for this basketball stalemate? It appears to be twofold: Essentially the same people vote on the major awards (writers or coaches or a combination), and the announcements of the winners are made one after the other right around the Final Four when the games dominate the sports page.

United Press International, on the verge of extinction in recent years, got it all started back in 1955. Four years later, the United States Basketball Writers Association (USBWA), having chosen All-American teams in each of the two previous seasons, added a Player of the Year award to its postseason honors. In recent years, the USBWA award was sponsored by Mercedes and then RCA.

The third oldest of the awards comes from the most dominant wire service, the Associated Press. Perhaps because of its vast network of media outlets, the AP award gets more print and broadcast attention than the other honors. The AP award started in 1961 before affiliating in 1972 with the Commonwealth Athletic Club of Lexington, Kentucky, which was looking for a way to honor Hall of Fame coach Adolph Rupp. The result of their merger is the Rupp Trophy.

The Atlanta Tipoff Club initially was associated with UPI before starting its own Naismith Award in 1969. Six years later, the National Association of Basketball Coaches initiated its award, which was sponsored from the outset by the Eastman Kodak Company. In 1977, the Los Angeles Athletic Club began the Wooden Award, in honor of Hall of Fame UCLA coach John Wooden.

NATIONAL PLAYER OF THE YEAR AWARDS

1955: Tom Gola, La Salle, 6-6, Sr. (24.2 ppg, 19.9 rpg/UPI)
The Explorers (26-5) were runner-ups in the NCAA Tournament.

1956: Bill Russell, San Francisco, 6-9, Sr. (20.6 ppg, 21 rpg, 51.3 FG%/UPI)
The Dons (29-0) captured the NCAA championship after winning all 14 of their conference games by more than 10 points.

1957: Chet Forte, Columbia, 5-9, Sr. (28.9 ppg, 4.5 rpg, 85.2 FT%/UPI)
The Lions (18-6) did not appear in postseason competition after finishing in a tie for third place in the Ivy League.

1958: Oscar Robertson, Cincinnati, 6-5, Soph. (35.1 ppg, 15.2 rpg, 57.1 FG%/UPI)

>The Bearcats (25-3) lost their NCAA Tournament opener after winning the Missouri Valley title (13-1 mark) in their first year in the conference.

1959: Oscar Robertson, Cincinnati, 6-5, Jr. (32.6 ppg, 16.3 rpg, 50.9 FG%/UPI, USBWA)

>The Bearcats (26-4) finished in third place in the NCAA Tournament after compiling a 13-1 Missouri Valley record to win the league title.

1960: Oscar Robertson, Cincinnati, 6-5, Sr. (33.7 ppg, 14.1 rpg, 52.6 FG%/UPI, USBWA)

>The Bearcats (28-2), third-place finisher in the NCAA Tournament, captured their third consecutive Missouri Valley title with a 13-1 record.

1961: Jerry Lucas, Ohio State, 6-8, Jr. (24.9 ppg, 17.4 rpg, 62.3 FG%/AP, UPI, USBWA)

>The Buckeyes (27-1) became the first team in 18 years to go undefeated in Big Ten competition (14-0) before finishing runner-up in the NCAA Tournament.

1962: Jerry Lucas, Ohio State, 6-8, Sr. (21.8 ppg, 17.8 rpg, 61.1 FG%/AP, UPI, USBWA)

>The Buckeyes (26-2) lost in the NCAA Championship Game after becoming the first Big Ten school to win three consecutive undisputed league titles since Wisconsin from 1912 to 1914.

1963: Art Heyman, Duke, 6-5, Sr. (24.9 ppg, 10.8 rpg/AP, UPI, USBWA)

>The Blue Devils (27-3), third-place finisher in the NCAA Tournament, went undefeated (14-0) in ACC competition.

1964: Gary Bradds, Ohio State, 6-8, Sr. (30.6 ppg, 13.4 rpg, 52.4 FG%/AP, UPI)

>The Buckeyes (16-8) did not participate in postseason competition after compiling an 11-3 Big Ten record to finish in a tie for first place with Michigan.

Walt Hazzard, UCLA, 6-2, Sr. (18.6 ppg, 4.7 rpg/USBWA)

>The NCAA champion Bruins (30-0) compiled a 15-0 record in the Athletic Association of Western Universities.

1965: Bill Bradley, Princeton, 6-5, Sr. (30.5 ppg, 11.8 rpg, 53.3 FG%, 88.6 FT%/AP, UPI, USBWA)

>The Tigers (23-6) finished in third place in the NCAA Tournament after winning the Ivy League title with a 13-1 mark.

1966: Cazzie Russell, Michigan, 6-5, Sr. (30.8 ppg, 8.4 rpg, 51.8 FG%, 82.5 FT%/AP, UPI, USBWA)

>The Wolverines (18-8) lost the NCAA Tournament Mideast Regional final after winning the Big Ten title with an 11-3 record.

1967: Lew Alcindor, UCLA, 7-2, Soph. (29 ppg, 15.5 rpg, 66.7 FG%/AP, UPI, USBWA)

>The NCAA champion Bruins (30-0) compiled a 14-0 record in the Pacific-8 Conference.

1968: Elvin Hayes, Houston, 6-8, Sr. (36.8 ppg, 18.9, 54.9 FG%/AP, UPI, USBWA)

>The independent Cougars (31-2) finished in fourth place in the NCAA Tournament.

1969: Lew Alcindor, UCLA, 7-2, Sr. (24 ppg, 14.7 rpg, 63.5 FG%/AP, UPI, USBWA, Naismith)

>The NCAA champion Bruins (29-1) compiled a 13-1 Pacific-8 record.

1970: Pete Maravich, Louisiana State, 6-5, Sr. (44.5 ppg, 5.3 rpg/AP, UPI, USBWA, Naismith)

>The Tigers (22-10), fourth-place finisher in the NIT, posted their highest SEC finish (runner-up with a 13-5 record) since going undefeated in league play in 1954.

1971: Austin Carr, Notre Dame, 6-3, Sr. (38 ppg, 7.4 rpg, 51.7 FG%, 81.1 FT%/AP, UPI, Naismith)

>The independent Irish (20-9) lost in the NCAA Tournament Midwest Regional semifinals.

Sidney Wicks, UCLA, 6-8, Sr. (21.3 ppg, 12.8 rpg, 52.4 FG%/USBWA)

>The NCAA champion Bruins (29-1) went undefeated (14-0) in Pacific-8 competition.

UCLA's Walt Hazzard (left) handles the ball against Duke.

1972: Bill Walton, UCLA, 6-11, Soph. (21.1 ppg, 15.5 rpg, 64.0 FG%/AP, UPI, USBWA, Naismith)

>The NCAA champion Bruins (30-0) compiled an unbeaten record (14-0) in Pacific-8 play.

1973: Bill Walton, UCLA, 6-11, Jr. (20.4 ppg, 16.9 rpg, 65.0 FG%/AP, UPI, USBWA, Naismith)

>The NCAA champion Bruins (30-0) went undefeated (14-0) in Pacific-8 competition for the seventh time in 10 years.

1974: Bill Walton, UCLA, 6-11, Sr. (19.3 ppg, 14.7 rpg, 66.5 FG%/UPI, USBWA, Naismith)

>The Bruins (26-4) finished in third place in the NCAA Tournament after winning the Pacific-8 title with a 12-2 record.

David Thompson, North Carolina State, 6-4, Jr. (26 ppg, 7.9 rpg, 54.7 FG%/AP)

>The Wolfpack (30-1) won the NCAA Tournament after becoming the only school to have back-to-back undefeated records in ACC competition.

1975: David Thompson, North Carolina State, 6-4, Sr. (29.9 ppg, 8.2 rpg, 54.6 FG%/AP, UPI, NABC, USBWA, Naismith)

>The Wolfpack (22-6) did not participate in national postseason play after finishing in a three-way tie for second place in the ACC and losing in the ACC Tournament final.

1976: Scott May, Indiana, 6-7, Sr. (23.5 ppg, 7.7 rpg, 52.7 FG%/AP, UPI, NABC, Naismith)

>The NCAA champion Hoosiers (32-0) captured their fourth consecutive Big Ten title.

Adrian Dantley, Notre Dame, 6-5, Jr. (28.6 ppg, 10.1 rpg, 58.8 FG%/USBWA)

>The independent Irish (23-6) lost in the NCAA Tournament Midwest Regional semifinals.

1977: Marques Johnson, UCLA, 6-7, Sr. (21.4 ppg, 11.1 rpg, 59.1 FG%/AP, UPI, NABC, USBWA, Naismith, Wooden)

The Bruins (24-5) lost in the NCAA Tournament West Regional semifinals after winning the Pacific-8 title with an 11-3 record.

1978: Phil Ford, North Carolina, 6-2, Sr. (20.8 ppg, 52.7 FG%, 81.0 FT%/NABC, USBWA, Wooden)

The Tar Heels (23-8) lost their NCAA Tournament West Regional opener after finishing atop the ACC standings with a 9-3 league record.

Butch Lee, Marquette, 6-2, Sr. (17.7 ppg, 3.1 rpg, 50.6 FG%, 87.9 FT%/AP, UPI, Naismith)

The independent Warriors (24-4) lost their NCAA Tournament Mideast Regional opener.

1979: Larry Bird, Indiana State, 6-9, Sr. (28.6 ppg, 14.9 rpg, 53.2 FG%, 83.1 FT%/AP, UPI, NABC, USBWA, Naismith, Wooden)

The Sycamores (33-1), NCAA Tournament runner-up, became the first Missouri Valley school to go undefeated in league competition (16-0) since Oklahoma A&M went 10-0 in 1948.

1980: Mark Aguirre, DePaul, 6-7, Soph. (26.8 ppg, 7.6 rpg, 54.0 FG%/AP, UPI, USBWA, Naismith)

The independent Blue Demons (26-2) lost their NCAA Tournament opener in the West Regional.

Michael Brooks, La Salle, 6-7, Sr. (24.1 ppg, 11.5 rpg, 52.4 FG%/NABC)

The Explorers (22-9) lost in the first round of the NCAA Tournament Mideast Regional after winning the East Coast Conference Tournament following a third-place finish in the ECC's Eastern Section.

Darrell Griffith, Louisville, 6-4, Sr. (22.9 ppg, 4.8 rpg, 55.3 FG%/Wooden).

The NCAA champion Cardinals (33-3) were undefeated in Metro Conference competition (12-0).

1981: Ralph Sampson, Virginia, 7-4, Soph. (17.7 ppg, 11.5 rpg, 55.7 FG%/AP, UPI, USBWA, Naismith)

The Cavaliers (29-4) lost in the NCAA Tournament national semifinals after winning their first ACC regular-season title with a 13-1 league record.

Danny Ainge, Brigham Young, 6-5, Sr. (24.4 ppg, 4.8 rpg, 51.8 FG%, 82.4 FT%/NABC, Wooden)

The Cougars (25-7) lost the NCAA Tournament East Regional final after finishing in third place in the WAC with a 12-4 league record.

1982: Ralph Sampson, Virginia, 7-4, Jr. (15.8 ppg, 11.4 rpg, 56.1 FG%/AP, UPI, NABC, USBWA, Naismith, Wooden)

The Cavaliers (30-4) lost in the NCAA Tournament Mideast Regional semifinals after tying North Carolina for first place in the ACC with a 12-2 record.

1983: Ralph Sampson, Virginia, 7-4, Sr. (19 ppg, 11.7 rpg, 60.4 FG%/AP, UPI, NABC, USBWA, Naismith, Wooden)

The Cavaliers (29-5) lost the NCAA Tournament West Regional final after tying North Carolina for first place in the ACC with a 12-2 record.

1984: Michael Jordan, North Carolina, 6-6, Jr. (19.6 ppg, 5.3 rpg, 55.1 FG%/AP, UPI, NABC, USBWA, Naismith, Wooden)

The Tar Heels (28-3) lost in the NCAA Tournament East Regional semifinals after becoming the first ACC team to go undefeated in league play (14-0) since North Carolina State in 1974.

1985: Chris Mullin, St. John's, 6-6, Sr. (19.8 ppg, 4.8 rpg, 52.1 FG%, 82.4 FT%/UPI, USBWA, Wooden)

The Redmen (31-4) lost in the NCAA Tournament national semifinals after winning the Big East title with a 15-1 mark.

Patrick Ewing, Georgetown, 7-0, Sr. (14.6 ppg, 9.2 rpg, 62.5 FG%/AP, NABC, Naismith)

The Hoyas (35-3) lost the NCAA Tournament final after finishing runner-up in the Big East standings with a 14-2 record.

1986: Walter Berry, St. John's, 6-8, Jr. (23 ppg, 11.1 rpg, 59.8 FG%/AP, UPI, NABC, USBWA, Wooden)

The Redmen (31-5) lost in the second round of the NCAA Tournament West Regional after tying for first place in the Big East with a 14-2 record.

Johnny Dawkins, Duke, 6-2, Sr. (20.2 ppg, 3.6 rpg, 54.9 FG%, 81.2 FT%/Naismith)

The Blue Devils (37-3) lost in the NCAA Tournament final after compiling a 12-2 ACC record to win their second regular-season league title in 20 years.

1987: David Robinson, Navy, 6-11, Sr. (28.2 ppg, 11.8 rpg, 59.1 FG%/AP, UPI, NABC, USBWA, Naismith, Wooden)

The Midshipmen (26-6) lost in the first round of the NCAA Tournament East Regional after winning the Colonial Athletic Association with a 13-1 mark.

1988: Hersey Hawkins, Bradley, 6-3, Sr. (36.3 ppg, 7.8 rpg, 52.4 FG%, 84.8 FT%/AP, UPI, USBWA)

The Braves (26-5) lost in the first round of the NCAA Tournament Southeast Regional after winning the Missouri Valley title with a 12-2 league record.

Danny Manning, Kansas, 6-10, Sr. (24.8 ppg, 9 rpg, 58.3 FG%/NABC, Naismith, Wooden)

The Jayhawks (27-11) won the NCAA Tournament after finishing in third place in the Big Eight with a 9-5 league record.

1989: Danny Ferry, Duke, 6-10, Sr. (22.6 ppg, 7.4 rpg, 52.2 FG%/UPI, USBWA, Naismith)

The Blue Devils (28-8) lost in the NCAA Tournament national semifinals after finishing in a three-way tie for first in the ACC standings with a 9-5 league record.

Sean Elliott, Arizona, 6-8, Sr. (22.3 ppg, 7.2 rpg, 84.1 FT%/AP, NABC, Wooden)

The Wildcats (29-4) lost in the NCAA Tournament West Regional semifinals after winning the Pacific-10 title with a 17-1 league record.

1990: Lionel Simmons, La Salle, 6-7, Sr. (26.5 ppg, 11.1 rpg, 51.3 FG%/AP, UPI, NABC, USBWA, Naismith, Wooden)

The Explorers (30-2) lost in the second round of the NCAA Tournament East Regional after compiling the best record in the Metro Atlantic Athletic Conference (16-0 in South Division).

1991: Larry Johnson, UNLV, 6-7, Sr. (22.7 ppg, 10.9 rpg, 66.2 FG%, 81.8 FT%/NABC, USBWA, Naismith, Wooden)

The Rebels (34-1) lost in the NCAA Tournament national semifinals after going undefeated (18-0) in the Big West Conference.

Shaquille O'Neal, Louisiana State, 7-1, Soph. (27.6 ppg, 14.7 rpg, 62.8 FG%/AP, UPI)

The Tigers (20-10) lost in the first round of the NCAA Tournament Midwest Regional after tying for first place in the SEC standings with a 13-5 league record.

1992: Christian Laettner, Duke, 6-11, Sr. (21.5 ppg, 7.9 rpg, 57.5 FG%, 81.5 FT%/AP, NABC, USBWA, Naismith, Wooden)

The Blue Devils (35-2) won the NCAA Tournament after winning the ACC regular-season title with a 14-2 league record.

Jim Jackson, Ohio State, 6-6, Jr. (22.4 ppg, 6.8 rpg, 81.1 FT%/UPI)

The Buckeyes (26-6) lost the NCAA Tournament Southeast Regional final after compiling a 15-3 Big Ten record to win their first undisputed league title since 1971.

1993: Calbert Cheaney, Indiana, 6-7, Sr. (22.4 ppg, 6.4 rpg, 54.9 FG%/AP, UPI, NABC, USBWA, Naismith, Wooden)

The Hoosiers (31-4) lost the NCAA Tournament Midwest Regional final after compiling the best record in Big Ten competition (17-1) since they went undefeated in 1976.

1994: Glenn Robinson, Purdue, 6-8, Jr. (30.3 ppg, 10.1 rpg/AP, UPI, NABC, USBWA, Naismith, Wooden)

The Boilermakers (29-5) lost the NCAA Tournament Southeast Regional final after winning the Big Ten championship with their first winning league record in four years (14-4).

1995 Ed O'Bannon, UCLA, 6-8, Sr. (20.4 ppg, 8.3 rpg, 1.9 spg, 53.3 FG%/USBWA, Wooden)

The Bruins (31-2) reached the Final Four for the first time since 1980 and captured the national title for the first time since 1975.

Shawn Respert, Michigan State, 6-3, Sr. (25.6 ppg, 4 rpg, 86.9 FT%, 47.4 3FG%/NABC)

The Spartans (22-6) finished at least eight games above .500 in Big Ten competition (14-4) for the first time since winning the NCAA championship with Magic Johnson in 1979.

Joe Smith, Maryland, 6-10, Soph. (20.8 ppg, 10.6 rpg, 2.9 bpg, 57.8 FG%/AP, UPI, Naismith)

The Terrapins (26-8) compiled a winning record in ACC competition (12-4) for the first time since 1985 en route to their first regular-season crown since 1980.

1996: Marcus Camby, Massachusetts, 6-11, Jr. (20.5 ppg, 8.1 rpg, 3.9 bpg/AP, NABC, Naismith, USBWA, Wooden)

The Minutemen (35-2) won 26 consecutive games in one stretch before reaching the Final Four for the first time in school history. Camby copped the honor despite missing four games after mysteriously collapsing before a contest in mid-January.

Ray Allen, Connecticut, 6-5, Jr. (23.4 ppg, 6.5 rpg/UPI)

The Huskies (32-3) became the first Big East team to post the league's undisputed best record in back-to-back seasons.

NATIONAL COACH OF THE YEAR AWARDS

1955: Phil Woolpert, San Francisco (28-1 overall record; 12-0 in California Basketball Association/UPI)

The Dons ascended to an NCAA title after absorbing three consecutive losing seasons from 1951 to 1953.

1956: Phil Woolpert, San Francisco (29-0; 14-0 in West Coast Athletic/UPI)

The Dons extended their winning streak to 55 consecutive games en route to another NCAA championship.

1957: Frank McGuire, North Carolina (27-0; 14-0 in ACC/UPI)

The Tar Heels captured their first ACC regular-season championship. They won 22 games by at least nine points.

1958: Tex Winter, Kansas State (22-5; 10-2 in Big Seven/UPI)

The Wildcats won the Big Seven championship one year before entering the NCAA Tournament ranked No. 1 in the country.

1959: Eddie Hickey, Marquette (23-6/USBWA)

The Warriors, after losing more than 10 games in 11 of their 12 previous seasons, had a 22-3 record in Hickey's first year at their helm until dropping three of their last four outings.

Adolph Rupp, Kentucky (24-3; 12-2 in SEC/UPI)

The Wildcats extended their streak of 20-win seasons to 14.

1960: Pete Newell, California (28-2; 11-1 in AAWU/UPI, USBWA)

The Bears' bid to win back-to-back NCAA championships was thwarted by Ohio State in the tourney final.

1961: Fred Taylor, Ohio State (27-1; 14-0 in Big Ten/UPI, USBWA)

The Buckeyes became the first team to go undefeated in Big Ten competition since Illinois in 1943.

1962: Fred Taylor, Ohio State (26-2; 13-1 in Big Ten/UPI, USBWA)

The Buckeyes captured their third of five consecutive Big Ten championships.

1963: Ed Jucker, Cincinnati (26-2; 11-1 in Missouri Valley/UPI, USBWA)

The Bearcats captured their sixth MVC championship in as many seasons as a member of the league.

1964: John Wooden, UCLA (30-0; 15-0 in AAWU/UPI, USBWA)

The Bruins went undefeated to capture their first of 10 NCAA championships.

1965: Dave Strack, Michigan (24-4; 13-1 in Big Ten/UPI)

The Wolverines won their first undisputed Big Ten title since 1948.

Butch van Breda Kolff, Princeton (23-6; 13-1 in Ivy League/USBWA)

The Tigers won their third consecutive conference title before reaching the Final Four.

1966: Adolph Rupp, Kentucky (27-2; 15-1 in SEC/UPI, USBWA)

The Wildcats' only regular-season defeat was at Tennessee before bowing to Texas Western in the NCAA Tournament final.

1967: John Wooden, UCLA (30-0; 14-0 in AAWU/AP, UPI, USBWA)

Only one of the Bruins' last 14 opponents scored more than 16 points.

1968: Guy Lewis, Houston (31-2/AP, UPI, NABC, USBWA)

The Cougars were ranked No. 1 in the country entering the NCAA Tournament.

1969: John Wooden, UCLA (29-1; 13-1 in Pacific-8/AP, UPI, NABC)

The Bruins' lone setback was to Southern Cal, 46-44.

Maury John, Drake (26-5; 13-3 in Missouri Valley/USBWA)

The Bulldogs set a school record for victories just two years after compiling an unsightly 9-16 mark.

1970: John Wooden, UCLA (28-2; 12-2 in Pacific-8/AP, UPI, NABC, USBWA)

The Bruins yielded 87.5 points per game while absorbing both of their losses in a late four-game stretch in league play before recovering.

1971: Al McGuire, Marquette (28-1/AP, UPI, USBWA)

The Warriors entered the NCAA Tournament undefeated before losing by one point to Ohio State.

Jack Kraft, Villanova (23-6/NABC)

The Wildcats reached the Final Four for the first time since 1939.

1972: John Wooden, UCLA (30-0; 14-0 in Pacific-8/AP, UPI, NABC, USBWA)

The Bruins scored at least 105 points in their first seven outings and never look back.

1973: John Wooden, UCLA (30-0; 14-0 in Pacific-8/AP, UPI, USBWA)

The Bruins, going undefeated for the fourth time in 10 years, captured their seventh consecutive NCAA championship.

Gene Bartow, Memphis State (24-6; 12-2 in Missouri Valley/NABC)

The Tigers reached the Final Four for the first time just three years after going 6-20.

1974: Al McGuire, Marquette (26-5/NABC)

The Warriors, with only one senior starter, ranked among the top five in both wire-service polls before finishing runner-up in the NCAA Tournament.

Digger Phelps, Notre Dame (26-3/UPI)

The Fighting Irish, two years after compiling a 6-20 record, won more than 25 games for one of only two times in school history.

Norman Sloan, North Carolina State (30-1; 12-0 in ACC/AP, USBWA)

The Wolfpack won the NCAA Tournament after going undefeated in ACC competition for the second consecutive season.

1975: Bob Knight, Indiana (31-1; 18-0 in Big Ten/AP, UPI, NABC, USBWA)

The Hoosiers were unbeaten until they were eliminated in the NCAA Tournament by Kentucky (92-90).

1976: Bob Knight, Indiana (32-0; 18-0 in Big Ten/AP, USBWA)

The Hoosiers became the last undefeated Division I team.

Johnny Orr, Michigan (25-7; 14-4 in Big Ten/NABC)

The Wolverines reached the NCAA Tournament championship game just three years after compiling a 6-8 league record.

Tom Young, Rutgers (31-2/UPI)

The Scarlet Knights arrived at the Final Four with an undefeated record.

1977: Bob Gaillard, San Francisco (29-2; 14-0 in WCAC/AP, UPI)

The Dons won their first 29 games before bowing to Notre Dame in their regular-season finale and UNLV in the opening round of the playoffs.

Dean Smith, North Carolina (28-5; 9-3 in ACC/NABC)

The Tar Heels reached the Final Four for the fifth time in 11 seasons.

Eddie Sutton, Arkansas (26-2; 16-0 in SWC/USBWA)

The Razorbacks became the first team to go undefeated in SWC competition since SMU in 1956.

1978: Eddie Sutton, Arkansas (32-4; 14-2 in SWC/AP, UPI)

The Razorbacks became the first SWC in 22 years to reach the Final Four.

Ray Meyer, DePaul (27-3/USBWA)

The Blue Demons won more than one NCAA Tournament game for the first time since 1960.

Bill Foster, Duke (27-7; 8-4 in ACC/shared NABC)

The Blue Devils compiled their first winning record in ACC competition since 1971 before making their first NCAA Tournament appearance since 1966.

Abe Lemons, Texas (26-5; 14-2 in SWC/shared NABC)

The NIT champion Longhorns won more than 25 games for the first time in school history.

1979: Bill Hodges, Indiana State (33-1; 16-0 in Missouri Valley/AP, UPI)

The Sycamores reached the championship game in its first NCAA Tournament appearance.

Ray Meyer, DePaul (26-6/NABC)

The Blue Demons reached the Final Four for the first time since 1943.

Dean Smith, North Carolina (23-6; 9-3 in ACC/USBWA)

The Tar Heels won their fourth consecutive ACC regular-season championship.

1980: Ray Meyer, DePaul (26-2/AP, UPI, USBWA)

The Blue Demons' only regular-season defeat was in double overtime at Notre Dame.

Lute Olson, Iowa (23-10; 10-8 in Big Ten/NABC)

The Hawkeyes reached the Final Four for the first time since 1956.

1981: Ralph Miller, Oregon State (26-2; 17-1 in Pacific-10/AP, UPI, shared NABC, USBWA)

The Beavers were undefeated until their regular-season finale.

Jack Hartman, Kansas State (24-9; 9-5 in Big Eight/shared NABC)

The Wildcats won their most games in a season since 1959.

1982: Ralph Miller, Oregon State (25-5; 16-2 in Pacific-10/AP)

The Beavers captured their third consecutive conference crown.

Don Monson, Idaho (27-3; 13-1 in Big Sky/NABC)

The Vandals' victories included decisions by at least 19 points away from home against Washington, Washington State, Iowa State, Oregon State, and Oregon.

Norm Stewart, Missouri (27-4; 12-2 in Big Eight/UPI)

The Tigers captured their third of four consecutive outright Big Eight Conference regular-season championships.

John Thompson, Georgetown (30-7; 10-4 in Big East/USBWA)

The Hoyas reached the Final Four for the first time since 1943.

1983: Lou Carnesecca, St. John's (28-5; 12-4 in Big East/NABC, USBWA)

The Redmen won at least 28 games for the first of three times in four seasons.

Guy Lewis, Houston (31-3; 16-0 in SWC/AP)

The Cougars won 26 consecutive games until they were upset in the NCAA Tournament final.

Jerry Tarkanian, UNLV (28-3; 15-1 in PCAA/UPI)

The Rebels won their first of 10 regular-season conference titles in as many years.

1984: Ray Meyer, DePaul (27-3/AP, UPI)

The Blue Demons, in Meyer's swan song, registered their seventh

Kansas State coach Jack Hartman.

consecutive season with more than 20 victories.

Marv Harshman, Washington (24-7; 15-3 in Pacific-10/NABC)

The Huskies won their first conference crown since 1953.

Gene Keady, Purdue (22-7; 15-3 in Big Ten/USBWA)

The Boilermakers compiled their 12th consecutive winning league record.

1985: Lou Carnesecca, St. John's (31-4; 15-1 in Big East/UPI, USBWA)

The Redmen captured their lone undisputed conference championship.

Bill Frieder, Michigan (26-4; 16-2 in Big Ten/AP)

The Wolverines won the Big Ten title just two years after compiling a 7-11 league record.

John Thompson, Georgetown (35-3; 14-2 in Big East/NABC)

The Hoyas won at least 30 games for the third time in four seasons.

1986: Eddie Sutton, Kentucky (32-4; 17-1 in SEC/AP, NABC)

Three of the Wildcats' four defeats were by a total of just nine points.

Mike Krzyzewski, Duke (37-3; 12-2 in ACC/UPI)

The Blue Devils established an ACC record for most victories in a single season.

Dick Versace, Bradley (32-3; 16-0 in Missouri Valley/USBWA)

The Braves won their first NCAA Tournament game in more than 30 years.

1987: John Chaney, Temple (32-4; 17-1 in Atlantic 10/USBWA)

The Owls became the first Atlantic 10 team to win more than 30 games in a single season.

Tom Davis, Iowa (30-5; 14-4 in Big Ten/AP)

The Hawkeyes set a school standard for victories just three years after compiling a losing record.

Bob Knight, Indiana (30-4; 15-3 in Big Ten/Naismith)

The Hoosiers finished among the top three in league standings for the seventh time in eight seasons.

Rick Pitino, Providence (25-9; 10-6 in Big East/NABC)

The Friars reached the Final Four two years after posting an 11-20 record.

John Thompson, Georgetown (29-5; 12-4 in Big East/UPI)

The Hoyas ranked among the top 10 in the final AP poll for one of six times in a nine-year span.

1988: John Chaney, Temple (32-2; 18-0 in Atlantic 10/AP, UPI, NABC, USBWA)

The Owls, leading the nation in field-goal percentage defense, won 32 games for the second consecutive campaign.

Larry Brown, Kansas (27-11; 9-5 in Big Eight/Naismith)

The Jayhawks finished at least four games above .500 in Big Eight play for the fifth time in as many seasons under Brown before becoming the first Big Eight team to win a Final Four game in more than 30 years.

1989: Bob Knight, Indiana (27-8; 15-3 in Big Ten/AP, UPI, USBWA)

The Hoosiers won 21 of 22 games in one stretch.

P. J. Carlesimo, Seton Hall (31-7; 11-5 in Big East/NABC)

The Pirates posted their first winning record in conference competition en route to reaching the NCAA Tournament championship game.

Mike Krzyzewski, Duke (28-8; 9-5 in ACC/Naismith)

The Blue Devils won at least 28 games for the second time in five consecutive seasons.

1990: Jim Calhoun, Connecticut (31-6; 12-4 in Big East/AP, UPI)

The Huskies, after finishing at least four games below .500 in league play the previous seven seasons, tied Syracuse for first place.

Bobby Cremins, Georgia Tech (28-7; 8-6 in ACC/Naismith)

The Yellow Jackets reached the Final Four for the only time in school history.

Jud Heathcote, Michigan State (28-6; 15-3 in Big Ten/NABC)

The Spartans won the Big Ten title just one year after finishing next to last place.

Roy Williams, Kansas (30-5; 11-3 in Big Eight/USBWA)

The Jayhawks reached the Final Four just one year after posting a losing record in league play.

1991: Randy Ayers, Ohio State (27-4; 15-3 in Big Ten/AP, Naismith, USBWA)

The Buckeyes captured their first league title since 1971.

Mike Krzyzewski, Duke (32-7; 11-3 in ACC/NABC)

The Blue Devils ended their streak of eight trips to the Final Four without a national championship.

Rick Majerus, Utah (30-4; 15-1 in WAC/UPI)

The Utes, 32-31 over the previous two years, became the only WAC team ever to win 30 games in a single season.

1992: Perry Clark, Tulane (21-8; 8-4 in Metro/UPI, USBWA)

The Green Wave won a conference title two years after compiling a 4-24 record.

Mike Krzyzewski, Duke (34-2; 14-2 in ACC/Naismith)

The Blue Devils reached the Final Four for the fifth consecutive season.

George Raveling, Southern Cal (24-6; 15-3 in Pacific-10/NABC)

The Trojans won more than 20 games for the first time since 1974.

Roy Williams, Kansas (27-5; 11-3 in Big Eight/AP)

The Jayhawks captured their first outright Big Eight crown since 1986.

1993: Eddie Fogler, Vanderbilt (28-6; 14-2 in SEC/AP, UPI, NABC, USBWA)

The Commodores shattered their school record for most victories in a single season.

Dean Smith, North Carolina (34-4; 14-2 in ACC/Naismith)

The Tar Heels won the NCAA title after reaching the Sweet 16 of the NCAA Tournament for the 13th consecutive season.

1994: Norm Stewart, Missouri (28-4; 14-0 in Big Eight/AP, UPI)

The Tigers became the first undefeated team in Big Eight competition since Kansas in 1971.

Nolan Richardson, Arkansas (31-3; 14-2 in SEC/Naismith, shared NABC)

The NCAA champion Razorbacks reached the 30-win plateau for the third time in five seasons.

Charlie Spoonhour, St. Louis (23-6; 8-4 in Great Midwest/USBWA)

The Billikens participated in the NCAA Tournament for the first time since 1957.

Gene Keady, Purdue (29-5; 14-4 in Big Ten/shared NABC)

The Boilermakers won the Big Ten title after three consecutive non-winning records in conference competition.

1995: Jim Harrick, UCLA (31-2; 16-2 in Pacific-10/NABC, Naismith)

The Bruins set a school record for most victories in a season en route to their first Final Four appearance since 1980.

Kelvin Sampson, Oklahoma (23-9; 9-5 in Big Eight/AP, USBWA)

The Sooners post their best league record (9-5) and overall mark since 1990.

Leonard Hamilton, Miami, Fla. (15-13; 9-9 in Big East/UPI)

The Hurricanes, winless in conference play the previous year, snap a 29-game league losing streak on the road en route to finishing with the greatest one-season turnaround in Big East history. Hamilton is the first coach of the year not to crack the 20-win plateau.

1996: Gene Keady, Purdue (26-6; 15-3 in Big Ten/AP, UPI, USBWA)

The Boilermakers become the first school since Ohio State in the early 1960s to win three consecutive Big Ten titles.

John Calipari, Massachusetts (35-2, 15-1 in Eastern Division of Atlantic 10/NABC, Naismith)

The Minutemen captured their fifth consecutive Allantic regular-season and conference tournament championship before reaching the Final Four for the first time in school history. It was light years removed from Calipari's first season as a head coach in 1988-89 when UMass registered its 11th consecutive losing record. He went to the pros after the '96 Final Four.

NCAA CONSENSUS FIRST-TEAM ALL-AMERICANS

1928-29: Tom Churchill, F-C, Jr., Oklahoma; Vern Corbin, F, Sr., California; Chuck Hyatt, F, Jr., Pittsburgh; Charles (Stretch) Murphy, C, Jr., Purdue; Joe Schaaf, F, Sr., Pennsylvania; John (Cat) Thompson, F, Jr., Montana State.

1929-30: Chuck Hyatt, F, Sr., Pittsburgh; Charles (Stretch) Murphy, C, Sr., Purdue; E. (Branch) McCracken, F, Sr., Indiana; John (Cat) Thompson, F, Sr., Montana State; Frank Ward, C, Sr., Montana State; John Wooden, G, Soph., Purdue.

1930-31: Wes Fesler, G, Sr., Ohio State; George Gregory, C, Sr., Columbia; Joe Reiff, F, Soph., Northwestern; Elwood (Woody) Romney, F-C, Jr., Brigham Young; John Wooden, G, Jr., Purdue.

1931-32: Louis (Bosey) Berger, F, Sr., Maryland; Ed (Moose) Krause, C, Soph., Notre Dame; Forest (Aggie) Sale, F-C, Jr., Kentucky; Les Witte, F, Soph., Wyoming; John Wooden, G, Sr., Purdue.

1932-33: Ed (Moose) Krause, C, Jr., Notre Dame; Elliott Loughlin, G, Sr., Navy; Jerry Nemer, F, Sr., Southern California; Joe Reiff, F, Sr., Northwestern; Forest (Aggie) Sale, F-C, Sr., Kentucky; Don Smith, G-F, Soph., Pittsburgh.

1933-34: Norm Cottom, F, Jr., Purdue; Claire Cribbs, G-C, Jr., Pittsburgh; Ed (Moose) Krause, C, Sr., Notre Dame; Hal Lee, G, Sr., Washington; Les Witte, F, Sr., Wyoming.

1934-35: Omar (Bud) Browning, G, Sr., Oklahoma; Claire Cribbs, G-C, Sr., Pittsburgh; LeRoy (Cowboy) Edwards, C, Soph., Kentucky; Jack Gray, F, Sr., Texas; Lee Guttero, C, Sr., Southern California.

1935-36: Vern Huffman, G, Jr., Indiana; Bob Kessler, F, Sr., Purdue; Bill Kinner, C-F, Sr., Utah; Hank Luisetti, F, Soph., Stanford; John Moir, F, Soph., Notre Dame; Paul Nowak, C, Soph., Notre Dame; H.L. (Ike) Poole, F-C, Sr., Arkansas.

1936-37: Jules Bender, G, Sr., Long Island; Hank Luisetti, F, Jr., Stanford; John Moir, F, Jr., Notre Dame; Paul Nowak, C, Jr., Notre Dame; Jewell Young, F, Jr., Purdue.

1937–38: Meyer "Mike" Bloom, C, Sr., Temple; Hank Luisetti, F, Sr., Stanford; John Moir, F, Sr., Notre Dame; Paul Nowak, C, Sr., Notre Dame; Fred Pralle, G, Sr., Kansas; Jewell Young, F, Sr., Purdue.

1938–39: Ernie Andres, G, Sr., Indiana; Jimmy Hull, F, Sr., Ohio State; Chet Jaworski, G, Sr., Rhode Island; Irving Torgoff, F, Sr., Long Island; Urgel "Slim" Wintermute, C, Sr., Oregon.

1939–40: Gus Broberg, G-F, Jr., Dartmouth; John Dick, F, Sr., Oregon; George Glamack, C, Jr., North Carolina; Bill Hapac, F, Sr., Illinois; Ralph Vaughn, F, Sr., Southern California.

1940–41: John Adams, F, Sr., Arkansas; Gus Broberg, G-F, Sr., Dartmouth; Howard Engleman, F, Sr., Kansas; Gene Englund, C, Sr., Wisconsin; George Glamack, C, Sr., North Carolina.

1941–42: Price Brookfield, C, Sr., West Texas State; Bob Davies, G, Sr., Seton Hall; Bob Kinney, C, Sr., Rice; John Kotz, F, Jr., Wisconsin; Andy Phillip, F, Soph., Illinois.

1942–43: Ed Beisser, C, Sr., Creighton; Charles Black, F, Soph., Kansas; Harry Boykoff, C, Soph., St. John's; Bill Closs, C, Sr., Rice; Andy Phillip, F, Jr., Illinois; George Senesky, F, Sr., St. Joseph's.

1943–44: Bob Brannum, C, Fr., Kentucky; Audley Brindley, C, Jr., Dartmouth; Otto Graham, F, Sr., Northwestern/Colgate; Leo Klier, F, Jr., Notre Dame; Bob Kurland, C, Soph., Oklahoma A&M; George Mikan, C, Soph., DePaul; Allie Paine, G, Jr., Oklahoma.

1944–45: Howie Dallmar, G, Soph., Penn; Arnie Ferrin, F, Soph., Utah; Wyndol Gray, F, Soph., Bowling Green; Billy Hassett, G, Jr., Notre Dame; Bill Henry, C, Sr., Rice; Walt Kirk, G, Jr., Illinois; Bob Kurland, C, Jr., Oklahoma A&M; George Mikan, C, Jr., DePaul.

1945–46: Leo Klier, F, Sr., Notre Dame; Bob Kurland, C, Sr., Oklahoma A&M; George Mikan, C, Sr., DePaul; Max Morris, F-C, Sr., Northwestern; Sid Tannenbaum, G, Jr., NYU.

1946–47: Ralph Beard, G, Soph., Kentucky; Alex Groza, C, Soph., Kentucky; Ralph Hamilton, F, Sr., Indiana; Sid Tannenbaum, G, Sr., NYU; Gerry Tucker, C, Sr., Oklahoma.

1947–48: Ralph Beard, G, Jr., Kentucky; Ed Macauley, C-F, Jr., St. Louis; Jim McIntyre, C, Jr., Minnesota; Kevin O'Shea, G, Soph., Notre Dame; Murray Wier, G, Sr., Iowa.

1948–49: Ralph Beard, G, Sr., Kentucky; Vince Boryla, F, Sr., Denver; Alex Groza, C, Sr., Kentucky; Tony Lavelli, G, Sr., Yale; Ed Macauley, C-F, Sr., St. Louis.

1949–50: Paul Arizin, F, Sr., Villanova; Bob Cousy, G, Sr., Holy Cross; Dick Schnittker, F, Sr., Ohio State; Bill Sharman, G, Sr., Southern California; Paul Unruh, F, Sr., Bradley.

1950–51: Clyde Lovellette, C, Jr., Kansas; Gene Melchiorre, G, Sr., Bradley; Bill Mlkvy, F, Jr., Temple; Sam Ranzino, F, Sr., North Carolina State; Bill Spivey, C, Jr., Kentucky.

1951–52: Chuck Darling, C, Sr., Iowa; Rod Fletcher, G, Sr., Illinois; Dick Groat, G, Sr., Duke; Cliff Hagan, F, Jr., Kentucky; Clyde Lovellette, C, Sr., Kansas.

1952–53: Ernie Beck, F, Sr., Penn; Walter Dukes, C, Jr., Seton Hall; Tom Gola, C-F, Soph., La Salle; Bob Houbregs, C, Sr., Washington; Johnny O'Brien, G, Sr., Seattle.

1953–54: Tom Gola, C-F, Jr., La Salle; Cliff Hagan, F, Sr., Kentucky; Bob Pettit, C, Sr., Louisiana State; Don Schlundt, C, Jr., Indiana; Frank Selvy, F, Sr., Furman.

1954–55: Dick Garmaker, F, Sr., Minnesota; Tom Gola, C-F, Sr., La Salle; Si Green, G, Jr., Duquesne; Dick Ricketts, F-C, Sr., Duquesne; Bill Russell, C, Jr., San Francisco.

1955–56: Robin Freeman, G, Sr., Ohio State; Si Green, G, Sr., Duquesne; Tom Heinsohn, F, Sr., Holy Cross; Bill Russell, C, Sr., San Francisco; Ron Shavlik, C, Sr., North Carolina State.

1956–57: Wilt Chamberlain, C, Soph., Kansas; Chet Forte, G, Sr., Columbia; Rod Hundley, G-F, Sr., West Virginia; Jim Krebs, C, Sr., Southern Methodist; Lennie Rosenbluth, F, Sr., North Carolina; Charlie Tyra, C, Sr., Louisville.

1957–58: Elgin Baylor, F-C, Jr., Seattle; Bob Boozer, F, Jr., Kansas State; Wilt Chamberlain, C, Jr., Kansas; Don Hennon, G, Jr., Pittsburgh; Oscar Robertson, F, Soph., Cincinnati; Guy Rodgers, G, Sr., Temple.

1958–59: Bob Boozer, F, Sr., Kansas State; Johnny Cox, F, Sr., Kentucky; Bailey Howell, F, Sr., Mississippi State; Oscar Robertson, F, Jr., Cincinnati; Jerry West, F, Jr., West Virginia.

1959–60: Darrall Imhoff, C, Sr., California; Jerry Lucas, C, Soph., Ohio State; Oscar Robertson, F, Sr., Cincinnati; Tom Stith, F, Jr., St. Bonaventure; Jerry West, F, Sr., West Virginia.

1989–90 All-American Syracuse forward Derrick Coleman brings down a rebound.

1960–61: Terry Dischinger, F, Jr., Purdue; Roger Kaiser, G, Sr., Georgia Tech; Jerry Lucas, C, Jr., Ohio State; Tom Stith, F, Sr., St. Bonaventure; Chet Walker, F, Jr., Bradley.

1961–62: Len Chappell, C, Sr., Wake Forest; Terry Dischinger, F, Sr., Purdue; Jerry Lucas, C, Sr., Ohio State; Billy McGill, C, Sr., Utah; Chet Walker, F, Sr., Bradley.

1962–63: Ron Bonham, F, Jr., Cincinnati; Jerry Harkness, F, Sr., Loyola (Ill.); Art Heyman, F, Sr., Duke; Barry Kramer, F, Jr., NYU; Tom Thacker, F-G, Sr., Cincinnati.

1963–64: Gary Bradds, C, Sr., Ohio State; Bill Bradley, F, Jr., Princeton; Walt Hazzard, G, Sr., UCLA; Cotton Nash, F, Sr., Kentucky; Dave Stallworth, F, Jr., Wichita State.

1964–65: Rick Barry, F, Sr., Miami (Fla.); Bill Bradley, F, Sr., Princeton; Gail Goodrich, G, Sr., UCLA; Fred Hetzel, F-C, Sr., Davidson; Cazzie Russell, G, Jr., Michigan.

1965–66: Dave Bing, G, Sr., Syracuse; Clyde Lee, C, Sr., Vanderbilt; Cazzie Russell, G, Sr., Michigan; Dave Schellhase, F, Sr., Purdue; Jimmy Walker, G, Jr., Providence.

1966–67: Lew Alcindor, C, Soph., UCLA; Clem Haskins, G-F, Sr., Western Kentucky; Elvin Hayes, F-C, Jr., Houston; Bob Lloyd, G, Sr., Rutgers; Wes Unseld, C, Jr., Louisville; Bob Verga, G, Sr., Duke; Jimmy Walker, G, Sr., Providence.

1967–68: Lew Alcindor, C, Jr., UCLA; Elvin Hayes, F-C, Sr., Houston; Pete Maravich, G, Soph., Louisiana State; Larry Miller, F, Sr., North Carolina; Wes Unseld, C, Sr., Louisville.

1968–69: Lew Alcindor, C, Sr., UCLA; Spencer Haywood, F-C, Jr., Detroit; Pete Maravich, G, Jr., Louisiana State; Rick Mount, G, Jr., Purdue; Calvin Murphy, G, Jr., Niagara.

1969–70: Dan Issel, F-C, Sr., Kentucky; Bob Lanier, C, Sr., St. Bonaventure; Pete Maravich, G, Sr., Louisiana State; Rick Mount, G, Sr., Purdue; Calvin Murphy, G, Sr., Niagara.

1970–71: Austin Carr, G, Sr., Notre Dame; Artis Gilmore, C, Sr., Jacksonville; Jim McDaniels, C, Sr., Western Kentucky; Dean Meminger, G, Sr., Marquette; Sidney Wicks, F, Sr., UCLA.

1971–72: Henry Bibby, G, Sr., UCLA; Jim Chones, C, Jr., Marquette; Bo Lamar, G, Jr., Southwestern Louisiana; Bob McAdoo, C, Jr., North Carolina; Ed Ratleff, F-G, Jr., Long Beach State; Tom Riker, C, Sr., South Carolina; Bill Walton, C, Soph., UCLA.

1972–73: Doug Collins, G, Sr., Illinois State; Ernie DiGregorio, G, Sr., Providence; Bo Lamar, G, Sr., Southwestern Louisiana; Ed Ratleff, F-G, Sr., Long Beach State; David Thompson, F, Soph., North Carolina State; Bill Walton, C, Jr., UCLA; Keith Wilkes, F, Jr., UCLA.

1973–74: Marvin Barnes, C, Sr., Providence; John Shumate, C-F, Soph., Notre Dame; David Thompson, F, Jr., North Carolina State; Bill Walton, C, Sr., UCLA; Keith Wilkes, F, Sr., UCLA.

1974–75: Adrian Dantley, F, Soph., Notre Dame; John Lucas, G, Jr., Maryland; Scott May, F, Jr., Indiana; Dave Meyers, F, Sr., UCLA; David Thompson, F, Sr., North Carolina State.

1975–76: Kent Benson, C, Jr., Indiana; Adrian Dantley, F, Jr., Notre Dame; John Lucas, G, Sr., Maryland; Scott May, F, Sr., Indiana; Richard Washington, C-F, Jr., UCLA.

1976–77: Kent Benson, C, Sr., Indiana; Otis Birdsong, G, Sr., Houston; Phil Ford, G, Jr., North Carolina; Rickey Green, G, Sr., Michigan; Marques Johnson, F, Sr., UCLA; Bernard King, F, Jr., Tennessee.

1977–78: Larry Bird, F, Jr., Indiana State; Phil Ford, G, Sr., North Carolina; David Greenwood, F, Jr., UCLA; Butch Lee, G, Sr., Marquette; Mychal Thompson, C, Sr., Minnesota.

1978–79: Larry Bird, F-C, Sr., Indiana State; Mike Gminski, C, Jr., Duke; David Greenwood, F, Sr., UCLA; Earvin "Magic" Johnson, G, Soph., Michigan State; Sidney Moncrief, G-F, Sr., Arkansas.

1979–80: Mark Aguirre, F, Soph., DePaul; Michael Brooks, F, Sr., La Salle; Joe Barry Carroll, C, Sr., Purdue; Darrell Griffith, G, Sr., Louisville; Kyle Macy, G, Sr., Kentucky.

1980–81: Mark Aguirre, F, Jr., DePaul; Danny Ainge, G, Sr., Brigham Young; Steve Johnson, C, Sr., Oregon State; Ralph Sampson, C, Soph., Virginia; Isiah Thomas, G, Soph., Indiana.

1981–82: Terry Cummings, F-C, Jr., DePaul; Quintin Dailey, G, Jr., San Francisco; Eric "Sleepy" Floyd, G, Sr., Georgetown; Ralph Sampson, C, Jr., Virginia; James Worthy, F, Jr., North Carolina.

1982–83: Dale Ellis, F, Sr., Tennessee; Patrick Ewing, C, Soph., Georgetown; Michael Jordan, G, Soph., North Carolina; Keith Lee, C, Soph., Memphis State; Sam Perkins, C, Jr., North Carolina; Ralph Sampson, C, Sr., Virginia; Wayman Tisdale, C-F, Fr., Oklahoma.

1983–84: Patrick Ewing, C, Jr., Georgetown; Michael Jordan, G, Jr., North Carolina; Hakeem Olajuwon, C, Jr., Houston; Sam Perkins, C, Sr., North Carolina; Wayman Tisdale, C-F, Soph., Oklahoma.

1984–85: Johnny Dawkins, G, Jr., Duke; Patrick Ewing, C, Sr., Georgetown; Keith Lee, C, Sr., Memphis State; Xavier McDaniel, F, Sr., Wichita State; Chris Mullin, G-F, Sr., St. John's; Wayman Tisdale, C-F, Jr., Oklahoma.

1985–86: Steve Alford, G, Jr., Indiana; Walter Berry, F, Jr., St. John's; Len Bias, F, Sr., Maryland; Johnny Dawkins, G, Sr., Duke; Kenny Walker, F, Sr., Kentucky.

1986–87: Steve Alford, G, Sr., Indiana; Danny Manning, F-C, Jr., Kansas; David Robinson, C, Sr., Navy, Kenny Smith, G, Sr., North Carolina; Reggie Williams, F-G, Sr., Georgetown.

1987–88: Sean Elliott, F, Jr., Arizona; Gary Grant, G, Sr., Michigan; Hersey Hawkins, G, Sr., Bradley; Danny Manning, F-C, Sr., Kansas; J. R. Reid, C, Soph., North Carolina.

1988–89: Sean Elliott, F, Sr., Arizona; Pervis Ellison, C, Sr., Louisville; Danny Ferry, F-C, Sr., Duke, Chris Jackson, G, Fr., Louisiana State, Stacey King, C, Sr., Oklahoma.

1989–90: Derrick Coleman, F, Sr., Syracuse; Chris Jackson, G, Soph., Louisiana State; Larry Johnson, F, Jr., UNLV; Gary Payton, G, Sr., Oregon State; Lionel Simmons, F, Sr., La Salle.

1990–91: Kenny Anderson, G, Soph., Georgia Tech; Jim Jackson, G-F, Soph., Ohio State; Larry Johnson, F, Sr., UNLV; Shaquille O'Neal, C, Soph., Louisiana State; Billy Owens, F, Jr., Syracuse.

1991–92: Jim Jackson, G-F, Jr., Ohio State; Christian Laettner, F-C, Sr., Duke; Harold Miner, G, Jr., Southern California; Alonzo Mourning, C, Sr., Georgetown; Shaquille O'Neal, C, Jr., Louisiana State.

1992–93: Calbert Cheaney, F, Sr., Indiana; Anfernee Hardaway, G, Jr., Memphis State; Bobby Hurley, G, Sr., Duke; Jamal Mashburn, F, Jr., Kentucky; Chris Webber, F, Soph., Michigan.

1995-96 All-American UMass center Marcus Camby.

1993–94: Grant Hill, F-G, Sr., Duke; Jason Kidd, G, Soph., California; Donyell Marshall, F, Jr., Connecticut; Glenn Robinson, F, Jr., Purdue; Clifford Rozier, C-F, Jr., Louisville.

1994-95: Ed O'Bannon, F, Sr., UCLA; Shawn Respert, G, Sr., Michigan State; Joe Smith, C, Soph., Maryland; Jerry Stackhouse, F, Soph., North Carolina; Damon Stoudamire, G, Sr., Arizona.

1995-96: Ray Allen, G-F, Jr., Connecticut; Marcus Camby, C, Jr., Massachusetts; Tim Duncan, C, Jr., Wake Forest; Allen Iverson, G, Soph., Georgetown; Kerry Kittles, G-F, Sr., Villanova.

SELECTIONS CITED FOR NCAA CONSENSUS ALL-AMERICAN TEAMS

Christy Walsh Syndicate: 1929 and 1930
College Humor Magazine: 1929–33, 1936
Helms Foundation: 1929–48
Converse Yearbook: 1932–48
Literary Digest Magazine: 1934
Omaha World Newspaper: 1937
Madison Square Garden: 1937–42
Newspaper Enterprises Association: 1938, 1953–63
Colliers (Basketball Coaches): 1939, 1949–56
Pic Magazine: 1942–44
The Sporting News: 1943–46
Argosy Magazine: 1945
True Magazine: 1946 and 1947
Associated Press: 1948–
Look Magazine: 1949–63
United Press International: 1949–
International News Service: 1950–58
National Association of Basketball Coaches: 1957–
United States Basketball Writers Association: 1960–

WHERE THE STARS ARE

College basketball undeniably was recognized as a "city" game in the 1950s and 1960s when New York (Lew Alcindor), Philadelphia (Wilt Chamberlain, Tom Gola and Guy Rodgers), Indianapolis (Oscar Robertson), Oakland (Bill Russell), Washington, D.C. (Elgin Baylor and Dave Bing), Chicago (Cazzie Russell), Detroit (Spencer Haywood) and Boston (Jimmy Walker) accounted for a majority of the biggest names in hoopdom.

The landscape changed somewhat in the next two decades when towns with populations of fewer than 60,000 supplied a high percentage of the NBA's premier players such as Charles Barkley (Leeds, Ala.), Larry Bird (French Lick, Ind.), Joe Dumars (Natchitoches, La.), Michael Jordan (Wilmington, N.C.), Karl Malone (Summerfield, La.), Moses Malone (Petersburg, Va.), Kevin McHale (Hibbing, Minn.), Dominique Wilkins (Washington, N.C.) and James Worthy (Gastonia, N.C.).

In the last couple of years, hamlets with little more than a post office and gas station furnished college standouts—Gans, Okla. (Oklahoma State center Bryant Reeves); Hammon, Okla. (Oklahoma forward Ryan Minor), and Pilot Knob, Mo. (Southern Illinois forward Chris Carr).

Whether or not the influence of big cities on big-time hoops might be waning is a subject for debate frequently hinging on provincialism.

"There are still more good players in the big cities," said New Yorker Howard Garfinkel, the creator of the prestigious Five Star Summer Camp. "We used to own the game, but we don't any longer. It's not like it was 40 to 50 years ago. It's no longer just a city game. Now it's national. It's everywhere."

Here is a state-by-state breakdown sizing up the high school hometowns of NCAA consensus first-team All-Americans since the 1928-29 season: Arizona (1), Arkansas (4), California (22), Colorado (3), Connecticut (4), District of Columbia (6), Florida (3), Georgia (4), Illinois (19), Indiana (27), Iowa (2), Kansas (4), Kentucky (11), Louisiana (4), Maryland (4), Massachusetts (4), Michigan (6), Minnesota (2), Mississippi (1), Missouri (5), Nebraska (2), New Jersey (8), New York (29), North Carolina (11), Ohio (13), Oklahoma (5), Oregon (4), Pennsylvania (25), Rhode Island (2), South Carolina (2), Tennessee (3), Texas (8), Utah (5), Virginia (7), Washington (3), West Virginia (2) and Wisconsin (3).

Fourteen states have never had an NCAA consensus All-American—Alabama, Alaska, Delaware, Hawaii, Idaho, Maine, Montana, Nevada, New Hampshire, New Mexico, North Dakota, South Dakota, Vermont and Wyoming.

Three NCAA consensus All-Americans have been from off the mainland U.S.—Tim Duncan (Virgin Islands), Hakeem Olajuwon (Nigeria) and Mychal Thompson (Bahamas).

18

NCAA RECORDS

ete Maravich might have been the most entertaining player in basketball history. He was a dazzling ballhandler, but his forte was putting points on the scoreboard for LSU.

Maravich never scored fewer than 30 points in back-to-back games and scored under 20 just once (17 at Tennessee as a sophomore) in his three varsity seasons. The son of LSU coach Press Maravich was outscored in just one game by a teammate (NIT opener vs. Georgetown in 1970). Maravich scored an amazing 48.2 percent of LSU's points in his three-year career en route to setting the following NCAA records:

• Most points (1,381) and highest scoring average (44.5 ppg) in a single season (1969-70).

• Most points (3,667) and highest scoring average (44.2 ppg) in a career (1967-68 through 1969-70).

• Most games in a career scoring at least 40 points (56).

• Most games in a single season scoring at least 50 points (10 in 1969-70).

• Most consecutive games scoring at least 50 points (three from Feb. 10-15).

• Most field goals made in a season (522 in 1969-70) and career (1,387).

• Most field-goal attempts in a season (1,168 in 1969-70) and a career (3,166).

• Most free throws made in a single game (30 of 31 attempts vs. Oregon State on Dec. 22, 1969).

• Most free throws made (893) and attempted (3,152) in a three-year career.

Maravich accumulated 28 50-point games, including scoring more than 50 points in four outings against both SEC power Kentucky and intra-state independent rival Tulane. The Tigers lost all six times to Kentucky by double-digit margins despite Maravich's firepower. Here is a breakdown of how he amassed a 44.1-point career scoring average and modest 28-26 record in 54 games against SEC competition:

SEC OPPONENT	AVERAGE	HIGH GAME	LOW GAME	W-L
Alabama	48.8 ppg	69	30	4-2
Auburn	49 ppg	55	44	3-3
Florida	44 ppg	52	32	4-2
Georgia	46 ppg	58	37	5-1
Kentucky	52 ppg	64	44	0-6
Mississippi	42.3 ppg	53	31	3-3
Miss. State	47.3 ppg	58	33	6-0
Tennessee	23 ppg	30	17	1-5
Vanderbilt	44.7 ppg	61	35	2-4

INDIVIDUAL—REGULAR SEASON

SCORING

Most points, game, vs. Division I opponent: 72, Kevin Bradshaw, U.S. International, vs. Loyola Marymount, Jan. 5, 1991.

Most points, game, vs. small-college opponent: 100, Frank Selvy, Furman, vs. Newberry, Feb. 13, 1954 (41 FGs, 18 FTs).

Most points, season: 1,381, Pete Maravich, Louisiana State, 1970 (522 FGs, 337 FTs, 31 games).

Most points, career: 3,667, Pete Maravich, Louisiana State, 1968–70.

Highest scoring average per game, season: 44.5, Pete Maravich, Louisiana State, 1970 (1,381 points in 31 games).

Highest scoring average, career: 44.2, Pete Maravich, Louisiana State, 1968–70 (3,667 points in 83 games).

Most combined points, game, two teammates, vs. Division I opponent: 92, Kevin Bradshaw (72) and Isaac Brown (20), U.S. International, vs. Loyola Marymount, Jan. 5, 1990.

Most combined points, game, two teammates, vs. non-Division I team: 125, Frank Selvy (100) and Darrell Floyd (25), Furman, vs. Newberry, Feb. 13, 1954.

Most combined points, game, two opposing players on Division I teams: 115, Pete Maravich (64), Louisiana State, and Dan Issel (51), Kentucky, Feb. 21, 1970.

Most games scoring at least 50 points, season: 10, Pete Maravich, Louisiana State, 1970.

Most games scoring at least 50 points, career: 28, Pete Maravich, Louisiana State 1968–70.

Most consecutive games scoring at least 50 points: 3, Pete Maravich, Louisiana State, Feb. 10–15, 1970.

Most games scoring in double figures, career: 132, Danny Manning, Kansas, 1985–88.

Most consecutive games scoring in double figures, career: 115, Lionel Simmons, La Salle, 1987–90.

FIELD GOALS

Most field goals, game: 41, Frank Selvy, Furman, vs. Newberry, Feb. 13, 1954.

Most field goals, season: 522, Pete Maravich, Louisiana State, 1970 (1,168 attempts, 44.7%).

Most field goals, career: 1,387, Pete Maravich, Louisiana State, 1968–70 (3,166 attempts).

Most consecutive field goals, game: 16, Doug Grayson, Kent, vs. North Carolina, Dec. 6, 1967 (18 of 19).

Most consecutive field goals, season: 25, Ray Voelkel, American, 1978 (during nine games, Nov. 24–Dec. 16).

Most field-goal attempts, game: 71, Jay Handlan, Washington & Lee, vs. Furman, Feb. 17, 1951 (made 30).

Most field-goal attempts, season: 1,168, Pete Maravich, Louisiana State, 1970 (522 made).

Most field-goal attempts, career: 3,166, Pete Maravich, Louisiana State, 1968–70 (made 1,387).

Most field goals without a miss, game: 15, Clifford Rozier, Louisville vs. Eastern Kentucky, Dec. 11, 1993..

Highest field-goal percentage, season: 74.6%, Steve Johnson, Oregon State, 1981 (235 of 315).

Highest field-goal percentage, career (min. 400 scored): 68.5%, Stephen Scheffler, Purdue, 1987–90 (408 of 596).

Highest field-goal percentage, career (min. 600 scored): 67.8%, Steve Johnson, Oregon State, 1977–81 (828 of 1,222).

THREE-POINT FIELD GOALS

Most three-point field goals, game: 14, Dave Jamerson, Ohio vs. Charleston, Dec. 21, 1989 (17 attempts); Askia Jones, Kansas State vs. Fresno State, Mar. 24, 1994 (18 attempts).

Most three-point field goals, season: 158, Darrin Fitzgerald, Butler, 1987 (362 attempts).

Highest three-point field-goal average, season: 5.64, Darrin Fitzgerald, Butler, 1987 (158 in 28 games).

Most three-point field goals, career: 401, Doug Day, Radford, 1990–93 (1,068 attempts).

Highest three-point field-goal average, career (min. 200 made): 4.57, Timothy Pollard, Mississippi Valley State, 1988–89 (256 in 56 games).

Most consecutive three-point field goals, game: 11, Gary Bossert, Niagara, vs. Siena, Jan. 7, 1987.

Most consecutive three-point field goals, season: 15, Todd Leslie, Northwestern, Dec. 1990 (during four games, Dec. 15–28).

Most consecutive games making a three-point field goal, season: 38, Steve Kerr, Arizona, Nov. 27, 1987 to April 2, 1988.

Most consecutive games making a three-point field goal, career: 73, Wally Lancaster, Virginia Tech, Dec. 30, 1986 to Mar. 4, 1989.

Most three-point field-goal attempts, game: 26, Lindsey Hunter, Jackson State, vs. Kansas, Dec. 27, 1992 (11 made).

Most three-point field-goal attempts, season: 362, Darrin Fitzgerald, Butler, 1987 (158 made).

Most three-point field-goal attempts, career: 940, Jeff Fryer, Loyola Marymount, 1987–90 (363 made).

Highest three-point field-goal attempt average per game, season: 12.9, Darrin Fitzgerald, Butler, 1987 (362 in 28 games).

Highest three-point field-goal attempt average per game, career: 7.8, Wally Lancaster, Virginia Tech, 1987–89 (694 in 89 games).

Most three-point field goals without a miss, game: 8, Tomas Thompson, San Francisco vs. Loyola Marymount, Mar. 7, 1992; Shawn Haughn, Dayton vs. St. Louis, Feb. 13, 1994.

Highest three-point field-goal percentage, season (min. 50 made): 63.4%, Glenn Tropf, Holy Cross, 1988 (52 of 82).

Highest three-point field-goal percentage, career (min. 200 made): 49.7%, Tony Bennett, Wisconsin-Green Bay, 1989–92 (290 of 584).

FREE THROWS

Most free throws, game: 30, Pete Maravich, Louisiana State, vs. Oregon State, Dec. 22, 1969 (31 attempts, 96.8%).

Most free throws, season: 355, Frank Selvy, Furman, 1954 (444 attempts, 80.0%).

Most free throws, career: 905, Dickie Hemric, Wake Forest, 1952–55 (1,359 attempts).

Most consecutive free throws, game: 24, Arlen Clark, Oklahoma State, vs. Colorado, Mar. 7, 1959 (24 of 24).

Most consecutive free throws, season: 64, Joe Dykstra, Western Illinois, 1981–82 (during eight games, Dec. 1–Jan. 4).

Most free-throw attempts, game: 36, Ed Tooley, Brown, vs. Amherst, Dec. 4, 1954 (23 made).

Most free-throw attempts, season: 444, Frank Selvy, Furman, 1954 (355 made).

Most free-throw attempts, career: 1,359, Dickie Hemric, Wake Forest, 1952–55 (905 made).

Most free throws without a miss, game: 24, Arlen Clark, Oklahoma State, vs. Colorado, Mar. 7, 1959.

Highest free-throw percentage, season: 95.9%, Craig Collins, Penn State, 1985 (94 of 98).

Highest free-throw percentage, career (min. 300 scored): 90.9%, Greg Starrick, Kentucky & Southern Ill. 1969–72 (341 of 375).

Highest free-throw percentage, career (min. 2.5 made per game): 92.3%, Dave Hildahl, Portland State, 1979–81 (131 of 142).

REBOUNDS

Most rebounds, game (before 1973): 51, Bill Chambers, William & Mary, vs. Virginia, Feb. 14, 1953.

Most rebounds, game (after 1973): 34, David Vaughn, Oral Roberts, vs. Brandeis, Jan. 8, 1973.

Most rebounds, season (before 1973): 734, Walter Dukes, Seton Hall (734 in 33 games).

Highest rebounding average, season (before 1973): 25.6, Charlie Slack, Marshall (538 in 21 games).

Most rebounds, season (since 1973): 597, Marvin Barnes, Providence (597 in 32 games).

Highest rebounding average, season (since 1973): 20, Kermit Washington, American (511 in 25 games).

Most rebounds, career (3 years): 1,751, Paul Silas, Creighton, 1962–64 (81 games).

Most rebounds, career (4 years): 2,201, Tom Gola, La Salle, 1952–55 (118 games).

Most rebounds, career (since 1973): 1,537, Derrick Coleman, Syracuse, 1987–90 (143 games).

Highest rebounding average, career (min. 800): 22.7, Artis Gilmore, Jacksonville, 1970–71 (1,224 in 54 games).

Highest rebounding average, career (since 1973): 15.2, Glenn Mosley, Seton Hall, 1974–77 (1,263 in 83 games).

ASSISTS

Most assists, game: 22, Tony Fairley, Charleston Southern, vs. Armstrong State, Feb. 9, 1987; Avery Johnson, Southern (La.), vs. Texas Southern, Jan. 25, 1988; and Sherman Douglas, Syracuse, vs. Providence, Jan. 28, 1989.

Most assists, season: 406, Mark Wade, UNLV, 1987 (38 games).

Highest assist average, season: 13.3, Avery Johnson, Southern (La.), 1988 (399 in 30 games).

Most assists, career: 1,076, Bobby Hurley, Duke, 1990–93 (140 games).

Highest average (min. 600 assists), career: 8.91, Avery Johnson, Cameron & Southern (La.), 1985 & 1987–88 (838 in 94 games).

BLOCKED SHOTS

Most blocked shots, game: 14, David Robinson, Navy, vs. N.C.-Wilmington, Jan. 4, 1986; and Shawn Bradley, Brigham Young, vs. Eastern Kentucky, Dec. 7, 1990.

Most blocked shots, season: 207, David Robinson, Navy, 1986 (35 games).

Highest blocked shot average, season: 5.91, David Robinson, Navy, 1986 (207 in 35 games).

Most blocked shots, career: 453, Alonzo Mourning, Georgetown, 1989–92 (120 games).

Highest blocked shot average (min. 200), career: 5.24, David Robinson, Navy, 1986–87 (351 in 67 games).

STEALS

Most steals, game: 13, Mookie Blaylock, Oklahoma, vs. Centenary, Dec. 12, 1987, and vs. Loyola Marymount, Dec. 17, 1988.

Most steals, season: 150, Mookie Blaylock, Oklahoma, 1988 (39 games).

Highest steal average, season: 4.96, Darron Brittman, Chicago State, 1986 (139 in 38 games).

Most steals, career: 376, Eric Murdock, Providence, 1988–91 (117 games).

Highest steal average (min. 200), career: 3.8, Mookie Blaylock, Oklahoma, 1988–89 (281 in 74 games).

SCORING

Most points, one team, one game: 186, Loyola Marymount, vs. U.S. International (140), Jan. 5, 1991.

Most points, two teams, one game: 331, Loyola Marymount (181) vs. U.S. International (150), Jan. 31, 1989.

Most points, one team, one half: 97, Oklahoma, vs. U.S. International, Nov. 29, 1989 (1st half).

Most points, two teams, one half: 172, Loyola Marymount (86) vs. Gonzaga (86), Feb. 18, 1989 (2nd half).

Most points, one team, one season: 4,012, Oklahoma, 1988 (39 games).

Highest scoring average per game, one season: 122.4, Loyola Marymount, 1990 (3,918 points in 32 games).

Highest average scoring margin, one season: 30.3, UCLA, 94.6-64.3, 1972.

Most games with at least 100 points, one season: 28, Loyola Marymount, 1990.

Largest lead before the opponent scores at the start of a game: 32-0, Connecticut, vs. New Hampshire, Dec. 12, 1990.

Largest halftime deficit overcome to win game: 29, Duke (74), vs. Tulane (72), Dec. 30, 1950 (trailed 56-27 at intermission).

Largest deficit before scoring that was overcome to win game: 28, New Mexico State (117), vs. Bradley (109), Jan. 27, 1977 (trailed 28-0 with 13:49 left in the first half).

Fewest points allowed, one team, one game (since 1938): 6, Tennessee (11), vs. Temple, Dec. 15, 1973; Kentucky (75), vs. Arkansas State, Jan. 8, 1945.

Fewest points, two teams, one game (since 1938): 17, Tennessee (11) vs. Temple (6), Dec. 15, 1973.

Widest margin of victory: 97, Southern, La. (154), vs. Patten (57), Dec. 26, 1993.

FIELD GOALS

Most field goals, one team, one game: 74, Houston, vs. Valparaiso, Feb. 24, 1968 (attempted 112, 66.1%).

Most field goals, two teams, one game: 130, Loyola Marymount (67) vs. U.S. International (63), Jan. 31, 1989.

Most field goals, one team, one half: 42, Oklahoma, vs. U.S. International, Nov. 29, 1989 (1st half).

Most field-goal attempts, one team, one game: 147, Oklahoma, vs. U.S. International, Nov. 29, 1989 (made 70).

Most field-goal attempts, two teams, one game: 245, Loyola Marymount (124) vs. U.S. International (121), Jan. 7, 1989.

Fewest field goals, one team, one game (since 1938): 2, Duke, vs. North Carolina State, Mar. 8, 1968 (attempted 11); and Arkansas State, vs. Kentucky, Jan. 8, 1945.

Fewest field-goal attempts, one team, one game (since 1938): 9, Pittsburgh, vs. Penn State, Mar. 1, 1952 (made 3).

Highest field-goal percentage, one team, one game (min. 15 made): 83.3%, Maryland, vs. South Carolina, Jan. 9, 1971 (15 of 18).

Highest field-goal percentage, one team, one game (min. 30 made): 81.4%, New Mexico, vs. Oregon State, Nov. 30, 1985 (35 of 43).

Highest field-goal percentage, one team, one half: 94.1%, North Carolina, vs. Virginia, Jan. 7, 1978 (16 of 17, 2nd half).

Most field goals made and attempted, one team, one season: 1,533, Oklahoma, 1988 (attempted 3,094, 49.5%).

Highest field goals-per-game-percentage, one team, one season: 46.3, UNLV, 1976.

Highest field-goal attempts-per-game percentage, one team, one season: 98.5, Oral Roberts, 1973 (2,659 in 27 games).

Highest field-goal percentage, one team, one season: 57.2%, Missouri, 1980 (936 of 1,635).

THREE-POINT FIELD GOALS

Most three-point field goals, one team, one game: 28, Troy State vs. George Mason, Dec. 10, 1994 (74 attempts); 21, Kentucky, vs. North Carolina, Dec. 27, 1989 (48 attempts); Loyola Marymount, vs. Michigan, Mar. 18, 1990 (40); and UNLV, vs. Nevada, Dec. 8, 1991 (46).

Most three-point field goals, two teams, one game: 44, Troy State (28) vs. George Mason (16), Dec. 10, 1994.

Most consecutive three-point field goals made without a miss, one team, one game: 11, Niagara, vs. Siena, Jan. 7, 1987; Eastern Kentucky, vs. N.C.-Asheville, Jan. 14, 1987.

Highest number of different players to score a three-point field goal, one team, one game: 9, Dartmouth, vs. Boston College, Nov. 30, 1993.

Most three-point field-goal attempts, one team, one game: 74, Troy State vs. George Mason, Dec. 10, 1994 (28 made).

Most three-point field-goal attempts, two teams, one game: 84, Kentucky (53) vs. Southwestern Louisiana (31), Dec. 23, 1989.

Highest three-point field-goal percentage (min. 10 scored), one team, one game: 90.9%, Duke, vs. Clemson, Feb. 1, 1988 (10 of 11).

Most three-point field goals made and attempted, one team, one season: 361 of 917, Arkansas, 1995.

Most three-point attempts without making one: 22, Canisius vs. St. Bonaventure, Jan. 21, 1995.

Highest three-point field goal percentage, one team, one season: 10.04, Kentucky, 1990 (281 3FGM in 28 games).

Highest three-point field-goal attempt percentage, one team, one season: 28.9, Kentucky, 1990 (810 in 28 games).

Highest three-point field-goal percentage (min. 100 scored), one team, one season: 50.8%, Indiana, 1987 (130 of 256).

FREE THROWS

Most free throws, one team, one game: 53, Morehead State, vs. Cincinnati, Feb. 11, 1956 (65 attempts); Miami (Ohio) vs. Central Michigan, Jan. 29, 1992 (64).

Most free throws, two teams, one game: 88, Morehead State (53) vs. Cincinnati (35), Feb. 11, 1956 (attempted 111).

Most free-throw attempts, one team, one game: 79, Northern Arizona, vs. Arizona, Jan. 26, 1953 (made 46).

Most free-throw attempts, two teams, one game: 130, Northern Arizona (79) vs. Arizona (51), Jan. 26, 1953 (made 78).

Most Free Throws Without a Miss (Min. 30 scored), one team, one game: UC Irvine, vs. Pacific, Feb. 21, 1981 (34 of 34); Samford, vs. Central Florida, Dec. 20, 1990 (34 of 34); Marshall, vs. Davidson, Dec. 17, 1979 (31 of 31); Indiana State, vs. Wichita State, Feb. 18, 1991 (31 of 31).

Most free throws without a miss, two teams, one game: Purdue (25-25) vs. Wisconsin (22-22), Feb. 7, 1976 (47 of 47).

Most free throws made and Attempted, one team, one season: 865 of 1,263, Bradley, 1954 (68.5%).

Most free throws per game, one team, one season: 28.9, Morehead State, 1956 (838 in 29 games).

Most consecutive free throws, one team, one season: 49, Indiana State, 1991 (during two games, Feb. 13–Feb. 18).

Highest free-throw attempts-per-game percentage, one team, one season: 41.0, Bradley, 1953 (1,107 attempts in 27 games).

Highest free-throw percentage, one team, one season: 82.2%, Harvard, 1984 (535 of 651).

REBOUNDS

Most rebounds, one team, one game: 108, Kentucky, vs. Mississippi, Feb. 8, 1964.

Most rebounds, two teams, one game: 152, Indiana (95) vs. Michigan (57), Mar. 11, 1961.

Highest rebound margin, one game: 84, Arizona (102), vs. Northern Arizona (18), Jan. 6, 1951.

Most rebounds, one team, one season: 2,074, Houston, 1968 (33 games).

Highest rebound average per game, one team, one season: 70.0, Connecticut, 1955 (1,751 in 25 games).

Highest average rebound margin, one season: 25.0, Morehead State, 1957 (64.3 offense, 39.3 defense).

ASSISTS

Most assists, one team, one game: 41, North Carolina, vs. Manhattan, Dec. 27, 1985; Weber State, vs. Northern Arizona, Mar. 2, 1991.

Most assists, two teams, one game: 65, Dayton (34), vs. Central Florida (31), Dec. 3, 1988.

Most assists, one team, one season: 926, UNLV, 1990 (average of 24.66 per game in 40 games).

BLOCKED SHOTS

Most blocked shots, one team, one game: 20, Iona, vs. Northern Illinois, Jan. 7, 1989.

Most blocked shots, two teams, one game: 29, Rider (17) vs. Fairleigh Dickinson (12), Jan. 9, 1989.

Most blocked shots, one team, one season: 309, Georgetown, 1989 (average of 9.09 per game in 34 games).

STEALS

Most steals, one team, one game: 34, Oklahoma, vs. Centenary, Dec. 12, 1987; Northwestern (La.) State, vs. LeTourneau, Jan. 20, 1992.

Most steals, two teams, one game: 44, Oklahoma (34) vs. Centenary (10), Dec. 12, 1987.

Most steals, one team, one season: 486, Oklahoma, 1988 (39 games).

Highest steals-per-game average, one team, one season: 14.83, Texas-San Antonio, 1991 (430 in 29 games).

PERSONAL FOULS

Most personal fouls, one team, one season: 966, Providence, 1987 (34 games).

Highest personal fouls-per-game percentage, one team, one season: 29.3, Indiana, 1952 (644 in 22 games).

Fewest personal fouls, one team, one season: 253, Air Force, 1962 (average of 11 per game in 23 games).

Most personal fouls, one team, one game: 50, Arizona, vs. Northern Arizona, Jan. 26, 1953.

Most personal fouls, two teams, one game: 84, Arizona (50) vs. Northern Arizona (34), Jan. 26, 1953.

Most players disqualified, one team, one game: 8, St. Joseph's, vs. Xavier, Jan. 10, 1976.

Most players disqualified, two teams, one game: 12, UNLV (6) vs. Hawaii (6), Jan. 19, 1979 (OT); Arizona (7) vs. West Texas State (5), Feb. 14, 1952.

DEFENSE

Lowest scoring average per game allowed, one season (since 1938): 25.7, Oklahoma State (27 games in 1939).

Lowest field goal percentage allowed, one season (since 1978): 36.45, UNLV (628 of 1,723 in 1992).

OVERTIMES

Most overtime periods, one game: 7, Cincinnati (75) at Bradley (73), Dec. 21, 1981.

Most points, one team, one overtime period: 25, Texas A&M, vs. North Carolina, Mar. 9, 1980; Wisconsin-Green Bay, vs. Cleveland State, Feb. 27, 1988; Old Dominion, vs. William & Mary, Feb. 1, 1992.

Most points, two teams, one overtime period: 40, Old Dominion (25) vs. William & Mary (15), Feb. 1, 1992.

Most points, one team, more than one overtime period: 39, Cleveland State, vs. Kent, Dec. 23, 1993 (4 OT).

Most points, two teams, more than one overtime period: 75, Cleveland State (39) vs. Kent (36), Dec. 23, 1993 (4 OT).

Largest winning margin in an overtime game: 18, Nebraska (85), vs. Iowa State (67), Dec. 30, 1949.

Most overtime games, one team, one season: 8, Western Kentucky, 1978 (won 5, lost 3); Portland, 1984 (won 4, lost 4).

Most consecutive overtime games, one team, one season: 4, Jacksonville, 1982 (won 3, lost 1); Illinois State, 1985 (won 3, lost 1); Dayton, 1988 (won 1, lost 3).

GENERAL RECORDS

Most games in a season, one team (since 1947–48): 40, Duke, 1986 (37-3); UNLV, 1990 (35-5).

Most victories, one season: 37, Duke, 1986 (37-3); UNLV, 1987 (37-2).

Most consecutive victories: 88, UCLA, Jan. 30, 1971–Jan. 17, 1974 (ended Jan. 19, 1974 at Notre Dame, 71-70; last UCLA defeat before streak also came at Notre Dame, 89-82).

Most consecutive homecourt victories: 129, Kentucky, Jan. 4, 1943–Jan. 8, 1955 (ended by Georgia Tech, 59-58).

Most consecutive regular-season victories: 76, UCLA, 1971–74 (NCAA, NIT, and CCA tourneys not included).

Most defeats in a season: 28, Prairie View, 1992 (0-28).

Most consecutive defeats: 37, The Citadel, Jan. 16, 1954–Dec. 12, 1955.

Most consecutive defeats on-the-road: 55, Cal State Sacramento, from Nov. 22, 1991, to Jan. 5, 1995 (ended at Loyola of Chicago, 68-56).

Most consecutive homecourt defeats: 32, New Hampshire, Feb. 9, 1988–Feb. 2, 1991 (ended vs. Holy Cross, 72-56).

Most consecutive 20-win seasons: 24, North Carolina, 1971–94.

Most consecutive non-losing seasons: 60, Kentucky, 1928–88 (did not play in 1953).

INDIVIDUAL—NCAA TOURNAMENT

SCORING

Most points, game: 61, Austin Carr, Notre Dame vs. Ohio, Southeast/Mideast Regional, 1st round, 1970.

Most points by two teammates, game: 85, Austin Carr (61) and Collis Jones (24), Notre Dame vs. Ohio, Southeast/Mideast Regional, 1st round, 1970.

Most points by two opposing players, game: 96, Austin Carr (52), Notre Dame, and Dan Issel (44), Kentucky, Southeast/Mideast Regional Semifinal Game, 1970.

Most points, series (three-game minimum): 184, Glen Rice, Michigan, 1989 (6 games).

Highest scoring average, series (three-game minimum): 52.7 (158 points), Austin Carr, Notre Dame, 1970 (3 games).

Most points, career (two-year minimum): 407, Christian Laettner, Duke, 1989-90-91-92 (23 games).

Highest scoring average (min. of 6 games), career (two-year minimum): 41.3 (289 points, Austin Carr, Notre Dame, 1969-70-71 (7 games).

FIELD GOALS

Most field goals made, game: 25, Austin Carr, Notre Dame vs. Ohio, Southeast/Mideast Regional, 1st round, 1970.

Most field-goal attempts, game: 44, Austin Carr, Notre Dame vs. Ohio, Southeast/Mideast Regional, 1st round, 1970.

Most field goals without a miss, game: 11-11, Kenny Walker, Kentucky vs. Western Kentucky, Southeast/Mideast Regional, 2d round, 1986.

Most field goals made, series (three-game minimum): 75, Glen Rice, Michigan, 1989 (6 games).

Most field-goal attempts, series (three-game minimum): 138, Jim McDaniels, Western Kentucky, 1971 (5 games).

Highest field-goal percentage (min. of 5 FGM per game), series (three-game minimum): 78.8% (26-33), Christian Laettner, Duke, 1989 (5 games).

Most field goals, career (two-year minimum): 152, Elvin Hayes, Houston, 1966-67-68 (13 games).

Most field-goal attempts, career (two-year minimum): 310, Elvin Hayes, Houston, 1966-67-68 (13 games).

Highest field-goal percentage (min. of 70 FGM), career (two-year minimum): 68.6% (109-159), Bill Walton, UCLA, 1972-73-74 (12 games).

THREE-POINT FIELD GOALS

Most three-point field goals, game: 11, Jeff Fryer, Loyola Marymount vs. Michigan, West/Far West Regional, 2d round, 1990.

Most three-point field-goal attempts, game: 22, Jeff Fryer, Loyola Marymount vs. Arkansas, Midwest Regional, 1st round, 1989.

Wyoming's Fennis Dembo is tied with Princeton's Bill Bradley for most free throws without a miss in an NCAA tournament game.

Most three-point field goals without a miss, game: 7-7, Sam Cassell, Florida State vs. Tulane, Southeast/Mideast Regional, 2d round, 1993.

Most three-point field goals, series (three-game minimum): 27, Glen Rice, Michigan, 1989 (6 games).

Most three-point field-goal attempts, series (three-game minimum): 65, Freddie Banks, UNLV, 1987 (5 games).

Highest three-point field-goal percentage (min. of 1.5 3FGM per game), series (three-game minimum): 100% (6-6), Ranzino Smith, North Carolina, 1987 (4 games).

Most three-point field goals, career (two-year minimum): 42, Bobby Hurley, Duke, 1990-91-92-93 (20).

Most three-point field-goal attempts, career (two-year minimum): 103, Anderson Hunt, UNLV, 1989-90-91 (15 games).

Highest three-point field-goal percentage (min. of 20 FGM), career (two-year minimum): 65.0% (26-40), William Scott, Kansas State, 1987-88 (5 games).

FREE THROWS

Most free throws made, game: 23, Bob Carney, Bradley vs. Colorado, Midwest Regional Regional Semifinal Game, 1954.

Most free-throw attempts, game: 27, David Robinson, Navy vs. Syracuse, East Regional, 2d round, 1986.

Most free throws without a miss, game: 16-16, Bill Bradley, Princeton vs. St. Joseph's, East Regional, 1st round, 1963; Fennis Dembo, Wyoming vs. UCLA, West/Far West Regional, 2d round, 1987.

Most free throws made, series (three-game minimum): 55, Bob Carney, Bradley, 1954 (5 games).

Most free-throw attempts, series (three-game minimum): 71, Jerry West, West Virginia, 1959 (5 games).

Most free throws without a miss, series (three-game minimum): 23-23, Richard Morgan, Virginia, 1989 (4 games).

Most free throws made, career (two-year minimum): 142, Christian Laettner, Duke, 1989-90-91-92 (23 games).

Most free-throw attempts, career (two-year minimum): 167, Christian Laettner, Duke, 1989-90-91-92 (23 games).

Highest free-throw percentage (min. of 30 FTM), career (two-year minimum): 95.7% (45-47), LaBradford Smith, Louisville, 1988-89-90 (8 games).

Highest free-throw percentage (min. of 50 FTM), career (two-year minimum): 90.6% (87-96), Bill Bradley, Princeton, 1963-64-65 (9 games); 90.6% (58-64), Steve Alford, Indiana, 1984-86-87 (10 games).

REBOUNDS

Most rebounds, game: 34, Fred Cohen, Temple vs. Connecticut, East Regional Semifinal Game, 1956.

Most rebounds, series (three-game minimum): 97, Elvin Hayes, Houston, 1968 (5 games).

Highest rebound average (min. of 3 games), series (three-game minimum): 23.3 (70 rebounds), Nate Thurmond, Bowling Green, 1963, (3 games).

Most rebounds, career (two-year minimum): 222, Elvin Hayes, Houston, 1966-67-68 (13 games).

Highest rebounding average (min. of 6 games), career (two-year minimum): 19.7 (118 rebounds), John Green, Michigan State, 1957-59 (6 games).

ASSISTS

Most assists, game: 18, Mark Wade, UNLV vs. Indiana, National Semifinal Game, 1987.

Most assists, series (three-game minimum): 61, Mark Wade, UNLV, 1987 (5 games).

Most assists, career (two-year minimum): 145, Bobby Hurley, Duke, 1990-91-92-93 (20 games).

BLOCKED SHOTS

Most blocked shots, game: 11, Shaquille O'Neal, Louisiana State vs. Brigham Young, West/Far West Regional, 1st round, 1992.

Most blocked shots, career (two-year minimum): 37, Alonzo Mourning, Georgetown, 1989-90-91-92 (10 games).

STEALS

Most steals, game: 8, Darrell Hawkins, Arkansas vs. Holy Cross, East Regional, 1st round, 1993; Grant Hill, Duke vs. California, Midwest Regional, 2d round, 1993.

Most steals, series (three-game minimum): 23, Mookie Blaylock, Oklahoma, 1988 (6 games).

Most steals, career (two-year minimum): 32, Mookie Blaylock, Oklahoma, 1988-89 (9 games); Christian Laettner, Duke, 1989-90-91-92 (23 games).

GENERAL RECORDS

Most games played, career (two-year minimum): 23, Christian Laettner, Duke, 1989-90-91-92.

TEAM—NCAA TOURNAMENT

SCORING

Most points, one team, one game: 149, Loyola Marymount, vs. Michigan (115), West/Far West Regional, 2d round, 1990.

Most points, one team, one tournament (three-game minimum): 571, UNLV, 1990 (6 games).

Highest scoring average, one team, one tournament (three-game minimum): 105.8, Loyola Marymount, 1990 (423 points in 4 games).

Most points, two teams, one game: 264, Loyola Marymount (149) vs. Michigan (115), West/Far West Regional, 2d round, 1990.

Fewest points, one team, one game: 20, North Carolina, vs. Pittsburgh (26), East Regional Final Game, 1941.

Largest winning margin, one team, one game: 69, Loyola of Chicago (111) vs. Tennessee Tech (42), Southeast/Mideast Regional, 1st round, 1963.

Most points scored by a losing team, one game: 120, Utah, vs. St. Joseph's (127), National Third Place Game, 1961 (4 OT).

Most players scoring in double figures, one team, one game: 7, Indiana, vs. George Mason, West/Far West Regional, 1st round, 1989; UNLV, vs. Arkansas-Little Rock, West/Far West Regional, 1st round, 1990.

Most players scoring in double figures, two teams, one game: 12, Notre Dame (6) vs. Houston (6), West/Far West Regional, 1st round, 1965.

Most players scoring, one team, one game: 14, Iowa, vs. Santa Clara, West/Far West Regional, 1st round, 1987.

Most players scoring, two teams, one game: 24, Brown (12) vs. Syracuse (12), East Regional, 1st round, 1986; Iowa (14) vs. Santa Clara (10), West/Far West Regional, 1st round, 1987.

Fewest players scoring, one team, one game: 3, Utah State, vs. San Francisco, West/Far West Regional Semifinal Game, 1964.

Fewest players scoring, two teams, one game: 9, Connecticut (4) vs. Temple (5), East Regional, 1st round, 1964; Michigan State (4) vs. Washington (5), Midwest Regional, 1st round, 1986.

FIELD GOALS

Most field goals, one team, one game: 52, Iowa, vs. Notre Dame, Southeast/Mideast Regional, Regional Third Place Game, 1970.

Most field-goal attempts, one team, one tournament (three-game minimum): 442, Western Kentucky, 1971 (5 games).

Most field goals made, two teams, one game: 97, Iowa (52) vs. Notre Dame (45), Southeast/Mideast Regional Third Place Game, 1970.

Fewest field goals, one team, one game: 8, Springfield, vs. Indiana, East Regional, 1st round, 1940.

Most field-goal attempts, one team, one game: 112, Marshall, vs. Southwestern Louisiana, Midwest Regional, 1st round, 1972.

Highest field-goal percentage, one team, one game: 80.0% (28-35), Oklahoma State, vs. Tulane, Southeast/Mideast Regional, 2d round, 1992.

Highest field-goal percentage, one team, one tournament (three-game minimum): 60.4% (113-187), North Carolina, 1975 (3 games).

Lowest field-goal percentage, one team, one game: 12.7% (8-63), Springfield, vs. Indiana, East Regional Semifinal Game, 1940.

THREE-POINT FIELD GOALS

Most three-point field goals, one team, one game: 21, Loyola Marymount, vs. Michigan, West/Far West Regional, 2d round, 1990.

Most three-point field goals made, one team, one tournament (three-game minimum): 60, Arkansas, 1995 (6 games).

Most three-point field goals made, two teams, one game: 27, Wisconsin (15) vs. Missouri (12), West/Far West Regional, 2d round, 1994.

Most three-point field-goal attempts, one team, one game: 41, Loyola Marymount, vs. UNLV, West Regional Final Game, 1990.

Most three-point field goal attempts, one team, one game (three-game minimum): 165, Arkansas, 1995 (6 games).

Most three-point field-goal attempts, one team, one tournament (three-game minimum): 137, Loyola Marymount, 1990 (4 games).

Most three-point field-goal attempts, two teams, one game: 62, Arkansas (34) vs. North Carolina (28), NSF, 1995.

Highest three-point field-goal percentage (min. of 7 3FGM), one team, one game: 88.9% (8-9), Kansas State, vs. Georgia, West/Far West Regional, 1st round, 1987.

Highest three-point field-goal percentage (min. of 12 3FGM), one team, one tournament (three-game minimum): 60.9% (14-23), Indiana, 1989 (3 games).

Highest three-point field-goal percentage (min. of 30 3FGM), one team, one tournament (three-game minimum): 51.9% (40-77), Kansas, 1993 (5 games).

FREE THROWS

Most free throws made, one team, one game: 41, Utah, vs. Santa Clara, West/Far West Regional, Regional Third Place Game, 1960; Navy, vs. Syracuse, East Regional, 2d round, 1986.

Most free throws made, one team, one tournament (three-game minimum): 146, Bradley, 1954 (5 games).

Most free throws made, two teams, one game: 69, Morehead State (37) vs. Pittsburgh (32), Southeast/Mideast Regional, 1st round, 1957.

Most free-throw attempts, one team, one game: 55, Texas-El Paso, vs. Tulsa, West/Far West Regional, 1st round, 1985.

Most free-throw attempts, one team, one tournament (three-game minimum): 194, Bradley, 1954 (5 games).

Highest free-throw percentage, one team, one tournament (three-game minimum): 87.0% (47-54), St. John's, 1969 (3 games).

Most free-throw attempts, two teams, one game: 105, Morehead State (53) vs. Iowa (52), Southeast/Mideast Regional Semifinal Game, 1956.

Most free throws without a miss, one team, one game: 22-22, Fordham, vs. South Carolina, East Regional Third Place Game, 1971.

REBOUNDS

Most rebounds, one team, one game: 86, Notre Dame, vs. Tennessee Tech, Southeast/Mideast Regional, 1st round, 1958.

Most rebounds, one team, one tournament (three-game minimum): 306, Houston, 1968 (5 games).

Most rebounds, two teams, one game: 134, Marshall (68) vs. Southwestern Louisiana (66), Midwest Regional, 1st round, 1972.

Largest rebound margin, one team, one game: 42, Notre Dame (86) vs. Tennessee Tech (44), Southeast/Mideast Regional, 1st round, 1958.

ASSISTS

Most assists, one team, one game: 36, North Carolina, vs. Loyola Marymount, West/Far West Regional, 2d round, 1988.

Most assists, one team, one tournament (three-game minimum): 140, UNLV, 1990 (6 games).

Most assists, two teams, one game: 58, UNLV (35) vs. Loyola Marymount (23), West Regional Final Game, 1990.

BLOCKED SHOTS

Most blocked shots, one team, one game: 13, Louisville, vs. Illinois, Midwest Regional Semifinal Game, 1989; Brigham Young, vs. Virginia, West Regional, 1st round, 1991.

Most blocked shots, one team, one tournament (three-game minimum): 37, Massachusetts, 1995 (4 games).

Most blocked shots, two teams, one game: 18, Iowa (10) vs. Duke (8), East Regional, 2d round, 1992.

STEALS

Most steals, one team, one game: 19, Providence, vs. Austin Peay State, Southeast/Mideast Regional, 2d round, 1987; Connecticut, vs. Boston U., East Regional, 1st round, 1990.

Most steals, one team, one tournament (three-game minimum): 72, Oklahoma, 1988 (6 games).

Most steals, two teams, one game: 28, North Carolina A&T (16) vs. Arkansas (12), Midwest Regional, 1st round, 1994.

Louisville's Denny Crum coached two of his teams to NCAA championships.

PERSONAL FOULS

Most personal fouls, one team, one game: 41, Dayton, vs. Illinois, East Regional Semifinal Game, 1952.

Most personal fouls, one team, one tournament (three-game minimum): 150, Pennsylvania, 1979 (6 games).

Most personal fouls, two teams, one game: 60, Seattle (31) vs. UCLA (29), West/Far West Regional Semifinal Game, 1964.

GENERAL RECORDS

Most players disqualified, one team, one game: 6, Kansas, vs. Notre Dame, Midwest Regional, 1st round, 1975.

Most players used, two teams, one game: 29, Arizona State (15) vs. Loyola Marymount (14), West/Far West Regional, 1st round, 1980.

HIT LIST   Here is a look at UCLA's 38-game winning streak in the NCAA Tournament during the Bruins' wonder years when they won nine national championships from 1964 through 1973 before losing to North Carolina State (80-77 in double overtime) at the 1974 Final Four.

1. Seattle, 95-90
2. San Francisco, 76-72
3. Kansas State, 90-84
4. Duke, 98-83
5. Brigham Young, 100-76
6. San Francisco, 101-93
7. Wichita State, 108-89
8. Michigan, 91-80
9. Wyoming, 109-60
10. Pacific, 80-64
11. Houston, 73-58
12. Dayton, 79-64
13. New Mexico State, 58-49
14. Santa Clara, 87-66
15. Houston, 101-69
16. North Carolina, 78-55
17. New Mexico State, 53-38
18. Santa Clara, 90-52
19. Drake, 85-82
20. Purdue, 92-72
21. Long Beach State, 88-65
22. Utah State, 101-79
23. New Mexico State, 93-77
24. Jacksonville, 80-69
25. Brigham Young, 91-73
26. Long Beach State, 57-55
27. Kansas, 68-60
28. Villanova, 68-62
29. Weber State, 90-58
30. Long Beach State, 73-57
31. Louisville, 96-77
32. Florida State, 81-76
33. Arizona State, 98-81
34. San Francisco, 54-39
35. Indiana, 70-59
36. Memphis State, 87-66
37. Dayton*, 111-100
38. San Francisco, 83-60

* Triple overtime.

OVERTIMES

Most overtime periods, one game: 4, Canisius (79) vs. North Carolina State (78), East Regional, 1st round, 1956; St. Joseph's (127) vs. Utah (120), National Third Place Game, 1961.

Most points in overtimes, one team: 38, St. Joseph's, vs. Utah, National Third Place Game, 1961 (4 OT).

Most points in overtimes, two teams: 69, St. Joseph's (38) vs. Utah (31), National Third Place Game, 1961 (4 OT).

NCAA TOURNAMENT FINAL FOUR RESULTS

YEAR	CHAMPION (COACH)	SCORE	RUNNER-UP	THIRD PLACE	FOURTH PLACE	MOST OUTSTANDING PLAYER	SITE OF FINALS
1939	Oregon (Howard Hobson)	46-33	Ohio State	*Oklahoma	*Villanova	None selected	Evanston, IL
1940	Indiana (Branch McCracken)	60-42	Kansas	*Duquesne	*Southern Cal	Marvin Huffman, Indiana	Kansas City
1941	Wisconsin (Bud Foster)	39-34	Washington State	*Pittsburgh	*Arkansas	John Kotz, Wisconsin	Kansas City
1942	Stanford (Everett Dean)	53-38	Dartmouth	*Colorado	*Kentucky	Howie Dallmar, Stanford	Kansas City
1943	Wyoming (Everett Shelton)	46-34	Georgetown	*Texas	*DePaul	Ken Sailors, Wyoming	New York City
1944	Utah (Vadal Peterson)	42-40 (OT)	Dartmouth	*Iowa State	*Ohio State	Arnie Ferrin, Utah	New York City
1945	Oklahoma State (Henry Iba)	49-45	New York University	*Arkansas	*Ohio State	Bob Kurland, Okla. State	New York City
1946	Oklahoma State (Henry Iba)	43-40	North Carolina	Ohio State	California	Bob Kurland, Okla. State	New York City
1947	Holy Cross (Doggie Julian)	58-47	Oklahoma	Texas	CCNY	George Kaftan, Holy Cross	New York City
1948	Kentucky (Adolph Rupp)	58-42	Baylor	Holy Cross	Kansas State	Alex Groza, Kentucky	New York City
1949	Kentucky (Adolph Rupp)	46-36	Oklahoma State	Illinois	Oregon State	Alex Groza, Kentucky	Seattle
1950	CCNY (Nat Holman)	71-68	Bradley	N.C. State	Baylor	Irwin Dambrot, CCNY	New York City
1951	Kentucky (Adolph Rupp)	68-58	Kansas State	Illinois	Okla. State	None selected	Minneapolis
1952	Kansas (Phog Allen)	80-63	St. John's	Illinois	Santa Clara	Clyde Lovellette, Kansas	Seattle
1953	Indiana (Branch McCracken)	69-68	Kansas	Washington	Louisiana St.	B.H. Born, Kansas	Kansas City
1954	La Salle (Ken Loeffler)	92-76	Bradley	Penn State	Southern Cal	Tom Gola, La Salle	Kansas City
1955	San Francisco (Phil Woolpert)	77-63	La Salle	Colorado	Iowa	Bill Russell, San Francisco	Kansas City
1956	San Francisco (Phil Woolpert)	83-71	Iowa	Temple	SMU	Hal Lear, Temple	Evanston, IL
1957	North Carolina (Frank McGuire)	54-53 (3 OT)	Kansas	San Francisco	Michigan State	Wilt Chamberlain, Kansas	Kansas City
1958	Kentucky (Adolph Rupp)	84-72	Seattle	Temple	Kansas State	Elgin Baylor, Seattle	Louisville, KY
1959	California (Pete Newell)	71-70	West Virginia	Cincinnati	Louisville	Jerry West, West Virginia	Louisville, KY
1960	Ohio State (Fred Taylor)	75-55	California	Cincinnati	New York Univ.	Jerry Lucas, Ohio State	San Francisco
1961	Cincinnati (Ed Jucker)	70-65 (OT)	Ohio State	St. Joseph's	Utah	Jerry Lucas, Ohio State	Kansas City
1962	Cincinnati (Ed Jucker)	71-59	Ohio State	Wake Forest	UCLA	Paul Hogue, Cincinnati	Louisville, KY
1963	Loyola, Ill. (George Ireland)	60-58 (OT)	Cincinnati	Duke	Oregon State	Art Heyman, Duke	Louisville, KY
1964	UCLA (John Wooden)	98-83	Duke	Michigan	Kansas State	Walt Hazzard, UCLA	Kansas City
1965	UCLA (John Wooden)	91-80	Michigan	Princeton	Wichita State	Bill Bradley, Princeton	Portland, OR
1966	Texas Western (Don Haskins)	72-65	Kentucky	Duke	Utah	Jerry Chambers, Utah	College Park, MD
1967	UCLA (John Wooden)	79-64	Dayton	Houston	North Carolina	Lew Alcindor, UCLA	Louisville, KY
1968	UCLA (John Wooden)	78-55	North Carolina	Ohio State	Houston	Lew Alcindor, UCLA	Los Angeles
1969	UCLA (John Wooden)	92-72	Purdue	Drake	North Carolina	Lew Alcindor, UCLA	Louisville, KY
1970	UCLA (John Wooden)	80-69	Jacksonville	New Mexico St.	St. Bonaventure	Sidney Wicks, UCLA	College Park, MD
1971	UCLA (John Wooden)	68-62	Villanova	Western Ky.	Kansas	Howard Porter, Villanova	Houston
1972	UCLA (John Wooden)	81-76	Florida State	North Carolina	Louisville	Bill Walton, UCLA	Los Angeles
1973	UCLA (John Wooden)	87-66	Memphis State	Indiana	Providence	Bill Walton, UCLA	St. Louis
1974	N.C. State (Norman Sloan)	76-64	Marquette	UCLA	Kansas	David Thompson, N.C. St.	Greensboro, NC
1975	UCLA (John Wooden)	92-85	Kentucky	Louisville	Syracuse	Richard Washington, UCLA	San Diego
1976	Indiana (Bob Knight)	86-68	Michigan	UCLA	Rutgers	Kent Benson, Indiana	Philadelphia
1977	Marquette (Al McGuire)	67-59	North Carolina	UNLV	UNC Charlotte	Butch Lee, Marquette	Atlanta
1978	Kentucky (Joe B. Hall)	94-88	Duke	Arkansas	Notre Dame	Jack Givens, Kentucky	St. Louis
1979	Michigan State (Jud Heathcote)	75-64	Indiana State	DePaul	Penn	Magic Johnson, Mich. St.	Salt Lake City
1980	Louisville (Denny Crum)	59-54	UCLA	Purdue	Iowa	Darrell Griffith, Louisville	Indianapolis
1981	Indiana (Bob Knight)	63-50	North Carolina	Virginia	Louisiana St.	Isiah Thomas, Indiana	Philadelphia
1982	North Carolina (Dean Smith)	63-62	Georgetown	*Houston	*Louisville	James Worthy, N. Carolina	New Orleans
1983	N.C. State (Jim Valvano)	54-52	Houston	*Louisville	*Georgia	Hakeem Olajuwon, Houston	Albuquerque, NM
1984	Georgetown (John Thompson)	84-75	Houston	*Kentucky	*Virginia	Patrick Ewing, Georgetown	Seattle
1985	Villanova (Rollie Massimino)	66-64	Georgetown	*St. John's	*Memphis State	Ed Pinckney, Villanova	Lexington, KY
1986	Louisville (Denny Crum)	72-69	Duke	*Kansas	*Louisiana St.	Pervis Ellison, Louisville	Dallas
1987	Indiana (Bob Knight)	74-73	Syracuse	*Providence	*UNLV	Keith Smart, Indiana	New Orleans
1988	Kansas (Larry Brown)	83-79	Oklahoma	*Arizona	*Duke	Danny Manning, Kansas	Kansas City
1989	Michigan (Steve Fisher)	80-79 (OT)	Seton Hall	*Duke	*Illinois	Glen Rice, Michigan	Seattle
1990	UNLV (Jerry Tarkanian)	103-73	Duke	*Arkansas	*Georgia Tech	Anderson Hunt, UNLV	Denver
1991	Duke (Mike Krzyzewski)	72-65	Kansas	*N. Carolina	*UNLV	Christian Laettner, Duke	Indianapolis
1992	Duke (Mike Krzyzewski)	71-51	Michigan	*Cincinnati	*Indiana	Bobby Hurley, Duke	Minneapolis
1993	North Carolina (Dean Smith)	77-71	Michigan	*Kansas	*Kentucky	Donald Williams, N. Caro.	New Orleans
1994	Arkansas (Nolan Richardson)	76-72	Duke	*Arizona	*Florida	Corliss Williamson, Ark.	Charlotte
1995	UCLA (Jim Harrick)	89-78	Arkansas	*North Carolina	*Okla. St.	Ed O'Bannon, UCLA	Seattle
1996	Kentucky (Rick Pitino)	76-67	Syracuse	*Massachusetts	*Miss. St.	Tony Delk, Kentucky	E. Rutherford

*Tied for third position because there was no consolation game.

Most Final Four Appearances by School: UCLA (15), North Carolina (12), Duke (11), Kentucky (11), Kansas (10), Ohio State (8), Indiana (7), Louisville (7), Arkansas (6), Cincinnati (6), Michigan (6).

Most Final Four victories by School: UCLA (25), Kentucky (14), Duke (11), Indiana (11), North Carolina (11), Kansas (8).

Most NCAA Tournament Appearances: Kentucky (37), UCLA (31), North Carolina (30), Louisville (26), Indiana (25), Kansas (25), Notre Dame (24), St. John's (23), Syracuse (23), Arkansas (22), Kansas State (22), Villanova(22).

Most NCAA Tournament Victories: UCLA (74), Kentucky (72), North Carolina (68), Duke (56), Kansas (54), Indiana (50), Louisville (50), Louisville (45), Michigan (40), Arkansas (37), Georgetown (36).

Most NCAA Tournament Championships: UCLA (11), Kentucky (6), Indiana (5), North Carolina (3).

UCLA'S 48-YEAR STREAK OF WINNING SEASONS

UCLA flopped in the NCAA Tournament last season as defending champion, but the Bruins extended their NCAA record of consecutive winning seasons. The streak started after the Bruins compiled a 12-13 record under coach Wilbur Johns in his final season in 1947-48. They had just two winning records in their previous 17 seasons before John Wooden assumed control of the program. Their average record in the last 48 years is 23-7.

SEASON	W.	L.	PCT.	COACH	LEADING SCORER (AVG.)
1948-49	22	7	.759	John Wooden	Carl Kraushaar (9.4 ppg)
1949-50	24	7	.774	John Wooden	Alan Sawyer (12.6)
1950-51	19	10	.655	John Wooden	Dick Ridgway (16.2)
1951-52	19	12	.613	John Wooden	Ron Livingston (10.1)
1952-53	16	8	.667	John Wooden	John Moore (12.2)
1953-54	18	7	.720	John Wooden	Ron Livingston (12.5)
1954-55	21	5	.808	John Wooden	John Moore (14.6)
1955-56	22	6	.786	John Wooden	Willie Naulls (23.6)
1956-57	22	4	.846	John Wooden	Dick Banton (14.1)
1957-58	16	10	.615	John Wooden	Ben Rogers (12.5)
1958-59	16	9	.640	John Wooden	Walt Torrence (21.5)
1959-60	14	12	.538	John Wooden	John Green (10.2)
1960-61	18	8	.692	John Wooden	Ron Lawson (13.7)
1961-62	18	11	.621	John Wooden	John Green (19.3)
1962-63	20	9	.690	John Wooden	Walt Hazzard (16.3)
1963-64	30	0	1.000	John Wooden	Gail Goodrich (21.5)
1964-65	28	2	.933	John Wooden	Gail Goodrich (24.8)
1965-66	18	8	.692	John Wooden	Mike Lynn (16.8)
1966-67	30	0	1.000	John Wooden	Lew Alcindor (29.0)
1967-68	29	1	.967	John Wooden	Lew Alcindor (26.2)
1968-69	29	1	.967	John Wooden	Lew Alcindor (24.0)
1969-70	28	2	.933	John Wooden	Sidney Wicks (18.6)
1970-71	29	1	.967	John Wooden	Sidney Wicks (21.3)
1971-72	30	0	1.000	John Wooden	Bill Walton (21.1)
1972-73	30	0	1.000	John Wooden	Bill Walton (20.4)
1973-74	26	4	.867	John Wooden	Bill Walton (19.3)
1974-75	28	3	.903	John Wooden	David Meyers (18.3)
1975-76	28	4	.875	Gene Bartow	Richard Washington (20.1)
1976-77	24	5	.831	Gene Bartow	Marques Johnson (21.4)
1977-78	25	3	.893	Gary Cunningham	David Greenwood (17.5)
1978-79	25	5	.833	Gary Cunningham	David Greenwood (19.9)
1979-80	22	10	.688	Larry Brown	Kiki Vandeweghe (19.5)
1980-81	20	7	.741	Larry Brown	Mike Sanders (15.4)
1981-82	21	6	.778	Larry Farmer	Mike Sanders (14.4)
1982-83	23	6	.793	Larry Farmer	Kenny Fields (18.0)
1983-84	17	11	.607	Larry Farmer	Kenny Fields (17.4)
1984-85	21	12	.636	Walt Hazzard	Reggie Miller (15.2)
1985-86	15	14	.517	Walt Hazzard	Reggie Miller (25.9)
1986-87	25	7	.781	Walt Hazzard	Reggie Miller (22.3)
1987-88	16	14	.533	Walt Hazzard	Trevor Wilson (15.4)
1988-89	21	10	.677	Jim Harrick	Don MacLean (18.6)
1989-90	22	11	.667	Jim Harrick	Don MacLean (19.9)
1990-91	23	9	.719	Jim Harrick	Don MacLean (23.0)
1991-92	28	5	.848	Jim Harrick	Tracy Murray (21.4)
1992-93	22	11	.667	Jim Harrick	Shon Tarver (17.2)
1993-94	21	7	.750	Jim Harrick	Ed O'Bannon (18.2)
1994-95	31	2	.939	Jim Harrick	Ed O'Bannon (20.4)
1995-96	23	8	.742	Jim Harrick	Toby Bailey (14.8)

KENTUCKY'S 60-YEAR STREAK OF NON-LOSING RECORDS

Kentucky, after compiling a 3-13 record under coach Basil Hayden in 1926-27, began a streak the next season that extended to 60 consecutive years without a losing mark until the Wildcats went 13-19 in 1988-89 under coach Eddie Sutton. They won 80 percent of their games (1,289-325) in the 60-year stretch. Kentucky had two .500 marks (13-13) in an eight-year span–1966-67 under Adolph Rupp (36th year as UK's coach) and 1973-74 under Joe B. Hall (2nd).

SEASON	W.	L.	PCT.	COACH	LEADING SCORER
1927-28	12	6	.667	John Mauer	Cecil Combs (186 points)
1928-29	12	5	.706	John Mauer	Stan Milward (116)
1929-30	16	3	.842	John Mauer	Cecil Combs (125)
1930-31	15	3	.833	Adolph Rupp	Carey Spicer (190)
1931-32	15	2	.882	Adolph Rupp	Aggie Sale (235)
1932-33	20	3	.870	Adolph Rupp	Aggie Sale (324)
1933-34	16	1	.941	Adolph Rupp	Frenchy DeMoisey (212)
1934-35	19	2	.905	Adolph Rupp	LeRoy Edwards (343)
1935-36	15	6	.714	Adolph Rupp	Ralph Carlisle (241)
1936-37	17	5	.773	Adolph Rupp	Ralph Carlisle (208)
1937-38	13	5	.722	Adolph Rupp	Joe Hagan (184)
1938-39	16	4	.800	Adolph Rupp	Fred Curtis (183)
1939-40	15	6	.714	Adolph Rupp	Mickey Rouse (175)
1940-41	17	8	.680	Adolph Rupp	Jim King (151)
1941-42	19	6	.760	Adolph Rupp	Marvin Akers (191)
1942-43	17	6	.739	Adolph Rupp	Milt Ticco (233)
1943-44	19	2	.905	Adolph Rupp	Bob Brannum (254)
1944-45	22	4	.846	Adolph Rupp	Jack Tingle (293)
1945-46	28	2	.933	Adolph Rupp	Jack Parkinson (11.3 ppg)
1946-47	34	3	.919	Adolph Rupp	Ralph Beard (10.9)
1947-48	36	3	.923	Adolph Rupp	Alex Groza (12.5)
1948-49	32	2	.941	Adolph Rupp	Alex Groza (20.5)
1949-50	25	5	.833	Adolph Rupp	Bill Spivey (19.3)
1950-51	32	2	.941	Adolph Rupp	Bill Spivey (19.2)
1951-52	29	3	.906	Adolph Rupp	Cliff Hagan (21.6)
1953-54	25	0	1.000	Adolph Rupp	Cliff Hagan (24.0)
1954-55	23	3	.885	Adolph Rupp	Bob Burrow (19.0)
1955-56	20	6	.769	Adolph Rupp	Bob Burrow (21.1)
1956-57	23	5	.821	Adolph Rupp	Johnny Cox (19.4)
1957-58	23	6	.793	Adolph Rupp	Vern Hatton (17.1)
1958-59	24	3	.889	Adolph Rupp	Johnny Cox (17.9)
1959-60	18	7	.680	Adolph Rupp	Billy Ray Lickert (14.4)
1960-61	19	9	.679	Adolph Rupp	Billy Ray Lickert (16.0)
1961-62	23	3	.885	Adolph Rupp	Cotton Nash (23.4)
1962-63	16	9	.640	Adolph Rupp	Cotton Nash (20.6)
1963-64	21	6	.778	Adolph Rupp	Cotton Nash (24.0)
1964-65	15	10	.600	Adolph Rupp	Louie Dampier (17.0)
1965-66	27	2	.931	Adolph Rupp	Pat Riley (21.9)
1966-67	13	13	.500	Adolph Rupp	Louie Dampier (20.6)
1967-68	22	5	.815	Adolph Rupp	Mike Casey (20.1)
1968-69	23	5	.821	Adolph Rupp	Dan Issel (26.6)
1969-70	26	2	.929	Adolph Rupp	Dan Issel (33.9)
1970-71	22	6	.786	Adolph Rupp	Tom Parker (17.6)
1971-72	21	7	.750	Adolph Rupp	Jim Andrews (21.5)
1972-73	20	8	.714	Joe B. Hall	Jim Andrews (20.1)
1973-74	13	13	.500	Joe B. Hall	Kevin Grevey (21.9)
1974-75	26	5	.839	Joe B. Hall	Kevin Grevey (23.6)
1975-76	20	10	.667	Joe B. Hall	Jack Givens (20.1)
1976-77	26	4	.867	Joe B. Hall	Jack Givens (18.9)
1977-78	30	2	.938	Joe B. Hall	Jack Givens (18.1)
1978-79	19	12	.613	Joe B. Hall	Kyle Macy (15.2)
1979-80	29	6	.829	Joe B. Hall	Kyle Macy (15.4)
1980-81	22	6	.786	Joe B. Hall	Sam Bowie (17.4)
1981-82	22	8	.733	Joe B. Hall	Derrick Hord (16.3)
1982-83	23	8	.742	Joe B. Hall	Melvin Turpin (15.1)
1983-84	29	5	.853	Joe B. Hall	Melvin Turpin (15.2)
1984-85	18	13	.581	Joe B. Hall	Kenny Walker (22.9)
1985-86	32	4	.889	Eddie Sutton	Kenny Walker (20.0)
1986-87	18	11	.621	Eddie Sutton	Rex Chapman (16.0)
1987-88	27	6	.818	Eddie Sutton	Rex Chapman (19.0)

NOTE: Kentucky was barred from playing competitive basketball during the 1952-53 season because of NCAA probation.

KENTUCKY'S 129-GAME HOMECOURT WINNING STREAK

Kentucky, two nights after losing to Ohio State, 45-40, in its first game in 1943, started a streak that went 11 years without dropping a homecourt game until bowing to Georgia Tech, 59-58, on Jan. 8, 1954. The setback also snapped a 70-game winning streak in SEC competition.

The first 84 of Kentucky's 129 consecutive homecourt victories were in Alumni Gym. The remainder were in Memorial Coliseum.

UK's average margin of victory during the streak was 31 points. Vanderbilt was involved in two of the three closest games–one-point loss in '43 and four-point setback in '50. The only other contest settled by fewer than five points during the streak was a 38-35 verdict against DePauw (Ind.) in 1944.

DATE/HOME GAME	UK	VISITING TEAM	
Jan. 4, 1943	64	Ft. Knox	43
Jan. 26, 1943	39	Vanderbilt	38
Feb. 6, 1943	67	Alabama	41
Feb. 8, 1943	48	Xavier	36
Feb. 13, 1943	53	Tennessee	29
Feb. 15, 1943	58	Georgia Tech	31
Dec. 1, 1943	51	Ft. Knox	18
Dec. 4, 1943	54	Berea (Naval V-12)	40
Dec. 18, 1943	58	Cincinnati	30
Jan. 15, 1944	61	Wright Field	28
Jan. 31, 1944	76	Ft. Knox A.R.C.	48
Feb. 5, 1944	38	DePauw (Ind.)	35
Feb. 7, 1944	51	Illinois	40
Feb. 26, 1944	51	Ohio University	35
Dec. 2, 1944	56	Ft. Knox	23
Dec. 4, 1944	56	Berea (Ky.)	32
Dec. 9, 1944	66	Cincinnati	24
Dec. 23, 1944	53	Ohio State	48
Jan. 6, 1945	59	Ohio University	46
Jan. 8, 1945	75	Arkansas State	6
Jan. 13, 1945	66	Michigan State	35
Jan. 29, 1945	73	Georgia	37
Feb. 3, 1945	51	Georgia Tech	32
Feb. 17, 1945	40	Tennessee	34
Dec. 1, 1945	59	Ft. Knox	36
Dec. 7, 1945	51	Western Ontario	42
Dec. 8, 1945	71	Western Ontario	28
Dec. 15, 1945	67	Cincinnati	31
Dec. 18, 1945	67	Arkansas	42
Dec. 21, 1945	43	Oklahoma	33
Jan. 5, 1946	57	Ohio University	48
Jan. 7, 1946	81	Ft. Benning	25
Jan. 28, 1946	54	Georgia Tech	26
Feb. 5, 1946	59	Michigan State	51
Feb. 16, 1946	54	Tennessee	34
Feb. 23, 1946	83	Xavier	40
Nov. 28, 1946	78	Indiana Central	36
Nov. 30, 1946	64	Tulane	35
Dec. 2, 1946	68	Ft. Knox	31
Dec. 9, 1946	65	Idaho	35
Dec. 14, 1946	83	Texas A&M	18
Dec. 16, 1946	62	Miami of Ohio	49
Dec. 23, 1946	75	Baylor	34
Dec. 28, 1946	96	Wabash (O.)	24
Jan. 4, 1947	46	Ohio University	36
Jan. 11, 1947	70	Dayton	29
Jan. 25, 1947	71	Xavier	34
Jan. 27, 1947	86	Michigan State	36
Feb. 10, 1947	81	Georgia	40
Feb. 15, 1947	61	Tennessee	46
Feb. 17, 1947	63	Alabama	33

Feb. 22, 1947	83	Georgia Tech	46
Nov. 9, 1947	80	Indiana Central	41
Dec. 1, 1947	80	Ft. Knox	41
Dec. 5, 1947	72	Tulsa	18
Dec. 6, 1947	71	Tulsa	22
Dec. 17, 1947	79	Xavier	37
Jan. 3, 1948	98	Western Ontario	41
Jan. 24, 1948	70	Cincinnati	43
Feb. 14, 1948	69	Tennessee	42
Feb. 16, 1948	63	Alabama	33
Feb. 20, 1948	79	Vanderbilt	43
Feb. 21, 1948	78	Georgia Tech	54
Nov. 29, 1948	74	Indiana Central	38
Dec. 10, 1948	81	Tulsa	27
Dec. 13, 1948	76	Arkansas	39
Feb. 8, 1949	71	Tennessee	56
Feb. 12, 1949	96	Xavier	50
Feb. 14, 1949	74	Alabama	32
Feb. 16, 1949	85	Mississippi	31
Feb. 19, 1949	78	Georgia Tech	32
Feb. 21, 1949	95	Georgia	40
Feb. 26, 1949	70	Vanderbilt	37
Dec. 3, 1949	84	Indiana Central	61
Dec. 10, 1949	90	Western Ontario	18
Jan. 9, 1950	83	North Carolina	44
Jan. 28, 1950	88	Georgia	56
Feb. 11, 1950	79	Tennessee	52
Feb. 13, 1950	77	Alabama	57
Feb. 15, 1950	90	Mississippi	50
Feb. 18, 1950	97	Georgia Tech	62
Feb. 23, 1950	58	Xavier	53
Feb. 25, 1950	70	Vanderbilt	66
Dec. 1, 1950	73	West Texas State	43
Dec. 9, 1950	70	Purdue	52
Dec. 14, 1950	85	Florida	37
Dec. 16, 1950	68	Kansas	39
Jan. 5, 1951	79	Auburn	35
Jan. 8, 1951	63	DePaul	55
Jan. 13, 1951	65	Alabama	48
Jan. 15, 1951	69	Notre Dame	44
Feb. 9, 1951	75	Georgia Tech	42
Feb. 13, 1951	78	Xavier	51
Feb. 17, 1951	86	Tennessee	61
Feb. 23, 1951	88	Georgia	41
Feb. 24, 1951	89	Vanderbilt	57
Mar. 13, 1951	97	Loyola of Chicago	61
Dec. 8, 1951	96	Washington & Lee	46
Dec. 17, 1951	81	St. John's	40
Dec. 20, 1951	98	DePaul	60
Dec. 26, 1951	84	UCLA	53
Jan. 5, 1952	57	Louisiana State	47
Jan. 7, 1952	83	Xavier	50
Jan. 12, 1952	99	Florida	52
Feb. 4, 1952	103	Tulane	54
Feb. 6, 1952	81	Mississippi	61
Feb. 9, 1952	93	Georgia Tech	42
Feb. 11, 1952	110	Mississippi State	66
Feb. 16, 1952	95	Tennessee	40
Feb. 21, 1952	75	Vanderbilt	45
Dec. 5, 1953	86	Temple	59
Dec. 14, 1953	101	Wake Forest	69
Dec. 21, 1953	85	Duke	69
Dec. 22, 1953	73	La Salle	60
Dec. 28, 1953	74	Minnesota	59
Jan. 4, 1953	77	Xavier	71
Jan. 9, 1953	105	Georgia Tech	53
Jan. 11, 1953	81	DePaul	63
Jan. 16, 1953	94	Tulane	43
Feb. 4, 1953	106	Georgia	55
Feb. 13, 1953	88	Mississippi	62
Feb. 15, 1953	81	Mississippi State	49
Feb. 18, 1953	90	Tennessee	63
Feb. 22, 1953	100	Vanderbilt	64
Dec. 4, 1953	74	Louisiana State	58
Dec. 18, 1953	79	Temple	61
Dec. 21, 1953	70	Utah	65
Dec. 22, 1953	63	La Salle	54
Dec. 30, 1953	82	St. Louis	65

Note: Kentucky was barred from playing competitive basketball during the 1952-53 season because of NCAA probation.

MOST VICTORIES IN A SINGLE SEASON

Neither Duke nor UNLV won the NCAA Tournament championship when they set the NCAA single-season record of 37 victories in back-to-back years. Both schools benefitted from playing extra games in the Preseason NIT.

Duke's three defeats were by a total of 13 points and UNLV's two setbacks were by a total of five points. Their reversals are in bold.

DUKE, (37-3 IN 1985-86)
COACH: MIKE KRZYZEWSKI

HOME: 15-0	ROAD: 11-2	NEUTRAL: 11-1

DUKE	OPPONENT
66	Lamar* 62
66	Alabama-Birmingham* 54
84	at William & Mary 61
71	at St. JohnÕs 70
92	Kansas* 86
98	East Carolina 66
84	at Vanderbilt 74
72	Virginia 64
69	at Davidson 52
88	Appalachian State 46
78	Northwestern 55
81	at Maryland 75
84	St. Louis 58
74	North Carolina State 64
87	at St. Joseph's 66
92	Wake Forest 63
92	**at North Carolina 95**
80	**at Georgia Tech 87**
80	Maryland 68
89	Harvard 52
89	Clemson 78
68	at Wake Forest 58
77	at Virginia 65
75	Georgia Tech 59
85	at Stetson 66
72	at North Carolina State 70
75	Notre Dame 74
104	Miami (Fla.) 82
93	Oklahoma 84
77	at Clemson 69
82	North Carolina 74

ACC TOURNAMENT

68	Wake Forest* 60
75	Virginia* 70
68	Georgia Tech* 67

NCAA TOURNAMENT

85	Miss. Valley State* 78
89	Old Dominion* 61
74	DePaul* 67
71	Navy* 50
71	Kansas* 67
69	**Louisville* 72**

*Neutral court games.

UNLV, (37-2 IN 1986-87)
COACH: JERRY TARKANIAN

HOME: 16-0	ROAD: 12-1	NEUTRAL: 9-1

UNLV	OPPONENT
92	Arizona 87
90	Oklahoma 81
78	Temple* 76
96	Western Kentucky* (2OT) 95
80	at Memphis State 77
99	at Nevada-Reno 88
115	Nevada-Reno 83
105	Ohio University 81
79	Louisiana Tech 75
103	Old Dominion 83
104	Navy 79
114	UC Irvine 72
89	San Jose State 77
117	Utah State 94
88	at UC Santa Barbara 74
88	**at Oklahoma 89**
73	at Cal State Fullerton 65
104	Long Beach State 74
85	New Mexico State 58
106	Fresno State 58
114	at UC Irvine 103
104	at Auburn 85
113	at Utah State 74
83	at San Jose State 74
73	at Pacific 59
74	Cal State Fullerton 64
86	UC Santa Barbara 76
86	at Long Beach State 66
80	at New Mexico State 69
82	Pacific 59
70	at Fresno State 59

BIG WEST TOURNAMENT

105	Long Beach State* 70
99	Cal State Fullerton* 65
94	San Jose State* 69

NCAA TOURNAMENT

95	Idaho State* 61
80	Kansas State* 78
92	Wyoming* 78
84	Iowa* 81
93	**Indiana* 97**

*Neutral court games.

19

STATISTICAL ODDS & ENDS

Longest streaks.... 1,000-point scorers.... Coaches who never had a losing record.... Winless teams.... Freshman statistics.... There are an abundance of statistics that just don't fit in anywhere, but are nonetheless valuable to the college basketball fanatic. These are statistics to wow your friends while downing a cold one at the local pub. They can answer a radio trivia question, thereby winning that ever-popular pizza "from our friends at...." They can rekindle memories of your favorite player from alma-mater days gone by. These are the statistical odds and ends of roundball.

PLAYERS WITH MORE THAN 900 POINTS IN EACH OF THREE SEASONS

Oscar Robertson, Cincinnati

1957–58	984 pts.
1958–59	978 pts.
1959–60	1,011 pts.

Pete Maravich, Louisiana State

1967–68	1,138 pts.
1968–69	1,148 pts.
1969–70	1,381 pts.

Larry Bird, Indiana State

1976–77	918 pts.
1977–78	959 pts.
1978–79	973 pts.

PLAYERS WHO AVERAGED MORE THAN 30 POINTS PER GAME IN EACH OF THREE SEASONS

Oscar Robertson, Cincinnati

1957–58	35.1 pts.
1958–59	32.6 pts.
1959–60	33.7 pts.

Pete Maravich, Louisiana State

1967–68	43.8 pts.
1968–69	44.2 pts.
1969–70	44.5 pts.

Freeman Williams, Portland State

1976–77	30.9 pts.
1977–78	38.8 pts.
1978–79	35.9 pts.

PLAYERS WHO AVERAGED 20 OR MORE POINTS PER GAME IN EACH OF FOUR SEASONS

George Dalton, John Carroll

1951–52	20.2 pts.
1952–53	24.8 pts.
1953–54	24.3 pts.
1954–55	23.9 pts.

Dickie Hemric, Wake Forest

1951–52	22.4 pts.
1952–53	24.9 pts.
1953–54	24.3 pts.
1954–55	27.6 pts.

Calvin Natt, Northeast Louisiana

1975–76	20.6 pts.
1976–77	29.0 pts.
1977–78	21.3 pts.
1978–79	24.4 pts.

Michael Brooks, La Salle

1976–77	20.0 pts.
1977–78	24.9 pts.
1978–79	23.3 pts.
1979–80	24.1 pts.

Ronnie Perry, Holy Cross

1976–77	23.0 pts.
1977–78	21.7 pts.
1978–79	25.0 pts.
1979–80	22.9 pts.

Andrew Toney, Southwestern Louisiana

1976–77	21.0 pts.
1977–78	24.5 pts.
1978–79	23.3 pts.
1979–80	26.1 pts.

Harry Kelly, Texas Southern

1979–80	29.0 pts.
1980–81	23.7 pts.
1981–82	29.7 pts.
1982–83	28.8 pts.

Lionel Simmons, La Salle

1986–87	20.3 pts.
1987–88	23.3 pts.
1988–89	28.4 pts.
1989–90	26.5 pts.

Alphonso Ford, Mississippi Valley St.

1989–90	29.9 pts.
1990–91	32.7 pts.
1991–92	27.5 pts.
1992–93	26.0 pts.

Note: Toney, Kelly, Simmons, and Ford are the only players to score more than 600 points in each of four seasons.

PLAYERS WITH AT LEAST 4,000 CAREER POINTS AND REBOUNDS

PLAYER, SCHOOL	YEARS	PTS.	REB.	TOTAL
Tom Gola, La Salle	1952–55	2,462	2,201	4,663
Lionel Simmons, La Salle	1987–90	3,217	1,429	4,646
Elvin Hayes, Houston	1966–68	2,884	1,602	4,486
Dickie Hemric, Wake Forest	1952–55	2,587	1,802	4,389
Oscar Robertson, Cincinnati	1958–60	2,973	1,338	4,311
Joe Holup, George Washington	1953–56	2,226	2,030	4,256
Pete Maravich, Louisiana St.	1968–70	3,667	528	4,195
Harry Kelly, Texas Southern	1980–83	3,066	1,085	4,151
Danny Manning, Kansas	1985–88	2,951	1,187	4,138
Larry Bird, Indiana State	1977–79	2,850	1,247	4,097
Elgin Baylor, CI/Seattle	1956–58	2,500	1,559	4,059
Michael Brooks, La Salle	1977–80	2,628	1,372	4,000

PERCENTAGE OF TEAM'S POINTS SCORED IN A SINGLE SEASON

PLAYER, SCHOOL	POINTS	SEASON	PCT.
Pete Maravich, Louisiana St.	1148/2316	1968–69	49.57%
Pete Maravich, Louisiana St.	1138/2308	1967–68	49.31%
Kevin Houston, Army	953/1957	1986–87	48.69%
Pete Maravich, Louisiana St.	1381/2985	1969–70	46.26%
Bill McGill, Utah	1009/2206	1961–62	45.73%
Frank Selvy, Furman	1209/2658	1953–54	45.49%
Arnold Short, Oklahoma City	696/1540	1953–54	45.19%
Dave Jamerson, Ohio University	874/1979	1989–90	44.16%
Vin Baker, Hartford	745/1704	1991–92	43.72%
Howard Komives, Bowling Green	844/1931	1963–64	43.71%
Freeman Williams, Portland St.	969/2217	1977–78	43.70%
Calvin Murphy, Niagara	916/2104	1967–68	43.54%
Freeman Williams, Portland St.	1010/2338	1976–77	43.20%
Bill Bradley, Princeton	936/2176	1963–64	43.01%

SCHOOLS WITH SEVEN PLAYERS ON THE SAME TEAM AVERAGING MORE THAN 10 POINTS PER GAME

SCHOOL (SEASON)	PLAYERS
Southern, La. (1987-88)	Kevin Florent (21)
	Darryl Battles (15.1)
	Derwyn Johnson (13.6)
	Avery Johnson (11.4)
	Patrick Garner (10.7)
	Carlos Sample (10.6)
	Rod Washington (10.5)
Troy State, Ala. (1995-96)	Rhodney Donaldson (16.3)
	Jermaine Ball (14.7)
	Jeff Black (13.2)
	Patrick Minifield (12.8)
	Matt Padgett (11.5)
	Derrick Bristol (11.4)
	Fred Spencer (10.6)

SCHOOLS WITH FOUR TEAMMATES AVERAGING OVER 17 POINTS PER GAME

SCHOOL (SEASON)	PLAYERS (PPG)
Iowa (1969-70)	John Johnson (27.9)
	Chad Calabria (19.1)
	Fred Brown (17.9)
	Glenn Vidnovic (17.3)
Loyola Marymount (1987-88)	Hank Gathers (22.5)
	Bo Kimble (22.2)
	Mike Yoest (17.6)
	Corey Gaines (17.4)

SCHOOLS WITH THREE TEAMMATES AVERAGING AT LEAST 20 POINTS PER GAME

SCHOOL (SEASON)	PLAYERS (PPG)
Marshall (1955–56)	Charlie Slack (22.5)
	Cebe Price (21.2)
	Paul Underwood (20.2)
Ohio State (1969–70)	Dave Sorenson (24.2)
	Jim Cleamons (21.6)
	Jody Finney (20.6)
Loyola Marymount (1989–90)	Bo Kimble (35.3)
	Hank Gathers (29)
	Jeff Fryer (22.7)
Georgia Tech (1989–90)	Dennis Scott (27.7)
	Brian Oliver (21.3)
	Kenny Anderson (20.6)
Iowa State (1993–94)	Loren Meyer (22.3)
	Fred Hoiberg (20.2)
	Julius Michalik (20)

SCHOOLS WITH TWO TEAMMATES AVERAGING AT LEAST 25 POINTS PER GAME

SCHOOL (SEASON)	PLAYERS (PPG)
Mississippi State (1956–57)	Jim Ashmore (28.3)
	Bailey Howell (25.9)
Oklahoma City (1972–73)	Ozzie Edwards (28.4)
	Marvin Rich (25.3)
Tennessee (1975–76)	Ernie Grunfeld (25.3)
	Bernard King (25.2)
Loyola Marymount (1989–90)	Bo Kimble (35.3)
	Hank Gathers (29)

PERCENTAGE OF TEAM'S POINTS SCORED IN A CAREER

PLAYER, SCHOOL	POINTS	SEASON	PCT.
Pete Maravich, Louisiana St.	3667/7609	1967-70	48.19%
Wilt Chamberlain, Kansas	1433/3492	1956-58	41.04%
Bill Bradley, Princeton	2503/6320	1962-65	39.60%
Oscar Roberston, Cincinnati	2973/7543	1986-87	39.41%
Calvin Murphy, Niagara	2548/6585	1967-70	38.69%
Frank Burgess, Gonzaga	2196/5782	1958-61	37.98%
Elgin Baylor, CI/Seattle	2500/6617	1954-58	37.78%

PLAYERS WITH THE HIGHEST SCORING AVERAGES AS A SENIOR

PLAYER, SCHOOL	SEASON	AVG.
Pete Maravich, Louisiana State	1969-70	44.5
Frank Selvy, Furman	1953-54	41.7
Billy McGill, Utah	1961-62	38.8
Austin Carr, Notre Dame	1970-71	38.0
Kevin Bradshaw, U.S. International	1990-91	37.6
Rick Barry, Miami (Fla.)	1964-65	37.4

PLAYERS WITH THE HIGHEST SCORING AVERAGES AS A JUNIOR

PLAYER, SCHOOL	SEASON	AVG.
Pete Maravich, Louisiana State	1968-69	44.2
Freeman Williams, Portland State	1976-77	38.8
Austin Carr, Notre Dame	1969-70	38.1
Dwight Lamar, Southwestern La.	1971-72	36.3
Richie Fuqua, Oral Roberts	1971-72	36.2

PLAYERS WITH THE HIGHEST SCORING AVERAGES AS A SOPHOMORE

PLAYER, SCHOOL	SEASON	AVG.
Pete Maravich, Louisiana State	1967-68	43.8
Johnny Neumann, Mississippi	1970-71	40.1
Calvin Murphy, Niagara	1967-68	38.2
Oscar Robertson, Cincinnati	1957-58	35.1
Larry Fogle, Canisius	1973-74	33.4

PLAYERS WITH 1,000 OR MORE POINTS AT TWO DIVISION I SCHOOLS

PLAYER	SCHOOL (POINTS, YEARS)
Jon Manning 1978-79	Oklahoma City (1,039 points in 1974-75 and 1975-76) North Texas State (1,090 points in 1977-78 and
Kenny Battle	Northern Illinois (1,072 points in 1984-85 and 1985-86) Illinois (1,112 points in 1987-88 and 1988-89)

Note: Manning is the only player to score more than 40 points for two different schools against Division I opponents—43 for OCU against Tulsa on January 20, 1975, and 41 for North Texas against Baylor on December 4, 1978.

MOST GAMES WITH 40 OR MORE POINTS VS. DIVISION I OPPONENTS

GAMES	PLAYER, SCHOOL (YEARS)
56	Pete Maravich, Louisiana State (1968-70)
21	Oscar Robertson, Cincinnati (1958-60)
21	Austin Carr, Notre Dame (1969-71)
16	Freeman Williams, Portland State (1975-78)
15	Elvin Hayes, Houston (1966-68)
14	Calvin Murphy, Niagara (1968-70)
14	Larry Bird, Indiana State (1977-79)

MOST POINTS FOR TWO TEAMMATES IN SAME GAME

92	Kevin Bradshaw (72) and Isaac Brown (20), U.S. International vs. Loyola Marymount, 12-5-90
91	Randy Woods (46) and Doug Overton (45), La Salle vs. Loyola Marymount, 12-31-90
91	Ronnie Schmitz (51) and Tony Dumas (40), Missouri-Kansas City vs. U.S. International, 3-4-91

MOST POINTS FOR TWO OPPOSING PLAYERS IN SAME GAME

115	Pete Maravich, Louisiana State (64), and Dan Issel, Kentucky (51), 2-21-70
109	Calvin Murphy, Niagara (68), and Bill Smith, Syracuse (41), 12-7-68
108	Chris Jackson, Louisiana State (55), and Gerald Glass, Mississippi (53), 3-4-89
101	Bo Kimble, Loyola Marymount (53), and Gary Payton, Oregon State (48), 12-19-89
100	Johnny Neumann, Mississippi (63), and Al Sanders, Louisiana State (37), 1-30-71

MOST POINTS FOR THREE TEAMMATES IN SAME GAME

120	Randy Woods (46), Doug Overton (45), and Jack Hurd (29), La Salle vs. Loyola Marymount, 12-31-90
118	Brent Price (56), Kermit Holmes (34), and Jeff Webster (28), Oklahoma vs. Loyola Marymount, 12-15-90

MOST PLAYERS WITH 40 OR MORE POINTS IN SAME GAME

3	Doug Spradley, Gonzaga (40), Hank Gathers, Loyola Marymount (40), and Bo Kimble, Loyola Marymount (40), 2-18-89
3	Ronnie Schmitz, UMKC (51), Tony Dumas, UMKC (40), and Kevin Bradshaw, U.S. International (43), 3-4-91

20/20 CLUB

Seven players have averaged at least 20 points and 20 rebounds per game in their careers (minimum of two seasons).

PLAYER	SCHOOL	SEASONS (CAREER AVERAGES)
Walt Dukes	Seton Hall	1952 and 1953 (23.5 ppg, 21.1 rpg)

Bill Russell	San Francisco	1954–56 (20.7 ppg, 20.3 rpg)
Elgin Baylor	College of Idaho and Seattle	1955, 1957, and 1958 (31.3 ppg, 20 rpg)
Paul Silas	Creighton	1962–64 (20.5 ppg, 21.6 rpg)
Julius Erving	Massachusetts	1970 and 1971 (26.3 ppg, 20.2 rpg)
Artis Gilmore	Jacksonville	1970 and 1971 (24.3 ppg, 22.7 rpg)
Kermit Washington	American	1971–73 (20.1 ppg, 20.2 rpg)

MOST POINTS IN A SEASON BY A FRESHMAN

PLAYER, TEAM	YEAR	G.	FG	3FG	FT	PTS.
Chris Jackson, Louisiana St.	1989	32	359	84	163	965
James Williams, Austin Peay	1973	29	360	–	134	854
Wayman Tisdale, Oklahoma	1983	33	338	–	134	810
Mark Aguirre, DePaul	1979	32	302	–	163	767
Harry Kelly, Texas Southern	1980	26	313	–	127	753

HIGHEST SEASON SCORING AVERAGE BY A FRESHMAN

PLAYER, TEAM	YEAR	G.	FG	3FG	FT	PTS.	AVG.
Chris Jackson, Louisiana St.	1989	32	359	84	163	965	30.2
James Williams, Austin Peay St.	1973	29	360	–	134	854	29.4
Harry Kelly, Texas Southern	1980	26	313	–	127	753	29.0
Bernard King, Tennessee	1975	25	273	–	115	661	26.4
Jacky Dorsey, Georgia	1975	25	267	–	112	646	25.8

HIGHEST SEASON FIELD-GOAL PERCENTAGE BY A FRESHMAN

PLAYER, TEAM	YEAR	G.	FG	FGA	PCT.
Sidney Moncrief, Arkansas	1976	28	149	224	66.5
Gary Trent, Ohio	1993	27	194	298	65.1
Ed Pinckney, Villanova	1982	32	169	264	64.0
Jimmy Lunsford, Alabama State	1993	22	142	223	63.7
Alexander Kovi, GWU	1995	32	160	253	63.2
Cedric Robinson, Nicholls St.	1983	24	146	231	63.2

HIGHEST SEASON THREE-POINT FIELD-GOAL PERCENTAGE BY A FRESHMAN

PLAYER, TEAM	YEAR	G.	3FG	3FGA	PCT.
Jay Edwards, Indiana	1988	23	59	110	53.6
Ross Richardson, LMU	1991	25	61	116	52.6
Lance Barker, Valparaiso	1992	26	61	117	52.1
Ed Peterson, Yale	1989	28	53	104	51.0
Willie Brand, UTA	1988	29	65	128	50.8

MOST THREE-POINT FIELD GOALS IN A SEASON BY A FRESHMAN

PLAYER, TEAM	YEAR	G.	3FG	AVG.
Keith Veney, Lamar	1993	27	106	3.93
Alphonso Ford, Miss. Valley	1990	27	104	3.85
Troy Green, SE Louis.	1996	27	98	3.63
Tony Ross, San Diego State	1987	28	104	3.71
Ronnie Schmitz, UMKC	1990	28	90	3.21

HIGHEST SEASON FREE-THROW PERCENTAGE BY A FRESHMAN

PLAYER, TEAM	YEAR	G.	FT	FTA	PCT.
Jim Barton, Dartmouth	1986	26	65	69	94.2
Steve Alford, Indiana	1984	31	137	150	91.3
Jay Edwards, Indiana	1988	23	69	76	90.8
LaBradford Smith, Louisville	1988	35	143	158	90.5
Geoff Billet, Rutgers	1996	26	72	80	90.0

MOST REBOUNDS IN A SEASON BY A FRESHMAN

PLAYER, TEAM	YEAR	G.	REB.
Pete Padgett, Nevada-Reno	1973	26	462
Kenny Miller, Loyola (Ill.)	1988	29	395
Shaquille O'Neal, LSU	1990	32	385
Ralph Sampson, Virginia	1980	34	381
Adonal Foyle, Colgate	1995	30	371

HIGHEST SEASON REBOUND AVERAGE BY A FRESHMAN

PLAYER, TEAM	YEAR	G.	REB.	AVG.
Pete Padgett, Nevada-Reno	1973	26	462	17.8
Glenn Mosley, Seton Hall	1974	21	299	14.2
Ira Terrell, SMU	1973	25	352	14.1
Kenny Miller, Loyola (Ill.)	1988	29	395	13.6
Bob Stephens, Drexel	1976	23	307	13.3
Michael Cage, San Diego State	1981	27	355	13.1

MOST ASSISTS IN A SEASON BY A FRESHMAN

PLAYER, TEAM	YEAR	G.	AST.
Bobby Hurley, Duke	1990	38	288
Kenny Anderson, Georgia Tech	1990	35	285
Andre LaFleur, Northeastern	1984	32	252
Orlando Smart, San Francisco	1991	29	237
Chris Corchiani, N.C. State	1988	32	235

HIGHEST SEASON ASSIST AVERAGE BY A FRESHMAN

PLAYER, TEAM	YEAR	G.	AST.	AVG.
Orlando Smart, San Francisco	1991	29	237	8.17
Kenny Anderson, Georgia Tech	1990	35	285	8.14
Taurence Chisholm, Delaware	1985	28	224	8.00
Andre LaFleur, Northeastern	1984	32	252	7.88
Marc Brown, Siena	1988	29	222	7.66
Jason Kidd, California	1993	29	222	7.66

MOST BLOCKED SHOTS IN A SEASON BY A FRESHMAN

PLAYER, TEAM	YEAR	G.	BLK.
Shawn Bradley, Brigham Young	1991	34	177
Alonzo Mourning, Georgetown	1989	34	169
Shaquille O'Neal, LSU	1990	32	115
Adonal Foyle, Colgate	1995	30	147
Keith Closs, Central Conn.	1995	26	139
Tim Duncan, Wake Forest	1994	33	124

HIGHEST SEASON BLOCKED SHOT AVERAGE BY A FRESHMAN

PLAYER, TEAM	YEAR	G.	BLK.	AVG.
Keith Closs, Central Conn.	1995	26	139	5.35
Shawn Bradley, Brigham Young	1991	34	177	5.21
Alonzo Mourning, Georgetown	1989	34	169	4.97
Adonal Foyle, Colgate	1995	30	147	4.90
Tim Duncan, Wake Forest	1994	33	124	3.76

MOST STEALS IN A SEASON BY A FRESHMAN

PLAYER, TEAM	YEAR	G.	ST.
Nadav Henefeld, Connecticut	1990	37	138
Jason Kidd, California	1993	29	110
Eric Murdock, Providence	1988	28	90
Pat Baldwin, Northwestern	1991	28	90
Clarence Ceasar, LSU	1992	31	90

HIGHEST SEASON STEAL AVERAGE BY A FRESHMAN

PLAYER, TEAM	YEAR	G.	ST.	AVG.
Jason Kidd, California	1993	29	110	3.79
Nadav Henefeld, Connecticut	1990	37	138	3.73
Ben Larson, Cal. Poly SLO	1996	29	100	3.45
Eric Murdock, Providence	1988	28	90	3.21
Pat Baldwin, Northwestern	1991	28	90	3.21
Jeff Myers, St. Francis (N.Y.)	1993	26	81	3.12

CENTERS OF ATTENTION

A statistical comparison of celebrated college centers sheds some light as to their impact. Here is how some of the premier pivotmen stack up statistically (winning percentages of their respective schools during their tenures are in parentheses):

STANDOUT CENTER, SCHOOL	COLLEGE CAREER AVERAGES
Lew Alcindor, UCLA (.978)	26.4 ppg, 15.5 rpg, 63.9 FG%
Bill Walton, UCLA (.956)	20.3 ppg, 15.7 rpg, 65.1 FG%
Bill Russell, San Francisco (.899)	20.7 ppg, 20.3 rpg, 51.6 FG%
Hakeem Olajuwon, Houston (.846)	13.3 ppg, 10.7 rpg, 63.9 FG%
Bob Lanier, St. Bonaventure (.844)	27.6 ppg, 15.7 rpg, 57.6 FG%
Pat Ewing, Georgetown (.8403)	15.3 ppg, 9.2 rpg, 62.0 FG%
Wilt Chamberlain, Kansas (.840)	29.9 ppg, 18.3 rpg, 47.0 FG%
Ralph Sampson, Virginia (.830)	16.9 ppg, 11.4 rpg, 56.8 FG%
David Robinson, Navy (.809)	21.0 ppg, 10.3 rpg, 61.3 FG%
Alonzo Mourning, Georgetown (.729)	16.7 ppg, 8.6 rpg, 56.6 FG%
Shaquille O'Neal, Louisiana State (.688)	21.6 ppg, 13.5 rpg, 61.0 FG%

WINNERS FROM THE START

Eight players have been members of teams that won a state high school championship, NCAA Tournament, and NBA title.

PLAYER HIGH SCHOOL	COLLEGE NBA TEAM
Lucius Allen Wyandotte (Kansas City, Mo.), 1965	UCLA, 1967-68 Milwaukee, 1971
Quinn Buckner Thornridge (Phoenix, Ill.), 1971-72	Indiana, 1976 Boston, 1984
Magic Johnson Lansing (Mich.), 1977	Michigan State, 1979 Los Angeles, 1980-82-85-87-88
Jerry Lucas Middletown (Ohio), 1958	Ohio State, 1960 New York, 1973
Rodney McCray Mt. Vernon (N.Y.), 1978-79	Louisville, 1980 Chicago, 1993
Rick Robey Brother Martin (New Orleans, La.), 1974	Kentucky, 1978 Boston, 1981
Billy Thompson Camden (N.J.), 1982	Louisville, 1986 Los Angeles, 1987-88
Milt Wagner Camden (N.J.), 1979	Louisville, 1986 Los Angeles, 1988

Notes: Buckner (1976 in Montreal), Johnson (1992 in Barcelona), and Lucas (1960 in Rome) constitute the unique group that also won an Olympic gold medal. McCray was a member of the 1980 U.S. team that boycotted the XXIInd Olympiad in Moscow after the Soviet Union's invasion of Afghanistan.

THE WIN CROWD

Twenty victories in a season has been a benchmark of success. But the parameters have been altered somewhat over the years with the advent of additional games on schedules and more pressure to win.

What would the select group of coaches look like if the standard of undeniable success in a season was increased to 25 triumphs? Here are the 11 major-college coaches with at least eight 25-win campaigns through 1995–96:

COACH (YEARS)	25-WIN SEASONS
*Dean Smith (33)	20
*Jerry Tarkanian (24)	12
John Wooden (29)	12
Ed Diddle (42)	11
*Jim Boeheim (18)	10
Hank Iba (41)	10
Adolph Rupp (41)	10
*Eddie Sutton (24)	9
Everett Case (19)	8
*Bob Knight (29)	8
Guy Lewis (30)	8

* Denotes active coaches.

WINNERS ALL THE WAY

Five major-college coaches had winning marks in college careers spanning more than 20 years through 1994.

COACH (SEASONS)	CLOSEST TO NON-WINNING RECORD
John Wooden (29)	14-12 with UCLA in 1959–60
Lou Carnesecca (24)	17-12 with St. John's in 1987–88
*Jerry Tarkanian (24)	16-12 with UNLV in 1980–81
Peck Hickman (23)	13-12 with Louisville in 1957–58
Ben Jobe (23)	12-10 with Alabama A&M in 1984–85

* Tarkanian also compiled seven more winning records in as many seasons for two community colleges in California, where he won five consecutive state championships after notching a 14-13 mark in 1961–62 at Riverside City College to begin his coaching odyssey.

EARLY ACHIEVERS–THE YOUNGEST TO COACH IN DIVISION I

NAME	SCHOOL YRS.	BIRTHDATE M.	FIRST GAME D.
Phog Allen	Kansas 22	11-18-1885 0	12-13-07 25
Branch McCracken	Ball State 22	06-09-08 5	12-06-30 27
Stan Morrison	Pacific 23	10-15-49 1	11-30-72 15
Bob Knight	Army 25	10-25-40 1	12-04-65 9
Rick Pitino	Boston Univ. 26	9-18-52 2	11-28-78 10
Fran McCaffery	Lehigh 26	5-26-59 5	1-25-85 29
John Griffin	Siena 26	5-17-56 6	11-27-82 10
Jim Valvano	Bucknell 26	3-10-46 8	12-02-72 22
Tates Locke	Army 26	2-26-37 9	12-04-63 8
Jack Armstrong	Niagara 26	N/A N/A	N/A N/A
Bob Davies	Seton Hall 26	1-15-20 N/A	12-02-46 N/A

Note: In the small college ranks, Allen was only 20 when he coached Baker in 1905, Valvano was 22 when he coached Johns Hopkins in 1968 and active coach Eldon Miller was only 23 when he coached Wittenberg in 1962.

RAGS TO RICHES

Here is a chronological list of the six coaches to go unbeaten in league competition the year after their school posted a losing conference record, since the start of national tournament competition:

SCHOOL (COACH)	UNDEFEATED LEAGUE	CONFERENCE REG.-SEASON	RECORD PREVIOUS SEASON
Iowa (Ralph Miller)			
	Big Ten	14-0 in '70	5-9 in '69 (T8th)
South Alabama (Cliff Ellis)			
	Sun Belt	10-0 in '79	3-7 in '78 (4th)
Northeastern (Jim Calhoun)			
	N. Atlantic	14-0 in '84	4-6 in '83 (6th)
Temple (John Chaney)			
	Atlantic 10	18-0 in '84	5-9 in '83 (E3d)
Loyola Marymount (Paul Westhead)			
	WCC	14-0 in '88	4-10 in '87 (8th)
Missouri (Norm Stewart)			
	Big Eight	14-0 in '94	5-9 in '93 (7th)

DOUBLE DUTY

Only five men have both played for and coached teams in the Final Four.

	FINAL FOUR EXPERIENCE	
NAME	AS PLAYER	AS HEAD COACH
Vic Bubas	N.C. State (1950)	Duke (1963-64-66)
Dick Harp	Kansas (1940)	Kansas (1957)
Bob Knight	Ohio St. (1960-61-62)	Indiana (1973-76-81-87-92)
Bones McKinney*	North Carolina (1946)	Wake Forest (1962)
Dean Smith	Kansas (1952-53)	N.C. (1967-68-69-72-77-81-82-91-93)

* McKinney played two seasons for North Carolina State prior to World War II military duty.

TRIPLE CROWN

Three coaches have won championships in the NCAA Tournament, NIT, and Summer Olympics.

COACH	NCAA	NIT	OLYMPICS (SITE)
Bob Knight	1976-81-87	1979	1984 (Los Angeles)
Pete Newell	1959	1949	1960 (Rome)
Dean Smith	1982	1971	1976 (Montreal)

Note: Knight and Smith won their NCAA and NIT titles with Indiana and North Carolina, respectively. Newell won the NCAA championship with California after capturing the NIT with San Francisco.

REGAL ROOKIES

Six coaches earned trips to the Final Four in their first college season.

FIRST-YEAR COACH	FINAL FOUR RECORD	TEAM (FINISH)	PREDECESSOR
Ray Meyer	19-5	DePaul '43 (T3d)	Bill Wendt
Gary Thompson	21-9	Wichita State '65 (4th)	Ralph Miller
Denny Crum	26-5	Louisville '72 (4th)	John Dromo
Bill Hodges	33-1	Indiana State '79 (2d)	Bob King
Larry Brown	22-10	UCLA '80 (2d)	Gary Cunningham
Steve Fisher	*6-0	Michigan '89 (1st)	Bill Frieder

* Michigan finished with an overall record of 30-7 after Fisher succeeded Frieder just before the start of the NCAA Tournament.

SCHOOLS WITH FOUR ACTIVE PLAYERS WITH OVER 1,200 POINTS

SEASON	SCHOOL	PLAYERS	GAMES	POINTS
1984–85	Alcorn State	Aaron Brandon	120	1,740
		Michael Phelps	114	1,664
		Tommy Collier	117	1,350
		Eddie Archer	120	1,248
1987–88	Southern Mississippi	Randolph Keys	121	1,626
		Casoy Fisher	121	1,599
		Derrick Hamilton	106	1,445
		John White	117	1,331
1990–91	UNLV	Stacey Augmon	145	2,011
		Greg Anthony	138	1,738
		Anderson Hunt*	109	1,632
		Larry Johnson	75	1,617
1990–91	Arkansas	Todd Day*	105	1,895
		Ron Huery	134	1,545
		Lee Mayberry*	105	1,422
		Oliver Miller*	103	1,216
1994-95	Coppin State	Sidney Goodman	119	1,416
		Stephen Stewart	90	1,393
		Keith Carmichael	118	1,315
		Tariq Saunders	112	1,220

* Denotes juniors.

SCHOOLS WITH FIVE ACTIVE PLAYERS WITH OVER 1,000 POINTS

SEASON	SCHOOL	PLAYERS	GAMES	POINTS
1986–87	Alabama1	Derrick McKey*	99	1,231
		Terry Coner	120	1,214
		Jim Farmer	111	1,197
		Mark Gottfried	126	1,061
		James Jackson	121	1,367
1990–91	East Tennessee State	Keith Jennings	127	1,988
		Greg Dennis	96	1,702
		Calvin Talford*	96	1,386
		Alvin West	126	1,115

1992–93	Florida State	Major Geer	126	1,094
		Doug Edwards	93	1,604
		Sam Cassell	66	1,211
		Rodney Dobard	122	1,058
		Chuck Graham	94	1,055
		Bob Sura**	65	1,055

* Denotes junior eligibility. **Denotes sophomore eligibility.

1. Gottfried and Jackson, transfers from other four-year schools, are listed but neither scored scored over 1,000 at Alabama. Their point totals include points scored at their previous school—Gottfried played one year at Oral Roberts and Jackson played two seasons at West Texas State. At Alabama, Gottfried scored 854 points and Jackson scored 354.

SCHOOLS WITH THREE OR MORE ACTIVE PLAYERS WITH OVER 1,500 POINTS

SEASON	SCHOOL	PLAYERS	GAMES	POINTS
1985–86	Duke	Johnny Dawkins	133	2,537
		Mark Alarie	133	2,136
		David Henderson	128	1,561
1980–81	Maryland	Albert King	118	2,058
		Ernest Graham	118	1,607
		Greg Manning	118	1,561
1989–90	Pepperdine[1]	Tom Lewis	114	2,050
		Craig Davis	121	1,619
		Dexter Howard	120	1,546
1989–90	Loyola Marymount[2]	Hank Gathers	117	2,723
		Bo Kimble	104	2,350
		Jeff Fryer	112	1,922
1990–91	UNLV[3]	Stacey Augmon	145	2,011
		Greg Anthony	138	1,738
		Anderson Hunt*	109	1,632
		Larry Johnson	75	1,617
1991–92	Arkansas	Todd Day	127	2,395
		Lee Mayberry	139	1,940
		Oliver Miller	137	1,674

* Denotes junior eligibility.

1. Lewis' totals include points scored at USC during his freshman year. His Pepperdine totals were 1,515 points in 87 games.

2. Gathers' totals include points scored at USC in his first season. Gathers' LMU totals are 2,490 points in 89 games. Kimble's totals include points scored at USC in his first season. Kimble's LMU totals are 2,010 points in 76 games.

3. Anthony's totals include points scored at Portland in his freshman year. His UNLV totals are 1,306 points in 110 games.

SCHOOLS WITH TWO ACTIVE PLAYERS WITH OVER 2,000 POINTS

SEASON	SCHOOL	PLAYERS	GAMES	POINTS
1980–81	Lamar	Mike Olliver	122	2,518
		B. B. Davis	119	2,084
1985–86	Duke	Johnny Dawkins	133	2,537
		Mark Alarie	133	2,136
1986–87	Oklahoma	Tim McAlister	136	2,275
		Darryl Kennedy	137	2,097
1989–90	Loyola Marymount	Hank Gathers	117	2,723
		Bo Kimble	104	2,350
1989–90	Texas Southern	Charles Price	116	2,119
		Fred West	118	2,066

Note: The point totals for Gathers (Southern Cal), Kimble (Southern Cal), and Price (Grambling) include freshman year at other schools.

SCHOOLS WITH SEVEN OR MORE PLAYERS WHO WOULD SCORE OVER 1,000 POINTS BEFORE ENDING THEIR MAJOR-COLLEGE CAREERS

SEASON	SCHOOL	PLAYERS	CL.
1977–78	Notre Dame	Dave Batton	Sr.
		Don Williams	Sr.
		Bruce Flowers	Jr.
		Rich Branning	So.
		Kelly Tripucka	Fr.
		Orlando Woolridge	Fr.
		Tracy Jackson	Fr.
1980–81	Wake Forest	Frank Johnson	Sr.
		Guy Morgan	Jr.
		Alvis Rogers	Jr.
		Mike Helms	Jr.
		Jim Johnstone	Jr.
		Danny Young	Fr.
		Anthony Teachey	Fr.
1985–86	Duke	Johnny Dawkins	Sr.
		Mark Alarie	Sr.
		David Henderson	Sr.
		Jay Bilas	Sr.
		Tommy Amaker	Jr.
		Kevin Strickland	So.
		Danny Ferry	Fr.
1986–87	Bucknell	Chris Seneca	Sr.
		Mark Atkinson	Sr.
		Mark Allsteadt	Sr.
		Mike Butts	So.
		Ted Aceto	So.
		Mike Joseph	Fr.
		Greg Leggett	Fr.
1987–88	Pittsburgh	Charles Smith	Sr.
		Demetreus Gore	Sr.
		Jerome Lane	Jr.
		Rod Brookin	So.
		Jason Matthews	Fr.
		Sean Miller	Fr.
		Bobby Martin	Fr.
		Darelle Porter	Fr.
1990–91	West Virginia	Chris Brooks	Sr.
		Tracy Shelton	Jr.
		Chris Leonard	Jr.
		Marsalis Basey	Fr.
		Mike Boyd	Fr.
		Pervires Greene	Fr.
		Ricky Robinson	Fr.

SCHOOLS WITH THREE PLAYERS WHO WOULD SCORE OVER 2,000 POINTS BEFORE ENDING THEIR CAREERS

SEASON	SCHOOL	PLAYERS	CL.
1977–78	Duke	Jim Spanarkel	Jr.
		Mike Gminski	So.
		Gene Banks	Fr.
1978–79	Duke	Jim Spanarkel	Sr.
		Mike Gminski	Jr.
		Gene Banks	So.
1983–84	Oklahoma	Wayman Tisdale	So.
		Tim McAlister	Fr.
		Darryl Kennedy	Fr.
1984–85	Oklahoma	Wayman Tisdale	Jr.
		Tim McAlister	So.
		Darryl Kennedy	So.
1985–86	Oklahoma	Tim McAlister	Jr.
		Darryl Kennedy	Jr.
		Stacey King	Fr.
1985–86	Duke	Johnny Dawkins	Sr.
		Mark Alarie	Sr.
		Danny Ferry	Fr.
1985–86	Southern Cal	Tom Lewis	Fr.
		Hank Gathers	Fr.
		Bo Kimble	Fr.
1986–87	Oklahoma	Tim McAlister	Sr.
		Darryl Kennedy	Sr.
		Stacey King	So.

Note: Neither Gathers, Lewis, nor Kimble remained at USC after their freshman season. Lewis transferred to Pepperdine, while Kimble and Gathers went to Loyola Marymount.

SCHOOLS WITH FIVE OR MORE PLAYERS WITH OVER 2,000 POINTS IN THEIR PLAYING CAREERS

SCHOOL	PLAYERS	YEARS	POINTS
Duke	Johnny Dawkins	83-86	2,537
	Christian Laettner	89-92	2,460
	Mike Gminski	77-80	2,323
	Danny Ferry	86-89	2,155
	Mark Alarie	83-86	2,136
	Gene Banks	78-81	2,079
	Jim Spanarkel	76-79	2,012
Villanova	Kerry Kittles	93-96	2,243
	Keith Herron	75-78	2,170
	Doug West	86-89	2,037
	Howard Porter	69-71	2,026
	John Pinone	80-83	2,024
	Bob Schafer	52-55	2,012
Georgia Tech	Rich Yunkus	69-71	2,232
	Mark Price	83-86	2,120
	Dennis Scott	88-90	2,115
	Tom Hammonds	86-89	2,081
	Travis Best	92-95	2,057
North Carolina	Phil Ford	75-78	2,290
	Sam Perkins	81-84	2,133
	Len Rosenbluth	55-57	2,045
	Al Wood	78-81	2,015
	Charlie Scott	68-70	2,007
Oklahoma	Wayman Tisdale	83-85	2,661
	Tim McAlister	84-87	2,275
	Jeff Webster	91-94	2,264
	Darryl Kennedy	84-87	2,097
	Stacey King	86-89	2,008
Tennessee	Allan Houston	90-93	2,801
	Ernie Grunfeld	74-77	2,249
	Tony White	84-87	2,219
	Reggie Johnson	77-80	2,103
	Dale Ellis	80-83	2,065

SCHOOLS WITH FOUR TEAMMATES WHO COMBINED TO AVERAGE OVER 80 POINTS PER GAME

AVG.	SCHOOL (SEASON)	PLAYERS (AVERAGE)
101.5	Loyola Marymount (1989–90)	Bo Kimble (35.3) Hank Gathers (29) Jeff Fryer (22.7) Terrell Lowery (14.5)
91.1	Loyola Marymount (1989–90)	Hank Gathers (41.7) Jeff Fryer (22.9) Enoch Simmons (18.7) Bo Kimble (16.8)
87.6	Furman (1953–54)	Frank Selvy (41.7) Darrell Floyd (24.3) Fred Fraley (11.8) Ken Deardorff (9.8)
84.4	Oklahoma City (1965–66)	Jerry Wells (27.1) Gary Gray (21.1) Charlie Hunter (19.6) James Ware (16.6)
83.8	Louisiana State (1969–70)	Pete Maravich (44.5) Danny Hester (16.1) Al Sanders (12) Bill Newton (11.2)
82.2	Iowa (1969-70)	John Johnson (27.9) Chad Calabria (19.1) Fred Brown (17.9) Glenn Vidnovic (17.3)

SCHOOLS WITH THREE TEAMMATES WHO COMBINED TO AVERAGE OVER 70 POINTS PER GAME

AVG.	SCHOOL (SEASON)	PLAYERS (AVERAGE)
87.0	Loyola Marymount (1989–90)	Bo Kimble (35.3) Hank Gathers (29) Jeff Fryer (22.7)
77.8	Furman (1953–54)	Frank Selvy (41.7) Darrell Floyd (24.3) Fred Fraley (11.8)
74.3	Loyola Marymount (1989–90)	Hank Gathers (32.7) Jeff Fryer (22.9) Enoch Simmons (18.7)
72.6	Louisiana State (1969–70)	Pete Maravich (44.5) Danny Hester (16.1) Al Sanders (12)
70.8	Notre Dame (1970–71)	Austin Carr (37.9) Collis Jones (23.1) Sid Catlett (9.8)

SCHOOLS WITH TWO TEAMMATES WHO COMBINED TO AVERAGE OVER 60 POINTS PER GAME

AVG.	SCHOOL (SEASON)	PLAYERS (AVERAGE)
66.0	Furman (1953–54)	Frank Selvy (41.7) Darrell Floyd (24.3)
64.3	Loyola Marymount (1989–90)	Bo Kimble (35.3) Hank Gathers (29)
61.0	Notre Dame (1970–71)	Austin Carr (37.9) Collis Jones (23.1)
60.6	Louisiana State (1969–70)	Pete Maravich (44.5) Danny Hester (16.1)

SCHOOLS WITH AT LEAST 65 VICTORIES IN TWO SUCCESSIVE SEASONS

SCHOOL (SEASONS)	RECORD
UNLV (1986 and 1987)	70-7
Georgetown (1984 and 1985)	69-6
UNLV (1990 and 1991)	69-6
Duke (1991 and 1992)	66-9
Oklahoma (1988 and 1989)	66-9
UNLV (1987 and 1988)	65-10

SCHOOLS WITH MORE THAN 90 VICTORIES IN THREE SUCCESSIVE SEASONS

SCHOOL (SEASONS)	RECORD
UNLV (1985–87)	98-11
UNLV (1989–91)	98-14
UNLV (1986–88)	98-15
UNLV (1990–92)	95-8
Duke (1990–92)	95-18
Georgetown (1984–86)	93-14
Oklahoma (1988–90)	93-14
Massachusetts (1994–96)	92-14
UNLV (1988–90)	92-21

SCHOOLS WITH MORE THAN 120 VICTORIES IN FOUR SUCCESSIVE SEASONS

SCHOOL (SEASONS)	RECORD
UNLV (1987–90)	129-23
UNLV (1984–87)	127-17
UNLV (1986–89)	127-23
UNLV (1985–88)	126-19
UNLV (1988–91)	126-22
UNLV (1989–92)	124-16
Duke (1989–92)	123-26
Georgetown (1984–87)	122-19
Georgetown (1982–85)	121-23

SCHOOLS WITH MORE THAN 150 VICTORIES IN FIVE SUCCESSIVE SEASONS

SCHOOL (SEASONS)	RECORD
UNLV (1987–91)	163-24
UNLV (1986–90)	162-28
UNLV (1983–87)	155-20
UNLV (1984–88)	155-25
UNLV (1985–89)	155-27
UNLV (1988–92)	152-24
Duke (1988–92)	151-33

SCHOOLS WITH MORE THAN 280 VICTORIES IN 10 SUCCESSIVE SEASONS

SCHOOL (SEASONS)	RECORD
UNLV (1983–92)	307-44
UNLV (1982–91)	301-52
UNLV (1984–93)	300-49
Duke (1985–94)	287-67
UCLA (1967–76)	286-17
UNLV (1981–90)	283-63
Duke (1984–93)	283-71
UCLA (1964–73)	281-15
UCLA (1968–77)	281-21
North Carolina (1980–89)	281-63
North Carolina (1982–91)	281-66
North Carolina (1981–90)	281-68

HIGHEST WINNING PERCENTAGE IN TWO SUCCESSIVE SEASONS SINCE 1950–51

SCHOOL (SEASONS)	RECORD	PCT.
UCLA (1972 and 1973)	60-0	1.000
Indiana (1975 and 1976)	63-1	.984
UCLA (1967 and 1968)	59-1	.983
UCLA (1971 and 1972)	59-1	.983
N.C. State (1973 and 1974)	57-1	.983
San Francisco (1955 and 1956)	57-1	.983
UCLA (1964 and 1965)	58-2	.967
UCLA (1968 and 1969)	58-2	.967
UNLV (1991 and 1992)	60-3	.952

HIGHEST WINNING PERCENTAGE IN THREE SUCCESSIVE SEASONS SINCE 1950–51

SCHOOL (SEASONS)	RECORD	PCT.
UCLA (1971–73)	89-1	.989
UCLA (1967–69)	88-2	.978
UCLA (1970–72)	87-3	.967
UCLA (1968–70)	86-4	.956
UCLA (1969–71)	86-4	.956

| UCLA (1972–74) | 86-4 | .956 |
| Indiana (1974–76) | 86-6 | .935 |

HIGHEST WINNING PERCENTAGE IN FOUR SUCCESSIVE SEASONS SINCE 1950–51

SCHOOL (SEASONS)	RECORD	PCT.
UCLA (1970–73)	117-3	.975
UCLA (1967–70)	116-4	.967
UCLA (1969–72)	116-4	.967
UCLA (1968–71)	115-5	.958
UCLA (1971–74)	115-5	.958
UCLA (1972–75)	114-7	.942
Cincinnati (1960–63)	110-9	.924

HIGHEST WINNING PERCENTAGE IN FIVE SUCCESSIVE SEASONS SINCE 1950–51

SCHOOL (SEASONS)	RECORD	PCT.
UCLA (1969–73)	146-4	.973
UCLA (1967–71)	145-5	.967
UCLA (1968–72)	145-5	.967
UCLA (1970–74)	143-7	.953
UCLA (1971–75)	143-8	.947

HIGHEST WINNING PERCENTAGE IN 10 SUCCESSIVE SEASONS SINCE 1950–51

SCHOOL (SEASONS)	RECORD	PCT.
UCLA (1964–73)	281-15	.949
UCLA (1967–76)	286-17	.944
UCLA (1965–74)	277-19	.936
UCLA (1966–75)	277-20	.933
UCLA (1968–77)	281-21	.930
UCLA (1969–78)	277-23	.923
UCLA (1970–79)	273-27	.910

HIGHEST NUMBER OF 20-WIN SEASONS SINCE 1950–51

SEASONS	SCHOOL
34	Kentucky
33	UCLA
30	Louisville
31	North Carolina
27	Duke
24	St. John's
24	Syracuse
23	North Carolina State
22	Kansas
22	Villanova
20	Notre Dame

HIGHEST NUMBER OF 25-WIN SEASONS SINCE 1950–51

SEASONS	SCHOOL
22	North Carolina
19	UCLA
17	Kentucky
13	UNLV
13	Kansas
11	Arkansas
11	Duke

HIGHEST NUMBER OF SUCCESSIVE 20-WIN SEASONS SINCE 1950–51

NO.	SEASONS	SCHOOL
26	1971–96	North Carolina
17	1967–83	UCLA
14	1945–59*	Kentucky
14	1971–84	Louisville
13	1967–79	Marquette
13	1978–90	Georgetown
12	1982–93	UNLV
12	1982–93	Oklahoma
12	1983–94	Syracuse
11	1984–94	Duke

* Kentucky did not compete during the 1953 season.

HIGHEST NUMBER OF SUCCESSIVE SEASONS WITH 27 OR MORE WINS SINCE 1950–51

NO.	SEASONS	SCHOOL
9	1983–91	UNLV
7	1983–89	North Carolina
7	1967–73	UCLA

UNBEATEN TEAMS SINCE 1937–38

YEAR	SCHOOL	RECORD
1939	Long Island	23-0
1940	Seton Hall	19-0
1944	Army	15-0
1954	Kentucky	25-0
1956	San Francisco	29-0
1957	North Carolina	32-0
1964	UCLA	30-0
1967	UCLA	30-0
1972	UCLA	30-0
1973	North Carolina St.	27-0
1973	UCLA	30-0
1976	Indiana	32-0

ALL-TIME WINLESS SEASONS (AT LEAST 10 GAMES)

YEAR	SCHOOL	RECORD
1992	Prairie View	0-28
1955	The Citadel	0-17
1945	Baylor	0-17
1944	Virginia Military	0-14
1943	Tulsa	0-10
1937	Middle Tenn. State	0-11
1937	William & Mary	0-18
1934	American	0-10
1932	Virginia Military	0-14
1927	St. Louis	0-14
1924	Northwestern	0-16
1918	Dartmouth	0-26
1917	Oregon	0-11
1910	Drake	0-10

PERFECT EXAMPLES

Three schools have gone unbeaten in league competition three consecutive seasons since the start of the NCAA Tournament.

SCHOOL (CONFERENCE)	COACH	UNBEATEN IN LEAGUE
Kentucky (SEC)	Adolph Rupp	1947, 1948, and 1949
West Virginia (Southern)	Fred Schaus	1957, 1958, and 1959
UCLA (Pacific-8)	John Wooden	1971, 1972, and 1973

RETURN ENGAGEMENTS

The eight schools that appeared in at least 10 consecutive NCAA Tournaments through 1996:

SCHOOL	NO.	YEARS
North Carolina	22	1975–96
UCLA	15	1967–81
Georgetown	14	1979–92
Arizona	12	1985–96
Duke	11	1984–94
Louisiana State	10	1984–93
Marquette	10	1971–80
Syracuse	10	1983–92

ALL TIED UP IN NOTS

Through 1996, the following 10 Division I schools had never won a regular-season title in their present conference despite membership in a league for at least 25 years:

SCHOOL	CONFERENCE(S)	YEARS
Harvard	Ivy League	66
Mississippi	Southeastern	64
The Citadel	Southern	60
Kent	Mid-American	45
San Jose State	Big West, WCC, WAC	44
Washington State	Pacific-10	43
Nebraska	Big Eight/Big 12	38
Oregon	Pacific-10	36
Texas-Arlington	Southland	32
UC Santa Barbara	Big West, WCC, WAC	30

Notes: Nebraska's drought is since the Big Eight went to eight members.... The dry spells for Washington State and Oregon are since the Pacific-10 Conference dropped a divisional format.

GROWTH OF FIELD OF DREAMS

Here is a time frame showing the expansion of the NCAA Tournament field from eight teams to 64 (number of schools classified as Division I at the time are in parentheses for designated years):

PLAYOFF ENTRANTS	YEARS (NUMBER OF DIVISION I SCHOOLS)
8 teams	1939 through 1950 (145 major colleges)
16 teams	1951 (153) and 1952 (156)
22–25 teams	1953 (158) through 1974 (233)
32 teams	1975 (233) through 1978 (254)
40 teams	1979 (257)
48 teams	1980 (261) through 1982 (272)
52 teams	1983 (274)
53 teams	1984 (276)
64 teams	since 1985 (282)

DUNKING FOR DOLLARS

The rapid growth of the NCAA Tournament after television became a key factor and the revenue a school generated are staggering. Each Final Four participant in 1990 received more than $1.47 million, a whopping increase of almost 3,000 percent in just 20 years.

Here is the cumulative payout in five-year increments from 1970 through 1990 to each Final Four school before the NCAA introduced a new revenue-sharing formula, beginning with the 1991 tournament:

YEAR	FINAL FOUR TEAM PAYOUT
1970	$49,576
1975	$133,381
1980	$326,378
1985	$751,899
1990	$1,472,339

THAT'S INCREDIBLE

Three schools won an NCAA Tournament one year after compiling a non-winning record.

CHAMPION, YEAR (W-L)	PREV. SEASON	GAMES IMPROVED
Wisconsin, 1941 (20-3)	5-15	+13
Ohio State, 1960 (25-3)	11-11	+11
Utah, 1944 (22-4)	10-12	+10

RECORDS IN FIRST SEASON OF DIVISION I

Includes schools that moved up to the major-college ranks after the first year of classification in 1948.

UNIVERSITY	YEAR	W	L	PCT.
Md.-Eastern Shore	1974	27	2	.931
Oral Roberts	1972	26	2	.929
Southwestern La.	1972	23	3	.885
Seattle	1953	29	4	.879
Old Dominion	1977	25	4	.862
Long Beach State	1970	24	5	.828
Southern (La.)	1978	23	5	.821
Hawaii	1971	23	5	.821
McNeese State	1974	20	5	.800
Jackson State	1978	19	5	.792
Alabama State	1983	22	6	.786
Alcorn State	1978	22	7	.759
Idaho State	1959	21	7	.750
Memphis State	1956	20	7	.741
Air Force	1958	17	6	.739
S.F. Austin State	1987	22	8	.733
Northeastern	1973	19	7	.731
Georgia Southern	1974	19	7	.731
Va. Commonwealth	1974	17	7	.708
Miami (Fla.)	1949	19	8	.704
Charleston	1992	19	8	.704
New Orleans	1976	18	8	.692
Weber State	1964	17	8	.680
George Mason	1979	17	8	.680
Florida A&M	1979	18	9	.667
Mercer	1974	16	8	.667
Tennessee Tech	1956	14	7	.667
American	1967	16	8	.667
Fairfield	1965	14	7	.667
Morehead State	1956	19	10	.655
UNLV	1970	17	9	.654
James Madison	1977	17	9	.654
Northwestern La.	1977	17	9	.654
Drexel	1974	15	9	.625
Northern Colorado	1974	15	9	.625
Lamar	1970	15	9	.625
Arkansas State	1971	15	9	.625
Abilene Christian	1971	15	9	.625
Massachusetts	1962	15	9	.625

UNIVERSITY	YEAR	W	L	PCT.
UC Santa Barbara	1964	18	11	.621
Delaware State	1974	18	11	.621
Illinois State	1972	16	10	.615
Northeast La.	1974	16	10	.615
North Carolina A&T	1974	16	10	.615
N.C.-Wilmington	1977	16	10	.615
Texas Southern	1978	16	10	.615
Austin Peay	1964	14	9	.609
Ala.-Birmingham	1980	18	12	.600
Southern Miss.	1969	15	10	.600
Chicago State	1985	16	11	.593
Tenn.-Chattanooga	1978	16	11	.593
Wright State	1988	16	11	.593
Loyola (La.)	1952	20	14	.588
N.C.-Asheville	1987	15	11	.577
San Jose State	1953	15	11	.577
Los Angeles State	1971	15	11	.577
New Mexico State	1951	19	14	.576
Sam Houston State	1987	16	12	.571
Radford	1985	16	12	.571
Kentucky Wesleyan	1957	16	12	.571
East Tenn. State	1959	13	10	.565
East Carolina	1965	12	10	.545
Southern Illinois	1968	13	11	.542
New Mexico	1951	13	11	.542
Cal State Fullerton	1975	13	11	.542
Boise State	1972	14	12	.538
Central Michigan	1974	14	12	.538
West Texas	1951	14	12	.538
Wisc.-Milwaukee	1974	14	12	.538
UNC Charlotte	1973	14	12	.538
Oklahoma City	1951	16	14	.533
Iona	1954	11	10	.524
Corpus Christi	1973	13	12	.520
Wisc.-Green Bay	1982	14	13	.519
Illinois-Chicago	1982	14	13	.519
Southeastern La.	1981	14	13	.519
Western Illinois	1982	14	13	.519
Eastern Illinois	1982	14	13	.519
Gonzaga	1953	15	14	.517
Catholic	1977	13	13	.500
Vermont	1962	12	12	.500
St. Peter's	1965	10	10	.500
Texas Tech	1951	14	14	.500
Centenary	1960	12	12	.500
Murray State	1954	15	16	.484
Hofstra	1967	12	13	.480
Tennessee State	1978	11	12	.478
Regis	1962	10	11	.476
Bethune-Cookman	1981	13	15	.464
South Carolina St.	1974	13	15	.464
Mo.-Kansas City	1990	13	15	.464
Southwest Mo. State	1983	13	15	.464
Hardin-Simmons	1951	13	15	.464
San Diego State	1971	12	14	.462
Marist	1982	12	14	.462
Maine	1962	11	13	.458
Fairleigh Dickinson	1968	10	12	.455
Mt. St. Mary's (Md.)	1989	12	15	.444
South Florida	1974	11	14	.440
Md.-Baltimore County	1987	12	16	.429
Coastal Carolina	1987	12	16	.429
Southeast Mo. State	1992	12	16	.429
West Chester	1974	11	15	.423
Howard	1974	11	15	.423
Grambling	1978	10	14	.417
St. Francis (Pa.)	1956	10	14	.417
Northern Illinois	1968	10	14	.417
Texas-El Paso	1951	10	15	.400
Delaware	1958	8	12	.400
Houston	1951	11	17	.393
Cleveland State	1973	9	14	.391
Louisiana Tech	1974	8	13	.381
Ball State	1972	9	15	.375
Rider	1968	9	15	.375
Campbell	1978	9	15	.375
Liberty	1989	10	17	.370
Coppin State	1986	10	17	.370
Southern Utah State	1989	10	18	.357
Central Florida	1985	10	18	.357
Loyola Marymount	1950	9	17	.346
Florida State	1957	9	17	.346
Pacific	1954	9	17	.346
Towson State	1980	9	17	.346

School	Year	W	L	Pct
Fresno State	1956	9	17	.346
Middle Tenn. State	1959	9	17	.346
U.S. International	1982	9	18	.333
Western Carolina	1977	8	16	.333
Fla. International	1988	9	19	.321
Portland State	1973	9	19	.321
Texas-Pan American	1969	8	17	.320
UC Irvine	1978	8	17	.320
Jacksonville	1967	8	17	.320
Portland	1954	6	13	.316
Texas-Arlington	1969	8	18	.308
Eastern Michigan	1974	8	18	.308
Texas-San Antonio	1982	8	19	.296
Arizona State	1951	8	19	.296
Northern Arizona	1951	8	19	.296
Northern Iowa	1981	8	19	.296
South Alabama	1972	7	17	.292
Cal State Northridge	1991	8	20	.286
Augusta	1985	8	20	.286
Winthrop	1987	8	20	.286
Central Conn. State	1987	8	21	.276
Providence	1949	7	19	.269
Robert Morris	1977	7	19	.269
Tenn.-Martin	1993	7	19	.269
Hartford	1985	7	21	.250
N.C.-Greensboro	1992	7	21	.250
Evansville*	1978	1	3	.250
Houston Baptist	1974	6	19	.240
Trinity (Tex.)	1971	5	16	.238
Ark.-Little Rock	1979	6	20	.231
Southwest Texas St.	1985	6	20	.231
Stetson	1972	6	20	.231
Monmouth (N.J.)	1984	6	21	.222
Armstrong State	1987	6	22	.214
Nicholls State	1981	6	22	.214
Appalachian State	1974	5	20	.200
Buffalo	1974	5	20	.200
San Diego	1980	5	20	.200
Baptist	1975	4	16	.200
Samford	1973	5	20	.200
Baltimore	1979	4	21	.160
Utica	1982	4	22	.154
Eastern Washington	1984	4	22	.154
Cal St. Sacramento	1992	4	24	.143
North Texas	1958	3	18	.143
New Hampshire	1962	3	20	.130
Wagner	1977	3	21	.125
Miss. Valley State	1980	3	24	.111
Morgan State	1985	3	25	.107
Prairie View	1981	2	22	.083
Pepperdine	1956	2	24	.077
Northeastern Ill.	1991	2	25	.074
Georgia State	1974	1	25	.038

* Evansville's season ended prematurely after a plane crash killed its coach and team.

MOST CONSECUTIVE WINNING SEASONS THROUGH 1996

WINS	SCHOOL	YEARS
48	UCLA	1949–96
46	Louisville	1945–90
38	Kentucky	1928–52, 54–66#
32	North Carolina	1965–96
31	St. John's	1923–53
30	Notre Dame	1926–55
30	St. John's	1964–93
26	Arkansas	1924–49
26	Princeton	1954–79
26	Toledo	1960–85

*–Kentucky did not play basketball during the 1953 season.

MOST CONSECUTIVE NON-LOSING SEASONS (INCLUDES .500 RECORD) THROUGH 1994

WINS	SCHOOL	YEARS
60	Kentucky	1928–52, 54–88# (2 .500 seasons)

48	UCLA	1949–94
47	Louisville	1944–90 (1)
34	Houston	1960–93 (2)
34	North Carolina	1963–94 (1)
33	Navy	1907–39 (3)
33	Duke	1940–72 (2)
32	Notre Dame	1924–55 (1)
32	Illinois	1929–60 (3)
31	St. John's	1923–53
31	Princeton	1954–84 (2)
31	Virginia Tech	1956–86 (2)
30	St. John's	1964–93

Kentucky did not play basketball during the 1953 season.

DEAD TEAMS WALKING

Seven schools never have posted a 20-win season despite being at the Division I level for at least 40 years:

SCHOOL	MOST VICTORIES
Air Force	17-6 record in 1957-58
Brown	17-9 in 1973-74
Colgate	18-10 in 1992-93
Harvard	19-3 in 1945-46
New Hampshire	19-9 in 1994-95
Northwestern	18-12 in 1982-83
Tennessee Tech	19-9 in 1984-85 and 1989-90

TEAMS INELIGIBLE FOR NCAA DIVISION I TOURNAMENT FOR AT LEAST THREE YEARS BECAUSE OF ENFORCEMENT SANCTIONS

(Listed Alphabetically)

Auburn: 1957, 1958, 1959, 1960, 1961, 1980, 1992 (7 years)
Centenary: 1970, 1971, 1973, 1974, 1975, 1976, 1977, 1978 (8)
Cincinnati: 1956, 1979, 1980, 1989 (4)
Clemson: 1976, 1977, 1978 (3)
Florida State: 1969, 1970, 1971 (3)
Illinois: 1968, 1969, 1975, 1991 (4)
Indiana: 1961, 1962, 1963, 1964 (4)
Kansas: 1961, 1962, 1973, 1989 (4)
Kentucky: 1953, 1990, 1991 (3)
Long Beach State: 1974, 1975, 1976 (3)
Louisiana Tech: 1974, 1975, 1976 (3)
Memphis State: 1958, 1959, 1980, 1987 (4)
Minnesota: 1976, 1977, 1978, 1988 (4)
Montana State: 1958, 1960, 1961 (3)
New Mexico State: 1963, 1964, 1973, 1974 (4)
North Carolina State: 1955, 1957, 1958, 1959, 1960, 1973, 1990 (7)
South Carolina: 1967, 1968, 1988 (3)
Texas-Pan American: 1969, 1974, 1975, 1993 (4)
UCLA: 1957, 1958, 1959, 1982 (4)
UNLV: 1978, 1979, 1992 (3)
Western Kentucky: 1973, 1974, 1975 (3)
Wichita State: 1974, 1975, 1982, 1983 (4)

HOW PLAYING RULES DIFFER

CATEGORY	LEAGUE
Bonus Free Throw	**COLLEGE:** 7th team foul per half* **INTL.:** 8th team foul per half **NBA:** 5th team foul per quarter
Game Duration	**COLLEGE:** Two 20-minute halves **INTL.:** Two 20-minute halves **NBA:** Four 12-minute quarters
Lane Width at Baseline	**COLLEGE:** 12' (rectangle) **INTL.:** 19'8.2" (trapezoid) **NBA:** 16' (rectangle)
Number of Timeouts	**COLLEGE:** Five per game (not including TV timeouts)

	INTL.: Two per half
	NBA: Seven per game
Player Foul Limit	COLLEGE: Five personals
	INTL.: Five personals
	NBA: Six personals
Shot Clock	COLLEGE: 35 seconds
	INTL.: 30 seconds
	NBA: 24 seconds
Three-Point Distance	COLLEGE: 19'9"
	INTL.: 20'6.1"
	NBA: 22'6"

* Beginning with tenth foul per half, player shoots two free throws.

SHOE WARS

Many schools have contracts with sneaker companies to wear their products exclusively. Which companies benefitted the most from Final Four exposure since the playoff field expanded to 64 teams in 1985?

1985: Nike 4 (Georgetown, Memphis State, St. John's, Villanova).
1986: Converse 2 (Louisville, LSU), Adidas 1 (Duke), Puma 1 (Kansas).
1987: Nike 2 (Syracuse, UNLV), Adidas 1 (Indiana), Converse 1 (Providence).
1988: Nike 2 (Arizona, Kansas), Converse 1 (Oklahoma), Adidas 1 (Duke).
1989: Nike 2 (Michigan, Seton Hall), Adidas 1 (Duke), Converse 1 (Illinois).
1990: Nike 2 (Georgia Tech, UNLV), Adidas 1 (Duke), Converse 1 (Arkansas).
1991: Converse 2 (Kansas, North Carolina), Adidas 1 (Duke), Nike 1 (UNLV).
1992: Adidas 2 (Duke, Indiana), Nike 2 (Cincinnati, Michigan).
1993: Converse 3 (Kansas, Kentucky, North Carolina), Nike 1 (Michigan).
1994: Nike 2 (Arizona, Duke), Converse 1 (Arkansas), Reebok 1 (Florida).
1995: Nike 2 (North Carolina, Oklahoma State), Converse 1 (Arkansas), Reebok 1 (UCLA).
1996: Nike 3 (Massachusetts, Mississippi State, Syracuse), Converse 1 (Kentucky).

Final Four Totals (1985–94): Nike 23, Converse 14, Adidas 8, Reebok 2, Puma 1,.

SEATING FROM A DIFFERENT VIEW

Eight schools currently play the majority of their home games in arenas with seating capacities of at least 20,000.

SCHOOL	ARENA	SEATING
Syracuse	Carrier Dome	33,000
Tennessee	Thompson-Boling Arena	24,535
North Carolina	Smith Center	24,063
Kentucky	Rupp Arena	23,000
Brigham Young	Marriott Center	22,700
Memphis	The Pyramid	20,142
Seton Hall	Meadowlands Arena	20,029
St. Louis	Kiel Center	20,000

TEN OLDEST ARENAS IN DIVISION I

UNIVERSITY	ARENA (CAPACITY)	LOCATION (YEAR OPENED)
Northeastern	Matthews Arena (6,000)	Boston, Mass. (1909)
Loyola (Ill.)	Alumni Gym (2,975)	Chicago, Ill. (1926)
Fordham	Rose Hill Gym (3,200)	Bronx, N.Y. (1926)
Harvard	Briggs Athletic Center (3,000)	Cambridge, Mass. (1926)
Oregon	McArthur Court (10,063)	Eugene, Ore. (1926)
Pennsylvania	The Palestra (8,700)	Philadelphia, Pa. (1927)
Washington	Edmundson Pavilion (8,000)	Seattle, Wash. (1927)
Butler	Hinkle Fieldhouse (11,000)	Indianapolis, Ind. (1928)
Minnesota	Williams Arena (14,395)	Minneapolis, Minn. (1928)
Wisconsin	Wisconsin Fieldhouse (11,500)	Madison, Wis. (1930)

PHOTO CREDITS

Photographs appearing in *Inside Sports College Basketball* were received from the following sources:

Bradley University, 306; City College of New York, 458; Dartmouth College, 54; DePaul University, 47, 280; Duke University, 340, 405, 442; Furman University, 83; Georgia Institute of Technology, 123, 323, 326 (right), 387, 492; Indiana University, 226 (left), 298, 341; Jacksonville University, 187; Kansas State University, 667; La Salle University, 81, 461; Louisiana Superdome, 211; Louisiana State University, photo by John Titchen, Star Bulletin Photo, 175; Louisiana Tech University, 415, 544, 583; Loyola Marymount University, 322; Marquette University, 232, 234, 239, 394 (bottom), 411, 462; Michigan State University, 244, 245, 485, 486 (right), 505(right); National Association of Basketball Coaches, 374, 470; National Association of Intercollegiate Athletics, 562, 566, 570, 571, 574; Niagara University, 185; North Atlantic Conference, 314; North Carolina State University, 213 (left), 323, 430 (left), 582; North Carolina State University, photo copyright Burnie Batchelor Studio, Inc., 111; North Carolina State University, photo by Simon Griffiths, 469 (left); Northeastern University, photo by J. D. Levine, 436; Oral Roberts University, 194; Oregon State University, 454; Pennsylvania State University, 84; Princeton University, 514; Providence College, 159, 389, 517; Providence College, photos by Thomas Maguire, Jr. 205, 209; Purdue University, 13, 130, 181, 353, 501; Purdue University, photo copyright Laughead Photographers, 494 (top); Rutgers, The State University of New Jersey, photo by Dean Nathans/*Scarlet Letter*, 226 (right); Rutgers, The State University of New Jersey, photo by F. J. Higgins, 469 (right); St. Bonaventure University, 169 (left); St. Joseph's University, 127; St. Louis University, 379; Southeastern Louisiana University, 537; Stanford University, 15, 38, 502; Syracuse University, 389 (bottom), 669; Syracuse University, photo by Stephen Parker 299; Temple University Libraries Photojournalism Collection, 580; University of Arizona, 260, 397, 481 (right); University of California, 348; University of California, Los Angeles (UCLA), 143, 147, 157, 163, 168, 191, 197, 213 (right), 217, 386, 389 (top), 401, 417, 432 (left), 433, 434 (left, bottom), 449, 470, 528, 533, 552, 664; University of California, Los Angeles (UCLA), photo by Norm Schindler, 434 (right, bottom); University of Cincinnati, 79, 110, 337; University of Connecticut, 354, 416 (right), 514; University of Dayton, photo by Ed Morris Photography, 160 (left); University of Denver, 513; University of Florida, 468; University of Houston, 160 (right), 169 (right), 271, 276, 292, 404, 420, 460, 580; University of Idaho, 139; University of Illinois, 475 (bottom), 497 (bottom), 510, 519; University of Iowa, 573; University of Kansas, 2, 116 (right), 116 (left), 310, 434 (top, right), University of Louisville, 166, 254, 294, 398 (middle), 403, 431, 685; University of Maryland, 475 (top), 520; University of Miami, 148; University of Mississippi, 480, 481 (left); University of Nevada, Las Vegas, 326 (left), 330, 332; University of North Carolina, 512, 539; University of Oklahoma, 286; University of Oregon, 30, 383;

University of Tennessee, 223, 230, 272, 348 (top), 406, 411, 484, 496 (left), 508; University of Texas at El Paso, 440; University of Utah, 44, 399 (right); University of Virginia, 425, 491, 438; University of Wisconsin, 505 (left); University of Wyoming, 40, 681; USA Basketball, 527, 542, 543, 545, 548, 549, 554; Vanderbilt University, 313; Villanova University, 547; Wake Forest University, 88, 118, 393 (top); West Virginia University, 98, 114; West Virginia University, photo copyright Laughead Photographers, 430 (right); Western Kentucky University, 380; Wichita State University, 136.

School logos appear courtesy of the individual school or conference.

INDEX

This index includes all persons, associations, leagues, and teams appearing in all sections of the *Inside Sports College Basketball,* except for box scores, individual and team sta-titistics boxes, long lists of names, and material of general statistical nature. **Boldfaced numerals** denote an entire section devoted to that subject.

A

AAU. *See* Amateur Athletic Union (AAU)

AAWU. *See* Athletic Association of Western Universities (AAWU)

Abdul-Jabbar, Kareem. *See* Alcindor, Lew

Abdul-Rahmad, Mahdi. *See* Hazzard, Walt

Abdul-Rauf, Mahmoud. *See* Jackson, Chris

Abernethy, Tom   138, 206, 220, 225, 227

ABFUSA. *See* Amateur Basketball Federation of the United States of America (ABFUSA)

Aces. *See* Evansville

Accounting Hall of Fame   514

Acre, Mark   473

Actwood, Walter   642

Adair, Jerry   106, 473

Adams, Robert B.   512

Adcock, Joe   474

Adkins, David   513, 521

AFC. *See* American Football Conference (AFC)

African-American players, issue of   13, 63, 138, 157, 180

Aggies. *See* New Mexico State; Texas A&M; Utah State

Aguirre, Mark   248, 252-254, 258, 262-263, 269, 386, 581, 584, 631, 670, 694
    player of the year award, 665

AIAW. *See* Association of Intercollegiate Athletics for Women (AIAW)

Ainge, Danny   258-259, 386, 618, 627, 670
    player of the year award, 665

Air Force Academy   61, 88, 139, 505, 623, 626

Akron Goodyears   415

Akron Pros   521

Alabama, University of   88, 93, 190, 229, 573, 623, 653, 657

Alabama-Birmingham, University of   127, 389, 391, 397, 416, 423, 430, 433-434, 582, 657, 705

Alarie, Mark   296, 697-698

Alaska-Anchorage, University of   280, 319, 572

Alcindor, Lew   117, 154, 156-157, 159-163, 165, 167, 169-170, 172-174, 176-177, 187, 201, 365, 512, 581, 609, 657, 669, 671, 687-688, 695
    player of the year award, 664

Alcorn State   66, 90, 100, 136, 265, 294, 395-396, 414, 474-477, 480-481, 483-489, 504, 520, 624, 626, 665, 667

Alcorn, Gary   633

Athletic scholarships   532, 568
Atkins, Doug   489
Atlanta Braves   475, 477, 480, 484, 486-487
Atlanta Falcons   505
Atlanta Hawks   407, 410, 413, 416, 432, 489, 520, 582
Atlantic Coast Conference (ACC)   77, 81-82, 88, 90, 93-94, 98, 100-101, 105, 107, 113, 117-119, 127, 129, 132, 135, 142-143, 150, 155, 160, 165-166, 176-177, 180-181, 187, 189, 192, 194-195, 202-203, 206, 208, 211, 216-217, 220, 229, 240-241, 245, 252, 258, 265, 271, 275-276, 278-283, 285, 289, 296, 299, 312-313, 321, 323-324, 330, 336, 343, 345, 351, 357, 361-362, 368-369, 375, 381, 439-440, 442-444, 449, 451, 457, 462, 468-469, 491, 536, 543-544, 548, 555, 580, 587-589, 629, 631, 633-634, 641, 645, 659, 664-668, 690
Atlantic 10 Conference   229, 281, 299, 301, 305, 321, 368, 381, 438-439, 449, 588, 590, 630, 632-634, 638, 641, 649-651, 655, 659, 661, 667-668, 696
Aubrey, Sam   51-52
Auburn University   29, 45, 94, 110, 118, 131, 143, 149, 172, 189, 202, 218, 238, 249, 253-254, 256, 287-288, 295, 299, 324, 347, 357, 363, 474-477, 479-480, 482, 486-488, 499, 512, 550, 569, 625, 629, 639, 641, 643, 648-649, 664-668, 673
Auerbach, Arnold Red,   33
Augmon, Stacey   328, 330, 332-333, 336, 581, 584, 658, 696-697
Auker, Eldon   474
Austin Peay State University   201, 204, 208-209, 230, 303, 499, 608, 625, 685
Averitt, William (Bird)   201, 388, 617
Awtrey, Dennis   173, 177, 652
Ayers, Randy   241, 330, 333-334, 341
    national coach of the year award, 668
Azary, John   70
Azzi, Jennifer   537, 539-542, 583, 585

B

BAA. *See* Basketball Association of America (BAA)
Badgers. *See* Wisconsin
Badgro, Morris (Red)   489
Baesler, Scotty   513
Bailey, Terrance   294, 607
Bainbridge NTC   49
Bajusz, John   630
Baker, Terry   138, 490
Baker University   10
Baker, Al (Bubba)   490

Baker, Dave   627
Baker, Richard T. (Dick)   514
Baker, Tay   156, 184, 466
Ball State University   165, 219-220, 235, 255, 278-279, 295, 298, 302, 313, 317, 334, 348, 362, 474, 476-481, 483-487, 490, 499, 502, 504, 506-507, 625, 638-639, 665
Ballard, Greg   232, 647
Baltimore Bullets   16, 391, 409, 417, 426, 430-431, 448, 519
Baltimore Colts   491, 495, 503
Baltimore Orioles   212, 473, 476, 480, 483, 485-487
Bando, Sal   489
Banks, Freddie   303, 681
Banks, Gene   243, 249, 697-698
Bantom, Mike   580-581, 584
Barber, John   75
Barber, Steve   474
Barker, Cliff   56, 58, 60-61, 578, 584
Barkley, Charles   273, 279, 388, 582, 584, 671
Barksdale, Don   42, 54, 578, 584, 657
Barmore, Leon   526, 528, 539-540, 549-550, 555-558
Barnes, Erich   490
Barnes, Jim
Bad News   141, 147, 388, 579, 584, 656
Barnes, Marvin   195, 204, 208-209, 214, 388, 649, 670, 676
Barnes, Roosevelt   490
Barnett, Dick   568, 570-571, 575
Barnett, J. D.   285, 288, 573
Barnhill, John   568, 570, 575
Barnstable, Dale   56, 58, 60-61
Baron of the Bluegrass   194
Barros, Dana   626
Barry, Jim   148
Barry, Rick   148, 388, 641, 669, 693
Barton, Jim   301, 305, 630, 694
Bartow, Gene   189, 199, 201, 204, 217, 225, 232, 235, 268, 288, 356, 371, 444, 448, 572, 688
    national coach of the year award, 666
Basketball Association of America (BAA)   386, 388, 396, 410, 414, 474, 483, 486, 506, 512, 515
Basketball Writers Association. *See* U.S. Basketball Writers Association (USBWA)
Bates, Billy Ray   568
Baton Rouge Open   509
Battles, Cliff   490
Baugh, Sammy   490
Baum, John   655
Bauman, Lorri   542
Baumholtz, Frankie   474

Bausch, Jim 509

Baylor University 50, 64, 120, 348, 350, 354, 474, 482, 489-497, 499, 501-502, 504-505, 507, 512, 572, 625, 627, 654, 666

Baylor, Elgin 63, 104, 106-107, 109, 341, 477, 503, 573, 662, 669, 671, 687, 692-694

BCA. *See* Black Coaches Association (BCA)

Beard, Butch 165

Beard, Ralph 46, 52-53, 55-56, 59-61, 388, 578, 584, 638, 669, 688

Bears. *See* Baylor University; Brown University; Southwest Missouri State

Beasley, Charles 165

Beavers. *See* Oregon State

Beaty, Zelmo 507, 568, 575

Beck, Ernie 63, 75-76, 389, 648, 669

Beckel, Bob 94, 109

Bee, Clair 15-16, 29, 32, 35, 38, 64, 67, 445, 448, 522

Beetsch, Dick 490

Begovich, Matty 15

Beisser, Ed 40-41, 630, 669

Bell, Melvin 172

Bellamy, Walt 123, 389, 584, 636

Belnap, Dutch 218, 240, 440

Beloit College 7, 19, 21, 69, 465, 569, 575, 578-579, 584

Belov, Aleksander 580

Bemus, Charles 5

Bender, Bob 243

Bender, Gary 564

Bender, Herb 564

Bender, Jules 16, 24, 639, 668

Bengals. *See* Idaho State

Bennett, Tony 602, 661, 675

Benson, Kent 220, 223, 226-227, 229, 389, 636, 670, 687

Benton, Eddie 354, 363, 369

Benton, Jim 491

Berenson, Senda 528

Berger, Louis (Bozey) 475

Berlin Olympic games. *See* Olympics (men's basketball team)—1936

Berman, Arnie 195, 627

Berry, Ricky 305, 652

Berry, Walter 292, 303, 320, 389, 651, 670
    player of the year award, 665

Bethune-Cookman 293, 330, 339, 438, 501, 573, 603, 701

Bias, Len 292, 298, 389, 641, 670

Bibby, Henry 183, 185, 192, 194, 198, 389, 657, 670

Big East Conference 245, 251-252, 265, 278, 285, 288, 290, 293, 295, 303, 305-306, 312, 316, 324, 332, 340, 343, 347, 350, 353-354, 359, 363, 368, 381-382, 437-439, 442-443, 445, 450, 464, 521, 545, 547, 554, 587, 591, 626, 630, 634, 641, 646, 648-652, 655, 658, 660, 665-668

Big Eight Conference 63, 72, 77, 98, 104, 133, 136, 143, 150, 175, 195, 235, 245, 251, 273-274, 299, 301, 305, 308, 312, 318, 333, 338, 343, 347, 351, 354, 368, 382, 444-447, 449, 452-453, 455, 458, 465-466, 470, 536, 549, 569, 587-588, 595, 619, 665, 667-668, 696, 700

Big Five Hall of Fame 547

Big Nasty 358

Big Nine 57, 64, 245, 594

Big Seven Conference 40, 52, 57, 67, 71, 74, 79, 253, 445, 447, 452-453, 470, 509, 519, 619-620, 666

Big Six Conference 28, 36, 38, 50, 247, 365, 444-446, 452-453, 509, 553, 619

Big Sky Conference 141, 143, 167, 174, 189, 202, 218, 455, 592, 619, 635, 643, 660, 667

Big South Conference 292, 347, 593

Big Ten Conference 8, 28, 32, 35, 37-41, 45, 48-50, 52-53, 55, 57, 67, 69-70, 72, 75, 78, 83, 88, 99, 105, 112, 117, 119, 123, 129, 133, 136, 141, 151, 162, 167, 174, 180-182, 184, 189, 195, 199, 208, 217, 223-224, 226, 231, 233, 235, 238, 240, 243, 245-247, 251-252, 255, 258, 261, 263, 268, 278, 281, 283, 287, 292, 298, 308, 312, 318-319, 324, 327, 334, 343, 345, 353, 359, 362, 365, 368, 370, 374, 381, 400, 423, 439-443, 447-448, 451, 453, 455-456, 460, 462-465, 467-470, 475, 477, 489-490, 492, 495, 497, 501, 503, 508-509, 517, 519, 542, 553-554, 562, 587, 594, 636, 642, 646, 648-649, 661, 664-668, 696

Big 12 Conference 321, 587, 595, 619, 621, 625, 629, 637, 643-644, 646-647, 656, 700

Big West Conference 180, 195, 201, 275, 321, 337, 442, 445, 470, 596, 619, 626-628, 635, 639, 644, 648, 658, 665, 690, 700

Biles, Willie 201, 209

Bing, Dave 154, 389, 655, 669, 671

Bird, Larry 180, 230, 237, 240, 243, 246, 248-249, 381, 390, 582, 584, 636, 670-671, 691-693
    player of the year award, 665

Birdsong, Otis 229, 231, 351, 390, 621, 635, 670

Black, W. O. 4

Black Athletic Clubs 12

Black Coaches Association (BCA) 321, 622

Black, Charles 26, 40, 390, 637, 669

Blackman, Rolando 262, 390, 581, 584

Blaik, Red 498, 501

Corzine, Dave 241, 243, 631
Cosic, Kresimir 192, 194, 516, 581
Costello, Larry 76
Cougars See Brigham Young University; Houston;
    Washington State
Coughran, John 195
Counts, Mel 133, 139, 579, 584, 647-648
Cousy, Bob 53, 58, 64, 66, 163, 176, 394, 635, 669
Cowan, Charlie 494
Cowden, Bill 39
Cowens, Dave 394, 633
Cox, Johnny 106-107, 109, 394, 638, 669, 688
Cox, Phil 658
Craig, Roger 476
Crawford Stanley, Marianne See Stanley, Marianne
    Crawford
Creech, Len 659
Creighton University 42, 54, 147, 630
Cremins, Bobby 181, 244, 288, 295, 322-323, 327,
    341, 348-349, 369, 439, 572
        national coach of the year award, 668
Cribbs, Claire 24, 394, 648, 668
Crichton, Michael 516
Crimson. See Harvard
Crimson Tide See Alabama
Crisler, Herbert (Fritz) 494
Crosthwaite, Ralph 660
Crum, Denny 196, 199, 212, 216, 218, 232, 240,
    246, 252, 254-255, 261, 268, 275, 281, 292, 295,
    308, 317, 327, 348, 356, 369, 439, 444, 446, 563,
    572, 685, 687, 696
Crusaders See Holy Cross
Culberson, Dick 48
Cummings, Terry 252, 265, 278, 395, 631, 670
Cunningham, Billy 143, 240, 395
Cunningham, Gary 240, 244, 246, 440, 688, 696
Cuomo, Mario 513
Curry, Denise 541, 543, 582-583, 585
Curtright, Guy 476
Cyclones. See Iowa State

D

Dabney, Mike 227
Dailey, Quintin 252, 265, 267, 395, 652, 670
Dallas Chaparrals 390, 514
Dallas Cowboys 133, 492, 495-497, 499, 503, 506,
    508
Dallas Diamonds 543, 545
Dallas Mavericks 386-387, 390, 398, 408, 410, 416,
    421-422

Dallas Texans 133, 494, 508
Dallmar, Howie 39, 48, 137, 218, 648, 669, 687
Daly, Chuck 199, 204, 218, 240, 245, 442, 582
Dampier, Louie 156, 395, 638, 688
Danforth, Roy 204, 218, 437
Daniel, Ken 650
Daniels, Mel 232, 395, 644
Dantley, Adrian 209, 216, 221, 223, 235, 395, 580,
    584, 646, 670
        player of the year award, 664
Danzig, Hal 627
Dare, Yinka 194, 366
Darling, Chuck 71, 395, 579, 584, 637, 669
Dartmouth College 44, 47, 630
Daugherty, Brad 395, 645
Davidson College 27, 36, 38, 48-51, 53-54, 57-59,
    61-67, 69-71, 74, 83, 87-88, 90, 93-94, 99, 101, 105-
    106, 109, 112, 118, 126, 133, 137, 142-143, 145, 150,
    157, 162, 177, 182, 185, 187-188, 191, 199, 202,
    218, 221, 227, 243, 246-247, 251, 278-279, 283, 288,
    290, 295, 312, 314, 324, 332, 338, 345, 349, 362-
    363, 369, 371, 476, 479, 481-482, 508, 514, 522,
    561-562, 624, 630, 637-638, 646, 658, 660, 665-667,
    688
Davies, Bob 33, 38, 52, 396, 573, 652, 669, 696
Davies, Charles (Chick) 57, 451
Davis, Charlie 173
Davis-Wrightsil, Clarissa 543
Davis, Ernie 494
Davis, Glenn 494
Davis, Lardie 38
Davis, Larry 38
Davis, Tom 298, 301, 308, 317, 348, 369, 439, 572-
    573, 603
        national coach of the year award, 667
Davis, Walter 208, 233, 396, 580, 584
Davis, Walter (Buddy) 510
Davis & Elkins College 11, 455-456, 570
Davis Cup 511
Davis-Wrightsil, Clarissa 543
Dawkins, Johnny 285, 292, 295-296, 298, 396, 589,
    631, 670, 697-698
        player of the year award, 665
Dawson, Len 494
Day, Todd 624, 696-697
Daye, Darren 256
Dayton, University of 36, 74, 78, 131, 163, 449,
    452, 486, 630, 706
Dean, Everett 30, 37-40, 447, 451, 687
Dean, Hal 516
DeBernardi, Forrest S. 12

Gola, Tom 63, 71, 75, 81, 83, 85, 87-88, 90, 92, 176, 384, 401, 638, 669, 671, 676, 687, 692
  player of the year award, 663
Golden Cyclones 530
Golden Eagles. *See* Marquette; Oral Roberts; Southern Mississippi; Tennessee Tech
Golden Flashes. *See* Kent
Golden Gophers. *See* Minnesota
Golden Griffins. *See* Canisius
Golden Hurricane. *See* Tulsa
Golden State Warriors 392-393, 402, 404, 419, 421, 424-425, 427, 433-434, 582
Goldon, Wayne 655
Goldwater, Barry 516
Gondrezick, Glen 235
Gonzaga University 634
Goodall, Bob 657
Goodrich, Gail, Jr. 28, 144
Goodrich, Gail, Sr. 148, 150, 669
Gordon, Bridgette 536, 539-541, 543, 583, 585
Gore, Al 518
Gore, Demetreus 306, 697
Governors. *See* Austin Peay State
Graham, Chuck 345, 697
Graham, Ernest 244, 697
Graham, Michael 281-282
Graham, Otto 402
Graham, Stedman 518
Grambling State University 614, 662
Grant, Gary 305, 402, 642, 670
Grant, Greg 658
Grant, Harry (Bud) 497
Grant, Harvey 563
Grant, Josh 658
Grant, Travis Machine Gun 568, 571, 575
Grate, Don 52, 402, 646
Graves, Butch 662
Graves, Ray 628
Grayer, Jeff 581, 584, 637
Grayson, Doug 159, 674
Great Lakes NTS 20, 49
Great Midwest Conference 336, 338, 441
Green, Cornell 133, 497, 658
Green, Dallas 478
Green, Litterial 634
Green, Mike 575, 639
Green, Rickey 227, 229, 235, 402, 642, 670
Green, Si 87, 92, 402, 632, 669
Green, Sidney 252, 658
Green Bay Packers 496, 499-500, 505, 507-508
Greenberg, Mel 527, 533

Green Wave. *See* Tulane
Greenwood, David 179, 237, 243, 249, 402, 657, 670, 688
Greer, Hal 402, 640
Greer, Hugh 120, 137, 454
Gregory, Claude 661
Gregory, George 6, 12, 24, 629, 668
Grekin, Norm 84, 384, 401
Grentz, Theresa Shank. *See* Shank Grentz, Theresa
Grevey, Kevin 220-221, 403, 638, 688
Grey Cup 508
Grider, Joshua 569
Griese, Bob 497
Griffin, Paul 660
Griffin, Rod 232, 403, 659
Griffith, Darrell 252, 254-256, 403, 640, 670, 687
  player of the year award, 665
Grimsley, Lou 564
Grizzlies. *See* Montana
Groat, Dick 63-64, 71-72, 403, 478, 631, 669
Grooms, Trent 638
Groza, Alex 26, 48, 50, 52-53, 56, 58-62, 403, 578, 584, 638, 669, 687-688
Grubar, Dick 177
Grunfeld, Ernie 210, 223-224, 580, 584, 655, 692, 698
GTE Academic All-American Hall of Fame 549
Guilford College 568-569, 571, 573, 575
Gulf South Classic 155
Gulf South Conference 501
Gulick, Luther 6
Gunter, Sue 550, 555-558, 582
Guziak, Ron 166
Gwynn, Tony 478

H

Haderlein, Jim 640
Haffner, Scott 317
Hagan, Cliff 70-72, 81, 83-84, 403, 638, 669, 688
Hagan, Jimmy 109, 118, 656
Hagan, Joe 27, 688
Hagan, Tom 173
Halas, George 497
Halbrook, Wade Swede 82
Halicki, Ed 478
Hall, Dale 45, 72, 404, 498, 625
Hall, Joe B. 61, 202, 204, 218, 223, 232, 237, 240, 255, 261, 268, 275, 281, 287-288, 454, 572, 687-688
Hall, Ray 628
Halsel, Mark 645

Hamilton, Lee H.   518
Hamilton, Leonard   299, 361, 572-573
　　national coach of the year award, 668
Hamilton, Lowell   318
Hamilton, Roy   235
Hamilton, Steve   99, 478, 643
Hamline College   5
Hammaker, Atlee   479
Hampton Institute   12
Handlan, Jay   68, 674
Hankins, Cecil   48
Hankins, Norm   57
Hankins, Steve   571
Hankinson, Phil   191
Hannon, Bill   72
Hanson, Victor A.   12
Hardaway, Anfernee   345, 404, 582, 584, 641, 670
Hardin, Wayne   498
Hardy, Kevin   498
Harkness, Jerry   135, 138, 404, 640, 669
Harlem Globetrotters   72, 109, 126, 364, 393, 397,
　　477, 519, 533, 549, 561, 567, 569
Harmon, Chuck   479
Harmon, Tom   498
Harp, Dick   99, 102, 105, 116, 443, 466, 696
Harper, Jerilynn   541, 544
Harper, Jerry   93, 623
Harper, Ron   287, 601, 641
Harrell, Billy   479
Harrick, Jim   295, 317, 327, 334, 341, 348, 356, 361,
　　364, 369, 440, 572-573, 687-688
　　national coach of the year award, 668
Harrington, Tom   109
Harris, Gene   129
Harris, Janet   535, 541, 544
Harris, Lucious   347, 596, 639
Harris, Steve   657
Harris Stewart, Lusia   544, 554
Harrison, Pops   48, 464
Harshman, Marv   225, 246, 278, 281, 287, 438, 444,
　　454-455
　　national coach of the year award, 667
Harstad, Bob   630
Hart, Tom   567
Hartman, Jack   159, 184, 199, 204, 218, 221, 232,
　　255, 258, 268, 455, 563
　　national coach of the year award, 667
Harvard University   88, 93, 190, 229, 623, 634-637,
　　640, 644, 646, 651, 657-658, 660
Haskell Institute   10

Haskins, Clem   148, 159, 165, 317, 327, 345, 348,
　　356, 382, 404, 660, 669
Haskins, Don   145, 154, 156, 163, 184, 199, 218,
　　281, 295, 301, 317, 341, 382, 440, 444, 572, 687
Haskins, Hal   569, 575
Hatchell, Sylvia   539, 555
Havana, University of   44
Haverford College   5
Havlicek, John   120-121, 126, 132-133, 404, 646
Hawaii, University of   635
Hawkins, Hersey   305-306, 308, 404, 581, 584, 605,
　　626, 670
　　player of the year award, 665
Hawkins, Robert Bubbles   209
Hawkins, Tom   110, 646
Hayes, E. C. Doc   163
Hayes, Elvin   157, 159-160, 162, 165, 169, 172, 404,
　　635, 669, 681-682, 692-693
　　player of the year award, 664
Hayes, Steve   235, 635
Haynes, Marques   72
Haynes, Willie   651
Haywood, Spencer   172-173, 179, 405, 563, 580,
　　584, 631, 669, 671
Hazzard, Walt   141, 143-145, 285, 287-288, 301,
　　303, 386, 405, 579, 584, 657, 669, 687-688
　　player of the year award, 664
Head Summit, Pat. *See* Summitt, Pat Head
Heathcote, George (Jud)   455
　　national coach of the year award, 668
Heinsohn, Tom   88, 92, 405, 635, 669
Heisman Trophy   138, 490, 492, 494, 496, 498-502,
　　504, 506-508, 523, 663
Heitz, Ken   162, 170, 174, 176
Helms, Joe   87
Helms Foundation   8, 12, 24, 446-447, 449, 459-
　　460, 462, 467, 477-478, 484, 492, 495, 497, 503,
　　510-511, 516, 670
Hemric, Ned (Dickie)   88, 405, 589, 659, 675, 691-
　　692
Henderson, Alan   351, 636
Henderson, Bill   50, 64, 455
Henderson, Cam   11, 444, 455
Henderson, David   296, 697
Henderson, Mel   644
Henderson, Phil   309, 327-328
Henderson, Skip   305, 612, 640
Hennessey, John   45
Hennier, Dick   566
Hennon, Don   63, 99, 104-105, 405, 648, 669

Messikomer, Ernie   461
Metro Atlantic Athletic Conference   265, 287, 295, 356, 600, 628, 633, 636, 640, 645, 651, 653, 665
Metro Conference   256, 261, 302, 313, 438-439, 441, 453, 628, 633, 636, 640, 645, 651, 653, 665
Metropolitan Basketball Writers Association   377, 486
Metropolitan Collegiate Conference   154, 620
Metropolitan Intercollegiate Basketball Association (MIBA)   377
Metropolitan Intercollegiate Basketball Committee   377
Metropolitan New York Basketball Writers Association   486
Metropolitan New York Conference   40, 486
Metzelaars, Pete   502
Mexican Olympic Team   30
Meyer, Joey   295, 301, 308, 334, 341
Meyer, Ray   28, 47, 78, 145, 225, 237, 240, 243, 246, 252, 255, 261, 263, 268, 278, 280-281, 444, 452, 463, 696
   national coach of the year award, 667
Meyers, Ann   533, 540-541, 546, 582, 585
Meyers, Dave   179, 206, 209, 216, 220, 417, 546, 657, 670
MIBA. *See* Metropolitan Inter-Collegiate Basketball Association (MIBA)
Miami Dolphins   493, 495, 497, 500
Miami (Fla.), University of   99, 148, 152, 190, 259, 340, 363, 641, 668
Miami Heat   418, 423, 429, 578
Miami (Ohio), University of   54, 61, 90, 99, 119, 166, 168, 174, 240-241, 281, 287, 363, 474, 490, 493-495, 500, 503-507, 601, 641, 689
Micheaux, Larry   278
Michigan, University of   58, 99, 149, 166, 226-227, 287, 317-319, 334, 349, 358, 374, 477, 482, 494-495, 498, 500, 641, 664, 666-667
Michigan State University   101-102, 189, 243-244, 246-247, 255, 293, 485, 493, 496, 499, 504-505, 509, 517, 523, 642, 652, 666, 668
Mid-American Conference (MAC)   15, 52, 64, 76, 123, 135, 141, 195, 261, 287, 301, 323, 447, 456-457, 468, 601-602, 604, 612, 625-626, 628, 632, 638, 641, 646, 656, 660, 700
Mid-Continent Conference   271, 287, 602, 620, 658
Mid-Eastern Athletic Conference   308, 382, 603
Middle Atlantic Conference   79, 109, 119, 216, 439, 450, 461, 469, 521, 620
Middle Tennessee State University   642
Midshipmen. *See* Navy

Midwestern City Conference   252, 261, 604
Midwestern Collegiate Conference   252, 261, 301, 317, 369, 452, 466, 604, 627, 629, 631, 640, 661
Mikan, George   7, 26, 43, 47-48, 50, 173, 384, 417, 631, 669
Mikan, Larry   173, 184
Mikkelsen, Vern   568-569, 575
Miller, Cheryl   525-526, 534, 538-541, 545-546, 555, 583, 585
Miller, Don   502
Miller, Kenny   306, 694
Miller, Larry   165, 170, 172, 418, 645, 669
Miller, Ralph   38, 137, 145, 168, 182, 184, 218, 255, 258, 261, 265, 268, 281, 317, 444, 463, 465, 696
   national coach of the year award, 667
Miller, Reggie   303, 384, 582, 584, 688
Miller, Sean   306, 697
Miller, Tony   195, 364
Millikan, Bud   83, 105, 184
Mills, Lew   438
Mills, Terry   298, 316
Milton, Alfred   624
Milwaukee Badgers   521
Milwaukee Braves   474, 476, 483, 485, 488
Milwaukee Brewers   483, 486
Milwaukee Bucks   386, 389, 398, 409, 417-418, 423-424, 466, 582
Milwaukee Hawks   406, 415, 420, 422, 485, 510
Mincy, Jerome   657
Miner, Harold   336, 338, 351, 418, 653, 670
Miners. *See* Texas-El Paso
Minneapolis Lakers   17, 28, 99, 388, 399-400, 412-413, 416, 421, 478, 497
Minnesota, University of   519, 642
Minnesota Muskies   395, 413
Minnesota School of Agriculture and Mining   5
Minnesota Timberwolves   412, 416, 582
Minnesota Twins   42, 474, 477, 481, 483, 485, 488
Minnesota Vikings   489-491, 494, 506
Minutemen. *See* Massachusetts
Misaka, Wat   46
Mississippi, University of   211, 218, 235, 237, 303, 312, 327, 330, 334, 336-337, 343, 361, 474, 477, 543, 642, 654, 657, 665, 667, 706
Mississippi State   94, 135, 176-177, 191, 195, 238, 334, 340, 348, 363, 369, 445, 492, 500, 506, 512, 551, 627-628, 631, 633-634, 639, 642, 662, 666
Mississippi Valley State   345, 369, 400, 614, 675
Missouri, University of   11, 29, 45, 94, 110, 118, 131, 143, 149, 172, 189, 202, 218, 238, 249, 253-254, 256, 287-288, 295, 299, 324, 347, 357, 363,

474-477, 479-480, 482, 486-488, 499, 512, 550, 569, 625, 629, 639, 641, 643, 648-649, 664-668, 673

Missouri Intercollegiate Athletic Association   448, 454, 458, 476, 489, 605, 619

Missouri Valley Conference   8, 10, 12, 28, 30-31, 36, 50, 55, 59, 67, 98, 117-118, 123, 126-127, 129, 133, 136, 141, 143, 152, 154, 180, 184, 216, 244, 254, 258, 265, 275, 305, 347, 439, 443, 447-448, 456-459, 461, 463-465, 468, 516, 519, 605, 619, 626, 630, 632, 636, 645, 654, 661, 664-667

Missouri Valley Intercollegiate Athletic Association   605, 619

Mitchell, Bobby   494

Mitchell, Mike   418, 625

Mitchell, Ron   635

Mitchell, Steve   657

Mitts, Billy   135

Mlkvy, Bill   63, 67-68, 72, 355, 418, 655, 669

Moccasins. See Tennessee-Chattanooga

Modzelewski, Stan   418, 429, 649

Moffett, Larry   235

Moir, John   24, 27-28, 418, 646, 668-669

Molinari, Jim   332, 573

Molinas, Jack   69, 77

Monarchs. See Old Dominion

Moncrief, Sidney   232, 243, 418, 624, 670, 694

Monday, Rick   489

Monroe, Earl The Pearl   567-568, 575

Monroe, Rodney   318, 645

Monson, Don   255, 265, 268
   national coach of the year award, 667

Montana, University of   156, 219, 643

Montana State University   474, 643, 646

Montgomery, Dave   659

Montreal Alouettes   504, 508

Montreal Expos   474, 484, 486

Montross, Eric   28, 349-350, 418, 645

Moore, Billie Jean   551, 556-557, 582

Moore, Donald (Dudey)   64, 72, 78, 83, 87, 90, 464

Moore, Jonathan   634

Moore, Leroy   507

Morehead State University   643

Morgan, Ralph   5-6, 13-14

Morgan, Tom   625

Morgernthaler, Elmore   50

Morris, Lon   562

Morris, Max   49-50, 419, 646, 669

Morris Harvey College. See Charleston, University of

Mortensen, Jesse   511

Mortimer, Jeff   477, 482

Morton, John   316-317

Moscow Red Army Team   549

Moss, Perry   268, 271

Most exciting playoff game finish, 338

Most incredible league tourney final, 211

Moten, Lawrence   655

Mount, Rick   117, 172, 174, 176-177, 180-182, 349, 419, 594, 649, 669

Mount Holyoke College   528

Mountain States Conference   32, 466-467, 469

Mountain States Intercollegiate Athletic Conference   620

Mountaineers. See West Virginia

Mourning, Alonzo   251, 315, 336-339, 419, 634, 670, 676, 682, 695

Mulkey Robertson, Kim   546

Mullin, Chris   285, 288, 290, 320, 419, 581-582, 584, 651, 670
   player of the year award, 665

Mullins, Jeff   144, 147, 579, 584, 631

Mullins, Peter   511

Murdock, Eric   332, 649, 676, 695

Murdock, Jackie   100

Murphy, Calvin   117, 166, 172, 180, 183, 185, 419, 645, 669, 692-693

Murphy, Charles (Stretch)   12, 24, 419, 649, 668

Murphy, Tod   627

Murray, Lamond   354, 366, 627

Murray State University   253, 643

Murrell, Red   105, 631

Musketeers. See Xavier

Musso, George   502

Mustangs. See Southern Methodist

Mutombo, Dikembe   194, 316

N

NABC. See National Association of Basketball Coaches (NABC)

NABC coach of the year awards. See National coach of the year awards (1955–96)

NABC player of the year awards. See National player of the year awards (1955–96)

NAIA. See National Association of Intercollegiate Athletics (NAIA)

Naismith coach of the year awards. See National coach of the year awards (1955–96)

Naismith player of the year awards. See National player of the year awards (1955–96)

Nance, Larry   419

Nance, Lynn   316, 573

New Jersey Nets   370, 374, 387, 394, 399, 401, 411, 420, 435, 466, 582

New Mexico, University of   90, 241, 255, 644

New Mexico A&M, University of   28, 30, 73, 93, 662

New Mexico School of Mines   50

New Mexico State University   30, 49, 51, 55, 59, 133, 275, 473, 480, 497, 510, 644, 656, 658

New Orleans, University of   644

New Orleans Buccaneers   508

New Orleans Saints   489, 500

New York Basketball Writers Association   43, 486

New York Clowns   125

New York Giants   475-477, 488, 490, 494, 499-500, 502-503, 505-508

New York Jets   495

New York Knicks   289, 388-389, 391, 393-394, 397-398, 404-408, 416-417, 423, 425, 427-428, 432, 443, 460, 476, 514, 520, 582

New York Mets   474, 476, 478-481

New York Nets   394, 450

New York University (NYU)   10-11, 14-15, 19-24, 26, 33, 38, 42-44, 49-52, 56-58, 70, 101, 106, 120-121, 129, 131, 135, 137, 139, 142, 190, 378, 411, 426, 429, 449-450, 475, 483, 487, 524, 578, 584, 620, 662, 669, 687

New York Yankees   12, 99, 475, 478-482, 484, 486-489, 504-505, 564

New Yorks Original Celtics   14

Newell, Pete   59, 61, 64, 99, 109, 112, 117, 120, 464, 470, 579, 687, 696

    national coach of the year award, 666

Newmann, John   650

Newmann, Johnny   420

Newsome, Manny   660

Newton, C. M.   70, 212, 218, 225, 232, 308, 317, 443

Niagara University   183, 644

Nichols, Deno   43

Nichols, Jack   57-58, 629, 660

Nielsen, Gifford   502

Nissen, Inge   533, 541, 543, 546

NIT. *See* National Invitational Tournament (NIT)

Nittany Lions. *See* Penn State

NJCAA. *See* National Junior College Athletic Association (NJCAA)

Nolan, Dick   41

Nordholz, Mike   160

Norfolk NAS   49

Norfolk NTS   49

Norman, Coniel   203, 221, 229

Norman, Ken   299, 563, 636

Norris, Eugene, education instructor   43

North Alabama, University of   573

North Atlantic Conference   252, 281, 314, 316, 354, 438, 443, 606, 626, 631, 645, 705

North Carolina, University of   37, 45, 69, 72, 77, 100-101, 105, 107, 112, 132, 155, 162, 176, 211, 217, 221, 229, 235, 245, 248, 251-252, 263, 268-269, 271, 275-276, 279, 283, 336, 340, 345, 349, 351, 356-357, 365, 444, 512, 522, 645, 665-668

    Undefeated team, 101

North Carolina A&T State University   210, 237, 293, 307-308, 575, 603, 685, 701

North Carolina-Asheville, University of   299

North Carolina-Charlotte, University of   37, 101, 147, 180, 203-204, 210, 212, 216, 219, 224, 230-233, 235, 237, 240, 249, 308, 340, 349, 384, 417, 462, 466-467, 498, 500, 503, 506, 509, 511, 517, 547, 579, 593, 597-598, 615, 620, 639, 657, 687, 701

North Carolina State University   54, 57, 66, 77, 111, 150, 203, 206, 212, 214, 216, 276, 278, 282, 326, 477, 487, 524, 555, 645, 664, 666

North Carolina-Wilmington, University of   292, 573

North Central Conference   444

North Dallas Forty   496

North Texas State University   118, 189, 209, 223, 230, 244, 273, 596, 605, 662, 693

Northeast Conference   231, 265, 301, 346-347, 354-355, 370, 420, 448, 476, 536, 541-542, 575, 580, 584, 607, 613, 616, 639, 645, 650, 691, 701

Northeastern Illinois University   324, 347, 361, 602, 620

Northeastern University   57, 82, 90, 125, 196, 216, 363, 476, 486, 488, 525, 545, 630, 645, 659, 666-668

Northern Arizona, University of   69, 76, 218, 365, 592, 619, 678-679, 702

Northern Illinois University   167, 188, 196, 209, 244, 325, 331-332, 491, 514, 555-556, 601-602, 604, 679, 693, 701

Northern Iowa, University of   12, 211, 493, 495, 523, 645, 648

Northwest College Conference   8

Northwest College Womens Sports Association   546

Northwestern University   27, 36, 38, 48-51, 53-54, 57-59, 61-67, 69-71, 74, 83, 87-88, 90, 93-94, 99, 101, 105-106, 109, 112, 118, 126, 133, 137, 142-143, 145, 150, 157, 162, 177, 182, 185, 187-188, 191, 199, 202, 218, 221, 227, 243, 246-247, 251, 278-279, 283, 288, 290, 295, 312, 314, 324, 332, 338, 345, 349, 362-363, 369, 371, 476, 479, 481-482, 508, 514,

Owens, R. C.   503
Owens, Ted   156, 163, 176, 190, 211-212, 240, 261, 438, 466
Owls. *See* Rice; Temple

P

Pacific, University of the   29, 45, 94, 110, 118, 131, 143, 149, 172, 189, 202, 218, 238, 249, 253-254, 256, 287-288, 295, 299, 324, 347, 357, 363, 474-477, 479-480, 482, 486-488, 499, 512, 550, 569, 625, 629, 639, 641, 643, 648-649, 664-668, 673
Pacific Coast Athletic Association   201, 232, 238, 443, 445, 596, 609
Pacific Coast Conference   16, 27-29, 34, 38, 54, 57, 64, 112, 448, 453-454, 457, 464, 476, 485, 499, 508, 511, 516, 609
Pacific-8 Conference   172, 180, 187, 192, 194, 201, 208, 216, 224, 227, 244, 455, 470, 609, 664-666, 700 *See also* Pacific-10 Conference
Pacific Lutheran   287, 454-455
Pacific-10 Conference   88, 159, 192, 208, 224, 244-245, 252, 285, 287, 292, 303, 330, 361, 364, 372, 439-440, 442-443, 448-449, 453-455, 464, 470, 536, 542, 551, 553, 587-588, 609, 624, 627, 647, 653, 655, 657, 659-660, 664-665, 667-668, 700 *See also* Pacific-8 Conference
Packer, Billy   77, 118, 384, 506
Page, H. O. Pat   8
Paladins. *See* Furman
Palestra   6, 14, 95, 154, 534, 648, 703
Pan American   166, 180, 184, 202, 208, 210, 219, 224, 230, 238, 247, 253, 263, 266, 293, 424, 455, 493, 510, 512, 521, 550, 566, 568-569, 575, 579, 584, 604, 644, 662
Pan American Games   180, 493, 510, 512, 521, 550
Panthers. *See* Northern Iowa; Pittsburgh
Panzer College   29
Parish, Robert   201, 225, 421
Parkhil, Barry   195, 659
Parkinson, Bruce   217
Parks, Cherokee   338, 342, 358-359
Parrack, Doyle   48, 78, 184
Parris, Antonio   632
Parseghian, Ara   503
Parsons, Pam   533, 535
Pasche, Alden   460
Paterno, Joe   503
Patriot League Conference   330, 353, 610, 625, 627, 629, 635, 638-639, 644
Patterson, Hal   503, 564

Patterson, Steve   174, 183, 187, 191-192
Patton College   354
Pauly, Steve   138, 511
Paxson, John   252, 421, 646
Payton, Gary   322-323, 421, 647-648, 670, 693
Payton, Walter   493
Peacocks. *See* St. Peter's
Pearson, Preston   503
Pelinka, Rob   316, 341
Pennefather, Shelly   540-541, 547
Penn State University. *See* Pennsylvania State University
Pennsylvania, University of   119, 191, 240, 245, 369, 524, 648
Pennsylvania State University   84, 503, 513, 545, 648
Pepperdine University   218, 356, 648
Perigo, Bill   468
Perkins, Sam   265, 269, 271, 278, 421, 581, 584, 645, 670, 698
Perry, Chana   536, 541
Perry, Curtis   575, 654
Perry, Ronnie   235, 635, 692
Person, Chuck   625
Person, Wesley   354
Peterson, Vadal   43, 47, 52, 78, 466, 687
Pettit, Bob   72, 81, 87, 422, 639, 669
Phelps, Derrick   349-350
Phelps, Digger   142, 190, 195, 208, 212, 218, 225, 232, 240, 246, 255, 261, 295, 301, 466, national coach of the year award, 666
Philadelphia Athletics   483, 488
Philadelphia College of Pharmacy   7, 11
Philadelphia Eagles   492, 495, 500, 506
Philadelphia NAMC   59
Philadelphia Phillies   52, 402, 474, 476, 478-482, 484-486, 488
Philadelphia 76ers   240, 388, 391-392, 394-395, 400, 404, 428
Philadelphia Warriors   40, 98, 387, 389, 393, 401, 418, 424-425, 461-462, 510, 512, 565
Phillip, Andy   26, 38, 40, 422, 636, 669
Phillips, Gene   183, 189, 654
Phillips, Mike   221, 241
Phoenix. *See* Wisconsin-Green Bay
Phoenix Cardinals   499
Phoenix Suns   396, 401, 415, 419, 424, 426-427, 432, 493, 572, 582
Pierce, John   572, 575
Pierce, Ricky   267, 563
Pilots. *See* Portland

T

Titans. *See* Cal State Fullerton; Detroit Mercy

Toledo, University of   163, 165, 173, 230, 294, 404-405, 414, 419-420, 422, 426, 430, 470, 479, 498, 504, 509, 582, 656

Tomjanovich, Rudy   166, 172, 430, 642

Tooley, Ed   88, 675

Toreros. *See* San Diego

Tormohlen, Gene   655

Toronto, University of   5

Toronto Blue Jays   386, 488

Torrance, Jack   512

Tower, Oswald   9

Townsend, John   28

Trabert, Tony   512

Track and Field Hall of Fame   509

Trans America Athletic Conf.   246, 252, 281, 317, 332, 374, 616, 619

Transylvania University   317, 466-467

Traveling   9, 59

Tribe. *See* William & Mary

Tri-Cities Blackhawks   415, 434, 510

Tri-Cities Hawks   426

Triche, Howard   303

Trinity College   7, 211, 613, 662, 702

Tripucka, Kelly   249, 253, 431, 646, 697

Tripucka, Tracy   638

Trojans. *See* Arkansas-Little Rock; Southern California, University of

Tropf, Glenn   305, 675

Trout, Monroe   522

Truesdale, Regan   628

Tsioropoulos, Lou   70, 83-84

Tubbs, Billy   251, 281, 288, 295, 301, 306, 308, 317, 327, 341, 446, 572-573

Tucker, Al   568

Tucker, Arnold   507

Tucker, Chad   627

Tucker, Gerry   26, 52-53, 431, 647, 669

Tucson Open   509

Tulane University   59, 64, 275, 657, 668

Tulsa, University of   657

Tunnell, Emlen   507

Turner, John   114

Turpin, Melvin   279, 283, 688

Two-shot penalty   92, 305

Twyman, Jack   431

Tyra, Charlie   94, 98, 384, 431, 640, 669

Tyson, Mike   510

U

UCLA   13, 21, 28-29, 38-39, 42, 54, 57, 59, 61, 64, 66, 69-70, 72, 83, 87, 90, 92, 94-95, 98-99, 104, 109, 112, 117, 119, 121, 123, 125, 127, 129, 131-133, 135, 137, 139, 141, 143-145, 147-155, 157, 159, 161-163, 165, 167-177, 179-180, 182-185, 187-188, 190-192, 194-199, 201-204, 206, 208-214, 216-221, 223, 225-227, 229, 232, 235, 237-238, 240, 243-244, 246-247, 249, 251-252, 255-256, 258, 261, 265-266, 268, 275, 285, 287-288, 290, 292-293, 301, 303, 315, 317, 327, 334, 336, 339-341, 348-349, 351, 356, 361, 363-366, 368-369, 371-372, 374, 380-382, 384, 386-387, 389, 398, 401-402, 405, 409, 417, 420, 425, 432-434, 439-440, 445, 448-449, 452, 470, 485, 500, 510, 512, 514-515, 519, 523, 532-533, 535, 539-541, 543-544, 546, 551-552, 556-559, 569, 572, 578-580, 582-585, 609, 657, 662-666, 668-670, 677, 680-682, 685-689, 695-696, 699-700, 702-703, 705

   Undefeated team, 144, 161, 198, 203, 209

UConn. *See* Connecticut

Utes. *See* Utah

Udall, Morris (Mo)   522

UMass. *See* Massachusetts

Umbricht, Jim   487

Undefeated teams, 33, 45, 84, 94, 101, 144, 161, 198, 203, 209, 225

Underwood, Paul   95, 692

Union University   12

University of. *See* specific geographic name

UNLV   657

Unruh, Paul   64, 431, 626, 669

Unseld, Wes   154, 159, 165-166, 172, 431, 640, 669

Upshaw, Cecil   487

Urzetta, Sam   57, 64

U.S. Basketball League   545

U.S. Basketball Writers Association (USBWA)   43, 190, 377, 386, 486, 514, 523, 546, 549, 551, 553-554, 622, 663, 670

U.S. International   293-294, 313-314, 325, 330-332, 674, 677, 693, 702

U.S. Jones Cup Team   555

U.S. Military Academy   12, 45, 503

U.S. Select Team   555

USA Basketball   539, 577, 622

U.S. Olympic team. *See* Olympics (men's basketball team); Olympics (women's basketball team)

Usilton, Jimmy   461

Utah, University of   44, 46, 49, 95, 127, 129, 133, 151, 203, 378, 466, 658, 668, 706

Warren, Mike   162, 169-170, 433, 523
Warrensburg Teachers College   10
Washburn College   23
Washington, Kenny   144-145, 150
Washington, Kermit   204, 433, 624, 676, 694
Washington, Richard   179, 219-221, 223, 229, 235, 433, 657, 670, 687-688
Washington, Stan   652
Washington, University of   57, 82, 90, 125, 196, 216, 363, 476, 486, 488, 525, 545, 630, 645, 659, 666-668
Washington Bullets   393, 415, 520
Washington Capitols   410, 426
Washington College   8
Washington Redskins   490, 493-494, 500, 504, 506-507
Washington Senators   121, 126, 475, 478-479, 483, 487-488
Washington State University   37-38, 45, 50, 78, 169-170, 174, 192, 269, 276, 278, 354, 476, 487, 511, 516, 626, 635, 660, 664-667
Watson, Bobby   70, 237
Watson, Deon   635
Watson, Lorenza   659
Watson, Lou   162, 206
Watts, Stan   67, 69, 99, 151, 154, 156, 190, 196, 199, 469
Waves. *See* Pepperdine
Wayland Baptist College   554
Weatherspoon, Clarence   654
Weatherspoon, Teresa   540-541, 549, 585
Webb, Spud   252, 563
Webber, Mayce (Chris)   342-343, 345, 349-351, 359, 366, 374, 433, 642, 670
Weber State College   27, 36, 38, 48-51, 53-54, 57-59, 61-67, 69-71, 74, 83, 87-88, 90, 93-94, 99, 101, 105-106, 109, 112, 118, 126, 133, 137, 142-143, 145, 150, 157, 162, 177, 182, 185, 187-188, 191, 199, 202, 218, 221, 227, 243, 246-247, 251, 278-279, 283, 288, 290, 295, 312, 314, 324, 332, 338, 345, 349, 362-363, 369, 371, 476, 479, 481-482, 508, 514, 522, 561-562, 624, 630, 637-638, 646, 658, 660, 665-667, 688
Weese, Dean   553-554
Weller, Chris   540, 554-558
Welp, Christian   660
Werber, Billy   488
Werkman, Nick   135, 141, 433
Werts, Melton   635
West, Jerry   107, 109, 112-114, 117-118, 121, 433, 484, 579, 584, 660, 669, 682, 687

West Chester (Pa.) State College   531
West Coast Athletic Association   543, 547, 617
West Coast Conference   112, 124, 131, 137, 151, 201, 218, 305, 322, 440, 445, 471, 634, 640, 648, 651-652
West Texas State University   38, 184, 229, 258, 295, 605, 619, 662, 669, 679, 689, 697
West Virginia, University of   11, 16, 28-29, 38-39, 45, 51, 54, 56, 58-60, 65, 68, 72-73, 90, 93, 95, 98-99, 105-107, 109, 111-114, 116-121, 124-126, 131-132, 136-137, 139, 151, 162, 166, 195-196, 211, 232, 240, 261, 268, 275, 289, 298-299, 315, 317, 368, 384, 407, 430, 433, 438, 441, 484, 493, 507, 515, 541, 556, 569-570, 575, 579, 584, 590-591, 619, 660, 669, 671, 682, 685, 687, 697, 700, 706
West Virginia State College   29, 232, 569
Western Athletic Conference (WAC)   132, 135, 142, 151, 154, 156-157, 189-190, 203, 221, 237, 294, 301, 321, 326, 333-334, 440-441, 445, 453, 469, 478, 553, 618-621, 623, 626, 629, 633, 635, 644, 649, 652, 654, 656-658, 661, 665, 668, 700
Western Carolina University   101, 237, 261, 266, 354, 362, 372, 508, 702
Western Conference   8, 12, 135, 261, 361, 451, 467, 485, 594, 623, 626, 629, 633, 635, 644, 649, 652, 654, 656-658, 661
Western Illinois State Teacher's College   13
Western Illinois University   13, 265-266, 273, 364, 570, 602, 675, 701
Western Kentucky   165, 660
Western League   8
Western Michigan University   61, 174, 189, 364, 501-502, 507, 509, 626, 652, 660
Westminster College   12
Westphal, Paul   434, 572
Whatley, James   508
White, Byron Whizzer   523
White, Jo Jo   159, 434, 580, 584, 637
White, Nera   531
White, Sammy   488
White, Sherman   67, 639
White, Tony   301, 347, 698
Whitehead, Jerome   229, 233
Whitman College   8
Whittenburg, Dereck   274, 276, 278
Whiz Kids   40
Wichita State University   136, 147, 149, 152, 263, 660
Wicks, Sidney   174, 183, 185, 187, 190-192, 434, 657, 670, 687-688
   player of the year award,